1993 PRICE GUIDE TO

BASEBALL CARDS

BY DR. JAMES BECKETT

TWELFTH EDITION

HOUSE OF COLLECTIBLES • NEW YORK

Published by: House of Collectibles
201 East 50th Street
New York, New York 10022

Distributed by Ballantine Books, a division of Random House, Inc., New York, and simultaneously in Canada by Random House of Canada Limited, Toronto.

Manufactured in the United States of America

Library of Congress Catalog Card Number: 84-645496

ISBN: 0-876-37881-5

Twelfth Edition: April 1992

10 9 8 7 6 5 4 3 2 1

Table of Contents

Advertisers

About the Author

Jim Beckett, the leading authority on sport card values in the United States, maintains a wide range of activities in the world of sports. He possesses one of the finest collections of sports cards and autographs in the world, has made numerous appearances on radio and television, and has been frequently cited in many national publications. He was awarded the first "Special Achievement Award" for Contributions to the Hobby by the National Sports Collectors Convention in 1980, the "Jock-Jasperson Award" for Hobby Dedication in 1983, and the "Buck Barker, Spirit of the Hobby" Award in 1991.

Dr. Beckett is the author of *The Sport Americana Baseball Card Price Guide, The Official Price Guide to Baseball Cards, The Sport Americana Price Guide to Baseball Collectibles, The Sport Americana Baseball Memorabilia and Autograph Price Guide, The Sport Americana Football Card Price Guide, The Official Price Guide to Football Cards, The Sport Americana Hockey Card Price Guide, The Official Price Guide to Hockey Cards, The Sport Americana Basketball Card Price Guide and Alphabetical Checklist, The Official Price Guide to Basketball Cards,* and *The Sport Americana Alphabetical Baseball Card Checklist.* In addition, he is the founder, publisher, and editor of *Beckett Baseball Card Monthly, Beckett Basketball Monthly, Beckett Football Card Monthly, Beckett Hockey Monthly,* and *Beckett Focus on Future Stars*, magazines dedicated to advancing the card collecting hobby.

Jim Beckett received his Ph.D. in Statistics from Southern Methodist University in 1975. Prior to starting Beckett Publications in 1984, Dr. Beckett served as an Associate Professor of Statistics at Bowling Green State University and as a Vice President of a consulting firm in Dallas, Texas. He currently resides in Dallas with his wife Patti and their daughters, Christina, Rebecca, and Melissa.

Preface

Isn't it great? Every year this book gets bigger and bigger with all the new sets coming out. But even more exciting is that every year there are more collectors, more shows, more stores, and more interest in the cards we love so much. This edition has been enhanced and expanded from the previous edition. The cards you collect — who they are, what they look like, where they are from, and (most important to many of you) what their current values are — are enumerated within. Many of the features contained in the other *Beckett Price Guides* have been incorporated into this volume since condition grading, nomenclature, and many other aspects of collecting are common to the card hobby in general. We hope you find the book both interesting and useful in your collecting pursuits.

The *Beckett Guide* has been successful where other attempts have failed because it is complete, current, and valid. This Price Guide contains not just one, but three prices by condition for all the baseball cards listed. These account for almost all the baseball cards in existence. The prices were added to the card lists just prior to printing and reflect not the author's opinions or desires but the going retail prices for each card, based on the marketplace (sports memorabilia conventions and shows, sports card shops, hobby papers, current mail order catalogs, local club meetings, auction results, and other firsthand reportings of actually realized prices).

What is the best price guide available (on the market) today? Of course card sellers will prefer the price guide with the highest prices as the best — while card buyers will naturally prefer the one with the lowest prices. Accuracy, however, is the true test. Use the price guide used by more collectors and dealers than all the others combined. Look for the Beckett name. I won't put my name on anything I won't stake my reputation on. Not the lowest and not the highest — but the most accurate, with integrity.

To facilitate your use of this book, read the complete introductory section in the pages following before going to the pricing pages. Every collectible field has its own terminology; we've tried to capture most of these terms and definitions in our glossary. Please read carefully the section on grading and the condition of your cards, as you will not be able to determine which price column is appropriate for a given card without first knowing its condition.

Welcome to the world of baseball cards.

Sincerely, Dr. James Beckett

Acknowledgments

A great deal of diligence, hard work, and dedicated effort went into this year's volume. However, the high standards to which we hold ourselves could not have been met without the expert input and generous amount of time contributed by many people. Our sincere thanks are extended to each and every one of you. Those who have worked closely with us on this and many other books have again proven themselves invaluable — Frank and Vivian Barning (Baseball Hobby News), Chris Benjamin, Sy Berger (Topps), Card Collectors Co., Peter Brennan, Cartophilium (Andrew Pywowarczuk), Ira Cetron, Barry Colla, Mike Cramer (Pacific Trading Cards), Bill and Diane Dodge, Doubleheaders (Wayne Varner, Mike Wheat, and Bill Zimpleman), Fleer Corporation (Paul Mullen, Vincent Murray, and Jeff Massien), Steve Freedman, Gervise Ford, Larry and Jeff Fritsch, Tony Galovich (American Card Exchange), Georgia Music and Sports (Dick DeCourcey), Dick Gilkeson, Steve Gold (AU Sports), Bill Goodwin (St. Louis Baseball Cards), Mike and Howard Gordon, George Grauer, John Greenwald, Wayne Grove, Bill Haber, Bill Henderson, Jay and Mary Kasper, Allan Kaye (Baseball Card News), Rick Keplinger, Michael Keyton, David Kohler (SportsCards Plus), Don Lepore, Paul Lewicki, Neil Lewis (Leaf), Lew Lipset, Norman and Ken Liss (Topps), Mark Macrae, Bill Madden, Major League Marketing (Dan Shedrick, Tom Day, and Julie Haddon), Mid-Atlantic Sports Cards (Bill Bossert), Dick Millerd, Brian Morris, B.A. Murry, Ralph Nozaki, Oldies and Goodies (Nigel Spill), Optigraphics/Score Group (Ed Fick), Jack Pollard, Jeff Prillaman, Gavin Riley, Alan Rosen (Mr. Mint), Clifton Rouse, John Rumierz, San Diego Sport Collectibles (Bill Goepner and Nacho Arredondo), Kevin Savage (Sports Gallery), Mike Schechter, Barry Sloate, John Spalding, Phil Spector (Scoreboard, Inc.), Sports Collectors Store, Frank Steele, Murvin Sterling, Lee Temanson, Ed Twombly (New England Bullpen), Gary Walter, Bill Wesslund (Portland Sports Card Co.), Craig Williamson, Scott Williard, Kit Young, and Ted Zanidakis. Of special help on this edition was B.A. Murry, who in early 1991 laid the groundwork for our Technical Services department before becoming our Senior Pricing Consultant. Finally we give a special acknowledgment to Dennis W. Eckes, "Mr. Sport Americana," whose untimely passing last year was a real loss to the hobby and to me personally. The success of the Beckett Price Guides has always been the result of a team effort.

I believe this year's Price Guide is our best yet. For that, you can thank all of the contributors nationwide (listed above and below) as well as our staff here in Dallas. Our company now boasts a substantial Technical Services team which has made (and is continuing to make) direct and important contributions to this work. Technical Services capably handled numerous technical details and provided able assistance in pricing for this edition of the annual guide. That effort was directed by Technical Services managers Jay Johnson and Pepper Hastings. They were assisted by Technical Services coordinator Mary Gregory, price guide analysts Theo Chen, Mike Hersh, Dan Hitt, Mary Huston, Rich Klein, Allan Muir, Grant Sandground and Dave Sliepka. Also contributing to our Technical Services functions were Jana Threatt, Wendy Jewell, Peter Tepp and Scott Layton, whose special assistance was invaluable in making this project a success. The price gathering and analytical talents of this fine group of hobbyists has helped make our Beckett team stronger, while making this guide and its companion monthly price guides even more widely recognized as the hobby's most reliable and relied upon sources of pricing information.

It is very difficult to be "accurate" — one can only do one's best. But this job is especially difficult since we're shooting at a moving target: Prices are fluctuating all the time. Having several full-time pricing experts has definitely proven to be better than just one, and I thank all of them for working together to provide you, our readers, with the most accurate prices possible.

Many people have provided price input, illustrative material, checklist verifications, errata, and/or background information. We should like to individually thank AbD Cards (Dale Wesolewski), Robert Abel, Carl Abrams, Dave Acker, Jeremy Ackerman, Jerry Adamic, Michael Adams, Ron Adelson, Tony Adkins, Andrew R. Aebi, A.J.'s Sport Stop, R.J. Albanese, Bob Alexander, Mike Alexander, Will Allison, All Star Sports Collectibles, J. Almeda, David Anderson, Dennis Anderson, Jason Anderson, T.M. Angell, Graham Anthony, Jim Anthony, Tom Antonowicz, Ric Apter, Jason Arasate, Mark Argo (Olde South Cards), William Arkell, Burl Armstrong, Neil Armstrong (World Series Cards), Brian Ashbach, Lester H. Auclair Jr., Robert August, Charles Austin, B & B Sales Co., B & F Sports Cards (Bill Bryda), Jeff Baas, Robert Baker, Ball Four Cards, Jason Ballek, John Barbier, George Barkwell, Youssef Barnetche, Joe Barney, Brent Barnhill, Ed Barry (Ed's Collectibles), Bob Bartosz (Baseball Card Shop), Nathan Basford, Nick Basso, David Bauers, Baxter's Cards, Bay State Cards (Lenny DeAngelico), Fred Beck, Andy Beisel, Joey Beland, Dennis Joe Belk, Scott Bell, Nick Belletto, Peter S. Bennett, Graham Benyman, Carl Berg, Ken Berg, Dave Berman, Bernie's Bullpen, Mildred Berteau, Beulah Sports, Seth Bienstock, Brian Bigelow, Steve Birchak, Josh Bird, Jack Bishop, Robert Bittner, Scott Bixby, Helga E. Blackford, Gilbert Blakey, Jim Bland, Karry and Levi Bleam, Brad Bliek, Steven Blosser, Bob Boffa, Bill Boiani, Cortland Bolles, Bernie Bond, Tim Bond (Tim's Cards & Comics), Jim Bosecker, Charlie Botello, Holly Bott, Andy Bowen, Chivous Bradley, Todd Brammer, Bill Brandt, Scott Brandt, Josh Brann, Brian Brannen, Shawn Bratt, Jim Braun, Jeff Breitenfield, James Brennan, Michael Brennan, Bob Bresnahan, Wes Brewer, Scott Bridge, John Brigandi, Chidozie Bright, William Brislin, Corey Broeckling, Philip Bronikowski, Chuck Brooks, Richard Brown, Dan Bruner, David Bryant, Martin Buchanan, Brad Buchta, Ngoc Bui, Steve Burchett, Gerald Burkett, T.J. Burner, Virgil Burns, Benjamin Burrell, Gary Bursae, Justin Bush, Patrick Buss, Jason Butler, Jim Butler, Al Cady, California Card Co., Allen Capeloto, Card Capital USA, The Card Mart, Danny Cariseo, Eric Carlson, Jim Carr, Patrick Carroll, Dale Cartwright, Carves Cards,

Ray Castelluccio Sr., Hector Castro, Joe Cavallo, Sandy Chan, Dwight Chapin, Ray Cherry, Peter Childs, Mike Chmielewski, Tim Chrisp, Bigg Wayne Christian, Dick Cianciotto, Cincinnati Baseball Cards, David Clark, Derrick Clark, Justin Clark, Clay Clement, Richard Clement, Nathanael Clemons, Bill Cochran, Ronald Coleman, Collectibles Unlimited (John Alward and Deb Ingram), Collection de Sport AZ (Ronald Villaneuve), The Collectory, Andrew T. Collier, Dan Collins, Ryan Collins, Jason T. Commerford, Joe Conkle, Charles Cook, Aaron Cooper, Curt and Steven Cooter, Pedro Cortes, Lou Costanzo (Champion Sports), Adam Cota, Michael Cotter, Tom Cox, Paul and Ryan Crabb, Steven C. Crane, Taylor Crane, Chad Cripe, James Critzer, Darrin Crow, Paul Curran, Allen Custer;

Ryan Dahlstrom, Gene Dalager, Dave Dame, Brett Daniel, Jason Daniel, William J. Danley, Jeff Daub, Brian David, James Davis, Roy Dawes, James Day, Travis Deaton, Gus DeLaFuente, Dakota Derr, Eric Devine, Diamond Jack's Sportcards, Gilberto Diaz, John Diaz, David DiGrezio, Ken Dinerman (California Cruizers), Discount Dorothy, Richard Dolloff (Dolloff Coin Center), Greg Douglass, Jon Dresher, Bobby Drumm, Richard Duglin (Baseball Cards-n-More), Rob Dunkel, Robert Dunn Jr., Gerald Dupire, F.J. Durkin, Robert Durocher, Mike Durr, Bill Dyer, Alan John Dykshorn, Bill Eddy, Ron Edge, Ken Edick (Home Plate of Utah), Adrian Edler, Danny Eggleston, John Ehm, Michael L. Ellis, David Elstein, Kevin Erhart, Leigh Erickson, Dallas Erle, Dave Estes, Cameron Evans, Doak Ewing, Bryan Failing, Gail Fairbrother, John Fales, Richard Faletti, Juan Faunce, John Faustmann, Don Ferguson, Chris Ferreira, Robert Ferrell, Chuck Ferrero, Angela Festa, David Festberg, The Fieldhouse, Anthony Fillizola, Financial Dynamics Corporation, Jay Finglass, Ross Fishman, Dan Foley, Fremont Fong, Perry Fong, Bobby Ford, Forever Young Sports Cards, Vern Forthun, Robert Fortney, Adam Foust, Ryan Fout, Clinton Fox, Linda Fox, Tommy Francavilla, Harold France, Craig Frank, Walter Franklin, Frank's Comics, John Franzatti, Rick Fray, Gary and Marilyn Frazier, Edward Freeland Sr., Matthew Fullerton, Bill Furman, Richard Galasso, Robert Gallagher, Stephen Gamblin, Glenn Garber, David Garzy, Bob Gavin, R. Genova, Willie George, Georgetown Card Exchange, Matt Gerig, Don Germaise, Tom Gerstmann, Larry Gevert, Randy Giefer, Mario Giordano, Mike Giovannoni, Herbert Gladhill, Bob Glassman, Patrick Gobble, Dick Goddard, Greg Goldstein (Dragon's Den), Jeff Goldstein, Ron Gomez, Jacob Goodman, Chris Goodrum, David Goss, Stephen J. Grauf, Bryan Greaves, Kenneth Greer Jr., Glen Gregson, Matt Griffin, Cameron Grimard, Bo Grimes, George Griswold, David Grogan, Bruce Gross, Mike Gunderson;

Michael Hagoe, LaRue Haigleratt, Hall's Nostalgia, Michael Hamel, Josh Hammer, Hershell Hanks, Joel Hansen, Gregg Hara, Zac Hargis, Mike Harper, Robert Harris, R. Winston Harris, Bryan and Renee Hart, Danny Hatchell, Pat Haven, Jacob Hawkins, Michael Head, Lucas Heck, Kevin Heimbigner, Jeremy W. Hekter, Joel Hellman, Rick Helmle, Chris Hendriksen, Gary Henry, David Herdman, Jim Hester, Scott Heuer, Kevin P. Hickey, Jonathan Hill, Ryan Hiney, Mary Hoagland, Robert Hodges, Ron Hodges, Ben Hodnett, Jason Hoffmann, C.

Robert Hofheinz, Gary Holcomb, Peter Holzhauer, Stephen Honsinger, Daniel R. Horn II, Frank Horrath, Reed Houchens, Bill House, Scott Howell, Dennis Hughes, Greg Hunt, Thomas Hurley, Rob Huscher, James Hwang, Shawn Ilg, Tom Imboden, Vern Isenberg, Steve Isler, Zachary Jacobs, Dave Janelt, Paul Jastrzembski, Forrest Jay, Nathan Jeffries, Donn Jennings Cards, Adam Jeske, JJ's Budget Baseball Cards, Chuck Johnson, Jan Johnson, June Johnson, Scott Johnson, Jason Johnston, Stewart W. Jones, W.L. Jordan, Dave Jurgensmeier, John Just;

Bruce Kalin, Drew Kalina, Doug Kane, Sam Kane, Max Kanter, Wayne Kardel, Bijan Karkouki, Jay Kasper, Frank Katen, Jerry I. Katz, Neil Katz, Bill Kaval, Gregory Keil, Karl Kelch, Nick Kerimi, Kevin's Kards, Tom Kladovasilakis, Jay Klippstein, Jeremy Knochel, Ernie Kohlstruk, Koinz and Kards (Tom Zmuda), Peter Kolch, Keith Komorny, Joshua Kouma, Ray Kramer, Kevin Kraus, Stephen Krauss, Joe Krieger, Justin Krile, Neil Krohn, Greg Kroll, Jeff Kroll, Thomas Kunnecke, Danny Kyle, John Kyranos, Beau Lalonde, Howard Landrum, Adam Laneuster, Jason Langham, Mitzi Lasiter, Jason Lassic, Allan Latawiec, Adalbert Lavature, Dan Lavin, William Lawrence, Tom Layberger, Tim Leatherwood, Brian Lee, Morley Leeking, Tommy Leffler, Mike Lehman, Tricia Leifhott, Cynthia Lemieux, William Lenhart, Irv Lerner, Michael LeTellier, David Levy, Caleb and Ben Lewis, Frank Liao, Kevin Lichtsinn, Dan Lindamood, Wade Lindsey, Bernice Lines, Andrew Ling, Leon Lipkovich, Mel Litroff, Litteral's, David Lloyd, Louie Locke, David Logsdon, Mike London, Ralph Long, Damian Lopez, Paul Lopresti Jr., Brett Love, Allan Lowenberg, David Loy, LSG Promotions, Bob Luce, Alan Lynn, Dan Mabey, David Macaray, Jim Macie, Shane Maerdele, Magoo's Sports Cards, John Mainor, Patrick Manary, Paul Marchant, Randy Mardus, Mark Twain Card Shop, Steve Marlin, Angelo Martignetti, Ernest Martinez, Tom Mason, Tony Mastrianni, Bill Mastro, Eric Mathison, Harold Matlock, Ronnie May, Paul Mazeika, Jack McAnlis, Pat McAulay (River City Trading Cards), Dr. William McAvoy, Jeff McCoy, Dan McCrory, McDag Productions Inc., Michael McDonald (The Sports Page), Terry McFarland, Jim McGee, Branson H. McKay, Scott McKevitt, Tony McLaughlin, Bill McMahon, Mendal Mearkle, Ken Melanson, Jeff Melaragno, Stephanie Melton, William Mendel, Marc Mendoza, Eric Meredith, Beverly Merry, Denise Merry, Randy Messel, Jeff Messler, Blake Meyer (Lone Star Sportscards), John Meyer, Keith Meyer, Joe Michalowicz, Elie Michaud Jr., Barry Miller, Cary Miller, Dan Miller, David (Otis) Miller, George Miller, Wayne Miller, Mitchell's Baseball Cards, Perry Miyashita, Douglas Mo, Peter Molick, Greg Mollo, George Moore, Rick Moore, Bruce Morehouse, Robert Morelli, Roger Morey, Jason Morgan, Ben Morrison, Dale Moseley, Jordan Moskovitz, Jeremy L. Muncy, Richard A. Muncy, Sandra J. Muncy, Bill Munn, Brian Murphy, Mark Murphy, John Musacchio, Jude Muses, Billy Myers, Michael Myers;

Andrew de Naray, Stephen Nardiello, National Sportscard Exchange, Edward Nazzaro (The Collector), Jeffrey Neumann, New England Card Promotions, William D. Newhand, New York Card Company, Royal Norman, Andrew Nunnally,

Bud Obermeyer, Mark Obert, Bob O'Brien, Mike O'Brien, John O'Hara, Keith Olbermann, Michael Oldham, Ryan Ollila, Patrick O'Neill, Tim Oord, Donovan Orbon, John Osborne, Ron Oser, Ed Osheskie, Brian Oster, Shawn Otterson, Federico Palazuelos, L.G. Pangle II, Mervin Parker, John Pash, Clay Pasternack, Eric Pauly, John Pawleska, Gary Pecherkiewicz Jr., Michael Perrotta, Doug and Trevor Perry, Russ Perry, Brian Peterson, Jon Peterson, Tom Pfirrmann, Lam Pham, Roger Pierce, Daniel Piscopo, Brian Pittman, David Pollack, Seth Poppel, Chris Port, Don Prestia, Eric Porteous, Kathleen Porter, Steve Pozgay, Andrew Prescott, J.P. Pritchard, Rich Pugh, Chris Quigley, Justin Quintana, Marco Quintana, Michael I. Raff, Bob Ragonese, Brighton Rain, Carol Ramstedt, Richard H. Ranck, Octavio Ranzola, Rick Rapa and Barry Sanders (Atlanta Sports Cards), Joe Raque, Jamie Ratliff, R.W. Ray, Brian Reed, Nancy Reed, Phil Regli, Paul Reichl, Tom Reid, John Revell, Barry Rickert, Stephen J. Riggins, Dave Ring, Greg Ritzer, Louis Rivers, Jeremy Robbins, Chad Roberts, Nathan Roberts, Dee Robinson, Matt Robinson, Bill Rodman, Doug Rodman, Michael Roedema, Fred Romanski, Steven J. Rondorf, Jon Rosen, Michael H. Rosen, Jerry Rosensewaike, Adam Rothans, Alan Rubenstein, Joseph A. Rushlaw, George Rusnak, Rust Inc.;

Terry Sack, Paul Sadows, Joe Sak, Jennifer Salems, Andrew Sanchez, Jon Sands, Charles Santee Jr., Merrill Santy, Reggie Sapida, Larry Saucier, Eric Saulnier, Kevin Savage, Gary Sawatzki, Joe Schaub, Rudy Scheithauer, Vince Schielack, A.J. Schmidt, Scott Schoeneberger, Aron Schor, Jack Schultz, Bruce Schwartz, Brian Schweitzer, Charlie Seaver, Michael N. Seikel, John Selsam, Rob Serfass, Jeff Sharp, Mary A. Shea, Paul Sheehan, Richard Sheldon, Travis Sheldon, Michael Shepherd, Craig Sherman, Nicholas Shiftan, Marcia Shipwash, Bob Sipos, Eugene Siuda, Randy Small, Art Smith, Eric Smith, Ray Smith, Fred M. Snyder, David Solka, Harry Sommer, Jim Sorensen, Paul Sorensen, Darrel Spalding, C. Specht, Jim Spickelmire, Gene Spielman, Sports Unlimited Card Company, Milton Spurlock, Adam Squiller, R. Dauer Stackpole, Charles Stahr, Dewayne Stanford, Joe Staviscak, Bob Stern, Ben Stodghill, Kelly Stohr, Robert Stone, Robert J. Stone, Sam Stone, Tim Strandberg (East Texas Sports Cards), Edward Strauss, Frankie Strigare, Richard Strobino, Eric Stubbs, Alan Sugahara, Scott Sullivan, Superior Sport Card, Jamie Sutherell, Gerry Swain, Richard Swales, Dusty Swenson, Roger Syferd, Josh Taft, David Talton, Maury Tasem, Ian Taylor, Norma Taylor, Lyle Telfer, Daniel Temmesfeld, Sam Tessier, John Thayer, Jason Thomas, Dave Thompson, Gerry Thompson, Jim D. Thompson, Carl Thrower, Jim Thurtell, Al Tom, Patrick Tomberlin, Bud Tompkins (Minnesota Connection), Lenny Tonozzi, Gregory Torres, Doug Traverso, Harold Trieb, Dr. Ralph Triplette, Tom Tsaldaris, Eric Unplanb, G.M. Vernidis Jr., Larry Paul Vonckx, Thomas Wagner, Brian Wagoner, Geoff Waidelich, G.E. Walker, Bob Wallace, Ed Wallar, Chris Walley, Gary Walter, John and Lori Ward, Matt Ward, Michael Ward, Mary Wassil, Scott Weberpal, Jack Welch, Richard West, David Westman, Bill White, Dave White, John White, Dan Whitehouse, Liz Wiechern,

Wild Pitch, Judd Wildman, Brandon W. Wilkins, John Willenborg, Ed Willett, Brandon Williams, Jeff Williams, Mark Willis, Brandon Willoughby, Michael Wilson, James Winner, Opry Winston, David Withers, Gary Wittman, John H. Wolf Jr., Jay Wolt (Cavalcade of Sports), John Wood, William Wood, Pete Wooten, Mike Worley, Jeff Wright, Frank Wunder, Steve Wymer, Lotay Yang, Yesterday's Heroes, Charles Yezak Jr., Joey Young, Wes Young, Robert Zanze, Mike Zinniel and Gary Zold.

Every year we make active solicitations for expert input. We are particularly appreciative of help (however extensive or cursory) provided for this volume. We receive many inquiries, comments and questions regarding material within this book. In fact, each and every one is read and digested. Time constraints, however, prevent us from personally replying. But keep sharing your knowledge. Your letters and input are part of the "big picture" of hobby information we can pass along to readers in our books and magazines. Even though we cannot respond to each letter, you are making significant contributions to the hobby through your interest and comments.

In the years since this guide debuted, Beckett Publications has grown beyond any rational expectation. A great many talented and hard working individuals have been instrumental in this growth and success. Our whole team is to be congratulated for what we together have accomplished. Our Beckett Publications team is led by Associate Publisher Claire Backus, Vice Presidents Joe Galindo and Fred Reed, and Director of Marketing Jeff Amano. They are ably assisted by Fernando Albieri, Theresa Anderson, Gena Andrews, Jeff Anthony, Patricia Bales, Airey Baringer II (special thanks to Airey for his late-night typesetting excellence), Barbara Barry, Nancy Bassi, Therese Bellar, Louise Bird, Wendy Bird, Cathryn Black, Terry Bloom, Lisa Borden, Amy Brougher, Chris Calandro, Mary Campana, Renata Campos, Sammy Cantrell, Susan Catka, Deana Chapman, Theo Chen, Lynne Chinn, Catherine Colbert, Tommy Collins, Belinda Cross, Billy Culbert, Randy Cummings, Patrick Cunningham, Gail Docekal, Andrew Drago, Louise Ebaugh, Mila Egusquiza, Susan Elliott, Daniel Evans, Bruce Felps, Jorge Field, Sara Field, Jean Paul Figari, Jeany Finch, Robson Fonseca, Kim Ford, Eric Ford, Gayle Gasperin, Anita Gonzalez, Mary Gonzalez-Davis, Jeff Greer, Mary Gregory, Julie Grove, Marcio Guimaraes, Karen Hall, Carmen Hand, Lori Harmeyer, Beth Harwell, Jenny Harwell, Mark Harwell, Pepper Hastings, Joanna Hayden, Mike Hersh, Barbara Hinkle, Tracy Hinton, Dan Hitt, Charlie Hodges, Heather Holland, E.J. Hradek, Rex Hudson, Rhonda Hughes, Mary Huston, Don James, Marion Jarrell, Sara Jenks, Julia Jernigan, Wendy Jewell, Jay Johnson, Michael Johnson Jr., Matt Keifer, Fran Keng, Monte King, Debbie Kingsbury, Amy Kirk, Rudy Klancnik, Rich Klein, Frances Knight, Jane Layton, Scott Layton, Tom Liggitt, Lori Lindsey, Mark Manning, Louis Marroquin, Kaki Matheson, Teri McGahey, Kirk McKinney, Omar Mediano, Edras Mendez, Stephen Moore, Glen Morante, Elizabeth Morris, Daniel Moscoso, Daniel Moscoso Jr., Mike Moss, Randy Mosty, Allan Muir, Hugh Murphy, Wendy

Neumann, Allen Neumann, LaQuita Norton, Robert Norton, Lisa O'Neill, Rich Olivieri, Abraham Pacheco, Guillermo Pacheco, Mike Payne, Suzee Payton, Ronda Pearson, Karen Penhollow, Julie Polomis, Reed Poole, Karen Quinn, Linda Rainwater, Roberto Ramirez, Nikki Renshaw, Patrick Richard, Jamile Romero, Grant Sandground, Gary Santaniello, Gabriel Santos, Maggie Seward, Carol Slawson, Steve Slawson, Dave Sliepka, Judi Smalling, Lisa Spaight, Mark Stokes, Cindy Struble, Peter Tepp, Jim Tereschuk, Christiann Thomas, Kimberly Thompson, Jana Threatt, Brett Tulloss, Valerie Voigt, Kim Whitesell, Mark Whitesell, Steve Wilson, Carol Ann Wurster, Robert Yearby. The whole Beckett Publications team has my thanks for jobs well done. Thank you, everyone.

I also thank my family, especially my wife, Patti, and daughters, Christina, Rebecca, and Melissa, for putting up with me again.

Errata

There are thousands of names, close to a half million prices, and untold other words in this book. There are going to be a few typographical errors, a few misspellings, and possibly, a number or two out of place. If you catch a blooper, drop me a note directly or in care of the publisher, and we will fix it up in the next year's edition.

Introduction

Welcome to the exciting world of baseball card collecting, America's fastest-growing avocation. You have made a good choice in buying this book, since it will open up to you the entire panorama of this field in the simplest, most concise way. It is estimated that a third of a million different baseball cards have been issued during the past century. And the number of total cards put out by all manufacturers last year has been estimated at several billion, with an initial retail value of more than $500 million. Sales of older cards by dealers may account for a like amount. With all that cardboard available in the marketplace, it should be no surprise that several million sports fans like you collect baseball cards today, and that number is growing by hundreds of thousands each year.

The growth of *Beckett Baseball Card Monthly* is another indication of this rising crescendo of popularity for baseball cards. Founded in 1984 by Dr. James Beckett, the author of this Price Guide, *Beckett Baseball Card Monthly* has grown to the pinnacle of the baseball card hobby with more than a million readers anxiously awaiting each enjoyable issue.

So collecting baseball cards — while still pursued as a hobby with youthful exuberance by kids in the neighborhood — has also taken on the trappings of an industry, with thousands of full- and part-time card dealers, as well as vendors of supplies, clubs and conventions. In fact, each year since 1980 thousands of hobbyists have assembled for a National Sports Collectors Convention, at which hundreds of dealers have displayed their wares, seminars have been conducted, autographs penned by sports notables, and millions of cards changed hands. These colossal affairs have been staged in Los Angeles, Detroit, St. Louis, Chicago, New York, Anaheim, Arlington (TX), San Francisco, Atlantic City, Chicago, Arlington (TX), Anaheim, and this year in Atlanta. So baseball card collecting really is national in scope!

This increasing interest has been reflected in card values. As more collectors compete for available supplies, card prices (especially for premium-grade cards) rise. A national publication indicated a "very strong advance" in baseball card prices during the past decade, and a quick perusal of prices in this book compared to the figures in earlier editions of this Price Guide will quickly confirm this. Which brings us back around again to the book you have in your hands. It is the best annual guide available to this exciting world of baseball cards. Read it and use it. May your enjoyment and your card collection increase in the coming months and years.

How to Collect

Each collection is personal and reflects the individuality of its owner. There are no set rules on how to collect cards. Since card collecting is a hobby or leisure pastime, what you collect, how much you collect, and how much time and money you spend collecting are entirely up to you. The funds you have available for collecting and your own personal taste should determine how you collect. Information and ideas presented here are intended to help you get the most enjoyment from this hobby.

It is impossible to collect every card ever produced. Therefore, beginners as well as intermediate and advanced collectors usually specialize in some way. One of the reasons this hobby is popular is that individual collectors can define and tailor their collecting methods to match their own tastes. To give you some ideas of the various approaches to collecting, we will list some of the more popular areas of specialization.

Many collectors select complete sets from particular years. For example, they may concentrate on assembling complete sets from all the years since their birth or since they became avid sports fans. They may try to collect a card for every player during that specified period of time. Many others wish to acquire only certain players. Usually such players are the superstars of the sport, but occasionally collectors will specialize in all the cards of players who attended a particular college or came from a certain town. Some collectors are only interested in the first cards or Rookie Cards of certain players. A handy guide for collectors interested in pursuing the hobby this way is the *Sport Americana Alphabetical Checklist No. 5.*

Another fun way to collect cards is by team. Most fans have a favorite team, and it is natural for that loyalty to be translated into a desire for cards of the players on that favorite team. For most of the recent years, team sets (all the cards from a given team for that year) are readily available at a reasonable price. The Sport Americana Team Baseball Card Checklist will open up this field to the collector.

Obtaining Cards

Several avenues are open to card collectors. Cards can be purchased in the traditional way at the local candy, grocery, or drug stores, with the bubble gum or other products included. For many years it has been possible to purchase complete sets of baseball cards through mail order advertisers found in traditional sports media publications, such as *The Sporting News, Baseball Digest, Street & Smith* yearbooks, and others. These sets are also advertised in the card collecting periodicals. Many collectors will begin by subscribing to at least one of the hobby periodicals, all with good up-to-date information. In fact, subscription offers can be found in the advertising section of this book. In addition, a great variety of cards (typically from all eras and all sports) can be obtained at the growing number of hobby retail stores dedicated to sports cards and memorabilia around the country.

Most serious card collectors obtain old (and new) cards from one or more of several main sources: (1) trading or buying from other collectors or dealers; (2) responding to sale or auction ads in the hobby publications; (3) buying at a local hobby store; and/or (4) attending sports collectibles shows or conventions. We advise that you try all four methods since each has its own distinct advantages: (1) trading is a great way to make new friends; (2) hobby periodicals help you keep up with what's going on in the hobby (including when and where the conventions are happening); (3) stores provide the opportunity for considering (any day of the week) a great diversity of material in a relaxed sports-oriented atmosphere that most fans love; and (4) shows provide enjoyment and the opportunity to view millions of collectibles under one roof, in addition to meeting some of the hundreds or even thousands of other collectors with similar interests who also attend the shows.

Preserving Your Cards

Cards are fragile. They must be handled properly in order to retain their value. Careless handling can easily result in creased or bent cards. It is, however, not recommended that tweezers or tongs be used to pick up your cards since such utensils might mar or indent card surfaces and thus reduce those cards' conditions and values. In general, your cards should be handled directly as little as possible. This is sometimes easier to say than to do. Although there are still many who use custom boxes, storage trays, or even shoe boxes, plastic sheets are the preferred method of storing cards. A collection stored in plastic pages in a three-ring album allows you to view your collection at any time without the need to touch the card itself. Cards can also be kept in single holders (of various types and thickness) designed for the enjoyment of each card individually. For a large collection, some collectors may use a combination of the above methods.

When purchasing plastic sheets for your cards, be sure that you find the pocket size that fits the cards snugly. Don't put your 1951 Bowmans in a sheet designed to fit 1981 Topps. Most hobby and collectibles shops and virtually all collectors' conventions will have these plastic pages available in quantity for the various sizes offered or you can purchase them directly from the advertisers in this book. Also remember that pocket size isn't the only factor to consider when looking for plastic sheets. Some collectors concerned with long-term storage of their cards in plastic sheets are cautious to avoid sheets containing PVC and request non-PVC sheets from their dealer.

Damp, sunny and/or hot conditions — no, this is not a weather forecast — are three elements to avoid in extremes if you are interested in preserving your collection. Too much (or too little) humidity can cause gradual deterioration of a card. Direct, bright sun (or fluorescent light) over time will bleach out the color of a card. Extreme heat accelerates the decomposition of the card. On the other hand, many cards have lasted more than 50 years without much scientific intervention. So be cautious, even if the above factors typically present a problem only when present in the extreme. It never hurts to be prudent.

Collecting vs. Investing

Collecting individual players and collecting complete sets are both popular vehicles for investment and speculation. Most investors and speculators stock up on complete sets or on quantities of players they think have good investment potential. There is obviously no guarantee in this book, or anywhere else for that matter, that cards will outperform the stock market or other investment alternatives in the future. After all, baseball cards do not pay quarterly dividends and cards cannot be sold at their "current values" as easily as stocks or bonds. Nevertheless, investors have noticed a favorable long-term trend in the past performance of baseball and other sports collectibles, and certain cards and sets have outperformed just about any other investment in some years. Many hobbyists maintain that the best investment is and always will be the building of a collection, which traditionally has held up better than outright speculation.

Some of the obvious questions are: Which cards? When to buy? When to sell? The best investment you can make is in your own education. The more you know about your collection and the hobby, the more informed the decisions you will be able to make. We're not selling investment tips. We're selling information about the current value of baseball cards. It's up to you to use that information to your best advantage.

Nomenclature

Each hobby has its own language to describe its area of interest. The nomenclature traditionally used for trading cards is derived from the *American Card Catalog*, published in 1960 by Nostalgia Press. That catalog, written by Jefferson Burdick (who is called the "Father of Card Collecting" for his pioneering work), uses letter and number designations for each separate set of cards. The letter used in the ACC designation refers to the generic type of card. While both sport and non-sport issues are classified in the ACC, we shall confine ourselves to the sport issues. The following list defines the letters and their meanings as used by the *American Card Catalog.*

(none) or N - 19th Century U.S. Tobacco
B - Blankets
D - Bakery Inserts Including Bread
E - Early Candy and Gum
F - Food Inserts
H - Advertising
M - Periodicals
PC - Postcards
R - Candy and Gum Cards 1930 to Present
T - 20th Century U.S. Tobacco
UO - Gas and Oil Inserts
V - Canadian Candy
W - Exhibits, Strip Cards, Team Issues

Following the letter prefix and an optional hyphen are one-, two-, or three-digit numbers, 1-999. These typically represent the company or entity issuing the cards. In several cases, the *ACC* number is extended by an additional hyphen and another one- or two-digit numerical suffix. For example, the 1957 Topps regular series baseball card issue carries an *ACC* designation of R414-11. The "R" indicates a Candy or Gum card produced since 1930. The "414" is the ACC designation for Topps Chewing Gum baseball card issues, and the "11" is the *ACC* designation for the 1957 regular issue (Topps' eleventh baseball set).

Like other traditional methods of identification, this system provides order to the process of cataloging cards; however, most serious collectors learn the *ACC* designation of the popular sets by repetition and familiarity, rather than by attempting to "figure out" what they might or should be.

From 1948 forward, collectors and dealers commonly refer to all sets by their year, maker, type of issue, and any other distinguishing characteristic. For example, such a characteristic could be an unusual issue or one of several regular issues put out by a specific maker in a single year. Regional issues are usually referred to by year, maker, and sometimes by title or theme of the set.

Glossary/Legend

Our glossary defines terms frequently used in the card collecting hobby. Many of these terms are also common to other types of sports memorabilia collecting. Some terms may have several meanings depending on use.

AAS - Action All Stars, a postcard-size set issued by Donruss during the mid-1980s.

ACC - Acronym for American Card Catalog.

ALP - Alphabetical checklist.

ANN - Announcer.

AS - All-Star card. A card portraying an All- Star Player of the previous year that says "All-Star" on its face.

ATG - All-Time Great card.

ATL - All-Time Leaders card.

AU - With autograph.

BC - Bonus Card (Used by Donruss for their team MVP bonus sets from 1988 through 1991).

BL - Blue letters.

BLANKET - A felt square (normally 5 to 6 inches, portraying a baseball player.

BOX - Card issued on a box or a card depicting a Boxer.

BRICK - A group of 50 or more cards having common characteristics that is intended to be bought, sold or traded as a unit.

CABINETS - Popular and highly valuable photographs on thick card stock produced in the 19th and early 20th century.

CHECKLIST - A list of the cards contained in a particular set. The list is always in numerical order if the cards are numbered. Some unnumbered sets are artificially numbered in alphabetical order, by team and alphabetically within the team, or by uniform number for convenience.

CL - Checklist card. A card that lists in order the cards and players in the set or series. Older checklist cards in Mint condition that have not been marked are very desirable and command premiums.

CO - Abbreviation for Coach.

COIN - A small disc of metal or plastic portraying a player in its center.

COLLECTOR - A person who engages in the hobby of collecting cards primarily for his own enjoyment, with any profit motive being secondary.

COLLECTOR ISSUE - A set produced for the sake of the card itself with no product or service sponsor. It derives its name from the fact that most of these sets are produced for sale directly to the hobby market.

COM - Card issued by the Post Cereal Company through their mail-in offer.

COMBINATION CARD - A single card depicting two or more players (but not a team card).

COMM - Commissioner.

COMMON CARD - The typical card of any set; it has no premium value accruing from subject matter, numerical scarcity, popular demand, or anomaly.

CONVENTION - A large weekend gathering of dealers and collectors at a single location for the purpose of buying, selling, and sometimes trading sports memorabilia items. Conventions are open to the public and sometimes feature autograph guests, door prizes, contests, seminars, etc. They are frequently referred to simply as "shows."

CONVENTION ISSUE - A set produced in conjunction with a sports collectibles convention to commemorate or promote the show.

COR - Corrected card.

COUPON - See Tab.

CREASE - A wrinkle on the card, usually caused by bending the card. Creases are a common (and serious) defect resulting from careless handling.

CY - Cy Young Award.

DC - Draft Choice.

DEALER - A person who engages in buying, selling, and trading sports collectibles or supplies. A dealer may also be a collector, but as a dealer, his main goal is to earn a profit.

DIE-CUT - A card with part of its stock partially cut, allowing one or more parts to be folded or removed. After removal or appropriate folding, the remaining part of the card can frequently be made to stand up.

DISC - A circular-shaped card.

DISPLAY CARD - A sheet, usually containing three to nine cards, that is printed and used by the manufacturer to advertise and/or display the packages containing his products and cards. The backs of display cards are blank or contain advertisements.

DK - Diamond King (artwork produced by Perez-Steele for Donruss).

DP - Double Print (a card that was printed in double the quantity compared to the other cards in the same series).

DT - Dream Team (produced by Score in 1990, 1991 and 1992).

EP - Elite Performer (1991 Fleer Ultra).

ERA - Earned Run Average.

ERR - Error card. A card with erroneous information, spelling, or depiction on either side of the card. Most errors are not corrected by the producing card company.

EXHIBIT - The generic name given to thick-stock, postcard-size cards with single color obverse pictures. The name is derived from the Exhibit Supply Co. of Chicago, the principal manufacturer of this type of card. These are also known as Arcade cards since they were found in many arcades.

FDP - First Draft Pick.

FOIL - Foil embossed stamp on card.

FRAN - The Franchise card (1991 Score).

FS - Father/son card.

FULL SHEET - A complete sheet of cards that has not been cut up into individual cards by the manufacturer. Also called an uncut sheet.

GL - Green letters.

HIGH NUMBER - The cards in the last series of numbers in a year in which such higher-numbered cards were printed or distributed in significantly lesser amounts than the lower-numbered cards. The high-number designation refers to a scarcity of the high-numbered cards. Not all years have high numbers in terms of this definition.

HL - Highlight card.

HOF - Hall of Fame, or a card that portrays a Hall of Famer (HOFer).

HOR - Horizontal pose on card as opposed to the standard vertical orientation found on most cards.

IA - In Action card.

IF - Infielder.

INSERT - A card of a different type or any other sports collectible (typically a poster or sticker) contained and sold in the same package along with a card or cards of a major set. An insert card is either unnumbered or not numbered in the same sequence as the major set. Sometimes the inserts are randomly distributed and are not found in every pack.

ISSUE - Synonymous with set, but usually used in conjunction with a manufacturer, e.g., a Topps issue.

K - Strikeout.

KM - K-Man (1991 Score).

KP - Kid Picture (a subset issued in the Topps Baseball sets of 1972 and 1973).

LAYERING - The separation or peeling of one or more layers of the card stock, usually at the corner of the card.

LEGITIMATE ISSUE - A set produced to promote or boost sales of a product or service, e.g., bubble gum, cereal, cigarettes, etc. Most collector issues are not legitimate issues in this sense.

LHP - Lefthanded pitcher.

LID - A circular-shaped card (possibly with tab) that forms the top of the container for the product being promoted.

LL - League leaders card or large letters on card.

MAJOR SET - A set produced by a national manufacturer of cards containing a large number of cards. Usually 100 or more different cards comprise a major set.

MB - Master Blaster (1991 Score).

MEM - Memorial card. For example, the 1990 Donruss and Topps Bart Giamatti cards.

MG - Manager.

MINI - A small card; for example, a 1975 Topps card of identical design but smaller dimensions than the regular Topps issue of 1975.

ML - Major League.

MVP - Most Valuable Player.

NAU - No autograph on card.

NH - No-Hitter card.

NNOF - No Name on Front (1949 Bowman).

NOF - Name on Front (1949 Bowman).

NON-SPORT CARD - A card from a set whose major theme is a subject other than a sports subject. A card of a sports figure or event that is part of a non-sport set is still a non-sport card, e.g., while the "Look 'N' See" non-sport card set contains a card of Babe Ruth, a sports figure, that card is a non-sport card.

NOTCHING - The grooving of the card, usually caused by fingernails, rubber bands, or bumping card edges against other objects.

OBVERSE - The front, face, or pictured side of the card.

OF - Outfield or Outfielder.

OLY - Olympics (see the 1985 Topps and 1988 Topps Traded sets; the members of the U.S. Olympic Baseball teams were featured subsets in both of these sets).

ORG - Organist.

P - Pitcher or Pitching pose.

P1 - First Printing.

P2 - Second Printing.

P3 - Third Printing.

PANEL - An extended card that is composed of two or more individual cards. Often the panel forms the back part of the container for the product being promoted, e.g., a Hostess panel, a Bazooka panel, an Esskay Meat panel.

PCL - Pacific Coast League.

PLASTIC SHEET - A clear, plastic page that is punched for insertion into a binder (with standard three-ring spacing) containing pockets for displaying cards. Many different styles of sheets exist with pockets of varying sizes to hold the many differing card formats. Also called a display sheet or storage sheet.

PREMIUM - A card, sometimes on photographic stock, that is purchased or obtained in conjunction with, or redemption for, another card or product. The premium is not packaged in the same unit as the primary item.

PUZZLE CARD - A card whose back contains a part of a picture which, when joined correctly with other puzzle cards, forms the completed picture.

PUZZLE PIECE - A die-cut piece designed to interlock with similar pieces.

PVC - Polyvinyl Chloride, a substance used to make many of the popular card display protective sheets. Non-PVC sheets are considered preferable for long-term storage of cards.

RARE - A card or series of cards of very limited availability. Unfortunately, "rare" is a subjective term frequently used indiscriminately to hype value. "Rare" cards are harder to obtain than "scarce" cards.

RB - Record Breaker card.

REGIONAL - A card or set of cards issued and distributed only in a limited geographical area of the country.

REVERSE - The back or narrative side of the card.

RHP - Righthanded pitcher.

RIF - Rifleman (1991 Score).

ROY - Rookie of the Year.

RP - Relief pitcher.

RR - Rated Rookies (a subset featured in Donruss sets).

SA - Super Action card.

SASE - Self-Addressed, Stamped Envelope.

SB - Stolen Bases.

SCARCE - A card or series of cards of limited availability. This subjective term is sometimes used indiscriminately to hype value. "Scarce" cards are not as difficult to obtain as "rare" cards.

SCR - Script name on back (1949 Bowman).

SEMI-HIGH - A card from the next to last series of a sequentially issued set. It has more value than an average card and generally less value than a high number. A card is not called a semi-high unless the next to last series in which it exists has an additional premium attached to it.

SERIES - The entire set of cards issued by a particular producer in a particular year, e.g., the 1971 Topps series. Also, within a particular set, series can refer to a group of (consecutively numbered) cards printed at the same time, e.g., the first series of the 1957 Topps issue (#1-#88).

SET - One each of the entire run of cards of the same type produced by a particular manufacturer during a single year. In other words, if you have a complete set of 1976 Topps then you have every card from #1 up to and including #660, i.e., all of the different cards that were produced.

SKIP-NUMBERED - A set that has many unissued card numbers between the lowest number in the set and the highest number in the set, e.g., the 1948 Leaf baseball set contains 98 cards skip-numbered from number 1 to number 168. A major set in which a few numbers were not printed is not considered to be skip-numbered.

SLUG - Silver Slugger card (1991 Bowman).

SP - Single or Short Print (a card which was printed in lesser quantity compared to the other cards in the same series; see also DP and TP).

SPECIAL CARD - A card that portrays something other than a single player or team, for example, a card that portrays the previous year's statistical leaders or the results from the previous year's World Series.

SS - Shortstop.

STAMP - Adhesive-backed papers depicting a player. The stamp may be individual or in a sheet of many stamps. Moisture must be applied to the adhesive in order for the stamp to be attached to another surface.

STAR CARD - A card that portrays a player of some repute, usually determined by his ability; however, sometimes referring to sheer popularity.

STICKER - A card with a removable layer that can be affixed to (stuck onto) another surface.

STOCK - The cardboard or paper on which the card is printed.

STRIP CARDS - A sheet or strip of cards, particularly popular in the 1920s and 1930s, with the individual cards usually separated by broken or dotted lines.

SUPERSTAR CARD - A card that portrays a superstar, e.g., a Hall of Famer or player with strong Hall of Fame potential.

SV - Super Veteran (see 1982 Topps).

TAB - A card portion set off from the rest of the card, usually with perforations, that may be removed without damaging the central character or event depicted by the card.

TBC - Turn Back the Clock cards.

TC - Team Checklist card.

TEAM CARD - A card that depicts an entire team.

TEST SET - A set, usually containing a small number of cards, issued by a national card producer and distributed in a limited section or sections of the country. Presumably, the purpose of a test set is to test market appeal for a particular type of card.

TL - Team Leader card.

TP - Triple Print (a card that was printed in triple the quantity compared to the other cards in the same series).

TRIMMED - A card cut down from its original size. Trimmed cards are undesirable to most collectors.

UER - Uncorrected Error.

UMP - Umpire.

USA - Team USA cards (see the 1991 Topps Traded set).

VAR - Variation card. One of two or more cards from the same series with the same number (or player with identical pose if the series is unnumbered) differing from one another by some aspect, the different feature stemming from the printing or stock of the card. This can be caused when the manufacturer of the cards notices an error in one or more of the cards, makes the changes, and then resumes the print run. In this case there will be two versions or variations of the same card. Sometimes one of the variations is relatively scarce.

VERT - Vertical pose on card.

WAS - Washington National League (1974 Topps).

WS - World Series card.

YL - Yellow Letters (1958 Topps).

YT - Yellow Team (1958 Topps).

History of Baseball Cards

Today's version of the baseball card, with its colorful and sometimes high tech fronts and backs, is a far cry from its earliest predecessors. The issue remains cloudy as to which was the very first baseball card ever produced, but the institution of baseball cards dates from the latter half of the 19th century, more than 100 years ago. Early issues, generally printed on heavy cardboard, were of poor quality, with photographs, drawings, and printing far short of today's standards.

Goodwin & Co., of New York, makers of Gypsy Queen, Old Judge, and other cigarette brands, is considered by many to be the first issuer of baseball and other sports cards. Their issues, predominantly in the 1 1/2" by 2 1/2" size, generally consisted of photographs of baseball players, boxers, wrestlers, and other subjects mounted on stiff cardboard. More than 2,000 different photos of baseball players alone have been identified. These "Old Judges," a collective name commonly used for the Goodwin & Co. cards, were issued from 1886 to 1890 and are treasured parts of many collections today.

Among the other cigarette companies which issued baseball cards that still attract attention today are Allen & Ginter, D. Buchner & Co. (Gold Coin Chewing Tobacco), and P.H. Mayo & Brother. Cards from the first two companies bore colored line drawings, while the Mayos are sepia photographs on black cardboard. In addition to the small-size cards from this era, several tobacco companies issued cabinet-size baseball cards. These "cabinets" were considerably larger than the small cards, usually about 4 1/4" by 6 1/2", and were printed on heavy stock. Goodwin & Co.'s Old Judge cabinets and the National Tobacco Works' "Newsboy" baseball photos are two that remain popular today.

By 1895 the American Tobacco Company began to dominate its competition. They discontinued baseball card inserts in their cigarette packages (actually slide boxes in those days). The lack of competition in the cigarette market had made these inserts unnecessary. This marked the end of the first era of baseball cards. At the dawn of the 20th century, few baseball cards were being issued. But once again it was the cigarette companies — particularly, the American Tobacco Company — followed to a lesser extent by the candy and gum makers that revived the practice of including baseball cards with their products. The bulk of these cards, identified in the American Card Catalog (designated hereafter as ACC) as T or E cards for 20th century "Tobacco" or "Early Candy and Gum" issues respectively, were released from 1909 to 1915.

This romantic and popular era of baseball card collecting produced many desirable items. The most outstanding is the fabled T-206 Honus Wagner card. Other perennial favorites among collectors are the T-206 Eddie Plank card, and the T-206 Magee error card. The former was once the second most valuable card and only recently relinquished that position to a more distinctive and aesthetically pleasing Napoleon Lajoie card from the 1933/34 Goudey Gum series. The latter misspells the player's name as "Magie," the most famous and valuable blooper card.

The ingenuity and distinctiveness of this era has yet to be surpassed. Highlights include the T-202 Hassan triple-folders, one of the best looking and the most distinctive cards ever issued; the durable T-201 Mecca double-folders, one of the first sets with players' records on the reverse; the T-3 Turkey Reds, the hobby's most popular cabinet card; the E-145 Cracker Jacks, the only major set containing Federal League player cards; and the T-204 Ramlys, with their distinctive black-and-white oval photos and ornate gold borders. These are but a few of the varieties issued during this period.

While the American Tobacco Company dominated the field, several other tobacco companies, as well as clothing manufacturers, newspapers and periodicals, game makers, and companies whose identities remain anonymous, also issued cards during this period. In fact, the Collins-McCarthy Candy Company, makers of Zeenuts Pacific Coast League baseball cards, issued cards yearly from 1911 to 1938. Their record for continuous annual card production has been exceeded only by the Topps Chewing Gum Company. The era of the tobacco card issues closed with the onset of World War I, with the exception of the Red Man chewing tobacco sets produced from 1952 to 1955.

The next flurry of card issues broke out in the roaring and prosperous 1920s, the era of the E card. The caramel companies (National Caramel, American Caramel, York Caramel) were the leading distributors of these E cards. In addition, the strip card, a continous strip with several cards divided by dotted lines or other sectioning features, flourished during this time. While the E cards and the strip cards generally are considered less imaginative than the T cards or the recent candy and gum issues, they still are sought after by many advanced collectors.

Another significant event of the 1920s was the introduction of the arcade card. Taking its designation from its issuer, the Exhibit Supply Company of Chicago, it is usually known as the "Exhibit" card. Once a trademark of the penny arcades, amusement parks and county fairs across the country, Exhibit machines dispensed nearly postcard-size photos on thick stock for one penny. These picture cards bore likenesses of a favorite cowboy, actor, actress or baseball player. Exhibit Supply and its associated companies produced baseball cards during a longer time span, although discontinuous, than any other manufacturer. Its first cards appeared in 1921, while its last issue was in 1966. In 1979, the Exhibit Supply Company was bought and somewhat revived by a collector/dealer who has since reprinted Exhibit photos of the past.

If the T card period, from 1909 to 1915, can be said to be the "Golden Age" of baseball card collecting, then perhaps the "Silver Age" commenced with the introduction of the Big League Gum series of 239 cards in 1933 (a 240th card was added in 1934). These are the forerunners of today's baseball gum cards, and the Goudey Gum Company of Boston is responsible for their success. This era spanned the period from the Depression days of 1933 to America's formal involvement in World War II in 1941.

Goudey's attractive designs, with full color line drawings on thick card stock, influenced greatly other cards being issued at that time. As a result, the most attractive and popular cards in collecting history were produced in this "Silver Age." The 1933 Goudey Big League Gum series also owes its popularity to the more than 40 Hall of Fame players in the set. These include four cards of Babe Ruth and two of Lou Gehrig. Goudey's reign continued in 1934 when it issued a 96-card set in color, together with the single remaining card from the 1933 series, #106, the Napoleon Lajoie card.

In addition to Goudey, several other bubblegum manufacturers issued baseball cards during this era. DeLong Gum Company issued an extremely attractive set in 1933. National Chicle Company's 192-card "Batter-Up" series of 1934-1936 became the largest die-cut set in card history. In addition, that company offered the popular "Diamond Stars" series during the same period. Other popular sets included the "Tattoo Orbit" set of 60 color cards issued in 1933 and Gum Products' 75-card "Double Play" set, featuring sepia depictions of two players per card.

In 1939 Gum Inc., which later became Bowman Gum, replaced Goudey Gum as the leading baseball card producer. In 1939 and the following year, it issued two important sets of black-and-white cards. In 1939 its "Play Ball America" set consisted of 162 cards. The larger, 240-card "Play Ball" set of 1940 still is considered by many to be the most attractive black-and-white cards ever produced. That firm introduced its only color set in 1941, consisting of 72 cards entitled "Play Ball Sports Hall of Fame." Many of these were colored repeats of poses from the black-and-white 1940 series.

In addition to regular gum cards, many manufacturers distributed premium issues during the 1930s. These premiums were printed on paper or photographic stock, rather than card stock. They were much larger than the regular cards and were sold for a penny across the counter with gum (which was packaged separately from the premium). They were often redeemed at the store or through the mail in exchange for the wrappers of previously purchased gum cards, a la proof-of-purchase box-top premiums today. The gum premiums are scarcer than the card issues of the 1930s and in most cases no manufacturer's name is present.

World War II brought an end to this popular era of card collecting when paper and rubber shortages curtailed the production of bubblegum baseball cards. They were resurrected again in 1948 by the Bowman Gum Company (the direct descendant of Gum, Inc.). This marked the beginning of the modern era of card collecting.

In 1948, Bowman Gum issued a 48-card set in black and white consisting of one card and one slab of gum in every one-cent pack. That same year, the Leaf Gum Company also issued a set of cards. Although rather poor in quality, these cards were issued in color. A squabble over the rights to use players' pictures developed between Bowman and Leaf. Eventually Leaf dropped out of the card market, but not before it had left a lasting heritage to the hobby by issuing some of the rarest cards now in existence. Leaf's baseball card series of 1948-49 contained 98 cards, skip numbered to #168 (not all numbers were printed). Of these 98 cards, 49 are relatively plentiful; however, the other 49 are rare and quite valuable.

Bowman continued its production of cards in 1949 with a color series of 240 cards. Because there are many scarce "high numbers," this series remains the most difficult Bowman regular issue to complete. Although the set was printed in color and commands great interest due to its scarcity, it is considered aesthetically inferior to the Goudey and National Chicle issues of the 1930s. In addition to the regular issue of 1949, Bowman also produced a set of 36 Pacific Coast League players. While this was not a regular issue, it still is prized by collectors. In fact, it has become the most valuable Bowman series.

In 1950 (representing Bowman's one-year monopoly of the baseball card market), the company began a string of top quality cards that continued until its demise in 1955. The 1950 series was itself something of an oddity because the "low" numbers, rather than the traditional high numbers, were the more difficult cards to obtain.

The year 1951 marked the beginning of the most competitive and perhaps the highest quality period of baseball card production. In that year Topps Chewing Gum Company of Brooklyn entered the market. Topps' 1951 series consisted of two sets of 52 cards each, one set with red backs and the other with blue backs. In addition, Topps also issued 31 insert cards, three of which remain the rarest Topps cards ("Current All-Stars" Konstanty, Roberts and Stanky). The 1951 Topps cards were unattractive and paled in comparison to the 1951 Bowman issues. However, they were successful, and Topps has continued to produce cards ever since.

Topps issued a larger and much more attractive card in 1952. This larger size became standard for the next five years. (Bowman followed with larger-size baseball cards in 1953.) This 1952 Topps set has become, like the 1933 Goudey series and the T-206 white border series, the classic set of its era. The 407-card set is a collector's dream of scarcities, rarities, errors and variations. It also contains the first Topps issues of Mickey Mantle and Willie Mays.

As with Bowman and Leaf in the late 1940s, competition over player rights arose. Ensuing court battles occurred between Topps and Bowman. The market split due to stiff competition, and in January 1956, Topps bought out Bowman. Topps remained essentially unchallenged as the primary producer of baseball cards through 1980. So, the story of major baseball card sets from 1956 through 1980 is by and large the story of Topps' issues. Notable exceptions include the small sets produced by Fleer Gum in 1959, 1960, 1961 and 1963, and more recently the Kellogg's Cereal and Hostess Cakes baseball cards issued to promote their products.

A court decision in 1980 paved the way for two other large gum companies to enter (or reenter, in Fleer's case) the baseball card arena. Fleer, which had last made photo cards in 1963, and the Donruss Company (then a division of General Mills) secured rights to produce baseball cards of current players, thus breaking Topps' monopoly. Each company issued major card sets in 1981 with bubblegum products.

Then a higher court decision in that year overturned the lower court ruling against Topps. It appeared that Topps had regained its sole position as a producer of baseball cards. Undaunted by the revocation ruling, Fleer and Donruss continued to issue cards in 1982 but without bubblegum or any other edible product. Fleer issued its current player baseball cards with "team logo stickers," while Donruss issued its cards with a piece of a baseball jigsaw puzzle. Since 1981, these three major baseball card producers have all thrived, sharing relatively equal recognition. Each has steadily increased its involvement in terms of numbers of issues per year. To the delight of collectors, their competition has generated novel, and in some cases exceptional, issues of current major league baseball players. Collectors also eagerly accepted the debut efforts of Score (1988) and Upper Deck (1989), the newest companies to enter the baseball card producing derby.

Upper Deck's successful entry into the market turned out to be very important. The company's card stock, photography, packaging and marketing gave baseball cards a new standard for quality, and began the "premium card" trend that continues today. The second premium baseball card set to be issued was the 1990 Leaf set, named for and issued by the parent company of Donruss. To gauge the significance of the premium card trend, one need only note that the two most valuable post-1986 regular-issue cards in the hobby are the 1989 Upper Deck Ken Griffey Jr. and 1990 Leaf Frank Thomas Rookie Cards. The impressive debut of Leaf in 1990 was followed by Leaf Studio, Fleer Ultra, O-Pee-Chee Premier and Topps Stadium Club in 1991. Of that quartet, Topps Stadium Club has made the biggest impact, although all four achieved at least modest success. In 1992, Donruss and Fleer abandoned the traditional 50-cent pack market and instead produced premium sets comparable to (and presumably designed to compete against) Upper Deck's set. Those moves, combined with the almost instantaneous spread of premium cards to the other major team sports cards, serve as strong indicators that premium cards are probably here to stay.

All current major card producers have become increasingly aware of the organized collecting market. While the drugstores and grocery stores down the street remain major outlets for card sales, an increasing number of issues have been directed to this organized hobby marketplace. In fact, many issues are now distributed exclusively through hobby channels. Although no one can ever say what the future will bring, one can only surmise that the hobby market will play a significant role in future plans of all the major baseball card producers.

The above has been a thumbnail sketch of card collecting from its inception in the 1880s to the present. It is difficult to tell the whole story in just a few pages

—there are several other good sources of information. Serious collectors should subscribe to at least one of the excellent hobby periodicals. We also suggest that collectors visit their local card shop(s) and also attend a sports collectibles show in their area. Card collecting is still a young and informal hobby. You can learn more about it in either place. After all, smart dealers realize that spending a few minutes teaching beginners about the hobby often pays off for them in the long run.

Business of Baseball Card Collecting

Determining Value

Why are some cards more valuable than others? Obviously, the economic laws of supply and demand are applicable to card collecting just as they are to any other field where a commodity is bought, sold or traded in a free, unregulated market.

Supply (the number of cards available on the market) is less than the total number of cards originally produced since attrition diminishes that original quantity. Each year a percentage of cards is typically thrown away, destroyed or otherwise lost to collectors. This percentage is much smaller today than it was in the past because more and more people have become increasingly aware of the value of their cards.

For those who collect only Mint condition cards, the supply of older cards can be quite small indeed. Until recently, collectors were not so conscious of the need to preserve the condition of their cards. For this reason, it is difficult to know exactly how many 1953 Topps are currently available, Mint or otherwise. It is generally accepted that there are fewer 1953 Topps available than 1963, 1973 or 1983 Topps cards. If demand were equal for each of these sets, the law of supply and demand would increase the price for the least available sets. Demand, however, is never equal for all sets, so price correlations can be complicated. The demand for a card is influenced by many factors. These include: (1) the age of the card; (2) the number of cards printed; (3) the player(s) portrayed on the card; (4) the attractiveness and popularity of the set; and perhaps most important, (5) the physical condition of the card.

In general, (1) the older the card, (2) the fewer the number of the cards printed, (3) the more famous the player, (4) the more attractive and popular the set, or (5) the better the condition of the card, the higher the value of the card will be. There are exceptions to all but one of these factors: the condition of the card. Given two cards similar in all respects except condition, the one in the best condition will always be valued higher.

While there are certain guidelines that help to establish the value of a card, the exceptions and peculiarities make any simple, direct mathematical formula to determine card values impossible.

Regional Variation

Two types of price variations exist among the sections of the country where a card is bought or sold. The first is the general price variation on all cards bought and sold in one geographical area as compared to another. Card prices are slightly higher on the East and West coasts, and slightly lower in the middle of the country. Although prices may vary from the East to the West, or from the Southwest to the Midwest, the prices listed in this guide are nonetheless presented as a consensus of all sections of this large and diverse country.

Still, prices for a particular player's cards may well be higher in his home team's area than in other regions. This exhibits the second type of regional price variation in which local players are favored over those from distant areas. For example, an Al Kaline card would be valued higher in Detroit than in Cincinnati because Kaline played in Detroit; therefore, the demand there for Al Kaline cards is higher than it is in Cincinnati. On the other hand, a Johnny Bench card would be priced higher in Cincinnati where he played than in Detroit for similar reasons. Frequently even common player cards command such a premium from hometown collectors.

Set Prices

A somewhat paradoxical situation exists in the price of a complete set versus the combined cost of the individual cards in the set. In nearly every case, the sum of the prices for the individual cards is higher than the cost for the complete set. This is especially prevalent in the cards of the past few years. The reasons for this apparent anomaly stem from the habits of collectors and from the carrying costs to dealers. Today each card in a set normally is produced in the same quantity as all others in its set.

However, many collectors pick up only stars, superstars and particular teams. As a result, the dealer is left with a shortage of certain player cards and an abundance of others. He therefore incurs an expense in simply "carrying" these less desirable cards in stock. On the other hand, if he sells a complete set, he gets rid of large numbers of cards at one time. For this reason, he generally is willing to receive less money for a complete set. By doing this, he recovers all of his costs and also makes a profit.

The disparity between the price of the complete set and that for the sum of the individual cards also has been influenced by the fact that the major manufacturers are now pre-collating card sets. Since "pulling" individual cards from the sets of all three manufacturers involves a specific type of labor (and cost), the singles or star card market is not affected significantly by pre-collation.

Set prices also do not include rare card varieties, unless specifically stated. Of course, the prices for sets do include one example of each type for the given set, but this is the least expensive variety.

Scarce Series

Scarce series occur because cards issued before 1974 were made available to the public each year in several series of finite numbers of cards, rather than all cards of the set being available for purchase at one time. At some point during the year, usually toward the end of the baseball season, interest in current year baseball cards waned. Consequently, the manufacturers produced smaller numbers of these later series of cards.

Nearly all nationwide issues from post-World War II manufacturers (1948 to 1973) exhibit these series variations. In the past, Topps, for example, may have issued series consisting of many different numbers of cards, including 55, 66, 80, 88 and others. Recently Topps has settled on what is now their standard sheet size of 132 cards, six of which comprise its 792-card set.

While the number of cards within a given series is usually the same as the number of cards on one printed sheet, this is not always the case. For example, Bowman used 36 cards on its standard printed sheets, but in 1948 substituted 12 cards during later print runs of that year's baseball cards. Twelve of the cards from the initial sheet of 36 cards were removed and replaced by 12 different cards giving, in effect, a first series of 36 cards and a second series of 12 new cards. This replacement produced a scarcity of 24 cards — the 12 cards removed from the original sheet and the 12 new cards added to the sheet. A full sheet of 1948 Bowman cards (second printing) shows that card numbers 37 through 48 have replaced 12 of the cards on the first printing sheet.

The Topps Company alsohas created scarcities and/or excesses of certain cards in many of their sets. Topps, however, has most frequently gone the other direction by double printing some of the cards. Double printing causes an abundance of cards of the players who are on the same sheet more than one time. During the years from 1978 to 1981, Topps double printed 66 cards out of their large 726-card set. The Topps practice of double printing cards in earlier years is the most logical explanation for the known scarcities of particular cards in some of these Topps sets.

From 1988 through 1990, Donruss short printed or doubleprinted certain cards in its major sets. Ostensibly this was because of their addition of bonus team MVP cards in their regular-issue wax packs.

We are always looking for information or photographs of printing sheets of cards for research. Each year we try to update the hobby's knowledge of distribution anomalies. Please let us know at the address in this book if you have first-hand knowledge that would be helpful in this pursuit.

Grading Your Cards

Each hobby has its own grading terminology — stamps, coins, comic books, beer cans, etc. Collectors of sports cards are no exception. The one invariable criterion for determining the value of a card is its condition: the better the condition of the card, the more valuable it is. However, condition grading is very subjective. Individual card dealers and collectors differ in the strictness of their grading, but the stated condition of a card should be determined without regard to whether it is being bought or sold.

The physical defects that lower the condition of a card are usually quite apparent, but each individual places his own estimation (negative value in this case) on these defects. We present the condition guide for use in determining values listed in this Price Guide in the hopes that excess subjectivity can be minimized.

The defects listed in the condition guide below are those either placed in the card at the time of printing — uneven borders, focus — or those defects that can occur to a card under normal handling — corner sharpness, gloss, edge wear, light creases — and finally, environmental conditions — browning. Other defects to cards are caused by human carelessness and in all cases should be noted separately and in addition to the condition grade. Among the more common alterations are heavy creases, tape, tape stains, rubber band marks, water damage, severe warping, smoke damage, trimming, paste, tears, writing, pin or tack holes, any back damage, and missing parts (tabs, tops, coupons, backgrounds).

Centering

It is important to define in words and pictures what is meant by certain frequently used hobby terms relating to grading cards. The adjacent pictures portray various stages of centering. Centering can range from well-centered to slightly off-center to off-center to badly off-center to miscut.

Slightly Off-Center (60/40): A slightly off-center card is one which upon close inspection is found to have one border bigger than the opposite border. This degree once was only offensive to purists, but now some hobbyists try to avoid cards that are anything other than perfectly centered.

Off-Center (70/30): An off-center card has one border which is noticeably more than twice as wide as the opposite border.

Badly Off-Center (80/20 or worse): A badly off-center card has virtually no border on one side of the card.

Miscut: A miscut card actually shows part of the adjacent card in its larger border and consequently a corresponding amount of its card is cut off.

Centering

Well-centered

Slightly Off-centered

Off-centered

Badly Off-centered

Miscut

Corner Wear

The partial cards shown at the right have been photographed at 300%. This was done in order to magnify each card's corner wear to such a degree that differences could be shown on a printed page.

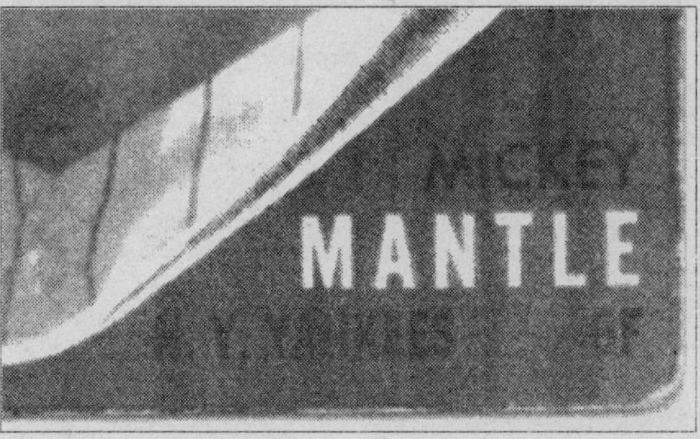

The 1962 Topps Mickey Mantle card definitely has a rounded corner. Some may say that this corner is badly rounded, but that is a judgment call.

The 1962 Topps Hank Aaron card has a slightly rounded corner. Note that there is definite corner wear evident by the fraying and that there is no longer a sharp point to which the corner converges.

The 1962 Topps Gil Hodges card has corner wear; it is slightly better than the Aaron card above. Nevertheless some collectors might classify this Hodges corner as slightly rounded.

The 1962 Topps Manager's Dream card showing Mantle and Mays has slight corner wear. This is not a fuzzy corner as very slight wear is noticeable on the card's photo surface.

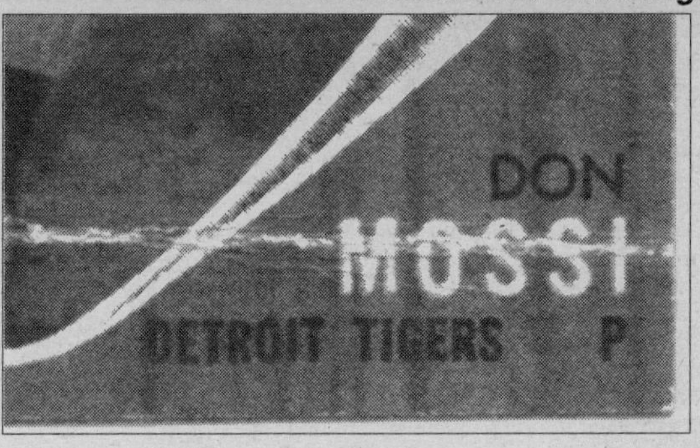

The 1962 Topps Don Mossi card has very slight corner wear such that it might be called a fuzzy corner. A close look at the original card shows that the corner is not perfect, but almost. However, note that corner wear is somewhat academic on this card. As you can plainly see, the heavy crease going across his name breaks through the photo surface.

Corner Wear

Degrees of corner wear generate several common terms useful to accurate grading. The wear on card corners can be expressed as fuzzy corners, corner wear or slightly rounded corners, rounded corners, badly rounded corners.

Fuzzy Corners: Fuzzy corners still come to a right angle (to a point) but the point has begun to fray slightly.

Corner Wear or Slightly Rounded Corners: The slight fraying of the corners has increased to where there is no longer a point to the corner. Nevertheless the corner is still reasonably sharp. There may be evidence of some slight loss of color in the corner also.

Rounded Corners: The corner is definitely no longer sharp but is not badly rounded.

Badly Rounded Corners: The corner is rounded to an objectionable degree. Excessive wear and rough handling are evident.

Creases

A third common defect is the crease. The degree of creasing in a card is very difficult to show in a drawing or picture. On giving the specific condition of an expensive card for sale, the seller should note any creases additionally. Creases can be categorized as to severity according to the following scale.

Light Crease: A light crease is a crease that is barely noticeable on close inspection. In fact when cards are in plastic sheets or holders, a light crease may not be seen (until the card is taken out of the holder). A light crease on the front is much more serious than a light crease on the card back only.

Medium Crease: A medium crease is noticeable when held and studied at arm's length by the naked eye, but does not overly detract from the appearance of the card. It is an obvious crease, but not one that breaks the picture surface of the card.

Heavy Crease: A heavy crease is one that has torn or broken through the card's picture surface, e.g., puts a tear in the photo surface.

Alterations

Deceptive Trimming: This occurs when someone alters the card in order (1) to shave off edge wear, (2) to improve the sharpness of the corners, or (3) to improve centering — obviously their objective is to falsely increase the perceived value of the card to an unsuspecting buyer. The shrinkage is usually only evident if the trimmed card is compared to an adjacent full-sized card or if the trimmed card is itself measured.

Obvious Trimming: Obvious trimming is noticeable and unfortunate. It is usually performed by non-collectors who give no thought to the present or future value of their cards.

Deceptively Retouched Borders: This occurs when the borders (especially on those cards with dark borders) are touched up on the edges and corners with magic marker of appropriate color in order to make the card appear to be Mint.

Categorization of Defects

A "Micro Defect" would be fuzzy corners, slight off-centering, printers' lines, printers' spots, slightly out of focus, or slight loss of original gloss. A NrMt card may have one micro defect. An ExMt card may have two or more micro defects.

A "Minor Defect" would be corner wear or slight rounding, off-centering, light crease on back, wax or gum stains on reverse, loss of original gloss, writing or tape marks on back, or rubber band marks. An Excellent card may have minor defects.

A "Major Defect" would be rounded corner(s), badly off-center borders, crease(s), deceptive trimming, deceptively retouched borders, pin hole, staple hole, incidental writing or tape marks on front, severe warping, water stains, medium crease(s), or sun fading. A Vg card may have one major defect. A Good card may have two or more major defects.

A "Catastrophic Defect" is the worst kind of defect and would include such defects as badly rounded corner(s), miscutting, heavy crease(s), obvious trimming, punch hole, tack hole, tear(s), corner missing or clipped, destructive writing on front. A Fair card may have one catastrophic defect. A Poor card has two or more catastrophic defects.

Condition Guide

Mint (Mt) - A card with no defects. The card has sharp corners, even borders, original gloss or shine on the surface, sharp focus of the picture, smooth edges, no signs of wear, and white borders. A Mint card does NOT have printers' lines or other printing defects or other serious quality control problems that should have been discovered by the card company before distribution. Note also that there is no allowance made for the age of the card.

Near Mint (NrMt) - A card with a micro defect. Any of the following would be sufficient to lower the grade of a card from Mint to the Near Mint category: layering at some of the corners (fuzzy corners), a very small amount of the original gloss lost, very minor wear on the edges, slightly off-center borders, slight wear visible only on close inspection, slight off-whiteness of the borders.

Excellent to Mint (ExMt) - A card with micro defects, but no minor defects. Two or three of the following would be sufficient to lower the grade of a card from Mint to the ExMt category: layering at some of the corners (fuzzy corners), a very small amount of the original gloss lost, minor wear on the edges, slightly off-center borders, slight wear visible only on close inspection, slight off-whiteness of the borders.

Excellent (Ex) - A card with minor defects. Any of the following would be sufficient to lower the grade of a card from Mint to the Excellent category: slight rounding at some of the corners, a small amount of the original gloss lost, minor wear on the edges, off-center borders, wear visible only on close inspection; off-whiteness of the borders.

Very Good (Vg) - A card that has been handled but not abused. Some rounding at all corners, slight layering or scuffing at one or two corners, slight notching on edges, gloss lost from the surface but not scuffed, borders might be somewhat uneven but some white is visible on all borders, noticeable yellowing or browning of borders, light crease(s), pictures may be slightly off focus.

Good (G) - A well-handled card, rounding and some layering at the corners, scuffing at the corners and minor scuffing on the face, borders noticeably uneven and browning, loss of gloss on the face, medium crease(s), notching on the edges.

Fair (F) - Round and layering corners, brown and dirty borders, frayed edges, noticeable scuffing on the face, white not visible on one or more borders, medium to heavy creases, cloudy focus.

Poor (P) - An abused card: The lowest grade of card, frequently some major physical alteration has been performed on the card, collectable only as a filler until a better-condition replacement can be obtained.

Categories between these major condition grades frequently are used, such as Very Good to Excellent (VG-E), Fair to Good (F-G), etc. Such grades indicate a card with all qualities at least in the lower of the two categories, but with several qualities in the higher of the two categories. In the case of ExMt, it essentially refers to a card that is halfway between Excellent and Mint.

Unopened packs, boxes and factory-collated sets are considered Mint in their unknown (and presumed perfect) state. However, once opened or broken out, each of these cards is graded (and valued) in its own right by taking into account any quality control defects (such as off-centering, printers' lines, machine creases or gum stains) that may be present in spite of the fact that the card has never been handled.

Cards before 1980 that are priced in the Price Guide in a top condition of NrMt are obviously worth an additional premium when offered in strict Mint condition. This additional premium increases relative to the age and scarcity of the card. For example, Mint cards from the late '70s may bring only a 10 percent premium for Mint (above NrMt), whereas high demand (or condition rarity) cards from early vintage sets can be sold for as much as double (and occasionally even more) the NrMt price when offered in strict Mint condition.

Cards before 1946 which are priced in the Price Guide in a top condition of ExMt, obviously are worth an additional premium when offered in strict Near Mint or better condition. This additional premium increases relative to the age and scarcity of the card.

Selling Your Cards

Just about every collector sells cards or will sell cards eventually. Someday you may be interested in selling your duplicates or maybe even your whole collection. You may sell to other collectors, friends or dealers. You may even sell cards you purchased from a certain dealer back to that same dealer. In any event, it helps to know some of the mechanics of the typical transaction between buyer and seller.

Dealers will buy cards in order to resell them to other collectors who are interested in the cards. Dealers will always pay a higher percentage for items which (in their opinion) can be resold quickly, and a much lower percentage for those items which are perceived as having low demand and hence are slow moving. In either case, dealers must buy at a price that allows for the expense of doing business and a margin for profit.

If you have cards for sale, the best advice we can give is that you get several offers for your cards — either from card shops or at a card show — and take the best offer, all things considered. Note, the "best" offer may not be the one for the highest amount. And remember, if a dealer really wants your cards, he won't let you get away without making his best competitive offer. Another alternative is to place your cards in an auction as one or several lots.

Many people think nothing of going into a department store and paying $15 for an item of clothing for which the store paid $5. But, if you were selling your $15 card to a dealer and he offered you only $5 for it, you might think his mark-up unreasonable. To complete the analogy: most department stores (and card dealers) that consistently pay $10 for $15 items eventually go out of business. An exception is when the dealer has lined up a willing buyer for the item(s) you are attempting to sell, or if the cards are so Hot that it's likely he'll only have to hold the cards for a short period of time.

In those cases, an offer of up to 75 percent of book value still will allow the dealer to make a reasonable profit considering the short time he will need to hold the merchandise. In general, however, most cards and collections will bring offers in the range of 25 to 50 percent of retail price. Also consider that most material from the past five to 10 years is very plentiful. If that's what you're selling, don't be surprised if your best offer is well below that range.

Interesting Notes

The first card numerically of an issue is the single card most likely to obtain excessive wear. Consequently, you typically will find the price on the #1 card (in NrMt or Mint condition) somewhat higher than might otherwise be the case.

Similarly, but to a lesser extent (because normally the less important, reverse side of the card is the one exposed), the last card numerically in an issue also is prone to abnormal wear. This extra wear and tear occurs because the first and last cards are exposed to the elements (human element included) more than any other cards. They are generally end cards in any brick formations, rubber bandings, stackings on wet surfaces, and like activities.

Sports cards have no intrinsic value. The value of a card, like the value of other collectibles, can be determined only by you and your enjoyment in viewing and possessing these cardboard swatches.

Remember, the buyer ultimately determines the price of each baseball card. You are the determining price factor because you have the ability to say "No" to the price of any card by not exchanging your hard-earned money for a given card. When the cost of a trading card exceeds the enjoyment you will receive from it, your answer should be "No." We assess and report the prices. You set them!

We are always interested in receiving the price input of collectors and dealers from around the country. We happily credit major contributors. We welcome your opinions, since your contributions assist us in ensuring a better guide each year. If you would like to join our survey list for the next editions of this book and others authored by Dr. Beckett, please send your name and address to Dr. James Beckett, 4887 Alpha Road, Suite 200, Dallas, Texas 75244.

Advertising

Within this Price Guide you will find advertisements for sports memorabilia material, mail order, and retail sports collectibles establishments. All advertisements were accepted in good faith based on the reputation of the advertiser; however, neither the author, the publisher, the distributors, nor the other advertisers in this Price Guide accept any responsibility for any particular advertiser not complying with the terms of his or her ad.

Readers also should be aware that prices in advertisements are subject to change over the annual period before a new edition of this volume is issued each spring. When replying to an advertisement late in the baseball year, the reader should take this into account, and contact the dealer by phone or in writing for up-to-date price information. Should you come into contact with any of the advertisers in this guide as a result of their advertisement herein, please mention to them this source as your contact.

Additional Reading

With the increase in popularity of the hobby in recent years, there has been a corresponding increase in available literature. Below is a list of the books and periodicals which receive our highest recommendation and which we hope will further advance your knowledge and enjoyment of our great hobby.

The Official Price Guide to Baseball Cards by Dr. James Beckett (Eleventh Edition, $5.95, released 1991, published by The House of Collectibles) — an abridgment of the Sport Americana Price Guide in a convenient and economical pocket-size format providing Dr. Beckett's pricing of the major baseball sets since 1948.

The Sport Americana Price Guide to Baseball Collectibles by Dr. James Beckett (Second Edition, $12.95, released 1988, published by Edgewater Book Company) — the complete guide/checklist with up-to-date values for box cards, coins, labels, Canadian cards, stamps, stickers, pins, etc.

The Sport Americana Football Card Price Guide by Dr. James Beckett (Eighth Edition, $14.95, released 1991, published by Edgewater Book Company) — the most comprehensive Price Guide and checklist ever issued on football cards. No serious football card hobbyist should be without it.

The Official Price Guide to Football Cards by Dr. James Beckett (Eleventh Edition, $5.99, released 1991, published by The House of Collectibles) — an abridgment of the Sport Americana Price Guide listed above in a convenient and economical pocket-size format providing Dr. Beckett's pricing of the major football sets since 1948.

The Sport Americana Hockey Card Price Guide by Dr. James Beckett (First Edition, $12.95, released 1991, published by Edgewater Book Company) — the most comprehensive Price Guide and checklist ever issued on hockey cards.

The Official Price Guide to Hockey Cards by Dr. James Beckett (First Edition, $5.99, released 1991, published by The House of Collectibles) — an abridgment of the Sport Americana Price Guide listed above in a convenient and economical pocket-size format providing Dr. Beckett's pricing of the major hockey sets since 1951.

The Sport Americana Basketball Card Price Guide and Alphabetical Checklist by Dr. James Beckett (First Edition, $12.95, released 1991, published by Edgewater Book Company) — the most comprehensive combination Price Guide and alphabetical checklist ever issued on basketball cards.

The Official Price Guide to Basketball Cards by Dr. James Beckett (First Edition, $5.99, released 1991, published by The House of Collectibles) — an abridgment of the Sport Americana Price Guide listed above in a convenient and economical pocket-size format providing Dr. Beckett's pricing of the major basketball sets since 1948.

The Sport Americana Alphabetical Baseball Card Checklist by Dr. James Beckett (Fourth Edition, $12.95, released 1990, published by Edgewater Book

Company) — an alphabetical listing, by the last name of the player portrayed on the card, of virtually all baseball cards (Major League and Minor League) produced up through the 1990 major sets.

The Sport Americana Price Guide to the Non-Sports Cards by Christopher Benjamin and Dennis W. Eckes (Third Edition [Part Two], $12.95, released 1988, published by Edgewater Book Company) — the definitive guide to all popular non-sports American tobacco and bubblegum cards. In addition to cards, illustrations and prices for wrappers are also included. Part Two covers non-sports cards from 1961 through 1987.

The Sport Americana Price Guide to the Non-Sports Cards 1930-1960 by Christopher Benjamin and Dennis W. Eckes ($14.95, released 1991, published by Edgewater Book Company) — the definitive guide to virtually all popular non-sports American tobacco and bubblegum cards issued between 1930 and 1960. In addition to cards, illustrations and prices for wrappers are also included.

The Sport Americana Baseball Address List by Jack Smalling and Dennis W. Eckes (Sixth Edition, $12.95, released 1990, published by Edgewater Book Company) — the definitive guide for autograph hunters, giving addresses and deceased information for virtually all major league baseball players past and present.

The Sport Americana Baseball Card Team Checklist by Jeff Fritsch and Dennis W. Eckes (Fifth Edition, $12.95, released 1990, published by Edgwater Book Company) — includes all Topps, Bowman, Donruss, Fleer, Score, Play Ball, Goudey, and Upper Deck cards, with the players portrayed on the cards listed with the teams for whom they played. The book is invaluable to the collector who specializes in an individual team because it is the most complete baseball card team checklist available.

The Encyclopedia of Baseball Cards, Volume I: 19th Century Cards by Lew Lipset ($11.95, released 1983, published by the author) — everything you ever wanted to know about 19th century cards.

The Encyclopedia of Baseball Cards, Volume II: Early Gum and Candy Cards by Lew Lipset ($10.95, released 1984, published by the author) — everything you ever wanted to know about Early Candy and Gum cards.

The Encyclopedia of Baseball Cards, Volume III: 20th Century Tobacco Cards, 1909-1932 by Lew Lipset ($12.95, released 1986, published by the author) — everything you ever wanted to know about old tobacco cards.

Beckett Baseball Card Monthly authored and edited by Dr. James Beckett — contains the most extensive and accepted monthly Price Guide, feature articles, "who's hot and who's not" section, convention calendar, and numerous letters to and responses from the editor. Published 12 times annually, it is the hobby's largest paid circulation periodical. *Beckett Football Card Monthly, Beckett Basketball Monthly, Beckett Hockey Monthly* and *Beckett Focus on Future Stars* are all similar to *Beckett Baseball Card Monthly* in style and content.

Prices in this Guide

Prices found in this guide reflect current retail rates just prior to the printing of this book. They do not reflect the FOR SALE prices of the author, the publisher, the distributors, the advertisers, or any card dealers associated with this guide. No one is obligated in any way to buy, sell or trade his or her cards based on these prices. The price listings were compiled by the author from actual buy/sell transactions at sports conventions, sports card shops, buy/sell advertisements in the hobby papers, for sale prices from dealer catalogs and price lists, and discussions with leading hobbyists in the U.S. and Canada. All prices are in U.S. dollars.

1948 Bowman

The 48-card Bowman set of 1948 was the first major set of the post-war period. Each 2 1/16" by 2 1/2" card had a black and white photo of a current player, with his biographical information printed in black ink on a gray back. Due to the printing process and the 36-card sheet size upon which Bowman was then printing, the 12 cards marked with an SP in the checklist are scarcer numerically, as they were removed from the printing sheet in order to make room for the 12 high numbers (37-48). Many cards are found with over-printed, transposed, or blank backs. The set features the Rookie Cards of Hall of Famers Yogi Berra, Ralph Kiner, Stan Musial, Red Schoendienst, and Warren Spahn. Half of the cards in the set feature New York players (Yankees or Giants).

	NRMT	VG-E	GOOD
COMPLETE SET (48)	3500.00	1500.00	350.00
COMMON PLAYER (1-36)	21.00	9.00	3.00
COMMON PLAYER (37-48)	28.00	12.50	4.00
COMMON PLAYER SP	35.00	15.75	5.25
☐ 1 Bob Elliott	95.00	15.00	3.00
☐ 2 Ewell Blackwell	42.00	18.00	5.00
☐ 3 Ralph Kiner	160.00	72.00	24.00
☐ 4 Johnny Mize	100.00	45.00	15.00
☐ 5 Bob Feller	225.00	100.00	33.00
☐ 6 Yogi Berra	525.00	225.00	75.00
☐ 7 Pete Reiser SP	56.00	26.00	6.00
☐ 8 Phil Rizzuto SP	240.00	100.00	30.00
☐ 9 Walker Cooper	21.00	9.00	3.00
☐ 10 Buddy Rosar	21.00	9.00	3.00
☐ 11 Johnny Lindell	21.00	9.00	3.00
☐ 12 Johnny Sain	50.00	22.50	7.50
☐ 13 Willard Marshall SP	36.00	16.25	5.50
☐ 14 Allie Reynolds	50.00	22.50	7.50
☐ 15 Eddie Joost	21.00	9.00	3.00
☐ 16 Jack Lohrke SP	36.00	16.25	5.50
☐ 17 Enos Slaughter	100.00	45.00	15.00
☐ 18 Warren Spahn	275.00	120.00	40.00
☐ 19 Tommy Henrich	28.00	12.50	4.00
☐ 20 Buddy Kerr SP	36.00	16.25	5.50
☐ 21 Ferris Fain	24.00	10.50	3.50
☐ 22 Floyd Bevens SP	38.00	17.00	4.50
☐ 23 Larry Jansen	24.00	10.50	3.50
☐ 24 Dutch Leonard SP	38.00	17.00	4.50
☐ 25 Barney McCosky	21.00	9.00	3.00
☐ 26 Frank Shea SP	36.00	16.25	5.50
☐ 27 Sid Gordon	21.00	9.00	3.00
☐ 28 Emil Verban SP	36.00	16.25	5.50
☐ 29 Joe Page SP	45.00	20.00	6.75
☐ 30 Whitey Lockman SP	42.00	18.00	5.25
☐ 31 Bill McCahan	21.00	9.00	3.00
☐ 32 Bill Rigney	24.00	10.50	3.50
☐ 33 Bill Johnson	21.00	9.00	3.00
☐ 34 Sheldon Jones SP	36.00	16.25	5.50
☐ 35 Snuffy Stirnweiss	24.00	10.50	3.50
☐ 36 Stan Musial	825.00	375.00	90.00
☐ 37 Clint Hartung	33.00	15.00	5.00
☐ 38 Red Schoendienst	150.00	67.50	22.50
☐ 39 Augie Galan	28.00	12.50	4.00
☐ 40 Marty Marion	75.00	34.00	11.25
☐ 41 Rex Barney	33.00	15.00	5.00
☐ 42 Ray Poat	28.00	12.50	4.00
☐ 43 Bruce Edwards	28.00	12.50	4.00
☐ 44 Johnny Wyrostek	28.00	12.50	4.00
☐ 45 Hank Sauer	40.00	18.00	6.00
☐ 46 Herman Wehmeier	28.00	12.50	4.00
☐ 47 Bobby Thomson	75.00	34.00	11.25
☐ 48 Dave Koslo	65.00	15.00	3.00

1949 Bowman

The cards in this 240-card set measure 2 1/16" by 2 1/2". In 1949 Bowman took an intermediate step between black and white and full color with this set of tinted photos on colored backgrounds. Collectors should note the series price variations, which reflect some inconsistencies in the printing process. There are four major varieties in name printing, which are noted in the checklist below: NOF: name on front; NNOF: no name on front; PR: printed name on back; and SCR: script name on back. These variations resulted when Bowman used twelve of the lower numbers to fill out the last press sheet of 36 cards, adding to numbers 217-240. Cards 1-3 and 5-73 can be found with either gray or white backs. The set features the Rookie Cards of Hall of Famers Roy

Campanella, Bob Lemon, Robin Roberts, Duke Snider, and Early Wynn as well as Rookie Cards of Richie Ashburn and Gil Hodges.

	NRMT	VG-E	GOOD
COMPLETE SET (240)	16000.00	7000.00	1750.00
COMMON CARD 1-3/5-36/73	17.00	7.25	2.50
COMMON CARD (37-72)	20.00	8.50	2.75
COMMON CARD (4/74-108)	17.00	7.25	2.50
COMMON CARD (109-144)	14.50	6.50	1.75
COMMON CARD (145-180)	90.00	40.00	13.50
COMMON CARD (181-216)	80.00	36.00	12.00
COMMON CARD (217-240)	80.00	36.00	12.00

	NRMT	VG-E	GOOD
☐ 1 Vern Bickford	80.00	12.00	2.00
☐ 2 Whitey Lockman	20.00	8.50	2.75
☐ 3 Bob Porterfield	17.00	7.25	2.50
☐ 4A Jerry Priddy NNOF	17.00	7.25	2.50
☐ 4B Jerry Priddy NOF	40.00	18.00	6.00
☐ 5 Hank Sauer	20.00	8.50	2.75
☐ 6 Phil Cavarretta	22.00	9.50	3.15
☐ 7 Joe Dobson	17.00	7.25	2.50
☐ 8 Murry Dickson	17.00	7.25	2.50
☐ 9 Ferris Fain	20.00	8.50	2.75
☐ 10 Ted Gray	17.00	7.25	2.50
☐ 11 Lou Boudreau MG	60.00	27.00	9.00
☐ 12 Cass Michaels	17.00	7.25	2.50
☐ 13 Bob Chesnes	17.00	7.25	2.50
☐ 14 Curt Simmons	27.00	12.00	4.00
☐ 15 Ned Garver	17.00	7.25	2.50
☐ 16 Al Kozar	17.00	7.25	2.50
☐ 17 Earl Torgeson	17.00	7.25	2.50
☐ 18 Bobby Thomson	30.00	13.50	4.50
☐ 19 Bobby Brown	50.00	22.50	7.50
☐ 20 Gene Hermanski	17.00	7.25	2.50
☐ 21 Frank Baumholtz	17.00	7.25	2.50
☐ 22 Peanuts Lowrey	17.00	7.25	2.50
☐ 23 Bobby Doerr	65.00	29.00	9.75
☐ 24 Stan Musial	500.00	225.00	75.00
☐ 25 Carl Scheib	17.00	7.25	2.50
☐ 26 George Kell	50.00	22.50	7.50
☐ 27 Bob Feller	160.00	72.00	24.00
☐ 28 Don Kolloway	17.00	7.25	2.50
☐ 29 Ralph Kiner	90.00	40.00	13.50
☐ 30 Andy Seminick	17.00	7.25	2.50
☐ 31 Dick Kokos	17.00	7.25	2.50
☐ 32 Eddie Yost	22.00	9.50	3.15
☐ 33 Warren Spahn	170.00	75.00	25.00
☐ 34 Dave Koslo	17.00	7.25	2.50
☐ 35 Vic Raschi	50.00	22.50	7.50
☐ 36 Pee Wee Reese	210.00	80.00	25.00
☐ 37 Johnny Wyrostek	20.00	8.50	2.75
☐ 38 Emil Verban	20.00	8.50	2.75
☐ 39 Billy Goodman	22.00	9.50	3.15
☐ 40 Red Munger	20.00	8.50	2.75
☐ 41 Lou Brissie	20.00	8.50	2.75
☐ 42 Hoot Evers	20.00	8.50	2.75
☐ 43 Dale Mitchell	22.00	9.50	3.15
☐ 44 Dave Philley	20.00	8.50	2.75
☐ 45 Wally Westlake	20.00	8.50	2.75
☐ 46 Robin Roberts	275.00	120.00	40.00
☐ 47 Johnny Sain	33.00	15.00	5.00
☐ 48 Willard Marshall	20.00	8.50	2.75
☐ 49 Frank Shea	20.00	8.50	2.75
☐ 50 Jackie Robinson	750.00	325.00	110.00
☐ 51 Herman Wehmeier	20.00	8.50	2.75
☐ 52 Johnny Schmitz	20.00	8.50	2.75
☐ 53 Jack Kramer	20.00	8.50	2.75
☐ 54 Marty Marion	27.00	12.00	4.00
☐ 55 Eddie Joost	20.00	8.50	2.75
☐ 56 Pat Mullin	20.00	8.50	2.75
☐ 57 Gene Bearden	22.00	9.50	3.15
☐ 58 Bob Elliott	22.00	9.50	3.15
☐ 59 Jack Lohrke	20.00	8.50	2.75
☐ 60 Yogi Berra	300.00	135.00	45.00
☐ 61 Rex Barney	20.00	8.50	2.75
☐ 62 Grady Hatton	20.00	8.50	2.75
☐ 63 Andy Pafko	22.00	9.50	3.15
☐ 64 Dom DiMaggio	27.00	12.00	4.00
☐ 65 Enos Slaughter	80.00	36.00	12.00
☐ 66 Elmer Valo	20.00	8.50	2.75
☐ 67 Alvin Dark	33.00	15.00	5.00
☐ 68 Sheldon Jones	20.00	8.50	2.75
☐ 69 Tommy Henrich	27.00	12.00	4.00
☐ 70 Carl Furillo	60.00	27.00	9.00
☐ 71 Vern Stephens	22.00	9.50	3.15
☐ 72 Tommy Holmes	22.00	9.50	3.15
☐ 73 Billy Cox	32.00	14.25	4.75
☐ 74 Tom McBride	17.00	7.25	2.50
☐ 75 Eddie Mayo	17.00	7.25	2.50
☐ 76 Bill Nicholson	20.00	8.50	2.75
☐ 77 Ernie Bonham	17.00	7.25	2.50
☐ 78A Sam Zoldak NNOF	17.00	7.25	2.50
☐ 78B Sam Zoldak NOF	40.00	18.00	6.00
☐ 79 Ron Northey	17.00	7.25	2.50
☐ 80 Bill McCahan	17.00	7.25	2.50
☐ 81 Virgil Stallcup	17.00	7.25	2.50
☐ 82 Joe Page	24.00	10.50	3.50
☐ 83A Bob Scheffing NNOF	17.00	7.25	2.50
☐ 83B Bob Scheffing NOF	40.00	18.00	6.00
☐ 84 Roy Campanella	675.00	300.00	90.00

☐ 85A Johnny Mize NNOF	75.00	34.00	11.25
☐ 85B Johnny Mize NOF	135.00	60.00	20.00
☐ 86 Johnny Pesky	24.00	10.50	3.50
☐ 87 Randy Gumpert	17.00	7.25	2.50
☐ 88A Bill Salkeld NNOF	17.00	7.25	2.50
☐ 88B Bill Salkeld NOF	40.00	18.00	6.00
☐ 89 Mizell Platt	17.00	7.25	2.50
☐ 90 Gil Coan	17.00	7.25	2.50
☐ 91 Dick Wakefield	17.00	7.25	2.50
☐ 92 Willie Jones	17.00	7.25	2.50
☐ 93 Ed Stevens	17.00	7.25	2.50
☐ 94 Mickey Vernon	32.00	14.25	4.75
☐ 95 Howie Pollet	20.00	8.50	2.75
☐ 96 Taft Wright	17.00	7.25	2.50
☐ 97 Danny Litwhiler	17.00	7.25	2.50
☐ 98A Phil Rizzuto NNOF	100.00	45.00	15.00
☐ 98B Phil Rizzuto NOF	200.00	90.00	30.00
☐ 99 Frank Gustine	17.00	7.25	2.50
☐ 100 Gil Hodges	210.00	80.00	25.00
☐ 101 Sid Gordon	17.00	7.25	2.50
☐ 102 Stan Spence	17.00	7.25	2.50
☐ 103 Joe Tipton	17.00	7.25	2.50
☐ 104 Eddie Stanky	27.00	12.00	4.00
☐ 105 Bill Kennedy	17.00	7.25	2.50
☐ 106 Jake Early	17.00	7.25	2.50
☐ 107 Eddie Lake	17.00	7.25	2.50
☐ 108 Ken Heintzelman	17.00	7.25	2.50
☐ 109A Ed Fitzgerald SCR	14.50	6.50	1.75
☐ 109B Ed Fitzgerald PR	36.00	16.25	5.50
☐ 110 Early Wynn	125.00	57.50	18.75
☐ 111 Red Schoendienst	75.00	34.00	11.25
☐ 112 Sam Chapman	14.50	6.50	1.75
☐ 113 Ray LaManno	14.50	6.50	1.75
☐ 114 Allie Reynolds	30.00	13.50	4.50
☐ 115 Dutch Leonard	14.50	6.50	1.75
☐ 116 Joe Hatton	14.50	6.50	1.75
☐ 117 Walker Cooper	14.50	6.50	1.75
☐ 118 Sam Mele	14.50	6.50	1.75
☐ 119 Floyd Baker	14.50	6.50	1.75
☐ 120 Cliff Fannin	14.50	6.50	1.75
☐ 121 Mark Christman	14.50	6.50	1.75
☐ 122 George Vico	14.50	6.50	1.75
☐ 123 Johnny Blatnick	14.50	6.50	1.75
☐ 124A Danny Murtaugh SCR	14.50	6.50	1.75
☐ 124B Danny Murtaugh PR	36.00	16.25	5.50
☐ 125 Ken Keltner	14.50	6.50	1.75
☐ 126A Al Brazle SCR	14.50	6.50	1.75
☐ 126B Al Brazle PR	36.00	16.25	5.50
☐ 127A Hank Majeski SCR	14.50	6.50	1.75
☐ 127B Hank Majeski PR	36.00	16.25	5.50
☐ 128 Johnny VanderMeer	25.00	11.00	3.50
☐ 129 Bill Johnson	14.50	6.50	1.75
☐ 130 Harry Walker	14.50	6.50	1.75
☐ 131 Paul Lehner	14.50	6.50	1.75
☐ 132A Al Evans SCR	14.50	6.50	1.75
☐ 132B Al Evans PR	36.00	16.25	5.50
☐ 133 Aaron Robinson	14.50	6.50	1.75
☐ 134 Hank Borowy	14.50	6.50	1.75

☐ 135 Stan Rojek	14.50	6.50	1.75
☐ 136 Hank Edwards	14.50	6.50	1.75
☐ 137 Ted Wilks	14.50	6.50	1.75
☐ 138 Buddy Rosar	14.50	6.50	1.75
☐ 139 Hank Arft	14.50	6.50	1.75
☐ 140 Ray Scarborough	14.50	6.50	1.75
☐ 141 Ulysses Lupien	14.50	6.50	1.75
☐ 142 Eddie Waitkus	18.00	7.50	2.50
☐ 143A Bob Dillinger SCR	14.50	6.50	1.75
☐ 143B Bob Dillinger PR	36.00	16.25	5.50
☐ 144 Mickey Haefner	14.50	6.50	1.75
☐ 145 Sylvester Donnelly	90.00	40.00	13.50
☐ 146 Mike McCormick	90.00	40.00	13.50
☐ 147 Bert Singleton	90.00	40.00	13.50
☐ 148 Bob Swift	90.00	40.00	13.50
☐ 149 Roy Partee	90.00	40.00	13.50
☐ 150 Allie Clark	90.00	40.00	13.50
☐ 151 Mickey Harris	90.00	40.00	13.50
☐ 152 Clarence Maddern	90.00	40.00	13.50
☐ 153 Phil Masi	90.00	40.00	13.50
☐ 154 Clint Hartung	90.00	40.00	13.50
☐ 155 Mickey Guerra	90.00	40.00	13.50
☐ 156 Al Zarilla	90.00	40.00	13.50
☐ 157 Walt Masterson	90.00	40.00	13.50
☐ 158 Harry Brecheen	100.00	45.00	15.00
☐ 159 Glen Moulder	90.00	40.00	13.50
☐ 160 Jim Blackburn	90.00	40.00	13.50
☐ 161 Jocko Thompson	90.00	40.00	13.50
☐ 162 Preacher Roe	140.00	63.00	21.00
☐ 163 Clyde McCullough	90.00	40.00	13.50
☐ 164 Vic Wertz	100.00	45.00	15.00
☐ 165 Snuffy Stirnweiss	100.00	45.00	15.00
☐ 166 Mike Tresh	90.00	40.00	13.50
☐ 167 Babe Martin	90.00	40.00	13.50
☐ 168 Doyle Lade	90.00	40.00	13.50
☐ 169 Jeff Heath	90.00	40.00	13.50
☐ 170 Bill Rigney	100.00	45.00	15.00
☐ 171 Dick Fowler	90.00	40.00	13.50
☐ 172 Eddie Pellagrini	90.00	40.00	13.50
☐ 173 Eddie Stewart	90.00	40.00	13.50
☐ 174 Terry Moore	115.00	50.00	15.00
☐ 175 Luke Appling	135.00	60.00	20.00
☐ 176 Ken Raffensberger	90.00	40.00	13.50
☐ 177 Stan Lopata	90.00	40.00	13.50
☐ 178 Tom Brown	90.00	40.00	13.50
☐ 179 Hugh Casey	100.00	45.00	15.00
☐ 180 Connie Berry	90.00	40.00	13.50
☐ 181 Gus Niarhos	80.00	36.00	12.00
☐ 182 Hal Peck	80.00	36.00	12.00
☐ 183 Lou Stringer	80.00	36.00	12.00
☐ 184 Bob Chipman	80.00	36.00	12.00
☐ 185 Pete Reiser	100.00	45.00	15.00
☐ 186 Buddy Kerr	80.00	36.00	12.00
☐ 187 Phil Marchildon	80.00	36.00	12.00
☐ 188 Karl Drews	80.00	36.00	12.00
☐ 189 Earl Wooten	80.00	36.00	12.00
☐ 190 Jim Hearn	80.00	36.00	12.00
☐ 191 Joe Haynes	80.00	36.00	12.00

□ 192 Harry Gumbert	80.00	36.00	12.00
□ 193 Ken Trinkle	80.00	36.00	12.00
□ 194 Ralph Branca	110.00	50.00	16.50
□ 195 Eddie Bockman	80.00	36.00	12.00
□ 196 Fred Hutchinson	100.00	45.00	15.00
□ 197 Johnny Lindell	80.00	36.00	12.00
□ 198 Steve Gromek	80.00	36.00	12.00
□ 199 Tex Hughson	80.00	36.00	12.00
□ 200 Jess Dobernic	80.00	36.00	12.00
□ 201 Sibby Sisti	80.00	36.00	12.00
□ 202 Larry Jansen	90.00	40.00	13.50
□ 203 Barney McCosky	80.00	36.00	12.00
□ 204 Bob Savage	80.00	36.00	12.00
□ 205 Dick Sisler	80.00	36.00	12.00
□ 206 Bruce Edwards	80.00	36.00	12.00
□ 207 Johnny Hopp	90.00	40.00	13.50
□ 208 Dizzy Trout	90.00	40.00	13.50
□ 209 Charlie Keller	110.00	50.00	16.50
□ 210 Joe Gordon	110.00	50.00	16.50
□ 211 Boo Ferriss	80.00	36.00	12.00
□ 212 Ralph Hamner	80.00	36.00	12.00
□ 213 Red Barrett	80.00	36.00	12.00
□ 214 Richie Ashburn	500.00	225.00	75.00
□ 215 Kirby Higbe	80.00	36.00	12.00
□ 216 Schoolboy Rowe	90.00	40.00	13.50
□ 217 Marino Pieretti	80.00	36.00	12.00
□ 218 Dick Kryhoski	80.00	36.00	12.00
□ 219 Virgil Fire Trucks	90.00	40.00	13.50
□ 220 Johnny McCarthy	80.00	36.00	12.00
□ 221 Bob Muncrief	80.00	36.00	12.00
□ 222 Alex Kellner	80.00	36.00	12.00
□ 223 Bobby Hofman	80.00	36.00	12.00
□ 224 Satchell Paige	1200.00	500.00	125.00
□ 225 Gerry Coleman	100.00	45.00	15.00
□ 226 Duke Snider	1100.00	500.00	125.00
□ 227 Fritz Ostermueller	80.00	36.00	12.00
□ 228 Jackie Mayo	80.00	36.00	12.00
□ 229 Ed Lopat	140.00	63.00	21.00
□ 230 Augie Galan	80.00	36.00	12.00
□ 231 Earl Johnson	80.00	36.00	12.00
□ 232 George McQuinn	80.00	36.00	12.00
□ 233 Larry Doby	175.00	80.00	27.00
□ 234 Rip Sewell	80.00	36.00	12.00
□ 235 Jim Russell	80.00	36.00	12.00
□ 236 Fred Sanford	80.00	36.00	12.00
□ 237 Monte Kennedy	80.00	36.00	12.00
□ 238 Bob Lemon	260.00	110.00	32.00
□ 239 Frank McCormick	90.00	40.00	13.50
□ 240 Babe Young UER (photo actually Bobby Young)	150.00	50.00	10.00

1950 Bowman

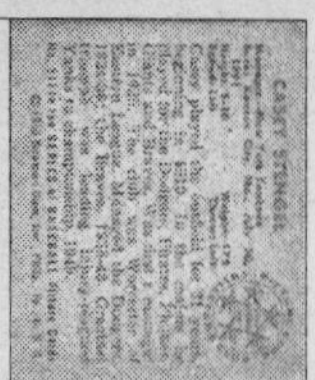

The cards in this 252-card set measure 2 1/16" by 2 1/2". This set, marketed in 1950 by Bowman, represented a major improvement in terms of quality over their previous efforts. Each card was a beautifully colored line drawing developed from a simple photograph. The first 72 cards are the scarcest in the set, while the final 72 cards may be found with or without the copyright line. This was the only Bowman sports set to carry the famous "5-Star" logo. Key rookies in this set are Hank Bauer, Don Newcombe, and Al Rosen.

	NRMT	VG-E	GOOD
COMPLETE SET (252)	9600.00	4500.00	1000.00
COMMON PLAYER (1-72)	55.00	25.00	8.25
COMMON PLAYER (73-216)	18.00	7.50	2.50
COMMON PLAYER (217-252)	20.00	8.50	2.75
□ 1 Mel Parnell	200.00	30.00	6.00
□ 2 Vern Stephens	60.00	27.00	9.00
□ 3 Dom DiMaggio	65.00	29.00	9.75
□ 4 Gus Zernial	65.00	29.00	9.75
□ 5 Bob Kuzava	55.00	25.00	8.25
□ 6 Bob Feller	180.00	80.00	27.00
□ 7 Jim Hegan	60.00	27.00	9.00
□ 8 George Kell	95.00	42.00	12.00
□ 9 Vic Wertz	60.00	27.00	9.00
□ 10 Tommy Henrich	65.00	29.00	9.75
□ 11 Phil Rizzuto	165.00	70.00	22.00
□ 12 Joe Page	65.00	29.00	9.75
□ 13 Ferris Fain	60.00	27.00	9.00
□ 14 Alex Kellner	55.00	25.00	8.25
□ 15 Al Kozar	55.00	25.00	8.25
□ 16 Roy Sievers	65.00	29.00	9.75
□ 17 Sid Hudson	55.00	25.00	8.25
□ 18 Eddie Robinson	55.00	25.00	8.25
□ 19 Warren Spahn	210.00	85.00	27.00
□ 20 Bob Elliott	60.00	27.00	9.00
□ 21 Pee Wee Reese	210.00	85.00	27.00
□ 22 Jackie Robinson	650.00	300.00	100.00

☐ 23	Don Newcombe	130.00	60.00	20.00
☐ 24	Johnny Schmitz	55.00	25.00	8.25
☐ 25	Hank Sauer	60.00	27.00	9.00
☐ 26	Grady Hatton	55.00	25.00	8.25
☐ 27	Herman Wehmeier	55.00	25.00	8.25
☐ 28	Bobby Thomson	65.00	29.00	9.75
☐ 29	Eddie Stanky	60.00	27.00	9.00
☐ 30	Eddie Waitkus	55.00	25.00	8.25
☐ 31	Del Ennis	65.00	29.00	9.75
☐ 32	Robin Roberts	140.00	63.00	21.00
☐ 33	Ralph Kiner	125.00	57.50	18.75
☐ 34	Murry Dickson	55.00	25.00	8.25
☐ 35	Enos Slaughter	125.00	57.50	18.75
☐ 36	Eddie Kazak	55.00	25.00	8.25
☐ 37	Luke Appling	75.00	34.00	11.25
☐ 38	Bill Wight	55.00	25.00	8.25
☐ 39	Larry Doby	70.00	32.00	10.50
☐ 40	Bob Lemon	110.00	50.00	16.50
☐ 41	Hoot Evers	55.00	25.00	8.25
☐ 42	Art Houtteman	55.00	25.00	8.25
☐ 43	Bobby Doerr	95.00	40.00	12.00
☐ 44	Joe Dobson	55.00	25.00	8.25
☐ 45	Al Zarilla	55.00	25.00	8.25
☐ 46	Yogi Berra	350.00	160.00	52.50
☐ 47	Jerry Coleman	65.00	29.00	9.75
☐ 48	Lou Brissie	55.00	25.00	8.25
☐ 49	Elmer Valo	55.00	25.00	8.25
☐ 50	Dick Kokos	55.00	25.00	8.25
☐ 51	Ned Garver	55.00	25.00	8.25
☐ 52	Sam Mele	55.00	25.00	8.25
☐ 53	Clyde Vollmer	55.00	25.00	8.25
☐ 54	Gil Coan	55.00	25.00	8.25
☐ 55	Buddy Kerr	55.00	25.00	8.25
☐ 56	Del Crandall	70.00	32.00	10.50
☐ 57	Vern Bickford	55.00	25.00	8.25
☐ 58	Carl Furillo	70.00	32.00	10.50
☐ 59	Ralph Branca	65.00	29.00	9.75
☐ 60	Andy Pafko	60.00	27.00	9.00
☐ 61	Bob Rush	55.00	25.00	8.25
☐ 62	Ted Kluszewski	90.00	40.00	13.50
☐ 63	Ewell Blackwell	60.00	27.00	9.00
☐ 64	Alvin Dark	65.00	29.00	9.75
☐ 65	Dave Koslo	55.00	25.00	8.25
☐ 66	Larry Jansen	60.00	27.00	9.00
☐ 67	Willie Jones	55.00	25.00	8.25
☐ 68	Curt Simmons	60.00	27.00	9.00
☐ 69	Wally Westlake	55.00	25.00	8.25
☐ 70	Bob Chesnes	55.00	25.00	8.25
☐ 71	Red Schoendienst	110.00	50.00	16.50
☐ 72	Howie Pollet	55.00	25.00	8.25
☐ 73	Willard Marshall	18.00	7.50	2.50
☐ 74	Johnny Antonelli	30.00	13.50	4.50
☐ 75	Roy Campanella	280.00	115.00	39.00
☐ 76	Rex Barney	18.00	7.50	2.50
☐ 77	Duke Snider	280.00	115.00	39.00
☐ 78	Mickey Owen	20.00	8.50	2.75
☐ 79	Johnny VanderMeer	26.00	11.50	3.75
☐ 80	Howard Fox	18.00	7.50	2.50
☐ 81	Ron Northey	18.00	7.50	2.50
☐ 82	Whitey Lockman	20.00	8.50	2.75
☐ 83	Sheldon Jones	18.00	7.50	2.50
☐ 84	Richie Ashburn	100.00	45.00	15.00
☐ 85	Ken Heintzelman	18.00	7.50	2.50
☐ 86	Stan Rojek	18.00	7.50	2.50
☐ 87	Bill Werle	18.00	7.50	2.50
☐ 88	Marty Marion	24.00	10.50	3.50
☐ 89	Red Munger	18.00	7.50	2.50
☐ 90	Harry Brecheen	20.00	8.50	2.75
☐ 91	Cass Michaels	18.00	7.50	2.50
☐ 92	Hank Majeski	18.00	7.50	2.50
☐ 93	Gene Bearden	20.00	8.50	2.75
☐ 94	Lou Boudreau	50.00	22.50	7.50
☐ 95	Aaron Robinson	18.00	7.50	2.50
☐ 96	Virgil Trucks	20.00	8.50	2.75
☐ 97	Maurice McDermott	18.00	7.50	2.50
☐ 98	Ted Williams	700.00	315.00	105.00
☐ 99	Billy Goodman	20.00	8.50	2.75
☐ 100	Vic Raschi	30.00	13.50	4.50
☐ 101	Bobby Brown	32.00	14.25	4.75
☐ 102	Billy Johnson	18.00	7.50	2.50
☐ 103	Eddie Joost	18.00	7.50	2.50
☐ 104	Sam Chapman	18.00	7.50	2.50
☐ 105	Bob Dillinger	18.00	7.50	2.50
☐ 106	Cliff Fannin	18.00	7.50	2.50
☐ 107	Sam Dente	18.00	7.50	2.50
☐ 108	Ray Scarborough	18.00	7.50	2.50
☐ 109	Sid Gordon	18.00	7.50	2.50
☐ 110	Tommy Holmes	20.00	8.50	2.75
☐ 111	Walker Cooper	18.00	7.50	2.50
☐ 112	Gil Hodges	100.00	45.00	15.00
☐ 113	Gene Hermanski	18.00	7.50	2.50
☐ 114	Wayne Terwilliger	20.00	8.50	2.75
☐ 115	Roy Smalley	18.00	7.50	2.50
☐ 116	Virgil Stallcup	18.00	7.50	2.50
☐ 117	Bill Rigney	18.00	7.50	2.50
☐ 118	Clint Hartung	18.00	7.50	2.50
☐ 119	Dick Sisler	18.00	7.50	2.50
☐ 120	John Thompson	18.00	7.50	2.50
☐ 121	Andy Seminick	18.00	7.50	2.50
☐ 122	Johnny Hopp	20.00	8.50	2.75
☐ 123	Dino Restelli	18.00	7.50	2.50
☐ 124	Clyde McCullough	18.00	7.50	2.50
☐ 125	Del Rice	18.00	7.50	2.50
☐ 126	Al Brazle	18.00	7.50	2.50
☐ 127	Dave Philley	18.00	7.50	2.50
☐ 128	Phil Masi	18.00	7.50	2.50
☐ 129	Joe Gordon	22.00	9.50	3.15
☐ 130	Dale Mitchell	20.00	8.50	2.75
☐ 131	Steve Gromek	18.00	7.50	2.50
☐ 132	Mickey Vernon	22.00	9.50	3.15
☐ 133	Don Kolloway	18.00	7.50	2.50
☐ 134	Paul Trout	18.00	7.50	2.50
☐ 135	Pat Mullin	18.00	7.50	2.50
☐ 136	Warren Rosar	18.00	7.50	2.50
☐ 137	Johnny Pesky	20.00	8.50	2.75
☐ 138	Allie Reynolds	30.00	13.50	4.50

☐ 139	Johnny Mize	70.00	32.00	10.50
☐ 140	Pete Suder	18.00	7.50	2.50
☐ 141	Joe Coleman	18.00	7.50	2.50
☐ 142	Sherm Lollar	24.00	10.50	3.50
☐ 143	Eddie Stewart	18.00	7.50	2.50
☐ 144	Al Evans	18.00	7.50	2.50
☐ 145	Jack Graham	18.00	7.50	2.50
☐ 146	Floyd Baker	18.00	7.50	2.50
☐ 147	Mike Garcia	24.00	10.50	3.50
☐ 148	Early Wynn	65.00	29.00	9.75
☐ 149	Bob Swift	18.00	7.50	2.50
☐ 150	George Vico	18.00	7.50	2.50
☐ 151	Fred Hutchinson	22.00	9.50	3.15
☐ 152	Ellis Kinder	18.00	7.50	2.50
☐ 153	Walt Masterson	18.00	7.50	2.50
☐ 154	Gus Niarhos	18.00	7.50	2.50
☐ 155	Frank Shea	18.00	7.50	2.50
☐ 156	Fred Sanford	18.00	7.50	2.50
☐ 157	Mike Guerra	18.00	7.50	2.50
☐ 158	Paul Lehner	18.00	7.50	2.50
☐ 159	Joe Tipton	18.00	7.50	2.50
☐ 160	Mickey Harris	18.00	7.50	2.50
☐ 161	Sherry Robertson	18.00	7.50	2.50
☐ 162	Eddie Yost	20.00	8.50	2.75
☐ 163	Earl Torgeson	18.00	7.50	2.50
☐ 164	Sibby Sisti	18.00	7.50	2.50
☐ 165	Bruce Edwards	18.00	7.50	2.50
☐ 166	Joe Hatton	18.00	7.50	2.50
☐ 167	Preacher Roe	30.00	13.50	4.50
☐ 168	Bob Scheffing	18.00	7.50	2.50
☐ 169	Hank Edwards	18.00	7.50	2.50
☐ 170	Dutch Leonard	20.00	8.50	2.75
☐ 171	Harry Gumbert	18.00	7.50	2.50
☐ 172	Peanuts Lowrey	18.00	7.50	2.50
☐ 173	Lloyd Merriman	18.00	7.50	2.50
☐ 174	Hank Thompson	22.00	9.50	3.15
☐ 175	Monte Kennedy	18.00	7.50	2.50
☐ 176	Sylvester Donnelly	18.00	7.50	2.50
☐ 177	Hank Borowy	18.00	7.50	2.50
☐ 178	Ed Fitzgerald	18.00	7.50	2.50
☐ 179	Chuck Diering	18.00	7.50	2.50
☐ 180	Harry Walker	18.00	7.50	2.50
☐ 181	Marino Pieretti	18.00	7.50	2.50
☐ 182	Sam Zoldak	18.00	7.50	2.50
☐ 183	Mickey Haefner	18.00	7.50	2.50
☐ 184	Randy Gumpert	18.00	7.50	2.50
☐ 185	Howie Judson	18.00	7.50	2.50
☐ 186	Ken Keltner	20.00	8.50	2.75
☐ 187	Lou Stringer	18.00	7.50	2.50
☐ 188	Earl Johnson	18.00	7.50	2.50
☐ 189	Owen Friend	18.00	7.50	2.50
☐ 190	Ken Wood	18.00	7.50	2.50
☐ 191	Dick Starr	18.00	7.50	2.50
☐ 192	Bob Chipman	18.00	7.50	2.50
☐ 193	Pete Reiser	22.00	9.50	3.15
☐ 194	Billy Cox	22.00	9.50	3.15
☐ 195	Phil Cavarretta	20.00	8.50	2.75
☐ 196	Doyle Lade	18.00	7.50	2.50
☐ 197	Johnny Wyrostek	18.00	7.50	2.50
☐ 198	Danny Litwhiler	18.00	7.50	2.50
☐ 199	Jack Kramer	18.00	7.50	2.50
☐ 200	Kirby Higbe	18.00	7.50	2.50
☐ 201	Pete Castiglione	18.00	7.50	2.50
☐ 202	Cliff Chambers	18.00	7.50	2.50
☐ 203	Danny Murtaugh	18.00	7.50	2.50
☐ 204	Granny Hamner	22.00	9.50	3.15
☐ 205	Mike Goliat	18.00	7.50	2.50
☐ 206	Stan Lopata	18.00	7.50	2.50
☐ 207	Max Lanier	18.00	7.50	2.50
☐ 208	Jim Hearn	18.00	7.50	2.50
☐ 209	Johnny Lindell	18.00	7.50	2.50
☐ 210	Ted Gray	18.00	7.50	2.50
☐ 211	Charley Keller	22.00	9.50	3.15
☐ 212	Jerry Priddy	18.00	7.50	2.50
☐ 213	Carl Scheib	18.00	7.50	2.50
☐ 214	Dick Fowler	18.00	7.50	2.50
☐ 215	Ed Lopat	30.00	13.50	4.50
☐ 216	Bob Porterfield	18.00	7.50	2.50
☐ 217	Casey Stengel MG	125.00	57.50	18.75
☐ 218	Cliff Mapes	22.00	9.50	3.15
☐ 219	Hank Bauer	75.00	34.00	11.25
☐ 220	Leo Durocher MG	60.00	27.00	9.00
☐ 221	Don Mueller	33.00	15.00	5.00
☐ 222	Bobby Morgan	20.00	8.50	2.75
☐ 223	Jim Russell	20.00	8.50	2.75
☐ 224	Jack Banta	20.00	8.50	2.75
☐ 225	Eddie Sawyer MG	22.00	9.50	3.15
☐ 226	Jim Konstanty	33.00	15.00	5.00
☐ 227	Bob Miller	20.00	8.50	2.75
☐ 228	Bill Nicholson	20.00	8.50	2.75
☐ 229	Frank Frisch	45.00	20.00	6.75
☐ 230	Bill Serena	20.00	8.50	2.75
☐ 231	Preston Ward	20.00	8.50	2.75
☐ 232	Al Rosen	60.00	27.00	9.00
☐ 233	Allie Clark	20.00	8.50	2.75
☐ 234	Bobby Shantz	27.00	12.00	4.00
☐ 235	Harold Gilbert	20.00	8.50	2.75
☐ 236	Bob Cain	20.00	8.50	2.75
☐ 237	Bill Salkeld	20.00	8.50	2.75
☐ 238	Vernal Jones	20.00	8.50	2.75
☐ 239	Bill Howerton	20.00	8.50	2.75
☐ 240	Eddie Lake	20.00	8.50	2.75
☐ 241	Neil Berry	20.00	8.50	2.75
☐ 242	Dick Kryhoski	20.00	8.50	2.75
☐ 243	Johnny Groth	20.00	8.50	2.75
☐ 244	Dale Coogan	20.00	8.50	2.75
☐ 245	Al Papai	20.00	8.50	2.75
☐ 246	Walt Dropo	27.00	12.00	4.00
☐ 247	Irv Noren	22.00	9.50	3.15
☐ 248	Sam Jethroe	22.00	9.50	3.15
☐ 249	Snuffy Stirnweiss	22.00	9.50	3.15
☐ 250	Ray Coleman	20.00	8.50	2.75
☐ 251	John Moss	20.00	8.50	2.75
☐ 252	Billy DeMars	85.00	15.00	3.00

1951 Bowman

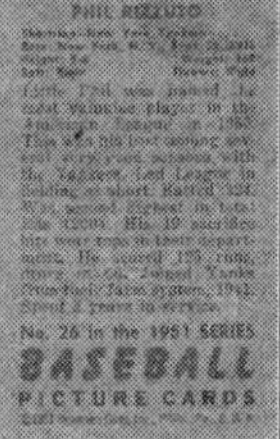

The cards in this 324-card set measure 2 1/16" by 3 1/8". Many of the obverses of the cards appearing in the 1951 Bowman set are enlargements of those appearing in the previous year. The high number series (253-324) is highly valued and contains the true "Rookie" cards of Mickey Mantle and Willie Mays. Card number 195 depicts Paul Richards in caricature. George Kell's card (number 46) incorrectly lists him as being in the "1941" Bowman series. Player names are found printed in a panel on the front of the card. These cards were supposedly also sold in sheets in variety stores in the Philadelphia area.

	NRMT	VG-E	GOOD
COMPLETE SET (324)	19000.00	8250.00	2000.00
COMMON PLAYER (1-36)	22.00	9.50	3.15
COMMON PLAYER (37-72)	18.00	7.50	2.50
COMMON PLAYER (73-252)	14.00	6.25	2.00
COMMON PLAYER (253-324)	65.00	29.00	9.75

Card	NRMT	VG-E	GOOD
☐ 1 Whitey Ford	1300.00	300.00	60.00
☐ 2 Yogi Berra	450.00	200.00	67.50
☐ 3 Robin Roberts	80.00	36.00	12.00
☐ 4 Del Ennis	27.00	12.00	4.00
☐ 5 Dale Mitchell	25.00	11.00	3.50
☐ 6 Don Newcombe	40.00	18.00	6.00
☐ 7 Gil Hodges	80.00	36.00	12.00
☐ 8 Paul Lehner	22.00	9.50	3.15
☐ 9 Sam Chapman	22.00	9.50	3.15
☐ 10 Red Schoendienst	75.00	34.00	11.25
☐ 11 Red Munger	22.00	9.50	3.15
☐ 12 Hank Majeski	22.00	9.50	3.15
☐ 13 Eddie Stanky	25.00	11.00	3.50
☐ 14 Alvin Dark	27.00	12.00	4.00
☐ 15 Johnny Pesky	25.00	11.00	3.50
☐ 16 Maurice McDermott	22.00	9.50	3.15
☐ 17 Pete Castiglione	22.00	9.50	3.15
☐ 18 Gil Coan	22.00	9.50	3.15
☐ 19 Sid Gordon	22.00	9.50	3.15
☐ 20 Del Crandell UER (sic, Crandall)	25.00	11.00	3.50
☐ 21 Snuffy Stirnweiss	25.00	11.00	3.50
☐ 22 Hank Sauer	25.00	11.00	3.50
☐ 23 Hoot Evers	22.00	9.50	3.15
☐ 24 Ewell Blackwell	27.00	12.00	4.00
☐ 25 Vic Raschi	32.00	14.25	4.75
☐ 26 Phil Rizzuto	100.00	45.00	15.00
☐ 27 Jim Konstanty	25.00	11.00	3.50
☐ 28 Eddie Waitkus	22.00	9.50	3.15
☐ 29 Allie Clark	22.00	9.50	3.15
☐ 30 Bob Feller	130.00	60.00	20.00
☐ 31 Roy Campanella	275.00	120.00	40.00
☐ 32 Duke Snider	250.00	110.00	37.50
☐ 33 Bob Hooper	22.00	9.50	3.15
☐ 34 Marty Marion	27.00	12.00	4.00
☐ 35 Al Zarilla	22.00	9.50	3.15
☐ 36 Joe Dobson	22.00	9.50	3.15
☐ 37 Whitey Lockman	20.00	8.50	2.75
☐ 38 Al Evans	18.00	7.50	2.50
☐ 39 Ray Scarborough	18.00	7.50	2.50
☐ 40 Gus Bell	27.00	12.00	4.00
☐ 41 Eddie Yost	18.00	7.50	2.50
☐ 42 Vern Bickford	18.00	7.50	2.50
☐ 43 Billy DeMars	18.00	7.50	2.50
☐ 44 Roy Smalley	18.00	7.50	2.50
☐ 45 Art Houtteman	18.00	7.50	2.50
☐ 46 George Kell 1941 UER	50.00	22.50	7.50
☐ 47 Grady Hatton	18.00	7.50	2.50
☐ 48 Ken Raffensberger	18.00	7.50	2.50
☐ 49 Jerry Coleman	20.00	8.50	2.75
☐ 50 Johnny Mize	55.00	25.00	8.25
☐ 51 Andy Seminick	18.00	7.50	2.50
☐ 52 Dick Sisler	18.00	7.50	2.50
☐ 53 Bob Lemon	50.00	22.50	7.50
☐ 54 Ray Boone	22.00	9.50	3.15
☐ 55 Gene Hermanski	18.00	7.50	2.50
☐ 56 Ralph Branca	27.00	12.00	4.00
☐ 57 Alex Kellner	18.00	7.50	2.50
☐ 58 Enos Slaughter	55.00	25.00	8.25
☐ 59 Randy Gumpert	18.00	7.50	2.50
☐ 60 Chico Carrasquel	18.00	7.50	2.50
☐ 61 Jim Hearn	18.00	7.50	2.50
☐ 62 Lou Boudreau	45.00	20.00	6.75
☐ 63 Bob Dillinger	18.00	7.50	2.50
☐ 64 Bill Werle	18.00	7.50	2.50
☐ 65 Mickey Vernon	20.00	8.50	2.75
☐ 66 Bob Elliott	20.00	8.50	2.75
☐ 67 Roy Sievers	20.00	8.50	2.75
☐ 68 Dick Kokos	18.00	7.50	2.50
☐ 69 Johnny Schmitz	18.00	7.50	2.50
☐ 70 Ron Northey	18.00	7.50	2.50
☐ 71 Jerry Priddy	18.00	7.50	2.50
☐ 72 Lloyd Merriman	18.00	7.50	2.50
☐ 73 Tommy Byrne	16.00	6.75	2.25

☐ 74	Billy Johnson	16.00	6.75	2.25
☐ 75	Russ Meyer	14.00	6.25	2.00
☐ 76	Stan Lopata	14.00	6.25	2.00
☐ 77	Mike Goliat	14.00	6.25	2.00
☐ 78	Early Wynn	48.00	22.00	5.50
☐ 79	Jim Hegan	16.00	6.75	2.25
☐ 80	Pee Wee Reese	145.00	65.00	18.00
☐ 81	Carl Furillo	35.00	15.75	5.25
☐ 82	Joe Tipton	14.00	6.25	2.00
☐ 83	Carl Scheib	14.00	6.25	2.00
☐ 84	Barney McCosky	14.00	6.25	2.00
☐ 85	Eddie Kazak	14.00	6.25	2.00
☐ 86	Harry Brecheen	16.00	6.75	2.25
☐ 87	Floyd Baker	14.00	6.25	2.00
☐ 88	Eddie Robinson	14.00	6.25	2.00
☐ 89	Hank Thompson	16.00	6.75	2.25
☐ 90	Dave Koslo	14.00	6.25	2.00
☐ 91	Clyde Vollmer	14.00	6.25	2.00
☐ 92	Vern Stephens	16.00	6.75	2.25
☐ 93	Danny O'Connell	14.00	6.25	2.00
☐ 94	Clyde McCullough	14.00	6.25	2.00
☐ 95	Sherry Robertson	14.00	6.25	2.00
☐ 96	Sandy Consuegra	14.00	6.25	2.00
☐ 97	Bob Kuzava	14.00	6.25	2.00
☐ 98	Willard Marshall	14.00	6.25	2.00
☐ 99	Earl Torgeson	14.00	6.25	2.00
☐ 100	Sherm Lollar	16.00	6.75	2.25
☐ 101	Owen Friend	14.00	6.25	2.00
☐ 102	Dutch Leonard	16.00	6.75	2.25
☐ 103	Andy Pafko	16.00	6.75	2.25
☐ 104	Virgil Trucks	16.00	6.75	2.25
☐ 105	Don Kolloway	14.00	6.25	2.00
☐ 106	Pat Mullin	14.00	6.25	2.00
☐ 107	Johnny Wyrostek	14.00	6.25	2.00
☐ 108	Virgil Stallcup	14.00	6.25	2.00
☐ 109	Allie Reynolds	30.00	13.50	4.50
☐ 110	Bobby Brown	30.00	13.50	4.50
☐ 111	Curt Simmons	16.00	6.75	2.25
☐ 112	Willie Jones	14.00	6.25	2.00
☐ 113	Bill Nicholson	14.00	6.25	2.00
☐ 114	Sam Zoldak	14.00	6.25	2.00
☐ 115	Steve Gromek	14.00	6.25	2.00
☐ 116	Bruce Edwards	14.00	6.25	2.00
☐ 117	Eddie Miksis	14.00	6.25	2.00
☐ 118	Preacher Roe	28.00	12.50	4.00
☐ 119	Eddie Joost	14.00	6.25	2.00
☐ 120	Joe Coleman	14.00	6.25	2.00
☐ 121	Jerry Staley	14.00	6.25	2.00
☐ 122	Joe Garagiola	150.00	67.50	22.50
☐ 123	Howie Judson	14.00	6.25	2.00
☐ 124	Gus Niarhos	14.00	6.25	2.00
☐ 125	Bill Rigney	14.00	6.25	2.00
☐ 126	Bobby Thomson	32.00	14.25	4.75
☐ 127	Sal Maglie	48.00	22.00	5.50
☐ 128	Ellis Kinder	14.00	6.25	2.00
☐ 129	Matt Batts	14.00	6.25	2.00
☐ 130	Tom Saffell	14.00	6.25	2.00
☐ 131	Cliff Chambers	14.00	6.25	2.00
☐ 132	Cass Michaels	14.00	6.25	2.00
☐ 133	Sam Dente	14.00	6.25	2.00
☐ 134	Warren Spahn	120.00	55.00	18.00
☐ 135	Walker Cooper	14.00	6.25	2.00
☐ 136	Ray Coleman	14.00	6.25	2.00
☐ 137	Dick Starr	14.00	6.25	2.00
☐ 138	Phil Cavarretta	16.00	6.75	2.25
☐ 139	Doyle Lade	14.00	6.25	2.00
☐ 140	Eddie Lake	14.00	6.25	2.00
☐ 141	Fred Hutchinson	16.00	6.75	2.25
☐ 142	Aaron Robinson	14.00	6.25	2.00
☐ 143	Ted Kluszewski	35.00	15.75	5.25
☐ 144	Herman Wehmeier	14.00	6.25	2.00
☐ 145	Fred Sanford	14.00	6.25	2.00
☐ 146	Johnny Hopp	16.00	6.75	2.25
☐ 147	Ken Heintzelman	14.00	6.25	2.00
☐ 148	Granny Hamner	14.00	6.25	2.00
☐ 149	Bubba Church	14.00	6.25	2.00
☐ 150	Mike Garcia	16.00	6.75	2.25
☐ 151	Larry Doby	30.00	13.50	4.50
☐ 152	Cal Abrams	14.00	6.25	2.00
☐ 153	Rex Barney	14.00	6.25	2.00
☐ 154	Pete Suder	14.00	6.25	2.00
☐ 155	Lou Brissie	14.00	6.25	2.00
☐ 156	Del Rice	14.00	6.25	2.00
☐ 157	Al Brazle	14.00	6.25	2.00
☐ 158	Chuck Diering	14.00	6.25	2.00
☐ 159	Eddie Stewart	14.00	6.25	2.00
☐ 160	Phil Masi	14.00	6.25	2.00
☐ 161	Wes Westrum	18.00	7.50	2.50
☐ 162	Larry Jansen	16.00	6.75	2.25
☐ 163	Monte Kennedy	14.00	6.25	2.00
☐ 164	Bill Wight	14.00	6.25	2.00
☐ 165	Ted Williams	600.00	270.00	90.00
☐ 166	Stan Rojek	14.00	6.25	2.00
☐ 167	Murry Dickson	14.00	6.25	2.00
☐ 168	Sam Mele	14.00	6.25	2.00
☐ 169	Sid Hudson	14.00	6.25	2.00
☐ 170	Sibby Sisti	14.00	6.25	2.00
☐ 171	Buddy Kerr	14.00	6.25	2.00
☐ 172	Ned Garver	14.00	6.25	2.00
☐ 173	Hank Arft	14.00	6.25	2.00
☐ 174	Mickey Owen	16.00	6.75	2.25
☐ 175	Wayne Terwilliger	14.00	6.25	2.00
☐ 176	Vic Wertz	16.00	6.75	2.25
☐ 177	Charlie Keller	16.00	6.75	2.25
☐ 178	Ted Gray	14.00	6.25	2.00
☐ 179	Danny Litwhiler	14.00	6.25	2.00
☐ 180	Howie Fox	14.00	6.25	2.00
☐ 181	Casey Stengel MG	100.00	45.00	15.00
☐ 182	Tom Ferrick	14.00	6.25	2.00
☐ 183	Hank Bauer	28.00	12.50	4.00
☐ 184	Eddie Sawyer MG	16.00	6.75	2.25
☐ 185	Jimmy Bloodworth	14.00	6.25	2.00
☐ 186	Richie Ashburn	60.00	27.00	9.00
☐ 187	Al Rosen	28.00	12.50	4.00
☐ 188	Bobby Avila	18.00	7.50	2.50
☐ 189	Erv Palica	14.00	6.25	2.00

☐ 190 Joe Hatton	14.00	6.25	2.00
☐ 191 Billy Hitchcock	14.00	6.25	2.00
☐ 192 Hank Wyse	14.00	6.25	2.00
☐ 193 Ted Wilks	14.00	6.25	2.00
☐ 194 Peanuts Lowrey	14.00	6.25	2.00
☐ 195 Paul Richards (caricature)	18.00	7.50	2.50
☐ 196 Billy Pierce	30.00	13.50	4.50
☐ 197 Bob Cain	14.00	6.25	2.00
☐ 198 Monte Irvin	110.00	50.00	16.50
☐ 199 Sheldon Jones	14.00	6.25	2.00
☐ 200 Jack Kramer	14.00	6.25	2.00
☐ 201 Steve O'Neill	14.00	6.25	2.00
☐ 202 Mike Guerra	14.00	6.25	2.00
☐ 203 Vernon Law	25.00	11.00	3.50
☐ 204 Vic Lombardi	14.00	6.25	2.00
☐ 205 Mickey Grasso	14.00	6.25	2.00
☐ 206 Conrado Marrero	14.00	6.25	2.00
☐ 207 Billy Southworth	14.00	6.25	2.00
☐ 208 Blix Donnelly	14.00	6.25	2.00
☐ 209 Ken Wood	14.00	6.25	2.00
☐ 210 Les Moss	14.00	6.25	2.00
☐ 211 Hal Jeffcoat	14.00	6.25	2.00
☐ 212 Bob Rush	14.00	6.25	2.00
☐ 213 Neil Berry	14.00	6.25	2.00
☐ 214 Bob Swift	14.00	6.25	2.00
☐ 215 Ken Peterson	14.00	6.25	2.00
☐ 216 Connie Ryan	14.00	6.25	2.00
☐ 217 Joe Page	20.00	8.50	2.75
☐ 218 Ed Lopat	28.00	12.50	4.00
☐ 219 Gene Woodling	33.00	15.00	5.00
☐ 220 Bob Miller	14.00	6.25	2.00
☐ 221 Dick Whitman	14.00	6.25	2.00
☐ 222 Thurman Tucker	14.00	6.25	2.00
☐ 223 Johnny VanderMeer	24.00	10.50	3.50
☐ 224 Billy Cox	16.00	6.75	2.25
☐ 225 Dan Bankhead	16.00	6.75	2.25
☐ 226 Jimmy Dykes	16.00	6.75	2.25
☐ 227 Bobby Schantz UER (sic, Shantz)	18.00	7.50	2.50
☐ 228 Cloyd Boyer	16.00	6.75	2.25
☐ 229 Bill Howerton	14.00	6.25	2.00
☐ 230 Max Lanier	14.00	6.25	2.00
☐ 231 Luis Aloma	14.00	6.25	2.00
☐ 232 Nelson Fox	135.00	60.00	20.00
☐ 233 Leo Durocher MG	50.00	22.50	7.50
☐ 234 Clint Hartung	14.00	6.25	2.00
☐ 235 Jack Lohrke	14.00	6.25	2.00
☐ 236 Warren Rosar	14.00	6.25	2.00
☐ 237 Billy Goodman	16.00	6.75	2.25
☐ 238 Pete Reiser	18.00	7.50	2.50
☐ 239 Bill MacDonald	14.00	6.25	2.00
☐ 240 Joe Haynes	14.00	6.25	2.00
☐ 241 Irv Noren	16.00	6.75	2.25
☐ 242 Sam Jethroe	16.00	6.75	2.25
☐ 243 Johnny Antonelli	16.00	6.75	2.25
☐ 244 Cliff Fannin	14.00	6.25	2.00
☐ 245 John Berardino	24.00	10.50	3.50
☐ 246 Bill Serena	14.00	6.25	2.00
☐ 247 Bob Ramazzotti	14.00	6.25	2.00
☐ 248 Johnny Klippstein	14.00	6.25	2.00
☐ 249 Johnny Groth	14.00	6.25	2.00
☐ 250 Hank Borowy	14.00	6.25	2.00
☐ 251 Willard Ramsdell	14.00	6.25	2.00
☐ 252 Dixie Howell	14.00	6.25	2.00
☐ 253 Mickey Mantle	7000.00	2750.00	750.00
☐ 254 Jackie Jensen	140.00	63.00	21.00
☐ 255 Milo Candini	65.00	29.00	9.75
☐ 256 Ken Sylvestri	65.00	29.00	9.75
☐ 257 Birdie Tebbetts	70.00	32.00	10.50
☐ 258 Luke Easter	70.00	32.00	10.50
☐ 259 Chuck Dressen MG	75.00	34.00	11.25
☐ 260 Carl Erskine	120.00	55.00	18.00
☐ 261 Wally Moses	70.00	32.00	10.50
☐ 262 Gus Zernial	70.00	32.00	10.50
☐ 263 Howie Pollet	65.00	29.00	9.75
☐ 264 Don Richmond	65.00	29.00	9.75
☐ 265 Steve Bilko	65.00	29.00	9.75
☐ 266 Harry Dorish	65.00	29.00	9.75
☐ 267 Ken Holcombe	65.00	29.00	9.75
☐ 268 Don Mueller	70.00	32.00	10.50
☐ 269 Ray Noble	65.00	29.00	9.75
☐ 270 Willard Nixon	65.00	29.00	9.75
☐ 271 Tommy Wright	65.00	29.00	9.75
☐ 272 Billy Meyer MG	65.00	29.00	9.75
☐ 273 Danny Murtaugh	65.00	29.00	9.75
☐ 274 George Metkovich	65.00	29.00	9.75
☐ 275 Bucky Harris MG	80.00	36.00	12.00
☐ 276 Frank Quinn	65.00	29.00	9.75
☐ 277 Roy Hartsfield	65.00	29.00	9.75
☐ 278 Norman Roy	65.00	29.00	9.75
☐ 279 Jim Delsing	65.00	29.00	9.75
☐ 280 Frank Overmire	65.00	29.00	9.75
☐ 281 Al Widmar	65.00	29.00	9.75
☐ 282 Frank Frisch	100.00	45.00	15.00
☐ 283 Walt Dubiel	65.00	29.00	9.75
☐ 284 Gene Bearden	70.00	32.00	10.50
☐ 285 Johnny Lipon	65.00	29.00	9.75
☐ 286 Bob Usher	65.00	29.00	9.75
☐ 287 Jim Blackburn	65.00	29.00	9.75
☐ 288 Bobby Adams	65.00	29.00	9.75
☐ 289 Cliff Mapes	70.00	32.00	10.50
☐ 290 Bill Dickey CO	175.00	80.00	27.00
☐ 291 Tommy Henrich CO	75.00	34.00	11.25
☐ 292 Eddie Pellegrini	65.00	29.00	9.75
☐ 293 Ken Johnson	65.00	29.00	9.75
☐ 294 Jocko Thompson	65.00	29.00	9.75
☐ 295 Al Lopez MG	110.00	50.00	16.50
☐ 296 Bob Kennedy	70.00	32.00	10.50
☐ 297 Dave Philley	65.00	29.00	9.75
☐ 298 Joe Astroth	65.00	29.00	9.75
☐ 299 Clyde King	70.00	32.00	10.50
☐ 300 Hal Rice	65.00	29.00	9.75
☐ 301 Tommy Glaviano	65.00	29.00	9.75
☐ 302 Jim Busby	65.00	29.00	9.75

Card	NRMT	VG-E	GOOD
☐ 303 Marv Rotblatt	65.00	29.00	9.75
☐ 304 Al Gettell	65.00	29.00	9.75
☐ 305 Willie Mays	2700.00	1000.00	250.00
☐ 306 Jim Piersall	120.00	55.00	18.00
☐ 307 Walt Masterson	65.00	29.00	9.75
☐ 308 Ted Beard	65.00	29.00	9.75
☐ 309 Mel Queen	65.00	29.00	9.75
☐ 310 Erv Dusak	65.00	29.00	9.75
☐ 311 Mickey Harris	65.00	29.00	9.75
☐ 312 Gene Mauch	80.00	36.00	12.00
☐ 313 Ray Mueller	65.00	29.00	9.75
☐ 314 Johnny Sain	80.00	36.00	12.00
☐ 315 Zack Taylor	65.00	29.00	9.75
☐ 316 Duane Pillette	65.00	29.00	9.75
☐ 317 Smoky Burgess	90.00	40.00	13.50
☐ 318 Warren Hacker	65.00	29.00	9.75
☐ 319 Red Rolfe	70.00	32.00	10.50
☐ 320 Hal White	65.00	29.00	9.75
☐ 321 Earl Johnson	65.00	29.00	9.75
☐ 322 Luke Sewell	70.00	32.00	10.50
☐ 323 Joe Adcock	100.00	45.00	15.00
☐ 324 Johnny Pramesa	120.00	40.00	8.00

1952 Bowman

The cards in this 252-card set measure 2 1/16" by 3 1/8". While the Bowman set of 1952 retained the card size introduced in 1951, it employed a modification of color tones from the two preceding years. The cards also appeared with a facsimile autograph on the front and, for the first time since 1949, premium advertising on the back. The 1952 set was sold in sheets as well as in gum packs. Artwork for 15 cards that were never issued was recently discovered. Notable rookies in this set are Lew Burdette, Gil McDougald, and Minnie Minoso.

	NRMT	VG-E	GOOD
COMPLETE SET (252)	9000.00	4200.00	1000.00
COMMON PLAYER (1-36)	20.00	8.50	2.75
COMMON PLAYER (37-72)	18.00	7.50	2.50
COMMON PLAYER (73-108)	15.00	6.50	2.15
COMMON PLAYER (109-144)	15.00	6.50	2.15
COMMON PLAYER (145-180)	14.00	6.25	2.00
COMMON PLAYER (181-216)	13.00	5.75	1.75
COMMON PLAYER (217-252)	30.00	13.50	4.50

Card	NRMT	VG-E	GOOD
☐ 1 Yogi Berra	600.00	150.00	30.00
☐ 2 Bobby Thomson	32.00	14.25	4.75
☐ 3 Fred Hutchinson	24.00	10.50	3.50
☐ 4 Robin Roberts	65.00	29.00	9.75
☐ 5 Minnie Minoso	100.00	45.00	15.00
☐ 6 Virgil Stallcup	20.00	8.50	2.75
☐ 7 Mike Garcia	22.00	9.50	3.15
☐ 8 Pee Wee Reese	110.00	50.00	16.50
☐ 9 Vern Stephens	22.00	9.50	3.15
☐ 10 Bob Hooper	20.00	8.50	2.75
☐ 11 Ralph Kiner	60.00	27.00	9.00
☐ 12 Max Surkont	20.00	8.50	2.75
☐ 13 Cliff Mapes	20.00	8.50	2.75
☐ 14 Cliff Chambers	20.00	8.50	2.75
☐ 15 Sam Mele	20.00	8.50	2.75
☐ 16 Turk Lown	20.00	8.50	2.75
☐ 17 Ed Lopat	33.00	15.00	5.00
☐ 18 Don Mueller	22.00	9.50	3.15
☐ 19 Bob Cain	20.00	8.50	2.75
☐ 20 Willie Jones	20.00	8.50	2.75
☐ 21 Nellie Fox	42.00	18.00	5.00
☐ 22 Willard Ramsdell	20.00	8.50	2.75
☐ 23 Bob Lemon	55.00	25.00	8.25
☐ 24 Carl Furillo	35.00	15.75	5.25
☐ 25 Mickey McDermott	20.00	8.50	2.75
☐ 26 Eddie Joost	20.00	8.50	2.75
☐ 27 Joe Garagiola	75.00	34.00	11.25
☐ 28 Roy Hartsfield	20.00	8.50	2.75
☐ 29 Ned Garver	20.00	8.50	2.75
☐ 30 Red Schoendienst	65.00	29.00	9.75
☐ 31 Eddie Yost	20.00	8.50	2.75
☐ 32 Eddie Miksis	20.00	8.50	2.75
☐ 33 Gil McDougald	65.00	29.00	9.75
☐ 34 Alvin Dark	24.00	10.50	3.50
☐ 35 Granny Hamner	20.00	8.50	2.75
☐ 36 Cass Michaels	20.00	8.50	2.75
☐ 37 Vic Raschi	24.00	10.50	3.50
☐ 38 Whitey Lockman	20.00	8.50	2.75
☐ 39 Vic Wertz	20.00	8.50	2.75
☐ 40 Bubba Church	18.00	7.50	2.50
☐ 41 Chico Carrasquel	18.00	7.50	2.50
☐ 42 Johnny Wyrostek	18.00	7.50	2.50
☐ 43 Bob Feller	110.00	50.00	16.50
☐ 44 Roy Campanella	210.00	85.00	27.00
☐ 45 Johnny Pesky	22.00	9.50	3.15
☐ 46 Carl Scheib	18.00	7.50	2.50
☐ 47 Pete Castiglione	18.00	7.50	2.50
☐ 48 Vern Bickford	18.00	7.50	2.50

☐ 49 Jim Hearn	18.00	7.50	2.50
☐ 50 Jerry Staley	18.00	7.50	2.50
☐ 51 Gil Coan	18.00	7.50	2.50
☐ 52 Phil Rizzuto	80.00	36.00	12.00
☐ 53 Richie Ashburn	55.00	25.00	8.25
☐ 54 Billy Pierce	24.00	10.50	3.50
☐ 55 Ken Raffensberger	18.00	7.50	2.50
☐ 56 Clyde King	18.00	7.50	2.50
☐ 57 Clyde Vollmer	18.00	7.50	2.50
☐ 58 Hank Majeski	18.00	7.50	2.50
☐ 59 Murry Dickson	18.00	7.50	2.50
☐ 60 Sid Gordon	18.00	7.50	2.50
☐ 61 Tommy Byrne	18.00	7.50	2.50
☐ 62 Joe Presko	18.00	7.50	2.50
☐ 63 Irv Noren	20.00	8.50	2.75
☐ 64 Roy Smalley	18.00	7.50	2.50
☐ 65 Hank Bauer	27.00	12.00	4.00
☐ 66 Sal Maglie	24.00	10.50	3.50
☐ 67 Johnny Groth	18.00	7.50	2.50
☐ 68 Jim Busby	18.00	7.50	2.50
☐ 69 Joe Adcock	24.00	10.50	3.50
☐ 70 Carl Erskine	27.00	12.00	4.00
☐ 71 Vernon Law	20.00	8.50	2.75
☐ 72 Earl Torgeson	18.00	7.50	2.50
☐ 73 Gerry Coleman	20.00	8.50	2.75
☐ 74 Wes Westrum	18.00	7.50	2.50
☐ 75 George Kell	42.00	18.00	5.00
☐ 76 Del Ennis	20.00	8.50	2.75
☐ 77 Eddie Robinson	15.00	6.50	2.15
☐ 78 Lloyd Merriman	15.00	6.50	2.15
☐ 79 Lou Brissie	15.00	6.50	2.15
☐ 80 Gil Hodges	65.00	29.00	9.75
☐ 81 Billy Goodman	18.00	7.50	2.50
☐ 82 Gus Zernial	18.00	7.50	2.50
☐ 83 Howie Pollet	15.00	6.50	2.15
☐ 84 Sam Jethroe	15.00	6.50	2.15
☐ 85 Marty Marion CO	20.00	8.50	2.75
☐ 86 Cal Abrams	15.00	6.50	2.15
☐ 87 Mickey Vernon	18.00	7.50	2.50
☐ 88 Bruce Edwards	15.00	6.50	2.15
☐ 89 Billy Hitchcock	15.00	6.50	2.15
☐ 90 Larry Jansen	18.00	7.50	2.50
☐ 91 Don Kolloway	15.00	6.50	2.15
☐ 92 Eddie Waitkus	15.00	6.50	2.15
☐ 93 Paul Richards	18.00	7.50	2.50
☐ 94 Luke Sewell	18.00	7.50	2.50
☐ 95 Luke Easter	18.00	7.50	2.50
☐ 96 Ralph Branca	20.00	8.50	2.75
☐ 97 Willard Marshall	15.00	6.50	2.15
☐ 98 Jimmy Dykes	18.00	7.50	2.50
☐ 99 Clyde McCullough	15.00	6.50	2.15
☐ 100 Sibby Sisti	15.00	6.50	2.15
☐ 101 Mickey Mantle	2000.00	800.00	200.00
☐ 102 Peanuts Lowrey	15.00	6.50	2.15
☐ 103 Joe Haynes	15.00	6.50	2.15
☐ 104 Hal Jeffcoat	15.00	6.50	2.15
☐ 105 Bobby Brown	25.00	11.00	3.50
☐ 106 Randy Gumpert	15.00	6.50	2.15
☐ 107 Del Rice	15.00	6.50	2.15
☐ 108 George Metkovich	15.00	6.50	2.15
☐ 109 Tom Morgan	15.00	6.50	2.15
☐ 110 Max Lanier	15.00	6.50	2.15
☐ 111 Hoot Evers	15.00	6.50	2.15
☐ 112 Smoky Burgess	18.00	7.50	2.50
☐ 113 Al Zarilla	15.00	6.50	2.15
☐ 114 Frank Hiller	15.00	6.50	2.15
☐ 115 Larry Doby	24.00	10.50	3.50
☐ 116 Duke Snider	190.00	85.00	28.50
☐ 117 Bill Wight	15.00	6.50	2.15
☐ 118 Ray Murray	15.00	6.50	2.15
☐ 119 Bill Howerton	15.00	6.50	2.15
☐ 120 Chet Nichols	15.00	6.50	2.15
☐ 121 Al Corwin	15.00	6.50	2.15
☐ 122 Billy Johnson	18.00	7.50	2.50
☐ 123 Sid Hudson	15.00	6.50	2.15
☐ 124 Birdie Tebbetts	18.00	7.50	2.50
☐ 125 Howie Fox	15.00	6.50	2.15
☐ 126 Phil Cavarretta	18.00	7.50	2.50
☐ 127 Dick Sisler	15.00	6.50	2.15
☐ 128 Don Newcombe	28.00	12.50	4.00
☐ 129 Gus Niarhos	15.00	6.50	2.15
☐ 130 Allie Clark	15.00	6.50	2.15
☐ 131 Bob Swift	15.00	6.50	2.15
☐ 132 Dave Cole	15.00	6.50	2.15
☐ 133 Dick Kryhoski	15.00	6.50	2.15
☐ 134 Al Brazle	15.00	6.50	2.15
☐ 135 Mickey Harris	15.00	6.50	2.15
☐ 136 Gene Hermanski	15.00	6.50	2.15
☐ 137 Stan Rojek	15.00	6.50	2.15
☐ 138 Ted Wilks	15.00	6.50	2.15
☐ 139 Jerry Priddy	15.00	6.50	2.15
☐ 140 Ray Scarborough	15.00	6.50	2.15
☐ 141 Hank Edwards	15.00	6.50	2.15
☐ 142 Early Wynn	45.00	20.00	6.75
☐ 143 Sandy Consuegra	15.00	6.50	2.15
☐ 144 Joe Hatton	15.00	6.50	2.15
☐ 145 Johnny Mize	50.00	22.50	7.50
☐ 146 Leo Durocher MG	42.00	18.00	5.00
☐ 147 Marlin Stuart	14.00	6.25	2.00
☐ 148 Ken Heintzelman	14.00	6.25	2.00
☐ 149 Howie Judson	14.00	6.25	2.00
☐ 150 Herman Wehmeier	14.00	6.25	2.00
☐ 151 Al Rosen	22.00	9.50	3.15
☐ 152 Billy Cox	18.00	7.50	2.50
☐ 153 Fred Hatfield	14.00	6.25	2.00
☐ 154 Ferris Fain	16.00	6.75	2.25
☐ 155 Billy Meyer	14.00	6.25	2.00
☐ 156 Warren Spahn	100.00	45.00	15.00
☐ 157 Jim Delsing	14.00	6.25	2.00
☐ 158 Bucky Harris MG	27.00	12.00	4.00
☐ 159 Dutch Leonard	16.00	6.75	2.25
☐ 160 Eddie Stanky	18.00	7.50	2.50
☐ 161 Jackie Jensen	30.00	13.50	4.50
☐ 162 Monte Irvin	45.00	20.00	6.75
☐ 163 Johnny Lipon	14.00	6.25	2.00
☐ 164 Connie Ryan	14.00	6.25	2.00

☐ 165	Saul Rogovin	14.00	6.25	2.00
☐ 166	Bobby Adams	14.00	6.25	2.00
☐ 167	Bobby Avila	16.00	6.75	2.25
☐ 168	Preacher Roe	27.00	12.00	4.00
☐ 169	Walt Dropo	16.00	6.75	2.25
☐ 170	Joe Astroth	14.00	6.25	2.00
☐ 171	Mel Queen	14.00	6.25	2.00
☐ 172	Ebba St.Claire	14.00	6.25	2.00
☐ 173	Gene Bearden	16.00	6.75	2.25
☐ 174	Mickey Grasso	14.00	6.25	2.00
☐ 175	Randy Jackson	14.00	6.25	2.00
☐ 176	Harry Brecheen	16.00	6.75	2.25
☐ 177	Gene Woodling	20.00	8.50	2.75
☐ 178	Dave Williams	18.00	7.50	2.50
☐ 179	Pete Suder	14.00	6.25	2.00
☐ 180	Ed Fitzgerald	14.00	6.25	2.00
☐ 181	Joe Collins	18.00	7.50	2.50
☐ 182	Dave Koslo	13.00	5.75	1.75
☐ 183	Pat Mullin	13.00	5.75	1.75
☐ 184	Curt Simmons	16.00	6.75	2.25
☐ 185	Eddie Stewart	13.00	5.75	1.75
☐ 186	Frank Smith	13.00	5.75	1.75
☐ 187	Jim Hegan	15.00	6.50	2.15
☐ 188	Charlie Dressen MG	16.00	6.75	2.25
☐ 189	Jim Piersall	20.00	8.50	2.75
☐ 190	Dick Fowler	13.00	5.75	1.75
☐ 191	Bob Friend	25.00	11.00	3.50
☐ 192	John Cusick	13.00	5.75	1.75
☐ 193	Bobby Young	13.00	5.75	1.75
☐ 194	Bob Porterfield	13.00	5.75	1.75
☐ 195	Frank Baumholtz	13.00	5.75	1.75
☐ 196	Stan Musial	500.00	225.00	75.00
☐ 197	Charlie Silvera	16.00	6.75	2.25
☐ 198	Chuck Diering	13.00	5.75	1.75
☐ 199	Ted Gray	13.00	5.75	1.75
☐ 200	Ken Silvestri	13.00	5.75	1.75
☐ 201	Ray Coleman	13.00	5.75	1.75
☐ 202	Harry Perkowski	13.00	5.75	1.75
☐ 203	Steve Gromek	13.00	5.75	1.75
☐ 204	Andy Pafko	15.00	6.50	2.15
☐ 205	Walt Masterson	13.00	5.75	1.75
☐ 206	Elmer Valo	13.00	5.75	1.75
☐ 207	George Strickland	13.00	5.75	1.75
☐ 208	Walker Cooper	13.00	5.75	1.75
☐ 209	Dick Littlefield	13.00	5.75	1.75
☐ 210	Archie Wilson	13.00	5.75	1.75
☐ 211	Paul Minner	13.00	5.75	1.75
☐ 212	Solly Hemus	13.00	5.75	1.75
☐ 213	Monte Kennedy	13.00	5.75	1.75
☐ 214	Ray Boone	15.00	6.50	2.15
☐ 215	Sheldon Jones	13.00	5.75	1.75
☐ 216	Matt Batts	13.00	5.75	1.75
☐ 217	Casey Stengel MG	165.00	72.00	20.00
☐ 218	Willie Mays	1000.00	400.00	100.00
☐ 219	Neil Berry	30.00	13.50	4.50
☐ 220	Russ Meyer	30.00	13.50	4.50
☐ 221	Lou Kretlow	30.00	13.50	4.50
☐ 222	Dixie Howell	30.00	13.50	4.50
☐ 223	Harry Simpson	30.00	13.50	4.50
☐ 224	Johnny Schmitz	30.00	13.50	4.50
☐ 225	Del Wilber	30.00	13.50	4.50
☐ 226	Alex Kellner	30.00	13.50	4.50
☐ 227	Clyde Sukeforth	30.00	13.50	4.50
☐ 228	Bob Chipman	30.00	13.50	4.50
☐ 229	Hank Arft	30.00	13.50	4.50
☐ 230	Frank Shea	30.00	13.50	4.50
☐ 231	Dee Fondy	30.00	13.50	4.50
☐ 232	Enos Slaughter	85.00	38.00	12.75
☐ 233	Bob Kuzava	30.00	13.50	4.50
☐ 234	Fred Fitzsimmons	30.00	13.50	4.50
☐ 235	Steve Souchock	30.00	13.50	4.50
☐ 236	Tommy Brown	30.00	13.50	4.50
☐ 237	Sherm Lollar	33.00	15.00	5.00
☐ 238	Roy McMillan	35.00	15.75	5.25
☐ 239	Dale Mitchell	33.00	15.00	5.00
☐ 240	Billy Loes	37.50	16.00	5.25
☐ 241	Mel Parnell	33.00	15.00	5.00
☐ 242	Everett Kell	30.00	13.50	4.50
☐ 243	Red Munger	30.00	13.50	4.50
☐ 244	Lew Burdette	60.00	27.00	9.00
☐ 245	George Schmees	30.00	13.50	4.50
☐ 246	Jerry Snyder	30.00	13.50	4.50
☐ 247	Johnny Pramesa	30.00	13.50	4.50
☐ 248	Bill Werle	30.00	13.50	4.50
☐ 249	Hank Thompson	33.00	15.00	5.00
☐ 250	Ike Delock	30.00	13.50	4.50
☐ 251	Jack Lohrke	30.00	13.50	4.50
☐ 252	Frank Crosetti CO	160.00	50.00	10.00

1953 Bowman Color

The cards in this 160-card set measure 2 1/2" by 3 3/4". The 1953 Bowman Color set, considered by many to be the best looking set of the modern era, contains Kodachrome photographs with no names or facsimile autographs on the face. Numbers 113 to 160 are somewhat more difficult to obtain, with numbers 113 to 128 being the most difficult. There are two cards of Al Corwin (126 and 149). There are no key rookie cards in this set.

	NRMT	VG-E	GOOD
COMPLETE SET (160)	11000.00	4500.00	1000.00
COMMON PLAYER (1-96)	33.00	15.00	5.00
COMMON PLAYER (97-112)	36.00	16.25	5.50
COMMON PLAYER (113-128)	55.00	25.00	8.25
COMMON PLAYER (129-160)	42.00	18.00	5.50

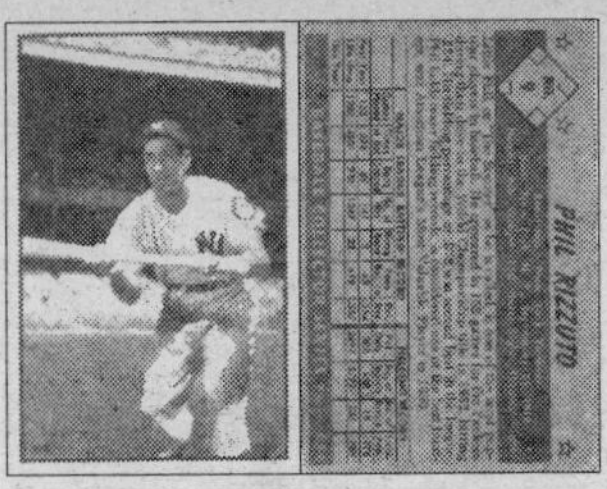

□ 1	Dave Williams	100.00	20.00	4.00
□ 2	Vic Wertz	36.00	16.25	5.50
□ 3	Sam Jethroe	33.00	15.00	5.00
□ 4	Art Houtteman	33.00	15.00	5.00
□ 5	Sid Gordon	33.00	15.00	5.00
□ 6	Joe Ginsberg	33.00	15.00	5.00
□ 7	Harry Chiti	33.00	15.00	5.00
□ 8	Al Rosen	45.00	20.00	6.75
□ 9	Phil Rizzuto	110.00	50.00	16.50
□ 10	Richie Ashburn	90.00	40.00	13.50
□ 11	Bobby Shantz	36.00	16.25	5.50
□ 12	Carl Erskine	42.00	18.00	5.50
□ 13	Gus Zernial	36.00	16.25	5.50
□ 14	Billy Loes	36.00	16.25	5.50
□ 15	Jim Busby	33.00	15.00	5.00
□ 16	Bob Friend	36.00	16.25	5.50
□ 17	Jerry Staley	33.00	15.00	5.00
□ 18	Nellie Fox	65.00	29.00	9.75
□ 19	Alvin Dark	36.00	16.25	5.50
□ 20	Don Lenhardt	33.00	15.00	5.00
□ 21	Joe Garagiola	80.00	36.00	12.00
□ 22	Bob Porterfield	33.00	15.00	5.00
□ 23	Herman Wehmeier	33.00	15.00	5.00
□ 24	Jackie Jensen	40.00	18.00	6.00
□ 25	Hoot Evers	33.00	15.00	5.00
□ 26	Roy McMillan	33.00	15.00	5.00
□ 27	Vic Raschi	40.00	18.00	6.00
□ 28	Smoky Burgess	36.00	16.25	5.50
□ 29	Bobby Avila	36.00	16.25	5.50
□ 30	Phil Cavarretta	36.00	16.25	5.50
□ 31	Jimmy Dykes	36.00	16.25	5.50
□ 32	Stan Musial	500.00	225.00	75.00
□ 33	Pee Wee Reese HOR	425.00	190.00	63.00
□ 34	Gil Coan	33.00	15.00	5.00
□ 35	Maurice McDermott	33.00	15.00	5.00
□ 36	Minnie Minoso	60.00	27.00	9.00
□ 37	Jim Wilson	33.00	15.00	5.00
□ 38	Harry Byrd	33.00	15.00	5.00
□ 39	Paul Richards MG	36.00	16.25	5.50
□ 40	Larry Doby	45.00	20.00	6.75
□ 41	Sammy White	33.00	15.00	5.00
□ 42	Tommy Brown	33.00	15.00	5.00
□ 43	Mike Garcia	36.00	16.25	5.50
□ 44	Berra/Bauer/Mantle	425.00	190.00	63.00
□ 45	Walt Dropo	36.00	16.25	5.50
□ 46	Roy Campanella	240.00	110.00	35.00
□ 47	Ned Garver	33.00	15.00	5.00
□ 48	Hank Sauer	36.00	16.25	5.50
□ 49	Eddie Stanky	36.00	16.25	5.50
□ 50	Lou Kretlow	33.00	15.00	5.00
□ 51	Monte Irvin	60.00	27.00	9.00
□ 52	Marty Marion	40.00	18.00	6.00
□ 53	Del Rice	33.00	15.00	5.00
□ 54	Chico Carrasquel	33.00	15.00	5.00
□ 55	Leo Durocher MG	60.00	27.00	9.00
□ 56	Bob Cain	33.00	15.00	5.00
□ 57	Lou Boudreau MG	50.00	22.50	7.50
□ 58	Willard Marshall	33.00	15.00	5.00
□ 59	Mickey Mantle	1750.00	700.00	200.00
□ 60	Granny Hamner	33.00	15.00	5.00
□ 61	George Kell	60.00	27.00	9.00
□ 62	Ted Kluszewski	60.00	27.00	9.00
□ 63	Gil McDougald	60.00	27.00	9.00
□ 64	Curt Simmons	36.00	16.25	5.50
□ 65	Robin Roberts	75.00	34.00	11.25
□ 66	Mel Parnell	36.00	16.25	5.50
□ 67	Mel Clark	33.00	15.00	5.00
□ 68	Allie Reynolds	45.00	20.00	6.75
□ 69	Charlie Grimm MG	36.00	16.25	5.50
□ 70	Clint Courtney	33.00	15.00	5.00
□ 71	Paul Minner	33.00	15.00	5.00
□ 72	Ted Gray	33.00	15.00	5.00
□ 73	Billy Pierce	40.00	18.00	6.00
□ 74	Don Mueller	36.00	16.25	5.50
□ 75	Saul Rogovin	33.00	15.00	5.00
□ 76	Jim Hearn	33.00	15.00	5.00
□ 77	Mickey Grasso	33.00	15.00	5.00
□ 78	Carl Furillo	50.00	22.50	7.50
□ 79	Ray Boone	36.00	16.25	5.50
□ 80	Ralph Kiner	80.00	36.00	12.00
□ 81	Enos Slaughter	75.00	34.00	11.25
□ 82	Joe Astroth	33.00	15.00	5.00
□ 83	Jack Daniels	33.00	15.00	5.00
□ 84	Hank Bauer	50.00	22.50	7.50
□ 85	Solly Hemus	33.00	15.00	5.00
□ 86	Harry Simpson	33.00	15.00	5.00
□ 87	Harry Perkowski	33.00	15.00	5.00
□ 88	Joe Dobson	33.00	15.00	5.00
□ 89	Sandy Consuegra	33.00	15.00	5.00
□ 90	Joe Nuxhall	36.00	16.25	5.50
□ 91	Steve Souchock	33.00	15.00	5.00
□ 92	Gil Hodges	120.00	55.00	18.00
□ 93	Phil Rizzuto and Billy Martin	210.00	90.00	27.00
□ 94	Bob Addis	33.00	15.00	5.00
□ 95	Wally Moses	36.00	16.25	5.50
□ 96	Sal Maglie	42.00	18.00	5.50
□ 97	Eddie Mathews	175.00	80.00	27.00
□ 98	Hector Rodriguez	36.00	16.25	5.50

☐ 99 Warren Spahn	150.00	67.50	22.50
☐ 100 Bill Wight	36.00	16.25	5.50
☐ 101 Red Schoendienst	85.00	38.00	12.75
☐ 102 Jim Hegan	40.00	18.00	6.00
☐ 103 Del Ennis	40.00	18.00	6.00
☐ 104 Luke Easter	40.00	18.00	6.00
☐ 105 Eddie Joost	36.00	16.25	5.50
☐ 106 Ken Raffensberger	36.00	16.25	5.50
☐ 107 Alex Kellner	36.00	16.25	5.50
☐ 108 Bobby Adams	36.00	16.25	5.50
☐ 109 Ken Wood	36.00	16.25	5.50
☐ 110 Bob Rush	36.00	16.25	5.50
☐ 111 Jim Dyck	36.00	16.25	5.50
☐ 112 Toby Atwell	36.00	16.25	5.50
☐ 113 Karl Drews	55.00	25.00	8.25
☐ 114 Bob Feller	300.00	135.00	45.00
☐ 115 Cloyd Boyer	60.00	27.00	9.00
☐ 116 Eddie Yost	60.00	27.00	9.00
☐ 117 Duke Snider	550.00	240.00	80.00
☐ 118 Billy Martin	300.00	135.00	45.00
☐ 119 Dale Mitchell	60.00	27.00	9.00
☐ 120 Marlin Stuart	55.00	25.00	8.25
☐ 121 Yogi Berra	550.00	240.00	80.00
☐ 122 Bill Serena	55.00	25.00	8.25
☐ 123 Johnny Lipon	55.00	25.00	8.25
☐ 124 Charlie Dressen MG	60.00	27.00	9.00
☐ 125 Fred Hatfield	55.00	25.00	8.25
☐ 126 Al Corwin	55.00	25.00	8.25
☐ 127 Dick Kryhoski	55.00	25.00	8.25
☐ 128 Whitey Lockman	60.00	27.00	9.00
☐ 129 Russ Meyer	42.00	18.00	5.50
☐ 130 Cass Michaels	42.00	18.00	5.50
☐ 131 Connie Ryan	42.00	18.00	5.50
☐ 132 Fred Hutchinson	45.00	20.00	6.75
☐ 133 Willie Jones	42.00	18.00	5.50
☐ 134 Johnny Pesky	45.00	20.00	6.75
☐ 135 Bobby Morgan	42.00	18.00	5.50
☐ 136 Jim Brideweser	42.00	18.00	5.50
☐ 137 Sam Dente	42.00	18.00	5.50
☐ 138 Bubba Church	42.00	18.00	5.50
☐ 139 Pete Runnels	45.00	20.00	6.75
☐ 140 Al Brazle	42.00	18.00	5.50
☐ 141 Frank Shea	42.00	18.00	5.50
☐ 142 Larry Miggins	42.00	18.00	5.50
☐ 143 Al Lopez MG	65.00	29.00	9.75
☐ 144 Warren Hacker	42.00	18.00	5.50
☐ 145 George Shuba	45.00	20.00	6.75
☐ 146 Early Wynn	120.00	55.00	18.00
☐ 147 Clem Koshorek	42.00	18.00	5.50
☐ 148 Billy Goodman	45.00	20.00	6.75
☐ 149 Al Corwin	42.00	18.00	5.50
☐ 150 Carl Scheib	42.00	18.00	5.50
☐ 151 Joe Adcock	50.00	22.50	7.50
☐ 152 Clyde Vollmer	42.00	18.00	5.50
☐ 153 Whitey Ford	450.00	200.00	67.50
☐ 154 Turk Lown	42.00	18.00	5.50
☐ 155 Allie Clark	42.00	18.00	5.50
☐ 156 Max Surkont	42.00	18.00	5.50
☐ 157 Sherm Lollar	45.00	20.00	6.75
☐ 158 Howard Fox	42.00	18.00	5.50
☐ 159 Mickey Vernon UER (photo actually Floyd Baker)	45.00	20.00	6.75
☐ 160 Cal Abrams	90.00	25.00	5.00

1953 Bowman B/W

The cards in this 64-card set measure 2 1/2" by 3 3/4". Some collectors believe that the high cost of producing the 1953 color series forced Bowman to issue this set in black and white, since the two sets are identical in design except for the element of color. This set was also produced in fewer numbers than its color counterpart, and is popular among collectors for the challenge involved in completing it. There are no key rookie cards in this set.

	NRMT	VG-E	GOOD
COMPLETE SET (64)	2500.00	1000.00	275.00
COMMON PLAYER (1-64)	35.00	15.75	5.25
☐ 1 Gus Bell	125.00	25.00	5.00
☐ 2 Willard Nixon	35.00	15.75	5.25
☐ 3 Bill Rigney	35.00	15.75	5.25
☐ 4 Pat Mullin	35.00	15.75	5.25
☐ 5 Dee Fondy	35.00	15.75	5.25
☐ 6 Ray Murray	35.00	15.75	5.25
☐ 7 Andy Seminick	35.00	15.75	5.25
☐ 8 Pete Suder	35.00	15.75	5.25
☐ 9 Walt Masterson	35.00	15.75	5.25
☐ 10 Dick Sisler	35.00	15.75	5.25
☐ 11 Dick Gernert	35.00	15.75	5.25

	NRMT	VG-E	GOOD
☐ 12 Randy Jackson	35.00	15.75	5.25
☐ 13 Joe Tipton	35.00	15.75	5.25
☐ 14 Bill Nicholson	35.00	15.75	5.25
☐ 15 Johnny Mize	130.00	60.00	20.00
☐ 16 Stu Miller	40.00	18.00	6.00
☐ 17 Virgil Trucks	40.00	18.00	6.00
☐ 18 Billy Hoeft	35.00	15.75	5.25
☐ 19 Paul LaPalme	35.00	15.75	5.25
☐ 20 Eddie Robinson	35.00	15.75	5.25
☐ 21 Clarence Podbielan	35.00	15.75	5.25
☐ 22 Matt Batts	35.00	15.75	5.25
☐ 23 Wilmer Mizell	35.00	15.75	5.25
☐ 24 Del Wilber	35.00	15.75	5.25
☐ 25 Johnny Sain	55.00	25.00	8.25
☐ 26 Preacher Roe	55.00	25.00	8.25
☐ 27 Bob Lemon	130.00	60.00	20.00
☐ 28 Hoyt Wilhelm	130.00	60.00	20.00
☐ 29 Sid Hudson	35.00	15.75	5.25
☐ 30 Walker Cooper	35.00	15.75	5.25
☐ 31 Gene Woodling	48.00	22.00	6.50
☐ 32 Rocky Bridges	35.00	15.75	5.25
☐ 33 Bob Kuzava	35.00	15.75	5.25
☐ 34 Ebba St.Claire	35.00	15.75	5.25
☐ 35 Johnny Wyrostek	35.00	15.75	5.25
☐ 36 Jim Piersall	48.00	22.00	6.50
☐ 37 Hal Jeffcoat	35.00	15.75	5.25
☐ 38 Dave Cole	35.00	15.75	5.25
☐ 39 Casey Stengel MG	325.00	150.00	50.00
☐ 40 Larry Jansen	35.00	15.75	5.25
☐ 41 Bob Ramazzotti	35.00	15.75	5.25
☐ 42 Howie Judson	35.00	15.75	5.25
☐ 43 Hal Bevan	35.00	15.75	5.25
☐ 44 Jim Delsing	35.00	15.75	5.25
☐ 45 Irv Noren	35.00	15.75	5.25
☐ 46 Bucky Harris	55.00	25.00	8.25
☐ 47 Jack Lohrke	35.00	15.75	5.25
☐ 48 Steve Ridzik	35.00	15.75	5.25
☐ 49 Floyd Baker	35.00	15.75	5.25
☐ 50 Dutch Leonard	35.00	15.75	5.25
☐ 51 Lou Burdette	48.00	22.00	6.50
☐ 52 Ralph Branca	40.00	18.00	6.00
☐ 53 Morrie Martin	35.00	15.75	5.25
☐ 54 Bill Miller	35.00	15.75	5.25
☐ 55 Don Johnson	35.00	15.75	5.25
☐ 56 Roy Smalley	35.00	15.75	5.25
☐ 57 Andy Pafko	35.00	15.75	5.25
☐ 58 Jim Konstanty	40.00	18.00	6.00
☐ 59 Duane Pillette	35.00	15.75	5.25
☐ 60 Billy Cox	40.00	18.00	6.00
☐ 61 Tom Gorman	35.00	15.75	5.25
☐ 62 Keith Thomas	35.00	15.75	5.25
☐ 63 Steve Gromek	35.00	15.75	5.25
☐ 64 Andy Hansen	50.00	20.00	4.00

1954 Bowman

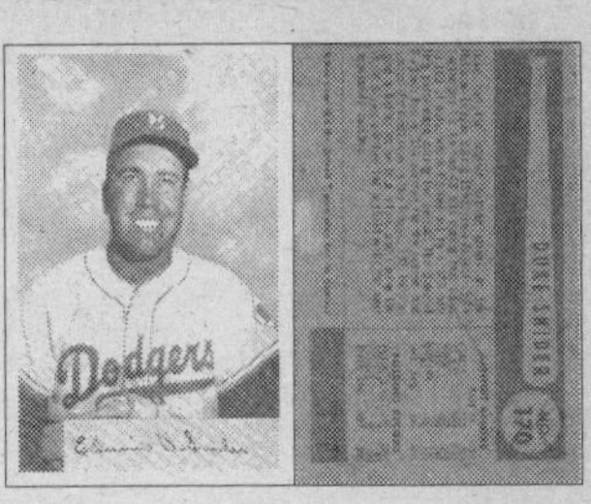

The cards in this 224-card set measure 2 1/2" by 3 3/4". A contractual problem apparently resulted in the deletion of the number 66 Ted Williams card from this Bowman set, thereby creating a scarcity that is highly valued among collectors. The set price below does NOT include number 66 Williams but does include number 66 Jim Piersall, the apparent replacement for Williams in spite of the fact that Piersall was already number 210 to appear later in the set. Many errors in players' statistics exist (and some were corrected) while a few players' names were printed on the front, instead of appearing as a facsimile autograph. The notable rookie cards in this set are Harvey Kuenn and Don Larsen.

	NRMT	VG-E	GOOD
COMPLETE SET (224)	4500.00	1800.00	475.00
COMMON PLAYER (1-128)	10.00	4.50	1.25
COMMON PLAYER (129-224)	14.00	6.25	2.00
☐ 1 Phil Rizzuto	135.00	35.00	7.00
☐ 2 Jackie Jensen	15.00	6.50	2.15
☐ 3 Marion Fricano	10.00	4.50	1.25
☐ 4 Bob Hooper	10.00	4.50	1.25
☐ 5 Billy Hunter	10.00	4.50	1.25
☐ 6 Nellie Fox	25.00	11.00	3.50
☐ 7 Walt Dropo	12.00	5.25	1.50
☐ 8 Jim Busby	10.00	4.50	1.25
☐ 9 Davey Williams	10.00	4.50	1.25
☐ 10 Carl Erskine	15.00	6.50	2.15
☐ 11 Sid Gordon	10.00	4.50	1.25
☐ 12 Roy McMillan	10.00	4.50	1.25
☐ 13 Paul Minner	10.00	4.50	1.25
☐ 14 Jerry Staley	10.00	4.50	1.25
☐ 15 Richie Ashburn	30.00	13.50	4.50
☐ 16 Jim Wilson	10.00	4.50	1.25

☐ 17 Tom Gorman 10.00 4.50 1.25
☐ 18 Hoot Evers 10.00 4.50 1.25
☐ 19 Bobby Shantz 12.00 5.25 1.50
☐ 20 Art Houtteman 10.00 4.50 1.25
☐ 21 Vic Wertz 12.00 5.25 1.50
☐ 22 Sam Mele 10.00 4.50 1.25
☐ 23 Harvey Kuenn 28.00 12.50 4.00
☐ 24 Bob Porterfield 10.00 4.50 1.25
☐ 25 Wes Westrum 10.00 4.50 1.25
☐ 26 Billy Cox 12.00 5.25 1.50
☐ 27 Dick Cole 10.00 4.50 1.25
☐ 28 Jim Greengrass 10.00 4.50 1.25
☐ 29 Johnny Klippstein 10.00 4.50 1.25
☐ 30 Del Rice 10.00 4.50 1.25
☐ 31 Smoky Burgess 12.00 5.25 1.50
☐ 32 Del Crandall 12.00 5.25 1.50
☐ 33A Vic Raschi 18.00 7.50 2.50
(no mention of
trade on back)
☐ 33B Vic Raschi 30.00 13.50 4.50
(traded to St.Louis)
☐ 34 Sammy White 10.00 4.50 1.25
☐ 35 Eddie Joost 10.00 4.50 1.25
☐ 36 George Strickland 10.00 4.50 1.25
☐ 37 Dick Kokos 10.00 4.50 1.25
☐ 38 Minnie Minoso 20.00 8.50 2.75
☐ 39 Ned Garver 10.00 4.50 1.25
☐ 40 Gil Coan 10.00 4.50 1.25
☐ 41 Alvin Dark 12.00 5.25 1.50
☐ 42 Billy Loes 12.00 5.25 1.50
☐ 43 Bob Friend 12.00 5.25 1.50
☐ 44 Harry Perkowski 10.00 4.50 1.25
☐ 45 Ralph Kiner 42.00 18.00 5.50
☐ 46 Rip Repulski 10.00 4.50 1.25
☐ 47 Granny Hamner 10.00 4.50 1.25
☐ 48 Jack Dittmer 10.00 4.50 1.25
☐ 49 Harry Byrd 10.00 4.50 1.25
☐ 50 George Kell 28.00 12.50 4.00
☐ 51 Alex Kellner 10.00 4.50 1.25
☐ 52 Joe Ginsberg 10.00 4.50 1.25
☐ 53 Don Lenhardt 10.00 4.50 1.25
☐ 54 Chico Carrasquel 10.00 4.50 1.25
☐ 55 Jim Delsing 10.00 4.50 1.25
☐ 56 Maurice McDermott 10.00 4.50 1.25
☐ 57 Hoyt Wilhelm 28.00 12.50 4.00
☐ 58 Pee Wee Reese 70.00 32.00 10.50
☐ 59 Bob Schultz 10.00 4.50 1.25
☐ 60 Fred Baczewski 10.00 4.50 1.25
☐ 61 Eddie Miksis 10.00 4.50 1.25
☐ 62 Enos Slaughter 42.00 18.00 5.50
☐ 63 Earl Torgeson 10.00 4.50 1.25
☐ 64 Eddie Mathews 65.00 29.00 9.75
☐ 65 Mickey Mantle 850.00 375.00 125.00
☐ 66A Ted Williams 4000.00 1500.00 300.00
☐ 66B Jim Piersall 100.00 45.00 15.00
☐ 67 Carl Scheib 10.00 4.50 1.25
☐ 68 Bobby Avila 10.00 4.50 1.25
☐ 69 Clint Courtney 10.00 4.50 1.25
☐ 70 Willard Marshall 10.00 4.50 1.25
☐ 71 Ted Gray 10.00 4.50 1.25
☐ 72 Eddie Yost 10.00 4.50 1.25
☐ 73 Don Mueller 12.00 5.25 1.50
☐ 74 Jim Gilliam 20.00 8.50 2.75
☐ 75 Max Surkont 10.00 4.50 1.25
☐ 76 Joe Nuxhall 12.00 5.25 1.50
☐ 77 Bob Rush 10.00 4.50 1.25
☐ 78 Sal Yvars 10.00 4.50 1.25
☐ 79 Curt Simmons 12.00 5.25 1.50
☐ 80 Johnny Logan 12.00 5.25 1.50
☐ 81 Jerry Coleman 12.00 5.25 1.50
☐ 82 Billy Goodman 12.00 5.25 1.50
☐ 83 Ray Murray 10.00 4.50 1.25
☐ 84 Larry Doby 15.00 6.50 2.15
☐ 85 Jim Dyck 10.00 4.50 1.25
☐ 86 Harry Dorish 10.00 4.50 1.25
☐ 87 Don Lund 10.00 4.50 1.25
☐ 88 Tom Umphlett 10.00 4.50 1.25
☐ 89 Willie Mays 350.00 160.00 52.50
☐ 90 Roy Campanella 135.00 60.00 20.00
☐ 91 Cal Abrams 10.00 4.50 1.25
☐ 92 Ken Raffensberger 10.00 4.50 1.25
☐ 93 Bill Serena 10.00 4.50 1.25
☐ 94 Solly Hemus 10.00 4.50 1.25
☐ 95 Robin Roberts 36.00 16.25 5.50
☐ 96 Joe Adcock 12.00 5.25 1.50
☐ 97 Gil McDougald 18.00 7.50 2.50
☐ 98 Ellis Kinder 10.00 4.50 1.25
☐ 99 Pete Suder 10.00 4.50 1.25
☐ 100 Mike Garcia 12.00 5.25 1.50
☐ 101 Don Larsen 35.00 15.75 5.25
☐ 102 Billy Pierce 12.00 5.25 1.50
☐ 103 Steve Souchock 10.00 4.50 1.25
☐ 104 Frank Shea 10.00 4.50 1.25
☐ 105 Sal Maglie 15.00 6.50 2.15
☐ 106 Clem Labine 12.00 5.25 1.50
☐ 107 Paul LaPalme 10.00 4.50 1.25
☐ 108 Bobby Adams 10.00 4.50 1.25
☐ 109 Roy Smalley 10.00 4.50 1.25
☐ 110 Red Schoendienst 36.00 16.25 5.50
☐ 111 Murry Dickson 10.00 4.50 1.25
☐ 112 Andy Pafko 12.00 5.25 1.50
☐ 113 Allie Reynolds 18.00 7.50 2.50
☐ 114 Willard Nixon 10.00 4.50 1.25
☐ 115 Don Bollweg 10.00 4.50 1.25
☐ 116 Luke Easter 10.00 4.50 1.25
☐ 117 Dick Kryhoski 10.00 4.50 1.25
☐ 118 Bob Boyd 10.00 4.50 1.25
☐ 119 Fred Hatfield 10.00 4.50 1.25
☐ 120 Mel Hoderlein 10.00 4.50 1.25
☐ 121 Ray Katt 10.00 4.50 1.25
☐ 122 Carl Furillo 20.00 8.50 2.75
☐ 123 Toby Atwell 10.00 4.50 1.25
☐ 124 Gus Bell 12.00 5.25 1.50
☐ 125 Warren Hacker 10.00 4.50 1.25
☐ 126 Cliff Chambers 10.00 4.50 1.25
☐ 127 Del Ennis 12.00 5.25 1.50

No.	Player			
☐	128 Ebba St.Claire	10.00	4.50	1.25
☐	129 Hank Bauer	21.00	9.00	3.00
☐	130 Milt Bolling	14.00	6.25	2.00
☐	131 Joe Astroth	14.00	6.25	2.00
☐	132 Bob Feller	90.00	40.00	13.50
☐	133 Duane Pillette	14.00	6.25	2.00
☐	134 Luis Aloma	14.00	6.25	2.00
☐	135 Johnny Pesky	16.00	6.75	2.25
☐	136 Clyde Vollmer	14.00	6.25	2.00
☐	137 Al Corwin	14.00	6.25	2.00
☐	138 Gil Hodges	65.00	29.00	9.75
☐	139 Preston Ward	14.00	6.25	2.00
☐	140 Saul Rogovin	14.00	6.25	2.00
☐	141 Joe Garagiola	48.00	22.00	6.00
☐	142 Al Brazle	14.00	6.25	2.00
☐	143 Willie Jones	14.00	6.25	2.00
☐	144 Ernie Johnson	18.00	7.50	2.50
☐	145 Billy Martin	70.00	32.00	10.50
☐	146 Dick Gernert	14.00	6.25	2.00
☐	147 Joe DeMaestri	14.00	6.25	2.00
☐	148 Dale Mitchell	16.00	6.75	2.25
☐	149 Bob Young	14.00	6.25	2.00
☐	150 Cass Michaels	14.00	6.25	2.00
☐	151 Pat Mullin	14.00	6.25	2.00
☐	152 Mickey Vernon	16.00	6.75	2.25
☐	153 Whitey Lockman	16.00	6.75	2.25
☐	154 Don Newcombe	24.00	10.50	3.50
☐	155 Frank Thomas	18.00	7.50	2.50
☐	156 Rocky Bridges	14.00	6.25	2.00
☐	157 Turk Lown	14.00	6.25	2.00
☐	158 Stu Miller	16.00	6.75	2.25
☐	159 Johnny Lindell	14.00	6.25	2.00
☐	160 Danny O'Connell	14.00	6.25	2.00
☐	161 Yogi Berra	175.00	80.00	27.00
☐	162 Ted Lepcio	14.00	6.25	2.00
☐	163A Dave Philley (no mention of trade on back)	16.00	6.75	2.25
☐	163B Dave Philley (traded to Cleveland)	24.00	10.50	3.50
☐	164 Early Wynn	42.00	18.00	5.75
☐	165 Johnny Groth	14.00	6.25	2.00
☐	166 Sandy Consuegra	14.00	6.25	2.00
☐	167 Billy Hoeft	14.00	6.25	2.00
☐	168 Ed Fitzgerald	14.00	6.25	2.00
☐	169 Larry Jansen	16.00	6.75	2.25
☐	170 Duke Snider	150.00	67.50	22.50
☐	171 Carlos Bernier	14.00	6.25	2.00
☐	172 Andy Seminick	14.00	6.25	2.00
☐	173 Dee Fondy	14.00	6.25	2.00
☐	174 Pete Castiglione	14.00	6.25	2.00
☐	175 Mel Clark	14.00	6.25	2.00
☐	176 Vern Bickford	14.00	6.25	2.00
☐	177 Whitey Ford	100.00	45.00	15.00
☐	178 Del Wilber	14.00	6.25	2.00
☐	179 Morrie Martin	14.00	6.25	2.00
☐	180 Joe Tipton	14.00	6.25	2.00
☐	181 Les Moss	14.00	6.25	2.00
☐	182 Sherm Lollar	16.00	6.75	2.25
☐	183 Matt Batts	14.00	6.25	2.00
☐	184 Mickey Grasso	14.00	6.25	2.00
☐	185 Daryl Spencer	14.00	6.25	2.00
☐	186 Russ Meyer	14.00	6.25	2.00
☐	187 Vernon Law	16.00	6.75	2.25
☐	188 Frank Smith	14.00	6.25	2.00
☐	189 Randy Jackson	14.00	6.25	2.00
☐	190 Joe Presko	14.00	6.25	2.00
☐	191 Karl Drews	14.00	6.25	2.00
☐	192 Lou Burdette	18.00	7.50	2.50
☐	193 Eddie Robinson	14.00	6.25	2.00
☐	194 Sid Hudson	14.00	6.25	2.00
☐	195 Bob Cain	14.00	6.25	2.00
☐	196 Bob Lemon	36.00	16.25	5.50
☐	197 Lou Kretlow	14.00	6.25	2.00
☐	198 Virgil Trucks	16.00	6.75	2.25
☐	199 Steve Gromek	14.00	6.25	2.00
☐	200 Conrado Marrero	14.00	6.25	2.00
☐	201 Bobby Thomson	18.00	7.50	2.50
☐	202 George Shuba	18.00	7.50	2.50
☐	203 Vic Janowicz	16.00	6.75	2.25
☐	204 Jack Collum	14.00	6.25	2.00
☐	205 Hal Jeffcoat	14.00	6.25	2.00
☐	206 Steve Bilko	14.00	6.25	2.00
☐	207 Stan Lopata	14.00	6.25	2.00
☐	208 Johnny Antonelli	16.00	6.75	2.25
☐	209 Gene Woodling	16.00	6.75	2.25
☐	210 Jim Piersall	18.00	7.50	2.50
☐	211 Al Robertson	14.00	6.25	2.00
☐	212 Owen Friend	14.00	6.25	2.00
☐	213 Dick Littlefield	14.00	6.25	2.00
☐	214 Ferris Fain	16.00	6.75	2.25
☐	215 Johnny Bucha	14.00	6.25	2.00
☐	216 Jerry Snyder	14.00	6.25	2.00
☐	217 Hank Thompson	16.00	6.75	2.25
☐	218 Preacher Roe	18.00	7.50	2.50
☐	219 Hal Rice	14.00	6.25	2.00
☐	220 Hobie Landrith	14.00	6.25	2.00
☐	221 Frank Baumholtz	14.00	6.25	2.00
☐	222 Memo Luna	14.00	6.25	2.00
☐	223 Steve Ridzik	14.00	6.25	2.00
☐	224 Bill Bruton	42.00	9.00	2.00

1955 Bowman

The cards in this 320-card set measure 2 1/2" by 3 3/4". The Bowman set of 1955 is known as the "TV set" because each player photograph is cleverly shown within a television set design. The set contains umpire

cards, some transposed pictures (e.g., Johnsons and Bollings), an incorrect spelling for Harvey Kuenn, and a traded line for Palica (all of which are noted in the checklist below). Some three-card advertising strips exist, the backs of these panels contain advertising for Bowman products. Advertising panels seen include Nellie Fox/Carl Furillo/ Carl Erskine and a panel including Early Wynn and Pee Wee Reese. The notable rookie cards in this set are Elston Howard and Don Zimmer.

	NRMT	VG-E	GOOD
COMPLETE SET (320)	5250.00	2350.00	550.00
COMMON PLAYER (1-96)	8.00	3.50	.80
COMMON PLAYER (97-224)	7.00	3.00	.70
COMMON PLAYER (225-320)	16.50	7.00	2.35
COMMON UMPIRES (225-320)	30.00	13.50	4.50
☐ 1 Hoyt Wilhelm	100.00	15.00	3.00
☐ 2 Alvin Dark	11.00	5.00	1.35
☐ 3 Joe Coleman	8.00	3.50	.80
☐ 4 Eddie Waitkus	8.00	3.50	.80
☐ 5 Jim Robertson	8.00	3.50	.80
☐ 6 Pete Suder	8.00	3.50	.80
☐ 7 Gene Baker	8.00	3.50	.80
☐ 8 Warren Hacker	8.00	3.50	.80
☐ 9 Gil McDougald	16.00	6.75	2.25
☐ 10 Phil Rizzuto	50.00	22.50	7.50
☐ 11 Bill Bruton	9.00	4.00	.90
☐ 12 Andy Pafko	9.00	4.00	.90
☐ 13 Clyde Vollmer	8.00	3.50	.80
☐ 14 Gus Keriazakos	8.00	3.50	.80
☐ 15 Frank Sullivan	8.00	3.50	.80
☐ 16 Jim Piersall	11.00	5.00	1.35
☐ 17 Del Ennis	9.00	4.00	.90
☐ 18 Stan Lopata	8.00	3.50	.80
☐ 19 Bobby Avila	8.00	3.50	.80
☐ 20 Al Smith	8.00	3.50	.80
☐ 21 Don Hoak	9.00	4.00	.90
☐ 22 Roy Campanella	110.00	50.00	16.50
☐ 23 Al Kaline	140.00	63.00	21.00
☐ 24 Al Aber	8.00	3.50	.80
☐ 25 Minnie Minoso	16.00	6.75	2.25
☐ 26 Virgil Trucks	9.00	4.00	.90
☐ 27 Preston Ward	8.00	3.50	.80
☐ 28 Dick Cole	8.00	3.50	.80
☐ 29 Red Schoendienst	27.00	12.00	4.00
☐ 30 Bill Sarni	8.00	3.50	.80
☐ 31 Johnny Temple	10.00	4.50	1.25
☐ 32 Wally Post	9.00	4.00	.90
☐ 33 Nellie Fox	22.00	9.50	3.15
☐ 34 Clint Courtney	8.00	3.50	.80
☐ 35 Bill Tuttle	8.00	3.50	.80
☐ 36 Wayne Belardi	8.00	3.50	.80
☐ 37 Pee Wee Reese	70.00	32.00	10.50
☐ 38 Early Wynn	27.00	12.00	4.00
☐ 39 Bob Darnell	8.00	3.50	.80
☐ 40 Vic Wertz	9.00	4.00	.90
☐ 41 Mel Clark	8.00	3.50	.80
☐ 42 Bob Greenwood	8.00	3.50	.80
☐ 43 Bob Buhl	9.00	4.00	.90
☐ 44 Danny O'Connell	8.00	3.50	.80
☐ 45 Tom Umphlett	8.00	3.50	.80
☐ 46 Mickey Vernon	9.00	4.00	.90
☐ 47 Sammy White	8.00	3.50	.80
☐ 48A Milt Bolling ERR (name on back is Frank Bolling)	10.00	4.50	1.25
☐ 48B Milt Bolling COR	25.00	11.00	3.50
☐ 49 Jim Greengrass	8.00	3.50	.80
☐ 50 Hobie Landrith	8.00	3.50	.80
☐ 51 Elvin Tappe	8.00	3.50	.80
☐ 52 Hal Rice	8.00	3.50	.80
☐ 53 Alex Kellner	8.00	3.50	.80
☐ 54 Don Bollweg	8.00	3.50	.80
☐ 55 Cal Abrams	8.00	3.50	.80
☐ 56 Billy Cox	9.00	4.00	.90
☐ 57 Bob Friend	9.00	4.00	.90
☐ 58 Frank Thomas	10.00	4.50	1.25
☐ 59 Whitey Ford	70.00	32.00	10.50
☐ 60 Enos Slaughter	27.00	12.00	4.00
☐ 61 Paul LaPalme	8.00	3.50	.80
☐ 62 Royce Lint	8.00	3.50	.80
☐ 63 Irv Noren	9.00	4.00	.90
☐ 64 Curt Simmons	9.00	4.00	.90
☐ 65 Don Zimmer	30.00	13.50	4.50
☐ 66 George Shuba	9.00	4.00	.90
☐ 67 Don Larsen	16.00	6.75	2.25
☐ 68 Elston Howard	65.00	29.00	9.75
☐ 69 Billy Hunter	8.00	3.50	.80
☐ 70 Lou Burdette	10.00	4.50	1.25
☐ 71 Dave Jolly	8.00	3.50	.80
☐ 72 Chet Nichols	8.00	3.50	.80
☐ 73 Eddie Yost	8.00	3.50	.80
☐ 74 Jerry Snyder	8.00	3.50	.80
☐ 75 Brooks Lawrence	8.00	3.50	.80
☐ 76 Tom Poholsky	8.00	3.50	.80
☐ 77 Jim McDonald	8.00	3.50	.80

☐ 78 Gil Coan	8.00	3.50	.80
☐ 79 Willie Miranda	8.00	3.50	.80
☐ 80 Lou Limmer	8.00	3.50	.80
☐ 81 Bobby Morgan	8.00	3.50	.80
☐ 82 Lee Walls	8.00	3.50	.80
☐ 83 Max Surkont	8.00	3.50	.80
☐ 84 George Freese	8.00	3.50	.80
☐ 85 Cass Michaels	8.00	3.50	.80
☐ 86 Ted Gray	8.00	3.50	.80
☐ 87 Randy Jackson	8.00	3.50	.80
☐ 88 Steve Bilko	8.00	3.50	.80
☐ 89 Lou Boudreau MG	22.00	9.50	3.15
☐ 90 Art Ditmar	8.00	3.50	.80
☐ 91 Dick Marlowe	8.00	3.50	.80
☐ 92 George Zuverink	8.00	3.50	.80
☐ 93 Andy Seminick	8.00	3.50	.80
☐ 94 Hank Thompson	9.00	4.00	.90
☐ 95 Sal Maglie	12.00	5.25	1.50
☐ 96 Ray Narleski	8.00	3.50	.80
☐ 97 Johnny Podres	16.00	6.75	2.25
☐ 98 Jim Gilliam	16.00	6.75	2.25
☐ 99 Jerry Coleman	9.00	4.00	.90
☐ 100 Tom Morgan	8.00	3.50	.80
☐ 101A Don Johnson ERR	10.00	4.50	1.25
(photo actually Ernie Johnson)			
☐ 101B Don Johnson COR	21.00	9.00	3.00
☐ 102 Bobby Thomson	11.00	5.00	1.35
☐ 103 Eddie Mathews	50.00	22.50	7.50
☐ 104 Bob Porterfield	7.00	3.00	.70
☐ 105 Johnny Schmitz	7.00	3.00	.70
☐ 106 Del Rice	7.00	3.00	.70
☐ 107 Solly Hemus	7.00	3.00	.70
☐ 108 Lou Kretlow	7.00	3.00	.70
☐ 109 Vern Stephens	8.00	3.50	.80
☐ 110 Bob Miller	7.00	3.00	.70
☐ 111 Steve Ridzik	7.00	3.00	.70
☐ 112 Granny Hamner	7.00	3.00	.70
☐ 113 Bob Hall	7.00	3.00	.70
☐ 114 Vic Janowicz	8.00	3.50	.80
☐ 115 Roger Bowman	7.00	3.00	.70
☐ 116 Sandy Consuegra	7.00	3.00	.70
☐ 117 Johnny Groth	7.00	3.00	.70
☐ 118 Bobby Adams	7.00	3.00	.70
☐ 119 Joe Astroth	7.00	3.00	.70
☐ 120 Ed Burtschy	7.00	3.00	.70
☐ 121 Rufus Crawford	7.00	3.00	.70
☐ 122 Al Corwin	7.00	3.00	.70
☐ 123 Marv Grissom	7.00	3.00	.70
☐ 124 Johnny Antonelli	9.00	4.00	.90
☐ 125 Paul Giel	7.00	3.00	.70
☐ 126 Billy Goodman	8.00	3.50	.80
☐ 127 Hank Majeski	7.00	3.00	.70
☐ 128 Mike Garcia	8.00	3.50	.80
☐ 129 Hal Naragon	7.00	3.00	.70
☐ 130 Richie Ashburn	24.00	10.50	3.50
☐ 131 Willard Marshall	7.00	3.00	.70
☐ 132A Harvey Kueen ERR	11.00	5.00	1.35
(sic, Kuenn)			

☐ 132B Harvey Kuenn COR	27.00	12.00	4.00
☐ 133 Charles King	7.00	3.00	.70
☐ 134 Bob Feller	60.00	27.00	9.00
☐ 135 Lloyd Merriman	7.00	3.00	.70
☐ 136 Rocky Bridges	7.00	3.00	.70
☐ 137 Bob Talbot	7.00	3.00	.70
☐ 138 Davey Williams	8.00	3.50	.80
☐ 139 Shantz Brothers	9.00	4.00	.90
Wilmer and Bobby			
☐ 140 Bobby Shantz	9.00	4.00	.90
☐ 141 Wes Westrum	7.00	3.00	.70
☐ 142 Rudy Regalado	7.00	3.00	.70
☐ 143 Don Newcombe	17.00	7.25	2.50
☐ 144 Art Houtteman	7.00	3.00	.70
☐ 145 Bob Nieman	7.00	3.00	.70
☐ 146 Don Liddle	7.00	3.00	.70
☐ 147 Sam Mele	7.00	3.00	.70
☐ 148 Bob Chakales	7.00	3.00	.70
☐ 149 Cloyd Boyer	7.00	3.00	.70
☐ 150 Billy Klaus	7.00	3.00	.70
☐ 151 Jim Brideweser	7.00	3.00	.70
☐ 152 Johnny Klippstein	7.00	3.00	.70
☐ 153 Eddie Robinson	7.00	3.00	.70
☐ 154 Frank Lary	10.00	4.50	1.25
☐ 155 Jerry Staley	7.00	3.00	.70
☐ 156 Jim Hughes	7.00	3.00	.70
☐ 157A Ernie Johnson ERR	10.00	4.50	1.25
(photo actually Don Johnson)			
☐ 157B Ernie Johnson COR	21.00	9.00	3.00
☐ 158 Gil Hodges	40.00	18.00	6.00
☐ 159 Harry Byrd	8.00	3.50	.80
☐ 160 Bill Skowron	22.00	9.50	3.15
☐ 161 Matt Batts	7.00	3.00	.70
☐ 162 Charlie Maxwell	8.00	3.50	.80
☐ 163 Sid Gordon	7.00	3.00	.70
☐ 164 Toby Atwell	7.00	3.00	.70
☐ 165 Maurice McDermott	7.00	3.00	.70
☐ 166 Jim Busby	7.00	3.00	.70
☐ 167 Bob Grim	12.00	5.25	1.50
☐ 168 Yogi Berra	95.00	42.00	12.00
☐ 169 Carl Furillo	16.00	6.75	2.25
☐ 170 Carl Erskine	15.00	6.50	2.15
☐ 171 Robin Roberts	25.00	11.00	3.50
☐ 172 Willie Jones	7.00	3.00	.70
☐ 173 Chico Carrasquel	7.00	3.00	.70
☐ 174 Sherm Lollar	8.00	3.50	.80
☐ 175 Wilmer Shantz	7.00	3.00	.70
☐ 176 Joe DeMaestri	7.00	3.00	.70
☐ 177 Willard Nixon	7.00	3.00	.70
☐ 178 Tom Brewer	7.00	3.00	.70
☐ 179 Hank Aaron	225.00	100.00	33.00
☐ 180 Johnny Logan	8.00	3.50	.80
☐ 181 Eddie Miksis	7.00	3.00	.70
☐ 182 Bob Rush	7.00	3.00	.70
☐ 183 Ray Katt	7.00	3.00	.70
☐ 184 Willie Mays	225.00	100.00	33.00
☐ 185 Vic Raschi	10.00	4.50	1.25

☐ 186 Alex Grammas	7.00	3.00	.70
☐ 187 Fred Hatfield	7.00	3.00	.70
☐ 188 Ned Garver	7.00	3.00	.70
☐ 189 Jack Collum	7.00	3.00	.70
☐ 190 Fred Baczewski	7.00	3.00	.70
☐ 191 Bob Lemon	25.00	11.00	3.50
☐ 192 George Strickland	7.00	3.00	.70
☐ 193 Howie Judson	7.00	3.00	.70
☐ 194 Joe Nuxhall	8.00	3.50	.80
☐ 195A Erv Palica (without trade)	8.00	3.50	.80
☐ 195B Erv Palica (with trade)	20.00	8.50	2.75
☐ 196 Russ Meyer	7.00	3.00	.70
☐ 197 Ralph Kiner	28.00	12.50	4.00
☐ 198 Dave Pope	7.00	3.00	.70
☐ 199 Vernon Law	8.00	3.50	.80
☐ 200 Dick Littlefield	7.00	3.00	.70
☐ 201 Allie Reynolds	15.00	6.50	2.15
☐ 202 Mickey Mantle	450.00	200.00	67.50
☐ 203 Steve Gromek	7.00	3.00	.70
☐ 204A Frank Bolling ERR (name on back is Milt Bolling)	9.00	4.00	.90
☐ 204B Frank Bolling COR	21.00	9.00	3.00
☐ 205 Rip Repulski	7.00	3.00	.70
☐ 206 Ralph Beard	7.00	3.00	.70
☐ 207 Frank Shea	7.00	3.00	.70
☐ 208 Ed Fitzgerald	7.00	3.00	.70
☐ 209 Smoky Burgess	9.00	4.00	.90
☐ 210 Earl Torgeson	7.00	3.00	.70
☐ 211 Sonny Dixon	7.00	3.00	.70
☐ 212 Jack Dittmer	7.00	3.00	.70
☐ 213 George Kell	20.00	8.50	2.75
☐ 214 Billy Pierce	10.00	4.50	1.25
☐ 215 Bob Kuzava	7.00	3.00	.70
☐ 216 Preacher Roe	12.00	5.25	1.50
☐ 217 Del Crandall	8.00	3.50	.80
☐ 218 Joe Adcock	9.00	4.00	.90
☐ 219 Whitey Lockman	8.00	3.50	.80
☐ 220 Jim Hearn	7.00	3.00	.70
☐ 221 Hector Brown	7.00	3.00	.70
☐ 222 Russ Kemmerer	7.00	3.00	.70
☐ 223 Hal Jeffcoat	7.00	3.00	.70
☐ 224 Dee Fondy	7.00	3.00	.70
☐ 225 Paul Richards	20.00	8.50	2.75
☐ 226 W. McKinley UMP	30.00	13.50	4.50
☐ 227 Frank Baumholtz	16.50	7.00	2.35
☐ 228 John Phillips	16.50	7.00	2.35
☐ 229 Jim Brosnan	20.00	8.50	2.75
☐ 230 Al Brazle	16.50	7.00	2.35
☐ 231 Jim Konstanty	20.00	8.50	2.75
☐ 232 Birdie Tebbetts	18.00	7.50	2.50
☐ 233 Bill Serena	16.50	7.00	2.35
☐ 234 Dick Bartell	18.00	7.50	2.50
☐ 235 J. Paparella UMP	30.00	13.50	4.50
☐ 236 Murry Dickson	16.50	7.00	2.35
☐ 237 Johnny Wyrostek	16.50	7.00	2.35
☐ 238 Eddie Stanky	20.00	8.50	2.75
☐ 239 Edwin Rommel UMP	30.00	13.50	4.50
☐ 240 Billy Loes	18.00	7.50	2.50
☐ 241 Johnny Pesky	18.00	7.50	2.50
☐ 242 Ernie Banks	350.00	160.00	52.50
☐ 243 Gus Bell	18.00	7.50	2.50
☐ 244 Duane Pillette	16.50	7.00	2.35
☐ 245 Bill Miller	16.50	7.00	2.35
☐ 246 Hank Bauer	36.00	16.25	5.50
☐ 247 Dutch Leonard	18.00	7.50	2.50
☐ 248 Harry Dorish	16.50	7.00	2.35
☐ 249 Billy Gardner	18.00	7.50	2.50
☐ 250 Larry Napp UMP	30.00	13.50	4.50
☐ 251 Stan Jok	16.50	7.00	2.35
☐ 252 Roy Smalley	16.50	7.00	2.35
☐ 253 Jim Wilson	16.50	7.00	2.35
☐ 254 Bennett Flowers	16.50	7.00	2.35
☐ 255 Pete Runnels	18.00	7.50	2.50
☐ 256 Owen Friend	16.50	7.00	2.35
☐ 257 Tom Alston	16.50	7.00	2.35
☐ 258 John Stevens UMP	30.00	13.50	4.50
☐ 259 Don Mossi	22.00	9.50	3.15
☐ 260 Edwin Hurley UMP	30.00	13.50	4.50
☐ 261 Walt Moryn	16.50	7.00	2.35
☐ 262 Jim Lemon	20.00	8.50	2.75
☐ 263 Eddie Joost	16.50	7.00	2.35
☐ 264 Bill Henry	16.50	7.00	2.35
☐ 265 Albert Barlick UMP	80.00	36.00	12.00
☐ 266 Mike Fornieles	16.50	7.00	2.35
☐ 267 Jim Honochick UMP	70.00	32.00	10.50
☐ 268 Roy Lee Hawes	16.50	7.00	2.35
☐ 269 Joe Amalfitano	16.50	7.00	2.35
☐ 270 Chico Fernandez	16.50	7.00	2.35
☐ 271 Bob Hooper	16.50	7.00	2.35
☐ 272 John Flaherty UMP	30.00	13.50	4.50
☐ 273 Bubba Church	16.50	7.00	2.35
☐ 274 Jim Delsing	16.50	7.00	2.35
☐ 275 William Grieve UMP	30.00	13.50	4.50
☐ 276 Ike Delock	16.50	7.00	2.35
☐ 277 Ed Runge UMP	35.00	15.75	5.25
☐ 278 Charlie Neal	30.00	13.50	4.50
☐ 279 Hank Soar UMP	30.00	13.50	4.50
☐ 280 Clyde McCullough	16.50	7.00	2.35
☐ 281 Charles Berry UMP	30.00	13.50	4.50
☐ 282 Phil Cavarretta	18.00	7.50	2.50
☐ 283 Nestor Chylak UMP	30.00	13.50	4.50
☐ 284 Bill Jackowski UMP	30.00	13.50	4.50
☐ 285 Walt Dropo	18.00	7.50	2.50
☐ 286 Frank Secory UMP	30.00	13.50	4.50
☐ 287 Ron Mrozinski	16.50	7.00	2.35
☐ 288 Dick Smith	16.50	7.00	2.35
☐ 289 Arthur Gore UMP	30.00	13.50	4.50
☐ 290 Hershell Freeman	16.50	7.00	2.35
☐ 291 Frank Dascoli UMP	30.00	13.50	4.50
☐ 292 Marv Blaylock	16.50	7.00	2.35
☐ 293 Thomas Gorman UMP	35.00	15.75	5.25
☐ 294 Wally Moses	18.00	7.50	2.50
☐ 295 Lee Ballanfant UMP	30.00	13.50	4.50

☐ 296 Bill Virdon	35.00	15.75	5.25
☐ 297 Dusty Boggess UMP	30.00	13.50	4.50
☐ 298 Charlie Grimm	18.00	7.50	2.50
☐ 299 Lon Warneke UMP	35.00	15.75	5.25
☐ 300 Tommy Byrne	18.00	7.50	2.50
☐ 301 William Engeln UMP	30.00	13.50	4.50
☐ 302 Frank Malzone	30.00	13.50	4.50
☐ 303 Jocko Conlan UMP	100.00	45.00	15.00
☐ 304 Harry Chiti	16.50	7.00	2.35
☐ 305 Frank Umont UMP	30.00	13.50	4.50
☐ 306 Bob Cerv	24.00	10.50	3.50
☐ 307 Babe Pinelli UMP	35.00	15.75	5.25
☐ 308 Al Lopez MG	45.00	20.00	6.75
☐ 309 Hal Dixon UMP	30.00	13.50	4.50
☐ 310 Ken Lehman	16.50	7.00	2.35
☐ 311 Lawrence Goetz UMP	30.00	13.50	4.50
☐ 312 Bill Wight	16.50	7.00	2.35
☐ 313 Augie Donatelli UMP	35.00	15.75	5.25
☐ 314 Dale Mitchell	18.00	7.50	2.50
☐ 315 Cal Hubbard UMP	85.00	38.00	12.75
☐ 316 Marion Fricano	16.50	7.00	2.35
☐ 317 William Summers UMP	30.00	13.50	4.50
☐ 318 Sid Hudson	16.50	7.00	2.35
☐ 319 Al Schroll	16.50	7.00	2.35
☐ 320 George Susce Jr.	50.00	10.00	2.00

1989 Bowman

The 1989 Bowman set, which was actually produced by Topps, contains 484 cards measuring 2 1/2" by 3 3/4". The fronts have white-bordered color photos with facsimile autographs and small Bowman logos. The backs are scarlet and feature charts detailing 1988 player performances vs. each team. The cards are checklisted below alphabetically according to teams in the AL and NL as follows: Baltimore Orioles (1-18), Boston Red Sox (19-36), California Angels (37-54), Chicago White Sox (55-72), Cleveland Indians (73-91), Detroit Tigers (92-109), Kansas City Royals (110-128), Milwaukee Brewers (129-146), Minnesota Twins (147-164), New York Yankees (165-183), Oakland Athletics (184-202), Seattle Mariners (203-220), Texas Rangers (221-238), Toronto Blue Jays (239-257), Atlanta Braves (262-279), Chicago Cubs (280-298), Cincinnati Reds (299-316), Houston Astros (317-334), Los Angeles Dodgers (335-352), Montreal Expos (353-370), New York Mets (371-389), Philadelphia Phillies (390-408), Pittsburgh Pirates (409-426), St. Louis Cardinals (427-444), San Diego Padres (445-462), and San Francisco Giants (463-480). Cards 258-261 form a father\son subset. The player selection is concentrated on prospects and "name" players. The cards were released in midseason 1989 in wax, rack, and cello pack formats. The key rookie cards in this set are Jim Abbott, Steve Avery, Ken Griffey Jr., Tino Martinez, and Jerome Walton. Topps also produced a limited Bowman "Tiffany" set with supposedly only 6,000 sets being produced. This Tiffany version is valued at approximately five times the values listed below.

	MINT	EXC	G-VG
COMPLETE SET (484)	17.00	7.25	2.50
COMMON PLAYER (1-484)	.03	.01	.00
☐ 1 Oswald Peraza	.06	.02	.00
☐ 2 Brian Holton	.03	.01	.00
☐ 3 Jose Bautista	.06	.02	.00
☐ 4 Pete Harnisch	.17	.07	.01
☐ 5 Dave Schmidt	.03	.01	.00
☐ 6 Gregg Olson	.40	.16	.04
☐ 7 Jeff Ballard	.06	.02	.00
☐ 8 Bob Melvin	.03	.01	.00
☐ 9 Cal Ripken	.30	.12	.03
☐ 10 Randy Milligan	.08	.03	.01
☐ 11 Juan Bell	.08	.03	.01
☐ 12 Billy Ripken	.03	.01	.00
☐ 13 Jim Traber	.03	.01	.00
☐ 14 Pete Stanicek	.03	.01	.00
☐ 15 Steve Finley	.25	.10	.02
☐ 16 Larry Sheets	.03	.01	.00
☐ 17 Phil Bradley	.03	.01	.00
☐ 18 Brady Anderson	.08	.03	.01
☐ 19 Lee Smith	.08	.03	.01
☐ 20 Tom Fischer	.06	.02	.00
☐ 21 Mike Boddicker	.03	.01	.00
☐ 22 Rob Murphy	.03	.01	.00
☐ 23 Wes Gardner	.03	.01	.00
☐ 24 John Dopson	.08	.03	.01

☐ 25 Bob Stanley .03 .01 .00
☐ 26 Roger Clemens .25 .10 .02
☐ 27 Rich Gedman .03 .01 .00
☐ 28 Marty Barrett .03 .01 .00
☐ 29 Luis Rivera .03 .01 .00
☐ 30 Jody Reed .06 .02 .00
☐ 31 Nick Esasky .03 .01 .00
☐ 32 Wade Boggs .18 .08 .01
☐ 33 Jim Rice .08 .03 .01
☐ 34 Mike Greenwell .12 .05 .01
☐ 35 Dwight Evans .08 .03 .01
☐ 36 Ellis Burks .12 .05 .01
☐ 37 Chuck Finley .10 .04 .01
☐ 38 Kirk McCaskill .03 .01 .00
☐ 39 Jim Abbott .90 .40 .09
☐ 40 Bryan Harvey .20 .08 .02
☐ 41 Bert Blyleven .08 .03 .01
☐ 42 Mike Witt .03 .01 .00
☐ 43 Bob McClure .03 .01 .00
☐ 44 Bill Schroeder .03 .01 .00
☐ 45 Lance Parrish .08 .03 .01
☐ 46 Dick Schofield .03 .01 .00
☐ 47 Wally Joyner .10 .04 .01
☐ 48 Jack Howell .03 .01 .00
☐ 49 Johnny Ray .03 .01 .00
☐ 50 Chili Davis .06 .02 .00
☐ 51 Tony Armas .03 .01 .00
☐ 52 Claudell Washington .03 .01 .00
☐ 53 Brian Downing .03 .01 .00
☐ 54 Devon White .08 .03 .01
☐ 55 Bobby Thigpen .08 .03 .01
☐ 56 Bill Long .03 .01 .00
☐ 57 Jerry Reuss .03 .01 .00
☐ 58 Shawn Hillegas .03 .01 .00
☐ 59 Melido Perez .06 .02 .00
☐ 60 Jeff Bittiger .06 .02 .00
☐ 61 Jack McDowell .15 .06 .01
☐ 62 Carlton Fisk .12 .05 .01
☐ 63 Steve Lyons .03 .01 .00
☐ 64 Ozzie Guillen .06 .02 .00
☐ 65 Robin Ventura 1.00 .40 .10
☐ 66 Fred Manrique .03 .01 .00
☐ 67 Dan Pasqua .03 .01 .00
☐ 68 Ivan Calderon .06 .02 .00
☐ 69 Ron Kittle .06 .02 .00
☐ 70 Daryl Boston .03 .01 .00
☐ 71 Dave Gallagher .08 .03 .01
☐ 72 Harold Baines .08 .03 .01
☐ 73 Charles Nagy .20 .08 .02
☐ 74 John Farrell .03 .01 .00
☐ 75 Kevin Wickander .06 .02 .00
☐ 76 Greg Swindell .06 .02 .00
☐ 77 Mike Walker .08 .03 .01
☐ 78 Doug Jones .03 .01 .00
☐ 79 Rich Yett .03 .01 .00
☐ 80 Tom Candiotti .06 .02 .00
☐ 81 Jesse Orosco .03 .01 .00
☐ 82 Bud Black .03 .01 .00
☐ 83 Andy Allanson .03 .01 .00
☐ 84 Pete O'Brien .03 .01 .00
☐ 85 Jerry Browne .03 .01 .00
☐ 86 Brook Jacoby .03 .01 .00
☐ 87 Mark Lewis .35 .15 .03
☐ 88 Luis Aguayo .03 .01 .00
☐ 89 Cory Snyder .06 .02 .00
☐ 90 Oddibe McDowell .03 .01 .00
☐ 91 Joe Carter .10 .04 .01
☐ 92 Frank Tanana .06 .02 .00
☐ 93 Jack Morris .10 .04 .01
☐ 94 Doyle Alexander .03 .01 .00
☐ 95 Steve Searcy .08 .03 .01
☐ 96 Randy Bockus .03 .01 .00
☐ 97 Jeff Robinson .03 .01 .00
☐ 98 Mike Henneman .03 .01 .00
☐ 99 Paul Gibson .03 .01 .00
☐ 100 Frank Williams .03 .01 .00
☐ 101 Matt Nokes .06 .02 .00
☐ 102 Rico Brogna UER .35 .15 .03
(Misspelled Ricco
on card back)
☐ 103 Lou Whitaker .08 .03 .01
☐ 104 Al Pedrique .03 .01 .00
☐ 105 Alan Trammell .12 .05 .01
☐ 106 Chris Brown .03 .01 .00
☐ 107 Pat Sheridan .03 .01 .00
☐ 108 Chet Lemon .03 .01 .00
☐ 109 Keith Moreland .03 .01 .00
☐ 110 Mel Stottlemyre Jr. .06 .02 .00
☐ 111 Bret Saberhagen .10 .04 .01
☐ 112 Floyd Bannister .03 .01 .00
☐ 113 Jeff Montgomery .06 .02 .00
☐ 114 Steve Farr .03 .01 .00
☐ 115 Tom Gordon UER .17 .07 .01
(front shows auto-
graph of Don Gordon)
☐ 116 Charlie Leibrandt .03 .01 .00
☐ 117 Mark Gubicza .06 .02 .00
☐ 118 Mike Macfarlane .10 .04 .01
☐ 119 Bob Boone .06 .02 .00
☐ 120 Kurt Stillwell .03 .01 .00
☐ 121 George Brett .12 .05 .01
☐ 122 Frank White .03 .01 .00
☐ 123 Kevin Seitzer .06 .02 .00
☐ 124 Willie Wilson .06 .02 .00
☐ 125 Pat Tabler .03 .01 .00
☐ 126 Bo Jackson .40 .16 .04
☐ 127 Hugh Walker .08 .03 .01
☐ 128 Danny Tartabull .10 .04 .01
☐ 129 Teddy Higuera .03 .01 .00
☐ 130 Don August .03 .01 .00
☐ 131 Juan Nieves .03 .01 .00
☐ 132 Mike Birkbeck .03 .01 .00
☐ 133 Dan Plesac .03 .01 .00
☐ 134 Chris Bosio .03 .01 .00
☐ 135 Bill Wegman .03 .01 .00
☐ 136 Chuck Crim .03 .01 .00

☐ 137	B.J. Surhoff	.06	.02	.00
☐ 138	Joey Meyer	.03	.01	.00
☐ 139	Dale Sveum	.03	.01	.00
☐ 140	Paul Molitor	.08	.03	.01
☐ 141	Jim Gantner	.03	.01	.00
☐ 142	Gary Sheffield	.25	.10	.02
☐ 143	Greg Brock	.03	.01	.00
☐ 144	Robin Yount	.12	.05	.01
☐ 145	Glenn Braggs	.03	.01	.00
☐ 146	Rob Deer	.06	.02	.00
☐ 147	Fred Toliver	.03	.01	.00
☐ 148	Jeff Reardon	.08	.03	.01
☐ 149	Allan Anderson	.03	.01	.00
☐ 150	Frank Viola	.08	.03	.01
☐ 151	Shane Rawley	.03	.01	.00
☐ 152	Juan Berenguer	.03	.01	.00
☐ 153	Johnny Ard	.12	.05	.01
☐ 154	Tim Laudner	.03	.01	.00
☐ 155	Brian Harper	.06	.02	.00
☐ 156	Al Newman	.03	.01	.00
☐ 157	Kent Hrbek	.08	.03	.01
☐ 158	Gary Gaetti	.06	.02	.00
☐ 159	Wally Backman	.03	.01	.00
☐ 160	Gene Larkin	.03	.01	.00
☐ 161	Greg Gagne	.03	.01	.00
☐ 162	Kirby Puckett	.25	.10	.02
☐ 163	Dan Gladden	.03	.01	.00
☐ 164	Randy Bush	.03	.01	.00
☐ 165	Dave LaPoint	.03	.01	.00
☐ 166	Andy Hawkins	.03	.01	.00
☐ 167	Dave Righetti	.06	.02	.00
☐ 168	Lance McCullers	.03	.01	.00
☐ 169	Jimmy Jones	.03	.01	.00
☐ 170	Al Leiter	.03	.01	.00
☐ 171	John Candelaria	.03	.01	.00
☐ 172	Don Slaught	.03	.01	.00
☐ 173	Jamie Quirk	.03	.01	.00
☐ 174	Rafael Santana	.03	.01	.00
☐ 175	Mike Pagliarulo	.03	.01	.00
☐ 176	Don Mattingly	.20	.08	.02
☐ 177	Ken Phelps	.03	.01	.00
☐ 178	Steve Sax	.08	.03	.01
☐ 179	Dave Winfield	.10	.04	.01
☐ 180	Stan Jefferson	.03	.01	.00
☐ 181	Rickey Henderson	.30	.12	.03
☐ 182	Bob Brower	.03	.01	.00
☐ 183	Roberto Kelly	.12	.05	.01
☐ 184	Curt Young	.03	.01	.00
☐ 185	Gene Nelson	.03	.01	.00
☐ 186	Bob Welch	.08	.03	.01
☐ 187	Rick Honeycutt	.03	.01	.00
☐ 188	Dave Stewart	.08	.03	.01
☐ 189	Mike Moore	.06	.02	.00
☐ 190	Dennis Eckersley	.08	.03	.01
☐ 191	Eric Plunk	.03	.01	.00
☐ 192	Storm Davis	.03	.01	.00
☐ 193	Terry Steinbach	.06	.02	.00
☐ 194	Ron Hassey	.03	.01	.00
☐ 195	Stan Royer	.12	.05	.01
☐ 196	Walt Weiss	.08	.03	.01
☐ 197	Mark McGwire	.12	.05	.01
☐ 198	Carney Lansford	.06	.02	.00
☐ 199	Glenn Hubbard	.03	.01	.00
☐ 200	Dave Henderson	.08	.03	.01
☐ 201	Jose Canseco	.45	.18	.04
☐ 202	Dave Parker	.08	.03	.01
☐ 203	Scott Bankhead	.06	.02	.00
☐ 204	Tom Niedenfuer	.03	.01	.00
☐ 205	Mark Langston	.08	.03	.01
☐ 206	Erik Hanson	.40	.16	.04
☐ 207	Mike Jackson	.03	.01	.00
☐ 208	Dave Valle	.03	.01	.00
☐ 209	Scott Bradley	.03	.01	.00
☐ 210	Harold Reynolds	.06	.02	.00
☐ 211	Tino Martinez	.60	.25	.06
☐ 212	Rich Renteria	.06	.02	.00
☐ 213	Rey Quinones	.03	.01	.00
☐ 214	Jim Presley	.03	.01	.00
☐ 215	Alvin Davis	.06	.02	.00
☐ 216	Edgar Martinez	.15	.06	.01
☐ 217	Darnell Coles	.03	.01	.00
☐ 218	Jeffrey Leonard	.03	.01	.00
☐ 219	Jay Buhner	.15	.06	.01
☐ 220	Ken Griffey Jr.	5.00	2.25	.50
☐ 221	Drew Hall	.03	.01	.00
☐ 222	Bobby Witt	.06	.02	.00
☐ 223	Jamie Moyer	.03	.01	.00
☐ 224	Charlie Hough	.03	.01	.00
☐ 225	Nolan Ryan	.45	.18	.04
☐ 226	Jeff Russell	.03	.01	.00
☐ 227	Jim Sundberg	.03	.01	.00
☐ 228	Julio Franco	.10	.04	.01
☐ 229	Buddy Bell	.06	.02	.00
☐ 230	Scott Fletcher	.03	.01	.00
☐ 231	Jeff Kunkel	.03	.01	.00
☐ 232	Steve Buechele	.03	.01	.00
☐ 233	Monty Fariss	.25	.10	.02
☐ 234	Rick Leach	.03	.01	.00
☐ 235	Ruben Sierra	.20	.08	.02
☐ 236	Cecil Espy	.06	.02	.00
☐ 237	Rafael Palmeiro	.12	.05	.01
☐ 238	Pete Incaviglia	.06	.02	.00
☐ 239	Dave Stieb	.08	.03	.01
☐ 240	Jeff Musselman	.03	.01	.00
☐ 241	Mike Flanagan	.06	.02	.00
☐ 242	Todd Stottlemyre	.12	.05	.01
☐ 243	Jimmy Key	.08	.03	.01
☐ 244	Tony Castillo	.08	.03	.01
☐ 245	Alex Sanchez	.08	.03	.01
☐ 246	Tom Henke	.06	.02	.00
☐ 247	John Cerutti	.03	.01	.00
☐ 248	Ernie Whitt	.03	.01	.00
☐ 249	Bob Brenly	.03	.01	.00
☐ 250	Rance Mulliniks	.03	.01	.00
☐ 251	Kelly Gruber	.08	.03	.01
☐ 252	Ed Sprague	.25	.10	.02

☐ 253 Fred McGriff	.15	.06	.01
☐ 254 Tony Fernandez	.06	.02	.00
☐ 255 Tom Lawless	.03	.01	.00
☐ 256 George Bell	.10	.04	.01
☐ 257 Jesse Barfield	.08	.03	.01
☐ 258 Roberto Alomar w/Dad	.20	.08	.02
☐ 259 Ken Griffey Jr./Sr.	1.00	.40	.10
☐ 260 Cal Ripken Jr./Sr.	.10	.04	.01
☐ 261 M.Stottlemyre Jr./Sr.	.06	.02	.00
☐ 262 Zane Smith	.06	.02	.00
☐ 263 Charlie Puleo	.03	.01	.00
☐ 264 Derek Lilliquist	.08	.03	.01
☐ 265 Paul Assenmacher	.03	.01	.00
☐ 266 John Smoltz	.45	.18	.04
☐ 267 Tom Glavine	.35	.15	.03
☐ 268 Steve Avery	1.50	.60	.15
☐ 269 Pete Smith	.06	.02	.00
☐ 270 Jody Davis	.03	.01	.00
☐ 271 Bruce Benedict	.03	.01	.00
☐ 272 Andres Thomas	.03	.01	.00
☐ 273 Gerald Perry	.03	.01	.00
☐ 274 Ron Gant	.35	.15	.03
☐ 275 Darrell Evans	.06	.02	.00
☐ 276 Dale Murphy	.10	.04	.01
☐ 277 Dion James	.03	.01	.00
☐ 278 Lonnie Smith	.06	.02	.00
☐ 279 Geronimo Berroa	.03	.01	.00
☐ 280 Steve Wilson	.08	.03	.01
☐ 281 Rick Sutcliffe	.06	.02	.00
☐ 282 Kevin Coffman	.03	.01	.00
☐ 283 Mitch Williams	.03	.01	.00
☐ 284 Greg Maddux	.08	.03	.01
☐ 285 Paul Kilgus	.03	.01	.00
☐ 286 Mike Harkey	.10	.04	.01
☐ 287 Lloyd McClendon	.03	.01	.00
☐ 288 Damon Berryhill	.06	.02	.00
☐ 289 Ty Griffin	.08	.03	.01
☐ 290 Ryne Sandberg	.30	.12	.03
☐ 291 Mark Grace	.25	.10	.02
☐ 292 Curt Wilkerson	.03	.01	.00
☐ 293 Vance Law	.03	.01	.00
☐ 294 Shawon Dunston	.08	.03	.01
☐ 295 Jerome Walton	.35	.15	.03
☐ 296 Mitch Webster	.03	.01	.00
☐ 297 Dwight Smith	.10	.04	.01
☐ 298 Andre Dawson	.12	.05	.01
☐ 299 Jeff Sellers	.03	.01	.00
☐ 300 Jose Rijo	.08	.03	.01
☐ 301 John Franco	.03	.01	.00
☐ 302 Rick Mahler	.03	.01	.00
☐ 303 Ron Robinson	.03	.01	.00
☐ 304 Danny Jackson	.06	.02	.00
☐ 305 Rob Dibble	.20	.08	.02
☐ 306 Tom Browning	.06	.02	.00
☐ 307 Bo Diaz	.03	.01	.00
☐ 308 Manny Trillo	.03	.01	.00
☐ 309 Chris Sabo	.50	.20	.05
☐ 310 Ron Oester	.03	.01	.00
☐ 311 Barry Larkin	.12	.05	.01
☐ 312 Todd Benzinger	.03	.01	.00
☐ 313 Paul O'Neill	.08	.03	.01
☐ 314 Kal Daniels	.08	.03	.01
☐ 315 Joel Youngblood	.03	.01	.00
☐ 316 Eric Davis	.10	.04	.01
☐ 317 Dave Smith	.03	.01	.00
☐ 318 Mark Portugal	.03	.01	.00
☐ 319 Brian Meyer	.06	.02	.00
☐ 320 Jim Deshaies	.03	.01	.00
☐ 321 Juan Agosto	.03	.01	.00
☐ 322 Mike Scott	.08	.03	.01
☐ 323 Rick Rhoden	.03	.01	.00
☐ 324 Jim Clancy	.03	.01	.00
☐ 325 Larry Andersen	.03	.01	.00
☐ 326 Alex Trevino	.03	.01	.00
☐ 327 Alan Ashby	.03	.01	.00
☐ 328 Craig Reynolds	.03	.01	.00
☐ 329 Bill Doran	.03	.01	.00
☐ 330 Rafael Ramirez	.03	.01	.00
☐ 331 Glenn Davis	.08	.03	.01
☐ 332 Willie Ansley	.15	.06	.01
☐ 333 Gerald Young	.03	.01	.00
☐ 334 Cameron Drew	.03	.01	.00
☐ 335 Jay Howell	.03	.01	.00
☐ 336 Tim Belcher	.08	.03	.01
☐ 337 Fernando Valenzuela	.08	.03	.01
☐ 338 Ricky Horton	.03	.01	.00
☐ 339 Tim Leary	.06	.02	.00
☐ 340 Bill Bene	.03	.01	.00
☐ 341 Orel Hershiser	.08	.03	.01
☐ 342 Mike Scioscia	.03	.01	.00
☐ 343 Rick Dempsey	.03	.01	.00
☐ 344 Willie Randolph	.06	.02	.00
☐ 345 Alfredo Griffin	.03	.01	.00
☐ 346 Eddie Murray	.10	.04	.01
☐ 347 Mickey Hatcher	.03	.01	.00
☐ 348 Mike Sharperson	.03	.01	.00
☐ 349 John Shelby	.03	.01	.00
☐ 350 Mike Marshall	.06	.02	.00
☐ 351 Kirk Gibson	.08	.03	.01
☐ 352 Mike Davis	.03	.01	.00
☐ 353 Bryn Smith	.03	.01	.00
☐ 354 Pascual Perez	.03	.01	.00
☐ 355 Kevin Gross	.03	.01	.00
☐ 356 Andy McGaffigan	.03	.01	.00
☐ 357 Brian Holman	.15	.06	.01
☐ 358 Dave Wainhouse	.08	.03	.01
☐ 359 Dennis Martinez	.06	.02	.00
☐ 360 Tim Burke	.03	.01	.00
☐ 361 Nelson Santovenia	.08	.03	.01
☐ 362 Tim Wallach	.06	.02	.00
☐ 363 Spike Owen	.03	.01	.00
☐ 364 Rex Hudler	.06	.02	.00
☐ 365 Andres Galarraga	.06	.02	.00
☐ 366 Otis Nixon	.06	.02	.00
☐ 367 Hubie Brooks	.06	.02	.00
☐ 368 Mike Aldrete	.03	.01	.00

☐ 369	Tim Raines	.08	.03	.01
☐ 370	Dave Martinez	.06	.02	.00
☐ 371	Bob Ojeda	.03	.01	.00
☐ 372	Ron Darling	.06	.02	.00
☐ 373	Wally Whitehurst	.08	.03	.01
☐ 374	Randy Myers	.03	.01	.00
☐ 375	David Cone	.08	.03	.01
☐ 376	Dwight Gooden	.12	.05	.01
☐ 377	Sid Fernandez	.06	.02	.00
☐ 378	Dave Proctor	.08	.03	.01
☐ 379	Gary Carter	.08	.03	.01
☐ 380	Keith Miller	.03	.01	.00
☐ 381	Gregg Jefferies	.25	.10	.02
☐ 382	Tim Teufel	.03	.01	.00
☐ 383	Kevin Elster	.03	.01	.00
☐ 384	Dave Magadan	.08	.03	.01
☐ 385	Keith Hernandez	.08	.03	.01
☐ 386	Mookie Wilson	.03	.01	.00
☐ 387	Darryl Strawberry	.30	.12	.03
☐ 388	Kevin McReynolds	.08	.03	.01
☐ 389	Mark Carreon	.06	.02	.00
☐ 390	Jeff Parrett	.03	.01	.00
☐ 391	Mike Maddux	.03	.01	.00
☐ 392	Don Carman	.03	.01	.00
☐ 393	Bruce Ruffin	.03	.01	.00
☐ 394	Ken Howell	.03	.01	.00
☐ 395	Steve Bedrosian	.06	.02	.00
☐ 396	Floyd Youmans	.03	.01	.00
☐ 397	Larry McWilliams	.03	.01	.00
☐ 398	Pat Combs	.10	.04	.01
☐ 399	Steve Lake	.03	.01	.00
☐ 400	Dickie Thon	.03	.01	.00
☐ 401	Ricky Jordan	.12	.05	.01
☐ 402	Mike Schmidt	.25	.10	.02
☐ 403	Tom Herr	.03	.01	.00
☐ 404	Chris James	.03	.01	.00
☐ 405	Juan Samuel	.06	.02	.00
☐ 406	Von Hayes	.06	.02	.00
☐ 407	Ron Jones	.08	.03	.01
☐ 408	Curt Ford	.03	.01	.00
☐ 409	Bob Walk	.03	.01	.00
☐ 410	Jeff Robinson	.03	.01	.00
☐ 411	Jim Gott	.03	.01	.00
☐ 412	Scott Medvin	.08	.03	.01
☐ 413	John Smiley	.08	.03	.01
☐ 414	Bob Kipper	.03	.01	.00
☐ 415	Brian Fisher	.03	.01	.00
☐ 416	Doug Drabek	.08	.03	.01
☐ 417	Mike LaValliere	.03	.01	.00
☐ 418	Ken Oberkfell	.03	.01	.00
☐ 419	Sid Bream	.03	.01	.00
☐ 420	Austin Manahan	.10	.04	.01
☐ 421	Jose Lind	.03	.01	.00
☐ 422	Bobby Bonilla	.17	.07	.01
☐ 423	Glenn Wilson	.03	.01	.00
☐ 424	Andy Van Slyke	.10	.04	.01
☐ 425	Gary Redus	.03	.01	.00
☐ 426	Barry Bonds	.20	.08	.02
☐ 427	Don Heinkel	.03	.01	.00
☐ 428	Ken Dayley	.03	.01	.00
☐ 429	Todd Worrell	.06	.02	.00
☐ 430	Brad DuVall	.08	.03	.01
☐ 431	Jose DeLeon	.03	.01	.00
☐ 432	Joe Magrane	.06	.02	.00
☐ 433	John Ericks	.12	.05	.01
☐ 434	Frank DiPino	.03	.01	.00
☐ 435	Tony Pena	.06	.02	.00
☐ 436	Ozzie Smith	.10	.04	.01
☐ 437	Terry Pendleton	.08	.03	.01
☐ 438	Jose Oquendo	.03	.01	.00
☐ 439	Tim Jones	.06	.02	.00
☐ 440	Pedro Guerrero	.08	.03	.01
☐ 441	Milt Thompson	.03	.01	.00
☐ 442	Willie McGee	.08	.03	.01
☐ 443	Vince Coleman	.08	.03	.01
☐ 444	Tom Brunansky	.06	.02	.00
☐ 445	Walt Terrell	.03	.01	.00
☐ 446	Eric Show	.03	.01	.00
☐ 447	Mark Davis	.06	.02	.00
☐ 448	Andy Benes	.45	.18	.04
☐ 449	Ed Whitson	.03	.01	.00
☐ 450	Dennis Rasmussen	.03	.01	.00
☐ 451	Bruce Hurst	.06	.02	.00
☐ 452	Pat Clements	.03	.01	.00
☐ 453	Benito Santiago	.08	.03	.01
☐ 454	Sandy Alomar Jr.	.35	.15	.03
☐ 455	Garry Templeton	.06	.02	.00
☐ 456	Jack Clark	.08	.03	.01
☐ 457	Tim Flannery	.03	.01	.00
☐ 458	Roberto Alomar	.40	.16	.04
☐ 459	Carmelo Martinez	.03	.01	.00
☐ 460	John Kruk	.03	.01	.00
☐ 461	Tony Gwynn	.15	.06	.01
☐ 462	Jerald Clark	.17	.07	.01
☐ 463	Don Robinson	.03	.01	.00
☐ 464	Craig Lefferts	.03	.01	.00
☐ 465	Kelly Downs	.03	.01	.00
☐ 466	Rick Reuschel	.06	.02	.00
☐ 467	Scott Garrelts	.03	.01	.00
☐ 468	Wil Tejada	.03	.01	.00
☐ 469	Kirt Manwaring	.03	.01	.00
☐ 470	Terry Kennedy	.03	.01	.00
☐ 471	Jose Uribe	.03	.01	.00
☐ 472	Royce Clayton	.45	.18	.04
☐ 473	Robby Thompson	.03	.01	.00
☐ 474	Kevin Mitchell	.15	.06	.01
☐ 475	Ernie Riles	.03	.01	.00
☐ 476	Will Clark	.40	.16	.04
☐ 477	Donell Nixon	.03	.01	.00
☐ 478	Candy Maldonado	.06	.02	.00
☐ 479	Tracy Jones	.03	.01	.00
☐ 480	Brett Butler	.08	.03	.01
☐ 481	Checklist Card	.06	.01	.00
☐ 482	Checklist Card	.06	.01	.00
☐ 483	Checklist Card	.06	.01	.00
☐ 484	Checklist Card	.06	.01	.00

1990 Bowman

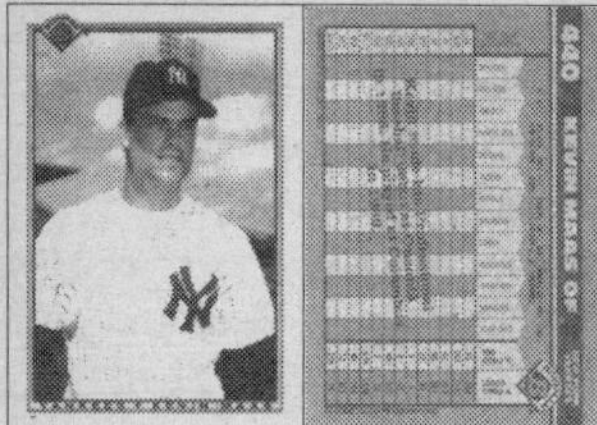

The 1990 Bowman set was issued in the standard card size of 2 1/2" by 3 1/2". This was the second issue by Topps using the Bowman name. The set consists of 528 cards, increased from 1989's edition of 484 cards. The cards feature a white border with the player's photo inside and the Bowman logo on top. Again, the Bowman cards were issued with the backs featuring team by team statistics. The card numbering is in team order with the teams themselves being ordered alphabetically within each league. The set numbering is as follows: Atlanta Braves (1-20), Chicago Cubs (21-40), Cincinnati Reds (41-60), Houston Astros (61-81), Los Angeles Dodgers (82-101), Montreal Expos (102-121), New York Mets (122-142), Philadelphia Phillies (143-162), Pittsburgh Pirates (163-182), St. Louis Cardinals (183-202), San Diego Padres (203-222), San Francisco Giants (223-242), Baltimore Orioles (243-262), Boston Red Sox (263-282), California Angels (283-302), Chicago White Sox (303-322), Cleveland Indians (323-342), Detroit Tigers (343-362), Kansas City Royals (363-383), Milwaukee Brewers (384-404), Minnesota Twins (405-424), New York Yankees (425-444), Oakland A's (445-464), Seattle Mariners (465-484), Texas Rangers (485-503), and Toronto Blue Jays (504-524). The key rookie cards in this set are Travis Fryman, Juan Gonzalez, Chuck Knoblauch, Ray Lankford, Kevin Maas, Ben McDonald, Jose Offerman, John Olerud, Frank Thomas, and Maurice Vaughn. Topps also produced a Bowman Tiffany glossy set. Production of these Tiffany Bowmans was reported to be approximately 3,000 sets. These Tiffany versions are valued at approximately eight times the values listed below.

	MINT	EXC	G-VG
COMPLETE SET (528)	17.00	7.25	2.50
COMMON PLAYER (1-528)	.03	.01	.00
☐ 1 Tommy Greene	.30	.10	.02
☐ 2 Tom Glavine	.15	.06	.01
☐ 3 Andy Nezelek	.03	.01	.00
☐ 4 Mike Stanton	.10	.04	.01
☐ 5 Rick Luecken	.08	.03	.01
☐ 6 Kent Mercker	.15	.06	.01
☐ 7 Derek Lilliquist	.03	.01	.00
☐ 8 Charlie Leibrandt	.03	.01	.00
☐ 9 Steve Avery	.50	.20	.05
☐ 10 John Smoltz	.17	.07	.01
☐ 11 Mark Lemke	.06	.02	.00
☐ 12 Lonnie Smith	.06	.02	.00
☐ 13 Oddibe McDowell	.03	.01	.00
☐ 14 Tyler Houston	.10	.04	.01
☐ 15 Jeff Blauser	.03	.01	.00
☐ 16 Ernie Whitt	.03	.01	.00
☐ 17 Alexis Infante	.06	.02	.00
☐ 18 Jim Presley	.03	.01	.00
☐ 19 Dale Murphy	.10	.04	.01
☐ 20 Nick Esasky	.03	.01	.00
☐ 21 Rick Sutcliffe	.06	.02	.00
☐ 22 Mike Bielecki	.03	.01	.00
☐ 23 Steve Wilson	.03	.01	.00
☐ 24 Kevin Blankenship	.03	.01	.00
☐ 25 Mitch Williams	.03	.01	.00
☐ 26 Dean Wilkins	.08	.03	.01
☐ 27 Greg Maddux	.08	.03	.01
☐ 28 Mike Harkey	.08	.03	.01
☐ 29 Mark Grace	.10	.04	.01
☐ 30 Ryne Sandberg	.25	.10	.02
☐ 31 Greg Smith	.08	.03	.01
☐ 32 Dwight Smith	.06	.02	.00
☐ 33 Damon Berryhill	.03	.01	.00
☐ 34 Earl Cunningham UER (Errant * by the word "in")	.12	.05	.01
☐ 35 Jerome Walton	.08	.03	.01
☐ 36 Lloyd McClendon	.03	.01	.00
☐ 37 Ty Griffin	.06	.02	.00
☐ 38 Shawon Dunston	.08	.03	.01
☐ 39 Andre Dawson	.10	.04	.01
☐ 40 Luis Salazar	.03	.01	.00
☐ 41 Tim Layana	.10	.04	.01
☐ 42 Rob Dibble	.08	.03	.01
☐ 43 Tom Browning	.06	.02	.00
☐ 44 Danny Jackson	.06	.02	.00
☐ 45 Jose Rijo	.08	.03	.01
☐ 46 Scott Scudder	.10	.04	.01
☐ 47 Randy Myers UER (Career ERA .274, should be 2.74)	.03	.01	.00
☐ 48 Brian Lane	.08	.03	.01
☐ 49 Paul O'Neill	.08	.03	.01
☐ 50 Barry Larkin	.10	.04	.01

☐ 51 Reggie Jefferson	.40	.16	.04
☐ 52 Jeff Branson	.10	.04	.01
☐ 53 Chris Sabo	.10	.04	.01
☐ 54 Joe Oliver	.08	.03	.01
☐ 55 Todd Benzinger	.03	.01	.00
☐ 56 Rolando Roomes	.03	.01	.00
☐ 57 Hal Morris	.35	.15	.03
☐ 58 Eric Davis	.10	.04	.01
☐ 59 Scott Bryant	.12	.05	.01
☐ 60 Ken Griffey Sr.	.08	.03	.01
☐ 61 Darryl Kile	.17	.07	.01
☐ 62 Dave Smith	.03	.01	.00
☐ 63 Mark Portugal	.03	.01	.00
☐ 64 Jeff Juden	.30	.12	.03
☐ 65 Bill Gullickson	.06	.02	.00
☐ 66 Danny Darwin	.03	.01	.00
☐ 67 Larry Andersen	.03	.01	.00
☐ 68 Jose Cano	.08	.03	.01
☐ 69 Dan Schatzeder	.03	.01	.00
☐ 70 Jim Deshaies	.03	.01	.00
☐ 71 Mike Scott	.08	.03	.01
☐ 72 Gerald Young	.03	.01	.00
☐ 73 Ken Caminiti	.03	.01	.00
☐ 74 Ken Oberkfell	.03	.01	.00
☐ 75 Dave Rohde	.08	.03	.01
☐ 76 Bill Doran	.03	.01	.00
☐ 77 Andujar Cedeno	.50	.20	.05
☐ 78 Craig Biggio	.08	.03	.01
☐ 79 Karl Rhodes	.12	.05	.01
☐ 80 Glenn Davis	.08	.03	.01
☐ 81 Eric Anthony	.17	.07	.01
☐ 82 John Wetteland	.08	.03	.01
☐ 83 Jay Howell	.03	.01	.00
☐ 84 Orel Hershiser	.08	.03	.01
☐ 85 Tim Belcher	.06	.02	.00
☐ 86 Kiki Jones	.15	.06	.01
☐ 87 Mike Hartley	.12	.05	.01
☐ 88 Ramon Martinez	.25	.10	.02
☐ 89 Mike Scioscia	.03	.01	.00
☐ 90 Willie Randolph	.06	.02	.00
☐ 91 Juan Samuel	.06	.02	.00
☐ 92 Jose Offerman	.20	.08	.02
☐ 93 Dave Hansen	.20	.08	.02
☐ 94 Jeff Hamilton	.03	.01	.00
☐ 95 Alfredo Griffin	.03	.01	.00
☐ 96 Tom Goodwin	.25	.10	.02
☐ 97 Kirk Gibson	.08	.03	.01
☐ 98 Jose Vizcaino	.10	.04	.01
☐ 99 Kal Daniels	.08	.03	.01
☐ 100 Hubie Brooks	.06	.02	.00
☐ 101 Eddie Murray	.10	.04	.01
☐ 102 Dennis Boyd	.03	.01	.00
☐ 103 Tim Burke	.03	.01	.00
☐ 104 Bill Sampen	.10	.04	.01
☐ 105 Brett Gideon	.03	.01	.00
☐ 106 Mark Gardner	.12	.05	.01
☐ 107 Howard Farmer	.10	.04	.01
☐ 108 Mel Rojas	.08	.03	.01
☐ 109 Kevin Gross	.03	.01	.00
☐ 110 Dave Schmidt	.03	.01	.00
☐ 111 Denny Martinez	.06	.02	.00
☐ 112 Jeff Goff	.06	.02	.00
☐ 113 Andres Galarraga	.06	.02	.00
☐ 114 Tim Wallach	.06	.02	.00
☐ 115 Marquis Grissom	.40	.16	.04
☐ 116 Spike Owen	.03	.01	.00
☐ 117 Larry Walker	.20	.08	.02
☐ 118 Tim Raines	.08	.03	.01
☐ 119 Delino DeShields	.40	.16	.04
☐ 120 Tom Foley	.03	.01	.00
☐ 121 Dave Martinez	.03	.01	.00
☐ 122 Frank Viola UER (Career ERA .384, should be 3.84)	.08	.03	.01
☐ 123 Julio Valera	.10	.04	.01
☐ 124 Alejandro Pena	.06	.02	.00
☐ 125 David Cone	.08	.03	.01
☐ 126 Dwight Gooden	.10	.04	.01
☐ 127 Kevin D. Brown	.10	.04	.01
☐ 128 John Franco	.03	.01	.00
☐ 129 Terry Bross	.10	.04	.01
☐ 130 Blaine Beatty	.10	.04	.01
☐ 131 Sid Fernandez	.06	.02	.00
☐ 132 Mike Marshall	.06	.02	.00
☐ 133 Howard Johnson	.08	.03	.01
☐ 134 Jaime Roseboro	.12	.05	.01
☐ 135 Alan Zinter	.08	.03	.01
☐ 136 Keith Miller	.03	.01	.00
☐ 137 Kevin Elster	.03	.01	.00
☐ 138 Kevin McReynolds	.08	.03	.01
☐ 139 Barry Lyons	.03	.01	.00
☐ 140 Gregg Jefferies	.10	.04	.01
☐ 141 Darryl Strawberry	.20	.08	.02
☐ 142 Todd Hundley	.30	.12	.03
☐ 143 Scott Service	.06	.02	.00
☐ 144 Chuck Malone	.08	.03	.01
☐ 145 Steve Ontiveros	.03	.01	.00
☐ 146 Roger McDowell	.03	.01	.00
☐ 147 Ken Howell	.03	.01	.00
☐ 148 Pat Combs	.08	.03	.01
☐ 149 Jeff Parrett	.03	.01	.00
☐ 150 Chuck McElroy	.10	.04	.01
☐ 151 Jason Grimsley	.10	.04	.01
☐ 152 Len Dykstra	.08	.03	.01
☐ 153 Mickey Morandini	.15	.06	.01
☐ 154 John Kruk	.03	.01	.00
☐ 155 Dickie Thon	.03	.01	.00
☐ 156 Ricky Jordan	.08	.03	.01
☐ 157 Jeff Jackson	.10	.04	.01
☐ 158 Darren Daulton	.03	.01	.00
☐ 159 Tom Herr	.03	.01	.00
☐ 160 Von Hayes	.06	.02	.00
☐ 161 Dave Hollins	.25	.10	.02
☐ 162 Carmelo Martinez	.03	.01	.00
☐ 163 Bob Walk	.03	.01	.00
☐ 164 Doug Drabek	.08	.03	.01

□ 165 Walt Terrell	.03	.01	.00
□ 166 Bill Landrum	.03	.01	.00
□ 167 Scott Ruskin	.10	.04	.01
□ 168 Bob Patterson	.03	.01	.00
□ 169 Bobby Bonilla	.12	.05	.01
□ 170 Jose Lind	.03	.01	.00
□ 171 Andy Van Slyke	.08	.03	.01
□ 172 Mike LaValliere	.03	.01	.00
□ 173 Willie Greene	.12	.05	.01
□ 174 Jay Bell	.03	.01	.00
□ 175 Sid Bream	.03	.01	.00
□ 176 Tom Prince	.03	.01	.00
□ 177 Wally Backman	.03	.01	.00
□ 178 Moises Alou	.10	.04	.01
□ 179 Steve Carter	.08	.03	.01
□ 180 Gary Redus	.03	.01	.00
□ 181 Barry Bonds	.15	.06	.01
□ 182 Don Slaught UER (Card back shows headings for a pitcher)	.03	.01	.00
□ 183 Joe Magrane	.03	.01	.00
□ 184 Bryn Smith	.03	.01	.00
□ 185 Todd Worrell	.03	.01	.00
□ 186 Jose DeLeon	.03	.01	.00
□ 187 Frank DiPino	.03	.01	.00
□ 188 John Tudor	.06	.02	.00
□ 189 Howard Hilton	.10	.04	.01
□ 190 John Ericks	.06	.02	.00
□ 191 Ken Dayley	.03	.01	.00
□ 192 Ray Lankford	.75	.30	.07
□ 193 Todd Zeile	.30	.12	.03
□ 194 Willie McGee	.08	.03	.01
□ 195 Ozzie Smith	.10	.04	.01
□ 196 Milt Thompson	.03	.01	.00
□ 197 Terry Pendleton	.08	.03	.01
□ 198 Vince Coleman	.08	.03	.01
□ 199 Paul Coleman	.15	.06	.01
□ 200 Jose Oquendo	.03	.01	.00
□ 201 Pedro Guerrero	.08	.03	.01
□ 202 Tom Brunansky	.06	.02	.00
□ 203 Roger Smithberg	.10	.04	.01
□ 204 Eddie Whitson	.03	.01	.00
□ 205 Dennis Rasmussen	.03	.01	.00
□ 206 Craig Lefferts	.03	.01	.00
□ 207 Andy Benes	.15	.06	.01
□ 208 Bruce Hurst	.06	.02	.00
□ 209 Eric Show	.03	.01	.00
□ 210 Rafael Valdez	.10	.04	.01
□ 211 Joey Cora	.03	.01	.00
□ 212 Thomas Howard	.12	.05	.01
□ 213 Rob Nelson	.03	.01	.00
□ 214 Jack Clark	.08	.03	.01
□ 215 Garry Templeton	.03	.01	.00
□ 216 Fred Lynn	.08	.03	.01
□ 217 Tony Gwynn	.12	.05	.01
□ 218 Benito Santiago	.08	.03	.01
□ 219 Mike Pagliarulo	.03	.01	.00
□ 220 Joe Carter	.10	.04	.01
□ 221 Roberto Alomar	.12	.05	.01
□ 222 Bip Roberts	.06	.02	.00
□ 223 Rick Reuschel	.06	.02	.00
□ 224 Russ Swan	.10	.04	.01
□ 225 Eric Gunderson	.12	.05	.01
□ 226 Steve Bedrosian	.06	.02	.00
□ 227 Mike Remlinger	.12	.05	.01
□ 228 Scott Garrelts	.03	.01	.00
□ 229 Ernie Camacho	.03	.01	.00
□ 230 Andres Santana	.20	.08	.02
□ 231 Will Clark	.25	.10	.02
□ 232 Kevin Mitchell	.10	.04	.01
□ 233 Robby Thompson	.03	.01	.00
□ 234 Bill Bathe	.03	.01	.00
□ 235 Tony Perezchica	.03	.01	.00
□ 236 Gary Carter	.08	.03	.01
□ 237 Brett Butler	.08	.03	.01
□ 238 Matt Williams	.15	.06	.01
□ 239 Earnie Riles	.03	.01	.00
□ 240 Kevin Bass	.03	.01	.00
□ 241 Terry Kennedy	.03	.01	.00
□ 242 Steve Hosey	.15	.06	.01
□ 243 Ben McDonald	.60	.25	.06
□ 244 Jeff Ballard	.03	.01	.00
□ 245 Joe Price	.03	.01	.00
□ 246 Curt Schilling	.03	.01	.00
□ 247 Pete Harnisch	.06	.02	.00
□ 248 Mark Williamson	.03	.01	.00
□ 249 Gregg Olson	.10	.04	.01
□ 250 Chris Myers	.10	.04	.01
□ 251A David Segui ERR (missing vital stats at top of card back under name)	.15	.06	.01
□ 251B David Segui COR	.15	.06	.01
□ 252 Joe Orsulak	.03	.01	.00
□ 253 Craig Worthington	.03	.01	.00
□ 254 Mickey Tettleton	.06	.02	.00
□ 255 Cal Ripken	.25	.10	.02
□ 256 Billy Ripken	.03	.01	.00
□ 257 Randy Milligan	.06	.02	.00
□ 258 Brady Anderson	.03	.01	.00
□ 259 Chris Hoiles	.20	.08	.02
□ 260 Mike Devereaux	.03	.01	.00
□ 261 Phil Bradley	.03	.01	.00
□ 262 Leo Gomez	.40	.16	.04
□ 263 Lee Smith	.06	.02	.00
□ 264 Mike Rochford	.03	.01	.00
□ 265 Jeff Reardon	.06	.02	.00
□ 266 Wes Gardner	.03	.01	.00
□ 267 Mike Boddicker	.03	.01	.00
□ 268 Roger Clemens	.25	.10	.02
□ 269 Rob Murphy	.03	.01	.00
□ 270 Mickey Pina	.10	.04	.01
□ 271 Tony Pena	.06	.02	.00
□ 272 Jody Reed	.06	.02	.00
□ 273 Kevin Romine	.03	.01	.00
□ 274 Mike Greenwell	.12	.05	.01

☐ 275 Maurice Vaughn .90 .40 .09
☐ 276 Danny Heep .03 .01 .00
☐ 277 Scott Cooper .30 .12 .03
☐ 278 Greg Blosser .15 .06 .01
☐ 279 Dwight Evans UER .08 .03 .01
(* by "1990 Team Breakdown")
☐ 280 Ellis Burks .08 .03 .01
☐ 281 Wade Boggs .12 .05 .01
☐ 282 Marty Barrett .03 .01 .00
☐ 283 Kirk McCaskill .03 .01 .00
☐ 284 Mark Langston .08 .03 .01
☐ 285 Bert Blyleven .06 .02 .00
☐ 286 Mike Fetters .08 .03 .01
☐ 287 Kyle Abbott .20 .08 .02
☐ 288 Jim Abbott .15 .06 .01
☐ 289 Chuck Finley .08 .03 .01
☐ 290 Gary DiSarcina .10 .04 .01
☐ 291 Dick Schofield .03 .01 .00
☐ 292 Devon White .06 .02 .00
☐ 293 Bobby Rose .10 .04 .01
☐ 294 Brian Downing .03 .01 .00
☐ 295 Lance Parrish .08 .03 .01
☐ 296 Jack Howell .03 .01 .00
☐ 297 Claudell Washington .03 .01 .00
☐ 298 John Orton .08 .03 .01
☐ 299 Wally Joyner .10 .04 .01
☐ 300 Lee Stevens .15 .06 .01
☐ 301 Chili Davis .06 .02 .00
☐ 302 Johnny Ray .03 .01 .00
☐ 303 Greg Hibbard .15 .06 .01
☐ 304 Eric King .03 .01 .00
☐ 305 Jack McDowell .12 .05 .01
☐ 306 Bobby Thigpen .08 .03 .01
☐ 307 Adam Peterson .03 .01 .00
☐ 308 Scott Radinsky .12 .05 .01
☐ 309 Wayne Edwards .08 .03 .01
☐ 310 Melido Perez .03 .01 .00
☐ 311 Robin Ventura .45 .18 .04
☐ 312 Sammy Sosa .20 .08 .02
☐ 313 Dan Pasqua .03 .01 .00
☐ 314 Carlton Fisk .12 .05 .01
☐ 315 Ozzie Guillen .06 .02 .00
☐ 316 Ivan Calderon .06 .02 .00
☐ 317 Daryl Boston .03 .01 .00
☐ 318 Craig Grebeck .08 .03 .01
☐ 319 Scott Fletcher .03 .01 .00
☐ 320 Frank Thomas 3.50 1.50 .35
☐ 321 Steve Lyons .03 .01 .00
☐ 322 Carlos Martinez .08 .03 .01
☐ 323 Joe Skalski .08 .03 .01
☐ 324 Tom Candiotti .06 .02 .00
☐ 325 Greg Swindell .06 .02 .00
☐ 326 Steve Olin .08 .03 .01
☐ 327 Kevin Wickander .03 .01 .00
☐ 328 Doug Jones .03 .01 .00
☐ 329 Jeff Shaw .10 .04 .01
☐ 330 Kevin Bearse .08 .03 .01
☐ 331 Dion James .03 .01 .00
☐ 332 Jerry Browne .03 .01 .00
☐ 333 Joey Belle .50 .20 .05
☐ 334 Felix Fermin .03 .01 .00
☐ 335 Candy Maldonado .06 .02 .00
☐ 336 Cory Snyder .06 .02 .00
☐ 337 Sandy Alomar Jr. .10 .04 .01
☐ 338 Mark Lewis .17 .07 .01
☐ 339 Carlos Baerga .35 .15 .03
☐ 340 Chris James .03 .01 .00
☐ 341 Brook Jacoby .03 .01 .00
☐ 342 Keith Hernandez .06 .02 .00
☐ 343 Frank Tanana .06 .02 .00
☐ 344 Scott Aldred .15 .06 .01
☐ 345 Mike Henneman .03 .01 .00
☐ 346 Steve Wapnick .08 .03 .01
☐ 347 Greg Gohr .15 .06 .01
☐ 348 Eric Stone .10 .04 .01
☐ 349 Brian DuBois .08 .03 .01
☐ 350 Kevin Ritz .08 .03 .01
☐ 351 Rico Brogna .12 .05 .01
☐ 352 Mike Heath .03 .01 .00
☐ 353 Alan Trammell .08 .03 .01
☐ 354 Chet Lemon .03 .01 .00
☐ 355 Dave Bergman .03 .01 .00
☐ 356 Lou Whitaker .06 .02 .00
☐ 357 Cecil Fielder UER .35 .15 .03
(* by "1990 Team Breakdown")
☐ 358 Milt Cuyler .30 .12 .03
☐ 359 Tony Phillips .03 .01 .00
☐ 360 Travis Fryman 1.00 .40 .10
☐ 361 Ed Romero .03 .01 .00
☐ 362 Lloyd Moseby .03 .01 .00
☐ 363 Mark Gubicza .06 .02 .00
☐ 364 Bret Saberhagen .08 .03 .01
☐ 365 Tom Gordon .08 .03 .01
☐ 366 Steve Farr .03 .01 .00
☐ 367 Kevin Appier .15 .06 .01
☐ 368 Storm Davis .03 .01 .00
☐ 369 Mark Davis .06 .02 .00
☐ 370 Jeff Montgomery .03 .01 .00
☐ 371 Frank White .03 .01 .00
☐ 372 Brent Mayne .17 .07 .01
☐ 373 Bob Boone .06 .02 .00
☐ 374 Jim Eisenreich .03 .01 .00
☐ 375 Danny Tartabull .10 .04 .01
☐ 376 Kurt Stillwell .03 .01 .00
☐ 377 Bill Pecota .03 .01 .00
☐ 378 Bo Jackson .35 .15 .03
☐ 379 Bob Hamelin .10 .04 .01
☐ 380 Kevin Seitzer .06 .02 .00
☐ 381 Rey Palacios .03 .01 .00
☐ 382 George Brett .10 .04 .01
☐ 383 Gerald Perry .03 .01 .00
☐ 384 Teddy Higuera .03 .01 .00
☐ 385 Tom Filer .03 .01 .00
☐ 386 Dan Plesac .03 .01 .00

☐ 387 Cal Eldred	.10	.04	.01
☐ 388 Jaime Navarro	.08	.03	.01
☐ 389 Chris Bosio	.03	.01	.00
☐ 390 Randy Veres	.06	.02	.00
☐ 391 Gary Sheffield	.08	.03	.01
☐ 392 George Canale	.10	.04	.01
☐ 393 B.J. Surhoff	.03	.01	.00
☐ 394 Tim McIntosh	.12	.05	.01
☐ 395 Greg Brock	.03	.01	.00
☐ 396 Greg Vaughn	.40	.16	.04
☐ 397 Darryl Hamilton	.08	.03	.01
☐ 398 Dave Parker	.08	.03	.01
☐ 399 Paul Molitor	.08	.03	.01
☐ 400 Jim Gantner	.03	.01	.00
☐ 401 Rob Deer	.06	.02	.00
☐ 402 Billy Spiers	.08	.03	.01
☐ 403 Glenn Braggs	.03	.01	.00
☐ 404 Robin Yount	.10	.04	.01
☐ 405 Rick Aguilera	.06	.02	.00
☐ 406 Johnny Ard	.06	.02	.00
☐ 407 Kevin Tapani	.25	.10	.02
☐ 408 Park Pittman	.10	.04	.01
☐ 409 Allan Anderson	.03	.01	.00
☐ 410 Juan Berenguer	.03	.01	.00
☐ 411 Willie Banks	.30	.12	.03
☐ 412 Rich Yett	.03	.01	.00
☐ 413 Dave West	.03	.01	.00
☐ 414 Greg Gagne	.03	.01	.00
☐ 415 Chuck Knoblauch	1.25	.50	.12
☐ 416 Randy Bush	.03	.01	.00
☐ 417 Gary Gaetti	.06	.02	.00
☐ 418 Kent Hrbek	.08	.03	.01
☐ 419 Al Newman	.03	.01	.00
☐ 420 Danny Gladden	.03	.01	.00
☐ 421 Paul Sorrento	.10	.04	.01
☐ 422 Derek Parks	.10	.04	.01
☐ 423 Scott Leius	.20	.08	.02
☐ 424 Kirby Puckett	.18	.08	.01
☐ 425 Willie Smith	.10	.04	.01
☐ 426 Dave Righetti	.06	.02	.00
☐ 427 Jeff Robinson	.03	.01	.00
☐ 428 Alan Mills	.10	.04	.01
☐ 429 Tim Leary	.06	.02	.00
☐ 430 Pascual Perez	.03	.01	.00
☐ 431 Alvaro Espinoza	.03	.01	.00
☐ 432 Dave Winfield	.10	.04	.01
☐ 433 Jesse Barfield	.08	.03	.01
☐ 434 Randy Velarde	.03	.01	.00
☐ 435 Rick Cerone	.03	.01	.00
☐ 436 Steve Balboni	.03	.01	.00
☐ 437 Mel Hall	.03	.01	.00
☐ 438 Bob Geren	.06	.02	.00
☐ 439 Bernie Williams	.35	.15	.03
☐ 440 Kevin Maas	1.25	.50	.12
☐ 441 Mike Blowers	.10	.04	.01
☐ 442 Steve Sax	.08	.03	.01
☐ 443 Don Mattingly	.20	.08	.02
☐ 444 Roberto Kelly	.08	.03	.01
☐ 445 Mike Moore	.06	.02	.00
☐ 446 Reggie Harris	.12	.05	.01
☐ 447 Scott Sanderson	.06	.02	.00
☐ 448 Dave Otto	.03	.01	.00
☐ 449 Dave Stewart	.08	.03	.01
☐ 450 Rick Honeycutt	.03	.01	.00
☐ 451 Dennis Eckersley	.08	.03	.01
☐ 452 Carney Lansford	.06	.02	.00
☐ 453 Scott Hemond	.10	.04	.01
☐ 454 Mark McGwire	.12	.05	.01
☐ 455 Felix Jose	.20	.08	.02
☐ 456 Terry Steinbach	.06	.02	.00
☐ 457 Rickey Henderson	.25	.10	.02
☐ 458 Dave Henderson	.08	.03	.01
☐ 459 Mike Gallego	.03	.01	.00
☐ 460 Jose Canseco	.35	.15	.03
☐ 461 Walt Weiss	.06	.02	.00
☐ 462 Ken Phelps	.03	.01	.00
☐ 463 Darren Lewis	.35	.15	.03
☐ 464 Ron Hassey	.03	.01	.00
☐ 465 Roger Salkeld	.45	.18	.04
☐ 466 Scott Bankhead	.03	.01	.00
☐ 467 Keith Comstock	.03	.01	.00
☐ 468 Randy Johnson	.12	.05	.01
☐ 469 Erik Hanson	.08	.03	.01
☐ 470 Mike Schooler	.06	.02	.00
☐ 471 Gary Eave	.08	.03	.01
☐ 472 Jeffrey Leonard	.03	.01	.00
☐ 473 Dave Valle	.03	.01	.00
☐ 474 Omar Vizquel	.03	.01	.00
☐ 475 Pete O'Brien	.03	.01	.00
☐ 476 Henry Cotto	.03	.01	.00
☐ 477 Jay Buhner	.10	.04	.01
☐ 478 Harold Reynolds	.06	.02	.00
☐ 479 Alvin Davis	.06	.02	.00
☐ 480 Darnell Coles	.03	.01	.00
☐ 481 Ken Griffey Jr.	1.50	.60	.15
☐ 482 Greg Briley	.06	.02	.00
☐ 483 Scott Bradley	.03	.01	.00
☐ 484 Tino Martinez	.35	.15	.03
☐ 485 Jeff Russell	.03	.01	.00
☐ 486 Nolan Ryan	.40	.16	.04
☐ 487 Robb Nen	.10	.04	.01
☐ 488 Kevin Brown	.06	.02	.00
☐ 489 Brian Bohanon	.10	.04	.01
☐ 490 Ruben Sierra	.17	.07	.01
☐ 491 Pete Incaviglia	.06	.02	.00
☐ 492 Juan Gonzalez	1.50	.60	.15
☐ 493 Steve Buechele	.03	.01	.00
☐ 494 Scott Coolbaugh	.08	.03	.01
☐ 495 Geno Petralli	.03	.01	.00
☐ 496 Rafael Palmeiro	.10	.04	.01
☐ 497 Julio Franco	.08	.03	.01
☐ 498 Gary Pettis	.03	.01	.00
☐ 499 Donald Harris	.10	.04	.01
☐ 500 Monty Fariss	.06	.02	.00
☐ 501 Harold Baines	.08	.03	.01
☐ 502 Cecil Espy	.03	.01	.00

□ 503 Jack Daugherty	.06	.02	.00
□ 504 Willie Blair	.06	.02	.00
□ 505 Dave Stieb	.08	.03	.01
□ 506 Tom Henke	.06	.02	.00
□ 507 John Cerutti	.03	.01	.00
□ 508 Paul Kilgus	.03	.01	.00
□ 509 Jimmy Key	.06	.02	.00
□ 510 John Olerud	.75	.30	.07
□ 511 Ed Sprague	.10	.04	.01
□ 512 Manny Lee	.03	.01	.00
□ 513 Fred McGriff	.10	.04	.01
□ 514 Glenallen Hill	.08	.03	.01
□ 515 George Bell	.08	.03	.01
□ 516 Mookie Wilson	.03	.01	.00
□ 517 Luis Sojo	.10	.04	.01
□ 518 Nelson Liriano	.03	.01	.00
□ 519 Kelly Gruber	.08	.03	.01
□ 520 Greg Myers	.03	.01	.00
□ 521 Pat Borders	.06	.02	.00
□ 522 Junior Felix	.08	.03	.01
□ 523 Eddie Zosky	.20	.08	.02
□ 524 Tony Fernandez	.06	.02	.00
□ 525 Checklist 1-132 UER (no copyright mark on the back)	.06	.01	.00
□ 526 Checklist 133-264	.06	.01	.00
□ 527 Checklist 265-396	.06	.01	.00
□ 528 Checklist 397-528	.08	.01	.00

1991 Bowman

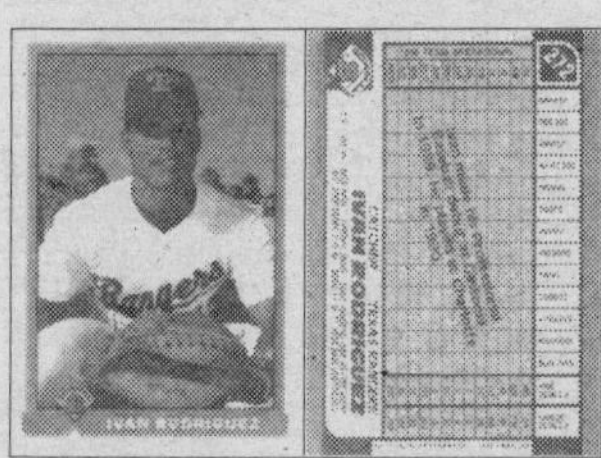

This 704-card standard size (2 1/2" by 3 1/2") set marked the third straight year that Topps issued a set using the Bowman name. The cards are arranged in team order by division as follows: AL East, AL West, NL East, and NL West. Some of the specials in the set include cards made for all the 1990 MVP's in each minor league, the leader sluggers by position (Silver Sluggers), and special cards commemorating long-time baseball figure Jimmie Reese, General Colin Powell, newly inducted Hall of Famer Rod Carew and Rickey Henderson's 938th Stolen Base. The cards themselves are designed just like the 1990 Bowman set while the backs again feature the innovative team by team breakdown of how the player did the previous year against a green background. The set numbering is as follows: Toronto Blue Jays (6-30), Milwaukee Brewers (31-56), Cleveland Indians (57-82), Baltimore Orioles (83-106), Boston Red Sox (107-130), Detroit Tigers (131-154), New York Yankees (155-179), California Angels (187-211), Oakland Athletics (212-238), Seattle Mariners (239-264), Texas Rangers (265-290), Kansas City Royals (291-316), Minnesota Twins (317-341), Chicago White Sox (342-366), St. Louis Cardinals (385-409), Chicago Cubs (411-433), Montreal Expos (434-459), New York Mets (460-484), Philadelphia Phillies (485-508), Pittsburgh Pirates (509-532), Houston Astros (539-565), Atlanta Braves (566-590), Los Angles Dodgers (591-615), San Fransico Giants (616-641), San Diego Padres (642-665), and Cincinnati Reds (666-691). Special subsets feature AL Silver Sluggers (367-375) and NL Silver Sluggers (376-384). There are two instances of misnumbering in the set; Ken Griffey (should be 255) and Ken Griffey Jr. are both numbered 246 and Donovan Osborne (should be 406) and Thomson/ Branca share number 410. The key rookie cards in this set are Jeff Bagwell, Jeromy Burnitz, Ryan Klesko, Phil Plantier, Ivan Rodriguez, and Todd Van Poppel.

	MINT	EXC	G-VG
COMPLETE SET (704)	18.00	7.50	2.50
COMMON PLAYER (1-704)	.03	.01	.00
□ 1 Rod Carew I	.15	.05	.01
□ 2 Rod Carew II	.10	.04	.01
□ 3 Rod Carew III	.10	.04	.01
□ 4 Rod Carew IV	.10	.04	.01
□ 5 Rod Carew V	.10	.04	.01
□ 6 Willie Fraser	.03	.01	.00
□ 7 John Olerud	.10	.04	.01
□ 8 William Suero	.12	.05	.01
□ 9 Roberto Alomar	.10	.04	.01
□ 10 Todd Stottlemyre	.06	.02	.00
□ 11 Joe Carter	.10	.04	.01
□ 12 Steve Karsay	.20	.08	.02
□ 13 Mark Whiten	.17	.07	.01
□ 14 Pat Borders	.06	.02	.00

☐ 15 Mike Timlin .12 .05 .01
☐ 16 Tom Henke .06 .02 .00
☐ 17 Eddie Zosky .06 .02 .00
☐ 18 Kelly Gruber .08 .03 .01
☐ 19 Jimmy Key .06 .02 .00
☐ 20 Jerry Schunk .08 .03 .01
☐ 21 Manny Lee .03 .01 .00
☐ 22 Dave Stieb .06 .02 .00
☐ 23 Pat Hentgen .10 .04 .01
☐ 24 Glenallen Hill .06 .02 .00
☐ 25 Rene Gonzales .03 .01 .00
☐ 26 Ed Sprague .08 .03 .01
☐ 27 Ken Dayley .03 .01 .00
☐ 28 Pat Tabler .03 .01 .00
☐ 29 Denis Boucher .10 .04 .01
☐ 30 Devon White .06 .02 .00
☐ 31 Dante Bichette .03 .01 .00
☐ 32 Paul Molitor .08 .03 .01
☐ 33 Greg Vaughn .08 .03 .01
☐ 34 Dan Plesac .03 .01 .00
☐ 35 Chris George .08 .03 .01
☐ 36 Tim McIntosh .03 .01 .00
☐ 37 Franklin Stubbs .03 .01 .00
☐ 38 Bo Dodson .17 .07 .01
☐ 39 Ron Robinson .03 .01 .00
☐ 40 Ed Nunez .03 .01 .00
☐ 41 Greg Brock .03 .01 .00
☐ 42 Jaime Navarro .03 .01 .00
☐ 43 Chris Bosio .03 .01 .00
☐ 44 B.J. Surhoff .03 .01 .00
☐ 45 Chris Johnson .10 .04 .01
☐ 46 Willie Randolph .06 .02 .00
☐ 47 Narciso Elvira .08 .03 .01
☐ 48 Jim Gantner .03 .01 .00
☐ 49 Kevin Brown .03 .01 .00
☐ 50 Julio Machado .03 .01 .00
☐ 51 Chuck Crim .03 .01 .00
☐ 52 Gary Sheffield .08 .03 .01
☐ 53 Angel Miranda .08 .03 .01
☐ 54 Teddy Higuera .03 .01 .00
☐ 55 Robin Yount .10 .04 .01
☐ 56 Cal Eldred .06 .02 .00
☐ 57 Sandy Alomar Jr. .08 .03 .01
☐ 58 Greg Swindell .06 .02 .00
☐ 59 Brook Jacoby .03 .01 .00
☐ 60 Efrain Valdez .08 .03 .01
☐ 61 Ever Magallanes .08 .03 .01
☐ 62 Tom Candiotti .06 .02 .00
☐ 63 Eric King .03 .01 .00
☐ 64 Alex Cole .08 .03 .01
☐ 65 Charles Nagy .08 .03 .01
☐ 66 Mitch Webster .03 .01 .00
☐ 67 Chris James .03 .01 .00
☐ 68 Jim Thome .35 .15 .03
☐ 69 Carlos Baerga .10 .04 .01
☐ 70 Mark Lewis .10 .04 .01
☐ 71 Jerry Browne .03 .01 .00
☐ 72 Jesse Orosco .03 .01 .00
☐ 73 Mike Huff .03 .01 .00
☐ 74 Jose Escobar .08 .03 .01
☐ 75 Jeff Manto .06 .02 .00
☐ 76 Turner Ward .10 .04 .01
☐ 77 Doug Jones .03 .01 .00
☐ 78 Bruce Egloff .08 .03 .01
☐ 79 Tim Costo .20 .08 .02
☐ 80 Beau Allred .08 .03 .01
☐ 81 Albert Belle .12 .05 .01
☐ 82 John Farrell .03 .01 .00
☐ 83 Glenn Davis .08 .03 .01
☐ 84 Joe Orsulak .03 .01 .00
☐ 85 Mark Williamson .03 .01 .00
☐ 86 Ben McDonald .08 .03 .01
☐ 87 Billy Ripken .03 .01 .00
☐ 88 Leo Gomez .10 .04 .01
☐ 89 Bob Melvin .03 .01 .00
☐ 90 Jeff Robinson .03 .01 .00
☐ 91 Jose Mesa .03 .01 .00
☐ 92 Gregg Olson .08 .03 .01
☐ 93 Mike Devereaux .03 .01 .00
☐ 94 Luis Mercedes .25 .10 .02
☐ 95 Arthur Rhodes .20 .08 .02
☐ 96 Juan Bell .03 .01 .00
☐ 97 Mike Mussina .30 .12 .03
☐ 98 Jeff Ballard .03 .01 .00
☐ 99 Chris Hoiles .06 .02 .00
☐ 100 Brady Anderson .03 .01 .00
☐ 101 Bob Milacki .03 .01 .00
☐ 102 David Segui .08 .03 .01
☐ 103 Dwight Evans .06 .02 .00
☐ 104 Cal Ripken .17 .07 .01
☐ 105 Mike Linskey .08 .03 .01
☐ 106 Jeff Tackett .10 .04 .01
☐ 107 Jeff Reardon .06 .02 .00
☐ 108 Dana Kiecker .06 .02 .00
☐ 109 Ellis Burks .08 .03 .01
☐ 110 Dave Owen .08 .03 .01
☐ 111 Danny Darwin .03 .01 .00
☐ 112 Mo Vaughn .20 .08 .02
☐ 113 Jeff McNeely .35 .15 .03
☐ 114 Tom Bolton .03 .01 .00
☐ 115 Greg Blosser .10 .04 .01
☐ 116 Mike Greenwell .10 .04 .01
☐ 117 Phil Plantier 1.25 .50 .12
☐ 118 Roger Clemens .15 .06 .01
☐ 119 John Marzano .03 .01 .00
☐ 120 Jody Reed .06 .02 .00
☐ 121 Scott Taylor .10 .04 .01
☐ 122 Jack Clark .08 .03 .01
☐ 123 Derek Livernois .10 .04 .01
☐ 124 Tony Pena .06 .02 .00
☐ 125 Tom Brunansky .06 .02 .00
☐ 126 Carlos Quintana .06 .02 .00
☐ 127 Tim Naehring .10 .04 .01
☐ 128 Matt Young .03 .01 .00
☐ 129 Wade Boggs .12 .05 .01
☐ 130 Kevin Morton .10 .04 .01

☐ 131	Pete Incaviglia	.06	.02	.00
☐ 132	Rob Deer	.06	.02	.00
☐ 133	Bill Gullickson	.06	.02	.00
☐ 134	Rico Brogna	.10	.04	.01
☐ 135	Lloyd Moseby	.03	.01	.00
☐ 136	Cecil Fielder	.15	.06	.01
☐ 137	Tony Phillips	.03	.01	.00
☐ 138	Mark Leiter	.10	.04	.01
☐ 139	John Cerutti	.03	.01	.00
☐ 140	Mickey Tettleton	.06	.02	.00
☐ 141	Milt Cuyler	.08	.03	.01
☐ 142	Greg Gohr	.06	.02	.00
☐ 143	Tony Bernazard	.03	.01	.00
☐ 144	Dan Gakeler	.08	.03	.01
☐ 145	Travis Fryman	.20	.08	.02
☐ 146	Dan Petry	.03	.01	.00
☐ 147	Scott Aldred	.03	.01	.00
☐ 148	John DeSilva	.10	.04	.01
☐ 149	Rusty Meacham	.10	.04	.01
☐ 150	Lou Whitaker	.06	.02	.00
☐ 151	Dave Haas	.08	.03	.01
☐ 152	Luis de los Santos	.03	.01	.00
☐ 153	Ivan Cruz	.10	.04	.01
☐ 154	Alan Trammell	.08	.03	.01
☐ 155	Pat Kelly	.25	.10	.02
☐ 156	Carl Everett	.25	.10	.02
☐ 157	Greg Cadaret	.03	.01	.00
☐ 158	Kevin Maas	.15	.06	.01
☐ 159	Jeff Johnson	.15	.06	.01
☐ 160	Willie Smith	.06	.02	.00
☐ 161	Gerald Williams	.25	.10	.02
☐ 162	Mike Humphreys	.15	.06	.01
☐ 163	Alvaro Espinoza	.03	.01	.00
☐ 164	Matt Nokes	.06	.02	.00
☐ 165	Wade Taylor	.12	.05	.01
☐ 166	Roberto Kelly	.08	.03	.01
☐ 167	John Habyan	.03	.01	.00
☐ 168	Steve Farr	.03	.01	.00
☐ 169	Jesse Barfield	.06	.02	.00
☐ 170	Steve Sax	.06	.02	.00
☐ 171	Jim Leyritz	.06	.02	.00
☐ 172	Robert Eenhoorn	.10	.04	.01
☐ 173	Bernie Williams	.12	.05	.01
☐ 174	Scott Lusader	.03	.01	.00
☐ 175	Torey Lovullo	.03	.01	.00
☐ 176	Chuck Cary	.03	.01	.00
☐ 177	Scott Sanderson	.03	.01	.00
☐ 178	Don Mattingly	.12	.05	.01
☐ 179	Mel Hall	.06	.02	.00
☐ 180	Juan Gonzalez Minor League MVP	.30	.12	.03
☐ 181	Hensley Meulens Minor League MVP	.06	.02	.00
☐ 182	Jose Offerman Minor League MVP	.08	.03	.01
☐ 183	Jeff Bagwell Minor League MVP	1.50	.60	.15
☐ 184	Jeff Conine Minor League MVP	.10	.04	.01
☐ 185	Henry Rodriguez Minor League MVP	.15	.06	.01
☐ 186	Jimmie Reese	.03	.01	.00
☐ 187	Kyle Abbott	.06	.02	.00
☐ 188	Lance Parrish	.06	.02	.00
☐ 189	Rafael Montalvo	.08	.03	.01
☐ 190	Floyd Bannister	.03	.01	.00
☐ 191	Dick Schofield	.03	.01	.00
☐ 192	Scott Lewis	.08	.03	.01
☐ 193	Jeff Robinson	.03	.01	.00
☐ 194	Kent Anderson	.03	.01	.00
☐ 195	Wally Joyner	.08	.03	.01
☐ 196	Chuck Finley	.08	.03	.01
☐ 197	Luis Sojo	.03	.01	.00
☐ 198	Jeff Richardson	.08	.03	.01
☐ 199	Dave Parker	.08	.03	.01
☐ 200	Jim Abbott	.10	.04	.01
☐ 201	Junior Felix	.03	.01	.00
☐ 202	Mark Langston	.06	.02	.00
☐ 203	Tim Salmon	.25	.10	.02
☐ 204	Cliff Young	.06	.02	.00
☐ 205	Scott Bailes	.03	.01	.00
☐ 206	Bobby Rose	.03	.01	.00
☐ 207	Gary Gaetti	.06	.02	.00
☐ 208	Ruben Amaro	.12	.05	.01
☐ 209	Luis Polonia	.03	.01	.00
☐ 210	Dave Winfield	.08	.03	.01
☐ 211	Bryan Harvey	.06	.02	.00
☐ 212	Mike Moore	.06	.02	.00
☐ 213	Rickey Henderson	.20	.08	.02
☐ 214	Steve Chitren	.08	.03	.01
☐ 215	Bob Welch	.06	.02	.00
☐ 216	Terry Steinbach	.03	.01	.00
☐ 217	Earnest Riles	.03	.01	.00
☐ 218	Todd Van Poppel	1.00	.40	.10
☐ 219	Mike Gallego	.03	.01	.00
☐ 220	Curt Young	.03	.01	.00
☐ 221	Todd Burns	.03	.01	.00
☐ 222	Vance Law	.03	.01	.00
☐ 223	Eric Show	.03	.01	.00
☐ 224	Don Peters	.12	.05	.01
☐ 225	Dave Stewart	.08	.03	.01
☐ 226	Dave Henderson	.08	.03	.01
☐ 227	Jose Canseco	.25	.10	.02
☐ 228	Walt Weiss	.06	.02	.00
☐ 229	Dann Howitt	.08	.03	.01
☐ 230	Willie Wilson	.06	.02	.00
☐ 231	Harold Baines	.06	.02	.00
☐ 232	Scott Hemond	.06	.02	.00
☐ 233	Joe Slusarski	.08	.03	.01
☐ 234	Mark McGwire	.10	.04	.01
☐ 235	Kirk Dressendorfer	.20	.08	.02
☐ 236	Craig Paquette	.15	.06	.01
☐ 237	Dennis Eckersley	.08	.03	.01
☐ 238	Dana Allison	.12	.05	.01
☐ 239	Scott Bradley	.03	.01	.00

☐ 240	Brian Holman	.03	.01	.00
☐ 241	Mike Schooler	.03	.01	.00
☐ 242	Rich DeLucia	.12	.05	.01
☐ 243	Edgar Martinez	.08	.03	.01
☐ 244	Henry Cotto	.03	.01	.00
☐ 245	Omar Vizquel	.03	.01	.00
☐ 246	Ken Griffey Jr. (See also 255)	.75	.30	.07
☐ 247	Jay Buhner	.08	.03	.01
☐ 248	Bill Krueger	.03	.01	.00
☐ 249	Dave Fleming	.10	.04	.01
☐ 250	Patrick Lennon	.20	.08	.02
☐ 251	Dave Valle	.03	.01	.00
☐ 252	Harold Reynolds	.06	.02	.00
☐ 253	Randy Johnson	.06	.02	.00
☐ 254	Scott Bankhead	.03	.01	.00
☐ 255	Ken Griffey Sr. UER (Card number is 246)	.08	.03	.01
☐ 256	Greg Briley	.03	.01	.00
☐ 257	Tino Martinez	.12	.05	.01
☐ 258	Alvin Davis	.06	.02	.00
☐ 259	Pete O'Brien	.03	.01	.00
☐ 260	Erik Hanson	.06	.02	.00
☐ 261	Bret Boone	.15	.06	.01
☐ 262	Roger Salkeld	.15	.06	.01
☐ 263	Dave Burba	.10	.04	.01
☐ 264	Kerry Woodson	.10	.04	.01
☐ 265	Julio Franco	.08	.03	.01
☐ 266	Dan Peltier	.10	.04	.01
☐ 267	Jeff Russell	.03	.01	.00
☐ 268	Steve Buechele	.03	.01	.00
☐ 269	Donald Harris	.06	.02	.00
☐ 270	Robb Nen	.03	.01	.00
☐ 271	Rich Gossage	.06	.02	.00
☐ 272	Ivan Rodriguez	1.50	.60	.15
☐ 273	Jeff Huson	.03	.01	.00
☐ 274	Kevin Brown	.06	.02	.00
☐ 275	Dan Smith	.10	.04	.01
☐ 276	Gary Pettis	.03	.01	.00
☐ 277	Jack Daugherty	.03	.01	.00
☐ 278	Mike Jeffcoat	.03	.01	.00
☐ 279	Brad Arnsberg	.03	.01	.00
☐ 280	Nolan Ryan	.30	.12	.03
☐ 281	Eric McCray	.10	.04	.01
☐ 282	Scott Chiamparino	.06	.02	.00
☐ 283	Ruben Sierra	.12	.05	.01
☐ 284	Geno Petralli	.03	.01	.00
☐ 285	Monty Fariss	.06	.02	.00
☐ 286	Rafael Palmeiro	.08	.03	.01
☐ 287	Bobby Witt	.06	.02	.00
☐ 288	Dean Palmer UER (Photo actually Dan Peltier)	.30	.12	.03
☐ 289	Tony Scruggs	.10	.04	.01
☐ 290	Kenny Rogers	.03	.01	.00
☐ 291	Bret Saberhagen	.08	.03	.01
☐ 292	Brian McRae	.35	.15	.03
☐ 293	Storm Davis	.03	.01	.00
☐ 294	Danny Tartabull	.08	.03	.01
☐ 295	David Howard	.10	.04	.01
☐ 296	Mike Boddicker	.03	.01	.00
☐ 297	Joel Johnston	.15	.06	.01
☐ 298	Tim Spehr	.15	.06	.01
☐ 299	Hector Wagner	.08	.03	.01
☐ 300	George Brett	.10	.04	.01
☐ 301	Mike Macfarlane	.03	.01	.00
☐ 302	Kirk Gibson	.08	.03	.01
☐ 303	Harvey Pulliam	.12	.05	.01
☐ 304	Jim Eisenreich	.03	.01	.00
☐ 305	Kevin Seitzer	.06	.02	.00
☐ 306	Mark Davis	.06	.02	.00
☐ 307	Kurt Stillwell	.03	.01	.00
☐ 308	Jeff Montgomery	.03	.01	.00
☐ 309	Kevin Appier	.06	.02	.00
☐ 310	Bob Hamelin	.03	.01	.00
☐ 311	Tom Gordon	.06	.02	.00
☐ 312	Kerwin Moore	.15	.06	.01
☐ 313	Hugh Walker	.03	.01	.00
☐ 314	Terry Shumpert	.06	.02	.00
☐ 315	Warren Cromartie	.03	.01	.00
☐ 316	Gary Thurman	.03	.01	.00
☐ 317	Steve Bedrosian	.03	.01	.00
☐ 318	Danny Gladden	.03	.01	.00
☐ 319	Jack Morris	.08	.03	.01
☐ 320	Kirby Puckett	.12	.05	.01
☐ 321	Kent Hrbek	.06	.02	.00
☐ 322	Kevin Tapani	.06	.02	.00
☐ 323	Denny Neagle	.30	.12	.03
☐ 324	Rich Garces	.10	.04	.01
☐ 325	Larry Casian	.08	.03	.01
☐ 326	Shane Mack	.06	.02	.00
☐ 327	Allan Anderson	.03	.01	.00
☐ 328	Junior Ortiz	.03	.01	.00
☐ 329	Paul Abbott	.08	.03	.01
☐ 330	Chuck Knoblauch	.20	.08	.02
☐ 331	Chili Davis	.06	.02	.00
☐ 332	Todd Ritchie	.15	.06	.01
☐ 333	Brian Harper	.06	.02	.00
☐ 334	Rick Aguilera	.06	.02	.00
☐ 335	Scott Erickson	.60	.25	.06
☐ 336	Pedro Munoz	.20	.08	.02
☐ 337	Scott Leius	.06	.02	.00
☐ 338	Greg Gagne	.03	.01	.00
☐ 339	Mike Pagliarulo	.03	.01	.00
☐ 340	Terry Leach	.03	.01	.00
☐ 341	Willie Banks	.08	.03	.01
☐ 342	Bobby Thigpen	.06	.02	.00
☐ 343	Roberto Hernandez	.15	.06	.01
☐ 344	Melido Perez	.03	.01	.00
☐ 345	Carlton Fisk	.10	.04	.01
☐ 346	Norberto Martin	.10	.04	.01
☐ 347	Johnny Ruffin	.10	.04	.01
☐ 348	Jeff Carter	.10	.04	.01
☐ 349	Lance Johnson	.03	.01	.00
☐ 350	Sammy Sosa	.08	.03	.01
☐ 351	Alex Fernandez	.17	.07	.01

☐ 352 Jack McDowell	.08	.03	.01
☐ 353 Bob Wickman	.08	.03	.01
☐ 354 Wilson Alvarez	.10	.04	.01
☐ 355 Charlie Hough	.03	.01	.00
☐ 356 Ozzie Guillen	.06	.02	.00
☐ 357 Cory Snyder	.06	.02	.00
☐ 358 Robin Ventura	.20	.08	.02
☐ 359 Scott Fletcher	.03	.01	.00
☐ 360 Cesar Bernhardt	.10	.04	.01
☐ 361 Dan Pasqua	.03	.01	.00
☐ 362 Tim Raines	.08	.03	.01
☐ 363 Brian Drahman	.08	.03	.01
☐ 364 Wayne Edwards	.03	.01	.00
☐ 365 Scott Radinsky	.06	.02	.00
☐ 366 Frank Thomas	.75	.30	.07
☐ 367 Cecil Fielder SLUG	.10	.04	.01
☐ 368 Julio Franco SLUG	.08	.03	.01
☐ 369 Kelly Gruber SLUG	.08	.03	.01
☐ 370 Alan Trammell SLUG	.08	.03	.01
☐ 371 Rickey Henderson SLUG	.12	.05	.01
☐ 372 Jose Canseco SLUG	.15	.06	.01
☐ 373 Ellis Burks SLUG	.08	.03	.01
☐ 374 Lance Parrish SLUG	.06	.02	.00
☐ 375 Dave Parker SLUG	.08	.03	.01
☐ 376 Eddie Murray SLUG	.08	.03	.01
☐ 377 Ryne Sandberg SLUG	.12	.05	.01
☐ 378 Matt Williams SLUG	.08	.03	.01
☐ 379 Barry Larkin SLUG	.08	.03	.01
☐ 380 Barry Bonds SLUG	.08	.03	.01
☐ 381 Bobby Bonilla SLUG	.08	.03	.01
☐ 382 Darryl Strawberry SLUG	.10	.04	.01
☐ 383 Benny Santiago SLUG	.08	.03	.01
☐ 384 Don Robinson SLUG	.03	.01	.00
☐ 385 Paul Coleman	.06	.02	.00
☐ 386 Milt Thompson	.03	.01	.00
☐ 387 Lee Smith	.06	.02	.00
☐ 388 Ray Lankford	.15	.06	.01
☐ 389 Tom Pagnozzi	.03	.01	.00
☐ 390 Ken Hill	.03	.01	.00
☐ 391 Jamie Moyer	.03	.01	.00
☐ 392 Greg Carmona	.10	.04	.01
☐ 393 John Ericks	.06	.02	.00
☐ 394 Bob Tewksbury	.03	.01	.00
☐ 395 Jose Oquendo	.03	.01	.00
☐ 396 Rheal Cormier	.35	.15	.03
☐ 397 Mike Milchin	.10	.04	.01
☐ 398 Ozzie Smith	.08	.03	.01
☐ 399 Aaron Holbert	.12	.05	.01
☐ 400 Jose DeLeon	.03	.01	.00
☐ 401 Felix Jose	.10	.04	.01
☐ 402 Juan Agosto	.03	.01	.00
☐ 403 Pedro Guerrero	.08	.03	.01
☐ 404 Todd Zeile	.10	.04	.01
☐ 405 Gerald Perry	.03	.01	.00
☐ 406 Donovan Osborne UER (Card number is 410)	.12	.05	.01
☐ 407 Bryn Smith	.03	.01	.00
☐ 408 Bernard Gilkey	.15	.06	.01
☐ 409 Rex Hudler	.03	.01	.00
☐ 410 Thomson/Branca Shot Bobby Thomson Ralph Branca (See also 406)	.08	.03	.01
☐ 411 Lance Dickson	.17	.07	.01
☐ 412 Danny Jackson	.03	.01	.00
☐ 413 Jerome Walton	.08	.03	.01
☐ 414 Sean Cheetham	.10	.04	.01
☐ 415 Joe Girardi	.03	.01	.00
☐ 416 Ryne Sandberg	.15	.06	.01
☐ 417 Mike Harkey	.06	.02	.00
☐ 418 George Bell	.08	.03	.01
☐ 419 Rick Wilkins	.17	.07	.01
☐ 420 Earl Cunningham	.06	.02	.00
☐ 421 Heathcliff Slocumb	.08	.03	.01
☐ 422 Mike Bielecki	.03	.01	.00
☐ 423 Jessie Hollins	.08	.03	.01
☐ 424 Shawon Dunston	.06	.02	.00
☐ 425 Dave Smith	.03	.01	.00
☐ 426 Greg Maddux	.06	.02	.00
☐ 427 Jose Vizcaino	.06	.02	.00
☐ 428 Luis Salazar	.03	.01	.00
☐ 429 Andre Dawson	.10	.04	.01
☐ 430 Rick Sutcliffe	.06	.02	.00
☐ 431 Paul Assenmacher	.03	.01	.00
☐ 432 Erik Pappas	.08	.03	.01
☐ 433 Mark Grace	.08	.03	.01
☐ 434 Dennis Martinez	.06	.02	.00
☐ 435 Marquis Grissom	.10	.04	.01
☐ 436 Wilfredo Cordero	.25	.10	.02
☐ 437 Tim Wallach	.06	.02	.00
☐ 438 Brian Barnes	.12	.05	.01
☐ 439 Barry Jones	.03	.01	.00
☐ 440 Ivan Calderon	.06	.02	.00
☐ 441 Stan Spencer	.10	.04	.01
☐ 442 Larry Walker	.06	.02	.00
☐ 443 Chris Haney	.12	.05	.01
☐ 444 Hector Rivera	.10	.04	.01
☐ 445 Delino DeSheilds	.08	.03	.01
☐ 446 Andres Galarraga	.06	.02	.00
☐ 447 Gilberto Reyes	.03	.01	.00
☐ 448 Willie Greene	.06	.02	.00
☐ 449 Greg Colbrunn	.12	.05	.01
☐ 450 Rondell White	.30	.12	.03
☐ 451 Steve Frey	.08	.03	.01
☐ 452 Shane Andrews	.15	.06	.01
☐ 453 Mike Fitzgerald	.03	.01	.00
☐ 454 Spike Owen	.03	.01	.00
☐ 455 Dave Martinez	.03	.01	.00
☐ 456 Dennis Boyd	.03	.01	.00
☐ 457 Eric Bullock	.03	.01	.00
☐ 458 Reid Cornelius	.20	.08	.02
☐ 459 Chris Nabholz	.08	.03	.01
☐ 460 David Cone	.06	.02	.00
☐ 461 Hubie Brooks	.06	.02	.00
☐ 462 Sid Fernandez	.06	.02	.00
☐ 463 Doug Simons	.08	.03	.01

☐ 464 Howard Johnson .08 .03 .01
☐ 465 Chris Donnels .20 .08 .02
☐ 466 Anthony Young .20 .08 .02
☐ 467 Todd Hundley .10 .04 .01
☐ 468 Rick Cerone .03 .01 .00
☐ 469 Kevin Elster .03 .01 .00
☐ 470 Wally Whitehurst .03 .01 .00
☐ 471 Vince Coleman .08 .03 .01
☐ 472 Dwight Gooden .08 .03 .01
☐ 473 Charlie O'Brien .03 .01 .00
☐ 474 Jeromy Burnitz .60 .25 .06
☐ 475 John Franco .03 .01 .00
☐ 476 Daryl Boston .03 .01 .00
☐ 477 Frank Viola .08 .03 .01
☐ 478 D.J. Dozier .10 .04 .01
☐ 479 Kevin McReynolds .06 .02 .00
☐ 480 Tom Herr .03 .01 .00
☐ 481 Gregg Jefferies .08 .03 .01
☐ 482 Pete Schourek .10 .04 .01
☐ 483 Ron Darling .06 .02 .00
☐ 484 Dave Magadan .06 .02 .00
☐ 485 Andy Ashby .10 .04 .01
☐ 486 Dale Murphy .08 .03 .01
☐ 487 Von Hayes .06 .02 .00
☐ 488 Kim Batiste .10 .04 .01
☐ 489 Tony Longmire .20 .08 .02
☐ 490 Wally Backman .03 .01 .00
☐ 491 Jeff Jackson .06 .02 .00
☐ 492 Mickey Morandini .08 .03 .01
☐ 493 Darrel Akerfelds .03 .01 .00
☐ 494 Ricky Jordan .06 .02 .00
☐ 495 Randy Ready .03 .01 .00
☐ 496 Darrin Fletcher .06 .02 .00
☐ 497 Chuck Malone .03 .01 .00
☐ 498 Pat Combs .06 .02 .00
☐ 499 Dickie Thon .03 .01 .00
☐ 500 Roger McDowell .03 .01 .00
☐ 501 Len Dykstra .06 .02 .00
☐ 502 Joe Boever .03 .01 .00
☐ 503 John Kruk .03 .01 .00
☐ 504 Terry Mulholland .06 .02 .00
☐ 505 Wes Chamberlain .40 .16 .04
☐ 506 Mike Lieberthal .12 .05 .01
☐ 507 Darren Daulton .03 .01 .00
☐ 508 Charlie Hayes .03 .01 .00
☐ 509 John Smiley .06 .02 .00
☐ 510 Gary Varsho .03 .01 .00
☐ 511 Curt Wilkerson .03 .01 .00
☐ 512 Orlando Merced .35 .15 .03
☐ 513 Barry Bonds .10 .04 .01
☐ 514 Mike LaValliere .03 .01 .00
☐ 515 Doug Drabek .06 .02 .00
☐ 516 Gary Redus .03 .01 .00
☐ 517 William Pennyfeather .15 .06 .01
☐ 518 Randy Tomlin .15 .06 .01
☐ 519 Mike Zimmerman .08 .03 .01
☐ 520 Jeff King .06 .02 .00
☐ 521 Kurt Miller .15 .06 .01
☐ 522 Jay Bell .03 .01 .00
☐ 523 Bill Landrum .03 .01 .00
☐ 524 Zane Smith .06 .02 .00
☐ 525 Bobby Bonilla .10 .04 .01
☐ 526 Bob Walk .03 .01 .00
☐ 527 Austin Manahan .06 .02 .00
☐ 528 Joe Ausanio .08 .03 .01
☐ 529 Andy Van Slyke .08 .03 .01
☐ 530 Jose Lind .03 .01 .00
☐ 531 Carlos Garcia .08 .03 .01
☐ 532 Don Slaught .03 .01 .00
☐ 533 Colin Powell .12 .05 .01
☐ 534 Frank Bolick .17 .07 .01
☐ 535 Gary Scott .25 .10 .02
☐ 536 Nikco Riesgo .35 .15 .03
☐ 537 Reggie Sanders .40 .16 .04
☐ 538 Tim Howard .20 .08 .02
☐ 539 Ryan Bowen .15 .06 .01
☐ 540 Eric Anthony .08 .03 .01
☐ 541 Jim Deshaies .03 .01 .00
☐ 542 Tom Nevers .15 .06 .01
☐ 543 Ken Caminiti .03 .01 .00
☐ 544 Karl Rhodes .06 .02 .00
☐ 545 Xavier Hernandez .06 .02 .00
☐ 546 Mike Scott .06 .02 .00
☐ 547 Jeff Juden .08 .03 .01
☐ 548 Darryl Kile .03 .01 .00
☐ 549 Willie Ansley .06 .02 .00
☐ 550 Luis Gonzalez .40 .16 .04
☐ 551 Mike Simms .12 .05 .01
☐ 552 Mark Portugal .03 .01 .00
☐ 553 Jimmy Jones .03 .01 .00
☐ 554 Jim Clancy .03 .01 .00
☐ 555 Pete Harnisch .06 .02 .00
☐ 556 Craig Biggio .08 .03 .01
☐ 557 Eric Yelding .03 .01 .00
☐ 558 Dave Rohde .03 .01 .00
☐ 559 Casey Candaele .03 .01 .00
☐ 560 Curt Schilling .03 .01 .00
☐ 561 Steve Finley .06 .02 .00
☐ 562 Javier Ortiz .08 .03 .01
☐ 563 Andujar Cedeno .20 .08 .02
☐ 564 Rafael Ramirez .03 .01 .00
☐ 565 Kenny Lofton .20 .08 .02
☐ 566 Steve Avery .30 .12 .03
☐ 567 Lonnie Smith .06 .02 .00
☐ 568 Kent Mercker .03 .01 .00
☐ 569 Chipper Jones .30 .12 .03
☐ 570 Terry Pendleton .08 .03 .01
☐ 571 Otis Nixon .06 .02 .00
☐ 572 Juan Berenguer .03 .01 .00
☐ 573 Charlie Leibrandt .03 .01 .00
☐ 574 David Justice .40 .16 .04
☐ 575 Keith Mitchell .35 .15 .03
☐ 576 Tom Glavine .12 .05 .01
☐ 577 Greg Olson .06 .02 .00
☐ 578 Rafael Belliard .03 .01 .00
☐ 579 Ben Rivera .08 .03 .01

Card			
☐ 580 John Smoltz	.10	.04	.01
☐ 581 Tyler Houston	.06	.02	.00
☐ 582 Mark Wohlers	.40	.16	.04
☐ 583 Ron Gant	.12	.05	.01
☐ 584 Ramon Caraballo	.08	.03	.01
☐ 585 Sid Bream	.03	.01	.00
☐ 586 Jeff Treadway	.03	.01	.00
☐ 587 Javier Lopez	.08	.03	.01
☐ 588 Deion Sanders	.08	.03	.01
☐ 589 Mike Heath	.03	.01	.00
☐ 590 Ryan Klesko	1.25	.50	.12
☐ 591 Bob Ojeda	.03	.01	.00
☐ 592 Alfredo Griffin	.03	.01	.00
☐ 593 Raul Mondesi	.20	.08	.02
☐ 594 Greg Smith	.03	.01	.00
☐ 595 Orel Hershiser	.08	.03	.01
☐ 596 Juan Samuel	.06	.02	.00
☐ 597 Brett Butler	.06	.02	.00
☐ 598 Gary Carter	.08	.03	.01
☐ 599 Stan Javier	.03	.01	.00
☐ 600 Kal Daniels	.06	.02	.00
☐ 601 Jamie McAndrew	.12	.05	.01
☐ 602 Mike Sharperson	.03	.01	.00
☐ 603 Jay Howell	.03	.01	.00
☐ 604 Eric Karros	.40	.16	.04
☐ 605 Tim Belcher	.06	.02	.00
☐ 606 Dan Opperman	.10	.04	.01
☐ 607 Lenny Harris	.03	.01	.00
☐ 608 Tom Goodwin	.06	.02	.00
☐ 609 Darryl Strawberry	.15	.06	.01
☐ 610 Ramon Martinez	.10	.04	.01
☐ 611 Kevin Gross	.03	.01	.00
☐ 612 Zakary Shinall	.08	.03	.01
☐ 613 Mike Scioscia	.03	.01	.00
☐ 614 Eddie Murray	.10	.04	.01
☐ 615 Ronnie Walden	.10	.04	.01
☐ 616 Will Clark	.20	.08	.02
☐ 617 Adam Hyzdu	.12	.05	.01
☐ 618 Matt Williams	.08	.03	.01
☐ 619 Don Robinson	.03	.01	.00
☐ 620 Jeff Brantley	.03	.01	.00
☐ 621 Greg Litton	.03	.01	.00
☐ 622 Steve Decker	.25	.10	.02
☐ 623 Robby Thompson	.03	.01	.00
☐ 624 Mark Leonard	.10	.04	.01
☐ 625 Kevin Bass	.03	.01	.00
☐ 626 Scott Garrelts	.03	.01	.00
☐ 627 Jose Uribe	.03	.01	.00
☐ 628 Eric Gunderson	.06	.02	.00
☐ 629 Steve Hosey	.06	.02	.00
☐ 630 Trevor Wilson	.03	.01	.00
☐ 631 Terry Kennedy	.03	.01	.00
☐ 632 Dave Righetti	.06	.02	.00
☐ 633 Kelly Downs	.03	.01	.00
☐ 634 Johnny Ard	.06	.02	.00
☐ 635 Eric Christopherson	.08	.03	.01
☐ 636 Kevin Mitchell	.10	.04	.01
☐ 637 John Burkett	.03	.01	.00
☐ 638 Kevin Rogers	.10	.04	.01
☐ 639 Bud Black	.03	.01	.00
☐ 640 Willie McGee	.08	.03	.01
☐ 641 Royce Clayton	.12	.05	.01
☐ 642 Tony Fernandez	.06	.02	.00
☐ 643 Ricky Bones	.10	.04	.01
☐ 644 Thomas Howard	.03	.01	.00
☐ 645 Dave Staton	.15	.06	.01
☐ 646 Jim Presley	.03	.01	.00
☐ 647 Tony Gwynn	.12	.05	.01
☐ 648 Marty Barrett	.03	.01	.00
☐ 649 Scott Coolbaugh	.03	.01	.00
☐ 650 Craig Lefferts	.03	.01	.00
☐ 651 Eddie Whitson	.03	.01	.00
☐ 652 Oscar Azocar	.06	.02	.00
☐ 653 Wes Gardner	.03	.01	.00
☐ 654 Bip Roberts	.03	.01	.00
☐ 655 Robbie Beckett	.10	.04	.01
☐ 656 Benito Santiago	.08	.03	.01
☐ 657 Greg W.Harris	.03	.01	.00
☐ 658 Jerald Clark	.03	.01	.00
☐ 659 Fred McGriff	.08	.03	.01
☐ 660 Larry Andersen	.03	.01	.00
☐ 661 Bruce Hurst	.06	.02	.00
☐ 662 Steve Martin	.10	.04	.01
☐ 663 Rafael Valdez	.03	.01	.00
☐ 664 Paul Faries	.08	.03	.01
☐ 665 Andy Benes	.06	.02	.00
☐ 666 Randy Myers	.03	.01	.00
☐ 667 Rob Dibble	.06	.02	.00
☐ 668 Glenn Sutko	.08	.03	.01
☐ 669 Glenn Braggs	.03	.01	.00
☐ 670 Billy Hatcher	.06	.02	.00
☐ 671 Joe Oliver	.03	.01	.00
☐ 672 Freddy Benavides	.08	.03	.01
☐ 673 Barry Larkin	.08	.03	.01
☐ 674 Chris Sabo	.08	.03	.01
☐ 675 Mariano Duncan	.03	.01	.00
☐ 676 Chris Jones	.15	.06	.01
☐ 677 Gino Minutelli	.15	.06	.01
☐ 678 Reggie Jefferson	.10	.04	.01
☐ 679 Jack Armstrong	.06	.02	.00
☐ 680 Chris Hammond	.08	.03	.01
☐ 681 Jose Rijo	.06	.02	.00
☐ 682 Bill Doran	.03	.01	.00
☐ 683 Terry Lee	.10	.04	.01
☐ 684 Tom Browning	.06	.02	.00
☐ 685 Paul O'Neill	.06	.02	.00
☐ 686 Eric Davis	.10	.04	.01
☐ 687 Dan Wilson	.15	.06	.01
☐ 688 Ted Power	.03	.01	.00
☐ 689 Tim Layana	.03	.01	.00
☐ 690 Norm Charlton	.03	.01	.00
☐ 691 Hal Morris	.08	.03	.01
☐ 692 Rickey Henderson	.15	.06	.01
☐ 693 Sam Militello Minor League MVP	.20	.08	.02

☐ 694 Matt Mieske Minor League MVP	.45	.18	.04
☐ 695 Paul Russo Minor League MVP	.15	.06	.01
☐ 696 Domingo Mota Minor League MVP	.20	.08	.02
☐ 697 Todd Guggiana Minor League MVP	.15	.06	.01
☐ 698 Marc Newfield Minor League MVP	.75	.30	.07
☐ 699 Checklist 1	.06	.01	.00
☐ 700 Checklist 2	.06	.01	.00
☐ 701 Checklist 3	.06	.01	.00
☐ 702 Checklist 4	.06	.01	.00
☐ 703 Checklist 5	.06	.01	.00
☐ 704 Checklist 6	.06	.01	.00

1981 Donruss

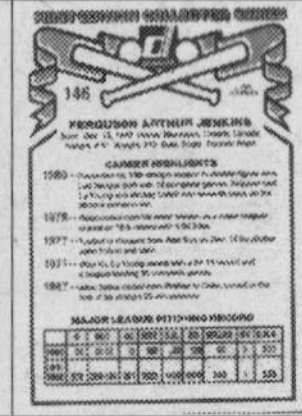

The cards in this 605-card set measure 2 1/2" by 3 1/2". In 1981 Donruss launched itself into the baseball card market with a set containing 600 numbered cards and five unnumbered checklists. Even though the five checklist cards are unnumbered, they are numbered below (601-605) for convenience in reference. The cards are printed on thin stock and more than one pose exists for several popular players. The numerous errors of the first print run were later corrected by the company. These are marked P1 and P2 in the checklist below. The key rookie cards in this set are Tim Raines and Jeff Reardon.

	MINT	EXC	G-VG
COMPLETE SET (605)	60.00	27.00	9.00
COMMON PLAYER (1-605)	.05	.02	.00

☐ 1 Ozzie Smith	2.50	.75	.15
☐ 2 Rollie Fingers	.75	.30	.07
☐ 3 Rick Wise	.05	.02	.00
☐ 4 Gene Richards	.05	.02	.00
☐ 5 Alan Trammell	1.00	.40	.10
☐ 6 Tom Brookens	.05	.02	.00
☐ 7A Duffy Dyer P1 (1980 batting average has decimal point)	.10	.04	.01
☐ 7B Duffy Dyer P2 (1980 batting average has no decimal point)	.10	.04	.01
☐ 8 Mark Fidrych	.15	.06	.01
☐ 9 Dave Rozema	.05	.02	.00
☐ 10 Ricky Peters	.05	.02	.00
☐ 11 Mike Schmidt	2.50	1.00	.25
☐ 12 Willie Stargell	.60	.25	.06
☐ 13 Tim Foli	.05	.02	.00
☐ 14 Manny Sanguillen	.10	.04	.01
☐ 15 Grant Jackson	.05	.02	.00
☐ 16 Eddie Solomon	.05	.02	.00
☐ 17 Omar Moreno	.05	.02	.00
☐ 18 Joe Morgan	.75	.30	.07
☐ 19 Rafael Landestoy	.05	.02	.00
☐ 20 Bruce Bochy	.05	.02	.00
☐ 21 Joe Sambito	.05	.02	.00
☐ 22 Manny Trillo	.05	.02	.00
☐ 23A Dave Smith P1 (Line box around stats is not complete)	.40	.16	.04
☐ 23B Dave Smith P2 (Box totally encloses stats at top)	.40	.16	.04
☐ 24 Terry Puhl	.05	.02	.00
☐ 25 Bump Wills	.05	.02	.00
☐ 26A John Ellis P1 ERR (Photo on front shows Danny Walton)	.50	.20	.05
☐ 26B John Ellis P2 COR	.10	.04	.01
☐ 27 Jim Kern	.05	.02	.00
☐ 28 Richie Zisk	.05	.02	.00
☐ 29 John Mayberry	.10	.04	.01
☐ 30 Bob Davis	.05	.02	.00
☐ 31 Jackson Todd	.05	.02	.00
☐ 32 Alvis Woods	.05	.02	.00
☐ 33 Steve Carlton	1.25	.50	.12
☐ 34 Lee Mazzilli	.05	.02	.00
☐ 35 John Stearns	.05	.02	.00
☐ 36 Roy Lee Jackson	.05	.02	.00
☐ 37 Mike Scott	.50	.20	.05
☐ 38 Lamar Johnson	.05	.02	.00
☐ 39 Kevin Bell	.05	.02	.00
☐ 40 Ed Farmer	.05	.02	.00
☐ 41 Ross Baumgarten	.05	.02	.00
☐ 42 Leo Sutherland	.05	.02	.00
☐ 43 Dan Meyer	.05	.02	.00
☐ 44 Ron Reed	.05	.02	.00
☐ 45 Mario Mendoza	.05	.02	.00

☐ 46 Rick Honeycutt	.05	.02	.00
☐ 47 Glenn Abbott	.05	.02	.00
☐ 48 Leon Roberts	.05	.02	.00
☐ 49 Rod Carew	1.50	.60	.15
☐ 50 Bert Campaneris	.10	.04	.01
☐ 51A Tom Donahue P1 ERR (Name on front misspelled Donahue)	.10	.04	.01
☐ 51B Tom Donohue P2 COR	.10	.04	.01
☐ 52 Dave Frost	.05	.02	.00
☐ 53 Ed Halicki	.05	.02	.00
☐ 54 Dan Ford	.05	.02	.00
☐ 55 Garry Maddox	.05	.02	.00
☐ 56A Steve Garvey P1 ("Surpassed 25 HR")	1.00	.40	.10
☐ 56B Steve Garvey P2 ("Surpassed 21 HR")	.75	.30	.07
☐ 57 Bill Russell	.10	.04	.01
☐ 58 Don Sutton	.50	.20	.05
☐ 59 Reggie Smith	.10	.04	.01
☐ 60 Rick Monday	.10	.04	.01
☐ 61 Ray Knight	.10	.04	.01
☐ 62 Johnny Bench	1.50	.60	.15
☐ 63 Mario Soto	.10	.04	.01
☐ 64 Doug Bair	.05	.02	.00
☐ 65 George Foster	.20	.08	.02
☐ 66 Jeff Burroughs	.05	.02	.00
☐ 67 Keith Hernandez	.35	.15	.03
☐ 68 Tom Herr	.10	.04	.01
☐ 69 Bob Forsch	.05	.02	.00
☐ 70 John Fulgham	.05	.02	.00
☐ 71A Bobby Bonds P1 ERR (986 lifetime HR)	.30	.12	.03
☐ 71B Bobby Bonds P2 COR (326 lifetime HR)	.15	.06	.01
☐ 72A Rennie Stennett P1 ("breaking broke leg")	.10	.04	.01
☐ 72B Rennie Stennett P2 (Word "broke" deleted)	.10	.04	.01
☐ 73 Joe Strain	.05	.02	.00
☐ 74 Ed Whitson	.10	.04	.01
☐ 75 Tom Griffin	.05	.02	.00
☐ 76 Billy North	.05	.02	.00
☐ 77 Gene Garber	.05	.02	.00
☐ 78 Mike Hargrove	.10	.04	.01
☐ 79 Dave Rosello	.05	.02	.00
☐ 80 Ron Hassey	.10	.04	.01
☐ 81 Sid Monge	.05	.02	.00
☐ 82A Joe Charboneau P1 ('78 highlights, "For some reason")	.10	.04	.01
☐ 82B Joe Charboneau P2 (Phrase "For some reason" deleted)	.10	.04	.01
☐ 83 Cecil Cooper	.15	.06	.01
☐ 84 Sal Bando	.10	.04	.01
☐ 85 Moose Haas	.05	.02	.00

☐ 86 Mike Caldwell	.05	.02	.00
☐ 87A Larry Hisle P1 ('77 highlights, line ends with "28 RBI")	.10	.04	.01
☐ 87B Larry Hisle P2 (Correct line "28 HR")	.10	.04	.01
☐ 88 Luis Gomez	.05	.02	.00
☐ 89 Larry Parrish	.05	.02	.00
☐ 90 Gary Carter	.90	.40	.09
☐ 91 Bill Gullickson	.50	.20	.05
☐ 92 Fred Norman	.05	.02	.00
☐ 93 Tommy Hutton	.05	.02	.00
☐ 94 Carl Yastrzemski	1.50	.60	.15
☐ 95 Glenn Hoffman	.05	.02	.00
☐ 96 Dennis Eckersley	.60	.25	.06
☐ 97A Tom Burgmeier P1 ERR (Throws: Right)	.10	.04	.01
☐ 97B Tom Burgmeier P2 COR (Throws: Left)	.10	.04	.01
☐ 98 Win Remmerswaal	.05	.02	.00
☐ 99 Bob Horner	.10	.04	.01
☐ 100 George Brett	2.50	1.00	.25
☐ 101 Dave Chalk	.05	.02	.00
☐ 102 Dennis Leonard	.05	.02	.00
☐ 103 Renie Martin	.05	.02	.00
☐ 104 Amos Otis	.10	.04	.01
☐ 105 Graig Nettles	.15	.06	.01
☐ 106 Eric Soderholm	.05	.02	.00
☐ 107 Tommy John	.20	.08	.02
☐ 108 Tom Underwood	.05	.02	.00
☐ 109 Lou Piniella	.15	.06	.01
☐ 110 Mickey Klutts	.05	.02	.00
☐ 111 Bobby Murcer	.15	.06	.01
☐ 112 Eddie Murray	2.50	1.00	.25
☐ 113 Rick Dempsey	.05	.02	.00
☐ 114 Scott McGregor	.05	.02	.00
☐ 115 Ken Singleton	.10	.04	.01
☐ 116 Gary Roenicke	.05	.02	.00
☐ 117 Dave Revering	.05	.02	.00
☐ 118 Mike Norris	.05	.02	.00
☐ 119 Rickey Henderson	18.00	7.50	2.50
☐ 120 Mike Heath	.05	.02	.00
☐ 121 Dave Cash	.05	.02	.00
☐ 122 Randy Jones	.05	.02	.00
☐ 123 Eric Rasmussen	.05	.02	.00
☐ 124 Jerry Mumphrey	.05	.02	.00
☐ 125 Richie Hebner	.05	.02	.00
☐ 126 Mark Wagner	.05	.02	.00
☐ 127 Jack Morris	1.00	.40	.10
☐ 128 Dan Petry	.10	.04	.01
☐ 129 Bruce Robbins	.05	.02	.00
☐ 130 Champ Summers	.05	.02	.00
☐ 131A Pete Rose P1 (Last line ends with "see card 251")	2.00	.80	.20
☐ 131B Pete Rose P2 (Last line corrected "see card 371")	1.75	.70	.17

□ 132 Willie Stargell .60 .25 .06
□ 133 Ed Ott .05 .02 .00
□ 134 Jim Bibby .05 .02 .00
□ 135 Bert Blyleven .25 .10 .02
□ 136 Dave Parker .60 .25 .06
□ 137 Bill Robinson .10 .04 .01
□ 138 Enos Cabell .05 .02 .00
□ 139 Dave Bergman .05 .02 .00
□ 140 J.R. Richard .10 .04 .01
□ 141 Ken Forsch .05 .02 .00
□ 142 Larry Bowa UER .15 .06 .01
(Shortshop on front)
□ 143 Frank LaCorte UER .05 .02 .00
(photo actually Randy Niemann)
□ 144 Denny Walling .05 .02 .00
□ 145 Buddy Bell .10 .04 .01
□ 146 Ferguson Jenkins .50 .20 .05
□ 147 Dannny Darwin .10 .04 .01
□ 148 John Grubb .05 .02 .00
□ 149 Alfredo Griffin .10 .04 .01
□ 150 Jerry Garvin .05 .02 .00
□ 151 Paul Mirabella .05 .02 .00
□ 152 Rick Bosetti .05 .02 .00
□ 153 Dick Ruthven .05 .02 .00
□ 154 Frank Taveras .05 .02 .00
□ 155 Craig Swan .05 .02 .00
□ 156 Jeff Reardon 3.50 1.50 .35
□ 157 Steve Henderson .05 .02 .00
□ 158 Jim Morrison .05 .02 .00
□ 159 Glenn Borgmann .05 .02 .00
□ 160 LaMarr Hoyt .15 .06 .01
□ 161 Rich Wortham .05 .02 .00
□ 162 Thad Bosley .05 .02 .00
□ 163 Julio Cruz .05 .02 .00
□ 164A Del Unser P1 .10 .04 .01
(No "3B" heading)
□ 164B Del Unser P2 .10 .04 .01
(Batting record on back corrected ("3B"))
□ 165 Jim Anderson .05 .02 .00
□ 166 Jim Beattie .05 .02 .00
□ 167 Shane Rawley .05 .02 .00
□ 168 Joe Simpson .05 .02 .00
□ 169 Rod Carew 1.50 .60 .15
□ 170 Fred Patek .05 .02 .00
□ 171 Frank Tanana .10 .04 .01
□ 172 Alfredo Martinez .05 .02 .00
□ 173 Chris Knapp .05 .02 .00
□ 174 Joe Rudi .10 .04 .01
□ 175 Greg Luzinski .15 .06 .01
□ 176 Steve Garvey .75 .30 .07
□ 177 Joe Ferguson .05 .02 .00
□ 178 Bob Welch .50 .20 .05
□ 179 Dusty Baker .10 .04 .01
□ 180 Rudy Law .05 .02 .00
□ 181 Dave Concepcion .20 .08 .02
□ 182 Johnny Bench 1.50 .60 .15
□ 183 Mike LaCoss .05 .02 .00
□ 184 Ken Griffey .30 .12 .03
□ 185 Dave Collins .05 .02 .00
□ 186 Brian Asselstine .05 .02 .00
□ 187 Garry Templeton .10 .04 .01
□ 188 Mike Phillips .05 .02 .00
□ 189 Pete Vuckovich .05 .02 .00
□ 190 John Urrea .05 .02 .00
□ 191 Tony Scott .05 .02 .00
□ 192 Darrell Evans .15 .06 .01
□ 193 Milt May .05 .02 .00
□ 194 Bob Knepper .05 .02 .00
□ 195 Randy Moffitt .05 .02 .00
□ 196 Larry Herndon .05 .02 .00
□ 197 Rick Camp .05 .02 .00
□ 198 Andre Thornton .10 .04 .01
□ 199 Tom Veryzer .05 .02 .00
□ 200 Gary Alexander .05 .02 .00
□ 201 Rick Waits .05 .02 .00
□ 202 Rick Manning .05 .02 .00
□ 203 Paul Molitor .60 .25 .06
□ 204 Jim Gantner .05 .02 .00
□ 205 Paul Mitchell .05 .02 .00
□ 206 Reggie Cleveland .05 .02 .00
□ 207 Sixto Lezcano .05 .02 .00
□ 208 Bruce Benedict .05 .02 .00
□ 209 Rodney Scott .05 .02 .00
□ 210 John Tamargo .05 .02 .00
□ 211 Bill Lee .05 .02 .00
□ 212 Andre Dawson UER 1.75 .70 .17
(Middle name Fernando, should be Nolan)
□ 213 Rowland Office .05 .02 .00
□ 214 Carl Yastrzemski 1.50 .60 .15
□ 215 Jerry Remy .05 .02 .00
□ 216 Mike Torrez .05 .02 .00
□ 217 Skip Lockwood .05 .02 .00
□ 218 Fred Lynn .20 .08 .02
□ 219 Chris Chambliss .10 .04 .01
□ 220 Willie Aikens .05 .02 .00
□ 221 John Wathan .10 .04 .01
□ 222 Dan Quisenberry .25 .10 .02
□ 223 Willie Wilson .20 .08 .02
□ 224 Clint Hurdle .05 .02 .00
□ 225 Bob Watson .05 .02 .00
□ 226 Jim Spencer .05 .02 .00
□ 227 Ron Guidry .25 .10 .02
□ 228 Reggie Jackson 2.50 1.00 .25
□ 229 Oscar Gamble .05 .02 .00
□ 230 Jeff Cox .05 .02 .00
□ 231 Luis Tiant .10 .04 .01
□ 232 Rich Dauer .05 .02 .00
□ 233 Dan Graham .05 .02 .00
□ 234 Mike Flanagan .10 .04 .01
□ 235 John Lowenstein .05 .02 .00
□ 236 Benny Ayala .05 .02 .00
□ 237 Wayne Gross .05 .02 .00
□ 238 Rick Langford .05 .02 .00

☐ 239 Tony Armas .05 .02 .00
☐ 240A Bob Lacy P1 ERR .20 .08 .02
(Name misspelled
Bob "Lacy")
☐ 240B Bob Lacey P2 COR .10 .04 .01
☐ 241 Gene Tenace .10 .04 .01
☐ 242 Bob Shirley .05 .02 .00
☐ 243 Gary Lucas .05 .02 .00
☐ 244 Jerry Turner .05 .02 .00
☐ 245 John Wockenfuss .05 .02 .00
☐ 246 Stan Papi .05 .02 .00
☐ 247 Milt Wilcox .05 .02 .00
☐ 248 Dan Schatzeder .05 .02 .00
☐ 249 Steve Kemp .05 .02 .00
☐ 250 Jim Lentine .05 .02 .00
☐ 251 Pete Rose 1.75 .70 .17
☐ 252 Bill Madlock .15 .06 .01
☐ 253 Dale Berra .05 .02 .00
☐ 254 Kent Tekulve .10 .04 .01
☐ 255 Enrique Romo .05 .02 .00
☐ 256 Mike Easler .05 .02 .00
☐ 257 Chuck Tanner MG .05 .02 .00
☐ 258 Art Howe .10 .04 .01
☐ 259 Alan Ashby .05 .02 .00
☐ 260 Nolan Ryan 6.25 2.75 .60
☐ 261A Vern Ruhle P1 ERR .50 .20 .05
(Photo on front
actually Ken Forsch)
☐ 261B Vern Ruhle P2 COR .10 .04 .01
☐ 262 Bob Boone .15 .06 .01
☐ 263 Cesar Cedeno .10 .04 .01
☐ 264 Jeff Leonard .10 .04 .01
☐ 265 Pat Putnam .05 .02 .00
☐ 266 Jon Matlack .05 .02 .00
☐ 267 Dave Rajsich .05 .02 .00
☐ 268 Billy Sample .05 .02 .00
☐ 269 Damaso Garcia .05 .02 .00
☐ 270 Tom Buskey .05 .02 .00
☐ 271 Joey McLaughlin .05 .02 .00
☐ 272 Barry Bonnell .05 .02 .00
☐ 273 Tug McGraw .15 .06 .01
☐ 274 Mike Jorgensen .05 .02 .00
☐ 275 Pat Zachry .05 .02 .00
☐ 276 Neil Allen .05 .02 .00
☐ 277 Joel Youngblood .05 .02 .00
☐ 278 Greg Pryor .05 .02 .00
☐ 279 Britt Burns .10 .04 .01
☐ 280 Rich Dotson .15 .06 .01
☐ 281 Chet Lemon .05 .02 .00
☐ 282 Rusty Kuntz .05 .02 .00
☐ 283 Ted Cox .05 .02 .00
☐ 284 Sparky Lyle .15 .06 .01
☐ 285 Larry Cox .05 .02 .00
☐ 286 Floyd Bannister .05 .02 .00
☐ 287 Byron McLaughlin .05 .02 .00
☐ 288 Rodney Craig .05 .02 .00
☐ 289 Bobby Grich .10 .04 .01
☐ 290 Dickie Thon .15 .06 .01
☐ 291 Mark Clear .05 .02 .00
☐ 292 Dave Lemanczyk .05 .02 .00
☐ 293 Jason Thompson .05 .02 .00
☐ 294 Rick Miller .05 .02 .00
☐ 295 Lonnie Smith .35 .15 .03
☐ 296 Ron Cey .15 .06 .01
☐ 297 Steve Yeager .05 .02 .00
☐ 298 Bobby Castillo .05 .02 .00
☐ 299 Manny Mota .10 .04 .01
☐ 300 Jay Johnstone .10 .04 .01
☐ 301 Dan Driessen .05 .02 .00
☐ 302 Joe Nolan .05 .02 .00
☐ 303 Paul Householder .05 .02 .00
☐ 304 Harry Spilman .05 .02 .00
☐ 305 Cesar Geronimo .05 .02 .00
☐ 306A Gary Mathews P1 ERR .20 .08 .02
(Name misspelled)
☐ 306B Gary Matthews P2 .10 .04 .01
COR
☐ 307 Ken Reitz .05 .02 .00
☐ 308 Ted Simmons .20 .08 .02
☐ 309 John Littlefield .05 .02 .00
☐ 310 George Frazier .05 .02 .00
☐ 311 Dane Iorg .05 .02 .00
☐ 312 Mike Ivie .05 .02 .00
☐ 313 Dennis Littlejohn .05 .02 .00
☐ 314 Gary Lavelle .05 .02 .00
☐ 315 Jack Clark .25 .10 .02
☐ 316 Jim Wohlford .05 .02 .00
☐ 317 Rick Matula .05 .02 .00
☐ 318 Toby Harrah .05 .02 .00
☐ 319A Dwane Kuiper P1 ERR .10 .04 .01
(Name misspelled)
☐ 319B Duane Kuiper P2 COR .10 .04 .01
☐ 320 Len Barker .05 .02 .00
☐ 321 Victor Cruz .05 .02 .00
☐ 322 Dell Alston .05 .02 .00
☐ 323 Robin Yount 2.50 1.00 .25
☐ 324 Charlie Moore .05 .02 .00
☐ 325 Lary Sorensen .05 .02 .00
☐ 326A Gorman Thomas P1 .20 .08 .02
(2nd line on back:
"30 HR mark 4th")
☐ 326B Gorman Thomas P2 .10 .04 .01
("30 HR mark 3rd")
☐ 327 Bob Rodgers MG .05 .02 .00
☐ 328 Phil Niekro .50 .20 .05
☐ 329 Chris Speier .05 .02 .00
☐ 330A Steve Rodgers P1 .20 .08 .02
ERR (Name misspelled)
☐ 330B Steve Rogers P2 COR .10 .04 .01
☐ 331 Woodie Fryman .05 .02 .00
☐ 332 Warren Cromartie .05 .02 .00
☐ 333 Jerry White .05 .02 .00
☐ 334 Tony Perez .35 .15 .03
☐ 335 Carlton Fisk 1.50 .60 .15
☐ 336 Dick Drago .05 .02 .00
☐ 337 Steve Renko .05 .02 .00

☐ 338 Jim Rice .25 .10 .02
☐ 339 Jerry Royster .05 .02 .00
☐ 340 Frank White .10 .04 .01
☐ 341 Jamie Quirk .05 .02 .00
☐ 342A Paul Spittorff P1 ERR .10 .04 .01
(Name misspelled)
☐ 342B Paul Splittorff .10 .04 .01
P2 COR
☐ 343 Marty Pattin .05 .02 .00
☐ 344 Pete LaCock .05 .02 .00
☐ 345 Willie Randolph .15 .06 .01
☐ 346 Rick Cerone .05 .02 .00
☐ 347 Rich Gossage .20 .08 .02
☐ 348 Reggie Jackson 2.50 1.00 .25
☐ 349 Ruppert Jones .05 .02 .00
☐ 350 Dave McKay .05 .02 .00
☐ 351 Yogi Berra CO .25 .10 .02
☐ 352 Doug DeCinces .05 .02 .00
☐ 353 Jim Palmer 1.00 .40 .10
☐ 354 Tippy Martinez .05 .02 .00
☐ 355 Al Bumbry .05 .02 .00
☐ 356 Earl Weaver MG .10 .04 .01
☐ 357A Bob Picciolo P1 ERR .10 .04 .01
(Name misspelled)
☐ 357B Rob Picciolo P2 COR .10 .04 .01
☐ 358 Matt Keough .05 .02 .00
☐ 359 Dwayne Murphy .05 .02 .00
☐ 360 Brian Kingman .05 .02 .00
☐ 361 Bill Fahey .05 .02 .00
☐ 362 Steve Mura .05 .02 .00
☐ 363 Dennis Kinney .05 .02 .00
☐ 364 Dave Winfield 1.25 .50 .12
☐ 365 Lou Whitaker .60 .25 .06
☐ 366 Lance Parrish .40 .16 .04
☐ 367 Tim Corcoran .05 .02 .00
☐ 368 Pat Underwood .05 .02 .00
☐ 369 Al Cowens .05 .02 .00
☐ 370 Sparky Anderson MG .10 .04 .01
☐ 371 Pete Rose 1.75 .70 .17
☐ 372 Phil Garner .10 .04 .01
☐ 373 Steve Nicosia .05 .02 .00
☐ 374 John Candelaria .10 .04 .01
☐ 375 Don Robinson .05 .02 .00
☐ 376 Lee Lacy .05 .02 .00
☐ 377 John Milner .05 .02 .00
☐ 378 Craig Reynolds .05 .02 .00
☐ 379A Luis Pujois P1 ERR .10 .04 .01
(Name misspelled)
☐ 379B Luis Pujols P2 COR .10 .04 .01
☐ 380 Joe Niekro .10 .04 .01
☐ 381 Joaquin Andujar .10 .04 .01
☐ 382 Keith Moreland .15 .06 .01
☐ 383 Jose Cruz .10 .04 .01
☐ 384 Bill Virdon MG .05 .02 .00
☐ 385 Jim Sundberg .05 .02 .00
☐ 386 Doc Medich .05 .02 .00
☐ 387 Al Oliver .10 .04 .01
☐ 388 Jim Norris .05 .02 .00
☐ 389 Bob Bailor .05 .02 .00
☐ 390 Ernie Whitt .05 .02 .00
☐ 391 Otto Velez .05 .02 .00
☐ 392 Roy Howell .05 .02 .00
☐ 393 Bob Walk .25 .10 .02
☐ 394 Doug Flynn .05 .02 .00
☐ 395 Pete Falcone .05 .02 .00
☐ 396 Tom Hausman .05 .02 .00
☐ 397 Elliott Maddox .05 .02 .00
☐ 398 Mike Squires .05 .02 .00
☐ 399 Marvis Foley .05 .02 .00
☐ 400 Steve Trout .05 .02 .00
☐ 401 Wayne Nordhagen .05 .02 .00
☐ 402 Tony LaRussa MG .10 .04 .01
☐ 403 Bruce Bochte .05 .02 .00
☐ 404 Bake McBride .05 .02 .00
☐ 405 Jerry Narron .05 .02 .00
☐ 406 Rob Dressler .05 .02 .00
☐ 407 Dave Heaverlo .05 .02 .00
☐ 408 Tom Paciorek .05 .02 .00
☐ 409 Carney Lansford .15 .06 .01
☐ 410 Brian Downing .10 .04 .01
☐ 411 Don Aase .05 .02 .00
☐ 412 Jim Barr .05 .02 .00
☐ 413 Don Baylor .15 .06 .01
☐ 414 Jim Fregosi .05 .02 .00
☐ 415 Dallas Green MG .05 .02 .00
☐ 416 Dave Lopes .10 .04 .01
☐ 417 Jerry Reuss .05 .02 .00
☐ 418 Rick Sutcliffe .15 .06 .01
☐ 419 Derrel Thomas .05 .02 .00
☐ 420 Tom Lasorda MG .10 .04 .01
☐ 421 Charles Leibrandt .50 .20 .05
☐ 422 Tom Seaver 1.50 .60 .15
☐ 423 Ron Oester .05 .02 .00
☐ 424 Junior Kennedy .05 .02 .00
☐ 425 Tom Seaver 1.50 .60 .15
☐ 426 Bobby Cox MG .05 .02 .00
☐ 427 Leon Durham .15 .06 .01
☐ 428 Terry Kennedy .10 .04 .01
☐ 429 Silvio Martinez .05 .02 .00
☐ 430 George Hendrick .05 .02 .00
☐ 431 Red Schoendienst MG .15 .06 .01
☐ 432 Johnnie LeMaster .05 .02 .00
☐ 433 Vida Blue .10 .04 .01
☐ 434 John Montefusco .05 .02 .00
☐ 435 Terry Whitfield .05 .02 .00
☐ 436 Dave Bristol MG .05 .02 .00
☐ 437 Dale Murphy 1.00 .40 .10
☐ 438 Jerry Dybzinski .05 .02 .00
☐ 439 Jorge Orta .05 .02 .00
☐ 440 Wayne Garland .05 .02 .00
☐ 441 Miguel Dilone .05 .02 .00
☐ 442 Dave Garcia MG .05 .02 .00
☐ 443 Don Money .05 .02 .00
☐ 444A Buck Martinez P1 ERR .10 .04 .01
(reverse negative)

☐ 444B Buck Martinez ....10 .04 .01
P2 COR
☐ 445 Jerry Augustine ....05 .02 .00
☐ 446 Ben Oglivie ....05 .02 .00
☐ 447 Jim Slaton ....05 .02 .00
☐ 448 Doyle Alexander ....05 .02 .00
☐ 449 Tony Bernazard ....05 .02 .00
☐ 450 Scott Sanderson ....10 .04 .01
☐ 451 David Palmer ....05 .02 .00
☐ 452 Stan Bahnsen ....05 .02 .00
☐ 453 Dick Williams MG ....05 .02 .00
☐ 454 Rick Burleson ....10 .04 .01
☐ 455 Gary Allenson ....05 .02 .00
☐ 456 Bob Stanley ....05 .02 .00
☐ 457A John Tudor P1 ERR .....50 .20 .05
(Lifetime W-L "9.7")
☐ 457B John Tudor P2 COR .....50 .20 .05
(Corrected "9-7")
☐ 458 Dwight Evans ....35 .15 .03
☐ 459 Glenn Hubbard ....05 .02 .00
☐ 460 U.L. Washington ....05 .02 .00
☐ 461 Larry Gura ....05 .02 .00
☐ 462 Rich Gale ....05 .02 .00
☐ 463 Hal McRae ....15 .06 .01
☐ 464 Jim Frey MG ....05 .02 .00
☐ 465 Bucky Dent ....10 .04 .01
☐ 466 Dennis Werth ....05 .02 .00
☐ 467 Ron Davis ....05 .02 .00
☐ 468 Reggie Jackson UER ... 2.50 1.00 .25
(32 HR in 1970,
should be 23)
☐ 469 Bobby Brown ....05 .02 .00
☐ 470 Mike Davis ....15 .06 .01
☐ 471 Gaylord Perry ....50 .20 .05
☐ 472 Mark Belanger ....10 .04 .01
☐ 473 Jim Palmer .... 1.00 .40 .10
☐ 474 Sammy Stewart ....05 .02 .00
☐ 475 Tim Stoddard ....05 .02 .00
☐ 476 Steve Stone ....05 .02 .00
☐ 477 Jeff Newman ....05 .02 .00
☐ 478 Steve McCatty ....05 .02 .00
☐ 479 Billy Martin MG ....20 .08 .02
☐ 480 Mitchell Page ....05 .02 .00
☐ 481 Cy Young Winner 1980 . .50 .20 .05
Steve Carlton
☐ 482 Bill Buckner ....10 .04 .01
☐ 483A Ivan DeJesus P1 ERR . .10 .04 .01
(Lifetime hits "702")
☐ 483B Ivan DeJesus P2 COR . .10 .04 .01
(Lifetime hits "642")
☐ 484 Cliff Johnson ....05 .02 .00
☐ 485 Lenny Randle ....05 .02 .00
☐ 486 Larry Milbourne ....05 .02 .00
☐ 487 Roy Smalley ....05 .02 .00
☐ 488 John Castino ....05 .02 .00
☐ 489 Ron Jackson ....05 .02 .00
☐ 490A Dave Roberts P1 ....10 .04 .01
(Career Highlights:
"Showed pop in")
☐ 490B Dave Roberts P2 ....10 .04 .01
("Declared himself")
☐ 491 MVP: George Brett ...... 1.50 .60 .15
☐ 492 Mike Cubbage ....05 .02 .00
☐ 493 Rob Wilfong ....05 .02 .00
☐ 494 Danny Goodwin ....05 .02 .00
☐ 495 Jose Morales ....05 .02 .00
☐ 496 Mickey Rivers ....10 .04 .01
☐ 497 Mike Edwards ....05 .02 .00
☐ 498 Mike Sadek ....05 .02 .00
☐ 499 Lenn Sakata ....05 .02 .00
☐ 500 Gene Michael MG ....05 .02 .00
☐ 501 Dave Roberts ....05 .02 .00
☐ 502 Steve Dillard ....05 .02 .00
☐ 503 Jim Essian ....10 .04 .01
☐ 504 Rance Mulliniks ....05 .02 .00
☐ 505 Darrell Porter ....05 .02 .00
☐ 506 Joe Torre MG ....15 .06 .01
☐ 507 Terry Crowley ....05 .02 .00
☐ 508 Bill Travers ....05 .02 .00
☐ 509 Nelson Norman ....05 .02 .00
☐ 510 Bob McClure ....05 .02 .00
☐ 511 Steve Howe ....10 .04 .01
☐ 512 Dave Rader ....05 .02 .00
☐ 513 Mick Kelleher ....05 .02 .00
☐ 514 Kiko Garcia ....05 .02 .00
☐ 515 Larry Biittner ....05 .02 .00
☐ 516A Willie Norwood P1 ......10 .04 .01
(Career Highlights
"Spent most of")
☐ 516B Willie Norwood P2 ......10 .04 .01
("Traded to Seattle")
☐ 517 Bo Diaz ....05 .02 .00
☐ 518 Juan Beniquez ....05 .02 .00
☐ 519 Scot Thompson ....05 .02 .00
☐ 520 Jim Tracy ....05 .02 .00
☐ 521 Carlos Lezcano ....05 .02 .00
☐ 522 Joe Amalfitano MG ....05 .02 .00
☐ 523 Preston Hanna ....05 .02 .00
☐ 524A Ray Burris P1 ....10 .04 .01
(Career Highlights:
"Went on ...")
☐ 524B Ray Burris P2 ....10 .04 .01
("Drafted by ...")
☐ 525 Broderick Perkins ....05 .02 .00
☐ 526 Mickey Hatcher ....10 .04 .01
☐ 527 John Goryl MG ....05 .02 .00
☐ 528 Dick Davis ....05 .02 .00
☐ 529 Butch Wynegar ....05 .02 .00
☐ 530 Sal Butera ....05 .02 .00
☐ 531 Jerry Koosman ....10 .04 .01
☐ 532A Geoff Zahn P1 ....10 .04 .01
(Career Highlights:
"Was 2nd in")
☐ 532B Geoff Zahn P2 ....10 .04 .01
("Signed a 3 year")
☐ 533 Dennis Martinez ....20 .08 .02

Card			
☐ 534 Gary Thomasson	.05	.02	.00
☐ 535 Steve Macko	.05	.02	.00
☐ 536 Jim Kaat	.20	.08	.02
☐ 537 Best Hitters George Brett Rod Carew	2.00	.80	.20
☐ 538 Tim Raines	5.50	2.50	.55
☐ 539 Keith Smith	.05	.02	.00
☐ 540 Ken Macha	.05	.02	.00
☐ 541 Burt Hooton	.05	.02	.00
☐ 542 Butch Hobson	.10	.04	.01
☐ 543 Bill Stein	.05	.02	.00
☐ 544 Dave Stapleton	.05	.02	.00
☐ 545 Bob Pate	.05	.02	.00
☐ 546 Doug Corbett	.05	.02	.00
☐ 547 Darrell Jackson	.05	.02	.00
☐ 548 Pete Redfern	.05	.02	.00
☐ 549 Roger Erickson	.05	.02	.00
☐ 550 Al Hrabosky	.05	.02	.00
☐ 551 Dick Tidrow	.05	.02	.00
☐ 552 Dave Ford	.05	.02	.00
☐ 553 Dave Kingman	.15	.06	.01
☐ 554A Mike Vail P1 (Career Highlights: "After two ...")	.10	.04	.01
☐ 554B Mike Vail P2 ("Traded to ...")	.10	.04	.01
☐ 555A Jerry Martin P1 (Career Highlights: "Overcame a ...")	.10	.04	.01
☐ 555B Jerry Martin P2 ("Traded to ...")	.10	.04	.01
☐ 556A Jesus Figueroa P1 (Career Highlights: "Had an ...")	.10	.04	.01
☐ 556B Jesus Figueroa P2 ("Traded to ...")	.10	.04	.01
☐ 557 Don Stanhouse	.05	.02	.00
☐ 558 Barry Foote	.05	.02	.00
☐ 559 Tim Blackwell	.05	.02	.00
☐ 560 Bruce Sutter	.20	.08	.02
☐ 561 Rick Reuschel	.15	.06	.01
☐ 562 Lynn McGlothen	.05	.02	.00
☐ 563A Bob Owchinko P1 (Career Highlights: "Traded to ...")	.10	.04	.01
☐ 563B Bob Owchinko P2 ("Involved in a ...")	.10	.04	.01
☐ 564 John Verhoeven	.05	.02	.00
☐ 565 Ken Landreaux	.05	.02	.00
☐ 566A Glen Adams P1 ERR (Name misspelled)	.10	.04	.01
☐ 566B Glenn Adams P2 COR	.10	.04	.01
☐ 567 Hosken Powell	.05	.02	.00
☐ 568 Dick Noles	.05	.02	.00
☐ 569 Danny Ainge	1.00	.40	.10
☐ 570 Bobby Mattick MG	.05	.02	.00
☐ 571 Joe Lefebvre	.05	.02	.00
☐ 572 Bobby Clark	.05	.02	.00
☐ 573 Dennis Lamp	.05	.02	.00
☐ 574 Randy Lerch	.05	.02	.00
☐ 575 Mookie Wilson	.60	.25	.06
☐ 576 Ron LeFlore	.05	.02	.00
☐ 577 Jim Dwyer	.05	.02	.00
☐ 578 Bill Castro	.05	.02	.00
☐ 579 Greg Minton	.05	.02	.00
☐ 580 Mark Littell	.05	.02	.00
☐ 581 Andy Hassler	.05	.02	.00
☐ 582 Dave Stieb	.60	.25	.06
☐ 583 Ken Oberkfell	.05	.02	.00
☐ 584 Larry Bradford	.05	.02	.00
☐ 585 Fred Stanley	.05	.02	.00
☐ 586 Bill Caudill	.05	.02	.00
☐ 587 Doug Capilla	.05	.02	.00
☐ 588 George Riley	.05	.02	.00
☐ 589 Willie Hernandez	.10	.04	.01
☐ 590 MVP: Mike Schmidt	1.50	.60	.15
☐ 591 Cy Young Winner 1980: Steve Stone	.05	.02	.00
☐ 592 Rick Sofield	.05	.02	.00
☐ 593 Bombo Rivera	.05	.02	.00
☐ 594 Gary Ward	.05	.02	.00
☐ 595A Dave Edwards P1 (Career Highlights: "Sidelined the")	.10	.04	.01
☐ 595B Dave Edwards P2 ("Traded to ...")	.10	.04	.01
☐ 596 Mike Proly	.05	.02	.00
☐ 597 Tommy Boggs	.05	.02	.00
☐ 598 Greg Gross	.05	.02	.00
☐ 599 Elias Sosa	.05	.02	.00
☐ 600 Pat Kelly	.05	.02	.00
☐ 601A Checklist 1 P1 ERR unnumbered (51 Donahue)	.15	.02	.00
☐ 601B Checklist 1 P2 COR unnumbered (51 Donohue)	.75	.07	.01
☐ 602 Checklist 2 unnumbered	.15	.02	.00
☐ 603A Checklist 3 P1 ERR unnumbered (306 Mathews)	.15	.02	.00
☐ 603B Checklist 3 P2 COR unnumbered (306 Matthews)	.15	.02	.00
☐ 604A Checklist 4 P1 ERR unnumbered (379 Pujois)	.15	.02	.00
☐ 604B Checklist 4 P2 COR unnumbered (379 Pujols)	.15	.02	.00
☐ 605A Checklist 5 P1 ERR unnumbered (566 Glen Adams)	.15	.02	.00

	MINT	EXC	G-VG
☐ 605B Checklist 5 P2 COR unnumbered (566 Glenn Adams)	.15	.02	.00

1982 Donruss

The 1982 Donruss set contains 653 numbered cards and the seven unnumbered checklists; each card measures 2 1/2" by 3 1/2". The first 26 cards of this set are entitled Donruss Diamond Kings (DK) and feature the artwork of Dick Perez of Perez-Steele Galleries. The set was marketed with puzzle pieces rather than with bubble gum. There are 63 pieces to the puzzle, which, when put together, make a collage of Babe Ruth entitled "Hall of Fame Diamond King." The card stock in this year's Donruss cards is considerably thicker than that of the 1981 cards. The seven unnumbered checklist cards are arbitrarily assigned numbers 654 through 660 and are listed at the end of the list below. The key rookie cards in this set are George Bell, Cal Ripken Jr., Steve Sax, Lee Smith, and Dave Stewart.

	MINT	EXC	G-VG
COMPLETE SET (660)	80.00	36.00	12.00
COMMON PLAYER (1-660)	.05	.02	.00
☐ 1 Pete Rose DK	1.50	.50	.10
☐ 2 Gary Carter DK	.35	.15	.03
☐ 3 Steve Garvey DK	.40	.16	.04
☐ 4 Vida Blue DK	.10	.04	.01
☐ 5A Alan Trammel DK ERR (name misspelled)	1.50	.60	.15
☐ 5B Alan Trammell DK COR	.40	.16	.04
☐ 6 Len Barker DK	.10	.04	.01
☐ 7 Dwight Evans DK	.15	.06	.01
☐ 8 Rod Carew DK	.60	.25	.06
☐ 9 George Hendrick DK	.10	.04	.01
☐ 10 Phil Niekro DK	.20	.08	.02
☐ 11 Richie Zisk DK	.10	.04	.01
☐ 12 Dave Parker DK	.30	.12	.03
☐ 13 Nolan Ryan DK	2.75	1.10	.27
☐ 14 Ivan DeJesus DK	.10	.04	.01
☐ 15 George Brett DK	.85	.35	.08
☐ 16 Tom Seaver DK	.70	.30	.07
☐ 17 Dave Kingman DK	.10	.04	.01
☐ 18 Dave Winfield DK	.55	.22	.05
☐ 19 Mike Norris DK	.10	.04	.01
☐ 20 Carlton Fisk DK	.70	.30	.07
☐ 21 Ozzie Smith DK	.75	.30	.07
☐ 22 Roy Smalley DK	.10	.04	.01
☐ 23 Buddy Bell DK	.10	.04	.01
☐ 24 Ken Singleton DK	.10	.04	.01
☐ 25 John Mayberry DK	.10	.04	.01
☐ 26 Gorman Thomas DK	.10	.04	.01
☐ 27 Earl Weaver MG	.10	.04	.01
☐ 28 Rollie Fingers	.50	.20	.05
☐ 29 Sparky Anderson MG	.10	.04	.01
☐ 30 Dennis Eckersley	.50	.20	.05
☐ 31 Dave Winfield	1.00	.40	.10
☐ 32 Burt Hooton	.05	.02	.00
☐ 33 Rick Waits	.05	.02	.00
☐ 34 George Brett	2.00	.80	.20
☐ 35 Steve McCatty	.05	.02	.00
☐ 36 Steve Rogers	.05	.02	.00
☐ 37 Bill Stein	.05	.02	.00
☐ 38 Steve Renko	.05	.02	.00
☐ 39 Mike Squires	.05	.02	.00
☐ 40 George Hendrick	.05	.02	.00
☐ 41 Bob Knepper	.05	.02	.00
☐ 42 Steve Carlton	1.00	.40	.10
☐ 43 Larry Biittner	.05	.02	.00
☐ 44 Chris Welsh	.05	.02	.00
☐ 45 Steve Nicosia	.05	.02	.00
☐ 46 Jack Clark	.25	.10	.02
☐ 47 Chris Chambliss	.10	.04	.01
☐ 48 Ivan DeJesus	.05	.02	.00
☐ 49 Lee Mazzilli	.05	.02	.00
☐ 50 Julio Cruz	.05	.02	.00
☐ 51 Pete Redfern	.05	.02	.00
☐ 52 Dave Stieb	.35	.15	.03
☐ 53 Doug Corbett	.05	.02	.00
☐ 54 Jorge Bell	8.00	3.50	.80
☐ 55 Joe Simpson	.05	.02	.00
☐ 56 Rusty Staub	.15	.06	.01
☐ 57 Hector Cruz	.05	.02	.00
☐ 58 Claudell Washington	.05	.02	.00
☐ 59 Enrique Romo	.05	.02	.00
☐ 60 Gary Lavelle	.05	.02	.00
☐ 61 Tim Flannery	.05	.02	.00
☐ 62 Joe Nolan	.05	.02	.00
☐ 63 Larry Bowa	.10	.04	.01
☐ 64 Sixto Lezcano	.05	.02	.00

☐ 65	Joe Sambito	.05	.02	.00
☐ 66	Bruce Kison	.05	.02	.00
☐ 67	Wayne Nordhagen	.05	.02	.00
☐ 68	Woodie Fryman	.05	.02	.00
☐ 69	Billy Sample	.05	.02	.00
☐ 70	Amos Otis	.05	.02	.00
☐ 71	Matt Keough	.05	.02	.00
☐ 72	Toby Harrah	.05	.02	.00
☐ 73	Dave Righetti	1.25	.50	.12
☐ 74	Carl Yastrzemski	1.25	.50	.12
☐ 75	Bob Welch	.35	.15	.03
☐ 76A	Alan Trammel ERR (name misspelled)	1.75	.70	.17
☐ 76B	Alan Trammell COR	.60	.25	.06
☐ 77	Rick Dempsey	.05	.02	.00
☐ 78	Paul Molitor	.50	.20	.05
☐ 79	Dennis Martinez	.15	.06	.01
☐ 80	Jim Slaton	.05	.02	.00
☐ 81	Champ Summers	.05	.02	.00
☐ 82	Carney Lansford	.15	.06	.01
☐ 83	Barry Foote	.05	.02	.00
☐ 84	Steve Garvey	.60	.25	.06
☐ 85	Rick Manning	.05	.02	.00
☐ 86	John Wathan	.05	.02	.00
☐ 87	Brian Kingman	.05	.02	.00
☐ 88	Andre Dawson UER (Middle name Fernando, should be Nolan)	1.25	.50	.12
☐ 89	Jim Kern	.05	.02	.00
☐ 90	Bobby Grich	.10	.04	.01
☐ 91	Bob Forsch	.05	.02	.00
☐ 92	Art Howe	.10	.04	.01
☐ 93	Marty Bystrom	.05	.02	.00
☐ 94	Ozzie Smith	1.50	.60	.15
☐ 95	Dave Parker	.50	.20	.05
☐ 96	Doyle Alexander	.05	.02	.00
☐ 97	Al Hrabosky	.05	.02	.00
☐ 98	Frank Taveras	.05	.02	.00
☐ 99	Tim Blackwell	.05	.02	.00
☐ 100	Floyd Bannister	.05	.02	.00
☐ 101	Alfredo Griffin	.05	.02	.00
☐ 102	Dave Engle	.05	.02	.00
☐ 103	Mario Soto	.05	.02	.00
☐ 104	Ross Baumgarten	.05	.02	.00
☐ 105	Ken Singleton	.10	.04	.01
☐ 106	Ted Simmons	.15	.06	.01
☐ 107	Jack Morris	.60	.25	.06
☐ 108	Bob Watson	.05	.02	.00
☐ 109	Dwight Evans	.25	.10	.02
☐ 110	Tom Lasorda MG	.10	.04	.01
☐ 111	Bert Blyleven	.25	.10	.02
☐ 112	Dan Quisenberry	.15	.06	.01
☐ 113	Rickey Henderson	6.00	2.50	.60
☐ 114	Gary Carter	.50	.20	.05
☐ 115	Brian Downing	.10	.04	.01
☐ 116	Al Oliver	.10	.04	.01
☐ 117	LaMarr Hoyt	.05	.02	.00
☐ 118	Cesar Cedeno	.10	.04	.01
☐ 119	Keith Moreland	.05	.02	.00
☐ 120	Bob Shirley	.05	.02	.00
☐ 121	Terry Kennedy	.05	.02	.00
☐ 122	Frank Pastore	.05	.02	.00
☐ 123	Gene Garber	.05	.02	.00
☐ 124	Tony Pena	.35	.15	.03
☐ 125	Allen Ripley	.05	.02	.00
☐ 126	Randy Martz	.05	.02	.00
☐ 127	Richie Zisk	.05	.02	.00
☐ 128	Mike Scott	.25	.10	.02
☐ 129	Lloyd Moseby	.15	.06	.01
☐ 130	Rob Wilfong	.05	.02	.00
☐ 131	Tim Stoddard	.05	.02	.00
☐ 132	Gorman Thomas	.10	.04	.01
☐ 133	Dan Petry	.05	.02	.00
☐ 134	Bob Stanley	.05	.02	.00
☐ 135	Lou Piniella	.10	.04	.01
☐ 136	Pedro Guerrero	.40	.16	.04
☐ 137	Len Barker	.05	.02	.00
☐ 138	Rich Gale	.05	.02	.00
☐ 139	Wayne Gross	.05	.02	.00
☐ 140	Tim Wallach	1.25	.50	.12
☐ 141	Gene Mauch MG	.05	.02	.00
☐ 142	Doc Medich	.05	.02	.00
☐ 143	Tony Bernazard	.05	.02	.00
☐ 144	Bill Virdon MG	.05	.02	.00
☐ 145	John Littlefield	.05	.02	.00
☐ 146	Dave Bergman	.05	.02	.00
☐ 147	Dick Davis	.05	.02	.00
☐ 148	Tom Seaver	1.25	.50	.12
☐ 149	Matt Sinatro	.05	.02	.00
☐ 150	Chuck Tanner MG	.05	.02	.00
☐ 151	Leon Durham	.05	.02	.00
☐ 152	Gene Tenace	.10	.04	.01
☐ 153	Al Bumbry	.05	.02	.00
☐ 154	Mark Brouhard	.05	.02	.00
☐ 155	Rick Peters	.05	.02	.00
☐ 156	Jerry Remy	.05	.02	.00
☐ 157	Rick Reuschel	.10	.04	.01
☐ 158	Steve Howe	.05	.02	.00
☐ 159	Alan Bannister	.05	.02	.00
☐ 160	U.L. Washington	.05	.02	.00
☐ 161	Rick Langford	.05	.02	.00
☐ 162	Bill Gullickson	.10	.04	.01
☐ 163	Mark Wagner	.05	.02	.00
☐ 164	Geoff Zahn	.05	.02	.00
☐ 165	Ron LeFlore	.05	.02	.00
☐ 166	Dane Iorg	.05	.02	.00
☐ 167	Joe Niekro	.10	.04	.01
☐ 168	Pete Rose	1.50	.60	.15
☐ 169	Dave Collins	.05	.02	.00
☐ 170	Rick Wise	.05	.02	.00
☐ 171	Jim Bibby	.05	.02	.00
☐ 172	Larry Herndon	.05	.02	.00
☐ 173	Bob Horner	.10	.04	.01
☐ 174	Steve Dillard	.05	.02	.00
☐ 175	Mookie Wilson	.10	.04	.01
☐ 176	Dan Meyer	.05	.02	.00

☐ 177 Fernando Arroyo	.05	.02	.00
☐ 178 Jackson Todd	.05	.02	.00
☐ 179 Darrell Jackson	.05	.02	.00
☐ 180 Alvis Woods	.05	.02	.00
☐ 181 Jim Anderson	.05	.02	.00
☐ 182 Dave Kingman	.15	.06	.01
☐ 183 Steve Henderson	.05	.02	.00
☐ 184 Brian Asselstine	.05	.02	.00
☐ 185 Rod Scurry	.05	.02	.00
☐ 186 Fred Breining	.05	.02	.00
☐ 187 Danny Boone	.05	.02	.00
☐ 188 Junior Kennedy	.05	.02	.00
☐ 189 Sparky Lyle	.10	.04	.01
☐ 190 Whitey Herzog MG	.10	.04	.01
☐ 191 Dave Smith	.10	.04	.01
☐ 192 Ed Ott	.05	.02	.00
☐ 193 Greg Luzinski	.10	.04	.01
☐ 194 Bill Lee	.05	.02	.00
☐ 195 Don Zimmer MG	.05	.02	.00
☐ 196 Hal McRae	.10	.04	.01
☐ 197 Mike Norris	.05	.02	.00
☐ 198 Duane Kuiper	.05	.02	.00
☐ 199 Rick Cerone	.05	.02	.00
☐ 200 Jim Rice	.25	.10	.02
☐ 201 Steve Yeager	.05	.02	.00
☐ 202 Tom Brookens	.05	.02	.00
☐ 203 Jose Morales	.05	.02	.00
☐ 204 Roy Howell	.05	.02	.00
☐ 205 Tippy Martinez	.05	.02	.00
☐ 206 Moose Haas	.05	.02	.00
☐ 207 Al Cowens	.05	.02	.00
☐ 208 Dave Stapleton	.05	.02	.00
☐ 209 Bucky Dent	.10	.04	.01
☐ 210 Ron Cey	.10	.04	.01
☐ 211 Jorge Orta	.05	.02	.00
☐ 212 Jamie Quirk	.05	.02	.00
☐ 213 Jeff Jones	.05	.02	.00
☐ 214 Tim Raines	1.25	.50	.12
☐ 215 Jon Matlack	.05	.02	.00
☐ 216 Rod Carew	1.25	.50	.12
☐ 217 Jim Kaat	.15	.06	.01
☐ 218 Joe Pittman	.05	.02	.00
☐ 219 Larry Christenson	.05	.02	.00
☐ 220 Juan Bonilla	.05	.02	.00
☐ 221 Mike Easler	.05	.02	.00
☐ 222 Vida Blue	.10	.04	.01
☐ 223 Rick Camp	.05	.02	.00
☐ 224 Mike Jorgensen	.05	.02	.00
☐ 225 Jody Davis	.15	.06	.01
☐ 226 Mike Parrott	.05	.02	.00
☐ 227 Jim Clancy	.05	.02	.00
☐ 228 Hosken Powell	.05	.02	.00
☐ 229 Tom Hume	.05	.02	.00
☐ 230 Britt Burns	.05	.02	.00
☐ 231 Jim Palmer	.90	.40	.09
☐ 232 Bob Rodgers MG	.05	.02	.00
☐ 233 Milt Wilcox	.05	.02	.00
☐ 234 Dave Revering	.05	.02	.00
☐ 235 Mike Torrez	.05	.02	.00
☐ 236 Robert Castillo	.05	.02	.00
☐ 237 Von Hayes	.60	.25	.06
☐ 238 Renie Martin	.05	.02	.00
☐ 239 Dwayne Murphy	.05	.02	.00
☐ 240 Rodney Scott	.05	.02	.00
☐ 241 Fred Patek	.05	.02	.00
☐ 242 Mickey Rivers	.10	.04	.01
☐ 243 Steve Trout	.05	.02	.00
☐ 244 Jose Cruz	.10	.04	.01
☐ 245 Manny Trillo	.05	.02	.00
☐ 246 Lary Sorensen	.05	.02	.00
☐ 247 Dave Edwards	.05	.02	.00
☐ 248 Dan Driessen	.05	.02	.00
☐ 249 Tommy Boggs	.05	.02	.00
☐ 250 Dale Berra	.05	.02	.00
☐ 251 Ed Whitson	.05	.02	.00
☐ 252 Lee Smith	3.00	1.25	.30
☐ 253 Tom Paciorek	.05	.02	.00
☐ 254 Pat Zachry	.05	.02	.00
☐ 255 Luis Leal	.05	.02	.00
☐ 256 John Castino	.05	.02	.00
☐ 257 Rich Dauer	.05	.02	.00
☐ 258 Cecil Cooper	.15	.06	.01
☐ 259 Dave Rozema	.05	.02	.00
☐ 260 John Tudor	.10	.04	.01
☐ 261 Jerry Mumphrey	.05	.02	.00
☐ 262 Jay Johnstone	.10	.04	.01
☐ 263 Bo Diaz	.05	.02	.00
☐ 264 Dennis Leonard	.05	.02	.00
☐ 265 Jim Spencer	.05	.02	.00
☐ 266 John Milner	.05	.02	.00
☐ 267 Don Aase	.05	.02	.00
☐ 268 Jim Sundberg	.05	.02	.00
☐ 269 Lamar Johnson	.05	.02	.00
☐ 270 Frank LaCorte	.05	.02	.00
☐ 271 Barry Evans	.05	.02	.00
☐ 272 Enos Cabell	.05	.02	.00
☐ 273 Del Unser	.05	.02	.00
☐ 274 George Foster	.15	.06	.01
☐ 275 Brett Butler	2.00	.80	.20
☐ 276 Lee Lacy	.05	.02	.00
☐ 277 Ken Reitz	.05	.02	.00
☐ 278 Keith Hernandez	.25	.10	.02
☐ 279 Doug DeCinces	.05	.02	.00
☐ 280 Charlie Moore	.05	.02	.00
☐ 281 Lance Parrish	.30	.12	.03
☐ 282 Ralph Houk MG	.05	.02	.00
☐ 283 Rich Gossage	.20	.08	.02
☐ 284 Jerry Reuss	.05	.02	.00
☐ 285 Mike Stanton	.05	.02	.00
☐ 286 Frank White	.05	.02	.00
☐ 287 Bob Owchinko	.05	.02	.00
☐ 288 Scott Sanderson	.10	.04	.01
☐ 289 Bump Wills	.05	.02	.00
☐ 290 Dave Frost	.05	.02	.00
☐ 291 Chet Lemon	.05	.02	.00
☐ 292 Tito Landrum	.05	.02	.00

☐ 293 Vern Ruhle	.05	.02	.00
☐ 294 Mike Schmidt	2.50	1.00	.25
☐ 295 Sam Mejias	.05	.02	.00
☐ 296 Gary Lucas	.05	.02	.00
☐ 297 John Candelaria	.05	.02	.00
☐ 298 Jerry Martin	.05	.02	.00
☐ 299 Dale Murphy	1.00	.40	.10
☐ 300 Mike Lum	.05	.02	.00
☐ 301 Tom Hausman	.05	.02	.00
☐ 302 Glenn Abbott	.05	.02	.00
☐ 303 Roger Erickson	.05	.02	.00
☐ 304 Otto Velez	.05	.02	.00
☐ 305 Danny Goodwin	.05	.02	.00
☐ 306 John Mayberry	.10	.04	.01
☐ 307 Lenny Randle	.05	.02	.00
☐ 308 Bob Bailor	.05	.02	.00
☐ 309 Jerry Morales	.05	.02	.00
☐ 310 Rufino Linares	.05	.02	.00
☐ 311 Kent Tekulve	.10	.04	.01
☐ 312 Joe Morgan	.60	.25	.06
☐ 313 John Urrea	.05	.02	.00
☐ 314 Paul Householder	.05	.02	.00
☐ 315 Garry Maddox	.05	.02	.00
☐ 316 Mike Ramsey	.05	.02	.00
☐ 317 Alan Ashby	.05	.02	.00
☐ 318 Bob Clark	.05	.02	.00
☐ 319 Tony LaRussa MG	.10	.04	.01
☐ 320 Charlie Lea	.05	.02	.00
☐ 321 Danny Darwin	.05	.02	.00
☐ 322 Cesar Geronimo	.05	.02	.00
☐ 323 Tom Underwood	.05	.02	.00
☐ 324 Andre Thornton	.10	.04	.01
☐ 325 Rudy May	.05	.02	.00
☐ 326 Frank Tanana	.10	.04	.01
☐ 327 Dave Lopes	.10	.04	.01
☐ 328 Richie Hebner	.05	.02	.00
☐ 329 Mike Flanagan	.10	.04	.01
☐ 330 Mike Caldwell	.05	.02	.00
☐ 331 Scott McGregor	.05	.02	.00
☐ 332 Jerry Augustine	.05	.02	.00
☐ 333 Stan Papi	.05	.02	.00
☐ 334 Rick Miller	.05	.02	.00
☐ 335 Graig Nettles	.15	.06	.01
☐ 336 Dusty Baker	.10	.04	.01
☐ 337 Dave Garcia MG	.05	.02	.00
☐ 338 Larry Gura	.05	.02	.00
☐ 339 Cliff Johnson	.05	.02	.00
☐ 340 Warren Cromartie	.05	.02	.00
☐ 341 Steve Comer	.05	.02	.00
☐ 342 Rick Burleson	.10	.04	.01
☐ 343 John Martin	.05	.02	.00
☐ 344 Craig Reynolds	.05	.02	.00
☐ 345 Mike Proly	.05	.02	.00
☐ 346 Ruppert Jones	.05	.02	.00
☐ 347 Omar Moreno	.05	.02	.00
☐ 348 Greg Minton	.05	.02	.00
☐ 349 Rick Mahler	.15	.06	.01
☐ 350 Alex Trevino	.05	.02	.00
☐ 351 Mike Krukow	.05	.02	.00
☐ 352A Shane Rawley ERR (photo actually Jim Anderson)	.75	.30	.07
☐ 352B Shane Rawley COR	.10	.04	.01
☐ 353 Garth Iorg	.05	.02	.00
☐ 354 Pete Mackanin	.05	.02	.00
☐ 355 Paul Moskau	.05	.02	.00
☐ 356 Richard Dotson	.05	.02	.00
☐ 357 Steve Stone	.05	.02	.00
☐ 358 Larry Hisle	.05	.02	.00
☐ 359 Aurelio Lopez	.05	.02	.00
☐ 360 Oscar Gamble	.05	.02	.00
☐ 361 Tom Burgmeier	.05	.02	.00
☐ 362 Terry Forster	.10	.04	.01
☐ 363 Joe Charboneau	.05	.02	.00
☐ 364 Ken Brett	.05	.02	.00
☐ 365 Tony Armas	.05	.02	.00
☐ 366 Chris Speier	.05	.02	.00
☐ 367 Fred Lynn	.20	.08	.02
☐ 368 Buddy Bell	.10	.04	.01
☐ 369 Jim Essian	.10	.04	.01
☐ 370 Terry Puhl	.05	.02	.00
☐ 371 Greg Gross	.05	.02	.00
☐ 372 Bruce Sutter	.15	.06	.01
☐ 373 Joe Lefebvre	.05	.02	.00
☐ 374 Ray Knight	.10	.04	.01
☐ 375 Bruce Benedict	.05	.02	.00
☐ 376 Tim Foli	.05	.02	.00
☐ 377 Al Holland	.05	.02	.00
☐ 378 Ken Kravec	.05	.02	.00
☐ 379 Jeff Burroughs	.05	.02	.00
☐ 380 Pete Falcone	.05	.02	.00
☐ 381 Ernie Whitt	.05	.02	.00
☐ 382 Brad Havens	.05	.02	.00
☐ 383 Terry Crowley	.05	.02	.00
☐ 384 Don Money	.05	.02	.00
☐ 385 Dan Schatzeder	.05	.02	.00
☐ 386 Gary Allenson	.05	.02	.00
☐ 387 Yogi Berra CO	.25	.10	.02
☐ 388 Ken Landreaux	.05	.02	.00
☐ 389 Mike Hargrove	.10	.04	.01
☐ 390 Darryl Motley	.05	.02	.00
☐ 391 Dave McKay	.05	.02	.00
☐ 392 Stan Bahnsen	.05	.02	.00
☐ 393 Ken Forsch	.05	.02	.00
☐ 394 Mario Mendoza	.05	.02	.00
☐ 395 Jim Morrison	.05	.02	.00
☐ 396 Mike Ivie	.05	.02	.00
☐ 397 Broderick Perkins	.05	.02	.00
☐ 398 Darrell Evans	.15	.06	.01
☐ 399 Ron Reed	.05	.02	.00
☐ 400 Johnny Bench	1.25	.50	.12
☐ 401 Steve Bedrosian	.50	.20	.05
☐ 402 Bill Robinson	.10	.04	.01
☐ 403 Bill Buckner	.10	.04	.01
☐ 404 Ken Oberkfell	.05	.02	.00
☐ 405 Cal Ripken Jr.	48.00	20.00	5.00

☐ 406 Jim Gantner .05 .02 .00
☐ 407 Kirk Gibson 1.25 .50 .12
☐ 408 Tony Perez .25 .10 .02
☐ 409 Tommy John UER .20 .08 .02
(Text says 52-56 as Yankee, should be 52-26)
☐ 410 Dave Stewart 5.50 2.50 .55
☐ 411 Dan Spillner .05 .02 .00
☐ 412 Willie Aikens .05 .02 .00
☐ 413 Mike Heath .05 .02 .00
☐ 414 Ray Burris .05 .02 .00
☐ 415 Leon Roberts .05 .02 .00
☐ 416 Mike Witt .25 .10 .02
☐ 417 Bob Molinaro .05 .02 .00
☐ 418 Steve Braun .05 .02 .00
☐ 419 Nolan Ryan UER 5.75 2.50 .55
(Nisnumbering of Nolan's no-hitters on card back)
☐ 420 Tug McGraw .15 .06 .01
☐ 421 Dave Concepcion .15 .06 .01
☐ 422A Juan Eichelberger .75 .30 .07
ERR (photo actually Gary Lucas)
☐ 422B Juan Eichelberger .10 .04 .01
COR
☐ 423 Rick Rhoden .05 .02 .00
☐ 424 Frank Robinson MG .25 .10 .02
☐ 425 Eddie Miller .05 .02 .00
☐ 426 Bill Caudill .05 .02 .00
☐ 427 Doug Flynn .05 .02 .00
☐ 428 Larry Andersen UER .05 .02 .00
(misspelled Anderson on card front)
☐ 429 Al Williams .05 .02 .00
☐ 430 Jerry Garvin .05 .02 .00
☐ 431 Glenn Adams .05 .02 .00
☐ 432 Barry Bonnell .05 .02 .00
☐ 433 Jerry Narron .05 .02 .00
☐ 434 John Stearns .05 .02 .00
☐ 435 Mike Tyson .05 .02 .00
☐ 436 Glenn Hubbard .05 .02 .00
☐ 437 Eddie Solomon .05 .02 .00
☐ 438 Jeff Leonard .05 .02 .00
☐ 439 Randy Bass .05 .02 .00
☐ 440 Mike LaCoss .05 .02 .00
☐ 441 Gary Matthews .05 .02 .00
☐ 442 Mark Littell .05 .02 .00
☐ 443 Don Sutton .40 .16 .04
☐ 444 John Harris .05 .02 .00
☐ 445 Vada Pinson CO .10 .04 .01
☐ 446 Elias Sosa .05 .02 .00
☐ 447 Charlie Hough .10 .04 .01
☐ 448 Willie Wilson .15 .06 .01
☐ 449 Fred Stanley .05 .02 .00
☐ 450 Tom Veryzer .05 .02 .00
☐ 451 Ron Davis .05 .02 .00
☐ 452 Mark Clear .05 .02 .00
☐ 453 Bill Russell .10 .04 .01
☐ 454 Lou Whitaker .40 .16 .04
☐ 455 Dan Graham .05 .02 .00
☐ 456 Reggie Cleveland .05 .02 .00
☐ 457 Sammy Stewart .05 .02 .00
☐ 458 Pete Vuckovich .05 .02 .00
☐ 459 John Wockenfuss .05 .02 .00
☐ 460 Glenn Hoffman .05 .02 .00
☐ 461 Willie Randolph .10 .04 .01
☐ 462 Fernando Valenzuela .60 .25 .06
☐ 463 Ron Hassey .05 .02 .00
☐ 464 Paul Splittorff .05 .02 .00
☐ 465 Rob Picciolo .05 .02 .00
☐ 466 Larry Parrish .05 .02 .00
☐ 467 Johnny Grubb .05 .02 .00
☐ 468 Dan Ford .05 .02 .00
☐ 469 Silvio Martinez .05 .02 .00
☐ 470 Kiko Garcia .05 .02 .00
☐ 471 Bob Boone .10 .04 .01
☐ 472 Luis Salazar .10 .04 .01
☐ 473 Randy Niemann .05 .02 .00
☐ 474 Tom Griffin .05 .02 .00
☐ 475 Phil Niekro .40 .16 .04
☐ 476 Hubie Brooks .60 .25 .06
☐ 477 Dick Tidrow .05 .02 .00
☐ 478 Jim Beattie .05 .02 .00
☐ 479 Damaso Garcia .05 .02 .00
☐ 480 Mickey Hatcher .05 .02 .00
☐ 481 Joe Price .05 .02 .00
☐ 482 Ed Farmer .05 .02 .00
☐ 483 Eddie Murray 1.50 .60 .15
☐ 484 Ben Oglivie .05 .02 .00
☐ 485 Kevin Saucier .05 .02 .00
☐ 486 Bobby Murcer .10 .04 .01
☐ 487 Bill Campbell .05 .02 .00
☐ 488 Reggie Smith .10 .04 .01
☐ 489 Wayne Garland .05 .02 .00
☐ 490 Jim Wright .05 .02 .00
☐ 491 Billy Martin MG .20 .08 .02
☐ 492 Jim Fanning MG .05 .02 .00
☐ 493 Don Baylor .15 .06 .01
☐ 494 Rick Honeycutt .05 .02 .00
☐ 495 Carlton Fisk 1.25 .50 .12
☐ 496 Denny Walling .05 .02 .00
☐ 497 Bake McBride .05 .02 .00
☐ 498 Darrell Porter .05 .02 .00
☐ 499 Gene Richards .05 .02 .00
☐ 500 Ron Oester .05 .02 .00
☐ 501 Ken Dayley .15 .06 .01
☐ 502 Jason Thompson .05 .02 .00
☐ 503 Milt May .05 .02 .00
☐ 504 Doug Bird .05 .02 .00
☐ 505 Bruce Bochte .05 .02 .00
☐ 506 Neil Allen .05 .02 .00
☐ 507 Joey McLaughlin .05 .02 .00
☐ 508 Butch Wynegar .05 .02 .00
☐ 509 Gary Roenicke .05 .02 .00

☐ 510 Robin Yount .... 2.00 .80 .20
☐ 511 Dave Tobik .... .05 .02 .00
☐ 512 Rich Gedman .... .20 .08 .02
☐ 513 Gene Nelson .... .05 .02 .00
☐ 514 Rick Monday .... .05 .02 .00
☐ 515 Miguel Dilone .... .05 .02 .00
☐ 516 Clint Hurdle .... .05 .02 .00
☐ 517 Jeff Newman .... .05 .02 .00
☐ 518 Grant Jackson .... .05 .02 .00
☐ 519 Andy Hassler .... .05 .02 .00
☐ 520 Pat Putnam .... .05 .02 .00
☐ 521 Greg Pryor .... .05 .02 .00
☐ 522 Tony Scott .... .05 .02 .00
☐ 523 Steve Mura .... .05 .02 .00
☐ 524 Johnnie LeMaster .... .05 .02 .00
☐ 525 Dick Ruthven .... .05 .02 .00
☐ 526 John McNamara MG ...... .05 .02 .00
☐ 527 Larry McWilliams .... .05 .02 .00
☐ 528 Johnny Ray .... .20 .08 .02
☐ 529 Pat Tabler .... .20 .08 .02
☐ 530 Tom Herr .... .10 .04 .01
☐ 531A San Diego Chicken .... 1.00 .40 .10
COR (with TM)
☐ 531B San Diego Chicken .... 1.00 .40 .10
ERR (without TM)
☐ 532 Sal Butera .... .05 .02 .00
☐ 533 Mike Griffin .... .05 .02 .00
☐ 534 Kelvin Moore .... .05 .02 .00
☐ 535 Reggie Jackson .... 1.75 .70 .17
☐ 536 Ed Romero .... .05 .02 .00
☐ 537 Derrel Thomas .... .05 .02 .00
☐ 538 Mike O'Berry .... .05 .02 .00
☐ 539 Jack O'Connor .... .05 .02 .00
☐ 540 Bob Ojeda .... .50 .20 .05
☐ 541 Roy Lee Jackson .... .05 .02 .00
☐ 542 Lynn Jones .... .05 .02 .00
☐ 543 Gaylord Perry .... .40 .16 .04
☐ 544A Phil Garner ERR .... .75 .30 .07
(Reverse negative)
☐ 544B Phil Garner COR .... .10 .04 .01
☐ 545 Garry Templeton .... .10 .04 .01
☐ 546 Rafael Ramirez .... .05 .02 .00
☐ 547 Jeff Reardon .... .75 .30 .07
☐ 548 Ron Guidry .... .25 .10 .02
☐ 549 Tim Laudner .... .10 .04 .01
☐ 550 John Henry Johnson ...... .05 .02 .00
☐ 551 Chris Bando .... .05 .02 .00
☐ 552 Bobby Brown .... .05 .02 .00
☐ 553 Larry Bradford .... .05 .02 .00
☐ 554 Scott Fletcher .... .25 .10 .02
☐ 555 Jerry Royster .... .05 .02 .00
☐ 556 Shooty Babitt UER .... .05 .02 .00
(Spelled Babbitt
on front)
☐ 557 Kent Hrbek .... 3.00 1.25 .30
☐ 558 Yankee Winners .... .15 .06 .01
Ron Guidry
Tommy John
☐ 559 Mark Bomback .... .05 .02 .00
☐ 560 Julio Valdez .... .05 .02 .00
☐ 561 Buck Martinez .... .05 .02 .00
☐ 562 Mike Marshall .... .35 .15 .03
(Dodger hitter)
☐ 563 Rennie Stennett .... .05 .02 .00
☐ 564 Steve Crawford .... .05 .02 .00
☐ 565 Bob Babcock .... .05 .02 .00
☐ 566 Johnny Podres CO .... .10 .04 .01
☐ 567 Paul Serna .... .05 .02 .00
☐ 568 Harold Baines .... 1.50 .60 .15
☐ 569 Dave LaRoche .... .05 .02 .00
☐ 570 Lee May .... .05 .02 .00
☐ 571 Gary Ward .... .05 .02 .00
☐ 572 John Denny .... .05 .02 .00
☐ 573 Roy Smalley .... .05 .02 .00
☐ 574 Bob Brenly .... .10 .04 .01
☐ 575 Bronx Bombers .... .90 .40 .09
Reggie Jackson
Dave Winfield
☐ 576 Luis Pujols .... .05 .02 .00
☐ 577 Butch Hobson .... .10 .04 .01
☐ 578 Harvey Kuenn MG .... .10 .04 .01
☐ 579 Cal Ripken Sr. CO .... .15 .06 .01
☐ 580 Juan Berenguer .... .05 .02 .00
☐ 581 Benny Ayala .... .05 .02 .00
☐ 582 Vance Law .... .10 .04 .01
☐ 583 Rick Leach .... .05 .02 .00
☐ 584 George Frazier .... .05 .02 .00
☐ 585 Phillies Finest .... 1.00 .40 .10
Pete Rose
Mike Schmidt
☐ 586 Joe Rudi .... .10 .04 .01
☐ 587 Juan Beniquez .... .05 .02 .00
☐ 588 Luis DeLeon .... .05 .02 .00
☐ 589 Craig Swan .... .05 .02 .00
☐ 590 Dave Chalk .... .05 .02 .00
☐ 591 Billy Gardner MG .... .05 .02 .00
☐ 592 Sal Bando .... .10 .04 .01
☐ 593 Bert Campaneris .... .10 .04 .01
☐ 594 Steve Kemp .... .05 .02 .00
☐ 595A Randy Lerch ERR .... .75 .30 .07
(Braves)
☐ 595B Randy Lerch COR .... .10 .04 .01
(Brewers)
☐ 596 Bryan Clark .... .05 .02 .00
☐ 597 Dave Ford .... .05 .02 .00
☐ 598 Mike Scioscia .... .40 .16 .04
☐ 599 John Lowenstein .... .05 .02 .00
☐ 600 Rene Lachemann MG ..... .05 .02 .00
☐ 601 Mick Kelleher .... .05 .02 .00
☐ 602 Ron Jackson .... .05 .02 .00
☐ 603 Jerry Koosman .... .10 .04 .01
☐ 604 Dave Goltz .... .05 .02 .00
☐ 605 Ellis Valentine .... .05 .02 .00
☐ 606 Lonnie Smith .... .25 .10 .02
☐ 607 Joaquin Andujar .... .10 .04 .01
☐ 608 Garry Hancock .... .05 .02 .00

Card	Player	MINT	EXC	G-VG
☐ 609	Jerry Turner	.05	.02	.00
☐ 610	Bob Bonner	.05	.02	.00
☐ 611	Jim Dwyer	.05	.02	.00
☐ 612	Terry Bulling	.05	.02	.00
☐ 613	Joel Youngblood	.05	.02	.00
☐ 614	Larry Milbourne	.05	.02	.00
☐ 615	Gene Roof UER (Name on front is Phil Roof)	.05	.02	.00
☐ 616	Keith Drumwright	.05	.02	.00
☐ 617	Dave Rosello	.05	.02	.00
☐ 618	Rickey Keeton	.05	.02	.00
☐ 619	Dennis Lamp	.05	.02	.00
☐ 620	Sid Monge	.05	.02	.00
☐ 621	Jerry White	.05	.02	.00
☐ 622	Luis Aguayo	.05	.02	.00
☐ 623	Jamie Easterly	.05	.02	.00
☐ 624	Steve Sax	3.50	1.50	.35
☐ 625	Dave Roberts	.05	.02	.00
☐ 626	Rick Bosetti	.05	.02	.00
☐ 627	Terry Francona	.05	.02	.00
☐ 628	Pride of Reds Tom Seaver Johnny Bench	.90	.40	.09
☐ 629	Paul Mirabella	.05	.02	.00
☐ 630	Rance Mulliniks	.05	.02	.00
☐ 631	Kevin Hickey	.05	.02	.00
☐ 632	Reid Nichols	.05	.02	.00
☐ 633	Dave Geisel	.05	.02	.00
☐ 634	Ken Griffey	.25	.10	.02
☐ 635	Bob Lemon MG	.10	.04	.01
☐ 636	Orlando Sanchez	.05	.02	.00
☐ 637	Bill Almon	.05	.02	.00
☐ 638	Danny Ainge	.35	.15	.03
☐ 639	Willie Stargell	.50	.20	.05
☐ 640	Bob Sykes	.05	.02	.00
☐ 641	Ed Lynch	.05	.02	.00
☐ 642	John Ellis	.05	.02	.00
☐ 643	Ferguson Jenkins	.40	.16	.04
☐ 644	Lenn Sakata	.05	.02	.00
☐ 645	Julio Gonzalez	.05	.02	.00
☐ 646	Jesse Orosco	.05	.02	.00
☐ 647	Jerry Dybzinski	.05	.02	.00
☐ 648	Tommy Davis CO	.10	.04	.01
☐ 649	Ron Gardenhire	.05	.02	.00
☐ 650	Felipe Alou CO	.10	.04	.01
☐ 651	Harvey Haddix CO	.05	.02	.00
☐ 652	Willie Upshaw	.05	.02	.00
☐ 653	Bill Madlock	.10	.04	.01
☐ 654A	DK Checklist ERR (unnumbered) (with Trammel)	.50	.10	.02
☐ 654B	DK Checklist COR (unnumbered) (with Trammell)	.15	.02	.00
☐ 655	Checklist 1 (unnumbered)	.15	.02	.00
☐ 656	Checklist 2 (unnumbered)	.15	.02	.00
☐ 657	Checklist 3 (unnumbered)	.15	.02	.00
☐ 658	Checklist 4 (unnumbered)	.15	.02	.00
☐ 659	Checklist 5 (unnumbered)	.15	.02	.00
☐ 660	Checklist 6 (unnumbered)	.15	.02	.00

1983 Donruss

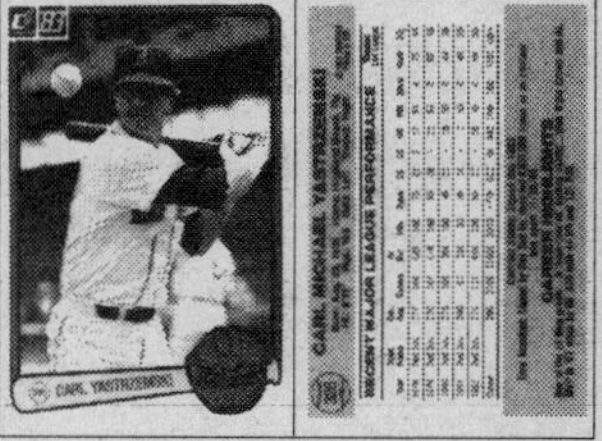

The cards in this 660-card set measure 2 1/2" by 3 1/2". The 1983 Donruss baseball set, issued with a 63-piece Diamond King puzzle, again leads off with a 26-card Diamond Kings (DK) series. Of the remaining 634 cards, two are combination cards, one portrays the San Diego Chicken, one shows the completed Ty Cobb puzzle, and seven are unnumbered checklist cards. The seven unnumbered checklist cards are arbitrarily assigned numbers 654 through 660 and are listed at the end of the list below. The Donruss logo and the year of issue are shown in the upper left corner of the obverse. The card backs have black print on yellow and white and are numbered on a small ball design. The complete set price below includes only the more common of each variation pair. The key rookie cards in this set are Wade Boggs, Julio Franco, Tony Gwynn, Howard Johnson, Willie McGee, Ryne Sandberg, and Frank Viola.

	MINT	EXC	G-VG
COMPLETE SET (660)	120.00	55.00	18.00

COMMON PLAYER (1-660) .... .05 .02 .00

☐ 1 Fernando Valenzuela DK .... .25 .08 .02
☐ 2 Rollie Fingers DK .... .20 .08 .02
☐ 3 Reggie Jackson DK .... .65 .25 .06
☐ 4 Jim Palmer DK .... .50 .20 .05
☐ 5 Jack Morris DK .... .30 .12 .03
☐ 6 George Foster DK .... .15 .06 .01
☐ 7 Jim Sundberg DK .... .10 .04 .01
☐ 8 Willie Stargell DK .... .30 .12 .03
☐ 9 Dave Stieb DK .... .15 .06 .01
☐ 10 Joe Niekro DK .... .10 .04 .01
☐ 11 Rickey Henderson DK ... 2.00 .80 .20
☐ 12 Dale Murphy DK .... .45 .18 .04
☐ 13 Toby Harrah DK .... .10 .04 .01
☐ 14 Bill Buckner DK .... .10 .04 .01
☐ 15 Willie Wilson DK .... .10 .04 .01
☐ 16 Steve Carlton DK .... .50 .20 .05
☐ 17 Ron Guidry DK .... .15 .06 .01
☐ 18 Steve Rogers DK .... .10 .04 .01
☐ 19 Kent Hrbek DK .... .30 .12 .03
☐ 20 Keith Hernandez DK .... .15 .06 .01
☐ 21 Floyd Bannister DK .... .10 .04 .01
☐ 22 Johnny Bench DK .... .65 .25 .06
☐ 23 Britt Burns DK .... .10 .04 .01
☐ 24 Joe Morgan DK .... .30 .12 .03
☐ 25 Carl Yastrzemski DK .... .60 .25 .06
☐ 26 Terry Kennedy DK .... .10 .04 .01
☐ 27 Gary Roenicke .... .05 .02 .00
☐ 28 Dwight Bernard .... .05 .02 .00
☐ 29 Pat Underwood .... .05 .02 .00
☐ 30 Gary Allenson .... .05 .02 .00
☐ 31 Ron Guidry .... .25 .10 .02
☐ 32 Burt Hooton .... .05 .02 .00
☐ 33 Chris Bando .... .05 .02 .00
☐ 34 Vida Blue .... .10 .04 .01
☐ 35 Rickey Henderson .... 5.00 2.25 .50
☐ 36 Ray Burris .... .05 .02 .00
☐ 37 John Butcher .... .05 .02 .00
☐ 38 Don Aase .... .05 .02 .00
☐ 39 Jerry Koosman .... .10 .04 .01
☐ 40 Bruce Sutter .... .15 .06 .01
☐ 41 Jose Cruz .... .10 .04 .01
☐ 42 Pete Rose .... 1.25 .50 .12
☐ 43 Cesar Cedeno .... .10 .04 .01
☐ 44 Floyd Chiffer .... .05 .02 .00
☐ 45 Larry McWilliams .... .05 .02 .00
☐ 46 Alan Fowlkes .... .05 .02 .00
☐ 47 Dale Murphy .... .75 .30 .07
☐ 48 Doug Bird .... .05 .02 .00
☐ 49 Hubie Brooks .... .25 .10 .02
☐ 50 Floyd Bannister .... .05 .02 .00
☐ 51 Jack O'Connor .... .05 .02 .00
☐ 52 Steve Senteney .... .05 .02 .00
☐ 53 Gary Gaetti .... 1.00 .40 .10
☐ 54 Damaso Garcia .... .05 .02 .00
☐ 55 Gene Nelson .... .05 .02 .00
☐ 56 Mookie Wilson .... .10 .04 .01
☐ 57 Allen Ripley .... .05 .02 .00
☐ 58 Bob Horner .... .10 .04 .01
☐ 59 Tony Pena .... .10 .04 .01
☐ 60 Gary Lavelle .... .05 .02 .00
☐ 61 Tim Lollar .... .05 .02 .00
☐ 62 Frank Pastore .... .05 .02 .00
☐ 63 Garry Maddox .... .05 .02 .00
☐ 64 Bob Forsch .... .05 .02 .00
☐ 65 Harry Spilman .... .05 .02 .00
☐ 66 Geoff Zahn .... .05 .02 .00
☐ 67 Salome Barojas .... .05 .02 .00
☐ 68 David Palmer .... .05 .02 .00
☐ 69 Charlie Hough .... .05 .02 .00
☐ 70 Dan Quisenberry .... .10 .04 .01
☐ 71 Tony Armas .... .05 .02 .00
☐ 72 Rick Sutcliffe .... .15 .06 .01
☐ 73 Steve Balboni .... .05 .02 .00
☐ 74 Jerry Remy .... .05 .02 .00
☐ 75 Mike Scioscia .... .10 .04 .01
☐ 76 John Wockenfuss .... .05 .02 .00
☐ 77 Jim Palmer .... .75 .30 .07
☐ 78 Rollie Fingers .... .45 .18 .04
☐ 79 Joe Nolan .... .05 .02 .00
☐ 80 Pete Vuckovich .... .05 .02 .00
☐ 81 Rick Leach .... .05 .02 .00
☐ 82 Rick Miller .... .05 .02 .00
☐ 83 Graig Nettles .... .10 .04 .01
☐ 84 Ron Cey .... .10 .04 .01
☐ 85 Miguel Dilone .... .05 .02 .00
☐ 86 John Wathan .... .05 .02 .00
☐ 87 Kelvin Moore .... .05 .02 .00
☐ 88A Byrn Smith ERR .... .20 .08 .02
(sic, Bryn)
☐ 88B Bryn Smith COR .... .60 .25 .06
☐ 89 Dave Hostetler .... .05 .02 .00
☐ 90 Rod Carew .... 1.00 .40 .10
☐ 91 Lonnie Smith .... .15 .06 .01
☐ 92 Bob Knepper .... .05 .02 .00
☐ 93 Marty Bystrom .... .05 .02 .00
☐ 94 Chris Welsh .... .05 .02 .00
☐ 95 Jason Thompson .... .05 .02 .00
☐ 96 Tom O'Malley .... .05 .02 .00
☐ 97 Phil Niekro .... .35 .15 .03
☐ 98 Neil Allen .... .05 .02 .00
☐ 99 Bill Buckner .... .10 .04 .01
☐ 100 Ed VandeBerg .... .05 .02 .00
☐ 101 Jim Clancy .... .05 .02 .00
☐ 102 Robert Castillo .... .05 .02 .00
☐ 103 Bruce Berenyi .... .05 .02 .00
☐ 104 Carlton Fisk .... 1.00 .40 .10
☐ 105 Mike Flanagan .... .10 .04 .01
☐ 106 Cecil Cooper .... .10 .04 .01
☐ 107 Jack Morris .... .60 .25 .06
☐ 108 Mike Morgan .... .10 .04 .01
☐ 109 Luis Aponte .... .05 .02 .00
☐ 110 Pedro Guerrero .... .35 .15 .03
☐ 111 Len Barker .... .05 .02 .00
☐ 112 Willie Wilson .... .10 .04 .01

☐ 113 Dave Beard .05 .02 .00
☐ 114 Mike Gates .05 .02 .00
☐ 115 Reggie Jackson 1.25 .50 .12
☐ 116 George Wright .05 .02 .00
☐ 117 Vance Law .10 .04 .01
☐ 118 Nolan Ryan 5.25 2.25 .50
☐ 119 Mike Krukow .05 .02 .00
☐ 120 Ozzie Smith 1.25 .50 .12
☐ 121 Broderick Perkins .05 .02 .00
☐ 122 Tom Seaver 1.00 .40 .10
☐ 123 Chris Chambliss .10 .04 .01
☐ 124 Chuck Tanner MG .05 .02 .00
☐ 125 Johnnie LeMaster .05 .02 .00
☐ 126 Mel Hall 1.00 .40 .10
☐ 127 Bruce Bochte .05 .02 .00
☐ 128 Charlie Puleo .05 .02 .00
☐ 129 Luis Leal .05 .02 .00
☐ 130 John Pacella .05 .02 .00
☐ 131 Glenn Gulliver .05 .02 .00
☐ 132 Don Money .05 .02 .00
☐ 133 Dave Rozema .05 .02 .00
☐ 134 Bruce Hurst .40 .16 .04
☐ 135 Rudy May .05 .02 .00
☐ 136 Tom Lasorda MG .10 .04 .01
☐ 137 Dan Spillner UER .10 .04 .01
(photo actually
Ed Whitson)
☐ 138 Jerry Martin .05 .02 .00
☐ 139 Mike Norris .05 .02 .00
☐ 140 Al Oliver .10 .04 .01
☐ 141 Daryl Sconiers .05 .02 .00
☐ 142 Lamar Johnson .05 .02 .00
☐ 143 Harold Baines .50 .20 .05
☐ 144 Alan Ashby .05 .02 .00
☐ 145 Garry Templeton .10 .04 .01
☐ 146 Al Holland .05 .02 .00
☐ 147 Bo Diaz .05 .02 .00
☐ 148 Dave Concepcion .10 .04 .01
☐ 149 Rick Camp .05 .02 .00
☐ 150 Jim Morrison .05 .02 .00
☐ 151 Randy Martz .05 .02 .00
☐ 152 Keith Hernandez .25 .10 .02
☐ 153 John Lowenstein .05 .02 .00
☐ 154 Mike Caldwell .05 .02 .00
☐ 155 Milt Wilcox .05 .02 .00
☐ 156 Rich Gedman .05 .02 .00
☐ 157 Rich Gossage .15 .06 .01
☐ 158 Jerry Reuss .05 .02 .00
☐ 159 Ron Hassey .05 .02 .00
☐ 160 Larry Gura .05 .02 .00
☐ 161 Dwayne Murphy .05 .02 .00
☐ 162 Woodie Fryman .05 .02 .00
☐ 163 Steve Comer .05 .02 .00
☐ 164 Ken Forsch .05 .02 .00
☐ 165 Dennis Lamp .05 .02 .00
☐ 166 David Green .05 .02 .00
☐ 167 Terry Puhl .05 .02 .00
☐ 168 Mike Schmidt 2.00 .80 .20
(wearing 37
rather than 20)
☐ 169 Eddie Milner .05 .02 .00
☐ 170 John Curtis .05 .02 .00
☐ 171 Don Robinson .05 .02 .00
☐ 172 Rich Gale .05 .02 .00
☐ 173 Steve Bedrosian .10 .04 .01
☐ 174 Willie Hernandez .05 .02 .00
☐ 175 Ron Gardenhire .05 .02 .00
☐ 176 Jim Beattie .05 .02 .00
☐ 177 Tim Laudner .05 .02 .00
☐ 178 Buck Martinez .05 .02 .00
☐ 179 Kent Hrbek .50 .20 .05
☐ 180 Alfredo Griffin .05 .02 .00
☐ 181 Larry Andersen .05 .02 .00
☐ 182 Pete Falcone .05 .02 .00
☐ 183 Jody Davis .05 .02 .00
☐ 184 Glenn Hubbard .05 .02 .00
☐ 185 Dale Berra .05 .02 .00
☐ 186 Greg Minton .05 .02 .00
☐ 187 Gary Lucas .05 .02 .00
☐ 188 Dave Van Gorder .05 .02 .00
☐ 189 Bob Dernier .05 .02 .00
☐ 190 Willie McGee 3.50 1.50 .35
☐ 191 Dickie Thon .10 .04 .01
☐ 192 Bob Boone .10 .04 .01
☐ 193 Britt Burns .05 .02 .00
☐ 194 Jeff Reardon .50 .20 .05
☐ 195 Jon Matlack .05 .02 .00
☐ 196 Don Slaught .35 .15 .03
☐ 197 Fred Stanley .05 .02 .00
☐ 198 Rick Manning .05 .02 .00
☐ 199 Dave Righetti .25 .10 .02
☐ 200 Dave Stapleton .05 .02 .00
☐ 201 Steve Yeager .05 .02 .00
☐ 202 Enos Cabell .05 .02 .00
☐ 203 Sammy Stewart .05 .02 .00
☐ 204 Moose Haas .05 .02 .00
☐ 205 Lenn Sakata .05 .02 .00
☐ 206 Charlie Moore .05 .02 .00
☐ 207 Alan Trammell .60 .25 .06
☐ 208 Jim Rice .25 .10 .02
☐ 209 Roy Smalley .05 .02 .00
☐ 210 Bill Russell .10 .04 .01
☐ 211 Andre Thornton .05 .02 .00
☐ 212 Willie Aikens .05 .02 .00
☐ 213 Dave McKay .05 .02 .00
☐ 214 Tim Blackwell .05 .02 .00
☐ 215 Buddy Bell .10 .04 .01
☐ 216 Doug DeCinces .10 .04 .01
☐ 217 Tom Herr .10 .04 .01
☐ 218 Frank LaCorte .05 .02 .00
☐ 219 Steve Carlton 1.00 .40 .10
☐ 220 Terry Kennedy .05 .02 .00
☐ 221 Mike Easler .05 .02 .00
☐ 222 Jack Clark .25 .10 .02
☐ 223 Gene Garber .05 .02 .00

☐ 224 Scott Holman .05 .02 .00
☐ 225 Mike Proly .05 .02 .00
☐ 226 Terry Bulling .05 .02 .00
☐ 227 Jerry Garvin .05 .02 .00
☐ 228 Ron Davis .05 .02 .00
☐ 229 Tom Hume .05 .02 .00
☐ 230 Marc Hill .05 .02 .00
☐ 231 Dennis Martinez .10 .04 .01
☐ 232 Jim Gantner .05 .02 .00
☐ 233 Larry Pashnick .05 .02 .00
☐ 234 Dave Collins .05 .02 .00
☐ 235 Tom Burgmeier .05 .02 .00
☐ 236 Ken Landreaux .05 .02 .00
☐ 237 John Denny .05 .02 .00
☐ 238 Hal McRae .10 .04 .01
☐ 239 Matt Keough .05 .02 .00
☐ 240 Doug Flynn .05 .02 .00
☐ 241 Fred Lynn .20 .08 .02
☐ 242 Billy Sample .05 .02 .00
☐ 243 Tom Paciorek .05 .02 .00
☐ 244 Joe Sambito .05 .02 .00
☐ 245 Sid Monge .05 .02 .00
☐ 246 Ken Oberkfell .05 .02 .00
☐ 247 Joe Pittman UER .10 .04 .01
(photo actually
Juan Eichelberger)
☐ 248 Mario Soto .05 .02 .00
☐ 249 Claudell Washington .05 .02 .00
☐ 250 Rick Rhoden .05 .02 .00
☐ 251 Darrell Evans .10 .04 .01
☐ 252 Steve Henderson .05 .02 .00
☐ 253 Manny Castillo .05 .02 .00
☐ 254 Craig Swan .05 .02 .00
☐ 255 Joey McLaughlin .05 .02 .00
☐ 256 Pete Redfern .05 .02 .00
☐ 257 Ken Singleton .10 .04 .01
☐ 258 Robin Yount 1.50 .60 .15
☐ 259 Elias Sosa .05 .02 .00
☐ 260 Bob Ojeda .10 .04 .01
☐ 261 Bobby Murcer .10 .04 .01
☐ 262 Candy Maldonado .50 .20 .05
☐ 263 Rick Waits .05 .02 .00
☐ 264 Greg Pryor .05 .02 .00
☐ 265 Bob Owchinko .05 .02 .00
☐ 266 Chris Speier .05 .02 .00
☐ 267 Bruce Kison .05 .02 .00
☐ 268 Mark Wagner .05 .02 .00
☐ 269 Steve Kemp .05 .02 .00
☐ 270 Phil Garner .10 .04 .01
☐ 271 Gene Richards .05 .02 .00
☐ 272 Renie Martin .05 .02 .00
☐ 273 Dave Roberts .05 .02 .00
☐ 274 Dan Driessen .05 .02 .00
☐ 275 Rufino Linares .05 .02 .00
☐ 276 Lee Lacy .05 .02 .00
☐ 277 Ryne Sandberg 35.00 15.75 5.25
☐ 278 Darrell Porter .05 .02 .00
☐ 279 Cal Ripken 12.50 5.50 1.65
☐ 280 Jamie Easterly .05 .02 .00
☐ 281 Bill Fahey .05 .02 .00
☐ 282 Glenn Hoffman .05 .02 .00
☐ 283 Willie Randolph .10 .04 .01
☐ 284 Fernando Valenzuela .25 .10 .02
☐ 285 Alan Bannister .05 .02 .00
☐ 286 Paul Splittorff .05 .02 .00
☐ 287 Joe Rudi .10 .04 .01
☐ 288 Bill Gullickson .10 .04 .01
☐ 289 Danny Darwin .05 .02 .00
☐ 290 Andy Hassler .05 .02 .00
☐ 291 Ernesto Escarrega .05 .02 .00
☐ 292 Steve Mura .05 .02 .00
☐ 293 Tony Scott .05 .02 .00
☐ 294 Manny Trillo .05 .02 .00
☐ 295 Greg Harris .05 .02 .00
☐ 296 Luis DeLeon .05 .02 .00
☐ 297 Kent Tekulve .05 .02 .00
☐ 298 Atlee Hammaker .05 .02 .00
☐ 299 Bruce Benedict .05 .02 .00
☐ 300 Fergie Jenkins .35 .15 .03
☐ 301 Dave Kingman .15 .06 .01
☐ 302 Bill Caudill .05 .02 .00
☐ 303 John Castino .05 .02 .00
☐ 304 Ernie Whitt .05 .02 .00
☐ 305 Randy Johnson .05 .02 .00
☐ 306 Garth Iorg .05 .02 .00
☐ 307 Gaylord Perry .35 .15 .03
☐ 308 Ed Lynch .05 .02 .00
☐ 309 Keith Moreland .05 .02 .00
☐ 310 Rafael Ramirez .05 .02 .00
☐ 311 Bill Madlock .10 .04 .01
☐ 312 Milt May .05 .02 .00
☐ 313 John Montefusco .05 .02 .00
☐ 314 Wayne Krenchicki .05 .02 .00
☐ 315 George Vukovich .05 .02 .00
☐ 316 Joaquin Andujar .10 .04 .01
☐ 317 Craig Reynolds .05 .02 .00
☐ 318 Rick Burleson .05 .02 .00
☐ 319 Richard Dotson .05 .02 .00
☐ 320 Steve Rogers .05 .02 .00
☐ 321 Dave Schmidt .10 .04 .01
☐ 322 Bud Black .40 .16 .04
☐ 323 Jeff Burroughs .05 .02 .00
☐ 324 Von Hayes .15 .06 .01
☐ 325 Butch Wynegar .05 .02 .00
☐ 326 Carl Yastrzemski 1.00 .40 .10
☐ 327 Ron Roenicke .05 .02 .00
☐ 328 Howard Johnson 10.00 4.50 1.25
☐ 329 Rick Dempsey UER .05 .02 .00
(posing as a left-
handed batter)
☐ 330A Jim Slaton .10 .04 .01
(bio printed
black on white)
☐ 330B Jim Slaton .15 .06 .01
(bio printed
black on yellow)

☐ 331 Benny Ayala	.05	.02	.00
☐ 332 Ted Simmons	.10	.04	.01
☐ 333 Lou Whitaker	.35	.15	.03
☐ 334 Chuck Rainey	.05	.02	.00
☐ 335 Lou Piniella	.10	.04	.01
☐ 336 Steve Sax	.50	.20	.05
☐ 337 Toby Harrah	.05	.02	.00
☐ 338 George Brett	1.50	.60	.15
☐ 339 Dave Lopes	.10	.04	.01
☐ 340 Gary Carter	.40	.16	.04
☐ 341 John Grubb	.05	.02	.00
☐ 342 Tim Foli	.05	.02	.00
☐ 343 Jim Kaat	.15	.06	.01
☐ 344 Mike LaCoss	.05	.02	.00
☐ 345 Larry Christenson	.05	.02	.00
☐ 346 Juan Bonilla	.05	.02	.00
☐ 347 Omar Moreno	.05	.02	.00
☐ 348 Chili Davis	.60	.25	.06
☐ 349 Tommy Boggs	.05	.02	.00
☐ 350 Rusty Staub	.15	.06	.01
☐ 351 Bump Wills	.05	.02	.00
☐ 352 Rick Sweet	.05	.02	.00
☐ 353 Jim Gott	.20	.08	.02
☐ 354 Terry Felton	.05	.02	.00
☐ 355 Jim Kern	.05	.02	.00
☐ 356 Bill Almon UER (Expos/Mets in 1983, not Padres/Mets)	.05	.02	.00
☐ 357 Tippy Martinez	.05	.02	.00
☐ 358 Roy Howell	.05	.02	.00
☐ 359 Dan Petry	.05	.02	.00
☐ 360 Jerry Mumphrey	.05	.02	.00
☐ 361 Mark Clear	.05	.02	.00
☐ 362 Mike Marshall	.10	.04	.01
☐ 363 Lary Sorensen	.05	.02	.00
☐ 364 Amos Otis	.10	.04	.01
☐ 365 Rick Langford	.05	.02	.00
☐ 366 Brad Mills	.05	.02	.00
☐ 367 Brian Downing	.10	.04	.01
☐ 368 Mike Richardt	.05	.02	.00
☐ 369 Aurelio Rodriguez	.05	.02	.00
☐ 370 Dave Smith	.05	.02	.00
☐ 371 Tug McGraw	.10	.04	.01
☐ 372 Doug Bair	.05	.02	.00
☐ 373 Ruppert Jones	.05	.02	.00
☐ 374 Alex Trevino	.05	.02	.00
☐ 375 Ken Dayley	.05	.02	.00
☐ 376 Rod Scurry	.05	.02	.00
☐ 377 Bob Brenly	.05	.02	.00
☐ 378 Scot Thompson	.05	.02	.00
☐ 379 Julio Cruz	.05	.02	.00
☐ 380 John Stearns	.05	.02	.00
☐ 381 Dale Murray	.05	.02	.00
☐ 382 Frank Viola	4.50	2.00	.45
☐ 383 Al Bumbry	.05	.02	.00
☐ 384 Ben Oglivie	.05	.02	.00
☐ 385 Dave Tobik	.05	.02	.00
☐ 386 Bob Stanley	.05	.02	.00
☐ 387 Andre Robertson	.05	.02	.00
☐ 388 Jorge Orta	.05	.02	.00
☐ 389 Ed Whitson	.05	.02	.00
☐ 390 Don Hood	.05	.02	.00
☐ 391 Tom Underwood	.05	.02	.00
☐ 392 Tim Wallach	.20	.08	.02
☐ 393 Steve Renko	.05	.02	.00
☐ 394 Mickey Rivers	.05	.02	.00
☐ 395 Greg Luzinski	.10	.04	.01
☐ 396 Art Howe	.10	.04	.01
☐ 397 Alan Wiggins	.05	.02	.00
☐ 398 Jim Barr	.05	.02	.00
☐ 399 Ivan DeJesus	.05	.02	.00
☐ 400 Tom Lawless	.05	.02	.00
☐ 401 Bob Walk	.05	.02	.00
☐ 402 Jimmy Smith	.05	.02	.00
☐ 403 Lee Smith	.60	.25	.06
☐ 404 George Hendrick	.05	.02	.00
☐ 405 Eddie Murray	1.25	.50	.12
☐ 406 Marshall Edwards	.05	.02	.00
☐ 407 Lance Parrish	.25	.10	.02
☐ 408 Carney Lansford	.10	.04	.01
☐ 409 Dave Winfield	.75	.30	.07
☐ 410 Bob Welch	.25	.10	.02
☐ 411 Larry Milbourne	.05	.02	.00
☐ 412 Dennis Leonard	.05	.02	.00
☐ 413 Dan Meyer	.05	.02	.00
☐ 414 Charlie Lea	.05	.02	.00
☐ 415 Rick Honeycutt	.05	.02	.00
☐ 416 Mike Witt	.05	.02	.00
☐ 417 Steve Trout	.05	.02	.00
☐ 418 Glenn Brummer	.05	.02	.00
☐ 419 Denny Walling	.05	.02	.00
☐ 420 Gary Matthews	.05	.02	.00
☐ 421 Charlie Leibrandt UER (Liebrandt on front of card)	.10	.04	.01
☐ 422 Juan Eichelberger UER (photo actually Joe Pittman)	.05	.02	.00
☐ 423 Cecilio Guante UER (listed as Matt on card)	.05	.02	.00
☐ 424 Bill Laskey	.05	.02	.00
☐ 425 Jerry Royster	.05	.02	.00
☐ 426 Dickie Noles	.05	.02	.00
☐ 427 George Foster	.15	.06	.01
☐ 428 Mike Moore	.90	.40	.09
☐ 429 Gary Ward	.05	.02	.00
☐ 430 Barry Bonnell	.05	.02	.00
☐ 431 Ron Washington	.05	.02	.00
☐ 432 Rance Mulliniks	.05	.02	.00
☐ 433 Mike Stanton	.05	.02	.00
☐ 434 Jesse Orosco	.05	.02	.00
☐ 435 Larry Bowa	.10	.04	.01
☐ 436 Biff Pocoroba	.05	.02	.00
☐ 437 Johnny Ray	.05	.02	.00
☐ 438 Joe Morgan	.50	.20	.05

☐ 439 Eric Show	.15	.06	.01
☐ 440 Larry Biittner	.05	.02	.00
☐ 441 Greg Gross	.05	.02	.00
☐ 442 Gene Tenace	.10	.04	.01
☐ 443 Danny Heep	.05	.02	.00
☐ 444 Bobby Clark	.05	.02	.00
☐ 445 Kevin Hickey	.05	.02	.00
☐ 446 Scott Sanderson	.10	.04	.01
☐ 447 Frank Tanana	.10	.04	.01
☐ 448 Cesar Geronimo	.05	.02	.00
☐ 449 Jimmy Sexton	.05	.02	.00
☐ 450 Mike Hargrove	.05	.02	.00
☐ 451 Doyle Alexander	.05	.02	.00
☐ 452 Dwight Evans	.25	.10	.02
☐ 453 Terry Forster	.05	.02	.00
☐ 454 Tom Brookens	.05	.02	.00
☐ 455 Rich Dauer	.05	.02	.00
☐ 456 Rob Picciolo	.05	.02	.00
☐ 457 Terry Crowley	.05	.02	.00
☐ 458 Ned Yost	.05	.02	.00
☐ 459 Kirk Gibson	.50	.20	.05
☐ 460 Reid Nichols	.05	.02	.00
☐ 461 Oscar Gamble	.05	.02	.00
☐ 462 Dusty Baker	.10	.04	.01
☐ 463 Jack Perconte	.05	.02	.00
☐ 464 Frank White	.05	.02	.00
☐ 465 Mickey Klutts	.05	.02	.00
☐ 466 Warren Cromartie	.05	.02	.00
☐ 467 Larry Parrish	.05	.02	.00
☐ 468 Bobby Grich	.10	.04	.01
☐ 469 Dane Iorg	.05	.02	.00
☐ 470 Joe Niekro	.10	.04	.01
☐ 471 Ed Farmer	.05	.02	.00
☐ 472 Tim Flannery	.05	.02	.00
☐ 473 Dave Parker	.40	.16	.04
☐ 474 Jeff Leonard	.05	.02	.00
☐ 475 Al Hrabosky	.05	.02	.00
☐ 476 Ron Hodges	.05	.02	.00
☐ 477 Leon Durham	.05	.02	.00
☐ 478 Jim Essian	.05	.02	.00
☐ 479 Roy Lee Jackson	.05	.02	.00
☐ 480 Brad Havens	.05	.02	.00
☐ 481 Joe Price	.05	.02	.00
☐ 482 Tony Bernazard	.05	.02	.00
☐ 483 Scott McGregor	.05	.02	.00
☐ 484 Paul Molitor	.40	.16	.04
☐ 485 Mike Ivie	.05	.02	.00
☐ 486 Ken Griffey	.25	.10	.02
☐ 487 Dennis Eckersley	.40	.16	.04
☐ 488 Steve Garvey	.50	.20	.05
☐ 489 Mike Fischlin	.05	.02	.00
☐ 490 U.L. Washington	.05	.02	.00
☐ 491 Steve McCatty	.05	.02	.00
☐ 492 Roy Johnson	.05	.02	.00
☐ 493 Don Baylor	.10	.04	.01
☐ 494 Bobby Johnson	.05	.02	.00
☐ 495 Mike Squires	.05	.02	.00
☐ 496 Bert Roberge	.05	.02	.00
☐ 497 Dick Ruthven	.05	.02	.00
☐ 498 Tito Landrum	.05	.02	.00
☐ 499 Sixto Lezcano	.05	.02	.00
☐ 500 Johnny Bench	1.00	.40	.10
☐ 501 Larry Whisenton	.05	.02	.00
☐ 502 Manny Sarmiento	.05	.02	.00
☐ 503 Fred Breining	.05	.02	.00
☐ 504 Bill Campbell	.05	.02	.00
☐ 505 Todd Cruz	.05	.02	.00
☐ 506 Bob Bailor	.05	.02	.00
☐ 507 Dave Stieb	.25	.10	.02
☐ 508 Al Williams	.05	.02	.00
☐ 509 Dan Ford	.05	.02	.00
☐ 510 Gorman Thomas	.10	.04	.01
☐ 511 Chet Lemon	.05	.02	.00
☐ 512 Mike Torrez	.05	.02	.00
☐ 513 Shane Rawley	.05	.02	.00
☐ 514 Mark Belanger	.10	.04	.01
☐ 515 Rodney Craig	.05	.02	.00
☐ 516 Onix Concepcion	.05	.02	.00
☐ 517 Mike Heath	.05	.02	.00
☐ 518 Andre Dawson UER (Middle name Fernando, should be Nolan)	1.25	.50	.12
☐ 519 Luis Sanchez	.05	.02	.00
☐ 520 Terry Bogener	.05	.02	.00
☐ 521 Rudy Law	.05	.02	.00
☐ 522 Ray Knight	.10	.04	.01
☐ 523 Joe Lefebvre	.05	.02	.00
☐ 524 Jim Wohlford	.05	.02	.00
☐ 525 Julio Franco	10.00	4.50	1.25
☐ 526 Ron Oester	.05	.02	.00
☐ 527 Rick Mahler	.05	.02	.00
☐ 528 Steve Nicosia	.05	.02	.00
☐ 529 Junior Kennedy	.05	.02	.00
☐ 530A Whitey Herzog MG (bio printed black on white)	.10	.04	.01
☐ 530B Whitey Herzog MG (bio printed black on yellow)	.10	.04	.01
☐ 531A Don Sutton (blue border on photo)	.35	.15	.03
☐ 531B Don Sutton (green border on photo)	.35	.15	.03
☐ 532 Mark Brouhard	.05	.02	.00
☐ 533A Sparky Anderson MG (bio printed black on white)	.10	.04	.01
☐ 533B Sparky Anderson MG (bio printed black on yellow)	.10	.04	.01
☐ 534 Roger LaFrancois	.05	.02	.00
☐ 535 George Frazier	.05	.02	.00
☐ 536 Tom Niedenfuer	.05	.02	.00
☐ 537 Ed Glynn	.05	.02	.00

☐ 538 Lee May .05 .02 .00
☐ 539 Bob Kearney .05 .02 .00
☐ 540 Tim Raines .60 .25 .06
☐ 541 Paul Mirabella .05 .02 .00
☐ 542 Luis Tiant .10 .04 .01
☐ 543 Ron LeFlore .05 .02 .00
☐ 544 Dave LaPoint .10 .04 .01
☐ 545 Randy Moffitt .05 .02 .00
☐ 546 Luis Aguayo .05 .02 .00
☐ 547 Brad Lesley .05 .02 .00
☐ 548 Luis Salazar .05 .02 .00
☐ 549 John Candelaria .05 .02 .00
☐ 550 Dave Bergman .05 .02 .00
☐ 551 Bob Watson .05 .02 .00
☐ 552 Pat Tabler .05 .02 .00
☐ 553 Brent Gaff .05 .02 .00
☐ 554 Al Cowens .05 .02 .00
☐ 555 Tom Brunansky .40 .16 .04
☐ 556 Lloyd Moseby .10 .04 .01
☐ 557A Pascual Perez ERR 2.00 .80 .20
(Twins in glove)
☐ 557B Pascual Perez COR .10 .04 .01
(Braves in glove)
☐ 558 Willie Upshaw .05 .02 .00
☐ 559 Richie Zisk .05 .02 .00
☐ 560 Pat Zachry .05 .02 .00
☐ 561 Jay Johnstone .10 .04 .01
☐ 562 Carlos Diaz .05 .02 .00
☐ 563 John Tudor .10 .04 .01
☐ 564 Frank Robinson MG .20 .08 .02
☐ 565 Dave Edwards .05 .02 .00
☐ 566 Paul Householder .05 .02 .00
☐ 567 Ron Reed .05 .02 .00
☐ 568 Mike Ramsey .05 .02 .00
☐ 569 Kiko Garcia .05 .02 .00
☐ 570 Tommy John .15 .06 .01
☐ 571 Tony LaRussa MG .10 .04 .01
☐ 572 Joel Youngblood .05 .02 .00
☐ 573 Wayne Tolleson .10 .04 .01
☐ 574 Keith Creel .05 .02 .00
☐ 575 Billy Martin MG .15 .06 .01
☐ 576 Jerry Dybzinski .05 .02 .00
☐ 577 Rick Cerone .05 .02 .00
☐ 578 Tony Perez .30 .12 .03
☐ 579 Greg Brock .10 .04 .01
☐ 580 Glenn Wilson .10 .04 .01
☐ 581 Tim Stoddard .05 .02 .00
☐ 582 Bob McClure .05 .02 .00
☐ 583 Jim Dwyer .05 .02 .00
☐ 584 Ed Romero .05 .02 .00
☐ 585 Larry Herndon .05 .02 .00
☐ 586 Wade Boggs 24.00 10.50 3.50
☐ 587 Jay Howell .10 .04 .01
☐ 588 Dave Stewart .75 .30 .07
☐ 589 Bert Blyleven .20 .08 .02
☐ 590 Dick Howser MG .05 .02 .00
☐ 591 Wayne Gross .05 .02 .00
☐ 592 Terry Francona .05 .02 .00
☐ 593 Don Werner .05 .02 .00
☐ 594 Bill Stein .05 .02 .00
☐ 595 Jesse Barfield .40 .16 .04
☐ 596 Bob Molinaro .05 .02 .00
☐ 597 Mike Vail .05 .02 .00
☐ 598 Tony Gwynn 23.00 10.00 3.35
☐ 599 Gary Rajsich .05 .02 .00
☐ 600 Jerry Ujdur .05 .02 .00
☐ 601 Cliff Johnson .05 .02 .00
☐ 602 Jerry White .05 .02 .00
☐ 603 Bryan Clark .05 .02 .00
☐ 604 Joe Ferguson .05 .02 .00
☐ 605 Guy Sularz .05 .02 .00
☐ 606A Ozzie Virgil .10 .04 .01
(green border
on photo)
☐ 606B Ozzie Virgil .10 .04 .01
(orange border
on photo)
☐ 607 Terry Harper .05 .02 .00
☐ 608 Harvey Kuenn MG .05 .02 .00
☐ 609 Jim Sundberg .05 .02 .00
☐ 610 Willie Stargell .50 .20 .05
☐ 611 Reggie Smith .10 .04 .01
☐ 612 Rob Wilfong .05 .02 .00
☐ 613 The Niekro Brothers .20 .08 .02
Joe Niekro
Phil Niekro
☐ 614 Lee Elia MG .05 .02 .00
☐ 615 Mickey Hatcher .05 .02 .00
☐ 616 Jerry Hairston .05 .02 .00
☐ 617 John Martin .05 .02 .00
☐ 618 Wally Backman .10 .04 .01
☐ 619 Storm Davis .25 .10 .02
☐ 620 Alan Knicely .05 .02 .00
☐ 621 John Stuper .05 .02 .00
☐ 622 Matt Sinatro .05 .02 .00
☐ 623 Geno Petralli .10 .04 .01
☐ 624 Duane Walker .05 .02 .00
☐ 625 Dick Williams MG .05 .02 .00
☐ 626 Pat Corrales MG .05 .02 .00
☐ 627 Vern Ruhle .05 .02 .00
☐ 628 Joe Torre MG .10 .04 .01
☐ 629 Anthony Johnson .05 .02 .00
☐ 630 Steve Howe .05 .02 .00
☐ 631 Gary Woods .05 .02 .00
☐ 632 LaMarr Hoyt .05 .02 .00
☐ 633 Steve Swisher .05 .02 .00
☐ 634 Terry Leach .10 .04 .01
☐ 635 Jeff Newman .05 .02 .00
☐ 636 Brett Butler .40 .16 .04
☐ 637 Gary Gray .05 .02 .00
☐ 638 Lee Mazzilli .05 .02 .00
☐ 639A Ron Jackson ERR 14.00 6.25 2.00
(A's in glove)
☐ 639B Ron Jackson COR .10 .04 .01
(Angels in glove,
red border on photo)

No.	Player	MINT	EXC	G-VG
☐ 639C	Ron Jackson COR (Angels in glove, green border on photo)	.50	.20	.05
☐ 640	Juan Beniquez	.05	.02	.00
☐ 641	Dave Rucker	.05	.02	.00
☐ 642	Luis Pujols	.05	.02	.00
☐ 643	Rick Monday	.05	.02	.00
☐ 644	Hosken Powell	.05	.02	.00
☐ 645	The Chicken	.25	.10	.02
☐ 646	Dave Engle	.05	.02	.00
☐ 647	Dick Davis	.05	.02	.00
☐ 648	Frank Robinson Vida Blue Joe Morgan	.30	.12	.03
☐ 649	Al Chambers	.05	.02	.00
☐ 650	Jesus Vega	.05	.02	.00
☐ 651	Jeff Jones	.05	.02	.00
☐ 652	Marvis Foley	.05	.02	.00
☐ 653	Ty Cobb Puzzle Card	.05	.02	.00
☐ 654A	Dick Perez/Diamond King Checklist (unnumbered) ERR (word "checklist" omitted from back)	.35	.05	.01
☐ 654B	Dick Perez/Diamond King Checklist (unnumbered) COR (word "checklist" is on back)	.35	.05	.01
☐ 655	Checklist 1 (unnumbered)	.15	.02	.00
☐ 656	Checklist 2 (unnumbered)	.15	.02	.00
☐ 657	Checklist 3 (unnumbered)	.15	.02	.00
☐ 658	Checklist 4 (unnumbered)	.15	.02	.00
☐ 659	Checklist 5 (unnumbered)	.15	.02	.00
☐ 660	Checklist 6 (unnumbered)	.15	.02	.00

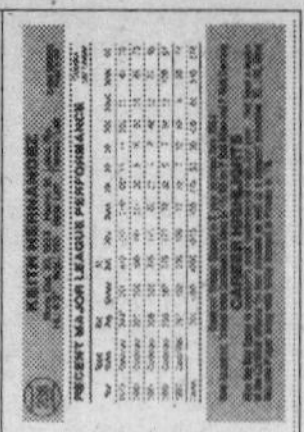

1984 Donruss

The 1984 Donruss set contains a total of 660 cards, each measuring 2 1/2" by 3 1/2"; however, only 658 are numbered. The first 26 cards in the set are again Diamond Kings (DK), although the drawings this year were styled differently and are easily differentiated from other DK issues. A new feature, Rated Rookies (RR), was introduced with this set with Bill Madden's 20 selections comprising numbers 27 through 46. Two "Living Legend" cards designated A (featuring Gaylord Perry and Rollie Fingers) and B (featuring Johnny Bench and Carl Yastrzemski) were issued as bonus cards in wax packs, but were not issued in the vending sets sold to hobby dealers. The seven unnumbered checklist cards are arbitrarily assigned numbers 652 through 658 and are listed at the end of the list below. The designs on the fronts of the Donruss cards changed considerably from the past two years. The backs contain statistics and are printed in green and black ink. The cards were distributed with a 63-piece puzzle of Duke Snider. There are no extra variation cards included in the complete set price below. The variation cards apparently resulted from a different printing for the factory sets as the Darling and Stenhouse no number variations as well as the Perez-Steel errors were corrected in the factory sets which were released later in the year. The key rookie cards in this set are Joe Carter, Ron Darling, Sid Fernandez, Tony Fernandez, Don Mattingly, Kevin McReynolds, Darryl Strawberry, and Andy Van Slyke.

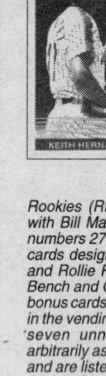

	MINT	EXC	G-VG
COMPLETE SET (658)	350.00	160.00	52.50
COMMON PLAYER (1-658)	.14	.06	.01

No.	Player	MINT	EXC	G-VG
☐ 1A	Robin Yount DK ERR (Perez Steel)	2.25	.75	.15
☐ 1B	Robin Yount DK COR	3.00	1.00	.20
☐ 2A	Dave Concepcion DK ERR (Perez Steel)	.25	.10	.02
☐ 2B	Dave Concepcion DK COR	.35	.15	.03
☐ 3A	Dwayne Murphy DK ERR (Perez Steel)	.20	.08	.02

☐ 3B	Dwayne Murphy DK COR	.30	.12	.03
☐ 4A	John Castino DK ERR (Perez Steel)	.20	.08	.02
☐ 4B	John Castino DK COR	.30	.12	.03
☐ 5A	Leon Durham DK ERR (Perez Steel)	.20	.08	.02
☐ 5B	Leon Durham DK COR	.30	.12	.03
☐ 6A	Rusty Staub DK ERR (Perez Steel)	.20	.08	.02
☐ 6B	Rusty Staub DK COR	.30	.12	.03
☐ 7A	Jack Clark DK ERR (Perez Steel)	.25	.10	.02
☐ 7B	Jack Clark DK COR	.35	.15	.03
☐ 8A	Dave Dravecky DK ERR (Perez Steel)	.20	.08	.02
☐ 8B	Dave Dravecky DK COR	.30	.12	.03
☐ 9A	Al Oliver DK ERR (Perez Steel)	.20	.08	.02
☐ 9B	Al Oliver DK COR	.30	.12	.03
☐ 10A	Dave Righetti DK ERR (Perez Steel)	.20	.08	.02
☐ 10B	Dave Righetti DK COR	.30	.12	.03
☐ 11A	Hal McRae DK ERR (Perez Steel)	.20	.08	.02
☐ 11B	Hal McRae DK COR	.30	.12	.03
☐ 12A	Ray Knight DK ERR (Perez Steel)	.20	.08	.02
☐ 12B	Ray Knight DK COR	.30	.12	.03
☐ 13A	Bruce Sutter DK ERR (Perez Steel)	.20	.08	.02
☐ 13B	Bruce Sutter DK COR	.30	.12	.03
☐ 14A	Bob Horner DK ERR (Perez Steel)	.20	.08	.02
☐ 14B	Bob Horner DK COR	.30	.12	.03
☐ 15A	Lance Parrish DK ERR (Perez Steel)	.35	.15	.03
☐ 15B	Lance Parrish DK COR	.50	.20	.05
☐ 16A	Matt Young DK ERR (Perez Steel)	.20	.08	.02
☐ 16B	Matt Young DK COR	.30	.12	.03
☐ 17A	Fred Lynn DK ERR (Perez Steel) (A's logo on back)	.25	.10	.02
☐ 17B	Fred Lynn DK COR	.35	.15	.03
☐ 18A	Ron Kittle DK ERR (Perez Steel)	.20	.08	.02
☐ 18B	Ron Kittle DK COR	.30	.12	.03
☐ 19A	Jim Clancy DK ERR (Perez Steel)	.20	.08	.02
☐ 19B	Jim Clancy DK COR	.30	.12	.03
☐ 20A	Bill Madlock DK ERR (Perez Steel)	.20	.08	.02
☐ 20B	Bill Madlock DK COR	.30	.12	.03
☐ 21A	Larry Parrish DK ERR (Perez Steel)	.20	.08	.02
☐ 21B	Larry Parrish DK COR	.30	.12	.03
☐ 22A	Eddie Murray DK ERR (Perez Steel)	1.25	.50	.12
☐ 22B	Eddie Murray DK COR	1.75	.70	.17
☐ 23A	Mike Schmidt DK ERR (Perez Steel)	2.50	1.00	.25
☐ 23B	Mike Schmidt DK COR	3.50	1.50	.35
☐ 24A	Pedro Guerrero DK ERR (Perez Steel)	.35	.15	.03
☐ 24B	Pedro Guerrero DK COR	.50	.20	.05
☐ 25A	Andre Thornton DK ERR (Perez Steel)	.20	.08	.02
☐ 25B	Andre Thornton DK COR	.30	.12	.03
☐ 26A	Wade Boggs DK ERR (Perez Steel)	3.50	1.50	.35
☐ 26B	Wade Boggs DK COR	4.50	2.00	.45
☐ 27	Joel Skinner RR	.20	.08	.02
☐ 28	Tommy Dunbar RR	.14	.06	.01
☐ 29A	Mike Stenhouse RR ERR (no number on back)	.20	.08	.02
☐ 29B	Mike Stenhouse RR COR (numbered on back)	2.50	1.00	.25
☐ 30A	Ron Darling RR ERR (no number on back)	3.00	1.25	.30
☐ 30B	Ron Darling RR COR (numbered on back)	18.00	7.50	2.50
☐ 31	Dion James RR	.20	.08	.02
☐ 32	Tony Fernandez RR	6.00	2.50	.60
☐ 33	Angel Salazar RR	.14	.06	.01
☐ 34	Kevin McReynolds RR	8.00	3.50	.80
☐ 35	Dick Schofield RR	.40	.16	.04
☐ 36	Brad Komminsk RR	.20	.08	.02
☐ 37	Tim Teufel RR	.50	.20	.05
☐ 38	Doug Frobel RR	.14	.06	.01
☐ 39	Greg Gagne RR	.75	.30	.07
☐ 40	Mike Fuentes RR	.14	.06	.01
☐ 41	Joe Carter RR	32.00	14.25	4.75
☐ 42	Mike Brown RR (Angels OF)	.14	.06	.01
☐ 43	Mike Jeffcoat RR	.20	.08	.02
☐ 44	Sid Fernandez RR	4.00	1.75	.40
☐ 45	Brian Dayett RR	.14	.06	.01
☐ 46	Chris Smith RR	.14	.06	.01
☐ 47	Eddie Murray	4.00	1.75	.40
☐ 48	Robin Yount	4.50	2.00	.45
☐ 49	Lance Parrish	.75	.30	.07
☐ 50	Jim Rice	.45	.18	.04
☐ 51	Dave Winfield	2.75	1.10	.27
☐ 52	Fernando Valenzuela	.50	.20	.05
☐ 53	George Brett	4.50	2.00	.45
☐ 54	Rickey Henderson	15.00	6.50	2.15

☐ 55 Gary Carter .... 1.25 .50 .12
☐ 56 Buddy Bell .... .20 .08 .02
☐ 57 Reggie Jackson .... 4.00 1.75 .40
☐ 58 Harold Baines .... .90 .40 .09
☐ 59 Ozzie Smith .... 3.25 1.35 .32
☐ 60 Nolan Ryan 17.00 7.25 2.50
☐ 61 Pete Rose .... 3.50 1.50 .35
☐ 62 Ron Oester .... .14 .06 .01
☐ 63 Steve Garvey .... 1.25 .50 .12
☐ 64 Jason Thompson .... .14 .06 .01
☐ 65 Jack Clark .... .40 .16 .04
☐ 66 Dale Murphy .... 2.50 1.00 .25
☐ 67 Leon Durham .... .14 .06 .01
☐ 68 Darryl Strawberry 65.00 29.00 9.75
☐ 69 Richie Zisk .... .14 .06 .01
☐ 70 Kent Hrbek .... .85 .35 .08
☐ 71 Dave Stieb .... .60 .25 .06
☐ 72 Ken Schrom .... .14 .06 .01
☐ 73 George Bell .... 3.00 1.25 .30
☐ 74 John Moses .... .20 .08 .02
☐ 75 Ed Lynch .... .14 .06 .01
☐ 76 Chuck Rainey .... .14 .06 .01
☐ 77 Biff Pocoroba .... .14 .06 .01
☐ 78 Cecilio Guante .... .14 .06 .01
☐ 79 Jim Barr .... .14 .06 .01
☐ 80 Kurt Bevacqua .... .14 .06 .01
☐ 81 Tom Foley .... .14 .06 .01
☐ 82 Joe Lefebvre .... .14 .06 .01
☐ 83 Andy Van Slyke .... 7.00 3.00 .70
☐ 84 Bob Lillis MG .... .14 .06 .01
☐ 85 Ricky Adams .... .14 .06 .01
☐ 86 Jerry Hairston .... .14 .06 .01
☐ 87 Bob James .... .14 .06 .01
☐ 88 Joe Altobelli MG .... .14 .06 .01
☐ 89 Ed Romero .... .14 .06 .01
☐ 90 John Grubb .... .14 .06 .01
☐ 91 John Henry Johnson .... .14 .06 .01
☐ 92 Juan Espino .... .14 .06 .01
☐ 93 Candy Maldonado .... .30 .12 .03
☐ 94 Andre Thornton .... .14 .06 .01
☐ 95 Onix Concepcion .... .14 .06 .01
☐ 96 Donnie Hill UER .... .25 .10 .02
(listed as P,
should be 2B)
☐ 97 Andre Dawson UER .... 4.00 1.75 .40
(wrong middle name,
should be Nolan)
☐ 98 Frank Tanana .... .20 .08 .02
☐ 99 Curt Wilkerson .... .14 .06 .01
☐ 100 Larry Gura .... .14 .06 .01
☐ 101 Dwayne Murphy .... .14 .06 .01
☐ 102 Tom Brennan .... .14 .06 .01
☐ 103 Dave Righetti .... .40 .16 .04
☐ 104 Steve Sax .... .80 .35 .08
☐ 105 Dan Petry .... .14 .06 .01
☐ 106 Cal Ripken 20.00 8.50 2.75
☐ 107 Paul Molitor UER .... .90 .40 .09
('83 stats should
say .270 BA, 608 AB,
and 164 hits)
☐ 108 Fred Lynn .... .35 .15 .03
☐ 109 Neil Allen .... .14 .06 .01
☐ 110 Joe Niekro .... .20 .08 .02
☐ 111 Steve Carlton .... 3.25 1.35 .32
☐ 112 Terry Kennedy .... .14 .06 .01
☐ 113 Bill Madlock .... .20 .08 .02
☐ 114 Chili Davis .... .30 .12 .03
☐ 115 Jim Gantner .... .14 .06 .01
☐ 116 Tom Seaver .... 5.25 2.25 .50
☐ 117 Bill Buckner .... .20 .08 .02
☐ 118 Bill Caudill .... .14 .06 .01
☐ 119 Jim Clancy .... .14 .06 .01
☐ 120 John Castino .... .14 .06 .01
☐ 121 Dave Concepcion .... .30 .12 .03
☐ 122 Greg Luzinski .... .20 .08 .02
☐ 123 Mike Boddicker .... .20 .08 .02
☐ 124 Pete Ladd .... .14 .06 .01
☐ 125 Juan Berenguer .... .14 .06 .01
☐ 126 John Montefusco .... .14 .06 .01
☐ 127 Ed Jurak .... .14 .06 .01
☐ 128 Tom Niedenfuer .... .14 .06 .01
☐ 129 Bert Blyleven .... .45 .18 .04
☐ 130 Bud Black .... .25 .10 .02
☐ 131 Gorman Heimueller .... .14 .06 .01
☐ 132 Dan Schatzeder .... .14 .06 .01
☐ 133 Ron Jackson .... .14 .06 .01
☐ 134 Tom Henke .... 1.25 .50 .12
☐ 135 Kevin Hickey .... .14 .06 .01
☐ 136 Mike Scott .... .40 .16 .04
☐ 137 Bo Diaz .... .14 .06 .01
☐ 138 Glenn Brummer .... .14 .06 .01
☐ 139 Sid Monge .... .14 .06 .01
☐ 140 Rich Gale .... .14 .06 .01
☐ 141 Brett Butler .... .75 .30 .07
☐ 142 Brian Harper .... 1.50 .60 .15
☐ 143 John Rabb .... .14 .06 .01
☐ 144 Gary Woods .... .14 .06 .01
☐ 145 Pat Putnam .... .14 .06 .01
☐ 146 Jim Acker .... .20 .08 .02
☐ 147 Mickey Hatcher .... .14 .06 .01
☐ 148 Todd Cruz .... .14 .06 .01
☐ 149 Tom Tellmann .... .14 .06 .01
☐ 150 John Wockenfuss .... .14 .06 .01
☐ 151 Wade Boggs 15.00 6.50 2.15
☐ 152 Don Baylor .... .20 .08 .02
☐ 153 Bob Welch .... .50 .20 .05
☐ 154 Alan Bannister .... .14 .06 .01
☐ 155 Willie Aikens .... .14 .06 .01
☐ 156 Jeff Burroughs .... .14 .06 .01
☐ 157 Bryan Little .... .14 .06 .01
☐ 158 Bob Boone .... .25 .10 .02
☐ 159 Dave Hostetler .... .14 .06 .01
☐ 160 Jerry Dybzinski .... .14 .06 .01
☐ 161 Mike Madden .... .14 .06 .01
☐ 162 Luis DeLeon .... .14 .06 .01
☐ 163 Willie Hernandez .... .20 .08 .02

☐ 164 Frank Pastore .14 .06 .01
☐ 165 Rick Camp .14 .06 .01
☐ 166 Lee Mazzilli .14 .06 .01
☐ 167 Scot Thompson .14 .06 .01
☐ 168 Bob Forsch .14 .06 .01
☐ 169 Mike Flanagan .20 .08 .02
☐ 170 Rick Manning .14 .06 .01
☐ 171 Chet Lemon .14 .06 .01
☐ 172 Jerry Remy .14 .06 .01
☐ 173 Ron Guidry .40 .16 .04
☐ 174 Pedro Guerrero .60 .25 .06
☐ 175 Willie Wilson .20 .08 .02
☐ 176 Carney Lansford .20 .08 .02
☐ 177 Al Oliver .20 .08 .02
☐ 178 Jim Sundberg .14 .06 .01
☐ 179 Bobby Grich .20 .08 .02
☐ 180 Rich Dotson .14 .06 .01
☐ 181 Joaquin Andujar .20 .08 .02
☐ 182 Jose Cruz .20 .08 .02
☐ 183 Mike Schmidt 13.00 5.75 1.75
☐ 184 Gary Redus .60 .25 .06
☐ 185 Garry Templeton .20 .08 .02
☐ 186 Tony Pena .25 .10 .02
☐ 187 Greg Minton .14 .06 .01
☐ 188 Phil Niekro .90 .40 .09
☐ 189 Ferguson Jenkins .90 .40 .09
☐ 190 Mookie Wilson .20 .08 .02
☐ 191 Jim Beattie .14 .06 .01
☐ 192 Gary Ward .14 .06 .01
☐ 193 Jesse Barfield .45 .18 .04
☐ 194 Pete Filson .14 .06 .01
☐ 195 Roy Lee Jackson .14 .06 .01
☐ 196 Rick Sweet .14 .06 .01
☐ 197 Jesse Orosco .14 .06 .01
☐ 198 Steve Lake .14 .06 .01
☐ 199 Ken Dayley .14 .06 .01
☐ 200 Manny Sarmiento .14 .06 .01
☐ 201 Mark Davis .30 .12 .03
☐ 202 Tim Flannery .14 .06 .01
☐ 203 Bill Scherrer .14 .06 .01
☐ 204 Al Holland .14 .06 .01
☐ 205 Dave Von Ohlen .14 .06 .01
☐ 206 Mike LaCoss .14 .06 .01
☐ 207 Juan Beniquez .14 .06 .01
☐ 208 Juan Agosto .20 .08 .02
☐ 209 Bobby Ramos .14 .06 .01
☐ 210 Al Bumbry .14 .06 .01
☐ 211 Mark Brouhard .14 .06 .01
☐ 212 Howard Bailey .14 .06 .01
☐ 213 Bruce Hurst .30 .12 .03
☐ 214 Bob Shirley .14 .06 .01
☐ 215 Pat Zachry .14 .06 .01
☐ 216 Julio Franco 5.00 2.25 .50
☐ 217 Mike Armstrong .14 .06 .01
☐ 218 Dave Beard .14 .06 .01
☐ 219 Steve Rogers .14 .06 .01
☐ 220 John Butcher .14 .06 .01
☐ 221 Mike Smithson .14 .06 .01
☐ 222 Frank White .14 .06 .01
☐ 223 Mike Heath .14 .06 .01
☐ 224 Chris Bando .14 .06 .01
☐ 225 Roy Smalley .14 .06 .01
☐ 226 Dusty Baker .20 .08 .02
☐ 227 Lou Whitaker .90 .40 .09
☐ 228 John Lowenstein .14 .06 .01
☐ 229 Ben Oglivie .14 .06 .01
☐ 230 Doug DeCinces .20 .08 .02
☐ 231 Lonnie Smith .30 .12 .03
☐ 232 Ray Knight .20 .08 .02
☐ 233 Gary Matthews .14 .06 .01
☐ 234 Juan Bonilla .14 .06 .01
☐ 235 Rod Scurry .14 .06 .01
☐ 236 Atlee Hammaker .14 .06 .01
☐ 237 Mike Caldwell .14 .06 .01
☐ 238 Keith Hernandez .50 .20 .05
☐ 239 Larry Bowa .20 .08 .02
☐ 240 Tony Bernazard .14 .06 .01
☐ 241 Damaso Garcia .14 .06 .01
☐ 242 Tom Brunansky .35 .15 .03
☐ 243 Dan Driessen .14 .06 .01
☐ 244 Ron Kittle .30 .12 .03
☐ 245 Tim Stoddard .14 .06 .01
☐ 246 Bob L. Gibson .14 .06 .01
(Brewers Pitcher)
☐ 247 Marty Castillo .14 .06 .01
☐ 248 Don Mattingly UER 60.00 27.00 9.00
("traiing" on back)
☐ 249 Jeff Newman .14 .06 .01
☐ 250 Alejandro Pena .90 .40 .09
☐ 251 Toby Harrah .14 .06 .01
☐ 252 Cesar Geronimo .14 .06 .01
☐ 253 Tom Underwood .14 .06 .01
☐ 254 Doug Flynn .14 .06 .01
☐ 255 Andy Hassler .14 .06 .01
☐ 256 Odell Jones .14 .06 .01
☐ 257 Rudy Law .14 .06 .01
☐ 258 Harry Spilman .14 .06 .01
☐ 259 Marty Bystrom .14 .06 .01
☐ 260 Dave Rucker .14 .06 .01
☐ 261 Ruppert Jones .14 .06 .01
☐ 262 Jeff R. Jones .14 .06 .01
(Reds OF)
☐ 263 Gerald Perry .60 .25 .06
☐ 264 Gene Tenace .20 .08 .02
☐ 265 Brad Wellman .14 .06 .01
☐ 266 Dickie Noles .14 .06 .01
☐ 267 Jamie Allen .14 .06 .01
☐ 268 Jim Gott .20 .08 .02
☐ 269 Ron Davis .14 .06 .01
☐ 270 Benny Ayala .14 .06 .01
☐ 271 Ned Yost .14 .06 .01
☐ 272 Dave Rozema .14 .06 .01
☐ 273 Dave Stapleton .14 .06 .01
☐ 274 Lou Piniella .25 .10 .02
☐ 275 Jose Morales .14 .06 .01
☐ 276 Broderick Perkins .14 .06 .01

☐ 277 Butch Davis .14 .06 .01
☐ 278 Tony Phillips 1.25 .50 .12
☐ 279 Jeff Reardon .90 .40 .09
☐ 280 Ken Forsch .14 .06 .01
☐ 281 Pete O'Brien .90 .40 .09
☐ 282 Tom Paciorek .14 .06 .01
☐ 283 Frank LaCorte .14 .06 .01
☐ 284 Tim Lollar .14 .06 .01
☐ 285 Greg Gross .14 .06 .01
☐ 286 Alex Trevino .14 .06 .01
☐ 287 Gene Garber .14 .06 .01
☐ 288 Dave Parker 1.25 .50 .12
☐ 289 Lee Smith .90 .40 .09
☐ 290 Dave LaPoint .14 .06 .01
☐ 291 John Shelby .40 .16 .04
☐ 292 Charlie Moore .14 .06 .01
☐ 293 Alan Trammell 2.50 1.00 .25
☐ 294 Tony Armas .14 .06 .01
☐ 295 Shane Rawley .14 .06 .01
☐ 296 Greg Brock .20 .08 .02
☐ 297 Hal McRae .20 .08 .02
☐ 298 Mike Davis .14 .06 .01
☐ 299 Tim Raines 1.25 .50 .12
☐ 300 Bucky Dent .20 .08 .02
☐ 301 Tommy John .35 .15 .03
☐ 302 Carlton Fisk 3.25 1.35 .32
☐ 303 Darrell Porter .14 .06 .01
☐ 304 Dickie Thon .20 .08 .02
☐ 305 Garry Maddox .14 .06 .01
☐ 306 Cesar Cedeno .20 .08 .02
☐ 307 Gary Lucas .14 .06 .01
☐ 308 Johnny Ray .14 .06 .01
☐ 309 Andy McGaffigan .14 .06 .01
☐ 310 Claudell Washington .20 .08 .02
☐ 311 Ryne Sandberg 25.00 11.00 3.50
☐ 312 George Foster .35 .15 .03
☐ 313 Spike Owen .50 .20 .05
☐ 314 Gary Gaetti .40 .16 .04
☐ 315 Willie Upshaw .14 .06 .01
☐ 316 Al Williams .14 .06 .01
☐ 317 Jorge Orta .14 .06 .01
☐ 318 Orlando Mercado .14 .06 .01
☐ 319 Junior Ortiz .14 .06 .01
☐ 320 Mike Proly .14 .06 .01
☐ 321 Randy Johnson UER .14 .06 .01
('72-'82 stats are
from one Randy Johnson
(Twins), '83 stats are
from the other (Braves)
☐ 322 Jim Morrison .14 .06 .01
☐ 323 Max Venable .14 .06 .01
☐ 324 Tony Gwynn 12.50 5.50 1.65
☐ 325 Duane Walker .14 .06 .01
☐ 326 Ozzie Virgil .14 .06 .01
☐ 327 Jeff Lahti .14 .06 .01
☐ 328 Bill Dawley .14 .06 .01
☐ 329 Rob Wilfong .14 .06 .01
☐ 330 Marc Hill .14 .06 .01
☐ 331 Ray Burris .14 .06 .01
☐ 332 Allan Ramirez .14 .06 .01
☐ 333 Chuck Porter .14 .06 .01
☐ 334 Wayne Krenchicki .14 .06 .01
☐ 335 Gary Allenson .14 .06 .01
☐ 336 Bobby Meacham .14 .06 .01
☐ 337 Joe Beckwith .14 .06 .01
☐ 338 Rick Sutcliffe .25 .10 .02
☐ 339 Mark Huismann .20 .08 .02
☐ 340 Tim Conroy .14 .06 .01
☐ 341 Scott Sanderson .20 .08 .02
☐ 342 Larry Biittner .14 .06 .01
☐ 343 Dave Stewart 1.75 .70 .17
☐ 344 Darryl Motley .14 .06 .01
☐ 345 Chris Codiroli .14 .06 .01
☐ 346 Rich Behenna .14 .06 .01
☐ 347 Andre Robertson .14 .06 .01
☐ 348 Mike Marshall .25 .10 .02
☐ 349 Larry Herndon .14 .06 .01
☐ 350 Rich Dauer .14 .06 .01
☐ 351 Cecil Cooper .20 .08 .02
☐ 352 Rod Carew 3.50 1.50 .35
☐ 353 Willie McGee 1.25 .50 .12
☐ 354 Phil Garner .20 .08 .02
☐ 355 Joe Morgan 1.50 .60 .15
☐ 356 Luis Salazar .14 .06 .01
☐ 357 John Candelaria .14 .06 .01
☐ 358 Bill Laskey .14 .06 .01
☐ 359 Bob McClure .14 .06 .01
☐ 360 Dave Kingman .25 .10 .02
☐ 361 Ron Cey .20 .08 .02
☐ 362 Matt Young .20 .08 .02
☐ 363 Lloyd Moseby .20 .08 .02
☐ 364 Frank Viola 2.00 .80 .20
☐ 365 Eddie Milner .14 .06 .01
☐ 366 Floyd Bannister .14 .06 .01
☐ 367 Dan Ford .14 .06 .01
☐ 368 Moose Haas .14 .06 .01
☐ 369 Doug Bair .14 .06 .01
☐ 370 Ray Fontenot .14 .06 .01
☐ 371 Luis Aponte .14 .06 .01
☐ 372 Jack Fimple .14 .06 .01
☐ 373 Neal Heaton .40 .16 .04
☐ 374 Greg Pryor .14 .06 .01
☐ 375 Wayne Gross .14 .06 .01
☐ 376 Charlie Lea .14 .06 .01
☐ 377 Steve Lubratich .14 .06 .01
☐ 378 Jon Matlack .14 .06 .01
☐ 379 Julio Cruz .14 .06 .01
☐ 380 John Mizerock .14 .06 .01
☐ 381 Kevin Gross .50 .20 .05
☐ 382 Mike Ramsey .14 .06 .01
☐ 383 Doug Gwosdz .14 .06 .01
☐ 384 Kelly Paris .14 .06 .01
☐ 385 Pete Falcone .14 .06 .01
☐ 386 Milt May .14 .06 .01
☐ 387 Fred Breining .14 .06 .01
☐ 388 Craig Lefferts .50 .20 .05

☐ 389 Steve Henderson	.14	.06	.01
☐ 390 Randy Moffitt	.14	.06	.01
☐ 391 Ron Washington	.14	.06	.01
☐ 392 Gary Roenicke	.14	.06	.01
☐ 393 Tom Candiotti	1.25	.50	.12
☐ 394 Larry Pashnick	.14	.06	.01
☐ 395 Dwight Evans	.60	.25	.06
☐ 396 Goose Gossage	.35	.15	.03
☐ 397 Derrel Thomas	.14	.06	.01
☐ 398 Juan Eichelberger	.14	.06	.01
☐ 399 Leon Roberts	.14	.06	.01
☐ 400 Dave Lopes	.20	.08	.02
☐ 401 Bill Gullickson	.20	.08	.02
☐ 402 Geoff Zahn	.14	.06	.01
☐ 403 Billy Sample	.14	.06	.01
☐ 404 Mike Squires	.14	.06	.01
☐ 405 Craig Reynolds	.14	.06	.01
☐ 406 Eric Show	.20	.08	.02
☐ 407 John Denny	.14	.06	.01
☐ 408 Dann Bilardello	.14	.06	.01
☐ 409 Bruce Benedict	.14	.06	.01
☐ 410 Kent Tekulve	.14	.06	.01
☐ 411 Mel Hall	.50	.20	.05
☐ 412 John Stuper	.14	.06	.01
☐ 413 Rick Dempsey	.14	.06	.01
☐ 414 Don Sutton	.90	.40	.09
☐ 415 Jack Morris	1.50	.60	.15
☐ 416 John Tudor	.30	.12	.03
☐ 417 Willie Randolph	.25	.10	.02
☐ 418 Jerry Reuss	.14	.06	.01
☐ 419 Don Slaught	.20	.08	.02
☐ 420 Steve McCatty	.14	.06	.01
☐ 421 Tim Wallach	.35	.15	.03
☐ 422 Larry Parrish	.14	.06	.01
☐ 423 Brian Downing	.20	.08	.02
☐ 424 Britt Burns	.14	.06	.01
☐ 425 David Green	.14	.06	.01
☐ 426 Jerry Mumphrey	.14	.06	.01
☐ 427 Ivan DeJesus	.14	.06	.01
☐ 428 Mario Soto	.14	.06	.01
☐ 429 Gene Richards	.14	.06	.01
☐ 430 Dale Berra	.14	.06	.01
☐ 431 Darrell Evans	.20	.08	.02
☐ 432 Glenn Hubbard	.14	.06	.01
☐ 433 Jody Davis	.14	.06	.01
☐ 434 Danny Heep	.14	.06	.01
☐ 435 Ed Nunez	.25	.10	.02
☐ 436 Bobby Castillo	.14	.06	.01
☐ 437 Ernie Whitt	.14	.06	.01
☐ 438 Scott Ullger	.14	.06	.01
☐ 439 Doyle Alexander	.14	.06	.01
☐ 440 Domingo Ramos	.14	.06	.01
☐ 441 Craig Swan	.14	.06	.01
☐ 442 Warren Brusstar	.14	.06	.01
☐ 443 Len Barker	.14	.06	.01
☐ 444 Mike Easler	.14	.06	.01
☐ 445 Renie Martin	.14	.06	.01
☐ 446 Dennis Rasmussen	.60	.25	.06
☐ 447 Ted Power	.20	.08	.02
☐ 448 Charles Hudson	.20	.08	.02
☐ 449 Danny Cox	.25	.10	.02
☐ 450 Kevin Bass	.20	.08	.02
☐ 451 Daryl Sconiers	.14	.06	.01
☐ 452 Scott Fletcher	.20	.08	.02
☐ 453 Bryn Smith	.20	.08	.02
☐ 454 Jim Dwyer	.14	.06	.01
☐ 455 Rob Picciolo	.14	.06	.01
☐ 456 Enos Cabell	.14	.06	.01
☐ 457 Dennis Boyd	.50	.20	.05
☐ 458 Butch Wynegar	.14	.06	.01
☐ 459 Burt Hooton	.14	.06	.01
☐ 460 Ron Hassey	.14	.06	.01
☐ 461 Danny Jackson	1.00	.40	.10
☐ 462 Bob Kearney	.14	.06	.01
☐ 463 Terry Francona	.14	.06	.01
☐ 464 Wayne Tolleson	.14	.06	.01
☐ 465 Mickey Rivers	.14	.06	.01
☐ 466 John Wathan	.14	.06	.01
☐ 467 Bill Almon	.14	.06	.01
☐ 468 George Vukovich	.14	.06	.01
☐ 469 Steve Kemp	.14	.06	.01
☐ 470 Ken Landreaux	.14	.06	.01
☐ 471 Milt Wilcox	.14	.06	.01
☐ 472 Tippy Martinez	.14	.06	.01
☐ 473 Ted Simmons	.20	.08	.02
☐ 474 Tim Foli	.14	.06	.01
☐ 475 George Hendrick	.14	.06	.01
☐ 476 Terry Puhl	.14	.06	.01
☐ 477 Von Hayes	.30	.12	.03
☐ 478 Bobby Brown	.14	.06	.01
☐ 479 Lee Lacy	.14	.06	.01
☐ 480 Joel Youngblood	.14	.06	.01
☐ 481 Jim Slaton	.14	.06	.01
☐ 482 Mike Fitzgerald	.14	.06	.01
☐ 483 Keith Moreland	.14	.06	.01
☐ 484 Ron Roenicke	.14	.06	.01
☐ 485 Luis Leal	.14	.06	.01
☐ 486 Bryan Oelkers	.14	.06	.01
☐ 487 Bruce Berenyi	.14	.06	.01
☐ 488 LaMarr Hoyt	.14	.06	.01
☐ 489 Joe Nolan	.14	.06	.01
☐ 490 Marshall Edwards	.14	.06	.01
☐ 491 Mike Laga	.14	.06	.01
☐ 492 Rick Cerone	.14	.06	.01
☐ 493 Rick Miller UER (listed as Mike on card front)	.14	.06	.01
☐ 494 Rick Honeycutt	.14	.06	.01
☐ 495 Mike Hargrove	.14	.06	.01
☐ 496 Joe Simpson	.14	.06	.01
☐ 497 Keith Atherton	.14	.06	.01
☐ 498 Chris Welsh	.14	.06	.01
☐ 499 Bruce Kison	.14	.06	.01
☐ 500 Bobby Johnson	.14	.06	.01
☐ 501 Jerry Koosman	.20	.08	.02
☐ 502 Frank DiPino	.14	.06	.01

☐ 503 Tony Perez	.65	.25	.06
☐ 504 Ken Oberkfell	.14	.06	.01
☐ 505 Mark Thurmond	.14	.06	.01
☐ 506 Joe Price	.14	.06	.01
☐ 507 Pascual Perez	.30	.12	.03
☐ 508 Marvell Wynne	.20	.08	.02
☐ 509 Mike Krukow	.14	.06	.01
☐ 510 Dick Ruthven	.14	.06	.01
☐ 511 Al Cowens	.14	.06	.01
☐ 512 Cliff Johnson	.14	.06	.01
☐ 513 Randy Bush	.25	.10	.02
☐ 514 Sammy Stewart	.14	.06	.01
☐ 515 Bill Schroeder	.14	.06	.01
☐ 516 Aurelio Lopez	.14	.06	.01
☐ 517 Mike Brown (Red Sox pitcher)	.14	.06	.01
☐ 518 Graig Nettles	.25	.10	.02
☐ 519 Dave Sax	.14	.06	.01
☐ 520 Jerry Willard	.20	.08	.02
☐ 521 Paul Splittorff	.14	.06	.01
☐ 522 Tom Burgmeier	.14	.06	.01
☐ 523 Chris Speier	.14	.06	.01
☐ 524 Bobby Clark	.14	.06	.01
☐ 525 George Wright	.14	.06	.01
☐ 526 Dennis Lamp	.14	.06	.01
☐ 527 Tony Scott	.14	.06	.01
☐ 528 Ed Whitson	.14	.06	.01
☐ 529 Ron Reed	.14	.06	.01
☐ 530 Charlie Puleo	.14	.06	.01
☐ 531 Jerry Royster	.14	.06	.01
☐ 532 Don Robinson	.14	.06	.01
☐ 533 Steve Trout	.14	.06	.01
☐ 534 Bruce Sutter	.30	.12	.03
☐ 535 Bob Horner	.25	.10	.02
☐ 536 Pat Tabler	.20	.08	.02
☐ 537 Chris Chambliss	.20	.08	.02
☐ 538 Bob Ojeda	.25	.10	.02
☐ 539 Alan Ashby	.14	.06	.01
☐ 540 Jay Johnstone	.20	.08	.02
☐ 541 Bob Dernier	.14	.06	.01
☐ 542 Brook Jacoby	1.00	.40	.10
☐ 543 U.L. Washington	.14	.06	.01
☐ 544 Danny Darwin	.14	.06	.01
☐ 545 Kiko Garcia	.14	.06	.01
☐ 546 Vance Law UER (listed as P on card front)	.14	.06	.01
☐ 547 Tug McGraw	.25	.10	.02
☐ 548 Dave Smith	.14	.06	.01
☐ 549 Len Matuszek	.14	.06	.01
☐ 550 Tom Hume	.14	.06	.01
☐ 551 Dave Dravecky	.45	.18	.04
☐ 552 Rick Rhoden	.14	.06	.01
☐ 553 Duane Kuiper	.14	.06	.01
☐ 554 Rusty Staub	.25	.10	.02
☐ 555 Bill Campbell	.14	.06	.01
☐ 556 Mike Torrez	.14	.06	.01
☐ 557 Dave Henderson	1.75	.70	.17
☐ 558 Len Whitehouse	.14	.06	.01
☐ 559 Barry Bonnell	.14	.06	.01
☐ 560 Rick Lysander	.14	.06	.01
☐ 561 Garth Iorg	.14	.06	.01
☐ 562 Bryan Clark	.14	.06	.01
☐ 563 Brian Giles	.14	.06	.01
☐ 564 Vern Ruhle	.14	.06	.01
☐ 565 Steve Bedrosian	.25	.10	.02
☐ 566 Larry McWilliams	.14	.06	.01
☐ 567 Jeff Leonard UER (listed as P on card front)	.20	.08	.02
☐ 568 Alan Wiggins	.14	.06	.01
☐ 569 Jeff Russell	.65	.25	.06
☐ 570 Salome Barojas	.14	.06	.01
☐ 571 Dane Iorg	.14	.06	.01
☐ 572 Bob Knepper	.14	.06	.01
☐ 573 Gary Lavelle	.14	.06	.01
☐ 574 Gorman Thomas	.20	.08	.02
☐ 575 Manny Trillo	.14	.06	.01
☐ 576 Jim Palmer	3.00	1.25	.30
☐ 577 Dale Murray	.14	.06	.01
☐ 578 Tom Brookens	.14	.06	.01
☐ 579 Rich Gedman	.14	.06	.01
☐ 580 Bill Doran	.90	.40	.09
☐ 581 Steve Yeager	.14	.06	.01
☐ 582 Dan Spillner	.14	.06	.01
☐ 583 Dan Quisenberry	.25	.10	.02
☐ 584 Rance Mulliniks	.14	.06	.01
☐ 585 Storm Davis	.20	.08	.02
☐ 586 Dave Schmidt	.14	.06	.01
☐ 587 Bill Russell	.20	.08	.02
☐ 588 Pat Sheridan	.20	.08	.02
☐ 589 Rafael Ramirez UER (A's on front)	.20	.08	.02
☐ 590 Bud Anderson	.14	.06	.01
☐ 591 George Frazier	.14	.06	.01
☐ 592 Lee Tunnell	.14	.06	.01
☐ 593 Kirk Gibson	1.25	.50	.12
☐ 594 Scott McGregor	.14	.06	.01
☐ 595 Bob Bailor	.14	.06	.01
☐ 596 Tommy Herr	.20	.08	.02
☐ 597 Luis Sanchez	.14	.06	.01
☐ 598 Dave Engle	.14	.06	.01
☐ 599 Craig McMurtry	.14	.06	.01
☐ 600 Carlos Diaz	.14	.06	.01
☐ 601 Tom O'Malley	.14	.06	.01
☐ 602 Nick Esasky	.40	.16	.04
☐ 603 Ron Hodges	.14	.06	.01
☐ 604 Ed VandeBerg	.14	.06	.01
☐ 605 Alfredo Griffin	.14	.06	.01
☐ 606 Glenn Hoffman	.14	.06	.01
☐ 607 Hubie Brooks	.40	.16	.04
☐ 608 Richard Barnes UER (photo actually Neal Heaton)	.14	.06	.01
☐ 609 Greg Walker	.25	.10	.02
☐ 610 Ken Singleton	.20	.08	.02

□ 611 Mark Clear	.14	.06	.01
□ 612 Buck Martinez	.14	.06	.01
□ 613 Ken Griffey	.35	.15	.03
□ 614 Reid Nichols	.14	.06	.01
□ 615 Doug Sisk	.14	.06	.01
□ 616 Bob Brenly	.14	.06	.01
□ 617 Joey McLaughlin	.14	.06	.01
□ 618 Glenn Wilson	.14	.06	.01
□ 619 Bob Stoddard	.14	.06	.01
□ 620 Lenn Sakata UER (listed as Len on card front)	.14	.06	.01
□ 621 Mike Young	.20	.08	.02
□ 622 John Stefero	.14	.06	.01
□ 623 Carmelo Martinez	.25	.10	.02
□ 624 Dave Bergman	.14	.06	.01
□ 625 Runnin' Reds UER (sic, Redbirds) David Green Willie McGee Lonnie Smith Ozzie Smith	.60	.25	.06
□ 626 Rudy May	.14	.06	.01
□ 627 Matt Keough	.14	.06	.01
□ 628 Jose DeLeon	.50	.20	.05
□ 629 Jim Essian	.20	.08	.02
□ 630 Darnell Coles	.25	.10	.02
□ 631 Mike Warren	.14	.06	.01
□ 632 Del Crandall MG	.14	.06	.01
□ 633 Dennis Martinez	.25	.10	.02
□ 634 Mike Moore	.40	.16	.04
□ 635 Lary Sorensen	.14	.06	.01
□ 636 Ricky Nelson	.14	.06	.01
□ 637 Omar Moreno	.14	.06	.01
□ 638 Charlie Hough	.14	.06	.01
□ 639 Dennis Eckersley	1.25	.50	.12
□ 640 Walt Terrell	.40	.16	.04
□ 641 Denny Walling	.14	.06	.01
□ 642 Dave Anderson	.25	.10	.02
□ 643 Jose Oquendo	.40	.16	.04
□ 644 Bob Stanley	.14	.06	.01
□ 645 Dave Geisel	.14	.06	.01
□ 646 Scott Garrelts	.50	.20	.05
□ 647 Gary Pettis	.40	.16	.04
□ 648 Duke Snider Puzzle Card	.20	.08	.02
□ 649 Johnnie LeMaster	.14	.06	.01
□ 650 Dave Collins	.14	.06	.01
□ 651 The Chicken	.35	.15	.03
□ 652 DK Checklist (unnumbered)	.20	.02	.00
□ 653 Checklist 1-130 (unnumbered)	.20	.02	.00
□ 654 Checklist 131-234 (unnumbered)	.20	.02	.00
□ 655 Checklist 235-338 (unnumbered)	.20	.02	.00
□ 656 Checklist 339-442 (unnumbered)	.20	.02	.00
□ 657 Checklist 443-546 (unnumbered)	.20	.02	.00
□ 658 Checklist 547-651 (unnumbered)	.20	.02	.00
□ A Living Legends A Gaylord Perry Rollie Fingers	5.50	2.50	.55
□ B Living Legends B Carl Yastrzemski Johnny Bench	8.50	3.75	.85

1985 Donruss

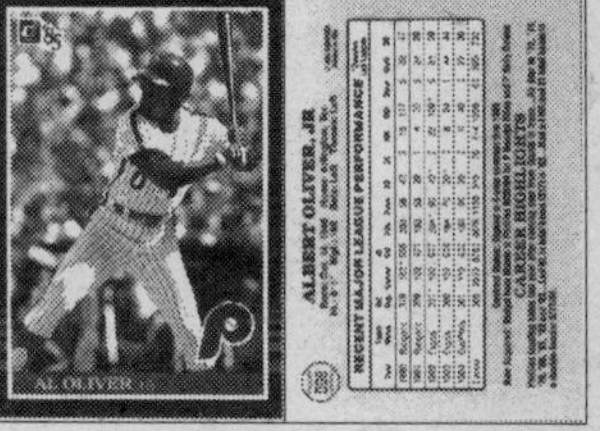

The cards in this 660-card set measure 2 1/2" by 3 1/2". The 1985 Donruss regular issue cards have fronts that feature jet black borders on which orange lines have been placed. The fronts contain the standard team logo, player's name, position, and Donruss logo. The cards were distributed with puzzle pieces from a Dick Perez rendition of Lou Gehrig. The first 26 cards of the set feature Diamond Kings (DK), for the fourth year in a row; the artwork on the Diamond Kings was again produced by the Perez-Steele Galleries. Cards 27-46 feature Rated Rookies (RR). The unnumbered checklist cards are arbitrarily numbered below as numbers 654 through 660. This set is noted for containing the Rookie Cards of Roger Clemens, Alvin Davis, Eric Davis, Shawon Dunston, Dwight Gooden, Orel Hershiser, Jimmy Key, Mark Langston, Terry Pendleton, Kirby Puckett, Jose Rijo, Bret Saberhagen, and Danny Tartabull.

	MINT	EXC	G-VG
COMPLETE SET (660)	180.00	80.00	27.00
COMMON PLAYER (1-660)	.08	.03	.01
☐ 1 Ryne Sandberg DK	3.00	.75	.15
☐ 2 Doug DeCinces DK	.12	.05	.01
☐ 3 Richard Dotson DK	.12	.05	.01
☐ 4 Bert Blyleven DK	.15	.06	.01
☐ 5 Lou Whitaker DK	.17	.07	.01
☐ 6 Dan Quisenberry DK	.15	.06	.01
☐ 7 Don Mattingly DK	3.50	1.50	.35
☐ 8 Carney Lansford DK	.12	.05	.01
☐ 9 Frank Tanana DK	.12	.05	.01
☐ 10 Willie Upshaw DK	.12	.05	.01
☐ 11 Claudell Washington DK	.12	.05	.01
☐ 12 Mike Marshall DK	.12	.05	.01
☐ 13 Joaquin Andujar DK	.12	.05	.01
☐ 14 Cal Ripken DK	3.00	1.25	.30
☐ 15 Jim Rice DK	.17	.07	.01
☐ 16 Don Sutton DK	.17	.07	.01
☐ 17 Frank Viola DK	.30	.12	.03
☐ 18 Alvin Davis DK	.35	.15	.03
☐ 19 Mario Soto DK	.12	.05	.01
☐ 20 Jose Cruz DK	.12	.05	.01
☐ 21 Charlie Lea DK	.12	.05	.01
☐ 22 Jesse Orosco DK	.12	.05	.01
☐ 23 Juan Samuel DK	.25	.10	.02
☐ 24 Tony Pena DK	.12	.05	.01
☐ 25 Tony Gwynn DK	1.25	.50	.12
☐ 26 Bob Brenly DK	.12	.05	.01
☐ 27 Danny Tartabull RR	7.50	3.25	.75
☐ 28 Mike Bielecki RR	.40	.16	.04
☐ 29 Steve Lyons RR	.35	.15	.03
☐ 30 Jeff Reed RR	.12	.05	.01
☐ 31 Tony Brewer RR	.08	.03	.01
☐ 32 John Morris RR	.15	.06	.01
☐ 33 Daryl Boston RR	.45	.18	.04
☐ 34 Al Pulido RR	.08	.03	.01
☐ 35 Steve Kiefer RR	.08	.03	.01
☐ 36 Larry Sheets RR	.15	.06	.01
☐ 37 Scott Bradley RR	.17	.07	.01
☐ 38 Calvin Schiraldi RR	.15	.06	.01
☐ 39 Shawon Dunston RR	5.50	2.50	.55
☐ 40 Charlie Mitchell RR	.08	.03	.01
☐ 41 Billy Hatcher RR	.90	.40	.09
☐ 42 Russ Stephans RR	.08	.03	.01
☐ 43 Alejandro Sanchez RR	.08	.03	.01
☐ 44 Steve Jeltz RR	.12	.05	.01
☐ 45 Jim Traber RR	.15	.06	.01
☐ 46 Doug Loman RR	.08	.03	.01
☐ 47 Eddie Murray	1.25	.50	.12
☐ 48 Robin Yount	1.50	.60	.15
☐ 49 Lance Parrish	.25	.10	.02
☐ 50 Jim Rice	.20	.08	.02
☐ 51 Dave Winfield	.85	.35	.08
☐ 52 Fernando Valenzuela	.17	.07	.01
☐ 53 George Brett	1.50	.60	.15
☐ 54 Dave Kingman	.15	.06	.01
☐ 55 Gary Carter	.40	.16	.04
☐ 56 Buddy Bell	.12	.05	.01
☐ 57 Reggie Jackson	1.25	.50	.12
☐ 58 Harold Baines	.35	.15	.03
☐ 59 Ozzie Smith	1.00	.40	.10
☐ 60 Nolan Ryan	6.50	2.75	.65
☐ 61 Mike Schmidt	3.50	1.50	.35
☐ 62 Dave Parker	.35	.15	.03
☐ 63 Tony Gwynn	4.25	1.75	.42
☐ 64 Tony Pena	.12	.05	.01
☐ 65 Jack Clark	.25	.10	.02
☐ 66 Dale Murphy	.75	.30	.07
☐ 67 Ryne Sandberg	7.00	3.00	.70
☐ 68 Keith Hernandez	.25	.10	.02
☐ 69 Alvin Davis	1.75	.70	.17
☐ 70 Kent Hrbek	.35	.15	.03
☐ 71 Willie Upshaw	.08	.03	.01
☐ 72 Dave Engle	.08	.03	.01
☐ 73 Alfredo Griffin	.08	.03	.01
☐ 74A Jack Perconte (Career Highlights takes four lines)	.12	.05	.01
☐ 74B Jack Perconte (Career Highlights takes three lines)	.12	.05	.01
☐ 75 Jesse Orosco	.08	.03	.01
☐ 76 Jody Davis	.08	.03	.01
☐ 77 Bob Horner	.12	.05	.01
☐ 78 Larry McWilliams	.08	.03	.01
☐ 79 Joel Youngblood	.08	.03	.01
☐ 80 Alan Wiggins	.08	.03	.01
☐ 81 Ron Oester	.08	.03	.01
☐ 82 Ozzie Virgil	.08	.03	.01
☐ 83 Ricky Horton	.15	.06	.01
☐ 84 Bill Doran	.15	.06	.01
☐ 85 Rod Carew	1.00	.40	.10
☐ 86 LaMarr Hoyt	.08	.03	.01
☐ 87 Tim Wallach	.15	.06	.01
☐ 88 Mike Flanagan	.12	.05	.01
☐ 89 Jim Sundberg	.08	.03	.01
☐ 90 Chet Lemon	.08	.03	.01
☐ 91 Bob Stanley	.08	.03	.01
☐ 92 Willie Randolph	.12	.05	.01
☐ 93 Bill Russell	.12	.05	.01
☐ 94 Julio Franco	1.25	.50	.12
☐ 95 Dan Quisenberry	.12	.05	.01
☐ 96 Bill Caudill	.08	.03	.01
☐ 97 Bill Gullickson	.12	.05	.01
☐ 98 Danny Darwin	.08	.03	.01
☐ 99 Curtis Wilkerson	.08	.03	.01
☐ 100 Bud Black	.12	.05	.01
☐ 101 Tony Phillips	.08	.03	.01
☐ 102 Tony Bernazard	.08	.03	.01
☐ 103 Jay Howell	.12	.05	.01
☐ 104 Burt Hooton	.08	.03	.01
☐ 105 Milt Wilcox	.08	.03	.01
☐ 106 Rich Dauer	.08	.03	.01
☐ 107 Don Sutton	.35	.15	.03

Card			
☐ 108 Mike Witt	.08	.03	.01
☐ 109 Bruce Sutter	.15	.06	.01
☐ 110 Enos Cabell	.08	.03	.01
☐ 111 John Denny	.08	.03	.01
☐ 112 Dave Dravecky	.15	.06	.01
☐ 113 Marvell Wynne	.08	.03	.01
☐ 114 Johnnie LeMaster	.08	.03	.01
☐ 115 Chuck Porter	.08	.03	.01
☐ 116 John Gibbons	.08	.03	.01
☐ 117 Keith Moreland	.08	.03	.01
☐ 118 Darnell Coles	.08	.03	.01
☐ 119 Dennis Lamp	.08	.03	.01
☐ 120 Ron Davis	.08	.03	.01
☐ 121 Nick Esasky	.12	.05	.01
☐ 122 Vance Law	.08	.03	.01
☐ 123 Gary Roenicke	.08	.03	.01
☐ 124 Bill Schroeder	.08	.03	.01
☐ 125 Dave Rozema	.08	.03	.01
☐ 126 Bobby Meacham	.08	.03	.01
☐ 127 Marty Barrett	.12	.05	.01
☐ 128 R.J. Reynolds	.20	.08	.02
☐ 129 Ernie Camacho UER (photo actually Rich Thompson)	.08	.03	.01
☐ 130 Jorge Orta	.08	.03	.01
☐ 131 Lary Sorensen	.08	.03	.01
☐ 132 Terry Francona	.08	.03	.01
☐ 133 Fred Lynn	.17	.07	.01
☐ 134 Bob Jones	.08	.03	.01
☐ 135 Jerry Hairston	.08	.03	.01
☐ 136 Kevin Bass	.12	.05	.01
☐ 137 Garry Maddox	.08	.03	.01
☐ 138 Dave LaPoint	.08	.03	.01
☐ 139 Kevin McReynolds	.90	.40	.09
☐ 140 Wayne Krenchicki	.08	.03	.01
☐ 141 Rafael Ramirez	.08	.03	.01
☐ 142 Rod Scurry	.08	.03	.01
☐ 143 Greg Minton	.08	.03	.01
☐ 144 Tim Stoddard	.08	.03	.01
☐ 145 Steve Henderson	.08	.03	.01
☐ 146 George Bell	.90	.40	.09
☐ 147 Dave Meier	.08	.03	.01
☐ 148 Sammy Stewart	.08	.03	.01
☐ 149 Mark Brouhard	.08	.03	.01
☐ 150 Larry Herndon	.08	.03	.01
☐ 151 Oil Can Boyd	.12	.05	.01
☐ 152 Brian Dayett	.08	.03	.01
☐ 153 Tom Niedenfuer	.08	.03	.01
☐ 154 Brook Jacoby	.15	.06	.01
☐ 155 Onix Concepcion	.08	.03	.01
☐ 156 Tim Conroy	.08	.03	.01
☐ 157 Joe Hesketh	.30	.12	.03
☐ 158 Brian Downing	.12	.05	.01
☐ 159 Tommy Dunbar	.08	.03	.01
☐ 160 Marc Hill	.08	.03	.01
☐ 161 Phil Garner	.12	.05	.01
☐ 162 Jerry Davis	.08	.03	.01
☐ 163 Bill Campbell	.08	.03	.01
☐ 164 John Franco	1.50	.60	.15
☐ 165 Len Barker	.08	.03	.01
☐ 166 Benny Distefano	.08	.03	.01
☐ 167 George Frazier	.08	.03	.01
☐ 168 Tito Landrum	.08	.03	.01
☐ 169 Cal Ripken	7.00	3.00	.70
☐ 170 Cecil Cooper	.12	.05	.01
☐ 171 Alan Trammell	.60	.25	.06
☐ 172 Wade Boggs	5.00	2.25	.50
☐ 173 Don Baylor	.15	.06	.01
☐ 174 Pedro Guerrero	.25	.10	.02
☐ 175 Frank White	.08	.03	.01
☐ 176 Rickey Henderson	5.00	2.25	.50
☐ 177 Charlie Lea	.08	.03	.01
☐ 178 Pete O'Brien	.12	.05	.01
☐ 179 Doug DeCinces	.08	.03	.01
☐ 180 Ron Kittle	.12	.05	.01
☐ 181 George Hendrick	.08	.03	.01
☐ 182 Joe Niekro	.12	.05	.01
☐ 183 Juan Samuel	1.00	.40	.10
☐ 184 Mario Soto	.08	.03	.01
☐ 185 Goose Gossage	.15	.06	.01
☐ 186 Johnny Ray	.08	.03	.01
☐ 187 Bob Brenly	.08	.03	.01
☐ 188 Craig McMurtry	.08	.03	.01
☐ 189 Leon Durham	.08	.03	.01
☐ 190 Dwight Gooden	13.00	5.75	1.75
☐ 191 Barry Bonnell	.08	.03	.01
☐ 192 Tim Teufel	.12	.05	.01
☐ 193 Dave Stieb	.17	.07	.01
☐ 194 Mickey Hatcher	.08	.03	.01
☐ 195 Jesse Barfield	.17	.07	.01
☐ 196 Al Cowens	.08	.03	.01
☐ 197 Hubie Brooks	.15	.06	.01
☐ 198 Steve Trout	.08	.03	.01
☐ 199 Glenn Hubbard	.08	.03	.01
☐ 200 Bill Madlock	.12	.05	.01
☐ 201 Jeff Robinson (Giants pitcher)	.15	.06	.01
☐ 202 Eric Show	.08	.03	.01
☐ 203 Dave Concepcion	.12	.05	.01
☐ 204 Ivan DeJesus	.08	.03	.01
☐ 205 Neil Allen	.08	.03	.01
☐ 206 Jerry Mumphrey	.08	.03	.01
☐ 207 Mike Brown (Angels OF)	.08	.03	.01
☐ 208 Carlton Fisk	1.00	.40	.10
☐ 209 Bryn Smith	.12	.05	.01
☐ 210 Tippy Martinez	.08	.03	.01
☐ 211 Dion James	.08	.03	.01
☐ 212 Willie Hernandez	.08	.03	.01
☐ 213 Mike Easler	.08	.03	.01
☐ 214 Ron Guidry	.17	.07	.01
☐ 215 Rick Honeycutt	.08	.03	.01
☐ 216 Brett Butler	.25	.10	.02
☐ 217 Larry Gura	.08	.03	.01
☐ 218 Ray Burris	.08	.03	.01
☐ 219 Steve Rogers	.08	.03	.01

☐ 220	Frank Tanana UER (Bats Left listed twice on card back)	.12	.05	.01
☐ 221	Ned Yost	.08	.03	.01
☐ 222	Bret Saberhagen UER (18 career IP on back)	8.00	3.50	.80
☐ 223	Mike Davis	.08	.03	.01
☐ 224	Bert Blyleven	.25	.10	.02
☐ 225	Steve Kemp	.08	.03	.01
☐ 226	Jerry Reuss	.08	.03	.01
☐ 227	Darrell Evans UER (80 homers in 1980)	.15	.06	.01
☐ 228	Wayne Gross	.08	.03	.01
☐ 229	Jim Gantner	.08	.03	.01
☐ 230	Bob Boone	.12	.05	.01
☐ 231	Lonnie Smith	.15	.06	.01
☐ 232	Frank DiPino	.08	.03	.01
☐ 233	Jerry Koosman	.12	.05	.01
☐ 234	Graig Nettles	.15	.06	.01
☐ 235	John Tudor	.15	.06	.01
☐ 236	John Rabb	.08	.03	.01
☐ 237	Rick Manning	.08	.03	.01
☐ 238	Mike Fitzgerald	.08	.03	.01
☐ 239	Gary Matthews	.08	.03	.01
☐ 240	Jim Presley	.20	.08	.02
☐ 241	Dave Collins	.08	.03	.01
☐ 242	Gary Gaetti	.15	.06	.01
☐ 243	Dann Bilardello	.08	.03	.01
☐ 244	Rudy Law	.08	.03	.01
☐ 245	John Lowenstein	.08	.03	.01
☐ 246	Tom Tellmann	.08	.03	.01
☐ 247	Howard Johnson	2.75	1.10	.27
☐ 248	Ray Fontenot	.08	.03	.01
☐ 249	Tony Armas	.08	.03	.01
☐ 250	Candy Maldonado	.15	.06	.01
☐ 251	Mike Jeffcoat	.12	.05	.01
☐ 252	Dane Iorg	.08	.03	.01
☐ 253	Bruce Bochte	.08	.03	.01
☐ 254	Pete Rose	1.25	.50	.12
☐ 255	Don Aase	.08	.03	.01
☐ 256	George Wright	.08	.03	.01
☐ 257	Britt Burns	.08	.03	.01
☐ 258	Mike Scott	.20	.08	.02
☐ 259	Len Matuszek	.08	.03	.01
☐ 260	Dave Rucker	.08	.03	.01
☐ 261	Craig Lefferts	.12	.05	.01
☐ 262	Jay Tibbs	.08	.03	.01
☐ 263	Bruce Benedict	.08	.03	.01
☐ 264	Don Robinson	.08	.03	.01
☐ 265	Gary Lavelle	.08	.03	.01
☐ 266	Scott Sanderson	.12	.05	.01
☐ 267	Matt Young	.08	.03	.01
☐ 268	Ernie Whitt	.08	.03	.01
☐ 269	Houston Jimenez	.08	.03	.01
☐ 270	Ken Dixon	.08	.03	.01
☐ 271	Pete Ladd	.08	.03	.01
☐ 272	Juan Berenguer	.08	.03	.01
☐ 273	Roger Clemens	37.50	15.00	4.00
☐ 274	Rick Cerone	.08	.03	.01
☐ 275	Dave Anderson	.08	.03	.01
☐ 276	George Vukovich	.08	.03	.01
☐ 277	Greg Pryor	.08	.03	.01
☐ 278	Mike Warren	.08	.03	.01
☐ 279	Bob James	.08	.03	.01
☐ 280	Bobby Grich	.12	.05	.01
☐ 281	Mike Mason	.08	.03	.01
☐ 282	Ron Reed	.08	.03	.01
☐ 283	Alan Ashby	.08	.03	.01
☐ 284	Mark Thurmond	.08	.03	.01
☐ 285	Joe Lefebvre	.08	.03	.01
☐ 286	Ted Power	.08	.03	.01
☐ 287	Chris Chambliss	.12	.05	.01
☐ 288	Lee Tunnell	.08	.03	.01
☐ 289	Rich Bordi	.08	.03	.01
☐ 290	Glenn Brummer	.08	.03	.01
☐ 291	Mike Boddicker	.08	.03	.01
☐ 292	Rollie Fingers	.35	.15	.03
☐ 293	Lou Whitaker	.35	.15	.03
☐ 294	Dwight Evans	.25	.10	.02
☐ 295	Don Mattingly	11.00	5.00	1.35
☐ 296	Mike Marshall	.12	.05	.01
☐ 297	Willie Wilson	.12	.05	.01
☐ 298	Mike Heath	.08	.03	.01
☐ 299	Tim Raines	.40	.16	.04
☐ 300	Larry Parrish	.08	.03	.01
☐ 301	Geoff Zahn	.08	.03	.01
☐ 302	Rich Dotson	.08	.03	.01
☐ 303	David Green	.08	.03	.01
☐ 304	Jose Cruz	.12	.05	.01
☐ 305	Steve Carlton	.90	.40	.09
☐ 306	Gary Redus	.12	.05	.01
☐ 307	Steve Garvey	.50	.20	.05
☐ 308	Jose DeLeon	.08	.03	.01
☐ 309	Randy Lerch	.08	.03	.01
☐ 310	Claudell Washington	.08	.03	.01
☐ 311	Lee Smith	.40	.16	.04
☐ 312	Darryl Strawberry	12.50	5.50	1.65
☐ 313	Jim Beattie	.08	.03	.01
☐ 314	John Butcher	.08	.03	.01
☐ 315	Damaso Garcia	.08	.03	.01
☐ 316	Mike Smithson	.08	.03	.01
☐ 317	Luis Leal	.08	.03	.01
☐ 318	Ken Phelps	.12	.05	.01
☐ 319	Wally Backman	.08	.03	.01
☐ 320	Ron Cey	.12	.05	.01
☐ 321	Brad Komminsk	.08	.03	.01
☐ 322	Jason Thompson	.08	.03	.01
☐ 323	Frank Williams	.08	.03	.01
☐ 324	Tim Lollar	.08	.03	.01
☐ 325	Eric Davis	13.50	6.00	1.85
☐ 326	Von Hayes	.15	.06	.01
☐ 327	Andy Van Slyke	.90	.40	.09
☐ 328	Craig Reynolds	.08	.03	.01
☐ 329	Dick Schofield	.12	.05	.01
☐ 330	Scott Fletcher	.08	.03	.01
☐ 331	Jeff Reardon	.40	.16	.04

☐ 332	Rick Dempsey	.08	.03	.01
☐ 333	Ben Oglivie	.08	.03	.01
☐ 334	Dan Petry	.08	.03	.01
☐ 335	Jackie Gutierrez	.08	.03	.01
☐ 336	Dave Righetti	.15	.06	.01
☐ 337	Alejandro Pena	.15	.06	.01
☐ 338	Mel Hall	.17	.07	.01
☐ 339	Pat Sheridan	.08	.03	.01
☐ 340	Keith Atherton	.08	.03	.01
☐ 341	David Palmer	.08	.03	.01
☐ 342	Gary Ward	.08	.03	.01
☐ 343	Dave Stewart	.60	.25	.06
☐ 344	Mark Gubicza	.75	.30	.07
☐ 345	Carney Lansford	.15	.06	.01
☐ 346	Jerry Willard	.08	.03	.01
☐ 347	Ken Griffey	.17	.07	.01
☐ 348	Franklin Stubbs	.50	.20	.05
☐ 349	Aurelio Lopez	.08	.03	.01
☐ 350	Al Bumbry	.08	.03	.01
☐ 351	Charlie Moore	.08	.03	.01
☐ 352	Luis Sanchez	.08	.03	.01
☐ 353	Darrell Porter	.08	.03	.01
☐ 354	Bill Dawley	.08	.03	.01
☐ 355	Charles Hudson	.08	.03	.01
☐ 356	Garry Templeton	.12	.05	.01
☐ 357	Cecilio Guante	.08	.03	.01
☐ 358	Jeff Leonard	.08	.03	.01
☐ 359	Paul Molitor	.40	.16	.04
☐ 360	Ron Gardenhire	.08	.03	.01
☐ 361	Larry Bowa	.12	.05	.01
☐ 362	Bob Kearney	.08	.03	.01
☐ 363	Garth Iorg	.08	.03	.01
☐ 364	Tom Brunansky	.15	.06	.01
☐ 365	Brad Gulden	.08	.03	.01
☐ 366	Greg Walker	.08	.03	.01
☐ 367	Mike Young	.08	.03	.01
☐ 368	Rick Waits	.08	.03	.01
☐ 369	Doug Bair	.08	.03	.01
☐ 370	Bob Shirley	.08	.03	.01
☐ 371	Bob Ojeda	.12	.05	.01
☐ 372	Bob Welch	.20	.08	.02
☐ 373	Neal Heaton	.08	.03	.01
☐ 374	Danny Jackson UER (photo actually Frank Wills)	.15	.06	.01
☐ 375	Donnie Hill	.08	.03	.01
☐ 376	Mike Stenhouse	.08	.03	.01
☐ 377	Bruce Kison	.08	.03	.01
☐ 378	Wayne Tolleson	.08	.03	.01
☐ 379	Floyd Bannister	.08	.03	.01
☐ 380	Vern Ruhle	.08	.03	.01
☐ 381	Tim Corcoran	.08	.03	.01
☐ 382	Kurt Kepshire	.08	.03	.01
☐ 383	Bobby Brown	.08	.03	.01
☐ 384	Dave Van Gorder	.08	.03	.01
☐ 385	Rick Mahler	.08	.03	.01
☐ 386	Lee Mazzilli	.08	.03	.01
☐ 387	Bill Laskey	.08	.03	.01
☐ 388	Thad Bosley	.08	.03	.01
☐ 389	Al Chambers	.08	.03	.01
☐ 390	Tony Fernandez	.60	.25	.06
☐ 391	Ron Washington	.08	.03	.01
☐ 392	Bill Swaggerty	.08	.03	.01
☐ 393	Bob L. Gibson	.08	.03	.01
☐ 394	Marty Castillo	.08	.03	.01
☐ 395	Steve Crawford	.08	.03	.01
☐ 396	Clay Christiansen	.08	.03	.01
☐ 397	Bob Bailor	.08	.03	.01
☐ 398	Mike Hargrove	.08	.03	.01
☐ 399	Charlie Leibrandt	.08	.03	.01
☐ 400	Tom Burgmeier	.08	.03	.01
☐ 401	Razor Shines	.08	.03	.01
☐ 402	Rob Wilfong	.08	.03	.01
☐ 403	Tom Henke	.17	.07	.01
☐ 404	Al Jones	.08	.03	.01
☐ 405	Mike LaCoss	.08	.03	.01
☐ 406	Luis DeLeon	.08	.03	.01
☐ 407	Greg Gross	.08	.03	.01
☐ 408	Tom Hume	.08	.03	.01
☐ 409	Rick Camp	.08	.03	.01
☐ 410	Milt May	.08	.03	.01
☐ 411	Henry Cotto	.15	.06	.01
☐ 412	David Von Ohlen	.08	.03	.01
☐ 413	Scott McGregor	.08	.03	.01
☐ 414	Ted Simmons	.12	.05	.01
☐ 415	Jack Morris	.60	.25	.06
☐ 416	Bill Buckner	.12	.05	.01
☐ 417	Butch Wynegar	.08	.03	.01
☐ 418	Steve Sax	.35	.15	.03
☐ 419	Steve Balboni	.08	.03	.01
☐ 420	Dwayne Murphy	.08	.03	.01
☐ 421	Andre Dawson	1.00	.40	.10
☐ 422	Charlie Hough	.08	.03	.01
☐ 423	Tommy John	.17	.07	.01
☐ 424A	Tom Seaver ERR (photo actually Floyd Bannister)	1.25	.50	.12
☐ 424B	Tom Seaver COR	25.00	11.00	3.50
☐ 425	Tommy Herr	.12	.05	.01
☐ 426	Terry Puhl	.08	.03	.01
☐ 427	Al Holland	.08	.03	.01
☐ 428	Eddie Milner	.08	.03	.01
☐ 429	Terry Kennedy	.08	.03	.01
☐ 430	John Candelaria	.08	.03	.01
☐ 431	Manny Trillo	.08	.03	.01
☐ 432	Ken Oberkfell	.08	.03	.01
☐ 433	Rick Sutcliffe	.12	.05	.01
☐ 434	Ron Darling	.30	.12	.03
☐ 435	Spike Owen	.08	.03	.01
☐ 436	Frank Viola	.60	.25	.06
☐ 437	Lloyd Moseby	.12	.05	.01
☐ 438	Kirby Puckett	30.00	13.50	4.50
☐ 439	Jim Clancy	.08	.03	.01
☐ 440	Mike Moore	.12	.05	.01
☐ 441	Doug Sisk	.08	.03	.01
☐ 442	Dennis Eckersley	.40	.16	.04

□ 443 Gerald Perry	.12	.05	.01
□ 444 Dale Berra	.08	.03	.01
□ 445 Dusty Baker	.12	.05	.01
□ 446 Ed Whitson	.08	.03	.01
□ 447 Cesar Cedeno	.12	.05	.01
□ 448 Rick Schu	.12	.05	.01
□ 449 Joaquin Andujar	.12	.05	.01
□ 450 Mark Bailey	.08	.03	.01
□ 451 Ron Romanick	.08	.03	.01
□ 452 Julio Cruz	.08	.03	.01
□ 453 Miguel Dilone	.08	.03	.01
□ 454 Storm Davis	.08	.03	.01
□ 455 Jaime Cocanower	.08	.03	.01
□ 456 Barbaro Garbey	.08	.03	.01
□ 457 Rich Gedman	.08	.03	.01
□ 458 Phil Niekro	.30	.12	.03
□ 459 Mike Scioscia	.12	.05	.01
□ 460 Pat Tabler	.08	.03	.01
□ 461 Darryl Motley	.08	.03	.01
□ 462 Chris Codiroli	.08	.03	.01
□ 463 Doug Flynn	.08	.03	.01
□ 464 Billy Sample	.08	.03	.01
□ 465 Mickey Rivers	.08	.03	.01
□ 466 John Wathan	.08	.03	.01
□ 467 Bill Krueger	.08	.03	.01
□ 468 Andre Thornton	.12	.05	.01
□ 469 Rex Hudler	.30	.12	.03
□ 470 Sid Bream	.75	.30	.07
□ 471 Kirk Gibson	.40	.16	.04
□ 472 John Shelby	.08	.03	.01
□ 473 Moose Haas	.08	.03	.01
□ 474 Doug Corbett	.08	.03	.01
□ 475 Willie McGee	.60	.25	.06
□ 476 Bob Knepper	.08	.03	.01
□ 477 Kevin Gross	.08	.03	.01
□ 478 Carmelo Martinez	.08	.03	.01
□ 479 Kent Tekulve	.08	.03	.01
□ 480 Chili Davis	.20	.08	.02
□ 481 Bobby Clark	.08	.03	.01
□ 482 Mookie Wilson	.12	.05	.01
□ 483 Dave Owen	.08	.03	.01
□ 484 Ed Nunez	.08	.03	.01
□ 485 Rance Mulliniks	.08	.03	.01
□ 486 Ken Schrom	.08	.03	.01
□ 487 Jeff Russell	.12	.05	.01
□ 488 Tom Paciorek	.08	.03	.01
□ 489 Dan Ford	.08	.03	.01
□ 490 Mike Caldwell	.08	.03	.01
□ 491 Scottie Earl	.08	.03	.01
□ 492 Jose Rijo	2.50	1.00	.25
□ 493 Bruce Hurst	.15	.06	.01
□ 494 Ken Landreaux	.08	.03	.01
□ 495 Mike Fischlin	.08	.03	.01
□ 496 Don Slaught	.08	.03	.01
□ 497 Steve McCatty	.08	.03	.01
□ 498 Gary Lucas	.08	.03	.01
□ 499 Gary Pettis	.12	.05	.01
□ 500 Marvis Foley	.08	.03	.01
□ 501 Mike Squires	.08	.03	.01
□ 502 Jim Pankovits	.08	.03	.01
□ 503 Luis Aguayo	.08	.03	.01
□ 504 Ralph Citarella	.08	.03	.01
□ 505 Bruce Bochy	.08	.03	.01
□ 506 Bob Owchinko	.08	.03	.01
□ 507 Pascual Perez	.12	.05	.01
□ 508 Lee Lacy	.08	.03	.01
□ 509 Atlee Hammaker	.08	.03	.01
□ 510 Bob Dernier	.08	.03	.01
□ 511 Ed VandeBerg	.08	.03	.01
□ 512 Cliff Johnson	.08	.03	.01
□ 513 Len Whitehouse	.08	.03	.01
□ 514 Dennis Martinez	.12	.05	.01
□ 515 Ed Romero	.08	.03	.01
□ 516 Rusty Kuntz	.08	.03	.01
□ 517 Rick Miller	.08	.03	.01
□ 518 Dennis Rasmussen	.12	.05	.01
□ 519 Steve Yeager	.08	.03	.01
□ 520 Chris Bando	.08	.03	.01
□ 521 U.L. Washington	.08	.03	.01
□ 522 Curt Young	.15	.06	.01
□ 523 Angel Salazar	.08	.03	.01
□ 524 Curt Kaufman	.08	.03	.01
□ 525 Odell Jones	.08	.03	.01
□ 526 Juan Agosto	.08	.03	.01
□ 527 Denny Walling	.08	.03	.01
□ 528 Andy Hawkins	.15	.06	.01
□ 529 Sixto Lezcano	.08	.03	.01
□ 530 Skeeter Barnes	.15	.06	.01
□ 531 Randy Johnson	.08	.03	.01
□ 532 Jim Morrison	.08	.03	.01
□ 533 Warren Brusstar	.08	.03	.01
□ 534A Jeff Pendleton ERR (wrong first name)	4.50	2.00	.45
□ 534B Terry Pendleton COR	12.00	5.25	1.50
□ 535 Vic Rodriguez	.12	.05	.01
□ 536 Bob McClure	.08	.03	.01
□ 537 Dave Bergman	.08	.03	.01
□ 538 Mark Clear	.08	.03	.01
□ 539 Mike Pagliarulo	.75	.30	.07
□ 540 Terry Whitfield	.08	.03	.01
□ 541 Joe Beckwith	.08	.03	.01
□ 542 Jeff Burroughs	.08	.03	.01
□ 543 Dan Schatzeder	.08	.03	.01
□ 544 Donnie Scott	.08	.03	.01
□ 545 Jim Slaton	.08	.03	.01
□ 546 Greg Luzinski	.12	.05	.01
□ 547 Mark Salas	.08	.03	.01
□ 548 Dave Smith	.08	.03	.01
□ 549 John Wockenfuss	.08	.03	.01
□ 550 Frank Pastore	.08	.03	.01
□ 551 Tim Flannery	.08	.03	.01
□ 552 Rick Rhoden	.08	.03	.01
□ 553 Mark Davis	.15	.06	.01
□ 554 Jeff Dedmon	.08	.03	.01
□ 555 Gary Woods	.08	.03	.01
□ 556 Danny Heep	.08	.03	.01

☐ 557	Mark Langston	4.50	2.00	.45
☐ 558	Darrell Brown	.08	.03	.01
☐ 559	Jimmy Key	2.00	.80	.20
☐ 560	Rick Lysander	.08	.03	.01
☐ 561	Doyle Alexander	.08	.03	.01
☐ 562	Mike Stanton	.08	.03	.01
☐ 563	Sid Fernandez	.35	.15	.03
☐ 564	Richie Hebner	.08	.03	.01
☐ 565	Alex Trevino	.08	.03	.01
☐ 566	Brian Harper	.30	.12	.03
☐ 567	Dan Gladden	.60	.25	.06
☐ 568	Luis Salazar	.08	.03	.01
☐ 569	Tom Foley	.08	.03	.01
☐ 570	Larry Andersen	.08	.03	.01
☐ 571	Danny Cox	.08	.03	.01
☐ 572	Joe Sambito	.08	.03	.01
☐ 573	Juan Beniquez	.08	.03	.01
☐ 574	Joel Skinner	.08	.03	.01
☐ 575	Randy St.Claire	.08	.03	.01
☐ 576	Floyd Rayford	.08	.03	.01
☐ 577	Roy Howell	.08	.03	.01
☐ 578	John Grubb	.08	.03	.01
☐ 579	Ed Jurak	.08	.03	.01
☐ 580	John Montefusco	.08	.03	.01
☐ 581	Orel Hershiser	5.00	2.25	.50
☐ 582	Tom Waddell	.08	.03	.01
☐ 583	Mark Huismann	.08	.03	.01
☐ 584	Joe Morgan	.40	.16	.04
☐ 585	Jim Wohlford	.08	.03	.01
☐ 586	Dave Schmidt	.08	.03	.01
☐ 587	Jeff Kunkel	.08	.03	.01
☐ 588	Hal McRae	.12	.05	.01
☐ 589	Bill Almon	.08	.03	.01
☐ 590	Carmen Castillo	.08	.03	.01
☐ 591	Omar Moreno	.08	.03	.01
☐ 592	Ken Howell	.15	.06	.01
☐ 593	Tom Brookens	.08	.03	.01
☐ 594	Joe Nolan	.08	.03	.01
☐ 595	Willie Lozado	.08	.03	.01
☐ 596	Tom Nieto	.08	.03	.01
☐ 597	Walt Terrell	.08	.03	.01
☐ 598	Al Oliver	.12	.05	.01
☐ 599	Shane Rawley	.08	.03	.01
☐ 600	Denny Gonzalez	.08	.03	.01
☐ 601	Mark Grant	.08	.03	.01
☐ 602	Mike Armstrong	.08	.03	.01
☐ 603	George Foster	.15	.06	.01
☐ 604	Dave Lopes	.12	.05	.01
☐ 605	Salome Barojas	.08	.03	.01
☐ 606	Roy Lee Jackson	.08	.03	.01
☐ 607	Pete Filson	.08	.03	.01
☐ 608	Duane Walker	.08	.03	.01
☐ 609	Glenn Wilson	.08	.03	.01
☐ 610	Rafael Santana	.15	.06	.01
☐ 611	Roy Smith	.12	.05	.01
☐ 612	Ruppert Jones	.08	.03	.01
☐ 613	Joe Cowley	.08	.03	.01
☐ 614	Al Nipper UER (photo actually Mike Brown)	.12	.05	.01

☐ 615	Gene Nelson	.08	.03	.01
☐ 616	Joe Carter	5.50	2.50	.55
☐ 617	Ray Knight	.12	.05	.01
☐ 618	Chuck Rainey	.08	.03	.01
☐ 619	Dan Driessen	.08	.03	.01
☐ 620	Daryl Sconiers	.08	.03	.01
☐ 621	Bill Stein	.08	.03	.01
☐ 622	Roy Smalley	.08	.03	.01
☐ 623	Ed Lynch	.08	.03	.01
☐ 624	Jeff Stone	.12	.05	.01
☐ 625	Bruce Berenyi	.08	.03	.01
☐ 626	Kelvin Chapman	.08	.03	.01
☐ 627	Joe Price	.08	.03	.01
☐ 628	Steve Bedrosian	.12	.05	.01
☐ 629	Vic Mata	.08	.03	.01
☐ 630	Mike Krukow	.08	.03	.01
☐ 631	Phil Bradley	.35	.15	.03
☐ 632	Jim Gott	.08	.03	.01
☐ 633	Randy Bush	.08	.03	.01
☐ 634	Tom Browning	1.75	.70	.17
☐ 635	Lou Gehrig Puzzle Card	.15	.06	.01
☐ 636	Reid Nichols	.08	.03	.01
☐ 637	Dan Pasqua	.75	.30	.07
☐ 638	German Rivera	.08	.03	.01
☐ 639	Don Schulze	.08	.03	.01
☐ 640A	Mike Jones (Career Highlights, takes five lines)	.12	.05	.01
☐ 640B	Mike Jones (Career Highlights, takes four lines)	.12	.05	.01
☐ 641	Pete Rose	1.25	.50	.12
☐ 642	Wade Rowdon	.08	.03	.01
☐ 643	Jerry Narron	.08	.03	.01
☐ 644	Darrell Miller	.12	.05	.01
☐ 645	Tim Hulett	.12	.05	.01
☐ 646	Andy McGaffigan	.08	.03	.01
☐ 647	Kurt Bevacqua	.08	.03	.01
☐ 648	John Russell	.12	.05	.01
☐ 649	Ron Robinson	.20	.08	.02
☐ 650	Donnie Moore	.08	.03	.01
☐ 651A	Two for the Title Dave Winfield Don Mattingly (yellow letters)	4.00	1.75	.40
☐ 651B	Two for the Title Dave Winfield Don Mattingly (white letters)	9.00	4.00	.90
☐ 652	Tim Laudner	.08	.03	.01
☐ 653	Steve Farr	.40	.16	.04
☐ 654	DK Checklist 1-26 (unnumbered)	.15	.02	.00
☐ 655	Checklist 27-130 (unnumbered)	.15	.02	.00

☐ 656	Checklist 131-234 (unnumbered)	.15	.02	.00
☐ 657	Checklist 235-338 (unnumbered)	.15	.02	.00
☐ 658	Checklist 339-442 (unnumbered)	.15	.02	.00
☐ 659	Checklist 443-546 (unnumbered)	.15	.02	.00
☐ 660	Checklist 547-653 (unnumbered)	.15	.02	.00

1986 Donruss

The cards in this 660-card set measure 2 1/2" by 3 1/2". The 1986 Donruss regular issue cards have fronts that feature blue borders. The fronts contain the standard team logo, player's name, position, and Donruss logo. The cards were distributed with puzzle pieces from a Dick Perez rendition of Hank Aaron. The first 26 cards of the set are Diamond Kings (DK), for the fifth year in a row; the artwork on the Diamond Kings was again produced by the Perez-Steele Galleries. Cards 27-46 again feature Rated Rookies (RR); Danny Tartabull is included in this subset for the second year in a row. The unnumbered checklist cards are arbitrarily numbered below as numbers 654 through 660. The key rookie cards in this set are Jose Canseco, Vince Coleman, Kal Daniels, Cecil Fielder, Fred McGriff, and Paul O'Neill.

		MINT	EXC	G-VG
	COMPLETE SET (660)	180.00	80.00	27.00
	COMMON PLAYER (1-660)	.07	.03	.01
☐ 1	Kirk Gibson DK	.30	.08	.02
☐ 2	Goose Gossage DK	.15	.06	.01
☐ 3	Willie McGee DK	.15	.06	.01
☐ 4	George Bell DK	.20	.08	.02
☐ 5	Tony Armas DK	.10	.04	.01
☐ 6	Chili Davis DK	.15	.06	.01
☐ 7	Cecil Cooper DK	.12	.05	.01
☐ 8	Mike Boddicker DK	.10	.04	.01
☐ 9	Dave Lopes DK	.10	.04	.01
☐ 10	Bill Doran DK	.10	.04	.01
☐ 11	Bret Saberhagen DK	.40	.16	.04
☐ 12	Brett Butler DK	.15	.06	.01
☐ 13	Harold Baines DK	.15	.06	.01
☐ 14	Mike Davis DK	.10	.04	.01
☐ 15	Tony Perez DK	.15	.06	.01
☐ 16	Willie Randolph DK	.12	.05	.01
☐ 17	Bob Boone DK	.12	.05	.01
☐ 18	Orel Hershiser DK	.35	.15	.03
☐ 19	Johnny Ray DK	.10	.04	.01
☐ 20	Gary Ward DK	.10	.04	.01
☐ 21	Rick Mahler DK	.10	.04	.01
☐ 22	Phil Bradley DK	.10	.04	.01
☐ 23	Jerry Koosman DK	.12	.05	.01
☐ 24	Tom Brunansky DK	.12	.05	.01
☐ 25	Andre Dawson DK	.35	.15	.03
☐ 26	Dwight Gooden DK	.65	.25	.06
☐ 27	Kal Daniels RR	3.25	1.35	.32
☐ 28	Fred McGriff RR	22.00	9.50	3.15
☐ 29	Cory Snyder RR	.50	.20	.05
☐ 30	Jose Guzman RR	.35	.15	.03
☐ 31	Ty Gainey RR	.10	.04	.01
☐ 32	Johnny Abrego RR	.07	.03	.01
☐ 33A	Andres Galarraga RR (no accent)	1.00	.40	.10
☐ 33B	Andrés Galarraga RR (accent over e)	2.00	.80	.20
☐ 34	Dave Shipanoff RR	.07	.03	.01
☐ 35	Mark McLemore RR	.10	.04	.01
☐ 36	Marty Clary RR	.10	.04	.01
☐ 37	Paul O'Neill RR	3.25	1.35	.32
☐ 38	Danny Tartabull RR	1.25	.50	.12
☐ 39	Jose Canseco RR	80.00	36.00	12.00
☐ 40	Juan Nieves RR	.12	.05	.01
☐ 41	Lance McCullers RR	.12	.05	.01
☐ 42	Rick Surhoff RR	.10	.04	.01
☐ 43	Todd Worrell RR	.17	.07	.01
☐ 44	Bob Kipper RR	.12	.05	.01
☐ 45	John Habyan RR	.10	.04	.01
☐ 46	Mike Woodard RR	.07	.03	.01
☐ 47	Mike Boddicker	.07	.03	.01
☐ 48	Robin Yount	.85	.35	.08
☐ 49	Lou Whitaker	.25	.10	.02
☐ 50	Oil Can Boyd	.07	.03	.01
☐ 51	Rickey Henderson	2.50	1.00	.25
☐ 52	Mike Marshall	.10	.04	.01
☐ 53	George Brett	.85	.35	.08
☐ 54	Dave Kingman	.12	.05	.01
☐ 55	Hubie Brooks	.12	.05	.01
☐ 56	Oddibe McDowell	.10	.04	.01

☐ 57 Doug DeCinces	.07	.03	.01
☐ 58 Britt Burns	.07	.03	.01
☐ 59 Ozzie Smith	.75	.30	.07
☐ 60 Jose Cruz	.10	.04	.01
☐ 61 Mike Schmidt	2.50	1.00	.25
☐ 62 Pete Rose	.80	.35	.08
☐ 63 Steve Garvey	.35	.15	.03
☐ 64 Tony Pena	.10	.04	.01
☐ 65 Chili Davis	.15	.06	.01
☐ 66 Dale Murphy	.50	.20	.05
☐ 67 Ryne Sandberg	3.75	1.60	.37
☐ 68 Gary Carter	.35	.15	.03
☐ 69 Alvin Davis	.15	.06	.01
☐ 70 Kent Hrbek	.20	.08	.02
☐ 71 George Bell	.50	.20	.05
☐ 72 Kirby Puckett	7.00	3.00	.70
☐ 73 Lloyd Moseby	.10	.04	.01
☐ 74 Bob Kearney	.07	.03	.01
☐ 75 Dwight Gooden	2.25	.90	.22
☐ 76 Gary Matthews	.07	.03	.01
☐ 77 Rick Mahler	.07	.03	.01
☐ 78 Benny Distefano	.07	.03	.01
☐ 79 Jeff Leonard	.07	.03	.01
☐ 80 Kevin McReynolds	.35	.15	.03
☐ 81 Ron Oester	.07	.03	.01
☐ 82 John Russell	.07	.03	.01
☐ 83 Tommy Herr	.10	.04	.01
☐ 84 Jerry Mumphrey	.07	.03	.01
☐ 85 Ron Romanick	.07	.03	.01
☐ 86 Daryl Boston	.10	.04	.01
☐ 87 Andre Dawson	.75	.30	.07
☐ 88 Eddie Murray	.75	.30	.07
☐ 89 Dion James	.07	.03	.01
☐ 90 Chet Lemon	.07	.03	.01
☐ 91 Bob Stanley	.07	.03	.01
☐ 92 Willie Randolph	.10	.04	.01
☐ 93 Mike Scioscia	.10	.04	.01
☐ 94 Tom Waddell	.07	.03	.01
☐ 95 Danny Jackson	.10	.04	.01
☐ 96 Mike Davis	.07	.03	.01
☐ 97 Mike Fitzgerald	.07	.03	.01
☐ 98 Gary Ward	.07	.03	.01
☐ 99 Pete O'Brien	.07	.03	.01
☐ 100 Bret Saberhagen	1.00	.40	.10
☐ 101 Alfredo Griffin	.07	.03	.01
☐ 102 Brett Butler	.15	.06	.01
☐ 103 Ron Guidry	.15	.06	.01
☐ 104 Jerry Reuss	.07	.03	.01
☐ 105 Jack Morris	.40	.16	.04
☐ 106 Rick Dempsey	.07	.03	.01
☐ 107 Ray Burris	.07	.03	.01
☐ 108 Brian Downing	.10	.04	.01
☐ 109 Willie McGee	.25	.10	.02
☐ 110 Bill Doran	.10	.04	.01
☐ 111 Kent Tekulve	.07	.03	.01
☐ 112 Tony Gwynn	2.00	.80	.20
☐ 113 Marvell Wynne	.07	.03	.01
☐ 114 David Green	.07	.03	.01

☐ 115 Jim Gantner	.07	.03	.01
☐ 116 George Foster	.12	.05	.01
☐ 117 Steve Trout	.07	.03	.01
☐ 118 Mark Langston	.60	.25	.06
☐ 119 Tony Fernandez	.20	.08	.02
☐ 120 John Butcher	.07	.03	.01
☐ 121 Ron Robinson	.07	.03	.01
☐ 122 Dan Spillner	.07	.03	.01
☐ 123 Mike Young	.07	.03	.01
☐ 124 Paul Molitor	.25	.10	.02
☐ 125 Kirk Gibson	.25	.10	.02
☐ 126 Ken Griffey	.15	.06	.01
☐ 127 Tony Armas	.07	.03	.01
☐ 128 Mariano Duncan	.35	.15	.03
☐ 129 Pat Tabler	.07	.03	.01
☐ 130 Frank White	.07	.03	.01
☐ 131 Carney Lansford	.10	.04	.01
☐ 132 Vance Law	.07	.03	.01
☐ 133 Dick Schofield	.07	.03	.01
☐ 134 Wayne Tolleson	.07	.03	.01
☐ 135 Greg Walker	.07	.03	.01
☐ 136 Denny Walling	.07	.03	.01
☐ 137 Ozzie Virgil	.07	.03	.01
☐ 138 Ricky Horton	.07	.03	.01
☐ 139 LaMarr Hoyt	.07	.03	.01
☐ 140 Wayne Krenchicki	.07	.03	.01
☐ 141 Glenn Hubbard	.07	.03	.01
☐ 142 Cecilio Guante	.07	.03	.01
☐ 143 Mike Krukow	.07	.03	.01
☐ 144 Lee Smith	.35	.15	.03
☐ 145 Edwin Nunez	.07	.03	.01
☐ 146 Dave Stieb	.15	.06	.01
☐ 147 Mike Smithson	.07	.03	.01
☐ 148 Ken Dixon	.07	.03	.01
☐ 149 Danny Darwin	.07	.03	.01
☐ 150 Chris Pittaro	.07	.03	.01
☐ 151 Bill Buckner	.10	.04	.01
☐ 152 Mike Pagliarulo	.10	.04	.01
☐ 153 Bill Russell	.10	.04	.01
☐ 154 Brook Jacoby	.10	.04	.01
☐ 155 Pat Sheridan	.07	.03	.01
☐ 156 Mike Gallego	.07	.03	.01
☐ 157 Jim Wohlford	.07	.03	.01
☐ 158 Gary Pettis	.07	.03	.01
☐ 159 Toby Harrah	.07	.03	.01
☐ 160 Richard Dotson	.07	.03	.01
☐ 161 Bob Knepper	.07	.03	.01
☐ 162 Dave Dravecky	.10	.04	.01
☐ 163 Greg Gross	.07	.03	.01
☐ 164 Eric Davis	2.50	1.00	.25
☐ 165 Gerald Perry	.10	.04	.01
☐ 166 Rick Rhoden	.07	.03	.01
☐ 167 Keith Moreland	.07	.03	.01
☐ 168 Jack Clark	.17	.07	.01
☐ 169 Storm Davis	.07	.03	.01
☐ 170 Cecil Cooper	.10	.04	.01
☐ 171 Alan Trammell	.45	.18	.04
☐ 172 Roger Clemens	8.00	3.50	.80

☐ 173 Don Mattingly .... 4.00 1.75 .40
☐ 174 Pedro Guerrero .... .20 .08 .02
☐ 175 Willie Wilson .... .12 .05 .01
☐ 176 Dwayne Murphy .... .07 .03 .01
☐ 177 Tim Raines .... .35 .15 .03
☐ 178 Larry Parrish .... .07 .03 .01
☐ 179 Mike Witt .... .07 .03 .01
☐ 180 Harold Baines .... .25 .10 .02
☐ 181 Vince Coleman UER .... 6.00 2.50 .60
(BA 2.67 on back)
☐ 182 Jeff Heathcock .... .07 .03 .01
☐ 183 Steve Carlton .... .60 .25 .06
☐ 184 Mario Soto .... .07 .03 .01
☐ 185 Goose Gossage .... .15 .06 .01
☐ 186 Johnny Ray .... .07 .03 .01
☐ 187 Dan Gladden .... .10 .04 .01
☐ 188 Bob Horner .... .12 .05 .01
☐ 189 Rick Sutcliffe .... .12 .05 .01
☐ 190 Keith Hernandez .... .17 .07 .01
☐ 191 Phil Bradley .... .10 .04 .01
☐ 192 Tom Brunansky .... .10 .04 .01
☐ 193 Jesse Barfield .... .15 .06 .01
☐ 194 Frank Viola .... .35 .15 .03
☐ 195 Willie Upshaw .... .07 .03 .01
☐ 196 Jim Beattie .... .07 .03 .01
☐ 197 Darryl Strawberry .... 4.75 2.00 .45
☐ 198 Ron Cey .... .10 .04 .01
☐ 199 Steve Bedrosian .... .10 .04 .01
☐ 200 Steve Kemp .... .07 .03 .01
☐ 201 Manny Trillo .... .07 .03 .01
☐ 202 Garry Templeton .... .10 .04 .01
☐ 203 Dave Parker .... .25 .10 .02
☐ 204 John Denny .... .07 .03 .01
☐ 205 Terry Pendleton .... .75 .30 .07
☐ 206 Terry Puhl .... .07 .03 .01
☐ 207 Bobby Grich .... .10 .04 .01
☐ 208 Ozzie Guillen .... 1.25 .50 .12
☐ 209 Jeff Reardon .... .35 .15 .03
☐ 210 Cal Ripken .... 4.00 1.75 .40
☐ 211 Bill Schroeder .... .07 .03 .01
☐ 212 Dan Petry .... .07 .03 .01
☐ 213 Jim Rice .... .15 .06 .01
☐ 214 Dave Righetti .... .12 .05 .01
☐ 215 Fernando Valenzuela ...... .15 .06 .01
☐ 216 Julio Franco .... .75 .30 .07
☐ 217 Darryl Motley .... .07 .03 .01
☐ 218 Dave Collins .... .07 .03 .01
☐ 219 Tim Wallach .... .10 .04 .01
☐ 220 George Wright .... .07 .03 .01
☐ 221 Tommy Dunbar .... .07 .03 .01
☐ 222 Steve Balboni .... .07 .03 .01
☐ 223 Jay Howell .... .07 .03 .01
☐ 224 Joe Carter .... 1.25 .50 .12
☐ 225 Ed Whitson .... .07 .03 .01
☐ 226 Orel Hershiser .... .75 .30 .07
☐ 227 Willie Hernandez .... .07 .03 .01
☐ 228 Lee Lacy .... .07 .03 .01
☐ 229 Rollie Fingers .... .30 .12 .03
☐ 230 Bob Boone .... .12 .05 .01
☐ 231 Joaquin Andujar .... .10 .04 .01
☐ 232 Craig Reynolds .... .07 .03 .01
☐ 233 Shane Rawley .... .07 .03 .01
☐ 234 Eric Show .... .07 .03 .01
☐ 235 Jose DeLeon .... .07 .03 .01
☐ 236 Jose Uribe .... .20 .08 .02
☐ 237 Moose Haas .... .07 .03 .01
☐ 238 Wally Backman .... .07 .03 .01
☐ 239 Dennis Eckersley .... .30 .12 .03
☐ 240 Mike Moore .... .10 .04 .01
☐ 241 Damaso Garcia .... .07 .03 .01
☐ 242 Tim Teufel .... .07 .03 .01
☐ 243 Dave Concepcion .... .12 .05 .01
☐ 244 Floyd Bannister .... .07 .03 .01
☐ 245 Fred Lynn .... .15 .06 .01
☐ 246 Charlie Moore .... .07 .03 .01
☐ 247 Walt Terrell .... .07 .03 .01
☐ 248 Dave Winfield .... .60 .25 .06
☐ 249 Dwight Evans .... .15 .06 .01
☐ 250 Dennis Powell .... .07 .03 .01
☐ 251 Andre Thornton .... .07 .03 .01
☐ 252 Onix Concepcion .... .07 .03 .01
☐ 253 Mike Heath .... .07 .03 .01
☐ 254A David Palmer ERR ...... .10 .04 .01
(position 2B)
☐ 254B David Palmer COR ...... .60 .25 .06
(position P)
☐ 255 Donnie Moore .... .07 .03 .01
☐ 256 Curtis Wilkerson .... .07 .03 .01
☐ 257 Julio Cruz .... .07 .03 .01
☐ 258 Nolan Ryan .... 4.25 1.75 .42
☐ 259 Jeff Stone .... .07 .03 .01
☐ 260 John Tudor .... .10 .04 .01
☐ 261 Mark Thurmond .... .07 .03 .01
☐ 262 Jay Tibbs .... .07 .03 .01
☐ 263 Rafael Ramirez .... .07 .03 .01
☐ 264 Larry McWilliams .... .07 .03 .01
☐ 265 Mark Davis .... .10 .04 .01
☐ 266 Bob Dernier .... .07 .03 .01
☐ 267 Matt Young .... .07 .03 .01
☐ 268 Jim Clancy .... .07 .03 .01
☐ 269 Mickey Hatcher .... .07 .03 .01
☐ 270 Sammy Stewart .... .07 .03 .01
☐ 271 Bob L. Gibson .... .07 .03 .01
☐ 272 Nelson Simmons .... .07 .03 .01
☐ 273 Rich Gedman .... .07 .03 .01
☐ 274 Butch Wynegar .... .07 .03 .01
☐ 275 Ken Howell .... .07 .03 .01
☐ 276 Mel Hall .... .12 .05 .01
☐ 277 Jim Sundberg .... .07 .03 .01
☐ 278 Chris Codiroli .... .07 .03 .01
☐ 279 Herm Winningham .... .07 .03 .01
☐ 280 Rod Carew .... .75 .30 .07
☐ 281 Don Slaught .... .07 .03 .01
☐ 282 Scott Fletcher .... .07 .03 .01
☐ 283 Bill Dawley .... .07 .03 .01
☐ 284 Andy Hawkins .... .07 .03 .01

☐ 285 Glenn Wilson	.07	.03	.01
☐ 286 Nick Esasky	.10	.04	.01
☐ 287 Claudell Washington	.07	.03	.01
☐ 288 Lee Mazzilli	.07	.03	.01
☐ 289 Jody Davis	.07	.03	.01
☐ 290 Darrell Porter	.07	.03	.01
☐ 291 Scott McGregor	.07	.03	.01
☐ 292 Ted Simmons	.10	.04	.01
☐ 293 Aurelio Lopez	.07	.03	.01
☐ 294 Marty Barrett	.07	.03	.01
☐ 295 Dale Berra	.07	.03	.01
☐ 296 Greg Brock	.07	.03	.01
☐ 297 Charlie Leibrandt	.07	.03	.01
☐ 298 Bill Krueger	.07	.03	.01
☐ 299 Bryn Smith	.07	.03	.01
☐ 300 Burt Hooton	.07	.03	.01
☐ 301 Stu Cliburn	.07	.03	.01
☐ 302 Luis Salazar	.07	.03	.01
☐ 303 Ken Dayley	.07	.03	.01
☐ 304 Frank DiPino	.07	.03	.01
☐ 305 Von Hayes	.12	.05	.01
☐ 306 Gary Redus	.07	.03	.01
☐ 307 Craig Lefferts	.07	.03	.01
☐ 308 Sammy Khalifa	.07	.03	.01
☐ 309 Scott Garrelts	.10	.04	.01
☐ 310 Rick Cerone	.07	.03	.01
☐ 311 Shawon Dunston	.75	.30	.07
☐ 312 Howard Johnson	.90	.40	.09
☐ 313 Jim Presley	.10	.04	.01
☐ 314 Gary Gaetti	.15	.06	.01
☐ 315 Luis Leal	.07	.03	.01
☐ 316 Mark Salas	.07	.03	.01
☐ 317 Bill Caudill	.07	.03	.01
☐ 318 Dave Henderson	.35	.15	.03
☐ 319 Rafael Santana	.07	.03	.01
☐ 320 Leon Durham	.07	.03	.01
☐ 321 Bruce Sutter	.12	.05	.01
☐ 322 Jason Thompson	.07	.03	.01
☐ 323 Bob Brenly	.07	.03	.01
☐ 324 Carmelo Martinez	.07	.03	.01
☐ 325 Eddie Milner	.07	.03	.01
☐ 326 Juan Samuel	.25	.10	.02
☐ 327 Tom Nieto	.07	.03	.01
☐ 328 Dave Smith	.07	.03	.01
☐ 329 Urbano Lugo	.07	.03	.01
☐ 330 Joel Skinner	.07	.03	.01
☐ 331 Bill Gullickson	.10	.04	.01
☐ 332 Floyd Rayford	.07	.03	.01
☐ 333 Ben Oglivie	.07	.03	.01
☐ 334 Lance Parrish	.17	.07	.01
☐ 335 Jackie Gutierrez	.07	.03	.01
☐ 336 Dennis Rasmussen	.07	.03	.01
☐ 337 Terry Whitfield	.07	.03	.01
☐ 338 Neal Heaton	.07	.03	.01
☐ 339 Jorge Orta	.07	.03	.01
☐ 340 Donnie Hill	.07	.03	.01
☐ 341 Joe Hesketh	.12	.05	.01
☐ 342 Charlie Hough	.07	.03	.01
☐ 343 Dave Rozema	.07	.03	.01
☐ 344 Greg Pryor	.07	.03	.01
☐ 345 Mickey Tettleton	1.25	.50	.12
☐ 346 George Vukovich	.07	.03	.01
☐ 347 Don Baylor	.12	.05	.01
☐ 348 Carlos Diaz	.07	.03	.01
☐ 349 Barbaro Garbey	.07	.03	.01
☐ 350 Larry Sheets	.07	.03	.01
☐ 351 Ted Higuera	.45	.18	.04
☐ 352 Juan Beniquez	.07	.03	.01
☐ 353 Bob Forsch	.07	.03	.01
☐ 354 Mark Bailey	.07	.03	.01
☐ 355 Larry Andersen	.07	.03	.01
☐ 356 Terry Kennedy	.07	.03	.01
☐ 357 Don Robinson	.07	.03	.01
☐ 358 Jim Gott	.07	.03	.01
☐ 359 Earnie Riles	.17	.07	.01
☐ 360 John Christensen	.07	.03	.01
☐ 361 Ray Fontenot	.07	.03	.01
☐ 362 Spike Owen	.07	.03	.01
☐ 363 Jim Acker	.07	.03	.01
☐ 364 Ron Davis	.07	.03	.01
☐ 365 Tom Hume	.07	.03	.01
☐ 366 Carlton Fisk	.75	.30	.07
☐ 367 Nate Snell	.07	.03	.01
☐ 368 Rick Manning	.07	.03	.01
☐ 369 Darrell Evans	.10	.04	.01
☐ 370 Ron Hassey	.07	.03	.01
☐ 371 Wade Boggs	2.50	1.00	.25
☐ 372 Rick Honeycutt	.07	.03	.01
☐ 373 Chris Bando	.07	.03	.01
☐ 374 Bud Black	.10	.04	.01
☐ 375 Steve Henderson	.07	.03	.01
☐ 376 Charlie Lea	.07	.03	.01
☐ 377 Reggie Jackson	.90	.40	.09
☐ 378 Dave Schmidt	.07	.03	.01
☐ 379 Bob James	.07	.03	.01
☐ 380 Glenn Davis	2.25	.90	.22
☐ 381 Tim Corcoran	.07	.03	.01
☐ 382 Danny Cox	.07	.03	.01
☐ 383 Tim Flannery	.07	.03	.01
☐ 384 Tom Browning	.25	.10	.02
☐ 385 Rick Camp	.07	.03	.01
☐ 386 Jim Morrison	.07	.03	.01
☐ 387 Dave LaPoint	.07	.03	.01
☐ 388 Dave Lopes	.10	.04	.01
☐ 389 Al Cowens	.07	.03	.01
☐ 390 Doyle Alexander	.07	.03	.01
☐ 391 Tim Laudner	.07	.03	.01
☐ 392 Don Aase	.07	.03	.01
☐ 393 Jaime Cocanower	.07	.03	.01
☐ 394 Randy O'Neal	.07	.03	.01
☐ 395 Mike Easler	.07	.03	.01
☐ 396 Scott Bradley	.07	.03	.01
☐ 397 Tom Niedenfuer	.07	.03	.01
☐ 398 Jerry Willard	.07	.03	.01
☐ 399 Lonnie Smith	.12	.05	.01
☐ 400 Bruce Bochte	.07	.03	.01

☐ 401	Terry Francona	.07	.03	.01
☐ 402	Jim Slaton	.07	.03	.01
☐ 403	Bill Stein	.07	.03	.01
☐ 404	Tim Hulett	.07	.03	.01
☐ 405	Alan Ashby	.07	.03	.01
☐ 406	Tim Stoddard	.07	.03	.01
☐ 407	Garry Maddox	.07	.03	.01
☐ 408	Ted Power	.07	.03	.01
☐ 409	Len Barker	.07	.03	.01
☐ 410	Denny Gonzalez	.07	.03	.01
☐ 411	George Frazier	.07	.03	.01
☐ 412	Andy Van Slyke	.35	.15	.03
☐ 413	Jim Dwyer	.07	.03	.01
☐ 414	Paul Householder	.07	.03	.01
☐ 415	Alejandro Sanchez	.07	.03	.01
☐ 416	Steve Crawford	.07	.03	.01
☐ 417	Dan Pasqua	.15	.06	.01
☐ 418	Enos Cabell	.07	.03	.01
☐ 419	Mike Jones	.07	.03	.01
☐ 420	Steve Kiefer	.07	.03	.01
☐ 421	Tim Burke	.20	.08	.02
☐ 422	Mike Mason	.07	.03	.01
☐ 423	Ruppert Jones	.07	.03	.01
☐ 424	Jerry Hairston	.07	.03	.01
☐ 425	Tito Landrum	.07	.03	.01
☐ 426	Jeff Calhoun	.07	.03	.01
☐ 427	Don Carman	.15	.06	.01
☐ 428	Tony Perez	.25	.10	.02
☐ 429	Jerry Davis	.07	.03	.01
☐ 430	Bob Walk	.07	.03	.01
☐ 431	Brad Wellman	.07	.03	.01
☐ 432	Terry Forster	.07	.03	.01
☐ 433	Billy Hatcher	.15	.06	.01
☐ 434	Clint Hurdle	.07	.03	.01
☐ 435	Ivan Calderon	2.00	.80	.20
☐ 436	Pete Filson	.07	.03	.01
☐ 437	Tom Henke	.12	.05	.01
☐ 438	Dave Engle	.07	.03	.01
☐ 439	Tom Filer	.07	.03	.01
☐ 440	Gorman Thomas	.10	.04	.01
☐ 441	Rick Aguilera	.90	.40	.09
☐ 442	Scott Sanderson	.10	.04	.01
☐ 443	Jeff Dedmon	.07	.03	.01
☐ 444	Joe Orsulak	.35	.15	.03
☐ 445	Atlee Hammaker	.07	.03	.01
☐ 446	Jerry Royster	.07	.03	.01
☐ 447	Buddy Bell	.10	.04	.01
☐ 448	Dave Rucker	.07	.03	.01
☐ 449	Ivan DeJesus	.07	.03	.01
☐ 450	Jim Pankovits	.07	.03	.01
☐ 451	Jerry Narron	.07	.03	.01
☐ 452	Bryan Little	.07	.03	.01
☐ 453	Gary Lucas	.07	.03	.01
☐ 454	Dennis Martinez	.10	.04	.01
☐ 455	Ed Romero	.07	.03	.01
☐ 456	Bob Melvin	.10	.04	.01
☐ 457	Glenn Hoffman	.07	.03	.01
☐ 458	Bob Shirley	.07	.03	.01
☐ 459	Bob Welch	.15	.06	.01
☐ 460	Carmen Castillo	.07	.03	.01
☐ 461	Dave Leeper (outfielder)	.07	.03	.01
☐ 462	Tim Birtsas	.10	.04	.01
☐ 463	Randy St.Claire	.07	.03	.01
☐ 464	Chris Welsh	.07	.03	.01
☐ 465	Greg Harris	.07	.03	.01
☐ 466	Lynn Jones	.07	.03	.01
☐ 467	Dusty Baker	.10	.04	.01
☐ 468	Roy Smith	.07	.03	.01
☐ 469	Andre Robertson	.07	.03	.01
☐ 470	Ken Landreaux	.07	.03	.01
☐ 471	Dave Bergman	.07	.03	.01
☐ 472	Gary Roenicke	.07	.03	.01
☐ 473	Pete Vuckovich	.07	.03	.01
☐ 474	Kirk McCaskill	.30	.12	.03
☐ 475	Jeff Lahti	.07	.03	.01
☐ 476	Mike Scott	.15	.06	.01
☐ 477	Darren Daulton	.35	.15	.03
☐ 478	Graig Nettles	.12	.05	.01
☐ 479	Bill Almon	.07	.03	.01
☐ 480	Greg Minton	.07	.03	.01
☐ 481	Randy Ready	.10	.04	.01
☐ 482	Len Dykstra	2.50	1.00	.25
☐ 483	Thad Bosley	.07	.03	.01
☐ 484	Harold Reynolds	.90	.40	.09
☐ 485	Al Oliver	.12	.05	.01
☐ 486	Roy Smalley	.07	.03	.01
☐ 487	John Franco	.15	.06	.01
☐ 488	Juan Agosto	.07	.03	.01
☐ 489	Al Pardo	.07	.03	.01
☐ 490	Bill Wegman	.25	.10	.02
☐ 491	Frank Tanana	.10	.04	.01
☐ 492	Brian Fisher	.10	.04	.01
☐ 493	Mark Clear	.07	.03	.01
☐ 494	Len Matuszek	.07	.03	.01
☐ 495	Ramon Romero	.07	.03	.01
☐ 496	John Wathan	.07	.03	.01
☐ 497	Rob Picciolo	.07	.03	.01
☐ 498	U.L. Washington	.07	.03	.01
☐ 499	John Candelaria	.07	.03	.01
☐ 500	Duane Walker	.07	.03	.01
☐ 501	Gene Nelson	.07	.03	.01
☐ 502	John Mizerock	.07	.03	.01
☐ 503	Luis Aguayo	.07	.03	.01
☐ 504	Kurt Kepshire	.07	.03	.01
☐ 505	Ed Wojna	.07	.03	.01
☐ 506	Joe Price	.07	.03	.01
☐ 507	Milt Thompson	.25	.10	.02
☐ 508	Junior Ortiz	.07	.03	.01
☐ 509	Vida Blue	.10	.04	.01
☐ 510	Steve Engel	.07	.03	.01
☐ 511	Karl Best	.07	.03	.01
☐ 512	Cecil Fielder	24.00	10.50	3.50
☐ 513	Frank Eufemia	.07	.03	.01
☐ 514	Tippy Martinez	.07	.03	.01
☐ 515	Billy Jo Robidoux	.07	.03	.01

☐ 516	Bill Scherrer	.07	.03	.01
☐ 517	Bruce Hurst	.10	.04	.01
☐ 518	Rich Bordi	.07	.03	.01
☐ 519	Steve Yeager	.07	.03	.01
☐ 520	Tony Bernazard	.07	.03	.01
☐ 521	Hal McRae	.10	.04	.01
☐ 522	Jose Rijo	.35	.15	.03
☐ 523	Mitch Webster	.17	.07	.01
☐ 524	Jack Howell	.15	.06	.01
☐ 525	Alan Bannister	.07	.03	.01
☐ 526	Ron Kittle	.10	.04	.01
☐ 527	Phil Garner	.10	.04	.01
☐ 528	Kurt Bevacqua	.07	.03	.01
☐ 529	Kevin Gross	.07	.03	.01
☐ 530	Bo Diaz	.07	.03	.01
☐ 531	Ken Oberkfell	.07	.03	.01
☐ 532	Rick Reuschel	.10	.04	.01
☐ 533	Ron Meridith	.07	.03	.01
☐ 534	Steve Braun	.07	.03	.01
☐ 535	Wayne Gross	.07	.03	.01
☐ 536	Ray Searage	.07	.03	.01
☐ 537	Tom Brookens	.07	.03	.01
☐ 538	Al Nipper	.07	.03	.01
☐ 539	Billy Sample	.07	.03	.01
☐ 540	Steve Sax	.25	.10	.02
☐ 541	Dan Quisenberry	.12	.05	.01
☐ 542	Tony Phillips	.10	.04	.01
☐ 543	Floyd Youmans	.10	.04	.01
☐ 544	Steve Buechele	.75	.30	.07
☐ 545	Craig Gerber	.07	.03	.01
☐ 546	Joe DeSa	.07	.03	.01
☐ 547	Brian Harper	.25	.10	.02
☐ 548	Kevin Bass	.10	.04	.01
☐ 549	Tom Foley	.07	.03	.01
☐ 550	Dave Van Gorder	.07	.03	.01
☐ 551	Bruce Bochy	.07	.03	.01
☐ 552	R.J. Reynolds	.07	.03	.01
☐ 553	Chris Brown	.10	.04	.01
☐ 554	Bruce Benedict	.07	.03	.01
☐ 555	Warren Brusstar	.07	.03	.01
☐ 556	Danny Heep	.07	.03	.01
☐ 557	Darnell Coles	.07	.03	.01
☐ 558	Greg Gagne	.12	.05	.01
☐ 559	Ernie Whitt	.07	.03	.01
☐ 560	Ron Washington	.07	.03	.01
☐ 561	Jimmy Key	.30	.12	.03
☐ 562	Billy Swift	.15	.06	.01
☐ 563	Ron Darling	.15	.06	.01
☐ 564	Dick Ruthven	.07	.03	.01
☐ 565	Zane Smith	.40	.16	.04
☐ 566	Sid Bream	.07	.03	.01
☐ 567A	Joel Youngblood ERR (position P)	.10	.04	.01
☐ 567B	Joel Youngblood COR (position IF)	.60	.25	.06
☐ 568	Mario Ramirez	.07	.03	.01
☐ 569	Tom Runnells	.15	.06	.01
☐ 570	Rick Schu	.07	.03	.01
☐ 571	Bill Campbell	.07	.03	.01
☐ 572	Dickie Thon	.10	.04	.01
☐ 573	Al Holland	.07	.03	.01
☐ 574	Reid Nichols	.07	.03	.01
☐ 575	Bert Roberge	.07	.03	.01
☐ 576	Mike Flanagan	.10	.04	.01
☐ 577	Tim Leary	.15	.06	.01
☐ 578	Mike Laga	.07	.03	.01
☐ 579	Steve Lyons	.07	.03	.01
☐ 580	Phil Niekro	.25	.10	.02
☐ 581	Gilberto Reyes	.20	.08	.02
☐ 582	Jamie Easterly	.07	.03	.01
☐ 583	Mark Gubicza	.15	.06	.01
☐ 584	Stan Javier	.25	.10	.02
☐ 585	Bill Laskey	.07	.03	.01
☐ 586	Jeff Russell	.10	.04	.01
☐ 587	Dickie Noles	.07	.03	.01
☐ 588	Steve Farr	.10	.04	.01
☐ 589	Steve Ontiveros	.07	.03	.01
☐ 590	Mike Hargrove	.07	.03	.01
☐ 591	Marty Bystrom	.07	.03	.01
☐ 592	Franklin Stubbs	.10	.04	.01
☐ 593	Larry Herndon	.07	.03	.01
☐ 594	Bill Swaggerty	.07	.03	.01
☐ 595	Carlos Ponce	.07	.03	.01
☐ 596	Pat Perry	.07	.03	.01
☐ 597	Ray Knight	.10	.04	.01
☐ 598	Steve Lombardozzi	.07	.03	.01
☐ 599	Brad Havens	.07	.03	.01
☐ 600	Pat Clements	.07	.03	.01
☐ 601	Joe Niekro	.10	.04	.01
☐ 602	Hank Aaron Puzzle Card	.10	.04	.01
☐ 603	Dwayne Henry	.15	.06	.01
☐ 604	Mookie Wilson	.10	.04	.01
☐ 605	Buddy Biancalana	.07	.03	.01
☐ 606	Rance Mulliniks	.07	.03	.01
☐ 607	Alan Wiggins	.07	.03	.01
☐ 608	Joe Cowley	.07	.03	.01
☐ 609A	Tom Seaver (green borders on name)	1.00	.40	.10
☐ 609B	Tom Seaver (yellow borders on name)	2.25	.90	.22
☐ 610	Neil Allen	.07	.03	.01
☐ 611	Don Sutton	.25	.10	.02
☐ 612	Fred Toliver	.10	.04	.01
☐ 613	Jay Baller	.07	.03	.01
☐ 614	Marc Sullivan	.07	.03	.01
☐ 615	John Grubb	.07	.03	.01
☐ 616	Bruce Kison	.07	.03	.01
☐ 617	Bill Madlock	.10	.04	.01
☐ 618	Chris Chambliss	.10	.04	.01
☐ 619	Dave Stewart	.35	.15	.03
☐ 620	Tim Lollar	.07	.03	.01
☐ 621	Gary Lavelle	.07	.03	.01
☐ 622	Charles Hudson	.07	.03	.01

☐ 623 Joel Davis	.10	.04	.01
☐ 624 Joe Johnson	.10	.04	.01
☐ 625 Sid Fernandez	.17	.07	.01
☐ 626 Dennis Lamp	.07	.03	.01
☐ 627 Terry Harper	.07	.03	.01
☐ 628 Jack Lazorko	.07	.03	.01
☐ 629 Roger McDowell	.35	.15	.03
☐ 630 Mark Funderburk	.07	.03	.01
☐ 631 Ed Lynch	.07	.03	.01
☐ 632 Rudy Law	.07	.03	.01
☐ 633 Roger Mason	.10	.04	.01
☐ 634 Mike Felder	.25	.10	.02
☐ 635 Ken Schrom	.07	.03	.01
☐ 636 Bob Ojeda	.10	.04	.01
☐ 637 Ed VandeBerg	.07	.03	.01
☐ 638 Bobby Meacham	.07	.03	.01
☐ 639 Cliff Johnson	.07	.03	.01
☐ 640 Garth Iorg	.07	.03	.01
☐ 641 Dan Driessen	.07	.03	.01
☐ 642 Mike Brown OF	.07	.03	.01
☐ 643 John Shelby	.07	.03	.01
☐ 644 Pete Rose (Ty-Breaking)	.40	.16	.04
☐ 645 The Knuckle Brothers Phil Niekro Joe Niekro	.12	.05	.01
☐ 646 Jesse Orosco	.07	.03	.01
☐ 647 Billy Beane	.10	.04	.01
☐ 648 Cesar Cedeno	.10	.04	.01
☐ 649 Bert Blyleven	.15	.06	.01
☐ 650 Max Venable	.07	.03	.01
☐ 651 Fleet Feet Vince Coleman Willie McGee	.50	.20	.05
☐ 652 Calvin Schiraldi	.07	.03	.01
☐ 653 King of Kings (Pete Rose)	.75	.30	.07
☐ 654 CL: Diamond Kings (unnumbered)	.15	.02	.00
☐ 655A CL 1: 27-130 (unnumbered) (45 Beane ERR)	.15	.02	.00
☐ 655B CL 1: 27-130 (unnumbered) (45 Habyan COR)	.50	.10	.02
☐ 656 CL 2: 131-234 (unnumbered)	.15	.02	.00
☐ 657 CL 3: 235-338 (unnumbered)	.15	.02	.00
☐ 658 CL 4: 339-442 (unnumbered)	.15	.02	.00
☐ 659 CL 5: 443-546 (unnumbered)	.15	.02	.00
☐ 660 CL 6: 547-653 (unnumbered)	.15	.02	.00

1986 Donruss Rookies

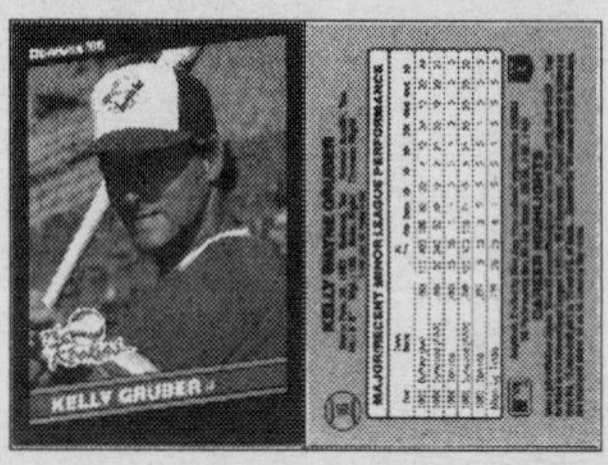

The 1986 Donruss "The Rookies" set features 56 cards plus a 15-piece puzzle of Hank Aaron. Cards are in full color and are standard size, 2 1/2" by 3 1/2". The set was distributed in a small green box with gold lettering. Although the set was wrapped in cellophane, the top card was number 1 Joyner, resulting in a percentage of the Joyner cards arriving in less than perfect condition. Donruss fixed the problem after it was called to their attention and even went so far as to include a customer service phone number in their second printing. Card fronts are similar in design to the 1986 Donruss regular issue except for the presence of "The Rookies" logo in the lower left corner and a bluish green border instead of a blue border. The key (extended) rookie cards in this set are Barry Bonds, Bobby Bonilla, Will Clark, Bo Jackson, Wally Joyner, Kevin Mitchell, and Ruben Sierra.

	MINT	EXC	G-VG
COMPLETE SET (56)	60.00	27.00	9.00
COMMON PLAYER (1-56)	.12	.05	.01
☐ 1 Wally Joyner	3.25	1.25	.25
☐ 2 Tracy Jones	.20	.08	.02
☐ 3 Allan Anderson	.20	.08	.02
☐ 4 Ed Correa	.12	.05	.01
☐ 5 Reggie Williams	.12	.05	.01
☐ 6 Charlie Kerfeld	.12	.05	.01
☐ 7 Andres Galarraga	.50	.20	.05
☐ 8 Bob Tewksbury	.20	.08	.02
☐ 9 Al Newman	.20	.08	.02
☐ 10 Andres Thomas	.20	.08	.02
☐ 11 Barry Bonds	8.50	3.75	.85

☐ 12 Juan Nieves	.20	.08	.02
☐ 13 Mark Eichhorn	.20	.08	.02
☐ 14 Dan Plesac	.20	.08	.02
☐ 15 Cory Snyder	.25	.10	.02
☐ 16 Kelly Gruber	2.50	1.00	.25
☐ 17 Kevin Mitchell	6.00	2.50	.60
☐ 18 Steve Lombardozzi	.20	.08	.02
☐ 19 Mitch Williams	.40	.16	.04
☐ 20 John Cerutti	.20	.08	.02
☐ 21 Todd Worrell	.20	.08	.02
☐ 22 Jose Canseco	12.00	5.25	1.50
☐ 23 Pete Incaviglia	.75	.30	.07
☐ 24 Jose Guzman	.25	.10	.02
☐ 25 Scott Bailes	.20	.08	.02
☐ 26 Greg Mathews	.12	.05	.01
☐ 27 Eric King	.20	.08	.02
☐ 28 Paul Assenmacher	.20	.08	.02
☐ 29 Jeff Sellers	.12	.05	.01
☐ 30 Bobby Bonilla	7.50	3.25	.75
☐ 31 Doug Drabek	1.50	.60	.15
☐ 32 Will Clark UER (Listed as throwing right, should be left)	13.50	6.00	1.85
☐ 33 Bip Roberts	.60	.25	.06
☐ 34 Jim Deshaies	.20	.08	.02
☐ 35 Mike LaValliere	.30	.12	.03
☐ 36 Scott Bankhead	.20	.08	.02
☐ 37 Dale Sveum	.20	.08	.02
☐ 38 Bo Jackson	11.00	5.00	1.35
☐ 39 Robby Thompson	.45	.18	.04
☐ 40 Eric Plunk	.20	.08	.02
☐ 41 Bill Bathe	.12	.05	.01
☐ 42 John Kruk	.45	.18	.04
☐ 43 Andy Allanson	.20	.08	.02
☐ 44 Mark Portugal	.25	.10	.02
☐ 45 Danny Tartabull	1.00	.40	.10
☐ 46 Bob Kipper	.20	.08	.02
☐ 47 Gene Walter	.20	.08	.02
☐ 48 Rey Quinones	.12	.05	.01
☐ 49 Bobby Witt	.60	.25	.06
☐ 50 Bill Mooneyham	.12	.05	.01
☐ 51 John Cangelosi	.12	.05	.01
☐ 52 Ruben Sierra	11.00	5.00	1.35
☐ 53 Rob Woodward	.12	.05	.01
☐ 54 Ed Hearn	.12	.05	.01
☐ 55 Joel McKeon	.12	.05	.01
☐ 56 Checklist Card	.12	.02	.00

1987 Donruss

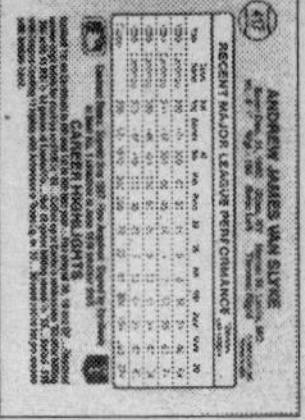

This 660-card set was distributed along with a puzzle of Roberto Clemente. The checklist cards are numbered throughout the set as multiples of 100. The wax pack boxes again contain four separate cards printed on the bottom of the box. Cards measure 2 1/2" by 3 1/2" and feature a black and gold border on the front; the backs are also done in black and gold on white card stock. The popular Diamond King subset returns for the sixth consecutive year. Some of the Diamond King (1-26) selections are repeats from prior years; Perez-Steele Galleries has indicated that a five-year rotation will be maintained in order to avoid depleting the pool of available worthy "kings" on some of the teams. Three of the Diamond Kings have a variation (on the reverse) where the yellow strip behind the words "Donruss Diamond Kings" is not printed and, hence, the background is white. The key rookie cards in this set are Barry Bonds, Bobby Bonilla, Will Clark, David Cone, Chuck Finley, Mike Greenwell, Bo Jackson, Wally Joyner, Barry Larkin, Dave Magadan, Kevin Mitchell, Rafael Palmiero, and Ruben Sierra. The backs of the cards in the factory sets are oriented differently than cards taken from wax packs, giving the appearance that one version or the other is upside down when sorting from the card backs.

	MINT	EXC	G-VG
COMPLETE SET (660)	65.00	27.00	3.00
COMMON PLAYER (1-660)	.05	.02	.00
☐ 1 Wally Joyner DK	.35	.15	.03
☐ 2 Roger Clemens DK	.65	.25	.06
☐ 3 Dale Murphy DK	.15	.06	.01
☐ 4 Darryl Strawberry DK	.50	.20	.05
☐ 5 Ozzie Smith DK	.15	.06	.01
☐ 6 Jose Canseco DK	1.25	.50	.12
☐ 7 Charlie Hough DK	.08	.03	.01
☐ 8 Brook Jacoby DK	.08	.03	.01
☐ 9 Fred Lynn DK	.12	.05	.01
☐ 10 Rick Rhoden DK	.08	.03	.01

☐ 11 Chris Brown DK	.08	.03	.01
☐ 12 Von Hayes DK	.10	.04	.01
☐ 13 Jack Morris DK	.15	.06	.01
☐ 14A Kevin McReynolds DK ERR (Yellow strip missing on back)	.50	.20	.05
☐ 14B Kevin McReynolds DK COR	.12	.05	.01
☐ 15 George Brett DK	.25	.10	.02
☐ 16 Ted Higuera DK	.08	.03	.01
☐ 17 Hubie Brooks DK	.08	.03	.01
☐ 18 Mike Scott DK	.10	.04	.01
☐ 19 Kirby Puckett DK	.50	.20	.05
☐ 20 Dave Winfield DK	.20	.08	.02
☐ 21 Lloyd Moseby DK	.08	.03	.01
☐ 22A Eric Davis DK ERR (Yellow strip missing on back)	1.00	.40	.10
☐ 22B Eric Davis DK COR	.25	.10	.02
☐ 23 Jim Presley DK	.08	.03	.01
☐ 24 Keith Moreland DK	.08	.03	.01
☐ 25A Greg Walker DK ERR (Yellow strip missing on back)	.45	.18	.04
☐ 25B Greg Walker DK COR	.10	.04	.01
☐ 26 Steve Sax DK	.12	.05	.01
☐ 27 DK Checklist 1-26	.07	.03	.01
☐ 28 B.J. Surhoff RR	.25	.10	.02
☐ 29 Randy Myers RR	.25	.10	.02
☐ 30 Ken Gerhart RR	.05	.02	.00
☐ 31 Benito Santiago RR	1.25	.50	.12
☐ 32 Greg Swindell RR	.75	.30	.07
☐ 33 Mike Birkbeck RR	.10	.04	.01
☐ 34 Terry Steinbach RR	.40	.16	.04
☐ 35 Bo Jackson RR	7.50	3.25	.75
☐ 36 Greg Maddux RR	1.25	.50	.12
☐ 37 Jim Lindeman RR	.08	.03	.01
☐ 38 Devon White RR	.90	.40	.09
☐ 39 Eric Bell RR	.08	.03	.01
☐ 40 Willie Fraser RR	.08	.03	.01
☐ 41 Jerry Browne RR	.20	.08	.02
☐ 42 Chris James RR	.35	.15	.03
☐ 43 Rafael Palmeiro RR	6.00	2.50	.60
☐ 44 Pat Dodson RR	.08	.03	.01
☐ 45 Duane Ward RR	.30	.12	.03
☐ 46 Mark McGwire RR	5.00	2.25	.50
☐ 47 Bruce Fields RR UER (Photo actually Darnell Coles)	.08	.03	.01
☐ 48 Eddie Murray	.40	.16	.04
☐ 49 Ted Higuera	.08	.03	.01
☐ 50 Kirk Gibson	.17	.07	.01
☐ 51 Oil Can Boyd	.05	.02	.00
☐ 52 Don Mattingly	1.00	.40	.10
☐ 53 Pedro Guerrero	.15	.06	.01
☐ 54 George Brett	.40	.16	.04
☐ 55 Jose Rijo	.17	.07	.01
☐ 56 Tim Raines	.20	.08	.02
☐ 57 Ed Correa	.05	.02	.00
☐ 58 Mike Witt	.05	.02	.00
☐ 59 Greg Walker	.05	.02	.00
☐ 60 Ozzie Smith	.35	.15	.03
☐ 61 Glenn Davis	.25	.10	.02
☐ 62 Glenn Wilson	.05	.02	.00
☐ 63 Tom Browning	.08	.03	.01
☐ 64 Tony Gwynn	.70	.30	.07
☐ 65 R.J. Reynolds	.05	.02	.00
☐ 66 Will Clark	10.00	4.50	1.25
☐ 67 Ozzie Virgil	.05	.02	.00
☐ 68 Rick Sutcliffe	.08	.03	.01
☐ 69 Gary Carter	.20	.08	.02
☐ 70 Mike Moore	.08	.03	.01
☐ 71 Bert Blyleven	.10	.04	.01
☐ 72 Tony Fernandez	.12	.05	.01
☐ 73 Kent Hrbek	.15	.06	.01
☐ 74 Lloyd Moseby	.05	.02	.00
☐ 75 Alvin Davis	.10	.04	.01
☐ 76 Keith Hernandez	.12	.05	.01
☐ 77 Ryne Sandberg	1.25	.50	.12
☐ 78 Dale Murphy	.30	.12	.03
☐ 79 Sid Bream	.05	.02	.00
☐ 80 Chris Brown	.05	.02	.00
☐ 81 Steve Garvey	.25	.10	.02
☐ 82 Mario Soto	.05	.02	.00
☐ 83 Shane Rawley	.05	.02	.00
☐ 84 Willie McGee	.12	.05	.01
☐ 85 Jose Cruz	.08	.03	.01
☐ 86 Brian Downing	.08	.03	.01
☐ 87 Ozzie Guillen	.15	.06	.01
☐ 88 Hubie Brooks	.10	.04	.01
☐ 89 Cal Ripken	1.50	.60	.15
☐ 90 Juan Nieves	.05	.02	.00
☐ 91 Lance Parrish	.10	.04	.01
☐ 92 Jim Rice	.12	.05	.01
☐ 93 Ron Guidry	.12	.05	.01
☐ 94 Fernando Valenzuela	.10	.04	.01
☐ 95 Andy Allanson	.05	.02	.00
☐ 96 Willie Wilson	.10	.04	.01
☐ 97 Jose Canseco	8.00	3.50	.80
☐ 98 Jeff Reardon	.12	.05	.01
☐ 99 Bobby Witt	.50	.20	.05
☐ 100 Checklist Card	.10	.01	.00
☐ 101 Jose Guzman	.08	.03	.01
☐ 102 Steve Balboni	.05	.02	.00
☐ 103 Tony Phillips	.05	.02	.00
☐ 104 Brook Jacoby	.08	.03	.01
☐ 105 Dave Winfield	.30	.12	.03
☐ 106 Orel Hershiser	.20	.08	.02
☐ 107 Lou Whitaker	.15	.06	.01
☐ 108 Fred Lynn	.12	.05	.01
☐ 109 Bill Wegman	.08	.03	.01
☐ 110 Donnie Moore	.05	.02	.00
☐ 111 Jack Clark	.15	.06	.01
☐ 112 Bob Knepper	.05	.02	.00
☐ 113 Von Hayes	.10	.04	.01
☐ 114 Bip Roberts	.40	.16	.04

☐ 115 Tony Pena	.08	.03	.01
☐ 116 Scott Garrelts	.05	.02	.00
☐ 117 Paul Molitor	.15	.06	.01
☐ 118 Darryl Strawberry	1.25	.50	.12
☐ 119 Shawon Dunston	.20	.08	.02
☐ 120 Jim Presley	.05	.02	.00
☐ 121 Jesse Barfield	.10	.04	.01
☐ 122 Gary Gaetti	.10	.04	.01
☐ 123 Kurt Stillwell	.20	.08	.02
☐ 124 Joel Davis	.05	.02	.00
☐ 125 Mike Boddicker	.05	.02	.00
☐ 126 Robin Yount	.45	.18	.04
☐ 127 Alan Trammell	.25	.10	.02
☐ 128 Dave Righetti	.10	.04	.01
☐ 129 Dwight Evans	.15	.06	.01
☐ 130 Mike Scioscia	.05	.02	.00
☐ 131 Julio Franco	.35	.15	.03
☐ 132 Bret Saberhagen	.30	.12	.03
☐ 133 Mike Davis	.05	.02	.00
☐ 134 Joe Hesketh	.08	.03	.01
☐ 135 Wally Joyner	2.00	.80	.20
☐ 136 Don Slaught	.05	.02	.00
☐ 137 Daryl Boston	.05	.02	.00
☐ 138 Nolan Ryan	2.00	.80	.20
☐ 139 Mike Schmidt	1.00	.40	.10
☐ 140 Tommy Herr	.05	.02	.00
☐ 141 Garry Templeton	.08	.03	.01
☐ 142 Kal Daniels	.20	.08	.02
☐ 143 Billy Sample	.05	.02	.00
☐ 144 Johnny Ray	.05	.02	.00
☐ 145 Rob Thompson	.25	.10	.02
☐ 146 Bob Dernier	.05	.02	.00
☐ 147 Danny Tartabull	.25	.10	.02
☐ 148 Ernie Whitt	.05	.02	.00
☐ 149 Kirby Puckett	1.75	.70	.17
☐ 150 Mike Young	.05	.02	.00
☐ 151 Ernest Riles	.05	.02	.00
☐ 152 Frank Tanana	.08	.03	.01
☐ 153 Rich Gedman	.05	.02	.00
☐ 154 Willie Randolph	.08	.03	.01
☐ 155 Bill Madlock	.08	.03	.01
☐ 156 Joe Carter	.50	.20	.05
☐ 157 Danny Jackson	.08	.03	.01
☐ 158 Carney Lansford	.10	.04	.01
☐ 159 Bryn Smith	.05	.02	.00
☐ 160 Gary Pettis	.05	.02	.00
☐ 161 Oddibe McDowell	.08	.03	.01
☐ 162 John Cangelosi	.05	.02	.00
☐ 163 Mike Scott	.10	.04	.01
☐ 164 Eric Show	.05	.02	.00
☐ 165 Juan Samuel	.15	.06	.01
☐ 166 Nick Esasky	.08	.03	.01
☐ 167 Zane Smith	.10	.04	.01
☐ 168 Mike Brown (Pirates OF)	.05	.02	.00
☐ 169 Keith Moreland	.05	.02	.00
☐ 170 John Tudor	.08	.03	.01
☐ 171 Ken Dixon	.05	.02	.00
☐ 172 Jim Gantner	.05	.02	.00
☐ 173 Jack Morris	.25	.10	.02
☐ 174 Bruce Hurst	.10	.04	.01
☐ 175 Dennis Rasmussen	.05	.02	.00
☐ 176 Mike Marshall	.08	.03	.01
☐ 177 Dan Quisenberry	.10	.04	.01
☐ 178 Eric Plunk	.05	.02	.00
☐ 179 Tim Wallach	.10	.04	.01
☐ 180 Steve Buechele	.08	.03	.01
☐ 181 Don Sutton	.15	.06	.01
☐ 182 Dave Schmidt	.05	.02	.00
☐ 183 Terry Pendleton	.20	.08	.02
☐ 184 Jim Deshaies	.15	.06	.01
☐ 185 Steve Bedrosian	.08	.03	.01
☐ 186 Pete Rose	.50	.20	.05
☐ 187 Dave Dravecky	.10	.04	.01
☐ 188 Rick Reuschel	.08	.03	.01
☐ 189 Dan Gladden	.05	.02	.00
☐ 190 Rick Mahler	.05	.02	.00
☐ 191 Thad Bosley	.05	.02	.00
☐ 192 Ron Darling	.10	.04	.01
☐ 193 Matt Young	.05	.02	.00
☐ 194 Tom Brunansky	.10	.04	.01
☐ 195 Dave Stieb	.10	.04	.01
☐ 196 Frank Viola	.20	.08	.02
☐ 197 Tom Henke	.08	.03	.01
☐ 198 Karl Best	.05	.02	.00
☐ 199 Dwight Gooden	.50	.20	.05
☐ 200 Checklist Card	.10	.01	.00
☐ 201 Steve Trout	.05	.02	.00
☐ 202 Rafael Ramirez	.05	.02	.00
☐ 203 Bob Walk	.05	.02	.00
☐ 204 Roger Mason	.05	.02	.00
☐ 205 Terry Kennedy	.05	.02	.00
☐ 206 Ron Oester	.05	.02	.00
☐ 207 John Russell	.05	.02	.00
☐ 208 Greg Mathews	.08	.03	.01
☐ 209 Charlie Kerfeld	.05	.02	.00
☐ 210 Reggie Jackson	.40	.16	.04
☐ 211 Floyd Bannister	.05	.02	.00
☐ 212 Vance Law	.05	.02	.00
☐ 213 Rich Bordi	.05	.02	.00
☐ 214 Dan Plesac	.15	.06	.01
☐ 215 Dave Collins	.05	.02	.00
☐ 216 Bob Stanley	.05	.02	.00
☐ 217 Joe Niekro	.08	.03	.01
☐ 218 Tom Niedenfuer	.05	.02	.00
☐ 219 Brett Butler	.12	.05	.01
☐ 220 Charlie Leibrandt	.05	.02	.00
☐ 221 Steve Ontiveros	.05	.02	.00
☐ 222 Tim Burke	.05	.02	.00
☐ 223 Curtis Wilkerson	.05	.02	.00
☐ 224 Pete Incaviglia	.35	.15	.03
☐ 225 Lonnie Smith	.10	.04	.01
☐ 226 Chris Codiroli	.05	.02	.00
☐ 227 Scott Bailes	.08	.03	.01
☐ 228 Rickey Henderson	1.00	.40	.10
☐ 229 Ken Howell	.05	.02	.00

☐ 230 Darnell Coles	.05	.02	.00
☐ 231 Don Aase	.05	.02	.00
☐ 232 Tim Leary	.10	.04	.01
☐ 233 Bob Boone	.10	.04	.01
☐ 234 Ricky Horton	.05	.02	.00
☐ 235 Mark Bailey	.05	.02	.00
☐ 236 Kevin Gross	.05	.02	.00
☐ 237 Lance McCullers	.05	.02	.00
☐ 238 Cecilio Guante	.05	.02	.00
☐ 239 Bob Melvin	.05	.02	.00
☐ 240 Billy Jo Robidoux	.05	.02	.00
☐ 241 Roger McDowell	.05	.02	.00
☐ 242 Leon Durham	.05	.02	.00
☐ 243 Ed Nunez	.05	.02	.00
☐ 244 Jimmy Key	.12	.05	.01
☐ 245 Mike Smithson	.05	.02	.00
☐ 246 Bo Diaz	.05	.02	.00
☐ 247 Carlton Fisk	.35	.15	.03
☐ 248 Larry Sheets	.05	.02	.00
☐ 249 Juan Castillo	.05	.02	.00
☐ 250 Eric King	.15	.06	.01
☐ 251 Doug Drabek	1.25	.50	.12
☐ 252 Wade Boggs	.75	.30	.07
☐ 253 Mariano Duncan	.08	.03	.01
☐ 254 Pat Tabler	.05	.02	.00
☐ 255 Frank White	.05	.02	.00
☐ 256 Alfredo Griffin	.05	.02	.00
☐ 257 Floyd Youmans	.05	.02	.00
☐ 258 Rob Wilfong	.05	.02	.00
☐ 259 Pete O'Brien	.05	.02	.00
☐ 260 Tim Hulett	.05	.02	.00
☐ 261 Dickie Thon	.05	.02	.00
☐ 262 Darren Daulton	.10	.04	.01
☐ 263 Vince Coleman	.50	.20	.05
☐ 264 Andy Hawkins	.05	.02	.00
☐ 265 Eric Davis	.50	.20	.05
☐ 266 Andres Thomas	.10	.04	.01
☐ 267 Mike Diaz	.05	.02	.00
☐ 268 Chili Davis	.10	.04	.01
☐ 269 Jody Davis	.05	.02	.00
☐ 270 Phil Bradley	.05	.02	.00
☐ 271 George Bell	.25	.10	.02
☐ 272 Keith Atherton	.05	.02	.00
☐ 273 Storm Davis	.05	.02	.00
☐ 274 Rob Deer	.15	.06	.01
☐ 275 Walt Terrell	.05	.02	.00
☐ 276 Roger Clemens	2.00	.80	.20
☐ 277 Mike Easler	.05	.02	.00
☐ 278 Steve Sax	.15	.06	.01
☐ 279 Andre Thornton	.05	.02	.00
☐ 280 Jim Sundberg	.05	.02	.00
☐ 281 Bill Bathe	.05	.02	.00
☐ 282 Jay Tibbs	.05	.02	.00
☐ 283 Dick Schofield	.05	.02	.00
☐ 284 Mike Mason	.05	.02	.00
☐ 285 Jerry Hairston	.05	.02	.00
☐ 286 Bill Doran	.05	.02	.00
☐ 287 Tim Flannery	.05	.02	.00
☐ 288 Gary Redus	.05	.02	.00
☐ 289 John Franco	.10	.04	.01
☐ 290 Paul Assenmacher	.05	.02	.00
☐ 291 Joe Orsulak	.08	.03	.01
☐ 292 Lee Smith	.15	.06	.01
☐ 293 Mike Laga	.05	.02	.00
☐ 294 Rick Dempsey	.05	.02	.00
☐ 295 Mike Felder	.08	.03	.01
☐ 296 Tom Brookens	.05	.02	.00
☐ 297 Al Nipper	.05	.02	.00
☐ 298 Mike Pagliarulo	.05	.02	.00
☐ 299 Franklin Stubbs	.08	.03	.01
☐ 300 Checklist Card	.10	.01	.00
☐ 301 Steve Farr	.08	.03	.01
☐ 302 Bill Mooneyham	.05	.02	.00
☐ 303 Andres Galarraga	.10	.04	.01
☐ 304 Scott Fletcher	.05	.02	.00
☐ 305 Jack Howell	.05	.02	.00
☐ 306 Russ Morman	.05	.02	.00
☐ 307 Todd Worrell	.10	.04	.01
☐ 308 Dave Smith	.05	.02	.00
☐ 309 Jeff Stone	.05	.02	.00
☐ 310 Ron Robinson	.05	.02	.00
☐ 311 Bruce Bochy	.05	.02	.00
☐ 312 Jim Winn	.05	.02	.00
☐ 313 Mark Davis	.08	.03	.01
☐ 314 Jeff Dedmon	.05	.02	.00
☐ 315 Jamie Moyer	.08	.03	.01
☐ 316 Wally Backman	.05	.02	.00
☐ 317 Ken Phelps	.05	.02	.00
☐ 318 Steve Lombardozzi	.05	.02	.00
☐ 319 Rance Mulliniks	.05	.02	.00
☐ 320 Tim Laudner	.05	.02	.00
☐ 321 Mark Eichhorn	.10	.04	.01
☐ 322 Lee Guetterman	.12	.05	.01
☐ 323 Sid Fernandez	.12	.05	.01
☐ 324 Jerry Mumphrey	.05	.02	.00
☐ 325 David Palmer	.05	.02	.00
☐ 326 Bill Almon	.05	.02	.00
☐ 327 Candy Maldonado	.08	.03	.01
☐ 328 John Kruk	.40	.16	.04
☐ 329 John Denny	.05	.02	.00
☐ 330 Milt Thompson	.08	.03	.01
☐ 331 Mike LaValliere	.25	.10	.02
☐ 332 Alan Ashby	.05	.02	.00
☐ 333 Doug Corbett	.05	.02	.00
☐ 334 Ron Karkovice	.08	.03	.01
☐ 335 Mitch Webster	.05	.02	.00
☐ 336 Lee Lacy	.05	.02	.00
☐ 337 Glenn Braggs	.30	.12	.03
☐ 338 Dwight Lowry	.05	.02	.00
☐ 339 Don Baylor	.08	.03	.01
☐ 340 Brian Fisher	.05	.02	.00
☐ 341 Reggie Williams	.05	.02	.00
☐ 342 Tom Candiotti	.10	.04	.01
☐ 343 Rudy Law	.05	.02	.00
☐ 344 Curt Young	.05	.02	.00
☐ 345 Mike Fitzgerald	.05	.02	.00

☐ 346 Ruben Sierra ... 8.50 3.75 .85
☐ 347 Mitch Williams ... .30 .12 .03
☐ 348 Jorge Orta ... .05 .02 .00
☐ 349 Mickey Tettleton ... .15 .06 .01
☐ 350 Ernie Camacho ... .05 .02 .00
☐ 351 Ron Kittle ... .08 .03 .01
☐ 352 Ken Landreaux ... .05 .02 .00
☐ 353 Chet Lemon ... .05 .02 .00
☐ 354 John Shelby ... .05 .02 .00
☐ 355 Mark Clear ... .05 .02 .00
☐ 356 Doug DeCinces ... .08 .03 .01
☐ 357 Ken Dayley ... .05 .02 .00
☐ 358 Phil Garner ... .08 .03 .01
☐ 359 Steve Jeltz ... .05 .02 .00
☐ 360 Ed Whitson ... .05 .02 .00
☐ 361 Barry Bonds ... 6.00 2.50 .60
☐ 362 Vida Blue ... .08 .03 .01
☐ 363 Cecil Cooper ... .08 .03 .01
☐ 364 Bob Ojeda ... .05 .02 .00
☐ 365 Dennis Eckersley ... .15 .06 .01
☐ 366 Mike Morgan ... .08 .03 .01
☐ 367 Willie Upshaw ... .05 .02 .00
☐ 368 Allan Anderson ... .17 .07 .01
☐ 369 Bill Gullickson ... .08 .03 .01
☐ 370 Bobby Thigpen ... 1.00 .40 .10
☐ 371 Juan Beniquez ... .05 .02 .00
☐ 372 Charlie Moore ... .05 .02 .00
☐ 373 Dan Petry ... .05 .02 .00
☐ 374 Rod Scurry ... .05 .02 .00
☐ 375 Tom Seaver ... .45 .18 .04
☐ 376 Ed VandeBerg ... .05 .02 .00
☐ 377 Tony Bernazard ... .05 .02 .00
☐ 378 Greg Pryor ... .05 .02 .00
☐ 379 Dwayne Murphy ... .05 .02 .00
☐ 380 Andy McGaffigan ... .05 .02 .00
☐ 381 Kirk McCaskill ... .05 .02 .00
☐ 382 Greg Harris ... .05 .02 .00
☐ 383 Rich Dotson ... .05 .02 .00
☐ 384 Craig Reynolds ... .05 .02 .00
☐ 385 Greg Gross ... .05 .02 .00
☐ 386 Tito Landrum ... .05 .02 .00
☐ 387 Craig Lefferts ... .05 .02 .00
☐ 388 Dave Parker ... .17 .07 .01
☐ 389 Bob Horner ... .10 .04 .01
☐ 390 Pat Clements ... .05 .02 .00
☐ 391 Jeff Leonard ... .05 .02 .00
☐ 392 Chris Speier ... .05 .02 .00
☐ 393 John Moses ... .05 .02 .00
☐ 394 Garth Iorg ... .05 .02 .00
☐ 395 Greg Gagne ... .05 .02 .00
☐ 396 Nate Snell ... .05 .02 .00
☐ 397 Bryan Clutterbuck ... .05 .02 .00
☐ 398 Darrell Evans ... .08 .03 .01
☐ 399 Steve Crawford ... .05 .02 .00
☐ 400 Checklist Card ... .10 .01 .00
☐ 401 Phil Lombardi ... .08 .03 .01
☐ 402 Rick Honeycutt ... .05 .02 .00
☐ 403 Ken Schrom ... .05 .02 .00
☐ 404 Bud Black ... .05 .02 .00
☐ 405 Donnie Hill ... .05 .02 .00
☐ 406 Wayne Krenchicki ... .05 .02 .00
☐ 407 Chuck Finley ... 2.00 .80 .20
☐ 408 Toby Harrah ... .05 .02 .00
☐ 409 Steve Lyons ... .05 .02 .00
☐ 410 Kevin Bass ... .05 .02 .00
☐ 411 Marvell Wynne ... .05 .02 .00
☐ 412 Ron Roenicke ... .05 .02 .00
☐ 413 Tracy Jones ... .12 .05 .01
☐ 414 Gene Garber ... .05 .02 .00
☐ 415 Mike Bielecki ... .10 .04 .01
☐ 416 Frank DiPino ... .05 .02 .00
☐ 417 Andy Van Slyke ... .20 .08 .02
☐ 418 Jim Dwyer ... .05 .02 .00
☐ 419 Ben Oglivie ... .05 .02 .00
☐ 420 Dave Bergman ... .05 .02 .00
☐ 421 Joe Sambito ... .05 .02 .00
☐ 422 Bob Tewksbury ... .08 .03 .01
☐ 423 Len Matuszek ... .05 .02 .00
☐ 424 Mike Kingery ... .08 .03 .01
☐ 425 Dave Kingman ... .10 .04 .01
☐ 426 Al Newman ... .08 .03 .01
☐ 427 Gary Ward ... .05 .02 .00
☐ 428 Ruppert Jones ... .05 .02 .00
☐ 429 Harold Baines ... .15 .06 .01
☐ 430 Pat Perry ... .05 .02 .00
☐ 431 Terry Puhl ... .05 .02 .00
☐ 432 Don Carman ... .05 .02 .00
☐ 433 Eddie Milner ... .05 .02 .00
☐ 434 LaMarr Hoyt ... .05 .02 .00
☐ 435 Rick Rhoden ... .05 .02 .00
☐ 436 Jose Uribe ... .05 .02 .00
☐ 437 Ken Oberkfell ... .05 .02 .00
☐ 438 Ron Davis ... .05 .02 .00
☐ 439 Jesse Orosco ... .05 .02 .00
☐ 440 Scott Bradley ... .05 .02 .00
☐ 441 Randy Bush ... .05 .02 .00
☐ 442 John Cerutti ... .12 .05 .01
☐ 443 Roy Smalley ... .05 .02 .00
☐ 444 Kelly Gruber ... 2.00 .80 .20
☐ 445 Bob Kearney ... .05 .02 .00
☐ 446 Ed Hearn ... .05 .02 .00
☐ 447 Scott Sanderson ... .08 .03 .01
☐ 448 Bruce Benedict ... .05 .02 .00
☐ 449 Junior Ortiz ... .05 .02 .00
☐ 450 Mike Aldrete ... .08 .03 .01
☐ 451 Kevin McReynolds ... .15 .06 .01
☐ 452 Rob Murphy ... .12 .05 .01
☐ 453 Kent Tekulve ... .05 .02 .00
☐ 454 Curt Ford ... .05 .02 .00
☐ 455 Dave Lopes ... .08 .03 .01
☐ 456 Bob Grich ... .08 .03 .01
☐ 457 Jose DeLeon ... .05 .02 .00
☐ 458 Andre Dawson ... .40 .16 .04
☐ 459 Mike Flanagan ... .08 .03 .01
☐ 460 Joey Meyer ... .10 .04 .01
☐ 461 Chuck Cary ... .10 .04 .01

☐ 462 Bill Buckner	.08	.03	.01
☐ 463 Bob Shirley	.05	.02	.00
☐ 464 Jeff Hamilton	.10	.04	.01
☐ 465 Phil Niekro	.17	.07	.01
☐ 466 Mark Gubicza	.10	.04	.01
☐ 467 Jerry Willard	.05	.02	.00
☐ 468 Bob Sebra	.08	.03	.01
☐ 469 Larry Parrish	.05	.02	.00
☐ 470 Charlie Hough	.05	.02	.00
☐ 471 Hal McRae	.08	.03	.01
☐ 472 Dave Leiper	.05	.02	.00
☐ 473 Mel Hall	.10	.04	.01
☐ 474 Dan Pasqua	.08	.03	.01
☐ 475 Bob Welch	.10	.04	.01
☐ 476 Johnny Grubb	.05	.02	.00
☐ 477 Jim Traber	.05	.02	.00
☐ 478 Chris Bosio	.25	.10	.02
☐ 479 Mark McLemore	.05	.02	.00
☐ 480 John Morris	.05	.02	.00
☐ 481 Billy Hatcher	.08	.03	.01
☐ 482 Dan Schatzeder	.05	.02	.00
☐ 483 Rich Gossage	.10	.04	.01
☐ 484 Jim Morrison	.05	.02	.00
☐ 485 Bob Brenly	.05	.02	.00
☐ 486 Bill Schroeder	.05	.02	.00
☐ 487 Mookie Wilson	.08	.03	.01
☐ 488 Dave Martinez	.40	.16	.04
☐ 489 Harold Reynolds	.10	.04	.01
☐ 490 Jeff Hearron	.05	.02	.00
☐ 491 Mickey Hatcher	.05	.02	.00
☐ 492 Barry Larkin	3.50	1.50	.35
☐ 493 Bob James	.05	.02	.00
☐ 494 John Habyan	.05	.02	.00
☐ 495 Jim Adduci	.05	.02	.00
☐ 496 Mike Heath	.05	.02	.00
☐ 497 Tim Stoddard	.05	.02	.00
☐ 498 Tony Armas	.05	.02	.00
☐ 499 Dennis Powell	.05	.02	.00
☐ 500 Checklist Card	.10	.01	.00
☐ 501 Chris Bando	.05	.02	.00
☐ 502 David Cone	2.25	.90	.22
☐ 503 Jay Howell	.05	.02	.00
☐ 504 Tom Foley	.05	.02	.00
☐ 505 Ray Chadwick	.05	.02	.00
☐ 506 Mike Loynd	.05	.02	.00
☐ 507 Neil Allen	.05	.02	.00
☐ 508 Danny Darwin	.05	.02	.00
☐ 509 Rick Schu	.05	.02	.00
☐ 510 Jose Oquendo	.05	.02	.00
☐ 511 Gene Walter	.05	.02	.00
☐ 512 Terry McGriff	.08	.03	.01
☐ 513 Ken Griffey	.12	.05	.01
☐ 514 Benny Distefano	.05	.02	.00
☐ 515 Terry Mulholland	.40	.16	.04
☐ 516 Ed Lynch	.05	.02	.00
☐ 517 Bill Swift	.08	.03	.01
☐ 518 Manny Lee	.05	.02	.00
☐ 519 Andre David	.05	.02	.00
☐ 520 Scott McGregor	.05	.02	.00
☐ 521 Rick Manning	.05	.02	.00
☐ 522 Willie Hernandez	.05	.02	.00
☐ 523 Marty Barrett	.05	.02	.00
☐ 524 Wayne Tolleson	.05	.02	.00
☐ 525 Jose Gonzalez	.10	.04	.01
☐ 526 Cory Snyder	.12	.05	.01
☐ 527 Buddy Biancalana	.05	.02	.00
☐ 528 Moose Haas	.05	.02	.00
☐ 529 Wilfredo Tejada	.05	.02	.00
☐ 530 Stu Cliburn	.05	.02	.00
☐ 531 Dale Mohorcic	.08	.03	.01
☐ 532 Ron Hassey	.05	.02	.00
☐ 533 Ty Gainey	.05	.02	.00
☐ 534 Jerry Royster	.05	.02	.00
☐ 535 Mike Maddux	.10	.04	.01
☐ 536 Ted Power	.05	.02	.00
☐ 537 Ted Simmons	.10	.04	.01
☐ 538 Rafael Belliard	.25	.10	.02
☐ 539 Chico Walker	.10	.04	.01
☐ 540 Bob Forsch	.05	.02	.00
☐ 541 John Stefero	.05	.02	.00
☐ 542 Dale Sveum	.08	.03	.01
☐ 543 Mark Thurmond	.05	.02	.00
☐ 544 Jeff Sellers	.08	.03	.01
☐ 545 Joel Skinner	.05	.02	.00
☐ 546 Alex Trevino	.05	.02	.00
☐ 547 Randy Kutcher	.05	.02	.00
☐ 548 Joaquin Andujar	.05	.02	.00
☐ 549 Casey Candaele	.08	.03	.01
☐ 550 Jeff Russell	.08	.03	.01
☐ 551 John Candelaria	.05	.02	.00
☐ 552 Joe Cowley	.05	.02	.00
☐ 553 Danny Cox	.05	.02	.00
☐ 554 Denny Walling	.05	.02	.00
☐ 555 Bruce Ruffin	.10	.04	.01
☐ 556 Buddy Bell	.08	.03	.01
☐ 557 Jimmy Jones	.15	.06	.01
☐ 558 Bobby Bonilla	5.50	2.50	.55
☐ 559 Jeff Robinson (Giants pitcher)	.08	.03	.01
☐ 560 Ed Olwine	.05	.02	.00
☐ 561 Glenallen Hill	.30	.12	.03
☐ 562 Lee Mazzilli	.05	.02	.00
☐ 563 Mike Brown (pitcher)	.05	.02	.00
☐ 564 George Frazier	.05	.02	.00
☐ 565 Mike Sharperson	.08	.03	.01
☐ 566 Mark Portugal	.15	.06	.01
☐ 567 Rick Leach	.05	.02	.00
☐ 568 Mark Langston	.25	.10	.02
☐ 569 Rafael Santana	.05	.02	.00
☐ 570 Manny Trillo	.05	.02	.00
☐ 571 Cliff Speck	.05	.02	.00
☐ 572 Bob Kipper	.05	.02	.00
☐ 573 Kelly Downs	.15	.06	.01
☐ 574 Randy Asadoor	.05	.02	.00
☐ 575 Dave Magadan	.75	.30	.07

□ 576	Marvin Freeman	.08	.03	.01
□ 577	Jeff Lahti	.05	.02	.00
□ 578	Jeff Calhoun	.05	.02	.00
□ 579	Gus Polidor	.05	.02	.00
□ 580	Gene Nelson	.05	.02	.00
□ 581	Tim Teufel	.05	.02	.00
□ 582	Odell Jones	.05	.02	.00
□ 583	Mark Ryal	.05	.02	.00
□ 584	Randy O'Neal	.05	.02	.00
□ 585	Mike Greenwell	6.00	2.50	.60
□ 586	Ray Knight	.08	.03	.01
□ 587	Ralph Bryant	.08	.03	.01
□ 588	Carmen Castillo	.05	.02	.00
□ 589	Ed Wojna	.05	.02	.00
□ 590	Stan Javier	.08	.03	.01
□ 591	Jeff Musselman	.08	.03	.01
□ 592	Mike Stanley	.12	.05	.01
□ 593	Darrell Porter	.05	.02	.00
□ 594	Drew Hall	.05	.02	.00
□ 595	Rob Nelson	.10	.04	.01
□ 596	Bryan Oelkers	.05	.02	.00
□ 597	Scott Nielsen	.10	.04	.01
□ 598	Brian Holton	.10	.04	.01
□ 599	Kevin Mitchell	5.00	2.25	.50
□ 600	Checklist Card	.10	.01	.00
□ 601	Jackie Gutierrez	.05	.02	.00
□ 602	Barry Jones	.12	.05	.01
□ 603	Jerry Narron	.05	.02	.00
□ 604	Steve Lake	.05	.02	.00
□ 605	Jim Pankovits	.05	.02	.00
□ 606	Ed Romero	.05	.02	.00
□ 607	Dave LaPoint	.05	.02	.00
□ 608	Don Robinson	.05	.02	.00
□ 609	Mike Krukow	.05	.02	.00
□ 610	Dave Valle	.05	.02	.00
□ 611	Len Dykstra	.30	.12	.03
□ 612	Roberto Clemente Puzzle Card	.10	.04	.01
□ 613	Mike Trujillo	.05	.02	.00
□ 614	Damaso Garcia	.05	.02	.00
□ 615	Neal Heaton	.05	.02	.00
□ 616	Juan Berenguer	.05	.02	.00
□ 617	Steve Carlton	.35	.15	.03
□ 618	Gary Lucas	.05	.02	.00
□ 619	Geno Petralli	.05	.02	.00
□ 620	Rick Aguilera	.15	.06	.01
□ 621	Fred McGriff	3.50	1.50	.35
□ 622	Dave Henderson	.15	.06	.01
□ 623	Dave Clark	.12	.05	.01
□ 624	Angel Salazar	.05	.02	.00
□ 625	Randy Hunt	.05	.02	.00
□ 626	John Gibbons	.05	.02	.00
□ 627	Kevin Brown	.50	.20	.05
□ 628	Bill Dawley	.05	.02	.00
□ 629	Aurelio Lopez	.05	.02	.00
□ 630	Charles Hudson	.05	.02	.00
□ 631	Ray Soff	.05	.02	.00
□ 632	Ray Hayward	.05	.02	.00
□ 633	Spike Owen	.05	.02	.00
□ 634	Glenn Hubbard	.05	.02	.00
□ 635	Kevin Elster	.15	.06	.01
□ 636	Mike LaCoss	.05	.02	.00
□ 637	Dwayne Henry	.05	.02	.00
□ 638	Rey Quinones	.05	.02	.00
□ 639	Jim Clancy	.05	.02	.00
□ 640	Larry Andersen	.05	.02	.00
□ 641	Calvin Schiraldi	.05	.02	.00
□ 642	Stan Jefferson	.08	.03	.01
□ 643	Marc Sullivan	.05	.02	.00
□ 644	Mark Grant	.05	.02	.00
□ 645	Cliff Johnson	.05	.02	.00
□ 646	Howard Johnson	.40	.16	.04
□ 647	Dave Sax	.05	.02	.00
□ 648	Dave Stewart	.20	.08	.02
□ 649	Danny Heep	.05	.02	.00
□ 650	Joe Johnson	.05	.02	.00
□ 651	Bob Brower	.08	.03	.01
□ 652	Rob Woodward	.05	.02	.00
□ 653	John Mizerock	.05	.02	.00
□ 654	Tim Pyznarski	.05	.02	.00
□ 655	Luis Aquino	.05	.02	.00
□ 656	Mickey Brantley	.08	.03	.01
□ 657	Doyle Alexander	.05	.02	.00
□ 658	Sammy Stewart	.05	.02	.00
□ 659	Jim Acker	.05	.02	.00
□ 660	Pete Ladd	.08	.03	.01

1987 Donruss Rookies

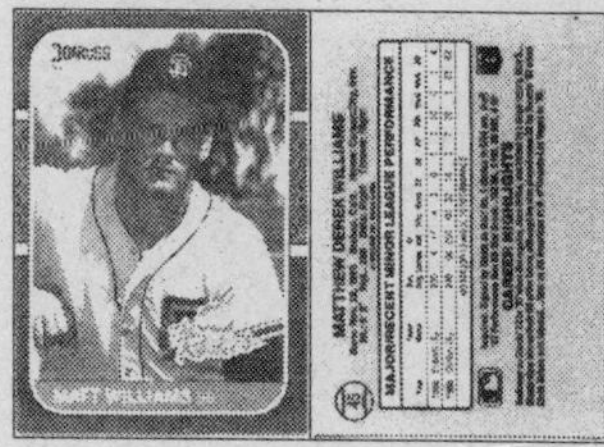

The 1987 Donruss "The Rookies" set features 56 cards plus a 15-piece puzzle of Roberto Clemente. Cards are in full color and are standard size, 2 1/2" by 3 1/2". The set was distributed in a small green and black box with

gold lettering. Card fronts are similar in design to the 1987 Donruss regular issue except for the presence of "The Rookies" logo in the lower left corner and a green border instead of a black border. The key (extended) rookie cards in this set are Ellis Burks, John Smiley, and Matt Williams.

	MINT	EXC	G-VG
COMPLETE SET (56)	20.00	8.50	2.75
COMMON PLAYER (1-56)	.07	.03	.01
☐ 1 Mark McGwire	2.00	.80	.20
☐ 2 Eric Bell	.07	.03	.01
☐ 3 Mark Williamson	.15	.06	.01
☐ 4 Mike Greenwell	2.50	1.00	.25
☐ 5 Ellis Burks	2.50	1.00	.25
☐ 6 DeWayne Buice	.10	.04	.01
☐ 7 Mark McLemore	.07	.03	.01
☐ 8 Devon White	.40	.16	.04
☐ 9 Willie Fraser	.07	.03	.01
☐ 10 Les Lancaster	.15	.06	.01
☐ 11 Ken Williams	.15	.06	.01
☐ 12 Matt Nokes	.60	.25	.06
☐ 13 Jeff Robinson (Tigers pitcher)	.12	.05	.01
☐ 14 Bo Jackson	3.50	1.50	.35
☐ 15 Kevin Seitzer	.20	.08	.02
☐ 16 Billy Ripken	.20	.08	.02
☐ 17 B.J. Surhoff	.15	.06	.01
☐ 18 Chuck Crim	.10	.04	.01
☐ 19 Mike Birkbeck	.07	.03	.01
☐ 20 Chris Bosio	.15	.06	.01
☐ 21 Les Straker	.10	.04	.01
☐ 22 Mark Davidson	.10	.04	.01
☐ 23 Gene Larkin	.25	.10	.02
☐ 24 Ken Gerhart	.07	.03	.01
☐ 25 Luis Polonia	.60	.25	.06
☐ 26 Terry Steinbach	.25	.10	.02
☐ 27 Mickey Brantley	.10	.04	.01
☐ 28 Mike Stanley	.10	.04	.01
☐ 29 Jerry Browne	.10	.04	.01
☐ 30 Todd Benzinger	.40	.16	.04
☐ 31 Fred McGriff	2.50	1.00	.25
☐ 32 Mike Henneman	.35	.15	.03
☐ 33 Casey Candaele	.10	.04	.01
☐ 34 Dave Magadan	.35	.15	.03
☐ 35 David Cone	.75	.30	.07
☐ 36 Mike Jackson	.25	.10	.02
☐ 37 John Mitchell	.10	.04	.01
☐ 38 Mike Dunne	.10	.04	.01
☐ 39 John Smiley	1.25	.50	.12
☐ 40 Joe Magrane	.20	.08	.02
☐ 41 Jim Lindeman	.10	.04	.01
☐ 42 Shane Mack	.30	.12	.03
☐ 43 Stan Jefferson	.10	.04	.01
☐ 44 Benito Santiago	.50	.20	.05
☐ 45 Matt Williams	5.50	2.50	.55
☐ 46 Dave Meads	.10	.04	.01
☐ 47 Rafael Palmeiro	2.50	1.00	.25
☐ 48 Bill Long	.12	.05	.01
☐ 49 Bob Brower	.10	.04	.01
☐ 50 James Steels	.07	.03	.01
☐ 51 Paul Noce	.07	.03	.01
☐ 52 Greg Maddux	.75	.30	.07
☐ 53 Jeff Musselman	.10	.04	.01
☐ 54 Brian Holton	.10	.04	.01
☐ 55 Chuck Jackson	.10	.04	.01
☐ 56 Checklist Card	.07	.01	.00

1988 Donruss

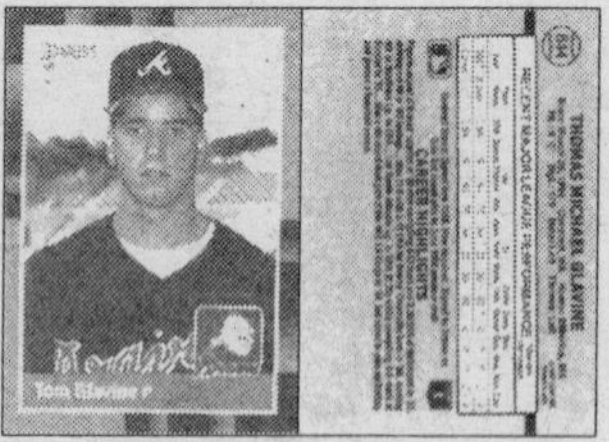

This 660-card set was distributed along with a puzzle of Stan Musial. The six regular checklist cards are numbered throughout the set as multiples of 100. Cards measure 2 1/2" by 3 1/2" and feature a distinctive black and blue border on the front. The popular Diamond King subset returns for the seventh consecutive year. Rated Rookies are featured again as cards 28-47. Cards marked as SP (short printed) from 648-660 are more difficult to find than the other 13 SP's in the lower 600s. These 26 cards listed as SP were apparently pulled from the printing sheet to make room for the 26 Bonus MVP cards. Six of the checklist cards were done two different ways to reflect the inclusion or exclusion of the Bonus MVP cards in the wax packs. In the checklist below, the A variations (for the checklist cards) are from the wax packs and the B variations are from the factory-collated sets. The key rookie cards in this set are Roberto Alomar, Ellis Burks, Ron Gant, Tom Glavine, Mark Grace, Gregg Jefferies, Roberto Kelly, and Matt Williams. There was also a Kirby Puckett card issued as the

package back of Donruss blister packs; it uses a different photo from both of Kirby's regular and Bonus MVP cards and is unnumbered on the back.

	MINT	EXC	G-VG
COMPLETE SET (660)	18.00	7.50	2.50
COMMON PLAYER (1-647)	.03	.01	.00
COMMON PLAYER (648-660)	.06	.02	.00
☐ 1 Mark McGwire DK	.17	.07	.01
☐ 2 Tim Raines DK	.08	.03	.01
☐ 3 Benito Santiago DK	.08	.03	.01
☐ 4 Alan Trammell DK	.10	.04	.01
☐ 5 Danny Tartabull DK	.10	.04	.01
☐ 6 Ron Darling DK	.08	.03	.01
☐ 7 Paul Molitor DK	.08	.03	.01
☐ 8 Devon White DK	.08	.03	.01
☐ 9 Andre Dawson DK	.10	.04	.01
☐ 10 Julio Franco DK	.10	.04	.01
☐ 11 Scott Fletcher DK	.06	.02	.00
☐ 12 Tony Fernandez DK	.08	.03	.01
☐ 13 Shane Rawley DK	.06	.02	.00
☐ 14 Kal Daniels DK	.08	.03	.01
☐ 15 Jack Clark DK	.08	.03	.01
☐ 16 Dwight Evans DK	.08	.03	.01
☐ 17 Tommy John DK	.08	.03	.01
☐ 18 Andy Van Slyke DK	.08	.03	.01
☐ 19 Gary Gaetti DK	.06	.02	.00
☐ 20 Mark Langston DK	.08	.03	.01
☐ 21 Will Clark DK	.25	.10	.02
☐ 22 Glenn Hubbard DK	.06	.02	.00
☐ 23 Billy Hatcher DK	.06	.02	.00
☐ 24 Bob Welch DK	.08	.03	.01
☐ 25 Ivan Calderon DK	.06	.02	.00
☐ 26 Cal Ripken DK	.20	.08	.02
☐ 27 DK Checklist 1-26	.06	.01	.00
☐ 28 Mackey Sasser RR	.15	.06	.01
☐ 29 Jeff Treadway RR	.20	.08	.02
☐ 30 Mike Campbell RR	.06	.02	.00
☐ 31 Lance Johnson RR	.15	.06	.01
☐ 32 Nelson Liriano RR	.08	.03	.01
☐ 33 Shawn Abner RR	.06	.02	.00
☐ 34 Roberto Alomar RR	3.00	1.25	.30
☐ 35 Shawn Hillegas RR	.08	.03	.01
☐ 36 Joey Meyer RR	.06	.02	.00
☐ 37 Kevin Elster RR	.06	.02	.00
☐ 38 Jose Lind RR	.20	.08	.02
☐ 39 Kirt Manwaring RR	.10	.04	.01
☐ 40 Mark Grace RR	1.50	.60	.15
☐ 41 Jody Reed RR	.30	.12	.03
☐ 42 John Farrell RR	.08	.03	.01
☐ 43 Al Leiter RR	.08	.03	.01
☐ 44 Gary Thurman RR	.10	.04	.01
☐ 45 Vicente Palacios RR	.10	.04	.01
☐ 46 Eddie Williams RR	.06	.02	.00
☐ 47 Jack McDowell RR	.50	.20	.05
☐ 48 Ken Dixon	.03	.01	.00
☐ 49 Mike Birkbeck	.03	.01	.00
☐ 50 Eric King	.03	.01	.00
☐ 51 Roger Clemens	.35	.15	.03
☐ 52 Pat Clements	.03	.01	.00
☐ 53 Fernando Valenzuela	.08	.03	.01
☐ 54 Mark Gubicza	.06	.02	.00
☐ 55 Jay Howell	.03	.01	.00
☐ 56 Floyd Youmans	.03	.01	.00
☐ 57 Ed Correa	.03	.01	.00
☐ 58 DeWayne Buice	.03	.01	.00
☐ 59 Jose DeLeon	.03	.01	.00
☐ 60 Danny Cox	.03	.01	.00
☐ 61 Nolan Ryan	.45	.18	.04
☐ 62 Steve Bedrosian	.06	.02	.00
☐ 63 Tom Browning	.06	.02	.00
☐ 64 Mark Davis	.06	.02	.00
☐ 65 R.J. Reynolds	.03	.01	.00
☐ 66 Kevin Mitchell	.25	.10	.02
☐ 67 Ken Oberkfell	.03	.01	.00
☐ 68 Rick Sutcliffe	.06	.02	.00
☐ 69 Dwight Gooden	.17	.07	.01
☐ 70 Scott Bankhead	.06	.02	.00
☐ 71 Bert Blyleven	.08	.03	.01
☐ 72 Jimmy Key	.08	.03	.01
☐ 73 Les Straker	.03	.01	.00
☐ 74 Jim Clancy	.03	.01	.00
☐ 75 Mike Moore	.06	.02	.00
☐ 76 Ron Darling	.08	.03	.01
☐ 77 Ed Lynch	.03	.01	.00
☐ 78 Dale Murphy	.15	.06	.01
☐ 79 Doug Drabek	.12	.05	.01
☐ 80 Scott Garrelts	.03	.01	.00
☐ 81 Ed Whitson	.03	.01	.00
☐ 82 Rob Murphy	.03	.01	.00
☐ 83 Shane Rawley	.03	.01	.00
☐ 84 Greg Mathews	.03	.01	.00
☐ 85 Jim Deshaies	.03	.01	.00
☐ 86 Mike Witt	.03	.01	.00
☐ 87 Donnie Hill	.03	.01	.00
☐ 88 Jeff Reed	.03	.01	.00
☐ 89 Mike Boddicker	.03	.01	.00
☐ 90 Ted Higuera	.06	.02	.00
☐ 91 Walt Terrell	.03	.01	.00
☐ 92 Bob Stanley	.03	.01	.00
☐ 93 Dave Righetti	.08	.03	.01
☐ 94 Orel Hershiser	.10	.04	.01
☐ 95 Chris Bando	.03	.01	.00
☐ 96 Bret Saberhagen	.12	.05	.01
☐ 97 Curt Young	.03	.01	.00
☐ 98 Tim Burke	.03	.01	.00
☐ 99 Charlie Hough	.03	.01	.00
☐ 100A Checklist 28-137	.06	.01	.00
☐ 100B Checklist 28-133	.06	.01	.00
☐ 101 Bobby Witt	.08	.03	.01
☐ 102 George Brett	.20	.08	.02
☐ 103 Mickey Tettleton	.08	.03	.01
☐ 104 Scott Bailes	.03	.01	.00
☐ 105 Mike Pagliarulo	.03	.01	.00

☐ 106	Mike Scioscia	.03	.01	.00
☐ 107	Tom Brookens	.03	.01	.00
☐ 108	Ray Knight	.06	.02	.00
☐ 109	Dan Plesac	.03	.01	.00
☐ 110	Wally Joyner	.15	.06	.01
☐ 111	Bob Forsch	.03	.01	.00
☐ 112	Mike Scott	.08	.03	.01
☐ 113	Kevin Gross	.03	.01	.00
☐ 114	Benito Santiago	.12	.05	.01
☐ 115	Bob Kipper	.03	.01	.00
☐ 116	Mike Krukow	.03	.01	.00
☐ 117	Chris Bosio	.06	.02	.00
☐ 118	Sid Fernandez	.08	.03	.01
☐ 119	Jody Davis	.03	.01	.00
☐ 120	Mike Morgan	.06	.02	.00
☐ 121	Mark Eichhorn	.03	.01	.00
☐ 122	Jeff Reardon	.10	.04	.01
☐ 123	John Franco	.06	.02	.00
☐ 124	Richard Dotson	.03	.01	.00
☐ 125	Eric Bell	.03	.01	.00
☐ 126	Juan Nieves	.03	.01	.00
☐ 127	Jack Morris	.12	.05	.01
☐ 128	Rick Rhoden	.03	.01	.00
☐ 129	Rich Gedman	.03	.01	.00
☐ 130	Ken Howell	.03	.01	.00
☐ 131	Brook Jacoby	.03	.01	.00
☐ 132	Danny Jackson	.06	.02	.00
☐ 133	Gene Nelson	.03	.01	.00
☐ 134	Neal Heaton	.03	.01	.00
☐ 135	Willie Fraser	.03	.01	.00
☐ 136	Jose Guzman	.06	.02	.00
☐ 137	Ozzie Guillen	.08	.03	.01
☐ 138	Bob Knepper	.03	.01	.00
☐ 139	Mike Jackson	.10	.04	.01
☐ 140	Joe Magrane	.12	.05	.01
☐ 141	Jimmy Jones	.06	.02	.00
☐ 142	Ted Power	.03	.01	.00
☐ 143	Ozzie Virgil	.03	.01	.00
☐ 144	Felix Fermin	.03	.01	.00
☐ 145	Kelly Downs	.03	.01	.00
☐ 146	Shawon Dunston	.10	.04	.01
☐ 147	Scott Bradley	.03	.01	.00
☐ 148	Dave Stieb	.08	.03	.01
☐ 149	Frank Viola	.10	.04	.01
☐ 150	Terry Kennedy	.03	.01	.00
☐ 151	Bill Wegman	.03	.01	.00
☐ 152	Matt Nokes	.25	.10	.02
☐ 153	Wade Boggs	.30	.12	.03
☐ 154	Wayne Tolleson	.03	.01	.00
☐ 155	Mariano Duncan	.03	.01	.00
☐ 156	Julio Franco	.15	.06	.01
☐ 157	Charlie Leibrandt	.03	.01	.00
☐ 158	Terry Steinbach	.08	.03	.01
☐ 159	Mike Fitzgerald	.03	.01	.00
☐ 160	Jack Lazorko	.03	.01	.00
☐ 161	Mitch Williams	.06	.02	.00
☐ 162	Greg Walker	.03	.01	.00
☐ 163	Alan Ashby	.03	.01	.00
☐ 164	Tony Gwynn	.25	.10	.02
☐ 165	Bruce Ruffin	.03	.01	.00
☐ 166	Ron Robinson	.03	.01	.00
☐ 167	Zane Smith	.08	.03	.01
☐ 168	Junior Ortiz	.03	.01	.00
☐ 169	Jamie Moyer	.03	.01	.00
☐ 170	Tony Pena	.06	.02	.00
☐ 171	Cal Ripken	.45	.18	.04
☐ 172	B.J. Surhoff	.06	.02	.00
☐ 173	Lou Whitaker	.10	.04	.01
☐ 174	Ellis Burks	.60	.25	.06
☐ 175	Ron Guidry	.08	.03	.01
☐ 176	Steve Sax	.10	.04	.01
☐ 177	Danny Tartabull	.15	.06	.01
☐ 178	Carney Lansford	.08	.03	.01
☐ 179	Casey Candaele	.03	.01	.00
☐ 180	Scott Fletcher	.03	.01	.00
☐ 181	Mark McLemore	.03	.01	.00
☐ 182	Ivan Calderon	.08	.03	.01
☐ 183	Jack Clark	.08	.03	.01
☐ 184	Glenn Davis	.10	.04	.01
☐ 185	Luis Aguayo	.03	.01	.00
☐ 186	Bo Diaz	.03	.01	.00
☐ 187	Stan Jefferson	.03	.01	.00
☐ 188	Sid Bream	.03	.01	.00
☐ 189	Bob Brenly	.03	.01	.00
☐ 190	Dion James	.03	.01	.00
☐ 191	Leon Durham	.03	.01	.00
☐ 192	Jesse Orosco	.03	.01	.00
☐ 193	Alvin Davis	.06	.02	.00
☐ 194	Gary Gaetti	.08	.03	.01
☐ 195	Fred McGriff	.30	.12	.03
☐ 196	Steve Lombardozzi	.03	.01	.00
☐ 197	Rance Mulliniks	.03	.01	.00
☐ 198	Rey Quinones	.03	.01	.00
☐ 199	Gary Carter	.08	.03	.01
☐ 200A	Checklist 138-247	.06	.01	.00
☐ 200B	Checklist 134-239	.06	.01	.00
☐ 201	Keith Moreland	.03	.01	.00
☐ 202	Ken Griffey	.10	.04	.01
☐ 203	Tommy Gregg	.08	.03	.01
☐ 204	Will Clark	.75	.30	.07
☐ 205	John Kruk	.06	.02	.00
☐ 206	Buddy Bell	.06	.02	.00
☐ 207	Von Hayes	.08	.03	.01
☐ 208	Tommy Herr	.03	.01	.00
☐ 209	Craig Reynolds	.03	.01	.00
☐ 210	Gary Pettis	.03	.01	.00
☐ 211	Harold Baines	.08	.03	.01
☐ 212	Vance Law	.03	.01	.00
☐ 213	Ken Gerhart	.03	.01	.00
☐ 214	Jim Gantner	.03	.01	.00
☐ 215	Chet Lemon	.03	.01	.00
☐ 216	Dwight Evans	.08	.03	.01
☐ 217	Don Mattingly	.25	.10	.02
☐ 218	Franklin Stubbs	.03	.01	.00
☐ 219	Pat Tabler	.03	.01	.00
☐ 220	Bo Jackson	.60	.25	.06

No.	Player			
☐ 221	Tony Phillips	.03	.01	.00
☐ 222	Tim Wallach	.06	.02	.00
☐ 223	Ruben Sierra	.35	.15	.03
☐ 224	Steve Buechele	.03	.01	.00
☐ 225	Frank White	.03	.01	.00
☐ 226	Alfredo Griffin	.03	.01	.00
☐ 227	Greg Swindell	.08	.03	.01
☐ 228	Willie Randolph	.06	.02	.00
☐ 229	Mike Marshall	.08	.03	.01
☐ 230	Alan Trammell	.15	.06	.01
☐ 231	Eddie Murray	.15	.06	.01
☐ 232	Dale Sveum	.03	.01	.00
☐ 233	Dick Schofield	.03	.01	.00
☐ 234	Jose Oquendo	.03	.01	.00
☐ 235	Bill Doran	.03	.01	.00
☐ 236	Milt Thompson	.03	.01	.00
☐ 237	Marvell Wynne	.03	.01	.00
☐ 238	Bobby Bonilla	.30	.12	.03
☐ 239	Chris Speier	.03	.01	.00
☐ 240	Glenn Braggs	.03	.01	.00
☐ 241	Wally Backman	.03	.01	.00
☐ 242	Ryne Sandberg	.35	.15	.03
☐ 243	Phil Bradley	.03	.01	.00
☐ 244	Kelly Gruber	.15	.06	.01
☐ 245	Tom Brunansky	.08	.03	.01
☐ 246	Ron Oester	.03	.01	.00
☐ 247	Bobby Thigpen	.10	.04	.01
☐ 248	Fred Lynn	.08	.03	.01
☐ 249	Paul Molitor	.10	.04	.01
☐ 250	Darrell Evans	.08	.03	.01
☐ 251	Gary Ward	.03	.01	.00
☐ 252	Bruce Hurst	.06	.02	.00
☐ 253	Bob Welch	.08	.03	.01
☐ 254	Joe Carter	.17	.07	.01
☐ 255	Willie Wilson	.06	.02	.00
☐ 256	Mark McGwire	.20	.08	.02
☐ 257	Mitch Webster	.03	.01	.00
☐ 258	Brian Downing	.06	.02	.00
☐ 259	Mike Stanley	.03	.01	.00
☐ 260	Carlton Fisk	.17	.07	.01
☐ 261	Billy Hatcher	.06	.02	.00
☐ 262	Glenn Wilson	.03	.01	.00
☐ 263	Ozzie Smith	.17	.07	.01
☐ 264	Randy Ready	.03	.01	.00
☐ 265	Kurt Stillwell	.06	.02	.00
☐ 266	David Palmer	.03	.01	.00
☐ 267	Mike Diaz	.03	.01	.00
☐ 268	Robby Thompson	.03	.01	.00
☐ 269	Andre Dawson	.15	.06	.01
☐ 270	Lee Guetterman	.03	.01	.00
☐ 271	Willie Upshaw	.03	.01	.00
☐ 272	Randy Bush	.03	.01	.00
☐ 273	Larry Sheets	.03	.01	.00
☐ 274	Rob Deer	.06	.02	.00
☐ 275	Kirk Gibson	.08	.03	.01
☐ 276	Marty Barrett	.03	.01	.00
☐ 277	Rickey Henderson	.25	.10	.02
☐ 278	Pedro Guerrero	.08	.03	.01
☐ 279	Brett Butler	.08	.03	.01
☐ 280	Kevin Seitzer	.08	.03	.01
☐ 281	Mike Davis	.03	.01	.00
☐ 282	Andres Galarraga	.08	.03	.01
☐ 283	Devon White	.10	.04	.01
☐ 284	Pete O'Brien	.03	.01	.00
☐ 285	Jerry Hairston	.03	.01	.00
☐ 286	Kevin Bass	.03	.01	.00
☐ 287	Carmelo Martinez	.03	.01	.00
☐ 288	Juan Samuel	.06	.02	.00
☐ 289	Kal Daniels	.08	.03	.01
☐ 290	Albert Hall	.03	.01	.00
☐ 291	Andy Van Slyke	.10	.04	.01
☐ 292	Lee Smith	.10	.04	.01
☐ 293	Vince Coleman	.10	.04	.01
☐ 294	Tom Niedenfuer	.03	.01	.00
☐ 295	Robin Yount	.20	.08	.02
☐ 296	Jeff Robinson (Tigers pitcher)	.08	.03	.01
☐ 297	Todd Benzinger	.20	.08	.02
☐ 298	Dave Winfield	.15	.06	.01
☐ 299	Mickey Hatcher	.03	.01	.00
☐ 300A	Checklist 248-357	.06	.01	.00
☐ 300B	Checklist 240-345	.06	.01	.00
☐ 301	Bud Black	.03	.01	.00
☐ 302	Jose Canseco	.75	.30	.07
☐ 303	Tom Foley	.03	.01	.00
☐ 304	Pete Incaviglia	.08	.03	.01
☐ 305	Bob Boone	.06	.02	.00
☐ 306	Bill Long	.03	.01	.00
☐ 307	Willie McGee	.08	.03	.01
☐ 308	Ken Caminiti	.17	.07	.01
☐ 309	Darren Daulton	.03	.01	.00
☐ 310	Tracy Jones	.03	.01	.00
☐ 311	Greg Booker	.03	.01	.00
☐ 312	Mike LaValliere	.03	.01	.00
☐ 313	Chili Davis	.06	.02	.00
☐ 314	Glenn Hubbard	.03	.01	.00
☐ 315	Paul Noce	.03	.01	.00
☐ 316	Keith Hernandez	.08	.03	.01
☐ 317	Mark Langston	.10	.04	.01
☐ 318	Keith Atherton	.03	.01	.00
☐ 319	Tony Fernandez	.08	.03	.01
☐ 320	Kent Hrbek	.10	.04	.01
☐ 321	John Cerutti	.03	.01	.00
☐ 322	Mike Kingery	.03	.01	.00
☐ 323	Dave Magadan	.08	.03	.01
☐ 324	Rafael Palmeiro	.30	.12	.03
☐ 325	Jeff Dedmon	.03	.01	.00
☐ 326	Barry Bonds	.35	.15	.03
☐ 327	Jeffrey Leonard	.03	.01	.00
☐ 328	Tim Flannery	.03	.01	.00
☐ 329	Dave Concepcion	.08	.03	.01
☐ 330	Mike Schmidt	.35	.15	.03
☐ 331	Bill Dawley	.03	.01	.00
☐ 332	Larry Andersen	.03	.01	.00
☐ 333	Jack Howell	.03	.01	.00
☐ 334	Ken Williams	.06	.02	.00

☐ 335 Bryn Smith	.03	.01	.00
☐ 336 Billy Ripken	.12	.05	.01
☐ 337 Greg Brock	.03	.01	.00
☐ 338 Mike Heath	.03	.01	.00
☐ 339 Mike Greenwell	.20	.08	.02
☐ 340 Claudell Washington	.03	.01	.00
☐ 341 Jose Gonzalez	.03	.01	.00
☐ 342 Mel Hall	.08	.03	.01
☐ 343 Jim Eisenreich	.06	.02	.00
☐ 344 Tony Bernazard	.03	.01	.00
☐ 345 Tim Raines	.10	.04	.01
☐ 346 Bob Brower	.03	.01	.00
☐ 347 Larry Parrish	.03	.01	.00
☐ 348 Thad Bosley	.03	.01	.00
☐ 349 Dennis Eckersley	.10	.04	.01
☐ 350 Cory Snyder	.08	.03	.01
☐ 351 Rick Cerone	.03	.01	.00
☐ 352 John Shelby	.03	.01	.00
☐ 353 Larry Herndon	.03	.01	.00
☐ 354 John Habyan	.03	.01	.00
☐ 355 Chuck Crim	.03	.01	.00
☐ 356 Gus Polidor	.03	.01	.00
☐ 357 Ken Dayley	.03	.01	.00
☐ 358 Danny Darwin	.03	.01	.00
☐ 359 Lance Parrish	.08	.03	.01
☐ 360 James Steels	.03	.01	.00
☐ 361 Al Pedrique	.03	.01	.00
☐ 362 Mike Aldrete	.03	.01	.00
☐ 363 Juan Castillo	.03	.01	.00
☐ 364 Len Dykstra	.08	.03	.01
☐ 365 Luis Quinones	.03	.01	.00
☐ 366 Jim Presley	.03	.01	.00
☐ 367 Lloyd Moseby	.03	.01	.00
☐ 368 Kirby Puckett	.30	.12	.03
☐ 369 Eric Davis	.15	.06	.01
☐ 370 Gary Redus	.03	.01	.00
☐ 371 Dave Schmidt	.03	.01	.00
☐ 372 Mark Clear	.03	.01	.00
☐ 373 Dave Bergman	.03	.01	.00
☐ 374 Charles Hudson	.03	.01	.00
☐ 375 Calvin Schiraldi	.03	.01	.00
☐ 376 Alex Trevino	.03	.01	.00
☐ 377 Tom Candiotti	.06	.02	.00
☐ 378 Steve Farr	.03	.01	.00
☐ 379 Mike Gallego	.03	.01	.00
☐ 380 Andy McGaffigan	.03	.01	.00
☐ 381 Kirk McCaskill	.03	.01	.00
☐ 382 Oddibe McDowell	.03	.01	.00
☐ 383 Floyd Bannister	.03	.01	.00
☐ 384 Denny Walling	.03	.01	.00
☐ 385 Don Carman	.03	.01	.00
☐ 386 Todd Worrell	.06	.02	.00
☐ 387 Eric Show	.03	.01	.00
☐ 388 Dave Parker	.10	.04	.01
☐ 389 Rick Mahler	.03	.01	.00
☐ 390 Mike Dunne	.03	.01	.00
☐ 391 Candy Maldonado	.06	.02	.00
☐ 392 Bob Dernier	.03	.01	.00
☐ 393 Dave Valle	.03	.01	.00
☐ 394 Ernie Whitt	.03	.01	.00
☐ 395 Juan Berenguer	.03	.01	.00
☐ 396 Mike Young	.03	.01	.00
☐ 397 Mike Felder	.03	.01	.00
☐ 398 Willie Hernandez	.03	.01	.00
☐ 399 Jim Rice	.08	.03	.01
☐ 400A Checklist 358-467	.06	.01	.00
☐ 400B Checklist 346-451	.06	.01	.00
☐ 401 Tommy John	.08	.03	.01
☐ 402 Brian Holton	.03	.01	.00
☐ 403 Carmen Castillo	.03	.01	.00
☐ 404 Jamie Quirk	.03	.01	.00
☐ 405 Dwayne Murphy	.03	.01	.00
☐ 406 Jeff Parrett	.06	.02	.00
☐ 407 Don Sutton	.10	.04	.01
☐ 408 Jerry Browne	.03	.01	.00
☐ 409 Jim Winn	.03	.01	.00
☐ 410 Dave Smith	.03	.01	.00
☐ 411 Shane Mack	.10	.04	.01
☐ 412 Greg Gross	.03	.01	.00
☐ 413 Nick Esasky	.03	.01	.00
☐ 414 Damaso Garcia	.03	.01	.00
☐ 415 Brian Fisher	.03	.01	.00
☐ 416 Brian Dayett	.03	.01	.00
☐ 417 Curt Ford	.03	.01	.00
☐ 418 Mark Williamson	.08	.03	.01
☐ 419 Bill Schroeder	.03	.01	.00
☐ 420 Mike Henneman	.15	.06	.01
☐ 421 John Marzano	.03	.01	.00
☐ 422 Ron Kittle	.06	.02	.00
☐ 423 Matt Young	.03	.01	.00
☐ 424 Steve Balboni	.03	.01	.00
☐ 425 Luis Polonia	.25	.10	.02
☐ 426 Randy St.Claire	.03	.01	.00
☐ 427 Greg Harris	.03	.01	.00
☐ 428 Johnny Ray	.03	.01	.00
☐ 429 Ray Searage	.03	.01	.00
☐ 430 Ricky Horton	.03	.01	.00
☐ 431 Gerald Young	.08	.03	.01
☐ 432 Rick Schu	.03	.01	.00
☐ 433 Paul O'Neill	.10	.04	.01
☐ 434 Rich Gossage	.08	.03	.01
☐ 435 John Cangelosi	.03	.01	.00
☐ 436 Mike LaCoss	.03	.01	.00
☐ 437 Gerald Perry	.03	.01	.00
☐ 438 Dave Martinez	.06	.02	.00
☐ 439 Darryl Strawberry	.35	.15	.03
☐ 440 John Moses	.03	.01	.00
☐ 441 Greg Gagne	.03	.01	.00
☐ 442 Jesse Barfield	.08	.03	.01
☐ 443 George Frazier	.03	.01	.00
☐ 444 Garth Iorg	.03	.01	.00
☐ 445 Ed Nunez	.03	.01	.00
☐ 446 Rick Aguilera	.06	.02	.00
☐ 447 Jerry Mumphrey	.03	.01	.00
☐ 448 Rafael Ramirez	.03	.01	.00
☐ 449 John Smiley	.45	.18	.04

☐ 450 Atlee Hammaker	.03	.01	.00
☐ 451 Lance McCullers	.03	.01	.00
☐ 452 Guy Hoffman	.03	.01	.00
☐ 453 Chris James	.08	.03	.01
☐ 454 Terry Pendleton	.12	.05	.01
☐ 455 Dave Meads	.04	.02	.00
☐ 456 Bill Buckner	.06	.02	.00
☐ 457 John Pawlowski	.04	.02	.00
☐ 458 Bob Sebra	.03	.01	.00
☐ 459 Jim Dwyer	.03	.01	.00
☐ 460 Jay Aldrich	.03	.01	.00
☐ 461 Frank Tanana	.06	.02	.00
☐ 462 Oil Can Boyd	.03	.01	.00
☐ 463 Dan Pasqua	.06	.02	.00
☐ 464 Tim Crews	.10	.04	.01
☐ 465 Andy Allanson	.03	.01	.00
☐ 466 Bill Pecota	.08	.03	.01
☐ 467 Steve Ontiveros	.03	.01	.00
☐ 468 Hubie Brooks	.08	.03	.01
☐ 469 Paul Kilgus	.06	.02	.00
☐ 470 Dale Mohorcic	.03	.01	.00
☐ 471 Dan Quisenberry	.08	.03	.01
☐ 472 Dave Stewart	.08	.03	.01
☐ 473 Dave Clark	.03	.01	.00
☐ 474 Joel Skinner	.03	.01	.00
☐ 475 Dave Anderson	.03	.01	.00
☐ 476 Dan Petry	.03	.01	.00
☐ 477 Carl Nichols	.03	.01	.00
☐ 478 Ernest Riles	.03	.01	.00
☐ 479 George Hendrick	.03	.01	.00
☐ 480 John Morris	.03	.01	.00
☐ 481 Manny Hernandez	.03	.01	.00
☐ 482 Jeff Stone	.03	.01	.00
☐ 483 Chris Brown	.03	.01	.00
☐ 484 Mike Bielecki	.06	.02	.00
☐ 485 Dave Dravecky	.08	.03	.01
☐ 486 Rick Manning	.03	.01	.00
☐ 487 Bill Almon	.03	.01	.00
☐ 488 Jim Sundberg	.03	.01	.00
☐ 489 Ken Phelps	.03	.01	.00
☐ 490 Tom Henke	.06	.02	.00
☐ 491 Dan Gladden	.03	.01	.00
☐ 492 Barry Larkin	.20	.08	.02
☐ 493 Fred Manrique	.06	.02	.00
☐ 494 Mike Griffin	.03	.01	.00
☐ 495 Mark Knudson	.10	.04	.01
☐ 496 Bill Madlock	.06	.02	.00
☐ 497 Tim Stoddard	.03	.01	.00
☐ 498 Sam Horn	.15	.06	.01
☐ 499 Tracy Woodson	.08	.03	.01
☐ 500A Checklist 468-577	.06	.01	.00
☐ 500B Checklist 452-557	.06	.01	.00
☐ 501 Ken Schrom	.03	.01	.00
☐ 502 Angel Salazar	.03	.01	.00
☐ 503 Eric Plunk	.03	.01	.00
☐ 504 Joe Hesketh	.06	.02	.00
☐ 505 Greg Minton	.03	.01	.00
☐ 506 Geno Petralli	.03	.01	.00
☐ 507 Bob James	.03	.01	.00
☐ 508 Robbie Wine	.03	.01	.00
☐ 509 Jeff Calhoun	.03	.01	.00
☐ 510 Steve Lake	.03	.01	.00
☐ 511 Mark Grant	.03	.01	.00
☐ 512 Frank Williams	.03	.01	.00
☐ 513 Jeff Blauser	.17	.07	.01
☐ 514 Bob Walk	.03	.01	.00
☐ 515 Craig Lefferts	.03	.01	.00
☐ 516 Manny Trillo	.03	.01	.00
☐ 517 Jerry Reed	.03	.01	.00
☐ 518 Rick Leach	.03	.01	.00
☐ 519 Mark Davidson	.08	.03	.01
☐ 520 Jeff Ballard	.08	.03	.01
☐ 521 Dave Stapleton	.03	.01	.00
☐ 522 Pat Sheridan	.03	.01	.00
☐ 523 Al Nipper	.03	.01	.00
☐ 524 Steve Trout	.03	.01	.00
☐ 525 Jeff Hamilton	.03	.01	.00
☐ 526 Tommy Hinzo	.03	.01	.00
☐ 527 Lonnie Smith	.08	.03	.01
☐ 528 Greg Cadaret	.10	.04	.01
☐ 529 Bob McClure UER ("Rob" on front)	.03	.01	.00
☐ 530 Chuck Finley	.15	.06	.01
☐ 531 Jeff Russell	.03	.01	.00
☐ 532 Steve Lyons	.03	.01	.00
☐ 533 Terry Puhl	.03	.01	.00
☐ 534 Eric Nolte	.06	.02	.00
☐ 535 Kent Tekulve	.03	.01	.00
☐ 536 Pat Pacillo	.06	.02	.00
☐ 537 Charlie Puleo	.03	.01	.00
☐ 538 Tom Prince	.06	.02	.00
☐ 539 Greg Maddux	.15	.06	.01
☐ 540 Jim Lindeman	.03	.01	.00
☐ 541 Pete Stanicek	.03	.01	.00
☐ 542 Steve Kiefer	.03	.01	.00
☐ 543A Jim Morrison ERR (no decimal before lifetime average)	.25	.10	.02
☐ 543B Jim Morrison COR	.06	.02	.00
☐ 544 Spike Owen	.03	.01	.00
☐ 545 Jay Buhner	.40	.16	.04
☐ 546 Mike Devereaux	.15	.06	.01
☐ 547 Jerry Don Gleaton	.03	.01	.00
☐ 548 Jose Rijo	.08	.03	.01
☐ 549 Dennis Martinez	.06	.02	.00
☐ 550 Mike Loynd	.03	.01	.00
☐ 551 Darrell Miller	.03	.01	.00
☐ 552 Dave LaPoint	.03	.01	.00
☐ 553 John Tudor	.06	.02	.00
☐ 554 Rocky Childress	.03	.01	.00
☐ 555 Wally Ritchie	.03	.01	.00
☐ 556 Terry McGriff	.03	.01	.00
☐ 557 Dave Leiper	.03	.01	.00
☐ 558 Jeff Robinson (Pirates pitcher)	.06	.02	.00
☐ 559 Jose Uribe	.03	.01	.00

☐ 560 Ted Simmons .08 .03 .01
☐ 561 Les Lancaster .08 .03 .01
☐ 562 Keith Miller .12 .05 .01
(New York Mets)
☐ 563 Harold Reynolds .06 .02 .00
☐ 564 Gene Larkin .12 .05 .01
☐ 565 Cecil Fielder .35 .15 .03
☐ 566 Roy Smalley .03 .01 .00
☐ 567 Duane Ward .03 .01 .00
☐ 568 Bill Wilkinson .06 .02 .00
☐ 569 Howard Johnson .15 .06 .01
☐ 570 Frank DiPino .03 .01 .00
☐ 571 Pete Smith .08 .03 .01
☐ 572 Darnell Coles .03 .01 .00
☐ 573 Don Robinson .03 .01 .00
☐ 574 Rob Nelson UER .03 .01 .00
(Career 0 RBI,
but 1 RBI in '87)
☐ 575 Dennis Rasmussen .03 .01 .00
☐ 576 Steve Jeltz UER .06 .02 .00
(Photo actually Juan
Samuel; Samuel noted
for one batting glove
and black bat)
☐ 577 Tom Pagnozzi .12 .05 .01
☐ 578 Ty Gainey .03 .01 .00
☐ 579 Gary Lucas .03 .01 .00
☐ 580 Ron Hassey .03 .01 .00
☐ 581 Herm Winningham .03 .01 .00
☐ 582 Rene Gonzales .06 .02 .00
☐ 583 Brad Komminsk .03 .01 .00
☐ 584 Doyle Alexander .03 .01 .00
☐ 585 Jeff Sellers .03 .01 .00
☐ 586 Bill Gullickson .06 .02 .00
☐ 587 Tim Belcher .12 .05 .01
☐ 588 Doug Jones .12 .05 .01
☐ 589 Melido Perez .15 .06 .01
☐ 590 Rick Honeycutt .03 .01 .00
☐ 591 Pascual Perez .03 .01 .00
☐ 592 Curt Wilkerson .03 .01 .00
☐ 593 Steve Howe .03 .01 .00
☐ 594 John Davis .06 .02 .00
☐ 595 Storm Davis .03 .01 .00
☐ 596 Sammy Stewart .03 .01 .00
☐ 597 Neil Allen .03 .01 .00
☐ 598 Alejandro Pena .06 .02 .00
☐ 599 Mark Thurmond .03 .01 .00
☐ 600A Checklist 578-BC26 .06 .01 .00
☐ 600B Checklist 558-660 .06 .01 .00
☐ 601 Jose Mesa .08 .03 .01
☐ 602 Don August .03 .01 .00
☐ 603 Terry Leach SP .06 .02 .00
☐ 604 Tom Newell .03 .01 .00
☐ 605 Randall Byers SP .10 .04 .01
☐ 606 Jim Gott .03 .01 .00
☐ 607 Harry Spilman .03 .01 .00
☐ 608 John Candelaria .03 .01 .00
☐ 609 Mike Brumley .08 .03 .01
☐ 610 Mickey Brantley .03 .01 .00
☐ 611 Jose Nunez SP .08 .03 .01
☐ 612 Tom Nieto .03 .01 .00
☐ 613 Rick Reuschel .06 .02 .00
☐ 614 Lee Mazzilli SP .06 .02 .00
☐ 615 Scott Lusader .06 .02 .00
☐ 616 Bobby Meacham .03 .01 .00
☐ 617 Kevin McReynolds SP .10 .04 .01
☐ 618 Gene Garber .03 .01 .00
☐ 619 Barry Lyons SP .10 .04 .01
☐ 620 Randy Myers .06 .02 .00
☐ 621 Donnie Moore .03 .01 .00
☐ 622 Domingo Ramos .03 .01 .00
☐ 623 Ed Romero .03 .01 .00
☐ 624 Greg Myers .10 .04 .01
☐ 625 Ripken Family .17 .07 .01
☐ 626 Pat Perry .03 .01 .00
☐ 627 Andres Thomas SP .06 .02 .00
☐ 628 Matt Williams SP 1.75 .70 .17
☐ 629 Dave Hengel .06 .02 .00
☐ 630 Jeff Musselman SP .06 .02 .00
☐ 631 Tim Laudner .03 .01 .00
☐ 632 Bob Ojeda SP .06 .02 .00
☐ 633 Rafael Santana .03 .01 .00
☐ 634 Wes Gardner .08 .03 .01
☐ 635 Roberto Kelly SP .75 .30 .07
☐ 636 Mike Flanagan SP .06 .02 .00
☐ 637 Jay Bell .30 .12 .03
☐ 638 Bob Melvin .03 .01 .00
☐ 639 Damon Berryhill UER .10 .04 .01
(Bats: Swithch)
☐ 640 David Wells SP .20 .08 .02
☐ 641 Puzzle Card .06 .02 .00
(Stan Musial)
☐ 642 Doug Sisk .03 .01 .00
☐ 643 Keith Hughes .06 .02 .00
☐ 644 Tom Glavine .90 .40 .09
☐ 645 Al Newman .03 .01 .00
☐ 646 Scott Sanderson .06 .02 .00
☐ 647 Scott Terry .06 .02 .00
☐ 648 Tim Teufel SP .06 .02 .00
☐ 649 Garry Templeton SP .06 .02 .00
☐ 650 Manny Lee SP .06 .02 .00
☐ 651 Roger McDowell SP .06 .02 .00
☐ 652 Mookie Wilson SP .06 .02 .00
☐ 653 David Cone SP .20 .08 .02
☐ 654 Ron Gant SP 3.50 1.50 .35
☐ 655 Joe Price SP .06 .02 .00
☐ 656 George Bell SP .15 .06 .01
☐ 657 Gregg Jefferies SP 1.50 .60 .15
☐ 658 Todd Stottlemyre SP .50 .20 .05
☐ 659 Geronimo Berroa SP .15 .06 .01
☐ 660 Jerry Royster SP .08 .03 .01

1988 Donruss Bonus MVP's

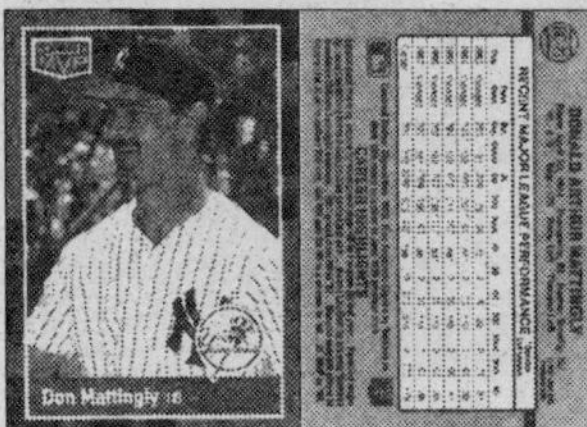

This 26-card set was distributed along with the regular 1988 Donruss issue as random inserts with the rack and wax packs. These bonus cards are numbered with the prefix BC for bonus cards and were supposedly produced in the same quantities as the other 660 regular issue cards. The "most valuable" player was selected from each of the 26 teams. Cards measure 2 1/2" by 3 1/2" and feature the same distinctive black and blue border on the front as the regular issue. The cards are distinguished by the MVP logo in the upper left corner of the obverse. The last 13 cards numerically are considered to be somewhat tougher to find than the first 13 cards.

	MINT	EXC	G-VG
COMPLETE SET (26)	3.00	1.25	.30
COMMON CARD (BC1-BC13)	.04	.02	.00
COMMON CARD (BC14-BC26)	.06	.02	.00

	MINT	EXC	G-VG
☐ BC1 Cal Ripken	.25	.10	.02
☐ BC2 Eric Davis	.08	.03	.01
☐ BC3 Paul Molitor	.08	.03	.01
☐ BC4 Mike Schmidt	.15	.06	.01
☐ BC5 Ivan Calderon	.04	.02	.00
☐ BC6 Tony Gwynn	.12	.05	.01
☐ BC7 Wade Boggs	.12	.05	.01
☐ BC8 Andy Van Slyke	.08	.03	.01
☐ BC9 Joe Carter	.08	.03	.01
☐ BC10 Andre Dawson	.10	.04	.01
☐ BC11 Alan Trammell	.10	.04	.01
☐ BC12 Mike Scott	.06	.02	.00
☐ BC13 Wally Joyner	.10	.04	.01
☐ BC14 Dale Murphy	.10	.04	.01
☐ BC15 Kirby Puckett	.20	.08	.02
☐ BC16 Pedro Guerrero	.08	.03	.01
☐ BC17 Kevin Seitzer	.08	.03	.01
☐ BC18 Tim Raines	.10	.04	.01
☐ BC19 George Bell	.12	.05	.01
☐ BC20 Darryl Strawberry	.25	.10	.02
☐ BC21 Don Mattingly	.20	.08	.02
☐ BC22 Ozzie Smith	.12	.05	.01
☐ BC23 Mark McGwire	.15	.06	.01
☐ BC24 Will Clark	.30	.12	.03
☐ BC25 Alvin Davis	.06	.02	.00
☐ BC26 Ruben Sierra	.25	.10	.02

1988 Donruss Rookies

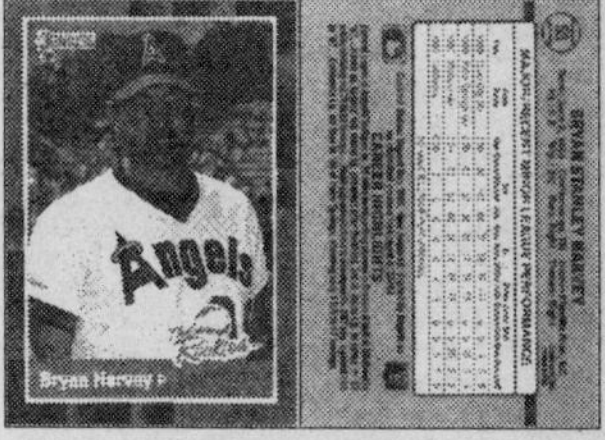

The 1988 Donruss "The Rookies" set features 56 cards plus a 15-piece puzzle of Stan Musial. Cards are in full color and are standard size, 2 1/2" by 3 1/2". The set was distributed in a small green and black box with gold lettering. Card fronts are similar in design to the 1988 Donruss regular issue except for the presence of "The Rookies" logo in the lower right corner and a green and black border instead of a blue and black border on the fronts. The key rookies in this set are ROY's, Chris Sabo and Walt Weiss.

	MINT	EXC	G-VG
COMPLETE SET (56)	12.00	5.25	1.50
COMMON PLAYER (1-56)	.07	.03	.01

	MINT	EXC	G-VG
☐ 1 Mark Grace	2.25	.75	.15
☐ 2 Mike Campbell	.07	.03	.01
☐ 3 Todd Frohwirth	.10	.04	.01

☐ 4 Dave Stapleton	.07	.03	.01
☐ 5 Shawn Abner	.10	.04	.01
☐ 6 Jose Cecena	.07	.03	.01
☐ 7 Dave Gallagher	.10	.04	.01
☐ 8 Mark Parent	.10	.04	.01
☐ 9 Cecil Espy	.12	.05	.01
☐ 10 Pete Smith	.10	.04	.01
☐ 11 Jay Buhner	.40	.16	.04
☐ 12 Pat Borders	.30	.12	.03
☐ 13 Doug Jennings	.12	.05	.01
☐ 14 Brady Anderson	.10	.04	.01
☐ 15 Pete Stanicek	.07	.03	.01
☐ 16 Roberto Kelly	.60	.25	.06
☐ 17 Jeff Treadway	.20	.08	.02
☐ 18 Walt Weiss	.25	.10	.02
☐ 19 Paul Gibson	.10	.04	.01
☐ 20 Tim Crews	.10	.04	.01
☐ 21 Melido Perez	.10	.04	.01
☐ 22 Steve Peters	.10	.04	.01
☐ 23 Craig Worthington	.10	.04	.01
☐ 24 John Trautwein	.07	.03	.01
☐ 25 DeWayne Vaughn	.07	.03	.01
☐ 26 David Wells	.12	.05	.01
☐ 27 Al Leiter	.10	.04	.01
☐ 28 Tim Belcher	.12	.05	.01
☐ 29 Johnny Paredes	.10	.04	.01
☐ 30 Chris Sabo	2.00	.80	.20
☐ 31 Damon Berryhill	.10	.04	.01
☐ 32 Randy Milligan	.35	.15	.03
☐ 33 Gary Thurman	.10	.04	.01
☐ 34 Kevin Elster	.12	.05	.01
☐ 35 Roberto Alomar	3.50	1.50	.35
☐ 36 Edgar Martinez UER (photo actually Edwin Nunez)	1.00	.40	.10
☐ 37 Todd Stottlemyre	.35	.15	.03
☐ 38 Joey Meyer	.10	.04	.01
☐ 39 Carl Nichols	.07	.03	.01
☐ 40 Jack McDowell	.45	.18	.04
☐ 41 Jose Bautista	.10	.04	.01
☐ 42 Sil Campusano	.12	.05	.01
☐ 43 John Dopson	.10	.04	.01
☐ 44 Jody Reed	.25	.10	.02
☐ 45 Darrin Jackson	.20	.08	.02
☐ 46 Mike Capel	.10	.04	.01
☐ 47 Ron Gant	2.25	.90	.22
☐ 48 John Davis	.07	.03	.01
☐ 49 Kevin Coffman	.07	.03	.01
☐ 50 Cris Carpenter	.20	.08	.02
☐ 51 Mackey Sasser	.15	.06	.01
☐ 52 Luis Alicea	.10	.04	.01
☐ 53 Bryan Harvey	.60	.25	.06
☐ 54 Steve Ellsworth	.10	.04	.01
☐ 55 Mike Macfarlane	.15	.06	.01
☐ 56 Checklist Card	.07	.01	.00

1989 Donruss

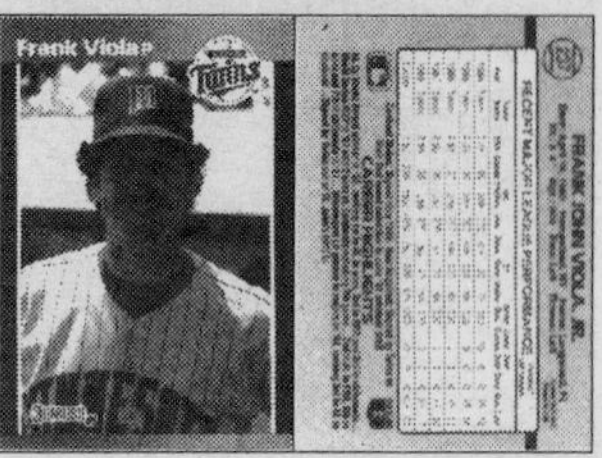

This 660-card set was distributed along with a puzzle of Warren Spahn. The six regular checklist cards are numbered throughout the set as multiples of 100. Cards measure 2 1/2" by 3 1/2" and feature a distinctive black side border with an alternating coating. The popular Diamond King subset returns for the eighth consecutive year. Rated Rookies are featured again as cards 28-47. The Donruss '89 logo appears in the lower left corner of every obverse. There are two variations that occur throughout most of the set. On the card backs "Denotes Led League" can be found with one asterisk to the left or with an asterisk on each side. On the card fronts the horizontal lines on the left and right borders can be glossy or non-glossy. Since both of these variation types are relatively minor and seem equally common, there is no premium value for either type. Rather than short-printing 26 cards in order to make room for printing the Bonus MVP's this year, Donruss apparently chose to double print 106 cards. These double prints are listed below by DP. The key rookie cards in this set are Sandy Alomar Jr., Ken Griffey Jr., Felix Jose, Ramon Martinez, Hal Morris, and Gary Sheffield.

	MINT	EXC	G-VG
COMPLETE SET (660)	17.00	7.25	2.50
COMMON PLAYER (1-660)	.03	.01	.00
☐ 1 Mike Greenwell DK	.08	.03	.01
☐ 2 Bobby Bonilla DK DP	.08	.03	.01
☐ 3 Pete Incaviglia DK	.06	.02	.00
☐ 4 Chris Sabo DK DP	.08	.03	.01
☐ 5 Robin Yount DK	.10	.04	.01
☐ 6 Tony Gwynn DK DP	.10	.04	.01

☐ 7 Carlton Fisk DK .10 .04 .01
(OF on back)
☐ 8 Cory Snyder DK .06 .02 .00
☐ 9 David Cone DK UER .08 .03 .01
(sic, "hurdlers")
☐ 10 Kevin Seitzer DK .06 .02 .00
☐ 11 Rick Reuschel DK .06 .02 .00
☐ 12 Johnny Ray DK .06 .02 .00
☐ 13 Dave Schmidt DK .06 .02 .00
☐ 14 Andres Galarraga DK .06 .02 .00
☐ 15 Kirk Gibson DK .08 .03 .01
☐ 16 Fred McGriff DK .10 .04 .01
☐ 17 Mark Grace DK .12 .05 .01
☐ 18 Jeff Robinson DT DK .06 .02 .00
☐ 19 Vince Coleman DK DP .08 .03 .01
☐ 20 Dave Henderson DK .06 .02 .00
☐ 21 Harold Reynolds DK .06 .02 .00
☐ 22 Gerald Perry DK .06 .02 .00
☐ 23 Frank Viola DK .08 .03 .01
☐ 24 Steve Bedrosian DK .06 .02 .00
☐ 25 Glenn Davis DK .08 .03 .01
☐ 26 Don Mattingly DK UER .12 .05 .01
(doesn't mention Don's previous DK in 1985)
☐ 27 DK Checklist DP .06 .01 .00
☐ 28 Sandy Alomar Jr. RR .40 .16 .04
☐ 29 Steve Searcy RR .08 .03 .01
☐ 30 Cameron Drew RR .03 .01 .00
☐ 31 Gary Sheffield RR .30 .12 .03
☐ 32 Erik Hanson RR .50 .20 .05
☐ 33 Ken Griffey Jr. RR 6.00 2.50 .60
☐ 34 Greg Harris RR .15 .06 .01
San Diego Padres
☐ 35 Gregg Jefferies RR .30 .12 .03
☐ 36 Luis Medina RR .08 .03 .01
☐ 37 Carlos Quintana RR .25 .10 .02
☐ 38 Felix Jose RR .75 .30 .07
☐ 39 Cris Carpenter RR .10 .04 .01
☐ 40 Ron Jones RR .08 .03 .01
☐ 41 Dave West RR .12 .05 .01
☐ 42 Randy Johnson RR .35 .15 .03
☐ 43 Mike Harkey RR .12 .05 .01
☐ 44 Pete Harnisch RR DP .17 .07 .01
☐ 45 Tom Gordon RR DP .17 .07 .01
☐ 46 Gregg Olson RR DP .40 .16 .04
☐ 47 Alex Sanchez RR DP .08 .03 .01
☐ 48 Ruben Sierra .25 .10 .02
☐ 49 Rafael Palmeiro .15 .06 .01
☐ 50 Ron Gant .45 .18 .04
☐ 51 Cal Ripken .35 .15 .03
☐ 52 Wally Joyner .12 .05 .01
☐ 53 Gary Carter .08 .03 .01
☐ 54 Andy Van Slyke .10 .04 .01
☐ 55 Robin Yount .15 .06 .01
☐ 56 Pete Incaviglia .06 .02 .00
☐ 57 Greg Brock .03 .01 .00
☐ 58 Melido Perez .06 .02 .00
☐ 59 Craig Lefferts .03 .01 .00
☐ 60 Gary Pettis .03 .01 .00
☐ 61 Danny Tartabull .10 .04 .01
☐ 62 Guillermo Hernandez .03 .01 .00
☐ 63 Ozzie Smith .12 .05 .01
☐ 64 Gary Gaetti .06 .02 .00
☐ 65 Mark Davis .06 .02 .00
☐ 66 Lee Smith .08 .03 .01
☐ 67 Dennis Eckersley .08 .03 .01
☐ 68 Wade Boggs .20 .08 .02
☐ 69 Mike Scott .08 .03 .01
☐ 70 Fred McGriff .15 .06 .01
☐ 71 Tom Browning .06 .02 .00
☐ 72 Claudell Washington .03 .01 .00
☐ 73 Mel Hall .06 .02 .00
☐ 74 Don Mattingly .20 .08 .02
☐ 75 Steve Bedrosian .06 .02 .00
☐ 76 Juan Samuel .06 .02 .00
☐ 77 Mike Scioscia .03 .01 .00
☐ 78 Dave Righetti .06 .02 .00
☐ 79 Alfredo Griffin .03 .01 .00
☐ 80 Eric Davis UER .10 .04 .01
(165 games in 1988, should be 135)
☐ 81 Juan Berenguer .03 .01 .00
☐ 82 Todd Worrell .06 .02 .00
☐ 83 Joe Carter .12 .05 .01
☐ 84 Steve Sax .10 .04 .01
☐ 85 Frank White .03 .01 .00
☐ 86 John Kruk .03 .01 .00
☐ 87 Rance Mulliniks .03 .01 .00
☐ 88 Alan Ashby .03 .01 .00
☐ 89 Charlie Leibrandt .03 .01 .00
☐ 90 Frank Tanana .06 .02 .00
☐ 91 Jose Canseco .50 .20 .05
☐ 92 Barry Bonds .25 .10 .02
☐ 93 Harold Reynolds .06 .02 .00
☐ 94 Mark McLemore .03 .01 .00
☐ 95 Mark McGwire .12 .05 .01
☐ 96 Eddie Murray .12 .05 .01
☐ 97 Tim Raines .10 .04 .01
☐ 98 Robby Thompson .03 .01 .00
☐ 99 Kevin McReynolds .08 .03 .01
☐ 100 Checklist Card .06 .01 .00
☐ 101 Carlton Fisk .15 .06 .01
☐ 102 Dave Martinez .03 .01 .00
☐ 103 Glenn Braggs .03 .01 .00
☐ 104 Dale Murphy .12 .05 .01
☐ 105 Ryne Sandberg .35 .15 .03
☐ 106 Dennis Martinez .06 .02 .00
☐ 107 Pete O'Brien .03 .01 .00
☐ 108 Dick Schofield .03 .01 .00
☐ 109 Henry Cotto .03 .01 .00
☐ 110 Mike Marshall .06 .02 .00
☐ 111 Keith Moreland .03 .01 .00
☐ 112 Tom Brunansky .06 .02 .00
☐ 113 Kelly Gruber UER .10 .04 .01
(wrong birthdate)
☐ 114 Brook Jacoby .03 .01 .00

☐ 115 Keith Brown	.06	.02	.00
☐ 116 Matt Nokes	.06	.02	.00
☐ 117 Keith Hernandez	.08	.03	.01
☐ 118 Bob Forsch	.03	.01	.00
☐ 119 Bert Blyleven UER (... 3000 strikeouts in 1987, should be 1986)	.08	.03	.01
☐ 120 Willie Wilson	.08	.03	.01
☐ 121 Tommy Gregg	.03	.01	.00
☐ 122 Jim Rice	.08	.03	.01
☐ 123 Bob Knepper	.03	.01	.00
☐ 124 Danny Jackson	.06	.02	.00
☐ 125 Eric Plunk	.03	.01	.00
☐ 126 Brian Fisher	.03	.01	.00
☐ 127 Mike Pagliarulo	.03	.01	.00
☐ 128 Tony Gwynn	.17	.07	.01
☐ 129 Lance McCullers	.03	.01	.00
☐ 130 Andres Galarraga	.06	.02	.00
☐ 131 Jose Uribe	.03	.01	.00
☐ 132 Kirk Gibson UER (wrong birthdate)	.08	.03	.01
☐ 133 David Palmer	.03	.01	.00
☐ 134 R.J. Reynolds	.03	.01	.00
☐ 135 Greg Walker	.03	.01	.00
☐ 136 Kirk McCaskill UER (wrong birthdate)	.03	.01	.00
☐ 137 Shawon Dunston	.08	.03	.01
☐ 138 Andy Allanson	.03	.01	.00
☐ 139 Rob Murphy	.03	.01	.00
☐ 140 Mike Aldrete	.03	.01	.00
☐ 141 Terry Kennedy	.03	.01	.00
☐ 142 Scott Fletcher	.03	.01	.00
☐ 143 Steve Balboni	.03	.01	.00
☐ 144 Bret Saberhagen	.10	.04	.01
☐ 145 Ozzie Virgil	.03	.01	.00
☐ 146 Dale Sveum	.03	.01	.00
☐ 147 Darryl Strawberry	.30	.12	.03
☐ 148 Harold Baines	.08	.03	.01
☐ 149 George Bell	.10	.04	.01
☐ 150 Dave Parker	.08	.03	.01
☐ 151 Bobby Bonilla	.20	.08	.02
☐ 152 Mookie Wilson	.03	.01	.00
☐ 153 Ted Power	.03	.01	.00
☐ 154 Nolan Ryan	.50	.20	.05
☐ 155 Jeff Reardon	.08	.03	.01
☐ 156 Tim Wallach	.06	.02	.00
☐ 157 Jamie Moyer	.03	.01	.00
☐ 158 Rich Gossage	.08	.03	.01
☐ 159 Dave Winfield	.12	.05	.01
☐ 160 Von Hayes	.06	.02	.00
☐ 161 Willie McGee	.08	.03	.01
☐ 162 Rich Gedman	.03	.01	.00
☐ 163 Tony Pena	.06	.02	.00
☐ 164 Mike Morgan	.06	.02	.00
☐ 165 Charlie Hough	.03	.01	.00
☐ 166 Mike Stanley	.03	.01	.00
☐ 167 Andre Dawson	.12	.05	.01
☐ 168 Joe Boever	.06	.02	.00
☐ 169 Pete Stanicek	.03	.01	.00
☐ 170 Bob Boone	.06	.02	.00
☐ 171 Ron Darling	.06	.02	.00
☐ 172 Bob Walk	.03	.01	.00
☐ 173 Rob Deer	.06	.02	.00
☐ 174 Steve Buechele	.03	.01	.00
☐ 175 Ted Higuera	.03	.01	.00
☐ 176 Ozzie Guillen	.06	.02	.00
☐ 177 Candy Maldonado	.06	.02	.00
☐ 178 Doyle Alexander	.03	.01	.00
☐ 179 Mark Gubicza	.06	.02	.00
☐ 180 Alan Trammell	.12	.05	.01
☐ 181 Vince Coleman	.10	.04	.01
☐ 182 Kirby Puckett	.25	.10	.02
☐ 183 Chris Brown	.03	.01	.00
☐ 184 Marty Barrett	.03	.01	.00
☐ 185 Stan Javier	.03	.01	.00
☐ 186 Mike Greenwell	.15	.06	.01
☐ 187 Billy Hatcher	.06	.02	.00
☐ 188 Jimmy Key	.06	.02	.00
☐ 189 Nick Esasky	.03	.01	.00
☐ 190 Don Slaught	.03	.01	.00
☐ 191 Cory Snyder	.06	.02	.00
☐ 192 John Candelaria	.03	.01	.00
☐ 193 Mike Schmidt	.35	.15	.03
☐ 194 Kevin Gross	.03	.01	.00
☐ 195 John Tudor	.06	.02	.00
☐ 196 Neil Allen	.03	.01	.00
☐ 197 Orel Hershiser	.08	.03	.01
☐ 198 Kal Daniels	.08	.03	.01
☐ 199 Kent Hrbek	.08	.03	.01
☐ 200 Checklist Card	.06	.01	.00
☐ 201 Joe Magrane	.06	.02	.00
☐ 202 Scott Bailes	.03	.01	.00
☐ 203 Tim Belcher	.06	.02	.00
☐ 204 George Brett	.15	.06	.01
☐ 205 Benito Santiago	.08	.03	.01
☐ 206 Tony Fernandez	.06	.02	.00
☐ 207 Gerald Young	.03	.01	.00
☐ 208 Bo Jackson	.50	.20	.05
☐ 209 Chet Lemon	.03	.01	.00
☐ 210 Storm Davis	.03	.01	.00
☐ 211 Doug Drabek	.08	.03	.01
☐ 212 Mickey Brantley UER (photo actually Nelson Simmons)	.06	.02	.00
☐ 213 Devon White	.06	.02	.00
☐ 214 Dave Stewart	.08	.03	.01
☐ 215 Dave Schmidt	.03	.01	.00
☐ 216 Bryn Smith	.03	.01	.00
☐ 217 Brett Butler	.08	.03	.01
☐ 218 Bob Ojeda	.03	.01	.00
☐ 219 Steve Rosenberg	.08	.03	.01
☐ 220 Hubie Brooks	.06	.02	.00
☐ 221 B.J. Surhoff	.06	.02	.00
☐ 222 Rick Mahler	.03	.01	.00
☐ 223 Rick Sutcliffe	.06	.02	.00
☐ 224 Neal Heaton	.03	.01	.00

☐ 225 Mitch Williams	.03	.01	.00
☐ 226 Chuck Finley	.08	.03	.01
☐ 227 Mark Langston	.08	.03	.01
☐ 228 Jesse Orosco	.03	.01	.00
☐ 229 Ed Whitson	.03	.01	.00
☐ 230 Terry Pendleton	.10	.04	.01
☐ 231 Lloyd Moseby	.03	.01	.00
☐ 232 Greg Swindell	.06	.02	.00
☐ 233 John Franco	.06	.02	.00
☐ 234 Jack Morris	.10	.04	.01
☐ 235 Howard Johnson	.12	.05	.01
☐ 236 Glenn Davis	.08	.03	.01
☐ 237 Frank Viola	.08	.03	.01
☐ 238 Kevin Seitzer	.06	.02	.00
☐ 239 Gerald Perry	.03	.01	.00
☐ 240 Dwight Evans	.08	.03	.01
☐ 241 Jim Deshaies	.03	.01	.00
☐ 242 Bo Diaz	.03	.01	.00
☐ 243 Carney Lansford	.06	.02	.00
☐ 244 Mike LaValliere	.03	.01	.00
☐ 245 Rickey Henderson	.35	.15	.03
☐ 246 Roberto Alomar	.45	.18	.04
☐ 247 Jimmy Jones	.03	.01	.00
☐ 248 Pascual Perez	.03	.01	.00
☐ 249 Will Clark	.40	.16	.04
☐ 250 Fernando Valenzuela	.08	.03	.01
☐ 251 Shane Rawley	.03	.01	.00
☐ 252 Sid Bream	.03	.01	.00
☐ 253 Steve Lyons	.03	.01	.00
☐ 254 Brian Downing	.03	.01	.00
☐ 255 Mark Grace	.25	.10	.02
☐ 256 Tom Candiotti	.06	.02	.00
☐ 257 Barry Larkin	.15	.06	.01
☐ 258 Mike Krukow	.03	.01	.00
☐ 259 Billy Ripken	.03	.01	.00
☐ 260 Cecilio Guante	.03	.01	.00
☐ 261 Scott Bradley	.03	.01	.00
☐ 262 Floyd Bannister	.03	.01	.00
☐ 263 Pete Smith	.03	.01	.00
☐ 264 Jim Gantner UER (wrong birtdate)	.03	.01	.00
☐ 265 Roger McDowell	.03	.01	.00
☐ 266 Bobby Thigpen	.08	.03	.01
☐ 267 Jim Clancy	.03	.01	.00
☐ 268 Terry Steinbach	.06	.02	.00
☐ 269 Mike Dunne	.03	.01	.00
☐ 270 Dwight Gooden	.10	.04	.01
☐ 271 Mike Heath	.03	.01	.00
☐ 272 Dave Smith	.03	.01	.00
☐ 273 Keith Atherton	.03	.01	.00
☐ 274 Tim Burke	.03	.01	.00
☐ 275 Damon Berryhill	.06	.02	.00
☐ 276 Vance Law	.03	.01	.00
☐ 277 Rich Dotson	.03	.01	.00
☐ 278 Lance Parrish	.08	.03	.01
☐ 279 Denny Walling	.03	.01	.00
☐ 280 Roger Clemens	.30	.12	.03
☐ 281 Greg Mathews	.03	.01	.00
☐ 282 Tom Niedenfuer	.03	.01	.00
☐ 283 Paul Kilgus	.03	.01	.00
☐ 284 Jose Guzman	.03	.01	.00
☐ 285 Calvin Schiraldi	.03	.01	.00
☐ 286 Charlie Puleo UER (career ERA 4.24, should be 4.23)	.03	.01	.00
☐ 287 Joe Orsulak	.03	.01	.00
☐ 288 Jack Howell	.03	.01	.00
☐ 289 Kevin Elster	.03	.01	.00
☐ 290 Jose Lind	.03	.01	.00
☐ 291 Paul Molitor	.10	.04	.01
☐ 292 Cecil Espy	.03	.01	.00
☐ 293 Bill Wegman	.03	.01	.00
☐ 294 Dan Pasqua	.06	.02	.00
☐ 295 Scott Garrelts UER (wrong birthdate)	.06	.02	.00
☐ 296 Walt Terrell	.03	.01	.00
☐ 297 Ed Hearn	.03	.01	.00
☐ 298 Lou Whitaker	.08	.03	.01
☐ 299 Ken Dayley	.03	.01	.00
☐ 300 Checklist Card	.06	.01	.00
☐ 301 Tommy Herr	.03	.01	.00
☐ 302 Mike Brumley	.03	.01	.00
☐ 303 Ellis Burks	.15	.06	.01
☐ 304 Curt Young UER (wrong birthdate)	.03	.01	.00
☐ 305 Jody Reed	.08	.03	.01
☐ 306 Bill Doran	.03	.01	.00
☐ 307 David Wells	.06	.02	.00
☐ 308 Ron Robinson	.03	.01	.00
☐ 309 Rafael Santana	.03	.01	.00
☐ 310 Julio Franco	.10	.04	.01
☐ 311 Jack Clark	.08	.03	.01
☐ 312 Chris James	.03	.01	.00
☐ 313 Milt Thompson	.03	.01	.00
☐ 314 John Shelby	.03	.01	.00
☐ 315 Al Leiter	.03	.01	.00
☐ 316 Mike Davis	.03	.01	.00
☐ 317 Chris Sabo	.60	.25	.06
☐ 318 Greg Gagne	.03	.01	.00
☐ 319 Jose Oquendo	.03	.01	.00
☐ 320 John Farrell	.03	.01	.00
☐ 321 Franklin Stubbs	.03	.01	.00
☐ 322 Kurt Stillwell	.03	.01	.00
☐ 323 Shawn Abner	.03	.01	.00
☐ 324 Mike Flanagan	.03	.01	.00
☐ 325 Kevin Bass	.03	.01	.00
☐ 326 Pat Tabler	.03	.01	.00
☐ 327 Mike Henneman	.03	.01	.00
☐ 328 Rick Honeycutt	.03	.01	.00
☐ 329 John Smiley	.06	.02	.00
☐ 330 Rey Quinones	.03	.01	.00
☐ 331 Johnny Ray	.03	.01	.00
☐ 332 Bob Welch	.08	.03	.01
☐ 333 Larry Sheets	.03	.01	.00
☐ 334 Jeff Parrett	.03	.01	.00

☐ 335 Rick Reuschel UER .06 .02 .00
(for Don Robinson, should be Jeff)
☐ 336 Randy Myers .06 .02 .00
☐ 337 Ken Williams .03 .01 .00
☐ 338 Andy McGaffigan .03 .01 .00
☐ 339 Joey Meyer .03 .01 .00
☐ 340 Dion James .03 .01 .00
☐ 341 Les Lancaster .03 .01 .00
☐ 342 Tom Foley .03 .01 .00
☐ 343 Geno Petralli .03 .01 .00
☐ 344 Dan Petry .03 .01 .00
☐ 345 Alvin Davis .06 .02 .00
☐ 346 Mickey Hatcher .03 .01 .00
☐ 347 Marvell Wynne .03 .01 .00
☐ 348 Danny Cox .03 .01 .00
☐ 349 Dave Stieb .08 .03 .01
☐ 350 Jay Bell .06 .02 .00
☐ 351 Jeff Treadway .06 .02 .00
☐ 352 Luis Salazar .03 .01 .00
☐ 353 Len Dykstra .08 .03 .01
☐ 354 Juan Agosto .03 .01 .00
☐ 355 Gene Larkin .06 .02 .00
☐ 356 Steve Farr .03 .01 .00
☐ 357 Paul Assenmacher .03 .01 .00
☐ 358 Todd Benzinger .03 .01 .00
☐ 359 Larry Andersen .03 .01 .00
☐ 360 Paul O'Neill .08 .03 .01
☐ 361 Ron Hassey .03 .01 .00
☐ 362 Jim Gott .03 .01 .00
☐ 363 Ken Phelps .03 .01 .00
☐ 364 Tim Flannery .03 .01 .00
☐ 365 Randy Ready .03 .01 .00
☐ 366 Nelson Santovenia .08 .03 .01
☐ 367 Kelly Downs .03 .01 .00
☐ 368 Danny Heep .03 .01 .00
☐ 369 Phil Bradley .03 .01 .00
☐ 370 Jeff Robinson .03 .01 .00
Pittsburgh Pirates
☐ 371 Ivan Calderon .06 .02 .00
☐ 372 Mike Witt .03 .01 .00
☐ 373 Greg Maddux .08 .03 .01
☐ 374 Carmen Castillo .03 .01 .00
☐ 375 Jose Rijo .08 .03 .01
☐ 376 Joe Price .03 .01 .00
☐ 377 Rene C. Gonzales .03 .01 .00
☐ 378 Oddibe McDowell .03 .01 .00
☐ 379 Jim Presley .03 .01 .00
☐ 380 Brad Wellman .03 .01 .00
☐ 381 Tom Glavine .35 .15 .03
☐ 382 Dan Plesac .03 .01 .00
☐ 383 Wally Backman .03 .01 .00
☐ 384 Dave Gallagher .08 .03 .01
☐ 385 Tom Henke .06 .02 .00
☐ 386 Luis Polonia .08 .03 .01
☐ 387 Junior Ortiz .03 .01 .00
☐ 388 David Cone .08 .03 .01
☐ 389 Dave Bergman .03 .01 .00
☐ 390 Danny Darwin .03 .01 .00
☐ 391 Dan Gladden .03 .01 .00
☐ 392 John Dopson .08 .03 .01
☐ 393 Frank DiPino .03 .01 .00
☐ 394 Al Nipper .03 .01 .00
☐ 395 Willie Randolph .06 .02 .00
☐ 396 Don Carman .03 .01 .00
☐ 397 Scott Terry .03 .01 .00
☐ 398 Rick Cerone .03 .01 .00
☐ 399 Tom Pagnozzi .03 .01 .00
☐ 400 Checklist Card .06 .01 .00
☐ 401 Mickey Tettleton .06 .02 .00
☐ 402 Curtis Wilkerson .03 .01 .00
☐ 403 Jeff Russell .03 .01 .00
☐ 404 Pat Perry .03 .01 .00
☐ 405 Jose Alvarez .06 .02 .00
☐ 406 Rick Schu .03 .01 .00
☐ 407 Sherman Corbett .03 .01 .00
☐ 408 Dave Magadan .08 .03 .01
☐ 409 Bob Kipper .03 .01 .00
☐ 410 Don August .03 .01 .00
☐ 411 Bob Brower .03 .01 .00
☐ 412 Chris Bosio .03 .01 .00
☐ 413 Jerry Reuss .03 .01 .00
☐ 414 Atlee Hammaker .03 .01 .00
☐ 415 Jim Walewander .03 .01 .00
☐ 416 Mike Macfarlane .10 .04 .01
☐ 417 Pat Sheridan .03 .01 .00
☐ 418 Pedro Guerrero .08 .03 .01
☐ 419 Allan Anderson .03 .01 .00
☐ 420 Mark Parent .08 .03 .01
☐ 421 Bob Stanley .03 .01 .00
☐ 422 Mike Gallego .03 .01 .00
☐ 423 Bruce Hurst .06 .02 .00
☐ 424 Dave Meads .03 .01 .00
☐ 425 Jesse Barfield .08 .03 .01
☐ 426 Rob Dibble .25 .10 .02
☐ 427 Joel Skinner .03 .01 .00
☐ 428 Ron Kittle .06 .02 .00
☐ 429 Rick Rhoden .03 .01 .00
☐ 430 Bob Dernier .03 .01 .00
☐ 431 Steve Jeltz .03 .01 .00
☐ 432 Rick Dempsey .03 .01 .00
☐ 433 Roberto Kelly .12 .05 .01
☐ 434 Dave Anderson .03 .01 .00
☐ 435 Herm Winningham .03 .01 .00
☐ 436 Al Newman .03 .01 .00
☐ 437 Jose DeLeon .03 .01 .00
☐ 438 Doug Jones .03 .01 .00
☐ 439 Brian Holton .03 .01 .00
☐ 440 Jeff Montgomery .06 .02 .00
☐ 441 Dickie Thon .03 .01 .00
☐ 442 Cecil Fielder .30 .12 .03
☐ 443 John Fishel .03 .01 .00
☐ 444 Jerry Don Gleaton .03 .01 .00
☐ 445 Paul Gibson .03 .01 .00
☐ 446 Walt Weiss .08 .03 .01
☐ 447 Glenn Wilson .03 .01 .00

☐ 448	Mike Moore	.06	.02	.00
☐ 449	Chili Davis	.06	.02	.00
☐ 450	Dave Henderson	.08	.03	.01
☐ 451	Jose Bautista	.08	.03	.01
☐ 452	Rex Hudler	.06	.02	.00
☐ 453	Bob Brenly	.03	.01	.00
☐ 454	Mackey Sasser	.06	.02	.00
☐ 455	Daryl Boston	.03	.01	.00
☐ 456	Mike Fitzgerald	.03	.01	.00
	Montreal Expos			
☐ 457	Jeffrey Leonard	.03	.01	.00
☐ 458	Bruce Sutter	.08	.03	.01
☐ 459	Mitch Webster	.03	.01	.00
☐ 460	Joe Hesketh	.06	.02	.00
☐ 461	Bobby Witt	.06	.02	.00
☐ 462	Stew Cliburn	.03	.01	.00
☐ 463	Scott Bankhead	.06	.02	.00
☐ 464	Ramon Martinez	1.25	.50	.12
☐ 465	Dave Leiper	.03	.01	.00
☐ 466	Luis Alicea	.03	.01	.00
☐ 467	John Cerutti	.03	.01	.00
☐ 468	Ron Washington	.03	.01	.00
☐ 469	Jeff Reed	.03	.01	.00
☐ 470	Jeff Robinson	.06	.02	.00
	Detroit Tigers			
☐ 471	Sid Fernandez	.06	.02	.00
☐ 472	Terry Puhl	.03	.01	.00
☐ 473	Charlie Lea	.03	.01	.00
☐ 474	Israel Sanchez	.06	.02	.00
☐ 475	Bruce Benedict	.03	.01	.00
☐ 476	Oil Can Boyd	.03	.01	.00
☐ 477	Craig Reynolds	.03	.01	.00
☐ 478	Frank Williams	.03	.01	.00
☐ 479	Greg Cadaret	.03	.01	.00
☐ 480	Randy Kramer	.08	.03	.01
☐ 481	Dave Eiland	.08	.03	.01
☐ 482	Eric Show	.03	.01	.00
☐ 483	Garry Templeton	.06	.02	.00
☐ 484	Wallace Johnson	.03	.01	.00
☐ 485	Kevin Mitchell	.15	.06	.01
☐ 486	Tim Crews	.03	.01	.00
☐ 487	Mike Maddux	.03	.01	.00
☐ 488	Dave LaPoint	.03	.01	.00
☐ 489	Fred Manrique	.03	.01	.00
☐ 490	Greg Minton	.03	.01	.00
☐ 491	Doug Dascenzo UER	.10	.04	.01
	(photo actually Damon Berryhill)			
☐ 492	Willie Upshaw	.03	.01	.00
☐ 493	Jack Armstrong	.10	.04	.01
☐ 494	Kirt Manwaring	.03	.01	.00
☐ 495	Jeff Ballard	.03	.01	.00
☐ 496	Jeff Kunkel	.03	.01	.00
☐ 497	Mike Campbell	.03	.01	.00
☐ 498	Gary Thurman	.03	.01	.00
☐ 499	Zane Smith	.06	.02	.00
☐ 500	Checklist Card DP	.06	.01	.00
☐ 501	Mike Birkbeck	.03	.01	.00
☐ 502	Terry Leach	.03	.01	.00
☐ 503	Shawn Hillegas	.03	.01	.00
☐ 504	Manny Lee	.03	.01	.00
☐ 505	Doug Jennings	.06	.02	.00
☐ 506	Ken Oberkfell	.03	.01	.00
☐ 507	Tim Teufel	.03	.01	.00
☐ 508	Tom Brookens	.03	.01	.00
☐ 509	Rafael Ramirez	.03	.01	.00
☐ 510	Fred Toliver	.03	.01	.00
☐ 511	Brian Holman	.15	.06	.01
☐ 512	Mike Bielecki	.03	.01	.00
☐ 513	Jeff Pico	.06	.02	.00
☐ 514	Charles Hudson	.03	.01	.00
☐ 515	Bruce Ruffin	.03	.01	.00
☐ 516	Larry McWilliams UER	.03	.01	.00
	(New Richland, should be North Richland)			
☐ 517	Jeff Sellers	.03	.01	.00
☐ 518	John Costello	.06	.02	.00
☐ 519	Brady Anderson	.08	.03	.01
☐ 520	Craig McMurtry	.03	.01	.00
☐ 521	Ray Hayward DP	.03	.01	.00
☐ 522	Drew Hall DP	.03	.01	.00
☐ 523	Mark Lemke DP	.17	.07	.01
☐ 524	Oswald Peraza DP	.06	.02	.00
☐ 525	Bryan Harvey DP	.17	.07	.01
☐ 526	Rick Aguilera DP	.03	.01	.00
☐ 527	Tom Prince DP	.03	.01	.00
☐ 528	Mark Clear DP	.03	.01	.00
☐ 529	Jerry Browne DP	.03	.01	.00
☐ 530	Juan Castillo DP	.03	.01	.00
☐ 531	Jack McDowell DP	.08	.03	.01
☐ 532	Chris Speier DP	.03	.01	.00
☐ 533	Darrell Evans DP	.06	.02	.00
☐ 534	Luis Aquino DP	.03	.01	.00
☐ 535	Eric King DP	.03	.01	.00
☐ 536	Ken Hill DP	.15	.06	.01
☐ 537	Randy Bush DP	.03	.01	.00
☐ 538	Shane Mack DP	.06	.02	.00
☐ 539	Tom Bolton DP	.06	.02	.00
☐ 540	Gene Nelson DP	.03	.01	.00
☐ 541	Wes Gardner DP	.03	.01	.00
☐ 542	Ken Caminiti DP	.03	.01	.00
☐ 543	Duane Ward DP	.03	.01	.00
☐ 544	Norm Charlton DP	.10	.04	.01
☐ 545	Hal Morris DP	.75	.30	.07
☐ 546	Rich Yett DP	.03	.01	.00
☐ 547	Hensley Meulens DP	.25	.10	.02
☐ 548	Greg Harris DP	.03	.01	.00
	Philadelphia Phillies			
☐ 549	Darren Daulton DP	.06	.02	.00
	(posing as right-handed hitter)			
☐ 550	Jeff Hamilton DP	.03	.01	.00
☐ 551	Luis Aguayo DP	.03	.01	.00
☐ 552	Tim Leary DP	.06	.02	.00
	(resembles M.Marshall)			
☐ 553	Ron Oester DP	.03	.01	.00

☐ 554 Steve Lombardozzi DP	.03	.01	.00
☐ 555 Tim Jones DP	.06	.02	.00
☐ 556 Bud Black DP	.03	.01	.00
☐ 557 Alejandro Pena DP	.03	.01	.00
☐ 558 Jose DeJesus DP	.10	.04	.01
☐ 559 Dennis Rasmussen DP	.03	.01	.00
☐ 560 Pat Borders DP	.10	.04	.01
☐ 561 Craig Biggio DP	.30	.12	.03
☐ 562 Luis De Los Santos DP	.08	.03	.01
☐ 563 Fred Lynn DP	.06	.02	.00
☐ 564 Todd Burns DP	.08	.03	.01
☐ 565 Felix Fermin DP	.03	.01	.00
☐ 566 Darnell Coles DP	.03	.01	.00
☐ 567 Willie Fraser DP	.03	.01	.00
☐ 568 Glenn Hubbard DP	.03	.01	.00
☐ 569 Craig Worthington DP	.08	.03	.01
☐ 570 Johnny Paredes DP	.08	.03	.01
☐ 571 Don Robinson DP	.03	.01	.00
☐ 572 Barry Lyons DP	.03	.01	.00
☐ 573 Bill Long DP	.03	.01	.00
☐ 574 Tracy Jones DP	.03	.01	.00
☐ 575 Juan Nieves DP	.03	.01	.00
☐ 576 Andres Thomas DP	.03	.01	.00
☐ 577 Rolando Roomes DP	.08	.03	.01
☐ 578 Luis Rivera UER DP (wrong birthdate)	.03	.01	.00
☐ 579 Chad Kreuter DP	.08	.03	.01
☐ 580 Tony Armas DP	.03	.01	.00
☐ 581 Jay Buhner	.15	.06	.01
☐ 582 Ricky Horton DP	.03	.01	.00
☐ 583 Andy Hawkins DP	.03	.01	.00
☐ 584 Sil Campusano	.10	.04	.01
☐ 585 Dave Clark	.03	.01	.00
☐ 586 Van Snider DP	.08	.03	.01
☐ 587 Todd Frohwirth DP	.03	.01	.00
☐ 588 Puzzle Card DP Warren Spahn	.06	.02	.00
☐ 589 William Brennan	.06	.02	.00
☐ 590 German Gonzalez	.06	.02	.00
☐ 591 Ernie Whitt DP	.03	.01	.00
☐ 592 Jeff Blauser	.03	.01	.00
☐ 593 Spike Owen DP	.03	.01	.00
☐ 594 Matt Williams	.20	.08	.02
☐ 595 Lloyd McClendon DP	.03	.01	.00
☐ 596 Steve Ontiveros	.03	.01	.00
☐ 597 Scott Medvin	.08	.03	.01
☐ 598 Hipolito Pena DP	.06	.02	.00
☐ 599 Jerald Clark DP	.15	.06	.01
☐ 600A Checklist Card DP 635 Kurt Schilling	.30	.10	.02
☐ 600B Checklist Card DP 635 Curt Schilling (MVP's not listed on checklist card)	.06	.01	.00
☐ 600C Checklist Card DP 635 Curt Schilling (MVP's listed following 660)	.06	.01	.00

☐ 601 Carmelo Martinez DP	.03	.01	.00
☐ 602 Mike LaCoss	.03	.01	.00
☐ 603 Mike Devereaux	.06	.02	.00
☐ 604 Alex Madrid DP	.06	.02	.00
☐ 605 Gary Redus DP	.03	.01	.00
☐ 606 Lance Johnson	.03	.01	.00
☐ 607 Terry Clark DP	.06	.02	.00
☐ 608 Manny Trillo DP	.03	.01	.00
☐ 609 Scott Jordan	.08	.03	.01
☐ 610 Jay Howell DP	.03	.01	.00
☐ 611 Francisco Melendez	.08	.03	.01
☐ 612 Mike Boddicker	.03	.01	.00
☐ 613 Kevin Brown DP	.08	.03	.01
☐ 614 Dave Valle	.03	.01	.00
☐ 615 Tim Laudner DP	.03	.01	.00
☐ 616 Andy Nezelek UER (wrong birthdate)	.08	.03	.01
☐ 617 Chuck Crim	.03	.01	.00
☐ 618 Jack Savage DP	.06	.02	.00
☐ 619 Adam Peterson	.06	.02	.00
☐ 620 Todd Stottlemyre	.15	.06	.01
☐ 621 Lance Blankenship	.08	.03	.01
☐ 622 Miguel Garcia DP	.08	.03	.01
☐ 623 Keith Miller DP New York Mets	.03	.01	.00
☐ 624 Ricky Jordan DP	.10	.04	.01
☐ 625 Ernest Riles DP	.03	.01	.00
☐ 626 John Moses DP	.03	.01	.00
☐ 627 Nelson Liriano DP	.03	.01	.00
☐ 628 Mike Smithson DP	.03	.01	.00
☐ 629 Scott Sanderson	.06	.02	.00
☐ 630 Dale Mohorcic	.03	.01	.00
☐ 631 Marvin Freeman DP	.03	.01	.00
☐ 632 Mike Young DP	.03	.01	.00
☐ 633 Dennis Lamp	.03	.01	.00
☐ 634 Dante Bichette DP	.15	.06	.01
☐ 635 Curt Schilling DP	.08	.03	.01
☐ 636 Scott May DP	.08	.03	.01
☐ 637 Mike Schooler	.12	.05	.01
☐ 638 Rick Leach	.03	.01	.00
☐ 639 Tom Lampkin UER (Throws Left, should be Throws Right)	.08	.03	.01
☐ 640 Brian Meyer	.08	.03	.01
☐ 641 Brian Harper	.06	.02	.00
☐ 642 John Smoltz	.50	.20	.05
☐ 643 Jose: 40/40 Club (Jose Canseco)	.20	.08	.02
☐ 644 Bill Schroeder	.03	.01	.00
☐ 645 Edgar Martinez	.20	.08	.02
☐ 646 Dennis Cook	.10	.04	.01
☐ 647 Barry Jones	.03	.01	.00
☐ 648 Orel: 59 and Counting (Orel Hershiser)	.08	.03	.01
☐ 649 Rod Nichols	.06	.02	.00
☐ 650 Jody Davis	.03	.01	.00
☐ 651 Bob Milacki	.15	.06	.01
☐ 652 Mike Jackson	.03	.01	.00

☐ 653 Derek Lilliquist	.08	.03	.01
☐ 654 Paul Mirabella	.03	.01	.00
☐ 655 Mike Diaz	.03	.01	.00
☐ 656 Jeff Musselman	.03	.01	.00
☐ 657 Jerry Reed	.03	.01	.00
☐ 658 Kevin Blankenship	.06	.02	.00
☐ 659 Wayne Tolleson	.03	.01	.00
☐ 660 Eric Hetzel	.08	.03	.01

1989 Donruss Bonus MVP's

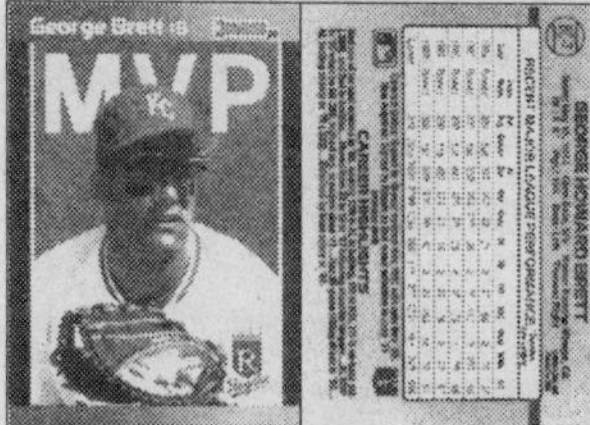

This 26-card set was distributed along with the regular 1989 Donruss issue as random inserts with the rack and wax packs. These bonus cards are numbered with the prefix BC for bonus cards and were supposedly produced in the same quantities as the other 660 regular issue cards. The "most valuable" player was selected from each of the 26 teams. Cards measure 2 1/2" by 3 1/2" and feature the same distinctive side border as the regular issue. The cards are distinguished by the bold MVP logo in the upper background of the obverse. Four of these cards were double printed with respect to the other cards in the set; these four are denoted by DP in the checklist below.

	MINT	EXC	G-VG
COMPLETE SET (26)	2.50	1.00	.25
COMMON CARD (BC1-BC26)	.05	.02	.00
☐ BC1 Kirby Puckett	.15	.06	.01
☐ BC2 Mike Scott	.08	.03	.01
☐ BC3 Joe Carter	.08	.03	.01
☐ BC4 Orel Hershiser	.08	.03	.01
☐ BC5 Jose Canseco	.20	.08	.02
☐ BC6 Darryl Strawberry	.15	.06	.01
☐ BC7 George Brett	.12	.05	.01
☐ BC8 Andre Dawson	.10	.04	.01
☐ BC9 Paul Molitor UER (Brewers logo missing the word Milwaukee)	.08	.03	.01
☐ BC10 Andy Van Slyke	.08	.03	.01
☐ BC11 Dave Winfield	.10	.04	.01
☐ BC12 Kevin Gross	.05	.02	.00
☐ BC13 Mike Greenwell	.08	.03	.01
☐ BC14 Ozzie Smith	.10	.04	.01
☐ BC15 Cal Ripken	.15	.06	.01
☐ BC16 Andres Galarraga	.08	.03	.01
☐ BC17 Alan Trammell	.10	.04	.01
☐ BC18 Kal Daniels	.08	.03	.01
☐ BC19 Fred McGriff	.10	.04	.01
☐ BC20 Tony Gwynn	.12	.05	.01
☐ BC21 Wally Joyner DP	.08	.03	.01
☐ BC22 Will Clark DP	.15	.06	.01
☐ BC23 Ozzie Guillen	.05	.02	.00
☐ BC24 Gerald Perry DP	.05	.02	.00
☐ BC25 Alvin Davis DP	.05	.02	.00
☐ BC26 Ruben Sierra	.12	.05	.01

1989 Donruss Rookies

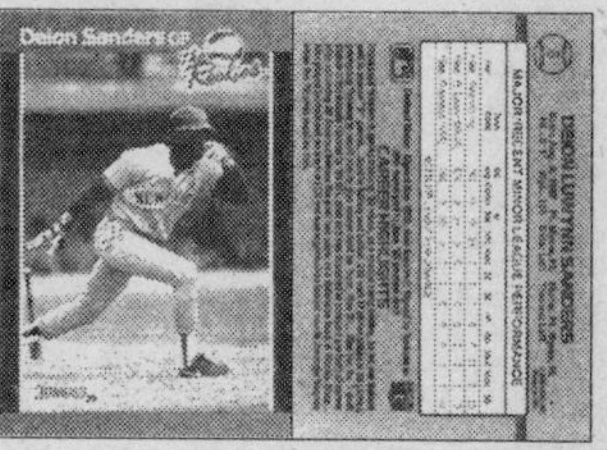

The 1989 Donruss Rookies set contains 56 standard-size (2 1/2" by 3 1/2") cards. The fronts have green and black borders; the backs are green and feature career highlights. The cards were distributed as a boxed set through the Donruss Dealer Network. The key rookie cards in this set are Jim Abbott,

Junior Felix, Deion Sanders, and Jerome Walton.

	MINT	EXC	G-VG
COMPLETE SET (56)	13.50	6.00	1.85
COMMON PLAYER (1-56)	.05	.02	.00

	MINT	EXC	G-VG
☐ 1 Gary Sheffield	.30	.12	.03
☐ 2 Gregg Jefferies	.30	.12	.03
☐ 3 Ken Griffey Jr.	7.50	3.25	.75
☐ 4 Tom Gordon	.25	.10	.02
☐ 5 Billy Spiers	.12	.05	.01
☐ 6 Deion Sanders	.60	.25	.06
☐ 7 Donn Pall	.08	.03	.01
☐ 8 Steve Carter	.08	.03	.01
☐ 9 Francisco Oliveras	.08	.03	.01
☐ 10 Steve Wilson	.08	.03	.01
☐ 11 Bob Geren	.08	.03	.01
☐ 12 Tony Castillo	.08	.03	.01
☐ 13 Kenny Rogers	.10	.04	.01
☐ 14 Carlos Martinez	.15	.06	.01
☐ 15 Edgar Martinez	.20	.08	.02
☐ 16 Jim Abbott	1.25	.50	.12
☐ 17 Torey Lovullo	.08	.03	.01
☐ 18 Mark Carreon	.08	.03	.01
☐ 19 Geronimo Berroa	.08	.03	.01
☐ 20 Luis Medina	.10	.04	.01
☐ 21 Sandy Alomar Jr.	.40	.16	.04
☐ 22 Bob Milacki	.15	.06	.01
☐ 23 Joe Girardi	.10	.04	.01
☐ 24 German Gonzalez	.08	.03	.01
☐ 25 Craig Worthington	.08	.03	.01
☐ 26 Jerome Walton	.40	.16	.04
☐ 27 Gary Wayne	.10	.04	.01
☐ 28 Tim Jones	.08	.03	.01
☐ 29 Dante Bichette	.08	.03	.01
☐ 30 Alexis Infante	.08	.03	.01
☐ 31 Ken Hill	.10	.04	.01
☐ 32 Dwight Smith	.12	.05	.01
☐ 33 Luis de los Santos	.08	.03	.01
☐ 34 Eric Yelding	.12	.05	.01
☐ 35 Gregg Olson	.45	.18	.04
☐ 36 Phil Stephenson	.08	.03	.01
☐ 37 Ken Patterson	.08	.03	.01
☐ 38 Rick Wrona	.08	.03	.01
☐ 39 Mike Brumley	.05	.02	.00
☐ 40 Cris Carpenter	.08	.03	.01
☐ 41 Jeff Brantley	.20	.08	.02
☐ 42 Ron Jones	.08	.03	.01
☐ 43 Randy Johnson	.10	.04	.01
☐ 44 Kevin Brown	.08	.03	.01
☐ 45 Ramon Martinez	1.25	.50	.12
☐ 46 Greg W.Harris	.10	.04	.01
☐ 47 Steve Finley	.35	.15	.03
☐ 48 Randy Kramer	.05	.02	.00
☐ 49 Erik Hanson	.45	.18	.04
☐ 50 Matt Merullo	.10	.04	.01
☐ 51 Mike Devereaux	.08	.03	.01
☐ 52 Clay Parker	.08	.03	.01
☐ 53 Omar Vizquel	.08	.03	.01
☐ 54 Derek Lilliquist	.05	.02	.00
☐ 55 Junior Felix	.15	.06	.01
☐ 56 Checklist Card	.05	.01	.00

1990 Donruss

The 1990 Donruss set contains 716 standard-size (2 1/2" by 3 1/2") cards. The front borders are bright red. The horizontally-oriented backs are amber. Cards numbered 1-26 are Diamond Kings; cards numbered 28-47 are Rated Rookies (RR). Card number 716 was added to the set shortly after the set's initial production, necessitating the checklist variation on card number 700. The set was the largest ever produced by Donruss, unfortunately it also had a large number of errors which were corrected after the cards were released. Every All-Star selection in the set has two versions, the statistical heading on the back is either "Recent Major League Performance" or "All-Star Game Performance." There are a number of cards that have been discovered to have minor printing flaws, which are insignificant variations, that collectors have found unworthy of price differentials. These very minor variations include numbers 1, 18, 154, 168, 206, 270, 321, 347, 405, 408, 425, 583, 585, 619, 637, 639, 699, 701, and 716. The factory sets were distributed without the Bonus Cards; thus there were again new checklist cards printed to reflect the exclusion of the Bonus Cards. These factory set checklist cards are the B variations below (except for 700C). The key rookie cards in this set are Delino

DeShields, Juan Gonzalez, Marquis Grissom, Dave Justice, Ben McDonald, John Olerud, and Dean Palmer. The unusual number of cards in the set (716 plus 26 BC's, i.e., not divisible by 132) apparently led to 50 double-printed numbers, which are indicated in the checklists below (1990 Donruss and 1990 Donruss Bonus MVP's) by DP.

	MINT	EXC	G-VG
COMPLETE SET (716)	18.00	7.50	2.50
COMMON PLAYER (1-716)	.03	.01	.00
☐ 1 Bo Jackson DK	.30	.12	.03
☐ 2 Steve Sax DK	.06	.02	.00
☐ 3A Ruben Sierra DK ERR (no small line on top border on card back)	1.00	.40	.10
☐ 3B Ruben Sierra DK COR	.10	.04	.01
☐ 4 Ken Griffey Jr. DK	.60	.25	.06
☐ 5 Mickey Tettleton DK	.06	.02	.00
☐ 6 Dave Stewart DK	.08	.03	.01
☐ 7 Jim Deshaies DK DP	.06	.02	.00
☐ 8 John Smoltz DK	.08	.03	.01
☐ 9 Mike Bielecki DK	.06	.02	.00
☐ 10A Brian Downing DK ERR (reverse negative on card front)	.65	.25	.06
☐ 10B Brian Downing DK COR	.08	.03	.01
☐ 11 Kevin Mitchell DK	.08	.03	.01
☐ 12 Kelly Gruber DK	.08	.03	.01
☐ 13 Joe Magrane DK	.06	.02	.00
☐ 14 John Franco DK	.06	.02	.00
☐ 15 Ozzie Guillen DK	.06	.02	.00
☐ 16 Lou Whitaker DK	.06	.02	.00
☐ 17 John Smiley DK	.06	.02	.00
☐ 18 Howard Johnson DK	.08	.03	.01
☐ 19 Willie Randolph DK	.06	.02	.00
☐ 20 Chris Bosio DK	.06	.02	.00
☐ 21 Tommy Herr DK DP	.06	.02	.00
☐ 22 Dan Gladden DK	.06	.02	.00
☐ 23 Ellis Burks DK	.08	.03	.01
☐ 24 Pete O'Brien DK	.06	.02	.00
☐ 25 Bryn Smith DK	.06	.02	.00
☐ 26 Ed Whitson DK DP	.06	.02	.00
☐ 27 DK Checklist DP (comments on Perez-Steele on back)	.06	.01	.00
☐ 28 Robin Ventura RR	.65	.25	.06
☐ 29 Todd Zeile RR	.35	.15	.03
☐ 30 Sandy Alomar Jr. RR	.10	.04	.01
☐ 31 Kent Mercker RR	.15	.06	.01
☐ 32 Ben McDonald RR	.75	.30	.07
☐ 33A Juan Gonzalez RR ERR (reverse negative)	4.00	1.75	.40
☐ 33B Juan Gonzalez RR COR	2.00	.80	.20
☐ 34 Eric Anthony RR	.17	.07	.01
☐ 35 Mike Fetters RR	.08	.03	.01
☐ 36 Marquis Grissom RR	.45	.18	.04
☐ 37 Greg Vaughn RR	.50	.20	.05
☐ 38 Brian Dubois RR	.10	.04	.01
☐ 39 Steve Avery RR UER (born in MI not NJ)	.90	.40	.09
☐ 40 Mark Gardner RR	.17	.07	.01
☐ 41 Andy Benes RR	.17	.07	.01
☐ 42 Delino DeShields RR	.40	.16	.04
☐ 43 Scott Coolbaugh RR	.10	.04	.01
☐ 44 Pat Combs RR DP	.06	.02	.00
☐ 45 Alex Sanchez RR DP	.06	.02	.00
☐ 46 Kelly Mann RR DP	.06	.02	.00
☐ 47 Julio Machado RR DP	.06	.02	.00
☐ 48 Pete Incaviglia	.06	.02	.00
☐ 49 Shawon Dunston	.08	.03	.01
☐ 50 Jeff Treadway	.03	.01	.00
☐ 51 Jeff Ballard	.03	.01	.00
☐ 52 Claudell Washington	.03	.01	.00
☐ 53 Juan Samuel	.06	.02	.00
☐ 54 John Smiley	.06	.02	.00
☐ 55 Rob Deer	.06	.02	.00
☐ 56 Geno Petralli	.03	.01	.00
☐ 57 Chris Bosio	.03	.01	.00
☐ 58 Carlton Fisk	.12	.05	.01
☐ 59 Kirt Manwaring	.03	.01	.00
☐ 60 Chet Lemon	.03	.01	.00
☐ 61 Bo Jackson	.40	.16	.04
☐ 62 Doyle Alexander	.03	.01	.00
☐ 63 Pedro Guerrero	.08	.03	.01
☐ 64 Allan Anderson	.03	.01	.00
☐ 65 Greg Harris	.03	.01	.00
☐ 66 Mike Greenwell	.12	.05	.01
☐ 67 Walt Weiss	.06	.02	.00
☐ 68 Wade Boggs	.15	.06	.01
☐ 69 Jim Clancy	.03	.01	.00
☐ 70 Junior Felix	.06	.02	.00
☐ 71 Barry Larkin	.12	.05	.01
☐ 72 Dave LaPoint	.03	.01	.00
☐ 73 Joel Skinner	.03	.01	.00
☐ 74 Jesse Barfield	.06	.02	.00
☐ 75 Tommy Herr	.03	.01	.00
☐ 76 Ricky Jordan	.06	.02	.00
☐ 77 Eddie Murray	.10	.04	.01
☐ 78 Steve Sax	.06	.02	.00
☐ 79 Tim Belcher	.06	.02	.00
☐ 80 Danny Jackson	.03	.01	.00
☐ 81 Kent Hrbek	.08	.03	.01
☐ 82 Milt Thompson	.03	.01	.00
☐ 83 Brook Jacoby	.03	.01	.00
☐ 84 Mike Marshall	.06	.02	.00
☐ 85 Kevin Seitzer	.06	.02	.00
☐ 86 Tony Gwynn	.15	.06	.01
☐ 87 Dave Stieb	.08	.03	.01
☐ 88 Dave Smith	.03	.01	.00
☐ 89 Bret Saberhagen	.08	.03	.01
☐ 90 Alan Trammell	.08	.03	.01
☐ 91 Tony Phillips	.03	.01	.00

☐ 92 Doug Drabek .08 .03 .01
☐ 93 Jeffrey Leonard .03 .01 .00
☐ 94 Wally Joyner .08 .03 .01
☐ 95 Carney Lansford .06 .02 .00
☐ 96 Cal Ripken .30 .12 .03
☐ 97 Andres Galarraga .06 .02 .00
☐ 98 Kevin Mitchell .10 .04 .01
☐ 99 Howard Johnson .08 .03 .01
☐ 100A Checklist Card .06 .01 .00
(28-129)
☐ 100B Checklist Card .06 .01 .00
(28-125)
☐ 101 Melido Perez .03
.01 .00
☐ 102 Spike Owen .03 .01 .00
☐ 103 Paul Molitor .08 .03 .01
☐ 104 Geronimo Berroa .03 .01 .00
☐ 105 Ryne Sandberg .30 .12 .03
☐ 106 Bryn Smith .03 .01 .00
☐ 107 Steve Buechele .03 .01 .00
☐ 108 Jim Abbott .17 .07 .01
☐ 109 Alvin Davis .06 .02 .00
☐ 110 Lee Smith .06 .02 .00
☐ 111 Roberto Alomar .15 .06 .01
☐ 112 Rick Reuschel .06 .02 .00
☐ 113A Kelly Gruber ERR .10 .04 .01
(born 2/22)
☐ 113B Kelly Gruber COR .10 .04 .01
(born 2/26; corrected in factory sets)
☐ 114 Joe Carter .10 .04 .01
☐ 115 Jose Rijo .08 .03 .01
☐ 116 Greg Minton .03 .01 .00
☐ 117 Bob Ojeda .03 .01 .00
☐ 118 Glenn Davis .08 .03 .01
☐ 119 Jeff Reardon .06 .02 .00
☐ 120 Kurt Stillwell .03 .01 .00
☐ 121 John Smoltz .15 .06 .01
☐ 122 Dwight Evans .06 .02 .00
☐ 123 Eric Yelding .06 .02 .00
☐ 124 John Franco .03 .01 .00
☐ 125 Jose Canseco .40 .16 .04
☐ 126 Barry Bonds .17 .07 .01
☐ 127 Lee Guetterman .03 .01 .00
☐ 128 Jack Clark .08 .03 .01
☐ 129 Dave Valle .03 .01 .00
☐ 130 Hubie Brooks .06 .02 .00
☐ 131 Ernest Riles .03 .01 .00
☐ 132 Mike Morgan .06 .02 .00
☐ 133 Steve Jeltz .03 .01 .00
☐ 134 Jeff Robinson .03 .01 .00
☐ 135 Ozzie Guillen .06 .02 .00
☐ 136 Chili Davis .06 .02 .00
☐ 137 Mitch Webster .03 .01 .00
☐ 138 Jerry Browne .03 .01 .00
☐ 139 Bo Diaz .03 .01 .00
☐ 140 Robby Thompson .03 .01 .00
☐ 141 Craig Worthington .03 .01 .00
☐ 142 Julio Franco .08 .03 .01
☐ 143 Brian Holman .03 .01 .00
☐ 144 George Brett .12 .05 .01
☐ 145 Tom Glavine .20 .08 .02
☐ 146 Robin Yount .12 .05 .01
☐ 147 Gary Carter .08 .03 .01
☐ 148 Ron Kittle .06 .02 .00
☐ 149 Tony Fernandez .06 .02 .00
☐ 150 Dave Stewart .08 .03 .01
☐ 151 Gary Gaetti .06 .02 .00
☐ 152 Kevin Elster .03 .01 .00
☐ 153 Gerald Perry .03 .01 .00
☐ 154 Jesse Orosco .03 .01 .00
☐ 155 Wally Backman .03 .01 .00
☐ 156 Dennis Martinez .06 .02 .00
☐ 157 Rick Sutcliffe .06 .02 .00
☐ 158 Greg Maddux .06 .02 .00
☐ 159 Andy Hawkins .03 .01 .00
☐ 160 John Kruk .03 .01 .00
☐ 161 Jose Oquendo .03 .01 .00
☐ 162 John Dopson .03 .01 .00
☐ 163 Joe Magrane .03 .01 .00
☐ 164 Bill Ripken .03 .01 .00
☐ 165 Fred Manrique .03 .01 .00
☐ 166 Nolan Ryan UER .50 .20 .05
(Did not lead NL in K's in '89 as he was in AL in '89)
☐ 167 Damon Berryhill .03 .01 .00
☐ 168 Dale Murphy .10 .04 .01
☐ 169 Mickey Tettleton .06 .02 .00
☐ 170A Kirk McCaskill ERR .06 .02 .00
(born 4/19)
☐ 170B Kirk McCaskill COR .06 .02 .00
(born 4/9; corrected in factory sets)
☐ 171 Dwight Gooden .10 .04 .01
☐ 172 Jose Lind .03 .01 .00
☐ 173 B.J. Surhoff .03 .01 .00
☐ 174 Ruben Sierra .20 .08 .02
☐ 175 Dan Plesac .03 .01 .00
☐ 176 Dan Pasqua .03 .01 .00
☐ 177 Kelly Downs .03 .01 .00
☐ 178 Matt Nokes .06 .02 .00
☐ 179 Luis Aquino .03 .01 .00
☐ 180 Frank Tanana .06 .02 .00
☐ 181 Tony Pena .06 .02 .00
☐ 182 Dan Gladden .03 .01 .00
☐ 183 Bruce Hurst .06 .02 .00
☐ 184 Roger Clemens .30 .12 .03
☐ 185 Mark McGwire .15 .06 .01
☐ 186 Rob Murphy .03 .01 .00
☐ 187 Jim Deshaies .03 .01 .00
☐ 188 Fred McGriff .12 .05 .01
☐ 189 Rob Dibble .06 .02 .00
☐ 190 Don Mattingly .20 .08 .02
☐ 191 Felix Fermin .03 .01 .00
☐ 192 Roberto Kelly .08 .03 .01
☐ 193 Dennis Cook .03 .01 .00

Card	Player	Mint	Ex	VG
☐ 194	Darren Daulton	.06	.02	.00
☐ 195	Alfredo Griffin	.03	.01	.00
☐ 196	Eric Plunk	.03	.01	.00
☐ 197	Orel Hershiser	.08	.03	.01
☐ 198	Paul O'Neill	.06	.02	.00
☐ 199	Randy Bush	.03	.01	.00
☐ 200A	Checklist Card (130-231)	.06	.01	.00
☐ 200B	Checklist Card (126-223)	.06	.01	.00
☐ 201	Ozzie Smith	.12	.05	.01
☐ 202	Pete O'Brien	.03	.01	.00
☐ 203	Jay Howell	.03	.01	.00
☐ 204	Mark Gubicza	.06	.02	.00
☐ 205	Ed Whitson	.03	.01	.00
☐ 206	George Bell	.08	.03	.01
☐ 207	Mike Scott	.08	.03	.01
☐ 208	Charlie Leibrandt	.03	.01	.00
☐ 209	Mike Heath	.03	.01	.00
☐ 210	Dennis Eckersley	.08	.03	.01
☐ 211	Mike LaValliere	.03	.01	.00
☐ 212	Darnell Coles	.03	.01	.00
☐ 213	Lance Parrish	.06	.02	.00
☐ 214	Mike Moore	.06	.02	.00
☐ 215	Steve Finley	.10	.04	.01
☐ 216	Tim Raines	.08	.03	.01
☐ 217A	Scott Garrelts ERR (born 10/20)	.06	.02	.00
☐ 217B	Scott Garrelts COR (born 10/30; corrected in factory sets)	.06	.02	.00
☐ 218	Kevin McReynolds	.08	.03	.01
☐ 219	Dave Gallagher	.03	.01	.00
☐ 220	Tim Wallach	.06	.02	.00
☐ 221	Chuck Crim	.03	.01	.00
☐ 222	Lonnie Smith	.06	.02	.00
☐ 223	Andre Dawson	.10	.04	.01
☐ 224	Nelson Santovenia	.03	.01	.00
☐ 225	Rafael Palmeiro	.12	.05	.01
☐ 226	Devon White	.06	.02	.00
☐ 227	Harold Reynolds	.06	.02	.00
☐ 228	Ellis Burks	.08	.03	.01
☐ 229	Mark Parent	.03	.01	.00
☐ 230	Will Clark	.30	.12	.03
☐ 231	Jimmy Key	.06	.02	.00
☐ 232	John Farrell	.03	.01	.00
☐ 233	Eric Davis	.10	.04	.01
☐ 234	Johnny Ray	.03	.01	.00
☐ 235	Darryl Strawberry	.25	.10	.02
☐ 236	Bill Doran	.03	.01	.00
☐ 237	Greg Gagne	.03	.01	.00
☐ 238	Jim Eisenreich	.03	.01	.00
☐ 239	Tommy Gregg	.03	.01	.00
☐ 240	Marty Barrett	.03	.01	.00
☐ 241	Rafael Ramirez	.03	.01	.00
☐ 242	Chris Sabo	.10	.04	.01
☐ 243	Dave Henderson	.06	.02	.00
☐ 244	Andy Van Slyke	.08	.03	.01
☐ 245	Alvaro Espinoza	.03	.01	.00
☐ 246	Garry Templeton	.03	.01	.00
☐ 247	Gene Harris	.06	.02	.00
☐ 248	Kevin Gross	.03	.01	.00
☐ 249	Brett Butler	.08	.03	.01
☐ 250	Willie Randolph	.06	.02	.00
☐ 251	Roger McDowell	.03	.01	.00
☐ 252	Rafael Belliard	.03	.01	.00
☐ 253	Steve Rosenberg	.03	.01	.00
☐ 254	Jack Howell	.03	.01	.00
☐ 255	Marvell Wynne	.03	.01	.00
☐ 256	Tom Candiotti	.06	.02	.00
☐ 257	Todd Benzinger	.03	.01	.00
☐ 258	Don Robinson	.03	.01	.00
☐ 259	Phil Bradley	.03	.01	.00
☐ 260	Cecil Espy	.03	.01	.00
☐ 261	Scott Bankhead	.06	.02	.00
☐ 262	Frank White	.03	.01	.00
☐ 263	Andres Thomas	.03	.01	.00
☐ 264	Glenn Braggs	.03	.01	.00
☐ 265	David Cone	.06	.02	.00
☐ 266	Bobby Thigpen	.08	.03	.01
☐ 267	Nelson Liriano	.03	.01	.00
☐ 268	Terry Steinbach	.06	.02	.00
☐ 269	Kirby Puckett UER (back doesn't consider Joe Torre's .363 in '71)	.20	.08	.02
☐ 270	Gregg Jefferies	.10	.04	.01
☐ 271	Jeff Blauser	.03	.01	.00
☐ 272	Cory Snyder	.06	.02	.00
☐ 273	Roy Smith	.03	.01	.00
☐ 274	Tom Foley	.03	.01	.00
☐ 275	Mitch Williams	.03	.01	.00
☐ 276	Paul Kilgus	.03	.01	.00
☐ 277	Don Slaught	.03	.01	.00
☐ 278	Von Hayes	.06	.02	.00
☐ 279	Vince Coleman	.08	.03	.01
☐ 280	Mike Boddicker	.03	.01	.00
☐ 281	Ken Dayley	.03	.01	.00
☐ 282	Mike Devereaux	.03	.01	.00
☐ 283	Kenny Rogers	.06	.02	.00
☐ 284	Jeff Russell	.03	.01	.00
☐ 285	Jerome Walton	.08	.03	.01
☐ 286	Derek Lilliquist	.03	.01	.00
☐ 287	Joe Orsulak	.03	.01	.00
☐ 288	Dick Schofield	.03	.01	.00
☐ 289	Ron Darling	.06	.02	.00
☐ 290	Bobby Bonilla	.15	.06	.01
☐ 291	Jim Gantner	.03	.01	.00
☐ 292	Bobby Witt	.06	.02	.00
☐ 293	Greg Brock	.03	.01	.00
☐ 294	Ivan Calderon	.06	.02	.00
☐ 295	Steve Bedrosian	.03	.01	.00
☐ 296	Mike Henneman	.03	.01	.00
☐ 297	Tom Gordon	.08	.03	.01
☐ 298	Lou Whitaker	.08	.03	.01
☐ 299	Terry Pendleton	.08	.03	.01

☐ 300A Checklist Card .06 .01 .00
(232-333)
☐ 300B Checklist Card .06 .01 .00
(224-321)
☐ 301 Juan Berenguer .03 .01 .00
☐ 302 Mark Davis .06 .02 .00
☐ 303 Nick Esasky .03 .01 .00
☐ 304 Rickey Henderson .25 .10 .02
☐ 305 Rick Cerone .03 .01 .00
☐ 306 Craig Biggio .10 .04 .01
☐ 307 Duane Ward .03 .01 .00
☐ 308 Tom Browning .06 .02 .00
☐ 309 Walt Terrell .03 .01 .00
☐ 310 Greg Swindell .06 .02 .00
☐ 311 Dave Righetti .06 .02 .00
☐ 312 Mike Maddux .03 .01 .00
☐ 313 Len Dykstra .08 .03 .01
☐ 314 Jose Gonzalez .03 .01 .00
☐ 315 Steve Balboni .03 .01 .00
☐ 316 Mike Scioscia .03 .01 .00
☐ 317 Ron Oester .03 .01 .00
☐ 318 Gary Wayne .06 .02 .00
☐ 319 Todd Worrell .03 .01 .00
☐ 320 Doug Jones .03 .01 .00
☐ 321 Jeff Hamilton .03 .01 .00
☐ 322 Danny Tartabull .08 .03 .01
☐ 323 Chris James .03 .01 .00
☐ 324 Mike Flanagan .03 .01 .00
☐ 325 Gerald Young .03 .01 .00
☐ 326 Bob Boone .06 .02 .00
☐ 327 Frank Williams .03 .01 .00
☐ 328 Dave Parker .08 .03 .01
☐ 329 Sid Bream .03 .01 .00
☐ 330 Mike Schooler .03 .01 .00
☐ 331 Bert Blyleven .08 .03 .01
☐ 332 Bob Welch .08 .03 .01
☐ 333 Bob Milacki .03 .01 .00
☐ 334 Tim Burke .03 .01 .00
☐ 335 Jose Uribe .03 .01 .00
☐ 336 Randy Myers .03 .01 .00
☐ 337 Eric King .03 .01 .00
☐ 338 Mark Langston .08 .03 .01
☐ 339 Teddy Higuera .03 .01 .00
☐ 340 Oddibe McDowell .03 .01 .00
☐ 341 Lloyd McClendon .03 .01 .00
☐ 342 Pascual Perez .03 .01 .00
☐ 343 Kevin Brown .06 .02 .00
(signed is misspelled
as signeed on back)
☐ 344 Chuck Finley .08 .03 .01
☐ 345 Erik Hanson .08 .03 .01
☐ 346 Rich Gedman .03 .01 .00
☐ 347 Bip Roberts .03 .01 .00
☐ 348 Matt Williams .15 .06 .01
☐ 349 Tom Henke .06 .02 .00
☐ 350 Brad Komminsk .03 .01 .00
☐ 351 Jeff Reed .03 .01 .00
☐ 352 Brian Downing .03 .01 .00
☐ 353 Frank Viola .08 .03 .01
☐ 354 Terry Puhl .03 .01 .00
☐ 355 Brian Harper .06 .02 .00
☐ 356 Steve Farr .03 .01 .00
☐ 357 Joe Boever .03 .01 .00
☐ 358 Danny Heep .03 .01 .00
☐ 359 Larry Andersen .03 .01 .00
☐ 360 Rolando Roomes .03 .01 .00
☐ 361 Mike Gallego .03 .01 .00
☐ 362 Bob Kipper .03 .01 .00
☐ 363 Clay Parker .03 .01 .00
☐ 364 Mike Pagliarulo .03 .01 .00
☐ 365 Ken Griffey Jr. UER 1.50 .60 .15
(signed through 1990,
should be 1991)
☐ 366 Rex Hudler .03 .01 .00
☐ 367 Pat Sheridan .03 .01 .00
☐ 368 Kirk Gibson .08 .03 .01
☐ 369 Jeff Parrett .03 .01 .00
☐ 370 Bob Walk .03 .01 .00
☐ 371 Ken Patterson .03 .01 .00
☐ 372 Bryan Harvey .03 .01 .00
☐ 373 Mike Bielecki .03 .01 .00
☐ 374 Tom Magrann .08 .03 .01
☐ 375 Rick Mahler .03 .01 .00
☐ 376 Craig Lefferts .03 .01 .00
☐ 377 Gregg Olson .12 .05 .01
☐ 378 Jamie Moyer .03 .01 .00
☐ 379 Randy Johnson .06 .02 .00
☐ 380 Jeff Montgomery .03 .01 .00
☐ 381 Marty Clary .03 .01 .00
☐ 382 Bill Spiers .06 .02 .00
☐ 383 Dave Magadan .06 .02 .00
☐ 384 Greg Hibbard .15 .06 .01
☐ 385 Ernie Whitt .03 .01 .00
☐ 386 Rick Honeycutt .03 .01 .00
☐ 387 Dave West .03 .01 .00
☐ 388 Keith Hernandez .06 .02 .00
☐ 389 Jose Alvarez .03 .01 .00
☐ 390 Joey Belle .60 .25 .06
☐ 391 Rick Aguilera .06 .02 .00
☐ 392 Mike Fitzgerald .03 .01 .00
☐ 393 Dwight Smith .06 .02 .00
☐ 394 Steve Wilson .06 .02 .00
☐ 395 Bob Geren .06 .02 .00
☐ 396 Randy Ready .03 .01 .00
☐ 397 Ken Hill .03 .01 .00
☐ 398 Jody Reed .06 .02 .00
☐ 399 Tom Brunansky .06 .02 .00
☐ 400A Checklist Card .06 .01 .00
(334-435)
☐ 400B Checklist Card .06 .01 .00
(322-419)
☐ 401 Rene Gonzales .03 .01 .00
☐ 402 Harold Baines .08 .03 .01
☐ 403 Cecilio Guante .03 .01 .00
☐ 404 Joe Girardi .06 .02 .00

☐ 405A Sergio Valdez ERR (card front shows black line crossing S in Sergio)	.30	.12	.03
☐ 405B Sergio Valdez COR	.10	.04	.01
☐ 406 Mark Williamson	.03	.01	.00
☐ 407 Glenn Hoffman	.03	.01	.00
☐ 408 Jeff Innis	.08	.03	.01
☐ 409 Randy Kramer	.03	.01	.00
☐ 410 Charlie O'Brien	.03	.01	.00
☐ 411 Charlie Hough	.03	.01	.00
☐ 412 Gus Polidor	.03	.01	.00
☐ 413 Ron Karkovice	.03	.01	.00
☐ 414 Trevor Wilson	.10	.04	.01
☐ 415 Kevin Ritz	.10	.04	.01
☐ 416 Gary Thurman	.03	.01	.00
☐ 417 Jeff Robinson	.03	.01	.00
☐ 418 Scott Terry	.03	.01	.00
☐ 419 Tim Laudner	.03	.01	.00
☐ 420 Dennis Rasmussen	.03	.01	.00
☐ 421 Luis Rivera	.03	.01	.00
☐ 422 Jim Corsi	.03	.01	.00
☐ 423 Dennis Lamp	.03	.01	.00
☐ 424 Ken Caminiti	.03	.01	.00
☐ 425 David Wells	.03	.01	.00
☐ 426 Norm Charlton	.03	.01	.00
☐ 427 Deion Sanders	.15	.06	.01
☐ 428 Dion James	.03	.01	.00
☐ 429 Chuck Cary	.03	.01	.00
☐ 430 Ken Howell	.03	.01	.00
☐ 431 Steve Lake	.03	.01	.00
☐ 432 Kal Daniels	.06	.02	.00
☐ 433 Lance McCullers	.03	.01	.00
☐ 434 Lenny Harris	.06	.02	.00
☐ 435 Scott Scudder	.12	.05	.01
☐ 436 Gene Larkin	.03	.01	.00
☐ 437 Dan Quisenberry	.06	.02	.00
☐ 438 Steve Olin	.08	.03	.01
☐ 439 Mickey Hatcher	.03	.01	.00
☐ 440 Willie Wilson	.06	.02	.00
☐ 441 Mark Grant	.03	.01	.00
☐ 442 Mookie Wilson	.03	.01	.00
☐ 443 Alex Trevino	.03	.01	.00
☐ 444 Pat Tabler	.03	.01	.00
☐ 445 Dave Bergman	.03	.01	.00
☐ 446 Todd Burns	.03	.01	.00
☐ 447 R.J. Reynolds	.03	.01	.00
☐ 448 Jay Buhner	.08	.03	.01
☐ 449 Lee Stevens	.15	.06	.01
☐ 450 Ron Hassey	.03	.01	.00
☐ 451 Bob Melvin	.03	.01	.00
☐ 452 Dave Martinez	.03	.01	.00
☐ 453 Greg Litton	.06	.02	.00
☐ 454 Mark Carreon	.03	.01	.00
☐ 455 Scott Fletcher	.03	.01	.00
☐ 456 Otis Nixon	.06	.02	.00
☐ 457 Tony Fossas	.03	.01	.00
☐ 458 John Russell	.03	.01	.00
☐ 459 Paul Assenmacher	.03	.01	.00
☐ 460 Zane Smith	.06	.02	.00
☐ 461 Jack Daugherty	.06	.02	.00
☐ 462 Rich Monteleone	.06	.02	.00
☐ 463 Greg Briley	.06	.02	.00
☐ 464 Mike Smithson	.03	.01	.00
☐ 465 Benito Santiago	.08	.03	.01
☐ 466 Jeff Brantley	.08	.03	.01
☐ 467 Jose Nunez	.03	.01	.00
☐ 468 Scott Bailes	.03	.01	.00
☐ 469 Ken Griffey Sr.	.08	.03	.01
☐ 470 Bob McClure	.03	.01	.00
☐ 471 Mackey Sasser	.03	.01	.00
☐ 472 Glenn Wilson	.03	.01	.00
☐ 473 Kevin Tapani	.30	.12	.03
☐ 474 Bill Buckner	.06	.02	.00
☐ 475 Ron Gant	.25	.10	.02
☐ 476 Kevin Romine	.03	.01	.00
☐ 477 Juan Agosto	.03	.01	.00
☐ 478 Herm Winningham	.03	.01	.00
☐ 479 Storm Davis	.03	.01	.00
☐ 480 Jeff King	.06	.02	.00
☐ 481 Kevin Mmahat	.10	.04	.01
☐ 482 Carmelo Martinez	.03	.01	.00
☐ 483 Omar Vizquel	.03	.01	.00
☐ 484 Jim Dwyer	.03	.01	.00
☐ 485 Bob Knepper	.03	.01	.00
☐ 486 Dave Anderson	.03	.01	.00
☐ 487 Ron Jones	.03	.01	.00
☐ 488 Jay Bell	.03	.01	.00
☐ 489 Sammy Sosa	.25	.10	.02
☐ 490 Kent Anderson	.06	.02	.00
☐ 491 Domingo Ramos	.03	.01	.00
☐ 492 Dave Clark	.03	.01	.00
☐ 493 Tim Birtsas	.03	.01	.00
☐ 494 Ken Oberkfell	.03	.01	.00
☐ 495 Larry Sheets	.03	.01	.00
☐ 496 Jeff Kunkel	.03	.01	.00
☐ 497 Jim Presley	.03	.01	.00
☐ 498 Mike Macfarlane	.03	.01	.00
☐ 499 Pete Smith	.03	.01	.00
☐ 500A Checklist Card DP (436-537)	.06	.01	.00
☐ 500B Checklist Card (420-517)	.06	.01	.00
☐ 501 Gary Sheffield	.08	.03	.01
☐ 502 Terry Bross	.10	.04	.01
☐ 503 Jerry Kutzler	.08	.03	.01
☐ 504 Lloyd Moseby	.03	.01	.00
☐ 505 Curt Young	.03	.01	.00
☐ 506 Al Newman	.03	.01	.00
☐ 507 Keith Miller	.03	.01	.00
☐ 508 Mike Stanton	.08	.03	.01
☐ 509 Rich Yett	.03	.01	.00
☐ 510 Tim Drummond	.08	.03	.01
☐ 511 Joe Hesketh	.06	.02	.00
☐ 512 Rick Wrona	.06	.02	.00
☐ 513 Luis Salazar	.03	.01	.00

☐ 514 Hal Morris .25 .10 .02
☐ 515 Terry Mulholland .06 .02 .00
☐ 516 John Morris .03 .01 .00
☐ 517 Carlos Quintana .08 .03 .01
☐ 518 Frank DiPino .03 .01 .00
☐ 519 Randy Milligan .06 .02 .00
☐ 520 Chad Kreuter .03 .01 .00
☐ 521 Mike Jeffcoat .03 .01 .00
☐ 522 Mike Harkey .06 .02 .00
☐ 523A Andy Nezelek ERR .17 .07 .01
(wrong birth year)
☐ 523B Andy Nezelek COR .06 .02 .00
(finally corrected
in factory sets)
☐ 524 Dave Schmidt .03 .01 .00
☐ 525 Tony Armas .03 .01 .00
☐ 526 Barry Lyons .03 .01 .00
☐ 527 Rick Reed .08 .03 .01
☐ 528 Jerry Reuss .03 .01 .00
☐ 529 Dean Palmer .75 .30 .07
☐ 530 Jeff Peterek .10 .04 .01
☐ 531 Carlos Martinez .06 .02 .00
☐ 532 Atlee Hammaker .03 .01 .00
☐ 533 Mike Brumley .03 .01 .00
☐ 534 Terry Leach .03 .01 .00
☐ 535 Doug Strange .08 .03 .01
☐ 536 Jose DeLeon .03
.01 .00
☐ 537 Shane Rawley .03 .01 .00
☐ 538 Joey Cora .03 .01 .00
☐ 539 Eric Hetzel .03 .01 .00
☐ 540 Gene Nelson .03 .01 .00
☐ 541 Wes Gardner .03 .01 .00
☐ 542 Mark Portugal .03 .01 .00
☐ 543 Al Leiter .03 .01 .00
☐ 544 Jack Armstrong .06 .02 .00
☐ 545 Greg Cadaret .03 .01 .00
☐ 546 Rod Nichols .03 .01 .00
☐ 547 Luis Polonia .03 .01 .00
☐ 548 Charlie Hayes .06 .02 .00
☐ 549 Dickie Thon .03 .01 .00
☐ 550 Tim Crews .03 .01 .00
☐ 551 Dave Winfield .10 .04 .01
☐ 552 Mike Davis .03 .01 .00
☐ 553 Ron Robinson .03 .01 .00
☐ 554 Carmen Castillo .03 .01 .00
☐ 555 John Costello .03 .01 .00
☐ 556 Bud Black .03 .01 .00
☐ 557 Rick Dempsey .03 .01 .00
☐ 558 Jim Acker .03 .01 .00
☐ 559 Eric Show .03 .01 .00
☐ 560 Pat Borders .03 .01 .00
☐ 561 Danny Darwin .03 .01 .00
☐ 562 Rick Luecken .08 .03 .01
☐ 563 Edwin Nunez .03 .01 .00
☐ 564 Felix Jose .20 .08 .02
☐ 565 John Cangelosi .03 .01 .00
☐ 566 Bill Swift .03 .01 .00
☐ 567 Bill Schroeder .03 .01 .00
☐ 568 Stan Javier .03 .01 .00
☐ 569 Jim Traber .03 .01 .00
☐ 570 Wallace Johnson .03 .01 .00
☐ 571 Donell Nixon .03 .01 .00
☐ 572 Sid Fernandez .06 .02 .00
☐ 573 Lance Johnson .03 .01 .00
☐ 574 Andy McGaffigan .03 .01 .00
☐ 575 Mark Knudson .03 .01 .00
☐ 576 Tommy Greene .25 .10 .02
☐ 577 Mark Grace .12 .05 .01
☐ 578 Larry Walker .25 .10 .02
☐ 579 Mike Stanley .03 .01 .00
☐ 580 Mike Witt DP .03 .01 .00
☐ 581 Scott Bradley .03 .01 .00
☐ 582 Greg Harris .03 .01 .00
☐ 583A Kevin Hickey ERR .17 .07 .01
☐ 583B Kevin Hickey COR .06 .02 .00
☐ 584 Lee Mazzilli .03 .01 .00
☐ 585 Jeff Pico .03 .01 .00
☐ 586 Joe Oliver .08 .03 .01
☐ 587 Willie Fraser DP .03 .01 .00
☐ 588 Carl Yastrzemski PUZ .06 .02 .00
Puzzle Card DP
☐ 589 Kevin Bass DP .03 .01 .00
☐ 590 John Moses DP .03 .01 .00
☐ 591 Tom Pagnozzi DP .03 .01 .00
☐ 592 Tony Castillo DP .03 .01 .00
☐ 593 Jerald Clark DP .03 .01 .00
☐ 594 Dan Schatzeder .03 .01 .00
☐ 595 Luis Quinones DP .03 .01 .00
☐ 596 Pete Harnisch DP .03 .01 .00
☐ 597 Gary Redus .03 .01 .00
☐ 598 Mel Hall .06 .02 .00
☐ 599 Rick Schu .03 .01 .00
☐ 600A Checklist Card .06 .01 .00
(538-639)
☐ 600B Checklist Card .06 .01 .00
(518-617)
☐ 601 Mike Kingery DP .03 .01 .00
☐ 602 Terry Kennedy DP .03 .01 .00
☐ 603 Mike Sharperson DP .03 .01 .00
☐ 604 Don Carman DP .03 .01 .00
☐ 605 Jim Gott .03 .01 .00
☐ 606 Donn Pall DP .03 .01 .00
☐ 607 Rance Mulliniks .03 .01 .00
☐ 608 Curt Wilkerson DP .03 .01 .00
☐ 609 Mike Felder DP .03 .01 .00
☐ 610 Guillermo Hernandez DP .03 .01 .00
☐ 611 Candy Maldonado DP .03 .01 .00
☐ 612 Mark Thurmond DP .03 .01 .00
☐ 613 Rick Leach DP .03 .01 .00
☐ 614 Jerry Reed DP .03 .01 .00
☐ 615 Franklin Stubbs .03 .01 .00
☐ 616 Billy Hatcher DP .03 .01 .00
☐ 617 Don August DP .03 .01 .00
☐ 618 Tim Teufel .03 .01 .00
☐ 619 Shawn Hillegas DP .03 .01 .00
☐ 620 Manny Lee .03 .01 .00

☐ 621 Gary Ward DP	.03	.01	.00
☐ 622 Mark Guthrie DP	.06	.02	.00
☐ 623 Jeff Musselman DP	.03	.01	.00
☐ 624 Mark Lemke DP	.06	.02	.00
☐ 625 Fernando Valenzuela	.08	.03	.01
☐ 626 Paul Sorrento DP	.10	.04	.01
☐ 627 Glenallen Hill DP	.06	.02	.00
☐ 628 Les Lancaster DP	.03	.01	.00
☐ 629 Vance Law DP	.03	.01	.00
☐ 630 Randy Velarde DP	.03	.01	.00
☐ 631 Todd Frohwirth DP	.03	.01	.00
☐ 632 Willie McGee	.08	.03	.01
☐ 633 Dennis Boyd DP	.03	.01	.00
☐ 634 Cris Carpenter DP	.03	.01	.00
☐ 635 Brian Holton	.03	.01	.00
☐ 636 Tracy Jones DP	.03	.01	.00
☐ 637A Terry Steinbach AS (Recent Major League Performance)	.10	.04	.01
☐ 637B Terry Steinbach AS (All-Star Game Performance)	.06	.02	.00
☐ 638 Brady Anderson	.03	.01	.00
☐ 639A Jack Morris ERR (card front shows black line crossing J in Jack)	.30	.12	.03
☐ 639B Jack Morris COR	.08	.03	.01
☐ 640 Jaime Navarro	.08	.03	.01
☐ 641 Darrin Jackson	.06	.02	.00
☐ 642 Mike Dyer	.10	.04	.01
☐ 643 Mike Schmidt	.25	.10	.02
☐ 644 Henry Cotto	.03	.01	.00
☐ 645 John Cerutti	.03	.01	.00
☐ 646 Francisco Cabrera	.10	.04	.01
☐ 647 Scott Sanderson	.03	.01	.00
☐ 648 Brian Meyer	.03	.01	.00
☐ 649 Ray Searage	.03	.01	.00
☐ 650A Bo Jackson AS (Recent Major League Performance)	.30	.12	.03
☐ 650B Bo Jackson AS (All-Star Game Performance)	.17	.07	.01
☐ 651 Steve Lyons	.03	.01	.00
☐ 652 Mike LaCoss	.03	.01	.00
☐ 653 Ted Power	.03	.01	.00
☐ 654A Howard Johnson AS (Recent Major League Performance)	.12	.05	.01
☐ 654B Howard Johnson AS (All-Star Game Performance)	.08	.03	.01
☐ 655 Mauro Gozzo	.10	.04	.01
☐ 656 Mike Blowers	.10	.04	.01
☐ 657 Paul Gibson	.03	.01	.00
☐ 658 Neal Heaton	.03	.01	.00
☐ 659A Nolan Ryan 5000K (665 King of Kings back) ERR	6.00	2.50	.60
☐ 659B Nolan Ryan 5000K COR (still an error as Ryan did not lead AL in K's in '75)	.75	.30	.07
☐ 660A Harold Baines AS (black line through star on front; Recent Major League Performance)	4.00	1.75	.40
☐ 660B Harold Baines AS (black line through star on front; All-Star Game Performance)	6.00	2.50	.60
☐ 660C Harold Baines AS (black line behind star on front; Recent Major League Performance)	2.00	.80	.20
☐ 660D Harold Baines AS (black line behind star on front; All-Star Game Performance)	.08	.03	.01
☐ 661 Gary Pettis	.03	.01	.00
☐ 662 Clint Zavaras	.08	.03	.01
☐ 663A Rick Reuschel AS (Recent Major League Performance)	.10	.04	.01
☐ 663B Rick Reuschel AS (All-Star Game Performance)	.06	.02	.00
☐ 664 Alejandro Pena	.06	.02	.00
☐ 665A Nolan Ryan KING (659 5000 K back) ERR	6.00	2.50	.60
☐ 665B Nolan Ryan KING COR	.75	.30	.07
☐ 665C Nolan Ryan KING ERR (no number on back; in factory sets)	2.50	1.00	.25
☐ 666 Ricky Horton	.03	.01	.00
☐ 667 Curt Schilling	.03	.01	.00
☐ 668 Bill Landrum	.03	.01	.00
☐ 669 Todd Stottlemyre	.08	.03	.01
☐ 670 Tim Leary	.06	.02	.00
☐ 671 John Wetteland	.08	.03	.01
☐ 672 Calvin Schiraldi	.03	.01	.00
☐ 673A Ruben Sierra AS (Recent Major League Performance)	.17	.07	.01
☐ 673B Ruben Sierra AS (All-Star Game Performance)	.12	.05	.01
☐ 674A Pedro Guerrero AS (Recent Major League Performance)	.10	.04	.01

Card			
☐ 674B Pedro Guerrero AS (All-Star Game Performance)	.06	.02	.00
☐ 675 Ken Phelps	.03	.01	.00
☐ 676A Cal Ripken AS (Recent Major League Performance)	.25	.10	.02
☐ 676B Cal Ripken AS (All-Star Game Performance)	.15	.06	.01
☐ 677 Denny Walling	.03	.01	.00
☐ 678 Goose Gossage	.06	.02	.00
☐ 679 Gary Mielke	.08	.03	.01
☐ 680 Bill Bathe	.03	.01	.00
☐ 681 Tom Lawless	.03	.01	.00
☐ 682 Xavier Hernandez	.08	.03	.01
☐ 683A Kirby Puckett AS (Recent Major League Performance)	.17	.07	.01
☐ 683B Kirby Puckett AS (All-Star Game Performance)	.12	.05	.01
☐ 684 Mariano Duncan	.03	.01	.00
☐ 685 Ramon Martinez	.25	.10	.02
☐ 686 Tim Jones	.03	.01	.00
☐ 687 Tom Filer	.03	.01	.00
☐ 688 Steve Lombardozzi	.03	.01	.00
☐ 689 Bernie Williams	.50	.20	.05
☐ 690 Chip Hale	.08	.03	.01
☐ 691 Beau Allred	.12	.05	.01
☐ 692A Ryne Sandberg AS (Recent Major League Performance)	.20	.08	.02
☐ 692B Ryne Sandberg AS (All-Star Game Performance)	.15	.06	.01
☐ 693 Jeff Huson	.08	.03	.01
☐ 694 Curt Ford	.03	.01	.00
☐ 695A Eric Davis AS (Recent Major League Performance)	.15	.06	.01
☐ 695B Eric Davis AS (All-Star Game Performance)	.10	.04	.01
☐ 696 Scott Lusader	.03	.01	.00
☐ 697A Mark McGwire AS (Recent Major League Performance)	.15	.06	.01
☐ 697B Mark McGwire AS (All-Star Game Performance)	.10	.04	.01
☐ 698 Steve Cummings	.08	.03	.01
☐ 699 George Canale	.10	.04	.01
☐ 700A Checklist Card (640-715/BC1-BC26)	.50	.10	.02
☐ 700B Checklist Card (640-716/BC1-BC26)	.10	.01	.00
☐ 700C Checklist Card (618-716)	.10	.01	.00
☐ 701A Julio Franco AS (Recent Major League Performance)	.12	.05	.01
☐ 701B Julio Franco AS (All-Star Game Performance)	.08	.03	.01
☐ 702 Dave Johnson (P)	.08	.03	.01
☐ 703A Dave Stewart AS (Recent Major League Performance)	.10	.04	.01
☐ 703B Dave Stewart AS (All-Star Game Performance)	.06	.02	.00
☐ 704 Dave Justice	2.50	1.00	.25
☐ 705A Tony Gwynn AS (Recent Major League Performance)	.17	.07	.01
☐ 705B Tony Gwynn AS (All-Star Game Performance)	.12	.05	.01
☐ 706 Greg Myers	.03	.01	.00
☐ 707A Will Clark AS (Recent Major League Performance)	.25	.10	.02
☐ 707B Will Clark AS (All-Star Game Performance)	.15	.06	.01
☐ 708A Benito Santiago AS (Recent Major League Performance)	.10	.04	.01
☐ 708B Benito Santiago AS (All-Star Game Performance)	.06	.02	.00
☐ 709 Larry McWilliams	.03	.01	.00
☐ 710A Ozzie Smith AS (Recent Major League Performance)	.12	.05	.01
☐ 710B Ozzie Smith AS (All-Star Game Performance)	.08	.03	.01
☐ 711 John Olerud	1.00	.40	.10
☐ 712A Wade Boggs AS (Recent Major League Performance)	.17	.07	.01
☐ 712B Wade Boggs AS (All-Star Game Performance)	.12	.05	.01
☐ 713 Gary Eave	.08	.03	.01
☐ 714 Bob Tewksbury	.03	.01	.00
☐ 715A Kevin Mitchell AS (Recent Major League Performance)	.12	.05	.01
☐ 715B Kevin Mitchell AS (All-Star Game Performance)	.08	.03	.01
☐ 716 Bart Giamatti	.15	.06	.01

1990 Donruss Bonus MVP's

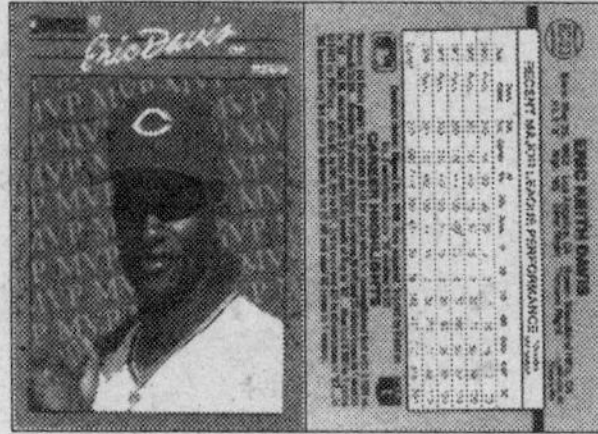

The 1990 Donruss Bonus MVP's set contains 26 standard-size (2 1/2" by 3 1/2") cards. The front borders are bright red. The horizontally oriented backs are amber. These cards were randomly distributed in all 1990 Donruss unopened pack formats. The selection of players in the set is Donruss' opinion of each team's MVP. The complete set price below does not include any variation cards. These Bonus MVP cards were printed with and distributed with the Donruss regular issue cards.

	MINT	EXC	G-VG
COMPLETE SET (26)	2.50	1.00	.25
COMMON CARD (BC1-BC26)	.05	.02	.00
☐ BC1 Bo Jackson	.25	.10	.02
☐ BC2 Howard Johnson	.08	.03	.01
☐ BC3 Dave Stewart	.08	.03	.01
☐ BC4 Tony Gwynn	.10	.04	.01
☐ BC5 Orel Hershiser	.08	.03	.01
☐ BC6 Pedro Guerrero	.08	.03	.01
☐ BC7 Tim Raines	.08	.03	.01
☐ BC8 Kirby Puckett	.10	.04	.01
☐ BC9 Alvin Davis	.05	.02	.00
☐ BC10 Ryne Sandberg	.12	.05	.01
☐ BC11 Kevin Mitchell	.08	.03	.01
☐ BC12A John Smoltz ERR (photo actually Tom Glavine)	.25	.10	.02
☐ BC12B John Smoltz COR	1.00	.40	.10
☐ BC13 George Bell	.08	.03	.01
☐ BC14 Julio Franco	.08	.03	.01
☐ BC15 Paul Molitor	.08	.03	.01
☐ BC16 Bobby Bonilla	.10	.04	.01
☐ BC17 Mike Greenwell	.08	.03	.01
☐ BC18 Cal Ripken	.15	.06	.01
☐ BC19 Carlton Fisk	.08	.03	.01
☐ BC20 Chili Davis	.05	.02	.00
☐ BC21 Glenn Davis	.08	.03	.01
☐ BC22 Steve Sax	.08	.03	.01
☐ BC23 Eric Davis DP	.08	.03	.01
☐ BC24 Greg Swindell DP	.05	.02	.00
☐ BC25 Von Hayes DP	.05	.02	.00
☐ BC26 Alan Trammell	.08	.03	.01

1990 Donruss Rookies

The 1990 Donruss Rookies set marked the fifth consecutive year that Donruss issued a boxed set honoring the best rookies of the season. This set, which used the 1990 Donruss design but featured a green border, was issued exclusively through the Donruss dealer network to hobby dealers. This 56-card, standard size, 2 1/2" by 3 1/2" set came in its own box and the words "The Rookies" are featured prominently on the front of the cards. The key rookie card in this set is Carlos Baerga.

	MINT	EXC	G-VG
COMPLETE SET (56)	9.00	4.00	.90
COMMON PLAYER (1-56)	.05	.02	.00
☐ 1 Sandy Alomar Jr. UER (No stitches on baseball on Donruss logo on card front)	.10	.04	.01
☐ 2 John Olerud	1.00	.40	.10

☐ 3 Pat Combs	.08	.03	.01
☐ 4 Brian DuBois	.08	.03	.01
☐ 5 Felix Jose	.20	.08	.02
☐ 6 Delino DeShields	.40	.16	.04
☐ 7 Mike Stanton	.08	.03	.01
☐ 8 Mike Munoz	.10	.04	.01
☐ 9 Craig Grebeck	.10	.04	.01
☐ 10 Joe Kraemer	.10	.04	.01
☐ 11 Jeff Huson	.08	.03	.01
☐ 12 Bill Sampen	.12	.05	.01
☐ 13 Brian Bohanon	.12	.05	.01
☐ 14 Dave Justice	2.50	1.00	.25
☐ 15 Robin Ventura	.65	.25	.06
☐ 16 Greg Vaughn	.50	.20	.05
☐ 17 Wayne Edwards	.10	.04	.01
☐ 18 Shawn Boskie	.12	.05	.01
☐ 19 Carlos Baerga	.40	.16	.04
☐ 20 Mark Gardner	.20	.08	.02
☐ 21 Kevin Appier	.20	.08	.02
☐ 22 Mike Harkey	.10	.04	.01
☐ 23 Tim Layana	.10	.04	.01
☐ 24 Glenallen Hill	.08	.03	.01
☐ 25 Jerry Kutzler	.08	.03	.01
☐ 26 Mike Blowers	.10	.04	.01
☐ 27 Scott Ruskin	.12	.05	.01
☐ 28 Dana Kiecker	.10	.04	.01
☐ 29 Willie Blair	.08	.03	.01
☐ 30 Ben McDonald	.75	.30	.07
☐ 31 Todd Zeile	.40	.16	.04
☐ 32 Scott Coolbaugh	.10	.04	.01
☐ 33 Xavier Hernandez	.05	.02	.00
☐ 34 Mike Hartley	.15	.06	.01
☐ 35 Kevin Tapani	.30	.12	.03
☐ 36 Kevin Wickander	.05	.02	.00
☐ 37 Carlos Hernandez	.10	.04	.01
☐ 38 Brian Traxler	.10	.04	.01
☐ 39 Marty Brown	.05	.02	.00
☐ 40 Scott Radinsky	.12	.05	.01
☐ 41 Julio Machado	.05	.02	.00
☐ 42 Steve Avery	.90	.40	.09
☐ 43 Mark Lemke	.10	.04	.01
☐ 44 Alan Mills	.10	.04	.01
☐ 45 Marquis Grissom	.45	.18	.04
☐ 46 Greg Olson	.20	.08	.02
☐ 47 Dave Hollins	.35	.15	.03
☐ 48 Jerald Clark	.08	.03	.01
☐ 49 Eric Anthony	.20	.08	.02
☐ 50 Tim Drummond	.10	.04	.01
☐ 51 John Burkett	.15	.06	.01
☐ 52 Brent Knackert	.12	.05	.01
☐ 53 Jeff Shaw	.10	.04	.01
☐ 54 John Orton	.10	.04	.01
☐ 55 Terry Shumpert	.12	.05	.01
☐ 56 Checklist Card	.05	.01	.00

1991 Donruss

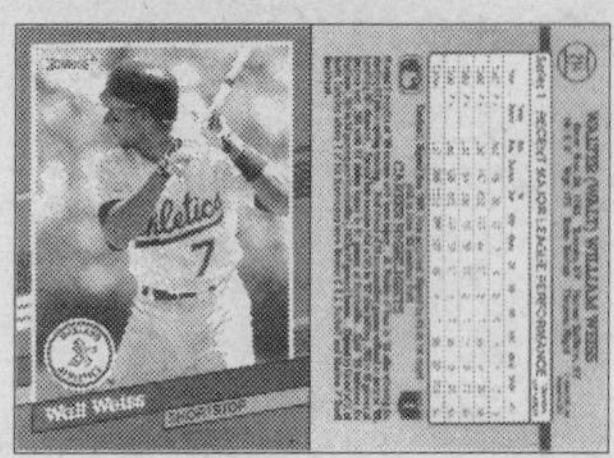

The 1991 Donruss set was issued in two separate series of 396 cards each. This set marked the first time Donruss has issued their cards in series. The cards feature a blue border with some stripes and the players name in white against a red background. The cards measure the standard size of 2 1/2" by 3 1/2". Series I contained 386 cards (numbered 1-386) and another ten cards numbered BC1-BC10. The cards again feature the artwork of Dick Perez drawing each team's Diamond King, which comprise the first 26 cards of the set. The first series also contains 20 Rated Rookie (RR) cards and nine All-Star cards (the AS cards are all American Leaguers in this first series). On cards 60, 70, 127, 182, 239, 294, 355, 368, and 377, the border stripes are red and yellow. As a separate promotion wax packs were also given away with six and 12-packs of Coke and Diet Coke. The key rookie cards in the set are Wes Chamberlain, Brian McRae, and Phil Plantier. The second series was issued approximately three months after the first series was issued. This series features the 26 MVP cards which Donruss had issued for the three previous years as their Bonus Cards, twenty more rated rookie cards and nine All-Star Cards (National Leaguers in this series). There were also special cards to honor the award winners and the heroes of the World Series. The 11 Bonus Cards pick up in time beginning with Valenzuela's no-hitter through the end of the season.

	MINT	EXC	G-VG
COMPLETE SET (792)	17.00	7.25	2.50
COMMON PLAYER (1-386)	.03	.01	.00
COMMON PLAYER (387-770)	.03	.01	.00

COMMON PLAYER (BC1-BC10) .05 .02 .00
COMMON PLAYER (BC11-BC22).05 .02 .00

☐ 1 Dave Stieb DK .... .06 .02 .00
☐ 2 Craig Biggio DK .... .06 .02 .00
☐ 3 Cecil Fielder DK .... .10 .04 .01
☐ 4 Barry Bonds DK .... .08 .03 .01
☐ 5 Barry Larkin DK .... .08 .03 .01
☐ 6 Dave Parker DK .... .06 .02 .00
☐ 7 Len Dykstra DK .... .06 .02 .00
☐ 8 Bobby Thigpen DK .... .06 .02 .00
☐ 9 Roger Clemens DK .... .10 .04 .01
☐ 10 Ron Gant DK UER .... .08 .03 .01
(no trademark on
team logo on back)
☐ 11 Delino DeShields DK .... .08 .03 .01
☐ 12 Roberto Alomar DK UER . .08 .03 .01
(no trademark on
team logo on back)
☐ 13 Sandy Alomar Jr. DK .... .06 .02 .00
☐ 14 Ryne Sandberg DK UER .. .12 .05 .01
(was DK in '85, not
'83 as shown)
☐ 15 Ramon Martinez DK .... .08 .03 .01
☐ 16 Edgar Martinez DK .... .06 .02 .00
☐ 17 Dave Magadan DK .... .06 .02 .00
☐ 18 Matt Williams DK .... .08 .03 .01
☐ 19 Rafael Palmeiro DK .... .08 .03 .01
UER (no trademark on
team logo on back)
☐ 20 Bob Welch DK .... .06 .02 .00
☐ 21 Dave Righetti DK .... .06 .02 .00
☐ 22 Brian Harper DK .... .06 .02 .00
☐ 23 Gregg Olson DK .... .06 .02 .00
☐ 24 Kurt Stillwell DK .... .06 .02 .00
☐ 25 Pedro Guerrero DK UER .. .06 .02 .00
(no trademark on
team logo on back)
☐ 26 Chuck Finley DK UER .... .06 .02 .00
(no trademark on
team logo on back)
☐ 27 DK Checklist .... .06 .01 .00
☐ 28 Tino Martinez RR .... .15 .06 .01
☐ 29 Mark Lewis RR .... .20 .08 .02
☐ 30 Bernard Gilkey RR .... .15 .06 .01
☐ 31 Hensley Meulens RR .... .08 .03 .01
☐ 32 Derek Bell RR .... .35 .15 .03
☐ 33 Jose Offerman RR .... .10 .04 .01
☐ 34 Terry Bross RR .... .06 .02 .00
☐ 35 Leo Gomez RR .... .25 .10 .02
☐ 36 Derrick May RR .... .08 .03 .01
☐ 37 Kevin Morton RR .... .15 .06 .01
☐ 38 Moises Alou RR .... .08 .03 .01
☐ 39 Julio Valera RR .... .08 .03 .01
☐ 40 Milt Cuyler RR .... .15 .06 .01
☐ 41 Phil Plantier RR .... 1.25 .50 .12
☐ 42 Scott Chiamparino RR .... .08 .03 .01
☐ 43 Ray Lankford RR .... .35 .15 .03
☐ 44 Mickey Morandini RR .... .10 .04 .01
☐ 45 Dave Hansen RR .... .10 .04 .01
☐ 46 Kevin Belcher RR .... .10 .04 .01
☐ 47 Darrin Fletcher RR .... .08 .03 .01
☐ 48 Steve Sax AS .... .06 .02 .00
☐ 49 Ken Griffey Jr. AS .... .30 .12 .03
☐ 50 Jose Canseco AS UER .... .15 .06 .01
(team in stat box
should be AL not A's)
☐ 51 Sandy Alomar AS .... .08 .03 .01
☐ 52 Cal Ripken AS .... .12 .05 .01
☐ 53 Rickey Henderson AS .... .12 .05 .01
☐ 54 Bob Welch AS .... .06 .02 .00
☐ 55 Wade Boggs AS .... .10 .04 .01
☐ 56 Mark McGwire AS .... .08 .03 .01
☐ 57 Jack McDowell UER .... .08 .03 .01
(career stats do
not include 1990)
☐ 58 Jose Lind .... .03 .01 .00
☐ 59 Alex Fernandez .... .20 .08 .02
☐ 60 Pat Combs .... .03 .01 .00
☐ 61 Mike Walker .... .06 .02 .00
☐ 62 Juan Samuel .... .06 .02 .00
☐ 63 Mike Blowers UER .... .06 .02 .00
(Last line has
aseball, not baseball)
☐ 64 Mark Guthrie .... .03 .01 .00
☐ 65 Mark Salas .... .03 .01 .00
☐ 66 Tim Jones .... .03 .01 .00
☐ 67 Tim Leary .... .06 .02 .00
☐ 68 Andres Galarraga .... .06 .02 .00
☐ 69 Bob Milacki .... .03 .01 .00
☐ 70 Tim Belcher .... .06 .02 .00
☐ 71 Todd Zeile .... .10 .04 .01
☐ 72 Jerome Walton .... .08 .03 .01
☐ 73 Kevin Seitzer .... .06 .02 .00
☐ 74 Jerald Clark .... .03 .01 .00
☐ 75 John Smoltz UER .... .10 .04 .01
(Born in Detroit,
not Warren)
☐ 76 Mike Henneman .... .03 .01 .00
☐ 77 Ken Griffey Jr. .... .75 .30 .07
☐ 78 Jim Abbott .... .10 .04 .01
☐ 79 Gregg Jefferies .... .08 .03 .01
☐ 80 Kevin Reimer .... .08 .03 .01
☐ 81 Roger Clemens .... .15 .06 .01
☐ 82 Mike Fitzgerald .... .03 .01 .00
☐ 83 Bruce Hurst UER .... .06 .02 .00
(Middle name is
Lee, not Vee)
☐ 84 Eric Davis .... .10 .04 .01
☐ 85 Paul Molitor .... .08 .03 .01
☐ 86 Will Clark .... .20 .08 .02
☐ 87 Mike Bielecki .... .03 .01 .00
☐ 88 Bret Saberhagen .... .08 .03 .01
☐ 89 Nolan Ryan .... .35 .15 .03
☐ 90 Bobby Thigpen .... .06 .02 .00
☐ 91 Dickie Thon .... .03 .01 .00

☐ 92 Duane Ward .03 .01 .00
☐ 93 Luis Polonia .03 .01 .00
☐ 94 Terry Kennedy .03 .01 .00
☐ 95 Kent Hrbek .06 .02 .00
☐ 96 Danny Jackson .03 .01 .00
☐ 97 Sid Fernandez .06 .02 .00
☐ 98 Jimmy Key .06 .02 .00
☐ 99 Franklin Stubbs .03 .01 .00
☐ 100 Checklist Card .06 .01 .00
☐ 101 R.J. Reynolds .03 .01 .00
☐ 102 Dave Stewart .08 .03 .01
☐ 103 Dan Pasqua .03 .01 .00
☐ 104 Dan Plesac .03 .01 .00
☐ 105 Mark McGwire .10 .04 .01
☐ 106 John Farrell .03 .01 .00
☐ 107 Don Mattingly .12 .05 .01
☐ 108 Carlton Fisk .10 .04 .01
☐ 109 Ken Oberkfell .03 .01 .00
☐ 110 Darrel Akerfelds .03 .01 .00
☐ 111 Gregg Olson .08 .03 .01
☐ 112 Mike Scioscia .03 .01 .00
☐ 113 Bryn Smith .03 .01 .00
☐ 114 Bob Geren .03 .01 .00
☐ 115 Tom Candiotti .06 .02 .00
☐ 116 Kevin Tapani .06 .02 .00
☐ 117 Jeff Treadway .03 .01 .00
☐ 118 Alan Trammell .08 .03 .01
☐ 119 Pete O'Brien .03 .01 .00
(Blue shading goes through stats)
☐ 120 Joel Skinner .03 .01 .00
☐ 121 Mike LaValliere .03 .01 .00
☐ 122 Dwight Evans .06 .02 .00
☐ 123 Jody Reed .06 .02 .00
☐ 124 Lee Guetterman .03 .01 .00
☐ 125 Tim Burke .03 .01 .00
☐ 126 Dave Johnson .03 .01 .00
☐ 127 Fernando Valenzuela .06 .02 .00
(Lower large stripe in yellow instead of blue) UER
☐ 128 Jose DeLeon .03 .01 .00
☐ 129 Andre Dawson .10 .04 .01
☐ 130 Gerald Perry .03 .01 .00
☐ 131 Greg Harris .03 .01 .00
☐ 132 Tom Glavine .08 .03 .01
☐ 133 Lance McCullers .03 .01 .00
☐ 134 Randy Johnson .03 .01 .00
☐ 135 Lance Parrish UER .06 .02 .00
(Born in McKeesport, not Clairton)
☐ 136 Mackey Sasser .03 .01 .00
☐ 137 Geno Petralli .03 .01 .00
☐ 138 Dennis Lamp .03 .01 .00
☐ 139 Dennis Martinez .06 .02 .00
☐ 140 Mike Pagliarulo .03 .01 .00
☐ 141 Hal Morris .10 .04 .01
☐ 142 Dave Parker .08 .03 .01
☐ 143 Brett Butler .06 .02 .00
☐ 144 Paul Assenmacher .03 .01 .00
☐ 145 Mark Gubicza .06 .02 .00
☐ 146 Charlie Hough .03 .01 .00
☐ 147 Sammy Sosa .08 .03 .01
☐ 148 Randy Ready .03 .01 .00
☐ 149 Kelly Gruber .08 .03 .01
☐ 150 Devon White .06 .02 .00
☐ 151 Gary Carter .08 .03 .01
☐ 152 Gene Larkin .03 .01 .00
☐ 153 Chris Sabo .08 .03 .01
☐ 154 David Cone .06 .02 .00
☐ 155 Todd Stottlemyre .06 .02 .00
☐ 156 Glenn Wilson .03 .01 .00
☐ 157 Bob Walk .03 .01 .00
☐ 158 Mike Gallego .03 .01 .00
☐ 159 Greg Hibbard .03 .01 .00
☐ 160 Chris Bosio .03 .01 .00
☐ 161 Mike Moore .06 .02 .00
☐ 162 Jerry Browne UER .03 .01 .00
(Born Christiansted, should be St. Croix)
☐ 163 Steve Sax UER .06 .02 .00
(No asterisk next to his 1989 At Bats)
☐ 164 Melido Perez .03 .01 .00
☐ 165 Danny Darwin .03 .01 .00
☐ 166 Roger McDowell .03 .01 .00
☐ 167 Bill Ripken .03 .01 .00
☐ 168 Mike Sharperson .03 .01 .00
☐ 169 Lee Smith .06 .02 .00
☐ 170 Matt Nokes .06 .02 .00
☐ 171 Jesse Orosco .03 .01 .00
☐ 172 Rick Aguilera .06 .02 .00
☐ 173 Jim Presley .03 .01 .00
☐ 174 Lou Whitaker .06 .02 .00
☐ 175 Harold Reynolds .06 .02 .00
☐ 176 Brook Jacoby .03 .01 .00
☐ 177 Wally Backman .03 .01 .00
☐ 178 Wade Boggs .12 .05 .01
☐ 179 Chuck Cary .03 .01 .00
(Comma after DOB, not on other cards)
☐ 180 Tom Foley .03 .01 .00
☐ 181 Pete Harnisch .03 .01 .00
☐ 182 Mike Morgan .06 .02 .00
☐ 183 Bob Tewksbury .03 .01 .00
☐ 184 Joe Girardi .03 .01 .00
☐ 185 Storm Davis .03 .01 .00
☐ 186 Ed Whitson .03 .01 .00
☐ 187 Steve Avery UER .30 .12 .03
(Born in New Jersey, should be Michigan)
☐ 188 Lloyd Moseby .03 .01 .00
☐ 189 Scott Bankhead .03 .01 .00
☐ 190 Mark Langston .06 .02 .00
☐ 191 Kevin McReynolds .06 .02 .00
☐ 192 Julio Franco .08 .03 .01

☐ 193 John Dopson .03 .01 .00
☐ 194 Oil Can Boyd .03 .01 .00
☐ 195 Bip Roberts .03 .01 .00
☐ 196 Billy Hatcher .03 .01 .00
☐ 197 Edgar Diaz .06 .02 .00
☐ 198 Greg Litton .03 .01 .00
☐ 199 Mark Grace .08 .03 .01
☐ 200 Checklist Card .06 .01 .00
☐ 201 George Brett .10 .04 .01
☐ 202 Jeff Russell .03 .01 .00
☐ 203 Ivan Calderon .06 .02 .00
☐ 204 Ken Howell .03 .01 .00
☐ 205 Tom Henke .06 .02 .00
☐ 206 Bryan Harvey .06 .02 .00
☐ 207 Steve Bedrosian .03 .01 .00
☐ 208 Al Newman .03 .01 .00
☐ 209 Randy Myers .03 .01 .00
☐ 210 Daryl Boston .03 .01 .00
☐ 211 Manny Lee .03 .01 .00
☐ 212 Dave Smith .03 .01 .00
☐ 213 Don Slaught .03 .01 .00
☐ 214 Walt Weiss .06 .02 .00
☐ 215 Donn Pall .03 .01 .00
☐ 216 Jaime Navarro .03 .01 .00
☐ 217 Willie Randolph .06 .02 .00
☐ 218 Rudy Seanez .10 .04 .01
☐ 219 Jim Leyritz .08 .03 .01
☐ 220 Ron Karkovice .03 .01 .00
☐ 221 Ken Caminiti .03 .01 .00
☐ 222 Von Hayes .06 .02 .00
☐ 223 Cal Ripken .20 .08 .02
☐ 224 Lenny Harris .03 .01 .00
☐ 225 Milt Thompson .03 .01 .00
☐ 226 Alvaro Espinoza .03 .01 .00
☐ 227 Chris James .03 .01 .00
☐ 228 Dan Gladden .03 .01 .00
☐ 229 Jeff Blauser .03 .01 .00
☐ 230 Mike Heath .03 .01 .00
☐ 231 Omar Vizquel .03 .01 .00
☐ 232 Doug Jones .03 .01 .00
☐ 233 Jeff King .03 .01 .00
☐ 234 Luis Rivera .03 .01 .00
☐ 235 Ellis Burks .08 .03 .01
☐ 236 Greg Cadaret .03 .01 .00
☐ 237 Dave Martinez .03 .01 .00
☐ 238 Mark Williamson .03 .01 .00
☐ 239 Stan Javier .03 .01 .00
☐ 240 Ozzie Smith .10 .04 .01
☐ 241 Shawn Boskie .06 .02 .00
☐ 242 Tom Gordon .06 .02 .00
☐ 243 Tony Gwynn .12 .05 .01
☐ 244 Tommy Gregg .03 .01 .00
☐ 245 Jeff Robinson .03 .01 .00
☐ 246 Keith Comstock .03 .01 .00
☐ 247 Jack Howell .03 .01 .00
☐ 248 Keith Miller .03 .01 .00
☐ 249 Bobby Witt .06 .02 .00
☐ 250 Rob Murphy UER .03 .01 .00
(shown as on Reds
in '89 in stats,
should be Red Sox)
☐ 251 Spike Owen .03 .01 .00
☐ 252 Garry Templeton .03 .01 .00
☐ 253 Glenn Braggs .03 .01 .00
☐ 254 Ron Robinson .03 .01 .00
☐ 255 Kevin Mitchell .10 .04 .01
☐ 256 Les Lancaster .03 .01 .00
☐ 257 Mel Stottlemyre Jr. .03 .01 .00
☐ 258 Kenny Rogers UER .03 .01 .00
(IP listed as 171,
should be 172)
☐ 259 Lance Johnson .03 .01 .00
☐ 260 John Kruk .03 .01 .00
☐ 261 Fred McGriff .08 .03 .01
☐ 262 Dick Schofield .03 .01 .00
☐ 263 Trevor Wilson .03 .01 .00
☐ 264 David West .03 .01 .00
☐ 265 Scott Scudder .06 .02 .00
☐ 266 Dwight Gooden .10 .04 .01
☐ 267 Willie Blair .03 .01 .00
☐ 268 Mark Portugal .03 .01 .00
☐ 269 Doug Drabek .06 .02 .00
☐ 270 Dennis Eckersley .08 .03 .01
☐ 271 Eric King .03 .01 .00
☐ 272 Robin Yount .10 .04 .01
☐ 273 Carney Lansford .06 .02 .00
☐ 274 Carlos Baerga .10 .04 .01
☐ 275 Dave Righetti .06 .02 .00
☐ 276 Scott Fletcher .03 .01 .00
☐ 277 Eric Yelding .03 .01 .00
☐ 278 Charlie Hayes .03 .01 .00
☐ 279 Jeff Ballard .03 .01 .00
☐ 280 Orel Hershiser .06 .02 .00
☐ 281 Jose Oquendo .03 .01 .00
☐ 282 Mike Witt .03 .01 .00
☐ 283 Mitch Webster .03 .01 .00
☐ 284 Greg Gagne .03 .01 .00
☐ 285 Greg Olson .06 .02 .00
☐ 286 Tony Phillips UER .03 .01 .00
(Born 4/15,
should be 4/25)
☐ 287 Scott Bradley .03 .01 .00
☐ 288 Cory Snyder UER .06 .02 .00
(In text, led is re-
peated and Inglewood is
misspelled as Englewood)
☐ 289 Jay Bell UER .03 .01 .00
(Born in Pensacola,
not Eglin AFB)
☐ 290 Kevin Romine .03 .01 .00
☐ 291 Jeff Robinson .03 .01 .00
☐ 292 Steve Frey UER .06 .02 .00
(Bats left,
should be right)
☐ 293 Craig Worthington .03 .01 .00

☐ 294	Tim Crews	.03	.01	.00
☐ 295	Joe Magrane	.03	.01	.00
☐ 296	Hector Villanueva	.03	.01	.00
☐ 297	Terry Shumpert	.03	.01	.00
☐ 298	Joe Carter	.08	.03	.01
☐ 299	Kent Mercker UER (IP listed as 53, should be 52)	.06	.02	.00
☐ 300	Checklist Card	.06	.01	.00
☐ 301	Chet Lemon	.03	.01	.00
☐ 302	Mike Schooler	.03	.01	.00
☐ 303	Dante Bichette	.03	.01	.00
☐ 304	Kevin Elster	.03	.01	.00
☐ 305	Jeff Huson	.03	.01	.00
☐ 306	Greg Harris	.03	.01	.00
☐ 307	Marquis Grissom UER (Middle name Deon, should be Dean)	.10	.04	.01
☐ 308	Calvin Schiraldi	.03	.01	.0C
☐ 309	Mariano Duncan	.03	.01	.00
☐ 310	Bill Spiers	.03	.01	.00
☐ 311	Scott Garrelts	.03	.01	.00
☐ 312	Mitch Williams	.03	.01	.00
☐ 313	Mike Macfarlane	.03	.01	.00
☐ 314	Kevin Brown	.03	.01	.00
☐ 315	Robin Ventura	.20	.08	.02
☐ 316	Darren Daulton	.03	.01	.00
☐ 317	Pat Borders	.03	.01	.00
☐ 318	Mark Eichhorn	.03	.01	.00
☐ 319	Jeff Brantley	.03	.01	.00
☐ 320	Shane Mack	.06	.02	.00
☐ 321	Rob Dibble	.06	.02	.00
☐ 322	John Franco	.03	.01	.00
☐ 323	Junior Felix	.06	.02	.00
☐ 324	Casey Candaele	.03	.01	.00
☐ 325	Bobby Bonilla	.10	.04	.01
☐ 326	Dave Henderson	.06	.02	.00
☐ 327	Wayne Edwards	.03	.01	.00
☐ 328	Mark Knudson	.03	.01	.00
☐ 329	Terry Steinbach	.03	.01	.00
☐ 330	Colby Ward UER (No comma between city and state)	.08	.03	.01
☐ 331	Oscar Azocar	.08	.03	.01
☐ 332	Scott Radinsky	.06	.02	.00
☐ 333	Eric Anthony	.08	.03	.01
☐ 334	Steve Lake	.03	.01	.00
☐ 335	Bob Melvin	.03	.01	.00
☐ 336	Kal Daniels	.06	.02	.00
☐ 337	Tom Pagnozzi	.03	.01	.00
☐ 338	Alan Mills	.03	.01	.00
☐ 339	Steve Olin	.03	.01	.00
☐ 340	Juan Berenguer	.03	.01	.00
☐ 341	Francisco Cabrera	.06	.02	.00
☐ 342	Dave Bergman	.03	.01	.00
☐ 343	Henry Cotto	.03	.01	.00
☐ 345	Bob Patterson	.03	.01	.00
☐ 346	John Marzano	.03	.01	.00
☐ 347	Dana Kiecker	.03	.01	.00
☐ 348	Dion James	.03	.01	.00
☐ 349	Hubie Brooks	.06	.02	.00
☐ 350	Bill Landrum	.03	.01	.00
☐ 351	Bill Sampen	.03	.01	.00
☐ 352	Greg Briley	.03	.01	.00
☐ 353	Paul Gibson	.03	.01	.00
☐ 354	Dave Eiland	.03	.01	.00
☐ 355	Steve Finley	.06	.02	.00
☐ 356	Bob Boone	.06	.02	.00
☐ 357	Steve Buechele	.03	.01	.00
☐ 358	Chris Hoiles	.10	.04	.01
☐ 359	Larry Walker	.06	.02	.00
☐ 360	Frank DiPino	.03	.01	.00
☐ 361	Mark Grant	.03	.01	.00
☐ 362	Dave Magadan	.06	.02	.00
☐ 363	Robby Thompson	.03	.01	.00
☐ 364	Lonnie Smith	.06	.02	.00
☐ 365	Steve Farr	.03	.01	.00
☐ 366	Dave Valle	.03	.01	.00
☐ 367	Tim Naehring	.10	.04	.01
☐ 368	Jim Acker	.03	.01	.00
☐ 369	Jeff Reardon UER (Born in Pittsfield, not Dalton)	.06	.02	.00
☐ 370	Tim Teufel	.03	.01	.00
☐ 371	Juan Gonzalez	.30	.12	.03
☐ 372	Luis Salazar	.03	.01	.00
☐ 373	Rick Honeycutt	.03	.01	.00
☐ 374	Greg Maddux	.06	.02	.00
☐ 375	Jose Uribe UER (Middle name Elta, should be Alta)	.03	.01	.00
☐ 376	Donnie Hill	.03	.01	.00
☐ 377	Don Carman	.03	.01	.00
☐ 378	Craig Grebeck	.03	.01	.00
☐ 379	Willie Fraser	.03	.01	.00
☐ 380	Glenallen Hill	.06	.02	.00
☐ 381	Joe Oliver	.03	.01	.00
☐ 382	Randy Bush	.03	.01	.00
☐ 383	Alex Cole	.08	.03	.01
☐ 384	Norm Charlton	.03	.01	.00
☐ 385	Gene Nelson	.03	.01	.00
☐ 386	Checklist Card	.06	.01	.00
☐ 387	Rickey Henderson MVP	.12	.05	.01
☐ 388	Lance Parrish MVP	.06	.02	.00
☐ 389	Fred McGriff MVP	.08	.03	.01
☐ 390	Dave Parker MVP	.08	.03	.01
☐ 391	Candy Maldonado MVP	.06	.02	.00
☐ 392	Ken Griffey Jr. MVP	.30	.12	.03
☐ 393	Gregg Olson MVP	.06	.02	.00
☐ 394	Rafael Palmeiro MVP	.08	.03	.01
☐ 395	Roger Clemens MVP	.10	.04	.01
☐ 396	George Brett MVP	.10	.04	.01
☐ 397	Cecil Fielder MVP	.10	.04	.01

☐ 398 Brian Harper MVP UER (Major League Performance, should be Career)	.03	.01	.00
☐ 399 Bobby Thigpen MVP	.06	.02	.00
☐ 400 Roberto Kelly MVP UER (Second Base on front and OF on back)	.06	.02	.00
☐ 401 Danny Darwin MVP	.03	.01	.00
☐ 402 Dave Justice MVP	.25	.10	.02
☐ 403 Lee Smith MVP	.06	.02	.00
☐ 404 Ryne Sandberg MVP	.12	.05	.01
☐ 405 Eddie Murray MVP	.08	.03	.01
☐ 406 Tim Wallach MVP	.06	.02	.00
☐ 407 Kevin Mitchell MVP	.08	.03	.01
☐ 408 Darryl Strawberry MVP	.10	.04	.01
☐ 409 Joe Carter MVP	.08	.03	.01
☐ 410 Len Dykstra MVP	.06	.02	.00
☐ 411 Doug Drabek MVP	.06	.02	.00
☐ 412 Chris Sabo MVP	.06	.02	.00
☐ 413 Paul Marak RR	.10	.04	.01
☐ 414 Tim McIntosh RR	.08	.03	.01
☐ 415 Brian Barnes RR	.10	.04	.01
☐ 416 Eric Gunderson RR	.08	.03	.01
☐ 417 Mike Gardiner RR	.15	.06	.01
☐ 418 Steve Carter RR	.03	.01	.00
☐ 419 Gerald Alexander RR	.10	.04	.01
☐ 420 Rich Garces RR	.10	.04	.01
☐ 421 Chuck Knoblauch RR	.40	.16	.04
☐ 422 Scott Aldred RR	.08	.03	.01
☐ 423 Wes Chamberlain RR	.45	.18	.04
☐ 424 Lance Dickson RR	.17	.07	.01
☐ 425 Greg Colbrunn RR	.12	.05	.01
☐ 426 Rich DeLucia RR	.15	.06	.01
☐ 427 Jeff Conine RR	.15	.06	.01
☐ 428 Steve Decker RR	.25	.10	.02
☐ 429 Turner Ward RR	.15	.06	.01
☐ 430 Mo Vaughn RR	.50	.20	.05
☐ 431 Steve Chitren RR	.10	.04	.01
☐ 432 Mike Benjamin RR	.08	.03	.01
☐ 433 Ryne Sandberg AS	.12	.05	.01
☐ 434 Len Dykstra AS	.06	.02	.00
☐ 435 Andre Dawson AS	.08	.03	.01
☐ 436A Mike Scioscia AS (White star by name)	.03	.01	.00
☐ 436B Mike Scioscia AS (Yellow star by name)	.03	.01	.00
☐ 437 Ozzie Smith AS	.08	.03	.01
☐ 438 Kevin Mitchell AS	.08	.03	.01
☐ 439 Jack Armstrong AS	.03	.01	.00
☐ 440 Chris Sabo AS	.06	.02	.00
☐ 441 Will Clark AS	.12	.05	.01
☐ 442 Mel Hall	.06	.02	.00
☐ 443 Mark Gardner	.03	.01	.00
☐ 444 Mike Devereaux	.03	.01	.00
☐ 445 Kirk Gibson	.06	.02	.00
☐ 446 Terry Pendleton	.08	.03	.01
☐ 447 Mike Harkey	.06	.02	.00
☐ 448 Jim Eisenreich	.03	.01	.00
☐ 449 Benito Santiago	.08	.03	.01
☐ 450 Oddibe McDowell	.03	.01	.00
☐ 451 Cecil Fielder	.15	.06	.01
☐ 452 Ken Griffey Sr.	.06	.02	.00
☐ 453 Bert Blyleven	.06	.02	.00
☐ 454 Howard Johnson	.08	.03	.01
☐ 455 Monty Fariss	.10	.04	.01
☐ 456 Tony Pena	.06	.02	.00
☐ 457 Tim Raines	.08	.03	.01
☐ 458 Dennis Rasmussen	.03	.01	.00
☐ 459 Luis Quinones	.03	.01	.00
☐ 460 B.J. Surhoff	.03	.01	.00
☐ 461 Ernest Riles	.03	.01	.00
☐ 462 Rick Sutcliffe	.06	.02	.00
☐ 463 Danny Tartabull	.08	.03	.01
☐ 464 Pete Incaviglia	.06	.02	.00
☐ 465 Carlos Martinez	.03	.01	.00
☐ 466 Ricky Jordan	.06	.02	.00
☐ 467 John Cerutti	.03	.01	.00
☐ 468 Dave Winfield	.10	.04	.01
☐ 469 Francisco Oliveras	.03	.01	.00
☐ 470 Roy Smith	.03	.01	.00
☐ 471 Barry Larkin	.08	.03	.01
☐ 472 Ron Darling	.06	.02	.00
☐ 473 David Wells	.03	.01	.00
☐ 474 Glenn Davis	.08	.03	.01
☐ 475 Neal Heaton	.03	.01	.00
☐ 476 Ron Hassey	.03	.01	.00
☐ 477 Frank Thomas	1.25	.50	.12
☐ 478 Greg Vaughn	.10	.04	.01
☐ 479 Todd Burns	.03	.01	.00
☐ 480 Candy Maldonado	.03	.01	.00
☐ 481 Dave LaPoint	.03	.01	.00
☐ 482 Alvin Davis	.06	.02	.00
☐ 483 Mike Scott	.06	.02	.00
☐ 484 Dale Murphy	.10	.04	.01
☐ 485 Ben McDonald	.10	.04	.01
☐ 486 Jay Howell	.03	.01	.00
☐ 487 Vince Coleman	.08	.03	.01
☐ 488 Alfredo Griffin	.03	.01	.00
☐ 489 Sandy Alomar Jr.	.08	.03	.01
☐ 490 Kirby Puckett	.12	.05	.01
☐ 491 Andres Thomas	.03	.01	.00
☐ 492 Jack Morris	.08	.03	.01
☐ 493 Matt Young	.03	.01	.00
☐ 494 Greg Myers	.03	.01	.00
☐ 495 Barry Bonds	.12	.05	.01
☐ 496 Scott Cooper UER (No BA for 1990 and career)	.17	.07	.01
☐ 497 Dan Schatzeder	.03	.01	.00
☐ 498 Jesse Barfield	.06	.02	.00
☐ 499 Jerry Goff	.08	.03	.01
☐ 500 Checklist Card	.06	.01	.00
☐ 501 Anthony Telford	.08	.03	.01

No.	Player			
☐ 502	Eddie Murray	.10	.04	.01
☐ 503	Omar Olivares	.10	.04	.01
☐ 504	Ryne Sandberg	.20	.08	.02
☐ 505	Jeff Montgomery	.03	.01	.00
☐ 506	Mark Parent	.03	.01	.00
☐ 507	Ron Gant	.12	.05	.01
☐ 508	Frank Tanana	.06	.02	.00
☐ 509	Jay Buhner	.06	.02	.00
☐ 510	Max Venable	.03	.01	.00
☐ 511	Wally Whitehurst	.03	.01	.00
☐ 512	Gary Pettis	.03	.01	.00
☐ 513	Tom Brunansky	.06	.02	.00
☐ 514	Tim Wallach	.06	.02	.00
☐ 515	Craig Lefferts	.03	.01	.00
☐ 516	Tim Layana	.03	.01	.00
☐ 517	Darryl Hamilton	.08	.03	.01
☐ 518	Rick Reuschel	.06	.02	.00
☐ 519	Steve Wilson	.03	.01	.00
☐ 520	Kurt Stillwell	.03	.01	.00
☐ 521	Rafael Palmeiro	.08	.03	.01
☐ 522	Ken Patterson	.03	.01	.00
☐ 523	Len Dykstra	.06	.02	.00
☐ 524	Tony Fernandez	.06	.02	.00
☐ 525	Kent Anderson	.03	.01	.00
☐ 526	Mark Leonard	.10	.04	.01
☐ 527	Allan Anderson	.03	.01	.00
☐ 528	Tom Browning	.06	.02	.00
☐ 529	Frank Viola	.08	.03	.01
☐ 530	John Olerud	.12	.05	.01
☐ 531	Juan Agosto	.03	.01	.00
☐ 532	Zane Smith	.06	.02	.00
☐ 533	Scott Sanderson	.03	.01	.00
☐ 534	Barry Jones	.03	.01	.00
☐ 535	Mike Felder	.03	.01	.00
☐ 536	Jose Canseco	.25	.10	.02
☐ 537	Felix Fermin	.03	.01	.00
☐ 538	Roberto Kelly	.08	.03	.01
☐ 539	Brian Holman	.03	.01	.00
☐ 540	Mark Davidson	.03	.01	.00
☐ 541	Terry Mulholland	.03	.01	.00
☐ 542	Randy Milligan	.06	.02	.00
☐ 543	Jose Gonzalez	.03	.01	.00
☐ 544	Craig Wilson	.10	.04	.01
☐ 545	Mike Hartley	.03	.01	.00
☐ 546	Greg Swindell	.06	.02	.00
☐ 547	Gary Gaetti	.06	.02	.00
☐ 548	Dave Justice	.50	.20	.05
☐ 549	Steve Searcy	.03	.01	.00
☐ 550	Erik Hansen	.06	.02	.00
☐ 551	Dave Stieb	.06	.02	.00
☐ 552	Andy Van Slyke	.08	.03	.01
☐ 553	Mike Greenwell	.10	.04	.01
☐ 554	Kevin Maas	.17	.07	.01
☐ 555	Delino DeShields	.10	.04	.01
☐ 556	Curt Schilling	.03	.01	.00
☐ 557	Ramon Martinez	.10	.04	.01
☐ 558	Pedro Guerrero	.06	.02	.00
☐ 559	Dwight Smith	.03	.01	.00
☐ 560	Mark Davis	.03	.01	.00
☐ 561	Shawn Abner	.03	.01	.00
☐ 562	Charlie Leibrandt	.03	.01	.00
☐ 563	John Shelby	.03	.01	.00
☐ 564	Bill Swift	.03	.01	.00
☐ 565	Mike Fetters	.03	.01	.00
☐ 566	Alejandro Pena	.06	.02	.00
☐ 567	Ruben Sierra	.12	.05	.01
☐ 568	Carlos Quintana	.06	.02	.00
☐ 569	Kevin Gross	.03	.01	.00
☐ 570	Derek Lilliquist	.03	.01	.00
☐ 571	Jack Armstrong	.06	.02	.00
☐ 572	Greg Brock	.03	.01	.00
☐ 573	Mike Kingery	.03	.01	.00
☐ 574	Greg Smith	.06	.02	.00
☐ 575	Brian McRae	.45	.18	.04
☐ 576	Jack Daugherty	.03	.01	.00
☐ 577	Ozzie Guillen	.06	.02	.00
☐ 578	Joe Boever	.03	.01	.00
☐ 579	Luis Sojo	.08	.03	.01
☐ 580	Chili Davis	.06	.02	.00
☐ 581	Don Robinson	.03	.01	.00
☐ 582	Brian Harper	.06	.02	.00
☐ 583	Paul O'Neill	.06	.02	.00
☐ 584	Bob Ojeda	.03	.01	.00
☐ 585	Mookie Wilson	.03	.01	.00
☐ 586	Rafael Ramirez	.03	.01	.00
☐ 587	Gary Redus	.03	.01	.00
☐ 588	Jamie Quirk	.03	.01	.00
☐ 589	Shawn Hillegas	.03	.01	.00
☐ 590	Tom Edens	.08	.03	.01
☐ 591	Joe Klink	.06	.02	.00
☐ 592	Charles Nagy	.10	.04	.01
☐ 593	Eric Plunk	.03	.01	.00
☐ 594	Tracy Jones	.03	.01	.00
☐ 595	Craig Biggio	.06	.02	.00
☐ 596	Jose DeJesus	.03	.01	.00
☐ 597	Mickey Tettleton	.06	.02	.00
☐ 598	Chris Gwynn	.03	.01	.00
☐ 599	Rex Hudler	.03	.01	.00
☐ 600	Checklist Card	.06	.01	.00
☐ 601	Jim Gott	.03	.01	.00
☐ 602	Jeff Manto	.06	.02	.00
☐ 603	Nelson Liriano	.03	.01	.00
☐ 604	Mark Lemke	.06	.02	.00
☐ 605	Clay Parker	.03	.01	.00
☐ 606	Edgar Martinez	.06	.02	.00
☐ 607	Mark Whiten	.20	.08	.02
☐ 608	Ted Power	.03	.01	.00
☐ 609	Tom Bolton	.03	.01	.00
☐ 610	Tom Herr	.03	.01	.00
☐ 611	Andy Hawkins UER (Pitched No-Hitter on 7/1, not 7/2)	.03	.01	.00
☐ 612	Scott Ruskin	.03	.01	.00
☐ 613	Ron Kittle	.06	.02	.00
☐ 614	John Wetteland	.06	.02	.00
☐ 615	Mike Perez	.10	.04	.01

Card			
☐ 616 Dave Clark	.03	.01	.00
☐ 617 Brent Mayne	.08	.03	.01
☐ 618 Jack Clark	.06	.02	.00
☐ 619 Marvin Freeman	.03	.01	.00
☐ 620 Edwin Nunez	.03	.01	.00
☐ 621 Russ Swan	.08	.03	.01
☐ 622 Johnny Ray	.03	.01	.00
☐ 623 Charlie O'Brien	.03	.01	.00
☐ 624 Joe Bitker	.08	.03	.01
☐ 625 Mike Marshall	.06	.02	.00
☐ 626 Otis Nixon	.06	.02	.00
☐ 627 Andy Benes	.08	.03	.01
☐ 628 Ron Oester	.03	.01	.00
☐ 629 Ted Higuera	.03	.01	.00
☐ 630 Kevin Bass	.03	.01	.00
☐ 631 Damon Berryhill	.03	.01	.00
☐ 632 Bo Jackson	.25	.10	.02
☐ 633 Brad Arnsberg	.03	.01	.00
☐ 634 Jerry Willard	.03	.01	.00
☐ 635 Tommy Greene	.06	.02	.00
☐ 636 Bob MacDonald	.10	.04	.01
☐ 637 Kirk McCaskill	.03	.01	.00
☐ 638 John Burkett	.06	.02	.00
☐ 639 Paul Abbott	.08	.03	.01
☐ 640 Todd Benzinger	.03	.01	.00
☐ 641 Todd Hundley	.10	.04	.01
☐ 642 George Bell	.08	.03	.01
☐ 643 Javier Ortiz	.08	.03	.01
☐ 644 Sid Bream	.03	.01	.00
☐ 645 Bob Welch	.06	.02	.00
☐ 646 Phil Bradley	.03	.01	.00
☐ 647 Bill Krueger	.03	.01	.00
☐ 648 Rickey Henderson	.20	.08	.02
☐ 649 Kevin Wickander	.03	.01	.00
☐ 650 Steve Balboni	.03	.01	.00
☐ 651 Gene Harris	.03	.01	.00
☐ 652 Jim Deshaies	.03	.01	.00
☐ 653 Jason Grimsley	.08	.03	.01
☐ 654 Joe Orsulak	.03	.01	.00
☐ 655 Jim Poole	.08	.03	.01
☐ 656 Felix Jose	.10	.04	.01
☐ 657 Denis Cook	.03	.01	.00
☐ 658 Tom Brookens	.03	.01	.00
☐ 659 Junior Ortiz	.03	.01	.00
☐ 660 Jeff Parrett	.03	.01	.00
☐ 661 Jerry Don Gleaton	.03	.01	.00
☐ 662 Brent Knackert	.06	.02	.00
☐ 663 Rance Mulliniks	.03	.01	.00
☐ 664 John Smiley	.06	.02	.00
☐ 665 Larry Andersen	.03	.01	.00
☐ 666 Willie McGee	.08	.03	.01
☐ 667 Chris Nabholz	.10	.04	.01
☐ 668 Brady Anderson	.03	.01	.00
☐ 669 Darren Holmes UER	.08	.03	.01
(19 CG's, should be 0)			
☐ 670 Ken Hill	.03	.01	.00
☐ 671 Gary Varsho	.03	.01	.00
☐ 672 Bill Pecota	.03	.01	.00
☐ 673 Fred Lynn	.06	.02	.00
☐ 674 Kevin Brown	.03	.01	.00
☐ 675 Dan Petry	.03	.01	.00
☐ 676 Mike Jackson	.03	.01	.00
☐ 677 Wally Joyner	.08	.03	.01
☐ 678 Danny Jackson	.03	.01	.00
☐ 679 Bill Haselman	.08	.03	.01
☐ 680 Mike Boddicker	.03	.01	.00
☐ 681 Mel Rojas	.08	.03	.01
☐ 682 Roberto Alomar	.10	.04	.01
☐ 683 Dave Justice ROY	.30	.12	.03
☐ 684 Chuck Crim	.03	.01	.00
☐ 685 Matt Williams	.10	.04	.01
☐ 686 Shawon Dunston	.06	.02	.00
☐ 687 Jeff Schulz	.08	.03	.01
☐ 688 John Barfield	.08	.03	.01
☐ 689 Gerald Young	.03	.01	.00
☐ 690 Luis Gonzalez	.45	.18	.04
☐ 691 Frank Wills	.06	.02	.00
☐ 692 Chuck Finley	.06	.02	.00
☐ 693 Sandy Alomar Jr. ROY	.08	.03	.01
☐ 694 Tim Drummond	.03	.01	.00
☐ 695 Herm Winningham	.03	.01	.00
☐ 696 Darryl Strawberry	.15	.06	.01
☐ 697 Al Leiter	.03	.01	.00
☐ 698 Karl Rhodes	.08	.03	.01
☐ 699 Stan Belinda	.08	.03	.01
☐ 700 Checklist Card	.06	.01	.00
☐ 701 Lance Blankenship	.03	.01	.00
☐ 702 Willie Stargell PUZ	.06	.02	.00
Puzzle Card			
☐ 703 Jim Gantner	.03	.01	.00
☐ 704 Reggie Harris	.08	.03	.01
☐ 705 Rob Ducey	.06	.02	.00
☐ 706 Tim Hulett	.03	.01	.00
☐ 707 Atlee Hammaker	.03	.01	.00
☐ 708 Xavier Hernandez	.03	.01	.00
☐ 709 Chuck McElroy	.06	.02	.00
☐ 710 John Mitchell	.03	.01	.00
☐ 711 Carlos Hernandez	.03	.01	.00
☐ 712 Geronimo Pena	.06	.02	.00
☐ 713 Jim Neidlinger	.10	.04	.01
☐ 714 John Orton	.06	.02	.00
☐ 715 Terry Leach	.03	.01	.00
☐ 716 Mike Stanton	.03	.01	.00
☐ 717 Walt Terrell	.03	.01	.00
☐ 718 Luis Aquino	.03	.01	.00
☐ 719 Bud Black	.03	.01	.00
(Blue Jays uniform, but Giants logo)			
☐ 720 Bob Kipper	.03	.01	.00
☐ 721 Jeff Gray	.08	.03	.01
☐ 722 Jose Rijo	.06	.02	.00
☐ 723 Curt Young	.03	.01	.00
☐ 724 Jose Vizcaino	.06	.02	.00
☐ 725 Randy Tomlin	.20	.08	.02
☐ 726 Junior Noboa	.06	.02	.00
☐ 727 Bob Welch CY	.06	.02	.00

Card			
☐ 728 Gary Ward	.03	.01	.00
☐ 729 Rob Deer	.06	.02	.00
(Brewers uniform,			
but Tigers logo)			
☐ 730 David Segui	.08	.03	.01
☐ 731 Mark Carreon	.03	.01	.00
☐ 732 Vicente Palacios	.03	.01	.00
☐ 733 Sam Horn	.06	.02	.00
☐ 734 Howard Farmer	.08	.03	.01
☐ 735 Ken Dayley	.03	.01	.00
(Cardinals uniform,			
but Blue Jays logo)			
☐ 736 Kelly Mann	.03	.01	.00
☐ 737 Joe Grahe	.08	.03	.01
☐ 738 Kelly Downs	.03	.01	.00
☐ 739 Jimmy Kremers	.08	.03	.01
☐ 740 Kevin Appier	.03	.01	.00
☐ 741 Jeff Reed	.03	.01	.00
☐ 742 Jose Rijo WS	.06	.02	.00
☐ 743 Dave Rohde	.06	.02	.00
☐ 744 Dr.Dirt/Mr.Clean	.06	.02	.00
Len Dykstra			
Dale Murphy			
UER (No '91 Donruss			
logo on card front)			
☐ 745 Paul Sorrento	.03	.01	.00
☐ 746 Thomas Howard	.08	.03	.01
☐ 747 Matt Stark	.12	.05	.01
☐ 748 Harold Baines	.06	.02	.00
☐ 749 Doug Dascenzo	.03	.01	.00
☐ 750 Doug Drabek CY	.06	.02	.00
☐ 751 Gary Sheffield	.08	.03	.01
☐ 752 Terry Lee	.10	.04	.01
☐ 753 Jim Vatcher	.08	.03	.01
☐ 754 Lee Stevens	.08	.03	.01
☐ 755 Randy Veres	.08	.03	.01
☐ 756 Bill Doran	.03	.01	.00
☐ 757 Gary Wayne	.03	.01	.00
☐ 758 Pedro Munoz	.17	.07	.01
☐ 759 Chris Hammond	.08	.03	.01
☐ 760 Checklist Card	.06	.01	.00
☐ 761 Rickey Henderson MVP	.12	.05	.01
☐ 762 Barry Bonds MVP	.08	.03	.01
☐ 763 Billy Hatcher WS	.03	.01	.00
UER (Line 13, on			
should be one)			
☐ 764 Julio Machado	.03	.01	.00
☐ 765 Jose Mesa	.03	.01	.00
☐ 766 Willie Randolph WS	.03	.01	.00
☐ 767 Scott Erickson	.75	.30	.07
☐ 768 Travis Fryman	.45	.18	.04
☐ 769 Rich Rodriguez	.08	.03	.01
☐ 770 Checklist Card	.06	.01	.00
☐ BC1 Langston/Witt	.05	.02	.00
No-Hits Mariners			
☐ BC2 Randy Johnson	.05	.02	.00
No-Hits Tigers			
☐ BC3 Nolan Ryan	.15	.06	.01
No-Hits A's			
☐ BC4 Dave Stewart	.08	.03	.01
No-Hits Blue Jays			
☐ BC5 Cecil Fielder	.10	.04	.01
50 Homer Club			
☐ BC6 Carlton Fisk	.08	.03	.01
Record Home Run			
☐ BC7 Ryne Sandberg	.10	.04	.01
Sets Fielding Records			
☐ BC8 Gary Carter	.08	.03	.01
Breaks Catching Mark			
☐ BC9 Mark McGwire	.10	.04	.01
Home Run Milestone			
(Back says First			
Baseman, others say			
only base)			
☐ BC10 Bo Jackson	.15	.06	.01
Four Consecutive HR's			
☐ BC11 Fernando Valenzuela	.08	.03	.01
No Hits Cardinals			
☐ BC12A Andy Hawkins ERR	1.00	.40	.10
Pitcher			
☐ BC12B Andy Hawkins COR	.05	.02	.00
No Hits White Sox			
☐ BC13 Melido Perez	.05	.02	.00
No Hits Yankees			
☐ BC14 Terry Mulholland	.05	.02	.00
No Hits Giants			
UER (Charlie Hayes is			
called Chris Hayes)			
☐ BC15 Nolan Ryan	.15	.06	.01
300th Win			
☐ BC16 Delino DeShields	.08	.03	.01
4 Hits in Debut			
☐ BC17 Cal Ripken	.12	.05	.01
Errorless Games			
☐ BC18 Eddie Murray	.08	.03	.01
Switch Hit Homers			
☐ BC19 George Brett	.08	.03	.01
3 Decade Champ			
☐ BC20 Bobby Thigpen	.05	.02	.00
Shatters Save Mark			
☐ BC21 Dave Stieb	.05	.02	.00
No Hits Indians			
☐ BC22 Willie McGee	.08	.03	.01
NL Batting Champ			

1991 Donruss Rookies

The 1991 Donruss Rookies set is a boxed set issued to honor the best rookies of the season. The cards measure the standard size (2 1/2" by 3 1/2"), and a mini puzzle featuring Hall of Famer Willie Stargell was included with the set. The fronts feature color action player photos, with white and red borders. Yellow and green stripes cut across the bottom of the card face, presenting the player's name and position. The words "The Rookies" and a baseball icon appear in the lower left corner of the picture. The horizontally oriented backs are printed in black on a green and white background, and present biography, statistics, and career highlights. The cards are numbered on the back. Outstanding rookies showcased in the set are Jeff Bagwell, Chito Martinez, Orlando Merced, Dean Palmer, Ivan Rodriguez, Todd Van Poppel, and Mo Vaughn.

	MINT	EXC	G-VG
COMPLETE SET (56)	8.50	3.75	.85
COMMON PLAYER (1-56)	.05	.02	.00
☐ 1 Pat Kelly	.30	.10	.02
☐ 2 Rich DeLucia	.10	.04	.01
☐ 3 Wes Chamberlain	.30	.12	.03
☐ 4 Scott Leius	.15	.06	.01
☐ 5 Darryl Kile	.15	.06	.01
☐ 6 Milt Cuyler	.12	.05	.01
☐ 7 Todd Van Poppel	1.00	.40	.10
☐ 8 Ray Lankford	.25	.10	.02
☐ 9 Brian Hunter	.75	.30	.07
☐ 10 Tony Perezchica	.05	.02	.00
☐ 11 Ced Landrum	.17	.07	.01
☐ 12 Dave Burba	.10	.04	.01
☐ 13 Ramon Garcia	.10	.04	.01
☐ 14 Ed Sprague	.10	.04	.01
☐ 15 Warren Newson	.20	.08	.02
☐ 16 Paul Faries	.10	.04	.01
☐ 17 Luis Gonzalez	.30	.12	.03
☐ 18 Charles Nagy	.10	.04	.01
☐ 19 Chris Hammond	.08	.03	.01
☐ 20 Frank Castillo	.15	.06	.01
☐ 21 Pedro Munoz	.20	.08	.02
☐ 22 Orlando Merced	.35	.15	.03
☐ 23 Jose Melendez	.12	.05	.01
☐ 24 Kirk Dressendorfer	.20	.08	.02
☐ 25 Heathcliff Slocumb	.10	.04	.01
☐ 26 Doug Simons	.12	.05	.01
☐ 27 Mike Timlin	.15	.06	.01
☐ 28 Jeff Fassaro	.15	.06	.01
☐ 29 Mark Leiter	.12	.05	.01
☐ 30 Jeff Bagwell	3.00	1.25	.30
☐ 31 Brian McRae	.35	.15	.03
☐ 32 Mark Whiten	.20	.08	.02
☐ 33 Ivan Rodriguez	2.00	.80	.20
☐ 34 Wade Taylor	.17	.07	.01
☐ 35 Darren Lewis	.17	.07	.01
☐ 36 Mo Vaughn	.45	.18	.04
☐ 37 Mike Remlinger	.12	.05	.01
☐ 38 Rick Wilkins	.17	.07	.01
☐ 39 Chuck Knoblauch	.40	.16	.04
☐ 40 Kevin Morton	.10	.04	.01
☐ 41 Carlos Rodriguez	.15	.06	.01
☐ 42 Mark Lewis	.20	.08	.02
☐ 43 Brent Mayne	.10	.04	.01
☐ 44 Chris Haney	.15	.06	.01
☐ 45 Denis Boucher	.15	.06	.01
☐ 46 Mike Gardiner	.10	.04	.01
☐ 47 Jeff Johnson	.20	.08	.02
☐ 48 Dean Palmer	.35	.15	.03
☐ 49 Chuck McElroy	.08	.03	.01
☐ 50 Chris Jones	.17	.07	.01
☐ 51 Scott Kamieniecki	.17	.07	.01
☐ 52 Al Osuna	.15	.06	.01
☐ 53 Rusty Meacham	.12	.05	.01
☐ 54 Chito Martinez	.50	.20	.05
☐ 55 Reggie Jefferson	.35	.15	.03
☐ 56 Checklist Card	.05	.01	.00

1992 Donruss I

The 1992 Donruss Series I contains 396 cards, measuring the standard size (2 1/2" by 3 1/2"). The front design features glossy color player photos with white borders. Two-toned blue stripes overlay the top and bottom of the

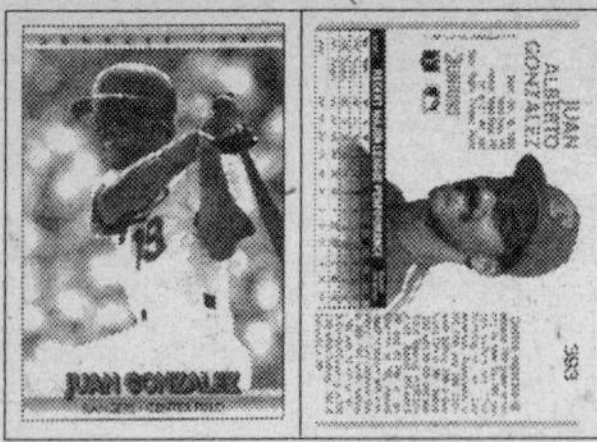

picture, with the player's name printed in silver-and-black lettering above the bottom stripe. The horizontally oriented backs have a color headshot of the player (except on subset cards listed below), biography, career highlights, and recent Major League performance statistics (no earlier than 1987). The set includes 20 Rated Rookies (1-20), ten All-Stars (21-30), five Highlight cards (33, 94, 154, 215, 276), and a puzzle of Hall of Famer Rod Carew. The cards are numbered on the back and checklisted below accordingly. Thirteen Diamond Kings cards featuring the artwork of Dick Perez are randomly inserted in foil packs. Also inserted in Series 1 and 2 foil and rack packs are 5,000 Cal Ripken autographed cards, 7,500 Legend cards of Rickey Henderson, and 10,000 Elite cards each of Wade Boggs, Joe Carter, Will Clark, Dwight Gooden, Ken Griffey Jr., Tony Gwynn, Howard Johnson, Terry Pendleton, Kirby Puckett, and Frank Thomas.

	MINT	EXC	G-VG
COMPLETE SET (396)	24.00	10.50	3.50
COMMON PLAYER (1-396)	.04	.02	.00
☐ 1 Mark Wohlers RR	.40	.16	.04
☐ 2 Wilfredo Cordero RR	.25	.10	.02
☐ 3 Kyle Abbott RR	.15	.06	.01
☐ 4 Dave Nilsson RR	.60	.25	.06
☐ 5 Kenny Lofton RR	.35	.15	.03
☐ 6 Luis Mercedes RR	.30	.12	.03
☐ 7 Roger Salkeld RR	.30	.12	.03
☐ 8 Eddie Zosky RR	.15	.06	.01
☐ 9 Todd Van Poppel RR	.75	.30	.07
☐ 10 Frank Seminara RR	.15	.06	.01
☐ 11 Andy Ashby RR	.10	.04	.01
☐ 12 Reggie Jefferson RR	.25	.10	.02
☐ 13 Ryan Klesko RR	2.00	.80	.20
☐ 14 Carlos Garcia RR	.07	.03	.01
☐ 15 John Ramos RR	.18	.08	.01
☐ 16 Eric Karros RR	.35	.15	.03
☐ 17 Patrick Lennon RR	.30	.12	.03
☐ 18 Eddie Taubensee RR	.25	.10	.02
☐ 19 Roberto Hernandez RR	.18	.08	.01
☐ 20 D.J. Dozier RR	.12	.05	.01
☐ 21 Dave Henderson AS	.07	.03	.01
☐ 22 Cal Ripken AS	.18	.08	.01
☐ 23 Wade Boggs AS	.12	.05	.01
☐ 24 Ken Griffey Jr. AS	.30	.12	.03
☐ 25 Jack Morris AS	.07	.03	.01
☐ 26 Danny Tartabull AS	.07	.03	.01
☐ 27 Cecil Fielder AS	.12	.05	.01
☐ 28 Roberto Alomar AS	.10	.04	.01
☐ 29 Sandy Alomar Jr. AS	.07	.03	.01
☐ 30 Rickey Henderson AS	.15	.06	.01
☐ 31 Ken Hill	.04	.02	.00
☐ 32 John Habyan	.04	.02	.00
☐ 33 Otis Nixon HL	.07	.03	.01
☐ 34 Tim Wallach	.07	.03	.01
☐ 35 Cal Ripken	.40	.16	.04
☐ 36 Gary Carter	.10	.04	.01
☐ 37 Juan Agosto	.04	.02	.00
☐ 38 Doug Dascenzo	.04	.02	.00
☐ 39 Kirk Gibson	.10	.04	.01
☐ 40 Benito Santiago	.10	.04	.01
☐ 41 Otis Nixon	.07	.03	.01
☐ 42 Andy Allanson	.04	.02	.00
☐ 43 Brian Holman	.04	.02	.00
☐ 44 Dick Schofield	.04	.02	.00
☐ 45 Dave Magadan	.07	.03	.01
☐ 46 Rafael Palmeiro	.12	.05	.01
☐ 47 Jody Reed	.07	.03	.01
☐ 48 Ivan Calderon	.07	.03	.01
☐ 49 Greg Harris	.04	.02	.00
☐ 50 Chris Sabo	.10	.04	.01
☐ 51 Paul Molitor	.10	.04	.01
☐ 52 Robby Thompson	.04	.02	.00
☐ 53 Dave Smith	.04	.02	.00
☐ 54 Mark Davis	.07	.03	.01
☐ 55 Kevin Brown	.07	.03	.01
☐ 56 Donn Pall	.04	.02	.00
☐ 57 Lenny Dykstra	.07	.03	.01
☐ 58 Roberto Alomar	.15	.06	.01
☐ 59 Jeff Robinson	.04	.02	.00
☐ 60 Willie McGee	.10	.04	.01
☐ 61 Jay Buhner	.07	.03	.01
☐ 62 Mike Pagliarulo	.04	.02	.00
☐ 63 Paul O'Neill	.07	.03	.01
☐ 64 Hubie Brooks	.07	.03	.01
☐ 65 Kelly Gruber	.10	.04	.01
☐ 66 Ken Caminiti	.07	.03	.01
☐ 67 Gary Redus	.04	.02	.00
☐ 68 Harold Baines	.07	.03	.01
☐ 69 Charlie Hough	.04	.02	.00
☐ 70 B.J. Surhoff	.07	.03	.01
☐ 71 Walt Weiss	.07	.03	.01
☐ 72 Shawn Hillegas	.04	.02	.00
☐ 73 Roberto Kelly	.10	.04	.01

☐ 74 Jeff Ballard	.04	.02	.00
☐ 75 Craig Biggio	.10	.04	.01
☐ 76 Pat Combs	.04	.02	.00
☐ 77 Jeff Robinson	.04	.02	.00
☐ 78 Tim Belcher	.07	.03	.01
☐ 79 Cris Carpenter	.04	.02	.00
☐ 80 Checklist Card	.07	.03	.01
☐ 81 Steve Avery	.30	.12	.03
☐ 82 Chris James	.04	.02	.00
☐ 83 Brian Harper	.04	.02	.00
☐ 84 Charlie Leibrandt	.04	.02	.00
☐ 85 Mickey Tettleton	.07	.03	.01
☐ 86 Pete O'Brien	.04	.02	.00
☐ 87 Danny Darwin	.04	.02	.00
☐ 88 Bob Walk	.04	.02	.00
☐ 89 Jeff Reardon	.07	.03	.01
☐ 90 Bobby Rose	.04	.02	.00
☐ 91 Danny Jackson	.04	.02	.00
☐ 92 John Morris	.04	.02	.00
☐ 93 Bud Black	.04	.02	.00
☐ 94 Tommy Greene HL	.07	.03	.01
☐ 95 Rick Aguilera	.04	.02	.00
☐ 96 Gary Gaetti	.07	.03	.01
☐ 97 David Cone	.10	.04	.01
☐ 98 John Olerud	.15	.06	.01
☐ 99 Joel Skinner	.04	.02	.00
☐ 100 Jay Bell	.04	.02	.00
☐ 101 Bob Milacki	.04	.02	.00
☐ 102 Norm Charlton	.04	.02	.00
☐ 103 Chuck Crim	.04	.02	.00
☐ 104 Terry Steinbach	.07	.03	.01
☐ 105 Juan Samuel	.07	.03	.01
☐ 106 Steve Howe	.04	.02	.00
☐ 107 Rafael Belliard	.04	.02	.00
☐ 108 Joey Cora	.04	.02	.00
☐ 109 Tommy Greene	.10	.04	.01
☐ 110 Gregg Olson	.10	.04	.01
☐ 111 Frank Tanana	.07	.03	.01
☐ 112 Lee Smith	.07	.03	.01
☐ 113 Greg Harris	.04	.02	.00
☐ 114 Dwayne Henry	.04	.02	.00
☐ 115 Chili Davis	.07	.03	.01
☐ 116 Kent Mercker	.07	.03	.01
☐ 117 Brian Barnes	.04	.02	.00
☐ 118 Rich DeLucia	.04	.02	.00
☐ 119 Andre Dawson	.12	.05	.01
☐ 120 Carlos Baerga	.12	.05	.01
☐ 121 Mike LaValliere	.04	.02	.00
☐ 122 Jeff Gray	.04	.02	.00
☐ 123 Bruce Hurst	.07	.03	.01
☐ 124 Alvin Davis	.07	.03	.01
☐ 125 John Candelaria	.04	.02	.00
☐ 126 Matt Nokes	.07	.03	.01
☐ 127 George Bell	.10	.04	.01
☐ 128 Bret Saberhagen	.10	.04	.01
☐ 129 Jeff Russell	.04	.02	.00
☐ 130 Jim Abbott	.12	.05	.01
☐ 131 Bill Gullickson	.04	.02	.00
☐ 132 Todd Zeile	.12	.05	.01
☐ 133 Dave Winfield	.12	.05	.01
☐ 134 Wally Whitehurst	.04	.02	.00
☐ 135 Matt Williams	.12	.05	.01
☐ 136 Tom Browning	.07	.03	.01
☐ 137 Marquis Grissom	.10	.04	.01
☐ 138 Erik Hanson	.07	.03	.01
☐ 139 Rob Dibble	.07	.03	.01
☐ 140 Don August	.04	.02	.00
☐ 141 Tom Henke	.04	.02	.00
☐ 142 Dan Pasqua	.04	.02	.00
☐ 143 George Brett	.15	.06	.01
☐ 144 Jerald Clark	.04	.02	.00
☐ 145 Robin Ventura	.30	.12	.03
☐ 146 Dale Murphy	.12	.05	.01
☐ 147 Dennis Eckersley	.10	.04	.01
☐ 148 Eric Yelding	.04	.02	.00
☐ 149 Mario Diaz	.04	.02	.00
☐ 150 Casey Candaele	.04	.02	.00
☐ 151 Steve Olin	.04	.02	.00
☐ 152 Luis Salazar	.04	.02	.00
☐ 153 Kevin Maas	.18	.08	.01
☐ 154 Nolan Ryan HL	.35	.15	.03
☐ 155 Barry Jones	.04	.02	.00
☐ 156 Chris Hoiles	.07	.03	.01
☐ 157 Bobby Ojeda	.04	.02	.00
☐ 158 Pedro Guerrero	.10	.04	.01
☐ 159 Paul Assenmacher	.04	.02	.00
☐ 160 Checklist Card	.07	.03	.01
☐ 161 Mike Macfarlane	.04	.02	.00
☐ 162 Craig Lefferts	.04	.02	.00
☐ 163 Brian Hunter	.60	.25	.06
☐ 164 Alan Trammell	.10	.04	.01
☐ 165 Ken Griffey Jr.	.75	.30	.07
☐ 166 Lance Parrish	.07	.03	.01
☐ 167 Brian Downing	.04	.02	.00
☐ 168 John Barfield	.04	.02	.00
☐ 169 Jack Clark	.07	.03	.01
☐ 170 Chris Nabholz	.04	.02	.00
☐ 171 Tim Teufel	.04	.02	.00
☐ 172 Chris Hammond	.07	.03	.01
☐ 173 Robin Yount	.15	.06	.01
☐ 174 Dave Righetti	.07	.03	.01
☐ 175 Joe Girardi	.04	.02	.00
☐ 176 Mike Boddicker	.04	.02	.00
☐ 177 Dean Palmer	.25	.10	.02
☐ 178 Greg Hibbard	.04	.02	.00
☐ 179 Randy Ready	.04	.02	.00
☐ 180 Devon White	.07	.03	.01
☐ 181 Mark Eichhorn	.04	.02	.00
☐ 182 Mike Felder	.04	.02	.00
☐ 183 Joe Klink	.04	.02	.00
☐ 184 Steve Bedrosian	.04	.02	.00
☐ 185 Barry Larkin	.12	.05	.01
☐ 186 John Franco	.04	.02	.00
☐ 187 Ed Sprague	.10	.04	.01
☐ 188 Mark Portugal	.04	.02	.00
☐ 189 Jose Lind	.04	.02	.00

☐ 190 Bob Welch .07 .03 .01
☐ 191 Alex Fernandez .12 .05 .01
☐ 192 Gary Sheffield .10 .04 .01
☐ 193 Rickey Henderson .25 .10 .02
☐ 194 Rod Nichols .04 .02 .00
☐ 195 Scott Kamieniecki .10 .04 .01
☐ 196 Mike Flanagan .07 .03 .01
☐ 197 Steve Finley .07 .03 .01
☐ 198 Darren Daulton .04 .02 .00
☐ 199 Leo Gomez .15 .06 .01
☐ 200 Mike Morgan .07 .03 .01
☐ 201 Bob Tewksbury .04 .02 .00
☐ 202 Sid Bream .04 .02 .00
☐ 203 Sandy Alomar Jr. .10 .04 .01
☐ 204 Greg Gagne .04 .02 .00
☐ 205 Juan Berenguer .04 .02 .00
☐ 206 Cecil Fielder .20 .08 .02
☐ 207 Randy Johnson .07 .03 .01
☐ 208 Tony Pena .07 .03 .01
☐ 209 Doug Drabek .07 .03 .01
☐ 210 Wade Boggs .20 .08 .02
☐ 211 Bryan Harvey .07 .03 .01
☐ 212 Jose Vizcaino .04 .02 .00
☐ 213 Alonzo Powell .10 .04 .01
☐ 214 Will Clark .25 .10 .02
☐ 215 Rickey Henderson HL .15 .06 .01
☐ 216 Jack Morris .10 .04 .01
☐ 217 Junior Felix .07 .03 .01
☐ 218 Vince Coleman .10 .04 .01
☐ 219 Jimmy Key .07 .03 .01
☐ 220 Alex Cole .07 .03 .01
☐ 221 Bill Landrum .04 .02 .00
☐ 222 Randy Milligan .04 .02 .00
☐ 223 Jose Rijo .07 .03 .01
☐ 224 Greg Vaughn .12 .05 .01
☐ 225 Dave Stewart .10 .04 .01
☐ 226 Lenny Harris .04 .02 .00
☐ 227 Scott Sanderson .04 .02 .00
☐ 228 Jeff Blauser .04 .02 .00
☐ 229 Ozzie Guillen .07 .03 .01
☐ 230 John Kruk .04 .02 .00
☐ 231 Bob Melvin .04 .02 .00
☐ 232 Milt Cuyler .12 .05 .01
☐ 233 Felix Jose .15 .06 .01
☐ 234 Ellis Burks .10 .04 .01
☐ 235 Pete Harnisch .07 .03 .01
☐ 236 Kevin Tapani .10 .04 .01
☐ 237 Terry Pendleton .10 .04 .01
☐ 238 Mark Gardner .04 .02 .00
☐ 239 Harold Reynolds .04 .02 .00
☐ 240 Checklist Card .07 .03 .01
☐ 241 Mike Harkey .04 .02 .00
☐ 242 Felix Fermin .04 .02 .00
☐ 243 Barry Bonds .18 .08 .01
☐ 244 Roger Clemens .25 .10 .02
☐ 245 Dennis Rasmussen .04 .02 .00
☐ 246 Jose DeLeon .04 .02 .00
☐ 247 Orel Hershiser .10 .04 .01
☐ 248 Mel Hall .07 .03 .01
☐ 249 Rick Wilkins .10 .04 .01
☐ 250 Tom Gordon .07 .03 .01
☐ 251 Kevin Reimer .07 .03 .01
☐ 252 Luis Polonia .07 .03 .01
☐ 253 Mike Henneman .04 .02 .00
☐ 254 Tom Pagnozzi .04 .02 .00
☐ 255 Chuck Finley .10 .04 .01
☐ 256 Mackey Sasser .04 .02 .00
☐ 257 John Burkett .04 .02 .00
☐ 258 Hal Morris .12 .05 .01
☐ 259 Larry Walker .07 .03 .01
☐ 260 Billy Swift .04 .02 .00
☐ 261 Joe Oliver .04 .02 .00
☐ 262 Julio Machado .04 .02 .00
☐ 263 Todd Stottlemyre .07 .03 .01
☐ 264 Matt Merullo .04 .02 .00
☐ 265 Brent Mayne .10 .04 .01
☐ 266 Thomas Howard .04 .02 .00
☐ 267 Lance Johnson .04 .02 .00
☐ 268 Terry Mulholland .04 .02 .00
☐ 269 Rick Honeycutt .04 .02 .00
☐ 270 Luis Gonzalez .18 .08 .01
☐ 271 Jose Guzman .04 .02 .00
☐ 272 Jimmy Jones .04 .02 .00
☐ 273 Mark Lewis .18 .08 .01
☐ 274 Rene Gonzales .04 .02 .00
☐ 275 Jeff Johnson .10 .04 .01
☐ 276 Dennis Martinez HL .07 .03 .01
☐ 277 Delino DeShields .10 .04 .01
☐ 278 Sam Horn .04 .02 .00
☐ 279 Kevin Gross .04 .02 .00
☐ 280 Jose Oquendo .04 .02 .00
☐ 281 Mark Grace .10 .04 .01
☐ 282 Mark Gubicza .07 .03 .01
☐ 283 Fred McGriff .12 .05 .01
☐ 284 Ron Gant .15 .06 .01
☐ 285 Lou Whitaker .07 .03 .01
☐ 286 Edgar Martinez .10 .04 .01
☐ 287 Ron Tingley .04 .02 .00
☐ 288 Kevin McReynolds .10 .04 .01
☐ 289 Ivan Rodriguez 1.00 .40 .10
☐ 290 Mike Gardiner .10 .04 .01
☐ 291 Chris Haney .10 .04 .01
☐ 292 Darrin Jackson .04 .02 .00
☐ 293 Bill Doran .04 .02 .00
☐ 294 Ted Higuera .04 .02 .00
☐ 295 Jeff Brantley .04 .02 .00
☐ 296 Les Lancaster .04 .02 .00
☐ 297 Jim Eisenreich .04 .02 .00
☐ 298 Ruben Sierra .20 .08 .02
☐ 299 Scott Radinsky .04 .02 .00
☐ 300 Jose DeJesus .04 .02 .00
☐ 301 Mike Timlin .10 .04 .01
☐ 302 Luis Sojo .04 .02 .00
☐ 303 Kelly Downs .04 .02 .00
☐ 304 Scott Bankhead .04 .02 .00
☐ 305 Pedro Munoz .15 .06 .01

☐ 306 Scott Scudder	.04	.02	.00
☐ 307 Kevin Elster	.04	.02	.00
☐ 308 Duane Ward	.04	.02	.00
☐ 309 Darryl Kile	.10	.04	.01
☐ 310 Orlando Merced	.20	.08	.02
☐ 311 Dave Henderson	.10	.04	.01
☐ 312 Tim Raines	.10	.04	.01
☐ 313 Mark Lee	.10	.04	.01
☐ 314 Mike Gallego	.04	.02	.00
☐ 315 Charles Nagy	.07	.03	.01
☐ 316 Jesse Barfield	.07	.03	.01
☐ 317 Todd Frohwirth	.04	.02	.00
☐ 318 Al Osuna	.04	.02	.00
☐ 319 Darrin Fletcher	.04	.02	.00
☐ 320 Checklist Card	.07	.03	.01
☐ 321 David Segui	.07	.03	.01
☐ 322 Stan Javier	.04	.02	.00
☐ 323 Bryn Smith	.04	.02	.00
☐ 324 Jeff Treadway	.04	.02	.00
☐ 325 Mark Whiten	.15	.06	.01
☐ 326 Kent Hrbek	.07	.03	.01
☐ 327 Dave Justice	.50	.20	.05
☐ 328 Tony Phillips	.04	.02	.00
☐ 329 Rob Murphy	.04	.02	.00
☐ 330 Kevin Morton	.10	.04	.01
☐ 331 John Smiley	.07	.03	.01
☐ 332 Luis Rivera	.04	.02	.00
☐ 333 Wally Joyner	.10	.04	.01
☐ 334 Heathcliff Slocumb	.04	.02	.00
☐ 335 Rick Cerone	.04	.02	.00
☐ 336 Mike Remlinger	.04	.02	.00
☐ 337 Mike Moore	.07	.03	.01
☐ 338 Lloyd McClendon	.04	.02	.00
☐ 339 Al Newman	.04	.02	.00
☐ 340 Kirk McCaskill	.04	.02	.00
☐ 341 Howard Johnson	.12	.05	.01
☐ 342 Greg Myers	.04	.02	.00
☐ 343 Kal Daniels	.10	.04	.01
☐ 344 Bernie Williams	.25	.10	.02
☐ 345 Shane Mack	.07	.03	.01
☐ 346 Gary Thurman	.04	.02	.00
☐ 347 Dante Bichette	.04	.02	.00
☐ 348 Mark McGwire	.15	.06	.01
☐ 349 Travis Fryman	.25	.10	.02
☐ 350 Ray Lankford	.17	.07	.01
☐ 351 Mike Jeffcoat	.04	.02	.00
☐ 352 Jack McDowell	.10	.04	.01
☐ 353 Mitch Williams	.07	.03	.01
☐ 354 Mike Devereaux	.04	.02	.00
☐ 355 Andres Galarraga	.07	.03	.01
☐ 356 Henry Cotto	.04	.02	.00
☐ 357 Scott Bailes	.04	.02	.00
☐ 358 Jeff Bagwell	1.50	.60	.15
☐ 359 Scott Leius	.07	.03	.01
☐ 360 Zane Smith	.04	.02	.00
☐ 361 Bill Pecota	.04	.02	.00
☐ 362 Tony Fernandez	.07	.03	.01
☐ 363 Glenn Braggs	.04	.02	.00
☐ 364 Bill Spiers	.04	.02	.00
☐ 365 Vicente Palacios	.04	.02	.00
☐ 366 Tim Burke	.04	.02	.00
☐ 367 Randy Tomlin	.10	.04	.01
☐ 368 Kenny Rogers	.04	.02	.00
☐ 369 Brett Butler	.07	.03	.01
☐ 370 Pat Kelly	.15	.06	.01
☐ 371 Bip Roberts	.04	.02	.00
☐ 372 Gregg Jefferies	.10	.04	.01
☐ 373 Kevin Bass	.04	.02	.00
☐ 374 Ron Karkovice	.04	.02	.00
☐ 375 Paul Gibson	.04	.02	.00
☐ 376 Bernard Gilkey	.12	.05	.01
☐ 377 Dave Gallagher	.04	.02	.00
☐ 378 Bill Wegman	.04	.02	.00
☐ 379 Pat Borders	.04	.02	.00
☐ 380 Ed Whitson	.04	.02	.00
☐ 381 Gilberto Reyes	.04	.02	.00
☐ 382 Russ Swan	.04	.02	.00
☐ 383 Andy Van Slyke	.10	.04	.01
☐ 384 Wes Chamberlain	.20	.08	.02
☐ 385 Steve Chitren	.04	.02	.00
☐ 386 Greg Olson	.04	.02	.00
☐ 387 Brian McRae	.18	.08	.01
☐ 388 Rich Rodriguez	.04	.02	.00
☐ 389 Steve Decker	.17	.07	.01
☐ 390 Chuck Knoblauch	.35	.15	.03
☐ 391 Bobby Witt	.07	.03	.01
☐ 392 Eddie Murray	.15	.06	.01
☐ 393 Juan Gonzalez	.40	.16	.04
☐ 394 Scott Ruskin	.04	.02	.00
☐ 395 Jay Howell	.04	.02	.00
☐ 396 Checklist Card	.07	.03	.01

1992 Donruss Diamond Kings

These standard-size (2 1/2" by 3 1/2") cards were randomly inserted in 1992 Donruss I foil packs (cards 1-13 and the checklist only) and in 1992 Donruss II foil packs (cards 14-26). The fronts feature player portraits by noted sports artist Dick Perez. The words "Donruss Diamond Kings" are superimposed at the card top in a gold-trimmed blue and black banner, with the player's name in a similarly designed black stripe at the card bottom. On a white background with a dark blue border, the backs present career summary. The cards are numbered on the back.

	MINT	EXC	G-VG
COMPLETE SET (27)	70.00	32.00	10.50
COMMON PLAYER (1-13/27)	2.00	.80	.20
COMMON PLAYER (14-26)	2.00	.80	.20
☐ DK1 Paul Molitor	2.25	.90	.22
☐ DK2 Will Clark	5.00	2.25	.50
☐ DK3 Joe Carter	2.50	1.00	.25
☐ DK4 Julio Franco	2.25	.90	.22
☐ DK5 Cal Ripken	6.00	2.50	.60
☐ DK6 Dave Justice	9.00	4.00	.90
☐ DK7 George Bell	2.25	.90	.22
☐ DK8 Frank Thomas	13.50	6.00	1.85
☐ DK9 Wade Boggs	4.00	1.75	.40
☐ DK10 Scott Sanderson	2.00	.80	.20
☐ DK11 Jeff Bagwell	7.50	3.25	.75
☐ DK12 John Kruk	2.00	.80	.20
☐ DK13 Felix Jose	2.50	1.00	.25
☐ DK14 Harold Baines	2.00	.80	.20
☐ DK15 Dwight Gooden	2.50	1.00	.25
☐ DK16 Brian McRae	3.00	1.25	.30
☐ DK17 Jay Bell	2.00	.80	.20
☐ DK18 Brett Butler	2.00	.80	.20
☐ DK19 Hal Morris	2.25	.90	.22
☐ DK20 Mark Langston	2.00	.80	.20
☐ DK21 Scott Erickson	4.00	1.75	.40
☐ DK22 Randy Johnson	2.00	.80	.20
☐ DK23 Greg Swindell	2.00	.80	.20
☐ DK24 Dennis Martinez	2.00	.80	.20
☐ DK25 Tony Phillips	2.00	.80	.20
☐ DK26 Fred McGriff	2.50	1.00	.25
☐ DK27 Checklist Card	2.00	.80	.20

1992 Donruss II

This 396-card set was the second series released by Donruss in 1992. The standard-size (2 1/2" by 3 1/2") cards have the same design as those in the first series. Special cards in the set focus on Rated Rookies (397-421), All-Stars (422-431), and Highlights (434, 495, 555, 616, 677). The cards are numbered on the back.

	MINT	EXC	G-VG
COMPLETE SET (396)	24.00	10.50	3.50
COMMON PLAYER (397-784)	.04	.02	.00
COMMON PLAYER (BC1-BC8)	.04	.02	.00
☐ 397 Royce Clayton RR	.25	.10	.02
☐ 398 John Jaha RR	.40	.16	.04
☐ 399 Dan Wilson RR	.12	.05	.01
☐ 400 Archie Corbin RR	.20	.08	.02
☐ 401 Barry Manuel RR	.20	.08	.02
☐ 402 Kim Batiste RR	.12	.05	.01
☐ 403 Pat Mahomes RR	.45	.18	.04
☐ 404 Dave Fleming RR	.30	.12	.03
☐ 405 Jeff Juden RR	.20	.08	.02
☐ 406 Jim Thome RR	.60	.25	.06
☐ 407 Sam Militello RR	.25	.10	.02
☐ 408 Jeff Nelson RR	.18	.08	.01
☐ 409 Anthony Young RR	.18	.08	.01
☐ 410 Tino Martinez RR	.15	.06	.01
☐ 411 Jeff Mutis RR	.20	.08	.02
☐ 412 Rey Sanchez RR	.12	.05	.01
☐ 413 Chris Gardner RR	.30	.12	.03
☐ 414 John VanderWal RR	.25	.10	.02
☐ 415 Reggie Sanders RR	.25	.10	.02
☐ 416 Brian Williams RR	.25	.10	.02
☐ 417 Mo Sanford RR	.20	.08	.02
☐ 418 David Weathers RR	.20	.08	.02
☐ 419 Hector Fajardo RR	.25	.10	.02
☐ 420 Steve Foster RR	.20	.08	.02

	Card			
☐ 421	Lance Dickson RR	.07	.03	.01
☐ 422	Andre Dawson AS	.07	.03	.01
☐ 423	Ozzie Smith AS	.07	.03	.01
☐ 424	Chris Sabo AS	.07	.03	.01
☐ 425	Tony Gwynn AS	.10	.04	.01
☐ 426	Tom Glavine AS	.07	.03	.01
☐ 427	Bobby Bonilla AS	.10	.04	.01
☐ 428	Will Clark AS	.15	.06	.01
☐ 429	Ryne Sandberg AS	.15	.06	.01
☐ 430	Benito Santiago AS	.07	.03	.01
☐ 431	Ivan Calderon AS	.07	.03	.01
☐ 432	Ozzie Smith	.12	.05	.01
☐ 433	Tim Leary	.07	.03	.01
☐ 434	Bret Saberhagen HL	.07	.03	.01
☐ 435	Mel Rojas	.07	.03	.01
☐ 436	Ben McDonald	.10	.04	.01
☐ 437	Tim Crews	.04	.02	.00
☐ 438	Rex Hudler	.04	.02	.00
☐ 439	Chico Walker	.04	.02	.00
☐ 440	Kurt Stillwell	.04	.02	.00
☐ 441	Tony Gwynn	.20	.08	.02
☐ 442	John Smoltz	.10	.04	.01
☐ 443	Lloyd Moseby	.04	.02	.00
☐ 444	Mike Schooler	.04	.02	.00
☐ 445	Joe Grahe	.07	.03	.01
☐ 446	Dwight Gooden	.12	.05	.01
☐ 447	Oil Can Boyd	.04	.02	.00
☐ 448	John Marzano	.04	.02	.00
☐ 449	Bret Barberie	.15	.06	.01
☐ 450	Mike Maddux	.04	.02	.00
☐ 451	Jeff Reed	.04	.02	.00
☐ 452	Dale Sveum	.04	.02	.00
☐ 453	Jose Uribe	.04	.02	.00
☐ 454	Bob Scanlan	.04	.02	.00
☐ 455	Kevin Appier	.07	.03	.01
☐ 456	Jeff Huson	.04	.02	.00
☐ 457	Ken Patterson	.04	.02	.00
☐ 458	Ricky Jordan	.07	.03	.01
☐ 459	Tom Candiotti	.07	.03	.01
☐ 460	Lee Stevens	.10	.04	.01
☐ 461	Rod Beck	.15	.06	.01
☐ 462	Dave Valle	.04	.02	.00
☐ 463	Scott Erickson	.45	.18	.04
☐ 464	Chris Jones	.07	.03	.01
☐ 465	Mark Carreon	.04	.02	.00
☐ 466	Rob Ducey	.04	.02	.00
☐ 467	Jim Corsi	.04	.02	.00
☐ 468	Jeff King	.04	.02	.00
☐ 469	Curt Young	.04	.02	.00
☐ 470	Bo Jackson	.35	.15	.03
☐ 471	Chris Bosio	.04	.02	.00
☐ 472	Jamie Quirk	.04	.02	.00
☐ 473	Jesse Orosco	.04	.02	.00
☐ 474	Alvaro Espinoza	.04	.02	.00
☐ 475	Joe Orsulak	.04	.02	.00
☐ 476	Checklist Card	.07	.03	.01
☐ 477	Gerald Young	.04	.02	.00
☐ 478	Wally Backman	.04	.02	.00

	Card			
☐ 479	Juan Bell	.04	.02	.00
☐ 480	Mike Scioscia	.04	.02	.00
☐ 481	Omar Olivares	.07	.03	.01
☐ 482	Francisco Cabrera	.04	.02	.00
☐ 483	Greg Swindell	.07	.03	.01
☐ 484	Terry Leach	.04	.02	.00
☐ 485	Tommy Gregg	.04	.02	.00
☐ 486	Scott Aldred	.04	.02	.00
☐ 487	Greg Briley	.04	.02	.00
☐ 488	Phil Plantier	.75	.30	.07
☐ 489	Curtis Wilkerson	.04	.02	.00
☐ 490	Tom Brunansky	.07	.03	.01
☐ 491	Mike Fetters	.04	.02	.00
☐ 492	Frank Castillo	.07	.03	.01
☐ 493	Joe Boever	.04	.02	.00
☐ 494	Kirt Manwaring	.04	.02	.00
☐ 495	Wilson Alvarez HL	.07	.03	.01
☐ 496	Gene Larkin	.04	.02	.00
☐ 497	Gary DiSarcina	.04	.02	.00
☐ 498	Frank Viola	.07	.03	.01
☐ 499	Manuel Lee	.04	.02	.00
☐ 500	Albert Belle	.15	.06	.01
☐ 501	Stan Belinda	.04	.02	.00
☐ 502	Dwight Evans	.07	.03	.01
☐ 503	Eric Davis	.12	.05	.01
☐ 504	Darren Holmes	.07	.03	.01
☐ 505	Mike Bordick	.07	.03	.01
☐ 506	Dave Hansen	.07	.03	.01
☐ 507	Lee Guetterman	.04	.02	.00
☐ 508	Keith Mitchell	.25	.10	.02
☐ 509	Melido Perez	.04	.02	.00
☐ 510	Dickie Thon	.07	.03	.01
☐ 511	Mark Williamson	.04	.02	.00
☐ 512	Mark Salas	.04	.02	.00
☐ 513	Milt Thompson	.04	.02	.00
☐ 514	Mo Vaughn	.35	.15	.03
☐ 515	Jim Deshaies	.04	.02	.00
☐ 516	Rich Garces	.04	.02	.00
☐ 517	Lonnie Smith	.07	.03	.01
☐ 518	Spike Owen	.04	.02	.00
☐ 519	Tracy Jones	.04	.02	.00
☐ 520	Greg Maddux	.07	.03	.01
☐ 521	Carlos Martinez	.04	.02	.00
☐ 522	Neal Heaton	.04	.02	.00
☐ 523	Mike Greenwell	.12	.05	.01
☐ 524	Andy Benes	.07	.03	.01
☐ 525	Jeff Schaefer	.04	.02	.00
☐ 526	Mike Sharperson	.04	.02	.00
☐ 527	Wade Taylor	.07	.03	.01
☐ 528	Jerome Walton	.07	.03	.01
☐ 529	Storm Davis	.04	.02	.00
☐ 530	Jose Hernandez	.18	.08	.01
☐ 531	Mark Langston	.07	.03	.01
☐ 532	Rob Deer	.04	.02	.00
☐ 533	Geronimo Pena	.04	.02	.00
☐ 534	Juan Guzman	.65	.25	.06
☐ 535	Pete Schourek	.07	.03	.01
☐ 536	Todd Benzinger	.04	.02	.00

☐ 537 Billy Hatcher	.07	.03	.01
☐ 538 Tom Foley	.04	.02	.00
☐ 539 Dave Cochrane	.04	.02	.00
☐ 540 Mariano Duncan	.04	.02	.00
☐ 541 Edwin Nunez	.04	.02	.00
☐ 542 Rance Mulliniks	.04	.02	.00
☐ 543 Carlton Fisk	.12	.05	.01
☐ 544 Luis Aquino	.04	.02	.00
☐ 545 Ricky Bones	.07	.03	.01
☐ 546 Craig Grebeck	.04	.02	.00
☐ 547 Charlie Hayes	.04	.02	.00
☐ 548 Jose Canseco	.35	.15	.03
☐ 549 Andujar Cedeno	.20	.08	.02
☐ 550 Geno Petralli	.04	.02	.00
☐ 551 Javier Ortiz	.04	.02	.00
☐ 552 Rudy Seanez	.04	.02	.00
☐ 553 Rich Gedman	.04	.02	.00
☐ 554 Eric Plunk	.04	.02	.00
☐ 555 Nolan Ryan HL Rich Gossage	.30	.12	.03
☐ 556 Checklist Card	.07	.03	.01
☐ 557 Greg Colbrunn	.07	.03	.01
☐ 558 Chito Martinez	.35	.15	.03
☐ 559 Darryl Strawberry	.25	.10	.02
☐ 560 Luis Alicea	.04	.02	.00
☐ 561 Dwight Smith	.07	.03	.01
☐ 562 Terry Shumpert	.04	.02	.00
☐ 563 Jim Vatcher	.04	.02	.00
☐ 564 Deion Sanders	.10	.04	.01
☐ 565 Walt Terrell	.04	.02	.00
☐ 566 Dave Burba	.04	.02	.00
☐ 567 Dave Howard	.07	.03	.01
☐ 568 Todd Hundley	.10	.04	.01
☐ 569 Jack Daugherty	.04	.02	.00
☐ 570 Scott Cooper	.15	.06	.01
☐ 571 Bill Sampen	.04	.02	.00
☐ 572 Jose Melendez	.07	.03	.01
☐ 573 Freddie Benavides	.04	.02	.00
☐ 574 Jim Gantner	.04	.02	.00
☐ 575 Trevor Wilson	.04	.02	.00
☐ 576 Ryne Sandberg	.30	.12	.03
☐ 577 Kevin Seitzer	.07	.03	.01
☐ 578 Gerald Alexander	.04	.02	.00
☐ 579 Mike Huff	.04	.02	.00
☐ 580 Von Hayes	.07	.03	.01
☐ 581 Derek Bell	.30	.12	.03
☐ 582 Mike Stanley	.04	.02	.00
☐ 583 Kevin Mitchell	.10	.04	.01
☐ 584 Mike Jackson	.04	.02	.00
☐ 585 Dan Gladden	.04	.02	.00
☐ 586 Ted Power	.04	.02	.00
☐ 587 Jeff Innis	.04	.02	.00
☐ 588 Bob MacDonald	.07	.03	.01
☐ 589 Jose Tolentino	.12	.05	.01
☐ 590 Bob Patterson	.04	.02	.00
☐ 591 Scott Brosius	.15	.06	.01
☐ 592 Frank Thomas	1.25	.50	.12
☐ 593 Darryl Hamilton	.07	.03	.01
☐ 594 Kirk Dressendorfer	.12	.05	.01
☐ 595 Jeff Shaw	.04	.02	.00
☐ 596 Don Mattingly	.20	.08	.02
☐ 597 Glenn Davis	.07	.03	.01
☐ 598 Andy Mota	.10	.04	.01
☐ 599 Jason Grimsley	.04	.02	.00
☐ 600 Jimmy Poole	.07	.03	.01
☐ 601 Jim Gott	.04	.02	.00
☐ 602 Stan Royer	.07	.03	.01
☐ 603 Marvin Freeman	.04	.02	.00
☐ 604 Denis Boucher	.07	.03	.01
☐ 605 Denny Neagle	.25	.10	.02
☐ 606 Mark Lemke	.07	.03	.01
☐ 607 Jerry Don Gleaton	.04	.02	.00
☐ 608 Brent Knackert	.04	.02	.00
☐ 609 Carlos Quintana	.07	.03	.01
☐ 610 Bobby Bonilla	.15	.06	.01
☐ 611 Joe Hesketh	.04	.02	.00
☐ 612 Daryl Boston	.04	.02	.00
☐ 613 Shawon Dunston	.07	.03	.01
☐ 614 Danny Cox	.04	.02	.00
☐ 615 Darren Lewis	.15	.06	.01
☐ 616 Alejandro Pena HL Kent Mercker Mark Wohlers	.12	.05	.01
☐ 617 Kirby Puckett	.20	.08	.02
☐ 618 Franklin Stubbs	.04	.02	.00
☐ 619 Chris Donnels	.15	.06	.01
☐ 620 David Wells	.04	.02	.00
☐ 621 Mike Aldrete	.04	.02	.00
☐ 622 Bob Kipper	.04	.02	.00
☐ 623 Anthony Telford	.04	.02	.00
☐ 624 Randy Myers	.04	.02	.00
☐ 625 Willie Randolph	.04	.02	.00
☐ 626 Joe Slusarski	.07	.03	.01
☐ 627 John Wetteland	.04	.02	.00
☐ 628 Greg Cadaret	.04	.02	.00
☐ 629 Tom Glavine	.10	.04	.01
☐ 630 Wilson Alvarez	.12	.05	.01
☐ 631 Wally Ritchie	.04	.02	.00
☐ 632 Mike Mussina	.20	.08	.02
☐ 633 Mark Leiter	.07	.03	.01
☐ 634 Gerald Perry	.04	.02	.00
☐ 635 Matt Young	.04	.02	.00
☐ 636 Checklist Card	.07	.03	.01
☐ 637 Scott Hemond	.04	.02	.00
☐ 638 David West	.04	.02	.00
☐ 639 Jim Clancy	.04	.02	.00
☐ 640 Doug Piatt	.10	.04	.01
☐ 641 Omar Vizquel	.04	.02	.00
☐ 642 Rick Sutcliffe	.07	.03	.01
☐ 643 Glenallen Hill	.07	.03	.01
☐ 644 Gary Varsho	.04	.02	.00
☐ 645 Tony Fossas	.04	.02	.00
☐ 646 Jack Howell	.04	.02	.00
☐ 647 Jim Campanis	.10	.04	.01
☐ 648 Chris Gwynn	.04	.02	.00
☐ 649 Jim Leyritz	.04	.02	.00

☐ 650 Chuck McElroy	.04	.02	.00
☐ 651 Sean Berry	.07	.03	.01
☐ 652 Donald Harris	.10	.04	.01
☐ 653 Don Slaught	.04	.02	.00
☐ 654 Rusty Meacham	.10	.04	.01
☐ 655 Scott Terry	.04	.02	.00
☐ 656 Ramon Martinez	.15	.06	.01
☐ 657 Keith Miller	.04	.02	.00
☐ 658 Ramon Garcia	.07	.03	.01
☐ 659 Milt Hill	.12	.05	.01
☐ 660 Steve Frey	.04	.02	.00
☐ 661 Bob McClure	.04	.02	.00
☐ 662 Ced Landrum	.10	.04	.01
☐ 663 Doug Henry	.25	.10	.02
☐ 664 Candy Maldonado	.04	.02	.00
☐ 665 Carl Willis	.04	.02	.00
☐ 666 Jeff Montgomery	.04	.02	.00
☐ 667 Craig Shipley	.12	.05	.01
☐ 668 Warren Newson	.12	.05	.01
☐ 669 Mickey Morandini	.07	.03	.01
☐ 670 Brook Jacoby	.04	.02	.00
☐ 671 Ryan Bowen	.12	.05	.01
☐ 672 Bill Krueger	.04	.02	.00
☐ 673 Rob Mallicoat	.04	.02	.00
☐ 674 Doug Jones	.04	.02	.00
☐ 675 Scott Livingstone	.18	.08	.01
☐ 676 Danny Tartabull	.10	.04	.01
☐ 677 Joe Carter HL	.07	.03	.01
☐ 678 Cecil Espy	.04	.02	.00
☐ 679 Randy Velarde	.04	.02	.00
☐ 680 Bruce Ruffin	.04	.02	.00
☐ 681 Ted Wood	.30	.12	.03
☐ 682 Dan Plesac	.04	.02	.00
☐ 683 Eric Bullock	.04	.02	.00
☐ 684 Junior Ortiz	.04	.02	.00
☐ 685 Dave Hollins	.04	.02	.00
☐ 686 Dennis Martinez	.07	.03	.01
☐ 687 Larry Andersen	.04	.02	.00
☐ 688 Doug Simons	.04	.02	.00
☐ 689 Tim Spehr	.10	.04	.01
☐ 690 Calvin Jones	.15	.06	.01
☐ 691 Mark Guthrie	.04	.02	.00
☐ 692 Alfredo Griffin	.04	.02	.00
☐ 693 Joe Carter	.12	.05	.01
☐ 694 Terry Mathews	.10	.04	.01
☐ 695 Pascual Perez	.04	.02	.00
☐ 696 Gene Nelson	.04	.02	.00
☐ 697 Gerald Williams	.25	.10	.02
☐ 698 Chris Cron	.15	.06	.01
☐ 699 Steve Buechele	.07	.03	.01
☐ 700 Paul McClellan	.07	.03	.01
☐ 701 Jim Lindeman	.04	.02	.00
☐ 702 Francisco Oliveras	.04	.02	.00
☐ 703 Rob Maurer	.35	.15	.03
☐ 704 Pat Hentgen	.10	.04	.01
☐ 705 Jaime Navarro	.04	.02	.00
☐ 706 Mike Magnante	.15	.06	.01
☐ 707 Nolan Ryan	.50	.20	.05
☐ 708 Bobby Thigpen	.07	.03	.01
☐ 709 John Cerutti	.04	.02	.00
☐ 710 Steve Wilson	.04	.02	.00
☐ 711 Hensley Meulens	.07	.03	.01
☐ 712 Rheal Cormier	.25	.10	.02
☐ 713 Scott Bradley	.04	.02	.00
☐ 714 Mitch Webster	.04	.02	.00
☐ 715 Roger Mason	.04	.02	.00
☐ 716 Checklist Card	.07	.03	.01
☐ 717 Jeff Fassero	.07	.03	.01
☐ 718 Cal Eldred	.04	.02	.00
☐ 719 Sid Fernandez	.07	.03	.01
☐ 720 Bob Zupcic	.20	.08	.02
☐ 721 Jose Offerman	.07	.03	.01
☐ 722 Cliff Brantley	.20	.08	.02
☐ 723 Ron Darling	.07	.03	.01
☐ 724 Dave Stieb	.07	.03	.01
☐ 725 Hector Villanueva	.07	.03	.01
☐ 726 Mike Hartley	.04	.02	.00
☐ 727 Arthur Rhodes	.20	.08	.02
☐ 728 Randy Bush	.04	.02	.00
☐ 729 Steve Sax	.07	.03	.01
☐ 730 Dave Otto	.04	.02	.00
☐ 731 John Wehner	.20	.08	.02
☐ 732 Dave Martinez	.04	.02	.00
☐ 733 Ruben Amaro	.10	.04	.01
☐ 734 Billy Ripken	.04	.02	.00
☐ 735 Steve Farr	.04	.02	.00
☐ 736 Shawn Abner	.04	.02	.00
☐ 737 Gil Heredia	.12	.05	.01
☐ 738 Ron Jones	.04	.02	.00
☐ 739 Tony Castillo	.04	.02	.00
☐ 740 Sammy Sosa	.07	.03	.01
☐ 741 Julio Franco	.07	.03	.01
☐ 742 Tim Naehring	.07	.03	.01
☐ 743 Steve Wapnick	.10	.04	.01
☐ 744 Craig Wilson	.07	.03	.01
☐ 745 Darrin Chapin	.15	.06	.01
☐ 746 Chris George	.15	.06	.01
☐ 747 Mike Simms	.07	.03	.01
☐ 748 Rosario Rodriguez	.07	.03	.01
☐ 749 Skeeter Barnes	.04	.02	.00
☐ 750 Roger McDowell	.04	.02	.00
☐ 751 Dann Howitt	.04	.02	.00
☐ 752 Paul Sorrento	.04	.02	.00
☐ 753 Braulio Castillo	.35	.15	.03
☐ 754 Yorkis Perez	.15	.06	.01
☐ 755 Willie Fraser	.04	.02	.00
☐ 756 Jeremy Hernandez	.20	.08	.02
☐ 757 Curt Schilling	.04	.02	.00
☐ 758 Steve Lyons	.04	.02	.00
☐ 759 Dave Anderson	.04	.02	.00
☐ 760 Willie Banks	.15	.06	.01
☐ 761 Mark Leonard	.04	.02	.00
☐ 762 Jack Armstrong	.07	.03	.01
☐ 763 Scott Servais	.07	.03	.01
☐ 764 Ray Stephens	.07	.03	.01
☐ 765 Junior Noboa	.04	.02	.00

☐ 766 Jim Olander	.18	.08	.01
☐ 767 Joe Magrane	.07	.03	.01
☐ 768 Lance Blankenship	.04	.02	.00
☐ 769 Mike Humphreys	.07	.03	.01
☐ 770 Jarvis Brown	.15	.06	.01
☐ 771 Damon Berryhill	.04	.02	.00
☐ 772 Alejandro Pena	.07	.03	.01
☐ 773 Jose Mesa	.04	.02	.00
☐ 774 Gary Cooper	.15	.06	.01
☐ 775 Carney Lansford	.07	.03	.01
☐ 776 Mike Bielecki	.04	.02	.00
☐ 777 Charlie O'Brien	.04	.02	.00
☐ 778 Carlos Hernandez	.04	.02	.00
☐ 779 Howard Farmer	.04	.02	.00
☐ 780 Mike Stanton	.04	.02	.00
☐ 781 Reggie Harris	.04	.02	.00
☐ 782 Xavier Hernandez	.04	.02	.00
☐ 783 Bryan Hickerson	.17	.07	.01
☐ 784 Checklist Card	.07	.03	.01
☐ BC1 Cal Ripken MVP	.15	.06	.01
☐ BC2 Terry Pendleton MVP	.07	.03	.01
☐ BC3 Roger Clemens CY	.15	.06	.01
☐ BC4 Tom Glavine CY	.07	.03	.01
☐ BC5 Chuck Knoblauch ROY	.15	.06	.01
☐ BC6 Jeff Bagwell ROY	.45	.18	.04
☐ BC7 Colorado Rockies	.15	.06	.01
☐ BC8 Florida Marlins	.15	.06	.01

1959 Fleer

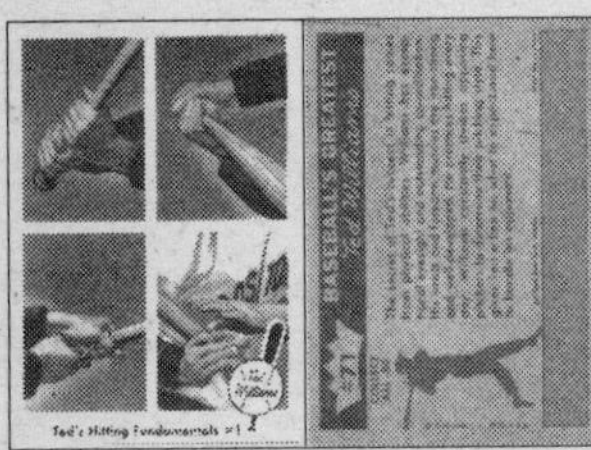

The cards in this 80-card set measure 2 1/2" by 3 1/2". The 1959 Fleer set, with a catalog designation of R418-1, portrays the life of Ted Williams. The wording of the wrapper, "Baseball's Greatest Series," has led to speculation that Fleer contemplated similar sets honoring other baseball immortals, but chose to develop instead the format of the 1960 and 1961 issues. Card number 68, which was withdrawn early in production, is considered scarce and has even been counterfeited; the fake has a rosy coloration and a cross-hatch pattern visible over the picture area.

	NRMT	VG-E	GOOD
COMPLETE SET (80)	1100.00	500.00	110.00
COMMON CARDS (1-80)	6.00	2.50	.60
☐ 1 The Early Years	35.00	5.00	1.00
☐ 2 Ted's Idol Babe Ruth	30.00	13.50	4.50
☐ 3 Practice Makes Perfect	6.00	2.50	.60
☐ 4 Learns Fine Points	6.00	2.50	.60
☐ 5 Ted's Fame Spreads	6.00	2.50	.60
☐ 6 Ted Turns Pro	6.00	2.50	.60
☐ 7 From Mound to Plate	6.00	2.50	.60
☐ 8 1937 First Full Season	6.00	2.50	.60
☐ 9 First Step to Majors	6.00	2.50	.60
☐ 10 Gunning as Pastime	6.00	2.50	.60
☐ 11 First Spring Training (with Jimmie Foxx)	12.50	5.50	1.65
☐ 12 Burning Up Minors	6.00	2.50	.60
☐ 13 1939 Shows Will Stay	6.00	2.50	.60
☐ 14 Outstanding Rookie '39	6.00	2.50	.60
☐ 15 Licks Sophomore Jinx	6.00	2.50	.60
☐ 16 1941 Greatest Year	6.00	2.50	.60
☐ 17 How Ted Hit .400	6.00	2.50	.60
☐ 18 1941 All Star Hero	6.00	2.50	.60
☐ 19 Ted Wins Triple Crown	6.00	2.50	.60
☐ 20 On to Naval Training	6.00	2.50	.60
☐ 21 Honors for Williams	6.00	2.50	.60
☐ 22 1944 Ted Solos	6.00	2.50	.60
☐ 23 Williams Wins Wings	6.00	2.50	.60
☐ 24 1945 Sharpshooter	6.00	2.50	.60
☐ 25 1945 Ted Discharged	6.00	2.50	.60
☐ 26 Off to Flying Start	6.00	2.50	.60
☐ 27 7/9/46 One Man Show	6.00	2.50	.60
☐ 28 The Williams Shift	6.00	2.50	.60
☐ 29 Ted Hits for Cycle	6.00	2.50	.60
☐ 30 Beating Williams Shift	6.00	2.50	.60
☐ 31 Sox Lose Series	6.00	2.50	.60
☐ 32 Most Valuable Player	6.00	2.50	.60
☐ 33 Another Triple Crown	6.00	2.50	.60
☐ 34 Runs Scored Record	6.00	2.50	.60
☐ 35 Sox Miss Pennant	6.00	2.50	.60
☐ 36 Banner Year for Ted	6.00	2.50	.60
☐ 37 1949 Sox Miss Again	6.00	2.50	.60
☐ 38 1949 Power Rampage	6.00	2.50	.60
☐ 39 1950 Great Start	6.00	2.50	.60
☐ 40 Ted Crashes into Wall	6.00	2.50	.60
☐ 41 1950 Ted Recovers	6.00	2.50	.60
☐ 42 Slowed by Injury	6.00	2.50	.60
☐ 43 Double Play Lead	6.00	2.50	.60

☐ 44 Back to Marines	6.00	2.50	.60
☐ 45 Farewell to Baseball	6.00	2.50	.60
☐ 46 Ready for Combat	6.00	2.50	.60
☐ 47 Ted Crash Lands Jet	6.00	2.50	.60
☐ 48 1953 Ted Returns	6.00	2.50	.60
☐ 49 Smash Return	6.00	2.50	.60
☐ 50 1954 Spring Injury	6.00	2.50	.60
☐ 51 Ted is Patched Up	6.00	2.50	.60
☐ 52 1954 Ted's Comeback	6.00	2.50	.60
☐ 53 Comeback is Success	6.00	2.50	.60
☐ 54 Ted Hooks Big One	6.00	2.50	.60
☐ 55 Retirement "No Go"	6.00	2.50	.60
☐ 56 2000th Hit	6.00	2.50	.60
☐ 57 400th Homer	6.00	2.50	.60
☐ 58 Williams Hits .388	6.00	2.50	.60
☐ 59 Hot September for Ted	6.00	2.50	.60
☐ 60 More Records for Ted	6.00	2.50	.60
☐ 61 1957 Outfielder Ted	6.00	2.50	.60
☐ 62 1958 Sixth Batting Title	6.00	2.50	.60
☐ 63 Ted's All-Star Record	6.00	2.50	.60
☐ 64 Daughter and Daddy	6.00	2.50	.60
☐ 65 1958 August 30	6.00	2.50	.60
☐ 66 1958 Powerhouse	6.00	2.50	.60
☐ 67 Two Famous Fishermen	12.50	5.50	1.65
☐ 68 Ted Signs for 1959	625.00	250.00	75.00
☐ 69 A Future Ted Williams	6.00	2.50	.60
☐ 70 Williams and Thorpe	15.00	6.50	2.15
☐ 71 Hitting Fund. 1	6.00	2.50	.60
☐ 72 Hitting Fund. 2	6.00	2.50	.60
☐ 73 Hitting Fund. 3	6.00	2.50	.60
☐ 74 Here's How	6.00	2.50	.60
☐ 75 Williams' Value to Sox	6.00	2.50	.60
☐ 76 On Base Record	6.00	2.50	.60
☐ 77 Ted Relaxes	6.00	2.50	.60
☐ 78 Honors for Williams	6.00	2.50	.60
☐ 79 Where Ted Stands	6.00	2.50	.60
☐ 80 Ted's Goals for 1959	15.00	5.00	1.00

1960 Fleer

The cards in this 79-card set measure 2 1/2" by 3 1/2". The cards from the 1960 Fleer series of Baseball Greats are sometimes mistaken for 1930s cards by collectors not familiar with this set. The cards each contain a tinted photo of a baseball immortal, and were issued in one series. There are no known scarcities, although a number 80 card (Pepper Martin reverse with either Eddie Collins or Lefty Grove obverse) exists (this is not considered part of the set). The catalog designation for 1960 Fleer is R418-2. The cards were printed on a 96-card sheet with 17 double prints. These are noted in the checklist below by DP. On the sheet the second Eddie Collins card is typically found in the number 80 position.

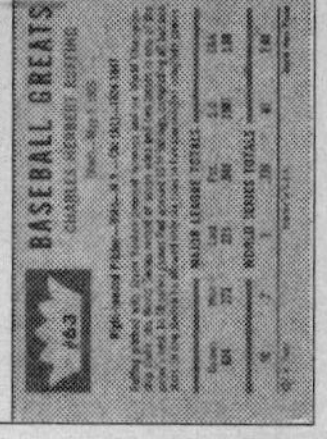

	NRMT	VG-E	GOOD
COMPLETE SET (79)	400.00	180.00	60.00
COMMON PLAYER (1-79)	3.00	1.25	.30
COMMON PLAYER DP	2.25	.90	.22
☐ 1 Napoleon Lajoie DP	15.00	3.00	.60
☐ 2 Christy Mathewson	9.00	4.00	.90
☐ 3 George H. Ruth	75.00	34.00	11.25
☐ 4 Carl Hubbell	5.00	2.25	.50
☐ 5 Grover Alexander	5.00	2.25	.50
☐ 6 Walter Johnson DP	6.00	2.50	.60
☐ 7 Charles A. Bender	3.00	1.25	.30
☐ 8 Roger P. Bresnahan	3.00	1.25	.30
☐ 9 Mordecai P. Brown	3.00	1.25	.30
☐ 10 Tristram Speaker	5.00	2.25	.50
☐ 11 Arky Vaughan DP	2.25	.90	.22
☐ 12 Zachariah Wheat	3.00	1.25	.30
☐ 13 George Sisler	3.00	1.25	.30
☐ 14 Connie Mack	5.00	2.25	.50
☐ 15 Clark C. Griffith	3.00	1.25	.30
☐ 16 Louis Boudreau DP	5.00	2.25	.50
☐ 17 Ernest Lombardi	3.00	1.25	.30
☐ 18 Henry Manush	3.00	1.25	.30
☐ 19 Martin Marion	3.00	1.25	.30
☐ 20 Edward Collins DP	2.25	.90	.22
☐ 21 James Maranville DP	2.25	.90	.22
☐ 22 Joseph Medwick	3.00	1.25	.30
☐ 23 Edward Barrow	3.00	1.25	.30
☐ 24 Gordon Cochrane	4.00	1.75	.40
☐ 25 James J. Collins	3.00	1.25	.30
☐ 26 Robert Feller DP	10.00	4.50	1.25
☐ 27 Lucius Appling	5.00	2.25	.50
☐ 28 Lou Gehrig	40.00	18.00	6.00
☐ 29 Charles Hartnett	3.00	1.25	.30

☐ 30 Charles Klein	3.00	1.25	.30
☐ 31 Anthony Lazzeri DP	3.00	1.25	.30
☐ 32 Aloysius Simmons	3.00	1.25	.30
☐ 33 Wilbert Robinson	3.00	1.25	.30
☐ 34 Edgar Rice	3.00	1.25	.30
☐ 35 Herbert Pennock	3.00	1.25	.30
☐ 36 Melvin Ott DP	4.00	1.75	.40
☐ 37 Frank O'Doul	3.00	1.25	.30
☐ 38 John Mize	6.00	2.50	.60
☐ 39 Edmund Miller	3.00	1.25	.30
☐ 40 Joseph Tinker	3.00	1.25	.30
☐ 41 John Baker DP	2.25	.90	.22
☐ 42 Tyrus Cobb	40.00	18.00	6.00
☐ 43 Paul Derringer	3.00	1.25	.30
☐ 44 Adrian Anson	3.00	1.25	.30
☐ 45 James Bottomley	3.00	1.25	.30
☐ 46 Edward S. Plank DP	3.00	1.25	.30
☐ 47 Denton (Cy) Young	7.50	3.25	.75
☐ 48 Hack Wilson	5.00	2.25	.50
☐ 49 Edward Walsh UER (photo actually Ed Walsh Jr.)	3.00	1.25	.30
☐ 50 Frank Chance	3.00	1.25	.30
☐ 51 Arthur Vance DP	2.25	.90	.22
☐ 52 William Terry	5.00	2.25	.50
☐ 53 James Foxx	6.50	2.75	.65
☐ 54 Vernon Gomez	5.00	2.25	.50
☐ 55 Branch Rickey	3.00	1.25	.30
☐ 56 Raymond Schalk DP	2.25	.90	.22
☐ 57 John Evers	3.00	1.25	.30
☐ 58 Charles Gehringer	5.00	2.25	.50
☐ 59 Burleigh Grimes	3.00	1.25	.30
☐ 60 Robert (Lefty) Grove	6.00	2.50	.60
☐ 61 George Waddell DP	2.25	.90	.22
☐ 62 John (Honus) Wagner	9.00	4.00	.90
☐ 63 Charles(Red) Ruffing	3.00	1.25	.30
☐ 64 Kenesaw M. Landis	3.00	1.25	.30
☐ 65 Harry Heilmann	3.00	1.25	.30
☐ 66 John McGraw DP	3.00	1.25	.30
☐ 67 Hugh Jennings	3.00	1.25	.30
☐ 68 Harold Newhouser	3.00	1.25	.30
☐ 69 Waite Hoyt	3.00	1.25	.30
☐ 70 Louis(Bobo) Newsom	3.00	1.25	.30
☐ 71 Earl Averill DP	2.25	.90	.22
☐ 72 Theodore Williams	60.00	27.00	9.00
☐ 73 Warren Giles	3.00	1.25	.30
☐ 74 Ford Frick	3.00	1.25	.30
☐ 75 Hazen (Kiki) Cuyler	3.00	1.25	.30
☐ 76 Paul Waner DP	2.25	.90	.22
☐ 77 Harold(Pie) Traynor	3.00	1.25	.30
☐ 78 Lloyd Waner	3.00	1.25	.30
☐ 79 Ralph Kiner	7.50	3.25	.75
☐ 80A Pepper Martin SP (Eddie Collins pictured on obverse)	1000.00	400.00	100.00
☐ 80B Pepper Martin SP (Lefty Grove pictured on obverse)	1000.00	400.00	100.00

1961 Fleer

The cards in this 154-card set measure 2 1/2" by 3 1/2". In 1961, Fleer continued its Baseball Greats format by issuing this series of cards. The set was released in two distinct series, 1-88 and 89-154 (of which the latter is more difficult to obtain). The players within each series are conveniently numbered in alphabetical order. It appears that this set continued to be issued the following year by Fleer. The catalog number for this set is F418-3. In each first series pack Fleer inserted a Major League team decal and a pennant sticker honoring past World Series winners.

	NRMT	VG-E	GOOD
COMPLETE SET (154)	800.00	350.00	120.00
COMMON PLAYER (1-88)	2.50	1.00	.25
COMMON PLAYER (89-154)	5.00	2.25	.50
☐ 1 Baker/Cobb/Wheat (checklist back)	25.00	5.00	1.00
☐ 2 Grover C. Alexander	5.00	2.25	.50
☐ 3 Nick Altrock	2.50	1.00	.25
☐ 4 Cap Anson	2.50	1.00	.25
☐ 5 Earl Averill	2.50	1.00	.25
☐ 6 Frank Baker	2.50	1.00	.25
☐ 7 Dave Bancroft	2.50	1.00	.25
☐ 8 Chief Bender	2.50	1.00	.25
☐ 9 Jim Bottomley	2.50	1.00	.25
☐ 10 Roger Bresnahan	2.50	1.00	.25
☐ 11 Mordecai Brown	2.50	1.00	.25
☐ 12 Max Carey	2.50	1.00	.25
☐ 13 Jack Chesbro	2.50	1.00	.25
☐ 14 Ty Cobb	35.00	15.75	5.25
☐ 15 Mickey Cochrane	4.00	1.75	.40
☐ 16 Eddie Collins	2.50	1.00	.25
☐ 17 Earle Combs	2.50	1.00	.25
☐ 18 Charles Comiskey	2.50	1.00	.25
☐ 19 Kiki Cuyler	2.50	1.00	.25

☐ 20 Paul Derringer	2.50	1.00	.25
☐ 21 Howard Ehmke	2.50	1.00	.25
☐ 22 W. Evans	2.50	1.00	.25
☐ 23 Johnny Evers	2.50	1.00	.25
☐ 24 Urban Faber	2.50	1.00	.25
☐ 25 Bob Feller	9.00	4.00	.90
☐ 26 Wes Ferrell	2.50	1.00	.25
☐ 27 Lew Fonseca	2.50	1.00	.25
☐ 28 Jimmy Foxx	6.00	2.50	.60
☐ 29 Ford Frick	2.50	1.00	.25
☐ 30 Frank Frisch	4.00	1.75	.40
☐ 31 Lou Gehrig	35.00	15.75	5.25
☐ 32 Charlie Gehringer	4.00	1.75	.40
☐ 33 Warren Giles	2.50	1.00	.25
☐ 34 Lefty Gomez	4.00	1.75	.40
☐ 35 Goose Goslin	2.50	1.00	.25
☐ 36 Clark Griffith	2.50	1.00	.25
☐ 37 Burleigh Grimes	2.50	1.00	.25
☐ 38 Lefty Grove	5.00	2.25	.50
☐ 39 Chick Hafey	2.50	1.00	.25
☐ 40 Jesse Haines	2.50	1.00	.25
☐ 41 Gabby Hartnett	2.50	1.00	.25
☐ 42 Harry Heilmann	2.50	1.00	.25
☐ 43 Rogers Hornsby	6.00	2.50	.60
☐ 44 Waite Hoyt	2.50	1.00	.25
☐ 45 Carl Hubbell	4.00	1.75	.40
☐ 46 Miller Huggins	2.50	1.00	.25
☐ 47 Hugh Jennings	2.50	1.00	.25
☐ 48 Ban Johnson	2.50	1.00	.25
☐ 49 Walter Johnson	9.00	4.00	.90
☐ 50 Ralph Kiner	6.00	2.50	.60
☐ 51 Chuck Klein	2.50	1.00	.25
☐ 52 Johnny Kling	2.50	1.00	.25
☐ 53 K.M. Landis	2.50	1.00	.25
☐ 54 Tony Lazzeri	2.50	1.00	.25
☐ 55 Ernie Lombardi	2.50	1.00	.25
☐ 56 Dolf Luque	2.50	1.00	.25
☐ 57 Heinie Manush	2.50	1.00	.25
☐ 58 Marty Marion	2.50	1.00	.25
☐ 59 Christy Mathewson	9.00	4.00	.90
☐ 60 John McGraw	4.00	1.75	.40
☐ 61 Joe Medwick	2.50	1.00	.25
☐ 62 E. (Bing) Miller	2.50	1.00	.25
☐ 63 Johnny Mize	5.00	2.25	.50
☐ 64 John Mostil	2.50	1.00	.25
☐ 65 Art Nehf	2.50	1.00	.25
☐ 66 Hal Newhouser	2.50	1.00	.25
☐ 67 D. (Bobo) Newsom	2.50	1.00	.25
☐ 68 Mel Ott	4.00	1.75	.40
☐ 69 Allie Reynolds	2.50	1.00	.25
☐ 70 Sam Rice	2.50	1.00	.25
☐ 71 Eppa Rixey	2.50	1.00	.25
☐ 72 Edd Roush	2.50	1.00	.25
☐ 73 Schoolboy Rowe	2.50	1.00	.25
☐ 74 Red Ruffing	2.50	1.00	.25
☐ 75 Babe Ruth	70.00	32.00	10.50
☐ 76 Joe Sewell	2.50	1.00	.25
☐ 77 Al Simmons	2.50	1.00	.25
☐ 78 George Sisler	2.50	1.00	.25
☐ 79 Tris Speaker	5.00	2.25	.50
☐ 80 Fred Toney	2.50	1.00	.25
☐ 81 Dazzy Vance	2.50	1.00	.25
☐ 82 Jim Vaughn	2.50	1.00	.25
☐ 83 Ed Walsh	2.50	1.00	.25
☐ 84 Lloyd Waner	2.50	1.00	.25
☐ 85 Paul Waner	2.50	1.00	.25
☐ 86 Zack Wheat	2.50	1.00	.25
☐ 87 Hack Wilson	4.00	1.75	.40
☐ 88 Jimmy Wilson	2.50	1.00	.25
☐ 89 Sisler and Traynor (checklist back)	20.00	5.00	1.00
☐ 90 Babe Adams	5.00	2.25	.50
☐ 91 Dale Alexander	5.00	2.25	.50
☐ 92 Jim Bagby	5.00	2.25	.50
☐ 93 Ossie Bluege	5.00	2.25	.50
☐ 94 Lou Boudreau	9.00	4.00	.90
☐ 95 Tom Bridges	5.00	2.25	.50
☐ 96 Donie Bush	5.00	2.25	.50
☐ 97 Dolph Camilli	5.00	2.25	.50
☐ 98 Frank Chance	7.50	3.25	.75
☐ 99 Jimmy Collins	7.50	3.25	.75
☐ 100 Stan Coveleskie	7.50	3.25	.75
☐ 101 Hugh Critz	5.00	2.25	.50
☐ 102 Alvin Crowder	5.00	2.25	.50
☐ 103 Joe Dugan	5.00	2.25	.50
☐ 104 Bibb Falk	5.00	2.25	.50
☐ 105 Rick Ferrell	7.50	3.25	.75
☐ 106 Art Fletcher	5.00	2.25	.50
☐ 107 Dennis Galehouse	5.00	2.25	.50
☐ 108 Chick Galloway	5.00	2.25	.50
☐ 109 Mule Haas	5.00	2.25	.50
☐ 110 Stan Hack	5.00	2.25	.50
☐ 111 Bump Hadley	5.00	2.25	.50
☐ 112 Billy B. Hamilton	7.50	3.25	.75
☐ 113 Joe Hauser	5.00	2.25	.50
☐ 114 Babe Herman	5.00	2.25	.50
☐ 115 Travis Jackson	9.00	4.00	.90
☐ 116 Eddie Joost	5.00	2.25	.50
☐ 117 Addie Joss	9.00	4.00	.90
☐ 118 Joe Judge	5.00	2.25	.50
☐ 119 Joe Kuhel	5.00	2.25	.50
☐ 120 Napoleon Lajoie	12.00	5.25	1.50
☐ 121 Dutch Leonard	5.00	2.25	.50
☐ 122 Ted Lyons	7.50	3.25	.75
☐ 123 Connie Mack	12.00	5.25	1.50
☐ 124 Rabbit Maranville	7.50	3.25	.75
☐ 125 Fred Marberry	5.00	2.25	.50
☐ 126 Joe McGinnity	9.00	4.00	.90
☐ 127 Oscar Melillo	5.00	2.25	.50
☐ 128 Ray Mueller	5.00	2.25	.50
☐ 129 Kid Nichols	7.50	3.25	.75
☐ 130 Lefty O'Doul	5.00	2.25	.50
☐ 131 Bob O'Farrell	5.00	2.25	.50
☐ 132 Roger Peckinpaugh	5.00	2.25	.50
☐ 133 Herb Pennock	7.50	3.25	.75
☐ 134 George Pipgras	5.00	2.25	.50

☐ 135 Eddie Plank	9.00	4.00	.90
☐ 136 Ray Schalk	7.50	3.25	.75
☐ 137 Hal Schumacher	5.00	2.25	.50
☐ 138 Luke Sewell	5.00	2.25	.50
☐ 139 Bob Shawkey	5.00	2.25	.50
☐ 140 Riggs Stephenson	5.00	2.25	.50
☐ 141 Billy Sullivan	5.00	2.25	.50
☐ 142 Bill Terry	12.00	5.25	1.50
☐ 143 Joe Tinker	7.50	3.25	.75
☐ 144 Pie Traynor	9.00	4.00	.90
☐ 145 Hal Trosky	5.00	2.25	.50
☐ 146 George Uhle	5.00	2.25	.50
☐ 147 Johnny VanderMeer	7.50	3.25	.75
☐ 148 Arky Vaughan	7.50	3.25	.75
☐ 149 Rube Waddell	7.50	3.25	.75
☐ 150 Honus Wagner	35.00	15.75	5.25
☐ 151 Dixie Walker	5.00	2.25	.50
☐ 152 Ted Williams	70.00	32.00	10.50
☐ 153 Cy Young	20.00	8.50	2.75
☐ 154 Ross Young	15.00	5.00	1.00

1963 Fleer

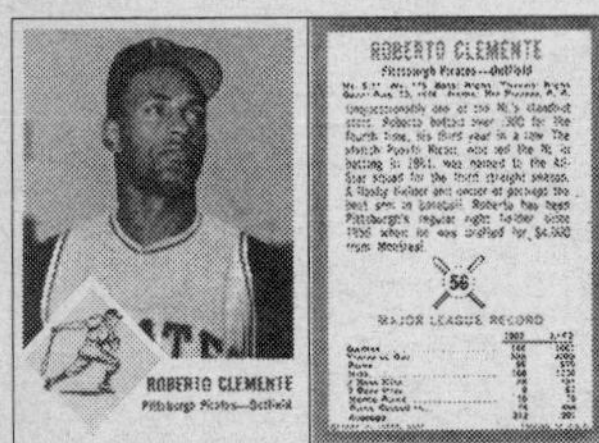

The cards in this 66-card set measure 2 1/2" by 3 1/2". The Fleer set of current baseball players was marketed in 1963 in a gum card-style waxed wrapper package which contained a cherry cookie instead of gum. The cards were printed in sheets of 66 with the scarce card of Adcock apparently being replaced by the unnumbered checklist card for the final press run. The complete set price includes the checklist card. The catalog designation for this set is R418-4. The key rookie card in this set is Maury Wills.

	NRMT	VG-E	GOOD
COMPLETE SET (67)	1100.00	500.00	100.00
COMMON PLAYER (1-66)	7.00	3.00	.70
☐ 1 Steve Barber	10.00	4.00	.80
☐ 2 Ron Hansen	7.00	3.00	.70
☐ 3 Milt Pappas	8.00	3.50	.80
☐ 4 Brooks Robinson	42.00	18.00	5.50
☐ 5 Willie Mays	90.00	40.00	13.50
☐ 6 Lou Clinton	7.00	3.00	.70
☐ 7 Bill Monbouquette	7.00	3.00	.70
☐ 8 Carl Yastrzemski	90.00	40.00	13.50
☐ 9 Ray Herbert	7.00	3.00	.70
☐ 10 Jim Landis	7.00	3.00	.70
☐ 11 Dick Donovan	7.00	3.00	.70
☐ 12 Tito Francona	7.00	3.00	.70
☐ 13 Jerry Kindall	7.00	3.00	.70
☐ 14 Frank Lary	8.00	3.50	.80
☐ 15 Dick Howser	8.00	3.50	.80
☐ 16 Jerry Lumpe	7.00	3.00	.70
☐ 17 Norm Siebern	7.00	3.00	.70
☐ 18 Don Lee	7.00	3.00	.70
☐ 19 Albie Pearson	7.00	3.00	.70
☐ 20 Bob Rodgers	8.00	3.50	.80
☐ 21 Leon Wagner	7.00	3.00	.70
☐ 22 Jim Kaat	11.00	5.00	1.35
☐ 23 Vic Power	7.00	3.00	.70
☐ 24 Rich Rollins	8.00	3.50	.80
☐ 25 Bobby Richardson	12.00	5.25	1.50
☐ 26 Ralph Terry	8.00	3.50	.80
☐ 27 Tom Cheney	7.00	3.00	.70
☐ 28 Chuck Cottier	7.00	3.00	.70
☐ 29 Jim Piersall	9.00	4.00	.90
☐ 30 Dave Stenhouse	7.00	3.00	.70
☐ 31 Glen Hobbie	7.00	3.00	.70
☐ 32 Ron Santo	11.00	5.00	1.35
☐ 33 Gene Freese	7.00	3.00	.70
☐ 34 Vada Pinson	11.00	5.00	1.35
☐ 35 Bob Purkey	7.00	3.00	.70
☐ 36 Joe Amalfitano	7.00	3.00	.70
☐ 37 Bob Aspromonte	7.00	3.00	.70
☐ 38 Dick Farrell	7.00	3.00	.70
☐ 39 Al Spangler	7.00	3.00	.70
☐ 40 Tommy Davis	9.00	4.00	.90
☐ 41 Don Drysdale	33.00	15.00	5.00
☐ 42 Sandy Koufax	110.00	50.00	16.50
☐ 43 Maury Wills	60.00	27.00	9.00
☐ 44 Frank Bolling	7.00	3.00	.70
☐ 45 Warren Spahn	30.00	13.50	4.50
☐ 46 Joe Adcock SP	140.00	63.00	21.00
☐ 47 Roger Craig	10.00	4.50	1.25
☐ 48 Al Jackson	7.00	3.00	.70
☐ 49 Rod Kanehl	7.00	3.00	.70
☐ 50 Ruben Amaro	7.00	3.00	.70
☐ 51 Johnny Callison	8.00	3.50	.80
☐ 52 Clay Dalrymple	7.00	3.00	.70
☐ 53 Don Demeter	7.00	3.00	.70
☐ 54 Art Mahaffey	7.00	3.00	.70
☐ 55 Smoky Burgess	8.00	3.50	.80
☐ 56 Roberto Clemente	90.00	40.00	13.50

☐ 57 Roy Face	9.00	4.00	.90
☐ 58 Vern Law	8.00	3.50	.80
☐ 59 Bill Mazeroski	11.00	5.00	1.35
☐ 60 Ken Boyer	14.00	6.25	2.00
☐ 61 Bob Gibson	32.00	14.25	4.75
☐ 62 Gene Oliver	7.00	3.00	.70
☐ 63 Bill White	12.00	5.25	1.50
☐ 64 Orlando Cepeda	14.00	6.25	2.00
☐ 65 Jim Davenport	7.00	3.00	.70
☐ 66 Billy O'Dell	9.00	4.00	.80
☐ xx Checklist card (unnumbered)	350.00	75.00	15.00

1981 Fleer

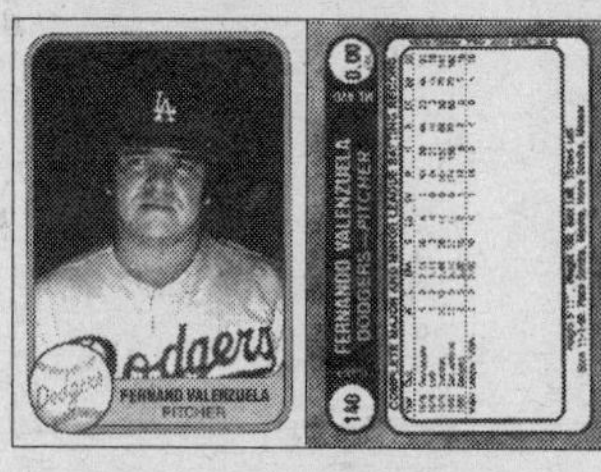

The cards in this 660-card set measure 2 1/2" by 3 1/2". This issue of cards marks Fleer's first entry into the current player baseball card market since 1963. Players from the same team are conveniently grouped together by number in the set. The teams are ordered (by 1980 standings) as follows: Philadelphia (1-27), Kansas City (28-50), Houston (51-78), New York Yankees (79-109), Los Angeles (110-141), Montreal (142-168), Baltimore (169-195), Cincinnati (196-220), Boston (221-241), Atlanta (242-267), California (268-290), Chicago Cubs (291-315), New York Mets (316-338), Chicago White Sox (339-350 and 352-359), Pittsburgh (360-386), Cleveland (387-408), Toronto (409-431), San Francisco (432-458), Detroit (459-483), San Diego (484-506), Milwaukee (507-527), St. Louis (528-550), Minnesota (551-571), Oakland (351 and 572-594), Seattle (595-616), and Texas (617-637). Cards 638-660 feature specials and checklists. The cards of pitchers in this set erroneously show a heading (on the card backs) of "Batting Record" over their career pitching statistics. There were three distinct printings: the two following the primary run were designed to correct numerous errors. The variations caused by these multiple printings are noted in the checklist below (P1, P2, or P3). The C. Nettles variation was corrected before the end of the first printing and thus is not included in the complete set consideration. The key rookie cards in this set are Kirk Gibson, Jeff Reardon, and Fernando Valenzuela, whose first name was erroneously spelled Fernand on the card front.

	MINT	EXC	G-VG
COMPLETE SET (660)	60.00	27.00	9.00
COMMON PLAYER (1-660)	.05	.02	.00
☐ 1 Pete Rose UER (270 hits in '63, should be 170)	2.00	.50	.10
☐ 2 Larry Bowa	.15	.06	.01
☐ 3 Manny Trillo	.05	.02	.00
☐ 4 Bob Boone	.15	.06	.01
☐ 5 Mike Schmidt See also 640A	2.50	1.00	.25
☐ 6A Steve Carlton P1 Pitcher of Year See also 660A Back "1066 Cardinals"	1.25	.50	.12
☐ 6B Steve Carlton P2 Pitcher of Year Back "1066 Cardinals"	1.25	.50	.12
☐ 6C Steve Carlton P3 "1966 Cardinals"	2.00	.80	.20
☐ 7 Tug McGraw See 657A	.15	.06	.01
☐ 8 Larry Christenson	.05	.02	.00
☐ 9 Bake McBride	.05	.02	.00
☐ 10 Greg Luzinski	.15	.06	.01
☐ 11 Ron Reed	.05	.02	.00
☐ 12 Dickie Noles	.05	.02	.00
☐ 13 Keith Moreland	.15	.06	.01
☐ 14 Bob Walk	.25	.10	.02
☐ 15 Lonnie Smith	.35	.15	.03
☐ 16 Dick Ruthven	.05	.02	.00
☐ 17 Sparky Lyle	.15	.06	.01
☐ 18 Greg Gross	.05	.02	.00
☐ 19 Garry Maddox	.05	.02	.00
☐ 20 Nino Espinosa	.05	.02	.00
☐ 21 George Vukovich	.05	.02	.00
☐ 22 John Vukovich	.05	.02	.00
☐ 23 Ramon Aviles	.05	.02	.00
☐ 24A Ken Saucier P1 (Name on back "Ken")	.05	.02	.00
☐ 24B Ken Saucier P2 (Name on back "Ken")	.05	.02	.00

☐ 24C	Kevin Saucier P3 (Name on back "Kevin")	.25	.10	.02
☐ 25	Randy Lerch	.05	.02	.00
☐ 26	Del Unser	.05	.02	.00
☐ 27	Tim McCarver	.15	.06	.01
☐ 28	George Brett See also 655A	2.50	1.00	.25
☐ 29	Willie Wilson	.20	.08	.02
☐ 30	Paul Splittorff	.05	.02	.00
☐ 31	Dan Quisenberry	.25	.10	.02
☐ 32A	Amos Otis P1 Batting Pose "Outfield" (32 on back)	.15	.06	.01
☐ 32B	Amos Otis P2 "Series Starter" (483 on back)	.15	.06	.01
☐ 33	Steve Busby	.10	.04	.01
☐ 34	U.L. Washington	.05	.02	.00
☐ 35	Dave Chalk	.05	.02	.00
☐ 36	Darrell Porter	.05	.02	.00
☐ 37	Marty Pattin	.05	.02	.00
☐ 38	Larry Gura	.05	.02	.00
☐ 39	Renie Martin	.05	.02	.00
☐ 40	Rich Gale	.05	.02	.00
☐ 41A	Hal McRae P1 "Royals" on front in black letters	.50	.20	.05
☐ 41B	Hal McRae P2 "Royals" on front in blue letters	.15	.06	.01
☐ 42	Dennis Leonard	.05	.02	.00
☐ 43	Willie Aikens	.05	.02	.00
☐ 44	Frank White	.10	.04	.01
☐ 45	Clint Hurdle	.05	.02	.00
☐ 46	John Wathan	.10	.04	.01
☐ 47	Pete LaCock	.05	.02	.00
☐ 48	Rance Mulliniks	.05	.02	.00
☐ 49	Jeff Twitty	.05	.02	.00
☐ 50	Jamie Quirk	.05	.02	.00
☐ 51	Art Howe	.10	.04	.01
☐ 52	Ken Forsch	.05	.02	.00
☐ 53	Vern Ruhle	.05	.02	.00
☐ 54	Joe Niekro	.10	.04	.01
☐ 55	Frank LaCorte	.05	.02	.00
☐ 56	J.R. Richard	.10	.04	.01
☐ 57	Nolan Ryan	6.25	2.75	.60
☐ 58	Enos Cabell	.05	.02	.00
☐ 59	Cesar Cedeno	.10	.04	.01
☐ 60	Jose Cruz	.10	.04	.01
☐ 61	Bill Virdon MG	.05	.02	.00
☐ 62	Terry Puhl	.05	.02	.00
☐ 63	Joaquin Andujar	.10	.04	.01
☐ 64	Alan Ashby	.05	.02	.00
☐ 65	Joe Sambito	.05	.02	.00
☐ 66	Denny Walling	.05	.02	.00
☐ 67	Jeff Leonard	.10	.04	.01
☐ 68	Luis Pujols	.05	.02	.00
☐ 69	Bruce Bochy	.05	.02	.00
☐ 70	Rafael Landestoy	.05	.02	.00
☐ 71	Dave Smith	.40	.16	.04
☐ 72	Danny Heep	.15	.06	.01
☐ 73	Julio Gonzalez	.05	.02	.00
☐ 74	Craig Reynolds	.05	.02	.00
☐ 75	Gary Woods	.05	.02	.00
☐ 76	Dave Bergman	.05	.02	.00
☐ 77	Randy Niemann	.05	.02	.00
☐ 78	Joe Morgan	.75	.30	.07
☐ 79	Reggie Jackson (See also 650A)	2.50	1.00	.25
☐ 80	Bucky Dent	.10	.04	.01
☐ 81	Tommy John	.20	.08	.02
☐ 82	Luis Tiant	.10	.04	.01
☐ 83	Rick Cerone	.05	.02	.00
☐ 84	Dick Howser MG	.05	.02	.00
☐ 85	Lou Piniella	.15	.06	.01
☐ 86	Ron Davis	.05	.02	.00
☐ 87A	Craig Nettles P1 ERR (Name on back misspelled "Craig")	11.00	5.00	1.35
☐ 87B	Graig Nettles P2 COR "Graig"	.35	.15	.03
☐ 88	Ron Guidry	.25	.10	.02
☐ 89	Rich Gossage	.20	.08	.02
☐ 90	Rudy May	.05	.02	.00
☐ 91	Gaylord Perry	.50	.20	.05
☐ 92	Eric Soderholm	.05	.02	.00
☐ 93	Bob Watson	.05	.02	.00
☐ 94	Bobby Murcer	.15	.06	.01
☐ 95	Bobby Brown	.05	.02	.00
☐ 96	Jim Spencer	.05	.02	.00
☐ 97	Tom Underwood	.05	.02	.00
☐ 98	Oscar Gamble	.05	.02	.00
☐ 99	Johnny Oates	.10	.04	.01
☐ 100	Fred Stanley	.05	.02	.00
☐ 101	Ruppert Jones	.05	.02	.00
☐ 102	Dennis Werth	.05	.02	.00
☐ 103	Joe Lefebvre	.05	.02	.00
☐ 104	Brian Doyle	.05	.02	.00
☐ 105	Aurelio Rodriguez	.05	.02	.00
☐ 106	Doug Bird	.05	.02	.00
☐ 107	Mike Griffin	.05	.02	.00
☐ 108	Tim Lollar	.05	.02	.00
☐ 109	Willie Randolph	.15	.06	.01
☐ 110	Steve Garvey	.75	.30	.07
☐ 111	Reggie Smith	.10	.04	.01
☐ 112	Don Sutton	.35	.15	.03
☐ 113	Burt Hooton	.05	.02	.00
☐ 114A	Dave Lopes P1 Small hand on back	.50	.20	.05
☐ 114B	Dave Lopes P2 No hand	.10	.04	.01
☐ 115	Dusty Baker	.10	.04	.01
☐ 116	Tom Lasorda MG	.10	.04	.01
☐ 117	Bill Russell	.10	.04	.01
☐ 118	Jerry Reuss	.10	.04	.01

Card			
☐ 119 Terry Forster	.10	.04	.01
☐ 120A Bob Welch P1	.50	.20	.05
Name on back is "Bob"			
☐ 120B Bob Welch P2	.50	.20	.05
Name on back is "Robert"			
☐ 121 Don Stanhouse	.05	.02	.00
☐ 122 Rick Monday	.10	.04	.01
☐ 123 Derrel Thomas	.05	.02	.00
☐ 124 Joe Ferguson	.05	.02	.00
☐ 125 Rick Sutcliffe	.15	.06	.01
☐ 126A Ron Cey P1	.50	.20	.05
Small hand on back			
☐ 126B Ron Cey P2	.15	.06	.01
No hand			
☐ 127 Dave Goltz	.05	.02	.00
☐ 128 Jay Johnstone	.10	.04	.01
☐ 129 Steve Yeager	.05	.02	.00
☐ 130 Gary Weiss	.05	.02	.00
☐ 131 Mike Scioscia	1.00	.40	.10
☐ 132 Vic Davalillo	.05	.02	.00
☐ 133 Doug Rau	.05	.02	.00
☐ 134 Pepe Frias	.05	.02	.00
☐ 135 Mickey Hatcher	.05	.02	.00
☐ 136 Steve Howe	.10	.04	.01
☐ 137 Robert Castillo	.05	.02	.00
☐ 138 Gary Thomasson	.05	.02	.00
☐ 139 Rudy Law	.05	.02	.00
☐ 140 Fernand Valenzuela	2.75	1.10	.27
UER (sic, Fernando)			
☐ 141 Manny Mota	.10	.04	.01
☐ 142 Gary Carter	.90	.40	.09
☐ 143 Steve Rogers	.05	.02	.00
☐ 144 Warren Cromartie	.05	.02	.00
☐ 145 Andre Dawson	1.75	.70	.17
☐ 146 Larry Parrish	.05	.02	.00
☐ 147 Rowland Office	.05	.02	.00
☐ 148 Ellis Valentine	.05	.02	.00
☐ 149 Dick Williams MG	.05	.02	.00
☐ 150 Bill Gullickson	.50	.20	.05
☐ 151 Elias Sosa	.05	.02	.00
☐ 152 John Tamargo	.05	.02	.00
☐ 153 Chris Speier	.05	.02	.00
☐ 154 Ron LeFlore	.05	.02	.00
☐ 155 Rodney Scott	.05	.02	.00
☐ 156 Stan Bahnsen	.05	.02	.00
☐ 157 Bill Lee	.05	.02	.00
☐ 158 Fred Norman	.05	.02	.00
☐ 159 Woodie Fryman	.05	.02	.00
☐ 160 David Palmer	.05	.02	.00
☐ 161 Jerry White	.05	.02	.00
☐ 162 Roberto Ramos	.05	.02	.00
☐ 163 John D'Acquisto	.05	.02	.00
☐ 164 Tommy Hutton	.05	.02	.00
☐ 165 Charlie Lea	.15	.06	.01
☐ 166 Scott Sanderson	.15	.06	.01
☐ 167 Ken Macha	.05	.02	.00
☐ 168 Tony Bernazard	.05	.02	.00
☐ 169 Jim Palmer	1.00	.40	.10
☐ 170 Steve Stone	.05	.02	.00
☐ 171 Mike Flanagan	.10	.04	.01
☐ 172 Al Bumbry	.05	.02	.00
☐ 173 Doug DeCinces	.05	.02	.00
☐ 174 Scott McGregor	.05	.02	.00
☐ 175 Mark Belanger	.10	.04	.01
☐ 176 Tim Stoddard	.05	.02	.00
☐ 177A Rick Dempsey P1	.50	.20	.05
Small hand on front			
☐ 177B Rick Dempsey P2	.10	.04	.01
No hand			
☐ 178 Earl Weaver MG	.10	.04	.01
☐ 179 Tippy Martinez	.05	.02	.00
☐ 180 Dennis Martinez	.20	.08	.02
☐ 181 Sammy Stewart	.05	.02	.00
☐ 182 Rich Dauer	.05	.02	.00
☐ 183 Lee May	.10	.04	.01
☐ 184 Eddie Murray	2.25	.90	.22
☐ 185 Benny Ayala	.05	.02	.00
☐ 186 John Lowenstein	.05	.02	.00
☐ 187 Gary Roenicke	.05	.02	.00
☐ 188 Ken Singleton	.10	.04	.01
☐ 189 Dan Graham	.05	.02	.00
☐ 190 Terry Crowley	.05	.02	.00
☐ 191 Kiko Garcia	.05	.02	.00
☐ 192 Dave Ford	.05	.02	.00
☐ 193 Mark Corey	.05	.02	.00
☐ 194 Lenn Sakata	.05	.02	.00
☐ 195 Doug DeCinces	.05	.02	.00
☐ 196 Johnny Bench	1.50	.60	.15
☐ 197 Dave Concepcion	.20	.08	.02
☐ 198 Ray Knight	.10	.04	.01
☐ 199 Ken Griffey	.30	.12	.03
☐ 200 Tom Seaver	1.50	.60	.15
☐ 201 Dave Collins	.05	.02	.00
☐ 202A George Foster P1	.20	.08	.02
Slugger			
Number on back 216			
☐ 202B George Foster P2	.20	.08	.02
Slugger			
Number on back 202			
☐ 203 Junior Kennedy	.05	.02	.00
☐ 204 Frank Pastore	.05	.02	.00
☐ 205 Dan Driessen	.05	.02	.00
☐ 206 Hector Cruz	.05	.02	.00
☐ 207 Paul Moskau	.05	.02	.00
☐ 208 Charlie Leibrandt	.50	.20	.05
☐ 209 Harry Spilman	.05	.02	.00
☐ 210 Joe Price	.05	.02	.00
☐ 211 Tom Hume	.05	.02	.00
☐ 212 Joe Nolan	.05	.02	.00
☐ 213 Doug Bair	.05	.02	.00
☐ 214 Mario Soto	.10	.04	.01
☐ 215A Bill Bonham P1	.50	.20	.05
Small hand on back			

☐ 215B Bill Bonham P2 .... .10 .04 .01
No hand
☐ 216 George Foster .... .20 .08 .02
(See 202)
☐ 217 Paul Householder .... .05 .02 .00
☐ 218 Ron Oester .... .05 .02 .00
☐ 219 Sam Mejias .... .05 .02 .00
☐ 220 Sheldon Burnside .... .05 .02 .00
☐ 221 Carl Yastrzemski .... 1.50 .60 .15
☐ 222 Jim Rice .... .25 .10 .02
☐ 223 Fred Lynn .... .20 .08 .02
☐ 224 Carlton Fisk .... 1.50 .60 .15
☐ 225 Rick Burleson .... .10 .04 .01
☐ 226 Dennis Eckersley .... .60 .25 .06
☐ 227 Butch Hobson .... .10 .04 .01
☐ 228 Tom Burgmeier .... .05 .02 .00
☐ 229 Garry Hancock .... .05 .02 .00
☐ 230 Don Zimmer MG .... .05 .02 .00
☐ 231 Steve Renko .... .05 .02 .00
☐ 232 Dwight Evans .... .35 .15 .03
☐ 233 Mike Torrez .... .05 .02 .00
☐ 234 Bob Stanley .... .05 .02 .00
☐ 235 Jim Dwyer .... .05 .02 .00
☐ 236 Dave Stapleton .... .05 .02 .00
☐ 237 Glenn Hoffman .... .05 .02 .00
☐ 238 Jerry Remy .... .05 .02 .00
☐ 239 Dick Drago .... .05 .02 .00
☐ 240 Bill Campbell .... .05 .02 .00
☐ 241 Tony Perez .... .35 .15 .03
☐ 242 Phil Niekro .... .50 .20 .05
☐ 243 Dale Murphy .... 1.00 .40 .10
☐ 244 Bob Horner .... .10 .04 .01
☐ 245 Jeff Burroughs .... .05 .02 .00
☐ 246 Rick Camp .... .05 .02 .00
☐ 247 Bobby Cox MG .... .05 .02 .00
☐ 248 Bruce Benedict .... .05 .02 .00
☐ 249 Gene Garber .... .05 .02 .00
☐ 250 Jerry Royster .... .05 .02 .00
☐ 251A Gary Matthews P1 .... .50 .20 .05
Small hand on back
☐ 251B Gary Matthews P2 .... .10 .04 .01
No hand
☐ 252 Chris Chambliss .... .10 .04 .01
☐ 253 Luis Gomez .... .05 .02 .00
☐ 254 Bill Nahorodny .... .05 .02 .00
☐ 255 Doyle Alexander .... .05 .02 .00
☐ 256 Brian Asselstine .... .05 .02 .00
☐ 257 Biff Pocoroba .... .05 .02 .00
☐ 258 Mike Lum .... .05 .02 .00
☐ 259 Charlie Spikes .... .05 .02 .00
☐ 260 Glenn Hubbard .... .05 .02 .00
☐ 261 Tommy Boggs .... .05 .02 .00
☐ 262 Al Hrabosky .... .05 .02 .00
☐ 263 Rick Matula .... .05 .02 .00
☐ 264 Preston Hanna .... .05 .02 .00
☐ 265 Larry Bradford .... .05 .02 .00
☐ 266 Rafael Ramirez .... .15 .06 .01
☐ 267 Larry McWilliams .... .05 .02 .00
☐ 268 Rod Carew .... 1.50 .60 .15
☐ 269 Bobby Grich .... .10 .04 .01
☐ 270 Carney Lansford .... .15 .06 .01
☐ 271 Don Baylor .... .15 .06 .01
☐ 272 Joe Rudi .... .10 .04 .01
☐ 273 Dan Ford .... .05 .02 .00
☐ 274 Jim Fregosi .... .05 .02 .00
☐ 275 Dave Frost .... .05 .02 .00
☐ 276 Frank Tanana .... .10 .04 .01
☐ 277 Dickie Thon .... .15 .06 .01
☐ 278 Jason Thompson .... .05 .02 .00
☐ 279 Rick Miller .... .05 .02 .00
☐ 280 Bert Campaneris .... .10 .04 .01
☐ 281 Tom Donohue .... .05 .02 .00
☐ 282 Brian Downing .... .10 .04 .01
☐ 283 Fred Patek .... .05 .02 .00
☐ 284 Bruce Kison .... .05 .02 .00
☐ 285 Dave LaRoche .... .05 .02 .00
☐ 286 Don Aase .... .05 .02 .00
☐ 287 Jim Barr .... .05 .02 .00
☐ 288 Alfredo Martinez .... .05 .02 .00
☐ 289 Larry Harlow .... .05 .02 .00
☐ 290 Andy Hassler .... .05 .02 .00
☐ 291 Dave Kingman .... .15 .06 .01
☐ 292 Bill Buckner .... .10 .04 .01
☐ 293 Rick Reuschel .... .15 .06 .01
☐ 294 Bruce Sutter .... .20 .08 .02
☐ 295 Jerry Martin .... .05 .02 .00
☐ 296 Scot Thompson .... .05 .02 .00
☐ 297 Ivan DeJesus .... .05 .02 .00
☐ 298 Steve Dillard .... .05 .02 .00
☐ 299 Dick Tidrow .... .05 .02 .00
☐ 300 Randy Martz .... .05 .02 .00
☐ 301 Lenny Randle .... .05 .02 .00
☐ 302 Lynn McGlothen .... .05 .02 .00
☐ 303 Cliff Johnson .... .05 .02 .00
☐ 304 Tim Blackwell .... .05 .02 .00
☐ 305 Dennis Lamp .... .05 .02 .00
☐ 306 Bill Caudill .... .05 .02 .00
☐ 307 Carlos Lezcano .... .05 .02 .00
☐ 308 Jim Tracy .... .05 .02 .00
☐ 309 Doug Capilla UER .... .05 .02 .00
(Cubs on front but
Braves on back)
☐ 310 Willie Hernandez .... .10 .04 .01
☐ 311 Mike Vail .... .05 .02 .00
☐ 312 Mike Krukow .... .05 .02 .00
☐ 313 Barry Foote .... .05 .02 .00
☐ 314 Larry Biittner .... .05 .02 .00
☐ 315 Mike Tyson .... .05 .02 .00
☐ 316 Lee Mazzilli .... .05 .02 .00
☐ 317 John Stearns .... .05 .02 .00
☐ 318 Alex Trevino .... .05 .02 .00
☐ 319 Craig Swan .... .05 .02 .00
☐ 320 Frank Taveras .... .05 .02 .00
☐ 321 Steve Henderson .... .05 .02 .00
☐ 322 Neil Allen .... .05 .02 .00
☐ 323 Mark Bomback .... .05 .02 .00

Card			
☐ 324 Mike Jorgensen	.05	.02	.00
☐ 325 Joe Torre MG	.10	.04	.01
☐ 326 Elliott Maddox	.05	.02	.00
☐ 327 Pete Falcone	.05	.02	.00
☐ 328 Ray Burris	.05	.02	.00
☐ 329 Claudell Washington	.05	.02	.00
☐ 330 Doug Flynn	.05	.02	.00
☐ 331 Joel Youngblood	.05	.02	.00
☐ 332 Bill Almon	.05	.02	.00
☐ 333 Tom Hausman	.05	.02	.00
☐ 334 Pat Zachry	.05	.02	.00
☐ 335 Jeff Reardon	3.50	1.50	.35
☐ 336 Wally Backman	.30	.12	.03
☐ 337 Dan Norman	.05	.02	.00
☐ 338 Jerry Morales	.05	.02	.00
☐ 339 Ed Farmer	.05	.02	.00
☐ 340 Bob Molinaro	.05	.02	.00
☐ 341 Todd Cruz	.05	.02	.00
☐ 342A Britt Burns P1 (Small hand on front)	.50	.20	.05
☐ 342B Britt Burns P2 (No hand)	.15	.06	.01
☐ 343 Kevin Bell	.05	.02	.00
☐ 344 Tony LaRussa MG	.10	.04	.01
☐ 345 Steve Trout	.05	.02	.00
☐ 346 Harold Baines	3.00	1.25	.30
☐ 347 Richard Wortham	.05	.02	.00
☐ 348 Wayne Nordhagen	.05	.02	.00
☐ 349 Mike Squires	.05	.02	.00
☐ 350 Lamar Johnson	.05	.02	.00
☐ 351 Rickey Henderson (Most Stolen Bases AL)	10.00	4.50	1.25
☐ 352 Francisco Barrios	.05	.02	.00
☐ 353 Thad Bosley	.05	.02	.00
☐ 354 Chet Lemon	.05	.02	.00
☐ 355 Bruce Kimm	.05	.02	.00
☐ 356 Richard Dotson	.15	.06	.01
☐ 357 Jim Morrison	.05	.02	.00
☐ 358 Mike Proly	.05	.02	.00
☐ 359 Greg Pryor	.05	.02	.00
☐ 360 Dave Parker	.60	.25	.06
☐ 361 Omar Moreno	.05	.02	.00
☐ 362A Kent Tekulve P1 (Back "1071 Waterbury" and "1078 Pirates")	.15	.06	.01
☐ 362B Kent Tekulve P2 ("1971 Waterbury" and "1978 Pirates")	.10	.04	.01
☐ 363 Willie Stargell	.60	.25	.06
☐ 364 Phil Garner	.10	.04	.01
☐ 365 Ed Ott	.05	.02	.00
☐ 366 Don Robinson	.05	.02	.00
☐ 367 Chuck Tanner MG	.05	.02	.00
☐ 368 Jim Rooker	.05	.02	.00
☐ 369 Dale Berra	.05	.02	.00
☐ 370 Jim Bibby	.05	.02	.00
☐ 371 Steve Nicosia	.05	.02	.00
☐ 372 Mike Easler	.05	.02	.00

Card			
☐ 373 Bill Robinson	.10	.04	.01
☐ 374 Lee Lacy	.05	.02	.00
☐ 375 John Candelaria	.10	.04	.01
☐ 376 Manny Sanguillen	.10	.04	.01
☐ 377 Rick Rhoden	.05	.02	.00
☐ 378 Grant Jackson	.05	.02	.00
☐ 379 Tim Foli	.05	.02	.00
☐ 380 Rod Scurry	.05	.02	.00
☐ 381 Bill Madlock	.10	.04	.01
☐ 382A Kurt Bevacqua P1 ERR (P on cap backwards)	.20	.08	.02
☐ 382B Kurt Bevacqua P2 COR	.10	.04	.01
☐ 383 Bert Blyleven	.25	.10	.02
☐ 384 Eddie Solomon	.05	.02	.00
☐ 385 Enrique Romo	.05	.02	.00
☐ 386 John Milner	.05	.02	.00
☐ 387 Mike Hargrove	.10	.04	.01
☐ 388 Jorge Orta	.05	.02	.00
☐ 389 Toby Harrah	.05	.02	.00
☐ 390 Tom Veryzer	.05	.02	.00
☐ 391 Miguel Dilone	.05	.02	.00
☐ 392 Dan Spillner	.05	.02	.00
☐ 393 Jack Brohamer	.05	.02	.00
☐ 394 Wayne Garland	.05	.02	.00
☐ 395 Sid Monge	.05	.02	.00
☐ 396 Rick Waits	.05	.02	.00
☐ 397 Joe Charboneau	.10	.04	.01
☐ 398 Gary Alexander	.05	.02	.00
☐ 399 Jerry Dybzinski	.05	.02	.00
☐ 400 Mike Stanton	.05	.02	.00
☐ 401 Mike Paxton	.05	.02	.00
☐ 402 Gary Gray	.05	.02	.00
☐ 403 Rick Manning	.05	.02	.00
☐ 404 Bo Diaz	.05	.02	.00
☐ 405 Ron Hassey	.10	.04	.01
☐ 406 Ross Grimsley	.05	.02	.00
☐ 407 Victor Cruz	.05	.02	.00
☐ 408 Len Barker	.05	.02	.00
☐ 409 Bob Bailor	.05	.02	.00
☐ 410 Otto Velez	.05	.02	.00
☐ 411 Ernie Whitt	.05	.02	.00
☐ 412 Jim Clancy	.05	.02	.00
☐ 413 Barry Bonnell	.05	.02	.00
☐ 414 Dave Stieb	.60	.25	.06
☐ 415 Damaso Garcia	.10	.04	.01
☐ 416 John Mayberry	.10	.04	.01
☐ 417 Roy Howell	.05	.02	.00
☐ 418 Danny Ainge	1.00	.40	.10
☐ 419A Jesse Jefferson P1 Back says Pirates	.10	.04	.01
☐ 419B Jesse Jefferson P2 Back says Pirates	.10	.04	.01
☐ 419C Jesse Jefferson P3 Back says Blue Jays	.25	.10	.02
☐ 420 Joey McLaughlin	.05	.02	.00
☐ 421 Lloyd Moseby	.35	.15	.03

☐ 422 Alvis Woods .05 .02 .00
☐ 423 Garth Iorg .05 .02 .00
☐ 424 Doug Ault .05 .02 .00
☐ 425 Ken Schrom .05 .02 .00
☐ 426 Mike Willis .05 .02 .00
☐ 427 Steve Braun .05 .02 .00
☐ 428 Bob Davis .05 .02 .00
☐ 429 Jerry Garvin .05 .02 .00
☐ 430 Alfredo Griffin .10 .04 .01
☐ 431 Bob Mattick MG .05 .02 .00
☐ 432 Vida Blue .10 .04 .01
☐ 433 Jack Clark .25 .10 .02
☐ 434 Willie McCovey .75 .30 .07
☐ 435 Mike Ivie .05 .02 .00
☐ 436A Darrel Evans P1 ERR .40 .16 .04
(Name on front "Darrel")
☐ 436B Darrell Evans P2 COR .15 .06 .01
(Name on front "Darrell")
☐ 437 Terry Whitfield .05 .02 .00
☐ 438 Rennie Stennett .05 .02 .00
☐ 439 John Montefusco .05 .02 .00
☐ 440 Jim Wohlford .05 .02 .00
☐ 441 Bill North .05 .02 .00
☐ 442 Milt May .05 .02 .00
☐ 443 Max Venable .05 .02 .00
☐ 444 Ed Whitson .05 .02 .00
☐ 445 Al Holland .05 .02 .00
☐ 446 Randy Moffitt .05 .02 .00
☐ 447 Bob Knepper .05 .02 .00
☐ 448 Gary Lavelle .05 .02 .00
☐ 449 Greg Minton .05 .02 .00
☐ 450 Johnnie LeMaster .05 .02 .00
☐ 451 Larry Herndon .05 .02 .00
☐ 452 Rich Murray .05 .02 .00
☐ 453 Joe Pettini .05 .02 .00
☐ 454 Allen Ripley .05 .02 .00
☐ 455 Dennis Littlejohn .05 .02 .00
☐ 456 Tom Griffin .05 .02 .00
☐ 457 Alan Hargesheimer .05 .02 .00
☐ 458 Joe Strain .05 .02 .00
☐ 459 Steve Kemp .05 .02 .00
☐ 460 Sparky Anderson MG .10 .04 .01
☐ 461 Alan Trammell 1.00 .40 .10
☐ 462 Mark Fidrych .10 .04 .01
☐ 463 Lou Whitaker .60 .25 .06
☐ 464 Dave Rozema .05 .02 .00
☐ 465 Milt Wilcox .05 .02 .00
☐ 466 Champ Summers .05 .02 .00
☐ 467 Lance Parrish .40 .16 .04
☐ 468 Dan Petry .10 .04 .01
☐ 469 Pat Underwood .05 .02 .00
☐ 470 Rick Peters .05 .02 .00
☐ 471 Al Cowens .05 .02 .00
☐ 472 John Wockenfuss .05 .02 .00
☐ 473 Tom Brookens .05 .02 .00
☐ 474 Richie Hebner .05 .02 .00
☐ 475 Jack Morris 1.00 .40 .10
☐ 476 Jim Lentine .05 .02 .00
☐ 477 Bruce Robbins .05 .02 .00
☐ 478 Mark Wagner .05 .02 .00
☐ 479 Tim Corcoran .05 .02 .00
☐ 480A Stan Papi P1 .15 .06 .01
(Front as Pitcher)
☐ 480B Stan Papi P2 .10 .04 .01
(Front as Shortstop)
☐ 481 Kirk Gibson 3.50 1.50 .35
☐ 482 Dan Schatzeder .05 .02 .00
☐ 483A Amos Otis P1 .10 .04 .01
(See card 32)
☐ 483B Amos Otis P2 .10 .04 .01
(See card 32)
☐ 484 Dave Winfield 1.25 .50 .12
☐ 485 Rollie Fingers .75 .30 .07
☐ 486 Gene Richards .05 .02 .00
☐ 487 Randy Jones .05 .02 .00
☐ 488 Ozzie Smith 2.50 1.00 .25
☐ 489 Gene Tenace .10 .04 .01
☐ 490 Bill Fahey .05 .02 .00
☐ 491 John Curtis .05 .02 .00
☐ 492 Dave Cash .05 .02 .00
☐ 493A Tim Flannery P1 .15 .06 .01
Batting right
☐ 493B Tim Flannery P2 .10 .04 .01
Batting left
☐ 494 Jerry Mumphrey .05 .02 .00
☐ 495 Bob Shirley .05 .02 .00
☐ 496 Steve Mura .05 .02 .00
☐ 497 Eric Rasmussen .05 .02 .00
☐ 498 Broderick Perkins .05 .02 .00
☐ 499 Barry Evans .05 .02 .00
☐ 500 Chuck Baker .05 .02 .00
☐ 501 Luis Salazar .15 .06 .01
☐ 502 Gary Lucas .05 .02 .00
☐ 503 Mike Armstrong .05 .02 .00
☐ 504 Jerry Turner .05 .02 .00
☐ 505 Dennis Kinney .05 .02 .00
☐ 506 Willie Montanez .05 .02 .00
☐ 507 Gorman Thomas .10 .04 .01
☐ 508 Ben Oglivie .05 .02 .00
☐ 509 Larry Hisle .05 .02 .00
☐ 510 Sal Bando .10 .04 .01
☐ 511 Robin Yount 2.50 1.00 .25
☐ 512 Mike Caldwell .05 .02 .00
☐ 513 Sixto Lezcano .05 .02 .00
☐ 514A Bill Travers P1 ERR .20 .08 .02
"Jerry Augustine" with Augustine back
☐ 514B Bill Travers P2 COR .10 .04 .01
☐ 515 Paul Molitor .60 .25 .06
☐ 516 Moose Haas .05 .02 .00
☐ 517 Bill Castro .05 .02 .00
☐ 518 Jim Slaton .05 .02 .00
☐ 519 Lary Sorensen .05 .02 .00
☐ 520 Bob McClure .05 .02 .00

☐ 521 Charlie Moore .... .05 .02 .00
☐ 522 Jim Gantner .... .05 .02 .00
☐ 523 Reggie Cleveland .... .05 .02 .00
☐ 524 Don Money .... .05 .02 .00
☐ 525 Bill Travers .... .05 .02 .00
☐ 526 Buck Martinez .... .05 .02 .00
☐ 527 Dick Davis .... .05 .02 .00
☐ 528 Ted Simmons .... .20 .08 .02
☐ 529 Garry Templeton .... .10 .04 .01
☐ 530 Ken Reitz .... .05 .02 .00
☐ 531 Tony Scott .... .05 .02 .00
☐ 532 Ken Oberkfell .... .05 .02 .00
☐ 533 Bob Sykes .... .05 .02 .00
☐ 534 Keith Smith .... .05 .02 .00
☐ 535 John Littlefield .... .05 .02 .00
☐ 536 Jim Kaat .... .20 .08 .02
☐ 537 Bob Forsch .... .05 .02 .00
☐ 538 Mike Phillips .... .05 .02 .00
☐ 539 Terry Landrum .... .05 .02 .00
☐ 540 Leon Durham .... .15 .06 .01
☐ 541 Terry Kennedy .... .10 .04 .01
☐ 542 George Hendrick .... .05 .02 .00
☐ 543 Dane Iorg .... .05 .02 .00
☐ 544 Mark Littell .... .05 .02 .00
☐ 545 Keith Hernandez .... .35 .15 .03
☐ 546 Silvio Martinez .... .05 .02 .00
☐ 547A Don Hood P1 ERR .... .20 .08 .02
("Pete Vuckovich"
with Vuckovich back)
☐ 547B Don Hood P2 COR .... .10 .04 .01
☐ 548 Bobby Bonds .... .15 .06 .01
☐ 549 Mike Ramsey .... .05 .02 .00
☐ 550 Tom Herr .... .15 .06 .01
☐ 551 Roy Smalley .... .05 .02 .00
☐ 552 Jerry Koosman .... .10 .04 .01
☐ 553 Ken Landreaux .... .05 .02 .00
☐ 554 John Castino .... .05 .02 .00
☐ 555 Doug Corbett .... .05 .02 .00
☐ 556 Bombo Rivera .... .05 .02 .00
☐ 557 Ron Jackson .... .05 .02 .00
☐ 558 Butch Wynegar .... .05 .02 .00
☐ 559 Hosken Powell .... .05 .02 .00
☐ 560 Pete Redfern .... .05 .02 .00
☐ 561 Roger Erickson .... .05 .02 .00
☐ 562 Glenn Adams .... .05 .02 .00
☐ 563 Rick Sofield .... .05 .02 .00
☐ 564 Geoff Zahn .... .05 .02 .00
☐ 565 Pete Mackanin .... .05 .02 .00
☐ 566 Mike Cubbage .... .05 .02 .00
☐ 567 Darrell Jackson .... .05 .02 .00
☐ 568 Dave Edwards .... .05 .02 .00
☐ 569 Rob Wilfong .... .05 .02 .00
☐ 570 Sal Butera .... .05 .02 .00
☐ 571 Jose Morales .... .05 .02 .00
☐ 572 Rick Langford .... .05 .02 .00
☐ 573 Mike Norris .... .05 .02 .00
☐ 574 Rickey Henderson 15.00 6.50 2.15
☐ 575 Tony Armas .... .05 .02 .00
☐ 576 Dave Revering .... .05 .02 .00
☐ 577 Jeff Newman .... .05 .02 .00
☐ 578 Bob Lacey .... .05 .02 .00
☐ 579 Brian Kingman .... .05 .02 .00
☐ 580 Mitchell Page .... .05 .02 .00
☐ 581 Billy Martin MG .... .20 .08 .02
☐ 582 Rob Picciolo .... .05 .02 .00
☐ 583 Mike Heath .... .05 .02 .00
☐ 584 Mickey Klutts .... .05 .02 .00
☐ 585 Orlando Gonzalez .... .05 .02 .00
☐ 586 Mike Davis .... .15 .06 .01
☐ 587 Wayne Gross .... .05 .02 .00
☐ 588 Matt Keough .... .05 .02 .00
☐ 589 Steve McCatty .... .05 .02 .00
☐ 590 Dwayne Murphy .... .05 .02 .00
☐ 591 Mario Guerrero .... .05 .02 .00
☐ 592 Dave McKay .... .05 .02 .00
☐ 593 Jim Essian .... .10 .04 .01
☐ 594 Dave Heaverlo .... .05 .02 .00
☐ 595 Maury Wills MG .... .10 .04 .01
☐ 596 Juan Beniquez .... .05 .02 .00
☐ 597 Rodney Craig .... .05 .02 .00
☐ 598 Jim Anderson .... .05 .02 .00
☐ 599 Floyd Bannister .... .05 .02 .00
☐ 600 Bruce Bochte .... .05 .02 .00
☐ 601 Julio Cruz .... .05 .02 .00
☐ 602 Ted Cox .... .05 .02 .00
☐ 603 Dan Meyer .... .05 .02 .00
☐ 604 Larry Cox .... .05 .02 .00
☐ 605 Bill Stein .... .05 .02 .00
☐ 606 Steve Garvey .... .75 .30 .07
☐ 607 Dave Roberts .... .05 .02 .00
☐ 608 Leon Roberts .... .05 .02 .00
☐ 609 Reggie Walton .... .05 .02 .00
☐ 610 Dave Edler .... .05 .02 .00
☐ 611 Larry Milbourne .... .05 .02 .00
☐ 612 Kim Allen .... .05 .02 .00
☐ 613 Mario Mendoza .... .05 .02 .00
☐ 614 Tom Paciorek .... .05 .02 .00
☐ 615 Glenn Abbott .... .05 .02 .00
☐ 616 Joe Simpson .... .05 .02 .00
☐ 617 Mickey Rivers .... .10 .04 .01
☐ 618 Jim Kern .... .05 .02 .00
☐ 619 Jim Sundberg .... .05 .02 .00
☐ 620 Richie Zisk .... .05 .02 .00
☐ 621 Jon Matlack .... .05 .02 .00
☐ 622 Ferguson Jenkins .... .50 .20 .05
☐ 623 Pat Corrales MG .... .05 .02 .00
☐ 624 Ed Figueroa .... .05 .02 .00
☐ 625 Buddy Bell .... .10 .04 .01
☐ 626 Al Oliver .... .10 .04 .01
☐ 627 Doc Medich .... .05 .02 .00
☐ 628 Bump Wills .... .05 .02 .00
☐ 629 Rusty Staub .... .15 .06 .01
☐ 630 Pat Putnam .... .05 .02 .00
☐ 631 John Grubb .... .05 .02 .00
☐ 632 Danny Darwin .... .10 .04 .01
☐ 633 Ken Clay .... .05 .02 .00

☐ 634 Jim Norris .05	.02	.00
☐ 635 John Butcher .05	.02	.00
☐ 636 Dave Roberts .05	.02	.00
☐ 637 Billy Sample .05	.02	.00
☐ 638 Carl Yastrzemski 1.50	.60	.15
☐ 639 Cecil Cooper .15	.06	.01
☐ 640A Mike Schmidt P1 2.00	.80	.20
(Portrait) "Third Base" (number on back 5)		
☐ 640B Mike Schmidt P2 2.00	.80	.20
"1980 Home Run King" (640 on back)		
☐ 641A CL: Phils/Royals P1 .15	.02	.00
41 is Hal McRae		
☐ 641B CL: Phils/Royals P2 .15	.02	.00
41 is Hal McRae, Double Threat		
☐ 642 CL: Astros/Yankees .15	.02	.00
☐ 643 CL: Expos/Dodgers .15	.02	.00
☐ 644A CL: Reds/Orioles P1 .15	.02	.00
202 is George Foster		
☐ 644B CL: Reds/Orioles P2 .15	.02	.00
202 is Foster Slugger		
☐ 645A Rose/Bowa/Schmidt 2.00	.80	.20
Triple Threat P1 (No number on back)		
☐ 645B Rose/Bowa/Schmidt 1.25	.50	.12
Triple Threat P2 (Back numbered 645)		
☐ 646 CL: Braves/Red Sox .15	.02	.00
☐ 647 CL: Cubs/Angels .15	.02	.00
☐ 648 CL: Mets/White Sox .15	.02	.00
☐ 649 CL: Indians/Pirates .15	.02	.00
☐ 650A Reggie Jackson 2.00	.80	.20
Mr. Baseball P1 Number on back 79		
☐ 650B Reggie Jackson 2.00	.80	.20
Mr. Baseball P2 Number on back 650		
☐ 651 CL: Giants/Blue Jays .15	.02	.00
☐ 652A CL: Tigers/Padres P1 .15	.02	.00
483 is listed		
☐ 652B CL: Tigers/Padres P2 .15	.02	.00
483 is deleted		
☐ 653A Willie Wilson P1 .20	.08	.02
Most Hits Most Runs Number on back 29		
☐ 653B Willie Wilson P2 .20	.08	.02
Most Hits Most Runs Number on back 653		
☐ 654A CL:Brewers/Cards P1 .15	.02	.00
514 Jerry Augustine 547 Pete Vuckovich		
☐ 654B CL:Brewers/Cards P2 .15	.02	.00
514 Billy Travers 547 Don Hood		
☐ 655A George Brett P1 1.75	.70	.17
.390 Average Number on back 28		
☐ 655B George Brett P2 1.75	.70	.17
.390 Average Number on back 655		
☐ 656 CL: Twins/Oakland A's .15	.02	.00
☐ 657A Tug McGraw P1 .15	.06	.01
Game Saver Number on back 7		
☐ 657B Tug McGraw P2 .15	.06	.01
Game Saver Number on back 657		
☐ 658 CL: Rangers/Mariners .15	.02	.00
☐ 659A Checklist P1 .15	.02	.00
of Special Cards Last lines on front Wilson Most Hits		
☐ 659B Checklist P2 .15	.02	.00
of Special Cards Last lines on front Otis Series Starter		
☐ 660A Steve Carlton P1 1.25	.50	.12
Golden Arm Back "1066 Cardinals" Number on back 6		
☐ 660B Steve Carlton P2 1.25	.50	.12
Golden Arm Number on back 660 Back "1066 Cardinals"		
☐ 660C Steve Carlton P3 2.00	.80	.20
Golden Arm "1966 Cardinals"		

1982 Fleer

The cards in this 660-card set measure 2 1/2" by 3 1/2". The 1982 Fleer set is again ordered by teams; in fact, the players within each team are listed in alphabetical order. The teams are ordered (by 1981 standings) as follows: Los Angeles (1-29), New York Yankees (30-56), Cincinnati (57-84), Oakland (85-109), St. Louis (110-132), Milwaukee (133-156), Baltimore (157-182), Montreal (183-211), Houston (212-237), Philadelphia (238-262), Detroit (263-286), Boston (287-312), Texas (313-334), Chicago White Sox (335-358), Cleveland (359-382), San Francisco (383-403), Kansas City (404-427), Atlanta (428-449), California (450-474), Pittsburgh (475-501), Seattle (502-519), New

York Mets (520-544), Minnesota (545-565), San Diego (566-585), Chicago Cubs (586-607), and Toronto (608-627). Cards numbered 628 through 646 are special cards highlighting some of the stars and leaders of the 1981 season. The last 14 cards in the set (647-660) are checklist cards. The backs feature player statistics and a full-color team logo in the upper right-hand corner of each card. The complete set price below does not include any of the more valuable variation cards listed. The key rookie cards in this set are George Bell, Cal Ripken Jr., Steve Sax, Lee Smith, and Dave Stewart.

	MINT	EXC	G-VG
COMPLETE SET (660)	80.00	36.00	12.00
COMMON PLAYER (1-660)	.05	.02	.00
☐ 1 Dusty Baker	.15	.05	.01
☐ 2 Robert Castillo	.05	.02	.00
☐ 3 Ron Cey	.10	.04	.01
☐ 4 Terry Forster	.10	.04	.01
☐ 5 Steve Garvey	.60	.25	.06
☐ 6 Dave Goltz	.05	.02	.00
☐ 7 Pedro Guerrero	.40	.16	.04
☐ 8 Burt Hooton	.05	.02	.00
☐ 9 Steve Howe	.05	.02	.00
☐ 10 Jay Johnstone	.10	.04	.01
☐ 11 Ken Landreaux	.05	.02	.00
☐ 12 Dave Lopes	.10	.04	.01
☐ 13 Mike Marshall (outfielder)	.35	.15	.03
☐ 14 Bobby Mitchell	.05	.02	.00
☐ 15 Rick Monday	.05	.02	.00
☐ 16 Tom Niedenfuer	.15	.06	.01
☐ 17 Ted Power	.15	.06	.01
☐ 18 Jerry Reuss	.05	.02	.00
☐ 19 Ron Roenicke	.05	.02	.00
☐ 20 Bill Russell	.10	.04	.01
☐ 21 Steve Sax	3.50	1.50	.35
☐ 22 Mike Scioscia	.35	.15	.03
☐ 23 Reggie Smith	.10	.04	.01
☐ 24 Dave Stewart	5.50	2.50	.55
☐ 25 Rick Sutcliffe	.15	.06	.01
☐ 26 Derrel Thomas	.05	.02	.00
☐ 27 Fernando Valenzuela	.40	.16	.04
☐ 28 Bob Welch	.35	.15	.03
☐ 29 Steve Yeager	.05	.02	.00
☐ 30 Bobby Brown	.05	.02	.00
☐ 31 Rick Cerone	.05	.02	.00
☐ 32 Ron Davis	.05	.02	.00
☐ 33 Bucky Dent	.10	.04	.01
☐ 34 Barry Foote	.05	.02	.00
☐ 35 George Frazier	.05	.02	.00
☐ 36 Oscar Gamble	.05	.02	.00
☐ 37 Rich Gossage	.20	.08	.02
☐ 38 Ron Guidry	.25	.10	.02
☐ 39 Reggie Jackson	1.75	.70	.17
☐ 40 Tommy John	.20	.08	.02
☐ 41 Rudy May	.05	.02	.00
☐ 42 Larry Milbourne	.05	.02	.00
☐ 43 Jerry Mumphrey	.05	.02	.00
☐ 44 Bobby Murcer	.10	.04	.01
☐ 45 Gene Nelson	.10	.04	.01
☐ 46 Graig Nettles	.15	.06	.01
☐ 47 Johnny Oates	.10	.04	.01
☐ 48 Lou Piniella	.10	.04	.01
☐ 49 Willie Randolph	.15	.06	.01
☐ 50 Rick Reuschel	.10	.04	.01
☐ 51 Dave Revering	.05	.02	.00
☐ 52 Dave Righetti	1.25	.50	.12
☐ 53 Aurelio Rodriguez	.05	.02	.00
☐ 54 Bob Watson	.05	.02	.00
☐ 55 Dennis Werth	.05	.02	.00
☐ 56 Dave Winfield	1.00	.40	.10
☐ 57 Johnny Bench	1.25	.50	.12
☐ 58 Bruce Berenyi	.05	.02	.00
☐ 59 Larry Biittner	.05	.02	.00
☐ 60 Scott Brown	.05	.02	.00
☐ 61 Dave Collins	.05	.02	.00
☐ 62 Geoff Combe	.05	.02	.00
☐ 63 Dave Concepcion	.15	.06	.01
☐ 64 Dan Driessen	.05	.02	.00
☐ 65 Joe Edelen	.05	.02	.00
☐ 66 George Foster	.15	.06	.01
☐ 67 Ken Griffey	.25	.10	.02
☐ 68 Paul Householder	.05	.02	.00
☐ 69 Tom Hume	.05	.02	.00
☐ 70 Junior Kennedy	.05	.02	.00
☐ 71 Ray Knight	.10	.04	.01
☐ 72 Mike LaCoss	.05	.02	.00
☐ 73 Rafael Landestoy	.05	.02	.00
☐ 74 Charlie Leibrandt	.10	.04	.01
☐ 75 Sam Mejias	.05	.02	.00
☐ 76 Paul Moskau	.05	.02	.00
☐ 77 Joe Nolan	.05	.02	.00
☐ 78 Mike O'Berry	.05	.02	.00
☐ 79 Ron Oester	.05	.02	.00
☐ 80 Frank Pastore	.05	.02	.00

☐ 81 Joe Price .05 .02 .00
☐ 82 Tom Seaver 1.25 .50 .12
☐ 83 Mario Soto .05 .02 .00
☐ 84 Mike Vail .05 .02 .00
☐ 85 Tony Armas .05 .02 .00
☐ 86 Shooty Babitt .05 .02 .00
☐ 87 Dave Beard .05 .02 .00
☐ 88 Rick Bosetti .05 .02 .00
☐ 89 Keith Drumwright .05 .02 .00
☐ 90 Wayne Gross .05 .02 .00
☐ 91 Mike Heath .05 .02 .00
☐ 92 Rickey Henderson 6.00 2.50 .60
☐ 93 Cliff Johnson .05 .02 .00
☐ 94 Jeff Jones .05 .02 .00
☐ 95 Matt Keough .05 .02 .00
☐ 96 Brian Kingman .05 .02 .00
☐ 97 Mickey Klutts .05 .02 .00
☐ 98 Rick Langford .05 .02 .00
☐ 99 Steve McCatty .05 .02 .00
☐ 100 Dave McKay .05 .02 .00
☐ 101 Dwayne Murphy .05 .02 .00
☐ 102 Jeff Newman .05 .02 .00
☐ 103 Mike Norris .05 .02 .00
☐ 104 Bob Owchinko .05 .02 .00
☐ 105 Mitchell Page .05 .02 .00
☐ 106 Rob Picciolo .05 .02 .00
☐ 107 Jim Spencer .05 .02 .00
☐ 108 Fred Stanley .05 .02 .00
☐ 109 Tom Underwood .05 .02 .00
☐ 110 Joaquin Andujar .10 .04 .01
☐ 111 Steve Braun .05 .02 .00
☐ 112 Bob Forsch .05 .02 .00
☐ 113 George Hendrick .05 .02 .00
☐ 114 Keith Hernandez .25 .10 .02
☐ 115 Tom Herr .10 .04 .01
☐ 116 Dane Iorg .05 .02 .00
☐ 117 Jim Kaat .15 .06 .01
☐ 118 Tito Landrum .05 .02 .00
☐ 119 Sixto Lezcano .05 .02 .00
☐ 120 Mark Littell .05 .02 .00
☐ 121 John Martin .05 .02 .00
☐ 122 Silvio Martinez .05 .02 .00
☐ 123 Ken Oberkfell .05 .02 .00
☐ 124 Darrell Porter .05 .02 .00
☐ 125 Mike Ramsey .05 .02 .00
☐ 126 Orlando Sanchez .05 .02 .00
☐ 127 Bob Shirley .05 .02 .00
☐ 128 Lary Sorensen .05 .02 .00
☐ 129 Bruce Sutter .15 .06 .01
☐ 130 Bob Sykes .05 .02 .00
☐ 131 Garry Templeton .10 .04 .01
☐ 132 Gene Tenace .10 .04 .01
☐ 133 Jerry Augustine .05 .02 .00
☐ 134 Sal Bando .10 .04 .01
☐ 135 Mark Brouhard .05 .02 .00
☐ 136 Mike Caldwell .05 .02 .00
☐ 137 Reggie Cleveland .05 .02 .00
☐ 138 Cecil Cooper .15 .06 .01
☐ 139 Jamie Easterly .05 .02 .00
☐ 140 Marshall Edwards .05 .02 .00
☐ 141 Rollie Fingers .50 .20 .05
☐ 142 Jim Gantner .05 .02 .00
☐ 143 Moose Haas .05 .02 .00
☐ 144 Larry Hisle .05 .02 .00
☐ 145 Roy Howell .05 .02 .00
☐ 146 Rickey Keeton .05 .02 .00
☐ 147 Randy Lerch .05 .02 .00
☐ 148 Paul Molitor .50 .20 .05
☐ 149 Don Money .05 .02 .00
☐ 150 Charlie Moore .05 .02 .00
☐ 151 Ben Oglivie .05 .02 .00
☐ 152 Ted Simmons .15 .06 .01
☐ 153 Jim Slaton .05 .02 .00
☐ 154 Gorman Thomas .10 .04 .01
☐ 155 Robin Yount 2.00 .80 .20
☐ 156 Pete Vuckovich .05 .02 .00
☐ 157 Benny Ayala .05 .02 .00
☐ 158 Mark Belanger .10 .04 .01
☐ 159 Al Bumbry .05 .02 .00
☐ 160 Terry Crowley .05 .02 .00
☐ 161 Rich Dauer .05 .02 .00
☐ 162 Doug DeCinces .05 .02 .00
☐ 163 Rick Dempsey .05 .02 .00
☐ 164 Jim Dwyer .05 .02 .00
☐ 165 Mike Flanagan .10 .04 .01
☐ 166 Dave Ford .05 .02 .00
☐ 167 Dan Graham .05 .02 .00
☐ 168 Wayne Krenchicki .05 .02 .00
☐ 169 John Lowenstein .05 .02 .00
☐ 170 Dennis Martinez .15 .06 .01
☐ 171 Tippy Martinez .05 .02 .00
☐ 172 Scott McGregor .05 .02 .00
☐ 173 Jose Morales .05 .02 .00
☐ 174 Eddie Murray 1.50 .60 .15
☐ 175 Jim Palmer .90 .40 .09
☐ 176 Cal Ripken 48.00 20.00 5.00
☐ 177 Gary Roenicke .05 .02 .00
☐ 178 Lenn Sakata .05 .02 .00
☐ 179 Ken Singleton .10 .04 .01
☐ 180 Sammy Stewart .05 .02 .00
☐ 181 Tim Stoddard .05 .02 .00
☐ 182 Steve Stone .05 .02 .00
☐ 183 Stan Bahnsen .05 .02 .00
☐ 184 Ray Burris .05 .02 .00
☐ 185 Gary Carter .50 .20 .05
☐ 186 Warren Cromartie .05 .02 .00
☐ 187 Andre Dawson 1.25 .50 .12
☐ 188 Terry Francona .05 .02 .00
☐ 189 Woodie Fryman .05 .02 .00
☐ 190 Bill Gullickson .10 .04 .01
☐ 191 Grant Jackson .05 .02 .00
☐ 192 Wallace Johnson .05 .02 .00
☐ 193 Charlie Lea .05 .02 .00
☐ 194 Bill Lee .05 .02 .00
☐ 195 Jerry Manuel .05 .02 .00
☐ 196 Brad Mills .05 .02 .00

No.	Player			
☐ 197	John Milner	.05	.02	.00
☐ 198	Rowland Office	.05	.02	.00
☐ 199	David Palmer	.05	.02	.00
☐ 200	Larry Parrish	.05	.02	.00
☐ 201	Mike Phillips	.05	.02	.00
☐ 202	Tim Raines	2.00	.80	.20
☐ 203	Bobby Ramos	.05	.02	.00
☐ 204	Jeff Reardon	.75	.30	.07
☐ 205	Steve Rogers	.05	.02	.00
☐ 206	Scott Sanderson	.10	.04	.01
☐ 207	Rodney Scott UER (photo actually Tim Raines)	.20	.08	.02
☐ 208	Elias Sosa	.05	.02	.00
☐ 209	Chris Speier	.05	.02	.00
☐ 210	Tim Wallach	1.25	.50	.12
☐ 211	Jerry White	.05	.02	.00
☐ 212	Alan Ashby	.05	.02	.00
☐ 213	Cesar Cedeno	.10	.04	.01
☐ 214	Jose Cruz	.10	.04	.01
☐ 215	Kiko Garcia	.05	.02	.00
☐ 216	Phil Garner	.10	.04	.01
☐ 217	Danny Heep	.05	.02	.00
☐ 218	Art Howe	.10	.04	.01
☐ 219	Bob Knepper	.05	.02	.00
☐ 220	Frank LaCorte	.05	.02	.00
☐ 221	Joe Niekro	.10	.04	.01
☐ 222	Joe Pittman	.05	.02	.00
☐ 223	Terry Puhl	.05	.02	.00
☐ 224	Luis Pujols	.05	.02	.00
☐ 225	Craig Reynolds	.05	.02	.00
☐ 226	J.R. Richard	.10	.04	.01
☐ 227	Dave Roberts	.05	.02	.00
☐ 228	Vern Ruhle	.05	.02	.00
☐ 229	Nolan Ryan	5.75	2.50	.55
☐ 230	Joe Sambito	.05	.02	.00
☐ 231	Tony Scott	.05	.02	.00
☐ 232	Dave Smith	.10	.04	.01
☐ 233	Harry Spilman	.05	.02	.00
☐ 234	Don Sutton	.40	.16	.04
☐ 235	Dickie Thon	.10	.04	.01
☐ 236	Denny Walling	.05	.02	.00
☐ 237	Gary Woods	.05	.02	.00
☐ 238	Luis Aguayo	.05	.02	.00
☐ 239	Ramon Aviles	.05	.02	.00
☐ 240	Bob Boone	.10	.04	.01
☐ 241	Larry Bowa	.10	.04	.01
☐ 242	Warren Brusstar	.05	.02	.00
☐ 243	Steve Carlton	1.00	.40	.10
☐ 244	Larry Christenson	.05	.02	.00
☐ 245	Dick Davis	.05	.02	.00
☐ 246	Greg Gross	.05	.02	.00
☐ 247	Sparky Lyle	.10	.04	.01
☐ 248	Garry Maddox	.05	.02	.00
☐ 249	Gary Matthews	.05	.02	.00
☐ 250	Bake McBride	.05	.02	.00
☐ 251	Tug McGraw	.10	.04	.01
☐ 252	Keith Moreland	.05	.02	.00
☐ 253	Dickie Noles	.05	.02	.00
☐ 254	Mike Proly	.05	.02	.00
☐ 255	Ron Reed	.05	.02	.00
☐ 256	Pete Rose	1.50	.60	.15
☐ 257	Dick Ruthven	.05	.02	.00
☐ 258	Mike Schmidt	2.50	1.00	.25
☐ 259	Lonnie Smith	.25	.10	.02
☐ 260	Manny Trillo	.05	.02	.00
☐ 261	Del Unser	.05	.02	.00
☐ 262	George Vukovich	.05	.02	.00
☐ 263	Tom Brookens	.05	.02	.00
☐ 264	George Cappuzzello	.05	.02	.00
☐ 265	Marty Castillo	.05	.02	.00
☐ 266	Al Cowens	.05	.02	.00
☐ 267	Kirk Gibson	.75	.30	.07
☐ 268	Richie Hebner	.05	.02	.00
☐ 269	Ron Jackson	.05	.02	.00
☐ 270	Lynn Jones	.05	.02	.00
☐ 271	Steve Kemp	.05	.02	.00
☐ 272	Rick Leach	.05	.02	.00
☐ 273	Aurelio Lopez	.05	.02	.00
☐ 274	Jack Morris	.60	.25	.06
☐ 275	Kevin Saucier	.05	.02	.00
☐ 276	Lance Parrish	.30	.12	.03
☐ 277	Rick Peters	.05	.02	.00
☐ 278	Dan Petry	.05	.02	.00
☐ 279	Dave Rozema	.05	.02	.00
☐ 280	Stan Papi	.05	.02	.00
☐ 281	Dan Schatzeder	.05	.02	.00
☐ 282	Champ Summers	.05	.02	.00
☐ 283	Alan Trammell	.60	.25	.06
☐ 284	Lou Whitaker	.40	.16	.04
☐ 285	Milt Wilcox	.05	.02	.00
☐ 286	John Wockenfuss	.05	.02	.00
☐ 287	Gary Allenson	.05	.02	.00
☐ 288	Tom Burgmeier	.05	.02	.00
☐ 289	Bill Campbell	.05	.02	.00
☐ 290	Mark Clear	.05	.02	.00
☐ 291	Steve Crawford	.05	.02	.00
☐ 292	Dennis Eckersley	.50	.20	.05
☐ 293	Dwight Evans	.25	.10	.02
☐ 294	Rich Gedman	.20	.08	.02
☐ 295	Garry Hancock	.05	.02	.00
☐ 296	Glenn Hoffman	.05	.02	.00
☐ 297	Bruce Hurst	.60	.25	.06
☐ 298	Carney Lansford	.15	.06	.01
☐ 299	Rick Miller	.05	.02	.00
☐ 300	Reid Nichols	.05	.02	.00
☐ 301	Bob Ojeda	.50	.20	.05
☐ 302	Tony Perez	.30	.12	.03
☐ 303	Chuck Rainey	.05	.02	.00
☐ 304	Jerry Remy	.05	.02	.00
☐ 305	Jim Rice	.25	.10	.02
☐ 306	Joe Rudi	.10	.04	.01
☐ 307	Bob Stanley	.05	.02	.00
☐ 308	Dave Stapleton	.05	.02	.00
☐ 309	Frank Tanana	.10	.04	.01
☐ 310	Mike Torrez	.05	.02	.00

☐ 311 John Tudor	.15	.06	.01
☐ 312 Carl Yastrzemski	1.25	.50	.12
☐ 313 Buddy Bell	.10	.04	.01
☐ 314 Steve Comer	.05	.02	.00
☐ 315 Danny Darwin	.05	.02	.00
☐ 316 John Ellis	.05	.02	.00
☐ 317 John Grubb	.05	.02	.00
☐ 318 Rick Honeycutt	.05	.02	.00
☐ 319 Charlie Hough	.10	.04	.01
☐ 320 Ferguson Jenkins	.40	.16	.04
☐ 321 John Henry Johnson	.05	.02	.00
☐ 322 Jim Kern	.05	.02	.00
☐ 323 Jon Matlack	.05	.02	.00
☐ 324 Doc Medich	.05	.02	.00
☐ 325 Mario Mendoza	.05	.02	.00
☐ 326 Al Oliver	.10	.04	.01
☐ 327 Pat Putnam	.05	.02	.00
☐ 328 Mickey Rivers	.10	.04	.01
☐ 329 Leon Roberts	.05	.02	.00
☐ 330 Billy Sample	.05	.02	.00
☐ 331 Bill Stein	.05	.02	.00
☐ 332 Jim Sundberg	.05	.02	.00
☐ 333 Mark Wagner	.05	.02	.00
☐ 334 Bump Wills	.05	.02	.00
☐ 335 Bill Almon	.05	.02	.00
☐ 336 Harold Baines	.75	.30	.07
☐ 337 Ross Baumgarten	.05	.02	.00
☐ 338 Tony Bernazard	.05	.02	.00
☐ 339 Britt Burns	.05	.02	.00
☐ 340 Richard Dotson	.05	.02	.00
☐ 341 Jim Essian	.10	.04	.01
☐ 342 Ed Farmer	.05	.02	.00
☐ 343 Carlton Fisk	1.25	.50	.12
☐ 344 Kevin Hickey	.05	.02	.00
☐ 345 LaMarr Hoyt	.05	.02	.00
☐ 346 Lamar Johnson	.05	.02	.00
☐ 347 Jerry Koosman	.10	.04	.01
☐ 348 Rusty Kuntz	.05	.02	.00
☐ 349 Dennis Lamp	.05	.02	.00
☐ 350 Ron LeFlore	.05	.02	.00
☐ 351 Chet Lemon	.05	.02	.00
☐ 352 Greg Luzinski	.10	.04	.01
☐ 353 Bob Molinaro	.05	.02	.00
☐ 354 Jim Morrison	.05	.02	.00
☐ 355 Wayne Nordhagen	.05	.02	.00
☐ 356 Greg Pryor	.05	.02	.00
☐ 357 Mike Squires	.05	.02	.00
☐ 358 Steve Trout	.05	.02	.00
☐ 359 Alan Bannister	.05	.02	.00
☐ 360 Len Barker	.05	.02	.00
☐ 361 Bert Blyleven	.25	.10	.02
☐ 362 Joe Charboneau	.05	.02	.00
☐ 363 John Denny	.05	.02	.00
☐ 364 Bo Diaz	.05	.02	.00
☐ 365 Miguel Dilone	.05	.02	.00
☐ 366 Jerry Dybzinski	.05	.02	.00
☐ 367 Wayne Garland	.05	.02	.00
☐ 368 Mike Hargrove	.10	.04	.01
☐ 369 Toby Harrah	.05	.02	.00
☐ 370 Ron Hassey	.05	.02	.00
☐ 371 Von Hayes	.60	.25	.06
☐ 372 Pat Kelly	.05	.02	.00
☐ 373 Duane Kuiper	.05	.02	.00
☐ 374 Rick Manning	.05	.02	.00
☐ 375 Sid Monge	.05	.02	.00
☐ 376 Jorge Orta	.05	.02	.00
☐ 377 Dave Rosello	.05	.02	.00
☐ 378 Dan Spillner	.05	.02	.00
☐ 379 Mike Stanton	.05	.02	.00
☐ 380 Andre Thornton	.10	.04	.01
☐ 381 Tom Veryzer	.05	.02	.00
☐ 382 Rick Waits	.05	.02	.00
☐ 383 Doyle Alexander	.05	.02	.00
☐ 384 Vida Blue	.10	.04	.01
☐ 385 Fred Breining	.05	.02	.00
☐ 386 Enos Cabell	.05	.02	.00
☐ 387 Jack Clark	.25	.10	.02
☐ 388 Darrell Evans	.10	.04	.01
☐ 389 Tom Griffin	.05	.02	.00
☐ 390 Larry Herndon	.05	.02	.00
☐ 391 Al Holland	.05	.02	.00
☐ 392 Gary Lavelle	.05	.02	.00
☐ 393 Johnnie LeMaster	.05	.02	.00
☐ 394 Jerry Martin	.05	.02	.00
☐ 395 Milt May	.05	.02	.00
☐ 396 Greg Minton	.05	.02	.00
☐ 397 Joe Morgan	.60	.25	.06
☐ 398 Joe Pettini	.05	.02	.00
☐ 399 Allen Ripley	.05	.02	.00
☐ 400 Billy Smith	.05	.02	.00
☐ 401 Rennie Stennett	.05	.02	.00
☐ 402 Ed Whitson	.05	.02	.00
☐ 403 Jim Wohlford	.05	.02	.00
☐ 404 Willie Aikens	.05	.02	.00
☐ 405 George Brett	2.00	.80	.20
☐ 406 Ken Brett	.05	.02	.00
☐ 407 Dave Chalk	.05	.02	.00
☐ 408 Rich Gale	.05	.02	.00
☐ 409 Cesar Geronimo	.05	.02	.00
☐ 410 Larry Gura	.05	.02	.00
☐ 411 Clint Hurdle	.05	.02	.00
☐ 412 Mike Jones	.05	.02	.00
☐ 413 Dennis Leonard	.05	.02	.00
☐ 414 Renie Martin	.05	.02	.00
☐ 415 Lee May	.05	.02	.00
☐ 416 Hal McRae	.10	.04	.01
☐ 417 Darryl Motley	.05	.02	.00
☐ 418 Rance Mulliniks	.05	.02	.00
☐ 419 Amos Otis	.10	.04	.01
☐ 420 Ken Phelps	.15	.06	.01
☐ 421 Jamie Quirk	.05	.02	.00
☐ 422 Dan Quisenberry	.15	.06	.01
☐ 423 Paul Splittorff	.05	.02	.00
☐ 424 U.L. Washington	.05	.02	.00
☐ 425 John Wathan	.05	.02	.00
☐ 426 Frank White	.05	.02	.00

☐ 427 Willie Wilson .... .15 .06 .01
☐ 428 Brian Asselstine .... .05 .02 .00
☐ 429 Bruce Benedict .... .05 .02 .00
☐ 430 Tommy Boggs .... .05 .02 .00
☐ 431 Larry Bradford .... .05 .02 .00
☐ 432 Rick Camp .... .05 .02 .00
☐ 433 Chris Chambliss .... .10 .04 .01
☐ 434 Gene Garber .... .05 .02 .00
☐ 435 Preston Hanna .... .05 .02 .00
☐ 436 Bob Horner .... .10 .04 .01
☐ 437 Glenn Hubbard .... .05 .02 .00
☐ 438A All Hrabosky ERR 20.00 8.50 2.75
(height 5'1",
All on reverse)
☐ 438B Al Hrabosky ERR ...... 1.00 .40 .10
(height 5'1")
☐ 438C Al Hrabosky .... .10 .04 .01
(height 5'10")
☐ 439 Rufino Linares .... .05 .02 .00
☐ 440 Rick Mahler .... .15 .06 .01
☐ 441 Ed Miller .... .05 .02 .00
☐ 442 John Montefusco .... .05 .02 .00
☐ 443 Dale Murphy .... 1.00 .40 .10
☐ 444 Phil Niekro .... .40 .16 .04
☐ 445 Gaylord Perry .... .40 .16 .04
☐ 446 Biff Pocoroba .... .05 .02 .00
☐ 447 Rafael Ramirez .... .05 .02 .00
☐ 448 Jerry Royster .... .05 .02 .00
☐ 449 Claudell Washington ...... .05 .02 .00
☐ 450 Don Aase .... .05 .02 .00
☐ 451 Don Baylor .... .15 .06 .01
☐ 452 Juan Beniquez .... .05 .02 .00
☐ 453 Rick Burleson .... .05 .02 .00
☐ 454 Bert Campaneris .... .10 .04 .01
☐ 455 Rod Carew .... 1.25 .50 .12
☐ 456 Bob Clark .... .05 .02 .00
☐ 457 Brian Downing .... .10 .04 .01
☐ 458 Dan Ford .... .05 .02 .00
☐ 459 Ken Forsch .... .05 .02 .00
☐ 460A Dave Frost (5 mm .... .30 .12 .03
space before ERA)
☐ 460B Dave Frost .... .10 .04 .01
(1 mm space)
☐ 461 Bobby Grich .... .10 .04 .01
☐ 462 Larry Harlow .... .05 .02 .00
☐ 463 John Harris .... .05 .02 .00
☐ 464 Andy Hassler .... .05 .02 .00
☐ 465 Butch Hobson .... .10 .04 .01
☐ 466 Jesse Jefferson .... .05 .02 .00
☐ 467 Bruce Kison .... .05 .02 .00
☐ 468 Fred Lynn .... .20 .08 .02
☐ 469 Angel Moreno .... .05 .02 .00
☐ 470 Ed Ott .... .05 .02 .00
☐ 471 Fred Patek .... .05 .02 .00
☐ 472 Steve Renko .... .05 .02 .00
☐ 473 Mike Witt .... .25 .10 .02
☐ 474 Geoff Zahn .... .05 .02 .00
☐ 475 Gary Alexander .... .05 .02 .00
☐ 476 Dale Berra .... .05 .02 .00
☐ 477 Kurt Bevacqua .... .05 .02 .00
☐ 478 Jim Bibby .... .05 .02 .00
☐ 479 John Candelaria .... .05 .02 .00
☐ 480 Victor Cruz .... .05 .02 .00
☐ 481 Mike Easler .... .05 .02 .00
☐ 482 Tim Foli .... .05 .02 .00
☐ 483 Lee Lacy .... .05 .02 .00
☐ 484 Vance Law .... .10 .04 .01
☐ 485 Bill Madlock .... .10 .04 .01
☐ 486 Willie Montanez .... .05 .02 .00
☐ 487 Omar Moreno .... .05 .02 .00
☐ 488 Steve Nicosia .... .05 .02 .00
☐ 489 Dave Parker .... .50 .20 .05
☐ 490 Tony Pena .... .35 .15 .03
☐ 491 Pascual Perez .... .15 .06 .01
☐ 492 Johnny Ray .... .20 .08 .02
☐ 493 Rick Rhoden .... .05 .02 .00
☐ 494 Bill Robinson .... .10 .04 .01
☐ 495 Don Robinson .... .05 .02 .00
☐ 496 Enrique Romo .... .05 .02 .00
☐ 497 Rod Scurry .... .05 .02 .00
☐ 498 Eddie Solomon .... .05 .02 .00
☐ 499 Willie Stargell .... .50 .20 .05
☐ 500 Kent Tekulve .... .10 .04 .01
☐ 501 Jason Thompson .... .05 .02 .00
☐ 502 Glenn Abbott .... .05 .02 .00
☐ 503 Jim Anderson .... .05 .02 .00
☐ 504 Floyd Bannister .... .05 .02 .00
☐ 505 Bruce Bochte .... .05 .02 .00
☐ 506 Jeff Burroughs .... .05 .02 .00
☐ 507 Bryan Clark .... .05 .02 .00
☐ 508 Ken Clay .... .05 .02 .00
☐ 509 Julio Cruz .... .05 .02 .00
☐ 510 Dick Drago .... .05 .02 .00
☐ 511 Gary Gray .... .05 .02 .00
☐ 512 Dan Meyer .... .05 .02 .00
☐ 513 Jerry Narron .... .05 .02 .00
☐ 514 Tom Paciorek .... .05 .02 .00
☐ 515 Casey Parsons .... .05 .02 .00
☐ 516 Lenny Randle .... .05 .02 .00
☐ 517 Shane Rawley .... .05 .02 .00
☐ 518 Joe Simpson .... .05 .02 .00
☐ 519 Richie Zisk .... .05 .02 .00
☐ 520 Neil Allen .... .05 .02 .00
☐ 521 Bob Bailor .... .05 .02 .00
☐ 522 Hubie Brooks .... .60 .25 .06
☐ 523 Mike Cubbage .... .05 .02 .00
☐ 524 Pete Falcone .... .05 .02 .00
☐ 525 Doug Flynn .... .05 .02 .00
☐ 526 Tom Hausman .... .05 .02 .00
☐ 527 Ron Hodges .... .05 .02 .00
☐ 528 Randy Jones .... .05 .02 .00
☐ 529 Mike Jorgensen .... .05 .02 .00
☐ 530 Dave Kingman .... .15 .06 .01
☐ 531 Ed Lynch .... .05 .02 .00
☐ 532 Mike Marshall .... .10 .04 .01
(screwball pitcher)

Card	Player			
☐ 533	Lee Mazzilli	.05	.02	.00
☐ 534	Dyar Miller	.05	.02	.00
☐ 535	Mike Scott	.25	.10	.02
☐ 536	Rusty Staub	.15	.06	.01
☐ 537	John Stearns	.05	.02	.00
☐ 538	Craig Swan	.05	.02	.00
☐ 539	Frank Taveras	.05	.02	.00
☐ 540	Alex Trevino	.05	.02	.00
☐ 541	Ellis Valentine	.05	.02	.00
☐ 542	Mookie Wilson	.15	.06	.01
☐ 543	Joel Youngblood	.05	.02	.00
☐ 544	Pat Zachry	.05	.02	.00
☐ 545	Glenn Adams	.05	.02	.00
☐ 546	Fernando Arroyo	.05	.02	.00
☐ 547	John Verhoeven	.05	.02	.00
☐ 548	Sal Butera	.05	.02	.00
☐ 549	John Castino	.05	.02	.00
☐ 550	Don Cooper	.05	.02	.00
☐ 551	Doug Corbett	.05	.02	.00
☐ 552	Dave Engle	.05	.02	.00
☐ 553	Roger Erickson	.05	.02	.00
☐ 554	Danny Goodwin	.05	.02	.00
☐ 555A	Darrell Jackson (black cap)	1.00	.40	.10
☐ 555B	Darrell Jackson (red cap with T)	.10	.04	.01
☐ 555C	Darrell Jackson (red cap, no emblem)	5.00	2.25	.50
☐ 556	Pete Mackanin	.05	.02	.00
☐ 557	Jack O'Connor	.05	.02	.00
☐ 558	Hosken Powell	.05	.02	.00
☐ 559	Pete Redfern	.05	.02	.00
☐ 560	Roy Smalley	.05	.02	.00
☐ 561	Chuck Baker UER (shortshop on front)	.05	.02	.00
☐ 562	Gary Ward	.05	.02	.00
☐ 563	Rob Wilfong	.05	.02	.00
☐ 564	Al Williams	.05	.02	.00
☐ 565	Butch Wynegar	.05	.02	.00
☐ 566	Randy Bass	.05	.02	.00
☐ 567	Juan Bonilla	.05	.02	.00
☐ 568	Danny Boone	.05	.02	.00
☐ 569	John Curtis	.05	.02	.00
☐ 570	Juan Eichelberger	.05	.02	.00
☐ 571	Barry Evans	.05	.02	.00
☐ 572	Tim Flannery	.05	.02	.00
☐ 573	Ruppert Jones	.05	.02	.00
☐ 574	Terry Kennedy	.05	.02	.00
☐ 575	Joe Lefebvre	.05	.02	.00
☐ 576A	John Littlefield ERR (left handed)	200.00	90.00	30.00
☐ 576B	John Littlefield COR (right handed)	.10	.04	.01
☐ 577	Gary Lucas	.05	.02	.00
☐ 578	Steve Mura	.05	.02	.00
☐ 579	Broderick Perkins	.05	.02	.00
☐ 580	Gene Richards	.05	.02	.00
☐ 581	Luis Salazar	.05	.02	.00
☐ 582	Ozzie Smith	1.50	.60	.15
☐ 583	John Urrea	.05	.02	.00
☐ 584	Chris Welsh	.05	.02	.00
☐ 585	Rick Wise	.05	.02	.00
☐ 586	Doug Bird	.05	.02	.00
☐ 587	Tim Blackwell	.05	.02	.00
☐ 588	Bobby Bonds	.10	.04	.01
☐ 589	Bill Buckner	.10	.04	.01
☐ 590	Bill Caudill	.05	.02	.00
☐ 591	Hector Cruz	.05	.02	.00
☐ 592	Jody Davis	.15	.06	.01
☐ 593	Ivan DeJesus	.05	.02	.00
☐ 594	Steve Dillard	.05	.02	.00
☐ 595	Leon Durham	.05	.02	.00
☐ 596	Rawly Eastwick	.05	.02	.00
☐ 597	Steve Henderson	.05	.02	.00
☐ 598	Mike Krukow	.05	.02	.00
☐ 599	Mike Lum	.05	.02	.00
☐ 600	Randy Martz	.05	.02	.00
☐ 601	Jerry Morales	.05	.02	.00
☐ 602	Ken Reitz	.05	.02	.00
☐ 603A	Lee Smith ERR (Cubs logo reversed)	3.25	1.35	.32
☐ 603B	Lee Smith COR	3.00	1.25	.30
☐ 604	Dick Tidrow	.05	.02	.00
☐ 605	Jim Tracy	.05	.02	.00
☐ 606	Mike Tyson	.05	.02	.00
☐ 607	Ty Waller	.05	.02	.00
☐ 608	Danny Ainge	.35	.15	.03
☐ 609	Jorge Bell	8.00	3.50	.80
☐ 610	Mark Bomback	.05	.02	.00
☐ 611	Barry Bonnell	.05	.02	.00
☐ 612	Jim Clancy	.05	.02	.00
☐ 613	Damaso Garcia	.05	.02	.00
☐ 614	Jerry Garvin	.05	.02	.00
☐ 615	Alfredo Griffin	.05	.02	.00
☐ 616	Garth Iorg	.05	.02	.00
☐ 617	Luis Leal	.05	.02	.00
☐ 618	Ken Macha	.05	.02	.00
☐ 619	John Mayberry	.10	.04	.01
☐ 620	Joey McLaughlin	.05	.02	.00
☐ 621	Lloyd Moseby	.10	.04	.01
☐ 622	Dave Stieb	.35	.15	.03
☐ 623	Jackson Todd	.05	.02	.00
☐ 624	Willie Upshaw	.05	.02	.00
☐ 625	Otto Velez	.05	.02	.00
☐ 626	Ernie Whitt	.05	.02	.00
☐ 627	Alvis Woods	.05	.02	.00
☐ 628	All Star Game Cleveland, Ohio	.05	.02	.00
☐ 629	All Star Infielders Frank White and Bucky Dent	.10	.04	.01
☐ 630	Big Red Machine Dan Driessen Dave Concepcion George Foster	.10	.04	.01

☐ 631 Bruce Sutter Top NL Relief Pitcher	.10	.04	.01
☐ 632 "Steve and Carlton" Steve Carlton and Carlton Fisk	.60	.25	.06
☐ 633 Carl Yastrzemski 3000th Game	.60	.25	.06
☐ 634 Dynamic Duo Johnny Bench and Tom Seaver	.90	.40	.09
☐ 635 West Meets East Fernando Valenzuela and Gary Carter	.20	.08	.02
☐ 636A Fernando Valenzuela: NL SO King ("he" NL)	.35	.15	.03
☐ 636B Fernando Valenzuela: NL SO King ("the" NL)	.15	.06	.01
☐ 637 Mike Schmidt Home Run King	1.00	.40	.10
☐ 638 NL All Stars Gary Carter and Dave Parker	.25	.10	.02
☐ 639 Perfect Game UER Len Barker and Bo Diaz (catcher actually Ron Hassey)	.10	.04	.01
☐ 640 Pete and Re-Pete Pete Rose and Son	1.75	.70	.17
☐ 641 Phillies Finest Lonnie Smith Mike Schmidt Steve Carlton	.60	.25	.06
☐ 642 Red Sox Reunion Fred Lynn and Dwight Evans	.10	.04	.01
☐ 643 Rickey Henderson Most Hits and Runs	2.50	1.00	.25
☐ 644 Rollie Fingers Most Saves AL	.25	.10	.02
☐ 645 Tom Seaver Most 1981 Wins	.75	.30	.07
☐ 646A Yankee Powerhouse Reggie Jackson and Dave Winfield (comma on back after outfielder)	1.00	.40	.10
☐ 646B Yankee Powerhouse Reggie Jackson and Dave Winfield (no comma)	.90	.40	.09
☐ 647 CL: Yankees/Dodgers	.15	.02	.00
☐ 648 CL: A's/Reds	.15	.02	.00
☐ 649 CL: Cards/Brewers	.15	.02	.00
☐ 650 CL: Expos/Orioles	.15	.02	.00
☐ 651 CL: Astros/Phillies	.15	.02	.00
☐ 652 CL: Tigers/Red Sox	.15	.02	.00
☐ 653 CL: Rangers/White Sox	.15	.02	.00
☐ 654 CL: Giants/Indians	.15	.02	.00
☐ 655 CL: Royals/Braves	.15	.02	.00
☐ 656 CL: Angels/Pirates	.15	.02	.00
☐ 657 CL: Mariners/Mets	.15	.02	.00
☐ 658 CL: Padres/Twins	.15	.02	.00
☐ 659 CL: Blue Jays/Cubs	.15	.02	.00
☐ 660 Specials Checklist	.15	.02	.00

1983 Fleer

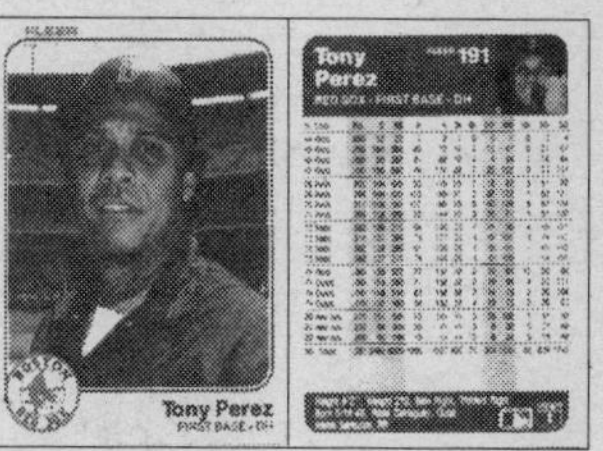

The cards in this 660-card set measure 2 1/2" by 3 1/2". In 1983, for the third straight year, Fleer has produced a baseball series numbering 660 cards. Of these, 1-628 are player cards, 629-646 are special cards, and 647-660 are checklist cards. The player cards are again ordered alphabetically within team. The team order relates back to each team's on-field performance during the previous year, i.e., World Champion Cardinals (1-25), AL Champion Brewers (26-51), Baltimore (52-75), California (76-103), Kansas City (104-128), Atlanta (129-152), Philadelphia (153-176), Boston (177-200), Los Angeles (201-227), Chicago White Sox (228-251), San Francisco (252-276), Montreal (277-301), Pittsburgh (302-326), Detroit (327-351), San Diego (352-375), New York Yankees (376-399), Cleveland (400-423), Toronto (424-444), Houston (445-469), Seattle (470-489), Chicago Cubs (490-512), Oakland (513-535), New York Mets (536-561), Texas (562-583), Cincinnati (584-606), and Minnesota (607-628). The front of each card has a colorful team logo at bottom left and the player's name and position at lower right. The reverses are done in shades of brown on white. The cards are numbered on the back next to a

small black and white photo of the player. The key rookie cards in this set are Wade Boggs, Tony Gwynn, Howard Johnson, Willie McGee, Ryne Sandberg, and Frank Viola.

	MINT	EXC	G-VG
COMPLETE SET (660)	120.00	55.00	18.00
COMMON PLAYER (1-660)	.05	.02	.00
☐ 1 Joaquin Andujar	.10	.04	.01
☐ 2 Doug Bair	.05	.02	.00
☐ 3 Steve Braun	.05	.02	.00
☐ 4 Glenn Brummer	.05	.02	.00
☐ 5 Bob Forsch	.05	.02	.00
☐ 6 David Green	.05	.02	.00
☐ 7 George Hendrick	.05	.02	.00
☐ 8 Keith Hernandez	.25	.10	.02
☐ 9 Tom Herr	.10	.04	.01
☐ 10 Dane Iorg	.05	.02	.00
☐ 11 Jim Kaat	.15	.06	.01
☐ 12 Jeff Lahti	.05	.02	.00
☐ 13 Tito Landrum	.05	.02	.00
☐ 14 Dave LaPoint	.10	.04	.01
☐ 15 Willie McGee	3.50	1.50	.35
☐ 16 Steve Mura	.05	.02	.00
☐ 17 Ken Oberkfell	.05	.02	.00
☐ 18 Darrell Porter	.05	.02	.00
☐ 19 Mike Ramsey	.05	.02	.00
☐ 20 Gene Roof	.05	.02	.00
☐ 21 Lonnie Smith	.15	.06	.01
☐ 22 Ozzie Smith	1.25	.50	.12
☐ 23 John Stuper	.05	.02	.00
☐ 24 Bruce Sutter	.15	.06	.01
☐ 25 Gene Tenace	.10	.04	.01
☐ 26 Jerry Augustine	.05	.02	.00
☐ 27 Dwight Bernard	.05	.02	.00
☐ 28 Mark Brouhard	.05	.02	.00
☐ 29 Mike Caldwell	.05	.02	.00
☐ 30 Cecil Cooper	.10	.04	.01
☐ 31 Jamie Easterly	.05	.02	.00
☐ 32 Marshall Edwards	.05	.02	.00
☐ 33 Rollie Fingers	.40	.16	.04
☐ 34 Jim Gantner	.05	.02	.00
☐ 35 Moose Haas	.05	.02	.00
☐ 36 Roy Howell	.05	.02	.00
☐ 37 Pete Ladd	.05	.02	.00
☐ 38 Bob McClure	.05	.02	.00
☐ 39 Doc Medich	.05	.02	.00
☐ 40 Paul Molitor	.40	.16	.04
☐ 41 Don Money	.05	.02	.00
☐ 42 Charlie Moore	.05	.02	.00
☐ 43 Ben Oglivie	.05	.02	.00
☐ 44 Ed Romero	.05	.02	.00
☐ 45 Ted Simmons	.10	.04	.01
☐ 46 Jim Slaton	.05	.02	.00
☐ 47 Don Sutton	.35	.15	.03
☐ 48 Gorman Thomas	.10	.04	.01
☐ 49 Pete Vuckovich	.05	.02	.00
☐ 50 Ned Yost	.05	.02	.00
☐ 51 Robin Yount	1.50	.60	.15
☐ 52 Benny Ayala	.05	.02	.00
☐ 53 Bob Bonner	.05	.02	.00
☐ 54 Al Bumbry	.05	.02	.00
☐ 55 Terry Crowley	.05	.02	.00
☐ 56 Storm Davis	.25	.10	.02
☐ 57 Rich Dauer	.05	.02	.00
☐ 58 Rick Dempsey UER (posing batting lefty)	.10	.04	.01
☐ 59 Jim Dwyer	.05	.02	.00
☐ 60 Mike Flanagan	.10	.04	.01
☐ 61 Dan Ford	.05	.02	.00
☐ 62 Glenn Gulliver	.05	.02	.00
☐ 63 John Lowenstein	.05	.02	.00
☐ 64 Dennis Martinez	.10	.04	.01
☐ 65 Tippy Martinez	.05	.02	.00
☐ 66 Scott McGregor	.05	.02	.00
☐ 67 Eddie Murray	1.25	.50	.12
☐ 68 Joe Nolan	.05	.02	.00
☐ 69 Jim Palmer	.75	.30	.07
☐ 70 Cal Ripken Jr.	12.50	5.50	1.65
☐ 71 Gary Roenicke	.05	.02	.00
☐ 72 Lenn Sakata	.05	.02	.00
☐ 73 Ken Singleton	.10	.04	.01
☐ 74 Sammy Stewart	.05	.02	.00
☐ 75 Tim Stoddard	.05	.02	.00
☐ 76 Don Aase	.05	.02	.00
☐ 77 Don Baylor	.10	.04	.01
☐ 78 Juan Beniquez	.05	.02	.00
☐ 79 Bob Boone	.10	.04	.01
☐ 80 Rick Burleson	.05	.02	.00
☐ 81 Rod Carew	1.00	.40	.10
☐ 82 Bobby Clark	.05	.02	.00
☐ 83 Doug Corbett	.05	.02	.00
☐ 84 John Curtis	.05	.02	.00
☐ 85 Doug DeCinces	.10	.04	.01
☐ 86 Brian Downing	.10	.04	.01
☐ 87 Joe Ferguson	.05	.02	.00
☐ 88 Tim Foli	.05	.02	.00
☐ 89 Ken Forsch	.05	.02	.00
☐ 90 Dave Goltz	.05	.02	.00
☐ 91 Bobby Grich	.10	.04	.01
☐ 92 Andy Hassler	.05	.02	.00
☐ 93 Reggie Jackson	1.25	.50	.12
☐ 94 Ron Jackson	.05	.02	.00
☐ 95 Tommy John	.15	.06	.01
☐ 96 Bruce Kison	.05	.02	.00
☐ 97 Fred Lynn	.20	.08	.02
☐ 98 Ed Ott	.05	.02	.00
☐ 99 Steve Renko	.05	.02	.00
☐ 100 Luis Sanchez	.05	.02	.00
☐ 101 Rob Wilfong	.05	.02	.00
☐ 102 Mike Witt	.05	.02	.00
☐ 103 Geoff Zahn	.05	.02	.00
☐ 104 Willie Aikens	.05	.02	.00
☐ 105 Mike Armstrong	.05	.02	.00
☐ 106 Vida Blue	.10	.04	.01

□ 107 Bud Black	.40	.16	.04
□ 108 George Brett	1.50	.60	.15
□ 109 Bill Castro	.05	.02	.00
□ 110 Onix Concepcion	.05	.02	.00
□ 111 Dave Frost	.05	.02	.00
□ 112 Cesar Geronimo	.05	.02	.00
□ 113 Larry Gura	.05	.02	.00
□ 114 Steve Hammond	.05	.02	.00
□ 115 Don Hood	.05	.02	.00
□ 116 Dennis Leonard	.05	.02	.00
□ 117 Jerry Martin	.05	.02	.00
□ 118 Lee May	.05	.02	.00
□ 119 Hal McRae	.10	.04	.01
□ 120 Amos Otis	.10	.04	.01
□ 121 Greg Pryor	.05	.02	.00
□ 122 Dan Quisenberry	.10	.04	.01
□ 123 Don Slaught	.35	.15	.03
□ 124 Paul Splittorff	.05	.02	.00
□ 125 U.L. Washington	.05	.02	.00
□ 126 John Wathan	.05	.02	.00
□ 127 Frank White	.05	.02	.00
□ 128 Willie Wilson	.10	.04	.01
□ 129 Steve Bedrosian	.15	.06	.01
□ 130 Bruce Benedict	.05	.02	.00
□ 131 Tommy Boggs	.05	.02	.00
□ 132 Brett Butler	.75	.30	.07
□ 133 Rick Camp	.05	.02	.00
□ 134 Chris Chambliss	.10	.04	.01
□ 135 Ken Dayley	.05	.02	.00
□ 136 Gene Garber	.05	.02	.00
□ 137 Terry Harper	.05	.02	.00
□ 138 Bob Horner	.10	.04	.01
□ 139 Glenn Hubbard	.05	.02	.00
□ 140 Rufino Linares	.05	.02	.00
□ 141 Rick Mahler	.05	.02	.00
□ 142 Dale Murphy	.75	.30	.07
□ 143 Phil Niekro	.35	.15	.03
□ 144 Pascual Perez	.10	.04	.01
□ 145 Biff Pocoroba	.05	.02	.00
□ 146 Rafael Ramirez	.05	.02	.00
□ 147 Jerry Royster	.05	.02	.00
□ 148 Ken Smith	.05	.02	.00
□ 149 Bob Walk	.05	.02	.00
□ 150 Claudell Washington	.05	.02	.00
□ 151 Bob Watson	.05	.02	.00
□ 152 Larry Whisenton	.05	.02	.00
□ 153 Porfirio Altamirano	.05	.02	.00
□ 154 Marty Bystrom	.05	.02	.00
□ 155 Steve Carlton	1.00	.40	.10
□ 156 Larry Christenson	.05	.02	.00
□ 157 Ivan DeJesus	.05	.02	.00
□ 158 John Denny	.05	.02	.00
□ 159 Bob Dernier	.05	.02	.00
□ 160 Bo Diaz	.05	.02	.00
□ 161 Ed Farmer	.05	.02	.00
□ 162 Greg Gross	.05	.02	.00
□ 163 Mike Krukow	.05	.02	.00
□ 164 Garry Maddox	.05	.02	.00
□ 165 Gary Matthews	.05	.02	.00
□ 166 Tug McGraw	.10	.04	.01
□ 167 Bob Molinaro	.05	.02	.00
□ 168 Sid Monge	.05	.02	.00
□ 169 Ron Reed	.05	.02	.00
□ 170 Bill Robinson	.10	.04	.01
□ 171 Pete Rose	1.25	.50	.12
□ 172 Dick Ruthven	.05	.02	.00
□ 173 Mike Schmidt	2.00	.80	.20
□ 174 Manny Trillo	.05	.02	.00
□ 175 Ozzie Virgil	.05	.02	.00
□ 176 George Vukovich	.05	.02	.00
□ 177 Gary Allenson	.05	.02	.00
□ 178 Luis Aponte	.05	.02	.00
□ 179 Wade Boggs	24.00	10.50	3.50
□ 180 Tom Burgmeier	.05	.02	.00
□ 181 Mark Clear	.05	.02	.00
□ 182 Dennis Eckersley	.40	.16	.04
□ 183 Dwight Evans	.25	.10	.02
□ 184 Rich Gedman	.05	.02	.00
□ 185 Glenn Hoffman	.05	.02	.00
□ 186 Bruce Hurst	.15	.06	.01
□ 187 Carney Lansford	.10	.04	.01
□ 188 Rick Miller	.05	.02	.00
□ 189 Reid Nichols	.05	.02	.00
□ 190 Bob Ojeda	.10	.04	.01
□ 191 Tony Perez	.30	.12	.03
□ 192 Chuck Rainey	.05	.02	.00
□ 193 Jerry Remy	.05	.02	.00
□ 194 Jim Rice	.25	.10	.02
□ 195 Bob Stanley	.05	.02	.00
□ 196 Dave Stapleton	.05	.02	.00
□ 197 Mike Torrez	.05	.02	.00
□ 198 John Tudor	.10	.04	.01
□ 199 Julio Valdez	.05	.02	.00
□ 200 Carl Yastrzemski	1.00	.40	.10
□ 201 Dusty Baker	.10	.04	.01
□ 202 Joe Beckwith	.05	.02	.00
□ 203 Greg Brock	.10	.04	.01
□ 204 Ron Cey	.10	.04	.01
□ 205 Terry Forster	.05	.02	.00
□ 206 Steve Garvey	.50	.20	.05
□ 207 Pedro Guerrero	.35	.15	.03
□ 208 Burt Hooton	.05	.02	.00
□ 209 Steve Howe	.05	.02	.00
□ 210 Ken Landreaux	.05	.02	.00
□ 211 Mike Marshall	.10	.04	.01
□ 212 Candy Maldonado	.50	.20	.05
□ 213 Rick Monday	.05	.02	.00
□ 214 Tom Niedenfuer	.05	.02	.00
□ 215 Jorge Orta	.05	.02	.00
□ 216 Jerry Reuss	.05	.02	.00
□ 217 Ron Roenicke	.05	.02	.00
□ 218 Vicente Romo	.05	.02	.00
□ 219 Bill Russell	.10	.04	.01
□ 220 Steve Sax	.50	.20	.05
□ 221 Mike Scioscia	.10	.04	.01
□ 222 Dave Stewart	.75	.30	.07

☐ 223 Derrel Thomas .05 .02 .00
☐ 224 Fernando Valenzuela .25 .10 .02
☐ 225 Bob Welch .25 .10 .02
☐ 226 Ricky Wright .05 .02 .00
☐ 227 Steve Yeager .05 .02 .00
☐ 228 Bill Almon .05 .02 .00
☐ 229 Harold Baines .50 .20 .05
☐ 230 Salome Barojas .05 .02 .00
☐ 231 Tony Bernazard .05 .02 .00
☐ 232 Britt Burns .05 .02 .00
☐ 233 Richard Dotson .05 .02 .00
☐ 234 Ernesto Escarrega .05 .02 .00
☐ 235 Carlton Fisk 1.00 .40 .10
☐ 236 Jerry Hairston .05 .02 .00
☐ 237 Kevin Hickey .05 .02 .00
☐ 238 LaMarr Hoyt .05 .02 .00
☐ 239 Steve Kemp .05 .02 .00
☐ 240 Jim Kern .05 .02 .00
☐ 241 Ron Kittle .40 .16 .04
☐ 242 Jerry Koosman .10 .04 .01
☐ 243 Dennis Lamp .05 .02 .00
☐ 244 Rudy Law .05 .02 .00
☐ 245 Vance Law .10 .04 .01
☐ 246 Ron LeFlore .05 .02 .00
☐ 247 Greg Luzinski .10 .04 .01
☐ 248 Tom Paciorek .05 .02 .00
☐ 249 Aurelio Rodriguez .05 .02 .00
☐ 250 Mike Squires .05 .02 .00
☐ 251 Steve Trout .05 .02 .00
☐ 252 Jim Barr .05 .02 .00
☐ 253 Dave Bergman .05 .02 .00
☐ 254 Fred Breining .05 .02 .00
☐ 255 Bob Brenly .05 .02 .00
☐ 256 Jack Clark .25 .10 .02
☐ 257 Chili Davis .60 .25 .06
☐ 258 Darrell Evans .10 .04 .01
☐ 259 Alan Fowlkes .05 .02 .00
☐ 260 Rich Gale .05 .02 .00
☐ 261 Atlee Hammaker .05 .02 .00
☐ 262 Al Holland .05 .02 .00
☐ 263 Duane Kuiper .05 .02 .00
☐ 264 Bill Laskey .05 .02 .00
☐ 265 Gary Lavelle .05 .02 .00
☐ 266 Johnnie LeMaster .05 .02 .00
☐ 267 Renie Martin .05 .02 .00
☐ 268 Milt May .05 .02 .00
☐ 269 Greg Minton .05 .02 .00
☐ 270 Joe Morgan .50 .20 .05
☐ 271 Tom O'Malley .05 .02 .00
☐ 272 Reggie Smith .10 .04 .01
☐ 273 Guy Sularz .05 .02 .00
☐ 274 Champ Summers .05 .02 .00
☐ 275 Max Venable .05 .02 .00
☐ 276 Jim Wohlford .05 .02 .00
☐ 277 Ray Burris .05 .02 .00
☐ 278 Gary Carter .40 .16 .04
☐ 279 Warren Cromartie .05 .02 .00
☐ 280 Andre Dawson 1.25 .50 .12
☐ 281 Terry Francona .05 .02 .00
☐ 282 Doug Flynn .05 .02 .00
☐ 283 Woodie Fryman .05 .02 .00
☐ 284 Bill Gullickson .10 .04 .01
☐ 285 Wallace Johnson .05 .02 .00
☐ 286 Charlie Lea .05 .02 .00
☐ 287 Randy Lerch .05 .02 .00
☐ 288 Brad Mills .05 .02 .00
☐ 289 Dan Norman .05 .02 .00
☐ 290 Al Oliver .10 .04 .01
☐ 291 David Palmer .05 .02 .00
☐ 292 Tim Raines .60 .25 .06
☐ 293 Jeff Reardon .50 .20 .05
☐ 294 Steve Rogers .05 .02 .00
☐ 295 Scott Sanderson .10 .04 .01
☐ 296 Dan Schatzeder .05 .02 .00
☐ 297 Bryn Smith .15 .06 .01
☐ 298 Chris Speier .05 .02 .00
☐ 299 Tim Wallach .20 .08 .02
☐ 300 Jerry White .05 .02 .00
☐ 301 Joel Youngblood .05 .02 .00
☐ 302 Ross Baumgarten .05 .02 .00
☐ 303 Dale Berra .05 .02 .00
☐ 304 John Candelaria .05 .02 .00
☐ 305 Dick Davis .05 .02 .00
☐ 306 Mike Easler .05 .02 .00
☐ 307 Richie Hebner .05 .02 .00
☐ 308 Lee Lacy .05 .02 .00
☐ 309 Bill Madlock .10 .04 .01
☐ 310 Larry McWilliams .05 .02 .00
☐ 311 John Milner .05 .02 .00
☐ 312 Omar Moreno .05 .02 .00
☐ 313 Jim Morrison .05 .02 .00
☐ 314 Steve Nicosia .05 .02 .00
☐ 315 Dave Parker .40 .16 .04
☐ 316 Tony Pena .10 .04 .01
☐ 317 Johnny Ray .05 .02 .00
☐ 318 Rick Rhoden .05 .02 .00
☐ 319 Don Robinson .05 .02 .00
☐ 320 Enrique Romo .05 .02 .00
☐ 321 Manny Sarmiento .05 .02 .00
☐ 322 Rod Scurry .05 .02 .00
☐ 323 Jimmy Smith .05 .02 .00
☐ 324 Willie Stargell .50 .20 .05
☐ 325 Jason Thompson .05 .02 .00
☐ 326 Kent Tekulve .05 .02 .00
☐ 327A Tom Brookens .05 .02 .00
(Short .375" brown box shaded in on card back)
☐ 327B Tom Brookens .05 .02 .00
(Longer 1.25" brown box shaded in on card back)
☐ 328 Enos Cabell .05 .02 .00
☐ 329 Kirk Gibson .50 .20 .05
☐ 330 Larry Herndon .05 .02 .00
☐ 331 Mike Ivie .05 .02 .00
☐ 332 Howard Johnson 10.00 4.50 1.25
☐ 333 Lynn Jones .05 .02 .00

No.	Player			
☐ 334	Rick Leach	.05	.02	.00
☐ 335	Chet Lemon	.05	.02	.00
☐ 336	Jack Morris	.60	.25	.06
☐ 337	Lance Parrish	.25	.10	.02
☐ 338	Larry Pashnick	.05	.02	.00
☐ 339	Dan Petry	.05	.02	.00
☐ 340	Dave Rozema	.05	.02	.00
☐ 341	Dave Rucker	.05	.02	.00
☐ 342	Elias Sosa	.05	.02	.00
☐ 343	Dave Tobik	.05	.02	.00
☐ 344	Alan Trammell	.60	.25	.06
☐ 345	Jerry Turner	.05	.02	.00
☐ 346	Jerry Ujdur	.05	.02	.00
☐ 347	Pat Underwood	.05	.02	.00
☐ 348	Lou Whitaker	.35	.15	.03
☐ 349	Milt Wilcox	.05	.02	.00
☐ 350	Glenn Wilson	.10	.04	.01
☐ 351	John Wockenfuss	.05	.02	.00
☐ 352	Kurt Bevacqua	.05	.02	.00
☐ 353	Juan Bonilla	.05	.02	.00
☐ 354	Floyd Chiffer	.05	.02	.00
☐ 355	Luis DeLeon	.05	.02	.00
☐ 356	Dave Dravecky	.50	.20	.05
☐ 357	Dave Edwards	.05	.02	.00
☐ 358	Juan Eichelberger	.05	.02	.00
☐ 359	Tim Flannery	.05	.02	.00
☐ 360	Tony Gwynn	23.00	10.00	3.35
☐ 361	Ruppert Jones	.05	.02	.00
☐ 362	Terry Kennedy	.05	.02	.00
☐ 363	Joe Lefebvre	.05	.02	.00
☐ 364	Sixto Lezcano	.05	.02	.00
☐ 365	Tim Lollar	.05	.02	.00
☐ 366	Gary Lucas	.05	.02	.00
☐ 367	John Montefusco	.05	.02	.00
☐ 368	Broderick Perkins	.05	.02	.00
☐ 369	Joe Pittman	.05	.02	.00
☐ 370	Gene Richards	.05	.02	.00
☐ 371	Luis Salazar	.05	.02	.00
☐ 372	Eric Show	.15	.06	.01
☐ 373	Garry Templeton	.10	.04	.01
☐ 374	Chris Welsh	.05	.02	.00
☐ 375	Alan Wiggins	.05	.02	.00
☐ 376	Rick Cerone	.05	.02	.00
☐ 377	Dave Collins	.05	.02	.00
☐ 378	Roger Erickson	.05	.02	.00
☐ 379	George Frazier	.05	.02	.00
☐ 380	Oscar Gamble	.05	.02	.00
☐ 381	Goose Gossage	.15	.06	.01
☐ 382	Ken Griffey	.25	.10	.02
☐ 383	Ron Guidry	.25	.10	.02
☐ 384	Dave LaRoche	.05	.02	.00
☐ 385	Rudy May	.05	.02	.00
☐ 386	John Mayberry	.10	.04	.01
☐ 387	Lee Mazzilli	.05	.02	.00
☐ 388	Mike Morgan	.10	.04	.01
☐ 389	Jerry Mumphrey	.05	.02	.00
☐ 390	Bobby Murcer	.10	.04	.01
☐ 391	Graig Nettles	.10	.04	.01
☐ 392	Lou Piniella	.10	.04	.01
☐ 393	Willie Randolph	.10	.04	.01
☐ 394	Shane Rawley	.05	.02	.00
☐ 395	Dave Righetti	.25	.10	.02
☐ 396	Andre Robertson	.05	.02	.00
☐ 397	Roy Smalley	.05	.02	.00
☐ 398	Dave Winfield	.75	.30	.07
☐ 399	Butch Wynegar	.05	.02	.00
☐ 400	Chris Bando	.05	.02	.00
☐ 401	Alan Bannister	.05	.02	.00
☐ 402	Len Barker	.05	.02	.00
☐ 403	Tom Brennan	.05	.02	.00
☐ 404	Carmelo Castillo	.05	.02	.00
☐ 405	Miguel Dilone	.05	.02	.00
☐ 406	Jerry Dybzinski	.05	.02	.00
☐ 407	Mike Fischlin	.05	.02	.00
☐ 408	Ed Glynn UER (photo actually Bud Anderson)	.05	.02	.00
☐ 409	Mike Hargrove	.05	.02	.00
☐ 410	Toby Harrah	.05	.02	.00
☐ 411	Ron Hassey	.05	.02	.00
☐ 412	Von Hayes	.15	.06	.01
☐ 413	Rick Manning	.05	.02	.00
☐ 414	Bake McBride	.05	.02	.00
☐ 415	Larry Milbourne	.05	.02	.00
☐ 416	Bill Nahorodny	.05	.02	.00
☐ 417	Jack Perconte	.05	.02	.00
☐ 418	Lary Sorensen	.05	.02	.00
☐ 419	Dan Spillner	.05	.02	.00
☐ 420	Rick Sutcliffe	.15	.06	.01
☐ 421	Andre Thornton	.05	.02	.00
☐ 422	Rick Waits	.05	.02	.00
☐ 423	Eddie Whitson	.05	.02	.00
☐ 424	Jesse Barfield	.40	.16	.04
☐ 425	Barry Bonnell	.05	.02	.00
☐ 426	Jim Clancy	.05	.02	.00
☐ 427	Damaso Garcia	.05	.02	.00
☐ 428	Jerry Garvin	.05	.02	.00
☐ 429	Alfredo Griffin	.05	.02	.00
☐ 430	Garth Iorg	.05	.02	.00
☐ 431	Roy Lee Jackson	.05	.02	.00
☐ 432	Luis Leal	.05	.02	.00
☐ 433	Buck Martinez	.05	.02	.00
☐ 434	Joey McLaughlin	.05	.02	.00
☐ 435	Lloyd Moseby	.10	.04	.01
☐ 436	Rance Mulliniks	.05	.02	.00
☐ 437	Dale Murray	.05	.02	.00
☐ 438	Wayne Nordhagen	.05	.02	.00
☐ 439	Geno Petralli	.10	.04	.01
☐ 440	Hosken Powell	.05	.02	.00
☐ 441	Dave Stieb	.25	.10	.02
☐ 442	Willie Upshaw	.05	.02	.00
☐ 443	Ernie Whitt	.05	.02	.00
☐ 444	Alvis Woods	.05	.02	.00
☐ 445	Alan Ashby	.05	.02	.00
☐ 446	Jose Cruz	.10	.04	.01
☐ 447	Kiko Garcia	.05	.02	.00

☐ 448	Phil Garner	.10	.04	.01
☐ 449	Danny Heep	.05	.02	.00
☐ 450	Art Howe	.10	.04	.01
☐ 451	Bob Knepper	.05	.02	.00
☐ 452	Alan Knicely	.05	.02	.00
☐ 453	Ray Knight	.10	.04	.01
☐ 454	Frank LaCorte	.05	.02	.00
☐ 455	Mike LaCoss	.05	.02	.00
☐ 456	Randy Moffitt	.05	.02	.00
☐ 457	Joe Niekro	.10	.04	.01
☐ 458	Terry Puhl	.05	.02	.00
☐ 459	Luis Pujols	.05	.02	.00
☐ 460	Craig Reynolds	.05	.02	.00
☐ 461	Bert Roberge	.05	.02	.00
☐ 462	Vern Ruhle	.05	.02	.00
☐ 463	Nolan Ryan	5.25	2.25	.50
☐ 464	Joe Sambito	.05	.02	.00
☐ 465	Tony Scott	.05	.02	.00
☐ 466	Dave Smith	.05	.02	.00
☐ 467	Harry Spilman	.05	.02	.00
☐ 468	Dickie Thon	.10	.04	.01
☐ 469	Denny Walling	.05	.02	.00
☐ 470	Larry Andersen	.05	.02	.00
☐ 471	Floyd Bannister	.05	.02	.00
☐ 472	Jim Beattie	.05	.02	.00
☐ 473	Bruce Bochte	.05	.02	.00
☐ 474	Manny Castillo	.05	.02	.00
☐ 475	Bill Caudill	.05	.02	.00
☐ 476	Bryan Clark	.05	.02	.00
☐ 477	Al Cowens	.05	.02	.00
☐ 478	Julio Cruz	.05	.02	.00
☐ 479	Todd Cruz	.05	.02	.00
☐ 480	Gary Gray	.05	.02	.00
☐ 481	Dave Henderson	1.25	.50	.12
☐ 482	Mike Moore	.90	.40	.09
☐ 483	Gaylord Perry	.35	.15	.03
☐ 484	Dave Revering	.05	.02	.00
☐ 485	Joe Simpson	.05	.02	.00
☐ 486	Mike Stanton	.05	.02	.00
☐ 487	Rick Sweet	.05	.02	.00
☐ 488	Ed VandeBerg	.05	.02	.00
☐ 489	Richie Zisk	.05	.02	.00
☐ 490	Doug Bird	.05	.02	.00
☐ 491	Larry Bowa	.10	.04	.01
☐ 492	Bill Buckner	.10	.04	.01
☐ 493	Bill Campbell	.05	.02	.00
☐ 494	Jody Davis	.05	.02	.00
☐ 495	Leon Durham	.05	.02	.00
☐ 496	Steve Henderson	.05	.02	.00
☐ 497	Willie Hernandez	.05	.02	.00
☐ 498	Ferguson Jenkins	.35	.15	.03
☐ 499	Jay Johnstone	.10	.04	.01
☐ 500	Junior Kennedy	.05	.02	.00
☐ 501	Randy Martz	.05	.02	.00
☐ 502	Jerry Morales	.05	.02	.00
☐ 503	Keith Moreland	.05	.02	.00
☐ 504	Dickie Noles	.05	.02	.00
☐ 505	Mike Proly	.05	.02	.00
☐ 506	Allen Ripley	.05	.02	.00
☐ 507	Ryne Sandberg UER (Should say High School in Spokane, Washington)	35.00	15.75	5.25
☐ 508	Lee Smith	.60	.25	.06
☐ 509	Pat Tabler	.10	.04	.01
☐ 510	Dick Tidrow	.05	.02	.00
☐ 511	Bump Wills	.05	.02	.00
☐ 512	Gary Woods	.05	.02	.00
☐ 513	Tony Armas	.05	.02	.00
☐ 514	Dave Beard	.05	.02	.00
☐ 515	Jeff Burroughs	.05	.02	.00
☐ 516	John D'Acquisto	.05	.02	.00
☐ 517	Wayne Gross	.05	.02	.00
☐ 518	Mike Heath	.05	.02	.00
☐ 519	Rickey Henderson UER (Brock record listed as 120 steals)	5.00	2.25	.50
☐ 520	Cliff Johnson	.05	.02	.00
☐ 521	Matt Keough	.05	.02	.00
☐ 522	Brian Kingman	.05	.02	.00
☐ 523	Rick Langford	.05	.02	.00
☐ 524	Dave Lopes	.10	.04	.01
☐ 525	Steve McCatty	.05	.02	.00
☐ 526	Dave McKay	.05	.02	.00
☐ 527	Dan Meyer	.05	.02	.00
☐ 528	Dwayne Murphy	.05	.02	.00
☐ 529	Jeff Newman	.05	.02	.00
☐ 530	Mike Norris	.05	.02	.00
☐ 531	Bob Owchinko	.05	.02	.00
☐ 532	Joe Rudi	.10	.04	.01
☐ 533	Jimmy Sexton	.05	.02	.00
☐ 534	Fred Stanley	.05	.02	.00
☐ 535	Tom Underwood	.05	.02	.00
☐ 536	Neil Allen	.05	.02	.00
☐ 537	Wally Backman	.10	.04	.01
☐ 538	Bob Bailor	.05	.02	.00
☐ 539	Hubie Brooks	.25	.10	.02
☐ 540	Carlos Diaz	.05	.02	.00
☐ 541	Pete Falcone	.05	.02	.00
☐ 542	George Foster	.15	.06	.01
☐ 543	Ron Gardenhire	.05	.02	.00
☐ 544	Brian Giles	.05	.02	.00
☐ 545	Ron Hodges	.05	.02	.00
☐ 546	Randy Jones	.05	.02	.00
☐ 547	Mike Jorgensen	.05	.02	.00
☐ 548	Dave Kingman	.15	.06	.01
☐ 549	Ed Lynch	.05	.02	.00
☐ 550	Jesse Orosco	.05	.02	.00
☐ 551	Rick Ownbey	.05	.02	.00
☐ 552	Charlie Puleo	.05	.02	.00
☐ 553	Gary Rajsich	.05	.02	.00
☐ 554	Mike Scott	.20	.08	.02
☐ 555	Rusty Staub	.10	.04	.01
☐ 556	John Stearns	.05	.02	.00
☐ 557	Craig Swan	.05	.02	.00
☐ 558	Ellis Valentine	.05	.02	.00
☐ 559	Tom Veryzer	.05	.02	.00

☐	560	Mookie Wilson	.10	.04	.01
☐	561	Pat Zachry	.05	.02	.00
☐	562	Buddy Bell	.10	.04	.01
☐	563	John Butcher	.05	.02	.00
☐	564	Steve Comer	.05	.02	.00
☐	565	Danny Darwin	.05	.02	.00
☐	566	Bucky Dent	.10	.04	.01
☐	567	John Grubb	.05	.02	.00
☐	568	Rick Honeycutt	.05	.02	.00
☐	569	Dave Hostetler	.05	.02	.00
☐	570	Charlie Hough	.05	.02	.00
☐	571	Lamar Johnson	.05	.02	.00
☐	572	Jon Matlack	.05	.02	.00
☐	573	Paul Mirabella	.05	.02	.00
☐	574	Larry Parrish	.05	.02	.00
☐	575	Mike Richardt	.05	.02	.00
☐	576	Mickey Rivers	.05	.02	.00
☐	577	Billy Sample	.05	.02	.00
☐	578	Dave Schmidt	.10	.04	.01
☐	579	Bill Stein	.05	.02	.00
☐	580	Jim Sundberg	.05	.02	.00
☐	581	Frank Tanana	.10	.04	.01
☐	582	Mark Wagner	.05	.02	.00
☐	583	George Wright	.05	.02	.00
☐	584	Johnny Bench	1.00	.40	.10
☐	585	Bruce Berenyi	.05	.02	.00
☐	586	Larry Biittner	.05	.02	.00
☐	587	Cesar Cedeno	.10	.04	.01
☐	588	Dave Concepcion	.10	.04	.01
☐	589	Dan Driessen	.05	.02	.00
☐	590	Greg Harris	.05	.02	.00
☐	591	Ben Hayes	.05	.02	.00
☐	592	Paul Householder	.05	.02	.00
☐	593	Tom Hume	.05	.02	.00
☐	594	Wayne Krenchicki	.05	.02	.00
☐	595	Rafael Landestoy	.05	.02	.00
☐	596	Charlie Leibrandt	.10	.04	.01
☐	597	Eddie Milner	.05	.02	.00
☐	598	Ron Oester	.05	.02	.00
☐	599	Frank Pastore	.05	.02	.00
☐	600	Joe Price	.05	.02	.00
☐	601	Tom Seaver	1.00	.40	.10
☐	602	Bob Shirley	.05	.02	.00
☐	603	Mario Soto	.05	.02	.00
☐	604	Alex Trevino	.05	.02	.00
☐	605	Mike Vail	.05	.02	.00
☐	606	Duane Walker	.05	.02	.00
☐	607	Tom Brunansky	.40	.16	.04
☐	608	Bobby Castillo	.05	.02	.00
☐	609	John Castino	.05	.02	.00
☐	610	Ron Davis	.05	.02	.00
☐	611	Lenny Faedo	.05	.02	.00
☐	612	Terry Felton	.05	.02	.00
☐	613	Gary Gaetti	1.00	.40	.10
☐	614	Mickey Hatcher	.05	.02	.00
☐	615	Brad Havens	.05	.02	.00
☐	616	Kent Hrbek	1.00	.40	.10
☐	617	Randy Johnson	.05	.02	.00
☐	618	Tim Laudner	.05	.02	.00
☐	619	Jeff Little	.05	.02	.00
☐	620	Bobby Mitchell	.05	.02	.00
☐	621	Jack O'Connor	.05	.02	.00
☐	622	John Pacella	.05	.02	.00
☐	623	Pete Redfern	.05	.02	.00
☐	624	Jesus Vega	.05	.02	.00
☐	625	Frank Viola	4.50	2.00	.45
☐	626	Ron Washington	.05	.02	.00
☐	627	Gary Ward	.05	.02	.00
☐	628	Al Williams	.05	.02	.00
☐	629	Red Sox All-Stars Carl Yastrzemski Dennis Eckersley Mark Clear	.30	.12	.03
☐	630	"300 Career Wins" Gaylord Perry and Terry Bulling 5/6/82	.10	.04	.01
☐	631	Pride of Venezuela Dave Concepcion and Manny Trillo	.10	.04	.01
☐	632	All-Star Infielders Robin Yount and Buddy Bell	.25	.10	.02
☐	633	Mr.Vet and Mr.Rookie Dave Winfield and Kent Hrbek	.25	.10	.02
☐	634	Fountain of Youth Willie Stargell and Pete Rose	.50	.20	.05
☐	635	Big Chiefs Toby Harrah and Andre Thornton	.10	.04	.01
☐	636	Smith Brothers Ozzie and Lonnie	.30	.12	.03
☐	637	Base Stealers' Threat Bo Diaz and Gary Carter	.10	.04	.01
☐	638	All-Star Catchers Carlton Fisk and Gary Carter	.20	.08	.02
☐	639	The Silver Shoe Rickey Henderson	2.00	.80	.20
☐	640	Home Run Threats Ben Oglivie and Reggie Jackson	.30	.12	.03
☐	641	Two Teams Same Day Joel Youngblood August 4, 1982	.10	.04	.01
☐	642	Last Perfect Game Ron Hassey and Len Barker	.10	.04	.01
☐	643	Black and Blue Vida Blue	.10	.04	.01
☐	644	Black and Blue Bud Black	.10	.04	.01
☐	645	Speed and Power Reggie Jackson	.40	.16	.04

□ 646 Speed and Power Rickey Henderson	1.25	.50	.12
□ 647 CL: Cards/Brewers	.15	.02	.00
□ 648 CL: Orioles/Angels	.15	.02	.00
□ 649 CL: Royals/Braves	.15	.02	.00
□ 650 CL: Phillies/Red Sox	.15	.02	.00
□ 651 CL: Dodgers/White Sox	.15	.02	.00
□ 652 CL: Giants/Expos	.15	.02	.00
□ 653 CL: Pirates/Tigers	.15	.02	.00
□ 654 CL: Padres/Yankees	.15	.02	.00
□ 655 CL: Indians/Blue Jays	.15	.02	.00
□ 656 CL: Astros/Mariners	.15	.02	.00
□ 657 CL: Cubs/A's	.15	.02	.00
□ 658 CL: Mets/Rangers	.15	.02	.00
□ 659 CL: Reds/Twins	.15	.02	.00
□ 660 CL: Specials/Teams	.15	.02	.00

1984 Fleer

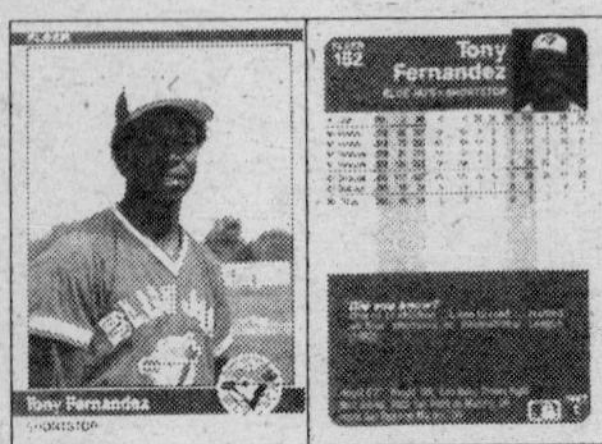

The cards in this 660-card set measure 2 1/2" by 3 1/2". The 1984 Fleer card set featured fronts with full-color team logos along with the player's name and position and the Fleer identification. The set features many imaginative photos, several multi-player cards, and many more action shots than the 1983 card set. The backs are quite similar to the 1983 backs except that blue rather than brown ink is used. The player cards are alphabetized within team and the teams are ordered by their 1983 season finish and won-lost record, e.g., Baltimore (1-23), Philadelphia (24-49), Chicago White Sox (50-73), Detroit (74-95), Los Angeles (96-118), New York Yankees (119-144), Toronto (145-169), Atlanta (170-193), Milwaukee (194-219), Houston (220-244), Pittsburgh (245-269), Montreal (270-293), San Diego (294-317), St. Louis (318-340), Kansas City (341-364), San Francisco (365-387), Boston (388-412), Texas (413-435), Oakland (436-461), Cincinnati (462-485), Chicago (486-507), California (508-532), Cleveland (533-555), Minnesota (556-579), New York Mets (580-603), and Seattle (604-625). Specials (626-646) and checklist cards (647-660) make up the end of the set. The key rookie cards in this set are Tony Fernandez, Don Mattingly, Kevin McReynolds, Juan Samuel, Darryl Strawberry, and Andy Van Slyke.

	MINT	EXC	G-VG
COMPLETE SET (660)	225.00	100.00	33.00
COMMON PLAYER (1-660)	.09	.04	.01
□ 1 Mike Boddicker	.25	.06	.01
□ 2 Al Bumbry	.09	.04	.01
□ 3 Todd Cruz	.09	.04	.01
□ 4 Rich Dauer	.09	.04	.01
□ 5 Storm Davis	.15	.06	.01
□ 6 Rick Dempsey	.09	.04	.01
□ 7 Jim Dwyer	.09	.04	.01
□ 8 Mike Flanagan	.15	.06	.01
□ 9 Dan Ford	.09	.04	.01
□ 10 John Lowenstein	.09	.04	.01
□ 11 Dennis Martinez	.15	.06	.01
□ 12 Tippy Martinez	.09	.04	.01
□ 13 Scott McGregor	.09	.04	.01
□ 14 Eddie Murray	2.50	1.00	.25
□ 15 Joe Nolan	.09	.04	.01
□ 16 Jim Palmer	2.00	.80	.20
□ 17 Cal Ripken	15.00	6.50	2.15
□ 18 Gary Roenicke	.09	.04	.01
□ 19 Lenn Sakata	.09	.04	.01
□ 20 John Shelby	.25	.10	.02
□ 21 Ken Singleton	.15	.06	.01
□ 22 Sammy Stewart	.09	.04	.01
□ 23 Tim Stoddard	.09	.04	.01
□ 24 Marty Bystrom	.09	.04	.01
□ 25 Steve Carlton	2.00	.80	.20
□ 26 Ivan DeJesus	.09	.04	.01
□ 27 John Denny	.09	.04	.01
□ 28 Bob Dernier	.09	.04	.01
□ 29 Bo Diaz	.09	.04	.01
□ 30 Kiko Garcia	.09	.04	.01
□ 31 Greg Gross	.09	.04	.01
□ 32 Kevin Gross	.35	.15	.03
□ 33 Von Hayes	.20	.08	.02
□ 34 Willie Hernandez	.15	.06	.01
□ 35 Al Holland	.09	.04	.01
□ 36 Charles Hudson	.15	.06	.01
□ 37 Joe Lefebvre	.09	.04	.01
□ 38 Sixto Lezcano	.09	.04	.01
□ 39 Garry Maddox	.09	.04	.01
□ 40 Gary Matthews	.09	.04	.01
□ 41 Len Matuszek	.09	.04	.01

No.	Player			
☐ 42	Tug McGraw	.15	.06	.01
☐ 43	Joe Morgan	1.00	.40	.10
☐ 44	Tony Perez	.50	.20	.05
☐ 45	Ron Reed	.09	.04	.01
☐ 46	Pete Rose	2.00	.80	.20
☐ 47	Juan Samuel	4.50	2.00	.45
☐ 48	Mike Schmidt	8.00	3.50	.80
☐ 49	Ozzie Virgil	.09	.04	.01
☐ 50	Juan Agosto	.15	.06	.01
☐ 51	Harold Baines	.60	.25	.06
☐ 52	Floyd Bannister	.09	.04	.01
☐ 53	Salome Barojas	.09	.04	.01
☐ 54	Britt Burns	.09	.04	.01
☐ 55	Julio Cruz	.09	.04	.01
☐ 56	Richard Dotson	.09	.04	.01
☐ 57	Jerry Dybzinski	.09	.04	.01
☐ 58	Carlton Fisk	2.00	.80	.20
☐ 59	Scott Fletcher	.15	.06	.01
☐ 60	Jerry Hairston	.09	.04	.01
☐ 61	Kevin Hickey	.09	.04	.01
☐ 62	Marc Hill	.09	.04	.01
☐ 63	LaMarr Hoyt	.09	.04	.01
☐ 64	Ron Kittle	.15	.06	.01
☐ 65	Jerry Koosman	.15	.06	.01
☐ 66	Dennis Lamp	.09	.04	.01
☐ 67	Rudy Law	.09	.04	.01
☐ 68	Vance Law	.15	.06	.01
☐ 69	Greg Luzinski	.15	.06	.01
☐ 70	Tom Paciorek	.09	.04	.01
☐ 71	Mike Squires	.09	.04	.01
☐ 72	Dick Tidrow	.09	.04	.01
☐ 73	Greg Walker	.15	.06	.01
☐ 74	Glenn Abbott	.09	.04	.01
☐ 75	Howard Bailey	.09	.04	.01
☐ 76	Doug Bair	.09	.04	.01
☐ 77	Juan Berenguer	.09	.04	.01
☐ 78	Tom Brookens	.09	.04	.01
☐ 79	Enos Cabell	.09	.04	.01
☐ 80	Kirk Gibson	.75	.30	.07
☐ 81	John Grubb	.09	.04	.01
☐ 82	Larry Herndon	.09	.04	.01
☐ 83	Wayne Krenchicki	.09	.04	.01
☐ 84	Rick Leach	.09	.04	.01
☐ 85	Chet Lemon	.09	.04	.01
☐ 86	Aurelio Lopez	.09	.04	.01
☐ 87	Jack Morris	1.00	.40	.10
☐ 88	Lance Parrish	.40	.16	.04
☐ 89	Dan Petry	.09	.04	.01
☐ 90	Dave Rozema	.09	.04	.01
☐ 91	Alan Trammell	1.50	.60	.15
☐ 92	Lou Whitaker	.60	.25	.06
☐ 93	Milt Wilcox	.09	.04	.01
☐ 94	Glenn Wilson	.09	.04	.01
☐ 95	John Wockenfuss	.09	.04	.01
☐ 96	Dusty Baker	.15	.06	.01
☐ 97	Joe Beckwith	.09	.04	.01
☐ 98	Greg Brock	.15	.06	.01
☐ 99	Jack Fimple	.09	.04	.01
☐ 100	Pedro Guerrero	.40	.16	.04
☐ 101	Rick Honeycutt	.09	.04	.01
☐ 102	Burt Hooton	.09	.04	.01
☐ 103	Steve Howe	.09	.04	.01
☐ 104	Ken Landreaux	.09	.04	.01
☐ 105	Mike Marshall	.15	.06	.01
☐ 106	Rick Monday	.09	.04	.01
☐ 107	Jose Morales	.09	.04	.01
☐ 108	Tom Niedenfuer	.09	.04	.01
☐ 109	Alejandro Pena	.60	.25	.06
☐ 110	Jerry Reuss	.09	.04	.01
☐ 111	Bill Russell	.15	.06	.01
☐ 112	Steve Sax	.50	.20	.05
☐ 113	Mike Scioscia	.15	.06	.01
☐ 114	Derrel Thomas	.09	.04	.01
☐ 115	Fernando Valenzuela	.35	.15	.03
☐ 116	Bob Welch	.35	.15	.03
☐ 117	Steve Yeager	.09	.04	.01
☐ 118	Pat Zachry	.09	.04	.01
☐ 119	Don Baylor	.15	.06	.01
☐ 120	Bert Campaneris	.15	.06	.01
☐ 121	Rick Cerone	.09	.04	.01
☐ 122	Ray Fontenot	.09	.04	.01
☐ 123	George Frazier	.09	.04	.01
☐ 124	Oscar Gamble	.09	.04	.01
☐ 125	Goose Gossage	.25	.10	.02
☐ 126	Ken Griffey	.25	.10	.02
☐ 127	Ron Guidry	.35	.15	.03
☐ 128	Jay Howell	.20	.08	.02
☐ 129	Steve Kemp	.09	.04	.01
☐ 130	Matt Keough	.09	.04	.01
☐ 131	Don Mattingly	38.00	17.00	4.00
☐ 132	John Montefusco	.09	.04	.01
☐ 133	Omar Moreno	.09	.04	.01
☐ 134	Dale Murray	.09	.04	.01
☐ 135	Graig Nettles	.20	.08	.02
☐ 136	Lou Piniella	.15	.06	.01
☐ 137	Willie Randolph	.15	.06	.01
☐ 138	Shane Rawley	.09	.04	.01
☐ 139	Dave Righetti	.30	.12	.03
☐ 140	Andre Robertson	.09	.04	.01
☐ 141	Bob Shirley	.09	.04	.01
☐ 142	Roy Smalley	.09	.04	.01
☐ 143	Dave Winfield	1.75	.70	.17
☐ 144	Butch Wynegar	.09	.04	.01
☐ 145	Jim Acker	.15	.06	.01
☐ 146	Doyle Alexander	.09	.04	.01
☐ 147	Jesse Barfield	.25	.10	.02
☐ 148	Jorge Bell	2.00	.80	.20
☐ 149	Barry Bonnell	.09	.04	.01
☐ 150	Jim Clancy	.09	.04	.01
☐ 151	Dave Collins	.09	.04	.01
☐ 152	Tony Fernandez	4.00	1.75	.40
☐ 153	Damaso Garcia	.09	.04	.01
☐ 154	Dave Geisel	.09	.04	.01
☐ 155	Jim Gott	.20	.08	.02
☐ 156	Alfredo Griffin	.09	.04	.01
☐ 157	Garth Iorg	.09	.04	.01

☐ 158 Roy Lee Jackson	.09	.04	.01
☐ 159 Cliff Johnson	.09	.04	.01
☐ 160 Luis Leal	.09	.04	.01
☐ 161 Buck Martinez	.09	.04	.01
☐ 162 Joey McLaughlin	.09	.04	.01
☐ 163 Randy Moffitt	.09	.04	.01
☐ 164 Lloyd Moseby	.15	.06	.01
☐ 165 Rance Mulliniks	.09	.04	.01
☐ 166 Jorge Orta	.09	.04	.01
☐ 167 Dave Stieb	.35	.15	.03
☐ 168 Willie Upshaw	.09	.04	.01
☐ 169 Ernie Whitt	.09	.04	.01
☐ 170 Len Barker	.09	.04	.01
☐ 171 Steve Bedrosian	.15	.06	.01
☐ 172 Bruce Benedict	.09	.04	.01
☐ 173 Brett Butler	.45	.18	.04
☐ 174 Rick Camp	.09	.04	.01
☐ 175 Chris Chambliss	.15	.06	.01
☐ 176 Ken Dayley	.09	.04	.01
☐ 177 Pete Falcone	.09	.04	.01
☐ 178 Terry Forster	.15	.06	.01
☐ 179 Gene Garber	.09	.04	.01
☐ 180 Terry Harper	.09	.04	.01
☐ 181 Bob Horner	.15	.06	.01
☐ 182 Glenn Hubbard	.09	.04	.01
☐ 183 Randy Johnson	.09	.04	.01
☐ 184 Craig McMurtry	.09	.04	.01
☐ 185 Donnie Moore	.09	.04	.01
☐ 186 Dale Murphy	1.50	.60	.15
☐ 187 Phil Niekro	.60	.25	.06
☐ 188 Pascual Perez	.20	.08	.02
☐ 189 Biff Pocoroba	.09	.04	.01
☐ 190 Rafael Ramirez	.09	.04	.01
☐ 191 Jerry Royster	.09	.04	.01
☐ 192 Claudell Washington	.09	.04	.01
☐ 193 Bob Watson	.09	.04	.01
☐ 194 Jerry Augustine	.09	.04	.01
☐ 195 Mark Brouhard	.09	.04	.01
☐ 196 Mike Caldwell	.09	.04	.01
☐ 197 Tom Candiotti	.75	.30	.07
☐ 198 Cecil Cooper	.15	.06	.01
☐ 199 Rollie Fingers	.50	.20	.05
☐ 200 Jim Gantner	.09	.04	.01
☐ 201 Bob L. Gibson	.09	.04	.01
☐ 202 Moose Haas	.09	.04	.01
☐ 203 Roy Howell	.09	.04	.01
☐ 204 Pete Ladd	.09	.04	.01
☐ 205 Rick Manning	.09	.04	.01
☐ 206 Bob McClure	.09	.04	.01
☐ 207 Paul Molitor UER ('83 stats should say .270 BA and 608 AB)	.50	.20	.05
☐ 208 Don Money	.09	.04	.01
☐ 209 Charlie Moore	.09	.04	.01
☐ 210 Ben Oglivie	.09	.04	.01
☐ 211 Chuck Porter	.09	.04	.01
☐ 212 Ed Romero	.09	.04	.01
☐ 213 Ted Simmons	.15	.06	.01
☐ 214 Jim Slaton	.09	.04	.01
☐ 215 Don Sutton	.60	.25	.06
☐ 216 Tom Tellmann	.09	.04	.01
☐ 217 Pete Vuckovich	.09	.04	.01
☐ 218 Ned Yost	.09	.04	.01
☐ 219 Robin Yount	3.25	1.35	.32
☐ 220 Alan Ashby	.09	.04	.01
☐ 221 Kevin Bass	.15	.06	.01
☐ 222 Jose Cruz	.15	.06	.01
☐ 223 Bill Dawley	.09	.04	.01
☐ 224 Frank DiPino	.09	.04	.01
☐ 225 Bill Doran	.60	.25	.06
☐ 226 Phil Garner	.15	.06	.01
☐ 227 Art Howe	.15	.06	.01
☐ 228 Bob Knepper	.09	.04	.01
☐ 229 Ray Knight	.15	.06	.01
☐ 230 Frank LaCorte	.09	.04	.01
☐ 231 Mike LaCoss	.09	.04	.01
☐ 232 Mike Madden	.09	.04	.01
☐ 233 Jerry Mumphrey	.09	.04	.01
☐ 234 Joe Niekro	.15	.06	.01
☐ 235 Terry Puhl	.09	.04	.01
☐ 236 Luis Pujols	.09	.04	.01
☐ 237 Craig Reynolds	.09	.04	.01
☐ 238 Vern Ruhle	.09	.04	.01
☐ 239 Nolan Ryan	11.00	5.00	1.35
☐ 240 Mike Scott	.25	.10	.02
☐ 241 Tony Scott	.09	.04	.01
☐ 242 Dave Smith	.09	.04	.01
☐ 243 Dickie Thon	.15	.06	.01
☐ 244 Denny Walling	.09	.04	.01
☐ 245 Dale Berra	.09	.04	.01
☐ 246 Jim Bibby	.09	.04	.01
☐ 247 John Candelaria	.09	.04	.01
☐ 248 Jose DeLeon	.35	.15	.03
☐ 249 Mike Easler	.09	.04	.01
☐ 250 Cecilio Guante	.09	.04	.01
☐ 251 Richie Hebner	.09	.04	.01
☐ 252 Lee Lacy	.09	.04	.01
☐ 253 Bill Madlock	.15	.06	.01
☐ 254 Milt May	.09	.04	.01
☐ 255 Lee Mazzilli	.09	.04	.01
☐ 256 Larry McWilliams	.09	.04	.01
☐ 257 Jim Morrison	.09	.04	.01
☐ 258 Dave Parker	.75	.30	.07
☐ 259 Tony Pena	.20	.08	.02
☐ 260 Johnny Ray	.09	.04	.01
☐ 261 Rick Rhoden	.09	.04	.01
☐ 262 Don Robinson	.09	.04	.01
☐ 263 Manny Sarmiento	.09	.04	.01
☐ 264 Rod Scurry	.09	.04	.01
☐ 265 Kent Tekulve	.09	.04	.01
☐ 266 Gene Tenace	.09	.04	.01
☐ 267 Jason Thompson	.09	.04	.01
☐ 268 Lee Tunnell	.09	.04	.01
☐ 269 Marvell Wynne	.15	.06	.01
☐ 270 Ray Burris	.09	.04	.01
☐ 271 Gary Carter	.75	.30	.07

☐ 272	Warren Cromartie	.09	.04	.01
☐ 273	Andre Dawson	2.50	1.00	.25
☐ 274	Doug Flynn	.09	.04	.01
☐ 275	Terry Francona	.09	.04	.01
☐ 276	Bill Gullickson	.15	.06	.01
☐ 277	Bob James	.09	.04	.01
☐ 278	Charlie Lea	.09	.04	.01
☐ 279	Bryan Little	.09	.04	.01
☐ 280	Al Oliver	.15	.06	.01
☐ 281	Tim Raines	.75	.30	.07
☐ 282	Bobby Ramos	.09	.04	.01
☐ 283	Jeff Reardon	.65	.25	.06
☐ 284	Steve Rogers	.09	.04	.01
☐ 285	Scott Sanderson	.15	.06	.01
☐ 286	Dan Schatzeder	.09	.04	.01
☐ 287	Bryn Smith	.15	.06	.01
☐ 288	Chris Speier	.09	.04	.01
☐ 289	Manny Trillo	.09	.04	.01
☐ 290	Mike Vail	.09	.04	.01
☐ 291	Tim Wallach	.25	.10	.02
☐ 292	Chris Welsh	.09	.04	.01
☐ 293	Jim Wohlford	.09	.04	.01
☐ 294	Kurt Bevacqua	.09	.04	.01
☐ 295	Juan Bonilla	.09	.04	.01
☐ 296	Bobby Brown	.09	.04	.01
☐ 297	Luis DeLeon	.09	.04	.01
☐ 298	Dave Dravecky	.20	.08	.02
☐ 299	Tim Flannery	.09	.04	.01
☐ 300	Steve Garvey	.80	.35	.08
☐ 301	Tony Gwynn	9.00	4.00	.90
☐ 302	Andy Hawkins	.35	.15	.03
☐ 303	Ruppert Jones	.09	.04	.01
☐ 304	Terry Kennedy	.09	.04	.01
☐ 305	Tim Lollar	.09	.04	.01
☐ 306	Gary Lucas	.09	.04	.01
☐ 307	Kevin McReynolds	5.50	2.50	.55
☐ 308	Sid Monge	.09	.04	.01
☐ 309	Mario Ramirez	.09	.04	.01
☐ 310	Gene Richards	.09	.04	.01
☐ 311	Luis Salazar	.09	.04	.01
☐ 312	Eric Show	.15	.06	.01
☐ 313	Elias Sosa	.09	.04	.01
☐ 314	Garry Templeton	.15	.06	.01
☐ 315	Mark Thurmond	.09	.04	.01
☐ 316	Ed Whitson	.09	.04	.01
☐ 317	Alan Wiggins	.09	.04	.01
☐ 318	Neil Allen	.09	.04	.01
☐ 319	Joaquin Andujar	.15	.06	.01
☐ 320	Steve Braun	.09	.04	.01
☐ 321	Glenn Brummer	.09	.04	.01
☐ 322	Bob Forsch	.09	.04	.01
☐ 323	David Green	.09	.04	.01
☐ 324	George Hendrick	.09	.04	.01
☐ 325	Tom Herr	.15	.06	.01
☐ 326	Dane Iorg	.09	.04	.01
☐ 327	Jeff Lahti	.09	.04	.01
☐ 328	Dave LaPoint	.09	.04	.01
☐ 329	Willie McGee	.90	.40	.09
☐ 330	Ken Oberkfell	.09	.04	.01
☐ 331	Darrell Porter	.09	.04	.01
☐ 332	Jamie Quirk	.09	.04	.01
☐ 333	Mike Ramsey	.09	.04	.01
☐ 334	Floyd Rayford	.09	.04	.01
☐ 335	Lonnie Smith	.25	.10	.02
☐ 336	Ozzie Smith	2.00	.80	.20
☐ 337	John Stuper	.09	.04	.01
☐ 338	Bruce Sutter	.20	.08	.02
☐ 339	Andy Van Slyke UER (Batting and throwing both wrong on card back)	4.50	2.00	.45
☐ 340	Dave Von Ohlen	.09	.04	.01
☐ 341	Willie Aikens	.09	.04	.01
☐ 342	Mike Armstrong	.09	.04	.01
☐ 343	Bud Black	.15	.06	.01
☐ 344	George Brett	3.00	1.25	.30
☐ 345	Onix Concepcion	.09	.04	.01
☐ 346	Keith Creel	.09	.04	.01
☐ 347	Larry Gura	.09	.04	.01
☐ 348	Don Hood	.09	.04	.01
☐ 349	Dennis Leonard	.09	.04	.01
☐ 350	Hal McRae	.15	.06	.01
☐ 351	Amos Otis	.15	.06	.01
☐ 352	Gaylord Perry	.60	.25	.06
☐ 353	Greg Pryor	.09	.04	.01
☐ 354	Dan Quisenberry	.20	.08	.02
☐ 355	Steve Renko	.09	.04	.01
☐ 356	Leon Roberts	.09	.04	.01
☐ 357	Pat Sheridan	.15	.06	.01
☐ 358	Joe Simpson	.09	.04	.01
☐ 359	Don Slaught	.15	.06	.01
☐ 360	Paul Splittorff	.09	.04	.01
☐ 361	U.L. Washington	.09	.04	.01
☐ 362	John Wathan	.09	.04	.01
☐ 363	Frank White	.09	.04	.01
☐ 364	Willie Wilson	.15	.06	.01
☐ 365	Jim Barr	.09	.04	.01
☐ 366	Dave Bergman	.09	.04	.01
☐ 367	Fred Breining	.09	.04	.01
☐ 368	Bob Brenly	.09	.04	.01
☐ 369	Jack Clark	.30	.12	.03
☐ 370	Chili Davis	.40	.16	.04
☐ 371	Mark Davis	.20	.08	.02
☐ 372	Darrell Evans	.15	.06	.01
☐ 373	Atlee Hammaker	.09	.04	.01
☐ 374	Mike Krukow	.09	.04	.01
☐ 375	Duane Kuiper	.09	.04	.01
☐ 376	Bill Laskey	.09	.04	.01
☐ 377	Gary Lavelle	.09	.04	.01
☐ 378	Johnnie LeMaster	.09	.04	.01
☐ 379	Jeff Leonard	.09	.04	.01
☐ 380	Randy Lerch	.09	.04	.01
☐ 381	Renie Martin	.09	.04	.01
☐ 382	Andy McGaffigan	.09	.04	.01
☐ 383	Greg Minton	.09	.04	.01
☐ 384	Tom O'Malley	.09	.04	.01
☐ 385	Max Venable	.09	.04	.01

No.	Player			
☐ 386	Brad Wellman	.09	.04	.01
☐ 387	Joel Youngblood	.09	.04	.01
☐ 388	Gary Allenson	.09	.04	.01
☐ 389	Luis Aponte	.09	.04	.01
☐ 390	Tony Armas	.09	.04	.01
☐ 391	Doug Bird	.09	.04	.01
☐ 392	Wade Boggs	10.00	4.50	1.25
☐ 393	Dennis Boyd	.35	.15	.03
☐ 394	Mike Brown UER (Red Sox pitcher, shown with record of 31-104)	.09	.04	.01
☐ 395	Mark Clear	.09	.04	.01
☐ 396	Dennis Eckersley	.80	.35	.08
☐ 397	Dwight Evans	.35	.15	.03
☐ 398	Rich Gedman	.09	.04	.01
☐ 399	Glenn Hoffman	.09	.04	.01
☐ 400	Bruce Hurst	.20	.08	.02
☐ 401	John Henry Johnson	.09	.04	.01
☐ 402	Ed Jurak	.09	.04	.01
☐ 403	Rick Miller	.09	.04	.01
☐ 404	Jeff Newman	.09	.04	.01
☐ 405	Reid Nichols	.09	.04	.01
☐ 406	Bob Ojeda	.15	.06	.01
☐ 407	Jerry Remy	.09	.04	.01
☐ 408	Jim Rice	.25	.10	.02
☐ 409	Bob Stanley	.09	.04	.01
☐ 410	Dave Stapleton	.09	.04	.01
☐ 411	John Tudor	.20	.08	.02
☐ 412	Carl Yastrzemski	2.00	.80	.20
☐ 413	Buddy Bell	.15	.06	.01
☐ 414	Larry Biittner	.09	.04	.01
☐ 415	John Butcher	.09	.04	.01
☐ 416	Danny Darwin	.09	.04	.01
☐ 417	Bucky Dent	.15	.06	.01
☐ 418	Dave Hostetler	.09	.04	.01
☐ 419	Charlie Hough	.09	.04	.01
☐ 420	Bobby Johnson	.09	.04	.01
☐ 421	Odell Jones	.09	.04	.01
☐ 422	Jon Matlack	.09	.04	.01
☐ 423	Pete O'Brien	.60	.25	.06
☐ 424	Larry Parrish	.09	.04	.01
☐ 425	Mickey Rivers	.09	.04	.01
☐ 426	Billy Sample	.09	.04	.01
☐ 427	Dave Schmidt	.09	.04	.01
☐ 428	Mike Smithson	.09	.04	.01
☐ 429	Bill Stein	.09	.04	.01
☐ 430	Dave Stewart	1.00	.40	.10
☐ 431	Jim Sundberg	.09	.04	.01
☐ 432	Frank Tanana	.15	.06	.01
☐ 433	Dave Tobik	.09	.04	.01
☐ 434	Wayne Tolleson	.09	.04	.01
☐ 435	George Wright	.09	.04	.01
☐ 436	Bill Almon	.09	.04	.01
☐ 437	Keith Atherton	.09	.04	.01
☐ 438	Dave Beard	.09	.04	.01
☐ 439	Tom Burgmeier	.09	.04	.01
☐ 440	Jeff Burroughs	.09	.04	.01
☐ 441	Chris Codiroli	.09	.04	.01
☐ 442	Tim Conroy	.09	.04	.01
☐ 443	Mike Davis	.09	.04	.01
☐ 444	Wayne Gross	.09	.04	.01
☐ 445	Garry Hancock	.09	.04	.01
☐ 446	Mike Heath	.09	.04	.01
☐ 447	Rickey Henderson	10.00	4.50	1.25
☐ 448	Donnie Hill	.15	.06	.01
☐ 449	Bob Kearney	.09	.04	.01
☐ 450	Bill Krueger	.15	.06	.01
☐ 451	Rick Langford	.09	.04	.01
☐ 452	Carney Lansford	.15	.06	.01
☐ 453	Dave Lopes	.15	.06	.01
☐ 454	Steve McCatty	.09	.04	.01
☐ 455	Dan Meyer	.09	.04	.01
☐ 456	Dwayne Murphy	.09	.04	.01
☐ 457	Mike Norris	.09	.04	.01
☐ 458	Ricky Peters	.09	.04	.01
☐ 459	Tony Phillips	.75	.30	.07
☐ 460	Tom Underwood	.09	.04	.01
☐ 461	Mike Warren	.09	.04	.01
☐ 462	Johnny Bench	2.00	.80	.20
☐ 463	Bruce Berenyi	.09	.04	.01
☐ 464	Dann Bilardello	.09	.04	.01
☐ 465	Cesar Cedeno	.15	.06	.01
☐ 466	Dave Concepcion	.20	.08	.02
☐ 467	Dan Driessen	.09	.04	.01
☐ 468	Nick Esasky	.25	.10	.02
☐ 469	Rich Gale	.09	.04	.01
☐ 470	Ben Hayes	.09	.04	.01
☐ 471	Paul Householder	.09	.04	.01
☐ 472	Tom Hume	.09	.04	.01
☐ 473	Alan Knicely	.09	.04	.01
☐ 474	Eddie Milner	.09	.04	.01
☐ 475	Ron Oester	.09	.04	.01
☐ 476	Kelly Paris	.09	.04	.01
☐ 477	Frank Pastore	.09	.04	.01
☐ 478	Ted Power	.15	.06	.01
☐ 479	Joe Price	.09	.04	.01
☐ 480	Charlie Puleo	.09	.04	.01
☐ 481	Gary Redus	.40	.16	.04
☐ 482	Bill Scherrer	.09	.04	.01
☐ 483	Mario Soto	.09	.04	.01
☐ 484	Alex Trevino	.09	.04	.01
☐ 485	Duane Walker	.09	.04	.01
☐ 486	Larry Bowa	.15	.06	.01
☐ 487	Warren Brusstar	.09	.04	.01
☐ 488	Bill Buckner	.15	.06	.01
☐ 489	Bill Campbell	.09	.04	.01
☐ 490	Ron Cey	.15	.06	.01
☐ 491	Jody Davis	.09	.04	.01
☐ 492	Leon Durham	.09	.04	.01
☐ 493	Mel Hall	.65	.25	.06
☐ 494	Ferguson Jenkins	.60	.25	.06
☐ 495	Jay Johnstone	.15	.06	.01
☐ 496	Craig Lefferts	.40	.16	.04
☐ 497	Carmelo Martinez	.20	.08	.02
☐ 498	Jerry Morales	.09	.04	.01

☐ 499 Keith Moreland .09 .04 .01
☐ 500 Dickie Noles .09 .04 .01
☐ 501 Mike Proly .09 .04 .01
☐ 502 Chuck Rainey .09 .04 .01
☐ 503 Dick Ruthven .09 .04 .01
☐ 504 Ryne Sandberg 18.00 7.50 2.50
☐ 505 Lee Smith .65 .25 .06
☐ 506 Steve Trout .09 .04 .01
☐ 507 Gary Woods .09 .04 .01
☐ 508 Juan Beniquez .09 .04 .01
☐ 509 Bob Boone .15 .06 .01
☐ 510 Rick Burleson .09 .04 .01
☐ 511 Rod Carew 2.00 .80 .20
☐ 512 Bobby Clark .09 .04 .01
☐ 513 John Curtis .09 .04 .01
☐ 514 Doug DeCinces .15 .06 .01
☐ 515 Brian Downing .15 .06 .01
☐ 516 Tim Foli .09 .04 .01
☐ 517 Ken Forsch .09 .04 .01
☐ 518 Bobby Grich .15 .06 .01
☐ 519 Andy Hassler .09 .04 .01
☐ 520 Reggie Jackson 2.50 1.00 .25
☐ 521 Ron Jackson .09 .04 .01
☐ 522 Tommy John .25 .10 .02
☐ 523 Bruce Kison .09 .04 .01
☐ 524 Steve Lubratich .09 .04 .01
☐ 525 Fred Lynn .25 .10 .02
☐ 526 Gary Pettis .30 .12 .03
☐ 527 Luis Sanchez .09 .04 .01
☐ 528 Daryl Sconiers .09 .04 .01
☐ 529 Ellis Valentine .09 .04 .01
☐ 530 Rob Wilfong .09 .04 .01
☐ 531 Mike Witt .09 .04 .01
☐ 532 Geoff Zahn .09 .04 .01
☐ 533 Bud Anderson .09 .04 .01
☐ 534 Chris Bando .09 .04 .01
☐ 535 Alan Bannister .09 .04 .01
☐ 536 Bert Blyleven .35 .15 .03
☐ 537 Tom Brennan .09 .04 .01
☐ 538 Jamie Easterly .09 .04 .01
☐ 539 Juan Eichelberger .09 .04 .01
☐ 540 Jim Essian .09 .04 .01
☐ 541 Mike Fischlin .09 .04 .01
☐ 542 Julio Franco 4.00 1.75 .40
☐ 543 Mike Hargrove .09 .04 .01
☐ 544 Toby Harrah .09 .04 .01
☐ 545 Ron Hassey .09 .04 .01
☐ 546 Neal Heaton .25 .10 .02
☐ 547 Bake McBride .09 .04 .01
☐ 548 Broderick Perkins .09 .04 .01
☐ 549 Lary Sorensen .09 .04 .01
☐ 550 Dan Spillner .09 .04 .01
☐ 551 Rick Sutcliffe .15 .06 .01
☐ 552 Pat Tabler .15 .06 .01
☐ 553 Gorman Thomas .15 .06 .01
☐ 554 Andre Thornton .09 .04 .01
☐ 555 George Vukovich .09 .04 .01
☐ 556 Darrell Brown .09 .04 .01
☐ 557 Tom Brunansky .25 .10 .02
☐ 558 Randy Bush .20 .08 .02
☐ 559 Bobby Castillo .09 .04 .01
☐ 560 John Castino .09 .04 .01
☐ 561 Ron Davis .09 .04 .01
☐ 562 Dave Engle .09 .04 .01
☐ 563 Lenny Faedo .09 .04 .01
☐ 564 Pete Filson .09 .04 .01
☐ 565 Gary Gaetti .30 .12 .03
☐ 566 Mickey Hatcher .09 .04 .01
☐ 567 Kent Hrbek .60 .25 .06
☐ 568 Rusty Kuntz .09 .04 .01
☐ 569 Tim Laudner .09 .04 .01
☐ 570 Rick Lysander .09 .04 .01
☐ 571 Bobby Mitchell .09 .04 .01
☐ 572 Ken Schrom .09 .04 .01
☐ 573 Ray Smith .09 .04 .01
☐ 574 Tim Teufel .35 .15 .03
☐ 575 Frank Viola 1.50 .60 .15
☐ 576 Gary Ward .09 .04 .01
☐ 577 Ron Washington .09 .04 .01
☐ 578 Len Whitehouse .09 .04 .01
☐ 579 Al Williams .09 .04 .01
☐ 580 Bob Bailor .09 .04 .01
☐ 581 Mark Bradley .09 .04 .01
☐ 582 Hubie Brooks .25 .10 .02
☐ 583 Carlos Diaz .09 .04 .01
☐ 584 George Foster .25 .10 .02
☐ 585 Brian Giles .09 .04 .01
☐ 586 Danny Heep .09 .04 .01
☐ 587 Keith Hernandez .35 .15 .03
☐ 588 Ron Hodges .09 .04 .01
☐ 589 Scott Holman .09 .04 .01
☐ 590 Dave Kingman .20 .08 .02
☐ 591 Ed Lynch .09 .04 .01
☐ 592 Jose Oquendo .30 .12 .03
☐ 593 Jesse Orosco .09 .04 .01
☐ 594 Junior Ortiz .15 .06 .01
☐ 595 Tom Seaver 3.50 1.50 .35
☐ 596 Doug Sisk .09 .04 .01
☐ 597 Rusty Staub .15 .06 .01
☐ 598 John Stearns .09 .04 .01
☐ 599 Darryl Strawberry 40.00 18.00 6.00
☐ 600 Craig Swan .09 .04 .01
☐ 601 Walt Terrell .25 .10 .02
☐ 602 Mike Torrez .09 .04 .01
☐ 603 Mookie Wilson .15 .06 .01
☐ 604 Jamie Allen .09 .04 .01
☐ 605 Jim Beattie .09 .04 .01
☐ 606 Tony Bernazard .09 .04 .01
☐ 607 Manny Castillo .09 .04 .01
☐ 608 Bill Caudill .09 .04 .01
☐ 609 Bryan Clark .09 .04 .01
☐ 610 Al Cowens .09 .04 .01
☐ 611 Dave Henderson .75 .30 .07
☐ 612 Steve Henderson .09 .04 .01
☐ 613 Orlando Mercado .09 .04 .01
☐ 614 Mike Moore .25 .10 .02

☐ 615	Ricky Nelson UER (Jamie Nelson's stats on back)	.15	.06	.01
☐ 616	Spike Owen	.35	.15	.03
☐ 617	Pat Putnam	.09	.04	.01
☐ 618	Ron Roenicke	.09	.04	.01
☐ 619	Mike Stanton	.09	.04	.01
☐ 620	Bob Stoddard	.09	.04	.01
☐ 621	Rick Sweet	.09	.04	.01
☐ 622	Roy Thomas	.09	.04	.01
☐ 623	Ed VandeBerg	.09	.04	.01
☐ 624	Matt Young	.15	.06	.01
☐ 625	Richie Zisk	.09	.04	.01
☐ 626	Fred Lynn 1982 AS Game RB	.15	.06	.01
☐ 627	Manny Trillo 1983 AS Game RB	.09	.04	.01
☐ 628	Steve Garvey NL Iron Man	.30	.12	.03
☐ 629	Rod Carew AL Batting Runner-Up	.50	.20	.05
☐ 630	Wade Boggs AL Batting Champion	1.00	.40	.10
☐ 631	Tim Raines: Letting Go of the Raines	.45	.18	.04
☐ 632	Al Oliver Double Trouble	.15	.06	.01
☐ 633	Steve Sax AS Second Base	.15	.06	.01
☐ 634	Dickie Thon AS Shortstop	.15	.06	.01
☐ 635	Ace Firemen Dan Quisenberry and Tippy Martinez	.15	.06	.01
☐ 636	Reds Reunited Joe Morgan Pete Rose Tony Perez	.60	.25	.06
☐ 637	Backstop Stars Lance Parrish Bob Boone	.15	.06	.01
☐ 638	Geo.Brett and G.Perry Pine Tar 7/24/83	.75	.30	.07
☐ 639	1983 No Hitters Dave Righetti Mike Warren Bob Forsch	.15	.06	.01
☐ 640	Bench and Yaz Retiring Superstars	2.50	1.00	.25
☐ 641	Gaylord Perry Going Out In Style	.30	.12	.03
☐ 642	Steve Carlton 300 Club and Strikeout Record	.50	.20	.05
☐ 643	Altobelli and Owens WS Managers	.09	.04	.01
☐ 644	Rick Dempsey World Series MVP	.09	.04	.01
☐ 645	Mike Boddicker WS Rookie Winner	.15	.06	.01
☐ 646	Scott McGregor WS Clincher	.09	.04	.01
☐ 647	CL: Orioles/Royals	.18	.02	.00
☐ 648	CL: Phillies/Giants	.18	.02	.00
☐ 649	CL: White Sox/Red Sox	.18	.02	.00
☐ 650	CL: Tigers/Rangers	.18	.02	.00
☐ 651	CL: Dodgers/A's	.18	.02	.00
☐ 652	CL: Yankees/Reds	.18	.02	.00
☐ 653	CL: Blue Jays/Cubs	.18	.02	.00
☐ 654	CL: Braves/Angels	.18	.02	.00
☐ 655	CL: Brewers/Indians	.18	.02	.00
☐ 656	CL: Astros/Twins	.18	.02	.00
☐ 657	CL: Pirates/Mets	.18	.02	.00
☐ 658	CL: Expos/Mariners	.18	.02	.00
☐ 659	CL: Padres/Specials	.18	.02	.00
☐ 660	CL: Cardinals/Teams	.18	.02	.00

1984 Fleer Update

The cards in this 132-card set measure 2 1/2" by 3 1/2". For the first time, the Fleer Gum Company issued a traded, extended, or update set. The purpose of the set was the same as the traded sets issued by Topps over the past four years, i.e., to portray players with their proper team for the current year and to portray rookies who were not in their regular issue. Like the Topps Traded sets of the past four years, the Fleer Update sets were distributed through hobby dealers only. The set was quite popular with collectors, and, apparently, the print run was relatively short, as the set was quickly in short supply and exhibited a rapid and dramatic price increase. The cards are numbered on the back with a U prefix; the order corresponds to the

alphabetical order of the subjects' names. The key (extended) rookie cards in this set are Roger Clemens, Alvin Davis, John Franco, Dwight Gooden, Jimmy Key, Mark Langston, Kirby Puckett, Jose Rijo, and Bret Saberhagen. Collectors are urged to be careful if purchasing single cards of Clemens, Darling, Gooden, Puckett, Rose, or Saberhagen as these specific cards have been illegally reprinted. These fakes are blurry when compared to the real thing.

	MINT	EXC	G-VG
COMPLETE SET (132)	625.00	250.00	75.00
COMMON PLAYER (1-132)	.30	.12	.03
☐ U1 Willie Aikens	.40	.16	.04
☐ U2 Luis Aponte	.30	.12	.03
☐ U3 Mark Bailey	.30	.12	.03
☐ U4 Bob Bailor	.30	.12	.03
☐ U5 Dusty Baker	.40	.16	.04
☐ U6 Steve Balboni	.40	.16	.04
☐ U7 Alan Bannister	.30	.12	.03
☐ U8 Marty Barrett	.60	.25	.06
☐ U9 Dave Beard	.30	.12	.03
☐ U10 Joe Beckwith	.30	.12	.03
☐ U11 Dave Bergman	.30	.12	.03
☐ U12 Tony Bernazard	.30	.12	.03
☐ U13 Bruce Bochte	.30	.12	.03
☐ U14 Barry Bonnell	.30	.12	.03
☐ U15 Phil Bradley	1.25	.50	.12
☐ U16 Fred Breining	.30	.12	.03
☐ U17 Mike Brown (Angels OF)	.30	.12	.03
☐ U18 Bill Buckner	.40	.16	.04
☐ U19 Ray Burris	.30	.12	.03
☐ U20 John Butcher	.30	.12	.03
☐ U21 Brett Butler	2.00	.80	.20
☐ U22 Enos Cabell	.30	.12	.03
☐ U23 Bill Campbell	.30	.12	.03
☐ U24 Bill Caudill	.30	.12	.03
☐ U25 Bobby Clark	.30	.12	.03
☐ U26 Bryan Clark	.30	.12	.03
☐ U27 Roger Clemens	250.00	110.00	37.50
☐ U28 Jaime Cocanower	.30	.12	.03
☐ U29 Ron Darling	6.00	2.50	.60
☐ U30 Alvin Davis	8.00	3.50	.80
☐ U31 Bob Dernier	.30	.12	.03
☐ U32 Carlos Diaz	.30	.12	.03
☐ U33 Mike Easler	.30	.12	.03
☐ U34 Dennis Eckersley	4.50	2.00	.45
☐ U35 Jim Essian	.40	.16	.04
☐ U36 Darrell Evans	.60	.25	.06
☐ U37 Mike Fitzgerald	.30	.12	.03
☐ U38 Tim Foli	.30	.12	.03
☐ U39 John Franco	9.00	4.00	.90
☐ U40 George Frazier	.30	.12	.03
☐ U41 Rich Gale	.30	.12	.03
☐ U42 Barbaro Garbey	.30	.12	.03
☐ U43 Dwight Gooden	120.00	55.00	18.00
☐ U44 Goose Gossage	1.00	.40	.10
☐ U45 Wayne Gross	.30	.12	.03
☐ U46 Mark Gubicza	4.00	1.75	.40
☐ U47 Jackie Gutierrez	.30	.12	.03
☐ U48 Toby Harrah	.40	.16	.04
☐ U49 Ron Hassey	.30	.12	.03
☐ U50 Richie Hebner	.30	.12	.03
☐ U51 Willie Hernandez	.40	.16	.04
☐ U52 Ed Hodge	.30	.12	.03
☐ U53 Ricky Horton	.40	.16	.04
☐ U54 Art Howe	.40	.16	.04
☐ U55 Dane Iorg	.30	.12	.03
☐ U56 Brook Jacoby	2.00	.80	.20
☐ U57 Dion James	.40	.16	.04
☐ U58 Mike Jeffcoat	.40	.16	.04
☐ U59 Ruppert Jones	.30	.12	.03
☐ U60 Bob Kearney	.30	.12	.03
☐ U61 Jimmy Key	10.00	4.50	1.25
☐ U62 Dave Kingman	.60	.25	.06
☐ U63 Brad Komminsk	.40	.16	.04
☐ U64 Jerry Koosman	.50	.20	.05
☐ U65 Wayne Krenchicki	.30	.12	.03
☐ U66 Rusty Kuntz	.30	.12	.03
☐ U67 Frank LaCorte	.30	.12	.03
☐ U68 Dennis Lamp	.30	.12	.03
☐ U69 Tito Landrum	.40	.16	.04
☐ U70 Mark Langston	22.00	9.50	3.15
☐ U71 Rick Leach	.30	.12	.03
☐ U72 Craig Lefferts	.60	.25	.06
☐ U73 Gary Lucas	.30	.12	.03
☐ U74 Jerry Martin	.30	.12	.03
☐ U75 Carmelo Martinez	.50	.20	.05
☐ U76 Mike Mason	.30	.12	.03
☐ U77 Gary Matthews	.40	.16	.04
☐ U78 Andy McGaffigan	.40	.16	.04
☐ U79 Joey McLaughlin	.30	.12	.03
☐ U80 Joe Morgan	5.00	2.25	.50
☐ U81 Darryl Motley	.30	.12	.03
☐ U82 Graig Nettles	.75	.30	.07
☐ U83 Phil Niekro	4.00	1.75	.40
☐ U84 Ken Oberkfell	.30	.12	.03
☐ U85 Al Oliver	.40	.16	.04
☐ U86 Jorge Orta	.30	.12	.03
☐ U87 Amos Otis	.40	.16	.04
☐ U88 Bob Owchinko	.30	.12	.03
☐ U89 Dave Parker	4.00	1.75	.40
☐ U90 Jack Perconte	.30	.12	.03
☐ U91 Tony Perez	4.50	2.00	.45
☐ U92 Gerald Perry	1.25	.50	.12
☐ U93 Kirby Puckett	225.00	100.00	33.00
☐ U94 Shane Rawley	.30	.12	.03
☐ U95 Floyd Rayford	.30	.12	.03
☐ U96 Ron Reed	.30	.12	.03
☐ U97 R.J. Reynolds	1.00	.40	.10
☐ U98 Gene Richards	.30	.12	.03
☐ U99 Jose Rijo	12.00	5.25	1.50

☐ U100 Jeff Robinson .... .40 .16 .04
(Giants pitcher)
☐ U101 Ron Romanick .... .30 .12 .03
☐ U102 Pete Rose 17.00 7.25 2.50
☐ U103 Bret Saberhagen 45.00 20.00 5.00
☐ U104 Scott Sanderson .... .60 .25 .06
☐ U105 Dick Schofield .... 1.00 .40 .10
☐ U106 Tom Seaver 21.00 9.00 3.00
☐ U107 Jim Slaton .... .30 .12 .03
☐ U108 Mike Smithson .... .30 .12 .03
☐ U109 Lary Sorensen .... .30 .12 .03
☐ U110 Tim Stoddard .... .30 .12 .03
☐ U111 Jeff Stone .... .40 .16 .04
☐ U112 Champ Summers .... .30 .12 .03
☐ U113 Jim Sundberg .... .30 .12 .03
☐ U114 Rick Sutcliffe .... .60 .25 .06
☐ U115 Craig Swan .... .40 .16 .04
☐ U116 Derrel Thomas .... .30 .12 .03
☐ U117 Gorman Thomas .... .40 .16 .04
☐ U118 Alex Trevino .... .30 .12 .03
☐ U119 Manny Trillo .... .30 .12 .03
☐ U120 John Tudor .... .50 .20 .05
☐ U121 Tom Underwood .... .30 .12 .03
☐ U122 Mike Vail .... .30 .12 .03
☐ U123 Tom Waddell .... .30 .12 .03
☐ U124 Gary Ward .... .30 .12 .03
☐ U125 Terry Whitfield .... .30 .12 .03
☐ U126 Curtis Wilkerson .... .30 .12 .03
☐ U127 Frank Williams .... .30 .12 .03
☐ U128 Glenn Wilson .... .30 .12 .03
☐ U129 John Wockenfuss .... .30 .12 .03
☐ U130 Ned Yost .... .30 .12 .03
☐ U131 Mike Young .... .40 .16 .04
☐ U132 Checklist: 1-132 .... .30 .10 .02

1985 Fleer

The cards in this 660-card set measure 2 1/2" by 3 1/2". The 1985 Fleer set features fronts that contain the team logo along with the player's name and position. The borders enclosing the photo are color-coded to correspond to the player's team. In each case, the color is one of the standard colors of that team, e.g., orange for Baltimore, red for St. Louis, etc. The backs feature the same name, number, and statistics format that Fleer has been using over the past few years. The cards are ordered alphabetically within team. The teams are ordered based on their respective performance during the prior year, e.g., World Champion Detroit Tigers (1-25), NL Champion San Diego (26-48), Chicago Cubs (49-71), New York Mets (72-95), Toronto (96-119), New York Yankees (120-147), Boston (148-169), Baltimore (170-195), Kansas City (196-218), St. Louis (219-243), Philadelphia (244-269), Minnesota (270-292), California (293-317), Atlanta (318-342), Houston (343-365), Los Angeles (366-391), Montreal (392-413), Oakland (414-436), Cleveland (437-460), Pittsburgh (461-481), Seattle (482-505), Chicago White Sox (506-530), Cincinnati (531-554), Texas (555-575), Milwaukee (576-601), and San Francisco (602-625). Specials (626-643), Major League Prospects (644-653), and checklist cards (654-660) complete the set. The black and white photo on the reverse is included for the third straight year. This set is noted for containing the Rookie Cards of Roger Clemens, Alvin Davis, Eric Davis, Glenn Davis, Shawon Dunston, Dwight Gooden, Kelly Gruber, Orel Hershiser, Jimmy Key, Mark Langston, Terry Pendleton, Kirby Puckett, Jose Rijo, Bret Saberhagen, and Danny Tartabull.

	MINT	EXC	G-VG
COMPLETE SET (660)	180.00	80.00	27.00
COMMON PLAYER (1-660)	.07	.03	.01

☐ 1 Doug Bair .... .12 .04 .01
☐ 2 Juan Berenguer .... .07 .03 .01
☐ 3 Dave Bergman .... .07 .03 .01
☐ 4 Tom Brookens .... .07 .03 .01
☐ 5 Marty Castillo .... .07 .03 .01
☐ 6 Darrell Evans .... .12 .05 .01
☐ 7 Barbaro Garbey .... .07 .03 .01
☐ 8 Kirk Gibson .... .35 .15 .03
☐ 9 John Grubb .... .07 .03 .01
☐ 10 Willie Hernandez .... .10 .04 .01
☐ 11 Larry Herndon .... .07 .03 .01
☐ 12 Howard Johnson .... 2.75 1.10 .27

☐ 13 Ruppert Jones .07 .03 .01
☐ 14 Rusty Kuntz .07 .03 .01
☐ 15 Chet Lemon .07 .03 .01
☐ 16 Aurelio Lopez .07 .03 .01
☐ 17 Sid Monge .07 .03 .01
☐ 18 Jack Morris .60 .25 .06
☐ 19 Lance Parrish .25 .10 .02
☐ 20 Dan Petry .07 .03 .01
☐ 21 Dave Rozema .07 .03 .01
☐ 22 Bill Scherrer .07 .03 .01
☐ 23 Alan Trammell .60 .25 .06
☐ 24 Lou Whitaker .40 .16 .04
☐ 25 Milt Wilcox .07 .03 .01
☐ 26 Kurt Bevacqua .07 .03 .01
☐ 27 Greg Booker .07 .03 .01
☐ 28 Bobby Brown .07 .03 .01
☐ 29 Luis DeLeon .07 .03 .01
☐ 30 Dave Dravecky .15 .06 .01
☐ 31 Tim Flannery .07 .03 .01
☐ 32 Steve Garvey .50 .20 .05
☐ 33 Goose Gossage .15 .06 .01
☐ 34 Tony Gwynn 4.25 1.75 .42
☐ 35 Greg Harris .07 .03 .01
☐ 36 Andy Hawkins .10 .04 .01
☐ 37 Terry Kennedy .07 .03 .01
☐ 38 Craig Lefferts .10 .04 .01
☐ 39 Tim Lollar .07 .03 .01
☐ 40 Carmelo Martinez .07 .03 .01
☐ 41 Kevin McReynolds .90 .40 .09
☐ 42 Graig Nettles .12 .05 .01
☐ 43 Luis Salazar .07 .03 .01
☐ 44 Eric Show .07 .03 .01
☐ 45 Garry Templeton .10 .04 .01
☐ 46 Mark Thurmond .07 .03 .01
☐ 47 Ed Whitson .07 .03 .01
☐ 48 Alan Wiggins .07 .03 .01
☐ 49 Rich Bordi .07 .03 .01
☐ 50 Larry Bowa .10 .04 .01
☐ 51 Warren Brusstar .07 .03 .01
☐ 52 Ron Cey .10 .04 .01
☐ 53 Henry Cotto .15 .06 .01
☐ 54 Jody Davis .07 .03 .01
☐ 55 Bob Dernier .07 .03 .01
☐ 56 Leon Durham .07 .03 .01
☐ 57 Dennis Eckersley .35 .15 .03
☐ 58 George Frazier .07 .03 .01
☐ 59 Richie Hebner .07 .03 .01
☐ 60 Dave Lopes .10 .04 .01
☐ 61 Gary Matthews .07 .03 .01
☐ 62 Keith Moreland .07 .03 .01
☐ 63 Rick Reuschel .12 .05 .01
☐ 64 Dick Ruthven .07 .03 .01
☐ 65 Ryne Sandberg 6.50 2.75 .65
☐ 66 Scott Sanderson .10 .04 .01
☐ 67 Lee Smith .40 .16 .04
☐ 68 Tim Stoddard .07 .03 .01
☐ 69 Rick Sutcliffe .12 .05 .01
☐ 70 Steve Trout .07 .03 .01
☐ 71 Gary Woods .07 .03 .01
☐ 72 Wally Backman .07 .03 .01
☐ 73 Bruce Berenyi .07 .03 .01
☐ 74 Hubie Brooks UER .15 .06 .01
(Kelvin Chapman's stats on card back)
☐ 75 Kelvin Chapman .07 .03 .01
☐ 76 Ron Darling .35 .15 .03
☐ 77 Sid Fernandez .50 .20 .05
☐ 78 Mike Fitzgerald .07 .03 .01
☐ 79 George Foster .15 .06 .01
☐ 80 Brent Gaff .07 .03 .01
☐ 81 Ron Gardenhire .07 .03 .01
☐ 82 Dwight Gooden 12.50 5.50 1.65
☐ 83 Tom Gorman .07 .03 .01
☐ 84 Danny Heep .07 .03 .01
☐ 85 Keith Hernandez .25 .10 .02
☐ 86 Ray Knight .10 .04 .01
☐ 87 Ed Lynch .07 .03 .01
☐ 88 Jose Oquendo .10 .04 .01
☐ 89 Jesse Orosco .07 .03 .01
☐ 90 Rafael Santana .12 .05 .01
☐ 91 Doug Sisk .07 .03 .01
☐ 92 Rusty Staub .12 .05 .01
☐ 93 Darryl Strawberry 12.50 5.50 1.65
☐ 94 Walt Terrell .07 .03 .01
☐ 95 Mookie Wilson .10 .04 .01
☐ 96 Jim Acker .07 .03 .01
☐ 97 Willie Aikens .07 .03 .01
☐ 98 Doyle Alexander .07 .03 .01
☐ 99 Jesse Barfield .17 .07 .01
☐ 100 George Bell .90 .40 .09
☐ 101 Jim Clancy .07 .03 .01
☐ 102 Dave Collins .07 .03 .01
☐ 103 Tony Fernandez .60 .25 .06
☐ 104 Damaso Garcia .07 .03 .01
☐ 105 Jim Gott .07 .03 .01
☐ 106 Alfredo Griffin .07 .03 .01
☐ 107 Garth Iorg .07 .03 .01
☐ 108 Roy Lee Jackson .07 .03 .01
☐ 109 Cliff Johnson .07 .03 .01
☐ 110 Jimmy Key 2.00 .80 .20
☐ 111 Dennis Lamp .07 .03 .01
☐ 112 Rick Leach .07 .03 .01
☐ 113 Luis Leal .07 .03 .01
☐ 114 Buck Martinez .07 .03 .01
☐ 115 Lloyd Moseby .10 .04 .01
☐ 116 Rance Mulliniks .07 .03 .01
☐ 117 Dave Stieb .20 .08 .02
☐ 118 Willie Upshaw .07 .03 .01
☐ 119 Ernie Whitt .07 .03 .01
☐ 120 Mike Armstrong .07 .03 .01
☐ 121 Don Baylor .12 .05 .01
☐ 122 Marty Bystrom .07 .03 .01
☐ 123 Rick Cerone .07 .03 .01
☐ 124 Joe Cowley .07 .03 .01
☐ 125 Brian Dayett .07 .03 .01
☐ 126 Tim Foli .07 .03 .01

☐ 127 Ray Fontenot	.07	.03	.01
☐ 128 Ken Griffey	.17	.07	.01
☐ 129 Ron Guidry	.20	.08	.02
☐ 130 Toby Harrah	.07	.03	.01
☐ 131 Jay Howell	.10	.04	.01
☐ 132 Steve Kemp	.07	.03	.01
☐ 133 Don Mattingly	10.00	4.50	1.25
☐ 134 Bobby Meacham	.07	.03	.01
☐ 135 John Montefusco	.07	.03	.01
☐ 136 Omar Moreno	.07	.03	.01
☐ 137 Dale Murray	.07	.03	.01
☐ 138 Phil Niekro	.30	.12	.03
☐ 139 Mike Pagliarulo	.60	.25	.06
☐ 140 Willie Randolph	.12	.05	.01
☐ 141 Dennis Rasmussen	.15	.06	.01
☐ 142 Dave Righetti	.15	.06	.01
☐ 143 Jose Rijo	2.50	1.00	.25
☐ 144 Andre Robertson	.07	.03	.01
☐ 145 Bob Shirley	.07	.03	.01
☐ 146 Dave Winfield	.80	.35	.08
☐ 147 Butch Wynegar	.07	.03	.01
☐ 148 Gary Allenson	.07	.03	.01
☐ 149 Tony Armas	.07	.03	.01
☐ 150 Marty Barrett	.10	.04	.01
☐ 151 Wade Boggs	5.00	2.25	.50
☐ 152 Dennis Boyd	.10	.04	.01
☐ 153 Bill Buckner	.10	.04	.01
☐ 154 Mark Clear	.07	.03	.01
☐ 155 Roger Clemens	37.50	16.00	4.00
☐ 156 Steve Crawford	.07	.03	.01
☐ 157 Mike Easler	.07	.03	.01
☐ 158 Dwight Evans	.20	.08	.02
☐ 159 Rich Gedman	.07	.03	.01
☐ 160 Jackie Gutierrez (W.Boggs on deck)	.15	.06	.01
☐ 161 Bruce Hurst	.12	.05	.01
☐ 162 John Henry Johnson	.07	.03	.01
☐ 163 Rick Miller	.07	.03	.01
☐ 164 Reid Nichols	.07	.03	.01
☐ 165 Al Nipper	.07	.03	.01
☐ 166 Bob Ojeda	.10	.04	.01
☐ 167 Jerry Remy	.07	.03	.01
☐ 168 Jim Rice	.20	.08	.02
☐ 169 Bob Stanley	.07	.03	.01
☐ 170 Mike Boddicker	.07	.03	.01
☐ 171 Al Bumbry	.07	.03	.01
☐ 172 Todd Cruz	.07	.03	.01
☐ 173 Rich Dauer	.07	.03	.01
☐ 174 Storm Davis	.07	.03	.01
☐ 175 Rick Dempsey	.07	.03	.01
☐ 176 Jim Dwyer	.07	.03	.01
☐ 177 Mike Flanagan	.10	.04	.01
☐ 178 Dan Ford	.07	.03	.01
☐ 179 Wayne Gross	.07	.03	.01
☐ 180 John Lowenstein	.07	.03	.01
☐ 181 Dennis Martinez	.12	.05	.01
☐ 182 Tippy Martinez	.07	.03	.01
☐ 183 Scott McGregor	.07	.03	.01
☐ 184 Eddie Murray	1.25	.50	.12
☐ 185 Joe Nolan	.07	.03	.01
☐ 186 Floyd Rayford	.07	.03	.01
☐ 187 Cal Ripken	7.00	3.00	.70
☐ 188 Gary Roenicke	.07	.03	.01
☐ 189 Lenn Sakata	.07	.03	.01
☐ 190 John Shelby	.07	.03	.01
☐ 191 Ken Singleton	.10	.04	.01
☐ 192 Sammy Stewart	.07	.03	.01
☐ 193 Bill Swaggerty	.07	.03	.01
☐ 194 Tom Underwood	.07	.03	.01
☐ 195 Mike Young	.07	.03	.01
☐ 196 Steve Balboni	.07	.03	.01
☐ 197 Joe Beckwith	.07	.03	.01
☐ 198 Bud Black	.10	.04	.01
☐ 199 George Brett	1.50	.60	.15
☐ 200 Onix Concepcion	.07	.03	.01
☐ 201 Mark Gubicza	.75	.30	.07
☐ 202 Larry Gura	.07	.03	.01
☐ 203 Mark Huismann	.07	.03	.01
☐ 204 Dane Iorg	.07	.03	.01
☐ 205 Danny Jackson	.20	.08	.02
☐ 206 Charlie Leibrandt	.07	.03	.01
☐ 207 Hal McRae	.10	.04	.01
☐ 208 Darryl Motley	.07	.03	.01
☐ 209 Jorge Orta	.07	.03	.01
☐ 210 Greg Pryor	.07	.03	.01
☐ 211 Dan Quisenberry	.12	.05	.01
☐ 212 Bret Saberhagen	8.00	3.50	.80
☐ 213 Pat Sheridan	.07	.03	.01
☐ 214 Don Slaught	.07	.03	.01
☐ 215 U.L. Washington	.07	.03	.01
☐ 216 John Wathan	.07	.03	.01
☐ 217 Frank White	.07	.03	.01
☐ 218 Willie Wilson	.12	.05	.01
☐ 219 Neil Allen	.07	.03	.01
☐ 220 Joaquin Andujar	.10	.04	.01
☐ 221 Steve Braun	.07	.03	.01
☐ 222 Danny Cox	.07	.03	.01
☐ 223 Bob Forsch	.07	.03	.01
☐ 224 David Green	.07	.03	.01
☐ 225 George Hendrick	.07	.03	.01
☐ 226 Tom Herr	.10	.04	.01
☐ 227 Ricky Horton	.15	.06	.01
☐ 228 Art Howe	.10	.04	.01
☐ 229 Mike Jorgensen	.07	.03	.01
☐ 230 Kurt Kepshire	.07	.03	.01
☐ 231 Jeff Lahti	.07	.03	.01
☐ 232 Tito Landrum	.07	.03	.01
☐ 233 Dave LaPoint	.07	.03	.01
☐ 234 Willie McGee	.60	.25	.06
☐ 235 Tom Nieto	.07	.03	.01
☐ 236 Terry Pendleton	4.50	2.00	.45
☐ 237 Darrell Porter	.07	.03	.01
☐ 238 Dave Rucker	.07	.03	.01
☐ 239 Lonnie Smith	.15	.06	.01
☐ 240 Ozzie Smith	1.00	.40	.10
☐ 241 Bruce Sutter	.12	.05	.01

☐ 242 Andy Van Slyke UER ...... .90 .40 .09
(Bats Right,
Throws Left)
☐ 243 Dave Von Ohlen .... .07 .03 .01
☐ 244 Larry Andersen .... .07 .03 .01
☐ 245 Bill Campbell .... .07 .03 .01
☐ 246 Steve Carlton .... .90 .40 .09
☐ 247 Tim Corcoran .... .07 .03 .01
☐ 248 Ivan DeJesus .... .07 .03 .01
☐ 249 John Denny .... .07 .03 .01
☐ 250 Bo Diaz .... .07 .03 .01
☐ 251 Greg Gross .... .07 .03 .01
☐ 252 Kevin Gross .... .10 .04 .01
☐ 253 Von Hayes .... .15 .06 .01
☐ 254 Al Holland .... .07 .03 .01
☐ 255 Charles Hudson .... .07 .03 .01
☐ 256 Jerry Koosman .... .10 .04 .01
☐ 257 Joe Lefebvre .... .07 .03 .01
☐ 258 Sixto Lezcano .... .07 .03 .01
☐ 259 Garry Maddox .... .07 .03 .01
☐ 260 Len Matuszek .... .07 .03 .01
☐ 261 Tug McGraw .... .12 .05 .01
☐ 262 Al Oliver .... .10 .04 .01
☐ 263 Shane Rawley .... .07 .03 .01
☐ 264 Juan Samuel .... .50 .20 .05
☐ 265 Mike Schmidt .... 3.50 1.50 .35
☐ 266 Jeff Stone .... .10 .04 .01
☐ 267 Ozzie Virgil .... .07 .03 .01
☐ 268 Glenn Wilson .... .07 .03 .01
☐ 269 John Wockenfuss .... .07 .03 .01
☐ 270 Darrell Brown .... .07 .03 .01
☐ 271 Tom Brunansky .... .15 .06 .01
☐ 272 Randy Bush .... .07 .03 .01
☐ 273 John Butcher .... .07 .03 .01
☐ 274 Bobby Castillo .... .07 .03 .01
☐ 275 Ron Davis .... .07 .03 .01
☐ 276 Dave Engle .... .07 .03 .01
☐ 277 Pete Filson .... .07 .03 .01
☐ 278 Gary Gaetti .... .15 .06 .01
☐ 279 Mickey Hatcher .... .07 .03 .01
☐ 280 Ed Hodge .... .07 .03 .01
☐ 281 Kent Hrbek .... .35 .15 .03
☐ 282 Houston Jimenez .... .07 .03 .01
☐ 283 Tim Laudner .... .07 .03 .01
☐ 284 Rick Lysander .... .07 .03 .01
☐ 285 Dave Meier .... .07 .03 .01
☐ 286 Kirby Puckett 30.00 13.50 4.50
☐ 287 Pat Putnam .... .07 .03 .01
☐ 288 Ken Schrom .... .07 .03 .01
☐ 289 Mike Smithson .... .07 .03 .01
☐ 290 Tim Teufel .... .10 .04 .01
☐ 291 Frank Viola .... .60 .25 .06
☐ 292 Ron Washington .... .07 .03 .01
☐ 293 Don Aase .... .07 .03 .01
☐ 294 Juan Beniquez .... .07 .03 .01
☐ 295 Bob Boone .... .12 .05 .01
☐ 296 Mike Brown .... .07 .03 .01
(Angels OF)
☐ 297 Rod Carew .... 1.00 .40 .10
☐ 298 Doug Corbett .... .07 .03 .01
☐ 299 Doug DeCinces .... .10 .04 .01
☐ 300 Brian Downing .... .10 .04 .01
☐ 301 Ken Forsch .... .07 .03 .01
☐ 302 Bobby Grich .... .10 .04 .01
☐ 303 Reggie Jackson .... 1.25 .50 .12
☐ 304 Tommy John .... .17 .07 .01
☐ 305 Curt Kaufman .... .07 .03 .01
☐ 306 Bruce Kison .... .07 .03 .01
☐ 307 Fred Lynn .... .17 .07 .01
☐ 308 Gary Pettis .... .10 .04 .01
☐ 309 Ron Romanick .... .07 .03 .01
☐ 310 Luis Sanchez .... .07 .03 .01
☐ 311 Dick Schofield .... .15 .06 .01
☐ 312 Daryl Sconiers .... .07 .03 .01
☐ 313 Jim Slaton .... .07 .03 .01
☐ 314 Derrel Thomas .... .07 .03 .01
☐ 315 Rob Wilfong .... .07 .03 .01
☐ 316 Mike Witt .... .07 .03 .01
☐ 317 Geoff Zahn .... .07 .03 .01
☐ 318 Len Barker .... .07 .03 .01
☐ 319 Steve Bedrosian .... .12 .05 .01
☐ 320 Bruce Benedict .... .07 .03 .01
☐ 321 Rick Camp .... .07 .03 .01
☐ 322 Chris Chambliss .... .10 .04 .01
☐ 323 Jeff Dedmon .... .07 .03 .01
☐ 324 Terry Forster .... .07 .03 .01
☐ 325 Gene Garber .... .07 .03 .01
☐ 326 Albert Hall .... .07 .03 .01
☐ 327 Terry Harper .... .07 .03 .01
☐ 328 Bob Horner .... .10 .04 .01
☐ 329 Glenn Hubbard .... .07 .03 .01
☐ 330 Randy Johnson .... .07 .03 .01
☐ 331 Brad Komminsk .... .07 .03 .01
☐ 332 Rick Mahler .... .07 .03 .01
☐ 333 Craig McMurtry .... .07 .03 .01
☐ 334 Donnie Moore .... .07 .03 .01
☐ 335 Dale Murphy .... .75 .30 .07
☐ 336 Ken Oberkfell .... .07 .03 .01
☐ 337 Pascual Perez .... .10 .04 .01
☐ 338 Gerald Perry .... .15 .06 .01
☐ 339 Rafael Ramirez .... .07 .03 .01
☐ 340 Jerry Royster .... .07 .03 .01
☐ 341 Alex Trevino .... .07 .03 .01
☐ 342 Claudell Washington ...... .07 .03 .01
☐ 343 Alan Ashby .... .07 .03 .01
☐ 344 Mark Bailey .... .07 .03 .01
☐ 345 Kevin Bass .... .10 .04 .01
☐ 346 Enos Cabell .... .07 .03 .01
☐ 347 Jose Cruz .... .10 .04 .01
☐ 348 Bill Dawley .... .07 .03 .01
☐ 349 Frank DiPino .... .07 .03 .01
☐ 350 Bill Doran .... .12 .05 .01
☐ 351 Phil Garner .... .10 .04 .01
☐ 352 Bob Knepper .... .07 .03 .01
☐ 353 Mike LaCoss .... .07 .03 .01
☐ 354 Jerry Mumphrey .... .07 .03 .01

☐ 355	Joe Niekro	.10	.04	.01
☐ 356	Terry Puhl	.07	.03	.01
☐ 357	Craig Reynolds	.07	.03	.01
☐ 358	Vern Ruhle	.07	.03	.01
☐ 359	Nolan Ryan	6.50	2.75	.65
☐ 360	Joe Sambito	.07	.03	.01
☐ 361	Mike Scott	.20	.08	.02
☐ 362	Dave Smith	.07	.03	.01
☐ 363	Julio Solano	.07	.03	.01
☐ 364	Dickie Thon	.07	.03	.01
☐ 365	Denny Walling	.07	.03	.01
☐ 366	Dave Anderson	.07	.03	.01
☐ 367	Bob Bailor	.07	.03	.01
☐ 368	Greg Brock	.07	.03	.01
☐ 369	Carlos Diaz	.07	.03	.01
☐ 370	Pedro Guerrero	.25	.10	.02
☐ 371	Orel Hershiser	5.00	2.25	.50
☐ 372	Rick Honeycutt	.07	.03	.01
☐ 373	Burt Hooton	.07	.03	.01
☐ 374	Ken Howell	.15	.06	.01
☐ 375	Ken Landreaux	.07	.03	.01
☐ 376	Candy Maldonado	.15	.06	.01
☐ 377	Mike Marshall	.10	.04	.01
☐ 378	Tom Niedenfuer	.07	.03	.01
☐ 379	Alejandro Pena	.07	.03	.01
☐ 380	Jerry Reuss	.07	.03	.01
☐ 381	R.J. Reynolds	.20	.08	.02
☐ 382	German Rivera	.07	.03	.01
☐ 383	Bill Russell	.07	.03	.01
☐ 384	Steve Sax	.35	.15	.03
☐ 385	Mike Scioscia	.10	.04	.01
☐ 386	Franklin Stubbs	.50	.20	.05
☐ 387	Fernando Valenzuela	.17	.07	.01
☐ 388	Bob Welch	.20	.08	.02
☐ 389	Terry Whitfield	.07	.03	.01
☐ 390	Steve Yeager	.07	.03	.01
☐ 391	Pat Zachry	.07	.03	.01
☐ 392	Fred Breining	.07	.03	.01
☐ 393	Gary Carter	.45	.18	.04
☐ 394	Andre Dawson	1.00	.40	.10
☐ 395	Miguel Dilone	.07	.03	.01
☐ 396	Dan Driessen	.07	.03	.01
☐ 397	Doug Flynn	.07	.03	.01
☐ 398	Terry Francona	.07	.03	.01
☐ 399	Bill Gullickson	.10	.04	.01
☐ 400	Bob James	.07	.03	.01
☐ 401	Charlie Lea	.07	.03	.01
☐ 402	Bryan Little	.07	.03	.01
☐ 403	Gary Lucas	.07	.03	.01
☐ 404	David Palmer	.07	.03	.01
☐ 405	Tim Raines	.40	.16	.04
☐ 406	Mike Ramsey	.07	.03	.01
☐ 407	Jeff Reardon	.40	.16	.04
☐ 408	Steve Rogers	.07	.03	.01
☐ 409	Dan Schatzeder	.07	.03	.01
☐ 410	Bryn Smith	.10	.04	.01
☐ 411	Mike Stenhouse	.07	.03	.01
☐ 412	Tim Wallach	.15	.06	.01
☐ 413	Jim Wohlford	.07	.03	.01
☐ 414	Bill Almon	.07	.03	.01
☐ 415	Keith Atherton	.07	.03	.01
☐ 416	Bruce Bochte	.07	.03	.01
☐ 417	Tom Burgmeier	.07	.03	.01
☐ 418	Ray Burris	.07	.03	.01
☐ 419	Bill Caudill	.07	.03	.01
☐ 420	Chris Codiroli	.07	.03	.01
☐ 421	Tim Conroy	.07	.03	.01
☐ 422	Mike Davis	.07	.03	.01
☐ 423	Jim Essian	.07	.03	.01
☐ 424	Mike Heath	.07	.03	.01
☐ 425	Rickey Henderson	5.00	2.25	.50
☐ 426	Donnie Hill	.07	.03	.01
☐ 427	Dave Kingman	.15	.06	.01
☐ 428	Bill Krueger	.07	.03	.01
☐ 429	Carney Lansford	.12	.05	.01
☐ 430	Steve McCatty	.07	.03	.01
☐ 431	Joe Morgan	.40	.16	.04
☐ 432	Dwayne Murphy	.07	.03	.01
☐ 433	Tony Phillips	.10	.04	.01
☐ 434	Lary Sorensen	.07	.03	.01
☐ 435	Mike Warren	.07	.03	.01
☐ 436	Curt Young	.15	.06	.01
☐ 437	Luis Aponte	.07	.03	.01
☐ 438	Chris Bando	.07	.03	.01
☐ 439	Tony Bernazard	.07	.03	.01
☐ 440	Bert Blyleven	.25	.10	.02
☐ 441	Brett Butler	.25	.10	.02
☐ 442	Ernie Camacho	.07	.03	.01
☐ 443	Joe Carter	6.50	2.75	.65
☐ 444	Carmelo Castillo	.07	.03	.01
☐ 445	Jamie Easterly	.07	.03	.01
☐ 446	Steve Farr	.35	.15	.03
☐ 447	Mike Fischlin	.07	.03	.01
☐ 448	Julio Franco	1.25	.50	.12
☐ 449	Mel Hall	.20	.08	.02
☐ 450	Mike Hargrove	.07	.03	.01
☐ 451	Neal Heaton	.10	.04	.01
☐ 452	Brook Jacoby	.17	.07	.01
☐ 453	Mike Jeffcoat	.07	.03	.01
☐ 454	Don Schulze	.10	.04	.01
☐ 455	Roy Smith	.07	.03	.01
☐ 456	Pat Tabler	.07	.03	.01
☐ 457	Andre Thornton	.10	.04	.01
☐ 458	George Vukovich	.07	.03	.01
☐ 459	Tom Waddell	.07	.03	.01
☐ 460	Jerry Willard	.07	.03	.01
☐ 461	Dale Berra	.07	.03	.01
☐ 462	John Candelaria	.07	.03	.01
☐ 463	Jose DeLeon	.07	.03	.01
☐ 464	Doug Frobel	.07	.03	.01
☐ 465	Cecilio Guante	.07	.03	.01
☐ 466	Brian Harper	.40	.16	.04
☐ 467	Lee Lacy	.07	.03	.01
☐ 468	Bill Madlock	.10	.04	.01
☐ 469	Lee Mazzilli	.07	.03	.01
☐ 470	Larry McWilliams	.07	.03	.01

☐ 471 Jim Morrison .07 .03 .01
☐ 472 Tony Pena .10 .04 .01
☐ 473 Johnny Ray .07 .03 .01
☐ 474 Rick Rhoden .07 .03 .01
☐ 475 Don Robinson .07 .03 .01
☐ 476 Rod Scurry .07 .03 .01
☐ 477 Kent Tekulve .07 .03 .01
☐ 478 Jason Thompson .07 .03 .01
☐ 479 John Tudor .12 .05 .01
☐ 480 Lee Tunnell .07 .03 .01
☐ 481 Marvell Wynne .07 .03 .01
☐ 482 Salome Barojas .07 .03 .01
☐ 483 Dave Beard .07 .03 .01
☐ 484 Jim Beattie .07 .03 .01
☐ 485 Barry Bonnell .07 .03 .01
☐ 486 Phil Bradley .35 .15 .03
☐ 487 Al Cowens .07 .03 .01
☐ 488 Alvin Davis 1.50 .60 .15
☐ 489 Dave Henderson .40 .16 .04
☐ 490 Steve Henderson .07 .03 .01
☐ 491 Bob Kearney .07 .03 .01
☐ 492 Mark Langston 4.50 2.00 .45
☐ 493 Larry Milbourne .07 .03 .01
☐ 494 Paul Mirabella .07 .03 .01
☐ 495 Mike Moore .12 .05 .01
☐ 496 Edwin Nunez .07 .03 .01
☐ 497 Spike Owen .07 .03 .01
☐ 498 Jack Perconte .07 .03 .01
☐ 499 Ken Phelps .07 .03 .01
☐ 500 Jim Presley .20 .08 .02
☐ 501 Mike Stanton .07 .03 .01
☐ 502 Bob Stoddard .07 .03 .01
☐ 503 Gorman Thomas .10 .04 .01
☐ 504 Ed VandeBerg .07 .03 .01
☐ 505 Matt Young .07 .03 .01
☐ 506 Juan Agosto .07 .03 .01
☐ 507 Harold Baines .35 .15 .03
☐ 508 Floyd Bannister .07 .03 .01
☐ 509 Britt Burns .07 .03 .01
☐ 510 Julio Cruz .07 .03 .01
☐ 511 Richard Dotson .07 .03 .01
☐ 512 Jerry Dybzinski .07 .03 .01
☐ 513 Carlton Fisk 1.00 .40 .10
☐ 514 Scott Fletcher .07 .03 .01
☐ 515 Jerry Hairston .07 .03 .01
☐ 516 Marc Hill .07 .03 .01
☐ 517 LaMarr Hoyt .07 .03 .01
☐ 518 Ron Kittle .12 .05 .01
☐ 519 Rudy Law .07 .03 .01
☐ 520 Vance Law .07 .03 .01
☐ 521 Greg Luzinski .12 .05 .01
☐ 522 Gene Nelson .07 .03 .01
☐ 523 Tom Paciorek .07 .03 .01
☐ 524 Ron Reed .07 .03 .01
☐ 525 Bert Roberge .07 .03 .01
☐ 526 Tom Seaver 1.00 .40 .10
☐ 527 Roy Smalley .07 .03 .01
☐ 528 Dan Spillner .07 .03 .01
☐ 529 Mike Squires .07 .03 .01
☐ 530 Greg Walker .07 .03 .01
☐ 531 Cesar Cedeno .10 .04 .01
☐ 532 Dave Concepcion .12 .05 .01
☐ 533 Eric Davis 13.50 6.00 1.85
☐ 534 Nick Esasky .10 .04 .01
☐ 535 Tom Foley .07 .03 .01
☐ 536 John Franco 1.50 .60 .15
☐ 537 Brad Gulden .07 .03 .01
☐ 538 Tom Hume .07 .03 .01
☐ 539 Wayne Krenchicki .07 .03 .01
☐ 540 Andy McGaffigan .07 .03 .01
☐ 541 Eddie Milner .07 .03 .01
☐ 542 Ron Oester .07 .03 .01
☐ 543 Bob Owchinko .07 .03 .01
☐ 544 Dave Parker .35 .15 .03
☐ 545 Frank Pastore .07 .03 .01
☐ 546 Tony Perez .20 .08 .02
☐ 547 Ted Power .07 .03 .01
☐ 548 Joe Price .07 .03 .01
☐ 549 Gary Redus .10 .04 .01
☐ 550 Pete Rose 1.25 .50 .12
☐ 551 Jeff Russell .20 .08 .02
☐ 552 Mario Soto .07 .03 .01
☐ 553 Jay Tibbs .07 .03 .01
☐ 554 Duane Walker .07 .03 .01
☐ 555 Alan Bannister .07 .03 .01
☐ 556 Buddy Bell .10 .04 .01
☐ 557 Danny Darwin .07 .03 .01
☐ 558 Charlie Hough .07 .03 .01
☐ 559 Bobby Jones .07 .03 .01
☐ 560 Odell Jones .07 .03 .01
☐ 561 Jeff Kunkel .07 .03 .01
☐ 562 Mike Mason .07 .03 .01
☐ 563 Pete O'Brien .10 .04 .01
☐ 564 Larry Parrish .07 .03 .01
☐ 565 Mickey Rivers .07 .03 .01
☐ 566 Billy Sample .07 .03 .01
☐ 567 Dave Schmidt .07 .03 .01
☐ 568 Donnie Scott .07 .03 .01
☐ 569 Dave Stewart .60 .25 .06
☐ 570 Frank Tanana .10 .04 .01
☐ 571 Wayne Tolleson .07 .03 .01
☐ 572 Gary Ward .07 .03 .01
☐ 573 Curtis Wilkerson .07 .03 .01
☐ 574 George Wright .07 .03 .01
☐ 575 Ned Yost .07 .03 .01
☐ 576 Mark Brouhard .07 .03 .01
☐ 577 Mike Caldwell .07 .03 .01
☐ 578 Bobby Clark .07 .03 .01
☐ 579 Jaime Cocanower .07 .03 .01
☐ 580 Cecil Cooper .12 .05 .01
☐ 581 Rollie Fingers .35 .15 .03
☐ 582 Jim Gantner .07 .03 .01
☐ 583 Moose Haas .07 .03 .01
☐ 584 Dion James .07 .03 .01
☐ 585 Pete Ladd .07 .03 .01
☐ 586 Rick Manning .07 .03 .01

□ 587 Bob McClure .07 .03 .01
□ 588 Paul Molitor .35 .15 .03
□ 589 Charlie Moore .07 .03 .01
□ 590 Ben Oglivie .07 .03 .01
□ 591 Chuck Porter .07 .03 .01
□ 592 Randy Ready .15 .06 .01
□ 593 Ed Romero .07 .03 .01
□ 594 Bill Schroeder .07 .03 .01
□ 595 Ray Searage .07 .03 .01
□ 596 Ted Simmons .12 .05 .01
□ 597 Jim Sundberg .07 .03 .01
□ 598 Don Sutton .35 .15 .03
□ 599 Tom Tellmann .07 .03 .01
□ 600 Rick Waits .07 .03 .01
□ 601 Robin Yount 1.50 .60 .15
□ 602 Dusty Baker .10 .04 .01
□ 603 Bob Brenly .07 .03 .01
□ 604 Jack Clark .25 .10 .02
□ 605 Chili Davis .20 .08 .02
□ 606 Mark Davis .12 .05 .01
□ 607 Dan Gladden .60 .25 .06
□ 608 Atlee Hammaker .07 .03 .01
□ 609 Mike Krukow .07 .03 .01
□ 610 Duane Kuiper .07 .03 .01
□ 611 Bob Lacey .07 .03 .01
□ 612 Bill Laskey .07 .03 .01
□ 613 Gary Lavelle .07 .03 .01
□ 614 Johnnie LeMaster .07 .03 .01
□ 615 Jeff Leonard .07 .03 .01
□ 616 Randy Lerch .07 .03 .01
□ 617 Greg Minton .07 .03 .01
□ 618 Steve Nicosia .07 .03 .01
□ 619 Gene Richards .07 .03 .01
□ 620 Jeff Robinson .15 .06 .01
(Giants pitcher)
□ 621 Scot Thompson .07 .03 .01
□ 622 Manny Trillo .07 .03 .01
□ 623 Brad Wellman .07 .03 .01
□ 624 Frank Williams .07 .03 .01
□ 625 Joel Youngblood .07 .03 .01
□ 626 Cal Ripken IA 2.50 1.00 .25
□ 627 Mike Schmidt IA 1.00 .40 .10
□ 628 Giving The Signs .10 .04 .01
Sparky Anderson
□ 629 AL Pitcher's Nightmare .80 .35 .08
Dave Winfield
Rickey Henderson
□ 630 NL Pitcher's Nightmare 1.25 .50 .12
Mike Schmidt
Ryne Sandberg
□ 631 NL All-Stars 1.00 .40 .10
Darryl Strawberry
Gary Carter
Steve Garvey
Ozzie Smith
□ 632 A-S Winning Battery .12 .05 .01
Gary Carter
Charlie Lea
□ 633 NL Pennant Clinchers .15 .06 .01
Steve Garvey
Goose Gossage
□ 634 NL Rookie Phenoms 1.25 .50 .12
Dwight Gooden
Juan Samuel
□ 635 Toronto's Big Guns .07 .03 .01
Willie Upshaw
□ 636 Toronto's Big Guns .07 .03 .01
Lloyd Moseby
□ 637 HOLLAND: Al Holland .07 .03 .01
□ 638 TUNNELL: Lee Tunnell .07 .03 .01
□ 639 500th Homer .40 .16 .04
Reggie Jackson
□ 640 4000th Hit .45 .18 .04
Pete Rose
□ 641 Father and Son 1.75 .70 .17
Cal Ripken Jr. and Sr.
□ 642 Cubs: Division Champs .07 .03 .01
□ 643 Two Perfect Games .12 .05 .01
and One No-Hitter:
Mike Witt
David Palmer
Jack Morris
□ 644 Willie Lozado and .10 .04 .01
Vic Mata
□ 645 Kelly Gruber and 9.50 4.25 1.00
Randy O'Neal
□ 646 Jose Roman and .10 .04 .01
Joel Skinner
□ 647 Steve Kiefer and 7.00 3.00 .70
Danny Tartabull
□ 648 Rob Deer and 1.75 .70 .17
Alejandro Sanchez
□ 649 Billy Hatcher and 6.00 2.50 .60
Shawon Dunston
□ 650 Ron Robinson and .60 .25 .06
Mike Bielecki
□ 651 Zane Smith and 1.25 .50 .12
Paul Zuvella
□ 652 Joe Hesketh and 9.00 4.00 .90
Glenn Davis
□ 653 John Russell and .15 .06 .01
Steve Jeltz
□ 654 CL: Tigers/Padres .15 .02 .00
and Cubs/Mets
□ 655 CL: Blue Jays/Yankees .15 .02 .00
and Red Sox/Orioles
□ 656 CL: Royals/Cardinals .15 .02 .00
and Phillies/Twins
□ 657 CL: Angels/Braves .15 .02 .00
and Astros/Dodgers
□ 658 CL: Expos/A's .15 .02 .00
and Indians/Pirates
□ 659 CL: Mariners/Wh.Sox .15 .02 .00
and Reds/Rangers
□ 660 CL: Brewers/Giants .15 .02 .00
and Special Cards

1985 Fleer Update

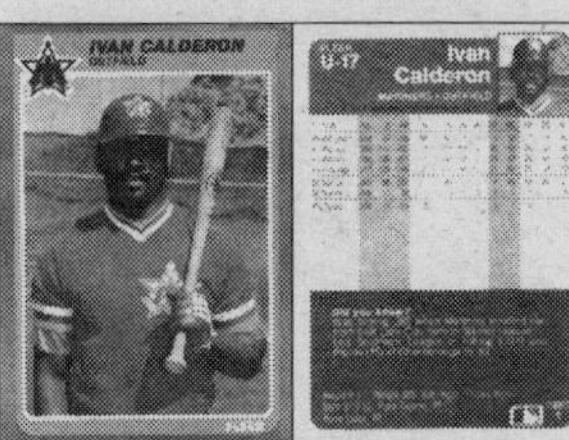

This 132-card set was issued late in the collecting year and features new players and players on new teams compared to the 1985 Fleer regular issue cards. Cards measure 2 1/2" by 3 1/2" and were distributed together as a complete set in a special box. The cards are numbered with a U prefix and are ordered alphabetically by the player's name. This set features the Extended Rookie Cards of Ivan Calderon, Vince Coleman, Ozzie Guillen, Teddy Higuera, and Mickey Tettleton.

	MINT	EXC	G-VG
COMPLETE SET (132)	30.00	13.50	4.50
COMMON PLAYER (1-132)	.10	.04	.01

	MINT	EXC	G-VG
☐ U1 Don Aase	.20	.06	.01
☐ U2 Bill Almon	.10	.04	.01
☐ U3 Dusty Baker	.15	.06	.01
☐ U4 Dale Berra	.10	.04	.01
☐ U5 Karl Best	.10	.04	.01
☐ U6 Tim Birtsas	.15	.06	.01
☐ U7 Vida Blue	.15	.06	.01
☐ U8 Rich Bordi	.10	.04	.01
☐ U9 Daryl Boston	.35	.15	.03
☐ U10 Hubie Brooks	.30	.12	.03
☐ U11 Chris Brown	.15	.06	.01
☐ U12 Tom Browning	1.50	.60	.15
☐ U13 Al Bumbry	.10	.04	.01
☐ U14 Tim Burke	.40	.16	.04
☐ U15 Ray Burris	.10	.04	.01
☐ U16 Jeff Burroughs	.10	.04	.01
☐ U17 Ivan Calderon	3.00	1.25	.30
☐ U18 Jeff Calhoun	.10	.04	.01
☐ U19 Bill Campbell	.10	.04	.01
☐ U20 Don Carman	.20	.08	.02
☐ U21 Gary Carter	.80	.35	.08
☐ U22 Bobby Castillo	.10	.04	.01
☐ U23 Bill Caudill	.10	.04	.01
☐ U24 Rick Cerone	.10	.04	.01
☐ U25 Jack Clark	.40	.16	.04
☐ U26 Pat Clements	.15	.06	.01
☐ U27 Stewart Cliburn	.10	.04	.01
☐ U28 Vince Coleman	11.00	5.00	1.35
☐ U29 Dave Collins	.10	.04	.01
☐ U30 Fritz Connally	.10	.04	.01
☐ U31 Henry Cotto	.15	.06	.01
☐ U32 Danny Darwin	.10	.04	.01
☐ U33 Darren Daulton	.45	.18	.04
☐ U34 Jerry Davis	.10	.04	.01
☐ U35 Brian Dayett	.10	.04	.01
☐ U36 Ken Dixon	.10	.04	.01
☐ U37 Tommy Dunbar	.10	.04	.01
☐ U38 Mariano Duncan	.75	.30	.07
☐ U39 Bob Fallon	.10	.04	.01
☐ U40 Brian Fisher	.15	.06	.01
☐ U41 Mike Fitzgerald	.10	.04	.01
☐ U42 Ray Fontenot	.10	.04	.01
☐ U43 Greg Gagne	.35	.15	.03
☐ U44 Oscar Gamble	.15	.06	.01
☐ U45 Jim Gott	.15	.06	.01
☐ U46 David Green	.10	.04	.01
☐ U47 Alfredo Griffin	.15	.06	.01
☐ U48 Ozzie Guillen	2.00	.80	.20
☐ U49 Toby Harrah	.15	.06	.01
☐ U50 Ron Hassey	.15	.06	.01
☐ U51 Rickey Henderson	5.00	2.25	.50
☐ U52 Steve Henderson	.10	.04	.01
☐ U53 George Hendrick	.15	.06	.01
☐ U54 Teddy Higuera	.60	.25	.06
☐ U55 Al Holland	.10	.04	.01
☐ U56 Burt Hooton	.10	.04	.01
☐ U57 Jay Howell	.15	.06	.01
☐ U58 LaMarr Hoyt	.10	.04	.01
☐ U59 Tim Hulett	.15	.06	.01
☐ U60 Bob James	.10	.04	.01
☐ U61 Cliff Johnson	.10	.04	.01
☐ U62 Howard Johnson	2.75	1.10	.27
☐ U63 Ruppert Jones	.10	.04	.01
☐ U64 Steve Kemp	.10	.04	.01
☐ U65 Bruce Kison	.10	.04	.01
☐ U66 Mike LaCoss	.10	.04	.01
☐ U67 Lee Lacy	.10	.04	.01
☐ U68 Dave LaPoint	.10	.04	.01
☐ U69 Gary Lavelle	.10	.04	.01
☐ U70 Vance Law	.15	.06	.01
☐ U71 Manny Lee	.30	.12	.03
☐ U72 Sixto Lezcano	.10	.04	.01
☐ U73 Tim Lollar	.10	.04	.01
☐ U74 Urbano Lugo	.10	.04	.01
☐ U75 Fred Lynn	.25	.10	.02
☐ U76 Steve Lyons	.25	.10	.02
☐ U77 Mickey Mahler	.10	.04	.01
☐ U78 Ron Mathis	.10	.04	.01
☐ U79 Len Matuszek	.10	.04	.01
☐ U80 Oddibe McDowell UER (part of bio actually Roger's)	.25	.10	.02

☐ U81 Roger McDowell UER (part of bio actually Oddibe's)	.50	.20	.05
☐ U82 Donnie Moore	.10	.04	.01
☐ U83 Ron Musselman	.10	.04	.01
☐ U84 Al Oliver	.20	.08	.02
☐ U85 Joe Orsulak	.40	.16	.04
☐ U86 Dan Pasqua	.50	.20	.05
☐ U87 Chris Pittaro	.10	.04	.01
☐ U88 Rick Reuschel	.20	.08	.02
☐ U89 Earnie Riles	.20	.08	.02
☐ U90 Jerry Royster	.10	.04	.01
☐ U91 Dave Rozema	.10	.04	.01
☐ U92 Dave Rucker	.10	.04	.01
☐ U93 Vern Ruhle	.10	.04	.01
☐ U94 Mark Salas	.15	.06	.01
☐ U95 Luis Salazar	.10	.04	.01
☐ U96 Joe Sambito	.10	.04	.01
☐ U97 Billy Sample	.15	.06	.01
☐ U98 Alejandro Sanchez	.10	.04	.01
☐ U99 Calvin Schiraldi	.20	.08	.02
☐ U100 Rick Schu	.20	.08	.02
☐ U101 Larry Sheets	.25	.10	.02
☐ U102 Ron Shephard	.10	.04	.01
☐ U103 Nelson Simmons	.15	.06	.01
☐ U104 Don Slaught	.10	.04	.01
☐ U105 Roy Smalley	.10	.04	.01
☐ U106 Lonnie Smith	.25	.10	.02
☐ U107 Nate Snell	.10	.04	.01
☐ U108 Lary Sorensen	.10	.04	.01
☐ U109 Chris Speier	.10	.04	.01
☐ U110 Mike Stenhouse	.10	.04	.01
☐ U111 Tim Stoddard	.10	.04	.01
☐ U112 John Stuper	.10	.04	.01
☐ U113 Jim Sundberg	.10	.04	.01
☐ U114 Bruce Sutter	.25	.10	.02
☐ U115 Don Sutton	.50	.20	.05
☐ U116 Bruce Tanner	.10	.04	.01
☐ U117 Kent Tekulve	.15	.06	.01
☐ U118 Walt Terrell	.15	.06	.01
☐ U119 Mickey Tettleton	2.00	.80	.20
☐ U120 Rich Thompson	.10	.04	.01
☐ U121 Louis Thornton	.10	.04	.01
☐ U122 Alex Trevino	.10	.04	.01
☐ U123 John Tudor	.20	.08	.02
☐ U124 Jose Uribe	.25	.10	.02
☐ U125 Dave Valle	.15	.06	.01
☐ U126 Dave Von Ohlen	.10	.04	.01
☐ U127 Curt Wardle	.10	.04	.01
☐ U128 U.L. Washington	.10	.04	.01
☐ U129 Ed Whitson	.15	.06	.01
☐ U130 Herm Winningham	.15	.06	.01
☐ U131 Rich Yett	.10	.04	.01
☐ U132 Checklist U1-U132	.10	.01	.00

1986 Fleer

The cards in this 660-card set measure 2 1/2" by 3 1/2". The 1986 Fleer set features fronts that contain the team logo along with the player's name and position. The player cards are alphabetized within team and the teams are ordered by their 1985 season finish and won-lost record, e.g., Kansas City (1-25), St. Louis (26-49), Toronto (50-73), New York Mets (74-97), New York Yankees (98-122), Los Angeles (123-147), California (148-171), Cincinnati (172-196), Chicago White Sox (197-220), Detroit (221-243), Montreal (244-267), Baltimore (268-291), Houston (292-314), San Diego (315-338), Boston (339-360), Chicago Cubs (361-385), Minnesota (386-409), Oakland (410-432), Philadelphia (433-457), Seattle (458-481), Milwaukee (482-506), Atlanta (507-532), San Francisco (533-555), Texas (556-578), Cleveland (579-601), and Pittsburgh (602-625). Specials (626-643), Major League Prospects (644-653), and checklist cards (654-660) complete the set. The border enclosing the photo is dark blue. The backs feature the same name, number, and statistics format that Fleer has been using over the past few years. The Dennis and Tippy Martinez cards were apparently switched in the set numbering, as their adjacent numbers (279 and 280) were reversed on the Orioles checklist card. The set includes the rookie cards of Jose Canseco, Vince Coleman, Kal Daniels, Len Dykstra, Cecil Fielder, and Benito Santiago.

	MINT	EXC	G-VG
COMPLETE SET (660)	135.00	60.00	12.50
COMMON PLAYER (1-660)	.06	.02	.00

☐ 1 Steve Balboni	.10	.03	.01

□ 2 Joe Beckwith	.06	.02	.00
□ 3 Buddy Biancalana	.06	.02	.00
□ 4 Bud Black	.10	.04	.01
□ 5 George Brett	.85	.35	.08
□ 6 Onix Concepcion	.06	.02	.00
□ 7 Steve Farr	.10	.04	.01
□ 8 Mark Gubicza	.15	.06	.01
□ 9 Dane Iorg	.06	.02	.00
□ 10 Danny Jackson	.12	.05	.01
□ 11 Lynn Jones	.06	.02	.00
□ 12 Mike Jones	.06	.02	.00
□ 13 Charlie Leibrandt	.06	.02	.00
□ 14 Hal McRae	.10	.04	.01
□ 15 Omar Moreno	.06	.02	.00
□ 16 Darryl Motley	.06	.02	.00
□ 17 Jorge Orta	.06	.02	.00
□ 18 Dan Quisenberry	.12	.05	.01
□ 19 Bret Saberhagen	1.00	.40	.10
□ 20 Pat Sheridan	.06	.02	.00
□ 21 Lonnie Smith	.12	.05	.01
□ 22 Jim Sundberg	.06	.02	.00
□ 23 John Wathan	.06	.02	.00
□ 24 Frank White	.06	.02	.00
□ 25 Willie Wilson	.10	.04	.01
□ 26 Joaquin Andujar	.06	.02	.00
□ 27 Steve Braun	.06	.02	.00
□ 28 Bill Campbell	.06	.02	.00
□ 29 Cesar Cedeno	.10	.04	.01
□ 30 Jack Clark	.17	.07	.01
□ 31 Vince Coleman	6.00	2.50	.60
□ 32 Danny Cox	.06	.02	.00
□ 33 Ken Dayley	.06	.02	.00
□ 34 Ivan DeJesus	.06	.02	.00
□ 35 Bob Forsch	.06	.02	.00
□ 36 Brian Harper	.20	.08	.02
□ 37 Tom Herr	.10	.04	.01
□ 38 Ricky Horton	.06	.02	.00
□ 39 Kurt Kepshire	.06	.02	.00
□ 40 Jeff Lahti	.06	.02	.00
□ 41 Tito Landrum	.06	.02	.00
□ 42 Willie McGee	.25	.10	.02
□ 43 Tom Nieto	.06	.02	.00
□ 44 Terry Pendleton	.75	.30	.07
□ 45 Darrell Porter	.06	.02	.00
□ 46 Ozzie Smith	.75	.30	.07
□ 47 John Tudor	.10	.04	.01
□ 48 Andy Van Slyke	.35	.15	.03
□ 49 Todd Worrell	.17	.07	.01
□ 50 Jim Acker	.06	.02	.00
□ 51 Doyle Alexander	.06	.02	.00
□ 52 Jesse Barfield	.15	.06	.01
□ 53 George Bell	.50	.20	.05
□ 54 Jeff Burroughs	.06	.02	.00
□ 55 Bill Caudill	.06	.02	.00
□ 56 Jim Clancy	.06	.02	.00
□ 57 Tony Fernandez	.20	.08	.02
□ 58 Tom Filer	.06	.02	.00
□ 59 Damaso Garcia	.06	.02	.00
□ 60 Tom Henke	.40	.16	.04
□ 61 Garth Iorg	.06	.02	.00
□ 62 Cliff Johnson	.06	.02	.00
□ 63 Jimmy Key	.30	.12	.03
□ 64 Dennis Lamp	.06	.02	.00
□ 65 Gary Lavelle	.06	.02	.00
□ 66 Buck Martinez	.06	.02	.00
□ 67 Lloyd Moseby	.10	.04	.01
□ 68 Rance Mulliniks	.06	.02	.00
□ 69 Al Oliver	.12	.05	.01
□ 70 Dave Stieb	.15	.06	.01
□ 71 Louis Thornton	.06	.02	.00
□ 72 Willie Upshaw	.06	.02	.00
□ 73 Ernie Whitt	.06	.02	.00
□ 74 Rick Aguilera	.90	.40	.09
□ 75 Wally Backman	.06	.02	.00
□ 76 Gary Carter	.30	.12	.03
□ 77 Ron Darling	.15	.06	.01
□ 78 Len Dykstra	2.50	1.00	.25
□ 79 Sid Fernandez	.17	.07	.01
□ 80 George Foster	.12	.05	.01
□ 81 Dwight Gooden	2.25	.90	.22
□ 82 Tom Gorman	.06	.02	.00
□ 83 Danny Heep	.06	.02	.00
□ 84 Keith Hernandez	.17	.07	.01
□ 85 Howard Johnson	.90	.40	.09
□ 86 Ray Knight	.10	.04	.01
□ 87 Terry Leach	.10	.04	.01
□ 88 Ed Lynch	.06	.02	.00
□ 89 Roger McDowell	.35	.15	.03
□ 90 Jesse Orosco	.06	.02	.00
□ 91 Tom Paciorek	.06	.02	.00
□ 92 Ronn Reynolds	.06	.02	.00
□ 93 Rafael Santana	.06	.02	.00
□ 94 Doug Sisk	.06	.02	.00
□ 95 Rusty Staub	.10	.04	.01
□ 96 Darryl Strawberry	5.00	2.25	.50
□ 97 Mookie Wilson	.10	.04	.01
□ 98 Neil Allen	.06	.02	.00
□ 99 Don Baylor	.10	.04	.01
□ 100 Dale Berra	.06	.02	.00
□ 101 Rich Bordi	.06	.02	.00
□ 102 Marty Bystrom	.06	.02	.00
□ 103 Joe Cowley	.06	.02	.00
□ 104 Brian Fisher	.10	.04	.01
□ 105 Ken Griffey	.15	.06	.01
□ 106 Ron Guidry	.15	.06	.01
□ 107 Ron Hassey	.06	.02	.00
□ 108 Rickey Henderson UER (SB Record of 120, sic)	2.50	1.00	.25
□ 109 Don Mattingly	4.00	1.75	.40
□ 110 Bobby Meacham	.06	.02	.00
□ 111 John Montefusco	.06	.02	.00
□ 112 Phil Niekro	.25	.10	.02
□ 113 Mike Pagliarulo	.10	.04	.01
□ 114 Dan Pasqua	.17	.07	.01
□ 115 Willie Randolph	.10	.04	.01
□ 116 Dave Righetti	.12	.05	.01

☐ 117 Andre Robertson	.06	.02	.00
☐ 118 Billy Sample	.06	.02	.00
☐ 119 Bob Shirley	.06	.02	.00
☐ 120 Ed Whitson	.06	.02	.00
☐ 121 Dave Winfield	.65	.25	.06
☐ 122 Butch Wynegar	.06	.02	.00
☐ 123 Dave Anderson	.06	.02	.00
☐ 124 Bob Bailor	.06	.02	.00
☐ 125 Greg Brock	.06	.02	.00
☐ 126 Enos Cabell	.06	.02	.00
☐ 127 Bobby Castillo	.06	.02	.00
☐ 128 Carlos Diaz	.06	.02	.00
☐ 129 Mariano Duncan	.35	.15	.03
☐ 130 Pedro Guerrero	.20	.08	.02
☐ 131 Orel Hershiser	.75	.30	.07
☐ 132 Rick Honeycutt	.06	.02	.00
☐ 133 Ken Howell	.06	.02	.00
☐ 134 Ken Landreaux	.06	.02	.00
☐ 135 Bill Madlock	.10	.04	.01
☐ 136 Candy Maldonado	.10	.04	.01
☐ 137 Mike Marshall	.10	.04	.01
☐ 138 Len Matuszek	.06	.02	.00
☐ 139 Tom Niedenfuer	.06	.02	.00
☐ 140 Alejandro Pena	.12	.05	.01
☐ 141 Jerry Reuss	.06	.02	.00
☐ 142 Bill Russell	.10	.04	.01
☐ 143 Steve Sax	.25	.10	.02
☐ 144 Mike Scioscia	.10	.04	.01
☐ 145 Fernando Valenzuela	.12	.05	.01
☐ 146 Bob Welch	.12	.05	.01
☐ 147 Terry Whitfield	.06	.02	.00
☐ 148 Juan Beniquez	.06	.02	.00
☐ 149 Bob Boone	.12	.05	.01
☐ 150 John Candelaria	.06	.02	.00
☐ 151 Rod Carew	.75	.30	.07
☐ 152 Stewart Cliburn	.06	.02	.00
☐ 153 Doug DeCinces	.10	.04	.01
☐ 154 Brian Downing	.10	.04	.01
☐ 155 Ken Forsch	.06	.02	.00
☐ 156 Craig Gerber	.06	.02	.00
☐ 157 Bobby Grich	.10	.04	.01
☐ 158 George Hendrick	.06	.02	.00
☐ 159 Al Holland	.06	.02	.00
☐ 160 Reggie Jackson	1.00	.40	.10
☐ 161 Ruppert Jones	.06	.02	.00
☐ 162 Urbano Lugo	.06	.02	.00
☐ 163 Kirk McCaskill	.30	.12	.03
☐ 164 Donnie Moore	.06	.02	.00
☐ 165 Gary Pettis	.06	.02	.00
☐ 166 Ron Romanick	.06	.02	.00
☐ 167 Dick Schofield	.06	.02	.00
☐ 168 Daryl Sconiers	.06	.02	.00
☐ 169 Jim Slaton	.06	.02	.00
☐ 170 Don Sutton	.25	.10	.02
☐ 171 Mike Witt	.06	.02	.00
☐ 172 Buddy Bell	.10	.04	.01
☐ 173 Tom Browning	.35	.15	.03
☐ 174 Dave Concepcion	.12	.05	.01
☐ 175 Eric Davis	2.50	1.00	.25
☐ 176 Bo Diaz	.06	.02	.00
☐ 177 Nick Esasky	.10	.04	.01
☐ 178 John Franco	.15	.06	.01
☐ 179 Tom Hume	.06	.02	.00
☐ 180 Wayne Krenchicki	.06	.02	.00
☐ 181 Andy McGaffigan	.06	.02	.00
☐ 182 Eddie Milner	.06	.02	.00
☐ 183 Ron Oester	.06	.02	.00
☐ 184 Dave Parker	.25	.10	.02
☐ 185 Frank Pastore	.06	.02	.00
☐ 186 Tony Perez	.25	.10	.02
☐ 187 Ted Power	.06	.02	.00
☐ 188 Joe Price	.06	.02	.00
☐ 189 Gary Redus	.06	.02	.00
☐ 190 Ron Robinson	.06	.02	.00
☐ 191 Pete Rose	.75	.30	.07
☐ 192 Mario Soto	.06	.02	.00
☐ 193 John Stuper	.06	.02	.00
☐ 194 Jay Tibbs	.06	.02	.00
☐ 195 Dave Van Gorder	.06	.02	.00
☐ 196 Max Venable	.06	.02	.00
☐ 197 Juan Agosto	.06	.02	.00
☐ 198 Harold Baines	.25	.10	.02
☐ 199 Floyd Bannister	.06	.02	.00
☐ 200 Britt Burns	.06	.02	.00
☐ 201 Julio Cruz	.06	.02	.00
☐ 202 Joel Davis	.10	.04	.01
☐ 203 Richard Dotson	.06	.02	.00
☐ 204 Carlton Fisk	.75	.30	.07
☐ 205 Scott Fletcher	.06	.02	.00
☐ 206 Ozzie Guillen	1.00	.40	.10
☐ 207 Jerry Hairston	.06	.02	.00
☐ 208 Tim Hulett	.06	.02	.00
☐ 209 Bob James	.06	.02	.00
☐ 210 Ron Kittle	.10	.04	.01
☐ 211 Rudy Law	.06	.02	.00
☐ 212 Bryan Little	.06	.02	.00
☐ 213 Gene Nelson	.06	.02	.00
☐ 214 Reid Nichols	.06	.02	.00
☐ 215 Luis Salazar	.06	.02	.00
☐ 216 Tom Seaver	.90	.40	.09
☐ 217 Dan Spillner	.06	.02	.00
☐ 218 Bruce Tanner	.06	.02	.00
☐ 219 Greg Walker	.06	.02	.00
☐ 220 Dave Wehrmeister	.06	.02	.00
☐ 221 Juan Berenguer	.06	.02	.00
☐ 222 Dave Bergman	.06	.02	.00
☐ 223 Tom Brookens	.06	.02	.00
☐ 224 Darrell Evans	.10	.04	.01
☐ 225 Barbaro Garbey	.06	.02	.00
☐ 226 Kirk Gibson	.25	.10	.02
☐ 227 John Grubb	.06	.02	.00
☐ 228 Willie Hernandez	.06	.02	.00
☐ 229 Larry Herndon	.06	.02	.00
☐ 230 Chet Lemon	.06	.02	.00
☐ 231 Aurelio Lopez	.06	.02	.00
☐ 232 Jack Morris	.40	.16	.04

Card			
☐ 233 Randy O'Neal	.06	.02	.00
☐ 234 Lance Parrish	.17	.07	.01
☐ 235 Dan Petry	.06	.02	.00
☐ 236 Alejandro Sanchez	.06	.02	.00
☐ 237 Bill Scherrer	.06	.02	.00
☐ 238 Nelson Simmons	.06	.02	.00
☐ 239 Frank Tanana	.10	.04	.01
☐ 240 Walt Terrell	.06	.02	.00
☐ 241 Alan Trammell	.50	.20	.05
☐ 242 Lou Whitaker	.25	.10	.02
☐ 243 Milt Wilcox	.06	.02	.00
☐ 244 Hubie Brooks	.12	.05	.01
☐ 245 Tim Burke	.20	.08	.02
☐ 246 Andre Dawson	.75	.30	.07
☐ 247 Mike Fitzgerald	.06	.02	.00
☐ 248 Terry Francona	.06	.02	.00
☐ 249 Bill Gullickson	.10	.04	.01
☐ 250 Joe Hesketh	.12	.05	.01
☐ 251 Bill Laskey	.06	.02	.00
☐ 252 Vance Law	.06	.02	.00
☐ 253 Charlie Lea	.06	.02	.00
☐ 254 Gary Lucas	.06	.02	.00
☐ 255 David Palmer	.06	.02	.00
☐ 256 Tim Raines	.35	.15	.03
☐ 257 Jeff Reardon	.35	.15	.03
☐ 258 Bert Roberge	.06	.02	.00
☐ 259 Dan Schatzeder	.06	.02	.00
☐ 260 Bryn Smith	.06	.02	.00
☐ 261 Randy St.Claire	.06	.02	.00
☐ 262 Scot Thompson	.06	.02	.00
☐ 263 Tim Wallach	.12	.05	.01
☐ 264 U.L. Washington	.06	.02	.00
☐ 265 Mitch Webster	.17	.07	.01
☐ 266 Herm Winningham	.06	.02	.00
☐ 267 Floyd Youmans	.10	.04	.01
☐ 268 Don Aase	.06	.02	.00
☐ 269 Mike Boddicker	.06	.02	.00
☐ 270 Rich Dauer	.06	.02	.00
☐ 271 Storm Davis	.06	.02	.00
☐ 272 Rick Dempsey	.06	.02	.00
☐ 273 Ken Dixon	.06	.02	.00
☐ 274 Jim Dwyer	.06	.02	.00
☐ 275 Mike Flanagan	.10	.04	.01
☐ 276 Wayne Gross	.06	.02	.00
☐ 277 Lee Lacy	.06	.02	.00
☐ 278 Fred Lynn	.12	.05	.01
☐ 279 Tippy Martinez	.06	.02	.00
☐ 280 Dennis Martinez	.10	.04	.01
☐ 281 Scott McGregor	.06	.02	.00
☐ 282 Eddie Murray	.75	.30	.07
☐ 283 Floyd Rayford	.06	.02	.00
☐ 284 Cal Ripken	4.00	1.75	.40
☐ 285 Gary Roenicke	.06	.02	.00
☐ 286 Larry Sheets	.10	.04	.01
☐ 287 John Shelby	.06	.02	.00
☐ 288 Nate Snell	.06	.02	.00
☐ 289 Sammy Stewart	.06	.02	.00
☐ 290 Alan Wiggins	.06	.02	.00
☐ 291 Mike Young	.06	.02	.00
☐ 292 Alan Ashby	.06	.02	.00
☐ 293 Mark Bailey	.06	.02	.00
☐ 294 Kevin Bass	.06	.02	.00
☐ 295 Jeff Calhoun	.06	.02	.00
☐ 296 Jose Cruz	.10	.04	.01
☐ 297 Glenn Davis	1.50	.60	.15
☐ 298 Bill Dawley	.06	.02	.00
☐ 299 Frank DiPino	.06	.02	.00
☐ 300 Bill Doran	.10	.04	.01
☐ 301 Phil Garner	.10	.04	.01
☐ 302 Jeff Heathcock	.06	.02	.00
☐ 303 Charlie Kerfeld	.06	.02	.00
☐ 304 Bob Knepper	.06	.02	.00
☐ 305 Ron Mathis	.06	.02	.00
☐ 306 Jerry Mumphrey	.06	.02	.00
☐ 307 Jim Pankovits	.06	.02	.00
☐ 308 Terry Puhl	.06	.02	.00
☐ 309 Craig Reynolds	.06	.02	.00
☐ 310 Nolan Ryan	4.25	1.75	.42
☐ 311 Mike Scott	.15	.06	.01
☐ 312 Dave Smith	.06	.02	.00
☐ 313 Dickie Thon	.06	.02	.00
☐ 314 Denny Walling	.06	.02	.00
☐ 315 Kurt Bevacqua	.06	.02	.00
☐ 316 Al Bumbry	.06	.02	.00
☐ 317 Jerry Davis	.06	.02	.00
☐ 318 Luis DeLeon	.06	.02	.00
☐ 319 Dave Dravecky	.12	.05	.01
☐ 320 Tim Flannery	.06	.02	.00
☐ 321 Steve Garvey	.35	.15	.03
☐ 322 Goose Gossage	.15	.06	.01
☐ 323 Tony Gwynn	2.00	.80	.20
☐ 324 Andy Hawkins	.06	.02	.00
☐ 325 LaMarr Hoyt	.06	.02	.00
☐ 326 Roy Lee Jackson	.06	.02	.00
☐ 327 Terry Kennedy	.06	.02	.00
☐ 328 Craig Lefferts	.06	.02	.00
☐ 329 Carmelo Martinez	.06	.02	.00
☐ 330 Lance McCullers	.12	.05	.01
☐ 331 Kevin McReynolds	.35	.15	.03
☐ 332 Graig Nettles	.10	.04	.01
☐ 333 Jerry Royster	.06	.02	.00
☐ 334 Eric Show	.06	.02	.00
☐ 335 Tim Stoddard	.06	.02	.00
☐ 336 Garry Templeton	.10	.04	.01
☐ 337 Mark Thurmond	.06	.02	.00
☐ 338 Ed Wojna	.06	.02	.00
☐ 339 Tony Armas	.06	.02	.00
☐ 340 Marty Barrett	.06	.02	.00
☐ 341 Wade Boggs	2.50	1.00	.25
☐ 342 Dennis Boyd	.06	.02	.00
☐ 343 Bill Buckner	.10	.04	.01
☐ 344 Mark Clear	.06	.02	.00
☐ 345 Roger Clemens	8.50	3.75	.85
☐ 346 Steve Crawford	.06	.02	.00
☐ 347 Mike Easler	.06	.02	.00
☐ 348 Dwight Evans	.15	.06	.01

☐ 349 Rich Gedman .06 .02 .00
☐ 350 Jackie Gutierrez .06 .02 .00
☐ 351 Glenn Hoffman .06 .02 .00
☐ 352 Bruce Hurst .10 .04 .01
☐ 353 Bruce Kison .06 .02 .00
☐ 354 Tim Lollar .06 .02 .00
☐ 355 Steve Lyons .06 .02 .00
☐ 356 Al Nipper .06 .02 .00
☐ 357 Bob Ojeda .10 .04 .01
☐ 358 Jim Rice .15 .06 .01
☐ 359 Bob Stanley .06 .02 .00
☐ 360 Mike Trujillo .06 .02 .00
☐ 361 Thad Bosley .06 .02 .00
☐ 362 Warren Brusstar .06 .02 .00
☐ 363 Ron Cey .10 .04 .01
☐ 364 Jody Davis .06 .02 .00
☐ 365 Bob Dernier .06 .02 .00
☐ 366 Shawon Dunston .75 .30 .07
☐ 367 Leon Durham .06 .02 .00
☐ 368 Dennis Eckersley .30 .12 .03
☐ 369 Ray Fontenot .06 .02 .00
☐ 370 George Frazier .06 .02 .00
☐ 371 Billy Hatcher .12 .05 .01
☐ 372 Dave Lopes .10 .04 .01
☐ 373 Gary Matthews .06 .02 .00
☐ 374 Ron Meredith .06 .02 .00
☐ 375 Keith Moreland .06 .02 .00
☐ 376 Reggie Patterson .06 .02 .00
☐ 377 Dick Ruthven .06 .02 .00
☐ 378 Ryne Sandberg 3.75 1.60 .37
☐ 379 Scott Sanderson .10 .04 .01
☐ 380 Lee Smith .35 .15 .03
☐ 381 Lary Sorensen .06 .02 .00
☐ 382 Chris Speier .06 .02 .00
☐ 383 Rick Sutcliffe .12 .05 .01
☐ 384 Steve Trout .06 .02 .00
☐ 385 Gary Woods .06 .02 .00
☐ 386 Bert Blyleven .15 .06 .01
☐ 387 Tom Brunansky .10 .04 .01
☐ 388 Randy Bush .06 .02 .00
☐ 389 John Butcher .06 .02 .00
☐ 390 Ron Davis .06 .02 .00
☐ 391 Dave Engle .06 .02 .00
☐ 392 Frank Eufemia .06 .02 .00
☐ 393 Pete Filson .06 .02 .00
☐ 394 Gary Gaetti .12 .05 .01
☐ 395 Greg Gagne .10 .04 .01
☐ 396 Mickey Hatcher .06 .02 .00
☐ 397 Kent Hrbek .20 .08 .02
☐ 398 Tim Laudner .06 .02 .00
☐ 399 Rick Lysander .06 .02 .00
☐ 400 Dave Meier .06 .02 .00
☐ 401 Kirby Puckett 7.00 3.00 .70
☐ 402 Mark Salas .06 .02 .00
☐ 403 Ken Schrom .06 .02 .00
☐ 404 Roy Smalley .06 .02 .00
☐ 405 Mike Smithson .06 .02 .00
☐ 406 Mike Stenhouse .06 .02 .00
☐ 407 Tim Teufel .10 .04 .01
☐ 408 Frank Viola .35 .15 .03
☐ 409 Ron Washington .06 .02 .00
☐ 410 Keith Atherton .06 .02 .00
☐ 411 Dusty Baker .10 .04 .01
☐ 412 Tim Birtsas .10 .04 .01
☐ 413 Bruce Bochte .06 .02 .00
☐ 414 Chris Codiroli .06 .02 .00
☐ 415 Dave Collins .06 .02 .00
☐ 416 Mike Davis .06 .02 .00
☐ 417 Alfredo Griffin .06 .02 .00
☐ 418 Mike Heath .06 .02 .00
☐ 419 Steve Henderson .06 .02 .00
☐ 420 Donnie Hill .06 .02 .00
☐ 421 Jay Howell .06 .02 .00
☐ 422 Tommy John .17 .07 .01
☐ 423 Dave Kingman .12 .05 .01
☐ 424 Bill Krueger .06 .02 .00
☐ 425 Rick Langford .06 .02 .00
☐ 426 Carney Lansford .12 .05 .01
☐ 427 Steve McCatty .06 .02 .00
☐ 428 Dwayne Murphy .06 .02 .00
☐ 429 Steve Ontiveros .06 .02 .00
☐ 430 Tony Phillips .10 .04 .01
☐ 431 Jose Rijo .35 .15 .03
☐ 432 Mickey Tettleton 1.25 .50 .12
☐ 433 Luis Aguayo .06 .02 .00
☐ 434 Larry Andersen .06 .02 .00
☐ 435 Steve Carlton .65 .25 .06
☐ 436 Don Carman .15 .06 .01
☐ 437 Tim Corcoran .06 .02 .00
☐ 438 Darren Daulton .30 .12 .03
☐ 439 John Denny .06 .02 .00
☐ 440 Tom Foley .06 .02 .00
☐ 441 Greg Gross .06 .02 .00
☐ 442 Kevin Gross .06 .02 .00
☐ 443 Von Hayes .12 .05 .01
☐ 444 Charles Hudson .06 .02 .00
☐ 445 Garry Maddox .06 .02 .00
☐ 446 Shane Rawley .06 .02 .00
☐ 447 Dave Rucker .06 .02 .00
☐ 448 John Russell .06 .02 .00
☐ 449 Juan Samuel .25 .10 .02
☐ 450 Mike Schmidt 2.50 1.00 .25
☐ 451 Rick Schu .06 .02 .00
☐ 452 Dave Shipanoff .06 .02 .00
☐ 453 Dave Stewart .35 .15 .03
☐ 454 Jeff Stone .06 .02 .00
☐ 455 Kent Tekulve .06 .02 .00
☐ 456 Ozzie Virgil .06 .02 .00
☐ 457 Glenn Wilson .06 .02 .00
☐ 458 Jim Beattie .06 .02 .00
☐ 459 Karl Best .06 .02 .00
☐ 460 Barry Bonnell .06 .02 .00
☐ 461 Phil Bradley .10 .04 .01
☐ 462 Ivan Calderon 2.00 .80 .20
☐ 463 Al Cowens .06 .02 .00
☐ 464 Alvin Davis .15 .06 .01

☐ 465 Dave Henderson	.35	.15	.03
☐ 466 Bob Kearney	.06	.02	.00
☐ 467 Mark Langston	.65	.25	.06
☐ 468 Bob Long	.06	.02	.00
☐ 469 Mike Moore	.10	.04	.01
☐ 470 Edwin Nunez	.06	.02	.00
☐ 471 Spike Owen	.06	.02	.00
☐ 472 Jack Perconte	.06	.02	.00
☐ 473 Jim Presley	.06	.02	.00
☐ 474 Donnie Scott	.06	.02	.00
☐ 475 Bill Swift	.12	.05	.01
☐ 476 Danny Tartabull	1.00	.40	.10
☐ 477 Gorman Thomas	.10	.04	.01
☐ 478 Roy Thomas	.06	.02	.00
☐ 479 Ed VandeBerg	.06	.02	.00
☐ 480 Frank Wills	.10	.04	.01
☐ 481 Matt Young	.06	.02	.00
☐ 482 Ray Burris	.06	.02	.00
☐ 483 Jaime Cocanower	.06	.02	.00
☐ 484 Cecil Cooper	.10	.04	.01
☐ 485 Danny Darwin	.06	.02	.00
☐ 486 Rollie Fingers	.25	.10	.02
☐ 487 Jim Gantner	.06	.02	.00
☐ 488 Bob L. Gibson	.06	.02	.00
☐ 489 Moose Haas	.06	.02	.00
☐ 490 Teddy Higuera	.45	.18	.04
☐ 491 Paul Householder	.06	.02	.00
☐ 492 Pete Ladd	.06	.02	.00
☐ 493 Rick Manning	.06	.02	.00
☐ 494 Bob McClure	.06	.02	.00
☐ 495 Paul Molitor	.25	.10	.02
☐ 496 Charlie Moore	.06	.02	.00
☐ 497 Ben Oglivie	.06	.02	.00
☐ 498 Randy Ready	.06	.02	.00
☐ 499 Earnie Riles	.15	.06	.01
☐ 500 Ed Romero	.06	.02	.00
☐ 501 Bill Schroeder	.06	.02	.00
☐ 502 Ray Searage	.06	.02	.00
☐ 503 Ted Simmons	.12	.05	.01
☐ 504 Pete Vuckovich	.06	.02	.00
☐ 505 Rick Waits	.06	.02	.00
☐ 506 Robin Yount	.80	.35	.08
☐ 507 Len Barker	.06	.02	.00
☐ 508 Steve Bedrosian	.10	.04	.01
☐ 509 Bruce Benedict	.06	.02	.00
☐ 510 Rick Camp	.06	.02	.00
☐ 511 Rick Cerone	.06	.02	.00
☐ 512 Chris Chambliss	.10	.04	.01
☐ 513 Jeff Dedmon	.06	.02	.00
☐ 514 Terry Forster	.06	.02	.00
☐ 515 Gene Garber	.06	.02	.00
☐ 516 Terry Harper	.06	.02	.00
☐ 517 Bob Horner	.10	.04	.01
☐ 518 Glenn Hubbard	.06	.02	.00
☐ 519 Joe Johnson	.10	.04	.01
☐ 520 Brad Komminsk	.06	.02	.00
☐ 521 Rick Mahler	.06	.02	.00
☐ 522 Dale Murphy	.50	.20	.05
☐ 523 Ken Oberkfell	.06	.02	.00
☐ 524 Pascual Perez	.10	.04	.01
☐ 525 Gerald Perry	.10	.04	.01
☐ 526 Rafael Ramirez	.06	.02	.00
☐ 527 Steve Shields	.06	.02	.00
☐ 528 Zane Smith	.35	.15	.03
☐ 529 Bruce Sutter	.12	.05	.01
☐ 530 Milt Thompson	.30	.12	.03
☐ 531 Claudell Washington	.06	.02	.00
☐ 532 Paul Zuvella	.06	.02	.00
☐ 533 Vida Blue	.10	.04	.01
☐ 534 Bob Brenly	.06	.02	.00
☐ 535 Chris Brown	.10	.04	.01
☐ 536 Chili Davis	.15	.06	.01
☐ 537 Mark Davis	.10	.04	.01
☐ 538 Rob Deer	.30	.12	.03
☐ 539 Dan Driessen	.06	.02	.00
☐ 540 Scott Garrelts	.12	.05	.01
☐ 541 Dan Gladden	.10	.04	.01
☐ 542 Jim Gott	.06	.02	.00
☐ 543 David Green	.06	.02	.00
☐ 544 Atlee Hammaker	.06	.02	.00
☐ 545 Mike Jeffcoat	.06	.02	.00
☐ 546 Mike Krukow	.06	.02	.00
☐ 547 Dave LaPoint	.06	.02	.00
☐ 548 Jeff Leonard	.06	.02	.00
☐ 549 Greg Minton	.06	.02	.00
☐ 550 Alex Trevino	.06	.02	.00
☐ 551 Manny Trillo	.06	.02	.00
☐ 552 Jose Uribe	.20	.08	.02
☐ 553 Brad Wellman	.06	.02	.00
☐ 554 Frank Williams	.06	.02	.00
☐ 555 Joel Youngblood	.06	.02	.00
☐ 556 Alan Bannister	.06	.02	.00
☐ 557 Glenn Brummer	.06	.02	.00
☐ 558 Steve Buechele	.65	.25	.06
☐ 559 Jose Guzman	.35	.15	.03
☐ 560 Toby Harrah	.06	.02	.00
☐ 561 Greg Harris	.06	.02	.00
☐ 562 Dwayne Henry	.15	.06	.01
☐ 563 Burt Hooton	.06	.02	.00
☐ 564 Charlie Hough	.06	.02	.00
☐ 565 Mike Mason	.06	.02	.00
☐ 566 Oddibe McDowell	.10	.04	.01
☐ 567 Dickie Noles	.06	.02	.00
☐ 568 Pete O'Brien	.06	.02	.00
☐ 569 Larry Parrish	.06	.02	.00
☐ 570 Dave Rozema	.06	.02	.00
☐ 571 Dave Schmidt	.06	.02	.00
☐ 572 Don Slaught	.06	.02	.00
☐ 573 Wayne Tolleson	.06	.02	.00
☐ 574 Duane Walker	.06	.02	.00
☐ 575 Gary Ward	.06	.02	.00
☐ 576 Chris Welsh	.06	.02	.00
☐ 577 Curtis Wilkerson	.06	.02	.00
☐ 578 George Wright	.06	.02	.00
☐ 579 Chris Bando	.06	.02	.00
☐ 580 Tony Bernazard	.06	.02	.00

☐ 581 Brett Butler	.17	.07	.01
☐ 582 Ernie Camacho	.06	.02	.00
☐ 583 Joe Carter	1.25	.50	.12
☐ 584 Carmen Castillo	.06	.02	.00
☐ 585 Jamie Easterly	.06	.02	.00
☐ 586 Julio Franco	.75	.30	.07
☐ 587 Mel Hall	.12	.05	.01
☐ 588 Mike Hargrove	.06	.02	.00
☐ 589 Neal Heaton	.06	.02	.00
☐ 590 Brook Jacoby	.10	.04	.01
☐ 591 Otis Nixon	.50	.20	.05
☐ 592 Jerry Reed	.06	.02	.00
☐ 593 Vern Ruhle	.06	.02	.00
☐ 594 Pat Tabler	.06	.02	.00
☐ 595 Rich Thompson	.06	.02	.00
☐ 596 Andre Thornton	.06	.02	.00
☐ 597 Dave Von Ohlen	.06	.02	.00
☐ 598 George Vukovich	.06	.02	.00
☐ 599 Tom Waddell	.06	.02	.00
☐ 600 Curt Wardle	.06	.02	.00
☐ 601 Jerry Willard	.06	.02	.00
☐ 602 Bill Almon	.06	.02	.00
☐ 603 Mike Bielecki	.10	.04	.01
☐ 604 Sid Bream	.10	.04	.01
☐ 605 Mike Brown OF	.06	.02	.00
☐ 606 Pat Clements	.06	.02	.00
☐ 607 Jose DeLeon	.06	.02	.00
☐ 608 Denny Gonzalez	.06	.02	.00
☐ 609 Cecilio Guante	.06	.02	.00
☐ 610 Steve Kemp	.06	.02	.00
☐ 611 Sammy Khalifa	.06	.02	.00
☐ 612 Lee Mazzilli	.06	.02	.00
☐ 613 Larry McWilliams	.06	.02	.00
☐ 614 Jim Morrison	.06	.02	.00
☐ 615 Joe Orsulak	.30	.12	.03
☐ 616 Tony Pena	.10	.04	.01
☐ 617 Johnny Ray	.06	.02	.00
☐ 618 Rick Reuschel	.10	.04	.01
☐ 619 R.J. Reynolds	.06	.02	.00
☐ 620 Rick Rhoden	.06	.02	.00
☐ 621 Don Robinson	.06	.02	.00
☐ 622 Jason Thompson	.06	.02	.00
☐ 623 Lee Tunnell	.06	.02	.00
☐ 624 Jim Winn	.06	.02	.00
☐ 625 Marvell Wynne	.06	.02	.00
☐ 626 Dwight Gooden IA	.60	.25	.06
☐ 627 Don Mattingly IA	1.25	.50	.12
☐ 628 4192 (Pete Rose)	.40	.16	.04
☐ 629 3000 Career Hits Rod Carew	.40	.16	.04
☐ 630 300 Career Wins Tom Seaver Phil Niekro	.30	.12	.03
☐ 631 Ouch (Don Baylor)	.10	.04	.01
☐ 632 Instant Offense Darryl Strawberry Tim Raines	.60	.25	.06
☐ 633 Shortstops Supreme Cal Ripken Alan Trammell	.75	.30	.07
☐ 634 Boggs and "Hero" Wade Boggs George Brett	.90	.40	.09
☐ 635 Braves Dynamic Duo Bob Horner Dale Murphy	.15	.06	.01
☐ 636 Cardinal Ignitors Willie McGee Vince Coleman	.50	.20	.05
☐ 637 Terror on Basepaths Vince Coleman	.60	.25	.06
☐ 638 Charlie Hustle / Dr.K Pete Rose Dwight Gooden	.75	.30	.07
☐ 639 1984 and 1985 AL Batting Champs Wade Boggs Don Mattingly	1.25	.50	.12
☐ 640 NL West Sluggers Dale Murphy Steve Garvey Dave Parker	.30	.12	.03
☐ 641 Staff Aces Fernando Valenzuela Dwight Gooden	.30	.12	.03
☐ 642 Blue Jay Stoppers Jimmy Key Dave Stieb	.12	.05	.01
☐ 643 AL All-Star Backstops Carlton Fisk Rich Gedman	.12	.05	.01
☐ 644 Gene Walter and Benito Santiago	4.00	1.75	.40
☐ 645 Mike Woodard and Collin Ward	.10	.04	.01
☐ 646 Kal Daniels and Paul O'Neill	5.50	2.50	.55
☐ 647 Andres Galarraga and Fred Toliver	1.00	.40	.10
☐ 648 Bob Kipper and Curt Ford	.10	.04	.01
☐ 649 Jose Canseco and Eric Plunk	40.00	18.00	6.00
☐ 650 Mark McLemore and Gus Polidor	.10	.04	.01
☐ 651 Rob Woodward and Mickey Brantley	.15	.06	.01
☐ 652 Billy Jo Robidoux and Mark Funderburk	.10	.04	.01
☐ 653 Cecil Fielder and Cory Snyder	18.00	7.50	2.50
☐ 654 CL: Royals/Cardinals Blue Jays/Mets	.15	.02	.00
☐ 655 CL: Yankees/Dodgers	.15	.02	.00

Angels/Reds UER (168 Darly Sconiers)			
☐ 656 CL: White Sox/Tigers	.15	.02	.00
Expos/Orioles (279 Dennis, 280 Tippy)			
☐ 657 CL: Astros/Padres	.15	.02	.00
Red Sox/Cubs			
☐ 658 CL: Twins/A's	.15	.02	.00
Phillies/Mariners			
☐ 659 CL: Brewers/Braves	.15	.02	.00
Giants/Rangers			
☐ 660 CL: Indians/Pirates	.15	.02	.00
Special Cards			

1986 Fleer Update

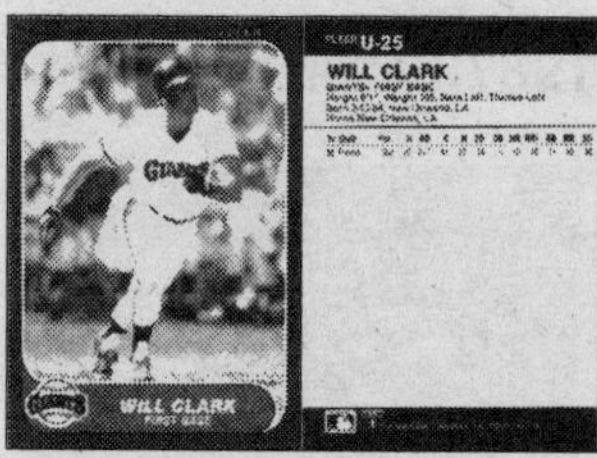

This 132-card set was distributed by Fleer to dealers as a complete set in a custom box. In addition to the complete set of 132 cards, the box also contains 25 Team Logo Stickers. The card fronts look very similar to the 1986 Fleer regular issue. The cards are numbered (with a U prefix) alphabetically according to player's last name. Cards measure the standard size, 2 1/2" by 3 1/2". The key (extended) rookie cards in this set are Barry Bonds, Bobby Bonilla, Will Clark, Wally Joyner, Kevin Mitchell, and Ruben Sierra.

	MINT	EXC	G-VG
COMPLETE SET (132)	32.00	14.25	4.75
COMMON PLAYER (1-132)	.07	.03	.01

☐ U1 Mike Aldrete	.15	.06	.01
☐ U2 Andy Allanson	.10	.04	.01
☐ U3 Neil Allen	.07	.03	.01
☐ U4 Joaquin Andujar	.10	.04	.01
☐ U5 Paul Assenmacher	.12	.05	.01
☐ U6 Scott Bailes	.12	.05	.01
☐ U7 Jay Baller	.10	.04	.01
☐ U8 Scott Bankhead	.20	.08	.02
☐ U9 Bill Bathe	.10	.04	.01
☐ U10 Don Baylor	.12	.05	.01
☐ U11 Billy Beane	.10	.04	.01
☐ U12 Steve Bedrosian	.10	.04	.01
☐ U13 Juan Beniquez	.07	.03	.01
☐ U14 Barry Bonds	6.50	2.75	.65
☐ U15 Bobby Bonilla UER (wrong birthday)	6.00	2.50	.60
☐ U16 Rich Bordi	.07	.03	.01
☐ U17 Bill Campbell	.07	.03	.01
☐ U18 Tom Candiotti	.15	.06	.01
☐ U19 John Cangelosi	.10	.04	.01
☐ U20 Jose Canseco UER (headings on back for a pitcher)	10.00	4.50	1.25
☐ U21 Chuck Cary	.15	.06	.01
☐ U22 Juan Castillo	.07	.03	.01
☐ U23 Rick Cerone	.07	.03	.01
☐ U24 John Cerutti	.15	.06	.01
☐ U25 Will Clark	12.00	5.25	1.50
☐ U26 Mark Clear	.07	.03	.01
☐ U27 Darnell Coles	.07	.03	.01
☐ U28 Dave Collins	.07	.03	.01
☐ U29 Tim Conroy	.07	.03	.01
☐ U30 Ed Correa	.10	.04	.01
☐ U31 Joe Cowley	.07	.03	.01
☐ U32 Bill Dawley	.07	.03	.01
☐ U33 Rob Deer	.25	.10	.02
☐ U34 John Denny	.07	.03	.01
☐ U35 Jim Deshaies	.17	.07	.01
☐ U36 Doug Drabek	1.25	.50	.12
☐ U37 Mike Easler	.07	.03	.01
☐ U38 Mark Eichhorn	.15	.06	.01
☐ U39 Dave Engle	.07	.03	.01
☐ U40 Mike Fischlin	.07	.03	.01
☐ U41 Scott Fletcher	.07	.03	.01
☐ U42 Terry Forster	.10	.04	.01
☐ U43 Terry Francona	.07	.03	.01
☐ U44 Andres Galarraga	.40	.16	.04
☐ U45 Lee Guetterman	.15	.06	.01
☐ U46 Bill Gullickson	.12	.05	.01
☐ U47 Jackie Gutierrez	.07	.03	.01
☐ U48 Moose Haas	.07	.03	.01
☐ U49 Billy Hatcher	.15	.06	.01
☐ U50 Mike Heath	.07	.03	.01
☐ U51 Guy Hoffman	.07	.03	.01
☐ U52 Tom Hume	.07	.03	.01
☐ U53 Pete Incaviglia	.60	.25	.06
☐ U54 Dane Iorg	.07	.03	.01
☐ U55 Chris James	.35	.15	.03
☐ U56 Stan Javier	.20	.08	.02

☐ U57 Tommy John	.17	.07	.01
☐ U58 Tracy Jones	.12	.05	.01
☐ U59 Wally Joyner	2.50	1.00	.25
☐ U60 Wayne Krenchicki	.07	.03	.01
☐ U61 John Kruk	.60	.25	.06
☐ U62 Mike LaCoss	.07	.03	.01
☐ U63 Pete Ladd	.07	.03	.01
☐ U64 Dave LaPoint	.07	.03	.01
☐ U65 Mike LaValliere	.30	.12	.03
☐ U66 Rudy Law	.07	.03	.01
☐ U67 Dennis Leonard	.10	.04	.01
☐ U68 Steve Lombardozzi	.10	.04	.01
☐ U69 Aurelio Lopez	.07	.03	.01
☐ U70 Mickey Mahler	.07	.03	.01
☐ U71 Candy Maldonado	.15	.06	.01
☐ U72 Roger Mason	.10	.04	.01
☐ U73 Greg Mathews	.12	.05	.01
☐ U74 Andy McGaffigan	.07	.03	.01
☐ U75 Joel McKeon	.10	.04	.01
☐ U76 Kevin Mitchell	5.25	2.25	.50
☐ U77 Bill Mooneyham	.07	.03	.01
☐ U78 Omar Moreno	.07	.03	.01
☐ U79 Jerry Mumphrey	.07	.03	.01
☐ U80 Al Newman	.12	.05	.01
☐ U81 Phil Niekro	.30	.12	.03
☐ U82 Randy Niemann	.07	.03	.01
☐ U83 Juan Nieves	.12	.05	.01
☐ U84 Bob Ojeda	.10	.04	.01
☐ U85 Rick Ownbey	.07	.03	.01
☐ U86 Tom Paciorek	.07	.03	.01
☐ U87 David Palmer	.07	.03	.01
☐ U88 Jeff Parrett	.12	.05	.01
☐ U89 Pat Perry	.10	.04	.01
☐ U90 Dan Plesac	.17	.07	.01
☐ U91 Darrell Porter	.07	.03	.01
☐ U92 Luis Quinones	.12	.05	.01
☐ U93 Rey Quinones	.07	.03	.01
☐ U94 Gary Redus	.07	.03	.01
☐ U95 Jeff Reed	.07	.03	.01
☐ U96 Bip Roberts	.50	.20	.05
☐ U97 Billy Jo Robidoux	.07	.03	.01
☐ U98 Gary Roenicke	.07	.03	.01
☐ U99 Ron Roenicke	.07	.03	.01
☐ U100 Angel Salazar	.07	.03	.01
☐ U101 Joe Sambito	.07	.03	.01
☐ U102 Billy Sample	.07	.03	.01
☐ U103 Dave Schmidt	.07	.03	.01
☐ U104 Ken Schrom	.07	.03	.01
☐ U105 Ruben Sierra	9.00	4.00	.90
☐ U106 Ted Simmons	.20	.08	.02
☐ U107 Sammy Stewart	.07	.03	.01
☐ U108 Kurt Stillwell	.30	.12	.03
☐ U109 Dale Sveum	.12	.05	.01
☐ U110 Tim Teufel	.10	.04	.01
☐ U111 Bob Tewksbury	.10	.04	.01
☐ U112 Andres Thomas	.12	.05	.01
☐ U113 Jason Thompson	.07	.03	.01
☐ U114 Milt Thompson	.10	.04	.01
☐ U115 Robby Thompson	.40	.16	.04
☐ U116 Jay Tibbs	.07	.03	.01
☐ U117 Fred Toliver	.10	.04	.01
☐ U118 Wayne Tolleson	.07	.03	.01
☐ U119 Alex Trevino	.07	.03	.01
☐ U120 Manny Trillo	.07	.03	.01
☐ U121 Ed VandeBerg	.07	.03	.01
☐ U122 Ozzie Virgil	.07	.03	.01
☐ U123 Tony Walker	.10	.04	.01
☐ U124 Gene Walter	.07	.03	.01
☐ U125 Duane Ward	.35	.15	.03
☐ U126 Jerry Willard	.07	.03	.01
☐ U127 Mitch Williams	.40	.16	.04
☐ U128 Reggie Williams	.10	.04	.01
☐ U129 Bobby Witt	.50	.20	.05
☐ U130 Marvell Wynne	.07	.03	.01
☐ U131 Steve Yeager	.07	.03	.01
☐ U132 Checklist 1-132	.07	.01	.00

1987 Fleer

This 660-card set features a distinctive blue border, which fades to white on the card fronts. The backs are printed in blue, red, and pink on white card stock. The bottom of the card back shows an innovative graph of the player's ability, e.g., "He's got the stuff" for pitchers and "How he's hitting 'em," for hitters. Cards are numbered on the back and are again the standard 2 1/2" by 3 1/2". Cards are again organized numerically by teams, i.e., World Champion Mets (1-25), Boston Red Sox (26-48), Houston Astros (49-72), California Angels (73-95), New York Yankees (96-120), Texas Rangers (121-143), Detroit Tigers (144-168), Philadelphia Phillies (169-192), Cincinnati Reds (193-218), Toronto Blue

Jays (219-240), Cleveland Indians (241-263), San Francisco Giants (264-288), St. Louis Cardinals (289-312), Montreal Expos (313-337), Milwaukee Brewers (338-361), Kansas City Royals (362-384), Oakland A's (385-410), San Diego Padres (411-435), Los Angeles Dodgers (436-460), Baltimore Orioles (461-483), Chicago White Sox (484-508), Atlanta Braves (509-532), Minnesota Twins (533-554), Chicago Cubs (555-578), Seattle Mariners (579-600), and Pittsburgh Pirates (601-624). The last 36 cards in the set consist of Specials (625-643), Rookie Pairs (644-653), and checklists (654-660). The key rookie cards in this set are Barry Bonds, Bobby Bonilla, Will Clark, Chuck Finley, Bo Jackson, Barry Larkin, Dave Magadan, Kevin Mitchell, Kevin Seitzer, and Ruben Sierra. Fleer also produced a "limited" edition version of this set with glossy coating and packaged in a "tin." However, this tin set was apparently not limited enough (estimated between 75,000 and 100,000 1987 tin sets produced by Fleer), since the price of the "tin" glossy cards is now the same as the regular set.

	MINT	EXC	G-VG
COMPLETE SET (660)	100.00	45.00	15.00
COMMON PLAYER (1-660)	.06	.02	.00
☐ 1 Rick Aguilera	.30	.08	.01
☐ 2 Richard Anderson	.06	.02	.00
☐ 3 Wally Backman	.06	.02	.00
☐ 4 Gary Carter	.30	.12	.03
☐ 5 Ron Darling	.15	.06	.01
☐ 6 Len Dykstra	.40	.16	.04
☐ 7 Kevin Elster	.25	.10	.02
☐ 8 Sid Fernandez	.15	.06	.01
☐ 9 Dwight Gooden	1.00	.40	.10
☐ 10 Ed Hearn	.06	.02	.00
☐ 11 Danny Heep	.06	.02	.00
☐ 12 Keith Hernandez	.20	.08	.02
☐ 13 Howard Johnson	.65	.25	.06
☐ 14 Ray Knight	.10	.04	.01
☐ 15 Lee Mazzilli	.06	.02	.00
☐ 16 Roger McDowell	.06	.02	.00
☐ 17 Kevin Mitchell	8.50	3.75	.85
☐ 18 Randy Niemann	.06	.02	.00
☐ 19 Bob Ojeda	.06	.02	.00
☐ 20 Jesse Orosco	.06	.02	.00
☐ 21 Rafael Santana	.06	.02	.00
☐ 22 Doug Sisk	.06	.02	.00
☐ 23 Darryl Strawberry	2.25	.90	.22
☐ 24 Tim Teufel	.06	.02	.00
☐ 25 Mookie Wilson	.10	.04	.01
☐ 26 Tony Armas	.06	.02	.00
☐ 27 Marty Barrett	.06	.02	.00
☐ 28 Don Baylor	.10	.04	.01
☐ 29 Wade Boggs	1.50	.60	.15
☐ 30 Oil Can Boyd	.06	.02	.00
☐ 31 Bill Buckner	.10	.04	.01
☐ 32 Roger Clemens	3.50	1.50	.35
☐ 33 Steve Crawford	.06	.02	.00
☐ 34 Dwight Evans	.20	.08	.02
☐ 35 Rich Gedman	.06	.02	.00
☐ 36 Dave Henderson	.25	.10	.02
☐ 37 Bruce Hurst	.12	.05	.01
☐ 38 Tim Lollar	.06	.02	.00
☐ 39 Al Nipper	.06	.02	.00
☐ 40 Spike Owen	.06	.02	.00
☐ 41 Jim Rice	.15	.06	.01
☐ 42 Ed Romero	.06	.02	.00
☐ 43 Joe Sambito	.06	.02	.00
☐ 44 Calvin Schiraldi	.06	.02	.00
☐ 45 Tom Seaver	.65	.25	.06
☐ 46 Jeff Sellers	.10	.04	.01
☐ 47 Bob Stanley	.06	.02	.00
☐ 48 Sammy Stewart	.06	.02	.00
☐ 49 Larry Andersen	.06	.02	.00
☐ 50 Alan Ashby	.06	.02	.00
☐ 51 Kevin Bass	.10	.04	.01
☐ 52 Jeff Calhoun	.06	.02	.00
☐ 53 Jose Cruz	.10	.04	.01
☐ 54 Danny Darwin	.06	.02	.00
☐ 55 Glenn Davis	.40	.16	.04
☐ 56 Jim Deshaies	.25	.10	.02
☐ 57 Bill Doran	.06	.02	.00
☐ 58 Phil Garner	.10	.04	.01
☐ 59 Billy Hatcher	.12	.05	.01
☐ 60 Charlie Kerfeld	.06	.02	.00
☐ 61 Bob Knepper	.06	.02	.00
☐ 62 Dave Lopes	.10	.04	.01
☐ 63 Aurelio Lopez	.06	.02	.00
☐ 64 Jim Pankovits	.06	.02	.00
☐ 65 Terry Puhl	.06	.02	.00
☐ 66 Craig Reynolds	.06	.02	.00
☐ 67 Nolan Ryan	3.00	1.25	.30
☐ 68 Mike Scott	.15	.06	.01
☐ 69 Dave Smith	.06	.02	.00
☐ 70 Dickie Thon	.06	.02	.00
☐ 71 Tony Walker	.06	.02	.00
☐ 72 Denny Walling	.06	.02	.00
☐ 73 Bob Boone	.12	.05	.01
☐ 74 Rick Burleson	.06	.02	.00
☐ 75 John Candelaria	.06	.02	.00
☐ 76 Doug Corbett	.06	.02	.00
☐ 77 Doug DeCinces	.10	.04	.01
☐ 78 Brian Downing	.10	.04	.01
☐ 79 Chuck Finley	4.00	1.75	.40
☐ 80 Terry Forster	.10	.04	.01
☐ 81 Bob Grich	.10	.04	.01
☐ 82 George Hendrick	.06	.02	.00
☐ 83 Jack Howell	.06	.02	.00
☐ 84 Reggie Jackson	.65	.25	.06
☐ 85 Ruppert Jones	.06	.02	.00
☐ 86 Wally Joyner	4.00	1.75	.40

☐ 87 Gary Lucas	.06	.02	.00
☐ 88 Kirk McCaskill	.06	.02	.00
☐ 89 Donnie Moore	.06	.02	.00
☐ 90 Gary Pettis	.06	.02	.00
☐ 91 Vern Ruhle	.06	.02	.00
☐ 92 Dick Schofield	.06	.02	.00
☐ 93 Don Sutton	.20	.08	.02
☐ 94 Rob Wilfong	.06	.02	.00
☐ 95 Mike Witt	.06	.02	.00
☐ 96 Doug Drabek	2.25	.90	.22
☐ 97 Mike Easler	.06	.02	.00
☐ 98 Mike Fischlin	.06	.02	.00
☐ 99 Brian Fisher	.06	.02	.00
☐ 100 Ron Guidry	.12	.05	.01
☐ 101 Rickey Henderson	2.00	.80	.20
☐ 102 Tommy John	.15	.06	.01
☐ 103 Ron Kittle	.10	.04	.01
☐ 104 Don Mattingly	2.00	.80	.20
☐ 105 Bobby Meacham	.06	.02	.00
☐ 106 Joe Niekro	.10	.04	.01
☐ 107 Mike Pagliarulo	.06	.02	.00
☐ 108 Dan Pasqua	.10	.04	.01
☐ 109 Willie Randolph	.10	.04	.01
☐ 110 Dennis Rasmussen	.06	.02	.00
☐ 111 Dave Righetti	.12	.05	.01
☐ 112 Gary Roenicke	.06	.02	.00
☐ 113 Rod Scurry	.06	.02	.00
☐ 114 Bob Shirley	.06	.02	.00
☐ 115 Joel Skinner	.06	.02	.00
☐ 116 Tim Stoddard	.06	.02	.00
☐ 117 Bob Tewksbury	.10	.04	.01
☐ 118 Wayne Tolleson	.06	.02	.00
☐ 119 Claudell Washington	.06	.02	.00
☐ 120 Dave Winfield	.50	.20	.05
☐ 121 Steve Buechele	.10	.04	.01
☐ 122 Ed Correa	.06	.02	.00
☐ 123 Scott Fletcher	.06	.02	.00
☐ 124 Jose Guzman	.10	.04	.01
☐ 125 Toby Harrah	.06	.02	.00
☐ 126 Greg Harris	.06	.02	.00
☐ 127 Charlie Hough	.06	.02	.00
☐ 128 Pete Incaviglia	.60	.25	.06
☐ 129 Mike Mason	.06	.02	.00
☐ 130 Oddibe McDowell	.10	.04	.01
☐ 131 Dale Mohorcic	.10	.04	.01
☐ 132 Pete O'Brien	.06	.02	.00
☐ 133 Tom Paciorek	.06	.02	.00
☐ 134 Larry Parrish	.06	.02	.00
☐ 135 Geno Petralli	.06	.02	.00
☐ 136 Darrell Porter	.06	.02	.00
☐ 137 Jeff Russell	.10	.04	.01
☐ 138 Ruben Sierra	15.00	6.50	2.15
☐ 139 Don Slaught	.06	.02	.00
☐ 140 Gary Ward	.06	.02	.00
☐ 141 Curtis Wilkerson	.06	.02	.00
☐ 142 Mitch Williams	.50	.20	.05
☐ 143 Bobby Witt	.90	.40	.09
☐ 144 Dave Bergman	.06	.02	.00
☐ 145 Tom Brookens	.06	.02	.00
☐ 146 Bill Campbell	.06	.02	.00
☐ 147 Chuck Cary	.12	.05	.01
☐ 148 Darnell Coles	.06	.02	.00
☐ 149 Dave Collins	.06	.02	.00
☐ 150 Darrell Evans	.12	.05	.01
☐ 151 Kirk Gibson	.25	.10	.02
☐ 152 John Grubb	.06	.02	.00
☐ 153 Willie Hernandez	.06	.02	.00
☐ 154 Larry Herndon	.06	.02	.00
☐ 155 Eric King	.20	.08	.02
☐ 156 Chet Lemon	.06	.02	.00
☐ 157 Dwight Lowry	.06	.02	.00
☐ 158 Jack Morris	.35	.15	.03
☐ 159 Randy O'Neal	.06	.02	.00
☐ 160 Lance Parrish	.12	.05	.01
☐ 161 Dan Petry	.06	.02	.00
☐ 162 Pat Sheridan	.06	.02	.00
☐ 163 Jim Slaton	.06	.02	.00
☐ 164 Frank Tanana	.10	.04	.01
☐ 165 Walt Terrell	.06	.02	.00
☐ 166 Mark Thurmond	.06	.02	.00
☐ 167 Alan Trammell	.40	.16	.04
☐ 168 Lou Whitaker	.20	.08	.02
☐ 169 Luis Aguayo	.06	.02	.00
☐ 170 Steve Bedrosian	.10	.04	.01
☐ 171 Don Carman	.06	.02	.00
☐ 172 Darren Daulton	.12	.05	.01
☐ 173 Greg Gross	.06	.02	.00
☐ 174 Kevin Gross	.06	.02	.00
☐ 175 Von Hayes	.12	.05	.01
☐ 176 Charles Hudson	.06	.02	.00
☐ 177 Tom Hume	.06	.02	.00
☐ 178 Steve Jeltz	.06	.02	.00
☐ 179 Mike Maddux	.12	.05	.01
☐ 180 Shane Rawley	.06	.02	.00
☐ 181 Gary Redus	.06	.02	.00
☐ 182 Ron Roenicke	.06	.02	.00
☐ 183 Bruce Ruffin	.10	.04	.01
☐ 184 John Russell	.06	.02	.00
☐ 185 Juan Samuel	.25	.10	.02
☐ 186 Dan Schatzeder	.06	.02	.00
☐ 187 Mike Schmidt	1.50	.60	.15
☐ 188 Rick Schu	.06	.02	.00
☐ 189 Jeff Stone	.06	.02	.00
☐ 190 Kent Tekulve	.06	.02	.00
☐ 191 Milt Thompson	.10	.04	.01
☐ 192 Glenn Wilson	.06	.02	.00
☐ 193 Buddy Bell	.10	.04	.01
☐ 194 Tom Browning	.12	.05	.01
☐ 195 Sal Butera	.06	.02	.00
☐ 196 Dave Concepcion	.12	.05	.01
☐ 197 Kal Daniels	.35	.15	.03
☐ 198 Eric Davis	1.00	.40	.10
☐ 199 John Denny	.06	.02	.00
☐ 200 Bo Diaz	.06	.02	.00
☐ 201 Nick Esasky	.10	.04	.01
☐ 202 John Franco	.10	.04	.01

No.	Player			
☐ 203	Bill Gullickson	.10	.04	.01
☐ 204	Barry Larkin	6.00	2.50	.60
☐ 205	Eddie Milner	.06	.02	.00
☐ 206	Rob Murphy	.15	.06	.01
☐ 207	Ron Oester	.06	.02	.00
☐ 208	Dave Parker	.25	.10	.02
☐ 209	Tony Perez	.20	.08	.02
☐ 210	Ted Power	.06	.02	.00
☐ 211	Joe Price	.06	.02	.00
☐ 212	Ron Robinson	.06	.02	.00
☐ 213	Pete Rose	.75	.30	.07
☐ 214	Mario Soto	.06	.02	.00
☐ 215	Kurt Stillwell	.35	.15	.03
☐ 216	Max Venable	.06	.02	.00
☐ 217	Chris Welsh	.06	.02	.00
☐ 218	Carl Willis	.15	.06	.01
☐ 219	Jesse Barfield	.15	.06	.01
☐ 220	George Bell	.40	.16	.04
☐ 221	Bill Caudill	.06	.02	.00
☐ 222	John Cerutti	.15	.06	.01
☐ 223	Jim Clancy	.06	.02	.00
☐ 224	Mark Eichhorn	.15	.06	.01
☐ 225	Tony Fernandez	.20	.08	.02
☐ 226	Damaso Garcia	.06	.02	.00
☐ 227	Kelly Gruber ERR (wrong birth year)	.75	.30	.07
☐ 228	Tom Henke	.12	.05	.01
☐ 229	Garth Iorg	.06	.02	.00
☐ 230	Joe Johnson	.06	.02	.00
☐ 231	Cliff Johnson	.06	.02	.00
☐ 232	Jimmy Key	.15	.06	.01
☐ 233	Dennis Lamp	.06	.02	.00
☐ 234	Rick Leach	.06	.02	.00
☐ 235	Buck Martinez	.06	.02	.00
☐ 236	Lloyd Moseby	.06	.02	.00
☐ 237	Rance Mulliniks	.06	.02	.00
☐ 238	Dave Stieb	.15	.06	.01
☐ 239	Willie Upshaw	.06	.02	.00
☐ 240	Ernie Whitt	.06	.02	.00
☐ 241	Andy Allanson	.06	.02	.00
☐ 242	Scott Bailes	.10	.04	.01
☐ 243	Chris Bando	.06	.02	.00
☐ 244	Tony Bernazard	.06	.02	.00
☐ 245	John Butcher	.06	.02	.00
☐ 246	Brett Butler	.15	.06	.01
☐ 247	Ernie Camacho	.06	.02	.00
☐ 248	Tom Candiotti	.12	.05	.01
☐ 249	Joe Carter	.75	.30	.07
☐ 250	Carmen Castillo	.06	.02	.00
☐ 251	Julio Franco	.60	.25	.06
☐ 252	Mel Hall	.12	.05	.01
☐ 253	Brook Jacoby	.10	.04	.01
☐ 254	Phil Niekro	.20	.08	.02
☐ 255	Otis Nixon	.17	.07	.01
☐ 256	Dickie Noles	.06	.02	.00
☐ 257	Bryan Oelkers	.06	.02	.00
☐ 258	Ken Schrom	.06	.02	.00
☐ 259	Don Schulze	.06	.02	.00
☐ 260	Cory Snyder	.17	.07	.01
☐ 261	Pat Tabler	.06	.02	.00
☐ 262	Andre Thornton	.06	.02	.00
☐ 263	Rich Yett	.06	.02	.00
☐ 264	Mike Aldrete	.10	.04	.01
☐ 265	Juan Berenguer	.06	.02	.00
☐ 266	Vida Blue	.10	.04	.01
☐ 267	Bob Brenly	.06	.02	.00
☐ 268	Chris Brown	.06	.02	.00
☐ 269	Will Clark	30.00	13.50	4.50
☐ 270	Chili Davis	.12	.05	.01
☐ 271	Mark Davis	.10	.04	.01
☐ 272	Kelly Downs	.25	.10	.02
☐ 273	Scott Garrelts	.10	.04	.01
☐ 274	Dan Gladden	.06	.02	.00
☐ 275	Mike Krukow	.06	.02	.00
☐ 276	Randy Kutcher	.06	.02	.00
☐ 277	Mike LaCoss	.06	.02	.00
☐ 278	Jeff Leonard	.06	.02	.00
☐ 279	Candy Maldonado	.10	.04	.01
☐ 280	Roger Mason	.06	.02	.00
☐ 281	Bob Melvin	.06	.02	.00
☐ 282	Greg Minton	.06	.02	.00
☐ 283	Jeff Robinson (Giants pitcher)	.10	.04	.01
☐ 284	Harry Spilman	.06	.02	.00
☐ 285	Robby Thompson	.40	.16	.04
☐ 286	Jose Uribe	.06	.02	.00
☐ 287	Frank Williams	.06	.02	.00
☐ 288	Joel Youngblood	.06	.02	.00
☐ 289	Jack Clark	.20	.08	.02
☐ 290	Vince Coleman	.75	.30	.07
☐ 291	Tim Conroy	.06	.02	.00
☐ 292	Danny Cox	.06	.02	.00
☐ 293	Ken Dayley	.06	.02	.00
☐ 294	Curt Ford	.06	.02	.00
☐ 295	Bob Forsch	.06	.02	.00
☐ 296	Tom Herr	.10	.04	.01
☐ 297	Ricky Horton	.06	.02	.00
☐ 298	Clint Hurdle	.06	.02	.00
☐ 299	Jeff Lahti	.06	.02	.00
☐ 300	Steve Lake	.06	.02	.00
☐ 301	Tito Landrum	.06	.02	.00
☐ 302	Mike LaValliere	.35	.15	.03
☐ 303	Greg Mathews	.10	.04	.01
☐ 304	Willie McGee	.20	.08	.02
☐ 305	Jose Oquendo	.06	.02	.00
☐ 306	Terry Pendleton	.35	.15	.03
☐ 307	Pat Perry	.06	.02	.00
☐ 308	Ozzie Smith	.60	.25	.06
☐ 309	Ray Soff	.06	.02	.00
☐ 310	John Tudor	.12	.05	.01
☐ 311	Andy Van Slyke UER (Bats R, Throws L)	.30	.12	.03
☐ 312	Todd Worrell	.12	.05	.01
☐ 313	Dann Bilardello	.06	.02	.00
☐ 314	Hubie Brooks	.12	.05	.01
☐ 315	Tim Burke	.06	.02	.00

☐ 316 Andre Dawson .65 .25 .06
☐ 317 Mike Fitzgerald .06 .02 .00
☐ 318 Tom Foley .06 .02 .00
☐ 319 Andres Galarraga .15 .06 .01
☐ 320 Joe Hesketh .12 .05 .01
☐ 321 Wallace Johnson .06 .02 .00
☐ 322 Wayne Krenchicki .06 .02 .00
☐ 323 Vance Law .06 .02 .00
☐ 324 Dennis Martinez .12 .05 .01
☐ 325 Bob McClure .06 .02 .00
☐ 326 Andy McGaffigan .06 .02 .00
☐ 327 Al Newman .12 .05 .01
☐ 328 Tim Raines .35 .15 .03
☐ 329 Jeff Reardon .25 .10 .02
☐ 330 Luis Rivera .06 .02 .00
☐ 331 Bob Sebra .06 .02 .00
☐ 332 Bryn Smith .06 .02 .00
☐ 333 Jay Tibbs .06 .02 .00
☐ 334 Tim Wallach .12 .05 .01
☐ 335 Mitch Webster .06 .02 .00
☐ 336 Jim Wohlford .06 .02 .00
☐ 337 Floyd Youmans .06 .02 .00
☐ 338 Chris Bosio .40 .16 .04
☐ 339 Glenn Braggs .40 .16 .04
☐ 340 Rick Cerone .06 .02 .00
☐ 341 Mark Clear .06 .02 .00
☐ 342 Bryan Clutterbuck .06 .02 .00
☐ 343 Cecil Cooper .10 .04 .01
☐ 344 Rob Deer .15 .06 .01
☐ 345 Jim Gantner .06 .02 .00
☐ 346 Ted Higuera .12 .05 .01
☐ 347 John Henry Johnson .06 .02 .00
☐ 348 Tim Leary .15 .06 .01
☐ 349 Rick Manning .06 .02 .00
☐ 350 Paul Molitor .25 .10 .02
☐ 351 Charlie Moore .06 .02 .00
☐ 352 Juan Nieves .10 .04 .01
☐ 353 Ben Oglivie .06 .02 .00
☐ 354 Dan Plesac .20 .08 .02
☐ 355 Ernest Riles .06 .02 .00
☐ 356 Billy Jo Robidoux .06 .02 .00
☐ 357 Bill Schroeder .06 .02 .00
☐ 358 Dale Sveum .10 .04 .01
☐ 359 Gorman Thomas .10 .04 .01
☐ 360 Bill Wegman .12 .05 .01
☐ 361 Robin Yount .75 .30 .07
☐ 362 Steve Balboni .06 .02 .00
☐ 363 Scott Bankhead .15 .06 .01
☐ 364 Buddy Biancalana .06 .02 .00
☐ 365 Bud Black .06 .02 .00
☐ 366 George Brett .75 .30 .07
☐ 367 Steve Farr .10 .04 .01
☐ 368 Mark Gubicza .12 .05 .01
☐ 369 Bo Jackson 20.00 8.50 2.75
☐ 370 Danny Jackson .10 .04 .01
☐ 371 Mike Kingery .10 .04 .01
☐ 372 Rudy Law .06 .02 .00
☐ 373 Charlie Leibrandt .06 .02 .00
☐ 374 Dennis Leonard .06 .02 .00
☐ 375 Hal McRae .10 .04 .01
☐ 376 Jorge Orta .06 .02 .00
☐ 377 Jamie Quirk .06 .02 .00
☐ 378 Dan Quisenberry .12 .05 .01
☐ 379 Bret Saberhagen .40 .16 .04
☐ 380 Angel Salazar .06 .02 .00
☐ 381 Lonnie Smith .12 .05 .01
☐ 382 Jim Sundberg .06 .02 .00
☐ 383 Frank White .06 .02 .00
☐ 384 Willie Wilson .10 .04 .01
☐ 385 Joaquin Andujar .06 .02 .00
☐ 386 Doug Bair .06 .02 .00
☐ 387 Dusty Baker .10 .04 .01
☐ 388 Bruce Bochte .06 .02 .00
☐ 389 Jose Canseco 11.00 5.00 1.35
☐ 390 Chris Codiroli .06 .02 .00
☐ 391 Mike Davis .06 .02 .00
☐ 392 Alfredo Griffin .06 .02 .00
☐ 393 Moose Haas .06 .02 .00
☐ 394 Donnie Hill .06 .02 .00
☐ 395 Jay Howell .06 .02 .00
☐ 396 Dave Kingman .12 .05 .01
☐ 397 Carney Lansford .12 .05 .01
☐ 398 Dave Leiper .06 .02 .00
☐ 399 Bill Mooneyham .06 .02 .00
☐ 400 Dwayne Murphy .06 .02 .00
☐ 401 Steve Ontiveros .06 .02 .00
☐ 402 Tony Phillips .06 .02 .00
☐ 403 Eric Plunk .06 .02 .00
☐ 404 Jose Rijo .25 .10 .02
☐ 405 Terry Steinbach .75 .30 .07
☐ 406 Dave Stewart .35 .15 .03
☐ 407 Mickey Tettleton .20 .08 .02
☐ 408 Dave Von Ohlen .06 .02 .00
☐ 409 Jerry Willard .06 .02 .00
☐ 410 Curt Young .06 .02 .00
☐ 411 Bruce Bochy .06 .02 .00
☐ 412 Dave Dravecky .12 .05 .01
☐ 413 Tim Flannery .06 .02 .00
☐ 414 Steve Garvey .40 .16 .04
☐ 415 Goose Gossage .15 .06 .01
☐ 416 Tony Gwynn 1.25 .50 .12
☐ 417 Andy Hawkins .06 .02 .00
☐ 418 LaMarr Hoyt .06 .02 .00
☐ 419 Terry Kennedy .06 .02 .00
☐ 420 John Kruk .75 .30 .07
☐ 421 Dave LaPoint .06 .02 .00
☐ 422 Craig Lefferts .06 .02 .00
☐ 423 Carmelo Martinez .06 .02 .00
☐ 424 Lance McCullers .06 .02 .00
☐ 425 Kevin McReynolds .25 .10 .02
☐ 426 Graig Nettles .10 .04 .01
☐ 427 Bip Roberts .65 .25 .06
☐ 428 Jerry Royster .06 .02 .00
☐ 429 Benito Santiago .60 .25 .06
☐ 430 Eric Show .06 .02 .00
☐ 431 Bob Stoddard .06 .02 .00

☐ 432 Garry Templeton .10 .04 .01
☐ 433 Gene Walter .06 .02 .00
☐ 434 Ed Whitson .06 .02 .00
☐ 435 Marvell Wynne .06 .02 .00
☐ 436 Dave Anderson .06 .02 .00
☐ 437 Greg Brock .06 .02 .00
☐ 438 Enos Cabell .06 .02 .00
☐ 439 Mariano Duncan .12 .05 .01
☐ 440 Pedro Guerrero .20 .08 .02
☐ 441 Orel Hershiser .35 .15 .03
☐ 442 Rick Honeycutt .06 .02 .00
☐ 443 Ken Howell .06 .02 .00
☐ 444 Ken Landreaux .06 .02 .00
☐ 445 Bill Madlock .10 .04 .01
☐ 446 Mike Marshall .10 .04 .01
☐ 447 Len Matuszek .06 .02 .00
☐ 448 Tom Niedenfuer .06 .02 .00
☐ 449 Alejandro Pena .12 .05 .01
☐ 450 Dennis Powell .06 .02 .00
☐ 451 Jerry Reuss .06 .02 .00
☐ 452 Bill Russell .10 .04 .01
☐ 453 Steve Sax .20 .08 .02
☐ 454 Mike Scioscia .06 .02 .00
☐ 455 Franklin Stubbs .06 .02 .00
☐ 456 Alex Trevino .06 .02 .00
☐ 457 Fernando Valenzuela .15 .06 .01
☐ 458 Ed VandeBerg .06 .02 .00
☐ 459 Bob Welch .15 .06 .01
☐ 460 Reggie Williams .06 .02 .00
☐ 461 Don Aase .06 .02 .00
☐ 462 Juan Beniquez .06 .02 .00
☐ 463 Mike Boddicker .06 .02 .00
☐ 464 Juan Bonilla .06 .02 .00
☐ 465 Rich Bordi .06 .02 .00
☐ 466 Storm Davis .06 .02 .00
☐ 467 Rick Dempsey .06 .02 .00
☐ 468 Ken Dixon .06 .02 .00
☐ 469 Jim Dwyer .06 .02 .00
☐ 470 Mike Flanagan .10 .04 .01
☐ 471 Jackie Gutierrez .06 .02 .00
☐ 472 Brad Havens .06 .02 .00
☐ 473 Lee Lacy .06 .02 .00
☐ 474 Fred Lynn .12 .05 .01
☐ 475 Scott McGregor .06 .02 .00
☐ 476 Eddie Murray .60 .25 .06
☐ 477 Tom O'Malley .06 .02 .00
☐ 478 Cal Ripken Jr. 2.50 1.00 .25
☐ 479 Larry Sheets .06 .02 .00
☐ 480 John Shelby .06 .02 .00
☐ 481 Nate Snell .06 .02 .00
☐ 482 Jim Traber .06 .02 .00
☐ 483 Mike Young .06 .02 .00
☐ 484 Neil Allen .06 .02 .00
☐ 485 Harold Baines .25 .10 .02
☐ 486 Floyd Bannister .06 .02 .00
☐ 487 Daryl Boston .06 .02 .00
☐ 488 Ivan Calderon .35 .15 .03
☐ 489 John Cangelosi .06 .02 .00
☐ 490 Steve Carlton .60 .25 .06
☐ 491 Joe Cowley .06 .02 .00
☐ 492 Julio Cruz .06 .02 .00
☐ 493 Bill Dawley .06 .02 .00
☐ 494 Jose DeLeon .06 .02 .00
☐ 495 Richard Dotson .06 .02 .00
☐ 496 Carlton Fisk .75 .30 .07
☐ 497 Ozzie Guillen .20 .08 .02
☐ 498 Jerry Hairston .06 .02 .00
☐ 499 Ron Hassey .06 .02 .00
☐ 500 Tim Hulett .06 .02 .00
☐ 501 Bob James .06 .02 .00
☐ 502 Steve Lyons .06 .02 .00
☐ 503 Joel McKeon .06 .02 .00
☐ 504 Gene Nelson .06 .02 .00
☐ 505 Dave Schmidt .06 .02 .00
☐ 506 Ray Searage .06 .02 .00
☐ 507 Bobby Thigpen 2.00 .80 .20
☐ 508 Greg Walker .06 .02 .00
☐ 509 Jim Acker .06 .02 .00
☐ 510 Doyle Alexander .06 .02 .00
☐ 511 Paul Assenmacher .06 .02 .00
☐ 512 Bruce Benedict .06 .02 .00
☐ 513 Chris Chambliss .10 .04 .01
☐ 514 Jeff Dedmon .06 .02 .00
☐ 515 Gene Garber .06 .02 .00
☐ 516 Ken Griffey .15 .06 .01
☐ 517 Terry Harper .06 .02 .00
☐ 518 Bob Horner .12 .05 .01
☐ 519 Glenn Hubbard .06 .02 .00
☐ 520 Rick Mahler .06 .02 .00
☐ 521 Omar Moreno .06 .02 .00
☐ 522 Dale Murphy .50 .20 .05
☐ 523 Ken Oberkfell .06 .02 .00
☐ 524 Ed Olwine .06 .02 .00
☐ 525 David Palmer .06 .02 .00
☐ 526 Rafael Ramirez .06 .02 .00
☐ 527 Billy Sample .06 .02 .00
☐ 528 Ted Simmons .12 .05 .01
☐ 529 Zane Smith .12 .05 .01
☐ 530 Bruce Sutter .12 .05 .01
☐ 531 Andres Thomas .15 .06 .01
☐ 532 Ozzie Virgil .06 .02 .00
☐ 533 Allan Anderson .25 .10 .02
☐ 534 Keith Atherton .06 .02 .00
☐ 535 Billy Beane .06 .02 .00
☐ 536 Bert Blyleven .15 .06 .01
☐ 537 Tom Brunansky .15 .06 .01
☐ 538 Randy Bush .06 .02 .00
☐ 539 George Frazier .06 .02 .00
☐ 540 Gary Gaetti .15 .06 .01
☐ 541 Greg Gagne .10 .04 .01
☐ 542 Mickey Hatcher .06 .02 .00
☐ 543 Neal Heaton .06 .02 .00
☐ 544 Kent Hrbek .17 .07 .01
☐ 545 Roy Lee Jackson .06 .02 .00
☐ 546 Tim Laudner .06 .02 .00
☐ 547 Steve Lombardozzi .06 .02 .00

☐ 548 Mark Portugal .25 .10 .02
☐ 549 Kirby Puckett 3.25 1.35 .32
☐ 550 Jeff Reed .06 .02 .00
☐ 551 Mark Salas .06 .02 .00
☐ 552 Roy Smalley .06 .02 .00
☐ 553 Mike Smithson .06 .02 .00
☐ 554 Frank Viola .30 .12 .03
☐ 555 Thad Bosley .06 .02 .00
☐ 556 Ron Cey .10 .04 .01
☐ 557 Jody Davis .06 .02 .00
☐ 558 Ron Davis .06 .02 .00
☐ 559 Bob Dernier .06 .02 .00
☐ 560 Frank DiPino .06 .02 .00
☐ 561 Shawon Dunston UER .30 .12 .03
(wrong birth year listed on card back)
☐ 562 Leon Durham .06 .02 .00
☐ 563 Dennis Eckersley .20 .08 .02
☐ 564 Terry Francona .06 .02 .00
☐ 565 Dave Gumpert .06 .02 .00
☐ 566 Guy Hoffman .06 .02 .00
☐ 567 Ed Lynch .06 .02 .00
☐ 568 Gary Matthews .06 .02 .00
☐ 569 Keith Moreland .06 .02 .00
☐ 570 Jamie Moyer .10 .04 .01
☐ 571 Jerry Mumphrey .06 .02 .00
☐ 572 Ryne Sandberg 2.25 .90 .22
☐ 573 Scott Sanderson .10 .04 .01
☐ 574 Lee Smith .25 .10 .02
☐ 575 Chris Speier .06 .02 .00
☐ 576 Rick Sutcliffe .10 .04 .01
☐ 577 Manny Trillo .06 .02 .00
☐ 578 Steve Trout .06 .02 .00
☐ 579 Karl Best .06 .02 .00
☐ 580 Scott Bradley .06 .02 .00
☐ 581 Phil Bradley .06 .02 .00
☐ 582 Mickey Brantley .06 .02 .00
☐ 583 Mike Brown .06 .02 .00
(Mariners pitcher)
☐ 584 Alvin Davis .15 .06 .01
☐ 585 Lee Guetterman .15 .06 .01
☐ 586 Mark Huismann .06 .02 .00
☐ 587 Bob Kearney .06 .02 .00
☐ 588 Pete Ladd .06 .02 .00
☐ 589 Mark Langston .35 .15 .03
☐ 590 Mike Moore .10 .04 .01
☐ 591 Mike Morgan .10 .04 .01
☐ 592 John Moses .06 .02 .00
☐ 593 Ken Phelps .06 .02 .00
☐ 594 Jim Presley .06 .02 .00
☐ 595 Rey Quinones UER .06 .02 .00
(Quinonez on front)
☐ 596 Harold Reynolds .20 .08 .02
☐ 597 Billy Swift .10 .04 .01
☐ 598 Danny Tartabull .45 .18 .04
☐ 599 Steve Yeager .06 .02 .00
☐ 600 Matt Young .06 .02 .00
☐ 601 Bill Almon .06 .02 .00
☐ 602 Rafael Belliard .40 .16 .04
☐ 603 Mike Bielecki .10 .04 .01
☐ 604 Barry Bonds 11.00 5.00 1.35
☐ 605 Bobby Bonilla 10.00 4.50 1.25
☐ 606 Sid Bream .06 .02 .00
☐ 607 Mike Brown .06 .02 .00
(Pirates OF)
☐ 608 Pat Clements .06 .02 .00
☐ 609 Mike Diaz .06 .02 .00
☐ 610 Cecilio Guante .06 .02 .00
☐ 611 Barry Jones .17 .07 .01
☐ 612 Bob Kipper .06 .02 .00
☐ 613 Larry McWilliams .06 .02 .00
☐ 614 Jim Morrison .06 .02 .00
☐ 615 Joe Orsulak .10 .04 .01
☐ 616 Junior Ortiz .06 .02 .00
☐ 617 Tony Pena .10 .04 .01
☐ 618 Johnny Ray .06 .02 .00
☐ 619 Rick Reuschel .10 .04 .01
☐ 620 R.J. Reynolds .06 .02 .00
☐ 621 Rick Rhoden .06 .02 .00
☐ 622 Don Robinson .06 .02 .00
☐ 623 Bob Walk .06 .02 .00
☐ 624 Jim Winn .06 .02 .00
☐ 625 Youthful Power .60 .25 .06
Pete Incaviglia
Jose Canseco
☐ 626 300 Game Winners .12 .05 .01
Don Sutton
Phil Niekro
☐ 627 AL Firemen .06 .02 .00
Dave Righetti
Don Aase
☐ 628 Rookie All-Stars 1.25 .50 .12
Wally Joyner
Jose Canseco
☐ 629 Magic Mets .50 .20 .05
Gary Carter
Sid Fernandez
Dwight Gooden
Keith Hernandez
Darryl Strawberry
☐ 630 NL Best Righties .10 .04 .01
Mike Scott
Mike Krukow
☐ 631 Sensational Southpaws .10 .04 .01
Fernando Valenzuela
John Franco
☐ 632 Count'Em .06 .02 .00
Bob Horner
☐ 633 AL Pitcher's Nightmare .75 .30 .07
Jose Canseco
Jim Rice
Kirby Puckett
☐ 634 All-Star Battery .35 .15 .03
Gary Carter
Roger Clemens

☐ 635 4000 Strikeouts .25 Steve Carlton	.10	.02
☐ 636 Big Bats at First .25 Glenn Davis Eddie Murray	.10	.02
☐ 637 On Base .25 Wade Boggs Keith Hernandez	.10	.02
☐ 638 Sluggers Left Side 1.00 Don Mattingly Darryl Strawberry	.40	.10
☐ 639 Former MVP's .25 Dave Parker Ryne Sandberg	.10	.02
☐ 640 Dr. K , Super K .75 Dwight Gooden Roger Clemens	.30	.07
☐ 641 AL West Stoppers .06 Mike Witt Charlie Hough	.02	.00
☐ 642 Doubles and Triples .12 Juan Samuel Tim Raines	.05	.01
☐ 643 Outfielders with Punch .10 Harold Baines Jesse Barfield	.04	.01
☐ 644 Dave Clark and 1.25 Greg Swindell	.50	.12
☐ 645 Ron Karkovice and .10 Russ Morman	.04	.01
☐ 646 Devon White and 1.50 Willie Fraser	.60	.15
☐ 647 Mike Stanley and .25 Jerry Browne	.10	.02
☐ 648 Dave Magadan and 1.50 Phil Lombardi	.60	.15
☐ 649 Jose Gonzalez and .12 Ralph Bryant	.05	.01
☐ 650 Jimmy Jones and .18 Randy Asadoor	.08	.01
☐ 651 Tracy Jones and .15 Marvin Freeman	.06	.01
☐ 652 John Stefero and .75 Kevin Seitzer	.30	.07
☐ 653 Rob Nelson and .12 Steve Fireovid	.05	.01
☐ 654 CL: Mets/Red Sox .10 Astros/Angels	.01	.00
☐ 655 CL: Yankees/Rangers .10 Tigers/Phillies	.01	.00
☐ 656 CL: Reds/Blue Jays .10 Indians/Giants ERR (230/231 wrong)	.01	.00
☐ 657 CL: Cardinals/Expos .10 Brewers/Royals	.01	.00
☐ 658 CL: A's/Padres .10 Dodgers/Orioles	.01	.00
☐ 659 CL: White Sox/Braves .10 Twins/Cubs	.01	.00
☐ 660 CL: Mariners/Pirates .10 Special Cards UER (580/581 wrong)	.01	.00

1987 Fleer Update

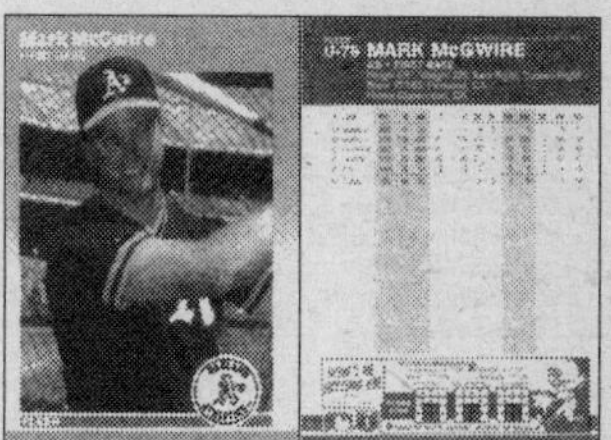

This 132-card set was distributed by Fleer to dealers as a complete set in a custom box. In addition to the complete set of 132 cards, the box also contains 25 Team Logo stickers. The card fronts look very similar to the 1987 Fleer regular issue. The cards are numbered (with a U prefix) alphabetically according to player's last name. Cards measure the standard size, 2 1/2" by 3 1/2". Fleer misalphabetized Jim Winn in their set numbering by putting him ahead of the next four players listed. The key (extended) rookie cards in this set are Ellis Burks, Mike Greenwell, Fred McGriff, Mark McGwire and Matt Williams. Fleer also produced a "limited" edition version of this set with glossy coating and packaged in a "tin." However, this tin set was apparently not limited enough (estimated between 75,000 and 100,000 1987 Update tin sets produced by Fleer), since the price of the "tin" glossy cards is now the same as the regular set.

	MINT	EXC	G-VG
COMPLETE SET (132)	14.00	6.25	2.00
COMMON PLAYER (1-132)	.05	.02	.00
☐ U1 Scott Bankhead	.15	.05	.01
☐ U2 Eric Bell	.10	.04	.01
☐ U3 Juan Beniquez	.05	.02	.00
☐ U4 Juan Berenguer	.05	.02	.00

☐ U5 Mike Birkbeck	.10	.04	.01
☐ U6 Randy Bockus	.10	.04	.01
☐ U7 Rod Booker	.05	.02	.00
☐ U8 Thad Bosley	.05	.02	.00
☐ U9 Greg Brock	.05	.02	.00
☐ U10 Bob Brower	.05	.02	.00
☐ U11 Chris Brown	.05	.02	.00
☐ U12 Jerry Browne	.10	.04	.01
☐ U13 Ralph Bryant	.10	.04	.01
☐ U14 DeWayne Buice	.05	.02	.00
☐ U15 Ellis Burks	2.00	.80	.20
☐ U16 Casey Candaele	.10	.04	.01
☐ U17 Steve Carlton	.25	.10	.02
☐ U18 Juan Castillo	.05	.02	.00
☐ U19 Chuck Crim	.10	.04	.01
☐ U20 Mark Davidson	.10	.04	.01
☐ U21 Mark Davis	.10	.04	.01
☐ U22 Storm Davis	.05	.02	.00
☐ U23 Bill Dawley	.05	.02	.00
☐ U24 Andre Dawson	.40	.16	.04
☐ U25 Brian Dayett	.05	.02	.00
☐ U26 Rick Dempsey	.05	.02	.00
☐ U27 Ken Dowell	.05	.02	.00
☐ U28 Dave Dravecky	.15	.06	.01
☐ U29 Mike Dunne	.10	.04	.01
☐ U30 Dennis Eckersley	.20	.08	.02
☐ U31 Cecil Fielder	2.50	1.00	.25
☐ U32 Brian Fisher	.10	.04	.01
☐ U33 Willie Fraser	.10	.04	.01
☐ U34 Ken Gerhart	.05	.02	.00
☐ U35 Jim Gott	.10	.04	.01
☐ U36 Dan Gladden	.10	.04	.01
☐ U37 Mike Greenwell	2.25	.90	.22
☐ U38 Cecilio Guante	.05	.02	.00
☐ U39 Albert Hall	.05	.02	.00
☐ U40 Atlee Hammaker	.05	.02	.00
☐ U41 Mickey Hatcher	.05	.02	.00
☐ U42 Mike Heath	.05	.02	.00
☐ U43 Neal Heaton	.05	.02	.00
☐ U44 Mike Henneman	.30	.12	.03
☐ U45 Guy Hoffman	.10	.04	.01
☐ U46 Charles Hudson	.05	.02	.00
☐ U47 Chuck Jackson	.10	.04	.01
☐ U48 Mike Jackson	.20	.08	.02
☐ U49 Reggie Jackson	.40	.16	.04
☐ U50 Chris James	.15	.06	.01
☐ U51 Dion James	.10	.04	.01
☐ U52 Stan Javier	.10	.04	.01
☐ U53 Stan Jefferson	.10	.04	.01
☐ U54 Jimmy Jones	.10	.04	.01
☐ U55 Tracy Jones	.10	.04	.01
☐ U56 Terry Kennedy	.05	.02	.00
☐ U57 Mike Kingery	.10	.04	.01
☐ U58 Ray Knight	.10	.04	.01
☐ U59 Gene Larkin	.20	.08	.02
☐ U60 Mike LaValliere	.10	.04	.01
☐ U61 Jack Lazorko	.05	.02	.00
☐ U62 Terry Leach	.10	.04	.01
☐ U63 Rick Leach	.05	.02	.00
☐ U64 Craig Lefferts	.05	.02	.00
☐ U65 Jim Lindeman	.10	.04	.01
☐ U66 Bill Long	.10	.04	.01
☐ U67 Mike Loynd	.05	.02	.00
☐ U68 Greg Maddux	.90	.40	.09
☐ U69 Bill Madlock	.12	.05	.01
☐ U70 Dave Magadan	.30	.12	.03
☐ U71 Joe Magrane	.20	.08	.02
☐ U72 Fred Manrique	.10	.04	.01
☐ U73 Mike Mason	.05	.02	.00
☐ U74 Lloyd McClendon	.15	.06	.01
☐ U75 Fred McGriff	2.50	1.00	.25
☐ U76 Mark McGwire	2.00	.80	.20
☐ U77 Mark McLemore	.05	.02	.00
☐ U78 Kevin McReynolds	.15	.06	.01
☐ U79 Dave Meads	.05	.02	.00
☐ U80 Greg Minton	.05	.02	.00
☐ U81 John Mitchell	.10	.04	.01
☐ U82 Kevin Mitchell	1.50	.60	.15
☐ U83 John Morris	.10	.04	.01
☐ U84 Jeff Musselman	.10	.04	.01
☐ U85 Randy Myers	.20	.08	.02
☐ U86 Gene Nelson	.05	.02	.00
☐ U87 Joe Niekro	.10	.04	.01
☐ U88 Tom Nieto	.05	.02	.00
☐ U89 Reid Nichols	.05	.02	.00
☐ U90 Matt Nokes	.50	.20	.05
☐ U91 Dickie Noles	.05	.02	.00
☐ U92 Edwin Nunez	.05	.02	.00
☐ U93 Jose Nunez	.10	.04	.01
☐ U94 Paul O'Neill	.35	.15	.03
☐ U95 Jim Paciorek	.10	.04	.01
☐ U96 Lance Parrish	.12	.05	.01
☐ U97 Bill Pecota	.15	.06	.01
☐ U98 Tony Pena	.12	.05	.01
☐ U99 Luis Polonia	.50	.20	.05
☐ U100 Randy Ready	.12	.05	.01
☐ U101 Jeff Reardon	.17	.07	.01
☐ U102 Gary Redus	.05	.02	.00
☐ U103 Rick Rhoden	.05	.02	.00
☐ U104 Wally Ritchie	.10	.04	.01
☐ U105 Jeff Robinson UER (wrong Jeff's stats on back)	.12	.05	.01
☐ U106 Mark Salas	.05	.02	.00
☐ U107 Dave Schmidt	.10	.04	.01
☐ U108 Kevin Seitzer UER (wrong birth year)	.15	.06	.01
☐ U109 John Shelby	.05	.02	.00
☐ U110 John Smiley	.90	.40	.09
☐ U111 Lary Sorensen	.05	.02	.00
☐ U112 Chris Speier	.05	.02	.00
☐ U113 Randy St.Claire	.05	.02	.00
☐ U114 Jim Sundberg	.05	.02	.00
☐ U115 B.J. Surhoff	.20	.08	.02
☐ U116 Greg Swindell	.35	.15	.03
☐ U117 Danny Tartabull	.25	.10	.02

☐ U118 Dorn Taylor	.10	.04	.01
☐ U119 Lee Tunnell	.05	.02	.00
☐ U120 Ed VandeBerg	.05	.02	.00
☐ U121 Andy Van Slyke	.17	.07	.01
☐ U122 Gary Ward	.05	.02	.00
☐ U123 Devon White	.35	.15	.03
☐ U124 Alan Wiggins	.05	.02	.00
☐ U125 Bill Wilkinson	.05	.02	.00
☐ U126 Jim Winn	.05	.02	.00
☐ U127 Frank Williams	.05	.02	.00
☐ U128 Ken Williams	.10	.04	.01
☐ U129 Matt Williams	4.50	2.00	.45
☐ U130 Herm Willingham	.05	.02	.00
☐ U131 Matt Young	.05	.02	.00
☐ U132 Checklist Card	.05	.01	.00

1988 Fleer

This 660-card set features a distinctive white background with red and blue diagonal stripes across the card. The backs are printed in gray and red on white card stock. The bottom of the card back shows an innovative breakdown of the player's demonstrated ability with respect to day, night, home, and road games. Cards are numbered on the back and are again the standard 2 1/2" by 3 1/2". Cards are again organized numerically by teams, i.e., World Champion Twins (1-25), St. Louis Cardinals (26-50), Detroit Tigers (51-75), San Francisco Giants (76-101), Toronto Blue Jays (102-126), New York Mets (127-154), Milwaukee Brewers (155-178), Montreal Expos (179-201), New York Yankees (202-226), Cincinnati Reds (227-250), Kansas City Royals (251-274), Oakland A's (275-296), Philadelphia Phillies (297-320), Pittsburgh Pirates (321-342), Boston Red Sox (343-367), Seattle Mariners (368-390), Chicago White Sox (391-413), Chicago Cubs (414-436), Houston Astros (437-460), Texas Rangers (461-483), California Angels (484-507), Los Angeles Dodgers (508-530), Atlanta Braves (531-552), Baltimore Orioles (553-575), San Diego Padres (576-599), and Cleveland Indians (600-621). The last 39 cards in the set consist of Specials (622-640), Rookie Pairs (641-653), and checklists (654-660). Cards 90 and 91 are incorrectly numbered on the checklist card number 654. The key rookie cards in this set are Ellis Burks, Ron Gant, Tom Glavine, Mark Grace, Gregg Jefferies, Roberto Kelly, Edgar Martinez, Jack McDowell, and Matt Williams. Fleer also produced a "limited" edition version of this set with glossy coating and packaged in a "tin." However, this tin set was apparently not limited enough (estimated between 40,000 and 60,000 1988 tin sets produced by Fleer), since the price of the "tin" glossy cards is now only double the price of the regular set.

	MINT	EXC	G-VG
COMPLETE SET (660)	36.00	16.00	3.25
COMMON PLAYER (1-660)	.04	.02	.00
☐ 1 Keith Atherton	.07	.03	.01
☐ 2 Don Baylor	.07	.03	.01
☐ 3 Juan Berenguer	.04	.02	.00
☐ 4 Bert Blyleven	.10	.04	.01
☐ 5 Tom Brunansky	.07	.03	.01
☐ 6 Randy Bush	.04	.02	.00
☐ 7 Steve Carlton	.25	.10	.02
☐ 8 Mark Davidson	.07	.03	.01
☐ 9 George Frazier	.04	.02	.00
☐ 10 Gary Gaetti	.07	.03	.01
☐ 11 Greg Gagne	.04	.02	.00
☐ 12 Dan Gladden	.04	.02	.00
☐ 13 Kent Hrbek	.12	.05	.01
☐ 14 Gene Larkin	.15	.06	.01
☐ 15 Tim Laudner	.04	.02	.00
☐ 16 Steve Lombardozzi	.04	.02	.00
☐ 17 Al Newman	.04	.02	.00
☐ 18 Joe Niekro	.07	.03	.01
☐ 19 Kirby Puckett	.65	.25	.06
☐ 20 Jeff Reardon	.15	.06	.01
☐ 21A Dan Schatzeder ERR (misspelled Schatzader on card front)	.10	.04	.01
☐ 21B Dan Schatzeder COR	.07	.03	.01
☐ 22 Roy Smalley	.04	.02	.00
☐ 23 Mike Smithson	.04	.02	.00
☐ 24 Les Straker	.04	.02	.00
☐ 25 Frank Viola	.12	.05	.01
☐ 26 Jack Clark	.10	.04	.01
☐ 27 Vince Coleman	.15	.06	.01

☐ 28 Danny Cox .04 .02 .00
☐ 29 Bill Dawley .04 .02 .00
☐ 30 Ken Dayley .04 .02 .00
☐ 31 Doug DeCinces .07 .03 .01
☐ 32 Curt Ford .04 .02 .00
☐ 33 Bob Forsch .04 .02 .00
☐ 34 David Green .04 .02 .00
☐ 35 Tom Herr .04 .02 .00
☐ 36 Ricky Horton .04 .02 .00
☐ 37 Lance Johnson .35 .15 .03
☐ 38 Steve Lake .04 .02 .00
☐ 39 Jim Lindeman .04 .02 .00
☐ 40 Joe Magrane .20 .08 .02
☐ 41 Greg Mathews .04 .02 .00
☐ 42 Willie McGee .10 .04 .01
☐ 43 John Morris .04 .02 .00
☐ 44 Jose Oquendo .04 .02 .00
☐ 45 Tony Pena .07 .03 .01
☐ 46 Terry Pendleton .20 .08 .02
☐ 47 Ozzie Smith .30 .12 .03
☐ 48 John Tudor .10 .04 .01
☐ 49 Lee Tunnell .04 .02 .00
☐ 50 Todd Worrell .07 .03 .01
☐ 51 Doyle Alexander .04 .02 .00
☐ 52 Dave Bergman .04 .02 .00
☐ 53 Tom Brookens .04 .02 .00
☐ 54 Darrell Evans .07 .03 .01
☐ 55 Kirk Gibson .15 .06 .01
☐ 56 Mike Heath .04 .02 .00
☐ 57 Mike Henneman .30 .12 .03
☐ 58 Willie Hernandez .04 .02 .00
☐ 59 Larry Herndon .04 .02 .00
☐ 60 Eric King .04 .02 .00
☐ 61 Chet Lemon .04 .02 .00
☐ 62 Scott Lusader .10 .04 .01
☐ 63 Bill Madlock .07 .03 .01
☐ 64 Jack Morris .17 .07 .01
☐ 65 Jim Morrison .04 .02 .00
☐ 66 Matt Nokes .60 .25 .06
☐ 67 Dan Petry .04 .02 .00
☐ 68A Jeff Robinson ERR .30 .12 .03
Detroit Tigers
(stats for other Jeff
Robinson on card back)
☐ 68B Jeff Robinson COR .10 .04 .01
Detroit Tigers
☐ 69 Pat Sheridan .04 .02 .00
☐ 70 Nate Snell .04 .02 .00
☐ 71 Frank Tanana .07 .03 .01
☐ 72 Walt Terrell .04 .02 .00
☐ 73 Mark Thurmond .04 .02 .00
☐ 74 Alan Trammell .20 .08 .02
☐ 75 Lou Whitaker .10 .04 .01
☐ 76 Mike Aldrete .04 .02 .00
☐ 77 Bob Brenly .04 .02 .00
☐ 78 Will Clark 3.00 1.25 .30
☐ 79 Chili Davis .10 .04 .01
☐ 80 Kelly Downs .07 .03 .01
☐ 81 Dave Dravecky .10 .04 .01
☐ 82 Scott Garrelts .04 .02 .00
☐ 83 Atlee Hammaker .04 .02 .00
☐ 84 Dave Henderson .15 .06 .01
☐ 85 Mike Krukow .04 .02 .00
☐ 86 Mike LaCoss .04 .02 .00
☐ 87 Craig Lefferts .04 .02 .00
☐ 88 Jeff Leonard .04 .02 .00
☐ 89 Candy Maldonado .07 .03 .01
☐ 90 Eddie Milner .04 .02 .00
☐ 91 Bob Melvin .04 .02 .00
☐ 92 Kevin Mitchell .75 .30 .07
☐ 93 Jon Perlman .04 .02 .00
☐ 94 Rick Reuschel .07 .03 .01
☐ 95 Don Robinson .04 .02 .00
☐ 96 Chris Speier .04 .02 .00
☐ 97 Harry Spilman .04 .02 .00
☐ 98 Robby Thompson .04 .02 .00
☐ 99 Jose Uribe .04 .02 .00
☐ 100 Mark Wasinger .07 .03 .01
☐ 101 Matt Williams 4.50 2.00 .45
☐ 102 Jesse Barfield .10 .04 .01
☐ 103 George Bell .17 .07 .01
☐ 104 Juan Beniquez .04 .02 .00
☐ 105 John Cerutti .04 .02 .00
☐ 106 Jim Clancy .04 .02 .00
☐ 107 Rob Ducey .12 .05 .01
☐ 108 Mark Eichhorn .07 .03 .01
☐ 109 Tony Fernandez .10 .04 .01
☐ 110 Cecil Fielder .90 .40 .09
☐ 111 Kelly Gruber .30 .12 .03
☐ 112 Tom Henke .07 .03 .01
☐ 113A Garth Iorg ERR .20 .08 .02
(misspelled Iorq
on card front)
☐ 113B Garth Iorg COR .07 .03 .01
☐ 114 Jimmy Key .10 .04 .01
☐ 115 Rick Leach .04 .02 .00
☐ 116 Manny Lee .04 .02 .00
☐ 117 Nelson Liriano .10 .04 .01
☐ 118 Fred McGriff 1.50 .60 .15
☐ 119 Lloyd Moseby .04 .02 .00
☐ 120 Rance Mulliniks .04 .02 .00
☐ 121 Jeff Musselman .04 .02 .00
☐ 122 Jose Nunez .07 .03 .01
☐ 123 Dave Stieb .10 .04 .01
☐ 124 Willie Upshaw .04 .02 .00
☐ 125 Duane Ward .10 .04 .01
☐ 126 Ernie Whitt .04 .02 .00
☐ 127 Rick Aguilera .07 .03 .01
☐ 128 Wally Backman .04 .02 .00
☐ 129 Mark Carreon .15 .06 .01
☐ 130 Gary Carter .12 .05 .01
☐ 131 David Cone .40 .16 .04
☐ 132 Ron Darling .10 .04 .01
☐ 133 Len Dykstra .12 .05 .01
☐ 134 Sid Fernandez .10 .04 .01
☐ 135 Dwight Gooden .25 .10 .02

☐ 136	Keith Hernandez	.10	.04	.01
☐ 137	Gregg Jefferies	2.75	1.10	.27
☐ 138	Howard Johnson	.35	.15	.03
☐ 139	Terry Leach	.04	.02	.00
☐ 140	Barry Lyons	.07	.03	.01
☐ 141	Dave Magadan	.10	.04	.01
☐ 142	Roger McDowell	.04	.02	.00
☐ 143	Kevin McReynolds	.12	.05	.01
☐ 144	Keith Miller (New York Mets)	.20	.08	.02
☐ 145	John Mitchell	.07	.03	.01
☐ 146	Randy Myers	.10	.04	.01
☐ 147	Bob Ojeda	.04	.02	.00
☐ 148	Jesse Orosco	.04	.02	.00
☐ 149	Rafael Santana	.04	.02	.00
☐ 150	Doug Sisk	.04	.02	.00
☐ 151	Darryl Strawberry	.75	.30	.07
☐ 152	Tim Teufel	.04	.02	.00
☐ 153	Gene Walter	.04	.02	.00
☐ 154	Mookie Wilson	.04	.02	.00
☐ 155	Jay Aldrich	.04	.02	.00
☐ 156	Chris Bosio	.07	.03	.01
☐ 157	Glenn Braggs	.04	.02	.00
☐ 158	Greg Brock	.04	.02	.00
☐ 159	Juan Castillo	.04	.02	.00
☐ 160	Mark Clear	.04	.02	.00
☐ 161	Cecil Cooper	.07	.03	.01
☐ 162	Chuck Crim	.04	.02	.00
☐ 163	Rob Deer	.07	.03	.01
☐ 164	Mike Felder	.04	.02	.00
☐ 165	Jim Gantner	.04	.02	.00
☐ 166	Ted Higuera	.07	.03	.01
☐ 167	Steve Kiefer	.04	.02	.00
☐ 168	Rick Manning	.04	.02	.00
☐ 169	Paul Molitor	.15	.06	.01
☐ 170	Juan Nieves	.04	.02	.00
☐ 171	Dan Plesac	.04	.02	.00
☐ 172	Earnest Riles	.04	.02	.00
☐ 173	Bill Schroeder	.04	.02	.00
☐ 174	Steve Stanicek	.04	.02	.00
☐ 175	B.J. Surhoff	.10	.04	.01
☐ 176	Dale Sveum	.04	.02	.00
☐ 177	Bill Wegman	.07	.03	.01
☐ 178	Robin Yount	.35	.15	.03
☐ 179	Hubie Brooks	.07	.03	.01
☐ 180	Tim Burke	.04	.02	.00
☐ 181	Casey Candaele	.04	.02	.00
☐ 182	Mike Fitzgerald	.04	.02	.00
☐ 183	Tom Foley	.04	.02	.00
☐ 184	Andres Galarraga	.10	.04	.01
☐ 185	Neal Heaton	.04	.02	.00
☐ 186	Wallace Johnson	.04	.02	.00
☐ 187	Vance Law	.04	.02	.00
☐ 188	Dennis Martinez	.07	.03	.01
☐ 189	Bob McClure	.04	.02	.00
☐ 190	Andy McGaffigan	.04	.02	.00
☐ 191	Reid Nichols	.04	.02	.00
☐ 192	Pascual Perez	.04	.02	.00
☐ 193	Tim Raines	.15	.06	.01
☐ 194	Jeff Reed	.04	.02	.00
☐ 195	Bob Sebra	.04	.02	.00
☐ 196	Bryn Smith	.04	.02	.00
☐ 197	Randy St.Claire	.04	.02	.00
☐ 198	Tim Wallach	.07	.03	.01
☐ 199	Mitch Webster	.04	.02	.00
☐ 200	Herm Winningham	.04	.02	.00
☐ 201	Floyd Youmans	.04	.02	.00
☐ 202	Brad Arnsberg	.10	.04	.01
☐ 203	Rick Cerone	.04	.02	.00
☐ 204	Pat Clements	.04	.02	.00
☐ 205	Henry Cotto	.04	.02	.00
☐ 206	Mike Easler	.04	.02	.00
☐ 207	Ron Guidry	.10	.04	.01
☐ 208	Bill Gullickson	.07	.03	.01
☐ 209	Rickey Henderson	.60	.25	.06
☐ 210	Charles Hudson	.04	.02	.00
☐ 211	Tommy John	.10	.04	.01
☐ 212	Roberto Kelly	1.25	.50	.12
☐ 213	Ron Kittle	.07	.03	.01
☐ 214	Don Mattingly	.60	.25	.06
☐ 215	Bobby Meacham	.04	.02	.00
☐ 216	Mike Pagliarulo	.04	.02	.00
☐ 217	Dan Pasqua	.04	.02	.00
☐ 218	Willie Randolph	.07	.03	.01
☐ 219	Rick Rhoden	.04	.02	.00
☐ 220	Dave Righetti	.07	.03	.01
☐ 221	Jerry Royster	.04	.02	.00
☐ 222	Tim Stoddard	.04	.02	.00
☐ 223	Wayne Tolleson	.04	.02	.00
☐ 224	Gary Ward	.04	.02	.00
☐ 225	Claudell Washington	.04	.02	.00
☐ 226	Dave Winfield	.25	.10	.02
☐ 227	Buddy Bell	.07	.03	.01
☐ 228	Tom Browning	.07	.03	.01
☐ 229	Dave Concepcion	.07	.03	.01
☐ 230	Kal Daniels	.10	.04	.01
☐ 231	Eric Davis	.25	.10	.02
☐ 232	Bo Diaz	.04	.02	.00
☐ 233	Nick Esasky (has a dollar sign before '87 SB totals)	.04	.02	.00
☐ 234	John Franco	.07	.03	.01
☐ 235	Guy Hoffman	.04	.02	.00
☐ 236	Tom Hume	.04	.02	.00
☐ 237	Tracy Jones	.04	.02	.00
☐ 238	Bill Landrum	.15	.06	.01
☐ 239	Barry Larkin	.60	.25	.06
☐ 240	Terry McGriff	.04	.02	.00
☐ 241	Rob Murphy	.04	.02	.00
☐ 242	Ron Oester	.04	.02	.00
☐ 243	Dave Parker	.15	.06	.01
☐ 244	Pat Perry	.04	.02	.00
☐ 245	Ted Power	.04	.02	.00
☐ 246	Dennis Rasmussen	.04	.02	.00
☐ 247	Ron Robinson	.04	.02	.00
☐ 248	Kurt Stillwell	.07	.03	.01

	No.	Player			
☐	249	Jeff Treadway	.40	.16	.04
☐	250	Frank Williams	.04	.02	.00
☐	251	Steve Balboni	.04	.02	.00
☐	252	Bud Black	.04	.02	.00
☐	253	Thad Bosley	.04	.02	.00
☐	254	George Brett	.35	.15	.03
☐	255	John Davis	.07	.03	.01
☐	256	Steve Farr	.04	.02	.00
☐	257	Gene Garber	.04	.02	.00
☐	258	Jerry Don Gleaton	.04	.02	.00
☐	259	Mark Gubicza	.07	.03	.01
☐	260	Bo Jackson	2.50	1.00	.25
☐	261	Danny Jackson	.07	.03	.01
☐	262	Ross Jones	.04	.02	.00
☐	263	Charlie Leibrandt	.04	.02	.00
☐	264	Bill Pecota	.10	.04	.01
☐	265	Melido Perez	.30	.12	.03
☐	266	Jamie Quirk	.04	.02	.00
☐	267	Dan Quisenberry	.07	.03	.01
☐	268	Bret Saberhagen	.20	.08	.02
☐	269	Angel Salazar	.04	.02	.00
☐	270	Kevin Seitzer UER (wrong birth year)	.10	.04	.01
☐	271	Danny Tartabull	.25	.10	.02
☐	272	Gary Thurman	.12	.05	.01
☐	273	Frank White	.04	.02	.00
☐	274	Willie Wilson	.07	.03	.01
☐	275	Tony Bernazard	.04	.02	.00
☐	276	Jose Canseco	2.50	1.00	.25
☐	277	Mike Davis	.04	.02	.00
☐	278	Storm Davis	.04	.02	.00
☐	279	Dennis Eckersley	.15	.06	.01
☐	280	Alfredo Griffin	.04	.02	.00
☐	281	Rick Honeycutt	.04	.02	.00
☐	282	Jay Howell	.04	.02	.00
☐	283	Reggie Jackson	.35	.15	.03
☐	284	Dennis Lamp	.04	.02	.00
☐	285	Carney Lansford	.07	.03	.01
☐	286	Mark McGwire	1.25	.50	.12
☐	287	Dwayne Murphy	.04	.02	.00
☐	288	Gene Nelson	.04	.02	.00
☐	289	Steve Ontiveros	.04	.02	.00
☐	290	Tony Phillips	.04	.02	.00
☐	291	Eric Plunk	.04	.02	.00
☐	292	Luis Polonia	.50	.20	.05
☐	293	Rick Rodriguez	.07	.03	.01
☐	294	Terry Steinbach	.10	.04	.01
☐	295	Dave Stewart	.12	.05	.01
☐	296	Curt Young	.04	.02	.00
☐	297	Luis Aguayo	.04	.02	.00
☐	298	Steve Bedrosian	.07	.03	.01
☐	299	Jeff Calhoun	.04	.02	.00
☐	300	Don Carman	.04	.02	.00
☐	301	Todd Frohwirth	.07	.03	.01
☐	302	Greg Gross	.04	.02	.00
☐	303	Kevin Gross	.04	.02	.00
☐	304	Von Hayes	.10	.04	.01
☐	305	Keith Hughes	.07	.03	.01
☐	306	Mike Jackson	.20	.08	.02
☐	307	Chris James	.10	.04	.01
☐	308	Steve Jeltz	.04	.02	.00
☐	309	Mike Maddux	.04	.02	.00
☐	310	Lance Parrish	.10	.04	.01
☐	311	Shane Rawley	.04	.02	.00
☐	312	Wally Ritchie	.04	.02	.00
☐	313	Bruce Ruffin	.04	.02	.00
☐	314	Juan Samuel	.07	.03	.01
☐	315	Mike Schmidt	.75	.30	.07
☐	316	Rick Schu	.04	.02	.00
☐	317	Jeff Stone	.04	.02	.00
☐	318	Kent Tekulve	.04	.02	.00
☐	319	Milt Thompson	.04	.02	.00
☐	320	Glenn Wilson	.04	.02	.00
☐	321	Rafael Belliard	.04	.02	.00
☐	322	Barry Bonds	1.00	.40	.10
☐	323	Bobby Bonilla UER (wrong birth year)	.90	.40	.09
☐	324	Sid Bream	.04	.02	.00
☐	325	John Cangelosi	.04	.02	.00
☐	326	Mike Diaz	.04	.02	.00
☐	327	Doug Drabek	.20	.08	.02
☐	328	Mike Dunne	.04	.02	.00
☐	329	Brian Fisher	.04	.02	.00
☐	330	Brett Gideon	.04	.02	.00
☐	331	Terry Harper	.04	.02	.00
☐	332	Bob Kipper	.04	.02	.00
☐	333	Mike LaValliere	.04	.02	.00
☐	334	Jose Lind	.40	.16	.04
☐	335	Junior Ortiz	.04	.02	.00
☐	336	Vicente Palacios	.15	.06	.01
☐	337	Bob Patterson	.07	.03	.01
☐	338	Al Pedrique	.04	.02	.00
☐	339	R.J. Reynolds	.04	.02	.00
☐	340	John Smiley	1.25	.50	.12
☐	341	Andy Van Slyke UER (wrong batting and throwing listed)	.17	.07	.01
☐	342	Bob Walk	.04	.02	.00
☐	343	Marty Barrett	.04	.02	.00
☐	344	Todd Benzinger	.40	.16	.04
☐	345	Wade Boggs	.50	.20	.05
☐	346	Tom Bolton	.12	.05	.01
☐	347	Oil Can Boyd	.04	.02	.00
☐	348	Ellis Burks	2.00	.80	.20
☐	349	Roger Clemens	1.00	.40	.10
☐	350	Steve Crawford	.07	.03	.01
☐	351	Dwight Evans	.10	.04	.01
☐	352	Wes Gardner	.10	.04	.01
☐	353	Rich Gedman	.04	.02	.00
☐	354	Mike Greenwell	1.25	.50	.12
☐	355	Sam Horn	.25	.10	.02
☐	356	Bruce Hurst	.07	.03	.01
☐	357	John Marzano	.07	.03	.01
☐	358	Al Nipper	.04	.02	.00
☐	359	Spike Owen	.04	.02	.00
☐	360	Jody Reed	.75	.30	.07

☐ 361 Jim Rice .10 .04 .01
☐ 362 Ed Romero .04 .02 .00
☐ 363 Kevin Romine .04 .02 .00
☐ 364 Joe Sambito .04 .02 .00
☐ 365 Calvin Schiraldi .04 .02 .00
☐ 366 Jeff Sellers .04 .02 .00
☐ 367 Bob Stanley .04 .02 .00
☐ 368 Scott Bankhead .07 .03 .01
☐ 369 Phil Bradley .04 .02 .00
☐ 370 Scott Bradley .04 .02 .00
☐ 371 Mickey Brantley .04 .02 .00
☐ 372 Mike Campbell .07 .03 .01
☐ 373 Alvin Davis .07 .03 .01
☐ 374 Lee Guetterman .04 .02 .00
☐ 375 Dave Hengel .07 .03 .01
☐ 376 Mike Kingery .04 .02 .00
☐ 377 Mark Langston .15 .06 .01
☐ 378 Edgar Martinez 1.25 .50 .12
☐ 379 Mike Moore .07 .03 .01
☐ 380 Mike Morgan .07 .03 .01
☐ 381 John Moses .04 .02 .00
☐ 382 Donnell Nixon .07 .03 .01
☐ 383 Edwin Nunez .04 .02 .00
☐ 384 Ken Phelps .04 .02 .00
☐ 385 Jim Presley .04 .02 .00
☐ 386 Rey Quinones .04 .02 .00
☐ 387 Jerry Reed .04 .02 .00
☐ 388 Harold Reynolds .07 .03 .01
☐ 389 Dave Valle .04 .02 .00
☐ 390 Bill Wilkinson .07 .03 .01
☐ 391 Harold Baines .10 .04 .01
☐ 392 Floyd Bannister .04 .02 .00
☐ 393 Daryl Boston .04 .02 .00
☐ 394 Ivan Calderon .10 .04 .01
☐ 395 Jose DeLeon .04 .02 .00
☐ 396 Richard Dotson .04 .02 .00
☐ 397 Carlton Fisk .35 .15 .03
☐ 398 Ozzie Guillen .10 .04 .01
☐ 399 Ron Hassey .04 .02 .00
☐ 400 Donnie Hill .04 .02 .00
☐ 401 Bob James .04 .02 .00
☐ 402 Dave LaPoint .04 .02 .00
☐ 403 Bill Lindsey .04 .02 .00
☐ 404 Bill Long .07 .03 .01
☐ 405 Steve Lyons .04 .02 .00
☐ 406 Fred Manrique .07 .03 .01
☐ 407 Jack McDowell 1.25 .50 .12
☐ 408 Gary Redus .04 .02 .00
☐ 409 Ray Searage .04 .02 .00
☐ 410 Bobby Thigpen .15 .06 .01
☐ 411 Greg Walker .04 .02 .00
☐ 412 Ken Williams .07 .03 .01
☐ 413 Jim Winn .04 .02 .00
☐ 414 Jody Davis .04 .02 .00
☐ 415 Andre Dawson .25 .10 .02
☐ 416 Brian Dayett .04 .02 .00
☐ 417 Bob Dernier .04 .02 .00
☐ 418 Frank DiPino .04 .02 .00
☐ 419 Shawon Dunston .12 .05 .01
☐ 420 Leon Durham .04 .02 .00
☐ 421 Les Lancaster .12 .05 .01
☐ 422 Ed Lynch .04 .02 .00
☐ 423 Greg Maddux .50 .20 .05
☐ 424 Dave Martinez .15 .06 .01
☐ 425A Keith Moreland ERR 2.00 .80 .20
(photo actually
Jody Davis)
☐ 425B Keith Moreland COR .12 .05 .01
(bat on shoulder)
☐ 426 Jamie Moyer .04 .02 .00
☐ 427 Jerry Mumphrey .04 .02 .00
☐ 428 Paul Noce .07 .03 .01
☐ 429 Rafael Palmeiro 1.50 .60 .15
☐ 430 Wade Rowdon .04 .02 .00
☐ 431 Ryne Sandberg 1.00 .40 .10
☐ 432 Scott Sanderson .07 .03 .01
☐ 433 Lee Smith .15 .06 .01
☐ 434 Jim Sundberg .04 .02 .00
☐ 435 Rick Sutcliffe .07 .03 .01
☐ 436 Manny Trillo .04 .02 .00
☐ 437 Juan Agosto .04 .02 .00
☐ 438 Larry Andersen .04 .02 .00
☐ 439 Alan Ashby .04 .02 .00
☐ 440 Kevin Bass .04 .02 .00
☐ 441 Ken Caminiti .45 .18 .04
☐ 442 Rocky Childress .04 .02 .00
☐ 443 Jose Cruz .07 .03 .01
☐ 444 Danny Darwin .04 .02 .00
☐ 445 Glenn Davis .12 .05 .01
☐ 446 Jim Deshaies .04 .02 .00
☐ 447 Bill Doran .04 .02 .00
☐ 448 Ty Gainey .04 .02 .00
☐ 449 Billy Hatcher .07 .03 .01
☐ 450 Jeff Heathcock .04 .02 .00
☐ 451 Bob Knepper .04 .02 .00
☐ 452 Rob Mallicoat .04 .02 .00
☐ 453 Dave Meads .04 .02 .00
☐ 454 Craig Reynolds .04 .02 .00
☐ 455 Nolan Ryan 1.50 .60 .15
☐ 456 Mike Scott .10 .04 .01
☐ 457 Dave Smith .04 .02 .00
☐ 458 Denny Walling .04 .02 .00
☐ 459 Robbie Wine .04 .02 .00
☐ 460 Gerald Young .12 .05 .01
☐ 461 Bob Brower .07 .03 .01
☐ 462A Jerry Browne ERR 2.00 .80 .20
(photo actually
Bob Brower,
white player)
☐ 462B Jerry Browne COR .12 .05 .01
(black player)
☐ 463 Steve Buechele .07 .03 .01
☐ 464 Edwin Correa .04 .02 .00
☐ 465 Cecil Espy .15 .06 .01
☐ 466 Scott Fletcher .04 .02 .00
☐ 467 Jose Guzman .07 .03 .01

☐ 468	Greg Harris	.04	.02	.00
☐ 469	Charlie Hough	.04	.02	.00
☐ 470	Pete Incaviglia	.10	.04	.01
☐ 471	Paul Kilgus	.07	.03	.01
☐ 472	Mike Loynd	.04	.02	.00
☐ 473	Oddibe McDowell	.04	.02	.00
☐ 474	Dale Mohorcic	.04	.02	.00
☐ 475	Pete O'Brien	.04	.02	.00
☐ 476	Larry Parrish	.04	.02	.00
☐ 477	Geno Petralli	.04	.02	.00
☐ 478	Jeff Russell	.04	.02	.00
☐ 479	Ruben Sierra	1.00	.40	.10
☐ 480	Mike Stanley	.04	.02	.00
☐ 481	Curtis Wilkerson	.04	.02	.00
☐ 482	Mitch Williams	.07	.03	.01
☐ 483	Bobby Witt	.10	.04	.01
☐ 484	Tony Armas	.04	.02	.00
☐ 485	Bob Boone	.07	.03	.01
☐ 486	Bill Buckner	.07	.03	.01
☐ 487	DeWayne Buice	.04	.02	.00
☐ 488	Brian Downing	.04	.02	.00
☐ 489	Chuck Finley	.30	.12	.03
☐ 490	Willie Fraser UER (wrong bio stats for George Hendrick)	.04	.02	.00
☐ 491	Jack Howell	.04	.02	.00
☐ 492	Ruppert Jones	.04	.02	.00
☐ 493	Wally Joyner	.30	.12	.03
☐ 494	Jack Lazorko	.04	.02	.00
☐ 495	Gary Lucas	.04	.02	.00
☐ 496	Kirk McCaskill	.04	.02	.00
☐ 497	Mark McLemore	.04	.02	.00
☐ 498	Darrell Miller	.04	.02	.00
☐ 499	Greg Minton	.04	.02	.00
☐ 500	Donnie Moore	.04	.02	.00
☐ 501	Gus Polidor	.04	.02	.00
☐ 502	Johnny Ray	.04	.02	.00
☐ 503	Mark Ryal	.04	.02	.00
☐ 504	Dick Schofield	.04	.02	.00
☐ 505	Don Sutton	.15	.06	.01
☐ 506	Devon White	.15	.06	.01
☐ 507	Mike Witt	.04	.02	.00
☐ 508	Dave Anderson	.04	.02	.00
☐ 509	Tim Belcher	.20	.08	.02
☐ 510	Ralph Bryant	.04	.02	.00
☐ 511	Tim Crews	.07	.03	.01
☐ 512	Mike Devereaux	.30	.12	.03
☐ 513	Mariano Duncan	.07	.03	.01
☐ 514	Pedro Guerrero	.10	.04	.01
☐ 515	Jeff Hamilton	.07	.03	.01
☐ 516	Mickey Hatcher	.04	.02	.00
☐ 517	Brad Havens	.04	.02	.00
☐ 518	Orel Hershiser	.17	.07	.01
☐ 519	Shawn Hillegas	.10	.04	.01
☐ 520	Ken Howell	.04	.02	.00
☐ 521	Tim Leary	.10	.04	.01
☐ 522	Mike Marshall	.10	.04	.01
☐ 523	Steve Sax	.12	.05	.01
☐ 524	Mike Scioscia	.04	.02	.00
☐ 525	Mike Sharperson	.07	.03	.01
☐ 526	John Shelby	.04	.02	.00
☐ 527	Franklin Stubbs	.04	.02	.00
☐ 528	Fernando Valenzuela	.10	.04	.01
☐ 529	Bob Welch	.10	.04	.01
☐ 530	Matt Young	.04	.02	.00
☐ 531	Jim Acker	.04	.02	.00
☐ 532	Paul Assenmacher	.04	.02	.00
☐ 533	Jeff Blauser	.40	.16	.04
☐ 534	Joe Boever	.10	.04	.01
☐ 535	Martin Clary	.04	.02	.00
☐ 536	Kevin Coffman	.04	.02	.00
☐ 537	Jeff Dedmon	.04	.02	.00
☐ 538	Ron Gant	6.00	2.50	.60
☐ 539	Tom Glavine	3.50	1.50	.35
☐ 540	Ken Griffey	.10	.04	.01
☐ 541	Albert Hall	.04	.02	.00
☐ 542	Glenn Hubbard	.04	.02	.00
☐ 543	Dion James	.04	.02	.00
☐ 544	Dale Murphy	.25	.10	.02
☐ 545	Ken Oberkfell	.04	.02	.00
☐ 546	David Palmer	.04	.02	.00
☐ 547	Gerald Perry	.04	.02	.00
☐ 548	Charlie Puleo	.04	.02	.00
☐ 549	Ted Simmons	.07	.03	.01
☐ 550	Zane Smith	.07	.03	.01
☐ 551	Andres Thomas	.04	.02	.00
☐ 552	Ozzie Virgil	.04	.02	.00
☐ 553	Don Aase	.04	.02	.00
☐ 554	Jeff Ballard	.10	.04	.01
☐ 555	Eric Bell	.04	.02	.00
☐ 556	Mike Boddicker	.04	.02	.00
☐ 557	Ken Dixon	.04	.02	.00
☐ 558	Jim Dwyer	.04	.02	.00
☐ 559	Ken Gerhart	.04	.02	.00
☐ 560	Rene Gonzales	.07	.03	.01
☐ 561	Mike Griffin	.04	.02	.00
☐ 562	John Habyan UER (misspelled Hayban on both sides of card)	.07	.03	.01
☐ 563	Terry Kennedy	.04	.02	.00
☐ 564	Ray Knight	.07	.03	.01
☐ 565	Lee Lacy	.04	.02	.00
☐ 566	Fred Lynn	.10	.04	.01
☐ 567	Eddie Murray	.30	.12	.03
☐ 568	Tom Niedenfuer	.04	.02	.00
☐ 569	Bill Ripken	.20	.08	.02
☐ 570	Cal Ripken	1.00	.40	.10
☐ 571	Dave Schmidt	.04	.02	.00
☐ 572	Larry Sheets	.04	.02	.00
☐ 573	Pete Stanicek	.04	.02	.00
☐ 574	Mark Williamson	.10	.04	.01
☐ 575	Mike Young	.04	.02	.00
☐ 576	Shawn Abner	.07	.03	.01
☐ 577	Greg Booker	.04	.02	.00
☐ 578	Chris Brown	.04	.02	.00
☐ 579	Keith Comstock	.07	.03	.01

No.	Player			
☐ 580	Joey Cora	.07	.03	.01
☐ 581	Mark Davis	.07	.03	.01
☐ 582	Tim Flannery (with surfboard)	.04	.02	.00
☐ 583	Goose Gossage	.10	.04	.01
☐ 584	Mark Grant	.04	.02	.00
☐ 585	Tony Gwynn	.45	.18	.04
☐ 586	Andy Hawkins	.04	.02	.00
☐ 587	Stan Jefferson	.07	.03	.01
☐ 588	Jimmy Jones	.07	.03	.01
☐ 589	John Kruk	.07	.03	.01
☐ 590	Shane Mack	.25	.10	.02
☐ 591	Carmelo Martinez	.04	.02	.00
☐ 592	Lance McCullers UER (6'11" tall)	.04	.02	.00
☐ 593	Eric Nolte	.07	.03	.01
☐ 594	Randy Ready	.04	.02	.00
☐ 595	Luis Salazar	.04	.02	.00
☐ 596	Benito Santiago	.20	.08	.02
☐ 597	Eric Show	.04	.02	.00
☐ 598	Garry Templeton	.07	.03	.01
☐ 599	Ed Whitson	.04	.02	.00
☐ 600	Scott Bailes	.04	.02	.00
☐ 601	Chris Bando	.04	.02	.00
☐ 602	Jay Bell	.75	.30	.07
☐ 603	Brett Butler	.12	.05	.01
☐ 604	Tom Candiotti	.07	.03	.01
☐ 605	Joe Carter	.35	.15	.03
☐ 606	Carmen Castillo	.04	.02	.00
☐ 607	Brian Dorsett	.07	.03	.01
☐ 608	John Farrell	.10	.04	.01
☐ 609	Julio Franco	.25	.10	.02
☐ 610	Mel Hall	.07	.03	.01
☐ 611	Tommy Hinzo	.04	.02	.00
☐ 612	Brook Jacoby	.04	.02	.00
☐ 613	Doug Jones	.25	.10	.02
☐ 614	Ken Schrom	.04	.02	.00
☐ 615	Cory Snyder	.10	.04	.01
☐ 616	Sammy Stewart	.04	.02	.00
☐ 617	Greg Swindell	.12	.05	.01
☐ 618	Pat Tabler	.04	.02	.00
☐ 619	Ed VandeBerg	.04	.02	.00
☐ 620	Eddie Williams	.07	.03	.01
☐ 621	Rich Yett	.04	.02	.00
☐ 622	Slugging Sophomores Wally Joyner Cory Snyder	.10	.04	.01
☐ 623	Dominican Dynamite George Bell Pedro Guerrero	.10	.04	.01
☐ 624	Oakland's Power Team Mark McGwire Jose Canseco	.50	.20	.05
☐ 625	Classic Relief Dave Righetti Dan Plesac	.07	.03	.01
☐ 626	All Star Righties Bret Saberhagen Mike Witt Jack Morris	.10	.04	.01
☐ 627	Game Closers John Franco Steve Bedrosian	.07	.03	.01
☐ 628	Masters/Double Play Ozzie Smith Ryne Sandberg	.35	.15	.03
☐ 629	Rookie Record Setter Mark McGwire	.25	.10	.02
☐ 630	Changing the Guard Mike Greenwell Ellis Burks Todd Benzinger	.20	.08	.02
☐ 631	NL Batting Champs Tony Gwynn Tim Raines	.15	.06	.01
☐ 632	Pitching Magic Mike Scott Orel Hershiser	.10	.04	.01
☐ 633	Big Bats at First Pat Tabler Mark McGwire	.12	.05	.01
☐ 634	Hitting King/Thief Tony Gwynn Vince Coleman	.20	.08	.02
☐ 635	Slugging Shortstops Tony Fernandez Cal Ripken Alan Trammell	.30	.12	.03
☐ 636	Tried/True Sluggers Mike Schmidt Gary Carter	.20	.08	.02
☐ 637	Crunch Time Darryl Strawberry Eric Davis	.25	.10	.02
☐ 638	AL All-Stars Matt Nokes Kirby Puckett	.15	.06	.01
☐ 639	NL All-Stars Keith Hernandez Dale Murphy	.10	.04	.01
☐ 640	The O's Brothers Billy Ripken Cal Ripken	.30	.12	.03
☐ 641	Mark Grace and Darrin Jackson	4.50	2.00	.45
☐ 642	Damon Berryhill and Jeff Montgomery	.35	.15	.03
☐ 643	Felix Fermin and Jesse Reid	.07	.03	.01
☐ 644	Greg Myers and Greg Tabor	.15	.06	.01
☐ 645	Joey Meyer and Jim Eppard	.10	.04	.01
☐ 646	Adam Peterson and Randy Velarde	.10	.04	.01

		MINT	EXC	G-VG
☐ 647	Peter Smith and Chris Gwynn	.25	.10	.02
☐ 648	Tom Newell and Greg Jelks	.07	.03	.01
☐ 649	Mario Diaz and Clay Parker	.12	.05	.01
☐ 650	Jack Savage and Todd Simmons	.07	.03	.01
☐ 651	John Burkett and Kirt Manwaring	.35	.15	.03
☐ 652	Dave Otto and Walt Weiss	.45	.18	.04
☐ 653	Jeff King and Randell Byers	.25	.10	.02
☐ 654	CL: Twins/Cards Tigers/Giants UER (90 Bob Melvin, 91 Eddie Milner)	.08	.01	.00
☐ 655	CL: Blue Jays/Mets Brewers/Expos UER (Mets listed before Blue Jays on card)	.08	.01	.00
☐ 656	CL: Yankees/Reds Royals/A's	.08	.01	.00
☐ 657	CL: Phillies/Pirates Red Sox/Mariners	.08	.01	.00
☐ 658	CL: White Sox/Cubs Astros/Rangers	.08	.01	.00
☐ 659	CL: Angels/Dodgers Braves/Orioles	.08	.01	.00
☐ 660	CL: Padres/Indians Rookies/Specials	.08	.01	.00

1988 Fleer Update

This 132-card set was distributed by Fleer to dealers as a complete set in a custom box. In addition to the complete set of 132 cards, the box also contains 25 Team Logo stickers. The card fronts look very similar to the 1988 Fleer regular issue. The cards are numbered (with a U prefix) alphabetically according to player's last name. Cards measure the standard size, 2 1/2" by 3 1/2". This was the first Fleer Update set to adopt the Fleer "alphabetical within team" numbering system. The key (extended) rookie cards in this set are Roberto Alomar, Craig Biggio, and Chris Sabo. Fleer also produced a "limited" edition version of this set with glossy coating and packaged in a "tin." However, this tin set was apparently not limited enough (estimated between 40,000

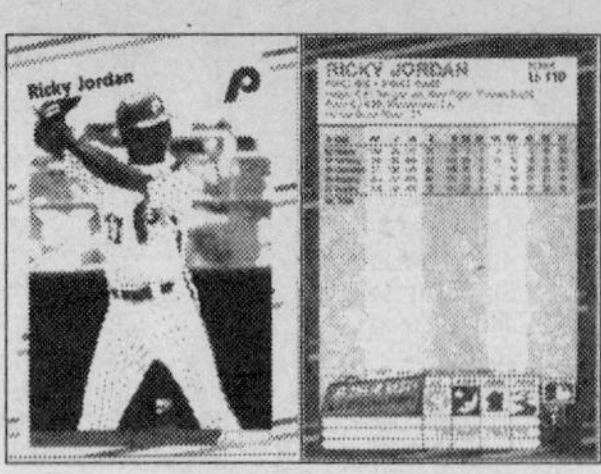

and 60,000 1988 Update tin sets produced by Fleer), since the price of the "tin" glossy cards is now only double the price of the regular set.

	MINT	EXC	G-VG
COMPLETE SET (132)	11.00	5.00	1.35
COMMON PLAYER (1-132)	.05	.02	.00

		MINT	EXC	G-VG
☐ U1	Jose Bautista	.10	.04	.01
☐ U2	Joe Orsulak	.10	.04	.01
☐ U3	Doug Sisk	.05	.02	.00
☐ U4	Craig Worthington	.10	.04	.01
☐ U5	Mike Boddicker	.10	.04	.01
☐ U6	Rick Cerone	.05	.02	.00
☐ U7	Larry Parrish	.05	.02	.00
☐ U8	Lee Smith	.12	.05	.01
☐ U9	Mike Smithson	.05	.02	.00
☐ U10	John Trautwein	.05	.02	.00
☐ U11	Sherman Corbett	.05	.02	.00
☐ U12	Chili Davis	.10	.04	.01
☐ U13	Jim Eppard	.05	.02	.00
☐ U14	Bryan Harvey	.60	.25	.06
☐ U15	John Davis	.05	.02	.00
☐ U16	Dave Gallagher	.10	.04	.01
☐ U17	Ricky Horton	.05	.02	.00
☐ U18	Dan Pasqua	.10	.04	.01
☐ U19	Melido Perez	.10	.04	.01
☐ U20	Jose Segura	.10	.04	.01
☐ U21	Andy Allanson	.05	.02	.00
☐ U22	Jon Perlman	.05	.02	.00
☐ U23	Domingo Ramos	.05	.02	.00
☐ U24	Rick Rodriguez	.05	.02	.00
☐ U25	Willie Upshaw	.05	.02	.00
☐ U26	Paul Gibson	.10	.04	.01
☐ U27	Don Heinkel	.05	.02	.00
☐ U28	Ray Knight	.10	.04	.01
☐ U29	Gary Pettis	.05	.02	.00
☐ U30	Luis Salazar	.05	.02	.00
☐ U31	Mike Macfarlane	.15	.06	.01
☐ U32	Jeff Montgomery	.15	.06	.01
☐ U33	Ted Power	.05	.02	.00
☐ U34	Israel Sanchez	.05	.02	.00

☐ U35	Kurt Stillwell	.10	.04	.01
☐ U36	Pat Tabler	.05	.02	.00
☐ U37	Don August	.10	.04	.01
☐ U38	Darryl Hamilton	.25	.10	.02
☐ U39	Jeff Leonard	.10	.04	.01
☐ U40	Joey Meyer	.10	.04	.01
☐ U41	Allan Anderson	.10	.04	.01
☐ U42	Brian Harper	.15	.06	.01
☐ U43	Tom Herr	.10	.04	.01
☐ U44	Charlie Lea	.05	.02	.00
☐ U45	John Moses (listed as Hohn on checklist card)	.05	.02	.00
☐ U46	John Candelaria	.05	.02	.00
☐ U47	Jack Clark	.10	.04	.01
☐ U48	Richard Dotson	.05	.02	.00
☐ U49	Al Leiter	.10	.04	.01
☐ U50	Rafael Santana	.05	.02	.00
☐ U51	Don Slaught	.05	.02	.00
☐ U52	Todd Burns	.10	.04	.01
☐ U53	Dave Henderson	.15	.06	.01
☐ U54	Doug Jennings	.10	.04	.01
☐ U55	Dave Parker	.15	.06	.01
☐ U56	Walt Weiss	.15	.06	.01
☐ U57	Bob Welch	.15	.06	.01
☐ U58	Henry Cotto	.05	.02	.00
☐ U59	Mario Diaz UER (listed as Marion on card front)	.10	.04	.01
☐ U60	Mike Jackson	.15	.06	.01
☐ U61	Bill Swift	.15	.06	.01
☐ U62	Jose Cecena	.10	.04	.01
☐ U63	Ray Hayward	.05	.02	.00
☐ U64	Jim Steels UER (listed as Jim Steele on card back)	.05	.02	.00
☐ U65	Pat Borders	.30	.12	.03
☐ U66	Sil Campusano	.12	.05	.01
☐ U67	Mike Flanagan	.10	.04	.01
☐ U68	Todd Stottlemyre	.75	.30	.07
☐ U69	David Wells	.20	.08	.02
☐ U70	Jose Alvarez	.10	.04	.01
☐ U71	Paul Runge	.05	.02	.00
☐ U72	Cesar Jimenez (card was intended for German Jiminez, it's his photo)	.05	.02	.00
☐ U73	Pete Smith	.10	.04	.01
☐ U74	John Smoltz	2.50	1.00	.25
☐ U75	Damon Berryhill	.10	.04	.01
☐ U76	Goose Gossage	.12	.05	.01
☐ U77	Mark Grace	2.25	.90	.22
☐ U78	Darrin Jackson	.15	.06	.01
☐ U79	Vance Law	.05	.02	.00
☐ U80	Jeff Pico	.10	.04	.01
☐ U81	Gary Varsho	.15	.06	.01
☐ U82	Tim Birtsas	.10	.04	.01
☐ U83	Rob Dibble	1.00	.40	.10
☐ U84	Danny Jackson	.10	.04	.01
☐ U85	Paul O'Neill	.12	.05	.01
☐ U86	Jose Rijo	.20	.08	.02
☐ U87	Chris Sabo	2.00	.80	.20
☐ U88	John Fishel	.05	.02	.00
☐ U89	Craig Biggio	1.25	.50	.12
☐ U90	Terry Puhl	.05	.02	.00
☐ U91	Rafael Ramirez	.05	.02	.00
☐ U92	Louie Meadows	.05	.02	.00
☐ U93	Kirk Gibson	.12	.05	.01
☐ U94	Alfredo Griffin	.05	.02	.00
☐ U95	Jay Howell	.10	.04	.01
☐ U96	Jesse Orosco	.05	.02	.00
☐ U97	Alejandro Pena	.12	.05	.01
☐ U98	Tracy Woodson	.10	.04	.01
☐ U99	John Dopson	.10	.04	.01
☐ U100	Brian Holman	.35	.15	.03
☐ U101	Rex Hudler	.15	.06	.01
☐ U102	Jeff Parrett	.10	.04	.01
☐ U103	Nelson Santovenia	.12	.05	.01
☐ U104	Kevin Elster	.10	.04	.01
☐ U105	Jeff Innis	.10	.04	.01
☐ U106	Mackey Sasser	.15	.06	.01
☐ U107	Phil Bradley	.10	.04	.01
☐ U108	Danny Clay	.05	.02	.00
☐ U109	Greg Harris	.05	.02	.00
☐ U110	Ricky Jordan	.30	.12	.03
☐ U111	David Palmer	.05	.02	.00
☐ U112	Jim Gott	.05	.02	.00
☐ U113	Tommy Gregg UER (photo actually Randy Milligan)	.10	.04	.01
☐ U114	Barry Jones	.10	.04	.01
☐ U115	Randy Milligan	.35	.15	.03
☐ U116	Luis Alicea	.10	.04	.01
☐ U117	Tom Brunansky	.10	.04	.01
☐ U118	John Costello	.10	.04	.01
☐ U119	Jose DeLeon	.05	.02	.00
☐ U120	Bob Horner	.10	.04	.01
☐ U121	Scott Terry	.10	.04	.01
☐ U122	Roberto Alomar	3.50	1.50	.35
☐ U123	Dave Leiper	.05	.02	.00
☐ U124	Keith Moreland	.05	.02	.00
☐ U125	Mark Parent	.10	.04	.01
☐ U126	Dennis Rasmussen	.05	.02	.00
☐ U127	Randy Bockus	.05	.02	.00
☐ U128	Brett Butler	.12	.05	.01
☐ U129	Donell Nixon	.05	.02	.00
☐ U130	Earnest Riles	.05	.02	.00
☐ U131	Roger Samuels	.05	.02	.00
☐ U132	Checklist U1-U132	.05	.01	.00

1989 Fleer

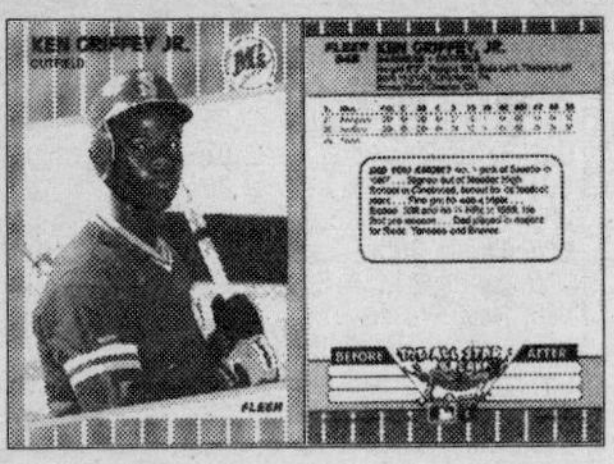

This 660-card set features a distinctive gray border background with white and yellow trim. The backs are printed in gray, black, and yellow on white card stock. The bottom of the card back shows an innovative breakdown of the player's demonstrated ability with respect to his performance before and after the All-Star break. Cards are numbered on the back and are again the standard 2 1/2" by 3 1/2". Cards are again organized numerically by teams and alphabetically within teams: Oakland A's (1-26), New York Mets (27-52), Los Angeles Dodgers (53-77), Boston Red Sox (78-101), Minnesota Twins (102-127), Detroit Tigers (128-151), Cincinnati Reds (152-175), Milwaukee Brewers (176-200), Pittsburgh Pirates (201-224), Toronto Blue Jays (225-248), New York Yankees (249-274), Kansas City Royals (275-298), San Diego Padres (299-322), San Francisco Giants (323-347), Houston Astros (348-370), Montreal Expos (371-395), Cleveland Indians (396-417), Chicago Cubs (418-442), St. Louis Cardinals (443-466), California Angels (467-490), Chicago White Sox (491-513), Texas Rangers (514-537), Seattle Mariners (538-561), Philadelphia Phillies (562-584), Atlanta Braves (585-605), and Baltimore Orioles (606-627). However, pairs 148/149, 153/154, 272/273, 283/284, and 367/368 were apparently mis-alphabetized by Fleer. The last 33 cards in the set consist of Specials (628-639), Rookie Pairs (640-653), and checklists (654-660). Due to the early beginning of production of this set, it seemed Fleer "presumed" that the A's would win the World Series, since they are listed as the first team in the numerical order; in fact, Fleer had the Mets over the underdog (but eventual World Champion) Dodgers as well. Fleer later reported that they merely arranged the teams according to team record due to the early printing date. Approximately half of the California Angels players have white rather than yellow halos. Certain Oakland A's player cards have red instead of green lines for front photo borders. Checklist cards are available either with or without positions listed for each player. The key rookies in this set are Sandy Alomar Jr., Ken Griffey Jr., Felix Jose, Ramon Martinez, Hal Morris, and Gary Sheffield. Fleer also produced the last of their three-year run of "limited" edition glossy, tin sets. This tin set was limited, but only compared to the previous year, as collector and dealer interest in the tin sets was apparently waning. It has been estimated that approximately 30,000 1989 tin sets were produced by Fleer; as a result, the price of the "tin" glossy cards is now about double the price of the regular set cards.

	MINT	EXC	G-VG
COMPLETE SET (660)	24.00	10.50	3.50
COMMON PLAYER (1-660)	.04	.02	.00
☐ 1 Don Baylor	.10	.04	.01
☐ 2 Lance Blankenship	.07	.03	.01
☐ 3 Todd Burns UER (Wrong birthdate; before/after All-Star stats missing)	.07	.03	.01
☐ 4 Greg Cadaret UER (All-Star Break stats show 3 losses, should be 2)	.07	.03	.01
☐ 5 Jose Canseco	.65	.25	.06
☐ 6 Storm Davis	.04	.02	.00
☐ 7 Dennis Eckersley	.10	.04	.01
☐ 8 Mike Gallego	.04	.02	.00
☐ 9 Ron Hassey	.04	.02	.00
☐ 10 Dave Henderson	.10	.04	.01
☐ 11 Rick Honeycutt	.04	.02	.00
☐ 12 Glenn Hubbard	.04	.02	.00
☐ 13 Stan Javier	.04	.02	.00
☐ 14 Doug Jennings	.07	.03	.01
☐ 15 Felix Jose	.90	.40	.09
☐ 16 Carney Lansford	.07	.03	.01
☐ 17 Mark McGwire	.15	.06	.01
☐ 18 Gene Nelson	.04	.02	.00
☐ 19 Dave Parker	.10	.04	.01
☐ 20 Eric Plunk	.04	.02	.00
☐ 21 Luis Polonia	.07	.03	.01
☐ 22 Terry Steinbach	.07	.03	.01
☐ 23 Dave Stewart	.10	.04	.01
☐ 24 Walt Weiss	.07	.03	.01
☐ 25 Bob Welch	.07	.03	.01
☐ 26 Curt Young	.04	.02	.00

Card			
☐ 27 Rick Aguilera	.07	.03	.01
☐ 28 Wally Backman	.04	.02	.00
☐ 29 Mark Carreon UER	.07	.03	.01
(after All-Star Break batting 7.14)			
☐ 30 Gary Carter	.07	.03	.01
☐ 31 David Cone	.10	.04	.01
☐ 32 Ron Darling	.07	.03	.01
☐ 33 Len Dykstra	.07	.03	.01
☐ 34 Kevin Elster	.04	.02	.00
☐ 35 Sid Fernandez	.07	.03	.01
☐ 36 Dwight Gooden	.15	.06	.01
☐ 37 Keith Hernandez	.10	.04	.01
☐ 38 Gregg Jefferies	.35	.15	.03
☐ 39 Howard Johnson	.15	.06	.01
☐ 40 Terry Leach	.04	.02	.00
☐ 41 Dave Magadan UER	.07	.03	.01
(Bio says 15 doubles, should be 13)			
☐ 42 Bob McClure	.04	.02	.00
☐ 43 Roger McDowell UER	.04	.02	.00
(Led Mets with 58, should be 62)			
☐ 44 Kevin McReynolds	.10	.04	.01
☐ 45 Keith Miller	.04	.02	.00
New York Mets			
☐ 46 Randy Myers	.07	.03	.01
☐ 47 Bob Ojeda	.04	.02	.00
☐ 48 Mackey Sasser	.07	.03	.01
☐ 49 Darryl Strawberry	.35	.15	.03
☐ 50 Tim Teufel	.04	.02	.00
☐ 51 Dave West	.15	.06	.01
☐ 52 Mookie Wilson	.04	.02	.00
☐ 53 Dave Anderson	.04	.02	.00
☐ 54 Tim Belcher	.10	.04	.01
☐ 55 Mike Davis	.04	.02	.00
☐ 56 Mike Devereaux	.07	.03	.01
☐ 57 Kirk Gibson	.10	.04	.01
☐ 58 Alfredo Griffin	.04	.02	.00
☐ 59 Chris Gwynn	.07	.03	.01
☐ 60 Jeff Hamilton	.04	.02	.00
☐ 61A Danny Heep	.40	.16	.04
(Home: Lake Hills)			
☐ 61B Danny Heep	.10	.04	.01
(Home: San Antonio)			
☐ 62 Orel Hershiser	.10	.04	.01
☐ 63 Brian Holton	.04	.02	.00
☐ 64 Jay Howell	.04	.02	.00
☐ 65 Tim Leary	.07	.03	.01
☐ 66 Mike Marshall	.07	.03	.01
☐ 67 Ramon Martinez	2.00	.80	.20
☐ 68 Jesse Orosco	.04	.02	.00
☐ 69 Alejandro Pena	.07	.03	.01
☐ 70 Steve Sax	.10	.04	.01
☐ 71 Mike Scioscia	.04	.02	.00
☐ 72 Mike Sharperson	.04	.02	.00
☐ 73 John Shelby	.04	.02	.00
☐ 74 Franklin Stubbs	.04	.02	.00

Card			
☐ 75 John Tudor	.07	.03	.01
☐ 76 Fernando Valenzuela	.10	.04	.01
☐ 77 Tracy Woodson	.07	.03	.01
☐ 78 Marty Barrett	.04	.02	.00
☐ 79 Todd Benzinger	.04	.02	.00
☐ 80 Mike Boddicker UER	.04	.02	.00
(Rochester in '76, should be '78)			
☐ 81 Wade Boggs	.25	.10	.02
☐ 82 Oil Can Boyd	.04	.02	.00
☐ 83 Ellis Burks	.17	.07	.01
☐ 84 Rick Cerone	.04	.02	.00
☐ 85 Roger Clemens	.40	.16	.04
☐ 86 Steve Curry	.07	.03	.01
☐ 87 Dwight Evans	.10	.04	.01
☐ 88 Wes Gardner	.04	.02	.00
☐ 89 Rich Gedman	.04	.02	.00
☐ 90 Mike Greenwell	.20	.08	.02
☐ 91 Bruce Hurst	.07	.03	.01
☐ 92 Dennis Lamp	.04	.02	.00
☐ 93 Spike Owen	.04	.02	.00
☐ 94 Larry Parrish UER	.04	.02	.00
(before All-Star Break batting 1.90)			
☐ 95 Carlos Quintana	.30	.12	.03
☐ 96 Jody Reed	.07	.03	.01
☐ 97 Jim Rice	.10	.04	.01
☐ 98A Kevin Romine ERR	.40	.16	.04
(photo actually Randy Kutcher batting)			
☐ 98B Kevin Romine COR	.10	.04	.01
(arms folded)			
☐ 99 Lee Smith	.10	.04	.01
☐ 100 Mike Smithson	.04	.02	.00
☐ 101 Bob Stanley	.04	.02	.00
☐ 102 Allan Anderson	.04	.02	.00
☐ 103 Keith Atherton	.04	.02	.00
☐ 104 Juan Berenguer	.04	.02	.00
☐ 105 Bert Blyleven	.10	.04	.01
☐ 106 Eric Bullock UER	.07	.03	.01
(Bats/Throws Right, should be Left)			
☐ 107 Randy Bush	.04	.02	.00
☐ 108 John Christensen	.04	.02	.00
☐ 109 Mark Davidson	.04	.02	.00
☐ 110 Gary Gaetti	.07	.03	.01
☐ 111 Greg Gagne	.04	.02	.00
☐ 112 Dan Gladden	.04	.02	.00
☐ 113 German Gonzalez	.07	.03	.01
☐ 114 Brian Harper	.07	.03	.01
☐ 115 Tom Herr	.04	.02	.00
☐ 116 Kent Hrbek	.10	.04	.01
☐ 117 Gene Larkin	.07	.03	.01
☐ 118 Tim Laudner	.04	.02	.00
☐ 119 Charlie Lea	.04	.02	.00
☐ 120 Steve Lombardozzi	.04	.02	.00
☐ 121A John Moses	.40	.16	.04
(Home: Tempe)			

No.	Player			
☐ 121B	John Moses (Home: Phoenix)	.10	.04	.01
☐ 122	Al Newman	.04	.02	.00
☐ 123	Mark Portugal	.04	.02	.00
☐ 124	Kirby Puckett	.35	.15	.03
☐ 125	Jeff Reardon	.10	.04	.01
☐ 126	Fred Toliver	.04	.02	.00
☐ 127	Frank Viola	.10	.04	.01
☐ 128	Doyle Alexander	.04	.02	.00
☐ 129	Dave Bergman	.04	.02	.00
☐ 130A	Tom Brookens ERR (Mike Heath back)	.75	.30	.07
☐ 130B	Tom Brookens COR	.07	.03	.01
☐ 131	Paul Gibson	.10	.04	.01
☐ 132A	Mike Heath ERR (Tom Brookens back)	.75	.30	.07
☐ 132B	Mike Heath COR	.07	.03	.01
☐ 133	Don Heinkel	.04	.02	.00
☐ 134	Mike Henneman	.04	.02	.00
☐ 135	Guillermo Hernandez	.04	.02	.00
☐ 136	Eric King	.04	.02	.00
☐ 137	Chet Lemon	.04	.02	.00
☐ 138	Fred Lynn UER ('74, '75 stats missing)	.07	.03	.01
☐ 139	Jack Morris	.10	.04	.01
☐ 140	Matt Nokes	.10	.04	.01
☐ 141	Gary Pettis	.04	.02	.00
☐ 142	Ted Power	.04	.02	.00
☐ 143	Jeff M. Robinson	.04	.02	.00
☐ 144	Luis Salazar	.04	.02	.00
☐ 145	Steve Searcy	.07	.03	.01
☐ 146	Pat Sheridan	.04	.02	.00
☐ 147	Frank Tanana	.07	.03	.01
☐ 148	Alan Trammell	.15	.06	.01
☐ 149	Walt Terrell	.04	.02	.00
☐ 150	Jim Walewander	.07	.03	.01
☐ 151	Lou Whitaker	.07	.03	.01
☐ 152	Tim Birtsas	.04	.02	.00
☐ 153	Tom Browning	.07	.03	.01
☐ 154	Keith Brown	.07	.03	.01
☐ 155	Norm Charlton	.15	.06	.01
☐ 156	Dave Concepcion	.07	.03	.01
☐ 157	Kal Daniels	.07	.03	.01
☐ 158	Eric Davis	.15	.06	.01
☐ 159	Bo Diaz	.04	.02	.00
☐ 160	Rob Dibble	.35	.15	.03
☐ 161	Nick Esasky	.04	.02	.00
☐ 162	John Franco	.04	.02	.00
☐ 163	Danny Jackson	.07	.03	.01
☐ 164	Barry Larkin	.17	.07	.01
☐ 165	Rob Murphy	.04	.02	.00
☐ 166	Paul O'Neill	.10	.04	.01
☐ 167	Jeff Reed	.04	.02	.00
☐ 168	Jose Rijo	.10	.04	.01
☐ 169	Ron Robinson	.04	.02	.00
☐ 170	Chris Sabo	.75	.30	.07
☐ 171	Candy Sierra	.07	.03	.01
☐ 172	Van Snider	.07	.03	.01
☐ 173A	Jeff Treadway (target registration mark above head on front in light blue)	10.00	4.50	1.25
☐ 173B	Jeff Treadway (no target on front)	.07	.03	.01
☐ 174	Frank Williams (after All-Star Break stats are jumbled)	.04	.02	.00
☐ 175	Herm Winningham	.04	.02	.00
☐ 176	Jim Adduci	.04	.02	.00
☐ 177	Don August	.04	.02	.00
☐ 178	Mike Birkbeck	.04	.02	.00
☐ 179	Chris Bosio	.04	.02	.00
☐ 180	Glenn Braggs	.04	.02	.00
☐ 181	Greg Brock	.04	.02	.00
☐ 182	Mark Clear	.04	.02	.00
☐ 183	Chuck Crim	.04	.02	.00
☐ 184	Rob Deer	.07	.03	.01
☐ 185	Tom Filer	.04	.02	.00
☐ 186	Jim Gantner	.04	.02	.00
☐ 187	Darryl Hamilton	.15	.06	.01
☐ 188	Ted Higuera	.04	.02	.00
☐ 189	Odell Jones	.04	.02	.00
☐ 190	Jeffrey Leonard	.04	.02	.00
☐ 191	Joey Meyer	.04	.02	.00
☐ 192	Paul Mirabella	.04	.02	.00
☐ 193	Paul Molitor	.12	.05	.01
☐ 194	Charlie O'Brien	.07	.03	.01
☐ 195	Dan Plesac	.04	.02	.00
☐ 196	Gary Sheffield	.40	.16	.04
☐ 197	B.J. Surhoff	.07	.03	.01
☐ 198	Dale Sveum	.04	.02	.00
☐ 199	Bill Wegman	.04	.02	.00
☐ 200	Robin Yount	.20	.08	.02
☐ 201	Rafael Belliard	.04	.02	.00
☐ 202	Barry Bonds	.30	.12	.03
☐ 203	Bobby Bonilla	.25	.10	.02
☐ 204	Sid Bream	.04	.02	.00
☐ 205	Benny Distefano	.04	.02	.00
☐ 206	Doug Drabek	.10	.04	.01
☐ 207	Mike Dunne	.04	.02	.00
☐ 208	Felix Fermin	.04	.02	.00
☐ 209	Brian Fisher	.04	.02	.00
☐ 210	Jim Gott	.04	.02	.00
☐ 211	Bob Kipper	.04	.02	.00
☐ 212	Dave LaPoint	.04	.02	.00
☐ 213	Mike LaValliere	.04	.02	.00
☐ 214	Jose Lind	.04	.02	.00
☐ 215	Junior Ortiz	.04	.02	.00
☐ 216	Vicente Palacios	.07	.03	.01
☐ 217	Tom Prince	.04	.02	.00
☐ 218	Gary Redus	.04	.02	.00
☐ 219	R.J. Reynolds	.04	.02	.00

- ☐ 220 Jeff Robinson .04 .02 .00
- ☐ 221 John Smiley .07 .03 .01
- ☐ 222 Andy Van Slyke .12 .05 .01
- ☐ 223 Bob Walk .04 .02 .00
- ☐ 224 Glenn Wilson .04 .02 .00
- ☐ 225 Jesse Barfield .10 .04 .01
- ☐ 226 George Bell .12 .05 .01
- ☐ 227 Pat Borders .17 .07 .01
- ☐ 228 John Cerutti .04 .02 .00
- ☐ 229 Jim Clancy .04 .02 .00
- ☐ 230 Mark Eichhorn .07 .03 .01
- ☐ 231 Tony Fernandez .07 .03 .01
- ☐ 232 Cecil Fielder .40 .16 .04
- ☐ 233 Mike Flanagan .04 .02 .00
- ☐ 234 Kelly Gruber .12 .05 .01
- ☐ 235 Tom Henke .07 .03 .01
- ☐ 236 Jimmy Key .07 .03 .01
- ☐ 237 Rick Leach .04 .02 .00
- ☐ 238 Manny Lee UER .07 .03 .01
  (bio says regular shortstop, sic, Tony Fernandez)
- ☐ 239 Nelson Liriano .04 .02 .00
- ☐ 240 Fred McGriff .20 .08 .02
- ☐ 241 Lloyd Moseby .04 .02 .00
- ☐ 242 Rance Mulliniks .04 .02 .00
- ☐ 243 Jeff Musselman .04 .02 .00
- ☐ 244 Dave Stieb .10 .04 .01
- ☐ 245 Todd Stottlemyre .20 .08 .02
- ☐ 246 Duane Ward .04 .02 .00
- ☐ 247 David Wells .12 .05 .01
- ☐ 248 Ernie Whitt UER .04 .02 .00
  (HR total 21, should be 121)
- ☐ 249 Luis Aguayo .04 .02 .00
- ☐ 250A Neil Allen .75 .30 .07
  (Home: Sarasota, FL)
- ☐ 250B Neil Allen .10 .04 .01
  (Home: Syosset, NY)
- ☐ 251 John Candelaria .04 .02 .00
- ☐ 252 Jack Clark .07 .03 .01
- ☐ 253 Richard Dotson .04 .02 .00
- ☐ 254 Rickey Henderson .40 .16 .04
- ☐ 255 Tommy John .10 .04 .01
- ☐ 256 Roberto Kelly .17 .07 .01
- ☐ 257 Al Leiter .04 .02 .00
- ☐ 258 Don Mattingly .30 .12 .03
- ☐ 259 Dale Mohorcic .04 .02 .00
- ☐ 260 Hal Morris 2.00 .80 .20
- ☐ 261 Scott Nielsen .04 .02 .00
- ☐ 262 Mike Pagliarulo UER .04 .02 .00
  (wrong birthdate)
- ☐ 263 Hipolito Pena .07 .03 .01
- ☐ 264 Ken Phelps .04 .02 .00
- ☐ 265 Willie Randolph .07 .03 .01
- ☐ 266 Rick Rhoden .04 .02 .00
- ☐ 267 Dave Righetti .07 .03 .01
- ☐ 268 Rafael Santana .04 .02 .00
- ☐ 269 Steve Shields .04 .02 .00
- ☐ 270 Joel Skinner .04 .02 .00
- ☐ 271 Don Slaught .04 .02 .00
- ☐ 272 Claudell Washington .04 .02 .00
- ☐ 273 Gary Ward .04 .02 .00
- ☐ 274 Dave Winfield .15 .06 .01
- ☐ 275 Luis Aquino .04 .02 .00
- ☐ 276 Floyd Bannister .04 .02 .00
- ☐ 277 George Brett .20 .08 .02
- ☐ 278 Bill Buckner .07 .03 .01
- ☐ 279 Nick Capra .04 .02 .00
- ☐ 280 Jose DeJesus .15 .06 .01
- ☐ 281 Steve Farr .04 .02 .00
- ☐ 282 Jerry Don Gleaton .04 .02 .00
- ☐ 283 Mark Gubicza .07 .03 .01
- ☐ 284 Tom Gordon UER .30 .12 .03
  (16.2 innings in '88, should be 15.2)
- ☐ 285 Bo Jackson .60 .25 .06
- ☐ 286 Charlie Leibrandt .04 .02 .00
- ☐ 287 Mike Macfarlane .12 .05 .01
- ☐ 288 Jeff Montgomery .07 .03 .01
- ☐ 289 Bill Pecota UER .07 .03 .01
  (photo actually Brad Wellman)
- ☐ 290 Jamie Quirk .04 .02 .00
- ☐ 291 Bret Saberhagen .12 .05 .01
- ☐ 292 Kevin Seitzer .07 .03 .01
- ☐ 293 Kurt Stillwell .04 .02 .00
- ☐ 294 Pat Tabler .04 .02 .00
- ☐ 295 Danny Tartabull .12 .05 .01
- ☐ 296 Gary Thurman .04 .02 .00
- ☐ 297 Frank White .04 .02 .00
- ☐ 298 Willie Wilson .07 .03 .01
- ☐ 299 Roberto Alomar .75 .30 .07
- ☐ 300 Sandy Alomar Jr. UER .60 .25 .06
  (wrong birthdate, says 6/16/66, should say 6/18/66)
- ☐ 301 Chris Brown .04 .02 .00
- ☐ 302 Mike Brumley UER .07 .03 .01
  (133 hits in '88, should be 134)
- ☐ 303 Mark Davis .07 .03 .01
- ☐ 304 Mark Grant .04 .02 .00
- ☐ 305 Tony Gwynn .20 .08 .02
- ☐ 306 Greg W. Harris .17 .07 .01
- ☐ 307 Andy Hawkins .04 .02 .00
- ☐ 308 Jimmy Jones .04 .02 .00
- ☐ 309 John Kruk .04 .02 .00
- ☐ 310 Dave Leiper .04 .02 .00
- ☐ 311 Carmelo Martinez .04 .02 .00
- ☐ 312 Lance McCullers .04 .02 .00
- ☐ 313 Keith Moreland .04 .02 .00
- ☐ 314 Dennis Rasmussen .04 .02 .00
- ☐ 315 Randy Ready UER .04 .02 .00

(1214 games in '88,
should be 114)

☐ 316 Benito Santiago .... .10 .04 .01
☐ 317 Eric Show .... .04 .02 .00
☐ 318 Todd Simmons .... .04 .02 .00
☐ 319 Garry Templeton .... .07 .03 .01
☐ 320 Dickie Thon .... .04 .02 .00
☐ 321 Ed Whitson .... .04 .02 .00
☐ 322 Marvell Wynne .... .04 .02 .00
☐ 323 Mike Aldrete .... .04 .02 .00
☐ 324 Brett Butler .... .10 .04 .01
☐ 325 Will Clark UER .... .60 .25 .06
(three consecutive
100 RBI seasons)
☐ 326 Kelly Downs UER .... .04 .02 .00
('88 stats missing)
☐ 327 Dave Dravecky .... .07 .03 .01
☐ 328 Scott Garrelts .... .04 .02 .00
☐ 329 Atlee Hammaker .... .04 .02 .00
☐ 330 Charlie Hayes .... .12 .05 .01
☐ 331 Mike Krukow .... .04 .02 .00
☐ 332 Craig Lefferts .... .04 .02 .00
☐ 333 Candy Maldonado .... .04 .02 .00
☐ 334 Kirt Manwaring UER .... .04 .02 .00
(Bats Rights)
☐ 335 Bob Melvin .... .04 .02 .00
☐ 336 Kevin Mitchell .... .20 .08 .02
☐ 337 Donell Nixon .... .04 .02 .00
☐ 338 Tony Perezchica .... .07 .03 .01
☐ 339 Joe Price .... .04 .02 .00
☐ 340 Rick Reuschel .... .07 .03 .01
☐ 341 Earnest Riles .... .04 .02 .00
☐ 342 Don Robinson .... .04 .02 .00
☐ 343 Chris Speier .... .04 .02 .00
☐ 344 Robby Thompson UER .... .04 .02 .00
(West Plam Beach)
☐ 345 Jose Uribe .... .04 .02 .00
☐ 346 Matt Williams .... .30 .12 .03
☐ 347 Trevor Wilson .... .15 .06 .01
☐ 348 Juan Agosto .... .04 .02 .00
☐ 349 Larry Andersen .... .04 .02 .00
☐ 350A Alan Ashby ERR .... 3.00 1.25 .30
(Throws Rig)
☐ 350B Alan Ashby COR .... .07 .03 .01
☐ 351 Kevin Bass .... .04 .02 .00
☐ 352 Buddy Bell .... .07 .03 .01
☐ 353 Craig Biggio .... .60 .25 .06
☐ 354 Danny Darwin .... .04 .02 .00
☐ 355 Glenn Davis .... .10 .04 .01
☐ 356 Jim Deshaies .... .04 .02 .00
☐ 357 Bill Doran .... .04 .02 .00
☐ 358 John Fishel .... .04 .02 .00
☐ 359 Billy Hatcher .... .07 .03 .01
☐ 360 Bob Knepper .... .04 .02 .00
☐ 361 Louie Meadows UER .... .07 .03 .01
(bio says 10 EBH's
and 6 SB's in '88,
should be 3 and 4)
☐ 362 Dave Meads .... .04 .02 .00
☐ 363 Jim Pankovits .... .04 .02 .00
☐ 364 Terry Puhl .... .04 .02 .00
☐ 365 Rafael Ramirez .... .04 .02 .00
☐ 366 Craig Reynolds .... .04 .02 .00
☐ 367 Mike Scott .... .10 .04 .01
(card number listed
as 368 on Astros CL)
☐ 368 Nolan Ryan .... .75 .30 .07
(card number listed
as 367 on Astros CL)
☐ 369 Dave Smith .... .04 .02 .00
☐ 370 Gerald Young .... .04 .02 .00
☐ 371 Hubie Brooks .... .07 .03 .01
☐ 372 Tim Burke .... .04 .02 .00
☐ 373 John Dopson .... .07 .03 .01
☐ 374 Mike Fitzgerald .... .04 .02 .00
☐ 375 Tom Foley .... .04 .02 .00
☐ 376 Andres Galarraga UER .... .07 .03 .01
(Home: Caracus)
☐ 377 Neal Heaton .... .04 .02 .00
☐ 378 Joe Hesketh .... .07 .03 .01
☐ 379 Brian Holman .... .20 .08 .02
☐ 380 Rex Hudler .... .07 .03 .01
☐ 381 Randy Johnson UER .... .35 .15 .03
(innings for '85 and
'86 shown as 27 and
120, should be 27.1
and 119.2)
☐ 382 Wallace Johnson .... .04 .02 .00
☐ 383 Tracy Jones .... .04 .02 .00
☐ 384 Dave Martinez .... .04 .02 .00
☐ 385 Dennis Martinez .... .07 .03 .01
☐ 386 Andy McGaffigan .... .04 .02 .00
☐ 387 Otis Nixon .... .07 .03 .01
☐ 388 Johnny Paredes .... .07 .03 .01
☐ 389 Jeff Parrett .... .04 .02 .00
☐ 390 Pascual Perez .... .04 .02 .00
☐ 391 Tim Raines .... .12 .05 .01
☐ 392 Luis Rivera .... .04 .02 .00
☐ 393 Nelson Santovenia .... .10 .04 .01
☐ 394 Bryn Smith .... .04 .02 .00
☐ 395 Tim Wallach .... .07 .03 .01
☐ 396 Andy Allanson UER .... .04 .02 .00
(1214 hits in '88,
should be 114)
☐ 397 Rod Allen .... .07 .03 .01
☐ 398 Scott Bailes .... .04 .02 .00
☐ 399 Tom Candiotti .... .07 .03 .01
☐ 400 Joe Carter .... .12 .05 .01
☐ 401 Carmen Castillo UER .... .04 .02 .00
(after All-Star Break
batting 2.50)
☐ 402 Dave Clark UER .... .07 .03 .01
(card front shows
position as Rookie;

after All-Star Break
batting 3.14)

☐ 403 John Farrell UER .04 .02 .00
(typo in runs
allowed in '88)

☐ 404 Julio Franco .12 .05 .01

☐ 405 Don Gordon .04 .02 .00

☐ 406 Mel Hall .07 .03 .01

☐ 407 Brad Havens .04 .02 .00

☐ 408 Brook Jacoby .04 .02 .00

☐ 409 Doug Jones .04 .02 .00

☐ 410 Jeff Kaiser .07 .03 .01

☐ 411 Luis Medina .10 .04 .01

☐ 412 Cory Snyder .07 .03 .01

☐ 413 Greg Swindell .07 .03 .01

☐ 414 Ron Tingley UER .07 .03 .01
(hit HR in first ML
at-bat, should be
first AL at-bat)

☐ 415 Willie Upshaw .04 .02 .00

☐ 416 Ron Washington .04 .02 .00

☐ 417 Rich Yett .04 .02 .00

☐ 418 Damon Berryhill .07 .03 .01

☐ 419 Mike Bielecki .07 .03 .01

☐ 420 Doug Dascenzo .10 .04 .01

☐ 421 Jody Davis UER .04 .02 .00
(Braves stats for
'88 missing)

☐ 422 Andre Dawson .15 .06 .01

☐ 423 Frank DiPino .04 .02 .00

☐ 424 Shawon Dunston .07 .03 .01

☐ 425 Rich Gossage .07 .03 .01

☐ 426 Mark Grace UER .40 .16 .04
(Minor League stats
for '88 missing)

☐ 427 Mike Harkey .15 .06 .01

☐ 428 Darrin Jackson .07 .03 .01

☐ 429 Les Lancaster .04 .02 .00

☐ 430 Vance Law .04 .02 .00

☐ 431 Greg Maddux .10 .04 .01

☐ 432 Jamie Moyer .04 .02 .00

☐ 433 Al Nipper .04 .02 .00

☐ 434 Rafael Palmeiro UER .20 .08 .02
(170 hits in '88,
should be 178)

☐ 435 Pat Perry .04 .02 .00

☐ 436 Jeff Pico .07 .03 .01

☐ 437 Ryne Sandberg .40 .16 .04

☐ 438 Calvin Schiraldi .04 .02 .00

☐ 439 Rick Sutcliffe .07 .03 .01

☐ 440A Manny Trillo ERR 3.00 1.25 .30
(Throws Rig)

☐ 440B Manny Trillo COR .07 .03 .01

☐ 441 Gary Varsho UER .07 .03 .01
(wrong birthdate;
.303 should be .302;
11/28 should be 9/19)

☐ 442 Mitch Webster .04 .02 .00

☐ 443 Luis Alicea .07 .03 .01

☐ 444 Tom Brunansky .07 .03 .01

☐ 445 Vince Coleman UER .12 .05 .01
(third straight with
83, should be fourth
straight with 81)

☐ 446 John Costello .04 .02 .00

☐ 447 Danny Cox .04 .02 .00

☐ 448 Ken Dayley .04 .02 .00

☐ 449 Jose DeLeon .04 .02 .00

☐ 450 Curt Ford .04 .02 .00

☐ 451 Pedro Guerrero .07 .03 .01

☐ 452 Bob Horner .07 .03 .01

☐ 453 Tim Jones .07 .03 .01

☐ 454 Steve Lake .04 .02 .00

☐ 455 Joe Magrane UER .07 .03 .01
(Des Moines, IO)

☐ 456 Greg Mathews .04 .02 .00

☐ 457 Willie McGee .07 .03 .01

☐ 458 Larry McWilliams .04 .02 .00

☐ 459 Jose Oquendo .04 .02 .00

☐ 460 Tony Pena .07 .03 .01

☐ 461 Terry Pendleton .12 .05 .01

☐ 462 Steve Peters UER .10 .04 .01
(Lives in Harrah,
not Harah)

☐ 463 Ozzie Smith .17 .07 .01

☐ 464 Scott Terry .04 .02 .00

☐ 465 Denny Walling .04 .02 .00

☐ 466 Todd Worrell .07 .03 .01

☐ 467 Tony Armas UER .04 .02 .00
(before All-Star Break
batting 2.39)

☐ 468 Dante Bichette .20 .08 .02

☐ 469 Bob Boone .07 .03 .01

☐ 470 Terry Clark .07 .03 .01

☐ 471 Stew Cliburn .04 .02 .00

☐ 472 Mike Cook UER .07 .03 .01
(TM near Angels logo
missing from front)

☐ 473 Sherman Corbett .04 .02 .00

☐ 474 Chili Davis .07 .03 .01

☐ 475 Brian Downing .04 .02 .00

☐ 476 Jim Eppard .04 .02 .00

☐ 477 Chuck Finley .10 .04 .01

☐ 478 Willie Fraser .04 .02 .00

☐ 479 Bryan Harvey UER .30 .12 .03
(ML record shows 0-0,
should be 7-5)

☐ 480 Jack Howell .04 .02 .00

☐ 481 Wally Joyner UER .15 .06 .01
(Yorba Linda, GA)

☐ 482 Jack Lazorko .04 .02 .00

☐ 483 Kirk McCaskill .04 .02 .00

☐ 484 Mark McLemore .04 .02 .00

☐ 485 Greg Minton .04 .02 .00

☐ 486 Dan Petry .04 .02 .00
☐ 487 Johnny Ray .04 .02 .00
☐ 488 Dick Schofield .04 .02 .00
☐ 489 Devon White .07 .03 .01
☐ 490 Mike Witt .04 .02 .00
☐ 491 Harold Baines .07 .03 .01
☐ 492 Daryl Boston .04 .02 .00
☐ 493 Ivan Calderon UER .07 .03 .01
('80 stats shifted)
☐ 494 Mike Diaz .04 .02 .00
☐ 495 Carlton Fisk .17 .07 .01
☐ 496 Dave Gallagher .10 .04 .01
☐ 497 Ozzie Guillen .07 .03 .01
☐ 498 Shawn Hillegas .04 .02 .00
☐ 499 Lance Johnson .04 .02 .00
☐ 500 Barry Jones .04 .02 .00
☐ 501 Bill Long .04 .02 .00
☐ 502 Steve Lyons .04 .02 .00
☐ 503 Fred Manrique .04 .02 .00
☐ 504 Jack McDowell .20 .08 .02
☐ 505 Donn Pall .07 .03 .01
☐ 506 Kelly Paris .04 .02 .00
☐ 507 Dan Pasqua .04 .02 .00
☐ 508 Ken Patterson .07 .03 .01
☐ 509 Melido Perez .07 .03 .01
☐ 510 Jerry Reuss .04 .02 .00
☐ 511 Mark Salas .04 .02 .00
☐ 512 Bobby Thigpen UER .10 .04 .01
('86 ERA 4.69,
should be 4.68)
☐ 513 Mike Woodard .04 .02 .00
☐ 514 Bob Brower .04 .02 .00
☐ 515 Steve Buechele .04 .02 .00
☐ 516 Jose Cecena .07 .03 .01
☐ 517 Cecil Espy .07 .03 .01
☐ 518 Scott Fletcher .04 .02 .00
☐ 519 Cecilio Guante .04 .02 .00
('87 Yankee stats
are off-centered)
☐ 520 Jose Guzman .04 .02 .00
☐ 521 Ray Hayward .07 .03 .01
☐ 522 Charlie Hough .04 .02 .00
☐ 523 Pete Incaviglia .10 .04 .01
☐ 524 Mike Jeffcoat .04 .02 .00
☐ 525 Paul Kilgus .04 .02 .00
☐ 526 Chad Kreuter .07 .03 .01
☐ 527 Jeff Kunkel .04 .02 .00
☐ 528 Oddibe McDowell .04 .02 .00
☐ 529 Pete O'Brien .04 .02 .00
☐ 530 Geno Petralli .04 .02 .00
☐ 531 Jeff Russell .04 .02 .00
☐ 532 Ruben Sierra .30 .12 .03
☐ 533 Mike Stanley .04 .02 .00
☐ 534A Ed VandeBerg ERR 3.00 1.25 .30
(Throws Lef)
☐ 534B Ed VandeBerg COR .07 .03 .01
☐ 535 Curtis Wilkerson ERR .04 .02 .00
(pitcher headings
at bottom)
☐ 536 Mitch Williams .04 .02 .00
☐ 537 Bobby Witt UER .07 .03 .01
('85 ERA .643,
should be 6.43)
☐ 538 Steve Balboni .04 .02 .00
☐ 539 Scott Bankhead .07 .03 .01
☐ 540 Scott Bradley .04 .02 .00
☐ 541 Mickey Brantley .04 .02 .00
☐ 542 Jay Buhner .17 .07 .01
☐ 543 Mike Campbell .04 .02 .00
☐ 544 Darnell Coles .04 .02 .00
☐ 545 Henry Cotto .04 .02 .00
☐ 546 Alvin Davis .07 .03 .01
☐ 547 Mario Diaz .04 .02 .00
☐ 548 Ken Griffey Jr. 9.00 4.00 .90
☐ 549 Erik Hanson .65 .25 .06
☐ 550 Mike Jackson UER .04 .02 .00
(Lifetime ERA 3.345,
should be 3.45)
☐ 551 Mark Langston .10 .04 .01
☐ 552 Edgar Martinez .17 .07 .01
☐ 553 Bill McGuire .04 .02 .00
☐ 554 Mike Moore .07 .03 .01
☐ 555 Jim Presley .04 .02 .00
☐ 556 Rey Quinones .04 .02 .00
☐ 557 Jerry Reed .04 .02 .00
☐ 558 Harold Reynolds .07 .03 .01
☐ 559 Mike Schooler .15 .06 .01
☐ 560 Bill Swift .07 .03 .01
☐ 561 Dave Valle .04 .02 .00
☐ 562 Steve Bedrosian .07 .03 .01
☐ 563 Phil Bradley .04 .02 .00
☐ 564 Don Carman .04 .02 .00
☐ 565 Bob Dernier .04 .02 .00
☐ 566 Marvin Freeman .04 .02 .00
☐ 567 Todd Frohwirth .04 .02 .00
☐ 568 Greg Gross .04 .02 .00
☐ 569 Kevin Gross .04 .02 .00
☐ 570 Greg Harris .04 .02 .00
☐ 571 Von Hayes .07 .03 .01
☐ 572 Chris James .04 .02 .00
☐ 573 Steve Jeltz .04 .02 .00
☐ 574 Ron Jones UER .07 .03 .01
(Led IL in '88 with
85, should be 75)
☐ 575 Ricky Jordan .15 .06 .01
☐ 576 Mike Maddux .04 .02 .00
☐ 577 David Palmer .04 .02 .00
☐ 578 Lance Parrish .07 .03 .01
☐ 579 Shane Rawley .04 .02 .00
☐ 580 Bruce Ruffin .04 .02 .00
☐ 581 Juan Samuel .07 .03 .01
☐ 582 Mike Schmidt .40 .16 .04
☐ 583 Kent Tekulve .04 .02 .00
☐ 584 Milt Thompson UER .04 .02 .00

Card	Price 1	Price 2	Price 3
(19 hits in '88, should be 109)			
☐ 585 Jose Alvarez	.07	.03	.01
☐ 586 Paul Assenmacher	.04	.02	.00
☐ 587 Bruce Benedict	.04	.02	.00
☐ 588 Jeff Blauser	.04	.02	.00
☐ 589 Terry Blocker	.07	.03	.01
☐ 590 Ron Gant	.50	.20	.05
☐ 591 Tom Glavine	.40	.16	.04
☐ 592 Tommy Gregg	.07	.03	.01
☐ 593 Albert Hall	.04	.02	.00
☐ 594 Dion James	.04	.02	.00
☐ 595 Rick Mahler	.04	.02	.00
☐ 596 Dale Murphy	.15	.06	.01
☐ 597 Gerald Perry	.04	.02	.00
☐ 598 Charlie Puleo	.04	.02	.00
☐ 599 Ted Simmons	.07	.03	.01
☐ 600 Pete Smith	.07	.03	.01
☐ 601 Zane Smith	.07	.03	.01
☐ 602 John Smoltz	.75	.30	.07
☐ 603 Bruce Sutter	.07	.03	.01
☐ 604 Andres Thomas	.04	.02	.00
☐ 605 Ozzie Virgil	.04	.02	.00
☐ 606 Brady Anderson	.07	.03	.01
☐ 607 Jeff Ballard	.04	.02	.00
☐ 608 Jose Bautista	.07	.03	.01
☐ 609 Ken Gerhart	.04	.02	.00
☐ 610 Terry Kennedy	.04	.02	.00
☐ 611 Eddie Murray	.15	.06	.01
☐ 612 Carl Nichols UER (before All-Star Break batting 1.88)	.07	.03	.01
☐ 613 Tom Niedenfuer	.04	.02	.00
☐ 614 Joe Orsulak	.04	.02	.00
☐ 615 Oswald Peraza UER (shown as Oswaldo)	.10	.04	.01
☐ 616A Bill Ripken ERR (Rick Face written on knob of bat)	9.00	4.00	.90
☐ 616B Bill Ripken (bat knob whited out)	30.00	13.50	4.50
☐ 616C Bill Ripken (words on bat knob scribbled out)	9.00	4.00	.90
☐ 616D Bill Ripken DP (black box covering bat knob)	.12	.05	.01
☐ 617 Cal Ripken	.50	.20	.05
☐ 618 Dave Schmidt	.04	.02	.00
☐ 619 Rick Schu	.04	.02	.00
☐ 620 Larry Sheets	.04	.02	.00
☐ 621 Doug Sisk	.04	.02	.00
☐ 622 Pete Stanicek	.04	.02	.00
☐ 623 Mickey Tettleton	.07	.03	.01
☐ 624 Jay Tibbs	.04	.02	.00
☐ 625 Jim Traber	.04	.02	.00

Card	Price 1	Price 2	Price 3
☐ 626 Mark Williamson	.04	.02	.00
☐ 627 Craig Worthington	.07	.03	.01
☐ 628 Speed/Power Jose Canseco	.25	.10	.02
☐ 629 Pitcher Perfect Tom Browning	.07	.03	.01
☐ 630 Like Father/Like Sons Roberto Alomar Sandy Alomar Jr. (names on card listed in wrong order) UER	.30	.12	.03
☐ 631 NL All Stars UER Will Clark Rafael Palmeiro (Gallaraga, sic; Clark 3 consecutive 100 RBI seasons; third with 102 RBI's)	.15	.06	.01
☐ 632 Homeruns - Coast to Coast UER Darryl Strawberry Will Clark (Homeruns should be two words)	.25	.10	.02
☐ 633 Hot Corners - Hot Hitters UER Wade Boggs Carney Lansford (Boggs hit .366 in '86, should be '88)	.15	.06	.01
☐ 634 Triple A's Jose Canseco Terry Steinbach Mark McGwire	.20	.08	.02
☐ 635 Dual Heat Mark Davis Dwight Gooden	.10	.04	.01
☐ 636 NL Pitching Power UER Danny Jackson David Cone (Hersheiser, sic)	.07	.03	.01
☐ 637 Cannon Arms UER Chris Sabo Bobby Bonilla (Bobby Bonds, sic)	.15	.06	.01
☐ 638 Double Trouble UER Andres Galarraga (misspelled Gallaraga on card back) Gerald Perry	.07	.03	.01
☐ 639 Power Center Kirby Puckett Eric Davis	.15	.06	.01
☐ 640 Steve Wilson and Cameron Drew	.10	.04	.01
☐ 641 Kevin Brown and Kevin Reimer	.50	.20	.05
☐ 642 Brad Pounders and	.25	.10	.02

Jerald Clark			
☐ 643 Mike Capel and Drew Hall	.12	.05	.01
☐ 644 Joe Girardi and Rolando Roomes	.12	.05	.01
☐ 645 Lenny Harris and Marty Brown	.20	.08	.02
☐ 646 Luis De Los Santos and Jim Campbell	.10	.04	.01
☐ 647 Randy Kramer and Miguel Garcia	.10	.04	.01
☐ 648 Torey Lovullo and Robert Palacios	.10	.04	.01
☐ 649 Jim Corsi and Bob Milacki	.17	.07	.01
☐ 650 Grady Hall and Mike Rochford	.10	.04	.01
☐ 651 Terry Taylor and Vance Lovelace	.10	.04	.01
☐ 652 Ken Hill and Dennis Cook	.25	.10	.02
☐ 653 Scott Service and Shane Turner	.10	.04	.01
☐ 654 CL: Oakland/Mets Dodgers/Red Sox (10 Henderson; 68 Jess Orosco)	.08	.01	.00
☐ 655A CL: Twins/Tigers ERR Reds/Brewers (179 Boslo and Twins/Tigers positions listed)	.08	.01	.00
☐ 655B CL: Twins/Tigers COR Reds/Brewers (179 Boslo but Twins/Tigers positions not listed)	.08	.01	.00
☐ 656 CL: Pirates/Blue Jays Yankees/Royals (225 Jess Barfield)	.08	.01	.00
☐ 657 CL: Padres/Giants Astros/Expos (367/368 wrong)	.08	.01	.00
☐ 658 CL: Indians/Cubs Cardinals/Angels (449 Deleon)	.08	.01	.00
☐ 659 CL: White Sox/Rangers Mariners/Phillies	.08	.01	.00
☐ 660 CL: Braves/Orioles Specials/Checklists (632 hyphenated differently and 650 Hali; 595 Rich Mahler; 619 Rich Schu)	.08	.01	.00

1989 Fleer Update

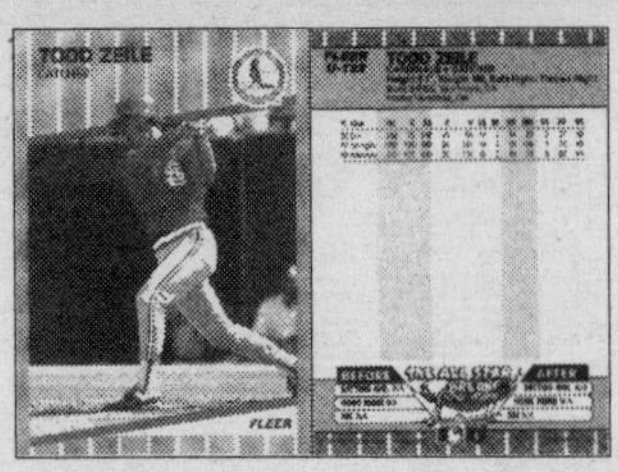

The 1989 Fleer Update set contains 132 standard-size (2 1/2" by 3 1/2") cards. The fronts are gray with white pinstripes. The vertically oriented backs show lifetime stats and performance "Before and After the All-Star Break." The set numbering is in team order with players within teams ordered alphabetically. The set does not include a card of 1989 AL Rookie of the Year Gregg Olson, but contains the first major card of Greg Vaughn and special cards for Nolan Ryan's 5,000th strikeout and Mike Schmidt's retirement. Other key rookies in this set are Joey (Albert) Belle, Junior Felix, Robin Ventura, Jerome Walton and Todd Zeile. Fleer did NOT produce a limited (tin) edition version of this set with glossy coating.

	MINT	EXC	G-VG
COMPLETE SET (132)	12.00	5.25	1.50
COMMON PLAYER (1-132)	.05	.02	.00
☐ U1 Phil Bradley	.10	.03	.01
☐ U2 Mike Devereaux	.10	.04	.01
☐ U3 Steve Finley	.35	.15	.03
☐ U4 Kevin Hickey	.05	.02	.00
☐ U5 Brian Holton	.08	.03	.01
☐ U6 Bob Milacki	.12	.05	.01
☐ U7 Randy Milligan	.08	.03	.01
☐ U8 John Dopson	.08	.03	.01
☐ U9 Nick Esasky	.08	.03	.01
☐ U10 Rob Murphy	.05	.02	.00
☐ U11 Jim Abbott	1.25	.50	.12
☐ U12 Bert Blyleven	.12	.05	.01
☐ U13 Jeff Manto	.15	.06	.01
☐ U14 Bob McClure	.05	.02	.00
☐ U15 Lance Parrish	.12	.05	.01
☐ U16 Lee Stevens	.65	.25	.06

☐ U17 Claudell Washington	.05	.02	.00
☐ U18 Mark Davis	.10	.04	.01
☐ U19 Eric King	.08	.03	.01
☐ U20 Ron Kittle	.08	.03	.01
☐ U21 Matt Merullo	.10	.04	.01
☐ U22 Steve Rosenberg	.08	.03	.01
☐ U23 Robin Ventura	2.25	.90	.22
☐ U24 Keith Atherton	.05	.02	.00
☐ U25 Joey Belle	2.00	.80	.20
☐ U26 Jerry Browne	.05	.02	.00
☐ U27 Felix Fermin	.05	.02	.00
☐ U28 Brad Komminsk	.05	.02	.00
☐ U29 Pete O'Brien	.05	.02	.00
☐ U30 Mike Brumley	.05	.02	.00
☐ U31 Tracy Jones	.08	.03	.01
☐ U32 Mike Schwabe	.08	.03	.01
☐ U33 Gary Ward	.05	.02	.00
☐ U34 Frank Williams	.05	.02	.00
☐ U35 Kevin Appier	.50	.20	.05
☐ U36 Bob Boone	.12	.05	.01
☐ U37 Luis de los Santos	.10	.04	.01
☐ U38 Jim Eisenreich	.10	.04	.01
☐ U39 Jaime Navarro	.35	.15	.03
☐ U40 Bill Spiers	.12	.05	.01
☐ U41 Greg Vaughn	2.00	.80	.20
☐ U42 Randy Veres	.08	.03	.01
☐ U43 Wally Backman	.05	.02	.00
☐ U44 Shane Rawley	.05	.02	.00
☐ U45 Steve Balboni	.05	.02	.00
☐ U46 Jesse Barfield	.10	.04	.01
☐ U47 Alvaro Espinoza	.10	.04	.01
☐ U48 Bob Geren	.08	.03	.01
☐ U49 Mel Hall	.10	.04	.01
☐ U50 Andy Hawkins	.05	.02	.00
☐ U51 Hensley Meulens	.40	.16	.04
☐ U52 Steve Sax	.12	.05	.01
☐ U53 Deion Sanders	.60	.25	.06
☐ U54 Rickey Henderson	.35	.15	.03
☐ U55 Mike Moore	.12	.05	.01
☐ U56 Tony Phillips	.08	.03	.01
☐ U57 Greg Briley	.15	.06	.01
☐ U58 Gene Harris	.10	.04	.01
☐ U59 Randy Johnson	.12	.05	.01
☐ U60 Jeffrey Leonard	.05	.02	.00
☐ U61 Dennis Powell	.05	.02	.00
☐ U62 Omar Vizquel	.08	.03	.01
☐ U63 Kevin Brown	.08	.03	.01
☐ U64 Julio Franco	.15	.06	.01
☐ U65 Jamie Moyer	.05	.02	.00
☐ U66 Rafael Palmeiro	.15	.06	.01
☐ U67 Nolan Ryan	1.50	.60	.15
☐ U68 Francisco Cabrera	.25	.10	.02
☐ U69 Junior Felix	.15	.06	.01
☐ U70 Al Leiter	.08	.03	.01
☐ U71 Alex Sanchez	.08	.03	.01
☐ U72 Geronimo Berroa	.05	.02	.00
☐ U73 Derek Lilliquist	.08	.03	.01
☐ U74 Lonnie Smith	.12	.05	.01
☐ U75 Jeff Treadway	.10	.04	.01
☐ U76 Paul Kilgus	.08	.03	.01
☐ U77 Lloyd McClendon	.08	.03	.01
☐ U78 Scott Sanderson	.08	.03	.01
☐ U79 Dwight Smith	.12	.05	.01
☐ U80 Jerome Walton	.40	.16	.04
☐ U81 Mitch Williams	.08	.03	.01
☐ U82 Steve Wilson	.08	.03	.01
☐ U83 Todd Benzinger	.08	.03	.01
☐ U84 Ken Griffey Sr.	.15	.06	.01
☐ U85 Rick Mahler	.05	.02	.00
☐ U86 Rolando Roomes	.08	.03	.01
☐ U87 Scott Scudder	.20	.08	.02
☐ U88 Jim Clancy	.05	.02	.00
☐ U89 Rick Rhoden	.05	.02	.00
☐ U90 Dan Schatzeder	.05	.02	.00
☐ U91 Mike Morgan	.08	.03	.01
☐ U92 Eddie Murray	.12	.05	.01
☐ U93 Willie Randolph	.10	.04	.01
☐ U94 Ray Searage	.05	.02	.00
☐ U95 Mike Aldrete	.05	.02	.00
☐ U96 Kevin Gross	.08	.03	.01
☐ U97 Mark Langston	.10	.04	.01
☐ U98 Spike Owen	.05	.02	.00
☐ U99 Zane Smith	.10	.04	.01
☐ U100 Don Aase	.05	.02	.00
☐ U101 Barry Lyons	.05	.02	.00
☐ U102 Juan Samuel	.10	.04	.01
☐ U103 Wally Whitehurst	.10	.04	.01
☐ U104 Dennis Cook	.08	.03	.01
☐ U105 Len Dykstra	.10	.04	.01
☐ U106 Charlie Hayes	.08	.03	.01
☐ U107 Tommy Herr	.08	.03	.01
☐ U108 Ken Howell	.08	.03	.01
☐ U109 John Kruk	.08	.03	.01
☐ U110 Roger McDowell	.08	.03	.01
☐ U111 Terry Mulholland	.10	.04	.01
☐ U112 Jeff Parrett	.05	.02	.00
☐ U113 Neal Heaton	.05	.02	.00
☐ U114 Jeff King	.10	.04	.01
☐ U115 Randy Kramer	.08	.03	.01
☐ U116 Bill Landrum	.08	.03	.01
☐ U117 Cris Carpenter	.08	.03	.01
☐ U118 Frank DiPino	.05	.02	.00
☐ U119 Ken Hill	.10	.04	.01
☐ U120 Dan Quisenberry	.10	.04	.01
☐ U121 Milt Thompson	.08	.03	.01
☐ U122 Todd Zeile	1.50	.60	.15
☐ U123 Jack Clark	.10	.04	.01
☐ U124 Bruce Hurst	.08	.03	.01
☐ U125 Mark Parent	.08	.03	.01
☐ U126 Bip Roberts	.12	.05	.01
☐ U127 Jeff Brantley UER (photo actually Joe Kmak)	.20	.08	.02
☐ U128 Terry Kennedy	.05	.02	.00

☐ U129 Mike LaCoss	.05	.02	.00
☐ U130 Greg Litton	.10	.04	.01
☐ U131 Mike Schmidt	.90	.40	.09
☐ U132 Checklist 1-132	.05	.01	.00

1990 Fleer

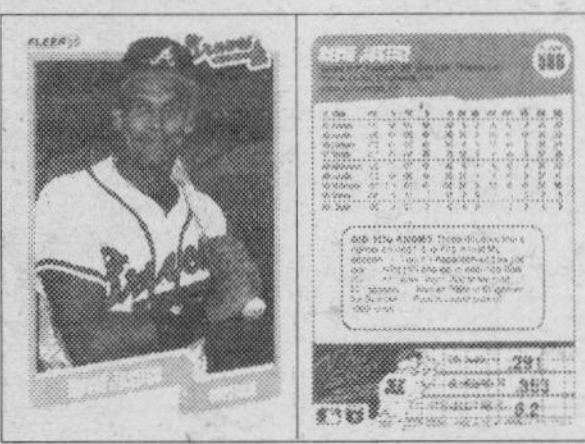

The 1990 Fleer set contains 660 standard-size (2 1/2" by 3 1/2") cards. The outer front borders are white; the inner, ribbon-like borders are different depending on the team. The vertically-oriented backs are white, red, pink, and navy. The set is again ordered numerically by teams, followed by combination cards, rookie prospect pairs, and checklists. Just as with the 1989 set, Fleer incorrectly anticipated the outcome of the 1989 Playoffs according to the team ordering. The A's, listed first, did win the World Series, but their opponents were the Giants, not the Cubs. Fleer later reported that they merely arranged the teams according to regular season team record due to the early printing date. The complete team ordering is as follows: Oakland A's (1-24), Chicago Cubs (25-49), San Francisco Giants (50-75), Toronto Blue Jays (76-99), Kansas City Royals (100-124), California Angels (125-148), San Diego Padres (149-171), Baltimore Orioles (172-195), New York Mets (196-219), Houston Astros (220-241), St. Louis Cardinals (242-265), Boston Red Sox (266-289), Texas Rangers (290-315), Milwaukee Brewers (316-340), Montreal Expos (341-364), Minnesota Twins (365-388), Los Angeles Dodgers (389-411), Cincinnati Reds (412-435), New York Yankees (436-458), Pittsburgh Pirates (459-482), Cleveland Indians (483-504), Seattle Mariners (505-528), Chicago White Sox (529-551), Philadelphia Phillies (552-573), Atlanta Braves (574-598), and Detroit Tigers (599-620). The key rookie cards in this set are Alex Cole, Delino DeShields, Juan Gonzalez, Marquis Grissom, Dave Justice, Kevin Maas, and Ben McDonald. The following five cards have minor printing differences, 6, 162, 260, 469, and 550; these differences are so minor that collectors have deemed them not significant enough to effect a price differential. Fleer also produced a separate set for Canada. The Canadian set only differs from the regular set in that it shows copyright "FLEER LTD./LTEE PTD. IN CANADA" on the card backs. Although these Canadian cards were undoubtedly produced in much lesser quantities compared to the U.S. issue, the fact that the versions are so similar has kept the demand (and the price differential) for the Canadian cards down.

	MINT	EXC	G-VG
COMPLETE SET (660)	18.00	7.50	2.50
COMMON PLAYER (1-660)	.03	.01	.00
☐ 1 Lance Blankenship	.06	.02	.00
☐ 2 Todd Burns	.03	.01	.00
☐ 3 Jose Canseco	.40	.16	.04
☐ 4 Jim Corsi	.03	.01	.00
☐ 5 Storm Davis	.03	.01	.00
☐ 6 Dennis Eckersley	.08	.03	.01
☐ 7 Mike Gallego	.03	.01	.00
☐ 8 Ron Hassey	.03	.01	.00
☐ 9 Dave Henderson	.08	.03	.01
☐ 10 Rickey Henderson	.25	.10	.02
☐ 11 Rick Honeycutt	.03	.01	.00
☐ 12 Stan Javier	.03	.01	.00
☐ 13 Felix Jose	.20	.08	.02
☐ 14 Carney Lansford	.06	.02	.00
☐ 15 Mark McGwire	.15	.06	.01
☐ 16 Mike Moore	.06	.02	.00
☐ 17 Gene Nelson	.03	.01	.00
☐ 18 Dave Parker	.08	.03	.01
☐ 19 Tony Phillips	.03	.01	.00
☐ 20 Terry Steinbach	.06	.02	.00
☐ 21 Dave Stewart	.08	.03	.01
☐ 22 Walt Weiss	.06	.02	.00
☐ 23 Bob Welch	.08	.03	.01
☐ 24 Curt Young	.03	.01	.00
☐ 25 Paul Assenmacher	.03	.01	.00
☐ 26 Damon Berryhill	.03	.01	.00
☐ 27 Mike Bielecki	.03	.01	.00
☐ 28 Kevin Blankenship	.03	.01	.00
☐ 29 Andre Dawson	.10	.04	.01
☐ 30 Shawon Dunston	.08	.03	.01
☐ 31 Joe Girardi	.03	.01	.00
☐ 32 Mark Grace	.12	.05	.01

Card			
☐ 33 Mike Harkey	.06	.02	.00
☐ 34 Paul Kilgus	.03	.01	.00
☐ 35 Les Lancaster	.03	.01	.00
☐ 36 Vance Law	.03	.01	.00
☐ 37 Greg Maddux	.06	.02	.00
☐ 38 Lloyd McClendon	.03	.01	.00
☐ 39 Jeff Pico	.03	.01	.00
☐ 40 Ryne Sandberg	.30	.12	.03
☐ 41 Scott Sanderson	.03	.01	.00
☐ 42 Dwight Smith	.06	.02	.00
☐ 43 Rick Sutcliffe	.06	.02	.00
☐ 44 Jerome Walton	.08	.03	.01
☐ 45 Mitch Webster	.03	.01	.00
☐ 46 Curt Wilkerson	.03	.01	.00
☐ 47 Dean Wilkins	.10	.04	.01
☐ 48 Mitch Williams	.03	.01	.00
☐ 49 Steve Wilson	.03	.01	.00
☐ 50 Steve Bedrosian	.03	.01	.00
☐ 51 Mike Benjamin	.10	.04	.01
☐ 52 Jeff Brantley	.08	.03	.01
☐ 53 Brett Butler	.08	.03	.01
☐ 54 Will Clark UER ("Did You Know" says first in runs, should say tied for first)	.30	.12	.03
☐ 55 Kelly Downs	.03	.01	.00
☐ 56 Scott Garrelts	.03	.01	.00
☐ 57 Atlee Hammaker	.03	.01	.00
☐ 58 Terry Kennedy	.03	.01	.00
☐ 59 Mike LaCoss	.03	.01	.00
☐ 60 Craig Lefferts	.03	.01	.00
☐ 61 Greg Litton	.03	.01	.00
☐ 62 Candy Maldonado	.03	.01	.00
☐ 63 Kirt Manwaring UER (no '88 Phoenix stats as noted in box)	.03	.01	.00
☐ 64 Randy McCament	.08	.03	.01
☐ 65 Kevin Mitchell	.10	.04	.01
☐ 66 Donell Nixon	.03	.01	.00
☐ 67 Ken Oberkfell	.03	.01	.00
☐ 68 Rick Reuschel	.06	.02	.00
☐ 69 Ernest Riles	.03	.01	.00
☐ 70 Don Robinson	.03	.01	.00
☐ 71 Pat Sheridan	.03	.01	.00
☐ 72 Chris Speier	.03	.01	.00
☐ 73 Robby Thompson	.03	.01	.00
☐ 74 Jose Uribe	.03	.01	.00
☐ 75 Matt Williams	.15	.06	.01
☐ 76 George Bell	.08	.03	.01
☐ 77 Pat Borders	.03	.01	.00
☐ 78 John Cerutti	.03	.01	.00
☐ 79 Junior Felix	.06	.02	.00
☐ 80 Tony Fernandez	.06	.02	.00
☐ 81 Mike Flanagan	.03	.01	.00
☐ 82 Mauro Gozzo	.08	.03	.01
☐ 83 Kelly Gruber	.08	.03	.01
☐ 84 Tom Henke	.06	.02	.00
☐ 85 Jimmy Key	.06	.02	.00
☐ 86 Manny Lee	.03	.01	.00
☐ 87 Nelson Liriano UER (should say "led the IL" instead of "led the TL")	.03	.01	.00
☐ 88 Lee Mazzilli	.03	.01	.00
☐ 89 Fred McGriff	.10	.04	.01
☐ 90 Lloyd Moseby	.03	.01	.00
☐ 91 Rance Mulliniks	.03	.01	.00
☐ 92 Alex Sanchez	.06	.02	.00
☐ 93 Dave Stieb	.08	.03	.01
☐ 94 Todd Stottlemyre	.08	.03	.01
☐ 95 Duane Ward UER (double line of '87 Syracuse stats)	.06	.02	.00
☐ 96 David Wells	.06	.02	.00
☐ 97 Ernie Whitt	.03	.01	.00
☐ 98 Frank Wills	.03	.01	.00
☐ 99 Mookie Wilson	.03	.01	.00
☐ 100 Kevin Appier	.15	.06	.01
☐ 101 Luis Aquino	.03	.01	.00
☐ 102 Bob Boone	.06	.02	.00
☐ 103 George Brett	.12	.05	.01
☐ 104 Jose DeJesus	.03	.01	.00
☐ 105 Luis De Los Santos	.03	.01	.00
☐ 106 Jim Eisenreich	.03	.01	.00
☐ 107 Steve Farr	.03	.01	.00
☐ 108 Tom Gordon	.06	.02	.00
☐ 109 Mark Gubicza	.06	.02	.00
☐ 110 Bo Jackson	.40	.16	.04
☐ 111 Terry Leach	.03	.01	.00
☐ 112 Charlie Leibrandt	.03	.01	.00
☐ 113 Rick Luecken	.08	.03	.01
☐ 114 Mike Macfarlane	.03	.01	.00
☐ 115 Jeff Montgomery	.03	.01	.00
☐ 116 Bret Saberhagen	.08	.03	.01
☐ 117 Kevin Seitzer	.06	.02	.00
☐ 118 Kurt Stillwell	.03	.01	.00
☐ 119 Pat Tabler	.03	.01	.00
☐ 120 Danny Tartabull	.08	.03	.01
☐ 121 Gary Thurman	.03	.01	.00
☐ 122 Frank White	.03	.01	.00
☐ 123 Willie Wilson	.06	.02	.00
☐ 124 Matt Winters	.10	.04	.01
☐ 125 Jim Abbott	.17	.07	.01
☐ 126 Tony Armas	.03	.01	.00
☐ 127 Dante Bichette	.06	.02	.00
☐ 128 Bert Blyleven	.08	.03	.01
☐ 129 Chili Davis	.06	.02	.00
☐ 130 Brian Downing	.03	.01	.00
☐ 131 Mike Fetters	.08	.03	.01
☐ 132 Chuck Finley	.08	.03	.01
☐ 133 Willie Fraser	.03	.01	.00
☐ 134 Bryan Harvey	.06	.02	.00
☐ 135 Jack Howell	.03	.01	.00
☐ 136 Wally Joyner	.08	.03	.01
☐ 137 Jeff Manto	.08	.03	.01
☐ 138 Kirk McCaskill	.03	.01	.00

□ 139 Bob McClure ....03 .01 .00
□ 140 Greg Minton ....03 .01 .00
□ 141 Lance Parrish ....08 .03 .01
□ 142 Dan Petry ....03 .01 .00
□ 143 Johnny Ray ....03 .01 .00
□ 144 Dick Schofield ....03 .01 .00
□ 145 Lee Stevens ....15 .06 .01
□ 146 Claudell Washington ......03 .01 .00
□ 147 Devon White ....06 .02 .00
□ 148 Mike Witt ....03 .01 .00
□ 149 Roberto Alomar ....15 .06 .01
□ 150 Sandy Alomar Jr. ....10 .04 .01
□ 151 Andy Benes ....15 .06 .01
□ 152 Jack Clark ....08 .03 .01
□ 153 Pat Clements ....03 .01 .00
□ 154 Joey Cora ....03 .01 .00
□ 155 Mark Davis ....06 .02 .00
□ 156 Mark Grant ....03 .01 .00
□ 157 Tony Gwynn ....15 .06 .01
□ 158 Greg W. Harris ....03 .01 .00
□ 159 Bruce Hurst ....06 .02 .00
□ 160 Darrin Jackson ....06 .02 .00
□ 161 Chris James ....06 .02 .00
□ 162 Carmelo Martinez ....03 .01 .00
□ 163 Mike Pagliarulo ....03 .01 .00
□ 164 Mark Parent ....03 .01 .00
□ 165 Dennis Rasmussen ....03 .01 .00
□ 166 Bip Roberts ....03 .01 .00
□ 167 Benito Santiago ....08 .03 .01
□ 168 Calvin Schiraldi ....03 .01 .00
□ 169 Eric Show ....03 .01 .00
□ 170 Garry Templeton ....03 .01 .00
□ 171 Ed Whitson ....03 .01 .00
□ 172 Brady Anderson ....03 .01 .00
□ 173 Jeff Ballard ....03 .01 .00
□ 174 Phil Bradley ....03 .01 .00
□ 175 Mike Devereaux ....03 .01 .00
□ 176 Steve Finley ....10 .04 .01
□ 177 Pete Harnisch ....06 .02 .00
□ 178 Kevin Hickey ....03 .01 .00
□ 179 Brian Holton ....03 .01 .00
□ 180 Ben McDonald ....75 .30 .07
□ 181 Bob Melvin ....03 .01 .00
□ 182 Bob Milacki ....03 .01 .00
□ 183 Randy Milligan UER ....06 .02 .00
(double line of
'87 stats)
□ 184 Gregg Olson ....15 .06 .01
□ 185 Joe Orsulak ....03 .01 .00
□ 186 Bill Ripken ....03 .01 .00
□ 187 Cal Ripken ....30 .12 .03
□ 188 Dave Schmidt ....03 .01 .00
□ 189 Larry Sheets ....03 .01 .00
□ 190 Mickey Tettleton ....06 .02 .00
□ 191 Mark Thurmond ....03 .01 .00
□ 192 Jay Tibbs ....03 .01 .00
□ 193 Jim Traber ....03 .01 .00
□ 194 Mark Williamson ....03 .01 .00
□ 195 Craig Worthington ....03 .01 .00
□ 196 Don Aase ....03 .01 .00
□ 197 Blaine Beatty ....08 .03 .01
□ 198 Mark Carreon ....03 .01 .00
□ 199 Gary Carter ....08 .03 .01
□ 200 David Cone ....06 .02 .00
□ 201 Ron Darling ....06 .02 .00
□ 202 Kevin Elster ....03 .01 .00
□ 203 Sid Fernandez ....06 .02 .00
□ 204 Dwight Gooden ....10 .04 .01
□ 205 Keith Hernandez ....06 .02 .00
□ 206 Jeff Innis ....08 .03 .01
□ 207 Gregg Jefferies ....10 .04 .01
□ 208 Howard Johnson ....08 .03 .01
□ 209 Barry Lyons UER ....03 .01 .00
(double line of
'87 stats)
□ 210 Dave Magadan ....06 .02 .00
□ 211 Kevin McReynolds ....08 .03 .01
□ 212 Jeff Musselman ....03 .01 .00
□ 213 Randy Myers ....03 .01 .00
□ 214 Bob Ojeda ....03 .01 .00
□ 215 Juan Samuel ....06 .02 .00
□ 216 Mackey Sasser ....03 .01 .00
□ 217 Darryl Strawberry ....25 .10 .02
□ 218 Tim Teufel ....03 .01 .00
□ 219 Frank Viola ....08 .03 .01
□ 220 Juan Agosto ....03 .01 .00
□ 221 Larry Andersen ....03 .01 .00
□ 222 Eric Anthony ....17 .07 .01
□ 223 Kevin Bass ....03 .01 .00
□ 224 Craig Biggio ....08 .03 .01
□ 225 Ken Caminiti ....03 .01 .00
□ 226 Jim Clancy ....03 .01 .00
□ 227 Danny Darwin ....03 .01 .00
□ 228 Glenn Davis ....08 .03 .01
□ 229 Jim Deshaies ....03 .01 .00
□ 230 Bill Doran ....03 .01 .00
□ 231 Bob Forsch ....03 .01 .00
□ 232 Brian Meyer ....06 .02 .00
□ 233 Terry Puhl ....03 .01 .00
□ 234 Rafael Ramirez ....03 .01 .00
□ 235 Rick Rhoden ....03 .01 .00
□ 236 Dan Schatzeder ....03 .01 .00
□ 237 Mike Scott ....08 .03 .01
□ 238 Dave Smith ....03 .01 .00
□ 239 Alex Trevino ....03 .01 .00
□ 240 Glenn Wilson ....03 .01 .00
□ 241 Gerald Young ....03 .01 .00
□ 242 Tom Brunansky ....06 .02 .00
□ 243 Cris Carpenter ....03 .01 .00
□ 244 Alex Cole ....30 .12 .03
□ 245 Vince Coleman ....08 .03 .01
□ 246 John Costello ....03 .01 .00
□ 247 Ken Dayley ....03 .01 .00
□ 248 Jose DeLeon ....03 .01 .00
□ 249 Frank DiPino ....03 .01 .00
□ 250 Pedro Guerrero ....08 .03 .01

☐ 251 Ken Hill	.03	.01	.00
☐ 252 Joe Magrane	.03	.01	.00
☐ 253 Willie McGee UER	.08	.03	.01
(no decimal point before 353)			
☐ 254 John Morris	.03	.01	.00
☐ 255 Jose Oquendo	.03	.01	.00
☐ 256 Tony Pena	.06	.02	.00
☐ 257 Terry Pendleton	.08	.03	.01
☐ 258 Ted Power	.03	.01	.00
☐ 259 Dan Quisenberry	.06	.02	.00
☐ 260 Ozzie Smith	.10	.04	.01
☐ 261 Scott Terry	.03	.01	.00
☐ 262 Milt Thompson	.03	.01	.00
☐ 263 Denny Walling	.03	.01	.00
☐ 264 Todd Worrell	.06	.02	.00
☐ 265 Todd Zeile	.40	.16	.04
☐ 266 Marty Barrett	.03	.01	.00
☐ 267 Mike Boddicker	.03	.01	.00
☐ 268 Wade Boggs	.15	.06	.01
☐ 269 Ellis Burks	.08	.03	.01
☐ 270 Rick Cerone	.03	.01	.00
☐ 271 Roger Clemens	.30	.12	.03
☐ 272 John Dopson	.03	.01	.00
☐ 273 Nick Esasky	.03	.01	.00
☐ 274 Dwight Evans	.06	.02	.00
☐ 275 Wes Gardner	.03	.01	.00
☐ 276 Rich Gedman	.03	.01	.00
☐ 277 Mike Greenwell	.12	.05	.01
☐ 278 Danny Heep	.03	.01	.00
☐ 279 Eric Hetzel	.03	.01	.00
☐ 280 Dennis Lamp	.03	.01	.00
☐ 281 Rob Murphy UER	.03	.01	.00
('89 stats say Reds, should say Red Sox)			
☐ 282 Joe Price	.03	.01	.00
☐ 283 Carlos Quintana	.08	.03	.01
☐ 284 Jody Reed	.06	.02	.00
☐ 285 Luis Rivera	.03	.01	.00
☐ 286 Kevin Romine	.03	.01	.00
☐ 287 Lee Smith	.06	.02	.00
☐ 288 Mike Smithson	.03	.01	.00
☐ 289 Bob Stanley	.03	.01	.00
☐ 290 Harold Baines	.08	.03	.01
☐ 291 Kevin Brown	.03	.01	.00
☐ 292 Steve Buechele	.03	.01	.00
☐ 293 Scott Coolbaugh	.10	.04	.01
☐ 294 Jack Daugherty	.08	.03	.01
☐ 295 Cecil Espy	.03	.01	.00
☐ 296 Julio Franco	.10	.04	.01
☐ 297 Juan Gonzalez	2.00	.80	.20
☐ 298 Cecilio Guante	.03	.01	.00
☐ 299 Drew Hall	.03	.01	.00
☐ 300 Charlie Hough	.03	.01	.00
☐ 301 Pete Incaviglia	.06	.02	.00
☐ 302 Mike Jeffcoat	.03	.01	.00
☐ 303 Chad Kreuter	.03	.01	.00
☐ 304 Jeff Kunkel	.03	.01	.00
☐ 305 Rick Leach	.03	.01	.00
☐ 306 Fred Manrique	.03	.01	.00
☐ 307 Jamie Moyer	.03	.01	.00
☐ 308 Rafael Palmeiro	.12	.05	.01
☐ 309 Geno Petralli	.03	.01	.00
☐ 310 Kevin Reimer	.03	.01	.00
☐ 311 Kenny Rogers	.06	.02	.00
☐ 312 Jeff Russell	.03	.01	.00
☐ 313 Nolan Ryan	.50	.20	.05
☐ 314 Ruben Sierra	.17	.07	.01
☐ 315 Bobby Witt	.06	.02	.00
☐ 316 Chris Bosio	.03	.01	.00
☐ 317 Glenn Braggs UER	.03	.01	.00
(stats say 111 K's, but bio says 117 K's)			
☐ 318 Greg Brock	.03	.01	.00
☐ 319 Chuck Crim	.03	.01	.00
☐ 320 Rob Deer	.06	.02	.00
☐ 321 Mike Felder	.03	.01	.00
☐ 322 Tom Filer	.03	.01	.00
☐ 323 Tony Fossas	.06	.02	.00
☐ 324 Jim Gantner	.03	.01	.00
☐ 325 Darryl Hamilton	.06	.02	.00
☐ 326 Teddy Higuera	.03	.01	.00
☐ 327 Mark Knudson	.03	.01	.00
☐ 328 Bill Krueger UER	.03	.01	.00
('86 stats missing)			
☐ 329 Tim McIntosh	.12	.05	.01
☐ 330 Paul Molitor	.08	.03	.01
☐ 331 Jaime Navarro	.06	.02	.00
☐ 332 Charlie O'Brien	.03	.01	.00
☐ 333 Jeff Peterek	.08	.03	.01
☐ 334 Dan Plesac	.03	.01	.00
☐ 335 Jerry Reuss	.03	.01	.00
☐ 336 Gary Sheffield UER	.08	.03	.01
(bio says played for 3 teams in '87, but stats say in '88)			
☐ 337 Bill Spiers	.06	.02	.00
☐ 338 B.J. Surhoff	.06	.02	.00
☐ 339 Greg Vaughn	.50	.20	.05
☐ 340 Robin Yount	.12	.05	.01
☐ 341 Hubie Brooks	.06	.02	.00
☐ 342 Tim Burke	.03	.01	.00
☐ 343 Mike Fitzgerald	.03	.01	.00
☐ 344 Tom Foley	.03	.01	.00
☐ 345 Andres Galarraga	.06	.02	.00
☐ 346 Damaso Garcia	.03	.01	.00
☐ 347 Marquis Grissom	.40	.16	.04
☐ 348 Kevin Gross	.03	.01	.00
☐ 349 Joe Hesketh	.03	.01	.00
☐ 350 Jeff Huson	.08	.03	.01
☐ 351 Wallace Johnson	.03	.01	.00
☐ 352 Mark Langston	.08	.03	.01
☐ 353A Dave Martinez	3.00	1.25	.30
(yellow on front)			
☐ 353B Dave Martinez	.06	.02	.00
(red on front)			

☐ 354 Dennis Martinez UER ..... .06 .02 .00
('87 ERA is 616,
should be 6.16)
☐ 355 Andy McGaffigan .... .03 .01 .00
☐ 356 Otis Nixon .... .06 .02 .00
☐ 357 Spike Owen .... .03 .01 .00
☐ 358 Pascual Perez .... .03 .01 .00
☐ 359 Tim Raines .... .08 .03 .01
☐ 360 Nelson Santovenia .... .03 .01 .00
☐ 361 Bryn Smith .... .03 .01 .00
☐ 362 Zane Smith .... .06 .02 .00
☐ 363 Larry Walker .... .25 .10 .02
☐ 364 Tim Wallach .... .06 .02 .00
☐ 365 Rick Aguilera .... .06 .02 .00
☐ 366 Allan Anderson .... .03 .01 .00
☐ 367 Wally Backman .... .03 .01 .00
☐ 368 Doug Baker .... .03 .01 .00
☐ 369 Juan Berenguer .... .03 .01 .00
☐ 370 Randy Bush .... .03 .01 .00
☐ 371 Carmen Castillo .... .03 .01 .00
☐ 372 Mike Dyer .... .08 .03 .01
☐ 373 Gary Gaetti .... .06 .02 .00
☐ 374 Greg Gagne .... .03 .01 .00
☐ 375 Dan Gladden .... .03 .01 .00
☐ 376 German Gonzalez UER ... .03 .01 .00
(bio says 31 saves in
'88, but stats say 30)
☐ 377 Brian Harper .... .03 .01 .00
☐ 378 Kent Hrbek .... .08 .03 .01
☐ 379 Gene Larkin .... .03 .01 .00
☐ 380 Tim Laudner UER .... .03 .01 .00
(no decimal point
before '85 BA of 238)
☐ 381 John Moses .... .03 .01 .00
☐ 382 Al Newman .... .03 .01 .00
☐ 383 Kirby Puckett .... .20 .08 .02
☐ 384 Shane Rawley .... .03 .01 .00
☐ 385 Jeff Reardon .... .06 .02 .00
☐ 386 Roy Smith .... .03 .01 .00
☐ 387 Gary Wayne .... .08 .03 .01
☐ 388 Dave West .... .03 .01 .00
☐ 389 Tim Belcher .... .06 .02 .00
☐ 390 Tim Crews UER .... .03 .01 .00
(stats say 163 IP for
'83, but bio says 136)
☐ 391 Mike Davis .... .03 .01 .00
☐ 392 Rick Dempsey .... .03 .01 .00
☐ 393 Kirk Gibson .... .08 .03 .01
☐ 394 Jose Gonzalez .... .03 .01 .00
☐ 395 Alfredo Griffin .... .03 .01 .00
☐ 396 Jeff Hamilton .... .03 .01 .00
☐ 397 Lenny Harris .... .03 .01 .00
☐ 398 Mickey Hatcher .... .03 .01 .00
☐ 399 Orel Hershiser .... .08 .03 .01
☐ 400 Jay Howell .... .03 .01 .00
☐ 401 Mike Marshall .... .06 .02 .00
☐ 402 Ramon Martinez .... .25 .10 .02
☐ 403 Mike Morgan .... .06 .02 .00
☐ 404 Eddie Murray .... .10 .04 .01
☐ 405 Alejandro Pena .... .06 .02 .00
☐ 406 Willie Randolph .... .06 .02 .00
☐ 407 Mike Scioscia .... .03 .01 .00
☐ 408 Ray Searage .... .03 .01 .00
☐ 409 Fernando Valenzuela ...... .08 .03 .01
☐ 410 Jose Vizcaino .... .12 .05 .01
☐ 411 John Wetteland .... .08 .03 .01
☐ 412 Jack Armstrong .... .08 .03 .01
☐ 413 Todd Benzinger UER ...... .03 .01 .00
(bio says .323 at
Pawtucket, but
stats say .321)
☐ 414 Tim Birtsas .... .03 .01 .00
☐ 415 Tom Browning .... .06 .02 .00
☐ 416 Norm Charlton .... .03 .01 .00
☐ 417 Eric Davis .... .10 .04 .01
☐ 418 Rob Dibble .... .06 .02 .00
☐ 419 John Franco .... .03 .01 .00
☐ 420 Ken Griffey Sr. .... .06 .02 .00
☐ 421 Chris Hammond .... .25 .10 .02
(no 1989 used for
"Did Not Play" stat,
actually did play for
Nashville in 1989)
☐ 422 Danny Jackson .... .03 .01 .00
☐ 423 Barry Larkin .... .12 .05 .01
☐ 424 Tim Leary .... .06 .02 .00
☐ 425 Rick Mahler .... .03 .01 .00
☐ 426 Joe Oliver .... .06 .02 .00
☐ 427 Paul O'Neill .... .06 .02 .00
☐ 428 Luis Quinones UER .... .03 .01 .00
('86-'88 stats are
omitted from card but
included in totals)
☐ 429 Jeff Reed .... .03 .01 .00
☐ 430 Jose Rijo .... .08 .03 .01
☐ 431 Ron Robinson .... .03 .01 .00
☐ 432 Rolando Roomes .... .03 .01 .00
☐ 433 Chris Sabo .... .10 .04 .01
☐ 434 Scott Scudder .... .06 .02 .00
☐ 435 Herm Winningham .... .03 .01 .00
☐ 436 Steve Balboni .... .03 .01 .00
☐ 437 Jesse Barfield .... .06 .02 .00
☐ 438 Mike Blowers .... .10 .04 .01
☐ 439 Tom Brookens .... .03 .01 .00
☐ 440 Greg Cadaret .... .03 .01 .00
☐ 441 Alvaro Espinoza UER .... .03 .01 .00
(career games say
218, should be 219)
☐ 442 Bob Geren .... .03 .01 .00
☐ 443 Lee Guetterman .... .03 .01 .00
☐ 444 Mel Hall .... .06 .02 .00
☐ 445 Andy Hawkins .... .03 .01 .00
☐ 446 Roberto Kelly .... .08 .03 .01
☐ 447 Don Mattingly .... .20 .08 .02
☐ 448 Lance McCullers .... .03 .01 .00
☐ 449 Hensley Meulens .... .12 .05 .01

□ 450 Dale Mohorcic	.03	.01	.00
□ 451 Clay Parker	.03	.01	.00
□ 452 Eric Plunk	.03	.01	.00
□ 453 Dave Righetti	.06	.02	.00
□ 454 Deion Sanders	.15	.06	.01
□ 455 Steve Sax	.06	.02	.00
□ 456 Don Slaught	.03	.01	.00
□ 457 Walt Terrell	.03	.01	.00
□ 458 Dave Winfield	.10	.04	.01
□ 459 Jay Bell	.03	.01	.00
□ 460 Rafael Belliard	.03	.01	.00
□ 461 Barry Bonds	.17	.07	.01
□ 462 Bobby Bonilla	.15	.06	.01
□ 463 Sid Bream	.03	.01	.00
□ 464 Benny Distefano	.03	.01	.00
□ 465 Doug Drabek	.06	.02	.00
□ 466 Jim Gott	.03	.01	.00
□ 467 Billy Hatcher UER (.1 hits for Cubs in 1984)	.06	.02	.00
□ 468 Neal Heaton	.03	.01	.00
□ 469 Jeff King	.06	.02	.00
□ 470 Bob Kipper	.03	.01	.00
□ 471 Randy Kramer	.03	.01	.00
□ 472 Bill Landrum	.03	.01	.00
□ 473 Mike LaValliere	.03	.01	.00
□ 474 Jose Lind	.03	.01	.00
□ 475 Junior Ortiz	.03	.01	.00
□ 476 Gary Redus	.03	.01	.00
□ 477 Rick Reed	.08	.03	.01
□ 478 R.J. Reynolds	.03	.01	.00
□ 479 Jeff Robinson	.03	.01	.00
□ 480 John Smiley	.06	.02	.00
□ 481 Andy Van Slyke	.08	.03	.01
□ 482 Bob Walk	.03	.01	.00
□ 483 Andy Allanson	.03	.01	.00
□ 484 Scott Bailes	.03	.01	.00
□ 485 Joey Belle UER (has Jay Bell "Did You Know")	.50	.20	.05
□ 486 Bud Black	.03	.01	.00
□ 487 Jerry Browne	.03	.01	.00
□ 488 Tom Candiotti	.06	.02	.00
□ 489 Joe Carter	.10	.04	.01
□ 490 Dave Clark (no '84 stats)	.03	.01	.00
□ 491 John Farrell	.03	.01	.00
□ 492 Felix Fermin	.03	.01	.00
□ 493 Brook Jacoby	.03	.01	.00
□ 494 Dion James	.03	.01	.00
□ 495 Doug Jones	.03	.01	.00
□ 496 Brad Komminsk	.03	.01	.00
□ 497 Rod Nichols	.03	.01	.00
□ 498 Pete O'Brien	.03	.01	.00
□ 499 Steve Olin	.08	.03	.01
□ 500 Jesse Orosco	.03	.01	.00
□ 501 Joel Skinner	.03	.01	.00
□ 502 Cory Snyder	.06	.02	.00
□ 503 Greg Swindell	.06	.02	.00
□ 504 Rich Yett	.03	.01	.00
□ 505 Scott Bankhead	.06	.02	.00
□ 506 Scott Bradley	.03	.01	.00
□ 507 Greg Briley UER (28 SB's in bio, but 27 in stats)	.06	.02	.00
□ 508 Jay Buhner	.08	.03	.01
□ 509 Darnell Coles	.03	.01	.00
□ 510 Keith Comstock	.03	.01	.00
□ 511 Henry Cotto	.03	.01	.00
□ 512 Alvin Davis	.06	.02	.00
□ 513 Ken Griffey Jr.	1.50	.60	.15
□ 514 Erik Hanson	.08	.03	.01
□ 515 Gene Harris	.06	.02	.00
□ 516 Brian Holman	.06	.02	.00
□ 517 Mike Jackson	.03	.01	.00
□ 518 Randy Johnson	.06	.02	.00
□ 519 Jeffrey Leonard	.03	.01	.00
□ 520 Edgar Martinez	.10	.04	.01
□ 521 Dennis Powell	.03	.01	.00
□ 522 Jim Presley	.03	.01	.00
□ 523 Jerry Reed	.03	.01	.00
□ 524 Harold Reynolds	.06	.02	.00
□ 525 Mike Schooler	.06	.02	.00
□ 526 Bill Swift	.03	.01	.00
□ 527 Dave Valle	.03	.01	.00
□ 528 Omar Vizquel	.03	.01	.00
□ 529 Ivan Calderon	.06	.02	.00
□ 530 Carlton Fisk UER (Bellow Falls, should be Bellows Falls)	.12	.05	.01
□ 531 Scott Fletcher	.03	.01	.00
□ 532 Dave Gallagher	.03	.01	.00
□ 533 Ozzie Guillen	.06	.02	.00
□ 534 Greg Hibbard	.15	.06	.01
□ 535 Shawn Hillegas	.03	.01	.00
□ 536 Lance Johnson	.03	.01	.00
□ 537 Eric King	.03	.01	.00
□ 538 Ron Kittle	.06	.02	.00
□ 539 Steve Lyons	.03	.01	.00
□ 540 Carlos Martinez	.06	.02	.00
□ 541 Tom McCarthy	.08	.03	.01
□ 542 Matt Merullo (had 5 ML runs scored entering '90, not 6)	.06	.02	.00
□ 543 Donn Pall UER (stats say pro career began in '85, bio says '88)	.03	.01	.00
□ 544 Dan Pasqua	.03	.01	.00
□ 545 Ken Patterson	.03	.01	.00
□ 546 Melido Perez	.03	.01	.00
□ 547 Steve Rosenberg	.06	.02	.00
□ 548 Sammy Sosa	.25	.10	.02
□ 549 Bobby Thigpen	.06	.02	.00
□ 550 Robin Ventura	.50	.20	.05
□ 551 Greg Walker	.03	.01	.00

☐ 552	Don Carman	.03	.01	.00
☐ 553	Pat Combs (6 walks for Phillies in '89 in stats, brief bio says 4)	.06	.02	.00
☐ 554	Dennis Cook	.03	.01	.00
☐ 555	Darren Daulton	.03	.01	.00
☐ 556	Len Dykstra	.06	.02	.00
☐ 557	Curt Ford	.03	.01	.00
☐ 558	Charlie Hayes	.03	.01	.00
☐ 559	Von Hayes	.06	.02	.00
☐ 560	Tommy Herr	.03	.01	.00
☐ 561	Ken Howell	.03	.01	.00
☐ 562	Steve Jeltz	.03	.01	.00
☐ 563	Ron Jones	.03	.01	.00
☐ 564	Ricky Jordan UER (duplicate line of statistics on back)	.06	.02	.00
☐ 565	John Kruk	.03	.01	.00
☐ 566	Steve Lake	.03	.01	.00
☐ 567	Roger McDowell	.03	.01	.00
☐ 568	Terry Mulholland UER ("Did You Know" refers to Dave Magadan)	.06	.02	.00
☐ 569	Dwayne Murphy	.03	.01	.00
☐ 570	Jeff Parrett	.03	.01	.00
☐ 571	Randy Ready	.03	.01	.00
☐ 572	Bruce Ruffin	.03	.01	.00
☐ 573	Dickie Thon	.03	.01	.00
☐ 574	Jose Alvarez UER ('78 and '79 stats are reversed)	.03	.01	.00
☐ 575	Geronimo Berroa	.03	.01	.00
☐ 576	Jeff Blauser	.03	.01	.00
☐ 577	Joe Boever	.03	.01	.00
☐ 578	Marty Clary UER (no comma between city and state)	.03	.01	.00
☐ 579	Jody Davis	.03	.01	.00
☐ 580	Mark Eichhorn	.03	.01	.00
☐ 581	Darrell Evans	.06	.02	.00
☐ 582	Ron Gant	.25	.10	.02
☐ 583	Tom Glavine	.20	.08	.02
☐ 584	Tommy Greene	.30	.12	.03
☐ 585	Tommy Gregg	.03	.01	.00
☐ 586	Dave Justice UER (Actually had 16 2B in Sumter in '86)	2.50	1.00	.25
☐ 587	Mark Lemke	.10	.04	.01
☐ 588	Derek Lilliquist	.03	.01	.00
☐ 589	Oddibe McDowell	.03	.01	.00
☐ 590	Kent Mercker ERA (bio says 2.75 ERA, stats say 2.68 ERA)	.15	.06	.01
☐ 591	Dale Murphy	.10	.04	.01
☐ 592	Gerald Perry	.03	.01	.00
☐ 593	Lonnie Smith	.06	.02	.00
☐ 594	Pete Smith	.03	.01	.00
☐ 595	John Smoltz	.15	.06	.01
☐ 596	Mike Stanton UER (no comma between city and state)	.08	.03	.01
☐ 597	Andres Thomas	.03	.01	.00
☐ 598	Jeff Treadway	.03	.01	.00
☐ 599	Doyle Alexander	.03	.01	.00
☐ 600	Dave Bergman	.03	.01	.00
☐ 601	Brian DuBois	.10	.04	.01
☐ 602	Paul Gibson	.03	.01	.00
☐ 603	Mike Heath	.03	.01	.00
☐ 604	Mike Henneman	.03	.01	.00
☐ 605	Guillermo Hernandez	.03	.01	.00
☐ 606	Shawn Holman	.08	.03	.01
☐ 607	Tracy Jones	.03	.01	.00
☐ 608	Chet Lemon	.03	.01	.00
☐ 609	Fred Lynn	.06	.02	.00
☐ 610	Jack Morris	.08	.03	.01
☐ 611	Matt Nokes	.03	.01	.00
☐ 612	Gary Pettis	.03	.01	.00
☐ 613	Kevin Ritz	.10	.04	.01
☐ 614	Jeff Robinson ('88 stats are not in line)	.03	.01	.00
☐ 615	Steve Searcy	.03	.01	.00
☐ 616	Frank Tanana	.06	.02	.00
☐ 617	Alan Trammell	.08	.03	.01
☐ 618	Gary Ward	.03	.01	.00
☐ 619	Lou Whitaker	.06	.02	.00
☐ 620	Frank Williams	.03	.01	.00
☐ 621A	George Brett '80 ERR (had 10 .390 hitting seasons)	2.00	.80	.20
☐ 621B	George Brett '80 COR	.08	.03	.01
☐ 622	Fern.Valenzuela '81	.06	.02	.00
☐ 623	Dale Murphy '82	.08	.03	.01
☐ 624A	Cal Ripken '83 ERR (misspelled Ripkin on card back)	3.00	1.25	.30
☐ 624B	Cal Ripken '83 COR	.12	.05	.01
☐ 625	Ryne Sandberg '84	.12	.05	.01
☐ 626	Don Mattingly '85	.12	.05	.01
☐ 627	Roger Clemens '86	.12	.05	.01
☐ 628	George Bell '87	.08	.03	.01
☐ 629	Jose Canseco '88 UER (Reggie won MVP in '83, should say '73)	.20	.08	.02
☐ 630A	Will Clark '89 ERR (32 total bases on card back)	2.00	.80	.20
☐ 630B	Will Clark '89 COR (321 total bases; technically still an error, listing only 24 runs)	.15	.06	.01
☐ 631	Game Savers Mark Davis	.06	.02	.00

	Mitch Williams			
☐ 632	Boston Igniters	.12	.05	.01
	Wade Boggs			
	Mike Greenwell			
☐ 633	Starter and Stopper	.06	.02	.00
	Mark Gubicza			
	Jeff Russell			
☐ 634	League's Best Shortstops	.15	.06	.01
	Tony Fernandez			
	Cal Ripken			
☐ 635	Human Dynamos	.20	.08	.02
	Kirby Puckett			
	Bo Jackson			
☐ 636	300 Strikeout Club	.20	.08	.02
	Nolan Ryan			
	Mike Scott			
☐ 637	The Dynamic Duo	.15	.06	.01
	Will Clark			
	Kevin Mitchell			
☐ 638	AL All-Stars	.15	.06	.01
	Don Mattingly			
	Mark McGwire			
☐ 639	NL East Rivals	.12	.05	.01
	Howard Johnson			
	Ryne Sandberg			
☐ 640	Rudy Seanez	.17	.07	.01
	Colin Charland			
☐ 641	George Canale	1.25	.50	.12
	Kevin Maas UER (Canale listed as INF on front, 1B on back)			
☐ 642	Kelly Mann	.25	.10	.02
	Dave Hansen			
☐ 643	Greg Smith	.10	.04	.01
	Stu Tate			
☐ 644	Tom Drees	.12	.05	.01
	Dann Howitt			
☐ 645	Mike Roesler	.15	.06	.01
	Derrick May			
☐ 646	Scott Hemond	.20	.08	.02
	Mark Gardner			
☐ 647	John Orton	.20	.08	.02
	Scott Leius			
☐ 648	Rich Monteleone	.10	.04	.01
	Dana Williams			
☐ 649	Mike Huff	.15	.06	.01
	Steve Frey			
☐ 650	Chuck McElroy	.17	.07	.01
	Moises Alou			
☐ 651	Bobby Rose	.15	.06	.01
	Mike Hartley			
☐ 652	Matt Kinzer	.10	.04	.01
	Wayne Edwards			
☐ 653	Delino DeShields	.45	.18	.04
	Jason Grimsley			
☐ 654	CL: A's/Cubs Giants/Blue Jays	.06	.01	.00
☐ 655	CL: Royals/Angels Padres/Orioles	.06	.01	.00
☐ 656	CL: Mets/Astros Cards/Red Sox	.06	.01	.00
☐ 657	CL: Rangers/Brewers Expos/Twins	.06	.01	.00
☐ 658	CL: Dodgers/Reds Yankees/Pirates	.06	.01	.00
☐ 659	CL: Indians/Mariners White Sox/Phillies	.06	.01	.00
☐ 660A	CL: Braves/Tigers Specials/Checklists (Checklist-660 in smaller print on card front)	.06	.01	.00
☐ 660B	CL: Braves/Tigers Specials/Checklists (Checklist-660 in normal print on card front)	.06	.01	.00

1990 Fleer Update

The 1990 Fleer Update set contains 132 standard-size (2 1/2" by 3 1/2") cards. This set marked the seventh consecutive year Fleer issued an end of season Update set. The set was issued exclusively as a boxed set through hobby dealers. The set is checklisted alphabetically by team for each league and then alphabetically within each team. The fronts are styled the same as the 1990 Fleer regular issue set. The backs are numbered with the prefix U for Update. The key rookies in this set are Alex Fernandez, Travis Fryman, Jose Offerman, John Olerud, Frank Thomas, and Mark Whiten.

	MINT	EXC	G-VG
COMPLETE SET (132)	10.00	4.50	1.25
COMMON PLAYER (1-132)	.05	.02	.00
☐ U1 Steve Avery	1.25	.30	.06
☐ U2 Francisco Cabrera	.10	.04	.01
☐ U3 Nick Esasky	.05	.02	.00
☐ U4 Jim Kremers	.10	.04	.01
☐ U5 Greg Olson	.20	.08	.02
☐ U6 Jim Presley	.05	.02	.00
☐ U7 Shawn Boskie	.12	.05	.01
☐ U8 Joe Kraemer	.10	.04	.01
☐ U9 Luis Salazar	.05	.02	.00
☐ U10 Hector Villanueva	.12	.05	.01
☐ U11 Glenn Braggs	.08	.03	.01
☐ U12 Mariano Duncan	.08	.03	.01
☐ U13 Billy Hatcher	.08	.03	.01
☐ U14 Tim Layana	.10	.04	.01
☐ U15 Hal Morris	.35	.15	.03
☐ U16 Javier Ortiz	.12	.05	.01
☐ U17 Dave Rohde	.10	.04	.01
☐ U18 Eric Yelding	.10	.04	.01
☐ U19 Hubie Brooks	.10	.04	.01
☐ U20 Kal Daniels	.08	.03	.01
☐ U21 Dave Hansen	.20	.08	.02
☐ U22 Mike Hartley	.10	.04	.01
☐ U23 Stan Javier	.05	.02	.00
☐ U24 Jose Offerman	.25	.10	.02
☐ U25 Juan Samuel	.10	.04	.01
☐ U26 Dennis Boyd	.05	.02	.00
☐ U27 Delino DeShields	.35	.15	.03
☐ U28 Steve Frey	.08	.03	.01
☐ U29 Mark Gardner	.10	.04	.01
☐ U30 Chris Nabholz	.20	.08	.02
☐ U31 Bill Sampen	.12	.05	.01
☐ U32 Dave Schmidt	.05	.02	.00
☐ U33 Daryl Boston	.08	.03	.01
☐ U34 Chuck Carr	.10	.04	.01
☐ U35 John Franco	.08	.03	.01
☐ U36 Todd Hundley	.30	.12	.03
☐ U37 Julio Machado	.05	.02	.00
☐ U38 Alejandro Pena	.08	.03	.01
☐ U39 Darren Reed	.12	.05	.01
☐ U40 Kelvin Torve	.05	.02	.00
☐ U41 Darrel Akerfelds	.05	.02	.00
☐ U42 Jose DeJesus	.10	.04	.01
☐ U43 Dave Hollins (misspelled Dane on card back)	.35	.15	.03
☐ U44 Carmelo Martinez	.05	.02	.00
☐ U45 Brad Moore	.10	.04	.01
☐ U46 Dale Murphy	.12	.05	.01
☐ U47 Wally Backman	.05	.02	.00
☐ U48 Stan Belinda	.12	.05	.01
☐ U49 Bob Patterson	.05	.02	.00
☐ U50 Ted Power	.05	.02	.00
☐ U51 Don Slaught	.05	.02	.00
☐ U52 Geronimo Pena	.12	.05	.01
☐ U53 Lee Smith	.12	.05	.01
☐ U54 John Tudor	.10	.04	.01
☐ U55 Joe Carter	.15	.06	.01
☐ U56 Tom Howard	.12	.05	.01
☐ U57 Craig Lefferts	.05	.02	.00
☐ U58 Rafael Valdez	.10	.04	.01
☐ U59 Dave Anderson	.05	.02	.00
☐ U60 Kevin Bass	.05	.02	.00
☐ U61 John Burkett	.15	.06	.01
☐ U62 Gary Carter	.10	.04	.01
☐ U63 Rick Parker	.08	.03	.01
☐ U64 Trevor Wilson	.08	.03	.01
☐ U65 Chris Hoiles	.20	.08	.02
☐ U66 Tim Hulett	.05	.02	.00
☐ U67 Dave Johnson	.10	.04	.01
☐ U68 Curt Schilling	.08	.03	.01
☐ U69 David Segui	.15	.06	.01
☐ U70 Tom Brunansky	.08	.03	.01
☐ U71 Greg Harris	.05	.02	.00
☐ U72 Dana Kiecker	.10	.04	.01
☐ U73 Tim Naehring	.25	.10	.02
☐ U74 Tony Pena	.08	.03	.01
☐ U75 Jeff Reardon	.10	.04	.01
☐ U76 Jerry Reed	.05	.02	.00
☐ U77 Mark Eichhorn	.08	.03	.01
☐ U78 Mark Langston	.10	.04	.01
☐ U79 John Orton	.08	.03	.01
☐ U80 Luis Polonia	.08	.03	.01
☐ U81 Dave Winfield	.12	.05	.01
☐ U82 Cliff Young	.12	.05	.01
☐ U83 Wayne Edwards	.08	.03	.01
☐ U84 Alex Fernandez	.75	.30	.07
☐ U85 Craig Grebeck	.10	.04	.01
☐ U86 Scott Radinsky	.12	.05	.01
☐ U87 Frank Thomas	5.50	2.50	.55
☐ U88 Beau Allred	.12	.05	.01
☐ U89 Sandy Alomar Jr.	.10	.04	.01
☐ U90 Carlos Baerga	.35	.15	.03
☐ U91 Kevin Bearse	.10	.04	.01
☐ U92 Chris James	.08	.03	.01
☐ U93 Candy Maldonado	.08	.03	.01
☐ U94 Jeff Manto	.08	.03	.01
☐ U95 Cecil Fielder	.35	.15	.03
☐ U96 Travis Fryman	1.25	.50	.12
☐ U97 Lloyd Moseby	.05	.02	.00
☐ U98 Edwin Nunez	.05	.02	.00
☐ U99 Tony Phillips	.05	.02	.00
☐ U100 Larry Sheets	.05	.02	.00
☐ U101 Mark Davis	.08	.03	.01
☐ U102 Storm Davis	.05	.02	.00
☐ U103 Gerald Perry	.05	.02	00
☐ U104 Terry Shumpert	12	.05	
☐ U105 Edgar Dia	10	.04	
☐ U106 Dave Parl	10	.04	
☐ U107 Tim Drun			
☐ U108 Junior O			
☐ U109 Park Pit			
☐ U110 Kevin Tapan			

☐ U111 Oscar Azocar	.12	.05	.01
☐ U112 Jim Leyritz	.10	.04	.01
☐ U113 Kevin Maas	1.25	.50	.12
☐ U114 Alan Mills	.12	.05	.01
☐ U115 Matt Nokes	.10	.04	.01
☐ U116 Pascual Perez	.08	.03	.01
☐ U117 Ozzie Canseco	.10	.04	.01
☐ U118 Scott Sanderson	.08	.03	.01
☐ U119 Tino Martinez	.50	.20	.05
☐ U120 Jeff Schneider	.10	.04	.01
☐ U121 Matt Young	.05	.02	.00
☐ U122 Brian Bohanon	.10	.04	.01
☐ U123 Jeff Huson	.08	.03	.01
☐ U124 Ramon Manon	.10	.04	.01
☐ U125 Gary Mielke UER (shown as Blue Jay on front)	.08	.03	.01
☐ U126 Willie Blair	.10	.04	.01
☐ U127 Glenallen Hill	.08	.03	.01
☐ U128 John Olerud	1.00	.40	.10
☐ U129 Luis Sojo	.12	.05	.01
☐ U130 Mark Whiten	.60	.25	.06
☐ U131 Nolan Ryan	.65	.25	.06
☐ U132 Checklist Card	.05	.01	.00

1991 Fleer

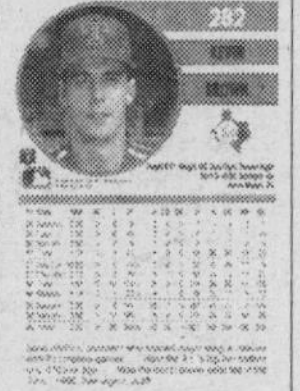

The 1991 Fleer set consists of 720 cards which measure the now standard size of 2 1/2" by 3 1/2". This set marks Fleer's eleventh consecutive year of issuing sets of current players. This set does not have what has been a Fleer tradition in recent years, the two-player rookie cards and there are less two-player special cards than in prior years. Apparently this was an attempt by Fleer to increase the number of single player cards in the set. The design features solid yellow borders with the information in black indicating name, position, and team. The backs feature beautiful full-color photos along with the career statistics and a biography for those players where there is room. The set is again ordered numerically by teams, followed by combination cards, rookie prospect pairs, and checklists. Again Fleer incorrectly anticipated the outcome of the 1990 Playoffs according to the team ordering. The A's, listed first, did not win the World Series and their opponents (and Series winners) were the Reds, not the Pirates. Fleer later reported that they merely arranged the teams according to regular season team record due to the early printing date. The complete team ordering is as follows: Oakland A's (1-28), Pittsburgh Pirates (29-54), Cincinnati Reds (55-82), Boston Red Sox (83-113), Chicago White Sox (114-139), New York Mets (140-166), Toronto Blue Jays (167-192), Los Angeles Dodgers (193-223), Montreal Expos (224-251), San Francisco Giants (252-277), Texas Rangers (278-304), California Angels (305-330), Detroit Tigers (331-357), Cleveland Indians (358-385), Philadelphia Phillies (386-412), Chicago Cubs (413-441), Seattle Mariners (442-465), Baltimore Orioles (466-496), Houston Astros (497-522) San Diego Padres (523-548), Kansas City Royals (549-575), Milwaukee Brewers (576-601), Minnesota Twins (602-627), St. Louis Cardinals (628-654), New York Yankees (655-680), and Atlanta Braves (681-708). A number of the cards in the set can be found with photos cropped (very slightly) differently as Fleer used two separate printers in their attempt to maximize production. The key rookie cards in this set are Wes Chamberlain, Luis Gonzalez, Brian McRae, and Phil Plantier.

	MINT	EXC	G-VG
COMPLETE SET (720)	18.00	7.50	2.50
COMMON PLAYER (1-720)	.03	.01	.00
☐ 1 Troy Afenir	.10	.03	.01
☐ 2 Harold Baines	.06	.02	.00
☐ 3 Lance Blankenship	.03	.01	.00
☐ 4 Todd Burns	.03	.01	.00
☐ 5 Jose Canseco	.25	.10	.02
☐ 6 Dennis Eckersley	.08	.03	.01
☐ 7 Mike Gallego	.03	.01	.00
☐ 8 Ron Hassey	.03	.01	.00
☐ 9 Dave Henderson	.06	.02	.00
☐ 10 Rickey Henderson	.20	.08	.02
☐ 11 Rick Honeycutt	.03	.01	.00
☐ 12 Doug Jennings	.03	.01	.00
☐ 13 Joe Klink	.06	.02	.00

No.	Player			
☐ 14	Carney Lansford	.06	.02	.00
☐ 15	Darren Lewis	.20	.08	.02
☐ 16	Willie McGee UER (Height 6'11")	.06	.02	.00
☐ 17	Mark McGwire UER (183 extra base hits in 1987)	.10	.04	.01
☐ 18	Mike Moore	.06	.02	.00
☐ 19	Gene Nelson	.03	.01	.00
☐ 20	Dave Otto	.03	.01	.00
☐ 21	Jamie Quirk	.03	.01	.00
☐ 22	Willie Randolph	.03	.01	.00
☐ 23	Scott Sanderson	.03	.01	.00
☐ 24	Terry Steinbach	.03	.01	.00
☐ 25	Dave Stewart	.08	.03	.01
☐ 26	Walt Weiss	.06	.02	.00
☐ 27	Bob Welch	.06	.02	.00
☐ 28	Curt Young	.03	.01	.00
☐ 29	Wally Backman	.03	.01	.00
☐ 30	Stan Belinda UER (Born in Huntington, should be State College)	.03	.01	.00
☐ 31	Jay Bell	.03	.01	.00
☐ 32	Rafael Belliard	.03	.01	.00
☐ 33	Barry Bonds	.12	.05	.01
☐ 34	Bobby Bonilla	.10	.04	.01
☐ 35	Sid Bream	.03	.01	.00
☐ 36	Doug Drabek	.06	.02	.00
☐ 37	Carlos Garcia	.08	.03	.01
☐ 38	Neal Heaton	.03	.01	.00
☐ 39	Jeff King	.06	.02	.00
☐ 40	Bob Kipper	.03	.01	.00
☐ 41	Bill Landrum	.03	.01	.00
☐ 42	Mike LaValliere	.03	.01	.00
☐ 43	Jose Lind	.03	.01	.00
☐ 44	Carmelo Martinez	.03	.01	.00
☐ 45	Bob Patterson	.03	.01	.00
☐ 46	Ted Power	.03	.01	.00
☐ 47	Gary Redus	.03	.01	.00
☐ 48	R.J. Reynolds	.03	.01	.00
☐ 49	Don Slaught	.03	.01	.00
☐ 50	John Smiley	.06	.02	.00
☐ 51	Zane Smith	.06	.02	.00
☐ 52	Randy Tomlin	.17	.07	.01
☐ 53	Andy Van Slyke	.08	.03	.01
☐ 54	Bob Walk	.03	.01	.00
☐ 55	Jack Armstrong	.06	.02	.00
☐ 56	Todd Benzinger	.03	.01	.00
☐ 57	Glenn Braggs	.03	.01	.00
☐ 58	Keith Brown	.03	.01	.00
☐ 59	Tom Browning	.06	.02	.00
☐ 60	Norm Charlton	.03	.01	.00
☐ 61	Eric Davis	.10	.04	.01
☐ 62	Rob Dibble	.06	.02	.00
☐ 63	Bill Doran	.03	.01	.00
☐ 64	Mariano Duncan	.03	.01	.00
☐ 65	Chris Hammond	.06	.02	.00
☐ 66	Billy Hatcher	.03	.01	.00
☐ 67	Danny Jackson	.03	.01	.00
☐ 68	Barry Larkin	.08	.03	.01
☐ 69	Tim Layana (Black line over made in first text line)	.03	.01	.00
☐ 70	Terry Lee	.08	.03	.01
☐ 71	Rick Mahler	.03	.01	.00
☐ 72	Hal Morris	.10	.04	.01
☐ 73	Randy Myers	.03	.01	.00
☐ 74	Ron Oester	.03	.01	.00
☐ 75	Joe Oliver	.03	.01	.00
☐ 76	Paul O'Neill	.06	.02	.00
☐ 77	Luis Quinones	.03	.01	.00
☐ 78	Jeff Reed	.03	.01	.00
☐ 79	Jose Rijo	.06	.02	.00
☐ 80	Chris Sabo	.08	.03	.01
☐ 81	Scott Scudder	.06	.02	.00
☐ 82	Herm Winningham	.03	.01	.00
☐ 83	Larry Andersen	.03	.01	.00
☐ 84	Marty Barrett	.03	.01	.00
☐ 85	Mike Boddicker	.03	.01	.00
☐ 86	Wade Boggs	.12	.05	.01
☐ 87	Tom Bolton	.03	.01	.00
☐ 88	Tom Brunansky	.06	.02	.00
☐ 89	Ellis Burks	.08	.03	.01
☐ 90	Roger Clemens	.15	.06	.01
☐ 91	Scott Cooper	.17	.07	.01
☐ 92	John Dopson	.03	.01	.00
☐ 93	Dwight Evans	.06	.02	.00
☐ 94	Wes Gardner	.03	.01	.00
☐ 95	Jeff Gray	.08	.03	.01
☐ 96	Mike Greenwell	.10	.04	.01
☐ 97	Greg Harris	.03	.01	.00
☐ 98	Daryl Irvine	.08	.03	.01
☐ 99	Dana Kiecker	.03	.01	.00
☐ 100	Randy Kutcher	.03	.01	.00
☐ 101	Dennis Lamp	.03	.01	.00
☐ 102	Mike Marshall	.06	.02	.00
☐ 103	John Marzano	.03	.01	.00
☐ 104	Rob Murphy	.03	.01	.00
☐ 105	Tim Naehring	.10	.04	.01
☐ 106	Tony Pena	.06	.02	.00
☐ 107	Phil Plantier	1.25	.50	.12
☐ 108	Carlos Quintana	.06	.02	.00
☐ 109	Jeff Reardon	.06	.02	.00
☐ 110	Jerry Reed	.03	.01	.00
☐ 111	Jody Reed	.06	.02	.00
☐ 112	Luis Rivera UER (Born 1/3/84)	.03	.01	.00
☐ 113	Kevin Romine	.03	.01	.00
☐ 114	Phil Bradley	.03	.01	.00
☐ 115	Ivan Calderon	.06	.02	.00
☐ 116	Wayne Edwards	.03	.01	.00
☐ 117	Alex Fernandez	.20	.08	.02
☐ 118	Carlton Fisk	.10	.04	.01
☐ 119	Scott Fletcher	.03	.01	.00
☐ 120	Craig Grebeck	.03	.01	.00
☐ 121	Ozzie Guillen	.06	.02	.00

☐ 122 Greg Hibbard .03 .01 .00
☐ 123 Lance Johnson UER .03 .01 .00
(Born Cincinnati, should be Lincoln Heights)
☐ 124 Barry Jones .03 .01 .00
☐ 125 Ron Karkovice .03 .01 .00
☐ 126 Eric King .03 .01 .00
☐ 127 Steve Lyons .03 .01 .00
☐ 128 Carlos Martinez .03 .01 .00
☐ 129 Jack McDowell UER .08 .03 .01
(Stanford misspelled as Standford on back)
☐ 130 Donn Pall .03 .01 .00
(No dots over any i's in text)
☐ 131 Dan Pasqua .03 .01 .00
☐ 132 Ken Patterson .03 .01 .00
☐ 133 Melido Perez .03 .01 .00
☐ 134 Adam Peterson .03 .01 .00
☐ 135 Scott Radinsky .06 .02 .00
☐ 136 Sammy Sosa .08 .03 .01
☐ 137 Bobby Thigpen .06 .02 .00
☐ 138 Frank Thomas 1.25 .50 .12
☐ 139 Robin Ventura .20 .08 .02
☐ 140 Daryl Boston .03 .01 .00
☐ 141 Chuck Carr .03 .01 .00
☐ 142 Mark Carreon .03 .01 .00
☐ 143 David Cone .06 .02 .00
☐ 144 Ron Darling .06 .02 .00
☐ 145 Kevin Elster .03 .01 .00
☐ 146 Sid Fernandez .06 .02 .00
☐ 147 John Franco .03 .01 .00
☐ 148 Dwight Gooden .10 .04 .01
☐ 149 Tom Herr .03 .01 .00
☐ 150 Todd Hundley .10 .04 .01
☐ 151 Gregg Jefferies .08 .03 .01
☐ 152 Howard Johnson .08 .03 .01
☐ 153 Dave Magadan .06 .02 .00
☐ 154 Kevin McReynolds .06 .02 .00
☐ 155 Keith Miller UER .03 .01 .00
(Text says Rochester in '87, stats say Tidewater, mixed up with other Keith Miller)
☐ 156 Bob Ojeda .03 .01 .00
☐ 157 Tom O'Malley .03 .01 .00
☐ 158 Alejandro Pena .06 .02 .00
☐ 159 Darren Reed .03 .01 .00
☐ 160 Mackey Sasser .03 .01 .00
☐ 161 Darryl Strawberry .15 .06 .01
☐ 162 Tim Teufel .03 .01 .00
☐ 163 Kelvin Torve .03 .01 .00
☐ 164 Julio Valera .08 .03 .01
☐ 165 Frank Viola .08 .03 .01
☐ 166 Wally Whitehurst .03 .01 .00
☐ 167 Jim Acker .03 .01 .00
☐ 168 Derek Bell .35 .15 .03
☐ 169 George Bell .08 .03 .01
☐ 170 Willie Blair .03 .01 .00
☐ 171 Pat Borders .03 .01 .00
☐ 172 John Cerutti .03 .01 .00
☐ 173 Junior Felix .06 .02 .00
☐ 174 Tony Fernandez .06 .02 .00
☐ 175 Kelly Gruber UER .08 .03 .01
(Born in Houston, should be Bellaire)
☐ 176 Tom Henke .06 .02 .00
☐ 177 Glenallen Hill .06 .02 .00
☐ 178 Jimmy Key .06 .02 .00
☐ 179 Manny Lee .03 .01 .00
☐ 180 Fred McGriff .08 .03 .01
☐ 181 Rance Mulliniks .03 .01 .00
☐ 182 Greg Myers .03 .01 .00
☐ 183 John Olerud .12 .05 .01
☐ 184 Luis Sojo .06 .02 .00
☐ 185 Dave Stieb .06 .02 .00
☐ 186 Todd Stottlemyre .06 .02 .00
☐ 187 Duane Ward .03 .01 .00
☐ 188 David Wells .03 .01 .00
☐ 189 Mark Whiten .17 .07 .01
☐ 190 Ken Williams .03 .01 .00
☐ 191 Frank Wills .03 .01 .00
☐ 192 Mookie Wilson .03 .01 .00
☐ 193 Don Aase .03 .01 .00
☐ 194 Tim Belcher UER .06 .02 .00
(Born Sparta, Ohio, should say Mt. Gilead)
☐ 195 Hubie Brooks .06 .02 .00
☐ 196 Dennis Cook .03 .01 .00
☐ 197 Tim Crews .03 .01 .00
☐ 198 Kal Daniels .06 .02 .00
☐ 199 Kirk Gibson .08 .03 .01
☐ 200 Jim Gott .03 .01 .00
☐ 201 Alfredo Griffin .03 .01 .00
☐ 202 Chris Gwynn .03 .01 .00
☐ 203 Dave Hansen .06 .02 .00
☐ 204 Lenny Harris .03 .01 .00
☐ 205 Mike Hartley .03 .01 .00
☐ 206 Mickey Hatcher .03 .01 .00
☐ 207 Carlos Hernandez .08 .03 .01
☐ 208 Orel Hershiser .08 .03 .01
☐ 209 Jay Howell UER .03 .01 .00
(No 1982 Yankee stats)
☐ 210 Mike Huff .06 .02 .00
☐ 211 Stan Javier .03 .01 .00
☐ 212 Ramon Martinez .10 .04 .01
☐ 213 Mike Morgan .03 .01 .00
☐ 214 Eddie Murray .10 .04 .01
☐ 215 Jim Neidlinger .10 .04 .01
☐ 216 Jose Offerman .10 .04 .01
☐ 217 Jim Poole .10 .04 .01
☐ 218 Juan Samuel .06 .02 .00
☐ 219 Mike Scioscia .03 .01 .00
☐ 220 Ray Searage .03 .01 .00
☐ 221 Mike Sharperson .03 .01 .00
☐ 222 Fernando Valenzuela .06 .02 .00

☐ 223 Jose Vizcaino .03 .01 .00
☐ 224 Mike Aldrete .03 .01 .00
☐ 225 Scott Anderson .08 .03 .01
☐ 226 Dennis Boyd .03 .01 .00
☐ 227 Tim Burke .03 .01 .00
☐ 228 Delino DeShields .10 .04 .01
☐ 229 Mike Fitzgerald .03 .01 .00
☐ 230 Tom Foley .03 .01 .00
☐ 231 Steve Frey .03 .01 .00
☐ 232 Andres Galarraga .06 .02 .00
☐ 233 Mark Gardner .06 .02 .00
☐ 234 Marquis Grissom .10 .04 .01
☐ 235 Kevin Gross .03 .01 .00
(No date given for
first Expos win)
☐ 236 Drew Hall .03 .01 .00
☐ 237 Dave Martinez .03 .01 .00
☐ 238 Dennis Martinez .06 .02 .00
☐ 239 Dale Mohorcic .03 .01 .00
☐ 240 Chris Nabholz .06 .02 .00
☐ 241 Otis Nixon .06 .02 .00
☐ 242 Junior Noboa .03 .01 .00
☐ 243 Spike Owen .03 .01 .00
☐ 244 Tim Raines .08 .03 .01
☐ 245 Mel Rojas UER .06 .02 .00
(Stats show 3.60 ERA,
bio says 3.19 ERA)
☐ 246 Scott Ruskin .08 .03 .01
☐ 247 Bill Sampen .03 .01 .00
☐ 248 Nelson Santovenia .03 .01 .00
☐ 249 Dave Schmidt .03 .01 .00
☐ 250 Larry Walker .08 .03 .01
☐ 251 Tim Wallach .06 .02 .00
☐ 252 Dave Anderson .03 .01 .00
☐ 253 Kevin Bass .03 .01 .00
☐ 254 Steve Bedrosian .03 .01 .00
☐ 255 Jeff Brantley .03 .01 .00
☐ 256 John Burkett .03 .01 .00
☐ 257 Brett Butler .06 .02 .00
☐ 258 Gary Carter .08 .03 .01
☐ 259 Will Clark .20 .08 .02
☐ 260 Steve Decker .25 .10 .02
☐ 261 Kelly Downs .03 .01 .00
☐ 262 Scott Garrelts .03 .01 .00
☐ 263 Terry Kennedy .03 .01 .00
☐ 264 Mike LaCoss .03 .01 .00
☐ 265 Mark Leonard .12 .05 .01
☐ 266 Greg Litton .03 .01 .00
☐ 267 Kevin Mitchell .10 .04 .01
☐ 268 Randy O'Neal .03 .01 .00
☐ 269 Rick Parker .03 .01 .00
☐ 270 Rick Reuschel .06 .02 .00
☐ 271 Ernest Riles .03 .01 .00
☐ 272 Don Robinson .03 .01 .00
☐ 273 Robby Thompson .03 .01 .00
☐ 274 Mark Thurmond .03 .01 .00
☐ 275 Jose Uribe .03 .01 .00
☐ 276 Matt Williams .10 .04 .01
☐ 277 Trevor Wilson .03 .01 .00
☐ 278 Gerald Alexander .10 .04 .01
☐ 279 Brad Arnsberg .03 .01 .00
☐ 280 Kevin Belcher .10 .04 .01
☐ 281 Joe Bitker .08 .03 .01
☐ 282 Kevin Brown .03 .01 .00
☐ 283 Steve Buechele .03 .01 .00
☐ 284 Jack Daugherty .03 .01 .00
☐ 285 Julio Franco .08 .03 .01
☐ 286 Juan Gonzalez .30 .12 .03
☐ 287 Bill Haselman .08 .03 .01
☐ 288 Charlie Hough .03 .01 .00
☐ 289 Jeff Huson .03 .01 .00
☐ 290 Pete Incaviglia .06 .02 .00
☐ 291 Mike Jeffcoat .03 .01 .00
☐ 292 Jeff Kunkel .03 .01 .00
☐ 293 Gary Mielke .03 .01 .00
☐ 294 Jamie Moyer .03 .01 .00
☐ 295 Rafael Palmeiro .10 .04 .01
☐ 296 Geno Petralli .03 .01 .00
☐ 297 Gary Pettis .03 .01 .00
☐ 298 Kevin Reimer .08 .03 .01
☐ 299 Kenny Rogers .03 .01 .00
☐ 300 Jeff Russell .03 .01 .00
☐ 301 John Russell .03 .01 .00
☐ 302 Nolan Ryan .35 .15 .03
☐ 303 Ruben Sierra .12 .05 .01
☐ 304 Bobby Witt .06 .02 .00
☐ 305 Jim Abbott .10 .04 .01
☐ 306 Kent Anderson .03 .01 .00
☐ 307 Dante Bichette .03 .01 .00
☐ 308 Bert Blyleven .06 .02 .00
☐ 309 Chili Davis .06 .02 .00
☐ 310 Brian Downing .03 .01 .00
☐ 311 Mark Eichhorn .03 .01 .00
☐ 312 Mike Fetters .03 .01 .00
☐ 313 Chuck Finley .06 .02 .00
☐ 314 Willie Fraser .03 .01 .00
☐ 315 Bryan Harvey .06 .02 .00
☐ 316 Donnie Hill .03 .01 .00
☐ 317 Wally Joyner .08 .03 .01
☐ 318 Mark Langston .06 .02 .00
☐ 319 Kirk McCaskill .03 .01 .00
☐ 320 John Orton .03 .01 .00
☐ 321 Lance Parrish .06 .02 .00
☐ 322 Luis Polonia UER .03 .01 .00
(1984 Madfison,
should be Madison)
☐ 323 Johnny Ray .03 .01 .00
☐ 324 Bobby Rose .03 .01 .00
☐ 325 Dick Schofield .03 .01 .00
☐ 326 Rick Schu .03 .01 .00
☐ 327 Lee Stevens .08 .03 .01
☐ 328 Devon White .06 .02 .00
☐ 329 Dave Winfield .10 .04 .01
☐ 330 Cliff Young .03 .01 .00
☐ 331 Dave Bergman .03 .01 .00
☐ 332 Phil Clark .15 .06 .01

☐ 333 Darnell Coles .03 .01 .00
☐ 334 Milt Cuyler .15 .06 .01
☐ 335 Cecil Fielder .15 .06 .01
☐ 336 Travis Fryman .40 .16 .04
☐ 337 Paul Gibson .03 .01 .00
☐ 338 Jerry Don Gleaton .03 .01 .00
☐ 339 Mike Heath .03 .01 .00
☐ 340 Mike Henneman .03 .01 .00
☐ 341 Chet Lemon .03 .01 .00
☐ 342 Lance McCullers .03 .01 .00
☐ 343 Jack Morris .08 .03 .01
☐ 344 Lloyd Moseby .03 .01 .00
☐ 345 Edwin Nunez .03 .01 .00
☐ 346 Clay Parker .03 .01 .00
☐ 347 Dan Petry .03 .01 .00
☐ 348 Tony Phillips .03 .01 .00
☐ 349 Jeff Robinson .03 .01 .00
☐ 350 Mark Salas .03 .01 .00
☐ 351 Mike Schwabe .03 .01 .00
☐ 352 Larry Sheets .03 .01 .00
☐ 353 John Shelby .03 .01 .00
☐ 354 Frank Tanana .06 .02 .00
☐ 355 Alan Trammell .08 .03 .01
☐ 356 Gary Ward .03 .01 .00
☐ 357 Lou Whitaker .06 .02 .00
☐ 358 Beau Allred .06 .02 .00
☐ 359 Sandy Alomar Jr. .08 .03 .01
☐ 360 Carlos Baerga .10 .04 .01
☐ 361 Kevin Bearse .03 .01 .00
☐ 362 Tom Brookens .03 .01 .00
☐ 363 Jerry Browne UER .03 .01 .00
(No dot over i in first text line)
☐ 364 Tom Candiotti .06 .02 .00
☐ 365 Alex Cole .08 .03 .01
☐ 366 John Farrell UER .03 .01 .00
(Born in Neptune, should be Monmouth)
☐ 367 Felix Fermin .03 .01 .00
☐ 368 Keith Hernandez .06 .02 .00
☐ 369 Brook Jacoby .03 .01 .00
☐ 370 Chris James .03 .01 .00
☐ 371 Dion James .03 .01 .00
☐ 372 Doug Jones .03 .01 .00
☐ 373 Candy Maldonado .03 .01 .00
☐ 374 Steve Olin .03 .01 .00
☐ 375 Jesse Orosco .03 .01 .00
☐ 376 Rudy Seanez .06 .02 .00
☐ 377 Joel Skinner .03 .01 .00
☐ 378 Cory Snyder .06 .02 .00
☐ 379 Greg Swindell .06 .02 .00
☐ 380 Sergio Valdez .06 .02 .00
☐ 381 Mike Walker .03 .01 .00
☐ 382 Colby Ward .08 .03 .01
☐ 383 Turner Ward .12 .05 .01
☐ 384 Mitch Webster .03 .01 .00
☐ 385 Kevin Wickander .03 .01 .00
☐ 386 Darrel Akerfelds .03 .01 .00
☐ 387 Joe Boever .03 .01 .00
☐ 388 Rod Booker .03 .01 .00
☐ 389 Sil Campusano .03 .01 .00
☐ 390 Don Carman .03 .01 .00
☐ 391 Wes Chamberlain .45 .18 .04
☐ 392 Pat Combs .03 .01 .00
☐ 393 Darren Daulton .03 .01 .00
☐ 394 Jose DeJesus .03 .01 .00
☐ 395 Len Dykstra .06 .02 .00
☐ 396 Jason Grimsley .03 .01 .00
☐ 397 Charlie Hayes .03 .01 .00
☐ 398 Von Hayes .06 .02 .00
☐ 399 David Hollins UER .08 .03 .01
(Atl-bats, should say at-bats)
☐ 400 Ken Howell .03 .01 .00
☐ 401 Ricky Jordan .06 .02 .00
☐ 402 John Kruk .03 .01 .00
☐ 403 Steve Lake .03 .01 .00
☐ 404 Chuck Malone .06 .02 .00
☐ 405 Roger McDowell UER .03 .01 .00
(Says Phillies is saves, should say in)
☐ 406 Chuck McElroy .03 .01 .00
☐ 407 Mickey Morandini .10 .04 .01
☐ 408 Terry Mulholland .03 .01 .00
☐ 409 Dale Murphy .10 .04 .01
☐ 410A Randy Ready ERR .06 .02 .00
(No Brewers stats listed for 1983)
☐ 410B Randy Ready COR .06 .02 .00
☐ 411 Bruce Ruffin .03 .01 .00
☐ 412 Dickie Thon .03 .01 .00
☐ 413 Paul Assenmacher .03 .01 .00
☐ 414 Damon Berryhill .03 .01 .00
☐ 415 Mike Bielecki .03 .01 .00
☐ 416 Shawn Boskie .03 .01 .00
☐ 417 Dave Clark .03 .01 .00
☐ 418 Doug Dascenzo .03 .01 .00
☐ 419A Andre Dawson ERR .12 .05 .01
(No stats for 1976)
☐ 419B Andre Dawson COR .12 .05 .01
☐ 420 Shawon Dunston .06 .02 .00
☐ 421 Joe Girardi .03 .01 .00
☐ 422 Mark Grace .08 .03 .01
☐ 423 Mike Harkey .06 .02 .00
☐ 424 Les Lancaster .03 .01 .00
☐ 425 Bill Long .03 .01 .00
☐ 426 Greg Maddux .06 .02 .00
☐ 427 Derrick May .08 .03 .01
☐ 428 Jeff Pico .03 .01 .00
☐ 429 Domingo Ramos .03 .01 .00
☐ 430 Luis Salazar .03 .01 .00
☐ 431 Ryne Sandberg .20 .08 .02
☐ 432 Dwight Smith .06 .02 .00
☐ 433 Greg Smith .03 .01 .00
☐ 434 Rick Sutcliffe .06 .02 .00
☐ 435 Gary Varsho .03 .01 .00

□ 436 Hector Villanueva .... .06 .02 .00
□ 437 Jerome Walton .... .08 .03 .01
□ 438 Curtis Wilkerson .... .03 .01 .00
□ 439 Mitch Williams .... .03 .01 .00
□ 440 Steve Wilson .... .03 .01 .00
□ 441 Marvell Wynne .... .03 .01 .00
□ 442 Scott Bankhead .... .03 .01 .00
□ 443 Scott Bradley .... .03 .01 .00
□ 444 Greg Briley .... .03 .01 .00
□ 445 Mike Brumley UER .... .03 .01 .00
(Text 40 SB's in 1988, stats say 41)
□ 446 Jay Buhner .... .06 .02 .00
□ 447 Dave Burba .... .10 .04 .01
□ 448 Henry Cotto .... .03 .01 .00
□ 449 Alvin Davis .... .06 .02 .00
□ 450A Ken Griffey Jr. .... .75 .30 .07
(Bat .300)
□ 450B Ken Griffey Jr. .... .75 .30 .07
(Bat around .300)
□ 451 Erik Hanson .... .06 .02 .00
□ 452 Gene Harris UER .... .03 .01 .00
(63 career runs, should be 73)
□ 453 Brian Holman .... .03 .01 .00
□ 454 Mike Jackson .... .03 .01 .00
□ 455 Randy Johnson .... .06 .02 .00
□ 456 Jeffrey Leonard .... .03 .01 .00
□ 457 Edgar Martinez .... .06 .02 .00
□ 458 Tino Martinez .... .15 .06 .01
□ 459 Pete O'Brien UER .... .03 .01 .00
(1987 BA .266, should be .286)
□ 460 Harold Reynolds .... .06 .02 .00
□ 461 Mike Schooler .... .03 .01 .00
□ 462 Bill Swift .... .03 .01 .00
□ 463 David Valle .... .03 .01 .00
□ 464 Omar Vizquel .... .03 .01 .00
□ 465 Matt Young .... .03 .01 .00
□ 466 Brady Anderson .... .03 .01 .00
□ 467 Jeff Ballard UER .... .03 .01 .00
(Missing top of right parenthesis after Saberhagen in last text line)
□ 468 Juan Bell .... .06 .02 .00
□ 469A Mike Devereaux .... .06 .02 .00
(First line of text ends with six)
□ 469B Mike Devereaux .... .06 .02 .00
(First line of text ends with runs)
□ 470 Steve Finley .... .06 .02 .00
□ 471 Dave Gallagher .... .03 .01 .00
□ 472 Leo Gomez .... .25 .10 .02
□ 473 Rene Gonzales .... .03 .01 .00
□ 474 Pete Harnisch .... .06 .02 .00
□ 475 Kevin Hickey .... .03 .01 .00
□ 476 Chris Hoiles .... .08 .03 .01
□ 477 Sam Horn .... .06 .02 .00
□ 478 Tim Hulett .... .03 .01 .00
(Photo shows National Leaguer sliding into second base)
□ 479 Dave Johnson .... .03 .01 .00
□ 480 Ron Kittle UER .... .06 .02 .00
(Edmonton misspelled as Edmundton)
□ 481 Ben McDonald .... .10 .04 .01
□ 482 Bob Melvin .... .03 .01 .00
□ 483 Bob Milacki .... .03 .01 .00
□ 484 Randy Milligan .... .06 .02 .00
□ 485 John Mitchell .... .03 .01 .00
□ 486 Gregg Olson .... .08 .03 .01
□ 487 Joe Orsulak .... .03 .01 .00
□ 488 Joe Price .... .03 .01 .00
□ 489 Bill Ripken .... .03 .01 .00
□ 490 Cal Ripken .... .20 .08 .02
□ 491 Curt Schilling .... .03 .01 .00
□ 492 David Segui .... .08 .03 .01
□ 493 Anthony Telford .... .08 .03 .01
□ 494 Mickey Tettleton .... .06 .02 .00
□ 495 Mark Williamson .... .03 .01 .00
□ 496 Craig Worthington .... .03 .01 .00
□ 497 Juan Agosto .... .03 .01 .00
□ 498 Eric Anthony .... .08 .03 .01
□ 499 Craig Biggio .... .06 .02 .00
□ 500 Ken Caminiti UER .... .03 .01 .00
(Born 4/4, should be 4/21)
□ 501 Casey Candaele .... .03 .01 .00
□ 502 Andujar Cedeno .... .35 .15 .03
□ 503 Danny Darwin .... .03 .01 .00
□ 504 Mark Davidson .... .03 .01 .00
□ 505 Glenn Davis .... .08 .03 .01
□ 506 Jim Deshaies .... .03 .01 .00
□ 507 Luis Gonzalez .... .40 .16 .04
□ 508 Bill Gullickson .... .06 .02 .00
□ 509 Xavier Hernandez .... .06 .02 .00
□ 510 Brian Meyer .... .03 .01 .00
□ 511 Ken Oberkfell .... .03 .01 .00
□ 512 Mark Portugal .... .03 .01 .00
□ 513 Rafael Ramirez .... .03 .01 .00
□ 514 Karl Rhodes .... .06 .02 .00
□ 515 Mike Scott .... .06 .02 .00
□ 516 Mike Simms .... .12 .05 .01
□ 517 Dave Smith .... .03 .01 .00
□ 518 Franklin Stubbs .... .03 .01 .00
□ 519 Glenn Wilson .... .03 .01 .00
□ 520 Eric Yelding UER .... .03 .01 .00
(Text has 63 steals, stats have 64, which is correct)
□ 521 Gerald Young .... .03 .01 .00
□ 522 Shawn Abner .... .03 .01 .00
□ 523 Roberto Alomar .... .10 .04 .01

☐ 524 Andy Benes	.08	.03	.01
☐ 525 Joe Carter	.08	.03	.01
☐ 526 Jack Clark	.06	.02	.00
☐ 527 Joey Cora	.03	.01	.00
☐ 528 Paul Faries	.08	.03	.01
☐ 529 Tony Gwynn	.12	.05	.01
☐ 530 Atlee Hammaker	.03	.01	.00
☐ 531 Greg Harris	.03	.01	.00
☐ 532 Thomas Howard	.03	.01	.00
☐ 533 Bruce Hurst	.06	.02	.00
☐ 534 Craig Lefferts	.03	.01	.00
☐ 535 Derek Lilliquist	.03	.01	.00
☐ 536 Fred Lynn	.06	.02	.00
☐ 537 Mike Pagliarulo	.03	.01	.00
☐ 538 Mark Parent	.03	.01	.00
☐ 539 Dennis Rasmussen	.03	.01	.00
☐ 540 Bip Roberts	.03	.01	.00
☐ 541 Richard Rodriguez	.03	.01	.00
☐ 542 Benito Santiago	.06	.02	.00
☐ 543 Calvin Schiraldi	.03	.01	.00
☐ 544 Eric Show	.03	.01	.00
☐ 545 Phil Stephenson	.03	.01	.00
☐ 546 Garry Templeton UER (Born 3/24/57, should be 3/24/56)	.03	.01	.00
☐ 547 Ed Whitson	.03	.01	.00
☐ 548 Eddie Williams	.03	.01	.00
☐ 549 Kevin Appier	.06	.02	.00
☐ 550 Luis Aquino	.03	.01	.00
☐ 551 Bob Boone	.06	.02	.00
☐ 552 George Brett	.10	.04	.01
☐ 553 Jeff Conine	.15	.06	.01
☐ 554 Steve Crawford	.03	.01	.00
☐ 555 Mark Davis	.03	.01	.00
☐ 556 Storm Davis	.03	.01	.00
☐ 557 Jim Eisenreich	.03	.01	.00
☐ 558 Steve Farr	.03	.01	.00
☐ 559 Tom Gordon	.06	.02	.00
☐ 560 Mark Gubicza	.06	.02	.00
☐ 561 Bo Jackson	.25	.10	.02
☐ 562 Mike Macfarlane	.03	.01	.00
☐ 563 Brian McRae	.45	.18	.04
☐ 564 Jeff Montgomery	.03	.01	.00
☐ 565 Bill Pecota	.03	.01	.00
☐ 566 Gerald Perry	.03	.01	.00
☐ 567 Bret Saberhagen	.08	.03	.01
☐ 568 Jeff Schulz	.10	.04	.01
☐ 569 Kevin Seitzer	.06	.02	.00
☐ 570 Terry Shumpert	.03	.01	.00
☐ 571 Kurt Stillwell	.03	.01	.00
☐ 572 Danny Tartabull	.08	.03	.01
☐ 573 Gary Thurman	.03	.01	.00
☐ 574 Frank White	.03	.01	.00
☐ 575 Willie Wilson	.06	.02	.00
☐ 576 Chris Bosio	.03	.01	.00
☐ 577 Greg Brock	.03	.01	.00
☐ 578 George Canale	.03	.01	.00
☐ 579 Chuck Crim	.03	.01	.00

☐ 580 Rob Deer	.06	.02	.00
☐ 581 Edgar Diaz	.06	.02	.00
☐ 582 Tom Edens	.08	.03	.01
☐ 583 Mike Felder	.03	.01	.00
☐ 584 Jim Gantner	.03	.01	.00
☐ 585 Darryl Hamilton	.03	.01	.00
☐ 586 Ted Higuera	.03	.01	.00
☐ 587 Mark Knudson	.03	.01	.00
☐ 588 Bill Krueger	.03	.01	.00
☐ 589 Tim McIntosh	.06	.02	.00
☐ 590 Paul Mirabella	.03	.01	.00
☐ 591 Paul Molitor	.08	.03	.01
☐ 592 Jaime Navarro	.03	.01	.00
☐ 593 Dave Parker	.08	.03	.01
☐ 594 Dan Plesac	.03	.01	.00
☐ 595 Ron Robinson	.03	.01	.00
☐ 596 Gary Sheffield	.08	.03	.01
☐ 597 Bill Spiers	.03	.01	.00
☐ 598 B.J. Surhoff	.03	.01	.00
☐ 599 Greg Vaughn	.10	.04	.01
☐ 600 Randy Veres	.03	.01	.00
☐ 601 Robin Yount	.10	.04	.01
☐ 602 Rick Aguilera	.03	.01	.00
☐ 603 Allan Anderson	.03	.01	.00
☐ 604 Juan Berenguer	.03	.01	.00
☐ 605 Randy Bush	.03	.01	.00
☐ 606 Carmen Castillo	.03	.01	.00
☐ 607 Tim Drummond	.03	.01	.00
☐ 608 Scott Erickson	.75	.30	.07
☐ 609 Gary Gaetti	.06	.02	.00
☐ 610 Greg Gagne	.03	.01	.00
☐ 611 Dan Gladden	.03	.01	.00
☐ 612 Mark Guthrie	.06	.02	.00
☐ 613 Brian Harper	.06	.02	.00
☐ 614 Kent Hrbek	.06	.02	.00
☐ 615 Gene Larkin	.03	.01	.00
☐ 616 Terry Leach	.03	.01	.00
☐ 617 Nelson Liriano	.03	.01	.00
☐ 618 Shane Mack	.06	.02	.00
☐ 619 John Moses	.03	.01	.00
☐ 620 Pedro Munoz	.17	.07	.01
☐ 621 Al Newman	.03	.01	.00
☐ 622 Junior Ortiz	.03	.01	.00
☐ 623 Kirby Puckett	.12	.05	.01
☐ 624 Roy Smith	.03	.01	.00
☐ 625 Kevin Tapani	.08	.03	.01
☐ 626 Gary Wayne	.03	.01	.00
☐ 627 David West	.03	.01	.00
☐ 628 Cris Carpenter	.03	.01	.00
☐ 629 Vince Coleman	.08	.03	.01
☐ 630 Ken Dayley	.03	.01	.00
☐ 631 Jose DeLeon	.03	.01	.00
☐ 632 Frank DiPino	.03	.01	.00
☐ 633 Bernard Gilkey	.15	.06	.01
☐ 634 Pedro Guerrero	.06	.02	.00
☐ 635 Ken Hill	.03	.01	.00
☐ 636 Felix Jose	.08	.03	.01
☐ 637 Ray Lankford	.35	.15	.03

☐ 638 Joe Magrane .03 .01 .00
☐ 639 Tom Niedenfuer .03 .01 .00
☐ 640 Jose Oquendo .03 .01 .00
☐ 641 Tom Pagnozzi .03 .01 .00
☐ 642 Terry Pendleton .08 .03 .01
☐ 643 Mike Perez .08 .03 .01
☐ 644 Bryn Smith .03 .01 .00
☐ 645 Lee Smith .06 .02 .00
☐ 646 Ozzie Smith .10 .04 .01
☐ 647 Scott Terry .03 .01 .00
☐ 648 Bob Tewksbury .03 .01 .00
☐ 649 Milt Thompson .03 .01 .00
☐ 650 John Tudor .06 .02 .00
☐ 651 Denny Walling .03 .01 .00
☐ 652 Craig Wilson .10 .04 .01
☐ 653 Todd Worrell .06 .02 .00
☐ 654 Todd Zeile .10 .04 .01
☐ 655 Oscar Azocar .06 .02 .00
☐ 656 Steve Balboni UER .03 .01 .00
(Born 1/5/57,
should be 1/16)
☐ 657 Jesse Barfield .06 .02 .00
☐ 658 Greg Cadaret .03 .01 .00
☐ 659 Chuck Cary .03 .01 .00
☐ 660 Rick Cerone .03 .01 .00
☐ 661 David Eiland .03 .01 .00
☐ 662 Alvaro Espinoza .03 .01 .00
☐ 663 Bob Geren .03 .01 .00
☐ 664 Lee Guetterman .03 .01 .00
☐ 665 Mel Hall .03 .01 .00
☐ 666 Andy Hawkins .03 .01 .00
☐ 667 Jimmy Jones .03 .01 .00
☐ 668 Roberto Kelly .08 .03 .01
☐ 669 Dave LaPoint UER .03 .01 .00
(No '81 Brewers stats,
totals also are wrong)
☐ 670 Tim Leary .06 .02 .00
☐ 671 Jim Leyritz .06 .02 .00
☐ 672 Kevin Maas .15 .06 .01
☐ 673 Don Mattingly .12 .05 .01
☐ 674 Matt Nokes .06 .02 .00
☐ 675 Pascual Perez .03 .01 .00
☐ 676 Eric Plunk .03 .01 .00
☐ 677 Dave Righetti .06 .02 .00
☐ 678 Jeff Robinson .03 .01 .00
☐ 679 Steve Sax .06 .02 .00
☐ 680 Mike Witt .03 .01 .00
☐ 681 Steve Avery UER .35 .15 .03
(Born in New Jersey,
should say Michigan)
☐ 682 Mike Bell .12 .05 .01
☐ 683 Jeff Blauser .03 .01 .00
☐ 684 Francisco Cabrera UER .06 .02 .00
(Born 10/16,
should say 10/10)
☐ 685 Tony Castillo .03 .01 .00
☐ 686 Marty Clary UER .03 .01 .00
(Shown pitching righty,
but bio has left)
☐ 687 Nick Esasky .03 .01 .00
☐ 688 Ron Gant .12 .05 .01
☐ 689 Tom Glavine .12 .05 .01
☐ 690 Mark Grant .03 .01 .00
☐ 691 Tommy Gregg .03 .01 .00
☐ 692 Dwayne Henry .03 .01 .00
☐ 693 Dave Justice .50 .20 .05
☐ 694 Jimmy Kremers .03 .01 .00
☐ 695 Charlie Leibrandt .03 .01 .00
☐ 696 Mark Lemke .06 .02 .00
☐ 697 Oddibe McDowell .06 .02 .00
☐ 698 Greg Olson .06 .02 .00
☐ 699 Jeff Parrett .03 .01 .00
☐ 700 Jim Presley .03 .01 .00
☐ 701 Victor Rosario .08 .03 .01
☐ 702 Lonnie Smith .06 .02 .00
☐ 703 Pete Smith .03 .01 .00
☐ 704 John Smoltz .08 .03 .01
☐ 705 Mike Stanton .03 .01 .00
☐ 706 Andres Thomas .03 .01 .00
☐ 707 Jeff Treadway .03 .01 .00
☐ 708 Jim Vatcher .08 .03 .01
☐ 709 Home Run Kings .15 .06 .01
Ryne Sandberg
Cecil Fielder
☐ 710 2nd Generation Stars .25 .10 .02
Barry Bonds
Ken Griffey Jr.
☐ 711 NLCS Team Leaders .08 .03 .01
Bobby Bonilla
Barry Larkin
☐ 712 Top Game Savers .06 .02 .00
Bobby Thigpen
John Franco
☐ 713 Chicago's 100 Club .10 .04 .01
Andre Dawson
Ryne Sandberg UER
(Ryno misspelled Rhino)
☐ 714 CL:A's/Pirates .06 .01 .00
Reds/Red Sox
☐ 715 CL:White Sox/Mets .06 .01 .00
Blue Jays/Dodgers
☐ 716 CL:Expos/Giants .06 .01 .00
Rangers/Angels
☐ 717 CL:Tigers/Indians .06 .01 .00
Phillies/Cubs
☐ 718 CL:Mariners/Orioles .06 .01 .00
Astros/Padres
☐ 719 CL:Royals/Brewers .06 .01 .00
Twins/Cardinals
☐ 720 CL:Yankees/Braves .06 .01 .00
Superstars/Specials

1991 Fleer Update

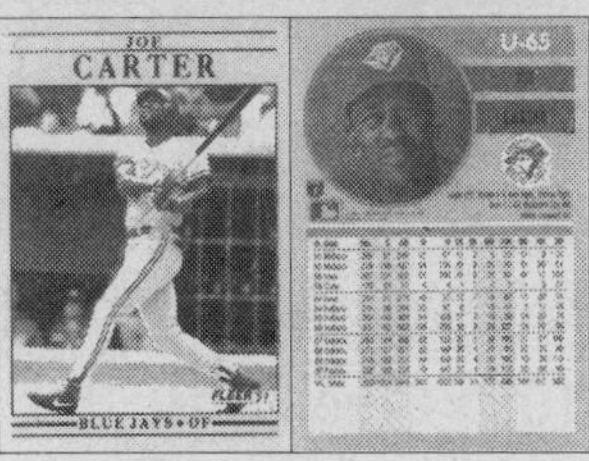

The 1991 Fleer Update set contains 132 cards measuring the standard size (2 1/2" by 3 1/2"). The glossy color action photos on the fronts are placed on a yellow card face and accentuated by black lines above and below. The backs have a head shot (circular format), biography, and complete Major League statistics. The cards are checklisted below alphabetically within and according to teams for each league as follows: Baltimore Orioles (1-3), Boston Red Sox (4-7), California Angels (8-10), Chicago White Sox (11-15), Cleveland Indians (16-21), Detroit Tigers (22-24), Kansas City Royals (25-28), Milwaukee Brewers (29-35), Minnesota Twins (36-41), New York Yankees (42-49), Oakland Athletics (50-51), Seattle Mariners (52-57), Texas Rangers (58-62), Toronto Blue Jays (63-69), Atlanta Braves (70-76), Chicago Cubs (77-83), Cincinnati Reds (84-86), Houston Astros (87-90), Los Angeles Dodgers (91-96), Montreal Expos (97-99), New York Mets (100-104), Philadelphia Phillies (105-110), Pittsburgh Pirates (111-115), St. Louis Cardinals (116-119), San Diego Padres (120-127), and San Francisco Giants (128-131). The key rookie cards in this set are Jeff Bagwell and Ivan Rodriguez.

	MINT	EXC	G-VG
COMPLETE SET (132)	10.00	4.50	1.25
COMMON PLAYER (U1-U132)	.05	.02	.00

	MINT	EXC	G-VG
☐ U1 Glenn Davis	.10	.04	.01
☐ U2 Dwight Evans	.08	.03	.01
☐ U3 Jose Mesa	.08	.03	.01
☐ U4 Jack Clark	.08	.03	.01
☐ U5 Danny Darwin	.05	.02	.00
☐ U6 Steve Lyons	.05	.02	.00
☐ U7 Mo Vaughn	.60	.25	.06
☐ U8 Floyd Bannister	.05	.02	.00
☐ U9 Gary Gaetti	.08	.03	.01
☐ U10 Dave Parker	.10	.04	.01
☐ U11 Joey Cora	.05	.02	.00
☐ U12 Charlie Hough	.05	.02	.00
☐ U13 Matt Merullo	.08	.03	.01
☐ U14 Warren Newson	.20	.08	.02
☐ U15 Tim Raines	.08	.03	.01
☐ U16 Albert Belle	.17	.07	.01
☐ U17 Glenallen Hill	.08	.03	.01
☐ U18 Shawn Hillegas	.05	.02	.00
☐ U19 Mark Lewis	.20	.08	.02
☐ U20 Charles Nagy	.10	.04	.01
☐ U21 Mark Whiten	.20	.08	.02
☐ U22 John Cerutti	.05	.02	.00
☐ U23 Rob Deer	.08	.03	.01
☐ U24 Mickey Tettleton	.08	.03	.01
☐ U25 Warren Cromartie	.05	.02	.00
☐ U26 Kirk Gibson	.08	.03	.01
☐ U27 David Howard	.12	.05	.01
☐ U28 Brent Mayne	.10	.04	.01
☐ U29 Dante Bichette	.05	.02	.00
☐ U30 Mark Lee	.10	.04	.01
☐ U31 Julio Machado	.05	.02	.00
☐ U32 Edwin Nunez	.05	.02	.00
☐ U33 Willie Randolph	.08	.03	.01
☐ U34 Franklin Stubbs	.05	.02	.00
☐ U35 Bill Wegman	.05	.02	.00
☐ U36 Chili Davis	.08	.03	.01
☐ U37 Chuck Knoblauch	.40	.16	.04
☐ U38 Scott Leius	.12	.05	.01
☐ U39 Jack Morris	.10	.04	.01
☐ U40 Mike Pagliarulo	.05	.02	.00
☐ U41 Lenny Webster	.12	.05	.01
☐ U42 John Habyan	.05	.02	.00
☐ U43 Steve Howe	.05	.02	.00
☐ U44 Jeff Johnson	.17	.07	.01
☐ U45 Scott Kamieniecki	.17	.07	.01
☐ U46 Pat Kelly	.25	.10	.02
☐ U47 Hensley Meulens	.08	.03	.01
☐ U48 Wade Taylor	.17	.07	.01
☐ U49 Bernie Williams	.25	.10	.02
☐ U50 Kirk Dressendorfer	.20	.08	.02
☐ U51 Ernest Riles	.05	.02	.00
☐ U52 Rich DeLucia	.12	.05	.01
☐ U53 Tracy Jones	.05	.02	.00
☐ U54 Bill Krueger	.05	.02	.00
☐ U55 Alonzo Powell	.12	.05	.01
☐ U56 Jeff Schaefer	.05	.02	.00
☐ U57 Russ Swan	.08	.03	.01
☐ U58 John Barfield	.08	.03	.01
☐ U59 Rich Gossage	.08	.03	.01
☐ U60 Jose Guzman	.08	.03	.01
☐ U61 Dean Palmer	.35	.15	.03
☐ U62 Ivan Rodriguez	2.00	.80	.20
☐ U63 Roberto Alomar	.12	.05	.01
☐ U64 Tom Candiotti	.08	.03	.01

☐ U65 Joe Carter	.10	.04	.01
☐ U66 Ed Sprague	.12	.05	.01
☐ U67 Pat Tabler	.05	.02	.00
☐ U68 Mike Timlin	.12	.05	.01
☐ U69 Devon White	.08	.03	.01
☐ U70 Rafael Belliard	.05	.02	.00
☐ U71 Juan Berenguer	.05	.02	.00
☐ U72 Sid Bream	.05	.02	.00
☐ U73 Marvin Freeman	.05	.02	.00
☐ U74 Kent Mercker	.08	.03	.01
☐ U75 Otis Nixon	.08	.03	.01
☐ U76 Terry Pendleton	.10	.04	.01
☐ U77 George Bell	.10	.04	.01
☐ U78 Danny Jackson	.08	.03	.01
☐ U79 Chuck McElroy	.08	.03	.01
☐ U80 Gary Scott	.25	.10	.02
☐ U81 Heathcliff Slocumb	.10	.04	.01
☐ U82 Dave Smith	.05	.02	.00
☐ U83 Rick Wilkins	.17	.07	.01
☐ U84 Freddie Benavides	.12	.05	.01
☐ U85 Ted Power	.05	.02	.00
☐ U86 Mo Sanford	.20	.08	.02
☐ U87 Jeff Bagwell	3.00	1.25	.30
☐ U88 Steve Finley	.08	.03	.01
☐ U89 Pete Harnisch	.08	.03	.01
☐ U90 Darryl Kile	.12	.05	.01
☐ U91 Brett Butler	.08	.03	.01
☐ U92 John Candelaria	.05	.02	.00
☐ U93 Gary Carter	.08	.03	.01
☐ U94 Kevin Gross	.05	.02	.00
☐ U95 Bob Ojeda	.05	.02	.00
☐ U96 Darryl Strawberry	.20	.08	.02
☐ U97 Ivan Calderon	.08	.03	.01
☐ U98 Ron Hassey	.05	.02	.00
☐ U99 Gilberto Reyes	.05	.02	.00
☐ U100 Hubie Brooks	.08	.03	.01
☐ U101 Rick Cerone	.05	.02	.00
☐ U102 Vince Coleman	.10	.04	.01
☐ U103 Jeff Innis	.05	.02	.00
☐ U104 Pete Schourek	.12	.05	.01
☐ U105 Andy Ashby	.12	.05	.01
☐ U106 Wally Backman	.05	.02	.00
☐ U107 Darrin Fletcher	.10	.04	.01
☐ U108 Tommy Greene	.08	.03	.01
☐ U109 John Morris	.05	.02	.00
☐ U110 Mitch Williams	.08	.03	.01
☐ U111 Lloyd McClendon	.05	.02	.00
☐ U112 Orlando Merced	.35	.15	.03
☐ U113 Vicente Palacios	.05	.02	.00
☐ U114 Gary Varsho	.05	.02	.00
☐ U115 John Wehner	.25	.10	.02
☐ U116 Rex Hudler	.08	.03	.01
☐ U117 Tim Jones	.05	.02	.00
☐ U118 Geronimo Pena	.05	.02	.00
☐ U119 Gerald Perry	.05	.02	.00
☐ U120 Larry Andersen	.05	.02	.00
☐ U121 Jerald Clark	.05	.02	.00
☐ U122 Scott Coolbaugh	.05	.02	.00
☐ U123 Tony Fernandez	.08	.03	.01
☐ U124 Darrin Jackson	.08	.03	.01
☐ U125 Fred McGriff	.10	.04	.01
☐ U126 Jose Mota	.17	.07	.01
☐ U127 Tim Teufel	.05	.02	.00
☐ U128 Bud Black	.05	.02	.00
☐ U129 Mike Felder	.05	.02	.00
☐ U130 Willie McGee	.08	.03	.01
☐ U131 Dave Righetti	.08	.03	.01
☐ U132 Checklist Card	.05	.01	.00

1991 Fleer Ultra

This 400-card standard size (2 1/2" by 3 1/2") set marked Fleer's first entry into the high-end premium card market. The set was released in wax packs and features the best players in the majors along with a good mix of young prospects. The cards feature full color action photography on the fronts and three full-color photos on the backs along with 1990 and career statistics. Fleer claimed in their original press release that there would only be 15 percent of Ultra issued as there was of the regular issue. Fleer also issued the sets in their now traditional alphabetical order as well as the teams in alphabetical order. The card numbering is as follows, Atlanta Braves (1-13), Baltimore Orioles (14-26), Boston Red Sox (27-42), California Angels (43-54), Chicago Cubs (55-71), Chicago White Sox (72-86), Cincinnati Reds (87-103), Cleveland Indians (104-119), Detroit Tigers (120-130), Houston Astros (131-142), Kansas City Royals (143-158), Los Angeles Dodgers (159-171), Milwaukee Brewers (172-184), Minnesota Twins (185-196), Montreal Expos (197-210), New York Mets (211-227), New

York Yankees (228-242), Oakland Athletics (243-257), Philadelphia Phillies (258-272), Pittsburgh Pirates (273-287), St. Louis Cardinals (288-299), San Diego Padres (300-313), San Francisco Giants (314-331), Seattle Mariners (332-345), Texas Rangers (346-357), Toronto Blue Jays (358-372), Major League Prospects (373-390), Elite Performance (391-396), and Checklists (397-400). The key rookie cards in this set are Wes Chamberlain, Brian McRae, and Phil Plantier.

	MINT	EXC	G-VG
COMPLETE SET (400)	40.00	18.00	6.00
COMMON PLAYER (1-400)	.06	.02	.00
☐ 1 Steve Avery	2.00	.50	.10
☐ 2 Jeff Blauser	.06	.02	.00
☐ 3 Francisco Cabrera	.06	.02	.00
☐ 4 Ron Gant	.30	.12	.03
☐ 5 Tom Glavine	.20	.08	.02
☐ 6 Tommy Gregg	.06	.02	.00
☐ 7 Dave Justice	2.50	1.00	.25
☐ 8 Oddibe McDowell	.06	.02	.00
☐ 9 Greg Olson	.10	.04	.01
☐ 10 Terry Pendleton	.15	.06	.01
☐ 11 Lonnie Smith	.10	.04	.01
☐ 12 John Smoltz	.15	.06	.01
☐ 13 Jeff Treadway	.06	.02	.00
☐ 14 Glenn Davis	.10	.04	.01
☐ 15 Mike Devereaux	.06	.02	.00
☐ 16 Leo Gomez	.50	.20	.05
☐ 17 Chris Hoiles	.10	.04	.01
☐ 18 Dave Johnson	.06	.02	.00
☐ 19 Ben McDonald	.20	.08	.02
☐ 20 Randy Milligan	.10	.04	.01
☐ 21 Gregg Olson	.10	.04	.01
☐ 22 Joe Orsulak	.06	.02	.00
☐ 23 Bill Ripken	.06	.02	.00
☐ 24 Cal Ripken	.75	.30	.07
☐ 25 David Segui	.12	.05	.01
☐ 26 Craig Worthington	.06	.02	.00
☐ 27 Wade Boggs	.25	.10	.02
☐ 28 Tom Bolton	.06	.02	.00
☐ 29 Tom Brunansky	.10	.04	.01
☐ 30 Ellis Burks	.12	.05	.01
☐ 31 Roger Clemens	.50	.20	.05
☐ 32 Mike Greenwell	.15	.06	.01
☐ 33 Greg Harris	.06	.02	.00
☐ 34 Daryl Irvine	.12	.05	.01
☐ 35 Mike Marshall UER (1990 in stats is shown as 990)	.10	.04	.01
☐ 36 Tim Naehring	.15	.06	.01
☐ 37 Tony Pena	.10	.04	.01
☐ 38 Phil Plantier	4.50	2.00	.45
☐ 39 Carlos Quintana	.10	.04	.01
☐ 40 Jeff Reardon	.12	.05	.01
☐ 41 Jody Reed	.10	.04	.01
☐ 42 Luis Rivera	.06	.02	.00
☐ 43 Jim Abbott	.20	.08	.02
☐ 44 Chuck Finley	.12	.05	.01
☐ 45 Bryan Harvey	.10	.04	.01
☐ 46 Donnie Hill	.06	.02	.00
☐ 47 Jack Howell	.06	.02	.00
☐ 48 Wally Joyner	.12	.05	.01
☐ 49 Mark Langston	.10	.04	.01
☐ 50 Kirk McCaskill	.06	.02	.00
☐ 51 Lance Parrish	.10	.04	.01
☐ 52 Dick Schofield	.06	.02	.00
☐ 53 Lee Stevens	.25	.10	.02
☐ 54 Dave Winfield	.17	.07	.01
☐ 55 George Bell	.12	.05	.01
☐ 56 Damon Berryhill	.06	.02	.00
☐ 57 Mike Bielecki	.06	.02	.00
☐ 58 Andre Dawson	.20	.08	.02
☐ 59 Shawon Dunston	.10	.04	.01
☐ 60 Joe Girardi UER (Bats right, LH hitter shown is Doug Dascenzo)	.06	.02	.00
☐ 61 Mark Grace	.15	.06	.01
☐ 62 Mike Harkey	.10	.04	.01
☐ 63 Les Lancaster	.06	.02	.00
☐ 64 Greg Maddux	.10	.04	.01
☐ 65 Derrick May	.12	.05	.01
☐ 66 Ryne Sandberg	.60	.25	.06
☐ 67 Luis Salazar	.06	.02	.00
☐ 68 Dwight Smith	.10	.04	.01
☐ 69 Hector Villanueva	.10	.04	.01
☐ 70 Jerome Walton	.10	.04	.01
☐ 71 Mitch Williams	.06	.02	.00
☐ 72 Carlton Fisk	.25	.10	.02
☐ 73 Scott Fletcher	.06	.02	.00
☐ 74 Ozzie Guillen	.10	.04	.01
☐ 75 Greg Hibbard	.06	.02	.00
☐ 76 Lance Johnson	.06	.02	.00
☐ 77 Steve Lyons	.06	.02	.00
☐ 78 Jack McDowell	.12	.05	.01
☐ 79 Dan Pasqua	.06	.02	.00
☐ 80 Melido Perez	.06	.02	.00
☐ 81 Tim Raines	.10	.04	.01
☐ 82 Sammy Sosa	.10	.04	.01
☐ 83 Cory Snyder	.10	.04	.01
☐ 84 Bobby Thigpen	.10	.04	.01
☐ 85 Frank Thomas (Card says he is an outfielder)	6.00	2.50	.60
☐ 86 Robin Ventura	.60	.25	.06
☐ 87 Todd Benzinger	.06	.02	.00
☐ 88 Glenn Braggs	.06	.02	.00
☐ 89 Tom Browning UER (Front photo actually Norm Charlton)	.10	.04	.01
☐ 90 Norm Charlton	.06	.02	.00
☐ 91 Eric Davis	.17	.07	.01
☐ 92 Rob Dibble	.10	.04	.01

Card			
☐ 93 Bill Doran	.06	.02	.00
☐ 94 Mariano Duncan UER (Right back photo is Billy Hatcher)	.06	.02	.00
☐ 95 Billy Hatcher	.10	.04	.01
☐ 96 Barry Larkin	.15	.06	.01
☐ 97 Randy Myers	.06	.02	.00
☐ 98 Hal Morris	.17	.07	.01
☐ 99 Joe Oliver	.06	.02	.00
☐ 100 Paul O'Neill	.10	.04	.01
☐ 101 Jeff Reed (See also 104)	.06	.02	.00
☐ 102 Jose Rijo	.10	.04	.01
☐ 103 Chris Sabo (See also 106)	.12	.05	.01
☐ 104 Beau Allred UER (Card number is 101)	.15	.06	.01
☐ 105 Sandy Alomar Jr.	.12	.05	.01
☐ 106 Carlos Baerga UER (Card number is 103)	.25	.10	.02
☐ 107 Albert Belle	.50	.20	.05
☐ 108 Jerry Browne	.06	.02	.00
☐ 109 Tom Candiotti	.10	.04	.01
☐ 110 Alex Cole	.10	.04	.01
☐ 111 John Farrell (See also 114)	.06	.02	.00
☐ 112 Felix Fermin	.06	.02	.00
☐ 113 Brook Jacoby	.06	.02	.00
☐ 114 Chris James UER (Card number is 111)	.06	.02	.00
☐ 115 Doug Jones	.06	.02	.00
☐ 116 Steve Olin (See also 119)	.06	.02	.00
☐ 117 Greg Swindell	.10	.04	.01
☐ 118 Turner Ward	.25	.10	.02
☐ 119 Mitch Webster UER (Card number is 116)	.06	.02	.00
☐ 120 Dave Bergman	.06	.02	.00
☐ 121 Cecil Fielder	.40	.16	.04
☐ 122 Travis Fryman	1.75	.70	.17
☐ 123 Mike Henneman	.06	.02	.00
☐ 124 Lloyd Moseby	.06	.02	.00
☐ 125 Dan Petry	.06	.02	.00
☐ 126 Tony Phillips	.06	.02	.00
☐ 127 Mark Salas	.06	.02	.00
☐ 128 Frank Tanana	.10	.04	.01
☐ 129 Alan Trammell	.15	.06	.01
☐ 130 Lou Whitaker	.12	.05	.01
☐ 131 Eric Anthony	.10	.04	.01
☐ 132 Craig Biggio	.10	.04	.01
☐ 133 Ken Caminiti	.06	.02	.00
☐ 134 Casey Candaele	.06	.02	.00
☐ 135 Andujar Cedeno	1.00	.40	.10
☐ 136 Mark Davidson	.06	.02	.00
☐ 137 Jim Deshaies	.06	.02	.00
☐ 138 Mark Portugal	.06	.02	.00
☐ 139 Rafael Ramirez	.06	.02	.00
☐ 140 Mike Scott	.10	.04	.01
☐ 141 Eric Yelding	.06	.02	.00
☐ 142 Gerald Young	.06	.02	.00
☐ 143 Kevin Appier	.10	.04	.01
☐ 144 George Brett	.20	.08	.02
☐ 145 Jeff Conine	.20	.08	.02
☐ 146 Jim Eisenreich	.06	.02	.00
☐ 147 Tom Gordon	.10	.04	.01
☐ 148 Mark Gubicza	.10	.04	.01
☐ 149 Bo Jackson	.60	.25	.06
☐ 150 Brent Mayne	.20	.08	.02
☐ 151 Mike Macfarlane	.06	.02	.00
☐ 152 Brian McRae	1.25	.50	.12
☐ 153 Jeff Montgomery	.06	.02	.00
☐ 154 Bret Saberhagen	.12	.05	.01
☐ 155 Kevin Seitzer	.10	.04	.01
☐ 156 Terry Shumpert	.06	.02	.00
☐ 157 Kurt Stillwell	.06	.02	.00
☐ 158 Danny Tartabull	.12	.05	.01
☐ 159 Tim Belcher	.10	.04	.01
☐ 160 Kal Daniels	.10	.04	.01
☐ 161 Alfredo Griffin	.06	.02	.00
☐ 162 Lenny Harris	.06	.02	.00
☐ 163 Jay Howell	.06	.02	.00
☐ 164 Ramon Martinez	.30	.12	.03
☐ 165 Mike Morgan	.10	.04	.01
☐ 166 Eddie Murray	.20	.08	.02
☐ 167 Jose Offerman	.12	.05	.01
☐ 168 Juan Samuel	.10	.04	.01
☐ 169 Mike Scioscia	.06	.02	.00
☐ 170 Mike Sharperson	.06	.02	.00
☐ 171 Darryl Strawberry	.40	.16	.04
☐ 172 Greg Brock	.06	.02	.00
☐ 173 Chuck Crim	.06	.02	.00
☐ 174 Jim Gantner	.06	.02	.00
☐ 175 Ted Higuera	.06	.02	.00
☐ 176 Mark Knudson	.06	.02	.00
☐ 177 Tim McIntosh	.06	.02	.00
☐ 178 Paul Molitor	.12	.05	.01
☐ 179 Dan Plesac	.06	.02	.00
☐ 180 Gary Sheffield	.10	.04	.01
☐ 181 Bill Spiers	.06	.02	.00
☐ 182 B.J. Surhoff	.06	.02	.00
☐ 183 Greg Vaughn	.20	.08	.02
☐ 184 Robin Yount	.25	.10	.02
☐ 185 Rick Aguilera	.10	.04	.01
☐ 186 Greg Gagne	.06	.02	.00
☐ 187 Dan Gladden	.06	.02	.00
☐ 188 Brian Harper	.10	.04	.01
☐ 189 Kent Hrbek	.12	.05	.01
☐ 190 Gene Larkin	.06	.02	.00
☐ 191 Shane Mack	.10	.04	.01
☐ 192 Pedro Munoz	.60	.25	.06
☐ 193 Al Newman	.06	.02	.00
☐ 194 Junior Ortiz	.06	.02	.00
☐ 195 Kirby Puckett	.25	.10	.02
☐ 196 Kevin Tapani	.12	.05	.01
☐ 197 Dennis Boyd	.06	.02	.00
☐ 198 Tim Burke	.06	.02	.00

☐ 199 Ivan Calderon	.10	.04	.01
☐ 200 Delino DeShields	.15	.06	.01
☐ 201 Mike Fitzgerald	.06	.02	.00
☐ 202 Steve Frey	.10	.04	.01
☐ 203 Andres Galarraga	.10	.04	.01
☐ 204 Marquis Grissom	.15	.06	.01
☐ 205 Dave Martinez	.06	.02	.00
☐ 206 Dennis Martinez	.10	.04	.01
☐ 207 Junior Noboa	.06	.02	.00
☐ 208 Spike Owen	.06	.02	.00
☐ 209 Scott Ruskin	.10	.04	.01
☐ 210 Tim Wallach	.10	.04	.01
☐ 211 Daryl Boston	.06	.02	.00
☐ 212 Vince Coleman	.12	.05	.01
☐ 213 David Cone	.10	.04	.01
☐ 214 Ron Darling	.10	.04	.01
☐ 215 Kevin Elster	.06	.02	.00
☐ 216 Sid Fernandez	.10	.04	.01
☐ 217 John Franco	.06	.02	.00
☐ 218 Dwight Gooden	.18	.08	.01
☐ 219 Tom Herr	.06	.02	.00
☐ 220 Todd Hundley	.10	.04	.01
☐ 221 Gregg Jefferies	.12	.05	.01
☐ 222 Howard Johnson	.15	.06	.01
☐ 223 Dave Magadan	.10	.04	.01
☐ 224 Kevin McReynolds	.10	.04	.01
☐ 225 Keith Miller	.06	.02	.00
☐ 226 Mackey Sasser	.06	.02	.00
☐ 227 Frank Viola	.10	.04	.01
☐ 228 Jesse Barfield	.10	.04	.01
☐ 229 Greg Cadaret	.06	.02	.00
☐ 230 Alvaro Espinoza	.06	.02	.00
☐ 231 Bob Geren	.06	.02	.00
☐ 232 Lee Guetterman	.06	.02	.00
☐ 233 Mel Hall	.06	.02	.00
☐ 234 Andy Hawkins UER (Back center photo is not him)	.06	.02	.00
☐ 235 Roberto Kelly	.10	.04	.01
☐ 236 Tim Leary	.10	.04	.01
☐ 237 Jim Leyritz	.06	.02	.00
☐ 238 Kevin Maas	.30	.12	.03
☐ 239 Don Mattingly	.30	.12	.03
☐ 240 Hensley Meulens	.12	.05	.01
☐ 241 Eric Plunk	.06	.02	.00
☐ 242 Steve Sax	.10	.04	.01
☐ 243 Todd Burns	.06	.02	.00
☐ 244 Jose Canseco	.75	.30	.07
☐ 245 Dennis Eckersley	.10	.04	.01
☐ 246 Mike Gallego	.06	.02	.00
☐ 247 Dave Henderson	.10	.04	.01
☐ 248 Rickey Henderson	.40	.16	.04
☐ 249 Rick Honeycutt	.06	.02	.00
☐ 250 Carney Lansford	.10	.04	.01
☐ 251 Mark McGwire	.15	.06	.01
☐ 252 Mike Moore	.10	.04	.01
☐ 253 Terry Steinbach	.06	.02	.00
☐ 254 Dave Stewart	.10	.04	.01
☐ 255 Walt Weiss	.10	.04	.01
☐ 256 Bob Welch	.10	.04	.01
☐ 257 Curt Young	.06	.02	.00
☐ 258 Wes Chamberlain	1.25	.50	.12
☐ 259 Pat Combs	.06	.02	.00
☐ 260 Darren Daulton	.06	.02	.00
☐ 261 Jose DeJesus	.06	.02	.00
☐ 262 Len Dykstra	.10	.04	.01
☐ 263 Charlie Hayes	.06	.02	.00
☐ 264 Von Hayes	.10	.04	.01
☐ 265 Ken Howell	.06	.02	.00
☐ 266 John Kruk	.06	.02	.00
☐ 267 Roger McDowell	.06	.02	.00
☐ 268 Mickey Morandini	.15	.06	.01
☐ 269 Terry Mulholland	.10	.04	.01
☐ 270 Dale Murphy	.15	.06	.01
☐ 271 Randy Ready	.06	.02	.00
☐ 272 Dickie Thon	.06	.02	.00
☐ 273 Stan Belinda	.06	.02	.00
☐ 274 Jay Bell	.06	.02	.00
☐ 275 Barry Bonds	.30	.12	.03
☐ 276 Bobby Bonilla	.20	.08	.02
☐ 277 Doug Drabek	.10	.04	.01
☐ 278 Carlos Garcia	.20	.08	.02
☐ 279 Neal Heaton	.06	.02	.00
☐ 280 Jeff King	.10	.04	.01
☐ 281 Bill Landrum	.06	.02	.00
☐ 282 Mike LaValliere	.06	.02	.00
☐ 283 Jose Lind	.06	.02	.00
☐ 284 Orlando Merced	.90	.40	.09
☐ 285 Gary Redus	.06	.02	.00
☐ 286 Don Slaught	.06	.02	.00
☐ 287 Andy Van Slyke	.10	.04	.01
☐ 288 Jose DeLeon	.06	.02	.00
☐ 289 Pedro Guerrero	.10	.04	.01
☐ 290 Ray Lankford	.60	.25	.06
☐ 291 Joe Magrane	.06	.02	.00
☐ 292 Jose Oquendo	.06	.02	.00
☐ 293 Tom Pagnozzi	.06	.02	.00
☐ 294 Bryn Smith	.06	.02	.00
☐ 295 Lee Smith	.10	.04	.01
☐ 296 Ozzie Smith UER (Born 12-26, 54, should have hyphen)	.25	.10	.02
☐ 297 Milt Thompson	.06	.02	.00
☐ 298 Craig Wilson	.15	.06	.01
☐ 299 Todd Zeile	.20	.08	.02
☐ 300 Shawn Abner	.06	.02	.00
☐ 301 Andy Benes	.15	.06	.01
☐ 302 Paul Faries	.12	.05	.01
☐ 303 Tony Gwynn	.25	.10	.02
☐ 304 Greg W. Harris	.06	.02	.00
☐ 305 Thomas Howard	.06	.02	.00
☐ 306 Bruce Hurst	.10	.04	.01
☐ 307 Craig Lefferts	.06	.02	.00
☐ 308 Fred McGriff	.15	.06	.01
☐ 309 Dennis Rasmussen	.06	.02	.00
☐ 310 Bip Roberts	.06	.02	.00

☐ 311 Benito Santiago	.10	.04	.01
☐ 312 Garry Templeton	.06	.02	.00
☐ 313 Ed Whitson	.06	.02	.00
☐ 314 Dave Anderson	.06	.02	.00
☐ 315 Kevin Bass	.06	.02	.00
☐ 316 Jeff Brantley	.06	.02	.00
☐ 317 John Burkett	.06	.02	.00
☐ 318 Will Clark	.60	.25	.06
☐ 319 Steve Decker	.40	.16	.04
☐ 320 Scott Garrelts	.06	.02	.00
☐ 321 Terry Kennedy	.06	.02	.00
☐ 322 Mark Leonard	.20	.08	.02
☐ 323 Darren Lewis	.60	.25	.06
☐ 324 Greg Litton	.06	.02	.00
☐ 325 Willie McGee	.10	.04	.01
☐ 326 Kevin Mitchell	.15	.06	.01
☐ 327 Don Robinson	.06	.02	.00
☐ 328 Andres Santana	.30	.12	.03
☐ 329 Robby Thompson	.06	.02	.00
☐ 330 Jose Uribe	.06	.02	.00
☐ 331 Matt Williams	.17	.07	.01
☐ 332 Scott Bradley	.06	.02	.00
☐ 333 Henry Cotto	.06	.02	.00
☐ 334 Alvin Davis	.10	.04	.01
☐ 335 Ken Griffey Sr.	.10	.04	.01
☐ 336 Ken Griffey Jr.	3.00	1.25	.30
☐ 337 Erik Hanson	.10	.04	.01
☐ 338 Brian Holman	.10	.04	.01
☐ 339 Randy Johnson	.10	.04	.01
☐ 340 Edgar Martinez UER (Listed as playing SS)	.10	.04	.01
☐ 341 Tino Martinez	.30	.12	.03
☐ 342 Pete O'Brien	.06	.02	.00
☐ 343 Harold Reynolds	.10	.04	.01
☐ 344 Dave Valle	.06	.02	.00
☐ 345 Omar Vizquel	.06	.02	.00
☐ 346 Brad Arnsberg	.06	.02	.00
☐ 347 Kevin Brown	.06	.02	.00
☐ 348 Julio Franco	.12	.05	.01
☐ 349 Jeff Huson	.06	.02	.00
☐ 350 Rafael Palmeiro	.17	.07	.01
☐ 351 Geno Petralli	.06	.02	.00
☐ 352 Gary Pettis	.06	.02	.00
☐ 353 Kenny Rogers	.06	.02	.00
☐ 354 Jeff Russell	.06	.02	.00
☐ 355 Nolan Ryan	1.25	.50	.12
☐ 356 Ruben Sierra	.30	.12	.03
☐ 357 Bobby Witt	.10	.04	.01
☐ 358 Roberto Alomar	.25	.10	.02
☐ 359 Pat Borders	.06	.02	.00
☐ 360 Joe Carter UER (Reverse negative on back photo)	.15	.06	.01
☐ 361 Kelly Gruber	.10	.04	.01
☐ 362 Tom Henke	.10	.04	.01
☐ 363 Glenallen Hill	.10	.04	.01
☐ 364 Jimmy Key	.10	.04	.01
☐ 365 Manny Lee	.06	.02	.00
☐ 366 Rance Mulliniks	.06	.02	.00
☐ 367 John Olerud UER (Throwing left on card; back has throws right)	.25	.10	.02
☐ 368 Dave Stieb	.10	.04	.01
☐ 369 Duane Ward	.06	.02	.00
☐ 370 David Wells	.06	.02	.00
☐ 371 Mark Whiten	.30	.12	.03
☐ 372 Mookie Wilson	.06	.02	.00
☐ 373 Willie Banks MLP	.40	.16	.04
☐ 374 Steve Carter MLP	.10	.04	.01
☐ 375 Scott Chiamparino MLP	.12	.05	.01
☐ 376 Steve Chitren MLP	.12	.05	.01
☐ 377 Darrin Fletcher MLP	.15	.06	.01
☐ 378 Rich Garces MLP	.15	.06	.01
☐ 379 Reggie Jefferson MLP	.75	.30	.07
☐ 380 Eric Karros MLP	.90	.40	.09
☐ 381 Pat Kelly MLP	.60	.25	.06
☐ 382 Chuck Knoblauch MLP	2.00	.80	.20
☐ 383 Denny Neagle MLP	.75	.30	.07
☐ 384 Dan Opperman MLP	.25	.10	.02
☐ 385 John Ramos MLP	.35	.15	.03
☐ 386 Henry Rodriguez MLP	.30	.12	.03
☐ 387 Maurice Vaughn MLP	1.50	.60	.15
☐ 388 Gerald Williams MLP	.60	.25	.06
☐ 389 Mike York MLP	.20	.08	.02
☐ 390 Eddie Zosky MLP	.25	.10	.02
☐ 391 Barry Bonds EP	.20	.08	.02
☐ 392 Cecil Fielder EP	.20	.08	.02
☐ 393 Rickey Henderson EP	.30	.12	.03
☐ 394 Dave Justice EP	.75	.30	.07
☐ 395 Nolan Ryan EP	.40	.16	.04
☐ 396 Bobby Thigpen EP	.10	.04	.01
☐ 397 Checklist Card Gregg Jefferies	.10	.04	.01
☐ 398 Checklist Card Von Hayes	.10	.04	.01
☐ 399 Checklist Card Terry Kennedy	.10	.04	.01
☐ 400 Checklist Card Nolan Ryan	.15	.06	.01

1991 Fleer Ultra Update

The 1991 Fleer Ultra Baseball Update set contains 120 cards and 20 team logo stickers. The set includes the year's hottest rookies and important veteran players traded after the original Ultra series was produced. The cards measure the standard size (2 1/2" by 3

1/2"). The front has a color action shot, while the back has a portrait photo and two full-figure action shots. The cards are numbered and checklisted below alphabetically within and according to teams for each league as follow: Baltimore Orioles (1-4), Boston Red Sox (5-7), California Angels (8-12), Chicago White Sox (13-18), Cleveland Indians (19-21), Detroit Tigers (22-24), Kansas City Royals (25-29), Milwaukee Brewers (30-33), Minnesota Twins (34-39), New York Yankees (40-44), Oakland Athletics (45-48), Seattle Mariners (49-53), Texas Rangers (54-58), Toronto Blue Jays (59-64), Atlanta Braves (65-69), Chicago Cubs (70-75), Cincinnati Reds (76-78), Houston Astros (79-84), Los Angeles Dodgers (85-89), Montreal Expos (90-93), New York Mets (94-97), Philadelphia Phillies (98-101), Pittsburgh Pirates (102-104), St. Louis Cardinals (105-109), San Diego Padres (110-114), and San Francisco Giants (115-119). The key rookie cards in this set are Jeff Bagwell and Ivan Rodriguez.

	MINT	EXC	G-VG
COMPLETE SET (120)	22.00	9.50	3.15
COMMON PLAYER (U1-U120)	.07	.03	.01
☐ U1 Dwight Evans	.10	.04	.01
☐ U2 Chito Martinez	1.25	.50	.12
☐ U3 Bob Melvin	.07	.03	.01
☐ U4 Mike Mussina	.75	.30	.07
☐ U5 Jack Clark	.12	.05	.01
☐ U6 Dana Kiecker	.07	.03	.01
☐ U7 Steve Lyons	.07	.03	.01
☐ U8 Gary Gaetti	.10	.04	.01
☐ U9 Dave Gallagher	.07	.03	.01
☐ U10 Dave Parker	.12	.05	.01
☐ U11 Luis Polonia	.10	.04	.01
☐ U12 Luis Sojo	.10	.04	.01
☐ U13 Wilson Alvarez	.17	.07	.01
☐ U14 Alex Fernandez	.40	.16	.04
☐ U15 Craig Grebeck	.07	.03	.01
☐ U16 Ron Karkovice	.07	.03	.01
☐ U17 Warren Newson	.30	.12	.03
☐ U18 Scott Radinsky	.10	.04	.01
☐ U19 Glenallen Hill	.10	.04	.01
☐ U20 Charles Nagy	.15	.06	.01
☐ U21 Mark Whiten	.30	.12	.03
☐ U22 Milt Cuyler	.30	.12	.03
☐ U23 Paul Gibson	.07	.03	.01
☐ U24 Mickey Tettleton	.10	.04	.01
☐ U25 Todd Benzinger	.07	.03	.01
☐ U26 Storm Davis	.07	.03	.01
☐ U27 Kirk Gibson	.12	.05	.01
☐ U28 Bill Pecota	.07	.03	.01
☐ U29 Gary Thurman	.07	.03	.01
☐ U30 Darryl Hamilton	.10	.04	.01
☐ U31 Jaime Navarro	.07	.03	.01
☐ U32 Willie Randolph	.10	.04	.01
☐ U33 Bill Wegman	.07	.03	.01
☐ U34 Randy Bush	.07	.03	.01
☐ U35 Chili Davis	.10	.04	.01
☐ U36 Scott Erickson	2.00	.80	.20
☐ U37 Chuck Knoblauch	1.00	.40	.10
☐ U38 Scott Leius	.12	.05	.01
☐ U39 Jack Morris	.15	.06	.01
☐ U40 John Habyan	.07	.03	.01
☐ U41 Pat Kelly	.50	.20	.05
☐ U42 Matt Nokes	.10	.04	.01
☐ U43 Scott Sanderson	.10	.04	.01
☐ U44 Bernie Williams	1.00	.40	.10
☐ U45 Harold Baines	.12	.05	.01
☐ U46 Brook Jacoby	.07	.03	.01
☐ U47 Earnest Riles	.07	.03	.01
☐ U48 Willie Wilson	.10	.04	.01
☐ U49 Jay Buhner	.12	.05	.01
☐ U50 Rich DeLucia	.25	.10	.02
☐ U51 Mike Jackson	.07	.03	.01
☐ U52 Bill Krueger	.07	.03	.01
☐ U53 Bill Swift	.10	.04	.01
☐ U54 Brian Downing	.10	.04	.01
☐ U55 Juan Gonzalez	2.50	1.00	.25
☐ U56 Dean Palmer	.75	.30	.07
☐ U57 Kevin Reimer	.15	.06	.01
☐ U58 Ivan Rodriguez	4.00	1.75	.40
☐ U59 Tom Candiotti	.10	.04	.01
☐ U60 Juan Guzman	1.25	.50	.12
☐ U61 Bob MacDonald	.17	.07	.01
☐ U62 Greg Myers	.07	.03	.01
☐ U63 Ed Sprague	.20	.08	.02
☐ U64 Devon White	.10	.04	.01
☐ U65 Rafael Belliard	.07	.03	.01
☐ U66 Juan Berenguer	.07	.03	.01
☐ U67 Brian Hunter	1.50	.60	.15
☐ U68 Kent Mercker	.10	.04	.01
☐ U69 Otis Nixon	.10	.04	.01
☐ U70 Danny Jackson	.10	.04	.01
☐ U71 Chuck McElroy	.10	.04	.01
☐ U72 Gary Scott	.45	.18	.04

☐ U73 Heathcliff Slocumb .... .15 .06 .01
☐ U74 Chico Walker .... .10 .04 .01
☐ U75 Rick Wilkins .... .35 .15 .03
☐ U76 Chris Hammond .... .15 .06 .01
☐ U77 Luis Quinones .... .07 .03 .01
☐ U78 Herm Winningham .... .07 .03 .01
☐ U79 Jeff Bagwell .... 5.00 2.25 .50
☐ U80 Jim Corsi .... .07 .03 .01
☐ U81 Steve Finley .... .12 .05 .01
☐ U82 Luis Gonzalez .... 1.50 .60 .15
☐ U83 Pete Harnisch .... .10 .04 .01
☐ U84 Darryl Kile .... .25 .10 .02
☐ U85 Brett Butler .... .12 .05 .01
☐ U86 Gary Carter .... .12 .05 .01
☐ U87 Tim Crews .... .07 .03 .01
☐ U88 Orel Hershiser .... .12 .05 .01
☐ U89 Bob Ojeda .... .07 .03 .01
☐ U90 Bret Barberie .... .50 .20 .05
☐ U91 Barry Jones .... .07 .03 .01
☐ U92 Gilberto Reyes .... .07 .03 .01
☐ U93 Larry Walker .... .15 .06 .01
☐ U94 Hubie Brooks .... .10 .04 .01
☐ U95 Tim Burke .... .07 .03 .01
☐ U96 Rick Cerone .... .07 .03 .01
☐ U97 Jeff Innis .... .07 .03 .01
☐ U98 Wally Backman .... .07 .03 .01
☐ U99 Tommy Greene .... .12 .05 .01
☐ U100 Ricky Jordan .... .10 .04 .01
☐ U101 Mitch Williams .... .10 .04 .01
☐ U102 John Smiley .... .12 .05 .01
☐ U103 Randy Tomlin .... .50 .20 .05
☐ U104 Gary Varsho .... .07 .03 .01
☐ U105 Cris Carpenter .... .07 .03 .01
☐ U106 Ken Hill .... .10 .04 .01
☐ U107 Felix Jose .... .20 .08 .02
☐ U108 Omar Olivares .... .25 .10 .02
☐ U109 Gerald Perry .... .07 .03 .01
☐ U110 Jerald Clark .... .10 .04 .01
☐ U111 Tony Fernandez .... .10 .04 .01
☐ U112 Darrin Jackson .... .10 .04 .01
☐ U113 Mike Maddux .... .10 .04 .01
☐ U114 Tim Teufel .... .10 .04 .01
☐ U115 Bud Black .... .07 .03 .01
☐ U116 Kelly Downs .... .07 .03 .01
☐ U117 Mike Felder .... .07 .03 .01
☐ U118 Willie McGee .... .12 .05 .01
☐ U119 Trevor Wilson .... .07 .03 .01
☐ U120 Checklist Card .... .07 .01 .00

1992 Fleer

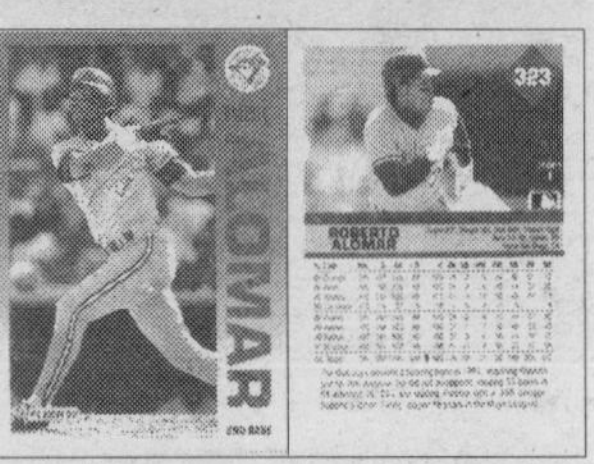

The 1992 Fleer set contains 720 cards measuring the standard size (2 1/2" by 3 1/2"). The card fronts shade from metallic pale green to white as one moves down the face. The team logo and player's name appear to the right of the picture, running the length of the card. The top portion of the backs has a different color player photo and biography, while the bottom portion includes statistics and player profile. The cards are checklisted below alphabetically within and according to teams for each league as follows: Baltimore Orioles (1-31), Boston Red Sox (32-49), California Angels (50-73), Chicago White Sox (74-101), Cleveland Indians (102-126), Detroit Tigers (127-149), Kansas City Royals (150-172), Milwaukee Brewers (173-194), Minnesota Twins (195-220), New York Yankees (221-247), Oakland Athletics (248-272), Seattle Mariners (273-296), Texas Rangers (297-321), Toronto Blue Jays (322-348), Atlanta Braves (349-374), Chicago Cubs (375-397), Cincinnati Reds (398-423), Houston Astros (424-446), Los Angeles Dodgers (447-471), Montreal Expos (472-494), New York Mets (495-520), Philadelphia Phillies (521-547), Pittsburgh Pirates (548-573), St. Louis Cardinals (574-596), San Diego Padres (597-624), and San Francisco Giants (625-651). Topical subsets feature Major League Prospects (652-680), Record Setters (681-687), League Leaders (688-697), Super Star Specials (698-707), Pro Visions (708-713), and Checklists (714-720).

	MINT	EXC	G-VG
COMPLETE SET (720)	36.00	16.25	5.50
COMMON PLAYER (1-720)	.04	.02	.00

☐ 1 Brady Anderson	.04	.02	.00
☐ 2 Jose Bautista	.04	.02	.00
☐ 3 Juan Bell	.04	.02	.00
☐ 4 Glenn Davis	.07	.03	.01
☐ 5 Mike Devereaux	.04	.02	.00
☐ 6 Dwight Evans	.07	.03	.01
☐ 7 Mike Flanagan	.07	.03	.01
☐ 8 Leo Gomez	.15	.06	.01
☐ 9 Chris Hoiles	.07	.03	.01
☐ 10 Sam Horn	.04	.02	.00
☐ 11 Tim Hulett	.04	.02	.00
☐ 12 Dave Johnson	.04	.02	.00
☐ 13 Chito Martinez	.30	.12	.03
☐ 14 Ben McDonald	.10	.04	.01
☐ 15 Bob Melvin	.04	.02	.00
☐ 16 Luis Mercedes	.20	.08	.02
☐ 17 Jose Mesa	.04	.02	.00
☐ 18 Bob Milacki	.04	.02	.00
☐ 19 Randy Milligan	.07	.03	.01
☐ 20 Mike Mussina	.20	.08	.02
☐ 21 Gregg Olson	.07	.03	.01
☐ 22 Joe Orsulak	.04	.02	.00
☐ 23 Jim Poole	.07	.03	.01
☐ 24 Arthur Rhodes	.25	.10	.02
☐ 25 Billy Ripken	.04	.02	.00
☐ 26 Cal Ripken	.40	.16	.04
☐ 27 David Segui	.07	.03	.01
☐ 28 Roy Smith	.04	.02	.00
☐ 29 Anthony Telford	.04	.02	.00
☐ 30 Mark Williamson	.04	.02	.00
☐ 31 Craig Worthington	.04	.02	.00
☐ 32 Wade Boggs	.20	.08	.02
☐ 33 Tom Bolton	.04	.02	.00
☐ 34 Tom Brunansky	.07	.03	.01
☐ 35 Ellis Burks	.07	.03	.01
☐ 36 Jack Clark	.07	.03	.01
☐ 37 Roger Clemens	.25	.10	.02
☐ 38 Danny Darwin	.04	.02	.00
☐ 39 Mike Greenwell	.12	.05	.01
☐ 40 Joe Hesketh	.04	.02	.00
☐ 41 Daryl Irvine	.04	.02	.00
☐ 42 Dennis Lamp	.04	.02	.00
☐ 43 Tony Pena	.07	.03	.01
☐ 44 Phil Plantier	.75	.30	.07
☐ 45 Carlos Quintana	.07	.03	.01
☐ 46 Jeff Reardon	.07	.03	.01
☐ 47 Jody Reed	.07	.03	.01
☐ 48 Luis Rivera	.04	.02	.00
☐ 49 Mo Vaughn	.35	.15	.03
☐ 50 Jim Abbott	.12	.05	.01
☐ 51 Kyle Abbott	.15	.06	.01
☐ 52 Ruben Amaro Jr.	.10	.04	.01
☐ 53 Scott Bailes	.04	.02	.00
☐ 54 Chris Beasley	.15	.06	.01
☐ 55 Mark Eichhorn	.04	.02	.00
☐ 56 Mike Fetters	.04	.02	.00
☐ 57 Chuck Finley	.07	.03	.01
☐ 58 Gary Gaetti	.07	.03	.01
☐ 59 Dave Gallagher	.04	.02	.00
☐ 60 Donnie Hill	.04	.02	.00
☐ 61 Bryan Harvey	.07	.03	.01
☐ 62 Wally Joyner	.07	.03	.01
☐ 63 Mark Langston	.07	.03	.01
☐ 64 Kirk McCaskill	.04	.02	.00
☐ 65 John Orton	.04	.02	.00
☐ 66 Lance Parrish	.07	.03	.01
☐ 67 Luis Polonia	.07	.03	.01
☐ 68 Bobby Rose	.04	.02	.00
☐ 69 Dick Schofield	.04	.02	.00
☐ 70 Luis Sojo	.04	.02	.00
☐ 71 Lee Stevens	.07	.03	.01
☐ 72 Dave Winfield	.12	.05	.01
☐ 73 Cliff Young	.04	.02	.00
☐ 74 Wilson Alvarez	.12	.05	.01
☐ 75 Esteban Beltre	.15	.06	.01
☐ 76 Joey Cora	.04	.02	.00
☐ 77 Brian Drahman	.07	.03	.01
☐ 78 Alex Fernandez	.12	.05	.01
☐ 79 Carlton Fisk	.12	.05	.01
☐ 80 Scott Fletcher	.04	.02	.00
☐ 81 Craig Grebeck	.04	.02	.00
☐ 82 Ozzie Guillen	.07	.03	.01
☐ 83 Greg Hibbard	.04	.02	.00
☐ 84 Charlie Hough	.04	.02	.00
☐ 85 Mike Huff	.04	.02	.00
☐ 86 Bo Jackson	.35	.15	.03
☐ 87 Lance Johnson	.04	.02	.00
☐ 88 Ron Karkovice	.04	.02	.00
☐ 89 Jack McDowell	.07	.03	.01
☐ 90 Matt Merullo	.04	.02	.00
☐ 91 Warren Newson	.07	.03	.01
☐ 92 Donn Pall UER (Called Dunn on card back)	.04	.02	.00
☐ 93 Dan Pasqua	.04	.02	.00
☐ 94 Ken Patterson	.04	.02	.00
☐ 95 Melido Perez	.04	.02	.00
☐ 96 Scott Radinsky	.04	.02	.00
☐ 97 Tim Raines	.07	.03	.01
☐ 98 Sammy Sosa	.07	.03	.01
☐ 99 Bobby Thigpen	.07	.03	.01
☐ 100 Frank Thomas	1.25	.50	.12
☐ 101 Robin Ventura	.25	.10	.02
☐ 102 Mike Aldrete	.04	.02	.00
☐ 103 Sandy Alomar Jr.	.07	.03	.01
☐ 104 Carlos Baerga	.12	.05	.01
☐ 105 Albert Belle	.15	.06	.01
☐ 106 Willie Blair	.04	.02	.00
☐ 107 Jerry Browne	.04	.02	.00
☐ 108 Alex Cole	.07	.03	.01
☐ 109 Felix Fermin	.04	.02	.00
☐ 110 Glenallen Hill	.07	.03	.01
☐ 111 Shawn Hillegas	.04	.02	.00
☐ 112 Chris James	.04	.02	.00
☐ 113 Reggie Jefferson	.20	.08	.02
☐ 114 Doug Jones	.04	.02	.00

	Player			
☐ 115	Eric King	.04	.02	.00
☐ 116	Mark Lewis	.15	.06	.01
☐ 117	Carlos Martinez	.04	.02	.00
☐ 118	Charles Nagy	.07	.03	.01
☐ 119	Rod Nichols	.04	.02	.00
☐ 120	Steve Olin	.04	.02	.00
☐ 121	Jesse Orosco	.04	.02	.00
☐ 122	Rudy Seanez	.04	.02	.00
☐ 123	Joel Skinner	.04	.02	.00
☐ 124	Greg Swindell	.07	.03	.01
☐ 125	Jim Thome	.60	.25	.06
☐ 126	Mark Whiten	.15	.06	.01
☐ 127	Scott Aldred	.04	.02	.00
☐ 128	Andy Allanson	.04	.02	.00
☐ 129	John Cerutti	.04	.02	.00
☐ 130	Milt Cuyler	.07	.03	.01
☐ 131	Mike Dalton	.15	.06	.01
☐ 132	Rob Deer	.04	.02	.00
☐ 133	Cecil Fielder	.25	.10	.02
☐ 134	Travis Fryman	.30	.12	.03
☐ 135	Dan Gakeler	.07	.03	.01
☐ 136	Paul Gibson	.04	.02	.00
☐ 137	Bill Gullickson	.04	.02	.00
☐ 138	Mike Henneman	.04	.02	.00
☐ 139	Pete Incaviglia	.07	.03	.01
☐ 140	Mark Leiter	.07	.03	.01
☐ 141	Scott Livingstone	.18	.08	.01
☐ 142	Lloyd Moseby	.04	.02	.00
☐ 143	Tony Phillips	.04	.02	.00
☐ 144	Mark Salas	.04	.02	.00
☐ 145	Frank Tanana	.07	.03	.01
☐ 146	Walt Terrell	.04	.02	.00
☐ 147	Mickey Tettleton	.07	.03	.01
☐ 148	Alan Trammell	.07	.03	.01
☐ 149	Lou Whitaker	.07	.03	.01
☐ 150	Kevin Appier	.07	.03	.01
☐ 151	Luis Aquino	.04	.02	.00
☐ 152	Todd Benzinger	.04	.02	.00
☐ 153	Mike Boddicker	.04	.02	.00
☐ 154	George Brett	.15	.06	.01
☐ 155	Storm Davis	.04	.02	.00
☐ 156	Jim Eisenreich	.04	.02	.00
☐ 157	Kirk Gibson	.07	.03	.01
☐ 158	Tom Gordon	.07	.03	.01
☐ 159	Mark Gubicza	.07	.03	.01
☐ 160	David Howard	.07	.03	.01
☐ 161	Mike Macfarlane	.04	.02	.00
☐ 162	Brent Mayne	.07	.03	.01
☐ 163	Brian McRae	.18	.08	.01
☐ 164	Jeff Montgomery	.04	.02	.00
☐ 165	Bill Pecota	.04	.02	.00
☐ 166	Harvey Pulliam	.20	.08	.02
☐ 167	Bret Saberhagen	.10	.04	.01
☐ 168	Kevin Seitzer	.07	.03	.01
☐ 169	Terry Shumpert	.04	.02	.00
☐ 170	Kurt Stillwell	.04	.02	.00
☐ 171	Danny Tartabull	.10	.04	.01
☐ 172	Gary Thurman	.04	.02	.00
☐ 173	Dante Bichette	.04	.02	.00
☐ 174	Kevin Brown	.07	.03	.01
☐ 175	Chuck Crim	.04	.02	.00
☐ 176	Jim Gantner	.04	.02	.00
☐ 177	Darryl Hamilton	.04	.02	.00
☐ 178	Ted Higuera	.04	.02	.00
☐ 179	Darren Holmes	.07	.03	.01
☐ 180	Mark Lee	.07	.03	.01
☐ 181	Julio Machado	.04	.02	.00
☐ 182	Paul Molitor	.07	.03	.01
☐ 183	Jaime Navarro	.04	.02	.00
☐ 184	Edwin Nunez	.04	.02	.00
☐ 185	Dan Plesac	.04	.02	.00
☐ 186	Willie Randolph	.04	.02	.00
☐ 187	Ron Robinson	.04	.02	.00
☐ 188	Gary Sheffield	.07	.03	.01
☐ 189	Bill Spiers	.04	.02	.00
☐ 190	B.J. Surhoff	.07	.03	.01
☐ 191	Dale Sveum	.04	.02	.00
☐ 192	Greg Vaughn	.07	.03	.01
☐ 193	Bill Wegman	.04	.02	.00
☐ 194	Robin Yount	.15	.06	.01
☐ 195	Rick Aguilera	.04	.02	.00
☐ 196	Allan Anderson	.04	.02	.00
☐ 197	Steve Bedrosian	.04	.02	.00
☐ 198	Randy Bush	.04	.02	.00
☐ 199	Larry Casian	.07	.03	.01
☐ 200	Chili Davis	.07	.03	.01
☐ 201	Scott Erickson	.45	.18	.04
☐ 202	Greg Gagne	.04	.02	.00
☐ 203	Dan Gladden	.04	.02	.00
☐ 204	Brian Harper	.04	.02	.00
☐ 205	Kent Hrbek	.07	.03	.01
☐ 206	Chuck Knoblauch	.35	.15	.03
☐ 207	Gene Larkin	.04	.02	.00
☐ 208	Terry Leach	.04	.02	.00
☐ 209	Scott Leius	.07	.03	.01
☐ 210	Shane Mack	.07	.03	.01
☐ 211	Jack Morris	.07	.03	.01
☐ 212	Pedro Munoz	.15	.06	.01
☐ 213	Denny Neagle	.25	.10	.02
☐ 214	Al Newman	.04	.02	.00
☐ 215	Junior Ortiz	.04	.02	.00
☐ 216	Mike Pagliarulo	.04	.02	.00
☐ 217	Kirby Puckett	.20	.08	.02
☐ 218	Paul Sorrento	.04	.02	.00
☐ 219	Kevin Tapani	.07	.03	.01
☐ 220	Lenny Webster	.07	.03	.01
☐ 221	Jesse Barfield	.07	.03	.01
☐ 222	Greg Cadaret	.04	.02	.00
☐ 223	Dave Eiland	.04	.02	.00
☐ 224	Alvaro Espinoza	.04	.02	.00
☐ 225	Steve Farr	.04	.02	.00
☐ 226	Bob Geren	.04	.02	.00
☐ 227	Lee Guetterman	.04	.02	.00
☐ 228	John Habyan	.04	.02	.00
☐ 229	Mel Hall	.07	.03	.01
☐ 230	Steve Howe	.04	.02	.00

☐ 231	Mike Humphreys	.07	.03	.01
☐ 232	Scott Kamieniecki	.07	.03	.01
☐ 233	Pat Kelly	.15	.06	.01
☐ 234	Roberto Kelly	.07	.03	.01
☐ 235	Tim Leary	.07	.03	.01
☐ 236	Kevin Maas	.18	.08	.01
☐ 237	Don Mattingly	.20	.08	.02
☐ 238	Hensley Meulens	.07	.03	.01
☐ 239	Matt Nokes	.07	.03	.01
☐ 240	Pascual Perez	.04	.02	.00
☐ 241	Eric Plunk	.04	.02	.00
☐ 242	John Ramos	.18	.08	.01
☐ 243	Scott Sanderson	.04	.02	.00
☐ 244	Steve Sax	.07	.03	.01
☐ 245	Wade Taylor	.07	.03	.01
☐ 246	Randy Velarde	.04	.02	.00
☐ 247	Bernie Williams	.25	.10	.02
☐ 248	Troy Afenir	.04	.02	.00
☐ 249	Harold Baines	.07	.03	.01
☐ 250	Lance Blankenship	.04	.02	.00
☐ 251	Mike Bordick	.07	.03	.01
☐ 252	Jose Canseco	.35	.15	.03
☐ 253	Steve Chitren	.04	.02	.00
☐ 254	Ron Darling	.04	.02	.00
☐ 255	Dennis Eckersley	.07	.03	.01
☐ 256	Mike Gallego	.04	.02	.00
☐ 257	Dave Henderson	.07	.03	.01
☐ 258	Rickey Henderson	.30	.12	.03
☐ 259	Rick Honeycutt	.04	.02	.00
☐ 260	Brook Jacoby	.04	.02	.00
☐ 261	Carney Lansford	.07	.03	.01
☐ 262	Mark McGwire	.12	.05	.01
☐ 263	Mike Moore	.07	.03	.01
☐ 264	Gene Nelson	.04	.02	.00
☐ 265	Jamie Quirk	.04	.02	.00
☐ 266	Joe Slusarski	.07	.03	.01
☐ 267	Terry Steinbach	.07	.03	.01
☐ 268	Dave Stewart	.07	.03	.01
☐ 269	Todd Van Poppel	.75	.30	.07
☐ 270	Walt Weiss	.07	.03	.01
☐ 271	Bob Welch	.07	.03	.01
☐ 272	Curt Young	.04	.02	.00
☐ 273	Scott Bradley	.04	.02	.00
☐ 274	Greg Briley	.04	.02	.00
☐ 275	Jay Buhner	.07	.03	.01
☐ 276	Henry Cotto	.04	.02	.00
☐ 277	Alvin Davis	.07	.03	.01
☐ 278	Rich DeLucia	.04	.02	.00
☐ 279	Ken Griffey Jr.	.75	.30	.07
☐ 280	Erik Hanson	.07	.03	.01
☐ 281	Brian Holman	.04	.02	.00
☐ 282	Mike Jackson	.04	.02	.00
☐ 283	Randy Johnson	.07	.03	.01
☐ 284	Tracy Jones	.04	.02	.00
☐ 285	Bill Krueger	.04	.02	.00
☐ 286	Edgar Martinez	.07	.03	.01
☐ 287	Tino Martinez	.15	.06	.01
☐ 288	Rob Murphy	.04	.02	.00
☐ 289	Pete O'Brien	.04	.02	.00
☐ 290	Alonzo Powell	.07	.03	.01
☐ 291	Harold Reynolds	.04	.02	.00
☐ 292	Mike Schooler	.04	.02	.00
☐ 293	Russ Swan	.04	.02	.00
☐ 294	Bill Swift	.04	.02	.00
☐ 295	Dave Valle	.04	.02	.00
☐ 296	Omar Vizquel	.04	.02	.00
☐ 297	Gerald Alexander	.04	.02	.00
☐ 298	Brad Arnsberg	.04	.02	.00
☐ 299	Kevin Brown	.07	.03	.01
☐ 300	Jack Daugherty	.04	.02	.00
☐ 301	Mario Diaz	.04	.02	.00
☐ 302	Brian Downing	.04	.02	.00
☐ 303	Julio Franco	.07	.03	.01
☐ 304	Juan Gonzalez	.35	.15	.03
☐ 305	Rich Gossage	.07	.03	.01
☐ 306	Jose Guzman	.04	.02	.00
☐ 307	Jose Hernandez	.18	.08	.01
☐ 308	Jeff Huson	.04	.02	.00
☐ 309	Mike Jeffcoat	.04	.02	.00
☐ 310	Terry Mathews	.10	.04	.01
☐ 311	Rafael Palmeiro	.12	.05	.01
☐ 312	Dean Palmer	.25	.10	.02
☐ 313	Geno Petralli	.04	.02	.00
☐ 314	Gary Pettis	.04	.02	.00
☐ 315	Kevin Reimer	.07	.03	.01
☐ 316	Ivan Rodriguez	.90	.40	.09
☐ 317	Kenny Rogers	.04	.02	.00
☐ 318	Wayne Rosenthal	.12	.05	.01
☐ 319	Jeff Russell	.04	.02	.00
☐ 320	Nolan Ryan	.50	.20	.05
☐ 321	Ruben Sierra	.20	.08	.02
☐ 322	Jim Acker	.04	.02	.00
☐ 323	Roberto Alomar	.12	.05	.01
☐ 324	Derek Bell	.35	.15	.03
☐ 325	Pat Borders	.04	.02	.00
☐ 326	Tom Candiotti	.07	.03	.01
☐ 327	Joe Carter	.10	.04	.01
☐ 328	Rob Ducey	.04	.02	.00
☐ 329	Kelly Gruber	.07	.03	.01
☐ 330	Juan Guzman	.65	.25	.06
☐ 331	Tom Henke	.04	.02	.00
☐ 332	Jimmy Key	.07	.03	.01
☐ 333	Manny Lee	.04	.02	.00
☐ 334	Al Leiter	.04	.02	.00
☐ 335	Bob MacDonald	.07	.03	.01
☐ 336	Candy Maldonado	.04	.02	.00
☐ 337	Rance Mulliniks	.04	.02	.00
☐ 338	Greg Myers	.04	.02	.00
☐ 339	John Olerud	.15	.06	.01
☐ 340	Ed Sprague	.10	.04	.01
☐ 341	Dave Stieb	.07	.03	.01
☐ 342	Todd Stottlemyre	.07	.03	.01
☐ 343	Mike Timlin	.07	.03	.01
☐ 344	Duane Ward	.04	.02	.00
☐ 345	David Wells	.04	.02	.00
☐ 346	Devon White	.07	.03	.01

□ 347	Mookie Wilson	.07	.03	.01
□ 348	Eddie Zosky	.12	.05	.01
□ 349	Steve Avery	.30	.12	.03
□ 350	Mike Bell	.07	.03	.01
□ 351	Rafael Belliard	.04	.02	.00
□ 352	Juan Berenguer	.04	.02	.00
□ 353	Jeff Blauser	.04	.02	.00
□ 354	Sid Bream	.04	.02	.00
□ 355	Francisco Cabrera	.04	.02	.00
□ 356	Marvin Freeman	.04	.02	.00
□ 357	Ron Gant	.15	.06	.01
□ 358	Tom Glavine	.10	.04	.01
□ 359	Brian Hunter	.60	.25	.06
□ 360	Dave Justice	.60	.25	.06
□ 361	Charlie Leibrandt	.04	.02	.00
□ 362	Mark Lemke	.04	.02	.00
□ 363	Kent Mercker	.04	.02	.00
□ 364	Keith Mitchell	.25	.10	.02
□ 365	Greg Olson	.04	.02	.00
□ 366	Terry Pendleton	.07	.03	.01
□ 367	Armando Reynoso	.12	.05	.01
□ 368	Deion Sanders	.10	.04	.01
□ 369	Lonnie Smith	.07	.03	.01
□ 370	Pete Smith	.04	.02	.00
□ 371	John Smoltz	.10	.04	.01
□ 372	Mike Stanton	.04	.02	.00
□ 373	Jeff Treadway	.04	.02	.00
□ 374	Mark Wohlers	.30	.12	.03
□ 375	Paul Assenmacher	.04	.02	.00
□ 376	George Bell	.07	.03	.01
□ 377	Shawn Boskie	.04	.02	.00
□ 378	Frank Castillo	.04	.02	.00
□ 379	Andre Dawson	.12	.05	.01
□ 380	Shawon Dunston	.07	.03	.01
□ 381	Mark Grace	.10	.04	.01
□ 382	Mike Harkey	.04	.02	.00
□ 383	Danny Jackson	.04	.02	.00
□ 384	Les Lancaster	.04	.02	.00
□ 385	Cedric Landrum	.10	.04	.01
□ 386	Greg Maddux	.07	.03	.01
□ 387	Derrick May	.07	.03	.01
□ 388	Chuck McElroy	.04	.02	.00
□ 389	Ryne Sandberg	.35	.15	.03
□ 390	Heathcliff Slocumb	.04	.02	.00
□ 391	Dave Smith	.04	.02	.00
□ 392	Dwight Smith	.07	.03	.01
□ 393	Rick Sutcliffe	.07	.03	.01
□ 394	Hector Villanueva	.07	.03	.01
□ 395	Chico Walker	.04	.02	.00
□ 396	Jerome Walton	.07	.03	.01
□ 397	Rick Wilkins	.10	.04	.01
□ 398	Jack Armstrong	.07	.03	.01
□ 399	Freddie Benavides	.04	.02	.00
□ 400	Glenn Braggs	.04	.02	.00
□ 401	Tom Browning	.07	.03	.01
□ 402	Norm Charlton	.04	.02	.00
□ 403	Eric Davis	.12	.05	.01
□ 404	Rob Dibble	.07	.03	.01
□ 405	Bill Doran	.04	.02	.00
□ 406	Mariano Duncan	.04	.02	.00
□ 407	Kip Gross	.15	.06	.01
□ 408	Chris Hammond	.07	.03	.01
□ 409	Billy Hatcher	.04	.02	.00
□ 410	Chris Jones	.07	.03	.01
□ 411	Barry Larkin	.12	.05	.01
□ 412	Hal Morris	.10	.04	.01
□ 413	Randy Myers	.04	.02	.00
□ 414	Joe Oliver	.04	.02	.00
□ 415	Paul O'Neill	.07	.03	.01
□ 416	Ted Power	.04	.02	.00
□ 417	Luis Quinones	.04	.02	.00
□ 418	Jeff Reed	.04	.02	.00
□ 419	Jose Rijo	.07	.03	.01
□ 420	Chris Sabo	.07	.03	.01
□ 421	Reggie Sanders	.25	.10	.02
□ 422	Scott Scudder	.04	.02	.00
□ 423	Glenn Sutko	.07	.03	.01
□ 424	Eric Anthony	.07	.03	.01
□ 425	Jeff Bagwell	1.25	.50	.12
□ 426	Craig Biggio	.07	.03	.01
□ 427	Ken Caminiti	.04	.02	.00
□ 428	Casey Candaele	.04	.02	.00
□ 429	Mike Capel	.04	.02	.00
□ 430	Andujar Cedeno	.20	.08	.02
□ 431	Jim Corsi	.04	.02	.00
□ 432	Mark Davidson	.04	.02	.00
□ 433	Steve Finley	.07	.03	.01
□ 434	Luis Gonzalez	.20	.08	.02
□ 435	Pete Harnisch	.07	.03	.01
□ 436	Dwayne Henry	.04	.02	.00
□ 437	Xavier Hernandez	.04	.02	.00
□ 438	Jimmy Jones	.04	.02	.00
□ 439	Darryl Kile	.10	.04	.01
□ 440	Rob Mallicoat	.04	.02	.00
□ 441	Andy Mota	.10	.04	.01
□ 442	Al Osuna	.04	.02	.00
□ 443	Mark Portugal	.04	.02	.00
□ 444	Scott Servais	.07	.03	.01
□ 445	Mike Simms	.07	.03	.01
□ 446	Gerald Young	.04	.02	.00
□ 447	Tim Belcher	.07	.03	.01
□ 448	Brett Butler	.07	.03	.01
□ 449	John Candelaria	.04	.02	.00
□ 450	Gary Carter	.07	.03	.01
□ 451	Dennis Cook	.04	.02	.00
□ 452	Tim Crews	.04	.02	.00
□ 453	Kal Daniels	.07	.03	.01
□ 454	Jim Gott	.04	.02	.00
□ 455	Alfredo Griffin	.04	.02	.00
□ 456	Kevin Gross	.04	.02	.00
□ 457	Chris Gwynn	.04	.02	.00
□ 458	Lenny Harris	.04	.02	.00
□ 459	Orel Hershiser	.07	.03	.01
□ 460	Jay Howell	.04	.02	.00
□ 461	Stan Javier	.04	.02	.00
□ 462	Eric Karros	.25	.10	.02

No.	Player			
☐ 463	Ramon Martinez	.15	.06	.01
☐ 464	Roger McDowell	.04	.02	.00
☐ 465	Mike Morgan	.07	.03	.01
☐ 466	Eddie Murray	.12	.05	.01
☐ 467	Jose Offerman	.07	.03	.01
☐ 468	Bob Ojeda	.04	.02	.00
☐ 469	Juan Samuel	.07	.03	.01
☐ 470	Mike Scioscia	.04	.02	.00
☐ 471	Darryl Strawberry	.25	.10	.02
☐ 472	Bret Barberie	.15	.06	.01
☐ 473	Brian Barnes	.04	.02	.00
☐ 474	Eric Bullock	.04	.02	.00
☐ 475	Ivan Calderon	.07	.03	.01
☐ 476	Delino DeShields	.07	.03	.01
☐ 477	Jeff Fassero	.07	.03	.01
☐ 478	Mike Fitzgerald	.04	.02	.00
☐ 479	Steve Frey	.04	.02	.00
☐ 480	Andres Galarraga	.07	.03	.01
☐ 481	Mark Gardner	.04	.02	.00
☐ 482	Marquis Grissom	.07	.03	.01
☐ 483	Chris Haney	.10	.04	.01
☐ 484	Barry Jones	.04	.02	.00
☐ 485	Dave Martinez	.04	.02	.00
☐ 486	Dennis Martinez	.07	.03	.01
☐ 487	Chris Nabholz	.04	.02	.00
☐ 488	Spike Owen	.04	.02	.00
☐ 489	Gilberto Reyes	.04	.02	.00
☐ 490	Mel Rojas	.07	.03	.01
☐ 491	Scott Ruskin	.04	.02	.00
☐ 492	Bill Sampen	.04	.02	.00
☐ 493	Larry Walker	.07	.03	.01
☐ 494	Tim Wallach	.07	.03	.01
☐ 495	Daryl Boston	.04	.02	.00
☐ 496	Hubie Brooks	.07	.03	.01
☐ 497	Tim Burke	.04	.02	.00
☐ 498	Mark Carreon	.04	.02	.00
☐ 499	Tony Castillo	.04	.02	.00
☐ 500	Vince Coleman	.07	.03	.01
☐ 501	David Cone	.07	.03	.01
☐ 502	Kevin Elster	.04	.02	.00
☐ 503	Sid Fernandez	.07	.03	.01
☐ 504	John Franco	.04	.02	.00
☐ 505	Dwight Gooden	.12	.05	.01
☐ 506	Todd Hundley	.10	.04	.01
☐ 507	Jeff Innis	.04	.02	.00
☐ 508	Gregg Jefferies	.10	.04	.01
☐ 509	Howard Johnson	.10	.04	.01
☐ 510	Dave Magadan	.07	.03	.01
☐ 511	Terry McDaniel	.12	.05	.01
☐ 512	Kevin McReynolds	.07	.03	.01
☐ 513	Keith Miller	.04	.02	.00
☐ 514	Charlie O'Brien	.04	.02	.00
☐ 515	Mackey Sasser	.04	.02	.00
☐ 516	Pete Schourek	.07	.03	.01
☐ 517	Julio Valera	.04	.02	.00
☐ 518	Frank Viola	.07	.03	.01
☐ 519	Wally Whitehurst	.04	.02	.00
☐ 520	Anthony Young	.17	.07	.01
☐ 521	Andy Ashby	.15	.06	.01
☐ 522	Kim Batiste	.12	.05	.01
☐ 523	Joe Boever	.04	.02	.00
☐ 524	Wes Chamberlain	.25	.10	.02
☐ 525	Pat Combs	.04	.02	.00
☐ 526	Danny Cox	.04	.02	.00
☐ 527	Darren Daulton	.04	.02	.00
☐ 528	Jose DeJesus	.04	.02	.00
☐ 529	Len Dykstra	.07	.03	.01
☐ 530	Darrin Fletcher	.04	.02	.00
☐ 531	Tommy Greene	.07	.03	.01
☐ 532	Jason Grimsley	.04	.02	.00
☐ 533	Charlie Hayes	.04	.02	.00
☐ 534	Von Hayes	.07	.03	.01
☐ 535	Dave Hollins	.04	.02	.00
☐ 536	Ricky Jordan	.07	.03	.01
☐ 537	John Kruk	.04	.02	.00
☐ 538	Jim Lindeman	.04	.02	.00
☐ 539	Mickey Morandini	.07	.03	.01
☐ 540	Terry Mulholland	.04	.02	.00
☐ 541	Dale Murphy	.10	.04	.01
☐ 542	Randy Ready	.04	.02	.00
☐ 543	Wally Ritchie	.04	.02	.00
☐ 544	Bruce Ruffin	.04	.02	.00
☐ 545	Steve Searcy	.04	.02	.00
☐ 546	Dickie Thon	.04	.02	.00
☐ 547	Mitch Williams	.04	.02	.00
☐ 548	Stan Belinda	.04	.02	.00
☐ 549	Jay Bell	.04	.02	.00
☐ 550	Barry Bonds	.18	.08	.01
☐ 551	Bobby Bonilla	.15	.06	.01
☐ 552	Steve Buechele	.07	.03	.01
☐ 553	Doug Drabek	.07	.03	.01
☐ 554	Neal Heaton	.04	.02	.00
☐ 555	Jeff King	.04	.02	.00
☐ 556	Bob Kipper	.04	.02	.00
☐ 557	Bill Landrum	.04	.02	.00
☐ 558	Mike LaValliere	.04	.02	.00
☐ 559	Jose Lind	.04	.02	.00
☐ 560	Lloyd McClendon	.04	.02	.00
☐ 561	Orlando Merced	.18	.08	.01
☐ 562	Bob Patterson	.04	.02	.00
☐ 563	Joe Redfield	.20	.08	.02
☐ 564	Gary Redus	.04	.02	.00
☐ 565	Rosario Rodriguez	.07	.03	.01
☐ 566	Don Slaught	.04	.02	.00
☐ 567	John Smiley	.07	.03	.01
☐ 568	Zane Smith	.04	.02	.00
☐ 569	Randy Tomlin	.07	.03	.01
☐ 570	Andy Van Slyke	.07	.03	.01
☐ 571	Gary Varsho	.04	.02	.00
☐ 572	Bob Walk	.04	.02	.00
☐ 573	John Wehner	.20	.08	.02
☐ 574	Juan Agosto	.04	.02	.00
☐ 575	Cris Carpenter	.04	.02	.00
☐ 576	Jose DeLeon	.04	.02	.00
☐ 577	Rich Gedman	.04	.02	.00
☐ 578	Bernard Gilkey	.12	.05	.01

☐ 579 Pedro Guerrero	.07	.03	.01
☐ 580 Ken Hill	.04	.02	.00
☐ 581 Rex Hudler	.04	.02	.00
☐ 582 Felix Jose	.10	.04	.01
☐ 583 Ray Lankford	.15	.06	.01
☐ 584 Omar Olivares	.07	.03	.01
☐ 585 Jose Oquendo	.04	.02	.00
☐ 586 Tom Pagnozzi	.04	.02	.00
☐ 587 Geronimo Pena	.04	.02	.00
☐ 588 Mike Perez	.04	.02	.00
☐ 589 Gerald Perry	.04	.02	.00
☐ 590 Bryn Smith	.04	.02	.00
☐ 591 Lee Smith	.07	.03	.01
☐ 592 Ozzie Smith	.12	.05	.01
☐ 593 Scott Terry	.04	.02	.00
☐ 594 Bob Tewksbury	.04	.02	.00
☐ 595 Milt Thompson	.04	.02	.00
☐ 596 Todd Zeile	.12	.05	.01
☐ 597 Larry Andersen	.04	.02	.00
☐ 598 Oscar Azocar	.04	.02	.00
☐ 599 Andy Benes	.07	.03	.01
☐ 600 Ricky Bones	.07	.03	.01
☐ 601 Jerald Clark	.04	.02	.00
☐ 602 Pat Clements	.04	.02	.00
☐ 603 Paul Faries	.04	.02	.00
☐ 604 Tony Fernandez	.07	.03	.01
☐ 605 Tony Gwynn	.20	.08	.02
☐ 606 Greg Harris	.04	.02	.00
☐ 607 Thomas Howard	.04	.02	.00
☐ 608 Bruce Hurst	.07	.03	.01
☐ 609 Darrin Jackson	.04	.02	.00
☐ 610 Tom Lampkin	.04	.02	.00
☐ 611 Craig Lefferts	.04	.02	.00
☐ 612 Jim Lewis	.12	.05	.01
☐ 613 Mike Maddux	.04	.02	.00
☐ 614 Fred McGriff	.12	.05	.01
☐ 615 Jose Melendez	.07	.03	.01
☐ 616 Jose Mota	.10	.04	.01
☐ 617 Dennis Rasmussen	.04	.02	.00
☐ 618 Bip Roberts	.04	.02	.00
☐ 619 Rich Rodriguez	.04	.02	.00
☐ 620 Benito Santiago	.07	.03	.01
☐ 621 Craig Shipley	.12	.05	.01
☐ 622 Tim Teufel	.04	.02	.00
☐ 623 Kevin Ward	.15	.06	.01
☐ 624 Ed Whitson	.04	.02	.00
☐ 625 Dave Anderson	.04	.02	.00
☐ 626 Kevin Bass	.04	.02	.00
☐ 627 Rod Beck	.12	.05	.01
☐ 628 Bud Black	.04	.02	.00
☐ 629 Jeff Brantley	.04	.02	.00
☐ 630 John Burkett	.04	.02	.00
☐ 631 Will Clark	.30	.12	.03
☐ 632 Royce Clayton	.25	.10	.02
☐ 633 Steve Decker	.15	.06	.01
☐ 634 Kelly Downs	.04	.02	.00
☐ 635 Mike Felder	.04	.02	.00
☐ 636 Scott Garrelts	.25	.10	.02
☐ 637 Eric Gunderson	.04	.02	.00
☐ 638 Bryan Hickerson	.17	.07	.01
☐ 639 Darren Lewis	.15	.06	.01
☐ 640 Greg Litton	.04	.02	.00
☐ 641 Kirt Manwaring	.04	.02	.00
☐ 642 Paul McClellan	.07	.03	.01
☐ 643 Willie McGee	.07	.03	.01
☐ 644 Kevin Mitchell	.10	.04	.01
☐ 645 Francisco Oliveras	.04	.02	.00
☐ 646 Mike Remlinger	.04	.02	.00
☐ 647 Dave Righetti	.07	.03	.01
☐ 648 Robby Thompson	.04	.02	.00
☐ 649 Jose Uribe	.04	.02	.00
☐ 650 Matt Williams	.12	.05	.01
☐ 651 Trevor Wilson	.04	.02	.00
☐ 652 Tom Goodwin	.18	.08	.01
☐ 653 Terry Bross	.04	.02	.00
☐ 654 Mike Christopher	.12	.05	.01
☐ 655 Kenny Lofton	.25	.10	.02
☐ 656 Chris Cron	.15	.06	.01
☐ 657 Willie Banks	.15	.06	.01
☐ 658 Pat Rice	.18	.08	.01
☐ 659 Rob Maurer	.35	.15	.03
☐ 660 Don Harris	.10	.04	.01
☐ 661 Henry Rodriguez	.07	.03	.01
☐ 662 Cliff Brantley	.20	.08	.02
☐ 663 Mike Linskey	.04	.02	.00
☐ 664 Gary Disarcina	.04	.02	.00
☐ 665 Gil Heredia	.12	.05	.01
☐ 666 Vinny Castilla	.12	.05	.01
☐ 667 Paul Abbott	.04	.02	.00
☐ 668 Monty Fariss	.10	.04	.01
☐ 669 Jarvis Brown	.15	.06	.01
☐ 670 Wayne Kirby	.15	.06	.01
☐ 671 Scott Brosius	.15	.06	.01
☐ 672 Bob Hamelin	.07	.03	.01
☐ 673 Joel Johnston	.15	.06	.01
☐ 674 Tim Spehr	.10	.04	.01
☐ 675 Jeff Gardner	.12	.05	.01
☐ 676 Rico Rossy	.15	.06	.01
☐ 677 Roberto Hernandez	.18	.08	.01
☐ 678 Ted Wood	.30	.12	.03
☐ 679 Cal Eldred	.10	.04	.01
☐ 680 Sean Berry	.07	.03	.01
☐ 681 Rickey Henderson RS	.15	.06	.01
☐ 682 Nolan Ryan RS	.30	.12	.03
☐ 683 Dennis Martinez RS	.07	.03	.01
☐ 684 Wilson Alvarez RS	.07	.03	.01
☐ 685 Joe Carter RS	.07	.03	.01
☐ 686 Dave Winfield RS	.10	.04	.01
☐ 687 David Cone RS	.07	.03	.01
☐ 688 Jose Canseco LL	.20	.08	.02
☐ 689 Howard Johnson LL	.07	.03	.01
☐ 690 Julio Franco LL	.07	.03	.01
☐ 691 Terry Pendleton LL	.07	.03	.01
☐ 692 Cecil Fielder LL	.12	.05	.01
☐ 693 Scott Erickson LL	.20	.08	.02
☐ 694 Tom Glavine LL	.07	.03	.01

☐ 695 Dennis Martinez LL	.07	.03	.01
☐ 696 Bryan Harvey LL	.07	.03	.01
☐ 697 Lee Smith LL	.07	.03	.01
☐ 698 Super Siblings	.10	.04	.01
Roberto Alomar			
Sandy Alomar Jr.			
☐ 699 The Indispensables	.18	.08	.01
Bobby Bonilla			
Will Clark			
☐ 700 Teamwork	.12	.05	.01
Mark Wohlers			
Kent Mercker			
Alejandro Pena			
☐ 701 Tiger Tandems	.30	.12	.03
Stacy Jones			
Bo Jackson			
Gregg Olson			
Frank Thomas			
☐ 702 The Ignitors	.07	.03	.01
Paul Molitor			
Brett Butler			
☐ 703 Indispensables II	.15	.06	.01
Cal Ripken			
Joe Carter			
☐ 704 Power Packs	.12	.05	.01
Barry Larkin			
Kirby Puckett			
☐ 705 Today and Tomorrow	.18	.08	.01
Mo Vaughn			
Cecil Fielder			
☐ 706 Teenage Sensations	.10	.04	.01
Ramon Martinez			
Ozzie Guillen			
☐ 707 Designated Hitters	.10	.04	.01
Harold Baines			
Wade Boggs			
☐ 708 Robin Yount PV	.10	.04	.01
☐ 709 Ken Griffey Jr. PV	.40	.16	.04
☐ 710 Nolan Ryan PV	.30	.12	.03
☐ 711 Cal Ripken PV	.20	.08	.02
☐ 712 Frank Thomas PV	.60	.25	.06
☐ 713 Dave Justice PV	.30	.12	.03
☐ 714 Checklist Card	.07	.03	.01
☐ 715 Checklist Card	.07	.03	.01
☐ 716 Checklist Card	.07	.03	.01
☐ 717 Checklist Card	.07	.03	.01
☐ 718 Checklist Card	.07	.03	.01
☐ 719 Checklist Card	.07	.03	.01
☐ 720 Checklist Card	.07	.03	.01

1948-49 Leaf

The cards in this 98-card set measure 2 3/8" by 2 7/8". The 1948-49 Leaf set was the first post-war baseball series issued in color. This effort was not entirely successful due to a lack of refinement which resulted in many color variations and cards out of register. In addition, the set was skip numbered from 1-168, with 49 of the 98 cards printed in limited quantities (marked with an asterisk in the checklist). Cards 102 and 136 have variations, and cards are sometimes found with overprinted or incorrect backs. The notable rookie cards in this set include Stan Musial, Satchel Paige, and Jackie Robinson.

	NRMT	VG-E	GOOD
COMPLETE SET (98)	28000.	12500.	3300.
COMMON NUMBERS	25.00	11.00	3.50
COMMON * NUMBERS	350.00	160.00	52.50
☐ 1 Joe DiMaggio	2000.00	750.00	150.00
☐ 3 Babe Ruth	2200.00	900.00	180.00
☐ 4 Stan Musial	750.00	325.00	110.00
☐ 5 Virgil Trucks *	400.00	180.00	60.00
☐ 8 Satchel Paige *	2100.00	900.00	180.00
☐ 10 Dizzy Trout	25.00	11.00	3.50
☐ 11 Phil Rizzuto	190.00	85.00	28.50
☐ 13 Cass Michaels *	350.00	160.00	52.50
☐ 14 Billy Johnson	25.00	11.00	3.50
☐ 17 Frank Overmire	25.00	11.00	3.50
☐ 19 Johnny Wyrostek *	350.00	160.00	52.50
☐ 20 Hank Sauer *	400.00	180.00	60.00
☐ 22 Al Evans	25.00	11.00	3.50
☐ 26 Sam Chapman	25.00	11.00	3.50
☐ 27 Mickey Harris	25.00	11.00	3.50
☐ 28 Jim Hegan	28.00	12.50	4.00
☐ 29 Elmer Valo	25.00	11.00	3.50
☐ 30 Billy Goodman *	350.00	160.00	52.50
☐ 31 Lou Brissie	25.00	11.00	3.50
☐ 32 Warren Spahn	275.00	120.00	40.00
☐ 33 Peanuts Lowrey *	350.00	160.00	52.50

☐ 36 Al Zarilla * 350.00 160.00 52.50
☐ 38 Ted Kluszewski 85.00 38.00 12.75
☐ 39 Ewell Blackwell 55.00 25.00 8.25
☐ 42 Kent Peterson 25.00 11.00 3.50
☐ 43 Ed Stevens * 350.00 160.00 52.50
☐ 45 Ken Keltner * 350.00 160.00 52.50
☐ 46 Johnny Mize 110.00 50.00 16.50
☐ 47 George Vico 25.00 11.00 3.50
☐ 48 Johnny Schmitz * 350.00 160.00 52.50
☐ 49 Del Ennis 38.00 16.00 4.00
☐ 50 Dick Wakefield 25.00 11.00 3.50
☐ 51 Al Dark * 450.00 200.00 67.50
☐ 53 Johnny VanderMeer 45.00 20.00 6.75
☐ 54 Bobby Adams * 350.00 160.00 52.50
☐ 55 Tommy Henrich * 450.00 200.00 67.50
☐ 56 Larry Jansen 28.00 12.50 4.00
☐ 57 Bob McCall 25.00 11.00 3.50
☐ 59 Luke Appling 90.00 40.00 13.50
☐ 61 Jake Early 25.00 11.00 3.50
☐ 62 Eddie Joost * 350.00 160.00 52.50
☐ 63 Barney McCosky * 350.00 160.00 52.50
☐ 65 Robert Elliott 35.00 15.75 5.25
(misspelled Elliot
on card front)
☐ 66 Orval Grove * 350.00 160.00 52.50
☐ 68 Eddie Miller * 350.00 160.00 52.50
☐ 70 Honus Wagner 280.00 115.00 35.00
☐ 72 Hank Edwards 25.00 11.00 3.50
☐ 73 Pat Seerey 25.00 11.00 3.50
☐ 75 Dom DiMaggio * 550.00 240.00 80.00
☐ 76 Ted Williams 650.00 300.00 100.00
☐ 77 Roy Smalley 25.00 11.00 3.50
☐ 78 Hoot Evers * 350.00 160.00 52.50
☐ 79 Jackie Robinson 700.00 315.00 105.00
☐ 81 Whitey Kurowski * 350.00 160.00 52.50
☐ 82 Johnny Lindell 25.00 11.00 3.50
☐ 83 Bobby Doerr 125.00 57.50 18.75
☐ 84 Sid Hudson 25.00 11.00 3.50
☐ 85 Dave Philley * 350.00 160.00 52.50
☐ 86 Ralph Weigel 25.00 11.00 3.50
☐ 88 Frank Gustine * 350.00 160.00 52.50
☐ 91 Ralph Kiner 185.00 80.00 25.00
☐ 93 Bob Feller * 1450.00 650.00 125.00
☐ 95 George Stirnweiss 30.00 13.50 4.50
☐ 97 Marty Marion 50.00 22.50 7.50
☐ 98 Hal Newhouser * 550.00 240.00 80.00
☐ 102A Gene Hermansk (sic)300.00135.00 45.00
☐ 102B Gene Hermanski 25.00 11.00 3.50
☐ 104 Eddie Stewart * 350.00 160.00 52.50
☐ 106 Lou Boudreau 110.00 50.00 16.50
☐ 108 Matt Batts * 350.00 160.00 52.50
☐ 111 Jerry Priddy 25.00 11.00 3.50
☐ 113 Dutch Leonard * 400.00 180.00 60.00
☐ 117 Joe Gordon 36.00 16.25 5.50
☐ 120 George Kell * 650.00 300.00 100.00
☐ 121 Johnny Pesky * 400.00 180.00 60.00
☐ 123 Cliff Fannin * 350.00 160.00 52.50
☐ 125 Andy Pafko 28.00 12.50 4.00
☐ 127 Enos Slaughter * 750.00 325.00 110.00
☐ 128 Buddy Rosar 25.00 11.00 3.50
☐ 129 Kirby Higbe * 350.00 160.00 52.50
☐ 131 Sid Gordon * 350.00 160.00 52.50
☐ 133 Tommy Holmes * 400.00 180.00 60.00
☐ 136A Cliff Aberson 25.00 11.00 3.50
(full sleeve)
☐ 136B Cliff Aberson 300.00 135.00 45.00
(short sleeve)
☐ 137 Harry Walker * 400.00 180.00 60.00
☐ 138 Larry Doby * 550.00 240.00 80.00
☐ 139 Johnny Hopp 28.00 12.50 4.00
☐ 142 Danny Murtaugh * 400.00 180.00 60.00
☐ 143 Dick Sisler * 400.00 180.00 60.00
☐ 144 Bob Dillinger * 350.00 160.00 52.50
☐ 146 Pete Reiser * 450.00 200.00 67.50
☐ 149 Hank Majeski * 350.00 160.00 52.50
☐ 153 Floyd Baker * 350.00 160.00 52.50
☐ 158 Harry Brecheen * 400.00 180.00 60.00
☐ 159 Mizell Platt 25.00 11.00 3.50
☐ 160 Bob Scheffing * 350.00 160.00 52.50
☐ 161 Vern Stephens * 400.00 180.00 60.00
☐ 163 Fred Hutchinson * 450.00 200.00 67.50
☐ 165 Dale Mitchell * 400.00 180.00 60.00
☐ 168 Phil Cavarretta * 450.00 200.00 67.50

1960 Leaf

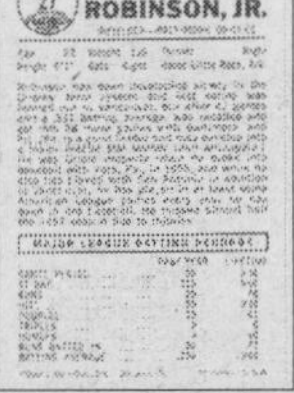

The cards in this 144-card set measure 2 1/2" by 3 1/2". The 1960 Leaf set was issued in a regular gum package style but with a marble instead of gum. The series was a joint production by Sports Novelties, Inc., and Leaf, two Chicago-based companies. Cards 73-144 are more difficult to find than the lower numbers. Photo variations exist (probably proof cards) for the seven cards listed with an asterisk and there is a well-known error card,

number 25 showing Brooks Lawrence (in a Reds uniform) with Jim Grant's name on front, and Grant's biography and record on back. The corrected version with Grant's photo is the more difficult variety. The only notable rookie card in this set is Dallas Green. The complete set price below includes both versions of Jim Grant.

	NRMT	VG-E	GOOD
COMPLETE SET (145)	1200.00	500.00	125.00
COMMON PLAYER (1-72)	2.25	.90	.22
COMMON PLAYER (73-144)	13.50	6.00	1.85
☐ 1 Luis Aparicio *	20.00	7.50	1.50
☐ 2 Woody Held	2.25	.90	.22
☐ 3 Frank Lary	3.00	1.25	.30
☐ 4 Camilo Pascual	3.00	1.25	.30
☐ 5 Pancho Herrera	2.25	.90	.22
☐ 6 Felipe Alou	4.00	1.75	.40
☐ 7 Benjamin Daniels	2.25	.90	.22
☐ 8 Roger Craig	4.50	2.00	.45
☐ 9 Eddie Kasko	2.25	.90	.22
☐ 10 Bob Grim	3.00	1.25	.30
☐ 11 Jim Busby	2.25	.90	.22
☐ 12 Ken Boyer	5.50	2.50	.55
☐ 13 Bob Boyd	2.25	.90	.22
☐ 14 Sam Jones	2.25	.90	.22
☐ 15 Larry Jackson	2.25	.90	.22
☐ 16 Elroy Face	4.00	1.75	.40
☐ 17 Walt Moryn *	2.25	.90	.22
☐ 18 Jim Gilliam	4.50	2.00	.45
☐ 19 Don Newcombe	4.00	1.75	.40
☐ 20 Glen Hobbie	2.25	.90	.22
☐ 21 Pedro Ramos	2.25	.90	.22
☐ 22 Ryne Duren	4.00	1.75	.40
☐ 23 Joey Jay *	2.25	.90	.22
☐ 24 Lou Berberet	2.25	.90	.22
☐ 25A Jim Grant ERR (photo actually Brooks Lawrence)	12.50	5.50	1.65
☐ 25B Jim Grant COR	18.00	7.50	2.50
☐ 26 Tom Borland	2.25	.90	.22
☐ 27 Brooks Robinson	28.00	12.50	4.00
☐ 28 Jerry Adair	2.25	.90	.22
☐ 29 Ron Jackson	2.25	.90	.22
☐ 30 George Strickland	2.25	.90	.22
☐ 31 Rocky Bridges	2.25	.90	.22
☐ 32 Bill Tuttle	2.25	.90	.22
☐ 33 Ken Hunt	2.25	.90	.22
☐ 34 Hal Griggs	2.25	.90	.22
☐ 35 Jim Coates *	2.25	.90	.22
☐ 36 Brooks Lawrence	2.25	.90	.22
☐ 37 Duke Snider	36.00	16.25	5.50
☐ 38 Al Spangler	2.25	.90	.22
☐ 39 Jim Owens	2.25	.90	.22
☐ 40 Bill Virdon	3.50	1.50	.35
☐ 41 Ernie Broglio	3.00	1.25	.30
☐ 42 Andre Rodgers	2.25	.90	.22
☐ 43 Julio Becquer	2.25	.90	.22
☐ 44 Tony Taylor	3.00	1.25	.30
☐ 45 Jerry Lynch	2.25	.90	.22
☐ 46 Cletis Boyer	3.50	1.50	.35
☐ 47 Jerry Lumpe	2.25	.90	.22
☐ 48 Charlie Maxwell	3.00	1.25	.30
☐ 49 Jim Perry	4.00	1.75	.40
☐ 50 Danny McDevitt	2.25	.90	.22
☐ 51 Juan Pizarro	2.25	.90	.22
☐ 52 Dallas Green	6.00	2.50	.60
☐ 53 Bob Friend	3.00	1.25	.30
☐ 54 Jack Sanford	3.00	1.25	.30
☐ 55 Jim Rivera	2.25	.90	.22
☐ 56 Ted Wills	2.25	.90	.22
☐ 57 Milt Pappas	3.00	1.25	.30
☐ 58 Hal Smith *	2.25	.90	.22
☐ 59 Bobby Avila	2.25	.90	.22
☐ 60 Clem Labine	3.00	1.25	.30
☐ 61 Norman Rehm *	2.25	.90	.22
☐ 62 John Gabler	2.25	.90	.22
☐ 63 John Tsitouris	2.25	.90	.22
☐ 64 Dave Sisler	2.25	.90	.22
☐ 65 Vic Power	2.25	.90	.22
☐ 66 Earl Battey	2.25	.90	.22
☐ 67 Bob Purkey	2.25	.90	.22
☐ 68 Moe Drabowsky	2.25	.90	.22
☐ 69 Hoyt Wilhelm	15.00	6.50	2.15
☐ 70 Humberto Robinson	2.25	.90	.22
☐ 71 Whitey Herzog	5.00	2.25	.50
☐ 72 Dick Donovan *	2.25	.90	.22
☐ 73 Gordon Jones	13.50	6.00	1.85
☐ 74 Joe Hicks	13.50	6.00	1.85
☐ 75 Ray Culp	15.00	6.50	2.15
☐ 76 Dick Drott	13.50	6.00	1.85
☐ 77 Bob Duliba	13.50	6.00	1.85
☐ 78 Art Ditmar	13.50	6.00	1.85
☐ 79 Steve Korcheck	13.50	6.00	1.85
☐ 80 Henry Mason	13.50	6.00	1.85
☐ 81 Harry Simpson	13.50	6.00	1.85
☐ 82 Gene Green	13.50	6.00	1.85
☐ 83 Bob Shaw	13.50	6.00	1.85
☐ 84 Howard Reed	13.50	6.00	1.85
☐ 85 Dick Stigman	13.50	6.00	1.85
☐ 86 Rip Repulski	13.50	6.00	1.85
☐ 87 Seth Morehead	13.50	6.00	1.85
☐ 88 Camilo Carreon	13.50	6.00	1.85
☐ 89 John Blanchard	15.00	6.50	2.15
☐ 90 Billy Hoeft	13.50	6.00	1.85
☐ 91 Fred Hopke	13.50	6.00	1.85
☐ 92 Joe Martin	13.50	6.00	1.85
☐ 93 Wally Shannon	13.50	6.00	1.85
☐ 94 Two Hal Smith's (Hal R. Smith, Hal W. Smith)	17.00	7.25	2.50
☐ 95 Al Schroll	13.50	6.00	1.85
☐ 96 John Kucks	13.50	6.00	1.85
☐ 97 Tom Morgan	13.50	6.00	1.85

☐ 98 Willie Jones 13.50 6.00 1.85
☐ 99 Marshall Renfroe 13.50 6.00 1.85
☐ 100 Willie Tasby 13.50 6.00 1.85
☐ 101 Irv Noren 13.50 6.00 1.85
☐ 102 Russ Snyder 13.50 6.00 1.85
☐ 103 Bob Turley 15.00 6.50 2.15
☐ 104 Jim Woods 13.50 6.00 1.85
☐ 105 Ronnie Kline 13.50 6.00 1.85
☐ 106 Steve Bilko 13.50 6.00 1.85
☐ 107 Elmer Valo 13.50 6.00 1.85
☐ 108 Tom McAvoy 13.50 6.00 1.85
☐ 109 Stan Williams 15.00 6.50 2.15
☐ 110 Earl Averill Jr. 13.50 6.00 1.85
☐ 111 Lee Walls 13.50 6.00 1.85
☐ 112 Paul Richards MG 15.00 6.50 2.15
☐ 113 Ed Sadowski 13.50 6.00 1.85
☐ 114 Stover McIlwain 13.50 6.00 1.85
☐ 115 Chuck Tanner 15.00 6.50 2.15
(photo actually
Ken Kuhn)
☐ 116 Lou Klimchock 13.50 6.00 1.85
☐ 117 Neil Chrisley 13.50 6.00 1.85
☐ 118 John Callison 15.00 6.50 2.15
☐ 119 Hal Smith 13.50 6.00 1.85
☐ 120 Carl Sawatski 13.50 6.00 1.85
☐ 121 Frank Leja 13.50 6.00 1.85
☐ 122 Earl Torgeson 13.50 6.00 1.85
☐ 123 Art Schult 13.50 6.00 1.85
☐ 124 Jim Brosnan 15.00 6.50 2.15
☐ 125 Sparky Anderson 35.00 15.75 5.25
☐ 126 Joe Pignatano 13.50 6.00 1.85
☐ 127 Rocky Nelson 13.50 6.00 1.85
☐ 128 Orlando Cepeda 45.00 20.00 6.75
☐ 129 Daryl Spencer 13.50 6.00 1.85
☐ 130 Ralph Lumenti 13.50 6.00 1.85
☐ 131 Sam Taylor 13.50 6.00 1.85
☐ 132 Harry Brecheen CO 15.00 6.50 2.15
☐ 133 Johnny Groth 13.50 6.00 1.85
☐ 134 Wayne Terwilliger 13.50 6.00 1.85
☐ 135 Kent Hadley 13.50 6.00 1.85
☐ 136 Faye Throneberry 13.50 6.00 1.85
☐ 137 Jack Meyer 13.50 6.00 1.85
☐ 138 Chuck Cottier 13.50 6.00 1.85
☐ 139 Joe DeMaestri 13.50 6.00 1.85
☐ 140 Gene Freese 13.50 6.00 1.85
☐ 141 Curt Flood 22.00 9.50 3.15
☐ 142 Gino Cimoli 13.50 6.00 1.85
☐ 143 Clay Dalrymple 13.50 6.00 1.85
☐ 144 Jim Bunning 50.00 17.50 3.50

1990 Leaf I

The 1990 Leaf set was another major, premium set introduced by Donruss in 1990. This set, which was produced on high quality paper stock, was issued in two separate series of 264 cards each. The cards are in the standard size of 2 1/2" by 3 1/2" and have full-color photos on both the front and the back of the cards. The first card of the set includes a brief history of the Leaf company and the checklists feature player photos in a style very reminiscent to the Topps checklists of the late 1960s. The card style is very similar to Upper Deck, but the Leaf sets were only distributed through hobby channels. The key rookie cards in this series are Delino DeShields, Marquis Grissom, Ben McDonald, John Olerud, Sammy Sosa, and Todd Zeile.

	MINT	EXC	G-VG
COMPLETE SET (264)	120.00	55.00	18.00
COMMON PLAYER (1-264)	.20	.08	.02

☐ 1 Introductory Card .... .20 .08 .02
☐ 2 Mike Henneman .... .20 .08 .02
☐ 3 Steve Bedrosian .... .20 .08 .02
☐ 4 Mike Scott .... .25 .10 .02
☐ 5 Allan Anderson .... .20 .08 .02
☐ 6 Rick Sutcliffe .... .25 .10 .02
☐ 7 Gregg Olson .... .75 .30 .07
☐ 8 Kevin Elster .... .20 .08 .02
☐ 9 Pete O'Brien .... .20 .08 .02
☐ 10 Carlton Fisk .... 1.00 .40 .10
☐ 11 Joe Magrane .... .20 .08 .02
☐ 12 Roger Clemens .... 2.25 .90 .22
☐ 13 Tom Glavine .... 1.25 .50 .12
☐ 14 Tom Gordon .... .25 .10 .02
☐ 15 Todd Benzinger .... .20 .08 .02
☐ 16 Hubie Brooks .... .20 .08 .02
☐ 17 Roberto Kelly .... .30 .12 .03

	Player			
☐ 18	Barry Larkin	.60	.25	.06
☐ 19	Mike Boddicker	.20	.08	.02
☐ 20	Roger McDowell	.20	.08	.02
☐ 21	Nolan Ryan	7.00	3.00	.70
☐ 22	John Farrell	.20	.08	.02
☐ 23	Bruce Hurst	.20	.08	.02
☐ 24	Wally Joyner	.40	.16	.04
☐ 25	Greg Maddux	.25	.10	.02
☐ 26	Chris Bosio	.20	.08	.02
☐ 27	John Cerutti	.20	.08	.02
☐ 28	Tim Burke	.20	.08	.02
☐ 29	Dennis Eckersley	.35	.15	.03
☐ 30	Glenn Davis	.30	.12	.03
☐ 31	Jim Abbott	1.75	.70	.17
☐ 32	Mike LaValliere	.20	.08	.02
☐ 33	Andres Thomas	.20	.08	.02
☐ 34	Lou Whitaker	.25	.10	.02
☐ 35	Alvin Davis	.25	.10	.02
☐ 36	Melido Perez	.20	.08	.02
☐ 37	Craig Biggio	.75	.30	.07
☐ 38	Rick Aguilera	.25	.10	.02
☐ 39	Pete Harnisch	.45	.18	.04
☐ 40	David Cone	.35	.15	.03
☐ 41	Scott Garrelts	.20	.08	.02
☐ 42	Jay Howell	.20	.08	.02
☐ 43	Eric King	.20	.08	.02
☐ 44	Pedro Guerrero	.30	.12	.03
☐ 45	Mike Bielecki	.20	.08	.02
☐ 46	Bob Boone	.25	.10	.02
☐ 47	Kevin Brown	.25	.10	.02
☐ 48	Jerry Browne	.20	.08	.02
☐ 49	Mike Scioscia	.20	.08	.02
☐ 50	Chuck Cary	.20	.08	.02
☐ 51	Wade Boggs	1.50	.60	.15
☐ 52	Von Hayes	.25	.10	.02
☐ 53	Tony Fernandez	.25	.10	.02
☐ 54	Dennis Martinez	.25	.10	.02
☐ 55	Tom Candiotti	.25	.10	.02
☐ 56	Andy Benes	1.50	.60	.15
☐ 57	Rob Dibble	.25	.10	.02
☐ 58	Chuck Crim	.20	.08	.02
☐ 59	John Smoltz	1.50	.60	.15
☐ 60	Mike Heath	.20	.08	.02
☐ 61	Kevin Gross	.20	.08	.02
☐ 62	Mark McGwire	.75	.30	.07
☐ 63	Bert Blyleven	.25	.10	.02
☐ 64	Bob Walk	.20	.08	.02
☐ 65	Mickey Tettleton	.25	.10	.02
☐ 66	Sid Fernandez	.25	.10	.02
☐ 67	Terry Kennedy	.20	.08	.02
☐ 68	Fernando Valenzuela	.25	.10	.02
☐ 69	Don Mattingly	1.50	.60	.15
☐ 70	Paul O'Neill	.25	.10	.02
☐ 71	Robin Yount	1.00	.40	.10
☐ 72	Bret Saberhagen	.40	.16	.04
☐ 73	Geno Petralli	.20	.08	.02
☐ 74	Brook Jacoby	.20	.08	.02
☐ 75	Roberto Alomar	1.50	.60	.15
☐ 76	Devon White	.25	.10	.02
☐ 77	Jose Lind	.20	.08	.02
☐ 78	Pat Combs	.20	.08	.02
☐ 79	Dave Stieb	.25	.10	.02
☐ 80	Tim Wallach	.25	.10	.02
☐ 81	Dave Stewart	.35	.15	.03
☐ 82	Eric Anthony	.60	.25	.06
☐ 83	Randy Bush	.20	.08	.02
☐ 84	Checklist Card (Rickey Henderson)	.35	.15	.03
☐ 85	Jaime Navarro	.30	.12	.03
☐ 86	Tommy Gregg	.20	.08	.02
☐ 87	Frank Tanana	.25	.10	.02
☐ 88	Omar Vizquel	.20	.08	.02
☐ 89	Ivan Calderon	.25	.10	.02
☐ 90	Vince Coleman	.35	.15	.03
☐ 91	Barry Bonds	1.25	.50	.12
☐ 92	Randy Milligan	.25	.10	.02
☐ 93	Frank Viola	.30	.12	.03
☐ 94	Matt Williams	.75	.30	.07
☐ 95	Alfredo Griffin	.20	.08	.02
☐ 96	Steve Sax	.25	.10	.02
☐ 97	Gary Gaetti	.25	.10	.02
☐ 98	Ryne Sandberg	3.00	1.25	.30
☐ 99	Danny Tartabull	.40	.16	.04
☐ 100	Rafael Palmeiro	.75	.30	.07
☐ 101	Jesse Orosco	.20	.08	.02
☐ 102	Garry Templeton	.20	.08	.02
☐ 103	Frank DiPino	.20	.08	.02
☐ 104	Tony Pena	.25	.10	.02
☐ 105	Dickie Thon	.20	.08	.02
☐ 106	Kelly Gruber	.30	.12	.03
☐ 107	Marquis Grissom	3.00	1.25	.30
☐ 108	Jose Canseco	3.75	1.60	.37
☐ 109	Mike Blowers	.30	.12	.03
☐ 110	Tom Browning	.20	.08	.02
☐ 111	Greg Vaughn	4.25	1.75	.42
☐ 112	Oddibe McDowell	.20	.08	.02
☐ 113	Gary Ward	.20	.08	.02
☐ 114	Jay Buhner	.30	.12	.03
☐ 115	Eric Show	.20	.08	.02
☐ 116	Bryan Harvey	.25	.10	.02
☐ 117	Andy Van Slyke	.35	.15	.03
☐ 118	Jeff Ballard	.20	.08	.02
☐ 119	Barry Lyons	.20	.08	.02
☐ 120	Kevin Mitchell	.75	.30	.07
☐ 121	Mike Gallego	.20	.08	.02
☐ 122	Dave Smith	.20	.08	.02
☐ 123	Kirby Puckett	1.75	.70	.17
☐ 124	Jerome Walton	.35	.15	.03
☐ 125	Bo Jackson	3.75	1.60	.37
☐ 126	Harold Baines	.25	.10	.02
☐ 127	Scott Bankhead	.20	.08	.02
☐ 128	Ozzie Guillen	.25	.10	.02
☐ 129	Jose Oquendo UER (League misspelled as Legue)	.20	.08	.02
☐ 130	John Dopson	.20	.08	.02

☐ 131 Charlie Hayes	.25	.10	.02
☐ 132 Fred McGriff	.75	.30	.07
☐ 133 Chet Lemon	.20	.08	.02
☐ 134 Gary Carter	.30	.12	.03
☐ 135 Rafael Ramirez	.20	.08	.02
☐ 136 Shane Mack	.25	.10	.02
☐ 137 Mark Grace UER (Card back has OB:L, should be B:L)	.60	.25	.06
☐ 138 Phil Bradley	.20	.08	.02
☐ 139 Dwight Gooden	.60	.25	.06
☐ 140 Harold Reynolds	.25	.10	.02
☐ 141 Scott Fletcher	.20	.08	.02
☐ 142 Ozzie Smith	.75	.30	.07
☐ 143 Mike Greenwell	.65	.25	.06
☐ 144 Pete Smith	.20	.08	.02
☐ 145 Mark Gubicza	.25	.10	.02
☐ 146 Chris Sabo	.60	.25	.06
☐ 147 Ramon Martinez	5.00	2.25	.50
☐ 148 Tim Leary	.25	.10	.02
☐ 149 Randy Myers	.20	.08	.02
☐ 150 Jody Reed	.25	.10	.02
☐ 151 Bruce Ruffin	.20	.08	.02
☐ 152 Jeff Russell	.20	.08	.02
☐ 153 Doug Jones	.20	.08	.02
☐ 154 Tony Gwynn	1.25	.50	.12
☐ 155 Mark Langston	.35	.15	.03
☐ 156 Mitch Williams	.20	.08	.02
☐ 157 Gary Sheffield	.35	.15	.03
☐ 158 Tom Henke	.25	.10	.02
☐ 159 Oil Can Boyd	.20	.08	.02
☐ 160 Rickey Henderson	2.50	1.00	.25
☐ 161 Bill Doran	.20	.08	.02
☐ 162 Chuck Finley	.40	.16	.04
☐ 163 Jeff King	.25	.10	.02
☐ 164 Nick Esasky	.20	.08	.02
☐ 165 Cecil Fielder	2.25	.90	.22
☐ 166 Dave Valle	.20	.08	.02
☐ 167 Robin Ventura	8.50	3.75	.85
☐ 168 Jim Deshaies	.20	.08	.02
☐ 169 Juan Berenguer	.20	.08	.02
☐ 170 Craig Worthington	.20	.08	.02
☐ 171 Gregg Jeffries	.45	.18	.04
☐ 172 Will Clark	3.00	1.25	.30
☐ 173 Kirk Gibson	.30	.12	.03
☐ 174 Checklist Card (Carlton Fisk)	.25	.10	.02
☐ 175 Bobby Thigpen	.25	.10	.02
☐ 176 John Tudor	.25	.10	.02
☐ 177 Andre Dawson	.65	.25	.06
☐ 178 George Brett	1.00	.40	.10
☐ 179 Steve Buechele	.20	.08	.02
☐ 180 Joey Belle	6.00	2.50	.60
☐ 181 Eddie Murray	.65	.25	.06
☐ 182 Bob Geren	.25	.10	.02
☐ 183 Rob Murphy	.20	.08	.02
☐ 184 Tom Herr	.25	.10	.02
☐ 185 George Bell	.50	.20	.05
☐ 186 Spike Owen	.20	.08	.02
☐ 187 Cory Snyder	.25	.10	.02
☐ 188 Fred Lynn	.25	.10	.02
☐ 189 Eric Davis	.60	.25	.06
☐ 190 Dave Parker	.30	.12	.03
☐ 191 Jeff Blauser	.20	.08	.02
☐ 192 Matt Nokes	.25	.10	.02
☐ 193 Delino DeShields	3.00	1.25	.30
☐ 194 Scott Sanderson	.20	.08	.02
☐ 195 Lance Parrish	.25	.10	.02
☐ 196 Bobby Bonilla	1.00	.40	.10
☐ 197 Cal Ripken	3.25	1.35	.32
☐ 198 Kevin McReynolds	.30	.12	.03
☐ 199 Robby Thompson	.20	.08	.02
☐ 200 Tim Belcher	.25	.10	.02
☐ 201 Jesse Barfield	.25	.10	.02
☐ 202 Mariano Duncan	.20	.08	.02
☐ 203 Bill Spiers	.25	.10	.02
☐ 204 Frank White	.25	.10	.02
☐ 205 Julio Franco	.40	.16	.04
☐ 206 Greg Swindell	.25	.10	.02
☐ 207 Benito Santiago	.30	.12	.03
☐ 208 Johnny Ray	.20	.08	.02
☐ 209 Gary Redus	.20	.08	.02
☐ 210 Jeff Parrett	.20	.08	.02
☐ 211 Jimmy Key	.25	.10	.02
☐ 212 Tim Raines	.35	.15	.03
☐ 213 Carney Lansford	.25	.10	.02
☐ 214 Gerald Young	.20	.08	.02
☐ 215 Gene Larkin	.20	.08	.02
☐ 216 Dan Plesac	.20	.08	.02
☐ 217 Lonnie Smith	.25	.10	.02
☐ 218 Alan Trammell	.45	.18	.04
☐ 219 Jeffrey Leonard	.20	.08	.02
☐ 220 Sammy Sosa	1.50	.60	.15
☐ 221 Todd Zeile	2.00	.80	.20
☐ 222 Bill Landrum	.20	.08	.02
☐ 223 Mike Devereaux	.20	.08	.02
☐ 224 Mike Marshall	.25	.10	.02
☐ 225 Jose Uribe	.20	.08	.02
☐ 226 Juan Samuel	.25	.10	.02
☐ 227 Mel Hall	.25	.10	.02
☐ 228 Kent Hrbek	.25	.10	.02
☐ 229 Shawon Dunston	.25	.10	.02
☐ 230 Kevin Seitzer	.25	.10	.02
☐ 231 Pete Incaviglia	.25	.10	.02
☐ 232 Sandy Alomar Jr.	.60	.25	.06
☐ 233 Bip Roberts	.25	.10	.02
☐ 234 Scott Terry	.20	.08	.02
☐ 235 Dwight Evans	.25	.10	.02
☐ 236 Ricky Jordan	.25	.10	.02
☐ 237 John Olerud	5.00	2.25	.50
☐ 238 Zane Smith	.25	.10	.02
☐ 239 Walt Weiss	.25	.10	.02
☐ 240 Alvaro Espinoza	.20	.08	.02
☐ 241 Billy Hatcher	.20	.08	.02
☐ 242 Paul Molitor	.35	.15	.03
☐ 243 Dale Murphy	.50	.20	.05

Card	MINT	EXC	G-VG
☐ 244 Dave Bergman	.20	.08	.02
☐ 245 Ken Griffey Jr.	22.00	9.50	3.15
☐ 246 Ed Whitson	.20	.08	.02
☐ 247 Kirk McCaskill	.20	.08	.02
☐ 248 Jay Bell	.20	.08	.02
☐ 249 Ben McDonald	4.00	1.75	.40
☐ 250 Darryl Strawberry	1.75	.70	.17
☐ 251 Brett Butler	.25	.10	.02
☐ 252 Terry Steinbach	.25	.10	.02
☐ 253 Ken Caminiti	.20	.08	.02
☐ 254 Dan Gladden	.20	.08	.02
☐ 255 Dwight Smith	.25	.10	.02
☐ 256 Kurt Stillwell	.20	.08	.02
☐ 257 Ruben Sierra	1.75	.70	.17
☐ 258 Mike Schooler	.25	.10	.02
☐ 259 Lance Johnson	.20	.08	.02
☐ 260 Terry Pendleton	.40	.16	.04
☐ 261 Ellis Burks	.45	.18	.04
☐ 262 Len Dykstra	.25	.10	.02
☐ 263 Mookie Wilson	.20	.08	.02
☐ 264 Checklist Card (Nolan Ryan) UER (No TM after Ranger logo)	.60	.25	.06

1990 Leaf II

This 264-card, standard size, 2 1/2" by 3 1/2" set was issued approximately six weeks after the release of the first series. The cards, which were in the same style as series one, were issued as more expensive Donruss cards and were not available in factory sets. The key rookies in the set are Carlos Baerga, Dave Justice, Kevin Maas, Jose Offerman, Kevin Tapani, Frank Thomas, and Mark Whiten.

	MINT	EXC	G-VG
COMPLETE SET (264)	160.00	72.00	24.00
COMMON PLAYER (265-528)	.20	.08	.02
☐ 265 No Hit King (Nolan Ryan)	2.00	.80	.20
☐ 266 Brian DuBois	.30	.12	.03
☐ 267 Don Robinson	.20	.08	.02
☐ 268 Glenn Wilson	.20	.08	.02
☐ 269 Kevin Tapani	3.00	1.25	.30
☐ 270 Marvell Wynne	.20	.08	.02
☐ 271 Billy Ripken	.20	.08	.02
☐ 272 Howard Johnson	.50	.20	.05
☐ 273 Brian Holman	.25	.10	.02
☐ 274 Dan Pasqua	.20	.08	.02
☐ 275 Ken Dayley	.20	.08	.02
☐ 276 Jeff Reardon	.25	.10	.02
☐ 277 Jim Presley	.20	.08	.02
☐ 278 Jim Eisenreich	.20	.08	.02
☐ 279 Danny Jackson	.25	.10	.02
☐ 280 Orel Hershiser	.35	.15	.03
☐ 281 Andy Hawkins	.20	.08	.02
☐ 282 Jose Rijo	.25	.10	.02
☐ 283 Luis Rivera	.20	.08	.02
☐ 284 John Kruk	.25	.10	.02
☐ 285 Jeff Huson	.25	.10	.02
☐ 286 Joel Skinner	.20	.08	.02
☐ 287 Jack Clark	.30	.12	.03
☐ 288 Chili Davis	.25	.10	.02
☐ 289 Joe Girardi	.25	.10	.02
☐ 290 B.J. Surhoff	.25	.10	.02
☐ 291 Luis Sojo	.35	.15	.03
☐ 292 Tom Foley	.20	.08	.02
☐ 293 Mike Moore	.25	.10	.02
☐ 294 Ken Oberkfell	.20	.08	.02
☐ 295 Luis Polonia	.25	.10	.02
☐ 296 Doug Drabek	.25	.10	.02
☐ 297 Dave Justice	36.00	16.25	5.50
☐ 298 Paul Gibson	.20	.08	.02
☐ 299 Edgar Martinez	.50	.20	.05
☐ 300 Frank Thomas UER (No B in front of birthdate)	65.00	29.00	9.75
☐ 301 Eric Yelding	.25	.10	.02
☐ 302 Greg Gagne	.20	.08	.02
☐ 303 Brad Komminsk	.20	.08	.02
☐ 304 Ron Darling	.25	.10	.02
☐ 305 Kevin Bass	.20	.08	.02
☐ 306 Jeff Hamilton	.20	.08	.02
☐ 307 Ron Karkovice	.20	.08	.02
☐ 308 Milt Thompson UER (Ray Lankford pictured on card back)	.25	.10	.02
☐ 309 Mike Harkey	.25	.10	.02
☐ 310 Mel Stottlemyre Jr.	.20	.08	.02
☐ 311 Kenny Rogers	.25	.10	.02
☐ 312 Mitch Webster	.20	.08	.02
☐ 313 Kal Daniels	.25	.10	.02

☐ 314 Matt Nokes .25 .10 .02
☐ 315 Dennis Lamp .20 .08 .02
☐ 316 Ken Howell .20 .08 .02
☐ 317 Glenallen Hill .25 .10 .02
☐ 318 Dave Martinez .20 .08 .02
☐ 319 Chris James .20 .08 .02
☐ 320 Mike Pagliarulo .20 .08 .02
☐ 321 Hal Morris 4.00 1.75 .40
☐ 322 Rob Deer .25 .10 .02
☐ 323 Greg Olson .65 .25 .06
☐ 324 Tony Phillips .20 .08 .02
☐ 325 Larry Walker 1.00 .40 .10
☐ 326 Ron Hassey .20 .08 .02
☐ 327 Jack Howell .20 .08 .02
☐ 328 John Smiley .25 .10 .02
☐ 329 Steve Finley .50 .20 .05
☐ 330 Dave Magadan .25 .10 .02
☐ 331 Greg Litton .25 .10 .02
☐ 332 Mickey Hatcher .20 .08 .02
☐ 333 Lee Guetterman .20 .08 .02
☐ 334 Norm Charlton .25 .10 .02
☐ 335 Edgar Diaz .25 .10 .02
☐ 336 Willie Wilson .25 .10 .02
☐ 337 Bobby Witt .25 .10 .02
☐ 338 Candy Maldonado .25 .10 .02
☐ 339 Craig Lefferts .20 .08 .02
☐ 340 Dante Bichette .35 .15 .03
☐ 341 Wally Backman .20 .08 .02
☐ 342 Dennis Cook .20 .08 .02
☐ 343 Pat Borders .25 .10 .02
☐ 344 Wallace Johnson .20 .08 .02
☐ 345 Willie Randolph .20 .08 .02
☐ 346 Danny Darwin .20 .08 .02
☐ 347 Al Newman .20 .08 .02
☐ 348 Mark Knudson .20 .08 .02
☐ 349 Joe Boever .20 .08 .02
☐ 350 Larry Sheets .20 .08 .02
☐ 351 Mike Jackson .20 .08 .02
☐ 352 Wayne Edwards .30 .12 .03
☐ 353 Bernard Gilkey 1.50 .60 .15
☐ 354 Don Slaught .20 .08 .02
☐ 355 Joe Orsulak .20 .08 .02
☐ 356 John Franco .20 .08 .02
☐ 357 Jeff Brantley .25 .10 .02
☐ 358 Mike Morgan .25 .10 .02
☐ 359 Deion Sanders 1.00 .40 .10
☐ 360 Terry Leach .20 .08 .02
☐ 361 Les Lancaster .20 .08 .02
☐ 362 Storm Davis .20 .08 .02
☐ 363 Scott Coolbaugh .30 .12 .03
☐ 364 Checklist Card .25 .10 .02
(Ozzie Smith)
☐ 365 Cecilio Guante .20 .08 .02
☐ 366 Joey Cora .20 .08 .02
☐ 367 Willie McGee .30 .12 .03
☐ 368 Jerry Reed .20 .08 .02
☐ 369 Darren Daulton .20 .08 .02
☐ 370 Manny Lee .20 .08 .02
☐ 371 Mark Gardner .45 .18 .04
☐ 372 Rick Honeycutt .20 .08 .02
☐ 373 Steve Balboni .20 .08 .02
☐ 374 Jack Armstrong .25 .10 .02
☐ 375 Charlie O'Brien .20 .08 .02
☐ 376 Ron Gant 1.50 .60 .15
☐ 377 Lloyd Moseby .20 .08 .02
☐ 378 Gene Harris .25 .10 .02
☐ 379 Joe Carter .65 .25 .06
☐ 380 Scott Bailes .20 .08 .02
☐ 381 R.J. Reynolds .20 .08 .02
☐ 382 Bob Melvin .20 .08 .02
☐ 383 Tim Teufel .20 .08 .02
☐ 384 John Burkett .35 .15 .03
☐ 385 Felix Jose 3.50 1.50 .35
☐ 386 Larry Andersen .20 .08 .02
☐ 387 David West .25 .10 .02
☐ 388 Luis Salazar .20 .08 .02
☐ 389 Mike Macfarlane .25 .10 .02
☐ 390 Charlie Hough .20 .08 .02
☐ 391 Greg Briley .25 .10 .02
☐ 392 Donn Pall .20 .08 .02
☐ 393 Bryn Smith .20 .08 .02
☐ 394 Carlos Quintana .45 .18 .04
☐ 395 Steve Lake .20 .08 .02
☐ 396 Mark Whiten 3.00 1.25 .30
☐ 397 Edwin Nunez .20 .08 .02
☐ 398 Rick Parker .25 .10 .02
☐ 399 Mark Portugal .20 .08 .02
☐ 400 Roy Smith .20 .08 .02
☐ 401 Hector Villanueva .30 .12 .03
☐ 402 Bob Milacki .25 .10 .02
☐ 403 Alejandro Pena .25 .10 .02
☐ 404 Scott Bradley .20 .08 .02
☐ 405 Ron Kittle .25 .10 .02
☐ 406 Bob Tewksbury .20 .08 .02
☐ 407 Wes Gardner .20 .08 .02
☐ 408 Ernie Whitt .20 .08 .02
☐ 409 Terry Shumpert .35 .15 .03
☐ 410 Tim Layana .30 .12 .03
☐ 411 Chris Gwynn .25 .10 .02
☐ 412 Jeff Robinson .20 .08 .02
☐ 413 Scott Scudder .35 .15 .03
☐ 414 Kevin Romine .20 .08 .02
☐ 415 Jose DeJesus .25 .10 .02
☐ 416 Mike Jeffcoat .20 .08 .02
☐ 417 Rudy Seanez .45 .18 .04
☐ 418 Mike Dunne .20 .08 .02
☐ 419 Dick Schofield .20 .08 .02
☐ 420 Steve Wilson .25 .10 .02
☐ 421 Bill Krueger .20 .08 .02
☐ 422 Junior Felix .25 .10 .02
☐ 423 Drew Hall .20 .08 .02
☐ 424 Curt Young .20 .08 .02
☐ 425 Franklin Stubbs .20 .08 .02
☐ 426 Dave Winfield .65 .25 .06
☐ 427 Rick Reed .25 .10 .02
☐ 428 Charlie Leibrandt .20 .08 .02

Card	Player			
□ 429	Jeff Robinson	.20	.08	.02
□ 430	Erik Hanson	.65	.25	.06
□ 431	Barry Jones	.20	.08	.02
□ 432	Alex Trevino	.20	.08	.02
□ 433	John Moses	.20	.08	.02
□ 434	Dave Johnson	.25	.10	.02
□ 435	Mackey Sasser	.25	.10	.02
□ 436	Rick Leach	.20	.08	.02
□ 437	Lenny Harris	.25	.10	.02
□ 438	Carlos Martinez	.25	.10	.02
□ 439	Rex Hudler	.20	.08	.02
□ 440	Domingo Ramos	.20	.08	.02
□ 441	Gerald Perry	.20	.08	.02
□ 442	Jeff Russell	.20	.08	.02
□ 443	Carlos Baerga	2.50	1.00	.25
□ 444	Checklist Card (Will Clark)	.40	.16	.04
□ 445	Stan Javier	.20	.08	.02
□ 446	Kevin Maas	7.50	3.25	.75
□ 447	Tom Brunansky	.25	.10	.02
□ 448	Carmelo Martinez	.20	.08	.02
□ 449	Willie Blair	.25	.10	.02
□ 450	Andres Galarraga	.25	.10	.02
□ 451	Bud Black	.20	.08	.02
□ 452	Greg Harris	.35	.15	.03
□ 453	Joe Oliver	.25	.10	.02
□ 454	Greg Brock	.20	.08	.02
□ 455	Jeff Treadway	.25	.10	.02
□ 456	Lance McCullers	.20	.08	.02
□ 457	Dave Schmidt	.20	.08	.02
□ 458	Todd Burns	.20	.08	.02
□ 459	Max Venable	.20	.08	.02
□ 460	Neal Heaton	.20	.08	.02
□ 461	Mark Williamson	.20	.08	.02
□ 462	Keith Miller	.20	.08	.02
□ 463	Mike LaCoss	.20	.08	.02
□ 464	Jose Offerman	1.25	.50	.12
□ 465	Jim Leyritz	.25	.10	.02
□ 466	Glenn Braggs	.20	.08	.02
□ 467	Ron Robinson	.20	.08	.02
□ 468	Mark Davis	.25	.10	.02
□ 469	Gary Pettis	.20	.08	.02
□ 470	Keith Hernandez	.25	.10	.02
□ 471	Dennis Rasmussen	.20	.08	.02
□ 472	Mark Eichhorn	.25	.10	.02
□ 473	Ted Power	.20	.08	.02
□ 474	Terry Mulholland	.25	.10	.02
□ 475	Todd Stottlemyre	.35	.15	.03
□ 476	Jerry Goff	.25	.10	.02
□ 477	Gene Nelson	.20	.08	.02
□ 478	Rich Gedman	.20	.08	.02
□ 479	Brian Harper	.25	.10	.02
□ 480	Mike Felder	.20	.08	.02
□ 481	Steve Avery	18.00	7.50	2.50
□ 482	Jack Morris	.40	.16	.04
□ 483	Randy Johnson	.75	.30	.07
□ 484	Scott Radinsky	.40	.16	.04
□ 485	Jose DeLeon	.20	.08	.02
□ 486	Stan Belinda	.35	.15	.03
□ 487	Brian Holton	.20	.08	.02
□ 488	Mark Carreon	.20	.08	.02
□ 489	Trevor Wilson	.30	.12	.03
□ 490	Mike Sharperson	.20	.08	.02
□ 491	Alan Mills	.35	.15	.03
□ 492	John Candelaria	.20	.08	.02
□ 493	Paul Assenmacher	.20	.08	.02
□ 494	Steve Crawford	.20	.08	.02
□ 495	Brad Arnsberg	.20	.08	.02
□ 496	Sergio Valdez	.25	.10	.02
□ 497	Mark Parent	.20	.08	.02
□ 498	Tom Pagnozzi	.20	.08	.02
□ 499	Greg Harris	.20	.08	.02
□ 500	Randy Ready	.20	.08	.02
□ 501	Duane Ward	.25	.10	.02
□ 502	Nelson Santovenia	.20	.08	.02
□ 503	Joe Klink	.35	.15	.03
□ 504	Eric Plunk	.20	.08	.02
□ 505	Jeff Reed	.20	.08	.02
□ 506	Ted Higuera	.25	.10	.02
□ 507	Joe Hesketh	.25	.10	.02
□ 508	Dan Petry	.20	.08	.02
□ 509	Matt Young	.20	.08	.02
□ 510	Jerald Clark	.25	.10	.02
□ 511	John Orton	.25	.10	.02
□ 512	Scott Ruskin	.35	.15	.03
□ 513	Chris Hoiles	.60	.25	.06
□ 514	Daryl Boston	.20	.08	.02
□ 515	Francisco Oliveras	.25	.10	.02
□ 516	Ozzie Canseco	.30	.12	.03
□ 517	Xavier Hernandez	.25	.10	.02
□ 518	Fred Manrique	.20	.08	.02
□ 519	Shawn Boskie	.35	.15	.03
□ 520	Jeff Montgomery	.25	.10	.02
□ 521	Jack Daugherty	.20	.08	.02
□ 522	Keith Comstock	.20	.08	.02
□ 523	Greg Hibbard	.60	.25	.06
□ 524	Lee Smith	.25	.10	.02
□ 525	Dana Kiecker	.25	.10	.02
□ 526	Darrel Akerfelds	.20	.08	.02
□ 527	Greg Myers	.20	.08	.02
□ 528	Checklist Card (Ryne Sandberg)	.40	.16	.04

1991 Leaf I

This 264-card standard size 2 1/2" by 3 1/2" set marks the second year Donruss has produced a premium set using the Leaf name. This set features a photo of the player which is surrounded by black and white borders.

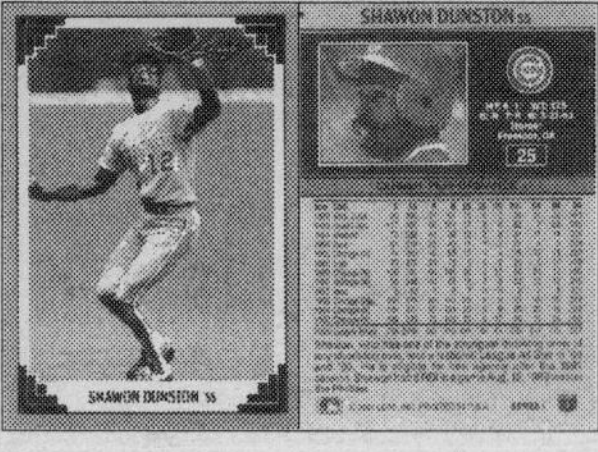

The whole card is framed in gray borders. The Leaf logo is in the upper right corner of the card. The back of the card features a gray, red and black back with white lettering on the black background and black lettering on the gray and red backgrounds. The backs of the cards also features biographical and statistical information along with a write-up when room is provided. The set was issued using the Donruss dealer distribution network with very little Leaf product being released in other fashions. The key rookie cards in this series are Wes Chamberlain and Brian McRae.

	MINT	EXC	G-VG
COMPLETE SET (264)	35.00	15.75	5.25
COMMON PLAYER (1-264)	.08	.03	.01
□ 1 The Leaf Card	.12	.05	.01
□ 2 Kurt Stillwell	.08	.03	.01
□ 3 Bobby Witt	.12	.05	.01
□ 4 Tony Phillips	.08	.03	.01
□ 5 Scott Garrelts	.08	.03	.01
□ 6 Greg Swindell	.12	.05	.01
□ 7 Billy Ripken	.08	.03	.01
□ 8 Dave Martinez	.08	.03	.01
□ 9 Kelly Gruber	.15	.06	.01
□ 10 Juan Samuel	.12	.05	.01
□ 11 Brian Holman	.08	.03	.01
□ 12 Craig Biggio	.17	.07	.01
□ 13 Lonnie Smith	.12	.05	.01
□ 14 Ron Robinson	.08	.03	.01
□ 15 Mike LaValliere	.08	.03	.01
□ 16 Mark Davis	.08	.03	.01
□ 17 Jack Daugherty	.08	.03	.01
□ 18 Mike Henneman	.08	.03	.01
□ 19 Mike Greenwell	.25	.10	.02
□ 20 Dave Magadan	.12	.05	.01
□ 21 Mark Williamson	.08	.03	.01
□ 22 Marquis Grissom	.25	.10	.02
□ 23 Pat Borders	.08	.03	.01
□ 24 Mike Scioscia	.08	.03	.01
□ 25 Shawon Dunston	.15	.06	.01
□ 26 Randy Bush	.08	.03	.01
□ 27 John Smoltz	.25	.10	.02
□ 28 Chuck Crim	.08	.03	.01
□ 29 Don Slaught	.08	.03	.01
□ 30 Mike Macfarlane	.08	.03	.01
□ 31 Wally Joyner	.20	.08	.02
□ 32 Pat Combs	.12	.05	.01
□ 33 Tony Pena	.12	.05	.01
□ 34 Howard Johnson	.25	.10	.02
□ 35 Leo Gomez	.75	.30	.07
□ 36 Spike Owen	.08	.03	.01
□ 37 Eric Davis	.30	.12	.03
□ 38 Roberto Kelly	.15	.06	.01
□ 39 Jerome Walton	.15	.06	.01
□ 40 Shane Mack	.12	.05	.01
□ 41 Kent Mercker	.12	.05	.01
□ 42 B.J. Surhoff	.08	.03	.01
□ 43 Jerry Browne	.08	.03	.01
□ 44 Lee Smith	.12	.05	.01
□ 45 Chuck Finley	.15	.06	.01
□ 46 Terry Mulholland	.12	.05	.01
□ 47 Tom Bolton	.08	.03	.01
□ 48 Tom Herr	.08	.03	.01
□ 49 Jim Deshaies	.08	.03	.01
□ 50 Walt Weiss	.12	.05	.01
□ 51 Hal Morris	.30	.12	.03
□ 52 Lee Guetterman	.08	.03	.01
□ 53 Paul Assenmacher	.08	.03	.01
□ 54 Brian Harper	.12	.05	.01
□ 55 Paul Gibson	.08	.03	.01
□ 56 John Burkett	.08	.03	.01
□ 57 Doug Jones	.08	.03	.01
□ 58 Jose Oquendo	.08	.03	.01
□ 59 Dick Schofield	.08	.03	.01
□ 60 Dickie Thon	.08	.03	.01
□ 61 Ramon Martinez	.60	.25	.06
□ 62 Jay Buhner	.15	.06	.01
□ 63 Mark Portugal	.08	.03	.01
□ 64 Bob Welch	.12	.05	.01
□ 65 Chris Sabo	.17	.07	.01
□ 66 Chuck Cary	.08	.03	.01
□ 67 Mark Langston	.15	.06	.01
□ 68 Joe Boever	.08	.03	.01
□ 69 Jody Reed	.12	.05	.01
□ 70 Alejandro Pena	.12	.05	.01
□ 71 Jeff King	.12	.05	.01
□ 72 Tom Pagnozzi	.08	.03	.01
□ 73 Joe Oliver	.08	.03	.01
□ 74 Mike Witt	.08	.03	.01
□ 75 Hector Villanueva	.12	.05	.01
□ 76 Dan Gladden	.08	.03	.01
□ 77 Dave Justice	4.00	1.75	.40
□ 78 Mike Gallego	.08	.03	.01
□ 79 Tom Candiotti	.12	.05	.01
□ 80 Ozzie Smith	.35	.15	.03
□ 81 Luis Polonia	.12	.05	.01
□ 82 Randy Ready	.08	.03	.01

Card	Player			
☐ 83	Greg Harris	.08	.03	.01
☐ 84	Checklist Card Dave Justice	.25	.10	.02
☐ 85	Kevin Mitchell	.30	.12	.03
☐ 86	Mark McLemore	.08	.03	.01
☐ 87	Terry Steinbach	.08	.03	.01
☐ 88	Tom Browning	.12	.05	.01
☐ 89	Matt Nokes	.12	.05	.01
☐ 90	Mike Harkey	.12	.05	.01
☐ 91	Omar Vizquel	.08	.03	.01
☐ 92	Dave Bergman	.08	.03	.01
☐ 93	Matt Williams	.30	.12	.03
☐ 94	Steve Olin	.08	.03	.01
☐ 95	Craig Wilson	.20	.08	.02
☐ 96	Dave Stieb	.12	.05	.01
☐ 97	Ruben Sierra	.50	.20	.05
☐ 98	Jay Howell	.08	.03	.01
☐ 99	Scott Bradley	.08	.03	.01
☐ 100	Eric Yelding	.08	.03	.01
☐ 101	Rickey Henderson	.75	.30	.07
☐ 102	Jeff Reed	.08	.03	.01
☐ 103	Jimmy Key	.12	.05	.01
☐ 104	Terry Shumpert	.12	.05	.01
☐ 105	Kenny Rogers	.08	.03	.01
☐ 106	Cecil Fielder	.75	.30	.07
☐ 107	Robby Thompson	.08	.03	.01
☐ 108	Alex Cole	.15	.06	.01
☐ 109	Randy Milligan	.12	.05	.01
☐ 110	Andres Galarraga	.12	.05	.01
☐ 111	Bill Spiers	.08	.03	.01
☐ 112	Kal Daniels	.15	.06	.01
☐ 113	Henry Cotto	.08	.03	.01
☐ 114	Casey Candaele	.08	.03	.01
☐ 115	Jeff Blauser	.08	.03	.01
☐ 116	Robin Yount	.35	.15	.03
☐ 117	Ben McDonald	.35	.15	.03
☐ 118	Bret Saberhagen	.15	.06	.01
☐ 119	Juan Gonzalez	4.00	1.75	.40
☐ 120	Lou Whitaker	.15	.06	.01
☐ 121	Ellis Burks	.17	.07	.01
☐ 122	Charlie O'Brien	.08	.03	.01
☐ 123	John Smiley	.12	.05	.01
☐ 124	Tim Burke	.08	.03	.01
☐ 125	John Olerud	.40	.16	.04
☐ 126	Eddie Murray	.30	.12	.03
☐ 127	Greg Maddux	.12	.05	.01
☐ 128	Kevin Tapani	.20	.08	.02
☐ 129	Ron Gant	.40	.16	.04
☐ 130	Jay Bell	.08	.03	.01
☐ 131	Chris Hoiles	.17	.07	.01
☐ 132	Tom Gordon	.12	.05	.01
☐ 133	Kevin Seitzer	.12	.05	.01
☐ 134	Jeff Huson	.08	.03	.01
☐ 135	Jerry Don Gleaton	.08	.03	.01
☐ 136	Jeff Brantley	.08	.03	.01
☐ 137	Felix Fermin	.08	.03	.01
☐ 138	Mike Devereaux	.08	.03	.01
☐ 139	Delino DeShields	.25	.10	.02
☐ 140	David Wells	.08	.03	.01
☐ 141	Tim Crews	.08	.03	.01
☐ 142	Erik Hanson	.12	.05	.01
☐ 143	Mark Davidson	.08	.03	.01
☐ 144	Tommy Gregg	.08	.03	.01
☐ 145	Jim Gantner	.08	.03	.01
☐ 146	Jose Lind	.08	.03	.01
☐ 147	Danny Tartabull	.15	.06	.01
☐ 148	Geno Petralli	.08	.03	.01
☐ 149	Travis Fryman	2.25	.90	.22
☐ 150	Tim Naehring	.15	.06	.01
☐ 151	Kevin McReynolds	.15	.06	.01
☐ 152	Joe Orsulak	.08	.03	.01
☐ 153	Steve Frey	.15	.06	.01
☐ 154	Duane Ward	.08	.03	.01
☐ 155	Stan Javier	.08	.03	.01
☐ 156	Damon Berryhill	.08	.03	.01
☐ 157	Gene Larkin	.08	.03	.01
☐ 158	Greg Olson	.12	.05	.01
☐ 159	Mark Knudson	.08	.03	.01
☐ 160	Carmelo Martinez	.08	.03	.01
☐ 161	Storm Davis	.08	.03	.01
☐ 162	Jim Abbott	.30	.12	.03
☐ 163	Len Dykstra	.15	.06	.01
☐ 164	Tom Brunansky	.12	.05	.01
☐ 165	Dwight Gooden	.30	.12	.03
☐ 166	Jose Mesa	.08	.03	.01
☐ 167	Oil Can Boyd	.08	.03	.01
☐ 168	Barry Larkin	.30	.12	.03
☐ 169	Scott Sanderson	.12	.05	.01
☐ 170	Mark Grace	.20	.08	.02
☐ 171	Mark Guthrie	.15	.06	.01
☐ 172	Tom Glavine	.30	.12	.03
☐ 173	Gary Sheffield	.15	.06	.01
☐ 174	Checklist Card Roger Clemens	.15	.06	.01
☐ 175	Chris James	.08	.03	.01
☐ 176	Milt Thompson	.08	.03	.01
☐ 177	Donnie Hill	.08	.03	.01
☐ 178	Wes Chamberlain	2.00	.80	.20
☐ 179	John Marzano	.08	.03	.01
☐ 180	Frank Viola	.15	.06	.01
☐ 181	Eric Anthony	.15	.06	.01
☐ 182	Jose Canseco	1.25	.50	.12
☐ 183	Scott Scudder	.12	.05	.01
☐ 184	Dave Eiland	.08	.03	.01
☐ 185	Luis Salazar	.08	.03	.01
☐ 186	Pedro Munoz	.75	.30	.07
☐ 187	Steve Searcy	.08	.03	.01
☐ 188	Don Robinson	.08	.03	.01
☐ 189	Sandy Alomar Jr.	.15	.06	.01
☐ 190	Jose DeLeon	.08	.03	.01
☐ 191	John Orton	.08	.03	.01
☐ 192	Darren Daulton	.12	.05	.01
☐ 193	Mike Morgan	.12	.05	.01
☐ 194	Greg Briley	.08	.03	.01
☐ 195	Karl Rhodes	.12	.05	.01
☐ 196	Harold Baines	.12	.05	.01

□ 197 Bill Doran	.08	.03	.01
□ 198 Alvaro Espinoza	.08	.03	.01
□ 199 Kirk McCaskill	.08	.03	.01
□ 200 Jose DeJesus	.08	.03	.01
□ 201 Jack Clark	.12	.05	.01
□ 202 Daryl Boston	.08	.03	.01
□ 203 Randy Tomlin	.60	.25	.06
□ 204 Pedro Guerrero	.12	.05	.01
□ 205 Billy Hatcher	.12	.05	.01
□ 206 Tim Leary	.12	.05	.01
□ 207 Ryne Sandberg	1.00	.40	.10
□ 208 Kirby Puckett	.50	.20	.05
□ 209 Charlie Leibrandt	.08	.03	.01
□ 210 Rick Honeycutt	.08	.03	.01
□ 211 Joel Skinner	.08	.03	.01
□ 212 Rex Hudler	.08	.03	.01
□ 213 Bryan Harvey	.12	.05	.01
□ 214 Charlie Hayes	.08	.03	.01
□ 215 Matt Young	.08	.03	.01
□ 216 Terry Kennedy	.08	.03	.01
□ 217 Carl Nichols	.08	.03	.01
□ 218 Mike Moore	.12	.05	.01
□ 219 Paul O'Neill	.12	.05	.01
□ 220 Steve Sax	.12	.05	.01
□ 221 Shawn Boskie	.12	.05	.01
□ 222 Rich DeLucia	.30	.12	.03
□ 223 Lloyd Moseby	.08	.03	.01
□ 224 Mike Kingery	.08	.03	.01
□ 225 Carlos Baerga	.30	.12	.03
□ 226 Bryn Smith	.08	.03	.01
□ 227 Todd Stottlemyre	.12	.05	.01
□ 228 Julio Franco	.20	.08	.02
□ 229 Jim Gott	.08	.03	.01
□ 230 Mike Schooler	.08	.03	.01
□ 231 Steve Finley	.12	.05	.01
□ 232 Dave Henderson	.15	.06	.01
□ 233 Luis Quinones	.08	.03	.01
□ 234 Mark Whiten	.35	.15	.03
□ 235 Brian McRae	2.00	.80	.20
□ 236 Rich Gossage	.12	.05	.01
□ 237 Rob Deer	.12	.05	.01
□ 238 Will Clark	1.00	.40	.10
□ 239 Albert Belle	.60	.25	.06
□ 240 Bob Melvin	.08	.03	.01
□ 241 Larry Walker	.12	.05	.01
□ 242 Dante Bichette	.08	.03	.01
□ 243 Orel Hershiser	.15	.06	.01
□ 244 Pete O'Brien	.08	.03	.01
□ 245 Pete Harnisch	.12	.05	.01
□ 246 Jeff Treadway	.08	.03	.01
□ 247 Julio Machado	.08	.03	.01
□ 248 Dave Johnson	.08	.03	.01
□ 249 Kirk Gibson	.15	.06	.01
□ 250 Kevin Brown	.08	.03	.01
□ 251 Milt Cuyler	.40	.16	.04
□ 252 Jeff Reardon	.15	.06	.01
□ 253 David Cone	.12	.05	.01
□ 254 Gary Redus	.08	.03	.01
□ 255 Junior Noboa	.08	.03	.01
□ 256 Greg Myers	.08	.03	.01
□ 257 Dennis Cook	.08	.03	.01
□ 258 Joe Girardi	.08	.03	.01
□ 259 Allan Anderson	.08	.03	.01
□ 260 Paul Marak	.15	.06	.01
□ 261 Barry Bonds	.50	.20	.05
□ 262 Juan Bell	.12	.05	.01
□ 263 Russ Morman	.08	.03	.01
□ 264 Checklist Card George Brett	.15	.06	.01

1991 Leaf II

The second series of the 1991 Leaf set contains 264 cards, measuring the standard size (2 1/2" by 3 1/2"). As with the first series, the glossy color player photos on the fronts are bordered in black and white, with a gray outer border framing the whole card. On a silver, red, and black background, the backs feature a color head shot, biography, and career performance statistics, with a career highlights when space allows. The cards are numbered on the back. The key rookie cards in this series are Orlando Merced and Denny Neagle.

	MINT	EXC	G-VG
COMPLETE SET (264)	40.00	18.00	6.00
COMMON PLAYER (265-528)	.08	.03	.01

□ 265 Jerald Clark	.12	.05	.01
□ 266 Dwight Evans	.12	.05	.01
□ 267 Roberto Alomar	.40	.16	.04
□ 268 Danny Jackson	.08	.03	.01
□ 269 Brian Downing	.08	.03	.01

☐ 270 John Cerutti	.08	.03	.01
☐ 271 Robin Ventura	1.25	.50	.12
☐ 272 Gerald Perry	.08	.03	.01
☐ 273 Wade Boggs	.50	.20	.05
☐ 274 Dennis Martinez	.12	.05	.01
☐ 275 Andy Benes	.20	.08	.02
☐ 276 Tony Fossas	.08	.03	.01
☐ 277 Franklin Stubbs	.08	.03	.01
☐ 278 John Kruk	.08	.03	.01
☐ 279 Kevin Gross	.08	.03	.01
☐ 280 Von Hayes	.12	.05	.01
☐ 281 Frank Thomas	8.00	3.50	.80
☐ 282 Rob Dibble	.15	.06	.01
☐ 283 Mel Hall	.12	.05	.01
☐ 284 Rick Mahler	.08	.03	.01
☐ 285 Dennis Eckersley	.15	.06	.01
☐ 286 Bernard Gilkey	.25	.10	.02
☐ 287 Dan Plesac	.08	.03	.01
☐ 288 Jason Grimsley	.15	.06	.01
☐ 289 Mark Lewis	.75	.30	.07
☐ 290 Tony Gwynn	.50	.20	.05
☐ 291 Jeff Russell	.08	.03	.01
☐ 292 Curt Schilling	.08	.03	.01
☐ 293 Pascual Perez	.08	.03	.01
☐ 294 Jack Morris	.15	.06	.01
☐ 295 Hubie Brooks	.12	.05	.01
☐ 296 Alex Fernandez	.60	.25	.06
☐ 297 Harold Reynolds	.12	.05	.01
☐ 298 Craig Worthington	.08	.03	.01
☐ 299 Willie Wilson	.12	.05	.01
☐ 300 Mike Maddux	.08	.03	.01
☐ 301 Dave Righetti	.12	.05	.01
☐ 302 Paul Molitor	.15	.06	.01
☐ 303 Gary Gaetti	.12	.05	.01
☐ 304 Terry Pendleton	.20	.08	.02
☐ 305 Kevin Elster	.08	.03	.01
☐ 306 Scott Fletcher	.08	.03	.01
☐ 307 Jeff Robinson	.08	.03	.01
☐ 308 Jesse Barfield	.12	.05	.01
☐ 309 Mike LaCoss	.08	.03	.01
☐ 310 Andy Van Slyke	.15	.06	.01
☐ 311 Glenallen Hill	.12	.05	.01
☐ 312 Bud Black	.08	.03	.01
☐ 313 Kent Hrbek	.15	.06	.01
☐ 314 Tim Teufel	.08	.03	.01
☐ 315 Tony Fernandez	.12	.05	.01
☐ 316 Beau Allred	.17	.07	.01
☐ 317 Curtis Wilkerson	.08	.03	.01
☐ 318 Bill Sampen	.12	.05	.01
☐ 319 Randy Johnson	.12	.05	.01
☐ 320 Mike Heath	.08	.03	.01
☐ 321 Sammy Sosa	.15	.06	.01
☐ 322 Mickey Tettleton	.12	.05	.01
☐ 323 Jose Vizcaino	.15	.06	.01
☐ 324 John Candelaria	.08	.03	.01
☐ 325 Dave Howard	.20	.08	.02
☐ 326 Jose Rijo	.12	.05	.01
☐ 327 Todd Zeile	.30	.12	.03
☐ 328 Gene Nelson	.08	.03	.01
☐ 329 Dwayne Henry	.08	.03	.01
☐ 330 Mike Boddicker	.08	.03	.01
☐ 331 Ozzie Guillen	.12	.05	.01
☐ 332 Sam Horn	.12	.05	.01
☐ 333 Wally Whitehurst	.08	.03	.01
☐ 334 Dave Parker	.15	.06	.01
☐ 335 George Brett	.35	.15	.03
☐ 336 Bobby Thigpen	.12	.05	.01
☐ 337 Ed Whitson	.08	.03	.01
☐ 338 Ivan Calderon	.12	.05	.01
☐ 339 Mike Pagliarulo	.08	.03	.01
☐ 340 Jack McDowell	.17	.07	.01
☐ 341 Dana Kiecker	.08	.03	.01
☐ 342 Fred McGriff	.25	.10	.02
☐ 343 Mark Lee	.20	.08	.02
☐ 344 Alfredo Griffin	.08	.03	.01
☐ 345 Scott Bankhead	.08	.03	.01
☐ 346 Darrin Jackson	.12	.05	.01
☐ 347 Rafael Palmeiro	.25	.10	.02
☐ 348 Steve Farr	.08	.03	.01
☐ 349 Hensley Meulens	.17	.07	.01
☐ 350 Danny Cox	.08	.03	.01
☐ 351 Alan Trammell	.20	.08	.02
☐ 352 Edwin Nunez	.08	.03	.01
☐ 353 Joe Carter	.25	.10	.02
☐ 354 Eric Show	.08	.03	.01
☐ 355 Vance Law	.08	.03	.01
☐ 356 Jeff Gray	.15	.06	.01
☐ 357 Bobby Bonilla	.40	.16	.04
☐ 358 Ernest Riles	.08	.03	.01
☐ 359 Ron Hassey	.08	.03	.01
☐ 360 Willie McGee	.15	.06	.01
☐ 361 Mackey Sasser	.08	.03	.01
☐ 362 Glenn Braggs	.08	.03	.01
☐ 363 Mario Diaz	.08	.03	.01
☐ 364 Checklist Card Barry Bonds	.12	.05	.01
☐ 365 Kevin Bass	.08	.03	.01
☐ 366 Pete Incaviglia	.12	.05	.01
☐ 367 Luis Sojo UER (1989 stats inter- spersed with 1990's)	.12	.05	.01
☐ 368 Lance Parrish	.12	.05	.01
☐ 369 Mark Leonard	.30	.12	.03
☐ 370 Heathcliff Slocumb	.17	.07	.01
☐ 371 Jimmy Jones	.08	.03	.01
☐ 372 Ken Griffey Jr.	5.00	2.25	.50
☐ 373 Chris Hammond	.15	.06	.01
☐ 374 Chili Davis	.12	.05	.01
☐ 375 Joey Cora	.08	.03	.01
☐ 376 Ken Hill	.08	.03	.01
☐ 377 Darryl Strawberry	.75	.30	.07
☐ 378 Ron Darling	.12	.05	.01
☐ 379 Sid Bream	.08	.03	.01
☐ 380 Bill Swift	.08	.03	.01
☐ 381 Shawn Abner	.08	.03	.01
☐ 382 Eric King	.08	.03	.01

□ 383 Mickey Morandini .... .17 .07 .01
□ 384 Carlton Fisk .... .35 .15 .03
□ 385 Steve Lake .... .08 .03 .01
□ 386 Mike Jeffcoat .... .08 .03 .01
□ 387 Darren Holmes .... .17 .07 .01
□ 388 Tim Wallach .... .12 .05 .01
□ 389 George Bell .... .20 .08 .02
□ 390 Craig Lefferts .... .08 .03 .01
□ 391 Ernie Whitt .... .08 .03 .01
□ 392 Felix Jose .... .30 .12 .03
□ 393 Kevin Maas .... .60 .25 .06
□ 394 Devon White .... .12 .05 .01
□ 395 Otis Nixon .... .12 .05 .01
□ 396 Chuck Knoblauch .... 2.50 1.00 .25
□ 397 Scott Coolbaugh .... .08 .03 .01
□ 398 Glenn Davis .... .15 .06 .01
□ 399 Manny Lee .... .08 .03 .01
□ 400 Andre Dawson .... .25 .10 .02
□ 401 Scott Chiamparino .... .15 .06 .01
□ 402 Bill Gullickson .... .12 .05 .01
□ 403 Lance Johnson .... .08 .03 .01
□ 404 Juan Agosto .... .08 .03 .01
□ 405 Danny Darwin .... .08 .03 .01
□ 406 Barry Jones .... .08 .03 .01
□ 407 Larry Andersen .... .08 .03 .01
□ 408 Luis Rivera .... .08 .03 .01
□ 409 Jaime Navarro .... .08 .03 .01
□ 410 Roger McDowell .... .08 .03 .01
□ 411 Brett Butler .... .12 .05 .01
□ 412 Dale Murphy .... .17 .07 .01
□ 413 Tim Raines UER .... .15 .06 .01
(Listed as hitting .500
in 1980, should be .050)
□ 414 Norm Charlton .... .08 .03 .01
□ 415 Greg Cadaret .... .08 .03 .01
□ 416 Chris Nabholz .... .15 .06 .01
□ 417 Dave Stewart .... .15 .06 .01
□ 418 Rich Gedman .... .08 .03 .01
□ 419 Willie Randolph .... .12 .05 .01
□ 420 Mitch Williams .... .12 .05 .01
□ 421 Brook Jacoby .... .08 .03 .01
□ 422 Greg Harris .... .08 .03 .01
□ 423 Nolan Ryan .... 2.50 1.00 .25
□ 424 Dave Rohde .... .15 .06 .01
□ 425 Don Mattingly .... .50 .20 .05
□ 426 Greg Gagne .... .08 .03 .01
□ 427 Vince Coleman .... .15 .06 .01
□ 428 Dan Pasqua .... .08 .03 .01
□ 429 Alvin Davis .... .12 .05 .01
□ 430 Cal Ripken .... 1.25 .50 .12
□ 431 Jamie Quirk .... .08 .03 .01
□ 432 Benito Santiago .... .15 .06 .01
□ 433 Jose Uribe .... .08 .03 .01
□ 434 Candy Maldonado .... .08 .03 .01
□ 435 Junior Felix .... .12 .05 .01
□ 436 Deion Sanders .... .20 .08 .02
□ 437 John Franco .... .08 .03 .01
□ 438 Greg Hibbard .... .08 .03 .01
□ 439 Floyd Bannister .... .08 .03 .01
□ 440 Steve Howe .... .08 .03 .01
□ 441 Steve Decker .... .50 .20 .05
□ 442 Vicente Palacios .... .08 .03 .01
□ 443 Pat Tabler .... .08 .03 .01
□ 444 Checklist Card .... .12 .05 .01
Darryl Strawberry
□ 445 Mike Felder .... .08 .03 .01
□ 446 Al Newman .... .08 .03 .01
□ 447 Chris Donnels .... .60 .25 .06
□ 448 Rich Rodriguez .... .15 .06 .01
□ 449 Turner Ward .... .30 .12 .03
□ 450 Bob Walk .... .08 .03 .01
□ 451 Gilberto Reyes .... .08 .03 .01
□ 452 Mike Jackson .... .08 .03 .01
□ 453 Rafael Belliard .... .08 .03 .01
□ 454 Wayne Edwards .... .08 .03 .01
□ 455 Andy Allanson .... .08 .03 .01
□ 456 Dave Smith .... .08 .03 .01
□ 457 Gary Carter .... .15 .06 .01
□ 458 Warren Cromartie .... .08 .03 .01
□ 459 Jack Armstrong .... .12 .05 .01
□ 460 Bob Tewksbury .... .08 .03 .01
□ 461 Joe Klink .... .08 .03 .01
□ 462 Xavier Hernandez .... .08 .03 .01
□ 463 Scott Radinsky .... .12 .05 .01
□ 464 Jeff Robinson .... .08 .03 .01
□ 465 Gregg Jefferies .... .20 .08 .02
□ 466 Denny Neagle .... .90 .40 .09
□ 467 Carmelo Martinez .... .08 .03 .01
□ 468 Donn Pall .... .08 .03 .01
□ 469 Bruce Hurst .... .12 .05 .01
□ 470 Eric Bullock .... .08 .03 .01
□ 471 Rick Aguilera .... .12 .05 .01
□ 472 Charlie Hough .... .08 .03 .01
□ 473 Carlos Quintana .... .12 .05 .01
□ 474 Marty Barrett .... .08 .03 .01
□ 475 Kevin Brown .... .08 .03 .01
□ 476 Bobby Ojeda .... .08 .03 .01
□ 477 Edgar Martinez .... .12 .05 .01
□ 478 Bip Roberts .... .08 .03 .01
□ 479 Mike Flanagan .... .12 .05 .01
□ 480 John Habyan .... .08 .03 .01
□ 481 Larry Casian .... .17 .07 .01
□ 482 Wally Backman .... .08 .03 .01
□ 483 Doug Dascenzo .... .08 .03 .01
□ 484 Rick Dempsey .... .08 .03 .01
□ 485 Ed Sprague .... .25 .10 .02
□ 486 Steve Chitren .... .15 .06 .01
□ 487 Mark McGwire .... .25 .10 .02
□ 488 Roger Clemens .... .75 .30 .07
□ 489 Orlando Merced .... 1.50 .60 .15
□ 490 Rene Gonzales .... .08 .03 .01
□ 491 Mike Stanton .... .08 .03 .01
□ 492 Al Osuna .... .30 .12 .03
□ 493 Rick Cerone .... .08 .03 .01
□ 494 Mariano Duncan .... .08 .03 .01
□ 495 Zane Smith .... .12 .05 .01

☐ 496 John Morris	.08	.03	.01
☐ 497 Frank Tanana	.12	.05	.01
☐ 498 Junior Ortiz	.08	.03	.01
☐ 499 Dave Winfield	.30	.12	.03
☐ 500 Gary Varsho	.08	.03	.01
☐ 501 Chico Walker	.08	.03	.01
☐ 502 Ken Caminiti	.08	.03	.01
☐ 503 Ken Griffey Sr.	.12	.05	.01
☐ 504 Randy Myers	.08	.03	.01
☐ 505 Steve Bedrosian	.12	.05	.01
☐ 506 Cory Snyder	.12	.05	.01
☐ 507 Cris Carpenter	.08	.03	.01
☐ 508 Tim Belcher	.12	.05	.01
☐ 509 Jeff Hamilton	.08	.03	.01
☐ 510 Steve Avery	2.50	1.00	.25
☐ 511 Dave Valle	.08	.03	.01
☐ 512 Tom Lampkin	.08	.03	.01
☐ 513 Shawn Hillegas	.08	.03	.01
☐ 514 Reggie Jefferson	1.25	.50	.12
☐ 515 Ron Karkovice	.08	.03	.01
☐ 516 Doug Drabek	.12	.05	.01
☐ 517 Tom Henke	.12	.05	.01
☐ 518 Chris Bosio	.08	.03	.01
☐ 519 Gregg Olson	.15	.06	.01
☐ 520 Bob Scanlan	.17	.07	.01
☐ 521 Alonzo Powell	.17	.07	.01
☐ 522 Jeff Ballard	.08	.03	.01
☐ 523 Ray Lankford	1.25	.50	.12
☐ 524 Tommy Greene	.15	.06	.01
☐ 525 Mike Timlin	.25	.10	.02
☐ 526 Juan Berenguer	.08	.03	.01
☐ 527 Scott Erickson	4.00	1.75	.40
☐ 528 Checklist Card Sandy Alomar Jr.	.12	.05	.01

1991 Leaf Gold Rookies

This 26-card standard size (2 1/2" by 3 1/2") set was issued by Leaf as an adjunct (inserted in packs) to their 1991 Leaf regular issue. The set features some of the most popular prospects active in baseball. This set marks the first time Leaf Inc. and/or Donruss had produced a card utilizing any of the first 24 young players. The first twelve cards were issued as random inserts in with the first series of 1991 Leaf foil packs. The rest were issued as random inserts in with the second series. The earliest Leaf Gold Rookie cards issued with the first series can sometimes be found with erroneous regular numbered backs 265 through 276 instead of the correct BC1 through BC12. These numbered variations are very tough to find and are valued at ten times the values listed below.

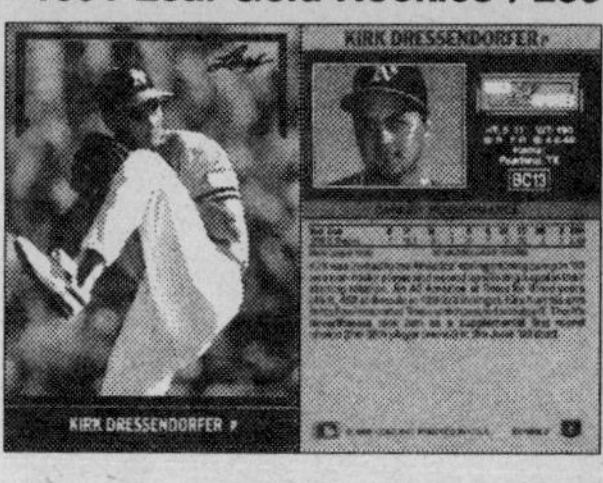

	MINT	EXC	G-VG
COMPLETE SET (26)	100.00	45.00	15.00
COMMON PLAYER (1-12)	1.50	.60	.15
COMMON PLAYER (13-26)	1.50	.60	.15
☐ BC1 Scott Leius	2.25	.90	.22
☐ BC2 Luis Gonzalez	5.00	2.25	.50
☐ BC3 Wilfredo Cordero	3.50	1.50	.35
☐ BC4 Gary Scott	3.00	1.25	.30
☐ BC5 Willie Banks	3.00	1.25	.30
☐ BC6 Arthur Rhodes	3.00	1.25	.30
☐ BC7 Mo Vaughn	7.00	3.00	.70
☐ BC8 Henry Rodriguez	2.00	.80	.20
☐ BC9 Todd Van Poppel	9.00	4.00	.90
☐ BC10 Reggie Sanders	5.00	2.25	.50
☐ BC11 Rico Brogna	4.00	1.75	.40
☐ BC12 Mike Mussina	5.00	2.25	.50
☐ BC13 Kirk Dressendorfer	3.00	1.25	.30
☐ BC14 Jeff Bagwell	14.00	6.25	2.00
☐ BC15 Pete Schourek	2.50	1.00	.25
☐ BC16 Wade Taylor	2.25	.90	.22
☐ BC17 Pat Kelly	3.50	1.50	.35
☐ BC18 Tim Costo	3.00	1.25	.30
☐ BC19 Roger Salkeld	5.00	2.25	.50
☐ BC20 Andujar Cedeno	5.00	2.25	.50
☐ BC21 Ryan Klesko UER (1990 Sumter BA .289; should be .368)	14.00	6.25	2.00
☐ BC22 Mike Huff	1.50	.60	.15
☐ BC23 Anthony Young	2.25	.90	.22
☐ BC24 Eddie Zosky	3.00	1.25	.30
☐ BC25 Nolan Ryan UER No Hitter 7 (Word other repeated in 7th line)	7.50	3.25	.75
☐ BC26 Rickey Henderson Record Steal	5.00	2.25	.50

1991 Leaf Studio

The 1991 Leaf Studio set contains 264 cards and a puzzle of recently inducted Hall of Famer Rod Carew. The Carew puzzle was issued on twenty-one 2 1/2" by 3 1/2" cards, with 3 puzzle pieces per card, for a total of 63 pieces. The player cards measure the standard-size (2 1/2" by 3 1/2"), and the fronts feature posed black and white head-and-shoulders player photos with mauve borders. The team logo, player's name, and position appear along the bottom of the card face. The backs are printed in black and white and have four categories of information: personal, career, hobbies and interests, and heroes. The cards are numbered on the back. The cards are checklisted below alphabetically within and according to teams for each league as follows: Baltimore Orioles (1-10), Boston Red Sox (11-20), California Angels (21-30), Chicago White Sox (31-40), Cleveland Indians (41-50), Detroit Tigers (51-60), Kansas City Royals (61-70), Milwaukee Brewers (71-80), Minnesota Twins (81-90), New York Yankees (91-100), Oakland Athletics (101-110), Seattle Mariners (111-120), Texas Rangers (121-130), Toronto Blue Jays (131-140), Atlanta Braves (141-150), Chicago Cubs (151-160), Cincinnati Reds (161-170), Houston Astros (171-180), Los Angeles Dodgers (181-190), Montreal Expos (191-200), New York Mets (201-210), Philadelphia Phillies (211-220), Pittsburgh Pirates (221-230), St. Louis Cardinals (231-240), San Diego Padres (241-250), and San Francisco Giants (251-260). The key rookie cards in the set are Jeff Bagwell, Wes Chamberlain, Phil Plantier, and Todd Van Poppel. Among the other notable cards are Frank Thomas and Dave Justice.

	MINT	EXC	G-VG
COMPLETE SET (264)	45.00	20.00	6.75
COMMON PLAYER (1-263)	.08	.03	.01
☐ 1 Glenn Davis	.15	.06	.01
☐ 2 Dwight Evans	.12	.05	.01
☐ 3 Leo Gomez	.75	.30	.07
☐ 4 Chris Hoiles	.20	.08	.02
☐ 5 Sam Horn	.12	.05	.01
☐ 6 Ben McDonald	.35	.15	.03
☐ 7 Randy Milligan	.12	.05	.01
☐ 8 Gregg Olson	.15	.06	.01
☐ 9 Cal Ripken	1.25	.50	.12
☐ 10 David Segui	.15	.06	.01
☐ 11 Wade Boggs	.50	.20	.05
☐ 12 Ellis Burks	.20	.08	.02
☐ 13 Jack Clark	.15	.06	.01
☐ 14 Roger Clemens	.75	.30	.07
☐ 15 Mike Greenwell	.30	.12	.03
☐ 16 Tim Naehring	.15	.06	.01
☐ 17 Tony Pena	.12	.05	.01
☐ 18 Phil Plantier	6.00	2.50	.60
☐ 19 Jeff Reardon	.15	.06	.01
☐ 20 Mo Vaughn	2.00	.80	.20
☐ 21 Jimmy Reese CO	.08	.03	.01
☐ 22 Jim Abbott	.30	.12	.03
☐ 23 Bert Blyleven	.15	.06	.01
☐ 24 Chuck Finley	.17	.07	.01
☐ 25 Gary Gaetti	.12	.05	.01
☐ 26 Wally Joyner	.20	.08	.02
☐ 27 Mark Langston	.15	.06	.01
☐ 28 Kirk McCaskill	.08	.03	.01
☐ 29 Lance Parrish	.12	.05	.01
☐ 30 Dave Winfield	.30	.12	.03
☐ 31 Alex Fernandez	.45	.18	.04
☐ 32 Carlton Fisk	.35	.15	.03
☐ 33 Scott Fletcher	.08	.03	.01
☐ 34 Greg Hibbard	.08	.03	.01
☐ 35 Charlie Hough	.08	.03	.01
☐ 36 Jack McDowell	.17	.07	.01
☐ 37 Tim Raines	.15	.06	.01
☐ 38 Sammy Sosa	.15	.06	.01
☐ 39 Bobby Thigpen	.12	.05	.01
☐ 40 Frank Thomas	7.50	3.25	.75
☐ 41 Sandy Alomar Jr.	.15	.06	.01
☐ 42 John Farrell	.08	.03	.01
☐ 43 Glenallen Hill	.08	.03	.01
☐ 44 Brook Jacoby	.08	.03	.01
☐ 45 Chris James	.08	.03	.01
☐ 46 Doug Jones	.08	.03	.01
☐ 47 Eric King	.08	.03	.01
☐ 48 Mark Lewis	.60	.25	.06
☐ 49 Greg Swindell UER (Photo actually Turner Ward)	.12	.05	.01
☐ 50 Mark Whiten	.35	.15	.03
☐ 51 Milt Cuyler	.35	.15	.03
☐ 52 Rob Deer	.12	.05	.01

No.	Player			
☐ 53	Cecil Fielder	.75	.30	.07
☐ 54	Travis Fryman	2.25	.90	.22
☐ 55	Bill Gullickson	.12	.05	.01
☐ 56	Lloyd Moseby	.08	.03	.01
☐ 57	Frank Tanana	.12	.05	.01
☐ 58	Mickey Tettleton	.12	.05	.01
☐ 59	Alan Trammell	.17	.07	.01
☐ 60	Lou Whitaker	.12	.05	.01
☐ 61	Mike Boddicker	.08	.03	.01
☐ 62	George Brett	.35	.15	.03
☐ 63	Jeff Conine	.25	.10	.02
☐ 64	Warren Cromartie	.08	.03	.01
☐ 65	Storm Davis	.08	.03	.01
☐ 66	Kirk Gibson	.15	.06	.01
☐ 67	Mark Gubicza	.12	.05	.01
☐ 68	Brian McRae	2.00	.80	.20
☐ 69	Bret Saberhagen	.17	.07	.01
☐ 70	Kurt Stillwell	.08	.03	.01
☐ 71	Tim McIntosh	.08	.03	.01
☐ 72	Candy Maldonado	.08	.03	.01
☐ 73	Paul Molitor	.15	.06	.01
☐ 74	Willie Randolph	.08	.03	.01
☐ 75	Ron Robinson	.08	.03	.01
☐ 76	Gary Sheffield	.15	.06	.01
☐ 77	Franklin Stubbs	.08	.03	.01
☐ 78	B.J. Surhoff	.08	.03	.01
☐ 79	Greg Vaughn	.35	.15	.03
☐ 80	Robin Yount	.40	.16	.04
☐ 81	Rick Aguilera	.12	.05	.01
☐ 82	Steve Bedrosian	.08	.03	.01
☐ 83	Scott Erickson	3.00	1.25	.30
☐ 84	Greg Gagne	.08	.03	.01
☐ 85	Dan Gladden	.08	.03	.01
☐ 86	Brian Harper	.12	.05	.01
☐ 87	Kent Hrbek	.15	.06	.01
☐ 88	Shane Mack	.12	.05	.01
☐ 89	Jack Morris	.17	.07	.01
☐ 90	Kirby Puckett	.50	.20	.05
☐ 91	Jesse Barfield	.12	.05	.01
☐ 92	Steve Farr	.08	.03	.01
☐ 93	Steve Howe	.08	.03	.01
☐ 94	Roberto Kelly	.15	.06	.01
☐ 95	Tim Leary	.12	.05	.01
☐ 96	Kevin Maas	.60	.25	.06
☐ 97	Don Mattingly	.50	.20	.05
☐ 98	Hensley Meulens	.15	.06	.01
☐ 99	Scott Sanderson	.08	.03	.01
☐ 100	Steve Sax	.12	.05	.01
☐ 101	Jose Canseco	1.25	.50	.12
☐ 102	Dennis Eckersley	.15	.06	.01
☐ 103	Dave Henderson	.15	.06	.01
☐ 104	Rickey Henderson	.75	.30	.07
☐ 105	Rick Honeycutt	.08	.03	.01
☐ 106	Mark McGwire	.25	.10	.02
☐ 107	Dave Stewart	.15	.06	.01
☐ 108	Eric Show	.08	.03	.01
☐ 109	Todd Van Poppel	4.00	1.75	.40
☐ 110	Bob Welch	.12	.05	.01
☐ 111	Alvin Davis	.12	.05	.01
☐ 112	Ken Griffey Jr.	5.00	2.25	.50
☐ 113	Ken Griffey Sr.	.15	.06	.01
☐ 114	Erik Hanson	.15	.06	.01
☐ 115	Brian Holman	.12	.05	.01
☐ 116	Randy Johnson	.12	.05	.01
☐ 117	Edgar Martinez	.15	.06	.01
☐ 118	Tino Martinez	.35	.15	.03
☐ 119	Harold Reynolds	.12	.05	.01
☐ 120	David Valle	.08	.03	.01
☐ 121	Kevin Belcher	.20	.08	.02
☐ 122	Scott Chiamparino	.15	.06	.01
☐ 123	Julio Franco	.20	.08	.02
☐ 124	Juan Gonzalez	4.00	1.75	.40
☐ 125	Rich Gossage	.12	.05	.01
☐ 126	Jeff Kunkel	.08	.03	.01
☐ 127	Rafael Palmeiro	.25	.10	.02
☐ 128	Nolan Ryan	2.50	1.00	.25
☐ 129	Ruben Sierra	.50	.20	.05
☐ 130	Bobby Witt	.12	.05	.01
☐ 131	Roberto Alomar	.40	.16	.04
☐ 132	Tom Candiotti	.12	.05	.01
☐ 133	Joe Carter	.30	.12	.03
☐ 134	Ken Dayley	.08	.03	.01
☐ 135	Kelly Gruber	.15	.06	.01
☐ 136	John Olerud	.35	.15	.03
☐ 137	Dave Stieb	.12	.05	.01
☐ 138	Turner Ward	.30	.12	.03
☐ 139	Devon White	.12	.05	.01
☐ 140	Mookie Wilson	.08	.03	.01
☐ 141	Steve Avery	2.50	1.00	.25
☐ 142	Sid Bream	.08	.03	.01
☐ 143	Nick Esasky	.08	.03	.01
☐ 144	Ron Gant	.35	.15	.03
☐ 145	Tom Glavine	.30	.12	.03
☐ 146	David Justice	4.00	1.75	.40
☐ 147	Kelly Mann	.08	.03	.01
☐ 148	Terry Pendleton	.17	.07	.01
☐ 149	John Smoltz	.20	.08	.02
☐ 150	Jeff Treadway	.08	.03	.01
☐ 151	George Bell	.20	.08	.02
☐ 152	Shawn Boskie	.12	.05	.01
☐ 153	Andre Dawson	.30	.12	.03
☐ 154	Lance Dickson	.50	.20	.05
☐ 155	Shawon Dunston	.15	.06	.01
☐ 156	Joe Girardi	.12	.05	.01
☐ 157	Mark Grace	.25	.10	.02
☐ 158	Ryne Sandberg	1.00	.40	.10
☐ 159	Gary Scott	.50	.20	.05
☐ 160	Dave Smith	.08	.03	.01
☐ 161	Tom Browning	.12	.05	.01
☐ 162	Eric Davis	.30	.12	.03
☐ 163	Rob Dibble	.15	.06	.01
☐ 164	Mariano Duncan	.08	.03	.01
☐ 165	Chris Hammond	.15	.06	.01
☐ 166	Billy Hatcher	.12	.05	.01
☐ 167	Barry Larkin	.30	.12	.03
☐ 168	Hal Morris	.30	.12	.03

☐ 169 Paul O'Neill .12 .05 .01
☐ 170 Chris Sabo .15 .06 .01
☐ 171 Eric Anthony .15 .06 .01
☐ 172 Jeff Bagwell 6.00 2.50 .60
☐ 173 Craig Biggio .20 .08 .02
☐ 174 Ken Caminiti .08 .03 .01
☐ 175 Jim Deshaies .08 .03 .01
☐ 176 Steve Finley .12 .05 .01
☐ 177 Pete Harnisch .12 .05 .01
☐ 178 Darryl Kile .25 .10 .02
☐ 179 Curt Schilling .08 .03 .01
☐ 180 Mike Scott .12 .05 .01
☐ 181 Brett Butler .12 .05 .01
☐ 182 Gary Carter .15 .06 .01
☐ 183 Orel Hershiser .15 .06 .01
☐ 184 Ramon Martinez .60 .25 .06
☐ 185 Eddie Murray .30 .12 .03
☐ 186 Jose Offerman .15 .06 .01
☐ 187 Bob Ojeda .08 .03 .01
☐ 188 Juan Samuel .12 .05 .01
☐ 189 Mike Scioscia .08 .03 .01
☐ 190 Darryl Strawberry .75 .30 .07
☐ 191 Moises Alou .15 .06 .01
☐ 192 Brian Barnes .25 .10 .02
☐ 193 Oil Can Boyd .08 .03 .01
☐ 194 Ivan Calderon .12 .05 .01
☐ 195 Delino DeShields .25 .10 .02
☐ 196 Mike Fitzgerald .08 .03 .01
☐ 197 Andres Galarraga .12 .05 .01
☐ 198 Marquis Grissom .25 .10 .02
☐ 199 Bill Sampen .15 .06 .01
☐ 200 Tim Wallach .12 .05 .01
☐ 201 Daryl Boston .08 .03 .01
☐ 202 Vince Coleman .15 .06 .01
☐ 203 John Franco .08 .03 .01
☐ 204 Dwight Gooden .30 .12 .03
☐ 205 Tom Herr .08 .03 .01
☐ 206 Gregg Jefferies .20 .08 .02
☐ 207 Howard Johnson .25 .10 .02
☐ 208 Dave Magadan UER .12 .05 .01
(Born 1862,
should be 1962)
☐ 209 Kevin McReynolds .15 .06 .01
☐ 210 Frank Viola .15 .06 .01
☐ 211 Wes Chamberlain 2.00 .80 .20
☐ 212 Darren Daulton .08 .03 .01
☐ 213 Lenny Dykstra .12 .05 .01
☐ 214 Charlie Hayes .08 .03 .01
☐ 215 Ricky Jordan .12 .05 .01
☐ 216 Steve Lake .08 .03 .01
(Pictured with parrot
on his shoulder)
☐ 217 Roger McDowell .08 .03 .01
☐ 218 Mickey Morandini .20 .08 .02
☐ 219 Terry Mulholland .12 .05 .01
☐ 220 Dale Murphy .20 .08 .02
☐ 221 Jay Bell .08 .03 .01
☐ 222 Barry Bonds .50 .20 .05
☐ 223 Bobby Bonilla .40 .16 .04
☐ 224 Doug Drabek .15 .06 .01
☐ 225 Bill Landrum .08 .03 .01
☐ 226 Mike LaValliere .08 .03 .01
☐ 227 Jose Lind .08 .03 .01
☐ 228 Don Slaught .08 .03 .01
☐ 229 John Smiley .12 .05 .01
☐ 230 Andy Van Slyke .15 .06 .01
☐ 231 Bernard Gilkey .25 .10 .02
☐ 232 Pedro Guerrero .15 .06 .01
☐ 233 Rex Hudler .08 .03 .01
☐ 234 Ray Lankford .90 .40 .09
☐ 235 Joe Magrane .08 .03 .01
☐ 236 Jose Oquendo .08 .03 .01
☐ 237 Lee Smith .12 .05 .01
☐ 238 Ozzie Smith .35 .15 .03
☐ 239 Milt Thompson .08 .03 .01
☐ 240 Todd Zeile .30 .12 .03
☐ 241 Larry Andersen .08 .03 .01
☐ 242 Andy Benes .20 .08 .02
☐ 243 Paul Faries .15 .06 .01
☐ 244 Tony Fernandez .12 .05 .01
☐ 245 Tony Gwynn .50 .20 .05
☐ 246 Atlee Hammaker .08 .03 .01
☐ 247 Fred McGriff .25 .10 .02
☐ 248 Bip Roberts .08 .03 .01
☐ 249 Bentio Santiago .15 .06 .01
☐ 250 Ed Whitson .08 .03 .01
☐ 251 Dave Anderson .08 .03 .01
☐ 252 Mike Benjamin .08 .03 .01
☐ 253 John Burkett UER .12 .05 .01
(Front photo actually
Trevor Wilson)
☐ 254 Will Clark 1.00 .40 .10
☐ 255 Scott Garrelts .08 .03 .01
☐ 256 Willie McGee .15 .06 .01
☐ 257 Kevin Mitchell .30 .12 .03
☐ 258 Dave Righetti .12 .05 .01
☐ 259 Matt Williams .30 .12 .03
☐ 260 Black and Decker .17 .07 .01
Bud Black
Steve Decker
☐ 261 Checklist Card 1-88 .12 .02 .00
Sparky Anderson MG
☐ 262 Checklist Card 89-176 .12 .02 .00
Tom Lasorda MG
☐ 263 Checklist Card 177-263 .12 .02 .00
Tony LaRussa MG
☐ xx Title Card .12 .05 .01
(unnumbered)

1991 O-Pee-Chee Premier

The 1991 O-Pee-Chee Premier set contains 132 standard-size (2 1/2" by 3 1/2") cards. The fronts feature color action player photos on a white card face. All the pictures are bordered in gold above, while the color of the border stripes on the other three sides varies from card to card. The player's name, team name, and position (the last item in English and French) appear below the picture. In a horizontal format, the backs have a color head shot and the team logo in a circular format. Biography and statistics (1990 and career) are presented on an orange and yellow striped background. The cards are arranged in alphabetical order and numbered on the back. Small packs of these cards were given out at the Fan Fest to commemorate the 1991 All-Star Game in Canada. The key rookie cards in this set are Lance Dickson, Kirk Dressendorfer, and Gary Scott.

	MINT	EXC	G-VG
COMPLETE SET (132)	45.00	20.00	6.75
COMMON PLAYER (1-132)	.08	.03	.01
☐ 1 Roberto Alomar	.50	.20	.05
☐ 2 Sandy Alomar Jr.	.20	.08	.02
☐ 3 Moises Alou	.12	.05	.01
☐ 4 Brian Barnes	.30	.12	.03
☐ 5 Steve Bedrosian	.08	.03	.01
☐ 6 George Bell	.30	.12	.03
☐ 7 Juan Bell	.12	.05	.01
☐ 8 Albert Belle	.90	.40	.09
☐ 9 Bud Black	.08	.03	.01
☐ 10 Mike Boddicker	.08	.03	.01
☐ 11 Wade Boggs	.75	.30	.07
☐ 12 Barry Bonds	.75	.30	.07
☐ 13 Denis Boucher	.30	.12	.03
☐ 14 George Brett	.50	.20	.05
☐ 15 Hubie Brooks	.12	.05	.01
☐ 16 Brett Butler	.12	.05	.01
☐ 17 Ivan Calderon	.12	.05	.01
☐ 18 Jose Canseco	2.00	.80	.20
☐ 19 Gary Carter	.17	.07	.01
☐ 20 Joe Carter	.35	.15	.03
☐ 21 Jack Clark	.17	.07	.01
☐ 22 Will Clark	1.50	.60	.15
☐ 23 Roger Clemens	1.25	.50	.12
☐ 24 Alex Cole	.17	.07	.01
☐ 25 Vince Coleman	.17	.07	.01
☐ 26 Jeff Conine	.30	.12	.03
☐ 27 Milt Cuyler	.50	.20	.05
☐ 28 Danny Darwin	.08	.03	.01
☐ 29 Eric Davis	.35	.15	.03
☐ 30 Glenn Davis	.17	.07	.01
☐ 31 Andre Dawson	.35	.15	.03
☐ 32 Ken Dayley	.08	.03	.01
☐ 33 Steve Decker	.60	.25	.06
☐ 34 Delino DeShields	.35	.15	.03
☐ 35 Lance Dickson	.50	.20	.05
☐ 36 Kirk Dressendorfer	.60	.25	.06
☐ 37 Shawon Dunston	.15	.06	.01
☐ 38 Dennis Eckersley	.17	.07	.01
☐ 39 Dwight Evans	.12	.05	.01
☐ 40 Howard Farmer	.15	.06	.01
☐ 41 Junior Felix	.12	.05	.01
☐ 42 Alex Fernandez	.50	.20	.05
☐ 43 Tony Fernandez	.12	.05	.01
☐ 44 Cecil Fielder	1.25	.50	.12
☐ 45 Carlton Fisk	.50	.20	.05
☐ 46 Willie Fraser	.08	.03	.01
☐ 47 Gary Gaetti	.12	.05	.01
☐ 48 Andres Galarraga	.12	.05	.01
☐ 49 Ron Gant	.50	.20	.05
☐ 50 Kirk Gibson	.15	.06	.01
☐ 51 Bernard Gilkey	.30	.12	.03
☐ 52 Leo Gomez	.90	.40	.09
☐ 53 Rene Gonzales	.08	.03	.01
☐ 54 Juan Gonzalez	5.00	2.25	.50
☐ 55 Dwight Gooden	.35	.15	.03
☐ 56 Ken Griffey Jr.	7.00	3.00	.70
☐ 57 Kelly Gruber	.15	.06	.01
☐ 58 Pedro Guerrero	.15	.06	.01
☐ 59 Tony Gwynn	.75	.30	.07
☐ 60 Chris Hammond	.20	.08	.02
☐ 61 Ron Hassey	.08	.03	.01
☐ 62 Rickey Henderson	1.25	.50	.12
☐ 63 Tom Henke	.12	.05	.01
☐ 64 Orel Hershiser	.20	.08	.02
☐ 65 Chris Hoiles	.20	.08	.02
☐ 66 Todd Hundley	.30	.12	.03
☐ 67 Pete Incaviglia	.12	.05	.01
☐ 68 Danny Jackson	.12	.05	.01
☐ 69 Barry Jones	.08	.03	.01

Card	Player	Mint	Exc	G-VG
□ 70	Dave Justice	6.00	2.50	.60
□ 71	Jimmy Key	.12	.05	.01
□ 72	Ray Lankford	1.00	.40	.10
□ 73	Darren Lewis	.75	.30	.07
□ 74	Kevin Maas	.75	.30	.07
□ 75	Denny Martinez	.12	.05	.01
□ 76	Tino Martinez	.50	.20	.05
□ 77	Don Mattingly	.75	.30	.07
□ 78	Willie McGee	.17	.07	.01
□ 79	Fred McGriff	.35	.15	.03
□ 80	Hensley Meulens	.20	.08	.02
□ 81	Kevin Mitchell	.35	.15	.03
□ 82	Paul Molitor	.20	.08	.02
□ 83	Mickey Morandini	.30	.12	.03
□ 84	Jack Morris	.20	.08	.02
□ 85	Dale Murphy	.30	.12	.03
□ 86	Eddie Murray	.35	.15	.03
□ 87	Chris Nabholz	.17	.07	.01
□ 88	Tim Naehring	.20	.08	.02
□ 89	Otis Nixon	.12	.05	.01
□ 90	Jose Offerman	.20	.08	.02
□ 91	Bob Ojeda	.08	.03	.01
□ 92	John Olerud	.60	.25	.06
□ 93	Gregg Olson	.15	.06	.01
□ 94	Dave Parker	.15	.06	.01
□ 95	Terry Pendleton	.20	.08	.02
□ 96	Kirby Puckett	.75	.30	.07
□ 97	Tim Raines	.20	.08	.02
□ 98	Jeff Reardon	.15	.06	.01
□ 99	Dave Righetti	.12	.05	.01
□ 100	Cal Ripken	2.00	.80	.20
□ 101	Mel Rojas	.08	.03	.01
□ 102	Nolan Ryan	6.00	2.50	.60
□ 103	Ryne Sandberg	1.50	.60	.15
□ 104	Scott Sanderson	.12	.05	.01
□ 105	Benny Santiago	.15	.06	.01
□ 106	Pete Schourek	.30	.12	.03
□ 107	Gary Scott	.60	.25	.06
□ 108	Terry Shumpert	.08	.03	.01
□ 109	Ruben Sierra	.75	.30	.07
□ 110	Doug Simons	.25	.10	.02
□ 111	Dave Smith	.08	.03	.01
□ 112	Ozzie Smith	.40	.16	.04
□ 113	Cory Snyder	.12	.05	.01
□ 114	Luis Sojo	.12	.05	.01
□ 115	Dave Stewart	.15	.06	.01
□ 116	Dave Stieb	.12	.05	.01
□ 117	Darryl Strawberry	1.25	.50	.12
□ 118	Pat Tabler	.08	.03	.01
□ 119	Wade Taylor	.30	.12	.03
□ 120	Bobby Thigpen	.12	.05	.01
□ 121	Frank Thomas	15.00	6.50	2.15
□ 122	Mike Timlin	.30	.12	.03
□ 123	Alan Trammell	.30	.12	.03
□ 124	Mo Vaughn	2.00	.80	.20
□ 125	Tim Wallach	.12	.05	.01
□ 126	Devon White	.12	.05	.01
□ 127	Mark Whiten	.60	.25	.06
□ 128	Bernie Williams	1.50	.60	.15
□ 129	Willie Wilson	.12	.05	.01
□ 130	Dave Winfield	.30	.12	.03
□ 131	Robin Yount	.50	.20	.05
□ 132	Checklist Card	.08	.01	.00

1988 Score

This 660-card set was distributed by Major League Marketing. Cards measure 2 1/2" by 3 1/2" and feature six distinctive border colors on the front. Highlights (652-660) and Rookie Prospects (623-647) are included in the set. Reggie Jackson's career is honored with a 5-card subset on cards 500-504. Card number 501, showing Reggie as a member of the Baltimore Orioles, is one of the few opportunities collectors have to visually remember (on a regular card) Reggie's one-year stay with the Orioles. The set is distinguished by the fact that each card back shows a full-color picture of the player. The key rookie cards in this set are Ellis Burks, Ron Gant, Tom Glavine, Gregg Jefferies, Roberto Kelly and Matt Williams. The company also produced a very limited "glossy" set, that is valued at eight times the value of the regular (non-glossy) set. Although exact production quantities of this glossy set are not known, it is generally accepted that the number of Score glossy sets produced in 1988 was much smaller (estimated only 10 percent to 15 percent as many) than the number of Topps Tiffany or Fleer Tin sets.

	MINT	EXC	G-VG
COMPLETE SET (660)	20.00	8.50	2.75

Card			
COMMON PLAYER (1-660)	.03	.01	.00
☐ 1 Don Mattingly	.30	.10	.02
☐ 2 Wade Boggs	.30	.12	.03
☐ 3 Tim Raines	.10	.04	.01
☐ 4 Andre Dawson	.15	.06	.01
☐ 5 Mark McGwire	.40	.16	.04
☐ 6 Kevin Seitzer	.08	.03	.01
☐ 7 Wally Joyner	.15	.06	.01
☐ 8 Jesse Barfield	.08	.03	.01
☐ 9 Pedro Guerrero	.08	.03	.01
☐ 10 Eric Davis	.15	.06	.01
☐ 11 George Brett	.20	.08	.02
☐ 12 Ozzie Smith	.17	.07	.01
☐ 13 Rickey Henderson	.30	.12	.03
☐ 14 Jim Rice	.08	.03	.01
☐ 15 Matt Nokes	.25	.10	.02
☐ 16 Mike Schmidt	.35	.15	.03
☐ 17 Dave Parker	.10	.04	.01
☐ 18 Eddie Murray	.15	.06	.01
☐ 19 Andres Galarraga	.08	.03	.01
☐ 20 Tony Fernandez	.08	.03	.01
☐ 21 Kevin McReynolds	.10	.04	.01
☐ 22 B.J. Surhoff	.08	.03	.01
☐ 23 Pat Tabler	.03	.01	.00
☐ 24 Kirby Puckett	.30	.12	.03
☐ 25 Benny Santiago	.12	.05	.01
☐ 26 Ryne Sandberg	.40	.16	.04
☐ 27 Kelly Downs (Will Clark in background, out of focus)	.08	.03	.01
☐ 28 Jose Cruz	.06	.02	.00
☐ 29 Pete O'Brien	.03	.01	.00
☐ 30 Mark Langston	.08	.03	.01
☐ 31 Lee Smith	.10	.04	.01
☐ 32 Juan Samuel	.08	.03	.01
☐ 33 Kevin Bass	.03	.01	.00
☐ 34 R.J. Reynolds	.03	.01	.00
☐ 35 Steve Sax	.10	.04	.01
☐ 36 John Kruk	.06	.02	.00
☐ 37 Alan Trammell	.15	.06	.01
☐ 38 Chris Bosio	.06	.02	.00
☐ 39 Brook Jacoby	.03	.01	.00
☐ 40 Willie McGee UER (Excited misspelled as excitd)	.08	.03	.01
☐ 41 Dave Magadan	.08	.03	.01
☐ 42 Fred Lynn	.08	.03	.01
☐ 43 Kent Hrbek	.10	.04	.01
☐ 44 Brian Downing	.06	.02	.00
☐ 45 Jose Canseco	.75	.30	.07
☐ 46 Jim Presley	.03	.01	.00
☐ 47 Mike Stanley	.03	.01	.00
☐ 48 Tony Pena	.06	.02	.00
☐ 49 David Cone	.20	.08	.02
☐ 50 Rick Sutcliffe	.06	.02	.00
☐ 51 Doug Drabek	.12	.05	.01
☐ 52 Bill Doran	.03	.01	.00
☐ 53 Mike Scioscia	.03	.01	.00
☐ 54 Candy Maldonado	.06	.02	.00
☐ 55 Dave Winfield	.15	.06	.01
☐ 56 Lou Whitaker	.10	.04	.01
☐ 57 Tom Henke	.06	.02	.00
☐ 58 Ken Gerhart	.03	.01	.00
☐ 59 Glenn Braggs	.03	.01	.00
☐ 60 Julio Franco	.15	.06	.01
☐ 61 Charlie Leibrandt	.03	.01	.00
☐ 62 Gary Gaetti	.08	.03	.01
☐ 63 Bob Boone	.08	.03	.01
☐ 64 Luis Polonia	.25	.10	.02
☐ 65 Dwight Evans	.08	.03	.01
☐ 66 Phil Bradley	.03	.01	.00
☐ 67 Mike Boddicker	.03	.01	.00
☐ 68 Vince Coleman	.10	.04	.01
☐ 69 Howard Johnson	.15	.06	.01
☐ 70 Tim Wallach	.08	.03	.01
☐ 71 Keith Moreland	.03	.01	.00
☐ 72 Barry Larkin	.20	.08	.02
☐ 73 Alan Ashby	.03	.01	.00
☐ 74 Rick Rhoden	.03	.01	.00
☐ 75 Darrell Evans	.06	.02	.00
☐ 76 Dave Stieb	.08	.03	.01
☐ 77 Dan Plesac	.03	.01	.00
☐ 78 Will Clark UER (Born 3/17/64, should be 3/13/64)	.75	.30	.07
☐ 79 Frank White	.03	.01	.00
☐ 80 Joe Carter	.20	.08	.02
☐ 81 Mike Witt	.03	.01	.00
☐ 82 Terry Steinbach	.08	.03	.01
☐ 83 Alvin Davis	.06	.02	.00
☐ 84 Tommy Herr (Will Clark shown sliding into second)	.08	.03	.01
☐ 85 Vance Law	.03	.01	.00
☐ 86 Kal Daniels	.08	.03	.01
☐ 87 Rick Honeycutt UER (wrong years for stats on back)	.03	.01	.00
☐ 88 Alfredo Griffin	.03	.01	.00
☐ 89 Bret Saberhagen	.12	.05	.01
☐ 90 Bert Blyleven	.08	.03	.01
☐ 91 Jeff Reardon	.10	.04	.01
☐ 92 Cory Snyder	.08	.03	.01
☐ 93A Greg Walker ERR (93 of 66)	4.00	1.75	.40
☐ 93B Greg Walker COR (93 of 660)	.06	.02	.00
☐ 94 Joe Magrane	.12	.05	.01
☐ 95 Rob Deer	.06	.02	.00
☐ 96 Ray Knight	.06	.02	.00
☐ 97 Casey Candaele	.03	.01	.00
☐ 98 John Cerutti	.03	.01	.00
☐ 99 Buddy Bell	.06	.02	.00
☐ 100 Jack Clark	.08	.03	.01
☐ 101 Eric Bell	.03	.01	.00

☐ 102 Willie Wilson .... .08 .03 .01
☐ 103 Dave Schmidt .... .03 .01 .00
☐ 104 Dennis Eckersley UER .... .10 .04 .01
(Complete games stats are wrong)
☐ 105 Don Sutton .... .10 .04 .01
☐ 106 Danny Tartabull .... .15 .06 .01
☐ 107 Fred McGriff .... .60 .25 .06
☐ 108 Les Straker .... .03 .01 .00
☐ 109 Lloyd Moseby .... .03 .01 .00
☐ 110 Roger Clemens .... .35 .15 .03
☐ 111 Glenn Hubbard .... .03 .01 .00
☐ 112 Ken Williams .... .06 .02 .00
☐ 113 Ruben Sierra .... .35 .15 .03
☐ 114 Stan Jefferson .... .06 .02 .00
☐ 115 Milt Thompson .... .03 .01 .00
☐ 116 Bobby Bonilla .... .30 .12 .03
☐ 117 Wayne Tolleson .... .03 .01 .00
☐ 118 Matt Williams .... 1.50 .60 .15
☐ 119 Chet Lemon .... .03 .01 .00
☐ 120 Dale Sveum .... .03 .01 .00
☐ 121 Dennis Boyd .... .03 .01 .00
☐ 122 Brett Butler .... .08 .03 .01
☐ 123 Terry Kennedy .... .03 .01 .00
☐ 124 Jack Howell .... .03 .01 .00
☐ 125 Curt Young .... .03 .01 .00
☐ 126A Dave Valle ERR .... .12 .05 .01
(misspelled Dale on card front)
☐ 126B Dave Valle COR .... .06 .02 .00
☐ 127 Curt Wilkerson .... .03 .01 .00
☐ 128 Tim Teufel .... .03 .01 .00
☐ 129 Ozzie Virgil .... .03 .01 .00
☐ 130 Brian Fisher .... .03 .01 .00
☐ 131 Lance Parrish .... .08 .03 .01
☐ 132 Tom Browning .... .06 .02 .00
☐ 133A Larry Andersen ERR .... .12 .05 .01
(misspelled Anderson on card front)
☐ 133B Larry Andersen COR .... .06 .02 .00
☐ 134A Bob Brenly ERR .... .12 .05 .01
(misspelled Brenley on card front)
☐ 134B Bob Brenly COR .... .06 .02 .00
☐ 135 Mike Marshall .... .06 .02 .00
☐ 136 Gerald Perry .... .03 .01 .00
☐ 137 Bobby Meacham .... .03 .01 .00
☐ 138 Larry Herndon .... .03 .01 .00
☐ 139 Fred Manrique .... .06 .02 .00
☐ 140 Charlie Hough .... .03 .01 .00
☐ 141 Ron Darling .... .08 .03 .01
☐ 142 Herm Winningham .... .03 .01 .00
☐ 143 Mike Diaz .... .03 .01 .00
☐ 144 Mike Jackson .... .10 .04 .01
☐ 145 Denny Walling .... .03 .01 .00
☐ 146 Robby Thompson .... .03 .01 .00
☐ 147 Franklin Stubbs .... .03 .01 .00
☐ 148 Albert Hall .... .03 .01 .00
☐ 149 Bobby Witt .... .08 .03 .01
☐ 150 Lance McCullers .... .03 .01 .00
☐ 151 Scott Bradley .... .03 .01 .00
☐ 152 Mark McLemore .... .03 .01 .00
☐ 153 Tim Laudner .... .03 .01 .00
☐ 154 Greg Swindell .... .08 .03 .01
☐ 155 Marty Barrett .... .03 .01 .00
☐ 156 Mike Heath .... .03 .01 .00
☐ 157 Gary Ward .... .03 .01 .00
☐ 158A Lee Mazzilli ERR .... .12 .05 .01
(misspelled Mazilli on card front)
☐ 158B Lee Mazzilli COR .... .06 .02 .00
☐ 159 Tom Foley .... .03 .01 .00
☐ 160 Robin Yount .... .20 .08 .02
☐ 161 Steve Bedrosian .... .06 .02 .00
☐ 162 Bob Walk .... .03 .01 .00
☐ 163 Nick Esasky .... .03 .01 .00
☐ 164 Ken Caminiti .... .20 .08 .02
☐ 165 Jose Uribe .... .03 .01 .00
☐ 166 Dave Anderson .... .03 .01 .00
☐ 167 Ed Whitson .... .03 .01 .00
☐ 168 Ernie Whitt .... .03 .01 .00
☐ 169 Cecil Cooper .... .06 .02 .00
☐ 170 Mike Pagliarulo .... .03 .01 .00
☐ 171 Pat Sheridan .... .03 .01 .00
☐ 172 Chris Bando .... .03 .01 .00
☐ 173 Lee Lacy .... .03 .01 .00
☐ 174 Steve Lombardozzi .... .03 .01 .00
☐ 175 Mike Greenwell .... .40 .16 .04
☐ 176 Greg Minton .... .03 .01 .00
☐ 177 Moose Haas .... .03 .01 .00
☐ 178 Mike Kingery .... .03 .01 .00
☐ 179 Greg A. Harris .... .03 .01 .00
☐ 180 Bo Jackson .... .60 .25 .06
☐ 181 Carmelo Martinez .... .03 .01 .00
☐ 182 Alex Trevino .... .03 .01 .00
☐ 183 Ron Oester .... .03 .01 .00
☐ 184 Danny Darwin .... .03 .01 .00
☐ 185 Mike Krukow .... .03 .01 .00
☐ 186 Rafael Palmeiro .... .50 .20 .05
☐ 187 Tim Burke .... .03 .01 .00
☐ 188 Roger McDowell .... .03 .01 .00
☐ 189 Garry Templeton .... .06 .02 .00
☐ 190 Terry Pendleton .... .12 .05 .01
☐ 191 Larry Parrish .... .03 .01 .00
☐ 192 Rey Quinones .... .03 .01 .00
☐ 193 Joaquin Andujar .... .03 .01 .00
☐ 194 Tom Brunansky .... .06 .02 .00
☐ 195 Donnie Moore .... .03 .01 .00
☐ 196 Dan Pasqua .... .06 .02 .00
☐ 197 Jim Gantner .... .03 .01 .00
☐ 198 Mark Eichhorn .... .06 .02 .00
☐ 199 John Grubb .... .03 .01 .00
☐ 200 Bill Ripken .... .12 .05 .01
☐ 201 Sam Horn .... .15 .06 .01
☐ 202 Todd Worrell .... .08 .03 .01
☐ 203 Terry Leach .... .03 .01 .00

☐ 204 Garth Iorg	.03	.01	.00
☐ 205 Brian Dayett	.03	.01	.00
☐ 206 Bo Diaz	.03	.01	.00
☐ 207 Craig Reynolds	.03	.01	.00
☐ 208 Brian Holton	.06	.02	.00
☐ 209 Marvell Wynne UER (misspelled Marvelle on card front)	.06	.02	.00
☐ 210 Dave Concepcion	.08	.03	.01
☐ 211 Mike Davis	.03	.01	.00
☐ 212 Devon White	.10	.04	.01
☐ 213 Mickey Brantley	.03	.01	.00
☐ 214 Greg Gagne	.03	.01	.00
☐ 215 Oddibe McDowell	.03	.01	.00
☐ 216 Jimmy Key	.06	.02	.00
☐ 217 Dave Bergman	.03	.01	.00
☐ 218 Calvin Schiraldi	.03	.01	.00
☐ 219 Larry Sheets	.03	.01	.00
☐ 220 Mike Easler	.03	.01	.00
☐ 221 Kurt Stillwell	.06	.02	.00
☐ 222 Chuck Jackson	.06	.02	.00
☐ 223 Dave Martinez	.08	.03	.01
☐ 224 Tim Leary	.08	.03	.01
☐ 225 Steve Garvey	.15	.06	.01
☐ 226 Greg Mathews	.03	.01	.00
☐ 227 Doug Sisk	.03	.01	.00
☐ 228 Dave Henderson	.08	.03	.01
☐ 229 Jimmy Dwyer	.03	.01	.00
☐ 230 Larry Owen	.03	.01	.00
☐ 231 Andre Thornton	.03	.01	.00
☐ 232 Mark Salas	.03	.01	.00
☐ 233 Tom Brookens	.03	.01	.00
☐ 234 Greg Brock	.03	.01	.00
☐ 235 Rance Mulliniks	.03	.01	.00
☐ 236 Bob Brower	.03	.01	.00
☐ 237 Joe Niekro	.06	.02	.00
☐ 238 Scott Bankhead	.06	.02	.00
☐ 239 Doug DeCinces	.03	.01	.00
☐ 240 Tommy John	.08	.03	.01
☐ 241 Rich Gedman	.03	.01	.00
☐ 242 Ted Power	.03	.01	.00
☐ 243 Dave Meads	.03	.01	.00
☐ 244 Jim Sundberg	.03	.01	.00
☐ 245 Ken Oberkfell	.03	.01	.00
☐ 246 Jimmy Jones	.06	.02	.00
☐ 247 Ken Landreaux	.03	.01	.00
☐ 248 Jose Oquendo	.03	.01	.00
☐ 249 John Mitchell	.06	.02	.00
☐ 250 Don Baylor	.08	.03	.01
☐ 251 Scott Fletcher	.03	.01	.00
☐ 252 Al Newman	.03	.01	.00
☐ 253 Carney Lansford	.08	.03	.01
☐ 254 Johnny Ray	.03	.01	.00
☐ 255 Gary Pettis	.03	.01	.00
☐ 256 Ken Phelps	.03	.01	.00
☐ 257 Rick Leach	.03	.01	.00
☐ 258 Tim Stoddard	.03	.01	.00
☐ 259 Ed Romero	.03	.01	.00
☐ 260 Sid Bream	.03	.01	.00
☐ 261A Tom Niedenfuer ERR (misspelled Neidenfuer on card front)	.12	.05	.01
☐ 261B Tom Niedenfuer COR	.06	.02	.00
☐ 262 Rick Dempsey	.03	.01	.00
☐ 263 Lonnie Smith	.08	.03	.01
☐ 264 Bob Forsch	.03	.01	.00
☐ 265 Barry Bonds	.35	.15	.03
☐ 266 Willie Randolph	.06	.02	.00
☐ 267 Mike Ramsey	.06	.02	.00
☐ 268 Don Slaught	.03	.01	.00
☐ 269 Mickey Tettleton	.08	.03	.01
☐ 270 Jerry Reuss	.03	.01	.00
☐ 271 Marc Sullivan	.03	.01	.00
☐ 272 Jim Morrison	.03	.01	.00
☐ 273 Steve Balboni	.03	.01	.00
☐ 274 Dick Schofield	.03	.01	.00
☐ 275 John Tudor	.08	.03	.01
☐ 276 Gene Larkin	.12	.05	.01
☐ 277 Harold Reynolds	.06	.02	.00
☐ 278 Jerry Browne	.03	.01	.00
☐ 279 Willie Upshaw	.03	.01	.00
☐ 280 Ted Higuera	.06	.02	.00
☐ 281 Terry McGriff	.03	.01	.00
☐ 282 Terry Puhl	.03	.01	.00
☐ 283 Mark Wasinger	.06	.02	.00
☐ 284 Luis Salazar	.03	.01	.00
☐ 285 Ted Simmons	.08	.03	.01
☐ 286 John Shelby	.03	.01	.00
☐ 287 John Smiley	.45	.18	.04
☐ 288 Curt Ford	.03	.01	.00
☐ 289 Steve Crawford	.03	.01	.00
☐ 290 Dan Quisenberry	.08	.03	.01
☐ 291 Alan Wiggins	.03	.01	.00
☐ 292 Randy Bush	.03	.01	.00
☐ 293 John Candelaria	.03	.01	.00
☐ 294 Tony Phillips	.03	.01	.00
☐ 295 Mike Morgan	.06	.02	.00
☐ 296 Bill Wegman	.03	.01	.00
☐ 297A Terry Francona ERR (misspelled Franconia on card front)	.12	.05	.01
☐ 297B Terry Francona COR	.06	.02	.00
☐ 298 Mickey Hatcher	.03	.01	.00
☐ 299 Andres Thomas	.03	.01	.00
☐ 300 Bob Stanley	.03	.01	.00
☐ 301 Al Pedrique	.03	.01	.00
☐ 302 Jim Lindeman	.03	.01	.00
☐ 303 Wally Backman	.03	.01	.00
☐ 304 Paul O'Neill	.12	.05	.01
☐ 305 Hubie Brooks	.08	.03	.01
☐ 306 Steve Buechele	.06	.02	.00
☐ 307 Bobby Thigpen	.10	.04	.01
☐ 308 George Hendrick	.03	.01	.00
☐ 309 John Moses	.03	.01	.00
☐ 310 Ron Guidry	.08	.03	.01
☐ 311 Bill Schroeder	.03	.01	.00

Card	Player			
☐ 312	Jose Nunez	.06	.02	.00
☐ 313	Bud Black	.03	.01	.00
☐ 314	Joe Sambito	.03	.01	.00
☐ 315	Scott McGregor	.03	.01	.00
☐ 316	Rafael Santana	.03	.01	.00
☐ 317	Frank Williams	.03	.01	.00
☐ 318	Mike Fitzgerald	.03	.01	.00
☐ 319	Rick Mahler	.03	.01	.00
☐ 320	Jim Gott	.03	.01	.00
☐ 321	Mariano Duncan	.03	.01	.00
☐ 322	Jose Guzman	.06	.02	.00
☐ 323	Lee Guetterman	.03	.01	.00
☐ 324	Dan Gladden	.03	.01	.00
☐ 325	Gary Carter	.08	.03	.01
☐ 326	Tracy Jones	.03	.01	.00
☐ 327	Floyd Youmans	.03	.01	.00
☐ 328	Bill Dawley	.03	.01	.00
☐ 329	Paul Noce	.06	.02	.00
☐ 330	Angel Salazar	.03	.01	.00
☐ 331	Goose Gossage	.08	.03	.01
☐ 332	George Frazier	.03	.01	.00
☐ 333	Ruppert Jones	.03	.01	.00
☐ 334	Billy Jo Robidoux	.03	.01	.00
☐ 335	Mike Scott	.08	.03	.01
☐ 336	Randy Myers	.06	.02	.00
☐ 337	Bob Sebra	.03	.01	.00
☐ 338	Eric Show	.03	.01	.00
☐ 339	Mitch Williams	.06	.02	.00
☐ 340	Paul Molitor	.10	.04	.01
☐ 341	Gus Polidor	.03	.01	.00
☐ 342	Steve Trout	.03	.01	.00
☐ 343	Jerry Don Gleaton	.03	.01	.00
☐ 344	Bob Knepper	.03	.01	.00
☐ 345	Mitch Webster	.03	.01	.00
☐ 346	John Morris	.03	.01	.00
☐ 347	Andy Hawkins	.03	.01	.00
☐ 348	Dave Leiper	.03	.01	.00
☐ 349	Ernest Riles	.03	.01	.00
☐ 350	Dwight Gooden	.15	.06	.01
☐ 351	Dave Righetti	.06	.02	.00
☐ 352	Pat Dodson	.06	.02	.00
☐ 353	John Habyan	.03	.01	.00
☐ 354	Jim Deshaies	.03	.01	.00
☐ 355	Butch Wynegar	.03	.01	.00
☐ 356	Bryn Smith	.03	.01	.00
☐ 357	Matt Young	.03	.01	.00
☐ 358	Tom Pagnozzi	.12	.05	.01
☐ 359	Floyd Rayford	.03	.01	.00
☐ 360	Darryl Strawberry	.35	.15	.03
☐ 361	Sal Butera	.03	.01	.00
☐ 362	Domingo Ramos	.03	.01	.00
☐ 363	Chris Brown	.03	.01	.00
☐ 364	Jose Gonzalez	.06	.02	.00
☐ 365	Dave Smith	.03	.01	.00
☐ 366	Andy McGaffigan	.03	.01	.00
☐ 367	Stan Javier	.03	.01	.00
☐ 368	Henry Cotto	.03	.01	.00
☐ 369	Mike Birkbeck	.03	.01	.00
☐ 370	Len Dykstra	.08	.03	.01
☐ 371	Dave Collins	.03	.01	.00
☐ 372	Spike Owen	.03	.01	.00
☐ 373	Geno Petralli	.03	.01	.00
☐ 374	Ron Karkovice	.03	.01	.00
☐ 375	Shane Rawley	.03	.01	.00
☐ 376	DeWayne Buice	.03	.01	.00
☐ 377	Bill Pecota	.08	.03	.01
☐ 378	Leon Durham	.03	.01	.00
☐ 379	Ed Olwine	.03	.01	.00
☐ 380	Bruce Hurst	.06	.02	.00
☐ 381	Bob McClure	.03	.01	.00
☐ 382	Mark Thurmond	.03	.01	.00
☐ 383	Buddy Biancalana	.03	.01	.00
☐ 384	Tim Conroy	.03	.01	.00
☐ 385	Tony Gwynn	.25	.10	.02
☐ 386	Greg Gross	.03	.01	.00
☐ 387	Barry Lyons	.08	.03	.01
☐ 388	Mike Felder	.06	.02	.00
☐ 389	Pat Clements	.03	.01	.00
☐ 390	Ken Griffey	.10	.04	.01
☐ 391	Mark Davis	.06	.02	.00
☐ 392	Jose Rijo	.10	.04	.01
☐ 393	Mike Young	.03	.01	.00
☐ 394	Willie Fraser	.03	.01	.00
☐ 395	Dion James	.03	.01	.00
☐ 396	Steve Shields	.03	.01	.00
☐ 397	Randy St.Claire	.03	.01	.00
☐ 398	Danny Jackson	.06	.02	.00
☐ 399	Cecil Fielder	.35	.15	.03
☐ 400	Keith Hernandez	.08	.03	.01
☐ 401	Don Carman	.03	.01	.00
☐ 402	Chuck Crim	.03	.01	.00
☐ 403	Rob Woodward	.03	.01	.00
☐ 404	Junior Ortiz	.03	.01	.00
☐ 405	Glenn Wilson	.03	.01	.00
☐ 406	Ken Howell	.03	.01	.00
☐ 407	Jeff Kunkel	.03	.01	.00
☐ 408	Jeff Reed	.03	.01	.00
☐ 409	Chris James	.08	.03	.01
☐ 410	Zane Smith	.08	.03	.01
☐ 411	Ken Dixon	.03	.01	.00
☐ 412	Ricky Horton	.03	.01	.00
☐ 413	Frank DiPino	.03	.01	.00
☐ 414	Shane Mack	.15	.06	.01
☐ 415	Danny Cox	.03	.01	.00
☐ 416	Andy Van Slyke	.10	.04	.01
☐ 417	Danny Heep	.03	.01	.00
☐ 418	John Cangelosi	.03	.01	.00
☐ 419A	John Christensen ERR (Christiansen on card front)	.12	.05	.01
☐ 419B	John Christensen COR	.06	.02	.00
☐ 420	Joey Cora	.06	.02	.00
☐ 421	Mike LaValliere	.03	.01	.00
☐ 422	Kelly Gruber	.15	.06	.01
☐ 423	Bruce Benedict	.03	.01	.00
☐ 424	Len Matuszek	.03	.01	.00

□ 425 Kent Tekulve .... .03 .01 .00
□ 426 Rafael Ramirez .... .03 .01 .00
□ 427 Mike Flanagan .... .06 .02 .00
□ 428 Mike Gallego .... .03 .01 .00
□ 429 Juan Castillo .... .03 .01 .00
□ 430 Neal Heaton .... .03 .01 .00
□ 431 Phil Garner .... .03 .01 .00
□ 432 Mike Dunne .... .03 .01 .00
□ 433 Wallace Johnson .... .03 .01 .00
□ 434 Jack O'Connor .... .03 .01 .00
□ 435 Steve Jeltz .... .03 .01 .00
□ 436 Donnell Nixon .... .06 .02 .00
□ 437 Jack Lazorko .... .03 .01 .00
□ 438 Keith Comstock .... .03 .01 .00
□ 439 Jeff D. Robinson .... .03 .01 .00
(Pirates pitcher)
□ 440 Graig Nettles .... .08 .03 .01
□ 441 Mel Hall .... .06 .02 .00
□ 442 Gerald Young .... .08 .03 .01
□ 443 Gary Redus .... .03 .01 .00
□ 444 Charlie Moore .... .03 .01 .00
□ 445 Bill Madlock .... .06 .02 .00
□ 446 Mark Clear .... .03 .01 .00
□ 447 Greg Booker .... .03 .01 .00
□ 448 Rick Schu .... .03 .01 .00
□ 449 Ron Kittle .... .06 .02 .00
□ 450 Dale Murphy .... .15 .06 .01
□ 451 Bob Dernier .... .03 .01 .00
□ 452 Dale Mohorcic .... .03 .01 .00
□ 453 Rafael Belliard .... .03 .01 .00
□ 454 Charlie Puleo .... .03 .01 .00
□ 455 Dwayne Murphy .... .03 .01 .00
□ 456 Jim Eisenreich .... .03 .01 .00
□ 457 David Palmer .... .03 .01 .00
□ 458 Dave Stewart .... .08 .03 .01
□ 459 Pascual Perez .... .03 .01 .00
□ 460 Glenn Davis .... .10 .04 .01
□ 461 Dan Petry .... .03 .01 .00
□ 462 Jim Winn .... .03 .01 .00
□ 463 Darrell Miller .... .03 .01 .00
□ 464 Mike Moore .... .06 .02 .00
□ 465 Mike LaCoss .... .03 .01 .00
□ 466 Steve Farr .... .03 .01 .00
□ 467 Jerry Mumphrey .... .03 .01 .00
□ 468 Kevin Gross .... .03 .01 .00
□ 469 Bruce Bochy .... .03 .01 .00
□ 470 Orel Hershiser .... .10 .04 .01
□ 471 Eric King .... .03 .01 .00
□ 472 Ellis Burks .... .60 .25 .06
□ 473 Darren Daulton .... .03 .01 .00
□ 474 Mookie Wilson .... .03 .01 .00
□ 475 Frank Viola .... .08 .03 .01
□ 476 Ron Robinson .... .03 .01 .00
□ 477 Bob Melvin .... .03 .01 .00
□ 478 Jeff Musselman .... .03 .01 .00
□ 479 Charlie Kerfeld .... .03 .01 .00
□ 480 Richard Dotson .... .03 .01 .00
□ 481 Kevin Mitchell .... .25 .10 .02
□ 482 Gary Roenicke .... .03 .01 .00
□ 483 Tim Flannery .... .03 .01 .00
□ 484 Rich Yett .... .03 .01 .00
□ 485 Pete Incaviglia .... .08 .03 .01
□ 486 Rick Cerone .... .03 .01 .00
□ 487 Tony Armas .... .03 .01 .00
□ 488 Jerry Reed .... .03 .01 .00
□ 489 Dave Lopes .... .06 .02 .00
□ 490 Frank Tanana .... .06 .02 .00
□ 491 Mike Loynd .... .03 .01 .00
□ 492 Bruce Ruffin .... .03 .01 .00
□ 493 Chris Speier .... .03 .01 .00
□ 494 Tom Hume .... .03 .01 .00
□ 495 Jesse Orosco .... .03 .01 .00
□ 496 Robbie Wine UER .... .03 .01 .00
(misspelled Robby
on card front)
□ 497 Jeff Montgomery .... .20 .08 .02
□ 498 Jeff Dedmon .... .03 .01 .00
□ 499 Luis Aguayo .... .03 .01 .00
□ 500 Reggie Jackson .... .20 .08 .02
(Oakland A's)
□ 501 Reggie Jackson .... .25 .10 .02
(Baltimore Orioles)
□ 502 Reggie Jackson .... .20 .08 .02
(New York Yankees)
□ 503 Reggie Jackson .... .20 .08 .02
(California Angels)
□ 504 Reggie Jackson .... .20 .08 .02
(Oakland A's)
□ 505 Billy Hatcher .... .06 .02 .00
□ 506 Ed Lynch .... .03 .01 .00
□ 507 Willie Hernandez .... .03 .01 .00
□ 508 Jose DeLeon .... .03 .01 .00
□ 509 Joel Youngblood .... .03 .01 .00
□ 510 Bob Welch .... .08 .03 .01
□ 511 Steve Ontiveros .... .03 .01 .00
□ 512 Randy Ready .... .03 .01 .00
□ 513 Juan Nieves .... .03 .01 .00
□ 514 Jeff Russell .... .03 .01 .00
□ 515 Von Hayes .... .08 .03 .01
□ 516 Mark Gubicza .... .06 .02 .00
□ 517 Ken Dayley .... .03 .01 .00
□ 518 Don Aase .... .03 .01 .00
□ 519 Rick Reuschel .... .06 .02 .00
□ 520 Mike Henneman .... .15 .06 .01
□ 521 Rick Aguilera .... .06 .02 .00
□ 522 Jay Howell .... .03 .01 .00
□ 523 Ed Correa .... .03 .01 .00
□ 524 Manny Trillo .... .03 .01 .00
□ 525 Kirk Gibson .... .08 .03 .01
□ 526 Wally Ritchie .... .03 .01 .00
□ 527 Al Nipper .... .03 .01 .00
□ 528 Atlee Hammaker .... .03 .01 .00
□ 529 Shawon Dunston .... .10 .04 .01
□ 530 Jim Clancy .... .03 .01 .00
□ 531 Tom Paciorek .... .03 .01 .00
□ 532 Joel Skinner .... .03 .01 .00

☐ 533 Scott Garrelts .03 .01 .00
☐ 534 Tom O'Malley .03 .01 .00
☐ 535 John Franco .06 .02 .00
☐ 536 Paul Kilgus .06 .02 .00
☐ 537 Darrell Porter .03 .01 .00
☐ 538 Walt Terrell .03 .01 .00
☐ 539 Bill Long .06 .02 .00
☐ 540 George Bell .12 .05 .01
☐ 541 Jeff Sellers .03 .01 .00
☐ 542 Joe Boever .08 .03 .01
☐ 543 Steve Howe .03 .01 .00
☐ 544 Scott Sanderson .06 .02 .00
☐ 545 Jack Morris .12 .05 .01
☐ 546 Todd Benzinger .20 .08 .02
☐ 547 Steve Henderson .03 .01 .00
☐ 548 Eddie Milner .03 .01 .00
☐ 549 Jeff M. Robinson .08 .03 .01
(Tigers pitcher)
☐ 550 Cal Ripken .40 .16 .04
☐ 551 Jody Davis .03 .01 .00
☐ 552 Kirk McCaskill .03 .01 .00
☐ 553 Craig Lefferts .03 .01 .00
☐ 554 Darnell Coles .03 .01 .00
☐ 555 Phil Niekro .15 .06 .01
☐ 556 Mike Aldrete .03 .01 .00
☐ 557 Pat Perry .03 .01 .00
☐ 558 Juan Agosto .03 .01 .00
☐ 559 Rob Murphy .03 .01 .00
☐ 560 Dennis Rasmussen .03 .01 .00
☐ 561 Manny Lee .03 .01 .00
☐ 562 Jeff Blauser .17 .07 .01
☐ 563 Bob Ojeda .03 .01 .00
☐ 564 Dave Dravecky .08 .03 .01
☐ 565 Gene Garber .03 .01 .00
☐ 566 Ron Roenicke .03 .01 .00
☐ 567 Tommy Hinzo .03 .01 .00
☐ 568 Eric Nolte .03 .01 .00
☐ 569 Ed Hearn .03 .01 .00
☐ 570 Mark Davidson .03 .01 .00
☐ 571 Jim Walewander .06 .02 .00
☐ 572 Donnie Hill .03 .01 .00
☐ 573 Jamie Moyer .03 .01 .00
☐ 574 Ken Schrom .03 .01 .00
☐ 575 Nolan Ryan .45 .18 .04
☐ 576 Jim Acker .03 .01 .00
☐ 577 Jamie Quirk .03 .01 .00
☐ 578 Jay Aldrich .03 .01 .00
☐ 579 Claudell Washington .03 .01 .00
☐ 580 Jeff Leonard .03 .01 .00
☐ 581 Carmen Castillo .03 .01 .00
☐ 582 Daryl Boston .03 .01 .00
☐ 583 Jeff DeWillis .03 .01 .00
☐ 584 John Marzano .03 .01 .00
☐ 585 Bill Gullickson .06 .02 .00
☐ 586 Andy Allanson .03 .01 .00
☐ 587 Lee Tunnell UER .03 .01 .00
(1987 stat line
reads .4.84 ERA)
☐ 588 Gene Nelson .03 .01 .00
☐ 589 Dave LaPoint .03 .01 .00
☐ 590 Harold Baines .08 .03 .01
☐ 591 Bill Buckner .06 .02 .00
☐ 592 Carlton Fisk .20 .08 .02
☐ 593 Rick Manning .03 .01 .00
☐ 594 Doug Jones .12 .05 .01
☐ 595 Tom Candiotti .06 .02 .00
☐ 596 Steve Lake .03 .01 .00
☐ 597 Jose Lind .20 .08 .02
☐ 598 Ross Jones .03 .01 .00
☐ 599 Gary Matthews .03 .01 .00
☐ 600 Fernando Valenzuela .08 .03 .01
☐ 601 Dennis Martinez .06 .02 .00
☐ 602 Les Lancaster .08 .03 .01
☐ 603 Ozzie Guillen .08 .03 .01
☐ 604 Tony Bernazard .03 .01 .00
☐ 605 Chili Davis .08 .03 .01
☐ 606 Roy Smalley .03 .01 .00
☐ 607 Ivan Calderon .08 .03 .01
☐ 608 Jay Tibbs .03 .01 .00
☐ 609 Guy Hoffman .03 .01 .00
☐ 610 Doyle Alexander .03 .01 .00
☐ 611 Mike Bielecki .03 .01 .00
☐ 612 Shawn Hillegas .08 .03 .01
☐ 613 Keith Atherton .03 .01 .00
☐ 614 Eric Plunk .03 .01 .00
☐ 615 Sid Fernandez .08 .03 .01
☐ 616 Dennis Lamp .03 .01 .00
☐ 617 Dave Engle .03 .01 .00
☐ 618 Harry Spilman .03 .01 .00
☐ 619 Don Robinson .03 .01 .00
☐ 620 John Farrell .08 .03 .01
☐ 621 Nelson Liriano .08 .03 .01
☐ 622 Floyd Bannister .03 .01 .00
☐ 623 Randy Milligan .35 .15 .03
☐ 624 Kevin Elster .06 .02 .00
☐ 625 Jody Reed .30 .12 .03
☐ 626 Shawn Abner .06 .02 .00
☐ 627 Kurt Manwaring .08 .03 .01
☐ 628 Pete Stanicek .06 .02 .00
☐ 629 Rob Ducey .10 .04 .01
☐ 630 Steve Kiefer .03 .01 .00
☐ 631 Gary Thurman .10 .04 .01
☐ 632 Darrel Akerfelds .08 .03 .01
☐ 633 Dave Clark .06 .02 .00
☐ 634 Roberto Kelly .60 .25 .06
☐ 635 Keith Hughes .06 .02 .00
☐ 636 John Davis .06 .02 .00
☐ 637 Mike Devereaux .15 .06 .01
☐ 638 Tom Glavine 1.00 .40 .10
☐ 639 Keith Miller .12 .05 .01
(New York Mets)
☐ 640 Chris Gwynn UER .15 .06 .01
(wrong batting and
throwing on back)
☐ 641 Tim Crews .06 .02 .00
☐ 642 Mackey Sasser .15 .06 .01

☐ 643 Vicente Palacios	.10	.04	.01
☐ 644 Kevin Romine	.03	.01	.00
☐ 645 Gregg Jefferies	1.00	.40	.10
☐ 646 Jeff Treadway	.20	.08	.02
☐ 647 Ron Gant	2.50	1.00	.25
☐ 648 Mark McGwire and Matt Nokes (Rookie Sluggers)	.08	.03	.01
☐ 649 Eric Davis and Tim Raines (Speed and Power)	.08	.03	.01
☐ 650 Don Mattingly and Jack Clark	.10	.04	.01
☐ 651 Tony Fernandez, Alan Trammell, and Cal Ripken	.20	.08	.02
☐ 652 Vince Coleman HL 100 Stolen Bases	.08	.03	.01
☐ 653 Kirby Puckett HL 10 Hits in a Row	.15	.06	.01
☐ 654 Benito Santiago HL Hitting Streak	.08	.03	.01
☐ 655 Juan Nieves HL No Hitter	.06	.02	.00
☐ 656 Steve Bedrosian HL Saves Record	.06	.02	.00
☐ 657 Mike Schmidt HL 500 Homers	.20	.08	.02
☐ 658 Don Mattingly HL Home Run Streak	.12	.05	.01
☐ 659 Mark McGwire HL Rookie HR Record	.10	.04	.01
☐ 660 Paul Molitor HL Hitting Streak	.08	.03	.01

1988 Score Traded

This 110-card set featured traded players (1-65) and rookies (66-110) for the 1988 season. The cards are distinguishable from the regular Score set by the orange borders and by the fact that the numbering on the back has a T suffix. The cards are standard size, 2 1/2" by 3 1/2", and were distributed by Score as a collated set in a special collector box along with some trivia cards. Score also produced a limited "glossy" Traded set, that is valued at one and a half times the value of the regular (non-glossy) set. It should be noted that the set itself (non-glossy) is now considered somewhat scarce. Apparently Score's first attempt at a Rookie/Traded set was produced very conservatively, resulting in a set which is now recognized as being much tougher to find than the other Rookie/Traded sets from the other major companies of that year. The key (extended) rookie cards in this set are Roberto Alomar, Craig Biggio, Rob Dibble, Mark Grace, Jack McDowell, Chris Sabo, and Walt Weiss.

	MINT	EXC	G-VG
COMPLETE SET (110)	60.00	27.00	9.00
COMMON PLAYER (1-65)	.12	.05	.01
COMMON PLAYER (66-110)	.12	.05	.01
☐ 1T Jack Clark	.30	.10	.02
☐ 2T Danny Jackson	.20	.08	.02
☐ 3T Brett Butler	.30	.12	.03
☐ 4T Kurt Stillwell	.20	.08	.02
☐ 5T Tom Brunansky	.20	.08	.02
☐ 6T Dennis Lamp	.12	.05	.01
☐ 7T Jose DeLeon	.12	.05	.01
☐ 8T Tom Herr	.12	.05	.01
☐ 9T Keith Moreland	.12	.05	.01
☐ 10T Kirk Gibson	.30	.12	.03
☐ 11T Bud Black	.20	.08	.02
☐ 12T Rafael Ramirez	.12	.05	.01
☐ 13T Luis Salazar	.12	.05	.01
☐ 14T Goose Gossage	.30	.12	.03
☐ 15T Bob Welch	.30	.12	.03
☐ 16T Vance Law	.12	.05	.01
☐ 17T Ray Knight	.20	.08	.02
☐ 18T Dan Quisenberry	.20	.08	.02
☐ 19T Don Slaught	.12	.05	.01
☐ 20T Lee Smith	.40	.16	.04
☐ 21T Rick Cerone	.12	.05	.01
☐ 22T Pat Tabler	.12	.05	.01
☐ 23T Larry McWilliams	.12	.05	.01
☐ 24T Ricky Horton	.12	.05	.01
☐ 25T Graig Nettles	.20	.08	.02
☐ 26T Dan Petry	.12	.05	.01
☐ 27T Jose Rijo	.30	.12	.03
☐ 28T Chili Davis	.30	.12	.03

☐ 29T Dickie Thon	.20	.08	.02
☐ 30T Mackey Sasser	.50	.20	.05
☐ 31T Mickey Tettleton	.30	.12	.03
☐ 32T Rick Dempsey	.12	.05	.01
☐ 33T Ron Hassey	.12	.05	.01
☐ 34T Phil Bradley	.12	.05	.01
☐ 35T Jay Howell	.12	.05	.01
☐ 36T Bill Buckner	.20	.08	.02
☐ 37T Alfredo Griffin	.12	.05	.01
☐ 38T Gary Pettis	.12	.05	.01
☐ 39T Calvin Schiraldi	.12	.05	.01
☐ 40T John Candelaria	.12	.05	.01
☐ 41T Joe Orsulak	.12	.05	.01
☐ 42T Willie Upshaw	.12	.05	.01
☐ 43T Herm Winningham	.12	.05	.01
☐ 44T Ron Kittle	.20	.08	.02
☐ 45T Bob Dernier	.12	.05	.01
☐ 46T Steve Balboni	.12	.05	.01
☐ 47T Steve Shields	.12	.05	.01
☐ 48T Henry Cotto	.12	.05	.01
☐ 49T Dave Henderson	.40	.16	.04
☐ 50T Dave Parker	.40	.16	.04
☐ 51T Mike Young	.12	.05	.01
☐ 52T Mark Salas	.12	.05	.01
☐ 53T Mike Davis	.12	.05	.01
☐ 54T Rafael Santana	.12	.05	.01
☐ 55T Don Baylor	.20	.08	.02
☐ 56T Dan Pasqua	.20	.08	.02
☐ 57T Ernest Riles	.12	.05	.01
☐ 58T Glenn Hubbard	.12	.05	.01
☐ 59T Mike Smithson	.12	.05	.01
☐ 60T Richard Dotson	.12	.05	.01
☐ 61T Jerry Reuss	.12	.05	.01
☐ 62T Mike Jackson	.20	.08	.02
☐ 63T Floyd Bannister	.12	.05	.01
☐ 64T Jesse Orosco	.12	.05	.01
☐ 65T Larry Parrish	.12	.05	.01
☐ 66T Jeff Bittiger	.20	.08	.02
☐ 67T Ray Hayward	.12	.05	.01
☐ 68T Ricky Jordan	1.00	.40	.10
☐ 69T Tommy Gregg	.25	.10	.02
☐ 70T Brady Anderson	.30	.12	.03
☐ 71T Jeff Montgomery	.25	.10	.02
☐ 72T Darryl Hamilton	.75	.30	.07
☐ 73T Cecil Espy	.30	.12	.03
☐ 74T Greg Briley	.60	.25	.06
☐ 75T Joey Meyer	.20	.08	.02
☐ 76T Mike Macfarlane	.40	.16	.04
☐ 77T Oswald Peraza	.20	.08	.02
☐ 78T Jack Armstrong	.60	.25	.06
☐ 79T Don Heinkel	.12	.05	.01
☐ 80T Mark Grace	15.00	6.50	2.15
☐ 81T Steve Curry	.20	.08	.02
☐ 82T Damon Berryhill	.25	.10	.02
☐ 83T Steve Ellsworth	.20	.08	.02
☐ 84T Pete Smith	.25	.10	.02
☐ 85T Jack McDowell	5.00	2.25	.50
☐ 86T Rob Dibble	4.00	1.75	.40
☐ 87T Bryan Harvey	2.00	.80	.20
☐ 88T John Dopson	.25	.10	.02
☐ 89T Dave Gallagher	.25	.10	.02
☐ 90T Todd Stottlemyre	3.00	1.25	.30
☐ 91T Mike Schooler	.60	.25	.06
☐ 92T Don Gordon	.12	.05	.01
☐ 93T Sil Campusano	.25	.10	.02
☐ 94T Jeff Pico	.20	.08	.02
☐ 95T Jay Buhner	3.00	1.25	.30
☐ 96T Nelson Santovenia	.25	.10	.02
☐ 97T Al Leiter	.20	.08	.02
☐ 98T Luis Aiicea	.20	.08	.02
☐ 99T Pat Borders	.90	.40	.09
☐ 100T Chris Sabo	8.00	3.50	.80
☐ 101T Tim Belcher	.50	.20	.05
☐ 102T Walt Weiss	1.00	.40	.10
☐ 103T Craig Biggio	4.50	2.00	.45
☐ 104T Don August	.20	.08	.02
☐ 105T Roberto Alomar	20.00	8.50	2.75
☐ 106T Todd Burns	.25	.10	.02
☐ 107T John Costello	.20	.08	.02
☐ 108T Melido Perez	.60	.25	.06
☐ 109T Darrin Jackson	.60	.25	.06
☐ 110T Orestes Destrade	.30	.10	.02

1989 Score

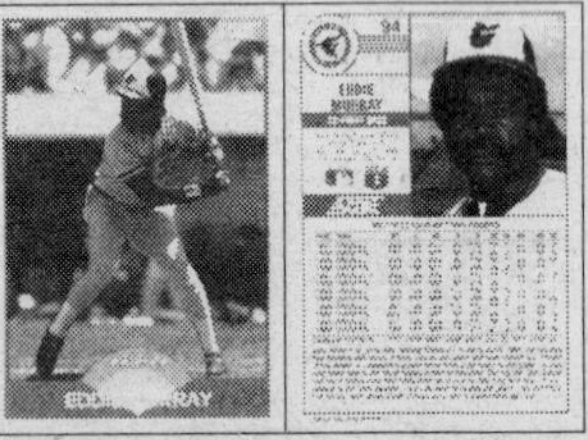

This 660-card set was distributed by Major League Marketing. Cards measure 2 1/2" by 3 1/2" and feature six distinctive inner border (inside a white outer border) colors on the front. Highlights (652-660) and Rookie Prospects (621-651) are included in the set. The set is distinguished by the fact that each card back shows a full-color picture (portrait) of the player. Score "missed" many of the mid-season and later trades; there are numerous examples of inconsistency with

regard to the treatment of these players. Study as examples of this inconsistency of handling of late trades, cards numbered 49, 71, 77, 83, 106, 126, 139, 145, 173, 177, 242, 348, 384, 420, 439, 488, 494, and 525. The key rookie cards in this set are Sandy Alomar Jr., Felix Jose, Ramon Martinez, Gary Sheffield, and John Smoltz.

	MINT	EXC	G-VG
COMPLETE SET (660)	18.00	7.50	2.50
COMMON PLAYER (1-660)	.03	.01	.00
☐ 1 Jose Canseco	.50	.20	.05
☐ 2 Andre Dawson	.12	.05	.01
☐ 3 Mark McGwire UER (Bio says 116 RBI's, should be 118)	.12	.05	.01
☐ 4 Benito Santiago	.08	.03	.01
☐ 5 Rick Reuschel	.06	.02	.00
☐ 6 Fred McGriff	.15	.06	.01
☐ 7 Kal Daniels	.08	.03	.01
☐ 8 Gary Gaetti	.06	.02	.00
☐ 9 Ellis Burks	.15	.06	.01
☐ 10 Darryl Strawberry	.30	.12	.03
☐ 11 Julio Franco	.10	.04	.01
☐ 12 Lloyd Moseby	.03	.01	.00
☐ 13 Jeff Pico	.06	.02	.00
☐ 14 Johnny Ray	.03	.01	.00
☐ 15 Cal Ripken	.35	.15	.03
☐ 16 Dick Schofield	.03	.01	.00
☐ 17 Mel Hall	.06	.02	.00
☐ 18 Bill Ripken	.03	.01	.00
☐ 19 Brook Jacoby	.03	.01	.00
☐ 20 Kirby Puckett	.30	.12	.03
☐ 21 Bill Doran	.03	.01	.00
☐ 22 Pete O'Brien	.03	.01	.00
☐ 23 Matt Nokes	.06	.02	.00
☐ 24 Brian Fisher	.03	.01	.00
☐ 25 Jack Clark	.08	.03	.01
☐ 26 Gary Pettis	.03	.01	.00
☐ 27 Dave Valle	.03	.01	.00
☐ 28 Willie Wilson	.06	.02	.00
☐ 29 Curt Young	.03	.01	.00
☐ 30 Dale Murphy	.12	.05	.01
☐ 31 Barry Larkin	.15	.06	.01
☐ 32 Dave Stewart	.08	.03	.01
☐ 33 Mike LaValliere	.03	.01	.00
☐ 34 Glenn Hubbard	.03	.01	.00
☐ 35 Ryne Sandberg	.35	.15	.03
☐ 36 Tony Pena	.06	.02	.00
☐ 37 Greg Walker	.03	.01	.00
☐ 38 Von Hayes	.06	.02	.00
☐ 39 Kevin Mitchell	.15	.06	.01
☐ 40 Tim Raines	.10	.04	.01
☐ 41 Keith Hernandez	.08	.03	.01
☐ 42 Keith Moreland	.03	.01	.00
☐ 43 Ruben Sierra	.25	.10	.02
☐ 44 Chet Lemon	.03	.01	.00
☐ 45 Willie Randolph	.06	.02	.00
☐ 46 Andy Allanson	.03	.01	.00
☐ 47 Candy Maldonado	.06	.02	.00
☐ 48 Sid Bream	.03	.01	.00
☐ 49 Denny Walling	.03	.01	.00
☐ 50 Dave Winfield	.12	.05	.01
☐ 51 Alvin Davis	.06	.02	.00
☐ 52 Cory Snyder	.06	.02	.00
☐ 53 Hubie Brooks	.06	.02	.00
☐ 54 Chili Davis	.06	.02	.00
☐ 55 Kevin Seitzer	.06	.02	.00
☐ 56 Jose Uribe	.03	.01	.00
☐ 57 Tony Fernandez	.06	.02	.00
☐ 58 Tim Teufel	.03	.01	.00
☐ 59 Oddibe McDowell	.03	.01	.00
☐ 60 Les Lancaster	.03	.01	.00
☐ 61 Billy Hatcher	.06	.02	.00
☐ 62 Dan Gladden	.03	.01	.00
☐ 63 Marty Barrett	.03	.01	.00
☐ 64 Nick Esasky	.03	.01	.00
☐ 65 Wally Joyner	.12	.05	.01
☐ 66 Mike Greenwell	.15	.06	.01
☐ 67 Ken Williams	.03	.01	.00
☐ 68 Bob Horner	.06	.02	.00
☐ 69 Steve Sax	.08	.03	.01
☐ 70 Rickey Henderson	.35	.15	.03
☐ 71 Mitch Webster	.03	.01	.00
☐ 72 Rob Deer	.06	.02	.00
☐ 73 Jim Presley	.03	.01	.00
☐ 74 Albert Hall	.03	.01	.00
☐ 75A George Brett ERR (at age 33)	.60	.25	.06
☐ 75B George Brett COR (at age 35)	.15	.06	.01
☐ 76 Brian Downing	.03	.01	.00
☐ 77 Dave Martinez	.03	.01	.00
☐ 78 Scott Fletcher	.03	.01	.00
☐ 79 Phil Bradley	.03	.01	.00
☐ 80 Ozzie Smith	.12	.05	.01
☐ 81 Larry Sheets	.03	.01	.00
☐ 82 Mike Aldrete	.03	.01	.00
☐ 83 Darnell Coles	.03	.01	.00
☐ 84 Len Dykstra	.08	.03	.01
☐ 85 Jim Rice	.08	.03	.01
☐ 86 Jeff Treadway	.03	.01	.00
☐ 87 Jose Lind	.03	.01	.00
☐ 88 Willie McGee	.08	.03	.01
☐ 89 Mickey Brantley	.03	.01	.00
☐ 90 Tony Gwynn	.17	.07	.01
☐ 91 R.J. Reynolds	.03	.01	.00
☐ 92 Milt Thompson	.03	.01	.00
☐ 93 Kevin McReynolds	.08	.03	.01
☐ 94 Eddie Murray UER ('86 batting .205, should be .305)	.12	.05	.01
☐ 95 Lance Parrish	.08	.03	.01
☐ 96 Ron Kittle	.06	.02	.00

Card			
☐ 97 Gerald Young	.03	.01	.00
☐ 98 Ernie Whitt	.03	.01	.00
☐ 99 Jeff Reed	.03	.01	.00
☐ 100 Don Mattingly	.20	.08	.02
☐ 101 Gerald Perry	.03	.01	.00
☐ 102 Vance Law	.03	.01	.00
☐ 103 John Shelby	.03	.01	.00
☐ 104 Chris Sabo	.60	.25	.06
☐ 105 Danny Tartabull	.10	.04	.01
☐ 106 Glenn Wilson	.03	.01	.00
☐ 107 Mark Davidson	.03	.01	.00
☐ 108 Dave Parker	.08	.03	.01
☐ 109 Eric Davis	.10	.04	.01
☐ 110 Alan Trammell	.12	.05	.01
☐ 111 Ozzie Virgil	.03	.01	.00
☐ 112 Frank Tanana	.06	.02	.00
☐ 113 Rafael Ramirez	.03	.01	.00
☐ 114 Dennis Martinez	.06	.02	.00
☐ 115 Jose DeLeon	.03	.01	.00
☐ 116 Bob Ojeda	.03	.01	.00
☐ 117 Doug Drabek	.08	.03	.01
☐ 118 Andy Hawkins	.03	.01	.00
☐ 119 Greg Maddux	.08	.03	.01
☐ 120 Cecil Fielder UER (photo on back reversed)	.30	.12	.03
☐ 121 Mike Scioscia	.03	.01	.00
☐ 122 Dan Petry	.03	.01	.00
☐ 123 Terry Kennedy	.03	.01	.00
☐ 124 Kelly Downs	.03	.01	.00
☐ 125 Greg Gross UER (Gregg on back)	.03	.01	.00
☐ 126 Fred Lynn	.08	.03	.01
☐ 127 Barry Bonds	.25	.10	.02
☐ 128 Harold Baines	.08	.03	.01
☐ 129 Doyle Alexander	.03	.01	.00
☐ 130 Kevin Elster	.03	.01	.00
☐ 131 Mike Heath	.03	.01	.00
☐ 132 Teddy Higuera	.03	.01	.00
☐ 133 Charlie Leibrandt	.03	.01	.00
☐ 134 Tim Laudner	.03	.01	.00
☐ 135A Ray Knight ERR (reverse negative)	.65	.25	.06
☐ 135B Ray Knight COR	.10	.04	.01
☐ 136 Howard Johnson	.12	.05	.01
☐ 137 Terry Pendleton	.10	.04	.01
☐ 138 Andy McGaffigan	.03	.01	.00
☐ 139 Ken Oberkfell	.03	.01	.00
☐ 140 Butch Wynegar	.03	.01	.00
☐ 141 Rob Murphy	.03	.01	.00
☐ 142 Rich Renteria	.06	.02	.00
☐ 143 Jose Guzman	.03	.01	.00
☐ 144 Andres Galarraga	.06	.02	.00
☐ 145 Ricky Horton	.03	.01	.00
☐ 146 Frank DiPino	.03	.01	.00
☐ 147 Glenn Braggs	.03	.01	.00
☐ 148 John Kruk	.03	.01	.00
☐ 149 Mike Schmidt	.35	.15	.03
☐ 150 Lee Smith	.08	.03	.01
☐ 151 Robin Yount	.15	.06	.01
☐ 152 Mark Eichhorn	.06	.02	.00
☐ 153 DeWayne Buice	.03	.01	.00
☐ 154 B.J. Surhoff	.06	.02	.00
☐ 155 Vince Coleman	.10	.04	.01
☐ 156 Tony Phillips	.03	.01	.00
☐ 157 Willie Fraser	.03	.01	.00
☐ 158 Lance McCullers	.03	.01	.00
☐ 159 Greg Gagne	.03	.01	.00
☐ 160 Jesse Barfield	.08	.03	.01
☐ 161 Mark Langston	.08	.03	.01
☐ 162 Kurt Stillwell	.03	.01	.00
☐ 163 Dion James	.03	.01	.00
☐ 164 Glenn Davis	.08	.03	.01
☐ 165 Walt Weiss	.08	.03	.01
☐ 166 Dave Concepcion	.06	.02	.00
☐ 167 Alfredo Griffin	.03	.01	.00
☐ 168 Don Heinkel	.03	.01	.00
☐ 169 Luis Rivera	.03	.01	.00
☐ 170 Shane Rawley	.03	.01	.00
☐ 171 Darrell Evans	.06	.02	.00
☐ 172 Robby Thompson	.03	.01	.00
☐ 173 Jody Davis	.03	.01	.00
☐ 174 Andy Van Slyke	.08	.03	.01
☐ 175 Wade Boggs UER (bio says .364, should be .356)	.20	.08	.02
☐ 176 Garry Templeton ('85 stats off-centered)	.06	.02	.00
☐ 177 Gary Redus	.03	.01	.00
☐ 178 Craig Lefferts	.03	.01	.00
☐ 179 Carney Lansford	.06	.02	.00
☐ 180 Ron Darling	.06	.02	.00
☐ 181 Kirk McCaskill	.03	.01	.00
☐ 182 Tony Armas	.03	.01	.00
☐ 183 Steve Farr	.03	.01	.00
☐ 184 Tom Brunansky	.06	.02	.00
☐ 185 Bryan Harvey UER ('87 games 47, should be 3)	.25	.10	.02
☐ 186 Mike Marshall	.06	.02	.00
☐ 187 Bo Diaz	.03	.01	.00
☐ 188 Willie Upshaw	.03	.01	.00
☐ 189 Mike Pagliarulo	.03	.01	.00
☐ 190 Mike Krukow	.03	.01	.00
☐ 191 Tommy Herr	.03	.01	.00
☐ 192 Jim Pankovits	.03	.01	.00
☐ 193 Dwight Evans	.06	.02	.00
☐ 194 Kelly Gruber	.10	.04	.01
☐ 195 Bobby Bonilla	.20	.08	.02
☐ 196 Wallace Johnson	.03	.01	.00
☐ 197 Dave Stieb	.08	.03	.01
☐ 198 Pat Borders	.15	.06	.01
☐ 199 Rafael Palmeiro	.15	.06	.01
☐ 200 Dwight Gooden	.12	.05	.01
☐ 201 Pete Incaviglia	.06	.02	.00

☐ 202 Chris James	.03	.01	.00
☐ 203 Marvell Wynne	.03	.01	.00
☐ 204 Pat Sheridan	.03	.01	.00
☐ 205 Don Baylor	.06	.02	.00
☐ 206 Paul O'Neill	.08	.03	.01
☐ 207 Pete Smith	.06	.02	.00
☐ 208 Mark McLemore	.03	.01	.00
☐ 209 Henry Cotto	.03	.01	.00
☐ 210 Kirk Gibson	.08	.03	.01
☐ 211 Claudell Washington	.03	.01	.00
☐ 212 Randy Bush	.03	.01	.00
☐ 213 Joe Carter	.12	.05	.01
☐ 214 Bill Buckner	.06	.02	.00
☐ 215 Bert Blyleven UER (wrong birth year)	.08	.03	.01
☐ 216 Brett Butler	.08	.03	.01
☐ 217 Lee Mazzilli	.03	.01	.00
☐ 218 Spike Owen	.03	.01	.00
☐ 219 Bill Swift	.03	.01	.00
☐ 220 Tim Wallach	.06	.02	.00
☐ 221 David Cone	.08	.03	.01
☐ 222 Don Carman	.03	.01	.00
☐ 223 Rich Gossage	.08	.03	.01
☐ 224 Bob Walk	.03	.01	.00
☐ 225 Dave Righetti	.06	.02	.00
☐ 226 Kevin Bass	.03	.01	.00
☐ 227 Kevin Gross	.03	.01	.00
☐ 228 Tim Burke	.03	.01	.00
☐ 229 Rick Mahler	.03	.01	.00
☐ 230 Lou Whitaker UER (252 games in '85, should be 152)	.08	.03	.01
☐ 231 Luis Alicea	.03	.01	.00
☐ 232 Roberto Alomar	.60	.25	.06
☐ 233 Bob Boone	.06	.02	.00
☐ 234 Dickie Thon	.03	.01	.00
☐ 235 Shawon Dunston	.08	.03	.01
☐ 236 Pete Stanicek	.03	.01	.00
☐ 237 Craig Biggio (inconsistent design, portrait on front)	.35	.15	.03
☐ 238 Dennis Boyd	.03	.01	.00
☐ 239 Tom Candiotti	.06	.02	.00
☐ 240 Gary Carter	.08	.03	.01
☐ 241 Mike Stanley	.03	.01	.00
☐ 242 Ken Phelps	.03	.01	.00
☐ 243 Chris Bosio	.03	.01	.00
☐ 244 Les Straker	.03	.01	.00
☐ 245 Dave Smith	.03	.01	.00
☐ 246 John Candelaria	.03	.01	.00
☐ 247 Joe Orsulak	.03	.01	.00
☐ 248 Storm Davis	.03	.01	.00
☐ 249 Floyd Bannister UER (ML Batting Record)	.03	.01	.00
☐ 250 Jack Morris	.10	.04	.01
☐ 251 Bret Saberhagen	.10	.04	.01
☐ 252 Tom Niedenfuer	.03	.01	.00
☐ 253 Neal Heaton	.03	.01	.00
☐ 254 Eric Show	.03	.01	.00
☐ 255 Juan Samuel	.06	.02	.00
☐ 256 Dale Sveum	.03	.01	.00
☐ 257 Jim Gott	.03	.01	.00
☐ 258 Scott Garrelts	.03	.01	.00
☐ 259 Larry McWilliams	.03	.01	.00
☐ 260 Steve Bedrosian	.06	.02	.00
☐ 261 Jack Howell	.03	.01	.00
☐ 262 Jay Tibbs	.03	.01	.00
☐ 263 Jamie Moyer	.03	.01	.00
☐ 264 Doug Sisk	.03	.01	.00
☐ 265 Todd Worrell	.06	.02	.00
☐ 266 John Farrell	.03	.01	.00
☐ 267 Dave Collins	.03	.01	.00
☐ 268 Sid Fernandez	.06	.02	.00
☐ 269 Tom Brookens	.03	.01	.00
☐ 270 Shane Mack	.08	.03	.01
☐ 271 Paul Kilgus	.03	.01	.00
☐ 272 Chuck Crim	.03	.01	.00
☐ 273 Bob Knepper	.03	.01	.00
☐ 274 Mike Moore	.06	.02	.00
☐ 275 Guillermo Hernandez	.03	.01	.00
☐ 276 Dennis Eckersley	.08	.03	.01
☐ 277 Graig Nettles	.06	.02	.00
☐ 278 Rich Dotson	.03	.01	.00
☐ 279 Larry Herndon	.03	.01	.00
☐ 280 Gene Larkin	.03	.01	.00
☐ 281 Roger McDowell	.03	.01	.00
☐ 282 Greg Swindell	.06	.02	.00
☐ 283 Juan Agosto	.03	.01	.00
☐ 284 Jeff M. Robinson Detroit Tigers	.03	.01	.00
☐ 285 Mike Dunne	.03	.01	.00
☐ 286 Greg Mathews	.03	.01	.00
☐ 287 Kent Tekulve	.03	.01	.00
☐ 288 Jerry Mumphrey	.03	.01	.00
☐ 289 Jack McDowell	.17	.07	.01
☐ 290 Frank Viola	.08	.03	.01
☐ 291 Mark Gubicza	.06	.02	.00
☐ 292 Dave Schmidt	.03	.01	.00
☐ 293 Mike Henneman	.03	.01	.00
☐ 294 Jimmy Jones	.03	.01	.00
☐ 295 Charlie Hough	.03	.01	.00
☐ 296 Rafael Santana	.03	.01	.00
☐ 297 Chris Speier	.03	.01	.00
☐ 298 Mike Witt	.03	.01	.00
☐ 299 Pascual Perez	.03	.01	.00
☐ 300 Nolan Ryan	.50	.20	.05
☐ 301 Mitch Williams	.03	.01	.00
☐ 302 Mookie Wilson	.03	.01	.00
☐ 303 Mackey Sasser	.06	.02	.00
☐ 304 John Cerutti	.03	.01	.00
☐ 305 Jeff Reardon	.08	.03	.01
☐ 306 Randy Myers UER (6 hits in '87, should be 61)	.03	.01	.00
☐ 307 Greg Brock	.03	.01	.00
☐ 308 Bob Welch	.08	.03	.01

☐ 309 Jeff D. Robinson	.03	.01	.00
Pittsburgh Pirates			
☐ 310 Harold Reynolds	.06	.02	.00
☐ 311 Jim Walewander	.03	.01	.00
☐ 312 Dave Magadan	.06	.02	.00
☐ 313 Jim Gantner	.03	.01	.00
☐ 314 Walt Terrell	.03	.01	.00
☐ 315 Wally Backman	.03	.01	.00
☐ 316 Luis Salazar	.03	.01	.00
☐ 317 Rick Rhoden	.03	.01	.00
☐ 318 Tom Henke	.06	.02	.00
☐ 319 Mike Macfarlane	.10	.04	.01
☐ 320 Dan Plesac	.03	.01	.00
☐ 321 Calvin Schiraldi	.03	.01	.00
☐ 322 Stan Javier	.03	.01	.00
☐ 323 Devon White	.06	.02	.00
☐ 324 Scott Bradley	.03	.01	.00
☐ 325 Bruce Hurst	.06	.02	.00
☐ 326 Manny Lee	.03	.01	.00
☐ 327 Rick Aguilera	.06	.02	.00
☐ 328 Bruce Ruffin	.03	.01	.00
☐ 329 Ed Whitson	.03	.01	.00
☐ 330 Bo Jackson	.50	.20	.05
☐ 331 Ivan Calderon	.06	.02	.00
☐ 332 Mickey Hatcher	.03	.01	.00
☐ 333 Barry Jones	.03	.01	.00
☐ 334 Ron Hassey	.03	.01	.00
☐ 335 Bill Wegman	.03	.01	.00
☐ 336 Damon Berryhill	.06	.02	.00
☐ 337 Steve Ontiveros	.03	.01	.00
☐ 338 Dan Pasqua	.03	.01	.00
☐ 339 Bill Pecota	.03	.01	.00
☐ 340 Greg Cadaret	.03	.01	.00
☐ 341 Scott Bankhead	.06	.02	.00
☐ 342 Ron Guidry	.08	.03	.01
☐ 343 Danny Heep	.03	.01	.00
☐ 344 Bob Brower	.03	.01	.00
☐ 345 Rich Gedman	.03	.01	.00
☐ 346 Nelson Santovenia	.08	.03	.01
☐ 347 George Bell	.10	.04	.01
☐ 348 Ted Power	.03	.01	.00
☐ 349 Mark Grant	.03	.01	.00
☐ 350A Roger Clemens ERR	4.00	1.75	.40
(778 career wins)			
☐ 350B Roger Clemens COR	.35	.15	.03
(78 career wins)			
☐ 351 Bill Long	.03	.01	.00
☐ 352 Jay Bell	.10	.04	.01
☐ 353 Steve Balboni	.03	.01	.00
☐ 354 Bob Kipper	.03	.01	.00
☐ 355 Steve Jeltz	.03	.01	.00
☐ 356 Jesse Orosco	.03	.01	.00
☐ 357 Bob Dernier	.03	.01	.00
☐ 358 Mickey Tettleton	.06	.02	.00
☐ 359 Duane Ward	.06	.02	.00
☐ 360 Darrin Jackson	.10	.04	.01
☐ 361 Rey Quinones	.03	.01	.00
☐ 362 Mark Grace	.30	.12	.03
☐ 363 Steve Lake	.03	.01	.00
☐ 364 Pat Perry	.03	.01	.00
☐ 365 Terry Steinbach	.06	.02	.00
☐ 366 Alan Ashby	.03	.01	.00
☐ 367 Jeff Montgomery	.06	.02	.00
☐ 368 Steve Buechele	.03	.01	.00
☐ 369 Chris Brown	.03	.01	.00
☐ 370 Orel Hershiser	.08	.03	.01
☐ 371 Todd Benzinger	.03	.01	.00
☐ 372 Ron Gant	.45	.18	.04
☐ 373 Paul Assenmacher	.03	.01	.00
☐ 374 Joey Meyer	.03	.01	.00
☐ 375 Neil Allen	.03	.01	.00
☐ 376 Mike Davis	.03	.01	.00
☐ 377 Jeff Parrett	.03	.01	.00
☐ 378 Jay Howell	.03	.01	.00
☐ 379 Rafael Belliard	.03	.01	.00
☐ 380 Luis Polonia UER	.08	.03	.01
(2 triples in '87,			
should be 10)			
☐ 381 Keith Atherton	.03	.01	.00
☐ 382 Kent Hrbek	.08	.03	.01
☐ 383 Bob Stanley	.03	.01	.00
☐ 384 Dave LaPoint	.03	.01	.00
☐ 385 Rance Mulliniks	.03	.01	.00
☐ 386 Melido Perez	.08	.03	.01
☐ 387 Doug Jones	.03	.01	.00
☐ 388 Steve Lyons	.03	.01	.00
☐ 389 Alejandro Pena	.06	.02	.00
☐ 390 Frank White	.03	.01	.00
☐ 391 Pat Tabler	.03	.01	.00
☐ 392 Eric Plunk	.03	.01	.00
☐ 393 Mike Maddux	.03	.01	.00
☐ 394 Allan Anderson	.03	.01	.00
☐ 395 Bob Brenly	.03	.01	.00
☐ 396 Rick Cerone	.03	.01	.00
☐ 397 Scott Terry	.03	.01	.00
☐ 398 Mike Jackson	.03	.01	.00
☐ 399 Bobby Thigpen UER	.08	.03	.01
(bio says 37 saves in			
'88, should be 34)			
☐ 400 Don Sutton	.10	.04	.01
☐ 401 Cecil Espy	.03	.01	.00
☐ 402 Junior Ortiz	.03	.01	.00
☐ 403 Mike Smithson	.03	.01	.00
☐ 404 Bud Black	.03	.01	.00
☐ 405 Tom Foley	.03	.01	.00
☐ 406 Andres Thomas	.03	.01	.00
☐ 407 Rick Sutcliffe	.06	.02	.00
☐ 408 Brian Harper	.06	.02	.00
☐ 409 John Smiley	.03	.01	.00
☐ 410 Juan Nieves	.03	.01	.00
☐ 411 Shawn Abner	.03	.01	.00
☐ 412 Wes Gardner	.03	.01	.00
☐ 413 Darren Daulton	.06	.02	.00
☐ 414 Juan Berenguer	.03	.01	.00
☐ 415 Charles Hudson	.03	.01	.00
☐ 416 Rick Honeycutt	.03	.01	.00

☐	417 Greg Booker	.03	.01	.00
☐	418 Tim Belcher	.10	.04	.01
☐	419 Don August	.03	.01	.00
☐	420 Dale Mohorcic	.03	.01	.00
☐	421 Steve Lombardozzi	.03	.01	.00
☐	422 Atlee Hammaker	.03	.01	.00
☐	423 Jerry Don Gleaton	.03	.01	.00
☐	424 Scott Bailes	.03	.01	.00
☐	425 Bruce Sutter	.08	.03	.01
☐	426 Randy Ready	.03	.01	.00
☐	427 Jerry Reed	.03	.01	.00
☐	428 Bryn Smith	.03	.01	.00
☐	429 Tim Leary	.06	.02	.00
☐	430 Mark Clear	.03	.01	.00
☐	431 Terry Leach	.03	.01	.00
☐	432 John Moses	.03	.01	.00
☐	433 Ozzie Guillen	.06	.02	.00
☐	434 Gene Nelson	.03	.01	.00
☐	435 Gary Ward	.03	.01	.00
☐	436 Luis Aguayo	.03	.01	.00
☐	437 Fernando Valenzuela	.08	.03	.01
☐	438 Jeff Russell UER (Saves total does not add up correctly)	.03	.01	.00
☐	439 Cecilio Guante	.03	.01	.00
☐	440 Don Robinson	.03	.01	.00
☐	441 Rick Anderson	.03	.01	.00
☐	442 Tom Glavine	.35	.15	.03
☐	443 Daryl Boston	.03	.01	.00
☐	444 Joe Price	.03	.01	.00
☐	445 Stewart Cliburn	.03	.01	.00
☐	446 Manny Trillo	.03	.01	.00
☐	447 Joel Skinner	.03	.01	.00
☐	448 Charlie Puleo	.03	.01	.00
☐	449 Carlton Fisk	.15	.06	.01
☐	450 Will Clark	.40	.16	.04
☐	451 Otis Nixon	.06	.02	.00
☐	452 Rick Schu	.03	.01	.00
☐	453 Todd Stottlemyre UER (ML Batting Record)	.15	.06	.01
☐	454 Tim Birtsas	.03	.01	.00
☐	455 Dave Gallagher	.08	.03	.01
☐	456 Barry Lyons	.03	.01	.00
☐	457 Fred Manrique	.03	.01	.00
☐	458 Ernest Riles	.03	.01	.00
☐	459 Doug Jennings	.06	.02	.00
☐	460 Joe Magrane	.06	.02	.00
☐	461 Jamie Quirk	.03	.01	.00
☐	462 Jack Armstrong	.10	.04	.01
☐	463 Bobby Witt	.06	.02	.00
☐	464 Keith Miller New York Mets	.06	.02	.00
☐	465 Todd Burns	.08	.03	.01
☐	466 John Dopson	.08	.03	.01
☐	467 Rich Yett	.03	.01	.00
☐	468 Craig Reynolds	.03	.01	.00
☐	469 Dave Bergman	.03	.01	.00
☐	470 Rex Hudler	.06	.02	.00
☐	471 Eric King	.03	.01	.00
☐	472 Joaquin Andujar	.03	.01	.00
☐	473 Sil Campusano	.08	.03	.01
☐	474 Terry Mulholland	.06	.02	.00
☐	475 Mike Flanagan	.03	.01	.00
☐	476 Greg A. Harris Philadelphia Phillies	.03	.01	.00
☐	477 Tommy John	.08	.03	.01
☐	478 Dave Anderson	.03	.01	.00
☐	479 Fred Toliver	.03	.01	.00
☐	480 Jimmy Key	.06	.02	.00
☐	481 Donell Nixon	.03	.01	.00
☐	482 Mark Portugal	.03	.01	.00
☐	483 Tom Pagnozzi	.03	.01	.00
☐	484 Jeff Kunkel	.03	.01	.00
☐	485 Frank Williams	.03	.01	.00
☐	486 Jody Reed	.08	.03	.01
☐	487 Roberto Kelly	.12	.05	.01
☐	488 Shawn Hillegas UER (165 innings in '87, should be 165.2)	.03	.01	.00
☐	489 Jerry Reuss	.03	.01	.00
☐	490 Mark Davis	.06	.02	.00
☐	491 Jeff Sellers	.03	.01	.00
☐	492 Zane Smith	.06	.02	.00
☐	493 Al Newman	.03	.01	.00
☐	494 Mike Young	.03	.01	.00
☐	495 Larry Parrish	.03	.01	.00
☐	496 Herm Winningham	.03	.01	.00
☐	497 Carmen Castillo	.03	.01	.00
☐	498 Joe Hesketh	.06	.02	.00
☐	499 Darrell Miller	.03	.01	.00
☐	500 Mike LaCoss	.03	.01	.00
☐	501 Charlie Lea	.03	.01	.00
☐	502 Bruce Benedict	.03	.01	.00
☐	503 Chuck Finley	.08	.03	.01
☐	504 Brad Wellman	.03	.01	.00
☐	505 Tim Crews	.03	.01	.00
☐	506 Ken Gerhart	.03	.01	.00
☐	507 Brian Holton UER (born 1/25/65 Denver, should be 11/29/59 in McKeesport)	.06	.02	.00
☐	508 Dennis Lamp	.03	.01	.00
☐	509 Bobby Meacham UER ('84 games 099)	.06	.02	.00
☐	510 Tracy Jones	.03	.01	.00
☐	511 Mike Fitzgerald Montreal Expos	.03	.01	.00
☐	512 Jeff Bittiger	.06	.02	.00
☐	513 Tim Flannery	.03	.01	.00
☐	514 Ray Hayward	.03	.01	.00
☐	515 Dave Leiper	.03	.01	.00
☐	516 Rod Scurry	.03	.01	.00
☐	517 Carmelo Martinez	.03	.01	.00
☐	518 Curtis Wilkerson	.03	.01	.00
☐	519 Stan Jefferson	.03	.01	.00
☐	520 Dan Quisenberry	.08	.03	.01

	No.	Player			
☐	521	Lloyd McClendon	.03	.01	.00
☐	522	Steve Trout	.03	.01	.00
☐	523	Larry Andersen	.03	.01	.00
☐	524	Don Aase	.03	.01	.00
☐	525	Bob Forsch	.03	.01	.00
☐	526	Geno Petralli	.03	.01	.00
☐	527	Angel Salazar	.03	.01	.00
☐	528	Mike Schooler	.12	.05	.01
☐	529	Jose Oquendo	.03	.01	.00
☐	530	Jay Buhner	.15	.06	.01
☐	531	Tom Bolton	.08	.03	.01
☐	532	Al Nipper	.03	.01	.00
☐	533	Dave Henderson	.08	.03	.01
☐	534	John Costello	.03	.01	.00
☐	535	Donnie Moore	.03	.01	.00
☐	536	Mike Laga	.03	.01	.00
☐	537	Mike Gallego	.03	.01	.00
☐	538	Jim Clancy	.03	.01	.00
☐	539	Joel Youngblood	.03	.01	.00
☐	540	Rick Leach	.03	.01	.00
☐	541	Kevin Romine	.03	.01	.00
☐	542	Mark Salas	.03	.01	.00
☐	543	Greg Minton	.03	.01	.00
☐	544	Dave Palmer	.03	.01	.00
☐	545	Dwayne Murphy UER (game-sinning)	.03	.01	.00
☐	546	Jim Deshaies	.03	.01	.00
☐	547	Don Gordon	.03	.01	.00
☐	548	Ricky Jordan	.12	.05	.01
☐	549	Mike Boddicker	.03	.01	.00
☐	550	Mike Scott	.08	.03	.01
☐	551	Jeff Ballard	.03	.01	.00
☐	552A	Jose Rijo ERR (uniform listed as 27 on back)	.65	.25	.06
☐	552B	Jose Rijo COR (uniform listed as 24 on back)	.15	.06	.01
☐	553	Danny Darwin	.03	.01	.00
☐	554	Tom Browning	.06	.02	.00
☐	555	Danny Jackson	.06	.02	.00
☐	556	Rick Dempsey	.03	.01	.00
☐	557	Jeffrey Leonard	.03	.01	.00
☐	558	Jeff Musselman	.03	.01	.00
☐	559	Ron Robinson	.03	.01	.00
☐	560	John Tudor	.06	.02	.00
☐	561	Don Slaught UER (237 games in 1987)	.03	.01	.00
☐	562	Dennis Rasmussen	.03	.01	.00
☐	563	Brady Anderson	.08	.03	.01
☐	564	Pedro Guerrero	.08	.03	.01
☐	565	Paul Molitor	.10	.04	.01
☐	566	Terry Clark	.06	.02	.00
☐	567	Terry Puhl	.03	.01	.00
☐	568	Mike Campbell	.03	.01	.00
☐	569	Paul Mirabella	.03	.01	.00
☐	570	Jeff Hamilton	.03	.01	.00
☐	571	Oswald Peraza	.06	.02	.00
☐	572	Bob McClure	.03	.01	.00
☐	573	Jose Bautista	.06	.02	.00
☐	574	Alex Trevino	.03	.01	.00
☐	575	John Franco	.03	.01	.00
☐	576	Mark Parent	.08	.03	.01
☐	577	Nelson Liriano	.03	.01	.00
☐	578	Steve Shields	.03	.01	.00
☐	579	Odell Jones	.03	.01	.00
☐	580	Al Leiter	.03	.01	.00
☐	581	Dave Stapleton	.06	.02	.00
☐	582	World Series '88 Orel Hershiser Jose Canseco Kirk Gibson Dave Stewart	.08	.03	.01
☐	583	Donnie Hill	.03	.01	.00
☐	584	Chuck Jackson	.03	.01	.00
☐	585	Rene Gonzales	.03	.01	.00
☐	586	Tracy Woodson	.03	.01	.00
☐	587	Jim Adduci	.03	.01	.00
☐	588	Mario Soto	.03	.01	.00
☐	589	Jeff Blauser	.03	.01	.00
☐	590	Jim Traber	.03	.01	.00
☐	591	Jon Perlman	.03	.01	.00
☐	592	Mark Williamson	.06	.02	.00
☐	593	Dave Meads	.03	.01	.00
☐	594	Jim Eisenreich	.03	.01	.00
☐	595A	Paul Gibson P1	1.00	.40	.10
☐	595B	Paul Gibson P2 (airbrushed leg on player in background)	.10	.04	.01
☐	596	Mike Birkbeck	.03	.01	.00
☐	597	Terry Francona	.03	.01	.00
☐	598	Paul Zuvella	.03	.01	.00
☐	599	Franklin Stubbs	.03	.01	.00
☐	600	Gregg Jefferies	.30	.12	.03
☐	601	John Cangelosi	.03	.01	.00
☐	602	Mike Sharperson	.03	.01	.00
☐	603	Mike Diaz	.03	.01	.00
☐	604	Gary Varsho	.08	.03	.01
☐	605	Terry Blocker	.06	.02	.00
☐	606	Charlie O'Brien	.06	.02	.00
☐	607	Jim Eppard	.03	.01	.00
☐	608	John Davis	.03	.01	.00
☐	609	Ken Griffey Sr.	.08	.03	.01
☐	610	Buddy Bell	.06	.02	.00
☐	611	Ted Simmons UER ('78 stats Cardinal)	.08	.03	.01
☐	612	Matt Williams	.20	.08	.02
☐	613	Danny Cox	.03	.01	.00
☐	614	Al Pedrique	.03	.01	.00
☐	615	Ron Oester	.03	.01	.00
☐	616	John Smoltz	.50	.20	.05
☐	617	Bob Melvin	.03	.01	.00
☐	618	Rob Dibble	.25	.10	.02
☐	619	Kirt Manwaring	.03	.01	.00
☐	620	Felix Fermin	.03	.01	.00
☐	621	Doug Dascenzo	.08	.03	.01

☐ 622 Bill Brennan	.06	.02	.00
☐ 623 Carlos Quintana	.25	.10	.02
☐ 624 Mike Harkey UER (13 and 31 walks in '88, should be 35 and 33)	.12	.05	.01
☐ 625 Gary Sheffield	.30	.12	.03
☐ 626 Tom Prince	.03	.01	.00
☐ 627 Steve Searcy	.08	.03	.01
☐ 628 Charlie Hayes (listed as outfielder)	.12	.05	.01
☐ 629 Felix Jose UER (Modesto misspelled as Modesta)	.75	.30	.07
☐ 630 Sandy Alomar Jr. (inconsistent design, portrait on front)	.40	.16	.04
☐ 631 Derek Lilliquist	.08	.03	.01
☐ 632 Geronimo Berroa	.06	.02	.00
☐ 633 Luis Medina	.10	.04	.01
☐ 634 Tom Gordon UER (height 6'0")	.20	.08	.02
☐ 635 Ramon Martinez	1.25	.50	.12
☐ 636 Craig Worthington	.08	.03	.01
☐ 637 Edgar Martinez	.20	.08	.02
☐ 638 Chad Kreuter	.08	.03	.01
☐ 639 Ron Jones	.08	.03	.01
☐ 640 Van Snider	.08	.03	.01
☐ 641 Lance Blankenship	.08	.03	.01
☐ 642 Dwight Smith UER (10 HR's in '87, should be 18)	.12	.05	.01
☐ 643 Cameron Drew	.03	.01	.00
☐ 644 Jerald Clark	.17	.07	.01
☐ 645 Randy Johnson	.35	.15	.03
☐ 646 Norm Charlton	.12	.05	.01
☐ 647 Todd Frohwirth UER (southpaw on back)	.06	.02	.00
☐ 648 Luis De Los Santos	.06	.02	.00
☐ 649 Tim Jones	.03	.01	.00
☐ 650 Dave West UER (ML hits 3, should be 6)	.10	.04	.01
☐ 651 Bob Milacki	.15	.06	.01
☐ 652 Wrigley Field HL (Let There Be Lights)	.03	.01	.00
☐ 653 Orel Hershiser HL (The Streak)	.08	.03	.01
☐ 654A Wade Boggs HL ERR (Wade Whacks 'Em) ("seaason" on back)	4.00	1.75	.40
☐ 654B Wade Boggs HL COR (Wade Whacks 'Em)	.12	.05	.01
☐ 655 Jose Canseco HL (One of a Kind)	.20	.08	.02
☐ 656 Doug Jones HL (Doug Sets Saves)	.03	.01	.00
☐ 657 Rickey Henderson HL (Rickey Rocks 'Em)	.17	.07	.01
☐ 658 Tom Browning HL (Tom Perfect Pitches)	.06	.02	.00
☐ 659 Mike Greenwell HL (Greenwell Gamers)	.08	.03	.01
☐ 660 Boston Red Sox HL (Joe Morgan MG, Sox Sock 'Em)	.06	.02	.00

1989 Score Traded

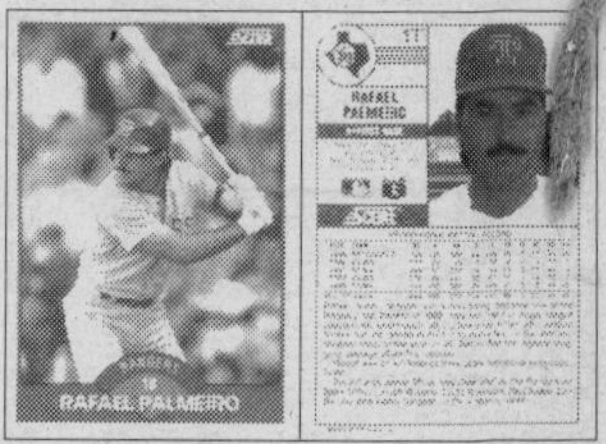

The 1989 Score Traded set contains 110 standard-size (2 1/2" by 3 1/2") cards. The fronts have coral green borders with pink diamonds at the bottom. The vertically-oriented backs have color facial shots, career stats, and biographical information. Cards 1-80 feature traded players; cards 81-110 feature 1989 rookies. The set was distributed in a blue box with 10 Magic Motion trivia cards. The key rookie cards in this set are Jim Abbott, Joey (Albert) Belle, Junior Felix, Ken Griffey Jr., and Jerome Walton.

	MINT	EXC	G-VG
COMPLETE SET (110)	12.00	5.25	1.50
COMMON PLAYER (1-80)	.05	.02	.00
COMMON PLAYER (81-110)	.05	.02	.00

☐ 1T Rafael Palmeiro	.15	.05	.01
☐ 2T Nolan Ryan	1.50	.60	.15
☐ 3T Jack Clark	.10	.04	.01
☐ 4T Dave LaPoint	.05	.02	.00
☐ 5T Mike Moore	.08	.03	.01
☐ 6T Pete O'Brien	.05	.02	.00
☐ 7T Jeffrey Leonard	.05	.02	.00
☐ 8T Rob Murphy	.05	.02	.00
☐ 9T Tom Herr	.05	.02	.00

☐ 10T Claudell Washington ...... .05 .02 .00
☐ 11T Mike Pagliarulo .... .05 .02 .00
☐ 12T Steve Lake .... .05 .02 .00
☐ 13T Spike Owen .... .05 .02 .00
☐ 14T Andy Hawkins .... .05 .02 .00
☐ 15T Todd Benzinger .... .05 .02 .00
☐ 16T Mookie Wilson .... .08 .03 .01
☐ 17T Bert Blyleven .... .10 .04 .01
☐ 18T Jeff Treadway .... .08 .03 .01
☐ 19T Bruce Hurst .... .10 .04 .01
☐ 20T Steve Sax .... .10 .04 .01
☐ 21T Juan Samuel .... .10 .04 .01
☐ 22T Jesse Barfield .... .10 .04 .01
☐ 23T Carmen Castillo .... .05 .02 .00
☐ 24T Terry Leach .... .05 .02 .00
☐ 25T Mark Langston .... .10 .04 .01
☐ 26T Eric King .... .08 .03 .01
☐ 27T Steve Balboni .... .05 .02 .00
☐ 28T Len Dykstra .... .10 .04 .01
☐ 29T Keith Moreland .... .05 .02 .00
☐ 30T Terry Kennedy .... .05 .02 .00
☐ 31T Eddie Murray .... .12 .05 .01
☐ 32T Mitch Williams .... .10 .04 .01
☐ 33T Jeff Parrett .... .05 .02 .00
☐ 34T Wally Backman .... .05 .02 .00
☐ 35T Julio Franco .... .12 .05 .01
☐ 36T Lance Parrish .... .10 .04 .01
☐ 37T Nick Esasky .... .05 .02 .00
☐ 38T Luis Polonia .... .08 .03 .01
☐ 39T Kevin Gross .... .05 .02 .00
☐ 40T John Dopson .... .05 .02 .00
☐ 41T Willie Randolph .... .08 .03 .01
☐ 42T Jim Clancy .... .05 .02 .00
☐ 43T Tracy Jones .... .05 .02 .00
☐ 44T Phil Bradley .... .05 .02 .00
☐ 45T Milt Thompson .... .05 .02 .00
☐ 46T Chris James .... .08 .03 .01
☐ 47T Scott Fletcher .... .05 .02 .00
☐ 48T Kal Daniels .... .10 .04 .01
☐ 49T Steve Bedrosian .... .08 .03 .01
☐ 50T Rickey Henderson .... .35 .15 .03
☐ 51T Dion James .... .05 .02 .00
☐ 52T Tim Leary .... .08 .03 .01
☐ 53T Roger McDowell .... .05 .02 .00
☐ 54T Mel Hall .... .08 .03 .01
☐ 55T Dickie Thon .... .08 .03 .01
☐ 56T Zane Smith .... .08 .03 .01
☐ 57T Danny Heep .... .05 .02 .00
☐ 58T Bob McClure .... .05 .02 .00
☐ 59T Brian Holton .... .05 .02 .00
☐ 60T Randy Ready .... .05 .02 .00
☐ 61T Bob Melvin .... .05 .02 .00
☐ 62T Harold Baines .... .10 .04 .01
☐ 63T Lance McCullers .... .05 .02 .00
☐ 64T Jody Davis .... .05 .02 .00
☐ 65T Darrell Evans .... .08 .03 .01
☐ 66T Joel Youngblood .... .05 .02 .00
☐ 67T Frank Viola .... .10 .04 .01
☐ 68T Mike Aldrete .... .05 .02 .00
☐ 69T Greg Cadaret .... .08 .03 .01
☐ 70T John Kruk .... .10 .04 .01
☐ 71T Pat Sheridan .... .05 .02 .00
☐ 72T Oddibe McDowell .... .05 .02 .00
☐ 73T Tom Brookens .... .05 .02 .00
☐ 74T Bob Boone .... .10 .04 .01
☐ 75T Walt Terrell .... .05 .02 .00
☐ 76T Joel Skinner .... .05 .02 .00
☐ 77T Randy Johnson .... .12 .05 .01
☐ 78T Felix Fermin .... .05 .02 .00
☐ 79T Rick Mahler .... .05 .02 .00
☐ 80T Richard Dotson .... .05 .02 .00
☐ 81T Cris Carpenter .... .10 .04 .01
☐ 82T Bill Spiers .... .12 .05 .01
☐ 83T Junior Felix .... .15 .06 .01
☐ 84T Joe Girardi .... .10 .04 .01
☐ 85T Jerome Walton .... .40 .16 .04
☐ 86T Greg Litton .... .10 .04 .01
☐ 87T Greg W.Harris .... .15 .06 .01
☐ 88T Jim Abbott .... 1.25 .50 .12
☐ 89T Kevin Brown .... .10 .04 .01
☐ 90T John Wetteland .... .15 .06 .01
☐ 91T Gary Wayne .... .10 .04 .01
☐ 92T Rich Monteleone .... .10 .04 .01
☐ 93T Bob Geren .... .10 .04 .01
☐ 94T Clay Parker .... .08 .03 .01
☐ 95T Steve Finley .... .35 .15 .03
☐ 96T Gregg Olson .... .60 .25 .06
☐ 97T Ken Patterson .... .08 .03 .01
☐ 98T Ken Hill .... .25 .10 .02
☐ 99T Scott Scudder .... .20 .08 .02
☐ 100T Ken Griffey Jr. .... 6.00 2.50 .60
☐ 101T Jeff Brantley .... .20 .08 .02
☐ 102T Donn Pall .... .08 .03 .01
☐ 103T Carlos Martinez .... .15 .06 .01
☐ 104T Joe Oliver .... .20 .08 .02
☐ 105T Omar Vizquel .... .08 .03 .01
☐ 106T Joey Belle .... 2.00 .80 .20
☐ 107T Kenny Rogers .... .10 .04 .01
☐ 108T Mark Carreon .... .10 .04 .01
☐ 109T Rolando Roomes .... .08 .03 .01
☐ 110T Pete Harnisch .... .25 .10 .02

1990 Score

The 1990 Score set contains 704 standard-size (2 1/2" by 3 1/2") cards. The front borders are red, blue, green or white. The vertically-oriented backs are white with borders that match the fronts, and feature color mugshots. Cards numbered 661-682 contain the first

round draft picks subset noted as DC for "draft choice" in the checklist below. Cards numbered 683-695 contain the "Dream Team" subset noted by DT in the checklist below. The key rookie cards in this set are Juan Gonzalez, Dave Justice, Chuck Knoblauch, Kevin Maas, Ben McDonald, John Olerud, and Frank Thomas.

	MINT	EXC	G-VG
COMPLETE SET (704)	20.00	8.50	2.75
COMMON PLAYER (1-704)	.03	.01	.00
☐ 1 Don Mattingly	.20	.08	.02
☐ 2 Cal Ripken	.30	.12	.03
☐ 3 Dwight Evans	.06	.02	.00
☐ 4 Barry Bonds	.17	.07	.01
☐ 5 Kevin McReynolds	.08	.03	.01
☐ 6 Ozzie Guillen	.06	.02	.00
☐ 7 Terry Kennedy	.03	.01	.00
☐ 8 Bryan Harvey	.06	.02	.00
☐ 9 Alan Trammell	.08	.03	.01
☐ 10 Cory Snyder	.06	.02	.00
☐ 11 Jody Reed	.06	.02	.00
☐ 12 Roberto Alomar	.15	.06	.01
☐ 13 Pedro Guerrero	.08	.03	.01
☐ 14 Gary Redus	.03	.01	.00
☐ 15 Marty Barrett	.03	.01	.00
☐ 16 Ricky Jordan	.06	.02	.00
☐ 17 Joe Magrane	.03	.01	.00
☐ 18 Sid Fernandez	.06	.02	.00
☐ 19 Richard Dotson	.03	.01	.00
☐ 20 Jack Clark	.08	.03	.01
☐ 21 Bob Walk	.03	.01	.00
☐ 22 Ron Karkovice	.03	.01	.00
☐ 23 Lenny Harris	.06	.02	.00
☐ 24 Phil Bradley	.03	.01	.00
☐ 25 Andres Galarraga	.06	.02	.00
☐ 26 Brian Downing	.03	.01	.00
☐ 27 Dave Martinez	.03	.01	.00
☐ 28 Eric King	.03	.01	.00
☐ 29 Barry Lyons	.03	.01	.00
☐ 30 Dave Schmidt	.03	.01	.00
☐ 31 Mike Boddicker	.03	.01	.00
☐ 32 Tom Foley	.03	.01	.00
☐ 33 Brady Anderson	.03	.01	.00
☐ 34 Jim Presley	.03	.01	.00
☐ 35 Lance Parrish	.06	.02	.00
☐ 36 Von Hayes	.06	.02	.00
☐ 37 Lee Smith	.06	.02	.00
☐ 38 Herm Winningham	.03	.01	.00
☐ 39 Alejandro Pena	.06	.02	.00
☐ 40 Mike Scott	.06	.02	.00
☐ 41 Joe Orsulak	.03	.01	.00
☐ 42 Rafael Ramirez	.03	.01	.00
☐ 43 Gerald Young	.03	.01	.00
☐ 44 Dick Schofield	.03	.01	.00
☐ 45 Dave Smith	.03	.01	.00
☐ 46 Dave Magadan	.06	.02	.00
☐ 47 Dennis Martinez	.03	.01	.00
☐ 48 Greg Minton	.03	.01	.00
☐ 49 Milt Thompson	.03	.01	.00
☐ 50 Orel Hershiser	.08	.03	.01
☐ 51 Bip Roberts	.03	.01	.00
☐ 52 Jerry Browne	.03	.01	.00
☐ 53 Bob Ojeda	.03	.01	.00
☐ 54 Fernando Valenzuela	.08	.03	.01
☐ 55 Matt Nokes	.06	.02	.00
☐ 56 Brook Jacoby	.03	.01	.00
☐ 57 Frank Tanana	.03	.01	.00
☐ 58 Scott Fletcher	.03	.01	.00
☐ 59 Ron Oester	.03	.01	.00
☐ 60 Bob Boone	.06	.02	.00
☐ 61 Dan Gladden	.03	.01	.00
☐ 62 Darnell Coles	.03	.01	.00
☐ 63 Gregg Olson	.12	.05	.01
☐ 64 Todd Burns	.03	.01	.00
☐ 65 Todd Benzinger	.03	.01	.00
☐ 66 Dale Murphy	.10	.04	.01
☐ 67 Mike Flanagan	.03	.01	.00
☐ 68 Jose Oquendo	.03	.01	.00
☐ 69 Cecil Espy	.03	.01	.00
☐ 70 Chris Sabo	.10	.04	.01
☐ 71 Shane Rawley	.03	.01	.00
☐ 72 Tom Brunansky	.06	.02	.00
☐ 73 Vance Law	.03	.01	.00
☐ 74 B.J. Surhoff	.06	.02	.00
☐ 75 Lou Whitaker	.06	.02	.00
☐ 76 Ken Caminiti UER (Euclid, Ohio should be Hanford, California)	.03	.01	.00
☐ 77 Nelson Liriano	.03	.01	.00
☐ 78 Tommy Gregg	.03	.01	.00
☐ 79 Don Slaught	.03	.01	.00
☐ 80 Eddie Murray	.10	.04	.01
☐ 81 Joe Boever	.03	.01	.00
☐ 82 Charlie Leibrandt	.03	.01	.00
☐ 83 Jose Lind	.03	.01	.00
☐ 84 Tony Phillips	.03	.01	.00
☐ 85 Mitch Webster	.03	.01	.00

Card	Player			
☐ 86	Dan Plesac	.03	.01	.00
☐ 87	Rick Mahler	.03	.01	.00
☐ 88	Steve Lyons	.03	.01	.00
☐ 89	Tony Fernandez	.06	.02	.00
☐ 90	Ryne Sandberg	.30	.12	.03
☐ 91	Nick Esasky	.03	.01	.00
☐ 92	Luis Salazar	.03	.01	.00
☐ 93	Pete Incaviglia	.06	.02	.00
☐ 94	Ivan Calderon	.06	.02	.00
☐ 95	Jeff Treadway	.03	.01	.00
☐ 96	Kurt Stillwell	.03	.01	.00
☐ 97	Gary Sheffield	.08	.03	.01
☐ 98	Jeffrey Leonard	.03	.01	.00
☐ 99	Andres Thomas	.03	.01	.00
☐ 100	Roberto Kelly	.08	.03	.01
☐ 101	Alvaro Espinoza	.03	.01	.00
☐ 102	Greg Gagne	.03	.01	.00
☐ 103	John Farrell	.03	.01	.00
☐ 104	Willie Wilson	.06	.02	.00
☐ 105	Glenn Braggs	.03	.01	.00
☐ 106	Chet Lemon	.03	.01	.00
☐ 107A	Jamie Moyer ERR (scintilating)	.06	.02	.00
☐ 107B	Jamie Moyer COR (scintillating)	.25	.10	.02
☐ 108	Chuck Crim	.03	.01	.00
☐ 109	Dave Valle	.03	.01	.00
☐ 110	Walt Weiss	.06	.02	.00
☐ 111	Larry Sheets	.03	.01	.00
☐ 112	Don Robinson	.03	.01	.00
☐ 113	Danny Heep	.03	.01	.00
☐ 114	Carmelo Martinez	.03	.01	.00
☐ 115	Dave Gallagher	.03	.01	.00
☐ 116	Mike LaValliere	.03	.01	.00
☐ 117	Bob McClure	.03	.01	.00
☐ 118	Rene Gonzales	.03	.01	.00
☐ 119	Mark Parent	.03	.01	.00
☐ 120	Wally Joyner	.08	.03	.01
☐ 121	Mark Gubicza	.06	.02	.00
☐ 122	Tony Pena	.06	.02	.00
☐ 123	Carmen Castillo	.03	.01	.00
☐ 124	Howard Johnson	.08	.03	.01
☐ 125	Steve Sax	.06	.02	.00
☐ 126	Tim Belcher	.06	.02	.00
☐ 127	Tim Burke	.03	.01	.00
☐ 128	Al Newman	.03	.01	.00
☐ 129	Dennis Rasmussen	.03	.01	.00
☐ 130	Doug Jones	.03	.01	.00
☐ 131	Fred Lynn	.06	.02	.00
☐ 132	Jeff Hamilton	.03	.01	.00
☐ 133	German Gonzalez	.03	.01	.00
☐ 134	John Morris	.03	.01	.00
☐ 135	Dave Parker	.08	.03	.01
☐ 136	Gary Pettis	.03	.01	.00
☐ 137	Dennis Boyd	.03	.01	.00
☐ 138	Candy Maldonado	.03	.01	.00
☐ 139	Rick Cerone	.03	.01	.00
☐ 140	George Brett	.12	.05	.01
☐ 141	Dave Clark	.03	.01	.00
☐ 142	Dickie Thon	.03	.01	.00
☐ 143	Junior Ortiz	.03	.01	.00
☐ 144	Don August	.03	.01	.00
☐ 145	Gary Gaetti	.06	.02	.00
☐ 146	Kirt Manwaring	.03	.01	.00
☐ 147	Jeff Reed	.03	.01	.00
☐ 148	Jose Alvarez	.03	.01	.00
☐ 149	Mike Schooler	.03	.01	.00
☐ 150	Mark Grace	.12	.05	.01
☐ 151	Geronimo Berroa	.03	.01	.00
☐ 152	Barry Jones	.03	.01	.00
☐ 153	Geno Petralli	.03	.01	.00
☐ 154	Jim Deshaies	.03	.01	.00
☐ 155	Barry Larkin	.12	.05	.01
☐ 156	Alfredo Griffin	.03	.01	.00
☐ 157	Tom Henke	.06	.02	.00
☐ 158	Mike Jeffcoat	.03	.01	.00
☐ 159	Bob Welch	.06	.02	.00
☐ 160	Julio Franco	.08	.03	.01
☐ 161	Henry Cotto	.03	.01	.00
☐ 162	Terry Steinbach	.06	.02	.00
☐ 163	Damon Berryhill	.03	.01	.00
☐ 164	Tim Crews	.03	.01	.00
☐ 165	Tom Browning	.06	.02	.00
☐ 166	Fred Manrique	.03	.01	.00
☐ 167	Harold Reynolds	.06	.02	.00
☐ 168A	Ron Hassey ERR (27 on back)	.06	.02	.00
☐ 168B	Ron Hassey COR (24 on back)	1.25	.50	.12
☐ 169	Shawon Dunston	.08	.03	.01
☐ 170	Bobby Bonilla	.15	.06	.01
☐ 171	Tommy Herr	.03	.01	.00
☐ 172	Mike Heath	.03	.01	.00
☐ 173	Rich Gedman	.03	.01	.00
☐ 174	Bill Ripken	.03	.01	.00
☐ 175	Pete O'Brien	.03	.01	.00
☐ 176A	Lloyd McClendon ERR (uniform number on back listed as 1)	.75	.30	.07
☐ 176B	Lloyd McClendon COR (uniform number on back listed as 10)	.06	.02	.00
☐ 177	Brian Holton	.03	.01	.00
☐ 178	Jeff Blauser	.03	.01	.00
☐ 179	Jim Eisenreich	.03	.01	.00
☐ 180	Bert Blyleven	.06	.02	.00
☐ 181	Rob Murphy	.03	.01	.00
☐ 182	Bill Doran	.03	.01	.00
☐ 183	Curt Ford	.03	.01	.00
☐ 184	Mike Henneman	.03	.01	.00
☐ 185	Eric Davis	.10	.04	.01
☐ 186	Lance McCullers	.03	.01	.00
☐ 187	Steve Davis	.08	.03	.01
☐ 188	Bill Wegman	.03	.01	.00
☐ 189	Brian Harper	.06	.02	.00
☐ 190	Mike Moore	.06	.02	.00

□ 191 Dale Mohorcic	.03	.01	.00
□ 192 Tim Wallach	.06	.02	.00
□ 193 Keith Hernandez	.06	.02	.00
□ 194 Dave Righetti	.06	.02	.00
□ 195A Bret Saberhagen ERR (joke)	.08	.03	.01
□ 195B Bret Saberhagen COR (joker)	.30	.12	.03
□ 196 Paul Kilgus	.03	.01	.00
□ 197 Bud Black	.03	.01	.00
□ 198 Juan Samuel	.06	.02	.00
□ 199 Kevin Seitzer	.06	.02	.00
□ 200 Darryl Strawberry	.25	.10	.02
□ 201 Dave Stieb	.06	.02	.00
□ 202 Charlie Hough	.03	.01	.00
□ 203 Jack Morris	.08	.03	.01
□ 204 Rance Mulliniks	.03	.01	.00
□ 205 Alvin Davis	.06	.02	.00
□ 206 Jack Howell	.03	.01	.00
□ 207 Ken Patterson	.03	.01	.00
□ 208 Terry Pendleton	.08	.03	.01
□ 209 Craig Lefferts	.03	.01	.00
□ 210 Kevin Brown UER (First mention of '89 Rangers should be '88)	.03	.01	.00
□ 211 Dan Petry	.03	.01	.00
□ 212 Dave Leiper	.03	.01	.00
□ 213 Daryl Boston	.03	.01	.00
□ 214 Kevin Hickey	.03	.01	.00
□ 215 Mike Krukow	.03	.01	.00
□ 216 Terry Francona	.03	.01	.00
□ 217 Kirk McCaskill	.03	.01	.00
□ 218 Scott Bailes	.03	.01	.00
□ 219 Bob Forsch	.03	.01	.00
□ 220A Mike Aldrete ERR (25 on back)	.06	.02	.00
□ 220B Mike Aldrete COR (24 on back)	.25	.10	.02
□ 221 Steve Buechele	.03	.01	.00
□ 222 Jesse Barfield	.06	.02	.00
□ 223 Juan Berenguer	.03	.01	.00
□ 224 Andy McGaffigan	.03	.01	.00
□ 225 Pete Smith	.03	.01	.00
□ 226 Mike Witt	.03	.01	.00
□ 227 Jay Howell	.03	.01	.00
□ 228 Scott Bradley	.03	.01	.00
□ 229 Jerome Walton	.08	.03	.01
□ 230 Greg Swindell	.06	.02	.00
□ 231 Atlee Hammaker	.03	.01	.00
□ 232A Mike Devereaux ERR (RF on front)	.06	.02	.00
□ 232B Mike Devereaux COR (CF on front)	1.25	.50	.12
□ 233 Ken Hill	.08	.03	.01
□ 234 Craig Worthington	.03	.01	.00
□ 235 Scott Terry	.03	.01	.00
□ 236 Brett Butler	.06	.02	.00
□ 237 Doyle Alexander	.03	.01	.00

□ 238 Dave Anderson	.03	.01	.00
□ 239 Bob Milacki	.03	.01	.00
□ 240 Dwight Smith	.06	.02	.00
□ 241 Otis Nixon	.03	.01	.00
□ 242 Pat Tabler	.03	.01	.00
□ 243 Derek Lilliquist	.03	.01	.00
□ 244 Danny Tartabull	.08	.03	.01
□ 245 Wade Boggs	.15	.06	.01
□ 246 Scott Garrelts (should say Relief Pitcher on front)	.03	.01	.00
□ 247 Spike Owen	.03	.01	.00
□ 248 Norm Charlton	.03	.01	.00
□ 249 Gerald Perry	.03	.01	.00
□ 250 Nolan Ryan	.50	.20	.05
□ 251 Kevin Gross	.03	.01	.00
□ 252 Randy Milligan	.06	.02	.00
□ 253 Mike LaCoss	.03	.01	.00
□ 254 Dave Bergman	.03	.01	.00
□ 255 Tony Gwynn	.15	.06	.01
□ 256 Felix Fermin	.03	.01	.00
□ 257 Greg W. Harris	.06	.02	.00
□ 258 Junior Felix	.06	.02	.00
□ 259 Mark Davis	.06	.02	.00
□ 260 Vince Coleman	.08	.03	.01
□ 261 Paul Gibson	.03	.01	.00
□ 262 Mitch Williams	.03	.01	.00
□ 263 Jeff Russell	.03	.01	.00
□ 264 Omar Vizquel	.03	.01	.00
□ 265 Andre Dawson	.10	.04	.01
□ 266 Storm Davis	.03	.01	.00
□ 267 Guillermo Hernandez	.03	.01	.00
□ 268 Mike Felder	.03	.01	.00
□ 269 Tom Candiotti	.06	.02	.00
□ 270 Bruce Hurst	.06	.02	.00
□ 271 Fred McGriff	.10	.04	.01
□ 272 Glenn Davis	.08	.03	.01
□ 273 John Franco	.03	.01	.00
□ 274 Rich Yett	.03	.01	.00
□ 275 Craig Biggio	.08	.03	.01
□ 276 Gene Larkin	.03	.01	.00
□ 277 Rob Dibble	.08	.03	.01
□ 278 Randy Bush	.03	.01	.00
□ 279 Kevin Bass	.03	.01	.00
□ 280A Bo Jackson ERR (Watham)	.40	.16	.04
□ 280B Bo Jackson COR (Wathan)	.75	.30	.07
□ 281 Wally Backman	.03	.01	.00
□ 282 Larry Andersen	.03	.01	.00
□ 283 Chris Bosio	.03	.01	.00
□ 284 Juan Agosto	.03	.01	.00
□ 285 Ozzie Smith	.12	.05	.01
□ 286 George Bell	.08	.03	.01
□ 287 Rex Hudler	.03	.01	.00
□ 288 Pat Borders	.03	.01	.00
□ 289 Danny Jackson	.03	.01	.00
□ 290 Carlton Fisk	.12	.05	.01

☐ 291 Tracy Jones .03 .01 .00

☐ 292 Allan Anderson .03 .01 .00

☐ 293 Johnny Ray .03 .01 .00

☐ 294 Lee Guetterman .03 .01 .00

☐ 295 Paul O'Neill .06 .02 .00

☐ 296 Carney Lansford .06 .02 .00

☐ 297 Tom Brookens .03 .01 .00

☐ 298 Claudell Washington .03 .01 .00

☐ 299 Hubie Brooks .03 .01 .00

☐ 300 Will Clark .30 .12 .03

☐ 301 Kenny Rogers .06 .02 .00

☐ 302 Darrell Evans .06 .02 .00

☐ 303 Greg Briley .06 .02 .00

☐ 304 Donn Pall .03 .01 .00

☐ 305 Teddy Higuera .03 .01 .00

☐ 306 Dan Pasqua .03 .01 .00

☐ 307 Dave Winfield .10 .04 .01

☐ 308 Dennis Powell .03 .01 .00

☐ 309 Jose DeLeon .03 .01 .00

☐ 310 Roger Clemens UER .30 .12 .03
(dominate, should
say dominant)

☐ 311 Melido Perez .03 .01 .00

☐ 312 Devon White .06 .02 .00

☐ 313 Dwight Gooden .10 .04 .01

☐ 314 Carlos Martinez .03 .01 .00

☐ 315 Dennis Eckersley .08 .03 .01

☐ 316 Clay Parker UER .03 .01 .00
(Height 6'11")

☐ 317 Rick Honeycutt .03 .01 .00

☐ 318 Tim Laudner .03 .01 .00

☐ 319 Joe Carter .10 .04 .01

☐ 320 Robin Yount .12 .05 .01

☐ 321 Felix Jose .20 .08 .02

☐ 322 Mickey Tettleton .06 .02 .00

☐ 323 Mike Gallego .03 .01 .00

☐ 324 Edgar Martinez .08 .03 .01

☐ 325 Dave Henderson .06 .02 .00

☐ 326 Chili Davis .06 .02 .00

☐ 327 Steve Balboni .03 .01 .00

☐ 328 Jody Davis .03 .01 .00

☐ 329 Shawn Hillegas .03 .01 .00

☐ 330 Jim Abbott .17 .07 .01

☐ 331 John Dopson .03 .01 .00

☐ 332 Mark Williamson .03 .01 .00

☐ 333 Jeff D. Robinson .03 .01 .00

☐ 334 John Smiley .06 .02 .00

☐ 335 Bobby Thigpen .06 .02 .00

☐ 336 Garry Templeton .03 .01 .00

☐ 337 Marvell Wynne .03 .01 .00

☐ 338A Ken Griffey Sr. ERR .10 .04 .01
(uniform number on
back listed as 25)

☐ 338B Ken Griffey Sr. COR 1.75 .70 .17
(uniform number on
back listed as 30)

☐ 339 Steve Finley .10 .04 .01

☐ 340 Ellis Burks .10 .04 .01

☐ 341 Frank Williams .03 .01 .00

☐ 342 Mike Morgan .03 .01 .00

☐ 343 Kevin Mitchell .10 .04 .01

☐ 344 Joel Youngblood .03 .01 .00

☐ 345 Mike Greenwell .12 .05 .01

☐ 346 Glenn Wilson .03 .01 .00

☐ 347 John Costello .03 .01 .00

☐ 348 Wes Gardner .03 .01 .00

☐ 349 Jeff Ballard .03 .01 .00

☐ 350 Mark Thurmond UER .03 .01 .00
(ERA is 192,
should be 1.92)

☐ 351 Randy Myers .03 .01 .00

☐ 352 Shawn Abner .03 .01 .00

☐ 353 Jesse Orosco .03 .01 .00

☐ 354 Greg Walker .03 .01 .00

☐ 355 Pete Harnisch .06 .02 .00

☐ 356 Steve Farr .03 .01 .00

☐ 357 Dave LaPoint .03 .01 .00

☐ 358 Willie Fraser .03 .01 .00

☐ 359 Mickey Hatcher .03 .01 .00

☐ 360 Rickey Henderson .25 .10 .02

☐ 361 Mike Fitzgerald .03 .01 .00

☐ 362 Bill Schroeder .03 .01 .00

☐ 363 Mark Carreon .03 .01 .00

☐ 364 Ron Jones .03 .01 .00

☐ 365 Jeff Montgomery .03 .01 .00

☐ 366 Bill Krueger .03 .01 .00

☐ 367 John Cangelosi .03 .01 .00

☐ 368 Jose Gonzalez .03 .01 .00

☐ 369 Greg Hibbard .15 .06 .01

☐ 370 John Smoltz .15 .06 .01

☐ 371 Jeff Brantley .08 .03 .01

☐ 372 Frank White .03 .01 .00

☐ 373 Ed Whitson .03 .01 .00

☐ 374 Willie McGee .08 .03 .01

☐ 375 Jose Canseco .40 .16 .04

☐ 376 Randy Ready .03 .01 .00

☐ 377 Don Aase .03 .01 .00

☐ 378 Tony Armas .03 .01 .00

☐ 379 Steve Bedrosian .03 .01 .00

☐ 380 Chuck Finley .06 .02 .00

☐ 381 Kent Hrbek .08 .03 .01

☐ 382 Jim Gantner .03 .01 .00

☐ 383 Mel Hall .06 .02 .00

☐ 384 Mike Marshall .06 .02 .00

☐ 385 Mark McGwire .15 .06 .01

☐ 386 Wayne Tolleson .03 .01 .00

☐ 387 Brian Holman .08 .03 .01

☐ 388 John Wetteland .06 .02 .00

☐ 389 Darren Daulton .03 .01 .00

☐ 390 Rob Deer .06 .02 .00

☐ 391 John Moses .03 .01 .00

☐ 392 Todd Worrell .06 .02 .00

☐ 393 Chuck Cary .03 .01 .00

☐ 394 Stan Javier .03 .01 .00

☐ 395 Willie Randolph .06 .02 .00

☐ 396 Bill Buckner .06 .02 .00

☐ 397 Robby Thompson	.03	.01	.00
☐ 398 Mike Scioscia	.03	.01	.00
☐ 399 Lonnie Smith	.06	.02	.00
☐ 400 Kirby Puckett	.20	.08	.02
☐ 401 Mark Langston	.08	.03	.01
☐ 402 Danny Darwin	.03	.01	.00
☐ 403 Greg Maddux	.06	.02	.00
☐ 404 Lloyd Moseby	.03	.01	.00
☐ 405 Rafael Palmeiro	.12	.05	.01
☐ 406 Chad Kreuter	.03	.01	.00
☐ 407 Jimmy Key	.06	.02	.00
☐ 408 Tim Birtsas	.03	.01	.00
☐ 409 Tim Raines	.08	.03	.01
☐ 410 Dave Stewart	.08	.03	.01
☐ 411 Eric Yelding	.06	.02	.00
☐ 412 Kent Anderson	.06	.02	.00
☐ 413 Les Lancaster	.03	.01	.00
☐ 414 Rick Dempsey	.03	.01	.00
☐ 415 Randy Johnson	.06	.02	.00
☐ 416 Gary Carter	.08	.03	.01
☐ 417 Rolando Roomes	.03	.01	.00
☐ 418 Dan Schatzeder	.03	.01	.00
☐ 419 Bryn Smith	.03	.01	.00
☐ 420 Ruben Sierra	.17	.07	.01
☐ 421 Steve Jeltz	.03	.01	.00
☐ 422 Ken Oberkfell	.03	.01	.00
☐ 423 Sid Bream	.03	.01	.00
☐ 424 Jim Clancy	.03	.01	.00
☐ 425 Kelly Gruber	.10	.04	.01
☐ 426 Rick Leach	.03	.01	.00
☐ 427 Len Dykstra	.08	.03	.01
☐ 428 Jeff Pico	.03	.01	.00
☐ 429 John Cerutti	.03	.01	.00
☐ 430 David Cone	.08	.03	.01
☐ 431 Jeff Kunkel	.03	.01	.00
☐ 432 Luis Aquino	.03	.01	.00
☐ 433 Ernie Whitt	.03	.01	.00
☐ 434 Bo Diaz	.03	.01	.00
☐ 435 Steve Lake	.03	.01	.00
☐ 436 Pat Perry	.03	.01	.00
☐ 437 Mike Davis	.03	.01	.00
☐ 438 Cecilio Guante	.03	.01	.00
☐ 439 Duane Ward	.03	.01	.00
☐ 440 Andy Van Slyke	.08	.03	.01
☐ 441 Gene Nelson	.03	.01	.00
☐ 442 Luis Polonia	.03	.01	.00
☐ 443 Kevin Elster	.03	.01	.00
☐ 444 Keith Moreland	.03	.01	.00
☐ 445 Roger McDowell	.03	.01	.00
☐ 446 Ron Darling	.06	.02	.00
☐ 447 Ernest Riles	.03	.01	.00
☐ 448 Mookie Wilson	.03	.01	.00
☐ 449A Billy Spiers ERR (no birth year)	.75	.30	.07
☐ 449B Billy Spiers COR (born in 1966)	.06	.02	.00
☐ 450 Rick Sutcliffe	.06	.02	.00
☐ 451 Nelson Santovenia	.03	.01	.00
☐ 452 Andy Allanson	.03	.01	.00
☐ 453 Bob Melvin	.03	.01	.00
☐ 454 Benito Santiago	.08	.03	.01
☐ 455 Jose Uribe	.03	.01	.00
☐ 456 Bill Landrum	.03	.01	.00
☐ 457 Bobby Witt	.06	.02	.00
☐ 458 Kevin Romine	.03	.01	.00
☐ 459 Lee Mazzilli	.03	.01	.00
☐ 460 Paul Molitor	.08	.03	.01
☐ 461 Ramon Martinez	.25	.10	.02
☐ 462 Frank DiPino	.03	.01	.00
☐ 463 Walt Terrell	.03	.01	.00
☐ 464 Bob Geren	.03	.01	.00
☐ 465 Rick Reuschel	.06	.02	.00
☐ 466 Mark Grant	.03	.01	.00
☐ 467 John Kruk	.03	.01	.00
☐ 468 Gregg Jefferies	.10	.04	.01
☐ 469 R.J. Reynolds	.03	.01	.00
☐ 470 Harold Baines	.08	.03	.01
☐ 471 Dennis Lamp	.03	.01	.00
☐ 472 Tom Gordon	.08	.03	.01
☐ 473 Terry Puhl	.03	.01	.00
☐ 474 Curt Wilkerson	.03	.01	.00
☐ 475 Dan Quisenberry	.06	.02	.00
☐ 476 Oddibe McDowell	.03	.01	.00
☐ 477 Zane Smith UER (Career ERA .393)	.06	.02	.00
☐ 478 Franklin Stubbs	.03	.01	.00
☐ 479 Wallace Johnson	.03	.01	.00
☐ 480 Jay Tibbs	.03	.01	.00
☐ 481 Tom Glavine	.20	.08	.02
☐ 482 Manny Lee	.03	.01	.00
☐ 483 Joe Hesketh UER (says Rookiess on back, should say Rookies)	.06	.02	.00
☐ 484 Mike Bielecki	.03	.01	.00
☐ 485 Greg Brock	.03	.01	.00
☐ 486 Pascual Perez	.03	.01	.00
☐ 487 Kirk Gibson	.08	.03	.01
☐ 488 Scott Sanderson	.03	.01	.00
☐ 489 Domingo Ramos	.03	.01	.00
☐ 490 Kal Daniels	.06	.02	.00
☐ 491A David Wells ERR (reverse negative photo on card back)	1.75	.70	.17
☐ 491B David Wells COR	.08	.03	.01
☐ 492 Jerry Reed	.03	.01	.00
☐ 493 Eric Show	.03	.01	.00
☐ 494 Mike Pagliarulo	.03	.01	.00
☐ 495 Ron Robinson	.03	.01	.00
☐ 496 Brad Komminsk	.03	.01	.00
☐ 497 Greg Litton	.03	.01	.00
☐ 498 Chris James	.03	.01	.00
☐ 499 Luis Quinones	.03	.01	.00
☐ 500 Frank Viola	.08	.03	.01
☐ 501 Tim Teufel UER (Twins '85, the s is lower case, should	.03	.01	.00

Card			
be upper case)			
☐ 502 Terry Leach	.03	.01	.00
☐ 503 Matt Williams	.15	.06	.01
☐ 504 Tim Leary	.06	.02	.00
☐ 505 Doug Drabek	.06	.02	.00
☐ 506 Mariano Duncan	.03	.01	.00
☐ 507 Charlie Hayes	.03	.01	.00
☐ 508 Joey Belle	.50	.20	.05
☐ 509 Pat Sheridan	.03	.01	.00
☐ 510 Mackey Sasser	.03	.01	.00
☐ 511 Jose Rijo	.06	.02	.00
☐ 512 Mike Smithson	.03	.01	.00
☐ 513 Gary Ward	.03	.01	.00
☐ 514 Dion James	.03	.01	.00
☐ 515 Jim Gott	.03	.01	.00
☐ 516 Drew Hall	.03	.01	.00
☐ 517 Doug Bair	.03	.01	.00
☐ 518 Scott Scudder	.08	.03	.01
☐ 519 Rick Aguilera	.06	.02	.00
☐ 520 Rafael Belliard	.03	.01	.00
☐ 521 Jay Buhner	.08	.03	.01
☐ 522 Jeff Reardon	.06	.02	.00
☐ 523 Steve Rosenberg	.06	.02	.00
☐ 524 Randy Velarde	.03	.01	.00
☐ 525 Jeff Musselman	.03	.01	.00
☐ 526 Bill Long	.03	.01	.00
☐ 527 Gary Wayne	.06	.02	.00
☐ 528 Dave Johnson (P)	.08	.03	.01
☐ 529 Ron Kittle	.06	.02	.00
☐ 530 Erik Hanson UER (5th line on back says seson, should say season)	.10	.04	.01
☐ 531 Steve Wilson	.03	.01	.00
☐ 532 Joey Meyer	.03	.01	.00
☐ 533 Curt Young	.03	.01	.00
☐ 534 Kelly Downs	.03	.01	.00
☐ 535 Joe Girardi	.03	.01	.00
☐ 536 Lance Blankenship	.03	.01	.00
☐ 537 Greg Mathews	.03	.01	.00
☐ 538 Donell Nixon	.03	.01	.00
☐ 539 Mark Knudson	.03	.01	.00
☐ 540 Jeff Wetherby	.08	.03	.01
☐ 541 Darrin Jackson	.06	.02	.00
☐ 542 Terry Mulholland	.06	.02	.00
☐ 543 Eric Hetzel	.03	.01	.00
☐ 544 Rick Reed	.08	.03	.01
☐ 545 Dennis Cook	.06	.02	.00
☐ 546 Mike Jackson	.03	.01	.00
☐ 547 Brian Fisher	.03	.01	.00
☐ 548 Gene Harris	.06	.02	.00
☐ 549 Jeff King	.06	.02	.00
☐ 550 Dave Dravecky	.06	.02	.00
☐ 551 Randy Kutcher	.03	.01	.00
☐ 552 Mark Portugal	.03	.01	.00
☐ 553 Jim Corsi	.03	.01	.00
☐ 554 Todd Stottlemyre	.08	.03	.01
☐ 555 Scott Bankhead	.06	.02	.00
☐ 556 Ken Dayley	.03	.01	.00
☐ 557 Rick Wrona	.06	.02	.00
☐ 558 Sammy Sosa	.25	.10	.02
☐ 559 Keith Miller	.03	.01	.00
☐ 560 Ken Griffey Jr.	1.50	.60	.15
☐ 561A Ryne Sandberg HL ERR (position on front listed as 3B)	9.00	4.00	.90
☐ 561B Ryne Sandberg HL COR	.15	.06	.01
☐ 562 Billy Hatcher	.03	.01	.00
☐ 563 Jay Bell	.03	.01	.00
☐ 564 Jack Daugherty	.06	.02	.00
☐ 565 Rich Monteleone	.03	.01	.00
☐ 566 Bo Jackson AS-MVP	.25	.10	.02
☐ 567 Tony Fossas	.06	.02	.00
☐ 568 Roy Smith	.03	.01	.00
☐ 569 Jaime Navarro	.06	.02	.00
☐ 570 Lance Johnson	.03	.01	.00
☐ 571 Mike Dyer	.08	.03	.01
☐ 572 Kevin Ritz	.08	.03	.01
☐ 573 Dave West	.03	.01	.00
☐ 574 Gary Mielke	.08	.03	.01
☐ 575 Scott Lusader	.03	.01	.00
☐ 576 Joe Oliver	.06	.02	.00
☐ 577 Sandy Alomar Jr.	.10	.04	.01
☐ 578 Andy Benes UER (extra comma between day and year)	.17	.07	.01
☐ 579 Tim Jones	.03	.01	.00
☐ 580 Randy McCament	.08	.03	.01
☐ 581 Curt Schilling	.03	.01	.00
☐ 582 John Orton	.08	.03	.01
☐ 583A Milt Cuyler ERR (998 games)	1.50	.60	.15
☐ 583B Milt Cuyler COR (98 games)	.50	.20	.05
☐ 584 Eric Anthony	.17	.07	.01
☐ 585 Greg Vaughn	.50	.20	.05
☐ 586 Deion Sanders	.20	.08	.02
☐ 587 Jose DeJesus	.03	.01	.00
☐ 588 Chip Hale	.08	.03	.01
☐ 589 John Olerud	1.00	.40	.10
☐ 590 Steve Olin	.10	.04	.01
☐ 591 Marquis Grissom	.45	.18	.04
☐ 592 Moises Alou	.12	.05	.01
☐ 593 Mark Lemke	.06	.02	.00
☐ 594 Dean Palmer	.75	.30	.07
☐ 595 Robin Ventura	.75	.30	.07
☐ 596 Tino Martinez	.50	.20	.05
☐ 597 Mike Huff	.12	.05	.01
☐ 598 Scott Hemond	.12	.05	.01
☐ 599 Wally Whitehurst	.06	.02	.00
☐ 600 Todd Zeile	.35	.15	.03
☐ 601 Glenallen Hill	.06	.02	.00
☐ 602 Hal Morris	.35	.15	.03
☐ 603 Juan Bell	.06	.02	.00
☐ 604 Bobby Rose	.10	.04	.01
☐ 605 Matt Merullo	.08	.03	.01

☐ 606 Kevin Maas .... 1.25 .50 .12
☐ 607 Randy Nosek .... .08 .03 .01
☐ 608A Billy Bates .... .10 .04 .01
(Text mentions 12
triples in tenth line)
☐ 608B Billy Bates .... .10 .04 .01
(Text has no mention
of triples)
☐ 609 Mike Stanton .... .10 .04 .01
☐ 610 Mauro Gozzo .... .10 .04 .01
☐ 611 Charles Nagy .... .20 .08 .02
☐ 612 Scott Coolbaugh .... .10 .04 .01
☐ 613 Jose Vizcaino .... .10 .04 .01
☐ 614 Greg Smith .... .10 .04 .01
☐ 615 Jeff Huson .... .08 .03 .01
☐ 616 Mickey Weston .... .08 .03 .01
☐ 617 John Pawlowski .... .06 .02 .00
☐ 618A Joe Skalski ERR .... .06 .02 .00
(27 on back)
☐ 618B Joe Skalski COR .... 1.25 .50 .12
(67 on back)
☐ 619 Bernie Williams .... .60 .25 .06
☐ 620 Shawn Holman .... .10 .04 .01
☐ 621 Gary Eave .... .08 .03 .01
☐ 622 Darrin Fletcher UER .... .15 .06 .01
(Elmherst, should
be Elmhurst)
☐ 623 Pat Combs .... .06 .02 .00
☐ 624 Mike Blowers .... .10 .04 .01
☐ 625 Kevin Appier .... .20 .08 .02
☐ 626 Pat Austin .... .08 .03 .01
☐ 627 Kelly Mann .... .08 .03 .01
☐ 628 Matt Kinzer .... .08 .03 .01
☐ 629 Chris Hammond .... .30 .12 .03
☐ 630 Dean Wilkins .... .10 .04 .01
☐ 631 Larry Walker UER .... .25 .10 .02
(Uniform number 55 on
front and 33 on back)
☐ 632 Blaine Beatty .... .10 .04 .01
☐ 633A Tommy Barrett ERR .... .08 .03 .01
(29 on back)
☐ 633B Tommy Barrett COR .... 3.50 1.50 .35
(14 on back)
☐ 634 Stan Belinda .... .12 .05 .01
☐ 635 Mike (Tex) Smith .... .08 .03 .01
☐ 636 Hensley Meulens .... .12 .05 .01
☐ 637 Juan Gonzalez .... 2.00 .80 .20
☐ 638 Lenny Webster .... .12 .05 .01
☐ 639 Mark Gardner .... .17 .07 .01
☐ 640 Tommy Greene .... .25 .10 .02
☐ 641 Mike Hartley .... .15 .06 .01
☐ 642 Phil Stephenson .... .06 .02 .00
☐ 643 Kevin Mmahat .... .10 .04 .01
☐ 644 Ed Whited .... .10 .04 .01
☐ 645 Delino DeShields .... .45 .18 .04
☐ 646 Kevin Blankenship .... .03 .01 .00
☐ 647 Paul Sorrento .... .10 .04 .01
☐ 648 Mike Roesler .... .10 .04 .01
☐ 649 Jason Grimsley .... .08 .03 .01
☐ 650 Dave Justice .... 2.50 1.00 .25
☐ 651 Scott Cooper .... .45 .18 .04
☐ 652 Dave Eiland .... .06 .02 .00
☐ 653 Mike Munoz .... .08 .03 .01
☐ 654 Jeff Fischer .... .08 .03 .01
☐ 655 Terry Jorgenson .... .08 .03 .01
☐ 656 George Canale .... .10 .04 .01
☐ 657 Brian DuBois .... .10 .04 .01
☐ 658 Carlos Quintana .... .06 .02 .00
☐ 659 Luis De Los Santos .... .03 .01 .00
☐ 660 Jerald Clark .... .03 .01 .00
☐ 661 Donald Harris DC .... .12 .05 .01
☐ 662 Paul Coleman DC .... .17 .07 .01
☐ 663 Frank Thomas DC .... 6.00 2.50 .60
☐ 664 Brent Mayne DC .... .20 .08 .02
☐ 665 Eddie Zosky DC .... .35 .15 .03
☐ 666 Steve Hosey DC .... .17 .07 .01
☐ 667 Scott Bryant DC .... .17 .07 .01
☐ 668 Tom Goodwin DC .... .35 .15 .03
☐ 669 Cal Eldred DC .... .12 .05 .01
☐ 670 Earl Cunningham DC .... .15 .06 .01
☐ 671 Alan Zinter DC .... .10 .04 .01
☐ 672 Chuck Knoblauch DC .... 2.00 .80 .20
☐ 673 Kyle Abbott DC .... .35 .15 .03
☐ 674 Roger Salkeld DC .... .75 .30 .07
☐ 675 Maurice Vaughn DC .... 1.50 .60 .15
☐ 676 Keith (Kiki) Jones DC .... .20 .08 .02
☐ 677 Tyler Houston DC .... .12 .05 .01
☐ 678 Jeff Jackson DC .... .10 .04 .01
☐ 679 Greg Gohr DC .... .20 .08 .02
☐ 680 Ben McDonald DC .... .75 .30 .07
☐ 681 Greg Blosser DC .... .25 .10 .02
☐ 682 Willie Green DC UER .... .15 .06 .01
(Name misspelled on
card, should be Greene)
☐ 683 Wade Boggs DT UER .... .10 .04 .01
(Text says 215 hits in
'89, should be 205)
☐ 684 Will Clark DT .... .15 .06 .01
☐ 685 Tony Gwynn DT UER .... .08 .03 .01
(Text reads battling
instead of batting)
☐ 686 Rickey Henderson DT .... .15 .06 .01
☐ 687 Bo Jackson DT .... .25 .10 .02
☐ 688 Mark Langston DT .... .06 .02 .00
☐ 689 Barry Larkin DT .... .08 .03 .01
☐ 690 Kirby Puckett DT .... .10 .04 .01
☐ 691 Ryne Sandberg DT .... .15 .06 .01
☐ 692 Mike Scott DT .... .06 .02 .00
☐ 693A Terry Steinbach DT .... .06 .02 .00
ERR (cathers)
☐ 693B Terry Steinbach DT .... .25 .10 .02
COR (catchers)
☐ 694 Bobby Thigpen DT .... .06 .02 .00
☐ 695 Mitch Williams DT .... .06 .02 .00
☐ 696 Nolan Ryan HL .... .25 .10 .02
☐ 697 Bo Jackson FB/BB .... 3.50 1.50 .35

Card	Player	MINT	EXC	G-VG
☐ 698	Rickey Henderson ALCS-MVP	.12	.05	.01
☐ 699	Will Clark NLCS-MVP	.12	.05	.01
☐ 700	WS Games 1/2	.06	.02	.00
☐ 701	Candlestick	.08	.03	.01
☐ 702	WS Game 3	.06	.02	.00
☐ 703	WS Wrap-up	.06	.02	.00
☐ 704	Wade Boggs HL	.10	.04	.01

1990 Score Dream Team Rookies

The 1990 Score Dream Team Rookies Insert contains ten standard-size (2 1/2" by 3 1/2") cards. The ten cards represent one player for each position and Bart Giamatti. The sets were inserted in the Score factory collated sets hobby dealers received early in 1990, but not the retail sets issued later in 1990. Card B1 is a special commemorative card of the late Commissioner A. Bartlett Giamatti.

	MINT	EXC	G-VG
COMPLETE SET (10)	10.00	4.50	1.25
COMMON PLAYER (B1-B10)	.25	.10	.02

Card	Player	MINT	EXC	G-VG
☐ B1	A.Bartlett Giamatti (late Commissioner)	1.00	.40	.10
☐ B2	Pat Combs	.35	.15	.03
☐ B3	Todd Zeile	2.00	.80	.20
☐ B4	Luis De Los Santos	.25	.10	.02
☐ B5	Mark Lemke	.60	.25	.06
☐ B6	Robin Ventura	5.00	2.25	.50
☐ B7	Jeff Huson	.25	.10	.02
☐ B8	Greg Vaughn	3.50	1.50	.35
☐ B9	Marquis Grissom	2.25	.90	.22
☐ B10	Eric Anthony	.60	.25	.06

1990 Score Traded

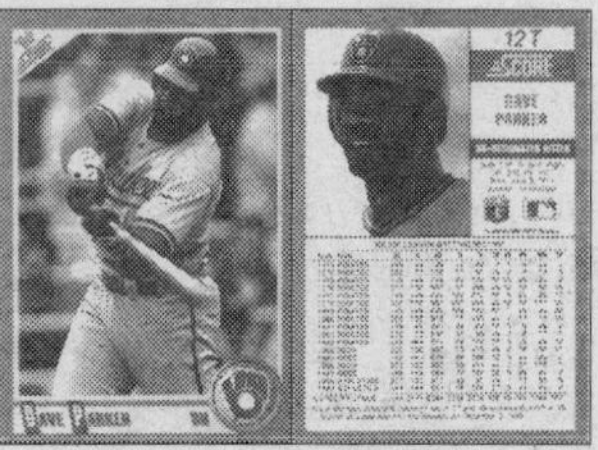

The 1990 Score Rookie/Traded set marks the fourth consecutive year Score has issued an end of the year set to mark trades and give rookies early cards. This now-standard set consists of 110 cards; cards measure the standard size of 2 1/2" by 3 1/2". The first 66 cards are traded players while the last 44 cards are rookie cards. Included in the rookie part of the set are cross-athletes Eric Lindros (hockey) and D.J. Dozier (football). The key baseball player rookie cards in the set are Derek Bell and Ray Lankford.

	MINT	EXC	G-VG
COMPLETE SET (110)	20.00	8.50	2.75
COMMON PLAYER (1-66)	.06	.02	.00
COMMON PLAYER (67-110)	.10	.04	.01

Card	Player	MINT	EXC	G-VG
☐ 1T	Dave Winfield	.15	.06	.01
☐ 2T	Kevin Bass	.06	.02	.00
☐ 3T	Nick Esasky	.06	.02	.00
☐ 4T	Mitch Webster	.06	.02	.00
☐ 5T	Pascual Perez	.06	.02	.00
☐ 6T	Gary Pettis	.06	.02	.00
☐ 7T	Tony Pena	.10	.04	.01
☐ 8T	Candy Maldonado	.10	.04	.01
☐ 9T	Cecil Fielder	.35	.15	.03
☐ 10T	Carmelo Martinez	.06	.02	.00
☐ 11T	Mark Langston	.10	.04	.01
☐ 12T	Dave Parker	.10	.04	.01
☐ 13T	Don Slaught	.06	.02	.00
☐ 14T	Tony Phillips	.06	.02	.00

☐ 15T John Franco .10 .04 .01
☐ 16T Randy Myers .10 .04 .01
☐ 17T Jeff Reardon .12 .05 .01
☐ 18T Sandy Alomar Jr. .15 .06 .01
☐ 19T Joe Carter .12 .05 .01
☐ 20T Fred Lynn .10 .04 .01
☐ 21T Storm Davis .06 .02 .00
☐ 22T Craig Lefferts .06 .02 .00
☐ 23T Pete O'Brien .06 .02 .00
☐ 24T Dennis Boyd .06 .02 .00
☐ 25T Lloyd Moseby .06 .02 .00
☐ 26T Mark Davis .10 .04 .01
☐ 27T Tim Leary .10 .04 .01
☐ 28T Gerald Perry .06 .02 .00
☐ 29T Don Aase .06 .02 .00
☐ 30T Ernie Whitt .06 .02 .00
☐ 31T Dale Murphy .12 .05 .01
☐ 32T Alejandro Pena .10 .04 .01
☐ 33T Juan Samuel .10 .04 .01
☐ 34T Hubie Brooks .10 .04 .01
☐ 35T Gary Carter .12 .05 .01
☐ 36T Jim Presley .06 .02 .00
☐ 37T Wally Backman .06 .02 .00
☐ 38T Matt Nokes .10 .04 .01
☐ 39T Dan Petry .06 .02 .00
☐ 40T Franklin Stubbs .06 .02 .00
☐ 41T Jeff Huson .10 .04 .01
☐ 42T Billy Hatcher .10 .04 .01
☐ 43T Terry Leach .06 .02 .00
☐ 44T Phil Bradley .06 .02 .00
☐ 45T Claudell Washington .06 .02 .00
☐ 46T Luis Polonia .06 .02 .00
☐ 47T Daryl Boston .06 .02 .00
☐ 48T Lee Smith .10 .04 .01
☐ 49T Tom Brunansky .10 .04 .01
☐ 50T Mike Witt .06 .02 .00
☐ 51T Willie Randolph .10 .04 .01
☐ 52T Stan Javier .06 .02 .00
☐ 53T Brad Komminsk .06 .02 .00
☐ 54T John Candelaria .06 .02 .00
☐ 55T Bryn Smith .06 .02 .00
☐ 56T Glenn Braggs .06 .02 .00
☐ 57T Keith Hernandez .12 .05 .01
☐ 58T Ken Oberkfell .06 .02 .00
☐ 59T Steve Jeltz .06 .02 .00
☐ 60T Chris James .10 .04 .01
☐ 61T Scott Sanderson .10 .04 .01
☐ 62T Bill Long .06 .02 .00
☐ 63T Rick Cerone .06 .02 .00
☐ 64T Scott Bailes .06 .02 .00
☐ 65T Larry Sheets .06 .02 .00
☐ 66T Junior Ortiz .06 .02 .00
☐ 67T Francisco Cabrera .12 .05 .01
☐ 68T Gary DiSarcina .12 .05 .01
☐ 69T Greg Olson .20 .08 .02
☐ 70T Beau Allred .12 .05 .01
☐ 71T Oscar Azocar .12 .05 .01
☐ 72T Kent Mercker .17 .07 .01
☐ 73T John Burkett .15 .06 .01
☐ 74T Carlos Baerga .60 .25 .06
☐ 75T Dave Hollins .40 .16 .04
☐ 76T Todd Hundley .50 .20 .05
☐ 77T Rick Parker .10 .04 .01
☐ 78T Steve Cummings .10 .04 .01
☐ 79T Bill Sampen .12 .05 .01
☐ 80T Jerry Kutzler .10 .04 .01
☐ 81T Derek Bell 2.50 1.00 .25
☐ 82T Kevin Tapani .60 .25 .06
☐ 83T Jim Leyritz .10 .04 .01
☐ 84T Ray Lankford 1.50 .60 .15
☐ 85T Wayne Edwards .10 .04 .01
☐ 86T Frank Thomas 9.00 4.00 .90
☐ 87T Tim Naehring .25 .10 .02
☐ 88T Willie Blair .10 .04 .01
☐ 89T Alan Mills .12 .05 .01
☐ 90T Scott Radinsky .12 .05 .01
☐ 91T Howard Farmer .12 .05 .01
☐ 92T Julio Machado .10 .04 .01
☐ 93T Rafael Valdez .10 .04 .01
☐ 94T Shawn Boskie .12 .05 .01
☐ 95T David Segui .17 .07 .01
☐ 96T Chris Hoiles .20 .08 .02
☐ 97T D.J. Dozier .40 .16 .04
☐ 98T Hector Villanueva .12 .05 .01
☐ 99T Eric Gunderson .17 .07 .01
☐ 100T Eric Lindros 6.50 2.75 .65
☐ 101T Dave Otto .10 .04 .01
☐ 102T Dana Kiecker .10 .04 .01
☐ 103T Tim Drummond .10 .04 .01
☐ 104T Mickey Pina .10 .04 .01
☐ 105T Craig Grebeck .10 .04 .01
☐ 106T Bernard Gilkey .50 .20 .05
☐ 107T Tim Layana .10 .04 .01
☐ 108T Scott Chiamparino .15 .06 .01
☐ 109T Steve Avery 3.00 1.25 .30
☐ 110T Terry Shumpert .12 .05 .01

1991 Score

The 1991 Score set contains 893 cards. The cards feature a solid color border framing the full-color photo of the cards. The cards measure the standard card size of 2 1/2" by 3 1/2" and also feature Score trademark full-color photos on the back. The backs also include a brief biography on each player. This set marks the fourth consecutive year that Score has issued a major set but the first time Score issued the set in two series. Score also reused their successful Dream Team concept

by using non-baseball photos of Today's stars. Series one contains 441 cards and ends with the Annie Leibowitz photo of Jose Canseco used in American Express ads. This first series also includes 49 Rookie prospects, 12 First Round Draft Picks and five each of the Master Blaster, K-Man, and Rifleman subsets. The All-Star sets in the first set are all American Leaguers (which are all caricatures). The key rookie cards in the first series are Jeromy Burnitz, Wes Chamberlain, Brian McRae, Marc Newfield, Phil Plantier, and Todd Van Poppel. There are a number of pitchers whose card backs show Innings Pitched totals which do not equal the added year-by-year total; the following card numbers were affected, 4, 24, 29, 30, 51, 81, 109, 111, 118, 141, 150, 156, 177, 204, 218, 232, 235, 255, 287, 289, 311, and 328. The second series was issued approximately three months after the release of Series One and included many of the special cards Score is noted for, e.g., the continuation of the Dream Team set begun in Series One, All-Star Cartoons featuring National Leaguers, a continuation of the 1990 first round draft picks, and 61 rookie prospects.

	MINT	EXC	G-VG
COMPLETE SET (893)	22.50	9.75	3.25
COMMON PLAYER (1-441)	.03	.01	.00
COMMON PLAYER (442-893)	.03	.01	.00
☐ 1 Jose Canseco	.25	.10	.02
☐ 2 Ken Griffey Jr.	.75	.30	.07
☐ 3 Ryne Sandberg	.20	.08	.02
☐ 4 Nolan Ryan	.35	.15	.03
☐ 5 Bo Jackson	.25	.10	.02
☐ 6 Bret Saberhagen UER (In bio, missed misspelled as mised)	.08	.03	.01
☐ 7 Will Clark	.20	.08	.02
☐ 8 Ellis Burks	.08	.03	.01
☐ 9 Joe Carter	.10	.04	.01
☐ 10 Rickey Henderson	.20	.08	.02
☐ 11 Ozzie Guillen	.06	.02	.00
☐ 12 Wade Boggs	.12	.05	.01
☐ 13 Jerome Walton	.08	.03	.01
☐ 14 John Franco	.03	.01	.00
☐ 15 Ricky Jordan UER (League misspelled as legue)	.06	.02	.00
☐ 16 Wally Backman	.03	.01	.00
☐ 17 Rob Dibble	.06	.02	.00
☐ 18 Glenn Braggs	.03	.01	.00
☐ 19 Cory Snyder	.06	.02	.00
☐ 20 Kal Daniels	.06	.02	.00
☐ 21 Mark Langston	.06	.02	.00
☐ 22 Kevin Gross	.03	.01	.00
☐ 23 Don Mattingly UER (First line, ' is missing from Yankee)	.12	.05	.01
☐ 24 Dave Righetti	.06	.02	.00
☐ 25 Roberto Alomar	.12	.05	.01
☐ 26 Robby Thompson	.03	.01	.00
☐ 27 Jack McDowell	.06	.02	.00
☐ 28 Bip Roberts UER (Bio reads playd)	.03	.01	.00
☐ 29 Jay Howell	.03	.01	.00
☐ 30 Dave Stieb UER (17 wins in bio, 18 in stats)	.06	.02	.00
☐ 31 Johnny Ray	.03	.01	.00
☐ 32 Steve Sax	.06	.02	.00
☐ 33 Terry Mulholland	.03	.01	.00
☐ 34 Lee Guetterman	.03	.01	.00
☐ 35 Tim Raines	.08	.03	.01
☐ 36 Scott Fletcher	.03	.01	.00
☐ 37 Lance Parrish	.06	.02	.00
☐ 38 Tony Phillips UER (Born 4/15, should be 4/25)	.03	.01	.00
☐ 39 Todd Stottlemyre	.06	.02	.00
☐ 40 Alan Trammell	.08	.03	.01
☐ 41 Todd Burns	.03	.01	.00
☐ 42 Mookie Wilson	.03	.01	.00
☐ 43 Chris Bosio	.03	.01	.00
☐ 44 Jeffrey Leonard	.03	.01	.00
☐ 45 Doug Jones	.03	.01	.00
☐ 46 Mike Scott UER (in first line, dominate should read dominating)	.06	.02	.00
☐ 47 Andy Hawkins	.03	.01	.00
☐ 48 Harold Reynolds	.06	.02	.00
☐ 49 Paul Molitor	.08	.03	.01
☐ 50 John Farrell	.03	.01	.00
☐ 51 Danny Darwin	.03	.01	.00
☐ 52 Jeff Blauser	.03	.01	.00

□ 53 John Tudor UER (41 wins in '81)	.06	.02	.00
□ 54 Milt Thompson	.03	.01	.00
□ 55 Dave Justice	.50	.20	.05
□ 56 Greg Olson	.06	.02	.00
□ 57 Willie Blair	.03	.01	.00
□ 58 Rick Parker	.03	.01	.00
□ 59 Shawn Boskie	.03	.01	.00
□ 60 Kevin Tapani	.06	.02	.00
□ 61 Dave Hollins	.08	.03	.01
□ 62 Scott Radinsky	.06	.02	.00
□ 63 Francisco Cabrera	.03	.01	.00
□ 64 Tim Layana	.03	.01	.00
□ 65 Jim Leyritz	.03	.01	.00
□ 66 Wayne Edwards	.03	.01	.00
□ 67 Lee Stevens	.08	.03	.01
□ 68 Bill Sampen UER (Fourth line, long is spelled along)	.03	.01	.00
□ 69 Craig Grebeck UER (Born in Cerritos, not Johnstown)	.03	.01	.00
□ 70 John Burkett	.03	.01	.00
□ 71 Hector Villanueva	.06	.02	.00
□ 72 Oscar Azocar	.03	.01	.00
□ 73 Alan Mills	.03	.01	.00
□ 74 Carlos Baerga	.10	.04	.01
□ 75 Charles Nagy	.10	.04	.01
□ 76 Tim Drummond	.03	.01	.00
□ 77 Dana Kiecker	.03	.01	.00
□ 78 Tom Edens	.08	.03	.01
□ 79 Kent Mercker	.06	.02	.00
□ 80 Steve Avery	.30	.12	.03
□ 81 Lee Smith	.06	.02	.00
□ 82 Dave Martinez	.03	.01	.00
□ 83 Dave Winfield	.10	.04	.01
□ 84 Bill Spiers	.03	.01	.00
□ 85 Dan Pasqua	.03	.01	.00
□ 86 Randy Milligan	.06	.02	.00
□ 87 Tracy Jones	.03	.01	.00
□ 88 Greg Myers	.03	.01	.00
□ 89 Keith Hernandez	.06	.02	.00
□ 90 Todd Benzinger	.03	.01	.00
□ 91 Mike Jackson	.03	.01	.00
□ 92 Mike Stanley	.03	.01	.00
□ 93 Candy Maldonado	.03	.01	.00
□ 94 John Kruk UER (No decimal point before 1990 BA)	.03	.01	.00
□ 95 Cal Ripken UER (Genius spelled genuis)	.20	.08	.02
□ 96 Willie Fraser	.03	.01	.00
□ 97 Mike Felder	.03	.01	.00
□ 98 Bill Landrum	.03	.01	.00
□ 99 Chuck Crim	.03	.01	.00
□ 100 Chuck Finley	.06	.02	.00
□ 101 Kirk Manwaring	.03	.01	.00
□ 102 Jaime Navarro	.03	.01	.00
□ 103 Dickie Thon	.03	.01	.00
□ 104 Brian Downing	.03	.01	.00
□ 105 Jim Abbott	.10	.04	.01
□ 106 Tom Brookens	.03	.01	.00
□ 107 Darryl Hamilton UER (Bio info is for Jeff Hamilton)	.03	.01	.00
□ 108 Bryan Harvey	.06	.02	.00
□ 109 Greg A. Harris UER (Shown pitching lefty, bio says righty)	.03	.01	.00
□ 110 Greg Swindell	.06	.02	.00
□ 111 Juan Berenguer	.03	.01	.00
□ 112 Mike Heath	.03	.01	.00
□ 113 Scott Bradley	.03	.01	.00
□ 114 Jack Morris	.08	.03	.01
□ 115 Barry Jones	.03	.01	.00
□ 116 Kevin Romine	.03	.01	.00
□ 117 Garry Templeton	.03	.01	.00
□ 118 Scott Sanderson	.03	.01	.00
□ 119 Roberto Kelly	.08	.03	.01
□ 120 George Brett	.10	.04	.01
□ 121 Oddibe McDowell	.03	.01	.00
□ 122 Jim Acker	.03	.01	.00
□ 123 Bill Swift UER (Born 12/27/61, should be 10/27)	.03	.01	.00
□ 124 Eric King	.03	.01	.00
□ 125 Jay Buhner	.06	.02	.00
□ 126 Matt Young	.03	.01	.00
□ 127 Alvaro Espinoza	.03	.01	.00
□ 128 Greg Hibbard	.03	.01	.00
□ 129 Jeff M. Robinson	.03	.01	.00
□ 130 Mike Greenwell	.10	.04	.01
□ 131 Dion James	.03	.01	.00
□ 132 Donn Pall UER (1988 ERA in stats 0.00)	.03	.01	.00
□ 133 Lloyd Moseby	.03	.01	.00
□ 134 Randy Velarde	.03	.01	.00
□ 135 Allan Anderson	.03	.01	.00
□ 136 Mark Davis	.03	.01	.00
□ 137 Eric Davis	.10	.04	.01
□ 138 Phil Stephenson	.03	.01	.00
□ 139 Felix Fermin	.03	.01	.00
□ 140 Pedro Guerrero	.06	.02	.00
□ 141 Charlie Hough	.03	.01	.00
□ 142 Mike Henneman	.03	.01	.00
□ 143 Jeff Montgomery	.03	.01	.00
□ 144 Lenny Harris	.03	.01	.00
□ 145 Bruce Hurst	.06	.02	.00
□ 146 Eric Anthony	.08	.03	.01
□ 147 Paul Assenmacher	.03	.01	.00
□ 148 Jesse Barfield	.06	.02	.00
□ 149 Carlos Quintana	.06	.02	.00
□ 150 Dave Stewart	.08	.03	.01
□ 151 Roy Smith	.03	.01	.00
□ 152 Paul Gibson	.03	.01	.00
□ 153 Mickey Hatcher	.03	.01	.00

☐ 154 Jim Eisenreich	.03	.01	.00
☐ 155 Kenny Rogers	.03	.01	.00
☐ 156 Dave Schmidt	.03	.01	.00
☐ 157 Lance Johnson	.03	.01	.00
☐ 158 Dave West	.03	.01	.00
☐ 159 Steve Balboni	.03	.01	.00
☐ 160 Jeff Brantley	.03	.01	.00
☐ 161 Craig Biggio	.06	.02	.00
☐ 162 Brook Jacoby	.03	.01	.00
☐ 163 Dan Gladden	.03	.01	.00
☐ 164 Jeff Reardon UER (Total IP shown as 943.2, should be 943.1)	.06	.02	.00
☐ 165 Mark Carreon	.03	.01	.00
☐ 166 Mel Hall	.03	.01	.00
☐ 167 Gary Mielke	.03	.01	.00
☐ 168 Cecil Fielder	.15	.06	.01
☐ 169 Darrin Jackson	.03	.01	.00
☐ 170 Rick Aguilera	.03	.01	.00
☐ 171 Walt Weiss	.06	.02	.00
☐ 172 Steve Farr	.03	.01	.00
☐ 173 Jody Reed	.06	.02	.00
☐ 174 Mike Jeffcoat	.03	.01	.00
☐ 175 Mark Grace	.08	.03	.01
☐ 176 Larry Sheets	.03	.01	.00
☐ 177 Bill Gullickson	.06	.02	.00
☐ 178 Chris Gwynn	.03	.01	.00
☐ 179 Melido Perez	.03	.01	.00
☐ 180 Sid Fernandez UER (779 runs in 1990)	.06	.02	.00
☐ 181 Tim Burke	.03	.01	.00
☐ 182 Gary Pettis	.03	.01	.00
☐ 183 Rob Murphy	.03	.01	.00
☐ 184 Craig Lefferts	.03	.01	.00
☐ 185 Howard Johnson	.08	.03	.01
☐ 186 Ken Caminiti	.03	.01	.00
☐ 187 Tim Belcher	.06	.02	.00
☐ 188 Greg Cadaret	.03	.01	.00
☐ 189 Matt Williams	.10	.04	.01
☐ 190 Dave Magadan	.06	.02	.00
☐ 191 Geno Petralli	.03	.01	.00
☐ 192 Jeff D. Robinson	.03	.01	.00
☐ 193 Jim Deshaies	.03	.01	.00
☐ 194 Willie Randolph	.03	.01	.00
☐ 195 George Bell	.08	.03	.01
☐ 196 Hubie Brooks	.06	.02	.00
☐ 197 Tom Gordon	.06	.02	.00
☐ 198 Mike Fitzgerald	.03	.01	.00
☐ 199 Mike Pagliarulo	.03	.01	.00
☐ 200 Kirby Puckett	.12	.05	.01
☐ 201 Shawon Dunston	.06	.02	.00
☐ 202 Dennis Boyd	.03	.01	.00
☐ 203 Junior Felix UER (Text has him in NL)	.06	.02	.00
☐ 204 Alejandro Pena	.06	.02	.00
☐ 205 Pete Smith	.03	.01	.00
☐ 206 Tom Glavine UER (Lefty spelled leftie)	.12	.05	.01
☐ 207 Luis Salazar	.03	.01	.00
☐ 208 John Smoltz	.10	.04	.01
☐ 209 Doug Dascenzo	.03	.01	.00
☐ 210 Tim Wallach	.06	.02	.00
☐ 211 Greg Gagne	.03	.01	.00
☐ 212 Mark Gubicza	.03	.01	.00
☐ 213 Mark Parent	.03	.01	.00
☐ 214 Ken Oberkfell	.03	.01	.00
☐ 215 Gary Carter	.08	.03	.01
☐ 216 Rafael Palmeiro	.10	.04	.01
☐ 217 Tom Niedenfuer	.03	.01	.00
☐ 218 Dave LaPoint	.03	.01	.00
☐ 219 Jeff Treadway	.03	.01	.00
☐ 220 Mitch Williams UER ('89 ERA shown as 2.76, should be 2.64)	.03	.01	.00
☐ 221 Jose DeLeon	.03	.01	.00
☐ 222 Mike LaValliere	.03	.01	.00
☐ 223 Darrel Akerfelds	.03	.01	.00
☐ 224A Kent Anderson ERR (first line, flachy should read flashy)	.03	.01	.00
☐ 224B Kent Anderson COR (corrected in factory sets)	.03	.01	.00
☐ 225 Dwight Evans	.06	.02	.00
☐ 226 Gary Redus	.03	.01	.00
☐ 227 Paul O'Neill	.06	.02	.00
☐ 228 Marty Barrett	.03	.01	.00
☐ 229 Tom Browning	.06	.02	.00
☐ 230 Terry Pendleton	.03	.01	.00
☐ 231 Jack Armstrong	.06	.02	.00
☐ 232 Mike Boddicker	.03	.01	.00
☐ 233 Neal Heaton	.03	.01	.00
☐ 234 Marquis Grissom	.10	.04	.01
☐ 235 Bert Blyleven	.06	.02	.00
☐ 236 Curt Young	.03	.01	.00
☐ 237 Don Carman	.03	.01	.00
☐ 238 Charlie Hayes	.03	.01	.00
☐ 239 Mark Knudson	.03	.01	.00
☐ 240 Todd Zeile	.10	.04	.01
☐ 241 Larry Walker UER (Maple River, should be Maple Ridge)	.06	.02	.00
☐ 242 Jerald Clark	.03	.01	.00
☐ 243 Jeff Ballard	.03	.01	.00
☐ 244 Jeff King	.03	.01	.00
☐ 245 Tom Brunansky	.06	.02	.00
☐ 246 Darren Daulton	.03	.01	.00
☐ 247 Scott Terry	.03	.01	.00
☐ 248 Rob Deer	.06	.02	.00
☐ 249 Brady Anderson UER (1990 Hagerstown 1 hit, should say 13 hits)	.03	.01	.00
☐ 250 Len Dykstra	.06	.02	.00
☐ 251 Greg W. Harris	.03	.01	.00
☐ 252 Mike Hartley	.03	.01	.00
☐ 253 Joey Cora	.03	.01	.00

☐ 254 Ivan Calderon	.06	.02	.00
☐ 255 Ted Power	.03	.01	.00
☐ 256 Sammy Sosa	.08	.03	.01
☐ 257 Steve Buechele	.03	.01	.00
☐ 258 Mike Devereaux UER (No comma between city and state)	.03	.01	.00
☐ 259 Brad Komminsk UER (Last text line, Ba should be BA)	.03	.01	.00
☐ 260 Teddy Higuera	.03	.01	.00
☐ 261 Shawn Abner	.03	.01	.00
☐ 262 Dave Valle	.03	.01	.00
☐ 263 Jeff Huson	.03	.01	.00
☐ 264 Edgar Martinez	.06	.02	.00
☐ 265 Carlton Fisk	.10	.04	.01
☐ 266 Steve Finley	.06	.02	.00
☐ 267 John Wetteland	.06	.02	.00
☐ 268 Kevin Appier	.06	.02	.00
☐ 269 Steve Lyons	.03	.01	.00
☐ 270 Mickey Tettleton	.06	.02	.00
☐ 271 Luis Rivera	.03	.01	.00
☐ 272 Steve Jeltz	.03	.01	.00
☐ 273 R.J. Reynolds	.03	.01	.00
☐ 274 Carlos Martinez	.03	.01	.00
☐ 275 Dan Plesac	.03	.01	.00
☐ 276 Mike Morgan UER (Total IP shown as 1149.1, should be 1149)	.03	.01	.00
☐ 277 Jeff Russell	.03	.01	.00
☐ 278 Pete Incaviglia	.06	.02	.00
☐ 279 Kevin Seitzer UER (Bio has 200 hits twice and .300 four times, should be once and three times)	.06	.02	.00
☐ 280 Bobby Thigpen	.06	.02	.00
☐ 281 Stan Javier UER (Born 1/9, should say 9/1)	.03	.01	.00
☐ 282 Henry Cotto	.03	.01	.00
☐ 283 Gary Wayne	.03	.01	.00
☐ 284 Shane Mack	.06	.02	.00
☐ 285 Brian Holman	.06	.02	.00
☐ 286 Gerald Perry	.03	.01	.00
☐ 287 Steve Crawford	.03	.01	.00
☐ 288 Nelson Liriano	.03	.01	.00
☐ 289 Don Aase	.03	.01	.00
☐ 290 Randy Johnson	.06	.02	.00
☐ 291 Harold Baines	.06	.02	.00
☐ 292 Kent Hrbek	.06	.02	.00
☐ 293A Les Lancaster ERR (No comma between Dallas and Texas)	.06	.02	.00
☐ 293B Les Lancaster COR (corrected in factory sets)	.06	.02	.00
☐ 294 Jeff Musselman	.03	.01	.00
☐ 295 Kurt Stillwell	.03	.01	.00
☐ 296 Stan Belinda	.03	.01	.00
☐ 297 Lou Whitaker	.06	.02	.00
☐ 298 Glenn Wilson	.03	.01	.00
☐ 299 Omar Vizquel UER (Born 5/15, should be 4/24, there is a decimal before GP total for '90)	.03	.01	.00
☐ 300 Ramon Martinez	.10	.04	.01
☐ 301 Dwight Smith	.03	.01	.00
☐ 302 Tim Crews	.03	.01	.00
☐ 303 Lance Blankenship	.03	.01	.00
☐ 304 Sid Bream	.03	.01	.00
☐ 305 Rafael Ramirez	.03	.01	.00
☐ 306 Steve Wilson	.03	.01	.00
☐ 307 Mackey Sasser	.03	.01	.00
☐ 308 Franklin Stubbs	.03	.01	.00
☐ 309 Jack Daugherty UER (Born 6/3/60, should say July)	.03	.01	.00
☐ 310 Eddie Murray	.10	.04	.01
☐ 311 Bob Welch	.06	.02	.00
☐ 312 Brian Harper	.06	.02	.00
☐ 313 Lance McCullers	.03	.01	.00
☐ 314 Dave Smith	.03	.01	.00
☐ 315 Bobby Bonilla	.10	.04	.01
☐ 316 Jerry Don Gleaton	.03	.01	.00
☐ 317 Greg Maddux	.06	.02	.00
☐ 318 Keith Miller	.03	.01	.00
☐ 319 Mark Portugal	.03	.01	.00
☐ 320 Robin Ventura	.20	.08	.02
☐ 321 Bob Ojeda	.03	.01	.00
☐ 322 Mike Harkey	.06	.02	.00
☐ 323 Jay Bell	.03	.01	.00
☐ 324 Mark McGwire	.10	.04	.01
☐ 325 Gary Gaetti	.06	.02	.00
☐ 326 Jeff Pico	.03	.01	.00
☐ 327 Kevin McReynolds	.06	.02	.00
☐ 328 Frank Tanana	.06	.02	.00
☐ 329 Eric Yelding UER (Listed as 6'3", should be 5'11")	.03	.01	.00
☐ 330 Barry Bonds	.12	.05	.01
☐ 331 Brian McRae RP UER (No comma between city and state)	.45	.18	.04
☐ 332 Pedro Munoz RP	.17	.07	.01
☐ 333 Daryl Irvine RP	.08	.03	.01
☐ 334 Chris Hoiles RP	.08	.03	.01
☐ 335 Thomas Howard RP	.10	.04	.01
☐ 336 Jeff Schulz RP	.10	.04	.01
☐ 337 Jeff Manto RP	.06	.02	.00
☐ 338 Beau Allred RP	.06	.02	.00
☐ 339 Mike Bordick RP	.10	.04	.01
☐ 340 Todd Hundley RP	.10	.04	.01
☐ 341 Jim Vatcher RP UER (Height 6'9", should be 5'9")	.08	.03	.01

☐ 342 Luis Sojo RP	.08	.03	.01
☐ 343 Jose Offerman RP UER (Born 1969, should say 1968)	.10	.04	.01
☐ 344 Pete Coachman RP	.12	.05	.01
☐ 345 Mike Benjamin RP	.08	.03	.01
☐ 346 Ozzie Canseco RP	.08	.03	.01
☐ 347 Tim McIntosh RP	.08	.03	.01
☐ 348 Phil Plantier RP	1.25	.50	.12
☐ 349 Terry Shumpert RP	.03	.01	.00
☐ 350 Darren Lewis RP	.20	.08	.02
☐ 351 David Walsh RP	.10	.04	.01
☐ 352A Scott Chiamparino RP ERR (Bats left, should be right)	.10	.04	.01
☐ 352B Scott Chiamparino RP COR (corrected in factory sets)	.10	.04	.01
☐ 353 Julio Valera RP UER (Progressed misspelled as progessed)	.08	.03	.01
☐ 354 Anthony Telford RP	.08	.03	.01
☐ 355 Kevin Wickander RP	.03	.01	.00
☐ 356 Tim Naehring RP	.10	.04	.01
☐ 357 Jim Poole RP	.10	.04	.01
☐ 358 Mark Whiten RP UER (Shown hitting lefty, bio says righty)	.20	.08	.02
☐ 359 Terry Wells RP	.08	.03	.01
☐ 360 Rafael Valdez RP	.06	.02	.00
☐ 361 Mel Stottlemyre Jr. RP	.03	.01	.00
☐ 362 David Segui RP	.08	.03	.01
☐ 363 Paul Abbott RP	.10	.04	.01
☐ 364 Steve Howard RP	.08	.03	.01
☐ 365 Karl Rhodes RP	.08	.03	.01
☐ 366 Rafael Novoa RP	.08	.03	.01
☐ 367 Joe Grahe RP	.08	.03	.01
☐ 368 Darren Reed RP	.08	.03	.01
☐ 369 Jeff McKnight RP	.08	.03	.01
☐ 370 Scott Leius RP	.10	.04	.01
☐ 371 Mark Dewey RP	.10	.04	.01
☐ 372 Mark Lee RP UER (Shown hitting lefty, bio says righty, born in Dakota, should say North Dakota)	.10	.04	.01
☐ 373 Rosario Rodriguez RP (Shown hitting lefty, bio says righty) UER	.10	.04	.01
☐ 374 Chuck McElroy RP	.08	.03	.01
☐ 375 Mike Bell RP	.10	.04	.01
☐ 376 Mickey Morandini RP	.10	.04	.01
☐ 377 Bill Haselman RP	.08	.03	.01
☐ 378 Dave Pavlas RP	.08	.03	.01
☐ 379 Derrick May RP	.08	.03	.01
☐ 380 Jeromy Burnitz FDP	.75	.30	.07
☐ 381 Donald Peters FDP	.15	.06	.01
☐ 382 Alex Fernandez FDP	.20	.08	.02
☐ 383 Michael Mussina FDP	.35	.15	.03
☐ 384 Daniel Smith FDP	.12	.05	.01
☐ 385 Lance Dickson FDP	.17	.07	.01
☐ 386 Carl Everett FDP	.25	.10	.02
☐ 387 Thomas Nevers FDP	.15	.06	.01
☐ 388 Adam Hyzdu FDP	.15	.06	.01
☐ 389 Todd Van Poppel FDP	1.25	.50	.12
☐ 390 Rondell White FDP	.40	.16	.04
☐ 391 Marc Newfield FDP	1.00	.40	.10
☐ 392 Julio Franco AS	.06	.02	.00
☐ 393 Wade Boggs AS	.08	.03	.01
☐ 394 Ozzie Guillen AS	.06	.02	.00
☐ 395 Cecil Fielder AS	.10	.04	.01
☐ 396 Ken Griffey Jr. AS	.30	.12	.03
☐ 397 Rickey Henderson AS	.12	.05	.01
☐ 398 Jose Canseco AS	.15	.06	.01
☐ 399 Roger Clemens AS	.10	.04	.01
☐ 400 Sandy Alomar Jr. AS	.08	.03	.01
☐ 401 Bobby Thigpen AS	.06	.02	.00
☐ 402 Bobby Bonilla MB	.08	.03	.01
☐ 403 Eric Davis MB	.08	.03	.01
☐ 404 Fred McGriff MB	.08	.03	.01
☐ 405 Glenn Davis MB	.06	.02	.00
☐ 406 Kevin Mitchell MB	.08	.03	.01
☐ 407 Rob Dibble KM	.06	.02	.00
☐ 408 Ramon Martinez KM	.08	.03	.01
☐ 409 David Cone KM	.06	.02	.00
☐ 410 Bobby Witt KM	.06	.02	.00
☐ 411 Mark Langston KM	.06	.02	.00
☐ 412 Bo Jackson RIF	.15	.06	.01
☐ 413 Shawon Dunston RIF UER (In the baseball, should say in baseball)	.06	.02	.00
☐ 414 Jesse Barfield RIF	.06	.02	.00
☐ 415 Ken Caminiti RIF	.03	.01	.00
☐ 416 Benito Santiago RIF	.06	.02	.00
☐ 417 Nolan Ryan HL	.20	.08	.02
☐ 418 Bobby Thigpen HL UER (Back refers to Hal McRae Jr., should say Brian McRae)	.06	.02	.00
☐ 419 Ramon Martinez HL	.08	.03	.01
☐ 420 Bo Jackson HL	.15	.06	.01
☐ 421 Carlton Fisk HL	.08	.03	.01
☐ 422 Jimmy Key	.06	.02	.00
☐ 423 Junior Noboa	.03	.01	.00
☐ 424 Al Newman	.03	.01	.00
☐ 425 Pat Borders	.03	.01	.00
☐ 426 Von Hayes	.06	.02	.00
☐ 427 Tim Teufel	.03	.01	.00
☐ 428 Eric Plunk UER (Text says Eric's had, no apostrophe needed)	.03	.01	.00
☐ 429 John Moses	.03	.01	.00
☐ 430 Mike Witt	.03	.01	.00
☐ 431 Otis Nixon	.06	.02	.00
☐ 432 Tony Fernandez	.06	.02	.00
☐ 433 Rance Mulliniks	.03	.01	.00

□ 434 Dan Petry	.03	.01	.00
□ 435 Bob Geren	.03	.01	.00
□ 436 Steve Frey	.06	.02	.00
□ 437 Jamie Moyer	.03	.01	.00
□ 438 Junior Ortiz	.03	.01	.00
□ 439 Tom O'Malley	.03	.01	.00
□ 440 Pat Combs	.03	.01	.00
□ 441 Jose Canseco DT	2.25	.90	.22
□ 442 Alfredo Griffin	.03	.01	.00
□ 443 Andres Galarraga	.06	.02	.00
□ 444 Bryn Smith	.03	.01	.00
□ 445 Andre Dawson	.10	.04	.01
□ 446 Juan Samuel	.06	.02	.00
□ 447 Mike Aldrete	.03	.01	.00
□ 448 Ron Gant	.12	.05	.01
□ 449 Fernando Valenzuela	.06	.02	.00
□ 450 Vince Coleman UER (Should say topped majors in steals four times, not three times)	.08	.03	.01
□ 451 Kevin Mitchell	.10	.04	.01
□ 452 Spike Owen	.03	.01	.00
□ 453 Mike Bielecki	.03	.01	.00
□ 454 Dennis Martinez	.06	.02	.00
□ 455 Brett Butler	.06	.02	.00
□ 456 Ron Darling	.06	.02	.00
□ 457 Dennis Rasmussen	.03	.01	.00
□ 458 Ken Howell	.03	.01	.00
□ 459 Steve Bedrosian	.03	.01	.00
□ 460 Frank Viola	.08	.03	.01
□ 461 Jose Lind	.03	.01	.00
□ 462 Chris Sabo	.08	.03	.01
□ 463 Dante Bichette	.03	.01	.00
□ 464 Rick Mahler	.03	.01	.00
□ 465 John Smiley	.03	.01	.00
□ 466 Devon White	.06	.02	.00
□ 467 John Orton	.03	.01	.00
□ 468 Mike Stanton	.03	.01	.00
□ 469 Billy Hatcher	.03	.01	.00
□ 470 Wally Joyner	.08	.03	.01
□ 471 Gene Larkin	.03	.01	.00
□ 472 Doug Drabek	.06	.02	.00
□ 473 Gary Sheffield	.08	.03	.01
□ 474 David Wells	.03	.01	.00
□ 475 Andy Van Slyke	.08	.03	.01
□ 476 Mike Gallego	.03	.01	.00
□ 477 B.J. Surhoff	.03	.01	.00
□ 478 Gene Nelson	.03	.01	.00
□ 479 Mariano Duncan	.03	.01	.00
□ 480 Fred McGriff	.08	.03	.01
□ 481 Jerry Browne	.03	.01	.00
□ 482 Alvin Davis	.06	.02	.00
□ 483 Bill Wegman	.03	.01	.00
□ 484 Dave Parker	.08	.03	.01
□ 485 Dennis Eckersley	.06	.02	.00
□ 486 Erik Hanson UER (Basketball misspelled as baseketball)	.06	.02	.00
□ 487 Bill Ripken	.03	.01	.00
□ 488 Tom Candiotti	.06	.02	.00
□ 489 Mike Schooler	.03	.01	.00
□ 490 Gregg Olson	.06	.02	.00
□ 491 Chris James	.03	.01	.00
□ 492 Pete Harnisch	.06	.02	.00
□ 493 Julio Franco	.08	.03	.01
□ 494 Greg Briley	.03	.01	.00
□ 495 Ruben Sierra	.12	.05	.01
□ 496 Steve Olin	.03	.01	.00
□ 497 Mike Fetters	.03	.01	.00
□ 498 Mark Williams	.08	.03	.01
□ 499 Bob Tewksbury	.03	.01	.00
□ 500 Tony Gwynn	.12	.05	.01
□ 501 Randy Myers	.03	.01	.00
□ 502 Keith Comstock	.03	.01	.00
□ 503 Craig Worthington UER (DeCinces misspelled DiCinces on back)	.03	.01	.00
□ 504 Mark Eichhorn UER (Stats incomplete, doesn't have '89 Braves stint)	.03	.01	.00
□ 505 Barry Larkin	.08	.03	.01
□ 506 Dave Johnson	.03	.01	.00
□ 507 Bobby Witt	.06	.02	.00
□ 508 Joe Orsulak	.03	.01	.00
□ 509 Pete O'Brien	.03	.01	.00
□ 510 Brad Arnsberg	.03	.01	.00
□ 511 Storm Davis	.03	.01	.00
□ 512 Bob Milacki	.03	.01	.00
□ 513 Bill Pecota	.03	.01	.00
□ 514 Glenallen Hill	.03	.01	.00
□ 515 Danny Tartabull	.08	.03	.01
□ 516 Mike Moore	.03	.01	.00
□ 517 Ron Robinson UER (577 K's in 1990)	.03	.01	.00
□ 518 Mark Gardner	.03	.01	.00
□ 519 Rick Wrona	.03	.01	.00
□ 520 Mike Scioscia	.03	.01	.00
□ 521 Frank Wills	.03	.01	.00
□ 522 Greg Brock	.03	.01	.00
□ 523 Jack Clark	.06	.02	.00
□ 524 Bruce Ruffin	.03	.01	.00
□ 525 Robin Yount	.10	.04	.01
□ 526 Tom Foley	.03	.01	.00
□ 527 Pat Perry	.03	.01	.00
□ 528 Greg Vaughn	.10	.04	.01
□ 529 Wally Whitehurst	.03	.01	.00
□ 530 Norm Charlton	.03	.01	.00
□ 531 Marvell Wynne	.03	.01	.00
□ 532 Jim Gantner	.03	.01	.00
□ 533 Greg Litton	.03	.01	.00
□ 534 Manny Lee	.03	.01	.00
□ 535 Scott Bailes	.03	.01	.00
□ 536 Charlie Leibrandt	.03	.01	.00
□ 537 Roger McDowell	.03	.01	.00
□ 538 Andy Benes	.08	.03	.01

No.	Player			
☐ 539	Rick Honeycutt	.03	.01	.00
☐ 540	Dwight Gooden	.10	.04	.01
☐ 541	Scott Garrelts	.03	.01	.00
☐ 542	Dave Clark	.03	.01	.00
☐ 543	Lonnie Smith	.06	.02	.00
☐ 544	Rick Reuschel	.06	.02	.00
☐ 545	Delino DeShields UER (Rockford misspelled as Rock Ford in '88)	.10	.04	.01
☐ 546	Mike Sharperson	.03	.01	.00
☐ 547	Mike Kingery	.03	.01	.00
☐ 548	Terry Kennedy	.03	.01	.00
☐ 549	David Cone	.08	.03	.01
☐ 550	Orel Hershiser	.08	.03	.01
☐ 551	Matt Nokes	.06	.02	.00
☐ 552	Eddie Williams	.03	.01	.00
☐ 553	Frank DiPino	.03	.01	.00
☐ 554	Fred Lynn	.06	.02	.00
☐ 555	Alex Cole	.08	.03	.01
☐ 556	Terry Leach	.03	.01	.00
☐ 557	Chet Lemon	.03	.01	.00
☐ 558	Paul Mirabella	.03	.01	.00
☐ 559	Bill Long	.03	.01	.00
☐ 560	Phil Bradley	.03	.01	.00
☐ 561	Duane Ward	.03	.01	.00
☐ 562	Dave Bergman	.03	.01	.00
☐ 563	Eric Show	.03	.01	.00
☐ 564	Xavier Hernandez	.06	.02	.00
☐ 565	Jeff Parrett	.03	.01	.00
☐ 566	Chuck Cary	.03	.01	.00
☐ 567	Ken Hill	.03	.01	.00
☐ 568	Bob Welch Hand (Complement should be compliment) UER	.06	.02	.00
☐ 569	John Mitchell	.03	.01	.00
☐ 570	Travis Fryman	.45	.18	.04
☐ 571	Derek Lilliquist	.03	.01	.00
☐ 572	Steve Lake	.03	.01	.00
☐ 573	John Barfield	.08	.03	.01
☐ 574	Randy Bush	.03	.01	.00
☐ 575	Joe Magrane	.03	.01	.00
☐ 576	Eddie Diaz	.08	.03	.01
☐ 577	Casey Candaele	.03	.01	.00
☐ 578	Jesse Orosco	.03	.01	.00
☐ 579	Tom Henke	.06	.02	.00
☐ 580	Rick Cerone UER (Actually his third go-round with Yankees)	.03	.01	.00
☐ 581	Drew Hall	.03	.01	.00
☐ 582	Tony Castillo	.06	.02	.00
☐ 583	Jimmy Jones	.03	.01	.00
☐ 584	Rick Reed	.03	.01	.00
☐ 585	Joe Girardi	.03	.01	.00
☐ 586	Jeff Gray	.08	.03	.01
☐ 587	Luis Polonia	.03	.01	.00
☐ 588	Joe Klink	.06	.02	.00
☐ 589	Rex Hudler	.03	.01	.00
☐ 590	Kirk McCaskill	.03	.01	.00
☐ 591	Juan Agosto	.03	.01	.00
☐ 592	Wes Gardner	.03	.01	.00
☐ 593	Rich Rodriguez	.08	.03	.01
☐ 594	Mitch Webster	.03	.01	.00
☐ 595	Kelly Gruber	.06	.02	.00
☐ 596	Dale Mohorcic	.03	.01	.00
☐ 597	Willie McGee	.06	.02	.00
☐ 598	Bill Krueger	.03	.01	.00
☐ 599	Bob Walk UER (Cards says he's 33, but actually he's 34)	.03	.01	.00
☐ 600	Kevin Maas	.15	.06	.01
☐ 601	Danny Jackson	.03	.01	.00
☐ 602	Craig McMurtry UER (Anonymously misspelled anonimously)	.03	.01	.00
☐ 603	Curtis Wilkerson	.03	.01	.00
☐ 604	Adam Peterson	.03	.01	.00
☐ 605	Sam Horn	.03	.01	.00
☐ 606	Tommy Gregg	.03	.01	.00
☐ 607	Ken Dayley	.03	.01	.00
☐ 608	Carmelo Castillo	.03	.01	.00
☐ 609	John Shelby	.03	.01	.00
☐ 610	Don Slaught	.03	.01	.00
☐ 611	Calvin Schiraldi	.03	.01	.00
☐ 612	Dennis Lamp	.03	.01	.00
☐ 613	Andres Thomas	.03	.01	.00
☐ 614	Jose Gonzalez	.03	.01	.00
☐ 615	Randy Ready	.03	.01	.00
☐ 616	Kevin Bass	.03	.01	.00
☐ 617	Mike Marshall	.06	.02	.00
☐ 618	Daryl Boston	.03	.01	.00
☐ 619	Andy McGaffigan	.03	.01	.00
☐ 620	Joe Oliver	.03	.01	.00
☐ 621	Jim Gott	.03	.01	.00
☐ 622	Jose Oquendo	.03	.01	.00
☐ 623	Jose DeJesus	.03	.01	.00
☐ 624	Mike Brumley	.03	.01	.00
☐ 625	John Olerud	.12	.05	.01
☐ 626	Ernest Riles	.03	.01	.00
☐ 627	Gene Harris	.03	.01	.00
☐ 628	Jose Uribe	.03	.01	.00
☐ 629	Darnell Coles	.03	.01	.00
☐ 630	Carney Lansford	.06	.02	.00
☐ 631	Tim Leary	.03	.01	.00
☐ 632	Tim Hulett	.03	.01	.00
☐ 633	Kevin Elster	.03	.01	.00
☐ 634	Tony Fossas	.03	.01	.00
☐ 635	Francisco Oliveras	.03	.01	.00
☐ 636	Bob Patterson	.03	.01	.00
☐ 637	Gary Ward	.03	.01	.00
☐ 638	Rene Gonzales	.03	.01	.00
☐ 639	Don Robinson	.03	.01	.00
☐ 640	Darryl Strawberry	.15	.06	.01
☐ 641	Dave Anderson	.03	.01	.00
☐ 642	Scott Scudder	.03	.01	.00

No.	Player			
☐ 643	Reggie Harris UER (Hepatitis misspelled as hepititis)	.08	.03	.01
☐ 644	Dave Henderson	.06	.02	.00
☐ 645	Ben McDonald	.10	.04	.01
☐ 646	Bob Kipper	.03	.01	.00
☐ 647	Hal Morris UER (It's should be its)	.10	.04	.01
☐ 648	Tim Birtsas	.03	.01	.00
☐ 649	Steve Searcy	.03	.01	.00
☐ 650	Dale Murphy	.10	.04	.01
☐ 651	Ron Oester	.03	.01	.00
☐ 652	Mike LaCoss	.03	.01	.00
☐ 653	Ron Jones	.03	.01	.00
☐ 654	Kelly Downs	.03	.01	.00
☐ 655	Roger Clemens	.15	.06	.01
☐ 656	Herm Winningham	.03	.01	.00
☐ 657	Trevor Wilson	.03	.01	.00
☐ 658	Jose Rijo	.06	.02	.00
☐ 659	Dann Bilardello UER (Bio has 13 games, 1 hit, and 32 AB, stats show 19, 2, and 37)	.03	.01	.00
☐ 660	Gregg Jefferies	.08	.03	.01
☐ 661	Doug Drabek AS UER (Through is mis-spelled though)	.06	.02	.00
☐ 662	Randy Myers AS	.03	.01	.00
☐ 663	Benny Santiago AS	.06	.02	.00
☐ 664	Will Clark AS	.12	.05	.01
☐ 665	Ryne Sandberg AS	.12	.05	.01
☐ 666	Barry Larkin AS UER (Line 13, coolly misspelled cooly)	.08	.03	.01
☐ 667	Matt Williams AS	.08	.03	.01
☐ 668	Barry Bonds AS	.08	.03	.01
☐ 669	Eric Davis AS	.08	.03	.01
☐ 670	Bobby Bonilla AS	.08	.03	.01
☐ 671	Chipper Jones FDP	.30	.12	.03
☐ 672	Eric Christopherson FDP	.12	.05	.01
☐ 673	Robbie Beckett FDP	.12	.05	.01
☐ 674	Shane Andrews FDP	.20	.08	.02
☐ 675	Steve Karsay FDP	.25	.10	.02
☐ 676	Aaron Holbert FDP	.15	.06	.01
☐ 677	Donovan Osborne FDP	.15	.06	.01
☐ 678	Todd Ritchie FDP	.15	.06	.01
☐ 679	Ron Walden FDP	.15	.06	.01
☐ 680	Tim Costo FDP	.25	.10	.02
☐ 681	Dan Wilson FDP	.20	.08	.02
☐ 682	Kurt Miller FDP	.17	.07	.01
☐ 683	Mike Lieberthal FDP	.12	.05	.01
☐ 684	Roger Clemens KM	.10	.04	.01
☐ 685	Doc Gooden KM	.08	.03	.01
☐ 686	Nolan Ryan KM	.20	.08	.02
☐ 687	Frank Viola KM	.06	.02	.00
☐ 688	Erik Hanson KM	.06	.02	.00
☐ 689	Matt Williams MB	.08	.03	.01
☐ 690	Jose Canseco MB UER (Mammoth misspelled as monmouth)	.15	.06	.01
☐ 691	Darryl Strawberry MB	.10	.04	.01
☐ 692	Bo Jackson MB	.15	.06	.01
☐ 693	Cecil Fielder MB	.10	.04	.01
☐ 694	Sandy Alomar Jr. RF	.08	.03	.01
☐ 695	Cory Snyder RF	.06	.02	.00
☐ 696	Eric Davis RF	.08	.03	.01
☐ 697	Ken Griffey Jr. RF	.30	.12	.03
☐ 698	Andy Van Slyke RF UER (Line 2, outfielders does not need)	.06	.02	.00
☐ 699	Langston/Witt NH Mark Langston Mike Witt	.06	.02	.00
☐ 700	Randy Johnson NH	.06	.02	.00
☐ 701	Nolan Ryan NH	.30	.12	.03
☐ 702	Dave Stewart NH	.06	.02	.00
☐ 703	Fernando Valenzuela NH	.06	.02	.00
☐ 704	Andy Hawkins NH	.03	.01	.00
☐ 705	Melido Perez NH	.03	.01	.00
☐ 706	Terry Mulholland NH	.03	.01	.00
☐ 707	Dave Stieb NH	.06	.02	.00
☐ 708	Brian Barnes RP	.12	.05	.01
☐ 709	Bernard Gilkey RP	.15	.06	.01
☐ 710	Steve Decker RP	.25	.10	.02
☐ 711	Paul Faries RP	.08	.03	.01
☐ 712	Paul Marak RP	.08	.03	.01
☐ 713	Wes Chamberlain RP	.45	.18	.04
☐ 714	Kevin Belcher RP	.10	.04	.01
☐ 715	Dan Boone RP UER (IP adds up to 101, but card has 101.2)	.03	.01	.00
☐ 716	Steve Adkins RP	.10	.04	.01
☐ 717	Geronimo Pena RP	.08	.03	.01
☐ 718	Howard Farmer RP	.03	.01	.00
☐ 719	Mark Leonard RP	.12	.05	.01
☐ 720	Tom Lampkin RP	.03	.01	.00
☐ 721	Mike Gardiner RP	.15	.06	.01
☐ 722	Jeff Conine RP	.15	.06	.01
☐ 723	Efrain Valdez RP	.08	.03	.01
☐ 724	Chuck Malone RP	.06	.02	.00
☐ 725	Leo Gomez RP	.25	.10	.02
☐ 726	Paul McClellan RP	.15	.06	.01
☐ 727	Mark Leiter RP	.12	.05	.01
☐ 728	Rich DeLucia RP UER (Line 2, all told is written alltold)	.12	.05	.01
☐ 729	Mel Rojas RP	.08	.03	.01
☐ 730	Hector Wagner RP	.10	.04	.01
☐ 731	Ray Lankford RP	.25	.10	.02
☐ 732	Turner Ward RP	.15	.06	.01
☐ 733	Gerald Alexander RP	.10	.04	.01
☐ 734	Scott Anderson RP	.08	.03	.01

☐	735 Tony Perezchica RP	.06	.02	.00
☐	736 Jimmy Kremers RP	.06	.02	.00
☐	737 American Flag (Pray for Peace)	.30	.12	.03
☐	738 Mike York RP	.10	.04	.01
☐	739 Mike Rochford RP	.06	.02	.00
☐	740 Scott Aldred RP	.08	.03	.01
☐	741 Rico Brogna RP	.25	.10	.02
☐	742 Dave Burba RP	.08	.03	.01
☐	743 Ray Stephens RP	.10	.04	.01
☐	744 Eric Gunderson RP	.06	.02	.00
☐	745 Troy Afenir RP	.08	.03	.01
☐	746 Jeff Shaw RP	.08	.03	.01
☐	747 Orlando Merced RP	.35	.15	.03
☐	748 Omar Olivares RP UER (Line 9, league is misspelled legaue)	.10	.04	.01
☐	749 Jerry Kutzler RP	.03	.01	.00
☐	750 Mo Vaughn RP UER (44 SB's in 1990)	.30	.12	.03
☐	751 Matt Stark RP	.12	.05	.01
☐	752 Randy Hennis RP	.08	.03	.01
☐	753 Andujar Cedeno RP	.35	.15	.03
☐	754 Kelvin Torve RP	.06	.02	.00
☐	755 Joe Kraemer RP	.06	.02	.00
☐	756 Phil Clark RP	.15	.06	.01
☐	757 Ed Vosberg RP	.08	.03	.01
☐	758 Mike Perez RP	.08	.03	.01
☐	759 Scott Lewis RP	.10	.04	.01
☐	760 Steve Chitren RP	.08	.03	.01
☐	761 Ray Young RP	.10	.04	.01
☐	762 Andres Santana RP	.15	.06	.01
☐	763 Rodney McCray RP	.10	.04	.01
☐	764 Sean Berry RP UER (Name misspelled Barry on card front)	.12	.05	.01
☐	765 Brent Mayne RP	.06	.02	.00
☐	766 Mike Simms RP	.12	.05	.01
☐	767 Glenn Sutko RP	.10	.04	.01
☐	768 Gary DiSarcina RP	.03	.01	.00
☐	769 George Brett HL	.08	.03	.01
☐	770 Cecil Fielder HL	.10	.04	.01
☐	771 Jim Presley	.03	.01	.00
☐	772 John Dopson	.03	.01	.00
☐	773 Bo Jackson Breaker	.25	.10	.02
☐	774 Brent Knackert UER (Born in 1954, shown throwing righty, but bio says lefty)	.06	.02	.00
☐	775 Bill Doran UER (Reds in NL East)	.03	.01	.00
☐	776 Dick Schofield	.03	.01	.00
☐	777 Nelson Santovenia	.03	.01	.00
☐	778 Mark Guthrie	.06	.02	.00
☐	779 Mark Lemke	.03	.01	.00
☐	780 Terry Steinbach	.03	.01	.00
☐	781 Tom Bolton	.03	.01	.00
☐	782 Randy Tomlin	.17	.07	.01
☐	783 Jeff Kunkel	.03	.01	.00
☐	784 Felix Jose	.10	.04	.01
☐	785 Rick Sutcliffe	.06	.02	.00
☐	786 John Cerutti	.03	.01	.00
☐	787 Jose Vizcaino UER (Offerman not Opperman)	.03	.01	.00
☐	788 Curt Schilling	.03	.01	.00
☐	789 Ed Whitson	.03	.01	.00
☐	790 Tony Pena	.06	.02	.00
☐	791 John Candelaria	.03	.01	.00
☐	792 Carmelo Martinez	.03	.01	.00
☐	793 Sandy Alomar Jr. UER (Indian's should say Indians')	.08	.03	.01
☐	794 Jim Neidlinger	.10	.04	.01
☐	795 Barry Larkin WS and Chris Sabo	.08	.03	.01
☐	796 Paul Sorrento	.03	.01	.00
☐	797 Tom Pagnozzi	.03	.01	.00
☐	798 Tino Martinez	.15	.06	.01
☐	799 Scott Ruskin UER (Text says first three seasons but lists averages for four)	.08	.03	.01
☐	800 Kirk Gibson	.06	.02	.00
☐	801 Walt Terrell	.03	.01	.00
☐	802 John Russell	.03	.01	.00
☐	803 Chili Davis	.06	.02	.00
☐	804 Chris Nabholz	.08	.03	.01
☐	805 Juan Gonzalez	.30	.12	.03
☐	806 Ron Hassey	.03	.01	.00
☐	807 Todd Worrell	.03	.01	.00
☐	808 Tommy Greene	.03	.01	.00
☐	809 Joel Skinner UER (Joel, not Bob, was drafted in 1979)	.03	.01	.00
☐	810 Benito Santiago	.06	.02	.00
☐	811 Pat Tabler UER (Line 3, always misspelled alway)	.03	.01	.00
☐	812 Scott Erickson UER (Record spelled rcord)	.75	.30	.07
☐	813 Moises Alou	.08	.03	.01
☐	814 Dale Sveum	.03	.01	.00
☐	815 Ryne Sandberg MANYR	.25	.10	.02
☐	816 Rick Dempsey	.03	.01	.00
☐	817 Scott Bankhead	.03	.01	.00
☐	818 Jason Grimsley	.03	.01	.00
☐	819 Doug Jennings	.03	.01	.00
☐	820 Tom Herr	.03	.01	.00
☐	821 Rob Ducey	.03	.01	.00
☐	822 Luis Quinones	.03	.01	.00
☐	823 Greg Minton	.03	.01	.00
☐	824 Mark Grant	.03	.01	.00
☐	825 Ozzie Smith UER (Shortstop misspelled shortsop)	.10	.04	.01
☐	826 Dave Eiland	.03	.01	.00

☐ 827 Danny Heep .03 .01 .00
☐ 828 Hensley Meulens .08 .03 .01
☐ 829 Charlie O'Brien .03 .01 .00
☐ 830 Glenn Davis .06 .02 .00
☐ 831 John Marzano UER .03 .01 .00
(International mis-
spelled Internaional)
☐ 832 Steve Ontiveros .03 .01 .00
☐ 833 Ron Karkovice .03 .01 .00
☐ 834 Jerry Goff .06 .02 .00
☐ 835 Ken Griffey Sr. .06 .02 .00
☐ 836 Kevin Reimer .08 .03 .01
☐ 837 Randy Kutcher UER .03 .01 .00
(Infectious mis-
spelled infectous)
☐ 838 Mike Blowers .03 .01 .00
☐ 839 Mike Macfarlane .03 .01 .00
☐ 840 Frank Thomas UER 1.25 .50 .12
(1989 Sarasota stats,
15 games but 188 AB)
☐ 841 The Griffeys 1.25 .50 .12
Ken Griffey Jr.
Ken Griffey Sr.
☐ 842 Jack Howell .03 .01 .00
☐ 843 Goose Gozzo .03 .01 .00
☐ 844 Gerald Young .03 .01 .00
☐ 845 Zane Smith .06 .02 .00
☐ 846 Kevin Brown .03 .01 .00
☐ 847 Sil Campusano .03 .01 .00
☐ 848 Larry Andersen .03 .01 .00
☐ 849 Cal Ripken FRAN .15 .06 .01
☐ 850 Roger Clemens FRAN .12 .05 .01
☐ 851 Sandy Alomar Jr. FRAN .08 .03 .01
☐ 852 Alan Trammell FRAN .08 .03 .01
☐ 853 George Brett FRAN .08 .03 .01
☐ 854 Robin Yount FRAN .08 .03 .01
☐ 855 Kirby Puckett FRAN .10 .04 .01
☐ 856 Don Mattingly FRAN .12 .05 .01
☐ 857 Rickey Henderson FRAN .20 .08 .02
☐ 858 Ken Griffey Jr. FRAN .60 .25 .06
☐ 859 Ruben Sierra FRAN .12 .05 .01
☐ 860 John Olerud FRAN .10 .04 .01
☐ 861 Dave Justice FRAN .50 .20 .05
☐ 862 Ryne Sandberg FRAN .25 .10 .02
☐ 863 Eric Davis FRAN .08 .03 .01
☐ 864 Darryl Strawberry FRAN .12 .05 .01
☐ 865 Tim Wallach FRAN .06 .02 .00
☐ 866 Doc Gooden FRAN .08 .03 .01
☐ 867 Len Dykstra FRAN .06 .02 .00
☐ 868 Barry Bonds FRAN .08 .03 .01
☐ 869 Todd Zeile FRAN UER .10 .04 .01
(Powerful misspelled
as poweful)
☐ 870 Benito Santiago FRAN .06 .02 .00
☐ 871 Will Clark FRAN .20 .08 .02
☐ 872 Craig Biggio FRAN .06 .02 .00
☐ 873 Wally Joyner FRAN .08 .03 .01
☐ 874 Frank Thomas FRAN .90 .40 .09
☐ 875 Rickey Henderson MVP .12 .05 .01
☐ 876 Barry Bonds MVP .08 .03 .01
☐ 877 Bob Welch CY .06 .02 .00
☐ 878 Doug Drabek CY .06 .02 .00
☐ 879 Sandy Alomar Jr ROY .08 .03 .01
☐ 880 Dave Justice ROY .30 .12 .03
☐ 881 Damon Berryhill .03 .01 .00
☐ 882 Frank Viola DT .12 .05 .01
☐ 883 Dave Stewart DT .15 .06 .01
☐ 884 Doug Jones DT .06 .02 .00
☐ 885 Randy Myers DT .06 .02 .00
☐ 886 Will Clark DT .40 .16 .04
☐ 887 Roberto Alomar DT .20 .08 .02
☐ 888 Barry Larkin DT .15 .06 .01
☐ 889 Wade Boggs DT .30 .12 .03
☐ 890 Rickey Henderson DT .90 .40 .09
☐ 891 Kirby Puckett DT .30 .12 .03
☐ 892 Ken Griffey Jr DT 1.50 .60 .15
☐ 893 Benny Santiago DT .15 .06 .01

1991 Score Cooperstown

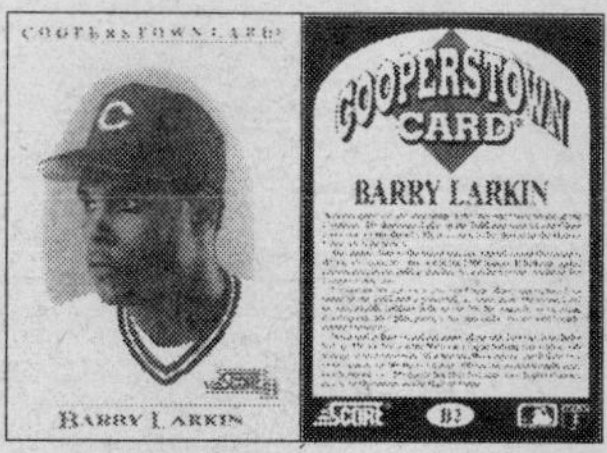

These standard-size (2 1/2" by 3 1/2") cards were available only as a set contained in factory sets, and their design is not like that of the regular Score issue. On a white card face, the fronts feature portraits of the players in an oval-shaped format. The words "Cooperstown Card" and a thin yellow stripe traverse the top of the card, while another yellow stripe and the player's name appears at the bottom. On a pale yellow background with green borders, the backs summarize the player's accomplishments. The cards are numbered on the back.

	MINT	VG-E	F-G
COMPLETE SET (7)	10.00	4.50	1.25
COMMON PLAYER (B1-B7)	.75	.30	.07
☐ B1 Wade Boggs	1.50	.60	.15
☐ B2 Barry Larkin	.75	.30	.07
☐ B3 Ken Griffey Jr.	4.00	1.75	.40
☐ B4 Rickey Henderson	2.00	.80	.20
☐ B5 George Brett	1.25	.50	.12
☐ B6 Will Clark	2.00	.80	.20
☐ B7 Nolan Ryan	3.00	1.25	.30

1991 Score Rookie/ Traded

The 1991 Score Rookie and Traded set contains 110 standard-size (2 1/2" by 3 1/2") player cards and 10 "World Series II" magic motion trivia cards. The front design features glossy color action photos, with white and purple borders on a mauve card face. The player's name, team, and position are given above the pictures. In a horizontal format, the left portion of the back has a color head shot and biography, while the right portion has statistics and player profile on a pale yellow background. The cards are numbered on the back. Cards 1-80 feature traded players, while cards 81-110 focus on rookies.

	MINT	EXC	G-VG
COMPLETE SET (110)	10.00	4.50	1.25
COMMON PLAYER (1T-80T)	.05	.02	.00
COMMON PLAYER (81T-110T)	.10	.04	.01
☐ 1T Bo Jackson	1.00	.40	.10
☐ 2T Mike Flanagan	.08	.03	.01
☐ 3T Pete Incaviglia	.08	.03	.01
☐ 4T Jack Clark	.10	.04	.01
☐ 5T Hubie Brooks	.08	.03	.01
☐ 6T Ivan Calderon	.08	.03	.01
☐ 7T Glenn Davis	.10	.04	.01
☐ 8T Wally Backman	.05	.02	.00
☐ 9T Dave Smith	.05	.02	.00
☐ 10T Tim Raines	.10	.04	.01
☐ 11T Joe Carter	.10	.04	.01
☐ 12T Sid Bream	.05	.02	.00
☐ 13T George Bell	.10	.04	.01
☐ 14T Steve Bedrosian	.08	.03	.01
☐ 15T Willie Wilson	.08	.03	.01
☐ 16T Darryl Strawberry	.20	.08	.02
☐ 17T Danny Jackson	.05	.02	.00
☐ 18T Kirk Gibson	.10	.04	.01
☐ 19T Willie McGee	.08	.03	.01
☐ 20T Junior Felix	.05	.02	.00
☐ 21T Steve Farr	.05	.02	.00
☐ 22T Pat Tabler	.05	.02	.00
☐ 23T Brett Butler	.08	.03	.01
☐ 24T Danny Darwin	.05	.02	.00
☐ 25T Mickey Tettleton	.08	.03	.01
☐ 26T Gary Carter	.10	.04	.01
☐ 27T Mitch Williams	.08	.03	.01
☐ 28T Candy Maldonado	.05	.02	.00
☐ 29T Otis Nixon	.08	.03	.01
☐ 30T Brian Downing	.05	.02	.00
☐ 31T Tom Candiotti	.08	.03	.01
☐ 32T John Candelaria	.05	.02	.00
☐ 33T Rob Murphy	.05	.02	.00
☐ 34T Deion Sanders	.12	.05	.01
☐ 35T Willie Randolph	.08	.03	.01
☐ 36T Pete Harnisch	.08	.03	.01
☐ 37T Dante Bichette	.05	.02	.00
☐ 38T Garry Templeton	.05	.02	.00
☐ 39T Gary Gaetti	.08	.03	.01
☐ 40T John Cerutti	.05	.02	.00
☐ 41T Rick Cerone	.05	.02	.00
☐ 42T Mike Pagliarulo	.05	.02	.00
☐ 43T Ron Hassey	.05	.02	.00
☐ 44T Roberto Alomar	.12	.05	.01
☐ 45T Mike Boddicker	.05	.02	.00
☐ 46T Bud Black	.05	.02	.00
☐ 47T Rob Deer	.08	.03	.01
☐ 48T Devon White	.08	.03	.01
☐ 49T Luis Sojo	.05	.02	.00
☐ 50T Terry Pendleton	.10	.04	.01
☐ 51T Kevin Gross	.05	.02	.00
☐ 52T Mike Huff	.05	.02	.00
☐ 53T Dave Righetti	.08	.03	.01
☐ 54T Matt Young	.05	.02	.00
☐ 55T Earnest Riles	.05	.02	.00
☐ 56T Bill Gullickson	.08	.03	.01
☐ 57T Vince Coleman	.10	.04	.01
☐ 58T Fred McGriff	.12	.05	.01
☐ 59T Franklin Stubbs	.05	.02	.00

☐ 60T Eric King	.05	.02	.00
☐ 61T Cory Snyder	.08	.03	.01
☐ 62T Dwight Evans	.08	.03	.01
☐ 63T Gerald Perry	.05	.02	.00
☐ 64T Eric Show	.05	.02	.00
☐ 65T Shawn Hillegas	.05	.02	.00
☐ 66T Tony Fernandez	.08	.03	.01
☐ 67T Tim Teufel	.05	.02	.00
☐ 68T Mitch Webster	.05	.02	.00
☐ 69T Mike Heath	.05	.02	.00
☐ 70T Chili Davis	.08	.03	.01
☐ 71T Larry Andersen	.05	.02	.00
☐ 72T Gary Varsho	.05	.02	.00
☐ 73T Juan Berenguer	.05	.02	.00
☐ 74T Jack Morris	.10	.04	.01
☐ 75T Barry Jones	.05	.02	.00
☐ 76T Rafael Belliard	.05	.02	.00
☐ 77T Steve Buechele	.05	.02	.00
☐ 78T Scott Sanderson	.05	.02	.00
☐ 79T Bob Ojeda	.05	.02	.00
☐ 80T Curt Schilling	.05	.02	.00
☐ 81T Brian Drahman	.10	.04	.01
☐ 82T Ivan Rodriguez	2.00	.80	.20
☐ 83T David Howard	.12	.05	.01
☐ 84T Heathcliff Slocumb	.12	.05	.01
☐ 85T Mike Timlin	.12	.05	.01
☐ 86T Darryl Kile	.12	.05	.01
☐ 87T Pete Schourek	.12	.05	.01
☐ 88T Bruce Walton	.12	.05	.01
☐ 89T Al Osuna	.15	.06	.01
☐ 90T Gary Scott	.25	.10	.02
☐ 91T Doug Simons	.12	.05	.01
☐ 92T Chris Jones	.15	.06	.01
☐ 93T Chuck Knoblauch	.40	.16	.04
☐ 94T Dana Allison	.15	.06	.01
☐ 95T Erik Pappas	.12	.05	.01
☐ 96T Jeff Bagwell	3.00	1.25	.30
☐ 97T Kirk Dressendorfer	.25	.10	.02
☐ 98T Freddie Benavides	.12	.05	.01
☐ 99T Luis Gonzalez	.45	.18	.04
☐ 100T Wade Taylor	.17	.07	.01
☐ 101T Ed Sprague	.12	.05	.01
☐ 102T Bob Scanlan	.12	.05	.01
☐ 103T Rick Wilkins	.17	.07	.01
☐ 104T Chris Donnels	.25	.10	.02
☐ 105T Joe Slusarski	.12	.05	.01
☐ 106T Mark Lewis	.20	.08	.02
☐ 107T Pat Kelly	.30	.12	.03
☐ 108T John Briscoe	.15	.06	.01
☐ 109T Luis Lopez	.20	.08	.02
☐ 110T Jeff Johnson	.20	.08	.02

1992 Score I

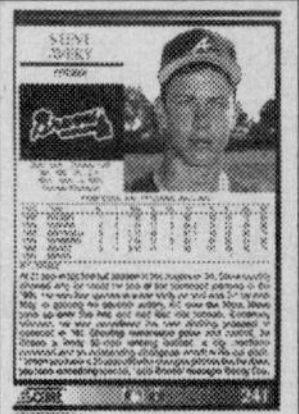

The 1992 Score I set contains 442 cards measuring the standard size (2 1/2" by 3 1/2"). The glossy color action photos on the fronts are bordered above and below by stripes of the same color, and a thicker, different color stripe runs the length of the card to one side of the picture. The backs have a color close-up shot in the upper right corner, with biography, complete career statistics, and player profile printed on a yellow background. Hall of Famer Joe DiMaggio is remembered in a five-card subset. He autographed 2,500 cards; 2,495 of these were randomly inserted in Series I packs, while the other five were given away through a mail-in sweepstakes. Another 150,000 unsigned DiMaggio cards were inserted in Series I Count Goods packs only. Score later extended its DiMaggio promotion to Series I blister packs; one hundred signed and twelve thousand unsigned cards were randomly inserted in these packs. Also a special "World Series II" trivia card was inserted into each pack. These cards highlight crucial games and heroes from past Octobers. Topical subsets included in the set focus on Rookie Prospects (395-424), No-Hit Club (425-428), Highlights (429-430), AL All-Stars (431-440; with color montages displaying Chris Greco's player caricatures), and Dream Team (441-442). The cards are numbered on the back.

	MINT	EXC	G-VG
COMPLETE SET (442)	13.50	6.00	1.85
COMMON PLAYER (1-442)	.03	.01	.00
☐ 1 Ken Griffey Jr.	.50	.20	.05
☐ 2 Nolan Ryan	.30	.12	.03
☐ 3 Will Clark	.20	.08	.02

☐ 4 Dave Justice	.30	.12	.03
☐ 5 Dave Henderson	.06	.02	.00
☐ 6 Bret Saberhagen	.08	.03	.01
☐ 7 Fred McGriff	.08	.03	.01
☐ 8 Erik Hanson	.06	.02	.00
☐ 9 Darryl Strawberry	.15	.06	.01
☐ 10 Dwight Gooden	.08	.03	.01
☐ 11 Juan Gonzalez	.25	.10	.02
☐ 12 Mark Langston	.06	.02	.00
☐ 13 Lonnie Smith	.03	.01	.00
☐ 14 Jeff Montgomery	.03	.01	.00
☐ 15 Roberto Alomar	.08	.03	.01
☐ 16 Delino DeShields	.06	.02	.00
☐ 17 Steve Bedrosian	.03	.01	.00
☐ 18 Terry Pendleton	.06	.02	.00
☐ 19 Mark Carreon	.03	.01	.00
☐ 20 Mark McGwire	.10	.04	.01
☐ 21 Roger Clemens	.15	.06	.01
☐ 22 Chuck Crim	.03	.01	.00
☐ 23 Don Mattingly	.12	.05	.01
☐ 24 Dickie Thon	.03	.01	.00
☐ 25 Ron Gant	.10	.04	.01
☐ 26 Milt Cuyler	.08	.03	.01
☐ 27 Mike Macfarlane	.03	.01	.00
☐ 28 Dan Gladden	.03	.01	.00
☐ 29 Melido Perez	.03	.01	.00
☐ 30 Willie Randolph	.03	.01	.00
☐ 31 Albert Belle	.12	.05	.01
☐ 32 Dave Winfield	.10	.04	.01
☐ 33 Jimmy Jones	.03	.01	.00
☐ 34 Kevin Gross	.03	.01	.00
☐ 35 Andres Galarraga	.06	.02	.00
☐ 36 Mike Devereaux	.03	.01	.00
☐ 37 Chris Bosio	.03	.01	.00
☐ 38 Mike LaValliere	.03	.01	.00
☐ 39 Gary Gaetti	.06	.02	.00
☐ 40 Felix Jose	.08	.03	.01
☐ 41 Alvaro Espinoza	.03	.01	.00
☐ 42 Rick Aguilera	.03	.01	.00
☐ 43 Mike Gallego	.03	.01	.00
☐ 44 Eric Davis	.10	.04	.01
☐ 45 George Bell	.08	.03	.01
☐ 46 Tom Brunansky	.06	.02	.00
☐ 47 Steve Farr	.03	.01	.00
☐ 48 Duane Ward	.03	.01	.00
☐ 49 David Wells	.03	.01	.00
☐ 50 Cecil Fielder	.15	.06	.01
☐ 51 Walt Weiss	.06	.02	.00
☐ 52 Todd Zeile	.10	.04	.01
☐ 53 Doug Jones	.03	.01	.00
☐ 54 Bob Walk	.03	.01	.00
☐ 55 Rafael Palmeiro	.08	.03	.01
☐ 56 Rob Deer	.03	.01	.00
☐ 57 Paul O'Neill	.06	.02	.00
☐ 58 Jeff Reardon	.06	.02	.00
☐ 59 Randy Ready	.03	.01	.00
☐ 60 Scott Erickson	.17	.07	.01
☐ 61 Paul Molitor	.08	.03	.01
☐ 62 Jack McDowell	.08	.03	.01
☐ 63 Jim Acker	.03	.01	.00
☐ 64 Jay Buhner	.06	.02	.00
☐ 65 Travis Fryman	.15	.06	.01
☐ 66 Marquis Grissom	.08	.03	.01
☐ 67 Mike Harkey	.06	.02	.00
☐ 68 Luis Polonia	.06	.02	.00
☐ 69 Ken Caminiti	.03	.01	.00
☐ 70 Chris Sabo	.08	.03	.01
☐ 71 Gregg Olson	.06	.02	.00
☐ 72 Carlton Fisk	.10	.04	.01
☐ 73 Juan Samuel	.06	.02	.00
☐ 74 Todd Stottlemyre	.06	.02	.00
☐ 75 Andre Dawson	.10	.04	.01
☐ 76 Alvin Davis	.06	.02	.00
☐ 77 Bill Doran	.03	.01	.00
☐ 78 B.J. Surhoff	.06	.02	.00
☐ 79 Kirk McCaskill	.03	.01	.00
☐ 80 Dale Murphy	.10	.04	.01
☐ 81 Jose DeLeon	.03	.01	.00
☐ 82 Alex Fernandez	.10	.04	.01
☐ 83 Ivan Calderon	.06	.02	.00
☐ 84 Brent Mayne	.06	.02	.00
☐ 85 Jody Reed	.06	.02	.00
☐ 86 Randy Tomlin	.08	.03	.01
☐ 87 Randy Milligan	.06	.02	.00
☐ 88 Pascual Perez	.03	.01	.00
☐ 89 Hensley Meulens	.06	.02	.00
☐ 90 Joe Carter	.08	.03	.01
☐ 91 Mike Moore	.06	.02	.00
☐ 92 Ozzie Guillen	.06	.02	.00
☐ 93 Shawn Hillegas	.03	.01	.00
☐ 94 Chili Davis	.06	.02	.00
☐ 95 Vince Coleman	.08	.03	.01
☐ 96 Jimmy Key	.06	.02	.00
☐ 97 Billy Ripken	.03	.01	.00
☐ 98 Dave Smith	.03	.01	.00
☐ 99 Tom Bolton	.03	.01	.00
☐ 100 Barry Larkin	.08	.03	.01
☐ 101 Kenny Rogers	.03	.01	.00
☐ 102 Mike Boddicker	.03	.01	.00
☐ 103 Kevin Elster	.03	.01	.00
☐ 104 Ken Hill	.03	.01	.00
☐ 105 Charlie Leibrandt	.03	.01	.00
☐ 106 Pat Combs	.03	.01	.00
☐ 107 Hubie Brooks	.06	.02	.00
☐ 108 Julio Franco	.08	.03	.01
☐ 109 Vicente Palacios	.03	.01	.00
☐ 110 Kal Daniels	.06	.02	.00
☐ 111 Bruce Hurst	.06	.02	.00
☐ 112 Willie McGee	.06	.02	.00
☐ 113 Ted Power	.03	.01	.00
☐ 114 Milt Thompson	.03	.01	.00
☐ 115 Doug Drabek	.06	.02	.00
☐ 116 Rafael Belliard	.03	.01	.00
☐ 117 Scott Garrelts	.03	.01	.00
☐ 118 Terry Mulholland	.03	.01	.00
☐ 119 Jay Howell	.03	.01	.00

☐ 120 Danny Jackson	.03	.01	.00
☐ 121 Scott Ruskin	.03	.01	.00
☐ 122 Robin Ventura	.15	.06	.01
☐ 123 Bip Roberts	.03	.01	.00
☐ 124 Jeff Russell	.03	.01	.00
☐ 125 Hal Morris	.08	.03	.01
☐ 126 Teddy Higuera	.03	.01	.00
☐ 127 Luis Sojo	.03	.01	.00
☐ 128 Carlos Baerga	.08	.03	.01
☐ 129 Jeff Ballard	.03	.01	.00
☐ 130 Tom Gordon	.06	.02	.00
☐ 131 Sid Bream	.03	.01	.00
☐ 132 Rance Mulliniks	.03	.01	.00
☐ 133 Andy Benes	.08	.03	.01
☐ 134 Mickey Tettleton	.06	.02	.00
☐ 135 Rich DeLucia	.03	.01	.00
☐ 136 Tom Pagnozzi	.03	.01	.00
☐ 137 Harold Baines	.06	.02	.00
☐ 138 Danny Darwin	.03	.01	.00
☐ 139 Kevin Bass	.03	.01	.00
☐ 140 Chris Nabholz	.03	.01	.00
☐ 141 Pete O'Brien	.03	.01	.00
☐ 142 Jeff Treadway	.03	.01	.00
☐ 143 Mickey Morandini	.06	.02	.00
☐ 144 Eric King	.03	.01	.00
☐ 145 Danny Tartabull	.08	.03	.01
☐ 146 Lance Johnson	.03	.01	.00
☐ 147 Casey Candaele	.03	.01	.00
☐ 148 Felix Fermin	.03	.01	.00
☐ 149 Rich Rodriguez	.06	.02	.00
☐ 150 Dwight Evans	.06	.02	.00
☐ 151 Joe Klink	.03	.01	.00
☐ 152 Kevin Reimer	.06	.02	.00
☐ 153 Orlando Merced	.12	.05	.01
☐ 154 Mel Hall	.06	.02	.00
☐ 155 Randy Myers	.03	.01	.00
☐ 156 Greg Harris	.03	.01	.00
☐ 157 Jeff Brantley	.03	.01	.00
☐ 158 Jim Eisenreich	.03	.01	.00
☐ 159 Luis Rivera	.03	.01	.00
☐ 160 Cris Carpenter	.03	.01	.00
☐ 161 Bruce Ruffin	.03	.01	.00
☐ 162 Omar Vizquel	.03	.01	.00
☐ 163 Gerald Alexander	.03	.01	.00
☐ 164 Mark Guthrie	.03	.01	.00
☐ 165 Scott Lewis	.08	.03	.01
☐ 166 Bill Sampen	.03	.01	.00
☐ 167 Dave Anderson	.03	.01	.00
☐ 168 Kevin McReynolds	.06	.02	.00
☐ 169 Jose Vizcaino	.03	.01	.00
☐ 170 Bob Geren	.03	.01	.00
☐ 171 Mike Morgan	.06	.02	.00
☐ 172 Jim Gott	.03	.01	.00
☐ 173 Mike Pagliarulo	.03	.01	.00
☐ 174 Mike Jeffcoat	.03	.01	.00
☐ 175 Craig Lefferts	.03	.01	.00
☐ 176 Steve Finley	.06	.02	.00
☐ 177 Wally Backman	.03	.01	.00
☐ 178 Kent Mercker	.03	.01	.00
☐ 179 John Cerutti	.03	.01	.00
☐ 180 Jay Bell	.03	.01	.00
☐ 181 Dale Sveum	.03	.01	.00
☐ 182 Greg Gagne	.03	.01	.00
☐ 183 Donnie Hill	.03	.01	.00
☐ 184 Rex Hudler	.03	.01	.00
☐ 185 Pat Kelly	.10	.04	.01
☐ 186 Jeff Robinson	.03	.01	.00
☐ 187 Jeff Gray	.03	.01	.00
☐ 188 Jerry Willard	.03	.01	.00
☐ 189 Carlos Quintana	.06	.02	.00
☐ 190 Dennis Eckersley	.06	.02	.00
☐ 191 Kelly Downs	.03	.01	.00
☐ 192 Gregg Jefferies	.08	.03	.01
☐ 193 Darrin Fletcher	.03	.01	.00
☐ 194 Mike Jackson	.03	.01	.00
☐ 195 Eddie Murray	.10	.04	.01
☐ 196 Bill Landrum	.03	.01	.00
☐ 197 Eric Yelding	.03	.01	.00
☐ 198 Devon White	.06	.02	.00
☐ 199 Larry Walker	.06	.02	.00
☐ 200 Ryne Sandberg	.18	.08	.01
☐ 201 Dave Magadan	.06	.02	.00
☐ 202 Steve Chitren	.03	.01	.00
☐ 203 Scott Fletcher	.03	.01	.00
☐ 204 Dwayne Henry	.03	.01	.00
☐ 205 Scott Coolbaugh	.03	.01	.00
☐ 206 Tracy Jones	.03	.01	.00
☐ 207 Von Hayes	.06	.02	.00
☐ 208 Bob Melvin	.03	.01	.00
☐ 209 Scott Scudder	.03	.01	.00
☐ 210 Luis Gonzalez	.12	.05	.01
☐ 211 Scott Sanderson	.03	.01	.00
☐ 212 Chris Donnels	.12	.05	.01
☐ 213 Heathcliff Slocumb	.03	.01	.00
☐ 214 Mike Timlin	.06	.02	.00
☐ 215 Brian Harper	.03	.01	.00
☐ 216 Juan Berenguer	.03	.01	.00
☐ 217 Mike Henneman	.03	.01	.00
☐ 218 Bill Spiers	.03	.01	.00
☐ 219 Scott Terry	.03	.01	.00
☐ 220 Frank Viola	.06	.02	.00
☐ 221 Mark Eichhorn	.03	.01	.00
☐ 222 Ernest Riles	.03	.01	.00
☐ 223 Ray Lankford	.10	.04	.01
☐ 224 Pete Harnisch	.06	.02	.00
☐ 225 Bobby Bonilla	.10	.04	.01
☐ 226 Mike Scioscia	.03	.01	.00
☐ 227 Joel Skinner	.03	.01	.00
☐ 228 Brian Holman	.03	.01	.00
☐ 229 Gilberto Reyes	.03	.01	.00
☐ 230 Matt Williams	.10	.04	.01
☐ 231 Jaime Navarro	.03	.01	.00
☐ 232 Jose Rijo	.06	.02	.00
☐ 233 Atlee Hammaker	.03	.01	.00
☐ 234 Tim Teufel	.03	.01	.00
☐ 235 John Kruk	.03	.01	.00

☐ 236 Kurt Stillwell .03 .01 .00
☐ 237 Dan Pasqua .03 .01 .00
☐ 238 Tim Crews .03 .01 .00
☐ 239 Dave Gallagher .03 .01 .00
☐ 240 Leo Gomez .10 .04 .01
☐ 241 Steve Avery .20 .08 .02
☐ 242 Bill Gullickson .03 .01 .00
☐ 243 Mark Portugal .03 .01 .00
☐ 244 Lee Guetterman .03 .01 .00
☐ 245 Benito Santiago .08 .03 .01
☐ 246 Jim Gantner .03 .01 .00
☐ 247 Robby Thompson .03 .01 .00
☐ 248 Terry Shumpert .03 .01 .00
☐ 249 Mike Bell .06 .02 .00
☐ 250 Harold Reynolds .03 .01 .00
☐ 251 Mike Felder .03 .01 .00
☐ 252 Bill Pecota .03 .01 .00
☐ 253 Bill Krueger .03 .01 .00
☐ 254 Alfredo Griffin .03 .01 .00
☐ 255 Lou Whitaker .06 .02 .00
☐ 256 Roy Smith .03 .01 .00
☐ 257 Jerald Clark .03 .01 .00
☐ 258 Sammy Sosa .06 .02 .00
☐ 259 Tim Naehring .06 .02 .00
☐ 260 Dave Righetti .06 .02 .00
☐ 261 Paul Gibson .03 .01 .00
☐ 262 Chris James .03 .01 .00
☐ 263 Larry Andersen .03 .01 .00
☐ 264 Storm Davis .03 .01 .00
☐ 265 Jose Lind .03 .01 .00
☐ 266 Greg Hibbard .03 .01 .00
☐ 267 Norm Charlton .03 .01 .00
☐ 268 Paul Kilgus .03 .01 .00
☐ 269 Greg Maddux .06 .02 .00
☐ 270 Ellis Burks .08 .03 .01
☐ 271 Frank Tanana .06 .02 .00
☐ 272 Gene Larkin .03 .01 .00
☐ 273 Ron Hassey .03 .01 .00
☐ 274 Jeff Robinson .03 .01 .00
☐ 275 Steve Howe .03 .01 .00
☐ 276 Daryl Boston .03 .01 .00
☐ 277 Mark Lee .06 .02 .00
☐ 278 Jose Segura .06 .02 .00
☐ 279 Lance Blankenship .03 .01 .00
☐ 280 Don Slaught .03 .01 .00
☐ 281 Russ Swan .03 .01 .00
☐ 282 Bob Tewksbury .03 .01 .00
☐ 283 Geno Petralli .03 .01 .00
☐ 284 Shane Mack .06 .02 .00
☐ 285 Bob Scanlan .06 .02 .00
☐ 286 Tim Leary .06 .02 .00
☐ 287 John Smoltz .08 .03 .01
☐ 288 Pat Borders .03 .01 .00
☐ 289 Mark Davidson .03 .01 .00
☐ 290 Sam Horn .03 .01 .00
☐ 291 Lenny Harris .03 .01 .00
☐ 292 Franklin Stubbs .03 .01 .00
☐ 293 Thomas Howard .03 .01 .00
☐ 294 Steve Lyons .03 .01 .00
☐ 295 Francisco Oliveras .03 .01 .00
☐ 296 Terry Leach .03 .01 .00
☐ 297 Barry Jones .03 .01 .00
☐ 298 Lance Parrish .06 .02 .00
☐ 299 Wally Whitehurst .03 .01 .00
☐ 300 Bob Welch .06 .02 .00
☐ 301 Charlie Hayes .03 .01 .00
☐ 302 Charlie Hough .03 .01 .00
☐ 303 Gary Redus .03 .01 .00
☐ 304 Scott Bradley .03 .01 .00
☐ 305 Jose Oquendo .03 .01 .00
☐ 306 Pete Incaviglia .06 .02 .00
☐ 307 Marvin Freeman .03 .01 .00
☐ 308 Gary Pettis .03 .01 .00
☐ 309 Joe Slusarski .06 .02 .00
☐ 310 Kevin Seitzer .06 .02 .00
☐ 311 Jeff Reed .03 .01 .00
☐ 312 Pat Tabler .03 .01 .00
☐ 313 Mike Maddux .03 .01 .00
☐ 314 Bob Milacki .03 .01 .00
☐ 315 Eric Anthony .06 .02 .00
☐ 316 Dante Bichette .03 .01 .00
☐ 317 Steve Decker .10 .04 .01
☐ 318 Jack Clark .06 .02 .00
☐ 319 Doug Dascenzo .03 .01 .00
☐ 320 Scott Leius .06 .02 .00
☐ 321 Jim Lindeman .03 .01 .00
☐ 322 Bryan Harvey .06 .02 .00
☐ 323 Spike Owen .03 .01 .00
☐ 324 Roberto Kelly .08 .03 .01
☐ 325 Stan Belinda .03 .01 .00
☐ 326 Joey Cora .03 .01 .00
☐ 327 Jeff Innis .03 .01 .00
☐ 328 Willie Wilson .06 .02 .00
☐ 329 Juan Agosto .03 .01 .00
☐ 330 Charles Nagy .06 .02 .00
☐ 331 Scott Bailes .03 .01 .00
☐ 332 Pete Schourek .06 .02 .00
☐ 333 Mike Flanagan .06 .02 .00
☐ 334 Omar Olivares .06 .02 .00
☐ 335 Dennis Lamp .03 .01 .00
☐ 336 Tommy Greene .06 .02 .00
☐ 337 Randy Velarde .03 .01 .00
☐ 338 Tom Lampkin .03 .01 .00
☐ 339 John Russell .03 .01 .00
☐ 340 Bob Kipper .03 .01 .00
☐ 341 Todd Burns .03 .01 .00
☐ 342 Ron Jones .03 .01 .00
☐ 343 Dave Valle .03 .01 .00
☐ 344 Mike Heath .03 .01 .00
☐ 345 John Olerud .10 .04 .01
☐ 346 Gerald Young .03 .01 .00
☐ 347 Ken Patterson .03 .01 .00
☐ 348 Les Lancaster .03 .01 .00
☐ 349 Steve Crawford .03 .01 .00
☐ 350 John Candelaria .03 .01 .00
☐ 351 Mike Aldrete .03 .01 .00

No.	Player			
☐ 352	Mariano Duncan	.03	.01	.00
☐ 353	Julio Machado	.03	.01	.00
☐ 354	Ken Williams	.03	.01	.00
☐ 355	Walt Terrell	.03	.01	.00
☐ 356	Mitch Williams	.03	.01	.00
☐ 357	Al Newman	.03	.01	.00
☐ 358	Bud Black	.03	.01	.00
☐ 359	Joe Hesketh	.03	.01	.00
☐ 360	Paul Assenmacher	.03	.01	.00
☐ 361	Bo Jackson	.25	.10	.02
☐ 362	Jeff Blauser	.03	.01	.00
☐ 363	Mike Brumley	.03	.01	.00
☐ 364	Jim Deshaies	.03	.01	.00
☐ 365	Brady Anderson	.03	.01	.00
☐ 366	Chuck McElroy	.03	.01	.00
☐ 367	Matt Merullo	.03	.01	.00
☐ 368	Tim Belcher	.06	.02	.00
☐ 369	Luis Aquino	.03	.01	.00
☐ 370	Joe Oliver	.03	.01	.00
☐ 371	Greg Swindell	.06	.02	.00
☐ 372	Lee Stevens	.06	.02	.00
☐ 373	Mark Knudson	.03	.01	.00
☐ 374	Bill Wegman	.03	.01	.00
☐ 375	Jerry Don Gleaton	.03	.01	.00
☐ 376	Pedro Guerrero	.06	.02	.00
☐ 377	Randy Bush	.03	.01	.00
☐ 378	Greg Harris	.03	.01	.00
☐ 379	Eric Plunk	.03	.01	.00
☐ 380	Jose DeJesus	.03	.01	.00
☐ 381	Bobby Witt	.06	.02	.00
☐ 382	Curtis Wilkerson	.03	.01	.00
☐ 383	Gene Nelson	.03	.01	.00
☐ 384	Wes Chamberlain	.12	.05	.01
☐ 385	Tom Henke	.03	.01	.00
☐ 386	Mark Lemke	.03	.01	.00
☐ 387	Greg Briley	.03	.01	.00
☐ 388	Rafael Ramirez	.03	.01	.00
☐ 389	Tony Fossas	.03	.01	.00
☐ 390	Henry Cotto	.03	.01	.00
☐ 391	Tim Hulett	.03	.01	.00
☐ 392	Dean Palmer	.17	.07	.01
☐ 393	Glenn Braggs	.03	.01	.00
☐ 394	Mark Salas	.03	.01	.00
☐ 395	Rusty Meacham	.08	.03	.01
☐ 396	Andy Ashby	.08	.03	.01
☐ 397	Jose Melendez	.08	.03	.01
☐ 398	Warren Newson	.08	.03	.01
☐ 399	Frank Castillo	.08	.03	.01
☐ 400	Chito Martinez	.25	.10	.02
☐ 401	Bernie Williams	.12	.05	.01
☐ 402	Derek Bell	.15	.06	.01
☐ 403	Javier Ortiz	.06	.02	.00
☐ 404	Tim Sherrill	.06	.02	.00
☐ 405	Rob MacDonald	.06	.02	.00
☐ 406	Phil Plantier	.30	.12	.03
☐ 407	Troy Afenir	.03	.01	.00
☐ 408	Gino Minutelli	.08	.03	.01
☐ 409	Reggie Jefferson	.15	.06	.01
☐ 410	Mike Remlinger	.03	.01	.00
☐ 411	Carlos Rodriguez	.06	.02	.00
☐ 412	Joe Redfield	.15	.06	.01
☐ 413	Alonzo Powell	.06	.02	.00
☐ 414	Scott Livingstone UER (Travis Fryman, not Woody, should be referenced on back)	.10	.04	.01
☐ 415	Scott Kamieniecki	.06	.02	.00
☐ 416	Tim Spehr	.08	.03	.01
☐ 417	Brian Hunter	.35	.15	.03
☐ 418	Ced Landrum	.08	.03	.01
☐ 419	Bret Barberie	.15	.06	.01
☐ 420	Kevin Morton	.06	.02	.00
☐ 421	Doug Henry	.12	.05	.01
☐ 422	Doug Piatt	.08	.03	.01
☐ 423	Pat Rice	.12	.05	.01
☐ 424	Juan Guzman	.17	.07	.01
☐ 425	Nolan Ryan NH	.18	.08	.01
☐ 426	Tommy Greene NH	.06	.02	.00
☐ 427	Bob Milacki and Mike Flanagan NH (Mark Williamson and Gregg Olson)	.06	.02	.00
☐ 428	Wilson Alvarez NH	.06	.02	.00
☐ 429	Otis Nixon HL	.06	.02	.00
☐ 430	Rickey Henderson HL	.12	.05	.01
☐ 431	Cecil Fielder AS	.10	.04	.01
☐ 432	Julio Franco AS	.06	.02	.00
☐ 433	Cal Ripken AS	.12	.05	.01
☐ 434	Wade Boggs AS	.10	.04	.01
☐ 435	Joe Carter AS	.08	.03	.01
☐ 436	Ken Griffey Jr. AS	.20	.08	.02
☐ 437	Ruben Sierra AS	.10	.04	.01
☐ 438	Scott Erickson AS	.10	.04	.01
☐ 439	Tom Henke AS	.03	.01	.00
☐ 440	Terry Steinbach AS	.03	.01	.00
☐ 441	Rickey Henderson DT	.20	.08	.02
☐ 442	Ryne Sandberg DT	.25	.10	.02

1992 Score II

The 1992 Score II set marks the second year that Score has released their set in two different series. Series II contains 451 standard size (2 1/2" by 3 1/2") cards. Topical subsets, some of which are continuations from the first series, focus on Rookies (736-772, 814-877), NL All-Stars (773-782), Highlights (783, 795-797), No-Hit Club (784-787), Draft Picks (799-810), Memorabilia (878-

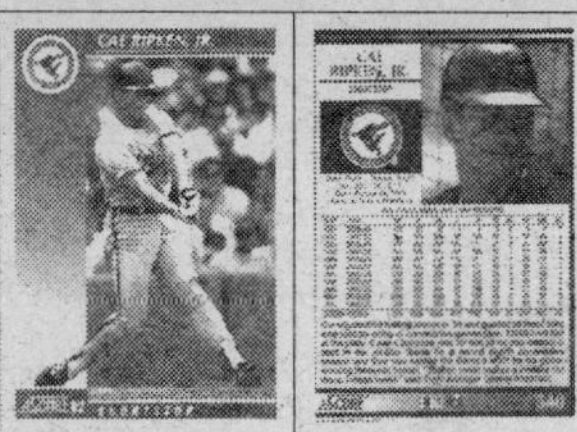

882), and Dream Team (883-893). The cards are numbered on the back.

	MINT	EXC	G-VG
COMPLETE SET (451)	13.50	6.00	1.85
COMMON PLAYER (443-893)	.03	.01	.00
☐ 443 Otis Nixon	.06	.02	.00
☐ 444 Scott Radinsky	.03	.01	.00
☐ 445 Mark Grace	.08	.03	.01
☐ 446 Tony Pena	.06	.02	.00
☐ 447 Billy Hatcher	.03	.01	.00
☐ 448 Glenallen Hill	.06	.02	.00
☐ 449 Chris Gwynn	.03	.01	.00
☐ 450 Tom Glavine	.08	.03	.01
☐ 451 John Habyan	.03	.01	.00
☐ 452 Al Osuna	.03	.01	.00
☐ 453 Tony Phillips	.03	.01	.00
☐ 454 Greg Cadaret	.03	.01	.00
☐ 455 Rob Dibble	.06	.02	.00
☐ 456 Rick Honeycutt	.03	.01	.00
☐ 457 Jerome Walton	.06	.02	.00
☐ 458 Mookie Wilson	.03	.01	.00
☐ 459 Mark Gubicza	.03	.01	.00
☐ 460 Craig Biggio	.06	.02	.00
☐ 461 Dave Cochrane	.03	.01	.00
☐ 462 Keith Miller	.03	.01	.00
☐ 463 Alex Cole	.06	.02	.00
☐ 464 Pete Smith	.03	.01	.00
☐ 465 Brett Butler	.06	.02	.00
☐ 466 Jeff Huson	.03	.01	.00
☐ 467 Steve Lake	.03	.01	.00
☐ 468 Lloyd Moseby	.03	.01	.00
☐ 469 Tim McIntosh	.03	.01	.00
☐ 470 Dennis Martinez	.06	.02	.00
☐ 471 Greg Myers	.03	.01	.00
☐ 472 Mackey Sasser	.03	.01	.00
☐ 473 Junior Ortiz	.03	.01	.00
☐ 474 Greg Olson	.03	.01	.00
☐ 475 Steve Sax	.06	.02	.00
☐ 476 Ricky Jordan	.03	.01	.00
☐ 477 Max Venable	.03	.01	.00
☐ 478 Brian McRae	.12	.05	.01
☐ 479 Doug Simons	.03	.01	.00
☐ 480 Rickey Henderson	.18	.08	.01
☐ 481 Gary Varsho	.03	.01	.00
☐ 482 Carl Willis	.03	.01	.00
☐ 483 Rick Wilkins	.08	.03	.01
☐ 484 Donn Pall	.03	.01	.00
☐ 485 Edgar Martinez	.06	.02	.00
☐ 486 Tom Foley	.03	.01	.00
☐ 487 Mark Williamson	.03	.01	.00
☐ 488 Jack Armstrong	.06	.02	.00
☐ 489 Gary Carter	.08	.03	.01
☐ 490 Ruben Sierra	.12	.05	.01
☐ 491 Gerald Perry	.03	.01	.00
☐ 492 Rob Murphy	.03	.01	.00
☐ 493 Zane Smith	.03	.01	.00
☐ 494 Darryl Kile	.08	.03	.01
☐ 495 Kelly Gruber	.06	.02	.00
☐ 496 Jerry Browne	.03	.01	.00
☐ 497 Darryl Hamilton	.03	.01	.00
☐ 498 Mike Stanton	.03	.01	.00
☐ 499 Mark Leonard	.03	.01	.00
☐ 500 Jose Canseco	.20	.08	.02
☐ 501 Dave Martinez	.03	.01	.00
☐ 502 Jose Guzman	.03	.01	.00
☐ 503 Terry Kennedy	.03	.01	.00
☐ 504 Ed Sprague	.08	.03	.01
☐ 505 Frank Thomas	.75	.30	.07
☐ 506 Darren Daulton	.06	.02	.00
☐ 507 Kevin Tapani	.06	.02	.00
☐ 508 Luis Salazar	.03	.01	.00
☐ 509 Paul Faries	.03	.01	.00
☐ 510 Sandy Alomar Jr.	.08	.03	.01
☐ 511 Jeff King	.03	.01	.00
☐ 512 Gary Thurman	.03	.01	.00
☐ 513 Chris Hammond	.06	.02	.00
☐ 514 Pedro Munoz	.10	.04	.01
☐ 515 Alan Trammell	.08	.03	.01
☐ 516 Geronimo Pena	.03	.01	.00
☐ 517 Rodney McCray	.03	.01	.00
☐ 518 Manny Lee	.03	.01	.00
☐ 519 Junior Felix	.06	.02	.00
☐ 520 Kirk Gibson	.06	.02	.00
☐ 521 Darrin Jackson	.03	.01	.00
☐ 522 John Burkett	.03	.01	.00
☐ 523 Jeff Johnson	.06	.02	.00
☐ 524 Jim Corsi	.03	.01	.00
☐ 525 Robin Yount	.10	.04	.01
☐ 526 Jamie Quirk	.03	.01	.00
☐ 527 Bob Ojeda	.03	.01	.00
☐ 528 Mark Lewis	.12	.05	.01
☐ 529 Bryn Smith	.03	.01	.00
☐ 530 Kent Hrbek	.06	.02	.00
☐ 531 Dennis Boyd	.03	.01	.00
☐ 532 Ron Karkovice	.03	.01	.00
☐ 533 Don August	.03	.01	.00
☐ 534 Todd Frohwirth	.03	.01	.00
☐ 535 Wally Joyner	.08	.03	.01

☐	536 Dennis Rasmussen	.03	.01	.00
☐	537 Andy Allanson	.03	.01	.00
☐	538 Goose Gossage	.06	.02	.00
☐	539 John Marzano	.03	.01	.00
☐	540 Cal Ripken	.20	.08	.02
☐	541 Bill Swift	.03	.01	.00
☐	542 Kevin Appier	.03	.01	.00
☐	543 Dave Bergman	.03	.01	.00
☐	544 Bernard Gilkey	.10	.04	.01
☐	545 Mike Greenwell	.10	.04	.01
☐	546 Jose Uribe	.03	.01	.00
☐	547 Jesse Orosco	.03	.01	.00
☐	548 Bob Patterson	.03	.01	.00
☐	549 Mike Stanley	.03	.01	.00
☐	550 Howard Johnson	.08	.03	.01
☐	551 Joe Orsulak	.03	.01	.00
☐	552 Dick Schofield	.03	.01	.00
☐	553 Dave Hollins	.06	.02	.00
☐	554 David Segui	.06	.02	.00
☐	555 Barry Bonds	.12	.05	.01
☐	556 Mo Vaughn	.25	.10	.02
☐	557 Craig Wilson	.08	.03	.01
☐	558 Bobby Rose	.03	.01	.00
☐	559 Rod Nichols	.03	.01	.00
☐	560 Len Dykstra	.06	.02	.00
☐	561 Craig Grebeck	.03	.01	.00
☐	562 Darren Lewis	.10	.04	.01
☐	563 Todd Benzinger	.03	.01	.00
☐	564 Ed Whitson	.03	.01	.00
☐	565 Jesse Barfield	.06	.02	.00
☐	566 Lloyd McClendon	.03	.01	.00
☐	567 Dan Plesac	.03	.01	.00
☐	568 Danny Cox	.03	.01	.00
☐	569 Skeeter Barnes	.03	.01	.00
☐	570 Bobby Thigpen	.06	.02	.00
☐	571 Deion Sanders	.08	.03	.01
☐	572 Chuck Knoblauch	.20	.08	.02
☐	573 Matt Nokes	.06	.02	.00
☐	574 Herm Winningham	.03	.01	.00
☐	575 Tom Candiotti	.06	.02	.00
☐	576 Jeff Bagwell	.75	.30	.07
☐	577 Brook Jacoby	.03	.01	.00
☐	578 Chico Walker	.03	.01	.00
☐	579 Brian Downing	.03	.01	.00
☐	580 Dave Stewart	.06	.02	.00
☐	581 Francisco Cabrera	.03	.01	.00
☐	582 Rene Gonzales	.03	.01	.00
☐	583 Stan Javier	.03	.01	.00
☐	584 Randy Johnson	.06	.02	.00
☐	585 Chuck Finley	.06	.02	.00
☐	586 Mark Gardner	.03	.01	.00
☐	587 Mark Whiten	.10	.04	.01
☐	588 Garry Templeton	.03	.01	.00
☐	589 Gary Sheffield	.08	.03	.01
☐	590 Ozzie Smith	.10	.04	.01
☐	591 Candy Maldonado	.03	.01	.00
☐	592 Mike Sharperson	.03	.01	.00
☐	593 Carlos Martinez	.03	.01	.00
☐	594 Scott Bankhead	.03	.01	.00
☐	595 Tim Wallach	.06	.02	.00
☐	596 Tino Martinez	.10	.04	.01
☐	597 Roger McDowell	.03	.01	.00
☐	598 Cory Snyder	.06	.02	.00
☐	599 Andujar Cedeno	.15	.06	.01
☐	600 Kirby Puckett	.12	.05	.01
☐	601 Rick Parker	.03	.01	.00
☐	602 Todd Hundley	.08	.03	.01
☐	603 Greg Litton	.03	.01	.00
☐	604 Dave Johnson	.03	.01	.00
☐	605 John Franco	.03	.01	.00
☐	606 Mike Fetters	.03	.01	.00
☐	607 Luis Alicea	.03	.01	.00
☐	608 Trevor Wilson	.03	.01	.00
☐	609 Rob Ducey	.03	.01	.00
☐	610 Ramon Martinez	.10	.04	.01
☐	611 Dave Burba	.03	.01	.00
☐	612 Dwight Smith	.06	.02	.00
☐	613 Kevin Maas	.12	.05	.01
☐	614 John Costello	.03	.01	.00
☐	615 Glenn Davis	.06	.02	.00
☐	616 Shawn Abner	.03	.01	.00
☐	617 Scott Hemond	.06	.02	.00
☐	618 Tom Prince	.03	.01	.00
☐	619 Wally Ritchie	.03	.01	.00
☐	620 Jim Abbott	.10	.04	.01
☐	621 Charlie O'Brien	.03	.01	.00
☐	622 Jack Daugherty	.03	.01	.00
☐	623 Tommy Gregg	.03	.01	.00
☐	624 Jeff Shaw	.03	.01	.00
☐	625 Tony Gwynn	.12	.05	.01
☐	626 Mark Leiter	.06	.02	.00
☐	627 Jim Clancy	.03	.01	.00
☐	628 Tim Layana	.03	.01	.00
☐	629 Jeff Schaefer	.03	.01	.00
☐	630 Lee Smith	.06	.02	.00
☐	631 Wade Taylor	.06	.02	.00
☐	632 Mike Simms	.06	.02	.00
☐	633 Terry Steinbach	.06	.02	.00
☐	634 Shawon Dunston	.06	.02	.00
☐	635 Tim Raines	.08	.03	.01
☐	636 Kirt Manwaring	.03	.01	.00
☐	637 Warren Cromartie	.03	.01	.00
☐	638 Luis Quinones	.03	.01	.00
☐	639 Greg Vaughn	.08	.03	.01
☐	640 Kevin Mitchell	.10	.04	.01
☐	641 Chris Hoiles	.06	.02	.00
☐	642 Tom Browning	.06	.02	.00
☐	643 Mitch Webster	.03	.01	.00
☐	644 Steve Olin	.03	.01	.00
☐	645 Tony Fernandez	.06	.02	.00
☐	646 Juan Bell	.03	.01	.00
☐	647 Joe Boever	.03	.01	.00
☐	648 Carney Lansford	.06	.02	.00
☐	649 Mike Benjamin	.03	.01	.00
☐	650 George Brett	.10	.04	.01
☐	651 Tim Burke	.03	.01	.00

☐ 652 Jack Morris	.06	.02	.00
☐ 653 Orel Hershiser	.06	.02	.00
☐ 654 Mike Schooler	.03	.01	.00
☐ 655 Andy Van Slyke	.06	.02	.00
☐ 656 Dave Stieb	.06	.02	.00
☐ 657 Dave Clark	.03	.01	.00
☐ 658 Ben McDonald	.08	.03	.01
☐ 659 John Smiley	.06	.02	.00
☐ 660 Wade Boggs	.12	.05	.01
☐ 661 Eric Bullock	.03	.01	.00
☐ 662 Eric Show	.03	.01	.00
☐ 663 Lenny Webster	.06	.02	.00
☐ 664 Mike Huff	.03	.01	.00
☐ 665 Rick Sutcliffe	.06	.02	.00
☐ 666 Jeff Manto	.03	.01	.00
☐ 667 Mike Fitzgerald	.03	.01	.00
☐ 668 Matt Young	.03	.01	.00
☐ 669 Dave West	.03	.01	.00
☐ 670 Mike Hartley	.03	.01	.00
☐ 671 Curt Schilling	.03	.01	.00
☐ 672 Brian Bohanon	.03	.01	.00
☐ 673 Cecil Espy	.03	.01	.00
☐ 674 Joe Grahe	.03	.01	.00
☐ 675 Sid Fernandez	.06	.02	.00
☐ 676 Edwin Nunez	.03	.01	.00
☐ 677 Hector Villanueva	.06	.02	.00
☐ 678 Sean Berry	.08	.03	.01
☐ 679 Dave Eiland	.03	.01	.00
☐ 680 Dave Cone	.08	.03	.01
☐ 681 Mike Bordick	.06	.02	.00
☐ 682 Tony Castillo	.03	.01	.00
☐ 683 John Barfield	.03	.01	.00
☐ 684 Jeff Hamilton	.03	.01	.00
☐ 685 Ken Dayley	.03	.01	.00
☐ 686 Carmelo Martinez	.03	.01	.00
☐ 687 Mike Capel	.03	.01	.00
☐ 688 Scott Chiamparino	.03	.01	.00
☐ 689 Rich Gedman	.03	.01	.00
☐ 690 Rich Monteleone	.03	.01	.00
☐ 691 Alejandro Pena	.03	.01	.00
☐ 692 Oscar Azocar	.03	.01	.00
☐ 693 Jim Poole	.06	.02	.00
☐ 694 Mike Gardiner	.06	.02	.00
☐ 695 Steve Buechele	.03	.01	.00
☐ 696 Rudy Seanez	.03	.01	.00
☐ 697 Paul Abbott	.03	.01	.00
☐ 698 Steve Searcy	.03	.01	.00
☐ 699 Jose Offerman	.06	.02	.00
☐ 700 Ivan Rodriguez	.60	.25	.06
☐ 701 Joe Girardi	.03	.01	.00
☐ 702 Tony Perezchica	.03	.01	.00
☐ 703 Paul McClellan	.06	.02	.00
☐ 704 David Howard	.06	.02	.00
☐ 705 Dan Petry	.03	.01	.00
☐ 706 Jack Howell	.03	.01	.00
☐ 707 Jose Mesa	.03	.01	.00
☐ 708 Randy St. Claire	.03	.01	.00
☐ 709 Kevin Brown	.06	.02	.00
☐ 710 Ron Darling	.03	.01	.00
☐ 711 Jason Grimsley	.03	.01	.00
☐ 712 John Orton	.03	.01	.00
☐ 713 Shawn Boskie	.03	.01	.00
☐ 714 Pat Clements	.03	.01	.00
☐ 715 Brian Barnes	.03	.01	.00
☐ 716 Luis Lopez	.08	.03	.01
☐ 717 Bob McClure	.03	.01	.00
☐ 718 Mark Davis	.03	.01	.00
☐ 719 Dann Bilardello	.03	.01	.00
☐ 720 Tom Edens	.03	.01	.00
☐ 721 Willie Fraser	.03	.01	.00
☐ 722 Curt Young	.03	.01	.00
☐ 723 Neal Heaton	.03	.01	.00
☐ 724 Craig Worthington	.03	.01	.00
☐ 725 Mel Rojas	.06	.02	.00
☐ 726 Daryl Irvine	.03	.01	.00
☐ 727 Roger Mason	.03	.01	.00
☐ 728 Kirk Dressendorfer	.08	.03	.01
☐ 729 Scott Aldred	.03	.01	.00
☐ 730 Willie Blair	.03	.01	.00
☐ 731 Allan Anderson	.03	.01	.00
☐ 732 Dana Kiecker	.03	.01	.00
☐ 733 Jose Gonzalez	.03	.01	.00
☐ 734 Brian Drahman	.06	.02	.00
☐ 735 Brad Komminsk	.03	.01	.00
☐ 736 Arthur Rhodes	.15	.06	.01
☐ 737 Terry Mathews	.10	.04	.01
☐ 738 Jeff Fassero	.06	.02	.00
☐ 739 Mike Magnante	.12	.05	.01
☐ 740 Kip Gross	.12	.05	.01
☐ 741 Jim Hunter	.10	.04	.01
☐ 742 Jose Mota	.08	.03	.01
☐ 743 Joe Bitker	.03	.01	.00
☐ 744 Tim Mauser	.10	.04	.01
☐ 745 Ramon Garcia	.06	.02	.00
☐ 746 Rod Beck	.12	.05	.01
☐ 747 Jim Austin	.10	.04	.01
☐ 748 Keith Mitchell	.15	.06	.01
☐ 749 Wayne Rosenthal	.10	.04	.01
☐ 750 Bryan Hickerson	.12	.05	.01
☐ 751 Bruce Egloff	.08	.03	.01
☐ 752 John Wehner	.12	.05	.01
☐ 753 Darren Holmes	.08	.03	.01
☐ 754 Dave Hansen	.06	.02	.00
☐ 755 Mike Mussina	.12	.05	.01
☐ 756 Anthony Young	.12	.05	.01
☐ 757 Ron Tingley	.03	.01	.00
☐ 758 Ricky Bones	.06	.02	.00
☐ 759 Mark Wohlers	.20	.08	.02
☐ 760 Wilson Alvarez	.08	.03	.01
☐ 761 Harvey Pulliam	.12	.05	.01
☐ 762 Ryan Bowen	.08	.03	.01
☐ 763 Terry Bross	.03	.01	.00
☐ 764 Joel Johnston	.08	.03	.01
☐ 765 Terry McDaniel	.12	.05	.01
☐ 766 Esteban Beltre	.10	.04	.01
☐ 767 Rob Maurer	.20	.08	.02

☐ 768 Ted Wood	.20	.08	.02
☐ 769 Mo Sanford	.15	.06	.01
☐ 770 Jeff Carter	.06	.02	.00
☐ 771 Gil Heredia	.12	.05	.01
☐ 772 Monty Fariss	.08	.03	.01
☐ 773 Will Clark AS	.12	.05	.01
☐ 774 Ryne Sandberg AS	.12	.05	.01
☐ 775 Barry Larkin AS	.08	.03	.01
☐ 776 Howard Johnson AS	.08	.03	.01
☐ 777 Barry Bonds AS	.10	.04	.01
☐ 778 Brett Butler AS	.06	.02	.00
☐ 779 Tony Gwynn AS	.10	.04	.01
☐ 780 Ramon Martinez AS	.08	.03	.01
☐ 781 Lee Smith AS	.06	.02	.00
☐ 782 Mike Scioscia AS	.03	.01	.00
☐ 783 Dennis Martinez HL	.06	.02	.00
☐ 784 Dennis Martinez No-Hit Club	.06	.02	.00
☐ 785 Mark Gardner No-Hit Club	.03	.01	.00
☐ 786 Bret Saberhagen No-Hit Club	.08	.03	.01
☐ 787 Kent Mercker Mark Wohlers Alejandro Pena No-Hit Club	.06	.02	.00
☐ 788 Cal Ripken MVP	.12	.05	.01
☐ 789 Terry Pendleton MVP	.06	.02	.00
☐ 790 Roger Clemens CY	.10	.04	.01
☐ 791 Tom Glavine CY	.08	.03	.01
☐ 792 Chuck Knoblauch ROY	.15	.06	.01
☐ 793 Jeff Bagwell ROY	.40	.16	.04
☐ 794 Cal Ripken Man of the Year	.12	.05	.01
☐ 795 David Cone HL	.08	.03	.01
☐ 796 Kirby Puckett HL	.10	.04	.01
☐ 797 Steve Avery HL	.12	.05	.01
☐ 798 Jack Morris HL	.08	.03	.01
☐ 799 Allen Watson Draft	.20	.08	.02
☐ 800 Manny Ramirez Draft	.40	.16	.04
☐ 801 Cliff Floyd Draft	.25	.10	.02
☐ 802 Al Shirley Draft	.30	.12	.03
☐ 803 Brian Barber Draft	.12	.05	.01
☐ 804 Jon Farrell Draft	.20	.08	.02
☐ 805 Brent Gates Draft	.12	.05	.01
☐ 806 Scott Ruffcorn Draft	.20	.08	.02
☐ 807 Tyrone Hill Draft	.25	.10	.02
☐ 808 Benji Gil Draft	.30	.12	.03
☐ 809 Aaron Sele Draft	.20	.08	.02
☐ 810 Tyler Green Draft	.40	.16	.04
☐ 811 Chris Jones	.03	.01	.00
☐ 812 Steve Wilson	.03	.01	.00
☐ 813 Cliff Young	.06	.02	.00
☐ 814 Don Wakamatsu	.10	.04	.01
☐ 815 Mike Humphreys	.08	.03	.01
☐ 816 Scott Servais	.08	.03	.01
☐ 817 Rico Rossy	.10	.04	.01
☐ 818 John Ramos	.12	.05	.01
☐ 819 Rob Mallicoat	.03	.01	.00
☐ 820 Milt Hill	.12	.05	.01
☐ 821 Carlos Garcia	.06	.02	.00
☐ 822 Stan Royer	.06	.02	.00
☐ 823 Jeff Plympton	.12	.05	.01
☐ 824 Braulio Castillo	.25	.10	.02
☐ 825 David Haas	.06	.02	.00
☐ 826 Luis Mercedes	.15	.06	.01
☐ 827 Eric Karros	.20	.08	.02
☐ 828 Shawn Hare	.12	.05	.01
☐ 829 Reggie Sanders	.15	.06	.01
☐ 830 Tom Goodwin	.12	.05	.01
☐ 831 Dan Gakeler	.08	.03	.01
☐ 832 Stacy Jones	.10	.04	.01
☐ 833 Kim Batiste	.08	.03	.01
☐ 834 Cal Eldred	.08	.03	.01
☐ 835 Chris George	.10	.04	.01
☐ 836 Wayne Housie	.12	.05	.01
☐ 837 Mike Ignasiak	.12	.05	.01
☐ 838 Josias Manzanillo	.12	.05	.01
☐ 839 Jim Olander	.12	.05	.01
☐ 840 Gary Cooper	.12	.05	.01
☐ 841 Royce Clayton	.15	.06	.01
☐ 842 Hector Fajardo	.20	.08	.02
☐ 843 Blaine Beatty	.03	.01	.00
☐ 844 Jorge Pedre	.12	.05	.01
☐ 845 Kenny Lofton	.20	.08	.02
☐ 846 Scott Brosius	.10	.04	.01
☐ 847 Chris Cron	.12	.05	.01
☐ 848 Denis Boucher	.06	.02	.00
☐ 849 Kyle Abbott	.10	.04	.01
☐ 850 Robert Zupcic	.18	.08	.01
☐ 851 Rheal Cormier	.15	.06	.01
☐ 852 Jim Lewis	.10	.04	.01
☐ 853 Anthony Telford	.03	.01	.00
☐ 854 Cliff Brantley	.12	.05	.01
☐ 855 Kevin Campbell	.12	.05	.01
☐ 856 Craig Shipley	.10	.04	.01
☐ 857 Chuck Carr	.03	.01	.00
☐ 858 Tony Eusebio	.12	.05	.01
☐ 859 Jim Thome	.30	.12	.03
☐ 860 Vinny Castilla	.10	.04	.01
☐ 861 Dann Howitt	.03	.01	.00
☐ 862 Kevin Ward	.10	.04	.01
☐ 863 Steve Wapnick	.06	.02	.00
☐ 864 Rod Brewer	.06	.02	.00
☐ 865 Todd Van Poppel	.45	.18	.04
☐ 866 Jose Hernandez	.10	.04	.01
☐ 867 Amalio Carreno	.10	.04	.01
☐ 868 Calvin Jones	.10	.04	.01
☐ 869 Jeff Gardner	.10	.04	.01
☐ 870 Jarvis Brown	.12	.05	.01
☐ 871 Eddie Taubensee	.15	.06	.01
☐ 872 Andy Mota	.08	.03	.01
☐ 873 Chris Haney	.06	.02	.00
☐ 874 Roberto Hernandez	.12	.05	.01
☐ 875 Laddie Renfroe	.10	.04	.01
☐ 876 Scott Cooper	.10	.04	.01

☐ 877 Armando Reynoso	.10	.04	.01
☐ 878 Ty Cobb (Memorabilia)	.25	.10	.02
☐ 879 Babe Ruth (Memorabilia)	.35	.15	.03
☐ 880 Honus Wagner (Memorabilia)	.15	.06	.01
☐ 881 Lou Gehrig (Memorabilia)	.25	.10	.02
☐ 882 Satchel Paige (Memorabilia)	.15	.06	.01
☐ 883 Will Clark DT	.25	.10	.02
☐ 884 Cal Ripken DT	.40	.16	.04
☐ 885 Wade Boggs DT	.20	.08	.02
☐ 886 Tony Gwynn DT	.20	.08	.02
☐ 887 Kirby Puckett DT	.20	.08	.02
☐ 888 Craig Biggio DT	.08	.03	.01
☐ 889 Scott Erickson DT	.35	.15	.03
☐ 890 Tom Glavine DT	.15	.06	.01
☐ 891 Rob Dibble DT	.08	.03	.01
☐ 892 Mitch Williams DT	.06	.02	.00
☐ 893 Frank Thomas DT	1.00	.40	.10

1951 Topps Blue Backs

The cards in this 52-card set measure 2" by 2 5/8". The 1951 Topps series of blue backed baseball cards could be used to play a baseball game by shuffling the cards and drawing them from a pile. These cards were marketed with a piece of caramel candy, which often melted or was squashed in such a way as to damage the card and wrapper (despite the fact that a paper shield was inserted between candy and card). Blue Backs are more difficult to obtain than the similarly styled Red Backs. The set is denoted on the cards as "Set B" and the Red Back set is correspondingly Set A. Appropriately leading off the set is Eddie Yost. The only notable rookie card in the set is Billy Pierce.

	NRMT	VG-E	GOOD
COMPLETE SET (52)	2100.00	900.00	200.00
COMMON PLAYER (1-52)	35.00	15.75	5.25
☐ 1 Eddie Yost	50.00	20.00	4.00
☐ 2 Hank Majeski	35.00	15.75	5.25
☐ 3 Richie Ashburn	165.00	75.00	22.50
☐ 4 Del Ennis	40.00	18.00	6.00
☐ 5 Johnny Pesky	40.00	18.00	6.00
☐ 6 Red Schoendienst	120.00	55.00	18.00
☐ 7 Gerry Staley	35.00	15.75	5.25
☐ 8 Dick Sisler	35.00	15.75	5.25
☐ 9 Johnny Sain	45.00	20.00	6.75
☐ 10 Joe Page	40.00	18.00	6.00
☐ 11 Johnny Groth	35.00	15.75	5.25
☐ 12 Sam Jethroe	35.00	15.75	5.25
☐ 13 Mickey Vernon	40.00	18.00	6.00
☐ 14 Red Munger	35.00	15.75	5.25
☐ 15 Eddie Joost	35.00	15.75	5.25
☐ 16 Murry Dickson	35.00	15.75	5.25
☐ 17 Roy Smalley	35.00	15.75	5.25
☐ 18 Ned Garver	35.00	15.75	5.25
☐ 19 Phil Masi	35.00	15.75	5.25
☐ 20 Ralph Branca	45.00	20.00	6.75
☐ 21 Billy Johnson	37.50	16.50	5.50
☐ 22 Bob Kuzava	35.00	15.75	5.25
☐ 23 Dizzy Trout	35.00	15.75	5.25
☐ 24 Sherman Lollar	37.50	16.50	5.50
☐ 25 Sam Mele	35.00	15.75	5.25
☐ 26 Chico Carrasquel	35.00	15.75	5.25
☐ 27 Andy Pafko	37.50	16.50	5.50
☐ 28 Harry Brecheen	37.50	16.50	5.50
☐ 29 Granville Hamner	35.00	15.75	5.25
☐ 30 Enos Slaughter	130.00	60.00	20.00
☐ 31 Lou Brissie	35.00	15.75	5.25
☐ 32 Bob Elliott	37.50	16.50	5.50
☐ 33 Don Lenhardt	35.00	15.75	5.25
☐ 34 Earl Torgeson	35.00	15.75	5.25
☐ 35 Tommy Byrne	37.50	16.50	5.50
☐ 36 Cliff Fannin	35.00	15.75	5.25
☐ 37 Bobby Doerr	110.00	50.00	16.50
☐ 38 Irv Noren	37.50	16.50	5.50
☐ 39 Ed Lopat	45.00	20.00	6.75
☐ 40 Vic Wertz	40.00	18.00	6.00
☐ 41 Johnny Schmitz	35.00	15.75	5.25
☐ 42 Bruce Edwards	35.00	15.75	5.25
☐ 43 Willie Jones	35.00	15.75	5.25
☐ 44 Johnny Wyrostek	35.00	15.75	5.25
☐ 45 Billy Pierce	45.00	20.00	6.75
☐ 46 Gerry Priddy	35.00	15.75	5.25
☐ 47 Herman Wehmeier	35.00	15.75	5.25
☐ 48 Billy Cox	40.00	18.00	6.00
☐ 49 Hank Sauer	37.50	16.50	5.50

☐ 50 Johnny Mize	140.00	63.00	21.00
☐ 51 Eddie Waitkus	35.00	15.75	5.25
☐ 52 Sam Chapman	50.00	20.00	4.00

1951 Topps Red Backs

The cards in this 52-card set measure 2" by 2 5/8". The 1951 Topps Red Back set is identical in style to the Blue Back set of the same year. The cards have rounded corners and were designed to be used as a baseball game. Zernial, number 36, is listed with either the White Sox or Athletics, and Holmes, number 52, with either the Braves or Hartford. The set is denoted on the cards as "Set A" and the Blue Back set is correspondingly Set B. The only notable rookie card in the set is Monte Irvin.

	NRMT	VG-E	GOOD
COMPLETE SET (54)	750.00	325.00	110.00
COMMON PLAYER (1-52)	7.00	3.00	.70
☐ 1 Yogi Berra	125.00	40.00	8.00
☐ 2 Sid Gordon	7.00	3.00	.70
☐ 3 Ferris Fain	8.00	3.50	.80
☐ 4 Vern Stephens	8.00	3.50	.80
☐ 5 Phil Rizzuto	33.00	15.00	5.00
☐ 6 Allie Reynolds	11.00	5.00	1.35
☐ 7 Howie Pollet	7.00	3.00	.70
☐ 8 Early Wynn	20.00	8.50	2.75
☐ 9 Roy Sievers	8.00	3.50	.80
☐ 10 Mel Parnell	8.00	3.50	.80
☐ 11 Gene Hermanski	7.00	3.00	.70
☐ 12 Jim Hegan	8.00	3.50	.80
☐ 13 Dale Mitchell	8.00	3.50	.80
☐ 14 Wayne Terwilliger	7.00	3.00	.70
☐ 15 Ralph Kiner	30.00	13.50	4.50
☐ 16 Preacher Roe	9.00	4.00	.90
☐ 17 Dave (Gus) Bell	9.00	4.00	.90
☐ 18 Gerry Coleman	9.00	4.00	.90
☐ 19 Dick Kokos	7.00	3.00	.70
☐ 20 Dom DiMaggio	12.00	5.25	1.50
☐ 21 Larry Jansen	8.00	3.50	.80
☐ 22 Bob Feller	45.00	20.00	6.75
☐ 23 Ray Boone	9.00	4.00	.90
☐ 24 Hank Bauer	13.00	5.75	1.75
☐ 25 Cliff Chambers	7.00	3.00	.70
☐ 26 Luke Easter	8.00	3.50	.80
☐ 27 Wally Westlake	7.00	3.00	.70
☐ 28 Elmer Valo	7.00	3.00	.70
☐ 29 Bob Kennedy	8.00	3.50	.80
☐ 30 Warren Spahn	45.00	20.00	6.75
☐ 31 Gil Hodges	33.00	15.00	5.00
☐ 32 Henry Thompson	8.00	3.50	.80
☐ 33 William Werle	7.00	3.00	.70
☐ 34 Grady Hatton	7.00	3.00	.70
☐ 35 Al Rosen	13.00	5.75	1.75
☐ 36A Gus Zernial (Chicago)	33.00	15.00	5.00
☐ 36B Gus Zernial (Philadelphia)	20.00	8.50	2.75
☐ 37 Wes Westrum	8.00	3.50	.80
☐ 38 Duke Snider	80.00	36.00	12.00
☐ 39 Ted Kluszewski	16.00	6.75	2.25
☐ 40 Mike Garcia	8.00	3.50	.80
☐ 41 Whitey Lockman	8.00	3.50	.80
☐ 42 Ray Scarborough	7.00	3.00	.70
☐ 43 Maurice McDermott	7.00	3.00	.70
☐ 44 Sid Hudson	7.00	3.00	.70
☐ 45 Andy Seminick	7.00	3.00	.70
☐ 46 Billy Goodman	8.00	3.50	.80
☐ 47 Tommy Glaviano	7.00	3.00	.70
☐ 48 Eddie Stanky	9.00	4.00	.90
☐ 49 Al Zarilla	7.00	3.00	.70
☐ 50 Monte Irvin	45.00	20.00	6.75
☐ 51 Eddie Robinson	7.00	3.00	.70
☐ 52A Tommy Holmes (Boston)	33.00	15.00	5.00
☐ 52B Tommy Holmes (Hartford)	20.00	8.50	2.75

1952 Topps

The cards in this 407-card set measure 2 5/8" by 3 3/4". The 1952 Topps set is Topps' first truly major set. Card numbers 1 to 80 were

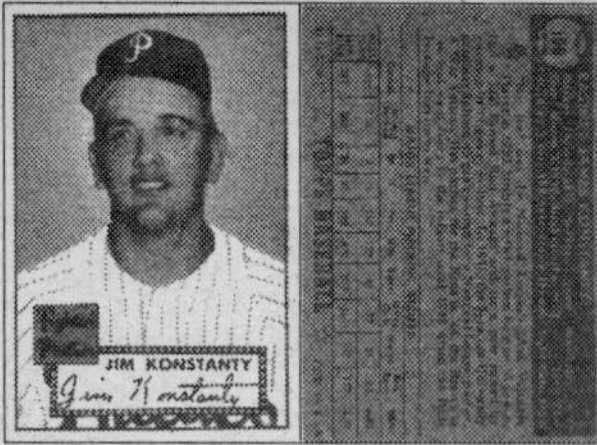

issued with red or black backs, both of which are less plentiful than card numbers 81 to 250. In fact, the first series is considered the most difficult with respect to finding perfect condition cards. Card number 48 (Joe Page) and number 49 (Johnny Sain) can be found with each other's write-up on their back. Card numbers 251 to 310 are somewhat scarce and numbers 311 to 407 are quite scarce. Cards 281-300 were single printed compared to the other cards in the next to last series. Cards 311-313 were double printed on the last high number printing sheet. The key card in the set is obviously Mickey Mantle, number 311, Mickey's first of many Topps cards. Although rarely seen, there exist salesman sample panels of three cards containing the fronts of regular cards with ad information on the back. Two such panels seen are Bob Mahoney/Robin Roberts/Sid Hudson and Wally Westlake/Dizzy Trout/Irv Noren. The key rookies in this set are Billy Martin, Eddie Mathews, and Hoyt Wilhelm.

	NRMT	VG-E	GOOD
COMPLETE SET (407)	60000.	22500.	7500.
COMMON PLAYER (1-80)	55.00	25.00	8.25
COMMON PLAYER (81-250)	27.00	12.00	4.00
COMMON PLAYER (251-280)	45.00	20.00	6.75
COMMON PLAYER (281-300)	55.00	25.00	8.25
COMMON PLAYER (301-310)	45.00	20.00	6.75
COMMON PLAYER (311-407)	175.00	80.00	27.00
☐ 1 Andy Pafko	1250.00	125.00	30.00
☐ 2 Pete Runnels	65.00	29.00	9.75
☐ 3 Hank Thompson	60.00	27.00	9.00
☐ 4 Don Lenhardt	55.00	25.00	8.25
☐ 5 Larry Jansen	60.00	27.00	9.00
☐ 6 Grady Hatton	55.00	25.00	8.25
☐ 7 Wayne Terwilliger	55.00	25.00	8.25
☐ 8 Fred Marsh	55.00	25.00	8.25
☐ 9 Robert Hogue	55.00	25.00	8.25
☐ 10 Al Rosen	90.00	40.00	13.50
☐ 11 Phil Rizzuto	180.00	80.00	27.00
☐ 12 Monty Basgall	55.00	25.00	8.25
☐ 13 Johnny Wyrostek	55.00	25.00	8.25
☐ 14 Bob Elliott	60.00	27.00	9.00
☐ 15 Johnny Pesky	65.00	29.00	9.75
☐ 16 Gene Hermanski	55.00	25.00	8.25
☐ 17 Jim Hegan	60.00	27.00	9.00
☐ 18 Merrill Combs	55.00	25.00	8.25
☐ 19 Johnny Bucha	55.00	25.00	8.25
☐ 20 Billy Loes	110.00	50.00	16.50
☐ 21 Ferris Fain	60.00	27.00	9.00
☐ 22 Dom DiMaggio	95.00	42.00	10.00
☐ 23 Billy Goodman	60.00	27.00	9.00
☐ 24 Luke Easter	60.00	27.00	9.00
☐ 25 Johnny Groth	55.00	25.00	8.25
☐ 26 Monte Irvin	110.00	50.00	16.50
☐ 27 Sam Jethroe	55.00	25.00	8.25
☐ 28 Jerry Priddy	55.00	25.00	8.25
☐ 29 Ted Kluszewski	100.00	45.00	15.00
☐ 30 Mel Parnell	60.00	27.00	9.00
☐ 31 Gus Zernial	65.00	29.00	9.75
☐ 32 Eddie Robinson	55.00	25.00	8.25
☐ 33 Warren Spahn	250.00	110.00	37.50
☐ 34 Elmer Valo	55.00	25.00	8.25
☐ 35 Hank Sauer	65.00	29.00	9.75
☐ 36 Gil Hodges	175.00	80.00	27.00
☐ 37 Duke Snider	300.00	135.00	45.00
☐ 38 Wally Westlake	55.00	25.00	8.25
☐ 39 Dizzy Trout	55.00	25.00	8.25
☐ 40 Irv Noren	55.00	25.00	8.25
☐ 41 Bob Wellman	55.00	25.00	8.25
☐ 42 Lou Kretlow	55.00	25.00	8.25
☐ 43 Ray Scarborough	55.00	25.00	8.25
☐ 44 Con Dempsey	55.00	25.00	8.25
☐ 45 Eddie Joost	55.00	25.00	8.25
☐ 46 Gordon Goldsberry	55.00	25.00	8.25
☐ 47 Willie Jones	55.00	25.00	8.25
☐ 48A Joe Page COR	75.00	34.00	11.25
☐ 48B Joe Page ERR (bio for Sain)	325.00	150.00	50.00
☐ 49A Johnny Sain COR	100.00	45.00	15.00
☐ 49B Johnny Sain ERR (bio for Page)	325.00	150.00	50.00
☐ 50 Marv Rickert	55.00	25.00	8.25
☐ 51 Jim Russell	55.00	25.00	8.25
☐ 52 Don Mueller	60.00	27.00	9.00
☐ 53 Chris Van Cuyk	55.00	25.00	8.25
☐ 54 Leo Kiely	55.00	25.00	8.25
☐ 55 Ray Boone	60.00	27.00	9.00
☐ 56 Tommy Glaviano	55.00	25.00	8.25
☐ 57 Ed Lopat	100.00	45.00	15.00
☐ 58 Bob Mahoney	55.00	25.00	8.25
☐ 59 Robin Roberts	140.00	63.00	21.00
☐ 60 Sid Hudson	55.00	25.00	8.25
☐ 61 Tookie Gilbert	55.00	25.00	8.25
☐ 62 Chuck Stobbs	55.00	25.00	8.25
☐ 63 Howie Pollet	55.00	25.00	8.25

☐ 64 Roy Sievers	60.00	27.00	9.00
☐ 65 Enos Slaughter	140.00	63.00	21.00
☐ 66 Preacher Roe	100.00	45.00	15.00
☐ 67 Allie Reynolds	100.00	45.00	15.00
☐ 68 Cliff Chambers	55.00	25.00	8.25
☐ 69 Virgil Stallcup	55.00	25.00	8.25
☐ 70 Al Zarilla	55.00	25.00	8.25
☐ 71 Tom Upton	55.00	25.00	8.25
☐ 72 Karl Olson	55.00	25.00	8.25
☐ 73 Bill Werle	55.00	25.00	8.25
☐ 74 Andy Hansen	55.00	25.00	8.25
☐ 75 Wes Westrum	55.00	25.00	8.25
☐ 76 Eddie Stanky	60.00	27.00	9.00
☐ 77 Bob Kennedy	55.00	25.00	8.25
☐ 78 Ellis Kinder	55.00	25.00	8.25
☐ 79 Gerry Staley	55.00	25.00	8.25
☐ 80 Herman Wehmeier	55.00	25.00	8.25
☐ 81 Vernon Law	32.00	14.25	4.75
☐ 82 Duane Pillette	27.00	12.00	4.00
☐ 83 Billy Johnson	30.00	13.50	4.50
☐ 84 Vern Stephens	32.00	14.25	4.75
☐ 85 Bob Kuzava	27.00	12.00	4.00
☐ 86 Ted Gray	27.00	12.00	4.00
☐ 87 Dale Coogan	27.00	12.00	4.00
☐ 88 Bob Feller	160.00	72.00	24.00
☐ 89 Johnny Lipon	27.00	12.00	4.00
☐ 90 Mickey Grasso	27.00	12.00	4.00
☐ 91 Red Schoendienst	80.00	36.00	12.00
☐ 92 Dale Mitchell	30.00	13.50	4.50
☐ 93 Al Sima	27.00	12.00	4.00
☐ 94 Sam Mele	27.00	12.00	4.00
☐ 95 Ken Holcombe	27.00	12.00	4.00
☐ 96 Willard Marshall	27.00	12.00	4.00
☐ 97 Earl Torgeson	27.00	12.00	4.00
☐ 98 Billy Pierce	32.00	14.25	4.75
☐ 99 Gene Woodling	60.00	27.00	9.00
☐ 100 Del Rice	27.00	12.00	4.00
☐ 101 Max Lanier	27.00	12.00	4.00
☐ 102 Bill Kennedy	27.00	12.00	4.00
☐ 103 Cliff Mapes	27.00	12.00	4.00
☐ 104 Don Kolloway	27.00	12.00	4.00
☐ 105 Johnny Pramesa	27.00	12.00	4.00
☐ 106 Mickey Vernon	30.00	13.50	4.50
☐ 107 Connie Ryan	27.00	12.00	4.00
☐ 108 Jim Konstanty	30.00	13.50	4.50
☐ 109 Ted Wilks	27.00	12.00	4.00
☐ 110 Dutch Leonard	30.00	13.50	4.50
☐ 111 Peanuts Lowrey	27.00	12.00	4.00
☐ 112 Hank Majeski	27.00	12.00	4.00
☐ 113 Dick Sisler	27.00	12.00	4.00
☐ 114 Willard Ramsdell	27.00	12.00	4.00
☐ 115 Red Munger	27.00	12.00	4.00
☐ 116 Carl Scheib	27.00	12.00	4.00
☐ 117 Sherm Lollar	30.00	13.50	4.50
☐ 118 Ken Raffensberger	27.00	12.00	4.00
☐ 119 Mickey McDermott	27.00	12.00	4.00
☐ 120 Bob Chakales	27.00	12.00	4.00
☐ 121 Gus Niarhos	27.00	12.00	4.00

☐ 122 Jackie Jensen	70.00	32.00	10.50
☐ 123 Eddie Yost	27.00	12.00	4.00
☐ 124 Monte Kennedy	27.00	12.00	4.00
☐ 125 Bill Rigney	27.00	12.00	4.00
☐ 126 Fred Hutchinson	30.00	13.50	4.50
☐ 127 Paul Minner	27.00	12.00	4.00
☐ 128 Don Bollweg	27.00	12.00	4.00
☐ 129 Johnny Mize	80.00	36.00	12.00
☐ 130 Sheldon Jones	27.00	12.00	4.00
☐ 131 Morrie Martin	27.00	12.00	4.00
☐ 132 Clyde Kluttz	27.00	12.00	4.00
☐ 133 Al Widmar	27.00	12.00	4.00
☐ 134 Joe Tipton	27.00	12.00	4.00
☐ 135 Dixie Howell	27.00	12.00	4.00
☐ 136 Johnny Schmitz	27.00	12.00	4.00
☐ 137 Roy McMillan	30.00	13.50	4.50
☐ 138 Bill MacDonald	27.00	12.00	4.00
☐ 139 Ken Wood	27.00	12.00	4.00
☐ 140 Johnny Antonelli	32.00	14.25	4.75
☐ 141 Clint Hartung	27.00	12.00	4.00
☐ 142 Harry Perkowski	27.00	12.00	4.00
☐ 143 Les Moss	27.00	12.00	4.00
☐ 144 Ed Blake	27.00	12.00	4.00
☐ 145 Joe Haynes	27.00	12.00	4.00
☐ 146 Frank House	27.00	12.00	4.00
☐ 147 Bob Young	27.00	12.00	4.00
☐ 148 Johnny Klippstein	27.00	12.00	4.00
☐ 149 Dick Kryhoski	27.00	12.00	4.00
☐ 150 Ted Beard	27.00	12.00	4.00
☐ 151 Wally Post	30.00	13.50	4.50
☐ 152 Al Evans	27.00	12.00	4.00
☐ 153 Bob Rush	27.00	12.00	4.00
☐ 154 Joe Muir	27.00	12.00	4.00
☐ 155 Frank Overmire	27.00	12.00	4.00
☐ 156 Frank Hiller	27.00	12.00	4.00
☐ 157 Bob Usher	27.00	12.00	4.00
☐ 158 Eddie Waitkus	27.00	12.00	4.00
☐ 159 Saul Rogovin	27.00	12.00	4.00
☐ 160 Owen Friend	27.00	12.00	4.00
☐ 161 Bud Byerly	27.00	12.00	4.00
☐ 162 Del Crandall	30.00	13.50	4.50
☐ 163 Stan Rojek	27.00	12.00	4.00
☐ 164 Walt Dubiel	27.00	12.00	4.00
☐ 165 Eddie Kazak	27.00	12.00	4.00
☐ 166 Paul LaPalme	27.00	12.00	4.00
☐ 167 Bill Howerton	27.00	12.00	4.00
☐ 168 Charlie Silvera	32.00	14.25	4.75
☐ 169 Howie Judson	27.00	12.00	4.00
☐ 170 Gus Bell	32.00	14.25	4.75
☐ 171 Ed Erautt	27.00	12.00	4.00
☐ 172 Eddie Miksis	27.00	12.00	4.00
☐ 173 Roy Smalley	27.00	12.00	4.00
☐ 174 Clarence Marshall	27.00	12.00	4.00
☐ 175 Billy Martin	350.00	160.00	52.50
☐ 176 Hank Edwards	27.00	12.00	4.00
☐ 177 Bill Wight	27.00	12.00	4.00
☐ 178 Cass Michaels	27.00	12.00	4.00
☐ 179 Frank Smith	27.00	12.00	4.00

No.	Player			
☐ 180	Charley Maxwell	30.00	13.50	4.50
☐ 181	Bob Swift	27.00	12.00	4.00
☐ 182	Billy Hitchcock	27.00	12.00	4.00
☐ 183	Erv Dusak	27.00	12.00	4.00
☐ 184	Bob Ramazzotti	27.00	12.00	4.00
☐ 185	Bill Nicholson	27.00	12.00	4.00
☐ 186	Walt Masterson	27.00	12.00	4.00
☐ 187	Bob Miller	27.00	12.00	4.00
☐ 188	Clarence Podbielan	27.00	12.00	4.00
☐ 189	Pete Reiser	35.00	15.75	5.25
☐ 190	Don Johnson	27.00	12.00	4.00
☐ 191	Yogi Berra	400.00	180.00	60.00
☐ 192	Myron Ginsberg	27.00	12.00	4.00
☐ 193	Harry Simpson	27.00	12.00	4.00
☐ 194	Joe Hatton	27.00	12.00	4.00
☐ 195	Minnie Minoso	120.00	55.00	18.00
☐ 196	Solly Hemus	27.00	12.00	4.00
☐ 197	George Strickland	27.00	12.00	4.00
☐ 198	Phil Haugstad	27.00	12.00	4.00
☐ 199	George Zuverink	27.00	12.00	4.00
☐ 200	Ralph Houk	65.00	29.00	9.75
☐ 201	Alex Kellner	27.00	12.00	4.00
☐ 202	Joe Collins	35.00	15.75	5.25
☐ 203	Curt Simmons	30.00	13.50	4.50
☐ 204	Ron Northey	27.00	12.00	4.00
☐ 205	Clyde King	27.00	12.00	4.00
☐ 206	Joe Ostrowski	27.00	12.00	4.00
☐ 207	Mickey Harris	27.00	12.00	4.00
☐ 208	Marlin Stuart	27.00	12.00	4.00
☐ 209	Howie Fox	27.00	12.00	4.00
☐ 210	Dick Fowler	27.00	12.00	4.00
☐ 211	Ray Coleman	27.00	12.00	4.00
☐ 212	Ned Garver	27.00	12.00	4.00
☐ 213	Nippy Jones	27.00	12.00	4.00
☐ 214	Johnny Hopp	30.00	13.50	4.50
☐ 215	Hank Bauer	48.00	22.00	5.50
☐ 216	Richie Ashburn	100.00	45.00	15.00
☐ 217	Snuffy Stirnweiss	32.00	14.25	4.75
☐ 218	Clyde McCullough	27.00	12.00	4.00
☐ 219	Bobby Shantz	35.00	15.75	5.25
☐ 220	Joe Presko	27.00	12.00	4.00
☐ 221	Granny Hamner	27.00	12.00	4.00
☐ 222	Hoot Evers	27.00	12.00	4.00
☐ 223	Del Ennis	32.00	14.25	4.75
☐ 224	Bruce Edwards	27.00	12.00	4.00
☐ 225	Frank Baumholtz	27.00	12.00	4.00
☐ 226	Dave Philley	27.00	12.00	4.00
☐ 227	Joe Garagiola	135.00	60.00	20.00
☐ 228	Al Brazle	27.00	12.00	4.00
☐ 229	Gene Bearden	30.00	13.50	4.50
☐ 230	Matt Batts	27.00	12.00	4.00
☐ 231	Sam Zoldak	27.00	12.00	4.00
☐ 232	Billy Cox	30.00	13.50	4.50
☐ 233	Bob Friend	32.00	14.25	4.75
☐ 234	Steve Souchock	27.00	12.00	4.00
☐ 235	Walt Dropo	30.00	13.50	4.50
☐ 236	Ed Fitzgerald	27.00	12.00	4.00
☐ 237	Jerry Coleman	32.00	14.25	4.75
☐ 238	Art Houtteman	27.00	12.00	4.00
☐ 239	Rocky Bridges	27.00	12.00	4.00
☐ 240	Jack Phillips	27.00	12.00	4.00
☐ 241	Tommy Byrne	27.00	12.00	4.00
☐ 242	Tom Poholsky	27.00	12.00	4.00
☐ 243	Larry Doby	40.00	18.00	6.00
☐ 244	Vic Wertz	30.00	13.50	4.50
☐ 245	Sherry Robertson	27.00	12.00	4.00
☐ 246	George Kell	75.00	34.00	11.25
☐ 247	Randy Gumpert	27.00	12.00	4.00
☐ 248	Frank Shea	27.00	12.00	4.00
☐ 249	Bobby Adams	27.00	12.00	4.00
☐ 250	Carl Erskine	65.00	29.00	9.75
☐ 251	Chico Carrasquel	45.00	20.00	6.75
☐ 252	Vern Bickford	45.00	20.00	6.75
☐ 253	Johnny Berardino	55.00	25.00	8.25
☐ 254	Joe Dobson	45.00	20.00	6.75
☐ 255	Clyde Vollmer	45.00	20.00	6.75
☐ 256	Pete Suder	45.00	20.00	6.75
☐ 257	Bobby Avila	50.00	22.50	7.50
☐ 258	Steve Gromek	45.00	20.00	6.75
☐ 259	Bob Addis	45.00	20.00	6.75
☐ 260	Pete Castiglione	45.00	20.00	6.75
☐ 261	Willie Mays	1750.00	700.00	175.00
☐ 262	Virgil Trucks	50.00	22.50	7.50
☐ 263	Harry Brecheen	50.00	22.50	7.50
☐ 264	Roy Hartsfield	45.00	20.00	6.75
☐ 265	Chuck Diering	45.00	20.00	6.75
☐ 266	Murry Dickson	45.00	20.00	6.75
☐ 267	Sid Gordon	45.00	20.00	6.75
☐ 268	Bob Lemon	175.00	80.00	27.00
☐ 269	Willard Nixon	45.00	20.00	6.75
☐ 270	Lou Brissie	45.00	20.00	6.75
☐ 271	Jim Delsing	45.00	20.00	6.75
☐ 272	Mike Garcia	50.00	22.50	7.50
☐ 273	Erv Palica	45.00	20.00	6.75
☐ 274	Ralph Branca	80.00	36.00	12.00
☐ 275	Pat Mullin	45.00	20.00	6.75
☐ 276	Jim Wilson	45.00	20.00	6.75
☐ 277	Early Wynn	175.00	80.00	27.00
☐ 278	Allie Clark	45.00	20.00	6.75
☐ 279	Eddie Stewart	45.00	20.00	6.75
☐ 280	Cloyd Boyer	50.00	22.50	7.50
☐ 281	Tommy Brown SP	55.00	25.00	8.25
☐ 282	Birdie Tebbetts SP	60.00	27.00	9.00
☐ 283	Phil Masi SP	55.00	25.00	8.25
☐ 284	Hank Arft SP	55.00	25.00	8.25
☐ 285	Cliff Fannin SP	55.00	25.00	8.25
☐ 286	Joe DeMaestri SP	55.00	25.00	8.25
☐ 287	Steve Bilko SP	55.00	25.00	8.25
☐ 288	Chet Nichols SP	55.00	25.00	8.25
☐ 289	Tommy Holmes SP	65.00	29.00	9.75
☐ 290	Joe Astroth SP	55.00	25.00	8.25
☐ 291	Gil Coan SP	55.00	25.00	8.25
☐ 292	Floyd Baker SP	55.00	25.00	8.25
☐ 293	Sibby Sisti SP	55.00	25.00	8.25
☐ 294	Walker Cooper SP	55.00	25.00	8.25
☐ 295	Phil Cavarretta SP	65.00	29.00	9.75

□ 296 Red Rolfe SP 65.00 29.00 9.75
□ 297 Andy Seminick SP 55.00 25.00 8.25
□ 298 Bob Ross SP 55.00 25.00 8.25
□ 299 Ray Murray SP 55.00 25.00 8.25
□ 300 Barney McCosky SP .. 55.00 25.00 8.25
□ 301 Bob Porterfield 45.00 20.00 6.75
□ 302 Max Surkont 45.00 20.00 6.75
□ 303 Harry Dorish 45.00 20.00 6.75
□ 304 Sam Dente 45.00 20.00 6.75
□ 305 Paul Richards 50.00 22.50 7.50
□ 306 Lou Sleater 45.00 20.00 6.75
□ 307 Frank Campos 45.00 20.00 6.75
□ 308 Luis Aloma 45.00 20.00 6.75
□ 309 Jim Busby 45.00 20.00 6.75
□ 310 George Metkovich 55.00 25.00 8.25
□ 311 Mickey Mantle DP 24000.00 7500.00 1500.00
□ 312 Jackie Robinson DP 1150.00 400.00 100.00
□ 313 Bobby Thomson DP 225.00 100.00 33.00
□ 314 Roy Campanella 1550.00 550.00 150.00
□ 315 Leo Durocher MG 350.00 160.00 52.50
□ 316 Dave Williams 200.00 90.00 30.00
□ 317 Conrado Marrero 175.00 80.00 27.00
□ 318 Harold Gregg 175.00 80.00 27.00
□ 319 Al Walker 175.00 80.00 27.00
□ 320 John Rutherford 175.00 80.00 27.00
□ 321 Joe Black 250.00 110.00 37.50
□ 322 Randy Jackson 175.00 80.00 27.00
□ 323 Bubba Church 175.00 80.00 27.00
□ 324 Warren Hacker 175.00 80.00 27.00
□ 325 Bill Serena 175.00 80.00 27.00
□ 326 George Shuba 200.00 90.00 30.00
□ 327 Al Wilson 175.00 80.00 27.00
□ 328 Bob Borkowski 175.00 80.00 27.00
□ 329 Ike Delock 175.00 80.00 27.00
□ 330 Turk Lown 175.00 80.00 27.00
□ 331 Tom Morgan 175.00 80.00 27.00
□ 332 Anthony Bartirome .. 175.00 80.00 27.00
□ 333 Pee Wee Reese 1050.00 375.00 90.00
□ 334 Wilmer Mizell 200.00 90.00 30.00
□ 335 Ted Lepcio 175.00 80.00 27.00
□ 336 Dave Koslo 175.00 80.00 27.00
□ 337 Jim Hearn 175.00 80.00 27.00
□ 338 Sal Yvars 175.00 80.00 27.00
□ 339 Russ Meyer 175.00 80.00 27.00
□ 340 Bob Hooper 175.00 80.00 27.00
□ 341 Hal Jeffcoat 175.00 80.00 27.00
□ 342 Clem Labine 225.00 100.00 33.00
□ 343 Dick Gernert 175.00 80.00 27.00
□ 344 Ewell Blackwell 200.00 90.00 30.00
□ 345 Sammy White 175.00 80.00 27.00
□ 346 George Spencer 175.00 80.00 27.00
□ 347 Joe Adcock 225.00 100.00 33.00
□ 348 Robert Kelly 175.00 80.00 27.00
□ 349 Bob Cain 175.00 80.00 27.00
□ 350 Cal Abrams 175.00 80.00 27.00
□ 351 Alvin Dark 225.00 100.00 33.00
□ 352 Karl Drews 175.00 80.00 27.00
□ 353 Bobby Del Greco 175.00 80.00 27.00
□ 354 Fred Hatfield 175.00 80.00 27.00
□ 355 Bobby Morgan 175.00 80.00 27.00
□ 356 Toby Atwell 175.00 80.00 27.00
□ 357 Smoky Burgess 225.00 100.00 33.00
□ 358 John Kucab 175.00 80.00 27.00
□ 359 Dee Fondy 175.00 80.00 27.00
□ 360 George Crowe 175.00 80.00 27.00
□ 361 William Posedel CO . 175.00 80.00 27.00
□ 362 Ken Heintzelman 175.00 80.00 27.00
□ 363 Dick Rozek 175.00 80.00 27.00
□ 364 Clyde Sukeforth CO . 175.00 80.00 27.00
□ 365 Cookie Lavagetto CO 175.00 80.00 27.00
□ 366 Dave Madison 175.00 80.00 27.00
□ 367 Ben Thorpe 175.00 80.00 27.00
□ 368 Ed Wright 175.00 80.00 27.00
□ 369 Dick Groat 300.00 135.00 45.00
□ 370 Billy Hoeft 175.00 80.00 27.00
□ 371 Bobby Hofman 175.00 80.00 27.00
□ 372 Gil McDougald 300.00 135.00 45.00
□ 373 Jim Turner CO 200.00 90.00 30.00
□ 374 John Benton 175.00 80.00 27.00
□ 375 John Merson 175.00 80.00 27.00
□ 376 Faye Throneberry 175.00 80.00 27.00
□ 377 Chuck Dressen MG . 200.00 90.00 30.00
□ 378 Leroy Fusselman 175.00 80.00 27.00
□ 379 Joe Rossi 175.00 80.00 27.00
□ 380 Clem Koshorek 175.00 80.00 27.00
□ 381 Milton Stock CO 175.00 80.00 27.00
□ 382 Sam Jones 200.00 90.00 30.00
□ 383 Del Wilber 175.00 80.00 27.00
□ 384 Frank Crosetti CO 250.00 110.00 37.50
□ 385 Herman Franks CO .. 200.00 90.00 30.00
□ 386 John Yuhas 175.00 80.00 27.00
□ 387 Billy Meyer MG 175.00 80.00 27.00
□ 388 Bob Chipman 175.00 80.00 27.00
□ 389 Ben Wade 175.00 80.00 27.00
□ 390 Glenn Nelson 175.00 80.00 27.00
□ 391 Ben Chapman UER .. 175.00 80.00 27.00
(photo actually
Sam Chapman)
□ 392 Hoyt Wilhelm 550.00 240.00 80.00
□ 393 Ebba St.Claire 175.00 80.00 27.00
□ 394 Billy Herman CO 250.00 110.00 37.50
□ 395 Jake Pitler CO 175.00 80.00 27.00
□ 396 Dick Williams 250.00 110.00 37.50
□ 397 Forrest Main 175.00 80.00 27.00
□ 398 Hal Rice 175.00 80.00 27.00
□ 399 Jim Fridley 175.00 80.00 27.00
□ 400 Bill Dickey CO 600.00 270.00 90.00
□ 401 Bob Schultz 175.00 80.00 27.00
□ 402 Earl Harrist 175.00 80.00 27.00
□ 403 Bill Miller 175.00 80.00 27.00
□ 404 Dick Brodowski 175.00 80.00 27.00
□ 405 Eddie Pellagrini 175.00 80.00 27.00
□ 406 Joe Nuxhall 225.00 100.00 33.00
□ 407 Eddie Mathews 2650.00 650.00 150.00

1953 Topps

The cards in this 274-card set measure 2 5/8" by 3 3/4". Although the last card is numbered 280, there are only 274 cards in the set since numbers 253, 261, 267, 268, 271, and 275 were never issued. The 1953 Topps series contains line drawings of players in full color. The name and team panel at the card base is easily damaged, making it very difficult to complete a mint set. The high number series, 221 to 280, was produced in shorter supply late in the year and hence is more difficult to complete than the lower numbers. The key cards in the set are Mickey Mantle (82) and Willie Mays (244). The key rookies in this set are Roy Face, Jim Gilliam, and Johnny Podres, all from the last series. There are a number of double-printed cards (actually not double but 50 percent more of each of these numbers were printed compared to the other cards in the series) indicated by DP in the checklist below. There were five players (10 Smoky Burgess, 44 Ellis Kinder, 61 Early Wynn, 72 Fred Hutchinson, and 81 Joe Black) held out of the first run of 1-85 (but printed in with numbers 86-165), who are each marked by SP in the checklist below. In addition, there are five numbers which were printed in with the more plentiful series 166-220; these cards (94, 107, 131, 145, and 156) are also indicated by DP in the checklist below. There were some three-card advertising panels produced by Topps; the players include Johnny Mize/Clem Koshorek/Toby Atwell and Mickey Mantle/Johnny Wyrostek/Sal Yvars. When cut apart, these advertising cards are distinguished by the non-standard card back, i.e., part of an advertisement for the 1953 Topps set instead of the typical statistics and biographical information about the player pictured.

	NRMT	VG-E	GOOD
COMPLETE SET (274)	13500.00	5000.00	1650.00
COMMON PLAYER (1-165)	25.00	11.00	3.50
COMMON DP (1-165)	15.00	6.50	2.15
COMMON PLAYER (166-220)	18.00	7.50	2.50
COMMON PLAYER (221-280)	95.00	42.00	10.00
COMMON DP (221-280)	45.00	20.00	6.75

	NRMT	VG-E	GOOD
□ 1 Jackie Robinson DP	600.00	150.00	30.00
□ 2 Luke Easter DP	18.00	7.50	2.50
□ 3 George Crowe	25.00	11.00	3.50
□ 4 Ben Wade	25.00	11.00	3.50
□ 5 Joe Dobson	25.00	11.00	3.50
□ 6 Sam Jones	25.00	11.00	3.50
□ 7 Bob Borkowski DP	15.00	6.50	2.15
□ 8 Clem Koshorek DP	15.00	6.50	2.15
□ 9 Joe Collins	30.00	13.50	4.50
□ 10 Smoky Burgess SP	38.00	16.00	5.00
□ 11 Sal Yvars	25.00	11.00	8.50
□ 12 Howie Judson DP	15.00	6.50	2.15
□ 13 Conrado Marrero DP	15.00	6.50	2.15
□ 14 Clem Labine DP	22.00	9.50	3.15
□ 15 Bobo Newsom DP	20.00	8.50	2.75
□ 16 Peanuts Lowrey DP	15.00	6.50	2.15
□ 17 Billy Hitchcock	25.00	11.00	3.50
□ 18 Ted Lepcio DP	15.00	6.50	2.15
□ 19 Mel Parnell DP	22.00	9.50	3.15
□ 20 Hank Thompson	27.00	12.00	4.00
□ 21 Billy Johnson	27.00	12.00	4.00
□ 22 Howie Fox	25.00	11.00	3.50
□ 23 Toby Atwell DP	15.00	6.50	2.15
□ 24 Ferris Fain	27.00	12.00	4.00
□ 25 Ray Boone	27.00	12.00	4.00
□ 26 Dale Mitchell DP	20.00	8.50	2.75
□ 27 Roy Campanella DP	210.00	90.00	25.00
□ 28 Eddie Pellagrini	25.00	11.00	3.50
□ 29 Hal Jeffcoat	25.00	11.00	3.50
□ 30 Willard Nixon	25.00	11.00	3.50
□ 31 Ewell Blackwell	42.00	17.00	5.50
□ 32 Clyde Vollmer	25.00	11.00	3.50
□ 33 Bob Kennedy DP	15.00	6.50	2.15
□ 34 George Shuba	27.00	12.00	4.00
□ 35 Irv Noren DP	18.00	7.50	2.50
□ 36 Johnny Groth DP	15.00	6.50	2.15
□ 37 Eddie Mathews DP	110.00	50.00	16.50
□ 38 Jim Hearn DP	15.00	6.50	2.15
□ 39 Eddie Miksis	25.00	11.00	3.50
□ 40 John Lipon	25.00	11.00	3.50
□ 41 Enos Slaughter	85.00	38.00	12.75
□ 42 Gus Zernial DP	18.00	7.50	2.50
□ 43 Gil McDougald	45.00	20.00	6.75
□ 44 Ellis Kinder SP	30.00	13.50	4.50
□ 45 Grady Hatton DP	15.00	6.50	2.15
□ 46 Johnny Klippstein DP	15.00	6.50	2.15

☐ 47 Bubba Church DP	15.00	6.50	2.15
☐ 48 Bob Del Greco DP	15.00	6.50	2.15
☐ 49 Faye Throneberry DP	15.00	6.50	2.15
☐ 50 Chuck Dressen MG DP	22.00	9.50	3.15
☐ 51 Frank Campos DP	15.00	6.50	2.15
☐ 52 Ted Gray DP	15.00	6.50	2.15
☐ 53 Sherm Lollar DP	18.00	7.50	2.50
☐ 54 Bob Feller DP	100.00	45.00	15.00
☐ 55 Maurice McDermott DP	15.00	6.50	2.15
☐ 56 Jerry Staley DP	15.00	6.50	2.15
☐ 57 Carl Scheib	25.00	11.00	3.50
☐ 58 George Metkovich	25.00	11.00	3.50
☐ 59 Karl Drews DP	15.00	6.50	2.15
☐ 60 Cloyd Boyer DP	15.00	6.50	2.15
☐ 61 Early Wynn SP	85.00	38.00	12.75
☐ 62 Monte Irvin DP	42.00	17.00	5.50
☐ 63 Gus Niarhos DP	15.00	6.50	2.15
☐ 64 Dave Philley	25.00	11.00	3.50
☐ 65 Earl Harrist	25.00	11.00	3.50
☐ 66 Minnie Minoso	45.00	20.00	6.75
☐ 67 Roy Sievers DP	18.00	7.50	2.50
☐ 68 Del Rice	25.00	11.00	3.50
☐ 69 Dick Brodowski	25.00	11.00	3.50
☐ 70 Ed Yuhas	25.00	11.00	3.50
☐ 71 Tony Bartirome	25.00	11.00	3.50
☐ 72 Fred Hutchinson SP	35.00	15.75	5.25
☐ 73 Eddie Robinson	25.00	11.00	3.50
☐ 74 Joe Rossi	25.00	11.00	3.50
☐ 75 Mike Garcia	27.00	12.00	4.00
☐ 76 Pee Wee Reese	140.00	63.00	21.00
☐ 77 Johnny Mize DP	60.00	27.00	9.00
☐ 78 Red Schoendienst	65.00	29.00	9.75
☐ 79 Johnny Wyrostek	25.00	11.00	3.50
☐ 80 Jim Hegan	27.00	12.00	4.00
☐ 81 Joe Black SP	60.00	27.00	9.00
☐ 82 Mickey Mantle	2500.00	750.00	200.00
☐ 83 Howie Pollet	25.00	11.00	3.50
☐ 84 Bob Hooper DP	15.00	6.50	2.15
☐ 85 Bobby Morgan DP	15.00	6.50	2.15
☐ 86 Billy Martin	140.00	63.00	21.00
☐ 87 Ed Lopat	40.00	18.00	6.00
☐ 88 Willie Jones DP	15.00	6.50	2.15
☐ 89 Chuck Stobbs DP	15.00	6.50	2.15
☐ 90 Hank Edwards DP	15.00	6.50	2.15
☐ 91 Ebba St.Claire DP	15.00	6.50	2.15
☐ 92 Paul Minner DP	15.00	6.50	2.15
☐ 93 Hal Rice DP	15.00	6.50	2.15
☐ 94 Bill Kennedy DP	18.00	7.50	2.50
☐ 95 Willard Marshall DP	15.00	6.50	2.15
☐ 96 Virgil Trucks	27.00	12.00	4.00
☐ 97 Don Kolloway DP	15.00	6.50	2.15
☐ 98 Cal Abrams DP	15.00	6.50	2.15
☐ 99 Dave Madison	25.00	11.00	3.50
☐ 100 Bill Miller	25.00	11.00	3.50
☐ 101 Ted Wilks	25.00	11.00	3.50
☐ 102 Connie Ryan DP	15.00	6.50	2.15
☐ 103 Joe Astroth DP	15.00	6.50	2.15
☐ 104 Yogi Berra	240.00	105.00	35.00
☐ 105 Joe Nuxhall DP	20.00	8.50	2.75
☐ 106 Johnny Antonelli	27.00	12.00	4.00
☐ 107 Danny O'Connell DP	18.00	7.50	2.50
☐ 108 Bob Porterfield DP	15.00	6.50	2.15
☐ 109 Alvin Dark	33.00	15.00	5.00
☐ 110 Herman Wehmeier DP	15.00	6.50	2.15
☐ 111 Hank Sauer DP	20.00	8.50	2.75
☐ 112 Ned Garver DP	15.00	6.50	2.15
☐ 113 Jerry Priddy	25.00	11.00	3.50
☐ 114 Phil Rizzuto	110.00	50.00	16.50
☐ 115 George Spencer	25.00	11.00	3.50
☐ 116 Frank Smith DP	15.00	6.50	2.15
☐ 117 Sid Gordon DP	15.00	6.50	2.15
☐ 118 Gus Bell DP	18.00	7.50	2.50
☐ 119 Johnny Sain SP	45.00	20.00	6.75
☐ 120 Davey Williams	30.00	13.50	4.50
☐ 121 Walt Dropo	27.00	12.00	4.00
☐ 122 Elmer Valo	25.00	11.00	3.50
☐ 123 Tommy Byrne DP	18.00	7.50	2.50
☐ 124 Sibby Sisti DP	15.00	6.50	2.15
☐ 125 Dick Williams DP	20.00	8.50	2.75
☐ 126 Bill Connelly DP	15.00	6.50	2.15
☐ 127 Clint Courtney DP	15.00	6.50	2.15
☐ 128 Wilmer Mizell DP	15.00	6.50	2.15
☐ 129 Keith Thomas	25.00	11.00	3.50
☐ 130 Turk Lown DP	15.00	6.50	2.15
☐ 131 Harry Byrd DP	18.00	7.50	2.50
☐ 132 Tom Morgan	25.00	11.00	3.50
☐ 133 Gil Coan	25.00	11.00	3.50
☐ 134 Rube Walker	27.00	12.00	4.00
☐ 135 Al Rosen DP	35.00	15.75	5.25
☐ 136 Ken Heintzelman DP	15.00	6.50	2.15
☐ 137 John Rutherford DP	15.00	6.50	2.15
☐ 138 George Kell	50.00	22.50	7.50
☐ 139 Sammy White	25.00	11.00	3.50
☐ 140 Tommy Glaviano	25.00	11.00	3.50
☐ 141 Allie Reynolds DP	35.00	15.75	5.25
☐ 142 Vic Wertz	27.00	12.00	4.00
☐ 143 Billy Pierce	32.00	14.25	4.75
☐ 144 Bob Schultz DP	15.00	6.50	2.15
☐ 145 Harry Dorish DP	18.00	7.50	2.50
☐ 146 Granny Hamner	25.00	11.00	3.50
☐ 147 Warren Spahn	130.00	60.00	20.00
☐ 148 Mickey Grasso	25.00	11.00	3.50
☐ 149 Dom DiMaggio DP	35.00	15.75	5.25
☐ 150 Harry Simpson DP	15.00	6.50	2.15
☐ 151 Hoyt Wilhelm	65.00	29.00	9.75
☐ 152 Bob Adams DP	15.00	6.50	2.15
☐ 153 Andy Seminick DP	15.00	6.50	2.15
☐ 154 Dick Groat	40.00	18.00	6.00
☐ 155 Dutch Leonard	25.00	11.00	3.50
☐ 156 Jim Rivera DP	18.00	7.50	2.50
☐ 157 Bob Addis DP	15.00	6.50	2.15
☐ 158 Johnny Logan	30.00	13.50	4.50
☐ 159 Wayne Terwilliger DP	15.00	6.50	2.15
☐ 160 Bob Young	25.00	11.00	3.50

- ☐ 161 Vern Bickford DP 15.00 6.50 2.15
- ☐ 162 Ted Kluszewski 48.00 22.00 6.00
- ☐ 163 Fred Hatfield DP 15.00 6.50 2.15
- ☐ 164 Frank Shea DP 15.00 6.50 2.15
- ☐ 165 Billy Hoeft 25.00 11.00 3.50
- ☐ 166 Billy Hunter 18.00 7.50 2.50
- ☐ 167 Art Schult 18.00 7.50 2.50
- ☐ 168 Willard Schmidt 18.00 7.50 2.50
- ☐ 169 Dizzy Trout 18.00 7.50 2.50
- ☐ 170 Bill Werle 18.00 7.50 2.50
- ☐ 171 Bill Glynn 18.00 7.50 2.50
- ☐ 172 Rip Repulski 18.00 7.50 2.50
- ☐ 173 Preston Ward 18.00 7.50 2.50
- ☐ 174 Billy Loes 22.00 9.50 3.15
- ☐ 175 Ron Kline 18.00 7.50 2.50
- ☐ 176 Don Hoak 25.00 11.00 3.50
- ☐ 177 Jim Dyck 18.00 7.50 2.50
- ☐ 178 Jim Waugh 18.00 7.50 2.50
- ☐ 179 Gene Hermanski 18.00 7.50 2.50
- ☐ 180 Virgil Stallcup 18.00 7.50 2.50
- ☐ 181 Al Zarilla 18.00 7.50 2.50
- ☐ 182 Bobby Hofman 18.00 7.50 2.50
- ☐ 183 Stu Miller 24.00 10.50 3.50
- ☐ 184 Hal Brown 18.00 7.50 2.50
- ☐ 185 Jim Pendleton 18.00 7.50 2.50
- ☐ 186 Charlie Bishop 18.00 7.50 2.50
- ☐ 187 Jim Fridley 18.00 7.50 2.50
- ☐ 188 Andy Carey 30.00 13.50 4.50
- ☐ 189 Ray Jablonski 18.00 7.50 2.50
- ☐ 190 Dixie Walker 18.00 7.50 2.50
- ☐ 191 Ralph Kiner 60.00 27.00 9.00
- ☐ 192 Wally Westlake 18.00 7.50 2.50
- ☐ 193 Mike Clark 18.00 7.50 2.50
- ☐ 194 Eddie Kazak 18.00 7.50 2.50
- ☐ 195 Ed McGhee 18.00 7.50 2.50
- ☐ 196 Bob Keegan 18.00 7.50 2.50
- ☐ 197 Del Crandall 20.00 8.50 2.75
- ☐ 198 Forrest Main 18.00 7.50 2.50
- ☐ 199 Marion Fricano 18.00 7.50 2.50
- ☐ 200 Gordon Goldsberry ... 18.00 7.50 2.50
- ☐ 201 Paul LaPalme 18.00 7.50 2.50
- ☐ 202 Carl Sawatski 18.00 7.50 2.50
- ☐ 203 Cliff Fannin 18.00 7.50 2.50
- ☐ 204 Dick Bokelman 18.00 7.50 2.50
- ☐ 205 Vern Benson 18.00 7.50 2.50
- ☐ 206 Ed Bailey 24.00 10.50 3.50
- ☐ 207 Whitey Ford 165.00 75.00 22.00
- ☐ 208 Jim Wilson 18.00 7.50 2.50
- ☐ 209 Jim Greengrass 18.00 7.50 2.50
- ☐ 210 Bob Cerv 27.00 12.00 4.00
- ☐ 211 J.W. Porter 18.00 7.50 2.50
- ☐ 212 Jack Dittmer 18.00 7.50 2.50
- ☐ 213 Ray Scarborough 18.00 7.50 2.50
- ☐ 214 Bill Bruton 22.00 9.50 3.15
- ☐ 215 Gene Conley 22.00 9.50 3.15
- ☐ 216 Jim Hughes 18.00 7.50 2.50
- ☐ 217 Murray Wall 18.00 7.50 2.50
- ☐ 218 Les Fusselman 18.00 7.50 2.50
- ☐ 219 Pete Runnels UER 22.00 9.50 3.15
  (photo actually
  Don Johnson)
- ☐ 220 Satchel Paige UER .. 450.00 200.00 67.50
  (misspelled Satchell
  on card front)
- ☐ 221 Bob Milliken 95.00 42.00 10.00
- ☐ 222 Vic Janowicz DP 50.00 22.50 7.50
- ☐ 223 Johnny O'Brien DP 50.00 22.50 7.50
- ☐ 224 Lou Sleater DP 45.00 20.00 6.75
- ☐ 225 Bobby Shantz 110.00 50.00 16.50
- ☐ 226 Ed Erautt 95.00 42.00 10.00
- ☐ 227 Morrie Martin 95.00 42.00 10.00
- ☐ 228 Hal Newhouser 110.00 50.00 16.50
- ☐ 229 Rocky Krsnich 95.00 42.00 10.00
- ☐ 230 Johnny Lindell DP 45.00 20.00 6.75
- ☐ 231 Solly Hemus DP 45.00 20.00 6.75
- ☐ 232 Dick Kokos 95.00 42.00 10.00
- ☐ 233 Al Aber 95.00 42.00 10.00
- ☐ 234 Ray Murray DP 45.00 20.00 6.75
- ☐ 235 John Hetki DP 45.00 20.00 6.75
- ☐ 236 Harry Perkowski DP .. 45.00 20.00 6.75
- ☐ 237 Bud Podbielan DP 45.00 20.00 6.75
- ☐ 238 Cal Hogue DP 45.00 20.00 6.75
- ☐ 239 Jim Delsing 95.00 42.00 10.00
- ☐ 240 Fred Marsh 95.00 42.00 10.00
- ☐ 241 Al Sima DP 45.00 20.00 6.75
- ☐ 242 Charlie Silvera 100.00 45.00 15.00
- ☐ 243 Carlos Bernier DP 45.00 20.00 6.75
- ☐ 244 Willie Mays 1875.00 700.00 175.00
- ☐ 245 Bill Norman 95.00 42.00 10.00
- ☐ 246 Roy Face DP 90.00 40.00 13.50
- ☐ 247 Mike Sandlock DP 45.00 20.00 6.75
- ☐ 248 Gene Stephens DP 45.00 20.00 6.75
- ☐ 249 Eddie O'Brien 95.00 42.00 10.00
- ☐ 250 Bob Wilson 95.00 42.00 10.00
- ☐ 251 Sid Hudson 95.00 42.00 10.00
- ☐ 252 Hank Foiles 95.00 42.00 10.00
- ☐ 253 Does not exist 00.00 00.00 00.00
- ☐ 254 Preacher Roe DP 90.00 40.00 13.50
- ☐ 255 Dixie Howell 95.00 42.00 10.00
- ☐ 256 Les Peden 95.00 42.00 10.00
- ☐ 257 Bob Boyd 95.00 42.00 10.00
- ☐ 258 Jim Gilliam 300.00 135.00 45.00
- ☐ 259 Roy McMillan DP 50.00 22.50 7.50
- ☐ 260 Sam Calderone 95.00 42.00 10.00
- ☐ 261 Does not exist 00.00 00.00 00.00
- ☐ 262 Bob Oldis 95.00 42.00 10.00
- ☐ 263 Johnny Podres 250.00 110.00 37.50
- ☐ 264 Gene Woodling DP 65.00 29.00 9.75
- ☐ 265 Jackie Jensen 110.00 50.00 16.50
- ☐ 266 Bob Cain 95.00 42.00 10.00
- ☐ 267 Does not exist 00.00 00.00 00.00
- ☐ 268 Does not exist 00.00 00.00 00.00
- ☐ 269 Duane Pillette 95.00 42.00 10.00
- ☐ 270 Vern Stephens 100.00 45.00 15.00
- ☐ 271 Does not exist 00.00 00.00 00.00
- ☐ 272 Bill Antonello 95.00 42.00 10.00

☐ 273 Harvey Haddix	120.00	55.00	18.00
☐ 274 John Riddle	95.00	42.00	10.00
☐ 275 Does not exist	00.00	00.00	00.00
☐ 276 Ken Raffensberger	95.00	42.00	10.00
☐ 277 Don Lund	95.00	42.00	10.00
☐ 278 Willie Miranda	95.00	42.00	10.00
☐ 279 Joe Coleman DP	45.00	20.00	6.75
☐ 280 Milt Bolling	325.00	75.00	15.00

1954 Topps

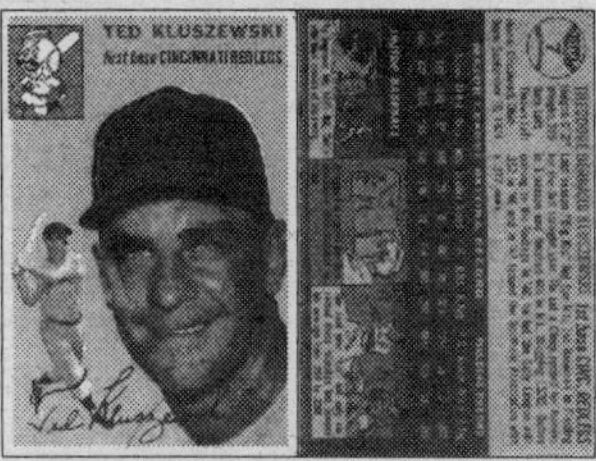

The cards in this 250-card set measure 2 5/8" by 3 3/4". Each of the cards in the 1954 Topps set contains a large "head" shot of the player in color plus a smaller full-length photo in black and white set against a color background. This series contains the rookie cards of Hank Aaron, Ernie Banks, and Al Kaline and two separate cards of Ted Williams (number 1 and number 250). Conspicuous by his absence is Mickey Mantle who apparently was the exclusive property of Bowman during 1954 (and 1955).

	NRMT	VG-E	GOOD
COMPLETE SET (250)	8000.00	3600.00	800.00
COMMON PLAYER (1-50)	14.00	6.25	2.00
COMMON PLAYER (51-75)	30.00	13.50	4.50
COMMON PLAYER (76-125)	14.00	6.25	2.00
COMMON PLAYER (126-250)	14.00	6.25	2.00

☐ 1 Ted Williams	600.00	200.00	40.00
☐ 2 Gus Zernial	16.00	6.75	2.25
☐ 3 Monte Irvin	33.00	15.00	5.00
☐ 4 Hank Sauer	16.00	6.75	2.25
☐ 5 Ed Lopat	22.00	9.50	3.15
☐ 6 Pete Runnels	16.00	6.75	2.25
☐ 7 Ted Kluszewski	28.00	12.50	4.00
☐ 8 Bob Young	14.00	6.25	2.00
☐ 9 Harvey Haddix	16.00	6.75	2.25
☐ 10 Jackie Robinson	275.00	120.00	40.00
☐ 11 Paul Leslie Smith	14.00	6.25	2.00
☐ 12 Del Crandall	16.00	6.75	2.25
☐ 13 Billy Martin	85.00	38.00	12.75
☐ 14 Preacher Roe	22.00	9.50	3.15
☐ 15 Al Rosen	22.00	9.50	3.15
☐ 16 Vic Janowicz	16.00	6.75	2.25
☐ 17 Phil Rizzuto	70.00	32.00	10.50
☐ 18 Walt Dropo	16.00	6.75	2.25
☐ 19 Johnny Lipon	14.00	6.25	2.00
☐ 20 Warren Spahn	100.00	45.00	15.00
☐ 21 Bobby Shantz	16.00	6.75	2.25
☐ 22 Jim Greengrass	14.00	6.25	2.00
☐ 23 Luke Easter	14.00	6.25	2.00
☐ 24 Granny Hamner	14.00	6.25	2.00
☐ 25 Harvey Kuenn	36.00	16.25	5.50
☐ 26 Ray Jablonski	14.00	6.25	2.00
☐ 27 Ferris Fain	16.00	6.75	2.25
☐ 28 Paul Minner	14.00	6.25	2.00
☐ 29 Jim Hegan	16.00	6.75	2.25
☐ 30 Eddie Mathews	100.00	45.00	15.00
☐ 31 Johnny Klippstein	14.00	6.25	2.00
☐ 32 Duke Snider	145.00	65.00	18.00
☐ 33 Johnny Schmitz	14.00	6.25	2.00
☐ 34 Jim Rivera	14.00	6.25	2.00
☐ 35 Jim Gilliam	27.00	12.00	4.00
☐ 36 Hoyt Wilhelm	40.00	18.00	6.00
☐ 37 Whitey Ford	110.00	50.00	16.50
☐ 38 Eddie Stanky	16.00	6.75	2.25
☐ 39 Sherm Lollar	16.00	6.75	2.25
☐ 40 Mel Parnell	16.00	6.75	2.25
☐ 41 Willie Jones	14.00	6.25	2.00
☐ 42 Don Mueller	16.00	6.75	2.25
☐ 43 Dick Groat	18.00	7.50	2.50
☐ 44 Ned Garver	14.00	6.25	2.00
☐ 45 Richie Ashburn	45.00	20.00	6.75
☐ 46 Ken Raffensberger	14.00	6.25	2.00
☐ 47 Ellis Kinder	14.00	6.25	2.00
☐ 48 Billy Hunter	14.00	6.25	2.00
☐ 49 Ray Murray	14.00	6.25	2.00
☐ 50 Yogi Berra	250.00	110.00	37.50
☐ 51 Johnny Lindell	30.00	13.50	4.50
☐ 52 Vic Power	33.00	15.00	5.00
☐ 53 Jack Dittmer	30.00	13.50	4.50
☐ 54 Vern Stephens	33.00	15.00	5.00
☐ 55 Phil Cavarretta MG	36.00	16.25	5.50
☐ 56 Willie Miranda	30.00	13.50	4.50
☐ 57 Luis Aloma	30.00	13.50	4.50
☐ 58 Bob Wilson	30.00	13.50	4.50
☐ 59 Gene Conley	33.00	15.00	5.00
☐ 60 Frank Baumholtz	30.00	13.50	4.50
☐ 61 Bob Cain	30.00	13.50	4.50
☐ 62 Eddie Robinson	33.00	15.00	5.00
☐ 63 Johnny Pesky	33.00	15.00	5.00
☐ 64 Hank Thompson	33.00	15.00	5.00

☐ 65	Bob Swift CO	30.00	13.50	4.50
☐ 66	Ted Lepcio	30.00	13.50	4.50
☐ 67	Jim Willis	30.00	13.50	4.50
☐ 68	Sam Calderone	30.00	13.50	4.50
☐ 69	Bud Podbielan	30.00	13.50	4.50
☐ 70	Larry Doby	70.00	32.00	10.50
☐ 71	Frank Smith	30.00	13.50	4.50
☐ 72	Preston Ward	30.00	13.50	4.50
☐ 73	Wayne Terwilliger	30.00	13.50	4.50
☐ 74	Bill Taylor	30.00	13.50	4.50
☐ 75	Fred Haney MG	30.00	13.50	4.50
☐ 76	Bob Scheffing CO	14.00	6.25	2.00
☐ 77	Ray Boone	16.00	6.75	2.25
☐ 78	Ted Kazanski	14.00	6.25	2.00
☐ 79	Andy Pafko	16.00	6.75	2.25
☐ 80	Jackie Jensen	22.00	9.50	3.15
☐ 81	Dave Hoskins	14.00	6.25	2.00
☐ 82	Milt Bolling	14.00	6.25	2.00
☐ 83	Joe Collins	18.00	7.50	2.50
☐ 84	Dick Cole	14.00	6.25	2.00
☐ 85	Bob Turley	28.00	12.50	4.00
☐ 86	Billy Herman CO	24.00	10.50	3.50
☐ 87	Roy Face	18.00	7.50	2.50
☐ 88	Matt Batts	14.00	6.25	2.00
☐ 89	Howie Pollet	14.00	6.25	2.00
☐ 90	Willie Mays	425.00	190.00	63.00
☐ 91	Bob Oldis	14.00	6.25	2.00
☐ 92	Wally Westlake	14.00	6.25	2.00
☐ 93	Sid Hudson	14.00	6.25	2.00
☐ 94	Ernie Banks	725.00	300.00	80.00
☐ 95	Hal Rice	14.00	6.25	2.00
☐ 96	Charlie Silvera	16.00	6.75	2.25
☐ 97	Jerald Hal Lane	14.00	6.25	2.00
☐ 98	Joe Black	22.00	9.50	3.15
☐ 99	Bobby Hofman	14.00	6.25	2.00
☐ 100	Bob Keegan	14.00	6.25	2.00
☐ 101	Gene Woodling	22.00	9.50	3.15
☐ 102	Gil Hodges	80.00	36.00	12.00
☐ 103	Jim Lemon	18.00	7.50	2.50
☐ 104	Mike Sandlock	14.00	6.25	2.00
☐ 105	Andy Carey	18.00	7.50	2.50
☐ 106	Dick Kokos	14.00	6.25	2.00
☐ 107	Duane Pillette	14.00	6.25	2.00
☐ 108	Thornton Kipper	14.00	6.25	2.00
☐ 109	Bill Bruton	16.00	6.75	2.25
☐ 110	Harry Dorish	14.00	6.25	2.00
☐ 111	Jim Delsing	14.00	6.25	2.00
☐ 112	Bill Renna	14.00	6.25	2.00
☐ 113	Bob Boyd	14.00	6.25	2.00
☐ 114	Dean Stone	14.00	6.25	2.00
☐ 115	Rip Repulski	14.00	6.25	2.00
☐ 116	Steve Bilko	14.00	6.25	2.00
☐ 117	Solly Hemus	14.00	6.25	2.00
☐ 118	Carl Scheib	14.00	6.25	2.00
☐ 119	Johnny Antonelli	16.00	6.75	2.25
☐ 120	Roy McMillan	14.00	6.25	2.00
☐ 121	Clem Labine	16.00	6.75	2.25
☐ 122	Johnny Logan	16.00	6.75	2.25
☐ 123	Bobby Adams	14.00	6.25	2.00
☐ 124	Marion Fricano	14.00	6.25	2.00
☐ 125	Harry Perkowski	14.00	6.25	2.00
☐ 126	Ben Wade	14.00	6.25	2.00
☐ 127	Steve O'Neill MG	14.00	6.25	2.00
☐ 128	Hank Aaron	1600.00	650.00	150.00
☐ 129	Forrest Jacobs	14.00	6.25	2.00
☐ 130	Hank Bauer	33.00	15.00	5.00
☐ 131	Reno Bertoia	14.00	6.25	2.00
☐ 132	Tom Lasorda	165.00	75.00	22.50
☐ 133	Dave Baker CO	14.00	6.25	2.00
☐ 134	Cal Hogue	14.00	6.25	2.00
☐ 135	Joe Presko	14.00	6.25	2.00
☐ 136	Connie Ryan	14.00	6.25	2.00
☐ 137	Wally Moon	27.00	12.00	4.00
☐ 138	Bob Borkowski	14.00	6.25	2.00
☐ 139	The O'Briens Johnny O'Brien Eddie O'Brien	30.00	13.50	4.50
☐ 140	Tom Wright	14.00	6.25	2.00
☐ 141	Joey Jay	16.00	6.75	2.25
☐ 142	Tom Poholsky	14.00	6.25	2.00
☐ 143	Rollie Hemsley CO	14.00	6.25	2.00
☐ 144	Bill Werle	14.00	6.25	2.00
☐ 145	Elmer Valo	14.00	6.25	2.00
☐ 146	Don Johnson	14.00	6.25	2.00
☐ 147	Johnny Riddle CO	14.00	6.25	2.00
☐ 148	Bob Trice	14.00	6.25	2.00
☐ 149	Al Robertson	14.00	6.25	2.00
☐ 150	Dick Kryhoski	14.00	6.25	2.00
☐ 151	Alex Grammas	14.00	6.25	2.00
☐ 152	Michael Blyzka	14.00	6.25	2.00
☐ 153	Al Walker	16.00	6.75	2.25
☐ 154	Mike Fornieles	14.00	6.25	2.00
☐ 155	Bob Kennedy	14.00	6.25	2.00
☐ 156	Joe Coleman	14.00	6.25	2.00
☐ 157	Don Lenhardt	14.00	6.25	2.00
☐ 158	Peanuts Lowrey	14.00	6.25	2.00
☐ 159	Dave Philley	14.00	6.25	2.00
☐ 160	Ralph Kress CO	14.00	6.25	2.00
☐ 161	John Hetki	14.00	6.25	2.00
☐ 162	Herman Wehmeier	14.00	6.25	2.00
☐ 163	Frank House	14.00	6.25	2.00
☐ 164	Stu Miller	16.00	6.75	2.25
☐ 165	Jim Pendleton	14.00	6.25	2.00
☐ 166	Johnny Podres	27.00	12.00	4.00
☐ 167	Don Lund	14.00	6.25	2.00
☐ 168	Morrie Martin	14.00	6.25	2.00
☐ 169	Jim Hughes	14.00	6.25	2.00
☐ 170	James(Dusty) Rhodes	18.00	7.50	2.50
☐ 171	Leo Kiely	14.00	6.25	2.00
☐ 172	Harold Brown	14.00	6.25	2.00
☐ 173	Jack Harshman	14.00	6.25	2.00
☐ 174	Tom Qualters	14.00	6.25	2.00
☐ 175	Frank Leja	18.00	7.50	2.50
☐ 176	Robert Keely CO	14.00	6.25	2.00
☐ 177	Bob Milliken	14.00	6.25	2.00
☐ 178	Bill Glynn	14.00	6.25	2.00

☐ 179 Gair Allie	14.00	6.25	2.00
☐ 180 Wes Westrum	14.00	6.25	2.00
☐ 181 Mel Roach	14.00	6.25	2.00
☐ 182 Chuck Harmon	14.00	6.25	2.00
☐ 183 Earle Combs CO	25.00	11.00	3.50
☐ 184 Ed Bailey	16.00	6.75	2.25
☐ 185 Chuck Stobbs	14.00	6.25	2.00
☐ 186 Karl Olson	14.00	6.25	2.00
☐ 187 Heinie Manush CO	25.00	11.00	3.50
☐ 188 Dave Jolly	14.00	6.25	2.00
☐ 189 Bob Ross	14.00	6.25	2.00
☐ 190 Ray Herbert	14.00	6.25	2.00
☐ 191 John(Dick) Schofield	16.00	6.75	2.25
☐ 192 Ellis Deal CO	14.00	6.25	2.00
☐ 193 Johnny Hopp CO	16.00	6.75	2.25
☐ 194 Bill Sarni	14.00	6.25	2.00
☐ 195 Billy Consolo	14.00	6.25	2.00
☐ 196 Stan Jok	14.00	6.25	2.00
☐ 197 Lynwood Rowe CO ("Schoolboy")	16.00	6.75	2.25
☐ 198 Carl Sawatski	14.00	6.25	2.00
☐ 199 Glenn(Rocky) Nelson	14.00	6.25	2.00
☐ 200 Larry Jansen	16.00	6.75	2.25
☐ 201 Al Kaline	725.00	300.00	80.00
☐ 202 Bob Purkey	14.00	6.25	2.00
☐ 203 Harry Brecheen CO	16.00	6.75	2.25
☐ 204 Angel Scull	14.00	6.25	2.00
☐ 205 Johnny Sain	28.00	12.50	4.00
☐ 206 Ray Crone	14.00	6.25	2.00
☐ 207 Tom Oliver CO	14.00	6.25	2.00
☐ 208 Grady Hatton	14.00	6.25	2.00
☐ 209 Chuck Thompson	14.00	6.25	2.00
☐ 210 Bob Buhl	18.00	7.50	2.50
☐ 211 Don Hoak	16.00	6.75	2.25
☐ 212 Bob Micelotta	14.00	6.25	2.00
☐ 213 Johnny Fitzpatrick CO	14.00	6.25	2.00
☐ 214 Arnie Portocarrero	14.00	6.25	2.00
☐ 215 Ed McGhee	14.00	6.25	2.00
☐ 216 Al Sima	14.00	6.25	2.00
☐ 217 Paul Schreiber CO	14.00	6.25	2.00
☐ 218 Fred Marsh	14.00	6.25	2.00
☐ 219 Chuck Kress	14.00	6.25	2.00
☐ 220 Ruben Gomez	14.00	6.25	2.00
☐ 221 Dick Brodowski	14.00	6.25	2.00
☐ 222 Bill Wilson	14.00	6.25	2.00
☐ 223 Joe Haynes	14.00	6.25	2.00
☐ 224 Dick Weik	14.00	6.25	2.00
☐ 225 Don Liddle	14.00	6.25	2.00
☐ 226 Jehosie Heard	14.00	6.25	2.00
☐ 227 Colonel Mills CO	14.00	6.25	2.00
☐ 228 Gene Hermanski	14.00	6.25	2.00
☐ 229 Bob Talbot	14.00	6.25	2.00
☐ 230 Bob Kuzava	16.00	6.75	2.25
☐ 231 Roy Smalley	14.00	6.25	2.00
☐ 232 Lou Limmer	14.00	6.25	2.00
☐ 233 Augie Galan CO	14.00	6.25	2.00
☐ 234 Jerry Lynch	16.00	6.75	2.25
☐ 235 Vernon Law	16.00	6.75	2.25
☐ 236 Paul Penson	14.00	6.25	2.00
☐ 237 Mike Ryba CO	14.00	6.25	2.00
☐ 238 Al Aber	14.00	6.25	2.00
☐ 239 Bill Skowron	85.00	38.00	12.75
☐ 240 Sam Mele	14.00	6.25	2.00
☐ 241 Robert Miller	14.00	6.25	2.00
☐ 242 Curt Roberts	14.00	6.25	2.00
☐ 243 Ray Blades CO	14.00	6.25	2.00
☐ 244 Leroy Wheat	14.00	6.25	2.00
☐ 245 Roy Sievers	16.00	6.75	2.25
☐ 246 Howie Fox	14.00	6.25	2.00
☐ 247 Ed Mayo CO	14.00	6.25	2.00
☐ 248 Al Smith	16.00	6.75	2.25
☐ 249 Wilmer Mizell	16.00	6.75	2.25
☐ 250 Ted Williams	700.00	200.00	40.00

1955 Topps

The cards in this 206-card set measure 2 5/8" by 3 3/4". Both the large "head" shot and the smaller full-length photos used on each card of the 1955 Topps set are in color. The card fronts were designed horizontally for the first time in Topps' history. The first card features Dusty Rhodes, hitting star for the Giants' 1954 World Series sweep over the Indians. A "high" series, 161 to 210, is more difficult to find than cards 1 to 160. Numbers 175, 186, 203, and 209 were never issued. To fill in for the four cards not issued in the high number series, Topps double printed four players, those appearing on cards 170, 172, 184, and 188. Although rarely seen, there exist salesman sample panels of three cards containing the fronts of regular cards with ad information for the 1955 Topps regular and the 1955 Topps Doubleheaders on the back.

One such ad panel depicts (from top to bottom) Danny Schell, Jake Thies, and Howie Pollet. The key rookies in this set are Ken Boyer, Roberto Clemente, Harmon Killebrew, and Sandy Koufax.

	NRMT	VG-E	GOOD
COMPLETE SET (206)	7500.00	3500.00	800.00
COMMON PLAYER (1-150)	9.00	4.00	.90
COMMON PLAYER (151-160)	18.00	7.50	2.50
COMMON PLAYER (161-210)	27.00	12.00	4.00
☐ 1 Dusty Rhodes	42.00	7.50	1.50
☐ 2 Ted Williams	400.00	180.00	60.00
☐ 3 Art Fowler	9.00	4.00	.90
☐ 4 Al Kaline	210.00	95.00	25.00
☐ 5 Jim Gilliam	14.00	6.25	2.00
☐ 6 Stan Hack	11.00	5.00	1.35
☐ 7 Jim Hegan	10.00	4.50	1.25
☐ 8 Harold Smith	9.00	4.00	.90
☐ 9 Robert Miller	9.00	4.00	.90
☐ 10 Bob Keegan	9.00	4.00	.90
☐ 11 Ferris Fain	10.00	4.50	1.25
☐ 12 Vernon(Jake) Thies	9.00	4.00	.90
☐ 13 Fred Marsh	9.00	4.00	.90
☐ 14 Jim Finigan	9.00	4.00	.90
☐ 15 Jim Pendleton	9.00	4.00	.90
☐ 16 Roy Sievers	10.00	4.50	1.25
☐ 17 Bobby Hofman	9.00	4.00	.90
☐ 18 Russ Kemmerer	9.00	4.00	.90
☐ 19 Billy Herman CO	14.00	6.25	2.00
☐ 20 Andy Carey	11.00	5.00	1.35
☐ 21 Alex Grammas	9.00	4.00	.90
☐ 22 Bill Skowron	21.00	9.00	3.00
☐ 23 Jack Parks	9.00	4.00	.90
☐ 24 Hal Newhouser	14.00	6.25	2.00
☐ 25 Johnny Podres	16.00	6.75	2.25
☐ 26 Dick Groat	11.00	5.00	1.35
☐ 27 Billy Gardner	10.00	4.50	1.25
☐ 28 Ernie Banks	200.00	90.00	30.00
☐ 29 Herman Wehmeier	9.00	4.00	.90
☐ 30 Vic Power	10.00	4.50	1.25
☐ 31 Warren Spahn	80.00	36.00	12.00
☐ 32 Warren McGhee	9.00	4.00	.90
☐ 33 Tom Qualters	9.00	4.00	.90
☐ 34 Wayne Terwilliger	9.00	4.00	.90
☐ 35 Dave Jolly	9.00	4.00	.90
☐ 36 Leo Kiely	9.00	4.00	.90
☐ 37 Joe Cunningham	11.00	5.00	1.35
☐ 38 Bob Turley	14.00	6.25	2.00
☐ 39 Bill Glynn	9.00	4.00	.90
☐ 40 Don Hoak	10.00	4.50	1.25
☐ 41 Chuck Stobbs	9.00	4.00	.90
☐ 42 John(Windy) McCall	9.00	4.00	.90
☐ 43 Harvey Haddix	10.00	4.50	1.25
☐ 44 Harold Valentine	9.00	4.00	.90
☐ 45 Hank Sauer	10.00	4.50	1.25
☐ 46 Ted Kazanski	9.00	4.00	.90
☐ 47 Hank Aaron UER (birth incorrectly listed as 2/10)	350.00	160.00	52.50
☐ 48 Bob Kennedy	9.00	4.00	.90
☐ 49 J.W. Porter	9.00	4.00	.90
☐ 50 Jackie Robinson	240.00	105.00	30.00
☐ 51 Jim Hughes	9.00	4.00	.90
☐ 52 Bill Tremel	9.00	4.00	.90
☐ 53 Bill Taylor	9.00	4.00	.90
☐ 54 Lou Limmer	9.00	4.00	.90
☐ 55 Rip Repulski	9.00	4.00	.90
☐ 56 Ray Jablonski	9.00	4.00	.90
☐ 57 Billy O'Dell	9.00	4.00	.90
☐ 58 Jim Rivera	9.00	4.00	.90
☐ 59 Gair Allie	9.00	4.00	.90
☐ 60 Dean Stone	9.00	4.00	.90
☐ 61 Forrest Jacobs	9.00	4.00	.90
☐ 62 Thornton Kipper	9.00	4.00	.90
☐ 63 Joe Collins	11.00	5.00	1.35
☐ 64 Gus Triandos	12.00	5.25	1.50
☐ 65 Ray Boone	10.00	4.50	1.25
☐ 66 Ron Jackson	9.00	4.00	.90
☐ 67 Wally Moon	11.00	5.00	1.35
☐ 68 Jim Davis	9.00	4.00	.90
☐ 69 Ed Bailey	10.00	4.50	1.25
☐ 70 Al Rosen	14.00	6.25	2.00
☐ 71 Ruben Gomez	9.00	4.00	.90
☐ 72 Karl Olson	9.00	4.00	.90
☐ 73 Jack Shepard	9.00	4.00	.90
☐ 74 Bob Borkowski	9.00	4.00	.90
☐ 75 Sandy Amoros	18.00	7.50	2.50
☐ 76 Howie Pollet	9.00	4.00	.90
☐ 77 Arnie Portocarrero	9.00	4.00	.90
☐ 78 Gordon Jones	9.00	4.00	.90
☐ 79 Clyde(Danny) Schell	9.00	4.00	.90
☐ 80 Bob Grim	15.00	6.50	2.15
☐ 81 Gene Conley	10.00	4.50	1.25
☐ 82 Chuck Harmon	9.00	4.00	.90
☐ 83 Tom Brewer	9.00	4.00	.90
☐ 84 Camilo Pascual	12.00	5.25	1.50
☐ 85 Don Mossi	16.00	6.75	2.25
☐ 86 Bill Wilson	9.00	4.00	.90
☐ 87 Frank House	9.00	4.00	.90
☐ 88 Bob Skinner	12.00	5.25	1.50
☐ 89 Joe Frazier	10.00	4.50	1.25
☐ 90 Karl Spooner	14.00	6.25	2.00
☐ 91 Milt Bolling	9.00	4.00	.90
☐ 92 Don Zimmer	36.00	16.25	5.50
☐ 93 Steve Bilko	9.00	4.00	.90
☐ 94 Reno Bertoia	9.00	4.00	.90
☐ 95 Preston Ward	9.00	4.00	.90
☐ 96 Chuck Bishop	9.00	4.00	.90
☐ 97 Carlos Paula	9.00	4.00	.90
☐ 98 John Riddle	9.00	4.00	.90
☐ 99 Frank Leja	9.00	4.00	.90
☐ 100 Monte Irvin	27.00	12.00	4.00
☐ 101 Johnny Gray	9.00	4.00	.90
☐ 102 Wally Westlake	9.00	4.00	.90

☐ 103 Chuck White	9.00	4.00	.90
☐ 104 Jack Harshman	9.00	4.00	.90
☐ 105 Chuck Diering	9.00	4.00	.90
☐ 106 Frank Sullivan	9.00	4.00	.90
☐ 107 Curt Roberts	9.00	4.00	.90
☐ 108 Al Walker	10.00	4.50	1.25
☐ 109 Ed Lopat	14.00	6.25	2.00
☐ 110 Gus Zernial	10.00	4.50	1.25
☐ 111 Bob Milliken	9.00	4.00	.90
☐ 112 Nelson King	9.00	4.00	.90
☐ 113 Harry Brecheen	10.00	4.50	1.25
☐ 114 Louis Ortiz	9.00	4.00	.90
☐ 115 Ellis Kinder	9.00	4.00	.90
☐ 116 Tom Hurd	9.00	4.00	.90
☐ 117 Mel Roach	9.00	4.00	.90
☐ 118 Bob Purkey	9.00	4.00	.90
☐ 119 Bob Lennon	9.00	4.00	.90
☐ 120 Ted Kluszewski	21.00	9.00	3.00
☐ 121 Bill Renna	9.00	4.00	.90
☐ 122 Carl Sawatski	9.00	4.00	.90
☐ 123 Sandy Koufax	1125.00	400.00	100.00
☐ 124 Harmon Killebrew	325.00	150.00	50.00
☐ 125 Ken Boyer	70.00	32.00	10.50
☐ 126 Dick Hall	9.00	4.00	.90
☐ 127 Dale Long	11.00	5.00	1.35
☐ 128 Ted Lepcio	9.00	4.00	.90
☐ 129 Elvin Tappe	9.00	4.00	.90
☐ 130 Mayo Smith MG	9.00	4.00	.90
☐ 131 Grady Hatton	9.00	4.00	.90
☐ 132 Bob Trice	9.00	4.00	.90
☐ 133 Dave Hoskins	9.00	4.00	.90
☐ 134 Joey Jay	10.00	4.50	1.25
☐ 135 Johnny O'Brien	9.00	4.00	.90
☐ 136 Veston(Bunky) Stewart	9.00	4.00	.90
☐ 137 Harry Elliott	9.00	4.00	.90
☐ 138 Ray Herbert	9.00	4.00	.90
☐ 139 Steve Kraly	9.00	4.00	.90
☐ 140 Mel Parnell	10.00	4.50	1.25
☐ 141 Tom Wright	9.00	4.00	.90
☐ 142 Jerry Lynch	10.00	4.50	1.25
☐ 143 John(Dick) Schofield	10.00	4.50	1.25
☐ 144 John(Joe) Amalfitano	9.00	4.00	.90
☐ 145 Elmer Valo	9.00	4.00	.90
☐ 146 Dick Donovan	11.00	5.00	1.35
☐ 147 Hugh Pepper	9.00	4.00	.90
☐ 148 Hector Brown	9.00	4.00	.90
☐ 149 Ray Crone	9.00	4.00	.90
☐ 150 Mike Higgins MG	9.00	4.00	.90
☐ 151 Ralph Kress CO	18.00	7.50	2.50
☐ 152 Harry Agganis	85.00	38.00	12.75
☐ 153 Bud Podbielan	18.00	7.50	2.50
☐ 154 Willie Miranda	18.00	7.50	2.50
☐ 155 Eddie Mathews	125.00	57.50	18.75
☐ 156 Joe Black	28.00	12.50	4.00
☐ 157 Robert Miller	18.00	7.50	2.50
☐ 158 Tommy Carroll	21.00	9.00	3.00
☐ 159 Johnny Schmitz	18.00	7.50	2.50
☐ 160 Ray Narleski	22.00	9.50	3.15

☐ 161 Chuck Tanner	32.00	14.25	4.75
☐ 162 Joe Coleman	27.00	12.00	4.00
☐ 163 Faye Throneberry	27.00	12.00	4.00
☐ 164 Roberto Clemente	1325.00	550.00	135.00
☐ 165 Don Johnson	27.00	12.00	4.00
☐ 166 Hank Bauer	50.00	22.50	7.50
☐ 167 Thomas Casagrande	27.00	12.00	4.00
☐ 168 Duane Pillette	27.00	12.00	4.00
☐ 169 Bob Oldis	27.00	12.00	4.00
☐ 170 Jim Pearce DP	12.00	5.25	1.50
☐ 171 Dick Brodowski	27.00	12.00	4.00
☐ 172 Frank Baumholtz DP	12.00	5.25	1.50
☐ 173 Bob Kline	27.00	12.00	4.00
☐ 174 Rudy Minarcin	27.00	12.00	4.00
☐ 175 Does not exist	00.00	00.00	0.00
☐ 176 Norm Zauchin	27.00	12.00	4.00
☐ 177 Al Robertson	27.00	12.00	4.00
☐ 178 Bobby Adams	27.00	12.00	4.00
☐ 179 Jim Bolger	27.00	12.00	4.00
☐ 180 Clem Labine	32.00	14.25	4.75
☐ 181 Roy McMillan	27.00	12.00	4.00
☐ 182 Humberto Robinson	27.00	12.00	4.00
☐ 183 Anthony Jacobs	27.00	12.00	4.00
☐ 184 Harry Perkowski DP	12.00	5.25	1.50
☐ 185 Don Ferrarese	27.00	12.00	4.00
☐ 186 Does not exist	00.00	00.00	0.00
☐ 187 Gil Hodges	145.00	65.00	18.00
☐ 188 Charlie Silvera DP	15.00	6.50	2.15
☐ 189 Phil Rizzuto	145.00	65.00	18.00
☐ 190 Gene Woodling	32.00	14.25	4.75
☐ 191 Eddie Stanky MG	32.00	14.25	4.75
☐ 192 Jim Delsing	27.00	12.00	4.00
☐ 193 Johnny Sain	36.00	16.25	5.50
☐ 194 Willie Mays	475.00	215.00	70.00
☐ 195 Ed Roebuck	32.00	14.25	4.75
☐ 196 Gale Wade	27.00	12.00	4.00
☐ 197 Al Smith	27.00	12.00	4.00
☐ 198 Yogi Berra	250.00	110.00	37.50
☐ 199 Odbert Hamric	27.00	12.00	4.00
☐ 200 Jackie Jensen	50.00	22.50	7.50
☐ 201 Sherm Lollar	32.00	14.25	4.75
☐ 202 Jim Owens	27.00	12.00	4.00
☐ 203 Does not exist	00.00	00.00	0.00
☐ 204 Frank Smith	27.00	12.00	4.00
☐ 205 Gene Freese	32.00	14.25	4.75
☐ 206 Pete Daley	27.00	12.00	4.00
☐ 207 Billy Consolo	27.00	12.00	4.00
☐ 208 Ray Moore	27.00	12.00	4.00
☐ 209 Does not exist	00.00	00.00	0.00
☐ 210 Duke Snider	525.00	125.00	25.00

1956 Topps

The cards in this 340-card set measure 2 5/8" by 3 3/4". Following up with another horizontally oriented card in 1956, Topps improved the format by layering the color "head" shot onto an actual action sequence involving the player. Cards 1 to 180 come with either white or gray backs: in the 1 to 100 sequence, gray backs are less common (worth about 10 percent more) and in the 101 to 180 sequence, white backs are less common (worth 30 percent more). The team cards, used for the first time in a regular set by Topps, are found dated 1955, or undated, with the team name appearing on either side. The dated team cards in the first series were not printed on the gray stock. The two unnumbered checklist cards are highly prized (must be unmarked to qualify as excellent or mint). The complete set price below does not include the unnumbered checklist cards or any of the variations. The key rookies in this set are Walt Alston, Luis Aparicio, and Roger Craig. There are ten double-printed cards in the first series as evidenced by the discovery of an uncut sheet of 110 cards (10 by 11); these DP's are listed below.

	NRMT	VG-E	GOOD
COMPLETE SET (340)	7500.00	3500.00	800.00
COMMON PLAYER (1-100)	8.00	3.50	.80
COMMON PLAYER (101-180)	11.00	5.00	1.35
COMMON PLAYER (181-260)	15.00	6.50	2.15
COMMON PLAYER (261-340)	11.00	5.00	1.35

	NRMT	VG-E	GOOD
☐ 1 William Harridge (AL President)	135.00	25.00	5.00
☐ 2 Warren Giles (NL President)	17.00	7.25	2.50
☐ 3 Elmer Valo	8.00	3.50	.80
☐ 4 Carlos Paula	8.00	3.50	.80
☐ 5 Ted Williams	275.00	120.00	40.00
☐ 6 Ray Boone	9.00	4.00	.90
☐ 7 Ron Negray	8.00	3.50	.80
☐ 8 Walter Alston MG	38.00	17.00	4.50
☐ 9 Ruben Gomez DP	8.00	3.50	.80
☐ 10 Warren Spahn	80.00	36.00	12.00
☐ 11A Chicago Cubs (centered)	30.00	13.50	4.50
☐ 11B Cubs Team (dated 1955)	60.00	27.00	9.00
☐ 11C Cubs Team (name at far left)	30.00	13.50	4.50
☐ 12 Andy Carey	10.00	4.50	1.25
☐ 13 Roy Face	10.00	4.50	1.25
☐ 14 Ken Boyer DP	15.00	6.50	2.15
☐ 15 Ernie Banks DP	90.00	40.00	13.50
☐ 16 Hector Lopez	11.00	5.00	1.35
☐ 17 Gene Conley	8.00	3.50	.80
☐ 18 Dick Donovan	8.00	3.50	.80
☐ 19 Chuck Diering	8.00	3.50	.80
☐ 20 Al Kaline	110.00	50.00	16.50
☐ 21 Joe Collins DP	8.00	3.50	.80
☐ 22 Jim Finigan	8.00	3.50	.80
☐ 23 Fred Marsh	8.00	3.50	.80
☐ 24 Dick Groat	11.00	5.00	1.35
☐ 25 Ted Kluszewski	21.00	9.00	3.00
☐ 26 Grady Hatton	8.00	3.50	.80
☐ 27 Nelson Burbrink	8.00	3.50	.80
☐ 28 Bobby Hofman	8.00	3.50	.80
☐ 29 Jack Harshman	8.00	3.50	.80
☐ 30 Jackie Robinson DP	160.00	72.00	24.00
☐ 31 Hank Aaron UER (small photo actually W.Mays)	240.00	105.00	32.00
☐ 32 Frank House	8.00	3.50	.80
☐ 33 Roberto Clemente	375.00	165.00	55.00
☐ 34 Tom Brewer	8.00	3.50	.80
☐ 35 Al Rosen	11.00	5.00	1.35
☐ 36 Rudy Minarcin	8.00	3.50	.80
☐ 37 Alex Grammas	8.00	3.50	.80
☐ 38 Bob Kennedy	8.00	3.50	.80
☐ 39 Don Mossi	9.00	4.00	.90
☐ 40 Bob Turley	11.00	5.00	1.35
☐ 41 Hank Sauer	9.00	4.00	.90
☐ 42 Sandy Amoros	10.00	4.50	1.25
☐ 43 Ray Moore	8.00	3.50	.80
☐ 44 Windy McCall	8.00	3.50	.80
☐ 45 Gus Zernial	9.00	4.00	.90
☐ 46 Gene Freese DP	8.00	3.50	.80
☐ 47 Art Fowler	8.00	3.50	.80
☐ 48 Jim Hegan	8.00	3.50	.80
☐ 49 Pedro Ramos	8.00	3.50	.80
☐ 50 Dusty Rhodes	9.00	4.00	.90
☐ 51 Ernie Oravetz	8.00	3.50	.80
☐ 52 Bob Grim	9.00	4.00	.90
☐ 53 Arnie Portocarrero	8.00	3.50	.80
☐ 54 Bob Keegan	8.00	3.50	.80

☐ 55 Wally Moon ... 10.00 4.50 1.25
☐ 56 Dale Long ... 9.00 4.00 .90
☐ 57 Duke Maas ... 8.00 3.50 .80
☐ 58 Ed Roebuck ... 9.00 4.00 .90
☐ 59 Jose Santiago ... 8.00 3.50 .80
☐ 60 Mayo Smith MG DP ... 8.00 3.50 .80
☐ 61 Bill Skowron ... 17.00 7.25 2.50
☐ 62 Hal Smith ... 8.00 3.50 .80
☐ 63 Roger Craig ... 30.00 13.50 4.50
☐ 64 Luis Arroyo ... 11.00 5.00 1.35
☐ 65 Johnny O'Brien ... 8.00 3.50 .80
☐ 66 Bob Speake ... 8.00 3.50 .80
☐ 67 Vic Power ... 8.00 3.50 .80
☐ 68 Chuck Stobbs ... 8.00 3.50 .80
☐ 69 Chuck Tanner ... 10.00 4.50 1.25
☐ 70 Jim Rivera ... 8.00 3.50 .80
☐ 71 Frank Sullivan ... 8.00 3.50 .80
☐ 72A Phillies Team ... 30.00 13.50 4.50
(centered)
☐ 72B Phillies Team ... 60.00 27.00 9.00
(dated 1955)
☐ 72C Phillies Team ... 30.00 13.50 4.50
(name at far left)
☐ 73 Wayne Terwilliger ... 8.00 3.50 .80
☐ 74 Jim King ... 8.00 3.50 .80
☐ 75 Roy Sievers DP ... 8.00 3.50 .80
☐ 76 Ray Crone ... 8.00 3.50 .80
☐ 77 Harvey Haddix ... 9.00 4.00 .90
☐ 78 Herman Wehmeier ... 8.00 3.50 .80
☐ 79 Sandy Koufax ... 375.00 165.00 55.00
☐ 80 Gus Triandos DP ... 8.00 3.50 .80
☐ 81 Wally Westlake ... 8.00 3.50 .80
☐ 82 Bill Renna ... 8.00 3.50 .80
☐ 83 Karl Spooner ... 9.00 4.00 .90
☐ 84 Babe Birrer ... 8.00 3.50 .80
☐ 85A Cleveland Indians ... 30.00 13.50 4.50
(centered)
☐ 85B Indians Team ... 60.00 27.00 9.00
(dated 1955)
☐ 85C Indians Team ... 30.00 13.50 4.50
(name at far left)
☐ 86 Ray Jablonski DP ... 8.00 3.50 .80
☐ 87 Dean Stone ... 8.00 3.50 .80
☐ 88 Johnny Kucks ... 10.00 4.50 1.25
☐ 89 Norm Zauchin ... 8.00 3.50 .80
☐ 90A Cincinnati Redlegs ... 30.00 13.50 4.50
Team (centered)
☐ 90B Reds Team ... 60.00 27.00 9.00
(dated 1955)
☐ 90C Reds Team ... 30.00 13.50 4.50
(name at far left)
☐ 91 Gail Harris ... 8.00 3.50 .80
☐ 92 Bob(Red) Wilson ... 8.00 3.50 .80
☐ 93 George Susce ... 8.00 3.50 .80
☐ 94 Ron Kline ... 8.00 3.50 .80
☐ 95A Milwaukee Braves ... 30.00 13.50 4.50
Team (centered)
☐ 95B Braves Team ... 60.00 27.00 9.00
(dated 1955)
☐ 95C Braves Team ... 30.00 13.50 4.50
(name at far left)
☐ 96 Bill Tremel ... 8.00 3.50 .80
☐ 97 Jerry Lynch ... 9.00 4.00 .90
☐ 98 Camilo Pascual ... 9.00 4.00 .90
☐ 99 Don Zimmer ... 16.00 6.75 2.25
☐ 100A Baltimore Orioles ... 30.00 13.50 4.50
Team (centered)
☐ 100B Orioles Team ... 60.00 27.00 9.00
(dated 1955)
☐ 100C Orioles Team ... 30.00 13.50 4.50
(name at far left)
☐ 101 Roy Campanella ... 125.00 57.50 18.75
☐ 102 Jim Davis ... 11.00 5.00 1.35
☐ 103 Willie Miranda ... 11.00 5.00 1.35
☐ 104 Bob Lennon ... 11.00 5.00 1.35
☐ 105 Al Smith ... 11.00 5.00 1.35
☐ 106 Joe Astroth ... 11.00 5.00 1.35
☐ 107 Eddie Mathews ... 60.00 27.00 9.00
☐ 108 Laurin Pepper ... 11.00 5.00 1.35
☐ 109 Enos Slaughter ... 30.00 13.50 4.50
☐ 110 Yogi Berra ... 140.00 63.00 21.00
☐ 111 Boston Red Sox ... 36.00 16.25 5.50
Team Card
☐ 112 Dee Fondy ... 11.00 5.00 1.35
☐ 113 Phil Rizzuto ... 50.00 22.50 7.50
☐ 114 Jim Owens ... 11.00 5.00 1.35
☐ 115 Jackie Jensen ... 14.00 6.25 2.00
☐ 116 Eddie O'Brien ... 11.00 5.00 1.35
☐ 117 Virgil Trucks ... 12.00 5.25 1.50
☐ 118 Nellie Fox ... 32.00 14.25 4.75
☐ 119 Larry Jackson ... 14.00 6.25 2.00
☐ 120 Richie Ashburn ... 33.00 15.00 5.00
☐ 121 Pittsburgh Pirates ... 36.00 16.25 5.50
Team Card
☐ 122 Willard Nixon ... 11.00 5.00 1.35
☐ 123 Roy McMillan ... 11.00 5.00 1.35
☐ 124 Don Kaiser ... 11.00 5.00 1.35
☐ 125 Minnie Minoso ... 21.00 9.00 3.00
☐ 126 Jim Brady ... 11.00 5.00 1.35
☐ 127 Willie Jones ... 11.00 5.00 1.35
☐ 128 Eddie Yost ... 11.00 5.00 1.35
☐ 129 Jake Martin ... 11.00 5.00 1.35
☐ 130 Willie Mays ... 300.00 135.00 45.00
☐ 131 Bob Roselli ... 11.00 5.00 1.35
☐ 132 Bobby Avila ... 12.00 5.25 1.50
☐ 133 Ray Narleski ... 11.00 5.00 1.35
☐ 134 St. Louis Cardinals ... 36.00 16.25 5.50
Team Card
☐ 135 Mickey Mantle ... 900.00 400.00 135.00
☐ 136 Johnny Logan ... 12.00 5.25 1.50
☐ 137 Al Silvera ... 11.00 5.00 1.35
☐ 138 Johnny Antonelli ... 12.00 5.25 1.50
☐ 139 Tommy Carroll ... 11.00 5.00 1.35
☐ 140 Herb Score ... 28.00 12.50 4.00
☐ 141 Joe Frazier ... 11.00 5.00 1.35
☐ 142 Gene Baker ... 11.00 5.00 1.35

☐ 143 Jim Piersall 15.00 6.50 2.15
☐ 144 Leroy Powell 11.00 5.00 1.35
☐ 145 Gil Hodges 48.00 22.00 6.00
☐ 146 Washington Nationals 32.00 14.25 4.75
Team Card
☐ 147 Earl Torgeson 11.00 5.00 1.35
☐ 148 Alvin Dark 14.00 6.25 2.00
☐ 149 Dixie Howell 11.00 5.00 1.35
☐ 150 Duke Snider 135.00 60.00 20.00
☐ 151 Spook Jacobs 11.00 5.00 1.35
☐ 152 Billy Hoeft 11.00 5.00 1.35
☐ 153 Frank Thomas 12.00 5.25 1.50
☐ 154 Dave Pope 11.00 5.00 1.35
☐ 155 Harvey Kuenn 15.00 6.50 2.15
☐ 156 Wes Westrum 11.00 5.00 1.35
☐ 157 Dick Brodowski 11.00 5.00 1.35
☐ 158 Wally Post 12.00 5.25 1.50
☐ 159 Clint Courtney 11.00 5.00 1.35
☐ 160 Billy Pierce 14.00 6.25 2.00
☐ 161 Joe DeMaestri 11.00 5.00 1.35
☐ 162 Dave(Gus) Bell 12.00 5.25 1.50
☐ 163 Gene Woodling 14.00 6.25 2.00
☐ 164 Harmon Killebrew ... 150.00 67.50 22.50
☐ 165 Red Schoendienst 30.00 13.50 4.50
☐ 166 Brooklyn Dodgers ... 190.00 85.00 28.50
Team Card
☐ 167 Harry Dorish 11.00 5.00 1.35
☐ 168 Sammy White 11.00 5.00 1.35
☐ 169 Bob Nelson 11.00 5.00 1.35
☐ 170 Bill Virdon 15.00 6.50 2.15
☐ 171 Jim Wilson 11.00 5.00 1.35
☐ 172 Frank Torre 14.00 6.25 2.00
☐ 173 Johnny Podres 15.00 6.50 2.15
☐ 174 Glen Gorbous 11.00 5.00 1.35
☐ 175 Del Crandall 12.00 5.25 1.50
☐ 176 Alex Kellner 11.00 5.00 1.35
☐ 177 Hank Bauer 20.00 8.50 2.75
☐ 178 Joe Black 14.00 6.25 2.00
☐ 179 Harry Chiti 11.00 5.00 1.35
☐ 180 Robin Roberts 32.00 14.25 4.75
☐ 181 Billy Martin 100.00 45.00 15.00
☐ 182 Paul Minner 15.00 6.50 2.15
☐ 183 Stan Lopata 15.00 6.50 2.15
☐ 184 Don Bessent 15.00 6.50 2.15
☐ 185 Bill Bruton 17.00 7.25 2.50
☐ 186 Ron Jackson 15.00 6.50 2.15
☐ 187 Early Wynn 35.00 15.75 5.25
☐ 188 Chicago White Sox 35.00 15.75 5.25
Team Card
☐ 189 Ned Garver 15.00 6.50 2.15
☐ 190 Carl Furillo 25.00 11.00 3.50
☐ 191 Frank Lary 18.00 7.50 2.50
☐ 192 Smoky Burgess 18.00 7.50 2.50
☐ 193 Wilmer Mizell 15.00 6.50 2.15
☐ 194 Monte Irvin 32.00 14.25 4.75
☐ 195 George Kell 30.00 13.50 4.50
☐ 196 Tom Poholsky 15.00 6.50 2.15
☐ 197 Granny Hamner 15.00 6.50 2.15
☐ 198 Ed Fitzgerald 15.00 6.50 2.15
☐ 199 Hank Thompson 18.00 7.50 2.50
☐ 200 Bob Feller 130.00 60.00 20.00
☐ 201 Rip Repulski 15.00 6.50 2.15
☐ 202 Jim Hearn 15.00 6.50 2.15
☐ 203 Bill Tuttle 15.00 6.50 2.15
☐ 204 Art Swanson 15.00 6.50 2.15
☐ 205 Whitey Lockman 18.00 7.50 2.50
☐ 206 Erv Palica 15.00 6.50 2.15
☐ 207 Jim Small 15.00 6.50 2.15
☐ 208 Elston Howard 48.00 22.00 6.00
☐ 209 Max Surkont 15.00 6.50 2.15
☐ 210 Mike Garcia 18.00 7.50 2.50
☐ 211 Murry Dickson 15.00 6.50 2.15
☐ 212 Johnny Temple 18.00 7.50 2.50
☐ 213 Detroit Tigers 48.00 22.00 6.00
Team Card
☐ 214 Bob Rush 15.00 6.50 2.15
☐ 215 Tommy Byrne 18.00 7.50 2.50
☐ 216 Jerry Schoonmaker ... 15.00 6.50 2.15
☐ 217 Billy Klaus 15.00 6.50 2.15
☐ 218 Joe Nuxall 18.00 7.50 2.50
(sic, Nuxhall)
☐ 219 Lew Burdette 20.00 8.50 2.75
☐ 220 Del Ennis 18.00 7.50 2.50
☐ 221 Bob Friend 18.00 7.50 2.50
☐ 222 Dave Philley 15.00 6.50 2.15
☐ 223 Randy Jackson 15.00 6.50 2.15
☐ 224 Bud Podbielan 15.00 6.50 2.15
☐ 225 Gil McDougald 27.00 12.00 4.00
☐ 226 New York Giants 70.00 32.00 10.50
Team Card
☐ 227 Russ Meyer 15.00 6.50 2.15
☐ 228 Mickey Vernon 18.00 7.50 2.50
☐ 229 Harry Brecheen 15.00 6.50 2.15
☐ 230 Chico Carrasquel 15.00 6.50 2.15
☐ 231 Bob Hale 15.00 6.50 2.15
☐ 232 Toby Atwell 15.00 6.50 2.15
☐ 233 Carl Erskine 24.00 10.50 3.50
☐ 234 Pete Runnels 18.00 7.50 2.50
☐ 235 Don Newcombe 48.00 22.00 6.00
☐ 236 Kansas City Athletics 27.00 12.00 4.00
Team Card
☐ 237 Jose Valdivielso 15.00 6.50 2.15
☐ 238 Walt Dropo 18.00 7.50 2.50
☐ 239 Harry Simpson 15.00 6.50 2.15
☐ 240 Whitey Ford 130.00 60.00 20.00
☐ 241 Don Mueller UER 18.00 7.50 2.50
(6" tall)
☐ 242 Hershell Freeman 15.00 6.50 2.15
☐ 243 Sherm Lollar 18.00 7.50 2.50
☐ 244 Bob Buhl 18.00 7.50 2.50
☐ 245 Billy Goodman 18.00 7.50 2.50
☐ 246 Tom Gorman 15.00 6.50 2.15
☐ 247 Bill Sarni 15.00 6.50 2.15
☐ 248 Bob Porterfield 15.00 6.50 2.15
☐ 249 Johnny Klippstein 15.00 6.50 2.15
☐ 250 Larry Doby 22.00 9.50 3.15

☐ 251	New York Yankees Team Card UER (Don Larsen misspelled as Larson on front)	225.00	100.00	33.00
☐ 252	Vern Law	18.00	7.50	2.50
☐ 253	Irv Noren	18.00	7.50	2.50
☐ 254	George Crowe	15.00	6.50	2.15
☐ 255	Bob Lemon	35.00	15.75	5.25
☐ 256	Tom Hurd	15.00	6.50	2.15
☐ 257	Bobby Thomson	21.00	9.00	3.00
☐ 258	Art Ditmar	18.00	7.50	2.50
☐ 259	Sam Jones	18.00	7.50	2.50
☐ 260	Pee Wee Reese	140.00	63.00	21.00
☐ 261	Bobby Shantz	15.00	6.50	2.15
☐ 262	Howie Pollet	11.00	5.00	1.35
☐ 263	Bob Miller	11.00	5.00	1.35
☐ 264	Ray Monzant	11.00	5.00	1.35
☐ 265	Sandy Consuegra	11.00	5.00	1.35
☐ 266	Don Ferrarese	11.00	5.00	1.35
☐ 267	Bob Nieman	11.00	5.00	1.35
☐ 268	Dale Mitchell	16.00	6.75	2.25
☐ 269	Jack Meyer	11.00	5.00	1.35
☐ 270	Billy Loes	14.00	6.25	2.00
☐ 271	Foster Castleman	11.00	5.00	1.35
☐ 272	Danny O'Connell	11.00	5.00	1.35
☐ 273	Walker Cooper	11.00	5.00	1.35
☐ 274	Frank Baumholtz	11.00	5.00	1.35
☐ 275	Jim Greengrass	11.00	5.00	1.35
☐ 276	George Zuverink	11.00	5.00	1.35
☐ 277	Daryl Spencer	11.00	5.00	1.35
☐ 278	Chet Nichols	11.00	5.00	1.35
☐ 279	Johnny Groth	11.00	5.00	1.35
☐ 280	Jim Gilliam	18.00	7.50	2.50
☐ 281	Art Houtteman	11.00	5.00	1.35
☐ 282	Warren Hacker	11.00	5.00	1.35
☐ 283	Hal Smith	11.00	5.00	1.35
☐ 284	Ike Delock	11.00	5.00	1.35
☐ 285	Eddie Miksis	11.00	5.00	1.35
☐ 286	Bill Wight	11.00	5.00	1.35
☐ 287	Bobby Adams	11.00	5.00	1.35
☐ 288	Bob Cerv	24.00	10.50	3.50
☐ 289	Hal Jeffcoat	11.00	5.00	1.35
☐ 290	Curt Simmons	14.00	6.25	2.00
☐ 291	Frank Kellert	11.00	5.00	1.35
☐ 292	Luis Aparicio	135.00	60.00	20.00
☐ 293	Stu Miller	14.00	6.25	2.00
☐ 294	Ernie Johnson	14.00	6.25	2.00
☐ 295	Clem Labine	14.00	6.25	2.00
☐ 296	Andy Seminick	11.00	5.00	1.35
☐ 297	Bob Skinner	14.00	6.25	2.00
☐ 298	Johnny Schmitz	11.00	5.00	1.35
☐ 299	Charlie Neal	25.00	11.00	3.50
☐ 300	Vic Wertz	14.00	6.25	2.00
☐ 301	Marv Grissom	11.00	5.00	1.35
☐ 302	Eddie Robinson	11.00	5.00	1.35
☐ 303	Jim Dyck	11.00	5.00	1.35
☐ 304	Frank Malzone	18.00	7.50	2.50
☐ 305	Brooks Lawrence	11.00	5.00	1.35
☐ 306	Curt Roberts	11.00	5.00	1.35
☐ 307	Hoyt Wilhelm	32.00	14.25	4.75
☐ 308	Chuck Harmon	11.00	5.00	1.35
☐ 309	Don Blasingame	11.00	5.00	1.35
☐ 310	Steve Gromek	11.00	5.00	1.35
☐ 311	Hal Naragon	11.00	5.00	1.35
☐ 312	Andy Pafko	12.00	5.25	1.50
☐ 313	Gene Stephens	11.00	5.00	1.35
☐ 314	Hobie Landrith	11.00	5.00	1.35
☐ 315	Milt Bolling	11.00	5.00	1.35
☐ 316	Jerry Coleman	14.00	6.25	2.00
☐ 317	Al Aber	11.00	5.00	1.35
☐ 318	Fred Hatfield	11.00	5.00	1.35
☐ 319	Jack Crimian	11.00	5.00	1.35
☐ 320	Joe Adcock	14.00	6.25	2.00
☐ 321	Jim Konstanty	12.00	5.25	1.50
☐ 322	Karl Olson	11.00	5.00	1.35
☐ 323	Willard Schmidt	11.00	5.00	1.35
☐ 324	Rocky Bridges	11.00	5.00	1.35
☐ 325	Don Liddle	11.00	5.00	1.35
☐ 326	Connie Johnson	11.00	5.00	1.35
☐ 327	Bob Wiesler	11.00	5.00	1.35
☐ 328	Preston Ward	11.00	5.00	1.35
☐ 329	Lou Berberet	11.00	5.00	1.35
☐ 330	Jim Busby	11.00	5.00	1.35
☐ 331	Dick Hall	11.00	5.00	1.35
☐ 332	Don Larsen	36.00	16.25	5.50
☐ 333	Rube Walker	12.00	5.25	1.50
☐ 334	Bob Miller	11.00	5.00	1.35
☐ 335	Don Hoak	12.00	5.25	1.50
☐ 336	Ellis Kinder	11.00	5.00	1.35
☐ 337	Bobby Morgan	11.00	5.00	1.35
☐ 338	Jim Delsing	11.00	5.00	1.35
☐ 339	Rance Pless	11.00	5.00	1.35
☐ 340	Mickey McDermott	50.00	7.50	1.50
☐ xx	Checklist 1/3 (unnumbered)	225.00	35.00	7.00
☐ xx	Checklist 2/4 (unnumbered)	225.00	35.00	7.00

1957 Topps

The cards in this 407-card set measure 2 1/2" by 3 1/2". In 1957, Topps returned to the vertical obverse, adopted what we now call the standard card size, and used a large, uncluttered color photo for the first time since 1952. Cards in the series 265 to 352 and the unnumbered checklist cards are scarcer than other cards in the set. However within this scarce series (265-352) there are 22 cards which were printed in double the quantity of

the other cards in the series; these 22 double prints are indicated by DP in the checklist below. The first star combination cards, cards 400 and 407, are quite popular with collectors. They feature the big stars of the previous season's World Series teams, the Dodgers (Furillo, Hodges, Campanella, and Snider) and Yankees (Berra and Mantle). The complete set price below does not include the unnumbered checklist cards. The key rookies in this set are Jim Bunning, Rocky Colavito, Don Drysdale, Whitey Herzog, Tony Kubek, Bobby Richardson, Brooks Robinson, and Frank Robinson.

	NRMT	VG-E	GOOD
COMPLETE SET (407)	7500.00	3500.00	800.00
COMMON PLAYER (1-88)	7.50	3.25	.75
COMMON PLAYER (89-176)	6.50	2.75	.65
COMMON PLAYER (177-264)	6.00	2.50	.60
COMMON PLAYER (265-352)	20.00	8.50	2.75
COMMON DP (265-352)	12.00	5.25	1.50
COMMON PLAYER (353-407)	6.00	2.50	.60
☐ 1 Ted Williams	450.00	125.00	25.00
☐ 2 Yogi Berra	145.00	65.00	18.00
☐ 3 Dale Long	9.00	4.00	.90
☐ 4 Johnny Logan	9.00	4.00	.90
☐ 5 Sal Maglie	11.00	5.00	1.35
☐ 6 Hector Lopez	9.00	4.00	.90
☐ 7 Luis Aparicio	36.00	16.25	5.50
☐ 8 Don Mossi	9.00	4.00	.90
☐ 9 Johnny Temple	9.00	4.00	.90
☐ 10 Willie Mays	225.00	100.00	33.00
☐ 11 George Zuverink	7.50	3.25	.75
☐ 12 Dick Groat	11.00	5.00	1.35
☐ 13 Wally Burnette	7.50	3.25	.75
☐ 14 Bob Nieman	7.50	3.25	.75
☐ 15 Robin Roberts	25.00	11.00	3.50
☐ 16 Walt Moryn	7.50	3.25	.75
☐ 17 Billy Gardner	7.50	3.25	.75
☐ 18 Don Drysdale	225.00	100.00	33.00
☐ 19 Bob Wilson	7.50	3.25	.75
☐ 20 Hank Aaron UER (reverse negative photo on front)	250.00	110.00	37.50
☐ 21 Frank Sullivan	7.50	3.25	.75
☐ 22 Jerry Snyder UER (photo actually Ed Fitzgerald)	7.50	3.25	.75
☐ 23 Sherm Lollar	9.00	4.00	.90
☐ 24 Bill Mazeroski	60.00	27.00	9.00
☐ 25 Whitey Ford	65.00	29.00	9.75
☐ 26 Bob Boyd	7.50	3.25	.75
☐ 27 Ted Kazanski	7.50	3.25	.75
☐ 28 Gene Conley	7.50	3.25	.75
☐ 29 Whitey Herzog	30.00	13.50	4.50
☐ 30 Pee Wee Reese	60.00	27.00	9.00
☐ 31 Ron Northey	7.50	3.25	.75
☐ 32 Hershell Freeman	7.50	3.25	.75
☐ 33 Jim Small	7.50	3.25	.75
☐ 34 Tom Sturdivant	7.50	3.25	.75
☐ 35 Frank Robinson	275.00	120.00	40.00
☐ 36 Bob Grim	9.00	4.00	.90
☐ 37 Frank Torre	9.00	4.00	.90
☐ 38 Nellie Fox	21.00	9.00	3.00
☐ 39 Al Worthington	7.50	3.25	.75
☐ 40 Early Wynn	22.00	9.50	3.15
☐ 41 Hal W. Smith	7.50	3.25	.75
☐ 42 Dee Fondy	7.50	3.25	.75
☐ 43 Connie Johnson	7.50	3.25	.75
☐ 44 Joe DeMaestri	7.50	3.25	.75
☐ 45 Carl Furillo	14.00	6.25	2.00
☐ 46 Robert J. Miller	7.50	3.25	.75
☐ 47 Don Blasingame	7.50	3.25	.75
☐ 48 Bill Bruton	9.00	4.00	.90
☐ 49 Daryl Spencer	7.50	3.25	.75
☐ 50 Herb Score	14.00	6.25	2.00
☐ 51 Clint Courtney	7.50	3.25	.75
☐ 52 Lee Walls	7.50	3.25	.75
☐ 53 Clem Labine	9.00	4.00	.90
☐ 54 Elmer Valo	7.50	3.25	.75
☐ 55 Ernie Banks	100.00	45.00	15.00
☐ 56 Dave Sisler	7.50	3.25	.75
☐ 57 Jim Lemon	7.50	3.25	.75
☐ 58 Ruben Gomez	7.50	3.25	.75
☐ 59 Dick Williams	9.00	4.00	.90
☐ 60 Billy Hoeft	7.50	3.25	.75
☐ 61 James(Dusty) Rhodes	9.00	4.00	.90
☐ 62 Billy Martin	50.00	22.50	7.50
☐ 63 Ike Delock	7.50	3.25	.75
☐ 64 Pete Runnels	9.00	4.00	.90
☐ 65 Wally Moon	9.00	4.00	.90
☐ 66 Brooks Lawrence	7.50	3.25	.75
☐ 67 Chico Carrasquel	7.50	3.25	.75
☐ 68 Ray Crone	7.50	3.25	.75
☐ 69 Roy McMillan	7.50	3.25	.75
☐ 70 Richie Ashburn	22.00	9.50	3.15
☐ 71 Murry Dickson	7.50	3.25	.75

☐ 72	Bill Tuttle	7.50	3.25	.75
☐ 73	George Crowe	7.50	3.25	.75
☐ 74	Vito Valentinetti	7.50	3.25	.75
☐ 75	Jim Piersall	11.00	5.00	1.35
☐ 76	Roberto Clemente	200.00	90.00	30.00
☐ 77	Paul Foytack	7.50	3.25	.75
☐ 78	Vic Wertz	9.00	4.00	.90
☐ 79	Lindy McDaniel	11.00	5.00	1.35
☐ 80	Gil Hodges	48.00	22.00	6.00
☐ 81	Herman Wehmeier	7.50	3.25	.75
☐ 82	Elston Howard	20.00	8.50	2.75
☐ 83	Lou Skizas	7.50	3.25	.75
☐ 84	Moe Drabowsky	7.50	3.25	.75
☐ 85	Larry Doby	11.00	5.00	1.35
☐ 86	Bill Sarni	7.50	3.25	.75
☐ 87	Tom Gorman	7.50	3.25	.75
☐ 88	Harvey Kuenn	11.00	5.00	1.35
☐ 89	Roy Sievers	7.50	3.25	.75
☐ 90	Warren Spahn	70.00	32.00	10.50
☐ 91	Mack Burk	6.50	2.75	.65
☐ 92	Mickey Vernon	7.50	3.25	.75
☐ 93	Hal Jeffcoat	6.50	2.75	.65
☐ 94	Bobby Del Greco	6.50	2.75	.65
☐ 95	Mickey Mantle	850.00	375.00	125.00
☐ 96	Hank Aguirre	6.50	2.75	.65
☐ 97	New York Yankees Team Card	50.00	22.50	7.50
☐ 98	Alvin Dark	8.50	3.75	.85
☐ 99	Bob Keegan	6.50	2.75	.65
☐ 100	Giles and Harridge League Presidents	11.00	5.00	1.35
☐ 101	Chuck Stobbs	6.50	2.75	.65
☐ 102	Ray Boone	7.50	3.25	.75
☐ 103	Joe Nuxhall	7.50	3.25	.75
☐ 104	Hank Foiles	6.50	2.75	.65
☐ 105	Johnny Antonelli	7.50	3.25	.75
☐ 106	Ray Moore	6.50	2.75	.65
☐ 107	Jim Rivera	6.50	2.75	.65
☐ 108	Tommy Byrne	7.50	3.25	.75
☐ 109	Hank Thompson	7.50	3.25	.75
☐ 110	Bill Virdon	8.50	3.75	.85
☐ 111	Hal R. Smith	6.50	2.75	.65
☐ 112	Tom Brewer	6.50	2.75	.65
☐ 113	Wilmer Mizell	6.50	2.75	.65
☐ 114	Milwaukee Braves Team Card	16.00	6.75	2.25
☐ 115	Jim Gilliam	12.00	5.25	1.50
☐ 116	Mike Fornieles	6.50	2.75	.65
☐ 117	Joe Adcock	8.50	3.75	.85
☐ 118	Bob Porterfield	6.50	2.75	.65
☐ 119	Stan Lopata	6.50	2.75	.65
☐ 120	Bob Lemon	22.00	9.50	3.15
☐ 121	Clete Boyer	17.00	7.25	2.50
☐ 122	Ken Boyer	13.00	5.75	1.75
☐ 123	Steve Ridzik	6.50	2.75	.65
☐ 124	Dave Philley	6.50	2.75	.65
☐ 125	Al Kaline	90.00	40.00	13.50
☐ 126	Bob Wiesler	6.50	2.75	.65
☐ 127	Bob Buhl	7.50	3.25	.75
☐ 128	Ed Bailey	7.50	3.25	.75
☐ 129	Saul Rogovin	6.50	2.75	.65
☐ 130	Don Newcombe	14.00	6.25	2.00
☐ 131	Milt Bolling	6.50	2.75	.65
☐ 132	Art Ditmar	6.50	2.75	.65
☐ 133	Del Crandall	7.50	3.25	.75
☐ 134	Don Kaiser	6.50	2.75	.65
☐ 135	Bill Skowron	13.00	5.75	1.75
☐ 136	Jim Hegan	7.50	3.25	.75
☐ 137	Bob Rush	6.50	2.75	.65
☐ 138	Minnie Minoso	13.00	5.75	1.75
☐ 139	Lou Kretlow	6.50	2.75	.65
☐ 140	Frank Thomas	7.50	3.25	.75
☐ 141	Al Aber	6.50	2.75	.65
☐ 142	Charley Thompson	6.50	2.75	.65
☐ 143	Andy Pafko	7.50	3.25	.75
☐ 144	Ray Narleski	6.50	2.75	.65
☐ 145	Al Smith	6.50	2.75	.65
☐ 146	Don Ferrarese	6.50	2.75	.65
☐ 147	Al Walker	6.50	2.75	.65
☐ 148	Don Mueller	7.50	3.25	.75
☐ 149	Bob Kennedy	6.50	2.75	.65
☐ 150	Bob Friend	7.50	3.25	.75
☐ 151	Willie Miranda	6.50	2.75	.65
☐ 152	Jack Harshman	6.50	2.75	.65
☐ 153	Karl Olson	6.50	2.75	.65
☐ 154	Red Schoendienst	21.00	9.00	3.00
☐ 155	Jim Brosnan	7.50	3.25	.75
☐ 156	Gus Triandos	7.50	3.25	.75
☐ 157	Wally Post	7.50	3.25	.75
☐ 158	Curt Simmons	7.50	3.25	.75
☐ 159	Solly Drake	6.50	2.75	.65
☐ 160	Billy Pierce	8.50	3.75	.85
☐ 161	Pittsburgh Pirates Team Card	13.50	6.00	1.85
☐ 162	Jack Meyer	6.50	2.75	.65
☐ 163	Sammy White	6.50	2.75	.65
☐ 164	Tommy Carroll	6.50	2.75	.65
☐ 165	Ted Kluszewski	30.00	13.50	4.50
☐ 166	Roy Face	8.50	3.75	.85
☐ 167	Vic Power	6.50	2.75	.65
☐ 168	Frank Lary	7.50	3.25	.75
☐ 169	Herb Plews	6.50	2.75	.65
☐ 170	Duke Snider	100.00	45.00	15.00
☐ 171	Boston Red Sox Team Card	13.50	6.00	1.85
☐ 172	Gene Woodling	8.50	3.75	.85
☐ 173	Roger Craig	14.00	6.25	2.00
☐ 174	Willie Jones	6.50	2.75	.65
☐ 175	Don Larsen	16.00	6.75	2.25
☐ 176A	Gene Baker ERR (misspelled Bakep on card back)	300.00	135.00	45.00
☐ 176B	Gene Baker COR	7.50	3.25	.75
☐ 177	Eddie Yost	6.00	2.50	.60
☐ 178	Don Bessent	6.00	2.50	.60
☐ 179	Ernie Oravetz	6.00	2.50	.60

☐ 180 Gus Bell 7.00 3.00 .70
☐ 181 Dick Donovan 6.00 2.50 .60
☐ 182 Hobie Landrith 6.00 2.50 .60
☐ 183 Chicago Cubs 13.50 6.00 1.85
Team Card
☐ 184 Tito Francona 9.00 4.00 .90
☐ 185 Johnny Kucks 7.00 3.00 .70
☐ 186 Jim King 6.00 2.50 .60
☐ 187 Virgil Trucks 7.00 3.00 .70
☐ 188 Felix Mantilla 8.00 3.50 .80
☐ 189 Willard Nixon 6.00 2.50 .60
☐ 190 Randy Jackson 6.00 2.50 .60
☐ 191 Joe Margoneri 6.00 2.50 .60
☐ 192 Jerry Coleman 7.00 3.00 .70
☐ 193 Del Rice 6.00 2.50 .60
☐ 194 Hal Brown 6.00 2.50 .60
☐ 195 Bobby Avila 6.00 2.50 .60
☐ 196 Larry Jackson 6.00 2.50 .60
☐ 197 Hank Sauer 7.00 3.00 .70
☐ 198 Detroit Tigers 13.50 6.00 1.85
Team Card
☐ 199 Vern Law 7.00 3.00 .70
☐ 200 Gil McDougald 13.00 5.75 1.75
☐ 201 Sandy Amoros 8.00 3.50 .80
☐ 202 Dick Gernert 6.00 2.50 .60
☐ 203 Hoyt Wilhelm 21.00 9.00 3.00
☐ 204 Kansas City Athletics 12.00 5.25 1.50
Team Card
☐ 205 Charlie Maxwell 7.00 3.00 .70
☐ 206 Willard Schmidt 6.00 2.50 .60
☐ 207 Gordon(Billy) Hunter 6.00 2.50 .60
☐ 208 Lou Burdette 9.00 4.00 .90
☐ 209 Bob Skinner 7.00 3.00 .70
☐ 210 Roy Campanella 100.00 45.00 15.00
☐ 211 Camilo Pascual 7.00 3.00 .70
☐ 212 Rocky Colavito 125.00 57.50 18.75
☐ 213 Les Moss 6.00 2.50 .60
☐ 214 Philadelphia Phillies 13.50 6.00 1.85
Team Card
☐ 215 Enos Slaughter 25.00 11.00 3.50
☐ 216 Marv Grissom 6.00 2.50 .60
☐ 217 Gene Stephens 6.00 2.50 .60
☐ 218 Ray Jablonski 6.00 2.50 .60
☐ 219 Tom Acker 6.00 2.50 .60
☐ 220 Jackie Jensen 11.00 5.00 1.35
☐ 221 Dixie Howell 6.00 2.50 .60
☐ 222 Alex Grammas 6.00 2.50 .60
☐ 223 Frank House 6.00 2.50 .60
☐ 224 Marv Blaylock 6.00 2.50 .60
☐ 225 Harry Simpson 6.00 2.50 .60
☐ 226 Preston Ward 6.00 2.50 .60
☐ 227 Jerry Staley 6.00 2.50 .60
☐ 228 Smoky Burgess UER 8.00 3.50 .80
(Misspelled Smokey
on card back)
☐ 229 George Susce 6.00 2.50 .60
☐ 230 George Kell 20.00 8.50 2.75
☐ 231 Solly Hemus 6.00 2.50 .60
☐ 232 Whitey Lockman 7.00 3.00 .70
☐ 233 Art Fowler 6.00 2.50 .60
☐ 234 Dick Cole 6.00 2.50 .60
☐ 235 Tom Poholsky 6.00 2.50 .60
☐ 236 Joe Ginsberg 6.00 2.50 .60
☐ 237 Foster Castleman 6.00 2.50 .60
☐ 238 Eddie Robinson 6.00 2.50 .60
☐ 239 Tom Morgan 6.00 2.50 .60
☐ 240 Hank Bauer 13.00 5.75 1.75
☐ 241 Joe Lonnett 6.00 2.50 .60
☐ 242 Charlie Neal 7.00 3.00 .70
☐ 243 St. Louis Cardinals 13.50 6.00 1.85
Team Card
☐ 244 Billy Loes 7.00 3.00 .70
☐ 245 Rip Repulski 6.00 2.50 .60
☐ 246 Jose Valdivielso 6.00 2.50 .60
☐ 247 Turk Lown 6.00 2.50 .60
☐ 248 Jim Finigan 6.00 2.50 .60
☐ 249 Dave Pope 6.00 2.50 .60
☐ 250 Eddie Mathews 40.00 18.00 6.00
☐ 251 Baltimore Orioles 13.50 6.00 1.85
Team Card
☐ 252 Carl Erskine 11.00 5.00 1.35
☐ 253 Gus Zernial 7.00 3.00 .70
☐ 254 Ron Negray 6.00 2.50 .60
☐ 255 Charlie Silvera 6.00 2.50 .60
☐ 256 Ron Kline 6.00 2.50 .60
☐ 257 Walt Dropo 7.00 3.00 .70
☐ 258 Steve Gromek 6.00 2.50 .60
☐ 259 Eddie O'Brien 6.00 2.50 .60
☐ 260 Del Ennis 7.00 3.00 .70
☐ 261 Bob Chakales 6.00 2.50 .60
☐ 262 Bobby Thomson 10.00 4.50 1.25
☐ 263 George Strickland 6.00 2.50 .60
☐ 264 Bob Turley 12.00 5.25 1.50
☐ 265 Harvey Haddix DP 15.00 6.50 2.15
☐ 266 Ken Kuhn DP 12.00 5.25 1.50
☐ 267 Danny Kravitz 20.00 8.50 2.75
☐ 268 Jack Collum 20.00 8.50 2.75
☐ 269 Bob Cerv 22.00 9.50 3.15
☐ 270 Washington Senators 45.00 20.00 6.75
Team Card
☐ 271 Danny O'Connell DP 12.00 5.25 1.50
☐ 272 Bobby Shantz 27.00 12.00 4.00
☐ 273 Jim Davis 20.00 8.50 2.75
☐ 274 Don Hoak 22.00 9.50 3.15
☐ 275 Cleveland Indians 45.00 20.00 6.75
Team Card
☐ 276 Jim Pyburn 20.00 8.50 2.75
☐ 277 Johnny Podres DP 50.00 22.50 7.50
☐ 278 Fred Hatfield DP 12.00 5.25 1.50
☐ 279 Bob Thurman 20.00 8.50 2.75
☐ 280 Alex Kellner 20.00 8.50 2.75
☐ 281 Gail Harris 20.00 8.50 2.75
☐ 282 Jack Dittmer DP 12.00 5.25 1.50
☐ 283 Wes Covington DP 15.00 6.50 2.15
☐ 284 Don Zimmer 30.00 13.50 4.50
☐ 285 Ned Garver 20.00 8.50 2.75

	Card	Player			
☐	286	Bobby Richardson	115.00	50.00	15.00
☐	287	Sam Jones	22.00	9.50	3.15
☐	288	Ted Lepcio	20.00	8.50	2.75
☐	289	Jim Bolger DP	12.00	5.25	1.50
☐	290	Andy Carey DP	15.00	6.50	2.15
☐	291	Windy McCall	20.00	8.50	2.75
☐	292	Billy Klaus	20.00	8.50	2.75
☐	293	Ted Abernathy	20.00	8.50	2.75
☐	294	Rocky Bridges DP	12.00	5.25	1.50
☐	295	Joe Collins DP	15.00	6.50	2.15
☐	296	Johnny Klippstein	20.00	8.50	2.75
☐	297	Jack Crimian	20.00	8.50	2.75
☐	298	Irv Noren DP	12.00	5.25	1.50
☐	299	Chuck Harmon	20.00	8.50	2.75
☐	300	Mike Garcia	22.00	9.50	3.15
☐	301	Sammy Esposito DP	12.00	5.25	1.50
☐	302	Sandy Koufax DP	325.00	150.00	50.00
☐	303	Billy Goodman	22.00	9.50	3.15
☐	304	Joe Cunningham	22.00	9.50	3.15
☐	305	Chico Fernandez	20.00	8.50	2.75
☐	306	Darrell Johnson DP	15.00	6.50	2.15
☐	307	Jack D. Phillips DP	12.00	5.25	1.50
☐	308	Dick Hall	20.00	8.50	2.75
☐	309	Jim Busby DP	12.00	5.25	1.50
☐	310	Max Surkont DP	12.00	5.25	1.50
☐	311	Al Pilarcik DP	12.00	5.25	1.50
☐	312	Tony Kubek DP	100.00	45.00	15.00
☐	313	Mel Parnell	22.00	9.50	3.15
☐	314	Ed Bouchee DP	12.00	5.25	1.50
☐	315	Lou Berberet DP	12.00	5.25	1.50
☐	316	Billy O'Dell	20.00	8.50	2.75
☐	317	New York Giants Team Card	50.00	22.50	7.50
☐	318	Mickey McDermott	20.00	8.50	2.75
☐	319	Gino Cimoli	22.00	9.50	3.15
☐	320	Neil Chrisley	20.00	8.50	2.75
☐	321	John(Red) Murff	20.00	8.50	2.75
☐	322	Cincinnati Reds Team Card	50.00	22.50	7.50
☐	323	Wes Westrum	22.00	9.50	3.15
☐	324	Brooklyn Dodgers Team Card	100.00	45.00	15.00
☐	325	Frank Bolling	20.00	8.50	2.75
☐	326	Pedro Ramos	20.00	8.50	2.75
☐	327	Jim Pendleton	20.00	8.50	2.75
☐	328	Brooks Robinson	400.00	180.00	60.00
☐	329	Chicago White Sox Team Card	45.00	20.00	6.75
☐	330	Jim Wilson	20.00	8.50	2.75
☐	331	Ray Katt	20.00	8.50	2.75
☐	332	Bob Bowman	20.00	8.50	2.75
☐	333	Ernie Johnson	22.00	9.50	3.15
☐	334	Jerry Schoonmaker	20.00	8.50	2.75
☐	335	Granny Hamner	20.00	8.50	2.75
☐	336	Haywood Sullivan	22.00	9.50	3.15
☐	337	Rene Valdes	20.00	8.50	2.75
☐	338	Jim Bunning	140.00	63.00	21.00
☐	339	Bob Speake	20.00	8.50	2.75
☐	340	Bill Wight	20.00	8.50	2.75
☐	341	Don Gross	20.00	8.50	2.75
☐	342	Gene Mauch	22.00	9.50	3.15
☐	343	Taylor Phillips	20.00	8.50	2.75
☐	344	Paul LaPalme	20.00	8.50	2.75
☐	345	Paul Smith	20.00	8.50	2.75
☐	346	Dick Littlefield	20.00	8.50	2.75
☐	347	Hal Naragon	20.00	8.50	2.75
☐	348	Jim Hearn	20.00	8.50	2.75
☐	349	Nellie King	20.00	8.50	2.75
☐	350	Eddie Miksis	20.00	8.50	2.75
☐	351	Dave Hillman	20.00	8.50	2.75
☐	352	Ellis Kinder	20.00	8.50	2.75
☐	353	Cal Neeman	6.00	2.50	.60
☐	354	W. (Rip) Coleman	6.00	2.50	.60
☐	355	Frank Malzone	8.00	3.50	.80
☐	356	Faye Throneberry	6.00	2.50	.60
☐	357	Earl Torgeson	6.00	2.50	.60
☐	358	Jerry Lynch	6.00	2.50	.60
☐	359	Tom Cheney	6.00	2.50	.60
☐	360	Johnny Groth	6.00	2.50	.60
☐	361	Curt Barclay	6.00	2.50	.60
☐	362	Roman Mejias	7.00	3.00	.70
☐	363	Eddie Kasko	6.00	2.50	.60
☐	364	Cal McLish	6.00	2.50	.60
☐	365	Ozzie Virgil	6.00	2.50	.60
☐	366	Ken Lehman	6.00	2.50	.60
☐	367	Ed Fitzgerald	6.00	2.50	.60
☐	368	Bob Purkey	6.00	2.50	.60
☐	369	Milt Graff	6.00	2.50	.60
☐	370	Warren Hacker	6.00	2.50	.60
☐	371	Bob Lennon	6.00	2.50	.60
☐	372	Norm Zauchin	6.00	2.50	.60
☐	373	Pete Whisenant	6.00	2.50	.60
☐	374	Don Cardwell	6.00	2.50	.60
☐	375	Jim Landis	6.00	2.50	.60
☐	376	Don Elston	6.00	2.50	.60
☐	377	Andre Rodgers	6.00	2.50	.60
☐	378	Elmer Singleton	6.00	2.50	.60
☐	379	Don Lee	6.00	2.50	.60
☐	380	Walker Cooper	6.00	2.50	.60
☐	381	Dean Stone	6.00	2.50	.60
☐	382	Jim Brideweser	6.00	2.50	.60
☐	383	Juan Pizarro	6.00	2.50	.60
☐	384	Bobby G. Smith	6.00	2.50	.60
☐	385	Art Houtteman	6.00	2.50	.60
☐	386	Lyle Luttrell	6.00	2.50	.60
☐	387	Jack Sanford	8.00	3.50	.80
☐	388	Pete Daley	6.00	2.50	.60
☐	389	Dave Jolly	6.00	2.50	.60
☐	390	Reno Bertoia	6.00	2.50	.60
☐	391	Ralph Terry	10.00	4.50	1.25
☐	392	Chuck Tanner	8.00	3.50	.80
☐	393	Raul Sanchez	6.00	2.50	.60
☐	394	Luis Arroyo	7.00	3.00	.70
☐	395	J.M.(Bubba) Phillips	6.00	2.50	.60
☐	396	K. (Casey) Wise	6.00	2.50	.60
☐	397	Roy Smalley	6.00	2.50	.60

☐ 398 Al Cicotte	7.00	3.00	.70
☐ 399 Billy Consolo	6.00	2.50	.60
☐ 400 Dodgers' Sluggers Carl Furillo Gil Hodges Roy Campanella Duke Snider	180.00	80.00	27.00
☐ 401 Earl Battey	8.00	3.50	.80
☐ 402 Jim Pisoni	6.00	2.50	.60
☐ 403 Dick Hyde	6.00	2.50	.60
☐ 404 Harry Anderson	6.00	2.50	.60
☐ 405 Duke Maas	6.00	2.50	.60
☐ 406 Bob Hale	6.00	2.50	.60
☐ 407 Yankee Power Hitters Mickey Mantle Yogi Berra	375.00	165.00	55.00
☐ xx Checklist 1/2 (unnumbered)	225.00	35.00	7.00
☐ xx Checklist 2/3 (unnumbered)	375.00	50.00	10.00
☐ xx Checklist 3/4 (unnumbered)	675.00	75.00	15.00
☐ xx Checklist 4/5 (unnumbered)	775.00	90.00	18.00

1958 Topps

The cards in this 494-card set measure 2 1/2" by 3 1/2". Although the last card is numbered 495, number 145 was not issued, bringing the set total to 494 cards. The 1958 Topps set contains the first Sport Magazine All-Star Selection series (475-495) and expanded use of combination cards. The team cards carried series checklists on back (Milwaukee, Detroit, Baltimore, and Cincinnati are also found with players listed alphabetically). Cards with the scarce yellow name (YL) or team (YT) lettering, as opposed to the common white lettering, are noted in the checklist. In the last series, cards of Stan Musial and Mickey Mantle were triple printed; the cards they replaced (443, 446, 450, and 462) on the printing sheet were hence printed in shorter supply than other cards in the last series and are marked with an SP in the list below. Technically the New York Giants team card (19) is an error as the Giants had already moved to San Francisco. The key rookies in this set are Orlando Cepeda, Curt Flood, Roger Maris, and Vada Pinson.

	NRMT	VG-E	GOOD
COMPLETE SET (494)	5250.00	2250.00	550.00
COMMON PLAYER (1-110)	7.25	3.25	1.00
COMMON PLAYER (111-198)	5.25	2.25	.50
COMMON PLAYER (199-352)	4.50	2.00	.45
COMMON PLAYER (353-440)	4.00	1.75	.40
COMMON PLAYER (441-474)	3.75	1.60	.37
COMMON PLAYER (475-495)	4.00	1.75	.40
☐ 1 Ted Williams	375.00	.00	.00
☐ 2A Bob Lemon	20.00	8.50	2.75
☐ 2B Bob Lemon YT	36.00	16.25	5.50
☐ 3 Alex Kellner	7.25	3.25	1.00
☐ 4 Hank Foiles	7.25	3.25	1.00
☐ 5 Willie Mays	185.00	80.00	24.00
☐ 6 George Zuverink	7.25	3.25	1.00
☐ 7 Dale Long	8.00	3.50	.80
☐ 8A Eddie Kasko	7.25	3.25	1.00
☐ 8B Eddie Kasko YL	25.00	11.00	3.50
☐ 9 Hank Bauer	12.00	5.25	1.50
☐ 10 Lou Burdette	10.00	4.50	1.25
☐ 11A Jim Rivera	7.25	3.25	1.00
☐ 11B Jim Rivera YT	21.00	9.00	3.00
☐ 12 George Crowe	7.25	3.25	1.00
☐ 13A Billy Hoeft	7.25	3.25	1.00
☐ 13B Billy Hoeft YL	25.00	11.00	3.50
☐ 14 Rip Repulski	7.25	3.25	1.00
☐ 15 Jim Lemon	8.00	3.50	.80
☐ 16 Charlie Neal	8.00	3.50	.80
☐ 17 Felix Mantilla	7.25	3.25	1.00
☐ 18 Frank Sullivan	7.25	3.25	1.00
☐ 19 New York Giants Team Card (checklist on back)	28.00	9.00	1.80
☐ 20A Gil McDougald	12.00	5.25	1.50
☐ 20B Gil McDougald YL	30.00	13.50	4.50
☐ 21 Curt Barclay	7.25	3.25	1.00
☐ 22 Hal Naragon	7.25	3.25	1.00
☐ 23A Bill Tuttle	7.25	3.25	1.00
☐ 23B Bill Tuttle YL	25.00	11.00	3.50
☐ 24A Hobie Landrith	7.25	3.25	1.00
☐ 24B Hobie Landrith YL	25.00	11.00	3.50
☐ 25 Don Drysdale	70.00	32.00	10.50
☐ 26 Ron Jackson	7.25	3.25	1.00

☐ 27 Bud Freeman 7.25 3.25 1.00
☐ 28 Jim Busby 7.25 3.25 1.00
☐ 29 Ted Lepcio 7.25 3.25 1.00
☐ 30A Hank Aaron 195.00 85.00 24.00
☐ 30B Hank Aaron YL 300.00 135.00 45.00
☐ 31 Tex Clevenger 7.25 3.25 1.00
☐ 32A J.W. Porter 7.25 3.25 1.00
☐ 32B J.W. Porter YL 25.00 11.00 3.50
☐ 33A Cal Neeman 7.25 3.25 1.00
☐ 33B Cal Neeman YT 21.00 9.00 3.00
☐ 34 Bob Thurman 7.25 3.25 1.00
☐ 35A Don Mossi .... 8.00 3.50 .80
☐ 35B Don Mossi YT 21.00 9.00 3.00
☐ 36 Ted Kazanski 7.25 3.25 1.00
☐ 37 Mike McCormick UER . 10.00 4.50 1.25
(photo actually
Ray Monzant)
☐ 38 Dick Gernert 7.25 3.25 1.00
☐ 39 Bob Martyn 7.25 3.25 1.00
☐ 40 George Kell 15.00 6.50 2.15
☐ 41 Dave Hillman 7.25 3.25 1.00
☐ 42 John Roseboro 12.00 5.25 1.50
☐ 43 Sal Maglie .... 9.00 4.00 .90
☐ 44 Washington Senators .. 16.50 6.00 1.25
Team Card
(checklist on back)
☐ 45 Dick Groat .... 9.00 4.00 .90
☐ 46A Lou Sleater 7.25 3.25 1.00
☐ 46B Lou Sleater YL 25.00 11.00 3.50
☐ 47 Roger Maris 350.00 160.00 52.50
☐ 48 Chuck Harmon 7.25 3.25 1.00
☐ 49 Smoky Burgess .... 9.00 4.00 .90
☐ 50A Billy Pierce .... 9.00 4.00 .90
☐ 50B Billy Pierce YT 25.00 11.00 3.50
☐ 51 Del Rice 7.25 3.25 1.00
☐ 52A Bob Clemente 165.00 75.00 22.50
☐ 52B Bob Clemente YT 275.00 120.00 40.00
☐ 53A Morrie Martin 7.25 3.25 1.00
☐ 53B Morrie Martin YL 25.00 11.00 3.50
☐ 54 Norm Siebern 7.25 3.25 1.00
☐ 55 Chico Carrasquel 7.25 3.25 1.00
☐ 56 Bill Fischer 7.25 3.25 1.00
☐ 57A Tim Thompson 7.25 3.25 1.00
☐ 57B Tim Thompson YL 25.00 11.00 3.50
☐ 58A Art Schult 7.25 3.25 1.00
☐ 58B Art Schult YT 21.00 9.00 3.00
☐ 59 Dave Sisler 7.25 3.25 1.00
☐ 60A Del Ennis .... 8.00 3.50 .80
☐ 60B Del Ennis YL 25.00 11.00 3.50
☐ 61A Darrell Johnson .... 8.00 3.50 .80
☐ 61B Darrell Johnson YL ... 25.00 11.00 3.50
☐ 62 Joe DeMaestri 7.25 3.25 1.00
☐ 63 Joe Nuxhall .... 8.00 3.50 .80
☐ 64 Joe Lonnett 7.25 3.25 1.00
☐ 65A Von McDaniel 7.25 3.25 1.00
☐ 65B Von McDaniel YL 25.00 11.00 3.50
☐ 66 Lee Walls 7.25 3.25 1.00
☐ 67 Joe Ginsberg 7.25 3.25 1.00
☐ 68 Daryl Spencer 7.25 3.25 1.00
☐ 69 Wally Burnette 7.25 3.25 1.00
☐ 70A Al Kaline 85.00 38.00 12.75
☐ 70B Al Kaline YL 135.00 60.00 20.00
☐ 71 Dodgers Team 38.00 12.50 2.50
(checklist on back)
☐ 72 Bud Byerly 7.25 3.25 1.00
☐ 73 Pete Daley 7.25 3.25 1.00
☐ 74 Roy Face .... 9.00 4.00 .90
☐ 75 Gus Bell .... 8.00 3.50 .80
☐ 76A Dick Farrell .... 8.00 3.50 .80
☐ 76B Dick Farrell YT 21.00 9.00 3.00
☐ 77A Don Zimmer 12.00 5.25 1.50
☐ 77B Don Zimmer YT 25.00 11.00 3.50
☐ 78A Ernie Johnson .... 8.00 3.50 .80
☐ 78B Ernie Johnson YL 25.00 11.00 3.50
☐ 79A Dick Williams .... 8.00 3.50 .80
☐ 79B Dick Williams YT 22.00 9.50 3.15
☐ 80 Dick Drott 7.25 3.25 1.00
☐ 81A Steve Boros .... 8.00 3.50 .80
☐ 81B Steve Boros YT 22.00 9.50 3.15
☐ 82 Ron Kline 7.25 3.25 1.00
☐ 83 Bob Hazle .... 8.00 3.50 .80
☐ 84 Billy O'Dell 7.25 3.25 1.00
☐ 85A Luis Aparicio 24.00 10.50 3.50
☐ 85B Luis Aparicio YT 42.00 18.00 5.50
☐ 86 Valmy Thomas 7.25 3.25 1.00
☐ 87 Johnny Kucks .... 8.00 3.50 .80
☐ 88 Duke Snider 75.00 34.00 11.25
☐ 89 Billy Klaus 7.25 3.25 1.00
☐ 90 Robin Roberts 20.00 8.50 2.75
☐ 91 Chuck Tanner .... 8.00 3.50 .80
☐ 92A Clint Courtney 7.25 3.25 1.00
☐ 92B Clint Courtney YL 25.00 11.00 3.50
☐ 93 Sandy Amoros .... 9.00 4.00 .90
☐ 94 Bob Skinner .... 8.00 3.50 .80
☐ 95 Frank Bolling 7.25 3.25 1.00
☐ 96 Joe Durham 7.25 3.25 1.00
☐ 97A Larry Jackson 7.25 3.25 1.00
☐ 97B Larry Jackson YL 25.00 11.00 3.50
☐ 98A Billy Hunter 7.25 3.25 1.00
☐ 98B Billy Hunter YL 25.00 11.00 3.50
☐ 99 Bobby Adams 7.25 3.25 1.00
☐ 100A Early Wynn 20.00 8.50 2.75
☐ 100B Early Wynn YT 36.00 16.25 5.50
☐ 101A Bobby Richardson .. 20.00 8.50 2.75
☐ 101B Bobby Richardson YL36.00 16.25 5.50
☐ 102 George Strickland 7.25 3.25 1.00
☐ 103 Jerry Lynch 7.25 3.25 1.00
☐ 104 Jim Pendleton 7.25 3.25 1.00
☐ 105 Billy Gardner 7.25 3.25 1.00
☐ 106 Dick Schofield 7.25 3.25 1.00
☐ 107 Ossie Virgil 7.25 3.25 1.00
☐ 108A Jim Landis 7.25 3.25 1.00
☐ 108B Jim Landis YT 21.00 9.00 3.00
☐ 109 Herb Plews 7.25 3.25 1.00
☐ 110 Johnny Logan .... 8.00 3.50 .80
☐ 111 Stu Miller .... 6.00 2.50 .60

☐ 112	Gus Zernial	6.00	2.50	.60
☐ 113	Jerry Walker	5.25	2.25	.50
☐ 114	Irv Noren	6.00	2.50	.60
☐ 115	Jim Bunning	20.00	8.50	2.75
☐ 116	Dave Philley	5.25	2.25	.50
☐ 117	Frank Torre	6.00	2.50	.60
☐ 118	Harvey Haddix	6.00	2.50	.60
☐ 119	Harry Chiti	5.25	2.25	.50
☐ 120	Johnny Podres	9.00	4.00	.90
☐ 121	Eddie Miksis	5.25	2.25	.50
☐ 122	Walt Moryn	5.25	2.25	.50
☐ 123	Dick Tomanek	5.25	2.25	.50
☐ 124	Bobby Usher	5.25	2.25	.50
☐ 125	Alvin Dark	7.00	3.00	.70
☐ 126	Stan Palys	5.25	2.25	.50
☐ 127	Tom Sturdivant	6.00	2.50	.60
☐ 128	Willie Kirkland	6.00	2.50	.60
☐ 129	Jim Derrington	5.25	2.25	.50
☐ 130	Jackie Jensen	10.00	4.50	1.25
☐ 131	Bob Henrich	5.25	2.25	.50
☐ 132	Vern Law	6.00	2.50	.60
☐ 133	Russ Nixon	7.00	3.00	.70
☐ 134	Philadelphia Phillies Team Card (checklist on back)	12.00	4.00	.80
☐ 135	Mike(Moe) Drabowsky	6.00	2.50	.60
☐ 136	Jim Finigan	5.25	2.25	.50
☐ 137	Russ Kemmerer	5.25	2.25	.50
☐ 138	Earl Torgeson	5.25	2.25	.50
☐ 139	George Brunet	5.25	2.25	.50
☐ 140	Wes Covington	6.00	2.50	.60
☐ 141	Ken Lehman	5.25	2.25	.50
☐ 142	Enos Slaughter	21.00	9.00	3.00
☐ 143	Billy Muffett	5.25	2.25	.50
☐ 144	Bobby Morgan	5.25	2.25	.50
☐ 145	Never issued	0.00	.00	.00
☐ 146	Dick Gray	5.25	2.25	.50
☐ 147	Don McMahon	7.00	3.00	.70
☐ 148	Billy Consolo	5.25	2.25	.50
☐ 149	Tom Acker	5.25	2.25	.50
☐ 150	Mickey Mantle	525.00	225.00	75.00
☐ 151	Buddy Pritchard	5.25	2.25	.50
☐ 152	Johnny Antonelli	6.00	2.50	.60
☐ 153	Les Moss	5.25	2.25	.50
☐ 154	Harry Byrd	5.25	2.25	.50
☐ 155	Hector Lopez	5.25	2.25	.50
☐ 156	Dick Hyde	5.25	2.25	.50
☐ 157	Dee Fondy	5.25	2.25	.50
☐ 158	Cleveland Indians Team Card (checklist on back)	12.00	5.25	1.50
☐ 159	Taylor Phillips	5.25	2.25	.50
☐ 160	Don Hoak	6.00	2.50	.60
☐ 161	Don Larsen	10.00	4.50	1.25
☐ 162	Gil Hodges	25.00	11.00	3.50
☐ 163	Jim Wilson	5.25	2.25	.50
☐ 164	Bob Taylor	5.25	2.25	.50
☐ 165	Bob Nieman	5.25	2.25	.50
☐ 166	Danny O'Connell	5.25	2.25	.50
☐ 167	Frank Baumann	5.25	2.25	.50
☐ 168	Joe Cunningham	6.00	2.50	.60
☐ 169	Ralph Terry	7.00	3.00	.70
☐ 170	Vic Wertz	6.00	2.50	.60
☐ 171	Harry Anderson	5.25	2.25	.50
☐ 172	Don Gross	5.25	2.25	.50
☐ 173	Eddie Yost	5.25	2.25	.50
☐ 174	Athletics Team (checklist on back)	11.00	4.00	.80
☐ 175	Marv Throneberry	10.00	4.50	1.25
☐ 176	Bob Buhl	6.00	2.50	.60
☐ 177	Al Smith	5.25	2.25	.50
☐ 178	Ted Kluszewski	11.00	5.00	1.35
☐ 179	Willie Miranda	5.25	2.25	.50
☐ 180	Lindy McDaniel	6.00	2.50	.60
☐ 181	Willie Jones	5.25	2.25	.50
☐ 182	Joe Caffie	5.25	2.25	.50
☐ 183	Dave Jolly	5.25	2.25	.50
☐ 184	Elvin Tappe	5.25	2.25	.50
☐ 185	Ray Boone	6.00	2.50	.60
☐ 186	Jack Meyer	5.25	2.25	.50
☐ 187	Sandy Koufax	180.00	80.00	27.00
☐ 188	Milt Bolling UER (photo actually Lou Berberet)	5.25	2.25	.50
☐ 189	George Susce	5.25	2.25	.50
☐ 190	Red Schoendienst	20.00	8.50	2.75
☐ 191	Art Ceccarelli	5.25	2.25	.50
☐ 192	Milt Graff	5.25	2.25	.50
☐ 193	Jerry Lumpe	7.00	3.00	.70
☐ 194	Roger Craig	9.00	4.00	.90
☐ 195	Whitey Lockman	6.00	2.50	.60
☐ 196	Mike Garcia	6.00	2.50	.60
☐ 197	Haywood Sullivan	6.00	2.50	.60
☐ 198	Bill Virdon	7.00	3.00	.70
☐ 199	Don Blasingame	4.50	2.00	.45
☐ 200	Bob Keegan	4.50	2.00	.45
☐ 201	Jim Bolger	4.50	2.00	.45
☐ 202	Woody Held	6.50	2.75	.65
☐ 203	Al Walker	4.50	2.00	.45
☐ 204	Leo Kiely	4.50	2.00	.45
☐ 205	Johnny Temple	5.50	2.50	.55
☐ 206	Bob Shaw	6.50	2.75	.65
☐ 207	Solly Hemus	4.50	2.00	.45
☐ 208	Cal McLish	4.50	2.00	.45
☐ 209	Bob Anderson	4.50	2.00	.45
☐ 210	Wally Moon	5.50	2.50	.55
☐ 211	Pete Burnside	4.50	2.00	.45
☐ 212	Bubba Phillips	4.50	2.00	.45
☐ 213	Red Wilson	4.50	2.00	.45
☐ 214	Willard Schmidt	4.50	2.00	.45
☐ 215	Jim Gilliam	9.00	4.00	.90
☐ 216	St. Louis Cardinals Team Card (checklist on back)	12.00	4.00	.80
☐ 217	Jack Harshman	4.50	2.00	.45
☐ 218	Dick Rand	4.50	2.00	.45

Card			
☐ 219 Camilo Pascual	5.50	2.50	.55
☐ 220 Tom Brewer	4.50	2.00	.45
☐ 221 Jerry Kindall	5.50	2.50	.55
☐ 222 Bud Daley	4.50	2.00	.45
☐ 223 Andy Pafko	5.50	2.50	.55
☐ 224 Bob Grim	5.50	2.50	.55
☐ 225 Billy Goodman	5.50	2.50	.55
☐ 226 Bob Smith	4.50	2.00	.45
☐ 227 Gene Stephens	4.50	2.00	.45
☐ 228 Duke Maas	4.50	2.00	.45
☐ 229 Frank Zupo	4.50	2.00	.45
☐ 230 Richie Ashburn	16.00	6.75	2.25
☐ 231 Lloyd Merritt	4.50	2.00	.45
☐ 232 Reno Bertoia	4.50	2.00	.45
☐ 233 Mickey Vernon	5.50	2.50	.55
☐ 234 Carl Sawatski	4.50	2.00	.45
☐ 235 Tom Gorman	4.50	2.00	.45
☐ 236 Ed Fitzgerald	4.50	2.00	.45
☐ 237 Bill Wight	4.50	2.00	.45
☐ 238 Bill Mazeroski	13.00	5.75	1.75
☐ 239 Chuck Stobbs	4.50	2.00	.45
☐ 240 Bill Skowron	12.00	5.25	1.50
☐ 241 Dick Littlefield	4.50	2.00	.45
☐ 242 Johnny Klippstein	4.50	2.00	.45
☐ 243 Larry Raines	4.50	2.00	.45
☐ 244 Don Demeter	4.50	2.00	.45
☐ 245 Frank Lary	5.50	2.50	.55
☐ 246 New York Yankees	40.00	12.50	2.50
Team Card			
(checklist on back)			
☐ 247 Casey Wise	4.50	2.00	.45
☐ 248 Herman Wehmeier	4.50	2.00	.45
☐ 249 Ray Moore	4.50	2.00	.45
☐ 250 Roy Sievers	5.50	2.50	.55
☐ 251 Warren Hacker	4.50	2.00	.45
☐ 252 Bob Trowbridge	4.50	2.00	.45
☐ 253 Don Mueller	5.50	2.50	.55
☐ 254 Alex Grammas	4.50	2.00	.45
☐ 255 Bob Turley	9.00	4.00	.90
☐ 256 Chicago White Sox	11.00	3.50	.75
Team Card			
(checklist on back)			
☐ 257 Hal Smith	4.50	2.00	.45
☐ 258 Carl Erskine	9.00	4.00	.90
☐ 259 Al Pilarcik	4.50	2.00	.45
☐ 260 Frank Malzone	5.50	2.50	.55
☐ 261 Turk Lown	4.50	2.00	.45
☐ 262 Johnny Groth	4.50	2.00	.45
☐ 263 Eddie Bressoud	4.50	2.00	.45
☐ 264 Jack Sanford	5.50	2.50	.55
☐ 265 Pete Runnels	5.50	2.50	.55
☐ 266 Connie Johnson	4.50	2.00	.45
☐ 267 Sherm Lollar	5.50	2.50	.55
☐ 268 Granny Hamner	4.50	2.00	.45
☐ 269 Paul Smith	4.50	2.00	.45
☐ 270 Warren Spahn	50.00	22.50	7.50
☐ 271 Billy Martin	20.00	8.50	2.75
☐ 272 Ray Crone	4.50	2.00	.45
☐ 273 Hal Smith	4.50	2.00	.45
☐ 274 Rocky Bridges	4.50	2.00	.45
☐ 275 Elston Howard	11.00	5.00	1.35
☐ 276 Bobby Avila	4.50	2.00	.45
☐ 277 Virgil Trucks	4.50	2.00	.45
☐ 278 Mack Burk	4.50	2.00	.45
☐ 279 Bob Boyd	4.50	2.00	.45
☐ 280 Jim Piersall	7.00	3.00	.70
☐ 281 Sammy Taylor	4.50	2.00	.45
☐ 282 Paul Foytack	4.50	2.00	.45
☐ 283 Ray Shearer	4.50	2.00	.45
☐ 284 Ray Katt	4.50	2.00	.45
☐ 285 Frank Robinson	85.00	38.00	12.75
☐ 286 Gino Cimoli	4.50	2.00	.45
☐ 287 Sam Jones	4.50	2.00	.45
☐ 288 Harmon Killebrew	80.00	36.00	12.00
☐ 289 Series Hurling Rivals	6.50	2.75	.65
Lou Burdette			
Bobby Shantz			
☐ 290 Dick Donovan	4.50	2.00	.45
☐ 291 Don Landrum	4.50	2.00	.45
☐ 292 Ned Garver	4.50	2.00	.45
☐ 293 Gene Freese	4.50	2.00	.45
☐ 294 Hal Jeffcoat	4.50	2.00	.45
☐ 295 Minnie Minoso	9.00	4.00	.90
☐ 296 Ryne Duren	9.00	4.00	.90
☐ 297 Don Buddin	4.50	2.00	.45
☐ 298 Jim Hearn	4.50	2.00	.45
☐ 299 Harry Simpson	4.50	2.00	.45
☐ 300 Harridge and Giles	8.00	3.50	.80
League Presidents			
☐ 301 Randy Jackson	4.50	2.00	.45
☐ 302 Mike Baxes	4.50	2.00	.45
☐ 303 Neil Chrisley	4.50	2.00	.45
☐ 304 Tigers' Big Bats	13.50	6.00	1.85
Harvey Kuenn			
Al Kaline			
☐ 305 Clem Labine	5.50	2.50	.55
☐ 306 Whammy Douglas	4.50	2.00	.45
☐ 307 Brooks Robinson	100.00	45.00	15.00
☐ 308 Paul Giel	5.50	2.50	.55
☐ 309 Gail Harris	4.50	2.00	.45
☐ 310 Ernie Banks	85.00	38.00	12.75
☐ 311 Bob Purkey	4.50	2.00	.45
☐ 312 Boston Red Sox	12.00	4.00	.80
Team Card			
(checklist on back)			
☐ 313 Bob Rush	4.50	2.00	.45
☐ 314 Dodgers' Boss and	21.00	9.00	3.00
Power: Duke Snider			
Walt Alston			
☐ 315 Bob Friend	5.50	2.50	.55
☐ 316 Tito Francona	4.50	2.00	.45
☐ 317 Albie Pearson	5.50	2.50	.55
☐ 318 Frank House	4.50	2.00	.45
☐ 319 Lou Skizas	4.50	2.00	.45
☐ 320 Whitey Ford	48.00	22.00	6.00
☐ 321 Sluggers Supreme	38.00	17.00	5.25

	Ted Kluszewski			
	Ted Williams			
☐ 322	Harding Peterson	4.50	2.00	.45
☐ 323	Elmer Valo	4.50	2.00	.45
☐ 324	Hoyt Wilhelm	18.00	7.50	2.50
☐ 325	Joe Adcock	5.50	2.50	.55
☐ 326	Bob Miller	4.50	2.00	.45
☐ 327	Chicago Cubs	12.00	4.00	.80
	Team Card			
	(checklist on back)			
☐ 328	Ike Delock	4.50	2.00	.45
☐ 329	Bob Cerv	5.50	2.50	.55
☐ 330	Ed Bailey	5.50	2.50	.55
☐ 331	Pedro Ramos	4.50	2.00	.45
☐ 332	Jim King	4.50	2.00	.45
☐ 333	Andy Carey	5.50	2.50	.55
☐ 334	Mound Aces	5.50	2.50	.55
	Bob Friend			
	Billy Pierce			
☐ 335	Ruben Gomez	4.50	2.00	.45
☐ 336	Bert Hamric	4.50	2.00	.45
☐ 337	Hank Aguirre	4.50	2.00	.45
☐ 338	Walt Dropo	4.50	2.00	.45
☐ 339	Fred Hatfield	4.50	2.00	.45
☐ 340	Don Newcombe	9.00	4.00	.90
☐ 341	Pittsburgh Pirates	12.00	4.00	.80
	Team Card			
	(checklist on back)			
☐ 342	Jim Brosnan	5.50	2.50	.55
☐ 343	Orlando Cepeda	70.00	32.00	10.50
☐ 344	Bob Porterfield	4.50	2.00	.45
☐ 345	Jim Hegan	4.50	2.00	.45
☐ 346	Steve Bilko	4.50	2.00	.45
☐ 347	Don Rudolph	4.50	2.00	.45
☐ 348	Chico Fernandez	4.50	2.00	.45
☐ 349	Murry Dickson	4.50	2.00	.45
☐ 350	Ken Boyer	11.00	5.00	1.35
☐ 351	Braves Fence Busters	25.00	11.00	3.50
	Del Crandall			
	Eddie Mathews			
	Hank Aaron			
	Joe Adcock			
☐ 352	Herb Score	7.50	3.25	.75
☐ 353	Stan Lopata	4.00	1.75	.40
☐ 354	Art Ditmar	4.00	1.75	.40
☐ 355	Bill Bruton	5.00	2.25	.50
☐ 356	Bob Malkmus	4.00	1.75	.40
☐ 357	Danny McDevitt	4.00	1.75	.40
☐ 358	Gene Baker	4.00	1.75	.40
☐ 359	Billy Loes	4.00	1.75	.40
☐ 360	Roy McMillan	4.00	1.75	.40
☐ 361	Mike Fornieles	4.00	1.75	.40
☐ 362	Ray Jablonski	4.00	1.75	.40
☐ 363	Don Elston	4.00	1.75	.40
☐ 364	Earl Battey	4.00	1.75	.40
☐ 365	Tom Morgan	4.00	1.75	.40
☐ 366	Gene Green	4.00	1.75	.40
☐ 367	Jack Urban	4.00	1.75	.40
☐ 368	Rocky Colavito	30.00	13.50	4.50
☐ 369	Ralph Lumenti	4.00	1.75	.40
☐ 370	Yogi Berra	95.00	42.00	11.00
☐ 371	Marty Keough	4.00	1.75	.40
☐ 372	Don Cardwell	4.00	1.75	.40
☐ 373	Joe Pignatano	4.00	1.75	.40
☐ 374	Brooks Lawrence	4.00	1.75	.40
☐ 375	Pee Wee Reese	55.00	25.00	8.25
☐ 376	Charley Rabe	4.00	1.75	.40
☐ 377A	Milwaukee Braves	12.00	5.00	1.00
	Team Card			
	(alphabetical)			
☐ 377B	Milwaukee Team	70.00	20.00	4.00
	numerical checklist			
☐ 378	Hank Sauer	5.00	2.25	.50
☐ 379	Ray Herbert	4.00	1.75	.40
☐ 380	Charley Maxwell	5.00	2.25	.50
☐ 381	Hal Brown	4.00	1.75	.40
☐ 382	Al Cicotte	4.00	1.75	.40
☐ 383	Lou Berberet	4.00	1.75	.40
☐ 384	John Goryl	4.00	1.75	.40
☐ 385	Wilmer Mizell	4.00	1.75	.40
☐ 386	Birdie's Sluggers	9.00	4.00	.90
	Ed Bailey			
	Birdie Tebbetts			
	Frank Robinson			
☐ 387	Wally Post	5.00	2.25	.50
☐ 388	Billy Moran	4.00	1.75	.40
☐ 389	Bill Taylor	4.00	1.75	.40
☐ 390	Del Crandall	5.00	2.25	.50
☐ 391	Dave Melton	4.00	1.75	.40
☐ 392	Bennie Daniels	4.00	1.75	.40
☐ 393	Tony Kubek	18.00	7.50	2.50
☐ 394	Jim Grant	6.00	2.50	.60
☐ 395	Willard Nixon	4.00	1.75	.40
☐ 396	Dutch Dotterer	4.00	1.75	.40
☐ 397A	Detroit Tigers	12.00	5.00	1.00
	Team Card			
	(alphabetical)			
☐ 397B	Detroit Team	70.00	20.00	4.00
	numerical checklist			
☐ 398	Gene Woodling	5.00	2.25	.50
☐ 399	Marv Grissom	4.00	1.75	.40
☐ 400	Nellie Fox	13.00	5.75	1.75
☐ 401	Don Bessent	4.00	1.75	.40
☐ 402	Bobby Gene Smith	4.00	1.75	.40
☐ 403	Steve Korcheck	4.00	1.75	.40
☐ 404	Curt Simmons	5.00	2.25	.50
☐ 405	Ken Aspromonte	4.00	1.75	.40
☐ 406	Vic Power	4.00	1.75	.40
☐ 407	Carlton Willey	4.00	1.75	.40
☐ 408A	Baltimore Orioles	12.00	4.00	.80
	Team Card			
	(alphabetical)			
☐ 408B	Baltimore Team	70.00	20.00	4.00
	numerical checklist			
☐ 409	Frank Thomas	5.00	2.25	.50
☐ 410	Murray Wall	4.00	1.75	.40

☐ 411 Tony Taylor .... 7.00 3.00 .70
☐ 412 Jerry Staley .... 4.00 1.75 .40
☐ 413 Jim Davenport .... 6.00 2.50 .60
☐ 414 Sammy White .... 4.00 1.75 .40
☐ 415 Bob Bowman .... 4.00 1.75 .40
☐ 416 Foster Castleman .... 4.00 1.75 .40
☐ 417 Carl Furillo .... 9.00 4.00 .90
☐ 418 World Series Batting 140.00 63.00 21.00
Foes: Mickey Mantle
Hank Aaron
☐ 419 Bobby Shantz .... 6.00 2.50 .60
☐ 420 Vada Pinson 25.00 11.00 3.50
☐ 421 Dixie Howell .... 4.00 1.75 .40
☐ 422 Norm Zauchin .... 4.00 1.75 .40
☐ 423 Phil Clark .... 4.00 1.75 .40
☐ 424 Larry Doby .... 6.00 2.50 .60
☐ 425 Sammy Esposito .... 4.00 1.75 .40
☐ 426 Johnny O'Brien .... 4.00 1.75 .40
☐ 427 Al Worthington .... 4.00 1.75 .40
☐ 428A Cincinnati Reds .... 12.00 4.00 .80
Team Card
(alphabetical)
☐ 428B Cincinnati Team 70.00 20.00 4.00
numerical checklist
☐ 429 Gus Triandos .... 5.00 2.25 .50
☐ 430 Bobby Thomson .... 6.00 2.50 .60
☐ 431 Gene Conley .... 4.00 1.75 .40
☐ 432 John Powers .... 4.00 1.75 .40
☐ 433A Pancho Herrer ERR 500.00 225.00 75.00
☐ 433B Pancho Herrera COR . 5.00 2.25 .50
☐ 434 Harvey Kuenn .... 6.00 2.50 .60
☐ 435 Ed Roebuck .... 5.00 2.25 .50
☐ 436 Rival Fence Busters ... 55.00 25.00 8.25
Willie Mays
Duke Snider
☐ 437 Bob Speake .... 4.00 1.75 .40
☐ 438 Whitey Herzog .... 7.00 3.00 .70
☐ 439 Ray Narleski .... 4.00 1.75 .40
☐ 440 Eddie Mathews 33.00 15.00 5.00
☐ 441 Jim Marshall .... 3.75 1.60 .37
☐ 442 Phil Paine .... 3.75 1.60 .37
☐ 443 Billy Harrell SP 12.00 5.25 1.50
☐ 444 Danny Kravitz .... 3.75 1.60 .37
☐ 445 Bob Smith .... 3.75 1.60 .37
☐ 446 Carroll Hardy SP 12.00 5.25 1.50
☐ 447 Ray Monzant .... 3.75 1.60 .37
☐ 448 Charlie Lau .... 7.00 3.00 .70
☐ 449 Gene Fodge .... 3.75 1.60 .37
☐ 450 Preston Ward SP 12.00 5.25 1.50
☐ 451 Joe Taylor .... 3.75 1.60 .37
☐ 452 Roman Mejias .... 3.75 1.60 .37
☐ 453 Tom Qualters .... 3.75 1.60 .37
☐ 454 Harry Hanebrink .... 3.75 1.60 .37
☐ 455 Hal Griggs .... 3.75 1.60 .37
☐ 456 Dick Brown .... 3.75 1.60 .37
☐ 457 Milt Pappas .... 7.00 3.00 .70
☐ 458 Julio Becquer .... 3.75 1.60 .37
☐ 459 Ron Blackburn .... 3.75 1.60 .37
☐ 460 Chuck Essegian .... 3.75 1.60 .37
☐ 461 Ed Mayer .... 3.75 1.60 .37
☐ 462 Gary Geiger SP 12.00 5.25 1.50
☐ 463 Vito Valentinetti .... 3.75 1.60 .37
☐ 464 Curt Flood 25.00 11.00 3.50
☐ 465 Arnie Portocarrero ...... 3.75 1.60 .37
☐ 466 Pete Whisenant .... 3.75 1.60 .37
☐ 467 Glen Hobbie .... 3.75 1.60 .37
☐ 468 Bob Schmidt .... 3.75 1.60 .37
☐ 469 Don Ferrarese .... 3.75 1.60 .37
☐ 470 R.C. Stevens .... 3.75 1.60 .37
☐ 471 Lenny Green .... 3.75 1.60 .37
☐ 472 Joey Jay .... 4.50 2.00 .45
☐ 473 Bill Renna .... 3.75 1.60 .37
☐ 474 Roman Semproch .... 3.75 1.60 .37
☐ 475 Haney/Stengel AS 18.00 7.50 1.50
(checklist back)
☐ 476 Stan Musial AS TP 36.00 16.25 5.50
☐ 477 Bill Skowron AS .... 6.00 2.50 .60
☐ 478 Johnny Temple AS ...... 4.00 1.75 .40
☐ 479 Nellie Fox AS .... 8.50 3.75 .85
☐ 480 Eddie Mathews AS 14.00 6.25 2.00
☐ 481 Frank Malzone AS .... 4.00 1.75 .40
☐ 482 Ernie Banks AS 21.00 9.00 3.00
☐ 483 Luis Aparicio AS 12.50 5.50 1.65
☐ 484 Frank Robinson AS ... 21.00 9.00 3.00
☐ 485 Ted Williams AS 65.00 29.00 9.75
☐ 486 Willie Mays AS 45.00 20.00 6.75
☐ 487 Mickey Mantle AS TP 100.00 45.00 15.00
☐ 488 Hank Aaron AS 45.00 20.00 6.75
☐ 489 Jackie Jensen AS .... 4.50 2.00 .45
☐ 490 Ed Bailey AS .... 4.00 1.75 .40
☐ 491 Sherm Lollar AS .... 4.00 1.75 .40
☐ 492 Bob Friend AS .... 4.00 1.75 .40
☐ 493 Bob Turley AS .... 4.50 2.00 .45
☐ 494 Warren Spahn AS 16.00 6.75 2.25
☐ 495 Herb Score AS .... 14.00 3.00 .60

1959 Topps

The cards in this 572-card set measure 2 1/2" by 3 1/2". The 1959 Topps set contains bust pictures of the players in a colored circle. Card numbers 551 to 572 are Sporting News All-Star Selections. High numbers 507 to 572 have the card number in a black background on the reverse rather than a green background as in the lower numbers. The high numbers are more difficult to obtain. Several cards in the 300s exist with or without an extra traded or option line on the back of the card. Cards 199 to 286 exist with either white or gray

backs. Cards 461 to 470 contain "Highlights" while cards 116 to 146 give an alphabetically ordered listing of "Rookie Prospects." These Rookie Prospects (RP) were Topps' first organized inclusion of untested "Rookie" cards. Card 440 features Lew Burdette erroneously posing as a left-handed pitcher. There were some three-card advertising panels produced by Topps; the players included are from the first series; one panel shows Don McMahon, Red Wilson, and Bob Boyd on the front with Ted Kluszewski's reverse on one of the backs. Another panel shows Billy Hunter, Chuck Stobbs, and Carl Sawatski on the front with Nellie Fox's reverse on one of the backs. When cut apart, these advertising cards are distinguished by the non-standard card back, i.e., part of an advertisement for the 1959 Topps set instead of the typical statistics and biographical information about the player pictured. The key rookies in this set are Sparky Anderson, Bob Gibson, and Bill White.

	NRMT	VG-E	GOOD
COMPLETE SET (572)	5250.00	2250.00	550.00
COMMON PLAYER (1-110)	6.00	2.50	.60
COMMON PLAYER (111-198)	3.75	1.60	.37
COMMON PLAYER (199-506)	3.25	1.35	.32
COMMON PLAYER (507-550)	16.00	6.75	2.25
COMMON PLAYER (551-572)	18.00	7.50	2.50

Card	NRMT	VG-E	GOOD
☐ 1 Ford Frick	75.00	15.00	3.00
(Commissioner)			
☐ 2 Eddie Yost	6.00	2.50	.60
☐ 3 Don McMahon	6.00	2.50	.60
☐ 4 Albie Pearson	6.00	2.50	.60
☐ 5 Dick Donovan	6.00	2.50	.60
☐ 6 Alex Grammas	6.00	2.50	.60
☐ 7 Al Pilarcik	6.00	2.50	.60
☐ 8 Phillies Team	30.00	10.00	2.00
(checklist on back)			
☐ 9 Paul Giel	6.00	2.50	.60
☐ 10 Mickey Mantle	400.00	180.00	60.00
☐ 11 Billy Hunter	6.00	2.50	.60
☐ 12 Vern Law	7.00	3.00	.70
☐ 13 Dick Gernert	6.00	2.50	.60
☐ 14 Pete Whisenant	6.00	2.50	.60
☐ 15 Dick Drott	6.00	2.50	.60
☐ 16 Joe Pignatano	6.00	2.50	.60
☐ 17 Danny's Stars	8.00	3.50	.80
Frank Thomas			
Danny Murtaugh			
Ted Kluszewski			
☐ 18 Jack Urban	6.00	2.50	.60
☐ 19 Eddie Bressoud	6.00	2.50	.60
☐ 20 Duke Snider	65.00	29.00	9.75
☐ 21 Connie Johnson	6.00	2.50	.60
☐ 22 Al Smith	6.00	2.50	.60
☐ 23 Murry Dickson	6.00	2.50	.60
☐ 24 Red Wilson	6.00	2.50	.60
☐ 25 Don Hoak	7.00	3.00	.70
☐ 26 Chuck Stobbs	6.00	2.50	.60
☐ 27 Andy Pafko	7.00	3.00	.70
☐ 28 Al Worthington	6.00	2.50	.60
☐ 29 Jim Bolger	6.00	2.50	.60
☐ 30 Nellie Fox	14.00	6.25	2.00
☐ 31 Ken Lehman	6.00	2.50	.60
☐ 32 Don Buddin	6.00	2.50	.60
☐ 33 Ed Fitzgerald	6.00	2.50	.60
☐ 34 Pitchers Beware	11.00	5.00	1.35
Al Kaline			
Charley Maxwell			
☐ 35 Ted Kluszewski	10.00	4.50	1.25
☐ 36 Hank Aguirre	6.00	2.50	.60
☐ 37 Gene Green	6.00	2.50	.60
☐ 38 Morrie Martin	6.00	2.50	.60
☐ 39 Ed Bouchee	6.00	2.50	.60
☐ 40A Warren Spahn ERR	50.00	22.50	7.50
(Born 1931)			
☐ 40B Warren Spahn ERR	100.00	45.00	12.50
(Born 1931, but three is partially obscured)			
☐ 40C Warren Spahn COR	50.00	22.50	7.50
(Born 1921)			
☐ 41 Bob Martyn	6.00	2.50	.60
☐ 42 Murray Wall	6.00	2.50	.60
☐ 43 Steve Bilko	6.00	2.50	.60
☐ 44 Vito Valentinetti	6.00	2.50	.60
☐ 45 Andy Carey	7.00	3.00	.70
☐ 46 Bill R. Henry	6.00	2.50	.60
☐ 47 Jim Finigan	6.00	2.50	.60
☐ 48 Orioles Team	18.00	6.00	1.20
(checklist on back)			
☐ 49 Bill Hall	6.00	2.50	.60
☐ 50 Willie Mays	150.00	67.50	22.50
☐ 51 Rip Coleman	6.00	2.50	.60
☐ 52 Coot Veal	6.00	2.50	.60
☐ 53 Stan Williams	8.00	3.50	.80
☐ 54 Mel Roach	6.00	2.50	.60

□ 55	Tom Brewer	6.00	2.50	.60
□ 56	Carl Sawatski	6.00	2.50	.60
□ 57	Al Cicotte	6.00	2.50	.60
□ 58	Eddie Miksis	6.00	2.50	.60
□ 59	Irv Noren	6.00	2.50	.60
□ 60	Bob Turley	9.00	4.00	.90
□ 61	Dick Brown	6.00	2.50	.60
□ 62	Tony Taylor	6.00	2.50	.60
□ 63	Jim Hearn	6.00	2.50	.60
□ 64	Joe DeMaestri	6.00	2.50	.60
□ 65	Frank Torre	6.00	2.50	.60
□ 66	Joe Ginsberg	6.00	2.50	.60
□ 67	Brooks Lawrence	6.00	2.50	.60
□ 68	Dick Schofield	6.00	2.50	.60
□ 69	Giants Team (checklist on back)	15.00	5.00	1.00
□ 70	Harvey Kuenn	9.00	4.00	.90
□ 71	Don Bessent	6.00	2.50	.60
□ 72	Bill Renna	6.00	2.50	.60
□ 73	Ron Jackson	6.00	2.50	.60
□ 74	Directing Power Jim Lemon Cookie Lavagetto Roy Sievers	7.00	3.00	.70
□ 75	Sam Jones	6.00	2.50	.60
□ 76	Bobby Richardson	16.00	6.75	2.25
□ 77	John Goryl	6.00	2.50	.60
□ 78	Pedro Ramos	6.00	2.50	.60
□ 79	Harry Chiti	6.00	2.50	.60
□ 80	Minnie Minoso	10.00	4.50	1.25
□ 81	Hal Jeffcoat	6.00	2.50	.60
□ 82	Bob Boyd	6.00	2.50	.60
□ 83	Bob Smith	6.00	2.50	.60
□ 84	Reno Bertoia	6.00	2.50	.60
□ 85	Harry Anderson	6.00	2.50	.60
□ 86	Bob Keegan	6.00	2.50	.60
□ 87	Danny O'Connell	6.00	2.50	.60
□ 88	Herb Score	9.00	4.00	.90
□ 89	Billy Gardner	6.00	2.50	.60
□ 90	Bill Skowron	11.00	5.00	1.35
□ 91	Herb Moford	6.00	2.50	.60
□ 92	Dave Philley	6.00	2.50	.60
□ 93	Julio Becquer	6.00	2.50	.60
□ 94	White Sox Team (checklist on back)	18.00	6.00	1.20
□ 95	Carl Willey	6.00	2.50	.60
□ 96	Lou Berberet	6.00	2.50	.60
□ 97	Jerry Lynch	6.00	2.50	.60
□ 98	Arnie Portocarrero	6.00	2.50	.60
□ 99	Ted Kazanski	6.00	2.50	.60
□ 100	Bob Cerv	7.00	3.00	.70
□ 101	Alex Kellner	6.00	2.50	.60
□ 102	Felipe Alou	12.00	5.25	1.50
□ 103	Billy Goodman	7.00	3.00	.70
□ 104	Del Rice	6.00	2.50	.60
□ 105	Lee Walls	6.00	2.50	.60
□ 106	Hal Woodeshick	6.00	2.50	.60
□ 107	Norm Larker	8.00	3.50	.80
□ 108	Zack Monroe	6.00	2.50	.60
□ 109	Bob Schmidt	6.00	2.50	.60
□ 110	George Witt	6.00	2.50	.60
□ 111	Redlegs Team (checklist on back)	10.00	3.50	.75
□ 112	Billy Consolo	3.75	1.60	.37
□ 113	Taylor Phillips	3.75	1.60	.37
□ 114	Earl Battey	3.75	1.60	.37
□ 115	Mickey Vernon	4.50	2.00	.45
□ 116	Bob Allison RP	7.50	3.25	.75
□ 117	John Blanchard RP	6.50	2.75	.65
□ 118	John Buzhardt RP	3.75	1.60	.37
□ 119	John Callison RP	6.50	2.75	.65
□ 120	Chuck Coles RP	3.75	1.60	.37
□ 121	Bob Conley RP	3.75	1.60	.37
□ 122	Bennie Daniels RP	3.75	1.60	.37
□ 123	Don Dillard RP	3.75	1.60	.37
□ 124	Dan Dobbek RP	3.75	1.60	.37
□ 125	Ron Fairly RP	6.50	2.75	.65
□ 126	Ed Haas RP	3.75	1.60	.37
□ 127	Kent Hadley RP	3.75	1.60	.37
□ 128	Bob Hartman RP	3.75	1.60	.37
□ 129	Frank Herrera RP	3.75	1.60	.37
□ 130	Lou Jackson RP	3.75	1.60	.37
□ 131	Deron Johnson RP	6.00	2.50	.60
□ 132	Don Lee RP	3.75	1.60	.37
□ 133	Bob Lillis RP	4.50	2.00	.45
□ 134	Jim McDaniel RP	3.75	1.60	.37
□ 135	Gene Oliver RP	3.75	1.60	.37
□ 136	Jim O'Toole RP	4.50	2.00	.45
□ 137	Dick Ricketts RP	3.75	1.60	.37
□ 138	John Romano RP	4.50	2.00	.45
□ 139	Ed Sadowski RP	3.75	1.60	.37
□ 140	Charlie Secrest RP	3.75	1.60	.37
□ 141	Joe Shipley RP	3.75	1.60	.37
□ 142	Dick Stigman RP	3.75	1.60	.37
□ 143	Willie Tasby RP	4.50	2.00	.45
□ 144	Jerry Walker RP	3.75	1.60	.37
□ 145	Dom Zanni RP	3.75	1.60	.37
□ 146	Jerry Zimmerman RP	3.75	1.60	.37
□ 147	Cubs Clubbers Dale Long Ernie Banks Walt Moryn	10.00	4.50	1.25
□ 148	Mike McCormick	4.50	2.00	.45
□ 149	Jim Bunning	11.00	5.00	1.35
□ 150	Stan Musial	150.00	67.50	22.50
□ 151	Bob Malkmus	3.75	1.60	.37
□ 152	Johnny Klippstein	3.75	1.60	.37
□ 153	Jim Marshall	3.75	1.60	.37
□ 154	Ray Herbert	3.75	1.60	.37
□ 155	Enos Slaughter	17.00	7.25	2.50
□ 156	Ace Hurlers Billy Pierce Robin Roberts	6.00	2.50	.60
□ 157	Felix Mantilla	3.75	1.60	.37
□ 158	Walt Dropo	3.75	1.60	.37
□ 159	Bob Shaw	4.50	2.00	.45

☐ 160 Dick Groat	6.00	2.50	.60
☐ 161 Frank Baumann	3.75	1.60	.37
☐ 162 Bobby G. Smith	3.75	1.60	.37
☐ 163 Sandy Koufax	145.00	65.00	18.00
☐ 164 Johnny Groth	3.75	1.60	.37
☐ 165 Bill Bruton	3.75	1.60	.37
☐ 166 Destruction Crew	6.00	2.50	.60
Minnie Minoso			
Rocky Colavito			
(misspelled Colovito			
on card back)			
Larry Doby			
☐ 167 Duke Maas	3.75	1.60	.37
☐ 168 Carroll Hardy	3.75	1.60	.37
☐ 169 Ted Abernathy	3.75	1.60	.37
☐ 170 Gene Woodling	5.00	2.25	.50
☐ 171 Willard Schmidt	3.75	1.60	.37
☐ 172 Athletics Team	10.00	3.50	.75
(checklist on back)			
☐ 173 Bill Monbouquette	3.75	1.60	.37
☐ 174 Jim Pendleton	3.75	1.60	.37
☐ 175 Dick Farrell	3.75	1.60	.37
☐ 176 Preston Ward	3.75	1.60	.37
☐ 177 John Briggs	3.75	1.60	.37
☐ 178 Ruben Amaro	3.75	1.60	.37
☐ 179 Don Rudolph	3.75	1.60	.37
☐ 180 Yogi Berra	85.00	38.00	12.75
☐ 181 Bob Porterfield	3.75	1.60	.37
☐ 182 Milt Graff	3.75	1.60	.37
☐ 183 Stu Miller	4.50	2.00	.45
☐ 184 Harvey Haddix	5.00	2.25	.50
☐ 185 Jim Busby	3.75	1.60	.37
☐ 186 Mudcat Grant	4.50	2.00	.45
☐ 187 Bubba Phillips	3.75	1.60	.37
☐ 188 Juan Pizarro	3.75	1.60	.37
☐ 189 Neil Chrisley	3.75	1.60	.37
☐ 190 Bill Virdon	5.00	2.25	.50
☐ 191 Russ Kemmerer	3.75	1.60	.37
☐ 192 Charlie Beamon	3.75	1.60	.37
☐ 193 Sammy Taylor	3.75	1.60	.37
☐ 194 Jim Brosnan	4.50	2.00	.45
☐ 195 Rip Repulski	3.75	1.60	.37
☐ 196 Billy Moran	3.75	1.60	.37
☐ 197 Ray Semproch	3.75	1.60	.37
☐ 198 Jim Davenport	4.50	2.00	.45
☐ 199 Leo Kiely	3.25	1.35	.32
☐ 200 Warren Giles	5.00	2.25	.50
(NL President)			
☐ 201 Tom Acker	3.25	1.35	.32
☐ 202 Roger Maris	145.00	65.00	18.00
☐ 203 Ossie Virgil	3.25	1.35	.32
☐ 204 Casey Wise	3.25	1.35	.32
☐ 205 Don Larsen	5.00	2.25	.50
☐ 206 Carl Furillo	5.50	2.50	.55
☐ 207 George Strickland	3.25	1.35	.32
☐ 208 Willie Jones	3.25	1.35	.32
☐ 209 Lenny Green	3.25	1.35	.32
☐ 210 Ed Bailey	4.00	1.75	.40
☐ 211 Bob Blaylock	3.25	1.35	.32
☐ 212 Fence Busters	36.00	16.25	5.50
Hank Aaron			
Eddie Mathews			
☐ 213 Jim Rivera	3.25	1.35	.32
☐ 214 Marcelino Solis	3.25	1.35	.32
☐ 215 Jim Lemon	4.00	1.75	.40
☐ 216 Andre Rodgers	3.25	1.35	.32
☐ 217 Carl Erskine	5.00	2.25	.50
☐ 218 Roman Mejias	3.25	1.35	.32
☐ 219 George Zuverink	3.25	1.35	.32
☐ 220 Frank Malzone	4.00	1.75	.40
☐ 221 Bob Bowman	3.25	1.35	.32
☐ 222 Bobby Shantz	4.50	2.00	.45
☐ 223 Cardinals Team	10.00	3.50	.75
(checklist on back)			
☐ 224 Claude Osteen	5.00	2.25	.50
☐ 225 Johnny Logan	4.00	1.75	.40
☐ 226 Art Ceccarelli	3.25	1.35	.32
☐ 227 Hal W. Smith	3.25	1.35	.32
☐ 228 Don Gross	3.25	1.35	.32
☐ 229 Vic Power	3.25	1.35	.32
☐ 230 Bill Fischer	3.25	1.35	.32
☐ 231 Ellis Burton	3.25	1.35	.32
☐ 232 Eddie Kasko	3.25	1.35	.32
☐ 233 Paul Foytack	3.25	1.35	.32
☐ 234 Chuck Tanner	4.00	1.75	.40
☐ 235 Valmy Thomas	3.25	1.35	.32
☐ 236 Ted Bowsfield	3.25	1.35	.32
☐ 237 Run Preventers	6.00	2.50	.60
Gil McDougald			
Bob Turley			
Bobby Richardson			
☐ 238 Gene Baker	3.25	1.35	.32
☐ 239 Bob Trowbridge	3.25	1.35	.32
☐ 240 Hank Bauer	5.00	2.25	.50
☐ 241 Billy Muffett	3.25	1.35	.32
☐ 242 Ron Samford	3.25	1.35	.32
☐ 243 Marv Grissom	3.25	1.35	.32
☐ 244 Ted Gray	3.25	1.35	.32
☐ 245 Ned Garver	3.25	1.35	.32
☐ 246 J.W. Porter	3.25	1.35	.32
☐ 247 Don Ferrarese	3.25	1.35	.32
☐ 248 Red Sox Team	10.00	3.50	.75
(checklist on back)			
☐ 249 Bobby Adams	3.25	1.35	.32
☐ 250 Billy O'Dell	3.25	1.35	.32
☐ 251 Clete Boyer	5.50	2.50	.55
☐ 252 Ray Boone	4.00	1.75	.40
☐ 253 Seth Morehead	3.25	1.35	.32
☐ 254 Zeke Bella	3.25	1.35	.32
☐ 255 Del Ennis	4.00	1.75	.40
☐ 256 Jerry Davie	3.25	1.35	.32
☐ 257 Leon Wagner	5.00	2.25	.50
☐ 258 Fred Kipp	3.25	1.35	.32
☐ 259 Jim Pisoni	3.25	1.35	.32
☐ 260 Early Wynn	14.00	6.25	2.00
☐ 261 Gene Stephens	3.25	1.35	.32

☐ 262 Hitters' Foes .... 6.00 2.50 .60
Johnny Podres
Clem Labine
Don Drysdale
☐ 263 Bud Daley .... 3.25 1.35 .32
☐ 264 Chico Carrasquel .... 3.25 1.35 .32
☐ 265 Ron Kline .... 3.25 1.35 .32
☐ 266 Woody Held .... 3.25 1.35 .32
☐ 267 John Romonosky .... 3.25 1.35 .32
☐ 268 Tito Francona .... 3.25 1.35 .32
☐ 269 Jack Meyer .... 3.25 1.35 .32
☐ 270 Gil Hodges 18.00 7.50 2.50
☐ 271 Orlando Pena .... 3.25 1.35 .32
☐ 272 Jerry Lumpe .... 3.25 1.35 .32
☐ 273 Joey Jay .... 3.25 1.35 .32
☐ 274 Jerry Kindall .... 3.25 1.35 .32
☐ 275 Jack Sanford .... 3.25 1.35 .32
☐ 276 Pete Daley .... 3.25 1.35 .32
☐ 277 Turk Lown .... 3.25 1.35 .32
☐ 278 Chuck Essegian .... 3.25 1.35 .32
☐ 279 Ernie Johnson .... 4.00 1.75 .40
☐ 280 Frank Bolling .... 3.25 1.35 .32
☐ 281 Walt Craddock .... 3.25 1.35 .32
☐ 282 R.C. Stevens .... 3.25 1.35 .32
☐ 283 Russ Heman .... 3.25 1.35 .32
☐ 284 Steve Korcheck .... 3.25 1.35 .32
☐ 285 Joe Cunningham .... 4.00 1.75 .40
☐ 286 Dean Stone .... 3.25 1.35 .32
☐ 287 Don Zimmer .... 4.50 2.00 .45
☐ 288 Dutch Dotterer .... 3.25 1.35 .32
☐ 289 Johnny Kucks .... 3.25 1.35 .32
☐ 290 Wes Covington .... 4.00 1.75 .40
☐ 291 Pitching Partners .... 4.00 1.75 .40
Pedro Ramos
Camilo Pascual
☐ 292 Dick Williams .... 4.00 1.75 .40
☐ 293 Ray Moore .... 3.25 1.35 .32
☐ 294 Hank Foiles .... 3.25 1.35 .32
☐ 295 Billy Martin 13.50 6.00 1.85
☐ 296 Ernie Broglio .... 4.50 2.00 .45
☐ 297 Jackie Brandt .... 3.25 1.35 .32
☐ 298 Tex Clevenger .... 3.25 1.35 .32
☐ 299 Billy Klaus .... 3.25 1.35 .32
☐ 300 Richie Ashburn 12.00 5.25 1.50
☐ 301 Earl Averill .... 3.25 1.35 .32
☐ 302 Don Mossi .... 4.00 1.75 .40
☐ 303 Marty Keough .... 3.25 1.35 .32
☐ 304 Cubs Team .... 10.00 3.50 .75
(checklist on back)
☐ 305 Curt Raydon .... 3.25 1.35 .32
☐ 306 Jim Gilliam .... 6.00 2.50 .60
☐ 307 Curt Barclay .... 3.25 1.35 .32
☐ 308 Norm Siebern .... 3.25 1.35 .32
☐ 309 Sal Maglie .... 4.50 2.00 .45
☐ 310 Luis Aparicio 17.00 7.25 2.50
☐ 311 Norm Zauchin .... 3.25 1.35 .32
☐ 312 Don Newcombe .... 5.00 2.25 .50
☐ 313 Frank House .... 3.25 1.35 .32
☐ 314 Don Cardwell .... 3.25 1.35 .32
☐ 315 Joe Adcock .... 4.50 2.00 .45
☐ 316A Ralph Lumenti UER .. 3.25 1.35 .32
(option)
(photo actually
Camilo Pascual)
☐ 316B Ralph Lumenti UER 95.00 42.00 11.00
(no option)
(photo actually
Camilo Pascual)
☐ 317 Hitting Kings 21.00 9.00 3.00
Willie Mays
Richie Ashburn
☐ 318 Rocky Bridges .... 3.25 1.35 .32
☐ 319 Dave Hillman .... 3.25 1.35 .32
☐ 320 Bob Skinner .... 4.00 1.75 .40
☐ 321A Bob Giallombardo ..... 3.25 1.35 .32
(option)
☐ 321B Bob Giallombardo ... 95.00 42.00 11.00
(no option)
☐ 322A Harry Hanebrink .... 3.25 1.35 .32
(traded)
☐ 322B Harry Hanebrink 95.00 42.00 11.00
(no trade)
☐ 323 Frank Sullivan .... 3.25 1.35 .32
☐ 324 Don Demeter .... 3.25 1.35 .32
☐ 325 Ken Boyer .... 7.50 3.25 .75
☐ 326 Marv Throneberry .... 4.50 2.00 .45
☐ 327 Gary Bell .... 3.25 1.35 .32
☐ 328 Lou Skizas .... 3.25 1.35 .32
☐ 329 Tigers Team .... 10.00 3.50 .75
(checklist on back)
☐ 330 Gus Triandos .... 4.00 1.75 .40
☐ 331 Steve Boros .... 3.25 1.35 .32
☐ 332 Ray Monzant .... 3.25 1.35 .32
☐ 333 Harry Simpson .... 3.25 1.35 .32
☐ 334 Glen Hobbie .... 3.25 1.35 .32
☐ 335 Johnny Temple .... 3.25 1.35 .32
☐ 336A Billy Loes .... 3.25 1.35 .32
(with traded line)
☐ 336B Billy Loes 95.00 42.00 11.00
(no trade)
☐ 337 George Crowe .... 3.25 1.35 .32
☐ 338 Sparky Anderson 36.00 16.25 5.50
☐ 339 Roy Face .... 5.00 2.25 .50
☐ 340 Roy Sievers .... 4.00 1.75 .40
☐ 341 Tom Qualters .... 3.25 1.35 .32
☐ 342 Ray Jablonski .... 3.25 1.35 .32
☐ 343 Billy Hoeft .... 3.25 1.35 .32
☐ 344 Russ Nixon .... 3.25 1.35 .32
☐ 345 Gil McDougald .... 6.50 2.75 .65
☐ 346 Batter Bafflers .... 3.25 1.35 .32
Dave Sisler
Tom Brewer
☐ 347 Bob Buhl .... 3.25 1.35 .32
☐ 348 Ted Lepcio .... 3.25 1.35 .32
☐ 349 Hoyt Wilhelm 16.00 6.75 2.25
☐ 350 Ernie Banks 65.00 29.00 9.75

☐ 351	Earl Torgeson	3.25	1.35	.32
☐ 352	Robin Roberts	15.00	6.50	2.15
☐ 353	Curt Flood	5.00	2.25	.50
☐ 354	Pete Burnside	3.25	1.35	.32
☐ 355	Jim Piersall	4.50	2.00	.45
☐ 356	Bob Mabe	3.25	1.35	.32
☐ 357	Dick Stuart	4.50	2.00	.45
☐ 358	Ralph Terry	4.00	1.75	.40
☐ 359	Bill White	25.00	11.00	3.50
☐ 360	Al Kaline	60.00	27.00	9.00
☐ 361	Willard Nixon	3.25	1.35	.32
☐ 362A	Dolan Nichols (with option line)	3.25	1.35	.32
☐ 362B	Dolan Nichols (no option)	95.00	42.00	11.00
☐ 363	Bobby Avila	3.25	1.35	.32
☐ 364	Danny McDevitt	3.25	1.35	.32
☐ 365	Gus Bell	4.00	1.75	.40
☐ 366	Humberto Robinson	3.25	1.35	.32
☐ 367	Cal Neeman	3.25	1.35	.32
☐ 368	Don Mueller	4.00	1.75	.40
☐ 369	Dick Tomanek	3.25	1.35	.32
☐ 370	Pete Runnels	4.00	1.75	.40
☐ 371	Dick Brodowski	3.25	1.35	.32
☐ 372	Jim Hegan	3.25	1.35	.32
☐ 373	Herb Plews	3.25	1.35	.32
☐ 374	Art Ditmar	3.25	1.35	.32
☐ 375	Bob Nieman	3.25	1.35	.32
☐ 376	Hal Naragon	3.25	1.35	.32
☐ 377	John Antonelli	4.00	1.75	.40
☐ 378	Gail Harris	3.25	1.35	.32
☐ 379	Bob Miller	3.25	1.35	.32
☐ 380	Hank Aaron	110.00	50.00	16.50
☐ 381	Mike Baxes	3.25	1.35	.32
☐ 382	Curt Simmons	4.00	1.75	.40
☐ 383	Words of Wisdom Don Larsen Casey Stengel	7.00	3.00	.70
☐ 384	Dave Sisler	3.25	1.35	.32
☐ 385	Sherm Lollar	4.00	1.75	.40
☐ 386	Jim Delsing	3.25	1.35	.32
☐ 387	Don Drysdale	40.00	18.00	6.00
☐ 388	Bob Will	3.25	1.35	.32
☐ 389	Joe Nuxhall	4.00	1.75	.40
☐ 390	Orlando Cepeda	20.00	8.50	2.75
☐ 391	Milt Pappas	4.00	1.75	.40
☐ 392	Whitey Herzog	5.00	2.25	.50
☐ 393	Frank Lary	4.00	1.75	.40
☐ 394	Randy Jackson	3.25	1.35	.32
☐ 395	Elston Howard	7.50	3.25	.75
☐ 396	Bob Rush	3.25	1.35	.32
☐ 397	Senators Team (checklist on back)	9.00	3.00	.60
☐ 398	Wally Post	3.25	1.35	.32
☐ 399	Larry Jackson	3.25	1.35	.32
☐ 400	Jackie Jensen	4.50	2.00	.45
☐ 401	Ron Blackburn	3.25	1.35	.32
☐ 402	Hector Lopez	3.25	1.35	.32
☐ 403	Clem Labine	4.00	1.75	.40
☐ 404	Hank Sauer	4.00	1.75	.40
☐ 405	Roy McMillan	3.25	1.35	.32
☐ 406	Solly Drake	3.25	1.35	.32
☐ 407	Moe Drabowsky	3.25	1.35	.32
☐ 408	Keystone Combo Nellie Fox Luis Aparicio	7.00	3.00	.70
☐ 409	Gus Zernial	4.00	1.75	.40
☐ 410	Billy Pierce	4.50	2.00	.45
☐ 411	Whitey Lockman	3.25	1.35	.32
☐ 412	Stan Lopata	3.25	1.35	.32
☐ 413	Camilo Pascual UER (listed as Camillo on front and Pasqual on back)	4.00	1.75	.40
☐ 414	Dale Long	4.00	1.75	.40
☐ 415	Bill Mazeroski	7.50	3.25	.75
☐ 416	Haywood Sullivan	4.00	1.75	.40
☐ 417	Virgil Trucks	3.25	1.35	.32
☐ 418	Gino Cimoli	3.25	1.35	.32
☐ 419	Braves Team (checklist on back)	10.00	3.50	.75
☐ 420	Rocky Colavito	18.00	7.50	2.50
☐ 421	Herman Wehmeier	3.25	1.35	.32
☐ 422	Hobie Landrith	3.25	1.35	.32
☐ 423	Bob Grim	3.25	1.35	.32
☐ 424	Ken Aspromonte	3.25	1.35	.32
☐ 425	Del Crandall	4.00	1.75	.40
☐ 426	Jerry Staley	3.25	1.35	.32
☐ 427	Charlie Neal	4.00	1.75	.40
☐ 428	Buc Hill Aces Ron Kline Bob Friend Vernon Law Roy Face	4.50	2.00	.45
☐ 429	Bobby Thomson	4.50	2.00	.45
☐ 430	Whitey Ford	40.00	18.00	6.00
☐ 431	Whammy Douglas	3.25	1.35	.32
☐ 432	Smoky Burgess	4.00	1.75	.40
☐ 433	Billy Harrell	3.25	1.35	.32
☐ 434	Hal Griggs	3.25	1.35	.32
☐ 435	Frank Robinson	45.00	20.00	6.75
☐ 436	Granny Hamner	3.25	1.35	.32
☐ 437	Ike Delock	3.25	1.35	.32
☐ 438	Sammy Esposito	3.25	1.35	.32
☐ 439	Brooks Robinson	50.00	22.50	7.50
☐ 440	Lou Burdette (posing as if lefthanded)	7.00	3.00	.70
☐ 441	John Roseboro	4.50	2.00	.45
☐ 442	Ray Narleski	3.25	1.35	.32
☐ 443	Daryl Spencer	3.25	1.35	.32
☐ 444	Ron Hansen	3.25	1.35	.32
☐ 445	Cal McLish	3.25	1.35	.32
☐ 446	Rocky Nelson	3.25	1.35	.32
☐ 447	Bob Anderson	3.25	1.35	.32
☐ 448	Vada Pinson UER	6.00	2.50	.60

(Born: 8/8/38, should be 8/11/38)

☐ 449 Tom Gorman .... 3.25 1.35 .32
☐ 450 Eddie Mathews 30.00 13.50 4.50
☐ 451 Jimmy Constable .... 3.25 1.35 .32
☐ 452 Chico Fernandez .... 3.25 1.35 .32
☐ 453 Les Moss .... 3.25 1.35 .32
☐ 454 Phil Clark .... 3.25 1.35 .32
☐ 455 Larry Doby .... 4.50 2.00 .45
☐ 456 Jerry Casale .... 3.25 1.35 .32
☐ 457 Dodgers Team 16.00 5.00 1.00
(checklist on back)
☐ 458 Gordon Jones .... 3.25 1.35 .32
☐ 459 Bill Tuttle .... 3.25 1.35 .32
☐ 460 Bob Friend .... 4.00 1.75 .40
☐ 461 Mantle Hits Homer 42.00 18.00 6.00
☐ 462 Colavito's Catch .... 8.50 3.75 .85
☐ 463 Kaline Batting Champ 14.00 6.25 2.00
☐ 464 Mays' Series Catch ... 21.00 9.00 3.00
☐ 465 Sievers Sets Mark .... 4.50 2.00 .45
☐ 466 Pierce All-Star .... 4.50 2.00 .45
☐ 467 Aaron Clubs Homer ... 20.00 8.50 2.75
☐ 468 Snider's Play 14.00 6.25 2.00
☐ 469 Hustler Banks 14.00 6.25 2.00
☐ 470 Musial's 3000 Hit 20.00 8.50 2.75
☐ 471 Tom Sturdivant .... 3.25 1.35 .32
☐ 472 Gene Freese .... 3.25 1.35 .32
☐ 473 Mike Fornieles .... 3.25 1.35 .32
☐ 474 Moe Thacker .... 3.25 1.35 .32
☐ 475 Jack Harshman .... 3.25 1.35 .32
☐ 476 Indians Team .... 9.00 3.00 .60
(checklist on back)
☐ 477 Barry Latman .... 3.25 1.35 .32
☐ 478 Bob Clemente 110.00 50.00 16.50
☐ 479 Lindy McDaniel .... 4.00 1.75 .40
☐ 480 Red Schoendienst 14.00 6.25 2.00
☐ 481 Charlie Maxwell .... 3.25 1.35 .32
☐ 482 Russ Meyer .... 3.25 1.35 .32
☐ 483 Clint Courtney .... 3.25 1.35 .32
☐ 484 Willie Kirkland .... 3.25 1.35 .32
☐ 485 Ryne Duren .... 4.50 2.00 .45
☐ 486 Sammy White .... 3.25 1.35 .32
☐ 487 Hal Brown .... 3.25 1.35 .32
☐ 488 Walt Moryn .... 3.25 1.35 .32
☐ 489 John Powers .... 3.25 1.35 .32
☐ 490 Frank Thomas .... 4.00 1.75 .40
☐ 491 Don Blasingame .... 3.25 1.35 .32
☐ 492 Gene Conley .... 3.25 1.35 .32
☐ 493 Jim Landis .... 3.25 1.35 .32
☐ 494 Don Pavletich .... 3.25 1.35 .32
☐ 495 Johnny Podres .... 4.50 2.00 .45
☐ 496 Wayne Terwilliger UER 3.25 1.35 .32
(Athlftics on front)
☐ 497 Hal R. Smith .... 3.25 1.35 .32
☐ 498 Dick Hyde .... 3.25 1.35 .32
☐ 499 Johnny O'Brien .... 3.25 1.35 .32
☐ 500 Vic Wertz .... 4.00 1.75 .40
☐ 501 Bob Tiefenauer .... 3.25 1.35 .32
☐ 502 Alvin Dark .... 4.50 2.00 .45
☐ 503 Jim Owens .... 3.25 1.35 .32
☐ 504 Ossie Alvarez .... 3.25 1.35 .32
☐ 505 Tony Kubek .... 9.00 4.00 .90
☐ 506 Bob Purkey .... 3.25 1.35 .32
☐ 507 Bob Hale 16.00 6.75 2.25
☐ 508 Art Fowler 16.00 6.75 2.25
☐ 509 Norm Cash 55.00 25.00 8.25
☐ 510 Yankees Team 70.00 20.00 4.00
(checklist on back)
☐ 511 George Susce 16.00 6.75 2.25
☐ 512 George Altman 16.00 6.75 2.25
☐ 513 Tommy Carroll 16.00 6.75 2.25
☐ 514 Bob Gibson 400.00 180.00 60.00
☐ 515 Harmon Killebrew ... 145.00 65.00 18.00
☐ 516 Mike Garcia 18.00 7.50 2.50
☐ 517 Joe Koppe 16.00 6.75 2.25
☐ 518 Mike Cueller UER 21.00 9.00 3.00
(sic, Cuellar)
☐ 519 Infield Power 18.00 7.50 2.50
Pete Runnels
Dick Gernert
Frank Malzone
☐ 520 Don Elston 16.00 6.75 2.25
☐ 521 Gary Geiger 16.00 6.75 2.25
☐ 522 Gene Snyder 16.00 6.75 2.25
☐ 523 Harry Bright 16.00 6.75 2.25
☐ 524 Larry Osborne 16.00 6.75 2.25
☐ 525 Jim Coates 16.00 6.75 2.25
☐ 526 Bob Speake 16.00 6.75 2.25
☐ 527 Solly Hemus 16.00 6.75 2.25
☐ 528 Pirates Team 42.00 15.00 3.00
(checklist on back)
☐ 529 George Bamberger 18.00 7.50 2.50
☐ 530 Wally Moon 18.00 7.50 2.50
☐ 531 Ray Webster 16.00 6.75 2.25
☐ 532 Mark Freeman 16.00 6.75 2.25
☐ 533 Darrell Johnson 18.00 7.50 2.50
☐ 534 Faye Throneberry 16.00 6.75 2.25
☐ 535 Ruben Gomez 16.00 6.75 2.25
☐ 536 Danny Kravitz 16.00 6.75 2.25
☐ 537 Rudolph Arias 16.00 6.75 2.25
☐ 538 Chick King 16.00 6.75 2.25
☐ 539 Gary Blaylock 16.00 6.75 2.25
☐ 540 Willie Miranda 16.00 6.75 2.25
☐ 541 Bob Thurman 16.00 6.75 2.25
☐ 542 Jim Perry 21.00 9.00 3.00
☐ 543 Corsair Trio 60.00 27.00 9.00
Bob Skinner
Bill Virdon
Roberto Clemente
☐ 544 Lee Tate 16.00 6.75 2.25
☐ 545 Tom Morgan 16.00 6.75 2.25
☐ 546 Al Schroll 16.00 6.75 2.25
☐ 547 Jim Baxes 16.00 6.75 2.25
☐ 548 Elmer Singleton 16.00 6.75 2.25
☐ 549 Howie Nunn 16.00 6.75 2.25
☐ 550 Roy Campanella 145.00 65.00 18.00

(Symbol of Courage)			
☐ 551 Fred Haney MG AS	18.00	7.50	2.50
☐ 552 Casey Stengel MG AS	35.00	15.75	5.25
☐ 553 Orlando Cepeda AS	22.00	9.50	3.15
☐ 554 Bill Skowron AS	20.00	8.50	2.75
☐ 555 Bill Mazeroski AS	20.00	8.50	2.75
☐ 556 Nellie Fox AS	22.00	9.50	3.15
☐ 557 Ken Boyer AS	20.00	8.50	2.75
☐ 558 Frank Malzone AS	18.00	7.50	2.50
☐ 559 Ernie Banks AS	50.00	22.50	7.50
☐ 560 Luis Aparicio AS	30.00	13.50	4.50
☐ 561 Hank Aaron AS	120.00	55.00	18.00
☐ 562 Al Kaline AS	50.00	22.50	7.50
☐ 563 Willie Mays AS	120.00	55.00	18.00
☐ 564 Mickey Mantle AS	250.00	110.00	37.50
☐ 565 Wes Covington AS	18.00	7.50	2.50
☐ 566 Roy Sievers AS	18.00	7.50	2.50
☐ 567 Del Crandall AS	18.00	7.50	2.50
☐ 568 Gus Triandos AS	18.00	7.50	2.50
☐ 569 Bob Friend AS	18.00	7.50	2.50
☐ 570 Bob Turley AS	18.00	7.50	2.50
☐ 571 Warren Spahn AS	36.00	16.25	5.50
☐ 572 Billy Pierce AS	32.00	12.00	2.50

1960 Topps

The cards in this 572-card set measure 2 1/2" by 3 1/2". The 1960 Topps set is the only Topps standard size issue to use a horizontally oriented front. World Series cards appeared for the first time (385 to 391), and there is a Rookie Prospect (RP) series (117-148), the most famous of which is Carl Yastrzemski, and a Sport Magazine All-Star Selection (AS) series (553-572). There are 16 manager cards listed alphabetically from 212 through 227. The coaching staff of each team was also afforded their own card in a 16-card subset (455-470). Cards 375 to 440 come with either gray or white backs, and the high series (507-572) were printed on a more limited basis than the rest of the set. The team cards have series checklists on the reverse. The key rookies in this set are Willie McCovey and Carl Yastrzemski.

	NRMT	VG-E	GOOD
COMPLETE SET (572)	4000.00	1650.00	350.00
COMMON PLAYER (1-110)	3.75	1.60	.37
COMMON PLAYER (111-198)	2.75	1.10	.27
COMMON PLAYER (199-286)	3.00	1.25	.30
COMMON PLAYER (287-440)	3.25	1.35	.32
COMMON PLAYER (441-506)	4.50	2.00	.45
COMMON PLAYER (507-552)	12.00	5.25	1.50
COMMON PLAYER (553-572)	14.00	6.25	2.00

☐ 1 Early Wynn	40.00	8.00	1.75
☐ 2 Roman Mejias	3.75	1.60	.37
☐ 3 Joe Adcock	4.50	2.00	.45
☐ 4 Bob Purkey	3.75	1.60	.37
☐ 5 Wally Moon	4.50	2.00	.45
☐ 6 Lou Berberet	3.75	1.60	.37
☐ 7 Master and Mentor	15.00	6.50	2.15
Willie Mays			
Bill Rigney			
☐ 8 Bud Daley	3.75	1.60	.37
☐ 9 Faye Throneberry	3.75	1.60	.37
☐ 10 Ernie Banks	48.00	22.00	6.00
☐ 11 Norm Siebern	3.75	1.60	.37
☐ 12 Milt Pappas	4.50	2.00	.45
☐ 13 Wally Post	3.75	1.60	.37
☐ 14 Jim Grant	3.75	1.60	.37
☐ 15 Pete Runnels	4.50	2.00	.45
☐ 16 Ernie Broglio	4.50	2.00	.45
☐ 17 Johnny Callison	4.50	2.00	.45
☐ 18 Dodgers Team	16.00	5.00	1.00
(checklist on back)			
☐ 19 Felix Mantilla	3.75	1.60	.37
☐ 20 Roy Face	5.00	2.25	.50
☐ 21 Dutch Dotterer	3.75	1.60	.37
☐ 22 Rocky Bridges	3.75	1.60	.37
☐ 23 Eddie Fisher	3.75	1.60	.37
☐ 24 Dick Gray	3.75	1.60	.37
☐ 25 Roy Sievers	4.50	2.00	.45
☐ 26 Wayne Terwilliger	3.75	1.60	.37
☐ 27 Dick Drott	3.75	1.60	.37
☐ 28 Brooks Robinson	48.00	22.00	6.00
☐ 29 Clem Labine	4.50	2.00	.45
☐ 30 Tito Francona	3.75	1.60	.37
☐ 31 Sammy Esposito	3.75	1.60	.37
☐ 32 Sophomore Stalwarts	4.50	2.00	.45
Jim O'Toole			
Vada Pinson			
☐ 33 Tom Morgan	3.75	1.60	.37
☐ 34 Sparky Anderson	9.00	4.00	.90
☐ 35 Whitey Ford	40.00	18.00	6.00

☐ 36 Russ Nixon .... 3.75 1.60 .37
☐ 37 Bill Bruton .... 3.75 1.60 .37
☐ 38 Jerry Casale .... 3.75 1.60 .37
☐ 39 Earl Averill .... 3.75 1.60 .37
☐ 40 Joe Cunningham .... 4.50 2.00 .45
☐ 41 Barry Latman .... 3.75 1.60 .37
☐ 42 Hobie Landrith .... 3.75 1.60 .37
☐ 43 Senators Team .... 7.50 2.50 .50
(checklist on back)
☐ 44 Bobby Locke .... 3.75 1.60 .37
☐ 45 Roy McMillan .... 3.75 1.60 .37
☐ 46 Jerry Fisher .... 3.75 1.60 .37
☐ 47 Don Zimmer .... 5.00 2.25 .50
☐ 48 Hal W. Smith .... 3.75 1.60 .37
☐ 49 Curt Raydon .... 3.75 1.60 .37
☐ 50 Al Kaline 48.00 22.00 6.00
☐ 51 Jim Coates .... 3.75 1.60 .37
☐ 52 Dave Philley .... 3.75 1.60 .37
☐ 53 Jackie Brandt .... 3.75 1.60 .37
☐ 54 Mike Fornieles .... 3.75 1.60 .37
☐ 55 Bill Mazeroski .... 6.00 2.50 .60
☐ 56 Steve Korcheck .... 3.75 1.60 .37
☐ 57 Win Savers .... 3.75 1.60 .37
Turk Lown
Jerry Staley
☐ 58 Gino Cimoli .... 3.75 1.60 .37
☐ 59 Juan Pizarro .... 3.75 1.60 .37
☐ 60 Gus Triandos .... 4.50 2.00 .45
☐ 61 Eddie Kasko .... 3.75 1.60 .37
☐ 62 Roger Craig .... 5.00 2.25 .50
☐ 63 George Strickland .... 3.75 1.60 .37
☐ 64 Jack Meyer .... 3.75 1.60 .37
☐ 65 Elston Howard .... 6.00 2.50 .60
☐ 66 Bob Trowbridge .... 3.75 1.60 .37
☐ 67 Jose Pagan .... 3.75 1.60 .37
☐ 68 Dave Hillman .... 3.75 1.60 .37
☐ 69 Billy Goodman .... 4.50 2.00 .45
☐ 70 Lew Burdette .... 5.00 2.25 .50
☐ 71 Marty Keough .... 3.75 1.60 .37
☐ 72 Tigers Team .... 8.00 2.50 .50
(checklist on back)
☐ 73 Bob Gibson 60.00 27.00 9.00
☐ 74 Walt Moryn .... 3.75 1.60 .37
☐ 75 Vic Power .... 3.75 1.60 .37
☐ 76 Bill Fischer .... 3.75 1.60 .37
☐ 77 Hank Foiles .... 3.75 1.60 .37
☐ 78 Bob Grim .... 3.75 1.60 .37
☐ 79 Walt Dropo .... 3.75 1.60 .37
☐ 80 Johnny Antonelli .... 4.50 2.00 .45
☐ 81 Russ Snyder .... 3.75 1.60 .37
☐ 82 Ruben Gomez .... 3.75 1.60 .37
☐ 83 Tony Kubek .... 6.50 2.75 .65
☐ 84 Hal R. Smith .... 3.75 1.60 .37
☐ 85 Frank Lary .... 4.50 2.00 .45
☐ 86 Dick Gernert .... 3.75 1.60 .37
☐ 87 John Romonosky .... 3.75 1.60 .37
☐ 88 John Roseboro .... 4.50 2.00 .45
☐ 89 Hal Brown .... 3.75 1.60 .37
☐ 90 Bobby Avila .... 3.75 1.60 .37
☐ 91 Bennie Daniels .... 3.75 1.60 .37
☐ 92 Whitey Herzog .... 5.00 2.25 .50
☐ 93 Art Schult .... 3.75 1.60 .37
☐ 94 Leo Kiely .... 3.75 1.60 .37
☐ 95 Frank Thomas .... 4.50 2.00 .45
☐ 96 Ralph Terry .... 4.50 2.00 .45
☐ 97 Ted Lepcio .... 3.75 1.60 .37
☐ 98 Gordon Jones .... 3.75 1.60 .37
☐ 99 Lenny Green .... 3.75 1.60 .37
☐ 100 Nellie Fox .... 8.50 3.75 .85
☐ 101 Bob Miller .... 3.75 1.60 .37
☐ 102 Kent Hadley .... 3.75 1.60 .37
☐ 103 Dick Farrell .... 3.75 1.60 .37
☐ 104 Dick Schofield .... 3.75 1.60 .37
☐ 105 Larry Sherry .... 5.00 2.25 .50
☐ 106 Billy Gardner .... 3.75 1.60 .37
☐ 107 Carlton Willey .... 3.75 1.60 .37
☐ 108 Pete Daley .... 3.75 1.60 .37
☐ 109 Clete Boyer .... 5.00 2.25 .50
☐ 110 Cal McLish .... 3.75 1.60 .37
☐ 111 Vic Wertz .... 3.50 1.50 .35
☐ 112 Jack Harshman .... 2.75 1.10 .27
☐ 113 Bob Skinner .... 3.50 1.50 .35
☐ 114 Ken Aspromonte .... 2.75 1.10 .27
☐ 115 Fork and Knuckler .... 5.00 2.25 .50
Roy Face
Hoyt Wilhelm
☐ 116 Jim Rivera .... 2.75 1.10 .27
☐ 117 Tom Borland RP .... 2.75 1.10 .27
☐ 118 Bob Bruce RP .... 2.75 1.10 .27
☐ 119 Chico Cardenas RP ..... 3.50 1.50 .35
☐ 120 Duke Carmel RP .... 2.75 1.10 .27
☐ 121 Camilo Carreon RP ...... 2.75 1.10 .27
☐ 122 Don Dillard RP .... 2.75 1.10 .27
☐ 123 Dan Dobbek RP .... 2.75 1.10 .27
☐ 124 Jim Donohue RP .... 2.75 1.10 .27
☐ 125 Dick Ellsworth RP .... 4.50 2.00 .45
☐ 126 Chuck Estrada RP .... 4.50 2.00 .45
☐ 127 Ron Hansen RP .... 2.75 1.10 .27
☐ 128 Bill Harris RP .... 2.75 1.10 .27
☐ 129 Bob Hartman RP .... 2.75 1.10 .27
☐ 130 Frank Herrera RP .... 2.75 1.10 .27
☐ 131 Ed Hobaugh RP .... 2.75 1.10 .27
☐ 132 Frank Howard RP 15.00 6.50 2.15
☐ 133 Manuel Javier RP .... 4.50 2.00 .45
(sic, Julian)
☐ 134 Deron Johnson RP ...... 3.50 1.50 .35
☐ 135 Ken Johnson RP .... 2.75 1.10 .27
☐ 136 Jim Kaat RP 35.00 15.75 5.25
☐ 137 Lou Klimchock RP ...... 2.75 1.10 .27
☐ 138 Art Mahaffey RP .... 3.50 1.50 .35
☐ 139 Carl Mathias RP .... 2.75 1.10 .27
☐ 140 Julio Navarro RP .... 3.50 1.50 .35
☐ 141 Jim Proctor RP .... 2.75 1.10 .27
☐ 142 Bill Short RP .... 3.50 1.50 .35
☐ 143 Al Spangler RP .... 2.75 1.10 .27
☐ 144 Al Stieglitz RP .... 2.75 1.10 .27

☐ 145 Jim Umbricht RP 2.75 1.10 .27
☐ 146 Ted Wieand RP 2.75 1.10 .27
☐ 147 Bob Will RP 2.75 1.10 .27
☐ 148 Carl Yastrzemski RP 350.00 160.00 52.50
☐ 149 Bob Nieman 2.75 1.10 .27
☐ 150 Billy Pierce 4.00 1.75 .40
☐ 151 Giants Team 7.50 2.50 .50
(checklist on back)
☐ 152 Gail Harris 2.75 1.10 .27
☐ 153 Bobby Thomson 4.00 1.75 .40
☐ 154 Jim Davenport 3.50 1.50 .35
☐ 155 Charlie Neal 3.50 1.50 .35
☐ 156 Art Ceccarelli 2.75 1.10 .27
☐ 157 Rocky Nelson 2.75 1.10 .27
☐ 158 Wes Covington 3.50 1.50 .35
☐ 159 Jim Piersall 4.00 1.75 .40
☐ 160 Rival All-Stars 50.00 22.50 7.50
Mickey Mantle
Ken Boyer
☐ 161 Ray Narleski 2.75 1.10 .27
☐ 162 Sammy Taylor 2.75 1.10 .27
☐ 163 Hector Lopez 2.75 1.10 .27
☐ 164 Reds Team 7.50 2.50 .50
(checklist on back)
☐ 165 Jack Sanford 3.50 1.50 .35
☐ 166 Chuck Essegian 2.75 1.10 .27
☐ 167 Valmy Thomas 2.75 1.10 .27
☐ 168 Alex Grammas 2.75 1.10 .27
☐ 169 Jake Striker 2.75 1.10 .27
☐ 170 Del Crandall 3.50 1.50 .35
☐ 171 Johnny Groth 2.75 1.10 .27
☐ 172 Willie Kirkland 2.75 1.10 .27
☐ 173 Billy Martin 11.00 5.00 1.35
☐ 174 Indians Team 7.50 2.50 .50
(checklist on back)
☐ 175 Pedro Ramos 2.75 1.10 .27
☐ 176 Vada Pinson 4.50 2.00 .45
☐ 177 Johnny Kucks 2.75 1.10 .27
☐ 178 Woody Held 2.75 1.10 .27
☐ 179 Rip Coleman 2.75 1.10 .27
☐ 180 Harry Simpson 2.75 1.10 .27
☐ 181 Billy Loes 2.75 1.10 .27
☐ 182 Glen Hobbie 2.75 1.10 .27
☐ 183 Eli Grba 2.75 1.10 .27
☐ 184 Gary Geiger 2.75 1.10 .27
☐ 185 Jim Owens 2.75 1.10 .27
☐ 186 Dave Sisler 2.75 1.10 .27
☐ 187 Jay Hook 2.75 1.10 .27
☐ 188 Dick Williams 3.50 1.50 .35
☐ 189 Don McMahon 2.75 1.10 .27
☐ 190 Gene Woodling 3.50 1.50 .35
☐ 191 Johnny Klippstein 2.75 1.10 .27
☐ 192 Danny O'Connell 2.75 1.10 .27
☐ 193 Dick Hyde 2.75 1.10 .27
☐ 194 Bobby Gene Smith 2.75 1.10 .27
☐ 195 Lindy McDaniel 3.50 1.50 .35
☐ 196 Andy Carey 3.50 1.50 .35
☐ 197 Ron Kline 2.75 1.10 .27
☐ 198 Jerry Lynch 2.75 1.10 .27
☐ 199 Dick Donovan 3.00 1.25 .30
☐ 200 Willie Mays 120.00 55.00 18.00
☐ 201 Larry Osborne 3.00 1.25 .30
☐ 202 Fred Kipp 3.00 1.25 .30
☐ 203 Sammy White 3.00 1.25 .30
☐ 204 Ryne Duren 4.00 1.75 .40
☐ 205 Johnny Logan 4.00 1.75 .40
☐ 206 Claude Osteen 4.00 1.75 .40
☐ 207 Bob Boyd 3.00 1.25 .30
☐ 208 White Sox Team 7.50 2.50 .50
(checklist on back)
☐ 209 Ron Blackburn 3.00 1.25 .30
☐ 210 Harmon Killebrew 30.00 13.50 4.50
☐ 211 Taylor Phillips 3.00 1.25 .30
☐ 212 Walt Alston MG 11.00 5.00 1.35
☐ 213 Chuck Dressen MG 3.50 1.50 .35
☐ 214 Jimmy Dykes MG 3.50 1.50 .35
☐ 215 Bob Elliott MG 3.00 1.25 .30
☐ 216 Joe Gordon MG 3.50 1.50 .35
☐ 217 Charlie Grimm MG 3.50 1.50 .35
☐ 218 Solly Hemus MG 3.00 1.25 .30
☐ 219 Fred Hutchinson MG 3.50 1.50 .35
☐ 220 Billy Jurges MG 3.00 1.25 .30
☐ 221 Cookie Lavagetto MG 3.00 1.25 .30
☐ 222 Al Lopez MG 6.50 2.75 .65
☐ 223 Danny Murtaugh MG 3.00 1.25 .30
☐ 224 Paul Richards MG 3.50 1.50 .35
☐ 225 Bill Rigney MG 3.00 1.25 .30
☐ 226 Eddie Sawyer MG 3.00 1.25 .30
☐ 227 Casey Stengel MG 17.00 7.25 2.50
☐ 228 Ernie Johnson 3.50 1.50 .35
☐ 229 Joe M. Morgan 5.00 2.25 .50
☐ 230 Mound Magicians 6.50 2.75 .65
Lou Burdette
Warren Spahn
Bob Buhl
☐ 231 Hal Naragon 3.00 1.25 .30
☐ 232 Jim Busby 3.00 1.25 .30
☐ 233 Don Elston 3.00 1.25 .30
☐ 234 Don Demeter 3.00 1.25 .30
☐ 235 Gus Bell 3.50 1.50 .35
☐ 236 Dick Ricketts 3.00 1.25 .30
☐ 237 Elmer Valo 3.00 1.25 .30
☐ 238 Danny Kravitz 3.00 1.25 .30
☐ 239 Joe Shipley 3.00 1.25 .30
☐ 240 Luis Aparicio 13.50 6.00 1.85
☐ 241 Albie Pearson 3.00 1.25 .30
☐ 242 Cardinals Team 7.50 2.50 .50
(checklist on back)
☐ 243 Bubba Phillips 3.00 1.25 .30
☐ 244 Hal Griggs 3.00 1.25 .30
☐ 245 Eddie Yost 3.00 1.25 .30
☐ 246 Lee Maye 3.00 1.25 .30
☐ 247 Gil McDougald 4.50 2.00 .45
☐ 248 Del Rice 3.00 1.25 .30
☐ 249 Earl Wilson 4.00 1.75 .40
☐ 250 Stan Musial 100.00 45.00 15.00

☐ 251	Bob Malkmus	3.00	1.25	.30
☐ 252	Ray Herbert	3.00	1.25	.30
☐ 253	Eddie Bressoud	3.00	1.25	.30
☐ 254	Arnie Portocarrero	3.00	1.25	.30
☐ 255	Jim Gilliam	4.50	2.00	.45
☐ 256	Dick Brown	3.00	1.25	.30
☐ 257	Gordy Coleman	4.00	1.75	.40
☐ 258	Dick Groat	4.50	2.00	.45
☐ 259	George Altman	3.00	1.25	.30
☐ 260	Power Plus Rocky Colavito Tito Francona	4.50	2.00	.45
☐ 261	Pete Burnside	3.00	1.25	.30
☐ 262	Hank Bauer	3.50	1.50	.35
☐ 263	Darrell Johnson	3.00	1.25	.30
☐ 264	Robin Roberts	12.50	5.50	1.65
☐ 265	Rip Repulski	3.00	1.25	.30
☐ 266	Joey Jay	3.00	1.25	.30
☐ 267	Jim Marshall	3.00	1.25	.30
☐ 268	Al Worthington	3.00	1.25	.30
☐ 269	Gene Green	3.00	1.25	.30
☐ 270	Bob Turley	4.00	1.75	.40
☐ 271	Julio Becquer	3.00	1.25	.30
☐ 272	Fred Green	3.00	1.25	.30
☐ 273	Neil Chrisley	3.00	1.25	.30
☐ 274	Tom Acker	3.00	1.25	.30
☐ 275	Curt Flood	4.50	2.00	.45
☐ 276	Ken McBride	3.00	1.25	.30
☐ 277	Harry Bright	3.00	1.25	.30
☐ 278	Stan Williams	3.00	1.25	.30
☐ 279	Chuck Tanner	3.50	1.50	.35
☐ 280	Frank Sullivan	3.00	1.25	.30
☐ 281	Ray Boone	3.50	1.50	.35
☐ 282	Joe Nuxhall	3.50	1.50	.35
☐ 283	John Blanchard	3.50	1.50	.35
☐ 284	Don Gross	3.00	1.25	.30
☐ 285	Harry Anderson	3.00	1.25	.30
☐ 286	Ray Semproch	3.00	1.25	.30
☐ 287	Felipe Alou	4.00	1.75	.40
☐ 288	Bob Mabe	3.25	1.35	.32
☐ 289	Willie Jones	3.25	1.35	.32
☐ 290	Jerry Lumpe	3.25	1.35	.32
☐ 291	Bob Keegan	3.25	1.35	.32
☐ 292	Dodger Backstops Joe Pignatano John Roseboro	4.00	1.75	.40
☐ 293	Gene Conley	3.25	1.35	.32
☐ 294	Tony Taylor	3.25	1.35	.32
☐ 295	Gil Hodges	16.00	6.75	2.25
☐ 296	Nelson Chittum	3.25	1.35	.32
☐ 297	Reno Bertoia	3.25	1.35	.32
☐ 298	George Witt	3.25	1.35	.32
☐ 299	Earl Torgeson	3.25	1.35	.32
☐ 300	Hank Aaron	120.00	55.00	18.00
☐ 301	Jerry Davie	3.25	1.35	.32
☐ 302	Phillies Team (checklist on back)	7.50	2.50	.50
☐ 303	Billy O'Dell	3.25	1.35	.32
☐ 304	Joe Ginsberg	3.25	1.35	.32
☐ 305	Richie Ashburn	9.00	4.00	.90
☐ 306	Frank Baumann	3.25	1.35	.32
☐ 307	Gene Oliver	3.25	1.35	.32
☐ 308	Dick Hall	3.25	1.35	.32
☐ 309	Bob Hale	3.25	1.35	.32
☐ 310	Frank Malzone	4.00	1.75	.40
☐ 311	Raul Sanchez	3.25	1.35	.32
☐ 312	Charley Lau	4.00	1.75	.40
☐ 313	Turk Lown	3.25	1.35	.32
☐ 314	Chico Fernandez	3.25	1.35	.32
☐ 315	Bobby Shantz	4.50	2.00	.45
☐ 316	Willie McCovey	240.00	105.00	32.00
☐ 317	Pumpsie Green	4.00	1.75	.40
☐ 318	Jim Baxes	3.25	1.35	.32
☐ 319	Joe Koppe	3.25	1.35	.32
☐ 320	Bob Allison	4.50	2.00	.45
☐ 321	Ron Fairly	4.50	2.00	.45
☐ 322	Willie Tasby	3.25	1.35	.32
☐ 323	John Romano	3.25	1.35	.32
☐ 324	Jim Perry	4.50	2.00	.45
☐ 325	Jim O'Toole	4.00	1.75	.40
☐ 326	Bob Clemente	120.00	55.00	18.00
☐ 327	Ray Sadecki	4.50	2.00	.45
☐ 328	Earl Battey	3.25	1.35	.32
☐ 329	Zack Monroe	3.25	1.35	.32
☐ 330	Harvey Kuenn	4.50	2.00	.45
☐ 331	Henry Mason	3.25	1.35	.32
☐ 332	Yankees Team (checklist on back)	25.00	7.50	2.50
☐ 333	Danny McDevitt	3.25	1.35	.32
☐ 334	Ted Abernathy	3.25	1.35	.32
☐ 335	Red Schoendienst	11.00	5.00	1.35
☐ 336	Ike Delock	3.25	1.35	.32
☐ 337	Cal Neeman	3.25	1.35	.32
☐ 338	Ray Monzant	3.25	1.35	.32
☐ 339	Harry Chiti	3.25	1.35	.32
☐ 340	Harvey Haddix	4.00	1.75	.40
☐ 341	Carroll Hardy	3.25	1.35	.32
☐ 342	Casey Wise	3.25	1.35	.32
☐ 343	Sandy Koufax	120.00	55.00	18.00
☐ 344	Clint Courtney	3.25	1.35	.32
☐ 345	Don Newcombe	4.50	2.00	.45
☐ 346	J.C. Martin UER (face actually Gary Peters)	3.25	1.35	.32
☐ 347	Ed Bouchee	3.25	1.35	.32
☐ 348	Barry Shetrone	3.25	1.35	.32
☐ 349	Moe Drabowsky	3.25	1.35	.32
☐ 350	Mickey Mantle	325.00	150.00	50.00
☐ 351	Don Nottebart	3.25	1.35	.32
☐ 352	Cincy Clouters Gus Bell Frank Robinson Jerry Lynch	5.50	2.50	.55
☐ 353	Don Larsen	4.00	1.75	.40
☐ 354	Bob Lillis	4.00	1.75	.40
☐ 355	Bill White	6.50	2.75	.65

	Card	Player			
☐	356	Joe Amalfitano	3.25	1.35	.32
☐	357	Al Schroll	3.25	1.35	.32
☐	358	Joe DeMaestri	3.25	1.35	.32
☐	359	Buddy Gilbert	3.25	1.35	.32
☐	360	Herb Score	4.50	2.00	.45
☐	361	Bob Oldis	3.25	1.35	.32
☐	362	Russ Kemmerer	3.25	1.35	.32
☐	363	Gene Stephens	3.25	1.35	.32
☐	364	Paul Foytack	3.25	1.35	.32
☐	365	Minnie Minoso	5.00	2.25	.50
☐	366	Dallas Green	9.00	4.00	.90
☐	367	Bill Tuttle	3.25	1.35	.32
☐	368	Daryl Spencer	3.25	1.35	.32
☐	369	Billy Hoeft	3.25	1.35	.32
☐	370	Bill Skowron	6.50	2.75	.65
☐	371	Bud Byerly	3.25	1.35	.32
☐	372	Frank House	3.25	1.35	.32
☐	373	Don Hoak	4.00	1.75	.40
☐	374	Bob Buhl	3.25	1.35	.32
☐	375	Dale Long	4.00	1.75	.40
☐	376	John Briggs	3.25	1.35	.32
☐	377	Roger Maris	110.00	50.00	16.50
☐	378	Stu Miller	3.25	1.35	.32
☐	379	Red Wilson	3.25	1.35	.32
☐	380	Bob Shaw	3.25	1.35	.32
☐	381	Braves Team (checklist on back)	7.50	2.50	.50
☐	382	Ted Bowsfield	3.25	1.35	.32
☐	383	Leon Wagner	3.25	1.35	.32
☐	384	Don Cardwell	3.25	1.35	.32
☐	385	World Series Game 1 Neal Steals Second	6.00	2.50	.60
☐	386	World Series Game 2 Neal Belts 2nd Homer	6.00	2.50	.60
☐	387	World Series Game 3 Furillo Breaks Game	6.00	2.50	.60
☐	388	World Series Game 4 Hodges' Homer	8.00	3.50	.80
☐	389	World Series Game 5 Luis Swipes Base	8.00	3.50	.80
☐	390	World Series Game 6 Scrambling After Ball	6.00	2.50	.60
☐	391	World Series Summary The Champs Celebrate	6.00	2.50	.60
☐	392	Tex Clevenger	3.25	1.35	.32
☐	393	Smoky Burgess	4.00	1.75	.40
☐	394	Norm Larker	3.25	1.35	.32
☐	395	Hoyt Wilhelm	12.00	5.25	1.50
☐	396	Steve Bilko	3.25	1.35	.32
☐	397	Don Blasingame	3.25	1.35	.32
☐	398	Mike Cuellar	4.00	1.75	.40
☐	399	Young Hill Stars Milt Pappas Jack Fisher Jerry Walker	4.00	1.75	.40
☐	400	Rocky Colavito	11.00	5.00	1.35
☐	401	Bob Duliba	3.25	1.35	.32
☐	402	Dick Stuart	4.00	1.75	.40
☐	403	Ed Sadowski	3.25	1.35	.32
☐	404	Bob Rush	3.25	1.35	.32
☐	405	Bobby Richardson	6.50	2.75	.65
☐	406	Billy Klaus	3.25	1.35	.32
☐	407	Gary Peters UER (face actually J.C. Martin)	4.00	1.75	.40
☐	408	Carl Furillo	4.50	2.00	.45
☐	409	Ron Samford	3.25	1.35	.32
☐	410	Sam Jones	3.25	1.35	.32
☐	411	Ed Bailey	4.00	1.75	.40
☐	412	Bob Anderson	3.25	1.35	.32
☐	413	Athletics Team (checklist on back)	7.00	2.50	.50
☐	414	Don Williams	3.25	1.35	.32
☐	415	Bob Cerv	4.00	1.75	.40
☐	416	Humberto Robinson	3.25	1.35	.32
☐	417	Chuck Cottier	3.25	1.35	.32
☐	418	Don Mossi	4.00	1.75	.40
☐	419	George Crowe	3.25	1.35	.32
☐	420	Eddie Mathews	32.00	14.25	4.75
☐	421	Duke Maas	3.25	1.35	.32
☐	422	John Powers	3.25	1.35	.32
☐	423	Ed Fitzgerald	3.25	1.35	.32
☐	424	Pete Whisenant	3.25	1.35	.32
☐	425	Johnny Podres	4.50	2.00	.45
☐	426	Ron Jackson	3.25	1.35	.32
☐	427	Al Grunwald	3.25	1.35	.32
☐	428	Al Smith	3.25	1.35	.32
☐	429	AL Kings Nellie Fox Harvey Kuenn	5.00	2.25	.50
☐	430	Art Ditmar	3.25	1.35	.32
☐	431	Andre Rodgers	3.25	1.35	.32
☐	432	Chuck Stobbs	3.25	1.35	.32
☐	433	Irv Noren	3.25	1.35	.32
☐	434	Brooks Lawrence	3.25	1.35	.32
☐	435	Gene Freese	3.25	1.35	.32
☐	436	Marv Throneberry	4.00	1.75	.40
☐	437	Bob Friend	4.00	1.75	.40
☐	438	Jim Coker	3.25	1.35	.32
☐	439	Tom Brewer	3.25	1.35	.32
☐	440	Jim Lemon	4.00	1.75	.40
☐	441	Gary Bell	4.50	2.00	.45
☐	442	Joe Pignatano	4.50	2.00	.45
☐	443	Charley Maxwell	5.00	2.25	.50
☐	444	Jerry Kindall	4.50	2.00	.45
☐	445	Warren Spahn	50.00	22.50	7.50
☐	446	Ellis Burton	4.50	2.00	.45
☐	447	Ray Moore	4.50	2.00	.45
☐	448	Jim Gentile	9.00	4.00	.90
☐	449	Jim Brosnan	5.00	2.25	.50
☐	450	Orlando Cepeda	15.00	6.50	2.15
☐	451	Curt Simmons	5.00	2.25	.50
☐	452	Ray Webster	4.50	2.00	.45
☐	453	Vern Law	6.50	2.75	.65
☐	454	Hal Woodeshick	4.50	2.00	.45
☐	455	Baltimore Coaches	5.50	2.50	.55

Eddie Robinson
Harry Brecheen
Luman Harris
☐ 456 Red Sox Coaches .... 6.50 2.75 .65
Rudy York
Billy Herman
Sal Maglie
Del Baker
☐ 457 Cubs Coaches .... 5.50 2.50 .55
Charlie Root
Lou Klein
Elvin Tappe
☐ 458 White Sox Coaches ..... 5.50 2.50 .55
Johnny Cooney
Don Gutteridge
Tony Cuccinello
Ray Berres
☐ 459 Reds Coaches .... 5.50 2.50 .55
Reggie Otero
Cot Deal
Wally Moses
☐ 460 Indians Coaches .... 6.50 2.75 .65
Mel Harder
Jo-Jo White
Bob Lemon
Ralph(Red) Kress
☐ 461 Tigers Coaches .... 6.50 2.75 .65
Tom Ferrick
Luke Appling
Billy Hitchcock
☐ 462 Athletics Coaches .... 5.50 2.50 .55
Fred Fitzsimmons
Don Heffner
Walker Cooper
☐ 463 Dodgers Coaches .... 6.50 2.75 .65
Bobby Bragan
Pete Reiser
Joe Becker
Greg Mulleavy
☐ 464 Braves Coaches .... 5.50 2.50 .55
Bob Scheffing
Whitlow Wyatt
Andy Pafko
George Myatt
☐ 465 Yankees Coaches 13.00 5.75 1.75
Bill Dickey
Ralph Houk
Frank Crosetti
Ed Lopat
☐ 466 Phillies Coaches .... 5.50 2.50 .55
Ken Silvestri
Dick Carter
Andy Cohen
☐ 467 Pirates Coaches .... 5.50 2.50 .55
Mickey Vernon
Frank Oceak
Sam Narron
Bill Burwell
☐ 468 Cardinals Coaches .... 5.50 2.50 .55
Johnny Keane
Howie Pollet
Ray Katt
Harry Walker
☐ 469 Giants Coaches .... 5.50 2.50 .55
Wes Westrum
Salty Parker
Bill Posedel
☐ 470 Senators Coaches .... 5.50 2.50 .55
Bob Swift
Ellis Clary
Sam Mele
☐ 471 Ned Garver .... 4.50 2.00 .45
☐ 472 Alvin Dark .... 5.50 2.50 .55
☐ 473 Al Cicotte .... 4.50 2.00 .45
☐ 474 Haywood Sullivan .... 4.00 1.75 .40
☐ 475 Don Drysdale 45.00 20.00 6.75
☐ 476 Lou Johnson .... 5.50 2.50 .55
☐ 477 Don Ferrarese .... 4.50 2.00 .45
☐ 478 Frank Torre .... 5.00 2.25 .50
☐ 479 Georges Maranda .... 4.50 2.00 .45
☐ 480 Yogi Berra 70.00 32.00 10.50
☐ 481 Wes Stock .... 4.50 2.00 .45
☐ 482 Frank Bolling .... 4.50 2.00 .45
☐ 483 Camilo Pascual .... 5.00 2.25 .50
☐ 484 Pirates Team 21.00 7.00 1.50
(checklist on back)
☐ 485 Ken Boyer .... 9.00 4.00 .90
☐ 486 Bobby Del Greco .... 4.50 2.00 .45
☐ 487 Tom Sturdivant .... 4.50 2.00 .45
☐ 488 Norm Cash .... 9.00 4.00 .90
☐ 489 Steve Ridzik .... 4.50 2.00 .45
☐ 490 Frank Robinson 55.00 25.00 8.25
☐ 491 Mel Roach .... 4.50 2.00 .45
☐ 492 Larry Jackson .... 4.50 2.00 .45
☐ 493 Duke Snider 60.00 27.00 9.00
☐ 494 Orioles Team .... 11.00 4.00 .80
(checklist on back)
☐ 495 Sherm Lollar .... 5.50 2.50 .55
☐ 496 Bill Virdon .... 6.00 2.50 .60
☐ 497 John Tsitouris .... 4.50 2.00 .45
☐ 498 Al Pilarcik .... 4.50 2.00 .45
☐ 499 Johnny James .... 4.50 2.00 .45
☐ 500 Johnny Temple .... 5.00 2.25 .50
☐ 501 Bob Schmidt .... 4.50 2.00 .45
☐ 502 Jim Bunning 10.00 4.50 1.25
☐ 503 Don Lee .... 4.50 2.00 .45
☐ 504 Seth Morehead .... 4.50 2.00 .45
☐ 505 Ted Kluszewski .... 9.00 4.00 .90
☐ 506 Lee Walls .... 4.50 2.00 .45
☐ 507 Dick Stigman 12.00 5.25 1.50
☐ 508 Billy Consolo 12.00 5.25 1.50
☐ 509 Tommy Davis 24.00 10.50 3.50
☐ 510 Jerry Staley 12.00 5.25 1.50
☐ 511 Ken Walters 12.00 5.25 1.50
☐ 512 Joe Gibbon 12.00 5.25 1.50
☐ 513 Chicago Cubs 32.00 10.00 2.00

		NRMT	VG-E	GOOD
	Team Card (checklist on back)			
☐ 514	Steve Barber	12.00	5.25	1.50
☐ 515	Stan Lopata	12.00	5.25	1.50
☐ 516	Marty Kutyna	12.00	5.25	1.50
☐ 517	Charlie James	12.00	5.25	1.50
☐ 518	Tony Gonzalez	12.00	5.25	1.50
☐ 519	Ed Roebuck	12.00	5.25	1.50
☐ 520	Don Buddin	12.00	5.25	1.50
☐ 521	Mike Lee	12.00	5.25	1.50
☐ 522	Ken Hunt	12.00	5.25	1.50
☐ 523	Clay Dalrymple	12.00	5.25	1.50
☐ 524	Bill Henry	12.00	5.25	1.50
☐ 525	Marv Breeding	12.00	5.25	1.50
☐ 526	Paul Giel	12.00	5.25	1.50
☐ 527	Jose Valdivielso	12.00	5.25	1.50
☐ 528	Ben Johnson	12.00	5.25	1.50
☐ 529	Norm Sherry	14.00	6.25	2.00
☐ 530	Mike McCormick	14.00	6.25	2.00
☐ 531	Sandy Amoros	14.00	6.25	2.00
☐ 532	Mike Garcia	14.00	6.25	2.00
☐ 533	Lu Clinton	12.00	5.25	1.50
☐ 534	Ken MacKenzie	12.00	5.25	1.50
☐ 535	Whitey Lockman	14.00	6.25	2.00
☐ 536	Wynn Hawkins	12.00	5.25	1.50
☐ 537	Boston Red Sox Team Card (checklist on back)	32.00	10.00	2.00
☐ 538	Frank Barnes	12.00	5.25	1.50
☐ 539	Gene Baker	12.00	5.25	1.50
☐ 540	Jerry Walker	12.00	5.25	1.50
☐ 541	Tony Curry	12.00	5.25	1.50
☐ 542	Ken Hamlin	12.00	5.25	1.50
☐ 543	Elio Chacon	12.00	5.25	1.50
☐ 544	Bill Monbouquette	14.00	6.25	2.00
☐ 545	Carl Sawatski	12.00	5.25	1.50
☐ 546	Hank Aguirre	12.00	5.25	1.50
☐ 547	Bob Aspromonte	12.00	5.25	1.50
☐ 548	Don Mincher	14.00	6.25	2.00
☐ 549	John Buzhardt	12.00	5.25	1.50
☐ 550	Jim Landis	12.00	5.25	1.50
☐ 551	Ed Rakow	12.00	5.25	1.50
☐ 552	Walt Bond	12.00	5.25	1.50
☐ 553	Bill Skowron AS	16.00	6.75	2.25
☐ 554	Willie McCovey AS	65.00	29.00	9.75
☐ 555	Nellie Fox AS	18.00	7.50	2.50
☐ 556	Charlie Neal AS	14.00	6.25	2.00
☐ 557	Frank Malzone AS	14.00	6.25	2.00
☐ 558	Eddie Mathews AS	32.00	14.25	4.75
☐ 559	Luis Aparicio AS	21.00	9.00	3.00
☐ 560	Ernie Banks AS	48.00	22.00	6.00
☐ 561	Al Kaline AS	48.00	22.00	6.00
☐ 562	Joe Cunningham AS	14.00	6.25	2.00
☐ 563	Mickey Mantle AS	250.00	110.00	37.50
☐ 564	Willie Mays AS	110.00	50.00	16.50
☐ 565	Roger Maris AS	110.00	50.00	16.50
☐ 566	Hank Aaron AS	110.00	50.00	16.50
☐ 567	Sherm Lollar AS	14.00	6.25	2.00
☐ 568	Del Crandall AS	14.00	6.25	2.00
☐ 569	Camilo Pascual AS	14.00	6.25	2.00
☐ 570	Don Drysdale AS	32.00	14.25	4.75
☐ 571	Billy Pierce AS	14.00	6.25	2.00
☐ 572	Johnny Antonelli AS	25.00	7.50	1.50

1961 Topps

The cards in this 587-card set measure 2 1/2" by 3 1/2". In 1961, Topps returned to the vertical obverse format. Introduced for the first time were "League Leaders" (41 to 50) and separate, numbered checklist cards. Two number 463s exist: the Braves team card carrying that number was meant to be number 426. There are three versions of the second series checklist card number 98; the variations are distinguished by the color of the "CHECKLIST" headline on the front of the card, the color of the printing of the card number on the bottom of the reverse, and the presence of the copyright notice running vertically on the card back. There are two groups of managers (131-139 and 219-226) as well as separate series of World Series cards (306-313), Baseball Thrills (401 to 410), previous MVP's (AL 471-478 and NL 479-486) and Sporting News All-Stars (566 to 589). The usual last series scarcity (523 to 589) exists. The set actually totals 587 cards since numbers 587 and 588 were never issued. The key rookies in this set are ex-Cubs Ron Santo and Billy Williams.

	NRMT	VG-E	GOOD
COMPLETE SET (587)	5750.00	2400.00	600.00
COMMON PLAYER (1-110)	2.50	1.00	.25
COMMON PLAYER (111-370)	3.00	1.25	.30

COMMON PLAYER (371-446) . 3.50 1.50 .35
COMMON PLAYER (447-522) . 4.75 2.00 .45
COMMON PLAYER (523-565) 30.00 13.50 4.50
COMMON PLAYER (566-589) 33.00 15.00 5.00

☐ 1 Dick Groat .... 20.00 2.50 .50
☐ 2 Roger Maris 160.00 40.00 8.00
☐ 3 John Buzhardt .... 2.50 1.00 .25
☐ 4 Lenny Green .... 2.50 1.00 .25
☐ 5 John Romano .... 2.50 1.00 .25
☐ 6 Ed Roebuck .... 2.50 1.00 .25
☐ 7 White Sox Team .... 6.00 2.50 .60
☐ 8 Dick Williams .... 3.00 1.25 .30
☐ 9 Bob Purkey .... 2.50 1.00 .25
☐ 10 Brooks Robinson 32.00 14.25 4.75
☐ 11 Curt Simmons .... 3.00 1.25 .30
☐ 12 Moe Thacker .... 2.50 1.00 .25
☐ 13 Chuck Cottier .... 2.50 1.00 .25
☐ 14 Don Mossi .... 3.00 1.25 .30
☐ 15 Willie Kirkland .... 2.50 1.00 .25
☐ 16 Billy Muffett .... 2.50 1.00 .25
☐ 17 Checklist 1 .... 10.00 1.00 .20
☐ 18 Jim Grant .... 2.50 1.00 .25
☐ 19 Clete Boyer .... 3.50 1.50 .35
☐ 20 Robin Roberts 11.00 5.00 1.35
☐ 21 Zorro Versalles UER ...... 4.00 1.75 .40
(first name should
be Zoilo)
☐ 22 Clem Labine .... 3.00 1.25 .30
☐ 23 Don Demeter .... 2.50 1.00 .25
☐ 24 Ken Johnson .... 2.50 1.00 .25
☐ 25 Reds' Heavy Artillery ..... 5.50 2.50 .55
Vada Pinson
Gus Bell
Frank Robinson
☐ 26 Wes Stock .... 2.50 1.00 .25
☐ 27 Jerry Kindall .... 2.50 1.00 .25
☐ 28 Hector Lopez .... 2.50 1.00 .25
☐ 29 Don Nottebart .... 2.50 1.00 .25
☐ 30 Nellie Fox .... 7.00 3.00 .70
☐ 31 Bob Schmidt .... 2.50 1.00 .25
☐ 32 Ray Sadecki .... 2.50 1.00 .25
☐ 33 Gary Geiger .... 2.50 1.00 .25
☐ 34 Wynn Hawkins .... 2.50 1.00 .25
☐ 35 Ron Santo 42.00 18.00 5.50
☐ 36 Jack Kralick .... 2.50 1.00 .25
☐ 37 Charley Maxwell .... 2.50 1.00 .25
☐ 38 Bob Lillis .... 2.50 1.00 .25
☐ 39 Leo Posada .... 2.50 1.00 .25
☐ 40 Bob Turley .... 3.50 1.50 .35
☐ 41 NL Batting Leaders .... 7.00 3.00 .70
Dick Groat
Norm Larker
Willie Mays
Roberto Clemente
☐ 42 AL Batting Leaders .... 4.00 1.75 .40
Pete Runnels
Al Smith
Minnie Minoso
Bill Skowron
☐ 43 NL Home Run Leaders .. 9.00 4.00 .90
Ernie Banks
Hank Aaron
Ed Mathews
Ken Boyer
☐ 44 AL Home Run Leaders 25.00 11.00 3.50
Mickey Mantle
Roger Maris
Jim Lemon
Rocky Colavito
☐ 45 NL ERA Leaders .... 4.00 1.75 .40
Mike McCormick
Ernie Broglio
Don Drysdale
Bob Friend
Stan Williams
☐ 46 AL ERA Leaders .... 4.00 1.75 .40
Frank Baumann
Jim Bunning
Art Ditmar
Hal Brown
☐ 47 NL Pitching Leaders ...... 4.50 2.00 .45
Ernie Broglio
Warren Spahn
Vern Law
Lou Burdette
☐ 48 AL Pitching Leaders ...... 4.00 1.75 .40
Chuck Estrada
Jim Perry
Bud Daley
Art Ditmar
Frank Lary
Milt Pappas
☐ 49 NL Strikeout Leaders .... 6.00 2.50 .60
Don Drysdale
Sandy Koufax
Sam Jones
Ernie Broglio
☐ 50 AL Strikeout Leaders ..... 4.50 2.00 .45
Jim Bunning
Pedro Ramos
Early Wynn
Frank Lary
☐ 51 Detroit Tigers .... 6.00 2.50 .60
Team Card
☐ 52 George Crowe .... 2.50 1.00 .25
☐ 53 Russ Nixon .... 2.50 1.00 .25
☐ 54 Earl Francis .... 2.50 1.00 .25
☐ 55 Jim Davenport .... 2.50 1.00 .25
☐ 56 Russ Kemmerer .... 2.50 1.00 .25
☐ 57 Marv Throneberry .... 3.50 1.50 .35
☐ 58 Joe Schaffernoth .... 2.50 1.00 .25
☐ 59 Jim Woods .... 2.50 1.00 .25
☐ 60 Woody Held .... 2.50 1.00 .25
☐ 61 Ron Piche .... 2.50 1.00 .25
☐ 62 Al Pilarcik .... 2.50 1.00 .25

☐ 63 Jim Kaat .... 8.00 3.50 .80
☐ 64 Alex Grammas .... 2.50 1.00 .25
☐ 65 Ted Kluszewski .... 5.00 2.25 .50
☐ 66 Bill Henry .... 2.50 1.00 .25
☐ 67 Ossie Virgil .... 2.50 1.00 .25
☐ 68 Deron Johnson .... 3.00 1.25 .30
☐ 69 Earl Wilson .... 2.50 1.00 .25
☐ 70 Bill Virdon .... 3.50 1.50 .35
☐ 71 Jerry Adair .... 2.50 1.00 .25
☐ 72 Stu Miller .... 2.50 1.00 .25
☐ 73 Al Spangler .... 2.50 1.00 .25
☐ 74 Joe Pignatano .... 2.50 1.00 .25
☐ 75 Lindy Shows Larry .... 3.00 1.25 .30
Lindy McDaniel
Larry Jackson
☐ 76 Harry Anderson .... 2.50 1.00 .25
☐ 77 Dick Stigman .... 2.50 1.00 .25
☐ 78 Lee Walls .... 2.50 1.00 .25
☐ 79 Joe Ginsberg .... 2.50 1.00 .25
☐ 80 Harmon Killebrew 21.00 9.00 3.00
☐ 81 Tracy Stallard .... 3.00 1.25 .30
☐ 82 Joe Christopher .... 2.50 1.00 .25
☐ 83 Bob Bruce .... 2.50 1.00 .25
☐ 84 Lee Maye .... 2.50 1.00 .25
☐ 85 Jerry Walker .... 2.50 1.00 .25
☐ 86 Los Angeles Dodgers .... 6.00 2.50 .60
Team Card
☐ 87 Joe Amalfitano .... 2.50 1.00 .25
☐ 88 Richie Ashburn .... 7.00 3.00 .70
☐ 89 Billy Martin .... 8.00 3.50 .80
☐ 90 Jerry Staley .... 2.50 1.00 .25
☐ 91 Walt Moryn .... 2.50 1.00 .25
☐ 92 Hal Naragon .... 2.50 1.00 .25
☐ 93 Tony Gonzalez .... 2.50 1.00 .25
☐ 94 Johnny Kucks .... 2.50 1.00 .25
☐ 95 Norm Cash .... 5.00 2.25 .50
☐ 96 Billy O'Dell .... 2.50 1.00 .25
☐ 97 Jerry Lynch .... 2.50 1.00 .25
☐ 98A Checklist 2 .... 10.00 1.00 .20
(red "Checklist",
98 black on white)
☐ 98B Checklist 2 .... 10.00 1.00 .20
(yellow "Checklist",
98 black on white)
☐ 98C Checklist 2 .... 10.00 1.00 .20
(yellow "Checklist",
98 white on black,
no copyright)
☐ 99 Don Buddin UER .... 2.50 1.00 .25
(66 HR's)
☐ 100 Harvey Haddix .... 3.50 1.50 .35
☐ 101 Bubba Phillips .... 2.50 1.00 .25
☐ 102 Gene Stephens .... 2.50 1.00 .25
☐ 103 Ruben Amaro .... 2.50 1.00 .25
☐ 104 John Blanchard .... 3.00 1.25 .30
☐ 105 Carl Willey .... 2.50 1.00 .25
☐ 106 Whitey Herzog .... 4.00 1.75 .40
☐ 107 Seth Morehead .... 2.50 1.00 .25
☐ 108 Dan Dobbek .... 2.50 1.00 .25
☐ 109 Johnny Podres .... 3.50 1.50 .35
☐ 110 Vada Pinson .... 4.00 1.75 .40
☐ 111 Jack Meyer .... 3.00 1.25 .30
☐ 112 Chico Fernandez .... 3.00 1.25 .30
☐ 113 Mike Fornieles .... 3.00 1.25 .30
☐ 114 Hobie Landrith .... 3.00 1.25 .30
☐ 115 Johnny Antonelli .... 3.50 1.50 .35
☐ 116 Joe DeMaestri .... 3.00 1.25 .30
☐ 117 Dale Long .... 3.50 1.50 .35
☐ 118 Chris Cannizzaro .... 3.00 1.25 .30
☐ 119 A's Big Armor .... 3.50 1.50 .35
Norm Siebern
Hank Bauer
Jerry Lumpe
☐ 120 Eddie Mathews 25.00 11.00 3.50
☐ 121 Eli Grba .... 3.00 1.25 .30
☐ 122 Chicago Cubs .... 6.00 2.50 .60
Team Card
☐ 123 Billy Gardner .... 3.00 1.25 .30
☐ 124 J.C. Martin .... 3.00 1.25 .30
☐ 125 Steve Barber .... 3.00 1.25 .30
☐ 126 Dick Stuart .... 3.50 1.50 .35
☐ 127 Ron Kline .... 3.00 1.25 .30
☐ 128 Rip Repulski .... 3.00 1.25 .30
☐ 129 Ed Hobaugh .... 3.00 1.25 .30
☐ 130 Norm Larker .... 3.50 1.50 .35
☐ 131 Paul Richards MG .... 3.50 1.50 .35
☐ 132 Al Lopez MG .... 4.50 2.00 .45
☐ 133 Ralph Houk MG .... 4.00 1.75 .40
☐ 134 Mickey Vernon MG .... 3.50 1.50 .35
☐ 135 Fred Hutchinson MG .... 3.50 1.50 .35
☐ 136 Walt Alston MG .... 5.50 2.50 .55
☐ 137 Chuck Dressen MG .... 3.50 1.50 .35
☐ 138 Danny Murtaugh MG .... 3.00 1.25 .30
☐ 139 Solly Hemus MG .... 3.00 1.25 .30
☐ 140 Gus Triandos .... 3.50 1.50 .35
☐ 141 Billy Williams 100.00 45.00 15.00
☐ 142 Luis Arroyo .... 3.50 1.50 .35
☐ 143 Russ Snyder .... 3.00 1.25 .30
☐ 144 Jim Coker .... 3.00 1.25 .30
☐ 145 Bob Buhl .... 3.00 1.25 .30
☐ 146 Marty Keough .... 3.00 1.25 .30
☐ 147 Ed Rakow .... 3.00 1.25 .30
☐ 148 Julian Javier .... 3.50 1.50 .35
☐ 149 Bob Oldis .... 3.00 1.25 .30
☐ 150 Willie Mays 110.00 50.00 16.50
☐ 151 Jim Donohue .... 3.00 1.25 .30
☐ 152 Earl Torgeson .... 3.00 1.25 .30
☐ 153 Don Lee .... 3.00 1.25 .30
☐ 154 Bobby Del Greco .... 3.00 1.25 .30
☐ 155 Johnny Temple .... 3.00 1.25 .30
☐ 156 Ken Hunt .... 3.00 1.25 .30
☐ 157 Cal McLish .... 3.00 1.25 .30
☐ 158 Pete Daley .... 3.00 1.25 .30
☐ 159 Orioles Team .... 6.00 2.50 .60
☐ 160 Whitey Ford UER 36.00 16.25 5.50
(incorrectly listed

as 5'0" tall)
☐ 161 Sherman Jones UER ... 3.00 1.25 .30
(photo actually
Eddie Fisher)
☐ 162 Jay Hook ... 3.00 1.25 .30
☐ 163 Ed Sadowski ... 3.00 1.25 .30
☐ 164 Felix Mantilla ... 3.00 1.25 .30
☐ 165 Gino Cimoli ... 3.00 1.25 .30
☐ 166 Danny Kravitz ... 3.00 1.25 .30
☐ 167 San Francisco Giants .. 6.00 2.50 .60
Team Card
☐ 168 Tommy Davis ... 5.00 2.25 .50
☐ 169 Don Elston ... 3.00 1.25 .30
☐ 170 Al Smith ... 3.00 1.25 .30
☐ 171 Paul Foytack ... 3.00 1.25 .30
☐ 172 Don Dillard ... 3.00 1.25 .30
☐ 173 Beantown Bombers ... 3.50 1.50 .35
Frank Malzone
Vic Wertz
Jackie Jensen
☐ 174 Ray Semproch ... 3.00 1.25 .30
☐ 175 Gene Freese ... 3.00 1.25 .30
☐ 176 Ken Aspromonte ... 3.00 1.25 .30
☐ 177 Don Larsen ... 3.50 1.50 .35
☐ 178 Bob Nieman ... 3.00 1.25 .30
☐ 179 Joe Koppe ... 3.00 1.25 .30
☐ 180 Bobby Richardson ... 6.50 2.75 .65
☐ 181 Fred Green ... 3.00 1.25 .30
☐ 182 Dave Nicholson ... 3.00 1.25 .30
☐ 183 Andre Rodgers ... 3.00 1.25 .30
☐ 184 Steve Bilko ... 3.00 1.25 .30
☐ 185 Herb Score ... 4.00 1.75 .40
☐ 186 Elmer Valo ... 3.00 1.25 .30
☐ 187 Billy Klaus ... 3.00 1.25 .30
☐ 188 Jim Marshall ... 3.00 1.25 .30
☐ 189A Checklist 3 ... 10.00 1.00 .20
(copyright symbol
almost adjacent to
263 Ken Hamlin)
☐ 189B Checklist 3 ... 10.00 1.00 .20
(copyright symbol
adjacent to
264 Glen Hobbie)
☐ 190 Stan Williams ... 3.00 1.25 .30
☐ 191 Mike De La Hoz ... 3.00 1.25 .30
☐ 192 Dick Brown ... 3.00 1.25 .30
☐ 193 Gene Conley ... 3.00 1.25 .30
☐ 194 Gordy Coleman ... 3.50 1.50 .35
☐ 195 Jerry Casale ... 3.00 1.25 .30
☐ 196 Ed Bouchee ... 3.00 1.25 .30
☐ 197 Dick Hall ... 3.00 1.25 .30
☐ 198 Carl Sawatski ... 3.00 1.25 .30
☐ 199 Bob Boyd ... 3.00 1.25 .30
☐ 200 Warren Spahn ... 30.00 13.50 4.50
☐ 201 Pete Whisenant ... 3.00 1.25 .30
☐ 202 Al Neiger ... 3.00 1.25 .30
☐ 203 Eddie Bressoud ... 3.00 1.25 .30
☐ 204 Bob Skinner ... 3.50 1.50 .35
☐ 205 Billy Pierce ... 4.00 1.75 .40
☐ 206 Gene Green ... 3.00 1.25 .30
☐ 207 Dodger Southpaws ... 18.00 7.50 2.50
Sandy Koufax
Johnny Podres
☐ 208 Larry Osborne ... 3.00 1.25 .30
☐ 209 Ken McBride ... 3.00 1.25 .30
☐ 210 Pete Runnels ... 3.50 1.50 .35
☐ 211 Bob Gibson ... 40.00 18.00 6.00
☐ 212 Haywood Sullivan ... 3.50 1.50 .35
☐ 213 Bill Stafford ... 3.00 1.25 .30
☐ 214 Danny Murphy ... 3.00 1.25 .30
☐ 215 Gus Bell ... 3.50 1.50 .35
☐ 216 Ted Bowsfield ... 3.00 1.25 .30
☐ 217 Mel Roach ... 3.00 1.25 .30
☐ 218 Hal Brown ... 3.00 1.25 .30
☐ 219 Gene Mauch MG ... 3.50 1.50 .35
☐ 220 Alvin Dark MG ... 3.50 1.50 .35
☐ 221 Mike Higgins MG ... 3.00 1.25 .30
☐ 222 Jimmy Dykes MG ... 3.50 1.50 .35
☐ 223 Bob Scheffing MG ... 3.00 1.25 .30
☐ 224 Joe Gordon MG ... 3.50 1.50 .35
☐ 225 Bill Rigney MG ... 3.00 1.25 .30
☐ 226 Harry Lavagetto MG ... 3.00 1.25 .30
☐ 227 Juan Pizarro ... 3.00 1.25 .30
☐ 228 New York Yankees ... 22.00 9.50 3.15
Team Card
☐ 229 Rudy Hernandez ... 3.00 1.25 .30
☐ 230 Don Hoak ... 3.50 1.50 .35
☐ 231 Dick Drott ... 3.00 1.25 .30
☐ 232 Bill White ... 5.00 2.25 .50
☐ 233 Joey Jay ... 3.00 1.25 .30
☐ 234 Ted Lepcio ... 3.00 1.25 .30
☐ 235 Camilo Pascual ... 3.50 1.50 .35
☐ 236 Don Gile ... 3.00 1.25 .30
☐ 237 Billy Loes ... 3.00 1.25 .30
☐ 238 Jim Gilliam ... 4.00 1.75 .40
☐ 239 Dave Sisler ... 3.00 1.25 .30
☐ 240 Ron Hansen ... 3.00 1.25 .30
☐ 241 Al Cicotte ... 3.00 1.25 .30
☐ 242 Hal Smith ... 3.00 1.25 .30
☐ 243 Frank Lary ... 3.50 1.50 .35
☐ 244 Chico Cardenas ... 3.50 1.50 .35
☐ 245 Joe Adcock ... 3.50 1.50 .35
☐ 246 Bob Davis ... 3.00 1.25 .30
☐ 247 Billy Goodman ... 3.00 1.25 .30
☐ 248 Ed Keegan ... 3.00 1.25 .30
☐ 249 Cincinnati Reds ... 6.00 2.50 .60
Team Card
☐ 250 Buc Hill Aces ... 3.50 1.50 .35
Vern Law
Roy Face
☐ 251 Bill Bruton ... 3.00 1.25 .30
☐ 252 Bill Short ... 3.00 1.25 .30
☐ 253 Sammy Taylor ... 3.00 1.25 .30
☐ 254 Ted Sadowski ... 3.00 1.25 .30
☐ 255 Vic Power ... 3.00 1.25 .30
☐ 256 Billy Hoeft ... 3.00 1.25 .30

☐ 257 Carroll Hardy	3.00	1.25	.30
☐ 258 Jack Sanford	3.00	1.25	.30
☐ 259 John Schaive	3.00	1.25	.30
☐ 260 Don Drysdale	25.00	11.00	3.50
☐ 261 Charlie Lau	3.50	1.50	.35
☐ 262 Tony Curry	3.00	1.25	.30
☐ 263 Ken Hamlin	3.00	1.25	.30
☐ 264 Glen Hobbie	3.00	1.25	.30
☐ 265 Tony Kubek	7.50	3.25	.75
☐ 266 Lindy McDaniel	3.50	1.50	.35
☐ 267 Norm Siebern	3.00	1.25	.30
☐ 268 Ike Delock	3.00	1.25	.30
☐ 269 Harry Chiti	3.00	1.25	.30
☐ 270 Bob Friend	3.50	1.50	.35
☐ 271 Jim Landis	3.00	1.25	.30
☐ 272 Tom Morgan	3.00	1.25	.30
☐ 273A Checklist 4 (copyright symbol adjacent to 336 Don Mincher)	15.00	1.50	.30
☐ 273B Checklist 4 (copyright symbol adjacent to 339 Gene Baker)	10.00	1.00	.20
☐ 274 Gary Bell	3.00	1.25	.30
☐ 275 Gene Woodling	3.50	1.50	.35
☐ 276 Ray Rippelmeyer	3.00	1.25	.30
☐ 277 Hank Foiles	3.00	1.25	.30
☐ 278 Don McMahon	3.00	1.25	.30
☐ 279 Jose Pagan	3.00	1.25	.30
☐ 280 Frank Howard	4.50	2.00	.45
☐ 281 Frank Sullivan	3.00	1.25	.30
☐ 282 Faye Throneberry	3.00	1.25	.30
☐ 283 Bob Anderson	3.00	1.25	.30
☐ 284 Dick Gernert	3.00	1.25	.30
☐ 285 Sherm Lollar	3.50	1.50	.35
☐ 286 George Witt	3.00	1.25	.30
☐ 287 Carl Yastrzemski	140.00	63.00	21.00
☐ 288 Albie Pearson	3.00	1.25	.30
☐ 289 Ray Moore	3.00	1.25	.30
☐ 290 Stan Musial	95.00	42.00	11.00
☐ 291 Tex Clevenger	3.00	1.25	.30
☐ 292 Jim Baumer	3.00	1.25	.30
☐ 293 Tom Sturdivant	3.00	1.25	.30
☐ 294 Don Blasingame	3.00	1.25	.30
☐ 295 Milt Pappas	3.50	1.50	.35
☐ 296 Wes Covington	3.50	1.50	.35
☐ 297 Athletics Team	6.00	2.50	.60
☐ 298 Jim Golden	3.00	1.25	.30
☐ 299 Clay Dalrymple	3.00	1.25	.30
☐ 300 Mickey Mantle	350.00	160.00	52.50
☐ 301 Chet Nichols	3.00	1.25	.30
☐ 302 Al Heist	3.00	1.25	.30
☐ 303 Gary Peters	3.50	1.50	.35
☐ 304 Rocky Nelson	3.00	1.25	.30
☐ 305 Mike McCormick	3.50	1.50	.35
☐ 306 World Series Game 1 Virdon Saves Game	7.00	3.00	.70
☐ 307 World Series Game 2 Mantle 2 Homers	32.00	14.25	4.75
☐ 308 World Series Game 3 Richardson is Hero	8.00	3.50	.80
☐ 309 World Series Game 4 Cimoli Safe	7.00	3.00	.70
☐ 310 World Series Game 5 Face Saves the Day	8.00	3.50	.80
☐ 311 World Series Game 6 Ford Second Shutout	9.00	4.00	.90
☐ 312 World Series Game 7 Mazeroski's Homer	10.00	4.50	1.25
☐ 313 World Series Summary Pirates Celebrate	7.00	3.00	.70
☐ 314 Bob Miller	3.00	1.25	.30
☐ 315 Earl Battey	3.00	1.25	.30
☐ 316 Bobby Gene Smith	3.00	1.25	.30
☐ 317 Jim Brewer	3.00	1.25	.30
☐ 318 Danny O'Connell	3.00	1.25	.30
☐ 319 Valmy Thomas	3.00	1.25	.30
☐ 320 Lou Burdette	4.00	1.75	.40
☐ 321 Marv Breeding	3.00	1.25	.30
☐ 322 Bill Kunkel	3.50	1.50	.35
☐ 323 Sammy Esposito	3.00	1.25	.30
☐ 324 Hank Aguirre	3.00	1.25	.30
☐ 325 Wally Moon	3.50	1.50	.35
☐ 326 Dave Hillman	3.00	1.25	.30
☐ 327 Matty Alou	5.50	2.50	.55
☐ 328 Jim O'Toole	3.50	1.50	.35
☐ 329 Julio Becquer	3.00	1.25	.30
☐ 330 Rocky Colavito	10.00	4.50	1.25
☐ 331 Ned Garver	3.00	1.25	.30
☐ 332 Dutch Dotterer UER (photo actually Tommy Dotterer, Dutch's brother)	3.00	1.25	.30
☐ 333 Fritz Brickell	3.00	1.25	.30
☐ 334 Walt Bond	3.00	1.25	.30
☐ 335 Frank Bolling	3.00	1.25	.30
☐ 336 Don Mincher	3.50	1.50	.35
☐ 337 Al's Aces Early Wynn Al Lopez Herb Score	5.00	2.25	.50
☐ 338 Don Landrum	3.00	1.25	.30
☐ 339 Gene Baker	3.00	1.25	.30
☐ 340 Vic Wertz	3.50	1.50	.35
☐ 341 Jim Owens	3.00	1.25	.30
☐ 342 Clint Courtney	3.00	1.25	.30
☐ 343 Earl Robinson	3.00	1.25	.30
☐ 344 Sandy Koufax	100.00	45.00	15.00
☐ 345 Jim Piersall	4.00	1.75	.40
☐ 346 Howie Nunn	3.00	1.25	.30
☐ 347 St. Louis Cardinals Team Card	6.00	2.50	.60
☐ 348 Steve Boros	3.00	1.25	.30
☐ 349 Danny McDevitt	3.00	1.25	.30
☐ 350 Ernie Banks	38.00	17.00	5.00

☐ 351 Jim King .... 3.00 1.25 .30
☐ 352 Bob Shaw .... 3.00 1.25 .30
☐ 353 Howie Bedell .... 3.00 1.25 .30
☐ 354 Billy Harrell .... 3.00 1.25 .30
☐ 355 Bob Allison .... 3.50 1.50 .35
☐ 356 Ryne Duren .... 3.50 1.50 .35
☐ 357 Daryl Spencer .... 3.00 1.25 .30
☐ 358 Earl Averill .... 3.00 1.25 .30
☐ 359 Dallas Green .... 4.00 1.75 .40
☐ 360 Frank Robinson 42.00 18.00 5.50
☐ 361A Checklist 5 .... 10.00 1.00 .20
(no ad on back)
☐ 361B Checklist 5 .... 15.00 1.50 .30
(Special Feature
ad on back)
☐ 362 Frank Funk .... 3.00 1.25 .30
☐ 363 John Roseboro .... 3.50 1.50 .35
☐ 364 Moe Drabowsky .... 3.00 1.25 .30
☐ 365 Jerry Lumpe .... 3.00 1.25 .30
☐ 366 Eddie Fisher .... 3.00 1.25 .30
☐ 367 Jim Rivera .... 3.00 1.25 .30
☐ 368 Bennie Daniels .... 3.00 1.25 .30
☐ 369 Dave Philley .... 3.00 1.25 .30
☐ 370 Roy Face .... 4.50 2.00 .45
☐ 371 Bill Skowron SP 35.00 15.75 5.25
☐ 372 Bob Hendley .... 3.50 1.50 .35
☐ 373 Boston Red Sox .... 7.50 3.25 .75
Team Card
☐ 374 Paul Giel .... 3.50 1.50 .35
☐ 375 Ken Boyer .... 5.50 2.50 .55
☐ 376 Mike Roarke .... 3.50 1.50 .35
☐ 377 Ruben Gomez .... 3.50 1.50 .35
☐ 378 Wally Post .... 4.00 1.75 .40
☐ 379 Bobby Shantz .... 4.50 2.00 .45
☐ 380 Minnie Minoso .... 5.00 2.25 .50
☐ 381 Dave Wickersham .... 3.50 1.50 .35
☐ 382 Frank Thomas .... 4.00 1.75 .40
☐ 383 Frisco First Liners .... 4.00 1.75 .40
Mike McCormick
Jack Sanford
Billy O'Dell
☐ 384 Chuck Essegian .... 3.50 1.50 .35
☐ 385 Jim Perry .... 4.50 2.00 .45
☐ 386 Joe Hicks .... 3.50 1.50 .35
☐ 387 Duke Maas .... 3.50 1.50 .35
☐ 388 Bob Clemente 95.00 42.00 11.00
☐ 389 Ralph Terry .... 4.50 2.00 .45
☐ 390 Del Crandall .... 4.00 1.75 .40
☐ 391 Winston Brown .... 3.50 1.50 .35
☐ 392 Reno Bertoia .... 3.50 1.50 .35
☐ 393 Batter Bafflers .... 3.50 1.50 .35
Don Cardwell
Glen Hobbie
☐ 394 Ken Walters .... 3.50 1.50 .35
☐ 395 Chuck Estrada .... 4.00 1.75 .40
☐ 396 Bob Aspromonte .... 3.50 1.50 .35
☐ 397 Hal Woodeshick .... 3.50 1.50 .35
☐ 398 Hank Bauer .... 4.50 2.00 .45
☐ 399 Cliff Cook .... 3.50 1.50 .35
☐ 400 Vern Law .... 4.50 2.00 .45
☐ 401 Ruth 60th Homer 25.00 11.00 3.50
☐ 402 Perfect Game 18.00 7.50 2.50
(Don Larsen)
☐ 403 26 Inning Tie .... 6.00 2.50 .60
☐ 404 Hornsby .424 Average . 8.00 3.50 .80
☐ 405 Gehrig's Streak 18.00 7.50 2.50
☐ 406 Mantle 565 Ft. Homer 45.00 20.00 6.75
☐ 407 Chesbro Wins 41 .... 6.00 2.50 .60
☐ 408 Mathewson Fans 267 .. 9.00 4.00 .90
☐ 409 Johnson Shutouts .... 9.00 4.00 .90
☐ 410 Haddix 12 Perfect .... 6.00 2.50 .60
Innings
☐ 411 Tony Taylor .... 3.50 1.50 .35
☐ 412 Larry Sherry .... 4.00 1.75 .40
☐ 413 Eddie Yost .... 3.50 1.50 .35
☐ 414 Dick Donovan .... 3.50 1.50 .35
☐ 415 Hank Aaron 125.00 57.50 18.75
☐ 416 Dick Howser .... 8.00 3.50 .80
☐ 417 Juan Marichal 145.00 65.00 18.00
☐ 418 Ed Bailey .... 4.00 1.75 .40
☐ 419 Tom Borland .... 3.50 1.50 .35
☐ 420 Ernie Broglio .... 4.00 1.75 .40
☐ 421 Ty Cline .... 3.50 1.50 .35
☐ 422 Bud Daley .... 3.50 1.50 .35
☐ 423 Charlie Neal SP .... 9.00 4.00 .90
☐ 424 Turk Lown .... 3.50 1.50 .35
☐ 425 Yogi Berra 75.00 34.00 11.25
☐ 426 Milwaukee Braves .... 9.00 4.00 .90
Team Card
(back numbered 463)
☐ 427 Dick Ellsworth .... 4.00 1.75 .40
☐ 428 Ray Barker SP .... 9.00 4.00 .90
☐ 429 Al Kaline 45.00 20.00 6.75
☐ 430 Bill Mazeroski SP 33.00 15.00 5.00
☐ 431 Chuck Stobbs .... 3.50 1.50 .35
☐ 432 Coot Veal .... 3.50 1.50 .35
☐ 433 Art Mahaffey .... 3.50 1.50 .35
☐ 434 Tom Brewer .... 3.50 1.50 .35
☐ 435 Orlando Cepeda UER . 10.00 4.50 1.25
(San Francis on
card front)
☐ 436 Jim Maloney .... 7.50 3.25 .75
☐ 437A Checklist 6 .... 15.00 1.50 .30
440 Louis Aparicio
☐ 437B Checklist 6 .... 15.00 1.50 .30
440 Luis Aparicio
☐ 438 Curt Flood .... 5.00 2.25 .50
☐ 439 Phil Regan .... 5.00 2.25 .50
☐ 440 Luis Aparicio 13.00 5.75 1.75
☐ 441 Dick Bertell .... 3.50 1.50 .35
☐ 442 Gordon Jones .... 3.50 1.50 .35
☐ 443 Duke Snider 45.00 20.00 6.75
☐ 444 Joe Nuxhall .... 4.00 1.75 .40
☐ 445 Frank Malzone .... 4.00 1.75 .40
☐ 446 Bob Taylor .... 3.50 1.50 .35
☐ 447 Harry Bright .... 4.75 2.00 .45

☐ 448 Del Rice .... 4.75 2.00 .45
☐ 449 Bob Bolin .... 4.75 2.00 .45
☐ 450 Jim Lemon .... 5.50 2.50 .55
☐ 451 Power for Ernie .... 5.50 2.50 .55
Daryl Spencer
Bill White
Ernie Broglio
☐ 452 Bob Allen .... 4.75 2.00 .45
☐ 453 Dick Schofield .... 4.75 2.00 .45
☐ 454 Pumpsie Green .... 4.75 2.00 .45
☐ 455 Early Wynn 13.50 6.00 1.85
☐ 456 Hal Bevan .... 4.75 2.00 .45
☐ 457 Johnny James .... 4.75 2.00 .45
(listed as Angel,
but wearing Yankee
uniform and cap)
☐ 458 Willie Tasby .... 4.75 2.00 .45
☐ 459 Terry Fox .... 4.75 2.00 .45
☐ 460 Gil Hodges 15.00 6.50 2.15
☐ 461 Smoky Burgess .... 5.50 2.50 .55
☐ 462 Lou Klimchock .... 4.75 2.00 .45
☐ 463 Jack Fisher .... 5.50 2.50 .55
(See also 426)
☐ 464 Lee Thomas .... 5.50 2.50 .55
(Pictured with Yankee
cap but listed as
Los Angeles Angel)
☐ 465 Roy McMillan .... 4.75 2.00 .45
☐ 466 Ron Moeller .... 4.75 2.00 .45
☐ 467 Cleveland Indians .... 9.00 4.00 .90
Team Card
☐ 468 John Callison .... 5.50 2.50 .55
☐ 469 Ralph Lumenti .... 4.75 2.00 .45
☐ 470 Roy Sievers .... 5.50 2.50 .55
☐ 471 Phil Rizzuto MVP 16.00 6.75 2.25
☐ 472 Yogi Berra MVP 48.00 22.00 6.00
☐ 473 Bob Shantz MVP .... 5.50 2.50 .55
☐ 474 Al Rosen MVP .... 6.50 2.75 .65
☐ 475 Mickey Mantle MVP 110.00 50.00 16.50
☐ 476 Jackie Jensen MVP ..... 5.50 2.50 .55
☐ 477 Nellie Fox MVP .... 7.50 3.25 .75
☐ 478 Roger Maris MVP 40.00 18.00 6.00
☐ 479 Jim Konstanty MVP ..... 5.50 2.50 .55
☐ 480 Roy Campanella MVP 30.00 13.50 4.50
☐ 481 Hank Sauer MVP .... 5.50 2.50 .55
☐ 482 Willie Mays MVP 42.00 18.00 5.50
☐ 483 Don Newcombe MVP .. 6.50 2.75 .65
☐ 484 Hank Aaron MVP 42.00 18.00 5.50
☐ 485 Ernie Banks MVP 25.00 11.00 3.50
☐ 486 Dick Groat MVP .... 5.50 2.50 .55
☐ 487 Gene Oliver .... 4.75 2.00 .45
☐ 488 Joe McClain .... 4.75 2.00 .45
☐ 489 Walt Dropo .... 4.75 2.00 .45
☐ 490 Jim Bunning .... 9.00 4.00 .90
☐ 491 Philadelphia Phillies .... 9.00 4.00 .90
Team Card
☐ 492 Ron Fairly .... 5.50 2.50 .55
☐ 493 Don Zimmer UER .... 6.50 2.75 .65
(Brooklyn A.L.)
☐ 494 Tom Cheney .... 4.75 2.00 .45
☐ 495 Elston Howard .... 8.50 3.75 .85
☐ 496 Ken MacKenzie .... 4.75 2.00 .45
☐ 497 Willie Jones .... 4.75 2.00 .45
☐ 498 Ray Herbert .... 4.75 2.00 .45
☐ 499 Chuck Schilling .... 4.75 2.00 .45
☐ 500 Harvey Kuenn .... 6.50 2.75 .65
☐ 501 John DeMerit .... 4.75 2.00 .45
☐ 502 Clarence Coleman .... 6.50 2.75 .65
☐ 503 Tito Francona .... 4.75 2.00 .45
☐ 504 Billy Consolo .... 4.75 2.00 .45
☐ 505 Red Schoendienst 15.00 6.50 2.15
☐ 506 Willie Davis 15.00 6.50 2.15
☐ 507 Pete Burnside .... 4.75 2.00 .45
☐ 508 Rocky Bridges .... 4.75 2.00 .45
☐ 509 Camilo Carreon .... 4.75 2.00 .45
☐ 510 Art Ditmar .... 4.75 2.00 .45
☐ 511 Joe M. Morgan .... 5.50 2.50 .55
☐ 512 Bob Will .... 4.75 2.00 .45
☐ 513 Jim Brosnan .... 5.50 2.50 .55
☐ 514 Jake Wood .... 4.75 2.00 .45
☐ 515 Jackie Brandt .... 4.75 2.00 .45
☐ 516 Checklist 7 .... 15.00 1.50 .30
☐ 517 Willie McCovey 55.00 25.00 8.25
☐ 518 Andy Carey .... 5.50 2.50 .55
☐ 519 Jim Pagliaroni .... 4.75 2.00 .45
☐ 520 Joe Cunningham .... 5.50 2.50 .55
☐ 521 Brother Battery .... 5.50 2.50 .55
Norm Sherry
Larry Sherry
☐ 522 Dick Farrell .... 5.50 2.50 .55
☐ 523 Joe Gibbon 30.00 13.50 4.50
☐ 524 Johnny Logan 33.00 15.00 5.00
☐ 525 Ron Perranoski 36.00 16.25 5.50
☐ 526 R.C. Stevens 30.00 13.50 4.50
☐ 527 Gene Leek 30.00 13.50 4.50
☐ 528 Pedro Ramos 30.00 13.50 4.50
☐ 529 Bob Roselli 30.00 13.50 4.50
☐ 530 Bob Malkmus 30.00 13.50 4.50
☐ 531 Jim Coates 30.00 13.50 4.50
☐ 532 Bob Hale 30.00 13.50 4.50
☐ 533 Jack Curtis 30.00 13.50 4.50
☐ 534 Eddie Kasko 30.00 13.50 4.50
☐ 535 Larry Jackson 30.00 13.50 4.50
☐ 536 Bill Tuttle 30.00 13.50 4.50
☐ 537 Bobby Locke 30.00 13.50 4.50
☐ 538 Chuck Hiller 30.00 13.50 4.50
☐ 539 Johnny Klippstein 30.00 13.50 4.50
☐ 540 Jackie Jensen 36.00 16.25 5.50
☐ 541 Roland Sheldon 30.00 13.50 4.50
☐ 542 Minnesota Twins 65.00 29.00 9.75
Team Card
☐ 543 Roger Craig 36.00 16.25 5.50
☐ 544 George Thomas 30.00 13.50 4.50
☐ 545 Hoyt Wilhelm 60.00 27.00 9.00
☐ 546 Marty Kutyna 30.00 13.50 4.50
☐ 547 Leon Wagner 30.00 13.50 4.50

☐ 548	Ted Wills	30.00	13.50	4.50
☐ 549	Hal R. Smith	30.00	13.50	4.50
☐ 550	Frank Baumann	30.00	13.50	4.50
☐ 551	George Altman	30.00	13.50	4.50
☐ 552	Jim Archer	30.00	13.50	4.50
☐ 553	Bill Fischer	30.00	13.50	4.50
☐ 554	Pittsburgh Pirates Team Card	65.00	29.00	9.75
☐ 555	Sam Jones	30.00	13.50	4.50
☐ 556	Ken R. Hunt	30.00	13.50	4.50
☐ 557	Jose Valdivielso	30.00	13.50	4.50
☐ 558	Don Ferrarese	30.00	13.50	4.50
☐ 559	Jim Gentile	36.00	16.25	5.50
☐ 560	Barry Latman	30.00	13.50	4.50
☐ 561	Charley James	30.00	13.50	4.50
☐ 562	Bill Monbouquette	33.00	15.00	5.00
☐ 563	Bob Cerv	36.00	16.25	5.50
☐ 564	Don Cardwell	30.00	13.50	4.50
☐ 565	Felipe Alou	33.00	15.00	5.00
☐ 566	Paul Richards MG AS	33.00	15.00	5.00
☐ 567	Danny Murtaugh MG AS	33.00	15.00	5.00
☐ 568	Bill Skowron AS	36.00	16.25	5.50
☐ 569	Frank Herrera AS	33.00	15.00	5.00
☐ 570	Nellie Fox AS	42.00	18.00	5.50
☐ 571	Bill Mazeroski AS	36.00	16.25	5.50
☐ 572	Brooks Robinson AS	95.00	42.00	11.00
☐ 573	Ken Boyer AS	36.00	16.25	5.50
☐ 574	Luis Aparicio AS	48.00	22.00	6.00
☐ 575	Ernie Banks AS	95.00	42.00	11.00
☐ 576	Roger Maris AS	135.00	60.00	20.00
☐ 577	Hank Aaron AS	160.00	72.00	24.00
☐ 578	Mickey Mantle AS	350.00	160.00	52.50
☐ 579	Willie Mays AS	160.00	72.00	24.00
☐ 580	Al Kaline AS	95.00	42.00	11.00
☐ 581	Frank Robinson AS	95.00	42.00	11.00
☐ 582	Earl Battey AS	33.00	15.00	5.00
☐ 583	Del Crandall AS	33.00	15.00	5.00
☐ 584	Jim Perry AS	33.00	15.00	5.00
☐ 585	Bob Friend AS	33.00	15.00	5.00
☐ 586	Whitey Ford AS	95.00	42.00	11.00
☐ 587	Does not exist	00.00	00.00	0.00
☐ 588	Does not exist	00.00	00.00	0.00
☐ 589	Warren Spahn AS	140.00	50.00	10.00

1962 Topps

The cards in this 598-card set measure 2 1/2" by 3 1/2". The 1962 Topps set contains a mini-series spotlighting Babe Ruth (135-144). Other subsets in the set include League Leaders (51-60), World Series cards (232-237), In Action cards (311-319), NL All Stars (390-399), AL All Stars (466-475), and Rookie Prospects (591-598). The All-Star selections were again provided by Sport Magazine, as in 1958 and 1960. The second series had two distinct printings which are distinguishable by numerous color and pose variations. Those cards with a distinctive "green tint" are valued at a slight premuim as they are basically the result of a flawed printing process occurring early in the second series run. Card number 139 exists as A: Babe Ruth Special card, B: Hal Reniff with arms over head, or C: Hal Reniff in the same pose as card number 159. In addition, two poses exist for players depicted on card numbers 129, 132, 134, 147, 174, 176, and 190. The high number series, 523 to 598, is somewhat more difficult to obtain than other cards in the set. Within the last series (523-598) there are 43 cards which were printed in lesser quantities; these are marked SP in the checklist below. The set price listed does not include the pose variations (see checklist below for individual values). The key rookies in this set are Lou Brock, Tim McCarver, Gaylord Perry, and Bob Uecker.

	NRMT	VG-E	GOOD
COMPLETE SET	5250.00	2000.00	500.00
COMMON PLAYER (1-109)	2.00	.80	.20
COMMON PLAYER (110-196)	2.25	.90	.22
COMMON PLAYER (197-283)	2.50	1.00	.25
COMMON PLAYER (284-370)	3.00	1.25	.30
COMMON PLAYER (371-446)	4.50	2.00	.45
COMMON PLAYER (447-522)	6.00	2.50	.60
COMMON PLAYER (523-590)	13.00	5.75	1.75
COMMON SP (523-590)	22.00	9.50	3.15
COMMON PLAYER (591-598)	30.00	13.50	4.50

☐ 1	Roger Maris	200.00	45.00	9.00
☐ 2	Jim Brosnan	2.50	1.00	.25
☐ 3	Pete Runnels	2.50	1.00	.25

☐ 4 John DeMerit .... 2.00 .80 .20
☐ 5 Sandy Koufax UER 110.00 50.00 16.50
(struck ou 18)
☐ 6 Marv Breeding .... 2.00 .80 .20
☐ 7 Frank Thomas .... 2.50 1.00 .25
☐ 8 Ray Herbert .... 2.00 .80 .20
☐ 9 Jim Davenport .... 2.00 .80 .20
☐ 10 Bob Clemente 100.00 45.00 15.00
☐ 11 Tom Morgan .... 2.00 .80 .20
☐ 12 Harry Craft MG .... 2.00 .80 .20
☐ 13 Dick Howser .... 2.50 1.00 .25
☐ 14 Bill White .... 4.00 1.75 .40
☐ 15 Dick Donovan .... 2.00 .80 .20
☐ 16 Darrell Johnson .... 2.00 .80 .20
☐ 17 John Callison .... 2.50 1.00 .25
☐ 18 Managers' Dream 100.00 45.00 15.00
Mickey Mantle
Willie Mays
☐ 19 Ray Washburn .... 2.00 .80 .20
☐ 20 Rocky Colavito .... 7.50 3.25 .75
☐ 21 Jim Kaat .... 5.50 2.50 .55
☐ 22A Checklist 1 ERR .... 9.00 .90 .20
(121-176 on back)
☐ 22B Checklist 1 COR .... 9.00 .90 .20
☐ 23 Norm Larker .... 2.50 1.00 .25
☐ 24 Tigers Team .... 5.00 2.25 .50
☐ 25 Ernie Banks 38.00 17.00 5.00
☐ 26 Chris Cannizzaro .... 2.00 .80 .20
☐ 27 Chuck Cottier .... 2.00 .80 .20
☐ 28 Minnie Minoso .... 4.00 1.75 .40
☐ 29 Casey Stengel MG 17.00 7.25 2.50
☐ 30 Eddie Mathews 20.00 8.50 2.75
☐ 31 Tom Tresh 12.00 5.25 1.50
☐ 32 John Roseboro .... 2.50 1.00 .25
☐ 33 Don Larsen .... 3.00 1.25 .30
☐ 34 Johnny Temple .... 2.00 .80 .20
☐ 35 Don Schwall .... 2.00 .80 .20
☐ 36 Don Leppert .... 2.00 .80 .20
☐ 37 Tribe Hill Trio .... 2.50 1.00 .25
Barry Latman
Dick Stigman
Jim Perry
☐ 38 Gene Stephens .... 2.00 .80 .20
☐ 39 Joe Koppe .... 2.00 .80 .20
☐ 40 Orlando Cepeda .... 8.00 3.50 .80
☐ 41 Cliff Cook .... 2.00 .80 .20
☐ 42 Jim King .... 2.00 .80 .20
☐ 43 Los Angeles Dodgers .... 6.00 2.50 .60
Team Card
☐ 44 Don Taussig .... 2.00 .80 .20
☐ 45 Brooks Robinson 33.00 15.00 5.00
☐ 46 Jack Baldschun .... 2.00 .80 .20
☐ 47 Bob Will .... 2.00 .80 .20
☐ 48 Ralph Terry .... 2.50 1.00 .25
☐ 49 Hal Jones .... 2.00 .80 .20
☐ 50 Stan Musial 100.00 45.00 15.00
☐ 51 AL Batting Leaders .... 4.00 1.75 .40
Norm Cash
Jim Piersall
Al Kaline
Elston Howard
☐ 52 NL Batting Leaders .... 5.50 2.50 .55
Bob Clemente
Vada Pinson
Ken Boyer
Wally Moon
☐ 53 AL Home Run Leaders 35.00 15.75 5.25
Roger Maris
Mickey Mantle
Jim Gentile
Harmon Killebrew
☐ 54 NL Home Run Leaders .. 5.50 2.50 .55
Orlando Cepeda
Willie Mays
Frank Robinson
☐ 55 AL ERA Leaders .... 3.50 1.50 .35
Dick Donovan
Bill Stafford
Don Mossi
Milt Pappas
☐ 56 NL ERA Leaders .... 4.00 1.75 .40
Warren Spahn
Jim O'Toole
Curt Simmons
Mike McCormick
☐ 57 AL Wins Leaders .... 4.00 1.75 .40
Whitey Ford
Frank Lary
Steve Barber
Jim Bunning
☐ 58 NL Wins Leaders .... 4.00 1.75 .40
Warren Spahn
Joe Jay
Jim O'Toole
☐ 59 AL Strikeout Leaders ..... 3.50 1.50 .35
Camilo Pascual
Whitey Ford
Jim Bunning
Juan Pizzaro
☐ 60 NL Strikeout Leaders .... 6.50 2.75 .65
Sandy Koufax
Stan Williams
Don Drysdale
Jim O'Toole
☐ 61 Cardinals Team .... 5.00 2.25 .50
☐ 62 Steve Boros .... 2.00 .80 .20
☐ 63 Tony Cloninger .... 3.00 1.25 .30
☐ 64 Russ Snyder .... 2.00 .80 .20
☐ 65 Bobby Richardson .... 5.50 2.50 .55
☐ 66 Cuno Barragan .... 2.00 .80 .20
☐ 67 Harvey Haddix .... 2.50 1.00 .25
☐ 68 Ken Hunt .... 2.00 .80 .20
☐ 69 Phil Ortega .... 2.00 .80 .20
☐ 70 Harmon Killebrew 20.00 8.50 2.75
☐ 71 Dick LeMay .... 2.00 .80 .20
☐ 72 Bob's Pupils .... 2.00 .80 .20

Steve Boros
Bob Scheffing
Jake Wood

☐ 73 Nellie Fox .... 6.00 2.50 .60
☐ 74 Bob Lillis .... 2.00 .80 .20
☐ 75 Milt Pappas .... 2.50 1.00 .25
☐ 76 Howie Bedell .... 2.00 .80 .20
☐ 77 Tony Taylor .... 2.00 .80 .20
☐ 78 Gene Green .... 2.00 .80 .20
☐ 79 Ed Hobaugh .... 2.00 .80 .20
☐ 80 Vada Pinson .... 3.50 1.50 .35
☐ 81 Jim Pagliaroni .... 2.00 .80 .20
☐ 82 Deron Johnson .... 2.00 .80 .20
☐ 83 Larry Jackson .... 2.00 .80 .20
☐ 84 Lenny Green .... 2.00 .80 .20
☐ 85 Gil Hodges 14.00 6.25 2.00
☐ 86 Donn Clendenon .... 3.00 1.25 .30
☐ 87 Mike Roarke .... 2.00 .80 .20
☐ 88 Ralph Houk MG .... 3.00 1.25 .30
(Berra in background)
☐ 89 Barney Schultz .... 2.00 .80 .20
☐ 90 Jim Piersall .... 3.00 1.25 .30
☐ 91 J.C. Martin .... 2.00 .80 .20
☐ 92 Sam Jones .... 2.00 .80 .20
☐ 93 John Blanchard .... 2.50 1.00 .25
☐ 94 Jay Hook .... 2.00 .80 .20
☐ 95 Don Hoak .... 2.50 1.00 .25
☐ 96 Eli Grba .... 2.00 .80 .20
☐ 97 Tito Francona .... 2.00 .80 .20
☐ 98 Checklist 2 .... 9.00 .90 .20
☐ 99 John (Boog) Powell 16.50 7.00 2.35
☐ 100 Warren Spahn 30.00 13.50 4.50
☐ 101 Carroll Hardy .... 2.00 .80 .20
☐ 102 Al Schroll .... 2.00 .80 .20
☐ 103 Don Blasingame .... 2.00 .80 .20
☐ 104 Ted Savage .... 2.00 .80 .20
☐ 105 Don Mossi .... 2.50 1.00 .25
☐ 106 Carl Sawatski .... 2.00 .80 .20
☐ 107 Mike McCormick .... 2.50 1.00 .25
☐ 108 Willie Davis .... 3.00 1.25 .30
☐ 109 Bob Shaw .... 2.00 .80 .20
☐ 110 Bill Skowron .... 4.00 1.75 .40
☐ 111 Dallas Green .... 3.50 1.50 .35
☐ 112 Hank Foiles .... 2.25 .90 .22
☐ 113 Chicago White Sox .... 5.00 2.25 .50
Team Card
☐ 114 Howie Koplitz .... 2.25 .90 .22
☐ 115 Bob Skinner .... 3.00 1.25 .30
☐ 116 Herb Score .... 3.50 1.50 .35
☐ 117 Gary Geiger .... 2.25 .90 .22
☐ 118 Julian Javier .... 2.25 .90 .22
☐ 119 Danny Murphy .... 2.25 .90 .22
☐ 120 Bob Purkey .... 2.25 .90 .22
☐ 121 Billy Hitchcock MG .... 2.25 .90 .22
☐ 122 Norm Bass .... 2.25 .90 .22
☐ 123 Mike de la Hoz .... 2.25 .90 .22
☐ 124 Bill Pleis .... 2.25 .90 .22
☐ 125 Gene Woodling .... 3.00 1.25 .30
☐ 126 Al Cicotte .... 2.25 .90 .22
☐ 127 Pride of A's .... 3.00 1.25 .30
Norm Siebern
Hank Bauer
Jerry Lumpe
☐ 128 Art Fowler .... 2.25 .90 .22
☐ 129A Lee Walls .... 2.25 .90 .22
(facing right)
☐ 129B Lee Walls 22.00 9.50 3.15
(facing left)
☐ 130 Frank Bolling .... 2.25 .90 .22
☐ 131 Pete Richert .... 2.25 .90 .22
☐ 132A Angels Team .... 6.00 2.50 .60
(without photo)
☐ 132B Angels Team 22.00 9.50 3.15
(with photo)
☐ 133 Felipe Alou .... 3.50 1.50 .35
☐ 134A Billy Hoeft .... 2.25 .90 .22
(facing right)
☐ 134B Billy Hoeft 22.00 9.50 3.15
(facing straight)
☐ 135 Babe Ruth Special 1 .. 14.00 6.25 2.00
Babe as a Boy
☐ 136 Babe Ruth Special 2 .. 14.00 6.25 2.00
Babe Joins Yanks
☐ 137 Babe Ruth Special 3 .. 14.00 6.25 2.00
Babe with Huggins
☐ 138 Babe Ruth Special 4 .. 14.00 6.25 2.00
Famous Slugger
☐ 139A Babe Ruth Special 5 16.00 6.75 2.25
Babe Hits 60
☐ 139B Hal Reniff PORT 12.50 5.50 1.65
☐ 139C Hal Reniff 55.00 25.00 8.25
(pitching)
☐ 140 Babe Ruth Special 6 .. 16.00 6.75 2.25
Gehrig and Ruth
☐ 141 Babe Ruth Special 7 .. 14.00 6.25 2.00
Twilight Years
☐ 142 Babe Ruth Special 8 .. 14.00 6.25 2.00
Coaching Dodgers
☐ 143 Babe Ruth Special 9 .. 14.00 6.25 2.00
Greatest Sports Hero
☐ 144 Babe Ruth Special 10 14.00 6.25 2.00
Farewell Speech
☐ 145 Barry Latman .... 2.25 .90 .22
☐ 146 Don Demeter .... 2.25 .90 .22
☐ 147A Bill Kunkel PORT .... 2.25 .90 .22
☐ 147B Bill Kunkel 22.00 9.50 3.15
(pitching pose)
☐ 148 Wally Post .... 2.25 .90 .22
☐ 149 Bob Duliba .... 2.25 .90 .22
☐ 150 Al Kaline 33.00 15.00 5.00
☐ 151 Johnny Klippstein .... 2.25 .90 .22
☐ 152 Mickey Vernon MG .... 3.00 1.25 .30
☐ 153 Pumpsie Green .... 2.25 .90 .22
☐ 154 Lee Thomas .... 3.00 1.25 .30
☐ 155 Stu Miller .... 2.25 .90 .22
☐ 156 Merritt Ranew .... 2.25 .90 .22

□ 157	Wes Covington	2.25	.90	.22
□ 158	Braves Team	5.00	2.25	.50
□ 159	Hal Reniff	3.00	1.25	.30
□ 160	Dick Stuart	3.00	1.25	.30
□ 161	Frank Baumann	2.25	.90	.22
□ 162	Sammy Drake	2.25	.90	.22
□ 163	Hot Corner Guard Billy Gardner Cletis Boyer	3.00	1.25	.30
□ 164	Hal Naragon	2.25	.90	.22
□ 165	Jackie Brandt	2.25	.90	.22
□ 166	Don Lee	2.25	.90	.22
□ 167	Tim McCarver	32.00	14.25	4.75
□ 168	Leo Posada	2.25	.90	.22
□ 169	Bob Cerv	3.00	1.25	.30
□ 170	Ron Santo	10.00	4.50	1.25
□ 171	Dave Sisler	2.25	.90	.22
□ 172	Fred Hutchinson MG	3.00	1.25	.30
□ 173	Chico Fernandez	2.25	.90	.22
□ 174A	Carl Willey (capless)	2.25	.90	.22
□ 174B	Carl Willey (with cap)	22.00	9.50	3.15
□ 175	Frank Howard	4.00	1.75	.40
□ 176A	Eddie Yost PORT	2.25	.90	.22
□ 176B	Eddie Yost BATTING	22.00	9.50	3.15
□ 177	Bobby Shantz	3.00	1.25	.30
□ 178	Camilo Carreon	2.25	.90	.22
□ 179	Tom Sturdivant	2.25	.90	.22
□ 180	Bob Allison	3.00	1.25	.30
□ 181	Paul Brown	2.25	.90	.22
□ 182	Bob Nieman	2.25	.90	.22
□ 183	Roger Craig	3.50	1.50	.35
□ 184	Haywood Sullivan	2.25	.90	.22
□ 185	Roland Sheldon	2.25	.90	.22
□ 186	Mack Jones	2.25	.90	.22
□ 187	Gene Conley	2.25	.90	.22
□ 188	Chuck Hiller	2.25	.90	.22
□ 189	Dick Hall	2.25	.90	.22
□ 190A	Wally Moon PORT	3.00	1.25	.30
□ 190B	Wally Moon BATTING	22.00	9.50	3.15
□ 191	Jim Brewer	2.25	.90	.22
□ 192A	Checklist 3 (without comma)	9.00	.90	.20
□ 192B	Checklist 3 (comma after Checklist)	12.50	1.25	.25
□ 193	Eddie Kasko	2.25	.90	.22
□ 194	Dean Chance	3.50	1.50	.35
□ 195	Joe Cunningham	3.00	1.25	.30
□ 196	Terry Fox	2.25	.90	.22
□ 197	Daryl Spencer	2.50	1.00	.25
□ 198	Johnny Keane MG	2.25	.90	.22
□ 199	Gaylord Perry	165.00	75.00	22.50
□ 200	Mickey Mantle	425.00	190.00	63.00
□ 201	Ike Delock	2.50	1.00	.25
□ 202	Carl Warwick	2.50	1.00	.25
□ 203	Jack Fisher	2.50	1.00	.25
□ 204	Johnny Weekly	2.50	1.00	.25
□ 205	Gene Freese	2.50	1.00	.25
□ 206	Senators Team	5.00	2.25	.50
□ 207	Pete Burnside	2.50	1.00	.25
□ 208	Billy Martin	6.50	2.75	.65
□ 209	Jim Fregosi	7.00	3.00	.70
□ 210	Roy Face	3.50	1.50	.35
□ 211	Midway Masters Frank Bolling Roy McMillan	3.00	1.25	.30
□ 212	Jim Owens	2.50	1.00	.25
□ 213	Richie Ashburn	9.00	4.00	.90
□ 214	Dom Zanni	2.50	1.00	.25
□ 215	Woody Held	2.50	1.00	.25
□ 216	Ron Kline	2.50	1.00	.25
□ 217	Walt Alston MG	5.00	2.25	.50
□ 218	Joe Torre	21.00	9.00	3.00
□ 219	Al Downing	4.50	2.00	.45
□ 220	Roy Sievers	3.00	1.25	.30
□ 221	Bill Short	2.50	1.00	.25
□ 222	Jerry Zimmerman	2.50	1.00	.25
□ 223	Alex Grammas	2.50	1.00	.25
□ 224	Don Rudolph	2.50	1.00	.25
□ 225	Frank Malzone	3.00	1.25	.30
□ 226	San Francisco Giants Team Card	5.00	2.25	.50
□ 227	Bob Tiefenauer	2.50	1.00	.25
□ 228	Dale Long	3.00	1.25	.30
□ 229	Jesus McFarlane	2.50	1.00	.25
□ 230	Camilo Pascual	3.00	1.25	.30
□ 231	Ernie Bowman	2.50	1.00	.25
□ 232	World Series Game 1 Yanks win opener	5.00	2.25	.50
□ 233	World Series Game 2 Jay ties it up	5.00	2.25	.50
□ 234	World Series Game 3 Maris wins in 9th	12.50	5.50	1.65
□ 235	World Series Game 4 Ford sets new mark	7.00	3.00	.70
□ 236	World Series Game 5 Yanks crush Reds	5.00	2.25	.50
□ 237	World Series Summary Yanks celebrate	5.00	2.25	.50
□ 238	Norm Sherry	2.50	1.00	.25
□ 239	Cecil Butler	2.50	1.00	.25
□ 240	George Altman	2.50	1.00	.25
□ 241	Johnny Kucks	2.50	1.00	.25
□ 242	Mel McGaha MG	2.50	1.00	.25
□ 243	Robin Roberts	11.00	5.00	1.35
□ 244	Don Gile	2.50	1.00	.25
□ 245	Ron Hansen	2.50	1.00	.25
□ 246	Art Ditmar	2.50	1.00	.25
□ 247	Joe Pignatano	2.50	1.00	.25
□ 248	Bob Aspromonte	2.50	1.00	.25
□ 249	Ed Keegan	2.50	1.00	.25
□ 250	Norm Cash	4.50	2.00	.45
□ 251	New York Yankees Team Card	18.00	7.50	2.50

☐ 252 Earl Francis 2.50 1.00 .25
☐ 253 Harry Chiti MG 2.50 1.00 .25
☐ 254 Gordon Windhorn 2.50 1.00 .25
☐ 255 Juan Pizarro 2.50 1.00 .25
☐ 256 Elio Chacon 2.50 1.00 .25
☐ 257 Jack Spring 2.50 1.00 .25
☐ 258 Marty Keough 2.50 1.00 .25
☐ 259 Lou Klimchock 2.50 1.00 .25
☐ 260 Billy Pierce 3.50 1.50 .35
☐ 261 George Alusik 2.50 1.00 .25
☐ 262 Bob Schmidt 2.50 1.00 .25
☐ 263 The Right Pitch 3.00 1.25 .30
Bob Purkey
Jim Turner
Joe Jay
☐ 264 Dick Ellsworth 2.50 1.00 .25
☐ 265 Joe Adcock 3.00 1.25 .30
☐ 266 John Anderson 2.50 1.00 .25
☐ 267 Dan Dobbek 2.50 1.00 .25
☐ 268 Ken McBride 2.50 1.00 .25
☐ 269 Bob Oldis 2.50 1.00 .25
☐ 270 Dick Groat 3.50 1.50 .35
☐ 271 Ray Rippelmeyer 2.50 1.00 .25
☐ 272 Earl Robinson 2.50 1.00 .25
☐ 273 Gary Bell 2.50 1.00 .25
☐ 274 Sammy Taylor 2.50 1.00 .25
☐ 275 Norm Siebern 2.50 1.00 .25
☐ 276 Hal Kolstad 2.50 1.00 .25
☐ 277 Checklist 4 9.00 .90 .20
☐ 278 Ken Johnson 2.50 1.00 .25
☐ 279 Hobie Landrith UER 2.50 1.00 .25
(wrong birthdate)
☐ 280 Johnny Podres 3.50 1.50 .35
☐ 281 Jake Gibbs 3.00 1.25 .30
☐ 282 Dave Hillman 2.50 1.00 .25
☐ 283 Charlie Smith 2.50 1.00 .25
☐ 284 Ruben Amaro 3.00 1.25 .30
☐ 285 Curt Simmons 3.50 1.50 .35
☐ 286 Al Lopez MG 4.50 2.00 .45
☐ 287 George Witt 3.00 1.25 .30
☐ 288 Billy Williams 36.00 16.25 5.50
☐ 289 Mike Krsnich 3.00 1.25 .30
☐ 290 Jim Gentile 4.50 2.00 .45
☐ 291 Hal Stowe 3.00 1.25 .30
☐ 292 Jerry Kindall 3.00 1.25 .30
☐ 293 Bob Miller 3.00 1.25 .30
☐ 294 Phillies Team 6.00 2.50 .60
☐ 295 Vern Law 4.00 1.75 .40
☐ 296 Ken Hamlin 3.00 1.25 .30
☐ 297 Ron Perranoski 3.50 1.50 .35
☐ 298 Bill Tuttle 3.00 1.25 .30
☐ 299 Don Wert 3.00 1.25 .30
☐ 300 Willie Mays 135.00 60.00 20.00
☐ 301 Galen Cisco 3.00 1.25 .30
☐ 302 Johnny Edwards 3.00 1.25 .30
☐ 303 Frank Torre 3.00 1.25 .30
☐ 304 Dick Farrell 3.00 1.25 .30
☐ 305 Jerry Lumpe 3.00 1.25 .30
☐ 306 Redbird Rippers 3.50 1.50 .35
Lindy McDaniel
Larry Jackson
☐ 307 Jim Grant 3.00 1.25 .30
☐ 308 Neil Chrisley 3.00 1.25 .30
☐ 309 Moe Morhardt 3.00 1.25 .30
☐ 310 Whitey Ford 36.00 16.25 5.50
☐ 311 Tony Kubek IA 5.00 2.25 .50
☐ 312 Warren Spahn IA 8.50 3.75 .85
☐ 313 Roger Maris IA 17.00 7.25 2.50
☐ 314 Rocky Colavito IA 5.50 2.50 .55
☐ 315 Whitey Ford IA 9.00 4.00 .90
☐ 316 Harmon Killebrew IA 8.50 3.75 .85
☐ 317 Stan Musial IA 18.00 7.50 2.50
☐ 318 Mickey Mantle IA 48.00 22.00 6.00
☐ 319 Mike McCormick IA 3.50 1.50 .35
☐ 320 Hank Aaron 135.00 60.00 20.00
☐ 321 Lee Stange 3.00 1.25 .30
☐ 322 Alvin Dark MG 3.50 1.50 .35
☐ 323 Don Landrum 3.00 1.25 .30
☐ 324 Joe McClain 3.00 1.25 .30
☐ 325 Luis Aparicio 12.50 5.50 1.65
☐ 326 Tom Parsons 3.00 1.25 .30
☐ 327 Ozzie Virgil 3.00 1.25 .30
☐ 328 Ken Walters 3.00 1.25 .30
☐ 329 Bob Bolin 3.00 1.25 .30
☐ 330 John Romano 3.00 1.25 .30
☐ 331 Moe Drabowsky 3.00 1.25 .30
☐ 332 Don Buddin 3.00 1.25 .30
☐ 333 Frank Cipriani 3.00 1.25 .30
☐ 334 Boston Red Sox 6.00 2.50 .60
Team Card
☐ 335 Bill Bruton 3.00 1.25 .30
☐ 336 Billy Muffett 3.00 1.25 .30
☐ 337 Jim Marshall 3.00 1.25 .30
☐ 338 Billy Gardner 3.00 1.25 .30
☐ 339 Jose Valdivielso 3.00 1.25 .30
☐ 340 Don Drysdale 36.00 16.25 5.50
☐ 341 Mike Hershberger 3.00 1.25 .30
☐ 342 Ed Rakow 3.00 1.25 .30
☐ 343 Albie Pearson 3.00 1.25 .30
☐ 344 Ed Bauta 3.00 1.25 .30
☐ 345 Chuck Schilling 3.00 1.25 .30
☐ 346 Jack Kralick 3.00 1.25 .30
☐ 347 Chuck Hinton 3.00 1.25 .30
☐ 348 Larry Burright 3.00 1.25 .30
☐ 349 Paul Foytack 3.00 1.25 .30
☐ 350 Frank Robinson 45.00 20.00 6.75
☐ 351 Braves' Backstops 5.00 2.25 .50
Joe Torre
Del Crandall
☐ 352 Frank Sullivan 3.00 1.25 .30
☐ 353 Bill Mazeroski 5.00 2.25 .50
☐ 354 Roman Mejias 3.00 1.25 .30
☐ 355 Steve Barber 3.00 1.25 .30
☐ 356 Tom Haller 4.00 1.75 .40
☐ 357 Jerry Walker 3.00 1.25 .30
☐ 358 Tommy Davis 5.00 2.25 .50

	Card			
☐	359 Bobby Locke	3.00	1.25	.30
☐	360 Yogi Berra	65.00	29.00	9.75
☐	361 Bob Hendley	3.00	1.25	.30
☐	362 Ty Cline	3.00	1.25	.30
☐	363 Bob Roselli	3.00	1.25	.30
☐	364 Ken Hunt	3.00	1.25	.30
☐	365 Charlie Neal	3.50	1.50	.35
☐	366 Phil Regan	3.50	1.50	.35
☐	367 Checklist 5	10.00	1.00	.20
☐	368 Bob Tillman	3.00	1.25	.30
☐	369 Ted Bowsfield	3.00	1.25	.30
☐	370 Ken Boyer	6.50	2.75	.65
☐	371 Earl Battey	4.50	2.00	.45
☐	372 Jack Curtis	4.50	2.00	.45
☐	373 Al Heist	4.50	2.00	.45
☐	374 Gene Mauch MG	5.00	2.25	.50
☐	375 Ron Fairly	5.00	2.25	.50
☐	376 Bud Daley	4.50	2.00	.45
☐	377 John Orsino	4.50	2.00	.45
☐	378 Bennie Daniels	4.50	2.00	.45
☐	379 Chuck Essegian	4.50	2.00	.45
☐	380 Lou Burdette	5.50	2.50	.55
☐	381 Chico Cardenas	4.50	2.00	.45
☐	382 Dick Williams	5.00	2.25	.50
☐	383 Ray Sadecki	4.50	2.00	.45
☐	384 K.C. Athletics	9.00	4.00	.90
	Team Card			
☐	385 Early Wynn	15.00	6.50	2.15
☐	386 Don Mincher	5.00	2.25	.50
☐	387 Lou Brock	200.00	90.00	30.00
☐	388 Ryne Duren	5.50	2.50	.55
☐	389 Smoky Burgess	5.00	2.25	.50
☐	390 Orlando Cepeda AS	6.50	2.75	.65
☐	391 Bill Mazeroski AS	6.00	2.50	.60
☐	392 Ken Boyer AS	6.00	2.50	.60
☐	393 Roy McMillan AS	5.00	2.25	.50
☐	394 Hank Aaron AS	33.00	15.00	5.00
☐	395 Willie Mays AS	33.00	15.00	5.00
☐	396 Frank Robinson AS	15.00	6.50	2.15
☐	397 John Roseboro AS	5.00	2.25	.50
☐	398 Don Drysdale AS	10.00	4.50	1.25
☐	399 Warren Spahn AS	10.00	4.50	1.25
☐	400 Elston Howard	9.00	4.00	.90
☐	401 AL/NL Homer Kings	33.00	15.00	5.00
	Roger Maris			
	Orlando Cepeda			
☐	402 Gino Cimoli	4.50	2.00	.45
☐	403 Chet Nichols	4.50	2.00	.45
☐	404 Tim Harkness	4.50	2.00	.45
☐	405 Jim Perry	5.00	2.25	.50
☐	406 Bob Taylor	4.50	2.00	.45
☐	407 Hank Aguirre	4.50	2.00	.45
☐	408 Gus Bell	5.00	2.25	.50
☐	409 Pittsburgh Pirates	9.00	4.00	.90
	Team Card			
☐	410 Al Smith	4.50	2.00	.45
☐	411 Danny O'Connell	4.50	2.00	.45
☐	412 Charlie James	4.50	2.00	.45

	Card			
☐	413 Matty Alou	5.50	2.50	.55
☐	414 Joe Gaines	4.50	2.00	.45
☐	415 Bill Virdon	5.50	2.50	.55
☐	416 Bob Scheffing MG	4.50	2.00	.45
☐	417 Joe Azcue	4.50	2.00	.45
☐	418 Andy Carey	4.50	2.00	.45
☐	419 Bob Bruce	4.50	2.00	.45
☐	420 Gus Triandos	5.00	2.25	.50
☐	421 Ken MacKenzie	4.50	2.00	.45
☐	422 Steve Bilko	4.50	2.00	.45
☐	423 Rival League	6.50	2.75	.65
	Relief Aces:			
	Roy Face			
	Hoyt Wilhelm			
☐	424 Al McBean	5.00	2.25	.50
☐	425 Carl Yastrzemski	240.00	105.00	32.00
☐	426 Bob Farley	4.50	2.00	.45
☐	427 Jake Wood	4.50	2.00	.45
☐	428 Joe Hicks	4.50	2.00	.45
☐	429 Billy O'Dell	4.50	2.00	.45
☐	430 Tony Kubek	9.00	4.00	.90
☐	431 Bob Rodgers	7.00	3.00	.70
☐	432 Jim Pendleton	4.50	2.00	.45
☐	433 Jim Archer	4.50	2.00	.45
☐	434 Clay Dalrymple	4.50	2.00	.45
☐	435 Larry Sherry	5.00	2.25	.50
☐	436 Felix Mantilla	4.50	2.00	.45
☐	437 Ray Moore	4.50	2.00	.45
☐	438 Dick Brown	4.50	2.00	.45
☐	439 Jerry Buchek	4.50	2.00	.45
☐	440 Joey Jay	4.50	2.00	.45
☐	441 Checklist 6	15.00	1.50	.30
☐	442 Wes Stock	4.50	2.00	.45
☐	443 Del Crandall	5.00	2.25	.50
☐	444 Ted Wills	4.50	2.00	.45
☐	445 Vic Power	4.50	2.00	.45
☐	446 Don Elston	4.50	2.00	.45
☐	447 Willie Kirkland	6.00	2.50	.60
☐	448 Joe Gibbon	6.00	2.50	.60
☐	449 Jerry Adair	6.00	2.50	.60
☐	450 Jim O'Toole	6.50	2.75	.65
☐	451 Jose Tartabull	6.50	2.75	.65
☐	452 Earl Averill Jr.	6.00	2.50	.60
☐	453 Cal McLish	6.00	2.50	.60
☐	454 Floyd Robinson	6.00	2.50	.60
☐	455 Luis Arroyo	6.50	2.75	.65
☐	456 Joe Amalfitano	6.00	2.50	.60
☐	457 Lou Clinton	6.00	2.50	.60
☐	458A Bob Buhl	6.00	2.50	.60
	(Braves emblem			
	on cap)			
☐	458B Bob Buhl	65.00	29.00	9.75
	(no emblem on cap)			
☐	459 Ed Bailey	6.50	2.75	.65
☐	460 Jim Bunning	10.00	4.50	1.25
☐	461 Ken Hubbs	18.00	7.50	2.50
☐	462A Willie Tasby	6.00	2.50	.60
	(Senators emblem			

on cap)
☐ 462B Willie Tasby 65.00 29.00 9.75
(no emblem on cap)
☐ 463 Hank Bauer MG .... 7.00 3.00 .70
☐ 464 Al Jackson .... 7.00 3.00 .70
☐ 465 Reds Team 12.00 5.25 1.50
☐ 466 Norm Cash AS .... 7.00 3.00 .70
☐ 467 Chuck Schilling AS ...... 6.50 2.75 .65
☐ 468 Brooks Robinson AS . 16.00 6.75 2.25
☐ 469 Luis Aparicio AS .... 9.00 4.00 .90
☐ 470 Al Kaline AS 16.00 6.75 2.25
☐ 471 Mickey Mantle AS ... 110.00 50.00 16.50
☐ 472 Rocky Colavito AS .... 7.50 3.25 .75
☐ 473 Elston Howard AS .... 7.50 3.25 .75
☐ 474 Frank Lary AS .... 6.50 2.75 .65
☐ 475 Whitey Ford AS 13.00 5.75 1.75
☐ 476 Orioles Team 12.00 5.25 1.50
☐ 477 Andre Rodgers .... 6.00 2.50 .60
☐ 478 Don Zimmer .... 7.00 3.00 .70
(Shown with Mets cap,
but listed as with
Cincinnati)
☐ 479 Joel Horlen .... 7.00 3.00 .70
☐ 480 Harvey Kuenn .... 7.00 3.00 .70
☐ 481 Vic Wertz .... 6.50 2.75 .65
☐ 482 Sam Mele MG .... 6.00 2.50 .60
☐ 483 Don McMahon .... 6.00 2.50 .60
☐ 484 Dick Schofield .... 6.00 2.50 .60
☐ 485 Pedro Ramos .... 6.00 2.50 .60
☐ 486 Jim Gilliam .... 8.00 3.50 .80
☐ 487 Jerry Lynch .... 6.00 2.50 .60
☐ 488 Hal Brown .... 6.00 2.50 .60
☐ 489 Julio Gotay .... 6.00 2.50 .60
☐ 490 Clete Boyer .... 7.00 3.00 .70
☐ 491 Leon Wagner .... 6.00 2.50 .60
☐ 492 Hal W. Smith .... 6.00 2.50 .60
☐ 493 Danny McDevitt .... 6.00 2.50 .60
☐ 494 Sammy White .... 6.00 2.50 .60
☐ 495 Don Cardwell .... 6.00 2.50 .60
☐ 496 Wayne Causey .... 6.00 2.50 .60
☐ 497 Ed Bouchee .... 6.00 2.50 .60
☐ 498 Jim Donohue .... 6.00 2.50 .60
☐ 499 Zoilo Versalles .... 6.00 2.50 .60
☐ 500 Duke Snider 50.00 22.50 7.50
☐ 501 Claude Osteen .... 6.50 2.75 .65
☐ 502 Hector Lopez .... 6.00 2.50 .60
☐ 503 Danny Murtaugh MG ... 6.00 2.50 .60
☐ 504 Eddie Bressoud .... 6.00 2.50 .60
☐ 505 Juan Marichal 38.00 17.00 5.00
☐ 506 Charlie Maxwell .... 6.00 2.50 .60
☐ 507 Ernie Broglio .... 6.00 2.50 .60
☐ 508 Gordy Coleman .... 6.50 2.75 .65
☐ 509 Dave Giusti .... 7.00 3.00 .70
☐ 510 Jim Lemon .... 6.50 2.75 .65
☐ 511 Bubba Phillips .... 6.00 2.50 .60
☐ 512 Mike Fornieles .... 6.00 2.50 .60
☐ 513 Whitey Herzog .... 7.00 3.00 .70
☐ 514 Sherm Lollar .... 6.50 2.75 .65
☐ 515 Stan Williams .... 6.00 2.50 .60
☐ 516 Checklist 7 .... 15.00 1.50 .30
☐ 517 Dave Wickersham .... 6.00 2.50 .60
☐ 518 Lee Maye .... 6.00 2.50 .60
☐ 519 Bob Johnson .... 6.00 2.50 .60
☐ 520 Bob Friend .... 6.50 2.75 .65
☐ 521 Jacke Davis UER .... 6.00 2.50 .60
(listed as OF on
front and P on back)
☐ 522 Lindy McDaniel .... 6.50 2.75 .65
☐ 523 Russ Nixon SP 22.00 9.50 3.15
☐ 524 Howie Nunn SP 22.00 9.50 3.15
☐ 525 George Thomas 13.00 5.75 1.75
☐ 526 Hal Woodeshick SP ... 22.00 9.50 3.15
☐ 527 Dick McAuliffe 18.00 7.50 2.50
☐ 528 Turk Lown 13.00 5.75 1.75
☐ 529 John Schaive SP 22.00 9.50 3.15
☐ 530 Bob Gibson SP 165.00 70.00 20.00
☐ 531 Bobby G. Smith 13.00 5.75 1.75
☐ 532 Dick Stigman 13.00 5.75 1.75
☐ 533 Charley Lau SP 22.00 9.50 3.15
☐ 534 Tony Gonzalez SP 22.00 9.50 3.15
☐ 535 Ed Roebuck 13.00 5.75 1.75
☐ 536 Dick Gernert 13.00 5.75 1.75
☐ 537 Cleveland Indians 30.00 13.50 4.50
Team Card
☐ 538 Jack Sanford 15.00 6.50 2.15
☐ 539 Billy Moran 13.00 5.75 1.75
☐ 540 Jim Landis SP 22.00 9.50 3.15
☐ 541 Don Nottebart SP 22.00 9.50 3.15
☐ 542 Dave Philley 13.00 5.75 1.75
☐ 543 Bob Allen SP 22.00 9.50 3.15
☐ 544 Willie McCovey SP .. 165.00 75.00 22.50
☐ 545 Hoyt Wilhelm SP 55.00 25.00 8.25
☐ 546 Moe Thacker SP 22.00 9.50 3.15
☐ 547 Don Ferrarese 13.00 5.75 1.75
☐ 548 Bobby Del Greco 13.00 5.75 1.75
☐ 549 Bill Rigney MG SP 22.00 9.50 3.15
☐ 550 Art Mahaffey SP 22.00 9.50 3.15
☐ 551 Harry Bright 13.00 5.75 1.75
☐ 552 Chicago Cubs SP 45.00 20.00 6.75
Team Card
☐ 553 Jim Coates 13.00 5.75 1.75
☐ 554 Bubba Morton SP 22.00 9.50 3.15
☐ 555 John Buzhardt SP 22.00 9.50 3.15
☐ 556 Al Spangler 13.00 5.75 1.75
☐ 557 Bob Anderson SP 22.00 9.50 3.15
☐ 558 John Goryl 13.00 5.75 1.75
☐ 559 Mike Higgins MG 13.00 5.75 1.75
☐ 560 Chuck Estrada SP 22.00 9.50 3.15
☐ 561 Gene Oliver SP 22.00 9.50 3.15
☐ 562 Bill Henry 13.00 5.75 1.75
☐ 563 Ken Aspromonte 13.00 5.75 1.75
☐ 564 Bob Grim 13.00 5.75 1.75
☐ 565 Jose Pagan 13.00 5.75 1.75
☐ 566 Marty Kutyna SP 22.00 9.50 3.15
☐ 567 Tracy Stallard SP 22.00 9.50 3.15
☐ 568 Jim Golden 13.00 5.75 1.75

☐ 569 Ed Sadowski SP	22.00	9.50	3.15
☐ 570 Bill Stafford SP	22.00	9.50	3.15
☐ 571 Billy Klaus SP	22.00	9.50	3.15
☐ 572 Bob G. Miller SP	28.00	12.50	4.00
☐ 573 Johnny Logan	15.00	6.50	2.15
☐ 574 Dean Stone	13.00	5.75	1.75
☐ 575 Red Schoendienst SP	50.00	22.50	7.50
☐ 576 Russ Kemmerer SP	22.00	9.50	3.15
☐ 577 Dave Nicholson SP	22.00	9.50	3.15
☐ 578 Jim Duffalo	13.00	5.75	1.75
☐ 579 Jim Schaffer SP	22.00	9.50	3.15
☐ 580 Bill Monbouquette	13.00	5.75	1.75
☐ 581 Mel Roach	13.00	5.75	1.75
☐ 582 Ron Piche	13.00	5.75	1.75
☐ 583 Larry Osborne	13.00	5.75	1.75
☐ 584 Minnesota Twins SP	42.00	18.00	5.50
Team Card			
☐ 585 Glen Hobbie SP	22.00	9.50	3.15
☐ 586 Sammy Esposito SP	22.00	9.50	3.15
☐ 587 Frank Funk SP	20.00	8.50	2.75
☐ 588 Birdie Tebbetts MG	13.00	5.75	1.75
☐ 589 Bob Turley	16.00	6.75	2.25
☐ 590 Curt Flood	20.00	8.50	2.75
☐ 591 Rookie Pitchers SP	55.00	25.00	8.25
Sam McDowell			
Ron Taylor			
Ron Nischwitz			
Art Quirk			
Dick Radatz			
☐ 592 Rookie Pitchers SP	65.00	29.00	9.75
Dan Pfister			
Bo Belinsky			
Dave Stenhouse			
Jim Bouton			
Joe Bonikowski			
☐ 593 Rookie Pitchers SP	35.00	15.75	5.25
Jack Lamabe			
Craig Anderson			
Jack Hamilton			
Bob Moorhead			
Bob Veale			
☐ 594 Rookie Catchers SP	120.00	55.00	18.00
Doc Edwards			
Ken Retzer			
Bob Uecker			
Doug Camilli			
Don Pavletich			
☐ 595 Rookie Infielders SP	30.00	13.50	4.50
Bob Sadowski			
Felix Torres			
Marlan Coughtry			
Ed Charles			
☐ 596 Rookie Infielders SP	65.00	29.00	9.75
Bernie Allen			
Joe Pepitone			
Phil Linz			
Rich Rollins			
☐ 597 Rookie Infielders SP	30.00	13.50	4.50
Jim McKnight			
Rod Kanehl			
Amado Samuel			
Denis Menke			
☐ 598 Rookie Outfielders SP	70.00	20.00	4.00
Al Luplow			
Manny Jimenez			
Howie Goss			
Jim Hickman			
Ed Olivares			

1963 Topps

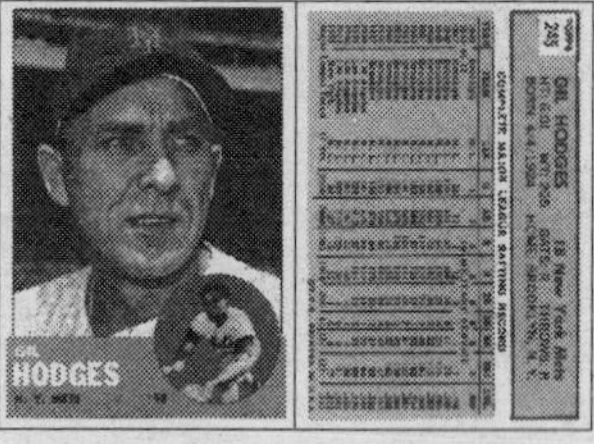

The cards in this 576-card set measure 2 1/2" by 3 1/2". The sharp color photographs of the 1963 set are a vivid contrast to the drab pictures of 1962. In addition to the "League Leaders" series (1-10) and World Series cards (142-148), the seventh and last series of cards (523-576) contains seven rookie cards (each depicting four players). There were some three-card advertising panels produced by Topps; the players included are from the first series; one panel shows Hoyt Wilhelm, Don Lock, and Bob Duliba on the front with a Stan Musial ad/endorsement on one of the backs. This set has gained special prominence in recent years since it contains the rookie card of Pete Rose (537). Other key rookies in this set are Tony Oliva, Willie Stargell, and Rusty Staub.

	NRMT	VG-E	GOOD
COMPLETE SET (576)	5250.00	2250.00	550.00
COMMON PLAYER (1-109)	2.00	.80	.20
COMMON PLAYER (110-196)	2.25	.90	.22
COMMON PLAYER (197-283)	2.75	1.10	.27
COMMON PLAYER (284-446)	3.75	1.60	.37

COMMON PLAYER (447-522) 13.00 5.75 1.75
COMMON PLAYER (523-576) . 9.00 4.00 .90

☐ 1 NL Batting Leaders 33.00 5.00 1.00
Tommy Davis
Frank Robinson
Stan Musial
Hank Aaron
Bill White
☐ 2 AL Batting Leaders 13.50 6.00 1.85
Pete Runnels
Mickey Mantle
Floyd Robinson
Norm Siebern
Chuck Hinton
☐ 3 NL Home Run Leaders .. 13.50 6.00 1.85
Willie Mays
Hank Aaron
Frank Robinson
Orlando Cepeda
Ernie Banks
☐ 4 AL Home Run Leaders .... 4.50 2.00 .45
Harmon Killebrew
Norm Cash
Rocky Colavito
Roger Maris
Jim Gentile
Leon Wagner
☐ 5 NL ERA Leaders .... 6.50 2.75 .65
Sandy Koufax
Bob Shaw
Bob Purkey
Bob Gibson
Don Drysdale
☐ 6 AL ERA Leaders .... 3.50 1.50 .35
Hank Aguirre
Robin Roberts
Whitey Ford
Eddie Fisher
Dean Chance
☐ 7 NL Pitching Leaders .... 3.50 1.50 .35
Don Drysdale
Jack Sanford
Bob Purkey
Billy O'Dell
Art Mahaffey
Joe Jay
☐ 8 AL Pitching Leaders .... 3.00 1.25 .30
Ralph Terry
Dick Donovan
Ray Herbert
Jim Bunning
Camilo Pascual
☐ 9 NL Strikeout Leaders ...... 6.50 2.75 .65
Don Drysdale
Sandy Koufax
Bob Gibson
Billy O'Dell
Dick Farrell
☐ 10 AL Strikeout Leaders ..... 3.00 1.25 .30
Camilo Pascual
Jim Bunning
Ralph Terry
Juan Pizarro
Jim Kaat
☐ 11 Lee Walls .... 2.00 .80 .20
☐ 12 Steve Barber .... 2.00 .80 .20
☐ 13 Philadelphia Phillies ...... 3.50 1.50 .35
Team Card
☐ 14 Pedro Ramos .... 2.00 .80 .20
☐ 15 Ken Hubbs .... 3.50 1.50 .35
☐ 16 Al Smith .... 2.00 .80 .20
☐ 17 Ryne Duren .... 2.50 1.00 .25
☐ 18 Buc Blasters 10.00 4.50 1.25
Smoky Burgess
Dick Stuart
Bob Clemente
Bob Skinner
☐ 19 Pete Burnside .... 2.00 .80 .20
☐ 20 Tony Kubek .... 4.00 1.75 .40
☐ 21 Marty Keough .... 2.00 .80 .20
☐ 22 Curt Simmons .... 2.50 1.00 .25
☐ 23 Ed Lopat MG .... 2.50 1.00 .25
☐ 24 Bob Bruce .... 2.00 .80 .20
☐ 25 Al Kaline 30.00 13.50 4.50
☐ 26 Ray Moore .... 2.00 .80 .20
☐ 27 Choo Choo Coleman ..... 2.00 .80 .20
☐ 28 Mike Fornieles .... 2.00 .80 .20
☐ 29A 1962 Rookie Stars ...... 6.00 2.50 .60
Sammy Ellis
Ray Culp
John Boozer
Jesse Gonder
☐ 29B 1963 Rookie Stars ...... 2.50 1.00 .25
Sammy Ellis
Ray Culp
John Boozer
Jesse Gonder
☐ 30 Harvey Kuenn .... 3.00 1.25 .30
☐ 31 Cal Koonce .... 2.00 .80 .20
☐ 32 Tony Gonzalez .... 2.00 .80 .20
☐ 33 Bo Belinsky .... 2.50 1.00 .25
☐ 34 Dick Schofield .... 2.00 .80 .20
☐ 35 John Buzhardt .... 2.00 .80 .20
☐ 36 Jerry Kindall .... 2.00 .80 .20
☐ 37 Jerry Lynch .... 2.00 .80 .20
☐ 38 Bud Daley .... 2.00 .80 .20
☐ 39 Angels Team .... 3.50 1.50 .35
☐ 40 Vic Power .... 2.00 .80 .20
☐ 41 Charley Lau .... 2.50 1.00 .25
☐ 42 Stan Williams .... 2.00 .80 .20
(listed as Yankee on
card but LA cap)
☐ 43 Veteran Masters .... 4.00 1.75 .40
Casey Stengel
Gene Woodling

☐ 44 Terry Fox	2.00	.80	.20
☐ 45 Bob Aspromonte	2.00	.80	.20
☐ 46 Tommy Aaron	2.50	1.00	.25
☐ 47 Don Lock	2.00	.80	.20
☐ 48 Birdie Tebbetts MG	2.00	.80	.20
☐ 49 Dal Maxvill	2.50	1.00	.25
☐ 50 Billy Pierce	2.50	1.00	.25
☐ 51 George Alusik	2.00	.80	.20
☐ 52 Chuck Schilling	2.00	.80	.20
☐ 53 Joe Moeller	2.00	.80	.20
☐ 54A 1962 Rookie Stars Nelson Mathews Harry Fanok Jack Cullen Dave DeBusschere	15.00	6.50	2.15
☐ 54B 1963 Rookie Stars Nelson Mathews Harry Fanok Jack Cullen Dave DeBusschere	5.50	2.50	.55
☐ 55 Bill Virdon	3.00	1.25	.30
☐ 56 Dennis Bennett	2.00	.80	.20
☐ 57 Billy Moran	2.00	.80	.20
☐ 58 Bob Will	2.00	.80	.20
☐ 59 Craig Anderson	2.00	.80	.20
☐ 60 Elston Howard	6.00	2.50	.60
☐ 61 Ernie Bowman	2.00	.80	.20
☐ 62 Bob Hendley	2.00	.80	.20
☐ 63 Reds Team	3.50	1.50	.35
☐ 64 Dick McAuliffe	2.50	1.00	.25
☐ 65 Jackie Brandt	2.00	.80	.20
☐ 66 Mike Joyce	2.00	.80	.20
☐ 67 Ed Charles	2.00	.80	.20
☐ 68 Friendly Foes Duke Snider Gil Hodges	10.00	4.50	1.25
☐ 69 Bud Zipfel	2.00	.80	.20
☐ 70 Jim O'Toole	2.00	.80	.20
☐ 71 Bobby Wine	2.00	.80	.20
☐ 72 Johnny Romano	2.00	.80	.20
☐ 73 Bobby Bragan MG	2.00	.80	.20
☐ 74 Denny Lemaster	2.00	.80	.20
☐ 75 Bob Allison	2.50	1.00	.25
☐ 76 Earl Wilson	2.00	.80	.20
☐ 77 Al Spangler	2.00	.80	.20
☐ 78 Marv Throneberry	2.50	1.00	.25
☐ 79 Checklist 1	9.00	.90	.20
☐ 80 Jim Gilliam	3.50	1.50	.35
☐ 81 Jim Schaffer	2.00	.80	.20
☐ 82 Ed Rakow	2.00	.80	.20
☐ 83 Charley James	2.00	.80	.20
☐ 84 Ron Kline	2.00	.80	.20
☐ 85 Tom Haller	2.00	.80	.20
☐ 86 Charley Maxwell	2.00	.80	.20
☐ 87 Bob Veale	2.50	1.00	.25
☐ 88 Ron Hansen	2.00	.80	.20
☐ 89 Dick Stigman	2.00	.80	.20
☐ 90 Gordy Coleman	2.00	.80	.20
☐ 91 Dallas Green	2.50	1.00	.25
☐ 92 Hector Lopez	2.00	.80	.20
☐ 93 Galen Cisco	2.00	.80	.20
☐ 94 Bob Schmidt	2.00	.80	.20
☐ 95 Larry Jackson	2.00	.80	.20
☐ 96 Lou Clinton	2.00	.80	.20
☐ 97 Bob Duliba	2.00	.80	.20
☐ 98 George Thomas	2.00	.80	.20
☐ 99 Jim Umbricht	2.00	.80	.20
☐ 100 Joe Cunningham	2.50	1.00	.25
☐ 101 Joe Gibbon	2.00	.80	.20
☐ 102A Checklist 2 (red on yellow)	9.00	.90	.20
☐ 102B Checklist 2 (white on red)	12.50	1.25	.25
☐ 103 Chuck Essegian	2.00	.80	.20
☐ 104 Lew Krausse	2.00	.80	.20
☐ 105 Ron Fairly	2.50	1.00	.25
☐ 106 Bobby Bolin	2.00	.80	.20
☐ 107 Jim Hickman	2.50	1.00	.25
☐ 108 Hoyt Wilhelm	9.00	4.00	.90
☐ 109 Lee Maye	2.00	.80	.20
☐ 110 Rich Rollins	3.00	1.25	.30
☐ 111 Al Jackson	2.25	.90	.22
☐ 112 Dick Brown	2.25	.90	.22
☐ 113 Don Landrum UER (photo actually Ron Santo)	3.00	1.25	.30
☐ 114 Dan Osinski	2.25	.90	.22
☐ 115 Carl Yastrzemski	75.00	34.00	11.25
☐ 116 Jim Brosnan	2.25	.90	.22
☐ 117 Jacke Davis	2.25	.90	.22
☐ 118 Sherm Lollar	2.25	.90	.22
☐ 119 Bob Lillis	2.25	.90	.22
☐ 120 Roger Maris	60.00	27.00	9.00
☐ 121 Jim Hannan	2.25	.90	.22
☐ 122 Julio Gotay	2.25	.90	.22
☐ 123 Frank Howard	3.50	1.50	.35
☐ 124 Dick Howser	3.00	1.25	.30
☐ 125 Robin Roberts	10.00	4.50	1.25
☐ 126 Bob Uecker	35.00	15.75	5.25
☐ 127 Bill Tuttle	2.25	.90	.22
☐ 128 Matty Alou	3.00	1.25	.30
☐ 129 Gary Bell	2.25	.90	.22
☐ 130 Dick Groat	3.00	1.25	.30
☐ 131 Washington Senators Team Card	4.00	1.75	.40
☐ 132 Jack Hamilton	2.25	.90	.22
☐ 133 Gene Freese	2.25	.90	.22
☐ 134 Bob Scheffing MG	2.25	.90	.22
☐ 135 Richie Ashburn	9.00	4.00	.90
☐ 136 Ike Delock	2.25	.90	.22
☐ 137 Mack Jones	2.25	.90	.22
☐ 138 Pride of NL Willie Mays Stan Musial	33.00	15.00	5.00
☐ 139 Earl Averill	2.25	.90	.22
☐ 140 Frank Lary	3.00	1.25	.30

□ 141 Manny Mota .... 5.50 2.50 .55
□ 142 World Series Game 1 .. 6.00 2.50 .60
Ford wins
series opener
□ 143 World Series Game 2 .. 5.00 2.25 .50
Sanford flashes
shutout magic
□ 144 World Series Game 3 10.00 4.50 1.25
Maris sparks
Yankee rally
□ 145 World Series Game 4 .. 5.00 2.25 .50
Hiller blasts
grand slammer
□ 146 World Series Game 5 .. 5.00 2.25 .50
Tresh's homer
defeats Giants
□ 147 World Series Game 6 .. 5.00 2.25 .50
Pierce stars in
3 hit victory
□ 148 World Series Game 7 .. 5.00 2.25 .50
Yanks celebrate
as Terry wins
□ 149 Marv Breeding .... 2.25 .90 .22
□ 150 Johnny Podres .... 3.00 1.25 .30
□ 151 Pirates Team .... 4.00 1.75 .40
□ 152 Ron Nischwitz .... 2.25 .90 .22
□ 153 Hal Smith .... 2.25 .90 .22
□ 154 Walt Alston MG .... 4.50 2.00 .45
□ 155 Bill Stafford .... 2.25 .90 .22
□ 156 Roy McMillan .... 2.25 .90 .22
□ 157 Diego Segui .... 2.25 .90 .22
□ 158 Rookie Stars .... 3.50 1.50 .35
Rogelio Alvares
Dave Roberts
Tommy Harper
Bob Saverine
□ 159 Jim Pagliaroni .... 2.25 .90 .22
□ 160 Juan Pizarro .... 2.25 .90 .22
□ 161 Frank Torre .... 2.25 .90 .22
□ 162 Twins Team .... 4.00 1.75 .40
□ 163 Don Larsen .... 3.00 1.25 .30
□ 164 Bubba Morton .... 2.25 .90 .22
□ 165 Jim Kaat .... 5.00 2.25 .50
□ 166 Johnny Keane MG .... 3.00 1.25 .30
□ 167 Jim Fregosi .... 3.00 1.25 .30
□ 168 Russ Nixon .... 2.25 .90 .22
□ 169 Rookie Stars 32.00 14.25 4.75
Dick Egan
Julio Navarro
Tommie Sisk
Gaylord Perry
□ 170 Joe Adcock .... 3.00 1.25 .30
□ 171 Steve Hamilton .... 2.25 .90 .22
□ 172 Gene Oliver .... 2.25 .90 .22
□ 173 Bombers' Best 55.00 25.00 8.25
Tom Tresh
Mickey Mantle
Bobby Richardson
□ 174 Larry Burright .... 2.25 .90 .22
□ 175 Bob Buhl .... 2.25 .90 .22
□ 176 Jim King .... 2.25 .90 .22
□ 177 Bubba Phillips .... 2.25 .90 .22
□ 178 Johnny Edwards .... 2.25 .90 .22
□ 179 Ron Piche .... 2.25 .90 .22
□ 180 Bill Skowron .... 3.50 1.50 .35
□ 181 Sammy Esposito .... 2.25 .90 .22
□ 182 Albie Pearson .... 2.25 .90 .22
□ 183 Joe Pepitone .... 3.50 1.50 .35
□ 184 Vern Law .... 3.00 1.25 .30
□ 185 Chuck Hiller .... 2.25 .90 .22
□ 186 Jerry Zimmerman .... 2.25 .90 .22
□ 187 Willie Kirkland .... 2.25 .90 .22
□ 188 Eddie Bressoud .... 2.25 .90 .22
□ 189 Dave Giusti .... 3.00 1.25 .30
□ 190 Minnie Minoso .... 3.50 1.50 .35
□ 191 Checklist 3 .... 9.00 .90 .20
□ 192 Clay Dalrymple .... 2.25 .90 .22
□ 193 Andre Rodgers .... 2.25 .90 .22
□ 194 Joe Nuxhall .... 3.00 1.25 .30
□ 195 Manny Jimenez .... 2.25 .90 .22
□ 196 Doug Camilli .... 2.25 .90 .22
□ 197 Roger Craig .... 3.50 1.50 .35
□ 198 Lenny Green .... 2.75 1.10 .27
□ 199 Joe Amalfitano .... 2.75 1.10 .27
□ 200 Mickey Mantle 350.00 160.00 52.50
□ 201 Cecil Butler .... 2.75 1.10 .27
□ 202 Boston Red Sox .... 5.50 2.50 .55
Team Card
□ 203 Chico Cardenas .... 2.75 1.10 .27
□ 204 Don Nottebart .... 2.75 1.10 .27
□ 205 Luis Aparicio 12.50 5.50 1.65
□ 206 Ray Washburn .... 2.75 1.10 .27
□ 207 Ken Hunt .... 2.75 1.10 .27
□ 208 Rookie Stars .... 2.75 1.10 .27
Ron Herbel
John Miller
Wally Wolf
Ron Taylor
□ 209 Hobie Landrith .... 2.75 1.10 .27
□ 210 Sandy Koufax 140.00 63.00 21.00
□ 211 Fred Whitfield .... 2.75 1.10 .27
□ 212 Glen Hobbie .... 2.75 1.10 .27
□ 213 Billy Hitchcock MG ...... 2.75 1.10 .27
□ 214 Orlando Pena .... 2.75 1.10 .27
□ 215 Bob Skinner .... 2.75 1.10 .27
□ 216 Gene Conley .... 2.75 1.10 .27
□ 217 Joe Christopher .... 2.75 1.10 .27
□ 218 Tiger Twirlers .... 3.50 1.50 .35
Frank Lary
Don Mossi
Jim Bunning
□ 219 Chuck Cottier .... 2.75 1.10 .27
□ 220 Camilo Pascual .... 3.50 1.50 .35
□ 221 Cookie Rojas .... 4.00 1.75 .40
□ 222 Cubs Team .... 5.50 2.50 .55
□ 223 Eddie Fisher .... 2.75 1.10 .27

☐ 224 Mike Roarke	2.75	1.10	.27
☐ 225 Joey Jay	2.75	1.10	.27
☐ 226 Julian Javier	2.75	1.10	.27
☐ 227 Jim Grant	2.75	1.10	.27
☐ 228 Rookie Stars	45.00	20.00	6.75
Max Alvis			
Bob Bailey			
Tony Oliva			
(listed as Pedro)			
Ed Kranepool			
☐ 229 Willie Davis	4.00	1.75	.40
☐ 230 Pete Runnels	3.50	1.50	.35
☐ 231 Eli Grba UER	2.75	1.10	.27
(large photo is			
Ryne Duren)			
☐ 232 Frank Malzone	3.50	1.50	.35
☐ 233 Casey Stengel MG	16.00	6.75	2.25
☐ 234 Dave Nicholson	2.75	1.10	.27
☐ 235 Billy O'Dell	2.75	1.10	.27
☐ 236 Bill Bryan	2.75	1.10	.27
☐ 237 Jim Coates	2.75	1.10	.27
☐ 238 Lou Johnson	2.75	1.10	.27
☐ 239 Harvey Haddix	3.50	1.50	.35
☐ 240 Rocky Colavito	8.00	3.50	.80
☐ 241 Bob Smith	2.75	1.10	.27
☐ 242 Power Plus	28.00	12.50	4.00
Ernie Banks			
Hank Aaron			
☐ 243 Don Leppert	2.75	1.10	.27
☐ 244 John Tsitouris	2.75	1.10	.27
☐ 245 Gil Hodges	17.00	7.25	2.50
☐ 246 Lee Stange	2.75	1.10	.27
☐ 247 Yankees Team	15.00	6.50	2.15
☐ 248 Tito Francona	2.75	1.10	.27
☐ 249 Leo Burke	2.75	1.10	.27
☐ 250 Stan Musial	110.00	50.00	16.50
☐ 251 Jack Lamabe	2.75	1.10	.27
☐ 252 Ron Santo	6.00	2.50	.60
☐ 253 Rookie Stars	2.75	1.10	.27
Len Gabrielson			
Pete Jernigan			
John Wojcik			
Deacon Jones			
☐ 254 Mike Hershberger	2.75	1.10	.27
☐ 255 Bob Shaw	2.75	1.10	.27
☐ 256 Jerry Lumpe	2.75	1.10	.27
☐ 257 Hank Aguirre	2.75	1.10	.27
☐ 258 Alvin Dark MG	3.50	1.50	.35
☐ 259 Johnny Logan	3.50	1.50	.35
☐ 260 Jim Gentile	3.50	1.50	.35
☐ 261 Bob Miller	2.75	1.10	.27
☐ 262 Ellis Burton	2.75	1.10	.27
☐ 263 Dave Stenhouse	2.75	1.10	.27
☐ 264 Phil Linz	3.50	1.50	.35
☐ 265 Vada Pinson	4.00	1.75	.40
☐ 266 Bob Allen	2.75	1.10	.27
☐ 267 Carl Sawatski	2.75	1.10	.27
☐ 268 Don Demeter	2.75	1.10	.27
☐ 269 Don Mincher	3.50	1.50	.35
☐ 270 Felipe Alou	3.50	1.50	.35
☐ 271 Dean Stone	2.75	1.10	.27
☐ 272 Danny Murphy	2.75	1.10	.27
☐ 273 Sammy Taylor	2.75	1.10	.27
☐ 274 Checklist 4	9.00	.90	.20
☐ 275 Eddie Mathews	20.00	8.50	2.75
☐ 276 Barry Shetrone	2.75	1.10	.27
☐ 277 Dick Farrell	2.75	1.10	.27
☐ 278 Chico Fernandez	2.75	1.10	.27
☐ 279 Wally Moon	3.50	1.50	.35
☐ 280 Bob Rodgers	4.00	1.75	.40
☐ 281 Tom Sturdivant	2.75	1.10	.27
☐ 282 Bobby Del Greco	2.75	1.10	.27
☐ 283 Roy Sievers	3.50	1.50	.35
☐ 284 Dave Sisler	3.75	1.60	.37
☐ 285 Dick Stuart	4.50	2.00	.45
☐ 286 Stu Miller	3.75	1.60	.37
☐ 287 Dick Bertell	3.75	1.60	.37
☐ 288 Chicago White Sox	7.50	3.25	.75
Team Card			
☐ 289 Hal Brown	3.75	1.60	.37
☐ 290 Bill White	5.00	2.25	.50
☐ 291 Don Rudolph	3.75	1.60	.37
☐ 292 Pumpsie Green	3.75	1.60	.37
☐ 293 Bill Pleis	3.75	1.60	.37
☐ 294 Bill Rigney MG	3.75	1.60	.37
☐ 295 Ed Roebuck	3.75	1.60	.37
☐ 296 Doc Edwards	3.75	1.60	.37
☐ 297 Jim Golden	3.75	1.60	.37
☐ 298 Don Dillard	3.75	1.60	.37
☐ 299 Rookie Stars	3.75	1.60	.37
Dave Morehead			
Bob Dustal			
Tom Butters			
Dan Schneider			
☐ 300 Willie Mays	140.00	63.00	21.00
☐ 301 Bill Fischer	3.75	1.60	.37
☐ 302 Whitey Herzog	5.00	2.25	.50
☐ 303 Earl Francis	3.75	1.60	.37
☐ 304 Harry Bright	3.75	1.60	.37
☐ 305 Don Hoak	4.50	2.00	.45
☐ 306 Star Receivers	4.50	2.00	.45
Earl Battey			
Elston Howard			
☐ 307 Chet Nichols	3.75	1.60	.37
☐ 308 Camilo Carreon	3.75	1.60	.37
☐ 309 Jim Brewer	3.75	1.60	.37
☐ 310 Tommy Davis	5.00	2.25	.50
☐ 311 Joe McClain	3.75	1.60	.37
☐ 312 Houston Colts	12.00	5.25	1.50
Team Card			
☐ 313 Ernie Broglio	4.50	2.00	.45
☐ 314 John Goryl	3.75	1.60	.37
☐ 315 Ralph Terry	4.50	2.00	.45
☐ 316 Norm Sherry	3.75	1.60	.37
☐ 317 Sam McDowell	5.00	2.25	.50
☐ 318 Gene Mauch MG	4.50	2.00	.45

	No.	Player			
☐	319	Joe Gaines	3.75	1.60	.37
☐	320	Warren Spahn	36.00	16.25	5.50
☐	321	Gino Cimoli	3.75	1.60	.37
☐	322	Bob Turley	4.50	2.00	.45
☐	323	Bill Mazeroski	5.00	2.25	.50
☐	324	Rookie Stars George Williams Pete Ward Phil Roof Vic Davalillo	5.00	2.25	.50
☐	325	Jack Sanford	3.75	1.60	.37
☐	326	Hank Foiles	3.75	1.60	.37
☐	327	Paul Foytack	3.75	1.60	.37
☐	328	Dick Williams	4.50	2.00	.45
☐	329	Lindy McDaniel	4.50	2.00	.45
☐	330	Chuck Hinton	3.75	1.60	.37
☐	331	Series Foes Bill Stafford Bill Pierce	4.50	2.00	.45
☐	332	Joel Horlen	3.75	1.60	.37
☐	333	Carl Warwick	3.75	1.60	.37
☐	334	Wynn Hawkins	3.75	1.60	.37
☐	335	Leon Wagner	3.75	1.60	.37
☐	336	Ed Bauta	3.75	1.60	.37
☐	337	Dodgers Team	11.00	5.00	1.35
☐	338	Russ Kemmerer	3.75	1.60	.37
☐	339	Ted Bowsfield	3.75	1.60	.37
☐	340	Yogi Berra (player/coach)	70.00	32.00	10.50
☐	341	Jack Baldschun	3.75	1.60	.37
☐	342	Gene Woodling	4.50	2.00	.45
☐	343	Johnny Pesky MG	4.50	2.00	.45
☐	344	Don Schwall	4.50	2.00	.45
☐	345	Brooks Robinson	45.00	20.00	6.75
☐	346	Billy Hoeft	3.75	1.60	.37
☐	347	Joe Torre	8.00	3.50	.80
☐	348	Vic Wertz	4.50	2.00	.45
☐	349	Zoilo Versalles	3.75	1.60	.37
☐	350	Bob Purkey	3.75	1.60	.37
☐	351	Al Luplow	3.75	1.60	.37
☐	352	Ken Johnson	3.75	1.60	.37
☐	353	Billy Williams	24.00	10.50	3.50
☐	354	Dom Zanni	3.75	1.60	.37
☐	355	Dean Chance	4.50	2.00	.45
☐	356	John Schaive	3.75	1.60	.37
☐	357	George Altman	3.75	1.60	.37
☐	358	Milt Pappas	4.50	2.00	.45
☐	359	Haywood Sullivan	3.75	1.60	.37
☐	360	Don Drysdale	35.00	15.75	5.25
☐	361	Clete Boyer	5.00	2.25	.50
☐	362	Checklist 5	9.00	.90	.20
☐	363	Dick Radatz	4.50	2.00	.45
☐	364	Howie Goss	3.75	1.60	.37
☐	365	Jim Bunning	8.00	3.50	.80
☐	366	Tony Taylor	3.75	1.60	.37
☐	367	Tony Cloninger	3.75	1.60	.37
☐	368	Ed Bailey	3.75	1.60	.37
☐	369	Jim Lemon MG	3.75	1.60	.37
☐	370	Dick Donovan	3.75	1.60	.37
☐	371	Rod Kanehl	4.00	1.75	.40
☐	372	Don Lee	4.00	1.75	.40
☐	373	Jim Campbell	4.00	1.75	.40
☐	374	Claude Osteen	4.50	2.00	.45
☐	375	Ken Boyer	6.50	2.75	.65
☐	376	John Wyatt	4.00	1.75	.40
☐	377	Baltimore Orioles Team Card	8.00	3.50	.80
☐	378	Bill Henry	4.00	1.75	.40
☐	379	Bob Anderson	4.00	1.75	.40
☐	380	Ernie Banks	50.00	22.50	7.50
☐	381	Frank Baumann	4.00	1.75	.40
☐	382	Ralph Houk MG	5.00	2.25	.50
☐	383	Pete Richert	4.00	1.75	.40
☐	384	Bob Tillman	4.00	1.75	.40
☐	385	Art Mahaffey	4.00	1.75	.40
☐	386	Rookie Stars Ed Kirkpatrick John Bateman Larry Bearnarth Garry Roggenburk	5.00	2.25	.50
☐	387	Al McBean	4.00	1.75	.40
☐	388	Jim Davenport	4.00	1.75	.40
☐	389	Frank Sullivan	4.00	1.75	.40
☐	390	Hank Aaron	140.00	63.00	21.00
☐	391	Bill Dailey	4.00	1.75	.40
☐	392	Tribe Thumpers Johnny Romano Tito Francona	4.50	2.00	.45
☐	393	Ken MacKenzie	4.00	1.75	.40
☐	394	Tim McCarver	14.00	6.25	2.00
☐	395	Don McMahon	4.00	1.75	.40
☐	396	Joe Koppe	4.00	1.75	.40
☐	397	Kansas City Athletics Team Card	7.50	3.25	.75
☐	398	Boog Powell	18.00	7.50	2.50
☐	399	Dick Ellsworth	4.50	2.00	.45
☐	400	Frank Robinson	42.00	18.00	5.50
☐	401	Jim Bouton	7.50	3.25	.75
☐	402	Mickey Vernon MG	4.50	2.00	.45
☐	403	Ron Perranoski	4.50	2.00	.45
☐	404	Bob Oldis	4.00	1.75	.40
☐	405	Floyd Robinson	4.00	1.75	.40
☐	406	Howie Koplitz	4.00	1.75	.40
☐	407	Rookie Stars Frank Kostro Chico Ruiz Larry Elliot Dick Simpson	4.50	2.00	.45
☐	408	Billy Gardner	4.00	1.75	.40
☐	409	Roy Face	5.00	2.25	.50
☐	410	Earl Battey	4.00	1.75	.40
☐	411	Jim Constable	4.00	1.75	.40
☐	412	Dodger Big Three Johnny Podres Don Drysdale Sandy Koufax	32.00	14.25	4.75

☐ 413	Jerry Walker	4.00	1.75	.40
☐ 414	Ty Cline	4.00	1.75	.40
☐ 415	Bob Gibson	38.00	17.00	5.00
☐ 416	Alex Grammas	4.00	1.75	.40
☐ 417	Giants Team	8.00	3.50	.80
☐ 418	John Orsino	4.00	1.75	.40
☐ 419	Tracy Stallard	4.00	1.75	.40
☐ 420	Bobby Richardson	7.50	3.25	.75
☐ 421	Tom Morgan	4.00	1.75	.40
☐ 422	Fred Hutchinson MG	4.50	2.00	.45
☐ 423	Ed Hobaugh	4.00	1.75	.40
☐ 424	Charlie Smith	4.00	1.75	.40
☐ 425	Smoky Burgess	4.50	2.00	.45
☐ 426	Barry Latman	4.00	1.75	.40
☐ 427	Bernie Allen	4.00	1.75	.40
☐ 428	Carl Boles	4.00	1.75	.40
☐ 429	Lou Burdette	5.00	2.25	.50
☐ 430	Norm Siebern	4.00	1.75	.40
☐ 431A	Checklist 6 (white on red)	10.00	1.00	.20
☐ 431B	Checklist 6 (black on orange)	15.00	1.50	.30
☐ 432	Roman Mejias	4.00	1.75	.40
☐ 433	Denis Menke	4.00	1.75	.40
☐ 434	John Callison	4.50	2.00	.45
☐ 435	Woody Held	4.00	1.75	.40
☐ 436	Tim Harkness	4.00	1.75	.40
☐ 437	Bill Bruton	4.50	2.00	.45
☐ 438	Wes Stock	4.00	1.75	.40
☐ 439	Don Zimmer	5.00	2.25	.50
☐ 440	Juan Marichal	24.00	10.50	3.50
☐ 441	Lee Thomas	4.50	2.00	.45
☐ 442	J.C. Hartman	4.00	1.75	.40
☐ 443	Jim Piersall	5.00	2.25	.50
☐ 444	Jim Maloney	4.50	2.00	.45
☐ 445	Norm Cash	5.50	2.50	.55
☐ 446	Whitey Ford	38.00	17.00	5.00
☐ 447	Felix Mantilla	13.00	5.75	1.75
☐ 448	Jack Kralick	13.00	5.75	1.75
☐ 449	Jose Tartabull	13.00	5.75	1.75
☐ 450	Bob Friend	15.00	6.50	2.15
☐ 451	Indians Team	24.00	10.50	3.50
☐ 452	Barney Schultz	13.00	5.75	1.75
☐ 453	Jake Wood	13.00	5.75	1.75
☐ 454A	Art Fowler (card number on white background)	13.00	5.75	1.75
☐ 454B	Art Fowler (card number on orange background)	20.00	8.50	2.75
☐ 455	Ruben Amaro	13.00	5.75	1.75
☐ 456	Jim Coker	13.00	5.75	1.75
☐ 457	Tex Clevenger	13.00	5.75	1.75
☐ 458	Al Lopez MG	17.00	7.25	2.50
☐ 459	Dick LeMay	13.00	5.75	1.75
☐ 460	Del Crandall	15.00	6.50	2.15
☐ 461	Norm Bass	13.00	5.75	1.75
☐ 462	Wally Post	13.00	5.75	1.75
☐ 463	Joe Schaffernoth	13.00	5.75	1.75
☐ 464	Ken Aspromonte	13.00	5.75	1.75
☐ 465	Chuck Estrada	15.00	6.50	2.15
☐ 466	Rookie Stars SP Nate Oliver Tony Martinez Bill Freehan Jerry Robinson	40.00	18.00	6.00
☐ 467	Phil Ortega	13.00	5.75	1.75
☐ 468	Carroll Hardy	13.00	5.75	1.75
☐ 469	Jay Hook	13.00	5.75	1.75
☐ 470	Tom Tresh SP	40.00	18.00	6.00
☐ 471	Ken Retzer	13.00	5.75	1.75
☐ 472	Lou Brock	140.00	63.00	21.00
☐ 473	New York Mets Team Card	90.00	40.00	13.50
☐ 474	Jack Fisher	13.00	5.75	1.75
☐ 475	Gus Triandos	15.00	6.50	2.15
☐ 476	Frank Funk	13.00	5.75	1.75
☐ 477	Donn Clendenon	15.00	6.50	2.15
☐ 478	Paul Brown	13.00	5.75	1.75
☐ 479	Ed Brinkman	13.00	5.75	1.75
☐ 480	Bill Monbouquette	13.00	5.75	1.75
☐ 481	Bob Taylor	13.00	5.75	1.75
☐ 482	Felix Torres	13.00	5.75	1.75
☐ 483	Jim Owens	13.00	5.75	1.75
☐ 484	Dale Long SP	22.00	9.50	3.15
☐ 485	Jim Landis	13.00	5.75	1.75
☐ 486	Ray Sadecki	13.00	5.75	1.75
☐ 487	John Roseboro	15.00	6.50	2.15
☐ 488	Jerry Adair	13.00	5.75	1.75
☐ 489	Paul Toth	13.00	5.75	1.75
☐ 490	Willie McCovey	125.00	57.50	18.75
☐ 491	Harry Craft MG	13.00	5.75	1.75
☐ 492	Dave Wickersham	13.00	5.75	1.75
☐ 493	Walt Bond	13.00	5.75	1.75
☐ 494	Phil Regan	15.00	6.50	2.15
☐ 495	Frank Thomas SP	22.00	9.50	3.15
☐ 496	Rookie Stars Steve Dalkowski Fred Newman Jack Smith Carl Bouldin	15.00	6.50	2.15
☐ 497	Bennie Daniels	13.00	5.75	1.75
☐ 498	Eddie Kasko	13.00	5.75	1.75
☐ 499	J.C. Martin	13.00	5.75	1.75
☐ 500	Harmon Killebrew SP	110.00	50.00	16.50
☐ 501	Joe Azcue	13.00	5.75	1.75
☐ 502	Daryl Spencer	13.00	5.75	1.75
☐ 503	Braves Team	32.00	14.25	4.75
☐ 504	Bob Johnson	13.00	5.75	1.75
☐ 505	Curt Flood	18.00	7.50	2.50
☐ 506	Gene Green	13.00	5.75	1.75
☐ 507	Roland Sheldon	13.00	5.75	1.75
☐ 508	Ted Savage	13.00	5.75	1.75
☐ 509A	Checklist 7 (copyright centered)	20.00	2.00	.40
☐ 509B	Checklist 7	20.00	2.00	.40

(copyright to right)
□ 510 Ken McBride 13.00 5.75 1.75
□ 511 Charlie Neal 15.00 6.50 2.15
□ 512 Cal McLish 13.00 5.75 1.75
□ 513 Gary Geiger 13.00 5.75 1.75
□ 514 Larry Osborne 13.00 5.75 1.75
□ 515 Don Elston 13.00 5.75 1.75
□ 516 Purnell Goldy 13.00 5.75 1.75
□ 517 Hal Woodeshick 13.00 5.75 1.75
□ 518 Don Blasingame 13.00 5.75 1.75
□ 519 Claude Raymond 13.00 5.75 1.75
□ 520 Orlando Cepeda 22.00 9.50 3.15
□ 521 Dan Pfister 13.00 5.75 1.75
□ 522 Rookie Stars 13.00 5.75 1.75
Mel Nelson
Gary Peters
Jim Roland
Art Quirk
□ 523 Bill Kunkel .... 9.00 4.00 .90
□ 524 Cardinals Team 18.00 7.50 2.50
□ 525 Nellie Fox 17.00 7.25 2.50
□ 526 Dick Hall .... 9.00 4.00 .90
□ 527 Ed Sadowski .... 9.00 4.00 .90
□ 528 Carl Willey .... 9.00 4.00 .90
□ 529 Wes Covington .... 9.00 4.00 .90
□ 530 Don Mossi 10.00 4.50 1.25
□ 531 Sam Mele MG .... 9.00 4.00 .90
□ 532 Steve Boros .... 9.00 4.00 .90
□ 533 Bobby Shantz 11.00 5.00 1.35
□ 534 Ken Walters .... 9.00 4.00 .90
□ 535 Jim Perry 11.00 5.00 1.35
□ 536 Norm Larker 10.00 4.50 1.25
□ 537 Rookie Stars 650.00 300.00 100.00
Pedro Gonzalez
Ken McMullen
Al Weis
Pete Rose
□ 538 George Brunet .... 9.00 4.00 .90
□ 539 Wayne Causey .... 9.00 4.00 .90
□ 540 Bob Clemente 180.00 80.00 27.00
□ 541 Ron Moeller .... 9.00 4.00 .90
□ 542 Lou Klimchock .... 9.00 4.00 .90
□ 543 Russ Snyder .... 9.00 4.00 .90
□ 544 Rookie Stars 36.00 16.25 5.50
Duke Carmel
Bill Haas
Rusty Staub
Dick Phillips
□ 545 Jose Pagan .... 9.00 4.00 .90
□ 546 Hal Reniff .... 9.00 4.00 .90
□ 547 Gus Bell 10.00 4.50 1.25
□ 548 Tom Satriano .... 9.00 4.00 .90
□ 549 Rookie Stars .... 9.00 4.00 .90
Marcelino Lopez
Pete Lovrich
Paul Ratliff
Elmo Plaskett
□ 550 Duke Snider 75.00 34.00 11.25
□ 551 Billy Klaus .... 9.00 4.00 .90
□ 552 Detroit Tigers 22.00 9.50 3.15
Team Card
□ 553 Rookie Stars 300.00 135.00 45.00
Brock Davis
Jim Gosger
Willie Stargell
John Herrnstein
□ 554 Hank Fischer .... 9.00 4.00 .90
□ 555 John Blanchard 10.00 4.50 1.25
□ 556 Al Worthington .... 9.00 4.00 .90
□ 557 Cuno Barragan .... 9.00 4.00 .90
□ 558 Rookie Stars 12.50 5.50 1.65
Bill Faul
Ron Hunt
Al Moran
Bob Lipski
□ 559 Danny Murtaugh MG .... 9.00 4.00 .90
□ 560 Ray Herbert .... 9.00 4.00 .90
□ 561 Mike De La Hoz .... 9.00 4.00 .90
□ 562 Rookie Stars 15.00 6.50 2.15
Randy Cardinal
Dave McNally
Ken Rowe
Don Rowe
□ 563 Mike McCormick 10.00 4.50 1.25
□ 564 George Banks .... 9.00 4.00 .90
□ 565 Larry Sherry 10.00 4.50 1.25
□ 566 Cliff Cook .... 9.00 4.00 .90
□ 567 Jim Duffalo .... 9.00 4.00 .90
□ 568 Bob Sadowski .... 9.00 4.00 .90
□ 569 Luis Arroyo 10.00 4.50 1.25
□ 570 Frank Bolling .... 9.00 4.00 .90
□ 571 Johnny Klippstein .... 9.00 4.00 .90
□ 572 Jack Spring .... 9.00 4.00 .90
□ 573 Coot Veal .... 9.00 4.00 .90
□ 574 Hal Kolstad .... 9.00 4.00 .90
□ 575 Don Cardwell .... 9.00 4.00 .90
□ 576 Johnny Temple 12.50 5.00 1.00

1964 Topps

The cards in this 587-card set measure 2 1/2" by 3 1/2". Players in the 1964 Topps baseball series were easy to sort by team due to the giant block lettering found at the top of each card. The name and position of the player are found underneath the picture, and the card is numbered in a ball design on the orange-colored back. The usual last series scarcity holds for this set (523 to 587). Subsets within this set include League Leaders (1-12) and

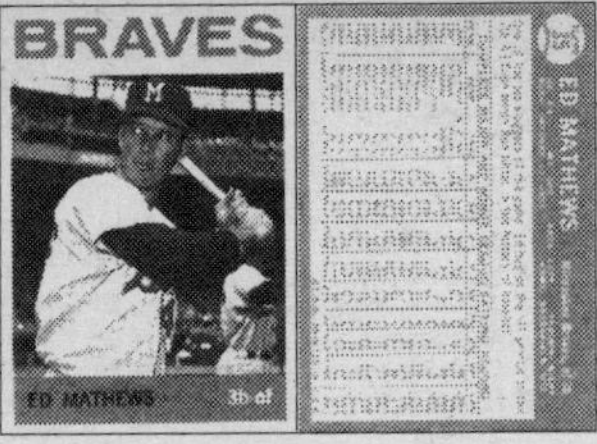

World Series cards (136-140). There were some three-card advertising panels produced by Topps; the players included are from the first series; one panel shows Walt Alston, Bill Henry, and Vada Pinson on the front with a Mickey Mantle card back on one of the backs. Another panel shows Carl Willey, White Sox Rookies, and Bob Friend on the front with a Mickey Mantle card back on one of the backs. The key rookie cards in this set are Richie Allen, Tommy John, Lou Piniella, and Phil Niekro.

	NRMT	VG-E	GOOD
COMPLETE SET (587)	3250.00	1350.00	350.00
COMMON PLAYER (1-196)	1.75	.70	.17
COMMON PLAYER (197-370)	3.00	1.25	.30
COMMON PLAYER (371-522)	4.50	2.00	.45
COMMON PLAYER (523-587)	8.50	3.75	.85

	NRMT	VG-E	GOOD
☐ 1 NL ERA Leaders	20.00	5.00	1.00
Sandy Koufax			
Dick Ellsworth			
Bob Friend			
☐ 2 AL ERA Leaders	3.00	1.25	.30
Gary Peters			
Juan Pizarro			
Camilo Pascual			
☐ 3 NL Pitching Leaders	9.00	4.00	.90
Sandy Koufax			
Juan Marichal			
Warren Spahn			
Jim Maloney			
☐ 4 AL Pitching Leaders	3.50	1.50	.35
Whitey Ford			
Camilo Pascual			
Jim Bouton			
☐ 5 NL Strikeout Leaders	7.00	3.00	.70
Sandy Koufax			
Jim Maloney			
Don Drysdale			
☐ 6 AL Strikeout Leaders	3.00	1.25	.30
Camilo Pascual			
Jim Bunning			
Dick Stigman			
☐ 7 NL Batting Leaders	6.50	2.75	.65
Tommy Davis			
Bob Clemente			
Dick Groat			
Hank Aaron			
☐ 8 AL Batting Leaders	6.50	2.75	.65
Carl Yastrzemski			
Al Kaline			
Rich Rollins			
☐ 9 NL Home Run Leaders	11.00	5.00	1.35
Hank Aaron			
Willie McCovey			
Willie Mays			
Orlando Cepeda			
☐ 10 AL Home Run Leaders	3.50	1.50	.35
Harmon Killebrew			
Dick Stuart			
Bob Allison			
☐ 11 NL RBI Leaders	6.00	2.50	.60
Hank Aaron			
Ken Boyer			
Bill White			
☐ 12 AL RBI Leaders	4.00	1.75	.40
Dick Stuart			
Al Kaline			
Harmon Killebrew			
☐ 13 Hoyt Wilhelm	8.50	3.75	.85
☐ 14 Dodgers Rookies	1.75	.70	.17
Dick Nen			
Nick Willhite			
☐ 15 Zoilo Versalles	1.75	.70	.17
☐ 16 John Boozer	1.75	.70	.17
☐ 17 Willie Kirkland	1.75	.70	.17
☐ 18 Billy O'Dell	1.75	.70	.17
☐ 19 Don Wert	1.75	.70	.17
☐ 20 Bob Friend	2.25	.90	.22
☐ 21 Yogi Berra MG	36.00	16.25	5.50
☐ 22 Jerry Adair	1.75	.70	.17
☐ 23 Chris Zachary	1.75	.70	.17
☐ 24 Carl Sawatski	1.75	.70	.17
☐ 25 Bill Monbouquette	1.75	.70	.17
☐ 26 Gino Cimoli	1.75	.70	.17
☐ 27 New York Mets	6.00	2.50	.60
Team Card			
☐ 28 Claude Osteen	2.25	.90	.22
☐ 29 Lou Brock	36.00	16.25	5.50
☐ 30 Ron Perranoski	2.25	.90	.22
☐ 31 Dave Nicholson	1.75	.70	.17
☐ 32 Dean Chance	2.25	.90	.22
☐ 33 Reds Rookies	2.25	.90	.22
Sammy Ellis			
Mel Queen			
☐ 34 Jim Perry	2.25	.90	.22
☐ 35 Eddie Mathews	20.00	8.50	2.75

☐ 36 Hal Reniff	1.75	.70	.17
☐ 37 Smoky Burgess	2.25	.90	.22
☐ 38 Jim Wynn	5.00	2.25	.50
☐ 39 Hank Aguirre	1.75	.70	.17
☐ 40 Dick Groat	2.75	1.10	.27
☐ 41 Friendly Foes Willie McCovey Leon Wagner	3.50	1.50	.35
☐ 42 Moe Drabowsky	1.75	.70	.17
☐ 43 Roy Sievers	2.25	.90	.22
☐ 44 Duke Carmel	1.75	.70	.17
☐ 45 Milt Pappas	2.25	.90	.22
☐ 46 Ed Brinkman	1.75	.70	.17
☐ 47 Giants Rookies Jesus Alou Ron Herbel	2.25	.90	.22
☐ 48 Bob Perry	1.75	.70	.17
☐ 49 Bill Henry	1.75	.70	.17
☐ 50 Mickey Mantle	190.00	85.00	28.50
☐ 51 Pete Richert	1.75	.70	.17
☐ 52 Chuck Hinton	1.75	.70	.17
☐ 53 Denis Menke	1.75	.70	.17
☐ 54 Sam Mele MG	1.75	.70	.17
☐ 55 Ernie Banks	25.00	11.00	3.50
☐ 56 Hal Brown	1.75	.70	.17
☐ 57 Tim Harkness	1.75	.70	.17
☐ 58 Don Demeter	1.75	.70	.17
☐ 59 Ernie Broglio	1.75	.70	.17
☐ 60 Frank Malzone	2.25	.90	.22
☐ 61 Angel Backstops Bob Rodgers Ed Sadowski	2.25	.90	.22
☐ 62 Ted Savage	1.75	.70	.17
☐ 63 John Orsino	1.75	.70	.17
☐ 64 Ted Abernathy	1.75	.70	.17
☐ 65 Felipe Alou	2.25	.90	.22
☐ 66 Eddie Fisher	1.75	.70	.17
☐ 67 Tigers Team	3.75	1.60	.37
☐ 68 Willie Davis	2.25	.90	.22
☐ 69 Clete Boyer	2.25	.90	.22
☐ 70 Joe Torre	3.75	1.60	.37
☐ 71 Jack Spring	1.75	.70	.17
☐ 72 Chico Cardenas	1.75	.70	.17
☐ 73 Jimmie Hall	2.25	.90	.22
☐ 74 Pirates Rookies Bob Priddy Tom Butters	1.75	.70	.17
☐ 75 Wayne Causey	1.75	.70	.17
☐ 76 Checklist 1	9.00	.90	.20
☐ 77 Jerry Walker	1.75	.70	.17
☐ 78 Merritt Ranew	1.75	.70	.17
☐ 79 Bob Heffner	1.75	.70	.17
☐ 80 Vada Pinson	3.25	1.35	.32
☐ 81 All-Star Vets Nellie Fox Harmon Killebrew	5.00	2.25	.50
☐ 82 Jim Davenport	1.75	.70	.17
☐ 83 Gus Triandos	2.25	.90	.22
☐ 84 Carl Willey	1.75	.70	.17
☐ 85 Pete Ward	1.75	.70	.17
☐ 86 Al Downing	2.25	.90	.22
☐ 87 St. Louis Cardinals Team Card	3.75	1.60	.37
☐ 88 John Roseboro	2.25	.90	.22
☐ 89 Boog Powell	4.50	2.00	.45
☐ 90 Earl Battey	1.75	.70	.17
☐ 91 Bob Bailey	1.75	.70	.17
☐ 92 Steve Ridzik	1.75	.70	.17
☐ 93 Gary Geiger	1.75	.70	.17
☐ 94 Braves Rookies Jim Britton Larry Maxie	1.75	.70	.17
☐ 95 George Altman	1.75	.70	.17
☐ 96 Bob Buhl	1.75	.70	.17
☐ 97 Jim Fregosi	2.25	.90	.22
☐ 98 Bill Bruton	1.75	.70	.17
☐ 99 Al Stanek	1.75	.70	.17
☐ 100 Elston Howard	4.50	2.00	.45
☐ 101 Walt Alston MG	3.75	1.60	.37
☐ 102 Checklist 2	9.00	.90	.20
☐ 103 Curt Flood	3.00	1.25	.30
☐ 104 Art Mahaffey	1.75	.70	.17
☐ 105 Woody Held	1.75	.70	.17
☐ 106 Joe Nuxhall	2.25	.90	.22
☐ 107 White Sox Rookies Bruce Howard Frank Kreutzer	1.75	.70	.17
☐ 108 John Wyatt	1.75	.70	.17
☐ 109 Rusty Staub	7.00	3.00	.70
☐ 110 Albie Pearson	1.75	.70	.17
☐ 111 Don Elston	1.75	.70	.17
☐ 112 Bob Tillman	1.75	.70	.17
☐ 113 Grover Powell	1.75	.70	.17
☐ 114 Don Lock	1.75	.70	.17
☐ 115 Frank Bolling	1.75	.70	.17
☐ 116 Twins Rookies Jay Ward Tony Oliva	15.00	6.50	2.15
☐ 117 Earl Francis	1.75	.70	.17
☐ 118 John Blanchard	2.25	.90	.22
☐ 119 Gary Kolb	1.75	.70	.17
☐ 120 Don Drysdale	20.00	8.50	2.75
☐ 121 Pete Runnels	2.25	.90	.22
☐ 122 Don McMahon	1.75	.70	.17
☐ 123 Jose Pagan	1.75	.70	.17
☐ 124 Orlando Pena	1.75	.70	.17
☐ 125 Pete Rose	175.00	80.00	27.00
☐ 126 Russ Snyder	1.75	.70	.17
☐ 127 Angels Rookies Aubrey Gatewood Dick Simpson	1.75	.70	.17
☐ 128 Mickey Lolich	15.00	6.50	2.15
☐ 129 Amado Samuel	1.75	.70	.17
☐ 130 Gary Peters	1.75	.70	.17
☐ 131 Steve Boros	1.75	.70	.17
☐ 132 Braves Team	3.75	1.60	.37

□ 133 Jim Grant .... 1.75 .70 .17
□ 134 Don Zimmer .... 2.25 .90 .22
□ 135 Johnny Callison .... 2.25 .90 .22
□ 136 World Series Game 1 11.00 5.00 1.35
Koufax strikes out 15
□ 137 World Series Game 2 .. 4.00 1.75 .40
Davis sparks rally
□ 138 World Series Game 3 .. 4.00 1.75 .40
LA 3 straight
□ 139 World Series Game 4 .. 4.00 1.75 .40
Sealing Yanks doom
□ 140 World Series Summary 4.00 1.75 .40
Dodgers celebrate
□ 141 Danny Murtaugh MG ... 1.75 .70 .17
□ 142 John Bateman .... 1.75 .70 .17
□ 143 Bubba Phillips .... 1.75 .70 .17
□ 144 Al Worthington .... 1.75 .70 .17
□ 145 Norm Siebern .... 1.75 .70 .17
□ 146 Indians Rookies 65.00 29.00 9.75
Tommy John
Bob Chance
□ 147 Ray Sadecki .... 1.75 .70 .17
□ 148 J.C. Martin .... 1.75 .70 .17
□ 149 Paul Foytack .... 1.75 .70 .17
□ 150 Willie Mays 95.00 42.00 11.00
□ 151 Athletics Team .... 3.00 1.25 .30
□ 152 Denny Lemaster .... 1.75 .70 .17
□ 153 Dick Williams .... 2.25 .90 .22
□ 154 Dick Tracewski .... 1.75 .70 .17
□ 155 Duke Snider 32.00 14.25 4.75
□ 156 Bill Dailey .... 1.75 .70 .17
□ 157 Gene Mauch MG .... 2.25 .90 .22
□ 158 Ken Johnson .... 1.75 .70 .17
□ 159 Charlie Dees .... 1.75 .70 .17
□ 160 Ken Boyer .... 5.00 2.25 .50
□ 161 Dave McNally .... 2.75 1.10 .27
□ 162 Hitting Area .... 2.25 .90 .22
Dick Sisler
Vada Pinson
□ 163 Donn Clendenon .... 2.25 .90 .22
□ 164 Bud Daley .... 1.75 .70 .17
□ 165 Jerry Lumpe .... 1.75 .70 .17
□ 166 Marty Keough .... 1.75 .70 .17
□ 167 Senators Rookies 24.00 10.50 3.50
Mike Brumley
Lou Piniella
□ 168 Al Weis .... 2.25 .90 .22
□ 169 Del Crandall .... 2.25 .90 .22
□ 170 Dick Radatz .... 2.25 .90 .22
□ 171 Ty Cline .... 1.75 .70 .17
□ 172 Indians Team .... 3.25 1.35 .32
□ 173 Ryne Duren .... 2.25 .90 .22
□ 174 Doc Edwards .... 2.25 .90 .22
□ 175 Billy Williams 15.00 6.50 2.15
□ 176 Tracy Stallard .... 1.75 .70 .17
□ 177 Harmon Killebrew 20.00 8.50 2.75
□ 178 Hank Bauer MG .... 2.25 .90 .22
□ 179 Carl Warwick .... 1.75 .70 .17
□ 180 Tommy Davis .... 2.50 1.00 .25
□ 181 Dave Wickersham .... 1.75 .70 .17
□ 182 Sox Sockers 11.00 5.00 1.35
Carl Yastrzemski
Chuck Schilling
□ 183 Ron Taylor .... 1.75 .70 .17
□ 184 Al Luplow .... 1.75 .70 .17
□ 185 Jim O'Toole .... 2.25 .90 .22
□ 186 Roman Mejias .... 1.75 .70 .17
□ 187 Ed Roebuck .... 1.75 .70 .17
□ 188 Checklist 3 .... 9.00 .90 .20
□ 189 Bob Hendley .... 1.75 .70 .17
□ 190 Bobby Richardson .... 4.50 2.00 .45
□ 191 Clay Dalrymple .... 1.75 .70 .17
□ 192 Cubs Rookies .... 1.75 .70 .17
John Boccabella
Billy Cowan
□ 193 Jerry Lynch .... 1.75 .70 .17
□ 194 John Goryl .... 1.75 .70 .17
□ 195 Floyd Robinson .... 1.75 .70 .17
□ 196 Jim Gentile .... 2.50 1.00 .25
□ 197 Frank Lary .... 3.00 1.25 .30
□ 198 Len Gabrielson .... 3.00 1.25 .30
□ 199 Joe Azcue .... 3.00 1.25 .30
□ 200 Sandy Koufax 95.00 42.00 11.00
□ 201 Orioles Rookies .... 3.50 1.50 .35
Sam Bowens
Wally Bunker
□ 202 Galen Cisco .... 3.00 1.25 .30
□ 203 John Kennedy .... 3.00 1.25 .30
□ 204 Matty Alou .... 3.50 1.50 .35
□ 205 Nellie Fox .... 5.00 2.25 .50
□ 206 Steve Hamilton .... 3.00 1.25 .30
□ 207 Fred Hutchinson MG ... 3.50 1.50 .35
□ 208 Wes Covington .... 3.00 1.25 .30
□ 209 Bob Allen .... 3.00 1.25 .30
□ 210 Carl Yastrzemski 75.00 34.00 11.25
□ 211 Jim Coker .... 3.00 1.25 .30
□ 212 Pete Lovrich .... 3.00 1.25 .30
□ 213 Angels Team .... 5.50 2.50 .55
□ 214 Ken McMullen .... 3.00 1.25 .30
□ 215 Ray Herbert .... 3.00 1.25 .30
□ 216 Mike de la Hoz .... 3.00 1.25 .30
□ 217 Jim King .... 3.00 1.25 .30
□ 218 Hank Fischer .... 3.00 1.25 .30
□ 219 Young Aces .... 4.00 1.75 .40
Al Downing
Jim Bouton
□ 220 Dick Ellsworth .... 3.50 1.50 .35
□ 221 Bob Saverine .... 3.00 1.25 .30
□ 222 Billy Pierce .... 3.50 1.50 .35
□ 223 George Banks .... 3.00 1.25 .30
□ 224 Tommie Sisk .... 3.00 1.25 .30
□ 225 Roger Maris 60.00 27.00 9.00
□ 226 Colts Rookies .... 4.00 1.75 .40
Gerald Grote
Larry Yellen
□ 227 Barry Latman .... 3.00 1.25 .30

No.	Player	Price 1	Price 2	Price 3
☐ 228	Felix Mantilla	3.00	1.25	.30
☐ 229	Charley Lau	3.50	1.50	.35
☐ 230	Brooks Robinson	32.00	14.25	4.75
☐ 231	Dick Calmus	3.00	1.25	.30
☐ 232	Al Lopez MG	4.50	2.00	.45
☐ 233	Hal Smith	3.00	1.25	.30
☐ 234	Gary Bell	3.00	1.25	.30
☐ 235	Ron Hunt	3.00	1.25	.30
☐ 236	Bill Faul	3.00	1.25	.30
☐ 237	Cubs Team	6.00	2.50	.60
☐ 238	Roy McMillan	3.00	1.25	.30
☐ 239	Herm Starrette	3.00	1.25	.30
☐ 240	Bill White	4.00	1.75	.40
☐ 241	Jim Owens	3.00	1.25	.30
☐ 242	Harvey Kuenn	4.00	1.75	.40
☐ 243	Phillies Rookies	20.00	8.50	2.75
	Richie Allen			
	John Herrnstein			
☐ 244	Tony LaRussa	12.00	5.25	1.50
☐ 245	Dick Stigman	3.00	1.25	.30
☐ 246	Manny Mota	4.00	1.75	.40
☐ 247	Dave DeBusschere	4.00	1.75	.40
☐ 248	Johnny Pesky MG	3.50	1.50	.35
☐ 249	Doug Camilli	3.00	1.25	.30
☐ 250	Al Kaline	30.00	13.50	4.50
☐ 251	Choo Choo Coleman	3.00	1.25	.30
☐ 252	Ken Aspromonte	3.00	1.25	.30
☐ 253	Wally Post	3.00	1.25	.30
☐ 254	Don Hoak	3.50	1.50	.35
☐ 255	Lee Thomas	3.50	1.50	.35
☐ 256	Johnny Weekly	3.00	1.25	.30
☐ 257	San Francisco Giants	6.00	2.50	.60
	Team Card			
☐ 258	Garry Roggenburk	3.00	1.25	.30
☐ 259	Harry Bright	3.00	1.25	.30
☐ 260	Frank Robinson	24.00	10.50	3.50
☐ 261	Jim Hannan	3.00	1.25	.30
☐ 262	Cards Rookies	5.00	2.25	.50
	Mike Shannon			
	Harry Fanok			
☐ 263	Chuck Estrada	3.50	1.50	.35
☐ 264	Jim Landis	3.00	1.25	.30
☐ 265	Jim Bunning	5.00	2.25	.50
☐ 266	Gene Freese	3.00	1.25	.30
☐ 267	Wilbur Wood	4.00	1.75	.40
☐ 268	Bill's Got It	3.50	1.50	.35
	Danny Murtaugh			
	Bill Virdon			
☐ 269	Ellis Burton	3.00	1.25	.30
☐ 270	Rich Rollins	3.50	1.50	.35
☐ 271	Bob Sadowski	3.00	1.25	.30
☐ 272	Jake Wood	3.00	1.25	.30
☐ 273	Mel Nelson	3.00	1.25	.30
☐ 274	Checklist 4	9.00	.90	.20
☐ 275	John Tsitouris	3.00	1.25	.30
☐ 276	Jose Tartabull	3.00	1.25	.30
☐ 277	Ken Retzer	3.00	1.25	.30
☐ 278	Bobby Shantz	3.50	1.50	.35
☐ 279	Joe Koppe UER	3.50	1.50	.35
	(Glove on wrong hand)			
☐ 280	Juan Marichal	11.00	5.00	1.35
☐ 281	Yankees Rookies	3.50	1.50	.35
	Jake Gibbs			
	Tom Metcalf			
☐ 282	Bob Bruce	3.00	1.25	.30
☐ 283	Tom McCraw	4.00	1.75	.40
☐ 284	Dick Schofield	3.00	1.25	.30
☐ 285	Robin Roberts	9.00	4.00	.90
☐ 286	Don Landrum	3.00	1.25	.30
☐ 287	Red Sox Rookies	25.00	11.00	3.50
	Tony Conigliaro			
	Bill Spanswick			
☐ 288	Al Moran	3.00	1.25	.30
☐ 289	Frank Funk	3.00	1.25	.30
☐ 290	Bob Allison	3.50	1.50	.35
☐ 291	Phil Ortega	3.00	1.25	.30
☐ 292	Mike Roarke	3.00	1.25	.30
☐ 293	Phillies Team	6.00	2.50	.60
☐ 294	Ken L. Hunt	3.00	1.25	.30
☐ 295	Roger Craig	4.00	1.75	.40
☐ 296	Ed Kirkpatrick	3.00	1.25	.30
☐ 297	Ken MacKenzie	3.00	1.25	.30
☐ 298	Harry Craft MG	3.00	1.25	.30
☐ 299	Bill Stafford	3.00	1.25	.30
☐ 300	Hank Aaron	95.00	42.00	11.00
☐ 301	Larry Brown	3.00	1.25	.30
☐ 302	Dan Pfister	3.00	1.25	.30
☐ 303	Jim Campbell	3.00	1.25	.30
☐ 304	Bob Johnson	3.00	1.25	.30
☐ 305	Jack Lamabe	3.00	1.25	.30
☐ 306	Giant Gunners	20.00	8.50	2.75
	Willie Mays			
	Orlando Cepeda			
☐ 307	Joe Gibbon	4.00	1.75	.40
☐ 308	Gene Stephens	3.00	1.25	.30
☐ 309	Paul Toth	3.00	1.25	.30
☐ 310	Jim Gilliam	4.00	1.75	.40
☐ 311	Tom Brown	3.00	1.25	.30
☐ 312	Tigers Rookies	3.50	1.50	.35
	Fritz Fisher			
	Fred Gladding			
☐ 313	Chuck Hiller	3.00	1.25	.30
☐ 314	Jerry Buchek	3.00	1.25	.30
☐ 315	Bo Belinsky	3.50	1.50	.35
☐ 316	Gene Oliver	3.00	1.25	.30
☐ 317	Al Smith	3.00	1.25	.30
☐ 318	Minnesota Twins	6.00	2.50	.60
	Team Card			
☐ 319	Paul Brown	3.00	1.25	.30
☐ 320	Rocky Colavito	6.50	2.75	.65
☐ 321	Bob Lillis	3.00	1.25	.30
☐ 322	George Brunet	3.00	1.25	.30
☐ 323	John Buzhardt	3.00	1.25	.30
☐ 324	Casey Stengel MG	15.00	6.50	2.15
☐ 325	Hector Lopez	3.00	1.25	.30
☐ 326	Ron Brand	3.00	1.25	.30

☐ 327	Don Blasingame	3.00	1.25	.30
☐ 328	Bob Shaw	3.00	1.25	.30
☐ 329	Russ Nixon	3.00	1.25	.30
☐ 330	Tommy Harper	3.50	1.50	.35
☐ 331	AL Bombers Roger Maris Norm Cash Mickey Mantle Al Kaline	95.00	42.00	11.00
☐ 332	Ray Washburn	3.00	1.25	.30
☐ 333	Billy Moran	3.00	1.25	.30
☐ 334	Lew Krausse	3.00	1.25	.30
☐ 335	Don Mossi	3.50	1.50	.35
☐ 336	Andre Rodgers	3.00	1.25	.30
☐ 337	Dodgers Rookies Al Ferrara Jeff Torborg	7.50	3.25	.75
☐ 338	Jack Kralick	3.00	1.25	.30
☐ 339	Walt Bond	3.00	1.25	.30
☐ 340	Joe Cunningham	3.50	1.50	.35
☐ 341	Jim Roland	3.00	1.25	.30
☐ 342	Willie Stargell	45.00	20.00	6.75
☐ 343	Senators Team	5.50	2.50	.55
☐ 344	Phil Linz	3.50	1.50	.35
☐ 345	Frank Thomas	3.50	1.50	.35
☐ 346	Joey Jay	3.50	1.50	.35
☐ 347	Bobby Wine	3.00	1.25	.30
☐ 348	Ed Lopat MG	3.50	1.50	.35
☐ 349	Art Fowler	3.00	1.25	.30
☐ 350	Willie McCovey	25.00	11.00	3.50
☐ 351	Dan Schneider	3.00	1.25	.30
☐ 352	Eddie Bressoud	3.00	1.25	.30
☐ 353	Wally Moon	3.50	1.50	.35
☐ 354	Dave Giusti	3.50	1.50	.35
☐ 355	Vic Power	3.00	1.25	.30
☐ 356	Reds Rookies Bill McCool Chico Ruiz	3.50	1.50	.35
☐ 357	Charley James	3.00	1.25	.30
☐ 358	Ron Kline	3.00	1.25	.30
☐ 359	Jim Schaffer	3.00	1.25	.30
☐ 360	Joe Pepitone	4.00	1.75	.40
☐ 361	Jay Hook	3.00	1.25	.30
☐ 362	Checklist 5	9.00	.90	.20
☐ 363	Dick McAuliffe	3.50	1.50	.35
☐ 364	Joe Gaines	3.00	1.25	.30
☐ 365	Cal McLish	3.00	1.25	.30
☐ 366	Nelson Mathews	3.00	1.25	.30
☐ 367	Fred Whitfield	3.00	1.25	.30
☐ 368	White Sox Rookies Fritz Ackley Don Buford	3.50	1.50	.35
☐ 369	Jerry Zimmerman	3.00	1.25	.30
☐ 370	Hal Woodeshick	3.00	1.25	.30
☐ 371	Frank Howard	5.50	2.50	.55
☐ 372	Howie Koplitz	4.50	2.00	.45
☐ 373	Pirates Team	9.00	4.00	.90
☐ 374	Bobby Bolin	4.50	2.00	.45
☐ 375	Ron Santo	6.00	2.50	.60
☐ 376	Dave Morehead	4.50	2.00	.45
☐ 377	Bob Skinner	4.50	2.00	.45
☐ 378	Braves Rookies Woody Woodward Jack Smith	5.50	2.50	.55
☐ 379	Tony Gonzalez	4.50	2.00	.45
☐ 380	Whitey Ford	28.00	12.50	4.00
☐ 381	Bob Taylor	4.50	2.00	.45
☐ 382	Wes Stock	4.50	2.00	.45
☐ 383	Bill Rigney MG	4.50	2.00	.45
☐ 384	Ron Hansen	4.50	2.00	.45
☐ 385	Curt Simmons	5.00	2.25	.50
☐ 386	Lenny Green	4.50	2.00	.45
☐ 387	Terry Fox	4.50	2.00	.45
☐ 388	A's Rookies John O'Donoghue George Williams	4.50	2.00	.45
☐ 389	Jim Umbricht (card back mentions his death)	4.50	2.00	.45
☐ 390	Orlando Cepeda	7.50	3.25	.75
☐ 391	Sam McDowell	5.00	2.25	.50
☐ 392	Jim Pagliaroni	4.50	2.00	.45
☐ 393	Casey Teaches Casey Stengel Ed Kranepool	5.50	2.50	.55
☐ 394	Bob Miller	4.50	2.00	.45
☐ 395	Tom Tresh	5.50	2.50	.55
☐ 396	Dennis Bennett	4.50	2.00	.45
☐ 397	Chuck Cottier	4.50	2.00	.45
☐ 398	Mets Rookies Bill Haas Dick Smith	4.50	2.00	.45
☐ 399	Jackie Brandt	4.50	2.00	.45
☐ 400	Warren Spahn	28.00	12.50	4.00
☐ 401	Charlie Maxwell	4.50	2.00	.45
☐ 402	Tom Sturdivant	4.50	2.00	.45
☐ 403	Reds Team	9.00	4.00	.90
☐ 404	Tony Martinez	4.50	2.00	.45
☐ 405	Ken McBride	4.50	2.00	.45
☐ 406	Al Spangler	4.50	2.00	.45
☐ 407	Bill Freehan	6.00	2.50	.60
☐ 408	Cubs Rookies Jim Stewart Fred Burdette	4.50	2.00	.45
☐ 409	Bill Fischer	4.50	2.00	.45
☐ 410	Dick Stuart	5.50	2.50	.55
☐ 411	Lee Walls	4.50	2.00	.45
☐ 412	Ray Culp	4.50	2.00	.45
☐ 413	Johnny Keane MG	4.50	2.00	.45
☐ 414	Jack Sanford	4.50	2.00	.45
☐ 415	Tony Kubek	6.50	2.75	.65
☐ 416	Lee Maye	4.50	2.00	.45
☐ 417	Don Cardwell	4.50	2.00	.45
☐ 418	Orioles Rookies Darold Knowles Les Narum	5.50	2.50	.55

☐ 419	Ken Harrelson	7.00	3.00	.70
☐ 420	Jim Maloney	5.50	2.50	.55
☐ 421	Camilo Carreon	4.50	2.00	.45
☐ 422	Jack Fisher	4.50	2.00	.45
☐ 423	Tops in NL Hank Aaron Willie Mays	90.00	40.00	13.50
☐ 424	Dick Bertell	4.50	2.00	.45
☐ 425	Norm Cash	6.00	2.50	.60
☐ 426	Bob Rodgers	5.50	2.50	.55
☐ 427	Don Rudolph	4.50	2.00	.45
☐ 428	Red Sox Rookies Archie Skeen Pete Smith (back states Archie has retired)	4.50	2.00	.45
☐ 429	Tim McCarver	8.50	3.75	.85
☐ 430	Juan Pizarro	4.50	2.00	.45
☐ 431	George Alusik	4.50	2.00	.45
☐ 432	Ruben Amaro	4.50	2.00	.45
☐ 433	Yankees Team	13.00	5.75	1.75
☐ 434	Don Nottebart	4.50	2.00	.45
☐ 435	Vic Davalillo	5.00	2.25	.50
☐ 436	Charlie Neal	5.00	2.25	.50
☐ 437	Ed Bailey	5.00	2.25	.50
☐ 438	Checklist 6	15.00	1.50	.30
☐ 439	Harvey Haddix	5.00	2.25	.50
☐ 440	Bob Clemente UER (1960 Pittsburfh)	130.00	60.00	20.00
☐ 441	Bob Duliba	4.50	2.00	.45
☐ 442	Pumpsie Green	4.50	2.00	.45
☐ 443	Chuck Dressen MG	5.00	2.25	.50
☐ 444	Larry Jackson	4.50	2.00	.45
☐ 445	Bill Skowron	5.50	2.50	.55
☐ 446	Julian Javier	4.50	2.00	.45
☐ 447	Ted Bowsfield	4.50	2.00	.45
☐ 448	Cookie Rojas	5.00	2.25	.50
☐ 449	Deron Johnson	5.00	2.25	.50
☐ 450	Steve Barber	4.50	2.00	.45
☐ 451	Joe Amalfitano	4.50	2.00	.45
☐ 452	Giants Rookies Gil Garrido Jim Ray Hart	6.00	2.50	.60
☐ 453	Frank Baumann	4.50	2.00	.45
☐ 454	Tommie Aaron	5.00	2.25	.50
☐ 455	Bernie Allen	4.50	2.00	.45
☐ 456	Dodgers Rookies Wes Parker John Werhas	6.00	2.50	.60
☐ 457	Jesse Gonder	4.50	2.00	.45
☐ 458	Ralph Terry	5.00	2.25	.50
☐ 459	Red Sox Rookies Pete Charton Dalton Jones	4.50	2.00	.45
☐ 460	Bob Gibson	36.00	16.25	5.50
☐ 461	George Thomas	4.50	2.00	.45
☐ 462	Birdie Tebbetts MG	4.50	2.00	.45
☐ 463	Don Leppert	4.50	2.00	.45
☐ 464	Dallas Green	5.50	2.50	.55
☐ 465	Mike Hershberger	4.50	2.00	.45
☐ 466	A's Rookies Dick Green Aurelio Monteagudo	4.50	2.00	.45
☐ 467	Bob Aspromonte	4.50	2.00	.45
☐ 468	Gaylord Perry	40.00	18.00	6.00
☐ 469	Cubs Rookies Fred Norman Sterling Slaughter	4.50	2.00	.45
☐ 470	Jim Bouton	6.00	2.50	.60
☐ 471	Gates Brown	6.00	2.50	.60
☐ 472	Vern Law	5.50	2.50	.55
☐ 473	Baltimore Orioles Team Card	9.00	4.00	.90
☐ 474	Larry Sherry	5.00	2.25	.50
☐ 475	Ed Charles	4.50	2.00	.45
☐ 476	Braves Rookies Rico Carty Dick Kelley	9.00	4.00	.90
☐ 477	Mike Joyce	4.50	2.00	.45
☐ 478	Dick Howser	5.00	2.25	.50
☐ 479	Cardinals Rookies Dave Bakenhaster Johnny Lewis	4.50	2.00	.45
☐ 480	Bob Purkey	4.50	2.00	.45
☐ 481	Chuck Schilling	4.50	2.00	.45
☐ 482	Phillies Rookies John Briggs Danny Cater	5.50	2.50	.55
☐ 483	Fred Valentine	4.50	2.00	.45
☐ 484	Bill Pleis	4.50	2.00	.45
☐ 485	Tom Haller	4.50	2.00	.45
☐ 486	Bob Kennedy MG	4.50	2.00	.45
☐ 487	Mike McCormick	5.00	2.25	.50
☐ 488	Yankees Rookies Pete Mikkelsen Bob Meyer	5.00	2.25	.50
☐ 489	Julio Navarro	4.50	2.00	.45
☐ 490	Ron Fairly	5.00	2.25	.50
☐ 491	Ed Rakow	4.50	2.00	.45
☐ 492	Colts Rookies Jim Beauchamp Mike White	4.50	2.00	.45
☐ 493	Don Lee	4.50	2.00	.45
☐ 494	Al Jackson	4.50	2.00	.45
☐ 495	Bill Virdon	5.50	2.50	.55
☐ 496	White Sox Team	9.00	4.00	.90
☐ 497	Jeoff Long	4.50	2.00	.45
☐ 498	Dave Stenhouse	4.50	2.00	.45
☐ 499	Indians Rookies Chico Salmon Gordon Seyfried	4.50	2.00	.45
☐ 500	Camilo Pascual	5.00	2.25	.50
☐ 501	Bob Veale	5.00	2.25	.50
☐ 502	Angels Rookies Bobby Knoop Bob Lee	5.50	2.50	.55

☐ 503 Earl Wilson .... 4.50 2.00 .45
☐ 504 Claude Raymond .... 4.50 2.00 .45
☐ 505 Stan Williams .... 4.50 2.00 .45
☐ 506 Bobby Bragan MG .... 4.50 2.00 .45
☐ 507 Johnny Edwards .... 4.50 2.00 .45
☐ 508 Diego Segui .... 4.50 2.00 .45
☐ 509 Pirates Rookies .... 6.00 2.50 .60
Gene Alley
Orlando McFarlane
☐ 510 Lindy McDaniel .... 5.00 2.25 .50
☐ 511 Lou Jackson .... 4.50 2.00 .45
☐ 512 Tigers Rookies .... 9.00 4.00 .90
Willie Horton
Joe Sparma
☐ 513 Don Larsen .... 5.00 2.25 .50
☐ 514 Jim Hickman .... 4.50 2.00 .45
☐ 515 Johnny Romano .... 4.50 2.00 .45
☐ 516 Twins Rookies .... 4.50 2.00 .45
Jerry Arrigo
Dwight Siebler
☐ 517A Checklist 7 ERR ...... 25.00 2.50 .50
(incorrect numbering
sequence on back)
☐ 517B Checklist 7 COR ...... 15.00 1.50 .30
(correct numbering
on back)
☐ 518 Carl Bouldin .... 4.50 2.00 .45
☐ 519 Charlie Smith .... 4.50 2.00 .45
☐ 520 Jack Baldschun .... 4.50 2.00 .45
☐ 521 Tom Satriano .... 4.50 2.00 .45
☐ 522 Bob Tiefenauer .... 4.50 2.00 .45
☐ 523 Lou Burdette UER 10.00 4.50 1.25
(pitching lefty)
☐ 524 Reds Rookies .... 8.50 3.75 .85
Jim Dickson
Bobby Klaus
☐ 525 Al McBean .... 8.50 3.75 .85
☐ 526 Lou Clinton .... 8.50 3.75 .85
☐ 527 Larry Bearnarth .... 8.50 3.75 .85
☐ 528 A's Rookies 11.00 5.00 1.35
Dave Duncan
Tommie Reynolds
☐ 529 Alvin Dark MG 10.00 4.50 1.25
☐ 530 Leon Wagner .... 8.50 3.75 .85
☐ 531 Los Angeles Dodgers 20.00 8.50 2.75
Team Card
☐ 532 Twins Rookies .... 8.50 3.75 .85
Bud Bloomfield
(Bloomfield photo
actually Jay Ward)
Joe Nossek
☐ 533 Johnny Klippstein .... 8.50 3.75 .85
☐ 534 Gus Bell 10.00 4.50 1.25
☐ 535 Phil Regan 10.00 4.50 1.25
☐ 536 Mets Rookies .... 8.50 3.75 .85
Larry Elliot
John Stephenson
☐ 537 Dan Osinski .... 8.50 3.75 .85
☐ 538 Minnie Minoso 11.00 5.00 1.35
☐ 539 Roy Face 11.00 5.00 1.35
☐ 540 Luis Aparicio 18.00 7.50 2.50
☐ 541 Braves Rookies 200.00 90.00 30.00
Phil Roof
Phil Niekro
☐ 542 Don Mincher 10.00 4.50 1.25
☐ 543 Bob Uecker 60.00 27.00 9.00
☐ 544 Colts Rookies 10.00 4.50 1.25
Steve Hertz
Joe Hoerner
☐ 545 Max Alvis .... 8.50 3.75 .85
☐ 546 Joe Christopher .... 8.50 3.75 .85
☐ 547 Gil Hodges 15.00 6.50 2.15
☐ 548 NL Rookies .... 8.50 3.75 .85
Wayne Schurr
Paul Speckenbach
☐ 549 Joe Moeller .... 8.50 3.75 .85
☐ 550 Ken Hubbs 21.00 9.00 3.00
(in memoriam)
☐ 551 Billy Hoeft .... 8.50 3.75 .85
☐ 552 Indians Rookies 10.00 4.50 1.25
Tom Kelley
Sonny Siebert
☐ 553 Jim Brewer .... 8.50 3.75 .85
☐ 554 Hank Foiles .... 8.50 3.75 .85
☐ 555 Lee Stange .... 8.50 3.75 .85
☐ 556 Mets Rookies .... 8.50 3.75 .85
Steve Dillon
Ron Locke
☐ 557 Leo Burke .... 8.50 3.75 .85
☐ 558 Don Schwall .... 8.50 3.75 .85
☐ 559 Dick Phillips .... 8.50 3.75 .85
☐ 560 Dick Farrell .... 8.50 3.75 .85
☐ 561 Phillies Rookies UER . 11.00 5.00 1.35
Dave Bennett
(19 ... is 18)
Rick Wise
☐ 562 Pedro Ramos .... 8.50 3.75 .85
☐ 563 Dal Maxvill .... 8.50 3.75 .85
☐ 564 AL Rookies .... 8.50 3.75 .85
Joe McCabe
Jerry McNertney
☐ 565 Stu Miller .... 8.50 3.75 .85
☐ 566 Ed Kranepool 10.00 4.50 1.25
☐ 567 Jim Kaat 12.50 5.50 1.65
☐ 568 NL Rookies .... 8.50 3.75 .85
Phil Gagliano
Cap Peterson
☐ 569 Fred Newman .... 8.50 3.75 .85
☐ 570 Bill Mazeroski 11.00 5.00 1.35
☐ 571 Gene Conley .... 8.50 3.75 .85
☐ 572 AL Rookies .... 8.50 3.75 .85
Dave Gray
Dick Egan
☐ 573 Jim Duffalo .... 8.50 3.75 .85
☐ 574 Manny Jimenez .... 8.50 3.75 .85
☐ 575 Tony Cloninger .... 8.50 3.75 .85

	NRMT	VG-E	GOOD
☐ 576 Mets Rookies	8.50	3.75	.85
Jerry Hinsley			
Bill Wakefield			
☐ 577 Gordy Coleman	8.50	3.75	.85
☐ 578 Glen Hobbie	8.50	3.75	.85
☐ 579 Red Sox Team	16.00	6.75	2.25
☐ 580 Johnny Podres	10.00	4.50	1.25
☐ 581 Yankees Rookies	8.50	3.75	.85
Pedro Gonzalez			
Archie Moore			
☐ 582 Rod Kanehl	8.50	3.75	.85
☐ 583 Tito Francona	8.50	3.75	.85
☐ 584 Joel Horlen	8.50	3.75	.85
☐ 585 Tony Taylor	8.50	3.75	.85
☐ 586 Jim Piersall	10.00	4.50	1.25
☐ 587 Bennie Daniels	12.00	5.00	1.00

1965 Topps

The cards in this 598-card set measure 2 1/2" by 3 1/2". The cards comprising the 1965 Topps set have team names located within a distinctive pennant design below the picture. The cards have blue borders on the reverse and were issued by series. Cards 523 to 598 are more difficult to obtain than all other series. Within this last series there are 44 cards that were printed in lesser quantities than the other cards in that series; these shorter-printed cards are marked by SP in the checklist below. In addition, the sixth series (447-522) is more difficult to obtain than series one through five. Featured subsets within this set include League Leaders (1-12) and World Series cards (132-139). Key cards in this set include Steve Carlton's rookie, Mickey Mantle, and Pete Rose. Other key rookies in this set are Jim Hunter, Joe Morgan, and Tony Perez.

	NRMT	VG-E	GOOD
COMPLETE SET (598)	3750.00	1750.00	400.00
COMMON PLAYER (1-196)	1.25	.50	.12
COMMON PLAYER (197-283)	2.00	.80	.20
COMMON PLAYER (284-370)	2.75	1.10	.27
COMMON PLAYER (371-446)	4.00	1.75	.40
COMMON PLAYER (447-522)	5.25	2.25	.50
COMMON PLAYER (523-598)	5.50	2.50	.55
COMMON SP (523-598)	11.00	5.00	1.35
☐ 1 AL Batting Leaders	15.00	3.00	.60
Tony Oliva			
Elston Howard			
Brooks Robinson			
☐ 2 NL Batting Leaders	7.50	3.25	.75
Bob Clemente			
Hank Aaron			
Rico Carty			
☐ 3 AL Home Run Leaders	12.50	5.50	1.65
Harmon Killebrew			
Mickey Mantle			
Boog Powell			
☐ 4 NL Home Run Leaders	6.00	2.50	.60
Willie Mays			
Billy Williams			
Jim Ray Hart			
Orlando Cepeda			
Johnny Callison			
☐ 5 AL RBI Leaders	12.50	5.50	1.65
Brooks Robinson			
Harmon Killebrew			
Mickey Mantle			
Dick Stuart			
☐ 6 NL RBI Leaders	4.00	1.75	.40
Ken Boyer			
Willie Mays			
Ron Santo			
☐ 7 AL ERA Leaders	2.50	1.00	.25
Dean Chance			
Joel Horlen			
☐ 8 NL ERA Leaders	7.50	3.25	.75
Sandy Koufax			
Don Drysdale			
☐ 9 AL Pitching Leaders	2.50	1.00	.25
Dean Chance			
Gary Peters			
Dave Wickersham			
Juan Pizarro			
Wally Bunker			
☐ 10 NL Pitching Leaders	2.50	1.00	.25
Larry Jackson			
Ray Sadecki			
Juan Marichal			
☐ 11 AL Strikeout Leaders	2.50	1.00	.25
Al Downing			
Dean Chance			
Camilo Pascual			

☐ 12 NL Strikeout Leaders .... 3.50 1.50 .35
Bob Veale
Don Drysdale
Bob Gibson
☐ 13 Pedro Ramos .... 1.25 .50 .12
☐ 14 Len Gabrielson .... 1.25 .50 .12
☐ 15 Robin Roberts .... 7.50 3.25 .75
☐ 16 Houston Rookies 175.00 80.00 27.00
Joe Morgan
Sonny Jackson
☐ 17 Johnny Romano .... 1.25 .50 .12
☐ 18 Bill McCool .... 1.25 .50 .12
☐ 19 Gates Brown .... 1.75 .70 .17
☐ 20 Jim Bunning .... 3.75 1.60 .37
☐ 21 Don Blasingame .... 1.25 .50 .12
☐ 22 Charlie Smith .... 1.25 .50 .12
☐ 23 Bob Tiefenauer .... 1.25 .50 .12
☐ 24 Minnesota Twins .... 3.00 1.25 .30
Team Card
☐ 25 Al McBean .... 1.25 .50 .12
☐ 26 Bobby Knoop .... 1.25 .50 .12
☐ 27 Dick Bertell .... 1.25 .50 .12
☐ 28 Barney Schultz .... 1.25 .50 .12
☐ 29 Felix Mantilla .... 1.25 .50 .12
☐ 30 Jim Bouton .... 2.50 1.00 .25
☐ 31 Mike White .... 1.25 .50 .12
☐ 32 Herman Franks MG .... 1.25 .50 .12
☐ 33 Jackie Brandt .... 1.25 .50 .12
☐ 34 Cal Koonce .... 1.25 .50 .12
☐ 35 Ed Charles .... 1.25 .50 .12
☐ 36 Bobby Wine .... 1.25 .50 .12
☐ 37 Fred Gladding .... 1.25 .50 .12
☐ 38 Jim King .... 1.25 .50 .12
☐ 39 Gerry Arrigo .... 1.25 .50 .12
☐ 40 Frank Howard .... 2.50 1.00 .25
☐ 41 White Sox Rookies .... 1.25 .50 .12
Bruce Howard
Marv Staehle
☐ 42 Earl Wilson .... 1.25 .50 .12
☐ 43 Mike Shannon .... 1.75 .70 .17
(Name in red, other
Cardinals in yellow)
☐ 44 Wade Blasingame .... 1.25 .50 .12
☐ 45 Roy McMillan .... 1.25 .50 .12
☐ 46 Bob Lee .... 1.25 .50 .12
☐ 47 Tommy Harper .... 1.75 .70 .17
☐ 48 Claude Raymond .... 1.25 .50 .12
☐ 49 Orioles Rookies .... 1.75 .70 .17
Curt Blefary
John Miller
☐ 50 Juan Marichal 9.50 4.25 1.00
☐ 51 Bill Bryan .... 1.25 .50 .12
☐ 52 Ed Roebuck .... 1.25 .50 .12
☐ 53 Dick McAuliffe .... 1.75 .70 .17
☐ 54 Joe Gibbon .... 1.25 .50 .12
☐ 55 Tony Conigliaro .... 8.00 3.50 .80
☐ 56 Ron Kline .... 1.25 .50 .12
☐ 57 Cardinals Team .... 2.50 1.00 .25
☐ 58 Fred Talbot .... 1.25 .50 .12
☐ 59 Nate Oliver .... 1.25 .50 .12
☐ 60 Jim O'Toole .... 1.25 .50 .12
☐ 61 Chris Cannizzaro .... 1.25 .50 .12
☐ 62 Jim Katt UER .... 4.50 2.00 .45
(sic, Kaat)
☐ 63 Ty Cline .... 1.25 .50 .12
☐ 64 Lou Burdette .... 1.75 .70 .17
☐ 65 Tony Kubek .... 3.00 1.25 .30
☐ 66 Bill Rigney MG .... 1.25 .50 .12
☐ 67 Harvey Haddix .... 1.75 .70 .17
☐ 68 Del Crandall .... 1.75 .70 .17
☐ 69 Bill Virdon .... 1.75 .70 .17
☐ 70 Bill Skowron .... 1.75 .70 .17
☐ 71 John O'Donoghue .... 1.25 .50 .12
☐ 72 Tony Gonzalez .... 1.25 .50 .12
☐ 73 Dennis Ribant .... 1.25 .50 .12
☐ 74 Red Sox Rookies .... 5.50 2.50 .55
Rico Petrocelli
Jerry Stephenson
☐ 75 Deron Johnson .... 1.25 .50 .12
☐ 76 Sam McDowell .... 1.75 .70 .17
☐ 77 Doug Camilli .... 1.25 .50 .12
☐ 78 Dal Maxvill .... 1.25 .50 .12
☐ 79 Checklist 1 .... 7.50 .75 .15
☐ 80 Turk Farrell .... 1.25 .50 .12
☐ 81 Don Buford .... 1.75 .70 .17
☐ 82 Braves Rookies .... 2.50 1.00 .25
Santos Alomar
John Braun
☐ 83 George Thomas .... 1.25 .50 .12
☐ 84 Ron Herbel .... 1.25 .50 .12
☐ 85 Willie Smith .... 1.25 .50 .12
☐ 86 Les Narum .... 1.25 .50 .12
☐ 87 Nelson Mathews .... 1.25 .50 .12
☐ 88 Jack Lamabe .... 1.25 .50 .12
☐ 89 Mike Hershberger .... 1.25 .50 .12
☐ 90 Rich Rollins .... 1.75 .70 .17
☐ 91 Cubs Team .... 2.50 1.00 .25
☐ 92 Dick Howser .... 1.75 .70 .17
☐ 93 Jack Fisher .... 1.25 .50 .12
☐ 94 Charlie Lau .... 1.75 .70 .17
☐ 95 Bill Mazeroski .... 3.00 1.25 .30
☐ 96 Sonny Siebert .... 1.25 .50 .12
☐ 97 Pedro Gonzalez .... 1.25 .50 .12
☐ 98 Bob Miller .... 1.25 .50 .12
☐ 99 Gil Hodges MG .... 6.00 2.50 .60
☐ 100 Ken Boyer .... 3.00 1.25 .30
☐ 101 Fred Newman .... 1.25 .50 .12
☐ 102 Steve Boros .... 1.25 .50 .12
☐ 103 Harvey Kuenn .... 1.75 .70 .17
☐ 104 Checklist 2 .... 7.50 .75 .15
☐ 105 Chico Salmon .... 1.25 .50 .12
☐ 106 Gene Oliver .... 1.25 .50 .12
☐ 107 Phillies Rookies .... 1.75 .70 .17
Pat Corrales
Costen Shockley
☐ 108 Don Mincher .... 1.75 .70 .17

☐ 109	Walt Bond	1.25	.50	.12
☐ 110	Ron Santo	3.00	1.25	.30
☐ 111	Lee Thomas	1.75	.70	.17
☐ 112	Derrell Griffith	1.25	.50	.12
☐ 113	Steve Barber	1.25	.50	.12
☐ 114	Jim Hickman	1.25	.50	.12
☐ 115	Bobby Richardson	3.00	1.25	.30
☐ 116	Cardinals Rookies Dave Dowling Bob Tolan	1.75	.70	.17
☐ 117	Wes Stock	1.25	.50	.12
☐ 118	Hal Lanier	1.75	.70	.17
☐ 119	John Kennedy	1.25	.50	.12
☐ 120	Frank Robinson	25.00	11.00	3.50
☐ 121	Gene Alley	1.75	.70	.17
☐ 122	Bill Pleis	1.25	.50	.12
☐ 123	Frank Thomas	1.75	.70	.17
☐ 124	Tom Satriano	1.25	.50	.12
☐ 125	Juan Pizarro	1.25	.50	.12
☐ 126	Dodgers Team	4.00	1.75	.40
☐ 127	Frank Lary	1.25	.50	.12
☐ 128	Vic Davalillo	1.25	.50	.12
☐ 129	Bennie Daniels	1.25	.50	.12
☐ 130	Al Kaline	25.00	11.00	3.50
☐ 131	Johnny Keane MG	1.25	.50	.12
☐ 132	World Series Game 1 Cards take opener	4.00	1.75	.40
☐ 133	World Series Game 2 Stottlemyre wins	4.00	1.75	.40
☐ 134	World Series Game 3 Mantle's homer	28.00	12.50	4.00
☐ 135	World Series Game 4 Boyer's grand-slam	4.50	2.00	.45
☐ 136	World Series Game 5 10th inning triumph	4.00	1.75	.40
☐ 137	World Series Game 6 Bouton wins again	4.50	2.00	.45
☐ 138	World Series Game 7 Gibson wins finale	6.00	2.50	.60
☐ 139	World Series Summary Cards celebrate	4.00	1.75	.40
☐ 140	Dean Chance	1.75	.70	.17
☐ 141	Charlie James	1.25	.50	.12
☐ 142	Bill Monbouquette	1.25	.50	.12
☐ 143	Pirates Rookies John Gelnar Jerry May	1.25	.50	.12
☐ 144	Ed Kranepool	1.75	.70	.17
☐ 145	Luis Tiant	12.00	5.25	1.50
☐ 146	Ron Hansen	1.25	.50	.12
☐ 147	Dennis Bennett	1.25	.50	.12
☐ 148	Willie Kirkland	1.25	.50	.12
☐ 149	Wayne Schurr	1.25	.50	.12
☐ 150	Brooks Robinson	25.00	11.00	3.50
☐ 151	Athletics Team	2.50	1.00	.25
☐ 152	Phil Ortega	1.25	.50	.12
☐ 153	Norm Cash	3.00	1.25	.30
☐ 154	Bob Humphreys	1.25	.50	.12
☐ 155	Roger Maris	50.00	22.50	7.50
☐ 156	Bob Sadowski	1.25	.50	.12
☐ 157	Zoilo Versalles	1.75	.70	.17
☐ 158	Dick Sisler	1.25	.50	.12
☐ 159	Jim Duffalo	1.25	.50	.12
☐ 160	Bob Clemente UER (1960 Pittsburfh)	75.00	34.00	11.25
☐ 161	Frank Baumann	1.25	.50	.12
☐ 162	Russ Nixon	1.25	.50	.12
☐ 163	Johnny Briggs	1.25	.50	.12
☐ 164	Al Spangler	1.25	.50	.12
☐ 165	Dick Ellsworth	1.25	.50	.12
☐ 166	Indians Rookies George Culver Tommie Agee	2.50	1.00	.25
☐ 167	Bill Wakefield	1.25	.50	.12
☐ 168	Dick Green	1.25	.50	.12
☐ 169	Dave Vineyard	1.25	.50	.12
☐ 170	Hank Aaron	90.00	40.00	13.50
☐ 171	Jim Roland	1.25	.50	.12
☐ 172	Jim Piersall	1.75	.70	.17
☐ 173	Detroit Tigers Team Card	2.50	1.00	.25
☐ 174	Joey Jay	1.25	.50	.12
☐ 175	Bob Aspromonte	1.25	.50	.12
☐ 176	Willie McCovey	18.00	7.50	2.50
☐ 177	Pete Mikkelsen	1.25	.50	.12
☐ 178	Dalton Jones	1.25	.50	.12
☐ 179	Hal Woodeshick	1.25	.50	.12
☐ 180	Bob Allison	1.75	.70	.17
☐ 181	Senators Rookies Don Loun Joe McCabe	1.25	.50	.12
☐ 182	Mike de la Hoz	1.25	.50	.12
☐ 183	Dave Nicholson	1.25	.50	.12
☐ 184	John Boozer	1.25	.50	.12
☐ 185	Max Alvis	1.25	.50	.12
☐ 186	Billy Cowan	1.25	.50	.12
☐ 187	Casey Stengel MG	12.50	5.50	1.65
☐ 188	Sam Bowens	1.25	.50	.12
☐ 189	Checklist 3	7.50	.75	.15
☐ 190	Bill White	2.50	1.00	.25
☐ 191	Phil Regan	1.25	.50	.12
☐ 192	Jim Coker	1.25	.50	.12
☐ 193	Gaylord Perry	20.00	8.50	2.75
☐ 194	Rookie Stars Bill Kelso Rick Reichardt	1.75	.70	.17
☐ 195	Bob Veale	1.75	.70	.17
☐ 196	Ron Fairly	1.75	.70	.17
☐ 197	Diego Segui	2.00	.80	.20
☐ 198	Smoky Burgess	2.50	1.00	.25
☐ 199	Bob Heffner	2.00	.80	.20
☐ 200	Joe Torre	3.50	1.50	.35
☐ 201	Twins Rookies Sandy Valdespino Cesar Tovar	2.50	1.00	.25
☐ 202	Leo Burke	2.00	.80	.20

□ 203	Dallas Green	2.50	1.00	.25
□ 204	Russ Snyder	2.00	.80	.20
□ 205	Warren Spahn	22.00	9.50	3.15
□ 206	Willie Horton	3.00	1.25	.30
□ 207	Pete Rose	160.00	72.00	24.00
□ 208	Tommy John	12.50	5.50	1.65
□ 209	Pirates Team	4.00	1.75	.40
□ 210	Jim Fregosi	3.00	1.25	.30
□ 211	Steve Ridzik	2.00	.80	.20
□ 212	Ron Brand	2.00	.80	.20
□ 213	Jim Davenport	2.00	.80	.20
□ 214	Bob Purkey	2.00	.80	.20
□ 215	Pete Ward	2.00	.80	.20
□ 216	Al Worthington	2.00	.80	.20
□ 217	Walt Alston MG	4.00	1.75	.40
□ 218	Dick Schofield	2.00	.80	.20
□ 219	Bob Meyer	2.00	.80	.20
□ 220	Billy Williams	12.50	5.50	1.65
□ 221	John Tsitouris	2.00	.80	.20
□ 222	Bob Tillman	2.00	.80	.20
□ 223	Dan Osinski	2.00	.80	.20
□ 224	Bob Chance	2.00	.80	.20
□ 225	Bo Belinsky	2.50	1.00	.25
□ 226	Yankees Rookies	2.50	1.00	.25
	Elvio Jimenez			
	Jake Gibbs			
□ 227	Bobby Klaus	2.00	.80	.20
□ 228	Jack Sanford	2.00	.80	.20
□ 229	Lou Clinton	2.00	.80	.20
□ 230	Ray Sadecki	2.00	.80	.20
□ 231	Jerry Adair	2.00	.80	.20
□ 232	Steve Blass	2.50	1.00	.25
□ 233	Don Zimmer	2.50	1.00	.25
□ 234	White Sox Team	4.00	1.75	.40
□ 235	Chuck Hinton	2.00	.80	.20
□ 236	Denny McLain	20.00	8.50	2.75
□ 237	Bernie Allen	2.00	.80	.20
□ 238	Joe Moeller	2.00	.80	.20
□ 239	Doc Edwards	2.00	.80	.20
□ 240	Bob Bruce	2.00	.80	.20
□ 241	Mack Jones	2.00	.80	.20
□ 242	George Brunet	2.00	.80	.20
□ 243	Reds Rookies	3.00	1.25	.30
	Ted Davidson			
	Tommy Helms			
□ 244	Lindy McDaniel	2.50	1.00	.25
□ 245	Joe Pepitone	3.00	1.25	.30
□ 246	Tom Butters	2.00	.80	.20
□ 247	Wally Moon	2.50	1.00	.25
□ 248	Gus Triandos	2.50	1.00	.25
□ 249	Dave McNally	2.50	1.00	.25
□ 250	Willie Mays	100.00	45.00	15.00
□ 251	Billy Herman MG	2.50	1.00	.25
□ 252	Pete Richert	2.00	.80	.20
□ 253	Danny Cater	2.50	1.00	.25
□ 254	Roland Sheldon	2.00	.80	.20
□ 255	Camilo Pascual	2.50	1.00	.25
□ 256	Tito Francona	2.00	.80	.20
□ 257	Jim Wynn	3.00	1.25	.30
□ 258	Larry Bearnarth	2.00	.80	.20
□ 259	Tigers Rookies	4.00	1.75	.40
	Jim Northrup			
	Ray Oyler			
□ 260	Don Drysdale	20.00	8.50	2.75
□ 261	Duke Carmel	2.00	.80	.20
□ 262	Bud Daley	2.00	.80	.20
□ 263	Marty Keough	2.00	.80	.20
□ 264	Bob Buhl	2.00	.80	.20
□ 265	Jim Pagliaroni	2.00	.80	.20
□ 266	Bert Campaneris	6.50	2.75	.65
□ 267	Senators Team	4.00	1.75	.40
□ 268	Ken McBride	2.00	.80	.20
□ 269	Frank Bolling	2.00	.80	.20
□ 270	Milt Pappas	2.50	1.00	.25
□ 271	Don Wert	2.00	.80	.20
□ 272	Chuck Schilling	2.00	.80	.20
□ 273	Checklist 4	7.50	.75	.15
□ 274	Lum Harris MG	2.00	.80	.20
□ 275	Dick Groat	2.50	1.00	.25
□ 276	Hoyt Wilhelm	7.50	3.25	.75
□ 277	Johnny Lewis	2.00	.80	.20
□ 278	Ken Retzer	2.00	.80	.20
□ 279	Dick Tracewski	2.00	.80	.20
□ 280	Dick Stuart	2.50	1.00	.25
□ 281	Bill Stafford	2.00	.80	.20
□ 282	Giants Rookies	4.00	1.75	.40
	Dick Estelle			
	Masanori Murakami			
□ 283	Fred Whitfield	2.00	.80	.20
□ 284	Nick Willhite	2.75	1.10	.27
□ 285	Ron Hunt	2.75	1.10	.27
□ 286	Athletics Rookies	2.75	1.10	.27
	Jim Dickson			
	Aurelio Monteagudo			
□ 287	Gary Kolb	2.75	1.10	.27
□ 288	Jack Hamilton	2.75	1.10	.27
□ 289	Gordy Coleman	3.25	1.35	.32
□ 290	Wally Bunker	3.25	1.35	.32
□ 291	Jerry Lynch	2.75	1.10	.27
□ 292	Larry Yellen	2.75	1.10	.27
□ 293	Angels Team	5.00	2.25	.50
□ 294	Tim McCarver	4.50	2.00	.45
□ 295	Dick Radatz	3.25	1.35	.32
□ 296	Tony Taylor	2.75	1.10	.27
□ 297	Dave DeBusschere	3.75	1.60	.37
□ 298	Jim Stewart	2.75	1.10	.27
□ 299	Jerry Zimmerman	2.75	1.10	.27
□ 300	Sandy Koufax	110.00	50.00	16.50
□ 301	Birdie Tebbetts MG	2.75	1.10	.27
□ 302	Al Stanek	2.75	1.10	.27
□ 303	John Orsino	2.75	1.10	.27
□ 304	Dave Stenhouse	2.75	1.10	.27
□ 305	Rico Carty	3.50	1.50	.35
□ 306	Bubba Phillips	2.75	1.10	.27
□ 307	Barry Latman	2.75	1.10	.27
□ 308	Mets Rookies	4.00	1.75	.40

Cleon Jones
Tom Parsons
□ 309 Steve Hamilton .... 2.75 1.10 .27
□ 310 Johnny Callison .... 3.50 1.50 .35
□ 311 Orlando Pena .... 2.75 1.10 .27
□ 312 Joe Nuxhall .... 3.50 1.50 .35
□ 313 Jim Schaffer .... 2.75 1.10 .27
□ 314 Sterling Slaughter .... 2.75 1.10 .27
□ 315 Frank Malzone .... 3.50 1.50 .35
□ 316 Reds Team .... 5.50 2.50 .55
□ 317 Don McMahon .... 2.75 1.10 .27
□ 318 Matty Alou .... 3.50 1.50 .35
□ 319 Ken McMullen .... 2.75 1.10 .27
□ 320 Bob Gibson 28.00 12.50 4.00
□ 321 Rusty Staub .... 4.00 1.75 .40
□ 322 Rick Wise .... 3.50 1.50 .35
□ 323 Hank Bauer MG .... 3.50 1.50 .35
□ 324 Bobby Locke .... 2.75 1.10 .27
□ 325 Donn Clendenon .... 3.50 1.50 .35
□ 326 Dwight Siebler .... 2.75 1.10 .27
□ 327 Denis Menke .... 2.75 1.10 .27
□ 328 Eddie Fisher .... 2.75 1.10 .27
□ 329 Hawk Taylor .... 2.75 1.10 .27
□ 330 Whitey Ford 25.00 11.00 3.50
□ 331 Dodgers Rookies .... 3.50 1.50 .35
Al Ferrara
John Purdin
□ 332 Ted Abernathy .... 2.75 1.10 .27
□ 333 Tom Reynolds .... 2.75 1.10 .27
□ 334 Vic Roznovsky .... 2.75 1.10 .27
□ 335 Mickey Lolich .... 4.50 2.00 .45
□ 336 Woody Held .... 2.75 1.10 .27
□ 337 Mike Cuellar .... 3.50 1.50 .35
□ 338 Philadelphia Phillies .... 5.50 2.50 .55
Team Card
□ 339 Ryne Duren .... 3.50 1.50 .35
□ 340 Tony Oliva .... 9.00 4.00 .90
□ 341 Bob Bolin .... 2.75 1.10 .27
□ 342 Bob Rodgers .... 3.50 1.50 .35
□ 343 Mike McCormick .... 3.50 1.50 .35
□ 344 Wes Parker .... 3.50 1.50 .35
□ 345 Floyd Robinson .... 2.75 1.10 .27
□ 346 Bobby Bragan MG .... 2.75 1.10 .27
□ 347 Roy Face .... 3.50 1.50 .35
□ 348 George Banks .... 2.75 1.10 .27
□ 349 Larry Miller .... 2.75 1.10 .27
□ 350 Mickey Mantle 400.00 180.00 60.00
□ 351 Jim Perry .... 3.50 1.50 .35
□ 352 Alex Johnson .... 3.50 1.50 .35
□ 353 Jerry Lumpe .... 2.75 1.10 .27
□ 354 Cubs Rookies .... 2.75 1.10 .27
Billy Ott
Jack Warner
□ 355 Vada Pinson .... 3.50 1.50 .35
□ 356 Bill Spanswick .... 2.75 1.10 .27
□ 357 Carl Warwick .... 2.75 1.10 .27
□ 358 Albie Pearson .... 2.75 1.10 .27
□ 359 Ken Johnson .... 2.75 1.10 .27
□ 360 Orlando Cepeda .... 7.00 3.00 .70
□ 361 Checklist 5 .... 9.00 .90 .20
□ 362 Don Schwall .... 2.75 1.10 .27
□ 363 Bob Johnson .... 2.75 1.10 .27
□ 364 Galen Cisco .... 2.75 1.10 .27
□ 365 Jim Gentile .... 3.50 1.50 .35
□ 366 Dan Schneider .... 2.75 1.10 .27
□ 367 Leon Wagner .... 2.75 1.10 .27
□ 368 White Sox Rookies ...... 3.50 1.50 .35
Ken Berry
Joel Gibson
□ 369 Phil Linz .... 3.50 1.50 .35
□ 370 Tommy Davis .... 3.50 1.50 .35
□ 371 Frank Kreutzer .... 4.00 1.75 .40
□ 372 Clay Dalrymple .... 4.00 1.75 .40
□ 373 Curt Simmons .... 4.50 2.00 .45
□ 374 Angels Rookies .... 4.50 2.00 .45
Jose Cardenal
Dick Simpson
□ 375 Dave Wickersham .... 4.00 1.75 .40
□ 376 Jim Landis .... 4.00 1.75 .40
□ 377 Willie Stargell 27.00 12.00 4.00
□ 378 Chuck Estrada .... 4.50 2.00 .45
□ 379 Giants Team .... 8.00 3.50 .80
□ 380 Rocky Colavito .... 7.50 3.25 .75
□ 381 Al Jackson .... 4.50 2.00 .45
□ 382 J.C. Martin .... 4.00 1.75 .40
□ 383 Felipe Alou .... 5.00 2.25 .50
□ 384 Johnny Klippstein .... 4.00 1.75 .40
□ 385 Carl Yastrzemski 85.00 38.00 12.75
□ 386 Cubs Rookies .... 4.50 2.00 .45
Paul Jaeckel
Fred Norman
□ 387 Johnny Podres .... 5.00 2.25 .50
□ 388 John Blanchard .... 4.50 2.00 .45
□ 389 Don Larsen .... 4.50 2.00 .45
□ 390 Bill Freehan .... 5.00 2.25 .50
□ 391 Mel McGaha MG .... 4.00 1.75 .40
□ 392 Bob Friend .... 4.50 2.00 .45
□ 393 Ed Kirkpatrick .... 4.00 1.75 .40
□ 394 Jim Hannan .... 4.00 1.75 .40
□ 395 Jim Ray Hart .... 4.50 2.00 .45
□ 396 Frank Bertaina .... 4.00 1.75 .40
□ 397 Jerry Buchek .... 4.00 1.75 .40
□ 398 Reds Rookies .... 4.50 2.00 .45
Dan Neville
Art Shamsky
□ 399 Ray Herbert .... 4.00 1.75 .40
□ 400 Harmon Killebrew 32.00 14.25 4.75
□ 401 Carl Willey .... 4.00 1.75 .40
□ 402 Joe Amalfitano .... 4.00 1.75 .40
□ 403 Boston Red Sox .... 8.00 3.50 .80
Team Card
□ 404 Stan Williams .... 4.00 1.75 .40
(listed as Indian
but Yankee cap)
□ 405 John Roseboro .... 4.50 2.00 .45
□ 406 Ralph Terry .... 4.50 2.00 .45

☐ 407	Lee Maye	4.00	1.75	.40
☐ 408	Larry Sherry	4.50	2.00	.45
☐ 409	Astros Rookies	5.00	2.25	.50
	Jim Beauchamp			
	Larry Dierker			
☐ 410	Luis Aparicio	10.00	4.50	1.25
☐ 411	Roger Craig	4.50	2.00	.45
☐ 412	Bob Bailey	4.00	1.75	.40
☐ 413	Hal Reniff	4.00	1.75	.40
☐ 414	Al Lopez MG	5.50	2.50	.55
☐ 415	Curt Flood	6.00	2.50	.60
☐ 416	Jim Brewer	4.00	1.75	.40
☐ 417	Ed Brinkman	4.00	1.75	.40
☐ 418	Johnny Edwards	4.00	1.75	.40
☐ 419	Ruben Amaro	4.00	1.75	.40
☐ 420	Larry Jackson	4.00	1.75	.40
☐ 421	Twins Rookies	4.00	1.75	.40
	Gary Dotter			
	Jay Ward			
☐ 422	Aubrey Gatewood	4.00	1.75	.40
☐ 423	Jesse Gonder	4.00	1.75	.40
☐ 424	Gary Bell	4.00	1.75	.40
☐ 425	Wayne Causey	4.00	1.75	.40
☐ 426	Braves Team	8.00	3.50	.80
☐ 427	Bob Saverine	4.00	1.75	.40
☐ 428	Bob Shaw	4.00	1.75	.40
☐ 429	Don Demeter	4.00	1.75	.40
☐ 430	Gary Peters	4.50	2.00	.45
☐ 431	Cards Rookies	6.00	2.50	.60
	Nelson Briles			
	Wayne Spiezio			
☐ 432	Jim Grant	4.00	1.75	.40
☐ 433	John Bateman	4.00	1.75	.40
☐ 434	Dave Morehead	4.00	1.75	.40
☐ 435	Willie Davis	5.00	2.25	.50
☐ 436	Don Elston	4.00	1.75	.40
☐ 437	Chico Cardenas	4.50	2.00	.45
☐ 438	Harry Walker MG	4.00	1.75	.40
☐ 439	Moe Drabowsky	4.00	1.75	.40
☐ 440	Tom Tresh	5.00	2.25	.50
☐ 441	Denny Lemaster	4.00	1.75	.40
☐ 442	Vic Power	4.00	1.75	.40
☐ 443	Checklist 6	12.50	1.25	.25
☐ 444	Bob Hendley	4.00	1.75	.40
☐ 445	Don Lock	4.00	1.75	.40
☐ 446	Art Mahaffey	4.00	1.75	.40
☐ 447	Julian Javier	5.25	2.25	.50
☐ 448	Lee Stange	5.25	2.25	.50
☐ 449	Mets Rookies	5.25	2.25	.50
	Jerry Hinsley			
	Gary Kroll			
☐ 450	Elston Howard	7.00	3.00	.70
☐ 451	Jim Owens	5.25	2.25	.50
☐ 452	Gary Geiger	5.25	2.25	.50
☐ 453	Dodgers Rookies	6.00	2.50	.60
	Willie Crawford			
	John Werhas			
☐ 454	Ed Rakow	5.25	2.25	.50
☐ 455	Norm Siebern	5.25	2.25	.50
☐ 456	Bill Henry	5.25	2.25	.50
☐ 457	Bob Kennedy MG	5.25	2.25	.50
☐ 458	John Buzhardt	5.25	2.25	.50
☐ 459	Frank Kostro	5.25	2.25	.50
☐ 460	Richie Allen	20.00	8.50	2.75
☐ 461	Braves Rookies	50.00	22.50	7.50
	Clay Carroll			
	Phil Niekro			
☐ 462	Lew Krausse UER	5.25	2.25	.50
	(photo actually			
	Pete Lovrich)			
☐ 463	Manny Mota	6.00	2.50	.60
☐ 464	Ron Piche	5.25	2.25	.50
☐ 465	Tom Haller	5.25	2.25	.50
☐ 466	Senators Rookies	5.25	2.25	.50
	Pete Craig			
	Dick Nen			
☐ 467	Ray Washburn	5.25	2.25	.50
☐ 468	Larry Brown	5.25	2.25	.50
☐ 469	Don Nottebart	5.25	2.25	.50
☐ 470	Yogi Berra P/CO	55.00	25.00	8.25
☐ 471	Billy Hoeft	5.25	2.25	.50
☐ 472	Don Pavletich	5.25	2.25	.50
☐ 473	Orioles Rookies	12.00	5.25	1.50
	Paul Blair			
	Dave Johnson			
☐ 474	Cookie Rojas	6.00	2.50	.60
☐ 475	Clete Boyer	6.00	2.50	.60
☐ 476	Billy O'Dell	5.25	2.25	.50
☐ 477	Cards Rookies	475.00	215.00	70.00
	Fritz Ackley			
	Steve Carlton			
☐ 478	Wilbur Wood	6.00	2.50	.60
☐ 479	Ken Harrelson	7.00	3.00	.70
☐ 480	Joel Horlen	6.00	2.50	.60
☐ 481	Cleveland Indians	11.00	5.00	1.35
	Team Card			
☐ 482	Bob Priddy	5.25	2.25	.50
☐ 483	George Smith	5.25	2.25	.50
☐ 484	Ron Perranoski	6.00	2.50	.60
☐ 485	Nellie Fox	10.00	4.50	1.25
☐ 486	Angels Rookies	6.00	2.50	.60
	Tom Egan			
	Pat Rogan			
☐ 487	Woody Woodward	6.00	2.50	.60
☐ 488	Ted Wills	5.25	2.25	.50
☐ 489	Gene Mauch MG	6.00	2.50	.60
☐ 490	Earl Battey	5.25	2.25	.50
☐ 491	Tracy Stallard	5.25	2.25	.50
☐ 492	Gene Freese	5.25	2.25	.50
☐ 493	Tigers Rookies	5.25	2.25	.50
	Bill Roman			
	Bruce Brubaker			
☐ 494	Jay Ritchie	5.25	2.25	.50
☐ 495	Joe Christopher	5.25	2.25	.50
☐ 496	Joe Cunningham	6.00	2.50	.60
☐ 497	Giants Rookies	7.00	3.00	.70

Ken Henderson
Jack Hiatt
☐ 498 Gene Stephens .... 5.25 2.25 .50
☐ 499 Stu Miller .... 5.25 2.25 .50
☐ 500 Eddie Mathews 32.00 14.25 4.75
☐ 501 Indians Rookies .... 5.25 2.25 .50
Ralph Gagliano
Jim Rittwage
☐ 502 Don Cardwell .... 5.25 2.25 .50
☐ 503 Phil Gagliano .... 5.25 2.25 .50
☐ 504 Jerry Grote .... 5.25 2.25 .50
☐ 505 Ray Culp .... 5.25 2.25 .50
☐ 506 Sam Mele MG .... 5.25 2.25 .50
☐ 507 Sammy Ellis .... 5.25 2.25 .50
☐ 508 Checklist 7 .... 15.00 1.50 .30
☐ 509 Red Sox Rookies .... 5.25 2.25 .50
Bob Guindon
Gerry Vezendy
☐ 510 Ernie Banks 70.00 32.00 10.50
☐ 511 Ron Locke .... 5.25 2.25 .50
☐ 512 Cap Peterson .... 5.25 2.25 .50
☐ 513 New York Yankees 14.00 6.25 2.00
Team Card
☐ 514 Joe Azcue .... 5.25 2.25 .50
☐ 515 Vern Law .... 6.00 2.50 .60
☐ 516 Al Weis .... 5.25 2.25 .50
☐ 517 Angels Rookies .... 5.25 2.25 .50
Paul Schaal
Jack Warner
☐ 518 Ken Rowe .... 5.25 2.25 .50
☐ 519 Bob Uecker UER 45.00 20.00 6.75
(posing as a left-
handed batter)
☐ 520 Tony Cloninger .... 5.25 2.25 .50
☐ 521 Phillies Rookies .... 5.25 2.25 .50
Dave Bennett
Morrie Stevens
☐ 522 Hank Aguirre .... 5.25 2.25 .50
☐ 523 Mike Brumley SP 11.00 5.00 1.35
☐ 524 Dave Giusti SP 12.00 5.25 1.50
☐ 525 Eddie Bressoud .... 5.50 2.50 .55
☐ 526 Athletics Rookies SP 160.00 72.00 24.00
Rene Lachemann
Johnny Odom
Jim Hunter ERR
("Tim" on back)
Skip Lockwood
☐ 527 Jeff Torborg SP 13.50 6.00 1.85
☐ 528 George Altman .... 5.50 2.50 .55
☐ 529 Jerry Fosnow SP 11.00 5.00 1.35
☐ 530 Jim Maloney .... 7.50 3.25 .75
☐ 531 Chuck Hiller .... 5.50 2.50 .55
☐ 532 Hector Lopez .... 5.50 2.50 .55
☐ 533 Mets Rookies SP 27.00 12.00 4.00
Dan Napoleon
Ron Swoboda
Tug McGraw
Jim Bethke
☐ 534 John Herrnstein .... 5.50 2.50 .55
☐ 535 Jack Kralick SP 11.00 5.00 1.35
☐ 536 Andre Rodgers SP 11.00 5.00 1.35
☐ 537 Angels Rookies .... 6.50 2.75 .65
Marcelino Lopez
Phil Roof
Rudy May
☐ 538 Chuck Dressen MG SP12.00 5.25 1.50
☐ 539 Herm Starrette .... 5.50 2.50 .55
☐ 540 Lou Brock SP 48.00 22.00 6.00
☐ 541 White Sox Rookies ...... 5.50 2.50 .55
Greg Bollo
Bob Locker
☐ 542 Lou Klimchock .... 5.50 2.50 .55
☐ 543 Ed Connolly SP 11.00 5.00 1.35
☐ 544 Howie Reed .... 5.50 2.50 .55
☐ 545 Jesus Alou SP 11.00 5.00 1.35
☐ 546 Indians Rookies .... 5.50 2.50 .55
Bill Davis
Mike Hedlund
Ray Barker
Floyd Weaver
☐ 547 Jake Wood SP 11.00 5.00 1.35
☐ 548 Dick Stigman .... 5.50 2.50 .55
☐ 549 Cubs Rookies SP 16.00 6.75 2.25
Roberto Pena
Glenn Beckert
☐ 550 Mel Stottlemyre SP ... 27.00 12.00 4.00
☐ 551 New York Mets SP 24.00 10.50 3.50
Team Card
☐ 552 Julio Gotay .... 5.50 2.50 .55
☐ 553 Astros Rookies .... 5.50 2.50 .55
Dan Coombs
Gene Ratliff
Jack McClure
☐ 554 Chico Ruiz SP 11.00 5.00 1.35
☐ 555 Jack Baldschun SP 11.00 5.00 1.35
☐ 556 Red Schoendienst 18.00 7.50 2.50
MG SP
☐ 557 Jose Santiago .... 5.50 2.50 .55
☐ 558 Tommie Sisk .... 5.50 2.50 .55
☐ 559 Ed Bailey SP 11.00 5.00 1.35
☐ 560 Boog Powell SP 16.00 6.75 2.25
☐ 561 Dodgers Rookies 12.00 5.25 1.50
Dennis Daboll
Mike Kekich
Hector Valle
Jim Lefebvre
☐ 562 Billy Moran .... 5.50 2.50 .55
☐ 563 Julio Navarro .... 5.50 2.50 .55
☐ 564 Mel Nelson .... 5.50 2.50 .55
☐ 565 Ernie Broglio SP 11.00 5.00 1.35
☐ 566 Yankees Rookies SP . 11.00 5.00 1.35
Gil Blanco
Ross Moschitto
Art Lopez
☐ 567 Tommie Aaron .... 6.50 2.75 .65
☐ 568 Ron Taylor SP 11.00 5.00 1.35

□ 569 Gino Cimoli SP 11.00 5.00 1.35
□ 570 Claude Osteen SP 12.00 5.25 1.50
□ 571 Ossie Virgil SP 11.00 5.00 1.35
□ 572 Baltimore Orioles SP . 21.00 9.00 3.00
Team Card
□ 573 Red Sox Rookies SP . 20.00 8.50 2.75
Jim Lonborg
Gerry Moses
Bill Schlesinger
Mike Ryan
□ 574 Roy Sievers .... 6.50 2.75 .65
□ 575 Jose Pagan .... 5.50 2.50 .55
□ 576 Terry Fox SP................ 11.00 5.00 1.35
□ 577 AL Rookie Stars SP ... 12.00 5.25 1.50
Darold Knowles
Don Buschhorn
Richie Scheinblum
□ 578 Camilo Carreon SP 11.00 5.00 1.35
□ 579 Dick Smith SP 11.00 5.00 1.35
□ 580 Jimmie Hall SP 12.00 5.25 1.50
□ 581 NL Rookie Stars SP 140.00 63.00 21.00
Tony Perez
Dave Ricketts
Kevin Collins
□ 582 Bob Schmidt SP 11.00 5.00 1.35
□ 583 Wes Covington SP 12.00 5.25 1.50
□ 584 Harry Bright .... 5.50 2.50 .55
□ 585 Hank Fischer .... 5.50 2.50 .55
□ 586 Tom McCraw SP 11.00 5.00 1.35
□ 587 Joe Sparma .... 5.50 2.50 .55
□ 588 Lenny Green .... 5.50 2.50 .55
□ 589 Giants Rookies SP 11.00 5.00 1.35
Frank Linzy
Bob Schroder
□ 590 John Wyatt .... 5.50 2.50 .55
□ 591 Bob Skinner SP 11.00 5.00 1.35
□ 592 Frank Bork SP 11.00 5.00 1.35
□ 593 Tigers Rookies SP 11.00 5.00 1.35
Jackie Moore
John Sullivan
□ 594 Joe Gaines .... 5.50 2.50 .55
□ 595 Don Lee .... 5.50 2.50 .55
□ 596 Don Landrum SP 11.00 5.00 1.35
□ 597 Twins Rookies .... 5.50 2.50 .55
Joe Nossek
John Sevcik
Dick Reese
□ 598 Al Downing SP 15.00 6.00 1.20

1966 Topps

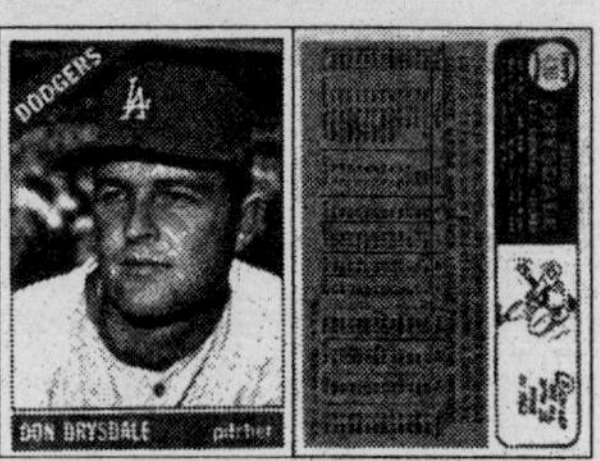

The cards in this 598-card set measure 2 1/2" by 3 1/2". There are the same number of cards as in the 1965 set. Once again, the seventh series cards (523 to 598) are considered more difficult to obtain than the cards of any other series in the set. Within this last series there are 43 cards that were printed in lesser quantities than the other cards in that series; these shorter-printed cards are marked by SP in the checklist below. The only featured subset within this set is League Leaders (215-226). Noteworthy rookie cards in the set include Jim Palmer (126), Ferguson Jenkins (254), and Don Sutton (288). Palmer is described in the bio (on his card back) as a left-hander.

	NRMT	VG-E	GOOD
COMPLETE SET (598)	4250.00	1750.00	450.00
COMMON PLAYER (1-109)	1.25	.50	.12
COMMON PLAYER (110-196) .	1.50	.60	.15
COMMON PLAYER (197-283) .	1.75	.70	.17
COMMON PLAYER (284-370) .	2.25	.90	.22
COMMON PLAYER (371-446) .	3.50	1.50	.35
COMMON PLAYER (447-522) .	6.00	2.50	.60
COMMON PLAYER (523-598)	14.00	6.25	2.00
COMMON SP (523-598)	28.00	12.50	4.00

□ 1 Willie Mays 175.00 50.00 10.00
□ 2 Ted Abernathy .... 1.25 .50 .12
□ 3 Sam Mele MG .... 1.25 .50 .12
□ 4 Ray Culp .... 1.25 .50 .12
□ 5 Jim Fregosi .... 1.75 .70 .17
□ 6 Chuck Schilling .... 1.25 .50 .12
□ 7 Tracy Stallard .... 1.25 .50 .12
□ 8 Floyd Robinson .... 1.25 .50 .12
□ 9 Clete Boyer .... 1.75 .70 .17
□ 10 Tony Cloninger .... 1.25 .50 .12
□ 11 Senators Rookies .... 1.25 .50 .12

Brant Alyea			
Pete Craig			
☐ 12 John Tsitouris	1.25	.50	.12
☐ 13 Lou Johnson	1.25	.50	.12
☐ 14 Norm Siebern	1.25	.50	.12
☐ 15 Vern Law	1.75	.70	.17
☐ 16 Larry Brown	1.25	.50	.12
☐ 17 John Stephenson	1.25	.50	.12
☐ 18 Roland Sheldon	1.25	.50	.12
☐ 19 San Francisco Giants	2.50	1.00	.25
Team Card			
☐ 20 Willie Horton	1.75	.70	.17
☐ 21 Don Nottebart	1.25	.50	.12
☐ 22 Joe Nossek	1.25	.50	.12
☐ 23 Jack Sanford	1.25	.50	.12
☐ 24 Don Kessinger	3.00	1.25	.30
☐ 25 Pete Ward	1.25	.50	.12
☐ 26 Ray Sadecki	1.25	.50	.12
☐ 27 Orioles Rookies	1.75	.70	.17
Darold Knowles			
Andy Etchebarren			
☐ 28 Phil Niekro	16.00	6.75	2.25
☐ 29 Mike Brumley	1.25	.50	.12
☐ 30 Pete Rose DP	42.00	18.00	5.50
☐ 31 Jack Cullen	1.25	.50	.12
☐ 32 Adolfo Phillips	1.25	.50	.12
☐ 33 Jim Pagliaroni	1.25	.50	.12
☐ 34 Checklist 1	7.50	.75	.15
☐ 35 Ron Swoboda	1.75	.70	.17
☐ 36 Jim Hunter	30.00	13.50	4.50
☐ 37 Billy Herman MG	2.00	.80	.20
☐ 38 Ron Nischwitz	1.25	.50	.12
☐ 39 Ken Henderson	1.25	.50	.12
☐ 40 Jim Grant	1.25	.50	.12
☐ 41 Don LeJohn	1.25	.50	.12
☐ 42 Aubrey Gatewood	1.25	.50	.12
☐ 43 Don Landrum	1.25	.50	.12
☐ 44 Indians Rookies	1.25	.50	.12
Bill Davis			
Tom Kelley			
☐ 45 Jim Gentile	1.75	.70	.17
☐ 46 Howie Koplitz	1.25	.50	.12
☐ 47 J.C. Martin	1.25	.50	.12
☐ 48 Paul Blair	1.75	.70	.17
☐ 49 Woody Woodward	1.75	.70	.17
☐ 50 Mickey Mantle DP	180.00	80.00	27.00
☐ 51 Gordon Richardson	1.25	.50	.12
☐ 52 Power Plus	1.25	.50	.12
Wes Covington			
Johnny Callison			
☐ 53 Bob Duliba	1.25	.50	.12
☐ 54 Jose Pagan	1.25	.50	.12
☐ 55 Ken Harrelson	1.75	.70	.17
☐ 56 Sandy Valdespino	1.25	.50	.12
☐ 57 Jim Lefebvre	1.75	.70	.17
☐ 58 Dave Wickersham	1.25	.50	.12
☐ 59 Reds Team	2.50	1.00	.25
☐ 60 Curt Flood	1.75	.70	.17
☐ 61 Bob Bolin	1.25	.50	.12
☐ 62A Merritt Ranew	1.25	.50	.12
(with sold line)			
☐ 62B Merritt Ranew	30.00	13.50	4.50
(without sold line)			
☐ 63 Jim Stewart	1.25	.50	.12
☐ 64 Bob Bruce	1.25	.50	.12
☐ 65 Leon Wagner	1.25	.50	.12
☐ 66 Al Weis	1.25	.50	.12
☐ 67 Mets Rookies	1.75	.70	.17
Cleon Jones			
Dick Selma			
☐ 68 Hal Reniff	1.25	.50	.12
☐ 69 Ken Hamlin	1.25	.50	.12
☐ 70 Carl Yastrzemski	42.00	18.00	5.00
☐ 71 Frank Carpin	1.25	.50	.12
☐ 72 Tony Perez	28.00	12.50	4.00
☐ 73 Jerry Zimmerman	1.25	.50	.12
☐ 74 Don Mossi	1.25	.50	.12
☐ 75 Tommy Davis	1.75	.70	.17
☐ 76 Red Schoendienst MG	4.00	1.75	.40
☐ 77 John Orsino	1.25	.50	.12
☐ 78 Frank Linzy	1.25	.50	.12
☐ 79 Joe Pepitone	1.75	.70	.17
☐ 80 Richie Allen	4.50	2.00	.45
☐ 81 Ray Oyler	1.25	.50	.12
☐ 82 Bob Hendley	1.25	.50	.12
☐ 83 Albie Pearson	1.25	.50	.12
☐ 84 Braves Rookies	1.25	.50	.12
Jim Beauchamp			
Dick Kelley			
☐ 85 Eddie Fisher	1.25	.50	.12
☐ 86 John Bateman	1.25	.50	.12
☐ 87 Dan Napoleon	1.25	.50	.12
☐ 88 Fred Whitfield	1.25	.50	.12
☐ 89 Ted Davidson	1.25	.50	.12
☐ 90 Luis Aparicio	7.00	3.00	.70
☐ 91A Bob Uecker	20.00	8.50	2.75
(with traded line)			
☐ 91B Bob Uecker	60.00	27.00	9.00
(no traded line)			
☐ 92 Yankees Team	3.50	1.50	.35
☐ 93 Jim Lonborg	2.25	.90	.22
☐ 94 Matty Alou	1.75	.70	.17
☐ 95 Pete Richert	1.25	.50	.12
☐ 96 Felipe Alou	1.75	.70	.17
☐ 97 Jim Merritt	1.25	.50	.12
☐ 98 Don Demeter	1.25	.50	.12
☐ 99 Buc Belters	3.50	1.50	.35
Willie Stargell			
Donn Clendenon			
☐ 100 Sandy Koufax	95.00	42.00	11.00
☐ 101A Checklist 2	15.00	1.50	.30
(115 W. Spahn) ERR			
☐ 101B Checklist 2	7.50	.75	.15
(115 Bill Henry) COR			
☐ 102 Ed Kirkpatrick	1.25	.50	.12
☐ 103A Dick Groat	2.00	.80	.20

(with traded line)
☐ 103B Dick Groat 32.00 14.25 4.75
(no traded line)
☐ 104A Alex Johnson .... 1.75 .70 .17
(with traded line)
☐ 104B Alex Johnson 30.00 13.50 4.50
(no traded line)
☐ 105 Milt Pappas .... 1.75 .70 .17
☐ 106 Rusty Staub .... 3.00 1.25 .30
☐ 107 A's Rookies .... 1.25 .50 .12
Larry Stahl
Ron Tompkins
☐ 108 Bobby Klaus .... 1.25 .50 .12
☐ 109 Ralph Terry .... 1.75 .70 .17
☐ 110 Ernie Banks 21.00 9.00 3.00
☐ 111 Gary Peters .... 1.50 .60 .15
☐ 112 Manny Mota .... 2.00 .80 .20
☐ 113 Hank Aguirre .... 1.50 .60 .15
☐ 114 Jim Gosger .... 1.50 .60 .15
☐ 115 Bill Henry .... 1.50 .60 .15
☐ 116 Walt Alston MG .... 3.50 1.50 .35
☐ 117 Jake Gibbs .... 1.50 .60 .15
☐ 118 Mike McCormick .... 2.00 .80 .20
☐ 119 Art Shamsky .... 1.50 .60 .15
☐ 120 Harmon Killebrew 18.00 7.50 2.50
☐ 121 Ray Herbert .... 1.50 .60 .15
☐ 122 Joe Gaines .... 1.50 .60 .15
☐ 123 Pirates Rookies .... 1.50 .60 .15
Frank Bork
Jerry May
☐ 124 Tug McGraw .... 4.00 1.75 .40
☐ 125 Lou Brock 21.00 9.00 3.00
☐ 126 Jim Palmer UER 250.00 110.00 37.50
(described as a
lefthander on
card back)
☐ 127 Ken Berry .... 1.50 .60 .15
☐ 128 Jim Landis .... 1.50 .60 .15
☐ 129 Jack Kralick .... 1.50 .60 .15
☐ 130 Joe Torre .... 3.00 1.25 .30
☐ 131 Angels Team .... 3.00 1.25 .30
☐ 132 Orlando Cepeda .... 5.00 2.25 .50
☐ 133 Don McMahon .... 1.50 .60 .15
☐ 134 Wes Parker .... 2.00 .80 .20
☐ 135 Dave Morehead .... 1.50 .60 .15
☐ 136 Woody Held .... 1.50 .60 .15
☐ 137 Pat Corrales .... 2.00 .80 .20
☐ 138 Roger Repoz .... 1.50 .60 .15
☐ 139 Cubs Rookies .... 1.50 .60 .15
Byron Browne
Don Young
☐ 140 Jim Maloney .... 2.00 .80 .20
☐ 141 Tom McCraw .... 1.50 .60 .15
☐ 142 Don Dennis .... 1.50 .60 .15
☐ 143 Jose Tartabull .... 1.50 .60 .15
☐ 144 Don Schwall .... 1.50 .60 .15
☐ 145 Bill Freehan .... 2.50 1.00 .25
☐ 146 George Altman .... 1.50 .60 .15
☐ 147 Lum Harris MG .... 1.50 .60 .15
☐ 148 Bob Johnson .... 1.50 .60 .15
☐ 149 Dick Nen .... 1.50 .60 .15
☐ 150 Rocky Colavito .... 4.50 2.00 .45
☐ 151 Gary Wagner .... 1.50 .60 .15
☐ 152 Frank Malzone .... 2.00 .80 .20
☐ 153 Rico Carty .... 2.50 1.00 .25
☐ 154 Chuck Hiller .... 1.50 .60 .15
☐ 155 Marcelino Lopez .... 1.50 .60 .15
☐ 156 Double Play Combo .... 2.00 .80 .20
Dick Schofield
Hal Lanier
☐ 157 Rene Lachemann .... 2.00 .80 .20
☐ 158 Jim Brewer .... 1.50 .60 .15
☐ 159 Chico Ruiz .... 1.50 .60 .15
☐ 160 Whitey Ford 21.00 9.00 3.00
☐ 161 Jerry Lumpe .... 1.50 .60 .15
☐ 162 Lee Maye .... 1.50 .60 .15
☐ 163 Tito Francona .... 1.50 .60 .15
☐ 164 White Sox Rookies ...... 2.00 .80 .20
Tommie Agee
Marv Staehle
☐ 165 Don Lock .... 1.50 .60 .15
☐ 166 Chris Krug .... 1.50 .60 .15
☐ 167 Boog Powell .... 3.50 1.50 .35
☐ 168 Dan Osinski .... 1.50 .60 .15
☐ 169 Duke Sims .... 1.50 .60 .15
☐ 170 Cookie Rojas .... 2.00 .80 .20
☐ 171 Nick Willhite .... 1.50 .60 .15
☐ 172 Mets Team .... 3.50 1.50 .35
☐ 173 Al Spangler .... 1.50 .60 .15
☐ 174 Ron Taylor .... 1.50 .60 .15
☐ 175 Bert Campaneris .... 2.00 .80 .20
☐ 176 Jim Davenport .... 1.50 .60 .15
☐ 177 Hector Lopez .... 1.50 .60 .15
☐ 178 Bob Tillman .... 1.50 .60 .15
☐ 179 Cards Rookies .... 2.00 .80 .20
Dennis Aust
Bob Tolan
☐ 180 Vada Pinson .... 2.50 1.00 .25
☐ 181 Al Worthington .... 1.50 .60 .15
☐ 182 Jerry Lynch .... 1.50 .60 .15
☐ 183 Checklist 3 .... 7.50 .75 .15
☐ 184 Denis Menke .... 1.50 .60 .15
☐ 185 Bob Buhl .... 1.50 .60 .15
☐ 186 Ruben Amaro .... 1.50 .60 .15
☐ 187 Chuck Dressen MG ..... 2.00 .80 .20
☐ 188 Al Luplow .... 1.50 .60 .15
☐ 189 John Roseboro .... 2.00 .80 .20
☐ 190 Jimmie Hall .... 2.00 .80 .20
☐ 191 Darrell Sutherland .... 1.50 .60 .15
☐ 192 Vic Power .... 1.50 .60 .15
☐ 193 Dave McNally .... 2.00 .80 .20
☐ 194 Senators Team .... 3.00 1.25 .30
☐ 195 Joe Morgan 42.00 18.00 5.50
☐ 196 Don Pavletich .... 1.50 .60 .15
☐ 197 Sonny Siebert .... 1.75 .70 .17
☐ 198 Mickey Stanley .... 3.00 1.25 .30

☐ 199 Chisox Clubbers .... 1.75 .70 .17
Bill Skowron
Johnny Romano
Floyd Robinson
☐ 200 Eddie Mathews 12.00 5.25 1.50
☐ 201 Jim Dickson .... 1.75 .70 .17
☐ 202 Clay Dalrymple .... 1.75 .70 .17
☐ 203 Jose Santiago .... 1.75 .70 .17
☐ 204 Cubs Team .... 3.50 1.50 .35
☐ 205 Tom Tresh .... 2.25 .90 .22
☐ 206 Al Jackson .... 1.75 .70 .17
☐ 207 Frank Quilici .... 1.75 .70 .17
☐ 208 Bob Miller .... 1.75 .70 .17
☐ 209 Tigers Rookies .... 3.00 1.25 .30
Fritz Fisher
John Hiller
☐ 210 Bill Mazeroski .... 3.50 1.50 .35
☐ 211 Frank Kreutzer .... 1.75 .70 .17
☐ 212 Ed Kranepool .... 2.25 .90 .22
☐ 213 Fred Newman .... 1.75 .70 .17
☐ 214 Tommy Harper .... 2.25 .90 .22
☐ 215 NL Batting Leaders ... 18.00 7.50 2.50
Bob Clemente
Hank Aaron
Willie Mays
☐ 216 AL Batting Leaders ...... 5.00 2.25 .50
Tony Oliva
Carl Yastrzemski
Vic Davalillo
☐ 217 NL Home Run Leaders12.00 5.25 1.50
Willie Mays
Willie McCovey
Billy Williams
☐ 218 AL Home Run Leaders 3.50 1.50 .35
Tony Conigliaro
Norm Cash
Willie Horton
☐ 219 NL RBI Leaders .... 5.00 2.25 .50
Deron Johnson
Frank Robinson
Willie Mays
☐ 220 AL RBI Leaders .... 3.50 1.50 .35
Rocky Colavito
Willie Horton
Tony Oliva
☐ 221 NL ERA Leaders .... 5.00 2.25 .50
Sandy Koufax
Juan Marichal
Vern Law
☐ 222 AL ERA Leaders .... 3.00 1.25 .30
Sam McDowell
Eddie Fisher
Sonny Siebert
☐ 223 NL Pitching Leaders .... 5.00 2.25 .50
Sandy Koufax
Tony Cloninger
Don Drysdale
☐ 224 AL Pitching Leaders .... 3.00 1.25 .30
Jim Grant
Mel Stottlemyre
Jim Kaat
☐ 225 NL Strikeout Leaders .. 5.00 2.25 .50
Sandy Koufax
Bob Veale
Bob Gibson
☐ 226 AL Strikeout Leaders ... 3.00 1.25 .30
Sam McDowell
Mickey Lolich
Dennis McLain
Sonny Siebert
☐ 227 Russ Nixon .... 1.75 .70 .17
☐ 228 Larry Dierker .... 1.75 .70 .17
☐ 229 Hank Bauer MG .... 2.25 .90 .22
☐ 230 Johnny Callison .... 2.25 .90 .22
☐ 231 Floyd Weaver .... 1.75 .70 .17
☐ 232 Glenn Beckert .... 2.25 .90 .22
☐ 233 Dom Zanni .... 1.75 .70 .17
☐ 234 Yankees Rookies .... 6.00 2.50 .60
Rich Beck
Roy White
☐ 235 Don Cardwell .... 1.75 .70 .17
☐ 236 Mike Hershberger .... 1.75 .70 .17
☐ 237 Billy O'Dell .... 1.75 .70 .17
☐ 238 Dodgers Team .... 3.50 1.50 .35
☐ 239 Orlando Pena .... 1.75 .70 .17
☐ 240 Earl Battey .... 1.75 .70 .17
☐ 241 Dennis Ribant .... 1.75 .70 .17
☐ 242 Jesus Alou .... 1.75 .70 .17
☐ 243 Nelson Briles .... 2.25 .90 .22
☐ 244 Astros Rookies .... 2.25 .90 .22
Chuck Harrison
Sonny Jackson
☐ 245 John Buzhardt .... 1.75 .70 .17
☐ 246 Ed Bailey .... 2.25 .90 .22
☐ 247 Carl Warwick .... 1.75 .70 .17
☐ 248 Pete Mikkelsen .... 1.75 .70 .17
☐ 249 Bill Rigney MG .... 1.75 .70 .17
☐ 250 Sammy Ellis .... 1.75 .70 .17
☐ 251 Ed Brinkman .... 1.75 .70 .17
☐ 252 Denny Lemaster .... 1.75 .70 .17
☐ 253 Don Wert .... 1.75 .70 .17
☐ 254 Phillies Rookies 120.00 55.00 18.00
Ferguson Jenkins
Bill Sorrell
☐ 255 Willie Stargell 18.00 7.50 2.50
☐ 256 Lew Krausse .... 1.75 .70 .17
☐ 257 Jeff Torborg .... 2.75 1.10 .27
☐ 258 Dave Giusti .... 2.25 .90 .22
☐ 259 Boston Red Sox .... 3.50 1.50 .35
Team Card
☐ 260 Bob Shaw .... 1.75 .70 .17
☐ 261 Ron Hansen .... 1.75 .70 .17
☐ 262 Jack Hamilton .... 1.75 .70 .17
☐ 263 Tom Egan .... 1.75 .70 .17
☐ 264 Twins Rookies .... 1.75 .70 .17
Andy Kosco

Ted Uhlaender
☐ 265 Stu Miller .... 1.75 .70 .17
☐ 266 Pedro Gonzalez UER ... 1.75 .70 .17
(misspelled Gonzales
on card back)
☐ 267 Joe Sparma .... 1.75 .70 .17
☐ 268 John Blanchard .... 2.25 .90 .22
☐ 269 Don Heffner MG .... 1.75 .70 .17
☐ 270 Claude Osteen .... 2.25 .90 .22
☐ 271 Hal Lanier .... 2.25 .90 .22
☐ 272 Jack Baldschun .... 1.75 .70 .17
☐ 273 Astro Aces .... 2.50 1.00 .25
Bob Aspromonte
Rusty Staub
☐ 274 Buster Narum .... 1.75 .70 .17
☐ 275 Tim McCarver .... 3.50 1.50 .35
☐ 276 Jim Bouton .... 2.75 1.10 .27
☐ 277 George Thomas .... 1.75 .70 .17
☐ 278 Cal Koonce .... 1.75 .70 .17
☐ 279 Checklist 4 .... 7.50 .75 .15
☐ 280 Bobby Knoop .... 1.75 .70 .17
☐ 281 Bruce Howard .... 1.75 .70 .17
☐ 282 Johnny Lewis .... 1.75 .70 .17
☐ 283 Jim Perry .... 2.25 .90 .22
☐ 284 Bobby Wine .... 2.25 .90 .22
☐ 285 Luis Tiant .... 3.50 1.50 .35
☐ 286 Gary Geiger .... 2.25 .90 .22
☐ 287 Jack Aker .... 2.25 .90 .22
☐ 288 Dodgers Rookies 130.00 60.00 20.00
Bill Singer
Don Sutton
☐ 289 Larry Sherry .... 2.25 .90 .22
☐ 290 Ron Santo .... 3.50 1.50 .35
☐ 291 Moe Drabowsky .... 2.25 .90 .22
☐ 292 Jim Coker .... 2.25 .90 .22
☐ 293 Mike Shannon .... 2.75 1.10 .27
☐ 294 Steve Ridzik .... 2.25 .90 .22
☐ 295 Jim Ray Hart .... 2.75 1.10 .27
☐ 296 Johnny Keane MG .... 2.25 .90 .22
☐ 297 Jim Owens .... 2.25 .90 .22
☐ 298 Rico Petrocelli .... 3.50 1.50 .35
☐ 299 Lou Burdette .... 3.00 1.25 .30
☐ 300 Bob Clemente 85.00 38.00 12.75
☐ 301 Greg Bollo .... 2.25 .90 .22
☐ 302 Ernie Bowman .... 2.25 .90 .22
☐ 303 Cleveland Indians .... 4.50 2.00 .45
Team Card
☐ 304 John Herrnstein .... 2.25 .90 .22
☐ 305 Camilo Pascual .... 2.75 1.10 .27
☐ 306 Ty Cline .... 2.25 .90 .22
☐ 307 Clay Carroll .... 2.75 1.10 .27
☐ 308 Tom Haller .... 2.75 1.10 .27
☐ 309 Diego Segui .... 2.25 .90 .22
☐ 310 Frank Robinson 40.00 18.00 6.00
☐ 311 Reds Rookies .... 2.75 1.10 .27
Tommy Helms
Dick Simpson
☐ 312 Bob Saverine .... 2.25 .90 .22
☐ 313 Chris Zachary .... 2.25 .90 .22
☐ 314 Hector Valle .... 2.25 .90 .22
☐ 315 Norm Cash .... 3.50 1.50 .35
☐ 316 Jack Fisher .... 2.25 .90 .22
☐ 317 Dalton Jones .... 2.25 .90 .22
☐ 318 Harry Walker MG .... 2.25 .90 .22
☐ 319 Gene Freese .... 2.25 .90 .22
☐ 320 Bob Gibson 24.00 10.50 3.50
☐ 321 Rick Reichardt .... 2.25 .90 .22
☐ 322 Bill Faul .... 2.25 .90 .22
☐ 323 Ray Barker .... 2.25 .90 .22
☐ 324 John Boozer .... 2.25 .90 .22
☐ 325 Vic Davalillo .... 2.25 .90 .22
☐ 326 Braves Team .... 4.50 2.00 .45
☐ 327 Bernie Allen .... 2.25 .90 .22
☐ 328 Jerry Grote .... 2.25 .90 .22
☐ 329 Pete Charton .... 2.25 .90 .22
☐ 330 Ron Fairly .... 2.75 1.10 .27
☐ 331 Ron Herbel .... 2.25 .90 .22
☐ 332 Bill Bryan .... 2.25 .90 .22
☐ 333 Senators Rookies .... 2.25 .90 .22
Joe Coleman
Jim French
☐ 334 Marty Keough .... 2.25 .90 .22
☐ 335 Juan Pizarro .... 2.25 .90 .22
☐ 336 Gene Alley .... 2.75 1.10 .27
☐ 337 Fred Gladding .... 2.25 .90 .22
☐ 338 Dal Maxvill .... 2.25 .90 .22
☐ 339 Del Crandall .... 2.75 1.10 .27
☐ 340 Dean Chance .... 2.75 1.10 .27
☐ 341 Wes Westrum MG .... 2.25 .90 .22
☐ 342 Bob Humphreys .... 2.25 .90 .22
☐ 343 Joe Christopher .... 2.25 .90 .22
☐ 344 Steve Blass .... 2.75 1.10 .27
☐ 345 Bob Allison .... 2.75 1.10 .27
☐ 346 Mike de la Hoz .... 2.25 .90 .22
☐ 347 Phil Regan .... 2.75 1.10 .27
☐ 348 Orioles Team .... 4.50 2.00 .45
☐ 349 Cap Peterson .... 2.25 .90 .22
☐ 350 Mel Stottlemyre .... 3.75 1.60 .37
☐ 351 Fred Valentine .... 2.25 .90 .22
☐ 352 Bob Aspromonte .... 2.25 .90 .22
☐ 353 Al McBean .... 2.25 .90 .22
☐ 354 Smoky Burgess .... 2.75 1.10 .27
☐ 355 Wade Blasingame .... 2.25 .90 .22
☐ 356 Red Sox Rookies .... 2.25 .90 .22
Owen Johnson
Ken Sanders
☐ 357 Gerry Arrigo .... 2.25 .90 .22
☐ 358 Charlie Smith .... 2.25 .90 .22
☐ 359 Johnny Briggs .... 2.25 .90 .22
☐ 360 Ron Hunt .... 2.25 .90 .22
☐ 361 Tom Satriano .... 2.25 .90 .22
☐ 362 Gates Brown .... 2.75 1.10 .27
☐ 363 Checklist 5 .... 9.00 .90 .20
☐ 364 Nate Oliver .... 2.25 .90 .22
☐ 365 Roger Maris 55.00 25.00 8.25
☐ 366 Wayne Causey .... 2.25 .90 .22

☐ 367 Mel Nelson	2.25	.90	.22
☐ 368 Charlie Lau	2.75	1.10	.27
☐ 369 Jim King	2.25	.90	.22
☐ 370 Chico Cardenas	2.25	.90	.22
☐ 371 Lee Stange	3.50	1.50	.35
☐ 372 Harvey Kuenn	4.50	2.00	.45
☐ 373 Giants Rookies Jack Hiatt Dick Estelle	4.00	1.75	.40
☐ 374 Bob Locker	3.50	1.50	.35
☐ 375 Donn Clendenon	4.00	1.75	.40
☐ 376 Paul Schaal	3.50	1.50	.35
☐ 377 Turk Farrell	3.50	1.50	.35
☐ 378 Dick Tracewski	3.50	1.50	.35
☐ 379 Cardinal Team	7.00	3.00	.70
☐ 380 Tony Conigliaro	7.50	3.25	.75
☐ 381 Hank Fischer	3.50	1.50	.35
☐ 382 Phil Roof	3.50	1.50	.35
☐ 383 Jackie Brandt	3.50	1.50	.35
☐ 384 Al Downing	4.00	1.75	.40
☐ 385 Ken Boyer	5.00	2.25	.50
☐ 386 Gil Hodges MG	6.50	2.75	.65
☐ 387 Howie Reed	3.50	1.50	.35
☐ 388 Don Mincher	4.00	1.75	.40
☐ 389 Jim O'Toole	3.50	1.50	.35
☐ 390 Brooks Robinson	28.00	12.50	4.00
☐ 391 Chuck Hinton	3.50	1.50	.35
☐ 392 Cubs Rookies Bill Hands Randy Hundley	4.50	2.00	.45
☐ 393 George Brunet	3.50	1.50	.35
☐ 394 Ron Brand	3.50	1.50	.35
☐ 395 Len Gabrielson	3.50	1.50	.35
☐ 396 Jerry Stephenson	3.50	1.50	.35
☐ 397 Bill White	5.00	2.25	.50
☐ 398 Danny Cater	3.50	1.50	.35
☐ 399 Ray Washburn	3.50	1.50	.35
☐ 400 Zoilo Versalles	3.50	1.50	.35
☐ 401 Ken McMullen	3.50	1.50	.35
☐ 402 Jim Hickman	3.50	1.50	.35
☐ 403 Fred Talbot	3.50	1.50	.35
☐ 404 Pittsburgh Pirates Team Card	7.00	3.00	.70
☐ 405 Elston Howard	6.00	2.50	.60
☐ 406 Joey Jay	3.50	1.50	.35
☐ 407 John Kennedy	3.50	1.50	.35
☐ 408 Lee Thomas	4.00	1.75	.40
☐ 409 Billy Hoeft	3.50	1.50	.35
☐ 410 Al Kaline	25.00	11.00	3.50
☐ 411 Gene Mauch MG	4.00	1.75	.40
☐ 412 Sam Bowens	3.50	1.50	.35
☐ 413 Johnny Romano	3.50	1.50	.35
☐ 414 Dan Coombs	3.50	1.50	.35
☐ 415 Max Alvis	3.50	1.50	.35
☐ 416 Phil Ortega	3.50	1.50	.35
☐ 417 Angels Rookies Jim McGlothlin Ed Sukla	4.00	1.75	.40
☐ 418 Phil Gagliano	3.50	1.50	.35
☐ 419 Mike Ryan	3.50	1.50	.35
☐ 420 Juan Marichal	12.50	5.50	1.65
☐ 421 Roy McMillan	3.50	1.50	.35
☐ 422 Ed Charles	3.50	1.50	.35
☐ 423 Ernie Broglio	3.50	1.50	.35
☐ 424 Reds Rookies Lee May Darrell Osteen	6.50	2.75	.65
☐ 425 Bob Veale	4.00	1.75	.40
☐ 426 White Sox Team	7.00	3.00	.70
☐ 427 John Miller	3.50	1.50	.35
☐ 428 Sandy Alomar	4.00	1.75	.40
☐ 429 Bill Monbouquette	3.50	1.50	.35
☐ 430 Don Drysdale	18.00	7.50	2.50
☐ 431 Walt Bond	3.50	1.50	.35
☐ 432 Bob Heffner	3.50	1.50	.35
☐ 433 Alvin Dark MG	4.00	1.75	.40
☐ 434 Willie Kirkland	3.50	1.50	.35
☐ 435 Jim Bunning	6.50	2.75	.65
☐ 436 Julian Javier	3.50	1.50	.35
☐ 437 Al Stanek	3.50	1.50	.35
☐ 438 Willie Smith	3.50	1.50	.35
☐ 439 Pedro Ramos	3.50	1.50	.35
☐ 440 Deron Johnson	3.50	1.50	.35
☐ 441 Tommie Sisk	3.50	1.50	.35
☐ 442 Orioles Rookies Ed Barnowski Eddie Watt	3.50	1.50	.35
☐ 443 Bill Wakefield	3.50	1.50	.35
☐ 444 Checklist 6	9.00	.90	.20
☐ 445 Jim Kaat	6.50	2.75	.65
☐ 446 Mack Jones	3.50	1.50	.35
☐ 447 Dick Ellsworth UER (photo actually Ken Hubbs)	7.00	3.00	.70
☐ 448 Eddie Stanky MG	7.00	3.00	.70
☐ 449 Joe Moeller	6.00	2.50	.60
☐ 450 Tony Oliva	9.00	4.00	.90
☐ 451 Barry Latman	6.00	2.50	.60
☐ 452 Joe Azcue	6.00	2.50	.60
☐ 453 Ron Kline	6.00	2.50	.60
☐ 454 Jerry Buchek	6.00	2.50	.60
☐ 455 Mickey Lolich	8.00	3.50	.80
☐ 456 Red Sox Rookies Darrell Brandon Joe Foy	6.00	2.50	.60
☐ 457 Joe Gibbon	6.00	2.50	.60
☐ 458 Manny Jiminez	6.00	2.50	.60
☐ 459 Bill McCool	6.00	2.50	.60
☐ 460 Curt Blefary	7.00	3.00	.70
☐ 461 Roy Face	7.00	3.00	.70
☐ 462 Bob Rodgers	7.00	3.00	.70
☐ 463 Philadelphia Phillies Team Card	12.00	5.25	1.50
☐ 464 Larry Bearnarth	6.00	2.50	.60
☐ 465 Don Buford	7.00	3.00	.70
☐ 466 Ken Johnson	6.00	2.50	.60

□ 467	Vic Roznovsky	6.00	2.50	.60
□ 468	Johnny Podres	7.00	3.00	.70
□ 469	Yankees Rookies	22.00	9.50	3.15
	Bobby Murcer			
	Dooley Womack			
□ 470	Sam McDowell	7.00	3.00	.70
□ 471	Bob Skinner	7.00	3.00	.70
□ 472	Terry Fox	6.00	2.50	.60
□ 473	Rich Rollins	7.00	3.00	.70
□ 474	Dick Schofield	6.00	2.50	.60
□ 475	Dick Radatz	7.00	3.00	.70
□ 476	Bobby Bragan MG	6.00	2.50	.60
□ 477	Steve Barber	6.00	2.50	.60
□ 478	Tony Gonzalez	6.00	2.50	.60
□ 479	Jim Hannan	6.00	2.50	.60
□ 480	Dick Stuart	7.00	3.00	.70
□ 481	Bob Lee	6.00	2.50	.60
□ 482	Cubs Rookies	6.00	2.50	.60
	John Boccabella			
	Dave Dowling			
□ 483	Joe Nuxhall	7.00	3.00	.70
□ 484	Wes Covington	6.00	2.50	.60
□ 485	Bob Bailey	6.00	2.50	.60
□ 486	Tommy John	12.50	5.50	1.65
□ 487	Al Ferrara	6.00	2.50	.60
□ 488	George Banks	6.00	2.50	.60
□ 489	Curt Simmons	7.00	3.00	.70
□ 490	Bobby Richardson	12.50	5.50	1.65
□ 491	Dennis Bennett	6.00	2.50	.60
□ 492	Athletics Team	11.00	5.00	1.35
□ 493	Johnny Klippstein	6.00	2.50	.60
□ 494	Gordy Coleman	7.00	3.00	.70
□ 495	Dick McAuliffe	7.00	3.00	.70
□ 496	Lindy McDaniel	7.00	3.00	.70
□ 497	Chris Cannizzaro	6.00	2.50	.60
□ 498	Pirates Rookies	7.00	3.00	.70
	Luke Walker			
	Woody Fryman			
□ 499	Wally Bunker	6.00	2.50	.60
□ 500	Hank Aaron	100.00	45.00	15.00
□ 501	John O'Donoghue	6.00	2.50	.60
□ 502	Lenny Green	6.00	2.50	.60
□ 503	Steve Hamilton	6.00	2.50	.60
□ 504	Grady Hatton MG	6.00	2.50	.60
□ 505	Jose Cardenal	6.00	2.50	.60
□ 506	Bo Belinsky	7.00	3.00	.70
□ 507	Johnny Edwards	6.00	2.50	.60
□ 508	Steve Hargan	7.00	3.00	.70
□ 509	Jake Wood	6.00	2.50	.60
□ 510	Hoyt Wilhelm	13.00	5.75	1.75
□ 511	Giants Rookies	7.00	3.00	.70
	Bob Barton			
	Tito Fuentes			
□ 512	Dick Stigman	6.00	2.50	.60
□ 513	Camilo Carreon	6.00	2.50	.60
□ 514	Hal Woodeshick	6.00	2.50	.60
□ 515	Frank Howard	8.00	3.50	.80
□ 516	Eddie Bressoud	6.00	2.50	.60

□ 517A	Checklist 7	15.00	1.50	.30
	529 White Sox Rookies			
	544 Cardinals Rookies			
□ 517B	Checklist 7	15.00	1.50	.30
	529 W. Sox Rookies			
	544 Cards Rookies			
□ 518	Braves Rookies	4.00	1.75	.40
	Herb Hippauf			
	Arnie Umbach			
□ 519	Bob Friend	7.00	3.00	.70
□ 520	Jim Wynn	8.00	3.50	.80
□ 521	John Wyatt	6.00	2.50	.60
□ 522	Phil Linz	7.00	3.00	.70
□ 523	Bob Sadowski	14.00	6.25	2.00
□ 524	Giants Rookies SP	28.00	12.50	4.00
	Ollie Brown			
	Don Mason			
□ 525	Gary Bell SP	28.00	12.50	4.00
□ 526	Twins Team SP	70.00	32.00	10.50
□ 527	Julio Navarro	14.00	6.25	2.00
□ 528	Jesse Gonder SP	28.00	12.50	4.00
□ 529	White Sox Rookies	18.00	7.50	2.50
	Lee Elia			
	Dennis Higgins			
	Bill Voss			
□ 530	Robin Roberts	40.00	18.00	6.00
□ 531	Joe Cunningham	14.00	6.25	2.00
□ 532	Aurelio Monteagudo SP	28.00	12.50	4.00
□ 533	Jerry Adair SP	28.00	12.50	4.00
□ 534	Mets Rookies	14.00	6.25	2.00
	Dave Eilers			
	Rob Gardner			
□ 535	Willie Davis SP	36.00	16.25	5.50
□ 536	Dick Egan	14.00	6.25	2.00
□ 537	Herman Franks MG	14.00	6.25	2.00
□ 538	Bob Allen SP	28.00	12.50	4.00
□ 539	Astros Rookies	14.00	6.25	2.00
	Bill Heath			
	Carroll Sembera			
□ 540	Denny McLain SP	55.00	25.00	8.25
□ 541	Gene Oliver SP	28.00	12.50	4.00
□ 542	George Smith	14.00	6.25	2.00
□ 543	Roger Craig SP	36.00	16.25	5.50
□ 544	Cardinals Rookies SP	30.00	13.50	4.50
	Joe Hoerner			
	George Kernek			
	Jimy Williams			
□ 545	Dick Green SP	28.00	12.50	4.00
□ 546	Dwight Siebler	14.00	6.25	2.00
□ 547	Horace Clarke SP	50.00	22.50	7.50
□ 548	Gary Kroll SP	28.00	12.50	4.00
□ 549	Senators Rookies	14.00	6.25	2.00
	Al Closter			
	Casey Cox			
□ 550	Willie McCovey SP	120.00	55.00	18.00
□ 551	Bob Purkey SP	28.00	12.50	4.00
□ 552	Birdie Tebbetts MG SP	28.00	12.50	4.00

□ 553	Rookie Stars	14.00	6.25	2.00
	Pat Garrett			
	Jackie Warner			
□ 554	Jim Northrup SP	30.00	13.50	4.50
□ 555	Ron Perranoski SP	30.00	13.50	4.50
□ 556	Mel Queen SP	28.00	12.50	4.00
□ 557	Felix Mantilla SP	28.00	12.50	4.00
□ 558	Red Sox Rookies	22.00	9.50	3.15
	Guido Grilli			
	Pete Magrini			
	George Scott			
□ 559	Roberto Pena SP	28.00	12.50	4.00
□ 560	Joel Horlen	14.00	6.25	2.00
□ 561	ChooChoo Coleman SP	42.00	18.00	5.50
□ 562	Russ Snyder	14.00	6.25	2.00
□ 563	Twins Rookies	14.00	6.25	2.00
	Pete Cimino			
	Cesar Tovar			
□ 564	Bob Chance SP	28.00	12.50	4.00
□ 565	Jim Piersall SP	36.00	16.25	5.50
□ 566	Mike Cuellar SP	30.00	13.50	4.50
□ 567	Dick Howser SP	30.00	13.50	4.50
□ 568	Athletics Rookies	16.00	6.75	2.25
	Paul Lindblad			
	Ron Stone			
□ 569	Orlando McFarlane SP	28.00	12.50	4.00
□ 570	Art Mahaffey SP	28.00	12.50	4.00
□ 571	Dave Roberts SP	28.00	12.50	4.00
□ 572	Bob Priddy	14.00	6.25	2.00
□ 573	Derrell Griffith	14.00	6.25	2.00
□ 574	Mets Rookies	14.00	6.25	2.00
	Bill Hepler			
	Bill Murphy			
□ 575	Earl Wilson	14.00	6.25	2.00
□ 576	Dave Nicholson SP	28.00	12.50	4.00
□ 577	Jack Lamabe SP	28.00	12.50	4.00
□ 578	Chi Chi Olivo SP	28.00	12.50	4.00
□ 579	Orioles Rookies	18.00	7.50	2.50
	Frank Bertaina			
	Gene Brabender			
	Dave Johnson			
□ 580	Billy Williams SP	95.00	42.00	11.00
□ 581	Tony Martinez	14.00	6.25	2.00
□ 582	Garry Roggenburk	14.00	6.25	2.00
□ 583	Tigers Team SP	130.00	60.00	20.00
□ 584	Yankees Rookies	14.00	6.25	2.00
	Frank Fernandez			
	Fritz Peterson			
□ 585	Tony Taylor	14.00	6.25	2.00
□ 586	Claude Raymond SP	28.00	12.50	4.00
□ 587	Dick Bertell	14.00	6.25	2.00
□ 588	Athletics Rookies	14.00	6.25	2.00
	Chuck Dobson			
	Ken Suarez			
□ 589	Lou Klimchock SP	28.00	12.50	4.00
□ 590	Bill Skowron SP	42.00	18.00	5.50
□ 591	NL Rookies SP	36.00	16.25	5.50
	Bart Shirley			
	Grant Jackson			
□ 592	Andre Rodgers	14.00	6.25	2.00
□ 593	Doug Camilli SP	28.00	12.50	4.00
□ 594	Chico Salmon	14.00	6.25	2.00
□ 595	Larry Jackson	14.00	6.25	2.00
□ 596	Astros Rookies SP	30.00	13.50	4.50
	Nate Colbert			
	Greg Sims			
□ 597	John Sullivan	14.00	6.25	2.00
□ 598	Gaylord Perry SP	300.00	75.00	15.00

1967 Topps

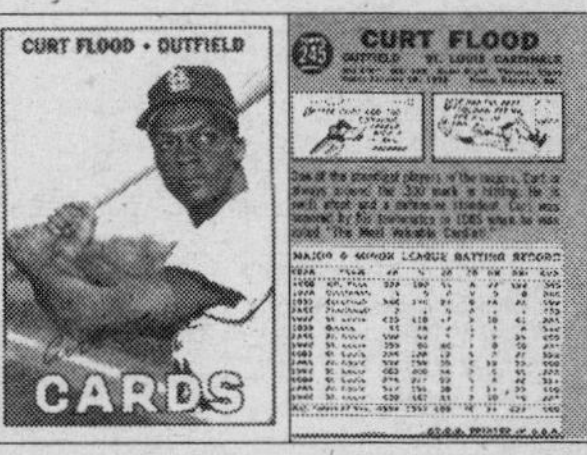

The cards in this 609-card set measure 2 1/2" by 3 1/2". The 1967 Topps series is considered by some collectors to be one of the company's finest accomplishments in baseball card production. Excellent color photographs are combined with easy-to-read backs. Cards 458 to 533 are slightly harder to find than numbers 1 to 457, and the inevitable (difficult to find) high series (534 to 609) exists. Each checklist card features a small circular picture of a popular player included in that series. Printing discrepancies resulted in some high series cards being in shorter supply. The checklist below identifies (by DP) 22 double-printed high numbers; of the 76 cards in the last series, 54 cards were short printed and the other 22 cards are much more plentiful. Featured subsets within this set include World Series cards (151-155) and League Leaders (233-244). Although there are several relatively expensive cards in this popular set, the key cards in the set are undoubtedly the Tom Seaver rookie card (581) and the Rod Carew rookie card (569). Although rarely seen, there exists a salesman's sample panel

of three cards, that pictures Earl Battey, Manny Mota, and Gene Brabender with ad information on the back about the "new" Topps cards.

	NRMT	VG-E	GOOD
COMPLETE SET (609)	5250.00	2300.00	650.00
COMMON PLAYER (1-109)	1.35	.55	.13
COMMON PLAYER (110-196)	1.75	.70	.17
COMMON PLAYER (197-283)	2.00	.80	.20
COMMON PLAYER (284-370)	2.50	1.00	.25
COMMON PLAYER (371-457)	3.00	1.25	.30
COMMON PLAYER (458-533)	6.00	2.50	.60
COMMON PLAYER (534-609)	18.00	7.50	2.50
COMMON DP (534-609)	9.00	4.00	.90

☐ 1 The Champs DP Frank Robinson Hank Bauer Brooks Robinson	21.00	5.00	1.00
☐ 2 Jack Hamilton	1.35	.55	.13
☐ 3 Duke Sims	1.35	.55	.13
☐ 4 Hal Lanier	1.75	.70	.17
☐ 5 Whitey Ford UER (1953 listed as 1933 in stats on back)	18.00	7.50	2.50
☐ 6 Dick Simpson	1.35	.55	.13
☐ 7 Don McMahon	1.35	.55	.13
☐ 8 Chuck Harrison	1.35	.55	.13
☐ 9 Ron Hansen	1.35	.55	.13
☐ 10 Matty Alou	1.75	.70	.17
☐ 11 Barry Moore	1.35	.55	.13
☐ 12 Dodgers Rookies Jim Campanis Bill Singer	1.75	.70	.17
☐ 13 Joe Sparma	1.35	.55	.13
☐ 14 Phil Linz	1.75	.70	.17
☐ 15 Earl Battey	1.35	.55	.13
☐ 16 Bill Hands	1.35	.55	.13
☐ 17 Jim Gosger	1.35	.55	.13
☐ 18 Gene Oliver	1.35	.55	.13
☐ 19 Jim McGlothlin	1.35	.55	.13
☐ 20 Orlando Cepeda	7.00	3.00	.70
☐ 21 Dave Bristol MG	1.35	.55	.13
☐ 22 Gene Brabender	1.35	.55	.13
☐ 23 Larry Elliot	1.35	.55	.13
☐ 24 Bob Allen	1.35	.55	.13
☐ 25 Elston Howard	3.50	1.50	.35
☐ 26A Bob Priddy (no traded line)	30.00	13.50	4.50
☐ 26B Bob Priddy (with traded line)	1.35	.55	.13
☐ 27 Bob Saverine	1.35	.55	.13
☐ 28 Barry Latman	1.35	.55	.13
☐ 29 Tom McCraw	1.35	.55	.13
☐ 30 Al Kaline DP	17.00	7.25	2.50
☐ 31 Jim Brewer	1.35	.55	.13
☐ 32 Bob Bailey	1.35	.55	.13
☐ 33 Athletic Rookies Sal Bando Randy Schwartz	3.00	1.25	.30
☐ 34 Pete Cimino	1.35	.55	.13
☐ 35 Rico Carty	2.00	.80	.20
☐ 36 Bob Tillman	1.35	.55	.13
☐ 37 Rick Wise	1.75	.70	.17
☐ 38 Bob Johnson	1.35	.55	.13
☐ 39 Curt Simmons	1.75	.70	.17
☐ 40 Rick Reichardt	1.35	.55	.13
☐ 41 Joe Hoerner	1.35	.55	.13
☐ 42 Mets Team	3.00	1.25	.30
☐ 43 Chico Salmon	1.35	.55	.13
☐ 44 Joe Nuxhall	1.75	.70	.17
☐ 45 Roger Maris	42.00	18.00	5.50
☐ 46 Lindy McDaniel	1.75	.70	.17
☐ 47 Ken McMullen	1.35	.55	.13
☐ 48 Bill Freehan	2.00	.80	.20
☐ 49 Roy Face	1.75	.70	.17
☐ 50 Tony Oliva	4.00	1.75	.40
☐ 51 Astros Rookies Dave Adlesh Wes Bales	1.35	.55	.13
☐ 52 Dennis Higgins	1.35	.55	.13
☐ 53 Clay Dalrymple	1.35	.55	.13
☐ 54 Dick Green	1.35	.55	.13
☐ 55 Don Drysdale	12.50	5.50	1.65
☐ 56 Jose Tartabull	1.35	.55	.13
☐ 57 Pat Jarvis	1.35	.55	.13
☐ 58 Paul Schaal	1.35	.55	.13
☐ 59 Ralph Terry	1.75	.70	.17
☐ 60 Luis Aparicio	6.50	2.75	.65
☐ 61 Gordy Coleman	1.35	.55	.13
☐ 62 Checklist 1 Frank Robinson	7.50	.75	.15
☐ 63 Cards' Clubbers Lou Brock Curt Flood	6.50	2.75	.65
☐ 64 Fred Valentine	1.35	.55	.13
☐ 65 Tom Haller	1.35	.55	.13
☐ 66 Manny Mota	1.75	.70	.17
☐ 67 Ken Berry	1.35	.55	.13
☐ 68 Bob Buhl	1.35	.55	.13
☐ 69 Vic Davalillo	1.35	.55	.13
☐ 70 Ron Santo	3.00	1.25	.30
☐ 71 Camilo Pascual	1.75	.70	.17
☐ 72 Tigers Rookies George Korince (Photo actually James Murray Brown) John (Tom) Matchick	1.35	.55	.13
☐ 73 Rusty Staub	2.50	1.00	.25
☐ 74 Wes Stock	1.35	.55	.13
☐ 75 George Scott	2.00	.80	.20
☐ 76 Jim Barbieri	1.35	.55	.13
☐ 77 Dooley Womack	1.35	.55	.13
☐ 78 Pat Corrales	1.75	.70	.17
☐ 79 Bubba Morton	1.35	.55	.13

	Card			
☐ 80	Jim Maloney	1.75	.70	.17
☐ 81	Eddie Stanky MG	1.75	.70	.17
☐ 82	Steve Barber	1.35	.55	.13
☐ 83	Ollie Brown	1.35	.55	.13
☐ 84	Tommie Sisk	1.35	.55	.13
☐ 85	Johnny Callison	1.75	.70	.17
☐ 86A	Mike McCormick	32.00	14.25	4.75
	(no traded line;			
	Senators on front			
	and Senators on back)			
☐ 86B	Mike McCormick	1.75	.70	.17
	(with traded line			
	at end of bio;			
	Senators on front			
	but Giants on back)			
☐ 87	George Altman	1.35	.55	.13
☐ 88	Mickey Lolich	3.00	1.25	.30
☐ 89	Felix Millan	1.35	.55	.13
☐ 90	Jim Nash	1.35	.55	.13
☐ 91	Johnny Lewis	1.35	.55	.13
☐ 92	Ray Washburn	1.35	.55	.13
☐ 93	Yankees Rookies	3.50	1.50	.35
	Stan Bahnsen			
	Bobby Murcer			
☐ 94	Ron Fairly	1.75	.70	.17
☐ 95	Sonny Siebert	1.35	.55	.13
☐ 96	Art Shamsky	1.35	.55	.13
☐ 97	Mike Cuellar	1.75	.70	.17
☐ 98	Rich Rollins	1.35	.55	.13
☐ 99	Lee Stange	1.35	.55	.13
☐ 100	Frank Robinson DP	17.00	7.25	2.50
☐ 101	Ken Johnson	1.35	.55	.13
☐ 102	Philadelphia Phillies	2.75	1.10	.27
	Team Card			
☐ 103	Checklist 2	9.00	1.25	.25
	Mickey Mantle			
☐ 104	Minnie Rojas	1.35	.55	.13
☐ 105	Ken Boyer	2.50	1.00	.25
☐ 106	Randy Hundley	1.75	.70	.17
☐ 107	Joel Horlen	1.35	.55	.13
☐ 108	Alex Johnson	1.75	.70	.17
☐ 109	Tribe Thumpers	2.25	.90	.22
	Rocky Colavito			
	Leon Wagner			
☐ 110	Jack Aker	1.75	.70	.17
☐ 111	John Kennedy	1.75	.70	.17
☐ 112	Dave Wickersham	1.75	.70	.17
☐ 113	Dave Nicholson	1.75	.70	.17
☐ 114	Jack Baldschun	1.75	.70	.17
☐ 115	Paul Casanova	1.75	.70	.17
☐ 116	Herman Franks MG	1.75	.70	.17
☐ 117	Darrell Brandon	1.75	.70	.17
☐ 118	Bernie Allen	1.75	.70	.17
☐ 119	Wade Blasingame	1.75	.70	.17
☐ 120	Floyd Robinson	1.75	.70	.17
☐ 121	Eddie Bressoud	1.75	.70	.17
☐ 122	George Brunet	1.75	.70	.17
☐ 123	Pirates Rookies	1.75	.70	.17
	Jim Price			
	Luke Walker			
☐ 124	Jim Stewart	1.75	.70	.17
☐ 125	Moe Drabowsky	1.75	.70	.17
☐ 126	Tony Taylor	1.75	.70	.17
☐ 127	John O'Donoghue	1.75	.70	.17
☐ 128	Ed Spiezio	1.75	.70	.17
☐ 129	Phil Roof	1.75	.70	.17
☐ 130	Phil Regan	2.25	.90	.22
☐ 131	Yankees Team	4.50	2.00	.45
☐ 132	Ozzie Virgil	1.75	.70	.17
☐ 133	Ron Kline	1.75	.70	.17
☐ 134	Gates Brown	2.25	.90	.22
☐ 135	Deron Johnson	1.75	.70	.17
☐ 136	Carroll Sembera	1.75	.70	.17
☐ 137	Twins Rookies	1.75	.70	.17
	Ron Clark			
	Jim Ollum			
☐ 138	Dick Kelley	1.75	.70	.17
☐ 139	Dalton Jones	1.75	.70	.17
☐ 140	Willie Stargell	17.00	7.25	2.50
☐ 141	John Miller	1.75	.70	.17
☐ 142	Jackie Brandt	1.75	.70	.17
☐ 143	Sox Sockers	2.25	.90	.22
	Pete Ward			
	Don Buford			
☐ 144	Bill Hepler	1.75	.70	.17
☐ 145	Larry Brown	1.75	.70	.17
☐ 146	Steve Carlton	110.00	50.00	16.50
☐ 147	Tom Egan	1.75	.70	.17
☐ 148	Adolfo Phillips	1.75	.70	.17
☐ 149	Joe Moeller	1.75	.70	.17
☐ 150	Mickey Mantle	210.00	90.00	25.00
☐ 151	World Series Game 1	3.50	1.50	.35
	Moe mows down 11			
☐ 152	World Series Game 2	5.50	2.50	.55
	Palmer blanks Dodgers			
☐ 153	World Series Game 3	3.50	1.50	.35
	Blair's homer			
	defeats L.A.			
☐ 154	World Series Game 4	3.50	1.50	.35
	Orioles 4 straight			
☐ 155	World Series Summary	3.50	1.50	.35
	Winners celebrate			
☐ 156	Ron Herbel	1.75	.70	.17
☐ 157	Danny Cater	1.75	.70	.17
☐ 158	Jimmie Coker	1.75	.70	.17
☐ 159	Bruce Howard	1.75	.70	.17
☐ 160	Willie Davis	2.25	.90	.22
☐ 161	Dick Williams MG	2.25	.90	.22
☐ 162	Billy O'Dell	1.75	.70	.17
☐ 163	Vic Roznovsky	1.75	.70	.17
☐ 164	Dwight Siebler	1.75	.70	.17
☐ 165	Cleon Jones	2.25	.90	.22
☐ 166	Eddie Mathews	12.00	5.25	1.50
☐ 167	Senators Rookies	1.75	.70	.17
	Joe Coleman			
	Tim Cullen			

☐ 168 Ray Culp .... 1.75 .70 .17
☐ 169 Horace Clarke .... 1.75 .70 .17
☐ 170 Dick McAuliffe .... 2.25 .90 .22
☐ 171 Cal Koonce .... 1.75 .70 .17
☐ 172 Bill Heath .... 1.75 .70 .17
☐ 173 St. Louis Cardinals ...... 3.50 1.50 .35
Team Card
☐ 174 Dick Radatz .... 2.25 .90 .22
☐ 175 Bobby Knoop .... 1.75 .70 .17
☐ 176 Sammy Ellis .... 1.75 .70 .17
☐ 177 Tito Fuentes .... 1.75 .70 .17
☐ 178 John Buzhardt .... 1.75 .70 .17
☐ 179 Braves Rookies .... 1.75 .70 .17
Charles Vaughan
Cecil Upshaw
☐ 180 Curt Blefary .... 2.25 .90 .22
☐ 181 Terry Fox .... 1.75 .70 .17
☐ 182 Ed Charles .... 1.75 .70 .17
☐ 183 Jim Pagliaroni .... 1.75 .70 .17
☐ 184 George Thomas .... 1.75 .70 .17
☐ 185 Ken Holtzman .... 3.00 1.25 .30
☐ 186 Mets Maulers .... 2.25 .90 .22
Ed Kranepool
Ron Swoboda
☐ 187 Pedro Ramos .... 1.75 .70 .17
☐ 188 Ken Harrelson .... 2.25 .90 .22
☐ 189 Chuck Hinton .... 1.75 .70 .17
☐ 190 Turk Farrell .... 1.75 .70 .17
☐ 191A Checklist 3 .... 7.50 .75 .15
(214 Tom Kelley)
(Willie Mays)
☐ 191B Checklist 3 .... 12.50 1.25 .25
(214 Dick Kelley)
(Willie Mays)
☐ 192 Fred Gladding .... 1.75 .70 .17
☐ 193 Jose Cardenal .... 1.75 .70 .17
☐ 194 Bob Allison .... 2.25 .90 .22
☐ 195 Al Jackson .... 1.75 .70 .17
☐ 196 Johnny Romano .... 1.75 .70 .17
☐ 197 Ron Perranoski .... 2.50 1.00 .25
☐ 198 Chuck Hiller .... 2.00 .80 .20
☐ 199 Billy Hitchcock MG ...... 2.00 .80 .20
☐ 200 Willie Mays UER 85.00 38.00 12.75
('63 Sna Francisco
on card back stats)
☐ 201 Hal Reniff .... 2.00 .80 .20
☐ 202 Johnny Edwards .... 2.00 .80 .20
☐ 203 Al McBean .... 2.00 .80 .20
☐ 204 Orioles Rookies .... 2.50 1.00 .25
Mike Epstein
Tom Phoebus
☐ 205 Dick Groat .... 2.50 1.00 .25
☐ 206 Dennis Bennett .... 2.00 .80 .20
☐ 207 John Orsino .... 2.00 .80 .20
☐ 208 Jack Lamabe .... 2.00 .80 .20
☐ 209 Joe Nossek .... 2.00 .80 .20
☐ 210 Bob Gibson 20.00 8.50 2.75
☐ 211 Twins Team .... 4.00 1.75 .40
☐ 212 Chris Zachary .... 2.00 .80 .20
☐ 213 Jay Johnstone .... 3.00 1.25 .30
☐ 214 Dick Kelley .... 2.00 .80 .20
☐ 215 Ernie Banks 20.00 8.50 2.75
☐ 216 Bengal Belters .... 7.50 3.25 .75
Norm Cash
Al Kaline
☐ 217 Rob Gardner .... 2.00 .80 .20
☐ 218 Wes Parker .... 2.50 1.00 .25
☐ 219 Clay Carroll .... 2.50 1.00 .25
☐ 220 Jim Ray Hart .... 2.50 1.00 .25
☐ 221 Woody Fryman .... 2.00 .80 .20
☐ 222 Reds Rookies .... 2.50 1.00 .25
Darrell Osteen
Lee May
☐ 223 Mike Ryan .... 2.00 .80 .20
☐ 224 Walt Bond .... 2.00 .80 .20
☐ 225 Mel Stottlemyre .... 2.50 1.00 .25
☐ 226 Julian Javier .... 2.00 .80 .20
☐ 227 Paul Lindblad .... 2.00 .80 .20
☐ 228 Gil Hodges MG .... 5.00 2.25 .50
☐ 229 Larry Jackson .... 2.00 .80 .20
☐ 230 Boog Powell .... 3.00 1.25 .30
☐ 231 John Bateman .... 2.00 .80 .20
☐ 232 Don Buford .... 2.50 1.00 .25
☐ 233 AL ERA Leaders .... 2.50 1.00 .25
Gary Peters
Joel Horlen
Steve Hargan
☐ 234 NL ERA Leaders .... 6.00 2.50 .60
Sandy Koufax
Mike Cuellar
Juan Marichal
☐ 235 AL Pitching Leaders .... 3.00 1.25 .30
Jim Kaat
Denny McLain
Earl Wilson
☐ 236 NL Pitching Leaders .. 12.00 5.25 1.50
Sandy Koufax
Juan Marichal
Bob Gibson
Gaylord Perry
☐ 237 AL Strikeout Leaders ... 2.50 1.00 .25
Sam McDowell
Jim Kaat
Earl Wilson
☐ 238 NL Strikeout Leaders .. 4.50 2.00 .45
Sandy Koufax
Jim Bunning
Bob Veale
☐ 239 AL Batting Leaders ...... 4.50 2.00 .45
Frank Robinson
Tony Oliva
Al Kaline
☐ 240 NL Batting Leaders ...... 3.00 1.25 .30
Matty Alou
Felipe Alou
Rico Carty

☐ 241	AL RBI Leaders Frank Robinson Harmon Killebrew Boog Powell	4.50	2.00	.45
☐ 242	NL RBI Leaders Hank Aaron Bob Clemente Richie Allen	7.50	3.25	.75
☐ 243	AL Home Run Leaders Frank Robinson Harmon Killebrew Boog Powell	4.50	2.00	.45
☐ 244	NL Home Run Leaders Hank Aaron Richie Allen Willie Mays	7.50	3.25	.75
☐ 245	Curt Flood	2.50	1.00	.25
☐ 246	Jim Perry	2.50	1.00	.25
☐ 247	Jerry Lumpe	2.00	.80	.20
☐ 248	Gene Mauch MG	2.50	1.00	.25
☐ 249	Nick Willhite	2.00	.80	.20
☐ 250	Hank Aaron UER (Second 1961 in stats should be 1962)	85.00	38.00	12.75
☐ 251	Woody Held	2.00	.80	.20
☐ 252	Bob Bolin	2.00	.80	.20
☐ 253	Indians Rookies Bill Davis Gus Gil	2.00	.80	.20
☐ 254	Milt Pappas	2.50	1.00	.25
☐ 255	Frank Howard	3.00	1.25	.30
☐ 256	Bob Hendley	2.00	.80	.20
☐ 257	Charlie Smith	2.00	.80	.20
☐ 258	Lee Maye	2.00	.80	.20
☐ 259	Don Dennis	2.00	.80	.20
☐ 260	Jim Lefebvre	2.50	1.00	.25
☐ 261	John Wyatt	2.00	.80	.20
☐ 262	Athletics Team	3.50	1.50	.35
☐ 263	Hank Aguirre	2.00	.80	.20
☐ 264	Ron Swoboda	2.50	1.00	.25
☐ 265	Lou Burdette	2.50	1.00	.25
☐ 266	Pitt Power Willie Stargell Donn Clendenon	4.00	1.75	.40
☐ 267	Don Schwall	2.00	.80	.20
☐ 268	Johnny Briggs	2.00	.80	.20
☐ 269	Don Nottebart	2.00	.80	.20
☐ 270	Zoilo Versalles	2.00	.80	.20
☐ 271	Eddie Watt	2.00	.80	.20
☐ 272	Cubs Rookies Bill Connors Dave Dowling	2.00	.80	.20
☐ 273	Dick Lines	2.00	.80	.20
☐ 274	Bob Aspromonte	2.00	.80	.20
☐ 275	Fred Whitfield	2.00	.80	.20
☐ 276	Bruce Brubaker	2.00	.80	.20
☐ 277	Steve Whitaker	2.00	.80	.20
☐ 278	Checklist 4 Jim Kaat	6.50	.75	.15
☐ 279	Frank Linzy	2.00	.80	.20
☐ 280	Tony Conigliaro	5.50	2.50	.55
☐ 281	Bob Rodgers	2.50	1.00	.25
☐ 282	John Odom	2.00	.80	.20
☐ 283	Gene Alley	2.50	1.00	.25
☐ 284	Johnny Podres	3.00	1.25	.30
☐ 285	Lou Brock	22.00	9.50	3.15
☐ 286	Wayne Causey	2.50	1.00	.25
☐ 287	Mets Rookies Greg Goossen Bart Shirley	2.50	1.00	.25
☐ 288	Denny Lemaster	2.50	1.00	.25
☐ 289	Tom Tresh	3.00	1.25	.30
☐ 290	Bill White	3.50	1.50	.35
☐ 291	Jim Hannan	2.50	1.00	.25
☐ 292	Don Pavletich	2.50	1.00	.25
☐ 293	Ed Kirkpatrick	2.50	1.00	.25
☐ 294	Walt Alston MG	3.50	1.50	.35
☐ 295	Sam McDowell	3.00	1.25	.30
☐ 296	Glenn Beckert	3.00	1.25	.30
☐ 297	Dave Morehead	2.50	1.00	.25
☐ 298	Ron Davis	2.50	1.00	.25
☐ 299	Norm Siebern	2.50	1.00	.25
☐ 300	Jim Kaat	4.00	1.75	.40
☐ 301	Jesse Gonder	2.50	1.00	.25
☐ 302	Orioles Team	5.00	2.25	.50
☐ 303	Gil Blanco	2.50	1.00	.25
☐ 304	Phil Gagliano	2.50	1.00	.25
☐ 305	Earl Wilson	2.50	1.00	.25
☐ 306	Bud Harrelson	3.50	1.50	.35
☐ 307	Jim Beauchamp	2.50	1.00	.25
☐ 308	Al Downing	3.00	1.25	.30
☐ 309	Hurlers Beware Johnny Callison Richie Allen	3.50	1.50	.35
☐ 310	Gary Peters	2.50	1.00	.25
☐ 311	Ed Brinkman	2.50	1.00	.25
☐ 312	Don Mincher	2.50	1.00	.25
☐ 313	Bob Lee	2.50	1.00	.25
☐ 314	Red Sox Rookies Mike Andrews Reggie Smith	7.50	3.25	.75
☐ 315	Billy Williams	11.00	5.00	1.35
☐ 316	Jack Kralick	2.50	1.00	.25
☐ 317	Cesar Tovar	2.50	1.00	.25
☐ 318	Dave Giusti	3.00	1.25	.30
☐ 319	Paul Blair	3.00	1.25	.30
☐ 320	Gaylord Perry	13.00	5.75	1.75
☐ 321	Mayo Smith MG	2.50	1.00	.25
☐ 322	Jose Pagan	2.50	1.00	.25
☐ 323	Mike Hershberger	2.50	1.00	.25
☐ 324	Hal Woodeshick	2.50	1.00	.25
☐ 325	Chico Cardenas	2.50	1.00	.25
☐ 326	Bob Uecker	22.00	9.50	3.15
☐ 327	California Angels Team Card	5.00	2.25	.50
☐ 328	Clete Boyer	3.00	1.25	.30

☐	329	Charlie Lau	3.00	1.25	.30
☐	330	Claude Osteen	3.00	1.25	.30
☐	331	Joe Foy	2.50	1.00	.25
☐	332	Jesus Alou	2.50	1.00	.25
☐	333	Fergie Jenkins	30.00	13.50	4.50
☐	334	Twin Terrors Bob Allison Harmon Killebrew	4.00	1.75	.40
☐	335	Bob Veale	3.00	1.25	.30
☐	336	Joe Azcue	2.50	1.00	.25
☐	337	Joe Morgan	25.00	11.00	3.50
☐	338	Bob Locker	2.50	1.00	.25
☐	339	Chico Ruiz	2.50	1.00	.25
☐	340	Joe Pepitone	3.00	1.25	.30
☐	341	Giants Rookies Dick Dietz Bill Sorrell	2.50	1.00	.25
☐	342	Hank Fischer	2.50	1.00	.25
☐	343	Tom Satriano	2.50	1.00	.25
☐	344	Ossie Chavarria	2.50	1.00	.25
☐	345	Stu Miller	2.50	1.00	.25
☐	346	Jim Hickman	2.50	1.00	.25
☐	347	Grady Hatton MG	2.50	1.00	.25
☐	348	Tug McGraw	3.50	1.50	.35
☐	349	Bob Chance	2.50	1.00	.25
☐	350	Joe Torre	3.50	1.50	.35
☐	351	Vern Law	3.00	1.25	.30
☐	352	Ray Oyler	2.50	1.00	.25
☐	353	Bill McCool	2.50	1.00	.25
☐	354	Cubs Team	5.00	2.25	.50
☐	355	Carl Yastrzemski	95.00	42.00	11.00
☐	356	Larry Jaster	2.50	1.00	.25
☐	357	Bill Skowron	3.00	1.25	.30
☐	358	Ruben Amaro	2.50	1.00	.25
☐	359	Dick Ellsworth	2.50	1.00	.25
☐	360	Leon Wagner	2.50	1.00	.25
☐	361	Checklist 5 Roberto Clemente	7.50	1.00	.25
☐	362	Darold Knowles	2.50	1.00	.25
☐	363	Dave Johnson	3.00	1.25	.30
☐	364	Claude Raymond	2.50	1.00	.25
☐	365	John Roseboro	3.00	1.25	.30
☐	366	Andy Kosco	2.50	1.00	.25
☐	367	Angels Rookies Bill Kelso Don Wallace	2.50	1.00	.25
☐	368	Jack Hiatt	2.50	1.00	.25
☐	369	Jim Hunter	20.00	8.50	2.75
☐	370	Tommy Davis	3.00	1.25	.30
☐	371	Jim Lonborg	4.00	1.75	.40
☐	372	Mike De La Hoz	3.00	1.25	.30
☐	373	White Sox Rookies DP Duane Josephson Fred Klages	3.00	1.25	.30
☐	374A	Mel Queen ERR DP (Incomplete stat line on back)	3.00	1.25	.30
☐	374B	Mel Queen COR DP (Complete stat line on back)	3.00	1.25	.30
☐	375	Jake Gibbs	3.00	1.25	.30
☐	376	Don Lock DP	3.00	1.25	.30
☐	377	Luis Tiant	4.50	2.00	.45
☐	378	Detroit Tigers Team Card UER (Willie Horton with 262 RBI's in 1966)	6.00	2.50	.60
☐	379	Jerry May DP	3.00	1.25	.30
☐	380	Dean Chance DP	3.50	1.50	.35
☐	381	Dick Schofield DP	3.00	1.25	.30
☐	382	Dave McNally	3.50	1.50	.35
☐	383	Ken Henderson DP	3.00	1.25	.30
☐	384	Cardinals Rookies Jim Cosman Dick Hughes	3.00	1.25	.30
☐	385	Jim Fregosi (batting wrong)	3.50	1.50	.35
☐	386	Dick Selma DP	3.00	1.25	.30
☐	387	Cap Peterson DP	3.00	1.25	.30
☐	388	Arnold Earley DP	3.00	1.25	.30
☐	389	Alvin Dark MG DP	3.50	1.50	.35
☐	390	Jim Wynn DP	4.00	1.75	.40
☐	391	Wilbur Wood DP	3.50	1.50	.35
☐	392	Tommy Harper DP	3.50	1.50	.35
☐	393	Jim Bouton DP	4.00	1.75	.40
☐	394	Jake Wood DP	3.00	1.25	.30
☐	395	Chris Short	3.00	1.25	.30
☐	396	Atlanta Aces Denis Menke Tony Cloninger	3.00	1.25	.30
☐	397	Willie Smith DP	3.00	1.25	.30
☐	398	Jeff Torborg	4.00	1.75	.40
☐	399	Al Worthington DP	3.00	1.25	.30
☐	400	Bob Clemente DP	65.00	29.00	9.75
☐	401	Jim Coates	3.00	1.25	.30
☐	402	Phillies Rookies DP Grant Jackson Billy Wilson	3.00	1.25	.30
☐	403	Dick Nen	3.00	1.25	.30
☐	404	Nelson Briles	3.50	1.50	.35
☐	405	Russ Snyder	3.00	1.25	.30
☐	406	Lee Elia DP	3.50	1.50	.35
☐	407	Reds Team	6.00	2.50	.60
☐	408	Jim Northrup DP	3.50	1.50	.35
☐	409	Ray Sadecki	3.00	1.25	.30
☐	410	Lou Johnson DP	3.00	1.25	.30
☐	411	Dick Howser DP	3.50	1.50	.35
☐	412	Astros Rookies Norm Miller Doug Rader	4.00	1.75	.40
☐	413	Jerry Grote	3.00	1.25	.30
☐	414	Casey Cox	3.00	1.25	.30
☐	415	Sonny Jackson	3.00	1.25	.30
☐	416	Roger Repoz	3.00	1.25	.30
☐	417A	Bob Bruce ERR DP (RBAVES on back)	30.00	13.50	4.50

☐ 417B Bob Bruce COR DP	3.00	1.25	.30
☐ 418 Sam Mele MG	3.00	1.25	.30
☐ 419 Don Kessinger DP	4.00	1.75	.40
☐ 420 Denny McLain	6.00	2.50	.60
☐ 421 Dal Maxvill DP	3.00	1.25	.30
☐ 422 Hoyt Wilhelm	8.00	3.50	.80
☐ 423 Fence Busters DP	20.00	8.50	2.75
Willie Mays			
Willie McCovey			
☐ 424 Pedro Gonzalez	3.00	1.25	.30
☐ 425 Pete Mikkelsen	3.00	1.25	.30
☐ 426 Lou Clinton	3.00	1.25	.30
☐ 427A Ruben Gomez ERR DP	3.00	1.25	.30
(Incomplete stat line on back)			
☐ 427B Ruben Gomez COR DP	3.00	1.25	.30
(Complete stat line on back)			
☐ 428 Dodgers Rookies DP	4.00	1.75	.40
Tom Hutton			
Gene Michael			
☐ 429 Garry Roggenburk DP	3.00	1.25	.30
☐ 430 Pete Rose	75.00	34.00	11.25
☐ 431 Ted Uhlaender	3.00	1.25	.30
☐ 432 Jimmie Hall DP	3.50	1.50	.35
☐ 433 Al Luplow DP	3.00	1.25	.30
☐ 434 Eddie Fisher DP	3.00	1.25	.30
☐ 435 Mack Jones DP	3.00	1.25	.30
☐ 436 Pete Ward	3.00	1.25	.30
☐ 437 Senators Team	6.00	2.50	.60
☐ 438 Chuck Dobson	3.00	1.25	.30
☐ 439 Byron Browne	3.00	1.25	.30
☐ 440 Steve Hargan	3.00	1.25	.30
☐ 441 Jim Davenport	3.00	1.25	.30
☐ 442 Yankees Rookies DP	4.50	2.00	.45
Bill Robinson			
Joe Verbanic			
☐ 443 Tito Francona DP	3.00	1.25	.30
☐ 444 George Smith	3.00	1.25	.30
☐ 445 Don Sutton	30.00	13.50	4.50
☐ 446 Russ Nixon DP	3.00	1.25	.30
☐ 447A Bo Belinsky ERR DP	3.50	1.50	.35
(Incomplete stat line on back)			
☐ 447B Bo Belinsky COR DP	3.50	1.50	.35
(Complete stat line on back)			
☐ 448 Harry Walker MG DP	3.00	1.25	.30
☐ 449 Orlando Pena	3.00	1.25	.30
☐ 450 Richie Allen	6.00	2.50	.60
☐ 451 Fred Newman DP	3.00	1.25	.30
☐ 452 Ed Kranepool	3.50	1.50	.35
☐ 453 Aurelio Monteagudo DP	3.00	1.25	.30
☐ 454A Checklist 6 DP	7.50	.75	.15
Juan Marichal			
(missing left ear)			
☐ 454B Checklist 6 DP	12.50	1.25	.25
Juan Marichal			
(left ear showing)			
☐ 455 Tommy Agee	3.50	1.50	.35
☐ 456 Phil Niekro	13.00	5.75	1.75
☐ 457 Andy Etchebarren DP	3.00	1.25	.30
☐ 458 Lee Thomas	7.00	3.00	.70
☐ 459 Senators Rookies	7.00	3.00	.70
Dick Bosman			
Pete Craig			
☐ 460 Harmon Killebrew	50.00	22.50	7.50
☐ 461 Bob Miller	6.00	2.50	.60
☐ 462 Bob Barton	6.00	2.50	.60
☐ 463 Hill Aces	7.00	3.00	.70
Sam McDowell			
Sonny Siebert			
☐ 464 Dan Coombs	6.00	2.50	.60
☐ 465 Willie Horton	7.00	3.00	.70
☐ 466 Bobby Wine	6.00	2.50	.60
☐ 467 Jim O'Toole	6.00	2.50	.60
☐ 468 Ralph Houk MG	7.00	3.00	.70
☐ 469 Len Gabrielson	6.00	2.50	.60
☐ 470 Bob Shaw	6.00	2.50	.60
☐ 471 Rene Lachemann	7.00	3.00	.70
☐ 472 Rookies Pirates	6.00	2.50	.60
John Gelnar			
George Spriggs			
☐ 473 Jose Santiago	6.00	2.50	.60
☐ 474 Bob Tolan	7.00	3.00	.70
☐ 475 Jim Palmer	110.00	50.00	16.50
☐ 476 Tony Perez SP	90.00	40.00	13.50
☐ 477 Braves Team	12.00	5.25	1.50
☐ 478 Bob Humphreys	6.00	2.50	.60
☐ 479 Gary Bell	6.00	2.50	.60
☐ 480 Willie McCovey	36.00	16.25	5.50
☐ 481 Leo Durocher MG	12.50	5.50	1.65
☐ 482 Bill Monbouquette	7.00	3.00	.70
☐ 483 Jim Landis	6.00	2.50	.60
☐ 484 Jerry Adair	6.00	2.50	.60
☐ 485 Tim McCarver	24.00	10.50	3.50
☐ 486 Twins Rookies	7.00	3.00	.70
Rich Reese			
Bill Whitby			
☐ 487 Tommie Reynolds	6.00	2.50	.60
☐ 488 Gerry Arrigo	6.00	2.50	.60
☐ 489 Doug Clemens	6.00	2.50	.60
☐ 490 Tony Cloninger	6.00	2.50	.60
☐ 491 Sam Bowens	6.00	2.50	.60
☐ 492 Pittsburgh Pirates	12.00	5.25	1.50
Team Card			
☐ 493 Phil Ortega	6.00	2.50	.60
☐ 494 Bill Rigney MG	6.00	2.50	.60
☐ 495 Fritz Peterson	6.00	2.50	.60
☐ 496 Orlando McFarlane	6.00	2.50	.60
☐ 497 Ron Campbell	6.00	2.50	.60
☐ 498 Larry Dierker	6.00	2.50	.60
☐ 499 Indians Rookies	6.00	2.50	.60
George Culver			
Jose Vidal			
☐ 500 Juan Marichal	25.00	11.00	3.50

☐ 501 Jerry Zimmerman	6.00	2.50	.60
☐ 502 Derrell Griffith	6.00	2.50	.60
☐ 503 Los Angeles Dodgers	12.00	5.25	1.50
Team Card			
☐ 504 Orlando Martinez	6.00	2.50	.60
☐ 505 Tommy Helms	7.00	3.00	.70
☐ 506 Smoky Burgess	7.00	3.00	.70
☐ 507 Orioles Rookies	6.00	2.50	.60
Ed Barnowski			
Larry Haney			
☐ 508 Dick Hall	6.00	2.50	.60
☐ 509 Jim King	6.00	2.50	.60
☐ 510 Bill Mazeroski	12.50	5.50	1.65
☐ 511 Don Wert	6.00	2.50	.60
☐ 512 Red Schoendienst MG	12.50	5.50	1.65
☐ 513 Marcelino Lopez	6.00	2.50	.60
☐ 514 John Werhas	6.00	2.50	.60
☐ 515 Bert Campaneris	7.00	3.00	.70
☐ 516 Giants Team	12.00	5.25	1.50
☐ 517 Fred Talbot	6.00	2.50	.60
☐ 518 Denis Menke	6.00	2.50	.60
☐ 519 Ted Davidson	6.00	2.50	.60
☐ 520 Max Alvis	6.00	2.50	.60
☐ 521 Bird Bombers	8.00	3.50	.80
Boog Powell			
Curt Blefary			
☐ 522 John Stephenson	6.00	2.50	.60
☐ 523 Jim Merritt	6.00	2.50	.60
☐ 524 Felix Mantilla	6.00	2.50	.60
☐ 525 Ron Hunt	6.00	2.50	.60
☐ 526 Tigers Rookies	8.00	3.50	.80
Pat Dobson			
George Korince			
(See 67T-72)			
☐ 527 Dennis Ribant	6.00	2.50	.60
☐ 528 Rico Petrocelli	8.00	3.50	.80
☐ 529 Gary Wagner	6.00	2.50	.60
☐ 530 Felipe Alou	7.00	3.00	.70
☐ 531 Checklist 7	12.50	1.25	.25
Brooks Robinson			
☐ 532 Jim Hicks	6.00	2.50	.60
☐ 533 Jack Fisher	6.00	2.50	.60
☐ 534 Hank Bauer MG DP	10.00	4.50	1.25
☐ 535 Donn Clendenon	22.00	9.50	3.15
☐ 536 Cubs Rookies	36.00	16.25	5.50
Joe Niekro			
Paul Popovich			
☐ 537 Chuck Estrada DP	9.00	4.00	.90
☐ 538 J.C. Martin	18.00	7.50	2.50
☐ 539 Dick Egan DP	9.00	4.00	.90
☐ 540 Norm Cash	42.00	18.00	5.50
☐ 541 Joe Gibbon	18.00	7.50	2.50
☐ 542 Athletics Rookies DP	11.00	5.00	1.35
Rick Monday			
Tony Pierce			
☐ 543 Dan Schneider	18.00	7.50	2.50
☐ 544 Cleveland Indians	33.00	15.00	5.00
Team Card			
☐ 545 Jim Grant	18.00	7.50	2.50
☐ 546 Woody Woodward	18.00	7.50	2.50
☐ 547 Red Sox Rookies DP	9.00	4.00	.90
Russ Gibson			
Bill Rohr			
☐ 548 Tony Gonzalez DP	9.00	4.00	.90
☐ 549 Jack Sanford	18.00	7.50	2.50
☐ 550 Vada Pinson DP	11.00	5.00	1.35
☐ 551 Doug Camilli DP	9.00	4.00	.90
☐ 552 Ted Savage	18.00	7.50	2.50
☐ 553 Yankees Rookies	32.00	14.25	4.75
Mike Hegan			
Thad Tillotson			
☐ 554 Andre Rodgers DP	9.00	4.00	.90
☐ 555 Don Cardwell	18.00	7.50	2.50
☐ 556 Al Weis DP	9.00	4.00	.90
☐ 557 Al Ferrara	18.00	7.50	2.50
☐ 558 Orioles Rookies	50.00	22.50	7.50
Mark Belanger			
Bill Dillman			
☐ 559 Dick Tracewski DP	9.00	4.00	.90
☐ 560 Jim Bunning	50.00	22.50	7.50
☐ 561 Sandy Alomar	20.00	8.50	2.75
☐ 562 Steve Blass DP	9.00	4.00	.90
☐ 563 Joe Adcock	22.00	9.50	3.15
☐ 564 Astros Rookies DP	9.00	4.00	.90
Alonzo Harris			
Aaron Pointer			
☐ 565 Lew Krausse	18.00	7.50	2.50
☐ 566 Gary Geiger DP	9.00	4.00	.90
☐ 567 Steve Hamilton	18.00	7.50	2.50
☐ 568 John Sullivan	18.00	7.50	2.50
☐ 569 AL Rookies DP	500.00	225.00	75.00
Rod Carew			
Hank Allen			
☐ 570 Maury Wills	95.00	42.00	11.00
☐ 571 Larry Sherry	18.00	7.50	2.50
☐ 572 Don Demeter	18.00	7.50	2.50
☐ 573 Chicago White Sox	32.00	14.25	4.75
Team Card UER			
(Indians team			
stats on back)			
☐ 574 Jerry Buchek	18.00	7.50	2.50
☐ 575 Dave Boswell	18.00	7.50	2.50
☐ 576 NL Rookies	22.00	9.50	3.15
Ramon Hernandez			
Norm Gigon			
☐ 577 Bill Short	18.00	7.50	2.50
☐ 578 John Boccabella	18.00	7.50	2.50
☐ 579 Bill Henry	18.00	7.50	2.50
☐ 580 Rocky Colavito	70.00	32.00	10.50
☐ 581 Mets Rookies	1200.00	500.00	150.00
Bill Denehy			
Tom Seaver			
☐ 582 Jim Owens DP	9.00	4.00	.90
☐ 583 Ray Barker	18.00	7.50	2.50
☐ 584 Jim Piersall	24.00	10.50	3.50
☐ 585 Wally Bunker	18.00	7.50	2.50

☐ 586 Manny Jimenez 18.00 7.50 2.50

☐ 587 NL Rookies 22.00 9.50 3.15
Don Shaw
Gary Sutherland

☐ 588 Johnny Klippstein DP .. 9.00 4.00 .90

☐ 589 Dave Ricketts DP .... 9.00 4.00 .90

☐ 590 Pete Richert 18.00 7.50 2.50

☐ 591 Ty Cline 18.00 7.50 2.50

☐ 592 NL Rookies 22.00 9.50 3.15
Jim Shellenback
Ron Willis

☐ 593 Wes Westrum MG 22.00 9.50 3.15

☐ 594 Dan Osinski 18.00 7.50 2.50

☐ 595 Cookie Rojas 22.00 9.50 3.15

☐ 596 Galen Cisco DP .... 9.00 4.00 .90

☐ 597 Ted Abernathy 18.00 7.50 2.50

☐ 598 White Sox Rookies 24.00 10.50 3.50
Walt Williams
Ed Stroud

☐ 599 Bob Duliba DP .... 9.00 4.00 .90

☐ 600 Brooks Robinson 250.00 110.00 37.50

☐ 601 Bill Bryan DP .... 9.00 4.00 .90

☐ 602 Juan Pizarro 18.00 7.50 2.50

☐ 603 Athletics Rookies 18.00 7.50 2.50
Tim Talton
Ramon Webster

☐ 604 Red Sox Team 125.00 57.50 18.75

☐ 605 Mike Shannon 45.00 20.00 6.75

☐ 606 Ron Taylor 18.00 7.50 2.50

☐ 607 Mickey Stanley 33.00 15.00 5.00

☐ 608 Cubs Rookies DP .... 9.00 4.00 .90
Rich Nye
John Upham

☐ 609 Tommy John 115.00 30.00 6.00

1968 Topps

The cards in this 598-card set measure 2 1/2" by 3 1/2". The 1968 Topps set includes Sporting News All-Star Selections as card numbers 361 to 380. Other subsets in the set include League Leaders (1-12) and World Series cards (151-158). The front of each checklist card features a picture of a popular player inside a circle. High numbers 534 to 598 are slightly more difficult to obtain. The first series looks different from the other series, as it has a lighter, wider mesh background on the card front. The later series all had a much darker, finer mesh pattern. Key cards in the set are the rookie cards of Johnny Bench (247) and Nolan Ryan (177).

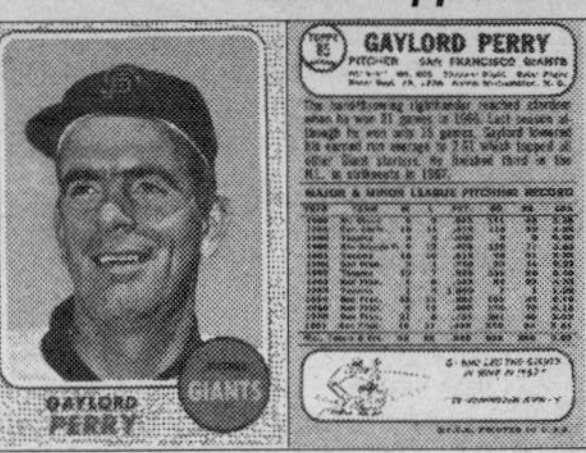

	NRMT	VG-E	GOOD
COMPLETE SET (598)	3300.00	1400.00	350.00
COMMON PLAYER (1-109)	1.35	.55	.13
COMMON PLAYER (110-196) .	1.35	.55	.13
COMMON PLAYER (197-283) .	1.35	.55	.13
COMMON PLAYER (284-370) .	1.35	.55	.13
COMMON PLAYER (371-457) .	1.35	.55	.13
COMMON PLAYER (458-533) :	3.00	1.25	.30
COMMON PLAYER (534-598) .	3.25	1.35	.32

☐ 1 NL Batting Leaders .... 15.00 3.00 .60
Bob Clemente
Tony Gonzalez
Matty Alou

☐ 2 AL Batting Leaders .... 9.00 4.00 .90
Carl Yastrzemski
Frank Robinson
Al Kaline

☐ 3 NL RBI Leaders .... 5.00 2.25 .50
Orlando Cepeda
Bob Clemente
Hank Aaron

☐ 4 AL RBI Leaders .... 9.00 4.00 .90
Carl Yastrzemski
Harmon Killebrew
Frank Robinson

☐ 5 NL Home Run Leaders .... 4.50 2.00 .45
Hank Aaron
Jim Wynn
Ron Santo
Willie McCovey

☐ 6 AL Home Run Leaders .... 6.00 2.50 .60
Carl Yastrzemski
Harmon Killebrew
Frank Howard

☐ 7 NL ERA Leaders .... 2.50 1.00 .25
Phil Niekro
Jim Bunning
Chris Short

☐ 8 AL ERA Leaders .... 2.25 .90 .22
Joel Horlen
Gary Peters

	Sonny Siebert			
☐ 9	NL Pitching Leaders	2.50	1.00	.25
	Mike McCormick			
	Ferguson Jenkins			
	Jim Bunning			
	Claude Osteen			
☐ 10A	AL Pitching Leaders	3.00	1.25	.30
	Jim Lonborg ERR (misspelled Lonberg on card back)			
	Earl Wilson			
	Dean Chance			
☐ 10B	AL Pitching Leaders	3.00	1.25	.30
	Jim Lonborg COR			
	Earl Wilson			
	Dean Chance			
☐ 11	NL Strikeout Leaders	3.50	1.50	.35
	Jim Bunning			
	Ferguson Jenkins			
	Gaylord Perry			
☐ 12	AL Strikeout Leaders	2.50	1.00	.25
	Jim Lonborg UER (misspelled Longberg on card back)			
	Sam McDowell			
	Dean Chance			
☐ 13	Chuck Hartenstein	1.35	.55	.13
☐ 14	Jerry McNertney	1.35	.55	.13
☐ 15	Ron Hunt	1.35	.55	.13
☐ 16	Indians Rookies	4.00	1.75	.40
	Lou Piniella			
	Richie Scheinblum			
☐ 17	Dick Hall	1.35	.55	.13
☐ 18	Mike Hershberger	1.35	.55	.13
☐ 19	Juan Pizarro	1.35	.55	.13
☐ 20	Brooks Robinson	21.00	9.00	3.00
☐ 21	Ron Davis	1.35	.55	.13
☐ 22	Pat Dobson	1.75	.70	.17
☐ 23	Chico Cardenas	1.35	.55	.13
☐ 24	Bobby Locke	1.35	.55	.13
☐ 25	Julian Javier	1.35	.55	.13
☐ 26	Darrell Brandon	1.35	.55	.13
☐ 27	Gil Hodges MG	7.00	3.00	.70
☐ 28	Ted Uhlaender	1.35	.55	.13
☐ 29	Joe Verbanic	1.35	.55	.13
☐ 30	Joe Torre	2.50	1.00	.25
☐ 31	Ed Stroud	1.35	.55	.13
☐ 32	Joe Gibbon	1.35	.55	.13
☐ 33	Pete Ward	1.35	.55	.13
☐ 34	Al Ferrara	1.35	.55	.13
☐ 35	Steve Hargan	1.35	.55	.13
☐ 36	Pirates Rookies	1.75	.70	.17
	Bob Moose			
	Bob Robertson			
☐ 37	Billy Williams	10.00	4.50	1.25
☐ 38	Tony Pierce	1.35	.55	.13
☐ 39	Cookie Rojas	1.35	.55	.13
☐ 40	Denny McLain	9.00	4.00	.90
☐ 41	Julio Gotay	1.35	.55	.13
☐ 42	Larry Haney	1.35	.55	.13
☐ 43	Gary Bell	1.35	.55	.13
☐ 44	Frank Kostro	1.35	.55	.13
☐ 45	Tom Seaver	200.00	90.00	30.00
☐ 46	Dave Ricketts	1.35	.55	.13
☐ 47	Ralph Houk MG	1.75	.70	.17
☐ 48	Ted Davidson	1.35	.55	.13
☐ 49A	Eddie Brinkman (white team name)	1.35	.55	.13
☐ 49B	Eddie Brinkman (yellow team name)	40.00	18.00	6.00
☐ 50	Willie Mays	60.00	27.00	9.00
☐ 51	Bob Locker	1.35	.55	.13
☐ 52	Hawk Taylor	1.35	.55	.13
☐ 53	Gene Alley	1.75	.70	.17
☐ 54	Stan Williams	1.35	.55	.13
☐ 55	Felipe Alou	1.75	.70	.17
☐ 56	Orioles Rookies	1.35	.55	.13
	Dave Leonhard			
	Dave May			
☐ 57	Dan Schneider	1.35	.55	.13
☐ 58	Eddie Mathews	9.00	4.00	.90
☐ 59	Don Lock	1.35	.55	.13
☐ 60	Ken Holtzman	1.75	.70	.17
☐ 61	Reggie Smith	2.00	.80	.20
☐ 62	Chuck Dobson	1.35	.55	.13
☐ 63	Dick Kenworthy	1.35	.55	.13
☐ 64	Jim Merritt	1.35	.55	.13
☐ 65	John Roseboro	1.35	.55	.13
☐ 66A	Casey Cox (white team name)	1.35	.55	.13
☐ 66B	Casey Cox (yellow team name)	100.00	45.00	15.00
☐ 67	Checklist 1	5.00	.50	.10
	Jim Kaat			
☐ 68	Ron Willis	1.35	.55	.13
☐ 69	Tom Tresh	1.75	.70	.17
☐ 70	Bob Veale	1.75	.70	.17
☐ 71	Vern Fuller	1.35	.55	.13
☐ 72	Tommy John	4.50	2.00	.45
☐ 73	Jim Ray Hart	1.75	.70	.17
☐ 74	Milt Pappas	1.75	.70	.17
☐ 75	Don Mincher	1.75	.70	.17
☐ 76	Braves Rookies	1.75	.70	.17
	Jim Britton			
	Ron Reed			
☐ 77	Don Wilson	1.35	.55	.13
☐ 78	Jim Northrup	1.75	.70	.17
☐ 79	Ted Kubiak	1.35	.55	.13
☐ 80	Rod Carew	150.00	67.50	22.50
☐ 81	Larry Jackson	1.35	.55	.13
☐ 82	Sam Bowens	1.35	.55	.13
☐ 83	John Stephenson	1.35	.55	.13
☐ 84	Bob Tolan	1.75	.70	.17
☐ 85	Gaylord Perry	11.00	5.00	1.35
☐ 86	Willie Stargell	11.00	5.00	1.35
☐ 87	Dick Williams MG	1.75	.70	.17

☐ 88 Phil Regan	1.75	.70	.17
☐ 89 Jake Gibbs	1.35	.55	.13
☐ 90 Vada Pinson	2.25	.90	.22
☐ 91 Jim Ollom	1.35	.55	.13
☐ 92 Ed Kranepool	1.75	.70	.17
☐ 93 Tony Cloninger	1.35	.55	.13
☐ 94 Lee Maye	1.35	.55	.13
☐ 95 Bob Aspromonte	1.35	.55	.13
☐ 96 Senator Rookies Frank Coggins Dick Nold	1.35	.55	.13
☐ 97 Tom Phoebus	1.35	.55	.13
☐ 98 Gary Sutherland	1.35	.55	.13
☐ 99 Rocky Colavito	3.50	1.50	.35
☐ 100 Bob Gibson	24.00	10.50	3.50
☐ 101 Glenn Beckert	1.75	.70	.17
☐ 102 Jose Cardenal	1.35	.55	.13
☐ 103 Don Sutton	10.00	4.50	1.25
☐ 104 Dick Dietz	1.35	.55	.13
☐ 105 Al Downing	1.75	.70	.17
☐ 106 Dalton Jones	1.35	.55	.13
☐ 107A Checklist 2 Juan Marichal (tan wide mesh)	5.00	.50	.10
☐ 107B Checklist 2 Juan Marichal (brown fine mesh)	5.00	.50	.10
☐ 108 Don Pavletich	1.35	.55	.13
☐ 109 Bert Campaneris	1.75	.70	.17
☐ 110 Hank Aaron	65.00	29.00	9.75
☐ 111 Rich Reese	1.35	.55	.13
☐ 112 Woodie Fryman	1.35	.55	.13
☐ 113 Tigers Rookies Tom Matchick Daryl Patterson	1.35	.55	.13
☐ 114 Ron Swoboda	1.75	.70	.17
☐ 115 Sam McDowell	1.75	.70	.17
☐ 116 Ken McMullen	1.35	.55	.13
☐ 117 Larry Jaster	1.35	.55	.13
☐ 118 Mark Belanger	1.75	.70	.17
☐ 119 Ted Savage	1.35	.55	.13
☐ 120 Mel Stottlemyre	2.00	.80	.20
☐ 121 Jimmie Hall	1.35	.55	.13
☐ 122 Gene Mauch MG	1.75	.70	.17
☐ 123 Jose Santiago	1.35	.55	.13
☐ 124 Nate Oliver	1.35	.55	.13
☐ 125 Joel Horlen	1.35	.55	.13
☐ 126 Bobby Etheridge	1.35	.55	.13
☐ 127 Paul Lindblad	1.35	.55	.13
☐ 128 Astros Rookies Tom Dukes Alonzo Harris	1.35	.55	.13
☐ 129 Mickey Stanley	1.75	.70	.17
☐ 130 Tony Perez	15.00	6.50	2.15
☐ 131 Frank Bertaina	1.35	.55	.13
☐ 132 Bud Harrelson	1.75	.70	.17
☐ 133 Fred Whitfield	1.35	.55	.13
☐ 134 Pat Jarvis	1.35	.55	.13
☐ 135 Paul Blair	1.75	.70	.17
☐ 136 Randy Hundley	1.75	.70	.17
☐ 137 Twins Team	2.50	1.00	.25
☐ 138 Ruben Amaro	1.35	.55	.13
☐ 139 Chris Short	1.35	.55	.13
☐ 140 Tony Conigliaro	4.50	2.00	.45
☐ 141 Dal Maxvill	1.35	.55	.13
☐ 142 White Sox Rookies Buddy Bradford Bill Voss	1.35	.55	.13
☐ 143 Pete Cimino	1.35	.55	.13
☐ 144 Joe Morgan	17.00	7.25	2.50
☐ 145 Don Drysdale	10.00	4.50	1.25
☐ 146 Sal Bando	1.75	.70	.17
☐ 147 Frank Linzy	1.35	.55	.13
☐ 148 Dave Bristol MG	1.35	.55	.13
☐ 149 Bob Saverine	1.35	.55	.13
☐ 150 Bob Clemente	50.00	22.50	7.50
☐ 151 World Series Game 1 Brock socks 4 hits in opener	6.00	2.50	.60
☐ 152 World Series Game 2 Yaz smashes 2 homers	8.00	3.50	.80
☐ 153 World Series Game 3 Briles cools Boston	3.50	1.50	.35
☐ 154 World Series Game 4 Gibson hurls shutout	6.00	2.50	.60
☐ 155 World Series Game 5 Lonborg wins again	3.50	1.50	.35
☐ 156 World Series Game 6 Petrocelli 2 homers	3.50	1.50	.35
☐ 157 World Series Game 7 St. Louis wins it	3.50	1.50	.35
☐ 158 World Series Summary Cardinals celebrate	3.50	1.50	.35
☐ 159 Don Kessinger	1.75	.70	.17
☐ 160 Earl Wilson	1.35	.55	.13
☐ 161 Norm Miller	1.35	.55	.13
☐ 162 Cards Rookies Hal Gilson Mike Torrez	1.75	.70	.17
☐ 163 Gene Brabender	1.35	.55	.13
☐ 164 Ramon Webster	1.35	.55	.13
☐ 165 Tony Oliva	3.50	1.50	.35
☐ 166 Claude Raymond	1.35	.55	.13
☐ 167 Elston Howard	3.00	1.25	.30
☐ 168 Dodgers Team	3.00	1.25	.30
☐ 169 Bob Bolin	1.35	.55	.13
☐ 170 Jim Fregosi	1.75	.70	.17
☐ 171 Don Nottebart	1.35	.55	.13
☐ 172 Walt Williams	1.35	.55	.13
☐ 173 John Boozer	1.35	.55	.13
☐ 174 Bob Tillman	1.35	.55	.13
☐ 175 Maury Wills	3.50	1.50	.35
☐ 176 Bob Allen	1.35	.55	.13
☐ 177 Mets Rookies Jerry Koosman Nolan Ryan	1500.00	650.00	175.00

☐ 178 Don Wert	1.35	.55	.13
☐ 179 Bill Stoneman	1.35	.55	.13
☐ 180 Curt Flood	1.75	.70	.17
☐ 181 Jerry Zimmerman	1.35	.55	.13
☐ 182 Dave Giusti	1.35	.55	.13
☐ 183 Bob Kennedy MG	1.35	.55	.13
☐ 184 Lou Johnson	1.35	.55	.13
☐ 185 Tom Haller	1.35	.55	.13
☐ 186 Eddie Watt	1.35	.55	.13
☐ 187 Sonny Jackson	1.35	.55	.13
☐ 188 Cap Peterson	1.35	.55	.13
☐ 189 Bill Landis	1.35	.55	.13
☐ 190 Bill White	2.00	.80	.20
☐ 191 Dan Frisella	1.35	.55	.13
☐ 192A Checklist 3	5.00	.50	.10
Carl Yastrzemski			
(Special Baseball			
Playing Card)			
☐ 192B Checklist 3	5.00	.50	.10
Carl Yastrzemski			
(Special Baseball			
Playing Card Game)			
☐ 193 Jack Hamilton	1.35	.55	.13
☐ 194 Don Buford	1.75	.70	.17
☐ 195 Joe Pepitone	1.75	.70	.17
☐ 196 Gary Nolan	1.75	.70	.17
☐ 197 Larry Brown	1.35	.55	.13
☐ 198 Roy Face	1.75	.70	.17
☐ 199 A's Rookies	1.35	.55	.13
Roberto Rodriquez			
Darrell Osteen			
☐ 200 Orlando Cepeda	4.50	2.00	.45
☐ 201 Mike Marshall	2.50	1.00	.25
☐ 202 Adolfo Phillips	1.35	.55	.13
☐ 203 Dick Kelley	1.35	.55	.13
☐ 204 Andy Etchebarren	1.35	.55	.13
☐ 205 Juan Marichal	7.50	3.25	.75
☐ 206 Cal Ermer MG	1.35	.55	.13
☐ 207 Carroll Sembera	1.35	.55	.13
☐ 208 Willie Davis	1.75	.70	.17
☐ 209 Tim Cullen	1.35	.55	.13
☐ 210 Gary Peters	1.35	.55	.13
☐ 211 J.C. Martin	1.35	.55	.13
☐ 212 Dave Morehead	1.35	.55	.13
☐ 213 Chico Ruiz	1.35	.55	.13
☐ 214 Yankees Rookies	1.75	.70	.17
Stan Bahnsen			
Frank Fernandez			
☐ 215 Jim Bunning	3.50	1.50	.35
☐ 216 Bubba Morton	1.35	.55	.13
☐ 217 Turk Farrell	1.35	.55	.13
☐ 218 Ken Suarez	1.35	.55	.13
☐ 219 Rob Gardner	1.35	.55	.13
☐ 220 Harmon Killebrew	14.00	6.25	2.00
☐ 221 Braves Team	2.75	1.10	.27
☐ 222 Jim Hardin	1.35	.55	.13
☐ 223 Ollie Brown	1.35	.55	.13
☐ 224 Jack Aker	1.35	.55	.13
☐ 225 Richie Allen	3.50	1.50	.35
☐ 226 Jimmie Price	1.35	.55	.13
☐ 227 Joe Hoerner	1.35	.55	.13
☐ 228 Dodgers Rookies	1.35	.55	.13
Jack Billingham			
Jim Fairey			
☐ 229 Fred Klages	1.35	.55	.13
☐ 230 Pete Rose	45.00	20.00	6.75
☐ 231 Dave Baldwin	1.35	.55	.13
☐ 232 Denis Menke	1.35	.55	.13
☐ 233 George Scott	1.75	.70	.17
☐ 234 Bill Monbouquette	1.35	.55	.13
☐ 235 Ron Santo	3.00	1.25	.30
☐ 236 Tug McGraw	3.00	1.25	.30
☐ 237 Alvin Dark MG	1.75	.70	.17
☐ 238 Tom Satriano	1.35	.55	.13
☐ 239 Bill Henry	1.35	.55	.13
☐ 240 Al Kaline	20.00	8.50	2.75
☐ 241 Felix Millan	1.35	.55	.13
☐ 242 Moe Drabowsky	1.35	.55	.13
☐ 243 Rich Rollins	1.35	.55	.13
☐ 244 John Donaldson	1.35	.55	.13
☐ 245 Tony Gonzalez	1.35	.55	.13
☐ 246 Fritz Peterson	1.35	.55	.13
☐ 247 Reds Rookies	300.00	135.00	45.00
Johnny Bench			
Ron Tompkins			
☐ 248 Fred Valentine	1.35	.55	.13
☐ 249 Bill Singer	1.75	.70	.17
☐ 250 Carl Yastrzemski	40.00	18.00	6.00
☐ 251 Manny Sanguillen	5.00	2.25	.50
☐ 252 Angels Team	2.75	1.10	.27
☐ 253 Dick Hughes	1.35	.55	.13
☐ 254 Cleon Jones	1.35	.55	.13
☐ 255 Dean Chance	1.75	.70	.17
☐ 256 Norm Cash	4.00	1.75	.40
☐ 257 Phil Niekro	6.50	2.75	.65
☐ 258 Cubs Rookies	1.35	.55	.13
Jose Arcia			
Bill Schlesinger			
☐ 259 Ken Boyer	2.25	.90	.22
☐ 260 Jim Wynn	1.75	.70	.17
☐ 261 Dave Duncan	1.75	.70	.17
☐ 262 Rick Wise	1.75	.70	.17
☐ 263 Horace Clarke	1.35	.55	.13
☐ 264 Ted Abernathy	1.35	.55	.13
☐ 265 Tommy Davis	1.75	.70	.17
☐ 266 Paul Popovich	1.35	.55	.13
☐ 267 Herman Franks MG	1.35	.55	.13
☐ 268 Bob Humphreys	1.35	.55	.13
☐ 269 Bob Tiefenauer	1.35	.55	.13
☐ 270 Matty Alou	1.75	.70	.17
☐ 271 Bobby Knoop	1.35	.55	.13
☐ 272 Ray Culp	1.35	.55	.13
☐ 273 Dave Johnson	1.75	.70	.17
☐ 274 Mike Cuellar	1.75	.70	.17
☐ 275 Tim McCarver	3.00	1.25	.30
☐ 276 Jim Roland	1.35	.55	.13

☐ 277 Jerry Buchek .... 1.35 .55 .13
☐ 278 Checklist 4 .... 5.00 .50 .10
Orlando Cepeda
☐ 279 Bill Hands .... 1.35 .55 .13
☐ 280 Mickey Mantle 180.00 80.00 27.00
☐ 281 Jim Campanis .... 1.35 .55 .13
☐ 282 Rick Monday .... 1.75 .70 .17
☐ 283 Mel Queen .... 1.35 .55 .13
☐ 284 Johnny Briggs .... 1.35 .55 .13
☐ 285 Dick McAuliffe .... 1.35 .55 .13
☐ 286 Cecil Upshaw .... 1.35 .55 .13
☐ 287 White Sox Rookies .... 1.35 .55 .13
Mickey Abarbanel
Cisco Carlos
☐ 288 Dave Wickersham .... 1.35 .55 .13
☐ 289 Woody Held .... 1.35 .55 .13
☐ 290 Willie McCovey 12.00 5.25 1.50
☐ 291 Dick Lines .... 1.35 .55 .13
☐ 292 Art Shamsky .... 1.35 .55 .13
☐ 293 Bruce Howard .... 1.35 .55 .13
☐ 294 Red Schoendienst MG 3.50 1.50 .35
☐ 295 Sonny Siebert .... 1.35 .55 .13
☐ 296 Byron Browne .... 1.35 .55 .13
☐ 297 Russ Gibson .... 1.35 .55 .13
☐ 298 Jim Brewer .... 1.35 .55 .13
☐ 299 Gene Michael .... 1.75 .70 .17
☐ 300 Rusty Staub .... 2.25 .90 .22
☐ 301 Twins Rookies .... 1.35 .55 .13
George Mitterwald
Rick Renick
☐ 302 Gerry Arrigo .... 1.35 .55 .13
☐ 303 Dick Green .... 1.35 .55 .13
☐ 304 Sandy Valdespino .... 1.35 .55 .13
☐ 305 Minnie Rojas .... 1.35 .55 .13
☐ 306 Mike Ryan .... 1.35 .55 .13
☐ 307 John Hiller .... 1.75 .70 .17
☐ 308 Pirates Team .... 2.75 1.10 .27
☐ 309 Ken Henderson .... 1.35 .55 .13
☐ 310 Luis Aparicio .... 6.00 2.50 .60
☐ 311 Jack Lamabe .... 1.35 .55 .13
☐ 312 Curt Blefary .... 1.35 .55 .13
☐ 313 Al Weis .... 1.35 .55 .13
☐ 314 Red Sox Rookies .... 1.35 .55 .13
Bill Rohr
George Spriggs
☐ 315 Zoilo Versalles .... 1.35 .55 .13
☐ 316 Steve Barber .... 1.35 .55 .13
☐ 317 Ron Brand .... 1.35 .55 .13
☐ 318 Chico Salmon .... 1.35 .55 .13
☐ 319 George Culver .... 1.35 .55 .13
☐ 320 Frank Howard .... 2.25 .90 .22
☐ 321 Leo Durocher MG .... 2.25 .90 .22
☐ 322 Dave Boswell .... 1.35 .55 .13
☐ 323 Deron Johnson .... 1.35 .55 .13
☐ 324 Jim Nash .... 1.35 .55 .13
☐ 325 Manny Mota .... 1.75 .70 .17
☐ 326 Dennis Ribant .... 1.35 .55 .13
☐ 327 Tony Taylor .... 1.35 .55 .13
☐ 328 Angels Rookies .... 1.35 .55 .13
Chuck Vinson
Jim Weaver
☐ 329 Duane Josephson .... 1.35 .55 .13
☐ 330 Roger Maris 36.00 16.25 5.50
☐ 331 Dan Osinski .... 1.35 .55 .13
☐ 332 Doug Rader .... 1.75 .70 .17
☐ 333 Ron Herbel .... 1.35 .55 .13
☐ 334 Orioles Team .... 2.75 1.10 .27
☐ 335 Bob Allison .... 1.75 .70 .17
☐ 336 John Purdin .... 1.35 .55 .13
☐ 337 Bill Robinson .... 2.00 .80 .20
☐ 338 Bob Johnson .... 1.35 .55 .13
☐ 339 Rich Nye .... 1.35 .55 .13
☐ 340 Max Alvis .... 1.35 .55 .13
☐ 341 Jim Lemon MG .... 1.35 .55 .13
☐ 342 Ken Johnson .... 1.35 .55 .13
☐ 343 Jim Gosger .... 1.35 .55 .13
☐ 344 Donn Clendenon .... 1.75 .70 .17
☐ 345 Bob Hendley .... 1.35 .55 .13
☐ 346 Jerry Adair .... 1.35 .55 .13
☐ 347 George Brunet .... 1.35 .55 .13
☐ 348 Phillies Rookies .... 1.35 .55 .13
Larry Colton
Dick Thoenen
☐ 349 Ed Spiezio .... 1.35 .55 .13
☐ 350 Hoyt Wilhelm .... 6.00 2.50 .60
☐ 351 Bob Barton .... 1.35 .55 .13
☐ 352 Jackie Hernandez .... 1.35 .55 .13
☐ 353 Mack Jones .... 1.35 .55 .13
☐ 354 Pete Richert .... 1.35 .55 .13
☐ 355 Ernie Banks 21.00 9.00 3.00
☐ 356A Checklist 5 .... 5.00 .50 .10
Ken Holtzman
(head centered
within circle)
☐ 356B Checklist 5 .... 5.00 .50 .10
Ken Holtzman
(head shifted right
within circle)
☐ 357 Len Gabrielson .... 1.35 .55 .13
☐ 358 Mike Epstein .... 1.35 .55 .13
☐ 359 Joe Moeller .... 1.35 .55 .13
☐ 360 Willie Horton .... 1.75 .70 .17
☐ 361 Harmon Killebrew AS .. 6.50 2.75 .65
☐ 362 Orlando Cepeda AS .... 2.50 1.00 .25
☐ 363 Rod Carew AS 13.00 5.75 1.75
☐ 364 Joe Morgan AS .... 8.00 3.50 .80
☐ 365 Brooks Robinson AS ... 8.00 3.50 .80
☐ 366 Ron Santo AS .... 2.00 .80 .20
☐ 367 Jim Fregosi AS .... 1.75 .70 .17
☐ 368 Gene Alley AS .... 1.75 .70 .17
☐ 369 Carl Yastrzemski AS .. 12.00 5.25 1.50
☐ 370 Hank Aaron AS 12.50 5.50 1.65
☐ 371 Tony Oliva AS .... 2.00 .80 .20
☐ 372 Lou Brock AS .... 7.50 3.25 .75
☐ 373 Frank Robinson AS .... 7.50 3.25 .75
☐ 374 Bob Clemente AS 12.50 5.50 1.65

☐ 375 Bill Freehan AS .... 1.75 .70 .17
☐ 376 Tim McCarver AS .... 2.00 .80 .20
☐ 377 Joel Horlen AS .... 1.35 .55 .13
☐ 378 Bob Gibson AS .... 9.00 4.00 .90
☐ 379 Gary Peters AS .... 1.35 .55 .13
☐ 380 Ken Holtzman AS .... 1.35 .55 .13
☐ 381 Boog Powell .... 2.50 1.00 .25
☐ 382 Ramon Hernandez .... 1.35 .55 .13
☐ 383 Steve Whitaker .... 1.35 .55 .13
☐ 384 Reds Rookies 10.00 4.50 1.25
Bill Henry
Hal McRae
☐ 385 Jim Hunter 12.00 5.25 1.50
☐ 386 Greg Goossen .... 1.35 .55 .13
☐ 387 Joe Foy .... 1.35 .55 .13
☐ 388 Ray Washburn .... 1.35 .55 .13
☐ 389 Jay Johnstone .... 1.75 .70 .17
☐ 390 Bill Mazeroski .... 2.50 1.00 .25
☐ 391 Bob Priddy .... 1.35 .55 .13
☐ 392 Grady Hatton MG .... 1.35 .55 .13
☐ 393 Jim Perry .... 1.75 .70 .17
☐ 394 Tommie Aaron .... 1.75 .70 .17
☐ 395 Camilo Pascual .... 1.75 .70 .17
☐ 396 Bobby Wine .... 1.35 .55 .13
☐ 397 Vic Davalillo .... 1.35 .55 .13
☐ 398 Jim Grant .... 1.35 .55 .13
☐ 399 Ray Oyler .... 1.35 .55 .13
☐ 400A Mike McCormick .... 1.75 .70 .17
(yellow letters)
☐ 400B Mike McCormick ... 100.00 45.00 15.00
(team name in
white letters)
☐ 401 Mets Team .... 3.00 1.25 .30
☐ 402 Mike Hegan .... 1.35 .55 .13
☐ 403 John Buzhardt .... 1.35 .55 .13
☐ 404 Floyd Robinson .... 1.35 .55 .13
☐ 405 Tommy Helms .... 1.75 .70 .17
☐ 406 Dick Ellsworth .... 1.35 .55 .13
☐ 407 Gary Kolb .... 1.35 .55 .13
☐ 408 Steve Carlton 50.00 22.50 7.50
☐ 409 Orioles Rookies .... 1.35 .55 .13
Frank Peters
Ron Stone
☐ 410 Fergie Jenkins 18.00 7.50 2.50
☐ 411 Ron Hansen .... 1.35 .55 .13
☐ 412 Clay Carroll .... 1.35 .55 .13
☐ 413 Tom McCraw .... 1.35 .55 .13
☐ 414 Mickey Lolich .... 3.50 1.50 .35
☐ 415 Johnny Callison .... 1.75 .70 .17
☐ 416 Bill Rigney MG .... 1.35 .55 .13
☐ 417 Willie Crawford .... 1.35 .55 .13
☐ 418 Eddie Fisher .... 1.35 .55 .13
☐ 419 Jack Hiatt .... 1.35 .55 .13
☐ 420 Cesar Tovar .... 1.35 .55 .13
☐ 421 Ron Taylor .... 1.35 .55 .13
☐ 422 Rene Lachemann .... 1.75 .70 .17
☐ 423 Fred Gladding .... 1.35 .55 .13
☐ 424 Chicago White Sox ...... 2.75 1.10 .27
Team Card
☐ 425 Jim Maloney .... 1.75 .70 .17
☐ 426 Hank Allen .... 1.35 .55 .13
☐ 427 Dick Calmus .... 1.35 .55 .13
☐ 428 Vic Roznovsky .... 1.35 .55 .13
☐ 429 Tommie Sisk .... 1.35 .55 .13
☐ 430 Rico Petrocelli .... 1.75 .70 .17
☐ 431 Dooley Womack .... 1.35 .55 .13
☐ 432 Indians Rookies .... 1.35 .55 .13
Bill Davis
Jose Vidal
☐ 433 Bob Rodgers .... 1.75 .70 .17
☐ 434 Ricardo Joseph .... 1.35 .55 .13
☐ 435 Ron Perranoski .... 1.75 .70 .17
☐ 436 Hal Lanier .... 1.75 .70 .17
☐ 437 Don Cardwell .... 1.35 .55 .13
☐ 438 Lee Thomas .... 1.75 .70 .17
☐ 439 Lum Harris MG .... 1.35 .55 .13
☐ 440 Claude Osteen .... 1.75 .70 .17
☐ 441 Alex Johnson .... 1.75 .70 .17
☐ 442 Dick Bosman .... 1.35 .55 .13
☐ 443 Joe Azcue .... 1.35 .55 .13
☐ 444 Jack Fisher .... 1.35 .55 .13
☐ 445 Mike Shannon .... 1.75 .70 .17
☐ 446 Ron Kline .... 1.35 .55 .13
☐ 447 Tigers Rookies .... 1.35 .55 .13
George Korince
Fred Lasher
☐ 448 Gary Wagner .... 1.35 .55 .13
☐ 449 Gene Oliver .... 1.35 .55 .13
☐ 450 Jim Kaat .... 3.50 1.50 .35
☐ 451 Al Spangler .... 1.35 .55 .13
☐ 452 Jesus Alou .... 1.35 .55 .13
☐ 453 Sammy Ellis .... 1.35 .55 .13
☐ 454A Checklist 6 .... 6.00 .60 .12
Frank Robinson
(cap complete
within circle)
☐ 454B Checklist 6 .... 6.00 .60 .12
Frank Robinson
(cap partially
within circle)
☐ 455 Rico Carty .... 2.00 .80 .20
☐ 456 John O'Donoghue .... 1.35 .55 .13
☐ 457 Jim Lefebvre .... 1.75 .70 .17
☐ 458 Lew Krausse .... 3.00 1.25 .30
☐ 459 Dick Simpson .... 3.00 1.25 .30
☐ 460 Jim Lonborg .... 3.50 1.50 .35
☐ 461 Chuck Hiller .... 3.00 1.25 .30
☐ 462 Barry Moore .... 3.00 1.25 .30
☐ 463 Jim Schaffer .... 3.00 1.25 .30
☐ 464 Don McMahon .... 3.00 1.25 .30
☐ 465 Tommie Agee .... 3.50 1.50 .35
☐ 466 Bill Dillman .... 3.00 1.25 .30
☐ 467 Dick Howser .... 3.50 1.50 .35
☐ 468 Larry Sherry .... 3.50 1.50 .35
☐ 469 Ty Cline .... 3.00 1.25 .30
☐ 470 Bill Freehan .... 4.00 1.75 .40

☐ 471	Orlando Pena	3.50	1.50	.35
☐ 472	Walt Alston MG	4.00	1.75	.40
☐ 473	Al Worthington	3.00	1.25	.30
☐ 474	Paul Schaal	3.00	1.25	.30
☐ 475	Joe Niekro	4.00	1.75	.40
☐ 476	Woody Woodward	3.00	1.25	.30
☐ 477	Philadelphia Phillies Team Card	6.00	2.50	.60
☐ 478	Dave McNally	3.50	1.50	.35
☐ 479	Phil Gagliano	3.00	1.25	.30
☐ 480	Manager's Dream Tony Oliva Chico Cardenas Bob Clemente	25.00	11.00	3.50
☐ 481	John Wyatt	3.00	1.25	.30
☐ 482	Jose Pagan	3.00	1.25	.30
☐ 483	Darold Knowles	3.00	1.25	.30
☐ 484	Phil Roof	3.00	1.25	.30
☐ 485	Ken Berry	3.00	1.25	.30
☐ 486	Cal Koonce	3.00	1.25	.30
☐ 487	Lee May	3.50	1.50	.35
☐ 488	Dick Tracewski	3.00	1.25	.30
☐ 489	Wally Bunker	3.00	1.25	.30
☐ 490	Super Stars Harmon Killebrew Willie Mays Mickey Mantle	90.00	40.00	13.50
☐ 491	Denny Lemaster	3.00	1.25	.30
☐ 492	Jeff Torborg	3.50	1.50	.35
☐ 493	Jim McGlothlin	3.00	1.25	.30
☐ 494	Ray Sadecki	3.00	1.25	.30
☐ 495	Leon Wagner	3.00	1.25	.30
☐ 496	Steve Hamilton	3.00	1.25	.30
☐ 497	Cardinals Team	6.00	2.50	.60
☐ 498	Bill Bryan	3.00	1.25	.30
☐ 499	Steve Blass	3.50	1.50	.35
☐ 500	Frank Robinson	24.00	10.50	3.50
☐ 501	John Odom	3.00	1.25	.30
☐ 502	Mike Andrews	3.00	1.25	.30
☐ 503	Al Jackson	3.00	1.25	.30
☐ 504	Russ Snyder	3.00	1.25	.30
☐ 505	Joe Sparma	3.50	1.50	.35
☐ 506	Clarence Jones	3.00	1.25	.30
☐ 507	Wade Blasingame	3.00	1.25	.30
☐ 508	Duke Sims	3.00	1.25	.30
☐ 509	Dennis Higgins	3.00	1.25	.30
☐ 510	Ron Fairly	3.50	1.50	.35
☐ 511	Bill Kelso	3.00	1.25	.30
☐ 512	Grant Jackson	3.00	1.25	.30
☐ 513	Hank Bauer MG	3.50	1.50	.35
☐ 514	Al McBean	3.00	1.25	.30
☐ 515	Russ Nixon	3.00	1.25	.30
☐ 516	Pete Mikkelsen	3.00	1.25	.30
☐ 517	Diego Segui	3.00	1.25	.30
☐ 518A	Checklist 7 ERR (539 AL Rookies) (Clete Boyer)	10.00	1.00	.20
☐ 518B	Checklist 7 COR (539 ML Rookies) (Clete Boyer)	6.00	.60	.12
☐ 519	Jerry Stephenson	3.00	1.25	.30
☐ 520	Lou Brock	25.00	11.00	3.50
☐ 521	Don Shaw	3.00	1.25	.30
☐ 522	Wayne Causey	3.00	1.25	.30
☐ 523	John Tsitouris	3.00	1.25	.30
☐ 524	Andy Kosco	3.00	1.25	.30
☐ 525	Jim Davenport	3.00	1.25	.30
☐ 526	Bill Denehy	3.00	1.25	.30
☐ 527	Tito Francona	3.00	1.25	.30
☐ 528	Tigers Team	56.00	24.00	8.00
☐ 529	Bruce Von Hoff	3.00	1.25	.30
☐ 530	Bird Belters Brooks Robinson Frank Robinson	10.00	4.50	1.25
☐ 531	Chuck Hinton	3.00	1.25	.30
☐ 532	Luis Tiant	4.00	1.75	.40
☐ 533	Wes Parker	3.50	1.50	.35
☐ 534	Bob Miller	3.25	1.35	.32
☐ 535	Danny Cater	3.25	1.35	.32
☐ 536	Bill Short	3.25	1.35	.32
☐ 537	Norm Siebern	3.25	1.35	.32
☐ 538	Manny Jimenez	3.25	1.35	.32
☐ 539	Major League Rookies Jim Ray Mike Ferraro	4.00	1.75	.40
☐ 540	Nelson Briles	3.25	1.35	.32
☐ 541	Sandy Alomar	4.00	1.75	.40
☐ 542	John Boccabella	3.25	1.35	.32
☐ 543	Bob Lee	3.25	1.35	.32
☐ 544	Mayo Smith MG	3.25	1.35	.32
☐ 545	Lindy McDaniel	3.25	1.35	.32
☐ 546	Roy White	4.00	1.75	.40
☐ 547	Dan Coombs	3.25	1.35	.32
☐ 548	Bernie Allen	3.25	1.35	.32
☐ 549	Orioles Rookies Curt Motton Roger Nelson	3.25	1.35	.32
☐ 550	Clete Boyer	4.00	1.75	.40
☐ 551	Darrell Sutherland	3.25	1.35	.32
☐ 552	Ed Kirkpatrick	3.25	1.35	.32
☐ 553	Hank Aguirre	3.25	1.35	.32
☐ 554	A's Team	6.50	2.75	.65
☐ 555	Jose Tartabull	3.25	1.35	.32
☐ 556	Dick Selma	3.25	1.35	.32
☐ 557	Frank Quilici	3.25	1.35	.32
☐ 558	Johnny Edwards	3.25	1.35	.32
☐ 559	Pirates Rookies Carl Taylor Luke Walker	4.00	1.75	.40
☐ 560	Paul Casanova	3.25	1.35	.32
☐ 561	Lee Elia	4.00	1.75	.40
☐ 562	Jim Bouton	4.50	2.00	.45
☐ 563	Ed Charles	3.25	1.35	.32
☐ 564	Eddie Stanky MG	4.00	1.75	.40
☐ 565	Larry Dierker	3.25	1.35	.32
☐ 566	Ken Harrelson	4.00	1.75	.40

☐ 567 Clay Dalrymple	3.25	1.35	.32
☐ 568 Willie Smith	3.25	1.35	.32
☐ 569 NL Rookies Ivan Murrell Les Rohr	3.25	1.35	.32
☐ 570 Rick Reichardt	3.25	1.35	.32
☐ 571 Tony LaRussa	4.50	2.00	.45
☐ 572 Don Bosch	3.25	1.35	.32
☐ 573 Joe Coleman	3.25	1.35	.32
☐ 574 Cincinnati Reds Team Card	6.50	2.75	.65
☐ 575 Jim Palmer	60.00	27.00	9.00
☐ 576 Dave Adlesh	3.25	1.35	.32
☐ 577 Fred Talbot	3.25	1.35	.32
☐ 578 Orlando Martinez	3.25	1.35	.32
☐ 579 NL Rookies Larry Hisle Mike Lum	4.00	1.75	.40
☐ 580 Bob Bailey	3.25	1.35	.32
☐ 581 Garry Roggenburk	3.25	1.35	.32
☐ 582 Jerry Grote	3.25	1.35	.32
☐ 583 Gates Brown	4.00	1.75	.40
☐ 584 Larry Shepard MG	3.25	1.35	.32
☐ 585 Wilbur Wood	4.00	1.75	.40
☐ 586 Jim Pagliaroni	3.25	1.35	.32
☐ 587 Roger Repoz	3.25	1.35	.32
☐ 588 Dick Schofield	3.25	1.35	.32
☐ 589 Twins Rookies Ron Clark Moe Ogier	3.25	1.35	.32
☐ 590 Tommy Harper	3.25	1.35	.32
☐ 591 Dick Nen	3.25	1.35	.32
☐ 592 John Bateman	3.25	1.35	.32
☐ 593 Lee Stange	3.25	1.35	.32
☐ 594 Phil Linz	4.00	1.75	.40
☐ 595 Phil Ortega	3.25	1.35	.32
☐ 596 Charlie Smith	3.25	1.35	.32
☐ 597 Bill McCool	3.25	1.35	.32
☐ 598 Jerry May	4.50	1.75	.35

1969 Topps

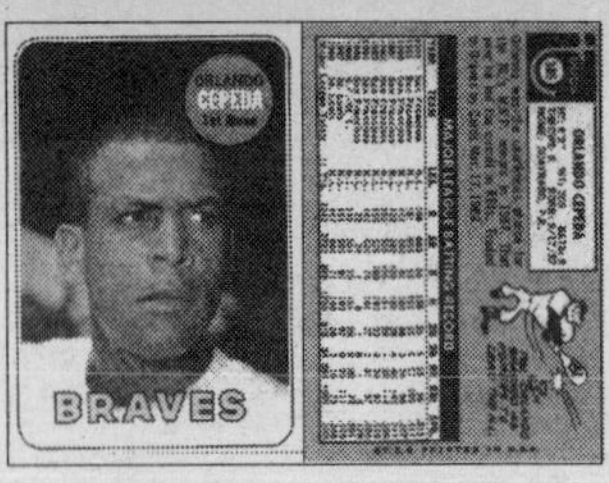

The cards in this 664-card set measure 2 1/2" by 3 1/2". The 1969 Topps set includes Sporting News All-Star Selections as card numbers 416 to 435. Other popular subsets within this set include League Leaders (1-12) and World Series cards (162-169). The fifth series contains several variations; the more difficult variety consists of cards with the player's first name, last name, and/or position in white letters instead of lettering in some other color. These are designated in the checklist below by WL (white letters). Each checklist card features a different popular player's picture inside a circle on the front of the checklist card. Two different poses of Clay Dalrymple and Donn Clendenon exist, as indicated in the checklist. The key rookie cards in this set are Rollie Fingers, Reggie Jackson, and Graig Nettles. This was the last year that Topps issued multi-player special star cards, ending a 13-year tradition, which they had begun in 1957. There were cropping differences in checklist cards 57, 214, and 412, due to their each being printed with two different series. The differences are difficult to explain and have not been greatly sought by collectors; hence they are not listed explicitly in the list below. The All-Star cards 426-435, when turned over and placed together, form a puzzle back of Pete Rose.

	NRMT	VG-E	GOOD
COMPLETE SET (664)	2500.00	1100.00	250.00
COMMON PLAYER (1-109)	1.35	.55	.13
COMMON PLAYER (110-218)	1.35	.55	.13
COMMON PLAYER (219-327)	2.25	.90	.22
COMMON PLAYER (328-425)	1.35	.55	.13
COMMON PLAYER (426-512)	1.35	.55	.13
COMMON PLAYER (513-588)	1.65	.70	.20
COMMON PLAYER (589-664)	2.25	.90	.22

☐ 1 AL Batting Leaders Carl Yastrzemski Danny Cater Tony Oliva	10.00	2.50	.50
☐ 2 NL Batting Leaders Pete Rose Matty Alou Felipe Alou	4.50	2.00	.45
☐ 3 AL RBI Leaders Ken Harrelson	2.50	1.00	.25

Card			
Frank Howard			
Jim Northrup			
☐ 4 NL RBI Leaders	3.50	1.50	.35
Willie McCovey			
Ron Santo			
Billy Williams			
☐ 5 AL Home Run Leaders	2.50	1.00	.25
Frank Howard			
Willie Horton			
Ken Harrelson			
☐ 6 NL Home Run Leaders	3.50	1.50	.35
Willie McCovey			
Richie Allen			
Ernie Banks			
☐ 7 AL ERA Leaders	2.50	1.00	.25
Luis Tiant			
Sam McDowell			
Dave McNally			
☐ 8 NL ERA Leaders	2.50	1.00	.25
Bob Gibson			
Bobby Bolin			
Bob Veale			
☐ 9 AL Pitching Leaders	2.50	1.00	.25
Denny McLain			
Dave McNally			
Luis Tiant			
Mel Stottlemyre			
☐ 10 NL Pitching Leaders	3.50	1.50	.35
Juan Marichal			
Bob Gibson			
Fergie Jenkins			
☐ 11 AL Strikeout Leaders	2.50	1.00	.25
Sam McDowell			
Denny McLain			
Luis Tiant			
☐ 12 NL Strikeout Leaders	3.00	1.25	.30
Bob Gibson			
Fergie Jenkins			
Bill Singer			
☐ 13 Mickey Stanley	1.75	.70	.17
☐ 14 Al McBean	1.35	.55	.13
☐ 15 Boog Powell	2.50	1.00	.25
☐ 16 Giants Rookies	1.35	.55	.13
Cesar Gutierrez			
Rich Robertson			
☐ 17 Mike Marshall	1.75	.70	.17
☐ 18 Dick Schofield	1.35	.55	.13
☐ 19 Ken Suarez	1.35	.55	.13
☐ 20 Ernie Banks	18.00	7.50	2.50
☐ 21 Jose Santiago	1.35	.55	.13
☐ 22 Jesus Alou	1.35	.55	.13
☐ 23 Lew Krausse	1.35	.55	.13
☐ 24 Walt Alston MG	2.50	1.00	.25
☐ 25 Roy White	1.75	.70	.17
☐ 26 Clay Carroll	1.35	.55	.13
☐ 27 Bernie Allen	1.35	.55	.13
☐ 28 Mike Ryan	1.35	.55	.13
☐ 29 Dave Morehead	1.35	.55	.13

Card			
☐ 30 Bob Allison	1.75	.70	.17
☐ 31 Mets Rookies	2.50	1.00	.25
Gary Gentry			
Amos Otis			
☐ 32 Sammy Ellis	1.35	.55	.13
☐ 33 Wayne Causey	1.35	.55	.13
☐ 34 Gary Peters	1.35	.55	.13
☐ 35 Joe Morgan	12.00	5.25	1.50
☐ 36 Luke Walker	1.35	.55	.13
☐ 37 Curt Motton	1.35	.55	.13
☐ 38 Zoilo Versalles	1.35	.55	.13
☐ 39 Dick Hughes	1.35	.55	.13
☐ 40 Mayo Smith MG	1.35	.55	.13
☐ 41 Bob Barton	1.35	.55	.13
☐ 42 Tommy Harper	1.35	.55	.13
☐ 43 Joe Niekro	1.75	.70	.17
☐ 44 Danny Cater	1.35	.55	.13
☐ 45 Maury Wills	2.50	1.00	.25
☐ 46 Fritz Peterson	1.35	.55	.13
☐ 47A Paul Popovich	1.35	.55	.13
(no helmet emblem)			
☐ 47B Paul Popovich	15.00	6.50	2.15
(C emblem on helmet)			
☐ 48 Brant Alyea	1.35	.55	.13
☐ 49A Royals Rookies COR	1.35	.55	.13
Steve Jones			
E. Rodriguez "g"			
☐ 49B Royals Rookies ERR	15.00	6.50	2.15
Steve Jones			
E. Rodriquez "q"			
☐ 50 Bob Clemente UER	48.00	22.00	6.00
(Bats Right listed twice)			
☐ 51 Woodie Fryman	1.35	.55	.13
☐ 52 Mike Andrews	1.35	.55	.13
☐ 53 Sonny Jackson	1.35	.55	.13
☐ 54 Cisco Carlos	1.35	.55	.13
☐ 55 Jerry Grote	1.35	.55	.13
☐ 56 Rich Reese	1.35	.55	.13
☐ 57 Checklist 1	4.50	.50	.10
Denny McLain			
☐ 58 Fred Gladding	1.35	.55	.13
☐ 59 Jay Johnstone	1.75	.70	.17
☐ 60 Nelson Briles	1.35	.55	.13
☐ 61 Jimmie Hall	1.35	.55	.13
☐ 62 Chico Salmon	1.35	.55	.13
☐ 63 Jim Hickman	1.35	.55	.13
☐ 64 Bill Monbouquette	1.35	.55	.13
☐ 65 Willie Davis	1.75	.70	.17
☐ 66 Orioles Rookies	1.75	.70	.17
Mike Adamson			
Merv Rettenmund			
☐ 67 Bill Stoneman	1.35	.55	.13
☐ 68 Dave Duncan	1.75	.70	.17
☐ 69 Steve Hamilton	1.35	.55	.13
☐ 70 Tommy Helms	1.75	.70	.17
☐ 71 Steve Whitaker	1.35	.55	.13
☐ 72 Ron Taylor	1.35	.55	.13

☐ 73 Johnny Briggs .... 1.35 .55 .13
☐ 74 Preston Gomez MG .... 1.35 .55 .13
☐ 75 Luis Aparicio .... 5.50 2.50 .55
☐ 76 Norm Miller .... 1.35 .55 .13
☐ 77A Ron Perranoski .... 1.75 .70 .17
(no emblem on cap)
☐ 77B Ron Perranoski 15.00 6.50 2.15
(LA on cap)
☐ 78 Tom Satriano .... 1.35 .55 .13
☐ 79 Milt Pappas .... 1.75 .70 .17
☐ 80 Norm Cash .... 2.50 1.00 .25
☐ 81 Mel Queen .... 1.35 .55 .13
☐ 82 Pirates Rookies 10.00 4.50 1.25
Rich Hebner
Al Oliver
☐ 83 Mike Ferraro .... 1.35 .55 .13
☐ 84 Bob Humphreys .... 1.35 .55 .13
☐ 85 Lou Brock 18.00 7.50 2.50
☐ 86 Pete Richert .... 1.35 .55 .13
☐ 87 Horace Clarke .... 1.35 .55 .13
☐ 88 Rich Nye .... 1.35 .55 .13
☐ 89 Russ Gibson .... 1.35 .55 .13
☐ 90 Jerry Koosman .... 5.00 2.25 .50
☐ 91 Alvin Dark MG .... 1.35 .55 .13
☐ 92 Jack Billingham .... 1.35 .55 .13
☐ 93 Joe Foy .... 1.35 .55 .13
☐ 94 Hank Aguirre .... 1.35 .55 .13
☐ 95 Johnny Bench 175.00 80.00 27.00
☐ 96 Denny Lemaster .... 1.35 .55 .13
☐ 97 Buddy Bradford .... 1.35 .55 .13
☐ 98 Dave Giusti .... 1.35 .55 .13
☐ 99A Twins Rookies 15.00 6.50 2.15
Danny Morris
Graig Nettles
(no loop)
☐ 99B Twins Rookies 24.00 10.50 3.50
(errant loop in
upper left corner
of obverse)
☐ 100 Hank Aaron 60.00 27.00 9.00
☐ 101 Daryl Patterson .... 1.35 .55 .13
☐ 102 Jim Davenport .... 1.35 .55 .13
☐ 103 Roger Repoz .... 1.35 .55 .13
☐ 104 Steve Blass .... 1.35 .55 .13
☐ 105 Rick Monday .... 1.75 .70 .17
☐ 106 Jim Hannan .... 1.35 .55 .13
☐ 107A Checklist 2 ERR .... 5.00 .50 .10
(161 Jim Purdin)
(Bob Gibson)
☐ 107B Checklist 2 COR .... 7.50 .75 .15
(161 John Purdin)
(Bob Gibson)
☐ 108 Tony Taylor .... 1.35 .55 .13
☐ 109 Jim Lonborg .... 1.75 .70 .17
☐ 110 Mike Shannon .... 1.75 .70 .17
☐ 111 Johnny Morris .... 1.35 .55 .13
☐ 112 J.C. Martin .... 1.35 .55 .13
☐ 113 Dave May .... 1.35 .55 .13
☐ 114 Yankees Rookies .... 1.35 .55 .13
Alan Closter
John Cumberland
☐ 115 Bill Hands .... 1.35 .55 .13
☐ 116 Chuck Harrison .... 1.35 .55 .13
☐ 117 Jim Fairey .... 1.35 .55 .13
☐ 118 Stan Williams .... 1.35 .55 .13
☐ 119 Doug Rader .... 1.75 .70 .17
☐ 120 Pete Rose 36.00 16.25 5.50
☐ 121 Joe Grzenda .... 1.35 .55 .13
☐ 122 Ron Fairly .... 1.75 .70 .17
☐ 123 Wilbur Wood .... 1.35 .55 .13
☐ 124 Hank Bauer MG .... 1.75 .70 .17
☐ 125 Ray Sadecki .... 1.35 .55 .13
☐ 126 Dick Tracewski .... 1.35 .55 .13
☐ 127 Kevin Collins .... 1.35 .55 .13
☐ 128 Tommie Aaron .... 1.75 .70 .17
☐ 129 Bill McCool .... 1.35 .55 .13
☐ 130 Carl Yastrzemski 28.00 12.50 4.00
☐ 131 Chris Cannizzaro .... 1.35 .55 .13
☐ 132 Dave Baldwin .... 1.35 .55 .13
☐ 133 Johnny Callison .... 1.75 .70 .17
☐ 134 Jim Weaver .... 1.35 .55 .13
☐ 135 Tommy Davis .... 1.75 .70 .17
☐ 136 Cards Rookies .... 1.75 .70 .17
Steve Huntz
Mike Torrez
☐ 137 Wally Bunker .... 1.75 .70 .17
☐ 138 John Bateman .... 1.35 .55 .13
☐ 139 Andy Kosco .... 1.35 .55 .13
☐ 140 Jim Lefebvre .... 1.75 .70 .17
☐ 141 Bill Dillman .... 1.35 .55 .13
☐ 142 Woody Woodward ...... 1.75 .70 .17
☐ 143 Joe Nossek .... 1.35 .55 .13
☐ 144 Bob Hendley .... 1.35 .55 .13
☐ 145 Max Alvis .... 1.35 .55 .13
☐ 146 Jim Perry .... 1.75 .70 .17
☐ 147 Leo Durocher MG .... 2.50 1.00 .25
☐ 148 Lee Stange .... 1.35 .55 .13
☐ 149 Ollie Brown .... 1.35 .55 .13
☐ 150 Denny McLain .... 5.00 2.25 .50
☐ 151A Clay Dalrymple .... 1.35 .55 .13
(Portrait, Orioles)
☐ 151B Clay Dalrymple 15.00 6.50 2.15
(Catching, Phillies)
☐ 152 Tommie Sisk .... 1.35 .55 .13
☐ 153 Ed Brinkman .... 1.35 .55 .13
☐ 154 Jim Britton .... 1.35 .55 .13
☐ 155 Pete Ward .... 1.35 .55 .13
☐ 156 Houston Rookies .... 1.35 .55 .13
Hal Gilson
Leon McFadden
☐ 157 Bob Rodgers .... 1.75 .70 .17
☐ 158 Joe Gibbon .... 1.35 .55 .13
☐ 159 Jerry Adair .... 1.35 .55 .13
☐ 160 Vada Pinson .... 2.00 .80 .20
☐ 161 John Purdin .... 1.35 .55 .13
☐ 162 World Series Game 1 .. 5.00 2.25 .50

Gibson fans 17
☐ 163 World Series Game 2 .. 3.50 1.50 .35
Tiger homers
deck the Cards
☐ 164 World Series Game 3 .. 5.00 2.25 .50
McCarver's homer
☐ 165 World Series Game 4 .. 5.00 2.25 .50
Brock lead-off homer
☐ 166 World Series Game 5 .. 6.00 2.50 .60
Kaline's key hit
☐ 167 World Series Game 6 .. 3.50 1.50 .35
Northrup grandslam
☐ 168 World Series Game 7 .. 5.00 2.25 .50
Lolich outduels
Bob Gibson
☐ 169 World Series Summary 3.50 1.50 .35
Tigers celebrate
☐ 170 Frank Howard .... 2.00 .80 .20
☐ 171 Glenn Beckert .... 1.75 .70 .17
☐ 172 Jerry Stephenson .... 1.35 .55 .13
☐ 173 White Sox Rookies ...... 1.35 .55 .13
Bob Christian
Gerry Nyman
☐ 174 Grant Jackson .... 1.35 .55 .13
☐ 175 Jim Bunning .... 3.00 1.25 .30
☐ 176 Joe Azcue .... 1.35 .55 .13
☐ 177 Ron Reed .... 1.35 .55 .13
☐ 178 Ray Oyler .... 1.35 .55 .13
☐ 179 Don Pavletich .... 1.35 .55 .13
☐ 180 Willie Horton .... 1.75 .70 .17
☐ 181 Mel Nelson .... 1.35 .55 .13
☐ 182 Bill Rigney MG .... 1.35 .55 .13
☐ 183 Don Shaw .... 1.35 .55 .13
☐ 184 Roberto Pena .... 1.35 .55 .13
☐ 185 Tom Phoebus .... 1.35 .55 .13
☐ 186 Johnny Edwards .... 1.35 .55 .13
☐ 187 Leon Wagner .... 1.35 .55 .13
☐ 188 Rick Wise .... 1.75 .70 .17
☐ 189 Red Sox Rookies .... 1.35 .55 .13
Joe Lahoud
John Thibodeau
☐ 190 Willie Mays 60.00 27.00 9.00
☐ 191 Lindy McDaniel .... 1.75 .70 .17
☐ 192 Jose Pagan .... 1.35 .55 .13
☐ 193 Don Cardwell .... 1.35 .55 .13
☐ 194 Ted Uhlaender .... 1.35 .55 .13
☐ 195 John Odom .... 1.35 .55 .13
☐ 196 Lum Harris MG .... 1.35 .55 .13
☐ 197 Dick Selma .... 1.35 .55 .13
☐ 198 Willie Smith .... 1.35 .55 .13
☐ 199 Jim French .... 1.35 .55 .13
☐ 200 Bob Gibson 13.50 6.00 1.85
☐ 201 Russ Snyder .... 1.35 .55 .13
☐ 202 Don Wilson .... 1.35 .55 .13
☐ 203 Dave Johnson .... 1.75 .70 .17
☐ 204 Jack Hiatt .... 1.35 .55 .13
☐ 205 Rick Reichardt .... 1.35 .55 .13
☐ 206 Phillies Rookies .... 1.75 .70 .17
Larry Hisle
Barry Lersch
☐ 207 Roy Face .... 1.75 .70 .17
☐ 208A Donn Clendenon .... 1.75 .70 .17
(Houston)
☐ 208B Donn Clendenon 15.00 6.50 2.15
(Expos)
☐ 209 Larry Haney UER .... 1.35 .55 .13
(reverse negative)
☐ 210 Felix Millan .... 1.35 .55 .13
☐ 211 Galen Cisco .... 1.35 .55 .13
☐ 212 Tom Tresh .... 1.75 .70 .17
☐ 213 Gerry Arrigo .... 1.35 .55 .13
☐ 214 Checklist 3 .... 4.00 .50 .10
With 69T deckle CL
on back (no player)
☐ 215 Rico Petrocelli .... 1.75 .70 .17
☐ 216 Don Sutton .... 8.00 3.50 .80
☐ 217 John Donaldson .... 1.35 .55 .13
☐ 218 John Roseboro .... 1.35 .55 .13
☐ 219 Freddie Patek .... 3.50 1.50 .35
☐ 220 Sam McDowell .... 2.75 1.10 .27
☐ 221 Art Shamsky .... 2.25 .90 .22
☐ 222 Duane Josephson .... 2.25 .90 .22
☐ 223 Tom Dukes .... 2.25 .90 .22
☐ 224 Angels Rookies .... 2.25 .90 .22
Bill Harrelson
Steve Kealey
☐ 225 Don Kessinger .... 2.75 1.10 .27
☐ 226 Bruce Howard .... 2.25 .90 .22
☐ 227 Frank Johnson .... 2.25 .90 .22
☐ 228 Dave Leonhard .... 2.25 .90 .22
☐ 229 Don Lock .... 2.25 .90 .22
☐ 230 Rusty Staub .... 3.50 1.50 .35
☐ 231 Pat Dobson .... 2.75 1.10 .27
☐ 232 Dave Ricketts .... 2.25 .90 .22
☐ 233 Steve Barber .... 2.25 .90 .22
☐ 234 Dave Bristol MG .... 2.25 .90 .22
☐ 235 Jim Hunter 13.00 5.75 1.75
☐ 236 Manny Mota .... 2.75 1.10 .27
☐ 237 Bobby Cox .... 3.50 1.50 .35
☐ 238 Ken Johnson .... 2.25 .90 .22
☐ 239 Bob Taylor .... 2.25 .90 .22
☐ 240 Ken Harrelson .... 2.75 1.10 .27
☐ 241 Jim Brewer .... 2.25 .90 .22
☐ 242 Frank Kostro .... 2.25 .90 .22
☐ 243 Ron Kline .... 2.25 .90 .22
☐ 244 Indians Rookies .... 2.75 1.10 .27
Ray Fosse
George Woodson
☐ 245 Ed Charles .... 2.25 .90 .22
☐ 246 Joe Coleman .... 2.25 .90 .22
☐ 247 Gene Oliver .... 2.25 .90 .22
☐ 248 Bob Priddy .... 2.25 .90 .22
☐ 249 Ed Spiezio .... 2.25 .90 .22
☐ 250 Frank Robinson 25.00 11.00 3.50
☐ 251 Ron Herbel .... 2.25 .90 .22
☐ 252 Chuck Cottier .... 2.25 .90 .22

☐ 253 Jerry Johnson .... 2.25 .90 .22
☐ 254 Joe Schultz .... 2.25 .90 .22
☐ 255 Steve Carlton 50.00 22.50 7.50
☐ 256 Gates Brown .... 2.75 1.10 .27
☐ 257 Jim Ray .... 2.25 .90 .22
☐ 258 Jackie Hernandez .... 2.25 .90 .22
☐ 259 Bill Short .... 2.25 .90 .22
☐ 260 Reggie Jackson 525.00 225.00 75.00
☐ 261 Bob Johnson .... 2.25 .90 .22
☐ 262 Mike Kekich .... 2.25 .90 .22
☐ 263 Jerry May .... 2.25 .90 .22
☐ 264 Bill Landis .... 2.25 .90 .22
☐ 265 Chico Cardenas .... 2.25 .90 .22
☐ 266 Dodger Rookies .... 2.25 .90 .22
Tom Hutton
Alan Foster
☐ 267 Vicente Romo .... 2.25 .90 .22
☐ 268 Al Spangler .... 2.25 .90 .22
☐ 269 Al Weis .... 2.25 .90 .22
☐ 270 Mickey Lolich .... 3.50 1.50 .35
☐ 271 Larry Stahl .... 2.25 .90 .22
☐ 272 Ed Stroud .... 2.25 .90 .22
☐ 273 Ron Willis .... 2.25 .90 .22
☐ 274 Clyde King MG .... 2.25 .90 .22
☐ 275 Vic Davalillo .... 2.25 .90 .22
☐ 276 Gary Wagner .... 2.25 .90 .22
☐ 277 Elrod Hendricks .... 2.25 .90 .22
☐ 278 Gary Geiger UER .... 2.25 .90 .22
(Batting wrong)
☐ 279 Roger Nelson .... 2.25 .90 .22
☐ 280 Alex Johnson .... 2.75 1.10 .27
☐ 281 Ted Kubiak .... 2.25 .90 .22
☐ 282 Pat Jarvis .... 2.25 .90 .22
☐ 283 Sandy Alomar .... 2.75 1.10 .27
☐ 284 Expos Rookies .... 2.25 .90 .22
Jerry Robertson
Mike Wegener
☐ 285 Don Mincher .... 2.75 1.10 .27
☐ 286 Dock Ellis .... 2.75 1.10 .27
☐ 287 Jose Tartabull .... 2.25 .90 .22
☐ 288 Ken Holtzman .... 2.75 1.10 .27
☐ 289 Bart Shirley .... 2.25 .90 .22
☐ 290 Jim Kaat .... 4.00 1.75 .40
☐ 291 Vern Fuller .... 2.25 .90 .22
☐ 292 Al Downing .... 2.75 1.10 .27
☐ 293 Dick Dietz .... 2.25 .90 .22
☐ 294 Jim Lemon MG .... 2.25 .90 .22
☐ 295 Tony Perez 12.50 5.50 1.65
☐ 296 Andy Messersmith .... 3.50 1.50 .35
☐ 297 Deron Johnson .... 2.25 .90 .22
☐ 298 Dave Nicholson .... 2.25 .90 .22
☐ 299 Mark Belanger .... 2.75 1.10 .27
☐ 300 Felipe Alou .... 2.75 1.10 .27
☐ 301 Darrell Brandon .... 2.25 .90 .22
☐ 302 Jim Pagliaroni .... 2.25 .90 .22
☐ 303 Cal Koonce .... 2.25 .90 .22
☐ 304 Padres Rookies .... 4.50 2.00 .45
Bill Davis
Clarence Gaston
☐ 305 Dick McAuliffe .... 2.25 .90 .22
☐ 306 Jim Grant .... 2.25 .90 .22
☐ 307 Gary Kolb .... 2.25 .90 .22
☐ 308 Wade Blasingame .... 2.25 .90 .22
☐ 309 Walt Williams .... 2.25 .90 .22
☐ 310 Tom Haller .... 2.25 .90 .22
☐ 311 Sparky Lyle 12.50 5.50 1.65
☐ 312 Lee Elia .... 2.75 1.10 .27
☐ 313 Bill Robinson .... 2.75 1.10 .27
☐ 314 Checklist 4 .... 4.50 .50 .10
Don Drysdale
☐ 315 Eddie Fisher .... 2.25 .90 .22
☐ 316 Hal Lanier .... 2.25 .90 .22
☐ 317 Bruce Look .... 2.25 .90 .22
☐ 318 Jack Fisher .... 2.25 .90 .22
☐ 319 Ken McMullen UER .... 2.25 .90 .22
(Headings on back
are for a pitcher)
☐ 320 Dal Maxvill .... 2.25 .90 .22
☐ 321 Jim McAndrew .... 2.25 .90 .22
☐ 322 Jose Vidal .... 2.25 .90 .22
☐ 323 Larry Miller .... 2.25 .90 .22
☐ 324 Tiger Rookies .... 2.25 .90 .22
Les Cain
Dave Campbell
☐ 325 Jose Cardenal .... 2.25 .90 .22
☐ 326 Gary Sutherland .... 2.25 .90 .22
☐ 327 Willie Crawford .... 2.25 .90 .22
☐ 328 Joel Horlen .... 1.35 .55 .13
☐ 329 Rick Joseph .... 1.35 .55 .13
☐ 330 Tony Conigliaro .... 3.00 1.25 .30
☐ 331 Braves Rookies .... 2.25 .90 .22
Gil Garrido
Tom House
☐ 332 Fred Talbot .... 1.35 .55 .13
☐ 333 Ivan Murrell .... 1.35 .55 .13
☐ 334 Phil Roof .... 1.35 .55 .13
☐ 335 Bill Mazeroski .... 2.25 .90 .22
☐ 336 Jim Roland .... 1.35 .55 .13
☐ 337 Marty Martinez .... 1.35 .55 .13
☐ 338 Del Unser .... 1.35 .55 .13
☐ 339 Reds Rookies .... 1.35 .55 .13
Steve Mingori
Jose Pena
☐ 340 Dave McNally .... 1.75 .70 .17
☐ 341 Dave Adlesh .... 1.35 .55 .13
☐ 342 Bubba Morton .... 1.35 .55 .13
☐ 343 Dan Frisella .... 1.35 .55 .13
☐ 344 Tom Matchick .... 1.35 .55 .13
☐ 345 Frank Linzy .... 1.35 .55 .13
☐ 346 Wayne Comer .... 1.35 .55 .13
☐ 347 Randy Hundley .... 1.75 .70 .17
☐ 348 Steve Hargan .... 1.35 .55 .13
☐ 349 Dick Williams MG .... 1.75 .70 .17
☐ 350 Richie Allen .... 3.00 1.25 .30
☐ 351 Carroll Sembera .... 1.35 .55 .13
☐ 352 Paul Schaal .... 1.35 .55 .13

☐ 353 Jeff Torborg	1.75	.70	.17
☐ 354 Nate Oliver	1.35	.55	.13
☐ 355 Phil Niekro	5.00	2.25	.50
☐ 356 Frank Quilici MG	1.35	.55	.13
☐ 357 Carl Taylor	1.35	.55	.13
☐ 358 Athletics Rookies	1.35	.55	.13
George Lauzerique			
Roberto Rodriquez			
☐ 359 Dick Kelley	1.35	.55	.13
☐ 360 Jim Wynn	1.75	.70	.17
☐ 361 Gary Holman	1.35	.55	.13
☐ 362 Jim Maloney	1.75	.70	.17
☐ 363 Russ Nixon	1.35	.55	.13
☐ 364 Tommie Agee	1.75	.70	.17
☐ 365 Jim Fregosi	1.75	.70	.17
☐ 366 Bo Belinsky	1.75	.70	.17
☐ 367 Lou Johnson	1.35	.55	.13
☐ 368 Vic Roznovsky	1.35	.55	.13
☐ 369 Bob Skinner	1.35	.55	.13
☐ 370 Juan Marichal	6.50	2.75	.65
☐ 371 Sal Bando	1.75	.70	.17
☐ 372 Adolfo Phillips	1.35	.55	.13
☐ 373 Fred Lasher	1.35	.55	.13
☐ 374 Bob Tillman	1.35	.55	.13
☐ 375 Harmon Killebrew	18.00	7.50	2.50
☐ 376 Royals Rookies	1.75	.70	.17
Mike Fiore			
Jim Rooker			
☐ 377 Gary Bell	1.35	.55	.13
☐ 378 Jose Herrera	1.35	.55	.13
☐ 379 Ken Boyer	2.25	.90	.22
☐ 380 Stan Bahnsen	1.35	.55	.13
☐ 381 Ed Kranepool	1.75	.70	.17
☐ 382 Pat Corrales	1.35	.55	.13
☐ 383 Casey Cox	1.35	.55	.13
☐ 384 Larry Shepard MG	1.35	.55	.13
☐ 385 Orlando Cepeda	3.00	1.25	.30
☐ 386 Jim McGlothlin	1.35	.55	.13
☐ 387 Bobby Klaus	1.35	.55	.13
☐ 388 Tom McCraw	1.35	.55	.13
☐ 389 Dan Coombs	1.35	.55	.13
☐ 390 Bill Freehan	2.00	.80	.20
☐ 391 Ray Culp	1.35	.55	.13
☐ 392 Bob Burda	1.35	.55	.13
☐ 393 Gene Brabender	1.35	.55	.13
☐ 394 Pilots Rookies	4.00	1.75	.40
Lou Piniella			
Marv Staehle			
☐ 395 Chris Short	1.35	.55	.13
☐ 396 Jim Campanis	1.35	.55	.13
☐ 397 Chuck Dobson	1.35	.55	.13
☐ 398 Tito Francona	1.35	.55	.13
☐ 399 Bob Bailey	1.35	.55	.13
☐ 400 Don Drysdale	10.00	4.50	1.25
☐ 401 Jake Gibbs	1.35	.55	.13
☐ 402 Ken Boswell	1.35	.55	.13
☐ 403 Bob Miller	1.35	.55	.13
☐ 404 Cubs Rookies	1.35	.55	.13
Vic LaRose			
Gary Ross			
☐ 405 Lee May	1.75	.70	.17
☐ 406 Phil Ortega	1.35	.55	.13
☐ 407 Tom Egan	1.35	.55	.13
☐ 408 Nate Colbert	1.35	.55	.13
☐ 409 Bob Moose	1.35	.55	.13
☐ 410 Al Kaline	18.00	7.50	2.50
☐ 411 Larry Dierker	1.35	.55	.13
☐ 412 Checklist 5 DP	7.50	1.00	.20
Mickey Mantle			
☐ 413 Roland Sheldon	1.35	.55	.13
☐ 414 Duke Sims	1.35	.55	.13
☐ 415 Ray Washburn	1.35	.55	.13
☐ 416 Willie McCovey AS	6.00	2.50	.60
☐ 417 Ken Harrelson AS	1.35	.55	.13
☐ 418 Tommy Helms AS	1.35	.55	.13
☐ 419 Rod Carew AS	10.00	4.50	1.25
☐ 420 Ron Santo AS	2.00	.80	.20
☐ 421 Brooks Robinson AS	6.50	2.75	.65
☐ 422 Don Kessinger AS	1.35	.55	.13
☐ 423 Bert Campaneris AS	1.35	.55	.13
☐ 424 Pete Rose AS	12.00	5.25	1.50
☐ 425 Carl Yastrzemski AS	12.00	5.25	1.50
☐ 426 Curt Flood AS DP	1.35	.55	.13
☐ 427 Tony Oliva AS DP	1.75	.70	.17
☐ 428 Lou Brock AS DP	6.00	2.50	.60
☐ 429 Willie Horton AS DP	1.35	.55	.13
☐ 430 Johnny Bench AS DP	13.50	6.00	1.85
☐ 431 Bill Freehan AS DP	1.35	.55	.13
☐ 432 Bob Gibson AS DP	5.00	2.25	.50
☐ 433 Denny McLain AS DP	1.75	.70	.17
☐ 434 Jerry Koosman AS DP	1.75	.70	.17
☐ 435 Sam McDowell AS DP	1.35	.55	.13
☐ 436 Gene Alley	1.75	.70	.17
☐ 437 Luis Alcaraz	1.35	.55	.13
☐ 438 Gary Waslewski	1.35	.55	.13
☐ 439 White Sox Rookies DP	1.35	.55	.13
Ed Herrmann			
Dan Lazar			
☐ 440A Willie McCovey	16.00	6.75	2.25
☐ 440B Willie McCovey WL	90.00	40.00	13.50
(McCovey white) DP			
☐ 441A Dennis Higgins	1.35	.55	.13
☐ 441B Dennis Higgins WL	20.00	8.50	2.75
(Higgins white)			
☐ 442 Ty Cline	1.35	.55	.13
☐ 443 Don Wert DP	1.35	.55	.13
☐ 444A Joe Moeller	1.35	.55	.13
☐ 444B Joe Moeller WL DP	15.00	6.50	2.15
(Moeller white)			
☐ 445 Bobby Knoop	1.35	.55	.13
☐ 446 Claude Raymond	1.35	.55	.13
☐ 447A Ralph Houk MG	1.75	.70	.17
☐ 447B Ralph Houk WL DP	15.00	6.50	2.15
MG (Houk white)			
☐ 448 Bob Tolan	1.35	.55	.13
☐ 449 Paul Lindblad DP	1.35	.55	.13

Card			
☐ 450 Billy Williams DP	6.50	2.75	.65
☐ 451A Rich Rollins	1.35	.55	.13
☐ 451B Rich Rollins WL	20.00	8.50	2.75
(Rich and 3B white)			
☐ 452A Al Ferrara	1.35	.55	.13
☐ 452B Al Ferrara WL	20.00	8.50	2.75
(Al and OF white)			
☐ 453 Mike Cuellar	1.75	.70	.17
☐ 454A Phillies Rookies	1.75	.70	.17
Larry Colton			
Don Money			
☐ 454B Phillies Rookies WL	20.00	8.50	2.75
Larry Colton			
Don Money			
(names in white)			
☐ 455 Sonny Siebert DP	1.35	.55	.13
☐ 456 Bud Harrelson DP	1.75	.70	.17
☐ 457 Dalton Jones DP	1.35	.55	.13
☐ 458 Curt Blefary	1.75	.70	.17
☐ 459 Dave Boswell DP	1.35	.55	.13
☐ 460 Joe Torre	2.25	.90	.22
☐ 461A Mike Epstein	1.35	.55	.13
☐ 461B Mike Epstein WL DP	15.00	6.50	2.15
(Epstein white)			
☐ 462 Red Schoendienst DP .	2.50	1.00	.25
MG			
☐ 463 Dennis Ribant DP	1.35	.55	.13
☐ 464A Dave Marshall	1.35	.55	.13
☐ 464B Dave Marshall WL DP	15.00	6.50	2.15
(Marshall white)			
☐ 465 Tommy John DP	4.00	1.75	.40
☐ 466 John Boccabella	1.35	.55	.13
☐ 467 Tommie Reynolds	1.35	.55	.13
☐ 468A Pirates Rookies	1.35	.55	.13
Bruce Dal Canton			
Bob Robertson			
☐ 468B Pirates Rookies WL	20.00	8.50	2.75
Bruce Dal Canton			
Bob Robertson			
(names in white)			
☐ 469 Chico Ruiz DP	1.35	.55	.13
☐ 470A Mel Stottlemyre	1.75	.70	.17
☐ 470B Mel Stottlemyre WL	21.00	9.00	3.00
(Stottlemyre white) DP			
☐ 471A Ted Savage	1.35	.55	.13
☐ 471B Ted Savage WL	20.00	8.50	2.75
(Savage white)			
☐ 472 Jim Price DP	1.35	.55	.13
☐ 473A Jose Arcia	1.35	.55	.13
☐ 473B Jose Arcia WL	20.00	8.50	2.75
(Jose and 2B white)			
☐ 474 Tom Murphy DP	1.35	.55	.13
☐ 475 Tim McCarver	2.50	1.00	.25
☐ 476A Boston Rookies	1.75	.70	.17
Ken Brett			
Gerry Moses			
☐ 476B Boston Rookies WL	20.00	8.50	2.75
Ken Brett			
Gerry Moses			
(names in white)			
☐ 477 Jeff James DP	1.35	.55	.13
☐ 478 Don Buford	1.75	.70	.17
☐ 479 Richie Scheinblum	1.35	.55	.13
☐ 480 Tom Seaver DP	125.00	57.50	18.75
☐ 481 Bill Melton	1.35	.55	.13
☐ 482A Jim Gosger	1.35	.55	.13
☐ 482B Jim Gosger WL	20.00	8.50	2.75
(Jim and OF white)			
☐ 483 Ted Abernathy	1.35	.55	.13
☐ 484 Joe Gordon MG	1.75	.70	.17
☐ 485A Gaylord Perry	10.00	4.50	1.25
☐ 485B Gaylord Perry WL ...	75.00	34.00	11.25
(Perry white)			
☐ 486A Paul Casanova	1.35	.55	.13
☐ 486B Paul Casanova WL DP	15.00	6.50	2.15
(Casanova white)			
☐ 487 Denis Menke	1.35	.55	.13
☐ 488 Joe Sparma	1.35	.55	.13
☐ 489 Clete Boyer DP	1.75	.70	.17
☐ 490 Matty Alou	1.75	.70	.17
☐ 491A Twins Rookies	1.35	.55	.13
Jerry Crider			
George Mitterwald			
☐ 491B Twins Rookies WL ..	20.00	8.50	2.75
Jerry Crider			
George Mitterwald			
(names in white)			
☐ 492 Tony Cloninger	1.35	.55	.13
☐ 493A Wes Parker	1.75	.70	.17
☐ 493B Wes Parker WL DP .	15.00	6.50	2.15
(Parker white)			
☐ 494 Ken Berry DP	1.35	.55	.13
☐ 495 Bert Campaneris	1.75	.70	.17
☐ 496 Larry Jaster	1.35	.55	.13
☐ 497 Julian Javier DP	1.35	.55	.13
☐ 498 Juan Pizarro	1.35	.55	.13
☐ 499 Astro Rookies DP	1.35	.55	.13
Don Bryant			
Steve Shea			
☐ 500A Mickey Mantle UER	200.00	90.00	30.00
(no Topps copy-right on card back)			
☐ 500B Mickey Mantle WL	600.00	270.00	90.00
(Mantle in white; no Topps copyright on card back) UER			
☐ 501A Tony Gonzalez	1.35	.55	.13
☐ 501B Tony Gonzalez WL ..	20.00	8.50	2.75
(Tony and OF white)			
☐ 502 Minnie Rojas DP	1.35	.55	.13
☐ 503 Larry Brown	1.35	.55	.13
☐ 504 Checklist 6	4.50	.50	.10
Brooks Robinson			
☐ 505A Bobby Bolin	1.35	.55	.13
☐ 505B Bobby Bolin WL DP	15.00	6.50	2.15
(Bolin white)			

☐ 506 Paul Blair DP	1.35	.55	.13
☐ 507 Cookie Rojas	1.35	.55	.13
☐ 508 Moe Drabowsky DP	1.35	.55	.13
☐ 509 Manny Sanguillen DP	1.75	.70	.17
☐ 510 Rod Carew	75.00	34.00	11.25
☐ 511A Diego Segui	1.35	.55	.13
☐ 511B Diego Segui WL	20.00	8.50	2.75
(Diego and P white)			
☐ 512 Cleon Jones	1.35	.55	.13
☐ 513 Camilo Pascual	2.00	.80	.20
☐ 514 Mike Lum	1.65	.70	.20
☐ 515 Dick Green	1.65	.70	.20
☐ 516 Earl Weaver MG	8.00	3.50	.80
☐ 517 Mike McCormick	2.00	.80	.20
☐ 518 Fred Whitfield	1.65	.70	.20
☐ 519 Yankees Rookies	1.65	.70	.20
Gerry Kenney			
Len Boehmer			
☐ 520 Bob Veale	2.00	.80	.20
☐ 521 George Thomas	1.65	.70	.20
☐ 522 Joe Hoerner	1.65	.70	.20
☐ 523 Bob Chance	1.65	.70	.20
☐ 524 Expos Rookies	1.65	.70	.20
Jose Laboy			
Floyd Wicker			
☐ 525 Earl Wilson	1.65	.70	.20
☐ 526 Hector Torres	1.65	.70	.20
☐ 527 Al Lopez MG	3.00	1.25	.30
☐ 528 Claude Osteen	1.65	.70	.20
☐ 529 Ed Kirkpatrick	1.65	.70	.20
☐ 530 Cesar Tovar	1.65	.70	.20
☐ 531 Dick Farrell	1.65	.70	.20
☐ 532 Bird Hill Aces	2.00	.80	.20
Tom Phoebus			
Jim Hardin			
Dave McNally			
Mike Cuellar			
☐ 533 Nolan Ryan	425.00	190.00	63.00
☐ 534 Jerry McNertney	1.65	.70	.20
☐ 535 Phil Regan	2.00	.80	.20
☐ 536 Padres Rookies	1.65	.70	.20
Danny Breeden			
Dave Roberts			
☐ 537 Mike Paul	1.65	.70	.20
☐ 538 Charlie Smith	1.65	.70	.20
☐ 539 Ted Shows How	5.00	2.25	.50
Mike Epstein			
Ted Williams			
☐ 540 Curt Flood	2.50	1.00	.25
☐ 541 Joe Verbanic	1.65	.70	.20
☐ 542 Bob Aspromonte	1.65	.70	.20
☐ 543 Fred Newman	1.65	.70	.20
☐ 544 Tigers Rookies	1.65	.70	.20
Mike Kilkenny			
Ron Woods			
☐ 545 Willie Stargell	12.50	5.50	1.65
☐ 546 Jim Nash	1.65	.70	.20
☐ 547 Billy Martin MG	5.00	2.25	.50
☐ 548 Bob Locker	1.65	.70	.20
☐ 549 Ron Brand	1.65	.70	.20
☐ 550 Brooks Robinson	18.00	7.50	2.50
☐ 551 Wayne Granger	1.65	.70	.20
☐ 552 Dodgers Rookies	2.00	.80	.20
Ted Sizemore			
Bill Sudakis			
☐ 553 Ron Davis	1.65	.70	.20
☐ 554 Frank Bertaina	1.65	.70	.20
☐ 555 Jim Ray Hart	2.00	.80	.20
☐ 556 A's Stars	2.00	.80	.20
Sal Bando			
Bert Campaneris			
Danny Cater			
☐ 557 Frank Fernandez	1.65	.70	.20
☐ 558 Tom Burgmeier	2.00	.80	.20
☐ 559 Cardinals Rookies	1.65	.70	.20
Joe Hague			
Jim Hicks			
☐ 560 Luis Tiant	2.50	1.00	.25
☐ 561 Ron Clark	1.65	.70	.20
☐ 562 Bob Watson	3.00	1.25	.30
☐ 563 Marty Pattin	1.65	.70	.20
☐ 564 Gil Hodges MG	7.50	3.25	.75
☐ 565 Hoyt Wilhelm	6.00	2.50	.60
☐ 566 Ron Hansen	1.65	.70	.20
☐ 567 Pirates Rookies	1.65	.70	.20
Elvio Jimenez			
Jim Shellenback			
☐ 568 Cecil Upshaw	1.65	.70	.20
☐ 569 Billy Harris	1.65	.70	.20
☐ 570 Ron Santo	4.00	1.75	.40
☐ 571 Cap Peterson	1.65	.70	.20
☐ 572 Giants Heroes	10.00	4.50	1.25
Willie McCovey			
Juan Marichal			
☐ 573 Jim Palmer	42.00	18.00	5.50
☐ 574 George Scott	2.00	.80	.20
☐ 575 Bill Singer	2.00	.80	.20
☐ 576 Phillies Rookies	1.65	.70	.20
Ron Stone			
Bill Wilson			
☐ 577 Mike Hegan	1.65	.70	.20
☐ 578 Don Bosch	1.65	.70	.20
☐ 579 Dave Nelson	2.00	.80	.20
☐ 580 Jim Northrup	2.00	.80	.20
☐ 581 Gary Nolan	1.65	.70	.20
☐ 582A Checklist 7	4.50	.50	.10
(white circle on back)			
(Tony Oliva)			
☐ 582B Checklist 7	7.50	.75	.15
(red circle on back)			
(Tony Oliva)			
☐ 583 Clyde Wright	1.65	.70	.20
☐ 584 Don Mason	1.65	.70	.20
☐ 585 Ron Swoboda	2.00	.80	.20
☐ 586 Tim Cullen	1.65	.70	.20
☐ 587 Joe Rudi	3.50	1.50	.35

☐ 588 Bill White	2.50	1.00	.25
☐ 589 Joe Pepitone	2.75	1.10	.27
☐ 590 Rico Carty	2.75	1.10	.27
☐ 591 Mike Hedlund	2.25	.90	.22
☐ 592 Padres Rookies Rafael Robles Al Santorini	2.25	.90	.22
☐ 593 Don Nottebart	2.25	.90	.22
☐ 594 Dooley Womack	2.25	.90	.22
☐ 595 Lee Maye	2.25	.90	.22
☐ 596 Chuck Hartenstein	2.25	.90	.22
☐ 597 A.L. Rookies Bob Floyd Larry Burchart Rollie Fingers	110.00	50.00	16.50
☐ 598 Ruben Amaro	2.25	.90	.22
☐ 599 John Boozer	2.25	.90	.22
☐ 600 Tony Oliva	4.50	2.00	.45
☐ 601 Tug McGraw	3.50	1.50	.35
☐ 602 Cubs Rookies Alec Distaso Don Young Jim Qualls	2.25	.90	.22
☐ 603 Joe Keough	2.25	.90	.22
☐ 604 Bobby Etheridge	2.25	.90	.22
☐ 605 Dick Ellsworth	2.25	.90	.22
☐ 606 Gene Mauch MG	2.75	1.10	.27
☐ 607 Dick Bosman	2.25	.90	.22
☐ 608 Dick Simpson	2.25	.90	.22
☐ 609 Phil Gagliano	2.25	.90	.22
☐ 610 Jim Hardin	2.25	.90	.22
☐ 611 Braves Rookies Bob Didier Walt Hriniak Gary Neibauer	2.75	1.10	.27
☐ 612 Jack Aker	2.25	.90	.22
☐ 613 Jim Beauchamp	2.25	.90	.22
☐ 614 Houston Rookies Tom Griffin Skip Guinn	2.25	.90	.22
☐ 615 Len Gabrielson	2.25	.90	.22
☐ 616 Don McMahon	2.25	.90	.22
☐ 617 Jesse Gonder	2.25	.90	.22
☐ 618 Ramon Webster	2.25	.90	.22
☐ 619 Royals Rookies Bill Butler Pat Kelly Juan Rios	2.75	1.10	.27
☐ 620 Dean Chance	2.75	1.10	.27
☐ 621 Bill Voss	2.25	.90	.22
☐ 622 Dan Osinski	2.25	.90	.22
☐ 623 Hank Allen	2.25	.90	.22
☐ 624 NL Rookies Darrel Chaney Duffy Dyer Terry Harmon	2.25	.90	.22
☐ 625 Mack Jones UER (Batting wrong)	2.25	.90	.22
☐ 626 Gene Michael	2.75	1.10	.27
☐ 627 George Stone	2.25	.90	.22
☐ 628 Red Sox Rookies Bill Conigliaro Syd O'Brien Fred Wenz	2.75	1.10	.27
☐ 629 Jack Hamilton	2.25	.90	.22
☐ 630 Bobby Bonds	32.00	14.25	4.75
☐ 631 John Kennedy	2.25	.90	.22
☐ 632 Jon Warden	2.25	.90	.22
☐ 633 Harry Walker MG	2.25	.90	.22
☐ 634 Andy Etchebarren	2.25	.90	.22
☐ 635 George Culver	2.25	.90	.22
☐ 636 Woody Held	2.25	.90	.22
☐ 637 Padres Rookies Jerry DaVanon Frank Reberger Clay Kirby	2.25	.90	.22
☐ 638 Ed Sprague	2.25	.90	.22
☐ 639 Barry Moore	2.25	.90	.22
☐ 640 Fergie Jenkins	17.00	7.25	2.50
☐ 641 NL Rookies Bobby Darwin John Miller Tommy Dean	2.75	1.10	.27
☐ 642 John Hiller	2.75	1.10	.27
☐ 643 Billy Cowan	2.25	.90	.22
☐ 644 Chuck Hinton	2.25	.90	.22
☐ 645 George Brunet	2.25	.90	.22
☐ 646 Expos Rookies Dan McGinn Carl Morton	2.75	1.10	.27
☐ 647 Dave Wickersham	2.25	.90	.22
☐ 648 Bobby Wine	2.25	.90	.22
☐ 649 Al Jackson	2.25	.90	.22
☐ 650 Ted Williams MG	10.00	4.50	1.25
☐ 651 Gus Gil	2.25	.90	.22
☐ 652 Eddie Watt	2.25	.90	.22
☐ 653 Aurelio Rodriguez UER (Photo actually Angels' batboy)	2.75	1.10	.27
☐ 654 White Sox Rookies Carlos May Don Secrist Rich Morales	3.50	1.50	.35
☐ 655 Mike Hershberger	2.25	.90	.22
☐ 656 Dan Schneider	2.25	.90	.22
☐ 657 Bobby Murcer	4.50	2.00	.45
☐ 658 AL Rookies Tom Hall Bill Burbach Jim Miles	2.75	1.10	.27
☐ 659 Johnny Podres	2.75	1.10	.27
☐ 660 Reggie Smith	3.50	1.50	.35
☐ 661 Jim Merritt	2.25	.90	.22
☐ 662 Royals Rookies Dick Drago George Spriggs	2.75	1.10	.27

Bob Oliver			
☐ 663 Dick Radatz	2.75	1.10	.27
☐ 664 Ron Hunt	3.50	1.25	.25

1970 Topps

The cards in this 720-card set measure 2 1/2" by 3 1/2". The Topps set for 1970 has color photos surrounded by white frame lines and gray borders. The backs have a blue biographical section and a yellow record section. All-Star selections are featured on cards 450 to 469. Other topical subsets within this set include League Leaders (61-72), Playoffs cards (195-202), and World Series cards (305-310). There are graduations of scarcity, terminating in the high series (634-720), which are outlined in the value summary. The key rookie card in this set is Thurman Munson.

	NRMT	VG-E	GOOD
COMPLETE SET (720)	2250.00	900.00	225.00
COMMON PLAYER (1-132)	.70	.30	.07
COMMON PLAYER (133-263)	.80	.35	.08
COMMON PLAYER (264-372)	1.00	.40	.10
COMMON PLAYER (373-459)	1.10	.45	.11
COMMON PLAYER (460-546)	1.60	.65	.16
COMMON PLAYER (547-633)	2.75	1.10	.27
COMMON PLAYER (634-720)	5.00	2.25	.50

☐ 1 New York Mets	12.00	2.50	.50
Team Card			
☐ 2 Diego Segui	.70	.30	.07
☐ 3 Darrel Chaney	.70	.30	.07
☐ 4 Tom Egan	.70	.30	.07
☐ 5 Wes Parker	1.00	.40	.10
☐ 6 Grant Jackson	.70	.30	.07
☐ 7 Indians Rookies	.70	.30	.07
Gary Boyd			
Russ Nagelson			
☐ 8 Jose Martinez	.70	.30	.07
☐ 9 Checklist 1	4.50	.50	.10
☐ 10 Carl Yastrzemski	30.00	13.50	4.50
☐ 11 Nate Colbert	.70	.30	.07
☐ 12 John Hiller	1.00	.40	.10
☐ 13 Jack Hiatt	.70	.30	.07
☐ 14 Hank Allen	.70	.30	.07
☐ 15 Larry Dierker	.70	.30	.07
☐ 16 Charlie Metro MG	.70	.30	.07
☐ 17 Hoyt Wilhelm	4.00	1.75	.40
☐ 18 Carlos May	.70	.30	.07
☐ 19 John Boccabella	.70	.30	.07
☐ 20 Dave McNally	1.00	.40	.10
☐ 21 A's Rookies	4.50	2.00	.45
Vida Blue			
Gene Tenace			
☐ 22 Ray Washburn	.70	.30	.07
☐ 23 Bill Robinson	1.00	.40	.10
☐ 24 Dick Selma	.70	.30	.07
☐ 25 Cesar Tovar	.70	.30	.07
☐ 26 Tug McGraw	1.50	.60	.15
☐ 27 Chuck Hinton	.70	.30	.07
☐ 28 Billy Wilson	.70	.30	.07
☐ 29 Sandy Alomar	.70	.30	.07
☐ 30 Matty Alou	1.00	.40	.10
☐ 31 Marty Pattin	.70	.30	.07
☐ 32 Harry Walker MG	.70	.30	.07
☐ 33 Don Wert	.70	.30	.07
☐ 34 Willie Crawford	.70	.30	.07
☐ 35 Joel Horlen	.70	.30	.07
☐ 36 Red Rookies	1.00	.40	.10
Danny Breeden			
Bernie Carbo			
☐ 37 Dick Drago	.70	.30	.07
☐ 38 Mack Jones	.70	.30	.07
☐ 39 Mike Nagy	.70	.30	.07
☐ 40 Rich Allen	1.75	.70	.17
☐ 41 George Lauzerique	.70	.30	.07
☐ 42 Tito Fuentes	.70	.30	.07
☐ 43 Jack Aker	.70	.30	.07
☐ 44 Roberto Pena	.70	.30	.07
☐ 45 Dave Johnson	1.00	.40	.10
☐ 46 Ken Rudolph	.70	.30	.07
☐ 47 Bob Miller	.70	.30	.07
☐ 48 Gil Garrido	.70	.30	.07
☐ 49 Tim Cullen	.70	.30	.07
☐ 50 Tommie Agee	1.00	.40	.10
☐ 51 Bob Christian	.70	.30	.07
☐ 52 Bruce Dal Canton	.70	.30	.07
☐ 53 John Kennedy	.70	.30	.07
☐ 54 Jeff Torborg	1.00	.40	.10
☐ 55 John Odom	.70	.30	.07
☐ 56 Phillies Rookies	.70	.30	.07
Joe Lis			
Scott Reid			

☐ 57 Pat Kelly .70 .30 .07
☐ 58 Dave Marshall .70 .30 .07
☐ 59 Dick Ellsworth .70 .30 .07
☐ 60 Jim Wynn 1.00 .40 .10
☐ 61 NL Batting Leaders 4.00 1.75 .40
Pete Rose
Bob Clemente
Cleon Jones
☐ 62 AL Batting Leaders 2.50 1.00 .25
Rod Carew
Reggie Smith
Tony Oliva
☐ 63 NL RBI Leaders 2.50 1.00 .25
Willie McCovey
Ron Santo
Tony Perez
☐ 64 AL RBI Leaders 3.00 1.25 .30
Harmon Killebrew
Boog Powell
Reggie Jackson
☐ 65 NL Home Run Leaders 3.00 1.25 .30
Willie McCovey
Hank Aaron
Lee May
☐ 66 AL Home Run Leaders 3.00 1.25 .30
Harmon Killebrew
Frank Howard
Reggie Jackson
☐ 67 NL ERA Leaders 4.00 1.75 .40
Juan Marichal
Steve Carlton
Bob Gibson
☐ 68 AL ERA Leaders 2.00 .80 .20
Dick Bosman
Jim Palmer
Mike Cuellar
☐ 69 NL Pitching Leaders 4.00 1.75 .40
Tom Seaver
Phil Niekro
Fergie Jenkins
Juan Marichal
☐ 70 AL Pitching Leaders 2.00 .80 .20
Dennis McLain
Mike Cuellar
Dave Boswell
Dave McNally
Jim Perry
Mel Stottlemyre
☐ 71 NL Strikeout Leaders 2.50 1.00 .25
Fergie Jenkins
Bob Gibson
Bill Singer
☐ 72 AL Strikeout Leaders 2.00 .80 .20
Sam McDowell
Mickey Lolich
Andy Messersmith
☐ 73 Wayne Granger .70 .30 .07
☐ 74 Angels Rookies .70 .30 .07
Greg Washburn
Wally Wolf
☐ 75 Jim Kaat 2.00 .80 .20
☐ 76 Carl Taylor .70 .30 .07
☐ 77 Frank Linzy .70 .30 .07
☐ 78 Joe Lahoud .70 .30 .07
☐ 79 Clay Kirby .70 .30 .07
☐ 80 Don Kessinger 1.00 .40 .10
☐ 81 Dave May .70 .30 .07
☐ 82 Frank Fernandez .70 .30 .07
☐ 83 Don Cardwell .70 .30 .07
☐ 84 Paul Casanova .70 .30 .07
☐ 85 Max Alvis .70 .30 .07
☐ 86 Lum Harris MG .70 .30 .07
☐ 87 Steve Renko .70 .30 .07
☐ 88 Pilots Rookies .70 .30 .07
Miguel Fuentes
Dick Baney
☐ 89 Juan Rios .70 .30 .07
☐ 90 Tim McCarver 1.50 .60 .15
☐ 91 Rich Morales .70 .30 .07
☐ 92 George Culver .70 .30 .07
☐ 93 Rick Renick .70 .30 .07
☐ 94 Freddie Patek 1.00 .40 .10
☐ 95 Earl Wilson .70 .30 .07
☐ 96 Cardinals Rookies 2.50 1.00 .25
Leron Lee
Jerry Reuss
☐ 97 Joe Moeller .70 .30 .07
☐ 98 Gates Brown 1.00 .40 .10
☐ 99 Bobby Pfeil .70 .30 .07
☐ 100 Mel Stottlemyre 1.25 .50 .12
☐ 101 Bobby Floyd .70 .30 .07
☐ 102 Joe Rudi 1.00 .40 .10
☐ 103 Frank Reberger .70 .30 .07
☐ 104 Gerry Moses .70 .30 .07
☐ 105 Tony Gonzalez .70 .30 .07
☐ 106 Darold Knowles .70 .30 .07
☐ 107 Bobby Etheridge .70 .30 .07
☐ 108 Tom Burgmeier .70 .30 .07
☐ 109 Expos Rookies .70 .30 .07
Garry Jestadt
Carl Morton
☐ 110 Bob Moose .70 .30 .07
☐ 111 Mike Hegan .70 .30 .07
☐ 112 Dave Nelson .70 .30 .07
☐ 113 Jim Ray .70 .30 .07
☐ 114 Gene Michael 1.00 .40 .10
☐ 115 Alex Johnson 1.00 .40 .10
☐ 116 Sparky Lyle 1.50 .60 .15
☐ 117 Don Young .70 .30 .07
☐ 118 George Mitterwald .70 .30 .07
☐ 119 Chuck Taylor .70 .30 .07
☐ 120 Sal Bando 1.00 .40 .10
☐ 121 Orioles Rookies 1.00 .40 .10
Fred Beene
Terry Crowley
☐ 122 George Stone .70 .30 .07

Card			
☐ 123 Don Gutteridge	.70	.30	.07
☐ 124 Larry Jaster	.70	.30	.07
☐ 125 Deron Johnson	.70	.30	.07
☐ 126 Marty Martinez	.70	.30	.07
☐ 127 Joe Coleman	.70	.30	.07
☐ 128A Checklist 2 ERR (226 R Perranoski)	4.50	.50	.10
☐ 128B Checklist 2 COR (226 R. Perranoski)	4.50	.50	.10
☐ 129 Jimmie Price	.70	.30	.07
☐ 130 Ollie Brown	.70	.30	.07
☐ 131 Dodgers Rookies Ray Lamb Bob Stinson	.70	.30	.07
☐ 132 Jim McGlothlin	.70	.30	.07
☐ 133 Clay Carroll	.80	.35	.08
☐ 134 Danny Walton	.80	.35	.08
☐ 135 Dick Dietz	.80	.35	.08
☐ 136 Steve Hargan	.80	.35	.08
☐ 137 Art Shamsky	.80	.35	.08
☐ 138 Joe Foy	.80	.35	.08
☐ 139 Rich Nye	.80	.35	.08
☐ 140 Reggie Jackson	150.00	67.50	22.50
☐ 141 Pirates Rookies Dave Cash Johnny Jeter	1.00	.40	.10
☐ 142 Fritz Peterson	.80	.35	.08
☐ 143 Phil Gagliano	.80	.35	.08
☐ 144 Ray Culp	.80	.35	.08
☐ 145 Rico Carty	1.00	.40	.10
☐ 146 Danny Murphy	.80	.35	.08
☐ 147 Angel Hermoso	.80	.35	.08
☐ 148 Earl Weaver MG	2.00	.80	.20
☐ 149 Billy Champion	.80	.35	.08
☐ 150 Harmon Killebrew	7.00	3.00	.70
☐ 151 Dave Roberts	.80	.35	.08
☐ 152 Ike Brown	.80	.35	.08
☐ 153 Gary Gentry	.80	.35	.08
☐ 154 Senators Rookies Jim Miles Jan Dukes	.80	.35	.08
☐ 155 Denis Menke	.80	.35	.08
☐ 156 Eddie Fisher	.80	.35	.08
☐ 157 Manny Mota	1.00	.40	.10
☐ 158 Jerry McNertney	.80	.35	.08
☐ 159 Tommy Helms	1.00	.40	.10
☐ 160 Phil Niekro	4.00	1.75	.40
☐ 161 Richie Scheinblum	.80	.35	.08
☐ 162 Jerry Johnson	.80	.35	.08
☐ 163 Syd O'Brien	.80	.35	.08
☐ 164 Ty Cline	.80	.35	.08
☐ 165 Ed Kirkpatrick	.80	.35	.08
☐ 166 Al Oliver	2.00	.80	.20
☐ 167 Bill Burbach	.80	.35	.08
☐ 168 Dave Watkins	.80	.35	.08
☐ 169 Tom Hall	.80	.35	.08
☐ 170 Billy Williams	6.00	2.50	.60
☐ 171 Jim Nash	.80	.35	.08
☐ 172 Braves Rookies Garry Hill Ralph Garr	2.50	1.00	.25
☐ 173 Jim Hicks	.80	.35	.08
☐ 174 Ted Sizemore	1.00	.40	.10
☐ 175 Dick Bosman	.80	.35	.08
☐ 176 Jim Ray Hart	1.00	.40	.10
☐ 177 Jim Northrup	1.00	.40	.10
☐ 178 Denny Lemaster	.80	.35	.08
☐ 179 Ivan Murrell	.80	.35	.08
☐ 180 Tommy John	2.50	1.00	.25
☐ 181 Sparky Anderson MG	1.50	.60	.15
☐ 182 Dick Hall	.80	.35	.08
☐ 183 Jerry Grote	.80	.35	.08
☐ 184 Ray Fosse	.80	.35	.08
☐ 185 Don Mincher	.80	.35	.08
☐ 186 Rick Joseph	.80	.35	.08
☐ 187 Mike Hedlund	.80	.35	.08
☐ 188 Manny Sanguillen	1.00	.40	.10
☐ 189 Yankees Rookies Thurman Munson Dave McDonald	100.00	45.00	15.00
☐ 190 Joe Torre	1.50	.60	.15
☐ 191 Vicente Romo	.80	.35	.08
☐ 192 Jim Qualls	.80	.35	.08
☐ 193 Mike Wegener	.80	.35	.08
☐ 194 Chuck Manuel	.80	.35	.08
☐ 195 NL Playoff Game 1 Seaver wins opener	6.50	2.75	.65
☐ 196 NL Playoff Game 2 Mets show muscle	2.00	.80	.20
☐ 197 NL Playoff Game 3 Ryan saves the day	15.00	6.50	2.15
☐ 198 NL Playoff Summary Mets celebrate (Ryan)	4.50	2.00	.45
☐ 199 AL Playoff Game 1 Orioles win squeaker (Cuellar)	2.00	.80	.20
☐ 200 AL Playoff Game 2 Powell scores winning run	2.50	1.00	.25
☐ 201 AL Playoff Game 3 Birds wrap it up	2.00	.80	.20
☐ 202 AL Playoff Summary Orioles celebrate	2.00	.80	.20
☐ 203 Rudy May	.80	.35	.08
☐ 204 Len Gabrielson	.80	.35	.08
☐ 205 Bert Campaneris	1.00	.40	.10
☐ 206 Clete Boyer	1.00	.40	.10
☐ 207 Tigers Rookies Norman McRae Bob Reed	.80	.35	.08
☐ 208 Fred Gladding	.80	.35	.08
☐ 209 Ken Suarez	.80	.35	.08
☐ 210 Juan Marichal	6.00	2.50	.60
☐ 211 Ted Williams MG	6.50	2.75	.65
☐ 212 Al Santorini	.80	.35	.08
☐ 213 Andy Etchebarren	.80	.35	.08

☐ 214 Ken Boswell	.80	.35	.08
☐ 215 Reggie Smith	1.25	.50	.12
☐ 216 Chuck Hartenstein	.80	.35	.08
☐ 217 Ron Hansen	.80	.35	.08
☐ 218 Ron Stone	.80	.35	.08
☐ 219 Jerry Kenney	.80	.35	.08
☐ 220 Steve Carlton	30.00	13.50	4.50
☐ 221 Ron Brand	.80	.35	.08
☐ 222 Jim Rooker	.80	.35	.08
☐ 223 Nate Oliver	.80	.35	.08
☐ 224 Steve Barber	.80	.35	.08
☐ 225 Lee May	1.00	.40	.10
☐ 226 Ron Perranoski	.80	.35	.08
☐ 227 Astros Rookies John Mayberry Bob Watkins	1.25	.50	.12
☐ 228 Aurelio Rodriguez	.80	.35	.08
☐ 229 Rich Robertson	.80	.35	.08
☐ 230 Brooks Robinson	11.00	5.00	1.35
☐ 231 Luis Tiant	1.50	.60	.15
☐ 232 Bob Didier	.80	.35	.08
☐ 233 Lew Krausse	.80	.35	.08
☐ 234 Tommy Dean	.80	.35	.08
☐ 235 Mike Epstein	.80	.35	.08
☐ 236 Bob Veale	.80	.35	.08
☐ 237 Russ Gibson	.80	.35	.08
☐ 238 Jose Laboy	.80	.35	.08
☐ 239 Ken Berry	.80	.35	.08
☐ 240 Fergie Jenkins	10.00	4.50	1.25
☐ 241 Royals Rookies Al Fitzmorris Scott Northey	.80	.35	.08
☐ 242 Walter Alston MG	1.50	.60	.15
☐ 243 Joe Sparma	.80	.35	.08
☐ 244A Checklist 3 (red bat on front)	4.50	.50	.10
☐ 244B Checklist 3 (brown bat on front)	4.50	.50	.10
☐ 245 Leo Cardenas	.80	.35	.08
☐ 246 Jim McAndrew	.80	.35	.08
☐ 247 Lou Klimchock	.80	.35	.08
☐ 248 Jesus Alou	.80	.35	.08
☐ 249 Bob Locker	.80	.35	.08
☐ 250 Willie McCovey UER (1963 San Francisci)	10.00	4.50	1.25
☐ 251 Dick Schofield	.80	.35	.08
☐ 252 Lowell Palmer	.80	.35	.08
☐ 253 Ron Woods	.80	.35	.08
☐ 254 Camilo Pascual	.80	.35	.08
☐ 255 Jim Spencer	.80	.35	.08
☐ 256 Vic Davalillo	.80	.35	.08
☐ 257 Dennis Higgins	.80	.35	.08
☐ 258 Paul Popovich	.80	.35	.08
☐ 259 Tommie Reynolds	.80	.35	.08
☐ 260 Claude Osteen	.80	.35	.08
☐ 261 Curt Motton	.80	.35	.08
☐ 262 Padres Rookies Jerry Morales Jim Williams	1.00	.40	.10
☐ 263 Duane Josephson	.80	.35	.08
☐ 264 Rich Hebner	1.25	.50	.12
☐ 265 Randy Hundley	1.25	.50	.12
☐ 266 Wally Bunker	1.00	.40	.10
☐ 267 Twins Rookies Herman Hill Paul Ratliff	1.00	.40	.10
☐ 268 Claude Raymond	1.00	.40	.10
☐ 269 Cesar Gutierrez	1.00	.40	.10
☐ 270 Chris Short	1.00	.40	.10
☐ 271 Greg Goossen	1.00	.40	.10
☐ 272 Hector Torres	1.00	.40	.10
☐ 273 Ralph Houk MG	1.25	.50	.12
☐ 274 Gerry Arrigo	1.00	.40	.10
☐ 275 Duke Sims	1.00	.40	.10
☐ 276 Ron Hunt	1.00	.40	.10
☐ 277 Paul Doyle	1.00	.40	.10
☐ 278 Tommie Aaron	1.25	.50	.12
☐ 279 Bill Lee	1.25	.50	.12
☐ 280 Donn Clendenon	1.25	.50	.12
☐ 281 Casey Cox	1.00	.40	.10
☐ 282 Steve Huntz	1.00	.40	.10
☐ 283 Angel Bravo	1.00	.40	.10
☐ 284 Jack Baldschun	1.00	.40	.10
☐ 285 Paul Blair	1.25	.50	.12
☐ 286 Dodgers Rookies Jack Jenkins Bill Buckner	8.50	3.75	.85
☐ 287 Fred Talbot	1.00	.40	.10
☐ 288 Larry Hisle	1.25	.50	.12
☐ 289 Gene Brabender	1.00	.40	.10
☐ 290 Rod Carew	50.00	22.50	7.50
☐ 291 Leo Durocher MG	1.75	.70	.17
☐ 292 Eddie Leon	1.00	.40	.10
☐ 293 Bob Bailey	1.00	.40	.10
☐ 294 Jose Azcue	1.00	.40	.10
☐ 295 Cecil Upshaw	1.00	.40	.10
☐ 296 Woody Woodward	1.25	.50	.12
☐ 297 Curt Blefary	1.00	.40	.10
☐ 298 Ken Henderson	1.00	.40	.10
☐ 299 Buddy Bradford	1.00	.40	.10
☐ 300 Tom Seaver	90.00	40.00	13.50
☐ 301 Chico Salmon	1.00	.40	.10
☐ 302 Jeff James	1.00	.40	.10
☐ 303 Brant Alyea	1.00	.40	.10
☐ 304 Bill Russell	3.00	1.25	.30
☐ 305 World Series Game 1 Buford leadoff homer	2.25	.90	.22
☐ 306 World Series Game 2 Clendenon's homer breaks ice	2.25	.90	.22
☐ 307 World Series Game 3 Agee's catch saves the day	2.25	.90	.22
☐ 308 World Series Game 4 Martin's bunt ends deadlock	2.25	.90	.22

□ 309 World Series Game 5 .. 3.00	1.25	.30	
Koosman shuts door			
□ 310 World Series Summary 3.00	1.25	.30	
Mets whoop it up			
□ 311 Dick Green 1.00	.40	.10	
□ 312 Mike Torrez 1.25	.50	.12	
□ 313 Mayo Smith MG 1.00	.40	.10	
□ 314 Bill McCool 1.00	.40	.10	
□ 315 Luis Aparicio 4.00	1.75	.40	
□ 316 Skip Guinn 1.00	.40	.10	
□ 317 Red Sox Rookies 1.25	.50	.12	
Billy Conigliaro			
Luis Alvarado			
□ 318 Willie Smith 1.00	.40	.10	
□ 319 Clay Dalrymple 1.00	.40	.10	
□ 320 Jim Maloney 1.25	.50	.12	
□ 321 Lou Piniella 2.00	.80	.20	
□ 322 Luke Walker 1.00	.40	.10	
□ 323 Wayne Comer 1.00	.40	.10	
□ 324 Tony Taylor 1.00	.40	.10	
□ 325 Dave Boswell 1.00	.40	.10	
□ 326 Bill Voss 1.00	.40	.10	
□ 327 Hal King 1.00	.40	.10	
□ 328 George Brunet 1.00	.40	.10	
□ 329 Chris Cannizzaro 1.00	.40	.10	
□ 330 Lou Brock 9.00	4.00	.90	
□ 331 Chuck Dobson 1.00	.40	.10	
□ 332 Bobby Wine 1.00	.40	.10	
□ 333 Bobby Murcer 1.75	.70	.17	
□ 334 Phil Regan 1.00	.40	.10	
□ 335 Bill Freehan 1.50	.60	.15	
□ 336 Del Unser 1.00	.40	.10	
□ 337 Mike McCormick 1.25	.50	.12	
□ 338 Paul Schaal 1.00	.40	.10	
□ 339 Johnny Edwards 1.00	.40	.10	
□ 340 Tony Conigliaro 1.75	.70	.17	
□ 341 Bill Sudakis 1.00	.40	.10	
□ 342 Wilbur Wood 1.25	.50	.12	
□ 343A Checklist 4 .... 4.50	.50	.10	
(red bat on front)			
□ 343B Checklist 4 .... 4.50	.50	.10	
(brown bat on front)			
□ 344 Marcelino Lopez 1.00	.40	.10	
□ 345 Al Ferrara 1.00	.40	.10	
□ 346 Red Schoendienst MG 1.75	.70	.17	
□ 347 Russ Snyder 1.00	.40	.10	
□ 348 Mets Rookies 1.25	.50	.12	
Mike Jorgensen			
Jesse Hudson			
□ 349 Steve Hamilton 1.00	.40	.10	
□ 350 Roberto Clemente 48.00	22.00	6.00	
□ 351 Tom Murphy 1.00	.40	.10	
□ 352 Bob Barton 1.00	.40	.10	
□ 353 Stan Williams 1.00	.40	.10	
□ 354 Amos Otis 1.50	.60	.15	
□ 355 Doug Rader 1.25	.50	.12	
□ 356 Fred Lasher 1.00	.40	.10	
□ 357 Bob Burda 1.00	.40	.10	
□ 358 Pedro Borbon 1.00	.40	.10	
□ 359 Phil Roof 1.00	.40	.10	
□ 360 Curt Flood 1.50	.60	.15	
□ 361 Ray Jarvis 1.00	.40	.10	
□ 362 Joe Hague 1.00	.40	.10	
□ 363 Tom Shopay 1.00	.40	.10	
□ 364 Dan McGinn 1.00	.40	.10	
□ 365 Zoilo Versalles 1.00	.40	.10	
□ 366 Barry Moore 1.00	.40	.10	
□ 367 Mike Lum 1.00	.40	.10	
□ 368 Ed Herrmann 1.00	.40	.10	
□ 369 Alan Foster 1.00	.40	.10	
□ 370 Tommy Harper 1.00	.40	.10	
□ 371 Rod Gaspar 1.00	.40	.10	
□ 372 Dave Giusti 1.00	.40	.10	
□ 373 Roy White 1.50	.60	.15	
□ 374 Tommie Sisk 1.10	.45	.11	
□ 375 Johnny Callison 1.10	.45	.11	
□ 376 Lefty Phillips MG 1.10	.45	.11	
□ 377 Bill Butler 1.10	.45	.11	
□ 378 Jim Davenport 1.10	.45	.11	
□ 379 Tom Tischinski 1.10	.45	.11	
□ 380 Tony Perez 7.50	3.25	.75	
□ 381 Athletics Rookies 1.10	.45	.11	
Bobby Brooks			
Mike Olivo			
□ 382 Jack DiLauro 1.10	.45	.11	
□ 383 Mickey Stanley 1.50	.60	.15	
□ 384 Gary Neibauer 1.10	.45	.11	
□ 385 George Scott 1.50	.60	.15	
□ 386 Bill Dillman 1.10	.45	.11	
□ 387 Baltimore Orioles 2.50	1.00	.25	
Team Card			
□ 388 Byron Browne 1.10	.45	.11	
□ 389 Jim Shellenback 1.10	.45	.11	
□ 390 Willie Davis 1.50	.60	.15	
□ 391 Larry Brown 1.10	.45	.11	
□ 392 Walt Hriniak 1.10	.45	.11	
□ 393 John Gelnar 1.10	.45	.11	
□ 394 Gil Hodges MG 4.00	1.75	.40	
□ 395 Walt Williams 1.10	.45	.11	
□ 396 Steve Blass 1.10	.45	.11	
□ 397 Roger Repoz 1.10	.45	.11	
□ 398 Bill Stoneman 1.10	.45	.11	
□ 399 New York Yankees 2.50	1.00	.25	
Team Card			
□ 400 Denny McLain 1.50	.60	.15	
□ 401 Giants Rookies 1.10	.45	.11	
John Harrell			
Bernie Williams			
□ 402 Ellie Rodriguez 1.10	.45	.11	
□ 403 Jim Bunning 2.50	1.00	.25	
□ 404 Rich Reese 1.10	.45	.11	
□ 405 Bill Hands 1.10	.45	.11	
□ 406 Mike Andrews 1.10	.45	.11	
□ 407 Bob Watson 1.50	.60	.15	
□ 408 Paul Lindblad 1.10	.45	.11	
□ 409 Bob Tolan 1.10	.45	.11	

☐ 410	Boog Powell	3.00	1.25	.30
☐ 411	Los Angeles Dodgers Team Card	2.50	1.00	.25
☐ 412	Larry Burchart	1.10	.45	.11
☐ 413	Sonny Jackson	1.10	.45	.11
☐ 414	Paul Edmondson	1.10	.45	.11
☐ 415	Julian Javier	1.10	.45	.11
☐ 416	Joe Verbanic	1.10	.45	.11
☐ 417	John Bateman	1.10	.45	.11
☐ 418	John Donaldson	1.10	.45	.11
☐ 419	Ron Taylor	1.10	.45	.11
☐ 420	Ken McMullen	1.10	.45	.11
☐ 421	Pat Dobson	1.10	.45	.11
☐ 422	Royals Team	2.50	1.00	.25
☐ 423	Jerry May	1.10	.45	.11
☐ 424	Mike Kilkenny (inconsistent design, card number in white circle)	1.10	.45	.11
☐ 425	Bobby Bonds	6.00	2.50	.60
☐ 426	Bill Rigney MG	1.10	.45	.11
☐ 427	Fred Norman	1.10	.45	.11
☐ 428	Don Buford	1.10	.45	.11
☐ 429	Cubs Rookies Randy Bobb Jim Cosman	1.10	.45	.11
☐ 430	Andy Messersmith	1.50	.60	.15
☐ 431	Ron Swoboda	1.50	.60	.15
☐ 432A	Checklist 5 ("Baseball" in yellow letters)	4.50	.50	.10
☐ 432B	Checklist 5 ("Baseball" in white letters)	4.50	.50	.10
☐ 433	Ron Bryant	1.10	.45	.11
☐ 434	Felipe Alou	1.50	.60	.15
☐ 435	Nelson Briles	1.10	.45	.11
☐ 436	Philadelphia Phillies Team Card	2.50	1.00	.25
☐ 437	Danny Cater	1.10	.45	.11
☐ 438	Pat Jarvis	1.10	.45	.11
☐ 439	Lee Maye	1.10	.45	.11
☐ 440	Bill Mazeroski	1.75	.70	.17
☐ 441	John O'Donoghue	1.10	.45	.11
☐ 442	Gene Mauch MG	1.10	.45	.11
☐ 443	Al Jackson	1.10	.45	.11
☐ 444	White Sox Rookies Billy Farmer John Matias	1.10	.45	.11
☐ 445	Vada Pinson	1.75	.70	.17
☐ 446	Billy Grabarkewitz	1.10	.45	.11
☐ 447	Lee Stange	1.10	.45	.11
☐ 448	Houston Astros Team Card	2.50	1.00	.25
☐ 449	Jim Palmer	21.00	9.00	3.00
☐ 450	Willie McCovey AS	4.50	2.00	.45
☐ 451	Boog Powell AS	1.50	.60	.15
☐ 452	Felix Millan AS	1.10	.45	.11
☐ 453	Rod Carew AS	6.50	2.75	.65
☐ 454	Ron Santo AS	1.50	.60	.15
☐ 455	Brooks Robinson AS	4.50	2.00	.45
☐ 456	Don Kessinger AS	1.10	.45	.11
☐ 457	Rico Petrocelli AS	1.10	.45	.11
☐ 458	Pete Rose AS	14.00	6.25	2.00
☐ 459	Reggie Jackson AS	21.00	9.00	3.00
☐ 460	Matty Alou AS	2.00	.80	.20
☐ 461	Carl Yastrzemski AS	11.00	5.00	1.35
☐ 462	Hank Aaron AS	13.00	5.75	1.75
☐ 463	Frank Robinson AS	6.00	2.50	.60
☐ 464	Johnny Bench AS	14.00	6.25	2.00
☐ 465	Bill Freehan AS	2.00	.80	.20
☐ 466	Juan Marichal AS	4.00	1.75	.40
☐ 467	Denny McLain AS	2.00	.80	.20
☐ 468	Jerry Koosman AS	2.00	.80	.20
☐ 469	Sam McDowell AS	2.00	.80	.20
☐ 470	Willie Stargell	9.00	4.00	.90
☐ 471	Chris Zachary	1.60	.65	.16
☐ 472	Braves Team	3.00	1.25	.30
☐ 473	Don Bryant	1.60	.65	.16
☐ 474	Dick Kelley	1.60	.65	.16
☐ 475	Dick McAuliffe	1.60	.65	.16
☐ 476	Don Shaw	1.60	.65	.16
☐ 477	Orioles Rookies Al Severinsen Roger Freed	1.60	.65	.16
☐ 478	Bobby Heise	1.60	.65	.16
☐ 479	Dick Woodson	1.60	.65	.16
☐ 480	Glenn Beckert	2.00	.80	.20
☐ 481	Jose Tartabull	1.60	.65	.16
☐ 482	Tom Hilgendorf	1.60	.65	.16
☐ 483	Gail Hopkins	1.60	.65	.16
☐ 484	Gary Nolan	2.00	.80	.20
☐ 485	Jay Johnstone	2.00	.80	.20
☐ 486	Terry Harmon	1.60	.65	.16
☐ 487	Cisco Carlos	1.60	.65	.16
☐ 488	J.C. Martin	1.60	.65	.16
☐ 489	Eddie Kasko MG	1.60	.65	.16
☐ 490	Bill Singer	2.00	.80	.20
☐ 491	Graig Nettles	5.00	2.25	.50
☐ 492	Astros Rookies Keith Lampard Scipio Spinks	1.60	.65	.16
☐ 493	Lindy McDaniel	1.60	.65	.16
☐ 494	Larry Stahl	1.60	.65	.16
☐ 495	Dave Morehead	1.60	.65	.16
☐ 496	Steve Whitaker	1.60	.65	.16
☐ 497	Eddie Watt	1.60	.65	.16
☐ 498	Al Weis	1.60	.65	.16
☐ 499	Skip Lockwood	1.60	.65	.16
☐ 500	Hank Aaron	48.00	22.00	6.00
☐ 501	Chicago White Sox Team Card	3.00	1.25	.30
☐ 502	Rollie Fingers	28.00	12.50	4.00
☐ 503	Dal Maxvill	1.60	.65	.16
☐ 504	Don Pavletich	1.60	.65	.16
☐ 505	Ken Holtzman	2.00	.80	.20

☐ 506 Ed Stroud	1.60	.65	.16
☐ 507 Pat Corrales	1.60	.65	.16
☐ 508 Joe Niekro	2.00	.80	.20
☐ 509 Montreal Expos Team Card	3.00	1.25	.30
☐ 510 Tony Oliva	3.00	1.25	.30
☐ 511 Joe Hoerner	1.60	.65	.16
☐ 512 Billy Harris	1.60	.65	.16
☐ 513 Preston Gomez MG	1.60	.65	.16
☐ 514 Steve Hovley	1.60	.65	.16
☐ 515 Don Wilson	1.60	.65	.16
☐ 516 Yankees Rookies John Ellis Jim Lyttle	1.60	.65	.16
☐ 517 Joe Gibbon	1.60	.65	.16
☐ 518 Bill Melton	1.60	.65	.16
☐ 519 Don McMahon	1.60	.65	.16
☐ 520 Willie Horton	2.00	.80	.20
☐ 521 Cal Koonce	1.60	.65	.16
☐ 522 Angels Team	3.00	1.25	.30
☐ 523 Jose Pena	1.60	.65	.16
☐ 524 Alvin Dark MG	2.00	.80	.20
☐ 525 Jerry Adair	1.60	.65	.16
☐ 526 Ron Herbel	1.60	.65	.16
☐ 527 Don Bosch	1.60	.65	.16
☐ 528 Elrod Hendricks	1.60	.65	.16
☐ 529 Bob Aspromonte	1.60	.65	.16
☐ 530 Bob Gibson	12.50	5.50	1.65
☐ 531 Ron Clark	1.60	.65	.16
☐ 532 Danny Murtaugh MG	1.60	.65	.16
☐ 533 Buzz Stephen	1.60	.65	.16
☐ 534 Minnesota Twins Team Card	3.00	1.25	.30
☐ 535 Andy Kosco	1.60	.65	.16
☐ 536 Mike Kekich	1.60	.65	.16
☐ 537 Joe Morgan	12.50	5.50	1.65
☐ 538 Bob Humphreys	1.60	.65	.16
☐ 539 Phillies Rookies Dennis Doyle Larry Bowa	4.00	1.75	.40
☐ 540 Gary Peters	1.60	.65	.16
☐ 541 Bill Heath	1.60	.65	.16
☐ 542 Checklist 6	4.50	.50	.10
☐ 543 Clyde Wright	1.60	.65	.16
☐ 544 Cincinnati Reds Team Card	3.25	1.35	.32
☐ 545 Ken Harrelson	2.25	.90	.22
☐ 546 Ron Reed	2.00	.80	.20
☐ 547 Rick Monday	3.50	1.50	.35
☐ 548 Howie Reed	2.75	1.10	.27
☐ 549 St. Louis Cardinals Team Card	5.50	2.50	.55
☐ 550 Frank Howard	4.00	1.75	.40
☐ 551 Dock Ellis	2.75	1.10	.27
☐ 552 Royals Rookies Don O'Riley Dennis Paepke Fred Rico	2.75	1.10	.27
☐ 553 Jim Lefebvre	3.50	1.50	.35
☐ 554 Tom Timmermann	2.75	1.10	.27
☐ 555 Orlando Cepeda	5.00	2.25	.50
☐ 556 Dave Bristol MG	2.75	1.10	.27
☐ 557 Ed Kranepool	3.50	1.50	.35
☐ 558 Vern Fuller	2.75	1.10	.27
☐ 559 Tommy Davis	3.50	1.50	.35
☐ 560 Gaylord Perry	12.50	5.50	1.65
☐ 561 Tom McCraw	2.75	1.10	.27
☐ 562 Ted Abernathy	2.75	1.10	.27
☐ 563 Boston Red Sox Team Card	5.50	2.50	.55
☐ 564 Johnny Briggs	2.75	1.10	.27
☐ 565 Jim Hunter	12.50	5.50	1.65
☐ 566 Gene Alley	2.75	1.10	.27
☐ 567 Bob Oliver	2.75	1.10	.27
☐ 568 Stan Bahnsen	2.75	1.10	.27
☐ 569 Cookie Rojas	2.75	1.10	.27
☐ 570 Jim Fregosi	3.50	1.50	.35
☐ 571 Jim Brewer	2.75	1.10	.27
☐ 572 Frank Quilici MG	2.75	1.10	.27
☐ 573 Padres Rookies Mike Corkins Rafael Robles Ron Slocum	2.75	1.10	.27
☐ 574 Bobby Bolin	2.75	1.10	.27
☐ 575 Cleon Jones	2.75	1.10	.27
☐ 576 Milt Pappas	3.50	1.50	.35
☐ 577 Bernie Allen	2.75	1.10	.27
☐ 578 Tom Griffin	2.75	1.10	.27
☐ 579 Detroit Tigers Team Card	5.50	2.50	.55
☐ 580 Pete Rose	75.00	34.00	11.25
☐ 581 Tom Satriano	2.75	1.10	.27
☐ 582 Mike Paul	2.75	1.10	.27
☐ 583 Hal Lanier	2.75	1.10	.27
☐ 584 Al Downing	3.50	1.50	.35
☐ 585 Rusty Staub	4.00	1.75	.40
☐ 586 Rickey Clark	2.75	1.10	.27
☐ 587 Jose Arcia	2.75	1.10	.27
☐ 588A Checklist 7 ERR (666 Adolfo)	7.50	.75	.15
☐ 588B Checklist 7 COR (666 Adolpho)	4.50	.50	.10
☐ 589 Joe Keough	2.75	1.10	.27
☐ 590 Mike Cuellar	3.50	1.50	.35
☐ 591 Mike Ryan	2.75	1.10	.27
☐ 592 Daryl Patterson	2.75	1.10	.27
☐ 593 Chicago Cubs Team Card	5.50	2.50	.55
☐ 594 Jake Gibbs	2.75	1.10	.27
☐ 595 Maury Wills	4.00	1.75	.40
☐ 596 Mike Hershberger	2.75	1.10	.27
☐ 597 Sonny Siebert	2.75	1.10	.27
☐ 598 Joe Pepitone	3.50	1.50	.35
☐ 599 Senators Rookies Dick Stelmaszek Gene Martin	2.75	1.10	.27

Dick Such
☐ 600 Willie Mays 70.00 32.00 10.50
☐ 601 Pete Richert .... 2.75 1.10 .27
☐ 602 Ted Savage .... 2.75 1.10 .27
☐ 603 Ray Oyler .... 2.75 1.10 .27
☐ 604 Clarence Gaston .... 3.50 1.50 .35
☐ 605 Rick Wise .... 3.50 1.50 .35
☐ 606 Chico Ruiz .... 2.75 1.10 .27
☐ 607 Gary Waslewski .... 2.75 1.10 .27
☐ 608 Pittsburgh Pirates .... 5.50 2.50 .55
Team Card
☐ 609 Buck Martinez .... 2.75 1.10 .27
(inconsistent design,
card number in
white circle)
☐ 610 Jerry Koosman .... 4.00 1.75 .40
☐ 611 Norm Cash .... 4.00 1.75 .40
☐ 612 Jim Hickman .... 2.75 1.10 .27
☐ 613 Dave Baldwin .... 2.75 1.10 .27
☐ 614 Mike Shannon .... 3.50 1.50 .35
☐ 615 Mark Belanger .... 3.50 1.50 .35
☐ 616 Jim Merritt .... 2.75 1.10 .27
☐ 617 Jim French .... 2.75 1.10 .27
☐ 618 Billy Wynne .... 2.75 1.10 .27
☐ 619 Norm Miller .... 2.75 1.10 .27
☐ 620 Jim Perry .... 4.00 1.75 .40
☐ 621 Braves Rookies 22.00 9.50 3.15
Mike McQueen
Darrell Evans
Rick Kester
☐ 622 Don Sutton 11.00 5.00 1.35
☐ 623 Horace Clarke .... 2.75 1.10 .27
☐ 624 Clyde King MG .... 2.75 1.10 .27
☐ 625 Dean Chance .... 3.50 1.50 .35
☐ 626 Dave Ricketts .... 2.75 1.10 .27
☐ 627 Gary Wagner .... 2.75 1.10 .27
☐ 628 Wayne Garrett .... 2.75 1.10 .27
☐ 629 Merv Rettenmund .... 2.75 1.10 .27
☐ 630 Ernie Banks 32.00 14.25 4.75
☐ 631 Oakland Athletics .... 5.50 2.50 .55
Team Card
☐ 632 Gary Sutherland .... 2.75 1.10 .27
☐ 633 Roger Nelson .... 2.75 1.10 .27
☐ 634 Bud Harrelson .... 6.00 2.50 .60
☐ 635 Bob Allison .... 6.00 2.50 .60
☐ 636 Jim Stewart .... 5.00 2.25 .50
☐ 637 Cleveland Indians 10.00 4.50 1.25
Team Card
☐ 638 Frank Bertaina .... 5.00 2.25 .50
☐ 639 Dave Campbell .... 5.00 2.25 .50
☐ 640 Al Kaline 48.00 22.00 6.00
☐ 641 Al McBean .... 5.00 2.25 .50
☐ 642 Angels Rookies .... 5.00 2.25 .50
Greg Garrett
Gordon Lund
Jarvis Tatum
☐ 643 Jose Pagan .... 5.00 2.25 .50
☐ 644 Gerry Nyman .... 5.00 2.25 .50
☐ 645 Don Money .... 6.00 2.50 .60
☐ 646 Jim Britton .... 5.00 2.25 .50
☐ 647 Tom Matchick .... 5.00 2.25 .50
☐ 648 Larry Haney .... 5.00 2.25 .50
☐ 649 Jimmie Hall .... 5.00 2.25 .50
☐ 650 Sam McDowell .... 6.00 2.50 .60
☐ 651 Jim Gosger .... 5.00 2.25 .50
☐ 652 Rich Rollins .... 5.00 2.25 .50
☐ 653 Moe Drabowsky .... 5.00 2.25 .50
☐ 654 NL Rookies .... 6.00 2.50 .60
Oscar Gamble
Boots Day
Angel Mangual
☐ 655 John Roseboro .... 5.00 2.25 .50
☐ 656 Jim Hardin .... 5.00 2.25 .50
☐ 657 San Diego Padres 10.00 4.50 1.25
Team Card
☐ 658 Ken Tatum .... 5.00 2.25 .50
☐ 659 Pete Ward .... 5.00 2.25 .50
☐ 660 Johnny Bench 165.00 75.00 22.50
☐ 661 Jerry Robertson .... 5.00 2.25 .50
☐ 662 Frank Lucchesi MG .... 5.00 2.25 .50
☐ 663 Tito Francona .... 5.00 2.25 .50
☐ 664 Bob Robertson .... 5.00 2.25 .50
☐ 665 Jim Lonborg .... 6.00 2.50 .60
☐ 666 Adolpho Phillips .... 5.00 2.25 .50
☐ 667 Bob Meyer .... 5.00 2.25 .50
☐ 668 Bob Tillman .... 5.00 2.25 .50
☐ 669 White Sox Rookies .... 5.00 2.25 .50
Bart Johnson
Dan Lazar
Mickey Scott
☐ 670 Ron Santo .... 7.00 3.00 .70
☐ 671 Jim Campanis .... 5.00 2.25 .50
☐ 672 Leon McFadden .... 5.00 2.25 .50
☐ 673 Ted Uhlaender .... 5.00 2.25 .50
☐ 674 Dave Leonhard .... 5.00 2.25 .50
☐ 675 Jose Cardenal .... 5.00 2.25 .50
☐ 676 Washington Senators 10.00 4.50 1.25
Team Card
☐ 677 Woodie Fryman .... 5.00 2.25 .50
☐ 678 Dave Duncan .... 6.00 2.50 .60
☐ 679 Ray Sadecki .... 5.00 2.25 .50
☐ 680 Rico Petrocelli .... 6.00 2.50 .60
☐ 681 Bob Garibaldi .... 5.00 2.25 .50
☐ 682 Dalton Jones .... 5.00 2.25 .50
☐ 683 Reds Rookies .... 7.00 3.00 .70
Vern Geishert
Hal McRae
Wayne Simpson
☐ 684 Jack Fisher .... 5.00 2.25 .50
☐ 685 Tom Haller .... 5.00 2.25 .50
☐ 686 Jackie Hernandez .... 5.00 2.25 .50
☐ 687 Bob Priddy .... 5.00 2.25 .50
☐ 688 Ted Kubiak .... 5.00 2.25 .50
☐ 689 Frank Tepedino .... 5.00 2.25 .50
☐ 690 Ron Fairly .... 6.00 2.50 .60
☐ 691 Joe Grzenda .... 5.00 2.25 .50

☐ 692 Duffy Dyer	5.00	2.25	.50
☐ 693 Bob Johnson	5.00	2.25	.50
☐ 694 Gary Ross	5.00	2.25	.50
☐ 695 Bobby Knoop	5.00	2.25	.50
☐ 696 San Francisco Giants Team Card	10.00	4.50	1.25
☐ 697 Jim Hannan	5.00	2.25	.50
☐ 698 Tom Tresh	6.00	2.50	.60
☐ 699 Hank Aguirre	5.00	2.25	.50
☐ 700 Frank Robinson	42.00	18.00	5.50
☐ 701 Jack Billingham	5.00	2.25	.50
☐ 702 AL Rookies Bob Johnson Ron Klimkowski Bill Zepp	5.00	2.25	.50
☐ 703 Lou Marone	5.00	2.25	.50
☐ 704 Frank Baker	5.00	2.25	.50
☐ 705 Tony Cloninger UER (Batter headings on card back)	5.00	2.25	.50
☐ 706 John McNamara MG	7.00	3.00	.70
☐ 707 Kevin Collins	5.00	2.25	.50
☐ 708 Jose Santiago	5.00	2.25	.50
☐ 709 Mike Fiore	5.00	2.25	.50
☐ 710 Felix Millan	5.00	2.25	.50
☐ 711 Ed Brinkman	5.00	2.25	.50
☐ 712 Nolan Ryan	450.00	200.00	67.50
☐ 713 Seattle Pilots Team Card	20.00	8.50	2.75
☐ 714 Al Spangler	5.00	2.25	.50
☐ 715 Mickey Lolich	7.00	3.00	.70
☐ 716 Cardinals Rookies Sal Campisi Reggie Cleveland Santiago Guzman	5.00	2.25	.50
☐ 717 Tom Phoebus	5.00	2.25	.50
☐ 718 Ed Spiezio	5.00	2.25	.50
☐ 719 Jim Roland	5.00	2.25	.50
☐ 720 Rick Reichardt	6.00	2.50	.50

1971 Topps

The cards in this 752-card set measure 2 1/2" by 3 1/2". The 1971 Topps set is a challenge to complete in strict mint condition because the black obverse border is easily scratched and damaged. An unusual feature of this set is that the player is also pictured in black and white on the back of the card. Featured subsets within this set include League Leaders (61-72), Playoffs cards (195-202), and World Series cards (327-332). Cards 524-643 and the last series (644-752) are somewhat scarce. The last series was printed in two sheets of 132. On the printing sheets 44 cards were printed in 50 percent greater quantity than the other 66 cards. These 66 (slightly) shorter-printed numbers are identified in the checklist below by SP. The key rookie cards in this set are the multi-player rookie card of Dusty Baker and Don Baylor and the individual cards of Bert Blyleven, Dave Concepcion, Steve Garvey, and Ted Simmons.

	NRMT	VG-E	GOOD
COMPLETE SET (752)	2250.00	900.00	275.00
COMMON PLAYER (1-132)	.80	.35	.08
COMMON PLAYER (133-263)	1.00	.40	.10
COMMON PLAYER (264-393)	1.00	.40	.10
COMMON PLAYER (394-523)	1.60	.65	.16
COMMON PLAYER (524-643)	3.50	1.50	.35
COMMON PLAYER (644-752)	5.25	2.25	.50
COMMON SP (644-752)	7.50	3.25	.75

☐ 1 Baltimore Orioles Team Card	12.00	2.00	.40
☐ 2 Dock Ellis	.80	.35	.08
☐ 3 Dick McAuliffe	.80	.35	.08
☐ 4 Vic Davalillo	.80	.35	.08
☐ 5 Thurman Munson	38.00	17.00	4.50
☐ 6 Ed Spiezio	.80	.35	.08
☐ 7 Jim Holt	.80	.35	.08
☐ 8 Mike McQueen	.80	.35	.08
☐ 9 George Scott	.80	.35	.08
☐ 10 Claude Osteen	.80	.35	.08
☐ 11 Elliott Maddox	.80	.35	.08
☐ 12 Johnny Callison	.80	.35	.08
☐ 13 White Sox Rookies Charlie Brinkman Dick Moloney	.80	.35	.08
☐ 14 Dave Concepcion	15.00	6.50	2.15
☐ 15 Andy Messersmith	.80	.35	.08
☐ 16 Ken Singleton	3.00	1.25	.30
☐ 17 Billy Sorrell	.80	.35	.08

☐ 18 Norm Miller .80 .35 .08
☐ 19 Skip Pitlock .80 .35 .08
☐ 20 Reggie Jackson 90.00 40.00 13.50
☐ 21 Dan McGinn .80 .35 .08
☐ 22 Phil Roof .80 .35 .08
☐ 23 Oscar Gamble .80 .35 .08
☐ 24 Rich Hand .80 .35 .08
☐ 25 Clarence Gaston 1.00 .40 .10
☐ 26 Bert Blyleven 45.00 20.00 6.75
☐ 27 Pirates Rookies .80 .35 .08
Fred Cambria
Gene Clines
☐ 28 Ron Klimkowski .80 .35 .08
☐ 29 Don Buford .80 .35 .08
☐ 30 Phil Niekro 4.00 1.75 .40
☐ 31 Eddie Kasko MG .80 .35 .08
☐ 32 Jerry DaVanon .80 .35 .08
☐ 33 Del Unser .80 .35 .08
☐ 34 Sandy Vance .80 .35 .08
☐ 35 Lou Piniella 1.50 .60 .15
☐ 36 Dean Chance 1.00 .40 .10
☐ 37 Rich McKinney .80 .35 .08
☐ 38 Jim Colborn .80 .35 .08
☐ 39 Tiger Rookies 1.25 .50 .12
Lerrin LaGrow
Gene Lamont
☐ 40 Lee May 1.00 .40 .10
☐ 41 Rick Austin .80 .35 .08
☐ 42 Boots Day .80 .35 .08
☐ 43 Steve Kealey .80 .35 .08
☐ 44 Johnny Edwards .80 .35 .08
☐ 45 Jim Hunter 6.50 2.75 .65
☐ 46 Dave Campbell .80 .35 .08
☐ 47 Johnny Jeter .80 .35 .08
☐ 48 Dave Baldwin .80 .35 .08
☐ 49 Don Money .80 .35 .08
☐ 50 Willie McCovey 8.50 3.75 .85
☐ 51 Steve Kline .80 .35 .08
☐ 52 Braves Rookies 1.00 .40 .10
Oscar Brown
Earl Williams
☐ 53 Paul Blair .80 .35 .08
☐ 54 Checklist 1 4.50 .50 .10
☐ 55 Steve Carlton 25.00 11.00 3.50
☐ 56 Duane Josephson .80 .35 .08
☐ 57 Von Joshua .80 .35 .08
☐ 58 Bill Lee .80 .35 .08
☐ 59 Gene Mauch MG .80 .35 .08
☐ 60 Dick Bosman .80 .35 .08
☐ 61 AL Batting Leaders 2.75 1.10 .27
Alex Johnson
Carl Yastrzemski
Tony Oliva
☐ 62 NL Batting Leaders 2.00 .80 .20
Rico Carty
Joe Torre
Manny Sanguillen
☐ 63 AL RBI Leaders 2.00 .80 .20
Frank Howard
Tony Conigliaro
Boog Powell
☐ 64 NL RBI Leaders 3.25 1.35 .32
Johnny Bench
Tony Perez
Billy Williams
☐ 65 AL HR Leaders 3.00 1.25 .30
Frank Howard
Harmon Killebrew
Carl Yastrzemski
☐ 66 NL HR Leaders 3.25 1.35 .32
Johnny Bench
Billy Williams
Tony Perez
☐ 67 AL ERA Leaders 2.00 .80 .20
Diego Segui
Jim Palmer
Clyde Wright
☐ 68 NL ERA Leaders 2.00 .80 .20
Tom Seaver
Wayne Simpson
Luke Walker
☐ 69 AL Pitching Leaders 2.00 .80 .20
Mike Cuellar
Dave McNally
Jim Perry
☐ 70 NL Pitching Leaders 3.25 1.35 .32
Bob Gibson
Gaylord Perry
Fergie Jenkins
☐ 71 AL Strikeout Leaders 1.75 .70 .17
Sam McDowell
Mickey Lolich
Bob Johnson
☐ 72 NL Strikeout Leaders 3.75 1.60 .37
Tom Seaver
Bob Gibson
Fergie Jenkins
☐ 73 George Brunet .80 .35 .08
☐ 74 Twins Rookies .80 .35 .08
Pete Hamm
Jim Nettles
☐ 75 Gary Nolan .80 .35 .08
☐ 76 Ted Savage .80 .35 .08
☐ 77 Mike Compton .80 .35 .08
☐ 78 Jim Spencer .80 .35 .08
☐ 79 Wade Blasingame .80 .35 .08
☐ 80 Bill Melton .80 .35 .08
☐ 81 Felix Millan .80 .35 .08
☐ 82 Casey Cox .80 .35 .08
☐ 83 Met Rookies 1.00 .40 .10
Tim Foli
Randy Bobb
☐ 84 Marcel Lachemann 1.00 .40 .10
☐ 85 Billy Grabarkewitz .80 .35 .08
☐ 86 Mike Kilkenny .80 .35 .08
☐ 87 Jack Heidemann .80 .35 .08

Card			
☐ 88 Hal King	.80	.35	.08
☐ 89 Ken Brett	.80	.35	.08
☐ 90 Joe Pepitone	1.00	.40	.10
☐ 91 Bob Lemon MG	1.75	.70	.17
☐ 92 Fred Wenz	.80	.35	.08
☐ 93 Senators Rookies	.80	.35	.08
Norm McRae			
Denny Riddleberger			
☐ 94 Don Hahn	.80	.35	.08
☐ 95 Luis Tiant	1.25	.50	.12
☐ 96 Joe Hague	.80	.35	.08
☐ 97 Floyd Wicker	.80	.35	.08
☐ 98 Joe Decker	.80	.35	.08
☐ 99 Mark Belanger	1.00	.40	.10
☐ 100 Pete Rose	45.00	20.00	6.75
☐ 101 Les Cain	.80	.35	.08
☐ 102 Astros Rookies	1.25	.50	.12
Ken Forsch			
Larry Howard			
☐ 103 Rich Severson	.80	.35	.08
☐ 104 Dan Frisella	.80	.35	.08
☐ 105 Tony Conigliaro	1.50	.60	.15
☐ 106 Tom Dukes	.80	.35	.08
☐ 107 Roy Foster	.80	.35	.08
☐ 108 John Cumberland	.80	.35	.08
☐ 109 Steve Hovley	.80	.35	.08
☐ 110 Bill Mazeroski	1.50	.60	.15
☐ 111 Yankee Rookies	.80	.35	.08
Loyd Colson			
Bobby Mitchell			
☐ 112 Manny Mota	1.00	.40	.10
☐ 113 Jerry Crider	.80	.35	.08
☐ 114 Billy Conigliaro	1.00	.40	.10
☐ 115 Donn Clendenon	.80	.35	.08
☐ 116 Ken Sanders	.80	.35	.08
☐ 117 Ted Simmons	15.00	6.50	2.15
☐ 118 Cookie Rojas	.80	.35	.08
☐ 119 Frank Lucchesi MG	.80	.35	.08
☐ 120 Willie Horton	1.00	.40	.10
☐ 121 Cubs Rookies	.80	.35	.08
Jim Dunegan			
Roe Skidmore			
☐ 122 Eddie Watt	.80	.35	.08
☐ 123A Checklist 2	4.50	.50	.10
(card number			
at bottom right)			
☐ 123B Checklist 2	4.50	.50	.10
(card number			
centered)			
☐ 124 Don Gullett	1.25	.50	.12
☐ 125 Ray Fosse	.80	.35	.08
☐ 126 Danny Coombs	.80	.35	.08
☐ 127 Danny Thompson	.80	.35	.08
☐ 128 Frank Johnson	.80	.35	.08
☐ 129 Aurelio Monteagudo	.80	.35	.08
☐ 130 Denis Menke	.80	.35	.08
☐ 131 Curt Blefary	.80	.35	.08
☐ 132 Jose Laboy	.80	.35	.08
☐ 133 Mickey Lolich	1.50	.60	.15
☐ 134 Jose Arcia	1.00	.40	.10
☐ 135 Rick Monday	1.25	.50	.12
☐ 136 Duffy Dyer	1.00	.40	.10
☐ 137 Marcelino Lopez	1.00	.40	.10
☐ 138 Phillies Rookies	1.25	.50	.12
Joe Lis			
Willie Montanez			
☐ 139 Paul Casanova	1.00	.40	.10
☐ 140 Gaylord Perry	7.50	3.25	.75
☐ 141 Frank Quilici	1.00	.40	.10
☐ 142 Mack Jones	1.00	.40	.10
☐ 143 Steve Blass	1.00	.40	.10
☐ 144 Jackie Hernandez	1.00	.40	.10
☐ 145 Bill Singer	1.00	.40	.10
☐ 146 Ralph Houk MG	1.00	.40	.10
☐ 147 Bob Priddy	1.00	.40	.10
☐ 148 John Mayberry	1.25	.50	.12
☐ 149 Mike Hershberger	1.00	.40	.10
☐ 150 Sam McDowell	1.00	.40	.10
☐ 151 Tommy Davis	1.25	.50	.12
☐ 152 Angels Rookies	1.00	.40	.10
Lloyd Allen			
Winston Llenas			
☐ 153 Gary Ross	1.00	.40	.10
☐ 154 Cesar Gutierrez	1.00	.40	.10
☐ 155 Ken Henderson	1.00	.40	.10
☐ 156 Bart Johnson	1.00	.40	.10
☐ 157 Bob Bailey	1.00	.40	.10
☐ 158 Jerry Reuss	1.25	.50	.12
☐ 159 Jarvis Tatum	1.00	.40	.10
☐ 160 Tom Seaver	50.00	22.50	7.50
☐ 161 Coin Checklist	3.50	.50	.10
☐ 162 Jack Billingham	1.00	.40	.10
☐ 163 Buck Martinez	1.00	.40	.10
☐ 164 Reds Rookies	1.25	.50	.12
Frank Duffy			
Milt Wilcox			
☐ 165 Cesar Tovar	1.00	.40	.10
☐ 166 Joe Hoerner	1.00	.40	.10
☐ 167 Tom Grieve	1.50	.60	.15
☐ 168 Bruce Dal Canton	1.00	.40	.10
☐ 169 Ed Herrmann	1.00	.40	.10
☐ 170 Mike Cuellar	1.00	.40	.10
☐ 171 Bobby Wine	1.00	.40	.10
☐ 172 Duke Sims	1.00	.40	.10
☐ 173 Gil Garrido	1.00	.40	.10
☐ 174 Dave LaRoche	1.00	.40	.10
☐ 175 Jim Hickman	1.00	.40	.10
☐ 176 Red Sox Rookies	1.00	.40	.10
Bob Montgomery			
Doug Griffin			
☐ 177 Hal McRae	1.75	.70	.17
☐ 178 Dave Duncan	1.00	.40	.10
☐ 179 Mike Corkins	1.00	.40	.10
☐ 180 Al Kaline UER	17.00	7.25	2.50
(Home instead			
of Birth)			

☐ 181 Hal Lanier	1.00	.40	.10
☐ 182 Al Downing	1.00	.40	.10
☐ 183 Gil Hodges MG	4.00	1.75	.40
☐ 184 Stan Bahnsen	1.00	.40	.10
☐ 185 Julian Javier	1.00	.40	.10
☐ 186 Bob Spence	1.00	.40	.10
☐ 187 Ted Abernathy	1.00	.40	.10
☐ 188 Dodgers Rookies	3.25	1.35	.32
Bob Valentine			
Mike Strahler			
☐ 189 George Mitterwald	1.00	.40	.10
☐ 190 Bob Tolan	1.00	.40	.10
☐ 191 Mike Andrews	1.00	.40	.10
☐ 192 Billy Wilson	1.00	.40	.10
☐ 193 Bob Grich	4.00	1.75	.40
☐ 194 Mike Lum	1.00	.40	.10
☐ 195 AL Playoff Game 1	2.25	.90	.22
Powell muscles Twins			
☐ 196 AL Playoff Game 2	2.00	.80	.20
McNally makes it two straight			
☐ 197 AL Playoff Game 3	3.50	1.50	.35
Palmer mows'em down			
☐ 198 AL Playoff Summary	2.00	.80	.20
Orioles celebrate			
☐ 199 NL Playoff Game 1	2.00	.80	.20
Cline pinch-triple decides it			
☐ 200 NL Playoff Game 2	2.00	.80	.20
Tolan scores for third time			
☐ 201 NL Playoff Game 3	2.00	.80	.20
Cline scores winning run			
☐ 202 NL Playoff Summary	2.00	.80	.20
Reds celebrate			
☐ 203 Larry Gura	1.25	.50	.12
☐ 204 Brewers Rookies	1.00	.40	.10
Bernie Smith			
George Kopacz			
☐ 205 Gerry Moses	1.00	.40	.10
☐ 206 Checklist 3	4.50	.50	.10
☐ 207 Alan Foster	1.00	.40	.10
☐ 208 Billy Martin MG	3.00	1.25	.30
☐ 209 Steve Renko	1.00	.40	.10
☐ 210 Rod Carew	42.00	18.00	5.50
☐ 211 Phil Hennigan	1.00	.40	.10
☐ 212 Rich Hebner	1.25	.50	.12
☐ 213 Frank Baker	1.00	.40	.10
☐ 214 Al Ferrara	1.00	.40	.10
☐ 215 Diego Segui	1.00	.40	.10
☐ 216 Cards Rookies	1.00	.40	.10
Reggie Cleveland			
Luis Melendez			
☐ 217 Ed Stroud	1.00	.40	.10
☐ 218 Tony Cloninger	1.00	.40	.10
☐ 219 Elrod Hendricks	1.00	.40	.10
☐ 220 Ron Santo	2.00	.80	.20
☐ 221 Dave Morehead	1.00	.40	.10
☐ 222 Bob Watson	1.25	.50	.12
☐ 223 Cecil Upshaw	1.00	.40	.10
☐ 224 Alan Gallagher	1.00	.40	.10
☐ 225 Gary Peters	1.00	.40	.10
☐ 226 Bill Russell	1.25	.50	.12
☐ 227 Floyd Weaver	1.00	.40	.10
☐ 228 Wayne Garrett	1.00	.40	.10
☐ 229 Jim Hannan	1.00	.40	.10
☐ 230 Willie Stargell	9.00	4.00	.90
☐ 231 Indians Rookies	1.25	.50	.12
Vince Colbert			
John Lowenstein			
☐ 232 John Strohmayer	1.00	.40	.10
☐ 233 Larry Bowa	1.75	.70	.17
☐ 234 Jim Lyttle	1.00	.40	.10
☐ 235 Nate Colbert	1.00	.40	.10
☐ 236 Bob Humphreys	1.00	.40	.10
☐ 237 Cesar Cedeno	3.00	1.25	.30
☐ 238 Chuck Dobson	1.00	.40	.10
☐ 239 Red Schoendienst MG	1.75	.70	.17
☐ 240 Clyde Wright	1.00	.40	.10
☐ 241 Dave Nelson	1.00	.40	.10
☐ 242 Jim Ray	1.00	.40	.10
☐ 243 Carlos May	1.00	.40	.10
☐ 244 Bob Tillman	1.00	.40	.10
☐ 245 Jim Kaat	2.25	.90	.22
☐ 246 Tony Taylor	1.00	.40	.10
☐ 247 Royals Rookies	1.25	.50	.12
Jerry Cram			
Paul Splittorff			
☐ 248 Hoyt Wilhelm	4.00	1.75	.40
☐ 249 Chico Salmon	1.00	.40	.10
☐ 250 Johnny Bench	50.00	22.50	7.50
☐ 251 Frank Reberger	1.00	.40	.10
☐ 252 Eddie Leon	1.00	.40	.10
☐ 253 Bill Sudakis	1.00	.40	.10
☐ 254 Cal Koonce	1.00	.40	.10
☐ 255 Bob Robertson	1.00	.40	.10
☐ 256 Tony Gonzalez	1.00	.40	.10
☐ 257 Nelson Briles	1.00	.40	.10
☐ 258 Dick Green	1.00	.40	.10
☐ 259 Dave Marshall	1.00	.40	.10
☐ 260 Tommy Harper	1.00	.40	.10
☐ 261 Darold Knowles	1.00	.40	.10
☐ 262 Padres Rookies	1.00	.40	.10
Jim Williams			
Dave Robinson			
☐ 263 John Ellis	1.00	.40	.10
☐ 264 Joe Morgan	9.00	4.00	.90
☐ 265 Jim Northrup	1.25	.50	.12
☐ 266 Bill Stoneman	1.00	.40	.10
☐ 267 Rich Morales	1.00	.40	.10
☐ 268 Philadelphia Phillies Team Card	2.00	.80	.20
☐ 269 Gail Hopkins	1.00	.40	.10
☐ 270 Rico Carty	1.25	.50	.12
☐ 271 Bill Zepp	1.00	.40	.10

Card	Player			
□ 272	Tommy Helms	1.25	.50	.12
□ 273	Pete Richert	1.00	.40	.10
□ 274	Ron Slocum	1.00	.40	.10
□ 275	Vada Pinson	1.50	.60	.15
□ 276	Giants Rookies	8.00	3.50	.80
	Mike Davison			
	George Foster			
□ 277	Gary Waslewski	1.00	.40	.10
□ 278	Jerry Grote	1.00	.40	.10
□ 279	Lefty Phillips MG	1.00	.40	.10
□ 280	Fergie Jenkins	11.00	5.00	1.35
□ 281	Danny Walton	1.00	.40	.10
□ 282	Jose Pagan	1.00	.40	.10
□ 283	Dick Such	1.00	.40	.10
□ 284	Jim Gosger	1.00	.40	.10
□ 285	Sal Bando	1.25	.50	.12
□ 286	Jerry McNertney	1.00	.40	.10
□ 287	Mike Fiore	1.00	.40	.10
□ 288	Joe Moeller	1.00	.40	.10
□ 289	Chicago White Sox	2.00	.80	.20
	Team Card			
□ 290	Tony Oliva	3.00	1.25	.30
□ 291	George Culver	1.00	.40	.10
□ 292	Jay Johnstone	1.25	.50	.12
□ 293	Pat Corrales	1.00	.40	.10
□ 294	Steve Dunning	1.00	.40	.10
□ 295	Bobby Bonds	4.00	1.75	.40
□ 296	Tom Timmermann	1.00	.40	.10
□ 297	Johnny Briggs	1.00	.40	.10
□ 298	Jim Nelson	1.00	.40	.10
□ 299	Ed Kirkpatrick	1.00	.40	.10
□ 300	Brooks Robinson	15.00	6.50	2.15
□ 301	Earl Wilson	1.00	.40	.10
□ 302	Phil Gagliano	1.00	.40	.10
□ 303	Lindy McDaniel	1.00	.40	.10
□ 304	Ron Brand	1.00	.40	.10
□ 305	Reggie Smith	1.75	.70	.17
□ 306	Jim Nash	1.00	.40	.10
□ 307	Don Wert	1.00	.40	.10
□ 308	St. Louis Cardinals	2.00	.80	.20
	Team Card			
□ 309	Dick Ellsworth	1.00	.40	.10
□ 310	Tommie Agee	1.00	.40	.10
□ 311	Lee Stange	1.00	.40	.10
□ 312	Harry Walker MG	1.00	.40	.10
□ 313	Tom Hall	1.00	.40	.10
□ 314	Jeff Torborg	1.25	.50	.12
□ 315	Ron Fairly	1.25	.50	.12
□ 316	Fred Scherman	1.00	.40	.10
□ 317	Athletic Rookies	1.00	.40	.10
	Jim Driscoll			
	Angel Mangual			
□ 318	Rudy May	1.00	.40	.10
□ 319	Ty Cline	1.00	.40	.10
□ 320	Dave McNally	1.25	.50	.12
□ 321	Tom Matchick	1.00	.40	.10
□ 322	Jim Beauchamp	1.00	.40	.10
□ 323	Billy Champion	1.00	.40	.10
□ 324	Graig Nettles	2.75	1.10	.27
□ 325	Juan Marichal	5.50	2.50	.55
□ 326	Richie Scheinblum	1.00	.40	.10
□ 327	World Series Game 1	2.00	.80	.20
	Powell homers to			
	opposite field			
□ 328	World Series Game 2	2.00	.80	.20
	Don Buford			
□ 329	World Series Game 3	3.00	1.25	.30
	Frank Robinson			
	shows muscle			
□ 330	World Series Game 4	2.00	.80	.20
	Reds stay alive			
□ 331	World Series Game 5	3.50	1.50	.35
	Brooks Robinson			
	commits robbery			
□ 332	World Series Summary	2.00	.80	.20
	Orioles celebrate			
□ 333	Clay Kirby	1.00	.40	.10
□ 334	Roberto Pena	1.00	.40	.10
□ 335	Jerry Koosman	2.00	.80	.20
□ 336	Detroit Tigers	2.00	.80	.20
	Team Card			
□ 337	Jesus Alou	1.00	.40	.10
□ 338	Gene Tenace	1.75	.70	.17
□ 339	Wayne Simpson	1.00	.40	.10
□ 340	Rico Petrocelli	1.25	.50	.12
□ 341	Steve Garvey	70.00	32.00	10.50
□ 342	Frank Tepedino	1.00	.40	.10
□ 343	Pirates Rookies	1.00	.40	.10
	Ed Acosta			
	Milt May			
□ 344	Ellie Rodriguez	1.00	.40	.10
□ 345	Joel Horlen	1.00	.40	.10
□ 346	Lum Harris MG	1.00	.40	.10
□ 347	Ted Uhlaender	1.00	.40	.10
□ 348	Fred Norman	1.00	.40	.10
□ 349	Rich Reese	1.00	.40	.10
□ 350	Billy Williams	6.00	2.50	.60
□ 351	Jim Shellenback	1.00	.40	.10
□ 352	Denny Doyle	1.00	.40	.10
□ 353	Carl Taylor	1.00	.40	.10
□ 354	Don McMahon	1.00	.40	.10
□ 355	Bud Harrelson	1.25	.50	.12
□ 356	Bob Locker	1.00	.40	.10
□ 357	Cincinnati Reds	2.00	.80	.20
	Team Card			
□ 358	Danny Cater	1.00	.40	.10
□ 359	Ron Reed	1.00	.40	.10
□ 360	Jim Fregosi	1.25	.50	.12
□ 361	Don Sutton	6.50	2.75	.65
□ 362	Orioles Rookies	1.00	.40	.10
	Mike Adamson			
	Roger Freed			
□ 363	Mike Nagy	1.00	.40	.10
□ 364	Tommy Dean	1.00	.40	.10
□ 365	Bob Johnson	1.00	.40	.10
□ 366	Ron Stone	1.00	.40	.10

No.	Player			
☐ 367	Dalton Jones	1.00	.40	.10
☐ 368	Bob Veale	1.00	.40	.10
☐ 369	Checklist 4	4.50	.50	.10
☐ 370	Joe Torre	3.50	1.50	.35
☐ 371	Jack Hiatt	1.00	.40	.10
☐ 372	Lew Krausse	1.00	.40	.10
☐ 373	Tom McCraw	1.00	.40	.10
☐ 374	Clete Boyer	1.25	.50	.12
☐ 375	Steve Hargan	1.00	.40	.10
☐ 376	Expos Rookies	1.00	.40	.10
	Clyde Mashore			
	Ernie McAnally			
☐ 377	Greg Garrett	1.00	.40	.10
☐ 378	Tito Fuentes	1.00	.40	.10
☐ 379	Wayne Granger	1.00	.40	.10
☐ 380	Ted Williams MG	6.50	2.75	.65
☐ 381	Fred Gladding	1.00	.40	.10
☐ 382	Jake Gibbs	1.00	.40	.10
☐ 383	Rod Gaspar	1.00	.40	.10
☐ 384	Rollie Fingers	12.50	5.50	1.65
☐ 385	Maury Wills	2.50	1.00	.25
☐ 386	Boston Red Sox	2.00	.80	.20
	Team Card			
☐ 387	Ron Herbel	1.00	.40	.10
☐ 388	Al Oliver	2.50	1.00	.25
☐ 389	Ed Brinkman	1.00	.40	.10
☐ 390	Glenn Beckert	1.25	.50	.12
☐ 391	Twins Rookies	1.25	.50	.12
	Steve Brye			
	Cotton Nash			
☐ 392	Grant Jackson	1.00	.40	.10
☐ 393	Merv Rettenmund	1.00	.40	.10
☐ 394	Clay Carroll	1.60	.65	.16
☐ 395	Roy White	2.00	.80	.20
☐ 396	Dick Schofield	1.60	.65	.16
☐ 397	Alvin Dark MG	2.00	.80	.20
☐ 398	Howie Reed	1.60	.65	.16
☐ 399	Jim French	1.60	.65	.16
☐ 400	Hank Aaron	45.00	20.00	6.75
☐ 401	Tom Murphy	1.60	.65	.16
☐ 402	Los Angeles Dodgers	3.25	1.35	.32
	Team Card			
☐ 403	Joe Coleman	1.60	.65	.16
☐ 404	Astros Rookies	1.60	.65	.16
	Buddy Harris			
	Roger Metzger			
☐ 405	Leo Cardenas	1.60	.65	.16
☐ 406	Ray Sadecki	1.60	.65	.16
☐ 407	Joe Rudi	2.00	.80	.20
☐ 408	Rafael Robles	1.60	.65	.16
☐ 409	Don Pavletich	1.60	.65	.16
☐ 410	Ken Holtzman	2.00	.80	.20
☐ 411	George Spriggs	1.60	.65	.16
☐ 412	Jerry Johnson	1.60	.65	.16
☐ 413	Pat Kelly	1.60	.65	.16
☐ 414	Woodie Fryman	1.60	.65	.16
☐ 415	Mike Hegan	1.60	.65	.16
☐ 416	Gene Alley	1.60	.65	.16
☐ 417	Dick Hall	1.60	.65	.16
☐ 418	Adolfo Phillips	1.60	.65	.16
☐ 419	Ron Hansen	1.60	.65	.16
☐ 420	Jim Merritt	1.60	.65	.16
☐ 421	John Stephenson	1.60	.65	.16
☐ 422	Frank Bertaina	1.60	.65	.16
☐ 423	Tigers Rookies	1.60	.65	.16
	Dennis Saunders			
	Tim Marting			
☐ 424	Roberto Rodriquez	1.60	.65	.16
☐ 425	Doug Rader	2.00	.80	.20
☐ 426	Chris Cannizzaro	1.60	.65	.16
☐ 427	Bernie Allen	1.60	.65	.16
☐ 428	Jim McAndrew	1.60	.65	.16
☐ 429	Chuck Hinton	1.60	.65	.16
☐ 430	Wes Parker	2.00	.80	.20
☐ 431	Tom Burgmeier	1.60	.65	.16
☐ 432	Bob Didier	1.60	.65	.16
☐ 433	Skip Lockwood	1.60	.65	.16
☐ 434	Gary Sutherland	1.60	.65	.16
☐ 435	Jose Cardenal	1.60	.65	.16
☐ 436	Wilbur Wood	2.00	.80	.20
☐ 437	Danny Murtaugh MG	1.60	.65	.16
☐ 438	Mike McCormick	2.00	.80	.20
☐ 439	Phillies Rookies	2.50	1.00	.25
	Greg Luzinski			
	Scott Reid			
☐ 440	Bert Campaneris	2.00	.80	.20
☐ 441	Milt Pappas	2.00	.80	.20
☐ 442	California Angels	3.25	1.35	.32
	Team Card			
☐ 443	Rich Robertson	1.60	.65	.16
☐ 444	Jimmie Price	1.60	.65	.16
☐ 445	Art Shamsky	1.60	.65	.16
☐ 446	Bobby Bolin	1.60	.65	.16
☐ 447	Cesar Geronimo	1.60	.65	.16
☐ 448	Dave Roberts	1.60	.65	.16
☐ 449	Brant Alyea	1.60	.65	.16
☐ 450	Bob Gibson	14.00	6.25	2.00
☐ 451	Joe Keough	1.60	.65	.16
☐ 452	John Boccabella	1.60	.65	.16
☐ 453	Terry Crowley	1.60	.65	.16
☐ 454	Mike Paul	1.60	.65	.16
☐ 455	Don Kessinger	2.00	.80	.20
☐ 456	Bob Meyer	1.60	.65	.16
☐ 457	Willie Smith	1.60	.65	.16
☐ 458	White Sox Rookies	1.60	.65	.16
	Ron Lolich			
	Dave Lemonds			
☐ 459	Jim Lefebvre	2.00	.80	.20
☐ 460	Fritz Peterson	1.60	.65	.16
☐ 461	Jim Ray Hart	2.00	.80	.20
☐ 462	Washington Senators	3.25	1.35	.32
	Team Card			
☐ 463	Tom Kelley	1.60	.65	.16
☐ 464	Aurelio Rodriguez	1.60	.65	.16
☐ 465	Tim McCarver	2.50	1.00	.25
☐ 466	Ken Berry	1.60	.65	.16

☐ 467 Al Santorini .... 1.60 .65 .16
☐ 468 Frank Fernandez .... 1.60 .65 .16
☐ 469 Bob Aspromonte .... 1.60 .65 .16
☐ 470 Bob Oliver .... 1.60 .65 .16
☐ 471 Tom Griffin .... 1.60 .65 .16
☐ 472 Ken Rudolph .... 1.60 .65 .16
☐ 473 Gary Wagner .... 1.60 .65 .16
☐ 474 Jim Fairey .... 1.60 .65 .16
☐ 475 Ron Perranoski .... 1.60 .65 .16
☐ 476 Dal Maxvill .... 1.60 .65 .16
☐ 477 Earl Weaver MG .... 2.25 .90 .22
☐ 478 Bernie Carbo .... 1.60 .65 .16
☐ 479 Dennis Higgins .... 1.60 .65 .16
☐ 480 Manny Sanguillen .... 2.00 .80 .20
☐ 481 Daryl Patterson .... 1.60 .65 .16
☐ 482 San Diego Padres .... 3.50 1.50 .35
Team Card
☐ 483 Gene Michael .... 2.00 .80 .20
☐ 484 Don Wilson .... 1.60 .65 .16
☐ 485 Ken McMullen .... 1.60 .65 .16
☐ 486 Steve Huntz .... 1.60 .65 .16
☐ 487 Paul Schaal .... 1.60 .65 .16
☐ 488 Jerry Stephenson .... 1.60 .65 .16
☐ 489 Luis Alvarado .... 1.60 .65 .16
☐ 490 Deron Johnson .... 1.60 .65 .16
☐ 491 Jim Hardin .... 1.60 .65 .16
☐ 492 Ken Boswell .... 1.60 .65 .16
☐ 493 Dave May .... 1.60 .65 .16
☐ 494 Braves Rookies .... 2.25 .90 .22
Ralph Garr
Rick Kester
☐ 495 Felipe Alou .... 2.00 .80 .20
☐ 496 Woody Woodward .... 2.00 .80 .20
☐ 497 Horacio Pina .... 1.60 .65 .16
☐ 498 John Kennedy .... 1.60 .65 .16
☐ 499 Checklist 5 .... 4.50 .50 .10
☐ 500 Jim Perry .... 2.00 .80 .20
☐ 501 Andy Etchebarren .... 1.60 .65 .16
☐ 502 Chicago Cubs .... 3.25 1.35 .32
Team Card
☐ 503 Gates Brown .... 2.00 .80 .20
☐ 504 Ken Wright .... 1.60 .65 .16
☐ 505 Ollie Brown .... 1.60 .65 .16
☐ 506 Bobby Knoop .... 1.60 .65 .16
☐ 507 George Stone .... 1.60 .65 .16
☐ 508 Roger Repoz .... 1.60 .65 .16
☐ 509 Jim Grant .... 1.60 .65 .16
☐ 510 Ken Harrelson .... 2.00 .80 .20
☐ 511 Chris Short .... 1.60 .65 .16
☐ 512 Red Sox Rookies .... 1.60 .65 .16
Dick Mills
Mike Garman
☐ 513 Nolan Ryan 190.00 80.00 16.00
☐ 514 Ron Woods .... 1.60 .65 .16
☐ 515 Carl Morton .... 1.60 .65 .16
☐ 516 Ted Kubiak .... 1.60 .65 .16
☐ 517 Charlie Fox MG .... 1.60 .65 .16
☐ 518 Joe Grzenda .... 1.60 .65 .16
☐ 519 Willie Crawford .... 1.60 .65 .16
☐ 520 Tommy John .... 4.00 1.75 .40
☐ 521 Leron Lee .... 1.60 .65 .16
☐ 522 Minnesota Twins .... 3.25 1.35 .32
Team Card
☐ 523 John Odom .... 1.60 .65 .16
☐ 524 Mickey Stanley .... 4.00 1.75 .40
☐ 525 Ernie Banks 33.00 15.00 5.00
☐ 526 Ray Jarvis .... 3.50 1.50 .35
☐ 527 Cleon Jones .... 3.50 1.50 .35
☐ 528 Wally Bunker .... 3.50 1.50 .35
☐ 529 NL Rookie Infielders ... 4.50 2.00 .45
Enzo Hernandez
Bill Buckner
Marty Perez
☐ 530 Carl Yastrzemski 40.00 18.00 6.00
☐ 531 Mike Torrez .... 3.50 1.50 .35
☐ 532 Bill Rigney MG .... 3.50 1.50 .35
☐ 533 Mike Ryan .... 3.50 1.50 .35
☐ 534 Luke Walker .... 3.50 1.50 .35
☐ 535 Curt Flood .... 4.50 2.00 .45
☐ 536 Claude Raymond .... 3.50 1.50 .35
☐ 537 Tom Egan .... 3.50 1.50 .35
☐ 538 Angel Bravo .... 3.50 1.50 .35
☐ 539 Larry Brown .... 3.50 1.50 .35
☐ 540 Larry Dierker .... 3.50 1.50 .35
☐ 541 Bob Burda .... 3.50 1.50 .35
☐ 542 Bob Miller .... 3.50 1.50 .35
☐ 543 New York Yankees .... 7.00 3.00 .70
Team Card
☐ 544 Vida Blue .... 5.00 2.25 .50
☐ 545 Dick Dietz .... 3.50 1.50 .35
☐ 546 John Matias .... 3.50 1.50 .35
☐ 547 Pat Dobson .... 3.50 1.50 .35
☐ 548 Don Mason .... 3.50 1.50 .35
☐ 549 Jim Brewer .... 3.50 1.50 .35
☐ 550 Harmon Killebrew 22.00 9.50 3.15
☐ 551 Frank Linzy .... 3.50 1.50 .35
☐ 552 Buddy Bradford .... 3.50 1.50 .35
☐ 553 Kevin Collins .... 3.50 1.50 .35
☐ 554 Lowell Palmer .... 3.50 1.50 .35
☐ 555 Walt Williams .... 3.50 1.50 .35
☐ 556 Jim McGlothlin .... 3.50 1.50 .35
☐ 557 Tom Satriano .... 3.50 1.50 .35
☐ 558 Hector Torres .... 3.50 1.50 .35
☐ 559 AL Rookie Pitchers .... 3.50 1.50 .35
Terry Cox
Bill Gogolewski
Gary Jones
☐ 560 Rusty Staub .... 4.50 2.00 .45
☐ 561 Syd O'Brien .... 3.50 1.50 .35
☐ 562 Dave Giusti .... 3.50 1.50 .35
☐ 563 San Francisco Giants .. 7.00 3.00 .70
Team Card
☐ 564 Al Fitzmorris .... 3.50 1.50 .35
☐ 565 Jim Wynn .... 4.50 2.00 .45
☐ 566 Tim Cullen .... 3.50 1.50 .35
☐ 567 Walt Alston MG .... 5.00 2.25 .50

☐ 568	Sal Campisi	3.50	1.50	.35
☐ 569	Ivan Murrell	3.50	1.50	.35
☐ 570	Jim Palmer	33.00	15.00	5.00
☐ 571	Ted Sizemore	3.50	1.50	.35
☐ 572	Jerry Kenney	3.50	1.50	.35
☐ 573	Ed Kranepool	4.00	1.75	.40
☐ 574	Jim Bunning	5.00	2.25	.50
☐ 575	Bill Freehan	4.50	2.00	.45
☐ 576	Cubs Rookies Adrian Garrett Brock Davis Garry Jestadt	3.50	1.50	.35
☐ 577	Jim Lonborg	4.00	1.75	.40
☐ 578	Ron Hunt	3.50	1.50	.35
☐ 579	Marty Pattin	3.50	1.50	.35
☐ 580	Tony Perez	11.00	5.00	1.35
☐ 581	Roger Nelson	3.50	1.50	.35
☐ 582	Dave Cash	3.50	1.50	.35
☐ 583	Ron Cook	3.50	1.50	.35
☐ 584	Cleveland Indians Team Card	7.00	3.00	.70
☐ 585	Willie Davis	4.00	1.75	.40
☐ 586	Dick Woodson	3.50	1.50	.35
☐ 587	Sonny Jackson	3.50	1.50	.35
☐ 588	Tom Bradley	3.50	1.50	.35
☐ 589	Bob Barton	3.50	1.50	.35
☐ 590	Alex Johnson	3.50	1.50	.35
☐ 591	Jackie Brown	3.50	1.50	.35
☐ 592	Randy Hundley	3.50	1.50	.35
☐ 593	Jack Aker	3.50	1.50	.35
☐ 594	Cards Rookies Bob Chlupsa Bob Stinson Al Hrabosky	5.00	2.25	.50
☐ 595	Dave Johnson	4.00	1.75	.40
☐ 596	Mike Jorgensen	3.50	1.50	.35
☐ 597	Ken Suarez	3.50	1.50	.35
☐ 598	Rick Wise	4.00	1.75	.40
☐ 599	Norm Cash	4.50	2.00	.45
☐ 600	Willie Mays	80.00	36.00	12.00
☐ 601	Ken Tatum	3.50	1.50	.35
☐ 602	Marty Martinez	3.50	1.50	.35
☐ 603	Pittsburgh Pirates Team Card	7.00	3.00	.70
☐ 604	John Gelnar	3.50	1.50	.35
☐ 605	Orlando Cepeda	5.00	2.25	.50
☐ 606	Chuck Taylor	3.50	1.50	.35
☐ 607	Paul Ratliff	3.50	1.50	.35
☐ 608	Mike Wegener	3.50	1.50	.35
☐ 609	Leo Durocher MG	4.50	2.00	.45
☐ 610	Amos Otis	4.00	1.75	.40
☐ 611	Tom Phoebus	3.50	1.50	.35
☐ 612	Indians Rookies Lou Camilli Ted Ford Steve Mingori	3.50	1.50	.35
☐ 613	Pedro Borbon	3.50	1.50	.35
☐ 614	Billy Cowan	3.50	1.50	.35
☐ 615	Mel Stottlemyre	4.00	1.75	.40
☐ 616	Larry Hisle	3.50	1.50	.35
☐ 617	Clay Dalrymple	3.50	1.50	.35
☐ 618	Tug McGraw	4.50	2.00	.45
☐ 619A	Checklist 6 ERR (no copyright)	7.50	.75	.15
☐ 619B	Checklist 6 COR (copyright on back)	4.50	.50	.10
☐ 620	Frank Howard	4.50	2.00	.45
☐ 621	Ron Bryant	3.50	1.50	.35
☐ 622	Joe Lahoud	3.50	1.50	.35
☐ 623	Pat Jarvis	3.50	1.50	.35
☐ 624	Oakland Athletics Team Card	7.50	3.25	.75
☐ 625	Lou Brock	28.00	12.50	4.00
☐ 626	Freddie Patek	4.00	1.75	.40
☐ 627	Steve Hamilton	3.50	1.50	.35
☐ 628	John Bateman	3.50	1.50	.35
☐ 629	John Hiller	4.00	1.75	.40
☐ 630	Roberto Clemente	60.00	27.00	9.00
☐ 631	Eddie Fisher	3.50	1.50	.35
☐ 632	Darrel Chaney	3.50	1.50	.35
☐ 633	AL Rookie Outfielders Bobby Brooks Pete Koegel Scott Northey	3.50	1.50	.35
☐ 634	Phil Regan	3.50	1.50	.35
☐ 635	Bobby Murcer	5.25	2.25	.50
☐ 636	Denny Lemaster	3.50	1.50	.35
☐ 637	Dave Bristol MG	3.50	1.50	.35
☐ 638	Stan Williams	3.50	1.50	.35
☐ 639	Tom Haller	3.50	1.50	.35
☐ 640	Frank Robinson	38.00	17.00	5.00
☐ 641	New York Mets Team Card	7.50	3.25	.75
☐ 642	Jim Roland	3.50	1.50	.35
☐ 643	Rick Reichardt	3.50	1.50	.35
☐ 644	Jim Stewart SP	7.50	3.25	.75
☐ 645	Jim Maloney SP	7.50	3.25	.75
☐ 646	Bobby Floyd SP	7.50	3.25	.75
☐ 647	Juan Pizarro	5.25	2.25	.50
☐ 648	Mets Rookies SP Rich Folkers Ted Martinez John Matlack	10.00	4.50	1.25
☐ 649	Sparky Lyle SP	10.00	4.50	1.25
☐ 650	Rich Allen SP	18.00	7.50	2.50
☐ 651	Jerry Robertson SP	7.50	3.25	.75
☐ 652	Atlanta Braves Team Card	10.00	4.50	1.25
☐ 653	Russ Snyder SP	7.50	3.25	.75
☐ 654	Don Shaw SP	7.50	3.25	.75
☐ 655	Mike Epstein SP	7.50	3.25	.75
☐ 656	Gerry Nyman SP	7.50	3.25	.75
☐ 657	Jose Azcue	5.25	2.25	.50
☐ 658	Paul Lindblad SP	7.50	3.25	.75
☐ 659	Byron Browne SP	7.50	3.25	.75
☐ 660	Ray Culp	5.25	2.25	.50

☐ 661 Chuck Tanner MG SP .. 7.50 3.25 .75
☐ 662 Mike Hedlund SP .... 7.50 3.25 .75
☐ 663 Marv Staehle .... 5.25 2.25 .50
☐ 664 Rookie Pitchers SP ..... 7.50 3.25 .75
Archie Reynolds
Bob Reynolds
Ken Reynolds
☐ 665 Ron Swoboda SP .... 8.50 3.75 .85
☐ 666 Gene Brabender SP ..... 7.50 3.25 .75
☐ 667 Pete Ward .... 5.25 2.25 .50
☐ 668 Gary Neibauer .... 5.25 2.25 .50
☐ 669 Ike Brown SP .... 7.50 3.25 .75
☐ 670 Bill Hands .... 5.25 2.25 .50
☐ 671 Bill Voss SP .... 7.50 3.25 .75
☐ 672 Ed Crosby SP .... 7.50 3.25 .75
☐ 673 Gerry Janeski SP .... 7.50 3.25 .75
☐ 674 Montreal Expos 10.00 4.50 1.25
Team Card
☐ 675 Dave Boswell .... 5.25 2.25 .50
☐ 676 Tommie Reynolds .... 5.25 2.25 .50
☐ 677 Jack DiLauro SP .... 7.50 3.25 .75
☐ 678 George Thomas .... 5.25 2.25 .50
☐ 679 Don O'Riley .... 5.25 2.25 .50
☐ 680 Don Mincher SP .... 7.50 3.25 .75
☐ 681 Bill Butler .... 5.25 2.25 .50
☐ 682 Terry Harmon .... 5.25 2.25 .50
☐ 683 Bill Burbach SP .... 7.50 3.25 .75
☐ 684 Curt Motton .... 5.25 2.25 .50
☐ 685 Moe Drabowsky .... 5.25 2.25 .50
☐ 686 Chico Ruiz SP .... 7.50 3.25 .75
☐ 687 Ron Taylor SP .... 7.50 3.25 .75
☐ 688 Sparky Anderson MG SP15.00 6.50 2.15
☐ 689 Frank Baker .... 5.25 2.25 .50
☐ 690 Bob Moose .... 5.25 2.25 .50
☐ 691 Bobby Heise .... 5.25 2.25 .50
☐ 692 AL Rookie Pitchers SP 7.50 3.25 .75
Hal Haydel
Rogelio Moret
Wayne Twitchell
☐ 693 Jose Pena SP .... 7.50 3.25 .75
☐ 694 Rick Renick SP .... 7.50 3.25 .75
☐ 695 Joe Niekro .... 6.50 2.75 .65
☐ 696 Jerry Morales .... 5.25 2.25 .50
☐ 697 Rickey Clark SP .... 7.50 3.25 .75
☐ 698 Milwaukee Brewers SP15.00 6.50 2.15
Team Card
☐ 699 Jim Britton .... 5.25 2.25 .50
☐ 700 Boog Powell SP 15.00 6.50 2.15
☐ 701 Bob Garibaldi .... 5.25 2.25 .50
☐ 702 Milt Ramirez .... 5.25 2.25 .50
☐ 703 Mike Kekich .... 5.25 2.25 .50
☐ 704 J.C. Martin SP .... 7.50 3.25 .75
☐ 705 Dick Selma SP .... 7.50 3.25 .75
☐ 706 Joe Foy SP .... 7.50 3.25 .75
☐ 707 Fred Lasher .... 5.25 2.25 .50
☐ 708 Russ Nagelson SP ...... 7.50 3.25 .75
☐ 709 Rookie Outfielders SP 38.00 17.00 5.00
Dusty Baker
Don Baylor
Tom Paciorek
☐ 710 Sonny Siebert .... 5.25 2.25 .50
☐ 711 Larry Stahl SP .... 7.50 3.25 .75
☐ 712 Jose Martinez .... 5.25 2.25 .50
☐ 713 Mike Marshall SP .... 7.50 3.25 .75
☐ 714 Dick Williams MG SP .. 8.50 3.75 .85
☐ 715 Horace Clarke SP .... 7.50 3.25 .75
☐ 716 Dave Leonhard .... 5.25 2.25 .50
☐ 717 Tommie Aaron SP .... 7.50 3.25 .75
☐ 718 Billy Wynne .... 5.25 2.25 .50
☐ 719 Jerry May SP .... 7.50 3.25 .75
☐ 720 Matty Alou .... 6.00 2.50 .60
☐ 721 John Morris .... 5.25 2.25 .50
☐ 722 Houston Astros SP 15.00 6.50 2.15
Team Card
☐ 723 Vicente Romo SP .... 7.50 3.25 .75
☐ 724 Tom Tischinski SP ...... 7.50 3.25 .75
☐ 725 Gary Gentry SP .... 7.50 3.25 .75
☐ 726 Paul Popovich .... 5.25 2.25 .50
☐ 727 Ray Lamb SP .... 7.50 3.25 .75
☐ 728 NL Rookie Outfielders . 5.25 2.25 .50
Wayne Redmond
Keith Lampard
Bernie Williams
☐ 729 Dick Billings .... 5.25 2.25 .50
☐ 730 Jim Rooker .... 5.25 2.25 .50
☐ 731 Jim Qualls SP .... 7.50 3.25 .75
☐ 732 Bob Reed .... 5.25 2.25 .50
☐ 733 Lee Maye SP .... 7.50 3.25 .75
☐ 734 Rob Gardner SP .... 7.50 3.25 .75
☐ 735 Mike Shannon SP .... 8.50 3.75 .85
☐ 736 Mel Queen SP .... 7.50 3.25 .75
☐ 737 Preston Gomez MG SP 7.50 3.25 .75
☐ 738 Russ Gibson SP .... 7.50 3.25 .75
☐ 739 Barry Lersch SP .... 7.50 3.25 .75
☐ 740 Luis Aparicio SP 18.00 7.50 2.50
☐ 741 Skip Guinn .... 5.25 2.25 .50
☐ 742 Kansas City Royals ... 10.00 4.50 1.25
Team Card
☐ 743 John O'Donoghue SP .. 7.50 3.25 .75
☐ 744 Chuck Manuel SP .... 7.50 3.25 .75
☐ 745 Sandy Alomar SP .... 7.50 3.25 .75
☐ 746 Andy Kosco .... 5.25 2.25 .50
☐ 747 NL Rookie Pitchers ..... 5.25 2.25 .50
Al Severinsen
Scipio Spinks
Balor Moore
☐ 748 John Purdin SP .... 7.50 3.25 .75
☐ 749 Ken Szotkiewicz .... 5.25 2.25 .50
☐ 750 Denny McLain SP 12.50 5.50 1.65
☐ 751 Al Weis SP 12.50 5.50 1.65
☐ 752 Dick Drago .... 7.50 3.00 .60

1972 Topps

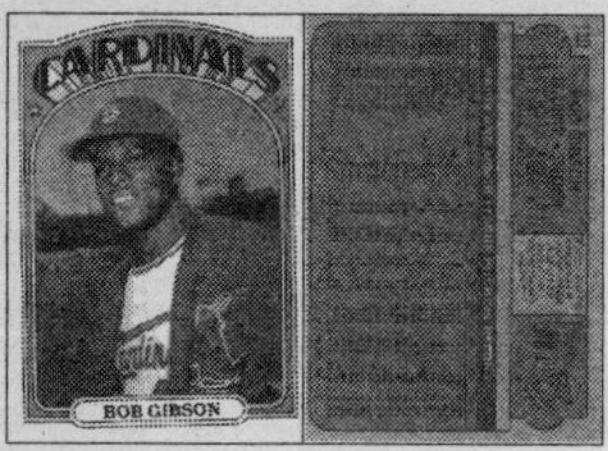

The cards in this 787-card set measure 2 1/2" by 3 1/2". The 1972 Topps set contained the most cards ever for a Topps set to that point in time. Features appearing for the first time were "Boyhood Photos" (KP: 341-348 and 491-498), Awards and Trophy cards (621-626), "In Action" (distributed throughout the set), and "Traded Cards" (TR: 751-757). Other subsets included League Leaders (85-96), Playoffs cards (221-222), and World Series cards (223-230). The curved lines of the color picture are a departure from the rectangular designs of other years. There is a series of intermediate scarcity (526-656) and the usual high numbers (657-787). The key rookie card in this set is Carlton Fisk.

	NRMT	VG-E	GOOD
COMPLETE SET (787)	2000.00	800.00	200.00
COMMON PLAYER (1-132)	.50	.20	.05
COMMON PLAYER (133-263)	.70	.30	.07
COMMON PLAYER (264-394)	.85	.35	.08
COMMON PLAYER (395-525)	1.25	.50	.12
COMMON PLAYER (526-656)	2.75	1.10	.27
COMMON PLAYER (657-787)	5.00	2.25	.50

	NRMT	VG-E	GOOD
☐ 1 Pittsburgh Pirates Team Card	7.00	1.25	.25
☐ 2 Ray Culp	.50	.20	.05
☐ 3 Bob Tolan	.50	.20	.05
☐ 4 Checklist 1	3.50	.35	.07
☐ 5 John Bateman	.50	.20	.05
☐ 6 Fred Scherman	.50	.20	.05
☐ 7 Enzo Hernandez	.50	.20	.05
☐ 8 Ron Swoboda	.75	.30	.07
☐ 9 Stan Williams	.50	.20	.05
☐ 10 Amos Otis	.75	.30	.07
☐ 11 Bobby Valentine	1.00	.40	.10
☐ 12 Jose Cardenal	.50	.20	.05
☐ 13 Joe Grzenda	.50	.20	.05
☐ 14 Phillies Rookies Pete Koegel Mike Anderson Wayne Twitchell	.50	.20	.05
☐ 15 Walt Williams	.50	.20	.05
☐ 16 Mike Jorgensen	.50	.20	.05
☐ 17 Dave Duncan	.50	.20	.05
☐ 18A Juan Pizarro (yellow underline C and S of Cubs)	.50	.20	.05
☐ 18B Juan Pizarro (green underline C and S of Cubs)	5.00	2.25	.50
☐ 19 Billy Cowan	.50	.20	.05
☐ 20 Don Wilson	.50	.20	.05
☐ 21 Atlanta Braves Team Card	1.25	.50	.12
☐ 22 Rob Gardner	.50	.20	.05
☐ 23 Ted Kubiak	.50	.20	.05
☐ 24 Ted Ford	.50	.20	.05
☐ 25 Bill Singer	.75	.30	.07
☐ 26 Andy Etchebarren	.50	.20	.05
☐ 27 Bob Johnson	.50	.20	.05
☐ 28 Twins Rookies Bob Gebhard Steve Brye Hal Haydel	.50	.20	.05
☐ 29A Bill Bonham (yellow underline C and S of Cubs)	.50	.20	.05
☐ 29B Bill Bonham (green underline C and S of Cubs)	5.00	2.25	.50
☐ 30 Rico Petrocelli	.75	.30	.07
☐ 31 Cleon Jones	.50	.20	.05
☐ 32 Jones In Action	.50	.20	.05
☐ 33 Billy Martin MG	3.25	1.35	.32
☐ 34 Martin In Action	1.50	.60	.15
☐ 35 Jerry Johnson	.50	.20	.05
☐ 36 Johnson In Action	.50	.20	.05
☐ 37 Carl Yastrzemski	15.00	6.50	2.15
☐ 38 Yastrzemski In Action	7.50	3.25	.75
☐ 39 Bob Barton	.50	.20	.05
☐ 40 Barton In Action	.50	.20	.05
☐ 41 Tommy Davis	.75	.30	.07
☐ 42 Davis In Action	.50	.20	.05
☐ 43 Rick Wise	.50	.20	.05
☐ 44 Wise In Action	.50	.20	.05
☐ 45A Glenn Beckert (yellow underline C and S of Cubs)	.50	.20	.05
☐ 45B Glenn Beckert (green underline C and S of Cubs)	5.00	2.25	.50
☐ 46 Beckert In Action	.50	.20	.05
☐ 47 John Ellis	.50	.20	.05
☐ 48 Ellis In Action	.50	.20	.05

□ 49 Willie Mays	25.00	11.00	3.50
□ 50 Mays In Action	12.50	5.50	1.65
□ 51 Harmon Killebrew	5.50	2.50	.55
□ 52 Killebrew In Action	2.50	1.00	.25
□ 53 Bud Harrelson	.75	.30	.07
□ 54 Harrelson In Action	.50	.20	.05
□ 55 Clyde Wright	.50	.20	.05
□ 56 Rich Chiles	.50	.20	.05
□ 57 Bob Oliver	.50	.20	.05
□ 58 Ernie McAnally	.50	.20	.05
□ 59 Fred Stanley	.50	.20	.05
□ 60 Manny Sanguillen	.75	.30	.07
□ 61 Cubs Rookies Burt Hooton Gene Hiser Earl Stephenson	1.00	.40	.10
□ 62 Angel Mangual	.50	.20	.05
□ 63 Duke Sims	.50	.20	.05
□ 64 Pete Broberg	.50	.20	.05
□ 65 Cesar Cedeno	1.00	.40	.10
□ 66 Ray Corbin	.50	.20	.05
□ 67 Red Schoendienst MG	1.25	.50	.12
□ 68 Jim York	.50	.20	.05
□ 69 Roger Freed	.50	.20	.05
□ 70 Mike Cuellar	.50	.20	.05
□ 71 California Angels Team Card	1.25	.50	.12
□ 72 Bruce Kison	1.00	.40	.10
□ 73 Steve Huntz	.50	.20	.05
□ 74 Cecil Upshaw	.50	.20	.05
□ 75 Bert Campaneris	.75	.30	.07
□ 76 Don Carrithers	.50	.20	.05
□ 77 Ron Theobald	.50	.20	.05
□ 78 Steve Arlin	.50	.20	.05
□ 79 Red Sox Rookies Mike Garman Cecil Cooper Carlton Fisk	125.00	57.50	18.75
□ 80 Tony Perez	3.50	1.50	.35
□ 81 Mike Hedlund	.50	.20	.05
□ 82 Ron Woods	.50	.20	.05
□ 83 Dalton Jones	.50	.20	.05
□ 84 Vince Colbert	.50	.20	.05
□ 85 NL Batting Leaders Joe Torre Ralph Garr Glenn Beckert	1.25	.50	.12
□ 86 AL Batting Leaders Tony Oliva Bobby Murcer Merv Rettenmund	1.25	.50	.12
□ 87 NL RBI Leaders Joe Torre Willie Stargell Hank Aaron	2.50	1.00	.25
□ 88 AL RBI Leaders Harmon Killebrew Frank Robinson Reggie Smith	2.25	.90	.22
□ 89 NL Home Run Leaders Willie Stargell Hank Aaron Lee May	2.00	.80	.20
□ 90 AL Home Run Leaders Bill Melton Norm Cash Reggie Jackson	1.75	.70	.17
□ 91 NL ERA Leaders Tom Seaver Dave Roberts UER (photo actually Danny Coombs) Don Wilson	1.75	.70	.17
□ 92 AL ERA Leaders Vida Blue Wilbur Wood Jim Palmer	1.25	.50	.12
□ 93 NL Pitching Leaders Fergie Jenkins Steve Carlton Al Downing Tom Seaver	2.00	.80	.20
□ 94 AL Pitching Leaders Mickey Lolich Vida Blue Wilbur Wood	1.25	.50	.12
□ 95 NL Strikeout Leaders Tom Seaver Fergie Jenkins Bill Stoneman	1.75	.70	.17
□ 96 AL Strikeout Leaders Mickey Lolich Vida Blue Joe Coleman	1.25	.50	.12
□ 97 Tom Kelley	.50	.20	.05
□ 98 Chuck Tanner MG	.50	.20	.05
□ 99 Ross Grimsley	.50	.20	.05
□ 100 Frank Robinson	5.50	2.50	.55
□ 101 Astros Rookies Bill Greif J.R. Richard Ray Busse	1.75	.70	.17
□ 102 Lloyd Allen	.50	.20	.05
□ 103 Checklist 2	3.50	.35	.07
□ 104 Toby Harrah	1.50	.60	.15
□ 105 Gary Gentry	.50	.20	.05
□ 106 Milwaukee Brewers Team Card	1.25	.50	.12
□ 107 Jose Cruz	1.75	.70	.17
□ 108 Gary Waslewski	.50	.20	.05
□ 109 Jerry May	.50	.20	.05
□ 110 Ron Hunt	.50	.20	.05
□ 111 Jim Grant	.50	.20	.05
□ 112 Greg Luzinski	1.00	.40	.10
□ 113 Rogelio Moret	.50	.20	.05
□ 114 Bill Buckner	2.00	.80	.20

☐ 115 Jim Fregosi .75 .30 .07
☐ 116 Ed Farmer .50 .20 .05
☐ 117A Cleo James .50 .20 .05
(yellow underline
C and S of Cubs)
☐ 117B Cleo James 5.00 2.25 .50
(green underline
C and S of Cubs)
☐ 118 Skip Lockwood .50 .20 .05
☐ 119 Marty Perez .50 .20 .05
☐ 120 Bill Freehan 1.00 .40 .10
☐ 121 Ed Sprague .50 .20 .05
☐ 122 Larry Biittner .50 .20 .05
☐ 123 Ed Acosta .50 .20 .05
☐ 124 Yankees Rookies .50 .20 .05
Alan Closter
Rusty Torres
Roger Hambright
☐ 125 Dave Cash .50 .20 .05
☐ 126 Bart Johnson .50 .20 .05
☐ 127 Duffy Dyer .50 .20 .05
☐ 128 Eddie Watt .50 .20 .05
☐ 129 Charlie Fox MG .50 .20 .05
☐ 130 Bob Gibson 5.50 2.50 .55
☐ 131 Jim Nettles .50 .20 .05
☐ 132 Joe Morgan 5.50 2.50 .55
☐ 133 Joe Keough .70 .30 .07
☐ 134 Carl Morton .70 .30 .07
☐ 135 Vada Pinson 1.00 .40 .10
☐ 136 Darrell Chaney .70 .30 .07
☐ 137 Dick Williams MG 1.00 .40 .10
☐ 138 Mike Kekich .70 .30 .07
☐ 139 Tim McCarver 1.25 .50 .12
☐ 140 Pat Dobson .70 .30 .07
☐ 141 Mets Rookies 1.00 .40 .10
Buzz Capra
Leroy Stanton
Jon Matlack
☐ 142 Chris Chambliss 2.50 1.00 .25
☐ 143 Garry Jestadt .70 .30 .07
☐ 144 Marty Pattin .70 .30 .07
☐ 145 Don Kessinger 1.00 .40 .10
☐ 146 Steve Kealey .70 .30 .07
☐ 147 Dave Kingman 6.50 2.75 .65
☐ 148 Dick Billings .70 .30 .07
☐ 149 Gary Neibauer .70 .30 .07
☐ 150 Norm Cash 1.25 .50 .12
☐ 151 Jim Brewer .70 .30 .07
☐ 152 Gene Clines .70 .30 .07
☐ 153 Rick Auerbach .70 .30 .07
☐ 154 Ted Simmons 2.50 1.00 .25
☐ 155 Larry Dierker .70 .30 .07
☐ 156 Minnesota Twins 1.50 .60 .15
Team Card
☐ 157 Don Gullett 1.00 .40 .10
☐ 158 Jerry Kenney .70 .30 .07
☐ 159 John Boccabella .70 .30 .07
☐ 160 Andy Messersmith .70 .30 .07
☐ 161 Brock Davis .70 .30 .07
☐ 162 Brewers Rookies UER 1.00 .40 .10
Jerry Bell
Darrell Porter
Bob Reynolds
(Porter and Bell
photos switched)
☐ 163 Tug McGraw 1.00 .40 .10
☐ 164 McGraw In Action .70 .30 .07
☐ 165 Chris Speier 1.00 .40 .10
☐ 166 Speier In Action .70 .30 .07
☐ 167 Deron Johnson .70 .30 .07
☐ 168 Johnson In Action .70 .30 .07
☐ 169 Vida Blue 1.00 .40 .10
☐ 170 Blue In Action .70 .30 .07
☐ 171 Darrell Evans 1.50 .60 .15
☐ 172 Evans In Action 1.00 .40 .10
☐ 173 Clay Kirby .70 .30 .07
☐ 174 Kirby In Action .70 .30 .07
☐ 175 Tom Haller .70 .30 .07
☐ 176 Haller In Action .70 .30 .07
☐ 177 Paul Schaal .70 .30 .07
☐ 178 Schaal In Action .70 .30 .07
☐ 179 Dock Ellis .70 .30 .07
☐ 180 Ellis In Action .70 .30 .07
☐ 181 Ed Kranepool .70 .30 .07
☐ 182 Kranepool In Action .70 .30 .07
☐ 183 Bill Melton .70 .30 .07
☐ 184 Melton In Action .70 .30 .07
☐ 185 Ron Bryant .70 .30 .07
☐ 186 Bryant In Action .70 .30 .07
☐ 187 Gates Brown .70 .30 .07
☐ 188 Frank Lucchesi MG .70 .30 .07
☐ 189 Gene Tenace 1.00 .40 .10
☐ 190 Dave Giusti .70 .30 .07
☐ 191 Jeff Burroughs 1.00 .40 .10
☐ 192 Chicago Cubs 1.50 .60 .15
Team Card
☐ 193 Kurt Bevacqua .70 .30 .07
☐ 194 Fred Norman .70 .30 .07
☐ 195 Orlando Cepeda 2.25 .90 .22
☐ 196 Mel Queen .70 .30 .07
☐ 197 Johnny Briggs .70 .30 .07
☐ 198 Dodgers Rookies 4.00 1.75 .40
Charlie Hough
Bob O'Brien
Mike Strahler
☐ 199 Mike Fiore .70 .30 .07
☐ 200 Lou Brock 5.50 2.50 .55
☐ 201 Phil Roof .70 .30 .07
☐ 202 Scipio Spinks .70 .30 .07
☐ 203 Ron Blomberg .70 .30 .07
☐ 204 Tommy Helms .70 .30 .07
☐ 205 Dick Drago .70 .30 .07
☐ 206 Dal Maxvill .70 .30 .07
☐ 207 Tom Egan .70 .30 .07
☐ 208 Milt Pappas .70 .30 .07
☐ 209 Joe Rudi 1.00 .40 .10

□ 210 Denny McLain 1.25 .50 .12
□ 211 Gary Sutherland .70 .30 .07
□ 212 Grant Jackson .70 .30 .07
□ 213 Angels Rookies .70 .30 .07
Billy Parker
Art Kusnyer
Tom Silverio
□ 214 Mike McQueen .70 .30 .07
□ 215 Alex Johnson .70 .30 .07
□ 216 Joe Niekro 1.00 .40 .10
□ 217 Roger Metzger .70 .30 .07
□ 218 Eddie Kasko MG .70 .30 .07
□ 219 Rennie Stennett 1.00 .40 .10
□ 220 Jim Perry 1.00 .40 .10
□ 221 NL Playoffs 1.25 .50 .12
Bucs champs
□ 222 AL Playoffs 1.75 .70 .17
Orioles champs
(Brooks Robinson)
□ 223 World Series Game 1 .. 1.25 .50 .12
(McNally pitching)
□ 224 World Series Game 2 .. 1.50 .60 .15
(Dave Johnson and
Mark Belanger)
□ 225 World Series Game 3 .. 1.25 .50 .12
(Sanguillen scoring)
□ 226 World Series Game 4 .. 2.75 1.10 .27
(Clemente on 2nd)
□ 227 World Series Game 5 .. 1.25 .50 .12
(Briles pitching)
□ 228 World Series Game 6 .. 1.50 .60 .15
(Frank Robinson and
Manny Sanguillen)
□ 229 World Series Game 7 .. 1.25 .50 .12
(Blass pitching)
□ 230 World Series Summary 1.25 .50 .12
(Pirates celebrate)
□ 231 Casey Cox .70 .30 .07
□ 232 Giants Rookies .70 .30 .07
Chris Arnold
Jim Barr
Dave Rader
□ 233 Jay Johnstone 1.00 .40 .10
□ 234 Ron Taylor .70 .30 .07
□ 235 Merv Rettenmund .70 .30 .07
□ 236 Jim McGlothlin .70 .30 .07
□ 237 New York Yankees 1.50 .60 .15
Team Card
□ 238 Leron Lee .70 .30 .07
□ 239 Tom Timmermann .70 .30 .07
□ 240 Rich Allen 2.50 1.00 .25
□ 241 Rollie Fingers 7.00 3.00 .70
□ 242 Don Mincher .70 .30 .07
□ 243 Frank Linzy .70 .30 .07
□ 244 Steve Braun .70 .30 .07
□ 245 Tommie Agee .70 .30 .07
□ 246 Tom Burgmeier .70 .30 .07
□ 247 Milt May .70 .30 .07
□ 248 Tom Bradley .70 .30 .07
□ 249 Harry Walker MG .70 .30 .07
□ 250 Boog Powell 1.25 .50 .12
□ 251 Checklist 3 3.50 .35 .07
□ 252 Ken Reynolds .70 .30 .07
□ 253 Sandy Alomar .70 .30 .07
□ 254 Boots Day .70 .30 .07
□ 255 Jim Lonborg 1.00 .40 .10
□ 256 George Foster 2.00 .80 .20
□ 257 Tigers Rookies .70 .30 .07
Jim Foor
Tim Hosley
Paul Jata
□ 258 Randy Hundley .70 .30 .07
□ 259 Sparky Lyle 1.00 .40 .10
□ 260 Ralph Garr 1.00 .40 .10
□ 261 Steve Mingori .70 .30 .07
□ 262 San Diego Padres 1.50 .60 .15
Team Card
□ 263 Felipe Alou 1.00 .40 .10
□ 264 Tommy John 2.00 .80 .20
□ 265 Wes Parker 1.00 .40 .10
□ 266 Bobby Bolin .85 .35 .08
□ 267 Dave Concepcion 3.00 1.25 .30
□ 268 A's Rookies .85 .35 .08
Dwain Anderson
Chris Floethe
□ 269 Don Hahn .85 .35 .08
□ 270 Jim Palmer 13.50 6.00 1.85
□ 271 Ken Rudolph .85 .35 .08
□ 272 Mickey Rivers 1.25 .50 .12
□ 273 Bobby Floyd .85 .35 .08
□ 274 Al Severinsen .85 .35 .08
□ 275 Cesar Tovar .85 .35 .08
□ 276 Gene Mauch MG .85 .35 .08
□ 277 Elliott Maddox .85 .35 .08
□ 278 Dennis Higgins .85 .35 .08
□ 279 Larry Brown .85 .35 .08
□ 280 Willie McCovey 6.00 2.50 .60
□ 281 Bill Parsons .85 .35 .08
□ 282 Houston Astros 1.75 .70 .17
Team Card
□ 283 Darrell Brandon .85 .35 .08
□ 284 Ike Brown .85 .35 .08
□ 285 Gaylord Perry 6.50 2.75 .65
□ 286 Gene Alley .85 .35 .08
□ 287 Jim Hardin .85 .35 .08
□ 288 Johnny Jeter .85 .35 .08
□ 289 Syd O'Brien .85 .35 .08
□ 290 Sonny Siebert .85 .35 .08
□ 291 Hal McRae 1.50 .60 .15
□ 292 McRae In Action 1.00 .40 .10
□ 293 Dan Frisella .85 .35 .08
□ 294 Frisella In Action .85 .35 .08
□ 295 Dick Dietz .85 .35 .08
□ 296 Dietz In Action .85 .35 .08
□ 297 Claude Osteen .85 .35 .08
□ 298 Osteen In Action .85 .35 .08

☐ 299	Hank Aaron	33.00	15.00	5.00
☐ 300	Aaron in Action	15.00	6.50	2.15
☐ 301	George Mitterwald	.85	.35	.08
☐ 302	Mitterwald In Action	.85	.35	.08
☐ 303	Joe Pepitone	1.00	.40	.10
☐ 304	Pepitone In Action	.85	.35	.08
☐ 305	Ken Boswell	.85	.35	.08
☐ 306	Boswell In Action	.85	.35	.08
☐ 307	Steve Renko	.85	.35	.08
☐ 308	Renko In Action	.85	.35	.08
☐ 309	Roberto Clemente	33.00	15.00	5.00
☐ 310	Clemente In Action	15.00	6.50	2.15
☐ 311	Clay Carroll	.85	.35	.08
☐ 312	Carroll In Action	.85	.35	.08
☐ 313	Luis Aparicio	3.00	1.25	.30
☐ 314	Aparicio In Action	1.50	.60	.15
☐ 315	Paul Splittorff	.85	.35	.08
☐ 316	Cardinals Rookies Jim Bibby Jorge Roque Santiago Guzman	1.25	.50	.12
☐ 317	Rich Hand	.85	.35	.08
☐ 318	Sonny Jackson	.85	.35	.08
☐ 319	Aurelio Rodriguez	.85	.35	.08
☐ 320	Steve Blass	.85	.35	.08
☐ 321	Joe Lahoud	.85	.35	.08
☐ 322	Jose Pena	.85	.35	.08
☐ 323	Earl Weaver MG	1.25	.50	.12
☐ 324	Mike Ryan	.85	.35	.08
☐ 325	Mel Stottlemyre	1.25	.50	.12
☐ 326	Pat Kelly	.85	.35	.08
☐ 327	Steve Stone	1.25	.50	.12
☐ 328	Boston Red Sox Team Card	1.75	.70	.17
☐ 329	Roy Foster	.85	.35	.08
☐ 330	Jim Hunter	4.50	2.00	.45
☐ 331	Stan Swanson	.85	.35	.08
☐ 332	Buck Martinez	.85	.35	.08
☐ 333	Steve Barber	.85	.35	.08
☐ 334	Rangers Rookies Bill Fahey Jim Mason Tom Ragland	.85	.35	.08
☐ 335	Bill Hands	.85	.35	.08
☐ 336	Marty Martinez	.85	.35	.08
☐ 337	Mike Kilkenny	.85	.35	.08
☐ 338	Bob Grich	1.25	.50	.12
☐ 339	Ron Cook	.85	.35	.08
☐ 340	Roy White	1.00	.40	.10
☐ 341	KP: Joe Torre	1.00	.40	.10
☐ 342	KP: Wilbur Wood	.85	.35	.08
☐ 343	KP: Willie Stargell	1.25	.50	.12
☐ 344	KP: Dave McNally	.85	.35	.08
☐ 345	KP: Rick Wise	.85	.35	.08
☐ 346	KP: Jim Fregosi	.85	.35	.08
☐ 347	KP: Tom Seaver	3.00	1.25	.30
☐ 348	KP: Sal Bando	.85	.35	.08
☐ 349	Al Fitzmorris	.85	.35	.08
☐ 350	Frank Howard	1.25	.50	.12
☐ 351	Braves Rookies Tom House Rick Kester Jimmy Britton	1.00	.40	.10
☐ 352	Dave LaRoche	.85	.35	.08
☐ 353	Art Shamsky	.85	.35	.08
☐ 354	Tom Murphy	.85	.35	.08
☐ 355	Bob Watson	1.00	.40	.10
☐ 356	Gerry Moses	.85	.35	.08
☐ 357	Woodie Fryman	.85	.35	.08
☐ 358	Sparky Anderson MG	1.25	.50	.12
☐ 359	Don Pavletich	.85	.35	.08
☐ 360	Dave Roberts	.85	.35	.08
☐ 361	Mike Andrews	.85	.35	.08
☐ 362	New York Mets Team Card	1.75	.70	.17
☐ 363	Ron Klimkowski	.85	.35	.08
☐ 364	Johnny Callison	.85	.35	.08
☐ 365	Dick Bosman	.85	.35	.08
☐ 366	Jimmy Rosario	.85	.35	.08
☐ 367	Ron Perranoski	.85	.35	.08
☐ 368	Danny Thompson	1.00	.40	.10
☐ 369	Jim Lefebvre	1.00	.40	.10
☐ 370	Don Buford	.85	.35	.08
☐ 371	Denny Lemaster	.85	.35	.08
☐ 372	Royals Rookies Lance Clemons Monty Montgomery	.85	.35	.08
☐ 373	John Mayberry	1.00	.40	.10
☐ 374	Jack Heidemann	.85	.35	.08
☐ 375	Reggie Cleveland	.85	.35	.08
☐ 376	Andy Kosco	.85	.35	.08
☐ 377	Terry Harmon	.85	.35	.08
☐ 378	Checklist 4	3.50	.35	.07
☐ 379	Ken Berry	.85	.35	.08
☐ 380	Earl Williams	.85	.35	.08
☐ 381	Chicago White Sox Team Card	1.75	.70	.17
☐ 382	Joe Gibbon	.85	.35	.08
☐ 383	Brant Alyea	.85	.35	.08
☐ 384	Dave Campbell	.85	.35	.08
☐ 385	Mickey Stanley	1.00	.40	.10
☐ 386	Jim Colborn	.85	.35	.08
☐ 387	Horace Clarke	.85	.35	.08
☐ 388	Charlie Williams	.85	.35	.08
☐ 389	Bill Rigney MG	.85	.35	.08
☐ 390	Willie Davis	1.00	.40	.10
☐ 391	Ken Sanders	.85	.35	.08
☐ 392	Pirates Rookies Fred Cambria Richie Zisk	1.25	.50	.12
☐ 393	Curt Motton	.85	.35	.08
☐ 394	Ken Forsch	.85	.35	.08
☐ 395	Matty Alou	1.50	.60	.15
☐ 396	Paul Lindblad	1.25	.50	.12
☐ 397	Philadelphia Phillies Team Card	2.50	1.00	.25

☐ 398 Larry Hisle	1.50	.60	.15
☐ 399 Milt Wilcox	1.25	.50	.12
☐ 400 Tony Oliva	2.00	.80	.20
☐ 401 Jim Nash	1.25	.50	.12
☐ 402 Bobby Heise	1.25	.50	.12
☐ 403 John Cumberland	1.25	.50	.12
☐ 404 Jeff Torborg	1.50	.60	.15
☐ 405 Ron Fairly	1.50	.60	.15
☐ 406 George Hendrick	1.75	.70	.17
☐ 407 Chuck Taylor	1.25	.50	.12
☐ 408 Jim Northrup	1.50	.60	.15
☐ 409 Frank Baker	1.25	.50	.12
☐ 410 Fergie Jenkins	6.50	2.75	.65
☐ 411 Bob Montgomery	1.25	.50	.12
☐ 412 Dick Kelley	1.25	.50	.12
☐ 413 White Sox Rookies Don Eddy Dave Lemonds	1.25	.50	.12
☐ 414 Bob Miller	1.25	.50	.12
☐ 415 Cookie Rojas	1.25	.50	.12
☐ 416 Johnny Edwards	1.25	.50	.12
☐ 417 Tom Hall	1.25	.50	.12
☐ 418 Tom Shopay	1.25	.50	.12
☐ 419 Jim Spencer	1.25	.50	.12
☐ 420 Steve Carlton	22.00	9.50	3.15
☐ 421 Ellie Rodriguez	1.25	.50	.12
☐ 422 Ray Lamb	1.25	.50	.12
☐ 423 Oscar Gamble	1.50	.60	.15
☐ 424 Bill Gogolewski	1.25	.50	.12
☐ 425 Ken Singleton	1.75	.70	.17
☐ 426 Singleton In Action	1.25	.50	.12
☐ 427 Tito Fuentes	1.25	.50	.12
☐ 428 Fuentes In Action	1.25	.50	.12
☐ 429 Bob Robertson	1.25	.50	.12
☐ 430 Robertson In Action	1.25	.50	.12
☐ 431 Clarence Gaston	1.75	.70	.17
☐ 432 Gaston In Action	1.25	.50	.12
☐ 433 Johnny Bench	42.00	18.00	5.50
☐ 434 Bench In Action	20.00	8.50	2.75
☐ 435 Reggie Jackson	42.00	18.00	5.50
☐ 436 Jackson In Action	20.00	8.50	2.75
☐ 437 Maury Wills	2.00	.80	.20
☐ 438 Wills In Action	1.50	.60	.15
☐ 439 Billy Williams	4.25	1.75	.42
☐ 440 Williams In Action	2.00	.80	.20
☐ 441 Thurman Munson	20.00	8.50	2.75
☐ 442 Munson In Action	10.00	4.50	1.25
☐ 443 Ken Henderson	1.25	.50	.12
☐ 444 Henderson In Action	1.25	.50	.12
☐ 445 Tom Seaver	32.00	14.25	4.75
☐ 446 Seaver In Action	16.00	6.75	2.25
☐ 447 Willie Stargell	5.00	2.25	.50
☐ 448 Stargell In Action	2.25	.90	.22
☐ 449 Bob Lemon MG	1.75	.70	.17
☐ 450 Mickey Lolich	1.75	.70	.17
☐ 451 Tony LaRussa	1.75	.70	.17
☐ 452 Ed Herrmann	1.25	.50	.12
☐ 453 Barry Lersch	1.25	.50	.12
☐ 454 Oakland A's Team Card	2.50	1.00	.25
☐ 455 Tommy Harper	1.25	.50	.12
☐ 456 Mark Belanger	1.50	.60	.15
☐ 457 Padres Rookies Darcy Fast Derrel Thomas Mike Ivie	1.25	.50	.12
☐ 458 Aurelio Monteagudo	1.25	.50	.12
☐ 459 Rick Renick	1.25	.50	.12
☐ 460 Al Downing	1.50	.60	.15
☐ 461 Tim Cullen	1.25	.50	.12
☐ 462 Rickey Clark	1.25	.50	.12
☐ 463 Bernie Carbo	1.25	.50	.12
☐ 464 Jim Roland	1.25	.50	.12
☐ 465 Gil Hodges MG	3.50	1.50	.35
☐ 466 Norm Miller	1.25	.50	.12
☐ 467 Steve Kline	1.25	.50	.12
☐ 468 Richie Scheinblum	1.25	.50	.12
☐ 469 Ron Herbel	1.25	.50	.12
☐ 470 Ray Fosse	1.50	.60	.15
☐ 471 Luke Walker	1.25	.50	.12
☐ 472 Phil Gagliano	1.25	.50	.12
☐ 473 Dan McGinn	1.25	.50	.12
☐ 474 Orioles Rookies Don Baylor Roric Harrison Johnny Oates	4.50	2.00	.45
☐ 475 Gary Nolan	1.50	.60	.15
☐ 476 Lee Richard	1.25	.50	.12
☐ 477 Tom Phoebus	1.25	.50	.12
☐ 478 Checklist 5	3.50	.35	.07
☐ 479 Don Shaw	1.25	.50	.12
☐ 480 Lee May	1.50	.60	.15
☐ 481 Billy Conigliaro	1.25	.50	.12
☐ 482 Joe Hoerner	1.25	.50	.12
☐ 483 Ken Suarez	1.25	.50	.12
☐ 484 Lum Harris MG	1.25	.50	.12
☐ 485 Phil Regan	1.25	.50	.12
☐ 486 John Lowenstein	1.25	.50	.12
☐ 487 Detroit Tigers Team Card	2.50	1.00	.25
☐ 488 Mike Nagy	1.25	.50	.12
☐ 489 Expos Rookies Terry Humphrey Keith Lampard	1.25	.50	.12
☐ 490 Dave McNally	1.50	.60	.15
☐ 491 KP: Lou Piniella	1.50	.60	.15
☐ 492 KP: Mel Stottlemyre	1.25	.50	.12
☐ 493 KP: Bob Bailey	1.25	.50	.12
☐ 494 KP: Willie Horton	1.25	.50	.12
☐ 495 KP: Bill Melton	1.25	.50	.12
☐ 496 KP: Bud Harrelson	1.25	.50	.12
☐ 497 KP: Jim Perry	1.25	.50	.12
☐ 498 KP: Brooks Robinson	2.00	.80	.20
☐ 499 Vicente Romo	1.25	.50	.12
☐ 500 Joe Torre	2.00	.80	.20
☐ 501 Pete Hamm	1.25	.50	.12

No.	Player			
☐ 502	Jackie Hernandez	1.25	.50	.12
☐ 503	Gary Peters	1.25	.50	.12
☐ 504	Ed Spiezio	1.25	.50	.12
☐ 505	Mike Marshall	1.50	.60	.15
☐ 506	Indians Rookies Terry Ley Jim Moyer Dick Tidrow	1.50	.60	.15
☐ 507	Fred Gladding	1.25	.50	.12
☐ 508	Elrod Hendricks	1.25	.50	.12
☐ 509	Don McMahon	1.25	.50	.12
☐ 510	Ted Williams MG	6.50	2.75	.65
☐ 511	Tony Taylor	1.25	.50	.12
☐ 512	Paul Popovich	1.25	.50	.12
☐ 513	Lindy McDaniel	1.25	.50	.12
☐ 514	Ted Sizemore	1.25	.50	.12
☐ 515	Bert Blyleven	11.00	5.00	1.35
☐ 516	Oscar Brown	1.25	.50	.12
☐ 517	Ken Brett	1.25	.50	.12
☐ 518	Wayne Garrett	1.25	.50	.12
☐ 519	Ted Abernathy	1.25	.50	.12
☐ 520	Larry Bowa	1.75	.70	.17
☐ 521	Alan Foster	1.25	.50	.12
☐ 522	Los Angeles Dodgers Team Card	2.50	1.00	.25
☐ 523	Chuck Dobson	1.25	.50	.12
☐ 524	Reds Rookies Ed Armbrister Mel Behney	1.25	.50	.12
☐ 525	Carlos May	1.25	.50	.12
☐ 526	Bob Bailey	2.75	1.10	.27
☐ 527	Dave Leonhard	2.75	1.10	.27
☐ 528	Ron Stone	2.75	1.10	.27
☐ 529	Dave Nelson	2.75	1.10	.27
☐ 530	Don Sutton	5.50	2.50	.55
☐ 531	Freddie Patek	3.25	1.35	.32
☐ 532	Fred Kendall	2.75	1.10	.27
☐ 533	Ralph Houk MG	3.25	1.35	.32
☐ 534	Jim Hickman	2.75	1.10	.27
☐ 535	Ed Brinkman	2.75	1.10	.27
☐ 536	Doug Rader	3.25	1.35	.32
☐ 537	Bob Locker	2.75	1.10	.27
☐ 538	Charlie Sands	2.75	1.10	.27
☐ 539	Terry Forster	3.25	1.35	.32
☐ 540	Felix Millan	2.75	1.10	.27
☐ 541	Roger Repoz	2.75	1.10	.27
☐ 542	Jack Billingham	2.75	1.10	.27
☐ 543	Duane Josephson	2.75	1.10	.27
☐ 544	Ted Martinez	2.75	1.10	.27
☐ 545	Wayne Granger	2.75	1.10	.27
☐ 546	Joe Hague	2.75	1.10	.27
☐ 547	Cleveland Indians Team Card	5.50	2.50	.55
☐ 548	Frank Reberger	2.75	1.10	.27
☐ 549	Dave May	2.75	1.10	.27
☐ 550	Brooks Robinson	21.00	9.00	3.00
☐ 551	Ollie Brown	2.75	1.10	.27
☐ 552	Brown In Action	2.75	1.10	.27
☐ 553	Wilbur Wood	2.75	1.10	.27
☐ 554	Wood In Action	2.75	1.10	.27
☐ 555	Ron Santo	3.75	1.60	.37
☐ 556	Santo In Action	3.25	1.35	.32
☐ 557	John Odom	2.75	1.10	.27
☐ 558	Odom In Action	2.75	1.10	.27
☐ 559	Pete Rose	45.00	20.00	6.75
☐ 560	Rose In Action	22.50	9.75	3.25
☐ 561	Leo Cardenas	2.75	1.10	.27
☐ 562	Cardenas In Action	2.75	1.10	.27
☐ 563	Ray Sadecki	2.75	1.10	.27
☐ 564	Sadecki In Action	2.75	1.10	.27
☐ 565	Reggie Smith	3.25	1.35	.32
☐ 566	Smith In Action	2.75	1.10	.27
☐ 567	Juan Marichal	6.50	2.75	.65
☐ 568	Marichal In Action	3.50	1.50	.35
☐ 569	Ed Kirkpatrick	2.75	1.10	.27
☐ 570	Kirkpatrick In Action	2.75	1.10	.27
☐ 571	Nate Colbert	2.75	1.10	.27
☐ 572	Colbert In Action	2.75	1.10	.27
☐ 573	Fritz Peterson	2.75	1.10	.27
☐ 574	Peterson In Action	2.75	1.10	.27
☐ 575	Al Oliver	3.50	1.50	.35
☐ 576	Leo Durocher MG	3.50	1.50	.35
☐ 577	Mike Paul	2.75	1.10	.27
☐ 578	Billy Grabarkewitz	2.75	1.10	.27
☐ 579	Doyle Alexander	3.50	1.50	.35
☐ 580	Lou Piniella	3.75	1.60	.37
☐ 581	Wade Blasingame	2.75	1.10	.27
☐ 582	Montreal Expos Team Card	5.50	2.50	.55
☐ 583	Darold Knowles	2.75	1.10	.27
☐ 584	Jerry McNertney	2.75	1.10	.27
☐ 585	George Scott	3.25	1.35	.32
☐ 586	Denis Menke	2.75	1.10	.27
☐ 587	Billy Wilson	2.75	1.10	.27
☐ 588	Jim Holt	2.75	1.10	.27
☐ 589	Hal Lanier	2.75	1.10	.27
☐ 590	Graig Nettles	3.50	1.50	.35
☐ 591	Paul Casanova	2.75	1.10	.27
☐ 592	Lew Krausse	2.75	1.10	.27
☐ 593	Rich Morales	2.75	1.10	.27
☐ 594	Jim Beauchamp	2.75	1.10	.27
☐ 595	Nolan Ryan	165.00	75.00	22.50
☐ 596	Manny Mota	3.25	1.35	.32
☐ 597	Jim Magnuson	2.75	1.10	.27
☐ 598	Hal King	2.75	1.10	.27
☐ 599	Billy Champion	2.75	1.10	.27
☐ 600	Al Kaline	22.00	9.50	3.15
☐ 601	George Stone	2.75	1.10	.27
☐ 602	Dave Bristol MG	2.75	1.10	.27
☐ 603	Jim Ray	2.75	1.10	.27
☐ 604A	Checklist 6 (copyright on back bottom right)	5.00	.50	.10
☐ 604B	Checklist 6 (copyright on back bottom left)	7.50	.75	.15

☐ 605	Nelson Briles	2.75	1.10	.27
☐ 606	Luis Melendez	2.75	1.10	.27
☐ 607	Frank Duffy	2.75	1.10	.27
☐ 608	Mike Corkins	2.75	1.10	.27
☐ 609	Tom Grieve	3.25	1.35	.32
☐ 610	Bill Stoneman	2.75	1.10	.27
☐ 611	Rich Reese	2.75	1.10	.27
☐ 612	Joe Decker	2.75	1.10	.27
☐ 613	Mike Ferraro	3.25	1.35	.32
☐ 614	Ted Uhlaender	2.75	1.10	.27
☐ 615	Steve Hargan	2.75	1.10	.27
☐ 616	Joe Ferguson	2.75	1.10	.27
☐ 617	Kansas City Royals Team Card	5.50	2.50	.55
☐ 618	Rich Robertson	2.75	1.10	.27
☐ 619	Rich McKinney	2.75	1.10	.27
☐ 620	Phil Niekro	5.50	2.50	.55
☐ 621	Commissioners Award	2.75	1.10	.27
☐ 622	MVP Award	2.75	1.10	.27
☐ 623	Cy Young Award	2.75	1.10	.27
☐ 624	Minor League Player	2.75	1.10	.27
☐ 625	Rookie of the Year	2.75	1.10	.27
☐ 626	Babe Ruth Award	3.00	1.25	.30
☐ 627	Moe Drabowsky	2.75	1.10	.27
☐ 628	Terry Crowley	2.75	1.10	.27
☐ 629	Paul Doyle	2.75	1.10	.27
☐ 630	Rich Hebner	2.75	1.10	.27
☐ 631	John Strohmayer	2.75	1.10	.27
☐ 632	Mike Hegan	2.75	1.10	.27
☐ 633	Jack Hiatt	2.75	1.10	.27
☐ 634	Dick Woodson	2.75	1.10	.27
☐ 635	Don Money	3.25	1.35	.32
☐ 636	Bill Lee	3.25	1.35	.32
☐ 637	Preston Gomez MG	2.75	1.10	.27
☐ 638	Ken Wright	2.75	1.10	.27
☐ 639	J.C. Martin	2.75	1.10	.27
☐ 640	Joe Coleman	2.75	1.10	.27
☐ 641	Mike Lum	2.75	1.10	.27
☐ 642	Dennis Riddleberger	2.75	1.10	.27
☐ 643	Russ Gibson	2.75	1.10	.27
☐ 644	Bernie Allen	2.75	1.10	.27
☐ 645	Jim Maloney	3.25	1.35	.32
☐ 646	Chico Salmon	2.75	1.10	.27
☐ 647	Bob Moose	2.75	1.10	.27
☐ 648	Jim Lyttle	2.75	1.10	.27
☐ 649	Pete Richert	2.75	1.10	.27
☐ 650	Sal Bando	3.25	1.35	.32
☐ 651	Cincinnati Reds Team Card	5.50	2.50	.55
☐ 652	Marcelino Lopez	2.75	1.10	.27
☐ 653	Jim Fairey	2.75	1.10	.27
☐ 654	Horacio Pina	2.75	1.10	.27
☐ 655	Jerry Grote	2.75	1.10	.27
☐ 656	Rudy May	2.75	1.10	.27
☐ 657	Bobby Wine	5.00	2.25	.50
☐ 658	Steve Dunning	5.00	2.25	.50
☐ 659	Bob Aspromonte	5.00	2.25	.50
☐ 660	Paul Blair	5.50	2.50	.55
☐ 661	Bill Virdon	6.00	2.50	.60
☐ 662	Stan Bahnsen	5.00	2.25	.50
☐ 663	Fran Healy	5.00	2.25	.50
☐ 664	Bobby Knoop	5.00	2.25	.50
☐ 665	Chris Short	5.00	2.25	.50
☐ 666	Hector Torres	5.00	2.25	.50
☐ 667	Ray Newman	5.00	2.25	.50
☐ 668	Texas Rangers Team Card	12.00	5.25	1.50
☐ 669	Willie Crawford	5.00	2.25	.50
☐ 670	Ken Holtzman	5.50	2.50	.55
☐ 671	Donn Clendenon	5.50	2.50	.55
☐ 672	Archie Reynolds	5.00	2.25	.50
☐ 673	Dave Marshall	5.00	2.25	.50
☐ 674	John Kennedy	5.00	2.25	.50
☐ 675	Pat Jarvis	5.00	2.25	.50
☐ 676	Danny Cater	5.00	2.25	.50
☐ 677	Ivan Murrell	5.00	2.25	.50
☐ 678	Steve Luebber	5.00	2.25	.50
☐ 679	Astros Rookies Bob Fenwick Bob Stinson	5.00	2.25	.50
☐ 680	Dave Johnson	6.00	2.50	.60
☐ 681	Bobby Pfeil	5.00	2.25	.50
☐ 682	Mike McCormick	5.50	2.50	.55
☐ 683	Steve Hovley	5.00	2.25	.50
☐ 684	Hal Breeden	5.00	2.25	.50
☐ 685	Joel Horlen	5.00	2.25	.50
☐ 686	Steve Garvey	75.00	34.00	11.25
☐ 687	Del Unser	5.00	2.25	.50
☐ 688	St. Louis Cardinals Team Card	10.00	4.50	1.25
☐ 689	Eddie Fisher	5.00	2.25	.50
☐ 690	Willie Montanez	6.00	2.50	.60
☐ 691	Curt Blefary	5.00	2.25	.50
☐ 692	Blefary In Action	5.00	2.25	.50
☐ 693	Alan Gallagher	5.00	2.25	.50
☐ 694	Gallagher In Action	5.00	2.25	.50
☐ 695	Rod Carew	100.00	45.00	15.00
☐ 696	Carew In Action	45.00	20.00	6.75
☐ 697	Jerry Koosman	12.50	5.50	1.65
☐ 698	Koosman In Action	8.00	3.50	.80
☐ 699	Bobby Murcer	12.50	5.50	1.65
☐ 700	Murcer In Action	8.00	3.50	.80
☐ 701	Jose Pagan	5.00	2.25	.50
☐ 702	Pagan In Action	5.00	2.25	.50
☐ 703	Doug Griffin	5.00	2.25	.50
☐ 704	Griffin In Action	5.00	2.25	.50
☐ 705	Pat Corrales	5.00	2.25	.50
☐ 706	Corrales In Action	5.00	2.25	.50
☐ 707	Tim Foli	5.00	2.25	.50
☐ 708	Foli In Action	5.00	2.25	.50
☐ 709	Jim Kaat	13.50	6.00	1.85
☐ 710	Kaat In Action	9.00	4.00	.90
☐ 711	Bobby Bonds	15.00	6.50	2.15
☐ 712	Bonds In Action	10.00	4.50	1.25
☐ 713	Gene Michael	5.00	2.25	.50
☐ 714	Michael In Action	5.00	2.25	.50

☐ 715 Mike Epstein .... 5.00 2.25 .50
☐ 716 Jesus Alou .... 5.00 2.25 .50
☐ 717 Bruce Dal Canton .... 5.00 2.25 .50
☐ 718 Del Rice MG .... 5.00 2.25 .50
☐ 719 Cesar Geronimo .... 5.00 2.25 .50
☐ 720 Sam McDowell .... 5.50 2.50 .55
☐ 721 Eddie Leon .... 5.00 2.25 .50
☐ 722 Bill Sudakis .... 5.00 2.25 .50
☐ 723 Al Santorini .... 5.00 2.25 .50
☐ 724 AL Rookie Pitchers ...... 5.50 2.50 .55
John Curtis
Rich Hinton
Mickey Scott
☐ 725 Dick McAuliffe .... 5.50 2.50 .55
☐ 726 Dick Selma .... 5.00 2.25 .50
☐ 727 Jose Laboy .... 5.00 2.25 .50
☐ 728 Gail Hopkins .... 5.00 2.25 .50
☐ 729 Bob Veale .... 5.50 2.50 .55
☐ 730 Rick Monday .... 5.50 2.50 .55
☐ 731 Baltimore Orioles 10.00 4.50 1.25
Team Card
☐ 732 George Culver .... 5.00 2.25 .50
☐ 733 Jim Ray Hart .... 5.50 2.50 .55
☐ 734 Bob Burda .... 5.00 2.25 .50
☐ 735 Diego Segui .... 5.00 2.25 .50
☐ 736 Bill Russell .... 6.50 2.75 .65
☐ 737 Len Randle .... 5.50 2.50 .55
☐ 738 Jim Merritt .... 5.00 2.25 .50
☐ 739 Don Mason .... 5.00 2.25 .50
☐ 740 Rico Carty .... 6.00 2.50 .60
☐ 741 Rookie First Basemen . 8.00 3.50 .80
Tom Hutton
John Milner
Rick Miller
☐ 742 Jim Rooker .... 5.50 2.50 .55
☐ 743 Cesar Gutierrez .... 5.00 2.25 .50
☐ 744 Jim Slaton .... 5.00 2.25 .50
☐ 745 Julian Javier .... 5.00 2.25 .50
☐ 746 Lowell Palmer .... 5.00 2.25 .50
☐ 747 Jim Stewart .... 5.00 2.25 .50
☐ 748 Phil Hennigan .... 5.00 2.25 .50
☐ 749 Walter Alston MG .... 9.00 4.00 .90
☐ 750 Willie Horton .... 6.00 2.50 .60
☐ 751 Steve Carlton TR 50.00 22.50 7.50
☐ 752 Joe Morgan TR 42.00 18.00 5.50
☐ 753 Denny McLain TR 11.00 5.00 1.35
☐ 754 Frank Robinson TR ... 33.00 15.00 5.00
☐ 755 Jim Fregosi TR .... 6.00 2.50 .60
☐ 756 Rick Wise TR .... 5.50 2.50 .55
☐ 757 Jose Cardenal TR .... 5.50 2.50 .55
☐ 758 Gil Garrido .... 5.00 2.25 .50
☐ 759 Chris Cannizzaro .... 5.00 2.25 .50
☐ 760 Bill Mazeroski .... 7.00 3.00 .70
☐ 761 Rookie Outfielders 18.00 7.50 2.50
Ben Oglivie
Ron Cey
Bernie Williams
☐ 762 Wayne Simpson .... 5.00 2.25 .50
☐ 763 Ron Hansen .... 5.00 2.25 .50
☐ 764 Dusty Baker .... 7.50 3.25 .75
☐ 765 Ken McMullen .... 5.00 2.25 .50
☐ 766 Steve Hamilton .... 5.00 2.25 .50
☐ 767 Tom McCraw .... 5.00 2.25 .50
☐ 768 Denny Doyle .... 5.00 2.25 .50
☐ 769 Jack Aker .... 5.00 2.25 .50
☐ 770 Jim Wynn .... 6.00 2.50 .60
☐ 771 San Francisco Giants 10.00 4.50 1.25
Team Card
☐ 772 Ken Tatum .... 5.00 2.25 .50
☐ 773 Ron Brand .... 5.00 2.25 .50
☐ 774 Luis Alvarado .... 5.00 2.25 .50
☐ 775 Jerry Reuss .... 6.00 2.50 .60
☐ 776 Bill Voss .... 5.00 2.25 .50
☐ 777 Hoyt Wilhelm 17.00 7.25 2.50
☐ 778 Twins Rookies .... 7.50 3.25 .75
Vic Albury
Rick Dempsey
Jim Strickland
☐ 779 Tony Cloninger .... 5.00 2.25 .50
☐ 780 Dick Green .... 5.00 2.25 .50
☐ 781 Jim McAndrew .... 5.00 2.25 .50
☐ 782 Larry Stahl .... 5.00 2.25 .50
☐ 783 Les Cain .... 5.00 2.25 .50
☐ 784 Ken Aspromonte .... 5.00 2.25 .50
☐ 785 Vic Davalillo .... 5.50 2.50 .55
☐ 786 Chuck Brinkman .... 5.00 2.25 .50
☐ 787 Ron Reed .... 6.50 2.75 .55

1973 Topps

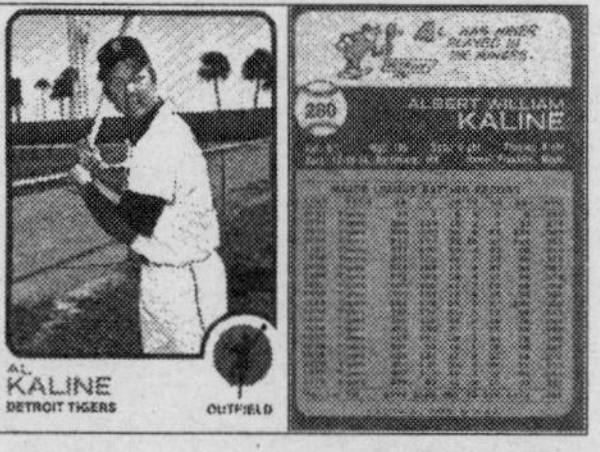

The cards in this 660-card set measure 2 1/2" by 3 1/2". The 1973 Topps set marked the last year in which Topps marketed baseball cards in consecutive series. The last series (529-660) is more difficult to obtain. Beginning in 1974, all Topps cards were printed at the

same time, thus eliminating the "high number" factor. The set features team leader cards with small individual pictures of the coaching staff members and a larger picture of the manager. The "background" variations below with respect to these leader cards are subtle and are best understood after a side-by-side comparison of the two varieties. An "All-Time Leaders" series (471-478) appeared for the first time in this set. Kid Pictures appeared again for the second year in a row (341-346). Other topical subsets within the set included League Leaders (61-68), Playoffs cards (201-202), World Series cards (203-210), and Rookie Prospects (601-616). The key rookie cards in this set are Bob Boone, Dwight Evans, and Mike Schmidt.

	NRMT	VG-E	GOOD
COMPLETE SET (660)	1150.00	450.00	135.00
COMMON PLAYER (1-132)	.45	.18	.04
COMMON PLAYER (133-264)	.45	.18	.04
COMMON PLAYER (265-396)	.60	.25	.06
COMMON PLAYER (397-528)	1.25	.50	.12
COMMON PLAYER (529-660)	2.75	1.10	.27

	NRMT	VG-E	GOOD
☐ 1 All-Time HR Leaders Babe Ruth 714 Hank Aaron 673 Willie Mays 654	25.00	6.00	1.25
☐ 2 Rich Hebner	.60	.25	.06
☐ 3 Jim Lonborg	.75	.30	.07
☐ 4 John Milner	.45	.18	.04
☐ 5 Ed Brinkman	.45	.18	.04
☐ 6 Mac Scarce	.45	.18	.04
☐ 7 Texas Rangers Team Card	1.00	.40	.10
☐ 8 Tom Hall	.45	.18	.04
☐ 9 Johnny Oates	.75	.30	.07
☐ 10 Don Sutton	2.50	1.00	.25
☐ 11 Chris Chambliss	.75	.30	.07
☐ 12A Padres Leaders Don Zimmer MG Dave Garcia CO Johnny Podres CO Bob Skinner CO Whitey Wietelmann CO (Podres no right ear)	.75	.30	.07
☐ 12B Padres Leaders (Podres has right ear)	1.50	.60	.15
☐ 13 George Hendrick	.75	.30	.07
☐ 14 Sonny Siebert	.45	.18	.04
☐ 15 Ralph Garr	.60	.25	.06
☐ 16 Steve Braun	.45	.18	.04
☐ 17 Fred Gladding	.45	.18	.04
☐ 18 Leroy Stanton	.45	.18	.04
☐ 19 Tim Foli	.45	.18	.04
☐ 20 Stan Bahnsen	.45	.18	.04
☐ 21 Randy Hundley	.45	.18	.04
☐ 22 Ted Abernathy	.45	.18	.04
☐ 23 Dave Kingman	1.50	.60	.15
☐ 24 Al Santorini	.45	.18	.04
☐ 25 Roy White	.75	.30	.07
☐ 26 Pittsburgh Pirates Team Card	1.00	.40	.10
☐ 27 Bill Gogolewski	.45	.18	.04
☐ 28 Hal McRae	1.00	.40	.10
☐ 29 Tony Taylor	.45	.18	.04
☐ 30 Tug McGraw	1.00	.40	.10
☐ 31 Buddy Bell	3.25	1.35	.32
☐ 32 Fred Norman	.45	.18	.04
☐ 33 Jim Breazeale	.45	.18	.04
☐ 34 Pat Dobson	.45	.18	.04
☐ 35 Willie Davis	.60	.25	.06
☐ 36 Steve Barber	.45	.18	.04
☐ 37 Bill Robinson	.75	.30	.07
☐ 38 Mike Epstein	.45	.18	.04
☐ 39 Dave Roberts	.45	.18	.04
☐ 40 Reggie Smith	.75	.30	.07
☐ 41 Tom Walker	.45	.18	.04
☐ 42 Mike Andrews	.45	.18	.04
☐ 43 Randy Moffitt	.45	.18	.04
☐ 44 Rick Monday	.60	.25	.06
☐ 45 Ellie Rodriguez UER (photo actually John Felske)	.45	.18	.04
☐ 46 Lindy McDaniel	.45	.18	.04
☐ 47 Luis Melendez	.45	.18	.04
☐ 48 Paul Splittorff	.45	.18	.04
☐ 49A Twins Leaders Frank Quilici MG Vern Morgan CO Bob Rodgers CO Ralph Rowe CO Al Worthington CO (solid backgrounds)	.75	.30	.07
☐ 49B Twins Leaders (natural backgrounds)	1.50	.60	.15
☐ 50 Roberto Clemente	30.00	13.50	4.50
☐ 51 Chuck Seelbach	.45	.18	.04
☐ 52 Denis Menke	.45	.18	.04
☐ 53 Steve Dunning	.45	.18	.04
☐ 54 Checklist 1	2.25	.25	.05
☐ 55 Jon Matlack	.60	.25	.06
☐ 56 Merv Rettenmund	.45	.18	.04
☐ 57 Derrel Thomas	.45	.18	.04
☐ 58 Mike Paul	.45	.18	.04
☐ 59 Steve Yeager	1.00	.40	.10
☐ 60 Ken Holtzman	.60	.25	.06
☐ 61 Batting Leaders Billy Williams Rod Carew	2.00	.80	.20
☐ 62 Home Run Leaders Johnny Bench Dick Allen	2.00	.80	.20
☐ 63 RBI Leaders	2.00	.80	.20

Card			
Johnny Bench			
Dick Allen			
☐ 64 Stolen Base Leaders	1.50	.60	.15
Lou Brock			
Bert Campaneris			
☐ 65 ERA Leaders	1.50	.60	.15
Steve Carlton			
Luis Tiant			
☐ 66 Victory Leaders	1.50	.60	.15
Steve Carlton			
Gaylord Perry			
Wilbur Wood			
☐ 67 Strikeout Leaders	6.50	2.75	.65
Steve Carlton			
Nolan Ryan			
☐ 68 Leading Firemen	1.00	.40	.10
Clay Carroll			
Sparky Lyle			
☐ 69 Phil Gagliano	.45	.18	.04
☐ 70 Milt Pappas	.60	.25	.06
☐ 71 Johnny Briggs	.45	.18	.04
☐ 72 Ron Reed	.45	.18	.04
☐ 73 Ed Herrmann	.45	.18	.04
☐ 74 Billy Champion	.45	.18	.04
☐ 75 Vada Pinson	.75	.30	.07
☐ 76 Doug Rader	.75	.30	.07
☐ 77 Mike Torrez	.45	.18	.04
☐ 78 Richie Scheinblum	.45	.18	.04
☐ 79 Jim Willoughby	.45	.18	.04
☐ 80 Tony Oliva UER	1.25	.50	.12
(Minnseota on front)			
☐ 81A Cubs Leaders	.75	.30	.07
Whitey Lockman MG			
Hank Aguirre CO			
Ernie Banks CO			
Larry Jansen CO			
Pete Reiser CO			
(solid backgrounds)			
☐ 81B Cubs Leaders	1.50	.60	.15
(natural backgrounds)			
☐ 82 Fritz Peterson	.45	.18	.04
☐ 83 Leron Lee	.45	.18	.04
☐ 84 Rollie Fingers	5.00	2.25	.50
☐ 85 Ted Simmons	1.75	.70	.17
☐ 86 Tom McCraw	.45	.18	.04
☐ 87 Ken Boswell	.45	.18	.04
☐ 88 Mickey Stanley	.60	.25	.06
☐ 89 Jack Billingham	.45	.18	.04
☐ 90 Brooks Robinson	6.00	2.50	.60
☐ 91 Los Angeles Dodgers	1.00	.40	.10
Team Card			
☐ 92 Jerry Bell	.45	.18	.04
☐ 93 Jesus Alou	.45	.18	.04
☐ 94 Dick Billings	.45	.18	.04
☐ 95 Steve Blass	.45	.18	.04
☐ 96 Doug Griffin	.45	.18	.04
☐ 97 Willie Montanez	.45	.18	.04
☐ 98 Dick Woodson	.45	.18	.04
☐ 99 Carl Taylor	.45	.18	.04
☐ 100 Hank Aaron	22.00	9.50	3.15
☐ 101 Ken Henderson	.45	.18	.04
☐ 102 Rudy May	.45	.18	.04
☐ 103 Celerino Sanchez	.45	.18	.04
☐ 104 Reggie Cleveland	.45	.18	.04
☐ 105 Carlos May	.45	.18	.04
☐ 106 Terry Humphrey	.45	.18	.04
☐ 107 Phil Hennigan	.45	.18	.04
☐ 108 Bill Russell	.75	.30	.07
☐ 109 Doyle Alexander	.60	.25	.06
☐ 110 Bob Watson	.60	.25	.06
☐ 111 Dave Nelson	.45	.18	.04
☐ 112 Gary Ross	.45	.18	.04
☐ 113 Jerry Grote	.45	.18	.04
☐ 114 Lynn McGlothen	.45	.18	.04
☐ 115 Ron Santo	.75	.30	.07
☐ 116A Yankees Leaders	.75	.30	.07
Ralph Houk MG			
Jim Hegan CO			
Elston Howard CO			
Dick Howser CO			
Jim Turner CO			
(solid backgrounds)			
☐ 116B Yankees Leaders	1.50	.60	.15
(natural backgrounds)			
☐ 117 Ramon Hernandez	.45	.18	.04
☐ 118 John Mayberry	.75	.30	.07
☐ 119 Larry Bowa	1.00	.40	.10
☐ 120 Joe Coleman	.45	.18	.04
☐ 121 Dave Rader	.45	.18	.04
☐ 122 Jim Strickland	.45	.18	.04
☐ 123 Sandy Alomar	.45	.18	.04
☐ 124 Jim Hardin	.45	.18	.04
☐ 125 Ron Fairly	.45	.18	.04
☐ 126 Jim Brewer	.45	.18	.04
☐ 127 Milwaukee Brewers	1.00	.40	.10
Team Card			
☐ 128 Ted Sizemore	.45	.18	.04
☐ 129 Terry Forster	.60	.25	.06
☐ 130 Pete Rose	18.00	7.50	2.50
☐ 131A Red Sox Leaders	.75	.30	.07
Eddie Kasko MG			
Doug Camilli CO			
Don Lenhardt CO			
Eddie Popowski CO			
(no right ear)			
Lee Stange CO			
☐ 131B Red Sox Leaders	1.50	.60	.15
(Popowski has right			
ear showing)			
☐ 132 Matty Alou	.45	.18	.04
☐ 133 Dave Roberts	.45	.18	.04
☐ 134 Milt Wilcox	.45	.18	.04
☐ 135 Lee May UER	.75	.30	.07
(career average .000)			
☐ 136A Orioles Leaders	.75	.30	.07
Earl Weaver MG			

George Bamberger CO Jim Frey CO Billy Hunter CO George Staller CO (orange backgrounds)			
☐ 136B Orioles Leaders 1.50	.60	.15	
(dark pale backgrounds)			
☐ 137 Jim Beauchamp .... .45	.18	.04	
☐ 138 Horacio Pina .... .45	.18	.04	
☐ 139 Carmen Fanzone .... .45	.18	.04	
☐ 140 Lou Piniella 1.00	.40	.10	
☐ 141 Bruce Kison .... .45	.18	.04	
☐ 142 Thurman Munson 10.00	4.50	1.25	
☐ 143 John Curtis .... .45	.18	.04	
☐ 144 Marty Perez .... .45	.18	.04	
☐ 145 Bobby Bonds 1.75	.70	.17	
☐ 146 Woodie Fryman .... .45	.18	.04	
☐ 147 Mike Anderson .... .45	.18	.04	
☐ 148 Dave Goltz .... .45	.18	.04	
☐ 149 Ron Hunt .... .45	.18	.04	
☐ 150 Wilbur Wood .... .60	.25	.06	
☐ 151 Wes Parker .... .60	.25	.06	
☐ 152 Dave May .... .45	.18	.04	
☐ 153 Al Hrabosky .... .75	.30	.07	
☐ 154 Jeff Torborg .... .75	.30	.07	
☐ 155 Sal Bando .... .75	.30	.07	
☐ 156 Cesar Geronimo .... .45	.18	.04	
☐ 157 Denny Riddleberger ...... .45	.18	.04	
☐ 158 Houston Astros 1.00	.40	.10	
Team Card			
☐ 159 Clarence Gaston .... .75	.30	.07	
☐ 160 Jim Palmer 11.00	5.00	1.35	
☐ 161 Ted Martinez .... .45	.18	.04	
☐ 162 Pete Broberg .... .45	.18	.04	
☐ 163 Vic Davalillo .... .45	.18	.04	
☐ 164 Monty Montgomery .... .45	.18	.04	
☐ 165 Luis Aparicio 2.75	1.10	.27	
☐ 166 Terry Harmon .... .45	.18	.04	
☐ 167 Steve Stone .... .60	.25	.06	
☐ 168 Jim Northrup .... .60	.25	.06	
☐ 169 Ron Schueler .... .45	.18	.04	
☐ 170 Harmon Killebrew 4.50	2.00	.45	
☐ 171 Bernie Carbo .... .45	.18	.04	
☐ 172 Steve Kline .... .45	.18	.04	
☐ 173 Hal Breeden .... .45	.18	.04	
☐ 174 Rich Gossage 15.00	6.50	2.15	
☐ 175 Frank Robinson 5.00	2.25	.50	
☐ 176 Chuck Taylor .... .45	.18	.04	
☐ 177 Bill Plummer .... .75	.30	.07	
☐ 178 Don Rose .... .45	.18	.04	
☐ 179A A's Leaders .... .75	.30	.07	
Dick Williams MG Jerry Adair CO Vern Hoscheit CO Irv Noren CO Wes Stock CO (Hoscheit left ear showing)			
☐ 179B A's Leaders 1.50	.60	.15	
(Hoscheit left ear not showing)			
☐ 180 Fergie Jenkins 4.00	1.75	.40	
☐ 181 Jack Brohamer .... .45	.18	.04	
☐ 182 Mike Caldwell .... .45	.18	.04	
☐ 183 Don Buford .... .45	.18	.04	
☐ 184 Jerry Koosman 1.00	.40	.10	
☐ 185 Jim Wynn .... .75	.30	.07	
☐ 186 Bill Fahey .... .45	.18	.04	
☐ 187 Luke Walker .... .45	.18	.04	
☐ 188 Cookie Rojas .... .45	.18	.04	
☐ 189 Greg Luzinski 1.00	.40	.10	
☐ 190 Bob Gibson 5.00	2.25	.50	
☐ 191 Detroit Tigers 1.00	.40	.10	
Team Card			
☐ 192 Pat Jarvis .... .45	.18	.04	
☐ 193 Carlton Fisk 36.00	16.25	5.50	
☐ 194 Jorge Orta .... .45	.18	.04	
☐ 195 Clay Carroll .... .45	.18	.04	
☐ 196 Ken McMullen .... .45	.18	.04	
☐ 197 Ed Goodson .... .45	.18	.04	
☐ 198 Horace Clarke .... .45	.18	.04	
☐ 199 Bert Blyleven 4.50	2.00	.45	
☐ 200 Billy Williams 3.50	1.50	.35	
☐ 201 A.L. Playoffs 1.00	.40	.10	
A's over Tigers; Hendrick scores winning run			
☐ 202 N.L. Playoffs 1.00	.40	.10	
Reds over Pirates Foster's run decides			
☐ 203 World Series Game 1 .. 1.00	.40	.10	
Tenace the Menace			
☐ 204 World Series Game 2 .. 1.00	.40	.10	
A's two straight			
☐ 205 World Series Game 3 .. 1.00	.40	.10	
Reds win squeeker			
☐ 206 World Series Game 4 .. 1.00	.40	.10	
Tenace singles in ninth			
☐ 207 World Series Game 5 .. 1.00	.40	.10	
Odom out at plate			
☐ 208 World Series Game 6 .. 1.00	.40	.10	
Reds' slugging ties series			
☐ 209 World Series Game 7 .. 1.00	.40	.10	
Campy stars winning rally			
☐ 210 World Series Summary 1.00	.40	.10	
World champions: A's Win			
☐ 211 Balor Moore .... .45	.18	.04	
☐ 212 Joe Lahoud .... .45	.18	.04	
☐ 213 Steve Garvey 15.00	6.50	2.15	
☐ 214 Steve Hamilton .... .45	.18	.04	
☐ 215 Dusty Baker .... .75	.30	.07	

☐ 216	Toby Harrah	.75	.30	.07
☐ 217	Don Wilson	.45	.18	.04
☐ 218	Aurelio Rodriguez	.45	.18	.04
☐ 219	St. Louis Cardinals Team Card	1.00	.40	.10
☐ 220	Nolan Ryan	70.00	32.00	10.50
☐ 221	Fred Kendall	.45	.18	.04
☐ 222	Rob Gardner	.45	.18	.04
☐ 223	Bud Harrelson	.60	.25	.06
☐ 224	Bill Lee	.45	.18	.04
☐ 225	Al Oliver	1.00	.40	.10
☐ 226	Ray Fosse	.45	.18	.04
☐ 227	Wayne Twitchell	.45	.18	.04
☐ 228	Bobby Darwin	.45	.18	.04
☐ 229	Roric Harrison	.45	.18	.04
☐ 230	Joe Morgan	5.00	2.25	.50
☐ 231	Bill Parsons	.45	.18	.04
☐ 232	Ken Singleton	.75	.30	.07
☐ 233	Ed Kirkpatrick	.45	.18	.04
☐ 234	Bill North	.45	.18	.04
☐ 235	Jim Hunter	3.75	1.60	.37
☐ 236	Tito Fuentes	.45	.18	.04
☐ 237A	Braves Leaders Eddie Mathews MG Lew Burdette CO Jim Busby CO Roy Hartsfield CO Ken Silvestri CO (Burdette right ear showing)	1.25	.50	.12
☐ 237B	Braves Leaders (Burdette right ear not showing)	2.50	1.00	.25
☐ 238	Tony Muser	.45	.18	.04
☐ 239	Pete Richert	.45	.18	.04
☐ 240	Bobby Murcer	.75	.30	.07
☐ 241	Dwain Anderson	.45	.18	.04
☐ 242	George Culver	.45	.18	.04
☐ 243	California Angels Team Card	1.00	.40	.10
☐ 244	Ed Acosta	.45	.18	.04
☐ 245	Carl Yastrzemski	15.00	6.50	2.15
☐ 246	Ken Sanders	.45	.18	.04
☐ 247	Del Unser	.45	.18	.04
☐ 248	Jerry Johnson	.45	.18	.04
☐ 249	Larry Biittner	.45	.18	.04
☐ 250	Manny Sanguillen	.75	.30	.07
☐ 251	Roger Nelson	.45	.18	.04
☐ 252A	Giants Leaders Charlie Fox MG Joe Amalfitano CO Andy Gilbert CO Don McMahon CO John McNamara CO (orange backgrounds)	.75	.30	.07
☐ 252B	Giants Leaders (dark pale backgrounds)	1.50	.60	.15
☐ 253	Mark Belanger	.75	.30	.07
☐ 254	Bill Stoneman	.45	.18	.04
☐ 255	Reggie Jackson	25.00	11.00	3.50
☐ 256	Chris Zachary	.45	.18	.04
☐ 257A	Mets Leaders Yogi Berra MG Roy McMillan CO Joe Pignatano CO Rube Walker CO Eddie Yost CO (orange backgrounds)	1.75	.70	.17
☐ 257B	Mets Leaders (dark pale backgrounds)	3.00	1.25	.30
☐ 258	Tommy John	1.50	.60	.15
☐ 259	Jim Holt	.45	.18	.04
☐ 260	Gary Nolan	.45	.18	.04
☐ 261	Pat Kelly	.45	.18	.04
☐ 262	Jack Aker	.45	.18	.04
☐ 263	George Scott	.60	.25	.06
☐ 264	Checklist 2	2.25	.25	.05
☐ 265	Gene Michael	.80	.35	.08
☐ 266	Mike Lum	.60	.25	.06
☐ 267	Lloyd Allen	.60	.25	.06
☐ 268	Jerry Morales	.60	.25	.06
☐ 269	Tim McCarver	1.00	.40	.10
☐ 270	Luis Tiant	1.00	.40	.10
☐ 271	Tom Hutton	.60	.25	.06
☐ 272	Ed Farmer	.60	.25	.06
☐ 273	Chris Speier	.60	.25	.06
☐ 274	Darold Knowles	.60	.25	.06
☐ 275	Tony Perez	3.00	1.25	.30
☐ 276	Joe Lovitto	.60	.25	.06
☐ 277	Bob Miller	.60	.25	.06
☐ 278	Baltimore Orioles Team Card	1.25	.50	.12
☐ 279	Mike Strahler	.60	.25	.06
☐ 280	Al Kaline	5.50	2.50	.55
☐ 281	Mike Jorgensen	.60	.25	.06
☐ 282	Steve Hovley	.60	.25	.06
☐ 283	Ray Sadecki	.60	.25	.06
☐ 284	Glenn Borgmann	.60	.25	.06
☐ 285	Don Kessinger	.80	.35	.08
☐ 286	Frank Linzy	.60	.25	.06
☐ 287	Eddie Leon	.60	.25	.06
☐ 288	Gary Gentry	.60	.25	.06
☐ 289	Bob Oliver	.60	.25	.06
☐ 290	Cesar Cedeno	.80	.35	.08
☐ 291	Rogelio Moret	.60	.25	.06
☐ 292	Jose Cruz	.80	.35	.08
☐ 293	Bernie Allen	.60	.25	.06
☐ 294	Steve Arlin	.60	.25	.06
☐ 295	Bert Campaneris	.80	.35	.08
☐ 296	Reds Leaders Sparky Anderson MG Alex Grammas CO Ted Kluszewski CO George Scherger CO	1.00	.40	.10

Larry Shepard CO
☐ 297 Walt Williams .60 .25 .06
☐ 298 Ron Bryant .60 .25 .06
☐ 299 Ted Ford .60 .25 .06
☐ 300 Steve Carlton 13.50 6.00 1.85
☐ 301 Billy Grabarkewitz .60 .25 .06
☐ 302 Terry Crowley .60 .25 .06
☐ 303 Nelson Briles .60 .25 .06
☐ 304 Duke Sims .60 .25 .06
☐ 305 Willie Mays 28.00 12.50 4.00
☐ 306 Tom Burgmeier .60 .25 .06
☐ 307 Boots Day .60 .25 .06
☐ 308 Skip Lockwood .60 .25 .06
☐ 309 Paul Popovich .60 .25 .06
☐ 310 Dick Allen 1.25 .50 .12
☐ 311 Joe Decker .60 .25 .06
☐ 312 Oscar Brown .60 .25 .06
☐ 313 Jim Ray .60 .25 .06
☐ 314 Ron Swoboda .80 .35 .08
☐ 315 John Odom .60 .25 .06
☐ 316 San Diego Padres 1.25 .50 .12
Team Card
☐ 317 Danny Cater .60 .25 .06
☐ 318 Jim McGlothlin .60 .25 .06
☐ 319 Jim Spencer .60 .25 .06
☐ 320 Lou Brock 5.00 2.25 .50
☐ 321 Rich Hinton .60 .25 .06
☐ 322 Garry Maddox 1.00 .40 .10
☐ 323 Tigers Leaders 1.00 .40 .10
Billy Martin MG
Art Fowler CO
Charlie Silvera CO
Dick Tracewski CO
☐ 324 Al Downing .80 .35 .08
☐ 325 Boog Powell 1.00 .40 .10
☐ 326 Darrell Brandon .60 .25 .06
☐ 327 John Lowenstein .60 .25 .06
☐ 328 Bill Bonham .60 .25 .06
☐ 329 Ed Kranepool .80 .35 .08
☐ 330 Rod Carew 16.00 6.75 2.25
☐ 331 Carl Morton .60 .25 .06
☐ 332 John Felske .60 .25 .06
☐ 333 Gene Clines .60 .25 .06
☐ 334 Freddie Patek .60 .25 .06
☐ 335 Bob Tolan .60 .25 .06
☐ 336 Tom Bradley .60 .25 .06
☐ 337 Dave Duncan .60 .25 .06
☐ 338 Checklist 3 2.25 .25 .05
☐ 339 Dick Tidrow .60 .25 .06
☐ 340 Nate Colbert .60 .25 .06
☐ 341 KP: Jim Palmer 1.75 .70 .17
☐ 342 KP: Sam McDowell .60 .25 .06
☐ 343 KP: Bobby Murcer 1.00 .40 .10
☐ 344 KP: Jim Hunter 1.25 .50 .12
☐ 345 KP: Chris Speier .60 .25 .06
☐ 346 KP: Gaylord Perry 1.25 .50 .12
☐ 347 Kansas City Royals 1.25 .50 .12
Team Card
☐ 348 Rennie Stennett .60 .25 .06
☐ 349 Dick McAuliffe .60 .25 .06
☐ 350 Tom Seaver 24.00 10.50 3.50
☐ 351 Jimmy Stewart .60 .25 .06
☐ 352 Don Stanhouse .60 .25 .06
☐ 353 Steve Brye .60 .25 .06
☐ 354 Billy Parker .60 .25 .06
☐ 355 Mike Marshall .60 .25 .06
☐ 356 White Sox Leaders 1.00 .40 .10
Chuck Tanner MG
Joe Lonnett CO
Jim Mahoney CO
Al Monchak CO
Johnny Sain CO
☐ 357 Ross Grimsley .60 .25 .06
☐ 358 Jim Nettles .60 .25 .06
☐ 359 Cecil Upshaw .60 .25 .06
☐ 360 Joe Rudi UER 1.00 .40 .10
(photo actually
Gene Tenace)
☐ 361 Fran Healy .60 .25 .06
☐ 362 Eddie Watt .60 .25 .06
☐ 363 Jackie Hernandez .60 .25 .06
☐ 364 Rick Wise .60 .25 .06
☐ 365 Rico Petrocelli .80 .35 .08
☐ 366 Brock Davis .60 .25 .06
☐ 367 Burt Hooton .80 .35 .08
☐ 368 Bill Buckner 1.00 .40 .10
☐ 369 Lerrin LaGrow .60 .25 .06
☐ 370 Willie Stargell 5.00 2.25 .50
☐ 371 Mike Kekich .60 .25 .06
☐ 372 Oscar Gamble .80 .35 .08
☐ 373 Clyde Wright .60 .25 .06
☐ 374 Darrell Evans 1.00 .40 .10
☐ 375 Larry Dierker .60 .25 .06
☐ 376 Frank Duffy .60 .25 .06
☐ 377 Expos Leaders 1.00 .40 .10
Gene Mauch MG
Dave Bristol CO
Larry Doby CO
Cal McLish CO
Jerry Zimmerman CO
☐ 378 Len Randle .60 .25 .06
☐ 379 Cy Acosta .60 .25 .06
☐ 380 Johnny Bench 24.00 10.50 3.50
☐ 381 Vicente Romo .60 .25 .06
☐ 382 Mike Hegan .60 .25 .06
☐ 383 Diego Segui .60 .25 .06
☐ 384 Don Baylor 1.75 .70 .17
☐ 385 Jim Perry .80 .35 .08
☐ 386 Don Money .60 .25 .06
☐ 387 Jim Barr .60 .25 .06
☐ 388 Ben Oglivie .80 .35 .08
☐ 389 New York Mets 2.00 .80 .20
Team Card
☐ 390 Mickey Lolich 1.00 .40 .10
☐ 391 Lee Lacy .80 .35 .08
☐ 392 Dick Drago .60 .25 .06

☐ 393 Jose Cardenal .60 .25 .06
☐ 394 Sparky Lyle 1.00 .40 .10
☐ 395 Roger Metzger .60 .25 .06
☐ 396 Grant Jackson .60 .25 .06
☐ 397 Dave Cash 1.25 .50 .12
☐ 398 Rich Hand 1.25 .50 .12
☐ 399 George Foster 2.00 .80 .20
☐ 400 Gaylord Perry 4.25 1.75 .42
☐ 401 Clyde Mashore 1.25 .50 .12
☐ 402 Jack Hiatt 1.25 .50 .12
☐ 403 Sonny Jackson 1.25 .50 .12
☐ 404 Chuck Brinkman 1.25 .50 .12
☐ 405 Cesar Tovar 1.25 .50 .12
☐ 406 Paul Lindblad 1.25 .50 .12
☐ 407 Felix Millan 1.25 .50 .12
☐ 408 Jim Colborn 1.25 .50 .12
☐ 409 Ivan Murrell 1.25 .50 .12
☐ 410 Willie McCovey 5.00 2.25 .50
(Bench behind plate)
☐ 411 Ray Corbin 1.25 .50 .12
☐ 412 Manny Mota 1.50 .60 .15
☐ 413 Tom Timmermann 1.25 .50 .12
☐ 414 Ken Rudolph 1.25 .50 .12
☐ 415 Marty Pattin 1.25 .50 .12
☐ 416 Paul Schaal 1.25 .50 .12
☐ 417 Scipio Spinks 1.25 .50 .12
☐ 418 Bob Grich 1.50 .60 .15
☐ 419 Casey Cox 1.25 .50 .12
☐ 420 Tommie Agee 1.25 .50 .12
☐ 421A Angels Leaders 1.50 .60 .15
Bobby Winkles MG
Tom Morgan CO
Salty Parker CO
Jimmie Reese CO
John Roseboro CO
(orange backgrounds)
☐ 421B Angels Leaders 3.00 1.25 .30
(dark pale
backgrounds)
☐ 422 Bob Robertson 1.25 .50 .12
☐ 423 Johnny Jeter 1.25 .50 .12
☐ 424 Denny Doyle 1.25 .50 .12
☐ 425 Alex Johnson 1.25 .50 .12
☐ 426 Dave LaRoche 1.25 .50 .12
☐ 427 Rick Auerbach 1.25 .50 .12
☐ 428 Wayne Simpson 1.25 .50 .12
☐ 429 Jim Fairey 1.25 .50 .12
☐ 430 Vida Blue 1.50 .60 .15
☐ 431 Gerry Moses 1.25 .50 .12
☐ 432 Dan Frisella 1.25 .50 .12
☐ 433 Willie Horton 1.50 .60 .15
☐ 434 San Francisco Giants 2.50 1.00 .25
Team Card
☐ 435 Rico Carty 1.75 .70 .17
☐ 436 Jim McAndrew 1.25 .50 .12
☐ 437 John Kennedy 1.25 .50 .12
☐ 438 Enzo Hernandez 1.25 .50 .12
☐ 439 Eddie Fisher 1.25 .50 .12
☐ 440 Glenn Beckert 1.50 .60 .15
☐ 441 Gail Hopkins 1.25 .50 .12
☐ 442 Dick Dietz 1.25 .50 .12
☐ 443 Danny Thompson 1.25 .50 .12
☐ 444 Ken Brett 1.25 .50 .12
☐ 445 Ken Berry 1.25 .50 .12
☐ 446 Jerry Reuss 1.50 .60 .15
☐ 447 Joe Hague 1.25 .50 .12
☐ 448 John Hiller 1.50 .60 .15
☐ 449A Indians Leaders 1.50 .60 .15
Ken Aspromonte MG
Rocky Colavito CO
Joe Lutz CO
Warren Spahn CO
(Spahn's right
ear pointed)
☐ 449B Indians Leaders 3.00 1.25 .30
(Spahn's right
ear round)
☐ 450 Joe Torre 1.75 .70 .17
☐ 451 John Vukovich 1.25 .50 .12
☐ 452 Paul Casanova 1.25 .50 .12
☐ 453 Checklist 4 2.25 .25 .05
☐ 454 Tom Haller 1.25 .50 .12
☐ 455 Bill Melton 1.25 .50 .12
☐ 456 Dick Green 1.25 .50 .12
☐ 457 John Strohmayer 1.25 .50 .12
☐ 458 Jim Mason 1.25 .50 .12
☐ 459 Jimmy Howarth 1.25 .50 .12
☐ 460 Bill Freehan 1.75 .70 .17
☐ 461 Mike Corkins 1.25 .50 .12
☐ 462 Ron Blomberg 1.25 .50 .12
☐ 463 Ken Tatum 1.25 .50 .12
☐ 464 Chicago Cubs 2.50 1.00 .25
Team Card
☐ 465 Dave Giusti 1.25 .50 .12
☐ 466 Jose Arcia 1.25 .50 .12
☐ 467 Mike Ryan 1.25 .50 .12
☐ 468 Tom Griffin 1.25 .50 .12
☐ 469 Dan Monzon 1.25 .50 .12
☐ 470 Mike Cuellar 1.25 .50 .12
☐ 471 Hits Leaders 4.25 1.75 .42
Ty Cobb 4191
☐ 472 Grand Slam Leaders 4.25 1.75 .42
Lou Gehrig 23
☐ 473 Total Bases Leaders 4.25 1.75 .42
Hank Aaron 6172
☐ 474 RBI Leaders 6.50 2.75 .65
Babe Ruth 2209
☐ 475 Batting Leaders 4.25 1.75 .42
Ty Cobb .367
☐ 476 Shutout Leaders 1.75 .70 .17
Walter Johnson 113
☐ 477 Victory Leaders 1.75 .70 .17
Cy Young 511
☐ 478 Strikeout Leaders 1.75 .70 .17
Walter Johnson 3508
☐ 479 Hal Lanier 1.25 .50 .12

☐ 480 Juan Marichal .... 3.75 1.60 .37
☐ 481 Chicago White Sox ...... 2.50 1.00 .25
Team Card
☐ 482 Rick Reuschel .... 4.50 2.00 .45
☐ 483 Dal Maxvill .... 1.25 .50 .12
☐ 484 Ernie McAnally .... 1.25 .50 .12
☐ 485 Norm Cash .... 1.25 .50 .12
☐ 486A Phillies Leaders .... 1.50 .60 .15
Danny Ozark MG
Carroll Beringer CO
Billy DeMars CO
Ray Rippelmeyer CO
Bobby Wine CO
(orange backgrounds)
☐ 486B Phillies Leaders .... 3.00 1.25 .30
(dark pale
backgrounds)
☐ 487 Bruce Dal Canton .... 1.25 .50 .12
☐ 488 Dave Campbell .... 1.25 .50 .12
☐ 489 Jeff Burroughs .... 1.50 .60 .15
☐ 490 Claude Osteen .... 1.25 .50 .12
☐ 491 Bob Montgomery .... 1.25 .50 .12
☐ 492 Pedro Borbon .... 1.25 .50 .12
☐ 493 Duffy Dyer .... 1.25 .50 .12
☐ 494 Rich Morales .... 1.25 .50 .12
☐ 495 Tommy Helms .... 1.25 .50 .12
☐ 496 Ray Lamb .... 1.25 .50 .12
☐ 497A Cardinals Leaders ..... 1.50 .60 .15
Red Schoendienst MG
Vern Benson CO
George Kissell CO
Barney Schultz CO
(orange backgrounds)
☐ 497B Cardinals Leaders ..... 3.00 1.25 .30
(dark pale
backgrounds)
☐ 498 Graig Nettles .... 2.50 1.00 .25
☐ 499 Bob Moose .... 1.25 .50 .12
☐ 500 Oakland A's .... 3.00 1.25 .30
Team Card
☐ 501 Larry Gura .... 1.50 .60 .15
☐ 502 Bobby Valentine .... 1.75 .70 .17
☐ 503 Phil Niekro .... 4.25 1.75 .42
☐ 504 Earl Williams .... 1.25 .50 .12
☐ 505 Bob Bailey .... 1.25 .50 .12
☐ 506 Bart Johnson .... 1.25 .50 .12
☐ 507 Darrel Chaney .... 1.25 .50 .12
☐ 508 Gates Brown .... 1.25 .50 .12
☐ 509 Jim Nash .... 1.2 .50 .12
☐ 510 Amos Otis .... 1.50 .60 .15
☐ 511 Sam McDowell .... 1.50 .60 .15
☐ 512 Dalton Jones .... 1.25 .50 .12
☐ 513 Dave Marshall .... 1.25 .50 .12
☐ 514 Jerry Kenney .... 1.25 .50 .12
☐ 515 Andy Messersmith ...... 1.50 .60 .15
☐ 516 Danny Walton .... 1.25 .50 .12
☐ 517A Pirates Leaders .... 1.50 .60 .15
Bill Virdon MG
Don Leppert CO
Bill Mazeroski CO
Dave Ricketts CO
Mel Wright CO
(Mazeroski has
no right ear)
☐ 517B Pirates Leaders .... 3.00 1.25 .30
(Mazeroski has
right ear)
☐ 518 Bob Veale .... 1.50 .60 .15
☐ 519 Johnny Edwards .... 1.25 .50 .12
☐ 520 Mel Stottlemyre .... 1.75 .70 .17
☐ 521 Atlanta Braves .... 2.50 1.00 .25
Team Card
☐ 522 Leo Cardenas .... 1.25 .50 .12
☐ 523 Wayne Granger .... 1.25 .50 .12
☐ 524 Gene Tenace .... 1.50 .60 .15
☐ 525 Jim Fregosi .... 1.50 .60 .15
☐ 526 Ollie Brown .... 1.25 .50 .12
☐ 527 Dan McGinn .... 1.25 .50 .12
☐ 528 Paul Blair .... 1.50 .60 .15
☐ 529 Milt May .... 2.75 1.10 .27
☐ 530 Jim Kaat .... 4.25 1.75 .42
☐ 531 Ron Woods .... 2.75 1.10 .27
☐ 532 Steve Mingori .... 2.75 1.10 .27
☐ 533 Larry Stahl .... 2.75 1.10 .27
☐ 534 Dave Lemonds .... 2.75 1.10 .27
☐ 535 Johnny Callison .... 3.25 1.35 .32
☐ 536 Philadelphia Phillies .... 5.50 2.50 .55
Team Card
☐ 537 Bill Slayback .... 2.75 1.10 .27
☐ 538 Jim Ray Hart .... 3.25 1.35 .32
☐ 539 Tom Murphy .... 2.75 1.10 .27
☐ 540 Cleon Jones .... 2.75 1.10 .27
☐ 541 Bob Bolin .... 2.75 1.10 .27
☐ 542 Pat Corrales .... 2.75 1.10 .27
☐ 543 Alan Foster .... 2.75 1.10 .27
☐ 544 Von Joshua .... 2.75 1.10 .27
☐ 545 Orlando Cepeda .... 4.25 1.75 .42
☐ 546 Jim York .... 2.75 1.10 .27
☐ 547 Bobby Heise .... 2.75 1.10 .27
☐ 548 Don Durham .... 2.75 1.10 .27
☐ 549 Rangers Leaders .... 3.75 1.60 .37
Whitey Herzog MG
Chuck Estrada CO
Chuck Hiller CO
Jackie Moore CO
☐ 550 Dave Johnson .... 3.25 1.35 .32
☐ 551 Mike Kilkenny .... 2.75 1.10 .27
☐ 552 J.C. Martin .... 2.75 1.10 .27
☐ 553 Mickey Scott .... 2.75 1.10 .27
☐ 554 Dave Concepcion .... 4.50 2.00 .45
☐ 555 Bill Hands .... 2.75 1.10 .27
☐ 556 New York Yankees ...... 6.50 2.75 .65
Team Card
☐ 557 Bernie Williams .... 2.75 1.10 .27
☐ 558 Jerry May .... 2.75 1.10 .27
☐ 559 Barry Lersch .... 2.75 1.10 .27

- ☐ 560 Frank Howard .... 4.25 1.75 .42
- ☐ 561 Jim Geddes .... 2.75 1.10 .27
- ☐ 562 Wayne Garrett .... 2.75 1.10 .27
- ☐ 563 Larry Haney .... 2.75 1.10 .27
- ☐ 564 Mike Thompson .... 2.75 1.10 .27
- ☐ 565 Jim Hickman .... 2.75 1.10 .27
- ☐ 566 Lew Krausse .... 2.75 1.10 .27
- ☐ 567 Bob Fenwick .... 2.75 1.10 .27
- ☐ 568 Ray Newman .... 2.75 1.10 .27
- ☐ 569 Dodgers Leaders .... 4.00 1.75 .40
  Walt Alston MG
  Red Adams CO
  Monty Basgall CO
  Jim Gilliam CO
  Tom Lasorda CO
- ☐ 570 Bill Singer .... 3.25 1.35 .32
- ☐ 571 Rusty Torres .... 2.75 1.10 .27
- ☐ 572 Gary Sutherland .... 2.75 1.10 .27
- ☐ 573 Fred Beene .... 2.75 1.10 .27
- ☐ 574 Bob Didier .... 2.75 1.10 .27
- ☐ 575 Dock Ellis .... 2.75 1.10 .27
- ☐ 576 Montreal Expos .... 5.50 2.50 .55
  Team Card
- ☐ 577 Eric Soderholm .... 2.75 1.10 .27
- ☐ 578 Ken Wright .... 2.75 1.10 .27
- ☐ 579 Tom Grieve .... 3.25 1.35 .32
- ☐ 580 Joe Pepitone .... 3.25 1.35 .32
- ☐ 581 Steve Kealey .... 2.75 1.10 .27
- ☐ 582 Darrell Porter .... 3.25 1.35 .32
- ☐ 583 Bill Grief .... 2.75 1.10 .27
- ☐ 584 Chris Arnold .... 2.75 1.10 .27
- ☐ 585 Joe Niekro .... 3.25 1.35 .32
- ☐ 586 Bill Sudakis .... 2.75 1.10 .27
- ☐ 587 Rich McKinney .... 2.75 1.10 .27
- ☐ 588 Checklist 5 .... 20.00 2.00 .40
- ☐ 589 Ken Forsch .... 2.75 1.10 .27
- ☐ 590 Deron Johnson .... 2.75 1.10 .27
- ☐ 591 Mike Hedlund .... 2.75 1.10 .27
- ☐ 592 John Boccabella .... 2.75 1.10 .27
- ☐ 593 Royals Leaders .... 3.25 1.35 .32
  Jack McKeon MG
  Galen Cisco CO
  Harry Dunlop CO
  Charlie Lau CO
- ☐ 594 Vic Harris .... 2.75 1.10 .27
- ☐ 595 Don Gullett .... 3.25 1.35 .32
- ☐ 596 Boston Red Sox .... 5.50 2.50 .55
  Team Card
- ☐ 597 Mickey Rivers .... 3.50 1.50 .35
- ☐ 598 Phil Roof .... 2.75 1.10 .27
- ☐ 599 Ed Crosby .... 2.75 1.10 .27
- ☐ 600 Dave McNally .... 3.25 1.35 .32
- ☐ 601 Rookie Catchers .... 2.75 1.10 .27
  Sergio Robles
  George Pena
  Rick Stelmaszek
- ☐ 602 Rookie Pitchers .... 2.75 1.10 .27
  Mel Behney
  Ralph Garcia
  Doug Rau
- ☐ 603 Rookie 3rd Basemen ... 2.75 1.10 .27
  Terry Hughes
  Bill McNulty
  Ken Reitz
- ☐ 604 Rookie Pitchers .... 2.75 1.10 .27
  Jesse Jefferson
  Dennis O'Toole
  Bob Strampe
- ☐ 605 Rookie 1st Basemen ... 2.75 1.10 .27
  Enos Cabell
  Pat Bourque
  Gonzalo Marquez
- ☐ 606 Rookie Outfielders .... 4.00 1.75 .40
  Gary Matthews
  Tom Paciorek
  Jorge Roque
- ☐ 607 Rookie Shortstops .... 2.75 1.10 .27
  Pepe Frias
  Ray Busse
  Mario Guerrero
- ☐ 608 Rookie Pitchers .... 3.25 1.35 .32
  Steve Busby
  Dick Colpaert
  George Medich
- ☐ 609 Rookie 2nd Basemen .. 4.50 2.00 .45
  Larvell Blanks
  Pedro Garcia
  Dave Lopes
- ☐ 610 Rookie Pitchers .... 3.75 1.60 .37
  Jimmy Freeman
  Charlie Hough
  Hank Webb
- ☐ 611 Rookie Outfielders .... 3.25 1.35 .32
  Rich Coggins
  Jim Wohlford
  Richie Zisk
- ☐ 612 Rookie Pitchers .... 2.75 1.10 .27
  Steve Lawson
  Bob Reynolds
  Brent Strom
- ☐ 613 Rookie Catchers 36.00 16.25 5.50
  Bob Boone
  Skip Jutze
  Mike Ivie
- ☐ 614 Rookie Outfielders 75.00 34.00 11.25
  Al Bumbry
  Dwight Evans
  Charlie Spikes
- ☐ 615 Rookie 3rd Basemen 450.00 150.00 35.00
  Ron Cey
  John Hilton
  Mike Schmidt
- ☐ 616 Rookie Pitchers .... 2.75 1.10 .27
  Norm Angelini
  Steve Blateric
  Mike Garman

☐ 617 Rich Chiles	2.75	1.10	.27
☐ 618 Andy Etchebarren	2.75	1.10	.27
☐ 619 Billy Wilson	2.75	1.10	.27
☐ 620 Tommy Harper	2.75	1.10	.27
☐ 621 Joe Ferguson	3.25	1.35	.32
☐ 622 Larry Hisle	3.25	1.35	.32
☐ 623 Steve Renko	2.75	1.10	.27
☐ 624 Astros Leaders Leo Durocher MG Preston Gomez CO Grady Hatton CO Hub Kittle CO Jim Owens CO	3.75	1.60	.37
☐ 625 Angel Mangual	2.75	1.10	.27
☐ 626 Bob Barton	2.75	1.10	.27
☐ 627 Luis Alvarado	2.75	1.10	.27
☐ 628 Jim Slaton	2.75	1.10	.27
☐ 629 Cleveland Indians Team Card	5.50	2.50	.55
☐ 630 Denny McLain	4.25	1.75	.42
☐ 631 Tom Matchick	2.75	1.10	.27
☐ 632 Dick Selma	2.75	1.10	.27
☐ 633 Ike Brown	2.75	1.10	.27
☐ 634 Alan Closter	2.75	1.10	.27
☐ 635 Gene Alley	2.75	1.10	.27
☐ 636 Rickey Clark	2.75	1.10	.27
☐ 637 Norm Miller	2.75	1.10	.27
☐ 638 Ken Reynolds	2.75	1.10	.27
☐ 639 Willie Crawford	2.75	1.10	.27
☐ 640 Dick Bosman	2.75	1.10	.27
☐ 641 Cincinnati Reds Team Card	5.50	2.50	.55
☐ 642 Jose LaBoy	2.75	1.10	.27
☐ 643 Al Fitzmorris	2.75	1.10	.27
☐ 644 Jack Heidemann	2.75	1.10	.27
☐ 645 Bob Locker	2.75	1.10	.27
☐ 646 Brewers Leaders Del Crandall MG Harvey Kuenn CO Joe Nossek CO Bob Shaw CO Jim Walton CO	3.25	1.35	.32
☐ 647 George Stone	2.75	1.10	.27
☐ 648 Tom Egan	2.75	1.10	.27
☐ 649 Rich Folkers	2.75	1.10	.27
☐ 650 Felipe Alou	3.25	1.35	.32
☐ 651 Don Carrithers	2.75	1.10	.27
☐ 652 Ted Kubiak	2.75	1.10	.27
☐ 653 Joe Hoerner	2.75	1.10	.27
☐ 654 Minnesota Twins Team Card	5.50	2.50	.55
☐ 655 Clay Kirby	2.75	1.10	.27
☐ 656 John Ellis	2.75	1.10	.27
☐ 657 Bob Johnson	2.75	1.10	.27
☐ 658 Elliott Maddox	2.75	1.10	.27
☐ 659 Jose Pagan	2.75	1.10	.27
☐ 660 Fred Scherman	3.75	1.50	.30

1974 Topps

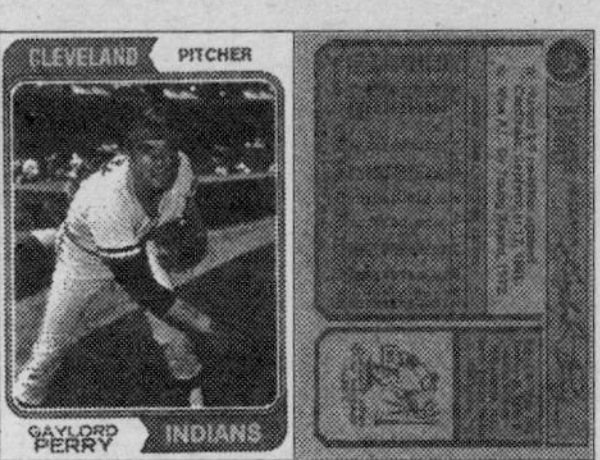

The cards in this 660-card set measure 2 1/2" by 3 1/2". This year marked the first time Topps issued all the cards of its baseball set at the same time rather than in series. Some interesting variations were created by the rumored move of the San Diego Padres to Washington. Fifteen cards (13 players, the team card, and the rookie card (599) of the Padres were printed either as "San Diego" (SD) or "Washington." The latter are the scarcer variety and are denoted in the checklist below by WAS. Each team's manager and his coaches again have a combined card with small pictures of each coach below the larger photo of the team's manager. The first six cards in the set (1-6) feature Hank Aaron and his illustrious career. Other topical subsets included in the set are League Leaders (201-208), All-Star selections (331-339), Playoffs cards (470-471), World Series cards (472-479), and Rookie Prospects (596-608). The card backs for the All-Stars (331-339) have no statistics, but form a picture puzzle of Bobby Bonds, the 1973 All-Star Game MVP. The key rookies in this set are Ken Griffey Sr., Dave Parker, and Dave Winfield.

	NRMT	VG-E	GOOD
COMPLETE SET (660)	625.00	275.00	75.00
COMMON PLAYER (1-660)	.40	.16	.04
☐ 1 Hank Aaron Complete ML record	30.00	6.00	1.25
☐ 2 Aaron Special 54-57 Records on back	6.00	2.50	.60
☐ 3 Aaron Special 58-61 Memorable homers	6.00	2.50	.60
☐ 4 Aaron Special 62-65 Life in ML's 1954-63	6.00	2.50	.60

Card	Price 1	Price 2	Price 3
☐ 5 Aaron Special 66-69	6.00	2.50	.60
Life in ML's 1964-73			
☐ 6 Aaron Special 70-73	6.00	2.50	.60
Milestone homers			
☐ 7 Jim Hunter	4.50	2.00	.45
☐ 8 George Theodore	.40	.16	.04
☐ 9 Mickey Lolich	.75	.30	.07
☐ 10 Johnny Bench	15.00	6.50	2.15
☐ 11 Jim Bibby	.40	.16	.04
☐ 12 Dave May	.40	.16	.04
☐ 13 Tom Hilgendorf	.40	.16	.04
☐ 14 Paul Popovich	.40	.16	.04
☐ 15 Joe Torre	1.00	.40	.10
☐ 16 Baltimore Orioles	.80	.35	.08
Team Card			
☐ 17 Doug Bird	.40	.16	.04
☐ 18 Gary Thomasson	.40	.16	.04
☐ 19 Gerry Moses	.40	.16	.04
☐ 20 Nolan Ryan	50.00	22.50	7.50
☐ 21 Bob Gallagher	.40	.16	.04
☐ 22 Cy Acosta	.40	.16	.04
☐ 23 Craig Robinson	.40	.16	.04
☐ 24 John Hiller	.60	.25	.06
☐ 25 Ken Singleton	.60	.25	.06
☐ 26 Bill Campbell	.40	.16	.04
☐ 27 George Scott	.60	.25	.06
☐ 28 Manny Sanguillen	.60	.25	.06
☐ 29 Phil Niekro	2.50	1.00	.25
☐ 30 Bobby Bonds	1.00	.40	.10
☐ 31 Astros Leaders	.60	.25	.06
Preston Gomez MG			
Roger Craig CO			
Hub Kittle CO			
Grady Hatton CO			
Bob Lillis CO			
☐ 32A Johnny Grubb SD	.40	.16	.04
☐ 32B Johnny Grubb WAS	5.00	2.25	.50
☐ 33 Don Newhauser	.40	.16	.04
☐ 34 Andy Kosco	.40	.16	.04
☐ 35 Gaylord Perry	3.50	1.50	.35
☐ 36 St. Louis Cardinals	.80	.35	.08
Team Card			
☐ 37 Dave Sells	.40	.16	.04
☐ 38 Don Kessinger	.60	.25	.06
☐ 39 Ken Suarez	.40	.16	.04
☐ 40 Jim Palmer	9.00	4.00	.90
☐ 41 Bobby Floyd	.40	.16	.04
☐ 42 Claude Osteen	.60	.25	.06
☐ 43 Jim Wynn	.60	.25	.06
☐ 44 Mel Stottlemyre	.75	.30	.07
☐ 45 Dave Johnson	.60	.25	.06
☐ 46 Pat Kelly	.40	.16	.04
☐ 47 Dick Ruthven	.40	.16	.04
☐ 48 Dick Sharon	.40	.16	.04
☐ 49 Steve Renko	.40	.16	.04
☐ 50 Rod Carew	13.00	5.75	1.75
☐ 51 Bobby Heise	.40	.16	.04
☐ 52 Al Oliver	1.00	.40	.10

Card	Price 1	Price 2	Price 3
☐ 53A Fred Kendall SD	.40	.16	.04
☐ 53B Fred Kendall WAS	5.00	2.25	.50
☐ 54 Elias Sosa	.40	.16	.04
☐ 55 Frank Robinson	5.00	2.25	.50
☐ 56 New York Mets	1.00	.40	.10
Team Card			
☐ 57 Darold Knowles	.40	.16	.04
☐ 58 Charlie Spikes	.40	.16	.04
☐ 59 Ross Grimsley	.40	.16	.04
☐ 60 Lou Brock	5.00	2.25	.50
☐ 61 Luis Aparicio	2.25	.90	.22
☐ 62 Bob Locker	.40	.16	.04
☐ 63 Bill Sudakis	.40	.16	.04
☐ 64 Doug Rau	.40	.16	.04
☐ 65 Amos Otis	.60	.25	.06
☐ 66 Sparky Lyle	.60	.25	.06
☐ 67 Tommy Helms	.60	.25	.06
☐ 68 Grant Jackson	.40	.16	.04
☐ 69 Del Unser	.40	.16	.04
☐ 70 Dick Allen	.75	.30	.07
☐ 71 Dan Frisella	.40	.16	.04
☐ 72 Aurelio Rodriguez	.40	.16	.04
☐ 73 Mike Marshall	.60	.25	.06
☐ 74 Minnesota Twins	.80	.35	.08
Team Card			
☐ 75 Jim Colborn	.40	.16	.04
☐ 76 Mickey Rivers	.60	.25	.06
☐ 77A Rich Troedson SD	.40	.16	.04
☐ 77B Rich Troedson WAS	5.00	2.25	.50
☐ 78 Giants Leaders	.60	.25	.06
Charlie Fox MG			
John McNamara CO			
Joe Amalfitano CO			
Andy Gilbert CO			
Don McMahon CO			
☐ 79 Gene Tenace	.60	.25	.06
☐ 80 Tom Seaver	17.00	7.25	2.50
☐ 81 Frank Duffy	.40	.16	.04
☐ 82 Dave Giusti	.40	.16	.04
☐ 83 Orlando Cepeda	1.25	.50	.12
☐ 84 Rick Wise	.40	.16	.04
☐ 85 Joe Morgan	5.00	2.25	.50
☐ 86 Joe Ferguson	.40	.16	.04
☐ 87 Fergie Jenkins	3.25	1.35	.32
☐ 88 Freddie Patek	.40	.16	.04
☐ 89 Jackie Brown	.40	.16	.04
☐ 90 Bobby Murcer	.75	.30	.07
☐ 91 Ken Forsch	.40	.16	.04
☐ 92 Paul Blair	.60	.25	.06
☐ 93 Rod Gilbreath	.40	.16	.04
☐ 94 Detroit Tigers	.80	.35	.08
Team Card			
☐ 95 Steve Carlton	9.00	4.00	.90
☐ 96 Jerry Hairston	.40	.16	.04
☐ 97 Bob Bailey	.40	.16	.04
☐ 98 Bert Blyleven	3.00	1.25	.30
☐ 99 Brewers Leaders	.60	.25	.06
Del Crandall MG			

Harvey Kuenn CO
Joe Nossek CO
Jim Walton CO
Al Widmar CO

☐ 100 Willie Stargell .... 4.00 1.75 .40
☐ 101 Bobby Valentine .... .60 .25 .06
☐ 102A Bill Greif SD .... .40 .16 .04
☐ 102B Bill Greif WAS .... 5.00 2.25 .50
☐ 103 Sal Bando .... .60 .25 .06
☐ 104 Ron Bryant .... .40 .16 .04
☐ 105 Carlton Fisk 21.00 9.00 3.00
☐ 106 Harry Parker .... .40 .16 .04
☐ 107 Alex Johnson .... .40 .16 .04
☐ 108 Al Hrabosky .... .60 .25 .06
☐ 109 Bob Grich .... .60 .25 .06
☐ 110 Billy Williams .... 3.00 1.25 .30
☐ 111 Clay Carroll .... .40 .16 .04
☐ 112 Dave Lopes .... .75 .30 .07
☐ 113 Dick Drago .... .40 .16 .04
☐ 114 Angels Team .... .80 .35 .08
☐ 115 Willie Horton .... .60 .25 .06
☐ 116 Jerry Reuss .... .60 .25 .06
☐ 117 Ron Blomberg .... .40 .16 .04
☐ 118 Bill Lee .... .60 .25 .06
☐ 119 Phillies Leaders .... .60 .25 .06
Danny Ozark MG
Ray Ripplemeyer CO
Bobby Wine CO
Carroll Beringer CO
Billy DeMars CO
☐ 120 Wilbur Wood .... .60 .25 .06
☐ 121 Larry Lintz .... .40 .16 .04
☐ 122 Jim Holt .... .40 .16 .04
☐ 123 Nelson Briles .... .40 .16 .04
☐ 124 Bobby Coluccio .... .40 .16 .04
☐ 125A Nate Colbert SD .... .40 .16 .04
☐ 125B Nate Colbert WAS ..... 5.00 2.25 .50
☐ 126 Checklist 1 .... 2.00 .20 .04
☐ 127 Tom Paciorek .... .40 .16 .04
☐ 128 John Ellis .... .40 .16 .04
☐ 129 Chris Speier .... .40 .16 .04
☐ 130 Reggie Jackson 21.00 9.00 3.00
☐ 131 Bob Boone .... 3.00 1.25 .30
☐ 132 Felix Millan .... .40 .16 .04
☐ 133 David Clyde .... .60 .25 .06
☐ 134 Denis Menke .... .40 .16 .04
☐ 135 Roy White .... .60 .25 .06
☐ 136 Rick Reuschel .... 1.00 .40 .10
☐ 137 Al Bumbry .... .40 .16 .04
☐ 138 Eddie Brinkman .... .40 .16 .04
☐ 139 Aurelio Monteagudo ...... .40 .16 .04
☐ 140 Darrell Evans .... .60 .25 .06
☐ 141 Pat Bourque .... .40 .16 .04
☐ 142 Pedro Garcia .... .40 .16 .04
☐ 143 Dick Woodson .... .40 .16 .04
☐ 144 Dodgers Leaders .... 1.50 .60 .15
Walter Alston MG
Tom Lasorda CO
Jim Gilliam CO
Red Adams CO
Monty Basgall CO
☐ 145 Dock Ellis .... .40 .16 .04
☐ 146 Ron Fairly .... .40 .16 .04
☐ 147 Bart Johnson .... .40 .16 .04
☐ 148A Dave Hilton SD .... .40 .16 .04
☐ 148B Dave Hilton WAS ...... 5.00 2.25 .50
☐ 149 Mac Scarce .... .40 .16 .04
☐ 150 John Mayberry .... .60 .25 .06
☐ 151 Diego Segui .... .40 .16 .04
☐ 152 Oscar Gamble .... .60 .25 .06
☐ 153 Jon Matlack .... .60 .25 .06
☐ 154 Houston Astros .... .80 .35 .08
Team Card
☐ 155 Bert Campaneris .... .60 .25 .06
☐ 156 Randy Moffitt .... .40 .16 .04
☐ 157 Vic Harris .... .40 .16 .04
☐ 158 Jack Billingham .... .40 .16 .04
☐ 159 Jim Ray Hart .... .60 .25 .06
☐ 160 Brooks Robinson .... 5.00 2.25 .50
☐ 161 Ray Burris UER .... .60 .25 .06
(card number is
printed sideways)
☐ 162 Bill Freehan .... .60 .25 .06
☐ 163 Ken Berry .... .40 .16 .04
☐ 164 Tom House .... .40 .16 .04
☐ 165 Willie Davis .... .60 .25 .06
☐ 166 Royals Leaders .... .60 .25 .06
Jack McKeon MG
Charlie Lau CO
Harry Dunlop CO
Galen Cisco CO
☐ 167 Luis Tiant .... .75 .30 .07
☐ 168 Danny Thompson .... .40 .16 .04
☐ 169 Steve Rogers .... .60 .25 .06
☐ 170 Bill Melton .... .40 .16 .04
☐ 171 Eduardo Rodriguez .... .40 .16 .04
☐ 172 Gene Clines .... .40 .16 .04
☐ 173A Randy Jones SD .... .75 .30 .07
☐ 173B Randy Jones WAS .... 7.00 3.00 .70
☐ 174 Bill Robinson .... .60 .25 .06
☐ 175 Reggie Cleveland .... .40 .16 .04
☐ 176 John Lowenstein .... .40 .16 .04
☐ 177 Dave Roberts .... .40 .16 .04
☐ 178 Garry Maddox .... .60 .25 .06
☐ 179 Mets Leaders .... 1.50 .60 .15
Yogi Berra MG
Rube Walker CO
Eddie Yost CO
Roy McMillan CO
Joe Pignatano CO
☐ 180 Ken Holtzman .... .60 .25 .06
☐ 181 Cesar Geronimo .... .40 .16 .04
☐ 182 Lindy McDaniel .... .40 .16 .04
☐ 183 Johnny Oates .... .60 .25 .06
☐ 184 Texas Rangers .... .80 .35 .08
Team Card

☐ 185	Jose Cardenal	.40	.16	.04
☐ 186	Fred Scherman	.40	.16	.04
☐ 187	Don Baylor	1.50	.60	.15
☐ 188	Rudy Meoli	.40	.16	.04
☐ 189	Jim Brewer	.40	.16	.04
☐ 190	Tony Oliva	1.00	.40	.10
☐ 191	Al Fitzmorris	.40	.16	.04
☐ 192	Mario Guerrero	.40	.16	.04
☐ 193	Tom Walker	.40	.16	.04
☐ 194	Darrell Porter	.40	.16	.04
☐ 195	Carlos May	.40	.16	.04
☐ 196	Jim Fregosi	.60	.25	.06
☐ 197A	Vicente Romo SD	.40	.16	.04
☐ 197B	Vicente Romo WAS	5.00	2.25	.50
☐ 198	Dave Cash	.40	.16	.04
☐ 199	Mike Kekich	.40	.16	.04
☐ 200	Cesar Cedeno	.60	.25	.06
☐ 201	Batting Leaders	4.25	1.75	.42
	Rod Carew			
	Pete Rose			
☐ 202	Home Run Leaders	2.75	1.10	.27
	Reggie Jackson			
	Willie Stargell			
☐ 203	RBI Leaders	2.75	1.10	.27
	Reggie Jackson			
	Willie Stargell			
☐ 204	Stolen Base Leaders	1.00	.40	.10
	Tommy Harper			
	Lou Brock			
☐ 205	Victory Leaders	.75	.30	.07
	Wilbur Wood			
	Ron Bryant			
☐ 206	ERA Leaders	3.00	1.25	.30
	Jim Palmer			
	Tom Seaver			
☐ 207	Strikeout Leaders	6.25	2.75	.60
	Nolan Ryan			
	Tom Seaver			
☐ 208	Leading Firemen	.75	.30	.07
	John Hiller			
	Mike Marshall			
☐ 209	Ted Sizemore	.40	.16	.04
☐ 210	Bill Singer	.40	.16	.04
☐ 211	Chicago Cubs Team	.80	.35	.08
☐ 212	Rollie Fingers	4.50	2.00	.45
☐ 213	Dave Rader	.40	.16	.04
☐ 214	Billy Grabarkewitz	.40	.16	.04
☐ 215	Al Kaline UER	5.00	2.25	.50
	(no copyright on back)			
☐ 216	Ray Sadecki	.40	.16	.04
☐ 217	Tim Foli	.40	.16	.04
☐ 218	Johnny Briggs	.40	.16	.04
☐ 219	Doug Griffin	.40	.16	.04
☐ 220	Don Sutton	2.50	1.00	.25
☐ 221	White Sox Leaders	.60	.25	.06
	Chuck Tanner MG			
	Jim Mahoney CO			
	Alex Monchak CO			
	Johnny Sain CO			
	Joe Lonnett CO			
☐ 222	Ramon Hernandez	.40	.16	.04
☐ 223	Jeff Burroughs	.60	.25	.06
☐ 224	Roger Metzger	.40	.16	.04
☐ 225	Paul Splittorff	.40	.16	.04
☐ 226A	Padres Team SD	1.00	.40	.10
☐ 226B	Padres Team WAS	5.00	2.25	.50
☐ 227	Mike Lum	.40	.16	.04
☐ 228	Ted Kubiak	.40	.16	.04
☐ 229	Fritz Peterson	.40	.16	.04
☐ 230	Tony Perez	3.50	1.50	.35
☐ 231	Dick Tidrow	.40	.16	.04
☐ 232	Steve Brye	.40	.16	.04
☐ 233	Jim Barr	.40	.16	.04
☐ 234	John Milner	.40	.16	.04
☐ 235	Dave McNally	.60	.25	.06
☐ 236	Cardinals Leaders	.75	.30	.07
	Red Schoendienst MG			
	Barney Schultz CO			
	George Kissell CO			
	Johnny Lewis CO			
	Vern Benson CO			
☐ 237	Ken Brett	.40	.16	.04
☐ 238	Fran Healy HOR	.60	.25	.06
	(Munson sliding			
	in background)			
☐ 239	Bill Russell	.60	.25	.06
☐ 240	Joe Coleman	.40	.16	.04
☐ 241A	Glenn Beckert SD	.60	.25	.06
☐ 241B	Glenn Beckert WAS	5.50	2.50	.55
☐ 242	Bill Gogolewski	.40	.16	.04
☐ 243	Bob Oliver	.40	.16	.04
☐ 244	Carl Morton	.40	.16	.04
☐ 245	Cleon Jones	.40	.16	.04
☐ 246	Oakland Athletics	1.00	.40	.10
	Team Card			
☐ 247	Rick Miller	.40	.16	.04
☐ 248	Tom Hall	.40	.16	.04
☐ 249	George Mitterwald	.40	.16	.04
☐ 250A	Willie McCovey SD	4.25	1.75	.42
☐ 250B	Willie McCovey WAS	25.00	11.00	3.50
☐ 251	Graig Nettles	2.00	.80	.20
☐ 252	Dave Parker	42.00	18.00	5.50
☐ 253	John Boccabella	.40	.16	.04
☐ 254	Stan Bahnsen	.40	.16	.04
☐ 255	Larry Bowa	.75	.30	.07
☐ 256	Tom Griffin	.40	.16	.04
☐ 257	Buddy Bell	1.00	.40	.10
☐ 258	Jerry Morales	.40	.16	.04
☐ 259	Bob Reynolds	.40	.16	.04
☐ 260	Ted Simmons	1.50	.60	.15
☐ 261	Jerry Bell	.40	.16	.04
☐ 262	Ed Kirkpatrick	.40	.16	.04
☐ 263	Checklist 2	2.00	.20	.04
☐ 264	Joe Rudi	.60	.25	.06
☐ 265	Tug McGraw	.75	.30	.07
☐ 266	Jim Northrup	.60	.25	.06

☐ 267	Andy Messersmith	.60	.25	.06
☐ 268	Tom Grieve	.60	.25	.06
☐ 269	Bob Johnson	.40	.16	.04
☐ 270	Ron Santo	.75	.30	.07
☐ 271	Bill Hands	.40	.16	.04
☐ 272	Paul Casanova	.40	.16	.04
☐ 273	Checklist 3	2.00	.20	.04
☐ 274	Fred Beene	.40	.16	.04
☐ 275	Ron Hunt	.40	.16	.04
☐ 276	Angels Leaders	.60	.25	.06
	Bobby Winkles MG			
	John Roseboro CO			
	Tom Morgan CO			
	Jimmie Reese CO			
	Salty Parker CO			
☐ 277	Gary Nolan	.40	.16	.04
☐ 278	Cookie Rojas	.40	.16	.04
☐ 279	Jim Crawford	.40	.16	.04
☐ 280	Carl Yastrzemski	12.00	5.25	1.50
☐ 281	San Francisco Giants	.80	.35	.08
	Team Card			
☐ 282	Doyle Alexander	.60	.25	.06
☐ 283	Mike Schmidt	100.00	45.00	15.00
☐ 284	Dave Duncan	.40	.16	.04
☐ 285	Reggie Smith	.60	.25	.06
☐ 286	Tony Muser	.40	.16	.04
☐ 287	Clay Kirby	.40	.16	.04
☐ 288	Gorman Thomas	1.75	.70	.17
☐ 289	Rick Auerbach	.40	.16	.04
☐ 290	Vida Blue	.60	.25	.06
☐ 291	Don Hahn	.40	.16	.04
☐ 292	Chuck Seelbach	.40	.16	.04
☐ 293	Milt May	.40	.16	.04
☐ 294	Steve Foucault	.40	.16	.04
☐ 295	Rick Monday	.60	.25	.06
☐ 296	Ray Corbin	.40	.16	.04
☐ 297	Hal Breeden	.40	.16	.04
☐ 298	Roric Harrison	.40	.16	.04
☐ 299	Gene Michael	.60	.25	.06
☐ 300	Pete Rose	12.50	5.50	1.65
☐ 301	Bob Montgomery	.40	.16	.04
☐ 302	Rudy May	.40	.16	.04
☐ 303	George Hendrick	.60	.25	.06
☐ 304	Don Wilson	.40	.16	.04
☐ 305	Tito Fuentes	.40	.16	.04
☐ 306	Orioles Leaders	.75	.30	.07
	Earl Weaver MG			
	Jim Frey CO			
	George Bamberger CO			
	Billy Hunter CO			
	George Staller CO			
☐ 307	Luis Melendez	.40	.16	.04
☐ 308	Bruce Dal Canton	.40	.16	.04
☐ 309A	Dave Roberts SD	.40	.16	.04
☐ 309B	Dave Roberts WAS	7.00	3.00	.70
☐ 310	Terry Forster	.60	.25	.06
☐ 311	Jerry Grote	.40	.16	.04
☐ 312	Deron Johnson	.40	.16	.04
☐ 313	Barry Lersch	.40	.16	.04
☐ 314	Milwaukee Brewers	.80	.35	.08
	Team Card			
☐ 315	Ron Cey	1.00	.40	.10
☐ 316	Jim Perry	.60	.25	.06
☐ 317	Richie Zisk	.40	.16	.04
☐ 318	Jim Merritt	.40	.16	.04
☐ 319	Randy Hundley	.40	.16	.04
☐ 320	Dusty Baker	.60	.25	.06
☐ 321	Steve Braun	.40	.16	.04
☐ 322	Ernie McAnally	.40	.16	.04
☐ 323	Richie Scheinblum	.40	.16	.04
☐ 324	Steve Kline	.40	.16	.04
☐ 325	Tommy Harper	.60	.25	.06
☐ 326	Reds Leaders	.75	.30	.07
	Sparky Anderson MG			
	Larry Shephard CO			
	George Scherger CO			
	Alex Grammas CO			
	Ted Kluszewski CO			
☐ 327	Tom Timmermann	.40	.16	.04
☐ 328	Skip Jutze	.40	.16	.04
☐ 329	Mark Belanger	.60	.25	.06
☐ 330	Juan Marichal	2.50	1.00	.25
☐ 331	All-Star Catchers	5.00	2.25	.50
	Carlton Fisk			
	Johnny Bench			
☐ 332	All-Star 1B	2.50	1.00	.25
	Dick Allen			
	Hank Aaron			
☐ 333	All-Star 2B	3.00	1.25	.30
	Rod Carew			
	Joe Morgan			
☐ 334	All-Star 3B	1.50	.60	.15
	Brooks Robinson			
	Ron Santo			
☐ 335	All-Star SS	.60	.25	.06
	Bert Campaneris			
	Chris Speier			
☐ 336	All-Star LF	2.50	1.00	.25
	Bobby Murcer			
	Pete Rose			
☐ 337	All-Star CF	.60	.25	.06
	Amos Otis			
	Cesar Cedeno			
☐ 338	All-Star RF	3.00	1.25	.30
	Reggie Jackson			
	Billy Williams			
☐ 339	All-Star Pitchers	.75	.30	.07
	Jim Hunter			
	Rick Wise			
☐ 340	Thurman Munson	7.50	3.25	.75
☐ 341	Dan Driessen	.75	.30	.07
☐ 342	Jim Lonborg	.60	.25	.06
☐ 343	Royals Team	.80	.35	.08
☐ 344	Mike Caldwell	.60	.25	.06
☐ 345	Bill North	.40	.16	.04
☐ 346	Ron Reed	.40	.16	.04

☐ 347 Sandy Alomar .40 .16 .04
☐ 348 Pete Richert .40 .16 .04
☐ 349 John Vukovich .40 .16 .04
☐ 350 Bob Gibson 4.50 2.00 .45
☐ 351 Dwight Evans 16.00 6.75 2.25
☐ 352 Bill Stoneman .40 .16 .04
☐ 353 Rich Coggins .40 .16 .04
☐ 354 Cubs Leaders .60 .25 .06
Whitey Lockman MG
J.C. Martin CO
Hank Aguirre CO
Al Spangler CO
Jim Marshall CO
☐ 355 Dave Nelson .40 .16 .04
☐ 356 Jerry Koosman .75 .30 .07
☐ 357 Buddy Bradford .40 .16 .04
☐ 358 Dal Maxvill .40 .16 .04
☐ 359 Brent Strom .40 .16 .04
☐ 360 Greg Luzinski .75 .30 .07
☐ 361 Don Carrithers .40 .16 .04
☐ 362 Hal King .40 .16 .04
☐ 363 New York Yankees .80 .35 .08
Team Card
☐ 364A Cito Gaston SD .75 .30 .07
☐ 364B Cito Gaston WAS 7.50 3.25 .75
☐ 365 Steve Busby .60 .25 .06
☐ 366 Larry Hisle .60 .25 .06
☐ 367 Norm Cash .75 .30 .07
☐ 368 Manny Mota .60 .25 .06
☐ 369 Paul Lindblad .40 .16 .04
☐ 370 Bob Watson .60 .25 .06
☐ 371 Jim Slaton .40 .16 .04
☐ 372 Ken Reitz .40 .16 .04
☐ 373 John Curtis .40 .16 .04
☐ 374 Marty Perez .40 .16 .04
☐ 375 Earl Williams .40 .16 .04
☐ 376 Jorge Orta .40 .16 .04
☐ 377 Ron Woods .40 .16 .04
☐ 378 Burt Hooton .60 .25 .06
☐ 379 Rangers Leaders 1.00 .40 .10
Billy Martin MG
Frank Lucchesi CO
Art Fowler CO
Charlie Silvera CO
Jackie Moore CO
☐ 380 Bud Harrelson .60 .25 .06
☐ 381 Charlie Sands .40 .16 .04
☐ 382 Bob Moose .40 .16 .04
☐ 383 Philadelphia Phillies .80 .35 .08
Team Card
☐ 384 Chris Chambliss .60 .25 .06
☐ 385 Don Gullett .60 .25 .06
☐ 386 Gary Matthews .60 .25 .06
☐ 387A Rich Morales SD .40 .16 .04
☐ 387B Rich Morales WAS 7.00 3.00 .70
☐ 388 Phil Roof .40 .16 .04
☐ 389 Gates Brown .60 .25 .06
☐ 390 Lou Piniella .75 .30 .07
☐ 391 Billy Champion .40 .16 .04
☐ 392 Dick Green .40 .16 .04
☐ 393 Orlando Pena .40 .16 .04
☐ 394 Ken Henderson .40 .16 .04
☐ 395 Doug Rader .60 .25 .06
☐ 396 Tommy Davis .60 .25 .06
☐ 397 George Stone .40 .16 .04
☐ 398 Duke Sims .40 .16 .04
☐ 399 Mike Paul .40 .16 .04
☐ 400 Harmon Killebrew 4.25 1.75 .42
☐ 401 Elliott Maddox .40 .16 .04
☐ 402 Jim Rooker .40 .16 .04
☐ 403 Red Sox Leaders .60 .25 .06
Darrell Johnson MG
Eddie Popowski CO
Lee Stange CO
Don Zimmer CO
Don Bryant CO
☐ 404 Jim Howarth .40 .16 .04
☐ 405 Ellie Rodriguez .40 .16 .04
☐ 406 Steve Arlin .40 .16 .04
☐ 407 Jim Wohlford .40 .16 .04
☐ 408 Charlie Hough .75 .30 .07
☐ 409 Ike Brown .40 .16 .04
☐ 410 Pedro Borbon .40 .16 .04
☐ 411 Frank Baker .40 .16 .04
☐ 412 Chuck Taylor .40 .16 .04
☐ 413 Don Money .40 .16 .04
☐ 414 Checklist 4 2.00 .20 .04
☐ 415 Gary Gentry .40 .16 .04
☐ 416 Chicago White Sox .80 .35 .08
Team Card
☐ 417 Rich Folkers .40 .16 .04
☐ 418 Walt Williams .40 .16 .04
☐ 419 Wayne Twitchell .40 .16 .04
☐ 420 Ray Fosse .40 .16 .04
☐ 421 Dan Fife .40 .16 .04
☐ 422 Gonzalo Marquez .40 .16 .04
☐ 423 Fred Stanley .40 .16 .04
☐ 424 Jim Beauchamp .40 .16 .04
☐ 425 Pete Broberg .40 .16 .04
☐ 426 Rennie Stennett .40 .16 .04
☐ 427 Bobby Bolin .40 .16 .04
☐ 428 Gary Sutherland .40 .16 .04
☐ 429 Dick Lange .40 .16 .04
☐ 430 Matty Alou .60 .25 .06
☐ 431 Gene Garber .60 .25 .06
☐ 432 Chris Arnold .40 .16 .04
☐ 433 Lerrin LaGrow .40 .16 .04
☐ 434 Ken McMullen .40 .16 .04
☐ 435 Dave Concepcion 1.75 .70 .17
☐ 436 Don Hood .40 .16 .04
☐ 437 Jim Lyttle .40 .16 .04
☐ 438 Ed Herrmann .40 .16 .04
☐ 439 Norm Miller .40 .16 .04
☐ 440 Jim Kaat 1.00 .40 .10
☐ 441 Tom Ragland .40 .16 .04
☐ 442 Alan Foster .40 .16 .04

- ☐ 443 Tom Hutton .40 .16 .04
- ☐ 444 Vic Davalillo .40 .16 .04
- ☐ 445 George Medich .40 .16 .04
- ☐ 446 Len Randle .40 .16 .04
- ☐ 447 Twins Leaders .60 .25 .06
  Frank Quilici MG
  Ralph Rowe CO
  Bob Rodgers CO
  Vern Morgan CO
- ☐ 448 Ron Hodges .40 .16 .04
- ☐ 449 Tom McCraw .40 .16 .04
- ☐ 450 Rich Hebner .40 .16 .04
- ☐ 451 Tommy John 1.75 .70 .17
- ☐ 452 Gene Hiser .40 .16 .04
- ☐ 453 Balor Moore .40 .16 .04
- ☐ 454 Kurt Bevacqua .40 .16 .04
- ☐ 455 Tom Bradley .40 .16 .04
- ☐ 456 Dave Winfield 80.00 36.00 12.00
- ☐ 457 Chuck Goggin .40 .16 .04
- ☐ 458 Jim Ray .40 .16 .04
- ☐ 459 Cincinnati Reds .80 .35 .08
  Team Card
- ☐ 460 Boog Powell .75 .30 .07
- ☐ 461 John Odom .40 .16 .04
- ☐ 462 Luis Alvarado .40 .16 .04
- ☐ 463 Pat Dobson .40 .16 .04
- ☐ 464 Jose Cruz .60 .25 .06
- ☐ 465 Dick Bosman .40 .16 .04
- ☐ 466 Dick Billings .40 .16 .04
- ☐ 467 Winston Llenas .40 .16 .04
- ☐ 468 Pepe Frias .40 .16 .04
- ☐ 469 Joe Decker .40 .16 .04
- ☐ 470 AL Playoffs 3.75 1.60 .37
  A's over Orioles
  (Reggie Jackson)
- ☐ 471 NL Playoffs 1.00 .40 .10
  Mets over Reds
  (Matlack pitching)
- ☐ 472 World Series Game 1 .. 1.00 .40 .10
  (Knowles pitching)
- ☐ 473 World Series Game 2 .. 4.00 1.75 .40
  (Willie Mays batting)
- ☐ 474 World Series Game 3 .. 1.00 .40 .10
  (Campaneris stealing)
- ☐ 475 World Series Game 4 .. 1.00 .40 .10
  (Staub batting)
- ☐ 476 World Series Game 5 .. 1.00 .40 .10
  Cleon Jones scoring)
- ☐ 477 World Series Game 6 .. 3.75 1.60 .37
  (Reggie Jackson)
- ☐ 478 World Series Game 7 .. 1.00 .40 .10
  (Campaneris batting)
- ☐ 479 World Series Summary 1.00 .40 .10
  A's celebrate; win
  2nd consecutive
  championship
- ☐ 480 Willie Crawford .40 .16 .04
- ☐ 481 Jerry Terrell .40 .16 .04
- ☐ 482 Bob Didier .40 .16 .04
- ☐ 483 Atlanta Braves .80 .35 .08
  Team Card
- ☐ 484 Carmen Fanzone .40 .16 .04
- ☐ 485 Felipe Alou .60 .25 .06
- ☐ 486 Steve Stone .60 .25 .06
- ☐ 487 Ted Martinez .40 .16 .04
- ☐ 488 Andy Etchebarren .40 .16 .04
- ☐ 489 Pirates Leaders .60 .25 .06
  Danny Murtaugh MG
  Don Osborn CO
  Don Leppert CO
  Bill Mazeroski CO
  Bob Skinner CO
- ☐ 490 Vada Pinson .75 .30 .07
- ☐ 491 Roger Nelson .40 .16 .04
- ☐ 492 Mike Rogodzinski .40 .16 .04
- ☐ 493 Joe Hoerner .40 .16 .04
- ☐ 494 Ed Goodson .40 .16 .04
- ☐ 495 Dick McAuliffe .40 .16 .04
- ☐ 496 Tom Murphy .40 .16 .04
- ☐ 497 Bobby Mitchell .40 .16 .04
- ☐ 498 Pat Corrales .40 .16 .04
- ☐ 499 Rusty Torres .40 .16 .04
- ☐ 500 Lee May .60 .25 .06
- ☐ 501 Eddie Leon .40 .16 .04
- ☐ 502 Dave LaRoche .40 .16 .04
- ☐ 503 Eric Soderholm .40 .16 .04
- ☐ 504 Joe Niekro .60 .25 .06
- ☐ 505 Bill Buckner .75 .30 .07
- ☐ 506 Ed Farmer .40 .16 .04
- ☐ 507 Larry Stahl .40 .16 .04
- ☐ 508 Montreal Expos .80 .35 .08
  Team Card
- ☐ 509 Jesse Jefferson .40 .16 .04
- ☐ 510 Wayne Garrett .40 .16 .04
- ☐ 511 Toby Harrah .60 .25 .06
- ☐ 512 Joe Lahoud .40 .16 .04
- ☐ 513 Jim Campanis .40 .16 .04
- ☐ 514 Paul Schaal .40 .16 .04
- ☐ 515 Willie Montanez .40 .16 .04
- ☐ 516 Horacio Pina .40 .16 .04
- ☐ 517 Mike Hegan .40 .16 .04
- ☐ 518 Derrel Thomas .40 .16 .04
- ☐ 519 Bill Sharp .40 .16 .04
- ☐ 520 Tim McCarver .75 .30 .07
- ☐ 521 Indians Leaders .60 .25 .06
  Ken Aspromonte MG
  Clay Bryant CO
  Tony Pacheco CO
- ☐ 522 J.R. Richard .60 .25 .06
- ☐ 523 Cecil Cooper 1.75 .70 .17
- ☐ 524 Bill Plummer .60 .25 .06
- ☐ 525 Clyde Wright .40 .16 .04
- ☐ 526 Frank Tepedino .40 .16 .04
- ☐ 527 Bobby Darwin .40 .16 .04
- ☐ 528 Bill Bonham .40 .16 .04
- ☐ 529 Horace Clarke .40 .16 .04

Card			
☐ 530 Mickey Stanley	.60	.25	.06
☐ 531 Expos Leaders	.60	.25	.06
Gene Mauch MG			
Dave Bristol CO			
Cal McLish CO			
Larry Doby CO			
Jerry Zimmerman CO			
☐ 532 Skip Lockwood	.40	.16	.04
☐ 533 Mike Phillips	.40	.16	.04
☐ 534 Eddie Watt	.40	.16	.04
☐ 535 Bob Tolan	.40	.16	.04
☐ 536 Duffy Dyer	.40	.16	.04
☐ 537 Steve Mingori	.40	.16	.04
☐ 538 Cesar Tovar	.40	.16	.04
☐ 539 Lloyd Allen	.40	.16	.04
☐ 540 Bob Robertson	.40	.16	.04
☐ 541 Cleveland Indians	.80	.35	.08
Team Card			
☐ 542 Rich Gossage	3.75	1.60	.37
☐ 543 Danny Cater	.40	.16	.04
☐ 544 Ron Schueler	.40	.16	.04
☐ 545 Billy Conigliaro	.40	.16	.04
☐ 546 Mike Corkins	.40	.16	.04
☐ 547 Glenn Borgmann	.40	.16	.04
☐ 548 Sonny Siebert	.40	.16	.04
☐ 549 Mike Jorgensen	.40	.16	.04
☐ 550 Sam McDowell	.60	.25	.06
☐ 551 Von Joshua	.40	.16	.04
☐ 552 Denny Doyle	.40	.16	.04
☐ 553 Jim Willoughby	.40	.16	.04
☐ 554 Tim Johnson	.40	.16	.04
☐ 555 Woodie Fryman	.40	.16	.04
☐ 556 Dave Campbell	.40	.16	.04
☐ 557 Jim McGlothlin	.40	.16	.04
☐ 558 Bill Fahey	.40	.16	.04
☐ 559 Darrell Chaney	.40	.16	.04
☐ 560 Mike Cuellar	.60	.25	.06
☐ 561 Ed Kranepool	.60	.25	.06
☐ 562 Jack Aker	.40	.16	.04
☐ 563 Hal McRae	.75	.30	.07
☐ 564 Mike Ryan	.40	.16	.04
☐ 565 Milt Wilcox	.40	.16	.04
☐ 566 Jackie Hernandez	.40	.16	.04
☐ 567 Boston Red Sox	.80	.35	.08
Team Card			
☐ 568 Mike Torrez	.60	.25	.06
☐ 569 Rick Dempsey	.60	.25	.06
☐ 570 Ralph Garr	.60	.25	.06
☐ 571 Rich Hand	.40	.16	.04
☐ 572 Enzo Hernandez	.40	.16	.04
☐ 573 Mike Adams	.40	.16	.04
☐ 574 Bill Parsons	.40	.16	.04
☐ 575 Steve Garvey	12.00	5.25	1.50
☐ 576 Scipio Spinks	.40	.16	.04
☐ 577 Mike Sadek	.40	.16	.04
☐ 578 Ralph Houk MG	.60	.25	.06
☐ 579 Cecil Upshaw	.40	.16	.04
☐ 580 Jim Spencer	.40	.16	.04

Card			
☐ 581 Fred Norman	.40	.16	.04
☐ 582 Bucky Dent	2.00	.80	.20
☐ 583 Marty Pattin	.40	.16	.04
☐ 584 Ken Rudolph	.40	.16	.04
☐ 585 Merv Rettenmund	.40	.16	.04
☐ 586 Jack Brohamer	.40	.16	.04
☐ 587 Larry Christenson	.40	.16	.04
☐ 588 Hal Lanier	.40	.16	.04
☐ 589 Boots Day	.40	.16	.04
☐ 590 Roger Moret	.40	.16	.04
☐ 591 Sonny Jackson	.40	.16	.04
☐ 592 Ed Bane	.40	.16	.04
☐ 593 Steve Yeager	.60	.25	.06
☐ 594 Leroy Stanton	.40	.16	.04
☐ 595 Steve Blass	.40	.16	.04
☐ 596 Rookie Pitchers	.40	.16	.04
Wayne Garland			
Fred Holdsworth			
Mark Littell			
Dick Pole			
☐ 597 Rookie Shortstops	.60	.25	.06
Dave Chalk			
John Gamble			
Pete MacKanin			
Manny Trillo			
☐ 598 Rookie Outfielders	22.00	9.50	3.15
Dave Augustine			
Ken Griffey			
Steve Ontiveros			
Jim Tyrone			
☐ 599A Rookie Pitchers WAS	.60	.25	.06
Ron Diorio			
Dave Freisleben			
Frank Riccelli			
Greg Shanahan			
☐ 599B Rookie Pitchers SD	3.00	1.25	.30
(SD in large print)			
☐ 599C Rookie Pitchers SD	5.00	2.25	.50
(SD in small print)			
☐ 600 Rookie Infielders	4.50	2.00	.45
Ron Cash			
Jim Cox			
Bill Madlock			
Reggie Sanders			
☐ 601 Rookie Outfielders	4.50	2.00	.45
Ed Armbrister			
Rich Bladt			
Brian Downing			
Bake McBride			
☐ 602 Rookie Pitchers	.60	.25	.06
Glen Abbott			
Rick Henninger			
Craig Swan			
Dan Vossler			
☐ 603 Rookie Catchers	.60	.25	.06
Barry Foote			
Tom Lundstedt			
Charlie Moore			

Sergio Robles
☐ 604 Rookie Infielders .... 4.50 2.00 .45
Terry Hughes
John Knox
Andy Thornton
Frank White
☐ 605 Rookie Pitchers .... 3.00 1.25 .30
Vic Albury
Ken Frailing
Kevin Kobel
Frank Tanana
☐ 606 Rookie Outfielders .... .40 .16 .04
Jim Fuller
Wilbur Howard
Tommy Smith
Otto Velez
☐ 607 Rookie Shortstops .... .40 .16 .04
Leo Foster
Tom Heintzelman
Dave Rosello
Frank Taveras
☐ 608A Rookie Pitchers: ERR 2.00 .80 .20
Bob Apodaco (sic)
Dick Baney
John D'Acquisto
Mike Wallace
☐ 608B Rookie Pitchers: COR .. .40 .16 .04
Bob Apodaca
Dick Baney
John D'Acquisto
Mike Wallace

☐ 609	Rico Petrocelli	.60	.25	.06
☐ 610	Dave Kingman	1.00	.40	.10
☐ 611	Rich Stelmaszek	.40	.16	.04
☐ 612	Luke Walker	.40	.16	.04
☐ 613	Dan Monzon	.40	.16	.04
☐ 614	Adrian Devine	.40	.16	.04
☐ 615	Johnny Jeter	.40	.16	.04
☐ 616	Larry Gura	.60	.25	.06
☐ 617	Ted Ford	.40	.16	.04
☐ 618	Jim Mason	.40	.16	.04
☐ 619	Mike Anderson	.40	.16	.04
☐ 620	Al Downing	.60	.25	.06
☐ 621	Bernie Carbo	.40	.16	.04
☐ 622	Phil Gagliano	.40	.16	.04
☐ 623	Celerino Sanchez	.40	.16	.04
☐ 624	Bob Miller	.40	.16	.04
☐ 625	Ollie Brown	.40	.16	.04
☐ 626	Pittsburgh Pirates .... Team Card	.80	.35	.08
☐ 627	Carl Taylor	.40	.16	.04
☐ 628	Ivan Murrell	.40	.16	.04
☐ 629	Rusty Staub	.75	.30	.07
☐ 630	Tommy Agee	.60	.25	.06
☐ 631	Steve Barber	.40	.16	.04
☐ 632	George Culver	.40	.16	.04
☐ 633	Dave Hamilton	.40	.16	.04
☐ 634	Braves Leaders	1.00	.40	.10

Eddie Mathews MG
Herm Starrette CO
Connie Ryan CO
Jim Busby CO
Ken Silvestri CO

☐ 635	Johnny Edwards	.40	.16	.04
☐ 636	Dave Goltz	.40	.16	.04
☐ 637	Checklist 5	2.00	.20	.04
☐ 638	Ken Sanders	.40	.16	.04
☐ 639	Joe Lovitto	.40	.16	.04
☐ 640	Milt Pappas	.60	.25	.06
☐ 641	Chuck Brinkman	.40	.16	.04
☐ 642	Terry Harmon	.40	.16	.04
☐ 643	Dodgers Team	.80	.35	.08
☐ 644	Wayne Granger	.40	.16	.04
☐ 645	Ken Boswell	.40	.16	.04
☐ 646	George Foster	1.50	.60	.15
☐ 647	Juan Beniquez	.60	.25	.06
☐ 648	Terry Crowley	.40	.16	.04
☐ 649	Fernando Gonzalez	.40	.16	.04
☐ 650	Mike Epstein	.40	.16	.04
☐ 651	Leron Lee	.40	.16	.04
☐ 652	Gail Hopkins	.40	.16	.04
☐ 653	Bob Stinson	.40	.16	.04
☐ 654A	Jesus Alou ERR .... (no position)	7.50	3.25	.75
☐ 654B	Jesus Alou COR .... (outfield)	.60	.25	.06
☐ 655	Mike Tyson	.40	.16	.04
☐ 656	Adrian Garrett	.40	.16	.04
☐ 657	Jim Shellenback	.40	.16	.04
☐ 658	Lee Lacy	.40	.16	.04
☐ 659	Joe Lis	.40	.16	.04
☐ 660	Larry Dierker	.60	.25	.06

1974 Topps Traded

The cards in this 44-card set measure 2 1/2" by 3 1/2". The 1974 Topps Traded set contains 43 player cards and one unnumbered checklist card. The obverses have the word "traded" in block letters and the backs are designed in newspaper style. Card numbers are the same as in the regular set except they are followed by a "T." No known scarcities exist for this set.

	NRMT	VG-E	GOOD
COMPLETE SET (44)	11.00	5.00	1.35
COMMON PLAYER	.25	.10	.02
☐ 23T Craig Robinson	.25	.10	.02
☐ 42T Claude Osteen	.35	.15	.03

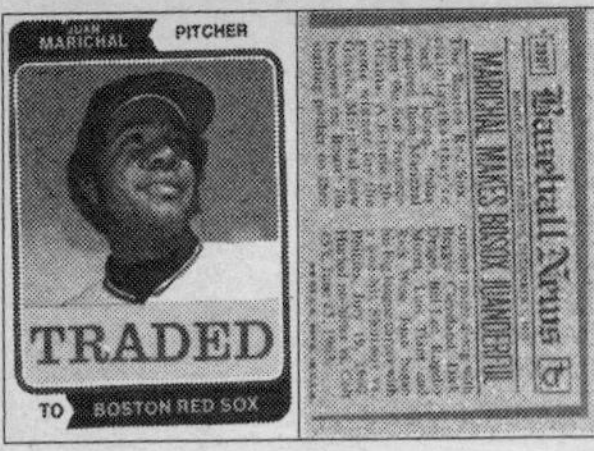

☐ 43T Jim Wynn	.35	.15	.03
☐ 51T Bobby Heise	.25	.10	.02
☐ 59T Ross Grimsley	.25	.10	.02
☐ 62T Bob Locker	.25	.10	.02
☐ 63T Bill Sudakis	.25	.10	.02
☐ 73T Mike Marshall	.50	.20	.05
☐ 123T Nelson Briles	.35	.15	.03
☐ 139T Aurelio Monteagudo	.25	.10	.02
☐ 151T Diego Segui	.25	.10	.02
☐ 165T Willie Davis	.35	.15	.03
☐ 175T Reggie Cleveland	.25	.10	.02
☐ 182T Lindy McDaniel	.25	.10	.02
☐ 186T Fred Scherman	.25	.10	.02
☐ 249T George Mitterwald	.25	.10	.02
☐ 262T Ed Kirkpatrick	.25	.10	.02
☐ 269T Bob Johnson	.25	.10	.02
☐ 270T Ron Santo	.60	.25	.06
☐ 313T Barry Lersch	.25	.10	.02
☐ 319T Randy Hundley	.35	.15	.03
☐ 330T Juan Marichal	2.00	.80	.20
☐ 348T Pete Richert	.25	.10	.02
☐ 373T John Curtis	.25	.10	.02
☐ 390T Lou Piniella	.60	.25	.06
☐ 428T Gary Sutherland	.25	.10	.02
☐ 454T Kurt Bevacqua	.25	.10	.02
☐ 458T Jim Ray	.25	.10	.02
☐ 485T Felipe Alou	.35	.15	.03
☐ 486T Steve Stone	.35	.15	.03
☐ 496T Tom Murphy	.25	.10	.02
☐ 516T Horacio Pina	.25	.10	.02
☐ 534T Eddie Watt	.25	.10	.02
☐ 538T Cesar Tovar	.25	.10	.02
☐ 544T Ron Schueler	.25	.10	.02
☐ 579T Cecil Upshaw	.25	.10	.02
☐ 585T Merv Rettenmund	.25	.10	.02
☐ 612T Luke Walker	.25	.10	.02
☐ 616T Larry Gura	.35	.15	.03
☐ 618T Jim Mason	.25	.10	.02
☐ 630T Tommie Agee	.35	.15	.03
☐ 648T Terry Crowley	.25	.10	.02
☐ 649T Fernando Gonzalez	.25	.10	.02
☐ xxxT Traded Checklist (unnumbered)	.65	.10	.02

1975 Topps

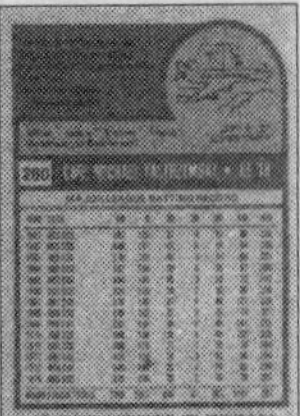

The cards in the 1975 Topps set were issued in two different sizes: a regular standard size (2 1/2" by 3 1/2") and a mini size (2 1/2" by 3 1/8") which was issued as a test in certain areas of the country. The 660-card Topps baseball set for 1975 was radically different in appearance from sets of the preceding years. The most prominent change was the use of a two-color frame surrounding the picture area rather than a single, subdued color. A facsimile autograph appears on the picture, and the backs are printed in red and green on gray. Cards 189-212 depict the MVP's of both leagues from 1951 through 1974. The first seven cards (1-7) feature players breaking records or achieving milestones during the previous season. Cards 306-313 picture league leaders in various statistical categories. Cards 459-466 depict the results of post-season action. Team cards feature a checklist back for players on that team and show a small inset photo of the manager on the front. The Phillies Team card number 46 erroneously lists Terry Harmon as number 339 instead of number 399. This set is quite popular with collectors, at least in part due to the fact that the rookie cards of Robin Yount, George Brett, Gary Carter, Jim Rice, Fred Lynn, and Keith Hernandez are all in the set. Topps minis have the same checklist and are worth approximately double the prices listed below.

	NRMT	VG-E	GOOD
COMPLETE SET (660)	825.00	375.00	95.00
COMMON PLAYER (1-132)	.40	.16	.04
COMMON PLAYER (133-264)	.40	.16	.04
COMMON PLAYER (265-660)	.40	.16	.04
☐ 1 RB: Hank Aaron	25.00	5.00	1.00

Sets Homer Mark
☐ 2 RB: Lou Brock .... 3.00 1.25 .30
118 Stolen Bases
☐ 3 RB: Bob Gibson .... 3.00 1.25 .30
3000th Strikeout
☐ 4 RB: Al Kaline .... 3.00 1.25 .30
3000 Hit Club
☐ 5 RB: Nolan Ryan 12.00 5.25 1.50
Fans 300 for
3rd Year in a Row
☐ 6 RB: Mike Marshall .... .60 .25 .06
Hurls 106 Games
☐ 7 No Hitters .... 3.00 1.25 .30
Steve Busby
Dick Bosman
Nolan Ryan
☐ 8 Rogelio Moret .... .40 .16 .04
☐ 9 Frank Tepedino .... .40 .16 .04
☐ 10 Willie Davis .... .60 .25 .06
☐ 11 Bill Melton .... .40 .16 .04
☐ 12 David Clyde .... .40 .16 .04
☐ 13 Gene Locklear .... .40 .16 .04
☐ 14 Milt Wilcox .... .40 .16 .04
☐ 15 Jose Cardenal .... .40 .16 .04
☐ 16 Frank Tanana .... 1.00 .40 .10
☐ 17 Dave Concepcion .... 1.50 .60 .15
☐ 18 Tigers: Team/Mgr. .... 1.25 .40 .08
Ralph Houk
(checklist back)
☐ 19 Jerry Koosman .... .75 .30 .07
☐ 20 Thurman Munson .... 8.00 3.50 .80
☐ 21 Rollie Fingers .... 4.25 1.75 .42
☐ 22 Dave Cash .... .40 .16 .04
☐ 23 Bill Russell .... .60 .25 .06
☐ 24 Al Fitzmorris .... .40 .16 .04
☐ 25 Lee May .... .60 .25 .06
☐ 26 Dave McNally .... .60 .25 .06
☐ 27 Ken Reitz .... .40 .16 .04
☐ 28 Tom Murphy .... .40 .16 .04
☐ 29 Dave Parker 12.00 5.25 1.50
☐ 30 Bert Blyleven .... 2.00 .80 .20
☐ 31 Dave Rader .... .40 .16 .04
☐ 32 Reggie Cleveland .... .40 .16 .04
☐ 33 Dusty Baker .... .60 .25 .06
☐ 34 Steve Renko .... .40 .16 .04
☐ 35 Ron Santo .... .75 .30 .07
☐ 36 Joe Lovitto .... .40 .16 .04
☐ 37 Dave Freisleben .... .40 .16 .04
☐ 38 Buddy Bell .... .75 .30 .07
☐ 39 Andre Thornton .... .60 .25 .06
☐ 40 Bill Singer .... .40 .16 .04
☐ 41 Cesar Geronimo .... .40 .16 .04
☐ 42 Joe Coleman .... .40 .16 .04
☐ 43 Cleon Jones .... .40 .16 .04
☐ 44 Pat Dobson .... .40 .16 .04
☐ 45 Joe Rudi .... .60 .25 .06
☐ 46 Phillies: Team/Mgr. .... 1.25 .40 .08
Danny Ozark UER
(checklist back)
☐ 47 Tommy John .... 1.75 .70 .17
☐ 48 Freddie Patek .... .40 .16 .04
☐ 49 Larry Dierker .... .40 .16 .04
☐ 50 Brooks Robinson .... 5.00 2.25 .50
☐ 51 Bob Forsch .... .75 .30 .07
☐ 52 Darrell Porter .... .40 .16 .04
☐ 53 Dave Giusti .... .40 .16 .04
☐ 54 Eric Soderholm .... .40 .16 .04
☐ 55 Bobby Bonds .... 1.00 .40 .10
☐ 56 Rick Wise .... .40 .16 .04
☐ 57 Dave Johnson .... .60 .25 .06
☐ 58 Chuck Taylor .... .40 .16 .04
☐ 59 Ken Henderson .... .40 .16 .04
☐ 60 Fergie Jenkins .... 3.25 1.35 .32
☐ 61 Dave Winfield 25.00 11.00 3.50
☐ 62 Fritz Peterson .... .40 .16 .04
☐ 63 Steve Swisher .... .40 .16 .04
☐ 64 Dave Chalk .... .40 .16 .04
☐ 65 Don Gullett .... .60 .25 .06
☐ 66 Willie Horton .... .60 .25 .06
☐ 67 Tug McGraw .... .75 .30 .07
☐ 68 Ron Blomberg .... .40 .16 .04
☐ 69 John Odom .... .40 .16 .04
☐ 70 Mike Schmidt 60.00 27.00 9.00
☐ 71 Charlie Hough .... .60 .25 .06
☐ 72 Royals: Team/Mgr. .... 1.25 .40 .08
Jack McKeon
(checklist back)
☐ 73 J.R. Richard .... .60 .25 .06
☐ 74 Mark Belanger .... .60 .25 .06
☐ 75 Ted Simmons .... 1.50 .60 .15
☐ 76 Ed Sprague .... .40 .16 .04
☐ 77 Richie Zisk .... .40 .16 .04
☐ 78 Ray Corbin .... .40 .16 .04
☐ 79 Gary Matthews .... .60 .25 .06
☐ 80 Carlton Fisk 16.00 6.75 2.25
☐ 81 Ron Reed .... .40 .16 .04
☐ 82 Pat Kelly .... .40 .16 .04
☐ 83 Jim Merritt .... .40 .16 .04
☐ 84 Enzo Hernandez .... .40 .16 .04
☐ 85 Bill Bonham .... .40 .16 .04
☐ 86 Joe Lis .... .40 .16 .04
☐ 87 George Foster .... 1.50 .60 .15
☐ 88 Tom Egan .... .40 .16 .04
☐ 89 Jim Ray .... .40 .16 .04
☐ 90 Rusty Staub .... .75 .30 .07
☐ 91 Dick Green .... .40 .16 .04
☐ 92 Cecil Upshaw .... .40 .16 .04
☐ 93 Dave Lopes .... .60 .25 .06
☐ 94 Jim Lonborg .... .60 .25 .06
☐ 95 John Mayberry .... .60 .25 .06
☐ 96 Mike Cosgrove .... .40 .16 .04
☐ 97 Earl Williams .... .40 .16 .04
☐ 98 Rich Folkers .... .40 .16 .04
☐ 99 Mike Hegan .... .40 .16 .04
☐ 100 Willie Stargell .... 3.50 1.50 .35
☐ 101 Expos: Team/Mgr. .... 1.25 .40 .08

Gene Mauch
(checklist back)
□ 102 Joe Decker .40 .16 .04
□ 103 Rick Miller .40 .16 .04
□ 104 Bill Madlock 1.25 .50 .12
□ 105 Buzz Capra .40 .16 .04
□ 106 Mike Hargrove .75 .30 .07
□ 107 Jim Barr .40 .16 .04
□ 108 Tom Hall .40 .16 .04
□ 109 George Hendrick .60 .25 .06
□ 110 Wilbur Wood .60 .25 .06
□ 111 Wayne Garrett .40 .16 .04
□ 112 Larry Hardy .40 .16 .04
□ 113 Elliott Maddox .40 .16 .04
□ 114 Dick Lange .40 .16 .04
□ 115 Joe Ferguson .40 .16 .04
□ 116 Lerrin LaGrow .40 .16 .04
□ 117 Orioles: Team/Mgr. 1.25 .40 .08
Earl Weaver
(checklist back)
□ 118 Mike Anderson .40 .16 .04
□ 119 Tommy Helms .60 .25 .06
□ 120 Steve Busby UER .60 .25 .06
(photo actually
Fran Healy)
□ 121 Bill North .40 .16 .04
□ 122 Al Hrabosky .40 .16 .04
□ 123 Johnny Briggs .40 .16 .04
□ 124 Jerry Reuss .60 .25 .06
□ 125 Ken Singleton .60 .25 .06
□ 126 Checklist 1-132 1.75 .20 .04
□ 127 Glenn Borgmann .40 .16 .04
□ 128 Bill Lee .60 .25 .06
□ 129 Rick Monday .60 .25 .06
□ 130 Phil Niekro 2.75 1.10 .27
□ 131 Toby Harrah .60 .25 .06
□ 132 Randy Moffitt .40 .16 .04
□ 133 Dan Driessen .40 .16 .04
□ 134 Ron Hodges .40 .16 .04
□ 135 Charlie Spikes .40 .16 .04
□ 136 Jim Mason .40 .16 .04
□ 137 Terry Forster .60 .25 .06
□ 138 Del Unser .40 .16 .04
□ 139 Horacio Pina .40 .16 .04
□ 140 Steve Garvey 8.50 3.75 .85
□ 141 Mickey Stanley .60 .25 .06
□ 142 Bob Reynolds .40 .16 .04
□ 143 Cliff Johnson .60 .25 .06
□ 144 Jim Wohlford .40 .16 .04
□ 145 Ken Holtzman .60 .25 .06
□ 146 Padres: Team/Mgr. 1.25 .40 .08
John McNamara
(checklist back)
□ 147 Pedro Garcia .40 .16 .04
□ 148 Jim Rooker .40 .16 .04
□ 149 Tim Foli .40 .16 .04
□ 150 Bob Gibson 4.25 1.75 .42
□ 151 Steve Brye .40 .16 .04
□ 152 Mario Guerrero .40 .16 .04
□ 153 Rick Reuschel .75 .30 .07
□ 154 Mike Lum .40 .16 .04
□ 155 Jim Bibby .40 .16 .04
□ 156 Dave Kingman 1.00 .40 .10
□ 157 Pedro Borbon .40 .16 .04
□ 158 Jerry Grote .40 .16 .04
□ 159 Steve Arlin .40 .16 .04
□ 160 Graig Nettles 1.50 .60 .15
□ 161 Stan Bahnsen .40 .16 .04
□ 162 Willie Montanez .40 .16 .04
□ 163 Jim Brewer .40 .16 .04
□ 164 Mickey Rivers .60 .25 .06
□ 165 Doug Rader .60 .25 .06
□ 166 Woodie Fryman .40 .16 .04
□ 167 Rich Coggins .40 .16 .04
□ 168 Bill Greif .40 .16 .04
□ 169 Cookie Rojas .40 .16 .04
□ 170 Bert Campaneris .60 .25 .06
□ 171 Ed Kirkpatrick .40 .16 .04
□ 172 Red Sox: Team/Mgr. 1.25 .40 .08
Darrell Johnson
(checklist back)
□ 173 Steve Rogers .40 .16 .04
□ 174 Bake McBride .60 .25 .06
□ 175 Don Money .40 .16 .04
□ 176 Burt Hooton .40 .16 .04
□ 177 Vic Correll .40 .16 .04
□ 178 Cesar Tovar .40 .16 .04
□ 179 Tom Bradley .40 .16 .04
□ 180 Joe Morgan 6.50 2.75 .65
□ 181 Fred Beene .40 .16 .04
□ 182 Don Hahn .40 .16 .04
□ 183 Mel Stottlemyre .75 .30 .07
□ 184 Jorge Orta .40 .16 .04
□ 185 Steve Carlton 8.50 3.75 .85
□ 186 Willie Crawford .40 .16 .04
□ 187 Denny Doyle .40 .16 .04
□ 188 Tom Griffin .40 .16 .04
□ 189 1951 MVP's 2.00 .80 .20
Larry (Yogi) Berra
Roy Campanella
(Campy never issued)
□ 190 1952 MVP's .60 .25 .06
Bobby Shantz
Hank Sauer
□ 191 1953 MVP's 1.00 .40 .10
Al Rosen
Roy Campanella
□ 192 1954 MVP's 2.00 .80 .20
Yogi Berra
Willie Mays
□ 193 1955 MVP's 2.00 .80 .20
Yogi Berra
Roy Campanella
(Campy card never
issued, pictured
with LA cap, sic)

☐ 194	1956 MVP's Mickey Mantle Don Newcombe	5.00	2.25	.50
☐ 195	1957 MVP's Mickey Mantle Hank Aaron	9.00	4.00	.90
☐ 196	1958 MVP's Jackie Jensen Ernie Banks	1.00	.40	.10
☐ 197	1959 MVP's Nellie Fox Ernie Banks	1.25	.50	.12
☐ 198	1960 MVP's Roger Maris Dick Groat	1.25	.50	.12
☐ 199	1961 MVP's Roger Maris Frank Robinson	2.00	.80	.20
☐ 200	1962 MVP's Mickey Mantle Maury Wills (Wills never issued)	5.00	2.25	.50
☐ 201	1963 MVP's Elston Howard Sandy Koufax	1.00	.40	.10
☐ 202	1964 MVP's Brooks Robinson Ken Boyer	1.00	.40	.10
☐ 203	1965 MVP's Zoilo Versalles Willie Mays	1.00	.40	.10
☐ 204	1966 MVP's Frank Robinson Bob Clemente	2.00	.80	.20
☐ 205	1967 MVP's Carl Yastrzemski Orlando Cepeda	1.25	.50	.12
☐ 206	1968 MVP's Denny McLain Bob Gibson	1.25	.50	.12
☐ 207	1969 MVP's Harmon Killebrew Willie McCovey	1.25	.50	.12
☐ 208	1970 MVP's Boog Powell Johnny Bench	1.00	.40	.10
☐ 209	1971 MVP's Vida Blue Joe Torre	.60	.25	.06
☐ 210	1972 MVP's Rich Allen Johnny Bench	1.00	.40	.10
☐ 211	1973 MVP's Reggie Jackson Pete Rose	4.00	1.75	.40
☐ 212	1974 MVP's Jeff Burroughs Steve Garvey	.75	.30	.07
☐ 213	Oscar Gamble	.60	.25	.06
☐ 214	Harry Parker	.40	.16	.04
☐ 215	Bobby Valentine	.60	.25	.06
☐ 216	Giants: Team/Mgr. Wes Westrum (checklist back)	1.25	.40	.08
☐ 217	Lou Piniella	.75	.30	.07
☐ 218	Jerry Johnson	.40	.16	.04
☐ 219	Ed Herrmann	.40	.16	.04
☐ 220	Don Sutton	2.50	1.00	.25
☐ 221	Aurelio Rodriguez	.40	.16	.04
☐ 222	Dan Spillner	.40	.16	.04
☐ 223	Robin Yount	195.00	80.00	16.00
☐ 224	Ramon Hernandez	.40	.16	.04
☐ 225	Bob Grich	.60	.25	.06
☐ 226	Bill Campbell	.40	.16	.04
☐ 227	Bob Watson	.60	.25	.06
☐ 228	George Brett	195.00	80.00	16.00
☐ 229	Barry Foote	.40	.16	.04
☐ 230	Jim Hunter	3.25	1.35	.32
☐ 231	Mike Tyson	.40	.16	.04
☐ 232	Diego Segui	.40	.16	.04
☐ 233	Billy Grabarkewitz	.40	.16	.04
☐ 234	Tom Grieve	.60	.25	.06
☐ 235	Jack Billingham	.40	.16	.04
☐ 236	Angels: Team/Mgr. Dick Williams (checklist back)	1.25	.40	.08
☐ 237	Carl Morton	.40	.16	.04
☐ 238	Dave Duncan	.40	.16	.04
☐ 239	George Stone	.40	.16	.04
☐ 240	Garry Maddox	.60	.25	.06
☐ 241	Dick Tidrow	.40	.16	.04
☐ 242	Jay Johnstone	.60	.25	.06
☐ 243	Jim Kaat	1.00	.40	.10
☐ 244	Bill Buckner	.75	.30	.07
☐ 245	Mickey Lolich	.75	.30	.07
☐ 246	Cardinals: Team/Mgr. Red Schoendienst (checklist back)	1.25	.40	.08
☐ 247	Enos Cabell	.40	.16	.04
☐ 248	Randy Jones	.60	.25	.06
☐ 249	Danny Thompson	.40	.16	.04
☐ 250	Ken Brett	.40	.16	.04
☐ 251	Fran Healy	.40	.16	.04
☐ 252	Fred Scherman	.40	.16	.04
☐ 253	Jesus Alou	.40	.16	.04
☐ 254	Mike Torrez	.40	.16	.04
☐ 255	Dwight Evans	7.00	3.00	.70
☐ 256	Billy Champion	.40	.16	.04
☐ 257	Checklist: 133-264	1.75	.20	.04
☐ 258	Dave LaRoche	.40	.16	.04
☐ 259	Len Randle	.40	.16	.04
☐ 260	Johnny Bench	13.50	6.00	1.85
☐ 261	Andy Hassler	.40	.16	.04
☐ 262	Rowland Office	.40	.16	.04
☐ 263	Jim Perry	.60	.25	.06
☐ 264	John Milner	.40	.16	.04

☐ 265	Ron Bryant	.40	.16	.0
☐ 266	Sandy Alomar	.40	.16	.04
☐ 267	Dick Ruthven	.40	.16	.04
☐ 268	Hal McRae	.75	.30	.07
☐ 269	Doug Rau	.40	.16	.04
☐ 270	Ron Fairly	.40	.16	.04
☐ 271	Gerry Moses	.40	.16	.04
☐ 272	Lynn McGlothen	.40	.16	.04
☐ 273	Steve Braun	.40	.16	.04
☐ 274	Vicente Romo	.40	.16	.04
☐ 275	Paul Blair	.60	.25	.06
☐ 276	White Sox Team/Mgr.	1.25	.40	.08
	Chuck Tanner			
	(checklist back)			
☐ 277	Frank Taveras	.40	.16	.04
☐ 278	Paul Lindblad	.40	.16	.04
☐ 279	Milt May	.40	.16	.04
☐ 280	Carl Yastrzemski	10.00	4.50	1.25
☐ 281	Jim Slaton	.40	.16	.04
☐ 282	Jerry Morales	.40	.16	.04
☐ 283	Steve Foucault	.40	.16	.04
☐ 284	Ken Griffey	3.75	1.60	.37
☐ 285	Ellie Rodriguez	.40	.16	.04
☐ 286	Mike Jorgensen	.40	.16	.04
☐ 287	Roric Harrison	.40	.16	.04
☐ 288	Bruce Ellingsen	.40	.16	.04
☐ 289	Ken Rudolph	.40	.16	.04
☐ 290	Jon Matlack	.60	.25	.06
☐ 291	Bill Sudakis	.40	.16	.04
☐ 292	Ron Schueler	.40	.16	.04
☐ 293	Dick Sharon	.40	.16	.04
☐ 294	Geoff Zahn	.40	.16	.04
☐ 295	Vada Pinson	.60	.25	.06
☐ 296	Alan Foster	.40	.16	.04
☐ 297	Craig Kusick	.40	.16	.04
☐ 298	Johnny Grubb	.40	.16	.04
☐ 299	Bucky Dent	.75	.30	.07
☐ 300	Reggie Jackson	18.00	7.50	2.50
☐ 301	Dave Roberts	.40	.16	.04
☐ 302	Rick Burleson	.60	.25	.06
☐ 303	Grant Jackson	.40	.16	.04
☐ 304	Pirates: Team/Mgr.	1.25	.40	.08
	Danny Murtaugh			
	(checklist back)			
☐ 305	Jim Colborn	.40	.16	.04
☐ 306	Batting Leaders	1.00	.40	.10
	Rod Carew			
	Ralph Garr			
☐ 307	Home Run Leaders	2.50	1.00	.25
	Dick Allen			
	Mike Schmidt			
☐ 308	RBI Leaders	1.00	.40	.10
	Jeff Burroughs			
	Johnny Bench			
☐ 309	Stolen Base Leaders	1.00	.40	.10
	Bill North			
	Lou Brock			
☐ 310	Victory Leaders	1.00	.40	.10
	Jim Hunter			
	Fergie Jenkins			
	Andy Messersmith			
	Phil Niekro			
☐ 311	ERA Leaders	1.00	.40	.10
	Jim Hunter			
	Buzz Capra			
☐ 312	Strikeout Leaders	7.00	3.00	.70
	Nolan Ryan			
	Steve Carlton			
☐ 313	Leading Firemen	.60	.25	.06
	Terry Forster			
	Mike Marshall			
☐ 314	Buck Martinez	.40	.16	.04
☐ 315	Don Kessinger	.60	.25	.06
☐ 316	Jackie Brown	.40	.16	.04
☐ 317	Joe Lahoud	.40	.16	.04
☐ 318	Ernie McAnally	.40	.16	.04
☐ 319	Johnny Oates	.60	.25	.06
☐ 320	Pete Rose	15.00	6.50	2.15
☐ 321	Rudy May	.40	.16	.04
☐ 322	Ed Goodson	.40	.16	.04
☐ 323	Fred Holdsworth	.40	.16	.04
☐ 324	Ed Kranepool	.60	.25	.06
☐ 325	Tony Oliva	1.00	.40	.10
☐ 326	Wayne Twitchell	.40	.16	.04
☐ 327	Jerry Hairston	.40	.16	.04
☐ 328	Sonny Siebert	.40	.16	.04
☐ 329	Ted Kubiak	.40	.16	.04
☐ 330	Mike Marshall	.60	.25	.06
☐ 331	Indians: Team/Mgr.	1.25	.40	.08
	Frank Robinson			
	(checklist back)			
☐ 332	Fred Kendall	.40	.16	.04
☐ 333	Dick Drago	.40	.16	.04
☐ 334	Greg Gross	.40	.16	.04
☐ 335	Jim Palmer	8.50	3.75	.85
☐ 336	Rennie Stennett	.40	.16	.04
☐ 337	Kevin Kobel	.40	.16	.04
☐ 338	Rich Stelmaszek	.40	.16	.04
☐ 339	Jim Fregosi	.60	.25	.06
☐ 340	Paul Splittorff	.40	.16	.04
☐ 341	Hal Breeden	.40	.16	.04
☐ 342	Leroy Stanton	.40	.16	.04
☐ 343	Danny Frisella	.40	.16	.04
☐ 344	Ben Oglivie	.60	.25	.06
☐ 345	Clay Carroll	.40	.16	.04
☐ 346	Bobby Darwin	.40	.16	.04
☐ 347	Mike Caldwell	.40	.16	.04
☐ 348	Tony Muser	.40	.16	.04
☐ 349	Ray Sadecki	.40	.16	.04
☐ 350	Bobby Murcer	.75	.30	.07
☐ 351	Bob Boone	1.25	.50	.12
☐ 352	Darold Knowles	.40	.16	.04
☐ 353	Luis Melendez	.40	.16	.04
☐ 354	Dick Bosman	.40	.16	.04
☐ 355	Chris Cannizzaro	.40	.16	.04
☐ 356	Rico Petrocelli	.60	.25	.06

Card	Player			
☐ 357	Ken Forsch	.40	.16	.04
☐ 358	Al Bumbry	.40	.16	.04
☐ 359	Paul Popovich	.40	.16	.04
☐ 360	George Scott	.60	.25	.06
☐ 361	Dodgers: Team/Mgr. Walter Alston (checklist back)	1.50	.50	.10
☐ 362	Steve Hargan	.40	.16	.04
☐ 363	Carmen Fanzone	.40	.16	.04
☐ 364	Doug Bird	.40	.16	.04
☐ 365	Bob Bailey	.40	.16	.04
☐ 366	Ken Sanders	.40	.16	.04
☐ 367	Craig Robinson	.40	.16	.04
☐ 368	Vic Albury	.40	.16	.04
☐ 369	Merv Rettenmund	.40	.16	.04
☐ 370	Tom Seaver	16.00	6.75	2.25
☐ 371	Gates Brown	.60	.25	.06
☐ 372	John D'Acquisto	.40	.16	.04
☐ 373	Bill Sharp	.40	.16	.04
☐ 374	Eddie Watt	.40	.16	.04
☐ 375	Roy White	.60	.25	.06
☐ 376	Steve Yeager	.60	.25	.06
☐ 377	Tom Hilgendorf	.40	.16	.04
☐ 378	Derrel Thomas	.40	.16	.04
☐ 379	Bernie Carbo	.40	.16	.04
☐ 380	Sal Bando	.60	.25	.06
☐ 381	John Curtis	.40	.16	.04
☐ 382	Don Baylor	1.50	.60	.15
☐ 383	Jim York	.40	.16	.04
☐ 384	Brewers: Team/Mgr. Del Crandall (checklist back)	1.25	.40	.08
☐ 385	Dock Ellis	.40	.16	.04
☐ 386	Checklist: 265-396	1.75	.20	.04
☐ 387	Jim Spencer	.40	.16	.04
☐ 388	Steve Stone	.60	.25	.06
☐ 389	Tony Solaita	.40	.16	.04
☐ 390	Ron Cey	.75	.30	.07
☐ 391	Don DeMola	.40	.16	.04
☐ 392	Bruce Bochte	.60	.25	.06
☐ 393	Gary Gentry	.40	.16	.04
☐ 394	Larvell Blanks	.40	.16	.04
☐ 395	Bud Harrelson	.60	.25	.06
☐ 396	Fred Norman	.40	.16	.04
☐ 397	Bill Freehan	.60	.25	.06
☐ 398	Elias Sosa	.40	.16	.04
☐ 399	Terry Harmon	.40	.16	.04
☐ 400	Dick Allen	.75	.30	.07
☐ 401	Mike Wallace	.40	.16	.04
☐ 402	Bob Tolan	.40	.16	.04
☐ 403	Tom Buskey	.40	.16	.04
☐ 404	Ted Sizemore	.40	.16	.04
☐ 405	John Montague	.40	.16	.04
☐ 406	Bob Gallagher	.40	.16	.04
☐ 407	Herb Washington	.40	.16	.04
☐ 408	Clyde Wright	.40	.16	.04
☐ 409	Bob Robertson	.40	.16	.04
☐ 410	Mike Cueller UER (sic, Cuellar)	.60	.25	.06
☐ 411	George Mitterwald	.40	.16	.04
☐ 412	Bill Hands	.40	.16	.04
☐ 413	Marty Pattin	.40	.16	.04
☐ 414	Manny Mota	.60	.25	.06
☐ 415	John Hiller	.60	.25	.06
☐ 416	Larry Lintz	.40	.16	.04
☐ 417	Skip Lockwood	.40	.16	.04
☐ 418	Leo Foster	.40	.16	.04
☐ 419	Dave Goltz	.40	.16	.04
☐ 420	Larry Bowa	.60	.25	.06
☐ 421	Mets: Team/Mgr. Yogi Berra (checklist back)	1.50	.50	.10
☐ 422	Brian Downing	1.00	.40	.10
☐ 423	Clay Kirby	.40	.16	.04
☐ 424	John Lowenstein	.40	.16	.04
☐ 425	Tito Fuentes	.40	.16	.04
☐ 426	George Medich	.40	.16	.04
☐ 427	Clarence Gaston	.60	.25	.06
☐ 428	Dave Hamilton	.40	.16	.04
☐ 429	Jim Dwyer	.40	.16	.04
☐ 430	Luis Tiant	.75	.30	.07
☐ 431	Rod Gilbreath	.40	.16	.04
☐ 432	Ken Berry	.40	.16	.04
☐ 433	Larry Demery	.40	.16	.04
☐ 434	Bob Locker	.40	.16	.04
☐ 435	Dave Nelson	.40	.16	.04
☐ 436	Ken Frailing	.40	.16	.04
☐ 437	Al Cowens	.60	.25	.06
☐ 438	Don Carrithers	.40	.16	.04
☐ 439	Ed Brinkman	.40	.16	.04
☐ 440	Andy Messersmith	.60	.25	.06
☐ 441	Bobby Heise	.40	.16	.04
☐ 442	Maximino Leon	.40	.16	.04
☐ 443	Twins: Team/Mgr. Frank Quilici (checklist back)	1.25	.40	.08
☐ 444	Gene Garber	.40	.16	.04
☐ 445	Felix Millan	.40	.16	.04
☐ 446	Bart Johnson	.40	.16	.04
☐ 447	Terry Crowley	.40	.16	.04
☐ 448	Frank Duffy	.40	.16	.04
☐ 449	Charlie Williams	.40	.16	.04
☐ 450	Willie McCovey	4.25	1.75	.42
☐ 451	Rick Dempsey	.60	.25	.06
☐ 452	Angel Mangual	.40	.16	.04
☐ 453	Claude Osteen	.60	.25	.06
☐ 454	Doug Griffin	.40	.16	.04
☐ 455	Don Wilson	.40	.16	.04
☐ 456	Bob Coluccio	.40	.16	.04
☐ 457	Mario Mendoza	.40	.16	.04
☐ 458	Ross Grimsley	.40	.16	.04
☐ 459	1974 AL Champs A's over Orioles (2B action pictured)	.75	.30	.07
☐ 460	1974 NL Champs Dodgers over Pirates	1.00	.40	.10

(Taveras/Garvey at 2B)			
☐ 461 World Series Game 1	2.50	1.00	.25
(Reggie Jackson)			
☐ 462 World Series Game 2	.75	.30	.07
(Dodger dugout)			
☐ 463 World Series Game 3	1.00	.40	.10
(Fingers pitching)			
☐ 464 World Series Game 4	.75	.30	.07
(A's batter)			
☐ 465 World Series Game 5	.75	.30	.07
(Rudi rounding third)			
☐ 466 World Series Summary	.75	.30	.07
A's do it again; win third straight (A's group picture)			
☐ 467 Ed Halicki	.40	.16	.04
☐ 468 Bobby Mitchell	.40	.16	.04
☐ 469 Tom Dettore	.40	.16	.04
☐ 470 Jeff Burroughs	.60	.25	.06
☐ 471 Bob Stinson	.40	.16	.04
☐ 472 Bruce Dal Canton	.40	.16	.04
☐ 473 Ken McMullen	.40	.16	.04
☐ 474 Luke Walker	.40	.16	.04
☐ 475 Darrell Evans	.60	.25	.06
☐ 476 Ed Figueroa	.40	.16	.04
☐ 477 Tom Hutton	.40	.16	.04
☐ 478 Tom Burgmeier	.40	.16	.04
☐ 479 Ken Boswell	.40	.16	.04
☐ 480 Carlos May	.40	.16	.04
☐ 481 Will McEnaney	.40	.16	.04
☐ 482 Tom McCraw	.40	.16	.04
☐ 483 Steve Ontiveros	.40	.16	.04
☐ 484 Glenn Beckert	.60	.25	.06
☐ 485 Sparky Lyle	.60	.25	.06
☐ 486 Ray Fosse	.40	.16	.04
☐ 487 Astros: Team/Mgr.	1.25	.40	.08
Preston Gomez (checklist back)			
☐ 488 Bill Travers	.40	.16	.04
☐ 489 Cecil Cooper	1.25	.50	.12
☐ 490 Reggie Smith	.75	.30	.07
☐ 491 Doyle Alexander	.40	.16	.04
☐ 492 Rich Hebner	.40	.16	.04
☐ 493 Don Stanhouse	.40	.16	.04
☐ 494 Pete LaCock	.40	.16	.04
☐ 495 Nelson Briles	.40	.16	.04
☐ 496 Pepe Frias	.40	.16	.04
☐ 497 Jim Nettles	.40	.16	.04
☐ 498 Al Downing	.60	.25	.06
☐ 499 Marty Perez	.40	.16	.04
☐ 500 Nolan Ryan	50.00	22.50	7.50
☐ 501 Bill Robinson	.60	.25	.06
☐ 502 Pat Bourque	.40	.16	.04
☐ 503 Fred Stanley	.40	.16	.04
☐ 504 Buddy Bradford	.40	.16	.04
☐ 505 Chris Speier	.40	.16	.04
☐ 506 Leron Lee	.40	.16	.04
☐ 507 Tom Carroll	.40	.16	.04
☐ 508 Bob Hansen	.40	.16	.04
☐ 509 Dave Hilton	.40	.16	.04
☐ 510 Vida Blue	.60	.25	.06
☐ 511 Rangers: Team/Mgr.	1.25	.40	.08
Billy Martin (checklist back)			
☐ 512 Larry Milbourne	.40	.16	.04
☐ 513 Dick Pole	.40	.16	.04
☐ 514 Jose Cruz	.60	.25	.06
☐ 515 Manny Sanguillen	.60	.25	.06
☐ 516 Don Hood	.40	.16	.04
☐ 517 Checklist: 397-528	1.75	.20	.04
☐ 518 Leo Cardenas	.40	.16	.04
☐ 519 Jim Todd	.40	.16	.04
☐ 520 Amos Otis	.60	.25	.06
☐ 521 Dennis Blair	.40	.16	.04
☐ 522 Gary Sutherland	.40	.16	.04
☐ 523 Tom Paciorek	.40	.16	.04
☐ 524 John Doherty	.40	.16	.04
☐ 525 Tom House	.40	.16	.04
☐ 526 Larry Hisle	.60	.25	.06
☐ 527 Mac Scarce	.40	.16	.04
☐ 528 Eddie Leon	.40	.16	.04
☐ 529 Gary Thomasson	.40	.16	.04
☐ 530 Gaylord Perry	3.25	1.35	.32
☐ 531 Reds: Team/Mgr.	1.50	.50	.10
Sparky Anderson (checklist back)			
☐ 532 Gorman Thomas	.60	.25	.06
☐ 533 Rudy Meoli	.40	.16	.04
☐ 534 Alex Johnson	.40	.16	.04
☐ 535 Gene Tenace	.60	.25	.06
☐ 536 Bob Moose	.40	.16	.04
☐ 537 Tommy Harper	.60	.25	.06
☐ 538 Duffy Dyer	.40	.16	.04
☐ 539 Jesse Jefferson	.40	.16	.04
☐ 540 Lou Brock	4.25	1.75	.42
☐ 541 Roger Metzger	.40	.16	.04
☐ 542 Pete Broberg	.40	.16	.04
☐ 543 Larry Biittner	.40	.16	.04
☐ 544 Steve Mingori	.40	.16	.04
☐ 545 Billy Williams	3.00	1.25	.30
☐ 546 John Knox	.40	.16	.04
☐ 547 Von Joshua	.40	.16	.04
☐ 548 Charlie Sands	.40	.16	.04
☐ 549 Bill Butler	.40	.16	.04
☐ 550 Ralph Garr	.60	.25	.06
☐ 551 Larry Christenson	.40	.16	.04
☐ 552 Jack Brohamer	.40	.16	.04
☐ 553 John Boccabella	.40	.16	.04
☐ 554 Rich Gossage	2.25	.90	.22
☐ 555 Al Oliver	.75	.30	.07
☐ 556 Tim Johnson	.40	.16	.04
☐ 557 Larry Gura	.40	.16	.04
☐ 558 Dave Roberts	.40	.16	.04
☐ 559 Bob Montgomery	.40	.16	.04
☐ 560 Tony Perez	3.00	1.25	.30
☐ 561 A's: Team/Mgr.	1.25	.40	.08

Alvin Dark
(checklist back)
☐ 562 Gary Nolan .... .40 .16 .04
☐ 563 Wilbur Howard .... .40 .16 .04
☐ 564 Tommy Davis .... .60 .25 .06
☐ 565 Joe Torre .... .75 .30 .07
☐ 566 Ray Burris .... .40 .16 .04
☐ 567 Jim Sundberg .... .75 .30 .07
☐ 568 Dale Murray .... .40 .16 .04
☐ 569 Frank White .... .75 .30 .07
☐ 570 Jim Wynn .... .60 .25 .06
☐ 571 Dave Lemanczyk .... .40 .16 .04
☐ 572 Roger Nelson .... .40 .16 .04
☐ 573 Orlando Pena .... .40 .16 .04
☐ 574 Tony Taylor .... .40 .16 .04
☐ 575 Gene Clines .... .40 .16 .04
☐ 576 Phil Roof .... .40 .16 .04
☐ 577 John Morris .... .40 .16 .04
☐ 578 Dave Tomlin .... .40 .16 .04
☐ 579 Skip Pitlock .... .40 .16 .04
☐ 580 Frank Robinson .... 4.25 1.75 .42
☐ 581 Darrel Chaney .... .40 .16 .04
☐ 582 Eduardo Rodriguez .... .40 .16 .04
☐ 583 Andy Etchebarren .... .40 .16 .04
☐ 584 Mike Garman .... .40 .16 .04
☐ 585 Chris Chambliss .... .60 .25 .06
☐ 586 Tim McCarver .... .75 .30 .07
☐ 587 Chris Ward .... .40 .16 .04
☐ 588 Rick Auerbach .... .40 .16 .04
☐ 589 Braves: Team/Mgr. .... 1.25 .40 .08
Clyde King
(checklist back)
☐ 590 Cesar Cedeno .... .60 .25 .06
☐ 591 Glenn Abbott .... .40 .16 .04
☐ 592 Balor Moore .... .40 .16 .04
☐ 593 Gene Lamont .... .60 .25 .06
☐ 594 Jim Fuller .... .40 .16 .04
☐ 595 Joe Niekro .... .60 .25 .06
☐ 596 Ollie Brown .... .40 .16 .04
☐ 597 Winston Llenas .... .40 .16 .04
☐ 598 Bruce Kison .... .40 .16 .04
☐ 599 Nate Colbert .... .40 .16 .04
☐ 600 Rod Carew 11.00 5.00 1.35
☐ 601 Juan Beniquez .... .60 .25 .06
☐ 602 John Vukovich .... .40 .16 .04
☐ 603 Lew Krausse .... .40 .16 .04
☐ 604 Oscar Zamora .... .40 .16 .04
☐ 605 John Ellis .... .40 .16 .04
☐ 606 Bruce Miller .... .40 .16 .04
☐ 607 Jim Holt .... .40 .16 .04
☐ 608 Gene Michael .... .60 .25 .06
☐ 609 Elrod Hendricks .... .40 .16 .04
☐ 610 Ron Hunt .... .40 .16 .04
☐ 611 Yankees: Team/Mgr. .... 1.50 .50 .10
Bill Virdon
(checklist back)
☐ 612 Terry Hughes .... .40 .16 .04
☐ 613 Bill Parsons .... .40 .16 .04
☐ 614 Rookie Pitchers .... .40 .16 .04
Jack Kucek
Dyar Miller
Vern Ruhle
Paul Siebert
☐ 615 Rookie Pitchers .... .75 .30 .07
Pat Darcy
Dennis Leonard
Tom Underwood
Hank Webb
☐ 616 Rookie Outfielders 24.00 10.50 3.50
Dave Augustine
Pepe Mangual
Jim Rice
John Scott
☐ 617 Rookie Infielders .... 1.75 .70 .17
Mike Cubbage
Doug DeCinces
Reggie Sanders
Manny Trillo
☐ 618 Rookie Pitchers .... 1.50 .60 .15
Jamie Easterly
Tom Johnson
Scott McGregor
Rick Rhoden
☐ 619 Rookie Outfielders .... .40 .16 .04
Benny Ayala
Nyls Nyman
Tommy Smith
Jerry Turner
☐ 620 Rookie Catcher/OF 42.00 18.00 5.50
Gary Carter
Marc Hill
Danny Meyer
Leon Roberts
☐ 621 Rookie Pitchers .... .60 .25 .06
John Denny
Rawly Eastwick
Jim Kern
Juan Veintidos
☐ 622 Rookie Outfielders 12.00 5.25 1.50
Ed Armbrister
Fred Lynn
Tom Poquette
Terry Whitfield UER
(listed as Ney York)
☐ 623 Rookie Infielders 20.00 8.50 2.75
Phil Garner
Keith Hernandez UER
(sic, bats right)
Bob Sheldon
Tom Veryzer
☐ 624 Rookie Pitchers .... .40 .16 .04
Doug Konieczny
Gary Lavelle
Jim Otten
Eddie Solomon
☐ 625 Boog Powell .... .75 .30 .07

	NRMT	VG-E	GOOD
☐ 626 Larry Haney UER (photo actually Dave Duncan)	.40	.16	.04
☐ 627 Tom Walker	.40	.16	.04
☐ 628 Ron LeFlore	.60	.25	.06
☐ 629 Joe Hoerner	.40	.16	.04
☐ 630 Greg Luzinski	.60	.25	.06
☐ 631 Lee Lacy	.40	.16	.04
☐ 632 Morris Nettles	.40	.16	.04
☐ 633 Paul Casanova	.40	.16	.04
☐ 634 Cy Acosta	.40	.16	.04
☐ 635 Chuck Dobson	.40	.16	.04
☐ 636 Charlie Moore	.40	.16	.04
☐ 637 Ted Martinez	.40	.16	.04
☐ 638 Cubs: Team/Mgr. Jim Marshall (checklist back)	1.25	.40	.08
☐ 639 Steve Kline	.40	.16	.04
☐ 640 Harmon Killebrew	4.25	1.75	.42
☐ 641 Jim Northrup	.60	.25	.06
☐ 642 Mike Phillips	.40	.16	.04
☐ 643 Brent Strom	.40	.16	.04
☐ 644 Bill Fahey	.40	.16	.04
☐ 645 Danny Cater	.40	.16	.04
☐ 646 Checklist: 529-660	1.75	.20	.04
☐ 647 Claudell Washington	1.25	.50	.12
☐ 648 Dave Pagan	.40	.16	.04
☐ 649 Jack Heidemann	.40	.16	.04
☐ 650 Dave May	.40	.16	.04
☐ 651 John Morlan	.40	.16	.04
☐ 652 Lindy McDaniel	.40	.16	.04
☐ 653 Lee Richard UER (listed as Richards on card front)	.40	.16	.04
☐ 654 Jerry Terrell	.40	.16	.04
☐ 655 Rico Carty	.60	.25	.06
☐ 656 Bill Plummer	.40	.16	.04
☐ 657 Bob Oliver	.40	.16	.04
☐ 658 Vic Harris	.40	.16	.04
☐ 659 Bob Apodaca	.40	.16	.04
☐ 660 Hank Aaron	25.00	7.50	1.50

1976 Topps

The 1976 Topps set of 660 cards (measuring 2 1/2" by 3 1/2") is known for its sharp color photographs and interesting presentation of subjects. Team cards feature a checklist back for players on that team and show a small inset photo of the manager on the front. A "Father and Son" series (66-70) spotlights five Major Leaguers whose fathers also made

the "Big Show." Other subseries include "All Time All Stars" (341-350), "Record Breakers" from the previous season (1-6), League Leaders (191-205), Post-season cards (461-462), and Rookie Prospects (589-599). The key rookies in this set are Dennis Eckersley, Ron Guidry, and Willie Randolph.

	NRMT	VG-E	GOOD
COMPLETE SET (660)	425.00	190.00	63.00
COMMON PLAYER (1-660)	.30	.12	.03
☐ 1 RB: Hank Aaron Most RBI's, 2262	15.00	4.00	.80
☐ 2 RB: Bobby Bonds Most leadoff HR's 32; plus three seasons 30 homers/30 steals	.60	.25	.06
☐ 3 RB: Mickey Lolich Lefthander, Most Strikeouts, 2679	.50	.20	.05
☐ 4 RB: Dave Lopes Most Consecutive SB attempts, 38	.40	.16	.04
☐ 5 RB: Tom Seaver Most Cons. seasons with 200 SO's, 8	3.00	1.25	.30
☐ 6 RB: Rennie Stennett Most Hits in a 9 inning game, 7	.40	.16	.04
☐ 7 Jim Umbarger	.30	.12	.03
☐ 8 Tito Fuentes	.30	.12	.03
☐ 9 Paul Lindblad	.30	.12	.03
☐ 10 Lou Brock	4.25	1.75	.42
☐ 11 Jim Hughes	.30	.12	.03
☐ 12 Richie Zisk	.30	.12	.03
☐ 13 John Wockenfuss	.30	.12	.03
☐ 14 Gene Garber	.30	.12	.03
☐ 15 George Scott	.40	.16	.04
☐ 16 Bob Apodaca	.30	.12	.03
☐ 17 New York Yankees Team Card;	1.00	.30	.06

Billy Martin MG
(checklist back)
- ☐ 18 Dale Murray .30 .12 .03
- ☐ 19 George Brett 48.00 22.00 6.50
- ☐ 20 Bob Watson .40 .16 .04
- ☐ 21 Dave LaRoche .30 .12 .03
- ☐ 22 Bill Russell .40 .16 .04
- ☐ 23 Brian Downing .60 .25 .06
- ☐ 24 Cesar Geronimo .30 .12 .03
- ☐ 25 Mike Torrez .30 .12 .03
- ☐ 26 Andre Thornton .40 .16 .04
- ☐ 27 Ed Figueroa .30 .12 .03
- ☐ 28 Dusty Baker .50 .20 .05
- ☐ 29 Rick Burleson .40 .16 .04
- ☐ 30 John Montefusco .40 .16 .04
- ☐ 31 Len Randle .30 .12 .03
- ☐ 32 Danny Frisella .30 .12 .03
- ☐ 33 Bill North .30 .12 .03
- ☐ 34 Mike Garman .30 .12 .03
- ☐ 35 Tony Oliva .90 .40 .09
- ☐ 36 Frank Taveras .30 .12 .03
- ☐ 37 John Hiller .40 .16 .04
- ☐ 38 Garry Maddox .40 .16 .04
- ☐ 39 Pete Broberg .30 .12 .03
- ☐ 40 Dave Kingman .90 .40 .09
- ☐ 41 Tippy Martinez .40 .16 .04
- ☐ 42 Barry Foote .30 .12 .03
- ☐ 43 Paul Splittorff .30 .12 .03
- ☐ 44 Doug Rader .40 .16 .04
- ☐ 45 Boog Powell .60 .25 .06
- ☐ 46 Los Angeles Dodgers 1.00 .30 .06
  Team Card;
  Walter Alston MG
  (checklist back)
- ☐ 47 Jesse Jefferson .30 .12 .03
- ☐ 48 Dave Concepcion .90 .40 .09
- ☐ 49 Dave Duncan .30 .12 .03
- ☐ 50 Fred Lynn 2.00 .80 .20
- ☐ 51 Ray Burris .30 .12 .03
- ☐ 52 Dave Chalk .30 .12 .03
- ☐ 53 Mike Beard .30 .12 .03
- ☐ 54 Dave Rader .30 .12 .03
- ☐ 55 Gaylord Perry 3.00 1.25 .30
- ☐ 56 Bob Tolan .30 .12 .03
- ☐ 57 Phil Garner .60 .25 .06
- ☐ 58 Ron Reed .30 .12 .03
- ☐ 59 Larry Hisle .40 .16 .04
- ☐ 60 Jerry Reuss .40 .16 .04
- ☐ 61 Ron LeFlore .40 .16 .04
- ☐ 62 Johnny Oates .40 .16 .04
- ☐ 63 Bobby Darwin .30 .12 .03
- ☐ 64 Jerry Koosman .50 .20 .05
- ☐ 65 Chris Chambliss .50 .20 .05
- ☐ 66 Father and Son .50 .20 .05
  Gus Bell
  Buddy Bell
- ☐ 67 Father and Son .60 .25 .06
  Ray Boone
  Bob Boone
- ☐ 68 Father and Son .40 .16 .04
  Joe Coleman
  Joe Coleman Jr.
- ☐ 69 Father and Son .40 .16 .04
  Jim Hegan
  Mike Hegan
- ☐ 70 Father and Son .40 .16 .04
  Roy Smalley
  Roy Smalley Jr.
- ☐ 71 Steve Rogers .30 .12 .03
- ☐ 72 Hal McRae .60 .25 .06
- ☐ 73 Baltimore Orioles 1.00 .30 .06
  Team Card;
  Earl Weaver MG
  (checklist back)
- ☐ 74 Oscar Gamble .40 .16 .04
- ☐ 75 Larry Dierker .30 .12 .03
- ☐ 76 Willie Crawford .30 .12 .03
- ☐ 77 Pedro Borbon .30 .12 .03
- ☐ 78 Cecil Cooper .75 .30 .07
- ☐ 79 Jerry Morales .30 .12 .03
- ☐ 80 Jim Kaat 1.00 .40 .10
- ☐ 81 Darrell Evans .60 .25 .06
- ☐ 82 Von Joshua .30 .12 .03
- ☐ 83 Jim Spencer .30 .12 .03
- ☐ 84 Brent Strom .30 .12 .03
- ☐ 85 Mickey Rivers .40 .16 .04
- ☐ 86 Mike Tyson .30 .12 .03
- ☐ 87 Tom Burgmeier .30 .12 .03
- ☐ 88 Duffy Dyer .30 .12 .03
- ☐ 89 Vern Ruhle .30 .12 .03
- ☐ 90 Sal Bando .50 .20 .05
- ☐ 91 Tom Hutton .30 .12 .03
- ☐ 92 Eduardo Rodriguez .30 .12 .03
- ☐ 93 Mike Phillips .30 .12 .03
- ☐ 94 Jim Dwyer .30 .12 .03
- ☐ 95 Brooks Robinson 4.25 1.75 .42
- ☐ 96 Doug Bird .30 .12 .03
- ☐ 97 Wilbur Howard .30 .12 .03
- ☐ 98 Dennis Eckersley 36.00 16.25 5.50
- ☐ 99 Lee Lacy .30 .12 .03
- ☐ 100 Jim Hunter 3.00 1.25 .30
- ☐ 101 Pete LaCock .30 .12 .03
- ☐ 102 Jim Willoughby .30 .12 .03
- ☐ 103 Biff Pocoroba .30 .12 .03
- ☐ 104 Cincinnati Reds 1.25 .40 .08
  Team Card;
  Sparky Anderson MG
  (checklist back)
- ☐ 105 Gary Lavelle .30 .12 .03
- ☐ 106 Tom Grieve .40 .16 .04
- ☐ 107 Dave Roberts .30 .12 .03
- ☐ 108 Don Kirkwood .30 .12 .03
- ☐ 109 Larry Lintz .30 .12 .03
- ☐ 110 Carlos May .30 .12 .03
- ☐ 111 Danny Thompson .30 .12 .03
- ☐ 112 Kent Tekulve 1.25 .50 .12

Card			
☐ 113 Gary Sutherland .30	.12	.03	
☐ 114 Jay Johnstone .40	.16	.04	
☐ 115 Ken Holtzman .40	.16	.04	
☐ 116 Charlie Moore .30	.12	.03	
☐ 117 Mike Jorgensen .30	.12	.03	
☐ 118 Boston Red Sox 1.00	.30	.06	
Team Card;			
Darrell Johnson MG			
(checklist back)			
☐ 119 Checklist 1-132 1.25	.15	.03	
☐ 120 Rusty Staub .60	.25	.06	
☐ 121 Tony Solaita .30	.12	.03	
☐ 122 Mike Cosgrove .30	.12	.03	
☐ 123 Walt Williams .30	.12	.03	
☐ 124 Doug Rau .30	.12	.03	
☐ 125 Don Baylor 1.00	.40	.10	
☐ 126 Tom Dettore .30	.12	.03	
☐ 127 Larvell Blanks .30	.12	.03	
☐ 128 Ken Griffey 2.25	.90	.22	
☐ 129 Andy Etchebarren .30	.12	.03	
☐ 130 Luis Tiant .50	.20	.05	
☐ 131 Bill Stein .30	.12	.03	
☐ 132 Don Hood .30	.12	.03	
☐ 133 Gary Matthews .40	.16	.04	
☐ 134 Mike Ivie .30	.12	.03	
☐ 135 Bake McBride .40	.16	.04	
☐ 136 Dave Goltz .30	.12	.03	
☐ 137 Bill Robinson .40	.16	.04	
☐ 138 Lerrin LaGrow .30	.12	.03	
☐ 139 Gorman Thomas .50	.20	.05	
☐ 140 Vida Blue .50	.20	.05	
☐ 141 Larry Parrish 1.00	.40	.10	
☐ 142 Dick Drago .30	.12	.03	
☐ 143 Jerry Grote .30	.12	.03	
☐ 144 Al Fitzmorris .30	.12	.03	
☐ 145 Larry Bowa .60	.25	.06	
☐ 146 George Medich .30	.12	.03	
☐ 147 Houston Astros 1.00	.30	.06	
Team Card;			
Bill Virdon MG			
(checklist back)			
☐ 148 Stan Thomas .30	.12	.03	
☐ 149 Tommy Davis .40	.16	.04	
☐ 150 Steve Garvey 6.00	2.50	.60	
☐ 151 Bill Bonham .30	.12	.03	
☐ 152 Leroy Stanton .30	.12	.03	
☐ 153 Buzz Capra .30	.12	.03	
☐ 154 Bucky Dent .60	.25	.06	
☐ 155 Jack Billingham .30	.12	.03	
☐ 156 Rico Carty .40	.16	.04	
☐ 157 Mike Caldwell .30	.12	.03	
☐ 158 Ken Reitz .30	.12	.03	
☐ 159 Jerry Terrell .30	.12	.03	
☐ 160 Dave Winfield 12.50	5.50	1.65	
☐ 161 Bruce Kison .30	.12	.03	
☐ 162 Jack Pierce .30	.12	.03	
☐ 163 Jim Slaton .30	.12	.03	
☐ 164 Pepe Mangual .30	.12	.03	
☐ 165 Gene Tenace .40	.16	.04	
☐ 166 Skip Lockwood .30	.12	.03	
☐ 167 Freddie Patek .30	.12	.03	
☐ 168 Tom Hilgendorf .30	.12	.03	
☐ 169 Graig Nettles 1.25	.50	.12	
☐ 170 Rick Wise .40	.16	.04	
☐ 171 Greg Gross .30	.12	.03	
☐ 172 Texas Rangers 1.00	.30	.06	
Team Card;			
Frank Lucchesi MG			
(checklist back)			
☐ 173 Steve Swisher .30	.12	.03	
☐ 174 Charlie Hough .40	.16	.04	
☐ 175 Ken Singleton .40	.16	.04	
☐ 176 Dick Lange .30	.12	.03	
☐ 177 Marty Perez .30	.12	.03	
☐ 178 Tom Buskey .30	.12	.03	
☐ 179 George Foster 1.00	.40	.10	
☐ 180 Rich Gossage 1.50	.60	.15	
☐ 181 Willie Montanez .30	.12	.03	
☐ 182 Harry Rasmussen .30	.12	.03	
☐ 183 Steve Braun .30	.12	.03	
☐ 184 Bill Greif .30	.12	.03	
☐ 185 Dave Parker 6.50	2.75	.65	
☐ 186 Tom Walker .30	.12	.03	
☐ 187 Pedro Garcia .30	.12	.03	
☐ 188 Fred Scherman .30	.12	.03	
☐ 189 Claudell Washington .40	.16	.04	
☐ 190 Jon Matlack .40	.16	.04	
☐ 191 NL Batting Leaders .60	.25	.06	
Bill Madlock			
Ted Simmons			
Manny Sanguillen			
☐ 192 AL Batting Leaders 2.00	.80	.20	
Rod Carew			
Fred Lynn			
Thurman Munson			
☐ 193 NL Home Run Leaders 1.25	.50	.12	
Mike Schmidt			
Dave Kingman			
Greg Luzinski			
☐ 194 AL Home Run Leaders 1.25	.50	.12	
Reggie Jackson			
George Scott			
John Mayberry			
☐ 195 NL RBI Leaders 1.25	.50	.12	
Greg Luzinski			
Johnny Bench			
Tony Perez			
☐ 196 AL RBI Leaders .60	.25	.06	
George Scott			
John Mayberry			
Fred Lynn			
☐ 197 NL Steals Leaders 1.25	.50	.12	
Dave Lopes			
Joe Morgan			
Lou Brock			
☐ 198 AL Steals Leaders .60	.25	.06	

Mickey Rivers
Claudell Washington
Amos Otis
☐ 199 NL Victory Leaders ...... 1.00 .40 .10
Tom Seaver
Randy Jones
Andy Messersmith
☐ 200 AL Victory Leaders ...... 1.25 .50 .12
Jim Hunter
Jim Palmer
Vida Blue
☐ 201 NL ERA Leaders .... .75 .30 .07
Randy Jones
Andy Messersmith
Tom Seaver
☐ 202 AL ERA Leaders .... 2.00 .80 .20
Jim Palmer
Jim Hunter
Dennis Eckersley
☐ 203 NL Strikeout Leaders ..... .75 .30 .07
Tom Seaver
John Montefusco
Andy Messersmith
☐ 204 AL Strikeout Leaders ...... .75 .30 .07
Frank Tanana
Bert Blyleven
Gaylord Perry
☐ 205 Leading Firemen .... .60 .25 .06
Al Hrabosky
Rich Gossage
☐ 206 Manny Trillo .... .30 .12 .03
☐ 207 Andy Hassler .... .30 .12 .03
☐ 208 Mike Lum .... .30 .12 .03
☐ 209 Alan Ashby .... .40 .16 .04
☐ 210 Lee May .... .40 .16 .04
☐ 211 Clay Carroll .... .30 .12 .03
☐ 212 Pat Kelly .... .30 .12 .03
☐ 213 Dave Heaverlo .... .30 .12 .03
☐ 214 Eric Soderholm .... .30 .12 .03
☐ 215 Reggie Smith .... .50 .20 .05
☐ 216 Montreal Expos .... 1.00 .30 .06
Team Card;
Karl Kuehl MG
(checklist back)
☐ 217 Dave Freisleben .... .30 .12 .03
☐ 218 John Knox .... .30 .12 .03
☐ 219 Tom Murphy .... .30 .12 .03
☐ 220 Manny Sanguillen .... .40 .16 .04
☐ 221 Jim Todd .... .30 .12 .03
☐ 222 Wayne Garrett .... .30 .12 .03
☐ 223 Ollie Brown .... .30 .12 .03
☐ 224 Jim York .... .30 .12 .03
☐ 225 Roy White .... .40 .16 .04
☐ 226 Jim Sundberg .... .40 .16 .04
☐ 227 Oscar Zamora .... .30 .12 .03
☐ 228 John Hale .... .30 .12 .03
☐ 229 Jerry Remy .... .40 .16 .04
☐ 230 Carl Yastrzemski .... 8.50 3.75 .85
☐ 231 Tom House .... .30 .12 .03
☐ 232 Frank Duffy .... .30 .12 .03
☐ 233 Grant Jackson .... .30 .12 .03
☐ 234 Mike Sadek .... .30 .12 .03
☐ 235 Bert Blyleven .... 1.50 .60 .15
☐ 236 Kansas City Royals ...... 1.00 .30 .06
Team Card;
Whitey Herzog MG
(checklist back)
☐ 237 Dave Hamilton .... .30 .12 .03
☐ 238 Larry Biittner .... .30 .12 .03
☐ 239 John Curtis .... .30 .12 .03
☐ 240 Pete Rose 12.00 5.25 1.50
☐ 241 Hector Torres .... .30 .12 .03
☐ 242 Dan Meyer .... .30 .12 .03
☐ 243 Jim Rooker .... .30 .12 .03
☐ 244 Bill Sharp .... .30 .12 .03
☐ 245 Felix Millan .... .30 .12 .03
☐ 246 Cesar Tovar .... .30 .12 .03
☐ 247 Terry Harmon .... .30 .12 .03
☐ 248 Dick Tidrow .... .30 .12 .03
☐ 249 Cliff Johnson .... .30 .12 .03
☐ 250 Fergie Jenkins .... 2.50 1.00 .25
☐ 251 Rick Monday .... .40 .16 .04
☐ 252 Tim Nordbrook .... .30 .12 .03
☐ 253 Bill Buckner .... .50 .20 .05
☐ 254 Rudy Meoli .... .30 .12 .03
☐ 255 Fritz Peterson .... .30 .12 .03
☐ 256 Rowland Office .... .30 .12 .03
☐ 257 Ross Grimsley .... .30 .12 .03
☐ 258 Nyls Nyman .... .30 .12 .03
☐ 259 Darrel Chaney .... .30 .12 .03
☐ 260 Steve Busby .... .40 .16 .04
☐ 261 Gary Thomasson .... .30 .12 .03
☐ 262 Checklist 133-264 .... 1.25 .15 .03
☐ 263 Lyman Bostock .... .50 .20 .05
☐ 264 Steve Renko .... .30 .12 .03
☐ 265 Willie Davis .... .40 .16 .04
☐ 266 Alan Foster .... .30 .12 .03
☐ 267 Aurelio Rodriguez .... .30 .12 .03
☐ 268 Del Unser .... .30 .12 .03
☐ 269 Rick Austin .... .30 .12 .03
☐ 270 Willie Stargell .... 3.25 1.35 .32
☐ 271 Jim Lonborg .... .40 .16 .04
☐ 272 Rick Dempsey .... .40 .16 .04
☐ 273 Joe Niekro .... .40 .16 .04
☐ 274 Tommy Harper .... .40 .16 .04
☐ 275 Rick Manning .... .30 .12 .03
☐ 276 Mickey Scott .... .30 .12 .03
☐ 277 Chicago Cubs .... 1.00 .30 .06
Team Card;
Jim Marshall MG
(checklist back)
☐ 278 Bernie Carbo .... .30 .12 .03
☐ 279 Roy Howell .... .30 .12 .03
☐ 280 Burt Hooton .... .40 .16 .04
☐ 281 Dave May .... .30 .12 .03
☐ 282 Dan Osborn .... .30 .12 .03

☐ 283 Merv Rettenmund .30 .12 .03
☐ 284 Steve Ontiveros .30 .12 .03
☐ 285 Mike Cuellar .40 .16 .04
☐ 286 Jim Wohlford .30 .12 .03
☐ 287 Pete Mackanin .30 .12 .03
☐ 288 Bill Campbell .30 .12 .03
☐ 289 Enzo Hernandez .30 .12 .03
☐ 290 Ted Simmons 1.00 .40 .10
☐ 291 Ken Sanders .30 .12 .03
☐ 292 Leon Roberts .30 .12 .03
☐ 293 Bill Castro .30 .12 .03
☐ 294 Ed Kirkpatrick .30 .12 .03
☐ 295 Dave Cash .30 .12 .03
☐ 296 Pat Dobson .30 .12 .03
☐ 297 Roger Metzger .30 .12 .03
☐ 298 Dick Bosman .30 .12 .03
☐ 299 Champ Summers .30 .12 .03
☐ 300 Johnny Bench 10.00 4.50 1.25
☐ 301 Jackie Brown .30 .12 .03
☐ 302 Rick Miller .30 .12 .03
☐ 303 Steve Foucault .30 .12 .03
☐ 304 California Angels 1.00 .30 .06
Team Card;
Dick Williams MG
(checklist back)
☐ 305 Andy Messersmith .40 .16 .04
☐ 306 Rod Gilbreath .30 .12 .03
☐ 307 Al Bumbry .30 .12 .03
☐ 308 Jim Barr .30 .12 .03
☐ 309 Bill Melton .30 .12 .03
☐ 310 Randy Jones .40 .16 .04
☐ 311 Cookie Rojas .30 .12 .03
☐ 312 Don Carrithers .30 .12 .03
☐ 313 Dan Ford .30 .12 .03
☐ 314 Ed Kranepool .40 .16 .04
☐ 315 Al Hrabosky .40 .16 .04
☐ 316 Robin Yount 48.00 22.00 6.50
☐ 317 John Candelaria 2.50 1.00 .25
☐ 318 Bob Boone 1.00 .40 .10
☐ 319 Larry Gura .30 .12 .03
☐ 320 Willie Horton .40 .16 .04
☐ 321 Jose Cruz .40 .16 .04
☐ 322 Glenn Abbott .30 .12 .03
☐ 323 Rob Sperring .30 .12 .03
☐ 324 Jim Bibby .30 .12 .03
☐ 325 Tony Perez 2.25 .90 .22
☐ 326 Dick Pole .30 .12 .03
☐ 327 Dave Moates .30 .12 .03
☐ 328 Carl Morton .30 .12 .03
☐ 329 Joe Ferguson .30 .12 .03
☐ 330 Nolan Ryan 42.00 18.00 5.50
☐ 331 San Diego Padres 1.00 .30 .06
Team Card;
John McNamara MG
(checklist back)
☐ 332 Charlie Williams .30 .12 .03
☐ 333 Bob Coluccio .30 .12 .03
☐ 334 Dennis Leonard .40 .16 .04
☐ 335 Bob Grich .40 .16 .04
☐ 336 Vic Albury .30 .12 .03
☐ 337 Bud Harrelson .40 .16 .04
☐ 338 Bob Bailey .30 .12 .03
☐ 339 John Denny .40 .16 .04
☐ 340 Jim Rice 6.50 2.75 .65
☐ 341 All-Time 1B 4.50 2.00 .45
Lou Gehrig
☐ 342 All-Time 2B 2.25 .90 .22
Rogers Hornsby
☐ 343 All-Time 3B 1.00 .40 .10
Pie Traynor
☐ 344 All-Time SS 3.00 1.25 .30
Honus Wagner
☐ 345 All-Time OF 7.50 3.25 .75
Babe Ruth
☐ 346 All-Time OF 4.50 2.00 .45
Ty Cobb
☐ 347 All-Time OF 4.50 2.00 .45
Ted Williams
☐ 348 All-Time C 1.00 .40 .10
Mickey Cochrane
☐ 349 All-Time RHP 2.25 .90 .22
Walter Johnson
☐ 350 All-Time LHP 1.50 .60 .15
Lefty Grove
☐ 351 Randy Hundley .30 .12 .03
☐ 352 Dave Giusti .30 .12 .03
☐ 353 Sixto Lezcano .30 .12 .03
☐ 354 Ron Blomberg .30 .12 .03
☐ 355 Steve Carlton 6.25 2.75 .60
☐ 356 Ted Martinez .30 .12 .03
☐ 357 Ken Forsch .30 .12 .03
☐ 358 Buddy Bell .50 .20 .05
☐ 359 Rick Reuschel .50 .20 .05
☐ 360 Jeff Burroughs .40 .16 .04
☐ 361 Detroit Tigers 1.00 .30 .06
Team Card;
Ralph Houk MG
(checklist back)
☐ 362 Will McEnaney .30 .12 .03
☐ 363 Dave Collins .75 .30 .07
☐ 364 Elias Sosa .30 .12 .03
☐ 365 Carlton Fisk 9.00 4.00 .90
☐ 366 Bobby Valentine .40 .16 .04
☐ 367 Bruce Miller .30 .12 .03
☐ 368 Wilbur Wood .40 .16 .04
☐ 369 Frank White .50 .20 .05
☐ 370 Ron Cey .60 .25 .06
☐ 371 Elrod Hendricks .30 .12 .03
☐ 372 Rick Baldwin .30 .12 .03
☐ 373 Johnny Briggs .30 .12 .03
☐ 374 Dan Warthen .30 .12 .03
☐ 375 Ron Fairly .30 .12 .03
☐ 376 Rich Hebner .30 .12 .03
☐ 377 Mike Hegan .30 .12 .03
☐ 378 Steve Stone .40 .16 .04
☐ 379 Ken Boswell .30 .12 .03

☐ 380	Bobby Bonds	.75	.30	.07
☐ 381	Denny Doyle	.30	.12	.03
☐ 382	Matt Alexander	.30	.12	.03
☐ 383	John Ellis	.30	.12	.03
☐ 384	Philadelphia Phillies Team Card; Danny Ozark MG (checklist back)	1.00	.30	.06
☐ 385	Mickey Lolich	.60	.25	.06
☐ 386	Ed Goodson	.30	.12	.03
☐ 387	Mike Miley	.30	.12	.03
☐ 388	Stan Perzanowski	.30	.12	.03
☐ 389	Glenn Adams	.30	.12	.03
☐ 390	Don Gullett	.40	.16	.04
☐ 391	Jerry Hairston	.30	.12	.03
☐ 392	Checklist 265-396	1.25	.15	.03
☐ 393	Paul Mitchell	.30	.12	.03
☐ 394	Fran Healy	.30	.12	.03
☐ 395	Jim Wynn	.40	.16	.04
☐ 396	Bill Lee	.40	.16	.04
☐ 397	Tim Foli	.30	.12	.03
☐ 398	Dave Tomlin	.30	.12	.03
☐ 399	Luis Melendez	.30	.12	.03
☐ 400	Rod Carew	8.00	3.50	.80
☐ 401	Ken Brett	.30	.12	.03
☐ 402	Don Money	.30	.12	.03
☐ 403	Geoff Zahn	.30	.12	.03
☐ 404	Enos Cabell	.30	.12	.03
☐ 405	Rollie Fingers	3.00	1.25	.30
☐ 406	Ed Herrmann	.30	.12	.03
☐ 407	Tom Underwood	.30	.12	.03
☐ 408	Charlie Spikes	.30	.12	.03
☐ 409	Dave Lemanczyk	.30	.12	.03
☐ 410	Ralph Garr	.40	.16	.04
☐ 411	Bill Singer	.40	.16	.04
☐ 412	Toby Harrah	.40	.16	.04
☐ 413	Pete Varney	.30	.12	.03
☐ 414	Wayne Garland	.30	.12	.03
☐ 415	Vada Pinson	.50	.20	.05
☐ 416	Tommy John	1.00	.40	.10
☐ 417	Gene Clines	.30	.12	.03
☐ 418	Jose Morales	.30	.12	.03
☐ 419	Reggie Cleveland	.30	.12	.03
☐ 420	Joe Morgan	5.00	2.25	.50
☐ 421	Oakland A's Team Card; (no MG on front; checklist back)	1.00	.30	.06
☐ 422	Johnny Grubb	.30	.12	.03
☐ 423	Ed Halicki	.30	.12	.03
☐ 424	Phil Roof	.30	.12	.03
☐ 425	Rennie Stennett	.30	.12	.03
☐ 426	Bob Forsch	.30	.12	.03
☐ 427	Kurt Bevacqua	.30	.12	.03
☐ 428	Jim Crawford	.30	.12	.03
☐ 429	Fred Stanley	.30	.12	.03
☐ 430	Jose Cardenal	.30	.12	.03
☐ 431	Dick Ruthven	.30	.12	.03
☐ 432	Tom Veryzer	.30	.12	.03
☐ 433	Rick Waits	.30	.12	.03
☐ 434	Morris Nettles	.30	.12	.03
☐ 435	Phil Niekro	2.00	.80	.20
☐ 436	Bill Fahey	.30	.12	.03
☐ 437	Terry Forster	.40	.16	.04
☐ 438	Doug DeCinces	.50	.20	.05
☐ 439	Rick Rhoden	.50	.20	.05
☐ 440	John Mayberry	.40	.16	.04
☐ 441	Gary Carter	10.00	4.50	1.25
☐ 442	Hank Webb	.30	.12	.03
☐ 443	San Francisco Giants Team Card; (no MG on front; checklist back)	1.00	.30	.06
☐ 444	Gary Nolan	.30	.12	.03
☐ 445	Rico Petrocelli	.40	.16	.04
☐ 446	Larry Haney	.30	.12	.03
☐ 447	Gene Locklear	.30	.12	.03
☐ 448	Tom Johnson	.30	.12	.03
☐ 449	Bob Robertson	.30	.12	.03
☐ 450	Jim Palmer	6.50	2.75	.65
☐ 451	Buddy Bradford	.30	.12	.03
☐ 452	Tom Hausman	.30	.12	.03
☐ 453	Lou Piniella	.60	.25	.06
☐ 454	Tom Griffin	.30	.12	.03
☐ 455	Dick Allen	.60	.25	.06
☐ 456	Joe Coleman	.30	.12	.03
☐ 457	Ed Crosby	.30	.12	.03
☐ 458	Earl Williams	.30	.12	.03
☐ 459	Jim Brewer	.30	.12	.03
☐ 460	Cesar Cedeno	.40	.16	.04
☐ 461	NL and AL Champs Reds sweep Bucs, Bosox surprise A's	.60	.25	.06
☐ 462	'75 World Series Reds Champs	.60	.25	.06
☐ 463	Steve Hargan	.30	.12	.03
☐ 464	Ken Henderson	.30	.12	.03
☐ 465	Mike Marshall	.40	.16	.04
☐ 466	Bob Stinson	.30	.12	.03
☐ 467	Woodie Fryman	.30	.12	.03
☐ 468	Jesus Alou	.30	.12	.03
☐ 469	Rawly Eastwick	.30	.12	.03
☐ 470	Bobby Murcer	.60	.25	.06
☐ 471	Jim Burton	.30	.12	.03
☐ 472	Bob Davis	.30	.12	.03
☐ 473	Paul Blair	.40	.16	.04
☐ 474	Ray Corbin	.30	.12	.03
☐ 475	Joe Rudi	.40	.16	.04
☐ 476	Bob Moose	.30	.12	.03
☐ 477	Cleveland Indians Team Card; Frank Robinson MG (checklist back)	1.00	.30	.06
☐ 478	Lynn McGlothen	.30	.12	.03
☐ 479	Bobby Mitchell	.30	.12	.03
☐ 480	Mike Schmidt	33.00	15.00	5.00

☐ 481 Rudy May	.30	.12	.03
☐ 482 Tim Hosley	.30	.12	.03
☐ 483 Mickey Stanley	.40	.16	.04
☐ 484 Eric Raich	.30	.12	.03
☐ 485 Mike Hargrove	.40	.16	.04
☐ 486 Bruce Dal Canton	.30	.12	.03
☐ 487 Leron Lee	.30	.12	.03
☐ 488 Claude Osteen	.40	.16	.04
☐ 489 Skip Jutze	.30	.12	.03
☐ 490 Frank Tanana	.50	.20	.05
☐ 491 Terry Crowley	.30	.12	.03
☐ 492 Marty Pattin	.30	.12	.03
☐ 493 Derrel Thomas	.30	.12	.03
☐ 494 Craig Swan	.30	.12	.03
☐ 495 Nate Colbert	.30	.12	.03
☐ 496 Juan Beniquez	.30	.12	.03
☐ 497 Joe McIntosh	.30	.12	.03
☐ 498 Glenn Borgmann	.30	.12	.03
☐ 499 Mario Guerrero	.30	.12	.03
☐ 500 Reggie Jackson	15.00	6.50	2.15
☐ 501 Billy Champion	.30	.12	.03
☐ 502 Tim McCarver	.50	.20	.05
☐ 503 Elliott Maddox	.30	.12	.03
☐ 504 Pittsburgh Pirates Team Card; Danny Murtaugh MG (checklist back)	1.00	.30	.06
☐ 505 Mark Belanger	.40	.16	.04
☐ 506 George Mitterwald	.30	.12	.03
☐ 507 Ray Bare	.30	.12	.03
☐ 508 Duane Kuiper	.30	.12	.03
☐ 509 Bill Hands	.30	.12	.03
☐ 510 Amos Otis	.40	.16	.04
☐ 511 Jamie Easterley	.30	.12	.03
☐ 512 Ellie Rodriguez	.30	.12	.03
☐ 513 Bart Johnson	.30	.12	.03
☐ 514 Dan Driessen	.40	.16	.04
☐ 515 Steve Yeager	.40	.16	.04
☐ 516 Wayne Granger	.30	.12	.03
☐ 517 John Milner	.30	.12	.03
☐ 518 Doug Flynn	.30	.12	.03
☐ 519 Steve Brye	.30	.12	.03
☐ 520 Willie McCovey	3.50	1.50	.35
☐ 521 Jim Colborn	.30	.12	.03
☐ 522 Ted Sizemore	.30	.12	.03
☐ 523 Bob Montgomery	.30	.12	.03
☐ 524 Pete Falcone	.30	.12	.03
☐ 525 Billy Williams	3.00	1.25	.30
☐ 526 Checklist 397-528	1.25	.15	.03
☐ 527 Mike Anderson	.30	.12	.03
☐ 528 Dock Ellis	.30	.12	.03
☐ 529 Deron Johnson	.30	.12	.03
☐ 530 Don Sutton	2.00	.80	.20
☐ 531 New York Mets Team Card; Joe Frazier MG (checklist back)	1.25	.40	.08
☐ 532 Milt May	.30	.12	.03
☐ 533 Lee Richard	.30	.12	.03
☐ 534 Stan Bahnsen	.30	.12	.03
☐ 535 Dave Nelson	.30	.12	.03
☐ 536 Mike Thompson	.30	.12	.03
☐ 537 Tony Muser	.30	.12	.03
☐ 538 Pat Darcy	.30	.12	.03
☐ 539 John Balaz	.30	.12	.03
☐ 540 Bill Freehan	.50	.20	.05
☐ 541 Steve Mingori	.30	.12	.03
☐ 542 Keith Hernandez	6.00	2.50	.60
☐ 543 Wayne Twitchell	.30	.12	.03
☐ 544 Pepe Frias	.30	.12	.03
☐ 545 Sparky Lyle	.50	.20	.05
☐ 546 Dave Rosello	.30	.12	.03
☐ 547 Roric Harrison	.30	.12	.03
☐ 548 Manny Mota	.40	.16	.04
☐ 549 Randy Tate	.30	.12	.03
☐ 550 Hank Aaron	18.00	7.50	2.50
☐ 551 Jerry DaVanon	.30	.12	.03
☐ 552 Terry Humphrey	.30	.12	.03
☐ 553 Randy Moffitt	.30	.12	.03
☐ 554 Ray Fosse	.30	.12	.03
☐ 555 Dyar Miller	.30	.12	.03
☐ 556 Minnesota Twins Team Card; Gene Mauch MG (checklist back)	1.00	.30	.06
☐ 557 Dan Spillner	.30	.12	.03
☐ 558 Clarence Gaston	.50	.20	.05
☐ 559 Clyde Wright	.30	.12	.03
☐ 560 Jorge Orta	.30	.12	.03
☐ 561 Tom Carroll	.30	.12	.03
☐ 562 Adrian Garrett	.30	.12	.03
☐ 563 Larry Demery	.30	.12	.03
☐ 564 Bubble Gum Champ Kurt Bevacqua	.40	.16	.04
☐ 565 Tug McGraw	.50	.20	.05
☐ 566 Ken McMullen	.30	.12	.03
☐ 567 George Stone	.30	.12	.03
☐ 568 Rob Andrews	.30	.12	.03
☐ 569 Nelson Briles	.30	.12	.03
☐ 570 George Hendrick	.40	.16	.04
☐ 571 Don DeMola	.30	.12	.03
☐ 572 Rich Coggins	.30	.12	.03
☐ 573 Bill Travers	.30	.12	.03
☐ 574 Don Kessinger	.40	.16	.04
☐ 575 Dwight Evans	3.50	1.50	.35
☐ 576 Maximino Leon	.30	.12	.03
☐ 577 Marc Hill	.30	.12	.03
☐ 578 Ted Kubiak	.30	.12	.03
☐ 579 Clay Kirby	.30	.12	.03
☐ 580 Bert Campaneris	.40	.16	.04
☐ 581 St. Louis Cardinals Team Card; Red Schoendienst MG (checklist back)	1.00	.30	.06
☐ 582 Mike Kekich	.30	.12	.03
☐ 583 Tommy Helms	.40	.16	.04

☐ 584 Stan Wall .30 .12 .03
☐ 585 Joe Torre .60 .25 .06
☐ 586 Ron Schueler .30 .12 .03
☐ 587 Leo Cardenas .30 .12 .03
☐ 588 Kevin Kobel .30 .12 .03
☐ 589 Rookie Pitchers 2.00 .80 .20
Santo Alcala
Mike Flanagan
Joe Pactwa
Pablo Torrealba
☐ 590 Rookie Outfielders .60 .25 .06
Henry Cruz
Chet Lemon
Ellis Valentine
Terry Whitfield
☐ 591 Rookie Pitchers .30 .12 .03
Steve Grilli
Craig Mitchell
Jose Sosa
George Throop
☐ 592 Rookie Infielders 7.00 3.00 .70
Willie Randolph
Dave McKay
Jerry Royster
Roy Staiger
☐ 593 Rookie Pitchers .40 .16 .04
Larry Anderson
Ken Crosby
Mark Littell
Butch Metzger
☐ 594 Rookie Catchers/OF .40 .16 .04
Andy Merchant
Ed Ott
Royle Stillman
Jerry White
☐ 595 Rookie Pitchers .40 .16 .04
Art DeFillipis
Randy Lerch
Sid Monge
Steve Barr
☐ 596 Rookie Infielders .50 .20 .05
Craig Reynolds
Lamar Johnson
Johnnie LeMaster
Jerry Manuel
☐ 597 Rookie Pitchers .60 .25 .06
Don Aase
Jack Kucek
Frank LaCorte
Mike Pazik
☐ 598 Rookie Outfielders .50 .20 .05
Hector Cruz
Jamie Quirk
Jerry Turner
Joe Wallis
☐ 599 Rookie Pitchers 10.00 4.50 1.25
Rob Dressler
Ron Guidry
Bob McClure
Pat Zachry
☐ 600 Tom Seaver 11.00 5.00 1.35
☐ 601 Ken Rudolph .30 .12 .03
☐ 602 Doug Konieczny .30 .12 .03
☐ 603 Jim Holt .30 .12 .03
☐ 604 Joe Lovitto .30 .12 .03
☐ 605 Al Downing .40 .16 .04
☐ 606 Milwaukee Brewers 1.00 .30 .06
Team Card;
Alex Grammas MG
(checklist back)
☐ 607 Rich Hinton .30 .12 .03
☐ 608 Vic Correll .30 .12 .03
☐ 609 Fred Norman .30 .12 .03
☐ 610 Greg Luzinski .50 .20 .05
☐ 611 Rich Folkers .30 .12 .03
☐ 612 Joe Lahoud .30 .12 .03
☐ 613 Tim Johnson .30 .12 .03
☐ 614 Fernando Arroyo .30 .12 .03
☐ 615 Mike Cubbage .30 .12 .03
☐ 616 Buck Martinez .30 .12 .03
☐ 617 Darold Knowles .30 .12 .03
☐ 618 Jack Brohamer .30 .12 .03
☐ 619 Bill Butler .30 .12 .03
☐ 620 Al Oliver .60 .25 .06
☐ 621 Tom Hall .30 .12 .03
☐ 622 Rick Auerbach .30 .12 .03
☐ 623 Bob Allietta .30 .12 .03
☐ 624 Tony Taylor .30 .12 .03
☐ 625 J.R. Richard .40 .16 .04
☐ 626 Bob Sheldon .30 .12 .03
☐ 627 Bill Plummer .40 .16 .04
☐ 628 John D'Acquisto .30 .12 .03
☐ 629 Sandy Alomar .30 .12 .03
☐ 630 Chris Speier .30 .12 .03
☐ 631 Atlanta Braves 1.00 .30 .06
Team Card;
Dave Bristol MG
(checklist back)
☐ 632 Rogelio Moret .30 .12 .03
☐ 633 John Stearns .40 .16 .04
☐ 634 Larry Christenson .30 .12 .03
☐ 635 Jim Fregosi .40 .16 .04
☐ 636 Joe Decker .30 .12 .03
☐ 637 Bruce Bochte .30 .12 .03
☐ 638 Doyle Alexander .30 .12 .03
☐ 639 Fred Kendall .30 .12 .03
☐ 640 Bill Madlock 1.00 .40 .10
☐ 641 Tom Paciorek .30 .12 .03
☐ 642 Dennis Blair .30 .12 .03
☐ 643 Checklist 529-660 1.25 .15 .03
☐ 644 Tom Bradley .30 .12 .03
☐ 645 Darrell Porter .30 .12 .03
☐ 646 John Lowenstein .30 .12 .03
☐ 647 Ramon Hernandez .30 .12 .03
☐ 648 Al Cowens .40 .16 .04
☐ 649 Dave Roberts .30 .12 .03

	NRMT	VG-E	GOOD
□ 650 Thurman Munson	7.00	3.00	.70
□ 651 John Odom	.30	.12	.03
□ 652 Ed Armbrister	.30	.12	.03
□ 653 Mike Norris	.40	.16	.04
□ 654 Doug Griffin	.30	.12	.03
□ 655 Mike Vail	.30	.12	.03
□ 656 Chicago White Sox Team Card; Chuck Tanner MG (checklist back)	1.00	.30	.06
□ 657 Roy Smalley	.50	.20	.05
□ 658 Jerry Johnson	.30	.12	.03
□ 659 Ben Oglivie	.40	.16	.04
□ 660 Dave Lopes	.75	.20	.04

1976 Topps Traded

The cards in this 44-card set measure 2 1/2" by 3 1/2". The 1976 Topps Traded set contains 43 players and one unnumbered checklist card. The individuals pictured were traded after the Topps regular set was printed. A "Sports Extra" heading design is found on each picture and is also used to introduce the biographical section of the reverse. Each card is numbered according to the player's regular 1976 card with the addition of "T" to indicate his new status.

	NRMT	VG-E	GOOD
COMPLETE SET (44)	10.00	4.50	1.25
COMMON PLAYER	.25	.10	.02
□ 27T Ed Figueroa	.25	.10	.02
□ 28T Dusty Baker	.35	.15	.03
□ 44T Doug Rader	.35	.15	.03
□ 58T Ron Reed	.25	.10	.02
□ 74T Oscar Gamble	.35	.15	.03
□ 80T Jim Kaat	.90	.40	.09
□ 83T Jim Spencer	.25	.10	.02
□ 85T Mickey Rivers	.35	.15	.03
□ 99T Lee Lacy	.25	.10	.02
□ 120T Rusty Staub	.50	.20	.05
□ 127T Larvell Blanks	.25	.10	.02
□ 146T George Medich	.25	.10	.02
□ 158T Ken Reitz	.25	.10	.02
□ 208T Mike Lum	.25	.10	.02
□ 211T Clay Carroll	.25	.10	.02
□ 231T Tom House	.25	.10	.02
□ 250T Fergie Jenkins	2.00	.80	.20
□ 259T Darrel Chaney	.25	.10	.02
□ 292T Leon Roberts	.25	.10	.02
□ 296T Pat Dobson	.25	.10	.02
□ 309T Bill Melton	.25	.10	.02
□ 338T Bob Bailey	.25	.10	.02
□ 380T Bobby Bonds	.50	.20	.05
□ 383T John Ellis	.25	.10	.02
□ 385T Mickey Lolich	.50	.20	.05
□ 401T Ken Brett	.25	.10	.02
□ 410T Ralph Garr	.35	.15	.03
□ 411T Bill Singer	.35	.15	.03
□ 428T Jim Crawford	.25	.10	.02
□ 434T Morris Nettles	.25	.10	.02
□ 464T Ken Henderson	.25	.10	.02
□ 497T Joe McIntosh	.25	.10	.02
□ 524T Pete Falcone	.25	.10	.02
□ 527T Mike Anderson	.25	.10	.02
□ 528T Dock Ellis	.25	.10	.02
□ 532T Milt May	.25	.10	.02
□ 554T Ray Fosse	.25	.10	.02
□ 579T Clay Kirby	.25	.10	.02
□ 583T Tommy Helms	.35	.15	.03
□ 592T Willie Randolph	2.50	1.00	.25
□ 618T Jack Brohamer	.25	.10	.02
□ 632T Rogelio Moret	.25	.10	.02
□ 649T Dave Roberts	.25	.10	.02
□ xxxT Traded Checklist (unnumbered)	.65	.10	.02

1977 Topps

The cards in this 660-card set measure 2 1/2" by 3 1/2". In 1977 for the fifth consecutive year, Topps produced a 660-card baseball set. The player's name, team affiliation, and his position are compactly arranged over the picture area and a facsimile autograph appears on the photo. Team cards feature a checklist of that team's players in the set and a small picture of the manager on the front of

the card. Appearing for the first time are the series "Brothers" (631-634) and "Turn Back the Clock" (433-437). Other subseries in the set are League Leaders (1-8), Record Breakers (231-234), Playoffs cards (276-277), World Series cards (411-413), and Rookie Prospects (472-479 and 487-494). The key cards in the set are the rookie cards of Dale Murphy (476) and Andre Dawson (473). Other notable rookie cards in the set include Jack Clark, Dennis Martinez, and Bruce Sutter. Cards numbered 23 or lower, that feature Yankees and do not follow the numbering checklisted below, are not necessarily error cards. They are undoubtedly Burger King cards, a separate set with its own pricing and mass distribution. Burger King cards are indistinguishable from the corresponding Topps cards except for the card numbering difference and the fact that Burger King cards do not have a printing sheet designation (such as A through F like the regular Topps) anywhere on the card back in very small print. There was an aluminum version of the Dale Murphy rookie card number 476 produced (legally) in the early '80s; proceeds from the sales (originally priced at 10.00) of this "card" went to the Huntington's Disease Foundation.

	NRMT	VG-E	GOOD
COMPLETE SET (660)	410.00	165.00	40.00
COMMON PLAYER (1-660)	.21	.09	.02
☐ 1 Batting Leaders George Brett Bill Madlock	4.00	.75	.15
☐ 2 Home Run Leaders Graig Nettles Mike Schmidt	1.00	.40	.10
☐ 3 RBI Leaders Lee May George Foster	.40	.16	.04
☐ 4 Stolen Base Leaders Bill North Dave Lopes	.30	.12	.03
☐ 5 Victory Leaders Jim Palmer Randy Jones	.50	.20	.05
☐ 6 Strikeout Leaders Nolan Ryan Tom Seaver	5.25	2.25	.50
☐ 7 ERA Leaders Mark Fidrych John Denny	.40	.16	.04
☐ 8 Leading Firemen Bill Campbell Rawly Eastwick	.30	.12	.03
☐ 9 Doug Rader	.30	.12	.03
☐ 10 Reggie Jackson	11.00	5.00	1.35
☐ 11 Rob Dressler	.21	.09	.02
☐ 12 Larry Haney	.21	.09	.02
☐ 13 Luis Gomez	.21	.09	.02
☐ 14 Tommy Smith	.21	.09	.02
☐ 15 Don Gullett	.30	.12	.03
☐ 16 Bob Jones	.21	.09	.02
☐ 17 Steve Stone	.30	.12	.03
☐ 18 Indians Team/Mgr. Frank Robinson (checklist back)	.90	.20	.04
☐ 19 John D'Acquisto	.21	.09	.02
☐ 20 Graig Nettles	.90	.40	.09
☐ 21 Ken Forsch	.21	.09	.02
☐ 22 Bill Freehan	.40	.16	.04
☐ 23 Dan Driessen	.21	.09	.02
☐ 24 Carl Morton	.21	.09	.02
☐ 25 Dwight Evans	2.75	1.10	.27
☐ 26 Ray Sadecki	.21	.09	.02
☐ 27 Bill Buckner	.40	.16	.04
☐ 28 Woodie Fryman	.21	.09	.02
☐ 29 Bucky Dent	.40	.16	.04
☐ 30 Greg Luzinski	.40	.16	.04
☐ 31 Jim Todd	.21	.09	.02
☐ 32 Checklist 1	1.00	.10	.02
☐ 33 Wayne Garland	.21	.09	.02
☐ 34 Angels Team/Mgr. Norm Sherry (checklist back)	.90	.20	.04
☐ 35 Rennie Stennett	.21	.09	.02
☐ 36 John Ellis	.21	.09	.02
☐ 37 Steve Hargan	.21	.09	.02
☐ 38 Craig Kusick	.21	.09	.02
☐ 39 Tom Griffin	.21	.09	.02
☐ 40 Bobby Murcer	.40	.16	.04
☐ 41 Jim Kern	.21	.09	.02
☐ 42 Jose Cruz	.30	.12	.03
☐ 43 Ray Bare	.21	.09	.02
☐ 44 Bud Harrelson	.30	.12	.03
☐ 45 Rawly Eastwick	.21	.09	.02
☐ 46 Buck Martinez	.21	.09	.02
☐ 47 Lynn McGlothen	.21	.09	.02

Card	Player			
☐ 48	Tom Paciorek	.21	.09	.02
☐ 49	Grant Jackson	.21	.09	.02
☐ 50	Ron Cey	.40	.16	.04
☐ 51	Brewers Team/Mgr. Alex Grammas (checklist back)	.90	.20	.04
☐ 52	Ellis Valentine	.21	.09	.02
☐ 53	Paul Mitchell	.21	.09	.02
☐ 54	Sandy Alomar	.21	.09	.02
☐ 55	Jeff Burroughs	.30	.12	.03
☐ 56	Rudy May	.21	.09	.02
☐ 57	Marc Hill	.21	.09	.02
☐ 58	Chet Lemon	.30	.12	.03
☐ 59	Larry Christenson	.21	.09	.02
☐ 60	Jim Rice	4.00	1.75	.40
☐ 61	Manny Sanguillen	.30	.12	.03
☐ 62	Eric Raich	.21	.09	.02
☐ 63	Tito Fuentes	.21	.09	.02
☐ 64	Larry Biittner	.21	.09	.02
☐ 65	Skip Lockwood	.21	.09	.02
☐ 66	Roy Smalley	.30	.12	.03
☐ 67	Joaquin Andujar	.60	.25	.06
☐ 68	Bruce Bochte	.21	.09	.02
☐ 69	Jim Crawford	.21	.09	.02
☐ 70	Johnny Bench	8.50	3.75	.85
☐ 71	Dock Ellis	.21	.09	.02
☐ 72	Mike Anderson	.21	.09	.02
☐ 73	Charlie Williams	.21	.09	.02
☐ 74	A's Team/Mgr. Jack McKeon (checklist back)	.90	.20	.04
☐ 75	Dennis Leonard	.30	.12	.03
☐ 76	Tim Foli	.21	.09	.02
☐ 77	Dyar Miller	.21	.09	.02
☐ 78	Bob Davis	.21	.09	.02
☐ 79	Don Money	.21	.09	.02
☐ 80	Andy Messersmith	.30	.12	.03
☐ 81	Juan Beniquez	.21	.09	.02
☐ 82	Jim Rooker	.21	.09	.02
☐ 83	Kevin Bell	.21	.09	.02
☐ 84	Ollie Brown	.21	.09	.02
☐ 85	Duane Kuiper	.21	.09	.02
☐ 86	Pat Zachry	.21	.09	.02
☐ 87	Glenn Borgmann	.21	.09	.02
☐ 88	Stan Wall	.21	.09	.02
☐ 89	Butch Hobson	.75	.30	.07
☐ 90	Cesar Cedeno	.30	.12	.03
☐ 91	John Verhoeven	.21	.09	.02
☐ 92	Dave Rosello	.21	.09	.02
☐ 93	Tom Poquette	.21	.09	.02
☐ 94	Craig Swan	.21	.09	.02
☐ 95	Keith Hernandez	2.75	1.10	.27
☐ 96	Lou Piniella	.40	.16	.04
☐ 97	Dave Heaverlo	.21	.09	.02
☐ 98	Milt May	.21	.09	.02
☐ 99	Tom Hausman	.21	.09	.02
☐ 100	Joe Morgan	3.50	1.50	.35
☐ 101	Dick Bosman	.21	.09	.02
☐ 102	Jose Morales	.21	.09	.02
☐ 103	Mike Bacsik	.21	.09	.02
☐ 104	Omar Moreno	.30	.12	.03
☐ 105	Steve Yeager	.30	.12	.03
☐ 106	Mike Flanagan	.40	.16	.04
☐ 107	Bill Melton	.21	.09	.02
☐ 108	Alan Foster	.21	.09	.02
☐ 109	Jorge Orta	.21	.09	.02
☐ 110	Steve Carlton	6.00	2.50	.60
☐ 111	Rico Petrocelli	.30	.12	.03
☐ 112	Bill Greif	.21	.09	.02
☐ 113	Blue Jays Leaders Roy Hartsfield MG Don Leppert CO Bob Miller CO Jackie Moore CO Harry Warner CO (checklist back)	.75	.20	.04
☐ 114	Bruce Dal Canton	.21	.09	.02
☐ 115	Rick Manning	.21	.09	.02
☐ 116	Joe Niekro	.30	.12	.03
☐ 117	Frank White	.30	.12	.03
☐ 118	Rick Jones	.21	.09	.02
☐ 119	John Stearns	.30	.12	.03
☐ 120	Rod Carew	7.50	3.25	.75
☐ 121	Gary Nolan	.21	.09	.02
☐ 122	Ben Oglivie	.30	.12	.03
☐ 123	Fred Stanley	.21	.09	.02
☐ 124	George Mitterwald	.21	.09	.02
☐ 125	Bill Travers	.21	.09	.02
☐ 126	Rod Gilbreath	.21	.09	.02
☐ 127	Ron Fairly	.21	.09	.02
☐ 128	Tommy John	1.00	.40	.10
☐ 129	Mike Sadek	.21	.09	.02
☐ 130	Al Oliver	.50	.20	.05
☐ 131	Orlando Ramirez	.21	.09	.02
☐ 132	Chip Lang	.21	.09	.02
☐ 133	Ralph Garr	.30	.12	.03
☐ 134	Padres Team/Mgr. John McNamara (checklist back)	.90	.20	.04
☐ 135	Mark Belanger	.30	.12	.03
☐ 136	Jerry Mumphrey	.30	.12	.03
☐ 137	Jeff Terpko	.21	.09	.02
☐ 138	Bob Stinson	.21	.09	.02
☐ 139	Fred Norman	.21	.09	.02
☐ 140	Mike Schmidt	22.00	9.50	3.15
☐ 141	Mark Littell	.21	.09	.02
☐ 142	Steve Dillard	.21	.09	.02
☐ 143	Ed Herrmann	.21	.09	.02
☐ 144	Bruce Sutter	4.00	1.75	.40
☐ 145	Tom Veryzer	.21	.09	.02
☐ 146	Dusty Baker	.30	.12	.03
☐ 147	Jackie Brown	.21	.09	.02
☐ 148	Fran Healy	.21	.09	.02
☐ 149	Mike Cubbage	.21	.09	.02
☐ 150	Tom Seaver	8.50	3.75	.85
☐ 151	Johnny LeMaster	.21	.09	.02

☐ 152 Gaylord Perry 2.50 1.00 .25
☐ 153 Ron Jackson .21 .09 .02
☐ 154 Dave Giusti .21 .09 .02
☐ 155 Joe Rudi .30 .12 .03
☐ 156 Pete Mackanin .21 .09 .02
☐ 157 Ken Brett .21 .09 .02
☐ 158 Ted Kubiak .21 .09 .02
☐ 159 Bernie Carbo .21 .09 .02
☐ 160 Will McEnaney .21 .09 .02
☐ 161 Garry Templeton 1.25 .50 .12
☐ 162 Mike Cuellar .30 .12 .03
☐ 163 Dave Hilton .21 .09 .02
☐ 164 Tug McGraw .40 .16 .04
☐ 165 Jim Wynn .30 .12 .03
☐ 166 Bill Campbell .21 .09 .02
☐ 167 Rich Hebner .21 .09 .02
☐ 168 Charlie Spikes .21 .09 .02
☐ 169 Darold Knowles .21 .09 .02
☐ 170 Thurman Munson 5.50 2.50 .55
☐ 171 Ken Sanders .21 .09 .02
☐ 172 John Milner .21 .09 .02
☐ 173 Chuck Scrivener .21 .09 .02
☐ 174 Nelson Briles .21 .09 .02
☐ 175 Butch Wynegar .40 .16 .04
☐ 176 Bob Robertson .21 .09 .02
☐ 177 Bart Johnson .21 .09 .02
☐ 178 Bombo Rivera .21 .09 .02
☐ 179 Paul Hartzell .21 .09 .02
☐ 180 Dave Lopes .30 .12 .03
☐ 181 Ken McMullen .21 .09 .02
☐ 182 Dan Spillner .21 .09 .02
☐ 183 Cardinals Team/Mgr. .90 .20 .04
Vern Rapp
(checklist back)
☐ 184 Bo McLaughlin .21 .09 .02
☐ 185 Sixto Lezcano .30 .12 .03
☐ 186 Doug Flynn .21 .09 .02
☐ 187 Dick Pole .21 .09 .02
☐ 188 Bob Tolan .21 .09 .02
☐ 189 Rick Dempsey .30 .12 .03
☐ 190 Ray Burris .21 .09 .02
☐ 191 Doug Griffin .21 .09 .02
☐ 192 Clarence Gaston .40 .16 .04
☐ 193 Larry Gura .21 .09 .02
☐ 194 Gary Matthews .30 .12 .03
☐ 195 Ed Figueroa .21 .09 .02
☐ 196 Len Randle .21 .09 .02
☐ 197 Ed Ott .21 .09 .02
☐ 198 Wilbur Wood .30 .12 .03
☐ 199 Pepe Frias .21 .09 .02
☐ 200 Frank Tanana .40 .16 .04
☐ 201 Ed Kranepool .30 .12 .03
☐ 202 Tom Johnson .21 .09 .02
☐ 203 Ed Armbrister .21 .09 .02
☐ 204 Jeff Newman .21 .09 .02
☐ 205 Pete Falcone .21 .09 .02
☐ 206 Boog Powell .50 .20 .05
☐ 207 Glenn Abbott .21 .09 .02
☐ 208 Checklist 2 1.00 .10 .02
☐ 209 Rob Andrews .21 .09 .02
☐ 210 Fred Lynn 1.50 .60 .15
☐ 211 Giants Team/Mgr. .90 .20 .04
Joe Altobelli
(checklist back)
☐ 212 Jim Mason .21 .09 .02
☐ 213 Maximino Leon .21 .09 .02
☐ 214 Darrell Porter .21 .09 .02
☐ 215 Butch Metzger .21 .09 .02
☐ 216 Doug DeCinces .30 .12 .03
☐ 217 Tom Underwood .21 .09 .02
☐ 218 John Wathan .90 .40 .09
☐ 219 Joe Coleman .21 .09 .02
☐ 220 Chris Chambliss .30 .12 .03
☐ 221 Bob Bailey .21 .09 .02
☐ 222 Francisco Barrios .21 .09 .02
☐ 223 Earl Williams .21 .09 .02
☐ 224 Rusty Torres .21 .09 .02
☐ 225 Bob Apodaca .21 .09 .02
☐ 226 Leroy Stanton .21 .09 .02
☐ 227 Joe Sambito .30 .12 .03
☐ 228 Twins Team/Mgr. .90 .20 .04
Gene Mauch
(checklist back)
☐ 229 Don Kessinger .30 .12 .03
☐ 230 Vida Blue .30 .12 .03
☐ 231 RB: George Brett 6.00 2.50 .60
Most cons. games
with 3 or more hits
☐ 232 RB: Minnie Minoso .40 .16 .04
Oldest to hit safely
☐ 233 RB: Jose Morales, Most .30 .12 .03
pinch-hits, season
☐ 234 RB: Nolan Ryan 7.50 3.25 .75
Most seasons, 300
or more strikeouts
☐ 235 Cecil Cooper .50 .20 .05
☐ 236 Tom Buskey .21 .09 .02
☐ 237 Gene Clines .21 .09 .02
☐ 238 Tippy Martinez .30 .12 .03
☐ 239 Bill Plummer .30 .12 .03
☐ 240 Ron LeFlore .30 .12 .03
☐ 241 Dave Tomlin .21 .09 .02
☐ 242 Ken Henderson .21 .09 .02
☐ 243 Ron Reed .21 .09 .02
☐ 244 John Mayberry .40 .16 .04
(cartoon mentions
T206 Wagner)
☐ 245 Rick Rhoden .30 .12 .03
☐ 246 Mike Vail .21 .09 .02
☐ 247 Chris Knapp .21 .09 .02
☐ 248 Wilbur Howard .21 .09 .02
☐ 249 Pete Redfern .21 .09 .02
☐ 250 Bill Madlock .60 .25 .06
☐ 251 Tony Muser .21 .09 .02
☐ 252 Dale Murray .21 .09 .02
☐ 253 John Hale .21 .09 .02

☐ 254	Doyle Alexander	.21	.09	.02
☐ 255	George Scott	.30	.12	.03
☐ 256	Joe Hoerner	.21	.09	.02
☐ 257	Mike Miley	.21	.09	.02
☐ 258	Luis Tiant	.40	.16	.04
☐ 259	Mets Team/Mgr.	.90	.20	.04
	Joe Frazier			
	(checklist back)			
☐ 260	J.R. Richard	.30	.12	.03
☐ 261	Phil Garner	.40	.16	.04
☐ 262	Al Cowens	.30	.12	.03
☐ 263	Mike Marshall	.30	.12	.03
☐ 264	Tom Hutton	.21	.09	.02
☐ 265	Mark Fidrych	1.00	.40	.10
☐ 266	Derrel Thomas	.21	.09	.02
☐ 267	Ray Fosse	.21	.09	.02
☐ 268	Rick Sawyer	.21	.09	.02
☐ 269	Joe Lis	.21	.09	.02
☐ 270	Dave Parker	4.50	2.00	.45
☐ 271	Terry Forster	.30	.12	.03
☐ 272	Lee Lacy	.21	.09	.02
☐ 273	Eric Soderholm	.21	.09	.02
☐ 274	Don Stanhouse	.21	.09	.02
☐ 275	Mike Hargrove	.30	.12	.03
☐ 276	AL Champs	.50	.20	.05
	Chambliss' homer			
	decides it			
☐ 277	NL Champs	.40	.16	.04
	Reds sweep Phillies			
☐ 278	Danny Frisella	.21	.09	.02
☐ 279	Joe Wallis	.21	.09	.02
☐ 280	Jim Hunter	2.25	.90	.22
☐ 281	Roy Staiger	.21	.09	.02
☐ 282	Sid Monge	.21	.09	.02
☐ 283	Jerry DaVanon	.21	.09	.02
☐ 284	Mike Norris	.21	.09	.02
☐ 285	Brooks Robinson	3.50	1.50	.35
☐ 286	Johnny Grubb	.21	.09	.02
☐ 287	Reds Team/Mgr.	.90	.20	.04
	Sparky Anderson			
	(checklist back)			
☐ 288	Bob Montgomery	.21	.09	.02
☐ 289	Gene Garber	.21	.09	.02
☐ 290	Amos Otis	.30	.12	.03
☐ 291	Jason Thompson	.30	.12	.03
☐ 292	Rogelio Moret	.21	.09	.02
☐ 293	Jack Brohamer	.21	.09	.02
☐ 294	George Medich	.21	.09	.02
☐ 295	Gary Carter	5.50	2.50	.55
☐ 296	Don Hood	.21	.09	.02
☐ 297	Ken Reitz	.21	.09	.02
☐ 298	Charlie Hough	.30	.12	.03
☐ 299	Otto Velez	.21	.09	.02
☐ 300	Jerry Koosman	.40	.16	.04
☐ 301	Toby Harrah	.30	.12	.03
☐ 302	Mike Garman	.21	.09	.02
☐ 303	Gene Tenace	.30	.12	.03
☐ 304	Jim Hughes	.21	.09	.02
☐ 305	Mickey Rivers	.30	.12	.03
☐ 306	Rick Waits	.21	.09	.02
☐ 307	Gary Sutherland	.21	.09	.02
☐ 308	Gene Pentz	.21	.09	.02
☐ 309	Red Sox Team/Mgr.	.90	.20	.04
	Don Zimmer			
	(checklist back)			
☐ 310	Larry Bowa	.40	.16	.04
☐ 311	Vern Ruhle	.21	.09	.02
☐ 312	Rob Belloir	.21	.09	.02
☐ 313	Paul Blair	.30	.12	.03
☐ 314	Steve Mingori	.21	.09	.02
☐ 315	Dave Chalk	.21	.09	.02
☐ 316	Steve Rogers	.21	.09	.02
☐ 317	Kurt Bevacqua	.21	.09	.02
☐ 318	Duffy Dyer	.21	.09	.02
☐ 319	Rich Gossage	1.00	.40	.10
☐ 320	Ken Griffey	1.50	.60	.15
☐ 321	Dave Goltz	.21	.09	.02
☐ 322	Bill Russell	.30	.12	.03
☐ 323	Larry Lintz	.21	.09	.02
☐ 324	John Curtis	.21	.09	.02
☐ 325	Mike Ivie	.21	.09	.02
☐ 326	Jesse Jefferson	.21	.09	.02
☐ 327	Astros Team/Mgr.	.90	.20	.04
	Bill Virdon			
	(checklist back)			
☐ 328	Tommy Boggs	.21	.09	.02
☐ 329	Ron Hodges	.21	.09	.02
☐ 330	George Hendrick	.30	.12	.03
☐ 331	Jim Colborn	.21	.09	.02
☐ 332	Elliott Maddox	.21	.09	.02
☐ 333	Paul Reuschel	.21	.09	.02
☐ 334	Bill Stein	.21	.09	.02
☐ 335	Bill Robinson	.30	.12	.03
☐ 336	Denny Doyle	.21	.09	.02
☐ 337	Ron Schueler	.21	.09	.02
☐ 338	Dave Duncan	.21	.09	.02
☐ 339	Adrian Devine	.21	.09	.02
☐ 340	Hal McRae	.40	.16	.04
☐ 341	Joe Kerrigan	.21	.09	.02
☐ 342	Jerry Remy	.21	.09	.02
☐ 343	Ed Halicki	.21	.09	.02
☐ 344	Brian Downing	.40	.16	.04
☐ 345	Reggie Smith	.40	.16	.04
☐ 346	Bill Singer	.30	.12	.03
☐ 347	George Foster	1.25	.50	.12
☐ 348	Brent Strom	.21	.09	.02
☐ 349	Jim Holt	.21	.09	.02
☐ 350	Larry Dierker	.21	.09	.02
☐ 351	Jim Sundberg	.30	.12	.03
☐ 352	Mike Phillips	.21	.09	.02
☐ 353	Stan Thomas	.21	.09	.02
☐ 354	Pirates Team/Mgr.	.90	.20	.04
	Chuck Tanner			
	(checklist back)			
☐ 355	Lou Brock	3.50	1.50	.35
☐ 356	Checklist 3	1.00	.10	.02

☐ 357 Tim McCarver	.40	.16	.04
☐ 358 Tom House	.21	.09	.02
☐ 359 Willie Randolph	2.00	.80	.20
☐ 360 Rick Monday	.30	.12	.03
☐ 361 Eduardo Rodriguez	.21	.09	.02
☐ 362 Tommy Davis	.30	.12	.03
☐ 363 Dave Roberts	.21	.09	.02
☐ 364 Vic Correll	.21	.09	.02
☐ 365 Mike Torrez	.21	.09	.02
☐ 366 Ted Sizemore	.21	.09	.02
☐ 367 Dave Hamilton	.21	.09	.02
☐ 368 Mike Jorgensen	.21	.09	.02
☐ 369 Terry Humphrey	.21	.09	.02
☐ 370 John Montefusco	.30	.12	.03
☐ 371 Royals Team/Mgr. Whitey Herzog (checklist back)	.90	.20	.04
☐ 372 Rich Folkers	.21	.09	.02
☐ 373 Bert Campaneris	.30	.12	.03
☐ 374 Kent Tekulve	.40	.16	.04
☐ 375 Larry Hisle	.30	.12	.03
☐ 376 Nino Espinosa	.21	.09	.02
☐ 377 Dave McKay	.21	.09	.02
☐ 378 Jim Umbarger	.21	.09	.02
☐ 379 Larry Cox	.21	.09	.02
☐ 380 Lee May	.30	.12	.03
☐ 381 Bob Forsch	.21	.09	.02
☐ 382 Charlie Moore	.21	.09	.02
☐ 383 Stan Bahnsen	.21	.09	.02
☐ 384 Darrel Chaney	.21	.09	.02
☐ 385 Dave LaRoche	.21	.09	.02
☐ 386 Manny Mota	.30	.12	.03
☐ 387 Yankees Team (checklist back)	.90	.20	.04
☐ 388 Terry Harmon	.21	.09	.02
☐ 389 Ken Kravec	.21	.09	.02
☐ 390 Dave Winfield	9.00	4.00	.90
☐ 391 Dan Warthen	.21	.09	.02
☐ 392 Phil Roof	.21	.09	.02
☐ 393 John Lowenstein	.21	.09	.02
☐ 394 Bill Laxton	.21	.09	.02
☐ 395 Manny Trillo	.21	.09	.02
☐ 396 Tom Murphy	.21	.09	.02
☐ 397 Larry Herndon	.30	.12	.03
☐ 398 Tom Burgmeier	.21	.09	.02
☐ 399 Bruce Boisclair	.21	.09	.02
☐ 400 Steve Garvey	4.00	1.75	.40
☐ 401 Mickey Scott	.21	.09	.02
☐ 402 Tommy Helms	.30	.12	.03
☐ 403 Tom Grieve	.30	.12	.03
☐ 404 Eric Rasmussen	.21	.09	.02
☐ 405 Claudell Washington	.30	.12	.03
☐ 406 Tim Johnson	.21	.09	.02
☐ 407 Dave Freisleben	.21	.09	.02
☐ 408 Cesar Tovar	.21	.09	.02
☐ 409 Pete Broberg	.21	.09	.02
☐ 410 Willie Montanez	.21	.09	.02
☐ 411 W.S. Games 1 and 2 Morgan homers opener; Bench stars as Reds take 2nd game	1.00	.40	.10
☐ 412 W.S. Games 3 and 4 Reds stop Yankees; Bench's two homers wrap it up	1.00	.40	.10
☐ 413 World Series Summary Cincy wins 2nd straight series	.60	.25	.06
☐ 414 Tommy Harper	.30	.12	.03
☐ 415 Jay Johnstone	.30	.12	.03
☐ 416 Chuck Hartenstein	.21	.09	.02
☐ 417 Wayne Garrett	.21	.09	.02
☐ 418 White Sox Team/Mgr. Bob Lemon (checklist back)	.90	.20	.04
☐ 419 Steve Swisher	.21	.09	.02
☐ 420 Rusty Staub	.40	.16	.04
☐ 421 Doug Rau	.21	.09	.02
☐ 422 Freddie Patek	.21	.09	.02
☐ 423 Gary Lavelle	.21	.09	.02
☐ 424 Steve Brye	.21	.09	.02
☐ 425 Joe Torre	.50	.20	.05
☐ 426 Dick Drago	.21	.09	.02
☐ 427 Dave Rader	.21	.09	.02
☐ 428 Rangers Team/Mgr. Frank Lucchesi (checklist back)	.90	.20	.04
☐ 429 Ken Boswell	.21	.09	.02
☐ 430 Fergie Jenkins	2.25	.90	.22
☐ 431 Dave Collins UER (photo actually Bobby Jones)	.30	.12	.03
☐ 432 Buzz Capra	.21	.09	.02
☐ 433 Turn back clock 1972 Nate Colbert	.30	.12	.03
☐ 434 Turn back clock 1967 Yaz Triple Crown	2.00	.80	.20
☐ 435 Turn back clock 1962 Wills 104 steals	.40	.16	.04
☐ 436 Turn back clock 1957 Keegan hurls Majors' only no-hitter	.30	.12	.03
☐ 437 Turn back clock 1952 Kiner leads NL HR's 7th straight year	.50	.20	.05
☐ 438 Marty Perez	.21	.09	.02
☐ 439 Gorman Thomas	.40	.16	.04
☐ 440 Jon Matlack	.30	.12	.03
☐ 441 Larvell Blanks	.21	.09	.02
☐ 442 Braves Team/Mgr. Dave Bristol (checklist back)	.90	.20	.04
☐ 443 Lamar Johnson	.21	.09	.02
☐ 444 Wayne Twitchell	.21	.09	.02
☐ 445 Ken Singleton	.30	.12	.03
☐ 446 Bill Bonham	.21	.09	.02

☐ 447	Jerry Turner	.21	.09	.02
☐ 448	Ellie Rodriguez	.21	.09	.02
☐ 449	Al Fitzmorris	.21	.09	.02
☐ 450	Pete Rose	9.00	4.00	.90
☐ 451	Checklist 4	1.00	.10	.02
☐ 452	Mike Caldwell	.21	.09	.02
☐ 453	Pedro Garcia	.21	.09	.02
☐ 454	Andy Etchebarren	.21	.09	.02
☐ 455	Rick Wise	.30	.12	.03
☐ 456	Leon Roberts	.21	.09	.02
☐ 457	Steve Luebber	.21	.09	.02
☐ 458	Leo Foster	.21	.09	.02
☐ 459	Steve Foucault	.21	.09	.02
☐ 460	Willie Stargell	2.75	1.10	.27
☐ 461	Dick Tidrow	.21	.09	.02
☐ 462	Don Baylor	.75	.30	.07
☐ 463	Jamie Quirk	.30	.12	.03
☐ 464	Randy Moffitt	.21	.09	.02
☐ 465	Rico Carty	.30	.12	.03
☐ 466	Fred Holdsworth	.21	.09	.02
☐ 467	Phillies Team/Mgr.	.90	.20	.04
	Danny Ozark			
	(checklist back)			
☐ 468	Ramon Hernandez	.21	.09	.02
☐ 469	Pat Kelly	.21	.09	.02
☐ 470	Ted Simmons	.75	.30	.07
☐ 471	Del Unser	.21	.09	.02
☐ 472	Rookie Pitchers	.40	.16	.04
	Don Aase			
	Bob McClure			
	Gil Patterson			
	Dave Wehrmeister			
☐ 473	Rookie Outfielders	65.00	29.00	9.75
	Andre Dawson			
	Gene Richards			
	John Scott			
	Denny Walling			
☐ 474	Rookie Shortstops	.30	.12	.03
	Bob Bailor			
	Kiko Garcia			
	Craig Reynolds			
	Alex Taveras			
☐ 475	Rookie Pitchers	.40	.16	.04
	Chris Batton			
	Rick Camp			
	Scott McGregor			
	Manny Sarmiento			
☐ 476	Rookie Catchers	45.00	20.00	6.75
	Gary Alexander			
	Rick Cerone			
	Dale Murphy			
	Kevin Pasley			
☐ 477	Rookie Infielders	.30	.12	.03
	Doug Ault			
	Rich Dauer			
	Orlando Gonzalez			
	Phil Mankowski			
☐ 478	Rookie Pitchers	.30	.12	.03
	Jim Gideon			
	Leon Hooten			
	Dave Johnson			
	Mark Lemongello			
☐ 479	Rookie Outfielders	.40	.16	.04
	Brian Asselstine			
	Wayne Gross			
	Sam Mejias			
	Alvis Woods			
☐ 480	Carl Yastrzemski	6.25	2.75	.60
☐ 481	Roger Metzger	.21	.09	.02
☐ 482	Tony Solaita	.21	.09	.02
☐ 483	Richie Zisk	.21	.09	.02
☐ 484	Burt Hooton	.21	.09	.02
☐ 485	Roy White	.30	.12	.03
☐ 486	Ed Bane	.21	.09	.02
☐ 487	Rookie Pitchers	.30	.12	.03
	Larry Anderson			
	Ed Glynn			
	Joe Henderson			
	Greg Terlecky			
☐ 488	Rookie Outfielders	15.00	6.50	2.15
	Jack Clark			
	Ruppert Jones			
	Lee Mazzilli			
	Dan Thomas			
☐ 489	Rookie Pitchers	.40	.16	.04
	Len Barker			
	Randy Lerch			
	Greg Minton			
	Mike Overy			
☐ 490	Rookie Shortstops	.30	.12	.03
	Billy Almon			
	Mickey Klutts			
	Tommy McMillan			
	Mark Wagner			
☐ 491	Rookie Pitchers	5.00	2.25	.50
	Mike Dupree			
	Dennis Martinez			
	Craig Mitchell			
	Bob Sykes			
☐ 492	Rookie Outfielders	.75	.30	.07
	Tony Armas			
	Steve Kemp			
	Carlos Lopez			
	Gary Woods			
☐ 493	Rookie Pitchers	.50	.20	.05
	Mike Krukow			
	Jim Otten			
	Gary Wheelock			
	Mike Willis			
☐ 494	Rookie Infielders	.75	.30	.07
	Juan Bernhardt			
	Mike Champion			
	Jim Gantner			
	Bump Wills			
☐ 495	Al Hrabosky	.30	.12	.03
☐ 496	Gary Thomasson	.21	.09	.02

No.	Player			
☐ 497	Clay Carroll	.21	.09	.02
☐ 498	Sal Bando	.30	.12	.03
☐ 499	Pablo Torrealba	.21	.09	.02
☐ 500	Dave Kingman	.50	.20	.05
☐ 501	Jim Bibby	.21	.09	.02
☐ 502	Randy Hundley	.21	.09	.02
☐ 503	Bill Lee	.30	.12	.03
☐ 504	Dodgers Team/Mgr. Tom Lasorda (checklist back)	.90	.20	.04
☐ 505	Oscar Gamble	.30	.12	.03
☐ 506	Steve Grilli	.21	.09	.02
☐ 507	Mike Hegan	.21	.09	.02
☐ 508	Dave Pagan	.21	.09	.02
☐ 509	Cookie Rojas	.21	.09	.02
☐ 510	John Candelaria	.60	.25	.06
☐ 511	Bill Fahey	.21	.09	.02
☐ 512	Jack Billingham	.21	.09	.02
☐ 513	Jerry Terrell	.21	.09	.02
☐ 514	Cliff Johnson	.21	.09	.02
☐ 515	Chris Speier	.21	.09	.02
☐ 516	Bake McBride	.21	.09	.02
☐ 517	Pete Vuckovich	.40	.16	.04
☐ 518	Cubs Team/Mgr. Herman Franks (checklist back)	.90	.20	.04
☐ 519	Don Kirkwood	.21	.09	.02
☐ 520	Garry Maddox	.30	.12	.03
☐ 521	Bob Grich	.30	.12	.03
☐ 522	Enzo Hernandez	.21	.09	.02
☐ 523	Rollie Fingers	2.50	1.00	.25
☐ 524	Rowland Office	.21	.09	.02
☐ 525	Dennis Eckersley	9.00	4.00	.90
☐ 526	Larry Parrish	.30	.12	.03
☐ 527	Dan Meyer	.21	.09	.02
☐ 528	Bill Castro	.21	.09	.02
☐ 529	Jim Essian	.50	.20	.05
☐ 530	Rick Reuschel	.40	.16	.04
☐ 531	Lyman Bostock	.30	.12	.03
☐ 532	Jim Willoughby	.21	.09	.02
☐ 533	Mickey Stanley	.30	.12	.03
☐ 534	Paul Splittorff	.21	.09	.02
☐ 535	Cesar Geronimo	.21	.09	.02
☐ 536	Vic Albury	.21	.09	.02
☐ 537	Dave Roberts	.21	.09	.02
☐ 538	Frank Taveras	.21	.09	.02
☐ 539	Mike Wallace	.21	.09	.02
☐ 540	Bob Watson	.30	.12	.03
☐ 541	John Denny	.30	.12	.03
☐ 542	Frank Duffy	.21	.09	.02
☐ 543	Ron Blomberg	.21	.09	.02
☐ 544	Gary Ross	.21	.09	.02
☐ 545	Bob Boone	.60	.25	.06
☐ 546	Orioles Team/Mgr. Earl Weaver (checklist back)	.90	.20	.04
☐ 547	Willie McCovey	3.00	1.25	.30
☐ 548	Joel Youngblood	.21	.09	.02
☐ 549	Jerry Royster	.21	.09	.02
☐ 550	Randy Jones	.30	.12	.03
☐ 551	Bill North	.21	.09	.02
☐ 552	Pepe Mangual	.21	.09	.02
☐ 553	Jack Heidemann	.21	.09	.02
☐ 554	Bruce Kimm	.21	.09	.02
☐ 555	Dan Ford	.21	.09	.02
☐ 556	Doug Bird	.21	.09	.02
☐ 557	Jerry White	.21	.09	.02
☐ 558	Elias Sosa	.21	.09	.02
☐ 559	Alan Bannister	.21	.09	.02
☐ 560	Dave Concepcion	.75	.30	.07
☐ 561	Pete LaCock	.21	.09	.02
☐ 562	Checklist 5	1.00	.10	.02
☐ 563	Bruce Kison	.21	.09	.02
☐ 564	Alan Ashby	.21	.09	.02
☐ 565	Mickey Lolich	.40	.16	.04
☐ 566	Rick Miller	.21	.09	.02
☐ 567	Enos Cabell	.21	.09	.02
☐ 568	Carlos May	.21	.09	.02
☐ 569	Jim Lonborg	.30	.12	.03
☐ 570	Bobby Bonds	.50	.20	.05
☐ 571	Darrell Evans	.50	.20	.05
☐ 572	Ross Grimsley	.21	.09	.02
☐ 573	Joe Ferguson	.21	.09	.02
☐ 574	Aurelio Rodriguez	.21	.09	.02
☐ 575	Dick Ruthven	.21	.09	.02
☐ 576	Fred Kendall	.21	.09	.02
☐ 577	Jerry Augustine	.21	.09	.02
☐ 578	Bob Randall	.21	.09	.02
☐ 579	Don Carrithers	.21	.09	.02
☐ 580	George Brett	24.00	10.50	3.50
☐ 581	Pedro Borbon	.21	.09	.02
☐ 582	Ed Kirkpatrick	.21	.09	.02
☐ 583	Paul Lindblad	.21	.09	.02
☐ 584	Ed Goodson	.21	.09	.02
☐ 585	Rick Burleson	.30	.12	.03
☐ 586	Steve Renko	.21	.09	.02
☐ 587	Rick Baldwin	.21	.09	.02
☐ 588	Dave Moates	.21	.09	.02
☐ 589	Mike Cosgrove	.21	.09	.02
☐ 590	Buddy Bell	.40	.16	.04
☐ 591	Chris Arnold	.21	.09	.02
☐ 592	Dan Briggs	.21	.09	.02
☐ 593	Dennis Blair	.21	.09	.02
☐ 594	Biff Pocoroba	.21	.09	.02
☐ 595	John Hiller	.30	.12	.03
☐ 596	Jerry Martin	.21	.09	.02
☐ 597	Mariners Leaders Darrell Johnson MG Don Bryant CO Jim Busby CO Vada Pinson CO Wes Stock CO (checklist back)	.75	.20	.04
☐ 598	Sparky Lyle	.50	.20	.05
☐ 599	Mike Tyson	.21	.09	.02
☐ 600	Jim Palmer	6.00	2.50	.60

☐ 601 Mike Lum .21 .09 .02
☐ 602 Andy Hassler .21 .09 .02
☐ 603 Willie Davis .30 .12 .03
☐ 604 Jim Slaton .21 .09 .02
☐ 605 Felix Millan .21 .09 .02
☐ 606 Steve Braun .21 .09 .02
☐ 607 Larry Demery .21 .09 .02
☐ 608 Roy Howell .21 .09 .02
☐ 609 Jim Barr .21 .09 .02
☐ 610 Jose Cardenal .21 .09 .02
☐ 611 Dave Lemanczyk .21 .09 .02
☐ 612 Barry Foote .21 .09 .02
☐ 613 Reggie Cleveland .21 .09 .02
☐ 614 Greg Gross .21 .09 .02
☐ 615 Phil Niekro 2.00 .80 .20
☐ 616 Tommy Sandt .21 .09 .02
☐ 617 Bobby Darwin .21 .09 .02
☐ 618 Pat Dobson .21 .09 .02
☐ 619 Johnny Oates .30 .12 .03
☐ 620 Don Sutton 2.00 .80 .20
☐ 621 Tigers Team/Mgr. .90 .20 .04
Ralph Houk
(checklist back)
☐ 622 Jim Wohlford .21 .09 .02
☐ 623 Jack Kucek .21 .09 .02
☐ 624 Hector Cruz .21 .09 .02
☐ 625 Ken Holtzman .30 .12 .03
☐ 626 Al Bumbry .21 .09 .02
☐ 627 Bob Myrick .21 .09 .02
☐ 628 Mario Guerrero .21 .09 .02
☐ 629 Bobby Valentine .30 .12 .03
☐ 630 Bert Blyleven 1.25 .50 .12
☐ 631 Big League Brothers 3.00 1.25 .30
George Brett
Ken Brett
☐ 632 Big League Brothers .30 .12 .03
Bob Forsch
Ken Forsch
☐ 633 Big League Brothers .30 .12 .03
Lee May
Carlos May
☐ 634 Big League Brothers .30 .12 .03
Paul Reuschel
Rick Reuschel UER
(photos switched)
☐ 635 Robin Yount 24.00 10.50 3.50
☐ 636 Santo Alcala .21 .09 .02
☐ 637 Alex Johnson .21 .09 .02
☐ 638 Jim Kaat .75 .30 .07
☐ 639 Jerry Morales .21 .09 .02
☐ 640 Carlton Fisk 6.50 2.75 .65
☐ 641 Dan Larson .21 .09 .02
☐ 642 Willie Crawford .21 .09 .02
☐ 643 Mike Pazik .21 .09 .02
☐ 644 Matt Alexander .21 .09 .02
☐ 645 Jerry Reuss .30 .12 .03
☐ 646 Andres Mora .21 .09 .02
☐ 647 Expos Team/Mgr. .90 .20 .04
Dick Williams
(checklist back)
☐ 648 Jim Spencer .21 .09 .02
☐ 649 Dave Cash .21 .09 .02
☐ 650 Nolan Ryan 30.00 13.50 4.50
☐ 651 Von Joshua .21 .09 .02
☐ 652 Tom Walker .21 .09 .02
☐ 653 Diego Segui .21 .09 .02
☐ 654 Ron Pruitt .21 .09 .02
☐ 655 Tony Perez 1.50 .60 .15
☐ 656 Ron Guidry 2.50 1.00 .25
☐ 657 Mick Kelleher .21 .09 .02
☐ 658 Marty Pattin .21 .09 .02
☐ 659 Merv Rettenmund .21 .09 .02
☐ 660 Willie Horton .50 .15 .03

1978 Topps

The cards in this 726-card set measure 2 1/2" by 3 1/2". The 1978 Topps set experienced an increase in number of cards from the previous five regular issue sets of 660. Cards 1 through 7 feature Record Breakers (RB) of the 1977 season. Other subsets within this set include League Leaders (201-208), Post-season cards (411-413), and Rookie Prospects (701-711). The key rookie cards in this set are the multi-player rookie card of Paul Molitor and Alan Trammell, Jack Morris, Eddie Murray, Lance Parrish, and Lou Whitaker. The manager cards in the set feature a "then and now" format on the card front showing the manager as he looked many years before, e.g., during his playing days. While no scarcities exist, 66 of the cards are more abundant in supply, as they were "double printed." These 66 double-printed cards are noted in the checklist by DP. Team cards

again feature a checklist of that team's players in the set on the back. Cards numbered 23 or lower, that feature Astros, Rangers, Tigers, or Yankees and do not follow the numbering checklisted below, are not necessarily error cards. They are undoubtedly Burger King cards, a separate set with its own pricing and mass distribution. Burger King cards are indistinguishable from the corresponding Topps cards except for the card numbering difference and the fact that Burger King cards do not have a printing sheet designation (such as A through F like the regular Topps) anywhere on the card back in very small print.

	NRMT	VG-E	GOOD
COMPLETE SET (726)	340.00	140.00	35.00
COMMON PLAYER (1-726)	.16	.07	.01
COMMON DP's (1-726)	.08	.03	.01
☐ 1 RB: Lou Brock Most steals, lifetime	3.00	.75	.15
☐ 2 RB: Sparky Lyle Most games, pure relief, lifetime	.25	.10	.02
☐ 3 RB: Willie McCovey Most times, 2 HR's in inning, lifetime	1.25	.50	.12
☐ 4 RB: Brooks Robinson Most consecutive seasons with one club	1.25	.50	.12
☐ 5 RB: Pete Rose Most hits, switch hitter, lifetime	2.50	1.00	.25
☐ 6 RB: Nolan Ryan Most games with 10 or more strikeouts, lifetime	6.00	2.50	.60
☐ 7 RB: Reggie Jackson Most homers, one World Series	3.00	1.25	.30
☐ 8 Mike Sadek	.16	.07	.01
☐ 9 Doug DeCinces	.25	.10	.02
☐ 10 Phil Niekro	1.50	.60	.15
☐ 11 Rick Manning	.16	.07	.01
☐ 12 Don Aase	.25	.10	.02
☐ 13 Art Howe	.50	.20	.05
☐ 14 Lerrin LaGrow	.16	.07	.01
☐ 15 Tony Perez DP	.60	.25	.06
☐ 16 Roy White	.25	.10	.02
☐ 17 Mike Krukow	.25	.10	.02
☐ 18 Bob Grich	.25	.10	.02
☐ 19 Darrell Porter	.16	.07	.01
☐ 20 Pete Rose DP	4.00	1.75	.40
☐ 21 Steve Kemp	.25	.10	.02
☐ 22 Charlie Hough	.25	.10	.02
☐ 23 Bump Wills	.16	.07	.01
☐ 24 Don Money DP	.08	.03	.01
☐ 25 Jon Matlack	.25	.10	.02
☐ 26 Rich Hebner	.16	.07	.01
☐ 27 Geoff Zahn	.16	.07	.01
☐ 28 Ed Ott	.16	.07	.01
☐ 29 Bob Lacey	.16	.07	.01
☐ 30 George Hendrick	.25	.10	.02
☐ 31 Glenn Abbott	.16	.07	.01
☐ 32 Garry Templeton	.35	.15	.03
☐ 33 Dave Lemanczyk	.16	.07	.01
☐ 34 Willie McCovey	2.75	1.10	.27
☐ 35 Sparky Lyle	.35	.15	.03
☐ 36 Eddie Murray	70.00	32.00	10.50
☐ 37 Rick Waits	.16	.07	.01
☐ 38 Willie Montanez	.16	.07	.01
☐ 39 Floyd Bannister	.60	.25	.06
☐ 40 Carl Yastrzemski	4.50	2.00	.45
☐ 41 Burt Hooton	.16	.07	.01
☐ 42 Jorge Orta	.16	.07	.01
☐ 43 Bill Atkinson	.16	.07	.01
☐ 44 Toby Harrah	.25	.10	.02
☐ 45 Mark Fidrych	.35	.15	.03
☐ 46 Al Cowens	.16	.07	.01
☐ 47 Jack Billingham	.16	.07	.01
☐ 48 Don Baylor	.50	.20	.05
☐ 49 Ed Kranepool	.25	.10	.02
☐ 50 Rick Reuschel	.35	.15	.03
☐ 51 Charlie Moore DP	.08	.03	.01
☐ 52 Jim Lonborg	.25	.10	.02
☐ 53 Phil Garner DP	.16	.07	.01
☐ 54 Tom Johnson	.16	.07	.01
☐ 55 Mitchell Page	.16	.07	.01
☐ 56 Randy Jones	.16	.07	.01
☐ 57 Dan Meyer	.16	.07	.01
☐ 58 Bob Forsch	.16	.07	.01
☐ 59 Otto Velez	.16	.07	.01
☐ 60 Thurman Munson	4.00	1.75	.40
☐ 61 Larvell Blanks	.16	.07	.01
☐ 62 Jim Barr	.16	.07	.01
☐ 63 Don Zimmer MG	.25	.10	.02
☐ 64 Gene Pentz	.16	.07	.01
☐ 65 Ken Singleton	.25	.10	.02
☐ 66 Chicago White Sox Team Card (checklist back)	.75	.15	.03
☐ 67 Claudell Washington	.25	.10	.02
☐ 68 Steve Foucault DP	.08	.03	.01
☐ 69 Mike Vail	.16	.07	.01
☐ 70 Rich Gossage	.75	.30	.07
☐ 71 Terry Humphrey	.16	.07	.01
☐ 72 Andre Dawson	15.00	6.50	2.15
☐ 73 Andy Hassler	.16	.07	.01
☐ 74 Checklist 1	.90	.10	.02
☐ 75 Dick Ruthven	.16	.07	.01
☐ 76 Steve Ontiveros	.16	.07	.01
☐ 77 Ed Kirkpatrick	.16	.07	.01
☐ 78 Pablo Torrealba	.16	.07	.01
☐ 79 Darrell Johnson DP	.08	.03	.01
☐ 80 Ken Griffey	1.00	.40	.10

□ 81 Pete Redfern	.16	.07	.01
□ 82 San Francisco Giants Team Card (checklist back)	.75	.15	.03
□ 83 Bob Montgomery	.16	.07	.01
□ 84 Kent Tekulve	.25	.10	.02
□ 85 Ron Fairly	.16	.07	.01
□ 86 Dave Tomlin	.16	.07	.01
□ 87 John Lowenstein	.16	.07	.01
□ 88 Mike Phillips	.16	.07	.01
□ 89 Ken Clay	.16	.07	.01
□ 90 Larry Bowa	.35	.15	.03
□ 91 Oscar Zamora	.16	.07	.01
□ 92 Adrian Devine	.16	.07	.01
□ 93 Bobby Cox DP	.08	.03	.01
□ 94 Chuck Scrivener	.16	.07	.01
□ 95 Jamie Quirk	.16	.07	.01
□ 96 Baltimore Orioles Team Card (checklist back)	.75	.15	.03
□ 97 Stan Bahnsen	.16	.07	.01
□ 98 Jim Essian	.25	.10	.02
□ 99 Willie Hernandez	.60	.25	.06
□ 100 George Brett	15.00	6.50	2.15
□ 101 Sid Monge	.16	.07	.01
□ 102 Matt Alexander	.16	.07	.01
□ 103 Tom Murphy	.16	.07	.01
□ 104 Lee Lacy	.16	.07	.01
□ 105 Reggie Cleveland	.16	.07	.01
□ 106 Bill Plummer	.25	.10	.02
□ 107 Ed Halicki	.16	.07	.01
□ 108 Von Joshua	.16	.07	.01
□ 109 Joe Torre	.35	.15	.03
□ 110 Richie Zisk	.16	.07	.01
□ 111 Mike Tyson	.16	.07	.01
□ 112 Houston Astros Team Card (checklist back)	.75	.15	.03
□ 113 Don Carrithers	.16	.07	.01
□ 114 Paul Blair	.25	.10	.02
□ 115 Gary Nolan	.16	.07	.01
□ 116 Tucker Ashford	.16	.07	.01
□ 117 John Montague	.16	.07	.01
□ 118 Terry Harmon	.16	.07	.01
□ 119 Dennis Martinez	1.00	.40	.10
□ 120 Gary Carter	3.50	1.50	.35
□ 121 Alvis Woods	.16	.07	.01
□ 122 Dennis Eckersley	4.50	2.00	.45
□ 123 Manny Trillo	.16	.07	.01
□ 124 Dave Rozema	.25	.10	.02
□ 125 George Scott	.25	.10	.02
□ 126 Paul Moskau	.16	.07	.01
□ 127 Chet Lemon	.25	.10	.02
□ 128 Bill Russell	.25	.10	.02
□ 129 Jim Colborn	.16	.07	.01
□ 130 Jeff Burroughs	.25	.10	.02
□ 131 Bert Blyleven	.75	.30	.07
□ 132 Enos Cabell	.16	.07	.01
□ 133 Jerry Augustine	.16	.07	.01
□ 134 Steve Henderson	.16	.07	.01
□ 135 Ron Guidry DP	.75	.30	.07
□ 136 Ted Sizemore	.16	.07	.01
□ 137 Craig Kusick	.16	.07	.01
□ 138 Larry Demery	.16	.07	.01
□ 139 Wayne Gross	.16	.07	.01
□ 140 Rollie Fingers	2.25	.90	.22
□ 141 Ruppert Jones	.16	.07	.01
□ 142 John Montefusco	.25	.10	.02
□ 143 Keith Hernandez	1.75	.70	.17
□ 144 Jesse Jefferson	.16	.07	.01
□ 145 Rick Monday	.25	.10	.02
□ 146 Doyle Alexander	.16	.07	.01
□ 147 Lee Mazzilli	.16	.07	.01
□ 148 Andre Thornton	.25	.10	.02
□ 149 Dale Murray	.16	.07	.01
□ 150 Bobby Bonds	.35	.15	.03
□ 151 Milt Wilcox	.16	.07	.01
□ 152 Ivan DeJesus	.16	.07	.01
□ 153 Steve Stone	.25	.10	.02
□ 154 Cecil Cooper DP	.16	.07	.01
□ 155 Butch Hobson	.35	.15	.03
□ 156 Andy Messersmith	.25	.10	.02
□ 157 Pete LaCock DP	.08	.03	.01
□ 158 Joaquin Andujar	.25	.10	.02
□ 159 Lou Piniella	.35	.15	.03
□ 160 Jim Palmer	4.50	2.00	.45
□ 161 Bob Boone	.50	.20	.05
□ 162 Paul Thormodsgard	.16	.07	.01
□ 163 Bill North	.16	.07	.01
□ 164 Bob Owchinko	.16	.07	.01
□ 165 Rennie Stennett	.16	.07	.01
□ 166 Carlos Lopez	.16	.07	.01
□ 167 Tim Foli	.16	.07	.01
□ 168 Reggie Smith	.35	.15	.03
□ 169 Jerry Johnson	.16	.07	.01
□ 170 Lou Brock	3.00	1.25	.30
□ 171 Pat Zachry	.16	.07	.01
□ 172 Mike Hargrove	.25	.10	.02
□ 173 Robin Yount	15.00	6.50	2.15
□ 174 Wayne Garland	.16	.07	.01
□ 175 Jerry Morales	.16	.07	.01
□ 176 Milt May	.16	.07	.01
□ 177 Gene Garber DP	.08	.03	.01
□ 178 Dave Chalk	.16	.07	.01
□ 179 Dick Tidrow	.16	.07	.01
□ 180 Dave Concepcion	.60	.25	.06
□ 181 Ken Forsch	.16	.07	.01
□ 182 Jim Spencer	.16	.07	.01
□ 183 Doug Bird	.16	.07	.01
□ 184 Checklist 2	.90	.10	.02
□ 185 Ellis Valentine	.16	.07	.01
□ 186 Bob Stanley DP	.25	.10	.02
□ 187 Jerry Royster DP	.08	.03	.01
□ 188 Al Bumbry	.16	.07	.01
□ 189 Tom Lasorda MG	.25	.10	.02
□ 190 John Candelaria	.35	.15	.03

☐ 191 Rodney Scott	.16	.07	.01
☐ 192 San Diego Padres Team Card (checklist back)	.75	.15	.03
☐ 193 Rich Chiles	.16	.07	.01
☐ 194 Derrel Thomas	.16	.07	.01
☐ 195 Larry Dierker	.16	.07	.01
☐ 196 Bob Bailor	.16	.07	.01
☐ 197 Nino Espinosa	.16	.07	.01
☐ 198 Ron Pruitt	.16	.07	.01
☐ 199 Craig Reynolds	.16	.07	.01
☐ 200 Reggie Jackson	7.50	3.25	.75
☐ 201 Batting Leaders Dave Parker Rod Carew	1.00	.40	.10
☐ 202 Home Run Leaders DP George Foster Jim Rice	.25	.10	.02
☐ 203 RBI Leaders George Foster Larry Hisle	.25	.10	.02
☐ 204 Steals Leaders DP Frank Taveras Freddie Patek	.16	.07	.01
☐ 205 Victory Leaders Steve Carlton Dave Goltz Dennis Leonard Jim Palmer	.75	.30	.07
☐ 206 Strikeout Leaders DP Phil Niekro Nolan Ryan	1.25	.50	.12
☐ 207 ERA Leaders DP John Candelaria Frank Tanana	.16	.07	.01
☐ 208 Top Firemen Rollie Fingers Bill Campbell	.25	.10	.02
☐ 209 Dock Ellis	.16	.07	.01
☐ 210 Jose Cardenal	.16	.07	.01
☐ 211 Earl Weaver MG DP	.16	.07	.01
☐ 212 Mike Caldwell	.16	.07	.01
☐ 213 Alan Bannister	.16	.07	.01
☐ 214 California Angels Team Card (checklist back)	.75	.15	.03
☐ 215 Darrell Evans	.35	.15	.03
☐ 216 Mike Paxton	.16	.07	.01
☐ 217 Rod Gilbreath	.16	.07	.01
☐ 218 Marty Pattin	.16	.07	.01
☐ 219 Mike Cubbage	.16	.07	.01
☐ 220 Pedro Borbon	.16	.07	.01
☐ 221 Chris Speier	.16	.07	.01
☐ 222 Jerry Martin	.16	.07	.01
☐ 223 Bruce Kison	.16	.07	.01
☐ 224 Jerry Tabb	.16	.07	.01
☐ 225 Don Gullett DP	.16	.07	.01
☐ 226 Joe Ferguson	.16	.07	.01
☐ 227 Al Fitzmorris	.16	.07	.01
☐ 228 Manny Mota DP	.16	.07	.01
☐ 229 Leo Foster	.16	.07	.01
☐ 230 Al Hrabosky	.16	.07	.01
☐ 231 Wayne Nordhagen	.16	.07	.01
☐ 232 Mickey Stanley	.25	.10	.02
☐ 233 Dick Pole	.16	.07	.01
☐ 234 Herman Franks MG	.16	.07	.01
☐ 235 Tim McCarver	.35	.15	.03
☐ 236 Terry Whitfield	.16	.07	.01
☐ 237 Rich Dauer	.16	.07	.01
☐ 238 Juan Beniquez	.16	.07	.01
☐ 239 Dyar Miller	.16	.07	.01
☐ 240 Gene Tenace	.25	.10	.02
☐ 241 Pete Vuckovich	.25	.10	.02
☐ 242 Barry Bonnell DP	.16	.07	.01
☐ 243 Bob McClure	.16	.07	.01
☐ 244 Montreal Expos Team Card DP (checklist back)	.35	.10	.02
☐ 245 Rick Burleson	.25	.10	.02
☐ 246 Dan Driessen	.16	.07	.01
☐ 247 Larry Christenson	.16	.07	.01
☐ 248 Frank White DP	.16	.07	.01
☐ 249 Dave Goltz DP	.08	.03	.01
☐ 250 Graig Nettles DP	.25	.10	.02
☐ 251 Don Kirkwood	.16	.07	.01
☐ 252 Steve Swisher DP	.08	.03	.01
☐ 253 Jim Kern	.16	.07	.01
☐ 254 Dave Collins	.25	.10	.02
☐ 255 Jerry Reuss	.25	.10	.02
☐ 256 Joe Altobelli MG	.16	.07	.01
☐ 257 Hector Cruz	.16	.07	.01
☐ 258 John Hiller	.25	.10	.02
☐ 259 Los Angeles Dodgers Team Card (checklist back)	.75	.15	.03
☐ 260 Bert Campaneris	.25	.10	.02
☐ 261 Tim Hosley	.16	.07	.01
☐ 262 Rudy May	.16	.07	.01
☐ 263 Danny Walton	.16	.07	.01
☐ 264 Jamie Easterly	.16	.07	.01
☐ 265 Sal Bando DP	.16	.07	.01
☐ 266 Bob Shirley	.16	.07	.01
☐ 267 Doug Ault	.16	.07	.01
☐ 268 Gil Flores	.16	.07	.01
☐ 269 Wayne Twitchell	.16	.07	.01
☐ 270 Carlton Fisk	5.00	2.25	.50
☐ 271 Randy Lerch DP	.08	.03	.01
☐ 272 Royle Stillman	.16	.07	.01
☐ 273 Fred Norman	.16	.07	.01
☐ 274 Freddie Patek	.16	.07	.01
☐ 275 Dan Ford	.16	.07	.01
☐ 276 Bill Bonham DP	.08	.03	.01
☐ 277 Bruce Boisclair	.16	.07	.01
☐ 278 Enrique Romo	.16	.07	.01
☐ 279 Bill Virdon MG	.25	.10	.02
☐ 280 Buddy Bell	.25	.10	.02

	Card			
☐ 281	Eric Rasmussen DP	.08	.03	.01
☐ 282	New York Yankees Team Card (checklist back)	1.00	.20	.04
☐ 283	Omar Moreno	.16	.07	.01
☐ 284	Randy Moffitt	.16	.07	.01
☐ 285	Steve Yeager DP	.16	.07	.01
☐ 286	Ben Oglivie	.25	.10	.02
☐ 287	Kiko Garcia	.16	.07	.01
☐ 288	Dave Hamilton	.16	.07	.01
☐ 289	Checklist 3	.90	.10	.02
☐ 290	Willie Horton	.25	.10	.02
☐ 291	Gary Ross	.16	.07	.01
☐ 292	Gene Richards	.16	.07	.01
☐ 293	Mike Willis	.16	.07	.01
☐ 294	Larry Parrish	.25	.10	.02
☐ 295	Bill Lee	.25	.10	.02
☐ 296	Biff Pocoroba	.16	.07	.01
☐ 297	Warren Brusstar DP	.08	.03	.01
☐ 298	Tony Armas	.25	.10	.02
☐ 299	Whitey Herzog MG	.25	.10	.02
☐ 300	Joe Morgan	3.00	1.25	.30
☐ 301	Buddy Schultz	.16	.07	.01
☐ 302	Chicago Cubs Team Card (checklist back)	.75	.15	.03
☐ 303	Sam Hinds	.16	.07	.01
☐ 304	John Milner	.16	.07	.01
☐ 305	Rico Carty	.25	.10	.02
☐ 306	Joe Niekro	.25	.10	.02
☐ 307	Glenn Borgmann	.16	.07	.01
☐ 308	Jim Rooker	.16	.07	.01
☐ 309	Cliff Johnson	.16	.07	.01
☐ 310	Don Sutton	2.00	.80	.20
☐ 311	Jose Baez DP	.08	.03	.01
☐ 312	Greg Minton	.25	.10	.02
☐ 313	Andy Etchebarren	.16	.07	.01
☐ 314	Paul Lindblad	.16	.07	.01
☐ 315	Mark Belanger	.25	.10	.02
☐ 316	Henry Cruz DP	.08	.03	.01
☐ 317	Dave Johnson	.25	.10	.02
☐ 318	Tom Griffin	.16	.07	.01
☐ 319	Alan Ashby	.16	.07	.01
☐ 320	Fred Lynn	1.00	.40	.10
☐ 321	Santo Alcala	.16	.07	.01
☐ 322	Tom Paciorek	.16	.07	.01
☐ 323	Jim Fregosi DP	.16	.07	.01
☐ 324	Vern Rapp MG	.16	.07	.01
☐ 325	Bruce Sutter	.75	.30	.07
☐ 326	Mike Lum DP	.08	.03	.01
☐ 327	Rick Langford DP	.08	.03	.01
☐ 328	Milwaukee Brewers Team Card (checklist back)	.75	.15	.03
☐ 329	John Verhoeven	.16	.07	.01
☐ 330	Bob Watson	.25	.10	.02
☐ 331	Mark Littell	.16	.07	.01
☐ 332	Duane Kuiper	.16	.07	.01
☐ 333	Jim Todd	.16	.07	.01
☐ 334	John Stearns	.16	.07	.01
☐ 335	Bucky Dent	.35	.15	.03
☐ 336	Steve Busby	.16	.07	.01
☐ 337	Tom Grieve	.25	.10	.02
☐ 338	Dave Heaverlo	.16	.07	.01
☐ 339	Mario Guerrero	.16	.07	.01
☐ 340	Bake McBride	.16	.07	.01
☐ 341	Mike Flanagan	.35	.15	.03
☐ 342	Aurelio Rodriguez	.16	.07	.01
☐ 343	John Wathan DP	.16	.07	.01
☐ 344	Sam Ewing	.16	.07	.01
☐ 345	Luis Tiant	.35	.15	.03
☐ 346	Larry Biittner	.16	.07	.01
☐ 347	Terry Forster	.25	.10	.02
☐ 348	Del Unser	.16	.07	.01
☐ 349	Rick Camp DP	.08	.03	.01
☐ 350	Steve Garvey	3.50	1.50	.35
☐ 351	Jeff Torborg	.25	.10	.02
☐ 352	Tony Scott	.16	.07	.01
☐ 353	Doug Bair	.16	.07	.01
☐ 354	Cesar Geronimo	.16	.07	.01
☐ 355	Bill Travers	.16	.07	.01
☐ 356	New York Mets Team Card (checklist back)	.90	.20	.04
☐ 357	Tom Poquette	.16	.07	.01
☐ 358	Mark Lemongello	.16	.07	.01
☐ 359	Marc Hill	.16	.07	.01
☐ 360	Mike Schmidt	15.00	6.50	2.15
☐ 361	Chris Knapp	.16	.07	.01
☐ 362	Dave May	.16	.07	.01
☐ 363	Bob Randall	.16	.07	.01
☐ 364	Jerry Turner	.16	.07	.01
☐ 365	Ed Figueroa	.16	.07	.01
☐ 366	Larry Milbourne DP	.08	.03	.01
☐ 367	Rick Dempsey	.25	.10	.02
☐ 368	Balor Moore	.16	.07	.01
☐ 369	Tim Nordbrook	.16	.07	.01
☐ 370	Rusty Staub	.35	.15	.03
☐ 371	Ray Burris	.16	.07	.01
☐ 372	Brian Asselstine	.16	.07	.01
☐ 373	Jim Willoughby	.16	.07	.01
☐ 374	Jose Morales	.16	.07	.01
☐ 375	Tommy John	.75	.30	.07
☐ 376	Jim Wohlford	.16	.07	.01
☐ 377	Manny Sarmiento	.16	.07	.01
☐ 378	Bobby Winkles MG	.16	.07	.01
☐ 379	Skip Lockwood	.16	.07	.01
☐ 380	Ted Simmons	.60	.25	.06
☐ 381	Philadelphia Phillies Team Card (checklist back)	.75	.15	.03
☐ 382	Joe Lahoud	.16	.07	.01
☐ 383	Mario Mendoza	.16	.07	.01
☐ 384	Jack Clark	4.00	1.75	.40
☐ 385	Tito Fuentes	.16	.07	.01
☐ 386	Bob Gorinski	.16	.07	.01

Card			
□ 387 Ken Holtzman	.25	.10	.02
□ 388 Bill Fahey DP	.08	.03	.01
□ 389 Julio Gonzalez	.16	.07	.01
□ 390 Oscar Gamble	.16	.07	.01
□ 391 Larry Haney	.16	.07	.01
□ 392 Billy Almon	.16	.07	.01
□ 393 Tippy Martinez	.16	.07	.01
□ 394 Roy Howell DP	.08	.03	.01
□ 395 Jim Hughes	.16	.07	.01
□ 396 Bob Stinson DP	.08	.03	.01
□ 397 Greg Gross	.16	.07	.01
□ 398 Don Hood	.16	.07	.01
□ 399 Pete Mackanin	.16	.07	.01
□ 400 Nolan Ryan	24.00	10.50	3.50
□ 401 Sparky Anderson MG	.25	.10	.02
□ 402 Dave Campbell	.16	.07	.01
□ 403 Bud Harrelson	.25	.10	.02
□ 404 Detroit Tigers Team Card (checklist back)	.75	.15	.03
□ 405 Rawly Eastwick	.16	.07	.01
□ 406 Mike Jorgensen	.16	.07	.01
□ 407 Odell Jones	.16	.07	.01
□ 408 Joe Zdeb	.16	.07	.01
□ 409 Ron Schueler	.16	.07	.01
□ 410 Bill Madlock	.50	.20	.05
□ 411 AL Champs Yankees rally to defeat Royals	.60	.25	.06
□ 412 NL Champs Dodgers overpower Phillies in four	.60	.25	.06
□ 413 World Series Reggie and Yankees reign supreme	2.25	.90	.22
□ 414 Darold Knowles DP	.08	.03	.01
□ 415 Ray Fosse	.16	.07	.01
□ 416 Jack Brohamer	.16	.07	.01
□ 417 Mike Garman DP	.08	.03	.01
□ 418 Tony Muser	.16	.07	.01
□ 419 Jerry Garvin	.16	.07	.01
□ 420 Greg Luzinski	.35	.15	.03
□ 421 Junior Moore	.16	.07	.01
□ 422 Steve Braun	.16	.07	.01
□ 423 Dave Rosello	.16	.07	.01
□ 424 Boston Red Sox Team Card (checklist back)	.75	.15	.03
□ 425 Steve Rogers DP	.08	.03	.01
□ 426 Fred Kendall	.16	.07	.01
□ 427 Mario Soto	.35	.15	.03
□ 428 Joel Youngblood	.16	.07	.01
□ 429 Mike Barlow	.16	.07	.01
□ 430 Al Oliver	.35	.15	.03
□ 431 Butch Metzger	.16	.07	.01
□ 432 Terry Bulling	.16	.07	.01
□ 433 Fernando Gonzalez	.16	.07	.01
□ 434 Mike Norris	.16	.07	.01
□ 435 Checklist 4	.90	.10	.02
□ 436 Vic Harris DP	.08	.03	.01
□ 437 Bo McLaughlin	.16	.07	.01
□ 438 John Ellis	.16	.07	.01
□ 439 Ken Kravec	.16	.07	.01
□ 440 Dave Lopes	.25	.10	.02
□ 441 Larry Gura	.16	.07	.01
□ 442 Elliott Maddox	.16	.07	.01
□ 443 Darrel Chaney	.16	.07	.01
□ 444 Roy Hartsfield MG	.16	.07	.01
□ 445 Mike Ivie	.16	.07	.01
□ 446 Tug McGraw	.35	.15	.03
□ 447 Leroy Stanton	.16	.07	.01
□ 448 Bill Castro	.16	.07	.01
□ 449 Tim Blackwell DP	.08	.03	.01
□ 450 Tom Seaver	5.00	2.25	.50
□ 451 Minnesota Twins Team Card (checklist back)	.75	.15	.03
□ 452 Jerry Mumphrey	.16	.07	.01
□ 453 Doug Flynn	.16	.07	.01
□ 454 Dave LaRoche	.16	.07	.01
□ 455 Bill Robinson	.25	.10	.02
□ 456 Vern Ruhle	.16	.07	.01
□ 457 Bob Bailey	.16	.07	.01
□ 458 Jeff Newman	.16	.07	.01
□ 459 Charlie Spikes	.16	.07	.01
□ 460 Jim Hunter	2.00	.80	.20
□ 461 Rob Andrews DP	.08	.03	.01
□ 462 Rogelio Moret	.16	.07	.01
□ 463 Kevin Bell	.16	.07	.01
□ 464 Jerry Grote	.16	.07	.01
□ 465 Hal McRae	.35	.15	.03
□ 466 Dennis Blair	.16	.07	.01
□ 467 Alvin Dark MG	.16	.07	.01
□ 468 Warren Cromartie	.35	.15	.03
□ 469 Rick Cerone	.25	.10	.02
□ 470 J.R. Richard	.25	.10	.02
□ 471 Roy Smalley	.16	.07	.01
□ 472 Ron Reed	.16	.07	.01
□ 473 Bill Buckner	.35	.15	.03
□ 474 Jim Slaton	.16	.07	.01
□ 475 Gary Matthews	.25	.10	.02
□ 476 Bill Stein	.16	.07	.01
□ 477 Doug Capilla	.16	.07	.01
□ 478 Jerry Remy	.16	.07	.01
□ 479 St. Louis Cardinals Team Card (checklist back)	.75	.15	.03
□ 480 Ron LeFlore	.25	.10	.02
□ 481 Jackson Todd	.16	.07	.01
□ 482 Rick Miller	.16	.07	.01
□ 483 Ken Macha	.16	.07	.01
□ 484 Jim Norris	.16	.07	.01
□ 485 Chris Chambliss	.25	.10	.02
□ 486 John Curtis	.16	.07	.01
□ 487 Jim Tyrone	.16	.07	.01
□ 488 Dan Spillner	.16	.07	.01

□ 489 Rudy Meoli	.16	.07	.01
□ 490 Amos Otis	.25	.10	.02
□ 491 Scott McGregor	.25	.10	.02
□ 492 Jim Sundberg	.16	.07	.01
□ 493 Steve Renko	.16	.07	.01
□ 494 Chuck Tanner MG	.16	.07	.01
□ 495 Dave Cash	.16	.07	.01
□ 496 Jim Clancy DP	.25	.10	.02
□ 497 Glenn Adams	.16	.07	.01
□ 498 Joe Sambito	.16	.07	.01
□ 499 Seattle Mariners Team Card (checklist back)	.75	.15	.03
□ 500 George Foster	.75	.30	.07
□ 501 Dave Roberts	.16	.07	.01
□ 502 Pat Rockett	.16	.07	.01
□ 503 Ike Hampton	.16	.07	.01
□ 504 Roger Freed	.16	.07	.01
□ 505 Felix Millan	.16	.07	.01
□ 506 Ron Blomberg	.16	.07	.01
□ 507 Willie Crawford	.16	.07	.01
□ 508 Johnny Oates	.25	.10	.02
□ 509 Brent Strom	.16	.07	.01
□ 510 Willie Stargell	2.50	1.00	.25
□ 511 Frank Duffy	.16	.07	.01
□ 512 Larry Herndon	.16	.07	.01
□ 513 Barry Foote	.16	.07	.01
□ 514 Rob Sperring	.16	.07	.01
□ 515 Tim Corcoran	.16	.07	.01
□ 516 Gary Beare	.16	.07	.01
□ 517 Andres Mora	.16	.07	.01
□ 518 Tommy Boggs DP	.08	.03	.01
□ 519 Brian Downing	.35	.15	.03
□ 520 Larry Hisle	.25	.10	.02
□ 521 Steve Staggs	.16	.07	.01
□ 522 Dick Williams MG	.16	.07	.01
□ 523 Donnie Moore	.25	.10	.02
□ 524 Bernie Carbo	.16	.07	.01
□ 525 Jerry Terrell	.16	.07	.01
□ 526 Cincinnati Reds Team Card (checklist back)	.75	.15	.03
□ 527 Vic Correll	.16	.07	.01
□ 528 Rob Picciolo	.16	.07	.01
□ 529 Paul Hartzell	.16	.07	.01
□ 530 Dave Winfield	6.25	2.75	.60
□ 531 Tom Underwood	.16	.07	.01
□ 532 Skip Jutze	.16	.07	.01
□ 533 Sandy Alomar	.16	.07	.01
□ 534 Wilbur Howard	.16	.07	.01
□ 535 Checklist 5	.90	.10	.02
□ 536 Roric Harrison	.16	.07	.01
□ 537 Bruce Bochte	.16	.07	.01
□ 538 Johnny LeMaster	.16	.07	.01
□ 539 Vic Davalillo DP	.08	.03	.01
□ 540 Steve Carlton	4.25	1.75	.42
□ 541 Larry Cox	.16	.07	.01
□ 542 Tim Johnson	.16	.07	.01

□ 543 Larry Harlow DP	.08	.03	.01
□ 544 Len Randle DP	.08	.03	.01
□ 545 Bill Campbell	.16	.07	.01
□ 546 Ted Martinez	.16	.07	.01
□ 547 John Scott	.16	.07	.01
□ 548 Billy Hunter MG DP	.08	.03	.01
□ 549 Joe Kerrigan	.16	.07	.01
□ 550 John Mayberry	.25	.10	.02
□ 551 Atlanta Braves Team Card (checklist back)	.75	.15	.03
□ 552 Francisco Barrios	.16	.07	.01
□ 553 Terry Puhl	.35	.15	.03
□ 554 Joe Coleman	.16	.07	.01
□ 555 Butch Wynegar	.16	.07	.01
□ 556 Ed Armbrister	.16	.07	.01
□ 557 Tony Solaita	.16	.07	.01
□ 558 Paul Mitchell	.16	.07	.01
□ 559 Phil Mankowski	.16	.07	.01
□ 560 Dave Parker	4.00	1.75	.40
□ 561 Charlie Williams	.16	.07	.01
□ 562 Glenn Burke	.16	.07	.01
□ 563 Dave Rader	.16	.07	.01
□ 564 Mick Kelleher	.16	.07	.01
□ 565 Jerry Koosman	.35	.15	.03
□ 566 Merv Rettenmund	.16	.07	.01
□ 567 Dick Drago	.16	.07	.01
□ 568 Tom Hutton	.16	.07	.01
□ 569 Lary Sorensen	.16	.07	.01
□ 570 Dave Kingman	.50	.20	.05
□ 571 Buck Martinez	.16	.07	.01
□ 572 Rick Wise	.25	.10	.02
□ 573 Luis Gomez	.16	.07	.01
□ 574 Bob Lemon MG	.35	.15	.03
□ 575 Pat Dobson	.16	.07	.01
□ 576 Sam Mejias	.16	.07	.01
□ 577 Oakland A's Team Card (checklist back)	.75	.15	.03
□ 578 Buzz Capra	.16	.07	.01
□ 579 Rance Mulliniks	.25	.10	.02
□ 580 Rod Carew	5.25	2.25	.50
□ 581 Lynn McGlothen	.16	.07	.01
□ 582 Fran Healy	.16	.07	.01
□ 583 George Medich	.16	.07	.01
□ 584 John Hale	.16	.07	.01
□ 585 Woodie Fryman DP	.08	.03	.01
□ 586 Ed Goodson	.16	.07	.01
□ 587 John Urrea	.16	.07	.01
□ 588 Jim Mason	.16	.07	.01
□ 589 Bob Knepper	.60	.25	.06
□ 590 Bobby Murcer	.35	.15	.03
□ 591 George Zeber	.16	.07	.01
□ 592 Bob Apodaca	.16	.07	.01
□ 593 Dave Skaggs	.16	.07	.01
□ 594 Dave Freisleben	.16	.07	.01
□ 595 Sixto Lezcano	.16	.07	.01
□ 596 Gary Wheelock	.16	.07	.01

☐ 597 Steve Dillard .16 .07 .01
☐ 598 Eddie Solomon .16 .07 .01
☐ 599 Gary Woods .16 .07 .01
☐ 600 Frank Tanana .25 .10 .02
☐ 601 Gene Mauch MG .16 .07 .01
☐ 602 Eric Soderholm .16 .07 .01
☐ 603 Will McEnaney .16 .07 .01
☐ 604 Earl Williams .16 .07 .01
☐ 605 Rick Rhoden .25 .10 .02
☐ 606 Pittsburgh Pirates .75 .15 .03
Team Card
(checklist back)
☐ 607 Fernando Arroyo .16 .07 .01
☐ 608 Johnny Grubb .16 .07 .01
☐ 609 John Denny .25 .10 .02
☐ 610 Garry Maddox .25 .10 .02
☐ 611 Pat Scanlon .16 .07 .01
☐ 612 Ken Henderson .16 .07 .01
☐ 613 Marty Perez .16 .07 .01
☐ 614 Joe Wallis .16 .07 .01
☐ 615 Clay Carroll .16 .07 .01
☐ 616 Pat Kelly .16 .07 .01
☐ 617 Joe Nolan .16 .07 .01
☐ 618 Tommy Helms .25 .10 .02
☐ 619 Thad Bosley DP .16 .07 .01
☐ 620 Willie Randolph .60 .25 .06
☐ 621 Craig Swan DP .16 .07 .01
☐ 622 Champ Summers .16 .07 .01
☐ 623 Eduardo Rodriguez .16 .07 .01
☐ 624 Gary Alexander DP .08 .03 .01
☐ 625 Jose Cruz .25 .10 .02
☐ 626 Toronto Blue Jays .35 .10 .02
Team Card DP
(checklist back)
☐ 627 David Johnson .16 .07 .01
☐ 628 Ralph Garr .16 .07 .01
☐ 629 Don Stanhouse .16 .07 .01
☐ 630 Ron Cey .35 .15 .03
☐ 631 Danny Ozark MG .16 .07 .01
☐ 632 Rowland Office .16 .07 .01
☐ 633 Tom Veryzer .16 .07 .01
☐ 634 Len Barker .16 .07 .01
☐ 635 Joe Rudi .25 .10 .02
☐ 636 Jim Bibby .16 .07 .01
☐ 637 Duffy Dyer .16 .07 .01
☐ 638 Paul Splittorff .16 .07 .01
☐ 639 Gene Clines .16 .07 .01
☐ 640 Lee May DP .16 .07 .01
☐ 641 Doug Rau .16 .07 .01
☐ 642 Denny Doyle .16 .07 .01
☐ 643 Tom House .16 .07 .01
☐ 644 Jim Dwyer .16 .07 .01
☐ 645 Mike Torrez .16 .07 .01
☐ 646 Rick Auerbach DP .08 .03 .01
☐ 647 Steve Dunning .16 .07 .01
☐ 648 Gary Thomasson .16 .07 .01
☐ 649 Moose Haas .25 .10 .02
☐ 650 Cesar Cedeno .25 .10 .02
☐ 651 Doug Rader .25 .10 .02
☐ 652 Checklist 6 .90 .10 .02
☐ 653 Ron Hodges DP .08 .03 .01
☐ 654 Pepe Frias .16 .07 .01
☐ 655 Lyman Bostock .25 .10 .02
☐ 656 Dave Garcia MG .16 .07 .01
☐ 657 Bombo Rivera .16 .07 .01
☐ 658 Manny Sanguillen .25 .10 .02
☐ 659 Texas Rangers .75 .15 .03
Team Card
(checklist back)
☐ 660 Jason Thompson .25 .10 .02
☐ 661 Grant Jackson .16 .07 .01
☐ 662 Paul Dade .16 .07 .01
☐ 663 Paul Reuschel .16 .07 .01
☐ 664 Fred Stanley .16 .07 .01
☐ 665 Dennis Leonard .25 .10 .02
☐ 666 Billy Smith .16 .07 .01
☐ 667 Jeff Byrd .16 .07 .01
☐ 668 Dusty Baker .25 .10 .02
☐ 669 Pete Falcone .16 .07 .01
☐ 670 Jim Rice 3.25 1.35 .32
☐ 671 Gary Lavelle .16 .07 .01
☐ 672 Don Kessinger .25 .10 .02
☐ 673 Steve Brye .16 .07 .01
☐ 674 Ray Knight 1.50 .60 .15
☐ 675 Jay Johnstone .25 .10 .02
☐ 676 Bob Myrick .16 .07 .01
☐ 677 Ed Herrmann .16 .07 .01
☐ 678 Tom Burgmeier .16 .07 .01
☐ 679 Wayne Garrett .16 .07 .01
☐ 680 Vida Blue .25 .10 .02
☐ 681 Rob Belloir .16 .07 .01
☐ 682 Ken Brett .16 .07 .01
☐ 683 Mike Champion .16 .07 .01
☐ 684 Ralph Houk MG .25 .10 .02
☐ 685 Frank Taveras .16 .07 .01
☐ 686 Gaylord Perry 2.25 .90 .22
☐ 687 Julio Cruz .25 .10 .02
☐ 688 George Mitterwald .16 .07 .01
☐ 689 Cleveland Indians .75 .15 .03
Team Card
(checklist back)
☐ 690 Mickey Rivers .25 .10 .02
☐ 691 Ross Grimsley .16 .07 .01
☐ 692 Ken Reitz .16 .07 .01
☐ 693 Lamar Johnson .16 .07 .01
☐ 694 Elias Sosa .16 .07 .01
☐ 695 Dwight Evans 1.75 .70 .17
☐ 696 Steve Mingori .16 .07 .01
☐ 697 Roger Metzger .16 .07 .01
☐ 698 Juan Bernhardt .16 .07 .01
☐ 699 Jackie Brown .16 .07 .01
☐ 700 Johnny Bench 4.50 2.00 .45
☐ 701 Rookie Pitchers .25 .10 .02
Tom Hume
Larry Landreth
Steve McCatty

Bruce Taylor
☐ 702 Rookie Catchers .... .16 .07 .01
Bill Nahorodny
Kevin Pasley
Rick Sweet
Don Werner
☐ 703 Rookie Pitchers DP ... 12.00 5.25 1.50
Larry Andersen
Tim Jones
Mickey Mahler
Jack Morris
☐ 704 Rookie 2nd Basemen 15.00 6.50 2.15
Garth Iorg
Dave Oliver
Sam Perlozzo
Lou Whitaker
☐ 705 Rookie Outfielders .... .50 .20 .05
Dave Bergman
Miguel Dilone
Clint Hurdle
Willie Norwood
☐ 706 Rookie 1st Basemen ...... .25 .10 .02
Wayne Cage
Ted Cox
Pat Putnam
Dave Revering
☐ 707 Rookie Shortstops 55.00 25.00 8.25
Mickey Klutts
Paul Molitor
Alan Trammell
U.L. Washington
☐ 708 Rookie Catchers 18.00 7.50 2.50
Bo Diaz
Dale Murphy
Lance Parrish
Ernie Whitt
☐ 709 Rookie Pitchers .... .35 .15 .03
Steve Burke
Matt Keough
Lance Rautzhan
Dan Schatzeder
☐ 710 Rookie Outfielders .... .60 .25 .06
Dell Alston
Rick Bosetti
Mike Easler
Keith Smith
☐ 711 Rookie Pitchers DP .... .16 .07 .01
Cardell Camper
Dennis Lamp
Craig Mitchell
Roy Thomas
☐ 712 Bobby Valentine .... .25 .10 .02
☐ 713 Bob Davis .... .16 .07 .01
☐ 714 Mike Anderson .... .16 .07 .01
☐ 715 Jim Kaat .... .75 .30 .07
☐ 716 Clarence Gaston .... .35 .15 .03
☐ 717 Nelson Briles .... .16 .07 .01
☐ 718 Ron Jackson .... .16 .07 .01
☐ 719 Randy Elliott .... .16 .07 .01
☐ 720 Fergie Jenkins .... 2.25 .90 .22
☐ 721 Billy Martin MG .... .60 .25 .06
☐ 722 Pete Broberg .... .16 .07 .01
☐ 723 John Wockenfuss .... .16 .07 .01
☐ 724 Kansas City Royals .... .75 .15 .03
Team Card
(checklist back)
☐ 725 Kurt Bevacqua .... .16 .07 .01
☐ 726 Wilbur Wood .... .25 .10 .02

1979 Topps

The cards in this 726-card set measure 2 1/2" by 3 1/2". Topps continued with the same number of cards as in 1978. Various series spotlight League Leaders (1-8), "Season and Career Record Holders" (411-418), "Record Breakers of 1978" (201-206), and one "Prospects" card for each team (701-726). Team cards feature a checklist on back of that team's players in the set and a small picture of the manager on the front of the card. There are 66 cards that were double printed and these are noted in the checklist by the abbreviation DP. Bump Wills (369) was initially depicted in a Ranger uniform but with a Blue Jays affiliation; later printings correctly labeled him with Texas. The set price listed does not include the scarcer Wills (Rangers) card. The key rookie cards in this set are Pedro Guerrero, Carney Lansford, Ozzie Smith, and Bob Welch. Cards numbered 23 or lower, which feature Phillies or Yankees and do not follow the numbering checklisted below, are not necessarily error cards. They are undoubtedly Burger King cards, separate sets for each team each with its own pricing

and mass distribution. Burger King cards are indistinguishable from the corresponding Topps cards except for the card numbering difference and the fact that Burger King cards do not have a printing sheet designation (such as A through F like the regular Topps) anywhere on the card back in very small print.

	NRMT	VG-E	GOOD
COMPLETE SET (726)	250.00	110.00	37.50
COMMON PLAYER (1-726)	.12	.05	.01
COMMON DP's (1-726)	.06	.02	.00

	NRMT	VG-E	GOOD
☐ 1 Batting Leaders Rod Carew Dave Parker	2.50	.50	.10
☐ 2 Home Run Leaders Jim Rice George Foster	.30	.12	.03
☐ 3 RBI Leaders Jim Rice George Foster	.30	.12	.03
☐ 4 Stolen Base Leaders Ron LeFlore Omar Moreno	.20	.08	.02
☐ 5 Victory Leaders Ron Guidry Gaylord Perry	.40	.16	.04
☐ 6 Strikeout Leaders Nolan Ryan J.R. Richard	2.75	1.10	.27
☐ 7 ERA Leaders Ron Guidry Craig Swan	.20	.08	.02
☐ 8 Leading Firemen Rich Gossage Rollie Fingers	.40	.16	.04
☐ 9 Dave Campbell	.12	.05	.01
☐ 10 Lee May	.20	.08	.02
☐ 11 Marc Hill	.12	.05	.01
☐ 12 Dick Drago	.12	.05	.01
☐ 13 Paul Dade	.12	.05	.01
☐ 14 Rafael Landestoy	.12	.05	.01
☐ 15 Ross Grimsley	.12	.05	.01
☐ 16 Fred Stanley	.12	.05	.01
☐ 17 Donnie Moore	.12	.05	.01
☐ 18 Tony Solaita	.12	.05	.01
☐ 19 Larry Gura DP	.12	.05	.01
☐ 20 Joe Morgan DP	1.25	.50	.12
☐ 21 Kevin Kobel	.12	.05	.01
☐ 22 Mike Jorgensen	.12	.05	.01
☐ 23 Terry Forster	.20	.08	.02
☐ 24 Paul Molitor	5.50	2.50	.55
☐ 25 Steve Carlton	3.50	1.50	.35
☐ 26 Jamie Quirk	.12	.05	.01
☐ 27 Dave Goltz	.12	.05	.01
☐ 28 Steve Brye	.12	.05	.01
☐ 29 Rick Langford	.12	.05	.01
☐ 30 Dave Winfield	5.00	2.25	.50
☐ 31 Tom House DP	.06	.02	.00
☐ 32 Jerry Mumphrey	.12	.05	.01
☐ 33 Dave Rozema	.12	.05	.01
☐ 34 Rob Andrews	.12	.05	.01
☐ 35 Ed Figueroa	.12	.05	.01
☐ 36 Alan Ashby	.12	.05	.01
☐ 37 Joe Kerrigan DP	.06	.02	.00
☐ 38 Bernie Carbo	.12	.05	.01
☐ 39 Dale Murphy	7.50	3.25	.75
☐ 40 Dennis Eckersley	3.00	1.25	.30
☐ 41 Twins Team/Mgr. Gene Mauch (checklist back)	.60	.12	.02
☐ 42 Ron Blomberg	.12	.05	.01
☐ 43 Wayne Twitchell	.12	.05	.01
☐ 44 Kurt Bevacqua	.12	.05	.01
☐ 45 Al Hrabosky	.12	.05	.01
☐ 46 Ron Hodges	.12	.05	.01
☐ 47 Fred Norman	.12	.05	.01
☐ 48 Merv Rettenmund	.12	.05	.01
☐ 49 Vern Ruhle	.12	.05	.01
☐ 50 Steve Garvey DP	1.50	.60	.15
☐ 51 Ray Fosse DP	.06	.02	.00
☐ 52 Randy Lerch	.12	.05	.01
☐ 53 Mick Kelleher	.12	.05	.01
☐ 54 Dell Alston DP	.06	.02	.00
☐ 55 Willie Stargell	2.25	.90	.22
☐ 56 John Hale	.12	.05	.01
☐ 57 Eric Rasmussen	.12	.05	.01
☐ 58 Bob Randall DP	.06	.02	.00
☐ 59 John Denny DP	.12	.05	.01
☐ 60 Mickey Rivers	.20	.08	.02
☐ 61 Bo Diaz	.20	.08	.02
☐ 62 Randy Moffitt	.12	.05	.01
☐ 63 Jack Brohamer	.12	.05	.01
☐ 64 Tom Underwood	.12	.05	.01
☐ 65 Mark Belanger	.20	.08	.02
☐ 66 Tigers Team/Mgr. Les Moss (checklist back)	.60	.12	.02
☐ 67 Jim Mason DP	.06	.02	.00
☐ 68 Joe Niekro DP	.12	.05	.01
☐ 69 Elliott Maddox	.12	.05	.01
☐ 70 John Candelaria	.30	.12	.03
☐ 71 Brian Downing	.30	.12	.03
☐ 72 Steve Mingori	.12	.05	.01
☐ 73 Ken Henderson	.12	.05	.01
☐ 74 Shane Rawley	.40	.16	.04
☐ 75 Steve Yeager	.20	.08	.02
☐ 76 Warren Cromartie	.20	.08	.02
☐ 77 Dan Briggs DP	.06	.02	.00
☐ 78 Elias Sosa	.12	.05	.01
☐ 79 Ted Cox	.12	.05	.01
☐ 80 Jason Thompson	.12	.05	.01
☐ 81 Roger Erickson	.12	.05	.01
☐ 82 Mets Team/Mgr. Joe Torre	.60	.12	.02

(checklist back)
☐ 83 Fred Kendall .12 .05 .01
☐ 84 Greg Minton .12 .05 .01
☐ 85 Gary Matthews .20 .08 .02
☐ 86 Rodney Scott .12 .05 .01
☐ 87 Pete Falcone .12 .05 .01
☐ 88 Bob Molinaro .12 .05 .01
☐ 89 Dick Tidrow .12 .05 .01
☐ 90 Bob Boone .40 .16 .04
☐ 91 Terry Crowley .12 .05 .01
☐ 92 Jim Bibby .12 .05 .01
☐ 93 Phil Mankowski .12 .05 .01
☐ 94 Len Barker .12 .05 .01
☐ 95 Robin Yount 9.00 4.00 .90
☐ 96 Indians Team/Mgr. .60 .12 .02
Jeff Torborg
(checklist back)
☐ 97 Sam Mejias .12 .05 .01
☐ 98 Ray Burris .12 .05 .01
☐ 99 John Wathan .20 .08 .02
☐ 100 Tom Seaver DP 3.00 1.25 .30
☐ 101 Roy Howell .12 .05 .01
☐ 102 Mike Anderson .12 .05 .01
☐ 103 Jim Todd .12 .05 .01
☐ 104 Johnny Oates DP .06 .02 .00
☐ 105 Rick Camp DP .06 .02 .00
☐ 106 Frank Duffy .12 .05 .01
☐ 107 Jesus Alou DP .06 .02 .00
☐ 108 Eduardo Rodriguez .12 .05 .01
☐ 109 Joel Youngblood .12 .05 .01
☐ 110 Vida Blue .20 .08 .02
☐ 111 Roger Freed .12 .05 .01
☐ 112 Phillies Team/Mgr. .60 .12 .02
Danny Ozark
(checklist back)
☐ 113 Pete Redfern .12 .05 .01
☐ 114 Cliff Johnson .12 .05 .01
☐ 115 Nolan Ryan 18.00 7.50 2.50
☐ 116 Ozzie Smith 65.00 29.00 9.75
☐ 117 Grant Jackson .12 .05 .01
☐ 118 Bud Harrelson .20 .08 .02
☐ 119 Don Stanhouse .12 .05 .01
☐ 120 Jim Sundberg .12 .05 .01
☐ 121 Checklist 1 DP .25 .03 .01
☐ 122 Mike Paxton .12 .05 .01
☐ 123 Lou Whitaker 4.50 2.00 .45
☐ 124 Dan Schatzeder .12 .05 .01
☐ 125 Rick Burleson .20 .08 .02
☐ 126 Doug Bair .12 .05 .01
☐ 127 Thad Bosley .12 .05 .01
☐ 128 Ted Martinez .12 .05 .01
☐ 129 Marty Pattin DP .06 .02 .00
☐ 130 Bob Watson DP .12 .05 .01
☐ 131 Jim Clancy .12 .05 .01
☐ 132 Rowland Office .12 .05 .01
☐ 133 Bill Castro .12 .05 .01
☐ 134 Alan Bannister .12 .05 .01
☐ 135 Bobby Murcer .30 .12 .03
☐ 136 Jim Kaat .40 .16 .04
☐ 137 Larry Wolfe DP .06 .02 .00
☐ 138 Mark Lee .12 .05 .01
☐ 139 Luis Pujols .12 .05 .01
☐ 140 Don Gullett .20 .08 .02
☐ 141 Tom Paciorek .12 .05 .01
☐ 142 Charlie Williams .12 .05 .01
☐ 143 Tony Scott .12 .05 .01
☐ 144 Sandy Alomar .12 .05 .01
☐ 145 Rick Rhoden .20 .08 .02
☐ 146 Duane Kuiper .12 .05 .01
☐ 147 Dave Hamilton .12 .05 .01
☐ 148 Bruce Boisclair .12 .05 .01
☐ 149 Manny Sarmiento .12 .05 .01
☐ 150 Wayne Cage .12 .05 .01
☐ 151 John Hiller .20 .08 .02
☐ 152 Rick Cerone .20 .08 .02
☐ 153 Dennis Lamp .12 .05 .01
☐ 154 Jim Gantner DP .12 .05 .01
☐ 155 Dwight Evans 1.50 .60 .15
☐ 156 Buddy Solomon .12 .05 .01
☐ 157 U.L. Washington UER .12 .05 .01
(sic, bats left,
should be right)
☐ 158 Joe Sambito .12 .05 .01
☐ 159 Roy White .20 .08 .02
☐ 160 Mike Flanagan .30 .12 .03
☐ 161 Barry Foote .12 .05 .01
☐ 162 Tom Johnson .12 .05 .01
☐ 163 Glenn Burke .12 .05 .01
☐ 164 Mickey Lolich .30 .12 .03
☐ 165 Frank Taveras .12 .05 .01
☐ 166 Leon Roberts .12 .05 .01
☐ 167 Roger Metzger DP .06 .02 .00
☐ 168 Dave Freisleben .12 .05 .01
☐ 169 Bill Nahorodny .12 .05 .01
☐ 170 Don Sutton 1.50 .60 .15
☐ 171 Gene Clines .12 .05 .01
☐ 172 Mike Bruhert .12 .05 .01
☐ 173 John Lowenstein .12 .05 .01
☐ 174 Rick Auerbach .12 .05 .01
☐ 175 George Hendrick .20 .08 .02
☐ 176 Aurelio Rodriguez .12 .05 .01
☐ 177 Ron Reed .12 .05 .01
☐ 178 Alvis Woods .12 .05 .01
☐ 179 Jim Beattie DP .12 .05 .01
☐ 180 Larry Hisle .12 .05 .01
☐ 181 Mike Garman .12 .05 .01
☐ 182 Tim Johnson .12 .05 .01
☐ 183 Paul Splittorff .12 .05 .01
☐ 184 Darrel Chaney .12 .05 .01
☐ 185 Mike Torrez .12 .05 .01
☐ 186 Eric Soderholm .12 .05 .01
☐ 187 Mark Lemongello .12 .05 .01
☐ 188 Pat Kelly .12 .05 .01
☐ 189 Eddie Whitson 1.00 .40 .10
☐ 190 Ron Cey .30 .12 .03
☐ 191 Mike Norris .12 .05 .01

☐ 192	Cardinals Team/Mgr.	.60	.12	.02
	Ken Boyer			
	(checklist back)			
☐ 193	Glenn Adams	.12	.05	.01
☐ 194	Randy Jones	.12	.05	.01
☐ 195	Bill Madlock	.40	.16	.04
☐ 196	Steve Kemp DP	.12	.05	.01
☐ 197	Bob Apodaca	.12	.05	.01
☐ 198	Johnny Grubb	.12	.05	.01
☐ 199	Larry Milbourne	.12	.05	.01
☐ 200	Johnny Bench DP	3.00	1.25	.30
☐ 201	RB: Mike Edwards	.12	.05	.01
	Most unassisted DP's,			
	second basemen			
☐ 202	RB: Ron Guidry, Most	.30	.12	.03
	strikeouts, lefthander,			
	nine inning game			
☐ 203	RB: J.R. Richard	.20	.08	.02
	Most strikeouts,			
	season, righthander			
☐ 204	RB: Pete Rose	1.50	.60	.15
	Most consecutive			
	games batting safely			
☐ 205	RB: John Stearns	.12	.05	.01
	Most SB's by			
	catcher, season			
☐ 206	RB: Sammy Stewart	.12	.05	.01
	7 straight SO's,			
	first ML game			
☐ 207	Dave Lemanczyk	.12	.05	.01
☐ 208	Clarence Gaston	.20	.08	.02
☐ 209	Reggie Cleveland	.12	.05	.01
☐ 210	Larry Bowa	.30	.12	.03
☐ 211	Denny Martinez	.60	.25	.06
☐ 212	Carney Lansford	5.00	2.25	.50
☐ 213	Bill Travers	.12	.05	.01
☐ 214	Red Sox Team/Mgr.	.60	.12	.02
	Don Zimmer			
	(checklist back)			
☐ 215	Willie McCovey	2.25	.90	.22
☐ 216	Wilbur Wood	.20	.08	.02
☐ 217	Steve Dillard	.12	.05	.01
☐ 218	Dennis Leonard	.20	.08	.02
☐ 219	Roy Smalley	.12	.05	.01
☐ 220	Cesar Geronimo	.12	.05	.01
☐ 221	Jesse Jefferson	.12	.05	.01
☐ 222	Bob Beall	.12	.05	.01
☐ 223	Kent Tekulve	.20	.08	.02
☐ 224	Dave Revering	.12	.05	.01
☐ 225	Rich Gossage	.75	.30	.07
☐ 226	Ron Pruitt	.12	.05	.01
☐ 227	Steve Stone	.20	.08	.02
☐ 228	Vic Davalillo	.12	.05	.01
☐ 229	Doug Flynn	.12	.05	.01
☐ 230	Bob Forsch	.12	.05	.01
☐ 231	John Wockenfuss	.12	.05	.01
☐ 232	Jimmy Sexton	.12	.05	.01
☐ 233	Paul Mitchell	.12	.05	.01
☐ 234	Toby Harrah	.20	.08	.02
☐ 235	Steve Rogers	.12	.05	.01
☐ 236	Jim Dwyer	.12	.05	.01
☐ 237	Billy Smith	.12	.05	.01
☐ 238	Balor Moore	.12	.05	.01
☐ 239	Willie Horton	.20	.08	.02
☐ 240	Rick Reuschel	.30	.12	.03
☐ 241	Checklist 2 DP	.25	.03	.01
☐ 242	Pablo Torrealba	.12	.05	.01
☐ 243	Buck Martinez DP	.06	.02	.00
☐ 244	Pirates Team/Mgr.	.60	.12	.02
	Chuck Tanner			
	(checklist back)			
☐ 245	Jeff Burroughs	.20	.08	.02
☐ 246	Darrell Jackson	.12	.05	.01
☐ 247	Tucker Ashford DP	.06	.02	.00
☐ 248	Pete LaCock	.12	.05	.01
☐ 249	Paul Thormodsgard	.12	.05	.01
☐ 250	Willie Randolph	.50	.20	.05
☐ 251	Jack Morris	4.50	2.00	.45
☐ 252	Bob Stinson	.12	.05	.01
☐ 253	Rick Wise	.20	.08	.02
☐ 254	Luis Gomez	.12	.05	.01
☐ 255	Tommy John	.75	.30	.07
☐ 256	Mike Sadek	.12	.05	.01
☐ 257	Adrian Devine	.12	.05	.01
☐ 258	Mike Phillips	.12	.05	.01
☐ 259	Reds Team/Mgr.	.60	.12	.02
	Sparky Anderson			
	(checklist back)			
☐ 260	Richie Zisk	.12	.05	.01
☐ 261	Mario Guerrero	.12	.05	.01
☐ 262	Nelson Briles	.12	.05	.01
☐ 263	Oscar Gamble	.12	.05	.01
☐ 264	Don Robinson	.60	.25	.06
☐ 265	Don Money	.12	.05	.01
☐ 266	Jim Willoughby	.12	.05	.01
☐ 267	Joe Rudi	.20	.08	.02
☐ 268	Julio Gonzalez	.12	.05	.01
☐ 269	Woodie Fryman	.12	.05	.01
☐ 270	Butch Hobson	.20	.08	.02
☐ 271	Rawly Eastwick	.12	.05	.01
☐ 272	Tim Corcoran	.12	.05	.01
☐ 273	Jerry Terrell	.12	.05	.01
☐ 274	Willie Norwood	.12	.05	.01
☐ 275	Junior Moore	.12	.05	.01
☐ 276	Jim Colborn	.12	.05	.01
☐ 277	Tom Grieve	.20	.08	.02
☐ 278	Andy Messersmith	.20	.08	.02
☐ 279	Jerry Grote DP	.06	.02	.00
☐ 280	Andre Thornton	.20	.08	.02
☐ 281	Vic Correll DP	.06	.02	.00
☐ 282	Blue Jays Team/Mgr.	.50	.12	.02
	Roy Hartsfield			
	(checklist back)			
☐ 283	Ken Kravec	.12	.05	.01
☐ 284	Johnnie LeMaster	.12	.05	.01
☐ 285	Bobby Bonds	.30	.12	.03

☐ 286 Duffy Dyer .12 .05 .01
☐ 287 Andres Mora .12 .05 .01
☐ 288 Milt Wilcox .12 .05 .01
☐ 289 Jose Cruz .20 .08 .02
☐ 290 Dave Lopes .20 .08 .02
☐ 291 Tom Griffin .12 .05 .01
☐ 292 Don Reynolds .12 .05 .01
☐ 293 Jerry Garvin .12 .05 .01
☐ 294 Pepe Frias .12 .05 .01
☐ 295 Mitchell Page .12 .05 .01
☐ 296 Preston Hanna .12 .05 .01
☐ 297 Ted Sizemore .12 .05 .01
☐ 298 Rich Gale .12 .05 .01
☐ 299 Steve Ontiveros .12 .05 .01
☐ 300 Rod Carew 3.50 1.50 .35
☐ 301 Tom Hume .12 .05 .01
☐ 302 Braves Team/Mgr. .60 .12 .02
Bobby Cox
(checklist back)
☐ 303 Lary Sorensen DP .06 .02 .00
☐ 304 Steve Swisher .12 .05 .01
☐ 305 Willie Montanez .12 .05 .01
☐ 306 Floyd Bannister .20 .08 .02
☐ 307 Larvell Blanks .12 .05 .01
☐ 308 Bert Blyleven .60 .25 .06
☐ 309 Ralph Garr .20 .08 .02
☐ 310 Thurman Munson 3.00 1.25 .30
☐ 311 Gary Lavelle .12 .05 .01
☐ 312 Bob Robertson .12 .05 .01
☐ 313 Dyar Miller .12 .05 .01
☐ 314 Larry Harlow .12 .05 .01
☐ 315 Jon Matlack .20 .08 .02
☐ 316 Milt May .12 .05 .01
☐ 317 Jose Cardenal .12 .05 .01
☐ 318 Bob Welch 10.00 4.50 1.25
☐ 319 Wayne Garrett .12 .05 .01
☐ 320 Carl Yastrzemski 3.75 1.60 .37
☐ 321 Gaylord Perry 2.00 .80 .20
☐ 322 Danny Goodwin .12 .05 .01
☐ 323 Lynn McGlothen .12 .05 .01
☐ 324 Mike Tyson .12 .05 .01
☐ 325 Cecil Cooper .40 .16 .04
☐ 326 Pedro Borbon .12 .05 .01
☐ 327 Art Howe DP .12 .05 .01
☐ 328 Oakland A's Team/Mgr. .60 .12 .02
Jack McKeon
(checklist back)
☐ 329 Joe Coleman .12 .05 .01
☐ 330 George Brett 10.00 4.50 1.25
☐ 331 Mickey Mahler .12 .05 .01
☐ 332 Gary Alexander .12 .05 .01
☐ 333 Chet Lemon .20 .08 .02
☐ 334 Craig Swan .12 .05 .01
☐ 335 Chris Chambliss .20 .08 .02
☐ 336 Bobby Thompson .12 .05 .01
☐ 337 John Montague .12 .05 .01
☐ 338 Vic Harris .12 .05 .01
☐ 339 Ron Jackson .12 .05 .01
☐ 340 Jim Palmer 3.00 1.25 .30
☐ 341 Willie Upshaw .20 .08 .02
☐ 342 Dave Roberts .12 .05 .01
☐ 343 Ed Glynn .12 .05 .01
☐ 344 Jerry Royster .12 .05 .01
☐ 345 Tug McGraw .30 .12 .03
☐ 346 Bill Buckner .30 .12 .03
☐ 347 Doug Rau .12 .05 .01
☐ 348 Andre Dawson 9.00 4.00 .90
☐ 349 Jim Wright .12 .05 .01
☐ 350 Garry Templeton .20 .08 .02
☐ 351 Wayne Nordhagen .06 .02 .00
☐ 352 Steve Renko .12 .05 .01
☐ 353 Checklist 3 .60 .06 .01
☐ 354 Bill Bonham .12 .05 .01
☐ 355 Lee Mazzilli .12 .05 .01
☐ 356 Giants Team/Mgr. .60 .12 .02
Joe Altobelli
(checklist back)
☐ 357 Jerry Augustine .12 .05 .01
☐ 358 Alan Trammell 12.50 5.50 1.65
☐ 359 Dan Spillner DP .06 .02 .00
☐ 360 Amos Otis .20 .08 .02
☐ 361 Tom Dixon .12 .05 .01
☐ 362 Mike Cubbage .12 .05 .01
☐ 363 Craig Skok .12 .05 .01
☐ 364 Gene Richards .12 .05 .01
☐ 365 Sparky Lyle .30 .12 .03
☐ 366 Juan Bernhardt .12 .05 .01
☐ 367 Dave Skaggs .12 .05 .01
☐ 368 Don Aase .12 .05 .01
☐ 369A Bump Wills ERR 3.00 1.25 .30
(Blue Jays)
☐ 369B Bump Wills COR 3.50 1.50 .35
(Rangers)
☐ 370 Dave Kingman .40 .16 .04
☐ 371 Jeff Holly .12 .05 .01
☐ 372 Lamar Johnson .12 .05 .01
☐ 373 Lance Rautzhan .12 .05 .01
☐ 374 Ed Herrmann .12 .05 .01
☐ 375 Bill Campbell .12 .05 .01
☐ 376 Gorman Thomas .20 .08 .02
☐ 377 Paul Moskau .12 .05 .01
☐ 378 Rob Picciolo DP .06 .02 .00
☐ 379 Dale Murray .12 .05 .01
☐ 380 John Mayberry .20 .08 .02
☐ 381 Astros Team/Mgr. .60 .12 .02
Bill Virdon
(checklist back)
☐ 382 Jerry Martin .12 .05 .01
☐ 383 Phil Garner .20 .08 .02
☐ 384 Tommy Boggs .12 .05 .01
☐ 385 Dan Ford .12 .05 .01
☐ 386 Francisco Barrios .12 .05 .01
☐ 387 Gary Thomasson .12 .05 .01
☐ 388 Jack Billingham .12 .05 .01
☐ 389 Joe Zdeb .12 .05 .01
☐ 390 Rollie Fingers 1.50 .60 .15

☐ 391 Al Oliver .30 .12 .03
☐ 392 Doug Ault .12 .05 .01
☐ 393 Scott McGregor .20 .08 .02
☐ 394 Randy Stein .12 .05 .01
☐ 395 Dave Cash .12 .05 .01
☐ 396 Bill Plummer .20 .08 .02
☐ 397 Sergio Ferrer .12 .05 .01
☐ 398 Ivan DeJesus .12 .05 .01
☐ 399 David Clyde .12 .05 .01
☐ 400 Jim Rice 2.00 .80 .20
☐ 401 Ray Knight .30 .12 .03
☐ 402 Paul Hartzell .12 .05 .01
☐ 403 Tim Foli .12 .05 .01
☐ 404 White Sox Team/Mgr .60 .12 .02
Don Kessinger
(checklist back)
☐ 405 Butch Wynegar DP .06 .02 .00
☐ 406 Joe Wallis DP .06 .02 .00
☐ 407 Pete Vuckovich .12 .05 .01
☐ 408 Charlie Moore DP .06 .02 .00
☐ 409 Willie Wilson 2.00 .80 .20
☐ 410 Darrell Evans .30 .12 .03
☐ 411 Hits Record .40 .16 .04
Season: G.Sisler
Career: Ty Cobb
☐ 412 RBI Record .40 .16 .04
Season: Hack Wilson
Career: Hank Aaron
☐ 413 Home Run Record .75 .30 .07
Season: Roger Maris
Career: Hank Aaron
☐ 414 Batting Record .40 .16 .04
Season: R.Hornsby
Career: Ty Cobb
☐ 415 Steals Record .50 .20 .05
Season: Lou Brock
Career: Lou Brock
☐ 416 Wins Record .20 .08 .02
Season: Jack Chesbro
Career: Cy Young
☐ 417 Strikeout Record DP .30 .12 .03
Season: Nolan Ryan
Career: W.Johnson
☐ 418 ERA Record DP .12 .05 .01
Season: Dutch Leonard
Career: W.Johnson
☐ 419 Dick Ruthven .12 .05 .01
☐ 420 Ken Griffey .75 .30 .07
☐ 421 Doug DeCinces .20 .08 .02
☐ 422 Ruppert Jones .12 .05 .01
☐ 423 Bob Montgomery .12 .05 .01
☐ 424 Angels Team/Mgr. .60 .12 .02
Jim Fregosi
(checklist back)
☐ 425 Rick Manning .12 .05 .01
☐ 426 Chris Speier .12 .05 .01
☐ 427 Andy Replogle .12 .05 .01
☐ 428 Bobby Valentine .20 .08 .02
☐ 429 John Urrea DP .06 .02 .00
☐ 430 Dave Parker 2.50 1.00 .25
☐ 431 Glenn Borgmann .12 .05 .01
☐ 432 Dave Heaverlo .12 .05 .01
☐ 433 Larry Biittner .12 .05 .01
☐ 434 Ken Clay .12 .05 .01
☐ 435 Gene Tenace .20 .08 .02
☐ 436 Hector Cruz .12 .05 .01
☐ 437 Rick Williams .12 .05 .01
☐ 438 Horace Speed .12 .05 .01
☐ 439 Frank White .20 .08 .02
☐ 440 Rusty Staub .30 .12 .03
☐ 441 Lee Lacy .12 .05 .01
☐ 442 Doyle Alexander .12 .05 .01
☐ 443 Bruce Bochte .12 .05 .01
☐ 444 Aurelio Lopez .20 .08 .02
☐ 445 Steve Henderson .12 .05 .01
☐ 446 Jim Lonborg .20 .08 .02
☐ 447 Manny Sanguillen .20 .08 .02
☐ 448 Moose Haas .12 .05 .01
☐ 449 Bombo Rivera .12 .05 .01
☐ 450 Dave Concepcion .50 .20 .05
☐ 451 Royals Team/Mgr. .60 .12 .02
Whitey Herzog
(checklist back)
☐ 452 Jerry Morales .12 .05 .01
☐ 453 Chris Knapp .12 .05 .01
☐ 454 Len Randle .12 .05 .01
☐ 455 Bill Lee DP .12 .05 .01
☐ 456 Chuck Baker .12 .05 .01
☐ 457 Bruce Sutter .75 .30 .07
☐ 458 Jim Essian .20 .08 .02
☐ 459 Sid Monge .12 .05 .01
☐ 460 Graig Nettles .50 .20 .05
☐ 461 Jim Barr DP .06 .02 .00
☐ 462 Otto Velez .12 .05 .01
☐ 463 Steve Comer .12 .05 .01
☐ 464 Joe Nolan .12 .05 .01
☐ 465 Reggie Smith .20 .08 .02
☐ 466 Mark Littell .12 .05 .01
☐ 467 Don Kessinger DP .12 .05 .01
☐ 468 Stan Bahnsen DP .06 .02 .00
☐ 469 Lance Parrish 3.50 1.50 .35
☐ 470 Garry Maddox DP .12 .05 .01
☐ 471 Joaquin Andujar .20 .08 .02
☐ 472 Craig Kusick .12 .05 .01
☐ 473 Dave Roberts .12 .05 .01
☐ 474 Dick Davis .12 .05 .01
☐ 475 Dan Driessen .12 .05 .01
☐ 476 Tom Poquette .12 .05 .01
☐ 477 Bob Grich .20 .08 .02
☐ 478 Juan Beniquez .12 .05 .01
☐ 479 Padres Team/Mgr. .60 .12 .02
Roger Craig
(checklist back)
☐ 480 Fred Lynn .75 .30 .07
☐ 481 Skip Lockwood .12 .05 .01
☐ 482 Craig Reynolds .12 .05 .01

- □ 483 Checklist 4 DP .25 .03 .01
- □ 484 Rick Waits .12 .05 .01
- □ 485 Bucky Dent .30 .12 .03
- □ 486 Bob Knepper .20 .08 .02
- □ 487 Miguel Dilone .12 .05 .01
- □ 488 Bob Owchinko .12 .05 .01
- □ 489 Larry Cox UER .12 .05 .01 (photo actually Dave Rader)
- □ 490 Al Cowens .12 .05 .01
- □ 491 Tippy Martinez .12 .05 .01
- □ 492 Bob Bailor .12 .05 .01
- □ 493 Larry Christenson .12 .05 .01
- □ 494 Jerry White .12 .05 .01
- □ 495 Tony Perez 1.00 .40 .10
- □ 496 Barry Bonnell DP .06 .02 .00
- □ 497 Glenn Abbott .12 .05 .01
- □ 498 Rich Chiles .12 .05 .01
- □ 499 Rangers Team/Mgr. .60 .12 .02 Pat Corrales (checklist back)
- □ 500 Ron Guidry 1.00 .40 .10
- □ 501 Junior Kennedy .12 .05 .01
- □ 502 Steve Braun .12 .05 .01
- □ 503 Terry Humphrey .12 .05 .01
- □ 504 Larry McWilliams .20 .08 .02
- □ 505 Ed Kranepool .12 .05 .01
- □ 506 John D'Acquisto .12 .05 .01
- □ 507 Tony Armas .20 .08 .02
- □ 508 Charlie Hough .20 .08 .02
- □ 509 Mario Mendoza .12 .05 .01
- □ 510 Ted Simmons .40 .16 .04
- □ 511 Paul Reuschel DP .06 .02 .00
- □ 512 Jack Clark 2.00 .80 .20
- □ 513 Dave Johnson .20 .08 .02
- □ 514 Mike Proly .12 .05 .01
- □ 515 Enos Cabell .12 .05 .01
- □ 516 Champ Summers DP .06 .02 .00
- □ 517 Al Bumbry .12 .05 .01
- □ 518 Jim Umbarger .12 .05 .01
- □ 519 Ben Oglivie .20 .08 .02
- □ 520 Gary Carter 3.00 1.25 .30
- □ 521 Sam Ewing .12 .05 .01
- □ 522 Ken Holtzman .20 .08 .02
- □ 523 John Milner .12 .05 .01
- □ 524 Tom Burgmeier .12 .05 .01
- □ 525 Freddie Patek .12 .05 .01
- □ 526 Dodgers Team/Mgr. .75 .15 .03 Tom Lasorda (checklist back)
- □ 527 Lerrin LaGrow .12 .05 .01
- □ 528 Wayne Gross DP .06 .02 .00
- □ 529 Brian Asselstine .12 .05 .01
- □ 530 Frank Tanana .20 .08 .02
- □ 531 Fernando Gonzalez .12 .05 .01
- □ 532 Buddy Schultz .12 .05 .01
- □ 533 Leroy Stanton .12 .05 .01
- □ 534 Ken Forsch .12 .05 .01
- □ 535 Ellis Valentine .12 .05 .01
- □ 536 Jerry Reuss .20 .08 .02
- □ 537 Tom Veryzer .12 .05 .01
- □ 538 Mike Ivie DP .06 .02 .00
- □ 539 John Ellis .12 .05 .01
- □ 540 Greg Luzinski .30 .12 .03
- □ 541 Jim Slaton .12 .05 .01
- □ 542 Rick Bosetti .12 .05 .01
- □ 543 Kiko Garcia .12 .05 .01
- □ 544 Fergie Jenkins 1.50 .60 .15
- □ 545 John Stearns .12 .05 .01
- □ 546 Bill Russell .20 .08 .02
- □ 547 Clint Hurdle .12 .05 .01
- □ 548 Enrique Romo .12 .05 .01
- □ 549 Bob Bailey .12 .05 .01
- □ 550 Sal Bando .20 .08 .02
- □ 551 Cubs Team/Mgr. .60 .12 .02 Herman Franks (checklist back)
- □ 552 Jose Morales .12 .05 .01
- □ 553 Denny Walling .12 .05 .01
- □ 554 Matt Keough .12 .05 .01
- □ 555 Biff Pocoroba .12 .05 .01
- □ 556 Mike Lum .12 .05 .01
- □ 557 Ken Brett .12 .05 .01
- □ 558 Jay Johnstone .20 .08 .02
- □ 559 Greg Pryor .12 .05 .01
- □ 560 John Montefusco .20 .08 .02
- □ 561 Ed Ott .12 .05 .01
- □ 562 Dusty Baker .20 .08 .02
- □ 563 Roy Thomas .12 .05 .01
- □ 564 Jerry Turner .12 .05 .01
- □ 565 Rico Carty .20 .08 .02
- □ 566 Nino Espinosa .12 .05 .01
- □ 567 Richie Hebner .12 .05 .01
- □ 568 Carlos Lopez .12 .05 .01
- □ 569 Bob Sykes .12 .05 .01
- □ 570 Cesar Cedeno .20 .08 .02
- □ 571 Darrell Porter .12 .05 .01
- □ 572 Rod Gilbreath .12 .05 .01
- □ 573 Jim Kern .12 .05 .01
- □ 574 Claudell Washington .20 .08 .02
- □ 575 Luis Tiant .30 .12 .03
- □ 576 Mike Parrott .12 .05 .01
- □ 577 Brewers Team/Mgr. .60 .12 .02 George Bamberger (checklist back)
- □ 578 Pete Broberg .12 .05 .01
- □ 579 Greg Gross .12 .05 .01
- □ 580 Ron Fairly .12 .05 .01
- □ 581 Darold Knowles .12 .05 .01
- □ 582 Paul Blair .20 .08 .02
- □ 583 Julio Cruz .12 .05 .01
- □ 584 Jim Rooker .12 .05 .01
- □ 585 Hal McRae .30 .12 .03
- □ 586 Bob Horner 1.00 .40 .10
- □ 587 Ken Reitz .12 .05 .01
- □ 588 Tom Murphy .12 .05 .01

☐ 589 Terry Whitfield .12 .05 .01
☐ 590 J.R. Richard .20 .08 .02
☐ 591 Mike Hargrove .20 .08 .02
☐ 592 Mike Krukow .20 .08 .02
☐ 593 Rick Dempsey .20 .08 .02
☐ 594 Bob Shirley .12 .05 .01
☐ 595 Phil Niekro 1.50 .60 .15
☐ 596 Jim Wohlford .12 .05 .01
☐ 597 Bob Stanley .12 .05 .01
☐ 598 Mark Wagner .12 .05 .01
☐ 599 Jim Spencer .12 .05 .01
☐ 600 George Foster .60 .25 .06
☐ 601 Dave LaRoche .12 .05 .01
☐ 602 Checklist 5 .60 .06 .01
☐ 603 Rudy May .12 .05 .01
☐ 604 Jeff Newman .12 .05 .01
☐ 605 Rick Monday DP .12 .05 .01
☐ 606 Expos Team/Mgr. .60 .12 .02
Dick Williams
(checklist back)
☐ 607 Omar Moreno .12 .05 .01
☐ 608 Dave McKay .12 .05 .01
☐ 609 Silvio Martinez .12 .05 .01
☐ 610 Mike Schmidt 9.00 4.00 .90
☐ 611 Jim Norris .12 .05 .01
☐ 612 Rick Honeycutt .60 .25 .06
☐ 613 Mike Edwards .12 .05 .01
☐ 614 Willie Hernandez .30 .12 .03
☐ 615 Ken Singleton .20 .08 .02
☐ 616 Billy Almon .12 .05 .01
☐ 617 Terry Puhl .12 .05 .01
☐ 618 Jerry Remy .12 .05 .01
☐ 619 Ken Landreaux .30 .12 .03
☐ 620 Bert Campaneris .20 .08 .02
☐ 621 Pat Zachry .12 .05 .01
☐ 622 Dave Collins .12 .05 .01
☐ 623 Bob McClure .12 .05 .01
☐ 624 Larry Herndon .12 .05 .01
☐ 625 Mark Fidrych .30 .12 .03
☐ 626 Yankees Team/Mgr. .75 .15 .03
Bob Lemon
(checklist back)
☐ 627 Gary Serum .12 .05 .01
☐ 628 Del Unser .12 .05 .01
☐ 629 Gene Garber .12 .05 .01
☐ 630 Bake McBride .12 .05 .01
☐ 631 Jorge Orta .12 .05 .01
☐ 632 Don Kirkwood .12 .05 .01
☐ 633 Rob Wilfong DP .06 .02 .00
☐ 634 Paul Lindblad .12 .05 .01
☐ 635 Don Baylor 1.00 .40 .10
☐ 636 Wayne Garland .12 .05 .01
☐ 637 Bill Robinson .20 .08 .02
☐ 638 Al Fitzmorris .12 .05 .01
☐ 639 Manny Trillo .12 .05 .01
☐ 640 Eddie Murray 18.00 7.50 2.50
☐ 641 Bobby Castillo .12 .05 .01
☐ 642 Wilbur Howard DP .06 .02 .00
☐ 643 Tom Hausman .12 .05 .01
☐ 644 Manny Mota .20 .08 .02
☐ 645 George Scott DP .12 .05 .01
☐ 646 Rick Sweet .12 .05 .01
☐ 647 Bob Lacey .12 .05 .01
☐ 648 Lou Piniella .30 .12 .03
☐ 649 John Curtis .12 .05 .01
☐ 650 Pete Rose 4.50 2.00 .45
☐ 651 Mike Caldwell .12 .05 .01
☐ 652 Stan Papi .12 .05 .01
☐ 653 Warren Brusstar DP .06 .02 .00
☐ 654 Rick Miller .12 .05 .01
☐ 655 Jerry Koosman .30 .12 .03
☐ 656 Hosken Powell .12 .05 .01
☐ 657 George Medich .12 .05 .01
☐ 658 Taylor Duncan .12 .05 .01
☐ 659 Mariners Team/Mgr. .60 .12 .02
Darrell Johnson
(checklist back)
☐ 660 Ron LeFlore DP .12 .05 .01
☐ 661 Bruce Kison .12 .05 .01
☐ 662 Kevin Bell .12 .05 .01
☐ 663 Mike Vail .12 .05 .01
☐ 664 Doug Bird .12 .05 .01
☐ 665 Lou Brock 2.25 .90 .22
☐ 666 Rich Dauer .12 .05 .01
☐ 667 Don Hood .12 .05 .01
☐ 668 Bill North .12 .05 .01
☐ 669 Checklist 6 .60 .06 .01
☐ 670 Jim Hunter DP .75 .30 .07
☐ 671 Joe Ferguson DP .06 .02 .00
☐ 672 Ed Halicki .12 .05 .01
☐ 673 Tom Hutton .12 .05 .01
☐ 674 Dave Tomlin .12 .05 .01
☐ 675 Tim McCarver .30 .12 .03
☐ 676 Johnny Sutton .12 .05 .01
☐ 677 Larry Parrish .20 .08 .02
☐ 678 Geoff Zahn .12 .05 .01
☐ 679 Derrel Thomas .12 .05 .01
☐ 680 Carlton Fisk 4.25 1.75 .42
☐ 681 John Henry Johnson .12 .05 .01
☐ 682 Dave Chalk .12 .05 .01
☐ 683 Dan Meyer DP .06 .02 .00
☐ 684 Jamie Easterly DP .06 .02 .00
☐ 685 Sixto Lezcano .12 .05 .01
☐ 686 Ron Schueler DP .06 .02 .00
☐ 687 Rennie Stennett .12 .05 .01
☐ 688 Mike Willis .12 .05 .01
☐ 689 Orioles Team/Mgr. .60 .12 .02
Earl Weaver
(checklist back)
☐ 690 Buddy Bell DP .12 .05 .01
☐ 691 Dock Ellis DP .06 .02 .00
☐ 692 Mickey Stanley .12 .05 .01
☐ 693 Dave Rader .12 .05 .01
☐ 694 Burt Hooton .12 .05 .01
☐ 695 Keith Hernandez 2.25 .90 .22
☐ 696 Andy Hassler .12 .05 .01

☐ 697 Dave Bergman .... .12 .05 .01
☐ 698 Bill Stein .... .12 .05 .01
☐ 699 Hal Dues .... .12 .05 .01
☐ 700 Reggie Jackson DP ..... 3.50 1.50 .35
☐ 701 Orioles Prospects .... .20 .08 .02
Mark Corey
John Flinn
Sammy Stewart
☐ 702 Red Sox Prospects .... .20 .08 .02
Joel Finch
Garry Hancock
Allen Ripley
☐ 703 Angels Prospects .... .12 .05 .01
Jim Anderson
Dave Frost
Bob Slater
☐ 704 White Sox Prospects ...... .12 .05 .01
Ross Baumgarten
Mike Colbern
Mike Squires
☐ 705 Indians Prospects .... .75 .30 .07
Alfredo Griffin
Tim Norrid
Dave Oliver
☐ 706 Tigers Prospects .... .12 .05 .01
Dave Stegman
Dave Tobik
Kip Young
☐ 707 Royals Prospects .... .30 .12 .03
Randy Bass
Jim Gaudet
Randy McGilberry
☐ 708 Brewers Prospects ...... 1.25 .50 .12
Kevin Bass
Eddie Romero
Ned Yost
☐ 709 Twins Prospects .... .12 .05 .01
Sam Perlozzo
Rick Sofield
Kevin Stanfield
☐ 710 Yankees Prospects .... .30 .12 .03
Brian Doyle
Mike Heath
Dave Rajsich
☐ 711 A's Prospects .... .30 .12 .03
Dwayne Murphy
Bruce Robinson
Alan Wirth
☐ 712 Mariners Prospects .... .12 .05 .01
Bud Anderson
Greg Biercevicz
Byron McLaughlin
☐ 713 Rangers Prospects .... .75 .30 .07
Danny Darwin
Pat Putnam
Billy Sample
☐ 714 Blue Jays Prospects .... .30 .12 .03
Victor Cruz
Pat Kelly
Ernie Whitt
☐ 715 Braves Prospects .... .30 .12 .03
Bruce Benedict
Glenn Hubbard
Larry Whisenton
☐ 716 Cubs Prospects .... .12 .05 .01
Dave Geisel
Karl Pagel
Scot Thompson
☐ 717 Reds Prospects .... .40 .16 .04
Mike LaCoss
Ron Oester
Harry Spilman
☐ 718 Astros Prospects .... .12 .05 .01
Bruce Bochy
Mike Fischlin
Don Pisker
☐ 719 Dodgers Prospects ..... 8.00 3.50 .80
Pedro Guerrero
Rudy Law
Joe Simpson
☐ 720 Expos Prospects .... 1.00 .40 .10
Jerry Fry
Jerry Pirtle
Scott Sanderson
☐ 721 Mets Prospects .... .30 .12 .03
Juan Berenguer
Dwight Bernard
Dan Norman
☐ 722 Phillies Prospects .... 2.25 .90 .22
Jim Morrison
Lonnie Smith
Jim Wright
☐ 723 Pirates Prospects .... .30 .12 .03
Dale Berra
Eugenio Cotes
Ben Wiltbank
☐ 724 Cardinals Prospects .... .60 .25 .06
Tom Bruno
George Frazier
Terry Kennedy
☐ 725 Padres Prospects .... .12 .05 .01
Jim Beswick
Steve Mura
Broderick Perkins
☐ 726 Giants Prospects .... .30 .12 .03
Greg Johnston
Joe Strain
John Tamargo

1980 Topps

The cards in this 726-card set measure 2 1/2" by 3 1/2". In 1980 Topps released another set of the same size and number of cards as the previous two years. As with those sets, Topps again has produced 66 double-printed cards in the set; they are noted by DP in the checklist below. The player's name appears over the picture and his position and team are found in pennant design. Every card carries a facsimile autograph. Team cards feature a team checklist of players in the set on the back and the manager's name on the front. Cards 1-6 show Highlights (HL) of the 1979 season, cards 201-207 are League Leaders, and cards 661-686 feature American and National League rookie "Future Stars," one card for each team showing three young prospects. The key rookie card in this set is Rickey Henderson; other noteworthy rookies included are Dave Stieb and Rick Sutcliffe.

	MINT	EXC	G-VG
COMPLETE SET (726)	290.00	110.00	30.00
COMMON PLAYER (1-726)	.10	.04	.01
COMMON DP's (1-726)	.05	.02	.00

	MINT	EXC	G-VG
☐ 1 HL: Brock and Yaz, Enter 3000 hit circle	2.50	.50	.10
☐ 2 HL: Willie McCovey, 512th homer sets new mark for NL lefties	.75	.30	.07
☐ 3 HL: Manny Mota, All-time pinch-hits, 145	.15	.06	.01
☐ 4 HL: Pete Rose, Career Record 10th season with 200 or more hits	1.50	.60	.15
☐ 5 HL: Garry Templeton, First with 100 hits from each side of plate	.15	.06	.01
☐ 6 HL: Del Unser, 3rd cons. pinch homer sets new ML standard	.10	.04	.01
☐ 7 Mike Lum	.10	.04	.01
☐ 8 Craig Swan	.10	.04	.01
☐ 9 Steve Braun	.10	.04	.01
☐ 10 Dennis Martinez	.40	.16	.04
☐ 11 Jimmy Sexton	.10	.04	.01
☐ 12 John Curtis DP	.05	.02	.00
☐ 13 Ron Pruitt	.10	.04	.01
☐ 14 Dave Cash	.10	.04	.01
☐ 15 Bill Campbell	.10	.04	.01
☐ 16 Jerry Narron	.10	.04	.01
☐ 17 Bruce Sutter	.60	.25	.06
☐ 18 Ron Jackson	.10	.04	.01
☐ 19 Balor Moore	.10	.04	.01
☐ 20 Dan Ford	.10	.04	.01
☐ 21 Manny Sarmiento	.10	.04	.01
☐ 22 Pat Putnam	.10	.04	.01
☐ 23 Derrel Thomas	.10	.04	.01
☐ 24 Jim Slaton	.10	.04	.01
☐ 25 Lee Mazzilli	.10	.04	.01
☐ 26 Marty Pattin	.10	.04	.01
☐ 27 Del Unser	.10	.04	.01
☐ 28 Bruce Kison	.10	.04	.01
☐ 29 Mark Wagner	.10	.04	.01
☐ 30 Vida Blue	.20	.08	.02
☐ 31 Jay Johnstone	.15	.06	.01
☐ 32 Julio Cruz DP	.10	.04	.01
☐ 33 Tony Scott	.10	.04	.01
☐ 34 Jeff Newman DP	.05	.02	.00
☐ 35 Luis Tiant	.25	.10	.02
☐ 36 Rusty Torres	.10	.04	.01
☐ 37 Kiko Garcia	.10	.04	.01
☐ 38 Dan Spillner DP	.05	.02	.00
☐ 39 Rowland Office	.10	.04	.01
☐ 40 Carlton Fisk	4.00	1.75	.40
☐ 41 Rangers Team/Mgr. Pat Corrales (checklist back)	.50	.10	.02
☐ 42 David Palmer	.20	.08	.02
☐ 43 Bombo Rivera	.10	.04	.01
☐ 44 Bill Fahey	.10	.04	.01
☐ 45 Frank White	.25	.10	.02
☐ 46 Rico Carty	.15	.06	.01
☐ 47 Bill Bonham DP	.05	.02	.00
☐ 48 Rick Miller	.10	.04	.01
☐ 49 Mario Guerrero	.10	.04	.01
☐ 50 J.R. Richard	.20	.08	.02
☐ 51 Joe Ferguson DP	.05	.02	.00
☐ 52 Warren Brusstar	.10	.04	.01
☐ 53 Ben Oglivie	.15	.06	.01
☐ 54 Dennis Lamp	.10	.04	.01
☐ 55 Bill Madlock	.35	.15	.03
☐ 56 Bobby Valentine	.20	.08	.02
☐ 57 Pete Vuckovich	.10	.04	.01
☐ 58 Doug Flynn	.10	.04	.01
☐ 59 Eddy Putman	.10	.04	.01

□ 60 Bucky Dent	.25	.10	.02
□ 61 Gary Serum	.10	.04	.01
□ 62 Mike Ivie	.10	.04	.01
□ 63 Bob Stanley	.10	.04	.01
□ 64 Joe Nolan	.10	.04	.01
□ 65 Al Bumbry	.10	.04	.01
□ 66 Royals Team/Mgr. Jim Frey (checklist back)	.50	.10	.02
□ 67 Doyle Alexander	.10	.04	.01
□ 68 Larry Harlow	.10	.04	.01
□ 69 Rick Williams	.10	.04	.01
□ 70 Gary Carter	2.50	1.00	.25
□ 71 John Milner DP	.05	.02	.00
□ 72 Fred Howard DP	.05	.02	.00
□ 73 Dave Collins	.10	.04	.01
□ 74 Sid Monge	.10	.04	.01
□ 75 Bill Russell	.15	.06	.01
□ 76 John Stearns	.10	.04	.01
□ 77 Dave Stieb	7.50	3.25	.75
□ 78 Ruppert Jones	.10	.04	.01
□ 79 Bob Owchinko	.10	.04	.01
□ 80 Ron LeFlore	.10	.04	.01
□ 81 Ted Sizemore	.10	.04	.01
□ 82 Astros Team/Mgr. Bill Virdon (checklist back)	.50	.10	.02
□ 83 Steve Trout	.20	.08	.02
□ 84 Gary Lavelle	.10	.04	.01
□ 85 Ted Simmons	.40	.16	.04
□ 86 Dave Hamilton	.10	.04	.01
□ 87 Pepe Frias	.10	.04	.01
□ 88 Ken Landreaux	.10	.04	.01
□ 89 Don Hood	.10	.04	.01
□ 90 Manny Trillo	.10	.04	.01
□ 91 Rick Dempsey	.15	.06	.01
□ 92 Rick Rhoden	.15	.06	.01
□ 93 Dave Roberts DP	.05	.02	.00
□ 94 Neil Allen	.20	.08	.02
□ 95 Cecil Cooper	.20	.08	.02
□ 96 A's Team/Mgr. Jim Marshall (checklist back)	.50	.10	.02
□ 97 Bill Lee	.15	.06	.01
□ 98 Jerry Terrell	.10	.04	.01
□ 99 Victor Cruz	.10	.04	.01
□ 100 Johnny Bench	3.50	1.50	.35
□ 101 Aurelio Lopez	.10	.04	.01
□ 102 Rich Dauer	.10	.04	.01
□ 103 Bill Caudill	.20	.08	.02
□ 104 Manny Mota	.15	.06	.01
□ 105 Frank Tanana	.20	.08	.02
□ 106 Jeff Leonard	.60	.25	.06
□ 107 Francisco Barrios	.10	.04	.01
□ 108 Bob Horner	.25	.10	.02
□ 109 Bill Travers	.10	.04	.01
□ 110 Fred Lynn DP	.25	.10	.02
□ 111 Bob Knepper	.15	.06	.01
□ 112 White Sox Team/Mgr. Tony LaRussa (checklist back)	.50	.10	.02
□ 113 Geoff Zahn	.10	.04	.01
□ 114 Juan Beniquez	.10	.04	.01
□ 115 Sparky Lyle	.20	.08	.02
□ 116 Larry Cox	.10	.04	.01
□ 117 Dock Ellis	.10	.04	.01
□ 118 Phil Garner	.15	.06	.01
□ 119 Sammy Stewart	.10	.04	.01
□ 120 Greg Luzinski	.20	.08	.02
□ 121 Checklist 1	.40	.05	.01
□ 122 Dave Rosello DP	.05	.02	.00
□ 123 Lynn Jones	.10	.04	.01
□ 124 Dave Lemanczyk	.10	.04	.01
□ 125 Tony Perez	.75	.30	.07
□ 126 Dave Tomlin	.10	.04	.01
□ 127 Gary Thomasson	.10	.04	.01
□ 128 Tom Burgmeier	.10	.04	.01
□ 129 Craig Reynolds	.10	.04	.01
□ 130 Amos Otis	.15	.06	.01
□ 131 Paul Mitchell	.10	.04	.01
□ 132 Biff Pocoroba	.10	.04	.01
□ 133 Jerry Turner	.10	.04	.01
□ 134 Matt Keough	.10	.04	.01
□ 135 Bill Buckner	.25	.10	.02
□ 136 Dick Ruthven	.10	.04	.01
□ 137 John Castino	.10	.04	.01
□ 138 Ross Baumgarten	.10	.04	.01
□ 139 Dane Iorg	.15	.06	.01
□ 140 Rich Gossage	.50	.20	.05
□ 141 Gary Alexander	.10	.04	.01
□ 142 Phil Huffman	.10	.04	.01
□ 143 Bruce Bochte DP	.10	.04	.01
□ 144 Steve Comer	.10	.04	.01
□ 145 Darrell Evans	.30	.12	.03
□ 146 Bob Welch	1.50	.60	.15
□ 147 Terry Puhl	.10	.04	.01
□ 148 Manny Sanguillen	.15	.06	.01
□ 149 Tom Hume	.10	.04	.01
□ 150 Jason Thompson	.10	.04	.01
□ 151 Tom Hausman DP	.05	.02	.00
□ 152 John Fulgham	.10	.04	.01
□ 153 Tim Blackwell	.10	.04	.01
□ 154 Lary Sorensen	.10	.04	.01
□ 155 Jerry Remy	.10	.04	.01
□ 156 Tony Brizzolara	.10	.04	.01
□ 157 Willie Wilson DP	.25	.10	.02
□ 158 Rob Picciolo DP	.05	.02	.00
□ 159 Ken Clay	.10	.04	.01
□ 160 Eddie Murray	9.00	4.00	.90
□ 161 Larry Christenson	.10	.04	.01
□ 162 Bob Randall	.10	.04	.01
□ 163 Steve Swisher	.10	.04	.01
□ 164 Greg Pryor	.10	.04	.01
□ 165 Omar Moreno	.10	.04	.01
□ 166 Glenn Abbott	.10	.04	.01
□ 167 Jack Clark	1.75	.70	.17

□ 168 Rick Waits .10 .04 .01
□ 169 Luis Gomez .10 .04 .01
□ 170 Burt Hooton .10 .04 .01
□ 171 Fernando Gonzalez .10 .04 .01
□ 172 Ron Hodges .10 .04 .01
□ 173 John Henry Johnson .10 .04 .01
□ 174 Ray Knight .20 .08 .02
□ 175 Rick Reuschel .25 .10 .02
□ 176 Champ Summers .10 .04 .01
□ 177 Dave Heaverlo .10 .04 .01
□ 178 Tim McCarver .25 .10 .02
□ 179 Ron Davis .20 .08 .02
□ 180 Warren Cromartie .15 .06 .01
□ 181 Moose Haas .10 .04 .01
□ 182 Ken Reitz .10 .04 .01
□ 183 Jim Anderson DP .05 .02 .00
□ 184 Steve Renko DP .05 .02 .00
□ 185 Hal McRae .25 .10 .02
□ 186 Junior Moore .10 .04 .01
□ 187 Alan Ashby .10 .04 .01
□ 188 Terry Crowley .10 .04 .01
□ 189 Kevin Kobel .10 .04 .01
□ 190 Buddy Bell .20 .08 .02
□ 191 Ted Martinez .10 .04 .01
□ 192 Braves Team/Mgr. .50 .10 .02
Bobby Cox
(checklist back)
□ 193 Dave Goltz .10 .04 .01
□ 194 Mike Easler .10 .04 .01
□ 195 John Montefusco .15 .06 .01
□ 196 Lance Parrish 2.00 .80 .20
□ 197 Byron McLaughlin .10 .04 .01
□ 198 Dell Alston DP .05 .02 .00
□ 199 Mike LaCoss .15 .06 .01
□ 200 Jim Rice 1.00 .40 .10
□ 201 Batting Leaders .25 .10 .02
Keith Hernandez
Fred Lynn
□ 202 Home Run Leaders .20 .08 .02
Dave Kingman
Gorman Thomas
□ 203 RBI Leaders .50 .20 .05
Dave Winfield
Don Baylor
□ 204 Stolen Base Leaders .20 .08 .02
Omar Moreno
Willie Wilson
□ 205 Victory Leaders .25 .10 .02
Joe Niekro
Phil Niekro
Mike Flanagan
□ 206 Strikeout Leaders 2.00 .80 .20
J.R. Richard
Nolan Ryan
□ 207 ERA Leaders .20 .08 .02
J.R. Richard
Ron Guidry
□ 208 Wayne Cage .10 .04 .01
□ 209 Von Joshua .10 .04 .01
□ 210 Steve Carlton 3.00 1.25 .30
□ 211 Dave Skaggs DP .05 .02 .00
□ 212 Dave Roberts .10 .04 .01
□ 213 Mike Jorgensen DP .05 .02 .00
□ 214 Angels Team/Mgr. .50 .10 .02
Jim Fregosi
(checklist back)
□ 215 Sixto Lezcano .10 .04 .01
□ 216 Phil Mankowski .10 .04 .01
□ 217 Ed Halicki .10 .04 .01
□ 218 Jose Morales .10 .04 .01
□ 219 Steve Mingori .10 .04 .01
□ 220 Dave Concepcion .35 .15 .03
□ 221 Joe Cannon .10 .04 .01
□ 222 Ron Hassey .40 .16 .04
□ 223 Bob Sykes .10 .04 .01
□ 224 Willie Montanez .10 .04 .01
□ 225 Lou Piniella .30 .12 .03
□ 226 Bill Stein .10 .04 .01
□ 227 Len Barker .10 .04 .01
□ 228 Johnny Oates .15 .06 .01
□ 229 Jim Bibby .10 .04 .01
□ 230 Dave Winfield 4.00 1.75 .40
□ 231 Steve McCatty .10 .04 .01
□ 232 Alan Trammell 4.50 2.00 .45
□ 233 LaRue Washington .10 .04 .01
□ 234 Vern Ruhle .10 .04 .01
□ 235 Andre Dawson 7.25 2.75 .90
□ 236 Marc Hill .10 .04 .01
□ 237 Scott McGregor .15 .06 .01
□ 238 Rob Wilfong .10 .04 .01
□ 239 Don Aase .10 .04 .01
□ 240 Dave Kingman .35 .15 .03
□ 241 Checklist 2 .40 .05 .01
□ 242 Lamar Johnson .10 .04 .01
□ 243 Jerry Augustine .10 .04 .01
□ 244 Cardinals Team/Mgr. .50 .10 .02
Ken Boyer
(checklist back)
□ 245 Phil Niekro 1.25 .50 .12
□ 246 Tim Foli DP .05 .02 .00
□ 247 Frank Riccelli .10 .04 .01
□ 248 Jamie Quirk .10 .04 .01
□ 249 Jim Clancy .10 .04 .01
□ 250 Jim Kaat .40 .16 .04
□ 251 Kip Young .10 .04 .01
□ 252 Ted Cox .10 .04 .01
□ 253 John Montague .10 .04 .01
□ 254 Paul Dade DP .05 .02 .00
□ 255 Dusty Baker DP .10 .04 .01
□ 256 Roger Erickson .10 .04 .01
□ 257 Larry Herndon .10 .04 .01
□ 258 Paul Moskau .10 .04 .01
□ 259 Mets Team/Mgr. .50 .10 .02
Joe Torre
(checklist back)
□ 260 Al Oliver .30 .12 .03

☐ 261 Dave Chalk	.10	.04	.01
☐ 262 Benny Ayala	.10	.04	.01
☐ 263 Dave LaRoche DP	.05	.02	.00
☐ 264 Bill Robinson	.15	.06	.01
☐ 265 Robin Yount	7.50	3.25	.75
☐ 266 Bernie Carbo	.10	.04	.01
☐ 267 Dan Schatzeder	.10	.04	.01
☐ 268 Rafael Landestoy	.10	.04	.01
☐ 269 Dave Tobik	.10	.04	.01
☐ 270 Mike Schmidt DP	4.50	2.00	.45
☐ 271 Dick Drago DP	.05	.02	.00
☐ 272 Ralph Garr	.10	.04	.01
☐ 273 Eduardo Rodriguez	.10	.04	.01
☐ 274 Dale Murphy	5.00	2.25	.50
☐ 275 Jerry Koosman	.25	.10	.02
☐ 276 Tom Veryzer	.10	.04	.01
☐ 277 Rick Bosetti	.10	.04	.01
☐ 278 Jim Spencer	.10	.04	.01
☐ 279 Rob Andrews	.10	.04	.01
☐ 280 Gaylord Perry	1.25	.50	.12
☐ 281 Paul Blair	.15	.06	.01
☐ 282 Mariners Team/Mgr. Darrell Johnson (checklist back)	.50	.10	.02
☐ 283 John Ellis	.10	.04	.01
☐ 284 Larry Murray DP	.05	.02	.00
☐ 285 Don Baylor	.40	.16	.04
☐ 286 Darold Knowles DP	.05	.02	.00
☐ 287 John Lowenstein	.10	.04	.01
☐ 288 Dave Rozema	.10	.04	.01
☐ 289 Bruce Bochy	.10	.04	.01
☐ 290 Steve Garvey	1.75	.70	.17
☐ 291 Randy Scarberry	.10	.04	.01
☐ 292 Dale Berra	.10	.04	.01
☐ 293 Elias Sosa	.10	.04	.01
☐ 294 Charlie Spikes	.10	.04	.01
☐ 295 Larry Gura	.10	.04	.01
☐ 296 Dave Rader	.10	.04	.01
☐ 297 Tim Johnson	.10	.04	.01
☐ 298 Ken Holtzman	.15	.06	.01
☐ 299 Steve Henderson	.10	.04	.01
☐ 300 Ron Guidry	.75	.30	.07
☐ 301 Mike Edwards	.10	.04	.01
☐ 302 Dodgers Team/Mgr. Tom Lasorda (checklist back)	.60	.12	.02
☐ 303 Bill Castro	.10	.04	.01
☐ 304 Butch Wynegar	.10	.04	.01
☐ 305 Randy Jones	.15	.06	.01
☐ 306 Denny Walling	.10	.04	.01
☐ 307 Rick Honeycutt	.15	.06	.01
☐ 308 Mike Hargrove	.15	.06	.01
☐ 309 Larry McWilliams	.10	.04	.01
☐ 310 Dave Parker	2.00	.80	.20
☐ 311 Roger Metzger	.10	.04	.01
☐ 312 Mike Barlow	.10	.04	.01
☐ 313 Johnny Grubb	.10	.04	.01
☐ 314 Tim Stoddard	.15	.06	.01
☐ 315 Steve Kemp	.15	.06	.01
☐ 316 Bob Lacey	.10	.04	.01
☐ 317 Mike Anderson DP	.05	.02	.00
☐ 318 Jerry Reuss	.15	.06	.01
☐ 319 Chris Speier	.10	.04	.01
☐ 320 Dennis Eckersley	1.50	.60	.15
☐ 321 Keith Hernandez	1.50	.60	.15
☐ 322 Claudell Washington	.15	.06	.01
☐ 323 Mick Kelleher	.10	.04	.01
☐ 324 Tom Underwood	.10	.04	.01
☐ 325 Dan Driessen	.10	.04	.01
☐ 326 Bo McLaughlin	.10	.04	.01
☐ 327 Ray Fosse DP	.05	.02	.00
☐ 328 Twins Team/Mgr. Gene Mauch (checklist back)	.50	.10	.02
☐ 329 Bert Roberge	.10	.04	.01
☐ 330 Al Cowens	.10	.04	.01
☐ 331 Richie Hebner	.10	.04	.01
☐ 332 Enrique Romo	.10	.04	.01
☐ 333 Jim Norris DP	.05	.02	.00
☐ 334 Jim Beattie	.10	.04	.01
☐ 335 Willie McCovey	1.75	.70	.17
☐ 336 George Medich	.10	.04	.01
☐ 337 Carney Lansford	.90	.40	.09
☐ 338 John Wockenfuss	.10	.04	.01
☐ 339 John D'Acquisto	.10	.04	.01
☐ 340 Ken Singleton	.15	.06	.01
☐ 341 Jim Essian	.15	.06	.01
☐ 342 Odell Jones	.10	.04	.01
☐ 343 Mike Vail	.10	.04	.01
☐ 344 Randy Lerch	.10	.04	.01
☐ 345 Larry Parrish	.15	.06	.01
☐ 346 Buddy Solomon	.10	.04	.01
☐ 347 Harry Chappas	.10	.04	.01
☐ 348 Checklist 3	.40	.05	.01
☐ 349 Jack Brohamer	.10	.04	.01
☐ 350 George Hendrick	.15	.06	.01
☐ 351 Bob Davis	.10	.04	.01
☐ 352 Dan Briggs	.10	.04	.01
☐ 353 Andy Hassler	.10	.04	.01
☐ 354 Rick Auerbach	.10	.04	.01
☐ 355 Gary Matthews	.15	.06	.01
☐ 356 Padres Team/Mgr. Jerry Coleman (checklist back)	.50	.10	.02
☐ 357 Bob McClure	.10	.04	.01
☐ 358 Lou Whitaker	2.50	1.00	.25
☐ 359 Randy Moffitt	.10	.04	.01
☐ 360 Darrell Porter DP	.10	.04	.01
☐ 361 Wayne Garland	.10	.04	.01
☐ 362 Danny Goodwin	.10	.04	.01
☐ 363 Wayne Gross	.10	.04	.01
☐ 364 Ray Burris	.10	.04	.01
☐ 365 Bobby Murcer	.30	.12	.03
☐ 366 Rob Dressler	.10	.04	.01
☐ 367 Billy Smith	.10	.04	.01
☐ 368 Willie Aikens	.20	.08	.02

☐ 369 Jim Kern	.10	.04	.01
☐ 370 Cesar Cedeno	.15	.06	.01
☐ 371 Jack Morris	2.50	1.00	.25
☐ 372 Joel Youngblood	.10	.04	.01
☐ 373 Dan Petry DP	.30	.12	.03
☐ 374 Jim Gantner	.20	.08	.02
☐ 375 Ross Grimsley	.10	.04	.01
☐ 376 Gary Allenson	.10	.04	.01
☐ 377 Junior Kennedy	.10	.04	.01
☐ 378 Jerry Mumphrey	.10	.04	.01
☐ 379 Kevin Bell	.10	.04	.01
☐ 380 Garry Maddox	.15	.06	.01
☐ 381 Cubs Team/Mgr. Preston Gomez (checklist back)	.50	.10	.02
☐ 382 Dave Freisleben	.10	.04	.01
☐ 383 Ed Ott	.10	.04	.01
☐ 384 Joey McLaughlin	.10	.04	.01
☐ 385 Enos Cabell	.10	.04	.01
☐ 386 Darrell Jackson	.10	.04	.01
☐ 387A Fred Stanley (yellow name on front)	1.00	.40	.10
☐ 387B Fred Stanley (red name on front)	.10	.04	.01
☐ 388 Mike Paxton	.10	.04	.01
☐ 389 Pete LaCock	.10	.04	.01
☐ 390 Fergie Jenkins	1.25	.50	.12
☐ 391 Tony Armas DP	.10	.04	.01
☐ 392 Milt Wilcox	.10	.04	.01
☐ 393 Ozzie Smith	12.50	5.50	1.65
☐ 394 Reggie Cleveland	.10	.04	.01
☐ 395 Ellis Valentine	.10	.04	.01
☐ 396 Dan Meyer	.10	.04	.01
☐ 397 Roy Thomas DP	.05	.02	.00
☐ 398 Barry Foote	.10	.04	.01
☐ 399 Mike Proly DP	.05	.02	.00
☐ 400 George Foster	.50	.20	.05
☐ 401 Pete Falcone	.10	.04	.01
☐ 402 Merv Rettenmund	.10	.04	.01
☐ 403 Pete Redfern DP	.05	.02	.00
☐ 404 Orioles Team/Mgr. Earl Weaver (checklist back)	.50	.10	.02
☐ 405 Dwight Evans	1.25	.50	.12
☐ 406 Paul Molitor	3.00	1.25	.30
☐ 407 Tony Solaita	.10	.04	.01
☐ 408 Bill North	.10	.04	.01
☐ 409 Paul Splittorff	.10	.04	.01
☐ 410 Bobby Bonds	.35	.15	.03
☐ 411 Frank LaCorte	.10	.04	.01
☐ 412 Thad Bosley	.10	.04	.01
☐ 413 Allen Ripley	.10	.04	.01
☐ 414 George Scott	.15	.06	.01
☐ 415 Bill Atkinson	.10	.04	.01
☐ 416 Tom Brookens	.10	.04	.01
☐ 417 Craig Chamberlain DP	.05	.02	.00
☐ 418 Roger Freed DP	.05	.02	.00
☐ 419 Vic Correll	.10	.04	.01
☐ 420 Butch Hobson	.20	.08	.02
☐ 421 Doug Bird	.10	.04	.01
☐ 422 Larry Milbourne	.10	.04	.01
☐ 423 Dave Frost	.10	.04	.01
☐ 424 Yankees Team/Mgr. Dick Howser (checklist back)	.50	.10	.02
☐ 425 Mark Belanger	.15	.06	.01
☐ 426 Grant Jackson	.10	.04	.01
☐ 427 Tom Hutton DP	.05	.02	.00
☐ 428 Pat Zachry	.10	.04	.01
☐ 429 Duane Kuiper	.10	.04	.01
☐ 430 Larry Hisle DP	.10	.04	.01
☐ 431 Mike Krukow	.15	.06	.01
☐ 432 Willie Norwood	.10	.04	.01
☐ 433 Rich Gale	.10	.04	.01
☐ 434 Johnnie LeMaster	.10	.04	.01
☐ 435 Don Gullett	.15	.06	.01
☐ 436 Billy Almon	.10	.04	.01
☐ 437 Joe Niekro	.20	.08	.02
☐ 438 Dave Revering	.10	.04	.01
☐ 439 Mike Phillips	.10	.04	.01
☐ 440 Don Sutton	1.25	.50	.12
☐ 441 Eric Soderholm	.10	.04	.01
☐ 442 Jorge Orta	.10	.04	.01
☐ 443 Mike Parrott	.10	.04	.01
☐ 444 Alvis Woods	.10	.04	.01
☐ 445 Mark Fidrych	.20	.08	.02
☐ 446 Duffy Dyer	.10	.04	.01
☐ 447 Nino Espinosa	.10	.04	.01
☐ 448 Jim Wohlford	.10	.04	.01
☐ 449 Doug Bair	.10	.04	.01
☐ 450 George Brett	9.00	4.00	.90
☐ 451 Indians Team/Mgr. Dave Garcia (checklist back)	.45	.10	.02
☐ 452 Steve Dillard	.10	.04	.01
☐ 453 Mike Bacsik	.10	.04	.01
☐ 454 Tom Donohue	.10	.04	.01
☐ 455 Mike Torrez	.10	.04	.01
☐ 456 Frank Taveras	.10	.04	.01
☐ 457 Bert Blyleven	.50	.20	.05
☐ 458 Billy Sample	.10	.04	.01
☐ 459 Mickey Lolich DP	.15	.06	.01
☐ 460 Willie Randolph	.40	.16	.04
☐ 461 Dwayne Murphy	.15	.06	.01
☐ 462 Mike Sadek DP	.05	.02	.00
☐ 463 Jerry Royster	.10	.04	.01
☐ 464 John Denny	.15	.06	.01
☐ 465 Rick Monday	.15	.06	.01
☐ 466 Mike Squires	.10	.04	.01
☐ 467 Jesse Jefferson	.10	.04	.01
☐ 468 Aurelio Rodriguez	.10	.04	.01
☐ 469 Randy Niemann DP	.05	.02	.00
☐ 470 Bob Boone	.35	.15	.03
☐ 471 Hosken Powell DP	.05	.02	.00
☐ 472 Willie Hernandez	.20	.08	.02
☐ 473 Bump Wills	.10	.04	.01

☐ 474 Steve Busby .15 .06 .01
☐ 475 Cesar Geronimo .10 .04 .01
☐ 476 Bob Shirley .10 .04 .01
☐ 477 Buck Martinez .10 .04 .01
☐ 478 Gil Flores .10 .04 .01
☐ 479 Expos Team/Mgr. .45 .10 .02
Dick Williams
(checklist back)
☐ 480 Bob Watson .15 .06 .01
☐ 481 Tom Paciorek .10 .04 .01
☐ 482 Rickey Henderson UER 150.00 67.50 22.50
(7 steals at Modesto,
should be at Fresno)
☐ 483 Bo Diaz .10 .04 .01
☐ 484 Checklist 4 .40 .05 .01
☐ 485 Mickey Rivers .15 .06 .01
☐ 486 Mike Tyson DP .05 .02 .00
☐ 487 Wayne Nordhagen .10 .04 .01
☐ 488 Roy Howell .10 .04 .01
☐ 489 Preston Hanna DP .05 .02 .00
☐ 490 Lee May .15 .06 .01
☐ 491 Steve Mura DP .05 .02 .00
☐ 492 Todd Cruz .10 .04 .01
☐ 493 Jerry Martin .10 .04 .01
☐ 494 Craig Minetto .10 .04 .01
☐ 495 Bake McBride .10 .04 .01
☐ 496 Silvio Martinez .10 .04 .01
☐ 497 Jim Mason .10 .04 .01
☐ 498 Danny Darwin .20 .08 .02
☐ 499 Giants Team/Mgr. .50 .10 .02
Dave Bristol
(checklist back)
☐ 500 Tom Seaver 3.50 1.50 .35
☐ 501 Rennie Stennett .10 .04 .01
☐ 502 Rich Wortham DP .05 .02 .00
☐ 503 Mike Cubbage .10 .04 .01
☐ 504 Gene Garber .10 .04 .01
☐ 505 Bert Campaneris .15 .06 .01
☐ 506 Tom Buskey .10 .04 .01
☐ 507 Leon Roberts .10 .04 .01
☐ 508 U.L. Washington .10 .04 .01
☐ 509 Ed Glynn .10 .04 .01
☐ 510 Ron Cey .30 .12 .03
☐ 511 Eric Wilkins .10 .04 .01
☐ 512 Jose Cardenal .10 .04 .01
☐ 513 Tom Dixon DP .05 .02 .00
☐ 514 Steve Ontiveros .10 .04 .01
☐ 515 Mike Caldwell .10 .04 .01
☐ 516 Hector Cruz .10 .04 .01
☐ 517 Don Stanhouse .10 .04 .01
☐ 518 Nelson Norman .10 .04 .01
☐ 519 Steve Nicosia .10 .04 .01
☐ 520 Steve Rogers .10 .04 .01
☐ 521 Ken Brett .10 .04 .01
☐ 522 Jim Morrison .10 .04 .01
☐ 523 Ken Henderson .10 .04 .01
☐ 524 Jim Wright DP .05 .02 .00
☐ 525 Clint Hurdle .10 .04 .01
☐ 526 Phillies Team/Mgr. .50 .10 .02
Dallas Green
(checklist back)
☐ 527 Doug Rau DP .05 .02 .00
☐ 528 Adrian Devine .10 .04 .01
☐ 529 Jim Barr .10 .04 .01
☐ 530 Jim Sundberg DP .10 .04 .01
☐ 531 Eric Rasmussen .10 .04 .01
☐ 532 Willie Horton .15 .06 .01
☐ 533 Checklist 5 .40 .05 .01
☐ 534 Andre Thornton .15 .06 .01
☐ 535 Bob Forsch .10 .04 .01
☐ 536 Lee Lacy .10 .04 .01
☐ 537 Alex Trevino .15 .06 .01
☐ 538 Joe Strain .10 .04 .01
☐ 539 Rudy May .10 .04 .01
☐ 540 Pete Rose 3.75 1.60 .37
☐ 541 Miguel Dilone .10 .04 .01
☐ 542 Joe Coleman .10 .04 .01
☐ 543 Pat Kelly .10 .04 .01
☐ 544 Rick Sutcliffe 2.00 .80 .20
☐ 545 Jeff Burroughs .10 .04 .01
☐ 546 Rick Langford .10 .04 .01
☐ 547 John Wathan .15 .06 .01
☐ 548 Dave Rajsich .10 .04 .01
☐ 549 Larry Wolfe .10 .04 .01
☐ 550 Ken Griffey .60 .25 .06
☐ 551 Pirates Team/Mgr. .50 .10 .02
Chuck Tanner
(checklist back)
☐ 552 Bill Nahorodny .10 .04 .01
☐ 553 Dick Davis .10 .04 .01
☐ 554 Art Howe .20 .08 .02
☐ 555 Ed Figueroa .10 .04 .01
☐ 556 Joe Rudi .15 .06 .01
☐ 557 Mark Lee .10 .04 .01
☐ 558 Alfredo Griffin .20 .08 .02
☐ 559 Dale Murray .10 .04 .01
☐ 560 Dave Lopes .15 .06 .01
☐ 561 Eddie Whitson .20 .08 .02
☐ 562 Joe Wallis .10 .04 .01
☐ 563 Will McEnaney .10 .04 .01
☐ 564 Rick Manning .10 .04 .01
☐ 565 Dennis Leonard .15 .06 .01
☐ 566 Bud Harrelson .15 .06 .01
☐ 567 Skip Lockwood .10 .04 .01
☐ 568 Gary Roenicke .15 .06 .01
☐ 569 Terry Kennedy .20 .08 .02
☐ 570 Roy Smalley .10 .04 .01
☐ 571 Joe Sambito .10 .04 .01
☐ 572 Jerry Morales DP .05 .02 .00
☐ 573 Kent Tekulve .15 .06 .01
☐ 574 Scot Thompson .10 .04 .01
☐ 575 Ken Kravec .10 .04 .01
☐ 576 Jim Dwyer .10 .04 .01
☐ 577 Blue Jays Team/Mgr. .45 .10 .02
Bobby Mattick
(checklist back)

□ 578 Scott Sanderson .30 .12 .03
□ 579 Charlie Moore .10 .04 .01
□ 580 Nolan Ryan 16.00 6.75 2.25
□ 581 Bob Bailor .10 .04 .01
□ 582 Brian Doyle .10 .04 .01
□ 583 Bob Stinson .10 .04 .01
□ 584 Kurt Bevacqua .10 .04 .01
□ 585 Al Hrabosky .15 .06 .01
□ 586 Mitchell Page .10 .04 .01
□ 587 Garry Templeton .20 .08 .02
□ 588 Greg Minton .10 .04 .01
□ 589 Chet Lemon .10 .04 .01
□ 590 Jim Palmer 3.00 1.25 .30
□ 591 Rick Cerone .10 .04 .01
□ 592 Jon Matlack .15 .06 .01
□ 593 Jesus Alou .10 .04 .01
□ 594 Dick Tidrow .10 .04 .01
□ 595 Don Money .10 .04 .01
□ 596 Rick Matula .10 .04 .01
□ 597 Tom Poquette .10 .04 .01
□ 598 Fred Kendall DP .05 .02 .00
□ 599 Mike Norris .10 .04 .01
□ 600 Reggie Jackson 5.25 2.25 .50
□ 601 Buddy Schultz .10 .04 .01
□ 602 Brian Downing .15 .06 .01
□ 603 Jack Billingham DP .05 .02 .00
□ 604 Glenn Adams .10 .04 .01
□ 605 Terry Forster .15 .06 .01
□ 606 Reds Team/Mgr. .50 .10 .02
John McNamara
(checklist back)
□ 607 Woodie Fryman .10 .04 .01
□ 608 Alan Bannister .10 .04 .01
□ 609 Ron Reed .10 .04 .01
□ 610 Willie Stargell 1.50 .60 .15
□ 611 Jerry Garvin DP .05 .02 .00
□ 612 Cliff Johnson .10 .04 .01
□ 613 Randy Stein .10 .04 .01
□ 614 John Hiller .15 .06 .01
□ 615 Doug DeCinces .15 .06 .01
□ 616 Gene Richards .10 .04 .01
□ 617 Joaquin Andujar .15 .06 .01
□ 618 Bob Montgomery DP .05 .02 .00
□ 619 Sergio Ferrer .10 .04 .01
□ 620 Richie Zisk .10 .04 .01
□ 621 Bob Grich .20 .08 .02
□ 622 Mario Soto .15 .06 .01
□ 623 Gorman Thomas .20 .08 .02
□ 624 Lerrin LaGrow .10 .04 .01
□ 625 Chris Chambliss .15 .06 .01
□ 626 Tigers Team/Mgr. .50 .10 .02
Sparky Anderson
(checklist back)
□ 627 Pedro Borbon .10 .04 .01
□ 628 Doug Capilla .10 .04 .01
□ 629 Jim Todd .10 .04 .01
□ 630 Larry Bowa .25 .10 .02
□ 631 Mark Littell .10 .04 .01
□ 632 Barry Bonnell .10 .04 .01
□ 633 Bob Apodaca .10 .04 .01
□ 634 Glenn Borgmann DP .05 .02 .00
□ 635 John Candelaria .20 .08 .02
□ 636 Toby Harrah .15 .06 .01
□ 637 Joe Simpson .10 .04 .01
□ 638 Mark Clear .15 .06 .01
□ 639 Larry Biittner .10 .04 .01
□ 640 Mike Flanagan .20 .08 .02
□ 641 Ed Kranepool .15 .06 .01
□ 642 Ken Forsch DP .10 .04 .01
□ 643 John Mayberry .15 .06 .01
□ 644 Charlie Hough .15 .06 .01
□ 645 Rick Burleson .15 .06 .01
□ 646 Checklist 6 .40 .05 .01
□ 647 Milt May .10 .04 .01
□ 648 Roy White .15 .06 .01
□ 649 Tom Griffin .10 .04 .01
□ 650 Joe Morgan 2.00 .80 .20
□ 651 Rollie Fingers 1.25 .50 .12
□ 652 Mario Mendoza .10 .04 .01
□ 653 Stan Bahnsen .10 .04 .01
□ 654 Bruce Boisclair DP .05 .02 .00
□ 655 Tug McGraw .30 .12 .03
□ 656 Larvell Blanks .10 .04 .01
□ 657 Dave Edwards .10 .04 .01
□ 658 Chris Knapp .10 .04 .01
□ 659 Brewers Team/Mgr. .50 .10 .02
George Bamberger
(checklist back)
□ 660 Rusty Staub .30 .12 .03
□ 661 Orioles Rookies .15 .06 .01
Mark Corey
Dave Ford
Wayne Krenchicki
□ 662 Red Sox Rookies .15 .06 .01
Joel Finch
Mike O'Berry
Chuck Rainey
□ 663 Angels Rookies .75 .30 .07
Ralph Botting
Bob Clark
Dickie Thon
□ 664 White Sox Rookies .15 .06 .01
Mike Colbern
Guy Hoffman
Dewey Robinson
□ 665 Indians Rookies .35 .15 .03
Larry Andersen
Bobby Cuellar
Sandy Wihtol
□ 666 Tigers Rookies .15 .06 .01
Mike Chris
Al Greene
Bruce Robbins
□ 667 Royals Rookies 1.75 .70 .17
Renie Martin
Bill Paschall

Dan Quisenberry
☐ 668 Brewers Rookies .15 .06 .01
Danny Boitano
Willie Mueller
Lenn Sakata
☐ 669 Twins Rookies .30 .12 .03
Dan Graham
Rick Sofield
Gary Ward
☐ 670 Yankees Rookies .15 .06 .01
Bobby Brown
Brad Gulden
Darryl Jones
☐ 671 A's Rookies 1.00 .40 .10
Derek Bryant
Brian Kingman
Mike Morgan
☐ 672 Mariners Rookies .15 .06 .01
Charlie Beamon
Rodney Craig
Rafael Vasquez
☐ 673 Rangers Rookies .15 .06 .01
Brian Allard
Jerry Don Gleaton
Greg Mahlberg
☐ 674 Blue Jays Rookies .15 .06 .01
Butch Edge
Pat Kelly
Ted Wilborn
☐ 675 Braves Rookies .15 .06 .01
Bruce Benedict
Larry Bradford
Eddie Miller
☐ 676 Cubs Rookies .15 .06 .01
Dave Geisel
Steve Macko
Karl Pagel
☐ 677 Reds Rookies .15 .06 .01
Art DeFreites
Frank Pastore
Harry Spilman
☐ 678 Astros Rookies .15 .06 .01
Reggie Baldwin
Alan Knicely
Pete Ladd
☐ 679 Dodgers Rookies .25 .10 .02
Joe Beckwith
Mickey Hatcher
Dave Patterson
☐ 680 Expos Rookies .25 .10 .02
Tony Bernazard
Randy Miller
John Tamargo
☐ 681 Mets Rookies 4.50 2.00 .45
Dan Norman
Jesse Orosco
Mike Scott
☐ 682 Phillies Rookies .15 .06 .01
Ramon Aviles
Dickie Noles
Kevin Saucier
☐ 683 Pirates Rookies .15 .06 .01
Dorian Boyland
Alberto Lois
Harry Saferight
☐ 684 Cardinals Rookies 1.00 .40 .10
George Frazier
Tom Herr
Dan O'Brien
☐ 685 Padres Rookies .25 .10 .02
Tim Flannery
Brian Greer
Jim Wilhelm
☐ 686 Giants Rookies .15 .06 .01
Greg Johnston
Dennis Littlejohn
Phil Nastu
☐ 687 Mike Heath DP .05 .02 .00
☐ 688 Steve Stone .15 .06 .01
☐ 689 Red Sox Team/Mgr. .50 .10 .02
Don Zimmer
(checklist back)
☐ 690 Tommy John .50 .20 .05
☐ 691 Ivan DeJesus .10 .04 .01
☐ 692 Rawly Eastwick DP .05 .02 .00
☐ 693 Craig Kusick .10 .04 .01
☐ 694 Jim Rooker .10 .04 .01
☐ 695 Reggie Smith .20 .08 .02
☐ 696 Julio Gonzalez .10 .04 .01
☐ 697 David Clyde .10 .04 .01
☐ 698 Oscar Gamble .10 .04 .01
☐ 699 Floyd Bannister .10 .04 .01
☐ 700 Rod Carew DP 1.75 .70 .17
☐ 701 Ken Oberkfell .25 .10 .02
☐ 702 Ed Farmer .10 .04 .01
☐ 703 Otto Velez .10 .04 .01
☐ 704 Gene Tenace .15 .06 .01
☐ 705 Freddie Patek .10 .04 .01
☐ 706 Tippy Martinez .10 .04 .01
☐ 707 Elliott Maddox .10 .04 .01
☐ 708 Bob Tolan .10 .04 .01
☐ 709 Pat Underwood .10 .04 .01
☐ 710 Graig Nettles .30 .12 .03
☐ 711 Bob Galasso .10 .04 .01
☐ 712 Rodney Scott .10 .04 .01
☐ 713 Terry Whitfield .10 .04 .01
☐ 714 Fred Norman .10 .04 .01
☐ 715 Sal Bando .15 .06 .01
☐ 716 Lynn McGlothen .10 .04 .01
☐ 717 Mickey Klutts DP .05 .02 .00
☐ 718 Greg Gross .10 .04 .01
☐ 719 Don Robinson .15 .06 .01
☐ 720 Carl Yastrzemski DP 1.75 .70 .17
☐ 721 Paul Hartzell .10 .04 .01
☐ 722 Jose Cruz .15 .06 .01
☐ 723 Shane Rawley .15 .06 .01

☐ 724 Jerry White	.10	.04	.01
☐ 725 Rick Wise	.15	.06	.01
☐ 726 Steve Yeager	.25	.10	.02

1981 Topps

The cards in this 726-card set measure 2 1/2" by 3 1/2". League Leaders (1-8), Record Breakers (201-208), and Post-season cards (401-404) are topical subsets found in this set marketed by Topps in 1981. The team cards are all grouped together (661-686) and feature team checklist backs and a very small photo of the team's manager in the upper right corner of the obverse. The obverses carry the player's position and team in a baseball cap design, and the company name is printed in a small baseball. The backs are red and gray. The 66 double-printed cards are noted in the checklist by DP. The set contains the rookie cards of Harold Baines, Mike Boddicker, Hubie Brooks, , Kirk Gibson, Bruce Hurst, Lloyd Moseby, Tony Pena, Tim Raines, Jeff Reardon, John Tudor, and Fernando Valenzuela.

	MINT	EXC	G-VG
COMPLETE SET (726)	110.00	45.00	10.00
COMMON PLAYER (1-726)	.09	.04	.01
COMMON DP's (1-726)	.05	.02	.00

☐ 1 Batting Leaders	1.50	.25	.05
George Brett			
Bill Buckner			
☐ 2 Home Run Leaders	.50	.20	.05
Reggie Jackson			
Ben Oglivie			
Mike Schmidt			
☐ 3 RBI Leaders	.35	.15	.03
Cecil Cooper			
Mike Schmidt			
☐ 4 Stolen Base Leaders	1.50	.60	.15
Rickey Henderson			
Ron LeFlore			
☐ 5 Victory Leaders	.20	.08	.02
Steve Stone			
Steve Carlton			
☐ 6 Strikeout Leaders	.20	.08	.02
Len Barker			
Steve Carlton			
☐ 7 ERA Leaders	.15	.06	.01
Rudy May			
Don Sutton			
☐ 8 Leading Firemen	.15	.06	.01
Dan Quisenberry			
Rollie Fingers			
Tom Hume			
☐ 9 Pete LaCock DP	.05	.02	.00
☐ 10 Mike Flanagan	.15	.06	.01
☐ 11 Jim Wohlford DP	.05	.02	.00
☐ 12 Mark Clear	.09	.04	.01
☐ 13 Joe Charboneau	.15	.06	.01
☐ 14 John Tudor	.90	.40	.09
☐ 15 Larry Parrish	.09	.04	.01
☐ 16 Ron Davis	.09	.04	.01
☐ 17 Cliff Johnson	.09	.04	.01
☐ 18 Glenn Adams	.09	.04	.01
☐ 19 Jim Clancy	.09	.04	.01
☐ 20 Jeff Burroughs	.15	.06	.01
☐ 21 Ron Oester	.09	.04	.01
☐ 22 Danny Darwin	.15	.06	.01
☐ 23 Alex Trevino	.09	.04	.01
☐ 24 Don Stanhouse	.09	.04	.01
☐ 25 Sixto Lezcano	.09	.04	.01
☐ 26 U.L. Washington	.09	.04	.01
☐ 27 Champ Summers DP	.05	.02	.00
☐ 28 Enrique Romo	.09	.04	.01
☐ 29 Gene Tenace	.15	.06	.01
☐ 30 Jack Clark	.50	.20	.05
☐ 31 Checklist 1-121 DP	.15	.02	.00
☐ 32 Ken Oberkfell	.09	.04	.01
☐ 33 Rick Honeycutt	.09	.04	.01
☐ 34 Aurelio Rodriguez	.09	.04	.01
☐ 35 Mitchell Page	.09	.04	.01
☐ 36 Ed Farmer	.09	.04	.01
☐ 37 Gary Roenicke	.09	.04	.01
☐ 38 Win Remmerswaal	.09	.04	.01
☐ 39 Tom Veryzer	.09	.04	.01
☐ 40 Tug McGraw	.20	.08	.02
☐ 41 Ranger Rookies	.15	.06	.01
Bob Babcock			
John Butcher			
Jerry Don Gleaton			
☐ 42 Jerry White DP	.05	.02	.00
☐ 43 Jose Morales	.09	.04	.01
☐ 44 Larry McWilliams	.09	.04	.01

☐ 45 Enos Cabell .09 .04 .01
☐ 46 Rick Bosetti .09 .04 .01
☐ 47 Ken Brett .09 .04 .01
☐ 48 Dave Skaggs .09 .04 .01
☐ 49 Bob Shirley .09 .04 .01
☐ 50 Dave Lopes .15 .06 .01
☐ 51 Bill Robinson DP .09 .04 .01
☐ 52 Hector Cruz .09 .04 .01
☐ 53 Kevin Saucier .09 .04 .01
☐ 54 Ivan DeJesus .09 .04 .01
☐ 55 Mike Norris .09 .04 .01
☐ 56 Buck Martinez .09 .04 .01
☐ 57 Dave Roberts .09 .04 .01
☐ 58 Joel Youngblood .09 .04 .01
☐ 59 Dan Petry .15 .06 .01
☐ 60 Willie Randolph .25 .10 .02
☐ 61 Butch Wynegar .09 .04 .01
☐ 62 Joe Pettini .09 .04 .01
☐ 63 Steve Renko DP .05 .02 .00
☐ 64 Brian Asselstine .09 .04 .01
☐ 65 Scott McGregor .09 .04 .01
☐ 66 Royals Rookies .15 .06 .01
Manny Castillo
Tim Ireland
Mike Jones
☐ 67 Ken Kravec .09 .04 .01
☐ 68 Matt Alexander DP .05 .02 .00
☐ 69 Ed Halicki .09 .04 .01
☐ 70 Al Oliver DP .15 .06 .01
☐ 71 Hal Dues .09 .04 .01
☐ 72 Barry Evans DP .05 .02 .00
☐ 73 Doug Bair .09 .04 .01
☐ 74 Mike Hargrove .15 .06 .01
☐ 75 Reggie Smith .15 .06 .01
☐ 76 Mario Mendoza .09 .04 .01
☐ 77 Mike Barlow .09 .04 .01
☐ 78 Steve Dillard .09 .04 .01
☐ 79 Bruce Robbins .09 .04 .01
☐ 80 Rusty Staub .25 .10 .02
☐ 81 Dave Stapleton .15 .06 .01
☐ 82 Astros Rookies DP .15 .06 .01
Danny Heep
Alan Knicely
Bobby Sprowl
☐ 83 Mike Proly .09 .04 .01
☐ 84 Johnnie LeMaster .09 .04 .01
☐ 85 Mike Caldwell .09 .04 .01
☐ 86 Wayne Gross .09 .04 .01
☐ 87 Rick Camp .09 .04 .01
☐ 88 Joe Lefebvre .09 .04 .01
☐ 89 Darrell Jackson .09 .04 .01
☐ 90 Bake McBride .09 .04 .01
☐ 91 Tim Stoddard DP .09 .04 .01
☐ 92 Mike Easler .09 .04 .01
☐ 93 Ed Glynn DP .05 .02 .00
☐ 94 Harry Spilman DP .05 .02 .00
☐ 95 Jim Sundberg .09 .04 .01
☐ 96 A's Rookies .15 .06 .01
Dave Beard
Ernie Camacho
Pat Dempsey
☐ 97 Chris Speier .09 .04 .01
☐ 98 Clint Hurdle .09 .04 .01
☐ 99 Eric Wilkins .09 .04 .01
☐ 100 Rod Carew 2.50 1.00 .25
☐ 101 Benny Ayala .09 .04 .01
☐ 102 Dave Tobik .09 .04 .01
☐ 103 Jerry Martin .09 .04 .01
☐ 104 Terry Forster .15 .06 .01
☐ 105 Jose Cruz .15 .06 .01
☐ 106 Don Money .09 .04 .01
☐ 107 Rich Wortham .09 .04 .01
☐ 108 Bruce Benedict .09 .04 .01
☐ 109 Mike Scott .65 .25 .06
☐ 110 Carl Yastrzemski 2.50 1.00 .25
☐ 111 Greg Minton .09 .04 .01
☐ 112 White Sox Rookies .15 .06 .01
Rusty Kuntz
Fran Mullin
Leo Sutherland
☐ 113 Mike Phillips .09 .04 .01
☐ 114 Tom Underwood .09 .04 .01
☐ 115 Roy Smalley .09 .04 .01
☐ 116 Joe Simpson .09 .04 .01
☐ 117 Pete Falcone .09 .04 .01
☐ 118 Kurt Bevacqua .09 .04 .01
☐ 119 Tippy Martinez .09 .04 .01
☐ 120 Larry Bowa .15 .06 .01
☐ 121 Larry Harlow .09 .04 .01
☐ 122 John Denny .09 .04 .01
☐ 123 Al Cowens .09 .04 .01
☐ 124 Jerry Garvin .09 .04 .01
☐ 125 Andre Dawson 3.50 1.50 .35
☐ 126 Charlie Leibrandt .75 .30 .07
☐ 127 Rudy Law .09 .04 .01
☐ 128 Gary Allenson DP .05 .02 .00
☐ 129 Art Howe .15 .06 .01
☐ 130 Larry Gura .09 .04 .01
☐ 131 Keith Moreland .20 .08 .02
☐ 132 Tommy Boggs .09 .04 .01
☐ 133 Jeff Cox .09 .04 .01
☐ 134 Steve Mura .09 .04 .01
☐ 135 Gorman Thomas .20 .08 .02
☐ 136 Doug Capilla .09 .04 .01
☐ 137 Hosken Powell .09 .04 .01
☐ 138 Rich Dotson DP .15 .06 .01
☐ 139 Oscar Gamble .09 .04 .01
☐ 140 Bob Forsch .09 .04 .01
☐ 141 Miguel Dilone .09 .04 .01
☐ 142 Jackson Todd .09 .04 .01
☐ 143 Dan Meyer .09 .04 .01
☐ 144 Allen Ripley .09 .04 .01
☐ 145 Mickey Rivers .15 .06 .01
☐ 146 Bobby Castillo .09 .04 .01
☐ 147 Dale Berra .09 .04 .01
☐ 148 Randy Niemann .09 .04 .01

☐ 149	Joe Nolan	.09	.04	.01
☐ 150	Mark Fidrych	.20	.08	.02
☐ 151	Claudell Washington	.15	.06	.01
☐ 152	John Urrea	.09	.04	.01
☐ 153	Tom Poquette	.09	.04	.01
☐ 154	Rick Langford	.09	.04	.01
☐ 155	Chris Chambliss	.15	.06	.01
☐ 156	Bob McClure	.09	.04	.01
☐ 157	John Wathan	.15	.06	.01
☐ 158	Fergie Jenkins	.75	.30	.07
☐ 159	Brian Doyle	.09	.04	.01
☐ 160	Garry Maddox	.09	.04	.01
☐ 161	Dan Graham	.09	.04	.01
☐ 162	Doug Corbett	.09	.04	.01
☐ 163	Bill Almon	.09	.04	.01
☐ 164	LaMarr Hoyt	.20	.08	.02
☐ 165	Tony Scott	.09	.04	.01
☐ 166	Floyd Bannister	.09	.04	.01
☐ 167	Terry Whitfield	.09	.04	.01
☐ 168	Don Robinson DP	.09	.04	.01
☐ 169	John Mayberry	.15	.06	.01
☐ 170	Ross Grimsley	.09	.04	.01
☐ 171	Gene Richards	.09	.04	.01
☐ 172	Gary Woods	.09	.04	.01
☐ 173	Bump Wills	.09	.04	.01
☐ 174	Doug Rau	.09	.04	.01
☐ 175	Dave Collins	.09	.04	.01
☐ 176	Mike Krukow	.09	.04	.01
☐ 177	Rick Peters	.09	.04	.01
☐ 178	Jim Essian DP	.09	.04	.01
☐ 179	Rudy May	.09	.04	.01
☐ 180	Pete Rose	3.50	1.50	.35
☐ 181	Elias Sosa	.09	.04	.01
☐ 182	Bob Grich	.15	.06	.01
☐ 183	Dick Davis DP	.05	.02	.00
☐ 184	Jim Dwyer	.09	.04	.01
☐ 185	Dennis Leonard	.09	.04	.01
☐ 186	Wayne Nordhagen	.09	.04	.01
☐ 187	Mike Parrott	.09	.04	.01
☐ 188	Doug DeCinces	.15	.06	.01
☐ 189	Craig Swan	.09	.04	.01
☐ 190	Cesar Cedeno	.15	.06	.01
☐ 191	Rick Sutcliffe	.20	.08	.02
☐ 192	Braves Rookies Terry Harper Ed Miller Rafael Ramirez	.20	.08	.02
☐ 193	Pete Vuckovich	.09	.04	.01
☐ 194	Rod Scurry	.09	.04	.01
☐ 195	Rich Murray	.09	.04	.01
☐ 196	Duffy Dyer	.09	.04	.01
☐ 197	Jim Kern	.09	.04	.01
☐ 198	Jerry Dybzinski	.09	.04	.01
☐ 199	Chuck Rainey	.09	.04	.01
☐ 200	George Foster	.25	.10	.02
☐ 201	RB: Johnny Bench Most homers, lifetime, catcher	.60	.25	.06
☐ 202	RB: Steve Carlton Most strikeouts, lefthander, lifetime	.50	.20	.05
☐ 203	RB: Bill Gullickson Most strikeouts, game, rookie	.20	.08	.02
☐ 204	RB: Ron LeFlore and Rodney Scott Most stolen bases, teammates, season	.15	.06	.01
☐ 205	RB: Pete Rose Most cons. seasons 600 or more at-bats	.75	.30	.07
☐ 206	RB: Mike Schmidt Most homers, third baseman, season	1.00	.40	.10
☐ 207	RB: Ozzie Smith Most assists, season, shortstop	.75	.30	.07
☐ 208	RB: Willie Wilson Most at-bats, season	.15	.06	.01
☐ 209	Dickie Thon DP	.15	.06	.01
☐ 210	Jim Palmer	1.75	.70	.17
☐ 211	Derrel Thomas	.09	.04	.01
☐ 212	Steve Nicosia	.09	.04	.01
☐ 213	Al Holland	.09	.04	.01
☐ 214	Angels Rookies Ralph Botting Jim Dorsey John Harris	.09	.04	.01
☐ 215	Larry Hisle	.09	.04	.01
☐ 216	John Henry Johnson	.09	.04	.01
☐ 217	Rich Hebner	.09	.04	.01
☐ 218	Paul Splittorff	.09	.04	.01
☐ 219	Ken Landreaux	.09	.04	.01
☐ 220	Tom Seaver	2.50	1.00	.25
☐ 221	Bob Davis	.09	.04	.01
☐ 222	Jorge Orta	.09	.04	.01
☐ 223	Roy Lee Jackson	.09	.04	.01
☐ 224	Pat Zachry	.09	.04	.01
☐ 225	Ruppert Jones	.09	.04	.01
☐ 226	Manny Sanguillen DP	.09	.04	.01
☐ 227	Fred Martinez	.09	.04	.01
☐ 228	Tom Paciorek	.09	.04	.01
☐ 229	Rollie Fingers	1.50	.60	.15
☐ 230	George Hendrick	.09	.04	.01
☐ 231	Joe Beckwith	.09	.04	.01
☐ 232	Mickey Klutts	.09	.04	.01
☐ 233	Skip Lockwood	.09	.04	.01
☐ 234	Lou Whitaker	1.00	.40	.10
☐ 235	Scott Sanderson	.25	.10	.02
☐ 236	Mike Ivie	.09	.04	.01
☐ 237	Charlie Moore	.09	.04	.01
☐ 238	Willie Hernandez	.15	.06	.01
☐ 239	Rick Miller DP	.05	.02	.00
☐ 240	Nolan Ryan	9.00	4.00	.90
☐ 241	Checklist 122-242 DP	.15	.02	.00
☐ 242	Chet Lemon	.09	.04	.01

No.	Player			
☐ 243	Sal Butera	.09	.04	.01
☐ 244	Cardinals Rookies	.15	.06	.01
	Tito Landrum			
	Al Olmsted			
	Andy Rincon			
☐ 245	Ed Figueroa	.09	.04	.01
☐ 246	Ed Ott DP	.05	.02	.00
☐ 247	Glenn Hubbard DP	.05	.02	.00
☐ 248	Joey McLaughlin	.09	.04	.01
☐ 249	Larry Cox	.09	.04	.01
☐ 250	Ron Guidry	.40	.16	.04
☐ 251	Tom Brookens	.09	.04	.01
☐ 252	Victor Cruz	.09	.04	.01
☐ 253	Dave Bergman	.09	.04	.01
☐ 254	Ozzie Smith	4.25	1.75	.42
☐ 255	Mark Littell	.09	.04	.01
☐ 256	Bombo Rivera	.09	.04	.01
☐ 257	Rennie Stennett	.09	.04	.01
☐ 258	Joe Price	.09	.04	.01
☐ 259	Mets Rookies	2.25	.90	.22
	Juan Berenguer			
	Hubie Brooks			
	Mookie Wilson			
☐ 260	Ron Cey	.25	.10	.02
☐ 261	Rickey Henderson	22.50	9.75	3.25
☐ 262	Sammy Stewart	.09	.04	.01
☐ 263	Brian Downing	.15	.06	.01
☐ 264	Jim Norris	.09	.04	.01
☐ 265	John Candelaria	.15	.06	.01
☐ 266	Tom Herr	.20	.08	.02
☐ 267	Stan Bahnsen	.09	.04	.01
☐ 268	Jerry Royster	.09	.04	.01
☐ 269	Ken Forsch	.09	.04	.01
☐ 270	Greg Luzinski	.20	.08	.02
☐ 271	Bill Castro	.09	.04	.01
☐ 272	Bruce Kimm	.09	.04	.01
☐ 273	Stan Papi	.09	.04	.01
☐ 274	Craig Chamberlain	.09	.04	.01
☐ 275	Dwight Evans	.60	.25	.06
☐ 276	Dan Spillner	.09	.04	.01
☐ 277	Alfredo Griffin	.15	.06	.01
☐ 278	Rick Sofield	.09	.04	.01
☐ 279	Bob Knepper	.09	.04	.01
☐ 280	Ken Griffey	.50	.20	.05
☐ 281	Fred Stanley	.09	.04	.01
☐ 282	Mariners Rookies	.15	.06	.01
	Rick Anderson			
	Greg Biercevicz			
	Rodney Craig			
☐ 283	Billy Sample	.09	.04	.01
☐ 284	Brian Kingman	.09	.04	.01
☐ 285	Jerry Turner	.09	.04	.01
☐ 286	Dave Frost	.09	.04	.01
☐ 287	Lenn Sakata	.09	.04	.01
☐ 288	Bob Clark	.09	.04	.01
☐ 289	Mickey Hatcher	.09	.04	.01
☐ 290	Bob Boone DP	.15	.06	.01
☐ 291	Aurelio Lopez	.09	.04	.01
☐ 292	Mike Squires	.09	.04	.01
☐ 293	Charlie Lea	.15	.06	.01
☐ 294	Mike Tyson DP	.05	.02	.00
☐ 295	Hal McRae	.20	.08	.02
☐ 296	Bill Nahorodny DP	.05	.02	.00
☐ 297	Bob Bailor	.09	.04	.01
☐ 298	Buddy Solomon	.09	.04	.01
☐ 299	Elliott Maddox	.09	.04	.01
☐ 300	Paul Molitor	1.00	.40	.10
☐ 301	Matt Keough	.09	.04	.01
☐ 302	Dodgers Rookies	5.00	2.25	.50
	Jack Perconte			
	Mike Scioscia			
	Fernando Valenzuela			
☐ 303	Johnny Oates	.15	.06	.01
☐ 304	John Castino	.09	.04	.01
☐ 305	Ken Clay	.09	.04	.01
☐ 306	Juan Beniquez DP	.05	.02	.00
☐ 307	Gene Garber	.09	.04	.01
☐ 308	Rick Manning	.09	.04	.01
☐ 309	Luis Salazar	.25	.10	.02
☐ 310	Vida Blue DP	.09	.04	.01
☐ 311	Freddie Patek	.09	.04	.01
☐ 312	Rick Rhoden	.09	.04	.01
☐ 313	Luis Pujols	.09	.04	.01
☐ 314	Rich Dauer	.09	.04	.01
☐ 315	Kirk Gibson	6.50	2.75	.65
☐ 316	Craig Minetto	.09	.04	.01
☐ 317	Lonnie Smith	.50	.20	.05
☐ 318	Steve Yeager	.09	.04	.01
☐ 319	Rowland Office	.09	.04	.01
☐ 320	Tom Burgmeier	.09	.04	.01
☐ 321	Leon Durham	.20	.08	.02
☐ 322	Neil Allen	.09	.04	.01
☐ 323	Jim Morrison DP	.09	.04	.01
☐ 324	Mike Willis	.09	.04	.01
☐ 325	Ray Knight	.20	.08	.02
☐ 326	Biff Pocoroba	.09	.04	.01
☐ 327	Moose Haas	.09	.04	.01
☐ 328	Twins Rookies	.15	.06	.01
	Dave Engle			
	Greg Johnston			
	Gary Ward			
☐ 329	Joaquin Andujar	.15	.06	.01
☐ 330	Frank White	.15	.06	.01
☐ 331	Dennis Lamp	.09	.04	.01
☐ 332	Lee Lacy DP	.09	.04	.01
☐ 333	Sid Monge	.09	.04	.01
☐ 334	Dane Iorg	.09	.04	.01
☐ 335	Rick Cerone	.09	.04	.01
☐ 336	Eddie Whitson	.09	.04	.01
☐ 337	Lynn Jones	.09	.04	.01
☐ 338	Checklist 243-363	.25	.03	.01
☐ 339	John Ellis	.09	.04	.01
☐ 340	Bruce Kison	.09	.04	.01
☐ 341	Dwayne Murphy	.09	.04	.01
☐ 342	Eric Rasmussen DP	.05	.02	.00
☐ 343	Frank Taveras	.09	.04	.01

☐ 344 Byron McLaughlin	.09	.04	.01
☐ 345 Warren Cromartie	.09	.04	.01
☐ 346 Larry Christenson DP	.05	.02	.00
☐ 347 Harold Baines	4.25	1.75	.42
☐ 348 Bob Sykes	.09	.04	.01
☐ 349 Glenn Hoffman	.09	.04	.01
☐ 350 J.R. Richard	.15	.06	.01
☐ 351 Otto Velez	.09	.04	.01
☐ 352 Dick Tidrow DP	.05	.02	.00
☐ 353 Terry Kennedy	.15	.06	.01
☐ 354 Mario Soto	.15	.06	.01
☐ 355 Bob Horner	.20	.08	.02
☐ 356 Padres Rookies George Stablein Craig Stimac Tom Tellmann	.09	.04	.01
☐ 357 Jim Slaton	.09	.04	.01
☐ 358 Mark Wagner	.09	.04	.01
☐ 359 Tom Hausman	.09	.04	.01
☐ 360 Willie Wilson	.25	.10	.02
☐ 361 Joe Strain	.09	.04	.01
☐ 362 Bo Diaz	.09	.04	.01
☐ 363 Geoff Zahn	.09	.04	.01
☐ 364 Mike Davis	.20	.08	.02
☐ 365 Graig Nettles DP	.15	.06	.01
☐ 366 Mike Ramsey	.09	.04	.01
☐ 367 Dennis Martinez	.25	.10	.02
☐ 368 Leon Roberts	.09	.04	.01
☐ 369 Frank Tanana	.15	.06	.01
☐ 370 Dave Winfield	2.00	.80	.20
☐ 371 Charlie Hough	.15	.06	.01
☐ 372 Jay Johnstone	.15	.06	.01
☐ 373 Pat Underwood	.09	.04	.01
☐ 374 Tommy Hutton	.09	.04	.01
☐ 375 Dave Concepcion	.25	.10	.02
☐ 376 Ron Reed	.09	.04	.01
☐ 377 Jerry Morales	.09	.04	.01
☐ 378 Dave Rader	.09	.04	.01
☐ 379 Lary Sorensen	.09	.04	.01
☐ 380 Willie Stargell	1.00	.40	.10
☐ 381 Cubs Rookies Carlos Lezcano Steve Macko Randy Martz	.15	.06	.01
☐ 382 Paul Mirabella	.09	.04	.01
☐ 383 Eric Soderholm DP	.05	.02	.00
☐ 384 Mike Sadek	.09	.04	.01
☐ 385 Joe Sambito	.09	.04	.01
☐ 386 Dave Edwards	.09	.04	.01
☐ 387 Phil Niekro	.75	.30	.07
☐ 388 Andre Thornton	.15	.06	.01
☐ 389 Marty Pattin	.09	.04	.01
☐ 390 Cesar Geronimo	.09	.04	.01
☐ 391 Dave Lemanczyk DP	.05	.02	.00
☐ 392 Lance Parrish	.75	.30	.07
☐ 393 Broderick Perkins	.09	.04	.01
☐ 394 Woodie Fryman	.09	.04	.01
☐ 395 Scot Thompson	.09	.04	.01
☐ 396 Bill Campbell	.09	.04	.01
☐ 397 Julio Cruz	.09	.04	.01
☐ 398 Ross Baumgarten	.09	.04	.01
☐ 399 Orioles Rookies Mike Boddicker Mark Corey Floyd Rayford	1.25	.50	.12
☐ 400 Reggie Jackson	3.50	1.50	.35
☐ 401 AL Champs Royals sweep Yanks (Brett swinging)	.65	.25	.06
☐ 402 NL Champs Phillies squeak past Astros	.25	.10	.02
☐ 403 1980 World Series Phillies beat Royals in six	.25	.10	.02
☐ 404 1980 World Series Phillies win first World Series	.25	.10	.02
☐ 405 Nino Espinosa	.09	.04	.01
☐ 406 Dickie Noles	.09	.04	.01
☐ 407 Ernie Whitt	.09	.04	.01
☐ 408 Fernando Arroyo	.09	.04	.01
☐ 409 Larry Herndon	.09	.04	.01
☐ 410 Bert Campaneris	.15	.06	.01
☐ 411 Terry Puhl	.09	.04	.01
☐ 412 Britt Burns	.15	.06	.01
☐ 413 Tony Bernazard	.09	.04	.01
☐ 414 John Pacella DP	.05	.02	.00
☐ 415 Ben Oglivie	.09	.04	.01
☐ 416 Gary Alexander	.09	.04	.01
☐ 417 Dan Schatzeder	.09	.04	.01
☐ 418 Bobby Brown	.09	.04	.01
☐ 419 Tom Hume	.09	.04	.01
☐ 420 Keith Hernandez	.50	.20	.05
☐ 421 Bob Stanley	.09	.04	.01
☐ 422 Dan Ford	.09	.04	.01
☐ 423 Shane Rawley	.09	.04	.01
☐ 424 Yankees Rookies Tim Lollar Bruce Robinson Dennis Werth	.09	.04	.01
☐ 425 Al Bumbry	.09	.04	.01
☐ 426 Warren Brusstar	.09	.04	.01
☐ 427 John D'Acquisto	.09	.04	.01
☐ 428 John Stearns	.09	.04	.01
☐ 429 Mick Kelleher	.09	.04	.01
☐ 430 Jim Bibby	.09	.04	.01
☐ 431 Dave Roberts	.09	.04	.01
☐ 432 Len Barker	.09	.04	.01
☐ 433 Rance Mulliniks	.09	.04	.01
☐ 434 Roger Erickson	.09	.04	.01
☐ 435 Jim Spencer	.09	.04	.01
☐ 436 Gary Lucas	.09	.04	.01
☐ 437 Mike Heath DP	.05	.02	.00
☐ 438 John Montefusco	.09	.04	.01
☐ 439 Denny Walling	.09	.04	.01

☐ 440 Jerry Reuss .09 .04 .01
☐ 441 Ken Reitz .09 .04 .01
☐ 442 Ron Pruitt .09 .04 .01
☐ 443 Jim Beattie DP .05 .02 .00
☐ 444 Garth Iorg .09 .04 .01
☐ 445 Ellis Valentine .09 .04 .01
☐ 446 Checklist 364-484 .25 .03 .01
☐ 447 Junior Kennedy DP .05 .02 .00
☐ 448 Tim Corcoran .09 .04 .01
☐ 449 Paul Mitchell .09 .04 .01
☐ 450 Dave Kingman DP .15 .06 .01
☐ 451 Indians Rookies .15 .06 .01
Chris Bando
Tom Brennan
Sandy Wihtol
☐ 452 Renie Martin .09 .04 .01
☐ 453 Rob Wilfong DP .05 .02 .00
☐ 454 Andy Hassler .09 .04 .01
☐ 455 Rick Burleson .15 .06 .01
☐ 456 Jeff Reardon 6.00 2.50 .60
☐ 457 Mike Lum .09 .04 .01
☐ 458 Randy Jones .09 .04 .01
☐ 459 Greg Gross .09 .04 .01
☐ 460 Rich Gossage .35 .15 .03
☐ 461 Dave McKay .09 .04 .01
☐ 462 Jack Brohamer .09 .04 .01
☐ 463 Milt May .09 .04 .01
☐ 464 Adrian Devine .09 .04 .01
☐ 465 Bill Russell .15 .06 .01
☐ 466 Bob Molinaro .09 .04 .01
☐ 467 Dave Stieb 1.00 .40 .10
☐ 468 John Wockenfuss .09 .04 .01
☐ 469 Jeff Leonard .20 .08 .02
☐ 470 Manny Trillo .09 .04 .01
☐ 471 Mike Vail .09 .04 .01
☐ 472 Dyar Miller DP .05 .02 .00
☐ 473 Jose Cardenal .09 .04 .01
☐ 474 Mike LaCoss .09 .04 .01
☐ 475 Buddy Bell .15 .06 .01
☐ 476 Jerry Koosman .15 .06 .01
☐ 477 Luis Gomez .09 .04 .01
☐ 478 Juan Eichelberger .09 .04 .01
☐ 479 Expos Rookies 9.00 4.00 .90
Tim Raines
Roberto Ramos
Bobby Pate
☐ 480 Carlton Fisk 2.50 1.00 .25
☐ 481 Bob Lacey DP .05 .02 .00
☐ 482 Jim Gantner .09 .04 .01
☐ 483 Mike Griffin .09 .04 .01
☐ 484 Max Venable DP .05 .02 .00
☐ 485 Garry Templeton .15 .06 .01
☐ 486 Marc Hill .09 .04 .01
☐ 487 Dewey Robinson .09 .04 .01
☐ 488 Damaso Garcia .15 .06 .01
☐ 489 John Littlefield .09 .04 .01
☐ 490 Eddie Murray 3.75 1.60 .37
☐ 491 Gordy Pladson .09 .04 .01
☐ 492 Barry Foote .09 .04 .01
☐ 493 Dan Quisenberry .35 .15 .03
☐ 494 Bob Walk .35 .15 .03
☐ 495 Dusty Baker .15 .06 .01
☐ 496 Paul Dade .09 .04 .01
☐ 497 Fred Norman .09 .04 .01
☐ 498 Pat Putnam .09 .04 .01
☐ 499 Frank Pastore .09 .04 .01
☐ 500 Jim Rice .50 .20 .05
☐ 501 Tim Foli DP .05 .02 .00
☐ 502 Giants Rookies .09 .04 .01
Chris Bourjos
Al Hargesheimer
Mike Rowland
☐ 503 Steve McCatty .09 .04 .01
☐ 504 Dale Murphy 1.75 .70 .17
☐ 505 Jason Thompson .09 .04 .01
☐ 506 Phil Huffman .09 .04 .01
☐ 507 Jamie Quirk .09 .04 .01
☐ 508 Rob Dressler .09 .04 .01
☐ 509 Pete Mackanin .09 .04 .01
☐ 510 Lee Mazzilli .09 .04 .01
☐ 511 Wayne Garland .09 .04 .01
☐ 512 Gary Thomasson .09 .04 .01
☐ 513 Frank LaCorte .09 .04 .01
☐ 514 George Riley .09 .04 .01
☐ 515 Robin Yount 4.00 1.75 .40
☐ 516 Doug Bird .09 .04 .01
☐ 517 Richie Zisk .09 .04 .01
☐ 518 Grant Jackson .09 .04 .01
☐ 519 John Tamargo DP .05 .02 .00
☐ 520 Steve Stone .09 .04 .01
☐ 521 Sam Mejias .09 .04 .01
☐ 522 Mike Colbern .09 .04 .01
☐ 523 John Fulgham .09 .04 .01
☐ 524 Willie Aikens .09 .04 .01
☐ 525 Mike Torrez .09 .04 .01
☐ 526 Phillies Rookies .15 .06 .01
Marty Bystrom
Jay Loviglio
Jim Wright
☐ 527 Danny Goodwin .09 .04 .01
☐ 528 Gary Matthews .15 .06 .01
☐ 529 Dave LaRoche .09 .04 .01
☐ 530 Steve Garvey 1.25 .50 .12
☐ 531 John Curtis .09 .04 .01
☐ 532 Bill Stein .09 .04 .01
☐ 533 Jesus Figueroa .09 .04 .01
☐ 534 Dave Smith .60 .25 .06
☐ 535 Omar Moreno .09 .04 .01
☐ 536 Bob Owchinko DP .05 .02 .00
☐ 537 Ron Hodges .09 .04 .01
☐ 538 Tom Griffin .09 .04 .01
☐ 539 Rodney Scott .09 .04 .01
☐ 540 Mike Schmidt DP 2.50 1.00 .25
☐ 541 Steve Swisher .09 .04 .01
☐ 542 Larry Bradford DP .05 .02 .00
☐ 543 Terry Crowley .09 .04 .01

☐ 544 Rich Gale .09 .04 .01
☐ 545 Johnny Grubb .09 .04 .01
☐ 546 Paul Moskau .09 .04 .01
☐ 547 Mario Guerrero .09 .04 .01
☐ 548 Dave Goltz .09 .04 .01
☐ 549 Jerry Remy .09 .04 .01
☐ 550 Tommy John .35 .15 .03
☐ 551 Pirates Rookies 1.50 .60 .15
Vance Law
Tony Pena
Pascual Perez
☐ 552 Steve Trout .09 .04 .01
☐ 553 Tim Blackwell .09 .04 .01
☐ 554 Bert Blyleven UER .50 .20 .05
(1 is missing from
1980 on card back)
☐ 555 Cecil Cooper .20 .08 .02
☐ 556 Jerry Mumphrey .09 .04 .01
☐ 557 Chris Knapp .09 .04 .01
☐ 558 Barry Bonnell .09 .04 .01
☐ 559 Willie Montanez .09 .04 .01
☐ 560 Joe Morgan 1.25 .50 .12
☐ 561 Dennis Littlejohn .09 .04 .01
☐ 562 Checklist 485-605 .25 .04 .01
☐ 563 Jim Kaat .25 .10 .02
☐ 564 Ron Hassey DP .09 .04 .01
☐ 565 Burt Hooton .09 .04 .01
☐ 566 Del Unser .09 .04 .01
☐ 567 Mark Bomback .09 .04 .01
☐ 568 Dave Revering .09 .04 .01
☐ 569 Al Williams DP .05 .02 .00
☐ 570 Ken Singleton .15 .06 .01
☐ 571 Todd Cruz .09 .04 .01
☐ 572 Jack Morris 1.75 .70 .17
☐ 573 Phil Garner .15 .06 .01
☐ 574 Bill Caudill .09 .04 .01
☐ 575 Tony Perez .50 .20 .05
☐ 576 Reggie Cleveland .09 .04 .01
☐ 577 Blue Jays Rookies .15 .06 .01
Luis Leal
Brian Milner
Ken Schrom
☐ 578 Bill Gullickson .75 .30 .07
☐ 579 Tim Flannery .09 .04 .01
☐ 580 Don Baylor .25 .10 .02
☐ 581 Roy Howell .09 .04 .01
☐ 582 Gaylord Perry .75 .30 .07
☐ 583 Larry Milbourne .09 .04 .01
☐ 584 Randy Lerch .09 .04 .01
☐ 585 Amos Otis .15 .06 .01
☐ 586 Silvio Martinez .09 .04 .01
☐ 587 Jeff Newman .09 .04 .01
☐ 588 Gary Lavelle .09 .04 .01
☐ 589 Lamar Johnson .09 .04 .01
☐ 590 Bruce Sutter .25 .10 .02
☐ 591 John Lowenstein .09 .04 .01
☐ 592 Steve Comer .09 .04 .01
☐ 593 Steve Kemp .09 .04 .01
☐ 594 Preston Hanna DP .05 .02 .00
☐ 595 Butch Hobson .15 .06 .01
☐ 596 Jerry Augustine .09 .04 .01
☐ 597 Rafael Landestoy .09 .04 .01
☐ 598 George Vukovich DP .05 .02 .00
☐ 599 Dennis Kinney .09 .04 .01
☐ 600 Johnny Bench 2.50 1.00 .25
☐ 601 Don Aase .09 .04 .01
☐ 602 Bobby Murcer .20 .08 .02
☐ 603 John Verhoeven .09 .04 .01
☐ 604 Rob Picciolo .09 .04 .01
☐ 605 Don Sutton .75 .30 .07
☐ 606 Reds Rookies DP .09 .04 .01
Bruce Berenyi
Geoff Combe
Paul Householder
☐ 607 David Palmer .09 .04 .01
☐ 608 Greg Pryor .09 .04 .01
☐ 609 Lynn McGlothen .09 .04 .01
☐ 610 Darrell Porter .09 .04 .01
☐ 611 Rick Matula DP .05 .02 .00
☐ 612 Duane Kuiper .09 .04 .01
☐ 613 Jim Anderson .09 .04 .01
☐ 614 Dave Rozema .09 .04 .01
☐ 615 Rick Dempsey .09 .04 .01
☐ 616 Rick Wise .09 .04 .01
☐ 617 Craig Reynolds .09 .04 .01
☐ 618 John Milner .09 .04 .01
☐ 619 Steve Henderson .09 .04 .01
☐ 620 Dennis Eckersley 1.00 .40 .10
☐ 621 Tom Donohue .09 .04 .01
☐ 622 Randy Moffitt .09 .04 .01
☐ 623 Sal Bando .15 .06 .01
☐ 624 Bob Welch .65 .25 .06
☐ 625 Bill Buckner .20 .08 .02
☐ 626 Tigers Rookies .15 .06 .01
Dave Steffen
Jerry Ujdur
Roger Weaver
☐ 627 Luis Tiant .15 .06 .01
☐ 628 Vic Correll .09 .04 .01
☐ 629 Tony Armas .09 .04 .01
☐ 630 Steve Carlton 2.00 .80 .20
☐ 631 Ron Jackson .09 .04 .01
☐ 632 Alan Bannister .09 .04 .01
☐ 633 Bill Lee .09 .04 .01
☐ 634 Doug Flynn .09 .04 .01
☐ 635 Bobby Bonds .20 .08 .02
☐ 636 Al Hrabosky .09 .04 .01
☐ 637 Jerry Narron .09 .04 .01
☐ 638 Checklist 606-726 .25 .04 .01
☐ 639 Carney Lansford .25 .10 .02
☐ 640 Dave Parker 1.00 .40 .10
☐ 641 Mark Belanger .15 .06 .01
☐ 642 Vern Ruhle .09 .04 .01
☐ 643 Lloyd Moseby .50 .20 .05
☐ 644 Ramon Aviles DP .05 .02 .00
☐ 645 Rick Reuschel .20 .08 .02

Card	Player	Mint	VG-E	F-G
☐ 646	Marvis Foley	.09	.04	.01
☐ 647	Dick Drago	.09	.04	.01
☐ 648	Darrell Evans	.25	.10	.02
☐ 649	Manny Sarmiento	.09	.04	.01
☐ 650	Bucky Dent	.15	.06	.01
☐ 651	Pedro Guerrero	1.00	.40	.10
☐ 652	John Montague	.09	.04	.01
☐ 653	Bill Fahey	.09	.04	.01
☐ 654	Ray Burris	.09	.04	.01
☐ 655	Dan Driessen	.09	.04	.01
☐ 656	Jon Matlack	.09	.04	.01
☐ 657	Mike Cubbage DP	.05	.02	.00
☐ 658	Milt Wilcox	.09	.04	.01
☐ 659	Brewers Rookies John Flinn Ed Romero Ned Yost	.15	.06	.01
☐ 660	Gary Carter	1.50	.60	.15
☐ 661	Orioles Team/Mgr. Earl Weaver (checklist back)	.25	.08	.02
☐ 662	Red Sox Team/Mgr. Ralph Houk (checklist back)	.25	.08	.02
☐ 663	Angels Team/Mgr. Jim Fregosi (checklist back)	.25	.08	.02
☐ 664	White Sox Team/Mgr. Tony LaRussa (checklist back)	.25	.08	.02
☐ 665	Indians Team/Mgr. Dave Garcia (checklist back)	.25	.08	.02
☐ 666	Tigers Team/Mgr. Sparky Anderson (checklist back)	.25	.08	.02
☐ 667	Royals Team/Mgr. Jim Frey (checklist back)	.25	.08	.02
☐ 668	Brewers Team/Mgr. Bob Rodgers (checklist back)	.25	.08	.02
☐ 669	Twins Team/Mgr. John Goryl (checklist back)	.25	.08	.02
☐ 670	Yankees Team/Mgr. Gene Michael (checklist back)	.25	.08	.02
☐ 671	A's Team/Mgr. Billy Martin (checklist back)	.25	.08	.02
☐ 672	Mariners Team/Mgr. Maury Wills (checklist back)	.25	.08	.02
☐ 673	Rangers Team/Mgr. Don Zimmer (checklist back)	.25	.08	.02
☐ 674	Blue Jays Team/Mgr. Bobby Mattick (checklist back)	.25	.08	.02
☐ 675	Braves Team/Mgr. Bobby Cox (checklist back)	.25	.08	.02
☐ 676	Cubs Team/Mgr. Joe Amalfitano (checklist back)	.25	.08	.02
☐ 677	Reds Team/Mgr. John McNamara (checklist back)	.25	.08	.02
☐ 678	Astros Team/Mgr. Bill Virdon (checklist back)	.25	.08	.02
☐ 679	Dodgers Team/Mgr. Tom Lasorda (checklist back)	.25	.08	.02
☐ 680	Expos Team/Mgr. Dick Williams (checklist back)	.25	.08	.02
☐ 681	Mets Team/Mgr. Joe Torre (checklist back)	.25	.08	.02
☐ 682	Phillies Team/Mgr. Dallas Green (checklist back)	.25	.08	.02
☐ 683	Pirates Team/Mgr. Chuck Tanner (checklist back)	.25	.08	.02
☐ 684	Cardinals Team/Mgr. Whitey Herzog (checklist back)	.25	.08	.02
☐ 685	Padres Team/Mgr. Frank Howard (checklist back)	.25	.08	.02
☐ 686	Giants Team/Mgr. Dave Bristol (checklist back)	.25	.08	.02
☐ 687	Jeff Jones	.09	.04	.01
☐ 688	Kiko Garcia	.09	.04	.01
☐ 689	Red Sox Rookies Bruce Hurst Keith MacWhorter Reid Nichols	2.00	.80	.20
☐ 690	Bob Watson	.09	.04	.01
☐ 691	Dick Ruthven	.09	.04	.01
☐ 692	Lenny Randle	.09	.04	.01
☐ 693	Steve Howe	.20	.08	.02
☐ 694	Bud Harrelson DP	.09	.04	.01
☐ 695	Kent Tekulve	.15	.06	.01
☐ 696	Alan Ashby	.09	.04	.01
☐ 697	Rick Waits	.09	.04	.01
☐ 698	Mike Jorgensen	.09	.04	.01
☐ 699	Glenn Abbott	.09	.04	.01
☐ 700	George Brett	4.00	1.75	.40
☐ 701	Joe Rudi	.15	.06	.01
☐ 702	George Medich	.09	.04	.01
☐ 703	Alvis Woods	.09	.04	.01

☐ 704 Bill Travers DP	.05	.02	.00
☐ 705 Ted Simmons	.25	.10	.02
☐ 706 Dave Ford	.09	.04	.01
☐ 707 Dave Cash	.09	.04	.01
☐ 708 Doyle Alexander	.09	.04	.01
☐ 709 Alan Trammell DP	.90	.40	.09
☐ 710 Ron LeFlore DP	.09	.04	.01
☐ 711 Joe Ferguson	.09	.04	.01
☐ 712 Bill Bonham	.09	.04	.01
☐ 713 Bill North	.09	.04	.01
☐ 714 Pete Redfern	.09	.04	.01
☐ 715 Bill Madlock	.15	.06	.01
☐ 716 Glenn Borgmann	.09	.04	.01
☐ 717 Jim Barr DP	.05	.02	.00
☐ 718 Larry Biittner	.09	.04	.01
☐ 719 Sparky Lyle	.15	.06	.01
☐ 720 Fred Lynn	.25	.10	.02
☐ 721 Toby Harrah	.15	.06	.01
☐ 722 Joe Niekro	.15	.06	.01
☐ 723 Bruce Bochte	.09	.04	.01
☐ 724 Lou Piniella	.15	.06	.01
☐ 725 Steve Rogers	.09	.04	.01
☐ 726 Rick Monday	.20	.08	.02

1981 Topps Traded

The cards in this 132-card set measure 2 1/2" by 3 1/2". For the first time since 1976, Topps issued a "traded" set in 1981. Unlike the small traded sets of 1974 and 1976, this set contains a larger number of cards and was sequentially numbered, alphabetically, from 727 to 858. Thus, this set gives the impression it is a continuation of their regular issue of this year. The sets were issued only through hobby card dealers and were boxed in complete sets of 132 cards. There are no key rookie cards in this set.

	MINT	EXC	G-VG
COMPLETE SET (132)	32.00	14.00	3.00
COMMON PLAYER (727-858)	.10	.04	.01
☐ 727 Danny Ainge	2.00	.80	.20
☐ 728 Doyle Alexander	.15	.06	.01
☐ 729 Gary Alexander	.10	.04	.01
☐ 730 Bill Almon	.10	.04	.01
☐ 731 Joaquin Andujar	.15	.06	.01
☐ 732 Bob Bailor	.10	.04	.01
☐ 733 Juan Beniquez	.10	.04	.01
☐ 734 Dave Bergman	.10	.04	.01
☐ 735 Tony Bernazard	.15	.06	.01
☐ 736 Larry Biittner	.10	.04	.01
☐ 737 Doug Bird	.10	.04	.01
☐ 738 Bert Blyleven	1.00	.40	.10
☐ 739 Mark Bomback	.10	.04	.01
☐ 740 Bobby Bonds	.25	.10	.02
☐ 741 Rick Bosetti	.10	.04	.01
☐ 742 Hubie Brooks	1.75	.70	.17
☐ 743 Rick Burleson	.15	.06	.01
☐ 744 Ray Burris	.10	.04	.01
☐ 745 Jeff Burroughs	.15	.06	.01
☐ 746 Enos Cabell	.10	.04	.01
☐ 747 Ken Clay	.10	.04	.01
☐ 748 Mark Clear	.10	.04	.01
☐ 749 Larry Cox	.10	.04	.01
☐ 750 Hector Cruz	.10	.04	.01
☐ 751 Victor Cruz	.10	.04	.01
☐ 752 Mike Cubbage	.10	.04	.01
☐ 753 Dick Davis	.10	.04	.01
☐ 754 Brian Doyle	.10	.04	.01
☐ 755 Dick Drago	.10	.04	.01
☐ 756 Leon Durham	.20	.08	.02
☐ 757 Jim Dwyer	.10	.04	.01
☐ 758 Dave Edwards	.10	.04	.01
☐ 759 Jim Essian	.20	.08	.02
☐ 760 Bill Fahey	.10	.04	.01
☐ 761 Rollie Fingers	2.50	1.00	.25
☐ 762 Carlton Fisk	5.50	2.50	.55
☐ 763 Barry Foote	.10	.04	.01
☐ 764 Ken Forsch	.10	.04	.01
☐ 765 Kiko Garcia	.10	.04	.01
☐ 766 Cesar Geronimo	.10	.04	.01
☐ 767 Gary Gray	.10	.04	.01
☐ 768 Mickey Hatcher	.15	.06	.01
☐ 769 Steve Henderson	.10	.04	.01
☐ 770 Marc Hill	.10	.04	.01
☐ 771 Butch Hobson	.20	.08	.02
☐ 772 Rick Honeycutt	.15	.06	.01
☐ 773 Roy Howell	.10	.04	.01
☐ 774 Mike Ivie	.10	.04	.01
☐ 775 Roy Lee Jackson	.10	.04	.01
☐ 776 Cliff Johnson	.10	.04	.01
☐ 777 Randy Jones	.15	.06	.01
☐ 778 Ruppert Jones	.10	.04	.01
☐ 779 Mick Kelleher	.10	.04	.01
☐ 780 Terry Kennedy	.20	.08	.02

☐ 781 Dave Kingman	.40	.16	.04
☐ 782 Bob Knepper	.10	.04	.01
☐ 783 Ken Kravec	.10	.04	.01
☐ 784 Bob Lacey	.10	.04	.01
☐ 785 Dennis Lamp	.10	.04	.01
☐ 786 Rafael Landestoy	.10	.04	.01
☐ 787 Ken Landreaux	.15	.06	.01
☐ 788 Carney Lansford	.65	.25	.06
☐ 789 Dave LaRoche	.10	.04	.01
☐ 790 Joe Lefebvre	.10	.04	.01
☐ 791 Ron LeFlore	.15	.06	.01
☐ 792 Randy Lerch	.10	.04	.01
☐ 793 Sixto Lezcano	.10	.04	.01
☐ 794 John Littlefield	.10	.04	.01
☐ 795 Mike Lum	.10	.04	.01
☐ 796 Greg Luzinski	.25	.10	.02
☐ 797 Fred Lynn	.60	.25	.06
☐ 798 Jerry Martin	.10	.04	.01
☐ 799 Buck Martinez	.10	.04	.01
☐ 800 Gary Matthews	.15	.06	.01
☐ 801 Mario Mendoza	.10	.04	.01
☐ 802 Larry Milbourne	.10	.04	.01
☐ 803 Rick Miller	.10	.04	.01
☐ 804 John Montefusco	.10	.04	.01
☐ 805 Jerry Morales	.10	.04	.01
☐ 806 Jose Morales	.10	.04	.01
☐ 807 Joe Morgan	2.50	1.00	.25
☐ 808 Jerry Mumphrey	.10	.04	.01
☐ 809 Gene Nelson	.20	.08	.02
☐ 810 Ed Ott	.10	.04	.01
☐ 811 Bob Owchinko	.10	.04	.01
☐ 812 Gaylord Perry	1.75	.70	.17
☐ 813 Mike Phillips	.10	.04	.01
☐ 814 Darrell Porter	.15	.06	.01
☐ 815 Mike Proly	.10	.04	.01
☐ 816 Tim Raines	12.00	5.25	1.50
☐ 817 Lenny Randle	.10	.04	.01
☐ 818 Doug Rau	.10	.04	.01
☐ 819 Jeff Reardon	5.50	2.50	.55
☐ 820 Ken Reitz	.10	.04	.01
☐ 821 Steve Renko	.10	.04	.01
☐ 822 Rick Reuschel	.30	.12	.03
☐ 823 Dave Revering	.10	.04	.01
☐ 824 Dave Roberts	.10	.04	.01
☐ 825 Leon Roberts	.10	.04	.01
☐ 826 Joe Rudi	.15	.06	.01
☐ 827 Kevin Saucier	.10	.04	.01
☐ 828 Tony Scott	.10	.04	.01
☐ 829 Bob Shirley	.10	.04	.01
☐ 830 Ted Simmons	.50	.20	.05
☐ 831 Lary Sorensen	.10	.04	.01
☐ 832 Jim Spencer	.10	.04	.01
☐ 833 Harry Spilman	.10	.04	.01
☐ 834 Fred Stanley	.10	.04	.01
☐ 835 Rusty Staub	.30	.12	.03
☐ 836 Bill Stein	.10	.04	.01
☐ 837 Joe Strain	.10	.04	.01
☐ 838 Bruce Sutter	.50	.20	.05
☐ 839 Don Sutton	1.75	.70	.17
☐ 840 Steve Swisher	.10	.04	.01
☐ 841 Frank Tanana	.25	.10	.02
☐ 842 Gene Tenace	.15	.06	.01
☐ 843 Jason Thompson	.10	.04	.01
☐ 844 Dickie Thon	.35	.15	.03
☐ 845 Bill Travers	.10	.04	.01
☐ 846 Tom Underwood	.10	.04	.01
☐ 847 John Urrea	.10	.04	.01
☐ 848 Mike Vail	.10	.04	.01
☐ 849 Ellis Valentine	.10	.04	.01
☐ 850 Fernando Valenzuela	4.00	1.75	.40
☐ 851 Pete Vuckovich	.15	.06	.01
☐ 852 Mark Wagner	.10	.04	.01
☐ 853 Bob Walk	.30	.12	.03
☐ 854 Claudell Washington	.20	.08	.02
☐ 855 Dave Winfield	5.00	2.25	.50
☐ 856 Geoff Zahn	.10	.04	.01
☐ 857 Richie Zisk	.15	.06	.01
☐ 858 Checklist 727-858	.10	.01	.00

1982 Topps

The cards in this 792-card set measure 2 1/2" by 3 1/2". The 1982 baseball series is the largest set Topps has ever issued at one printing. The 66-card increase from the previous year's total eliminated the "double print" practice, that had occurred in every regular issue since 1978. Cards 1-6 depict Highlights (HL) of the 1981 season, cards 161-168 picture League Leaders, and there are mini-series of AL (547-557) and NL (337-347) All-Stars (AS). The abbreviation "SA" in the checklist is given for the 40 "Super Action" cards introduced in this set. The team cards are actually Team Leader (TL) cards picturing the batting and pitching leader for that team

with a checklist back. The key rookie cards in this set are George Bell, Cal Ripken Jr., Steve Sax, Lee Smith, and Dave Stewart.

	MINT	EXC	G-VG
COMPLETE SET (792)	140.00	63.00	21.00
COMMON PLAYER (1-792)	.08	.03	.01
☐ 1 HL: Steve Carlton	.60	.15	.03
Sets new NL strikeout record			
☐ 2 HL: Ron Davis	.08	.03	.01
Fans 8 straight in relief			
☐ 3 HL: Tim Raines	.35	.15	.03
Swipes 71 bases as rookie			
☐ 4 HL: Pete Rose	.75	.30	.07
Sets NL career hits mark			
☐ 5 HL: Nolan Ryan	2.25	.90	.22
Pitches fifth career no-hitter			
☐ 6 HL: Fern. Valenzuela	.20	.08	.02
8 shutouts as rookie			
☐ 7 Scott Sanderson	.15	.06	.01
☐ 8 Rich Dauer	.08	.03	.01
☐ 9 Ron Guidry	.35	.15	.03
☐ 10 SA: Ron Guidry	.20	.08	.02
☐ 11 Gary Alexander	.08	.03	.01
☐ 12 Moose Haas	.08	.03	.01
☐ 13 Lamar Johnson	.08	.03	.01
☐ 14 Steve Howe	.08	.03	.01
☐ 15 Ellis Valentine	.08	.03	.01
☐ 16 Steve Comer	.08	.03	.01
☐ 17 Darrell Evans	.15	.06	.01
☐ 18 Fernando Arroyo	.08	.03	.01
☐ 19 Ernie Whitt	.08	.03	.01
☐ 20 Garry Maddox	.08	.03	.01
☐ 21 Orioles Rookies	65.00	29.00	9.75
Bob Bonner			
Cal Ripken			
Jeff Schneider			
☐ 22 Jim Beattie	.08	.03	.01
☐ 23 Willie Hernandez	.15	.06	.01
☐ 24 Dave Frost	.08	.03	.01
☐ 25 Jerry Remy	.08	.03	.01
☐ 26 Jorge Orta	.08	.03	.01
☐ 27 Tom Herr	.15	.06	.01
☐ 28 John Urrea	.08	.03	.01
☐ 29 Dwayne Murphy	.08	.03	.01
☐ 30 Tom Seaver	1.75	.70	.17
☐ 31 SA: Tom Seaver	.80	.35	.08
☐ 32 Gene Garber	.08	.03	.01
☐ 33 Jerry Morales	.08	.03	.01
☐ 34 Joe Sambito	.08	.03	.01
☐ 35 Willie Aikens	.08	.03	.01
☐ 36 Rangers TL	.20	.05	.01
Batting: Al Oliver			
Pitching: Doc Medich			
☐ 37 Dan Graham	.08	.03	.01
☐ 38 Charlie Lea	.08	.03	.01
☐ 39 Lou Whitaker	.60	.25	.06
☐ 40 Dave Parker	.80	.35	.08
☐ 41 SA: Dave Parker	.35	.15	.03
☐ 42 Rick Sofield	.08	.03	.01
☐ 43 Mike Cubbage	.08	.03	.01
☐ 44 Britt Burns	.08	.03	.01
☐ 45 Rick Cerone	.08	.03	.01
☐ 46 Jerry Augustine	.08	.03	.01
☐ 47 Jeff Leonard	.08	.03	.01
☐ 48 Bobby Castillo	.08	.03	.01
☐ 49 Alvis Woods	.08	.03	.01
☐ 50 Buddy Bell	.15	.06	.01
☐ 51 Cubs Rookies	.35	.15	.03
Jay Howell			
Carlos Lezcano			
Ty Waller			
☐ 52 Larry Andersen	.08	.03	.01
☐ 53 Greg Gross	.08	.03	.01
☐ 54 Ron Hassey	.08	.03	.01
☐ 55 Rick Burleson	.08	.03	.01
☐ 56 Mark Littell	.08	.03	.01
☐ 57 Craig Reynolds	.08	.03	.01
☐ 58 John D'Acquisto	.08	.03	.01
☐ 59 Rich Gedman	.25	.10	.02
☐ 60 Tony Armas	.08	.03	.01
☐ 61 Tommy Boggs	.08	.03	.01
☐ 62 Mike Tyson	.08	.03	.01
☐ 63 Mario Soto	.08	.03	.01
☐ 64 Lynn Jones	.08	.03	.01
☐ 65 Terry Kennedy	.08	.03	.01
☐ 66 Astros TL	.60	.20	.04
Batting: Art Howe			
Pitching: Nolan Ryan			
☐ 67 Rich Gale	.08	.03	.01
☐ 68 Roy Howell	.08	.03	.01
☐ 69 Al Williams	.08	.03	.01
☐ 70 Tim Raines	2.00	.80	.20
☐ 71 Roy Lee Jackson	.08	.03	.01
☐ 72 Rick Auerbach	.08	.03	.01
☐ 73 Buddy Solomon	.08	.03	.01
☐ 74 Bob Clark	.08	.03	.01
☐ 75 Tommy John	.30	.12	.03
☐ 76 Greg Pryor	.08	.03	.01
☐ 77 Miguel Dilone	.08	.03	.01
☐ 78 George Medich	.08	.03	.01
☐ 79 Bob Bailor	.08	.03	.01
☐ 80 Jim Palmer	1.50	.60	.15
☐ 81 SA: Jim Palmer	.75	.30	.07
☐ 82 Bob Welch	.50	.20	.05
☐ 83 Yankees Rookies	.15	.06	.01
Steve Balboni			
Andy McGaffigan			
Andre Robertson			
☐ 84 Rennie Stennett	.08	.03	.01

☐ 85 Lynn McGlothen	.08	.03	.01
☐ 86 Dane Iorg	.08	.03	.01
☐ 87 Matt Keough	.08	.03	.01
☐ 88 Biff Pocoroba	.08	.03	.01
☐ 89 Steve Henderson	.08	.03	.01
☐ 90 Nolan Ryan	7.50	3.25	.75
☐ 91 Carney Lansford	.25	.10	.02
☐ 92 Brad Havens	.08	.03	.01
☐ 93 Larry Hisle	.08	.03	.01
☐ 94 Andy Hassler	.08	.03	.01
☐ 95 Ozzie Smith	2.25	.90	.22
☐ 96 Royals TL	.30	.10	.02
Batting: George Brett			
Pitching: Larry Gura			
☐ 97 Paul Moskau	.08	.03	.01
☐ 98 Terry Bulling	.08	.03	.01
☐ 99 Barry Bonnell	.08	.03	.01
☐ 100 Mike Schmidt	3.50	1.50	.35
☐ 101 SA: Mike Schmidt	1.50	.60	.15
☐ 102 Dan Briggs	.08	.03	.01
☐ 103 Bob Lacey	.08	.03	.01
☐ 104 Rance Mulliniks	.08	.03	.01
☐ 105 Kirk Gibson	1.25	.50	.12
☐ 106 Enrique Romo	.08	.03	.01
☐ 107 Wayne Krenchicki	.08	.03	.01
☐ 108 Bob Sykes	.08	.03	.01
☐ 109 Dave Revering	.08	.03	.01
☐ 110 Carlton Fisk	1.75	.70	.17
☐ 111 SA: Carlton Fisk	.90	.40	.09
☐ 112 Billy Sample	.08	.03	.01
☐ 113 Steve McCatty	.08	.03	.01
☐ 114 Ken Landreaux	.08	.03	.01
☐ 115 Gaylord Perry	.60	.25	.06
☐ 116 Jim Wohlford	.08	.03	.01
☐ 117 Rawly Eastwick	.08	.03	.01
☐ 118 Expos Rookies	.50	.20	.05
Terry Francona			
Brad Mills			
Bryn Smith			
☐ 119 Joe Pittman	.08	.03	.01
☐ 120 Gary Lucas	.08	.03	.01
☐ 121 Ed Lynch	.08	.03	.01
☐ 122 Jamie Easterly UER	.08	.03	.01
(photo actually			
Reggie Cleveland)			
☐ 123 Danny Goodwin	.08	.03	.01
☐ 124 Reid Nichols	.08	.03	.01
☐ 125 Danny Ainge	.75	.30	.07
☐ 126 Braves TL	.20	.05	.01
Batting: C.Washington			
Pitching: Rick Mahler			
☐ 127 Lonnie Smith	.30	.12	.03
☐ 128 Frank Pastore	.08	.03	.01
☐ 129 Checklist 1-132	.15	.02	.00
☐ 130 Julio Cruz	.08	.03	.01
☐ 131 Stan Bahnsen	.08	.03	.01
☐ 132 Lee May	.08	.03	.01
☐ 133 Pat Underwood	.08	.03	.01
☐ 134 Dan Ford	.08	.03	.01
☐ 135 Andy Rincon	.08	.03	.01
☐ 136 Lenn Sakata	.08	.03	.01
☐ 137 George Cappuzzello	.08	.03	.01
☐ 138 Tony Pena	.30	.12	.03
☐ 139 Jeff Jones	.08	.03	.01
☐ 140 Ron LeFlore	.08	.03	.01
☐ 141 Indians Rookies	1.00	.40	.10
Chris Bando			
Tom Brennan			
Von Hayes			
☐ 142 Dave LaRoche	.08	.03	.01
☐ 143 Mookie Wilson	.20	.08	.02
☐ 144 Fred Breining	.08	.03	.01
☐ 145 Bob Horner	.15	.06	.01
☐ 146 Mike Griffin	.08	.03	.01
☐ 147 Denny Walling	.08	.03	.01
☐ 148 Mickey Klutts	.08	.03	.01
☐ 149 Pat Putnam	.08	.03	.01
☐ 150 Ted Simmons	.20	.08	.02
☐ 151 Dave Edwards	.08	.03	.01
☐ 152 Ramon Aviles	.08	.03	.01
☐ 153 Roger Erickson	.08	.03	.01
☐ 154 Dennis Werth	.08	.03	.01
☐ 155 Otto Velez	.08	.03	.01
☐ 156 Oakland A's TL	.75	.25	.05
Batting: R.Henderson			
Pitching: S. McCatty			
☐ 157 Steve Crawford	.08	.03	.01
☐ 158 Brian Downing	.15	.06	.01
☐ 159 Larry Biittner	.08	.03	.01
☐ 160 Luis Tiant	.15	.06	.01
☐ 161 Batting Leaders	.15	.06	.01
Bill Madlock			
Carney Lansford			
☐ 162 Home Run Leaders	.35	.15	.03
Mike Schmidt			
Tony Armas			
Dwight Evans			
Bobby Grich			
Eddie Murray			
☐ 163 RBI Leaders	.60	.25	.06
Mike Schmidt			
Eddie Murray			
☐ 164 Stolen Base Leaders	1.50	.60	.15
Tim Raines			
Rickey Henderson			
☐ 165 Victory Leaders	.20	.08	.02
Tom Seaver			
Denny Martinez			
Steve McCatty			
Jack Morris			
Pete Vuckovich			
☐ 166 Strikeout Leaders	.15	.06	.01
Fernando Valenzuela			
Len Barker			
☐ 167 ERA Leaders	.90	.40	.09
Nolan Ryan			

	Steve McCatty			
☐ 168	Leading Firemen	.20	.08	.02
	Bruce Sutter			
	Rollie Fingers			
☐ 169	Charlie Leibrandt	.15	.06	.01
☐ 170	Jim Bibby	.08	.03	.01
☐ 171	Giants Rookies	2.50	1.00	.25
	Bob Brenly			
	Chili Davis			
	Bob Tufts			
☐ 172	Bill Gullickson	.20	.08	.02
☐ 173	Jamie Quirk	.08	.03	.01
☐ 174	Dave Ford	.08	.03	.01
☐ 175	Jerry Mumphrey	.08	.03	.01
☐ 176	Dewey Robinson	.08	.03	.01
☐ 177	John Ellis	.08	.03	.01
☐ 178	Dyar Miller	.08	.03	.01
☐ 179	Steve Garvey	.90	.40	.09
☐ 180	SA: Steve Garvey	.45	.18	.04
☐ 181	Silvio Martinez	.08	.03	.01
☐ 182	Larry Herndon	.08	.03	.01
☐ 183	Mike Proly	.08	.03	.01
☐ 184	Mick Kelleher	.08	.03	.01
☐ 185	Phil Niekro	.60	.25	.06
☐ 186	Cardinals TL	.20	.05	.01
	Batting: K. Hernandez			
	Pitching: Bob Forsch			
☐ 187	Jeff Newman	.08	.03	.01
☐ 188	Randy Martz	.08	.03	.01
☐ 189	Glenn Hoffman	.08	.03	.01
☐ 190	J.R. Richard	.15	.06	.01
☐ 191	Tim Wallach	1.75	.70	.17
☐ 192	Broderick Perkins	.08	.03	.01
☐ 193	Darrell Jackson	.08	.03	.01
☐ 194	Mike Vail	.08	.03	.01
☐ 195	Paul Molitor	.75	.30	.07
☐ 196	Willie Upshaw	.08	.03	.01
☐ 197	Shane Rawley	.08	.03	.01
☐ 198	Chris Speier	.08	.03	.01
☐ 199	Don Aase	.08	.03	.01
☐ 200	George Brett	2.75	1.10	.27
☐ 201	SA: George Brett	1.25	.50	.12
☐ 202	Rick Manning	.08	.03	.01
☐ 203	Blue Jays Rookies	1.75	.70	.17
	Jesse Barfield			
	Brian Milner			
	Boomer Wells			
☐ 204	Gary Roenicke	.08	.03	.01
☐ 205	Neil Allen	.08	.03	.01
☐ 206	Tony Bernazard	.08	.03	.01
☐ 207	Rod Scurry	.08	.03	.01
☐ 208	Bobby Murcer	.15	.06	.01
☐ 209	Gary Lavelle	.08	.03	.01
☐ 210	Keith Hernandez	.40	.16	.04
☐ 211	Dan Petry	.08	.03	.01
☐ 212	Mario Mendoza	.08	.03	.01
☐ 213	Dave Stewart	7.50	3.25	.75
☐ 214	Brian Asselstine	.08	.03	.01
☐ 215	Mike Krukow	.08	.03	.01
☐ 216	White Sox TL	.20	.05	.01
	Batting: Chet Lemon			
	Pitching: Dennis Lamp			
☐ 217	Bo McLaughlin	.08	.03	.01
☐ 218	Dave Roberts	.08	.03	.01
☐ 219	John Curtis	.08	.03	.01
☐ 220	Manny Trillo	.08	.03	.01
☐ 221	Jim Slaton	.08	.03	.01
☐ 222	Butch Wynegar	.08	.03	.01
☐ 223	Lloyd Moseby	.15	.06	.01
☐ 224	Bruce Bochte	.08	.03	.01
☐ 225	Mike Torrez	.08	.03	.01
☐ 226	Checklist 133-264	.15	.02	.00
☐ 227	Ray Burris	.08	.03	.01
☐ 228	Sam Mejias	.08	.03	.01
☐ 229	Geoff Zahn	.08	.03	.01
☐ 230	Willie Wilson	.20	.08	.02
☐ 231	Phillies Rookies	.40	.16	.04
	Mark Davis			
	Bob Dernier			
	Ozzie Virgil			
☐ 232	Terry Crowley	.08	.03	.01
☐ 233	Duane Kuiper	.08	.03	.01
☐ 234	Ron Hodges	.08	.03	.01
☐ 235	Mike Easler	.08	.03	.01
☐ 236	John Martin	.08	.03	.01
☐ 237	Rusty Kuntz	.08	.03	.01
☐ 238	Kevin Saucier	.08	.03	.01
☐ 239	Jon Matlack	.08	.03	.01
☐ 240	Bucky Dent	.15	.06	.01
☐ 241	SA: Bucky Dent	.08	.03	.01
☐ 242	Milt May	.08	.03	.01
☐ 243	Bob Owchinko	.08	.03	.01
☐ 244	Rufino Linares	.08	.03	.01
☐ 245	Ken Reitz	.08	.03	.01
☐ 246	New York Mets TL	.20	.05	.01
	Batting: Hubie Brooks			
	Pitching: Mike Scott			
☐ 247	Pedro Guerrero	.60	.25	.06
☐ 248	Frank LaCorte	.08	.03	.01
☐ 249	Tim Flannery	.08	.03	.01
☐ 250	Tug McGraw	.15	.06	.01
☐ 251	Fred Lynn	.30	.12	.03
☐ 252	SA: Fred Lynn	.15	.06	.01
☐ 253	Chuck Baker	.08	.03	.01
☐ 254	Jorge Bell	11.00	5.00	1.35
☐ 255	Tony Perez	.45	.18	.04
☐ 256	SA: Tony Perez	.20	.08	.02
☐ 257	Larry Harlow	.08	.03	.01
☐ 258	Bo Diaz	.08	.03	.01
☐ 259	Rodney Scott	.08	.03	.01
☐ 260	Bruce Sutter	.20	.08	.02
☐ 261	Tigers Rookies UER	.15	.06	.01
	Howard Bailey			
	Marty Castillo			
	Dave Rucker			
	(Rucker photo act-			

ally Roger Weaver)

☐ 262 Doug Bair	.08	.03	.01
☐ 263 Victor Cruz	.08	.03	.01
☐ 264 Dan Quisenberry	.25	.10	.02
☐ 265 Al Bumbry	.08	.03	.01
☐ 266 Rick Leach	.08	.03	.01
☐ 267 Kurt Bevacqua	.08	.03	.01
☐ 268 Rickey Keeton	.08	.03	.01
☐ 269 Jim Essian	.15	.06	.01
☐ 270 Rusty Staub	.20	.08	.02
☐ 271 Larry Bradford	.08	.03	.01
☐ 272 Bump Wills	.08	.03	.01
☐ 273 Doug Bird	.08	.03	.01
☐ 274 Bob Ojeda	.75	.30	.07
☐ 275 Bob Watson	.08	.03	.01
☐ 276 Angels TL	.25	.07	.02
Batting: Rod Carew			
Pitching: Ken Forsch			
☐ 277 Terry Puhl	.08	.03	.01
☐ 278 John Littlefield	.08	.03	.01
☐ 279 Bill Russell	.15	.06	.01
☐ 280 Ben Oglivie	.08	.03	.01
☐ 281 John Verhoeven	.08	.03	.01
☐ 282 Ken Macha	.08	.03	.01
☐ 283 Brian Allard	.08	.03	.01
☐ 284 Bob Grich	.15	.06	.01
☐ 285 Sparky Lyle	.15	.06	.01
☐ 286 Bill Fahey	.08	.03	.01
☐ 287 Alan Bannister	.08	.03	.01
☐ 288 Garry Templeton	.15	.06	.01
☐ 289 Bob Stanley	.08	.03	.01
☐ 290 Ken Singleton	.15	.06	.01
☐ 291 Pirates Rookies	.30	.12	.03
Vance Law			
Bob Long			
Johnny Ray			
☐ 292 David Palmer	.08	.03	.01
☐ 293 Rob Picciolo	.08	.03	.01
☐ 294 Mike LaCoss	.08	.03	.01
☐ 295 Jason Thompson	.08	.03	.01
☐ 296 Bob Walk	.08	.03	.01
☐ 297 Clint Hurdle	.08	.03	.01
☐ 298 Danny Darwin	.08	.03	.01
☐ 299 Steve Trout	.08	.03	.01
☐ 300 Reggie Jackson	2.50	1.00	.25
☐ 301 SA: Reggie Jackson	1.25	.50	.12
☐ 302 Doug Flynn	.08	.03	.01
☐ 303 Bill Caudill	.08	.03	.01
☐ 304 Johnnie LeMaster	.08	.03	.01
☐ 305 Don Sutton	.60	.25	.06
☐ 306 SA: Don Sutton	.30	.12	.03
☐ 307 Randy Bass	.08	.03	.01
☐ 308 Charlie Moore	.08	.03	.01
☐ 309 Pete Redfern	.08	.03	.01
☐ 310 Mike Hargrove	.15	.06	.01
☐ 311 Dodgers TL	.20	.05	.01
Batting: Dusty Baker			
Pitching: Burt Hooton			
☐ 312 Lenny Randle	.08	.03	.01
☐ 313 John Harris	.08	.03	.01
☐ 314 Buck Martinez	.08	.03	.01
☐ 315 Burt Hooton	.08	.03	.01
☐ 316 Steve Braun	.08	.03	.01
☐ 317 Dick Ruthven	.08	.03	.01
☐ 318 Mike Heath	.08	.03	.01
☐ 319 Dave Rozema	.08	.03	.01
☐ 320 Chris Chambliss	.15	.06	.01
☐ 321 SA: Chris Chambliss	.08	.03	.01
☐ 322 Garry Hancock	.08	.03	.01
☐ 323 Bill Lee	.08	.03	.01
☐ 324 Steve Dillard	.08	.03	.01
☐ 325 Jose Cruz	.15	.06	.01
☐ 326 Pete Falcone	.08	.03	.01
☐ 327 Joe Nolan	.08	.03	.01
☐ 328 Ed Farmer	.08	.03	.01
☐ 329 U.L. Washington	.08	.03	.01
☐ 330 Rick Wise	.08	.03	.01
☐ 331 Benny Ayala	.08	.03	.01
☐ 332 Don Robinson	.08	.03	.01
☐ 333 Brewers Rookies	.15	.06	.01
Frank DiPino			
Marshall Edwards			
Chuck Porter			
☐ 334 Aurelio Rodriguez	.08	.03	.01
☐ 335 Jim Sundberg	.08	.03	.01
☐ 336 Mariners TL	.15	.05	.01
Batting: Tom Paciorek			
Pitching: Glenn Abbott			
☐ 337 Pete Rose AS	.75	.30	.07
☐ 338 Dave Lopes AS	.08	.03	.01
☐ 339 Mike Schmidt AS	.90	.40	.09
☐ 340 Dave Concepcion AS	.15	.06	.01
☐ 341 Andre Dawson AS	.50	.20	.05
☐ 342A George Foster AS	.20	.08	.02
(with autograph)			
☐ 342B George Foster AS	1.50	.60	.15
(w/o autograph)			
☐ 343 Dave Parker AS	.25	.10	.02
☐ 344 Gary Carter AS	.25	.10	.02
☐ 345 Fern. Valenzuela AS	.15	.06	.01
☐ 346A Tom Seaver AS ERR	1.00	.40	.10
("t ed")			
☐ 346B Tom Seaver AS COR	.50	.20	.05
("tied")			
☐ 347 Bruce Sutter AS	.15	.06	.01
☐ 348 Derrel Thomas	.08	.03	.01
☐ 349 George Frazier	.08	.03	.01
☐ 350 Thad Bosley	.08	.03	.01
☐ 351 Reds Rookies	.15	.06	.01
Scott Brown			
Geoff Coumbe			
Paul Householder			
☐ 352 Dick Davis	.08	.03	.01
☐ 353 Jack O'Connor	.08	.03	.01
☐ 354 Roberto Ramos	.08	.03	.01
☐ 355 Dwight Evans	.35	.15	.03

☐ 356	Denny Lewallyn	.08	.03	.01
☐ 357	Butch Hobson	.15	.06	.01
☐ 358	Mike Parrott	.08	.03	.01
☐ 359	Jim Dwyer	.08	.03	.01
☐ 360	Len Barker	.08	.03	.01
☐ 361	Rafael Landestoy	.08	.03	.01
☐ 362	Jim Wright UER	.08	.03	.01
	(wrong Jim Wright pictured)			
☐ 363	Bob Molinaro	.08	.03	.01
☐ 364	Doyle Alexander	.08	.03	.01
☐ 365	Bill Madlock	.15	.06	.01
☐ 366	Padres TL	.15	.05	.01
	Batting: Luis Salazar			
	Pitching: Eichelberger			
☐ 367	Jim Kaat	.20	.08	.02
☐ 368	Alex Trevino	.08	.03	.01
☐ 369	Champ Summers	.08	.03	.01
☐ 370	Mike Norris	.08	.03	.01
☐ 371	Jerry Don Gleaton	.08	.03	.01
☐ 372	Luis Gomez	.08	.03	.01
☐ 373	Gene Nelson	.15	.06	.01
☐ 374	Tim Blackwell	.08	.03	.01
☐ 375	Dusty Baker	.15	.06	.01
☐ 376	Chris Welsh	.08	.03	.01
☐ 377	Kiko Garcia	.08	.03	.01
☐ 378	Mike Caldwell	.08	.03	.01
☐ 379	Rob Wilfong	.08	.03	.01
☐ 380	Dave Stieb	.60	.25	.06
☐ 381	Red Sox Rookies	.60	.25	.06
	Bruce Hurst			
	Dave Schmidt			
	Julio Valdez			
☐ 382	Joe Simpson	.08	.03	.01
☐ 383A	Pascual Perez ERR	30.00	13.50	4.50
	(no position on front)			
☐ 383B	Pascual Perez COR	.15	.06	.01
☐ 384	Keith Moreland	.08	.03	.01
☐ 385	Ken Forsch	.08	.03	.01
☐ 386	Jerry White	.08	.03	.01
☐ 387	Tom Veryzer	.08	.03	.01
☐ 388	Joe Rudi	.15	.06	.01
☐ 389	George Vukovich	.08	.03	.01
☐ 390	Eddie Murray	2.25	.90	.22
☐ 391	Dave Tobik	.08	.03	.01
☐ 392	Rick Bosetti	.08	.03	.01
☐ 393	Al Hrabosky	.08	.03	.01
☐ 394	Checklist 265-396	.15	.02	.00
☐ 395	Omar Moreno	.08	.03	.01
☐ 396	Twins TL	.15	.05	.01
	Batting: John Castino			
	Pitching: F. Arroyo			
☐ 397	Ken Brett	.08	.03	.01
☐ 398	Mike Squires	.08	.03	.01
☐ 399	Pat Zachry	.08	.03	.01
☐ 400	Johnny Bench	1.75	.70	.17
☐ 401	SA: Johnny Bench	.80	.35	.08
☐ 402	Bill Stein	.08	.03	.01
☐ 403	Jim Tracy	.08	.03	.01
☐ 404	Dickie Thon	.15	.06	.01
☐ 405	Rick Reuschel	.15	.06	.01
☐ 406	Al Holland	.08	.03	.01
☐ 407	Danny Boone	.08	.03	.01
☐ 408	Ed Romero	.08	.03	.01
☐ 409	Don Cooper	.08	.03	.01
☐ 410	Ron Cey	.15	.06	.01
☐ 411	SA: Ron Cey	.08	.03	.01
☐ 412	Luis Leal	.08	.03	.01
☐ 413	Dan Meyer	.08	.03	.01
☐ 414	Elias Sosa	.08	.03	.01
☐ 415	Don Baylor	.15	.06	.01
☐ 416	Marty Bystrom	.08	.03	.01
☐ 417	Pat Kelly	.08	.03	.01
☐ 418	Rangers Rookies	.20	.08	.02
	John Butcher			
	Bobby Johnson			
	Dave Schmidt			
☐ 419	Steve Stone	.08	.03	.01
☐ 420	George Hendrick	.08	.03	.01
☐ 421	Mark Clear	.08	.03	.01
☐ 422	Cliff Johnson	.08	.03	.01
☐ 423	Stan Papi	.08	.03	.01
☐ 424	Bruce Benedict	.08	.03	.01
☐ 425	John Candelaria	.08	.03	.01
☐ 426	Orioles TL	.25	.07	.02
	Batting: Eddie Murray			
	Pitching: Sam Stewart			
☐ 427	Ron Oester	.08	.03	.01
☐ 428	LaMarr Hoyt	.08	.03	.01
☐ 429	John Wathan	.08	.03	.01
☐ 430	Vida Blue	.15	.06	.01
☐ 431	SA: Vida Blue	.08	.03	.01
☐ 432	Mike Scott	.40	.16	.04
☐ 433	Alan Ashby	.08	.03	.01
☐ 434	Joe Lefebvre	.08	.03	.01
☐ 435	Robin Yount	2.75	1.10	.27
☐ 436	Joe Strain	.08	.03	.01
☐ 437	Juan Berenguer	.08	.03	.01
☐ 438	Pete Mackanin	.08	.03	.01
☐ 439	Dave Righetti	2.00	.80	.20
☐ 440	Jeff Burroughs	.08	.03	.01
☐ 441	Astros Rookies	.15	.06	.01
	Danny Heep			
	Billy Smith			
	Bobby Sprowl			
☐ 442	Bruce Kison	.08	.03	.01
☐ 443	Mark Wagner	.08	.03	.01
☐ 444	Terry Forster	.15	.06	.01
☐ 445	Larry Parrish	.08	.03	.01
☐ 446	Wayne Garland	.08	.03	.01
☐ 447	Darrell Porter	.08	.03	.01
☐ 448	SA: Darrell Porter	.08	.03	.01
☐ 449	Luis Aguayo	.08	.03	.01
☐ 450	Jack Morris	1.00	.40	.10
☐ 451	Ed Miller	.08	.03	.01

☐ 452 Lee Smith 4.50 2.00 .45
☐ 453 Art Howe .15 .06 .01
☐ 454 Rick Langford .08 .03 .01
☐ 455 Tom Burgmeier .08 .03 .01
☐ 456 Chicago Cubs TL .15 .05 .01
Batting: Bill Buckner
Pitching: Randy Martz
☐ 457 Tim Stoddard .08 .03 .01
☐ 458 Willie Montanez .08 .03 .01
☐ 459 Bruce Berenyi .08 .03 .01
☐ 460 Jack Clark .40 .16 .04
☐ 461 Rich Dotson .08 .03 .01
☐ 462 Dave Chalk .08 .03 .01
☐ 463 Jim Kern .08 .03 .01
☐ 464 Juan Bonilla .08 .03 .01
☐ 465 Lee Mazzilli .08 .03 .01
☐ 466 Randy Lerch .08 .03 .01
☐ 467 Mickey Hatcher .08 .03 .01
☐ 468 Floyd Bannister .08 .03 .01
☐ 469 Ed Ott .08 .03 .01
☐ 470 John Mayberry .15 .06 .01
☐ 471 Royals Rookies .15 .06 .01
Atlee Hammaker
Mike Jones
Darryl Motley
☐ 472 Oscar Gamble .08 .03 .01
☐ 473 Mike Stanton .08 .03 .01
☐ 474 Ken Oberkfell .08 .03 .01
☐ 475 Alan Trammell 1.00 .40 .10
☐ 476 Brian Kingman .08 .03 .01
☐ 477 Steve Yeager .08 .03 .01
☐ 478 Ray Searage .08 .03 .01
☐ 479 Rowland Office .08 .03 .01
☐ 480 Steve Carlton 1.50 .60 .15
☐ 481 SA: Steve Carlton .75 .30 .07
☐ 482 Glenn Hubbard .08 .03 .01
☐ 483 Gary Woods .08 .03 .01
☐ 484 Ivan DeJesus .08 .03 .01
☐ 485 Kent Tekulve .08 .03 .01
☐ 486 Yankees TL .20 .05 .01
Batting: J. Mumphrey
Pitching: Tommy John
☐ 487 Bob McClure .08 .03 .01
☐ 488 Ron Jackson .08 .03 .01
☐ 489 Rick Dempsey .08 .03 .01
☐ 490 Dennis Eckersley .75 .30 .07
☐ 491 Checklist 397-528 .15 .02 .00
☐ 492 Joe Price .08 .03 .01
☐ 493 Chet Lemon .08 .03 .01
☐ 494 Hubie Brooks .60 .25 .06
☐ 495 Dennis Leonard .08 .03 .01
☐ 496 Johnny Grubb .08 .03 .01
☐ 497 Jim Anderson .08 .03 .01
☐ 498 Dave Bergman .08 .03 .01
☐ 499 Paul Mirabella .08 .03 .01
☐ 500 Rod Carew 1.75 .70 .17
☐ 501 SA: Rod Carew .80 .35 .08
☐ 502 Braves Rookies 2.50 1.00 .25
Steve Bedrosian UER
(photo actually
Larry Owen)
Brett Butler
Larry Owen
☐ 503 Julio Gonzalez .08 .03 .01
☐ 504 Rick Peters .08 .03 .01
☐ 505 Graig Nettles .20 .08 .02
☐ 506 SA: Graig Nettles .15 .06 .01
☐ 507 Terry Harper .08 .03 .01
☐ 508 Jody Davis .20 .08 .02
☐ 509 Harry Spilman .08 .03 .01
☐ 510 Fernando Valenzuela .60 .25 .06
☐ 511 Ruppert Jones .08 .03 .01
☐ 512 Jerry Dybzinski .08 .03 .01
☐ 513 Rick Rhoden .08 .03 .01
☐ 514 Joe Ferguson .08 .03 .01
☐ 515 Larry Bowa .15 .06 .01
☐ 516 SA: Larry Bowa .08 .03 .01
☐ 517 Mark Brouhard .08 .03 .01
☐ 518 Garth Iorg .08 .03 .01
☐ 519 Glenn Adams .08 .03 .01
☐ 520 Mike Flanagan .15 .06 .01
☐ 521 Bill Almon .08 .03 .01
☐ 522 Chuck Rainey .08 .03 .01
☐ 523 Gary Gray .08 .03 .01
☐ 524 Tom Hausman .08 .03 .01
☐ 525 Ray Knight .15 .06 .01
☐ 526 Expos TL .15 .05 .01
Batting: W.Cromartie
Pitching: B.Gullickson
☐ 527 John Henry Johnson .08 .03 .01
☐ 528 Matt Alexander .08 .03 .01
☐ 529 Allen Ripley .08 .03 .01
☐ 530 Dickie Noles .08 .03 .01
☐ 531 A's Rookies .08 .03 .01
Rich Bordi
Mark Budaska
Kelvin Moore
☐ 532 Toby Harrah .08 .03 .01
☐ 533 Joaquin Andujar .15 .06 .01
☐ 534 Dave McKay .08 .03 .01
☐ 535 Lance Parrish .50 .20 .05
☐ 536 Rafael Ramirez .08 .03 .01
☐ 537 Doug Capilla .08 .03 .01
☐ 538 Lou Piniella .15 .06 .01
☐ 539 Vern Ruhle .08 .03 .01
☐ 540 Andre Dawson 2.00 .80 .20
☐ 541 Barry Evans .08 .03 .01
☐ 542 Ned Yost .08 .03 .01
☐ 543 Bill Robinson .15 .06 .01
☐ 544 Larry Christenson .08 .03 .01
☐ 545 Reggie Smith .15 .06 .01
☐ 546 SA: Reggie Smith .08 .03 .01
☐ 547 Rod Carew AS .50 .20 .05
☐ 548 Willie Randolph AS .08 .03 .01
☐ 549 George Brett AS .65 .25 .06
☐ 550 Bucky Dent AS .08 .03 .01

- ☐ 551 Reggie Jackson AS .... .65 .25 .06
- ☐ 552 Ken Singleton AS .... .08 .03 .01
- ☐ 553 Dave Winfield AS .... .40 .16 .04
- ☐ 554 Carlton Fisk AS .... .50 .20 .05
- ☐ 555 Scott McGregor AS .... .08 .03 .01
- ☐ 556 Jack Morris AS .... .30 .12 .03
- ☐ 557 Rich Gossage AS .... .15 .06 .01
- ☐ 558 John Tudor .... .15 .06 .01
- ☐ 559 Indians TL .... .15 .05 .01
  Batting: Mike Hargrove
  Pitching: Bert Blyleven
- ☐ 560 Doug Corbett .... .08 .03 .01
- ☐ 561 Cardinals Rookies .... .15 .06 .01
  Glenn Brummer
  Luis DeLeon
  Gene Roof
- ☐ 562 Mike O'Berry .... .08 .03 .01
- ☐ 563 Ross Baumgarten .... .08 .03 .01
- ☐ 564 Doug DeCinces .... .08 .03 .01
- ☐ 565 Jackson Todd .... .08 .03 .01
- ☐ 566 Mike Jorgensen .... .08 .03 .01
- ☐ 567 Bob Babcock .... .08 .03 .01
- ☐ 568 Joe Pettini .... .08 .03 .01
- ☐ 569 Willie Randolph .... .15 .06 .01
- ☐ 570 SA: Willie Randolph .... .08 .03 .01
- ☐ 571 Glenn Abbott .... .08 .03 .01
- ☐ 572 Juan Beniquez .... .08 .03 .01
- ☐ 573 Rick Waits .... .08 .03 .01
- ☐ 574 Mike Ramsey .... .08 .03 .01
- ☐ 575 Al Cowens .... .08 .03 .01
- ☐ 576 Giants TL .... .15 .05 .01
  Batting: Milt May
  Pitching: Vida Blue
- ☐ 577 Rick Monday .... .08 .03 .01
- ☐ 578 Shooty Babitt .... .08 .03 .01
- ☐ 579 Rick Mahler .... .25 .10 .02
- ☐ 580 Bobby Bonds .... .15 .06 .01
- ☐ 581 Ron Reed .... .08 .03 .01
- ☐ 582 Luis Pujols .... .08 .03 .01
- ☐ 583 Tippy Martinez .... .08 .03 .01
- ☐ 584 Hosken Powell .... .08 .03 .01
- ☐ 585 Rollie Fingers .... .75 .30 .07
- ☐ 586 SA: Rollie Fingers .... .35 .15 .03
- ☐ 587 Tim Lollar .... .08 .03 .01
- ☐ 588 Dale Berra .... .08 .03 .01
- ☐ 589 Dave Stapleton .... .08 .03 .01
- ☐ 590 Al Oliver .... .15 .06 .01
- ☐ 591 SA: Al Oliver .... .08 .03 .01
- ☐ 592 Craig Swan .... .08 .03 .01
- ☐ 593 Billy Smith .... .08 .03 .01
- ☐ 594 Renie Martin .... .08 .03 .01
- ☐ 595 Dave Collins .... .08 .03 .01
- ☐ 596 Damaso Garcia .... .08 .03 .01
- ☐ 597 Wayne Nordhagen .... .08 .03 .01
- ☐ 598 Bob Galasso .... .08 .03 .01
- ☐ 599 White Sox Rookies .... .08 .03 .01
  Jay Loviglio
  Reggie Patterson
  Leo Sutherland
- ☐ 600 Dave Winfield .... 1.50 .60 .15
- ☐ 601 Sid Monge .... .08 .03 .01
- ☐ 602 Freddie Patek .... .08 .03 .01
- ☐ 603 Rich Hebner .... .08 .03 .01
- ☐ 604 Orlando Sanchez .... .08 .03 .01
- ☐ 605 Steve Rogers .... .08 .03 .01
- ☐ 606 Blue Jays TL .... .15 .05 .01
  Batting: J.Mayberry
  Pitching: Dave Stieb
- ☐ 607 Leon Durham .... .08 .03 .01
- ☐ 608 Jerry Royster .... .08 .03 .01
- ☐ 609 Rick Sutcliffe .... .20 .08 .02
- ☐ 610 Rickey Henderson .... 9.00 4.00 .90
- ☐ 611 Joe Niekro .... .15 .06 .01
- ☐ 612 Gary Ward .... .08 .03 .01
- ☐ 613 Jim Gantner .... .08 .03 .01
- ☐ 614 Juan Eichelberger .... .08 .03 .01
- ☐ 615 Bob Boone .... .15 .06 .01
- ☐ 616 SA: Bob Boone .... .08 .03 .01
- ☐ 617 Scott McGregor .... .08 .03 .01
- ☐ 618 Tim Foli .... .08 .03 .01
- ☐ 619 Bill Campbell .... .08 .03 .01
- ☐ 620 Ken Griffey .... .40 .16 .04
- ☐ 621 SA: Ken Griffey .... .20 .08 .02
- ☐ 622 Dennis Lamp .... .08 .03 .01
- ☐ 623 Mets Rookies .... .50 .20 .05
  Ron Gardenhire
  Terry Leach
  Tim Leary
- ☐ 624 Fergie Jenkins .... .60 .25 .06
- ☐ 625 Hal McRae .... .15 .06 .01
- ☐ 626 Randy Jones .... .08 .03 .01
- ☐ 627 Enos Cabell .... .08 .03 .01
- ☐ 628 Bill Travers .... .08 .03 .01
- ☐ 629 John Wockenfuss .... .08 .03 .01
- ☐ 630 Joe Charboneau .... .08 .03 .01
- ☐ 631 Gene Tenace .... .15 .06 .01
- ☐ 632 Bryan Clark .... .08 .03 .01
- ☐ 633 Mitchell Page .... .08 .03 .01
- ☐ 634 Checklist 529-660 .... .15 .02 .00
- ☐ 635 Ron Davis .... .08 .03 .01
- ☐ 636 Phillies TL .... .40 .15 .03
  Batting: Pete Rose
  Pitching: S.Carlton
- ☐ 637 Rick Camp .... .08 .03 .01
- ☐ 638 John Milner .... .08 .03 .01
- ☐ 639 Ken Kravec .... .08 .03 .01
- ☐ 640 Cesar Cedeno .... .15 .06 .01
- ☐ 641 Steve Mura .... .08 .03 .01
- ☐ 642 Mike Scioscia .... .40 .16 .04
- ☐ 643 Pete Vuckovich .... .08 .03 .01
- ☐ 644 John Castino .... .08 .03 .01
- ☐ 645 Frank White .... .08 .03 .01
- ☐ 646 SA: Frank White .... .08 .03 .01
- ☐ 647 Warren Brusstar .... .08 .03 .01
- ☐ 648 Jose Morales .... .08 .03 .01
- ☐ 649 Ken Clay .... .08 .03 .01

☐ 650 Carl Yastrzemski .... 1.75 .70 .17
☐ 651 SA: Carl Yastrzemski ...... .80 .35 .08
☐ 652 Steve Nicosia .... .08 .03 .01
☐ 653 Angels Rookies .... 1.25 .50 .12
Tom Brunansky
Luis Sanchez
Daryl Sconiers
☐ 654 Jim Morrison .... .08 .03 .01
☐ 655 Joel Youngblood .... .08 .03 .01
☐ 656 Eddie Whitson .... .08 .03 .01
☐ 657 Tom Poquette .... .08 .03 .01
☐ 658 Tito Landrum .... .08 .03 .01
☐ 659 Fred Martinez .... .08 .03 .01
☐ 660 Dave Concepcion .... .20 .08 .02
☐ 661 SA: Dave Concepcion ..... .15 .06 .01
☐ 662 Luis Salazar .... .08 .03 .01
☐ 663 Hector Cruz .... .08 .03 .01
☐ 664 Dan Spillner .... .08 .03 .01
☐ 665 Jim Clancy .... .08 .03 .01
☐ 666 Tigers TL .... .15 .05 .01
Batting: Steve Kemp
Pitching: Dan Petry
☐ 667 Jeff Reardon .... 1.25 .50 .12
☐ 668 Dale Murphy .... 1.50 .60 .15
☐ 669 Larry Milbourne .... .08 .03 .01
☐ 670 Steve Kemp .... .08 .03 .01
☐ 671 Mike Davis .... .08 .03 .01
☐ 672 Bob Knepper .... .08 .03 .01
☐ 673 Keith Drumwright .... .08 .03 .01
☐ 674 Dave Goltz .... .08 .03 .01
☐ 675 Cecil Cooper .... .20 .08 .02
☐ 676 Sal Butera .... .08 .03 .01
☐ 677 Alfredo Griffin .... .08 .03 .01
☐ 678 Tom Paciorek .... .08 .03 .01
☐ 679 Sammy Stewart .... .08 .03 .01
☐ 680 Gary Matthews .... .08 .03 .01
☐ 681 Dodgers Rookies .... 5.00 2.25 .50
Mike Marshall
Ron Roenicke
Steve Sax
☐ 682 Jesse Jefferson .... .08 .03 .01
☐ 683 Phil Garner .... .15 .06 .01
☐ 684 Harold Baines .... 1.25 .50 .12
☐ 685 Bert Blyleven .... .35 .15 .03
☐ 686 Gary Allenson .... .08 .03 .01
☐ 687 Greg Minton .... .08 .03 .01
☐ 688 Leon Roberts .... .08 .03 .01
☐ 689 Lary Sorensen .... .08 .03 .01
☐ 690 Dave Kingman .... .20 .08 .02
☐ 691 Dan Schatzeder .... .08 .03 .01
☐ 692 Wayne Gross .... .08 .03 .01
☐ 693 Cesar Geronimo .... .08 .03 .01
☐ 694 Dave Wehrmeister .... .08 .03 .01
☐ 695 Warren Cromartie .... .08 .03 .01
☐ 696 Pirates TL .... .15 .05 .01
Batting: Bill Madlock
Pitching:Eddie Solomon
☐ 697 John Montefusco .... .08 .03 .01
☐ 698 Tony Scott .... .08 .03 .01
☐ 699 Dick Tidrow .... .08 .03 .01
☐ 700 George Foster .... .30 .12 .03
☐ 701 SA: George Foster .... .15 .06 .01
☐ 702 Steve Renko .... .08 .03 .01
☐ 703 Brewers TL .... .15 .05 .01
Batting: Cecil Cooper
Pitching: P.Vuckovich
☐ 704 Mickey Rivers .... .08 .03 .01
☐ 705 SA: Mickey Rivers .... .08 .03 .01
☐ 706 Barry Foote .... .08 .03 .01
☐ 707 Mark Bomback .... .08 .03 .01
☐ 708 Gene Richards .... .08 .03 .01
☐ 709 Don Money .... .08 .03 .01
☐ 710 Jerry Reuss .... .08 .03 .01
☐ 711 Mariners Rookies .... 4.00 1.75 .40
Dave Edler
Dave Henderson
Reggie Walton
☐ 712 Dennis Martinez .... .20 .08 .02
☐ 713 Del Unser .... .08 .03 .01
☐ 714 Jerry Koosman .... .15 .06 .01
☐ 715 Willie Stargell .... .75 .30 .07
☐ 716 SA: Willie Stargell .... .35 .15 .03
☐ 717 Rick Miller .... .08 .03 .01
☐ 718 Charlie Hough .... .15 .06 .01
☐ 719 Jerry Narron .... .08 .03 .01
☐ 720 Greg Luzinski .... .15 .06 .01
☐ 721 SA: Greg Luzinski .... .08 .03 .01
☐ 722 Jerry Martin .... .08 .03 .01
☐ 723 Junior Kennedy .... .08 .03 .01
☐ 724 Dave Rosello .... .08 .03 .01
☐ 725 Amos Otis .... .15 .06 .01
☐ 726 SA: Amos Otis .... .08 .03 .01
☐ 727 Sixto Lezcano .... .08 .03 .01
☐ 728 Aurelio Lopez .... .08 .03 .01
☐ 729 Jim Spencer .... .08 .03 .01
☐ 730 Gary Carter .... .80 .35 .08
☐ 731 Padres Rookies .... .08 .03 .01
Mike Armstrong
Doug Gwosdz
Fred Kuhaulua
☐ 732 Mike Lum .... .08 .03 .01
☐ 733 Larry McWilliams .... .08 .03 .01
☐ 734 Mike Ivie .... .08 .03 .01
☐ 735 Rudy May .... .08 .03 .01
☐ 736 Jerry Turner .... .08 .03 .01
☐ 737 Reggie Cleveland .... .08 .03 .01
☐ 738 Dave Engle .... .08 .03 .01
☐ 739 Joey McLaughlin .... .08 .03 .01
☐ 740 Dave Lopes .... .15 .06 .01
☐ 741 SA: Dave Lopes .... .08 .03 .01
☐ 742 Dick Drago .... .08 .03 .01
☐ 743 John Stearns .... .08 .03 .01
☐ 744 Mike Witt .... .40 .16 .04
☐ 745 Bake McBride .... .08 .03 .01
☐ 746 Andre Thornton .... .15 .06 .01
☐ 747 John Lowenstein .... .08 .03 .01

☐ 748 Marc Hill	.08	.03	.01
☐ 749 Bob Shirley	.08	.03	.01
☐ 750 Jim Rice	.40	.16	.04
☐ 751 Rick Honeycutt	.08	.03	.01
☐ 752 Lee Lacy	.08	.03	.01
☐ 753 Tom Brookens	.08	.03	.01
☐ 754 Joe Morgan	.90	.40	.09
☐ 755 SA: Joe Morgan	.40	.16	.04
☐ 756 Reds TL Batting: Ken Griffey Pitching: Tom Seaver	.30	.10	.02
☐ 757 Tom Underwood	.08	.03	.01
☐ 758 Claudell Washington	.08	.03	.01
☐ 759 Paul Splittorff	.08	.03	.01
☐ 760 Bill Buckner	.15	.06	.01
☐ 761 Dave Smith	.15	.06	.01
☐ 762 Mike Phillips	.08	.03	.01
☐ 763 Tom Hume	.08	.03	.01
☐ 764 Steve Swisher	.08	.03	.01
☐ 765 Gorman Thomas	.15	.06	.01
☐ 766 Twins Rookies Lenny Faedo Kent Hrbek Tim Laudner	4.00	1.75	.40
☐ 767 Roy Smalley	.08	.03	.01
☐ 768 Jerry Garvin	.08	.03	.01
☐ 769 Richie Zisk	.08	.03	.01
☐ 770 Rich Gossage	.25	.10	.02
☐ 771 SA: Rich Gossage	.15	.06	.01
☐ 772 Bert Campaneris	.15	.06	.01
☐ 773 John Denny	.08	.03	.01
☐ 774 Jay Johnstone	.15	.06	.01
☐ 775 Bob Forsch	.08	.03	.01
☐ 776 Mark Belanger	.15	.06	.01
☐ 777 Tom Griffin	.08	.03	.01
☐ 778 Kevin Hickey	.08	.03	.01
☐ 779 Grant Jackson	.08	.03	.01
☐ 780 Pete Rose	2.25	.90	.22
☐ 781 SA: Pete Rose	1.00	.40	.10
☐ 782 Frank Taveras	.08	.03	.01
☐ 783 Greg Harris	.25	.10	.02
☐ 784 Milt Wilcox	.08	.03	.01
☐ 785 Dan Driessen	.08	.03	.01
☐ 786 Red Sox TL Batting: C.Lansford Pitching: Mike Torrez	.15	.05	.01
☐ 787 Fred Stanley	.08	.03	.01
☐ 788 Woodie Fryman	.08	.03	.01
☐ 789 Checklist 661-792	.15	.02	.00
☐ 790 Larry Gura	.08	.03	.01
☐ 791 Bobby Brown	.08	.03	.01
☐ 792 Frank Tanana	.20	.08	.02

1982 Topps Traded

The cards in this 132-card set measure 2 1/2" by 3 1/2". The 1982 Topps Traded or extended series is distinguished by a "T" printed after the number (located on the reverse). This was the first time Topps began a new tradition of newly numbering (and alphabetizing) their traded series from 1T to 132T. Of the total cards, 70 players represent the American League and 61 represent the National League, with the remaining card a numbered checklist (132T). The Cubs lead the pack with 12 changes, while the Red Sox are the only team in either league to have no new additions. All 131 player photos used in the set are completely new. Of this total, 112 individuals are seen in the uniform of their new team, 11 others have been elevated to single card status from "Future Stars" cards, and eight more are entirely new to the 1982 Topps lineup. The backs are almost completely red in color with black print. There are no key rookie cards in this set. Although the Cal Ripken card is this set's most valuable card, it is not his Rookie Card since he had already been included in the 1982 regular set, albeit on a multi-player card.

	MINT	EXC	G-VG
COMPLETE SET (132)	190.00	80.00	20.00
COMMON PLAYER (1-132)	.15	.06	.01

☐ 1T Doyle Alexander	.25	.10	.02
☐ 2T Jesse Barfield	2.50	1.00	.25
☐ 3T Ross Baumgarten	.15	.06	.01
☐ 4T Steve Bedrosian	.60	.25	.06
☐ 5T Mark Belanger	.25	.10	.02
☐ 6T Kurt Bevacqua	.15	.06	.01
☐ 7T Tim Blackwell	.15	.06	.01
☐ 8T Vida Blue	.25	.10	.02

☐ 9T Bob Boone	.35	.15	.03
☐ 10T Larry Bowa	.25	.10	.02
☐ 11T Dan Briggs	.15	.06	.01
☐ 12T Bobby Brown	.15	.06	.01
☐ 13T Tom Brunansky	2.50	1.00	.25
☐ 14T Jeff Burroughs	.25	.10	.02
☐ 15T Enos Cabell	.15	.06	.01
☐ 16T Bill Campbell	.15	.06	.01
☐ 17T Bobby Castillo	.15	.06	.01
☐ 18T Bill Caudill	.15	.06	.01
☐ 19T Cesar Cedeno	.25	.10	.02
☐ 20T Dave Collins	.15	.06	.01
☐ 21T Doug Corbett	.15	.06	.01
☐ 22T Al Cowens	.15	.06	.01
☐ 23T Chili Davis	3.50	1.50	.35
☐ 24T Dick Davis	.15	.06	.01
☐ 25T Ron Davis	.15	.06	.01
☐ 26T Doug DeCinces	.25	.10	.02
☐ 27T Ivan DeJesus	.15	.06	.01
☐ 28T Bob Dernier	.25	.10	.02
☐ 29T Bo Diaz	.15	.06	.01
☐ 30T Roger Erickson	.15	.06	.01
☐ 31T Jim Essian	.25	.10	.02
☐ 32T Ed Farmer	.15	.06	.01
☐ 33T Doug Flynn	.15	.06	.01
☐ 34T Tim Foli	.15	.06	.01
☐ 35T Dan Ford	.15	.06	.01
☐ 36T George Foster	.60	.25	.06
☐ 37T Dave Frost	.15	.06	.01
☐ 38T Rich Gale	.15	.06	.01
☐ 39T Ron Gardenhire	.15	.06	.01
☐ 40T Ken Griffey	.75	.30	.07
☐ 41T Greg Harris	.35	.15	.03
☐ 42T Von Hayes	1.50	.60	.15
☐ 43T Larry Herndon	.15	.06	.01
☐ 44T Kent Hrbek	5.00	2.25	.50
☐ 45T Mike Ivie	.15	.06	.01
☐ 46T Grant Jackson	.15	.06	.01
☐ 47T Reggie Jackson	7.50	3.25	.75
☐ 48T Ron Jackson	.15	.06	.01
☐ 49T Fergie Jenkins	1.50	.60	.15
☐ 50T Lamar Johnson	.15	.06	.01
☐ 51T Randy Johnson	.15	.06	.01
☐ 52T Jay Johnstone	.25	.10	.02
☐ 53T Mick Kelleher	.15	.06	.01
☐ 54T Steve Kemp	.15	.06	.01
☐ 55T Junior Kennedy	.15	.06	.01
☐ 56T Jim Kern	.15	.06	.01
☐ 57T Ray Knight	.35	.15	.03
☐ 58T Wayne Krenchicki	.15	.06	.01
☐ 59T Mike Krukow	.15	.06	.01
☐ 60T Duane Kuiper	.15	.06	.01
☐ 61T Mike LaCoss	.15	.06	.01
☐ 62T Chet Lemon	.15	.06	.01
☐ 63T Sixto Lezcano	.15	.06	.01
☐ 64T Dave Lopes	.25	.10	.02
☐ 65T Jerry Martin	.15	.06	.01
☐ 66T Renie Martin	.15	.06	.01
☐ 67T John Mayberry	.25	.10	.02
☐ 68T Lee Mazzilli	.15	.06	.01
☐ 69T Bake McBride	.15	.06	.01
☐ 70T Dan Meyer	.15	.06	.01
☐ 71T Larry Milbourne	.15	.06	.01
☐ 72T Eddie Milner	.15	.06	.01
☐ 73T Sid Monge	.15	.06	.01
☐ 74T John Montefusco	.15	.06	.01
☐ 75T Jose Morales	.15	.06	.01
☐ 76T Keith Moreland	.15	.06	.01
☐ 77T Jim Morrison	.15	.06	.01
☐ 78T Rance Mulliniks	.15	.06	.01
☐ 79T Steve Mura	.15	.06	.01
☐ 80T Gene Nelson	.25	.10	.02
☐ 81T Joe Nolan	.15	.06	.01
☐ 82T Dickie Noles	.15	.06	.01
☐ 83T Al Oliver	.35	.15	.03
☐ 84T Jorge Orta	.15	.06	.01
☐ 85T Tom Paciorek	.15	.06	.01
☐ 86T Larry Parrish	.25	.10	.02
☐ 87T Jack Perconte	.15	.06	.01
☐ 88T Gaylord Perry	1.50	.60	.15
☐ 89T Rob Picciolo	.15	.06	.01
☐ 90T Joe Pittman	.15	.06	.01
☐ 91T Hosken Powell	.15	.06	.01
☐ 92T Mike Proly	.15	.06	.01
☐ 93T Greg Pryor	.15	.06	.01
☐ 94T Charlie Puleo	.15	.06	.01
☐ 95T Shane Rawley	.15	.06	.01
☐ 96T Johnny Ray	.50	.20	.05
☐ 97T Dave Revering	.15	.06	.01
☐ 98T Cal Ripken	160.00	60.00	12.50
☐ 99T Allen Ripley	.15	.06	.01
☐ 100T Bill Robinson	.25	.10	.02
☐ 101T Aurelio Rodriguez	.15	.06	.01
☐ 102T Joe Rudi	.25	.10	.02
☐ 103T Steve Sax	6.50	2.75	.65
☐ 104T Dan Schatzeder	.15	.06	.01
☐ 105T Bob Shirley	.15	.06	.01
☐ 106T Eric Show	.35	.15	.03
☐ 107T Roy Smalley	.15	.06	.01
☐ 108T Lonnie Smith	.35	.15	.03
☐ 109T Ozzie Smith	12.00	5.25	1.50
☐ 110T Reggie Smith	.25	.10	.02
☐ 111T Lary Sorensen	.15	.06	.01
☐ 112T Elias Sosa	.15	.06	.01
☐ 113T Mike Stanton	.15	.06	.01
☐ 114T Steve Stroughter	.15	.06	.01
☐ 115T Champ Summers	.15	.06	.01
☐ 116T Rick Sutcliffe	.35	.15	.03
☐ 117T Frank Tanana	.25	.10	.02
☐ 118T Frank Taveras	.15	.06	.01
☐ 119T Garry Templeton	.25	.10	.02
☐ 120T Alex Trevino	.15	.06	.01
☐ 121T Jerry Turner	.15	.06	.01
☐ 122T Ed VandeBerg	.15	.06	.01
☐ 123T Tom Veryzer	.15	.06	.01
☐ 124T Ron Washington	.15	.06	.01

☐ 125T	Bob Watson	.25	.10	.02
☐ 126T	Dennis Werth	.15	.06	.01
☐ 127T	Eddie Whitson	.25	.10	.02
☐ 128T	Rob Wilfong	.15	.06	.01
☐ 129T	Bump Wills	.15	.06	.01
☐ 130T	Gary Woods	.15	.06	.01
☐ 131T	Butch Wynegar	.15	.06	.01
☐ 132T	Checklist: 1-132	.15	.02	.00

1983 Topps

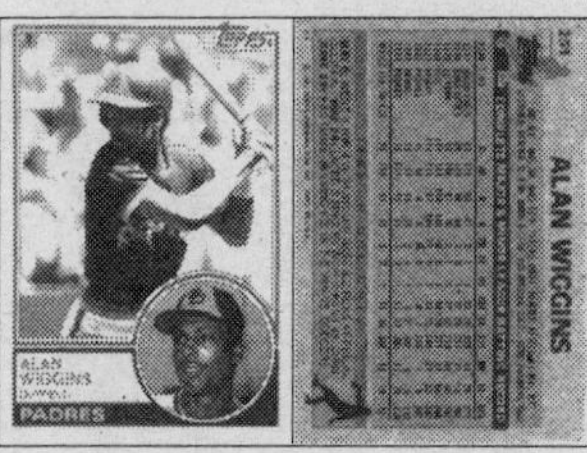

The cards in this 792-card set measure 2 1/2" by 3 1/2". Each regular card of the Topps set for 1983 features a large action shot of a player with a small cameo portrait at bottom right. There are special series for AL and NL All Stars (386-407), League Leaders (701-708), and Record Breakers (1-6). In addition, there are 34 "Super Veteran" (SV) cards and six numbered checklist cards. The Super Veteran cards are oriented horizontally and show two pictures of the featured player, a recent picture and a picture showing the player as a rookie when he broke in. The cards are numbered on the reverse at the upper left corner. The team cards are actually Team Leader (TL) cards picturing the batting and pitching leader for that team with a checklist back. The key rookie cards in this set are Wade Boggs, Tony Gwynn, Willie McGee, Ryne Sandberg, and Frank Viola.

	MINT	EXC	G-VG
COMPLETE SET (792)	165.00	75.00	15.00
COMMON PLAYER (1-792)	.08	.03	.01

☐ 1	RB: Tony Armas 11 putouts by rightfielder	.20	.05	.01
☐ 2	RB: Rickey Henderson Sets modern record for steals, season	1.50	.60	.15
☐ 3	RB: Greg Minton 269 1/3 homerless innings streak	.08	.03	.01
☐ 4	RB: Lance Parrish Threw out three baserunners in All-Star game	.15	.06	.01
☐ 5	RB: Manny Trillo 479 consecutive errorless chances, second baseman	.08	.03	.01
☐ 6	RB: John Wathan ML steals record for catchers, 31	.08	.03	.01
☐ 7	Gene Richards	.08	.03	.01
☐ 8	Steve Balboni	.08	.03	.01
☐ 9	Joey McLaughlin	.08	.03	.01
☐ 10	Gorman Thomas	.15	.06	.01
☐ 11	Billy Gardner MG	.08	.03	.01
☐ 12	Paul Mirabella	.08	.03	.01
☐ 13	Larry Herndon	.08	.03	.01
☐ 14	Frank LaCorte	.08	.03	.01
☐ 15	Ron Cey	.15	.06	.01
☐ 16	George Vukovich	.08	.03	.01
☐ 17	Kent Tekulve	.08	.03	.01
☐ 18	SV: Kent Tekulve	.08	.03	.01
☐ 19	Oscar Gamble	.08	.03	.01
☐ 20	Carlton Fisk	1.50	.60	.15
☐ 21	Baltimore Orioles TL BA: Eddie Murray ERA: Jim Palmer	.30	.10	.02
☐ 22	Randy Martz	.08	.03	.01
☐ 23	Mike Heath	.08	.03	.01
☐ 24	Steve Mura	.08	.03	.01
☐ 25	Hal McRae	.15	.06	.01
☐ 26	Jerry Royster	.08	.03	.01
☐ 27	Doug Corbett	.08	.03	.01
☐ 28	Bruce Bochte	.08	.03	.01
☐ 29	Randy Jones	.08	.03	.01
☐ 30	Jim Rice	.35	.15	.03
☐ 31	Bill Gullickson	.15	.06	.01
☐ 32	Dave Bergman	.08	.03	.01
☐ 33	Jack O'Connor	.08	.03	.01
☐ 34	Paul Householder	.08	.03	.01
☐ 35	Rollie Fingers	.65	.25	.06
☐ 36	SV: Rollie Fingers	.35	.15	.03
☐ 37	Darrell Johnson MG	.08	.03	.01
☐ 38	Tim Flannery	.08	.03	.01
☐ 39	Terry Puhl	.08	.03	.01
☐ 40	Fernando Valenzuela	.40	.16	.04
☐ 41	Jerry Turner	.08	.03	.01
☐ 42	Dale Murray	.08	.03	.01
☐ 43	Bob Dernier	.08	.03	.01
☐ 44	Don Robinson	.08	.03	.01

☐ 45 John Mayberry .15 .06 .01
☐ 46 Richard Dotson .08 .03 .01
☐ 47 Dave McKay .08 .03 .01
☐ 48 Lary Sorensen .08 .03 .01
☐ 49 Willie McGee 5.50 2.50 .55
☐ 50 Bob Horner UER .15 .06 .01
('82 RBI total 7)
☐ 51 Chicago Cubs TL .20 .07 .01
BA: Leon Durham
ERA: Fergie Jenkins
☐ 52 Onix Concepcion .08 .03 .01
☐ 53 Mike Witt .08 .03 .01
☐ 54 Jim Maler .08 .03 .01
☐ 55 Mookie Wilson .15 .06 .01
☐ 56 Chuck Rainey .08 .03 .01
☐ 57 Tim Blackwell .08 .03 .01
☐ 58 Al Holland .08 .03 .01
☐ 59 Benny Ayala .08 .03 .01
☐ 60 Johnny Bench 1.50 .60 .15
☐ 61 SV: Johnny Bench .75 .30 .07
☐ 62 Bob McClure .08 .03 .01
☐ 63 Rick Monday .08 .03 .01
☐ 64 Bill Stein .08 .03 .01
☐ 65 Jack Morris .90 .40 .09
☐ 66 Bob Lillis MG .08 .03 .01
☐ 67 Sal Butera .08 .03 .01
☐ 68 Eric Show .25 .10 .02
☐ 69 Lee Lacy .08 .03 .01
☐ 70 Steve Carlton 1.50 .60 .15
☐ 71 SV: Steve Carlton .75 .30 .07
☐ 72 Tom Paciorek .08 .03 .01
☐ 73 Allen Ripley .08 .03 .01
☐ 74 Julio Gonzalez .08 .03 .01
☐ 75 Amos Otis .15 .06 .01
☐ 76 Rick Mahler .08 .03 .01
☐ 77 Hosken Powell .08 .03 .01
☐ 78 Bill Caudill .08 .03 .01
☐ 79 Mick Kelleher .08 .03 .01
☐ 80 George Foster .25 .10 .02
☐ 81 Yankees TL .15 .06 .01
BA: Jerry Mumphrey
ERA: Dave Righetti
☐ 82 Bruce Hurst .25 .10 .02
☐ 83 Ryne Sandberg 50.00 22.50 7.50
☐ 84 Milt May .08 .03 .01
☐ 85 Ken Singleton .15 .06 .01
☐ 86 Tom Hume .08 .03 .01
☐ 87 Joe Rudi .15 .06 .01
☐ 88 Jim Gantner .08 .03 .01
☐ 89 Leon Roberts .08 .03 .01
☐ 90 Jerry Reuss .08 .03 .01
☐ 91 Larry Milbourne .08 .03 .01
☐ 92 Mike LaCoss .08 .03 .01
☐ 93 John Castino .08 .03 .01
☐ 94 Dave Edwards .08 .03 .01
☐ 95 Alan Trammell 1.00 .40 .10
☐ 96 Dick Howser MG .08 .03 .01
☐ 97 Ross Baumgarten .08 .03 .01
☐ 98 Vance Law .15 .06 .01
☐ 99 Dickie Noles .08 .03 .01
☐ 100 Pete Rose 2.00 .80 .20
☐ 101 SV: Pete Rose 1.00 .40 .10
☐ 102 Dave Beard .08 .03 .01
☐ 103 Darrell Porter .08 .03 .01
☐ 104 Bob Walk .08 .03 .01
☐ 105 Don Baylor .15 .06 .01
☐ 106 Gene Nelson .08 .03 .01
☐ 107 Mike Jorgensen .08 .03 .01
☐ 108 Glenn Hoffman .08 .03 .01
☐ 109 Luis Leal .08 .03 .01
☐ 110 Ken Griffey .35 .15 .03
☐ 111 Montreal Expos TL .15 .06 .01
BA: Al Oliver
ERA: Steve Rogers
☐ 112 Bob Shirley .08 .03 .01
☐ 113 Ron Roenicke .08 .03 .01
☐ 114 Jim Slaton .08 .03 .01
☐ 115 Chili Davis .60 .25 .06
☐ 116 Dave Schmidt .15 .06 .01
☐ 117 Alan Knicely .08 .03 .01
☐ 118 Chris Welsh .08 .03 .01
☐ 119 Tom Brookens .08 .03 .01
☐ 120 Len Barker .08 .03 .01
☐ 121 Mickey Hatcher .08 .03 .01
☐ 122 Jimmy Smith .08 .03 .01
☐ 123 George Frazier .08 .03 .01
☐ 124 Marc Hill .08 .03 .01
☐ 125 Leon Durham .08 .03 .01
☐ 126 Joe Torre MG .15 .06 .01
☐ 127 Preston Hanna .08 .03 .01
☐ 128 Mike Ramsey .08 .03 .01
☐ 129 Checklist: 1-132 .15 .02 .00
☐ 130 Dave Stieb .35 .15 .03
☐ 131 Ed Ott .08 .03 .01
☐ 132 Todd Cruz .08 .03 .01
☐ 133 Jim Barr .08 .03 .01
☐ 134 Hubie Brooks .35 .15 .03
☐ 135 Dwight Evans .40 .16 .04
☐ 136 Willie Aikens .08 .03 .01
☐ 137 Woodie Fryman .08 .03 .01
☐ 138 Rick Dempsey .08 .03 .01
☐ 139 Bruce Berenyi .08 .03 .01
☐ 140 Willie Randolph .15 .06 .01
☐ 141 Indians TL .15 .06 .01
BA: Toby Harrah
ERA: Rick Sutcliffe
☐ 142 Mike Caldwell .08 .03 .01
☐ 143 Joe Pettini .08 .03 .01
☐ 144 Mark Wagner .08 .03 .01
☐ 145 Don Sutton .50 .20 .05
☐ 146 SV: Don Sutton .25 .10 .02
☐ 147 Rick Leach .08 .03 .01
☐ 148 Dave Roberts .08 .03 .01
☐ 149 Johnny Ray .08 .03 .01
☐ 150 Bruce Sutter .20 .08 .02
☐ 151 SV: Bruce Sutter .15 .06 .01

☐ 152 Jay Johnstone	.15	.06	.01
☐ 153 Jerry Koosman	.15	.06	.01
☐ 154 Johnnie LeMaster	.08	.03	.01
☐ 155 Dan Quisenberry	.15	.06	.01
☐ 156 Billy Martin MG	.15	.06	.01
☐ 157 Steve Bedrosian	.15	.06	.01
☐ 158 Rob Wilfong	.08	.03	.01
☐ 159 Mike Stanton	.08	.03	.01
☐ 160 Dave Kingman	.15	.06	.01
☐ 161 SV: Dave Kingman	.08	.03	.01
☐ 162 Mark Clear	.08	.03	.01
☐ 163 Cal Ripken	18.00	7.50	2.50
☐ 164 David Palmer	.08	.03	.01
☐ 165 Dan Driessen	.08	.03	.01
☐ 166 John Pacella	.08	.03	.01
☐ 167 Mark Brouhard	.08	.03	.01
☐ 168 Juan Eichelberger	.08	.03	.01
☐ 169 Doug Flynn	.08	.03	.01
☐ 170 Steve Howe	.08	.03	.01
☐ 171 Giants TL	.20	.07	.01
BA: Joe Morgan			
ERA: Bill Laskey			
☐ 172 Vern Ruhle	.08	.03	.01
☐ 173 Jim Morrison	.08	.03	.01
☐ 174 Jerry Ujdur	.08	.03	.01
☐ 175 Bo Diaz	.08	.03	.01
☐ 176 Dave Righetti	.35	.15	.03
☐ 177 Harold Baines	.75	.30	.07
☐ 178 Luis Tiant	.15	.06	.01
☐ 179 SV: Luis Tiant	.08	.03	.01
☐ 180 Rickey Henderson	7.50	3.25	.75
☐ 181 Terry Felton	.08	.03	.01
☐ 182 Mike Fischlin	.08	.03	.01
☐ 183 Ed VandeBerg	.08	.03	.01
☐ 184 Bob Clark	.08	.03	.01
☐ 185 Tim Lollar	.08	.03	.01
☐ 186 Whitey Herzog MG	.15	.06	.01
☐ 187 Terry Leach	.15	.06	.01
☐ 188 Rick Miller	.08	.03	.01
☐ 189 Dan Schatzeder	.08	.03	.01
☐ 190 Cecil Cooper	.15	.06	.01
☐ 191 Joe Price	.08	.03	.01
☐ 192 Floyd Rayford	.08	.03	.01
☐ 193 Harry Spilman	.08	.03	.01
☐ 194 Cesar Geronimo	.08	.03	.01
☐ 195 Bob Stoddard	.08	.03	.01
☐ 196 Bill Fahey	.08	.03	.01
☐ 197 Jim Eisenreich	.50	.20	.05
☐ 198 Kiko Garcia	.08	.03	.01
☐ 199 Marty Bystrom	.08	.03	.01
☐ 200 Rod Carew	1.50	.60	.15
☐ 201 SV: Rod Carew	.75	.30	.07
☐ 202 Blue Jays TL	.15	.06	.01
BA: Damaso Garcia			
ERA: Dave Stieb			
☐ 203 Mike Morgan	.15	.06	.01
☐ 204 Junior Kennedy	.08	.03	.01
☐ 205 Dave Parker	.65	.25	.06
☐ 206 Ken Oberkfell	.08	.03	.01
☐ 207 Rick Camp	.08	.03	.01
☐ 208 Dan Meyer	.08	.03	.01
☐ 209 Mike Moore	1.50	.60	.15
☐ 210 Jack Clark	.35	.15	.03
☐ 211 John Denny	.08	.03	.01
☐ 212 John Stearns	.08	.03	.01
☐ 213 Tom Burgmeier	.08	.03	.01
☐ 214 Jerry White	.08	.03	.01
☐ 215 Mario Soto	.08	.03	.01
☐ 216 Tony LaRussa MG	.15	.06	.01
☐ 217 Tim Stoddard	.08	.03	.01
☐ 218 Roy Howell	.08	.03	.01
☐ 219 Mike Armstrong	.08	.03	.01
☐ 220 Dusty Baker	.15	.06	.01
☐ 221 Joe Niekro	.15	.06	.01
☐ 222 Damaso Garcia	.08	.03	.01
☐ 223 John Montefusco	.08	.03	.01
☐ 224 Mickey Rivers	.08	.03	.01
☐ 225 Enos Cabell	.08	.03	.01
☐ 226 Enrique Romo	.08	.03	.01
☐ 227 Chris Bando	.08	.03	.01
☐ 228 Joaquin Andujar	.15	.06	.01
☐ 229 Phillies TL	.20	.07	.01
BA: Bo Diaz			
ERA: Steve Carlton			
☐ 230 Fergie Jenkins	.50	.20	.05
☐ 231 SV: Fergie Jenkins	.25	.10	.02
☐ 232 Tom Brunansky	.35	.15	.03
☐ 233 Wayne Gross	.08	.03	.01
☐ 234 Larry Andersen	.08	.03	.01
☐ 235 Claudell Washington	.08	.03	.01
☐ 236 Steve Renko	.08	.03	.01
☐ 237 Dan Norman	.08	.03	.01
☐ 238 Bud Black	.60	.25	.06
☐ 239 Dave Stapleton	.08	.03	.01
☐ 240 Rich Gossage	.20	.08	.02
☐ 241 SV: Rich Gossage	.15	.06	.01
☐ 242 Joe Nolan	.08	.03	.01
☐ 243 Duane Walker	.08	.03	.01
☐ 244 Dwight Bernard	.08	.03	.01
☐ 245 Steve Sax	.75	.30	.07
☐ 246 George Bamberger MG	.08	.03	.01
☐ 247 Dave Smith	.08	.03	.01
☐ 248 Bake McBride	.08	.03	.01
☐ 249 Checklist: 133-264	.15	.02	.00
☐ 250 Bill Buckner	.15	.06	.01
☐ 251 Alan Wiggins	.08	.03	.01
☐ 252 Luis Aguayo	.08	.03	.01
☐ 253 Larry McWilliams	.08	.03	.01
☐ 254 Rick Cerone	.08	.03	.01
☐ 255 Gene Garber	.08	.03	.01
☐ 256 SV: Gene Garber	.08	.03	.01
☐ 257 Jesse Barfield	.40	.16	.04
☐ 258 Manny Castillo	.08	.03	.01
☐ 259 Jeff Jones	.08	.03	.01
☐ 260 Steve Kemp	.08	.03	.01
☐ 261 Tigers TL	.15	.06	.01

No.	Player			
	BA: Larry Herndon			
	ERA: Dan Petry			
☐ 262	Ron Jackson	.08	.03	.01
☐ 263	Renie Martin	.08	.03	.01
☐ 264	Jamie Quirk	.08	.03	.01
☐ 265	Joel Youngblood	.08	.03	.01
☐ 266	Paul Boris	.08	.03	.01
☐ 267	Terry Francona	.08	.03	.01
☐ 268	Storm Davis	.40	.16	.04
☐ 269	Ron Oester	.08	.03	.01
☐ 270	Dennis Eckersley	.60	.25	.06
☐ 271	Ed Romero	.08	.03	.01
☐ 272	Frank Tanana	.15	.06	.01
☐ 273	Mark Belanger	.15	.06	.01
☐ 274	Terry Kennedy	.08	.03	.01
☐ 275	Ray Knight	.15	.06	.01
☐ 276	Gene Mauch MG	.08	.03	.01
☐ 277	Rance Mulliniks	.08	.03	.01
☐ 278	Kevin Hickey	.08	.03	.01
☐ 279	Greg Gross	.08	.03	.01
☐ 280	Bert Blyleven	.30	.12	.03
☐ 281	Andre Robertson	.08	.03	.01
☐ 282	Reggie Smith	.30	.12	.03
	(Ryne Sandberg			
	ducking back)			
☐ 283	SV: Reggie Smith	.08	.03	.01
☐ 284	Jeff Lahti	.08	.03	.01
☐ 285	Lance Parrish	.35	.15	.03
☐ 286	Rick Langford	.08	.03	.01
☐ 287	Bobby Brown	.08	.03	.01
☐ 288	Joe Cowley	.08	.03	.01
☐ 289	Jerry Dybzinski	.08	.03	.01
☐ 290	Jeff Reardon	.75	.30	.07
☐ 291	Pirates TL	.15	.06	.01
	BA: Bill Madlock			
	ERA: John Candelaria			
☐ 292	Craig Swan	.08	.03	.01
☐ 293	Glenn Gulliver	.08	.03	.01
☐ 294	Dave Engle	.08	.03	.01
☐ 295	Jerry Remy	.08	.03	.01
☐ 296	Greg Harris	.08	.03	.01
☐ 297	Ned Yost	.08	.03	.01
☐ 298	Floyd Chiffer	.08	.03	.01
☐ 299	George Wright	.08	.03	.01
☐ 300	Mike Schmidt	3.00	1.25	.30
☐ 301	SV: Mike Schmidt	1.50	.60	.15
☐ 302	Ernie Whitt	.08	.03	.01
☐ 303	Miguel Dilone	.08	.03	.01
☐ 304	Dave Rucker	.08	.03	.01
☐ 305	Larry Bowa	.15	.06	.01
☐ 306	Tom Lasorda MG	.15	.06	.01
☐ 307	Lou Piniella	.15	.06	.01
☐ 308	Jesus Vega	.08	.03	.01
☐ 309	Jeff Leonard	.08	.03	.01
☐ 310	Greg Luzinski	.15	.06	.01
☐ 311	Glenn Brummer	.08	.03	.01
☐ 312	Brian Kingman	.08	.03	.01
☐ 313	Gary Gray	.08	.03	.01
☐ 314	Ken Dayley	.08	.03	.01
☐ 315	Rick Burleson	.08	.03	.01
☐ 316	Paul Splittorff	.08	.03	.01
☐ 317	Gary Rajsich	.08	.03	.01
☐ 318	John Tudor	.15	.06	.01
☐ 319	Lenn Sakata	.08	.03	.01
☐ 320	Steve Rogers	.08	.03	.01
☐ 321	Brewers TL	.20	.07	.01
	BA: Robin Yount			
	ERA: Pete Vuckovich			
☐ 322	Dave Van Gorder	.08	.03	.01
☐ 323	Luis DeLeon	.08	.03	.01
☐ 324	Mike Marshall	.15	.06	.01
☐ 325	Von Hayes	.25	.10	.02
☐ 326	Garth Iorg	.08	.03	.01
☐ 327	Bobby Castillo	.08	.03	.01
☐ 328	Craig Reynolds	.08	.03	.01
☐ 329	Randy Niemann	.08	.03	.01
☐ 330	Buddy Bell	.15	.06	.01
☐ 331	Mike Krukow	.08	.03	.01
☐ 332	Glenn Wilson	.15	.06	.01
☐ 333	Dave LaRoche	.08	.03	.01
☐ 334	SV: Dave LaRoche	.08	.03	.01
☐ 335	Steve Henderson	.08	.03	.01
☐ 336	Rene Lachemann MG	.08	.03	.01
☐ 337	Tito Landrum	.08	.03	.01
☐ 338	Bob Owchinko	.08	.03	.01
☐ 339	Terry Harper	.08	.03	.01
☐ 340	Larry Gura	.08	.03	.01
☐ 341	Doug DeCinces	.08	.03	.01
☐ 342	Atlee Hammaker	.08	.03	.01
☐ 343	Bob Bailor	.08	.03	.01
☐ 344	Roger LaFrancois	.08	.03	.01
☐ 345	Jim Clancy	.08	.03	.01
☐ 346	Joe Pittman	.08	.03	.01
☐ 347	Sammy Stewart	.08	.03	.01
☐ 348	Alan Bannister	.08	.03	.01
☐ 349	Checklist: 265-396	.15	.02	.00
☐ 350	Robin Yount	2.00	.80	.20
☐ 351	Reds TL	.15	.06	.01
	BA: Cesar Cedeno			
	ERA: Mario Soto			
☐ 352	Mike Scioscia	.15	.06	.01
☐ 353	Steve Comer	.08	.03	.01
☐ 354	Randy Johnson	.08	.03	.01
☐ 355	Jim Bibby	.08	.03	.01
☐ 356	Gary Woods	.08	.03	.01
☐ 357	Len Matuszek	.08	.03	.01
☐ 358	Jerry Garvin	.08	.03	.01
☐ 359	Dave Collins	.08	.03	.01
☐ 360	Nolan Ryan	7.00	3.00	.70
☐ 361	SV: Nolan Ryan	3.25	1.35	.32
☐ 362	Bill Almon	.08	.03	.01
☐ 363	John Stuper	.08	.03	.01
☐ 364	Brett Butler	.60	.25	.06
☐ 365	Dave Lopes	.15	.06	.01
☐ 366	Dick Williams MG	.08	.03	.01
☐ 367	Bud Anderson	.08	.03	.01

☐ 368 Richie Zisk	.08	.03	.01
☐ 369 Jesse Orosco	.08	.03	.01
☐ 370 Gary Carter	.65	.25	.06
☐ 371 Mike Richardt	.08	.03	.01
☐ 372 Terry Crowley	.08	.03	.01
☐ 373 Kevin Saucier	.08	.03	.01
☐ 374 Wayne Krenchicki	.08	.03	.01
☐ 375 Pete Vuckovich	.08	.03	.01
☐ 376 Ken Landreaux	.08	.03	.01
☐ 377 Lee May	.08	.03	.01
☐ 378 SV: Lee May	.08	.03	.01
☐ 379 Guy Sularz	.08	.03	.01
☐ 380 Ron Davis	.08	.03	.01
☐ 381 Red Sox TL BA: Jim Rice ERA: Bob Stanley	.15	.06	.01
☐ 382 Bob Knepper	.08	.03	.01
☐ 383 Ozzie Virgil	.08	.03	.01
☐ 384 Dave Dravecky	.75	.30	.07
☐ 385 Mike Easler	.08	.03	.01
☐ 386 Rod Carew AS	.45	.18	.04
☐ 387 Bob Grich AS	.15	.06	.01
☐ 388 George Brett AS	.60	.25	.06
☐ 389 Robin Yount AS	.60	.25	.06
☐ 390 Reggie Jackson AS	.50	.20	.05
☐ 391 Rickey Henderson AS	2.00	.80	.20
☐ 392 Fred Lynn AS	.15	.06	.01
☐ 393 Carlton Fisk AS	.40	.16	.04
☐ 394 Pete Vuckovich AS	.08	.03	.01
☐ 395 Larry Gura AS	.08	.03	.01
☐ 396 Dan Quisenberry AS	.15	.06	.01
☐ 397 Pete Rose AS	.60	.25	.06
☐ 398 Manny Trillo AS	.08	.03	.01
☐ 399 Mike Schmidt AS	.60	.25	.06
☐ 400 Dave Concepcion AS	.15	.06	.01
☐ 401 Dale Murphy AS	.35	.15	.03
☐ 402 Andre Dawson AS	.40	.16	.04
☐ 403 Tim Raines AS	.30	.12	.03
☐ 404 Gary Carter AS	.25	.10	.02
☐ 405 Steve Rogers AS	.08	.03	.01
☐ 406 Steve Carlton AS	.40	.16	.04
☐ 407 Bruce Sutter AS	.15	.06	.01
☐ 408 Rudy May	.08	.03	.01
☐ 409 Marvis Foley	.08	.03	.01
☐ 410 Phil Niekro	.50	.20	.05
☐ 411 SV: Phil Niekro	.25	.10	.02
☐ 412 Rangers TL BA: Buddy Bell ERA: Charlie Hough	.15	.06	.01
☐ 413 Matt Keough	.08	.03	.01
☐ 414 Julio Cruz	.08	.03	.01
☐ 415 Bob Forsch	.08	.03	.01
☐ 416 Joe Ferguson	.08	.03	.01
☐ 417 Tom Hausman	.08	.03	.01
☐ 418 Greg Pryor	.08	.03	.01
☐ 419 Steve Crawford	.08	.03	.01
☐ 420 Al Oliver	.15	.06	.01
☐ 421 SV: Al Oliver	.08	.03	.01
☐ 422 George Cappuzzello	.08	.03	.01
☐ 423 Tom Lawless	.08	.03	.01
☐ 424 Jerry Augustine	.08	.03	.01
☐ 425 Pedro Guerrero	.50	.20	.05
☐ 426 Earl Weaver MG	.15	.06	.01
☐ 427 Roy Lee Jackson	.08	.03	.01
☐ 428 Champ Summers	.08	.03	.01
☐ 429 Eddie Whitson	.08	.03	.01
☐ 430 Kirk Gibson	.75	.30	.07
☐ 431 Gary Gaetti	1.75	.70	.17
☐ 432 Porfirio Altamirano	.08	.03	.01
☐ 433 Dale Berra	.08	.03	.01
☐ 434 Dennis Lamp	.08	.03	.01
☐ 435 Tony Armas	.08	.03	.01
☐ 436 Bill Campbell	.08	.03	.01
☐ 437 Rick Sweet	.08	.03	.01
☐ 438 Dave LaPoint	.15	.06	.01
☐ 439 Rafael Ramirez	.08	.03	.01
☐ 440 Ron Guidry	.35	.15	.03
☐ 441 Astros TL BA: Ray Knight ERA: Joe Niekro	.15	.06	.01
☐ 442 Brian Downing	.15	.06	.01
☐ 443 Don Hood	.08	.03	.01
☐ 444 Wally Backman	.15	.06	.01
☐ 445 Mike Flanagan	.15	.06	.01
☐ 446 Reid Nichols	.08	.03	.01
☐ 447 Bryn Smith	.15	.06	.01
☐ 448 Darrell Evans	.15	.06	.01
☐ 449 Eddie Milner	.08	.03	.01
☐ 450 Ted Simmons	.15	.06	.01
☐ 451 SV: Ted Simmons	.08	.03	.01
☐ 452 Lloyd Moseby	.15	.06	.01
☐ 453 Lamar Johnson	.08	.03	.01
☐ 454 Bob Welch	.40	.16	.04
☐ 455 Sixto Lezcano	.08	.03	.01
☐ 456 Lee Elia MG	.08	.03	.01
☐ 457 Milt Wilcox	.08	.03	.01
☐ 458 Ron Washington	.08	.03	.01
☐ 459 Ed Farmer	.08	.03	.01
☐ 460 Roy Smalley	.08	.03	.01
☐ 461 Steve Trout	.08	.03	.01
☐ 462 Steve Nicosia	.08	.03	.01
☐ 463 Gaylord Perry	.50	.20	.05
☐ 464 SV: Gaylord Perry	.25	.10	.02
☐ 465 Lonnie Smith	.20	.08	.02
☐ 466 Tom Underwood	.08	.03	.01
☐ 467 Rufino Linares	.08	.03	.01
☐ 468 Dave Goltz	.08	.03	.01
☐ 469 Ron Gardenhire	.08	.03	.01
☐ 470 Greg Minton	.08	.03	.01
☐ 471 K.C. Royals TL BA: Willie Wilson ERA: Vida Blue	.15	.06	.01
☐ 472 Gary Allenson	.08	.03	.01
☐ 473 John Lowenstein	.08	.03	.01
☐ 474 Ray Burris	.08	.03	.01
☐ 475 Cesar Cedeno	.15	.06	.01

☐ 476 Rob Picciolo .08 .03 .01
☐ 477 Tom Niedenfuer .08 .03 .01
☐ 478 Phil Garner .15 .06 .01
☐ 479 Charlie Hough .08 .03 .01
☐ 480 Toby Harrah .08 .03 .01
☐ 481 Scot Thompson .08 .03 .01
☐ 482 Tony Gwynn UER 33.00 15.00 5.00
(no Topps logo under
card number on back)
☐ 483 Lynn Jones .08 .03 .01
☐ 484 Dick Ruthven .08 .03 .01
☐ 485 Omar Moreno .08 .03 .01
☐ 486 Clyde King MG .08 .03 .01
☐ 487 Jerry Hairston .08 .03 .01
☐ 488 Alfredo Griffin .08 .03 .01
☐ 489 Tom Herr .15 .06 .01
☐ 490 Jim Palmer 1.25 .50 .12
☐ 491 SV: Jim Palmer .60 .25 .06
☐ 492 Paul Serna .08 .03 .01
☐ 493 Steve McCatty .08 .03 .01
☐ 494 Bob Brenly .08 .03 .01
☐ 495 Warren Cromartie .08 .03 .01
☐ 496 Tom Veryzer .08 .03 .01
☐ 497 Rick Sutcliffe .20 .08 .02
☐ 498 Wade Boggs 36.00 16.25 5.50
☐ 499 Jeff Little .08 .03 .01
☐ 500 Reggie Jackson 2.00 .80 .20
☐ 501 SV: Reggie Jackson 1.00 .40 .10
☐ 502 Atlanta Braves TL .20 .07 .01
BA: Dale Murphy
ERA: Phil Niekro
☐ 503 Moose Haas .08 .03 .01
☐ 504 Don Werner .08 .03 .01
☐ 505 Garry Templeton .15 .06 .01
☐ 506 Jim Gott .30 .12 .03
☐ 507 Tony Scott .08 .03 .01
☐ 508 Tom Filer .08 .03 .01
☐ 509 Lou Whitaker .50 .20 .05
☐ 510 Tug McGraw .15 .06 .01
☐ 511 SV: Tug McGraw .08 .03 .01
☐ 512 Doyle Alexander .08 .03 .01
☐ 513 Fred Stanley .08 .03 .01
☐ 514 Rudy Law .08 .03 .01
☐ 515 Gene Tenace .15 .06 .01
☐ 516 Bill Virdon MG .08 .03 .01
☐ 517 Gary Ward .08 .03 .01
☐ 518 Bill Laskey .08 .03 .01
☐ 519 Terry Bulling .08 .03 .01
☐ 520 Fred Lynn .30 .12 .03
☐ 521 Bruce Benedict .08 .03 .01
☐ 522 Pat Zachry .08 .03 .01
☐ 523 Carney Lansford .15 .06 .01
☐ 524 Tom Brennan .08 .03 .01
☐ 525 Frank White .08 .03 .01
☐ 526 Checklist: 397-528 .15 .02 .00
☐ 527 Larry Biittner .08 .03 .01
☐ 528 Jamie Easterly .08 .03 .01
☐ 529 Tim Laudner .08 .03 .01
☐ 530 Eddie Murray 2.00 .80 .20
☐ 531 Oakland A's TL .40 .12 .02
BA: Rickey Henderson
ERA: Rick Langford
☐ 532 Dave Stewart 1.25 .50 .12
☐ 533 Luis Salazar .08 .03 .01
☐ 534 John Butcher .08 .03 .01
☐ 535 Manny Trillo .08 .03 .01
☐ 536 John Wockenfuss .08 .03 .01
☐ 537 Rod Scurry .08 .03 .01
☐ 538 Danny Heep .08 .03 .01
☐ 539 Roger Erickson .08 .03 .01
☐ 540 Ozzie Smith 1.75 .70 .17
☐ 541 Britt Burns .08 .03 .01
☐ 542 Jody Davis .08 .03 .01
☐ 543 Alan Fowlkes .08 .03 .01
☐ 544 Larry Whisenton .08 .03 .01
☐ 545 Floyd Bannister .08 .03 .01
☐ 546 Dave Garcia MG .08 .03 .01
☐ 547 Geoff Zahn .08 .03 .01
☐ 548 Brian Giles .08 .03 .01
☐ 549 Charlie Puleo .08 .03 .01
☐ 550 Carl Yastrzemski 1.50 .60 .15
☐ 551 SV: Carl Yastrzemski .75 .30 .07
☐ 552 Tim Wallach .30 .12 .03
☐ 553 Dennis Martinez .15 .06 .01
☐ 554 Mike Vail .08 .03 .01
☐ 555 Steve Yeager .08 .03 .01
☐ 556 Willie Upshaw .08 .03 .01
☐ 557 Rick Honeycutt .08 .03 .01
☐ 558 Dickie Thon .15 .06 .01
☐ 559 Pete Redfern .08 .03 .01
☐ 560 Ron LeFlore .08 .03 .01
☐ 561 Cardinals TL .15 .06 .01
BA: Lonnie Smith
ERA: Joaquin Andujar
☐ 562 Dave Rozema .08 .03 .01
☐ 563 Juan Bonilla .08 .03 .01
☐ 564 Sid Monge .08 .03 .01
☐ 565 Bucky Dent .15 .06 .01
☐ 566 Manny Sarmiento .08 .03 .01
☐ 567 Joe Simpson .08 .03 .01
☐ 568 Willie Hernandez .08 .03 .01
☐ 569 Jack Perconte .08 .03 .01
☐ 570 Vida Blue .15 .06 .01
☐ 571 Mickey Klutts .08 .03 .01
☐ 572 Bob Watson .08 .03 .01
☐ 573 Andy Hassler .08 .03 .01
☐ 574 Glenn Adams .08 .03 .01
☐ 575 Neil Allen .08 .03 .01
☐ 576 Frank Robinson MG .20 .08 .02
☐ 577 Luis Aponte .08 .03 .01
☐ 578 David Green .08 .03 .01
☐ 579 Rich Dauer .08 .03 .01
☐ 580 Tom Seaver 1.50 .60 .15
☐ 581 SV: Tom Seaver .75 .30 .07
☐ 582 Marshall Edwards .08 .03 .01
☐ 583 Terry Forster .15 .06 .01

☐ 584 Dave Hostetler .08 .03 .01
☐ 585 Jose Cruz .15 .06 .01
☐ 586 Frank Viola 7.50 3.25 .75
☐ 587 Ivan DeJesus .08 .03 .01
☐ 588 Pat Underwood .08 .03 .01
☐ 589 Alvis Woods .08 .03 .01
☐ 590 Tony Pena .15 .06 .01
☐ 591 White Sox TL .15 .06 .01
BA: Greg Luzinski
ERA: LaMarr Hoyt
☐ 592 Shane Rawley .08 .03 .01
☐ 593 Broderick Perkins .08 .03 .01
☐ 594 Eric Rasmussen .08 .03 .01
☐ 595 Tim Raines 1.00 .40 .10
☐ 596 Randy Johnson .08 .03 .01
☐ 597 Mike Proly .08 .03 .01
☐ 598 Dwayne Murphy .08 .03 .01
☐ 599 Don Aase .08 .03 .01
☐ 600 George Brett 2.00 .80 .20
☐ 601 Ed Lynch .08 .03 .01
☐ 602 Rich Gedman .08 .03 .01
☐ 603 Joe Morgan .75 .30 .07
☐ 604 SV: Joe Morgan .35 .15 .03
☐ 605 Gary Roenicke .08 .03 .01
☐ 606 Bobby Cox MG .08 .03 .01
☐ 607 Charlie Leibrandt .15 .06 .01
☐ 608 Don Money .08 .03 .01
☐ 609 Danny Darwin .08 .03 .01
☐ 610 Steve Garvey .75 .30 .07
☐ 611 Bert Roberge .08 .03 .01
☐ 612 Steve Swisher .08 .03 .01
☐ 613 Mike Ivie .08 .03 .01
☐ 614 Ed Glynn .08 .03 .01
☐ 615 Garry Maddox .08 .03 .01
☐ 616 Bill Nahorodny .08 .03 .01
☐ 617 Butch Wynegar .08 .03 .01
☐ 618 LaMarr Hoyt .08 .03 .01
☐ 619 Keith Moreland .08 .03 .01
☐ 620 Mike Norris .08 .03 .01
☐ 621 New York Mets TL .15 .06 .01
BA: Mookie Wilson
ERA: Craig Swan
☐ 622 Dave Edler .08 .03 .01
☐ 623 Luis Sanchez .08 .03 .01
☐ 624 Glenn Hubbard .08 .03 .01
☐ 625 Ken Forsch .08 .03 .01
☐ 626 Jerry Martin .08 .03 .01
☐ 627 Doug Bair .08 .03 .01
☐ 628 Julio Valdez .08 .03 .01
☐ 629 Charlie Lea .08 .03 .01
☐ 630 Paul Molitor .60 .25 .06
☐ 631 Tippy Martinez .08 .03 .01
☐ 632 Alex Trevino .08 .03 .01
☐ 633 Vicente Romo .08 .03 .01
☐ 634 Max Venable .08 .03 .01
☐ 635 Graig Nettles .15 .06 .01
☐ 636 SV: Graig Nettles .08 .03 .01
☐ 637 Pat Corrales MG .08 .03 .01
☐ 638 Dan Petry .08 .03 .01
☐ 639 Art Howe .15 .06 .01
☐ 640 Andre Thornton .08 .03 .01
☐ 641 Billy Sample .08 .03 .01
☐ 642 Checklist: 529-660 .15 .02 .00
☐ 643 Bump Wills .08 .03 .01
☐ 644 Joe Lefebvre .08 .03 .01
☐ 645 Bill Madlock .15 .06 .01
☐ 646 Jim Essian .08 .03 .01
☐ 647 Bobby Mitchell .08 .03 .01
☐ 648 Jeff Burroughs .08 .03 .01
☐ 649 Tommy Boggs .08 .03 .01
☐ 650 George Hendrick .08 .03 .01
☐ 651 Angels TL .20 .07 .01
BA: Rod Carew
ERA: Mike Witt
☐ 652 Butch Hobson .15 .06 .01
☐ 653 Ellis Valentine .08 .03 .01
☐ 654 Bob Ojeda .15 .06 .01
☐ 655 Al Bumbry .08 .03 .01
☐ 656 Dave Frost .08 .03 .01
☐ 657 Mike Gates .08 .03 .01
☐ 658 Frank Pastore .08 .03 .01
☐ 659 Charlie Moore .08 .03 .01
☐ 660 Mike Hargrove .15 .06 .01
☐ 661 Bill Russell .15 .06 .01
☐ 662 Joe Sambito .08 .03 .01
☐ 663 Tom O'Malley .08 .03 .01
☐ 664 Bob Molinaro .08 .03 .01
☐ 665 Jim Sundberg .08 .03 .01
☐ 666 Sparky Anderson MG .15 .06 .01
☐ 667 Dick Davis .08 .03 .01
☐ 668 Larry Christenson .08 .03 .01
☐ 669 Mike Squires .08 .03 .01
☐ 670 Jerry Mumphrey .08 .03 .01
☐ 671 Lenny Faedo .08 .03 .01
☐ 672 Jim Kaat .20 .08 .02
☐ 673 SV: Jim Kaat .15 .06 .01
☐ 674 Kurt Bevacqua .08 .03 .01
☐ 675 Jim Beattie .08 .03 .01
☐ 676 Biff Pocoroba .08 .03 .01
☐ 677 Dave Revering .08 .03 .01
☐ 678 Juan Beniquez .08 .03 .01
☐ 679 Mike Scott .25 .10 .02
☐ 680 Andre Dawson 1.75 .70 .17
☐ 681 Dodgers Leaders .15 .06 .01
BA: Pedro Guerrero
ERA: Fern.Valenzuela
☐ 682 Bob Stanley .08 .03 .01
☐ 683 Dan Ford .08 .03 .01
☐ 684 Rafael Landestoy .08 .03 .01
☐ 685 Lee Mazzilli .08 .03 .01
☐ 686 Randy Lerch .08 .03 .01
☐ 687 U.L. Washington .08 .03 .01
☐ 688 Jim Wohlford .08 .03 .01
☐ 689 Ron Hassey .08 .03 .01
☐ 690 Kent Hrbek .75 .30 .07
☐ 691 Dave Tobik .08 .03 .01

☐ 692 Denny Walling .08 .03 .01
☐ 693 Sparky Lyle .15 .06 .01
☐ 694 SV: Sparky Lyle .08 .03 .01
☐ 695 Ruppert Jones .08 .03 .01
☐ 696 Chuck Tanner MG .08 .03 .01
☐ 697 Barry Foote .08 .03 .01
☐ 698 Tony Bernazard .08 .03 .01
☐ 699 Lee Smith 1.00 .40 .10
☐ 700 Keith Hernandez .35 .15 .03
☐ 701 Batting Leaders .15 .06 .01
AL: Willie Wilson
NL: Al Oliver
☐ 702 Home Run Leaders .20 .08 .02
AL: Reggie Jackson
AL: Gorman Thomas
NL: Dave Kingman
☐ 703 RBI Leaders .20 .08 .02
AL: Hal McRae
NL: Dale Murphy
NL: Al Oliver
☐ 704 SB Leaders .90 .40 .09
AL: Rickey Henderson
NL: Tim Raines
☐ 705 Victory Leaders .15 .06 .01
AL: LaMarr Hoyt
NL: Steve Carlton
☐ 706 Strikeout Leaders .15 .06 .01
AL: Floyd Bannister
NL: Steve Carlton
☐ 707 ERA Leaders .08 .03 .01
AL: Rick Sutcliffe
NL: Steve Rogers
☐ 708 Leading Firemen .15 .06 .01
AL: Dan Quisenberry
NL: Bruce Sutter
☐ 709 Jimmy Sexton .08 .03 .01
☐ 710 Willie Wilson .15 .06 .01
☐ 711 Mariners TL .15 .06 .01
BA: Bruce Bochte
ERA: Jim Beattie
☐ 712 Bruce Kison .08 .03 .01
☐ 713 Ron Hodges .08 .03 .01
☐ 714 Wayne Nordhagen .08 .03 .01
☐ 715 Tony Perez .40 .16 .04
☐ 716 SV: Tony Perez .20 .08 .02
☐ 717 Scott Sanderson .15 .06 .01
☐ 718 Jim Dwyer .08 .03 .01
☐ 719 Rich Gale .08 .03 .01
☐ 720 Dave Concepcion .15 .06 .01
☐ 721 John Martin .08 .03 .01
☐ 722 Jorge Orta .08 .03 .01
☐ 723 Randy Moffitt .08 .03 .01
☐ 724 Johnny Grubb .08 .03 .01
☐ 725 Dan Spillner .08 .03 .01
☐ 726 Harvey Kuenn MG .08 .03 .01
☐ 727 Chet Lemon .08 .03 .01
☐ 728 Ron Reed .08 .03 .01
☐ 729 Jerry Morales .08 .03 .01
☐ 730 Jason Thompson .08 .03 .01
☐ 731 Al Williams .08 .03 .01
☐ 732 Dave Henderson .75 .30 .07
☐ 733 Buck Martinez .08 .03 .01
☐ 734 Steve Braun .08 .03 .01
☐ 735 Tommy John .25 .10 .02
☐ 736 SV: Tommy John .15 .06 .01
☐ 737 Mitchell Page .08 .03 .01
☐ 738 Tim Foli .08 .03 .01
☐ 739 Rick Ownbey .08 .03 .01
☐ 740 Rusty Staub .15 .06 .01
☐ 741 SV: Rusty Staub .08 .03 .01
☐ 742 Padres TL .15 .06 .01
BA: Terry Kennedy
ERA: Tim Lollar
☐ 743 Mike Torrez .08 .03 .01
☐ 744 Brad Mills .08 .03 .01
☐ 745 Scott McGregor .08 .03 .01
☐ 746 John Wathan .08 .03 .01
☐ 747 Fred Breining .08 .03 .01
☐ 748 Derrel Thomas .08 .03 .01
☐ 749 Jon Matlack .08 .03 .01
☐ 750 Ben Oglivie .08 .03 .01
☐ 751 Brad Havens .08 .03 .01
☐ 752 Luis Pujols .08 .03 .01
☐ 753 Elias Sosa .08 .03 .01
☐ 754 Bill Robinson .15 .06 .01
☐ 755 John Candelaria .08 .03 .01
☐ 756 Russ Nixon MG .08 .03 .01
☐ 757 Rick Manning .08 .03 .01
☐ 758 Aurelio Rodriguez .08 .03 .01
☐ 759 Doug Bird .08 .03 .01
☐ 760 Dale Murphy 1.25 .50 .12
☐ 761 Gary Lucas .08 .03 .01
☐ 762 Cliff Johnson .08 .03 .01
☐ 763 Al Cowens .08 .03 .01
☐ 764 Pete Falcone .08 .03 .01
☐ 765 Bob Boone .15 .06 .01
☐ 766 Barry Bonnell .08 .03 .01
☐ 767 Duane Kuiper .08 .03 .01
☐ 768 Chris Speier .08 .03 .01
☐ 769 Checklist: 661-792 .15 .02 .00
☐ 770 Dave Winfield 1.25 .50 .12
☐ 771 Twins TL .15 .06 .01
BA: Kent Hrbek
ERA: Bobby Castillo
☐ 772 Jim Kern .08 .03 .01
☐ 773 Larry Hisle .08 .03 .01
☐ 774 Alan Ashby .08 .03 .01
☐ 775 Burt Hooton .08 .03 .01
☐ 776 Larry Parrish .08 .03 .01
☐ 777 John Curtis .08 .03 .01
☐ 778 Rich Hebner .08 .03 .01
☐ 779 Rick Waits .08 .03 .01
☐ 780 Gary Matthews .08 .03 .01
☐ 781 Rick Rhoden .08 .03 .01
☐ 782 Bobby Murcer .15 .06 .01
☐ 783 SV: Bobby Murcer .08 .03 .01

☐ 784 Jeff Newman	.08	.03	.01
☐ 785 Dennis Leonard	.08	.03	.01
☐ 786 Ralph Houk MG	.08	.03	.01
☐ 787 Dick Tidrow	.08	.03	.01
☐ 788 Dane Iorg	.08	.03	.01
☐ 789 Bryan Clark	.08	.03	.01
☐ 790 Bob Grich	.15	.06	.01
☐ 791 Gary Lavelle	.08	.03	.01
☐ 792 Chris Chambliss	.15	.06	.01

1983 Topps Traded

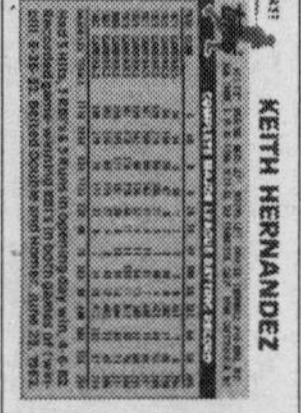

The cards in this 132-card set measure 2 1/2" by 3 1/2". For the third year in a row, Topps issued a 132-card Traded (or extended) set featuring some of the year's top rookies and players who had changed teams during the year, but were featured with their old team in the Topps regular issue of 1983. The cards were available through hobby dealers only and were printed in Ireland by the Topps affiliate in that country. The set is numbered alphabetically by the last name of the player of the card. The Darryl Strawberry card number 108 can be found with either one or two asterisks (in the lower left corner of the reverse). The key (extended) rookie card in this set is obviously Darryl Strawberry. Also noteworthy is Julio Franco's first Topps (extended) card.

	MINT	EXC	G-VG
COMPLETE SET (132)	125.00	57.50	18.75
COMMON PLAYER (1-132)	.12	.05	.01

☐ 1T Neil Allen	.20	.08	.02
☐ 2T Bill Almon	.12	.05	.01
☐ 3T Joe Altobelli MG	.12	.05	.01
☐ 4T Tony Armas	.12	.05	.01
☐ 5T Doug Bair	.12	.05	.01
☐ 6T Steve Baker	.12	.05	.01
☐ 7T Floyd Bannister	.12	.05	.01
☐ 8T Don Baylor	.25	.10	.02
☐ 9T Tony Bernazard	.12	.05	.01
☐ 10T Larry Biittner	.12	.05	.01
☐ 11T Dann Bilardello	.12	.05	.01
☐ 12T Doug Bird	.12	.05	.01
☐ 13T Steve Boros MG	.12	.05	.01
☐ 14T Greg Brock	.20	.08	.02
☐ 15T Mike Brown (Red Sox pitcher)	.12	.05	.01
☐ 16T Tom Burgmeier	.12	.05	.01
☐ 17T Randy Bush	.25	.10	.02
☐ 18T Bert Campaneris	.20	.08	.02
☐ 19T Ron Cey	.20	.08	.02
☐ 20T Chris Codiroli	.12	.05	.01
☐ 21T Dave Collins	.12	.05	.01
☐ 22T Terry Crowley	.12	.05	.01
☐ 23T Julio Cruz	.12	.05	.01
☐ 24T Mike Davis	.12	.05	.01
☐ 25T Frank DiPino	.12	.05	.01
☐ 26T Bill Doran	1.00	.40	.10
☐ 27T Jerry Dybzinski	.12	.05	.01
☐ 28T Jamie Easterly	.12	.05	.01
☐ 29T Juan Eichelberger	.12	.05	.01
☐ 30T Jim Essian	.20	.08	.02
☐ 31T Pete Falcone	.12	.05	.01
☐ 32T Mike Ferraro MG	.12	.05	.01
☐ 33T Terry Forster	.20	.08	.02
☐ 34T Julio Franco	11.00	5.00	1.35
☐ 35T Rich Gale	.12	.05	.01
☐ 36T Kiko Garcia	.12	.05	.01
☐ 37T Steve Garvey	1.25	.50	.12
☐ 38T Johnny Grubb	.12	.05	.01
☐ 39T Mel Hall	1.50	.60	.15
☐ 40T Von Hayes	.50	.20	.05
☐ 41T Danny Heep	.20	.08	.02
☐ 42T Steve Henderson	.12	.05	.01
☐ 43T Keith Hernandez	.75	.30	.07
☐ 44T Leo Hernandez	.12	.05	.01
☐ 45T Willie Hernandez	.20	.08	.02
☐ 46T Al Holland	.12	.05	.01
☐ 47T Frank Howard MG	.20	.08	.02
☐ 48T Bobby Johnson	.12	.05	.01
☐ 49T Cliff Johnson	.12	.05	.01
☐ 50T Odell Jones	.12	.05	.01
☐ 51T Mike Jorgensen	.12	.05	.01
☐ 52T Bob Kearney	.12	.05	.01
☐ 53T Steve Kemp	.20	.08	.02
☐ 54T Matt Keough	.12	.05	.01
☐ 55T Ron Kittle	.50	.20	.05
☐ 56T Mickey Klutts	.12	.05	.01
☐ 57T Alan Knicely	.12	.05	.01
☐ 58T Mike Krukow	.12	.05	.01
☐ 59T Rafael Landestoy	.12	.05	.01
☐ 60T Carney Lansford	.35	.15	.03

□ 61T Joe Lefebvre	.12	.05	.01
□ 62T Bryan Little	.12	.05	.01
□ 63T Aurelio Lopez	.12	.05	.01
□ 64T Mike Madden	.12	.05	.01
□ 65T Rick Manning	.12	.05	.01
□ 66T Billy Martin MG	.30	.12	.03
□ 67T Lee Mazzilli	.12	.05	.01
□ 68T Andy McGaffigan	.12	.05	.01
□ 69T Craig McMurtry	.12	.05	.01
□ 70T John McNamara MG	.12	.05	.01
□ 71T Orlando Mercado	.12	.05	.01
□ 72T Larry Milbourne	.12	.05	.01
□ 73T Randy Moffitt	.12	.05	.01
□ 74T Sid Monge	.12	.05	.01
□ 75T Jose Morales	.12	.05	.01
□ 76T Omar Moreno	.12	.05	.01
□ 77T Joe Morgan	2.50	1.00	.25
□ 78T Mike Morgan	.30	.12	.03
□ 79T Dale Murray	.12	.05	.01
□ 80T Jeff Newman	.12	.05	.01
□ 81T Pete O'Brien	1.00	.40	.10
□ 82T Jorge Orta	.12	.05	.01
□ 83T Alejandro Pena	1.25	.50	.12
□ 84T Pascual Perez	.30	.12	.03
□ 85T Tony Perez	1.25	.50	.12
□ 86T Broderick Perkins	.12	.05	.01
□ 87T Tony Phillips	1.25	.50	.12
□ 88T Charlie Puleo	.12	.05	.01
□ 89T Pat Putnam	.12	.05	.01
□ 90T Jamie Quirk	.12	.05	.01
□ 91T Doug Rader MG	.20	.08	.02
□ 92T Chuck Rainey	.12	.05	.01
□ 93T Bobby Ramos	.12	.05	.01
□ 94T Gary Redus	.65	.25	.06
□ 95T Steve Renko	.12	.05	.01
□ 96T Leon Roberts	.12	.05	.01
□ 97T Aurelio Rodriguez	.12	.05	.01
□ 98T Dick Ruthven	.12	.05	.01
□ 99T Daryl Sconiers	.12	.05	.01
□ 100T Mike Scott	.50	.20	.05
□ 101T Tom Seaver	5.50	2.50	.55
□ 102T John Shelby	.30	.12	.03
□ 103T Bob Shirley	.12	.05	.01
□ 104T Joe Simpson	.12	.05	.01
□ 105T Doug Sisk	.12	.05	.01
□ 106T Mike Smithson	.12	.05	.01
□ 107T Elias Sosa	.12	.05	.01
□ 108T Darryl Strawberry	100.00	45.00	15.00
□ 109T Tom Tellmann	.12	.05	.01
□ 110T Gene Tenace	.20	.08	.02
□ 111T Gorman Thomas	.25	.10	.02
□ 112T Dick Tidrow	.12	.05	.01
□ 113T Dave Tobik	.12	.05	.01
□ 114T Wayne Tolleson	.12	.05	.01
□ 115T Mike Torrez	.12	.05	.01
□ 116T Manny Trillo	.12	.05	.01
□ 117T Steve Trout	.12	.05	.01
□ 118T Lee Tunnell	.12	.05	.01
□ 119T Mike Vail	.12	.05	.01
□ 120T Ellis Valentine	.12	.05	.01
□ 121T Tom Veryzer	.12	.05	.01
□ 122T George Vukovich	.12	.05	.01
□ 123T Rick Waits	.12	.05	.01
□ 124T Greg Walker	.25	.10	.02
□ 125T Chris Welsh	.12	.05	.01
□ 126T Len Whitehouse	.12	.05	.01
□ 127T Eddie Whitson	.20	.08	.02
□ 128T Jim Wohlford	.12	.05	.01
□ 129T Matt Young	.20	.08	.02
□ 130T Joel Youngblood	.12	.05	.01
□ 131T Pat Zachry	.12	.05	.01
□ 132T Checklist 1T-132T	.12	.02	.00

1984 Topps

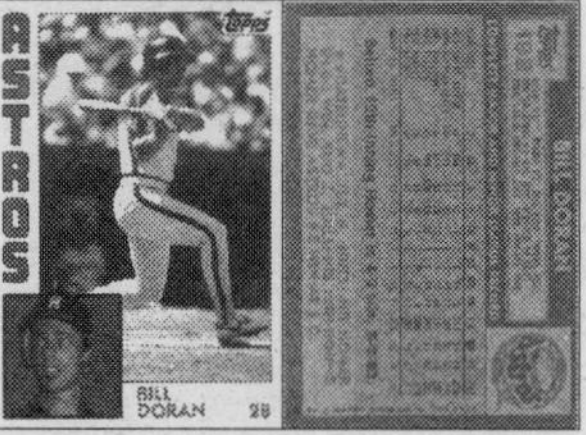

The cards in this 792-card set measure 2 1/2" by 3 1/2". For the second year in a row, Topps utilized a dual picture on the front of the card. A portrait is shown in a square insert and an action shot is featured in the main photo. Card numbers 1-6 feature 1983 Highlights (HL), cards 131-138 depict League Leaders, card numbers 386-407 feature All-Stars, and card numbers 701-718 feature active Major League career leaders in various statistical categories. Each team leader (TL) card features the team's leading hitter and pitcher pictured on the front with a team checklist back. There are six numerical checklist cards in the set. The player cards feature team logos in the upper right corner of the reverse. The key rookie cards in this set are Don Mattingly, Darryl Strawberry, and Andy Van Slyke. Topps also produced a specially boxed "glossy" edition, frequently referred to as the Topps Tiffany set. There were supposedly

only 10,000 sets of the Tiffany cards produced; they were marketed to hobby dealers. The checklist of cards (792 regular and 132 Traded) is identical to that of the normal non-glossy cards. There are two primary distinguishing features of the Tiffany cards, white card stock reverses and high gloss obverses. These Tiffany cards are valued at approximately five times the values listed below. Topps tested a special send-in offer in Michigan and a few other states whereby collectors could obtain direct from Topps ten cards of their choice. Needless to say most people ordered the key (most valuable) players necessitating the printing of a special sheet to keep up with the demand. The special sheet had five cards of Darryl Strawberry, three cards of Don Mattingly, etc. The test was apparently a failure in Topps' eyes as they have never tried it again.

	MINT	EXC	G-VG
COMPLETE SET (792)	100.00	45.00	15.00
COMMON PLAYER (1-792)	.06	.02	.00
☐ 1 HL: Steve Carlton 300th win and all-time SO king	.40	.16	.04
☐ 2 HL: Rickey Henderson 100 stolen bases, three times	1.00	.40	.10
☐ 3 HL: Dan Quisenberry Sets save record	.10	.04	.01
☐ 4 HL: Nolan Ryan, Steve Carlton, and Gaylord Perry (All surpass Johnson)	.50	.20	.05
☐ 5 HL: Dave Righetti, Bob Forsch, and Mike Warren (All pitch no-hitters)	.10	.04	.01
☐ 6 HL: Johnny Bench, Gaylord Perry, and Carl Yastrzemski (Superstars retire)	.35	.15	.03
☐ 7 Gary Lucas	.06	.02	.00
☐ 8 Don Mattingly	20.00	8.50	2.75
☐ 9 Jim Gott	.10	.04	.01
☐ 10 Robin Yount	1.25	.50	.12
☐ 11 Minnesota Twins TL Kent Hrbek Ken Schrom	.10	.04	.01
☐ 12 Billy Sample	.06	.02	.00
☐ 13 Scott Holman	.06	.02	.00
☐ 14 Tom Brookens	.06	.02	.00
☐ 15 Burt Hooton	.06	.02	.00
☐ 16 Omar Moreno	.06	.02	.00
☐ 17 John Denny	.06	.02	.00
☐ 18 Dale Berra	.06	.02	.00
☐ 19 Ray Fontenot	.06	.02	.00
☐ 20 Greg Luzinski	.10	.04	.01
☐ 21 Joe Altobelli MG	.06	.02	.00
☐ 22 Bryan Clark	.06	.02	.00
☐ 23 Keith Moreland	.06	.02	.00
☐ 24 John Martin	.06	.02	.00
☐ 25 Glenn Hubbard	.06	.02	.00
☐ 26 Bud Black	.10	.04	.01
☐ 27 Daryl Sconiers	.06	.02	.00
☐ 28 Frank Viola	.75	.30	.07
☐ 29 Danny Heep	.06	.02	.00
☐ 30 Wade Boggs	5.00	2.25	.50
☐ 31 Andy McGaffigan	.06	.02	.00
☐ 32 Bobby Ramos	.06	.02	.00
☐ 33 Tom Burgmeier	.06	.02	.00
☐ 34 Eddie Milner	.06	.02	.00
☐ 35 Don Sutton	.35	.15	.03
☐ 36 Denny Walling	.06	.02	.00
☐ 37 Texas Rangers TL Buddy Bell Rick Honeycutt	.10	.04	.01
☐ 38 Luis DeLeon	.06	.02	.00
☐ 39 Garth Iorg	.06	.02	.00
☐ 40 Dusty Baker	.10	.04	.01
☐ 41 Tony Bernazard	.06	.02	.00
☐ 42 Johnny Grubb	.06	.02	.00
☐ 43 Ron Reed	.06	.02	.00
☐ 44 Jim Morrison	.06	.02	.00
☐ 45 Jerry Mumphrey	.06	.02	.00
☐ 46 Ray Smith	.06	.02	.00
☐ 47 Rudy Law	.06	.02	.00
☐ 48 Julio Franco	3.00	1.25	.30
☐ 49 John Stuper	.06	.02	.00
☐ 50 Chris Chambliss	.10	.04	.01
☐ 51 Jim Frey MG	.06	.02	.00
☐ 52 Paul Splittorff	.06	.02	.00
☐ 53 Juan Beniquez	.06	.02	.00
☐ 54 Jesse Orosco	.06	.02	.00
☐ 55 Dave Concepcion	.10	.04	.01
☐ 56 Gary Allenson	.06	.02	.00
☐ 57 Dan Schatzeder	.06	.02	.00
☐ 58 Max Venable	.06	.02	.00
☐ 59 Sammy Stewart	.06	.02	.00
☐ 60 Paul Molitor UER ('83 stats .272, 613, 167; should be .270, 608, 164)	.30	.12	.03
☐ 61 Chris Codiroli	.06	.02	.00
☐ 62 Dave Hostetler	.06	.02	.00
☐ 63 Ed VandeBerg	.06	.02	.00
☐ 64 Mike Scioscia	.10	.04	.01
☐ 65 Kirk Gibson	.40	.16	.04
☐ 66 Houston Astros TL Jose Cruz Nolan Ryan	.30	.12	.03
☐ 67 Gary Ward	.06	.02	.00
☐ 68 Luis Salazar	.06	.02	.00

☐ 69	Rod Scurry	.06	.02	.00
☐ 70	Gary Matthews	.06	.02	.00
☐ 71	Leo Hernandez	.06	.02	.00
☐ 72	Mike Squires	.06	.02	.00
☐ 73	Jody Davis	.06	.02	.00
☐ 74	Jerry Martin	.06	.02	.00
☐ 75	Bob Forsch	.06	.02	.00
☐ 76	Alfredo Griffin	.06	.02	.00
☐ 77	Brett Butler	.30	.12	.03
☐ 78	Mike Torrez	.06	.02	.00
☐ 79	Rob Wilfong	.06	.02	.00
☐ 80	Steve Rogers	.06	.02	.00
☐ 81	Billy Martin MG	.15	.06	.01
☐ 82	Doug Bird	.06	.02	.00
☐ 83	Richie Zisk	.06	.02	.00
☐ 84	Lenny Faedo	.06	.02	.00
☐ 85	Atlee Hammaker	.06	.02	.00
☐ 86	John Shelby	.15	.06	.01
☐ 87	Frank Pastore	.06	.02	.00
☐ 88	Rob Picciolo	.06	.02	.00
☐ 89	Mike Smithson	.06	.02	.00
☐ 90	Pedro Guerrero	.25	.10	.02
☐ 91	Dan Spillner	.06	.02	.00
☐ 92	Lloyd Moseby	.10	.04	.01
☐ 93	Bob Knepper	.06	.02	.00
☐ 94	Mario Ramirez	.06	.02	.00
☐ 95	Aurelio Lopez	.06	.02	.00
☐ 96	K.C. Royals TL	.10	.04	.01
	Hal McRae			
	Larry Gura			
☐ 97	LaMarr Hoyt	.06	.02	.00
☐ 98	Steve Nicosia	.06	.02	.00
☐ 99	Craig Lefferts	.20	.08	.02
☐ 100	Reggie Jackson	1.00	.40	.10
☐ 101	Porfirio Altamirano	.06	.02	.00
☐ 102	Ken Oberkfell	.06	.02	.00
☐ 103	Dwayne Murphy	.06	.02	.00
☐ 104	Ken Dayley	.06	.02	.00
☐ 105	Tony Armas	.06	.02	.00
☐ 106	Tim Stoddard	.06	.02	.00
☐ 107	Ned Yost	.06	.02	.00
☐ 108	Randy Moffitt	.06	.02	.00
☐ 109	Brad Wellman	.06	.02	.00
☐ 110	Ron Guidry	.25	.10	.02
☐ 111	Bill Virdon MG	.06	.02	.00
☐ 112	Tom Niedenfuer	.06	.02	.00
☐ 113	Kelly Paris	.06	.02	.00
☐ 114	Checklist 1-132	.12	.02	.00
☐ 115	Andre Thornton	.10	.04	.01
☐ 116	George Bjorkman	.06	.02	.00
☐ 117	Tom Veryzer	.06	.02	.00
☐ 118	Charlie Hough	.06	.02	.00
☐ 119	John Wockenfuss	.06	.02	.00
☐ 120	Keith Hernandez	.25	.10	.02
☐ 121	Pat Sheridan	.10	.04	.01
☐ 122	Cecilio Guante	.06	.02	.00
☐ 123	Butch Wynegar	.06	.02	.00
☐ 124	Damaso Garcia	.06	.02	.00
☐ 125	Britt Burns	.06	.02	.00
☐ 126	Atlanta Braves TL	.15	.06	.01
	Dale Murphy			
	Craig McMurtry			
☐ 127	Mike Madden	.06	.02	.00
☐ 128	Rick Manning	.06	.02	.00
☐ 129	Bill Laskey	.06	.02	.00
☐ 130	Ozzie Smith	1.00	.40	.10
☐ 131	Batting Leaders	.45	.18	.04
	Bill Madlock			
	Wade Boggs			
☐ 132	Home Run Leaders	.25	.10	.02
	Mike Schmidt			
	Jim Rice			
☐ 133	RBI Leaders	.20	.08	.02
	Dale Murphy			
	Cecil Cooper			
	Jim Rice			
☐ 134	Stolen Base Leaders	.60	.25	.06
	Tim Raines			
	Rickey Henderson			
☐ 135	Victory Leaders	.10	.04	.01
	John Denny			
	LaMarr Hoyt			
☐ 136	Strikeout Leaders	.25	.10	.02
	Steve Carlton			
	Jack Morris			
☐ 137	ERA Leaders	.10	.04	.01
	Atlee Hammaker			
	Rick Honeycutt			
☐ 138	Leading Firemen	.10	.04	.01
	Al Holland			
	Dan Quisenberry			
☐ 139	Bert Campaneris	.10	.04	.01
☐ 140	Storm Davis	.10	.04	.01
☐ 141	Pat Corrales MG	.06	.02	.00
☐ 142	Rich Gale	.06	.02	.00
☐ 143	Jose Morales	.06	.02	.00
☐ 144	Brian Harper	.60	.25	.06
☐ 145	Gary Lavelle	.06	.02	.00
☐ 146	Ed Romero	.06	.02	.00
☐ 147	Dan Petry	.06	.02	.00
☐ 148	Joe Lefebvre	.06	.02	.00
☐ 149	Jon Matlack	.06	.02	.00
☐ 150	Dale Murphy	.75	.30	.07
☐ 151	Steve Trout	.06	.02	.00
☐ 152	Glenn Brummer	.06	.02	.00
☐ 153	Dick Tidrow	.06	.02	.00
☐ 154	Dave Henderson	.40	.16	.04
☐ 155	Frank White	.06	.02	.00
☐ 156	Oakland A's TL	.25	.10	.02
	Rickey Henderson			
	Tim Conroy			
☐ 157	Gary Gaetti	.15	.06	.01
☐ 158	John Curtis	.06	.02	.00
☐ 159	Darryl Cias	.06	.02	.00
☐ 160	Mario Soto	.06	.02	.00
☐ 161	Junior Ortiz	.10	.04	.01

☐ 162 Bob Ojeda .10 .04 .01
☐ 163 Lorenzo Gray .06 .02 .00
☐ 164 Scott Sanderson .10 .04 .01
☐ 165 Ken Singleton .10 .04 .01
☐ 166 Jamie Nelson .06 .02 .00
☐ 167 Marshall Edwards .06 .02 .00
☐ 168 Juan Bonilla .06 .02 .00
☐ 169 Larry Parrish .06 .02 .00
☐ 170 Jerry Reuss .06 .02 .00
☐ 171 Frank Robinson MG .15 .06 .01
☐ 172 Frank DiPino .06 .02 .00
☐ 173 Marvell Wynne .10 .04 .01
☐ 174 Juan Berenguer .06 .02 .00
☐ 175 Graig Nettles .15 .06 .01
☐ 176 Lee Smith .40 .16 .04
☐ 177 Jerry Hairston .06 .02 .00
☐ 178 Bill Krueger .10 .04 .01
☐ 179 Buck Martinez .06 .02 .00
☐ 180 Manny Trillo .06 .02 .00
☐ 181 Roy Thomas .06 .02 .00
☐ 182 Darryl Strawberry 21.00 9.00 3.00
☐ 183 Al Williams .06 .02 .00
☐ 184 Mike O'Berry .06 .02 .00
☐ 185 Sixto Lezcano .06 .02 .00
☐ 186 Cardinal TL .10 .04 .01
Lonnie Smith
John Stuper
☐ 187 Luis Aponte .06 .02 .00
☐ 188 Bryan Little .06 .02 .00
☐ 189 Tim Conroy .06 .02 .00
☐ 190 Ben Oglivie .06 .02 .00
☐ 191 Mike Boddicker .06 .02 .00
☐ 192 Nick Esasky .15 .06 .01
☐ 193 Darrell Brown .06 .02 .00
☐ 194 Domingo Ramos .06 .02 .00
☐ 195 Jack Morris .60 .25 .06
☐ 196 Don Slaught .15 .06 .01
☐ 197 Garry Hancock .06 .02 .00
☐ 198 Bill Doran .30 .12 .03
☐ 199 Willie Hernandez .10 .04 .01
☐ 200 Andre Dawson 1.00 .40 .10
☐ 201 Bruce Kison .06 .02 .00
☐ 202 Bobby Cox MG .06 .02 .00
☐ 203 Matt Keough .06 .02 .00
☐ 204 Bobby Meacham .06 .02 .00
☐ 205 Greg Minton .06 .02 .00
☐ 206 Andy Van Slyke 2.50 1.00 .25
☐ 207 Donnie Moore .06 .02 .00
☐ 208 Jose Oquendo .20 .08 .02
☐ 209 Manny Sarmiento .06 .02 .00
☐ 210 Joe Morgan .40 .16 .04
☐ 211 Rick Sweet .06 .02 .00
☐ 212 Broderick Perkins .06 .02 .00
☐ 213 Bruce Hurst .15 .06 .01
☐ 214 Paul Householder .06 .02 .00
☐ 215 Tippy Martinez .06 .02 .00
☐ 216 White Sox TL .15 .06 .01
Carlton Fisk
Richard Dotson
☐ 217 Alan Ashby .06 .02 .00
☐ 218 Rick Waits .06 .02 .00
☐ 219 Joe Simpson .06 .02 .00
☐ 220 Fernando Valenzuela .20 .08 .02
☐ 221 Cliff Johnson .06 .02 .00
☐ 222 Rick Honeycutt .06 .02 .00
☐ 223 Wayne Krenchicki .06 .02 .00
☐ 224 Sid Monge .06 .02 .00
☐ 225 Lee Mazzilli .06 .02 .00
☐ 226 Juan Eichelberger .06 .02 .00
☐ 227 Steve Braun .06 .02 .00
☐ 228 John Rabb .06 .02 .00
☐ 229 Paul Owens MG .06 .02 .00
☐ 230 Rickey Henderson 5.00 2.25 .50
☐ 231 Gary Woods .06 .02 .00
☐ 232 Tim Wallach .15 .06 .01
☐ 233 Checklist 133-264 .12 .02 .00
☐ 234 Rafael Ramirez .06 .02 .00
☐ 235 Matt Young .10 .04 .01
☐ 236 Ellis Valentine .06 .02 .00
☐ 237 John Castino .06 .02 .00
☐ 238 Reid Nichols .06 .02 .00
☐ 239 Jay Howell .10 .04 .01
☐ 240 Eddie Murray 1.25 .50 .12
☐ 241 Bill Almon .06 .02 .00
☐ 242 Alex Trevino .06 .02 .00
☐ 243 Pete Ladd .06 .02 .00
☐ 244 Candy Maldonado .20 .08 .02
☐ 245 Rick Sutcliffe .10 .04 .01
☐ 246 New York Mets TL .20 .08 .02
Mookie Wilson
Tom Seaver
☐ 247 Onix Concepcion .06 .02 .00
☐ 248 Bill Dawley .06 .02 .00
☐ 249 Jay Johnstone .10 .04 .01
☐ 250 Bill Madlock .10 .04 .01
☐ 251 Tony Gwynn 4.50 2.00 .45
☐ 252 Larry Christenson .06 .02 .00
☐ 253 Jim Wohlford .06 .02 .00
☐ 254 Shane Rawley .06 .02 .00
☐ 255 Bruce Benedict .06 .02 .00
☐ 256 Dave Geisel .06 .02 .00
☐ 257 Julio Cruz .06 .02 .00
☐ 258 Luis Sanchez .06 .02 .00
☐ 259 Sparky Anderson MG .10 .04 .01
☐ 260 Scott McGregor .06 .02 .00
☐ 261 Bobby Brown .06 .02 .00
☐ 262 Tom Candiotti .40 .16 .04
☐ 263 Jack Fimple .06 .02 .00
☐ 264 Doug Frobel .06 .02 .00
☐ 265 Donnie Hill .10 .04 .01
☐ 266 Steve Lubratich .06 .02 .00
☐ 267 Carmelo Martinez .15 .06 .01
☐ 268 Jack O'Connor .06 .02 .00
☐ 269 Aurelio Rodriguez .06 .02 .00
☐ 270 Jeff Russell .30 .12 .03
☐ 271 Moose Haas .06 .02 .00

☐ 272 Rick Dempsey	.06	.02	.00
☐ 273 Charlie Puleo	.06	.02	.00
☐ 274 Rick Monday	.06	.02	.00
☐ 275 Len Matuszek	.06	.02	.00
☐ 276 Angels TL	.15	.06	.01
Rod Carew			
Geoff Zahn			
☐ 277 Eddie Whitson	.06	.02	.00
☐ 278 Jorge Bell	1.00	.40	.10
☐ 279 Ivan DeJesus	.06	.02	.00
☐ 280 Floyd Bannister	.06	.02	.00
☐ 281 Larry Milbourne	.06	.02	.00
☐ 282 Jim Barr	.06	.02	.00
☐ 283 Larry Biittner	.06	.02	.00
☐ 284 Howard Bailey	.06	.02	.00
☐ 285 Darrell Porter	.06	.02	.00
☐ 286 Lary Sorensen	.06	.02	.00
☐ 287 Warren Cromartie	.06	.02	.00
☐ 288 Jim Beattie	.06	.02	.00
☐ 289 Randy Johnson	.06	.02	.00
☐ 290 Dave Dravecky	.15	.06	.01
☐ 291 Chuck Tanner MG	.06	.02	.00
☐ 292 Tony Scott	.06	.02	.00
☐ 293 Ed Lynch	.06	.02	.00
☐ 294 U.L. Washington	.06	.02	.00
☐ 295 Mike Flanagan	.10	.04	.01
☐ 296 Jeff Newman	.06	.02	.00
☐ 297 Bruce Berenyi	.06	.02	.00
☐ 298 Jim Gantner	.06	.02	.00
☐ 299 John Butcher	.06	.02	.00
☐ 300 Pete Rose	1.00	.40	.10
☐ 301 Frank LaCorte	.06	.02	.00
☐ 302 Barry Bonnell	.06	.02	.00
☐ 303 Marty Castillo	.06	.02	.00
☐ 304 Warren Brusstar	.06	.02	.00
☐ 305 Roy Smalley	.06	.02	.00
☐ 306 Dodgers TL	.15	.06	.01
Pedro Guerrero			
Bob Welch			
☐ 307 Bobby Mitchell	.06	.02	.00
☐ 308 Ron Hassey	.06	.02	.00
☐ 309 Tony Phillips	.35	.15	.03
☐ 310 Willie McGee	.40	.16	.04
☐ 311 Jerry Koosman	.10	.04	.01
☐ 312 Jorge Orta	.06	.02	.00
☐ 313 Mike Jorgensen	.06	.02	.00
☐ 314 Orlando Mercado	.06	.02	.00
☐ 315 Bob Grich	.10	.04	.01
☐ 316 Mark Bradley	.06	.02	.00
☐ 317 Greg Pryor	.06	.02	.00
☐ 318 Bill Gullickson	.10	.04	.01
☐ 319 Al Bumbry	.06	.02	.00
☐ 320 Bob Stanley	.06	.02	.00
☐ 321 Harvey Kuenn MG	.06	.02	.00
☐ 322 Ken Schrom	.06	.02	.00
☐ 323 Alan Knicely	.06	.02	.00
☐ 324 Alejandro Pena	.30	.12	.03
☐ 325 Darrell Evans	.15	.06	.01
☐ 326 Bob Kearney	.06	.02	.00
☐ 327 Ruppert Jones	.06	.02	.00
☐ 328 Vern Ruhle	.06	.02	.00
☐ 329 Pat Tabler	.10	.04	.01
☐ 330 John Candelaria	.06	.02	.00
☐ 331 Bucky Dent	.10	.04	.01
☐ 332 Kevin Gross	.20	.08	.02
☐ 333 Larry Herndon	.06	.02	.00
☐ 334 Chuck Rainey	.06	.02	.00
☐ 335 Don Baylor	.10	.04	.01
☐ 336 Seattle Mariners TL	.10	.04	.01
Pat Putnam			
Matt Young			
☐ 337 Kevin Hagen	.06	.02	.00
☐ 338 Mike Warren	.06	.02	.00
☐ 339 Roy Lee Jackson	.06	.02	.00
☐ 340 Hal McRae	.10	.04	.01
☐ 341 Dave Tobik	.06	.02	.00
☐ 342 Tim Foli	.06	.02	.00
☐ 343 Mark Davis	.10	.04	.01
☐ 344 Rick Miller	.06	.02	.00
☐ 345 Kent Hrbek	.35	.15	.03
☐ 346 Kurt Bevacqua	.06	.02	.00
☐ 347 Allan Ramirez	.06	.02	.00
☐ 348 Toby Harrah	.06	.02	.00
☐ 349 Bob L. Gibson	.06	.02	.00
(Brewers Pitcher)			
☐ 350 George Foster	.15	.06	.01
☐ 351 Russ Nixon MG	.06	.02	.00
☐ 352 Dave Stewart	.50	.20	.05
☐ 353 Jim Anderson	.06	.02	.00
☐ 354 Jeff Burroughs	.06	.02	.00
☐ 355 Jason Thompson	.06	.02	.00
☐ 356 Glenn Abbott	.06	.02	.00
☐ 357 Ron Cey	.10	.04	.01
☐ 358 Bob Dernier	.06	.02	.00
☐ 359 Jim Acker	.10	.04	.01
☐ 360 Willie Randolph	.10	.04	.01
☐ 361 Dave Smith	.06	.02	.00
☐ 362 David Green	.06	.02	.00
☐ 363 Tim Laudner	.06	.02	.00
☐ 364 Scott Fletcher	.10	.04	.01
☐ 365 Steve Bedrosian	.10	.04	.01
☐ 366 Padres TL	.12	.05	.01
Terry Kennedy			
Dave Dravecky			
☐ 367 Jamie Easterly	.06	.02	.00
☐ 368 Hubie Brooks	.15	.06	.01
☐ 369 Steve McCatty	.06	.02	.00
☐ 370 Tim Raines	.40	.16	.04
☐ 371 Dave Gumpert	.06	.02	.00
☐ 372 Gary Roenicke	.06	.02	.00
☐ 373 Bill Scherrer	.06	.02	.00
☐ 374 Don Money	.06	.02	.00
☐ 375 Dennis Leonard	.06	.02	.00
☐ 376 Dave Anderson	.10	.04	.01
☐ 377 Danny Darwin	.06	.02	.00
☐ 378 Bob Brenly	.06	.02	.00

☐ 379 Checklist 265-396 .12 .02 .00
☐ 380 Steve Garvey .45 .18 .04
☐ 381 Ralph Houk MG .06 .02 .00
☐ 382 Chris Nyman .06 .02 .00
☐ 383 Terry Puhl .06 .02 .00
☐ 384 Lee Tunnell .06 .02 .00
☐ 385 Tony Perez .25 .10 .02
☐ 386 George Hendrick AS .06 .02 .00
☐ 387 Johnny Ray AS .06 .02 .00
☐ 388 Mike Schmidt AS .50 .20 .05
☐ 389 Ozzie Smith AS .30 .12 .03
☐ 390 Tim Raines AS .15 .06 .01
☐ 391 Dale Murphy AS .25 .10 .02
☐ 392 Andre Dawson AS .35 .15 .03
☐ 393 Gary Carter AS .15 .06 .01
☐ 394 Steve Rogers AS .06 .02 .00
☐ 395 Steve Carlton AS .25 .10 .02
☐ 396 Jesse Orosco AS .06 .02 .00
☐ 397 Eddie Murray AS .40 .16 .04
☐ 398 Lou Whitaker AS .15 .06 .01
☐ 399 George Brett AS .40 .16 .04
☐ 400 Cal Ripken AS 1.25 .50 .12
☐ 401 Jim Rice AS .15 .06 .01
☐ 402 Dave Winfield AS .25 .10 .02
☐ 403 Lloyd Moseby AS .06 .02 .00
☐ 404 Ted Simmons AS .10 .04 .01
☐ 405 LaMarr Hoyt AS .06 .02 .00
☐ 406 Ron Guidry AS .10 .04 .01
☐ 407 Dan Quisenberry AS .10 .04 .01
☐ 408 Lou Piniella .10 .04 .01
☐ 409 Juan Agosto .10 .04 .01
☐ 410 Claudell Washington .06 .02 .00
☐ 411 Houston Jimenez .06 .02 .00
☐ 412 Doug Rader MG .06 .02 .00
☐ 413 Spike Owen .25 .10 .02
☐ 414 Mitchell Page .06 .02 .00
☐ 415 Tommy John .20 .08 .02
☐ 416 Dane Iorg .06 .02 .00
☐ 417 Mike Armstrong .06 .02 .00
☐ 418 Ron Hodges .06 .02 .00
☐ 419 John Henry Johnson .06 .02 .00
☐ 420 Cecil Cooper .10 .04 .01
☐ 421 Charlie Lea .06 .02 .00
☐ 422 Jose Cruz .10 .04 .01
☐ 423 Mike Morgan .10 .04 .01
☐ 424 Dann Bilardello .06 .02 .00
☐ 425 Steve Howe .06 .02 .00
☐ 426 Orioles TL .60 .25 .06
Cal Ripken
Mike Boddicker
☐ 427 Rick Leach .06 .02 .00
☐ 428 Fred Breining .06 .02 .00
☐ 429 Randy Bush .15 .06 .01
☐ 430 Rusty Staub .10 .04 .01
☐ 431 Chris Bando .06 .02 .00
☐ 432 Charles Hudson .10 .04 .01
☐ 433 Rich Hebner .06 .02 .00
☐ 434 Harold Baines .35 .15 .03
☐ 435 Neil Allen .06 .02 .00
☐ 436 Rick Peters .06 .02 .00
☐ 437 Mike Proly .06 .02 .00
☐ 438 Biff Pocoroba .06 .02 .00
☐ 439 Bob Stoddard .06 .02 .00
☐ 440 Steve Kemp .06 .02 .00
☐ 441 Bob Lillis MG .06 .02 .00
☐ 442 Byron McLaughlin .06 .02 .00
☐ 443 Benny Ayala .06 .02 .00
☐ 444 Steve Renko .06 .02 .00
☐ 445 Jerry Remy .06 .02 .00
☐ 446 Luis Pujols .06 .02 .00
☐ 447 Tom Brunansky .15 .06 .01
☐ 448 Ben Hayes .06 .02 .00
☐ 449 Joe Pettini .06 .02 .00
☐ 450 Gary Carter .40 .16 .04
☐ 451 Bob Jones .06 .02 .00
☐ 452 Chuck Porter .06 .02 .00
☐ 453 Willie Upshaw .06 .02 .00
☐ 454 Joe Beckwith .06 .02 .00
☐ 455 Terry Kennedy .06 .02 .00
☐ 456 Chicago Cubs TL .12 .05 .01
Keith Moreland
Fergie Jenkins
☐ 457 Dave Rozema .06 .02 .00
☐ 458 Kiko Garcia .06 .02 .00
☐ 459 Kevin Hickey .06 .02 .00
☐ 460 Dave Winfield .80 .35 .08
☐ 461 Jim Maler .06 .02 .00
☐ 462 Lee Lacy .06 .02 .00
☐ 463 Dave Engle .06 .02 .00
☐ 464 Jeff A. Jones .06 .02 .00
(A's Pitcher)
☐ 465 Mookie Wilson .10 .04 .01
☐ 466 Gene Garber .06 .02 .00
☐ 467 Mike Ramsey .06 .02 .00
☐ 468 Geoff Zahn .06 .02 .00
☐ 469 Tom O'Malley .06 .02 .00
☐ 470 Nolan Ryan 5.50 2.50 .55
☐ 471 Dick Howser MG .06 .02 .00
☐ 472 Mike Brown .06 .02 .00
(Red Sox Pitcher)
☐ 473 Jim Dwyer .06 .02 .00
☐ 474 Greg Bargar .06 .02 .00
☐ 475 Gary Redus .25 .10 .02
☐ 476 Tom Tellmann .06 .02 .00
☐ 477 Rafael Landestoy .06 .02 .00
☐ 478 Alan Bannister .06 .02 .00
☐ 479 Frank Tanana .10 .04 .01
☐ 480 Ron Kittle .10 .04 .01
☐ 481 Mark Thurmond .06 .02 .00
☐ 482 Enos Cabell .06 .02 .00
☐ 483 Fergie Jenkins .35 .15 .03
☐ 484 Ozzie Virgil .06 .02 .00
☐ 485 Rick Rhoden .06 .02 .00
☐ 486 N.Y. Yankees TL .12 .05 .01
Don Baylor
Ron Guidry

☐ 487 Ricky Adams .06 .02 .00
☐ 488 Jesse Barfield .20 .08 .02
☐ 489 Dave Von Ohlen .06 .02 .00
☐ 490 Cal Ripken 7.50 3.25 .75
☐ 491 Bobby Castillo .06 .02 .00
☐ 492 Tucker Ashford .06 .02 .00
☐ 493 Mike Norris .06 .02 .00
☐ 494 Chili Davis .20 .08 .02
☐ 495 Rollie Fingers .40 .16 .04
☐ 496 Terry Francona .06 .02 .00
☐ 497 Bud Anderson .06 .02 .00
☐ 498 Rich Gedman .06 .02 .00
☐ 499 Mike Witt .06 .02 .00
☐ 500 George Brett 1.50 .60 .15
☐ 501 Steve Henderson .06 .02 .00
☐ 502 Joe Torre MG .10 .04 .01
☐ 503 Elias Sosa .06 .02 .00
☐ 504 Mickey Rivers .06 .02 .00
☐ 505 Pete Vuckovich .06 .02 .00
☐ 506 Ernie Whitt .06 .02 .00
☐ 507 Mike LaCoss .06 .02 .00
☐ 508 Mel Hall .40 .16 .04
☐ 509 Brad Havens .06 .02 .00
☐ 510 Alan Trammell .65 .25 .06
☐ 511 Marty Bystrom .06 .02 .00
☐ 512 Oscar Gamble .06 .02 .00
☐ 513 Dave Beard .06 .02 .00
☐ 514 Floyd Rayford .06 .02 .00
☐ 515 Gorman Thomas .10 .04 .01
☐ 516 Montreal Expos TL .10 .04 .01
Al Oliver
Charlie Lea
☐ 517 John Moses .10 .04 .01
☐ 518 Greg Walker .10 .04 .01
☐ 519 Ron Davis .06 .02 .00
☐ 520 Bob Boone .10 .04 .01
☐ 521 Pete Falcone .06 .02 .00
☐ 522 Dave Bergman .06 .02 .00
☐ 523 Glenn Hoffman .06 .02 .00
☐ 524 Carlos Diaz .06 .02 .00
☐ 525 Willie Wilson .10 .04 .01
☐ 526 Ron Oester .06 .02 .00
☐ 527 Checklist 397-528 .12 .02 .00
☐ 528 Mark Brouhard .06 .02 .00
☐ 529 Keith Atherton .06 .02 .00
☐ 530 Dan Ford .06 .02 .00
☐ 531 Steve Boros MG .06 .02 .00
☐ 532 Eric Show .10 .04 .01
☐ 533 Ken Landreaux .06 .02 .00
☐ 534 Pete O'Brien .35 .15 .03
☐ 535 Bo Diaz .06 .02 .00
☐ 536 Doug Bair .06 .02 .00
☐ 537 Johnny Ray .06 .02 .00
☐ 538 Kevin Bass .10 .04 .01
☐ 539 George Frazier .06 .02 .00
☐ 540 George Hendrick .06 .02 .00
☐ 541 Dennis Lamp .06 .02 .00
☐ 542 Duane Kuiper .06 .02 .00
☐ 543 Craig McMurtry .06 .02 .00
☐ 544 Cesar Geronimo .06 .02 .00
☐ 545 Bill Buckner .10 .04 .01
☐ 546 Indians TL .10 .04 .01
Mike Hargrove
Lary Sorensen
☐ 547 Mike Moore .15 .06 .01
☐ 548 Ron Jackson .06 .02 .00
☐ 549 Walt Terrell .15 .06 .01
☐ 550 Jim Rice .15 .06 .01
☐ 551 Scott Ullger .06 .02 .00
☐ 552 Ray Burris .06 .02 .00
☐ 553 Joe Nolan .06 .02 .00
☐ 554 Ted Power .10 .04 .01
☐ 555 Greg Brock .10 .04 .01
☐ 556 Joey McLaughlin .06 .02 .00
☐ 557 Wayne Tolleson .06 .02 .00
☐ 558 Mike Davis .06 .02 .00
☐ 559 Mike Scott .15 .06 .01
☐ 560 Carlton Fisk 1.00 .40 .10
☐ 561 Whitey Herzog MG .06 .02 .00
☐ 562 Manny Castillo .06 .02 .00
☐ 563 Glenn Wilson .06 .02 .00
☐ 564 Al Holland .06 .02 .00
☐ 565 Leon Durham .06 .02 .00
☐ 566 Jim Bibby .06 .02 .00
☐ 567 Mike Heath .06 .02 .00
☐ 568 Pete Filson .06 .02 .00
☐ 569 Bake McBride .06 .02 .00
☐ 570 Dan Quisenberry .10 .04 .01
☐ 571 Bruce Bochy .06 .02 .00
☐ 572 Jerry Royster .06 .02 .00
☐ 573 Dave Kingman .15 .06 .01
☐ 574 Brian Downing .10 .04 .01
☐ 575 Jim Clancy .06 .02 .00
☐ 576 Giants TL .10 .04 .01
Jeff Leonard
Atlee Hammaker
☐ 577 Mark Clear .06 .02 .00
☐ 578 Lenn Sakata .06 .02 .00
☐ 579 Bob James .06 .02 .00
☐ 580 Lonnie Smith .15 .06 .01
☐ 581 Jose DeLeon .20 .08 .02
☐ 582 Bob McClure .06 .02 .00
☐ 583 Derrel Thomas .06 .02 .00
☐ 584 Dave Schmidt .06 .02 .00
☐ 585 Dan Driessen .06 .02 .00
☐ 586 Joe Niekro .10 .04 .01
☐ 587 Von Hayes .10 .04 .01
☐ 588 Milt Wilcox .06 .02 .00
☐ 589 Mike Easler .06 .02 .00
☐ 590 Dave Stieb .20 .08 .02
☐ 591 Tony LaRussa MG .10 .04 .01
☐ 592 Andre Robertson .06 .02 .00
☐ 593 Jeff Lahti .06 .02 .00
☐ 594 Gene Richards .06 .02 .00
☐ 595 Jeff Reardon .35 .15 .03
☐ 596 Ryne Sandberg 9.00 4.00 .90

☐ 597	Rick Camp	.06	.02	.00
☐ 598	Rusty Kuntz	.06	.02	.00
☐ 599	Doug Sisk	.06	.02	.00
☐ 600	Rod Carew	1.00	.40	.10
☐ 601	John Tudor	.15	.06	.01
☐ 602	John Wathan	.06	.02	.00
☐ 603	Renie Martin	.06	.02	.00
☐ 604	John Lowenstein	.06	.02	.00
☐ 605	Mike Caldwell	.06	.02	.00
☐ 606	Blue Jays TL Lloyd Moseby Dave Stieb	.12	.05	.01
☐ 607	Tom Hume	.06	.02	.00
☐ 608	Bobby Johnson	.06	.02	.00
☐ 609	Dan Meyer	.06	.02	.00
☐ 610	Steve Sax	.35	.15	.03
☐ 611	Chet Lemon	.06	.02	.00
☐ 612	Harry Spilman	.06	.02	.00
☐ 613	Greg Gross	.06	.02	.00
☐ 614	Len Barker	.06	.02	.00
☐ 615	Garry Templeton	.10	.04	.01
☐ 616	Don Robinson	.06	.02	.00
☐ 617	Rick Cerone	.06	.02	.00
☐ 618	Dickie Noles	.06	.02	.00
☐ 619	Jerry Dybzinski	.06	.02	.00
☐ 620	Al Oliver	.10	.04	.01
☐ 621	Frank Howard MG	.06	.02	.00
☐ 622	Al Cowens	.06	.02	.00
☐ 623	Ron Washington	.06	.02	.00
☐ 624	Terry Harper	.06	.02	.00
☐ 625	Larry Gura	.06	.02	.00
☐ 626	Bob Clark	.06	.02	.00
☐ 627	Dave LaPoint	.06	.02	.00
☐ 628	Ed Jurak	.06	.02	.00
☐ 629	Rick Langford	.06	.02	.00
☐ 630	Ted Simmons	.10	.04	.01
☐ 631	Dennis Martinez	.10	.04	.01
☐ 632	Tom Foley	.06	.02	.00
☐ 633	Mike Krukow	.06	.02	.00
☐ 634	Mike Marshall	.10	.04	.01
☐ 635	Dave Righetti	.15	.06	.01
☐ 636	Pat Putnam	.06	.02	.00
☐ 637	Phillies TL Gary Matthews John Denny	.10	.04	.01
☐ 638	George Vukovich	.06	.02	.00
☐ 639	Rick Lysander	.06	.02	.00
☐ 640	Lance Parrish	.25	.10	.02
☐ 641	Mike Richardt	.06	.02	.00
☐ 642	Tom Underwood	.06	.02	.00
☐ 643	Mike Brown (Angels OF)	.06	.02	.00
☐ 644	Tim Lollar	.06	.02	.00
☐ 645	Tony Pena	.10	.04	.01
☐ 646	Checklist 529-660	.12	.02	.00
☐ 647	Ron Roenicke	.06	.02	.00
☐ 648	Len Whitehouse	.06	.02	.00
☐ 649	Tom Herr	.10	.04	.01
☐ 650	Phil Niekro	.30	.12	.03
☐ 651	John McNamara MG	.06	.02	.00
☐ 652	Rudy May	.06	.02	.00
☐ 653	Dave Stapleton	.06	.02	.00
☐ 654	Bob Bailor	.06	.02	.00
☐ 655	Amos Otis	.10	.04	.01
☐ 656	Bryn Smith	.10	.04	.01
☐ 657	Thad Bosley	.06	.02	.00
☐ 658	Jerry Augustine	.06	.02	.00
☐ 659	Duane Walker	.06	.02	.00
☐ 660	Ray Knight	.10	.04	.01
☐ 661	Steve Yeager	.06	.02	.00
☐ 662	Tom Brennan	.06	.02	.00
☐ 663	Johnnie LeMaster	.06	.02	.00
☐ 664	Dave Stegman	.06	.02	.00
☐ 665	Buddy Bell	.10	.04	.01
☐ 666	Detroit Tigers TL Lou Whitaker Jack Morris	.15	.06	.01
☐ 667	Vance Law	.06	.02	.00
☐ 668	Larry McWilliams	.06	.02	.00
☐ 669	Dave Lopes	.10	.04	.01
☐ 670	Rich Gossage	.15	.06	.01
☐ 671	Jamie Quirk	.06	.02	.00
☐ 672	Ricky Nelson	.06	.02	.00
☐ 673	Mike Walters	.06	.02	.00
☐ 674	Tim Flannery	.06	.02	.00
☐ 675	Pascual Perez	.10	.04	.01
☐ 676	Brian Giles	.06	.02	.00
☐ 677	Doyle Alexander	.06	.02	.00
☐ 678	Chris Speier	.06	.02	.00
☐ 679	Art Howe	.10	.04	.01
☐ 680	Fred Lynn	.15	.06	.01
☐ 681	Tom Lasorda MG	.10	.04	.01
☐ 682	Dan Morogiello	.06	.02	.00
☐ 683	Marty Barrett	.15	.06	.01
☐ 684	Bob Shirley	.06	.02	.00
☐ 685	Willie Aikens	.06	.02	.00
☐ 686	Joe Price	.06	.02	.00
☐ 687	Roy Howell	.06	.02	.00
☐ 688	George Wright	.06	.02	.00
☐ 689	Mike Fischlin	.06	.02	.00
☐ 690	Jack Clark	.20	.08	.02
☐ 691	Steve Lake	.06	.02	.00
☐ 692	Dickie Thon	.10	.04	.01
☐ 693	Alan Wiggins	.06	.02	.00
☐ 694	Mike Stanton	.06	.02	.00
☐ 695	Lou Whitaker	.35	.15	.03
☐ 696	Pirates TL Bill Madlock Rick Rhoden	.10	.04	.01
☐ 697	Dale Murray	.06	.02	.00
☐ 698	Marc Hill	.06	.02	.00
☐ 699	Dave Rucker	.06	.02	.00
☐ 700	Mike Schmidt	2.25	.90	.22
☐ 701	NL Active Batting Bill Madlock Pete Rose	.20	.08	.02

Dave Parker
☐ 702 NL Active Hits .... .20 .08 .02
Pete Rose
Rusty Staub
Tony Perez
☐ 703 NL Active Home Run ...... .20 .08 .02
Mike Schmidt
Tony Perez
Dave Kingman
☐ 704 NL Active RBI .... .10 .04 .01
Tony Perez
Rusty Staub
Al Oliver
☐ 705 NL Active Steals .... .10 .04 .01
Joe Morgan
Cesar Cedeno
Larry Bowa
☐ 706 NL Active Victory .... .25 .10 .02
Steve Carlton
Fergie Jenkins
Tom Seaver
☐ 707 NL Active Strikeout .... .50 .20 .05
Steve Carlton
Nolan Ryan
Tom Seaver
☐ 708 NL Active ERA .... .20 .08 .02
Tom Seaver
Steve Carlton
Steve Rogers
☐ 709 NL Active Save .... .10 .04 .01
Bruce Sutter
Tug McGraw
Gene Garber
☐ 710 AL Active Batting .... .20 .08 .02
Rod Carew
George Brett
Cecil Cooper
☐ 711 AL Active Hits .... .20 .08 .02
Rod Carew
Bert Campaneris
Reggie Jackson
☐ 712 AL Active Home Run ...... .20 .08 .02
Reggie Jackson
Graig Nettles
Greg Luzinski
☐ 713 AL Active RBI .... .20 .08 .02
Reggie Jackson
Ted Simmons
Graig Nettles
☐ 714 AL Active Steals .... .10 .04 .01
Bert Campaneris
Dave Lopes
Omar Moreno
☐ 715 AL Active Victory .... .20 .08 .02
Jim Palmer
Don Sutton
Tommy John
☐ 716 AL Active Strikeout .... .15 .06 .01
Don Sutton
Bert Blyleven
Jerry Koosman
☐ 717 AL Active ERA .... .20 .08 .02
Jim Palmer
Rollie Fingers
Ron Guidry
☐ 718 AL Active Save .... .15 .06 .01
Rollie Fingers
Rich Gossage
Dan Quisenberry
☐ 719 Andy Hassler .... .06 .02 .00
☐ 720 Dwight Evans .... .20 .08 .02
☐ 721 Del Crandall MG .... .06 .02 .00
☐ 722 Bob Welch .... .20 .08 .02
☐ 723 Rich Dauer .... .06 .02 .00
☐ 724 Eric Rasmussen .... .06 .02 .00
☐ 725 Cesar Cedeno .... .10 .04 .01
☐ 726 Brewers TL .... .10 .04 .01
Ted Simmons
Moose Haas
☐ 727 Joel Youngblood .... .06 .02 .00
☐ 728 Tug McGraw .... .10 .04 .01
☐ 729 Gene Tenace .... .10 .04 .01
☐ 730 Bruce Sutter .... .15 .06 .01
☐ 731 Lynn Jones .... .06 .02 .00
☐ 732 Terry Crowley .... .06 .02 .00
☐ 733 Dave Collins .... .06 .02 .00
☐ 734 Odell Jones .... .06 .02 .00
☐ 735 Rick Burleson .... .06 .02 .00
☐ 736 Dick Ruthven .... .06 .02 .00
☐ 737 Jim Essian .... .06 .02 .00
☐ 738 Bill Schroeder .... .06 .02 .00
☐ 739 Bob Watson .... .06 .02 .00
☐ 740 Tom Seaver .... 1.25 .50 .12
☐ 741 Wayne Gross .... .06 .02 .00
☐ 742 Dick Williams MG .... .06 .02 .00
☐ 743 Don Hood .... .06 .02 .00
☐ 744 Jamie Allen .... .06 .02 .00
☐ 745 Dennis Eckersley .... .40 .16 .04
☐ 746 Mickey Hatcher .... .06 .02 .00
☐ 747 Pat Zachry .... .06 .02 .00
☐ 748 Jeff Leonard .... .06 .02 .00
☐ 749 Doug Flynn .... .06 .02 .00
☐ 750 Jim Palmer .... .90 .40 .09
☐ 751 Charlie Moore .... .06 .02 .00
☐ 752 Phil Garner .... .10 .04 .01
☐ 753 Doug Gwosdz .... .06 .02 .00
☐ 754 Kent Tekulve .... .06 .02 .00
☐ 755 Garry Maddox .... .06 .02 .00
☐ 756 Reds TL .... .10 .04 .01
Ron Oester
Mario Soto
☐ 757 Larry Bowa .... .10 .04 .01
☐ 758 Bill Stein .... .06 .02 .00
☐ 759 Richard Dotson .... .06 .02 .00
☐ 760 Bob Horner .... .10 .04 .01
☐ 761 John Montefusco .... .06 .02 .00

☐ 762 Rance Mulliniks	.06	.02	.00
☐ 763 Craig Swan	.06	.02	.00
☐ 764 Mike Hargrove	.06	.02	.00
☐ 765 Ken Forsch	.06	.02	.00
☐ 766 Mike Vail	.06	.02	.00
☐ 767 Carney Lansford	.10	.04	.01
☐ 768 Champ Summers	.06	.02	.00
☐ 769 Bill Caudill	.06	.02	.00
☐ 770 Ken Griffey	.15	.06	.01
☐ 771 Billy Gardner MG	.06	.02	.00
☐ 772 Jim Slaton	.06	.02	.00
☐ 773 Todd Cruz	.06	.02	.00
☐ 774 Tom Gorman	.06	.02	.00
☐ 775 Dave Parker	.35	.15	.03
☐ 776 Craig Reynolds	.06	.02	.00
☐ 777 Tom Paciorek	.06	.02	.00
☐ 778 Andy Hawkins	.20	.08	.02
☐ 779 Jim Sundberg	.06	.02	.00
☐ 780 Steve Carlton	.75	.30	.07
☐ 781 Checklist 661-792	.12	.02	.00
☐ 782 Steve Balboni	.06	.02	.00
☐ 783 Luis Leal	.06	.02	.00
☐ 784 Leon Roberts	.06	.02	.00
☐ 785 Joaquin Andujar	.10	.04	.01
☐ 786 Red Sox TL Wade Boggs Bob Ojeda	.40	.16	.04
☐ 787 Bill Campbell	.06	.02	.00
☐ 788 Milt May	.06	.02	.00
☐ 789 Bert Blyleven	.20	.08	.02
☐ 790 Doug DeCinces	.10	.04	.01
☐ 791 Terry Forster	.06	.02	.00
☐ 792 Bill Russell	.15	.06	.01

1984 Topps Traded

The cards in this 132-card set measure 2 1/2" by 3 1/2". In its now standard procedure, Topps issued its Traded (or extended) set for the fourth year in a row. Because all photos and statistics of its regular set for the year were developed during the fall and winter months of the preceding year, players who changed teams during the fall, winter, and spring months are portrayed with the teams they were with in 1983. The Traded set amends the shortcomings of the regular set by presenting the players with their proper teams for the current year. Sevral of 1984's top rookies not contained in the regular set are picked up in the Traded set. The key (extended) rookie cards in this set are Alvin Davis, Dwight Gooden, Mark Langston, Jose Rijo, and Bret Saberhagen. Again this year, the Topps affiliate in Ireland printed the cards, and the cards were available through hobby channels only. Topps also produced a specially boxed "glossy" edition, frequently referred to as the Topps Traded Tiffany set. There were supposedly only 10,000 sets of the Tiffany cards produced; they were marketed to hobby dealers. The checklist of cards is identical to that of the normal non-glossy cards. There are two primary distinguishing features of the Tiffany cards, white card stock reverses and high gloss obverses. These Tiffany cards are valued at approximately five times the values listed below.

	MINT	EXC	G-VG
COMPLETE SET (132)	100.00	45.00	15.00
COMMON PLAYER (1-132)	.12	.05	.01
☐ 1T Willie Aikens	.20	.08	.02
☐ 2T Luis Aponte	.12	.05	.01
☐ 3T Mike Armstrong	.12	.05	.01
☐ 4T Bob Bailor	.12	.05	.01
☐ 5T Dusty Baker	.20	.08	.02
☐ 6T Steve Balboni	.20	.08	.02
☐ 7T Alan Bannister	.12	.05	.01
☐ 8T Dave Beard	.12	.05	.01
☐ 9T Joe Beckwith	.12	.05	.01
☐ 10T Bruce Berenyi	.12	.05	.01
☐ 11T Dave Bergman	.12	.05	.01
☐ 12T Tony Bernazard	.12	.05	.01
☐ 13T Yogi Berra MG	.40	.16	.04
☐ 14T Barry Bonnell	.12	.05	.01
☐ 15T Phil Bradley	.60	.25	.06
☐ 16T Fred Breining	.12	.05	.01
☐ 17T Bill Buckner	.25	.10	.02
☐ 18T Ray Burris	.12	.05	.01
☐ 19T John Butcher	.12	.05	.01
☐ 20T Brett Butler	.75	.30	.07

□ 21T	Enos Cabell	.12	.05	.01
□ 22T	Bill Campbell	.12	.05	.01
□ 23T	Bill Caudill	.12	.05	.01
□ 24T	Bob Clark	.12	.05	.01
□ 25T	Bryan Clark	.12	.05	.01
□ 26T	Jaime Cocanower	.12	.05	.01
□ 27T	Ron Darling	3.00	1.25	.30
□ 28T	Alvin Davis	4.00	1.75	.40
□ 29T	Ken Dayley	.20	.08	.02
□ 30T	Jeff Dedmon	.12	.05	.01
□ 31T	Bob Dernier	.12	.05	.01
□ 32T	Carlos Diaz	.12	.05	.01
□ 33T	Mike Easler	.12	.05	.01
□ 34T	Dennis Eckersley	2.00	.80	.20
□ 35T	Jim Essian	.20	.08	.02
□ 36T	Darrell Evans	.30	.12	.03
□ 37T	Mike Fitzgerald	.12	.05	.01
□ 38T	Tim Foli	.12	.05	.01
□ 39T	George Frazier	.12	.05	.01
□ 40T	Rich Gale	.12	.05	.01
□ 41T	Barbaro Garbey	.12	.05	.01
□ 42T	Dwight Gooden	40.00	18.00	6.00
□ 43T	Rich Gossage	.50	.20	.05
□ 44T	Wayne Gross	.12	.05	.01
□ 45T	Mark Gubicza	2.00	.80	.20
□ 46T	Jackie Gutierrez	.12	.05	.01
□ 47T	Mel Hall	.40	.16	.04
□ 48T	Toby Harrah	.20	.08	.02
□ 49T	Ron Hassey	.20	.08	.02
□ 50T	Rich Hebner	.12	.05	.01
□ 51T	Willie Hernandez	.25	.10	.02
□ 52T	Ricky Horton	.20	.08	.02
□ 53T	Art Howe	.20	.08	.02
□ 54T	Dane Iorg	.12	.05	.01
□ 55T	Brook Jacoby	1.00	.40	.10
□ 56T	Mike Jeffcoat	.20	.08	.02
□ 57T	Dave Johnson MG	.25	.10	.02
□ 58T	Lynn Jones	.12	.05	.01
□ 59T	Ruppert Jones	.12	.05	.01
□ 60T	Mike Jorgensen	.12	.05	.01
□ 61T	Bob Kearney	.12	.05	.01
□ 62T	Jimmy Key	5.00	2.25	.50
□ 63T	Dave Kingman	.30	.12	.03
□ 64T	Jerry Koosman	.25	.10	.02
□ 65T	Wayne Krenchicki	.12	.05	.01
□ 66T	Rusty Kuntz	.12	.05	.01
□ 67T	Rene Lachemann MG	.12	.05	.01
□ 68T	Frank LaCorte	.12	.05	.01
□ 69T	Dennis Lamp	.12	.05	.01
□ 70T	Mark Langston	11.00	5.00	1.35
□ 71T	Rick Leach	.12	.05	.01
□ 72T	Craig Lefferts	.30	.12	.03
□ 73T	Gary Lucas	.12	.05	.01
□ 74T	Jerry Martin	.12	.05	.01
□ 75T	Carmelo Martinez	.20	.08	.02
□ 76T	Mike Mason	.12	.05	.01
□ 77T	Gary Matthews	.20	.08	.02
□ 78T	Andy McGaffigan	.20	.08	.02
□ 79T	Larry Milbourne	.12	.05	.01
□ 80T	Sid Monge	.12	.05	.01
□ 81T	Jackie Moore MG	.12	.05	.01
□ 82T	Joe Morgan	2.50	1.00	.25
□ 83T	Graig Nettles	.40	.16	.04
□ 84T	Phil Niekro	1.75	.70	.17
□ 85T	Ken Oberkfell	.12	.05	.01
□ 86T	Mike O'Berry	.12	.05	.01
□ 87T	Al Oliver	.30	.12	.03
□ 88T	Jorge Orta	.12	.05	.01
□ 89T	Amos Otis	.20	.08	.02
□ 90T	Dave Parker	1.75	.70	.17
□ 91T	Tony Perez	1.00	.40	.10
□ 92T	Gerald Perry	.60	.25	.06
□ 93T	Gary Pettis	.40	.16	.04
□ 94T	Rob Picciolo	.12	.05	.01
□ 95T	Vern Rapp MG	.12	.05	.01
□ 96T	Floyd Rayford	.12	.05	.01
□ 97T	Randy Ready	.30	.12	.03
□ 98T	Ron Reed	.12	.05	.01
□ 99T	Gene Richards	.12	.05	.01
□ 100T	Jose Rijo	6.00	2.50	.60
□ 101T	Jeff Robinson (Giants pitcher)	.20	.08	.02
□ 102T	Ron Romanick	.12	.05	.01
□ 103T	Pete Rose	8.00	3.50	.80
□ 104T	Bret Saberhagen	21.00	9.00	3.00
□ 105T	Juan Samuel	4.00	1.75	.40
□ 106T	Scott Sanderson	.30	.12	.03
□ 107T	Dick Schofield	.40	.16	.04
□ 108T	Tom Seaver	7.50	3.25	.75
□ 109T	Jim Slaton	.12	.05	.01
□ 110T	Mike Smithson	.12	.05	.01
□ 111T	Lary Sorensen	.12	.05	.01
□ 112T	Tim Stoddard	.12	.05	.01
□ 113T	Champ Summers	.12	.05	.01
□ 114T	Jim Sundberg	.12	.05	.01
□ 115T	Rick Sutcliffe	.30	.12	.03
□ 116T	Craig Swan	.12	.05	.01
□ 117T	Tim Teufel	.45	.18	.04
□ 118T	Derrel Thomas	.12	.05	.01
□ 119T	Gorman Thomas	.25	.10	.02
□ 120T	Alex Trevino	.12	.05	.01
□ 121T	Manny Trillo	.12	.05	.01
□ 122T	John Tudor	.25	.10	.02
□ 123T	Tom Underwood	.12	.05	.01
□ 124T	Mike Vail	.12	.05	.01
□ 125T	Tom Waddell	.12	.05	.01
□ 126T	Gary Ward	.12	.05	.01
□ 127T	Curt Wilkerson	.12	.05	.01
□ 128T	Frank Williams	.12	.05	.01
□ 129T	Glenn Wilson	.12	.05	.01
□ 130T	John Wockenfuss	.12	.05	.01
□ 131T	Ned Yost	.12	.05	.01
□ 132T	Checklist 1-132	.12	.01	.00

1985 Topps

The cards in this 792-card set measure 2 1/2" by 3 1/2". The 1985 Topps set contains full color cards. The fronts feature both the Topps and team logos along with the team name, player's name, and his position. The backs feature player statistics with ink colors of light green and maroon on a gray stock. A trivia quiz is included on the lower portion of the backs. The first ten cards (1-10) are Record Breakers (RB), cards 131-143 are Father and Son (FS) cards, and cards 701 to 722 portray All-Star selections (AS). Cards 271 to 282 represent "First Draft Picks" still active in professional baseball and cards 389-404 feature the coach and players on the 1984 U.S. Olympic Baseball Team. The manager cards in the set are important in that they contain the checklist of that team's players on the back. The key rookie cards in this set are Roger Clemens, Eric Davis, Shawon Dunston, Dwight Gooden, Orel Hershiser, Mark Langston, Mark McGwire, Terry Pendleton, Kirby Puckett, Jose Rijo, and Bret Saberhagen. Topps also produced a specially boxed "glossy" edition, frequently referred to as the Topps Tiffany set. There were supposedly only 8,000 sets of the Tiffany cards produced; they were marketed to hobby dealers. The checklist of cards (792 regular and 132 Traded) is identical to that of the normal non-glossy cards. There are two primary distinguishing features of the Tiffany cards, white card stock reverses and high gloss obverses. These Tiffany cards are valued at approximately five times the values listed below.

	MINT	EXC	G-VG
COMPLETE SET (792)	100.00	45.00	15.00
COMMON PLAYER (1-792)	.05	.02	.00
□ 1 Carlton Fisk RB Longest game by catcher	.35	.10	.02
□ 2 Steve Garvey RB Consecutive error- less games, 1B	.15	.06	.01
□ 3 Dwight Gooden RB Most strikeouts, rookie, season	.90	.40	.09
□ 4 Cliff Johnson RB Most pinch homers, lifetime	.05	.02	.00
□ 5 Joe Morgan RB Most homers, 2B, lifetime	.15	.06	.01
□ 6 Pete Rose RB Most singles, lifetime	.35	.15	.03
□ 7 Nolan Ryan RB Most strikeouts, lifetime	1.00	.40	.10
□ 8 Juan Samuel RB Most stolen bases, rookie, season	.17	.07	.01
□ 9 Bruce Sutter RB Most saves, season, NL	.08	.03	.01
□ 10 Don Sutton RB Most seasons, 100 or more K's	.15	.06	.01
□ 11 Ralph Houk MG (checklist back)	.08	.03	.01
□ 12 Dave Lopes	.08	.03	.01
□ 13 Tim Lollar	.05	.02	.00
□ 14 Chris Bando	.05	.02	.00
□ 15 Jerry Koosman	.08	.03	.01
□ 16 Bobby Meacham	.05	.02	.00
□ 17 Mike Scott	.12	.05	.01
□ 18 Mickey Hatcher	.05	.02	.00
□ 19 George Frazier	.05	.02	.00
□ 20 Chet Lemon	.05	.02	.00
□ 21 Lee Tunnell	.05	.02	.00
□ 22 Duane Kuiper	.05	.02	.00
□ 23 Bret Saberhagen	4.00	1.75	.40
□ 24 Jesse Barfield	.15	.06	.01
□ 25 Steve Bedrosian	.10	.04	.01
□ 26 Roy Smalley	.05	.02	.00
□ 27 Bruce Berenyi	.05	.02	.00
□ 28 Dann Bilardello	.05	.02	.00
□ 29 Odell Jones	.05	.02	.00
□ 30 Cal Ripken	3.50	1.50	.35
□ 31 Terry Whitfield	.05	.02	.00
□ 32 Chuck Porter	.05	.02	.00
□ 33 Tito Landrum	.05	.02	.00
□ 34 Ed Nunez	.05	.02	.00
□ 35 Graig Nettles	.10	.04	.01

☐ 36 Fred Breining	.05	.02	.00
☐ 37 Reid Nichols	.05	.02	.00
☐ 38 Jackie Moore MG	.08	.03	.01
(checklist back)			
☐ 39 John Wockenfuss	.05	.02	.00
☐ 40 Phil Niekro	.20	.08	.02
☐ 41 Mike Fischlin	.05	.02	.00
☐ 42 Luis Sanchez	.05	.02	.00
☐ 43 Andre David	.05	.02	.00
☐ 44 Dickie Thon	.08	.03	.01
☐ 45 Greg Minton	.05	.02	.00
☐ 46 Gary Woods	.05	.02	.00
☐ 47 Dave Rozema	.05	.02	.00
☐ 48 Tony Fernandez	.75	.30	.07
☐ 49 Butch Davis	.05	.02	.00
☐ 50 John Candelaria	.05	.02	.00
☐ 51 Bob Watson	.05	.02	.00
☐ 52 Jerry Dybzinski	.05	.02	.00
☐ 53 Tom Gorman	.05	.02	.00
☐ 54 Cesar Cedeno	.08	.03	.01
☐ 55 Frank Tanana	.08	.03	.01
☐ 56 Jim Dwyer	.05	.02	.00
☐ 57 Pat Zachry	.05	.02	.00
☐ 58 Orlando Mercado	.05	.02	.00
☐ 59 Rick Waits	.05	.02	.00
☐ 60 George Hendrick	.05	.02	.00
☐ 61 Curt Kaufman	.05	.02	.00
☐ 62 Mike Ramsey	.05	.02	.00
☐ 63 Steve McCatty	.05	.02	.00
☐ 64 Mark Bailey	.05	.02	.00
☐ 65 Bill Buckner	.10	.04	.01
☐ 66 Dick Williams MG	.08	.03	.01
(checklist back)			
☐ 67 Rafael Santana	.10	.04	.01
☐ 68 Von Hayes	.12	.05	.01
☐ 69 Jim Winn	.05	.02	.00
☐ 70 Don Baylor	.10	.04	.01
☐ 71 Tim Laudner	.05	.02	.00
☐ 72 Rick Sutcliffe	.10	.04	.01
☐ 73 Rusty Kuntz	.05	.02	.00
☐ 74 Mike Krukow	.05	.02	.00
☐ 75 Willie Upshaw	.05	.02	.00
☐ 76 Alan Bannister	.05	.02	.00
☐ 77 Joe Beckwith	.05	.02	.00
☐ 78 Scott Fletcher	.05	.02	.00
☐ 79 Rick Mahler	.05	.02	.00
☐ 80 Keith Hernandez	.12	.05	.01
☐ 81 Lenn Sakata	.05	.02	.00
☐ 82 Joe Price	.05	.02	.00
☐ 83 Charlie Moore	.05	.02	.00
☐ 84 Spike Owen	.05	.02	.00
☐ 85 Mike Marshall	.10	.04	.01
☐ 86 Don Aase	.05	.02	.00
☐ 87 David Green	.05	.02	.00
☐ 88 Bryn Smith	.08	.03	.01
☐ 89 Jackie Gutierrez	.05	.02	.00
☐ 90 Rich Gossage	.12	.05	.01
☐ 91 Jeff Burroughs	.05	.02	.00
☐ 92 Paul Owens MG	.08	.03	.01
(checklist back)			
☐ 93 Don Schulze	.05	.02	.00
☐ 94 Toby Harrah	.05	.02	.00
☐ 95 Jose Cruz	.08	.03	.01
☐ 96 Johnny Ray	.05	.02	.00
☐ 97 Pete Filson	.05	.02	.00
☐ 98 Steve Lake	.05	.02	.00
☐ 99 Milt Wilcox	.05	.02	.00
☐ 100 George Brett	.80	.35	.08
☐ 101 Jim Acker	.05	.02	.00
☐ 102 Tommy Dunbar	.05	.02	.00
☐ 103 Randy Lerch	.05	.02	.00
☐ 104 Mike Fitzgerald	.05	.02	.00
☐ 105 Ron Kittle	.10	.04	.01
☐ 106 Pascual Perez	.08	.03	.01
☐ 107 Tom Foley	.05	.02	.00
☐ 108 Darnell Coles	.08	.03	.01
☐ 109 Gary Roenicke	.05	.02	.00
☐ 110 Alejandro Pena	.10	.04	.01
☐ 111 Doug DeCinces	.08	.03	.01
☐ 112 Tom Tellmann	.05	.02	.00
☐ 113 Tom Herr	.08	.03	.01
☐ 114 Bob James	.05	.02	.00
☐ 115 Rickey Henderson	2.50	1.00	.25
☐ 116 Dennis Boyd	.12	.05	.01
☐ 117 Greg Gross	.05	.02	.00
☐ 118 Eric Show	.05	.02	.00
☐ 119 Pat Corrales MG	.08	.03	.01
(checklist back)			
☐ 120 Steve Kemp	.05	.02	.00
☐ 121 Checklist: 1-132	.12	.02	.00
☐ 122 Tom Brunansky	.12	.05	.01
☐ 123 Dave Smith	.05	.02	.00
☐ 124 Rich Hebner	.05	.02	.00
☐ 125 Kent Tekulve	.05	.02	.00
☐ 126 Ruppert Jones	.05	.02	.00
☐ 127 Mark Gubicza	.40	.16	.04
☐ 128 Ernie Whitt	.05	.02	.00
☐ 129 Gene Garber	.05	.02	.00
☐ 130 Al Oliver	.10	.04	.01
☐ 131 Buddy/Gus Bell FS	.08	.03	.01
☐ 132 Dale/Yogi Berra FS	.15	.06	.01
☐ 133 Bob/Ray Boone FS	.08	.03	.01
☐ 134 Terry/Tito Francona FS	.05	.02	.00
☐ 135 Terry/Bob Kennedy FS	.05	.02	.00
☐ 136 Jeff/Bill Kunkel FS	.05	.02	.00
☐ 137 Vance/Vern Law FS	.05	.02	.00
☐ 138 Dick/Dick Schofield FS	.05	.02	.00
☐ 139 Joel/Bob Skinner FS	.05	.02	.00
☐ 140 Roy/Roy Smalley FS	.05	.02	.00
☐ 141 Mike/D.Stenhouse FS	.05	.02	.00
☐ 142 Steve/Dizzy Trout FS	.05	.02	.00
☐ 143 Ozzie/Ossie Virgil FS	.05	.02	.00
☐ 144 Ron Gardenhire	.05	.02	.00
☐ 145 Alvin Davis	.75	.30	.07
☐ 146 Gary Redus	.08	.03	.01
☐ 147 Bill Swaggerty	.05	.02	.00

☐ 148 Steve Yeager	.05	.02	.00
☐ 149 Dickie Noles	.05	.02	.00
☐ 150 Jim Rice	.15	.06	.01
☐ 151 Moose Haas	.05	.02	.00
☐ 152 Steve Braun	.05	.02	.00
☐ 153 Frank LaCorte	.05	.02	.00
☐ 154 Argenis Salazar	.05	.02	.00
☐ 155 Yogi Berra MG (checklist back)	.15	.06	.01
☐ 156 Craig Reynolds	.05	.02	.00
☐ 157 Tug McGraw	.10	.04	.01
☐ 158 Pat Tabler	.05	.02	.00
☐ 159 Carlos Diaz	.05	.02	.00
☐ 160 Lance Parrish	.15	.06	.01
☐ 161 Ken Schrom	.05	.02	.00
☐ 162 Benny Distefano	.08	.03	.01
☐ 163 Dennis Eckersley	.25	.10	.02
☐ 164 Jorge Orta	.05	.02	.00
☐ 165 Dusty Baker	.08	.03	.01
☐ 166 Keith Atherton	.05	.02	.00
☐ 167 Rufino Linares	.05	.02	.00
☐ 168 Garth Iorg	.05	.02	.00
☐ 169 Dan Spillner	.05	.02	.00
☐ 170 George Foster	.12	.05	.01
☐ 171 Bill Stein	.05	.02	.00
☐ 172 Jack Perconte	.05	.02	.00
☐ 173 Mike Young	.05	.02	.00
☐ 174 Rick Honeycutt	.05	.02	.00
☐ 175 Dave Parker	.25	.10	.02
☐ 176 Bill Schroeder	.05	.02	.00
☐ 177 Dave Von Ohlen	.05	.02	.00
☐ 178 Miguel Dilone	.05	.02	.00
☐ 179 Tommy John	.15	.06	.01
☐ 180 Dave Winfield	.40	.16	.04
☐ 181 Roger Clemens	20.00	8.50	2.75
☐ 182 Tim Flannery	.05	.02	.00
☐ 183 Larry McWilliams	.05	.02	.00
☐ 184 Carmen Castillo	.05	.02	.00
☐ 185 Al Holland	.05	.02	.00
☐ 186 Bob Lillis MG (checklist back)	.08	.03	.01
☐ 187 Mike Walters	.05	.02	.00
☐ 188 Greg Pryor	.05	.02	.00
☐ 189 Warren Brusstar	.05	.02	.00
☐ 190 Rusty Staub	.10	.04	.01
☐ 191 Steve Nicosia	.05	.02	.00
☐ 192 Howard Johnson	3.50	1.50	.35
☐ 193 Jimmy Key	1.00	.40	.10
☐ 194 Dave Stegman	.05	.02	.00
☐ 195 Glenn Hubbard	.05	.02	.00
☐ 196 Pete O'Brien	.08	.03	.01
☐ 197 Mike Warren	.05	.02	.00
☐ 198 Eddie Milner	.05	.02	.00
☐ 199 Dennis Martinez	.10	.04	.01
☐ 200 Reggie Jackson	.65	.25	.06
☐ 201 Burt Hooton	.05	.02	.00
☐ 202 Gorman Thomas	.08	.03	.01
☐ 203 Bob McClure	.05	.02	.00
☐ 204 Art Howe	.08	.03	.01
☐ 205 Steve Rogers	.05	.02	.00
☐ 206 Phil Garner	.08	.03	.01
☐ 207 Mark Clear	.05	.02	.00
☐ 208 Champ Summers	.05	.02	.00
☐ 209 Bill Campbell	.05	.02	.00
☐ 210 Gary Matthews	.05	.02	.00
☐ 211 Clay Christiansen	.05	.02	.00
☐ 212 George Vukovich	.05	.02	.00
☐ 213 Billy Gardner MG (checklist back)	.08	.03	.01
☐ 214 John Tudor	.10	.04	.01
☐ 215 Bob Brenly	.05	.02	.00
☐ 216 Jerry Don Gleaton	.05	.02	.00
☐ 217 Leon Roberts	.05	.02	.00
☐ 218 Doyle Alexander	.05	.02	.00
☐ 219 Gerald Perry	.10	.04	.01
☐ 220 Fred Lynn	.12	.05	.01
☐ 221 Ron Reed	.05	.02	.00
☐ 222 Hubie Brooks	.12	.05	.01
☐ 223 Tom Hume	.05	.02	.00
☐ 224 Al Cowens	.05	.02	.00
☐ 225 Mike Boddicker	.05	.02	.00
☐ 226 Juan Beniquez	.05	.02	.00
☐ 227 Danny Darwin	.05	.02	.00
☐ 228 Dion James	.05	.02	.00
☐ 229 Dave LaPoint	.05	.02	.00
☐ 230 Gary Carter	.25	.10	.02
☐ 231 Dwayne Murphy	.05	.02	.00
☐ 232 Dave Beard	.05	.02	.00
☐ 233 Ed Jurak	.05	.02	.00
☐ 234 Jerry Narron	.05	.02	.00
☐ 235 Garry Maddox	.05	.02	.00
☐ 236 Mark Thurmond	.05	.02	.00
☐ 237 Julio Franco	.60	.25	.06
☐ 238 Jose Rijo	1.25	.50	.12
☐ 239 Tim Teufel	.12	.05	.01
☐ 240 Dave Stieb	.15	.06	.01
☐ 241 Jim Frey MG (checklist back)	.08	.03	.01
☐ 242 Greg Harris	.05	.02	.00
☐ 243 Barbaro Garbey	.05	.02	.00
☐ 244 Mike Jones	.05	.02	.00
☐ 245 Chili Davis	.15	.06	.01
☐ 246 Mike Norris	.05	.02	.00
☐ 247 Wayne Tolleson	.05	.02	.00
☐ 248 Terry Forster	.05	.02	.00
☐ 249 Harold Baines	.20	.08	.02
☐ 250 Jesse Orosco	.05	.02	.00
☐ 251 Brad Gulden	.05	.02	.00
☐ 252 Dan Ford	.05	.02	.00
☐ 253 Sid Bream	.35	.15	.03
☐ 254 Pete Vuckovich	.05	.02	.00
☐ 255 Lonnie Smith	.10	.04	.01
☐ 256 Mike Stanton	.05	.02	.00
☐ 257 Bryan Little	.05	.02	.00
☐ 258 Mike Brown (Angels OF)	.05	.02	.00

	No.	Player			
☐	259	Gary Allenson	.05	.02	.00
☐	260	Dave Righetti	.12	.05	.01
☐	261	Checklist: 133-264	.12	.02	.00
☐	262	Greg Booker	.05	.02	.00
☐	263	Mel Hall	.15	.06	.01
☐	264	Joe Sambito	.05	.02	.00
☐	265	Juan Samuel	.45	.18	.04
☐	266	Frank Viola	.30	.12	.03
☐	267	Henry Cotto	.12	.05	.01
☐	268	Chuck Tanner MG (checklist back)	.08	.03	.01
☐	269	Doug Baker	.05	.02	.00
☐	270	Dan Quisenberry	.10	.04	.01
☐	271	Tim Foli FDP68	.05	.02	.00
☐	272	Jeff Burroughs FDP69	.05	.02	.00
☐	273	Bill Almon FDP74	.05	.02	.00
☐	274	Floyd Bannister FDP76	.05	.02	.00
☐	275	Harold Baines FDP77	.12	.05	.01
☐	276	Bob Horner FDP78	.10	.04	.01
☐	277	Al Chambers FDP79	.05	.02	.00
☐	278	D.Strawberry FDP80	2.00	.80	.20
☐	279	Mike Moore FDP81	.10	.04	.01
☐	280	Sh.Dunston FDP82	2.75	1.10	.27
☐	281	Tim Belcher FDP83	1.00	.40	.10
☐	282	Shawn Abner FDP84	.20	.08	.02
☐	283	Fran Mullins	.05	.02	.00
☐	284	Marty Bystrom	.05	.02	.00
☐	285	Dan Driessen	.05	.02	.00
☐	286	Rudy Law	.05	.02	.00
☐	287	Walt Terrell	.05	.02	.00
☐	288	Jeff Kunkel	.05	.02	.00
☐	289	Tom Underwood	.05	.02	.00
☐	290	Cecil Cooper	.10	.04	.01
☐	291	Bob Welch	.15	.06	.01
☐	292	Brad Komminsk	.05	.02	.00
☐	293	Curt Young	.12	.05	.01
☐	294	Tom Nieto	.05	.02	.00
☐	295	Joe Niekro	.08	.03	.01
☐	296	Ricky Nelson	.05	.02	.00
☐	297	Gary Lucas	.05	.02	.00
☐	298	Marty Barrett	.08	.03	.01
☐	299	Andy Hawkins	.08	.03	.01
☐	300	Rod Carew	.60	.25	.06
☐	301	John Montefusco	.05	.02	.00
☐	302	Tim Corcoran	.05	.02	.00
☐	303	Mike Jeffcoat	.05	.02	.00
☐	304	Gary Gaetti	.12	.05	.01
☐	305	Dale Berra	.05	.02	.00
☐	306	Rick Reuschel	.08	.03	.01
☐	307	Sparky Anderson MG (checklist back)	.08	.03	.01
☐	308	John Wathan	.05	.02	.00
☐	309	Mike Witt	.05	.02	.00
☐	310	Manny Trillo	.05	.02	.00
☐	311	Jim Gott	.05	.02	.00
☐	312	Marc Hill	.05	.02	.00
☐	313	Dave Schmidt	.05	.02	.00
☐	314	Ron Oester	.05	.02	.00
☐	315	Doug Sisk	.05	.02	.00
☐	316	John Lowenstein	.05	.02	.00
☐	317	Jack Lazorko	.05	.02	.00
☐	318	Ted Simmons	.10	.04	.01
☐	319	Jeff Jones	.05	.02	.00
☐	320	Dale Murphy	.40	.16	.04
☐	321	Ricky Horton	.12	.05	.01
☐	322	Dave Stapleton	.05	.02	.00
☐	323	Andy McGaffigan	.05	.02	.00
☐	324	Bruce Bochy	.05	.02	.00
☐	325	John Denny	.05	.02	.00
☐	326	Kevin Bass	.08	.03	.01
☐	327	Brook Jacoby	.15	.06	.01
☐	328	Bob Shirley	.05	.02	.00
☐	329	Ron Washington	.05	.02	.00
☐	330	Leon Durham	.05	.02	.00
☐	331	Bill Laskey	.05	.02	.00
☐	332	Brian Harper	.20	.08	.02
☐	333	Willie Hernandez	.08	.03	.01
☐	334	Dick Howser MG (checklist back)	.08	.03	.01
☐	335	Bruce Benedict	.05	.02	.00
☐	336	Rance Mulliniks	.05	.02	.00
☐	337	Billy Sample	.05	.02	.00
☐	338	Britt Burns	.05	.02	.00
☐	339	Danny Heep	.05	.02	.00
☐	340	Robin Yount	.80	.35	.08
☐	341	Floyd Rayford	.05	.02	.00
☐	342	Ted Power	.05	.02	.00
☐	343	Bill Russell	.08	.03	.01
☐	344	Dave Henderson	.20	.08	.02
☐	345	Charlie Lea	.05	.02	.00
☐	346	Terry Pendleton	2.00	.80	.20
☐	347	Rick Langford	.05	.02	.00
☐	348	Bob Boone	.10	.04	.01
☐	349	Domingo Ramos	.05	.02	.00
☐	350	Wade Boggs	2.50	1.00	.25
☐	351	Juan Agosto	.05	.02	.00
☐	352	Joe Morgan	.25	.10	.02
☐	353	Julio Solano	.05	.02	.00
☐	354	Andre Robertson	.05	.02	.00
☐	355	Bert Blyleven	.15	.06	.01
☐	356	Dave Meier	.05	.02	.00
☐	357	Rich Bordi	.05	.02	.00
☐	358	Tony Pena	.08	.03	.01
☐	359	Pat Sheridan	.05	.02	.00
☐	360	Steve Carlton	.50	.20	.05
☐	361	Alfredo Griffin	.05	.02	.00
☐	362	Craig McMurtry	.05	.02	.00
☐	363	Ron Hodges	.05	.02	.00
☐	364	Richard Dotson	.05	.02	.00
☐	365	Danny Ozark MG (checklist back)	.08	.03	.01
☐	366	Todd Cruz	.05	.02	.00
☐	367	Keefe Cato	.05	.02	.00
☐	368	Dave Bergman	.05	.02	.00
☐	369	R.J. Reynolds	.15	.06	.01
☐	370	Bruce Sutter	.10	.04	.01

□ 371 Mickey Rivers	.05	.02	.00
□ 372 Roy Howell	.05	.02	.00
□ 373 Mike Moore	.10	.04	.01
□ 374 Brian Downing	.08	.03	.01
□ 375 Jeff Reardon	.20	.08	.02
□ 376 Jeff Newman	.05	.02	.00
□ 377 Checklist: 265-396	.12	.02	.00
□ 378 Alan Wiggins	.05	.02	.00
□ 379 Charles Hudson	.05	.02	.00
□ 380 Ken Griffey	.15	.06	.01
□ 381 Roy Smith	.05	.02	.00
□ 382 Denny Walling	.05	.02	.00
□ 383 Rick Lysander	.05	.02	.00
□ 384 Jody Davis	.05	.02	.00
□ 385 Jose DeLeon	.05	.02	.00
□ 386 Dan Gladden	.35	.15	.03
□ 387 Buddy Biancalana	.08	.03	.01
□ 388 Bert Roberge	.05	.02	.00
□ 389 Rod Dedeaux OLY CO	.05	.02	.00
□ 390 Sid Akins OLY	.05	.02	.00
□ 391 Flavio Alfaro OLY	.05	.02	.00
□ 392 Don August OLY	.10	.04	.01
□ 393 Scott Bankhead OLY	.30	.12	.03
□ 394 Bob Caffrey OLY	.05	.02	.00
□ 395 Mike Dunne OLY	.10	.04	.01
□ 396 Gary Green OLY	.10	.04	.01
□ 397 John Hoover OLY	.10	.04	.01
□ 398 Shane Mack OLY	1.00	.40	.10
□ 399 John Marzano OLY	.15	.06	.01
□ 400 Oddibe McDowell OLY	.20	.08	.02
□ 401 Mark McGwire OLY	11.00	5.00	1.35
□ 402 Pat Pacillo OLY	.10	.04	.01
□ 403 Cory Snyder OLY	.90	.40	.09
□ 404 Billy Swift OLY	.25	.10	.02
□ 405 Tom Veryzer	.05	.02	.00
□ 406 Len Whitehouse	.05	.02	.00
□ 407 Bobby Ramos	.05	.02	.00
□ 408 Sid Monge	.05	.02	.00
□ 409 Brad Wellman	.05	.02	.00
□ 410 Bob Horner	.10	.04	.01
□ 411 Bobby Cox MG (checklist back)	.08	.03	.01
□ 412 Bud Black	.08	.03	.01
□ 413 Vance Law	.05	.02	.00
□ 414 Gary Ward	.05	.02	.00
□ 415 Ron Darling UER (no trivia answer)	.15	.06	.01
□ 416 Wayne Gross	.05	.02	.00
□ 417 John Franco	.75	.30	.07
□ 418 Ken Landreaux	.05	.02	.00
□ 419 Mike Caldwell	.05	.02	.00
□ 420 Andre Dawson	.60	.25	.06
□ 421 Dave Rucker	.05	.02	.00
□ 422 Carney Lansford	.10	.04	.01
□ 423 Barry Bonnell	.05	.02	.00
□ 424 Al Nipper	.05	.02	.00
□ 425 Mike Hargrove	.05	.02	.00
□ 426 Vern Ruhle	.05	.02	.00
□ 427 Mario Ramirez	.05	.02	.00
□ 428 Larry Andersen	.05	.02	.00
□ 429 Rick Cerone	.05	.02	.00
□ 430 Ron Davis	.05	.02	.00
□ 431 U.L. Washington	.05	.02	.00
□ 432 Thad Bosley	.05	.02	.00
□ 433 Jim Morrison	.05	.02	.00
□ 434 Gene Richards	.05	.02	.00
□ 435 Dan Petry	.05	.02	.00
□ 436 Willie Aikens	.05	.02	.00
□ 437 Al Jones	.05	.02	.00
□ 438 Joe Torre MG (checklist back)	.10	.04	.01
□ 439 Junior Ortiz	.05	.02	.00
□ 440 Fernando Valenzuela	.12	.05	.01
□ 441 Duane Walker	.05	.02	.00
□ 442 Ken Forsch	.05	.02	.00
□ 443 George Wright	.05	.02	.00
□ 444 Tony Phillips	.08	.03	.01
□ 445 Tippy Martinez	.05	.02	.00
□ 446 Jim Sundberg	.05	.02	.00
□ 447 Jeff Lahti	.05	.02	.00
□ 448 Derrel Thomas	.05	.02	.00
□ 449 Phil Bradley	.25	.10	.02
□ 450 Steve Garvey	.35	.15	.03
□ 451 Bruce Hurst	.10	.04	.01
□ 452 John Castino	.05	.02	.00
□ 453 Tom Waddell	.05	.02	.00
□ 454 Glenn Wilson	.05	.02	.00
□ 455 Bob Knepper	.05	.02	.00
□ 456 Tim Foli	.05	.02	.00
□ 457 Cecilio Guante	.05	.02	.00
□ 458 Randy Johnson	.05	.02	.00
□ 459 Charlie Leibrandt	.05	.02	.00
□ 460 Ryne Sandberg	3.00	1.25	.30
□ 461 Marty Castillo	.05	.02	.00
□ 462 Gary Lavelle	.05	.02	.00
□ 463 Dave Collins	.05	.02	.00
□ 464 Mike Mason	.05	.02	.00
□ 465 Bob Grich	.08	.03	.01
□ 466 Tony LaRussa MG (checklist back)	.08	.03	.01
□ 467 Ed Lynch	.05	.02	.00
□ 468 Wayne Krenchicki	.05	.02	.00
□ 469 Sammy Stewart	.05	.02	.00
□ 470 Steve Sax	.25	.10	.02
□ 471 Pete Ladd	.05	.02	.00
□ 472 Jim Essian	.05	.02	.00
□ 473 Tim Wallach	.10	.04	.01
□ 474 Kurt Kepshire	.05	.02	.00
□ 475 Andre Thornton	.08	.03	.01
□ 476 Jeff Stone	.08	.03	.01
□ 477 Bob Ojeda	.08	.03	.01
□ 478 Kurt Bevacqua	.05	.02	.00
□ 479 Mike Madden	.05	.02	.00
□ 480 Lou Whitaker	.25	.10	.02
□ 481 Dale Murray	.05	.02	.00
□ 482 Harry Spilman	.05	.02	.00

☐ 483 Mike Smithson .05 .02 .00
☐ 484 Larry Bowa .08 .03 .01
☐ 485 Matt Young .05 .02 .00
☐ 486 Steve Balboni .05 .02 .00
☐ 487 Frank Williams .05 .02 .00
☐ 488 Joel Skinner .05 .02 .00
☐ 489 Bryan Clark .05 .02 .00
☐ 490 Jason Thompson .05 .02 .00
☐ 491 Rick Camp .05 .02 .00
☐ 492 Dave Johnson MG (checklist back) .08 .03 .01
☐ 493 Orel Hershiser 2.25 .90 .22
☐ 494 Rich Dauer .05 .02 .00
☐ 495 Mario Soto .05 .02 .00
☐ 496 Donnie Scott .05 .02 .00
☐ 497 Gary Pettis UER (photo actually Gary's little brother, Lynn) .12 .05 .01
☐ 498 Ed Romero .05 .02 .00
☐ 499 Danny Cox .08 .03 .01
☐ 500 Mike Schmidt 1.25 .50 .12
☐ 501 Dan Schatzeder .05 .02 .00
☐ 502 Rick Miller .05 .02 .00
☐ 503 Tim Conroy .05 .02 .00
☐ 504 Jerry Willard .05 .02 .00
☐ 505 Jim Beattie .05 .02 .00
☐ 506 Franklin Stubbs .25 .10 .02
☐ 507 Ray Fontenot .05 .02 .00
☐ 508 John Shelby .05 .02 .00
☐ 509 Milt May .05 .02 .00
☐ 510 Kent Hrbek .17 .07 .01
☐ 511 Lee Smith .25 .10 .02
☐ 512 Tom Brookens .05 .02 .00
☐ 513 Lynn Jones .05 .02 .00
☐ 514 Jeff Cornell .05 .02 .00
☐ 515 Dave Concepcion .10 .04 .01
☐ 516 Roy Lee Jackson .05 .02 .00
☐ 517 Jerry Martin .05 .02 .00
☐ 518 Chris Chambliss .08 .03 .01
☐ 519 Doug Rader MG (checklist back) .08 .03 .01
☐ 520 LaMarr Hoyt .05 .02 .00
☐ 521 Rick Dempsey .05 .02 .00
☐ 522 Paul Molitor .20 .08 .02
☐ 523 Candy Maldonado .15 .06 .01
☐ 524 Rob Wilfong .05 .02 .00
☐ 525 Darrell Porter .05 .02 .00
☐ 526 David Palmer .05 .02 .00
☐ 527 Checklist: 397-528 .12 .02 .00
☐ 528 Bill Krueger .05 .02 .00
☐ 529 Rich Gedman .05 .02 .00
☐ 530 Dave Dravecky .10 .04 .01
☐ 531 Joe Lefebvre .05 .02 .00
☐ 532 Frank DiPino .05 .02 .00
☐ 533 Tony Bernazard .05 .02 .00
☐ 534 Brian Dayett .05 .02 .00
☐ 535 Pat Putnam .05 .02 .00
☐ 536 Kirby Puckett 16.00 6.75 2.25
☐ 537 Don Robinson .05 .02 .00
☐ 538 Keith Moreland .05 .02 .00
☐ 539 Aurelio Lopez .05 .02 .00
☐ 540 Claudell Washington .05 .02 .00
☐ 541 Mark Davis .10 .04 .01
☐ 542 Don Slaught .05 .02 .00
☐ 543 Mike Squires .05 .02 .00
☐ 544 Bruce Kison .05 .02 .00
☐ 545 Lloyd Moseby .08 .03 .01
☐ 546 Brent Gaff .05 .02 .00
☐ 547 Pete Rose MG (checklist back) .50 .20 .05
☐ 548 Larry Parrish .05 .02 .00
☐ 549 Mike Scioscia .08 .03 .01
☐ 550 Scott McGregor .05 .02 .00
☐ 551 Andy Van Slyke .45 .18 .04
☐ 552 Chris Codiroli .05 .02 .00
☐ 553 Bob Clark .05 .02 .00
☐ 554 Doug Flynn .05 .02 .00
☐ 555 Bob Stanley .05 .02 .00
☐ 556 Sixto Lezcano .05 .02 .00
☐ 557 Len Barker .05 .02 .00
☐ 558 Carmelo Martinez .05 .02 .00
☐ 559 Jay Howell .05 .02 .00
☐ 560 Bill Madlock .08 .03 .01
☐ 561 Darryl Motley .05 .02 .00
☐ 562 Houston Jimenez .05 .02 .00
☐ 563 Dick Ruthven .05 .02 .00
☐ 564 Alan Ashby .05 .02 .00
☐ 565 Kirk Gibson .25 .10 .02
☐ 566 Ed VandeBerg .05 .02 .00
☐ 567 Joel Youngblood .05 .02 .00
☐ 568 Cliff Johnson .05 .02 .00
☐ 569 Ken Oberkfell .05 .02 .00
☐ 570 Darryl Strawberry 5.00 2.25 .50
☐ 571 Charlie Hough .05 .02 .00
☐ 572 Tom Paciorek .05 .02 .00
☐ 573 Jay Tibbs .05 .02 .00
☐ 574 Joe Altobelli MG (checklist back) .08 .03 .01
☐ 575 Pedro Guerrero .17 .07 .01
☐ 576 Jaime Cocanower .05 .02 .00
☐ 577 Chris Speier .05 .02 .00
☐ 578 Terry Francona .05 .02 .00
☐ 579 Ron Romanick .05 .02 .00
☐ 580 Dwight Evans .15 .06 .01
☐ 581 Mark Wagner .05 .02 .00
☐ 582 Ken Phelps .08 .03 .01
☐ 583 Bobby Brown .05 .02 .00
☐ 584 Kevin Gross .05 .02 .00
☐ 585 Butch Wynegar .05 .02 .00
☐ 586 Bill Scherrer .05 .02 .00
☐ 587 Doug Frobel .05 .02 .00
☐ 588 Bobby Castillo .05 .02 .00
☐ 589 Bob Dernier .05 .02 .00
☐ 590 Ray Knight .08 .03 .01
☐ 591 Larry Herndon .05 .02 .00

☐ 592 Jeff Robinson (Giants pitcher)	.12	.05	.01
☐ 593 Rick Leach	.05	.02	.00
☐ 594 Curt Wilkerson	.05	.02	.00
☐ 595 Larry Gura	.05	.02	.00
☐ 596 Jerry Hairston	.05	.02	.00
☐ 597 Brad Lesley	.05	.02	.00
☐ 598 Jose Oquendo	.05	.02	.00
☐ 599 Storm Davis	.05	.02	.00
☐ 600 Pete Rose	.75	.30	.07
☐ 601 Tom Lasorda MG (checklist back)	.08	.03	.01
☐ 602 Jeff Dedmon	.05	.02	.00
☐ 603 Rick Manning	.05	.02	.00
☐ 604 Daryl Sconiers	.05	.02	.00
☐ 605 Ozzie Smith	.50	.20	.05
☐ 606 Rich Gale	.05	.02	.00
☐ 607 Bill Almon	.05	.02	.00
☐ 608 Craig Lefferts	.08	.03	.01
☐ 609 Broderick Perkins	.05	.02	.00
☐ 610 Jack Morris	.40	.16	.04
☐ 611 Ozzie Virgil	.05	.02	.00
☐ 612 Mike Armstrong	.05	.02	.00
☐ 613 Terry Puhl	.05	.02	.00
☐ 614 Al Williams	.05	.02	.00
☐ 615 Marvell Wynne	.05	.02	.00
☐ 616 Scott Sanderson	.08	.03	.01
☐ 617 Willie Wilson	.10	.04	.01
☐ 618 Pete Falcone	.05	.02	.00
☐ 619 Jeff Leonard	.05	.02	.00
☐ 620 Dwight Gooden	7.50	3.25	.75
☐ 621 Marvis Foley	.05	.02	.00
☐ 622 Luis Leal	.05	.02	.00
☐ 623 Greg Walker	.05	.02	.00
☐ 624 Benny Ayala	.05	.02	.00
☐ 625 Mark Langston	2.50	1.00	.25
☐ 626 German Rivera	.05	.02	.00
☐ 627 Eric Davis	8.00	3.50	.80
☐ 628 Rene Lachemann MG (checklist back)	.08	.03	.01
☐ 629 Dick Schofield	.12	.05	.01
☐ 630 Tim Raines	.25	.10	.02
☐ 631 Bob Forsch	.05	.02	.00
☐ 632 Bruce Bochte	.05	.02	.00
☐ 633 Glenn Hoffman	.05	.02	.00
☐ 634 Bill Dawley	.05	.02	.00
☐ 635 Terry Kennedy	.05	.02	.00
☐ 636 Shane Rawley	.05	.02	.00
☐ 637 Brett Butler	.15	.06	.01
☐ 638 Mike Pagliarulo	.35	.15	.03
☐ 639 Ed Hodge	.05	.02	.00
☐ 640 Steve Henderson	.05	.02	.00
☐ 641 Rod Scurry	.05	.02	.00
☐ 642 Dave Owen	.05	.02	.00
☐ 643 Johnny Grubb	.05	.02	.00
☐ 644 Mark Huismann	.05	.02	.00
☐ 645 Damaso Garcia	.05	.02	.00
☐ 646 Scot Thompson	.05	.02	.00
☐ 647 Rafael Ramirez	.05	.02	.00
☐ 648 Bob Jones	.05	.02	.00
☐ 649 Sid Fernandez	.35	.15	.03
☐ 650 Greg Luzinski	.10	.04	.01
☐ 651 Jeff Russell	.12	.05	.01
☐ 652 Joe Nolan	.05	.02	.00
☐ 653 Mark Brouhard	.05	.02	.00
☐ 654 Dave Anderson	.05	.02	.00
☐ 655 Joaquin Andujar	.08	.03	.01
☐ 656 Chuck Cottier MG (checklist back)	.08	.03	.01
☐ 657 Jim Slaton	.05	.02	.00
☐ 658 Mike Stenhouse	.05	.02	.00
☐ 659 Checklist: 529-660	.12	.02	.00
☐ 660 Tony Gwynn	2.25	.90	.22
☐ 661 Steve Crawford	.05	.02	.00
☐ 662 Mike Heath	.05	.02	.00
☐ 663 Luis Aguayo	.05	.02	.00
☐ 664 Steve Farr	.25	.10	.02
☐ 665 Don Mattingly	4.50	2.00	.45
☐ 666 Mike LaCoss	.05	.02	.00
☐ 667 Dave Engle	.05	.02	.00
☐ 668 Steve Trout	.05	.02	.00
☐ 669 Lee Lacy	.05	.02	.00
☐ 670 Tom Seaver	.50	.20	.05
☐ 671 Dane Iorg	.05	.02	.00
☐ 672 Juan Berenguer	.05	.02	.00
☐ 673 Buck Martinez	.05	.02	.00
☐ 674 Atlee Hammaker	.05	.02	.00
☐ 675 Tony Perez	.17	.07	.01
☐ 676 Albert Hall	.05	.02	.00
☐ 677 Wally Backman	.05	.02	.00
☐ 678 Joey McLaughlin	.05	.02	.00
☐ 679 Bob Kearney	.05	.02	.00
☐ 680 Jerry Reuss	.05	.02	.00
☐ 681 Ben Oglivie	.05	.02	.00
☐ 682 Doug Corbett	.05	.02	.00
☐ 683 Whitey Herzog MG (checklist back)	.08	.03	.01
☐ 684 Bill Doran	.08	.03	.01
☐ 685 Bill Caudill	.05	.02	.00
☐ 686 Mike Easler	.05	.02	.00
☐ 687 Bill Gullickson	.08	.03	.01
☐ 688 Len Matuszek	.05	.02	.00
☐ 689 Luis DeLeon	.05	.02	.00
☐ 690 Alan Trammell	.40	.16	.04
☐ 691 Dennis Rasmussen	.12	.05	.01
☐ 692 Randy Bush	.05	.02	.00
☐ 693 Tim Stoddard	.05	.02	.00
☐ 694 Joe Carter	3.50	1.50	.35
☐ 695 Rick Rhoden	.05	.02	.00
☐ 696 John Rabb	.05	.02	.00
☐ 697 Onix Concepcion	.05	.02	.00
☐ 698 Jorge Bell	.45	.18	.04
☐ 699 Donnie Moore	.05	.02	.00
☐ 700 Eddie Murray	.60	.25	.06
☐ 701 Eddie Murray AS	.20	.08	.02
☐ 702 Damaso Garcia AS	.05	.02	.00

Card			
☐ 703 George Brett AS	.25	.10	.02
☐ 704 Cal Ripken AS	.75	.30	.07
☐ 705 Dave Winfield AS	.20	.08	.02
☐ 706 Rickey Henderson AS	.50	.20	.05
☐ 707 Tony Armas AS	.05	.02	.00
☐ 708 Lance Parrish AS	.10	.04	.01
☐ 709 Mike Boddicker AS	.05	.02	.00
☐ 710 Frank Viola AS	.12	.05	.01
☐ 711 Dan Quisenberry AS	.08	.03	.01
☐ 712 Keith Hernandez AS	.12	.05	.01
☐ 713 Ryne Sandberg AS	.65	.25	.06
☐ 714 Mike Schmidt AS	.40	.16	.04
☐ 715 Ozzie Smith AS	.17	.07	.01
☐ 716 Dale Murphy AS	.20	.08	.02
☐ 717 Tony Gwynn AS	.35	.15	.03
☐ 718 Jeff Leonard AS	.05	.02	.00
☐ 719 Gary Carter AS	.15	.06	.01
☐ 720 Rick Sutcliffe AS	.08	.03	.01
☐ 721 Bob Knepper AS	.05	.02	.00
☐ 722 Bruce Sutter AS	.08	.03	.01
☐ 723 Dave Stewart	.30	.12	.03
☐ 724 Oscar Gamble	.05	.02	.00
☐ 725 Floyd Bannister	.05	.02	.00
☐ 726 Al Bumbry	.05	.02	.00
☐ 727 Frank Pastore	.05	.02	.00
☐ 728 Bob Bailor	.05	.02	.00
☐ 729 Don Sutton	.20	.08	.02
☐ 730 Dave Kingman	.10	.04	.01
☐ 731 Neil Allen	.05	.02	.00
☐ 732 John McNamara MG (checklist back)	.08	.03	.01
☐ 733 Tony Scott	.05	.02	.00
☐ 734 John Henry Johnson	.05	.02	.00
☐ 735 Garry Templeton	.08	.03	.01
☐ 736 Jerry Mumphrey	.05	.02	.00
☐ 737 Bo Diaz	.05	.02	.00
☐ 738 Omar Moreno	.05	.02	.00
☐ 739 Ernie Camacho	.05	.02	.00
☐ 740 Jack Clark	.15	.06	.01
☐ 741 John Butcher	.05	.02	.00
☐ 742 Ron Hassey	.05	.02	.00
☐ 743 Frank White	.05	.02	.00
☐ 744 Doug Bair	.05	.02	.00
☐ 745 Buddy Bell	.08	.03	.01
☐ 746 Jim Clancy	.05	.02	.00
☐ 747 Alex Trevino	.05	.02	.00
☐ 748 Lee Mazzilli	.05	.02	.00
☐ 749 Julio Cruz	.05	.02	.00
☐ 750 Rollie Fingers	.20	.08	.02
☐ 751 Kelvin Chapman	.05	.02	.00
☐ 752 Bob Owchinko	.05	.02	.00
☐ 753 Greg Brock	.05	.02	.00
☐ 754 Larry Milbourne	.05	.02	.00
☐ 755 Ken Singleton	.08	.03	.01
☐ 756 Rob Picciolo	.05	.02	.00
☐ 757 Willie McGee	.30	.12	.03
☐ 758 Ray Burris	.05	.02	.00
☐ 759 Jim Fanning MG (checklist back)	.08	.03	.01
☐ 760 Nolan Ryan	3.75	1.60	.37
☐ 761 Jerry Remy	.05	.02	.00
☐ 762 Eddie Whitson	.05	.02	.00
☐ 763 Kiko Garcia	.05	.02	.00
☐ 764 Jamie Easterly	.05	.02	.00
☐ 765 Willie Randolph	.08	.03	.01
☐ 766 Paul Mirabella	.05	.02	.00
☐ 767 Darrell Brown	.05	.02	.00
☐ 768 Ron Cey	.08	.03	.01
☐ 769 Joe Cowley	.05	.02	.00
☐ 770 Carlton Fisk	.50	.20	.05
☐ 771 Geoff Zahn	.05	.02	.00
☐ 772 Johnnie LeMaster	.05	.02	.00
☐ 773 Hal McRae	.08	.03	.01
☐ 774 Dennis Lamp	.05	.02	.00
☐ 775 Mookie Wilson	.08	.03	.01
☐ 776 Jerry Royster	.05	.02	.00
☐ 777 Ned Yost	.05	.02	.00
☐ 778 Mike Davis	.05	.02	.00
☐ 779 Nick Esasky	.08	.03	.01
☐ 780 Mike Flanagan	.08	.03	.01
☐ 781 Jim Gantner	.05	.02	.00
☐ 782 Tom Niedenfuer	.05	.02	.00
☐ 783 Mike Jorgensen	.05	.02	.00
☐ 784 Checklist: 661-792	.12	.02	.00
☐ 785 Tony Armas	.05	.02	.00
☐ 786 Enos Cabell	.05	.02	.00
☐ 787 Jim Wohlford	.05	.02	.00
☐ 788 Steve Comer	.05	.02	.00
☐ 789 Luis Salazar	.05	.02	.00
☐ 790 Ron Guidry	.15	.06	.01
☐ 791 Ivan DeJesus	.05	.02	.00
☐ 792 Darrell Evans	.15	.06	.01

1985 Topps Traded

The cards in this 132-card set measure 2 1/2" by 3 1/2". In its now standard procedure, Topps issued its Traded (or extended) set for the fifth year in a row. Topps did however test on a limited basis the issuance of these Traded cards in wax packs. Because all photos and statistics of its regular set for the year were developed during the fall and winter months of the preceding year, players who changed teams during the fall, winter, and spring months are portrayed in the 1985 regular issue set with the teams they were with in 1984. The Traded set amends the shortcomings of the regular set by presenting the players with their proper teams for the

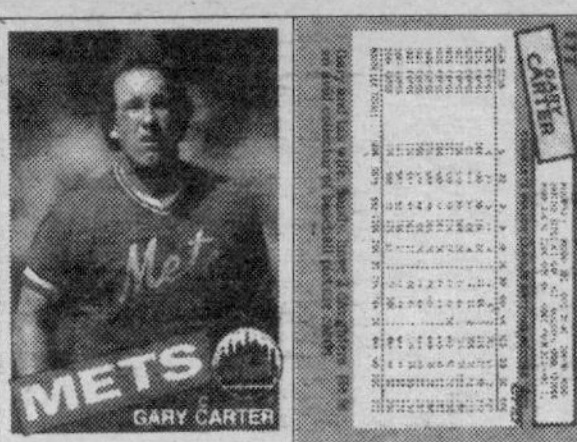

current year. Most of 1985's top rookies not contained in the regular set are picked up in the Traded set. The key (extended) rookie cards in this set are Vince Coleman, Ozzie Guillen, and Mickey Tettleton. Again this year, the Topps affiliate in Ireland printed the cards, and the cards were available through hobby channels only. Topps also produced a specially boxed "glossy" edition, frequently referred to as the Topps Traded Tiffany set. There were supposedly only 8,000 sets of the Tiffany cards produced; they were marketed to hobby dealers. The checklist of cards is identical to that of the normal non-glossy cards. There are two primary distinguishing features of the Tiffany cards, white card stock reverses and high gloss obverses. These Tiffany cards are valued at approximately five times the values listed below.

	MINT	EXC	G-VG
COMPLETE SET (132)	30.00	13.50	4.50
COMMON PLAYER (1-132)	.10	.04	.01
☐ 1T Don Aase	.15	.05	.01
☐ 2T Bill Almon	.10	.04	.01
☐ 3T Benny Ayala	.10	.04	.01
☐ 4T Dusty Baker	.15	.06	.01
☐ 5T Geo.Bamberger MG	.10	.04	.01
☐ 6T Dale Berra	.10	.04	.01
☐ 7T Rich Bordi	.10	.04	.01
☐ 8T Daryl Boston	.35	.15	.03
☐ 9T Hubie Brooks	.30	.12	.03
☐ 10T Chris Brown	.15	.06	.01
☐ 11T Tom Browning	1.50	.60	.15
☐ 12T Al Bumbry	.10	.04	.01
☐ 13T Ray Burris	.10	.04	.01
☐ 14T Jeff Burroughs	.10	.04	.01
☐ 15T Bill Campbell	.10	.04	.01
☐ 16T Don Carman	.20	.08	.02
☐ 17T Gary Carter	.80	.35	.08
☐ 18T Bobby Castillo	.10	.04	.01
☐ 19T Bill Caudill	.10	.04	.01
☐ 20T Rick Cerone	.10	.04	.01
☐ 21T Bryan Clark	.10	.04	.01
☐ 22T Jack Clark	.40	.16	.04
☐ 23T Pat Clements	.10	.04	.01
☐ 24T Vince Coleman	11.00	5.00	1.35
☐ 25T Dave Collins	.10	.04	.01
☐ 26T Danny Darwin	.15	.06	.01
☐ 27T Jim Davenport MG	.10	.04	.01
☐ 28T Jerry Davis	.10	.04	.01
☐ 29T Brian Dayett	.10	.04	.01
☐ 30T Ivan DeJesus	.10	.04	.01
☐ 31T Ken Dixon	.10	.04	.01
☐ 32T Mariano Duncan	.75	.30	.07
☐ 33T John Felske MG	.10	.04	.01
☐ 34T Mike Fitzgerald	.10	.04	.01
☐ 35T Ray Fontenot	.10	.04	.01
☐ 36T Greg Gagne	.35	.15	.03
☐ 37T Oscar Gamble	.15	.06	.01
☐ 38T Scott Garrelts	.30	.12	.03
☐ 39T Bob L. Gibson	.10	.04	.01
☐ 40T Jim Gott	.15	.06	.01
☐ 41T David Green	.10	.04	.01
☐ 42T Alfredo Griffin	.15	.06	.01
☐ 43T Ozzie Guillen	2.00	.80	.20
☐ 44T Eddie Haas MG	.10	.04	.01
☐ 45T Terry Harper	.10	.04	.01
☐ 46T Toby Harrah	.15	.06	.01
☐ 47T Greg Harris	.10	.04	.01
☐ 48T Ron Hassey	.15	.06	.01
☐ 49T Rickey Henderson	5.00	2.25	.50
☐ 50T Steve Henderson	.10	.04	.01
☐ 51T George Hendrick	.15	.06	.01
☐ 52T Joe Hesketh	.35	.15	.03
☐ 53T Teddy Higuera	.60	.25	.06
☐ 54T Donnie Hill	.10	.04	.01
☐ 55T Al Holland	.10	.04	.01
☐ 56T Burt Hooton	.10	.04	.01
☐ 57T Jay Howell	.15	.06	.01
☐ 58T Ken Howell	.20	.08	.02
☐ 59T LaMarr Hoyt	.10	.04	.01
☐ 60T Tim Hulett	.15	.06	.01
☐ 61T Bob James	.10	.04	.01
☐ 62T Steve Jeltz	.10	.04	.01
☐ 63T Cliff Johnson	.10	.04	.01
☐ 64T Howard Johnson	2.75	1.10	.27
☐ 65T Ruppert Jones	.10	.04	.01
☐ 66T Steve Kemp	.10	.04	.01
☐ 67T Bruce Kison	.10	.04	.01
☐ 68T Alan Knicely	.10	.04	.01
☐ 69T Mike LaCoss	.10	.04	.01
☐ 70T Lee Lacy	.10	.04	.01
☐ 71T Dave LaPoint	.10	.04	.01
☐ 72T Gary Lavelle	.10	.04	.01
☐ 73T Vance Law	.10	.04	.01
☐ 74T Johnnie LeMaster	.10	.04	.01
☐ 75T Sixto Lezcano	.10	.04	.01
☐ 76T Tim Lollar	.10	.04	.01

☐ 77T Fred Lynn .25 .10 .02
☐ 78T Billy Martin MG .20 .08 .02
☐ 79T Ron Mathis .10 .04 .01
☐ 80T Len Matuszek .10 .04 .01
☐ 81T Gene Mauch MG .10 .04 .01
☐ 82T Oddibe McDowell .20 .08 .02
☐ 83T Roger McDowell .50 .20 .05
☐ 84T John McNamara MG .15 .06 .01
☐ 85T Donnie Moore .10 .04 .01
☐ 86T Gene Nelson .15 .06 .01
☐ 87T Steve Nicosia .10 .04 .01
☐ 88T Al Oliver .20 .08 .02
☐ 89T Joe Orsulak .40 .16 .04
☐ 90T Rob Picciolo .10 .04 .01
☐ 91T Chris Pittaro .10 .04 .01
☐ 92T Jim Presley .20 .08 .02
☐ 93T Rick Reuschel .20 .08 .02
☐ 94T Bert Roberge .10 .04 .01
☐ 95T Bob Rodgers MG .15 .06 .01
☐ 96T Jerry Royster .10 .04 .01
☐ 97T Dave Rozema .10 .04 .01
☐ 98T Dave Rucker .10 .04 .01
☐ 99T Vern Ruhle .10 .04 .01
☐ 100T Paul Runge .10 .04 .01
☐ 101T Mark Salas .15 .06 .01
☐ 102T Luis Salazar .10 .04 .01
☐ 103T Joe Sambito .10 .04 .01
☐ 104T Rick Schu .15 .06 .01
☐ 105T Donnie Scott .10 .04 .01
☐ 106T Larry Sheets .20 .08 .02
☐ 107T Don Slaught .10 .04 .01
☐ 108T Roy Smalley .10 .04 .01
☐ 109T Lonnie Smith .25 .10 .02
☐ 110T Nate Snell UER .15 .06 .01
(headings on back
for a batter)
☐ 111T Chris Speier .10 .04 .01
☐ 112T Mike Stenhouse .10 .04 .01
☐ 113T Tim Stoddard .10 .04 .01
☐ 114T Jim Sundberg .10 .04 .01
☐ 115T Bruce Sutter .25 .10 .02
☐ 116T Don Sutton .50 .20 .05
☐ 117T Kent Tekulve .15 .06 .01
☐ 118T Tom Tellmann .10 .04 .01
☐ 119T Walt Terrell .15 .06 .01
☐ 120T Mickey Tettleton 2.00 .80 .20
☐ 121T Derrel Thomas .10 .04 .01
☐ 122T Rich Thompson .10 .04 .01
☐ 123T Alex Trevino .10 .04 .01
☐ 124T John Tudor .20 .08 .02
☐ 125T Jose Uribe .25 .10 .02
☐ 126T Bobby Valentine MG .20 .08 .02
☐ 127T Dave Von Ohlen .10 .04 .01
☐ 128T U.L. Washington .10 .04 .01
☐ 129T Earl Weaver MG .15 .06 .01
☐ 130T Eddie Whitson .15 .06 .01
☐ 131T Herm Winningham .15 .06 .01
☐ 132T Checklist 1-132 .10 .01 .00

1986 Topps

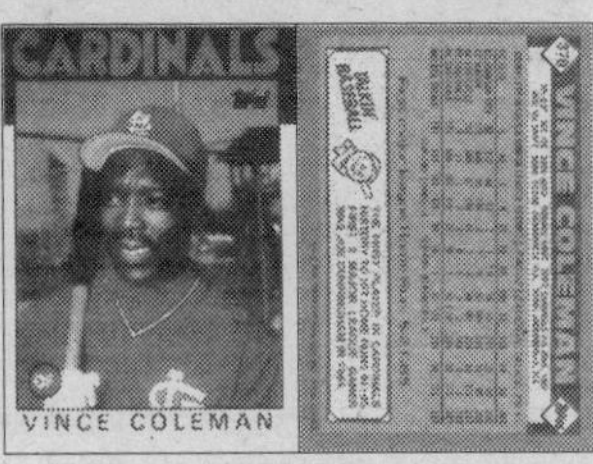

The cards in this 792-card set are standard-size (2 1/2" by 3 1/2"). The first seven cards are a tribute to Pete Rose and his career. Cards 2-7 show small photos of Pete's Topps cards of the given years on the front with biographical information pertaining to those years on the back. The team leader cards were done differently with a simple player action shot on a white background; the player pictured is dubbed the "Dean" of that team, i.e., the player with the longest continuous service with that team. Topps again features a "Turn Back the Clock" series (401-405). Record breakers of the previous year are acknowledged on cards 201 to 207. Cards 701-722 feature All-Star selections from each league. Manager cards feature the team checklist on the reverse. Ryne Sandberg (690) is the only player card in the set without a Topps logo on the front of the card; this omission was never corrected by Topps. There are two other uncorrected errors involving misnumbered cards; see card numbers 51, 57, 141, and 171 in the checklist below. The backs of all the cards have a distinctive red background. The key rookie cards in this set are Vince Coleman, Len Dykstra and Cecil Fielder. Topps also produced a specially boxed "glossy" edition, frequently referred to as the Topps Tiffany set. There were supposedly only 5,000 sets of the Tiffany cards produced; they were marketed to hobby dealers. The checklist of cards (792 regular and 132 Traded) is identical to that of the normal non-glossy cards. There are two primary distinguishing features of the Tiffany cards, white card stock reverses and high gloss obverses. These Tiffany cards are

valued at approximately five times the values listed below.

	MINT	EXC	G-VG
COMPLETE SET (792)	36.00	16.25	5.50
COMMON PLAYER (1-792)	.04	.02	.00
☐ 1 Pete Rose	1.00	.20	.04
☐ 2 Rose Special: '63-'66	.30	.12	.03
☐ 3 Rose Special: '67-'70	.30	.12	.03
☐ 4 Rose Special: '71-'74	.30	.12	.03
☐ 5 Rose Special: '75-'78	.30	.12	.03
☐ 6 Rose Special: '79-'82	.30	.12	.03
☐ 7 Rose Special: '83-'85	.30	.12	.03
☐ 8 Dwayne Murphy	.04	.02	.00
☐ 9 Roy Smith	.04	.02	.00
☐ 10 Tony Gwynn	1.00	.40	.10
☐ 11 Bob Ojeda	.04	.02	.00
☐ 12 Jose Uribe	.12	.05	.01
☐ 13 Bob Kearney	.04	.02	.00
☐ 14 Julio Cruz	.04	.02	.00
☐ 15 Eddie Whitson	.04	.02	.00
☐ 16 Rick Schu	.07	.03	.01
☐ 17 Mike Stenhouse	.04	.02	.00
☐ 18 Brent Gaff	.04	.02	.00
☐ 19 Rich Hebner	.04	.02	.00
☐ 20 Lou Whitaker	.15	.06	.01
☐ 21 George Bamberger MG (checklist back)	.07	.03	.01
☐ 22 Duane Walker	.04	.02	.00
☐ 23 Manny Lee	.10	.04	.01
☐ 24 Len Barker	.04	.02	.00
☐ 25 Willie Wilson	.07	.03	.01
☐ 26 Frank DiPino	.04	.02	.00
☐ 27 Ray Knight	.07	.03	.01
☐ 28 Eric Davis	1.25	.50	.12
☐ 29 Tony Phillips	.07	.03	.01
☐ 30 Eddie Murray	.45	.18	.04
☐ 31 Jamie Easterly	.04	.02	.00
☐ 32 Steve Yeager	.04	.02	.00
☐ 33 Jeff Lahti	.04	.02	.00
☐ 34 Ken Phelps	.04	.02	.00
☐ 35 Jeff Reardon	.17	.07	.01
☐ 36 Tigers Leaders Lance Parrish	.10	.04	.01
☐ 37 Mark Thurmond	.04	.02	.00
☐ 38 Glenn Hoffman	.04	.02	.00
☐ 39 Dave Rucker	.04	.02	.00
☐ 40 Ken Griffey	.12	.05	.01
☐ 41 Brad Wellman	.04	.02	.00
☐ 42 Geoff Zahn	.04	.02	.00
☐ 43 Dave Engle	.04	.02	.00
☐ 44 Lance McCullers	.10	.04	.01
☐ 45 Damaso Garcia	.04	.02	.00
☐ 46 Billy Hatcher	.12	.05	.01
☐ 47 Juan Berenguer	.04	.02	.00
☐ 48 Bill Almon	.04	.02	.00
☐ 49 Rick Manning	.04	.02	.00
☐ 50 Dan Quisenberry	.10	.04	.01
☐ 51 Bobby Wine MG ERR (checklist back) (number of card on back is actually 57)	.10	.04	.01
☐ 52 Chris Welsh	.04	.02	.00
☐ 53 Len Dykstra	1.25	.50	.12
☐ 54 John Franco	.10	.04	.01
☐ 55 Fred Lynn	.12	.05	.01
☐ 56 Tom Niedenfuer	.04	.02	.00
☐ 57 Bill Doran (see also 51)	.07	.03	.01
☐ 58 Bill Krueger	.04	.02	.00
☐ 59 Andre Thornton	.04	.02	.00
☐ 60 Dwight Evans	.12	.05	.01
☐ 61 Karl Best	.04	.02	.00
☐ 62 Bob Boone	.07	.03	.01
☐ 63 Ron Roenicke	.04	.02	.00
☐ 64 Floyd Bannister	.04	.02	.00
☐ 65 Dan Driessen	.04	.02	.00
☐ 66 Cardinals Leaders Bob Forsch	.04	.02	.00
☐ 67 Carmelo Martinez	.04	.02	.00
☐ 68 Ed Lynch	.04	.02	.00
☐ 69 Luis Aguayo	.04	.02	.00
☐ 70 Dave Winfield	.35	.15	.03
☐ 71 Ken Schrom	.04	.02	.00
☐ 72 Shawon Dunston	.35	.15	.03
☐ 73 Randy O'Neal	.04	.02	.00
☐ 74 Rance Mulliniks	.04	.02	.00
☐ 75 Jose DeLeon	.04	.02	.00
☐ 76 Dion James	.04	.02	.00
☐ 77 Charlie Leibrandt	.04	.02	.00
☐ 78 Bruce Benedict	.04	.02	.00
☐ 79 Dave Schmidt	.04	.02	.00
☐ 80 Darryl Strawberry	2.00	.80	.20
☐ 81 Gene Mauch MG (checklist back)	.07	.03	.01
☐ 82 Tippy Martinez	.04	.02	.00
☐ 83 Phil Garner	.07	.03	.01
☐ 84 Curt Young	.04	.02	.00
☐ 85 Tony Perez (Eric Davis also shown on card)	.15	.06	.01
☐ 86 Tom Waddell	.04	.02	.00
☐ 87 Candy Maldonado	.10	.04	.01
☐ 88 Tom Nieto	.04	.02	.00
☐ 89 Randy St.Claire	.04	.02	.00
☐ 90 Garry Templeton	.07	.03	.01
☐ 91 Steve Crawford	.04	.02	.00
☐ 92 Al Cowens	.04	.02	.00
☐ 93 Scot Thompson	.04	.02	.00
☐ 94 Rich Bordi	.04	.02	.00
☐ 95 Ozzie Virgil	.04	.02	.00
☐ 96 Blue Jays Leaders Jim Clancy	.04	.02	.00
☐ 97 Gary Gaetti	.10	.04	.01
☐ 98 Dick Ruthven	.04	.02	.00

☐ 99 Buddy Biancalana	.04	.02	.00
☐ 100 Nolan Ryan	2.25	.90	.22
☐ 101 Dave Bergman	.04	.02	.00
☐ 102 Joe Orsulak	.20	.08	.02
☐ 103 Luis Salazar	.04	.02	.00
☐ 104 Sid Fernandez	.12	.05	.01
☐ 105 Gary Ward	.04	.02	.00
☐ 106 Ray Burris	.04	.02	.00
☐ 107 Rafael Ramirez	.04	.02	.00
☐ 108 Ted Power	.04	.02	.00
☐ 109 Len Matuszek	.04	.02	.00
☐ 110 Scott McGregor	.04	.02	.00
☐ 111 Roger Craig MG	.07	.03	.01
(checklist back)			
☐ 112 Bill Campbell	.04	.02	.00
☐ 113 U.L. Washington	.04	.02	.00
☐ 114 Mike Brown	.04	.02	.00
(Pirates OF)			
☐ 115 Jay Howell	.04	.02	.00
☐ 116 Brook Jacoby	.07	.03	.01
☐ 117 Bruce Kison	.04	.02	.00
☐ 118 Jerry Royster	.04	.02	.00
☐ 119 Barry Bonnell	.04	.02	.00
☐ 120 Steve Carlton	.35	.15	.03
☐ 121 Nelson Simmons	.04	.02	.00
☐ 122 Pete Filson	.04	.02	.00
☐ 123 Greg Walker	.04	.02	.00
☐ 124 Luis Sanchez	.04	.02	.00
☐ 125 Dave Lopes	.07	.03	.01
☐ 126 Mets Leaders	.04	.02	.00
Mookie Wilson			
☐ 127 Jack Howell	.10	.04	.01
☐ 128 John Wathan	.04	.02	.00
☐ 129 Jeff Dedmon	.04	.02	.00
☐ 130 Alan Trammell	.25	.10	.02
☐ 131 Checklist: 1-132	.10	.01	.00
☐ 132 Razor Shines	.04	.02	.00
☐ 133 Andy McGaffigan	.04	.02	.00
☐ 134 Carney Lansford	.10	.04	.01
☐ 135 Joe Niekro	.07	.03	.01
☐ 136 Mike Hargrove	.04	.02	.00
☐ 137 Charlie Moore	.04	.02	.00
☐ 138 Mark Davis	.07	.03	.01
☐ 139 Daryl Boston	.12	.05	.01
☐ 140 John Candelaria	.04	.02	.00
☐ 141 Chuck Cottier MG	.07	.03	.01
(checklist back)			
(see also 171)			
☐ 142 Bob Jones	.04	.02	.00
☐ 143 Dave Van Gorder	.04	.02	.00
☐ 144 Doug Sisk	.04	.02	.00
☐ 145 Pedro Guerrero	.12	.05	.01
☐ 146 Jack Perconte	.04	.02	.00
☐ 147 Larry Sheets	.04	.02	.00
☐ 148 Mike Heath	.04	.02	.00
☐ 149 Brett Butler	.12	.05	.01
☐ 150 Joaquin Andujar	.04	.02	.00
☐ 151 Dave Stapleton	.04	.02	.00
☐ 152 Mike Morgan	.07	.03	.01
☐ 153 Ricky Adams	.04	.02	.00
☐ 154 Bert Roberge	.04	.02	.00
☐ 155 Bob Grich	.07	.03	.01
☐ 156 White Sox Leaders	.04	.02	.00
Richard Dotson			
☐ 157 Ron Hassey	.04	.02	.00
☐ 158 Derrel Thomas	.04	.02	.00
☐ 159 Orel Hershiser UER	.35	.15	.03
(82 Alburquerque)			
☐ 160 Chet Lemon	.04	.02	.00
☐ 161 Lee Tunnell	.04	.02	.00
☐ 162 Greg Gagne	.07	.03	.01
☐ 163 Pete Ladd	.04	.02	.00
☐ 164 Steve Balboni	.04	.02	.00
☐ 165 Mike Davis	.04	.02	.00
☐ 166 Dickie Thon	.04	.02	.00
☐ 167 Zane Smith	.25	.10	.02
☐ 168 Jeff Burroughs	.04	.02	.00
☐ 169 George Wright	.04	.02	.00
☐ 170 Gary Carter	.20	.08	.02
☐ 171 Bob Rodgers MG ERR	.12	.05	.01
(checklist back)			
(number of card on			
back actually 141)			
☐ 172 Jerry Reed	.04	.02	.00
☐ 173 Wayne Gross	.04	.02	.00
☐ 174 Brian Snyder	.04	.02	.00
☐ 175 Steve Sax	.15	.06	.01
☐ 176 Jay Tibbs	.04	.02	.00
☐ 177 Joel Youngblood	.04	.02	.00
☐ 178 Ivan DeJesus	.04	.02	.00
☐ 179 Stu Cliburn	.04	.02	.00
☐ 180 Don Mattingly	1.75	.70	.17
☐ 181 Al Nipper	.04	.02	.00
☐ 182 Bobby Brown	.04	.02	.00
☐ 183 Larry Andersen	.04	.02	.00
☐ 184 Tim Laudner	.04	.02	.00
☐ 185 Rollie Fingers	.15	.06	.01
☐ 186 Astros Leaders	.04	.02	.00
Jose Cruz			
☐ 187 Scott Fletcher	.04	.02	.00
☐ 188 Bob Dernier	.04	.02	.00
☐ 189 Mike Mason	.04	.02	.00
☐ 190 George Hendrick	.04	.02	.00
☐ 191 Wally Backman	.04	.02	.00
☐ 192 Milt Wilcox	.04	.02	.00
☐ 193 Daryl Sconiers	.04	.02	.00
☐ 194 Craig McMurtry	.04	.02	.00
☐ 195 Dave Concepcion	.10	.04	.01
☐ 196 Doyle Alexander	.04	.02	.00
☐ 197 Enos Cabell	.04	.02	.00
☐ 198 Ken Dixon	.04	.02	.00
☐ 199 Dick Howser MG	.07	.03	.01
(checklist back)			
☐ 200 Mike Schmidt	1.00	.40	.10
☐ 201 RB: Vince Coleman	.30	.12	.03
Most stolen bases,			

season, rookie
☐ 202 RB: Dwight Gooden .30 .12 .03
Youngest 20 game
winner
☐ 203 RB: Keith Hernandez .10 .04 .01
Most game-winning
RBI's
☐ 204 RB: Phil Niekro .10 .04 .01
Oldest shutout
pitcher
☐ 205 RB: Tony Perez .10 .04 .01
Oldest grand slammer
☐ 206 RB: Pete Rose .35 .15 .03
Most hits, lifetime
☐ 207 RB: Fern.Valenzuela .10 .04 .01
Most cons. innings,
start of season,
no earned runs
☐ 208 Ramon Romero .04 .02 .00
☐ 209 Randy Ready .07 .03 .01
☐ 210 Calvin Schiraldi .04 .02 .00
☐ 211 Ed Wojna .04 .02 .00
☐ 212 Chris Speier .04 .02 .00
☐ 213 Bob Shirley .04 .02 .00
☐ 214 Randy Bush .04 .02 .00
☐ 215 Frank White .04 .02 .00
☐ 216 A's Leaders .04 .02 .00
Dwayne Murphy
☐ 217 Bill Scherrer .04 .02 .00
☐ 218 Randy Hunt .04 .02 .00
☐ 219 Dennis Lamp .04 .02 .00
☐ 220 Bob Horner .07 .03 .01
☐ 221 Dave Henderson .17 .07 .01
☐ 222 Craig Gerber .04 .02 .00
☐ 223 Atlee Hammaker .04 .02 .00
☐ 224 Cesar Cedeno .07 .03 .01
☐ 225 Ron Darling .10 .04 .01
☐ 226 Lee Lacy .04 .02 .00
☐ 227 Al Jones .04 .02 .00
☐ 228 Tom Lawless .04 .02 .00
☐ 229 Bill Gullickson .07 .03 .01
☐ 230 Terry Kennedy .04 .02 .00
☐ 231 Jim Frey MG .07 .03 .01
(checklist back)
☐ 232 Rick Rhoden .04 .02 .00
☐ 233 Steve Lyons .04 .02 .00
☐ 234 Doug Corbett .04 .02 .00
☐ 235 Butch Wynegar .04 .02 .00
☐ 236 Frank Eufemia .04 .02 .00
☐ 237 Ted Simmons .07 .03 .01
☐ 238 Larry Parrish .04 .02 .00
☐ 239 Joel Skinner .04 .02 .00
☐ 240 Tommy John .12 .05 .01
☐ 241 Tony Fernandez .12 .05 .01
☐ 242 Rich Thompson .04 .02 .00
☐ 243 Johnny Grubb .04 .02 .00
☐ 244 Craig Lefferts .04 .02 .00
☐ 245 Jim Sundberg .04 .02 .00
☐ 246 Phillies Leaders .15 .06 .01
Steve Carlton
☐ 247 Terry Harper .04 .02 .00
☐ 248 Spike Owen .04 .02 .00
☐ 249 Rob Deer .30 .12 .03
☐ 250 Dwight Gooden 1.00 .40 .10
☐ 251 Rich Dauer .04 .02 .00
☐ 252 Bobby Castillo .04 .02 .00
☐ 253 Dann Bilardello .04 .02 .00
☐ 254 Ozzie Guillen .60 .25 .06
☐ 255 Tony Armas .04 .02 .00
☐ 256 Kurt Kepshire .04 .02 .00
☐ 257 Doug DeCinces .04 .02 .00
☐ 258 Tim Burke .12 .05 .01
☐ 259 Dan Pasqua .12 .05 .01
☐ 260 Tony Pena .07 .03 .01
☐ 261 Bobby Valentine MG .07 .03 .01
(checklist back)
☐ 262 Mario Ramirez .04 .02 .00
☐ 263 Checklist: 133-264 .10 .01 .00
☐ 264 Darren Daulton .25 .10 .02
☐ 265 Ron Davis .04 .02 .00
☐ 266 Keith Moreland .04 .02 .00
☐ 267 Paul Molitor .15 .06 .01
☐ 268 Mike Scott .10 .04 .01
☐ 269 Dane Iorg .04 .02 .00
☐ 270 Jack Morris .25 .10 .02
☐ 271 Dave Collins .04 .02 .00
☐ 272 Tim Tolman .04 .02 .00
☐ 273 Jerry Willard .04 .02 .00
☐ 274 Ron Gardenhire .04 .02 .00
☐ 275 Charlie Hough .04 .02 .00
☐ 276 Yankees Leaders .07 .03 .01
Willie Randolph
☐ 277 Jaime Cocanower .04 .02 .00
☐ 278 Sixto Lezcano .04 .02 .00
☐ 279 Al Pardo .04 .02 .00
☐ 280 Tim Raines .20 .08 .02
☐ 281 Steve Mura .04 .02 .00
☐ 282 Jerry Mumphrey .04 .02 .00
☐ 283 Mike Fischlin .04 .02 .00
☐ 284 Brian Dayett .04 .02 .00
☐ 285 Buddy Bell .07 .03 .01
☐ 286 Luis DeLeon .04 .02 .00
☐ 287 John Christensen .04 .02 .00
☐ 288 Don Aase .04 .02 .00
☐ 289 Johnnie LeMaster .04 .02 .00
☐ 290 Carlton Fisk .35 .15 .03
☐ 291 Tom Lasorda MG .10 .04 .01
(checklist back)
☐ 292 Chuck Porter .04 .02 .00
☐ 293 Chris Chambliss .07 .03 .01
☐ 294 Danny Cox .04 .02 .00
☐ 295 Kirk Gibson .20 .08 .02
☐ 296 Geno Petralli .04 .02 .00
☐ 297 Tim Lollar .04 .02 .00
☐ 298 Craig Reynolds .04 .02 .00
☐ 299 Bryn Smith .04 .02 .00

Card			
☐ 300 George Brett	.40	.16	.04
☐ 301 Dennis Rasmussen	.04	.02	.00
☐ 302 Greg Gross	.04	.02	.00
☐ 303 Curt Wardle	.04	.02	.00
☐ 304 Mike Gallego	.07	.03	.01
☐ 305 Phil Bradley	.07	.03	.01
☐ 306 Padres Leaders Terry Kennedy	.04	.02	.00
☐ 307 Dave Sax	.04	.02	.00
☐ 308 Ray Fontenot	.04	.02	.00
☐ 309 John Shelby	.04	.02	.00
☐ 310 Greg Minton	.04	.02	.00
☐ 311 Dick Schofield	.04	.02	.00
☐ 312 Tom Filer	.04	.02	.00
☐ 313 Joe DeSa	.04	.02	.00
☐ 314 Frank Pastore	.04	.02	.00
☐ 315 Mookie Wilson	.07	.03	.01
☐ 316 Sammy Khalifa	.04	.02	.00
☐ 317 Ed Romero	.04	.02	.00
☐ 318 Terry Whitfield	.04	.02	.00
☐ 319 Rick Camp	.04	.02	.00
☐ 320 Jim Rice	.10	.04	.01
☐ 321 Earl Weaver MG (checklist back)	.07	.03	.01
☐ 322 Bob Forsch	.04	.02	.00
☐ 323 Jerry Davis	.04	.02	.00
☐ 324 Dan Schatzeder	.04	.02	.00
☐ 325 Juan Beniquez	.04	.02	.00
☐ 326 Kent Tekulve	.04	.02	.00
☐ 327 Mike Pagliarulo	.07	.03	.01
☐ 328 Pete O'Brien	.04	.02	.00
☐ 329 Kirby Puckett	3.50	1.50	.35
☐ 330 Rick Sutcliffe	.10	.04	.01
☐ 331 Alan Ashby	.04	.02	.00
☐ 332 Darryl Motley	.04	.02	.00
☐ 333 Tom Henke	.25	.10	.02
☐ 334 Ken Oberkfell	.04	.02	.00
☐ 335 Don Sutton	.17	.07	.01
☐ 336 Indians Leaders Andre Thornton	.04	.02	.00
☐ 337 Darnell Coles	.04	.02	.00
☐ 338 Jorge Bell	.30	.12	.03
☐ 339 Bruce Berenyi	.04	.02	.00
☐ 340 Cal Ripken	2.00	.80	.20
☐ 341 Frank Williams	.04	.02	.00
☐ 342 Gary Redus	.04	.02	.00
☐ 343 Carlos Diaz	.04	.02	.00
☐ 344 Jim Wohlford	.04	.02	.00
☐ 345 Donnie Moore	.04	.02	.00
☐ 346 Bryan Little	.04	.02	.00
☐ 347 Teddy Higuera	.20	.08	.02
☐ 348 Cliff Johnson	.04	.02	.00
☐ 349 Mark Clear	.04	.02	.00
☐ 350 Jack Clark	.12	.05	.01
☐ 351 Chuck Tanner MG (checklist back)	.07	.03	.01
☐ 352 Harry Spilman	.04	.02	.00
☐ 353 Keith Atherton	.04	.02	.00
☐ 354 Tony Bernazard	.04	.02	.00
☐ 355 Lee Smith	.17	.07	.01
☐ 356 Mickey Hatcher	.04	.02	.00
☐ 357 Ed VandeBerg	.04	.02	.00
☐ 358 Rick Dempsey	.04	.02	.00
☐ 359 Mike LaCoss	.04	.02	.00
☐ 360 Lloyd Moseby	.07	.03	.01
☐ 361 Shane Rawley	.04	.02	.00
☐ 362 Tom Paciorek	.04	.02	.00
☐ 363 Terry Forster	.04	.02	.00
☐ 364 Reid Nichols	.04	.02	.00
☐ 365 Mike Flanagan	.07	.03	.01
☐ 366 Reds Leaders Dave Concepcion	.07	.03	.01
☐ 367 Aurelio Lopez	.04	.02	.00
☐ 368 Greg Brock	.04	.02	.00
☐ 369 Al Holland	.04	.02	.00
☐ 370 Vince Coleman	2.25	.90	.22
☐ 371 Bill Stein	.04	.02	.00
☐ 372 Ben Oglivie	.04	.02	.00
☐ 373 Urbano Lugo	.04	.02	.00
☐ 374 Terry Francona	.04	.02	.00
☐ 375 Rich Gedman	.04	.02	.00
☐ 376 Bill Dawley	.04	.02	.00
☐ 377 Joe Carter	.65	.25	.06
☐ 378 Bruce Bochte	.04	.02	.00
☐ 379 Bobby Meacham	.04	.02	.00
☐ 380 LaMarr Hoyt	.04	.02	.00
☐ 381 Ray Miller MG (checklist back)	.07	.03	.01
☐ 382 Ivan Calderon	1.00	.40	.10
☐ 383 Chris Brown	.07	.03	.01
☐ 384 Steve Trout	.04	.02	.00
☐ 385 Cecil Cooper	.07	.03	.01
☐ 386 Cecil Fielder	7.50	3.25	.75
☐ 387 Steve Kemp	.04	.02	.00
☐ 388 Dickie Noles	.04	.02	.00
☐ 389 Glenn Davis	1.00	.40	.10
☐ 390 Tom Seaver	.50	.20	.05
☐ 391 Julio Franco	.35	.15	.03
☐ 392 John Russell	.04	.02	.00
☐ 393 Chris Pittaro	.04	.02	.00
☐ 394 Checklist: 265-396	.10	.01	.00
☐ 395 Scott Garrelts	.10	.04	.01
☐ 396 Red Sox Leaders Dwight Evans	.10	.04	.01
☐ 397 Steve Buechele	.35	.15	.03
☐ 398 Earnie Riles	.12	.05	.01
☐ 399 Bill Swift	.07	.03	.01
☐ 400 Rod Carew	.40	.16	.04
☐ 401 Turn Back 5 Years Fern.Valenzuela '81	.10	.04	.01
☐ 402 Turn Back 10 Years Tom Seaver '76	.15	.06	.01
☐ 403 Turn Back 15 Years Willie Mays '71	.15	.06	.01
☐ 404 Turn Back 20 Years Frank Robinson '66	.12	.05	.01

☐ 405 Turn Back 25 Years .15 .06 .01
Roger Maris '61
☐ 406 Scott Sanderson .07 .03 .01
☐ 407 Sal Butera .04 .02 .00
☐ 408 Dave Smith .04 .02 .00
☐ 409 Paul Runge .04 .02 .00
☐ 410 Dave Kingman .10 .04 .01
☐ 411 Sparky Anderson MG .07 .03 .01
(checklist back)
☐ 412 Jim Clancy .04 .02 .00
☐ 413 Tim Flannery .04 .02 .00
☐ 414 Tom Gorman .04 .02 .00
☐ 415 Hal McRae .07 .03 .01
☐ 416 Dennis Martinez .07 .03 .01
☐ 417 R.J. Reynolds .04 .02 .00
☐ 418 Alan Knicely .04 .02 .00
☐ 419 Frank Wills .04 .02 .00
☐ 420 Von Hayes .10 .04 .01
☐ 421 David Palmer .04 .02 .00
☐ 422 Mike Jorgensen .04 .02 .00
☐ 423 Dan Spillner .04 .02 .00
☐ 424 Rick Miller .04 .02 .00
☐ 425 Larry McWilliams .04 .02 .00
☐ 426 Brewers Leaders .04 .02 .00
Charlie Moore
☐ 427 Joe Cowley .04 .02 .00
☐ 428 Max Venable .04 .02 .00
☐ 429 Greg Booker .04 .02 .00
☐ 430 Kent Hrbek .15 .06 .01
☐ 431 George Frazier .04 .02 .00
☐ 432 Mark Bailey .04 .02 .00
☐ 433 Chris Codiroli .04 .02 .00
☐ 434 Curt Wilkerson .04 .02 .00
☐ 435 Bill Caudill .04 .02 .00
☐ 436 Doug Flynn .04 .02 .00
☐ 437 Rick Mahler .04 .02 .00
☐ 438 Clint Hurdle .04 .02 .00
☐ 439 Rick Honeycutt .04 .02 .00
☐ 440 Alvin Davis .10 .04 .01
☐ 441 Whitey Herzog MG .07 .03 .01
(checklist back)
☐ 442 Ron Robinson .07 .03 .01
☐ 443 Bill Buckner .07 .03 .01
☐ 444 Alex Trevino .04 .02 .00
☐ 445 Bert Blyleven .10 .04 .01
☐ 446 Lenn Sakata .04 .02 .00
☐ 447 Jerry Don Gleaton .04 .02 .00
☐ 448 Herm Winningham .04 .02 .00
☐ 449 Rod Scurry .04 .02 .00
☐ 450 Graig Nettles .07 .03 .01
☐ 451 Mark Brown .04 .02 .00
☐ 452 Bob Clark .04 .02 .00
☐ 453 Steve Jeltz .04 .02 .00
☐ 454 Burt Hooton .04 .02 .00
☐ 455 Willie Randolph .07 .03 .01
☐ 456 Braves Leaders .10 .04 .01
Dale Murphy
☐ 457 Mickey Tettleton .60 .25 .06
☐ 458 Kevin Bass .07 .03 .01
☐ 459 Luis Leal .04 .02 .00
☐ 460 Leon Durham .04 .02 .00
☐ 461 Walt Terrell .04 .02 .00
☐ 462 Domingo Ramos .04 .02 .00
☐ 463 Jim Gott .04 .02 .00
☐ 464 Ruppert Jones .04 .02 .00
☐ 465 Jesse Orosco .04 .02 .00
☐ 466 Tom Foley .04 .02 .00
☐ 467 Bob James .04 .02 .00
☐ 468 Mike Scioscia .07 .03 .01
☐ 469 Storm Davis .04 .02 .00
☐ 470 Bill Madlock .07 .03 .01
☐ 471 Bobby Cox MG .07 .03 .01
(checklist back)
☐ 472 Joe Hesketh .10 .04 .01
☐ 473 Mark Brouhard .04 .02 .00
☐ 474 John Tudor .10 .04 .01
☐ 475 Juan Samuel .15 .06 .01
☐ 476 Ron Mathis .04 .02 .00
☐ 477 Mike Easler .04 .02 .00
☐ 478 Andy Hawkins .04 .02 .00
☐ 479 Bob Melvin .07 .03 .01
☐ 480 Oddibe McDowell .07 .03 .01
☐ 481 Scott Bradley .07 .03 .01
☐ 482 Rick Lysander .04 .02 .00
☐ 483 George Vukovich .04 .02 .00
☐ 484 Donnie Hill .04 .02 .00
☐ 485 Gary Matthews .04 .02 .00
☐ 486 Angels Leaders .07 .03 .01
Bobby Grich
☐ 487 Bret Saberhagen .50 .20 .05
☐ 488 Lou Thornton .04 .02 .00
☐ 489 Jim Winn .04 .02 .00
☐ 490 Jeff Leonard .04 .02 .00
☐ 491 Pascual Perez .07 .03 .01
☐ 492 Kelvin Chapman .04 .02 .00
☐ 493 Gene Nelson .04 .02 .00
☐ 494 Gary Roenicke .04 .02 .00
☐ 495 Mark Langston .30 .12 .03
☐ 496 Jay Johnstone .07 .03 .01
☐ 497 John Stuper .04 .02 .00
☐ 498 Tito Landrum .04 .02 .00
☐ 499 Bob L. Gibson .04 .02 .00
☐ 500 Rickey Henderson 1.25 .50 .12
☐ 501 Dave Johnson MG .07 .03 .01
(checklist back)
☐ 502 Glen Cook .04 .02 .00
☐ 503 Mike Fitzgerald .04 .02 .00
☐ 504 Denny Walling .04 .02 .00
☐ 505 Jerry Koosman .07 .03 .01
☐ 506 Bill Russell .04 .02 .00
☐ 507 Steve Ontiveros .04 .02 .00
☐ 508 Alan Wiggins .04 .02 .00
☐ 509 Ernie Camacho .04 .02 .00
☐ 510 Wade Boggs 1.25 .50 .12
☐ 511 Ed Nunez .04 .02 .00
☐ 512 Thad Bosley .04 .02 .00

☐ 513 Ron Washington .04 .02 .00
☐ 514 Mike Jones .04 .02 .00
☐ 515 Darrell Evans .07 .03 .01
☐ 516 Giants Leaders .04 .02 .00
Greg Minton
☐ 517 Milt Thompson .17 .07 .01
☐ 518 Buck Martinez .04 .02 .00
☐ 519 Danny Darwin .04 .02 .00
☐ 520 Keith Hernandez .12 .05 .01
☐ 521 Nate Snell .04 .02 .00
☐ 522 Bob Bailor .04 .02 .00
☐ 523 Joe Price .04 .02 .00
☐ 524 Darrell Miller .04 .02 .00
☐ 525 Marvell Wynne .04 .02 .00
☐ 526 Charlie Lea .04 .02 .00
☐ 527 Checklist: 397-528 .10 .01 .00
☐ 528 Terry Pendleton .35 .15 .03
☐ 529 Marc Sullivan .04 .02 .00
☐ 530 Rich Gossage .10 .04 .01
☐ 531 Tony LaRussa MG .07 .03 .01
(checklist back)
☐ 532 Don Carman .10 .04 .01
☐ 533 Billy Sample .04 .02 .00
☐ 534 Jeff Calhoun .04 .02 .00
☐ 535 Toby Harrah .04 .02 .00
☐ 536 Jose Rijo .20 .08 .02
☐ 537 Mark Salas .04 .02 .00
☐ 538 Dennis Eckersley .15 .06 .01
☐ 539 Glenn Hubbard .04 .02 .00
☐ 540 Dan Petry .04 .02 .00
☐ 541 Jorge Orta .04 .02 .00
☐ 542 Don Schulze .04 .02 .00
☐ 543 Jerry Narron .04 .02 .00
☐ 544 Eddie Milner .04 .02 .00
☐ 545 Jimmy Key .15 .06 .01
☐ 546 Mariners Leaders .07 .03 .01
Dave Henderson
☐ 547 Roger McDowell .17 .07 .01
☐ 548 Mike Young .04 .02 .00
☐ 549 Bob Welch .10 .04 .01
☐ 550 Tom Herr .07 .03 .01
☐ 551 Dave LaPoint .04 .02 .00
☐ 552 Marc Hill .04 .02 .00
☐ 553 Jim Morrison .04 .02 .00
☐ 554 Paul Householder .04 .02 .00
☐ 555 Hubie Brooks .10 .04 .01
☐ 556 John Denny .04 .02 .00
☐ 557 Gerald Perry .07 .03 .01
☐ 558 Tim Stoddard .04 .02 .00
☐ 559 Tommy Dunbar .04 .02 .00
☐ 560 Dave Righetti .10 .04 .01
☐ 561 Bob Lillis MG .07 .03 .01
(checklist back)
☐ 562 Joe Beckwith .04 .02 .00
☐ 563 Alejandro Sanchez .04 .02 .00
☐ 564 Warren Brusstar .04 .02 .00
☐ 565 Tom Brunansky .10 .04 .01
☐ 566 Alfredo Griffin .04 .02 .00

☐ 567 Jeff Barkley .04 .02 .00
☐ 568 Donnie Scott .04 .02 .00
☐ 569 Jim Acker .04 .02 .00
☐ 570 Rusty Staub .07 .03 .01
☐ 571 Mike Jeffcoat .04 .02 .00
☐ 572 Paul Zuvella .04 .02 .00
☐ 573 Tom Hume .04 .02 .00
☐ 574 Ron Kittle .07 .03 .01
☐ 575 Mike Boddicker .04 .02 .00
☐ 576 Expos Leaders .10 .04 .01
Andre Dawson
☐ 577 Jerry Reuss .04 .02 .00
☐ 578 Lee Mazzilli .04 .02 .00
☐ 579 Jim Slaton .04 .02 .00
☐ 580 Willie McGee .15 .06 .01
☐ 581 Bruce Hurst .07 .03 .01
☐ 582 Jim Gantner .04 .02 .00
☐ 583 Al Bumbry .04 .02 .00
☐ 584 Brian Fisher .07 .03 .01
☐ 585 Garry Maddox .04 .02 .00
☐ 586 Greg Harris .04 .02 .00
☐ 587 Rafael Santana .04 .02 .00
☐ 588 Steve Lake .04 .02 .00
☐ 589 Sid Bream .04 .02 .00
☐ 590 Bob Knepper .04 .02 .00
☐ 591 Jackie Moore MG .07 .03 .01
(checklist back)
☐ 592 Frank Tanana .07 .03 .01
☐ 593 Jesse Barfield .10 .04 .01
☐ 594 Chris Bando .04 .02 .00
☐ 595 Dave Parker .15 .06 .01
☐ 596 Onix Concepcion .04 .02 .00
☐ 597 Sammy Stewart .04 .02 .00
☐ 598 Jim Presley .07 .03 .01
☐ 599 Rick Aguilera .40 .16 .04
☐ 600 Dale Murphy .25 .10 .02
☐ 601 Gary Lucas .04 .02 .00
☐ 602 Mariano Duncan .20 .08 .02
☐ 603 Bill Laskey .04 .02 .00
☐ 604 Gary Pettis .04 .02 .00
☐ 605 Dennis Boyd .04 .02 .00
☐ 606 Royals Leaders .07 .03 .01
Hal McRae
☐ 607 Ken Dayley .04 .02 .00
☐ 608 Bruce Bochy .04 .02 .00
☐ 609 Barbaro Garbey .04 .02 .00
☐ 610 Ron Guidry .10 .04 .01
☐ 611 Gary Woods .04 .02 .00
☐ 612 Richard Dotson .04 .02 .00
☐ 613 Roy Smalley .04 .02 .00
☐ 614 Rick Waits .04 .02 .00
☐ 615 Johnny Ray .04 .02 .00
☐ 616 Glenn Brummer .04 .02 .00
☐ 617 Lonnie Smith .10 .04 .01
☐ 618 Jim Pankovits .04 .02 .00
☐ 619 Danny Heep .04 .02 .00
☐ 620 Bruce Sutter .10 .04 .01
☐ 621 John Felske MG .07 .03 .01

(checklist back)
□ 622 Gary Lavelle .04 .02 .00
□ 623 Floyd Rayford .04 .02 .00
□ 624 Steve McCatty .04 .02 .00
□ 625 Bob Brenly .04 .02 .00
□ 626 Roy Thomas .04 .02 .00
□ 627 Ron Oester .04 .02 .00
□ 628 Kirk McCaskill .17 .07 .01
□ 629 Mitch Webster .12 .05 .01
□ 630 Fernando Valenzuela .10 .04 .01
□ 631 Steve Braun .04 .02 .00
□ 632 Dave Von Ohlen .04 .02 .00
□ 633 Jackie Gutierrez .04 .02 .00
□ 634 Roy Lee Jackson .04 .02 .00
□ 635 Jason Thompson .04 .02 .00
□ 636 Cubs Leaders .10 .04 .01
Lee Smith
□ 637 Rudy Law .04 .02 .00
□ 638 John Butcher .04 .02 .00
□ 639 Bo Diaz .04 .02 .00
□ 640 Jose Cruz .07 .03 .01
□ 641 Wayne Tolleson .04 .02 .00
□ 642 Ray Searage .04 .02 .00
□ 643 Tom Brookens .04 .02 .00
□ 644 Mark Gubicza .10 .04 .01
□ 645 Dusty Baker .07 .03 .01
□ 646 Mike Moore .07 .03 .01
□ 647 Mel Hall .07 .03 .01
□ 648 Steve Bedrosian .07 .03 .01
□ 649 Ronn Reynolds .04 .02 .00
□ 650 Dave Stieb .12 .05 .01
□ 651 Billy Martin MG .12 .05 .01
(checklist back)
□ 652 Tom Browning .20 .08 .02
□ 653 Jim Dwyer .04 .02 .00
□ 654 Ken Howell .07 .03 .01
□ 655 Manny Trillo .04 .02 .00
□ 656 Brian Harper .15 .06 .01
□ 657 Juan Agosto .04 .02 .00
□ 658 Rob Wilfong .04 .02 .00
□ 659 Checklist: 529-660 .10 .01 .00
□ 660 Steve Garvey .25 .10 .02
□ 661 Roger Clemens 4.00 1.75 .40
□ 662 Bill Schroeder .04 .02 .00
□ 663 Neil Allen .04 .02 .00
□ 664 Tim Corcoran .04 .02 .00
□ 665 Alejandro Pena .04 .02 .00
□ 666 Rangers Leaders .04 .02 .00
Charlie Hough
□ 667 Tim Teufel .04 .02 .00
□ 668 Cecilio Guante .04 .02 .00
□ 669 Ron Cey .07 .03 .01
□ 670 Willie Hernandez .04 .02 .00
□ 671 Lynn Jones .04 .02 .00
□ 672 Rob Picciolo .04 .02 .00
□ 673 Ernie Whitt .04 .02 .00
□ 674 Pat Tabler .04 .02 .00
□ 675 Claudell Washington .04 .02 .00
□ 676 Matt Young .04 .02 .00
□ 677 Nick Esasky .04 .02 .00
□ 678 Dan Gladden .04 .02 .00
□ 679 Britt Burns .04 .02 .00
□ 680 George Foster .10 .04 .01
□ 681 Dick Williams MG .07 .03 .01
(checklist back)
□ 682 Junior Ortiz .04 .02 .00
□ 683 Andy Van Slyke .20 .08 .02
□ 684 Bob McClure .04 .02 .00
□ 685 Tim Wallach .10 .04 .01
□ 686 Jeff Stone .04 .02 .00
□ 687 Mike Trujillo .04 .02 .00
□ 688 Larry Herndon .04 .02 .00
□ 689 Dave Stewart .20 .08 .02
□ 690 Ryne Sandberg UER 2.00 .80 .20
(no Topps logo
on front)
□ 691 Mike Madden .04 .02 .00
□ 692 Dale Berra .04 .02 .00
□ 693 Tom Tellmann .04 .02 .00
□ 694 Garth Iorg .04 .02 .00
□ 695 Mike Smithson .04 .02 .00
□ 696 Dodgers Leaders .07 .03 .01
Bill Russell
□ 697 Bud Black .04 .02 .00
□ 698 Brad Komminsk .04 .02 .00
□ 699 Pat Corrales MG .07 .03 .01
(checklist back)
□ 700 Reggie Jackson .50 .20 .05
□ 701 Keith Hernandez AS .10 .04 .01
□ 702 Tom Herr AS .07 .03 .01
□ 703 Tim Wallach AS .07 .03 .01
□ 704 Ozzie Smith AS .15 .06 .01
□ 705 Dale Murphy AS .15 .06 .01
□ 706 Pedro Guerrero AS .10 .04 .01
□ 707 Willie McGee AS .07 .03 .01
□ 708 Gary Carter AS .12 .05 .01
□ 709 Dwight Gooden AS .30 .12 .03
□ 710 John Tudor AS .07 .03 .01
□ 711 Jeff Reardon AS .10 .04 .01
□ 712 Don Mattingly AS .40 .16 .04
□ 713 Damaso Garcia AS .04 .02 .00
□ 714 George Brett AS .20 .08 .02
□ 715 Cal Ripken AS .50 .20 .05
□ 716 Rickey Henderson AS .35 .15 .03
□ 717 Dave Winfield AS .15 .06 .01
□ 718 George Bell AS .12 .05 .01
□ 719 Carlton Fisk AS .15 .06 .01
□ 720 Bret Saberhagen AS .15 .06 .01
□ 721 Ron Guidry AS .07 .03 .01
□ 722 Dan Quisenberry AS .07 .03 .01
□ 723 Marty Bystrom .04 .02 .00
□ 724 Tim Hulett .04 .02 .00
□ 725 Mario Soto .04 .02 .00
□ 726 Orioles Leaders .04 .02 .00
Rick Dempsey
□ 727 David Green .04 .02 .00

☐ 728 Mike Marshall	.07	.03	.01
☐ 729 Jim Beattie	.04	.02	.00
☐ 730 Ozzie Smith	.40	.16	.04
☐ 731 Don Robinson	.04	.02	.00
☐ 732 Floyd Youmans	.07	.03	.01
☐ 733 Ron Romanick	.04	.02	.00
☐ 734 Marty Barrett	.04	.02	.00
☐ 735 Dave Dravecky	.07	.03	.01
☐ 736 Glenn Wilson	.04	.02	.00
☐ 737 Pete Vuckovich	.04	.02	.00
☐ 738 Andre Robertson	.04	.02	.00
☐ 739 Dave Rozema	.04	.02	.00
☐ 740 Lance Parrish	.12	.05	.01
☐ 741 Pete Rose MG (checklist back)	.35	.15	.03
☐ 742 Frank Viola	.17	.07	.01
☐ 743 Pat Sheridan	.04	.02	.00
☐ 744 Lary Sorensen	.04	.02	.00
☐ 745 Willie Upshaw	.04	.02	.00
☐ 746 Denny Gonzalez	.04	.02	.00
☐ 747 Rick Cerone	.04	.02	.00
☐ 748 Steve Henderson	.04	.02	.00
☐ 749 Ed Jurak	.04	.02	.00
☐ 750 Gorman Thomas	.07	.03	.01
☐ 751 Howard Johnson	.45	.18	.04
☐ 752 Mike Krukow	.04	.02	.00
☐ 753 Dan Ford	.04	.02	.00
☐ 754 Pat Clements	.04	.02	.00
☐ 755 Harold Baines	.15	.06	.01
☐ 756 Pirates Leaders Rick Rhoden	.04	.02	.00
☐ 757 Darrell Porter	.04	.02	.00
☐ 758 Dave Anderson	.04	.02	.00
☐ 759 Moose Haas	.04	.02	.00
☐ 760 Andre Dawson	.40	.16	.04
☐ 761 Don Slaught	.04	.02	.00
☐ 762 Eric Show	.04	.02	.00
☐ 763 Terry Puhl	.04	.02	.00
☐ 764 Kevin Gross	.04	.02	.00
☐ 765 Don Baylor	.10	.04	.01
☐ 766 Rick Langford	.04	.02	.00
☐ 767 Jody Davis	.04	.02	.00
☐ 768 Vern Ruhle	.04	.02	.00
☐ 769 Harold Reynolds	.50	.20	.05
☐ 770 Vida Blue	.07	.03	.01
☐ 771 John McNamara MG (checklist back)	.07	.03	.01
☐ 772 Brian Downing	.07	.03	.01
☐ 773 Greg Pryor	.04	.02	.00
☐ 774 Terry Leach	.07	.03	.01
☐ 775 Al Oliver	.07	.03	.01
☐ 776 Gene Garber	.04	.02	.00
☐ 777 Wayne Krenchicki	.04	.02	.00
☐ 778 Jerry Hairston	.04	.02	.00
☐ 779 Rick Reuschel	.07	.03	.01
☐ 780 Robin Yount	.40	.16	.04
☐ 781 Joe Nolan	.04	.02	.00
☐ 782 Ken Landreaux	.04	.02	.00
☐ 783 Ricky Horton	.04	.02	.00
☐ 784 Alan Bannister	.04	.02	.00
☐ 785 Bob Stanley	.04	.02	.00
☐ 786 Twins Leaders Mickey Hatcher	.04	.02	.00
☐ 787 Vance Law	.04	.02	.00
☐ 788 Marty Castillo	.04	.02	.00
☐ 789 Kurt Bevacqua	.04	.02	.00
☐ 790 Phil Niekro	.17	.07	.01
☐ 791 Checklist: 661-792	.10	.01	.00
☐ 792 Charles Hudson	.07	.03	.01

1986 Topps Traded

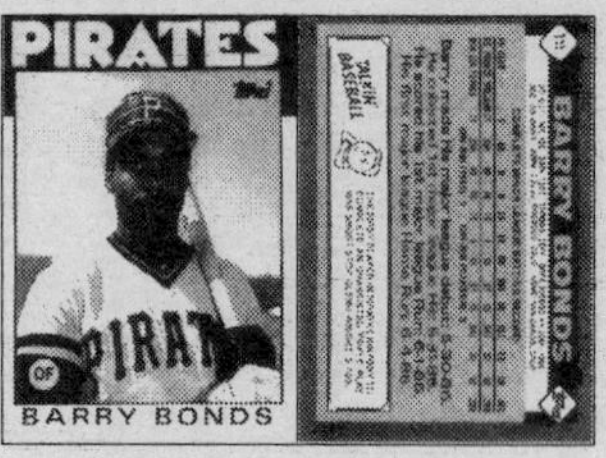

This 132-card Traded or extended set was distributed by Topps to dealers in a special red and white box as a complete set. The card fronts are identical in style to the Topps regular issue and are also 2 1/2" by 3 1/2". The backs are printed in red and black on white card stock. Cards are numbered (with a T suffix) alphabetically according to the name of the player. The key (extended) rookie cards in this set are Barry Bonds, Bobby Bonilla, Jose Canseco, Will Clark, Bo Jackson, and Kevin Mitchell. Topps also produced a specially boxed "glossy" edition frequently referred to as the Topps Traded Tiffany set. There were supposedly only 5,000 sets of the Tiffany cards produced; they were marketed to hobby dealers. The checklist of cards is identical to that of the normal non-glossy cards. There are two primary distinguishing features of the Tiffany cards, white card stock reverses and high gloss obverses. These Tiffany cards are valued at approximately five times the values listed below.

	MINT	EXC	G-VG
COMPLETE SET (132)	26.00	11.00	2.50
COMMON PLAYER (1-132)	.06	.02	.00

	MINT	EXC	G-VG
☐ 1T Andy Allanson	.12	.04	.01
☐ 2T Neil Allen	.06	.02	.00
☐ 3T Joaquin Andujar	.10	.04	.01
☐ 4T Paul Assenmacher	.12	.05	.01
☐ 5T Scott Bailes	.12	.05	.01
☐ 6T Don Baylor	.12	.05	.01
☐ 7T Steve Bedrosian	.10	.04	.01
☐ 8T Juan Beniquez	.06	.02	.00
☐ 9T Juan Berenguer	.06	.02	.00
☐ 10T Mike Bielecki	.15	.06	.01
☐ 11T Barry Bonds	3.75	1.60	.37
☐ 12T Bobby Bonilla	3.50	1.50	.35
☐ 13T Juan Bonilla	.06	.02	.00
☐ 14T Rich Bordi	.06	.02	.00
☐ 15T Steve Boros MG	.06	.02	.00
☐ 16T Rick Burleson	.10	.04	.01
☐ 17T Bill Campbell	.06	.02	.00
☐ 18T Tom Candiotti	.15	.06	.01
☐ 19T John Cangelosi	.10	.04	.01
☐ 20T Jose Canseco	9.00	4.00	.90
☐ 21T Carmen Castillo	.06	.02	.00
☐ 22T Rick Cerone	.06	.02	.00
☐ 23T John Cerutti	.12	.05	.01
☐ 24T Will Clark	9.00	4.00	.90
☐ 25T Mark Clear	.06	.02	.00
☐ 26T Darnell Coles	.06	.02	.00
☐ 27T Dave Collins	.06	.02	.00
☐ 28T Tim Conroy	.06	.02	.00
☐ 29T Joe Cowley	.06	.02	.00
☐ 30T Joel Davis	.10	.04	.01
☐ 31T Rob Deer	.15	.06	.01
☐ 32T John Denny	.06	.02	.00
☐ 33T Mike Easler	.06	.02	.00
☐ 34T Mark Eichhorn	.12	.05	.01
☐ 35T Steve Farr	.12	.05	.01
☐ 36T Scott Fletcher	.06	.02	.00
☐ 37T Terry Forster	.10	.04	.01
☐ 38T Terry Francona	.06	.02	.00
☐ 39T Jim Fregosi MG	.10	.04	.01
☐ 40T Andres Galarraga	.35	.15	.03
☐ 41T Ken Griffey	.25	.10	.02
☐ 42T Bill Gullickson	.12	.05	.01
☐ 43T Jose Guzman	.25	.10	.02
☐ 44T Moose Haas	.06	.02	.00
☐ 45T Billy Hatcher	.12	.05	.01
☐ 46T Mike Heath	.06	.02	.00
☐ 47T Tom Hume	.06	.02	.00
☐ 48T Pete Incaviglia	.35	.15	.03
☐ 49T Dane Iorg	.06	.02	.00
☐ 50T Bo Jackson	7.00	3.00	.70
☐ 51T Wally Joyner	1.50	.60	.15
☐ 52T Charlie Kerfeld	.06	.02	.00
☐ 53T Eric King	.15	.06	.01
☐ 54T Bob Kipper	.10	.04	.01
☐ 55T Wayne Krenchicki	.06	.02	.00
☐ 56T John Kruk	.40	.16	.04
☐ 57T Mike LaCoss	.06	.02	.00
☐ 58T Pete Ladd	.06	.02	.00
☐ 59T Mike Laga	.10	.04	.01
☐ 60T Hal Lanier MG	.06	.02	.00
☐ 61T Dave LaPoint	.06	.02	.00
☐ 62T Rudy Law	.06	.02	.00
☐ 63T Rick Leach	.06	.02	.00
☐ 64T Tim Leary	.15	.06	.01
☐ 65T Dennis Leonard	.10	.04	.01
☐ 66T Jim Leyland MG	.15	.06	.01
☐ 67T Steve Lyons	.10	.04	.01
☐ 68T Mickey Mahler	.06	.02	.00
☐ 69T Candy Maldonado	.15	.06	.01
☐ 70T Roger Mason	.10	.04	.01
☐ 71T Bob McClure	.06	.02	.00
☐ 72T Andy McGaffigan	.06	.02	.00
☐ 73T Gene Michael MG	.06	.02	.00
☐ 74T Kevin Mitchell	3.25	1.35	.32
☐ 75T Omar Moreno	.06	.02	.00
☐ 76T Jerry Mumphrey	.06	.02	.00
☐ 77T Phil Niekro	.25	.10	.02
☐ 78T Randy Niemann	.06	.02	.00
☐ 79T Juan Nieves	.12	.05	.01
☐ 80T Otis Nixon	.25	.10	.02
☐ 81T Bob Ojeda	.12	.05	.01
☐ 82T Jose Oquendo	.10	.04	.01
☐ 83T Tom Paciorek	.06	.02	.00
☐ 84T David Palmer	.06	.02	.00
☐ 85T Frank Pastore	.06	.02	.00
☐ 86T Lou Piniella MG	.12	.05	.01
☐ 87T Dan Plesac	.17	.07	.01
☐ 88T Darrell Porter	.06	.02	.00
☐ 89T Rey Quinones	.06	.02	.00
☐ 90T Gary Redus	.06	.02	.00
☐ 91T Bip Roberts	.30	.12	.03
☐ 92T Billy Jo Robidoux	.10	.04	.01
☐ 93T Jeff Robinson (Giants pitcher)	.10	.04	.01
☐ 94T Gary Roenicke	.06	.02	.00
☐ 95T Ed Romero	.06	.02	.00
☐ 96T Argenis Salazar	.06	.02	.00
☐ 97T Joe Sambito	.06	.02	.00
☐ 98T Billy Sample	.06	.02	.00
☐ 99T Dave Schmidt	.10	.04	.01
☐ 100T Ken Schrom	.06	.02	.00
☐ 101T Tom Seaver	.45	.18	.04
☐ 102T Ted Simmons	.15	.06	.01
☐ 103T Sammy Stewart	.06	.02	.00
☐ 104T Kurt Stillwell	.25	.10	.02
☐ 105T Franklin Stubbs	.12	.05	.01
☐ 106T Dale Sveum	.12	.05	.01
☐ 107T Chuck Tanner MG	.06	.02	.00
☐ 108T Danny Tartabull	.80	.35	.08
☐ 109T Tim Teufel	.12	.05	.01
☐ 110T Bob Tewksbury	.10	.04	.01
☐ 111T Andres Thomas	.10	.04	.01

☐ 112T Milt Thompson	.12	.05	.01
☐ 113T Robby Thompson	.30	.12	.03
☐ 114T Jay Tibbs	.06	.02	.00
☐ 115T Wayne Tolleson	.06	.02	.00
☐ 116T Alex Trevino	.06	.02	.00
☐ 117T Manny Trillo	.06	.02	.00
☐ 118T Ed VandeBerg	.06	.02	.00
☐ 119T Ozzie Virgil	.06	.02	.00
☐ 120T Bob Walk	.06	.02	.00
☐ 121T Gene Walter	.06	.02	.00
☐ 122T Claudell Washington	.10	.04	.01
☐ 123T Bill Wegman	.15	.06	.01
☐ 124T Dick Williams MG	.06	.02	.00
☐ 125T Mitch Williams	.25	.10	.02
☐ 126T Bobby Witt	.30	.12	.03
☐ 127T Todd Worrell	.12	.05	.01
☐ 128T George Wright	.06	.02	.00
☐ 129T Ricky Wright	.06	.02	.00
☐ 130T Steve Yeager	.06	.02	.00
☐ 131T Paul Zuvella	.06	.02	.00
☐ 132T Checklist 1-132	.06	.01	.00

1987 Topps

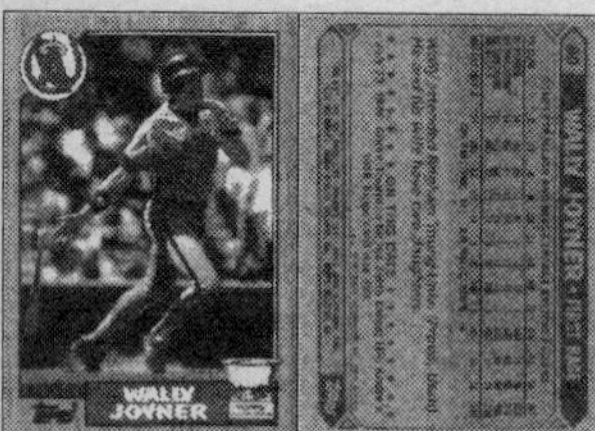

This 792-card set is reminiscent of the 1962 Topps baseball cards with their simulated wood grain borders. The backs are printed in yellow and blue on gray card stock. The manager cards contain a checklist of the respective team's players on the back. Subsets in the set include Record Breakers (1-7), Turn Back the Clock (311-315), and All-Star selections (595-616). The Team Leader cards typically show players conferring on the mound inside a white cloud. The wax pack wrapper gives details of "Spring Fever Baseball" where a lucky collector can win a trip for four to Spring Training. The key rookie cards in this set are Barry Bonds, Bobby Bonilla, Will Clark, Mike Greenwell, Bo Jackson, Barry Larkin, Dave Magadan, Kevin Mitchell, Rafael Palmiero, and Ruben Sierra. Topps also produced a specially boxed "glossy" edition, frequently referred to as the Topps Tiffany set. This year Topps did not disclose the number of sets they produced or sold. It is apparent from the availability that there were many more sets produced this year compared to the 1984-86 Tiffany sets, perhaps 30,000 sets, more than three times as many. The checklist of cards (792 regular and 132 Traded) is identical to that of the normal non-glossy cards. There are two primary distinguishing features of the Tiffany cards, white card stock reverses and high gloss obverses. These Tiffany cards are valued at approximately three times the values listed below.

	MINT	EXC	G-VG
COMPLETE SET (792)	32.00	14.25	4.75
COMMON PLAYER (1-792)	.03	.01	.00

☐ 1 RB: Roger Clemens Most strikeouts, nine inning game	.35	.10	.02
☐ 2 RB: Jim Deshaies Most cons. K's, start of game	.06	.02	.00
☐ 3 RB: Dwight Evans Earliest home run, season	.08	.03	.01
☐ 4 RB: Davey Lopes Most steals, season, 40-year-old	.06	.02	.00
☐ 5 RB: Dave Righetti Most saves, season	.08	.03	.01
☐ 6 RB: Ruben Sierra Youngest player to switch hit homers in game	.30	.12	.03
☐ 7 RB: Todd Worrell Most saves, season, rookie	.06	.02	.00
☐ 8 Terry Pendleton	.15	.06	.01
☐ 9 Jay Tibbs	.03	.01	.00
☐ 10 Cecil Cooper	.08	.03	.01
☐ 11 Indians Team (mound conference)	.03	.01	.00
☐ 12 Jeff Sellers	.06	.02	.00
☐ 13 Nick Esasky	.06	.02	.00
☐ 14 Dave Stewart	.15	.06	.01
☐ 15 Claudell Washington	.03	.01	.00
☐ 16 Pat Clements	.03	.01	.00
☐ 17 Pete O'Brien	.03	.01	.00
☐ 18 Dick Howser MG	.06	.02	.00

Card			
(checklist back)			
☐ 19 Matt Young	.03	.01	.00
☐ 20 Gary Carter	.15	.06	.01
☐ 21 Mark Davis	.08	.03	.01
☐ 22 Doug DeCinces	.06	.02	.00
☐ 23 Lee Smith	.12	.05	.01
☐ 24 Tony Walker	.06	.02	.00
☐ 25 Bert Blyleven	.08	.03	.01
☐ 26 Greg Brock	.03	.01	.00
☐ 27 Joe Cowley	.03	.01	.00
☐ 28 Rick Dempsey	.03	.01	.00
☐ 29 Jimmy Key	.08	.03	.01
☐ 30 Tim Raines	.15	.06	.01
☐ 31 Braves Team	.03	.01	.00
(Hubbard/Ramirez)			
☐ 32 Tim Leary	.06	.02	.00
☐ 33 Andy Van Slyke	.15	.06	.01
☐ 34 Jose Rijo	.12	.05	.01
☐ 35 Sid Bream	.03	.01	.00
☐ 36 Eric King	.10	.04	.01
☐ 37 Marvell Wynne	.03	.01	.00
☐ 38 Dennis Leonard	.03	.01	.00
☐ 39 Marty Barrett	.03	.01	.00
☐ 40 Dave Righetti	.08	.03	.01
☐ 41 Bo Diaz	.03	.01	.00
☐ 42 Gary Redus	.03	.01	.00
☐ 43 Gene Michael MG	.06	.02	.00
(checklist back)			
☐ 44 Greg Harris	.03	.01	.00
☐ 45 Jim Presley	.03	.01	.00
☐ 46 Dan Gladden	.03	.01	.00
☐ 47 Dennis Powell	.03	.01	.00
☐ 48 Wally Backman	.03	.01	.00
☐ 49 Terry Harper	.03	.01	.00
☐ 50 Dave Smith	.03	.01	.00
☐ 51 Mel Hall	.08	.03	.01
☐ 52 Keith Atherton	.03	.01	.00
☐ 53 Ruppert Jones	.03	.01	.00
☐ 54 Bill Dawley	.03	.01	.00
☐ 55 Tim Wallach	.08	.03	.01
☐ 56 Brewers Team	.03	.01	.00
(mound conference)			
☐ 57 Scott Nielsen	.06	.02	.00
☐ 58 Thad Bosley	.03	.01	.00
☐ 59 Ken Dayley	.03	.01	.00
☐ 60 Tony Pena	.06	.02	.00
☐ 61 Bobby Thigpen	.50	.20	.05
☐ 62 Bobby Meacham	.03	.01	.00
☐ 63 Fred Toliver	.03	.01	.00
☐ 64 Harry Spilman	.03	.01	.00
☐ 65 Tom Browning	.08	.03	.01
☐ 66 Marc Sullivan	.03	.01	.00
☐ 67 Bill Swift	.06	.02	.00
☐ 68 Tony LaRussa MG	.06	.02	.00
(checklist back)			
☐ 69 Lonnie Smith	.08	.03	.01
☐ 70 Charlie Hough	.03	.01	.00
☐ 71 Mike Aldrete	.06	.02	.00
☐ 72 Walt Terrell	.03	.01	.00
☐ 73 Dave Anderson	.03	.01	.00
☐ 74 Dan Pasqua	.06	.02	.00
☐ 75 Ron Darling	.08	.03	.01
☐ 76 Rafael Ramirez	.03	.01	.00
☐ 77 Bryan Oelkers	.03	.01	.00
☐ 78 Tom Foley	.03	.01	.00
☐ 79 Juan Nieves	.06	.02	.00
☐ 80 Wally Joyner	.75	.30	.07
☐ 81 Padres Team	.03	.01	.00
(Hawkins/Kennedy)			
☐ 82 Rob Murphy	.10	.04	.01
☐ 83 Mike Davis	.03	.01	.00
☐ 84 Steve Lake	.03	.01	.00
☐ 85 Kevin Bass	.03	.01	.00
☐ 86 Nate Snell	.03	.01	.00
☐ 87 Mark Salas	.03	.01	.00
☐ 88 Ed Wojna	.03	.01	.00
☐ 89 Ozzie Guillen	.10	.04	.01
☐ 90 Dave Stieb	.10	.04	.01
☐ 91 Harold Reynolds	.08	.03	.01
☐ 92A Urbano Lugo	.20	.08	.02
ERR (no trademark)			
☐ 92B Urbano Lugo COR	.06	.02	.00
☐ 93 Jim Leyland MG	.06	.02	.00
(checklist back)			
☐ 94 Calvin Schiraldi	.03	.01	.00
☐ 95 Oddibe McDowell	.03	.01	.00
☐ 96 Frank Williams	.03	.01	.00
☐ 97 Glenn Wilson	.03	.01	.00
☐ 98 Bill Scherrer	.03	.01	.00
☐ 99 Darryl Motley	.03	.01	.00
☐ 100 Steve Garvey	.20	.08	.02
☐ 101 Carl Willis	.10	.04	.01
☐ 102 Paul Zuvella	.03	.01	.00
☐ 103 Rick Aguilera	.10	.04	.01
☐ 104 Billy Sample	.03	.01	.00
☐ 105 Floyd Youmans	.03	.01	.00
☐ 106 Blue Jays Team	.12	.05	.01
(Bell/Barfield)			
☐ 107 John Butcher	.03	.01	.00
☐ 108 Jim Gantner UER	.06	.02	.00
(Brewers logo reversed)			
☐ 109 R.J. Reynolds	.03	.01	.00
☐ 110 John Tudor	.08	.03	.01
☐ 111 Alfredo Griffin	.03	.01	.00
☐ 112 Alan Ashby	.03	.01	.00
☐ 113 Neil Allen	.03	.01	.00
☐ 114 Billy Beane	.03	.01	.00
☐ 115 Donnie Moore	.03	.01	.00
☐ 116 Bill Russell	.06	.02	.00
☐ 117 Jim Beattie	.03	.01	.00
☐ 118 Bobby Valentine MG	.06	.02	.00
(checklist back)			
☐ 119 Ron Robinson	.06	.02	.00
☐ 120 Eddie Murray	.30	.12	.03
☐ 121 Kevin Romine	.06	.02	.00

☐ 122 Jim Clancy .03 .01 .00
☐ 123 John Kruk .25 .10 .02
☐ 124 Ray Fontenot .03 .01 .00
☐ 125 Bob Brenly .03 .01 .00
☐ 126 Mike Loynd .03 .01 .00
☐ 127 Vance Law .03 .01 .00
☐ 128 Checklist 1-132 .08 .01 .00
☐ 129 Rick Cerone .03 .01 .00
☐ 130 Dwight Gooden .30 .12 .03
☐ 131 Pirates Team .03 .01 .00
(Bream/Pena)
☐ 132 Paul Assenmacher .03 .01 .00
☐ 133 Jose Oquendo .03 .01 .00
☐ 134 Rich Yett .03 .01 .00
☐ 135 Mike Easler .03 .01 .00
☐ 136 Ron Romanick .03 .01 .00
☐ 137 Jerry Willard .03 .01 .00
☐ 138 Roy Lee Jackson .03 .01 .00
☐ 139 Devon White .45 .18 .04
☐ 140 Bret Saberhagen .17 .07 .01
☐ 141 Herm Winningham .03 .01 .00
☐ 142 Rick Sutcliffe .06 .02 .00
☐ 143 Steve Boros MG .06 .02 .00
(checklist back)
☐ 144 Mike Scioscia .03 .01 .00
☐ 145 Charlie Kerfeld .03 .01 .00
☐ 146 Tracy Jones .08 .03 .01
☐ 147 Randy Niemann .03 .01 .00
☐ 148 Dave Collins .03 .01 .00
☐ 149 Ray Searage .03 .01 .00
☐ 150 Wade Boggs .40 .16 .04
☐ 151 Mike LaCoss .03 .01 .00
☐ 152 Toby Harrah .03 .01 .00
☐ 153 Duane Ward .20 .08 .02
☐ 154 Tom O'Malley .03 .01 .00
☐ 155 Eddie Whitson .03 .01 .00
☐ 156 Mariners Team .03 .01 .00
(mound conference)
☐ 157 Danny Darwin .03 .01 .00
☐ 158 Tim Teufel .03 .01 .00
☐ 159 Ed Olwine .03 .01 .00
☐ 160 Julio Franco .25 .10 .02
☐ 161 Steve Ontiveros .03 .01 .00
☐ 162 Mike LaValliere .15 .06 .01
☐ 163 Kevin Gross .03 .01 .00
☐ 164 Sammy Khalifa .03 .01 .00
☐ 165 Jeff Reardon .12 .05 .01
☐ 166 Bob Boone .08 .03 .01
☐ 167 Jim Deshaies .15 .06 .01
☐ 168 Lou Piniella MG .08 .03 .01
(checklist back)
☐ 169 Ron Washington .03 .01 .00
☐ 170 Bo Jackson 3.25 1.35 .32
☐ 171 Chuck Cary .10 .04 .01
☐ 172 Ron Oester .03 .01 .00
☐ 173 Alex Trevino .03 .01 .00
☐ 174 Henry Cotto .03 .01 .00
☐ 175 Bob Stanley .03 .01 .00
☐ 176 Steve Buechele .03 .01 .00
☐ 177 Keith Moreland .03 .01 .00
☐ 178 Cecil Fielder 1.25 .50 .12
☐ 179 Bill Wegman .08 .03 .01
☐ 180 Chris Brown .03 .01 .00
☐ 181 Cardinals Team .03 .01 .00
(mound conference)
☐ 182 Lee Lacy .03 .01 .00
☐ 183 Andy Hawkins .03 .01 .00
☐ 184 Bobby Bonilla 1.75 .70 .17
☐ 185 Roger McDowell .03 .01 .00
☐ 186 Bruce Benedict .03 .01 .00
☐ 187 Mark Huismann .03 .01 .00
☐ 188 Tony Phillips .03 .01 .00
☐ 189 Joe Hesketh .06 .02 .00
☐ 190 Jim Sundberg .03 .01 .00
☐ 191 Charles Hudson .03 .01 .00
☐ 192 Cory Snyder .08 .03 .01
☐ 193 Roger Craig MG .06 .02 .00
(checklist back)
☐ 194 Kirk McCaskill .03 .01 .00
☐ 195 Mike Pagliarulo .03 .01 .00
☐ 196 Randy O'Neal UER .03 .01 .00
(wrong ML career
W-L totals)
☐ 197 Mark Bailey .03 .01 .00
☐ 198 Lee Mazzilli .03 .01 .00
☐ 199 Mariano Duncan .08 .03 .01
☐ 200 Pete Rose .35 .15 .03
☐ 201 John Cangelosi .03 .01 .00
☐ 202 Ricky Wright .03 .01 .00
☐ 203 Mike Kingery .03 .01 .00
☐ 204 Sammy Stewart .03 .01 .00
☐ 205 Graig Nettles .08 .03 .01
☐ 206 Twins Team .06 .02 .00
(Frank Viola and
Tim Laudner)
☐ 207 George Frazier .03 .01 .00
☐ 208 John Shelby .03 .01 .00
☐ 209 Rick Schu .03 .01 .00
☐ 210 Lloyd Moseby .03 .01 .00
☐ 211 John Morris .03 .01 .00
☐ 212 Mike Fitzgerald .03 .01 .00
☐ 213 Randy Myers .15 .06 .01
☐ 214 Omar Moreno .03 .01 .00
☐ 215 Mark Langston .17 .07 .01
☐ 216 B.J. Surhoff .15 .06 .01
☐ 217 Chris Codiroli .03 .01 .00
☐ 218 Sparky Anderson MG .06 .02 .00
(checklist back)
☐ 219 Cecilio Guante .03 .01 .00
☐ 220 Joe Carter .30 .12 .03
☐ 221 Vern Ruhle .03 .01 .00
☐ 222 Denny Walling .03 .01 .00
☐ 223 Charlie Leibrandt .03 .01 .00
☐ 224 Wayne Tolleson .03 .01 .00
☐ 225 Mike Smithson .03 .01 .00
☐ 226 Max Venable .03 .01 .00

□ 227	Jamie Moyer	.08	.03	.01
□ 228	Curt Wilkerson	.03	.01	.00
□ 229	Mike Birkbeck	.06	.02	.00
□ 230	Don Baylor	.08	.03	.01
□ 231	Giants Team (Bob Brenly and Jim Gott)	.03	.01	.00
□ 232	Reggie Williams	.03	.01	.00
□ 233	Russ Morman	.03	.01	.00
□ 234	Pat Sheridan	.03	.01	.00
□ 235	Alvin Davis	.08	.03	.01
□ 236	Tommy John	.10	.04	.01
□ 237	Jim Morrison	.03	.01	.00
□ 238	Bill Krueger	.03	.01	.00
□ 239	Juan Espino	.03	.01	.00
□ 240	Steve Balboni	.03	.01	.00
□ 241	Danny Heep	.03	.01	.00
□ 242	Rick Mahler	.03	.01	.00
□ 243	Whitey Herzog MG (checklist back)	.06	.02	.00
□ 244	Dickie Noles	.03	.01	.00
□ 245	Willie Upshaw	.03	.01	.00
□ 246	Jim Dwyer	.03	.01	.00
□ 247	Jeff Reed	.03	.01	.00
□ 248	Gene Walter	.03	.01	.00
□ 249	Jim Pankovits	.03	.01	.00
□ 250	Teddy Higuera	.06	.02	.00
□ 251	Rob Wilfong	.03	.01	.00
□ 252	Dennis Martinez	.08	.03	.01
□ 253	Eddie Milner	.03	.01	.00
□ 254	Bob Tewksbury	.06	.02	.00
□ 255	Juan Samuel	.10	.04	.01
□ 256	Royals Team (Brett/F.White)	.10	.04	.01
□ 257	Bob Forsch	.03	.01	.00
□ 258	Steve Yeager	.03	.01	.00
□ 259	Mike Greenwell	1.50	.60	.15
□ 260	Vida Blue	.06	.02	.00
□ 261	Ruben Sierra	2.50	1.00	.25
□ 262	Jim Winn	.03	.01	.00
□ 263	Stan Javier	.06	.02	.00
□ 264	Checklist 133-264	.08	.01	.00
□ 265	Darrell Evans	.08	.03	.01
□ 266	Jeff Hamilton	.08	.03	.01
□ 267	Howard Johnson	.25	.10	.02
□ 268	Pat Corrales MG (checklist back)	.06	.02	.00
□ 269	Cliff Speck	.03	.01	.00
□ 270	Jody Davis	.03	.01	.00
□ 271	Mike Brown (Mariners pitcher)	.03	.01	.00
□ 272	Andres Galarraga	.10	.04	.01
□ 273	Gene Nelson	.03	.01	.00
□ 274	Jeff Hearron UER (duplicate 1986 stat line on back)	.03	.01	.00
□ 275	LaMarr Hoyt	.03	.01	.00
□ 276	Jackie Gutierrez	.03	.01	.00
□ 277	Juan Agosto	.03	.01	.00
□ 278	Gary Pettis	.03	.01	.00
□ 279	Dan Plesac	.10	.04	.01
□ 280	Jeff Leonard	.03	.01	.00
□ 281	Reds Team (Pete Rose, Bo Diaz, and Bill Gullickson)	.10	.04	.01
□ 282	Jeff Calhoun	.03	.01	.00
□ 283	Doug Drabek	.60	.25	.06
□ 284	John Moses	.03	.01	.00
□ 285	Dennis Boyd	.03	.01	.00
□ 286	Mike Woodard	.03	.01	.00
□ 287	Dave Von Ohlen	.03	.01	.00
□ 288	Tito Landrum	.03	.01	.00
□ 289	Bob Kipper	.03	.01	.00
□ 290	Leon Durham	.03	.01	.00
□ 291	Mitch Williams	.17	.07	.01
□ 292	Franklin Stubbs	.03	.01	.00
□ 293	Bob Rodgers MG (checklist back)	.06	.02	.00
□ 294	Steve Jeltz	.03	.01	.00
□ 295	Len Dykstra	.17	.07	.01
□ 296	Andres Thomas	.06	.02	.00
□ 297	Don Schulze	.03	.01	.00
□ 298	Larry Herndon	.03	.01	.00
□ 299	Joel Davis	.03	.01	.00
□ 300	Reggie Jackson	.30	.12	.03
□ 301	Luis Aquino UER (no trademark, never corrected)	.06	.02	.00
□ 302	Bill Schroeder	.03	.01	.00
□ 303	Juan Berenguer	.03	.01	.00
□ 304	Phil Garner	.06	.02	.00
□ 305	John Franco	.08	.03	.01
□ 306	Red Sox Team (Tom Seaver, John McNamara, and Rich Gedman)	.08	.03	.01
□ 307	Lee Guetterman	.10	.04	.01
□ 308	Don Slaught	.03	.01	.00
□ 309	Mike Young	.03	.01	.00
□ 310	Frank Viola	.15	.06	.01
□ 311	Turn Back 1982 Rickey Henderson	.15	.06	.01
□ 312	Turn Back 1977 Reggie Jackson	.12	.05	.01
□ 313	Turn Back 1972 Roberto Clemente	.12	.05	.01
□ 314	Turn Back 1967 UER Carl Yastrzemski (sic, 112 RBI's on back)	.12	.05	.01
□ 315	Turn Back 1962 Maury Wills	.06	.02	.00
□ 316	Brian Fisher	.03	.01	.00
□ 317	Clint Hurdle	.03	.01	.00
□ 318	Jim Fregosi MG (checklist back)	.06	.02	.00

☐ 319 Greg Swindell .35 .15 .03
☐ 320 Barry Bonds 2.00 .80 .20
☐ 321 Mike Laga .03 .01 .00
☐ 322 Chris Bando .03 .01 .00
☐ 323 Al Newman .06 .02 .00
☐ 324 David Palmer .03 .01 .00
☐ 325 Garry Templeton .06 .02 .00
☐ 326 Mark Gubicza .08 .03 .01
☐ 327 Dale Sveum .08 .03 .01
☐ 328 Bob Welch .08 .03 .01
☐ 329 Ron Roenicke .03 .01 .00
☐ 330 Mike Scott .08 .03 .01
☐ 331 Mets Team .15 .06 .01
(Gary Carter and
Darryl Strawberry)
☐ 332 Joe Price .03 .01 .00
☐ 333 Ken Phelps .03 .01 .00
☐ 334 Ed Correa .03 .01 .00
☐ 335 Candy Maldonado .08 .03 .01
☐ 336 Allan Anderson .15 .06 .01
☐ 337 Darrell Miller .03 .01 .00
☐ 338 Tim Conroy .03 .01 .00
☐ 339 Donnie Hill .03 .01 .00
☐ 340 Roger Clemens 1.00 .40 .10
☐ 341 Mike Brown .03 .01 .00
(Pirates OF)
☐ 342 Bob James .03 .01 .00
☐ 343 Hal Lanier MG .06 .02 .00
(checklist back)
☐ 344A Joe Niekro .10 .04 .01
(copyright inside
righthand border)
☐ 344B Joe Niekro .35 .15 .03
(copyright outside
righthand border)
☐ 345 Andre Dawson .25 .10 .02
☐ 346 Shawon Dunston .12 .05 .01
☐ 347 Mickey Brantley .06 .02 .00
☐ 348 Carmelo Martinez .03 .01 .00
☐ 349 Storm Davis .03 .01 .00
☐ 350 Keith Hernandez .10 .04 .01
☐ 351 Gene Garber .03 .01 .00
☐ 352 Mike Felder .06 .02 .00
☐ 353 Ernie Camacho .03 .01 .00
☐ 354 Jamie Quirk .03 .01 .00
☐ 355 Don Carman .03 .01 .00
☐ 356 White Sox Team .03 .01 .00
(mound conference)
☐ 357 Steve Fireovid .03 .01 .00
☐ 358 Sal Butera .03 .01 .00
☐ 359 Doug Corbett .03 .01 .00
☐ 360 Pedro Guerrero .10 .04 .01
☐ 361 Mark Thurmond .03 .01 .00
☐ 362 Luis Quinones .06 .02 .00
☐ 363 Jose Guzman .06 .02 .00
☐ 364 Randy Bush .03 .01 .00
☐ 365 Rick Rhoden .03 .01 .00
☐ 366 Mark McGwire 1.25 .50 .12
☐ 367 Jeff Lahti .03 .01 .00
☐ 368 John McNamara MG .06 .02 .00
(checklist back)
☐ 369 Brian Dayett .03 .01 .00
☐ 370 Fred Lynn .08 .03 .01
☐ 371 Mark Eichhorn .08 .03 .01
☐ 372 Jerry Mumphrey .03 .01 .00
☐ 373 Jeff Dedmon .03 .01 .00
☐ 374 Glenn Hoffman .03 .01 .00
☐ 375 Ron Guidry .08 .03 .01
☐ 376 Scott Bradley .03 .01 .00
☐ 377 John Henry Johnson .03 .01 .00
☐ 378 Rafael Santana .03 .01 .00
☐ 379 John Russell .03 .01 .00
☐ 380 Rich Gossage .08 .03 .01
☐ 381 Expos Team .03 .01 .00
(mound conference)
☐ 382 Rudy Law .03 .01 .00
☐ 383 Ron Davis .03 .01 .00
☐ 384 Johnny Grubb .03 .01 .00
☐ 385 Orel Hershiser .15 .06 .01
☐ 386 Dickie Thon .03 .01 .00
☐ 387 T.R. Bryden .03 .01 .00
☐ 388 Geno Petralli .03 .01 .00
☐ 389 Jeff Robinson .06 .02 .00
(Giants pitcher)
☐ 390 Gary Matthews .03 .01 .00
☐ 391 Jay Howell .03 .01 .00
☐ 392 Checklist 265-396 .08 .01 .00
☐ 393 Pete Rose MG .25 .10 .02
(checklist back)
☐ 394 Mike Bielecki .06 .02 .00
☐ 395 Damaso Garcia .03 .01 .00
☐ 396 Tim Lollar .03 .01 .00
☐ 397 Greg Walker .03 .01 .00
☐ 398 Brad Havens .03 .01 .00
☐ 399 Curt Ford .03 .01 .00
☐ 400 George Brett .25 .10 .02
☐ 401 Billy Jo Robidoux .03 .01 .00
☐ 402 Mike Trujillo .03 .01 .00
☐ 403 Jerry Royster .03 .01 .00
☐ 404 Doug Sisk .03 .01 .00
☐ 405 Brook Jacoby .06 .02 .00
☐ 406 Yankees Team .20 .08 .02
(Henderson/Mattingly)
☐ 407 Jim Acker .03 .01 .00
☐ 408 John Mizerock .03 .01 .00
☐ 409 Milt Thompson .06 .02 .00
☐ 410 Fernando Valenzuela .08 .03 .01
☐ 411 Darnell Coles .03 .01 .00
☐ 412 Eric Davis .30 .12 .03
☐ 413 Moose Haas .03 .01 .00
☐ 414 Joe Orsulak .03 .01 .00
☐ 415 Bobby Witt .25 .10 .02
☐ 416 Tom Nieto .03 .01 .00
☐ 417 Pat Perry .03 .01 .00
☐ 418 Dick Williams MG .06 .02 .00
(checklist back)

☐ 419 Mark Portugal .... .12 .05 .01
☐ 420 Will Clark .... 3.50 1.50 .35
☐ 421 Jose DeLeon .... .03 .01 .00
☐ 422 Jack Howell .... .03 .01 .00
☐ 423 Jaime Cocanower .... .03 .01 .00
☐ 424 Chris Speier .... .03 .01 .00
☐ 425 Tom Seaver .... .35 .15 .03
☐ 426 Floyd Rayford .... .03 .01 .00
☐ 427 Edwin Nunez .... .03 .01 .00
☐ 428 Bruce Bochy .... .03 .01 .00
☐ 429 Tim Pyznarski .... .03 .01 .00
☐ 430 Mike Schmidt .... .60 .25 .06
☐ 431 Dodgers Team .... .06 .02 .00
(mound conference)
☐ 432 Jim Slaton .... .03 .01 .00
☐ 433 Ed Hearn .... .03 .01 .00
☐ 434 Mike Fischlin .... .03 .01 .00
☐ 435 Bruce Sutter .... .08 .03 .01
☐ 436 Andy Allanson .... .03 .01 .00
☐ 437 Ted Power .... .03 .01 .00
☐ 438 Kelly Downs .... .10 .04 .01
☐ 439 Karl Best .... .03 .01 .00
☐ 440 Willie McGee .... .10 .04 .01
☐ 441 Dave Leiper .... .03 .01 .00
☐ 442 Mitch Webster .... .03 .01 .00
☐ 443 John Felske MG .... .06 .02 .00
(checklist back)
☐ 444 Jeff Russell .... .06 .02 .00
☐ 445 Dave Lopes .... .06 .02 .00
☐ 446 Chuck Finley .... .75 .30 .07
☐ 447 Bill Almon .... .03 .01 .00
☐ 448 Chris Bosio .... .15 .06 .01
☐ 449 Pat Dodson .... .06 .02 .00
☐ 450 Kirby Puckett .... .90 .40 .09
☐ 451 Joe Sambito .... .03 .01 .00
☐ 452 Dave Henderson .... .10 .04 .01
☐ 453 Scott Terry .... .06 .02 .00
☐ 454 Luis Salazar .... .03 .01 .00
☐ 455 Mike Boddicker .... .03 .01 .00
☐ 456 A's Team .... .03 .01 .00
(mound conference)
☐ 457 Len Matuszek .... .03 .01 .00
☐ 458 Kelly Gruber .... .75 .30 .07
☐ 459 Dennis Eckersley .... .12 .05 .01
☐ 460 Darryl Strawberry .... .75 .30 .07
☐ 461 Craig McMurtry .... .03 .01 .00
☐ 462 Scott Fletcher .... .03 .01 .00
☐ 463 Tom Candiotti .... .08 .03 .01
☐ 464 Butch Wynegar .... .03 .01 .00
☐ 465 Todd Worrell .... .08 .03 .01
☐ 466 Kal Daniels .... .17 .07 .01
☐ 467 Randy St.Claire .... .03 .01 .00
☐ 468 George Bamberger MG .. .06 .02 .00
(checklist back)
☐ 469 Mike Diaz .... .03 .01 .00
☐ 470 Dave Dravecky .... .08 .03 .01
☐ 471 Ronn Reynolds .... .03 .01 .00
☐ 472 Bill Doran .... .03 .01 .00
☐ 473 Steve Farr .... .06 .02 .00
☐ 474 Jerry Narron .... .03 .01 .00
☐ 475 Scott Garrelts .... .03 .01 .00
☐ 476 Danny Tartabull .... .40 .16 .04
☐ 477 Ken Howell .... .03 .01 .00
☐ 478 Tim Laudner .... .03 .01 .00
☐ 479 Bob Sebra .... .03 .01 .00
☐ 480 Jim Rice .... .10 .04 .01
☐ 481 Phillies Team .... .06 .02 .00
(Glenn Wilson,
Juan Samuel, and
Von Hayes)
☐ 482 Daryl Boston .... .03 .01 .00
☐ 483 Dwight Lowry .... .03 .01 .00
☐ 484 Jim Traber .... .03 .01 .00
☐ 485 Tony Fernandez .... .10 .04 .01
☐ 486 Otis Nixon .... .10 .04 .01
☐ 487 Dave Gumpert .... .03 .01 .00
☐ 488 Ray Knight .... .06 .02 .00
☐ 489 Bill Gullickson .... .06 .02 .00
☐ 490 Dale Murphy .... .20 .08 .02
☐ 491 Ron Karkovice .... .06 .02 .00
☐ 492 Mike Heath .... .03 .01 .00
☐ 493 Tom Lasorda MG .... .08 .03 .01
(checklist back)
☐ 494 Barry Jones .... .10 .04 .01
☐ 495 Gorman Thomas .... .06 .02 .00
☐ 496 Bruce Bochte .... .03 .01 .00
☐ 497 Dale Mohorcic .... .06 .02 .00
☐ 498 Bob Kearney .... .03 .01 .00
☐ 499 Bruce Ruffin .... .06 .02 .00
☐ 500 Don Mattingly .... .50 .20 .05
☐ 501 Craig Lefferts .... .03 .01 .00
☐ 502 Dick Schofield .... .03 .01 .00
☐ 503 Larry Andersen .... .03 .01 .00
☐ 504 Mickey Hatcher .... .03 .01 .00
☐ 505 Bryn Smith .... .03 .01 .00
☐ 506 Orioles Team .... .03 .01 .00
(mound conference)
☐ 507 Dave Stapleton .... .03 .01 .00
(infielder)
☐ 508 Scott Bankhead .... .06 .02 .00
☐ 509 Enos Cabell .... .03 .01 .00
☐ 510 Tom Henke .... .08 .03 .01
☐ 511 Steve Lyons .... .03 .01 .00
☐ 512 Dave Magadan .... .35 .15 .03
☐ 513 Carmen Castillo .... .03 .01 .00
☐ 514 Orlando Mercado .... .03 .01 .00
☐ 515 Willie Hernandez .... .03 .01 .00
☐ 516 Ted Simmons .... .08 .03 .01
☐ 517 Mario Soto .... .03 .01 .00
☐ 518 Gene Mauch MG .... .06 .02 .00
(checklist back)
☐ 519 Curt Young .... .03 .01 .00
☐ 520 Jack Clark .... .10 .04 .01
☐ 521 Rick Reuschel .... .06 .02 .00
☐ 522 Checklist 397-528 .... .08 .01 .00
☐ 523 Earnie Riles .... .03 .01 .00

☐ 524 Bob Shirley .03 .01 .00
☐ 525 Phil Bradley .03 .01 .00
☐ 526 Roger Mason .03 .01 .00
☐ 527 Jim Wohlford .03 .01 .00
☐ 528 Ken Dixon .03 .01 .00
☐ 529 Alvaro Espinoza .17 .07 .01
☐ 530 Tony Gwynn .40 .16 .04
☐ 531 Astros Team .10 .04 .01
(Y.Berra conference)
☐ 532 Jeff Stone .03 .01 .00
☐ 533 Argenis Salazar .03 .01 .00
☐ 534 Scott Sanderson .06 .02 .00
☐ 535 Tony Armas .03 .01 .00
☐ 536 Terry Mulholland .25 .10 .02
☐ 537 Rance Mulliniks .03 .01 .00
☐ 538 Tom Niedenfuer .03 .01 .00
☐ 539 Reid Nichols .03 .01 .00
☐ 540 Terry Kennedy .03 .01 .00
☐ 541 Rafael Belliard .17 .07 .01
☐ 542 Ricky Horton .03 .01 .00
☐ 543 Dave Johnson MG .08 .03 .01
(checklist back)
☐ 544 Zane Smith .10 .04 .01
☐ 545 Buddy Bell .06 .02 .00
☐ 546 Mike Morgan .06 .02 .00
☐ 547 Rob Deer .10 .04 .01
☐ 548 Bill Mooneyham .03 .01 .00
☐ 549 Bob Melvin .03 .01 .00
☐ 550 Pete Incaviglia .17 .07 .01
☐ 551 Frank Wills .06 .02 .00
☐ 552 Larry Sheets .03 .01 .00
☐ 553 Mike Maddux .06 .02 .00
☐ 554 Buddy Biancalana .03 .01 .00
☐ 555 Dennis Rasmussen .03 .01 .00
☐ 556 Angels Team .06 .02 .00
(Lachemann, Witt,
and Boone)
☐ 557 John Cerutti .10 .04 .01
☐ 558 Greg Gagne .06 .02 .00
☐ 559 Lance McCullers .03 .01 .00
☐ 560 Glenn Davis .17 .07 .01
☐ 561 Rey Quinones .03 .01 .00
☐ 562 Bryan Clutterbuck .03 .01 .00
☐ 563 John Stefero .03 .01 .00
☐ 564 Larry McWilliams .03 .01 .00
☐ 565 Dusty Baker .06 .02 .00
☐ 566 Tim Hulett .03 .01 .00
☐ 567 Greg Mathews .06 .02 .00
☐ 568 Earl Weaver MG .08 .03 .01
(checklist back)
☐ 569 Wade Rowdon .03 .01 .00
☐ 570 Sid Fernandez .10 .04 .01
☐ 571 Ozzie Virgil .03 .01 .00
☐ 572 Pete Ladd .03 .01 .00
☐ 573 Hal McRae .06 .02 .00
☐ 574 Manny Lee .06 .02 .00
☐ 575 Pat Tabler .03 .01 .00
☐ 576 Frank Pastore .03 .01 .00
☐ 577 Dann Bilardello .03 .01 .00
☐ 578 Billy Hatcher .08 .03 .01
☐ 579 Rick Burleson .03 .01 .00
☐ 580 Mike Krukow .03 .01 .00
☐ 581 Cubs Team .03 .01 .00
(Cey/Trout)
☐ 582 Bruce Berenyi .03 .01 .00
☐ 583 Junior Ortiz .03 .01 .00
☐ 584 Ron Kittle .06 .02 .00
☐ 585 Scott Bailes .06 .02 .00
☐ 586 Ben Oglivie .03 .01 .00
☐ 587 Eric Plunk .03 .01 .00
☐ 588 Wallace Johnson .03 .01 .00
☐ 589 Steve Crawford .03 .01 .00
☐ 590 Vince Coleman .25 .10 .02
☐ 591 Spike Owen .03 .01 .00
☐ 592 Chris Welsh .03 .01 .00
☐ 593 Chuck Tanner MG .06 .02 .00
(checklist back)
☐ 594 Rick Anderson .03 .01 .00
☐ 595 Keith Hernandez AS .08 .03 .01
☐ 596 Steve Sax AS .08 .03 .01
☐ 597 Mike Schmidt AS .25 .10 .02
☐ 598 Ozzie Smith AS .10 .04 .01
☐ 599 Tony Gwynn AS .17 .07 .01
☐ 600 Dave Parker AS .08 .03 .01
☐ 601 Darryl Strawberry AS .25 .10 .02
☐ 602 Gary Carter AS .08 .03 .01
☐ 603A Dwight Gooden AS .50 .20 .05
ERR (no trademark)
☐ 603B Dwight Gooden AS COR .12 .05 .01
☐ 604 Fern. Valenzuela AS .08 .03 .01
☐ 605 Todd Worrell AS .06 .02 .00
☐ 606A Don Mattingly AS 1.00 .40 .10
ERR (no trademark)
☐ 606B Don Mattingly AS COR .20 .08 .02
☐ 607 Tony Bernazard AS .06 .02 .00
☐ 608 Wade Boggs AS .20 .08 .02
☐ 609 Cal Ripken AS .30 .12 .03
☐ 610 Jim Rice AS .08 .03 .01
☐ 611 Kirby Puckett AS .35 .15 .03
☐ 612 George Bell AS .08 .03 .01
☐ 613 Lance Parrish AS UER .06 .02 .00
(Pitcher heading
on back)
☐ 614 Roger Clemens AS .35 .15 .03
☐ 615 Teddy Higuera AS .06 .02 .00
☐ 616 Dave Righetti AS .08 .03 .01
☐ 617 Al Nipper .03 .01 .00
☐ 618 Tom Kelly MG .08 .03 .01
(checklist back)
☐ 619 Jerry Reed .03 .01 .00
☐ 620 Jose Canseco 3.00 1.25 .30
☐ 621 Danny Cox .03 .01 .00
☐ 622 Glenn Braggs .17 .07 .01
☐ 623 Kurt Stillwell .15 .06 .01
☐ 624 Tim Burke .03 .01 .00
☐ 625 Mookie Wilson .03 .01 .00

	No.	Player			
☐	626	Joel Skinner	.03	.01	.00
☐	627	Ken Oberkfell	.03	.01	.00
☐	628	Bob Walk	.03	.01	.00
☐	629	Larry Parrish	.03	.01	.00
☐	630	John Candelaria	.03	.01	.00
☐	631	Tigers Team (mound conference)	.03	.01	.00
☐	632	Rob Woodward	.03	.01	.00
☐	633	Jose Uribe	.03	.01	.00
☐	634	Rafael Palmeiro	1.50	.60	.15
☐	635	Ken Schrom	.03	.01	.00
☐	636	Darren Daulton	.08	.03	.01
☐	637	Bip Roberts	.30	.12	.03
☐	638	Rich Bordi	.03	.01	.00
☐	639	Gerald Perry	.03	.01	.00
☐	640	Mark Clear	.03	.01	.00
☐	641	Domingo Ramos	.03	.01	.00
☐	642	Al Pulido	.03	.01	.00
☐	643	Ron Shepherd	.03	.01	.00
☐	644	John Denny	.03	.01	.00
☐	645	Dwight Evans	.10	.04	.01
☐	646	Mike Mason	.03	.01	.00
☐	647	Tom Lawless	.03	.01	.00
☐	648	Barry Larkin	1.50	.60	.15
☐	649	Mickey Tettleton	.10	.04	.01
☐	650	Hubie Brooks	.08	.03	.01
☐	651	Benny Distefano	.03	.01	.00
☐	652	Terry Forster	.06	.02	.00
☐	653	Kevin Mitchell	1.50	.60	.15
☐	654	Checklist 529-660	.08	.01	.00
☐	655	Jesse Barfield	.10	.04	.01
☐	656	Rangers Team (Valentine/R.Wright)	.03	.01	.00
☐	657	Tom Waddell	.03	.01	.00
☐	658	Robby Thompson	.15	.06	.01
☐	659	Aurelio Lopez	.03	.01	.00
☐	660	Bob Horner	.08	.03	.01
☐	661	Lou Whitaker	.12	.05	.01
☐	662	Frank DiPino	.03	.01	.00
☐	663	Cliff Johnson	.03	.01	.00
☐	664	Mike Marshall	.08	.03	.01
☐	665	Rod Scurry	.03	.01	.00
☐	666	Von Hayes	.08	.03	.01
☐	667	Ron Hassey	.03	.01	.00
☐	668	Juan Bonilla	.03	.01	.00
☐	669	Bud Black	.03	.01	.00
☐	670	Jose Cruz	.06	.02	.00
☐	671A	Ray Soff ERR (no D* before copyright line)	.08	.03	.01
☐	671B	Ray Soff COR (D* before copyright line)	.08	.03	.01
☐	672	Chili Davis	.08	.03	.01
☐	673	Don Sutton	.12	.05	.01
☐	674	Bill Campbell	.03	.01	.00
☐	675	Ed Romero	.03	.01	.00
☐	676	Charlie Moore	.03	.01	.00
☐	677	Bob Grich	.06	.02	.00
☐	678	Carney Lansford	.08	.03	.01
☐	679	Kent Hrbek	.12	.05	.01
☐	680	Ryne Sandberg	.75	.30	.07
☐	681	George Bell	.20	.08	.02
☐	682	Jerry Reuss	.03	.01	.00
☐	683	Gary Roenicke	.03	.01	.00
☐	684	Kent Tekulve	.03	.01	.00
☐	685	Jerry Hairston	.03	.01	.00
☐	686	Doyle Alexander	.03	.01	.00
☐	687	Alan Trammell	.17	.07	.01
☐	688	Juan Beniquez	.03	.01	.00
☐	689	Darrell Porter	.03	.01	.00
☐	690	Dane Iorg	.03	.01	.00
☐	691	Dave Parker	.15	.06	.01
☐	692	Frank White	.03	.01	.00
☐	693	Terry Puhl	.03	.01	.00
☐	694	Phil Niekro	.12	.05	.01
☐	695	Chico Walker	.08	.03	.01
☐	696	Gary Lucas	.03	.01	.00
☐	697	Ed Lynch	.03	.01	.00
☐	698	Ernie Whitt	.03	.01	.00
☐	699	Ken Landreaux	.03	.01	.00
☐	700	Dave Bergman	.03	.01	.00
☐	701	Willie Randolph	.06	.02	.00
☐	702	Greg Gross	.03	.01	.00
☐	703	Dave Schmidt	.03	.01	.00
☐	704	Jesse Orosco	.03	.01	.00
☐	705	Bruce Hurst	.08	.03	.01
☐	706	Rick Manning	.03	.01	.00
☐	707	Bob McClure	.03	.01	.00
☐	708	Scott McGregor	.03	.01	.00
☐	709	Dave Kingman	.08	.03	.01
☐	710	Gary Gaetti	.08	.03	.01
☐	711	Ken Griffey	.10	.04	.01
☐	712	Don Robinson	.03	.01	.00
☐	713	Tom Brookens	.03	.01	.00
☐	714	Dan Quisenberry	.08	.03	.01
☐	715	Bob Dernier	.03	.01	.00
☐	716	Rick Leach	.03	.01	.00
☐	717	Ed VandeBerg	.03	.01	.00
☐	718	Steve Carlton	.25	.10	.02
☐	719	Tom Hume	.03	.01	.00
☐	720	Richard Dotson	.03	.01	.00
☐	721	Tom Herr	.03	.01	.00
☐	722	Bob Knepper	.03	.01	.00
☐	723	Brett Butler	.10	.04	.01
☐	724	Greg Minton	.03	.01	.00
☐	725	George Hendrick	.03	.01	.00
☐	726	Frank Tanana	.06	.02	.00
☐	727	Mike Moore	.06	.02	.00
☐	728	Tippy Martinez	.03	.01	.00
☐	729	Tom Paciorek	.03	.01	.00
☐	730	Eric Show	.03	.01	.00
☐	731	Dave Concepcion	.08	.03	.01
☐	732	Manny Trillo	.03	.01	.00
☐	733	Bill Caudill	.03	.01	.00
☐	734	Bill Madlock	.08	.03	.01

☐ 735 Rickey Henderson	.50	.20	.05
☐ 736 Steve Bedrosian	.06	.02	.00
☐ 737 Floyd Bannister	.03	.01	.00
☐ 738 Jorge Orta	.03	.01	.00
☐ 739 Chet Lemon	.03	.01	.00
☐ 740 Rich Gedman	.03	.01	.00
☐ 741 Paul Molitor	.12	.05	.01
☐ 742 Andy McGaffigan	.03	.01	.00
☐ 743 Dwayne Murphy	.03	.01	.00
☐ 744 Roy Smalley	.03	.01	.00
☐ 745 Glenn Hubbard	.03	.01	.00
☐ 746 Bob Ojeda	.03	.01	.00
☐ 747 Johnny Ray	.03	.01	.00
☐ 748 Mike Flanagan	.06	.02	.00
☐ 749 Ozzie Smith	.20	.08	.02
☐ 750 Steve Trout	.03	.01	.00
☐ 751 Garth Iorg	.03	.01	.00
☐ 752 Dan Petry	.03	.01	.00
☐ 753 Rick Honeycutt	.03	.01	.00
☐ 754 Dave LaPoint	.03	.01	.00
☐ 755 Luis Aguayo	.03	.01	.00
☐ 756 Carlton Fisk	.25	.10	.02
☐ 757 Nolan Ryan	1.00	.40	.10
☐ 758 Tony Bernazard	.03	.01	.00
☐ 759 Joel Youngblood	.03	.01	.00
☐ 760 Mike Witt	.03	.01	.00
☐ 761 Greg Pryor	.03	.01	.00
☐ 762 Gary Ward	.03	.01	.00
☐ 763 Tim Flannery	.03	.01	.00
☐ 764 Bill Buckner	.06	.02	.00
☐ 765 Kirk Gibson	.12	.05	.01
☐ 766 Don Aase	.03	.01	.00
☐ 767 Ron Cey	.06	.02	.00
☐ 768 Dennis Lamp	.03	.01	.00
☐ 769 Steve Sax	.12	.05	.01
☐ 770 Dave Winfield	.20	.08	.02
☐ 771 Shane Rawley	.03	.01	.00
☐ 772 Harold Baines	.12	.05	.01
☐ 773 Robin Yount	.30	.12	.03
☐ 774 Wayne Krenchicki	.03	.01	.00
☐ 775 Joaquin Andujar	.03	.01	.00
☐ 776 Tom Brunansky	.08	.03	.01
☐ 777 Chris Chambliss	.06	.02	.00
☐ 778 Jack Morris	.15	.06	.01
☐ 779 Craig Reynolds	.03	.01	.00
☐ 780 Andre Thornton	.03	.01	.00
☐ 781 Atlee Hammaker	.03	.01	.00
☐ 782 Brian Downing	.06	.02	.00
☐ 783 Willie Wilson	.08	.03	.01
☐ 784 Cal Ripken	.90	.40	.09
☐ 785 Terry Francona	.03	.01	.00
☐ 786 Jimy Williams MG (checklist back)	.06	.02	.00
☐ 787 Alejandro Pena	.08	.03	.01
☐ 788 Tim Stoddard	.03	.01	.00
☐ 789 Dan Schatzeder	.03	.01	.00
☐ 790 Julio Cruz	.03	.01	.00
☐ 791 Lance Parrish UER (no trademark, never corrected)	.15	.06	.01
☐ 792 Checklist 661-792	.10	.01	.00

1987 Topps Traded

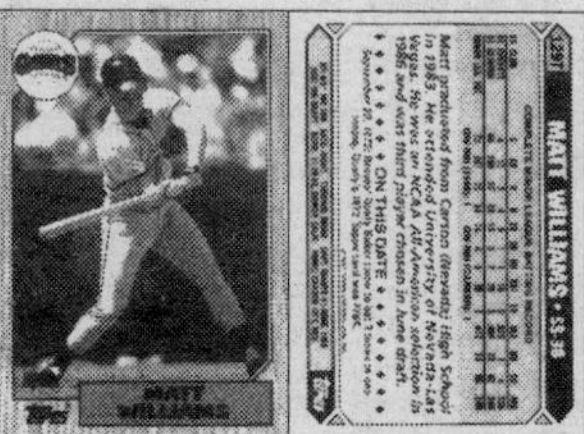

This 132-card Traded or extended set was distributed by Topps to dealers in a special green and white box as a complete set. The card fronts are identical in style to the Topps regular issue and are also 2 1/2" by 3 1/2". The backs are printed in yellow and blue on white card stock. Cards are numbered (with a T suffix) alphabetically according to the name of the player. The key (extended) rookies in this set (without any prior cards) are Ellis Burks and Matt Williams. Topps also produced a specially boxed "glossy" edition, frequently referred to as the Topps Traded Tiffany set. This year Topps did not disclose the number of sets they produced or sold. It is apparent from the availability that there were many more sets produced this year compared to the 1984-86 Tiffany sets, perhaps 30,000 sets, more than three times as many. The checklist of cards is identical to that of the normal non-glossy cards. There are two primary distinguishing features of the Tiffany cards, white card stock reverses and high gloss obverses. These Tiffany cards are valued at approximately three times the values listed below.

	MINT	EXC	G-VG
COMPLETE SET (132)	10.00	4.50	1.25
COMMON PLAYER (1-132)	.05	.02	.00

☐ 1T Bill Almon	.10	.03	.01

☐ 2T Scott Bankhead	.10	.04	.01
☐ 3T Eric Bell	.10	.04	.01
☐ 4T Juan Beniquez	.05	.02	.00
☐ 5T Juan Berenguer	.05	.02	.00
☐ 6T Greg Booker	.05	.02	.00
☐ 7T Thad Bosley	.05	.02	.00
☐ 8T Larry Bowa MG	.10	.04	.01
☐ 9T Greg Brock	.05	.02	.00
☐ 10T Bob Brower	.05	.02	.00
☐ 11T Jerry Browne	.12	.05	.01
☐ 12T Ralph Bryant	.10	.04	.01
☐ 13T DeWayne Buice	.05	.02	.00
☐ 14T Ellis Burks	1.50	.60	.15
☐ 15T Ivan Calderon	.15	.06	.01
☐ 16T Jeff Calhoun	.05	.02	.00
☐ 17T Casey Candaele	.10	.04	.01
☐ 18T John Cangelosi	.05	.02	.00
☐ 19T Steve Carlton	.20	.08	.02
☐ 20T Juan Castillo	.05	.02	.00
☐ 21T Rick Cerone	.05	.02	.00
☐ 22T Ron Cey	.10	.04	.01
☐ 23T John Christensen	.05	.02	.00
☐ 24T David Cone	1.00	.40	.10
☐ 25T Chuck Crim	.10	.04	.01
☐ 26T Storm Davis	.05	.02	.00
☐ 27T Andre Dawson	.25	.10	.02
☐ 28T Rick Dempsey	.05	.02	.00
☐ 29T Doug Drabek	.35	.15	.03
☐ 30T Mike Dunne	.10	.04	.01
☐ 31T Dennis Eckersley	.20	.08	.02
☐ 32T Lee Elia MG	.05	.02	.00
☐ 33T Brian Fisher	.05	.02	.00
☐ 34T Terry Francona	.05	.02	.00
☐ 35T Willie Fraser	.05	.02	.00
☐ 36T Billy Gardner MG	.05	.02	.00
☐ 37T Ken Gerhart	.05	.02	.00
☐ 38T Dan Gladden	.10	.04	.01
☐ 39T Jim Gott	.10	.04	.01
☐ 40T Cecilio Guante	.05	.02	.00
☐ 41T Albert Hall	.05	.02	.00
☐ 42T Terry Harper	.05	.02	.00
☐ 43T Mickey Hatcher	.05	.02	.00
☐ 44T Brad Havens	.05	.02	.00
☐ 45T Neal Heaton	.05	.02	.00
☐ 46T Mike Henneman	.25	.10	.02
☐ 47T Donnie Hill	.05	.02	.00
☐ 48T Guy Hoffman	.05	.02	.00
☐ 49T Brian Holton	.10	.04	.01
☐ 50T Charles Hudson	.05	.02	.00
☐ 51T Danny Jackson	.10	.04	.01
☐ 52T Reggie Jackson	.40	.16	.04
☐ 53T Chris James	.15	.06	.01
☐ 54T Dion James	.10	.04	.01
☐ 55T Stan Jefferson	.10	.04	.01
☐ 56T Joe Johnson	.05	.02	.00
☐ 57T Terry Kennedy	.05	.02	.00
☐ 58T Mike Kingery	.10	.04	.01
☐ 59T Ray Knight	.10	.04	.01
☐ 60T Gene Larkin	.15	.06	.01
☐ 61T Mike LaValliere	.10	.04	.01
☐ 62T Jack Lazorko	.05	.02	.00
☐ 63T Terry Leach	.10	.04	.01
☐ 64T Tim Leary	.15	.06	.01
☐ 65T Jim Lindeman	.10	.04	.01
☐ 66T Steve Lombardozzi	.10	.04	.01
☐ 67T Bill Long	.10	.04	.01
☐ 68T Barry Lyons	.10	.04	.01
☐ 69T Shane Mack	.17	.07	.01
☐ 70T Greg Maddux	.75	.30	.07
☐ 71T Bill Madlock	.10	.04	.01
☐ 72T Joe Magrane	.15	.06	.01
☐ 73T Dave Martinez	.30	.12	.03
☐ 74T Fred McGriff	2.00	.80	.20
☐ 75T Mark McLemore	.05	.02	.00
☐ 76T Kevin McReynolds	.20	.08	.02
☐ 77T Dave Meads	.05	.02	.00
☐ 78T Eddie Milner	.05	.02	.00
☐ 79T Greg Minton	.05	.02	.00
☐ 80T John Mitchell	.10	.04	.01
☐ 81T Kevin Mitchell	1.00	.40	.10
☐ 82T Charlie Moore	.05	.02	.00
☐ 83T Jeff Musselman	.10	.04	.01
☐ 84T Gene Nelson	.05	.02	.00
☐ 85T Graig Nettles	.15	.06	.01
☐ 86T Al Newman	.10	.04	.01
☐ 87T Reid Nichols	.05	.02	.00
☐ 88T Tom Niedenfuer	.05	.02	.00
☐ 89T Joe Niekro	.10	.04	.01
☐ 90T Tom Nieto	.05	.02	.00
☐ 91T Matt Nokes	.50	.20	.05
☐ 92T Dickie Noles	.05	.02	.00
☐ 93T Pat Pacillo	.10	.04	.01
☐ 94T Lance Parrish	.15	.06	.01
☐ 95T Tony Pena	.15	.06	.01
☐ 96T Luis Polonia	.45	.18	.04
☐ 97T Randy Ready	.12	.05	.01
☐ 98T Jeff Reardon	.20	.08	.02
☐ 99T Gary Redus	.05	.02	.00
☐ 100T Jeff Reed	.05	.02	.00
☐ 101T Rick Rhoden	.05	.02	.00
☐ 102T Cal Ripken Sr. MG	.10	.04	.01
☐ 103T Wally Ritchie	.10	.04	.01
☐ 104T Jeff Robinson (Tigers pitcher)	.10	.04	.01
☐ 105T Gary Roenicke	.05	.02	.00
☐ 106T Jerry Royster	.05	.02	.00
☐ 107T Mark Salas	.05	.02	.00
☐ 108T Luis Salazar	.05	.02	.00
☐ 109T Benny Santiago	.50	.20	.05
☐ 110T Dave Schmidt	.10	.04	.01
☐ 111T Kevin Seitzer	.17	.07	.01
☐ 112T John Shelby	.05	.02	.00
☐ 113T Steve Shields	.05	.02	.00
☐ 114T John Smiley	.75	.30	.07
☐ 115T Chris Speier	.05	.02	.00
☐ 116T Mike Stanley	.10	.04	.01

☐ 117T Terry Steinbach	.35	.15	.03
☐ 118T Les Straker	.10	.04	.01
☐ 119T Jim Sundberg	.05	.02	.00
☐ 120T Danny Tartabull	.25	.10	.02
☐ 121T Tom Trebelhorn MG	.10	.04	.01
☐ 122T Dave Valle	.05	.02	.00
☐ 123T Ed VandeBerg	.05	.02	.00
☐ 124T Andy Van Slyke	.17	.07	.01
☐ 125T Gary Ward	.05	.02	.00
☐ 126T Alan Wiggins	.05	.02	.00
☐ 127T Bill Wilkinson	.10	.04	.01
☐ 128T Frank Williams	.05	.02	.00
☐ 129T Matt Williams	3.25	1.35	.32
☐ 130T Jim Winn	.05	.02	.00
☐ 131T Matt Young	.05	.02	.00
☐ 132T Checklist 1T-132T	.05	.01	.00

1988 Topps

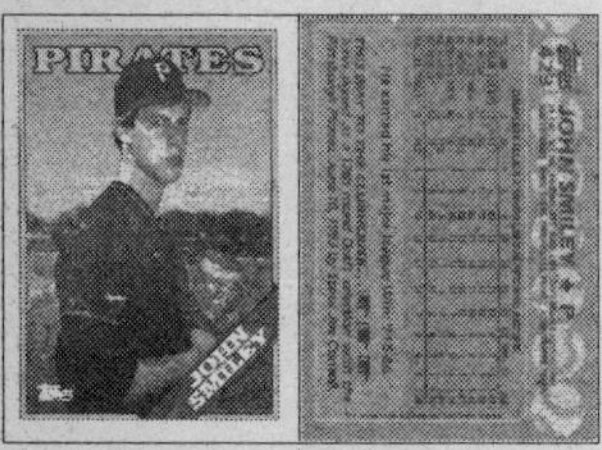

This 792-card set features backs that are printed in orange and black on gray card stock. The manager cards contain a checklist of the respective team's players on the back. Subsets in the set include Record Breakers (1-7), Turn Back the Clock (661-665), and All-Star selections (386-407). The Team Leader cards typically show two players together inside a white cloud. The key rookie cards in this set are Ellis Burks, Tom Glavine, and Matt Williams. Topps also produced a specially boxed "glossy" edition, frequently referred to as the Topps Tiffany set. This year, again, Topps did not disclose the number of Tiffany sets they produced or sold. It is apparent from the availability that there were many more sets produced this year compared to the 1984-86 Tiffany sets, perhaps 25,000 sets. The checklist of cards (792 regular and 132 Traded) is identical to that of the normal non-glossy cards. There are two primary distinguishing features of the Tiffany cards, white card stock reverses and high gloss obverses. These Tiffany cards are valued at approximately four times the values listed below.

	MINT	EXC	G-VG
COMPLETE SET (792)	18.00	7.50	2.50
COMMON PLAYER (1-792)	.03	.01	.00
☐ 1 Vince Coleman RB 100 Steals for Third Cons. Season	.10	.04	.01
☐ 2 Don Mattingly RB Six Grand Slams	.12	.05	.01
☐ 3A Mark McGwire RB Rookie Homer Record (white spot behind left foot)	.20	.08	.02
☐ 3B Mark McGwire RB Rookie Homer Record (no white spot)	.10	.04	.01
☐ 4A Eddie Murray RB Switch Home Runs, Two Straight Games (caption in box on card front)	.50	.20	.05
☐ 4B Eddie Murray RB Switch Home Runs, Two Straight Games (no caption on front)	.10	.04	.01
☐ 5 Phil/Joe Niekro RB Brothers Win Record	.06	.02	.00
☐ 6 Nolan Ryan RB 11th Season with 200 Strikeouts	.25	.10	.02
☐ 7 Benito Santiago RB 34-Game Hitting Streak, Rookie Record	.06	.02	.00
☐ 8 Kevin Elster	.06	.02	.00
☐ 9 Andy Hawkins	.03	.01	.00
☐ 10 Ryne Sandberg	.40	.16	.04
☐ 11 Mike Young	.03	.01	.00
☐ 12 Bill Schroeder	.03	.01	.00
☐ 13 Andres Thomas	.03	.01	.00
☐ 14 Sparky Anderson MG (checklist back)	.06	.02	.00
☐ 15 Chili Davis	.06	.02	.00
☐ 16 Kirk McCaskill	.03	.01	.00
☐ 17 Ron Oester	.03	.01	.00
☐ 18A Al Leiter ERR (photo actually Steve George, right ear visible)	.20	.08	.02
☐ 18B Al Leiter COR (left ear visible)	.10	.04	.01

☐ 19 Mark Davidson	.06	.02	.00
☐ 20 Kevin Gross	.03	.01	.00
☐ 21 Red Sox TL	.08	.03	.01
Wade Boggs and			
Spike Owen			
☐ 22 Greg Swindell	.08	.03	.01
☐ 23 Ken Landreaux	.03	.01	.00
☐ 24 Jim Deshaies	.03	.01	.00
☐ 25 Andres Galarraga	.08	.03	.01
☐ 26 Mitch Williams	.06	.02	.00
☐ 27 R.J. Reynolds	.03	.01	.00
☐ 28 Jose Nunez	.06	.02	.00
☐ 29 Argenis Salazar	.03	.01	.00
☐ 30 Sid Fernandez	.08	.03	.01
☐ 31 Bruce Bochy	.03	.01	.00
☐ 32 Mike Morgan	.03	.01	.00
☐ 33 Rob Deer	.06	.02	.00
☐ 34 Ricky Horton	.03	.01	.00
☐ 35 Harold Baines	.08	.03	.01
☐ 36 Jamie Moyer	.03	.01	.00
☐ 37 Ed Romero	.03	.01	.00
☐ 38 Jeff Calhoun	.03	.01	.00
☐ 39 Gerald Perry	.03	.01	.00
☐ 40 Orel Hershiser	.10	.04	.01
☐ 41 Bob Melvin	.03	.01	.00
☐ 42 Bill Landrum	.10	.04	.01
☐ 43 Dick Schofield	.03	.01	.00
☐ 44 Lou Piniella MG	.06	.02	.00
(checklist back)			
☐ 45 Kent Hrbek	.10	.04	.01
☐ 46 Darnell Coles	.03	.01	.00
☐ 47 Joaquin Andujar	.03	.01	.00
☐ 48 Alan Ashby	.03	.01	.00
☐ 49 Dave Clark	.03	.01	.00
☐ 50 Hubie Brooks	.06	.02	.00
☐ 51 Orioles TL	.20	.08	.02
Eddie Murray and			
Cal Ripken			
☐ 52 Don Robinson	.03	.01	.00
☐ 53 Curt Wilkerson	.03	.01	.00
☐ 54 Jim Clancy	.03	.01	.00
☐ 55 Phil Bradley	.03	.01	.00
☐ 56 Ed Hearn	.03	.01	.00
☐ 57 Tim Crews	.06	.02	.00
☐ 58 Dave Magadan	.08	.03	.01
☐ 59 Danny Cox	.03	.01	.00
☐ 60 Rickey Henderson	.30	.12	.03
☐ 61 Mark Knudson	.06	.02	.00
☐ 62 Jeff Hamilton	.03	.01	.00
☐ 63 Jimmy Jones	.06	.02	.00
☐ 64 Ken Caminiti	.17	.07	.01
☐ 65 Leon Durham	.03	.01	.00
☐ 66 Shane Rawley	.03	.01	.00
☐ 67 Ken Oberkfell	.03	.01	.00
☐ 68 Dave Dravecky	.08	.03	.01
☐ 69 Mike Hart	.03	.01	.00
☐ 70 Roger Clemens	.35	.15	.03
☐ 71 Gary Pettis	.03	.01	.00
☐ 72 Dennis Eckersley	.10	.04	.01
☐ 73 Randy Bush	.03	.01	.00
☐ 74 Tom Lasorda MG	.08	.03	.01
(checklist back)			
☐ 75 Joe Carter	.17	.07	.01
☐ 76 Dennis Martinez	.06	.02	.00
☐ 77 Tom O'Malley	.03	.01	.00
☐ 78 Dan Petry	.03	.01	.00
☐ 79 Ernie Whitt	.03	.01	.00
☐ 80 Mark Langston	.08	.03	.01
☐ 81 Reds TL	.03	.01	.00
Ron Robinson			
and John Franco			
☐ 82 Darrel Akerfelds	.03	.01	.00
☐ 83 Jose Oquendo	.03	.01	.00
☐ 84 Cecilio Guante	.03	.01	.00
☐ 85 Howard Johnson	.15	.06	.01
☐ 86 Ron Karkovice	.03	.01	.00
☐ 87 Mike Mason	.03	.01	.00
☐ 88 Earnie Riles	.03	.01	.00
☐ 89 Gary Thurman	.08	.03	.01
☐ 90 Dale Murphy	.15	.06	.01
☐ 91 Joey Cora	.06	.02	.00
☐ 92 Len Matuszek	.03	.01	.00
☐ 93 Bob Sebra	.03	.01	.00
☐ 94 Chuck Jackson	.06	.02	.00
☐ 95 Lance Parrish	.08	.03	.01
☐ 96 Todd Benzinger	.17	.07	.01
☐ 97 Scott Garrelts	.03	.01	.00
☐ 98 Rene Gonzales	.03	.01	.00
☐ 99 Chuck Finley	.12	.05	.01
☐ 100 Jack Clark	.08	.03	.01
☐ 101 Allan Anderson	.03	.01	.00
☐ 102 Barry Larkin	.20	.08	.02
☐ 103 Curt Young	.03	.01	.00
☐ 104 Dick Williams MG	.06	.02	.00
(checklist back)			
☐ 105 Jesse Orosco	.03	.01	.00
☐ 106 Jim Walewander	.03	.01	.00
☐ 107 Scott Bailes	.03	.01	.00
☐ 108 Steve Lyons	.03	.01	.00
☐ 109 Joel Skinner	.03	.01	.00
☐ 110 Teddy Higuera	.06	.02	.00
☐ 111 Expos TL	.03	.01	.00
Hubie Brooks and			
Vance Law			
☐ 112 Les Lancaster	.08	.03	.01
☐ 113 Kelly Gruber	.15	.06	.01
☐ 114 Jeff Russell	.03	.01	.00
☐ 115 Johnny Ray	.03	.01	.00
☐ 116 Jerry Don Gleaton	.03	.01	.00
☐ 117 James Steels	.03	.01	.00
☐ 118 Bob Welch	.08	.03	.01
☐ 119 Robbie Wine	.03	.01	.00
☐ 120 Kirby Puckett	.30	.12	.03
☐ 121 Checklist 1-132	.06	.01	.00
☐ 122 Tony Bernazard	.03	.01	.00
☐ 123 Tom Candiotti	.06	.02	.00

☐ 124 Ray Knight	.06	.02	.00
☐ 125 Bruce Hurst	.06	.02	.00
☐ 126 Steve Jeltz	.03	.01	.00
☐ 127 Jim Gott	.03	.01	.00
☐ 128 Johnny Grubb	.03	.01	.00
☐ 129 Greg Minton	.03	.01	.00
☐ 130 Buddy Bell	.06	.02	.00
☐ 131 Don Schulze	.03	.01	.00
☐ 132 Donnie Hill	.03	.01	.00
☐ 133 Greg Mathews	.03	.01	.00
☐ 134 Chuck Tanner MG (checklist back)	.06	.02	.00
☐ 135 Dennis Rasmussen	.03	.01	.00
☐ 136 Brian Dayett	.03	.01	.00
☐ 137 Chris Bosio	.03	.01	.00
☐ 138 Mitch Webster	.03	.01	.00
☐ 139 Jerry Browne	.06	.02	.00
☐ 140 Jesse Barfield	.08	.03	.01
☐ 141 Royals TL George Brett and Bret Saberhagen	.15	.06	.01
☐ 142 Andy Van Slyke	.10	.04	.01
☐ 143 Mickey Tettleton	.06	.02	.00
☐ 144 Don Gordon	.03	.01	.00
☐ 145 Bill Madlock	.06	.02	.00
☐ 146 Donnell Nixon	.06	.02	.00
☐ 147 Bill Buckner	.06	.02	.00
☐ 148 Carmelo Martinez	.03	.01	.00
☐ 149 Ken Howell	.03	.01	.00
☐ 150 Eric Davis	.15	.06	.01
☐ 151 Bob Knepper	.03	.01	.00
☐ 152 Jody Reed	.25	.10	.02
☐ 153 John Habyan	.03	.01	.00
☐ 154 Jeff Stone	.03	.01	.00
☐ 155 Bruce Sutter	.08	.03	.01
☐ 156 Gary Matthews	.03	.01	.00
☐ 157 Atlee Hammaker	.03	.01	.00
☐ 158 Tim Hulett	.03	.01	.00
☐ 159 Brad Arnsberg	.08	.03	.01
☐ 160 Willie McGee	.08	.03	.01
☐ 161 Bryn Smith	.03	.01	.00
☐ 162 Mark McLemore	.03	.01	.00
☐ 163 Dale Mohorcic	.03	.01	.00
☐ 164 Dave Johnson MG (checklist back)	.06	.02	.00
☐ 165 Robin Yount	.20	.08	.02
☐ 166 Rick Rodriquez	.06	.02	.00
☐ 167 Rance Mulliniks	.03	.01	.00
☐ 168 Barry Jones	.03	.01	.00
☐ 169 Ross Jones	.03	.01	.00
☐ 170 Rich Gossage	.08	.03	.01
☐ 171 Cubs TL Shawon Dunston and Manny Trillo	.06	.02	.00
☐ 172 Lloyd McClendon	.06	.02	.00
☐ 173 Eric Plunk	.03	.01	.00
☐ 174 Phil Garner	.06	.02	.00
☐ 175 Kevin Bass	.03	.01	.00
☐ 176 Jeff Reed	.03	.01	.00
☐ 177 Frank Tanana	.06	.02	.00
☐ 178 Dwayne Henry	.06	.02	.00
☐ 179 Charlie Puleo	.03	.01	.00
☐ 180 Terry Kennedy	.03	.01	.00
☐ 181 David Cone	.20	.08	.02
☐ 182 Ken Phelps	.03	.01	.00
☐ 183 Tom Lawless	.03	.01	.00
☐ 184 Ivan Calderon	.08	.03	.01
☐ 185 Rick Rhoden	.03	.01	.00
☐ 186 Rafael Palmeiro	.30	.12	.03
☐ 187 Steve Kiefer	.03	.01	.00
☐ 188 John Russell	.03	.01	.00
☐ 189 Wes Gardner	.06	.02	.00
☐ 190 Candy Maldonado	.06	.02	.00
☐ 191 John Cerutti	.03	.01	.00
☐ 192 Devon White	.10	.04	.01
☐ 193 Brian Fisher	.03	.01	.00
☐ 194 Tom Kelly MG (checklist back)	.06	.02	.00
☐ 195 Dan Quisenberry	.08	.03	.01
☐ 196 Dave Engle	.03	.01	.00
☐ 197 Lance McCullers	.03	.01	.00
☐ 198 Franklin Stubbs	.03	.01	.00
☐ 199 Dave Meads	.03	.01	.00
☐ 200 Wade Boggs	.30	.12	.03
☐ 201 Rangers TL Bobby Valentine, Pete O'Brien, Pete Incaviglia, and Steve Buechele	.06	.02	.00
☐ 202 Glenn Hoffman	.03	.01	.00
☐ 203 Fred Toliver	.03	.01	.00
☐ 204 Paul O'Neill	.12	.05	.01
☐ 205 Nelson Liriano	.08	.03	.01
☐ 206 Domingo Ramos	.03	.01	.00
☐ 207 John Mitchell	.06	.02	.00
☐ 208 Steve Lake	.03	.01	.00
☐ 209 Richard Dotson	.03	.01	.00
☐ 210 Willie Randolph	.06	.02	.00
☐ 211 Frank DiPino	.03	.01	.00
☐ 212 Greg Brock	.03	.01	.00
☐ 213 Albert Hall	.03	.01	.00
☐ 214 Dave Schmidt	.03	.01	.00
☐ 215 Von Hayes	.06	.02	.00
☐ 216 Jerry Reuss	.03	.01	.00
☐ 217 Harry Spilman	.03	.01	.00
☐ 218 Dan Schatzeder	.03	.01	.00
☐ 219 Mike Stanley	.03	.01	.00
☐ 220 Tom Henke	.06	.02	.00
☐ 221 Rafael Belliard	.03	.01	.00
☐ 222 Steve Farr	.03	.01	.00
☐ 223 Stan Jefferson	.03	.01	.00
☐ 224 Tom Trebelhorn MG (checklist back)	.06	.02	.00
☐ 225 Mike Scioscia	.03	.01	.00
☐ 226 Dave Lopes	.06	.02	.00
☐ 227 Ed Correa	.03	.01	.00

☐ 228	Wallace Johnson	.03	.01	.00
☐ 229	Jeff Musselman	.03	.01	.00
☐ 230	Pat Tabler	.03	.01	.00
☐ 231	Pirates TL Barry Bonds and Bobby Bonilla	.15	.06	.01
☐ 232	Bob James	.03	.01	.00
☐ 233	Rafael Santana	.03	.01	.00
☐ 234	Ken Dayley	.03	.01	.00
☐ 235	Gary Ward	.03	.01	.00
☐ 236	Ted Power	.03	.01	.00
☐ 237	Mike Heath	.03	.01	.00
☐ 238	Luis Polonia	.25	.10	.02
☐ 239	Roy Smalley	.03	.01	.00
☐ 240	Lee Smith	.10	.04	.01
☐ 241	Damaso Garcia	.03	.01	.00
☐ 242	Tom Niedenfuer	.03	.01	.00
☐ 243	Mark Ryal	.03	.01	.00
☐ 244	Jeff D. Robinson (Pirates pitcher)	.06	.02	.00
☐ 245	Rich Gedman	.03	.01	.00
☐ 246	Mike Campbell	.06	.02	.00
☐ 247	Thad Bosley	.03	.01	.00
☐ 248	Storm Davis	.03	.01	.00
☐ 249	Mike Marshall	.06	.02	.00
☐ 250	Nolan Ryan	.45	.18	.04
☐ 251	Tom Foley	.03	.01	.00
☐ 252	Bob Brower	.03	.01	.00
☐ 253	Checklist 133-264	.06	.01	.00
☐ 254	Lee Elia MG (checklist back)	.06	.02	.00
☐ 255	Mookie Wilson	.03	.01	.00
☐ 256	Ken Schrom	.03	.01	.00
☐ 257	Jerry Royster	.03	.01	.00
☐ 258	Ed Nunez	.03	.01	.00
☐ 259	Ron Kittle	.06	.02	.00
☐ 260	Vince Coleman	.10	.04	.01
☐ 261	Giants TL (five players)	.03	.01	.00
☐ 262	Drew Hall	.06	.02	.00
☐ 263	Glenn Braggs	.03	.01	.00
☐ 264	Les Straker	.03	.01	.00
☐ 265	Bo Diaz	.03	.01	.00
☐ 266	Paul Assenmacher	.03	.01	.00
☐ 267	Billy Bean	.06	.02	.00
☐ 268	Bruce Ruffin	.03	.01	.00
☐ 269	Ellis Burks	.60	.25	.06
☐ 270	Mike Witt	.03	.01	.00
☐ 271	Ken Gerhart	.03	.01	.00
☐ 272	Steve Ontiveros	.03	.01	.00
☐ 273	Garth Iorg	.03	.01	.00
☐ 274	Junior Ortiz	.03	.01	.00
☐ 275	Kevin Seitzer	.08	.03	.01
☐ 276	Luis Salazar	.03	.01	.00
☐ 277	Alejandro Pena	.06	.02	.00
☐ 278	Jose Cruz	.06	.02	.00
☐ 279	Randy St.Claire	.03	.01	.00
☐ 280	Pete Incaviglia	.08	.03	.01

☐ 281	Jerry Hairston	.03	.01	.00
☐ 282	Pat Perry	.03	.01	.00
☐ 283	Phil Lombardi	.06	.02	.00
☐ 284	Larry Bowa MG (checklist back)	.06	.02	.00
☐ 285	Jim Presley	.03	.01	.00
☐ 286	Chuck Crim	.03	.01	.00
☐ 287	Manny Trillo	.03	.01	.00
☐ 288	Pat Pacillo (Chris Sabo in background of photo)	.06	.02	.00
☐ 289	Dave Bergman	.03	.01	.00
☐ 290	Tony Fernandez	.08	.03	.01
☐ 291	Astros TL Billy Hatcher and Kevin Bass	.06	.02	.00
☐ 292	Carney Lansford	.08	.03	.01
☐ 293	Doug Jones	.12	.05	.01
☐ 294	Al Pedrique	.03	.01	.00
☐ 295	Bert Blyleven	.08	.03	.01
☐ 296	Floyd Rayford	.03	.01	.00
☐ 297	Zane Smith	.06	.02	.00
☐ 298	Milt Thompson	.03	.01	.00
☐ 299	Steve Crawford	.03	.01	.00
☐ 300	Don Mattingly	.25	.10	.02
☐ 301	Bud Black	.03	.01	.00
☐ 302	Jose Uribe	.03	.01	.00
☐ 303	Eric Show	.03	.01	.00
☐ 304	George Hendrick	.03	.01	.00
☐ 305	Steve Sax	.10	.04	.01
☐ 306	Billy Hatcher	.06	.02	.00
☐ 307	Mike Trujillo	.03	.01	.00
☐ 308	Lee Mazzilli	.03	.01	.00
☐ 309	Bill Long	.06	.02	.00
☐ 310	Tom Herr	.03	.01	.00
☐ 311	Scott Sanderson	.06	.02	.00
☐ 312	Joey Meyer	.06	.02	.00
☐ 313	Bob McClure	.03	.01	.00
☐ 314	Jimy Williams MG (checklist back)	.06	.02	.00
☐ 315	Dave Parker	.10	.04	.01
☐ 316	Jose Rijo	.08	.03	.01
☐ 317	Tom Nieto	.03	.01	.00
☐ 318	Mel Hall	.06	.02	.00
☐ 319	Mike Loynd	.03	.01	.00
☐ 320	Alan Trammell	.15	.06	.01
☐ 321	White Sox TL Harold Baines and Carlton Fisk	.15	.06	.01
☐ 322	Vicente Palacios	.10	.04	.01
☐ 323	Rick Leach	.03	.01	.00
☐ 324	Danny Jackson	.06	.02	.00
☐ 325	Glenn Hubbard	.03	.01	.00
☐ 326	Al Nipper	.03	.01	.00
☐ 327	Larry Sheets	.03	.01	.00
☐ 328	Greg Cadaret	.10	.04	.01
☐ 329	Chris Speier	.03	.01	.00
☐ 330	Eddie Whitson	.03	.01	.00

Card	Price 1	Price 2	Price 3
□ 331 Brian Downing	.06	.02	.00
□ 332 Jerry Reed	.03	.01	.00
□ 333 Wally Backman	.03	.01	.00
□ 334 Dave LaPoint	.03	.01	.00
□ 335 Claudell Washington	.03	.01	.00
□ 336 Ed Lynch	.03	.01	.00
□ 337 Jim Gantner	.03	.01	.00
□ 338 Brian Holton UER (1987 ERA .389, should be 3.89)	.08	.03	.01
□ 339 Kurt Stillwell	.06	.02	.00
□ 340 Jack Morris	.12	.05	.01
□ 341 Carmen Castillo	.03	.01	.00
□ 342 Larry Andersen	.03	.01	.00
□ 343 Greg Gagne	.03	.01	.00
□ 344 Tony LaRussa MG (checklist back)	.06	.02	.00
□ 345 Scott Fletcher	.03	.01	.00
□ 346 Vance Law	.03	.01	.00
□ 347 Joe Johnson	.03	.01	.00
□ 348 Jim Eisenreich	.03	.01	.00
□ 349 Bob Walk	.03	.01	.00
□ 350 Will Clark	.75	.30	.07
□ 351 Cardinals TL Red Schoendienst and Tony Pena	.06	.02	.00
□ 352 Billy Ripken	.12	.05	.01
□ 353 Ed Olwine	.03	.01	.00
□ 354 Marc Sullivan	.03	.01	.00
□ 355 Roger McDowell	.03	.01	.00
□ 356 Luis Aguayo	.03	.01	.00
□ 357 Floyd Bannister	.03	.01	.00
□ 358 Rey Quinones	.03	.01	.00
□ 359 Tim Stoddard	.03	.01	.00
□ 360 Tony Gwynn	.25	.10	.02
□ 361 Greg Maddux	.20	.08	.02
□ 362 Juan Castillo	.03	.01	.00
□ 363 Willie Fraser	.03	.01	.00
□ 364 Nick Esasky	.03	.01	.00
□ 365 Floyd Youmans	.03	.01	.00
□ 366 Chet Lemon	.03	.01	.00
□ 367 Tim Leary	.06	.02	.00
□ 368 Gerald Young	.08	.03	.01
□ 369 Greg Harris	.03	.01	.00
□ 370 Jose Canseco	.75	.30	.07
□ 371 Joe Hesketh	.06	.02	.00
□ 372 Matt Williams	1.50	.60	.15
□ 373 Checklist 265-396	.06	.01	.00
□ 374 Doc Edwards MG (checklist back)	.06	.02	.00
□ 375 Tom Brunansky	.06	.02	.00
□ 376 Bill Wilkinson	.06	.02	.00
□ 377 Sam Horn	.12	.05	.01
□ 378 Todd Frohwirth	.06	.02	.00
□ 379 Rafael Ramirez	.03	.01	.00
□ 380 Joe Magrane	.12	.05	.01
□ 381 Angels TL Wally Joyner and Jack Howell	.10	.04	.01
□ 382 Keith Miller (New York Mets)	.12	.05	.01
□ 383 Eric Bell	.03	.01	.00
□ 384 Neil Allen	.03	.01	.00
□ 385 Carlton Fisk	.17	.07	.01
□ 386 Don Mattingly AS	.12	.05	.01
□ 387 Willie Randolph AS	.06	.02	.00
□ 388 Wade Boggs AS	.15	.06	.01
□ 389 Alan Trammell AS	.10	.04	.01
□ 390 George Bell AS	.10	.04	.01
□ 391 Kirby Puckett AS	.15	.06	.01
□ 392 Dave Winfield AS	.10	.04	.01
□ 393 Matt Nokes AS	.08	.03	.01
□ 394 Roger Clemens AS	.17	.07	.01
□ 395 Jimmy Key AS	.06	.02	.00
□ 396 Tom Henke AS	.06	.02	.00
□ 397 Jack Clark AS	.06	.02	.00
□ 398 Juan Samuel AS	.06	.02	.00
□ 399 Tim Wallach AS	.06	.02	.00
□ 400 Ozzie Smith AS	.12	.05	.01
□ 401 Andre Dawson AS	.12	.05	.01
□ 402 Tony Gwynn AS	.15	.06	.01
□ 403 Tim Raines AS	.08	.03	.01
□ 404 Benny Santiago AS	.08	.03	.01
□ 405 Dwight Gooden AS	.08	.03	.01
□ 406 Shane Rawley AS	.06	.02	.00
□ 407 Steve Bedrosian AS	.06	.02	.00
□ 408 Dion James	.03	.01	.00
□ 409 Joel McKeon	.03	.01	.00
□ 410 Tony Pena	.06	.02	.00
□ 411 Wayne Tolleson	.03	.01	.00
□ 412 Randy Myers	.06	.02	.00
□ 413 John Christensen	.03	.01	.00
□ 414 John McNamara MG (checklist back)	.06	.02	.00
□ 415 Don Carman	.03	.01	.00
□ 416 Keith Moreland	.03	.01	.00
□ 417 Mark Ciardi	.06	.02	.00
□ 418 Joel Youngblood	.03	.01	.00
□ 419 Scott McGregor	.03	.01	.00
□ 420 Wally Joyner	.15	.06	.01
□ 421 Ed VandeBerg	.03	.01	.00
□ 422 Dave Concepcion	.06	.02	.00
□ 423 John Smiley	.45	.18	.04
□ 424 Dwayne Murphy	.03	.01	.00
□ 425 Jeff Reardon	.10	.04	.01
□ 426 Randy Ready	.03	.01	.00
□ 427 Paul Kilgus	.06	.02	.00
□ 428 John Shelby	.03	.01	.00
□ 429 Tigers TL Alan Trammell and Kirk Gibson	.15	.06	.01
□ 430 Glenn Davis	.08	.03	.01
□ 431 Casey Candaele	.03	.01	.00
□ 432 Mike Moore	.06	.02	.00
□ 433 Bill Pecota	.08	.03	.01
□ 434 Rick Aguilera	.06	.02	.00

☐ 435 Mike Pagliarulo .03 .01 .00
☐ 436 Mike Bielecki .06 .02 .00
☐ 437 Fred Manrique .06 .02 .00
☐ 438 Rob Ducey .10 .04 .01
☐ 439 Dave Martinez .12 .05 .01
☐ 440 Steve Bedrosian .06 .02 .00
☐ 441 Rick Manning .03 .01 .00
☐ 442 Tom Bolton .10 .04 .01
☐ 443 Ken Griffey .10 .04 .01
☐ 444 Cal Ripken, Sr. MG .08 .03 .01
(checklist back)
UER (two copyrights)
☐ 445 Mike Krukow .03 .01 .00
☐ 446 Doug DeCinces .06 .02 .00
☐ 447 Jeff Montgomery .20 .08 .02
☐ 448 Mike Davis .03 .01 .00
☐ 449 Jeff M. Robinson .08 .03 .01
(Tigers pitcher)
☐ 450 Barry Bonds .35 .15 .03
☐ 451 Keith Atherton .03 .01 .00
☐ 452 Willie Wilson .06 .02 .00
☐ 453 Dennis Powell .03 .01 .00
☐ 454 Marvell Wynne .03 .01 .00
☐ 455 Shawn Hillegas .08 .03 .01
☐ 456 Dave Anderson .03 .01 .00
☐ 457 Terry Leach .03 .01 .00
☐ 458 Ron Hassey .03 .01 .00
☐ 459 Yankees TL .10 .04 .01
Dave Winfield and
Willie Randolph
☐ 460 Ozzie Smith .15 .06 .01
☐ 461 Danny Darwin .03 .01 .00
☐ 462 Don Slaught .03 .01 .00
☐ 463 Fred McGriff .60 .25 .06
☐ 464 Jay Tibbs .03 .01 .00
☐ 465 Paul Molitor .10 .04 .01
☐ 466 Jerry Mumphrey .03 .01 .00
☐ 467 Don Aase .03 .01 .00
☐ 468 Darren Daulton .06 .02 .00
☐ 469 Jeff Dedmon .03 .01 .00
☐ 470 Dwight Evans .08 .03 .01
☐ 471 Donnie Moore .03 .01 .00
☐ 472 Robby Thompson .03 .01 .00
☐ 473 Joe Niekro .06 .02 .00
☐ 474 Tom Brookens .03 .01 .00
☐ 475 Pete Rose MG .20 .08 .02
(checklist back)
☐ 476 Dave Stewart .08 .03 .01
☐ 477 Jamie Quirk .03 .01 .00
☐ 478 Sid Bream .03 .01 .00
☐ 479 Brett Butler .08 .03 .01
☐ 480 Dwight Gooden .15 .06 .01
☐ 481 Mariano Duncan .06 .02 .00
☐ 482 Mark Davis .06 .02 .00
☐ 483 Rod Booker .03 .01 .00
☐ 484 Pat Clements .03 .01 .00
☐ 485 Harold Reynolds .06 .02 .00
☐ 486 Pat Keedy .03 .01 .00
☐ 487 Jim Pankovits .03 .01 .00
☐ 488 Andy McGaffigan .03 .01 .00
☐ 489 Dodgers TL .08 .03 .01
Pedro Guerrero and
Fernando Valenzuela
☐ 490 Larry Parrish .03 .01 .00
☐ 491 B.J. Surhoff .06 .02 .00
☐ 492 Doyle Alexander .03 .01 .00
☐ 493 Mike Greenwell .20 .08 .02
☐ 494 Wally Ritchie .03 .01 .00
☐ 495 Eddie Murray .15 .06 .01
☐ 496 Guy Hoffman .03 .01 .00
☐ 497 Kevin Mitchell .25 .10 .02
☐ 498 Bob Boone .06 .02 .00
☐ 499 Eric King .03 .01 .00
☐ 500 Andre Dawson .15 .06 .01
☐ 501 Tim Birtsas .03 .01 .00
☐ 502 Dan Gladden .03 .01 .00
☐ 503 Junior Noboa .03 .01 .00
☐ 504 Bob Rodgers MG .06 .02 .00
(checklist back)
☐ 505 Willie Upshaw .03 .01 .00
☐ 506 John Cangelosi .03 .01 .00
☐ 507 Mark Gubicza .06 .02 .00
☐ 508 Tim Teufel .03 .01 .00
☐ 509 Bill Dawley .03 .01 .00
☐ 510 Dave Winfield .15 .06 .01
☐ 511 Joel Davis .03 .01 .00
☐ 512 Alex Trevino .03 .01 .00
☐ 513 Tim Flannery .03 .01 .00
☐ 514 Pat Sheridan .03 .01 .00
☐ 515 Juan Nieves .03 .01 .00
☐ 516 Jim Sundberg .03 .01 .00
☐ 517 Ron Robinson .03 .01 .00
☐ 518 Greg Gross .03 .01 .00
☐ 519 Mariners TL .06 .02 .00
Harold Reynolds and
Phil Bradley
☐ 520 Dave Smith .03 .01 .00
☐ 521 Jim Dwyer .03 .01 .00
☐ 522 Bob Patterson .06 .02 .00
☐ 523 Gary Roenicke .03 .01 .00
☐ 524 Gary Lucas .03 .01 .00
☐ 525 Marty Barrett .03 .01 .00
☐ 526 Juan Berenguer .03 .01 .00
☐ 527 Steve Henderson .03 .01 .00
☐ 528A Checklist 397-528 .40 .10 .02
ERR (455 S. Carlton)
☐ 528B Checklist 397-528 .10 .01 .00
COR (455 S. Hillegas)
☐ 529 Tim Burke .03 .01 .00
☐ 530 Gary Carter .08 .03 .01
☐ 531 Rich Yett .03 .01 .00
☐ 532 Mike Kingery .03 .01 .00
☐ 533 John Farrell .08 .03 .01
☐ 534 John Wathan MG .06 .02 .00
(checklist back)
☐ 535 Ron Guidry .08 .03 .01

☐ 536 John Morris .03 .01 .00
☐ 537 Steve Buechele .06 .02 .00
☐ 538 Bill Wegman .03 .01 .00
☐ 539 Mike LaValliere .03 .01 .00
☐ 540 Bret Saberhagen .12 .05 .01
☐ 541 Juan Beniquez .03 .01 .00
☐ 542 Paul Noce .06 .02 .00
☐ 543 Kent Tekulve .03 .01 .00
☐ 544 Jim Traber .03 .01 .00
☐ 545 Don Baylor .06 .02 .00
☐ 546 John Candelaria .03 .01 .00
☐ 547 Felix Fermin .03 .01 .00
☐ 548 Shane Mack .08 .03 .01
☐ 549 Braves TL .08 .03 .01
Albert Hall,
Dale Murphy,
Ken Griffey,
and Dion James
☐ 550 Pedro Guerrero .08 .03 .01
☐ 551 Terry Steinbach .08 .03 .01
☐ 552 Mark Thurmond .03 .01 .00
☐ 553 Tracy Jones .03 .01 .00
☐ 554 Mike Smithson .03 .01 .00
☐ 555 Brook Jacoby .03 .01 .00
☐ 556 Stan Clarke .03 .01 .00
☐ 557 Craig Reynolds .03 .01 .00
☐ 558 Bob Ojeda .03 .01 .00
☐ 559 Ken Williams .06 .02 .00
☐ 560 Tim Wallach .06 .02 .00
☐ 561 Rick Cerone .03 .01 .00
☐ 562 Jim Lindeman .03 .01 .00
☐ 563 Jose Guzman .03 .01 .00
☐ 564 Frank Lucchesi MG .06 .02 .00
(checklist back)
☐ 565 Lloyd Moseby .03 .01 .00
☐ 566 Charlie O'Brien .08 .03 .01
☐ 567 Mike Diaz .03 .01 .00
☐ 568 Chris Brown .03 .01 .00
☐ 569 Charlie Leibrandt .03 .01 .00
☐ 570 Jeffrey Leonard .03 .01 .00
☐ 571 Mark Williamson .08 .03 .01
☐ 572 Chris James .08 .03 .01
☐ 573 Bob Stanley .03 .01 .00
☐ 574 Graig Nettles .08 .03 .01
☐ 575 Don Sutton .10 .04 .01
☐ 576 Tommy Hinzo .03 .01 .00
☐ 577 Tom Browning .06 .02 .00
☐ 578 Gary Gaetti .06 .02 .00
☐ 579 Mets TL .08 .03 .01
Gary Carter and
Kevin McReynolds
☐ 580 Mark McGwire .20 .08 .02
☐ 581 Tito Landrum .03 .01 .00
☐ 582 Mike Henneman .15 .06 .01
☐ 583 Dave Valle .06 .02 .00
☐ 584 Steve Trout .03 .01 .00
☐ 585 Ozzie Guillen .06 .02 .00
☐ 586 Bob Forsch .03 .01 .00
☐ 587 Terry Puhl .03 .01 .00
☐ 588 Jeff Parrett .06 .02 .00
☐ 589 Geno Petralli .03 .01 .00
☐ 590 George Bell .12 .05 .01
☐ 591 Doug Drabek .12 .05 .01
☐ 592 Dale Sveum .03 .01 .00
☐ 593 Bob Tewksbury .03 .01 .00
☐ 594 Bobby Valentine MG .06 .02 .00
(checklist back)
☐ 595 Frank White .03 .01 .00
☐ 596 John Kruk .06 .02 .00
☐ 597 Gene Garber .03 .01 .00
☐ 598 Lee Lacy .03 .01 .00
☐ 599 Calvin Schiraldi .03 .01 .00
☐ 600 Mike Schmidt .35 .15 .03
☐ 601 Jack Lazorko .03 .01 .00
☐ 602 Mike Aldrete .03 .01 .00
☐ 603 Rob Murphy .03 .01 .00
☐ 604 Chris Bando .03 .01 .00
☐ 605 Kirk Gibson .08 .03 .01
☐ 606 Moose Haas .03 .01 .00
☐ 607 Mickey Hatcher .03 .01 .00
☐ 608 Charlie Kerfeld .03 .01 .00
☐ 609 Twins TL .08 .03 .01
Gary Gaetti and
Kent Hrbek
☐ 610 Keith Hernandez .08 .03 .01
☐ 611 Tommy John .08 .03 .01
☐ 612 Curt Ford .03 .01 .00
☐ 613 Bobby Thigpen .10 .04 .01
☐ 614 Herm Winningham .03 .01 .00
☐ 615 Jody Davis .03 .01 .00
☐ 616 Jay Aldrich .03 .01 .00
☐ 617 Oddibe McDowell .03 .01 .00
☐ 618 Cecil Fielder .35 .15 .03
☐ 619 Mike Dunne .06 .02 .00
(inconsistent design,
black name on front)
☐ 620 Cory Snyder .08 .03 .01
☐ 621 Gene Nelson .03 .01 .00
☐ 622 Kal Daniels .08 .03 .01
☐ 623 Mike Flanagan .06 .02 .00
☐ 624 Jim Leyland MG .06 .02 .00
(checklist back)
☐ 625 Frank Viola .08 .03 .01
☐ 626 Glenn Wilson .03 .01 .00
☐ 627 Joe Boever .06 .02 .00
☐ 628 Dave Henderson .08 .03 .01
☐ 629 Kelly Downs .03 .01 .00
☐ 630 Darrell Evans .06 .02 .00
☐ 631 Jack Howell .03 .01 .00
☐ 632 Steve Shields .03 .01 .00
☐ 633 Barry Lyons .08 .03 .01
☐ 634 Jose DeLeon .03 .01 .00
☐ 635 Terry Pendleton .12 .05 .01
☐ 636 Charles Hudson .03 .01 .00
☐ 637 Jay Bell .30 .12 .03
☐ 638 Steve Balboni .03 .01 .00

☐ 639	Brewers TL Glenn Braggs and Tony Muser CO	.03	.01	.00
☐ 640	Garry Templeton (inconsistent design, green border)	.06	.02	.00
☐ 641	Rick Honeycutt	.03	.01	.00
☐ 642	Bob Dernier	.03	.01	.00
☐ 643	Rocky Childress	.03	.01	.00
☐ 644	Terry McGriff	.03	.01	.00
☐ 645	Matt Nokes	.25	.10	.02
☐ 646	Checklist 529-660	.06	.01	.00
☐ 647	Pascual Perez	.03	.01	.00
☐ 648	Al Newman	.03	.01	.00
☐ 649	DeWayne Buice	.03	.01	.00
☐ 650	Cal Ripken	.35	.15	.03
☐ 651	Mike Jackson	.10	.04	.01
☐ 652	Bruce Benedict	.03	.01	.00
☐ 653	Jeff Sellers	.03	.01	.00
☐ 654	Roger Craig MG (checklist back)	.06	.02	.00
☐ 655	Len Dykstra	.08	.03	.01
☐ 656	Lee Guetterman	.03	.01	.00
☐ 657	Gary Redus	.03	.01	.00
☐ 658	Tim Conroy (inconsistent design, name in white)	.03	.01	.00
☐ 659	Bobby Meacham	.03	.01	.00
☐ 660	Rick Reuschel	.06	.02	.00
☐ 661	Turn Back Clock 1983 Nolan Ryan	.17	.07	.01
☐ 662	Turn Back Clock 1978 Jim Rice	.08	.03	.01
☐ 663	Turn Back Clock 1973 Ron Blomberg	.03	.01	.00
☐ 664	Turn Back Clock 1968 Bob Gibson	.10	.04	.01
☐ 665	Turn Back Clock 1963 Stan Musial	.12	.05	.01
☐ 666	Mario Soto	.03	.01	.00
☐ 667	Luis Quinones	.03	.01	.00
☐ 668	Walt Terrell	.03	.01	.00
☐ 669	Phillies TL Lance Parrish and Mike Ryan CO	.06	.02	.00
☐ 670	Dan Plesac	.03	.01	.00
☐ 671	Tim Laudner	.03	.01	.00
☐ 672	John Davis	.06	.02	.00
☐ 673	Tony Phillips	.03	.01	.00
☐ 674	Mike Fitzgerald	.03	.01	.00
☐ 675	Jim Rice	.08	.03	.01
☐ 676	Ken Dixon	.03	.01	.00
☐ 677	Eddie Milner	.03	.01	.00
☐ 678	Jim Acker	.03	.01	.00
☐ 679	Darrell Miller	.03	.01	.00
☐ 680	Charlie Hough	.03	.01	.00
☐ 681	Bobby Bonilla	.30	.12	.03
☐ 682	Jimmy Key	.08	.03	.01
☐ 683	Julio Franco	.15	.06	.01
☐ 684	Hal Lanier MG (checklist back)	.06	.02	.00
☐ 685	Ron Darling	.08	.03	.01
☐ 686	Terry Francona	.03	.01	.00
☐ 687	Mickey Brantley	.06	.02	.00
☐ 688	Jim Winn	.03	.01	.00
☐ 689	Tom Pagnozzi	.12	.05	.01
☐ 690	Jay Howell	.03	.01	.00
☐ 691	Dan Pasqua	.06	.02	.00
☐ 692	Mike Birkbeck	.03	.01	.00
☐ 693	Benito Santiago	.12	.05	.01
☐ 694	Eric Nolte	.06	.02	.00
☐ 695	Shawon Dunston	.10	.04	.01
☐ 696	Duane Ward	.06	.02	.00
☐ 697	Steve Lombardozzi	.03	.01	.00
☐ 698	Brad Havens	.03	.01	.00
☐ 699	Padres TL Benito Santiago and Tony Gwynn	.12	.05	.01
☐ 700	George Brett	.20	.08	.02
☐ 701	Sammy Stewart	.03	.01	.00
☐ 702	Mike Gallego	.03	.01	.00
☐ 703	Bob Brenly	.03	.01	.00
☐ 704	Dennis Boyd	.03	.01	.00
☐ 705	Juan Samuel	.08	.03	.01
☐ 706	Rick Mahler	.03	.01	.00
☐ 707	Fred Lynn	.08	.03	.01
☐ 708	Gus Polidor	.03	.01	.00
☐ 709	George Frazier	.03	.01	.00
☐ 710	Darryl Strawberry	.35	.15	.03
☐ 711	Bill Gullickson	.06	.02	.00
☐ 712	John Moses	.03	.01	.00
☐ 713	Willie Hernandez	.03	.01	.00
☐ 714	Jim Fregosi MG (checklist back)	.06	.02	.00
☐ 715	Todd Worrell	.06	.02	.00
☐ 716	Lenn Sakata	.03	.01	.00
☐ 717	Jay Baller	.03	.01	.00
☐ 718	Mike Felder	.03	.01	.00
☐ 719	Denny Walling	.03	.01	.00
☐ 720	Tim Raines	.10	.04	.01
☐ 721	Pete O'Brien	.03	.01	.00
☐ 722	Manny Lee	.03	.01	.00
☐ 723	Bob Kipper	.03	.01	.00
☐ 724	Danny Tartabull	.15	.06	.01
☐ 725	Mike Boddicker	.03	.01	.00
☐ 726	Alfredo Griffin	.03	.01	.00
☐ 727	Greg Booker	.03	.01	.00
☐ 728	Andy Allanson	.03	.01	.00
☐ 729	Blue Jays TL George Bell and Fred McGriff	.10	.04	.01
☐ 730	John Franco	.06	.02	.00
☐ 731	Rick Schu	.03	.01	.00
☐ 732	David Palmer	.03	.01	.00
☐ 733	Spike Owen	.03	.01	.00
☐ 734	Craig Lefferts	.03	.01	.00

☐ 735 Kevin McReynolds	.10	.04	.01
☐ 736 Matt Young	.03	.01	.00
☐ 737 Butch Wynegar	.03	.01	.00
☐ 738 Scott Bankhead	.06	.02	.00
☐ 739 Daryl Boston	.03	.01	.00
☐ 740 Rick Sutcliffe	.06	.02	.00
☐ 741 Mike Easler	.03	.01	.00
☐ 742 Mark Clear	.03	.01	.00
☐ 743 Larry Herndon	.03	.01	.00
☐ 744 Whitey Herzog MG (checklist back)	.06	.02	.00
☐ 745 Bill Doran	.03	.01	.00
☐ 746 Gene Larkin	.12	.05	.01
☐ 747 Bobby Witt	.08	.03	.01
☐ 748 Reid Nichols	.03	.01	.00
☐ 749 Mark Eichhorn	.06	.02	.00
☐ 750 Bo Jackson	.60	.25	.06
☐ 751 Jim Morrison	.03	.01	.00
☐ 752 Mark Grant	.03	.01	.00
☐ 753 Danny Heep	.03	.01	.00
☐ 754 Mike LaCoss	.03	.01	.00
☐ 755 Ozzie Virgil	.03	.01	.00
☐ 756 Mike Maddux	.03	.01	.00
☐ 757 John Marzano	.06	.02	.00
☐ 758 Eddie Williams	.06	.02	.00
☐ 759 A's TL Mark McGwire and Jose Canseco	.17	.07	.01
☐ 760 Mike Scott	.08	.03	.01
☐ 761 Tony Armas	.03	.01	.00
☐ 762 Scott Bradley	.03	.01	.00
☐ 763 Doug Sisk	.03	.01	.00
☐ 764 Greg Walker	.03	.01	.00
☐ 765 Neal Heaton	.03	.01	.00
☐ 766 Henry Cotto	.03	.01	.00
☐ 767 Jose Lind	.20	.08	.02
☐ 768 Dickie Noles	.03	.01	.00
☐ 769 Cecil Cooper	.06	.02	.00
☐ 770 Lou Whitaker	.08	.03	.01
☐ 771 Ruben Sierra	.35	.15	.03
☐ 772 Sal Butera	.03	.01	.00
☐ 773 Frank Williams	.03	.01	.00
☐ 774 Gene Mauch MG (checklist back)	.06	.02	.00
☐ 775 Dave Stieb	.08	.03	.01
☐ 776 Checklist 661-792	.06	.01	.00
☐ 777 Lonnie Smith	.08	.03	.01
☐ 778A Keith Comstock ERR (white "Padres")	2.50	1.00	.25
☐ 778B Keith Comstock COR (blue "Padres")	.08	.03	.01
☐ 779 Tom Glavine	1.00	.40	.10
☐ 780 Fernando Valenzuela	.08	.03	.01
☐ 781 Keith Hughes	.06	.02	.00
☐ 782 Jeff Ballard	.08	.03	.01
☐ 783 Ron Roenicke	.03	.01	.00
☐ 784 Joe Sambito	.03	.01	.00
☐ 785 Alvin Davis	.06	.02	.00
☐ 786 Joe Price (inconsistent design, orange team name)	.03	.01	.00
☐ 787 Bill Almon	.03	.01	.00
☐ 788 Ray Searage	.03	.01	.00
☐ 789 Indians' TL Joe Carter and Cory Snyder	.08	.03	.01
☐ 790 Dave Righetti	.08	.03	.01
☐ 791 Ted Simmons	.08	.03	.01
☐ 792 John Tudor	.10	.04	.01

1988 Topps Traded

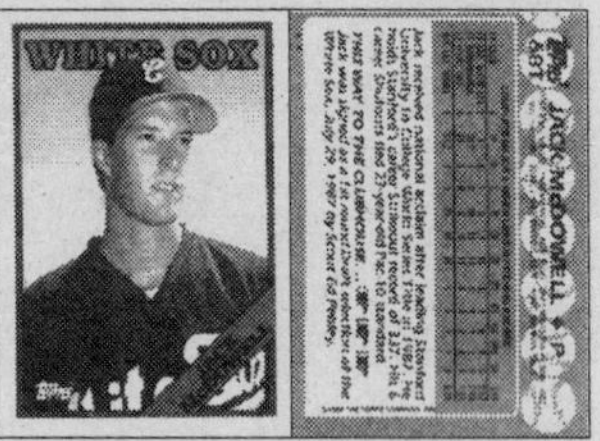

This 132-card Traded or extended set was distributed by Topps to dealers in a special blue and white box as a complete set. The card fronts are identical in style to the Topps regular issue and are also 2 1/2" by 3 1/2". The backs are printed in orange and black on white card stock. Cards are numbered (with a T suffix) alphabetically according to the name of the player. This set has generated additional interest due to the inclusion of the 1988 U.S. Olympic baseball team members. These Olympians are indicated in the checklist below by OLY. The key (extended) rookie cards in this set are Jim Abbott, Roberto Alomar, Andy Benes, Ron Gant, Mark Grace, Tino Martinez, Jack McDowell, Chris Sabo, Robin Ventura, and Walt Weiss. Topps also produced a specially boxed "glossy" edition, frequently referred to as the Topps Traded Tiffany set. This year, again, Topps did not disclose the number of Tiffany sets they produced or sold. It is apparent from the availability that there were many more sets produced this year compared to the 1984-86 Tiffany sets, perhaps

25,000 sets. The checklist of cards is identical to that of the normal non-glossy cards. There are two primary distinguishing features of the Tiffany cards, white card stock reverses and high gloss obverses. These Tiffany cards are valued at approximately four times the values listed below.

	MINT	EXC	G-VG
COMPLETE SET (132)	28.00	12.50	4.00
COMMON PLAYER (1-132)	.06	.02	.00
☐ 1T Jim Abbott OLY	6.00	1.50	.30
☐ 2T Juan Agosto	.06	.02	.00
☐ 3T Luis Alicea	.10	.04	.01
☐ 4T Roberto Alomar	3.50	1.50	.35
☐ 5T Brady Anderson	.10	.04	.01
☐ 6T Jack Armstrong	.20	.08	.02
☐ 7T Don August	.10	.04	.01
☐ 8T Floyd Bannister	.06	.02	.00
☐ 9T Bret Barberie OLY	.60	.25	.06
☐ 10T Jose Bautista	.10	.04	.01
☐ 11T Don Baylor	.10	.04	.01
☐ 12T Tim Belcher	.12	.05	.01
☐ 13T Buddy Bell	.10	.04	.01
☐ 14T Andy Benes OLY	3.00	1.25	.30
☐ 15T Damon Berryhill	.10	.04	.01
☐ 16T Bud Black	.06	.02	.00
☐ 17T Pat Borders	.30	.12	.03
☐ 18T Phil Bradley	.06	.02	.00
☐ 19T Jeff Branson OLY	.20	.08	.02
☐ 20T Tom Brunansky	.10	.04	.01
☐ 21T Jay Buhner	.60	.25	.06
☐ 22T Brett Butler	.12	.05	.01
☐ 23T Jim Campanis OLY	.20	.08	.02
☐ 24T Sil Campusano	.12	.05	.01
☐ 25T John Candelaria	.06	.02	.00
☐ 26T Jose Cecena	.10	.04	.01
☐ 27T Rick Cerone	.06	.02	.00
☐ 28T Jack Clark	.10	.04	.01
☐ 29T Kevin Coffman	.06	.02	.00
☐ 30T Pat Combs OLY	.25	.10	.02
☐ 31T Henry Cotto	.06	.02	.00
☐ 32T Chili Davis	.12	.05	.01
☐ 33T Mike Davis	.06	.02	.00
☐ 34T Jose DeLeon	.06	.02	.00
☐ 35T Richard Dotson	.06	.02	.00
☐ 36T Cecil Espy	.12	.05	.01
☐ 37T Tom Filer	.06	.02	.00
☐ 38T Mike Fiore OLY	.20	.08	.02
☐ 39T Ron Gant	2.50	1.00	.25
☐ 40T Kirk Gibson	.12	.05	.01
☐ 41T Rich Gossage	.12	.05	.01
☐ 42T Mark Grace	2.25	.90	.22
☐ 43T Alfredo Griffin	.06	.02	.00
☐ 44T Ty Griffin OLY	.15	.06	.01
☐ 45T Bryan Harvey	.60	.25	.06
☐ 46T Ron Hassey	.06	.02	.00
☐ 47T Ray Hayward	.06	.02	.00
☐ 48T Dave Henderson	.12	.05	.01
☐ 49T Tom Herr	.10	.04	.01
☐ 50T Bob Horner	.10	.04	.01
☐ 51T Ricky Horton	.06	.02	.00
☐ 52T Jay Howell	.06	.02	.00
☐ 53T Glenn Hubbard	.06	.02	.00
☐ 54T Jeff Innis	.10	.04	.01
☐ 55T Danny Jackson	.10	.04	.01
☐ 56T Darrin Jackson	.20	.08	.02
☐ 57T Roberto Kelly	.75	.30	.07
☐ 58T Ron Kittle	.10	.04	.01
☐ 59T Ray Knight	.10	.04	.01
☐ 60T Vance Law	.06	.02	.00
☐ 61T Jeffrey Leonard	.06	.02	.00
☐ 62T Mike Macfarlane	.15	.06	.01
☐ 63T Scotti Madison	.10	.04	.01
☐ 64T Kirt Manwaring	.10	.04	.01
☐ 65T Mark Marquess OLY CO	.06	.02	.00
☐ 66T Tino Martinez OLY	3.00	1.25	.30
☐ 67T Billy Masse OLY	.20	.08	.02
☐ 68T Jack McDowell	1.00	.40	.10
☐ 69T Jack McKeon MG	.06	.02	.00
☐ 70T Larry McWilliams	.06	.02	.00
☐ 71T Mickey Morandini OLY	.50	.20	.05
☐ 72T Keith Moreland	.06	.02	.00
☐ 73T Mike Morgan	.10	.04	.01
☐ 74T Charles Nagy OLY	.60	.25	.06
☐ 75T Al Nipper	.06	.02	.00
☐ 76T Russ Nixon MG	.06	.02	.00
☐ 77T Jesse Orosco	.06	.02	.00
☐ 78T Joe Orsulak	.06	.02	.00
☐ 79T Dave Palmer	.06	.02	.00
☐ 80T Mark Parent	.10	.04	.01
☐ 81T Dave Parker	.15	.06	.01
☐ 82T Dan Pasqua	.10	.04	.01
☐ 83T Melido Perez	.20	.08	.02
☐ 84T Steve Peters	.10	.04	.01
☐ 85T Dan Petry	.06	.02	.00
☐ 86T Gary Pettis	.06	.02	.00
☐ 87T Jeff Pico	.10	.04	.01
☐ 88T Jim Poole OLY	.20	.08	.02
☐ 89T Ted Power	.06	.02	.00
☐ 90T Rafael Ramirez	.06	.02	.00
☐ 91T Dennis Rasmussen	.06	.02	.00
☐ 92T Jose Rijo	.20	.08	.02
☐ 93T Ernie Riles	.06	.02	.00
☐ 94T Luis Rivera	.10	.04	.01
☐ 95T Doug Robbins OLY	.15	.06	.01
☐ 96T Frank Robinson MG	.15	.06	.01
☐ 97T Cookie Rojas MG	.06	.02	.00
☐ 98T Chris Sabo	2.00	.80	.20
☐ 99T Mark Salas	.06	.02	.00
☐ 100T Luis Salazar	.06	.02	.00
☐ 101T Rafael Santana	.06	.02	.00
☐ 102T Nelson Santovenia	.12	.05	.01
☐ 103T Mackey Sasser	.15	.06	.01

☐ 104T Calvin Schiraldi	.06	.02	.00
☐ 105T Mike Schooler	.20	.08	.02
☐ 106T Scott Servais OLY	.20	.08	.02
☐ 107T Dave Silvestri OLY	.15	.06	.01
☐ 108T Don Slaught	.06	.02	.00
☐ 109T Joe Slusarski OLY	.40	.16	.04
☐ 110T Lee Smith	.12	.05	.01
☐ 111T Pete Smith	.10	.04	.01
☐ 112T Jim Snyder MG	.06	.02	.00
☐ 113T Ed Sprague OLY	.50	.20	.05
☐ 114T Pete Stanicek	.10	.04	.01
☐ 115T Kurt Stillwell	.10	.04	.01
☐ 116T Todd Stottlemyre	.75	.30	.07
☐ 117T Bill Swift	.15	.06	.01
☐ 118T Pat Tabler	.06	.02	.00
☐ 119T Scott Terry	.06	.02	.00
☐ 120T Mickey Tettleton	.15	.06	.01
☐ 121T Dickie Thon	.10	.04	.01
☐ 122T Jeff Treadway	.25	.10	.02
☐ 123T Willie Upshaw	.06	.02	.00
☐ 124T Robin Ventura OLY	9.00	4.00	.90
☐ 125T Ron Washington	.06	.02	.00
☐ 126T Walt Weiss	.30	.12	.03
☐ 127T Bob Welch	.20	.08	.02
☐ 128T David Wells	.20	.08	.02
☐ 129T Glenn Wilson	.06	.02	.00
☐ 130T Ted Wood OLY	.35	.15	.03
☐ 131T Don Zimmer MG	.06	.02	.00
☐ 132T Checklist 1T-132T	.06	.01	.00

1989 Topps

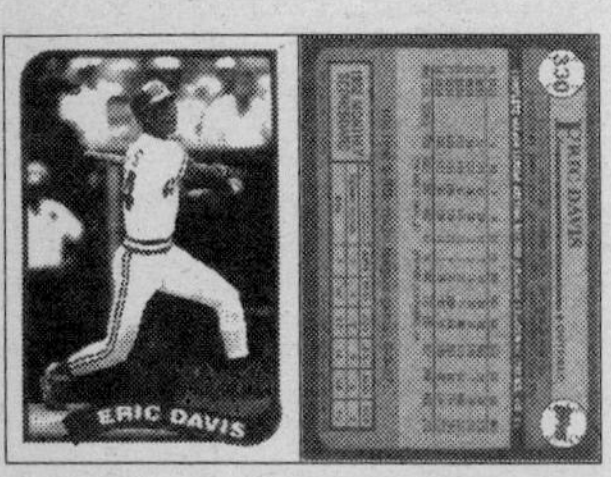

This 792-card set features backs that are printed in pink and black on gray card stock. The manager cards contain a checklist of the respective team's players on the back. Subsets in the set include Record Breakers (1-7), Turn Back the Clock (661-665), and All-Star selections (386-407). The bonus cards distributed throughout the set, which are indicated on the Topps checklist cards, are actually Team Leader (TL) cards. Also sprinkled throughout the set are Future Stars (FS) and First Draft Picks (FDP). There are subtle variations found in the Future Stars cards with respect to the placement of photo and type on the card; in fact, each card has at least two varieties but they are difficult to detect (requiring precise measurement) as well as difficult to explain. The key rookies in this set are Jim Abbott, Sandy Alomar Jr., Steve Avery, Andy Benes, Ramon Martinez, Robin Ventura, and Gary Sheffield. Topps also produced a specially boxed "glossy" edition, frequently referred to as the Topps Tiffany set. This year, again, Topps did not disclose the number of Tiffany sets they produced or sold but it seems that production quantities were roughly similar (or slightly smaller, approximately 15,000 sets) to the previous two years. The checklist of cards (792 regular and 132 Traded) is identical to that of the normal non-glossy cards. There are two primary distinguishing features of the Tiffany cards, white card stock reverses and high gloss obverses. These Tiffany cards are valued at approximately four times the values listed below.

	MINT	EXC	G-VG
COMPLETE SET (792)	20.00	8.50	2.75
COMMON PLAYER (1-792)	.03	.01	.00
☐ 1 George Bell RB Slams 3 HR on Opening Day	.10	.04	.01
☐ 2 Wade Boggs RB Gets 200 Hits 6th Straight Season	.10	.04	.01
☐ 3 Gary Carter RB Sets Record for Career Putouts	.06	.02	.00
☐ 4 Andre Dawson RB Logs Double Figures in HR and SB	.08	.03	.01
☐ 5 Orel Hershiser RB Pitches 59 Scoreless Innings	.06	.02	.00
☐ 6 Doug Jones RB UER Earns His 15th Straight Save (photo actually Chris Codiroli)	.03	.01	.00
☐ 7 Kevin McReynolds RB Steals 21 Without Being Caught	.06	.02	.00

☐ 8 Dave Eiland .08 .03 .01
☐ 9 Tim Teufel .03 .01 .00
☐ 10 Andre Dawson .12 .05 .01
☐ 11 Bruce Sutter .06 .02 .00
☐ 12 Dale Sveum .03 .01 .00
☐ 13 Doug Sisk .03 .01 .00
☐ 14 Tom Kelly MG .06 .02 .00
(team checklist back)
☐ 15 Robby Thompson .03 .01 .00
☐ 16 Ron Robinson .03 .01 .00
☐ 17 Brian Downing .03 .01 .00
☐ 18 Rick Rhoden .03 .01 .00
☐ 19 Greg Gagne .03 .01 .00
☐ 20 Steve Bedrosian .06 .02 .00
☐ 21 Chicago White Sox TL .03 .01 .00
Greg Walker
☐ 22 Tim Crews .03 .01 .00
☐ 23 Mike Fitzgerald .03 .01 .00
Montreal Expos
☐ 24 Larry Andersen .03 .01 .00
☐ 25 Frank White .03 .01 .00
☐ 26 Dale Mohorcic .03 .01 .00
☐ 27A Orestes Destrade .15 .06 .01
(F* next to copyright)
☐ 27B Orestes Destrade .15 .06 .01
(E*F* next to
copyright)
☐ 28 Mike Moore .06 .02 .00
☐ 29 Kelly Gruber .10 .04 .01
☐ 30 Dwight Gooden .10 .04 .01
☐ 31 Terry Francona .03 .01 .00
☐ 32 Dennis Rasmussen .03 .01 .00
☐ 33 B.J. Surhoff .06 .02 .00
☐ 34 Ken Williams .03 .01 .00
☐ 35 John Tudor UER .06 .02 .00
('84 Pirates record,
should be Red Sox)
☐ 36 Mitch Webster .03 .01 .00
☐ 37 Bob Stanley .03 .01 .00
☐ 38 Paul Runge .03 .01 .00
☐ 39 Mike Maddux .03 .01 .00
☐ 40 Steve Sax .08 .03 .01
☐ 41 Terry Mulholland .06 .02 .00
☐ 42 Jim Eppard .03 .01 .00
☐ 43 Guillermo Hernandez .03 .01 .00
☐ 44 Jim Snyder MG .06 .02 .00
(team checklist back)
☐ 45 Kal Daniels .08 .03 .01
☐ 46 Mark Portugal .03 .01 .00
☐ 47 Carney Lansford .06 .02 .00
☐ 48 Tim Burke .03 .01 .00
☐ 49 Craig Biggio .35 .15 .03
☐ 50 George Bell .10 .04 .01
☐ 51 California Angels TL .03 .01 .00
Mark McLemore
☐ 52 Bob Brenly .03 .01 .00
☐ 53 Ruben Sierra .25 .10 .02
☐ 54 Steve Trout .03 .01 .00
☐ 55 Julio Franco .12 .05 .01
☐ 56 Pat Tabler .03 .01 .00
☐ 57 Alejandro Pena .06 .02 .00
☐ 58 Lee Mazzilli .03 .01 .00
☐ 59 Mark Davis .06 .02 .00
☐ 60 Tom Brunansky .06 .02 .00
☐ 61 Neil Allen .03 .01 .00
☐ 62 Alfredo Griffin .03 .01 .00
☐ 63 Mark Clear .03 .01 .00
☐ 64 Alex Trevino .03 .01 .00
☐ 65 Rick Reuschel .06 .02 .00
☐ 66 Manny Trillo .03 .01 .00
☐ 67 Dave Palmer .03 .01 .00
☐ 68 Darrell Miller .03 .01 .00
☐ 69 Jeff Ballard .03 .01 .00
☐ 70 Mark McGwire .12 .05 .01
☐ 71 Mike Boddicker .03 .01 .00
☐ 72 John Moses .03 .01 .00
☐ 73 Pascual Perez .03 .01 .00
☐ 74 Nick Leyva MG .06 .02 .00
(team checklist back)
☐ 75 Tom Henke .06 .02 .00
☐ 76 Terry Blocker .06 .02 .00
☐ 77 Doyle Alexander .03 .01 .00
☐ 78 Jim Sundberg .03 .01 .00
☐ 79 Scott Bankhead .03 .01 .00
☐ 80 Cory Snyder .06 .02 .00
☐ 81 Montreal Expos TL .06 .02 .00
Tim Raines
☐ 82 Dave Leiper .03 .01 .00
☐ 83 Jeff Blauser .08 .03 .01
☐ 84 Bill Bene FDP .03 .01 .00
☐ 85 Kevin McReynolds .08 .03 .01
☐ 86 Al Nipper .03 .01 .00
☐ 87 Larry Owen .03 .01 .00
☐ 88 Darryl Hamilton .12 .05 .01
☐ 89 Dave LaPoint .03 .01 .00
☐ 90 Vince Coleman UER .10 .04 .01
(wrong birth year)
☐ 91 Floyd Youmans .03 .01 .00
☐ 92 Jeff Kunkel .03 .01 .00
☐ 93 Ken Howell .03 .01 .00
☐ 94 Chris Speier .03 .01 .00
☐ 95 Gerald Young .03 .01 .00
☐ 96 Rick Cerone .06 .02 .00
(Ellis Burks in
background of photo)
☐ 97 Greg Mathews .03 .01 .00
☐ 98 Larry Sheets .03 .01 .00
☐ 99 Sherman Corbett .03 .01 .00
☐ 100 Mike Schmidt .35 .15 .03
☐ 101 Les Straker .03 .01 .00
☐ 102 Mike Gallego .03 .01 .00
☐ 103 Tim Birtsas .03 .01 .00
☐ 104 Dallas Green MG .06 .02 .00
(team checklist back)
☐ 105 Ron Darling .06 .02 .00
☐ 106 Willie Upshaw .03 .01 .00

☐ 107 Jose DeLeon .03 .01 .00
☐ 108 Fred Manrique .03 .01 .00
☐ 109 Hipolito Pena .03 .01 .00
☐ 110 Paul Molitor .10 .04 .01
☐ 111 Cincinnati Reds TL .08 .03 .01
Eric Davis
(swinging bat)
☐ 112 Jim Presley .03 .01 .00
☐ 113 Lloyd Moseby .03 .01 .00
☐ 114 Bob Kipper .03 .01 .00
☐ 115 Jody Davis .03 .01 .00
☐ 116 Jeff Montgomery .06 .02 .00
☐ 117 Dave Anderson .03 .01 .00
☐ 118 Checklist 1-132 .06 .01 .00
☐ 119 Terry Puhl .03 .01 .00
☐ 120 Frank Viola .08 .03 .01
☐ 121 Garry Templeton .06 .02 .00
☐ 122 Lance Johnson .08 .03 .01
☐ 123 Spike Owen .03 .01 .00
☐ 124 Jim Traber .03 .01 .00
☐ 125 Mike Krukow .03 .01 .00
☐ 126 Sid Bream .03 .01 .00
☐ 127 Walt Terrell .03 .01 .00
☐ 128 Milt Thompson .03 .01 .00
☐ 129 Terry Clark .06 .02 .00
☐ 130 Gerald Perry .03 .01 .00
☐ 131 Dave Otto .06 .02 .00
☐ 132 Curt Ford .03 .01 .00
☐ 133 Bill Long .03 .01 .00
☐ 134 Don Zimmer MG .06 .02 .00
(team checklist back)
☐ 135 Jose Rijo .08 .03 .01
☐ 136 Joey Meyer .03 .01 .00
☐ 137 Geno Petralli .03 .01 .00
☐ 138 Wallace Johnson .03 .01 .00
☐ 139 Mike Flanagan .03 .01 .00
☐ 140 Shawon Dunston .08 .03 .01
☐ 141 Cleveland Indians TL .03 .01 .00
Brook Jacoby
☐ 142 Mike Diaz .03 .01 .00
☐ 143 Mike Campbell .03 .01 .00
☐ 144 Jay Bell .06 .02 .00
☐ 145 Dave Stewart .08 .03 .01
☐ 146 Gary Pettis .03 .01 .00
☐ 147 DeWayne Buice .03 .01 .00
☐ 148 Bill Pecota .03 .01 .00
☐ 149 Doug Dascenzo .08 .03 .01
☐ 150 Fernando Valenzuela .08 .03 .01
☐ 151 Terry McGriff .03 .01 .00
☐ 152 Mark Thurmond .03 .01 .00
☐ 153 Jim Pankovits .03 .01 .00
☐ 154 Don Carman .03 .01 .00
☐ 155 Marty Barrett .03 .01 .00
☐ 156 Dave Gallagher .08 .03 .01
☐ 157 Tom Glavine .35 .15 .03
☐ 158 Mike Aldrete .03 .01 .00
☐ 159 Pat Clements .03 .01 .00
☐ 160 Jeffrey Leonard .03 .01 .00
☐ 161 Gregg Olson FDP UER .60 .25 .06
(born Scribner, NE,
should be Omaha, NE)
☐ 162 John Davis .03 .01 .00
☐ 163 Bob Forsch .03 .01 .00
☐ 164 Hal Lanier MG .06 .02 .00
(team checklist back)
☐ 165 Mike Dunne .03 .01 .00
☐ 166 Doug Jennings .08 .03 .01
☐ 167 Steve Searcy FS .08 .03 .01
☐ 168 Willie Wilson .06 .02 .00
☐ 169 Mike Jackson .03 .01 .00
☐ 170 Tony Fernandez .06 .02 .00
☐ 171 Atlanta Braves TL .03 .01 .00
Andres Thomas
☐ 172 Frank Williams .03 .01 .00
☐ 173 Mel Hall .06 .02 .00
☐ 174 Todd Burns .08 .03 .01
☐ 175 John Shelby .03 .01 .00
☐ 176 Jeff Parrett .03 .01 .00
☐ 177 Monty Fariss FDP .30 .12 .03
☐ 178 Mark Grant .03 .01 .00
☐ 179 Ozzie Virgil .03 .01 .00
☐ 180 Mike Scott .08 .03 .01
☐ 181 Craig Worthington .08 .03 .01
☐ 182 Bob McClure .03 .01 .00
☐ 183 Oddibe McDowell .03 .01 .00
☐ 184 John Costello .03 .01 .00
☐ 185 Claudell Washington .03 .01 .00
☐ 186 Pat Perry .03 .01 .00
☐ 187 Darren Daulton .06 .02 .00
☐ 188 Dennis Lamp .03 .01 .00
☐ 189 Kevin Mitchell .15 .06 .01
☐ 190 Mike Witt .03 .01 .00
☐ 191 Sil Campusano .10 .04 .01
☐ 192 Paul Mirabella .03 .01 .00
☐ 193 Sparky Anderson MG .06 .02 .00
(team checklist back)
UER (553 Salazer)
☐ 194 Greg W. Harris .15 .06 .01
San Diego Padres
☐ 195 Ozzie Guillen .06 .02 .00
☐ 196 Denny Walling .03 .01 .00
☐ 197 Neal Heaton .03 .01 .00
☐ 198 Danny Heep .03 .01 .00
☐ 199 Mike Schooler .12 .05 .01
☐ 200 George Brett .15 .06 .01
☐ 201 Blue Jays TL .06 .02 .00
Kelly Gruber
☐ 202 Brad Moore .08 .03 .01
☐ 203 Rob Ducey .03 .01 .00
☐ 204 Brad Havens .03 .01 .00
☐ 205 Dwight Evans .08 .03 .01
☐ 206 Roberto Alomar .45 .18 .04
☐ 207 Terry Leach .03 .01 .00
☐ 208 Tom Pagnozzi .03 .01 .00
☐ 209 Jeff Bittiger .06 .02 .00
☐ 210 Dale Murphy .12 .05 .01

□ 211 Mike Pagliarulo .03 .01 .00
□ 212 Scott Sanderson .06 .02 .00
□ 213 Rene Gonzales .03 .01 .00
□ 214 Charlie O'Brien .03 .01 .00
□ 215 Kevin Gross .03 .01 .00
□ 216 Jack Howell .03 .01 .00
□ 217 Joe Price .03 .01 .00
□ 218 Mike LaValliere .03 .01 .00
□ 219 Jim Clancy .03 .01 .00
□ 220 Gary Gaetti .06 .02 .00
□ 221 Cecil Espy .03 .01 .00
□ 222 Mark Lewis FDP .60 .25 .06
□ 223 Jay Buhner .15 .06 .01
□ 224 Tony LaRussa MG .06 .02 .00
(team checklist back)
□ 225 Ramon Martinez 1.25 .50 .12
□ 226 Bill Doran .03 .01 .00
□ 227 John Farrell .03 .01 .00
□ 228 Nelson Santovenia .08 .03 .01
□ 229 Jimmy Key .06 .02 .00
□ 230 Ozzie Smith .12 .05 .01
□ 231 San Diego Padres TL .10 .04 .01
Roberto Alomar
(G.Carter at plate)
□ 232 Ricky Horton .03 .01 .00
□ 233 Gregg Jefferies FS .30 .12 .03
□ 234 Tom Browning .06 .02 .00
□ 235 John Kruk .03 .01 .00
□ 236 Charles Hudson .03 .01 .00
□ 237 Glenn Hubbard .03 .01 .00
□ 238 Eric King .03 .01 .00
□ 239 Tim Laudner .03 .01 .00
□ 240 Greg Maddux .08 .03 .01
□ 241 Brett Butler .08 .03 .01
□ 242 Ed VandeBerg .03 .01 .00
□ 243 Bob Boone .06 .02 .00
□ 244 Jim Acker .03 .01 .00
□ 245 Jim Rice .08 .03 .01
□ 246 Rey Quinones .03 .01 .00
□ 247 Shawn Hillegas .03 .01 .00
□ 248 Tony Phillips .03 .01 .00
□ 249 Tim Leary .06 .02 .00
□ 250 Cal Ripken .35 .15 .03
□ 251 John Dopson .08 .03 .01
□ 252 Billy Hatcher .03 .01 .00
□ 253 Jose Alvarez .06 .02 .00
□ 254 Tom Lasorda MG .06 .02 .00
(team checklist back)
□ 255 Ron Guidry .08 .03 .01
□ 256 Benny Santiago .08 .03 .01
□ 257 Rick Aguilera .03 .01 .00
□ 258 Checklist 133-264 .06 .01 .00
□ 259 Larry McWilliams .03 .01 .00
□ 260 Dave Winfield .12 .05 .01
□ 261 St.Louis Cardinals TL .06 .02 .00
Tom Brunansky
(with Luis Alicea)
□ 262 Jeff Pico .06 .02 .00
□ 263 Mike Felder .03 .01 .00
□ 264 Rob Dibble .25 .10 .02
□ 265 Kent Hrbek .08 .03 .01
□ 266 Luis Aquino .03 .01 .00
□ 267 Jeff Robinson .06 .02 .00
Detroit Tigers
□ 268 Keith Miller .06 .02 .00
Philadelphia Phillies
□ 269 Tom Bolton .03 .01 .00
□ 270 Wally Joyner .12 .05 .01
□ 271 Jay Tibbs .03 .01 .00
□ 272 Ron Hassey .03 .01 .00
□ 273 Jose Lind .03 .01 .00
□ 274 Mark Eichhorn .06 .02 .00
□ 275 Danny Tartabull UER .10 .04 .01
(Born San Juan, PR
should be Miami, FL)
□ 276 Paul Kilgus .03 .01 .00
□ 277 Mike Davis .03 .01 .00
□ 278 Andy McGaffigan .03 .01 .00
□ 279 Scott Bradley .03 .01 .00
□ 280 Bob Knepper .03 .01 .00
□ 281 Gary Redus .03 .01 .00
□ 282 Cris Carpenter .08 .03 .01
□ 283 Andy Allanson .03 .01 .00
□ 284 Jim Leyland MG .06 .02 .00
(team checklist back)
□ 285 John Candelaria .03 .01 .00
□ 286 Darrin Jackson .08 .03 .01
□ 287 Juan Nieves .03 .01 .00
□ 288 Pat Sheridan .03 .01 .00
□ 289 Ernie Whitt .03 .01 .00
□ 290 John Franco .03 .01 .00
□ 291 New York Mets TL .08 .03 .01
Darryl Strawberry
(with K.Hernandez
and K.McReynolds)
□ 292 Jim Corsi .06 .02 .00
□ 293 Glenn Wilson .03 .01 .00
□ 294 Juan Berenguer .03 .01 .00
□ 295 Scott Fletcher .03 .01 .00
□ 296 Ron Gant .40 .16 .04
□ 297 Oswald Peraza .06 .02 .00
□ 298 Chris James .03 .01 .00
□ 299 Steve Ellsworth .06 .02 .00
□ 300 Darryl Strawberry .30 .12 .03
□ 301 Charlie Leibrandt .03 .01 .00
□ 302 Gary Ward .03 .01 .00
□ 303 Felix Fermin .03 .01 .00
□ 304 Joel Youngblood .03 .01 .00
□ 305 Dave Smith .03 .01 .00
□ 306 Tracy Woodson .03 .01 .00
□ 307 Lance McCullers .03 .01 .00
□ 308 Ron Karkovice .03 .01 .00
□ 309 Mario Diaz .06 .02 .00
□ 310 Rafael Palmeiro .12 .05 .01
□ 311 Chris Bosio .03 .01 .00
□ 312 Tom Lawless .03 .01 .00

☐ 313 Dennis Martinez .... .06 .02 .00
☐ 314 Bobby Valentine MG ...... .06 .02 .00
(team checklist back)
☐ 315 Greg Swindell .... .06 .02 .00
☐ 316 Walt Weiss .... .08 .03 .01
☐ 317 Jack Armstrong .... .10 .04 .01
☐ 318 Gene Larkin .... .03 .01 .00
☐ 319 Greg Booker .... .03 .01 .00
☐ 320 Lou Whitaker .... .08 .03 .01
☐ 321 Boston Red Sox TL .... .06 .02 .00
Jody Reed
☐ 322 John Smiley .... .06 .02 .00
☐ 323 Gary Thurman .... .03 .01 .00
☐ 324 Bob Milacki .... .15 .06 .01
☐ 325 Jesse Barfield .... .08 .03 .01
☐ 326 Dennis Boyd .... .03 .01 .00
☐ 327 Mark Lemke .... .15 .06 .01
☐ 328 Rick Honeycutt .... .03 .01 .00
☐ 329 Bob Melvin .... .03 .01 .00
☐ 330 Eric Davis .... .10 .04 .01
☐ 331 Curt Wilkerson .... .03 .01 .00
☐ 332 Tony Armas .... .03 .01 .00
☐ 333 Bob Ojeda .... .03 .01 .00
☐ 334 Steve Lyons .... .03 .01 .00
☐ 335 Dave Righetti .... .06 .02 .00
☐ 336 Steve Balboni .... .03 .01 .00
☐ 337 Calvin Schiraldi .... .03 .01 .00
☐ 338 Jim Adduci .... .03 .01 .00
☐ 339 Scott Bailes .... .03 .01 .00
☐ 340 Kirk Gibson .... .08 .03 .01
☐ 341 Jim Deshaies .... .03 .01 .00
☐ 342 Tom Brookens .... .03 .01 .00
☐ 343 Gary Sheffield FS .... .30 .12 .03
☐ 344 Tom Trebelhorn MG ...... .06 .02 .00
(team checklist back)
☐ 345 Charlie Hough .... .03 .01 .00
☐ 346 Rex Hudler .... .03 .01 .00
☐ 347 John Cerutti .... .03 .01 .00
☐ 348 Ed Hearn .... .03 .01 .00
☐ 349 Ron Jones .... .08 .03 .01
☐ 350 Andy Van Slyke .... .08 .03 .01
☐ 351 San Fran. Giants TL .... .03 .01 .00
Bob Melvin
(with Bill Fahey CO)
☐ 352 Rick Schu .... .03 .01 .00
☐ 353 Marvell Wynne .... .03 .01 .00
☐ 354 Larry Parrish .... .03 .01 .00
☐ 355 Mark Langston .... .08 .03 .01
☐ 356 Kevin Elster .... .03 .01 .00
☐ 357 Jerry Reuss .... .03 .01 .00
☐ 358 Ricky Jordan .... .12 .05 .01
☐ 359 Tommy John .... .08 .03 .01
☐ 360 Ryne Sandberg .... .35 .15 .03
☐ 361 Kelly Downs .... .03 .01 .00
☐ 362 Jack Lazorko .... .03 .01 .00
☐ 363 Rich Yett .... .03 .01 .00
☐ 364 Rob Deer .... .06 .02 .00
☐ 365 Mike Henneman .... .03 .01 .00
☐ 366 Herm Winningham .... .03 .01 .00
☐ 367 Johnny Paredes .... .06 .02 .00
☐ 368 Brian Holton .... .03 .01 .00
☐ 369 Ken Caminiti .... .03 .01 .00
☐ 370 Dennis Eckersley .... .08 .03 .01
☐ 371 Manny Lee .... .03 .01 .00
☐ 372 Craig Lefferts .... .03 .01 .00
☐ 373 Tracy Jones .... .03 .01 .00
☐ 374 John Wathan MG .... .06 .02 .00
(team checklist back)
☐ 375 Terry Pendleton .... .10 .04 .01
☐ 376 Steve Lombardozzi .... .03 .01 .00
☐ 377 Mike Smithson .... .03 .01 .00
☐ 378 Checklist 265-396 .... .06 .01 .00
☐ 379 Tim Flannery .... .03 .01 .00
☐ 380 Rickey Henderson .... .35 .15 .03
☐ 381 Baltimore Orioles TL ...... .03 .01 .00
Larry Sheets
☐ 382 John Smoltz .... .50 .20 .05
☐ 383 Howard Johnson .... .12 .05 .01
☐ 384 Mark Salas .... .03 .01 .00
☐ 385 Von Hayes .... .06 .02 .00
☐ 386 Andres Galarraga AS ...... .06 .02 .00
☐ 387 Ryne Sandberg AS .... .15 .06 .01
☐ 388 Bobby Bonilla AS .... .10 .04 .01
☐ 389 Ozzie Smith AS .... .10 .04 .01
☐ 390 Darryl Strawberry AS ..... .15 .06 .01
☐ 391 Andre Dawson AS .... .10 .04 .01
☐ 392 Andy Van Slyke AS .... .08 .03 .01
☐ 393 Gary Carter AS .... .08 .03 .01
☐ 394 Orel Hershiser AS .... .08 .03 .01
☐ 395 Danny Jackson AS .... .06 .02 .00
☐ 396 Kirk Gibson AS .... .08 .03 .01
☐ 397 Don Mattingly AS .... .12 .05 .01
☐ 398 Julio Franco AS .... .08 .03 .01
☐ 399 Wade Boggs AS .... .10 .04 .01
☐ 400 Alan Trammell AS .... .08 .03 .01
☐ 401 Jose Canseco AS .... .20 .08 .02
☐ 402 Mike Greenwell AS .... .08 .03 .01
☐ 403 Kirby Puckett AS .... .12 .05 .01
☐ 404 Bob Boone AS .... .06 .02 .00
☐ 405 Roger Clemens AS .... .12 .05 .01
☐ 406 Frank Viola AS .... .06 .02 .00
☐ 407 Dave Winfield AS .... .10 .04 .01
☐ 408 Greg Walker .... .03 .01 .00
☐ 409 Ken Dayley .... .03 .01 .00
☐ 410 Jack Clark .... .08 .03 .01
☐ 411 Mitch Williams .... .03 .01 .00
☐ 412 Barry Lyons .... .03 .01 .00
☐ 413 Mike Kingery .... .03 .01 .00
☐ 414 Jim Fregosi MG .... .06 .02 .00
(team checklist back)
☐ 415 Rich Gossage .... .08 .03 .01
☐ 416 Fred Lynn .... .08 .03 .01
☐ 417 Mike LaCoss .... .03 .01 .00
☐ 418 Bob Dernier .... .03 .01 .00
☐ 419 Tom Filer .... .03 .01 .00
☐ 420 Joe Carter .... .10 .04 .01

☐ 421 Kirk McCaskill	.03	.01	.00
☐ 422 Bo Diaz	.03	.01	.00
☐ 423 Brian Fisher	.03	.01	.00
☐ 424 Luis Polonia UER (wrong birthdate)	.06	.02	.00
☐ 425 Jay Howell	.03	.01	.00
☐ 426 Dan Gladden	.03	.01	.00
☐ 427 Eric Show	.03	.01	.00
☐ 428 Craig Reynolds	.03	.01	.00
☐ 429 Minnesota Twins TL Greg Gagne (taking throw at 2nd)	.03	.01	.00
☐ 430 Mark Gubicza	.06	.02	.00
☐ 431 Luis Rivera	.03	.01	.00
☐ 432 Chad Kreuter	.06	.02	.00
☐ 433 Albert Hall	.03	.01	.00
☐ 434 Ken Patterson	.06	.02	.00
☐ 435 Len Dykstra	.08	.03	.01
☐ 436 Bobby Meacham	.03	.01	.00
☐ 437 Andy Benes FDP	.50	.20	.05
☐ 438 Greg Gross	.03	.01	.00
☐ 439 Frank DiPino	.03	.01	.00
☐ 440 Bobby Bonilla	.20	.08	.02
☐ 441 Jerry Reed	.03	.01	.00
☐ 442 Jose Oquendo	.03	.01	.00
☐ 443 Rod Nichols	.06	.02	.00
☐ 444 Moose Stubing MG (team checklist back)	.06	.02	.00
☐ 445 Matt Nokes	.06	.02	.00
☐ 446 Rob Murphy	.03	.01	.00
☐ 447 Donell Nixon	.03	.01	.00
☐ 448 Eric Plunk	.03	.01	.00
☐ 449 Carmelo Martinez	.03	.01	.00
☐ 450 Roger Clemens	.30	.12	.03
☐ 451 Mark Davidson	.03	.01	.00
☐ 452 Israel Sanchez	.06	.02	.00
☐ 453 Tom Prince	.03	.01	.00
☐ 454 Paul Assenmacher	.03	.01	.00
☐ 455 Johnny Ray	.03	.01	.00
☐ 456 Tim Belcher	.06	.02	.00
☐ 457 Mackey Sasser	.06	.02	.00
☐ 458 Donn Pall	.06	.02	.00
☐ 459 Seattle Mariners TL Dave Valle	.03	.01	.00
☐ 460 Dave Stieb	.08	.03	.01
☐ 461 Buddy Bell	.06	.02	.00
☐ 462 Jose Guzman	.03	.01	.00
☐ 463 Steve Lake	.03	.01	.00
☐ 464 Bryn Smith	.03	.01	.00
☐ 465 Mark Grace	.30	.12	.03
☐ 466 Chuck Crim	.03	.01	.00
☐ 467 Jim Walewander	.03	.01	.00
☐ 468 Henry Cotto	.03	.01	.00
☐ 469 Jose Bautista	.06	.02	.00
☐ 470 Lance Parrish	.08	.03	.01
☐ 471 Steve Curry	.06	.02	.00
☐ 472 Brian Harper	.06	.02	.00
☐ 473 Don Robinson	.03	.01	.00
☐ 474 Bob Rodgers MG (team checklist back)	.06	.02	.00
☐ 475 Dave Parker	.08	.03	.01
☐ 476 Jon Perlman	.03	.01	.00
☐ 477 Dick Schofield	.03	.01	.00
☐ 478 Doug Drabek	.08	.03	.01
☐ 479 Mike Macfarlane	.10	.04	.01
☐ 480 Keith Hernandez	.08	.03	.01
☐ 481 Chris Brown	.03	.01	.00
☐ 482 Steve Peters	.08	.03	.01
☐ 483 Mickey Hatcher	.03	.01	.00
☐ 484 Steve Shields	.03	.01	.00
☐ 485 Hubie Brooks	.06	.02	.00
☐ 486 Jack McDowell	.17	.07	.01
☐ 487 Scott Lusader	.03	.01	.00
☐ 488 Kevin Coffman ("Now with Cubs")	.03	.01	.00
☐ 489 Phila. Phillies TL Mike Schmidt	.12	.05	.01
☐ 490 Chris Sabo	.60	.25	.06
☐ 491 Mike Birkbeck	.03	.01	.00
☐ 492 Alan Ashby	.03	.01	.00
☐ 493 Todd Benzinger	.03	.01	.00
☐ 494 Shane Rawley	.03	.01	.00
☐ 495 Candy Maldonado	.06	.02	.00
☐ 496 Dwayne Henry	.03	.01	.00
☐ 497 Pete Stanicek	.03	.01	.00
☐ 498 Dave Valle	.03	.01	.00
☐ 499 Don Heinkel	.03	.01	.00
☐ 500 Jose Canseco	.50	.20	.05
☐ 501 Vance Law	.03	.01	.00
☐ 502 Duane Ward	.06	.02	.00
☐ 503 Al Newman	.03	.01	.00
☐ 504 Bob Walk	.03	.01	.00
☐ 505 Pete Rose MG (team checklist back)	.15	.06	.01
☐ 506 Kirt Manwaring	.03	.01	.00
☐ 507 Steve Farr	.03	.01	.00
☐ 508 Wally Backman	.03	.01	.00
☐ 509 Bud Black	.03	.01	.00
☐ 510 Bob Horner	.06	.02	.00
☐ 511 Richard Dotson	.03	.01	.00
☐ 512 Donnie Hill	.03	.01	.00
☐ 513 Jesse Orosco	.03	.01	.00
☐ 514 Chet Lemon	.03	.01	.00
☐ 515 Barry Larkin	.15	.06	.01
☐ 516 Eddie Whitson	.03	.01	.00
☐ 517 Greg Brock	.03	.01	.00
☐ 518 Bruce Ruffin	.03	.01	.00
☐ 519 New York Yankees TL Willie Randolph	.06	.02	.00
☐ 520 Rick Sutcliffe	.06	.02	.00
☐ 521 Mickey Tettleton	.06	.02	.00
☐ 522 Randy Kramer	.06	.02	.00
☐ 523 Andres Thomas	.03	.01	.00
☐ 524 Checklist 397-528	.06	.01	.00
☐ 525 Chili Davis	.06	.02	.00
☐ 526 Wes Gardner	.03	.01	.00

☐ 527	Dave Henderson	.08	.03	.01
☐ 528	Luis Medina (lower left front has white triangle)	.08	.03	.01
☐ 529	Tom Foley	.03	.01	.00
☐ 530	Nolan Ryan	.50	.20	.05
☐ 531	Dave Hengel	.06	.02	.00
☐ 532	Jerry Browne	.03	.01	.00
☐ 533	Andy Hawkins	.03	.01	.00
☐ 534	Doc Edwards MG (team checklist back)	.06	.02	.00
☐ 535	Todd Worrell UER (4 wins in '88, should be 5)	.06	.02	.00
☐ 536	Joel Skinner	.03	.01	.00
☐ 537	Pete Smith	.06	.02	.00
☐ 538	Juan Castillo	.03	.01	.00
☐ 539	Barry Jones	.03	.01	.00
☐ 540	Bo Jackson	.50	.20	.05
☐ 541	Cecil Fielder	.30	.12	.03
☐ 542	Todd Frohwirth	.03	.01	.00
☐ 543	Damon Berryhill	.03	.01	.00
☐ 544	Jeff Sellers	.03	.01	.00
☐ 545	Mookie Wilson	.03	.01	.00
☐ 546	Mark Williamson	.03	.01	.00
☐ 547	Mark McLemore	.03	.01	.00
☐ 548	Bobby Witt	.06	.02	.00
☐ 549	Chicago Cubs TL Jamie Moyer (pitching)	.03	.01	.00
☐ 550	Orel Hershiser	.08	.03	.01
☐ 551	Randy Ready	.03	.01	.00
☐ 552	Greg Cadaret	.03	.01	.00
☐ 553	Luis Salazar	.03	.01	.00
☐ 554	Nick Esasky	.03	.01	.00
☐ 555	Bert Blyleven	.08	.03	.01
☐ 556	Bruce Fields	.03	.01	.00
☐ 557	Keith Miller New York Mets	.06	.02	.00
☐ 558	Dan Pasqua	.03	.01	.00
☐ 559	Juan Agosto	.03	.01	.00
☐ 560	Tim Raines	.10	.04	.01
☐ 561	Luis Aguayo	.03	.01	.00
☐ 562	Danny Cox	.03	.01	.00
☐ 563	Bill Schroeder	.03	.01	.00
☐ 564	Russ Nixon MG (team checklist back)	.06	.02	.00
☐ 565	Jeff Russell	.03	.01	.00
☐ 566	Al Pedrique	.03	.01	.00
☐ 567	David Wells UER (Complete Pitching Recor)	.08	.03	.01
☐ 568	Mickey Brantley	.03	.01	.00
☐ 569	German Jimenez	.06	.02	.00
☐ 570	Tony Gwynn UER ('88 average should be italicized as league leader)	.17	.07	.01
☐ 571	Billy Ripken	.03	.01	.00
☐ 572	Atlee Hammaker	.03	.01	.00
☐ 573	Jim Abbott FDP	1.25	.50	.12
☐ 574	Dave Clark	.03	.01	.00
☐ 575	Juan Samuel	.06	.02	.00
☐ 576	Greg Minton	.03	.01	.00
☐ 577	Randy Bush	.03	.01	.00
☐ 578	John Morris	.03	.01	.00
☐ 579	Houston Astros TL Glenn Davis (batting stance)	.06	.02	.00
☐ 580	Harold Reynolds	.06	.02	.00
☐ 581	Gene Nelson	.03	.01	.00
☐ 582	Mike Marshall	.06	.02	.00
☐ 583	Paul Gibson	.08	.03	.01
☐ 584	Randy Velarde UER (signed 1935, should be 1985)	.06	.02	.00
☐ 585	Harold Baines	.08	.03	.01
☐ 586	Joe Boever	.03	.01	.00
☐ 587	Mike Stanley	.03	.01	.00
☐ 588	Luis Alicea	.06	.02	.00
☐ 589	Dave Meads	.03	.01	.00
☐ 590	Andres Galarraga	.06	.02	.00
☐ 591	Jeff Musselman	.03	.01	.00
☐ 592	John Cangelosi	.03	.01	.00
☐ 593	Drew Hall	.03	.01	.00
☐ 594	Jimy Williams MG (team checklist back)	.06	.02	.00
☐ 595	Teddy Higuera	.03	.01	.00
☐ 596	Kurt Stillwell	.03	.01	.00
☐ 597	Terry Taylor	.08	.03	.01
☐ 598	Ken Gerhart	.03	.01	.00
☐ 599	Tom Candiotti	.06	.02	.00
☐ 600	Wade Boggs	.20	.08	.02
☐ 601	Dave Dravecky	.08	.03	.01
☐ 602	Devon White	.06	.02	.00
☐ 603	Frank Tanana	.06	.02	.00
☐ 604	Paul O'Neill	.08	.03	.01
☐ 605A	Bob Welch ERR (missing line on back, "Complete M.L. Pitching Record")	3.00	1.25	.30
☐ 605B	Bob Welch COR	.10	.04	.01
☐ 606	Rick Dempsey	.03	.01	.00
☐ 607	Willie Ansley FDP	.20	.08	.02
☐ 608	Phil Bradley	.03	.01	.00
☐ 609	Detroit Tigers TL Frank Tanana (with Alan Trammell and Mike Heath)	.06	.02	.00
☐ 610	Randy Myers	.03	.01	.00
☐ 611	Don Slaught	.03	.01	.00
☐ 612	Dan Quisenberry	.08	.03	.01
☐ 613	Gary Varsho	.06	.02	.00
☐ 614	Joe Hesketh	.06	.02	.00
☐ 615	Robin Yount	.15	.06	.01
☐ 616	Steve Rosenberg	.08	.03	.01

☐ 617 Mark Parent .... .06 .02 .00
☐ 618 Rance Mulliniks .... .03 .01 .00
☐ 619 Checklist 529-660 .... .06 .01 .00
☐ 620 Barry Bonds .... .25 .10 .02
☐ 621 Rick Mahler .... .03 .01 .00
☐ 622 Stan Javier .... .03 .01 .00
☐ 623 Fred Toliver .... .03 .01 .00
☐ 624 Jack McKeon MG .... .06 .02 .00
(team checklist back)
☐ 625 Eddie Murray .... .12 .05 .01
☐ 626 Jeff Reed .... .03 .01 .00
☐ 627 Greg Harris .... .03 .01 .00
Philadelphia Phillies
☐ 628 Matt Williams .... .20 .08 .02
☐ 629 Pete O'Brien .... .03 .01 .00
☐ 630 Mike Greenwell .... .15 .06 .01
☐ 631 Dave Bergman .... .03 .01 .00
☐ 632 Bryan Harvey .... .25 .10 .02
☐ 633 Daryl Boston .... .03 .01 .00
☐ 634 Marvin Freeman .... .03 .01 .00
☐ 635 Willie Randolph .... .06 .02 .00
☐ 636 Bill Wilkinson .... .03 .01 .00
☐ 637 Carmen Castillo .... .03 .01 .00
☐ 638 Floyd Bannister .... .03 .01 .00
☐ 639 Oakland A's TL .... .06 .02 .00
Walt Weiss
☐ 640 Willie McGee .... .08 .03 .01
☐ 641 Curt Young .... .03 .01 .00
☐ 642 Argenis Salazar .... .03 .01 .00
☐ 643 Louie Meadows .... .03 .01 .00
☐ 644 Lloyd McClendon .... .03 .01 .00
☐ 645 Jack Morris .... .10 .04 .01
☐ 646 Kevin Bass .... .03 .01 .00
☐ 647 Randy Johnson .... .35 .15 .03
☐ 648 Sandy Alomar FS .... .40 .16 .04
☐ 649 Stewart Cliburn .... .03 .01 .00
☐ 650 Kirby Puckett .... .30 .12 .03
☐ 651 Tom Niedenfuer .... .03 .01 .00
☐ 652 Rich Gedman .... .03 .01 .00
☐ 653 Tommy Barrett .... .06 .02 .00
☐ 654 Whitey Herzog MG .... .06 .02 .00
(team checklist back)
☐ 655 Dave Magadan .... .08 .03 .01
☐ 656 Ivan Calderon .... .06 .02 .00
☐ 657 Joe Magrane .... .06 .02 .00
☐ 658 R.J. Reynolds .... .03 .01 .00
☐ 659 Al Leiter .... .03 .01 .00
☐ 660 Will Clark .... .40 .16 .04
☐ 661 Dwight Gooden TBC84 .. .08 .03 .01
☐ 662 Lou Brock TBC79 .... .08 .03 .01
☐ 663 Hank Aaron TBC74 .... .10 .04 .01
☐ 664 Gil Hodges TBC69 .... .06 .02 .00
☐ 665A Tony Oliva TBC64 ..... 2.00 .80 .20
ERR (fabricated card
is enlarged version
of Oliva's 64T card;
Topps copyright
missing)
☐ 665B Tony Oliva TBC64 .... .06 .02 .00
COR (fabricated
card)
☐ 666 Randy St.Claire .... .03 .01 .00
☐ 667 Dwayne Murphy .... .03 .01 .00
☐ 668 Mike Bielecki .... .06 .02 .00
☐ 669 L.A. Dodgers TL .... .06 .02 .00
Orel Hershiser
(mound conference
with Mike Scioscia)
☐ 670 Kevin Seitzer .... .06 .02 .00
☐ 671 Jim Gantner .... .03 .01 .00
☐ 672 Allan Anderson .... .03 .01 .00
☐ 673 Don Baylor .... .06 .02 .00
☐ 674 Otis Nixon .... .06 .02 .00
☐ 675 Bruce Hurst .... .06 .02 .00
☐ 676 Ernie Riles .... .03 .01 .00
☐ 677 Dave Schmidt .... .03 .01 .00
☐ 678 Dion James .... .03 .01 .00
☐ 679 Willie Fraser .... .03 .01 .00
☐ 680 Gary Carter .... .08 .03 .01
☐ 681 Jeff Robinson .... .03 .01 .00
Pittsburgh Pirates
☐ 682 Rick Leach .... .03 .01 .00
☐ 683 Jose Cecena .... .03 .01 .00
☐ 684 Dave Johnson MG .... .06 .02 .00
(team checklist back)
☐ 685 Jeff Treadway .... .08 .03 .01
☐ 686 Scott Terry .... .03 .01 .00
☐ 687 Alvin Davis .... .06 .02 .00
☐ 688 Zane Smith .... .06 .02 .00
☐ 689A Stan Jefferson .... .08 .03 .01
(pink triangle on
front bottom left)
☐ 689B Stan Jefferson .... .08 .03 .01
(violet triangle on
front bottom left)
☐ 690 Doug Jones .... .03 .01 .00
☐ 691 Roberto Kelly UER .... .15 .06 .01
(83 Oneonita)
☐ 692 Steve Ontiveros .... .03 .01 .00
☐ 693 Pat Borders .... .15 .06 .01
☐ 694 Les Lancaster .... .03 .01 .00
☐ 695 Carlton Fisk .... .15 .06 .01
☐ 696 Don August .... .03 .01 .00
☐ 697A Franklin Stubbs .... .08 .03 .01
(team name on front
in white)
☐ 697B Franklin Stubbs .... .08 .03 .01
(team name on front
in gray)
☐ 698 Keith Atherton .... .03 .01 .00
☐ 699 Pittsburgh Pirates TL ..... .06 .02 .00
Al Pedrique
(Tony Gwynn sliding)
☐ 700 Don Mattingly .... .20 .08 .02
☐ 701 Storm Davis .... .03 .01 .00
☐ 702 Jamie Quirk .... .03 .01 .00

☐ 703 Scott Garrelts .03 .01 .00
☐ 704 Carlos Quintana .25 .10 .02
☐ 705 Terry Kennedy .03 .01 .00
☐ 706 Pete Incaviglia .06 .02 .00
☐ 707 Steve Jeltz .03 .01 .00
☐ 708 Chuck Finley .08 .03 .01
☐ 709 Tom Herr .03 .01 .00
☐ 710 David Cone .08 .03 .01
☐ 711 Candy Sierra .06 .02 .00
☐ 712 Bill Swift .06 .02 .00
☐ 713 Ty Griffin FDP .10 .04 .01
☐ 714 Joe Morgan MG .06 .02 .00
(team checklist back)
☐ 715 Tony Pena .06 .02 .00
☐ 716 Wayne Tolleson .03 .01 .00
☐ 717 Jamie Moyer .03 .01 .00
☐ 718 Glenn Braggs .03 .01 .00
☐ 719 Danny Darwin .03 .01 .00
☐ 720 Tim Wallach .06 .02 .00
☐ 721 Ron Tingley .06 .02 .00
☐ 722 Todd Stottlemyre .15 .06 .01
☐ 723 Rafael Belliard .03 .01 .00
☐ 724 Jerry Don Gleaton .03 .01 .00
☐ 725 Terry Steinbach .06 .02 .00
☐ 726 Dickie Thon .03 .01 .00
☐ 727 Joe Orsulak .03 .01 .00
☐ 728 Charlie Puleo .03 .01 .00
☐ 729 Texas Rangers TL .03 .01 .00
Steve Buechele
(inconsistent design,
team name on front
surrounded by black,
should be white)
☐ 730 Danny Jackson .06 .02 .00
☐ 731 Mike Young .03 .01 .00
☐ 732 Steve Buechele .03 .01 .00
☐ 733 Randy Bockus .03 .01 .00
☐ 734 Jody Reed .06 .02 .00
☐ 735 Roger McDowell .03 .01 .00
☐ 736 Jeff Hamilton .03 .01 .00
☐ 737 Norm Charlton .12 .05 .01
☐ 738 Darnell Coles .03 .01 .00
☐ 739 Brook Jacoby .03 .01 .00
☐ 740 Dan Plesac .03 .01 .00
☐ 741 Ken Phelps .03 .01 .00
☐ 742 Mike Harkey FS .12 .05 .01
☐ 743 Mike Heath .03 .01 .00
☐ 744 Roger Craig MG .06 .02 .00
(team checklist back)
☐ 745 Fred McGriff .15 .06 .01
☐ 746 German Gonzalez UER .06 .02 .00
(wrong birthdate)
☐ 747 Wil Tejada .03 .01 .00
☐ 748 Jimmy Jones .03 .01 .00
☐ 749 Rafael Ramirez .03 .01 .00
☐ 750 Bret Saberhagen .10 .04 .01
☐ 751 Ken Oberkfell .03 .01 .00
☐ 752 Jim Gott .03 .01 .00
☐ 753 Jose Uribe .03 .01 .00
☐ 754 Bob Brower .03 .01 .00
☐ 755 Mike Scioscia .03 .01 .00
☐ 756 Scott Medvin .08 .03 .01
☐ 757 Brady Anderson .08 .03 .01
☐ 758 Gene Walter .03 .01 .00
☐ 759 Milwaukee Brewers TL .06 .02 .00
Rob Deer
☐ 760 Lee Smith .08 .03 .01
☐ 761 Dante Bichette .17 .07 .01
☐ 762 Bobby Thigpen .08 .03 .01
☐ 763 Dave Martinez .03 .01 .00
☐ 764 Robin Ventura FDP 1.50 .60 .15
☐ 765 Glenn Davis .08 .03 .01
☐ 766 Cecilio Guante .03 .01 .00
☐ 767 Mike Capel .06 .02 .00
☐ 768 Bill Wegman .03 .01 .00
☐ 769 Junior Ortiz .03 .01 .00
☐ 770 Alan Trammell .10 .04 .01
☐ 771 Ron Kittle .06 .02 .00
☐ 772 Ron Oester .03 .01 .00
☐ 773 Keith Moreland .03 .01 .00
☐ 774 Frank Robinson MG .10 .04 .01
(team checklist back)
☐ 775 Jeff Reardon .08 .03 .01
☐ 776 Nelson Liriano .03 .01 .00
☐ 777 Ted Power .03 .01 .00
☐ 778 Bruce Benedict .03 .01 .00
☐ 779 Craig McMurtry .03 .01 .00
☐ 780 Pedro Guerrero .08 .03 .01
☐ 781 Greg Briley .15 .06 .01
☐ 782 Checklist 661-792 .06 .01 .00
☐ 783 Trevor Wilson .10 .04 .01
☐ 784 Steve Avery FDP 2.00 .80 .20
☐ 785 Ellis Burks .15 .06 .01
☐ 786 Melido Perez .08 .03 .01
☐ 787 Dave West .12 .05 .01
☐ 788 Mike Morgan .06 .02 .00
☐ 789 Kansas City Royals TL .10 .04 .01
Bo Jackson
(throwing)
☐ 790 Sid Fernandez .06 .02 .00
☐ 791 Jim Lindeman .03 .01 .00
☐ 792 Rafael Santana .06 .02 .00

1989 Topps Traded

The 1989 Topps Traded set contains 132 standard-size (2 1/2" by 3 1/2") cards. The fronts have white borders; the horizontally-oriented backs are red and pink. From the front the cards' style is indistinguishable from

the 1989 Topps regular issue. The cards were distributed as a boxed set. The key rookies in this set are Ken Griffey Jr., Deion Sanders, and Jerome Walton. Topps also produced a specially boxed "glossy" edition frequently referred to as the Topps Traded Tiffany set. This year, again, Topps did not disclose the number of Tiffany sets they produced or sold but it seems that production quantities were roughly similar (or slightly smaller, 15,000 sets) to the previous two years. The checklist of cards is identical to that of the normal non-glossy cards. There are two primary distinguishing features of the Tiffany cards, white card stock reverses and high gloss obverses. These Tiffany cards are valued at approximately four times the values listed below.

	MINT	EXC	G-VG
COMPLETE SET (132)	9.00	4.00	.90
COMMON PLAYER (1-132)	.05	.02	.00
☐ 1T Don Aase	.10	.04	.01
☐ 2T Jim Abbott	.90	.40	.09
☐ 3T Kent Anderson	.10	.04	.01
☐ 4T Keith Atherton	.05	.02	.00
☐ 5T Wally Backman	.05	.02	.00
☐ 6T Steve Balboni	.05	.02	.00
☐ 7T Jesse Barfield	.10	.04	.01
☐ 8T Steve Bedrosian	.08	.03	.01
☐ 9T Todd Benzinger	.08	.03	.01
☐ 10T Geronimo Berroa	.05	.02	.00
☐ 11T Bert Blyleven	.12	.05	.01
☐ 12T Bob Boone	.12	.05	.01
☐ 13T Phil Bradley	.05	.02	.00
☐ 14T Jeff Brantley	.20	.08	.02
☐ 15T Kevin Brown	.08	.03	.01
☐ 16T Jerry Browne	.05	.02	.00
☐ 17T Chuck Cary	.05	.02	.00
☐ 18T Carmen Castillo	.05	.02	.00
☐ 19T Jim Clancy	.05	.02	.00
☐ 20T Jack Clark	.10	.04	.01
☐ 21T Bryan Clutterbuck	.05	.02	.00
☐ 22T Jody Davis	.05	.02	.00
☐ 23T Mike Devereaux	.08	.03	.01
☐ 24T Frank DiPino	.05	.02	.00
☐ 25T Benny Distefano	.05	.02	.00
☐ 26T John Dopson	.08	.03	.01
☐ 27T Len Dykstra	.10	.04	.01
☐ 28T Jim Eisenreich	.05	.02	.00
☐ 29T Nick Esasky	.05	.02	.00
☐ 30T Alvaro Espinoza	.08	.03	.01
☐ 31T Darrell Evans UER (Stat headings on back are for a pitcher)	.10	.04	.01
☐ 32T Junior Felix	.15	.06	.01
☐ 33T Felix Fermin	.05	.02	.00
☐ 34T Julio Franco	.12	.05	.01
☐ 35T Terry Francona	.05	.02	.00
☐ 36T Cito Gaston MG	.08	.03	.01
☐ 37T Bob Geren UER (Photo actually Mike Fennell)	.10	.04	.01
☐ 38T Tom Gordon	.20	.08	.02
☐ 39T Tommy Gregg	.08	.03	.01
☐ 40T Ken Griffey Sr.	.12	.05	.01
☐ 41T Ken Griffey Jr.	6.00	2.50	.60
☐ 42T Kevin Gross	.05	.02	.00
☐ 43T Lee Guetterman	.05	.02	.00
☐ 44T Mel Hall	.10	.04	.01
☐ 45T Erik Hanson	.50	.20	.05
☐ 46T Gene Harris	.10	.04	.01
☐ 47T Andy Hawkins	.05	.02	.00
☐ 48T Rickey Henderson	.35	.15	.03
☐ 49T Tom Herr	.08	.03	.01
☐ 50T Ken Hill	.25	.10	.02
☐ 51T Brian Holman	.17	.07	.01
☐ 52T Brian Holton	.08	.03	.01
☐ 53T Art Howe MG	.05	.02	.00
☐ 54T Ken Howell	.05	.02	.00
☐ 55T Bruce Hurst	.08	.03	.01
☐ 56T Chris James	.08	.03	.01
☐ 57T Randy Johnson	.12	.05	.01
☐ 58T Jimmy Jones	.05	.02	.00
☐ 59T Terry Kennedy	.05	.02	.00
☐ 60T Paul Kilgus	.05	.02	.00
☐ 61T Eric King	.05	.02	.00
☐ 62T Ron Kittle	.08	.03	.01
☐ 63T John Kruk	.08	.03	.01
☐ 64T Randy Kutcher	.05	.02	.00
☐ 65T Steve Lake	.05	.02	.00
☐ 66T Mark Langston	.10	.04	.01
☐ 67T Dave LaPoint	.05	.02	.00
☐ 68T Rick Leach	.05	.02	.00
☐ 69T Terry Leach	.05	.02	.00
☐ 70T Jim Lefebvre MG	.05	.02	.00
☐ 71T Al Leiter	.08	.03	.01
☐ 72T Jeffrey Leonard	.05	.02	.00
☐ 73T Derek Lilliquist	.08	.03	.01

□ 74T Rick Mahler	.05	.02	.00
□ 75T Tom McCarthy	.10	.04	.01
□ 76T Lloyd McClendon	.10	.04	.01
□ 77T Lance McCullers	.05	.02	.00
□ 78T Oddibe McDowell	.05	.02	.00
□ 79T Roger McDowell	.08	.03	.01
□ 80T Larry McWilliams	.05	.02	.00
□ 81T Randy Milligan	.10	.04	.01
□ 82T Mike Moore	.10	.04	.01
□ 83T Keith Moreland	.05	.02	.00
□ 84T Mike Morgan	.08	.03	.01
□ 85T Jamie Moyer	.05	.02	.00
□ 86T Rob Murphy	.05	.02	.00
□ 87T Eddie Murray	.12	.05	.01
□ 88T Pete O'Brien	.05	.02	.00
□ 89T Gregg Olson	.50	.20	.05
□ 90T Steve Ontiveros	.05	.02	.00
□ 91T Jesse Orosco	.05	.02	.00
□ 92T Spike Owen	.05	.02	.00
□ 93T Rafael Palmeiro	.15	.06	.01
□ 94T Clay Parker	.08	.03	.01
□ 95T Jeff Parrett	.05	.02	.00
□ 96T Lance Parrish	.10	.04	.01
□ 97T Dennis Powell	.05	.02	.00
□ 98T Rey Quinones	.05	.02	.00
□ 99T Doug Rader MG	.05	.02	.00
□ 100T Willie Randolph	.08	.03	.01
□ 101T Shane Rawley	.05	.02	.00
□ 102T Randy Ready	.05	.02	.00
□ 103T Bip Roberts	.12	.05	.01
□ 104T Kenny Rogers	.12	.05	.01
□ 105T Ed Romero	.05	.02	.00
□ 106T Nolan Ryan	1.50	.60	.15
□ 107T Luis Salazar	.05	.02	.00
□ 108T Juan Samuel	.10	.04	.01
□ 109T Alex Sanchez	.10	.04	.01
□ 110T Deion Sanders	.60	.25	.06
□ 111T Steve Sax	.12	.05	.01
□ 112T Rick Schu	.05	.02	.00
□ 113T Dwight Smith	.12	.05	.01
□ 114T Lonnie Smith	.10	.04	.01
□ 115T Billy Spiers	.12	.05	.01
□ 116T Kent Tekulve	.05	.02	.00
□ 117T Walt Terrell	.05	.02	.00
□ 118T Milt Thompson	.05	.02	.00
□ 119T Dickie Thon	.05	.02	.00
□ 120T Jeff Torborg MG	.05	.02	.00
□ 121T Jeff Treadway	.08	.03	.01
□ 122T Omar Vizquel	.10	.04	.01
□ 123T Jerome Walton	.40	.16	.04
□ 124T Gary Ward	.05	.02	.00
□ 125T Claudell Washington	.05	.02	.00
□ 126T Curt Wilkerson	.05	.02	.00
□ 127T Eddie Williams	.05	.02	.00
□ 128T Frank Williams	.05	.02	.00
□ 129T Ken Williams	.08	.03	.01
□ 130T Mitch Williams	.10	.04	.01
□ 131T Steve Wilson	.10	.04	.01
□ 132T Checklist 1T-132T	.05	.01	.00

1990 Topps

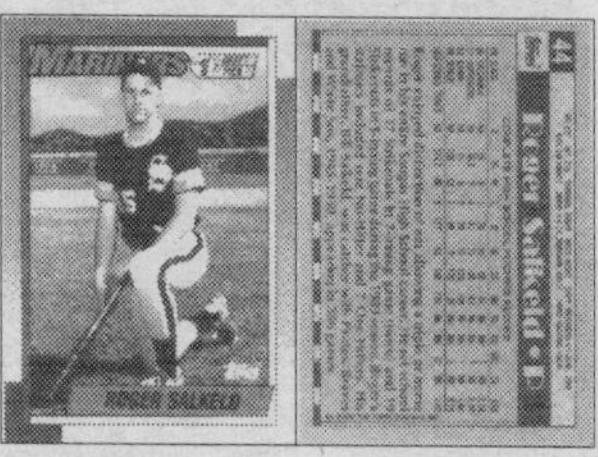

The 1990 Topps set contains 792 standard-size (2 1/2" by 3 1/2") cards. The front borders are various colors. The horizontally-oriented backs are yellowish green. Cards 385-407 contain the All-Stars. Cards 661-665 contain the Turn Back the Clock cards. The manager cards this year contain information that had been on the backs of the Team Leader cards in the past few years; the Team Leader cards were discontinued, apparently in order to allow better individual player card selection. Topps really concentrated on individual player cards in this set with 725, the most ever in a baseball card set. The checklist cards are oriented alphabetically by team name and player name. The key rookie cards in this set are Juan Gonzalez, Ben McDonald, and Frank Thomas. Topps also produced a specially boxed "glossy" edition frequently referred to as the Topps Tiffany set. This year, again, Topps did not disclose the number of Tiffany sets they produced or sold but it seems that production quantities were roughly similar (approximately 15,000 sets) to the previous year. The checklist of cards is identical to that of the normal non-glossy cards. There are two primary distinguishing features of the Tiffany cards, white card stock reverses and high gloss obverses. These Tiffany cards are valued at approximately four times the values listed below.

	MINT	EXC	G-VG
COMPLETE SET (792)	20.00	8.50	2.75
COMMON PLAYER (1-792)	.03	.01	.00
□ 1 Nolan Ryan	.50	.12	.02
□ 2 Nolan Ryan Salute New York Mets	.20	.08	.02
□ 3 Nolan Ryan Salute California Angels	.20	.08	.02
□ 4 Nolan Ryan Salute Houston Astros	.20	.08	.02
□ 5 Nolan Ryan Salute Texas Rangers UER (says Texas Stadium rather than Arlington Stadium)	.20	.08	.02
□ 6 Vince Coleman RB (50 consecutive stolen bases)	.06	.02	.00
□ 7 Rickey Henderson RB (40 career leadoff home runs)	.10	.04	.01
□ 8 Cal Ripken RB (20 or more homers for 8 consecutive years, record for shortstops)	.10	.04	.01
□ 9 Eric Plunk	.03	.01	.00
□ 10 Barry Larkin	.10	.04	.01
□ 11 Paul Gibson	.03	.01	.00
□ 12 Joe Girardi	.03	.01	.00
□ 13 Mark Williamson	.03	.01	.00
□ 14 Mike Fetters	.08	.03	.01
□ 15 Teddy Higuera	.03	.01	.00
□ 16 Kent Anderson	.03	.01	.00
□ 17 Kelly Downs	.03	.01	.00
□ 18 Carlos Quintana	.08	.03	.01
□ 19 Al Newman	.03	.01	.00
□ 20 Mark Gubicza	.06	.02	.00
□ 21 Jeff Torborg MG	.03	.01	.00
□ 22 Bruce Ruffin	.03	.01	.00
□ 23 Randy Velarde	.03	.01	.00
□ 24 Joe Hesketh	.03	.01	.00
□ 25 Willie Randolph	.06	.02	.00
□ 26 Don Slaught	.03	.01	.00
□ 27 Rick Leach	.03	.01	.00
□ 28 Duane Ward	.03	.01	.00
□ 29 John Cangelosi	.03	.01	.00
□ 30 David Cone	.08	.03	.01
□ 31 Henry Cotto	.03	.01	.00
□ 32 John Farrell	.03	.01	.00
□ 33 Greg Walker	.03	.01	.00
□ 34 Tony Fossas	.06	.02	.00
□ 35 Benito Santiago	.08	.03	.01
□ 36 John Costello	.03	.01	.00
□ 37 Domingo Ramos	.03	.01	.00
□ 38 Wes Gardner	.03	.01	.00
□ 39 Curt Ford	.03	.01	.00
□ 40 Jay Howell	.03	.01	.00
□ 41 Matt Williams	.15	.06	.01
□ 42 Jeff M. Robinson	.03	.01	.00
□ 43 Dante Bichette	.06	.02	.00
□ 44 Roger Salkeld FDP	.45	.18	.04
□ 45 Dave Parker UER (born in Jackson, not Calhoun)	.08	.03	.01
□ 46 Rob Dibble	.06	.02	.00
□ 47 Brian Harper	.06	.02	.00
□ 48 Zane Smith	.06	.02	.00
□ 49 Tom Lawless	.03	.01	.00
□ 50 Glenn Davis	.08	.03	.01
□ 51 Doug Rader MG	.03	.01	.00
□ 52 Jack Daugherty	.06	.02	.00
□ 53 Mike LaCoss	.03	.01	.00
□ 54 Joel Skinner	.03	.01	.00
□ 55 Darrell Evans UER (HR total should be 414, not 424)	.06	.02	.00
□ 56 Franklin Stubbs	.03	.01	.00
□ 57 Greg Vaughn	.45	.18	.04
□ 58 Keith Miller	.03	.01	.00
□ 59 Ted Power	.03	.01	.00
□ 60 George Brett	.12	.05	.01
□ 61 Deion Sanders	.15	.06	.01
□ 62 Ramon Martinez	.25	.10	.02
□ 63 Mike Pagliarulo	.03	.01	.00
□ 64 Danny Darwin	.03	.01	.00
□ 65 Devon White	.06	.02	.00
□ 66 Greg Litton	.06	.02	.00
□ 67 Scott Sanderson	.03	.01	.00
□ 68 Dave Henderson	.06	.02	.00
□ 69 Todd Frohwirth	.03	.01	.00
□ 70 Mike Greenwell	.12	.05	.01
□ 71 Allan Anderson	.03	.01	.00
□ 72 Jeff Huson	.08	.03	.01
□ 73 Bob Milacki	.03	.01	.00
□ 74 Jeff Jackson FDP	.10	.04	.01
□ 75 Doug Jones	.03	.01	.00
□ 76 Dave Valle	.03	.01	.00
□ 77 Dave Bergman	.03	.01	.00
□ 78 Mike Flanagan	.03	.01	.00
□ 79 Ron Kittle	.06	.02	.00
□ 80 Jeff Russell	.03	.01	.00
□ 81 Bob Rodgers MG	.03	.01	.00
□ 82 Scott Terry	.03	.01	.00
□ 83 Hensley Meulens	.12	.05	.01
□ 84 Ray Searage	.03	.01	.00
□ 85 Juan Samuel	.06	.02	.00
□ 86 Paul Kilgus	.03	.01	.00
□ 87 Rick Luecken	.08	.03	.01
□ 88 Glenn Braggs	.03	.01	.00
□ 89 Clint Zavaras	.08	.03	.01
□ 90 Jack Clark	.06	.02	.00
□ 91 Steve Frey	.08	.03	.01
□ 92 Mike Stanley	.03	.01	.00
□ 93 Shawn Hillegas	.03	.01	.00
□ 94 Herm Winningham	.03	.01	.00

☐ 95 Todd Worrell	.06	.02	.00
☐ 96 Jody Reed	.06	.02	.00
☐ 97 Curt Schilling	.06	.02	.00
☐ 98 Jose Gonzalez	.03	.01	.00
☐ 99 Rich Monteleone	.06	.02	.00
☐ 100 Will Clark	.30	.12	.03
☐ 101 Shane Rawley	.03	.01	.00
☐ 102 Stan Javier	.03	.01	.00
☐ 103 Marvin Freeman	.03	.01	.00
☐ 104 Bob Knepper	.03	.01	.00
☐ 105 Randy Myers	.03	.01	.00
☐ 106 Charlie O'Brien	.03	.01	.00
☐ 107 Fred Lynn	.06	.02	.00
☐ 108 Rod Nichols	.03	.01	.00
☐ 109 Roberto Kelly	.08	.03	.01
☐ 110 Tommy Helms MG	.03	.01	.00
☐ 111 Ed Whited	.08	.03	.01
☐ 112 Glenn Wilson	.03	.01	.00
☐ 113 Manny Lee	.03	.01	.00
☐ 114 Mike Bielecki	.03	.01	.00
☐ 115 Tony Pena	.06	.02	.00
☐ 116 Floyd Bannister	.03	.01	.00
☐ 117 Mike Sharperson	.03	.01	.00
☐ 118 Erik Hanson	.08	.03	.01
☐ 119 Billy Hatcher	.03	.01	.00
☐ 120 John Franco	.03	.01	.00
☐ 121 Robin Ventura	.50	.20	.05
☐ 122 Shawn Abner	.03	.01	.00
☐ 123 Rich Gedman	.03	.01	.00
☐ 124 Dave Dravecky	.06	.02	.00
☐ 125 Kent Hrbek	.06	.02	.00
☐ 126 Randy Kramer	.03	.01	.00
☐ 127 Mike Devereaux	.03	.01	.00
☐ 128 Checklist 1	.06	.01	.00
☐ 129 Ron Jones	.03	.01	.00
☐ 130 Bert Blyleven	.06	.02	.00
☐ 131 Matt Nokes	.06	.02	.00
☐ 132 Lance Blankenship	.03	.01	.00
☐ 133 Ricky Horton	.03	.01	.00
☐ 134 Earl Cunningham FDP	.15	.06	.01
☐ 135 Dave Magadan	.06	.02	.00
☐ 136 Kevin Brown	.03	.01	.00
☐ 137 Marty Pevey	.08	.03	.01
☐ 138 Al Leiter	.03	.01	.00
☐ 139 Greg Brock	.03	.01	.00
☐ 140 Andre Dawson	.10	.04	.01
☐ 141 John Hart MG	.03	.01	.00
☐ 142 Jeff Wetherby	.08	.03	.01
☐ 143 Rafael Belliard	.03	.01	.00
☐ 144 Bud Black	.03	.01	.00
☐ 145 Terry Steinbach	.03	.01	.00
☐ 146 Rob Richie	.03	.01	.00
☐ 147 Chuck Finley	.06	.02	.00
☐ 148 Edgar Martinez	.08	.03	.01
☐ 149 Steve Farr	.03	.01	.00
☐ 150 Kirk Gibson	.08	.03	.01
☐ 151 Rick Mahler	.03	.01	.00
☐ 152 Lonnie Smith	.06	.02	.00
☐ 153 Randy Milligan	.06	.02	.00
☐ 154 Mike Maddux	.03	.01	.00
☐ 155 Ellis Burks	.08	.03	.01
☐ 156 Ken Patterson	.03	.01	.00
☐ 157 Craig Biggio	.08	.03	.01
☐ 158 Craig Lefferts	.03	.01	.00
☐ 159 Mike Felder	.03	.01	.00
☐ 160 Dave Righetti	.06	.02	.00
☐ 161 Harold Reynolds	.06	.02	.00
☐ 162 Todd Zeile	.35	.15	.03
☐ 163 Phil Bradley	.03	.01	.00
☐ 164 Jeff Juden FDP	.35	.15	.03
☐ 165 Walt Weiss	.06	.02	.00
☐ 166 Bobby Witt	.06	.02	.00
☐ 167 Kevin Appier	.20	.08	.02
☐ 168 Jose Lind	.03	.01	.00
☐ 169 Richard Dotson	.03	.01	.00
☐ 170 George Bell	.08	.03	.01
☐ 171 Russ Nixon MG	.03	.01	.00
☐ 172 Tom Lampkin	.03	.01	.00
☐ 173 Tim Belcher	.06	.02	.00
☐ 174 Jeff Kunkel	.03	.01	.00
☐ 175 Mike Moore	.06	.02	.00
☐ 176 Luis Quinones	.03	.01	.00
☐ 177 Mike Henneman	.03	.01	.00
☐ 178 Chris James	.06	.02	.00
☐ 179 Brian Holton	.03	.01	.00
☐ 180 Tim Raines	.08	.03	.01
☐ 181 Juan Agosto	.03	.01	.00
☐ 182 Mookie Wilson	.03	.01	.00
☐ 183 Steve Lake	.03	.01	.00
☐ 184 Danny Cox	.03	.01	.00
☐ 185 Ruben Sierra	.17	.07	.01
☐ 186 Dave LaPoint	.03	.01	.00
☐ 187 Rick Wrona	.06	.02	.00
☐ 188 Mike Smithson	.03	.01	.00
☐ 189 Dick Schofield	.03	.01	.00
☐ 190 Rick Reuschel	.06	.02	.00
☐ 191 Pat Borders	.03	.01	.00
☐ 192 Don August	.03	.01	.00
☐ 193 Andy Benes	.15	.06	.01
☐ 194 Glenallen Hill	.06	.02	.00
☐ 195 Tim Burke	.03	.01	.00
☐ 196 Gerald Young	.03	.01	.00
☐ 197 Doug Drabek	.06	.02	.00
☐ 198 Mike Marshall	.06	.02	.00
☐ 199 Sergio Valdez	.08	.03	.01
☐ 200 Don Mattingly	.20	.08	.02
☐ 201 Cito Gaston MG	.06	.02	.00
☐ 202 Mike Macfarlane	.03	.01	.00
☐ 203 Mike Roesler	.08	.03	.01
☐ 204 Bob Dernier	.03	.01	.00
☐ 205 Mark Davis	.06	.02	.00
☐ 206 Nick Esasky	.03	.01	.00
☐ 207 Bob Ojeda	.03	.01	.00
☐ 208 Brook Jacoby	.03	.01	.00
☐ 209 Greg Mathews	.03	.01	.00
☐ 210 Ryne Sandberg	.30	.12	.03

□ 211 John Cerutti	.03	.01	.00
□ 212 Joe Orsulak	.03	.01	.00
□ 213 Scott Bankhead	.03	.01	.00
□ 214 Terry Francona	.03	.01	.00
□ 215 Kirk McCaskill	.03	.01	.00
□ 216 Ricky Jordan	.06	.02	.00
□ 217 Don Robinson	.03	.01	.00
□ 218 Wally Backman	.03	.01	.00
□ 219 Donn Pall	.03	.01	.00
□ 220 Barry Bonds	.15	.06	.01
□ 221 Gary Mielke	.08	.03	.01
□ 222 Kurt Stillwell UER (Graduate misspelled as gradute)	.03	.01	.00
□ 223 Tommy Gregg	.03	.01	.00
□ 224 Delino DeShields	.40	.16	.04
□ 225 Jim Deshaies	.03	.01	.00
□ 226 Mickey Hatcher	.03	.01	.00
□ 227 Kevin Tapani	.35	.15	.03
□ 228 Dave Martinez	.03	.01	.00
□ 229 David Wells	.03	.01	.00
□ 230 Keith Hernandez	.06	.02	.00
□ 231 Jack McKeon MG	.03	.01	.00
□ 232 Darnell Coles	.03	.01	.00
□ 233 Ken Hill	.06	.02	.00
□ 234 Mariano Duncan	.03	.01	.00
□ 235 Jeff Reardon	.06	.02	.00
□ 236 Hal Morris	.35	.15	.03
□ 237 Kevin Ritz	.08	.03	.01
□ 238 Felix Jose	.20	.08	.02
□ 239 Eric Show	.03	.01	.00
□ 240 Mark Grace	.12	.05	.01
□ 241 Mike Krukow	.03	.01	.00
□ 242 Fred Manrique	.03	.01	.00
□ 243 Barry Jones	.03	.01	.00
□ 244 Bill Schroeder	.03	.01	.00
□ 245 Roger Clemens	.30	.12	.03
□ 246 Jim Eisenreich	.03	.01	.00
□ 247 Jerry Reed	.03	.01	.00
□ 248 Dave Anderson	.03	.01	.00
□ 249 Mike Smith	.06	.02	.00
□ 250 Jose Canseco	.40	.16	.04
□ 251 Jeff Blauser	.03	.01	.00
□ 252 Otis Nixon	.06	.02	.00
□ 253 Mark Portugal	.03	.01	.00
□ 254 Francisco Cabrera	.10	.04	.01
□ 255 Bobby Thigpen	.06	.02	.00
□ 256 Marvell Wynne	.03	.01	.00
□ 257 Jose DeLeon	.03	.01	.00
□ 258 Barry Lyons	.03	.01	.00
□ 259 Lance McCullers	.03	.01	.00
□ 260 Eric Davis	.10	.04	.01
□ 261 Whitey Herzog MG	.03	.01	.00
□ 262 Checklist 2	.06	.01	.00
□ 263 Mel Stottlemyre Jr.	.03	.01	.00
□ 264 Bryan Clutterbuck	.03	.01	.00
□ 265 Pete O'Brien	.03	.01	.00
□ 266 German Gonzalez	.03	.01	.00
□ 267 Mark Davidson	.03	.01	.00
□ 268 Rob Murphy	.03	.01	.00
□ 269 Dickie Thon	.03	.01	.00
□ 270 Dave Stewart	.08	.03	.01
□ 271 Chet Lemon	.03	.01	.00
□ 272 Bryan Harvey	.06	.02	.00
□ 273 Bobby Bonilla	.15	.06	.01
□ 274 Mauro Gozzo	.08	.03	.01
□ 275 Mickey Tettleton	.06	.02	.00
□ 276 Gary Thurman	.03	.01	.00
□ 277 Lenny Harris	.06	.02	.00
□ 278 Pascual Perez	.03	.01	.00
□ 279 Steve Buechele	.03	.01	.00
□ 280 Lou Whitaker	.06	.02	.00
□ 281 Kevin Bass	.03	.01	.00
□ 282 Derek Lilliquist	.03	.01	.00
□ 283 Joey Belle	.60	.25	.06
□ 284 Mark Gardner	.15	.06	.01
□ 285 Willie McGee	.08	.03	.01
□ 286 Lee Guetterman	.03	.01	.00
□ 287 Vance Law	.03	.01	.00
□ 288 Greg Briley	.03	.01	.00
□ 289 Norm Charlton	.03	.01	.00
□ 290 Robin Yount	.12	.05	.01
□ 291 Dave Johnson MG	.03	.01	.00
□ 292 Jim Gott	.03	.01	.00
□ 293 Mike Gallego	.03	.01	.00
□ 294 Craig McMurtry	.03	.01	.00
□ 295 Fred McGriff	.10	.04	.01
□ 296 Jeff Ballard	.03	.01	.00
□ 297 Tommy Herr	.03	.01	.00
□ 298 Dan Gladden	.03	.01	.00
□ 299 Adam Peterson	.03	.01	.00
□ 300 Bo Jackson	.40	.16	.04
□ 301 Don Aase	.03	.01	.00
□ 302 Marcus Lawton	.10	.04	.01
□ 303 Rick Cerone	.03	.01	.00
□ 304 Marty Clary	.03	.01	.00
□ 305 Eddie Murray	.10	.04	.01
□ 306 Tom Niedenfuer	.03	.01	.00
□ 307 Bip Roberts	.03	.01	.00
□ 308 Jose Guzman	.03	.01	.00
□ 309 Eric Yelding	.06	.02	.00
□ 310 Steve Bedrosian	.03	.01	.00
□ 311 Dwight Smith	.06	.02	.00
□ 312 Dan Quisenberry	.06	.02	.00
□ 313 Gus Polidor	.03	.01	.00
□ 314 Donald Harris FDP	.12	.05	.01
□ 315 Bruce Hurst	.06	.02	.00
□ 316 Carney Lansford	.06	.02	.00
□ 317 Mark Guthrie	.08	.03	.01
□ 318 Wallace Johnson	.03	.01	.00
□ 319 Dion James	.03	.01	.00
□ 320 Dave Stieb	.06	.02	.00
□ 321 Joe Morgan MG	.03	.01	.00
□ 322 Junior Ortiz	.03	.01	.00
□ 323 Willie Wilson	.06	.02	.00
□ 324 Pete Harnisch	.06	.02	.00

- ☐ 325 Robby Thompson .... .03 .01 .00
- ☐ 326 Tom McCarthy .... .06 .02 .00
- ☐ 327 Ken Williams .... .03 .01 .00
- ☐ 328 Curt Young .... .03 .01 .00
- ☐ 329 Oddibe McDowell .... .03 .01 .00
- ☐ 330 Ron Darling .... .06 .02 .00
- ☐ 331 Juan Gonzalez .... 1.75 .70 .17
- ☐ 332 Paul O'Neill .... .06 .02 .00
- ☐ 333 Bill Wegman .... .03 .01 .00
- ☐ 334 Johnny Ray .... .03 .01 .00
- ☐ 335 Andy Hawkins .... .03 .01 .00
- ☐ 336 Ken Griffey Jr. .... 1.50 .60 .15
- ☐ 337 Lloyd McClendon .... .03 .01 .00
- ☐ 338 Dennis Lamp .... .03 .01 .00
- ☐ 339 Dave Clark .... .03 .01 .00
- ☐ 340 Fernando Valenzuela .... .08 .03 .01
- ☐ 341 Tom Foley .... .03 .01 .00
- ☐ 342 Alex Trevino .... .03 .01 .00
- ☐ 343 Frank Tanana .... .06 .02 .00
- ☐ 344 George Canale .... .10 .04 .01
- ☐ 345 Harold Baines .... .08 .03 .01
- ☐ 346 Jim Presley .... .03 .01 .00
- ☐ 347 Junior Felix .... .06 .02 .00
- ☐ 348 Gary Wayne .... .08 .03 .01
- ☐ 349 Steve Finley .... .10 .04 .01
- ☐ 350 Bret Saberhagen .... .08 .03 .01
- ☐ 351 Roger Craig MG .... .03 .01 .00
- ☐ 352 Bryn Smith .... .03 .01 .00
- ☐ 353 Sandy Alomar Jr. .... .10 .04 .01
  (not listed as Jr.
  on card front)
- ☐ 354 Stan Belinda .... .12 .05 .01
- ☐ 355 Marty Barrett .... .03 .01 .00
- ☐ 356 Randy Ready .... .03 .01 .00
- ☐ 357 Dave West .... .03 .01 .00
- ☐ 358 Andres Thomas .... .03 .01 .00
- ☐ 359 Jimmy Jones .... .03 .01 .00
- ☐ 360 Paul Molitor .... .08 .03 .01
- ☐ 361 Randy McCament .... .06 .02 .00
- ☐ 362 Damon Berryhill .... .03 .01 .00
- ☐ 363 Dan Petry .... .03 .01 .00
- ☐ 364 Rolando Roomes .... .03 .01 .00
- ☐ 365 Ozzie Guillen .... .06 .02 .00
- ☐ 366 Mike Heath .... .03 .01 .00
- ☐ 367 Mike Morgan .... .03 .01 .00
- ☐ 368 Bill Doran .... .03 .01 .00
- ☐ 369 Todd Burns .... .03 .01 .00
- ☐ 370 Tim Wallach .... .06 .02 .00
- ☐ 371 Jimmy Key .... .06 .02 .00
- ☐ 372 Terry Kennedy .... .03 .01 .00
- ☐ 373 Alvin Davis .... .06 .02 .00
- ☐ 374 Steve Cummings .... .08 .03 .01
- ☐ 375 Dwight Evans .... .06 .02 .00
- ☐ 376 Checklist 3 UER .... .06 .01 .00
  (Higuera misalphabet-
  ized in Brewer list)
- ☐ 377 Mickey Weston .... .08 .03 .01
- ☐ 378 Luis Salazar .... .03 .01 .00
- ☐ 379 Steve Rosenberg .... .03 .01 .00
- ☐ 380 Dave Winfield .... .10 .04 .01
- ☐ 381 Frank Robinson MG .... .08 .03 .01
- ☐ 382 Jeff Musselman .... .03 .01 .00
- ☐ 383 John Morris .... .03 .01 .00
- ☐ 384 Pat Combs .... .06 .02 .00
- ☐ 385 Fred McGriff AS .... .08 .03 .01
- ☐ 386 Julio Franco AS .... .08 .03 .01
- ☐ 387 Wade Boggs AS .... .10 .04 .01
- ☐ 388 Cal Ripken AS .... .12 .05 .01
- ☐ 389 Robin Yount AS .... .08 .03 .01
- ☐ 390 Ruben Sierra AS .... .10 .04 .01
- ☐ 391 Kirby Puckett AS .... .10 .04 .01
- ☐ 392 Carlton Fisk AS .... .08 .03 .01
- ☐ 393 Bret Saberhagen AS .... .08 .03 .01
- ☐ 394 Jeff Ballard AS .... .03 .01 .00
- ☐ 395 Jeff Russell AS .... .03 .01 .00
- ☐ 396 A.Bartlett Giamatti .... .12 .05 .01
  (commemorative)
- ☐ 397 Will Clark AS .... .15 .06 .01
- ☐ 398 Ryne Sandberg AS .... .12 .05 .01
- ☐ 399 Howard Johnson AS .... .08 .03 .01
- ☐ 400 Ozzie Smith AS .... .08 .03 .01
- ☐ 401 Kevin Mitchell AS .... .08 .03 .01
- ☐ 402 Eric Davis AS .... .08 .03 .01
- ☐ 403 Tony Gwynn AS .... .08 .03 .01
- ☐ 404 Craig Biggio AS .... .06 .02 .00
- ☐ 405 Mike Scott AS .... .06 .02 .00
- ☐ 406 Joe Magrane AS .... .03 .01 .00
- ☐ 407 Mark Davis AS .... .03 .01 .00
- ☐ 408 Trevor Wilson .... .03 .01 .00
- ☐ 409 Tom Brunansky .... .06 .02 .00
- ☐ 410 Joe Boever .... .03 .01 .00
- ☐ 411 Ken Phelps .... .03 .01 .00
- ☐ 412 Jamie Moyer .... .03 .01 .00
- ☐ 413 Brian Dubois .... .08 .03 .01
- ☐ 414A Frank Thomas FDP .... 4.00 1.75 .40
  ERR (Name missing
  on card front)
- ☐ 414B Frank Thomas FDP COR4.00 1.75 .40
- ☐ 415 Shawon Dunston .... .08 .03 .01
- ☐ 416 Dave Johnson (P) .... .08 .03 .01
- ☐ 417 Jim Gantner .... .03 .01 .00
- ☐ 418 Tom Browning .... .06 .02 .00
- ☐ 419 Beau Allred .... .12 .05 .01
- ☐ 420 Carlton Fisk .... .12 .05 .01
- ☐ 421 Greg Minton .... .03 .01 .00
- ☐ 422 Pat Sheridan .... .03 .01 .00
- ☐ 423 Fred Toliver .... .03 .01 .00
- ☐ 424 Jerry Reuss .... .03 .01 .00
- ☐ 425 Bill Landrum .... .03 .01 .00
- ☐ 426 Jeff Hamilton .... .03 .01 .00
- ☐ 427 Carmen Castillo .... .03 .01 .00
- ☐ 428 Steve Davis .... .08 .03 .01
- ☐ 429 Tom Kelly MG .... .03 .01 .00
- ☐ 430 Pete Incaviglia .... .06 .02 .00
- ☐ 431 Randy Johnson .... .06 .02 .00
- ☐ 432 Damaso Garcia .... .03 .01 .00

□ 433 Steve Olin	.08	.03	.01
□ 434 Mark Carreon	.03	.01	.00
□ 435 Kevin Seitzer	.06	.02	.00
□ 436 Mel Hall	.06	.02	.00
□ 437 Les Lancaster	.03	.01	.00
□ 438 Greg Myers	.03	.01	.00
□ 439 Jeff Parrett	.03	.01	.00
□ 440 Alan Trammell	.08	.03	.01
□ 441 Bob Kipper	.03	.01	.00
□ 442 Jerry Browne	.03	.01	.00
□ 443 Cris Carpenter	.03	.01	.00
□ 444 Kyle Abbott FDP	.25	.10	.02
□ 445 Danny Jackson	.03	.01	.00
□ 446 Dan Pasqua	.03	.01	.00
□ 447 Atlee Hammaker	.03	.01	.00
□ 448 Greg Gagne	.03	.01	.00
□ 449 Dennis Rasmussen	.03	.01	.00
□ 450 Rickey Henderson	.25	.10	.02
□ 451 Mark Lemke	.06	.02	.00
□ 452 Luis De Los Santos	.03	.01	.00
□ 453 Jody Davis	.03	.01	.00
□ 454 Jeff King	.06	.02	.00
□ 455 Jeffrey Leonard	.03	.01	.00
□ 456 Chris Gwynn	.03	.01	.00
□ 457 Gregg Jefferies	.10	.04	.01
□ 458 Bob McClure	.03	.01	.00
□ 459 Jim Lefebvre MG	.03	.01	.00
□ 460 Mike Scott	.06	.02	.00
□ 461 Carlos Martinez	.06	.02	.00
□ 462 Denny Walling	.03	.01	.00
□ 463 Drew Hall	.03	.01	.00
□ 464 Jerome Walton	.08	.03	.01
□ 465 Kevin Gross	.03	.01	.00
□ 466 Rance Mulliniks	.03	.01	.00
□ 467 Juan Nieves	.03	.01	.00
□ 468 Bill Ripken	.03	.01	.00
□ 469 John Kruk	.03	.01	.00
□ 470 Frank Viola	.08	.03	.01
□ 471 Mike Brumley	.03	.01	.00
□ 472 Jose Uribe	.03	.01	.00
□ 473 Joe Price	.03	.01	.00
□ 474 Rich Thompson	.03	.01	.00
□ 475 Bob Welch	.06	.02	.00
□ 476 Brad Komminsk	.03	.01	.00
□ 477 Willie Fraser	.03	.01	.00
□ 478 Mike LaValliere	.03	.01	.00
□ 479 Frank White	.03	.01	.00
□ 480 Sid Fernandez	.06	.02	.00
□ 481 Garry Templeton	.03	.01	.00
□ 482 Steve Carter	.06	.02	.00
□ 483 Alejandro Pena	.06	.02	.00
□ 484 Mike Fitzgerald	.03	.01	.00
□ 485 John Candelaria	.03	.01	.00
□ 486 Jeff Treadway	.03	.01	.00
□ 487 Steve Searcy	.03	.01	.00
□ 488 Ken Oberkfell	.03	.01	.00
□ 489 Nick Leyva MG	.03	.01	.00
□ 490 Dan Plesac	.03	.01	.00
□ 491 Dave Cochrane	.08	.03	.01
□ 492 Ron Oester	.03	.01	.00
□ 493 Jason Grimsley	.08	.03	.01
□ 494 Terry Puhl	.03	.01	.00
□ 495 Lee Smith	.06	.02	.00
□ 496 Cecil Espy UER ('89 stats have 3 SB's, should be 33)	.03	.01	.00
□ 497 Dave Schmidt	.03	.01	.00
□ 498 Rick Schu	.03	.01	.00
□ 499 Bill Long	.03	.01	.00
□ 500 Kevin Mitchell	.10	.04	.01
□ 501 Matt Young	.03	.01	.00
□ 502 Mitch Webster	.03	.01	.00
□ 503 Randy St.Claire	.03	.01	.00
□ 504 Tom O'Malley	.03	.01	.00
□ 505 Kelly Gruber	.08	.03	.01
□ 506 Tom Glavine	.20	.08	.02
□ 507 Gary Redus	.03	.01	.00
□ 508 Terry Leach	.03	.01	.00
□ 509 Tom Pagnozzi	.03	.01	.00
□ 510 Dwight Gooden	.10	.04	.01
□ 511 Clay Parker	.03	.01	.00
□ 512 Gary Pettis	.03	.01	.00
□ 513 Mark Eichhorn	.03	.01	.00
□ 514 Andy Allanson	.03	.01	.00
□ 515 Len Dykstra	.06	.02	.00
□ 516 Tim Leary	.06	.02	.00
□ 517 Roberto Alomar	.15	.06	.01
□ 518 Bill Krueger	.03	.01	.00
□ 519 Bucky Dent MG	.06	.02	.00
□ 520 Mitch Williams	.03	.01	.00
□ 521 Craig Worthington	.03	.01	.00
□ 522 Mike Dunne	.03	.01	.00
□ 523 Jay Bell	.03	.01	.00
□ 524 Daryl Boston	.03	.01	.00
□ 525 Wally Joyner	.08	.03	.01
□ 526 Checklist 4	.06	.01	.00
□ 527 Ron Hassey	.03	.01	.00
□ 528 Kevin Wickander	.06	.02	.00
□ 529 Greg Harris	.03	.01	.00
□ 530 Mark Langston	.06	.02	.00
□ 531 Ken Caminiti	.03	.01	.00
□ 532 Cecilio Guante	.03	.01	.00
□ 533 Tim Jones	.03	.01	.00
□ 534 Louie Meadows	.03	.01	.00
□ 535 John Smoltz	.15	.06	.01
□ 536 Bob Geren	.03	.01	.00
□ 537 Mark Grant	.03	.01	.00
□ 538 Bill Spiers UER (photo actually George Canale)	.08	.03	.01
□ 539 Neal Heaton	.03	.01	.00
□ 540 Danny Tartabull	.08	.03	.01
□ 541 Pat Perry	.03	.01	.00
□ 542 Darren Daulton	.06	.02	.00
□ 543 Nelson Liriano	.03	.01	.00
□ 544 Dennis Boyd	.03	.01	.00

Card	Player			
☐ 545	Kevin McReynolds	.08	.03	.01
☐ 546	Kevin Hickey	.03	.01	.00
☐ 547	Jack Howell	.03	.01	.00
☐ 548	Pat Clements	.03	.01	.00
☐ 549	Don Zimmer MG	.03	.01	.00
☐ 550	Julio Franco	.08	.03	.01
☐ 551	Tim Crews	.03	.01	.00
☐ 552	Mike Smith	.06	.02	.00
☐ 553	Scott Scudder UER (Cedar Rap1ds)	.10	.04	.01
☐ 554	Jay Buhner	.08	.03	.01
☐ 555	Jack Morris	.08	.03	.01
☐ 556	Gene Larkin	.03	.01	.00
☐ 557	Jeff Innis	.10	.04	.01
☐ 558	Rafael Ramirez	.03	.01	.00
☐ 559	Andy McGaffigan	.03	.01	.00
☐ 560	Steve Sax	.08	.03	.01
☐ 561	Ken Dayley	.03	.01	.00
☐ 562	Chad Kreuter	.03	.01	.00
☐ 563	Alex Sanchez	.06	.02	.00
☐ 564	Tyler Houston FDP	.12	.05	.01
☐ 565	Scott Fletcher	.03	.01	.00
☐ 566	Mark Knudson	.03	.01	.00
☐ 567	Ron Gant	.25	.10	.02
☐ 568	John Smiley	.06	.02	.00
☐ 569	Ivan Calderon	.06	.02	.00
☐ 570	Cal Ripken	.30	.12	.03
☐ 571	Brett Butler	.06	.02	.00
☐ 572	Greg A. Harris	.03	.01	.00
☐ 573	Danny Heep	.03	.01	.00
☐ 574	Bill Swift	.03	.01	.00
☐ 575	Lance Parrish	.06	.02	.00
☐ 576	Mike Dyer	.08	.03	.01
☐ 577	Charlie Hayes	.06	.02	.00
☐ 578	Joe Magrane	.03	.01	.00
☐ 579	Art Howe MG	.03	.01	.00
☐ 580	Joe Carter	.10	.04	.01
☐ 581	Ken Griffey Sr.	.08	.03	.01
☐ 582	Rick Honeycutt	.03	.01	.00
☐ 583	Bruce Benedict	.03	.01	.00
☐ 584	Phil Stephenson	.06	.02	.00
☐ 585	Kal Daniels	.06	.02	.00
☐ 586	Edwin Nunez	.03	.01	.00
☐ 587	Lance Johnson	.03	.01	.00
☐ 588	Rick Rhoden	.03	.01	.00
☐ 589	Mike Aldrete	.03	.01	.00
☐ 590	Ozzie Smith	.10	.04	.01
☐ 591	Todd Stottlemyre	.08	.03	.01
☐ 592	R.J. Reynolds	.03	.01	.00
☐ 593	Scott Bradley	.03	.01	.00
☐ 594	Luis Sojo	.10	.04	.01
☐ 595	Greg Swindell	.06	.02	.00
☐ 596	Jose DeJesus	.03	.01	.00
☐ 597	Chris Bosio	.03	.01	.00
☐ 598	Brady Anderson	.03	.01	.00
☐ 599	Frank Williams	.03	.01	.00
☐ 600	Darryl Strawberry	.25	.10	.02
☐ 601	Luis Rivera	.03	.01	.00
☐ 602	Scott Garrelts	.03	.01	.00
☐ 603	Tony Armas	.03	.01	.00
☐ 604	Ron Robinson	.03	.01	.00
☐ 605	Mike Scioscia	.03	.01	.00
☐ 606	Storm Davis	.03	.01	.00
☐ 607	Steve Jeltz	.03	.01	.00
☐ 608	Eric Anthony	.17	.07	.01
☐ 609	Sparky Anderson MG	.06	.02	.00
☐ 610	Pedro Guerrero	.06	.02	.00
☐ 611	Walt Terrell	.03	.01	.00
☐ 612	Dave Gallagher	.03	.01	.00
☐ 613	Jeff Pico	.03	.01	.00
☐ 614	Nelson Santovenia	.03	.01	.00
☐ 615	Rob Deer	.06	.02	.00
☐ 616	Brian Holman	.08	.03	.01
☐ 617	Geronimo Berroa	.03	.01	.00
☐ 618	Ed Whitson	.03	.01	.00
☐ 619	Rob Ducey	.03	.01	.00
☐ 620	Tony Castillo	.03	.01	.00
☐ 621	Melido Perez	.03	.01	.00
☐ 622	Sid Bream	.03	.01	.00
☐ 623	Jim Corsi	.03	.01	.00
☐ 624	Darrin Jackson	.03	.01	.00
☐ 625	Roger McDowell	.03	.01	.00
☐ 626	Bob Melvin	.03	.01	.00
☐ 627	Jose Rijo	.06	.02	.00
☐ 628	Candy Maldonado	.03	.01	.00
☐ 629	Eric Hetzel	.03	.01	.00
☐ 630	Gary Gaetti	.06	.02	.00
☐ 631	John Wetteland	.08	.03	.01
☐ 632	Scott Lusader	.03	.01	.00
☐ 633	Dennis Cook	.06	.02	.00
☐ 634	Luis Polonia	.03	.01	.00
☐ 635	Brian Downing	.03	.01	.00
☐ 636	Jesse Orosco	.03	.01	.00
☐ 637	Craig Reynolds	.03	.01	.00
☐ 638	Jeff Montgomery	.03	.01	.00
☐ 639	Tony LaRussa MG	.06	.02	.00
☐ 640	Rick Sutcliffe	.06	.02	.00
☐ 641	Doug Strange	.08	.03	.01
☐ 642	Jack Armstrong	.06	.02	.00
☐ 643	Alfredo Griffin	.03	.01	.00
☐ 644	Paul Assenmacher	.03	.01	.00
☐ 645	Jose Oquendo	.03	.01	.00
☐ 646	Checklist 5	.06	.01	.00
☐ 647	Rex Hudler	.03	.01	.00
☐ 648	Jim Clancy	.03	.01	.00
☐ 649	Dan Murphy	.08	.03	.01
☐ 650	Mike Witt	.03	.01	.00
☐ 651	Rafael Santana	.03	.01	.00
☐ 652	Mike Boddicker	.03	.01	.00
☐ 653	John Moses	.03	.01	.00
☐ 654	Paul Coleman FDP	.17	.07	.01
☐ 655	Gregg Olson	.12	.05	.01
☐ 656	Mackey Sasser	.03	.01	.00
☐ 657	Terry Mulholland	.06	.02	.00
☐ 658	Donell Nixon	.03	.01	.00
☐ 659	Greg Cadaret	.03	.01	.00

☐ 660 Vince Coleman	.08	.03	.01
☐ 661 Dick Howser TBC'85 UER (Seaver's 300th on 7/11/85, should be 8/4/85)	.03	.01	.00
☐ 662 Mike Schmidt TBC'80	.10	.04	.01
☐ 663 Fred Lynn TBC'75	.06	.02	.00
☐ 664 Johnny Bench TBC'70	.08	.03	.01
☐ 665 Sandy Koufax TBC'65	.08	.03	.01
☐ 666 Brian Fisher	.03	.01	.00
☐ 667 Curt Wilkerson	.03	.01	.00
☐ 668 Joe Oliver	.08	.03	.01
☐ 669 Tom Lasorda MG	.06	.02	.00
☐ 670 Dennis Eckersley	.08	.03	.01
☐ 671 Bob Boone	.06	.02	.00
☐ 672 Roy Smith	.03	.01	.00
☐ 673 Joey Meyer	.03	.01	.00
☐ 674 Spike Owen	.03	.01	.00
☐ 675 Jim Abbott	.17	.07	.01
☐ 676 Randy Kutcher	.03	.01	.00
☐ 677 Jay Tibbs	.03	.01	.00
☐ 678 Kirt Manwaring UER ('88 Phoenix stats repeated)	.03	.01	.00
☐ 679 Gary Ward	.03	.01	.00
☐ 680 Howard Johnson	.08	.03	.01
☐ 681 Mike Schooler	.03	.01	.00
☐ 682 Dann Bilardello	.03	.01	.00
☐ 683 Kenny Rogers	.06	.02	.00
☐ 684 Julio Machado	.08	.03	.01
☐ 685 Tony Fernandez	.06	.02	.00
☐ 686 Carmelo Martinez	.03	.01	.00
☐ 687 Tim Birtsas	.03	.01	.00
☐ 688 Milt Thompson	.03	.01	.00
☐ 689 Rich Yett	.03	.01	.00
☐ 690 Mark McGwire	.15	.06	.01
☐ 691 Chuck Cary	.03	.01	.00
☐ 692 Sammy Sosa	.25	.10	.02
☐ 693 Calvin Schiraldi	.03	.01	.00
☐ 694 Mike Stanton	.08	.03	.01
☐ 695 Tom Henke	.06	.02	.00
☐ 696 B.J. Surhoff	.03	.01	.00
☐ 697 Mike Davis	.03	.01	.00
☐ 698 Omar Vizquel	.03	.01	.00
☐ 699 Jim Leyland MG	.03	.01	.00
☐ 700 Kirby Puckett	.20	.08	.02
☐ 701 Bernie Williams	.50	.20	.05
☐ 702 Tony Phillips	.03	.01	.00
☐ 703 Jeff Brantley	.08	.03	.01
☐ 704 Chip Hale	.08	.03	.01
☐ 705 Claudell Washington	.03	.01	.00
☐ 706 Geno Petralli	.03	.01	.00
☐ 707 Luis Aquino	.03	.01	.00
☐ 708 Larry Sheets	.03	.01	.00
☐ 709 Juan Berenguer	.03	.01	.00
☐ 710 Von Hayes	.06	.02	.00
☐ 711 Rick Aguilera	.03	.01	.00
☐ 712 Todd Benzinger	.03	.01	.00
☐ 713 Tim Drummond	.08	.03	.01
☐ 714 Marquis Grissom	.40	.16	.04
☐ 715 Greg Maddux	.06	.02	.00
☐ 716 Steve Balboni	.03	.01	.00
☐ 717 Ron Karkovice	.03	.01	.00
☐ 718 Gary Sheffield	.08	.03	.01
☐ 719 Wally Whitehurst	.06	.02	.00
☐ 720 Andres Galarraga	.06	.02	.00
☐ 721 Lee Mazzilli	.03	.01	.00
☐ 722 Felix Fermin	.03	.01	.00
☐ 723 Jeff D. Robinson	.03	.01	.00
☐ 724 Juan Bell	.06	.02	.00
☐ 725 Terry Pendleton	.08	.03	.01
☐ 726 Gene Nelson	.03	.01	.00
☐ 727 Pat Tabler	.03	.01	.00
☐ 728 Jim Acker	.03	.01	.00
☐ 729 Bobby Valentine MG	.03	.01	.00
☐ 730 Tony Gwynn	.15	.06	.01
☐ 731 Don Carman	.03	.01	.00
☐ 732 Ernest Riles	.03	.01	.00
☐ 733 John Dopson	.03	.01	.00
☐ 734 Kevin Elster	.03	.01	.00
☐ 735 Charlie Hough	.03	.01	.00
☐ 736 Rick Dempsey	.03	.01	.00
☐ 737 Chris Sabo	.10	.04	.01
☐ 738 Gene Harris	.06	.02	.00
☐ 739 Dale Sveum	.03	.01	.00
☐ 740 Jesse Barfield	.06	.02	.00
☐ 741 Steve Wilson	.03	.01	.00
☐ 742 Ernie Whitt	.03	.01	.00
☐ 743 Tom Candiotti	.06	.02	.00
☐ 744 Kelly Mann	.08	.03	.01
☐ 745 Hubie Brooks	.03	.01	.00
☐ 746 Dave Smith	.03	.01	.00
☐ 747 Randy Bush	.03	.01	.00
☐ 748 Doyle Alexander	.03	.01	.00
☐ 749 Mark Parent UER ('87 BA .80, should be .080)	.03	.01	.00
☐ 750 Dale Murphy	.10	.04	.01
☐ 751 Steve Lyons	.03	.01	.00
☐ 752 Tom Gordon	.08	.03	.01
☐ 753 Chris Speier	.03	.01	.00
☐ 754 Bob Walk	.03	.01	.00
☐ 755 Rafael Palmeiro	.12	.05	.01
☐ 756 Ken Howell	.03	.01	.00
☐ 757 Larry Walker	.25	.10	.02
☐ 758 Mark Thurmond	.03	.01	.00
☐ 759 Tom Trebelhorn MG	.03	.01	.00
☐ 760 Wade Boggs	.15	.06	.01
☐ 761 Mike Jackson	.03	.01	.00
☐ 762 Doug Dascenzo	.03	.01	.00
☐ 763 Dennis Martinez	.06	.02	.00
☐ 764 Tim Teufel	.03	.01	.00
☐ 765 Chili Davis	.06	.02	.00
☐ 766 Brian Meyer	.06	.02	.00
☐ 767 Tracy Jones	.03	.01	.00
☐ 768 Chuck Crim	.03	.01	.00

☐ 769 Greg Hibbard	.15	.06	.01
☐ 770 Cory Snyder	.06	.02	.00
☐ 771 Pete Smith	.03	.01	.00
☐ 772 Jeff Reed	.03	.01	.00
☐ 773 Dave Leiper	.03	.01	.00
☐ 774 Ben McDonald	.75	.30	.07
☐ 775 Andy Van Slyke	.08	.03	.01
☐ 776 Charlie Leibrandt	.03	.01	.00
☐ 777 Tim Laudner	.03	.01	.00
☐ 778 Mike Jeffcoat	.03	.01	.00
☐ 779 Lloyd Moseby	.03	.01	.00
☐ 780 Orel Hershiser	.08	.03	.01
☐ 781 Mario Diaz	.03	.01	.00
☐ 782 Jose Alvarez	.03	.01	.00
☐ 783 Checklist 6	.06	.01	.00
☐ 784 Scott Bailes	.03	.01	.00
☐ 785 Jim Rice	.08	.03	.01
☐ 786 Eric King	.03	.01	.00
☐ 787 Rene Gonzales	.03	.01	.00
☐ 788 Frank DiPino	.03	.01	.00
☐ 789 John Wathan MG	.03	.01	.00
☐ 790 Gary Carter	.08	.03	.01
☐ 791 Alvaro Espinoza	.03	.01	.00
☐ 792 Gerald Perry	.06	.02	.00

1990 Topps Traded

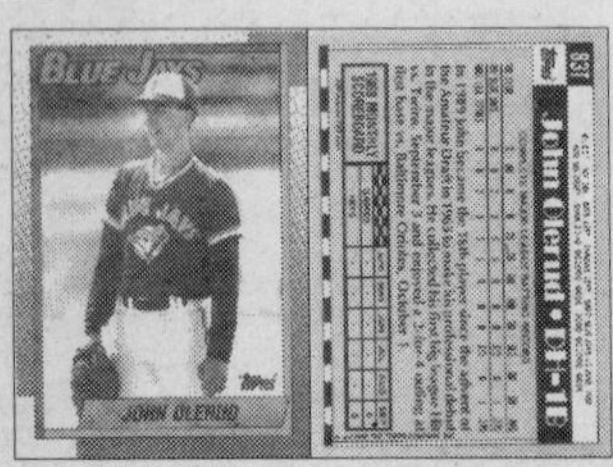

The 1990 Topps Traded Set was the tenth consecutive year Topps issued a set at the end of the year. This 132-card standard size set of 2 1/2" by 3 1/2" was arranged alphabetically by player and includes a mix of traded players and rookies for whom Topps did not include a card in the regular set. The key rookie cards in this set are Scott Erickson, Travis Fryman, Dave Justice, Kevin Maas, and John Olerud. Also for the first time, Topps not only issued the set in a special collector boxes (made in Ireland) but distributed (on a significant basis) the set via their own wax packs. The wax pack cards were produced Topps' Duryea, Pennsylvania plant. There were seven cards in the packs and the wrapper highlighted the set as containing promising rookies, players who changed teams, and new managers. The cards differ in that the Irish-made cards have the whiter-type backs typical of the cards made in Ireland while the American cards have the typical Topps gray-type card stock on the back. Topps also produced a specially boxed "glossy" edition frequently referred to as the Topps Traded Tiffany set. This year, again, Topps did not disclose the number of Tiffany sets they produced or sold but it seems that production quantities were roughly similar (approximately 15,000 sets) to the previous year. The checklist of cards is identical to that of the normal non-glossy cards. There are two primary distinguishing features of the Tiffany cards, white card stock reverses and high gloss obverses. These Tiffany cards are valued at approximately four times the values listed below.

	MINT	EXC	G-VG
COMPLETE SET (132)	10.00	4.50	1.25
COMMON PLAYER (1T-132T)	.05	.02	.00
☐ 1T Darrel Akerfelds	.05	.02	.00
☐ 2T Sandy Alomar Jr.	.12	.05	.01
☐ 3T Brad Arnsberg	.10	.04	.01
☐ 4T Steve Avery	.90	.40	.09
☐ 5T Wally Backman	.05	.02	.00
☐ 6T Carlos Baerga	.40	.16	.04
☐ 7T Kevin Bass	.08	.03	.01
☐ 8T Willie Blair	.08	.03	.01
☐ 9T Mike Blowers	.10	.04	.01
☐ 10T Shawn Boskie	.12	.05	.01
☐ 11T Daryl Boston	.05	.02	.00
☐ 12T Dennis Boyd	.05	.02	.00
☐ 13T Glenn Braggs	.05	.02	.00
☐ 14T Hubie Brooks	.08	.03	.01
☐ 15T Tom Brunansky	.08	.03	.01
☐ 16T John Burkett	.15	.06	.01
☐ 17T Casey Candaele	.05	.02	.00
☐ 18T John Candelaria	.05	.02	.00
☐ 19T Gary Carter	.10	.04	.01
☐ 20T Joe Carter	.12	.05	.01
☐ 21T Rick Cerone	.05	.02	.00
☐ 22T Scott Coolbaugh	.12	.05	.01
☐ 23T Bobby Cox MG	.05	.02	.00
☐ 24T Mark Davis	.10	.04	.01
☐ 25T Storm Davis	.05	.02	.00
☐ 26T Edgar Diaz	.10	.04	.01
☐ 27T Wayne Edwards	.10	.04	.01

☐ 28T Mark Eichhorn .08 .03 .01
☐ 29T Scott Erickson 3.00 1.25 .30
☐ 30T Nick Esasky .05 .02 .00
☐ 31T Cecil Fielder .35 .15 .03
☐ 32T John Franco .08 .03 .01
☐ 33T Travis Fryman 1.25 .50 .12
☐ 34T Bill Gullickson .08 .03 .01
☐ 35T Darryl Hamilton .10 .04 .01
☐ 36T Mike Harkey .12 .05 .01
☐ 37T Bud Harrelson MG .08 .03 .01
☐ 38T Billy Hatcher .08 .03 .01
☐ 39T Keith Hernandez .10 .04 .01
☐ 40T Joe Hesketh .08 .03 .01
☐ 41T Dave Hollins .35 .15 .03
☐ 42T Sam Horn .10 .04 .01
☐ 43T Steve Howard .15 .06 .01
☐ 44T Todd Hundley .35 .15 .03
☐ 45T Jeff Huson .10 .04 .01
☐ 46T Chris James .08 .03 .01
☐ 47T Stan Javier .05 .02 .00
☐ 48T Dave Justice 2.50 1.00 .25
☐ 49T Jeff Kaiser .08 .03 .01
☐ 50T Dana Kiecker .10 .04 .01
☐ 51T Joe Klink .12 .05 .01
☐ 52T Brent Knackert .12 .05 .01
☐ 53T Brad Komminsk .05 .02 .00
☐ 54T Mark Langston .10 .04 .01
☐ 55T Tim Layana .10 .04 .01
☐ 56T Rick Leach .05 .02 .00
☐ 57T Terry Leach .05 .02 .00
☐ 58T Tim Leary .10 .04 .01
☐ 59T Craig Lefferts .05 .02 .00
☐ 60T Charlie Leibrandt .05 .02 .00
☐ 61T Jim Leyritz .10 .04 .01
☐ 62T Fred Lynn .10 .04 .01
☐ 63T Kevin Maas 1.25 .50 .12
☐ 64T Shane Mack .12 .05 .01
☐ 65T Candy Maldonado .08 .03 .01
☐ 66T Fred Manrique .05 .02 .00
☐ 67T Mike Marshall .08 .03 .01
☐ 68T Carmelo Martinez .05 .02 .00
☐ 69T John Marzano .08 .03 .01
☐ 70T Ben McDonald .75 .30 .07
☐ 71T Jack McDowell .15 .06 .01
☐ 72T John McNamara MG .05 .02 .00
☐ 73T Orlando Mercado .05 .02 .00
☐ 74T Stump Merrill MG .08 .03 .01
☐ 75T Alan Mills .10 .04 .01
☐ 76T Hal Morris .35 .15 .03
☐ 77T Lloyd Moseby .05 .02 .00
☐ 78T Randy Myers .08 .03 .01
☐ 79T Tim Naehring .25 .10 .02
☐ 80T Junior Noboa .08 .03 .01
☐ 81T Matt Nokes .10 .04 .01
☐ 82T Pete O'Brien .05 .02 .00
☐ 83T John Olerud 1.00 .40 .10
☐ 84T Greg Olson .20 .08 .02
☐ 85T Junior Ortiz .05 .02 .00
☐ 86T Dave Parker .10 .04 .01
☐ 87T Rick Parker .10 .04 .01
☐ 88T Bob Patterson .05 .02 .00
☐ 89T Alejandro Pena .08 .03 .01
☐ 90T Tony Pena .08 .03 .01
☐ 91T Pascual Perez .08 .03 .01
☐ 92T Gerald Perry .05 .02 .00
☐ 93T Dan Petry .05 .02 .00
☐ 94T Gary Pettis .05 .02 .00
☐ 95T Tony Phillips .05 .02 .00
☐ 96T Lou Piniella MG .10 .04 .01
☐ 97T Luis Polonia .08 .03 .01
☐ 98T Jim Presley .05 .02 .00
☐ 99T Scott Radinsky .12 .05 .01
☐ 100T Willie Randolph .08 .03 .01
☐ 101T Jeff Reardon .10 .04 .01
☐ 102T Greg Riddoch MG .10 .04 .01
☐ 103T Jeff Robinson .05 .02 .00
☐ 104T Ron Robinson .05 .02 .00
☐ 105T Kevin Romine .05 .02 .00
☐ 106T Scott Ruskin .12 .05 .01
☐ 107T John Russell .05 .02 .00
☐ 108T Bill Sampen .12 .05 .01
☐ 109T Juan Samuel .08 .03 .01
☐ 110T Scott Sanderson .08 .03 .01
☐ 111T Jack Savage .08 .03 .01
☐ 112T Dave Schmidt .05 .02 .00
☐ 113T Red Schoendienst MG .10 .04 .01
☐ 114T Terry Shumpert .12 .05 .01
☐ 115T Matt Sinatro .05 .02 .00
☐ 116T Don Slaught .05 .02 .00
☐ 117T Bryn Smith .05 .02 .00
☐ 118T Lee Smith .10 .04 .01
☐ 119T Paul Sorrento .12 .05 .01
☐ 120T Franklin Stubbs UER .08 .03 .01
('84 says '99 and has
the same stats as '89,
'83 stats are missing)
☐ 121T Russ Swan .12 .05 .01
☐ 122T Bob Tewksbury .05 .02 .00
☐ 123T Wayne Tolleson .05 .02 .00
☐ 124T John Tudor .08 .03 .01
☐ 125T Randy Veres .08 .03 .01
☐ 126T Hector Villanueva .12 .05 .01
☐ 127T Mitch Webster .05 .02 .00
☐ 128T Ernie Whitt .05 .02 .00
☐ 129T Frank Wills .05 .02 .00
☐ 130T Dave Winfield .12 .05 .01
☐ 131T Matt Young .05 .02 .00
☐ 132T Checklist Card .05 .01 .00

1991 Topps

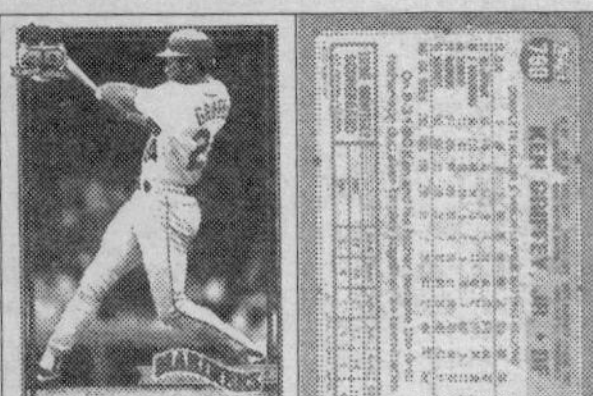

The 1991 Topps Set consists of 792 cards in the now standard size of 2 1/2" by 3 1/2". This set marks Topps 10th consecutive year of issuing a 792-card set. Topps also commemorated their fortieth anniversary by including a "Topps 40" logo on the front of each card. Virtually all of the cards have been discovered without the 40th logo. As a special promotion Topps inserted (randomly) into their wax packs one of every previous card they ever issued. Topps again issued their checklists in team order (and alphabetically within team) and included a special 22-card All-Star set (386-407). There are five players listed as Future Stars, 114 Lance Dickson, 211 Brian Barnes, 561 Tim McIntosh, 587 Jose Offerman, and 594 Rich Garces. There are nine players listed as First Draft Picks, 74 Shane Andrews, 103 Tim Costo, 113 Carl Everett, 278 Alex Fernandez, 471 Mike Lieberthal, 491 Kurt Miller, 529 Marc Newfield, 596 Ronnie Walden, and 767 Dan Wilson. The key rookie cards in this set are Wes Chamberlain, Brian McRae, Marc Newfield, and Phil Plantier. The complete 1991 Topps set was also issued as a factory set of micro baseball cards with cards measuring approximately one-fourth the size of the regular size cards but identical in other respects. The set was also issued with a gold "Operation Desert Shield" emblem stamped on the cards. It has been reported that Topps sent wax cases (equivalent to 6,313 sets) as gifts to U.S. troops stationed in the Persian Gulf. These Desert Shield cards are quite valuable in comparison to the regular issue of Topps; but one must be careful as counterfeits of these cards are known. Due to the scarcity of these Desert Shield cards, they are usually sold at one hundred times the value of the corresponding regular card.

	MINT	EXC	G-VG
COMPLETE SET (792)	21.00	9.00	3.00
COMMON PLAYER (1-792)	.03	.01	.00
☐ 1 Nolan Ryan	.35	.15	.03
☐ 2 George Brett RB	.08	.03	.01
☐ 3 Carlton Fisk RB	.08	.03	.01
☐ 4 Kevin Maas RB	.10	.04	.01
☐ 5 Cal Ripken RB	.12	.05	.01
☐ 6 Nolan Ryan RB	.20	.08	.02
☐ 7 Ryne Sandberg RB	.12	.05	.01
☐ 8 Bobby Thigpen RB	.06	.02	.00
☐ 9 Darrin Fletcher	.08	.03	.01
☐ 10 Gregg Olson	.06	.02	.00
☐ 11 Roberto Kelly	.08	.03	.01
☐ 12 Paul Assenmacher	.03	.01	.00
☐ 13 Mariano Duncan	.03	.01	.00
☐ 14 Dennis Lamp	.03	.01	.00
☐ 15 Von Hayes	.06	.02	.00
☐ 16 Mike Heath	.03	.01	.00
☐ 17 Jeff Brantley	.03	.01	.00
☐ 18 Nelson Liriano	.03	.01	.00
☐ 19 Jeff Robinson New York Yankees	.03	.01	.00
☐ 20 Pedro Guerrero	.06	.02	.00
☐ 21 Joe Morgan MG	.06	.02	.00
☐ 22 Storm Davis	.03	.01	.00
☐ 23 Jim Gantner	.03	.01	.00
☐ 24 Dave Martinez	.03	.01	.00
☐ 25 Tim Belcher	.06	.02	.00
☐ 26 Luis Sojo UER (Born in Barquisimento, not Carquis)	.06	.02	.00
☐ 27 Bobby Witt	.03	.01	.00
☐ 28 Alvaro Espinoza	.03	.01	.00
☐ 29 Bob Walk	.03	.01	.00
☐ 30 Gregg Jefferies	.08	.03	.01
☐ 31 Colby Ward	.08	.03	.01
☐ 32 Mike Simms	.12	.05	.01
☐ 33 Barry Jones	.03	.01	.00
☐ 34 Atlee Hammaker	.03	.01	.00
☐ 35 Greg Maddux	.06	.02	.00
☐ 36 Donnie Hill	.03	.01	.00
☐ 37 Tom Bolton	.03	.01	.00
☐ 38 Scott Bradley	.03	.01	.00
☐ 39 Jim Neidlinger	.10	.04	.01
☐ 40 Kevin Mitchell	.10	.04	.01
☐ 41 Ken Dayley	.03	.01	.00
☐ 42 Chris Hoiles	.10	.04	.01
☐ 43 Roger McDowell	.03	.01	.00
☐ 44 Mike Felder	.03	.01	.00
☐ 45 Chris Sabo	.08	.03	.01
☐ 46 Tim Drummond	.03	.01	.00
☐ 47 Brook Jacoby	.03	.01	.00

☐ 48 Dennis Boyd .03 .01 .00
☐ 49A Pat Borders ERR .25 .10 .02
(40 steals at
Kinston in '86)
☐ 49B Pat Borders COR .06 .02 .00
(0 steals at
Kinston in '86)
☐ 50 Bob Welch .06 .02 .00
☐ 51 Art Howe MG .03 .01 .00
☐ 52 Francisco Oliveras .03 .01 .00
☐ 53 Mike Sharperson UER .03 .01 .00
(Born in 1961, not 1960)
☐ 54 Gary Mielke .03 .01 .00
☐ 55 Jeffrey Leonard .03 .01 .00
☐ 56 Jeff Parrett .03 .01 .00
☐ 57 Jack Howell .03 .01 .00
☐ 58 Mel Stottlemyre Jr. .03 .01 .00
☐ 59 Eric Yelding .03 .01 .00
☐ 60 Frank Viola .06 .02 .00
☐ 61 Stan Javier .03 .01 .00
☐ 62 Lee Guetterman .03 .01 .00
☐ 63 Milt Thompson .03 .01 .00
☐ 64 Tom Herr .03 .01 .00
☐ 65 Bruce Hurst .06 .02 .00
☐ 66 Terry Kennedy .03 .01 .00
☐ 67 Rick Honeycutt .03 .01 .00
☐ 68 Gary Sheffield .08 .03 .01
☐ 69 Steve Wilson .03 .01 .00
☐ 70 Ellis Burks .08 .03 .01
☐ 71 Jim Acker .03 .01 .00
☐ 72 Junior Ortiz .03 .01 .00
☐ 73 Craig Worthington .03 .01 .00
☐ 74 Shane Andrews .17 .07 .01
☐ 75 Jack Morris .08 .03 .01
☐ 76 Jerry Browne .03 .01 .00
☐ 77 Drew Hall .03 .01 .00
☐ 78 Geno Petralli .03 .01 .00
☐ 79 Frank Thomas 1.00 .40 .10
☐ 80A Fernando Valenzuela .30 .12 .03
ERR (104 earned runs
in '90 tied for
league lead)
☐ 80B Fernando Valenzuela .08 .03 .01
COR (104 earned runs
in '90 led league, 20
CG's in 1986 now
italicized)
☐ 81 Cito Gaston MG .06 .02 .00
☐ 82 Tom Glavine .12 .05 .01
☐ 83 Daryl Boston .03 .01 .00
☐ 84 Bob McClure .03 .01 .00
☐ 85 Jesse Barfield .06 .02 .00
☐ 86 Les Lancaster .03 .01 .00
☐ 87 Tracy Jones .03 .01 .00
☐ 88 Bob Tewksbury .03 .01 .00
☐ 89 Darren Daulton .03 .01 .00
☐ 90 Danny Tartabull .08 .03 .01
☐ 91 Greg Colbrunn .12 .05 .01
☐ 92 Danny Jackson .03 .01 .00
☐ 93 Ivan Calderon .06 .02 .00
☐ 94 John Dopson .03 .01 .00
☐ 95 Paul Molitor .08 .03 .01
☐ 96 Trevor Wilson .03 .01 .00
☐ 97A Brady Anderson ERR .25 .10 .02
(September, 2 RBI and
3 hits, should be 3
RBI and 14 hits
☐ 97B Brady Anderson COR .06 .02 .00
☐ 98 Sergio Valdez .03 .01 .00
☐ 99 Chris Gwynn .03 .01 .00
☐ 100A Don Mattingly ERR .75 .30 .07
(10 hits in 1990)
☐ 100B Don Mattingly COR .15 .06 .01
(101 hits in 1990)
☐ 101 Rob Ducey .03 .01 .00
☐ 102 Gene Larkin .03 .01 .00
☐ 103 Tim Costo .25 .10 .02
☐ 104 Don Robinson .03 .01 .00
☐ 105 Kevin McReynolds .06 .02 .00
☐ 106 Ed Nunez .03 .01 .00
☐ 107 Luis Polonia .03 .01 .00
☐ 108 Matt Young .03 .01 .00
☐ 109 Greg Riddoch MG .03 .01 .00
☐ 110 Tom Henke .06 .02 .00
☐ 111 Andres Thomas .03 .01 .00
☐ 112 Frank DiPino .03 .01 .00
☐ 113 Carl Everett .25 .10 .02
☐ 114 Lance Dickson .17 .07 .01
☐ 115 Hubie Brooks .03 .01 .00
☐ 116 Mark Davis .03 .01 .00
☐ 117 Dion James .03 .01 .00
☐ 118 Tom Edens .08 .03 .01
☐ 119 Carl Nichols .03 .01 .00
☐ 120 Joe Carter .08 .03 .01
☐ 121 Eric King .03 .01 .00
☐ 122 Paul O'Neill .06 .02 .00
☐ 123 Greg A. Harris .03 .01 .00
☐ 124 Randy Bush .03 .01 .00
☐ 125 Steve Bedrosian .03 .01 .00
☐ 126 Bernard Gilkey .15 .06 .01
☐ 127 Joe Price .03 .01 .00
☐ 128 Travis Fryman .40 .16 .04
(Front has SS,
back has SS-3B)
☐ 129 Mark Eichhorn .03 .01 .00
☐ 130 Ozzie Smith .10 .04 .01
☐ 131A Checklist 1 ERR .15 .02 .00
727 Phil Bradley
☐ 131B Checklist 1 COR .06 .01 .00
717 Phil Bradley
☐ 132 Jamie Quirk .03 .01 .00
☐ 133 Greg Briley .03 .01 .00
☐ 134 Kevin Elster .03 .01 .00
☐ 135 Jerome Walton .08 .03 .01
☐ 136 Dave Schmidt .03 .01 .00
☐ 137 Randy Ready .03 .01 .00

☐ 138 Jamie Moyer .03 .01 .00
☐ 139 Jeff Treadway .03 .01 .00
☐ 140 Fred McGriff .08 .03 .01
☐ 141 Nick Leyva MG .03 .01 .00
☐ 142 Curt Wilkerson .03 .01 .00
☐ 143 John Smiley .06 .02 .00
☐ 144 Dave Henderson .06 .02 .00
☐ 145 Lou Whitaker .06 .02 .00
☐ 146 Dan Plesac .03 .01 .00
☐ 147 Carlos Baerga .10 .04 .01
☐ 148 Rey Palacios .03 .01 .00
☐ 149 Al Osuna UER .12 .05 .01
(Shown throwing right,
but bio says lefty)
☐ 150 Cal Ripken .20 .08 .02
☐ 151 Tom Browning .06 .02 .00
☐ 152 Mickey Hatcher .03 .01 .00
☐ 153 Bryan Harvey .06 .02 .00
☐ 154 Jay Buhner .06 .02 .00
☐ 155A Dwight Evans ERR .25 .10 .02
(led league with
162 games in '82)
☐ 155B Dwight Evans COR .06 .02 .00
(tied for lead with
162 games in '82)
☐ 156 Carlos Martinez .03 .01 .00
☐ 157 John Smoltz .08 .03 .01
☐ 158 Jose Uribe .03 .01 .00
☐ 159 Joe Boever .03 .01 .00
☐ 160 Vince Coleman UER .08 .03 .01
(Wrong birth year,
born 9/22/60)
☐ 161 Tim Leary .06 .02 .00
☐ 162 Ozzie Canseco .08 .03 .01
☐ 163 Dave Johnson .03 .01 .00
☐ 164 Edgar Diaz .06 .02 .00
☐ 165 Sandy Alomar Jr. .08 .03 .01
☐ 166 Harold Baines .06 .02 .00
☐ 167A Randy Tomlin ERR .50 .20 .05
(Harriburg)
☐ 167B Randy Tomlin COR .20 .08 .02
(Harrisburg)
☐ 168 John Olerud .12 .05 .01
☐ 169 Luis Aquino .03 .01 .00
☐ 170 Carlton Fisk .10 .04 .01
☐ 171 Tony LaRussa MG .06 .02 .00
☐ 172 Pete Incaviglia .06 .02 .00
☐ 173 Jason Grimsley .03 .01 .00
☐ 174 Ken Caminiti .03 .01 .00
☐ 175 Jack Armstrong .06 .02 .00
☐ 176 John Orton .03 .01 .00
☐ 177 Reggie Harris .08 .03 .01
☐ 178 Dave Valle .03 .01 .00
☐ 179 Pete Harnisch .03 .01 .00
☐ 180 Tony Gwynn .12 .05 .01
☐ 181 Duane Ward .03 .01 .00
☐ 182 Junior Noboa .03 .01 .00
☐ 183 Clay Parker .03 .01 .00
☐ 184 Gary Green .03 .01 .00
☐ 185 Joe Magrane .03 .01 .00
☐ 186 Rod Booker .03 .01 .00
☐ 187 Greg Cadaret .03 .01 .00
☐ 188 Damon Berryhill .03 .01 .00
☐ 189 Daryl Irvine .08 .03 .01
☐ 190 Matt Williams .10 .04 .01
☐ 191 Willie Blair .03 .01 .00
☐ 192 Rob Deer .06 .02 .00
☐ 193 Felix Fermin .03 .01 .00
☐ 194 Xavier Hernandez .06 .02 .00
☐ 195 Wally Joyner .08 .03 .01
☐ 196 Jim Vatcher .08 .03 .01
☐ 197 Chris Nabholz .08 .03 .01
☐ 198 R.J. Reynolds .03 .01 .00
☐ 199 Mike Hartley .06 .02 .00
☐ 200 Darryl Strawberry .15 .06 .01
☐ 201 Tom Kelly MG .03 .01 .00
☐ 202 Jim Leyritz .03 .01 .00
☐ 203 Gene Harris .03 .01 .00
☐ 204 Herm Winningham .03 .01 .00
☐ 205 Mike Perez .08 .03 .01
☐ 206 Carlos Quintana .06 .02 .00
☐ 207 Gary Wayne .03 .01 .00
☐ 208 Willie Wilson .06 .02 .00
☐ 209 Ken Howell .03 .01 .00
☐ 210 Lance Parrish .06 .02 .00
☐ 211 Brian Barnes .10 .04 .01
☐ 212 Steve Finley .06 .02 .00
☐ 213 Frank Wills .03 .01 .00
☐ 214 Joe Girardi .03 .01 .00
☐ 215 Dave Smith .03 .01 .00
☐ 216 Greg Gagne .03 .01 .00
☐ 217 Chris Bosio .03 .01 .00
☐ 218 Rick Parker .03 .01 .00
☐ 219 Jack McDowell .08 .03 .01
☐ 220 Tim Wallach .06 .02 .00
☐ 221 Don Slaught .03 .01 .00
☐ 222 Brian McRae .40 .16 .04
☐ 223 Allan Anderson .03 .01 .00
☐ 224 Juan Gonzalez .30 .12 .03
☐ 225 Randy Johnson .03 .01 .00
☐ 226 Alfredo Griffin .03 .01 .00
☐ 227 Steve Avery .30 .12 .03
☐ 228 Rex Hudler .03 .01 .00
☐ 229 Rance Mulliniks .03 .01 .00
☐ 230 Sid Fernandez .06 .02 .00
☐ 231 Doug Rader MG .03 .01 .00
☐ 232 Jose DeJesus .03 .01 .00
☐ 233 Al Leiter .03 .01 .00
☐ 234 Scott Erickson .60 .25 .06
☐ 235 Dave Parker .08 .03 .01
☐ 236A Frank Tanana ERR .25 .10 .02
(tied for lead with
269 K's in '75)
☐ 236B Frank Tanana COR .06 .02 .00
(led league with
269 K's in '75)

☐ 237 Rick Cerone	.03	.01	.00
☐ 238 Mike Dunne	.03	.01	.00
☐ 239 Darren Lewis	.20	.08	.02
☐ 240 Mike Scott	.06	.02	.00
☐ 241 Dave Clark UER (Career totals 19 HR and 5 3B, should be 22 and 3)	.03	.01	.00
☐ 242 Mike LaCoss	.03	.01	.00
☐ 243 Lance Johnson	.03	.01	.00
☐ 244 Mike Jeffcoat	.03	.01	.00
☐ 245 Kal Daniels	.06	.02	.00
☐ 246 Kevin Wickander	.03	.01	.00
☐ 247 Jody Reed	.03	.01	.00
☐ 248 Tom Gordon	.06	.02	.00
☐ 249 Bob Melvin	.03	.01	.00
☐ 250 Dennis Eckersley	.06	.02	.00
☐ 251 Mark Lemke	.06	.02	.00
☐ 252 Mel Rojas	.06	.02	.00
☐ 253 Garry Templeton	.03	.01	.00
☐ 254 Shawn Boskie	.03	.01	.00
☐ 255 Brian Downing	.03	.01	.00
☐ 256 Greg Hibbard	.03	.01	.00
☐ 257 Tom O'Malley	.03	.01	.00
☐ 258 Chris Hammond	.08	.03	.01
☐ 259 Hensley Meulens	.08	.03	.01
☐ 260 Harold Reynolds	.06	.02	.00
☐ 261 Bud Harrelson MG	.03	.01	.00
☐ 262 Tim Jones	.03	.01	.00
☐ 263 Checklist 2	.06	.01	.00
☐ 264 Dave Hollins	.08	.03	.01
☐ 265 Mark Gubicza	.03	.01	.00
☐ 266 Carmelo Castillo	.03	.01	.00
☐ 267 Mark Knudson	.03	.01	.00
☐ 268 Tom Brookens	.03	.01	.00
☐ 269 Joe Hesketh	.03	.01	.00
☐ 270A Mark McGwire ERR (1987 Slugging Pctg. listed as 618)	.30	.12	.03
☐ 270B Mark McGwire COR (1987 Slugging Pctg. listed as .618)	.10	.04	.01
☐ 271 Omar Olivares	.10	.04	.01
☐ 272 Jeff King	.06	.02	.00
☐ 273 Johnny Ray	.03	.01	.00
☐ 274 Ken Williams	.03	.01	.00
☐ 275 Alan Trammell	.08	.03	.01
☐ 276 Bill Swift	.03	.01	.00
☐ 277 Scott Coolbaugh	.03	.01	.00
☐ 278 Alex Fernandez UER (No '90 White Sox stats)	.20	.08	.02
☐ 279A Jose Gonzalez ERR (photo actually Billy Bean)	.25	.10	.02
☐ 279B Jose Gonzalez COR	.06	.02	.00
☐ 280 Bret Saberhagen	.08	.03	.01
☐ 281 Larry Sheets	.03	.01	.00
☐ 282 Don Carman	.03	.01	.00

☐ 283 Marquis Grissom	.10	.04	.01
☐ 284 Billy Spiers	.03	.01	.00
☐ 285 Jim Abbott	.10	.04	.01
☐ 286 Ken Oberkfell	.03	.01	.00
☐ 287 Mark Grant	.03	.01	.00
☐ 288 Derrick May	.08	.03	.01
☐ 289 Tim Birtsas	.03	.01	.00
☐ 290 Steve Sax	.06	.02	.00
☐ 291 John Wathan MG	.03	.01	.00
☐ 292 Bud Black	.03	.01	.00
☐ 293 Jay Bell	.03	.01	.00
☐ 294 Mike Moore	.03	.01	.00
☐ 295 Rafael Palmeiro	.08	.03	.01
☐ 296 Mark Williamson	.03	.01	.00
☐ 297 Manny Lee	.03	.01	.00
☐ 298 Omar Vizquel	.03	.01	.00
☐ 299 Scott Radinsky	.06	.02	.00
☐ 300 Kirby Puckett	.12	.05	.01
☐ 301 Steve Farr	.03	.01	.00
☐ 302 Tim Teufel	.03	.01	.00
☐ 303 Mike Boddicker	.03	.01	.00
☐ 304 Kevin Reimer	.08	.03	.01
☐ 305 Mike Scioscia	.03	.01	.00
☐ 306A Lonnie Smith ERR (136 games in '90)	.25	.10	.02
☐ 306B Lonnie Smith COR (135 games in '90)	.06	.02	.00
☐ 307 Andy Benes	.08	.03	.01
☐ 308 Tom Pagnozzi	.03	.01	.00
☐ 309 Norm Charlton	.03	.01	.00
☐ 310 Gary Carter	.08	.03	.01
☐ 311 Jeff Pico	.03	.01	.00
☐ 312 Charlie Hayes	.03	.01	.00
☐ 313 Ron Robinson	.03	.01	.00
☐ 314 Gary Pettis	.03	.01	.00
☐ 315 Roberto Alomar	.10	.04	.01
☐ 316 Gene Nelson	.03	.01	.00
☐ 317 Mike Fitzgerald	.03	.01	.00
☐ 318 Rick Aguilera	.03	.01	.00
☐ 319 Jeff McKnight	.06	.02	.00
☐ 320 Tony Fernandez	.06	.02	.00
☐ 321 Bob Rodgers MG	.03	.01	.00
☐ 322 Terry Shumpert	.03	.01	.00
☐ 323 Cory Snyder	.06	.02	.00
☐ 324A Ron Kittle ERR (Set another standard ...)	.25	.10	.02
☐ 324B Ron Kittle COR (Tied another standard ...)	.06	.02	.00
☐ 325 Brett Butler	.06	.02	.00
☐ 326 Ken Patterson	.03	.01	.00
☐ 327 Ron Hassey	.03	.01	.00
☐ 328 Walt Terrell	.03	.01	.00
☐ 329 Dave Justice UER (Drafted third round on card, should say fourth pick)	.50	.20	.05

Card	Player			
☐ 330	Dwight Gooden	.10	.04	.01
☐ 331	Eric Anthony	.08	.03	.01
☐ 332	Kenny Rogers	.03	.01	.00
☐ 333	Chipper Jones FDP	.30	.12	.03
☐ 334	Todd Benzinger	.03	.01	.00
☐ 335	Mitch Williams	.03	.01	.00
☐ 336	Matt Nokes	.06	.02	.00
☐ 337A	Keith Comstock ERR (Cubs logo on front)	.25	.10	.02
☐ 337B	Keith Comstock COR (Mariners logo on front)	.06	.02	.00
☐ 338	Luis Rivera	.03	.01	.00
☐ 339	Larry Walker	.08	.03	.01
☐ 340	Ramon Martinez	.10	.04	.01
☐ 341	John Moses	.03	.01	.00
☐ 342	Mickey Morandini	.08	.03	.01
☐ 343	Jose Oquendo	.03	.01	.00
☐ 344	Jeff Russell	.03	.01	.00
☐ 345	Len Dykstra	.06	.02	.00
☐ 346	Jesse Orosco	.03	.01	.00
☐ 347	Greg Vaughn	.08	.03	.01
☐ 348	Todd Stottlemyre	.06	.02	.00
☐ 349	Dave Gallagher	.03	.01	.00
☐ 350	Glenn Davis	.06	.02	.00
☐ 351	Joe Torre MG	.06	.02	.00
☐ 352	Frank White	.03	.01	.00
☐ 353	Tony Castillo	.03	.01	.00
☐ 354	Sid Bream	.03	.01	.00
☐ 355	Chili Davis	.06	.02	.00
☐ 356	Mike Marshall	.06	.02	.00
☐ 357	Jack Savage	.03	.01	.00
☐ 358	Mark Parent	.03	.01	.00
☐ 359	Chuck Cary	.03	.01	.00
☐ 360	Tim Raines	.06	.02	.00
☐ 361	Scott Garrelts	.03	.01	.00
☐ 362	Hector Villenueva	.06	.02	.00
☐ 363	Rick Mahler	.03	.01	.00
☐ 364	Dan Pasqua	.03	.01	.00
☐ 365	Mike Schooler	.03	.01	.00
☐ 366A	Checklist 3 ERR 19 Carl Nichols	.15	.02	.00
☐ 366B	Checklist 3 COR 119 Carl Nichols	.06	.01	.00
☐ 367	Dave Walsh	.10	.04	.01
☐ 368	Felix Jose	.08	.03	.01
☐ 369	Steve Searcy	.03	.01	.00
☐ 370	Kelly Gruber	.06	.02	.00
☐ 371	Jeff Montgomery	.03	.01	.00
☐ 372	Spike Owen	.03	.01	.00
☐ 373	Darrin Jackson	.03	.01	.00
☐ 374	Larry Casian	.08	.03	.01
☐ 375	Tony Pena	.06	.02	.00
☐ 376	Mike Harkey	.06	.02	.00
☐ 377	Rene Gonzales	.03	.01	.00
☐ 378A	Wilson Alvarez ERR ('89 Port Charlotte and '90 Birmingham stat lines omitted)	.45	.18	.04
☐ 378B	Wilson Alvarez COR (Text still says 143 K's in 1988, whereas stats say 134)	.12	.05	.01
☐ 379	Randy Velarde	.03	.01	.00
☐ 380	Willie McGee	.06	.02	.00
☐ 381	Jim Leyland MG	.03	.01	.00
☐ 382	Mackey Sasser	.03	.01	.00
☐ 383	Pete Smith	.03	.01	.00
☐ 384	Gerald Perry	.03	.01	.00
☐ 385	Mickey Tettleton	.06	.02	.00
☐ 386	Cecil Fielder AS	.10	.04	.01
☐ 387	Julio Franco AS	.06	.02	.00
☐ 388	Kelly Gruber AS	.06	.02	.00
☐ 389	Alan Trammell AS	.08	.03	.01
☐ 390	Jose Canseco AS	.15	.06	.01
☐ 391	Rickey Henderson AS	.12	.05	.01
☐ 392	Ken Griffey Jr. AS	.30	.12	.03
☐ 393	Carlton Fisk AS	.08	.03	.01
☐ 394	Bob Welch AS	.06	.02	.00
☐ 395	Chuck Finley AS	.06	.02	.00
☐ 396	Bobby Thigpen AS	.06	.02	.00
☐ 397	Eddie Murray AS	.08	.03	.01
☐ 398	Ryne Sandberg AS	.12	.05	.01
☐ 399	Matt Williams AS	.08	.03	.01
☐ 400	Barry Larkin AS	.08	.03	.01
☐ 401	Barry Bonds AS	.08	.03	.01
☐ 402	Darryl Strawbery AS	.10	.04	.01
☐ 403	Bobby Bonilla AS	.08	.03	.01
☐ 404	Mike Scioscia AS	.03	.01	.00
☐ 405	Doug Drabek AS	.06	.02	.00
☐ 406	Frank Viola AS	.06	.02	.00
☐ 407	John Franco AS	.03	.01	.00
☐ 408	Earnie Riles	.03	.01	.00
☐ 409	Mike Stanley	.03	.01	.00
☐ 410	Dave Righetti	.06	.02	.00
☐ 411	Lance Blankenship	.03	.01	.00
☐ 412	Dave Bergman	.03	.01	.00
☐ 413	Terry Mulholland	.03	.01	.00
☐ 414	Sammy Sosa	.08	.03	.01
☐ 415	Rick Sutcliffe	.06	.02	.00
☐ 416	Randy Milligan	.06	.02	.00
☐ 417	Bill Krueger	.03	.01	.00
☐ 418	Nick Esasky	.03	.01	.00
☐ 419	Jeff Reed	.03	.01	.00
☐ 420	Bobby Thigpen	.06	.02	.00
☐ 421	Alex Cole	.08	.03	.01
☐ 422	Rick Reuschel	.06	.02	.00
☐ 423	Rafael Ramirez UER (Born 1959, not 1958)	.03	.01	.00
☐ 424	Calvin Schiraldi	.03	.01	.00
☐ 425	Andy Van Slyke	.08	.03	.01
☐ 426	Joe Grahe	.08	.03	.01
☐ 427	Rick Dempsey	.03	.01	.00
☐ 428	John Barfield	.08	.03	.01
☐ 429	Stump Merrill MG	.03	.01	.00
☐ 430	Gary Gaetti	.06	.02	.00
☐ 431	Paul Gibson	.03	.01	.00

☐ 432 Delino DeShields .10 .04 .01
☐ 433 Pat Tabler .03 .01 .00
☐ 434 Julio Machado .03 .01 .00
☐ 435 Kevin Maas .15 .06 .01
☐ 436 Scott Bankhead .03 .01 .00
☐ 437 Doug Dascenzo .03 .01 .00
☐ 438 Vicente Palacios .03 .01 .00
☐ 439 Dickie Thon .03 .01 .00
☐ 440 George Bell .08 .03 .01
☐ 441 Zane Smith .03 .01 .00
☐ 442 Charlie O'Brien .03 .01 .00
☐ 443 Jeff Innis .03 .01 .00
☐ 444 Glenn Braggs .03 .01 .00
☐ 445 Greg Swindell .06 .02 .00
☐ 446 Craig Grebeck .06 .02 .00
☐ 447 John Burkett .03 .01 .00
☐ 448 Craig Lefferts .03 .01 .00
☐ 449 Juan Berenguer .03 .01 .00
☐ 450 Wade Boggs .12 .05 .01
☐ 451 Neal Heaton .03 .01 .00
☐ 452 Bill Schroeder .03 .01 .00
☐ 453 Lenny Harris .03 .01 .00
☐ 454A Kevin Appier ERR .25 .10 .02
('90 Omaha stat
line omitted)
☐ 454B Kevin Appier COR .06 .02 .00
☐ 455 Walt Weiss .06 .02 .00
☐ 456 Charlie Leibrandt .03 .01 .00
☐ 457 Todd Hundley .10 .04 .01
☐ 458 Brian Holman .03 .01 .00
☐ 459 Tom Trebelhorn MG UER .03 .01 .00
(Pitching and batting
columns switched)
☐ 460 Dave Stieb .06 .02 .00
☐ 461 Robin Ventura .20 .08 .02
☐ 462 Steve Frey .03 .01 .00
☐ 463 Dwight Smith .03 .01 .00
☐ 464 Steve Buechele .03 .01 .00
☐ 465 Ken Griffey Sr. .06 .02 .00
☐ 466 Charles Nagy .08 .03 .01
☐ 467 Dennis Cook .03 .01 .00
☐ 468 Tim Hulett .03 .01 .00
☐ 469 Chet Lemon .03 .01 .00
☐ 470 Howard Johnson .08 .03 .01
☐ 471 Mike Lieberthal .10 .04 .01
☐ 472 Kirt Manwaring .03 .01 .00
☐ 473 Curt Young .03 .01 .00
☐ 474 Phil Plantier 1.25 .50 .12
☐ 475 Teddy Higuera .03 .01 .00
☐ 476 Glenn Wilson .03 .01 .00
☐ 477 Mike Fetters .03 .01 .00
☐ 478 Kurt Stillwell .03 .01 .00
☐ 479 Bob Patterson UER .03 .01 .00
(Has a decimal point
between 7 and 9)
☐ 480 Dave Magadan .06 .02 .00
☐ 481 Eddie Whitson .03 .01 .00
☐ 482 Tino Martinez .15 .06 .01
☐ 483 Mike Aldrete .03 .01 .00
☐ 484 Dave LaPoint .03 .01 .00
☐ 485 Terry Pendleton .08 .03 .01
☐ 486 Tommy Greene .08 .03 .01
☐ 487 Rafael Belliard .03 .01 .00
☐ 488 Jeff Manto .06 .02 .00
☐ 489 Bobby Valentine MG .03 .01 .00
☐ 490 Kirk Gibson .06 .02 .00
☐ 491 Kurt Miller .15 .06 .01
☐ 492 Ernie Whitt .03 .01 .00
☐ 493 Jose Rijo .06 .02 .00
☐ 494 Chris James .03 .01 .00
☐ 495 Charlie Hough .03 .01 .00
☐ 496 Marty Barrett .03 .01 .00
☐ 497 Ben McDonald .10 .04 .01
☐ 498 Mark Salas .03 .01 .00
☐ 499 Melido Perez .03 .01 .00
☐ 500 Will Clark .10 .04 .01
☐ 501 Mike Bielecki .03 .01 .00
☐ 502 Carney Lansford .06 .02 .00
☐ 503 Roy Smith .03 .01 .00
☐ 504 Julio Valera .06 .02 .00
☐ 505 Chuck Finley .06 .02 .00
☐ 506 Darnell Coles .03 .01 .00
☐ 507 Steve Jeltz .03 .01 .00
☐ 508 Mike York .08 .03 .01
☐ 509 Glenallen Hill .06 .02 .00
☐ 510 John Franco .03 .01 .00
☐ 511 Steve Balboni .03 .01 .00
☐ 512 Jose Mesa .03 .01 .00
☐ 513 Jerald Clark .03 .01 .00
☐ 514 Mike Stanton .03 .01 .00
☐ 515 Alvin Davis .06 .02 .00
☐ 516 Karl Rhodes .08 .03 .01
☐ 517 Joe Oliver .03 .01 .00
☐ 518 Cris Carpenter .03 .01 .00
☐ 519 Sparky Anderson MG .06 .02 .00
☐ 520 Mark Grace .08 .03 .01
☐ 521 Joe Orsulak .03 .01 .00
☐ 522 Stan Belinda .03 .01 .00
☐ 523 Rodney McCray .08 .03 .01
☐ 524 Darrel Akerfelds .03 .01 .00
☐ 525 Willie Randolph .03 .01 .00
☐ 526A Moises Alou ERR .35 .15 .03
(37 runs in 2 games
for '90 Pirates)
☐ 526B Moises Alou COR .08 .03 .01
(0 runs in 2 games
for '90 Pirates)
☐ 527A Checklist 4 ERR .15 .02 .00
105 Keith Miller
719 Kevin McReynolds
☐ 527B Checklist 4 COR .06 .01 .00
105 Kevin McReynolds
719 Keith Miller
☐ 528 Denny Martinez .06 .02 .00
☐ 529 Marc Newfield .90 .40 .09
☐ 530 Roger Clemens .15 .06 .01

☐ 531 Dave Rohde .08 .03 .01
☐ 532 Kirk McCaskill .03 .01 .00
☐ 533 Oddibe McDowell .03 .01 .00
☐ 534 Mike Jackson .03 .01 .00
☐ 535 Ruben Sierra UER .12 .05 .01
(Back reads 100 Runs amd 100 RBI's)
☐ 536 Mike Witt .03 .01 .00
☐ 537 Jose Lind .03 .01 .00
☐ 538 Bip Roberts .03 .01 .00
☐ 539 Scott Terry .03 .01 .00
☐ 540 George Brett .10 .04 .01
☐ 541 Domingo Ramos .03 .01 .00
☐ 542 Rob Murphy .03 .01 .00
☐ 543 Junior Felix .06 .02 .00
☐ 544 Alejandro Pena .06 .02 .00
☐ 545 Dale Murphy .10 .04 .01
☐ 546 Jeff Ballard .03 .01 .00
☐ 547 Mike Pagliarulo .03 .01 .00
☐ 548 Jaime Navarro .03 .01 .00
☐ 549 John McNamara MG .03 .01 .00
☐ 550 Eric Davis .10 .04 .01
☐ 551 Bob Kipper .03 .01 .00
☐ 552 Jeff Hamilton .03 .01 .00
☐ 553 Joe Klink .06 .02 .00
☐ 554 Brian Harper .06 .02 .00
☐ 555 Turner Ward .12 .05 .01
☐ 556 Gary Ward .03 .01 .00
☐ 557 Wally Whitehurst .03 .01 .00
☐ 558 Otis Nixon .06 .02 .00
☐ 559 Adam Peterson .03 .01 .00
☐ 560 Greg Smith .06 .02 .00
☐ 561 Tim McIntosh .08 .03 .01
☐ 562 Jeff Kunkel .03 .01 .00
☐ 563 Brent Knackert .03 .01 .00
☐ 564 Dante Bichette .03 .01 .00
☐ 565 Craig Biggio .06 .02 .00
☐ 566 Craig Wilson .10 .04 .01
☐ 567 Dwayne Henry .03 .01 .00
☐ 568 Ron Karkovice .03 .01 .00
☐ 569 Curt Schilling .03 .01 .00
☐ 570 Barry Bonds .12 .05 .01
☐ 571 Pat Combs .03 .01 .00
☐ 572 Dave Anderson .03 .01 .00
☐ 573 Rich Rodriguez .08 .03 .01
☐ 574 John Marzano .03 .01 .00
☐ 575 Robin Yount .10 .04 .01
☐ 576 Jeff Kaiser .03 .01 .00
☐ 577 Bill Doran .03 .01 .00
☐ 578 Dave West .03 .01 .00
☐ 579 Roger Craig MG .03 .01 .00
☐ 580 Dave Stewart .06 .02 .00
☐ 581 Luis Quinones .03 .01 .00
☐ 582 Marty Clary .03 .01 .00
☐ 583 Tony Phillips .03 .01 .00
☐ 584 Kevin Brown .03 .01 .00
☐ 585 Pete O'Brien .03 .01 .00
☐ 586 Fred Lynn .06 .02 .00
☐ 587 Jose Offerman UER .10 .04 .01
(Text says he signed 7/24/86, but bio says 1988)
☐ 588 Mark Whiten .20 .08 .02
☐ 589 Scott Ruskin .03 .01 .00
☐ 590 Eddie Murray .10 .04 .01
☐ 591 Ken Hill .03 .01 .00
☐ 592 B.J. Surhoff .03 .01 .00
☐ 593A Mike Walker ERR .25 .10 .02
('90 Canton-Akron stat line omitted)
☐ 593B Mike Walker COR .08 .03 .01
☐ 594 Rich Garces .10 .04 .01
☐ 595 Bill Landrum .03 .01 .00
☐ 596 Ronnie Walden .15 .06 .01
☐ 597 Jerry Don Gleaton .03 .01 .00
☐ 598 Sam Horn .03 .01 .00
☐ 599A Greg Myers ERR .25 .10 .02
('90 Syracuse stat line omitted)
☐ 599B Greg Myers COR .06 .02 .00
☐ 600 Bo Jackson .25 .10 .02
☐ 601 Bob Ojeda .03 .01 .00
☐ 602 Casey Candaele .03 .01 .00
☐ 603A Wes Chamberlain ERR 1.50 .60 .15
(photo actually Louie Meadows)
☐ 603B Wes Chamberlain COR .45 .18 .04
☐ 604 Billy Hatcher .03 .01 .00
☐ 605 Jeff Reardon .06 .02 .00
☐ 606 Jim Gott .03 .01 .00
☐ 607 Edgar Martinez .06 .02 .00
☐ 608 Todd Burns .03 .01 .00
☐ 609 Jeff Torborg MG .03 .01 .00
☐ 610 Andres Galarraga .06 .02 .00
☐ 611 Dave Eiland .03 .01 .00
☐ 612 Steve Lyons .03 .01 .00
☐ 613 Eric Show .03 .01 .00
☐ 614 Luis Salazar .03 .01 .00
☐ 615 Bert Blyleven .06 .02 .00
☐ 616 Todd Zeile .10 .04 .01
☐ 617 Bill Wegman .03 .01 .00
☐ 618 Sil Campusano .03 .01 .00
☐ 619 David Wells .03 .01 .00
☐ 620 Ozzie Guillen .06 .02 .00
☐ 621 Ted Power .03 .01 .00
☐ 622 Jack Daugherty .03 .01 .00
☐ 623 Jeff Blauser .03 .01 .00
☐ 624 Tom Candiotti .06 .02 .00
☐ 625 Terry Steinbach .03 .01 .00
☐ 626 Gerald Young .03 .01 .00
☐ 627 Tim Layana .03 .01 .00
☐ 628 Greg Litton .03 .01 .00
☐ 629 Wes Gardner .03 .01 .00
☐ 630 Dave Winfield .10 .04 .01
☐ 631 Mike Morgan .06 .02 .00
☐ 632 Lloyd Moseby .03 .01 .00

☐ 633 Kevin Tapani .... .06 .02 .00
☐ 634 Henry Cotto .... .03 .01 .00
☐ 635 Andy Hawkins .... .03 .01 .00
☐ 636 Geronimo Pena .... .08 .03 .01
☐ 637 Bruce Ruffin .... .03 .01 .00
☐ 638 Mike Macfarlane .... .03 .01 .00
☐ 639 Frank Robinson MG .... .08 .03 .01
☐ 640 Andre Dawson .... .10 .04 .01
☐ 641 Mike Henneman .... .03 .01 .00
☐ 642 Hal Morris .... .10 .04 .01
☐ 643 Jim Presley .... .03 .01 .00
☐ 644 Chuck Crim .... .03 .01 .00
☐ 645 Juan Samuel .... .06 .02 .00
☐ 646 Andujar Cedeno .... .35 .15 .03
☐ 647 Mark Portugal .... .03 .01 .00
☐ 648 Lee Stevens .... .10 .04 .01
☐ 649 Bill Sampen .... .03 .01 .00
☐ 650 Jack Clark .... .06 .02 .00
☐ 651 Alan Mills .... .03 .01 .00
☐ 652 Kevin Romine .... .03 .01 .00
☐ 653 Anthony Telford .... .08 .03 .01
☐ 654 Paul Sorrento .... .03 .01 .00
☐ 655 Erik Hanson .... .06 .02 .00
☐ 656A Checklist 5 ERR .... .15 .02 .00
348 Vicente Palacios
381 Jose Lind
537 Mike LaValliere
665 Jim Leyland
☐ 656B Checklist 5 COR .... .06 .01 .00
438 Vicente Palacios
537 Jose Lind
665 Mike LaValliere
381 Jim Leyland
☐ 657 Mike Kingery .... .03 .01 .00
☐ 658 Scott Aldred .... .08 .03 .01
☐ 659 Oscar Azocar .... .06 .02 .00
☐ 660 Lee Smith .... .06 .02 .00
☐ 661 Steve Lake .... .03 .01 .00
☐ 662 Ron Dibble .... .06 .02 .00
☐ 663 Greg Brock .... .03 .01 .00
☐ 664 John Farrell .... .03 .01 .00
☐ 665 Mike LaValliere .... .03 .01 .00
☐ 666 Danny Darwin .... .03 .01 .00
☐ 667 Kent Anderson .... .03 .01 .00
☐ 668 Bill Long .... .03 .01 .00
☐ 669 Lou Piniella MG .... .06 .02 .00
☐ 670 Rickey Henderson .... .20 .08 .02
☐ 671 Andy McGaffigan .... .03 .01 .00
☐ 672 Shane Mack .... .06 .02 .00
☐ 673 Greg Olson UER .... .03 .01 .00
(6 RBI in '88 at Tidewater and 2 RBI in '87, should be 48 and 15)
☐ 674A Kevin Gross ERR .... .25 .10 .02
(89 BB with Phillies in '88 tied for league lead)
☐ 674B Kevin Gross COR .... .06 .02 .00
(89 BB with Phillies in '88 led league)
☐ 675 Tom Brunansky .... .06 .02 .00
☐ 676 Scott Chiamparino .... .08 .03 .01
☐ 677 Billy Ripken .... .03 .01 .00
☐ 678 Mark Davidson .... .03 .01 .00
☐ 679 Bill Bathe .... .03 .01 .00
☐ 680 David Cone .... .06 .02 .00
☐ 681 Jeff Schaefer .... .06 .02 .00
☐ 682 Ray Lankford .... .30 .12 .03
☐ 683 Derek Lilliquist .... .03 .01 .00
☐ 684 Milt Cuyler .... .17 .07 .01
☐ 685 Doug Drabek .... .06 .02 .00
☐ 686 Mike Gallego .... .03 .01 .00
☐ 687A John Cerutti ERR .... .25 .10 .02
(4.46 ERA in '90)
☐ 687B John Cerutti COR .... .06 .02 .00
(4.76 ERA in '90)
☐ 688 Rosario Rodriguez .... .08 .03 .01
☐ 689 John Kruk .... .03 .01 .00
☐ 690 Orel Hershiser .... .06 .02 .00
☐ 691 Mike Blowers .... .03 .01 .00
☐ 692A Efrain Valdez ERR .... .30 .12 .03
(born 6/11/66)
☐ 692B Efrain Valdez COR .... .10 .04 .01
(born 7/11/66 and two lines of text added)
☐ 693 Francisco Cabrera .... .03 .01 .00
☐ 694 Randy Veres .... .03 .01 .00
☐ 695 Kevin Seitzer .... .06 .02 .00
☐ 696 Steve Olin .... .03 .01 .00
☐ 697 Shawn Abner .... .03 .01 .00
☐ 698 Mark Guthrie .... .03 .01 .00
☐ 699 Jim Lefebvre MG .... .03 .01 .00
☐ 700 Jose Canseco .... .25 .10 .02
☐ 701 Pascual Perez .... .03 .01 .00
☐ 702 Tim Naehring .... .10 .04 .01
☐ 703 Juan Agosto .... .03 .01 .00
☐ 704 Devon White .... .06 .02 .00
☐ 705 Robby Thompson .... .03 .01 .00
☐ 706A Brad Arnsberg ERR .... .25 .10 .02
(68.2 IP in '90)
☐ 706B Brad Arnsberg COR .... .06 .02 .00
(62.2 IP in '90)
☐ 707 Jim Eisenreich .... .03 .01 .00
☐ 708 John Mitchell .... .03 .01 .00
☐ 709 Matt Sinatro .... .03 .01 .00
☐ 710 Kent Hrbek .... .06 .02 .00
☐ 711 Jose DeLeon .... .03 .01 .00
☐ 712 Ricky Jordan .... .06 .02 .00
☐ 713 Scott Scudder .... .06 .02 .00
☐ 714 Marvell Wynne .... .03 .01 .00
☐ 715 Tim Burke .... .03 .01 .00
☐ 716 Bob Geren .... .03 .01 .00
☐ 717 Phil Bradley .... .03 .01 .00
☐ 718 Steve Crawford .... .03 .01 .00
☐ 719 Keith Miller .... .03 .01 .00
☐ 720 Cecil Fielder .... .15 .06 .01

☐ 721 Mark Lee	.10	.04	.01
☐ 722 Wally Backman	.03	.01	.00
☐ 723 Candy Maldonado	.03	.01	.00
☐ 724 David Segui	.08	.03	.01
☐ 725 Ron Gant	.12	.05	.01
☐ 726 Phil Stephenson	.03	.01	.00
☐ 727 Mookie Wilson	.03	.01	.00
☐ 728 Scott Sanderson	.03	.01	.00
☐ 729 Don Zimmer MG	.03	.01	.00
☐ 730 Barry Larkin	.08	.03	.01
☐ 731 Jeff Gray	.08	.03	.01
☐ 732 Franklin Stubbs	.03	.01	.00
☐ 733 Kelly Downs	.03	.01	.00
☐ 734 John Russell	.03	.01	.00
☐ 735 Ron Darling	.06	.02	.00
☐ 736 Dick Schofield	.03	.01	.00
☐ 737 Tim Crews	.03	.01	.00
☐ 738 Mel Hall	.03	.01	.00
☐ 739 Russ Swan	.06	.02	.00
☐ 740 Ryne Sandberg	.20	.08	.02
☐ 741 Jimmy Key	.06	.02	.00
☐ 742 Tommy Gregg	.03	.01	.00
☐ 743 Bryn Smith	.03	.01	.00
☐ 744 Nelson Santovenia	.03	.01	.00
☐ 745 Doug Jones	.03	.01	.00
☐ 746 John Shelby	.03	.01	.00
☐ 747 Tony Fossas	.03	.01	.00
☐ 748 Al Newman	.03	.01	.00
☐ 749 Greg W. Harris	.03	.01	.00
☐ 750 Bobby Bonilla	.10	.04	.01
☐ 751 Wayne Edwards	.03	.01	.00
☐ 752 Kevin Bass	.03	.01	.00
☐ 753 Paul Marak	.08	.03	.01
☐ 754 Bill Pecota	.03	.01	.00
☐ 755 Mark Langston	.06	.02	.00
☐ 756 Jeff Huson	.03	.01	.00
☐ 757 Mark Gardner	.06	.02	.00
☐ 758 Mike Devereaux	.03	.01	.00
☐ 759 Bobby Cox MG	.03	.01	.00
☐ 760 Benny Santiago	.06	.02	.00
☐ 761 Larry Andersen	.03	.01	.00
☐ 762 Mitch Webster	.03	.01	.00
☐ 763 Dana Kiecker	.03	.01	.00
☐ 764 Mark Carreon	.03	.01	.00
☐ 765 Shawon Dunston	.06	.02	.00
☐ 766 Jeff Robinson	.03	.01	.00
☐ 767 Dan Wilson	.15	.06	.01
☐ 768 Don Pall	.03	.01	.00
☐ 769 Tim Sherrill	.08	.03	.01
☐ 770 Jay Howell	.03	.01	.00
☐ 771 Gary Redus UER (Born in Tanner, should say Athens)	.03	.01	.00
☐ 772 Kent Mercker (Born in Indianapolis, should say Dublin, Ohio)	.08	.03	.01
☐ 773 Tom Foley	.03	.01	.00
☐ 774 Dennis Rasmussen	.03	.01	.00
☐ 775 Julio Franco	.08	.03	.01
☐ 776 Brent Mayne	.08	.03	.01
☐ 777 John Candelaria	.03	.01	.00
☐ 778 Dan Gladden	.03	.01	.00
☐ 779 Carmelo Martinez	.03	.01	.00
☐ 780A Randy Myers ERR (15 career losses)	.25	.10	.02
☐ 780B Randy Myers COR (19 career losses)	.06	.02	.00
☐ 781 Darryl Hamilton	.03	.01	.00
☐ 782 Jim Deshaies	.03	.01	.00
☐ 783 Joel Skinner	.03	.01	.00
☐ 784 Willie Fraser	.03	.01	.00
☐ 785 Scott Fletcher	.03	.01	.00
☐ 786 Eric Plunk	.03	.01	.00
☐ 787 Checklist 6	.06	.01	.00
☐ 788 Bob Milacki	.03	.01	.00
☐ 789 Tom Lasorda MG	.06	.02	.00
☐ 790 Ken Griffey Jr.	.75	.30	.07
☐ 791 Mike Benjamin	.06	.02	.00
☐ 792 Mike Greenwell	.10	.04	.01

1991 Topps Traded

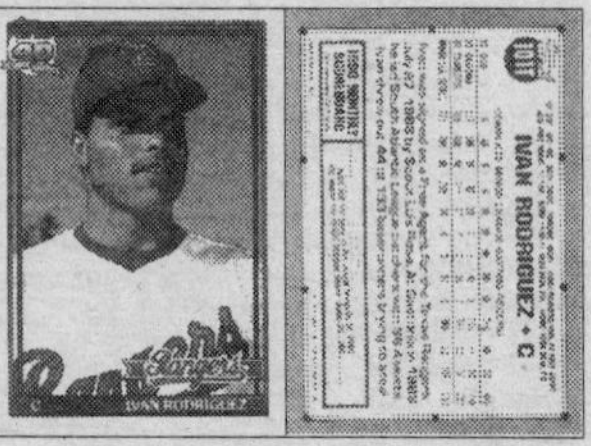

The 1991 Topps Traded set contains 132 cards measuring the standard size (2 1/2 by 3 1/2"). The set includes a Team U.S.A. subset, featuring 25 of America's top collegiate players; these players are indicated in the checklist below by USA. The cards were sold in wax packs as well as factory sets. The cards in the wax packs (gray backs) and collated factory sets (white backs) are from different card stock. The fronts have color action player photos, with two different color borders on a white card face. The player's position and name are given in the thicker border below the picture. In blue print on a

pink and gray background, the horizontally oriented backs have biographical information and statistics. The cards are numbered on the back in the upper left corner; the set numbering corresponds to alphabetical order. The key rookie cards in this set are Jeff Bagwell and Ivan Rodriguez.

	MINT	EXC	G-VG
COMPLETE SET (132)	11.00	5.00	1.35
COMMON PLAYER (1T-132T)	.05	.02	.00
☐ 1T Juan Agosto	.05	.02	.00
☐ 2T Roberto Alomar	.12	.05	.01
☐ 3T Wally Backman	.05	.02	.00
☐ 4T Jeff Bagwell	3.00	1.25	.30
☐ 5T Skeeter Barnes	.08	.03	.01
☐ 6T Steve Bedrosian	.05	.02	.00
☐ 7T Derek Bell	.35	.15	.03
☐ 8T George Bell	.10	.04	.01
☐ 9T Rafael Belliard	.05	.02	.00
☐ 10T Dante Bichette	.05	.02	.00
☐ 11T Bud Black	.05	.02	.00
☐ 12T Mike Boddicker	.08	.03	.01
☐ 13T Sid Bream	.05	.02	.00
☐ 14T Hubie Brooks	.08	.03	.01
☐ 15T Brett Butler	.08	.03	.01
☐ 16T Ivan Calderon	.08	.03	.01
☐ 17T John Candelaria	.05	.02	.00
☐ 18T Tom Candiotti	.08	.03	.01
☐ 19T Gary Carter	.08	.03	.01
☐ 20T Joe Carter	.10	.04	.01
☐ 21T Rick Cerone	.05	.02	.00
☐ 22T Jack Clark	.08	.03	.01
☐ 23T Vince Coleman	.08	.03	.01
☐ 24T Scott Coolbaugh	.05	.02	.00
☐ 25T Danny Cox	.05	.02	.00
☐ 26T Danny Darwin	.05	.02	.00
☐ 27T Chili Davis	.08	.03	.01
☐ 28T Glenn Davis	.10	.04	.01
☐ 29T Steve Decker	.25	.10	.02
☐ 30T Rob Deer	.08	.03	.01
☐ 31T Rich DeLucia	.12	.05	.01
☐ 32T John Dettmer USA	.12	.05	.01
☐ 33T Brian Downing	.05	.02	.00
☐ 34T Darren Dreifort USA	.12	.05	.01
☐ 35T Kirk Dressendorfer	.20	.08	.02
☐ 36T Jim Essian MG	.05	.02	.00
☐ 37T Dwight Evans	.08	.03	.01
☐ 38T Steve Farr	.05	.02	.00
☐ 39T Jeff Fassero	.12	.05	.01
☐ 40T Junior Felix	.08	.03	.01
☐ 41T Tony Fernandez	.08	.03	.01
☐ 42T Steve Finley	.08	.03	.01
☐ 43T Jim Fregosi MG	.05	.02	.00
☐ 44T Gary Gaetti	.08	.03	.01
☐ 45T Jason Giambi USA	.20	.08	.02
☐ 46T Kirk Gibson	.10	.04	.01
☐ 47T Leo Gomez	.25	.10	.02
☐ 48T Luis Gonzalez	.40	.16	.04
☐ 49T Jeff Granger USA	.30	.12	.03
☐ 50T Todd Greene USA	.15	.06	.01
☐ 51T Jeffrey Hammonds USA	.40	.16	.04
☐ 52T Mike Hargrove MG	.05	.02	.00
☐ 53T Pete Harnisch	.08	.03	.01
☐ 54T Rick Helling USA UER (Misspelled Hellings on card back)	.15	.06	.01
☐ 55T Glenallen Hill	.08	.03	.01
☐ 56T Charlie Hough	.05	.02	.00
☐ 57T Pete Incaviglia	.08	.03	.01
☐ 58T Bo Jackson	1.00	.40	.10
☐ 59T Danny Jackson	.08	.03	.01
☐ 60T Reggie Jefferson	.40	.16	.04
☐ 61T Charles Johnson USA	.40	.16	.04
☐ 62T Jeff Johnson	.20	.08	.02
☐ 63T Todd Johnson USA	.15	.06	.01
☐ 64T Barry Jones	.05	.02	.00
☐ 65T Chris Jones	.15	.06	.01
☐ 66T Scott Kamieniecki	.15	.06	.01
☐ 67T Pat Kelly	.30	.12	.03
☐ 68T Darryl Kile	.12	.05	.01
☐ 69T Chuck Knoblauch	.40	.16	.04
☐ 70T Bill Krueger	.05	.02	.00
☐ 71T Scott Leius	.12	.05	.01
☐ 72T Donnie Leshnock USA	.12	.05	.01
☐ 73T Mark Lewis	.20	.08	.02
☐ 74T Candy Maldonado	.08	.03	.01
☐ 75T Jason McDonald USA	.12	.05	.01
☐ 76T Willie McGee	.08	.03	.01
☐ 77T Fred McGriff	.10	.04	.01
☐ 78T Billy McMillon USA	.15	.06	.01
☐ 79T Hal McRae MG	.08	.03	.01
☐ 80T Dan Melendez USA	.20	.08	.02
☐ 81T Orlando Merced	.40	.16	.04
☐ 82T Jack Morris	.10	.04	.01
☐ 83T Phil Nevin USA	.20	.08	.02
☐ 84T Otis Nixon	.08	.03	.01
☐ 85T Johnny Oates MG	.05	.02	.00
☐ 86T Bob Ojeda	.05	.02	.00
☐ 87T Mike Pagliarulo	.05	.02	.00
☐ 88T Dean Palmer	.35	.15	.03
☐ 89T Dave Parker	.10	.04	.01
☐ 90T Terry Pendleton	.10	.04	.01
☐ 91T Tony Phillips (P) USA	.15	.06	.01
☐ 92T Doug Piatt	.15	.06	.01
☐ 93T Ron Polk USA CO	.05	.02	.00
☐ 94T Tim Raines	.10	.04	.01
☐ 95T Willie Randolph	.08	.03	.01
☐ 96T Dave Righetti	.08	.03	.01
☐ 97T Ernie Riles	.05	.02	.00
☐ 98T Chris Roberts USA	.40	.16	.04
☐ 99T Jeff D. Robinson	.05	.02	.00
☐ 100T Jeff M. Robinson	.05	.02	.00
☐ 101T Ivan Rodriguez	2.00	.80	.20
☐ 102T Steve Rodriguez USA	.15	.06	.01

		MINT	EXC	G-VG
☐ 103T	Tom Runnells MG	.05	.02	.00
☐ 104T	Scott Sanderson	.08	.03	.01
☐ 105T	Bob Scanlan	.12	.05	.01
☐ 106T	Pete Schourek	.12	.05	.01
☐ 107T	Gary Scott	.25	.10	.02
☐ 108T	Paul Shuey USA	.12	.05	.01
☐ 109T	Doug Simons	.12	.05	.01
☐ 110T	Dave Smith	.05	.02	.00
☐ 111T	Cory Snyder	.08	.03	.01
☐ 112T	Luis Sojo	.08	.03	.01
☐ 113T	Kennie Steenstra USA	.15	.06	.01
☐ 114T	Darryl Strawberry	.20	.08	.02
☐ 115T	Franklin Stubbs	.05	.02	.00
☐ 116T	Todd Taylor USA	.12	.05	.01
☐ 117T	Wade Taylor	.17	.07	.01
☐ 118T	Garry Templeton	.05	.02	.00
☐ 119T	Mickey Tettleton	.08	.03	.01
☐ 120T	Tim Teufel	.05	.02	.00
☐ 121T	Mike Timlin	.12	.05	.01
☐ 122T	David Tuttle USA	.15	.06	.01
☐ 123T	Mo Vaughn	.60	.25	.06
☐ 124T	Jeff Ware USA	.25	.10	.02
☐ 125T	Devon White	.08	.03	.01
☐ 126T	Mark Whiten	.20	.08	.02
☐ 127T	Mitch Williams	.08	.03	.01
☐ 128T	Craig Wilson USA	.15	.06	.01
☐ 129T	Willie Wilson	.08	.03	.01
☐ 130T	Chris Wimmer	.15	.06	.01
☐ 131T	Ivan Zweig USA	.15	.06	.01
☐ 132T	Checklist Card	.05	.01	.00

1991 Topps Stadium Club I

This 300-card standard size (2 1/2" by 3 1/2") set marked Topps first entry into the mass market with a premium quality set. The set features borderless full-color action photos on the front with the name of the player and the Topps Stadium club logo on the bottom of the card, while the back of the card has the basic biographical information as well as making use of the Fastball Bars system and an inset photo of the player's Topps rookie card. The key rookie cards in this series are Lance Dickson and Randy Tomlin.

	MINT	EXC	G-VG
COMPLETE SET (300)	165.00	75.00	15.00
COMMON PLAYER (1-300)	.20	.08	.02

		MINT	EXC	G-VG
☐ 1	Dave Stewart (Wearing Tuxedo)	1.50	.60	.15
☐ 2	Wally Joyner	.40	.16	.04
☐ 3	Shawon Dunston	.30	.12	.03
☐ 4	Darren Daulton	.20	.08	.02
☐ 5	Will Clark	3.25	1.35	.32
☐ 6	Sammy Sosa	.35	.15	.03
☐ 7	Dan Plesac	.20	.08	.02
☐ 8	Marquis Grissom	.75	.30	.07
☐ 9	Erik Hanson	.30	.12	.03
☐ 10	Geno Petralli	.20	.08	.02
☐ 11	Jose Rijo	.25	.10	.02
☐ 12	Carlos Quintana	.25	.10	.02
☐ 13	Junior Ortiz	.20	.08	.02
☐ 14	Bob Walk	.20	.08	.02
☐ 15	Mike Macfarlane	.20	.08	.02
☐ 16	Eric Yelding	.20	.08	.02
☐ 17	Bryn Smith	.20	.08	.02
☐ 18	Bip Roberts	.25	.10	.02
☐ 19	Mike Scioscia	.20	.08	.02
☐ 20	Mark Williamson	.20	.08	.02
☐ 21	Don Mattingly	1.50	.60	.15
☐ 22	John Franco	.25	.10	.02
☐ 23	Chet Lemon	.20	.08	.02
☐ 24	Tom Henke	.25	.10	.02
☐ 25	Jerry Browne	.20	.08	.02
☐ 26	Dave Justice	12.00	5.25	1.50
☐ 27	Mark Langston	.40	.16	.04
☐ 28	Damon Berryhill	.20	.08	.02
☐ 29	Kevin Bass	.20	.08	.02
☐ 30	Scott Fletcher	.20	.08	.02
☐ 31	Moises Alou	.25	.10	.02
☐ 32	Dave Valle	.20	.08	.02
☐ 33	Jody Reed	.25	.10	.02
☐ 34	Dave West	.25	.10	.02
☐ 35	Kevin McReynolds	.30	.12	.03
☐ 36	Pat Combs	.25	.10	.02
☐ 37	Eric Davis	.75	.30	.07
☐ 38	Bret Saberhagen	.40	.16	.04
☐ 39	Stan Javier	.20	.08	.02
☐ 40	Chuck Cary	.20	.08	.02
☐ 41	Tony Phillips	.20	.08	.02

□ 42 Lee Smith	.25	.10	.02
□ 43 Tim Teufel	.20	.08	.02
□ 44 Lance Dickson	1.00	.40	.10
□ 45 Greg Litton	.20	.08	.02
□ 46 Teddy Higuera	.25	.10	.02
□ 47 Edgar Martinez	.30	.12	.03
□ 48 Steve Avery	8.00	3.50	.80
□ 49 Walt Weiss	.25	.10	.02
□ 50 David Segui	.30	.12	.03
□ 51 Andy Benes	.40	.16	.04
□ 52 Karl Rhodes	.30	.12	.03
□ 53 Neal Heaton	.20	.08	.02
□ 54 Danny Gladden	.20	.08	.02
□ 55 Luis Rivera	.20	.08	.02
□ 56 Kevin Brown	.25	.10	.02
□ 57 Frank Thomas	30.00	13.50	4.50
□ 58 Terry Mulholland	.25	.10	.02
□ 59 Dick Schofield	.20	.08	.02
□ 60 Ron Darling	.25	.10	.02
□ 61 Sandy Alomar Jr.	.40	.16	.04
□ 62 Dave Stieb	.25	.10	.02
□ 63 Alan Trammell	.45	.18	.04
□ 64 Matt Nokes	.25	.10	.02
□ 65 Lenny Harris	.20	.08	.02
□ 66 Milt Thompson	.20	.08	.02
□ 67 Storm Davis	.20	.08	.02
□ 68 Joe Oliver	.20	.08	.02
□ 69 Andres Galarraga	.25	.10	.02
□ 70 Ozzie Guillen	.25	.10	.02
□ 71 Ken Howell	.20	.08	.02
□ 72 Garry Templeton	.20	.08	.02
□ 73 Derrick May	.25	.10	.02
□ 74 Xavier Hernandez	.20	.08	.02
□ 75 Dave Parker	.30	.12	.03
□ 76 Rick Aguilera	.25	.10	.02
□ 77 Robby Thompson	.20	.08	.02
□ 78 Pete Incaviglia	.25	.10	.02
□ 79 Bob Welch	.25	.10	.02
□ 80 Randy Milligan	.25	.10	.02
□ 81 Chuck Finley	.30	.12	.03
□ 82 Alvin Davis	.25	.10	.02
□ 83 Tim Naehring	.35	.15	.03
□ 84 Jay Bell	.20	.08	.02
□ 85 Joe Magrane	.20	.08	.02
□ 86 Howard Johnson	.60	.25	.06
□ 87 Jack McDowell	.35	.15	.03
□ 88 Kevin Seitzer	.25	.10	.02
□ 89 Bruce Ruffin	.20	.08	.02
□ 90 Fernando Valenzuela	.25	.10	.02
□ 91 Terry Kennedy	.20	.08	.02
□ 92 Barry Larkin	.75	.30	.07
□ 93 Larry Walker	.35	.15	.03
□ 94 Luis Salazar	.20	.08	.02
□ 95 Gary Sheffield	.30	.12	.03
□ 96 Bobby Witt	.25	.10	.02
□ 97 Lonnie Smith	.25	.10	.02
□ 98 Bryan Harvey	.25	.10	.02
□ 99 Mookie Wilson	.25	.10	.02
□ 100 Dwight Gooden	.75	.30	.07
□ 101 Lou Whitaker	.25	.10	.02
□ 102 Ron Karkovice	.20	.08	.02
□ 103 Jesse Barfield	.25	.10	.02
□ 104 Jose DeJesus	.20	.08	.02
□ 105 Benito Santiago	.30	.12	.03
□ 106 Brian Holman	.25	.10	.02
□ 107 Rafael Ramirez	.20	.08	.02
□ 108 Ellis Burks	.40	.16	.04
□ 109 Mike Bielecki	.20	.08	.02
□ 110 Kirby Puckett	1.50	.60	.15
□ 111 Terry Shumpert	.25	.10	.02
□ 112 Chuck Crim	.20	.08	.02
□ 113 Todd Benzinger	.20	.08	.02
□ 114 Brian Barnes	.45	.18	.04
□ 115 Carlos Baerga	.85	.35	.08
□ 116 Kal Daniels	.25	.10	.02
□ 117 Dave Johnson	.20	.08	.02
□ 118 Andy Van Slyke	.30	.12	.03
□ 119 John Burkett	.20	.08	.02
□ 120 Rickey Henderson	2.50	1.00	.25
□ 121 Tim Jones	.20	.08	.02
□ 122 Daryl Irvine	.30	.12	.03
□ 123 Ruben Sierra	1.50	.60	.15
□ 124 Jim Abbott	1.00	.40	.10
□ 125 Daryl Boston	.20	.08	.02
□ 126 Greg Maddux	.25	.10	.02
□ 127 Von Hayes	.25	.10	.02
□ 128 Mike Fitzgerald	.20	.08	.02
□ 129 Wayne Edwards	.20	.08	.02
□ 130 Greg Briley	.20	.08	.02
□ 131 Rob Dibble	.25	.10	.02
□ 132 Gene Larkin	.20	.08	.02
□ 133 David Wells	.20	.08	.02
□ 134 Steve Balboni	.20	.08	.02
□ 135 Greg Vaughn	1.25	.50	.12
□ 136 Mark Davis	.25	.10	.02
□ 137 Dave Rhode	.25	.10	.02
□ 138 Eric Show	.20	.08	.02
□ 139 Bobby Bonilla	1.00	.40	.10
□ 140 Dana Kiecker	.20	.08	.02
□ 141 Gary Pettis	.20	.08	.02
□ 142 Dennis Boyd	.20	.08	.02
□ 143 Mike Benjamin	.20	.08	.02
□ 144 Luis Polonia	.25	.10	.02
□ 145 Doug Jones	.20	.08	.02
□ 146 Al Newman	.20	.08	.02
□ 147 Alex Fernandez	.90	.40	.09
□ 148 Bill Doran	.20	.08	.02
□ 149 Kevin Elster	.20	.08	.02
□ 150 Len Dykstra	.30	.12	.03
□ 151 Mike Gallego	.20	.08	.02
□ 152 Tim Belcher	.25	.10	.02
□ 153 Jay Buhner	.30	.12	.03
□ 154 Ozzie Smith UER (Rookie card is 1979, but card back says '78)	.80	.35	.08
□ 155 Jose Canseco	4.00	1.75	.40

□ 156	Gregg Olson	.30	.12	.03
□ 157	Charlie O'Brien	.20	.08	.02
□ 158	Frank Tanana	.25	.10	.02
□ 159	George Brett	.90	.40	.09
□ 160	Jeff Huson	.20	.08	.02
□ 161	Kevin Tapani	.45	.18	.04
□ 162	Jerome Walton	.25	.10	.02
□ 163	Charlie Hayes	.20	.08	.02
□ 164	Chris Bosio	.20	.08	.02
□ 165	Chris Sabo	.35	.15	.03
□ 166	Lance Parrish	.25	.10	.02
□ 167	Don Robinson	.20	.08	.02
□ 168	Manny Lee	.20	.08	.02
□ 169	Dennis Rasmussen	.20	.08	.02
□ 170	Wade Boggs	1.50	.60	.15
□ 171	Bob Geren	.20	.08	.02
□ 172	Mackey Sasser	.20	.08	.02
□ 173	Julio Franco	.45	.18	.04
□ 174	Otis Nixon	.25	.10	.02
□ 175	Bert Blyleven	.25	.10	.02
□ 176	Craig Biggio	.35	.15	.03
□ 177	Eddie Murray	.60	.25	.06
□ 178	Randy Tomlin	1.25	.50	.12
□ 179	Tino Martinez	1.00	.40	.10
□ 180	Carlton Fisk	.90	.40	.09
□ 181	Dwight Smith	.25	.10	.02
□ 182	Scott Garrelts	.20	.08	.02
□ 183	Jim Gantner	.20	.08	.02
□ 184	Dickie Thon	.20	.08	.02
□ 185	John Farrell	.20	.08	.02
□ 186	Cecil Fielder	2.25	.90	.22
□ 187	Glenn Braggs	.20	.08	.02
□ 188	Allan Anderson	.20	.08	.02
□ 189	Kurt Stillwell	.20	.08	.02
□ 190	Jose Oquendo	.20	.08	.02
□ 191	Joe Orsulak	.20	.08	.02
□ 192	Ricky Jordan	.25	.10	.02
□ 193	Kelly Downs	.20	.08	.02
□ 194	Delino DeShields	.75	.30	.07
□ 195	Omar Vizquel	.20	.08	.02
□ 196	Mark Carreon	.20	.08	.02
□ 197	Mike Harkey	.25	.10	.02
□ 198	Jack Howell	.20	.08	.02
□ 199	Lance Johnson	.20	.08	.02
□ 200	Nolan Ryan (Wearing Tuxedo)	15.00	6.50	2.15
□ 201	John Marzano	.20	.08	.02
□ 202	Doug Drabek	.30	.12	.03
□ 203	Mark Lemke	.30	.12	.03
□ 204	Steve Sax	.30	.12	.03
□ 205	Greg Harris	.20	.08	.02
□ 206	B.J. Surhoff	.25	.10	.02
□ 207	Todd Burns	.20	.08	.02
□ 208	Jose Gonzalez	.20	.08	.02
□ 209	Mike Scott	.25	.10	.02
□ 210	Dave Magadan	.25	.10	.02
□ 211	Dante Bichette	.20	.08	.02
□ 212	Trevor Wilson	.20	.08	.02
□ 213	Hector Villanueva	.25	.10	.02
□ 214	Dan Pasqua	.20	.08	.02
□ 215	Greg Colbrunn	.40	.16	.04
□ 216	Mike Jeffcoat	.20	.08	.02
□ 217	Harold Reynolds	.25	.10	.02
□ 218	Paul O'Neill	.25	.10	.02
□ 219	Mark Guthrie	.20	.08	.02
□ 220	Barry Bonds	1.25	.50	.12
□ 221	Jimmy Key	.25	.10	.02
□ 222	Billy Ripken	.20	.08	.02
□ 223	Tom Pagnozzi	.20	.08	.02
□ 224	Bo Jackson	4.00	1.75	.40
□ 225	Sid Fernandez	.25	.10	.02
□ 226	Mike Marshall	.25	.10	.02
□ 227	John Kruk	.20	.08	.02
□ 228	Mike Fetters	.20	.08	.02
□ 229	Eric Anthony	.30	.12	.03
□ 230	Ryne Sandberg	3.25	1.35	.32
□ 231	Carney Lansford	.25	.10	.02
□ 232	Melido Perez	.20	.08	.02
□ 233	Jose Lind	.20	.08	.02
□ 234	Darryl Hamilton	.25	.10	.02
□ 235	Tom Browning	.25	.10	.02
□ 236	Spike Owen	.20	.08	.02
□ 237	Juan Gonzalez	11.00	5.00	1.35
□ 238	Felix Fermin	.20	.08	.02
□ 239	Keith Miller	.20	.08	.02
□ 240	Mark Gubicza	.25	.10	.02
□ 241	Kent Anderson	.20	.08	.02
□ 242	Alvaro Espinoza	.20	.08	.02
□ 243	Dale Murphy	.50	.20	.05
□ 244	Orel Hershiser	.40	.16	.04
□ 245	Paul Molitor	.40	.16	.04
□ 246	Eddie Whitson	.20	.08	.02
□ 247	Joe Girardi	.25	.10	.02
□ 248	Kent Hrbek	.25	.10	.02
□ 249	Bill Sampen	.25	.10	.02
□ 250	Kevin Mitchell	.75	.30	.07
□ 251	Mariano Duncan	.20	.08	.02
□ 252	Scott Bradley	.20	.08	.02
□ 253	Mike Greenwell	.60	.25	.06
□ 254	Tom Gordon	.25	.10	.02
□ 255	Todd Zeile	.90	.40	.09
□ 256	Bobby Thigpen	.25	.10	.02
□ 257	Gregg Jefferies	.40	.16	.04
□ 258	Kenny Rogers	.20	.08	.02
□ 259	Shane Mack	.25	.10	.02
□ 260	Zane Smith	.25	.10	.02
□ 261	Mitch Williams	.20	.08	.02
□ 262	Jim Deshaies	.20	.08	.02
□ 263	Dave Winfield	.60	.25	.06
□ 264	Ben McDonald	1.25	.50	.12
□ 265	Randy Ready	.20	.08	.02
□ 266	Pat Borders	.25	.10	.02
□ 267	Jose Uribe	.20	.08	.02
□ 268	Derek Lilliquist	.20	.08	.02
□ 269	Greg Brock	.20	.08	.02
□ 270	Ken Griffey Jr.	16.00	6.75	2.25

☐ 271 Jeff Gray	.30	.12	.03
☐ 272 Danny Tartabull	.40	.16	.04
☐ 273 Denny Martinez	.25	.10	.02
☐ 274 Robin Ventura	3.00	1.25	.30
☐ 275 Randy Myers	.25	.10	.02
☐ 276 Jack Daugherty	.20	.08	.02
☐ 277 Greg Gagne	.20	.08	.02
☐ 278 Jay Howell	.20	.08	.02
☐ 279 Mike LaValliere	.20	.08	.02
☐ 280 Rex Hudler	.20	.08	.02
☐ 281 Mike Simms	.60	.25	.06
☐ 282 Kevin Maas	2.50	1.00	.25
☐ 283 Jeff Ballard	.20	.08	.02
☐ 284 Dave Henderson	.30	.12	.03
☐ 285 Pete O'Brien	.20	.08	.02
☐ 286 Brook Jacoby	.20	.08	.02
☐ 287 Mike Henneman	.20	.08	.02
☐ 288 Greg Olson	.25	.10	.02
☐ 289 Greg Myers	.20	.08	.02
☐ 290 Mark Grace	.50	.20	.05
☐ 291 Shawn Abner	.20	.08	.02
☐ 292 Frank Viola	.30	.12	.03
☐ 293 Lee Stevens	.50	.20	.05
☐ 294 Jason Grimsley	.25	.10	.02
☐ 295 Matt Williams	.75	.30	.07
☐ 296 Ron Robinson	.20	.08	.02
☐ 297 Tom Brunansky	.25	.10	.02
☐ 298 Checklist 1-100	.20	.03	.01
☐ 299 Checklist 101-200	.20	.03	.01
☐ 300 Checklist 201-300	.20	.03	.01

1991 Topps Stadium Club II

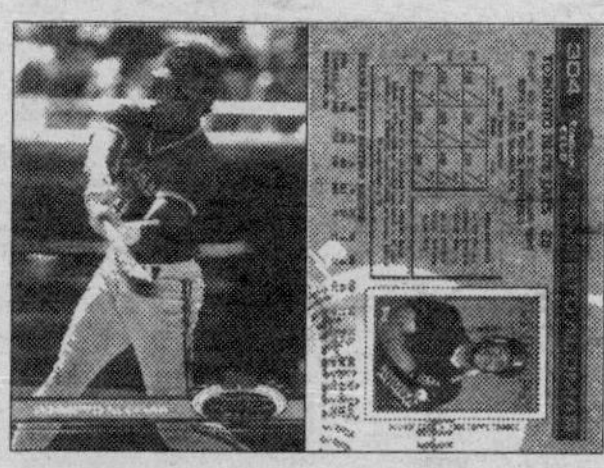

The 1991 Topps Stadium Club Series II set contains 300 cards measuring the standard size (2 1/2" by 3 1/2"). Series II cards were also available at McDonald's restaurants in the Northeast at three cards per pack. The front design has borderless high glossy color player photos. At the bottom of the card face, the player's name appears in an aqua stripe bounded by gold stripes. The "Topps Stadium Club" insignia overlays the stripe. In a horizontal format, the backs have a miniature reproduction of the player's rookie card, biography, Fastball BARS system, evaluation, and major league batting record, on a painted background consisting of a baseball and playing field. The cards are numbered on the back. The key rookie cards in this series are Jeff Bagwell, Wes Chamberlain, and Phil Plantier.

	MINT	EXC	G-VG
COMPLETE SET (300)	100.00	45.00	15.00
COMMON PLAYER (301-600)	.20	.08	.02
☐ 301 Darryl Strawberry	2.25	.90	.22
☐ 302 Bud Black	.20	.08	.02
☐ 303 Harold Baines	.25	.10	.02
☐ 304 Roberto Alomar	1.00	.40	.10
☐ 305 Norm Charlton	.25	.10	.02
☐ 306 Gary Thurman	.20	.08	.02
☐ 307 Mike Felder	.20	.08	.02
☐ 308 Tony Gwynn	1.50	.60	.15
☐ 309 Roger Clemens	2.25	.90	.22
☐ 310 Andre Dawson	.60	.25	.06
☐ 311 Scott Radinsky	.25	.10	.02
☐ 312 Bob Melvin	.20	.08	.02
☐ 313 Kirk McCaskill	.20	.08	.02
☐ 314 Pedro Guerrero	.30	.12	.03
☐ 315 Walt Terrell	.20	.08	.02
☐ 316 Sam Horn	.20	.08	.02
☐ 317 Wes Chamberlain	4.00	1.75	.40
☐ 318 Pedro Munoz	1.25	.50	.12
☐ 319 Roberto Kelly	.35	.15	.03
☐ 320 Mark Portugal	.20	.08	.02
☐ 321 Tim McIntosh	.25	.10	.02
☐ 322 Jesse Orosco	.20	.08	.02
☐ 323 Gary Green	.20	.08	.02
☐ 324 Greg Harris	.20	.08	.02
☐ 325 Hubie Brooks	.25	.10	.02
☐ 326 Chris Nabholz	.30	.12	.03
☐ 327 Terry Pendleton	.35	.15	.03
☐ 328 Eric King	.20	.08	.02
☐ 329 Chili Davis	.25	.10	.02
☐ 330 Anthony Telford	.30	.12	.03
☐ 331 Kelly Gruber	.30	.12	.03
☐ 332 Dennis Eckersley	.30	.12	.03
☐ 333 Mel Hall	.25	.10	.02
☐ 334 Bob Kipper	.20	.08	.02
☐ 335 Willie McGee	.25	.10	.02
☐ 336 Steve Olin	.20	.08	.02
☐ 337 Steve Buechele	.20	.08	.02

☐ 338 Scott Leius	.40	.16	.04
☐ 339 Hal Morris	1.00	.40	.10
☐ 340 Jose Offerman	.40	.16	.04
☐ 341 Kent Mercker	.25	.10	.02
☐ 342 Ken Griffey Sr.	.30	.12	.03
☐ 343 Pete Harnisch	.25	.10	.02
☐ 344 Kirk Gibson	.30	.12	.03
☐ 345 Dave Smith	.20	.08	.02
☐ 346 Dave Martinez	.20	.08	.02
☐ 347 Atlee Hammaker	.20	.08	.02
☐ 348 Brian Downing	.20	.08	.02
☐ 349 Todd Hundley	.60	.25	.06
☐ 350 Candy Maldonado	.20	.08	.02
☐ 351 Dwight Evans	.25	.10	.02
☐ 352 Steve Searcy	.20	.08	.02
☐ 353 Gary Gaetti	.25	.10	.02
☐ 354 Jeff Reardon	.30	.12	.03
☐ 355 Travis Fryman	4.25	1.75	.42
☐ 356 Dave Righetti	.25	.10	.02
☐ 357 Fred McGriff	.60	.25	.06
☐ 358 Don Slaught	.20	.08	.02
☐ 359 Gene Nelson	.20	.08	.02
☐ 360 Billy Spiers	.20	.08	.02
☐ 361 Lee Guetterman	.20	.08	.02
☐ 362 Darren Lewis	1.25	.50	.12
☐ 363 Duane Ward	.20	.08	.02
☐ 364 Lloyd Moseby	.20	.08	.02
☐ 365 John Smoltz	.45	.18	.04
☐ 366 Felix Jose	.75	.30	.07
☐ 367 David Cone	.30	.12	.03
☐ 368 Wally Backman	.20	.08	.02
☐ 369 Jeff Montgomery	.25	.10	.02
☐ 370 Rich Garces	.40	.16	.04
☐ 371 Billy Hatcher	.25	.10	.02
☐ 372 Bill Swift	.20	.08	.02
☐ 373 Jim Eisenreich	.20	.08	.02
☐ 374 Rob Ducey	.20	.08	.02
☐ 375 Tim Crews	.20	.08	.02
☐ 376 Steve Finley	.25	.10	.02
☐ 377 Jeff Blauser	.20	.08	.02
☐ 378 Willie Wilson	.25	.10	.02
☐ 379 Gerald Perry	.20	.08	.02
☐ 380 Jose Mesa	.20	.08	.02
☐ 381 Pat Kelly	1.75	.70	.17
☐ 382 Matt Merullo	.25	.10	.02
☐ 383 Ivan Calderon	.25	.10	.02
☐ 384 Scott Chiamparino	.30	.12	.03
☐ 385 Lloyd McClendon	.20	.08	.02
☐ 386 Dave Bergman	.20	.08	.02
☐ 387 Ed Sprague	.60	.25	.06
☐ 388 Jeff Bagwell	12.00	5.25	1.50
☐ 389 Brett Butler	.30	.12	.03
☐ 390 Larry Andersen	.20	.08	.02
☐ 391 Glenn Davis	.30	.12	.03
☐ 392 Alex Cole UER (Front photo actually Otis Nixon)	.35	.15	.03
☐ 393 Mike Heath	.20	.08	.02
☐ 394 Danny Darwin	.20	.08	.02
☐ 395 Steve Lake	.20	.08	.02
☐ 396 Tim Layana	.20	.08	.02
☐ 397 Terry Leach	.20	.08	.02
☐ 398 Bill Wegman	.20	.08	.02
☐ 399 Mark McGwire	.60	.25	.06
☐ 400 Mike Boddicker	.20	.08	.02
☐ 401 Steve Howe	.20	.08	.02
☐ 402 Bernard Gilkey	.60	.25	.06
☐ 403 Thomas Howard	.25	.10	.02
☐ 404 Rafael Belliard	.20	.08	.02
☐ 405 Tom Candiotti	.25	.10	.02
☐ 406 Rene Gonzalez	.20	.08	.02
☐ 407 Chuck McElroy	.25	.10	.02
☐ 408 Paul Sorrento	.25	.10	.02
☐ 409 Randy Johnson	.30	.12	.03
☐ 410 Brady Anderson	.20	.08	.02
☐ 411 Dennis Cook	.20	.08	.02
☐ 412 Mickey Tettleton	.25	.10	.02
☐ 413 Mike Stanton	.20	.08	.02
☐ 414 Ken Oberkfell	.20	.08	.02
☐ 415 Rick Honeycutt	.20	.08	.02
☐ 416 Nelson Santovenia	.20	.08	.02
☐ 417 Bob Tewksbury	.20	.08	.02
☐ 418 Brent Mayne	.35	.15	.03
☐ 419 Steve Farr	.20	.08	.02
☐ 420 Phil Stephenson	.20	.08	.02
☐ 421 Jeff Russell	.20	.08	.02
☐ 422 Chris James	.20	.08	.02
☐ 423 Tim Leary	.25	.10	.02
☐ 424 Gary Carter	.35	.15	.03
☐ 425 Glenallen Hill	.25	.10	.02
☐ 426 Matt Young UER (Card mentions 83T/Tr as RC, but 84T shown)	.20	.08	.02
☐ 427 Sid Bream	.20	.08	.02
☐ 428 Greg Swindell	.25	.10	.02
☐ 429 Scott Aldred	.30	.12	.03
☐ 430 Cal Ripken	4.00	1.75	.40
☐ 431 Bill Landrum	.20	.08	.02
☐ 432 Earnest Riles	.20	.08	.02
☐ 433 Danny Jackson	.25	.10	.02
☐ 434 Casey Candaele	.20	.08	.02
☐ 435 Ken Hill	.25	.10	.02
☐ 436 Jaime Navarro	.25	.10	.02
☐ 437 Lance Blankenship	.20	.08	.02
☐ 438 Randy Velarde	.20	.08	.02
☐ 439 Frank DiPino	.20	.08	.02
☐ 440 Carl Nichols	.20	.08	.02
☐ 441 Jeff M. Robinson	.20	.08	.02
☐ 442 Deion Sanders	.50	.20	.05
☐ 443 Vicente Palacios	.20	.08	.02
☐ 444 Devon White	.25	.10	.02
☐ 445 John Cerutti	.20	.08	.02
☐ 446 Tracy Jones	.20	.08	.02
☐ 447 Jack Morris	.35	.15	.03
☐ 448 Mitch Webster	.20	.08	.02
☐ 449 Bob Ojeda	.20	.08	.02

☐ 450 Oscar Azocar .20 .08 .02
☐ 451 Luis Aquino .20 .08 .02
☐ 452 Mark Whiten 1.25 .50 .12
☐ 453 Stan Belinda .25 .10 .02
☐ 454 Ron Gant 1.00 .40 .10
☐ 455 Jose DeLeon .20 .08 .02
☐ 456 Mark Salas UER .20 .08 .02
(Back has 85T photo, but calls it 86T)
☐ 457 Junior Felix .25 .10 .02
☐ 458 Wally Whitehurst .20 .08 .02
☐ 459 Phil Plantier 12.00 5.25 1.50
☐ 460 Juan Berenguer .20 .08 .02
☐ 461 Franklin Stubbs .20 .08 .02
☐ 462 Joe Boever .20 .08 .02
☐ 463 Tim Wallach .25 .10 .02
☐ 464 Mike Moore .25 .10 .02
☐ 465 Albert Belle 1.50 .60 .15
☐ 466 Mike Witt .20 .08 .02
☐ 467 Craig Worthington .20 .08 .02
☐ 468 Jerald Clark .25 .10 .02
☐ 469 Scott Terry .20 .08 .02
☐ 470 Milt Cuyler 1.00 .40 .10
☐ 471 John Smiley .30 .12 .03
☐ 472 Charles Nagy .40 .16 .04
☐ 473 Alan Mills .25 .10 .02
☐ 474 John Russell .20 .08 .02
☐ 475 Bruce Hurst .25 .10 .02
☐ 476 Andujar Cedeno 3.00 1.25 .30
☐ 477 Dave Eiland .20 .08 .02
☐ 478 Brian McRae 3.50 1.50 .35
☐ 479 Mike LaCoss .20 .08 .02
☐ 480 Chris Gwynn .20 .08 .02
☐ 481 Jamie Moyer .20 .08 .02
☐ 482 John Olerud 1.25 .50 .12
☐ 483 Efrain Valdez .30 .12 .03
☐ 484 Sil Campusano .20 .08 .02
☐ 485 Pascual Perez .25 .10 .02
☐ 486 Gary Redus .20 .08 .02
☐ 487 Andy Hawkins .20 .08 .02
☐ 488 Cory Snyder .25 .10 .02
☐ 489 Chris Hoiles .35 .15 .03
☐ 490 Ron Hassey .20 .08 .02
☐ 491 Gary Wayne .20 .08 .02
☐ 492 Mark Lewis 1.25 .50 .12
☐ 493 Scott Coolbaugh .25 .10 .02
☐ 494 Gerald Young .20 .08 .02
☐ 495 Juan Samuel .25 .10 .02
☐ 496 Willie Fraser .20 .08 .02
☐ 497 Jeff Treadway .20 .08 .02
☐ 498 Vince Coleman .35 .15 .03
☐ 499 Cris Carpenter .20 .08 .02
☐ 500 Jack Clark .25 .10 .02
☐ 501 Kevin Appier .25 .10 .02
☐ 502 Rafael Palmeiro .75 .30 .07
☐ 503 Hensley Meulens .40 .16 .04
☐ 504 George Bell .50 .20 .05
☐ 505 Tony Pena .25 .10 .02
☐ 506 Roger McDowell .20 .08 .02
☐ 507 Luis Sojo .25 .10 .02
☐ 508 Mike Schooler .20 .08 .02
☐ 509 Robin Yount .90 .40 .09
☐ 510 Jack Armstrong .25 .10 .02
☐ 511 Rick Cerone .20 .08 .02
☐ 512 Curt Wilkerson .20 .08 .02
☐ 513 Joe Carter .60 .25 .06
☐ 514 Tim Burke .20 .08 .02
☐ 515 Tony Fernandez .25 .10 .02
☐ 516 Ramon Martinez 1.25 .50 .12
☐ 517 Tim Hulett .20 .08 .02
☐ 518 Terry Steinbach .25 .10 .02
☐ 519 Pete Smith .20 .08 .02
☐ 520 Ken Caminiti .20 .08 .02
☐ 521 Shawn Boskie .25 .10 .02
☐ 522 Mike Pagliarulo .20 .08 .02
☐ 523 Tim Raines .35 .15 .03
☐ 524 Alfredo Griffin .20 .08 .02
☐ 525 Henry Cotto .20 .08 .02
☐ 526 Mike Stanley .20 .08 .02
☐ 527 Charlie Leibrandt .20 .08 .02
☐ 528 Jeff King .25 .10 .02
☐ 529 Eric Plunk .20 .08 .02
☐ 530 Tom Lampkin .20 .08 .02
☐ 531 Steve Bedrosian .25 .10 .02
☐ 532 Tom Herr .20 .08 .02
☐ 533 Craig Lefferts .20 .08 .02
☐ 534 Jeff Reed .20 .08 .02
☐ 535 Mickey Morandini .45 .18 .04
☐ 536 Greg Cadaret .20 .08 .02
☐ 537 Ray Lankford 2.00 .80 .20
☐ 538 John Candelaria .20 .08 .02
☐ 539 Rob Deer .25 .10 .02
☐ 540 Brad Arnsberg .20 .08 .02
☐ 541 Mike Sharperson .20 .08 .02
☐ 542 Jeff D. Robinson .20 .08 .02
☐ 543 Mo Vaughn 3.75 1.60 .37
☐ 544 Jeff Parrett .20 .08 .02
☐ 545 Willie Randolph .25 .10 .02
☐ 546 Herm Winningham .20 .08 .02
☐ 547 Jeff Innis .20 .08 .02
☐ 548 Chuck Knoblauch 5.50 2.50 .55
☐ 549 Tommy Greene UER .30 .12 .03
(Born in North Carolina, not South Carolina)
☐ 550 Jeff Hamilton .20 .08 .02
☐ 551 Barry Jones .20 .08 .02
☐ 552 Ken Dayley .20 .08 .02
☐ 553 Rick Dempsey .20 .08 .02
☐ 554 Greg Smith .20 .08 .02
☐ 555 Mike Devereaux .20 .08 .02
☐ 556 Keith Comstock .20 .08 .02
☐ 557 Paul Faries .30 .12 .03
☐ 558 Tom Glavine .75 .30 .07
☐ 559 Craig Grebeck .25 .10 .02
☐ 560 Scott Erickson 7.00 3.00 .70
☐ 561 Joel Skinner .20 .08 .02

□ 562 Mike Morgan	.25	.10	.02
□ 563 Dave Gallagher	.20	.08	.02
□ 564 Todd Stottlemyre	.30	.12	.03
□ 565 Rich Rodriguez	.30	.12	.03
□ 566 Craig Wilson	.35	.15	.03
□ 567 Jeff Brantley	.25	.10	.02
□ 568 Scott Kameniecki	.45	.18	.04
□ 569 Steve Decker	.90	.40	.09
□ 570 Juan Agosto	.20	.08	.02
□ 571 Tommy Gregg	.20	.08	.02
□ 572 Kevin Wickander	.20	.08	.02
□ 573 Jamie Quirk UER (Rookie card is 1976, but card back is 1990)	.20	.08	.02
□ 574 Jerry Don Gleaton	.20	.08	.02
□ 575 Chris Hammond	.60	.25	.06
□ 576 Luis Gonzalez	3.50	1.50	.35
□ 577 Russ Swan	.25	.10	.02
□ 578 Jeff Conine	.40	.16	.04
□ 579 Charlie Hough	.20	.08	.02
□ 580 Jeff Kunkel	.20	.08	.02
□ 581 Darrel Akerfelds	.20	.08	.02
□ 582 Jeff Manto	.25	.10	.02
□ 583 Alejandro Pena	.25	.10	.02
□ 584 Mark Davidson	.20	.08	.02
□ 585 Bob MacDonald	.30	.12	.03
□ 586 Paul Assenmacher	.20	.08	.02
□ 587 Dan Wilson	.70	.30	.07
□ 588 Tom Bolton	.20	.08	.02
□ 589 Brian Harper	.25	.10	.02
□ 590 John Habyan	.20	.08	.02
□ 591 John Orton	.20	.08	.02
□ 592 Mark Gardner	.25	.10	.02
□ 593 Turner Ward	.45	.18	.04
□ 594 Bob Patterson	.20	.08	.02
□ 595 Ed Nunez	.20	.08	.02
□ 596 Gary Scott UER (Major League Batting Record should be Minor League)	.90	.40	.09
□ 597 Scott Bankhead	.20	.08	.02
□ 598 Checklist 301-400	.20	.03	.01
□ 599 Checklist 401-500	.20	.03	.01
□ 600 Checklist 501-600	.20	.03	.01

1992 Topps

The 1992 Topps set contains 792 cards measuring the standard size (2 1/2" by 3 1/2"). The fronts have either posed or action color player photos on a white card face. Different color stripes frame the pictures, and the player's name and team name appear in two short color stripes respectively at the bottom. In a horizontal format, the backs have biography and complete career batting or pitching record. In addition, some of the cards have a picture of a baseball field and stadium on the back. Special subsets included are Record Breakers (2-5), Prospects (58, 126, 179, 473, 551, 591, 618, 656, 676), and All-Stars (386-407). The cards are numbered on the back. These cards were not issued with bubble gum and feature white card stock.

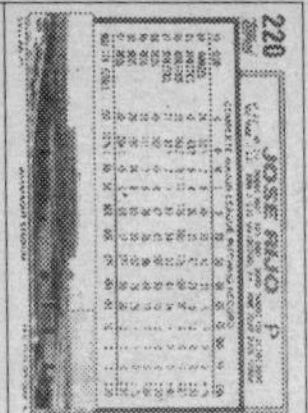

	MINT	EXC	G-VG
COMPLETE SET (792)	24.00	10.50	3.50
COMMON PLAYER (1-792)	.03	.01	.00
□ 1 Nolan Ryan	.35	.15	.03
□ 2 Ricky Henderson RB	.10	.04	.01
□ 3 Jeff Reardon RB	.03	.01	.00
□ 4 Nolan Ryan RB	.18	.08	.01
□ 5 Dave Winfield RB	.06	.02	.00
□ 6 Brien Taylor	1.00	.40	.10
□ 7 Jim Olander	.18	.08	.01
□ 8 Bryan Hickerson	.12	.05	.01
□ 9 Jon Farrell	.18	.08	.01
□ 10 Wade Boggs	.12	.05	.01
□ 11 Jack McDowell	.06	.02	.00
□ 12 Luis Gonzalez	.12	.05	.01
□ 13 Mike Scioscia	.03	.01	.00
□ 14 Wes Chamberlain	.12	.05	.01
□ 15 Dennis Martinez	.03	.01	.00
□ 16 Jeff Montgomery	.03	.01	.00
□ 17 Randy Milligan	.03	.01	.00
□ 18 Greg Cadaret	.03	.01	.00
□ 19 Jamie Quirk	.03	.01	.00
□ 20 Bip Roberts	.03	.01	.00
□ 21 Buck Rogers MG	.03	.01	.00
□ 22 Bill Wegman	.03	.01	.00
□ 23 Chuck Knoblauch	.15	.06	.01
□ 24 Randy Myers	.03	.01	.00

□ 25 Ron Gant	.10	.04	.01
□ 26 Mike Bielecki	.03	.01	.00
□ 27 Juan Gonzalez	.25	.10	.02
□ 28 Mike Schooler	.03	.01	.00
□ 29 Mickey Tettleton	.03	.01	.00
□ 30 John Kruk	.03	.01	.00
□ 31 Bryn Smith	.03	.01	.00
□ 32 Chris Nabholz	.03	.01	.00
□ 33 Carlos Baerga	.10	.04	.01
□ 34 Jeff Juden	.10	.04	.01
□ 35 Dave Righetti	.06	.02	.00
□ 36 Scott Ruffcorn	.15	.06	.01
□ 37 Luis Polonia	.06	.02	.00
□ 38 Tom Candiotti	.06	.02	.00
□ 39 Greg Olson	.03	.01	.00
□ 40 Cal Ripken	.20	.08	.02
□ 41 Craig Lefferts	.03	.01	.00
□ 42 Mike Macfarlane	.03	.01	.00
□ 43 Jose Lind	.03	.01	.00
□ 44 Rick Aguilera	.03	.01	.00
□ 45 Gary Carter	.06	.02	.00
□ 46 Steve Farr	.03	.01	.00
□ 47 Rex Hudler	.03	.01	.00
□ 48 Scott Scudder	.03	.01	.00
□ 49 Damon Berryhill	.03	.01	.00
□ 50 Ken Griffey Jr.	.50	.20	.05
□ 51 Tom Runnells MG	.03	.01	.00
□ 52 Juan Bell	.03	.01	.00
□ 53 Tommy Gregg	.03	.01	.00
□ 54 David Wells	.03	.01	.00
□ 55 Rafael Palmeiro	.08	.03	.01
□ 56 Charlie O'Brien	.03	.01	.00
□ 57 Donn Pall	.03	.01	.00
□ 58 1992 Prospects C	.45	.18	.04
Brad Ausmus			
Jim Campanis Jr.			
Dave Nilsson			
Doug Robbins			
□ 59 Mo Vaughn	.20	.08	.02
□ 60 Tony Fernandez	.06	.02	.00
□ 61 Paul O'Neill	.06	.02	.00
□ 62 Gene Nelson	.03	.01	.00
□ 63 Randy Ready	.03	.01	.00
□ 64 Bob Kipper	.03	.01	.00
□ 65 Willie McGee	.06	.02	.00
□ 66 Scott Stahoviak	.25	.10	.02
□ 67 Luis Salazar	.03	.01	.00
□ 68 Marvin Freeman	.03	.01	.00
□ 69 Kenny Lofton	.17	.07	.01
□ 70 Gary Gaetti	.06	.02	.00
□ 71 Erik Hanson	.06	.02	.00
□ 72 Eddie Zosky	.10	.04	.01
□ 73 Brian Barnes	.06	.02	.00
□ 74 Scott Leius	.06	.02	.00
□ 75 Bret Saberhagen	.08	.03	.01
□ 76 Mike Gallego	.03	.01	.00
□ 77 Jack Armstrong	.03	.01	.00
□ 78 Ivan Rodriguez	.50	.20	.05
□ 79 Jesse Orosco	.03	.01	.00
□ 80 David Justice	.35	.15	.03
□ 81 Ced Landrum	.08	.03	.01
□ 82 Doug Simons	.06	.02	.00
□ 83 Tommy Greene	.06	.02	.00
□ 84 Leo Gomez	.10	.04	.01
□ 85 Jose DeLeon	.03	.01	.00
□ 86 Steve Finley	.06	.02	.00
□ 87 Bob MacDonald	.06	.02	.00
□ 88 Darrin Jackson	.03	.01	.00
□ 89 Neal Heaton	.03	.01	.00
□ 90 Robin Yount	.10	.04	.01
□ 91 Jeff Reed	.03	.01	.00
□ 92 Lenny Harris	.03	.01	.00
□ 93 Reggie Jefferson	.10	.04	.01
□ 94 Sammy Sosa	.06	.02	.00
□ 95 Scott Bailes	.03	.01	.00
□ 96 Tom McKinnon	.15	.06	.01
□ 97 Luis Rivera	.03	.01	.00
□ 98 Mike Harkey	.03	.01	.00
□ 99 Jeff Treadway	.03	.01	.00
□ 100 Jose Canseco	.20	.08	.02
□ 101 Omar Vizquel	.03	.01	.00
□ 102 Scott Kamieniecki	.06	.02	.00
□ 103 Ricky Jordan	.06	.02	.00
□ 104 Jeff Ballard	.03	.01	.00
□ 105 Felix Jose	.08	.03	.01
□ 106 Mike Boddicker	.03	.01	.00
□ 107 Dan Pasqua	.03	.01	.00
□ 108 Mike Timlin	.06	.02	.00
□ 109 Roger Craig MG	.03	.01	.00
□ 110 Ryne Sandberg	.18	.08	.01
□ 111 Mark Carreon	.03	.01	.00
□ 112 Oscar Azocar	.03	.01	.00
□ 113 Mike Greenwell	.10	.04	.01
□ 114 Mark Portugal	.03	.01	.00
□ 115 Terry Pendleton	.08	.03	.01
□ 116 Willie Randolph	.03	.01	.00
□ 117 Scott Terry	.03	.01	.00
□ 118 Chili Davis	.06	.02	.00
□ 119 Mark Gardner	.03	.01	.00
□ 120 Alan Trammell	.08	.03	.01
□ 121 Derek Bell	.17	.07	.01
□ 122 Gary Varsho	.03	.01	.00
□ 123 Bob Ojeda	.03	.01	.00
□ 124 Shawn Livsey	.15	.06	.01
□ 125 Chris Hoiles	.06	.02	.00
□ 126 1992 Prospects 1B	1.50	.60	.15
Ryan Klesko			
John Jaha			
Rico Brogna			
Dave Staton			
□ 127 Carlos Quintana	.06	.02	.00
□ 128 Kurt Stillwell	.03	.01	.00
□ 129 Melido Perez	.03	.01	.00
□ 130 Alvin Davis	.06	.02	.00
□ 131 Checklist 1-132	.06	.02	.00
□ 132 Eric Show	.03	.01	.00

☐ 133 Rance Mulliniks	.03	.01	.00
☐ 134 Darryl Kile	.08	.03	.01
☐ 135 Von Hayes	.06	.02	.00
☐ 136 Bill Doran	.03	.01	.00
☐ 137 Jeff Robinson	.03	.01	.00
☐ 138 Monty Fariss	.06	.02	.00
☐ 139 Jeff Innis	.03	.01	.00
☐ 140 Mark Grace	.08	.03	.01
☐ 141 Jim Leyland MG	.03	.01	.00
☐ 142 Todd Van Poppel	.45	.18	.04
☐ 143 Paul Gibson	.03	.01	.00
☐ 144 Bill Swift	.03	.01	.00
☐ 145 Danny Tartabull	.08	.03	.01
☐ 146 Al Newman	.03	.01	.00
☐ 147 Cris Carpenter	.03	.01	.00
☐ 148 Anthony Young	.08	.03	.01
☐ 149 Brian Bohanon	.03	.01	.00
☐ 150 Roger Clemens	.15	.06	.01
☐ 151 Jeff Hamilton	.03	.01	.00
☐ 152 Charlie Leibrandt	.03	.01	.00
☐ 153 Ron Karkovice	.03	.01	.00
☐ 154 Hensley Meulens	.06	.02	.00
☐ 155 Scott Bankhead	.03	.01	.00
☐ 156 Manny Ramirez	.40	.16	.04
☐ 157 Keith Miller	.03	.01	.00
☐ 158 Todd Frohwirth	.03	.01	.00
☐ 159 Darrin Fletcher	.03	.01	.00
☐ 160 Bobby Bonilla	.10	.04	.01
☐ 161 Casey Candaele	.03	.01	.00
☐ 162 Paul Faries	.03	.01	.00
☐ 163 Dana Kiecker	.03	.01	.00
☐ 164 Shane Mack	.06	.02	.00
☐ 165 Mark Langston	.06	.02	.00
☐ 166 Geronimo Pena	.03	.01	.00
☐ 167 Andy Allanson	.03	.01	.00
☐ 168 Dwight Smith	.06	.02	.00
☐ 169 Chuck Crim	.03	.01	.00
☐ 170 Alex Cole	.06	.02	.00
☐ 171 Bill Plummer MG	.03	.01	.00
☐ 172 Juan Berenguer	.03	.01	.00
☐ 173 Brian Downing	.03	.01	.00
☐ 174 Steve Frey	.03	.01	.00
☐ 175 Orel Hershiser	.06	.02	.00
☐ 176 Ramon Garcia	.06	.02	.00
☐ 177 Dan Gladden	.03	.01	.00
☐ 178 Jim Acker	.03	.01	.00
☐ 179 1992 Prospects 2B Bobby DeJardin Cesar Bernhardt Armando Moreno Andy Stankiewicz	.25	.10	.02
☐ 180 Kevin Mitchell	.08	.03	.01
☐ 181 Hector Villanueva	.03	.01	.00
☐ 182 Jeff Reardon	.06	.02	.00
☐ 183 Brent Mayne	.06	.02	.00
☐ 184 Jimmy Jones	.03	.01	.00
☐ 185 Benito Santiago	.06	.02	.00
☐ 186 Cliff Floyd	.25	.10	.02
☐ 187 Ernie Riles	.03	.01	.00
☐ 188 Jose Guzman	.03	.01	.00
☐ 189 Junior Felix	.06	.02	.00
☐ 190 Glenn Davis	.08	.03	.01
☐ 191 Charlie Hough	.03	.01	.00
☐ 192 Dave Fleming	.06	.02	.00
☐ 193 Omar Olivares	.06	.02	.00
☐ 194 Eric Karros	.20	.08	.02
☐ 195 David Cone	.08	.03	.01
☐ 196 Frank Castillo	.06	.02	.00
☐ 197 Glenn Braggs	.03	.01	.00
☐ 198 Scott Aldred	.03	.01	.00
☐ 199 Jeff Blauser	.03	.01	.00
☐ 200 Len Dykstra	.06	.02	.00
☐ 201 Buck Showalter MG	.06	.02	.00
☐ 202 Rick Honeycutt	.03	.01	.00
☐ 203 Greg Myers	.03	.01	.00
☐ 204 Trevor Wilson	.03	.01	.00
☐ 205 Jay Howell	.03	.01	.00
☐ 206 Luis Sojo	.03	.01	.00
☐ 207 Jack Clark	.06	.02	.00
☐ 208 Julio Machado	.03	.01	.00
☐ 209 Lloyd McClendon	.03	.01	.00
☐ 210 Ozzie Guillen	.06	.02	.00
☐ 211 Jeremy Hernandez	.12	.05	.01
☐ 212 Randy Velarde	.03	.01	.00
☐ 213 Les Lancaster	.03	.01	.00
☐ 214 Andy Mota	.10	.04	.01
☐ 215 Rich Gossage	.06	.02	.00
☐ 216 Brent Gates	.20	.08	.02
☐ 217 Brian Harper	.03	.01	.00
☐ 218 Mike Flanagan	.06	.02	.00
☐ 219 Jerry Browne	.03	.01	.00
☐ 220 Jose Rijo	.06	.02	.00
☐ 221 Skeeter Barnes	.03	.01	.00
☐ 222 Jaime Navarro	.03	.01	.00
☐ 223 Mel Hall	.03	.01	.00
☐ 224 Bret Barberie	.15	.06	.01
☐ 225 Roberto Alomar	.10	.04	.01
☐ 226 Pete Smith	.03	.01	.00
☐ 227 Daryl Boston	.03	.01	.00
☐ 228 Eddie Whitson	.03	.01	.00
☐ 229 Shawn Boskie	.03	.01	.00
☐ 230 Dick Schofield	.03	.01	.00
☐ 231 Brian Drahman	.06	.02	.00
☐ 232 John Smiley	.06	.02	.00
☐ 233 Mitch Webster	.03	.01	.00
☐ 234 Terry Steinbach	.03	.01	.00
☐ 235 Jack Morris	.06	.02	.00
☐ 236 Bill Pecota	.03	.01	.00
☐ 237 Jose Hernandez	.12	.05	.01
☐ 238 Greg Litton	.03	.01	.00
☐ 239 Brian Holman	.03	.01	.00
☐ 240 Andres Galarraga	.06	.02	.00
☐ 241 Gerald Young	.03	.01	.00
☐ 242 Mike Mussina	.12	.05	.01
☐ 243 Alvaro Espinoza	.03	.01	.00
☐ 244 Darren Daulton	.03	.01	.00

☐ 245 John Smoltz	.08	.03	.01
☐ 246 Jason Pruitt	.15	.06	.01
☐ 247 Chuck Finley	.06	.02	.00
☐ 248 Jim Gantner	.03	.01	.00
☐ 249 Tony Fossas	.03	.01	.00
☐ 250 Ken Griffey Sr.	.06	.02	.00
☐ 251 Kevin Elster	.03	.01	.00
☐ 252 Dennis Rasmussen	.03	.01	.00
☐ 253 Terry Kennedy	.03	.01	.00
☐ 254 Ryan Bowen	.06	.02	.00
☐ 255 Robin Ventura	.15	.06	.01
☐ 256 Mike Aldrete	.03	.01	.00
☐ 257 Jeff Russell	.03	.01	.00
☐ 258 Jim Lindeman	.03	.01	.00
☐ 259 Ron Darling	.06	.02	.00
☐ 260 Devon White	.06	.02	.00
☐ 261 Tom Lasorda MG	.06	.02	.00
☐ 262 Terry Lee	.06	.02	.00
☐ 263 Bob Patterson	.03	.01	.00
☐ 264 Checklist 133-264	.06	.02	.00
☐ 265 Teddy Higuera	.03	.01	.00
☐ 266 Roberto Kelly	.08	.03	.01
☐ 267 Steve Bedrosian	.03	.01	.00
☐ 268 Brady Anderson	.03	.01	.00
☐ 269 Ruben Amaro Jr.	.08	.03	.01
☐ 270 Tony Gwynn	.12	.05	.01
☐ 271 Tracy Jones	.03	.01	.00
☐ 272 Jerry Don Gleaton	.03	.01	.00
☐ 273 Craig Grebeck	.03	.01	.00
☐ 274 Bob Scanlan	.06	.02	.00
☐ 275 Todd Zeile	.10	.04	.01
☐ 276 Shawn Green	.20	.08	.02
☐ 277 Scott Chiamparino	.03	.01	.00
☐ 278 Darryl Hamilton	.03	.01	.00
☐ 279 Jim Clancy	.03	.01	.00
☐ 280 Carlos Martinez	.03	.01	.00
☐ 281 Kevin Appier	.03	.01	.00
☐ 282 John Wehner	.10	.04	.01
☐ 283 Reggie Sanders	.15	.06	.01
☐ 284 Gene Larkin	.03	.01	.00
☐ 285 Bob Welch	.06	.02	.00
☐ 286 Gilberto Reyes	.03	.01	.00
☐ 287 Pete Schourek	.06	.02	.00
☐ 288 Andujar Cedeno	.15	.06	.01
☐ 289 Mike Morgan	.06	.02	.00
☐ 290 Bo Jackson	.25	.10	.02
☐ 291 Phil Garner MG	.03	.01	.00
☐ 292 Ray Lankford	.10	.04	.01
☐ 293 Mike Henneman	.03	.01	.00
☐ 294 Dave Valle	.03	.01	.00
☐ 295 Alonzo Powell	.06	.02	.00
☐ 296 Tom Brunansky	.06	.02	.00
☐ 297 Kevin Brown	.03	.01	.00
☐ 298 Kelly Gruber	.06	.02	.00
☐ 299 Charles Nagy	.03	.01	.00
☐ 300 Don Mattingly	.12	.05	.01
☐ 301 Kirk McCaskill	.03	.01	.00
☐ 302 Joey Cora	.03	.01	.00
☐ 303 Dan Plesac	.03	.01	.00
☐ 304 Joe Oliver	.03	.01	.00
☐ 305 Tom Glavine	.08	.03	.01
☐ 306 Al Shirley	.30	.12	.03
☐ 307 Bruce Ruffin	.03	.01	.00
☐ 308 Craig Shipley	.12	.05	.01
☐ 309 Dave Martinez	.03	.01	.00
☐ 310 Jose Mesa	.03	.01	.00
☐ 311 Henry Cotto	.03	.01	.00
☐ 312 Mike LaValliere	.03	.01	.00
☐ 313 Kevin Tapani	.06	.02	.00
☐ 314 Jeff Huson	.03	.01	.00
☐ 315 Juan Samuel	.06	.02	.00
☐ 316 Curt Schilling	.03	.01	.00
☐ 317 Mike Bordick	.06	.02	.00
☐ 318 Steve Howe	.03	.01	.00
☐ 319 Tony Phillips	.03	.01	.00
☐ 320 George Bell	.08	.03	.01
☐ 321 Lou Piniella MG	.06	.02	.00
☐ 322 Tim Burke	.03	.01	.00
☐ 323 Milt Thompson	.03	.01	.00
☐ 324 Danny Darwin	.03	.01	.00
☐ 325 Joe Orsulak	.03	.01	.00
☐ 326 Eric King	.03	.01	.00
☐ 327 Jay Buhner	.06	.02	.00
☐ 328 Joel Johnston	.08	.03	.01
☐ 329 Franklin Stubbs	.03	.01	.00
☐ 330 Will Clark	.18	.08	.01
☐ 331 Steve Lake	.03	.01	.00
☐ 332 Chris Jones	.06	.02	.00
☐ 333 Pat Tabler	.03	.01	.00
☐ 334 Kevin Gross	.03	.01	.00
☐ 335 Dave Henderson	.06	.02	.00
☐ 336 Greg Anthony	.12	.05	.01
☐ 337 Alejandro Pena	.06	.02	.00
☐ 338 Shawn Abner	.03	.01	.00
☐ 339 Tom Browning	.03	.01	.00
☐ 340 Otis Nixon	.03	.01	.00
☐ 341 Bob Geren	.03	.01	.00
☐ 342 Tim Spehr	.08	.03	.01
☐ 343 John Vander Wal	.20	.08	.02
☐ 344 Jack Daugherty	.03	.01	.00
☐ 345 Zane Smith	.03	.01	.00
☐ 346 Rheal Cormier	.12	.05	.01
☐ 347 Kent Hrbek	.06	.02	.00
☐ 348 Rick Wilkins	.08	.03	.01
☐ 349 Steve Lyons	.03	.01	.00
☐ 350 Gregg Olson	.06	.02	.00
☐ 351 Greg Riddoch MG	.03	.01	.00
☐ 352 Ed Nunez	.03	.01	.00
☐ 353 Braulio Castillo	.25	.10	.02
☐ 354 Dave Bergman	.03	.01	.00
☐ 355 Warren Newson	.08	.03	.01
☐ 356 Luis Quinones	.03	.01	.00
☐ 357 Mike Witt	.03	.01	.00
☐ 358 Ted Wood	.15	.06	.01
☐ 359 Mike Moore	.06	.02	.00
☐ 360 Lance Parrish	.06	.02	.00

☐ 361 Barry Jones	.03	.01	.00
☐ 362 Javier Ortiz	.03	.01	.00
☐ 363 John Candelaria	.03	.01	.00
☐ 364 Glenallen Hill	.06	.02	.00
☐ 365 Duane Ward	.03	.01	.00
☐ 366 Checklist 265-396	.06	.02	.00
☐ 367 Rafael Belliard	.03	.01	.00
☐ 368 Bill Krueger	.03	.01	.00
☐ 369 Steve Whitaker	.15	.06	.01
☐ 370 Shawon Dunston	.06	.02	.00
☐ 371 Dante Bichette	.03	.01	.00
☐ 372 Kip Gross	.12	.05	.01
☐ 373 Don Robinson	.03	.01	.00
☐ 374 Bernie Williams	.12	.05	.01
☐ 375 Bert Blyleven	.06	.02	.00
☐ 376 Chris Donnels	.10	.04	.01
☐ 377 Bob Zupcic	.18	.08	.01
☐ 378 Joel Skinner	.03	.01	.00
☐ 379 Steve Chitren	.03	.01	.00
☐ 380 Barry Bonds	.12	.05	.01
☐ 381 Sparky Anderson MG	.03	.01	.00
☐ 382 Sid Fernandez	.06	.02	.00
☐ 383 Dave Hollins	.06	.02	.00
☐ 384 Mark Lee	.06	.02	.00
☐ 385 Tim Wallach	.06	.02	.00
☐ 386 Will Clark AS	.12	.05	.01
☐ 387 Ryne Sandberg AS	.12	.05	.01
☐ 388 Howard Johnson AS	.08	.03	.01
☐ 389 Barry Larkin AS	.08	.03	.01
☐ 390 Barry Bonds AS	.10	.04	.01
☐ 391 Ron Gant AS	.08	.03	.01
☐ 392 Bobby Bonilla AS	.08	.03	.01
☐ 393 Craig Biggio AS	.06	.02	.00
☐ 394 Dennis Martinez AS	.06	.02	.00
☐ 395 Tom Glavine AS	.08	.03	.01
☐ 396 Ozzie Smith AS	.08	.03	.01
☐ 397 Cecil Fielder AS	.10	.04	.01
☐ 398 Julio Franco AS	.08	.03	.01
☐ 399 Wade Boggs AS	.10	.04	.01
☐ 400 Cal Ripken AS	.12	.05	.01
☐ 401 Jose Canseco AS	.12	.05	.01
☐ 402 Joe Carter AS	.08	.03	.01
☐ 403 Ruben Sierra AS	.10	.04	.01
☐ 404 Matt Nokes AS	.06	.02	.00
☐ 405 Roger Clemens AS	.10	.04	.01
☐ 406 Jim Abbott AS	.08	.03	.01
☐ 407 Bryan Harvey AS	.06	.02	.00
☐ 408 Bob Milacki	.03	.01	.00
☐ 409 Geno Petralli	.03	.01	.00
☐ 410 Dave Stewart	.06	.02	.00
☐ 411 Mike Jackson	.03	.01	.00
☐ 412 Luis Aquino	.03	.01	.00
☐ 413 Tim Teufel	.03	.01	.00
☐ 414 Jeff Ware	.08	.03	.01
☐ 415 Jim Deshaies	.03	.01	.00
☐ 416 Ellis Burks	.08	.03	.01
☐ 417 Allan Anderson	.03	.01	.00
☐ 418 Alfredo Griffin	.03	.01	.00
☐ 419 Wally Whitehurst	.03	.01	.00
☐ 420 Sandy Alomar Jr.	.08	.03	.01
☐ 421 Juan Agosto	.03	.01	.00
☐ 422 Sam Horn	.03	.01	.00
☐ 423 Jeff Fassero	.06	.02	.00
☐ 424 Paul McClellan	.06	.02	.00
☐ 425 Cecil Fielder	.15	.06	.01
☐ 426 Tim Raines	.08	.03	.01
☐ 427 Eddie Taubensee	.15	.06	.01
☐ 428 Dennis Boyd	.03	.01	.00
☐ 429 Tony LaRussa MG	.03	.01	.00
☐ 430 Steve Sax	.06	.02	.00
☐ 431 Tom Gordon	.06	.02	.00
☐ 432 Billy Hatcher	.03	.01	.00
☐ 433 Cal Eldred	.06	.02	.00
☐ 434 Wally Backman	.03	.01	.00
☐ 435 Mark Eichhorn	.03	.01	.00
☐ 436 Mookie Wilson	.03	.01	.00
☐ 437 Scott Servais	.06	.02	.00
☐ 438 Mike Maddux	.03	.01	.00
☐ 439 Chico Walker	.03	.01	.00
☐ 440 Doug Drabek	.06	.02	.00
☐ 441 Rob Deer	.03	.01	.00
☐ 442 Dave West	.03	.01	.00
☐ 443 Spike Owen	.03	.01	.00
☐ 444 Tyrone Hill	.25	.10	.02
☐ 445 Matt Williams	.10	.04	.01
☐ 446 Mark Lewis	.12	.05	.01
☐ 447 David Segui	.06	.02	.00
☐ 448 Tom Pagnozzi	.03	.01	.00
☐ 449 Jeff Johnson	.06	.02	.00
☐ 450 Mark McGwire	.10	.04	.01
☐ 451 Tom Henke	.03	.01	.00
☐ 452 Wilson Alvarez	.06	.02	.00
☐ 453 Gary Redus	.03	.01	.00
☐ 454 Darren Holmes	.06	.02	.00
☐ 455 Pete O'Brien	.03	.01	.00
☐ 456 Pat Combs	.03	.01	.00
☐ 457 Hubie Brooks	.06	.02	.00
☐ 458 Frank Tanana	.06	.02	.00
☐ 459 Tom Kelly MG	.03	.01	.00
☐ 460 Andre Dawson	.10	.04	.01
☐ 461 Doug Jones	.03	.01	.00
☐ 462 Rich Rodriguez	.06	.02	.00
☐ 463 Mike Simms	.06	.02	.00
☐ 464 Mike Jeffcoat	.03	.01	.00
☐ 465 Barry Larkin	.08	.03	.01
☐ 466 Stan Belinda	.03	.01	.00
☐ 467 Lonnie Smith	.03	.01	.00
☐ 468 Greg Harris	.03	.01	.00
☐ 469 Jim Eisenreich	.03	.01	.00
☐ 470 Pedro Guerrero	.06	.02	.00
☐ 471 Jose DeJesus	.03	.01	.00
☐ 472 Rich Rowland	.10	.04	.01
☐ 473 1992 Prospects 3B Frank Bolick Craig Paquette Tom Redington	.30	.12	.03

Paul Russo			
☐ 474 Mike Rossiter	.15	.06	.01
☐ 475 Robby Thompson	.03	.01	.00
☐ 476 Randy Bush	.03	.01	.00
☐ 477 Greg Hibbard	.03	.01	.00
☐ 478 Dale Sveum	.03	.01	.00
☐ 479 Chito Martinez	.15	.06	.01
☐ 480 Scott Sanderson	.03	.01	.00
☐ 481 Tino Martinez	.12	.05	.01
☐ 482 Jimmy Key	.06	.02	.00
☐ 483 Terry Shumpert	.03	.01	.00
☐ 484 Mike Hartley	.03	.01	.00
☐ 485 Chris Sabo	.08	.03	.01
☐ 486 Bob Walk	.03	.01	.00
☐ 487 John Cerutti	.03	.01	.00
☐ 488 Scott Cooper	.10	.04	.01
☐ 489 Bobby Cox MG	.03	.01	.00
☐ 490 Julio Franco	.08	.03	.01
☐ 491 Jeff Brantley	.03	.01	.00
☐ 492 Mike Devereaux	.03	.01	.00
☐ 493 Jose Offerman	.08	.03	.01
☐ 494 Gary Thurman	.03	.01	.00
☐ 495 Carney Lansford	.06	.02	.00
☐ 496 Joe Grahe	.03	.01	.00
☐ 497 Andy Ashby	.08	.03	.01
☐ 498 Gerald Perry	.03	.01	.00
☐ 499 Dave Otto	.03	.01	.00
☐ 500 Vince Coleman	.08	.03	.01
☐ 501 Rob Mallicoat	.03	.01	.00
☐ 502 Greg Briley	.03	.01	.00
☐ 503 Pascual Perez	.03	.01	.00
☐ 504 Aaron Sele	.20	.08	.02
☐ 505 Bobby Thigpen	.06	.02	.00
☐ 506 Todd Benzinger	.03	.01	.00
☐ 507 Candy Maldonado	.03	.01	.00
☐ 508 Bill Gullickson	.03	.01	.00
☐ 509 Doug Dascenzo	.03	.01	.00
☐ 510 Frank Viola	.06	.02	.00
☐ 511 Kenny Rogers	.03	.01	.00
☐ 512 Mike Heath	.03	.01	.00
☐ 513 Kevin Bass	.03	.01	.00
☐ 514 Kim Batiste	.06	.02	.00
☐ 515 Delino DeShields	.06	.02	.00
☐ 516 Ed Sprague	.06	.02	.00
☐ 517 Jim Gott	.03	.01	.00
☐ 518 Jose Melendez	.06	.02	.00
☐ 519 Hal McRae MG	.03	.01	.00
☐ 520 Jeff Bagwell	.75	.30	.07
☐ 521 Joe Hesketh	.03	.01	.00
☐ 522 Milt Cuyler	.10	.04	.01
☐ 523 Shawn Hillegas	.03	.01	.00
☐ 524 Don Slaught	.03	.01	.00
☐ 525 Randy Johnson	.06	.02	.00
☐ 526 Doug Piatt	.08	.03	.01
☐ 527 Checklist 397-528	.06	.02	.00
☐ 528 Steve Foster	.15	.06	.01
☐ 529 Joe Girardi	.03	.01	.00
☐ 530 Jim Abbott	.10	.04	.01
☐ 531 Larry Walker	.06	.02	.00
☐ 532 Mike Huff	.03	.01	.00
☐ 533 Mackey Sasser	.03	.01	.00
☐ 534 Benji Gil	.30	.12	.03
☐ 535 Dave Stieb	.06	.02	.00
☐ 536 Willie Wilson	.06	.02	.00
☐ 537 Mark Leiter	.06	.02	.00
☐ 538 Jose Uribe	.03	.01	.00
☐ 539 Thomas Howard	.03	.01	.00
☐ 540 Ben McDonald	.08	.03	.01
☐ 541 Jose Tolentino	.15	.06	.01
☐ 542 Keith Mitchell	.20	.08	.02
☐ 543 Jerome Walton	.06	.02	.00
☐ 544 Cliff Brantley	.12	.05	.01
☐ 545 Andy Van Slyke	.06	.02	.00
☐ 546 Paul Sorrento	.03	.01	.00
☐ 547 Herm Winningham	.03	.01	.00
☐ 548 Mark Guthrie	.03	.01	.00
☐ 549 Joe Torre MG	.03	.01	.00
☐ 550 Darryl Strawberry	.15	.06	.01
☐ 551 1992 Prospects SS	.45	.18	.04
Wilfredo Cordero			
Chipper Jones			
Manny Alexander			
Alex Arias			
☐ 552 Dave Gallagher	.03	.01	.00
☐ 553 Edgar Martinez	.06	.02	.00
☐ 554 Donald Harris	.06	.02	.00
☐ 555 Frank Thomas	.60	.25	.06
☐ 556 Storm Davis	.03	.01	.00
☐ 557 Dickie Thon	.03	.01	.00
☐ 558 Scott Garrelts	.03	.01	.00
☐ 559 Steve Olin	.03	.01	.00
☐ 560 Rickey Henderson	.18	.08	.01
☐ 561 Jose Vizcaino	.03	.01	.00
☐ 562 Wade Taylor	.06	.02	.00
☐ 563 Pat Borders	.03	.01	.00
☐ 564 Jimmy Gonzalez	.12	.05	.01
☐ 565 Lee Smith	.06	.02	.00
☐ 566 Bill Sampen	.03	.01	.00
☐ 567 Dean Palmer	.17	.07	.01
☐ 568 Bryan Harvey	.06	.02	.00
☐ 569 Tony Pena	.06	.02	.00
☐ 570 Lou Whitaker	.06	.02	.00
☐ 571 Randy Tomlin	.06	.02	.00
☐ 572 Greg Vaughn	.08	.03	.01
☐ 573 Kelly Downs	.03	.01	.00
☐ 574 Steve Avery	.20	.08	.02
☐ 575 Kirby Puckett	.12	.05	.01
☐ 576 Heathcliff Slocumb	.03	.01	.00
☐ 577 Kevin Seitzer	.06	.02	.00
☐ 578 Lee Guetterman	.03	.01	.00
☐ 579 Johnny Oates MG	.03	.01	.00
☐ 580 Greg Maddux	.06	.02	.00
☐ 581 Stan Javier	.03	.01	.00
☐ 582 Vicente Palacios	.03	.01	.00
☐ 583 Mel Rojas	.03	.01	.00
☐ 584 Wayne Rosenthal	.10	.04	.01

☐ 585 Lenny Webster .03 .01 .00
☐ 586 Rod Nichols .03 .01 .00
☐ 587 Mickey Morandini .06 .02 .00
☐ 588 Russ Swan .03 .01 .00
☐ 589 Mariano Duncan .03 .01 .00
☐ 590 Howard Johnson .08 .03 .01
☐ 591 1992 Prospects OF .50 .20 .05
Jeromy Burnitz
Jacob Brumfield
Alan Cockrell
D.J. Dozier
☐ 592 Denny Neagle .12 .05 .01
☐ 593 Steve Decker .10 .04 .01
☐ 594 Brian Barber .12 .05 .01
☐ 595 Bruce Hurst .06 .02 .00
☐ 596 Kent Mercker .06 .02 .00
☐ 597 Mike Magnante .15 .06 .01
☐ 598 Jody Reed .06 .02 .00
☐ 599 Steve Searcy .03 .01 .00
☐ 600 Paul Molitor .08 .03 .01
☐ 601 Dave Smith .03 .01 .00
☐ 602 Mike Fetters .03 .01 .00
☐ 603 Luis Mercedes .15 .06 .01
☐ 604 Chris Gwynn .03 .01 .00
☐ 605 Scott Erickson .15 .06 .01
☐ 606 Brook Jacoby .03 .01 .00
☐ 607 Todd Stottlemyre .06 .02 .00
☐ 608 Scott Bradley .03 .01 .00
☐ 609 Mike Hargrove MG .03 .01 .00
☐ 610 Eric Davis .10 .04 .01
☐ 611 Brian Hunter .35 .15 .03
☐ 612 Pat Kelly .10 .04 .01
☐ 613 Pedro Munoz .10 .04 .01
☐ 614 Al Osuna .06 .02 .00
☐ 615 Matt Merullo .03 .01 .00
☐ 616 Larry Andersen .03 .01 .00
☐ 617 Junior Ortiz .03 .01 .00
☐ 618 1992 Prospects OF .40 .16 .04
Cesar Hernandez
Steve Hosey
Jeff McNeely
Dan Peltier
☐ 619 Danny Jackson .03 .01 .00
☐ 620 George Brett .10 .04 .01
☐ 621 Dan Gakeler .06 .02 .00
☐ 622 Steve Buechele .03 .01 .00
☐ 623 Bob Tewksbury .03 .01 .00
☐ 624 Shawn Estes .15 .06 .01
☐ 625 Kevin McReynolds .06 .02 .00
☐ 626 Chris Haney .06 .02 .00
☐ 627 Mike Sharperson .03 .01 .00
☐ 628 Mark Williamson .03 .01 .00
☐ 629 Wally Joyner .08 .03 .01
☐ 630 Carlton Fisk .10 .04 .01
☐ 631 Armando Reynoso .10 .04 .01
☐ 632 Felix Fermin .03 .01 .00
☐ 633 Mitch Williams .03 .01 .00
☐ 634 Manuel Lee .03 .01 .00
☐ 635 Harold Baines .06 .02 .00
☐ 636 Greg Harris .03 .01 .00
☐ 637 Orlando Merced .10 .04 .01
☐ 638 Chris Bosio .03 .01 .00
☐ 639 Wayne Housie .15 .06 .01
☐ 640 Xavier Hernandez .03 .01 .00
☐ 641 David Howard .06 .02 .00
☐ 642 Tim Crews .03 .01 .00
☐ 643 Rick Cerone .03 .01 .00
☐ 644 Terry Leach .03 .01 .00
☐ 645 Deion Sanders .08 .03 .01
☐ 646 Craig Wilson .08 .03 .01
☐ 647 Marquis Grissom .08 .03 .01
☐ 648 Scott Fletcher .03 .01 .00
☐ 649 Norm Charlton .03 .01 .00
☐ 650 Jesse Barfield .06 .02 .00
☐ 651 Joe Slusarski .06 .02 .00
☐ 652 Bobby Rose .03 .01 .00
☐ 653 Dennis Lamp .03 .01 .00
☐ 654 Allen Watson .18 .08 .01
☐ 655 Brett Butler .06 .02 .00
☐ 656 1992 Prospects OF .45 .18 .04
Rudy Pemberton
Henry Rodriguez
Lee Tinsley
Gerald Williams
☐ 657 Dave Johnson .03 .01 .00
☐ 658 Checklist 529-660 .06 .02 .00
☐ 659 Brian McRae .12 .05 .01
☐ 660 Fred McGriff .08 .03 .01
☐ 661 Bill Landrum .03 .01 .00
☐ 662 Juan Guzman .15 .06 .01
☐ 663 Greg Gagne .03 .01 .00
☐ 664 Ken Hill .03 .01 .00
☐ 665 Dave Haas .08 .03 .01
☐ 666 Tom Foley .03 .01 .00
☐ 667 Roberto Hernandez .10 .04 .01
☐ 668 Dwayne Henry .03 .01 .00
☐ 669 Jim Fregosi MG .03 .01 .00
☐ 670 Harold Reynolds .03 .01 .00
☐ 671 Mark Whiten .08 .03 .01
☐ 672 Eric Plunk .03 .01 .00
☐ 673 Todd Hundley .06 .02 .00
☐ 674 Mo Sanford .15 .06 .01
☐ 675 Bobby Witt .03 .01 .00
☐ 676 1992 Prospects P .45 .18 .04
Sam Militello
Pat Mahomes
Turk Wendell
Roger Salkeld
☐ 677 John Marzano .03 .01 .00
☐ 678 Joe Klink .03 .01 .00
☐ 679 Pete Incaviglia .06 .02 .00
☐ 680 Dale Murphy .10 .04 .01
☐ 681 Rene Gonzales .03 .01 .00
☐ 682 Andy Benes .08 .03 .01
☐ 683 Jim Poole .03 .01 .00
☐ 684 Trever Miller .12 .05 .01

☐ 685 Scott Livingstone	.10	.04	.01
☐ 686 Rich DeLucia	.03	.01	.00
☐ 687 Harvey Pulliam	.08	.03	.01
☐ 688 Tim Belcher	.06	.02	.00
☐ 689 Mark Lemke	.03	.01	.00
☐ 690 John Franco	.03	.01	.00
☐ 691 Walt Weiss	.06	.02	.00
☐ 692 Scott Ruskin	.03	.01	.00
☐ 693 Jeff King	.03	.01	.00
☐ 694 Mike Gardiner	.06	.02	.00
☐ 695 Gary Sheffield	.08	.03	.01
☐ 696 Joe Boever	.03	.01	.00
☐ 697 Mike Felder	.03	.01	.00
☐ 698 John Habyan	.03	.01	.00
☐ 699 Cito Gaston MG	.03	.01	.00
☐ 700 Ruben Sierra	.12	.05	.01
☐ 701 Scott Radinsky	.03	.01	.00
☐ 702 Lee Stevens	.06	.02	.00
☐ 703 Mark Wohlers	.18	.08	.01
☐ 704 Curt Young	.03	.01	.00
☐ 705 Dwight Evans	.06	.02	.00
☐ 706 Rob Murphy	.03	.01	.00
☐ 707 Gregg Jefferies	.08	.03	.01
☐ 708 Tom Bolton	.03	.01	.00
☐ 709 Chris James	.03	.01	.00
☐ 710 Kevin Maas	.12	.05	.01
☐ 711 Ricky Bones	.06	.02	.00
☐ 712 Curt Wilkerson	.03	.01	.00
☐ 713 Roger McDowell	.03	.01	.00
☐ 714 Calvin Reese	.35	.15	.03
☐ 715 Craig Biggio	.06	.02	.00
☐ 716 Kirk Dressendorfer	.08	.03	.01
☐ 717 Ken Dayley	.03	.01	.00
☐ 718 B.J. Surhoff	.03	.01	.00
☐ 719 Terry Mulholland	.03	.01	.00
☐ 720 Kirk Gibson	.06	.02	.00
☐ 721 Mike Pagliarulo	.03	.01	.00
☐ 722 Walt Terrell	.03	.01	.00
☐ 723 Jose Oquendo	.03	.01	.00
☐ 724 Kevin Morton	.06	.02	.00
☐ 725 Dwight Gooden	.10	.04	.01
☐ 726 Kirt Manwaring	.03	.01	.00
☐ 727 Chuck McElroy	.03	.01	.00
☐ 728 Dave Burba	.06	.02	.00
☐ 729 Art Howe MG	.03	.01	.00
☐ 730 Ramon Martinez	.10	.04	.01
☐ 731 Donnie Hill	.03	.01	.00
☐ 732 Nelson Santovenia	.03	.01	.00
☐ 733 Bob Melvin	.03	.01	.00
☐ 734 Scott Hatteberg	.15	.06	.01
☐ 735 Greg Swindell	.06	.02	.00
☐ 736 Lance Johnson	.03	.01	.00
☐ 737 Kevin Reimer	.03	.01	.00
☐ 738 Dennis Eckersley	.08	.03	.01
☐ 739 Rob Ducey	.03	.01	.00
☐ 740 Ken Caminiti	.03	.01	.00
☐ 741 Mark Gubicza	.03	.01	.00
☐ 742 Billy Spiers	.03	.01	.00
☐ 743 Darren Lewis	.06	.02	.00
☐ 744 Chris Hammond	.06	.02	.00
☐ 745 Dave Magadan	.06	.02	.00
☐ 746 Bernard Gilkey	.10	.04	.01
☐ 747 Willie Banks	.08	.03	.01
☐ 748 Matt Nokes	.06	.02	.00
☐ 749 Jerald Clark	.03	.01	.00
☐ 750 Travis Fryman	.15	.06	.01
☐ 751 Steve Wilson	.03	.01	.00
☐ 752 Billy Ripken	.03	.01	.00
☐ 753 Paul Assenmacher	.03	.01	.00
☐ 754 Charlie Hayes	.03	.01	.00
☐ 755 Alex Fernandez	.10	.04	.01
☐ 756 Gary Pettis	.03	.01	.00
☐ 757 Rob Dibble	.06	.02	.00
☐ 758 Tim Naehring	.06	.02	.00
☐ 759 Jeff Torborg MG	.03	.01	.00
☐ 760 Ozzie Smith	.10	.04	.01
☐ 761 Mike Fitzgerald	.03	.01	.00
☐ 762 John Burkett	.03	.01	.00
☐ 763 Kyle Abbott	.08	.03	.01
☐ 764 Tyler Green	.45	.18	.04
☐ 765 Pete Harnisch	.06	.02	.00
☐ 766 Mark Davis	.03	.01	.00
☐ 767 Kal Daniels	.06	.02	.00
☐ 768 Jim Thome	.30	.12	.03
☐ 769 Jack Howell	.03	.01	.00
☐ 770 Sid Bream	.03	.01	.00
☐ 771 Arthur Rhodes	.15	.06	.01
☐ 772 Garry Templeton	.03	.01	.00
☐ 773 Hal Morris	.08	.03	.01
☐ 774 Bud Black	.03	.01	.00
☐ 775 Ivan Calderon	.06	.02	.00
☐ 776 Doug Henry	.12	.05	.01
☐ 777 John Olerud	.10	.04	.01
☐ 778 Tim Leary	.03	.01	.00
☐ 779 Jay Bell	.03	.01	.00
☐ 780 Eddie Murray	.10	.04	.01
☐ 781 Paul Abbott	.08	.03	.01
☐ 782 Phil Plantier	.35	.15	.03
☐ 783 Joe Magrane	.03	.01	.00
☐ 784 Ken Patterson	.03	.01	.00
☐ 785 Albert Belle	.12	.05	.01
☐ 786 Royce Clayton	.12	.05	.01
☐ 787 Checklist 661-792	.06	.02	.00
☐ 788 Mike Stanton	.03	.01	.00
☐ 789 Bobby Valentine MG	.03	.01	.00
☐ 790 Joe Carter	.08	.03	.01
☐ 791 Danny Cox	.03	.01	.00
☐ 792 Dave Winfield	.10	.04	.01

1989 Upper Deck

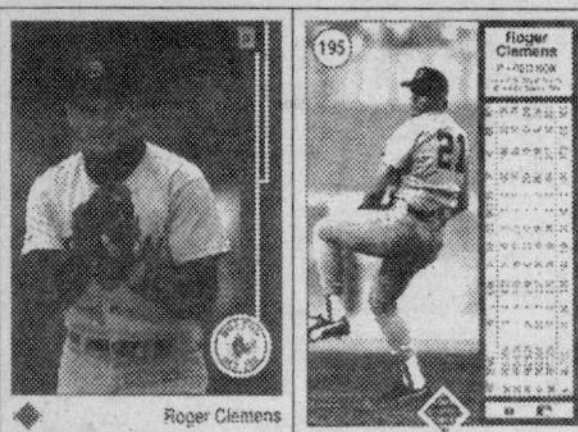

This attractive set was introduced in 1989 as an additional major card set. The cards feature full color on both the front and the back. The cards are distinguished by the fact that each card has a hologram on the reverse, thus making the cards essentially copy proof. Cards 668-693 feature a "Collector's Choice" (CC) colorful drawing of a player (by artist Vernon Wells) on the card front and a checklist of that team on the card back. Cards 1-26 are designated "Rookie Stars" by Upper Deck. On many cards "Rookie" and team logos can be found with either a "TM" or (R). Cards with missing or duplicate holograms appear to be relatively common and hence there is little, if any, premium value on these "variations." The more significant variations involving changed photos or changed type are listed below. According to the company, the Murphy and Sheridan cards were corrected very early, after only 2 percent of the cards had been produced. This means, for example, that out of 1,000,000 Dale Murphy '89 Upper Deck cards produced, there are only 20,000 Murphy error cards. Similarly, the Sheffield was corrected after 15 percent had been printed; Varsho, Gallego, and Schroeder were corrected after 20 percent; and Holton, Manrique, and Winningham were corrected 30 percent of the way through. Collectors should also note that many dealers consider that Upper Deck's "planned" production of 1,000,000 of each player was increased (perhaps even doubled) later in the year due to the explosion in popularity of the Upper Deck cards. The key rookie cards in this set are Sandy Alomar Jr., Ken Griffey Jr., Felix Jose, Ramon Martinez, Gary Sheffield, and John Smoltz.

	MINT	EXC	G-VG
COMPLETE SET (700)	150.00	67.50	22.50
COMMON PLAYER (1-700)	.08	.03	.01
☐ 1 Ken Griffey Jr.	60.00	15.00	3.00
☐ 2 Luis Medina	.15	.06	.01
☐ 3 Tony Chance	.12	.05	.01
☐ 4 Dave Otto	.12	.05	.01
☐ 5 Sandy Alomar Jr. UER (Born 6/16/66, should be 6/18/66)	2.00	.80	.20
☐ 6 Rolando Roomes	.12	.05	.01
☐ 7 Dave West	.25	.10	.02
☐ 8 Cris Carpenter	.20	.08	.02
☐ 9 Gregg Jefferies	1.00	.40	.10
☐ 10 Doug Dascenzo	.15	.06	.01
☐ 11 Ron Jones	.15	.06	.01
☐ 12 Luis De Los Santos	.12	.05	.01
☐ 13A Gary Sheffield ERR (SS upside down on card front)	1.75	.70	.17
☐ 13B Gary Sheffield COR	1.50	.60	.15
☐ 14 Mike Harkey	.30	.12	.03
☐ 15 Lance Blankenship	.12	.05	.01
☐ 16 William Brennan	.12	.05	.01
☐ 17 John Smoltz	2.75	1.10	.27
☐ 18 Ramon Martinez	7.50	3.25	.75
☐ 19 Mark Lemke	.50	.20	.05
☐ 20 Juan Bell	.15	.06	.01
☐ 21 Rey Palacios	.12	.05	.01
☐ 22 Felix Jose	4.50	2.00	.45
☐ 23 Van Snider	.15	.06	.01
☐ 24 Dante Bichette	.40	.16	.04
☐ 25 Randy Johnson	1.25	.50	.12
☐ 26 Carlos Quintana	.90	.40	.09
☐ 27 Star Rookie CL	.12	.02	.00
☐ 28 Mike Schooler	.30	.12	.03
☐ 29 Randy St.Claire	.08	.03	.01
☐ 30 Jerald Clark	.50	.20	.05
☐ 31 Kevin Gross	.08	.03	.01
☐ 32 Dan Firova	.08	.03	.01
☐ 33 Jeff Calhoun	.08	.03	.01
☐ 34 Tommy Hinzo	.08	.03	.01
☐ 35 Ricky Jordan	.35	.15	.03
☐ 36 Larry Parrish	.08	.03	.01
☐ 37 Bret Saberhagen UER (hit total 931, should be 1031)	.35	.15	.03
☐ 38 Mike Smithson	.08	.03	.01
☐ 39 Dave Dravecky	.12	.05	.01
☐ 40 Ed Romero	.08	.03	.01
☐ 41 Jeff Musselman	.08	.03	.01
☐ 42 Ed Hearn	.08	.03	.01
☐ 43 Rance Mulliniks	.08	.03	.01
☐ 44 Jim Eisenreich	.08	.03	.01
☐ 45 Sil Campusano	.15	.06	.01
☐ 46 Mike Krukow	.08	.03	.01
☐ 47 Paul Gibson	.15	.06	.01

	Player			
☐ 48	Mike LaCoss	.08	.03	.01
☐ 49	Larry Herndon	.08	.03	.01
☐ 50	Scott Garrelts	.08	.03	.01
☐ 51	Dwayne Henry	.08	.03	.01
☐ 52	Jim Acker	.08	.03	.01
☐ 53	Steve Sax	.15	.06	.01
☐ 54	Pete O'Brien	.08	.03	.01
☐ 55	Paul Runge	.08	.03	.01
☐ 56	Rick Rhoden	.08	.03	.01
☐ 57	John Dopson	.12	.05	.01
☐ 58	Casey Candaele UER (no stats for Astros for '88 season)	.08	.03	.01
☐ 59	Dave Righetti	.12	.05	.01
☐ 60	Joe Hesketh	.12	.05	.01
☐ 61	Frank DiPino	.08	.03	.01
☐ 62	Tim Laudner	.08	.03	.01
☐ 63	Jamie Moyer	.08	.03	.01
☐ 64	Fred Toliver	.08	.03	.01
☐ 65	Mitch Webster	.08	.03	.01
☐ 66	John Tudor	.12	.05	.01
☐ 67	John Cangelosi	.08	.03	.01
☐ 68	Mike Devereaux	.12	.05	.01
☐ 69	Brian Fisher	.08	.03	.01
☐ 70	Mike Marshall	.12	.05	.01
☐ 71	Zane Smith	.12	.05	.01
☐ 72A	Brian Holton ERR (photo actually Shawn Hillegas)	1.50	.60	.15
☐ 72B	Brian Holton COR	.30	.12	.03
☐ 73	Jose Guzman	.08	.03	.01
☐ 74	Rick Mahler	.08	.03	.01
☐ 75	John Shelby	.08	.03	.01
☐ 76	Jim Deshaies	.08	.03	.01
☐ 77	Bobby Meacham	.08	.03	.01
☐ 78	Bryn Smith	.08	.03	.01
☐ 79	Joaquin Andujar	.08	.03	.01
☐ 80	Richard Dotson	.08	.03	.01
☐ 81	Charlie Lea	.08	.03	.01
☐ 82	Calvin Schiraldi	.08	.03	.01
☐ 83	Les Straker	.08	.03	.01
☐ 84	Les Lancaster	.08	.03	.01
☐ 85	Allan Anderson	.08	.03	.01
☐ 86	Junior Ortiz	.08	.03	.01
☐ 87	Jesse Orosco	.08	.03	.01
☐ 88	Felix Fermin	.08	.03	.01
☐ 89	Dave Anderson	.08	.03	.01
☐ 90	Rafael Belliard UER (Born '61, not '51)	.08	.03	.01
☐ 91	Franklin Stubbs	.08	.03	.01
☐ 92	Cecil Espy	.08	.03	.01
☐ 93	Albert Hall	.08	.03	.01
☐ 94	Tim Leary	.12	.05	.01
☐ 95	Mitch Williams	.12	.05	.01
☐ 96	Tracy Jones	.08	.03	.01
☐ 97	Danny Darwin	.08	.03	.01
☐ 98	Gary Ward	.08	.03	.01
☐ 99	Neal Heaton	.08	.03	.01
☐ 100	Jim Pankovits	.08	.03	.01
☐ 101	Bill Doran	.08	.03	.01
☐ 102	Tim Wallach	.12	.05	.01
☐ 103	Joe Magrane	.12	.05	.01
☐ 104	Ozzie Virgil	.08	.03	.01
☐ 105	Alvin Davis	.12	.05	.01
☐ 106	Tom Brookens	.08	.03	.01
☐ 107	Shawon Dunston	.15	.06	.01
☐ 108	Tracy Woodson	.08	.03	.01
☐ 109	Nelson Liriano	.08	.03	.01
☐ 110	Devon White UER (doubles total 46, should be 56)	.12	.05	.01
☐ 111	Steve Balboni	.08	.03	.01
☐ 112	Buddy Bell	.12	.05	.01
☐ 113	German Jimenez	.08	.03	.01
☐ 114	Ken Dayley	.08	.03	.01
☐ 115	Andres Galarraga	.12	.05	.01
☐ 116	Mike Scioscia	.08	.03	.01
☐ 117	Gary Pettis	.08	.03	.01
☐ 118	Ernie Whitt	.08	.03	.01
☐ 119	Bob Boone	.12	.05	.01
☐ 120	Ryne Sandberg	1.50	.60	.15
☐ 121	Bruce Benedict	.08	.03	.01
☐ 122	Hubie Brooks	.12	.05	.01
☐ 123	Mike Moore	.12	.05	.01
☐ 124	Wallace Johnson	.08	.03	.01
☐ 125	Bob Horner	.12	.05	.01
☐ 126	Chili Davis	.12	.05	.01
☐ 127	Manny Trillo	.08	.03	.01
☐ 128	Chet Lemon	.08	.03	.01
☐ 129	John Cerutti	.08	.03	.01
☐ 130	Orel Hershiser	.17	.07	.01
☐ 131	Terry Pendleton	.25	.10	.02
☐ 132	Jeff Blauser	.17	.07	.01
☐ 133	Mike Fitzgerald	.08	.03	.01
☐ 134	Henry Cotto	.08	.03	.01
☐ 135	Gerald Young	.08	.03	.01
☐ 136	Luis Salazar	.08	.03	.01
☐ 137	Alejandro Pena	.12	.05	.01
☐ 138	Jack Howell	.08	.03	.01
☐ 139	Tony Fernandez	.12	.05	.01
☐ 140	Mark Grace	1.00	.40	.10
☐ 141	Ken Caminiti	.08	.03	.01
☐ 142	Mike Jackson	.08	.03	.01
☐ 143	Larry McWilliams	.08	.03	.01
☐ 144	Andres Thomas	.08	.03	.01
☐ 145	Nolan Ryan (triple exposure)	3.50	1.50	.35
☐ 146	Mike Davis	.08	.03	.01
☐ 147	DeWayne Buice	.08	.03	.01
☐ 148	Jody Davis	.08	.03	.01
☐ 149	Jesse Barfield	.12	.05	.01
☐ 150	Matt Nokes	.12	.05	.01
☐ 151	Jerry Reuss	.08	.03	.01
☐ 152	Rick Cerone	.08	.03	.01
☐ 153	Storm Davis	.08	.03	.01
☐ 154	Marvell Wynne	.08	.03	.01

☐ 155 Will Clark	2.00	.80	.20
☐ 156 Luis Aguayo	.08	.03	.01
☐ 157 Willie Upshaw	.08	.03	.01
☐ 158 Randy Bush	.08	.03	.01
☐ 159 Ron Darling	.12	.05	.01
☐ 160 Kal Daniels	.15	.06	.01
☐ 161 Spike Owen	.08	.03	.01
☐ 162 Luis Polonia	.17	.07	.01
☐ 163 Kevin Mitchell UER ('88/total HR's 18/52, should be 19/53)	.50	.20	.05
☐ 164 Dave Gallagher	.15	.06	.01
☐ 165 Benito Santiago	.15	.06	.01
☐ 166 Greg Gagne	.08	.03	.01
☐ 167 Ken Phelps	.08	.03	.01
☐ 168 Sid Fernandez	.12	.05	.01
☐ 169 Bo Diaz	.08	.03	.01
☐ 170 Cory Snyder	.12	.05	.01
☐ 171 Eric Show	.08	.03	.01
☐ 172 Robby Thompson	.08	.03	.01
☐ 173 Marty Barrett	.08	.03	.01
☐ 174 Dave Henderson	.17	.07	.01
☐ 175 Ozzie Guillen	.12	.05	.01
☐ 176 Barry Lyons	.08	.03	.01
☐ 177 Kelvin Torve	.12	.05	.01
☐ 178 Don Slaught	.08	.03	.01
☐ 179 Steve Lombardozzi	.08	.03	.01
☐ 180 Chris Sabo	1.75	.70	.17
☐ 181 Jose Uribe	.08	.03	.01
☐ 182 Shane Mack	.15	.06	.01
☐ 183 Ron Karkovice	.08	.03	.01
☐ 184 Todd Benzinger	.08	.03	.01
☐ 185 Dave Stewart	.15	.06	.01
☐ 186 Julio Franco	.35	.15	.03
☐ 187 Ron Robinson	.08	.03	.01
☐ 188 Wally Backman	.08	.03	.01
☐ 189 Randy Velarde	.08	.03	.01
☐ 190 Joe Carter	.40	.16	.04
☐ 191 Bob Welch	.17	.07	.01
☐ 192 Kelly Paris	.08	.03	.01
☐ 193 Chris Brown	.08	.03	.01
☐ 194 Rick Reuschel	.12	.05	.01
☐ 195 Roger Clemens	1.50	.60	.15
☐ 196 Dave Concepcion	.12	.05	.01
☐ 197 Al Newman	.08	.03	.01
☐ 198 Brook Jacoby	.08	.03	.01
☐ 199 Mookie Wilson	.08	.03	.01
☐ 200 Don Mattingly	.90	.40	.09
☐ 201 Dick Schofield	.08	.03	.01
☐ 202 Mark Gubicza	.12	.05	.01
☐ 203 Gary Gaetti	.12	.05	.01
☐ 204 Dan Pasqua	.08	.03	.01
☐ 205 Andre Dawson	.45	.18	.04
☐ 206 Chris Speier	.08	.03	.01
☐ 207 Kent Tekulve	.08	.03	.01
☐ 208 Rod Scurry	.08	.03	.01
☐ 209 Scott Bailes	.08	.03	.01
☐ 210 Rickey Henderson UER (Throws Right)	1.50	.60	.15
☐ 211 Harold Baines	.17	.07	.01
☐ 212 Tony Armas	.08	.03	.01
☐ 213 Kent Hrbek	.17	.07	.01
☐ 214 Darrin Jackson	.12	.05	.01
☐ 215 George Brett	.65	.25	.06
☐ 216 Rafael Santana	.08	.03	.01
☐ 217 Andy Allanson	.08	.03	.01
☐ 218 Brett Butler	.15	.06	.01
☐ 219 Steve Jeltz	.08	.03	.01
☐ 220 Jay Buhner	.50	.20	.05
☐ 221 Bo Jackson	2.25	.90	.22
☐ 222 Angel Salazar	.08	.03	.01
☐ 223 Kirk McCaskill	.08	.03	.01
☐ 224 Steve Lyons	.08	.03	.01
☐ 225 Bert Blyleven	.15	.06	.01
☐ 226 Scott Bradley	.08	.03	.01
☐ 227 Bob Melvin	.08	.03	.01
☐ 228 Ron Kittle	.12	.05	.01
☐ 229 Phil Bradley	.08	.03	.01
☐ 230 Tommy John	.15	.06	.01
☐ 231 Greg Walker	.08	.03	.01
☐ 232 Juan Berenguer	.08	.03	.01
☐ 233 Pat Tabler	.08	.03	.01
☐ 234 Terry Clark	.12	.05	.01
☐ 235 Rafael Palmeiro	.50	.20	.05
☐ 236 Paul Zuvella	.08	.03	.01
☐ 237 Willie Randolph	.12	.05	.01
☐ 238 Bruce Fields	.08	.03	.01
☐ 239 Mike Aldrete	.08	.03	.01
☐ 240 Lance Parrish	.15	.06	.01
☐ 241 Greg Maddux	.30	.12	.03
☐ 242 John Moses	.08	.03	.01
☐ 243 Melido Perez	.15	.06	.01
☐ 244 Willie Wilson	.12	.05	.01
☐ 245 Mark McLemore	.08	.03	.01
☐ 246 Von Hayes	.12	.05	.01
☐ 247 Matt Williams	.75	.30	.07
☐ 248 John Candelaria UER (listed as Yankee for part of '87, should be Mets)	.08	.03	.01
☐ 249 Harold Reynolds	.12	.05	.01
☐ 250 Greg Swindell	.12	.05	.01
☐ 251 Juan Agosto	.08	.03	.01
☐ 252 Mike Felder	.08	.03	.01
☐ 253 Vince Coleman	.25	.10	.02
☐ 254 Larry Sheets	.08	.03	.01
☐ 255 George Bell	.35	.15	.03
☐ 256 Terry Steinbach	.12	.05	.01
☐ 257 Jack Armstrong	.30	.12	.03
☐ 258 Dickie Thon	.08	.03	.01
☐ 259 Ray Knight	.12	.05	.01
☐ 260 Darryl Strawberry	1.25	.50	.12
☐ 261 Doug Sisk	.08	.03	.01
☐ 262 Alex Trevino	.08	.03	.01
☐ 263 Jeffrey Leonard	.08	.03	.01
☐ 264 Tom Henke	.12	.05	.01

No.	Player			
☐ 265	Ozzie Smith	.50	.20	.05
☐ 266	Dave Bergman	.08	.03	.01
☐ 267	Tony Phillips	.08	.03	.01
☐ 268	Mark Davis	.12	.05	.01
☐ 269	Kevin Elster	.08	.03	.01
☐ 270	Barry Larkin	.45	.18	.04
☐ 271	Manny Lee	.08	.03	.01
☐ 272	Tom Brunansky	.12	.05	.01
☐ 273	Craig Biggio	1.50	.60	.15
☐ 274	Jim Gantner	.08	.03	.01
☐ 275	Eddie Murray	.50	.20	.05
☐ 276	Jeff Reed	.08	.03	.01
☐ 277	Tim Teufel	.08	.03	.01
☐ 278	Rick Honeycutt	.08	.03	.01
☐ 279	Guillermo Hernandez	.08	.03	.01
☐ 280	John Kruk	.08	.03	.01
☐ 281	Luis Alicea	.08	.03	.01
☐ 282	Jim Clancy	.08	.03	.01
☐ 283	Billy Ripken	.08	.03	.01
☐ 284	Craig Reynolds	.08	.03	.01
☐ 285	Robin Yount	.60	.25	.06
☐ 286	Jimmy Jones	.08	.03	.01
☐ 287	Ron Oester	.08	.03	.01
☐ 288	Terry Leach	.08	.03	.01
☐ 289	Dennis Eckersley	.20	.08	.02
☐ 290	Alan Trammell	.35	.15	.03
☐ 291	Jimmy Key	.15	.06	.01
☐ 292	Chris Bosio	.08	.03	.01
☐ 293	Jose DeLeon	.08	.03	.01
☐ 294	Jim Traber	.08	.03	.01
☐ 295	Mike Scott	.15	.06	.01
☐ 296	Roger McDowell	.08	.03	.01
☐ 297	Garry Templeton	.08	.03	.01
☐ 298	Doyle Alexander	.08	.03	.01
☐ 299	Nick Esasky	.08	.03	.01
☐ 300	Mark McGwire UER (doubles total 52, should be 51)	.50	.20	.05
☐ 301	Darryl Hamilton	.35	.15	.03
☐ 302	Dave Smith	.08	.03	.01
☐ 303	Rick Sutcliffe	.12	.05	.01
☐ 304	Dave Stapleton	.12	.05	.01
☐ 305	Alan Ashby	.08	.03	.01
☐ 306	Pedro Guerrero	.17	.07	.01
☐ 307	Ron Guidry	.15	.06	.01
☐ 308	Steve Farr	.08	.03	.01
☐ 309	Curt Ford	.08	.03	.01
☐ 310	Claudell Washington	.08	.03	.01
☐ 311	Tom Prince	.08	.03	.01
☐ 312	Chad Kreuter	.12	.05	.01
☐ 313	Ken Oberkfell	.08	.03	.01
☐ 314	Jerry Browne	.08	.03	.01
☐ 315	R.J. Reynolds	.08	.03	.01
☐ 316	Scott Bankhead	.12	.05	.01
☐ 317	Milt Thompson	.08	.03	.01
☐ 318	Mario Diaz	.12	.05	.01
☐ 319	Bruce Ruffin	.08	.03	.01
☐ 320	Dave Valle	.08	.03	.01

No.	Player			
☐ 321A	Gary Varsho ERR (back photo actually Mike Bielecki bunting)	2.50	1.00	.25
☐ 321B	Gary Varsho COR (in road uniform)	.15	.06	.01
☐ 322	Paul Mirabella	.08	.03	.01
☐ 323	Chuck Jackson	.12	.05	.01
☐ 324	Drew Hall	.08	.03	.01
☐ 325	Don August	.08	.03	.01
☐ 326	Israel Sanchez	.12	.05	.01
☐ 327	Denny Walling	.08	.03	.01
☐ 328	Joel Skinner	.08	.03	.01
☐ 329	Danny Tartabull	.30	.12	.03
☐ 330	Tony Pena	.12	.05	.01
☐ 331	Jim Sundberg	.08	.03	.01
☐ 332	Jeff D. Robinson Pittsburgh Pirates	.08	.03	.01
☐ 333	Oddibe McDowell	.08	.03	.01
☐ 334	Jose Lind	.08	.03	.01
☐ 335	Paul Kilgus	.08	.03	.01
☐ 336	Juan Samuel	.12	.05	.01
☐ 337	Mike Campbell	.08	.03	.01
☐ 338	Mike Maddux	.08	.03	.01
☐ 339	Darnell Coles	.08	.03	.01
☐ 340	Bob Dernier	.08	.03	.01
☐ 341	Rafael Ramirez	.08	.03	.01
☐ 342	Scott Sanderson	.12	.05	.01
☐ 343	B.J. Surhoff	.12	.05	.01
☐ 344	Billy Hatcher	.12	.05	.01
☐ 345	Pat Perry	.08	.03	.01
☐ 346	Jack Clark	.15	.06	.01
☐ 347	Gary Thurman	.08	.03	.01
☐ 348	Tim Jones	.08	.03	.01
☐ 349	Dave Winfield	.40	.16	.04
☐ 350	Frank White	.08	.03	.01
☐ 351	Dave Collins	.08	.03	.01
☐ 352	Jack Morris	.30	.12	.03
☐ 353	Eric Plunk	.08	.03	.01
☐ 354	Leon Durham	.08	.03	.01
☐ 355	Ivan DeJesus	.08	.03	.01
☐ 356	Brian Holman	.35	.15	.03
☐ 357A	Dale Murphy ERR (front has reverse negative)	60.00	27.00	9.00
☐ 357B	Dale Murphy COR	.40	.16	.04
☐ 358	Mark Portugal	.08	.03	.01
☐ 359	Andy McGaffigan	.08	.03	.01
☐ 360	Tom Glavine	1.25	.50	.12
☐ 361	Keith Moreland	.08	.03	.01
☐ 362	Todd Stottlemyre	.35	.15	.03
☐ 363	Dave Leiper	.08	.03	.01
☐ 364	Cecil Fielder	1.25	.50	.12
☐ 365	Carmelo Martinez	.08	.03	.01
☐ 366	Dwight Evans	.15	.06	.01
☐ 367	Kevin McReynolds	.15	.06	.01
☐ 368	Rich Gedman	.08	.03	.01
☐ 369	Len Dykstra	.15	.06	.01
☐ 370	Jody Reed	.15	.06	.01

Card			
☐ 371 Jose Canseco UER (strikeout total 391, should be 491)	2.25	.90	.22
☐ 372 Rob Murphy	.08	.03	.01
☐ 373 Mike Henneman	.08	.03	.01
☐ 374 Walt Weiss	.15	.06	.01
☐ 375 Rob Dibble	.90	.40	.09
☐ 376 Kirby Puckett (Mark McGwire in background)	1.00	.40	.10
☐ 377 Dennis Martinez	.12	.05	.01
☐ 378 Ron Gant	2.00	.80	.20
☐ 379 Brian Harper	.12	.05	.01
☐ 380 Nelson Santovenia	.17	.07	.01
☐ 381 Lloyd Moseby	.08	.03	.01
☐ 382 Lance McCullers	.08	.03	.01
☐ 383 Dave Stieb	.15	.06	.01
☐ 384 Tony Gwynn	.65	.25	.06
☐ 385 Mike Flanagan	.08	.03	.01
☐ 386 Bob Ojeda	.08	.03	.01
☐ 387 Bruce Hurst	.12	.05	.01
☐ 388 Dave Magadan	.15	.06	.01
☐ 389 Wade Boggs	.75	.30	.07
☐ 390 Gary Carter	.20	.08	.02
☐ 391 Frank Tanana	.12	.05	.01
☐ 392 Curt Young	.08	.03	.01
☐ 393 Jeff Treadway	.17	.07	.01
☐ 394 Darrell Evans	.12	.05	.01
☐ 395 Glenn Hubbard	.08	.03	.01
☐ 396 Chuck Cary	.08	.03	.01
☐ 397 Frank Viola	.17	.07	.01
☐ 398 Jeff Parrett	.08	.03	.01
☐ 399 Terry Blocker	.08	.03	.01
☐ 400 Dan Gladden	.08	.03	.01
☐ 401 Louie Meadows	.08	.03	.01
☐ 402 Tim Raines	.17	.07	.01
☐ 403 Joey Meyer	.08	.03	.01
☐ 404 Larry Andersen	.08	.03	.01
☐ 405 Rex Hudler	.12	.05	.01
☐ 406 Mike Schmidt	1.75	.70	.17
☐ 407 John Franco	.08	.03	.01
☐ 408 Brady Anderson	.15	.06	.01
☐ 409 Don Carman	.08	.03	.01
☐ 410 Eric Davis	.40	.16	.04
☐ 411 Bob Stanley	.08	.03	.01
☐ 412 Pete Smith	.12	.05	.01
☐ 413 Jim Rice	.15	.06	.01
☐ 414 Bruce Sutter	.15	.06	.01
☐ 415 Oil Can Boyd	.08	.03	.01
☐ 416 Ruben Sierra	1.00	.40	.10
☐ 417 Mike LaValliere	.08	.03	.01
☐ 418 Steve Buechele	.08	.03	.01
☐ 419 Gary Redus	.08	.03	.01
☐ 420 Scott Fletcher	.08	.03	.01
☐ 421 Dale Sveum	.08	.03	.01
☐ 422 Bob Knepper	.08	.03	.01
☐ 423 Luis Rivera	.08	.03	.01
☐ 424 Ted Higuera	.08	.03	.01
☐ 425 Kevin Bass	.08	.03	.01
☐ 426 Ken Gerhart	.08	.03	.01
☐ 427 Shane Rawley	.08	.03	.01
☐ 428 Paul O'Neill	.15	.06	.01
☐ 429 Joe Orsulak	.08	.03	.01
☐ 430 Jackie Gutierrez	.08	.03	.01
☐ 431 Gerald Perry	.08	.03	.01
☐ 432 Mike Greenwell	.50	.20	.05
☐ 433 Jerry Royster	.08	.03	.01
☐ 434 Ellis Burks	.50	.20	.05
☐ 435 Ed Olwine	.08	.03	.01
☐ 436 Dave Rucker	.08	.03	.01
☐ 437 Charlie Hough	.08	.03	.01
☐ 438 Bob Walk	.08	.03	.01
☐ 439 Bob Brower	.08	.03	.01
☐ 440 Barry Bonds	.80	.35	.08
☐ 441 Tom Foley	.08	.03	.01
☐ 442 Rob Deer	.12	.05	.01
☐ 443 Glenn Davis	.20	.08	.02
☐ 444 Dave Martinez	.08	.03	.01
☐ 445 Bill Wegman	.08	.03	.01
☐ 446 Lloyd McClendon	.08	.03	.01
☐ 447 Dave Schmidt	.08	.03	.01
☐ 448 Darren Daulton	.12	.05	.01
☐ 449 Frank Williams	.08	.03	.01
☐ 450 Don Aase	.08	.03	.01
☐ 451 Lou Whitaker	.17	.07	.01
☐ 452 Goose Gossage	.15	.06	.01
☐ 453 Ed Whitson	.08	.03	.01
☐ 454 Jim Walewander	.08	.03	.01
☐ 455 Damon Berryhill	.12	.05	.01
☐ 456 Tim Burke	.08	.03	.01
☐ 457 Barry Jones	.08	.03	.01
☐ 458 Joel Youngblood	.08	.03	.01
☐ 459 Floyd Youmans	.08	.03	.01
☐ 460 Mark Salas	.08	.03	.01
☐ 461 Jeff Russell	.08	.03	.01
☐ 462 Darrell Miller	.08	.03	.01
☐ 463 Jeff Kunkel	.08	.03	.01
☐ 464 Sherman Corbett	.08	.03	.01
☐ 465 Curtis Wilkerson	.08	.03	.01
☐ 466 Bud Black	.08	.03	.01
☐ 467 Cal Ripken	1.75	.70	.17
☐ 468 John Farrell	.08	.03	.01
☐ 469 Terry Kennedy	.08	.03	.01
☐ 470 Tom Candiotti	.12	.05	.01
☐ 471 Roberto Alomar	1.75	.70	.17
☐ 472 Jeff M. Robinson Detroit Tigers	.12	.05	.01
☐ 473 Vance Law	.08	.03	.01
☐ 474 Randy Ready UER (strikeout total 136, should be 115)	.08	.03	.01
☐ 475 Walt Terrell	.08	.03	.01
☐ 476 Kelly Downs	.08	.03	.01
☐ 477 Johnny Paredes	.12	.05	.01
☐ 478 Shawn Hillegas	.08	.03	.01
☐ 479 Bob Brenly	.08	.03	.01

☐ 480	Otis Nixon	.12	.05	.01
☐ 481	Johnny Ray	.08	.03	.01
☐ 482	Geno Petralli	.08	.03	.01
☐ 483	Stu Cliburn	.08	.03	.01
☐ 484	Pete Incaviglia	.12	.05	.01
☐ 485	Brian Downing	.08	.03	.01
☐ 486	Jeff Stone	.08	.03	.01
☐ 487	Carmen Castillo	.08	.03	.01
☐ 488	Tom Niedenfuer	.08	.03	.01
☐ 489	Jay Bell	.30	.12	.03
☐ 490	Rick Schu	.08	.03	.01
☐ 491	Jeff Pico	.12	.05	.01
☐ 492	Mark Parent	.12	.05	.01
☐ 493	Eric King	.08	.03	.01
☐ 494	Al Nipper	.08	.03	.01
☐ 495	Andy Hawkins	.08	.03	.01
☐ 496	Daryl Boston	.08	.03	.01
☐ 497	Ernie Riles	.08	.03	.01
☐ 498	Pascual Perez	.08	.03	.01
☐ 499	Bill Long UER (games started total 70, should be 44)	.08	.03	.01
☐ 500	Kirt Manwaring	.08	.03	.01
☐ 501	Chuck Crim	.08	.03	.01
☐ 502	Candy Maldonado	.12	.05	.01
☐ 503	Dennis Lamp	.08	.03	.01
☐ 504	Glenn Braggs	.08	.03	.01
☐ 505	Joe Price	.08	.03	.01
☐ 506	Ken Williams	.08	.03	.01
☐ 507	Bill Pecota	.12	.05	.01
☐ 508	Rey Quinones	.08	.03	.01
☐ 509	Jeff Bittiger	.12	.05	.01
☐ 510	Kevin Seitzer	.12	.05	.01
☐ 511	Steve Bedrosian	.12	.05	.01
☐ 512	Todd Worrell	.12	.05	.01
☐ 513	Chris James	.12	.05	.01
☐ 514	Jose Oquendo	.08	.03	.01
☐ 515	David Palmer	.08	.03	.01
☐ 516	John Smiley	.15	.06	.01
☐ 517	Dave Clark	.08	.03	.01
☐ 518	Mike Dunne	.08	.03	.01
☐ 519	Ron Washington	.08	.03	.01
☐ 520	Bob Kipper	.08	.03	.01
☐ 521	Lee Smith	.15	.06	.01
☐ 522	Juan Castillo	.08	.03	.01
☐ 523	Don Robinson	.08	.03	.01
☐ 524	Kevin Romine	.08	.03	.01
☐ 525	Paul Molitor	.20	.08	.02
☐ 526	Mark Langston	.17	.07	.01
☐ 527	Donnie Hill	.08	.03	.01
☐ 528	Larry Owen	.08	.03	.01
☐ 529	Jerry Reed	.08	.03	.01
☐ 530	Jack McDowell	.75	.30	.07
☐ 531	Greg Mathews	.08	.03	.01
☐ 532	John Russell	.08	.03	.01
☐ 533	Dan Quisenberry	.15	.06	.01
☐ 534	Greg Gross	.08	.03	.01
☐ 535	Danny Cox	.08	.03	.01

☐ 536	Terry Francona	.08	.03	.01
☐ 537	Andy Van Slyke	.25	.10	.02
☐ 538	Mel Hall	.12	.05	.01
☐ 539	Jim Gott	.08	.03	.01
☐ 540	Doug Jones	.08	.03	.01
☐ 541	Craig Lefferts	.08	.03	.01
☐ 542	Mike Boddicker	.08	.03	.01
☐ 543	Greg Brock	.08	.03	.01
☐ 544	Atlee Hammaker	.08	.03	.01
☐ 545	Tom Bolton	.12	.05	.01
☐ 546	Mike Macfarlane	.17	.07	.01
☐ 547	Rich Renteria	.12	.05	.01
☐ 548	John Davis	.08	.03	.01
☐ 549	Floyd Bannister	.08	.03	.01
☐ 550	Mickey Brantley	.08	.03	.01
☐ 551	Duane Ward	.12	.05	.01
☐ 552	Dan Petry	.08	.03	.01
☐ 553	Mickey Tettleton UER (walks total 175, should be 136)	.15	.06	.01
☐ 554	Rick Leach	.08	.03	.01
☐ 555	Mike Witt	.08	.03	.01
☐ 556	Sid Bream	.08	.03	.01
☐ 557	Bobby Witt	.15	.06	.01
☐ 558	Tommy Herr	.08	.03	.01
☐ 559	Randy Milligan	.25	.10	.02
☐ 560	Jose Cecena	.12	.05	.01
☐ 561	Mackey Sasser	.17	.07	.01
☐ 562	Carney Lansford	.12	.05	.01
☐ 563	Rick Aguilera	.12	.05	.01
☐ 564	Ron Hassey	.08	.03	.01
☐ 565	Dwight Gooden	.40	.16	.04
☐ 566	Paul Assenmacher	.08	.03	.01
☐ 567	Neil Allen	.08	.03	.01
☐ 568	Jim Morrison	.08	.03	.01
☐ 569	Mike Pagliarulo	.08	.03	.01
☐ 570	Ted Simmons	.15	.06	.01
☐ 571	Mark Thurmond	.08	.03	.01
☐ 572	Fred McGriff	.60	.25	.06
☐ 573	Wally Joyner	.35	.15	.03
☐ 574	Jose Bautista	.12	.05	.01
☐ 575	Kelly Gruber	.30	.12	.03
☐ 576	Cecilio Guante	.08	.03	.01
☐ 577	Mark Davidson	.08	.03	.01
☐ 578	Bobby Bonilla UER (total steals 2 in '87, should be 3)	.75	.30	.07
☐ 579	Mike Stanley	.08	.03	.01
☐ 580	Gene Larkin	.08	.03	.01
☐ 581	Stan Javier	.08	.03	.01
☐ 582	Howard Johnson	.35	.15	.03
☐ 583A	Mike Gallego ERR (front reversed negative)	1.25	.50	.12
☐ 583B	Mike Gallego COR	.12	.05	.01
☐ 584	David Cone	.20	.08	.02
☐ 585	Doug Jennings	.15	.06	.01
☐ 586	Charles Hudson	.08	.03	.01

☐ 587 Dion James ....08 .03 .01
☐ 588 Al Leiter ....08 .03 .01
☐ 589 Charlie Puleo ....08 .03 .01
☐ 590 Roberto Kelly ....40 .16 .04
☐ 591 Thad Bosley ....08 .03 .01
☐ 592 Pete Stanicek ....08 .03 .01
☐ 593 Pat Borders ....30 .12 .03
☐ 594 Bryan Harvey ....75 .30 .07
☐ 595 Jeff Ballard ....12 .05 .01
☐ 596 Jeff Reardon ....15 .06 .01
☐ 597 Doug Drabek ....15 .06 .01
☐ 598 Edwin Correa ....08 .03 .01
☐ 599 Keith Atherton ....08 .03 .01
☐ 600 Dave LaPoint ....08 .03 .01
☐ 601 Don Baylor ....12 .05 .01
☐ 602 Tom Pagnozzi ....08 .03 .01
☐ 603 Tim Flannery ....08 .03 .01
☐ 604 Gene Walter ....08 .03 .01
☐ 605 Dave Parker ....17 .07 .01
☐ 606 Mike Diaz ....08 .03 .01
☐ 607 Chris Gwynn ....12 .05 .01
☐ 608 Odell Jones ....08 .03 .01
☐ 609 Carlton Fisk ....50 .20 .05
☐ 610 Jay Howell ....08 .03 .01
☐ 611 Tim Crews ....08 .03 .01
☐ 612 Keith Hernandez ....15 .06 .01
☐ 613 Willie Fraser ....08 .03 .01
☐ 614 Jim Eppard ....08 .03 .01
☐ 615 Jeff Hamilton ....08 .03 .01
☐ 616 Kurt Stillwell ....12 .05 .01
☐ 617 Tom Browning ....12 .05 .01
☐ 618 Jeff Montgomery ....15 .06 .01
☐ 619 Jose Rijo ....17 .07 .01
☐ 620 Jamie Quirk ....08 .03 .01
☐ 621 Willie McGee ....17 .07 .01
☐ 622 Mark Grant UER ....08 .03 .01
(glove on wrong hand)
☐ 623 Bill Swift ....12 .05 .01
☐ 624 Orlando Mercado ....08 .03 .01
☐ 625 John Costello ....08 .03 .01
☐ 626 Jose Gonzalez ....08 .03 .01
☐ 627A Bill Schroeder ERR ... 1.50 .60 .15
(back photo actually Ronn Reynolds buckling shin guards)
☐ 627B Bill Schroeder COR ......20 .08 .02
☐ 628A Fred Manrique ERR ......35 .15 .03
(back photo actually Ozzie Guillen throwing)
☐ 628B Fred Manrique COR .....12 .05 .01
(swinging bat on back)
☐ 629 Ricky Horton ....08 .03 .01
☐ 630 Dan Plesac ....08 .03 .01
☐ 631 Alfredo Griffin ....08 .03 .01
☐ 632 Chuck Finley ....35 .15 .03
☐ 633 Kirk Gibson ....17 .07 .01
☐ 634 Randy Myers ....12 .05 .01
☐ 635 Greg Minton ....08 .03 .01
☐ 636A Herm Winningham ....35 .15 .03
ERR (W1nningham on back)
☐ 636B Herm Winningham ....12 .05 .01
COR
☐ 637 Charlie Leibrandt ....08 .03 .01
☐ 638 Tim Birtsas ....08 .03 .01
☐ 639 Bill Buckner ....12 .05 .01
☐ 640 Danny Jackson ....12 .05 .01
☐ 641 Greg Booker ....08 .03 .01
☐ 642 Jim Presley ....08 .03 .01
☐ 643 Gene Nelson ....08 .03 .01
☐ 644 Rod Booker ....08 .03 .01
☐ 645 Dennis Rasmussen ....08 .03 .01
☐ 646 Juan Nieves ....08 .03 .01
☐ 647 Bobby Thigpen ....17 .07 .01
☐ 648 Tim Belcher ....20 .08 .02
☐ 649 Mike Young ....08 .03 .01
☐ 650 Ivan Calderon ....12 .05 .01
☐ 651 Oswaldo Peraza ....12 .05 .01
☐ 652A Pat Sheridan ERR ... 20.00 8.50 2.75
(no position on front)
☐ 652B Pat Sheridan COR ....12 .05 .01
☐ 653 Mike Morgan ....12 .05 .01
☐ 654 Mike Heath ....08 .03 .01
☐ 655 Jay Tibbs ....08 .03 .01
☐ 656 Fernando Valenzuela ......15 .06 .01
☐ 657 Lee Mazzilli ....08 .03 .01
☐ 658 AL CY:Frank Viola ....12 .05 .01
☐ 659A AL MVP:J.Canseco ......45 .18 .04
(eagle logo in black)
☐ 659B AL MVP:J.Canseco ......45 .18 .04
(eagle logo in blue)
☐ 660 AL ROY:Walt Weiss ....12 .05 .01
☐ 661 NL CY:Orel Hershiser .....15 .06 .01
☐ 662 NL MVP:Kirk Gibson ......12 .05 .01
☐ 663 NL ROY:Chris Sabo ....15 .06 .01
☐ 664 ALCS MVP:D.Eckersley ..12 .05 .01
☐ 665 NLCS MVP:O.Hershiser .15 .06 .01
☐ 666 Great WS Moment ....12 .05 .01
(Kirk Gibson's homer)
☐ 667 WS MVP:O.Hershiser .....15 .06 .01
☐ 668 Angels Checklist ....12 .05 .01
Wally Joyner
☐ 669 Astros Checklist ....60 .25 .06
Nolan Ryan
☐ 670 Athletics Checklist ....40 .16 .04
Jose Canseco
☐ 671 Blue Jays Checklist ....15 .06 .01
Fred McGriff
☐ 672 Braves Checklist ....15 .06 .01
Dale Murphy
☐ 673 Brewers Checklist ....12 .05 .01
Paul Molitor
☐ 674 Cardinals Checklist ....15 .06 .01
Ozzie Smith
☐ 675 Cubs Checklist ....30 .12 .03
Ryne Sandberg

☐ 676 Dodgers Checklist	.12	.05	.01
Kirk Gibson			
☐ 677 Expos Checklist	.12	.05	.01
Andres Galaragga			
☐ 678 Giants Checklist	.40	.16	.04
Will Clark			
☐ 679 Indians Checklist	.12	.05	.01
Cory Snyder			
☐ 680 Mariners Checklist	.12	.05	.01
Alvin Davis			
☐ 681 Mets Checklist	.30	.12	.03
Darryl Strawberry			
☐ 682 Orioles Checklist	.35	.15	.03
Cal Ripken			
☐ 683 Padres Checklist	.15	.06	.01
Tony Gwynn			
☐ 684 Phillies Checklist	.35	.15	.03
Mike Schmidt			
☐ 685 Pirates Checklist	.12	.05	.01
Andy Van Slyke			
UER (96 Junior Ortiz)			
☐ 686 Rangers Checklist	.20	.08	.02
Ruben Sierra			
☐ 687 Red Sox Checklist	.17	.07	.01
Wade Boggs			
☐ 688 Reds Checklist	.15	.06	.01
Eric Davis			
☐ 689 Royals Checklist	.15	.06	.01
George Brett			
☐ 690 Tigers Checklist	.15	.06	.01
Alan Trammell			
☐ 691 Twins Checklist	.12	.05	.01
Frank Viola			
☐ 692 White Sox Checklist	.12	.05	.01
Harold Baines			
☐ 693 Yankees Checklist	.20	.08	.02
Don Mattingly			
☐ 694 Checklist 1-100	.12	.01	.00
☐ 695 Checklist 101-200	.12	.01	.00
☐ 696 Checklist 201-300	.12	.01	.00
☐ 697 Checklist 301-400	.12	.01	.00
☐ 698 Checklist 401-500 UER	.12	.01	.00
467 Cal Ripkin Jr.			
☐ 699 Checklist 501-600 UER	.12	.01	.00
543 Greg Booker			
☐ 700 Checklist 601-700	.12	.01	.00

1989 Upper Deck Extended

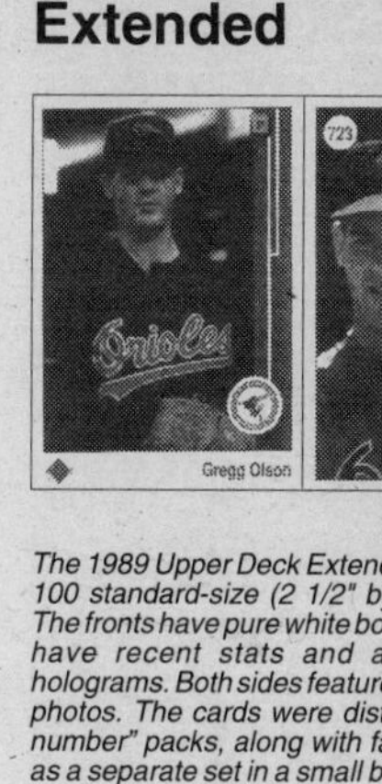

The 1989 Upper Deck Extended set contains 100 standard-size (2 1/2" by 3 1/2") cards. The fronts have pure white borders; the backs have recent stats and anti-counterfeit holograms. Both sides feature attractive color photos. The cards were distributed in "high number" packs, along with factory sets, and as a separate set in a small blue custom box. The key rookie cards in this set are Jim Abbott, Jerome Walton, and Todd Zeile.

	MINT	EXC	G-VG
COMPLETE SET (100)	16.50	7.50	1.50
COMMON PLAYER (701-800)	.08	.03	.01
☐ 701 Checklist 701-800	.12	.01	.00
☐ 702 Jesse Barfield	.12	.05	.01
☐ 703 Walt Terrell	.08	.03	.01
☐ 704 Dickie Thon	.08	.03	.01
☐ 705 Al Leiter	.08	.03	.01
☐ 706 Dave LaPoint	.08	.03	.01
☐ 707 Charlie Hayes	.25	.10	.02
☐ 708 Andy Hawkins	.08	.03	.01
☐ 709 Mickey Hatcher	.08	.03	.01
☐ 710 Lance McCullers	.08	.03	.01
☐ 711 Ron Kittle	.12	.05	.01
☐ 712 Bert Blyleven	.15	.06	.01
☐ 713 Rick Dempsey	.08	.03	.01
☐ 714 Ken Williams	.08	.03	.01
☐ 715 Steve Rosenberg	.12	.05	.01
☐ 716 Joe Skalski	.12	.05	.01
☐ 717 Spike Owen	.08	.03	.01
☐ 718 Todd Burns	.15	.06	.01
☐ 719 Kevin Gross	.08	.03	.01
☐ 720 Tommy Herr	.08	.03	.01
☐ 721 Rob Ducey	.12	.05	.01

☐ 722 Gary Green .12 .05 .01
☐ 723 Gregg Olson 1.50 .60 .15
☐ 724 Greg W. Harris .40 .16 .04
☐ 725 Craig Worthington .15 .06 .01
☐ 726 Tom Howard .30 .12 .03
☐ 727 Dale Mohorcic .08 .03 .01
☐ 728 Rich Yett .08 .03 .01
☐ 729 Mel Hall .12 .05 .01
☐ 730 Floyd Youmans .08 .03 .01
☐ 731 Lonnie Smith .15 .06 .01
☐ 732 Wally Backman .08 .03 .01
☐ 733 Trevor Wilson .35 .15 .03
☐ 734 Jose Alvarez .12 .05 .01
☐ 735 Bob Milacki .35 .15 .03
☐ 736 Tom Gordon .80 .35 .08
☐ 737 Wally Whitehurst .17 .07 .01
☐ 738 Mike Aldrete .08 .03 .01
☐ 739 Keith Miller .15 .06 .01
☐ 740 Randy Milligan .17 .07 .01
☐ 741 Jeff Parrett .08 .03 .01
☐ 742 Steve Finley .75 .30 .07
☐ 743 Junior Felix .35 .15 .03
☐ 744 Pete Harnisch .60 .25 .06
☐ 745 Bill Spiers .30 .12 .03
☐ 746 Hensley Meulens 1.00 .40 .10
☐ 747 Juan Bell .15 .06 .01
☐ 748 Steve Sax .15 .06 .01
☐ 749 Phil Bradley .08 .03 .01
☐ 750 Rey Quinones .08 .03 .01
☐ 751 Tommy Gregg .08 .03 .01
☐ 752 Kevin Brown .15 .06 .01
☐ 753 Derek Lilliquist .12 .05 .01
☐ 754 Todd Zeile 3.50 1.50 .35
☐ 755 Jim Abbott 3.50 1.50 .35
(triple exposure)
☐ 756 Ozzie Canseco .20 .08 .02
☐ 757 Nick Esasky .08 .03 .01
☐ 758 Mike Moore .12 .05 .01
☐ 759 Rob Murphy .08 .03 .01
☐ 760 Rick Mahler .08 .03 .01
☐ 761 Fred Lynn .15 .06 .01
☐ 762 Kevin Blankenship .12 .05 .01
☐ 763 Eddie Murray .35 .15 .03
☐ 764 Steve Searcy .15 .06 .01
☐ 765 Jerome Walton 1.00 .40 .10
☐ 766 Erik Hanson 1.50 .60 .15
☐ 767 Bob Boone .15 .06 .01
☐ 768 Edgar Martinez 1.00 .40 .10
☐ 769 Jose DeJesus .17 .07 .01
☐ 770 Greg Briley .35 .15 .03
☐ 771 Steve Peters .12 .05 .01
☐ 772 Rafael Palmeiro .35 .15 .03
☐ 773 Jack Clark .15 .06 .01
☐ 774 Nolan Ryan 3.50 1.50 .35
(throwing football)
☐ 775 Lance Parrish .15 .06 .01
☐ 776 Joe Girardi .15 .06 .01
☐ 777 Willie Randolph .12 .05 .01
☐ 778 Mitch Williams .12 .05 .01
☐ 779 Dennis Cook .17 .07 .01
☐ 780 Dwight Smith .30 .12 .03
☐ 781 Lenny Harris .40 .16 .04
☐ 782 Torey Lovullo .12 .05 .01
☐ 783 Norm Charlton .30 .12 .03
☐ 784 Chris Brown .08 .03 .01
☐ 785 Todd Benzinger .12 .05 .01
☐ 786 Shane Rawley .08 .03 .01
☐ 787 Omar Vizquel .15 .06 .01
☐ 788 LaVel Freeman .25 .10 .02
☐ 789 Jeffrey Leonard .08 .03 .01
☐ 790 Eddie Williams .08 .03 .01
☐ 791 Jamie Moyer .08 .03 .01
☐ 792 Bruce Hurst UER .12 .05 .01
(Workd Series)
☐ 793 Julio Franco .30 .12 .03
☐ 794 Claudell Washington .08 .03 .01
☐ 795 Jody Davis .08 .03 .01
☐ 796 Oddibe McDowell .08 .03 .01
☐ 797 Paul Kilgus .08 .03 .01
☐ 798 Tracy Jones .08 .03 .01
☐ 799 Steve Wilson .15 .06 .01
☐ 800 Pete O'Brien .12 .05 .01

1990 Upper Deck

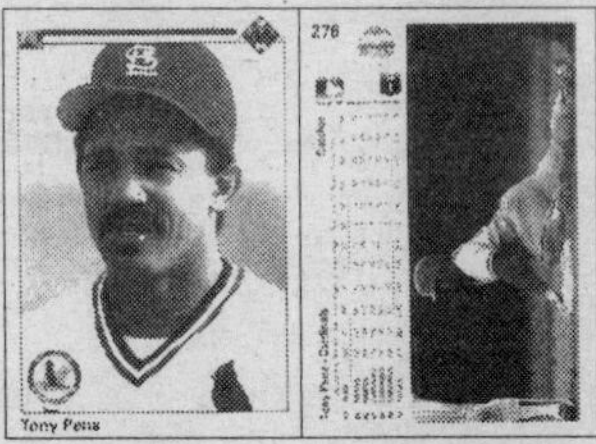

The 1990 Upper Deck set contains 700 standard-size (2 1/2" by 3 1/2") cards. The front and back borders are white, and both sides feature full-color photos. The horizontally oriented backs have recent stats and anti-counterfeiting holograms. Unlike the 1989 Upper Deck set, the team checklist cards are not grouped numerically at the end of the set, but are mixed in with the first 100 cards. The key rookie cards in this set are Juan Gonzalez, Kevin Maas, Ben McDonald, John Olerud,

and Dean Palmer. Cards 101 through 199 have two minor varieties in that the cards either show or omit "Copyright 1990 Upper Deck Co. Printed in USA below the two licensing logos. Those without are considered minor errors; they were found in the High Number foil packs.

	MINT	EXC	G-VG
COMPLETE SET (700)	35.00	15.75	5.25
COMMON PLAYER (1-700)	.05	.02	.00

	MINT	EXC	G-VG
☐ 1 Star Rookie Checklist	.10	.01	.00
☐ 2 Randy Nosek	.10	.04	.01
☐ 3 Tom Drees UER (11th line, hulred, should be hurled)	.10	.04	.01
☐ 4 Curt Young	.05	.02	.00
☐ 5 Devon White TC California Angels	.08	.03	.01
☐ 6 Luis Salazar	.05	.02	.00
☐ 7 Von Hayes TC Philadelphia Phillies	.08	.03	.01
☐ 8 Jose Bautista	.05	.02	.00
☐ 9 Marquis Grissom	1.00	.40	.10
☐ 10 Orel Hershiser TC Los Angeles Dodgers	.08	.03	.01
☐ 11 Rick Aguilera	.08	.03	.01
☐ 12 Benito Santiago TC San Diego Padres	.08	.03	.01
☐ 13 Deion Sanders	.35	.15	.03
☐ 14 Marvell Wynne	.05	.02	.00
☐ 15 Dave West	.05	.02	.00
☐ 16 Bobby Bonilla TC Pittsburgh Pirates	.10	.04	.01
☐ 17 Sammy Sosa	.50	.20	.05
☐ 18 Steve Sax TC New York Yankees	.08	.03	.01
☐ 19 Jack Howell	.05	.02	.00
☐ 20 Mike Schmidt Special UER (Suprising, should be surprising)	.50	.20	.05
☐ 21 Robin Ventura UER (Samta Maria)	2.25	.90	.22
☐ 22 Brian Meyer	.10	.04	.01
☐ 23 Blaine Beatty	.15	.06	.01
☐ 24 Ken Griffey Jr. TC Seattle Mariners	.75	.30	.07
☐ 25 Greg Vaughn UER (Association misspelled as assiocation)	1.25	.50	.12
☐ 26 Xavier Hernandez	.10	.04	.01
☐ 27 Jason Grimsley	.12	.05	.01
☐ 28 Eric Anthony UER (Ashville, should be Asheville)	.35	.15	.03
☐ 29 Tim Raines TC Montreal Expos	.08	.03	.01
UER (Wallach listed before Walker)			
☐ 30 David Wells	.08	.03	.01
☐ 31 Hal Morris	1.25	.50	.12
☐ 32 Bo Jackson TC Kansas City Royals	.35	.15	.03
☐ 33 Kelly Mann	.15	.06	.01
☐ 34 Nolan Ryan Special	1.00	.40	.10
☐ 35 Scott Service UER (Born Cincinatti on 7/27/67, should be Cincinnati 2/27)	.10	.04	.01
☐ 36 Mark McGwire TC Oakland A's	.10	.04	.01
☐ 37 Tino Martinez	1.50	.60	.15
☐ 38 Chili Davis	.08	.03	.01
☐ 39 Scott Sanderson	.05	.02	.00
☐ 40 Kevin Mitchell TC San Francisco Giants	.08	.03	.01
☐ 41 Lou Whitaker TC Detroit Tigers	.08	.03	.01
☐ 42 Scott Coolbaugh UER (Definately)	.12	.05	.01
☐ 43 Jose Cano UER (Born 9/7/62, should be 3/7/62)	.10	.04	.01
☐ 44 Jose Vizcaino	.17	.07	.01
☐ 45 Bob Hamelin	.17	,07	.01
☐ 46 Jose Offerman UER (Posesses)	.50	.20	.05
☐ 47 Kevin Blankenship	.05	.02	.00
☐ 48 Kirby Puckett TC Minnesota Twins	.12	.05	.01
☐ 49 Tommy Greene UER (Livest, should be liveliest)	.60	.25	.06
☐ 50 Will Clark Special UER (Perenial, should be perennial)	.40	.16	.04
☐ 51 Rob Nelson	.05	.02	.00
☐ 52 Chris Hammond UER (Chatanooga)	.45	.18	.04
☐ 53 Joe Carter TC Cleveland Indians	.08	.03	.01
☐ 54A Ben McDonald ERR (no Rookie designation on card front)	20.00	8.50	2.75
☐ 54B Ben McDonald COR	1.50	.60	.15
☐ 55 Andy Benes UER (Whichita)	.50	.20	.05
☐ 56 John Olerud	2.50	1.00	.25
☐ 57 Roger Clemens TC Boston Red Sox	.15	.06	.01
☐ 58 Tony Armas	.05	.02	.00
☐ 59 George Canale	.17	.07	.01
☐ 60A Mickey Tettleton TC Baltimore Orioles (683 Jamie Weston)	3.00	1.25	.30

☐ 60B Mickey Tettleton TC .... .12 .05 .01
Baltimore Orioles
(683 Mickey Weston)
☐ 61 Mike Stanton .... .25 .10 .02
☐ 62 Dwight Gooden TC .... .10 .04 .01
New York Mets
☐ 63 Kent Mercker UER .... .25 .10 .02
(Albuguerque)
☐ 64 Francisco Cabrera .... .20 .08 .02
☐ 65 Steve Avery UER .... 3.50 1.50 .35
(born NJ, should be MI,
Merker should be Mercker)
☐ 66 Jose Canseco .... .75 .30 .07
☐ 67 Matt Merullo .... .10 .04 .01
☐ 68 Vince Coleman TC .... .08 .03 .01
St. Louis Cardinals
UER (Guererro)
☐ 69 Ron Karkovice .... .05 .02 .00
☐ 70 Kevin Maas .... 3.50 1.50 .35
☐ 71 Dennis Cook UER .... .08 .03 .01
(Shown with righty
glove on card back)
☐ 72 Juan Gonzalez UER .... 7.00 3.00 .70
(135 games for Tulsa
in '89, should be 133)
☐ 73 Andre Dawson TC .... .08 .03 .01
Chicago Cubs
☐ 74 Dean Palmer UER .... 2.25 .90 .22
(Permanent misspelled
as perminant)
☐ 75 Bo Jackson Special .... .40 .16 .04
UER (Monsterous,
should be monstrous)
☐ 76 Rob Richie .... .05 .02 .00
☐ 77 Bobby Rose UER .... .15 .06 .01
(Pickin, should
be pick in)
☐ 78 Brian Dubois UER .... .12 .05 .01
(Commiting)
☐ 79 Ozzie Guillen TC .... .08 .03 .01
Chicago White Sox
☐ 80 Gene Nelson .... .05 .02 .00
☐ 81 Bob McClure .... .05 .02 .00
☐ 82 Julio Franco TC .... .08 .03 .01
Texas Rangers
☐ 83 Greg Minton .... .05 .02 .00
☐ 84 John Smoltz TC UER .... .10 .04 .01
Atlanta Braves
(Oddibe not Odibbe)
☐ 85 Willie Fraser .... .05 .02 .00
☐ 86 Neal Heaton .... .05 .02 .00
☐ 87 Kevin Tapani .... .75 .30 .07
☐ 88 Mike Scott TC .... .08 .03 .01
Houston Astros
☐ 89A Jim Gott ERR .... 6.50 2.75 .65
(photo actually
Rick Reed)
☐ 89B Jim Gott COR .... .08 .03 .01
☐ 90 Lance Johnson .... .08 .03 .01
☐ 91 Robin Yount TC UER .... .10 .04 .01
Milwaukee Brewers
(Checklist on back has
178 Rob Deer and
176 Mike Felder)
☐ 92 Jeff Parrett .... .05 .02 .00
☐ 93 Julio Machado UER .... .10 .04 .01
(Valenzuelan, should
be Venezuelan)
☐ 94 Ron Jones .... .05 .02 .00
☐ 95 George Bell TC .... .08 .03 .01
Toronto Blue Jays
☐ 96 Jerry Reuss .... .05 .02 .00
☐ 97 Brian Fisher .... .05 .02 .00
☐ 98 Kevin Ritz UER .... .12 .05 .01
(Amercian)
☐ 99 Barry Larkin TC .... .08 .03 .01
Cincinnati Reds
☐ 100 Checklist 1-100 .... .08 .01 .00
☐ 101 Gerald Perry .... .05 .02 .00
☐ 102 Kevin Appier .... .40 .16 .04
☐ 103 Julio Franco .... .12 .05 .01
☐ 104 Craig Biggio .... .15 .06 .01
☐ 105 Bo Jackson UER .... .75 .30 .07
('89 BA wrong,
should be .256)
☐ 106 Junior Felix .... .10 .04 .01
☐ 107 Mike Harkey .... .08 .03 .01
☐ 108 Fred McGriff .... .15 .06 .01
☐ 109 Rick Sutcliffe .... .08 .03 .01
☐ 110 Pete O'Brien .... .05 .02 .00
☐ 111 Kelly Gruber .... .10 .04 .01
☐ 112 Dwight Evans .... .08 .03 .01
☐ 113 Pat Borders .... .05 .02 .00
☐ 114 Dwight Gooden .... .17 .07 .01
☐ 115 Kevin Batiste .... .12 .05 .01
☐ 116 Eric Davis .... .15 .06 .01
☐ 117 Kevin Mitchell UER .... .15 .06 .01
(Career HR total 99,
should be 100)
☐ 118 Ron Oester .... .05 .02 .00
☐ 119 Brett Butler .... .08 .03 .01
☐ 120 Danny Jackson .... .08 .03 .01
☐ 121 Tommy Gregg .... .05 .02 .00
☐ 122 Ken Caminiti .... .05 .02 .00
☐ 123 Kevin Brown .... .05 .02 .00
☐ 124 George Brett UER .... .20 .08 .02
(133 runs, should
be 1300)
☐ 125 Mike Scott .... .08 .03 .01
☐ 126 Cory Snyder .... .08 .03 .01
☐ 127 George Bell .... .12 .05 .01
☐ 128 Mark Grace .... .20 .08 .02
☐ 129 Devon White .... .08 .03 .01
☐ 130 Tony Fernandez .... .08 .03 .01
☐ 131 Don Aase .... .05 .02 .00
☐ 132 Rance Mulliniks .... .05 .02 .00

☐ 133 Marty Barrett	.05	.02	.00
☐ 134 Nelson Liriano	.05	.02	.00
☐ 135 Mark Carreon	.05	.02	.00
☐ 136 Candy Maldonado	.05	.02	.00
☐ 137 Tim Birtsas	.05	.02	.00
☐ 138 Tom Brookens	.05	.02	.00
☐ 139 John Franco	.05	.02	.00
☐ 140 Mike LaCoss	.05	.02	.00
☐ 141 Jeff Treadway	.05	.02	.00
☐ 142 Pat Tabler	.05	.02	.00
☐ 143 Darrell Evans	.08	.03	.01
☐ 144 Rafael Ramirez	.05	.02	.00
☐ 145 Oddibe McDowell UER (misspelled Odibbe)	.05	.02	.00
☐ 146 Brian Downing	.05	.02	.00
☐ 147 Curt Wilkerson	.05	.02	.00
☐ 148 Ernie Whitt	.05	.02	.00
☐ 149 Bill Schroeder	.05	.02	.00
☐ 150 Domingo Ramos UER (Says throws right, but shows him throwing lefty)	.05	.02	.00
☐ 151 Rick Honeycutt	.05	.02	.00
☐ 152 Don Slaught	.05	.02	.00
☐ 153 Mitch Webster	.05	.02	.00
☐ 154 Tony Phillips	.05	.02	.00
☐ 155 Paul Kilgus	.05	.02	.00
☐ 156 Ken Griffey Jr. UER (Simultaniously)	5.00	2.25	.50
☐ 157 Gary Sheffield	.12	.05	.01
☐ 158 Wally Backman	.05	.02	.00
☐ 159 B.J. Surhoff	.05	.02	.00
☐ 160 Louie Meadows	.05	.02	.00
☐ 161 Paul O'Neill	.08	.03	.01
☐ 162 Jeff McKnight	.12	.05	.01
☐ 163 Alvaro Espinoza	.05	.02	.00
☐ 164 Scott Scudder	.20	.08	.02
☐ 165 Jeff Reed	.05	.02	.00
☐ 166 Gregg Jefferies	.15	.06	.01
☐ 167 Barry Larkin	.17	.07	.01
☐ 168 Gary Carter	.10	.04	.01
☐ 169 Robby Thompson	.05	.02	.00
☐ 170 Rolando Roomes	.05	.02	.00
☐ 171 Mark McGwire UER (Total games 427 and hits 479, should be 467 and 427)	.20	.08	.02
☐ 172 Steve Sax	.08	.03	.01
☐ 173 Mark Williamson	.05	.02	.00
☐ 174 Mitch Williams	.05	.02	.00
☐ 175 Brian Holton	.05	.02	.00
☐ 176 Rob Deer	.08	.03	.01
☐ 177 Tim Raines	.10	.04	.01
☐ 178 Mike Felder	.05	.02	.00
☐ 179 Harold Reynolds	.08	.03	.01
☐ 180 Terry Francona	.05	.02	.00
☐ 181 Chris Sabo	.15	.06	.01
☐ 182 Darryl Strawberry	.35	.15	.03
☐ 183 Willie Randolph	.08	.03	.01
☐ 184 Bill Ripken	.05	.02	.00
☐ 185 Mackey Sasser	.05	.02	.00
☐ 186 Todd Benzinger	.05	.02	.00
☐ 187 Kevin Elster	.05	.02	.00
☐ 188 Jose Uribe	.05	.02	.00
☐ 189 Tom Browning	.08	.03	.01
☐ 190 Keith Miller	.05	.02	.00
☐ 191 Don Mattingly	.30	.12	.03
☐ 192 Dave Parker	.10	.04	.01
☐ 193 Roberto Kelly UER 96 RBI, should be 62)	.12	.05	.01
☐ 194 Phil Bradley	.05	.02	.00
☐ 195 Ron Hassey	.05	.02	.00
☐ 196 Gerald Young	.05	.02	.00
☐ 197 Hubie Brooks	.08	.03	.01
☐ 198 Bill Doran	.05	.02	.00
☐ 199 Al Newman	.05	.02	.00
☐ 200 Checklist 101-200	.08	.01	.00
☐ 201 Terry Puhl	.05	.02	.00
☐ 202 Frank DiPino	.05	.02	.00
☐ 203 Jim Clancy	.05	.02	.00
☐ 204 Bob Ojeda	.05	.02	.00
☐ 205 Alex Trevino	.05	.02	.00
☐ 206 Dave Henderson	.10	.04	.01
☐ 207 Henry Cotto	.05	.02	.00
☐ 208 Rafael Belliard UER (Born 1961, not 1951)	.05	.02	.00
☐ 209 Stan Javier	.05	.02	.00
☐ 210 Jerry Reed	.05	.02	.00
☐ 211 Doug Dascenzo	.05	.02	.00
☐ 212 Andres Thomas	.05	.02	.00
☐ 213 Greg Maddux	.08	.03	.01
☐ 214 Mike Schooler	.05	.02	.00
☐ 215 Lonnie Smith	.08	.03	.01
☐ 216 Jose Rijo	.08	.03	.01
☐ 217 Greg Gagne	.05	.02	.00
☐ 218 Jim Gantner	.05	.02	.00
☐ 219 Allan Anderson	.05	.02	.00
☐ 220 Rick Mahler	.05	.02	.00
☐ 221 Jim Deshaies	.05	.02	.00
☐ 222 Keith Hernandez	.08	.03	.01
☐ 223 Vince Coleman	.10	.04	.01
☐ 224 David Cone	.10	.04	.01
☐ 225 Ozzie Smith	.17	.07	.01
☐ 226 Matt Nokes	.08	.03	.01
☐ 227 Barry Bonds	.25	.10	.02
☐ 228 Felix Jose	.35	.15	.03
☐ 229 Dennis Powell	.05	.02	.00
☐ 230 Mike Gallego	.05	.02	.00
☐ 231 Shawon Dunston UER ('89 stats are Andre Dawson's)	.10	.04	.01
☐ 232 Ron Gant	.40	.16	.04
☐ 233 Omar Vizquel	.05	.02	.00
☐ 234 Derek Lilliquist	.05	.02	.00
☐ 235 Erik Hanson	.12	.05	.01
☐ 236 Kirby Puckett UER	.35	.15	.03

(824 games, should be 924)
☐ 237 Bill Spiers .... .08 .03 .01
☐ 238 Dan Gladden .... .05 .02 .00
☐ 239 Bryan Clutterbuck .... .05 .02 .00
☐ 240 John Moses .... .05 .02 .00
☐ 241 Ron Darling .... .08 .03 .01
☐ 242 Joe Magrane .... .05 .02 .00
☐ 243 Dave Magadan .... .08 .03 .01
☐ 244 Pedro Guerrero UER .... .08 .03 .01
(Misspelled Guererro)
☐ 245 Glenn Davis .... .10 .04 .01
☐ 246 Terry Steinbach .... .05 .02 .00
☐ 247 Fred Lynn .... .08 .03 .01
☐ 248 Gary Redus .... .05 .02 .00
☐ 249 Ken Williams .... .05 .02 .00
☐ 250 Sid Bream .... .05 .02 .00
☐ 251 Bob Welch UER .... .08 .03 .01
(2587 career strike-outs, should be 1587)
☐ 252 Bill Buckner .... .08 .03 .01
☐ 253 Carney Lansford .... .08 .03 .01
☐ 254 Paul Molitor .... .10 .04 .01
☐ 255 Jose DeJesus .... .05 .02 .00
☐ 256 Orel Hershiser .... .10 .04 .01
☐ 257 Tom Brunansky .... .08 .03 .01
☐ 258 Mike Davis .... .05 .02 .00
☐ 259 Jeff Ballard .... .05 .02 .00
☐ 260 Scott Terry .... .05 .02 .00
☐ 261 Sid Fernandez .... .08 .03 .01
☐ 262 Mike Marshall .... .08 .03 .01
☐ 263 Howard Johnson UER .... .12 .05 .01
(192 SO, should be 592)
☐ 264 Kirk Gibson UER .... .10 .04 .01
(659 runs, should be 669)
☐ 265 Kevin McReynolds .... .10 .04 .01
☐ 266 Cal Ripken .... .50 .20 .05
☐ 267 Ozzie Guillen UER .... .08 .03 .01
(Career triples 27, should be 29)
☐ 268 Jim Traber .... .05 .02 .00
☐ 269 Bobby Thigpen .... .08 .03 .01
☐ 270 Joe Orsulak .... .05 .02 .00
☐ 271 Bob Boone .... .08 .03 .01
☐ 272 Dave Stewart UER .... .10 .04 .01
(Totals wrong due to omission of '86 stats)
☐ 273 Tim Wallach .... .08 .03 .01
☐ 274 Luis Aquino UER .... .05 .02 .00
(Says throws lefty, but shows him throwing righty)
☐ 275 Mike Moore .... .08 .03 .01
☐ 276 Tony Pena .... .08 .03 .01
☐ 277 Eddie Murray UER .... .15 .06 .01
(Several typos in career total stats)
☐ 278 Milt Thompson .... .05 .02 .00
☐ 279 Alejandro Pena .... .08 .03 .01
☐ 280 Ken Dayley .... .05 .02 .00
☐ 281 Carmen Castillo .... .05 .02 .00
☐ 282 Tom Henke .... .08 .03 .01
☐ 283 Mickey Hatcher .... .05 .02 .00
☐ 284 Roy Smith .... .05 .02 .00
☐ 285 Manny Lee .... .05 .02 .00
☐ 286 Dan Pasqua .... .05 .02 .00
☐ 287 Larry Sheets .... .05 .02 .00
☐ 288 Garry Templeton .... .05 .02 .00
☐ 289 Eddie Williams .... .05 .02 .00
☐ 290 Brady Anderson .... .05 .02 .00
☐ 291 Spike Owen .... .05 .02 .00
☐ 292 Storm Davis .... .05 .02 .00
☐ 293 Chris Bosio .... .05 .02 .00
☐ 294 Jim Eisenreich .... .05 .02 .00
☐ 295 Don August .... .05 .02 .00
☐ 296 Jeff Hamilton .... .05 .02 .00
☐ 297 Mickey Tettleton .... .08 .03 .01
☐ 298 Mike Scioscia .... .05 .02 .00
☐ 299 Kevin Hickey .... .05 .02 .00
☐ 300 Checklist 201-300 .... .08 .01 .00
☐ 301 Shawn Abner .... .05 .02 .00
☐ 302 Kevin Bass .... .05 .02 .00
☐ 303 Bip Roberts .... .05 .02 .00
☐ 304 Joe Girardi .... .08 .03 .01
☐ 305 Danny Darwin .... .05 .02 .00
☐ 306 Mike Heath .... .05 .02 .00
☐ 307 Mike Macfarlane .... .05 .02 .00
☐ 308 Ed Whitson .... .05 .02 .00
☐ 309 Tracy Jones .... .05 .02 .00
☐ 310 Scott Fletcher .... .05 .02 .00
☐ 311 Darnell Coles .... .05 .02 .00
☐ 312 Mike Brumley .... .05 .02 .00
☐ 313 Bill Swift .... .05 .02 .00
☐ 314 Charlie Hough .... .05 .02 .00
☐ 315 Jim Presley .... .05 .02 .00
☐ 316 Luis Polonia .... .05 .02 .00
☐ 317 Mike Morgan .... .05 .02 .00
☐ 318 Lee Guetterman .... .05 .02 .00
☐ 319 Jose Oquendo .... .05 .02 .00
☐ 320 Wayne Tolleson .... .05 .02 .00
☐ 321 Jody Reed .... .08 .03 .01
☐ 322 Damon Berryhill .... .05 .02 .00
☐ 323 Roger Clemens .... .40 .16 .04
☐ 324 Ryne Sandberg .... .45 .18 .04
☐ 325 Benito Santiago UER .... .10 .04 .01
(Misspelled Santago on card back)
☐ 326 Bret Saberhagen UER .... .12 .05 .01
(1140 hits, should be 1240; 56 CG, should be 52)
☐ 327 Lou Whitaker .... .08 .03 .01
☐ 328 Dave Gallagher .... .05 .02 .00
☐ 329 Mike Pagliarulo .... .05 .02 .00
☐ 330 Doyle Alexander .... .05 .02 .00

□ 331	Jeffrey Leonard	.05	.02	.00
□ 332	Torey Lovullo	.05	.02	.00
□ 333	Pete Incaviglia	.08	.03	.01
□ 334	Rickey Henderson	.40	.16	.04
□ 335	Rafael Palmeiro	.17	.07	.01
□ 336	Ken Hill	.12	.05	.01
□ 337	Dave Winfield UER (1418 RBI, should be 1438)	.15	.06	.01
□ 338	Alfredo Griffin	.05	.02	.00
□ 339	Andy Hawkins	.05	.02	.00
□ 340	Ted Power	.05	.02	.00
□ 341	Steve Wilson	.08	.03	.01
□ 342	Jack Clark UER (916 BB, should be 1006; 1142 SO, should be 1130)	.10	.04	.01
□ 343	Ellis Burks	.12	.05	.01
□ 344	Tony Gwynn UER (Doubles stats on card back are wrong)	.25	.10	.02
□ 345	Jerome Walton UER (Total At Bats 476, should be 475)	.12	.05	.01
□ 346	Roberto Alomar UER (61 doubles, should be 51)	.35	.15	.03
□ 347	Carlos Martinez UER (Born 8/11/64, should be 8/11/65)	.08	.03	.01
□ 348	Chet Lemon	.05	.02	.00
□ 349	Willie Wilson	.08	.03	.01
□ 350	Greg Walker	.05	.02	.00
□ 351	Tom Bolton	.05	.02	.00
□ 352	German Gonzalez	.05	.02	.00
□ 353	Harold Baines	.08	.03	.01
□ 354	Mike Greenwell	.17	.07	.01
□ 355	Ruben Sierra	.35	.15	.03
□ 356	Andres Galarraga	.08	.03	.01
□ 357	Andre Dawson	.12	.05	.01
□ 358	Jeff Brantley	.12	.05	.01
□ 359	Mike Bielecki	.05	.02	.00
□ 360	Ken Oberkfell	.05	.02	.00
□ 361	Kurt Stillwell	.05	.02	.00
□ 362	Brian Holman	.08	.03	.01
□ 363	Kevin Seitzer	.08	.03	.01
□ 364	Alvin Davis	.08	.03	.01
□ 365	Tom Gordon	.10	.04	.01
□ 366	Bobby Bonilla	.20	.08	.02
□ 367	Carlton Fisk	.17	.07	.01
□ 368	Steve Carter UER (Charlotesville)	.08	.03	.01
□ 369	Joel Skinner	.05	.02	.00
□ 370	John Cangelosi	.05	.02	.00
□ 371	Cecil Espy	.05	.02	.00
□ 372	Gary Wayne	.08	.03	.01
□ 373	Jim Rice	.10	.04	.01
□ 374	Mike Dyer	.12	.05	.01
□ 375	Joe Carter	.12	.05	.01
□ 376	Dwight Smith	.08	.03	.01
□ 377	John Wetteland	.12	.05	.01
□ 378	Earnie Riles	.05	.02	.00
□ 379	Otis Nixon	.08	.03	.01
□ 380	Vance Law	.05	.02	.00
□ 381	Dave Bergman	.05	.02	.00
□ 382	Frank White	.05	.02	.00
□ 383	Scott Bradley	.05	.02	.00
□ 384	Israel Sanchez UER (totals don't include '89 stats)	.05	.02	.00
□ 385	Gary Pettis	.05	.02	.00
□ 386	Donn Pall	.05	.02	.00
□ 387	John Smiley	.08	.03	.01
□ 388	Tom Candiotti	.08	.03	.01
□ 389	Junior Ortiz	.05	.02	.00
□ 390	Steve Lyons	.05	.02	.00
□ 391	Brian Harper	.08	.03	.01
□ 392	Fred Manrique	.05	.02	.00
□ 393	Lee Smith	.08	.03	.01
□ 394	Jeff Kunkel	.05	.02	.00
□ 395	Claudell Washington	.05	.02	.00
□ 396	John Tudor	.08	.03	.01
□ 397	Terry Kennedy UER (Career totals all wrong)	.05	.02	.00
□ 398	Lloyd McClendon	.05	.02	.00
□ 399	Craig Lefferts	.05	.02	.00
□ 400	Checklist 301-400	.08	.01	.00
□ 401	Keith Moreland	.05	.02	.00
□ 402	Rich Gedman	.05	.02	.00
□ 403	Jeff D. Robinson	.05	.02	.00
□ 404	Randy Ready	.05	.02	.00
□ 405	Rick Cerone	.05	.02	.00
□ 406	Jeff Blauser	.05	.02	.00
□ 407	Larry Andersen	.05	.02	.00
□ 408	Joe Boever	.05	.02	.00
□ 409	Felix Fermin	.05	.02	.00
□ 410	Glenn Wilson	.05	.02	.00
□ 411	Rex Hudler	.05	.02	.00
□ 412	Mark Grant	.05	.02	.00
□ 413	Dennis Martinez	.08	.03	.01
□ 414	Darrin Jackson	.05	.02	.00
□ 415	Mike Aldrete	.05	.02	.00
□ 416	Roger McDowell	.05	.02	.00
□ 417	Jeff Reardon	.08	.03	.01
□ 418	Darren Daulton	.08	.03	.01
□ 419	Tim Laudner	.05	.02	.00
□ 420	Don Carman	.05	.02	.00
□ 421	Lloyd Moseby	.05	.02	.00
□ 422	Doug Drabek	.08	.03	.01
□ 423	Lenny Harris UER (Walks 2 in '89, should be 20)	.08	.03	.01
□ 424	Jose Lind	.05	.02	.00
□ 425	Dave Johnson (P)	.10	.04	.01
□ 426	Jerry Browne	.05	.02	.00

☐ 427 Eric Yelding	.08	.03	.01
☐ 428 Brad Komminsk	.05	.02	.00
☐ 429 Jody Davis	.05	.02	.00
☐ 430 Mariano Duncan	.05	.02	.00
☐ 431 Mark Davis	.08	.03	.01
☐ 432 Nelson Santovenia	.05	.02	.00
☐ 433 Bruce Hurst	.08	.03	.01
☐ 434 Jeff Huson	.10	.04	.01
☐ 435 Chris James	.05	.02	.00
☐ 436 Mark Guthrie	.10	.04	.01
☐ 437 Charlie Hayes	.08	.03	.01
☐ 438 Shane Rawley	.05	.02	.00
☐ 439 Dickie Thon	.05	.02	.00
☐ 440 Juan Berenguer	.05	.02	.00
☐ 441 Kevin Romine	.05	.02	.00
☐ 442 Bill Landrum	.05	.02	.00
☐ 443 Todd Frohwirth	.05	.02	.00
☐ 444 Craig Worthington	.05	.02	.00
☐ 445 Fernando Valenzuela	.10	.04	.01
☐ 446 Joey Belle	1.50	.60	.15
☐ 447 Ed Whited UER (Ashville, should be Asheville)	.15	.06	.01
☐ 448 Dave Smith	.05	.02	.00
☐ 449 Dave Clark	.05	.02	.00
☐ 450 Juan Agosto	.05	.02	.00
☐ 451 Dave Valle	.05	.02	.00
☐ 452 Kent Hrbek	.10	.04	.01
☐ 453 Von Hayes	.08	.03	.01
☐ 454 Gary Gaetti	.08	.03	.01
☐ 455 Greg Briley	.08	.03	.01
☐ 456 Glenn Braggs	.05	.02	.00
☐ 457 Kirt Manwaring	.05	.02	.00
☐ 458 Mel Hall	.05	.02	.00
☐ 459 Brook Jacoby	.05	.02	.00
☐ 460 Pat Sheridan	.05	.02	.00
☐ 461 Rob Murphy	.05	.02	.00
☐ 462 Jimmy Key	.08	.03	.01
☐ 463 Nick Esasky	.05	.02	.00
☐ 464 Rob Ducey	.05	.02	.00
☐ 465 Carlos Quintana UER (Internatinoal)	.12	.05	.01
☐ 466 Larry Walker	.45	.18	.04
☐ 467 Todd Worrell	.08	.03	.01
☐ 468 Kevin Gross	.05	.02	.00
☐ 469 Terry Pendleton	.10	.04	.01
☐ 470 Dave Martinez	.05	.02	.00
☐ 471 Gene Larkin	.05	.02	.00
☐ 472 Len Dykstra UER ('89 and total runs understated by 10)	.10	.04	.01
☐ 473 Barry Lyons	.05	.02	.00
☐ 474 Terry Mulholland	.08	.03	.01
☐ 475 Chip Hale	.10	.04	.01
☐ 476 Jesse Barfield	.08	.03	.01
☐ 477 Dan Plesac	.05	.02	.00
☐ 478A Scott Garrelts ERR (photo actually Bill Bathe)	4.00	1.75	.40
☐ 478B Scott Garrelts COR	.08	.03	.01
☐ 479 Dave Righetti	.08	.03	.01
☐ 480 Gus Polidor UER (Wearing 14 on front, but 10 on back)	.05	.02	.00
☐ 481 Mookie Wilson	.05	.02	.00
☐ 482 Luis Rivera	.05	.02	.00
☐ 483 Mike Flanagan	.05	.02	.00
☐ 484 Dennis Boyd	.05	.02	.00
☐ 485 John Cerutti	.05	.02	.00
☐ 486 John Costello	.05	.02	.00
☐ 487 Pascual Perez	.05	.02	.00
☐ 488 Tommy Herr	.05	.02	.00
☐ 489 Tom Foley	.05	.02	.00
☐ 490 Curt Ford	.05	.02	.00
☐ 491 Steve Lake	.05	.02	.00
☐ 492 Tim Teufel	.05	.02	.00
☐ 493 Randy Bush	.05	.02	.00
☐ 494 Mike Jackson	.05	.02	.00
☐ 495 Steve Jeltz	.05	.02	.00
☐ 496 Paul Gibson	.05	.02	.00
☐ 497 Steve Balboni	.05	.02	.00
☐ 498 Bud Black	.05	.02	.00
☐ 499 Dale Sveum	.05	.02	.00
☐ 500 Checklist 401-500	.08	.01	.00
☐ 501 Tim Jones	.05	.02	.00
☐ 502 Mark Portugal	.05	.02	.00
☐ 503 Ivan Calderon	.08	.03	.01
☐ 504 Rick Rhoden	.05	.02	.00
☐ 505 Willie McGee	.10	.04	.01
☐ 506 Kirk McCaskill	.05	.02	.00
☐ 507 Dave LaPoint	.05	.02	.00
☐ 508 Jay Howell	.05	.02	.00
☐ 509 Johnny Ray	.05	.02	.00
☐ 510 Dave Anderson	.05	.02	.00
☐ 511 Chuck Crim	.05	.02	.00
☐ 512 Joe Hesketh	.05	.02	.00
☐ 513 Dennis Eckersley	.10	.04	.01
☐ 514 Greg Brock	.05	.02	.00
☐ 515 Tim Burke	.05	.02	.00
☐ 516 Frank Tanana	.08	.03	.01
☐ 517 Jay Bell	.05	.02	.00
☐ 518 Guillermo Hernandez	.05	.02	.00
☐ 519 Randy Kramer UER (Codiroli misspelled as Codoroli)	.08	.03	.01
☐ 520 Charles Hudson	.05	.02	.00
☐ 521 Jim Corsi (word "originally" is misspelled on back)	.05	.02	.00
☐ 522 Steve Rosenberg	.05	.02	.00
☐ 523 Cris Carpenter	.05	.02	.00
☐ 524 Matt Winters	.12	.05	.01
☐ 525 Melido Perez	.05	.02	.00
☐ 526 Chris Gwynn UER (Albeguergue)	.05	.02	.00
☐ 527 Bert Blyleven UER	.08	.03	.01

(Games career total is wrong, should be 644)
☐ 528 Chuck Cary .05 .02 .00
☐ 529 Daryl Boston .05 .02 .00
☐ 530 Dale Mohorcic .05 .02 .00
☐ 531 Geronimo Berroa .05 .02 .00
☐ 532 Edgar Martinez .12 .05 .01
☐ 533 Dale Murphy .15 .06 .01
☐ 534 Jay Buhner .10 .04 .01
☐ 535 John Smoltz UER .30 .12 .03
(HEA Stadium)
☐ 536 Andy Van Slyke .10 .04 .01
☐ 537 Mike Henneman .05 .02 .00
☐ 538 Miguel Garcia .08 .03 .01
☐ 539 Frank Williams .05 .02 .00
☐ 540 R.J. Reynolds .05 .02 .00
☐ 541 Shawn Hillegas .05 .02 .00
☐ 542 Walt Weiss .08 .03 .01
☐ 543 Greg Hibbard .30 .12 .03
☐ 544 Nolan Ryan 1.00 .40 .10
☐ 545 Todd Zeile .75 .30 .07
☐ 546 Hensley Meulens .20 .08 .02
☐ 547 Tim Belcher .08 .03 .01
☐ 548 Mike Witt .05 .02 .00
☐ 549 Greg Cadaret UER .05 .02 .00
(Aquiring, should be Acquiring)
☐ 550 Franklin Stubbs .05 .02 .00
☐ 551 Tony Castillo .05 .02 .00
☐ 552 Jeff M. Robinson .05 .02 .00
☐ 553 Steve Olin .15 .06 .01
☐ 554 Alan Trammell .12 .05 .01
☐ 555 Wade Boggs 4X .30 .12 .03
(Bo Jackson in background)
☐ 556 Will Clark .50 .20 .05
☐ 557 Jeff King .10 .04 .01
☐ 558 Mike Fitzgerald .05 .02 .00
☐ 559 Ken Howell .05 .02 .00
☐ 560 Bob Kipper .05 .02 .00
☐ 561 Scott Bankhead .05 .02 .00
☐ 562A Jeff Innis ERR 3.00 1.25 .30
(photo actually David West)
☐ 562B Jeff Innis COR .10 .04 .01
☐ 563 Randy Johnson .10 .04 .01
☐ 564 Wally Whitehurst .05 .02 .00
☐ 565 Gene Harris .10 .04 .01
☐ 566 Norm Charlton .10 .04 .01
☐ 567 Robin Yount UER .20 .08 .02
(7602 career hits, should be 2606)
☐ 568 Joe Oliver UER .12 .05 .01
(Fl.orida)
☐ 569 Mark Parent .05 .02 .00
☐ 570 John Farrell UER .05 .02 .00
(Loss total added wrong)
☐ 571 Tom Glavine .35 .15 .03
☐ 572 Rod Nichols .10 .04 .01
☐ 573 Jack Morris .12 .05 .01
☐ 574 Greg Swindell .08 .03 .01
☐ 575 Steve Searcy .05 .02 .00
☐ 576 Ricky Jordan .08 .03 .01
☐ 577 Matt Williams .25 .10 .02
☐ 578 Mike LaValliere .05 .02 .00
☐ 579 Bryn Smith .05 .02 .00
☐ 580 Bruce Ruffin .05 .02 .00
☐ 581 Randy Myers .05 .02 .00
☐ 582 Rick Wrona .10 .04 .01
☐ 583 Juan Samuel .08 .03 .01
☐ 584 Les Lancaster .05 .02 .00
☐ 585 Jeff Musselman .05 .02 .00
☐ 586 Rob Dibble .15 .06 .01
☐ 587 Eric Show .05 .02 .00
☐ 588 Jesse Orosco .05 .02 .00
☐ 589 Herm Winningham .05 .02 .00
☐ 590 Andy Allanson .05 .02 .00
☐ 591 Dion James .05 .02 .00
☐ 592 Carmelo Martinez .05 .02 .00
☐ 593 Luis Quinones .05 .02 .00
☐ 594 Dennis Rasmussen .05 .02 .00
☐ 595 Rich Yett .05 .02 .00
☐ 596 Bob Walk .05 .02 .00
☐ 597A Andy McGaffigan ERR .40 .16 .04
(photo actually Rich Thompson)
☐ 597B Andy McGaffigan COR .10 .04 .01
☐ 598 Billy Hatcher .08 .03 .01
☐ 599 Bob Knepper .05 .02 .00
☐ 600 Checklist 501-600 UER .08 .01 .00
(599 Bob Kneppers)
☐ 601 Joey Cora .08 .03 .01
☐ 602 Steve Finley .15 .06 .01
☐ 603 Kal Daniels UER .10 .04 .01
(12 hits in '87, should be 123; 335 runs, should be 235)
☐ 604 Gregg Olson .17 .07 .01
☐ 605 Dave Stieb .10 .04 .01
☐ 606 Kenny Rogers .08 .03 .01
(Shown catching football)
☐ 607 Zane Smith .08 .03 .01
☐ 608 Bob Geren UER .08 .03 .01
(Origionally)
☐ 609 Chad Kreuter .05 .02 .00
☐ 610 Mike Smithson .05 .02 .00
☐ 611 Jeff Wetherby .10 .04 .01
☐ 612 Gary Mielke .10 .04 .01
☐ 613 Pete Smith .05 .02 .00
☐ 614 Jack Daugherty UER .10 .04 .01
(Born 7/30/60, should be 7/3/60; origionally)
☐ 615 Lance McCullers .05 .02 .00
☐ 616 Don Robinson .05 .02 .00
☐ 617 Jose Guzman .05 .02 .00

☐ 618 Steve Bedrosian .05 .02 .00
☐ 619 Jamie Moyer .05 .02 .00
☐ 620 Atlee Hammaker .05 .02 .00
☐ 621 Rick Luecken UER .10 .04 .01
(Innings pitched wrong)
☐ 622 Greg W. Harris .05 .02 .00
☐ 623 Pete Harnisch .08 .03 .01
☐ 624 Jerald Clark .08 .03 .01
☐ 625 Jack McDowell .05 .02 .00
☐ 626 Frank Viola .10 .04 .01
☐ 627 Teddy Higuera .05 .02 .00
☐ 628 Marty Pevey .10 .04 .01
☐ 629 Bill Wegman .05 .02 .00
☐ 630 Eric Plunk .05 .02 .00
☐ 631 Drew Hall .05 .02 .00
☐ 632 Doug Jones .05 .02 .00
☐ 633 Geno Petralli .05 .02 .00
☐ 634 Jose Alvarez .05 .02 .00
☐ 635 Bob Milacki .08 .03 .01
☐ 636 Bobby Witt .08 .03 .01
☐ 637 Trevor Wilson .08 .03 .01
☐ 638 Jeff Russell UER .05 .02 .00
(Shutout stats wrong)
☐ 639 Mike Krukow .05 .02 .00
☐ 640 Rick Leach .05 .02 .00
☐ 641 Dave Schmidt .05 .02 .00
☐ 642 Terry Leach .05 .02 .00
☐ 643 Calvin Schiraldi .05 .02 .00
☐ 644 Bob Melvin .05 .02 .00
☐ 645 Jim Abbott .35 .15 .03
☐ 646 Jaime Navarro .15 .06 .01
☐ 647 Mark Langston UER .08 .03 .01
(Several errors in stats totals)
☐ 648 Juan Nieves .05 .02 .00
☐ 649 Damaso Garcia .05 .02 .00
☐ 650 Charlie O'Brien .05 .02 .00
☐ 651 Eric King .05 .02 .00
☐ 652 Mike Boddicker .05 .02 .00
☐ 653 Duane Ward .08 .03 .01
☐ 654 Bob Stanley .05 .02 .00
☐ 655 Sandy Alomar Jr. .15 .06 .01
☐ 656 Danny Tartabull UER .12 .05 .01
(395 BB, should be 295)
☐ 657 Randy McCament .10 .04 .01
☐ 658 Charlie Leibrandt .05 .02 .00
☐ 659 Dan Quisenberry .08 .03 .01
☐ 660 Paul Assenmacher .05 .02 .00
☐ 661 Walt Terrell .05 .02 .00
☐ 662 Tim Leary .08 .03 .01
☐ 663 Randy Milligan .08 .03 .01
☐ 664 Bo Diaz .05 .02 .00
☐ 665 Mark Lemke UER .05 .02 .00
(Richmond misspelled as Richomond)
☐ 666 Jose Gonzalez .05 .02 .00
☐ 667 Chuck Finley UER .12 .05 .01
(Born 11/16/62, should be 11/26/62)
☐ 668 John Kruk .05 .02 .00
☐ 669 Dick Schofield .05 .02 .00
☐ 670 Tim Crews .05 .02 .00
☐ 671 John Dopson .05 .02 .00
☐ 672 John Orton .12 .05 .01
☐ 673 Eric Hetzel .05 .02 .00
☐ 674 Lance Parrish .10 .04 .01
☐ 675 Ramon Martinez .90 .40 .09
☐ 676 Mark Gubicza .08 .03 .01
☐ 677 Greg Litton .08 .03 .01
☐ 678 Greg Mathews .05 .02 .00
☐ 679 Dave Dravecky .10 .04 .01
☐ 680 Steve Farr .05 .02 .00
☐ 681 Mike Devereaux .05 .02 .00
☐ 682 Ken Griffey Sr. .10 .04 .01
☐ 683A Mickey Weston ERR 3.50 1.50 .35
(listed as Jamie on card)
☐ 683B Mickey Weston COR .10 .04 .01
(technically still an error as birthdate is listed as 3/26/81)
☐ 684 Jack Armstrong .08 .03 .01
☐ 685 Steve Buechele .05 .02 .00
☐ 686 Bryan Harvey .08 .03 .01
☐ 687 Lance Blankenship .05 .02 .00
☐ 688 Dante Bichette .08 .03 .01
☐ 689 Todd Burns .05 .02 .00
☐ 690 Dan Petry .05 .02 .00
☐ 691 Kent Anderson .08 .03 .01
☐ 692 Todd Stottlemyre .12 .05 .01
☐ 693 Wally Joyner UER .15 .06 .01
(Several stats errors)
☐ 694 Mike Rochford .05 .02 .00
☐ 695 Floyd Bannister .05 .02 .00
☐ 696 Rick Reuschel .08 .03 .01
☐ 697 Jose DeLeon .05 .02 .00
☐ 698 Jeff Montgomery .05 .02 .00
☐ 699 Kelly Downs .05 .02 .00
☐ 700A Checklist 601-700 3.00 .50 .10
(683 Jamie Weston)
☐ 700B Checklist 601-700 .10 .01 .00
(683 Mickey Weston)

1990 Upper Deck Extended

The 1990 Upper Deck Extended Set was issued in July 1990. These cards which are in the same style as the first 700 cards of the

1990 Upper Deck set and were issued either as a separate set in its own collectors box, as part of the complete 1-800 factory set, as well as mixed in with the earlier numbered Upper Deck cards in late-season wax packs. This 100-card set which measures the standard size 2 1/2" by 3 1/2" also has a Nolan Ryan variation. All cards produced before August 12th only discuss Ryan's sixth no-hitter while the later-issue cards include a stripe honoring Ryan's 300th victory. The key rookie cards in this set are Carlos Baerga, Alex Cole, Delino DeShields, Dave Justice, and Ray Lankford. Card 702 was originally scheduled to be Mike Witt. A few 702 Witt cards and checklist cards showing 702 Witt escaped into early packs; they are characterized by a black rectangle covering much of the card's back.

	MINT	EXC	G-VG
COMPLETE SET (100)	12.50	5.50	1.65
COMMON PLAYER (1-100)	.06	.02	.00
□ 701 Jim Gott	.06	.02	.00
□ 702 Rookie Threats Delino DeShields Marquis Grissom Larry Walker	.50	.20	.05
□ 703 Alejandro Pena	.10	.04	.01
□ 704 Willie Randolph	.10	.04	.01
□ 705 Tim Leary	.10	.04	.01
□ 706 Chuck McElroy	.20	.08	.02
□ 707 Gerald Perry	.06	.02	.00
□ 708 Tom Brunansky	.10	.04	.01
□ 709 John Franco	.10	.04	.01
□ 710 Mark Davis	.10	.04	.01
□ 711 Dave Justice	8.50	3.75	.85
□ 712 Storm Davis	.06	.02	.00
□ 713 Scott Ruskin	.20	.08	.02
□ 714 Glenn Braggs	.06	.02	.00
□ 715 Kevin Bearse	.15	.06	.01
□ 716 Jose Nunez	.06	.02	.00
□ 717 Tim Layana	.15	.06	.01
□ 718 Greg Myers	.06	.02	.00
□ 719 Pete O'Brien	.06	.02	.00
□ 720 John Candelaria	.06	.02	.00
□ 721 Craig Grebeck	.15	.06	.01
□ 722 Shawn Boskie	.20	.08	.02
□ 723 Jim Leyritz	.12	.05	.01
□ 724 Bill Sampen	.15	.06	.01
□ 725 Scott Radinsky	.20	.08	.02
□ 726 Todd Hundley	.60	.25	.06
□ 727 Scott Hemond	.17	.07	.01
□ 728 Lenny Webster	.20	.08	.02
□ 729 Jeff Reardon	.12	.05	.01
□ 730 Mitch Webster	.06	.02	.00
□ 731 Brian Bohanon	.17	.07	.01
□ 732 Rick Parker	.10	.04	.01
□ 733 Terry Shumpert	.17	.07	.01
□ 734A Ryan's 6th No-Hitter (no stripe on front)	9.00	4.00	.90
□ 734B Ryan's 6th No-Hitter (stripe added on card front for 300th win)	1.25	.50	.12
□ 735 John Burkett	.25	.10	.02
□ 736 Derrick May	.25	.10	.02
□ 737 Carlos Baerga	.75	.30	.07
□ 738 Greg Smith	.12	.05	.01
□ 739 Scott Sanderson	.10	.04	.01
□ 740 Joe Kraemer	.12	.05	.01
□ 741 Hector Villanueva	.17	.07	.01
□ 742 Mike Fetters	.10	.04	.01
□ 743 Mark Gardner	.30	.12	.03
□ 744 Matt Nokes	.10	.04	.01
□ 745 Dave Winfield	.15	.06	.01
□ 746 Delino DeShields	1.00	.40	.10
□ 747 Dann Howitt	.20	.08	.02
□ 748 Tony Pena	.10	.04	.01
□ 749 Oil Can Boyd	.06	.02	.00
□ 750 Mike Benjamin	.17	.07	.01
□ 751 Alex Cole	.65	.25	.06
□ 752 Eric Gunderson	.25	.10	.02
□ 753 Howard Farmer	.17	.07	.01
□ 754 Joe Carter	.15	.06	.01
□ 755 Ray Lankford	2.00	.80	.20
□ 756 Sandy Alomar Jr.	.20	.08	.02
□ 757 Alex Sanchez	.10	.04	.01
□ 758 Nick Esasky	.06	.02	.00
□ 759 Stan Belinda	.20	.08	.02
□ 760 Jim Presley	.06	.02	.00
□ 761 Gary DiSarcina	.15	.06	.01
□ 762 Wayne Edwards	.12	.05	.01
□ 763 Pat Combs	.10	.04	.01
□ 764 Mickey Pina	.15	.06	.01
□ 765 Wilson Alvarez	.50	.20	.05
□ 766 Dave Parker	.10	.04	.01
□ 767 Mike Blowers	.15	.06	.01
□ 768 Tony Phillips	.06	.02	.00
□ 769 Pascual Perez	.06	.02	.00
□ 770 Gary Pettis	.06	.02	.00

□ 771 Fred Lynn	.10	.04	.01
□ 772 Mel Rojas	.12	.05	.01
□ 773 David Segui	.25	.10	.02
□ 774 Gary Carter	.12	.05	.01
□ 775 Rafael Valdez	.15	.06	.01
□ 776 Glenallen Hill	.10	.04	.01
□ 777 Keith Hernandez	.12	.05	.01
□ 778 Billy Hatcher	.10	.04	.01
□ 779 Marty Clary	.06	.02	.00
□ 780 Candy Maldonado	.10	.04	.01
□ 781 Mike Marshall	.10	.04	.01
□ 782 Billy Jo Robidoux	.06	.02	.00
□ 783 Mark Langston	.10	.04	.01
□ 784 Paul Sorrento	.17	.07	.01
□ 785 Dave Hollins	.60	.25	.06
□ 786 Cecil Fielder	.75	.30	.07
□ 787 Matt Young	.06	.02	.00
□ 788 Jeff Huson	.10	.04	.01
□ 789 Lloyd Moseby	.06	.02	.00
□ 790 Ron Kittle	.10	.04	.01
□ 791 Hubie Brooks	.10	.04	.01
□ 792 Craig Lefferts	.06	.02	.00
□ 793 Kevin Bass	.06	.02	.00
□ 794 Bryn Smith	.06	.02	.00
□ 795 Juan Samuel	.10	.04	.01
□ 796 Sam Horn	.10	.04	.01
□ 797 Randy Myers	.10	.04	.01
□ 798 Chris James	.10	.04	.01
□ 799 Bill Gullickson	.10	.04	.01
□ 800 Checklist 701-800	.06	.01	.00

1991 Upper Deck

This set marks the third year Upper Deck has issued a 700-card set in January. These cards measure 2 1/2" by 3 1/2". The set features 26 star rookies to lead off the set as well as other special cards featuring multi-players. The set is made on the typical Upper Deck card stock and features full-color photos on both the front and the back. The team checklist (TC) cards in the set feature an attractive Vernon Wells drawing of a featured player for that particular team. A special Michael Jordan card (numbered SP1) was randomly included in packs on a somewhat limited basis. This Jordan card is not included in the set price below. The key rookie cards in this set include Wes Chamberlain, Luis Gonzalez, Brian McRae, Phil Plantier, and Todd Van Poppel.

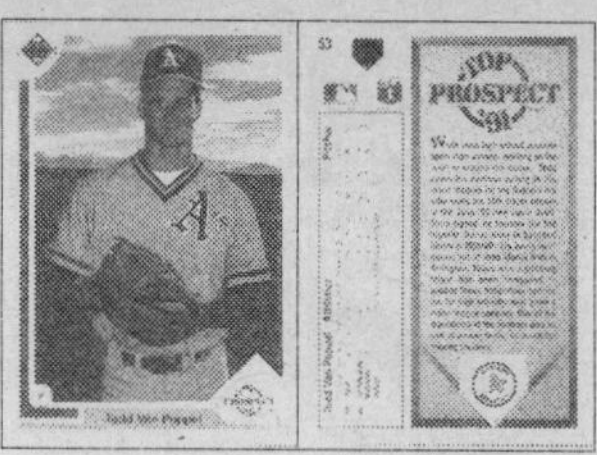

	MINT	EXC	G-VG
COMPLETE SET (700)	28.00	12.50	4.00
COMMON PLAYER (1-700)	.05	.02	.00
□ 1 Star Rookie Checklist	.10	.02	.00
□ 2 Phil Plantier	3.75	1.60	.37
□ 3 D.J. Dozier	.20	.08	.02
□ 4 Dave Hansen	.25	.10	.02
□ 5 Maurice Vaughn	1.25	.50	.12
□ 6 Leo Gomez	.50	.20	.05
□ 7 Scott Aldred	.15	.06	.01
□ 8 Scott Chiamparino	.10	.04	.01
□ 9 Lance Dickson	.35	.15	.03
□ 10 Sean Berry	.20	.08	.02
□ 11 Bernie Williams	.90	.40	.09
□ 12 Brian Barnes UER (Photo either not him or in wrong jersey)	.20	.08	.02
□ 13 Narciso Elvira	.12	.05	.01
□ 14 Mike Gardiner	.25	.10	.02
□ 15 Greg Colbrunn	.20	.08	.02
□ 16 Bernard Gilkey	.25	.10	.02
□ 17 Mark Lewis	.50	.20	.05
□ 18 Mickey Morandini	.15	.06	.01
□ 19 Charles Nagy	.17	.07	.01
□ 20 Geronimo Pena	.15	.06	.01
□ 21 Henry Rodriguez	.25	.10	.02
□ 22 Scott Cooper	.40	.16	.04
□ 23 Andujar Cedeno UER (Shown batting left, back says right)	.90	.40	.09
□ 24 Eric Karros	.75	.30	.07
□ 25 Steve Decker UER (Lewis-Clark State College, not Lewis and Clark)	.40	.16	.04
□ 26 Kevin Belcher	.15	.06	.01
□ 27 Jeff Conine	.20	.08	.02
□ 28 Oakland Athletics TC Dave Stewart	.08	.03	.01
□ 29 Chicago White Sox TC Carlton Fisk	.08	.03	.01

Card			
☐ 30 Texas Rangers TC	.08	.03	.01
Rafael Palmeiro			
☐ 31 California Angels TC	.08	.03	.01
Chuck Finley			
☐ 32 Seattle Mariners TC	.05	.02	.00
Harold Reynolds			
☐ 33 Kansas City Royals TC	.08	.03	.01
Bret Saberhagen			
☐ 34 Minnesota Twins TC	.08	.03	.01
Gary Gaetti			
☐ 35 Scott Leius	.17	.07	.01
☐ 36 Neal Heaton	.05	.02	.00
☐ 37 Terry Lee	.12	.05	.01
☐ 38 Gary Redus	.05	.02	.00
☐ 39 Barry Jones	.05	.02	.00
☐ 40 Chuck Knoblauch	2.00	.80	.20
☐ 41 Larry Andersen	.05	.02	.00
☐ 42 Darryl Hamilton	.08	.03	.01
☐ 43 Boston Red Sox TC	.08	.03	.01
Mike Greenwell			
☐ 44 Toronto Blue Jays TC	.08	.03	.01
Kelly Gruber			
☐ 45 Detroit Tigers TC	.08	.03	.01
Jack Morris			
☐ 46 Cleveland Indians TC	.08	.03	.01
Sandy Alomar Jr.			
☐ 47 Baltimore Orioles TC	.08	.03	.01
Gregg Olson			
☐ 48 Milwaukee Brewers TC	.08	.03	.01
Dave Parker			
☐ 49 New York Yankees TC	.08	.03	.01
Roberto Kelly			
☐ 50 Top Prospect Checklist	.05	.01	.00
☐ 51 Kyle Abbott	.25	.10	.02
☐ 52 Jeff Juden	.40	.16	.04
☐ 53 Todd Van Poppel UER	2.50	1.00	.25
(Born Arlington and attended John Martin HS, should say Hinsdale and James Martin HS)			
☐ 54 Steve Karsay	.40	.16	.04
☐ 55 Chipper Jones	.65	.25	.06
☐ 56 Chris Johnson UER	.12	.05	.01
(Called Tim on back)			
☐ 57 John Ericks	.12	.05	.01
☐ 58 Gary Scott	.40	.16	.04
☐ 59 Kiki Jones	.20	.08	.02
☐ 60 Wilfredo Cordero	.50	.20	.05
☐ 61 Royce Clayton	.90	.40	.09
☐ 62 Tim Costo	.45	.18	.04
☐ 63 Roger Salkeld	.70	.30	.07
☐ 64 Brook Fordyce	.20	.08	.02
☐ 65 Mike Mussina	.75	.30	.07
☐ 66 Dave Staton	.35	.15	.03
☐ 67 Mike Lieberthal	.25	.10	.02
☐ 68 Kurt Miller	.30	.12	.03
☐ 69 Dan Peltier	.20	.08	.02
☐ 70 Greg Blosser	.25	.10	.02
☐ 71 Reggie Sanders	.90	.40	.09
☐ 72 Brent Mayne	.15	.06	.01
☐ 73 Rico Brogna	.50	.20	.05
☐ 74 Willie Banks	.35	.15	.03
☐ 75 Len Brutcher	.12	.05	.01
☐ 76 Pat Kelly	.50	.20	.05
☐ 77 Cincinnati Reds TC	.08	.03	.01
Chris Sabo			
☐ 78 Los Angeles Dodgers TC	.08	.03	.01
Ramon Martinez			
☐ 79 San Fran. Giants TC	.08	.03	.01
Matt Williams			
☐ 80 San Diego Padres TC	.08	.03	.01
Roberto Alomar			
☐ 81 Houston Astros TC	.08	.03	.01
Glenn Davis			
☐ 82 Atlanta Braves TC	.08	.03	.01
Ron Gant			
☐ 83 Fielder's Feat	.20	.08	.02
Cecil Fielder			
☐ 84 Orlando Merced	.80	.35	.08
☐ 85 Domingo Ramos	.05	.02	.00
☐ 86 Tom Bolton	.05	.02	.00
☐ 87 Andres Santana	.25	.10	.02
☐ 88 John Dopson	.05	.02	.00
☐ 89 Kenny Williams	.05	.02	.00
☐ 90 Marty Barrett	.05	.02	.00
☐ 91 Tom Pagnozzi	.05	.02	.00
☐ 92 Carmelo Martinez	.05	.02	.00
☐ 93 Save Master	.08	.03	.01
(Bobby Thigpen)			
☐ 94 Pittsburgh Pirates TC	.12	.05	.01
Barry Bonds			
☐ 95 New York Mets TC	.08	.03	.01
Gregg Jefferies			
☐ 96 Montreal Expos TC	.05	.02	.00
Tim Wallach			
☐ 97 Phila. Phillies TC	.08	.03	.01
Len Dykstra			
☐ 98 St.Louis Cardinals TC	.08	.03	.01
Pedro Guerrero			
☐ 99 Chicago Cubs TC	.08	.03	.01
Mark Grace			
☐ 100 Checklist 1-100	.05	.01	.00
☐ 101 Kevin Elster	.05	.02	.00
☐ 102 Tom Brookens	.05	.02	.00
☐ 103 Mackey Sasser	.05	.02	.00
☐ 104 Felix Fermin	.05	.02	.00
☐ 105 Kevin McReynolds	.08	.03	.01
☐ 106 Dave Stieb	.08	.03	.01
☐ 107 Jeffrey Leonard	.05	.02	.00
☐ 108 Dave Henderson	.08	.03	.01
☐ 109 Sid Bream	.05	.02	.00
☐ 110 Henry Cotto	.05	.02	.00
☐ 111 Shawon Dunston	.08	.03	.01
☐ 112 Mariano Duncan	.05	.02	.00
☐ 113 Joe Girardi	.05	.02	.00
☐ 114 Billy Hatcher	.05	.02	.00

☐ 115 Greg Maddux	.08	.03	.01
☐ 116 Jerry Browne	.05	.02	.00
☐ 117 Juan Samuel	.08	.03	.01
☐ 118 Steve Olin	.05	.02	.00
☐ 119 Alfredo Griffin	.05	.02	.00
☐ 120 Mitch Webster	.05	.02	.00
☐ 121 Joel Skinner	.05	.02	.00
☐ 122 Frank Viola	.10	.04	.01
☐ 123 Cory Snyder	.08	.03	.01
☐ 124 Howard Johnson	.12	.05	.01
☐ 125 Carlos Baerga	.20	.08	.02
☐ 126 Tony Fernandez	.08	.03	.01
☐ 127 Dave Stewart	.08	.03	.01
☐ 128 Jay Buhner	.08	.03	.01
☐ 129 Mike LaValliere	.05	.02	.00
☐ 130 Scott Bradley	.05	.02	.00
☐ 131 Tony Phillips	.05	.02	.00
☐ 132 Ryne Sandberg	.35	.15	.03
☐ 133 Paul O'Neill	.08	.03	.01
☐ 134 Mark Grace	.10	.04	.01
☐ 135 Chris Sabo	.08	.03	.01
☐ 136 Ramon Martinez	.17	.07	.01
☐ 137 Brook Jacoby	.05	.02	.00
☐ 138 Candy Maldonado	.05	.02	.00
☐ 139 Mike Scioscia	.05	.02	.00
☐ 140 Chris James	.05	.02	.00
☐ 141 Craig Worthington	.05	.02	.00
☐ 142 Manny Lee	.05	.02	.00
☐ 143 Tim Raines	.08	.03	.01
☐ 144 Sandy Alomar Jr.	.08	.03	.01
☐ 145 John Olerud	.17	.07	.01
☐ 146 Ozzie Canseco (With Jose)	.12	.05	.01
☐ 147 Pat Borders	.05	.02	.00
☐ 148 Harold Reynolds	.05	.02	.00
☐ 149 Tom Henke	.05	.02	.00
☐ 150 R.J. Reynolds	.05	.02	.00
☐ 151 Mike Gallego	.05	.02	.00
☐ 152 Bobby Bonilla	.17	.07	.01
☐ 153 Terry Steinbach	.05	.02	.00
☐ 154 Barry Bonds	.20	.08	.02
☐ 155 Jose Canseco	.40	.16	.04
☐ 156 Gregg Jefferies	.10	.04	.01
☐ 157 Matt Williams	.15	.06	.01
☐ 158 Craig Biggio	.08	.03	.01
☐ 159 Daryl Boston	.05	.02	.00
☐ 160 Ricky Jordan	.05	.02	.00
☐ 161 Stan Belinda	.05	.02	.00
☐ 162 Ozzie Smith	.15	.06	.01
☐ 163 Tom Brunansky	.08	.03	.01
☐ 164 Todd Zeile	.15	.06	.01
☐ 165 Mike Greenwell	.15	.06	.01
☐ 166 Kal Daniels	.08	.03	.01
☐ 167 Kent Hrbek	.08	.03	.01
☐ 168 Franklin Stubbs	.05	.02	.00
☐ 169 Dick Schofield	.05	.02	.00
☐ 170 Junior Ortiz	.05	.02	.00
☐ 171 Hector Villanueva	.08	.03	.01
☐ 172 Dennis Eckersley	.08	.03	.01
☐ 173 Mitch Williams	.05	.02	.00
☐ 174 Mark McGwire	.12	.05	.01
☐ 175 Fernando Valenzuela 3X	.08	.03	.01
☐ 176 Gary Carter	.08	.03	.01
☐ 177 Dave Magadan	.08	.03	.01
☐ 178 Robby Thompson	.05	.02	.00
☐ 179 Bob Ojeda	.05	.02	.00
☐ 180 Ken Caminiti	.05	.02	.00
☐ 181 Don Slaught	.05	.02	.00
☐ 182 Luis Rivera	.05	.02	.00
☐ 183 Jay Bell	.05	.02	.00
☐ 184 Jody Reed	.05	.02	.00
☐ 185 Wally Backman	.05	.02	.00
☐ 186 Dave Martinez	.05	.02	.00
☐ 187 Luis Polonia	.05	.02	.00
☐ 188 Shane Mack	.08	.03	.01
☐ 189 Spike Owen	.05	.02	.00
☐ 190 Scott Bailes	.05	.02	.00
☐ 191 John Russell	.05	.02	.00
☐ 192 Walt Weiss	.08	.03	.01
☐ 193 Jose Oquendo	.05	.02	.00
☐ 194 Carney Lansford	.08	.03	.01
☐ 195 Jeff Huson	.05	.02	.00
☐ 196 Keith Miller	.05	.02	.00
☐ 197 Eric Yelding	.05	.02	.00
☐ 198 Ron Darling	.08	.03	.01
☐ 199 John Kruk	.05	.02	.00
☐ 200 Checklist 101-200	.05	.01	.00
☐ 201 John Shelby	.05	.02	.00
☐ 202 Bob Geren	.05	.02	.00
☐ 203 Lance McCullers	.05	.02	.00
☐ 204 Alvaro Espinoza	.05	.02	.00
☐ 205 Mark Salas	.05	.02	.00
☐ 206 Mike Pagliarulo	.05	.02	.00
☐ 207 Jose Uribe	.05	.02	.00
☐ 208 Jim Deshaies	.05	.02	.00
☐ 209 Ron Karkovice	.05	.02	.00
☐ 210 Rafael Ramirez	.05	.02	.00
☐ 211 Donnie Hill	.05	.02	.00
☐ 212 Brian Harper	.08	.03	.01
☐ 213 Jack Howell	.05	.02	.00
☐ 214 Wes Gardner	.05	.02	.00
☐ 215 Tim Burke	.05	.02	.00
☐ 216 Doug Jones	.05	.02	.00
☐ 217 Hubie Brooks	.08	.03	.01
☐ 218 Tom Candiotti	.08	.03	.01
☐ 219 Gerald Perry	.05	.02	.00
☐ 220 Jose DeLeon	.05	.02	.00
☐ 221 Wally Whitehurst	.05	.02	.00
☐ 222 Alan Mills	.08	.03	.01
☐ 223 Alan Trammell	.10	.04	.01
☐ 224 Dwight Gooden	.15	.06	.01
☐ 225 Travis Fryman	1.25	.50	.12
☐ 226 Joe Carter	.10	.04	.01
☐ 227 Julio Franco	.10	.04	.01
☐ 228 Craig Lefferts	.05	.02	.00
☐ 229 Gary Pettis	.05	.02	.00

□ 230 Dennis Rasmussen	.05	.02	.00
□ 231A Brian Downing ERR (No position on front)	.20	.08	.02
□ 231B Brian Downing COR (DH on front)	.45	.18	.04
□ 232 Carlos Quintana	.08	.03	.01
□ 233 Gary Gaetti	.08	.03	.01
□ 234 Mark Langston	.08	.03	.01
□ 235 Tim Wallach	.08	.03	.01
□ 236 Greg Swindell	.08	.03	.01
□ 237 Eddie Murray	.15	.06	.01
□ 238 Jeff Manto	.05	.02	.00
□ 239 Lenny Harris	.05	.02	.00
□ 240 Jesse Orosco	.05	.02	.00
□ 241 Scott Lusader	.05	.02	.00
□ 242 Sid Fernandez	.08	.03	.01
□ 243 Jim Leyritz	.05	.02	.00
□ 244 Cecil Fielder	.25	.10	.02
□ 245 Darryl Strawberry	.30	.12	.03
□ 246 Frank Thomas UER (Comiskey Park misspelled Comisky)	4.00	1.75	.40
□ 247 Kevin Mitchell	.12	.05	.01
□ 248 Lance Johnson	.05	.02	.00
□ 249 Rick Reuschel	.08	.03	.01
□ 250 Mark Portugal	.05	.02	.00
□ 251 Derek Lilliquist	.05	.02	.00
□ 252 Brian Holman	.05	.02	.00
□ 253 Rafael Valdez UER (Born 4/17/68, should be 12/17/67)	.05	.02	.00
□ 254 B.J. Surhoff	.05	.02	.00
□ 255 Tony Gwynn	.17	.07	.01
□ 256 Andy Van Slyke	.08	.03	.01
□ 257 Todd Stottlemyre	.08	.03	.01
□ 258 Jose Lind	.05	.02	.00
□ 259 Greg Myers	.05	.02	.00
□ 260 Jeff Ballard	.05	.02	.00
□ 261 Bobby Thigpen	.08	.03	.01
□ 262 Jimmy Kremers	.08	.03	.01
□ 263 Robin Ventura	.40	.16	.04
□ 264 John Smoltz	.12	.05	.01
□ 265 Sammy Sosa	.08	.03	.01
□ 266 Gary Sheffield	.08	.03	.01
□ 267 Len Dykstra	.08	.03	.01
□ 268 Bill Spiers	.05	.02	.00
□ 269 Charlie Hayes	.05	.02	.00
□ 270 Brett Butler	.08	.03	.01
□ 271 Bip Roberts	.05	.02	.00
□ 272 Rob Deer	.08	.03	.01
□ 273 Fred Lynn	.08	.03	.01
□ 274 Dave Parker	.08	.03	.01
□ 275 Andy Benes	.12	.05	.01
□ 276 Glenallen Hill	.08	.03	.01
□ 277 Steve Howard	.10	.04	.01
□ 278 Doug Drabek	.08	.03	.01
□ 279 Joe Oliver	.05	.02	.00
□ 280 Todd Benzinger	.05	.02	.00

□ 281 Eric King	.05	.02	.00
□ 282 Jim Presley	.05	.02	.00
□ 283 Ken Patterson	.05	.02	.00
□ 284 Jack Daugherty	.05	.02	.00
□ 285 Ivan Calderon	.08	.03	.01
□ 286 Edgar Diaz	.08	.03	.01
□ 287 Kevin Bass	.05	.02	.00
□ 288 Don Carman	.05	.02	.00
□ 289 Greg Brock	.05	.02	.00
□ 290 John Franco	.05	.02	.00
□ 291 Joey Cora	.05	.02	.00
□ 292 Bill Wegman	.05	.02	.00
□ 293 Eric Show	.05	.02	.00
□ 294 Scott Bankhead	.05	.02	.00
□ 295 Garry Templeton	.05	.02	.00
□ 296 Mickey Tettleton	.08	.03	.01
□ 297 Luis Sojo	.08	.03	.01
□ 298 Jose Rijo	.08	.03	.01
□ 299 Dave Johnson	.05	.02	.00
□ 300 Checklist 201-300	.05	.01	.00
□ 301 Mark Grant	.05	.02	.00
□ 302 Pete Harnisch	.08	.03	.01
□ 303 Greg Olson	.10	.04	.01
□ 304 Anthony Telford	.12	.05	.01
□ 305 Lonnie Smith	.08	.03	.01
□ 306 Chris Hoiles	.15	.06	.01
□ 307 Bryn Smith	.05	.02	.00
□ 308 Mike Devereaux	.05	.02	.00
□ 309A Milt Thompson ERR (Under yr information has print dot)	.25	.10	.02
□ 309B Milt Thompson COR (Under yr information says 86)	.05	.02	.00
□ 310 Bob Melvin	.05	.02	.00
□ 311 Luis Salazar	.05	.02	.00
□ 312 Ed Whitson	.05	.02	.00
□ 313 Charlie Hough	.05	.02	.00
□ 314 Dave Clark	.05	.02	.00
□ 315 Eric Gunderson	.05	.02	.00
□ 316 Dan Petry	.05	.02	.00
□ 317 Dante Bichette UER (Assists misspelled as assissts)	.05	.02	.00
□ 318 Mike Heath	.05	.02	.00
□ 319 Damon Berryhill	.05	.02	.00
□ 320 Walt Terrell	.05	.02	.00
□ 321 Scott Fletcher	.05	.02	.00
□ 322 Dan Plesac	.05	.02	.00
□ 323 Jack McDowell	.10	.04	.01
□ 324 Paul Molitor	.10	.04	.01
□ 325 Ozzie Guillen	.08	.03	.01
□ 326 Gregg Olson	.08	.03	.01
□ 327 Pedro Guerrero	.08	.03	.01
□ 328 Bob Milacki	.05	.02	.00
□ 329 John Tudor UER ('90 Cardinals, should be '90 Dodgers)	.08	.03	.01

☐ 330	Steve Finley UER (Born 3/12/65, should be 5/12)	.08	.03	.01
☐ 331	Jack Clark	.08	.03	.01
☐ 332	Jerome Walton	.08	.03	.01
☐ 333	Andy Hawkins	.05	.02	.00
☐ 334	Derrick May	.10	.04	.01
☐ 335	Roberto Alomar	.15	.06	.01
☐ 336	Jack Morris	.10	.04	.01
☐ 337	Dave Winfield	.12	.05	.01
☐ 338	Steve Searcy	.05	.02	.00
☐ 339	Chili Davis	.08	.03	.01
☐ 340	Larry Sheets	.05	.02	.00
☐ 341	Ted Higuera	.05	.02	.00
☐ 342	David Segui	.10	.04	.01
☐ 343	Greg Cadaret	.05	.02	.00
☐ 344	Robin Yount	.15	.06	.01
☐ 345	Nolan Ryan	.60	.25	.06
☐ 346	Ray Lankford	.40	.16	.04
☐ 347	Cal Ripken	.40	.16	.04
☐ 348	Lee Smith	.08	.03	.01
☐ 349	Brady Anderson	.05	.02	.00
☐ 350	Frank DiPino	.05	.02	.00
☐ 351	Hal Morris	.12	.05	.01
☐ 352	Deion Sanders	.12	.05	.01
☐ 353	Barry Larkin	.12	.05	.01
☐ 354	Don Mattingly	.20	.08	.02
☐ 355	Eric Davis	.15	.06	.01
☐ 356	Jose Offerman	.12	.05	.01
☐ 357	Mel Rojas	.08	.03	.01
☐ 358	Rudy Seanez	.15	.06	.01
☐ 359	Oil Can Boyd	.05	.02	.00
☐ 360	Nelson Liriano	.05	.02	.00
☐ 361	Ron Gant	.20	.08	.02
☐ 362	Howard Farmer	.08	.03	.01
☐ 363	David Justice	1.25	.50	.12
☐ 364	Delino DeShields	.12	.05	.01
☐ 365	Steve Avery	.75	.30	.07
☐ 366	David Cone	.08	.03	.01
☐ 367	Lou Whitaker	.08	.03	.01
☐ 368	Von Hayes	.08	.03	.01
☐ 369	Frank Tanana	.05	.02	.00
☐ 370	Tim Teufel	.05	.02	.00
☐ 371	Randy Myers	.05	.02	.00
☐ 372	Roberto Kelly	.08	.03	.01
☐ 373	Jack Armstrong	.08	.03	.01
☐ 374	Kelly Gruber	.08	.03	.01
☐ 375	Kevin Maas	.30	.12	.03
☐ 376	Randy Johnson	.08	.03	.01
☐ 377	David West	.05	.02	.00
☐ 378	Brent Knackert	.12	.05	.01
☐ 379	Rick Honeycutt	.05	.02	.00
☐ 380	Kevin Gross	.05	.02	.00
☐ 381	Tom Foley	.05	.02	.00
☐ 382	Jeff Blauser	.05	.02	.00
☐ 383	Scott Ruskin	.08	.03	.01
☐ 384	Andres Thomas	.05	.02	.00
☐ 385	Dennis Martinez	.08	.03	.01
☐ 386	Mike Henneman	.05	.02	.00
☐ 387	Felix Jose	.12	.05	.01
☐ 388	Alejandro Pena	.08	.03	.01
☐ 389	Chet Lemon	.05	.02	.00
☐ 390	Craig Wilson	.12	.05	.01
☐ 391	Chuck Crim	.05	.02	.00
☐ 392	Mel Hall	.05	.02	.00
☐ 393	Mark Knudson	.05	.02	.00
☐ 394	Norm Charlton	.05	.02	.00
☐ 395	Mike Felder	.05	.02	.00
☐ 396	Tim Layana	.05	.02	.00
☐ 397	Steve Frey	.08	.03	.01
☐ 398	Bill Doran	.05	.02	.00
☐ 399	Dion James	.05	.02	.00
☐ 400	Checklist 301-400	.05	.01	.00
☐ 401	Ron Hassey	.05	.02	.00
☐ 402	Don Robinson	.05	.02	.00
☐ 403	Gene Nelson	.05	.02	.00
☐ 404	Terry Kennedy	.05	.02	.00
☐ 405	Todd Burns	.05	.02	.00
☐ 406	Roger McDowell	.05	.02	.00
☐ 407	Bob Kipper	.05	.02	.00
☐ 408	Darren Daulton	.05	.02	.00
☐ 409	Chuck Cary	.05	.02	.00
☐ 410	Bruce Ruffin	.05	.02	.00
☐ 411	Juan Berenguer	.05	.02	.00
☐ 412	Gary Ward	.05	.02	.00
☐ 413	Al Newman	.05	.02	.00
☐ 414	Danny Jackson	.05	.02	.00
☐ 415	Greg Gagne	.05	.02	.00
☐ 416	Tom Herr	.05	.02	.00
☐ 417	Jeff Parrett	.05	.02	.00
☐ 418	Jeff Reardon	.08	.03	.01
☐ 419	Mark Lemke	.08	.03	.01
☐ 420	Charlie O'Brien	.05	.02	.00
☐ 421	Willie Randolph	.05	.02	.00
☐ 422	Steve Bedrosian	.05	.02	.00
☐ 423	Mike Moore	.05	.02	.00
☐ 424	Jeff Brantley	.05	.02	.00
☐ 425	Bob Welch	.08	.03	.01
☐ 426	Terry Mulholland	.05	.02	.00
☐ 427	Willie Blair	.08	.03	.01
☐ 428	Darrin Fletcher	.10	.04	.01
☐ 429	Mike Witt	.05	.02	.00
☐ 430	Joe Boever	.05	.02	.00
☐ 431	Tom Gordon	.08	.03	.01
☐ 432	Pedro Munoz	.50	.20	.05
☐ 433	Kevin Seitzer	.08	.03	.01
☐ 434	Kevin Tapani	.08	.03	.01
☐ 435	Bret Saberhagen	.10	.04	.01
☐ 436	Ellis Burks	.10	.04	.01
☐ 437	Chuck Finley	.08	.03	.01
☐ 438	Mike Boddicker	.05	.02	.00
☐ 439	Francisco Cabrera	.08	.03	.01
☐ 440	Todd Hundley	.15	.06	.01
☐ 441	Kelly Downs	.05	.02	.00
☐ 442	Dann Howitt	.10	.04	.01
☐ 443	Scott Garrelts	.05	.02	.00

☐ 444 Rickey Henderson 3X .35 .15 .03
☐ 445 Will Clark .35 .15 .03
☐ 446 Ben McDonald .15 .06 .01
☐ 447 Dale Murphy .12 .05 .01
☐ 448 Dave Righetti .08 .03 .01
☐ 449 Dickie Thon .05 .02 .00
☐ 450 Ted Power .05 .02 .00
☐ 451 Scott Coolbaugh .05 .02 .00
☐ 452 Dwight Smith .08 .03 .01
☐ 453 Pete Incaviglia .08 .03 .01
☐ 454 Andre Dawson .15 .06 .01
☐ 455 Ruben Sierra .20 .08 .02
☐ 456 Andres Galarraga .08 .03 .01
☐ 457 Alvin Davis .08 .03 .01
☐ 458 Tony Castillo .05 .02 .00
☐ 459 Pete O'Brien .05 .02 .00
☐ 460 Charlie Leibrandt .05 .02 .00
☐ 461 Vince Coleman .10 .04 .01
☐ 462 Steve Sax .08 .03 .01
☐ 463 Omar Olivares .15 .06 .01
☐ 464 Oscar Azocar .08 .03 .01
☐ 465 Joe Magrane .05 .02 .00
☐ 466 Karl Rhodes .08 .03 .01
☐ 467 Benito Santiago .08 .03 .01
☐ 468 Joe Klink .10 .04 .01
☐ 469 Sil Campusano .05 .02 .00
☐ 470 Mark Parent .05 .02 .00
☐ 471 Shawn Boskie UER .08 .03 .01
(Depleted misspelled
as depleated)
☐ 472 Kevin Brown .05 .02 .00
☐ 473 Rick Sutcliffe .08 .03 .01
☐ 474 Rafael Palmeiro .15 .06 .01
☐ 475 Mike Harkey .08 .03 .01
☐ 476 Jaime Navarro .08 .03 .01
☐ 477 Marquis Grissom UER .12 .05 .01
(DeShields misspelled
as DeSheilds)
☐ 478 Marty Clary .05 .02 .00
☐ 479 Greg Briley .05 .02 .00
☐ 480 Tom Glavine .17 .07 .01
☐ 481 Lee Guetterman .05 .02 .00
☐ 482 Rex Hudler .05 .02 .00
☐ 483 Dave LaPoint .05 .02 .00
☐ 484 Terry Pendleton .12 .05 .01
☐ 485 Jesse Barfield .08 .03 .01
☐ 486 Jose DeJesus .05 .02 .00
☐ 487 Paul Abbott .12 .05 .01
☐ 488 Ken Howell .05 .02 .00
☐ 489 Greg W. Harris .05 .02 .00
☐ 490 Roy Smith .05 .02 .00
☐ 491 Paul Assenmacher .05 .02 .00
☐ 492 Geno Petralli .05 .02 .00
☐ 493 Steve Wilson .05 .02 .00
☐ 494 Kevin Reimer .17 .07 .01
☐ 495 Bill Long .05 .02 .00
☐ 496 Mike Jackson .05 .02 .00
☐ 497 Oddibe McDowell .05 .02 .00
☐ 498 Bill Swift .05 .02 .00
☐ 499 Jeff Treadway .05 .02 .00
☐ 500 Checklist 401-500 .05 .01 .00
☐ 501 Gene Larkin .05 .02 .00
☐ 502 Bob Boone .08 .03 .01
☐ 503 Allan Anderson .05 .02 .00
☐ 504 Luis Aquino .05 .02 .00
☐ 505 Mark Guthrie .05 .02 .00
☐ 506 Joe Orsulak .05 .02 .00
☐ 507 Dana Kiecker .08 .03 .01
☐ 508 Dave Gallagher .05 .02 .00
☐ 509 Greg A. Harris .05 .02 .00
☐ 510 Mark Williamson .05 .02 .00
☐ 511 Casey Candaele .05 .02 .00
☐ 512 Mookie Wilson .05 .02 .00
☐ 513 Dave Smith .05 .02 .00
☐ 514 Chuck Carr .08 .03 .01
☐ 515 Glenn Wilson .05 .02 .00
☐ 516 Mike Fitzgerald .05 .02 .00
☐ 517 Devon White .08 .03 .01
☐ 518 Dave Hollins .10 .04 .01
☐ 519 Mark Eichhorn .05 .02 .00
☐ 520 Otis Nixon .08 .03 .01
☐ 521 Terry Shumpert .05 .02 .00
☐ 522 Scott Erickson 3.00 1.25 .30
☐ 523 Danny Tartabull .10 .04 .01
☐ 524 Orel Hershiser .08 .03 .01
☐ 525 George Brett .15 .06 .01
☐ 526 Greg Vaughn .15 .06 .01
☐ 527 Tim Naehring .12 .05 .01
☐ 528 Curt Schilling .05 .02 .00
☐ 529 Chris Bosio .05 .02 .00
☐ 530 Sam Horn .05 .02 .00
☐ 531 Mike Scott .08 .03 .01
☐ 532 George Bell .10 .04 .01
☐ 533 Eric Anthony .10 .04 .01
☐ 534 Julio Valera .08 .03 .01
☐ 535 Glenn Davis .08 .03 .01
☐ 536 Larry Walker UER .10 .04 .01
(Should have comma
after Expos in text)
☐ 537 Pat Combs .05 .02 .00
☐ 538 Chris Nabholz .10 .04 .01
☐ 539 Kirk McCaskill .05 .02 .00
☐ 540 Randy Ready .05 .02 .00
☐ 541 Mark Gubicza .05 .02 .00
☐ 542 Rick Aguilera .05 .02 .00
☐ 543 Brian McRae 1.00 .40 .10
☐ 544 Kirby Puckett .20 .08 .02
☐ 545 Bo Jackson .35 .15 .03
☐ 546 Wade Boggs .20 .08 .02
☐ 547 Tim McIntosh .10 .04 .01
☐ 548 Randy Milligan .08 .03 .01
☐ 549 Dwight Evans .08 .03 .01
☐ 550 Billy Ripken .05 .02 .00
☐ 551 Erik Hanson .08 .03 .01
☐ 552 Lance Parrish .08 .03 .01
☐ 553 Tino Martinez .25 .10 .02

☐ 554 Jim Abbott .15 .06 .01
☐ 555 Ken Griffey Jr. UER 1.25 .50 .12
(Second most votes for
1991 All-Star Game)
☐ 556 Milt Cuyler .35 .15 .03
☐ 557 Mark Leonard .20 .08 .02
☐ 558 Jay Howell .05 .02 .00
☐ 559 Lloyd Moseby .05 .02 .00
☐ 560 Chris Gwynn .05 .02 .00
☐ 561 Mark Whiten .40 .16 .04
☐ 562 Harold Baines .08 .03 .01
☐ 563 Junior Felix .08 .03 .01
☐ 564 Darren Lewis .45 .18 .04
☐ 565 Fred McGriff .15 .06 .01
☐ 566 Kevin Appier .08 .03 .01
☐ 567 Luis Gonzalez 1.00 .40 .10
☐ 568 Frank White .05 .02 .00
☐ 569 Juan Agosto .05 .02 .00
☐ 570 Mike Macfarlane .05 .02 .00
☐ 571 Bert Blyleven .08 .03 .01
☐ 572 Ken Griffey Sr. .08 .03 .01
☐ 573 Lee Stevens .25 .10 .02
☐ 574 Edgar Martinez .08 .03 .01
☐ 575 Wally Joyner .10 .04 .01
☐ 576 Tim Belcher .08 .03 .01
☐ 577 John Burkett .05 .02 .00
☐ 578 Mike Morgan .05 .02 .00
☐ 579 Paul Gibson .05 .02 .00
☐ 580 Jose Vizcaino .05 .02 .00
☐ 581 Duane Ward .05 .02 .00
☐ 582 Scott Sanderson .05 .02 .00
☐ 583 David Wells .05 .02 .00
☐ 584 Willie McGee .08 .03 .01
☐ 585 John Cerutti .05 .02 .00
☐ 586 Danny Darwin .05 .02 .00
☐ 587 Kurt Stillwell .05 .02 .00
☐ 588 Rich Gedman .05 .02 .00
☐ 589 Mark Davis .05 .02 .00
☐ 590 Bill Gullickson .05 .02 .00
☐ 591 Matt Young .05 .02 .00
☐ 592 Bryan Harvey .08 .03 .01
☐ 593 Omar Vizquel .05 .02 .00
☐ 594 Scott Lewis .12 .05 .01
☐ 595 Dave Valle .05 .02 .00
☐ 596 Tim Crews .05 .02 .00
☐ 597 Mike Bielecki .05 .02 .00
☐ 598 Mike Sharperson .05 .02 .00
☐ 599 Dave Bergman .05 .02 .00
☐ 600 Checklist 501-600 .05 .01 .00
☐ 601 Steve Lyons .05 .02 .00
☐ 602 Bruce Hurst .08 .03 .01
☐ 603 Donn Pall .05 .02 .00
☐ 604 Jim Vatcher .10 .04 .01
☐ 605 Dan Pasqua .05 .02 .00
☐ 606 Kenny Rogers .05 .02 .00
☐ 607 Jeff Schulz .12 .05 .01
☐ 608 Brad Arnsberg .05 .02 .00
☐ 609 Willie Wilson .08 .03 .01
☐ 610 Jamie Moyer .05 .02 .00
☐ 611 Ron Oester .05 .02 .00
☐ 612 Dennis Cook .05 .02 .00
☐ 613 Rick Mahler .05 .02 .00
☐ 614 Bill Landrum .05 .02 .00
☐ 615 Scott Scudder .08 .03 .01
☐ 616 Tom Edens .12 .05 .01
☐ 617 1917 Revisited .10 .04 .01
(White Sox in vin-
tage uniforms)
☐ 618 Jim Gantner .05 .02 .00
☐ 619 Darrel Akerfelds .05 .02 .00
☐ 620 Ron Robinson .05 .02 .00
☐ 621 Scott Radinsky .08 .03 .01
☐ 622 Pete Smith .05 .02 .00
☐ 623 Melido Perez .05 .02 .00
☐ 624 Jerald Clark .05 .02 .00
☐ 625 Carlos Martinez .05 .02 .00
☐ 626 Wes Chamberlain 1.00 .40 .10
☐ 627 Bobby Witt .05 .02 .00
☐ 628 Ken Dayley .05 .02 .00
☐ 629 John Barfield .10 .04 .01
☐ 630 Bob Tewksbury .05 .02 .00
☐ 631 Glenn Braggs .05 .02 .00
☐ 632 Jim Neidlinger .12 .05 .01
☐ 633 Tom Browning .08 .03 .01
☐ 634 Kirk Gibson .08 .03 .01
☐ 635 Rob Dibble .08 .03 .01
☐ 636A Stolen Base Leaders .25 .10 .02
(Rickey Henderson and
Lou Brock in tuxedos
and no date on card)
☐ 636B Stolen Base Leaders .50 .20 .05
(Dated May 1, 1991
on card front)
☐ 637 Jeff Montgomery .05 .02 .00
☐ 638 Mike Schooler .05 .02 .00
☐ 639 Storm Davis .05 .02 .00
☐ 640 Rich Rodriguez .12 .05 .01
☐ 641 Phil Bradley .05 .02 .00
☐ 642 Kent Mercker .10 .04 .01
☐ 643 Carlton Fisk .15 .06 .01
☐ 644 Mike Bell .12 .05 .01
☐ 645 Alex Fernandez .40 .16 .04
☐ 646 Juan Gonzalez .90 .40 .09
☐ 647 Ken Hill .05 .02 .00
☐ 648 Jeff Russell .05 .02 .00
☐ 649 Chuck Malone .08 .03 .01
☐ 650 Steve Buechele .05 .02 .00
☐ 651 Mike Benjamin .05 .02 .00
☐ 652 Tony Pena .08 .03 .01
☐ 653 Trevor Wilson .05 .02 .00
☐ 654 Alex Cole .10 .04 .01
☐ 655 Roger Clemens .30 .12 .03
☐ 656 The Bashing Years .12 .05 .01
(Mark McGwire)
☐ 657 Joe Grahe .10 .04 .01
☐ 658 Jim Eisenreich .05 .02 .00

☐ 659 Dan Gladden	.05	.02	.00
☐ 660 Steve Farr	.05	.02	.00
☐ 661 Bill Sampen	.05	.02	.00
☐ 662 Dave Rohde	.08	.03	.01
☐ 663 Mark Gardner	.05	.02	.00
☐ 664 Mike Simms	.30	.12	.03
☐ 665 Moises Alou	.10	.04	.01
☐ 666 Mickey Hatcher	.05	.02	.00
☐ 667 Jimmy Key	.08	.03	.01
☐ 668 John Wetteland	.08	.03	.01
☐ 669 John Smiley	.08	.03	.01
☐ 670 Jim Acker	.05	.02	.00
☐ 671 Pascual Perez	.05	.02	.00
☐ 672 Reggie Harris UER (Opportunity misspelled as oppurtinty)	.15	.06	.01
☐ 673 Matt Nokes	.08	.03	.01
☐ 674 Rafael Novoa	.12	.05	.01
☐ 675 Hensley Meulens	.10	.04	.01
☐ 676 Jeff M. Robinson	.05	.02	.00
☐ 677 Ground Breaking (new Comiskey Park; Carlton Fisk and Robin Ventura)	.15	.06	.01
☐ 678 Johnny Ray	.05	.02	.00
☐ 679 Greg Hibbard	.05	.02	.00
☐ 680 Paul Sorrento	.05	.02	.00
☐ 681 Mike Marshall	.08	.03	.01
☐ 682 Jim Clancy	.05	.02	.00
☐ 683 Rob Murphy	.05	.02	.00
☐ 684 Dave Schmidt	.05	.02	.00
☐ 685 Jeff Gray	.10	.04	.01
☐ 686 Mike Hartley	.10	.04	.01
☐ 687 Jeff King	.08	.03	.01
☐ 688 Stan Javier	.05	.02	.00
☐ 689 Bob Walk	.05	.02	.00
☐ 690 Jim Gott	.05	.02	.00
☐ 691 Mike LaCoss	.05	.02	.00
☐ 692 John Farrell	.05	.02	.00
☐ 693 Tim Leary	.08	.03	.01
☐ 694 Mike Walker	.05	.02	.00
☐ 695 Eric Plunk	.05	.02	.00
☐ 696 Mike Fetters	.05	.02	.00
☐ 697 Wayne Edwards	.05	.02	.00
☐ 698 Tim Drummond	.10	.04	.01
☐ 699 Willie Fraser	.05	.02	.00
☐ 700 Checklist 601-700	.10	.04	.01
☐ SP1 Michael Jordan SP (Shown batting in White Sox uniform)	11.00	5.00	1.35

1991 Upper Deck Silver Sluggers

The Upper Deck Silver Slugger set features nine players from each league, representing the nine batting positions on the team. The cards measure the standard size (2 1/2" by 3 1/2"). The fronts have glossy color action player photos, with white borders on three sides and a "Silver Slugger" bat serving as the border on the left side. The player's name appears in a tan stripe below the picture, with the team logo superimposed at the lower right corner. Two-thirds of the back are occupied by another color action photo, with career highlights in a horizontally oriented rectangle to the left of the picture. The cards are numbered on the back.

	MINT	EXC	G-VG
COMPLETE SET (18)	45.00	20.00	6.75
COMMON PLAYER (SS1-SS18)	1.50	.60	.15

☐ SS1 Julio Franco	2.25	.90	.22
☐ SS2 Alan Trammell	2.00	.80	.20
☐ SS3 Rickey Henderson	5.50	2.50	.55
☐ SS4 Jose Canseco	8.00	3.50	.80
☐ SS5 Barry Bonds	4.00	1.75	.40
☐ SS6 Eddie Murray	2.50	1.00	.25
☐ SS7 Kelly Gruber	1.75	.70	.17
☐ SS8 Ryne Sandberg	6.00	2.50	.60
☐ SS9 Darryl Strawberry	5.00	2.25	.50
☐ SS10 Ellis Burks	1.75	.70	.17
☐ SS11 Lance Parrish	1.50	.60	.15
☐ SS12 Cecil Fielder	5.00	2.25	.50
☐ SS13 Matt Williams	2.50	1.00	.25
☐ SS14 Dave Parker	1.75	.70	.17
☐ SS15 Bobby Bonilla	4.00	1.75	.40
☐ SS16 Don Robinson	1.50	.60	.15

☐ SS17 Benito Santiago	1.75	.70	.17
☐ SS18 Barry Larkin	2.25	.90	.22

1991 Upper Deck Extended

This 100-card standard size (2 1/2" by 3 1/2") series was issued by Upper Deck several months after the release of their major series. The set features rookie players as well as players who switched teams between seasons. In the extended wax packs were low number cards, special cards featuring Hank Aaron as the next featured player in their baseball heroes series, and a special card honoring the May 1st exploits of Rickey Henderson and Nolan Ryan. For the first time in Upper Deck's three year history, they did not issue a factory Extended set. The key rookie card in this set is Jeff Bagwell.

	MINT	EXC	G-VG
COMPLETE SET (100)	10.00	4.50	1.25
COMMON PLAYER (701-800)	.05	.02	.00
☐ 701 Mike Heath	.05	.02	.00
☐ 702 Rookie Threats	1.00	.40	.10
Luis Gonzalez			
Karl Rhodes			
Jeff Bagwell			
☐ 703 Jose Mesa	.05	.02	.00
☐ 704 Dave Smith	.05	.02	.00
☐ 705 Danny Darwin	.05	.02	.00
☐ 706 Rafael Belliard	.05	.02	.00
☐ 707 Rob Murphy	.05	.02	.00
☐ 708 Terry Pendleton	.15	.06	.01
☐ 709 Mike Pagliarulo	.05	.02	.00
☐ 710 Sid Bream	.05	.02	.00
☐ 711 Junior Felix	.08	.03	.01
☐ 712 Dante Bichette	.05	.02	.00
☐ 713 Kevin Gross	.05	.02	.00
☐ 714 Luis Sojo	.08	.03	.01
☐ 715 Bob Ojeda	.05	.02	.00
☐ 716 Julio Machado	.05	.02	.00
☐ 717 Steve Farr	.05	.02	.00
☐ 718 Franklin Stubbs	.05	.02	.00
☐ 719 Mike Boddicker	.05	.02	.00
☐ 720 Willie Randolph	.05	.02	.00
☐ 721 Willie McGee	.08	.03	.01
☐ 722 Chili Davis	.08	.03	.01
☐ 723 Danny Jackson	.05	.02	.00
☐ 724 Cory Snyder	.08	.03	.01
☐ 725 MVP Lineup	.30	.12	.03
Andre Dawson			
George Bell			
Ryne Sandberg			
☐ 726 Rob Deer	.08	.03	.01
☐ 727 Rich DeLucia	.17	.07	.01
☐ 728 Mike Perez	.12	.05	.01
☐ 729 Mickey Tettleton	.08	.03	.01
☐ 730 Mike Blowers	.05	.02	.00
☐ 731 Gary Gaetti	.08	.03	.01
☐ 732 Brett Butler	.08	.03	.01
☐ 733 Dave Parker	.10	.04	.01
☐ 734 Eddie Zosky	.25	.10	.02
☐ 735 Jack Clark	.08	.03	.01
☐ 736 Jack Morris	.10	.04	.01
☐ 737 Kirk Gibson	.10	.04	.01
☐ 738 Steve Bedrosian	.05	.02	.00
☐ 739 Candy Maldonado	.05	.02	.00
☐ 740 Matt Young	.05	.02	.00
☐ 741 Rich Garces	.12	.05	.01
☐ 742 George Bell	.10	.04	.01
☐ 743 Deion Sanders	.17	.07	.01
☐ 744 Bo Jackson	1.50	.60	.15
☐ 745 Luis Mercedes	.45	.18	.04
☐ 746 Reggie Jefferson UER	.75	.30	.07
(Throwing left on card; back has throws right)			
☐ 747 Pete Incaviglia	.08	.03	.01
☐ 748 Chris Hammond	.12	.05	.01
☐ 749 Mike Stanton	.05	.02	.00
☐ 750 Scott Sanderson	.05	.02	.00
☐ 751 Paul Faries	.10	.04	.01
☐ 752 Al Osuna	.17	.07	.01
☐ 753 Steve Chitren	.12	.05	.01
☐ 754 Tony Fernandez	.08	.03	.01
☐ 755 Jeff Bagwell UER	4.00	1.75	.40
(Strikeout and walk totals reversed)			
☐ 756 Kirk Dressendorfer	.35	.15	.03
☐ 757 Glenn Davis	.08	.03	.01
☐ 758 Gary Carter	.08	.03	.01
☐ 759 Zane Smith	.05	.02	.00

	MINT	EXC	G-VG
☐ 760 Vance Law	.05	.02	.00
☐ 761 Denis Boucher	.20	.08	.02
☐ 762 Turner Ward	.25	.10	.02
☐ 763 Roberto Alomar	.17	.07	.01
☐ 764 Albert Belle	.35	.15	.03
☐ 765 Joe Carter	.12	.05	.01
☐ 766 Pete Schourek	.20	.08	.02
☐ 767 Heathcliff Slocumb	.12	.05	.01
☐ 768 Vince Coleman	.10	.04	.01
☐ 769 Mitch Williams	.05	.02	.00
☐ 770 Brian Downing	.05	.02	.00
☐ 771 Dana Allison	.17	.07	.01
☐ 772 Pete Harnisch	.05	.02	.00
☐ 773 Tim Raines	.08	.03	.01
☐ 774 Darryl Kile	.17	.07	.01
☐ 775 Fred McGriff	.12	.05	.01
☐ 776 Dwight Evans	.08	.03	.01
☐ 777 Joe Slusarski	.15	.06	.01
☐ 778 Dave Righetti	.08	.03	.01
☐ 779 Jeff Hamilton	.05	.02	.00
☐ 780 Ernest Riles	.05	.02	.00
☐ 781 Ken Dayley	.05	.02	.00
☐ 782 Eric King	.05	.02	.00
☐ 783 Devon White	.08	.03	.01
☐ 784 Beau Allred	.12	.05	.01
☐ 785 Mike Timlin	.17	.07	.01
☐ 786 Ivan Calderon	.08	.03	.01
☐ 787 Hubie Brooks	.08	.03	.01
☐ 788 Juan Agosto	.05	.02	.00
☐ 789 Barry Jones	.05	.02	.00
☐ 790 Wally Backman	.05	.02	.00
☐ 791 Jim Presley	.05	.02	.00
☐ 792 Charlie Hough	.05	.02	.00
☐ 793 Larry Andersen	.05	.02	.00
☐ 794 Steve Finley	.08	.03	.01
☐ 795 Shawn Abner	.05	.02	.00
☐ 796 Jeff M. Robinson	.05	.02	.00
☐ 797 Joe Bitker	.05	.02	.00
☐ 798 Eric Show	.05	.02	.00
☐ 799 Bud Black	.05	.02	.00
☐ 800 Checklist 701-800	.05	.01	.00
☐ HH1 Hank Aaron Hologram	9.00	4.00	.90
☐ SP2 Henderson/Ryan (Rickey and Nolan)	9.00	4.00	.90

1991 Upper Deck Final Edition

The 1991 Upper Deck Final Edition boxed set contains 100 cards and showcases players who made major contributions during their team's late-season pennant drive. In addition to the late season traded and impact rookie cards (22-78), the set includes two special subsets: Diamond Skills cards (1-21), depicting the best Minor League prospects, and All-Star cards (80-99). Six assorted hologram cards were issued with each set. The cards measure the standard size (2 1/2" by 3 1/2"). The fronts feature posed or action color player photos on a white card face, with the upper left corner of the picture cut out to provide space for the Upper Deck logo. The pictures are bordered in green on the left, with the player's name in a tan border below the picture. Two-thirds of the back are occupied by another color action photo, with biography, statistics, and career highlights in a horizontally oriented red rectangle to the left of the picture. The cards are numbered on the back. Among the outstanding rookie cards in this set are Ryan Klesko, Marc Newfield, Frankie Rodriguez, and Ivan Rodriguez.

	MINT	EXC	G-VG
COMPLETE SET (100)	16.00	6.75	2.25
COMMON PLAYER (1-100)	.05	.02	.00
☐ 1F Diamond Skills Checklist Card (Ryan Klesko and Reggie Sanders)	.75	.30	.07
☐ 2F Pedro Martinez	1.75	.70	.17
☐ 3F Lance Dickson	.15	.06	.01
☐ 4F Royce Clayton	.35	.15	.03
☐ 5F Scott Bryant	.17	.07	.01
☐ 6F Dan Wilson	.25	.10	.02
☐ 7F Dmitri Young	1.50	.60	.15
☐ 8F Ryan Klesko	4.00	1.75	.40
☐ 9F Tom Goodwin	.25	.10	.02
☐ 10F Rondell White	.90	.40	.09
☐ 11F Reggie Sanders	.35	.15	.03
☐ 12F Todd Van Poppel	.75	.30	.07

- ☐ 13F Arthur Rhodes .45 .18 .04
- ☐ 14F Eddie Zosky .17 .07 .01
- ☐ 15F Gerald Williams .60 .25 .06
- ☐ 16F Robert Eenhoorn .20 .08 .02
- ☐ 17F Jim Thome 1.50 .60 .15
- ☐ 18F Marc Newfield 2.00 .80 .20
- ☐ 19F Kerwin Moore .40 .16 .04
- ☐ 20F Jeff McNeely .90 .40 .09
- ☐ 21F Frankie Rodriguez 2.50 1.00 .25
- ☐ 22F Andy Mota .25 .10 .02
- ☐ 23F Chris Haney .25 .10 .02
- ☐ 24F Kenny Lofton .50 .20 .05
- ☐ 25F Dave Nilsson .75 .30 .07
- ☐ 26F Derek Bell 1.25 .50 .12
- ☐ 27F Frank Castillo .20 .08 .02
- ☐ 28F Candy Maldonado .05 .02 .00
- ☐ 29F Chuck McElroy .05 .02 .00
- ☐ 30F Chito Martinez 1.00 .40 .10
- ☐ 31F Steve Howe .05 .02 .00
- ☐ 32F Freddie Benavides .15 .06 .01
- ☐ 33F Scott Kamieniecki .20 .08 .02
- ☐ 34F Denny Neagle .60 .25 .06
- ☐ 35F Mike Humphreys .25 .10 .02
- ☐ 36F Mike Remlinger .20 .08 .02
- ☐ 37F Scott Coolbaugh .05 .02 .00
- ☐ 38F Darren Lewis .25 .10 .02
- ☐ 39F Thomas Howard .08 .03 .01
- ☐ 40F John Candelaria .05 .02 .00
- ☐ 41F Todd Benzinger .05 .02 .00
- ☐ 42F Wilson Alvarez .12 .05 .01
- ☐ 43F Patrick Lennon .50 .20 .05
- ☐ 44F Rusty Meacham .20 .08 .02
- ☐ 45F Ryan Bowen .30 .12 .03
- ☐ 46F Rick Wilkins .30 .12 .03
- ☐ 47F Ed Sprague .20 .08 .02
- ☐ 48F Bob Scanlan .15 .06 .01
- ☐ 49F Tom Candiotti .08 .03 .01
- ☐ 50F Perfecto (Dennis Martinez) .08 .03 .01
- ☐ 51F Oil Can Boyd .05 .02 .00
- ☐ 52F Glenallen Hill .08 .03 .01
- ☐ 53F Scott Livingstone .40 .16 .04
- ☐ 54F Brian Hunter 1.50 .60 .15
- ☐ 55F Ivan Rodriguez 3.50 1.50 .35
- ☐ 56F Keith Mitchell .75 .30 .07
- ☐ 57F Roger McDowell .05 .02 .00
- ☐ 58F Otis Nixon .08 .03 .01
- ☐ 59F Juan Bell .08 .03 .01
- ☐ 60F Bill Krueger .05 .02 .00
- ☐ 61F Chris Donnels .35 .15 .03
- ☐ 62F Tommy Greene .10 .04 .01
- ☐ 63F Doug Simons .17 .07 .01
- ☐ 64F Andy Ashby .17 .07 .01
- ☐ 65F Anthony Young .35 .15 .03
- ☐ 66F Kevin Morton .25 .10 .02
- ☐ 67F Bret Barberie .45 .18 .04
- ☐ 68F Scott Servais .15 .06 .01
- ☐ 69F Ron Darling .08 .03 .01
- ☐ 70F Tim Burke .05 .02 .00
- ☐ 71F Vicente Palacios .05 .02 .00
- ☐ 72F Gerald Alexander .15 .06 .01
- ☐ 73F Reggie Jefferson .30 .12 .03
- ☐ 74F Dean Palmer .50 .20 .05
- ☐ 75F Mark Whiten .20 .08 .02
- ☐ 76F Randy Tomlin .30 .12 .03
- ☐ 77F Mark Wohlers .75 .30 .07
- ☐ 78F Brook Jacoby .05 .02 .00
- ☐ 79F All-Star Checklist (Ken Griffey Jr. and Ryne Sandberg) .75 .30 .07
- ☐ 80F Jack Morris AS .10 .04 .01
- ☐ 81F Sandy Alomar Jr. AS .08 .03 .01
- ☐ 82F Cecil Fielder AS .17 .07 .01
- ☐ 83F Roberto Alomar AS .12 .05 .01
- ☐ 84F Wade Boggs AS .15 .06 .01
- ☐ 85F Cal Ripken AS .35 .15 .03
- ☐ 86F Rickey Henderson AS .25 .10 .02
- ☐ 87F Ken Griffey Jr. AS .60 .25 .06
- ☐ 88F Dave Henderson AS .08 .03 .01
- ☐ 89F Danny Tartabull AS .08 .03 .01
- ☐ 90F Tom Glavine AS .08 .03 .01
- ☐ 91F Benito Santiago AS .08 .03 .01
- ☐ 92F Will Clark AS .25 .10 .02
- ☐ 93F Ryne Sandberg AS .25 .10 .02
- ☐ 94F Chris Sabo AS .08 .03 .01
- ☐ 95F Ozzie Smith AS .10 .04 .01
- ☐ 96F Ivan Calderon AS .08 .03 .01
- ☐ 97F Tony Gwynn AS .12 .05 .01
- ☐ 98F Andre Dawson AS .10 .04 .01
- ☐ 99F Bobby Bonilla AS .10 .04 .01
- ☐ 100F Checklist 1-100 .05 .01 .00

1992 Upper Deck

The 1992 Upper Deck set contains 700 standard-size (2 1/2" by 3 1/2") cards. Special subsets included in the set are Star Rookies (1-27; SR), Team Checklists (29-40, 86-99; TC), with player portraits by Vernon Wells; Top Prospects (52-77; TP); Bloodlines (79-85), and Diamond Skills (640-650; DS). Moreover, a nine-card Baseball Heroes subset (randomly inserted in packs) focuses on the career of Ted Williams. He autographed and numbered 2,500 cards, which were randomly inserted in low series foil packs. The cards are numbered on the back.

	MINT	EXC	G-VG
COMPLETE SET (700)	36.00	16.25	5.50
COMMON PLAYER (1-700)	.04	.02	.00
☐ 1 Star Rookie Checklist Ryan Klesko Jim Thome	.40	.10	.02
☐ 2 Royce Clayton SR	.15	.06	.01
☐ 3 Brian Jordan SR	.25	.10	.02
☐ 4 Dave Fleming SR	.10	.04	.01
☐ 5 Jim Thome SR	.30	.12	.03
☐ 6 Jeff Juden SR	.15	.06	.01
☐ 7 Roberto Hernandez SR	.10	.04	.01
☐ 8 Kyle Abbott SR	.15	.06	.01
☐ 9 Chris George SR	.10	.04	.01
☐ 10 Rob Maurer SR	.25	.10	.02
☐ 11 Donald Harris SR	.10	.04	.01
☐ 12 Ted Wood SR	.20	.08	.02
☐ 13 Patrick Lennon SR	.20	.08	.02
☐ 14 Willie Banks SR	.10	.04	.01
☐ 15 Roger Salkeld SR	.30	.12	.03
☐ 16 Wilfredo Cordero SR	.15	.06	.01
☐ 17 Arthur Rhodes SR	.20	.08	.02
☐ 18 Pedro Martinez SR	.50	.20	.05
☐ 19 Andy Ashby SR	.12	.05	.01
☐ 20 Tom Goodwin SR	.12	.05	.01
☐ 21 Braulio Castillo SR	.35	.15	.03
☐ 22 Todd Van Poppel SR	.50	.20	.05
☐ 23 Brian Williams SR	.20	.08	.02
☐ 24 Ryan Klesko SR	1.25	.50	.12
☐ 25 Kenny Lofton SR	.25	.10	.02
☐ 26 Derek Bell SR	.25	.10	.02
☐ 27 Reggie Sanders SR	.20	.08	.02
☐ 28 Dave Winfield's 400th	.10	.04	.01
☐ 29 Atlanta TC Dave Justice	.20	.08	.02
☐ 30 Cincinnati TC Rob Dibble	.07	.03	.01
☐ 31 Houston TC Craig Biggio	.07	.03	.01
☐ 32 Los Angeles TC Eddie Murray	.10	.04	.01
☐ 33 San Diego TC Fred McGriff	.10	.04	.01
☐ 34 San Francisco TC Willie McGee	.07	.03	.01
☐ 35 Chicago TC Shawon Dunston	.07	.03	.01
☐ 36 Montreal TC Delino DeShields	.07	.03	.01
☐ 37 New York TC Howard Johnson	.07	.03	.01
☐ 38 Philadelphia TC John Kruk	.07	.03	.01
☐ 39 Pittsburgh TC Doug Drabek	.07	.03	.01
☐ 40 St. Louis TC Todd Zeile	.10	.04	.01
☐ 41 Playoff Perfection Steve Avery	.15	.06	.01
☐ 42 Jeremy Hernandez	.17	.07	.01
☐ 43 Doug Henry	.17	.07	.01
☐ 44 Chris Donnels	.15	.06	.01
☐ 45 Mo Sanford	.10	.04	.01
☐ 46 Scott Kamieniecki	.10	.04	.01
☐ 47 Mark Lemke	.04	.02	.00
☐ 48 Steve Farr	.04	.02	.00
☐ 49 Francisco Oliveras	.04	.02	.00
☐ 50 Ced Landrum	.10	.04	.01
☐ 51 Top Prospect Checklist Rondell White Craig Griffey	.20	.08	.02
☐ 52 Eduardo Perez TP	.50	.20	.05
☐ 53 Tom Nevers TP	.12	.05	.01
☐ 54 David Zancanaro TP	.20	.08	.02
☐ 55 Shawn Green TP	.25	.10	.02
☐ 56 Mark Wohlers TP	.20	.08	.02
☐ 57 Dave Nilsson TP	.40	.16	.04
☐ 58 Dmitri Young TP	.40	.16	.04
☐ 59 Ryan Hawblitzel TP	.20	.08	.02
☐ 60 Raul Mondesi TP	.25	.10	.02
☐ 61 Rondell White TP	.25	.10	.02
☐ 62 Steve Hosey TP	.10	.04	.01
☐ 63 Manny Ramirez TP	.50	.20	.05
☐ 64 Marc Newfield TP	.50	.20	.05
☐ 65 Jeromy Burnitz TP	.40	.16	.04
☐ 66 Mark Smith TP	.15	.06	.01
☐ 67 Joey Hamilton TP	.20	.08	.02
☐ 68 Tyler Green TP	.50	.20	.05
☐ 69 Jon Farrell TP	.20	.08	.02
☐ 70 Kurt Miller TP	.12	.05	.01
☐ 71 Jeff Plympton TP	.15	.06	.01
☐ 72 Dan Wilson TP	.10	.04	.01
☐ 73 Joe Vitiello TP	.50	.20	.05
☐ 74 Rico Brogna TP	.12	.05	.01
☐ 75 David McCarty TP	.75	.30	.07
☐ 76 Bob Wickman TP	.10	.04	.01
☐ 77 Carlos Rodriguez TP	.10	.04	.01
☐ 78 Stay In School Jim Abbott	.10	.04	.01

Card			
☐ 79 Ramon Martinez	.15	.06	.01
Pedro Martinez			
☐ 80 Kevin Mitchell	.18	.08	.01
Keith Mitchell			
☐ 81 Sandy Alomar Jr.	.12	.05	.01
Roberto Alomar			
☐ 82 Cal Ripken	.12	.05	.01
Billy Ripken			
☐ 83 Tony Gwynn	.12	.05	.01
Chris Gwynn			
☐ 84 Dwight Gooden	.12	.05	.01
Gary Sheffield			
☐ 85 Ken Griffey Sr.	.50	.20	.05
Ken Griffey Jr.			
Craig Griffey			
☐ 86 California TC	.10	.04	.01
Jim Abbott			
☐ 87 Chicago TC	.35	.15	.03
Frank Thomas			
☐ 88 Kansas City TC	.07	.03	.01
Danny Tartabull			
☐ 89 Minnesota TC	.15	.06	.01
Scott Erickson			
☐ 90 Oakland TC	.15	.06	.01
Rickey Henderson			
☐ 91 Seattle TC	.07	.03	.01
Edgar Martinez			
☐ 92 Texas TC	.30	.12	.03
Nolan Ryan			
☐ 93 Baltimore TC	.10	.04	.01
Ben McDonald			
☐ 94 Boston TC	.10	.04	.01
Ellis Burks			
☐ 95 Cleveland TC	.07	.03	.01
Greg Swindell			
☐ 96 Detroit TC	.12	.05	.01
Cecil Fielder			
☐ 97 Milwaukee TC	.10	.04	.01
Greg Vaughn			
☐ 98 New York TC	.12	.05	.01
Kevin Maas			
☐ 99 Toronto Checklist	.07	.03	.01
Dave Stieb			
☐ 100 Checklist 1-100	.07	.03	.01
☐ 101 Joe Oliver	.04	.02	.00
☐ 102 Hector Villanueva	.04	.02	.00
☐ 103 Ed Whitson	.04	.02	.00
☐ 104 Danny Jackson	.04	.02	.00
☐ 105 Chris Hammond	.07	.03	.01
☐ 106 Ricky Jordan	.07	.03	.01
☐ 107 Kevin Bass	.04	.02	.00
☐ 108 Darrin Fletcher	.04	.02	.00
☐ 109 Junior Ortiz	.04	.02	.00
☐ 110 Tom Bolton	.04	.02	.00
☐ 111 Jeff King	.04	.02	.00
☐ 112 Dave Magadan	.07	.03	.01
☐ 113 Mike LaValliere	.04	.02	.00
☐ 114 Hubie Brooks	.07	.03	.01
☐ 115 Jay Bell	.04	.02	.00
☐ 116 David Wells	.04	.02	.00
☐ 117 Jim Leyritz	.04	.02	.00
☐ 118 Manuel Lee	.04	.02	.00
☐ 119 Alvaro Espinoza	.04	.02	.00
☐ 120 B.J. Surhoff	.04	.02	.00
☐ 121 Hal Morris	.12	.05	.01
☐ 122 Shawon Dawson	.07	.03	.01
☐ 123 Chris Sabo	.07	.03	.01
☐ 124 Andre Dawson	.15	.06	.01
☐ 125 Eric Davis	.15	.06	.01
☐ 126 Chili Davis	.07	.03	.01
☐ 127 Dale Murphy	.12	.05	.01
☐ 128 Kirk McCaskill	.04	.02	.00
☐ 129 Terry Mulholland	.04	.02	.00
☐ 130 Rick Aguilera	.04	.02	.00
☐ 131 Vince Coleman	.10	.04	.01
☐ 132 Andy Van Slyke	.07	.03	.01
☐ 133 Gregg Jefferies	.10	.04	.01
☐ 134 Barry Bonds	.18	.08	.01
☐ 135 Dwight Gooden	.12	.05	.01
☐ 136 Dave Stieb	.07	.03	.01
☐ 137 Albert Belle	.15	.06	.01
☐ 138 Teddy Higuera	.04	.02	.00
☐ 139 Jesse Barfield	.07	.03	.01
☐ 140 Pat Borders	.04	.02	.00
☐ 141 Bip Roberts	.04	.02	.00
☐ 142 Rob Dibble	.07	.03	.01
☐ 143 Mark Grace	.10	.04	.01
☐ 144 Barry Larkin	.12	.05	.01
☐ 145 Ryne Sandberg	.25	.10	.02
☐ 146 Scott Erickson	.17	.07	.01
☐ 147 Luis Polonia	.07	.03	.01
☐ 148 John Burkett	.04	.02	.00
☐ 149 Luis Sojo	.04	.02	.00
☐ 150 Dickie Thon	.04	.02	.00
☐ 151 Walt Weiss	.07	.03	.01
☐ 152 Mike Scioscia	.04	.02	.00
☐ 153 Mark McGwire	.12	.05	.01
☐ 154 Matt Williams	.12	.05	.01
☐ 155 Rickey Henderson	.30	.12	.03
☐ 156 Sandy Alomar Jr.	.10	.04	.01
☐ 157 Brian McRae	.18	.08	.01
☐ 158 Harold Baines	.07	.03	.01
☐ 159 Kevin Appier	.04	.02	.00
☐ 160 Felix Fermin	.04	.02	.00
☐ 161 Leo Gomez	.12	.05	.01
☐ 162 Craig Biggio	.10	.04	.01
☐ 163 Ben McDonald	.12	.05	.01
☐ 164 Randy Johnson	.07	.03	.01
☐ 165 Cal Ripken	.30	.12	.03
☐ 166 Frank Thomas	.75	.30	.07
☐ 167 Delino DeShields	.10	.04	.01
☐ 168 Greg Gagne	.04	.02	.00
☐ 169 Ron Karkovice	.04	.02	.00
☐ 170 Charlie Leibrandt	.04	.02	.00
☐ 171 Dave Righetti	.07	.03	.01
☐ 172 Dave Henderson	.07	.03	.01

No.	Player			
☐ 173	Steve Decker	.12	.05	.01
☐ 174	Darryl Strawberry	.25	.10	.02
☐ 175	Will Clark	.30	.12	.03
☐ 176	Ruben Sierra	.20	.08	.02
☐ 177	Ozzie Smith	.12	.05	.01
☐ 178	Charles Nagy	.04	.02	.00
☐ 179	Gary Pettis	.04	.02	.00
☐ 180	Kirk Gibson	.07	.03	.01
☐ 181	Randy Milligan	.04	.02	.00
☐ 182	Dave Valle	.04	.02	.00
☐ 183	Chris Hoiles	.07	.03	.01
☐ 184	Tony Phillips	.04	.02	.00
☐ 185	Brady Anderson	.04	.02	.00
☐ 186	Scott Fletcher	.04	.02	.00
☐ 187	Gene Larkin	.04	.02	.00
☐ 188	Lance Johnson	.04	.02	.00
☐ 189	Greg Olson	.04	.02	.00
☐ 190	Melido Perez	.04	.02	.00
☐ 191	Lenny Harris	.04	.02	.00
☐ 192	Terry Kennedy	.04	.02	.00
☐ 193	Mike Gallego	.04	.02	.00
☐ 194	Willie McGee	.07	.03	.01
☐ 195	Juan Samuel	.07	.03	.01
☐ 196	Jeff Huson	.04	.02	.00
☐ 197	Alex Cole	.07	.03	.01
☐ 198	Ron Robinson	.04	.02	.00
☐ 199	Joel Skinner	.04	.02	.00
☐ 200	Checklist 101-200	.07	.03	.01
☐ 201	Kevin Reimer	.04	.02	.00
☐ 202	Stan Belinda	.04	.02	.00
☐ 203	Pat Tabler	.04	.02	.00
☐ 204	Jose Guzman	.04	.02	.00
☐ 205	Jose Lind	.04	.02	.00
☐ 206	Spike Owen	.04	.02	.00
☐ 207	Joe Orsulak	.04	.02	.00
☐ 208	Charlie Hayes	.04	.02	.00
☐ 209	Mike Devereaux	.04	.02	.00
☐ 210	Mike Fitzgerald	.04	.02	.00
☐ 211	Willie Randolph	.04	.02	.00
☐ 212	Rod Nichols	.04	.02	.00
☐ 213	Mike Boddicker	.04	.02	.00
☐ 214	Bill Spiers	.04	.02	.00
☐ 215	Steve Olin	.04	.02	.00
☐ 216	David Howard	.07	.03	.01
☐ 217	Gary Varsho	.04	.02	.00
☐ 218	Mike Harkey	.04	.02	.00
☐ 219	Luis Aquino	.04	.02	.00
☐ 220	Chuck McElroy	.04	.02	.00
☐ 221	Doug Drabek	.07	.03	.01
☐ 222	Dave Winfield	.12	.05	.01
☐ 223	Rafael Palmeiro	.12	.05	.01
☐ 224	Joe Carter	.10	.04	.01
☐ 225	Bobby Bonilla	.15	.06	.01
☐ 226	Ivan Calderon	.07	.03	.01
☐ 227	Gregg Olson	.07	.03	.01
☐ 228	Tim Wallach	.07	.03	.01
☐ 229	Terry Pendleton	.10	.04	.01
☐ 230	Gilberto Reyes	.04	.02	.00
☐ 231	Carlos Baerga	.12	.05	.01
☐ 232	Greg Vaughn	.12	.05	.01
☐ 233	Bret Saberhagen	.10	.04	.01
☐ 234	Gary Sheffield	.10	.04	.01
☐ 235	Mark Lewis	.15	.06	.01
☐ 236	George Bell	.10	.04	.01
☐ 237	Danny Tartabull	.10	.04	.01
☐ 238	Willie Wilson	.07	.03	.01
☐ 239	Doug Dascenzo	.04	.02	.00
☐ 240	Bill Pecota	.04	.02	.00
☐ 241	Julio Franco	.10	.04	.01
☐ 242	Ed Sprague	.12	.05	.01
☐ 243	Juan Gonzalez	.35	.15	.03
☐ 244	Chuck Finley	.10	.04	.01
☐ 245	Ivan Rodriguez	.75	.30	.07
☐ 246	Len Dykstra	.07	.03	.01
☐ 247	Deion Sanders	.12	.05	.01
☐ 248	Dwight Evans	.07	.03	.01
☐ 249	Larry Walker	.07	.03	.01
☐ 250	Billy Ripken	.04	.02	.00
☐ 251	Mickey Tettleton	.07	.03	.01
☐ 252	Tony Pena	.07	.03	.01
☐ 253	Benito Santiago	.10	.04	.01
☐ 254	Kirby Puckett	.15	.06	.01
☐ 255	Cecil Fielder	.25	.10	.02
☐ 256	Howard Johnson	.12	.05	.01
☐ 257	Andujar Cedeno	.20	.08	.02
☐ 258	Jose Rijo	.07	.03	.01
☐ 259	Al Osuna	.10	.04	.01
☐ 260	Todd Hundley	.07	.03	.01
☐ 261	Orel Hershiser	.10	.04	.01
☐ 262	Ray Lankford	.15	.06	.01
☐ 263	Robin Ventura	.25	.10	.02
☐ 264	Felix Jose	.15	.06	.01
☐ 265	Eddie Murray	.15	.06	.01
☐ 266	Kevin Mitchell	.12	.05	.01
☐ 267	Gary Carter	.10	.04	.01
☐ 268	Mike Benjamin	.04	.02	.00
☐ 269	Dick Schofield	.04	.02	.00
☐ 270	Jose Uribe	.04	.02	.00
☐ 271	Pete Incaviglia	.07	.03	.01
☐ 272	Tony Fernandez	.07	.03	.01
☐ 273	Alan Trammell	.10	.04	.01
☐ 274	Tony Gwynn	.17	.07	.01
☐ 275	Mike Greenwell	.12	.05	.01
☐ 276	Jeff Bagwell	1.25	.50	.12
☐ 277	Frank Viola	.10	.04	.01
☐ 278	Randy Myers	.04	.02	.00
☐ 279	Ken Caminiti	.04	.02	.00
☐ 280	Bill Doran	.04	.02	.00
☐ 281	Dan Pasqua	.04	.02	.00
☐ 282	Alfredo Griffin	.04	.02	.00
☐ 283	Jose Oquendo	.04	.02	.00
☐ 284	Kal Daniels	.07	.03	.01
☐ 285	Bobby Thigpen	.07	.03	.01
☐ 286	Robby Thompson	.04	.02	.00
☐ 287	Mark Eichhorn	.04	.02	.00
☐ 288	Mike Felder	.04	.02	.00

□ 289 Dave Gallagher .04 .02 .00
□ 290 Dave Anderson .04 .02 .00
□ 291 Mel Hall .04 .02 .00
□ 292 Jerald Clark .04 .02 .00
□ 293 Al Newman .04 .02 .00
□ 294 Rob Deer .04 .02 .00
□ 295 Matt Nokes .07 .03 .01
□ 296 Jack Armstrong .04 .02 .00
□ 297 Jim Deshaies .04 .02 .00
□ 298 Jeff Innis .04 .02 .00
□ 299 Jeff Reed .04 .02 .00
□ 300 Checklist 201-300 .07 .03 .01
□ 301 Lonnie Smith .04 .02 .00
□ 302 Jimmy Key .07 .03 .01
□ 303 Junior Felix .07 .03 .01
□ 304 Mike Heath .04 .02 .00
□ 305 Mark Langston .07 .03 .01
□ 306 Greg W. Harris .04 .02 .00
□ 307 Brett Butler .07 .03 .01
□ 308 Luis Rivera .04 .02 .00
□ 309 Bruce Ruffin .04 .02 .00
□ 310 Paul Faries .04 .02 .00
□ 311 Terry Leach .04 .02 .00
□ 312 Scott Brosius .15 .06 .01
□ 313 Scott Leius .07 .03 .01
□ 314 Harold Reynolds .04 .02 .00
□ 315 Jack Morris .10 .04 .01
□ 316 David Segui .07 .03 .01
□ 317 Bill Gullickson .04 .02 .00
□ 318 Todd Frohwirth .04 .02 .00
□ 319 Mark Leiter .07 .03 .01
□ 320 Jeff M. Robinson .04 .02 .00
□ 321 Gary Gaetti .07 .03 .01
□ 322 John Smoltz .10 .04 .01
□ 323 Andy Benes .10 .04 .01
□ 324 Kelly Gruber .10 .04 .01
□ 325 Jim Abbott .12 .05 .01
□ 326 John Kruk .04 .02 .00
□ 327 Kevin Seitzer .07 .03 .01
□ 328 Darrin Jackson .04 .02 .00
□ 329 Kurt Stillwell .04 .02 .00
□ 330 Mike Maddux .04 .02 .00
□ 331 Dennis Eckersley .10 .04 .01
□ 332 Dan Gladden .04 .02 .00
□ 333 Jose Canseco .30 .12 .03
□ 334 Kent Hrbek .07 .03 .01
□ 335 Ken Griffey Sr. .07 .03 .01
□ 336 Greg Swindell .07 .03 .01
□ 337 Trevor Wilson .04 .02 .00
□ 338 Sam Horn .04 .02 .00
□ 339 Mike Henneman .04 .02 .00
□ 340 Jerry Browne .04 .02 .00
□ 341 Glenn Braggs .04 .02 .00
□ 342 Tom Glavine .12 .05 .01
□ 343 Wally Joyner .10 .04 .01
□ 344 Fred McGriff .12 .05 .01
□ 345 Ron Gant .15 .06 .01
□ 346 Ramon Martinez .15 .06 .01
□ 347 Wes Chamberlain .20 .08 .02
□ 348 Terry Shumpert .04 .02 .00
□ 349 Tim Teufel .04 .02 .00
□ 350 Wally Backman .04 .02 .00
□ 351 Joe Girardi .04 .02 .00
□ 352 Devon White .07 .03 .01
□ 353 Greg Maddux .07 .03 .01
□ 354 Ryan Bowen .10 .04 .01
□ 355 Roberto Alomar .15 .06 .01
□ 356 Don Mattingly .20 .08 .02
□ 357 Pedro Guerrero .07 .03 .01
□ 358 Steve Sax .07 .03 .01
□ 359 Joey Cora .04 .02 .00
□ 360 Jim Gantner .04 .02 .00
□ 361 Brian Barnes .07 .03 .01
□ 362 Kevin McReynolds .07 .03 .01
□ 363 Bret Barberie .20 .08 .02
□ 364 David Cone .10 .04 .01
□ 365 Dennis Martinez .07 .03 .01
□ 366 Brian Hunter .40 .16 .04
□ 367 Edgar Martinez .07 .03 .01
□ 368 Steve Finley .07 .03 .01
□ 369 Greg Briley .04 .02 .00
□ 370 Jeff Blauser .04 .02 .00
□ 371 Todd Stottlemyre .07 .03 .01
□ 372 Luis Gonzalez .20 .08 .02
□ 373 Rick Wilkins .10 .04 .01
□ 374 Darryl Kile .10 .04 .01
□ 375 John Olerud .15 .06 .01
□ 376 Lee Smith .07 .03 .01
□ 377 Kevin Maas .20 .08 .02
□ 378 Dante Bichette .04 .02 .00
□ 379 Tom Pagnozzi .04 .02 .00
□ 380 Mike Flanagan .07 .03 .01
□ 381 Charlie O'Brien .04 .02 .00
□ 382 Dave Martinez .04 .02 .00
□ 383 Keith Miller .04 .02 .00
□ 384 Scott Ruskin .04 .02 .00
□ 385 Kevin Elster .04 .02 .00
□ 386 Alvin Davis .04 .02 .00
□ 387 Casey Candaele .04 .02 .00
□ 388 Pete O'Brien .04 .02 .00
□ 389 Jeff Treadway .04 .02 .00
□ 390 Scott Bradley .04 .02 .00
□ 391 Mookie Wilson .04 .02 .00
□ 392 Jimmy Jones .04 .02 .00
□ 393 Candy Maldonado .04 .02 .00
□ 394 Eric Yelding .04 .02 .00
□ 395 Tom Henke .04 .02 .00
□ 396 Franklin Stubbs .04 .02 .00
□ 397 Milt Thompson .04 .02 .00
□ 398 Mark Carreon .04 .02 .00
□ 399 Randy Velarde .04 .02 .00
□ 400 Checklist 301-400 .07 .03 .01
□ 401 Omar Vizquel .04 .02 .00
□ 402 Joe Boever .04 .02 .00
□ 403 Bill Krueger .04 .02 .00
□ 404 Jody Reed .07 .03 .01

Card	Player	Price 1	Price 2	Price 3
☐ 405	Mike Schooler	.04	.02	.00
☐ 406	Jason Grimsley	.04	.02	.00
☐ 407	Greg Myers	.04	.02	.00
☐ 408	Randy Ready	.04	.02	.00
☐ 409	Mike Timlin	.07	.03	.01
☐ 410	Mitch Williams	.04	.02	.00
☐ 411	Garry Templeton	.04	.02	.00
☐ 412	Greg Cadaret	.04	.02	.00
☐ 413	Donnie Hill	.04	.02	.00
☐ 414	Wally Whitehurst	.04	.02	.00
☐ 415	Scott Sanderson	.04	.02	.00
☐ 416	Thomas Howard	.04	.02	.00
☐ 417	Neal Heaton	.04	.02	.00
☐ 418	Charlie Hough	.04	.02	.00
☐ 419	Jack Howell	.04	.02	.00
☐ 420	Greg Hibbard	.04	.02	.00
☐ 421	Carlos Quintana	.07	.03	.01
☐ 422	Kim Batiste	.10	.04	.01
☐ 423	Paul Molitor	.10	.04	.01
☐ 424	Ken Griffey Jr.	.90	.40	.09
☐ 425	Phil Plantier	.40	.16	.04
☐ 426	Denny Neagle	.15	.06	.01
☐ 427	Von Hayes	.07	.03	.01
☐ 428	Shane Mack	.07	.03	.01
☐ 429	Darren Daulton	.04	.02	.00
☐ 430	Dwayne Henry	.04	.02	.00
☐ 431	Lance Parrish	.07	.03	.01
☐ 432	Mike Humphreys	.10	.04	.01
☐ 433	Tim Burke	.04	.02	.00
☐ 434	Bryan Harvey	.07	.03	.01
☐ 435	Pat Kelly	.15	.06	.01
☐ 436	Ozzie Guillen	.07	.03	.01
☐ 437	Bruce Hurst	.07	.03	.01
☐ 438	Sammy Sosa	.07	.03	.01
☐ 439	Dennis Rasmussen	.04	.02	.00
☐ 440	Ken Patterson	.04	.02	.00
☐ 441	Jay Buhner	.07	.03	.01
☐ 442	Pat Combs	.04	.02	.00
☐ 443	Wade Boggs	.20	.08	.02
☐ 444	George Brett	.15	.06	.01
☐ 445	Mo Vaughn	.30	.12	.03
☐ 446	Chuck Knoblauch	.30	.12	.03
☐ 447	Tom Candiotti	.07	.03	.01
☐ 448	Mark Portugal	.04	.02	.00
☐ 449	Mickey Morandini	.07	.03	.01
☐ 450	Duane Ward	.04	.02	.00
☐ 451	Otis Nixon	.04	.02	.00
☐ 452	Bob Welch	.07	.03	.01
☐ 453	Rusty Meacham	.07	.03	.01
☐ 454	Keith Mitchell	.25	.10	.02
☐ 455	Marquis Grissom	.10	.04	.01
☐ 456	Robin Yount	.15	.06	.01
☐ 457	Harvey Pulliam	.10	.04	.01
☐ 458	Jose DeLeon	.04	.02	.00
☐ 459	Mark Gubicza	.04	.02	.00
☐ 460	Darryl Hamilton	.04	.02	.00
☐ 461	Tom Browning	.04	.02	.00
☐ 462	Monty Fariss	.07	.03	.01
☐ 463	Jerome Walton	.07	.03	.01
☐ 464	Paul O'Neill	.07	.03	.01
☐ 465	Dean Palmer	.20	.08	.02
☐ 466	Travis Fryman	.25	.10	.02
☐ 467	John Smiley	.07	.03	.01
☐ 468	Lloyd Moseby	.04	.02	.00
☐ 469	John Wehner	.15	.06	.01
☐ 470	Skeeter Barnes	.04	.02	.00
☐ 471	Steve Chitren	.04	.02	.00
☐ 472	Kent Mercker	.04	.02	.00
☐ 473	Terry Steinbach	.04	.02	.00
☐ 474	Andres Galarraga	.07	.03	.01
☐ 475	Steve Avery	.40	.16	.04
☐ 476	Tom Gordon	.07	.03	.01
☐ 477	Cal Eldred	.07	.03	.01
☐ 478	Omar Olivares	.07	.03	.01
☐ 479	Julio Machado	.04	.02	.00
☐ 480	Bob Milacki	.04	.02	.00
☐ 481	Les Lancaster	.04	.02	.00
☐ 482	John Candelaria	.04	.02	.00
☐ 483	Brian Downing	.04	.02	.00
☐ 484	Roger McDowell	.04	.02	.00
☐ 485	Scott Scudder	.04	.02	.00
☐ 486	Zane Smith	.04	.02	.00
☐ 487	John Cerutti	.04	.02	.00
☐ 488	Steve Buechele	.04	.02	.00
☐ 489	Paul Gibson	.04	.02	.00
☐ 490	Curtis Wilkerson	.04	.02	.00
☐ 491	Marvin Freeman	.04	.02	.00
☐ 492	Tom Foley	.04	.02	.00
☐ 493	Juan Berenguer	.04	.02	.00
☐ 494	Ernest Riles	.04	.02	.00
☐ 495	Sid Bream	.04	.02	.00
☐ 496	Chuck Crim	.04	.02	.00
☐ 497	Mike Macfarlane	.04	.02	.00
☐ 498	Dale Sveum	.04	.02	.00
☐ 499	Storm Davis	.04	.02	.00
☐ 500	Checklist 401-500	.07	.03	.01
☐ 501	Jeff Reardon	.07	.03	.01
☐ 502	Shawn Abner	.04	.02	.00
☐ 503	Tony Fossas	.04	.02	.00
☐ 504	Cory Snyder	.07	.03	.01
☐ 505	Matt Young	.04	.02	.00
☐ 506	Allan Anderson	.04	.02	.00
☐ 507	Mark Lee	.07	.03	.01
☐ 508	Gene Nelson	.04	.02	.00
☐ 509	Mike Pagliarulo	.04	.02	.00
☐ 510	Rafael Belliard	.04	.02	.00
☐ 511	Jay Howell	.04	.02	.00
☐ 512	Bob Tewksbury	.04	.02	.00
☐ 513	Mike Morgan	.07	.03	.01
☐ 514	John Franco	.04	.02	.00
☐ 515	Kevin Gross	.04	.02	.00
☐ 516	Lou Whitaker	.07	.03	.01
☐ 517	Orlando Merced	.15	.06	.01
☐ 518	Todd Benzinger	.04	.02	.00
☐ 519	Gary Redus	.04	.02	.00
☐ 520	Walt Terrell	.04	.02	.00

☐ 521 Jack Clark	.07	.03	.01
☐ 522 Dave Parker	.07	.03	.01
☐ 523 Tim Naehring	.07	.03	.01
☐ 524 Mark Whiten	.15	.06	.01
☐ 525 Ellis Burks	.10	.04	.01
☐ 526 Frank Castillo	.07	.03	.01
☐ 527 Brian Harper	.04	.02	.00
☐ 528 Brook Jacoby	.04	.02	.00
☐ 529 Rick Sutcliffe	.07	.03	.01
☐ 530 Joe Klink	.04	.02	.00
☐ 531 Terry Bross	.04	.02	.00
☐ 532 Jose Offerman	.10	.04	.01
☐ 533 Todd Zeile	.12	.05	.01
☐ 534 Eric Karros	.30	.12	.03
☐ 535 Anthony Young	.15	.06	.01
☐ 536 Milt Cuyler	.12	.05	.01
☐ 537 Randy Tomlin	.10	.04	.01
☐ 538 Scott Livingstone	.15	.06	.01
☐ 539 Jim Eisenreich	.04	.02	.00
☐ 540 Don Slaught	.04	.02	.00
☐ 541 Scott Cooper	.15	.06	.01
☐ 542 Joe Grahe	.04	.02	.00
☐ 543 Tom Brunansky	.07	.03	.01
☐ 544 Eddie Zosky	.15	.06	.01
☐ 545 Roger Clemens	.25	.10	.02
☐ 546 David Justice	.75	.30	.07
☐ 547 Dave Stewart	.07	.03	.01
☐ 548 David West	.04	.02	.00
☐ 549 Dave Smith	.04	.02	.00
☐ 550 Dan Plesac	.04	.02	.00
☐ 551 Alex Fernandez	.15	.06	.01
☐ 552 Bernard Gilkey	.12	.05	.01
☐ 553 Jack McDowell	.10	.04	.01
☐ 554 Tino Martinez	.20	.08	.02
☐ 555 Bo Jackson	.35	.15	.03
☐ 556 Bernie Williams	.20	.08	.02
☐ 557 Mark Gardner	.04	.02	.00
☐ 558 Glenallen Hill	.07	.03	.01
☐ 559 Oil Can Boyd	.04	.02	.00
☐ 560 Chris James	.04	.02	.00
☐ 561 Scott Servais	.10	.04	.01
☐ 562 Rey Sanchez	.15	.06	.01
☐ 563 Paul McClellan	.10	.04	.01
☐ 564 Andy Mota	.15	.06	.01
☐ 565 Darren Lewis	.07	.03	.01
☐ 566 Jose Melendez	.10	.04	.01
☐ 567 Tommy Greene	.10	.04	.01
☐ 568 Rich Rodriguez	.07	.03	.01
☐ 569 Heathcliff Slocumb	.04	.02	.00
☐ 570 Joe Hesketh	.04	.02	.00
☐ 571 Carlton Fisk	.12	.05	.01
☐ 572 Erik Hanson	.07	.03	.01
☐ 573 Wilson Alvarez	.07	.03	.01
☐ 574 Rheal Cormier	.15	.06	.01
☐ 575 Tim Raines	.10	.04	.01
☐ 576 Bobby Witt	.04	.02	.00
☐ 577 Roberto Kelly	.10	.04	.01
☐ 578 Kevin Brown	.04	.02	.00
☐ 579 Chris Nabholz	.07	.03	.01
☐ 580 Jesse Orosco	.04	.02	.00
☐ 581 Jeff Brantley	.04	.02	.00
☐ 582 Rafael Ramirez	.04	.02	.00
☐ 583 Kelly Downs	.04	.02	.00
☐ 584 Mike Simms	.10	.04	.01
☐ 585 Mike Remlinger	.04	.02	.00
☐ 586 Dave Hollins	.07	.03	.01
☐ 587 Larry Andersen	.04	.02	.00
☐ 588 Mike Gardiner	.10	.04	.01
☐ 589 Craig Lefferts	.04	.02	.00
☐ 590 Paul Assenmacher	.04	.02	.00
☐ 591 Bryn Smith	.04	.02	.00
☐ 592 Donn Pall	.04	.02	.00
☐ 593 Mike Jackson	.04	.02	.00
☐ 594 Scott Radinsky	.04	.02	.00
☐ 595 Brian Holman	.04	.02	.00
☐ 596 Geronimo Pena	.04	.02	.00
☐ 597 Mike Jeffcoat	.04	.02	.00
☐ 598 Carlos Martinez	.04	.02	.00
☐ 599 Geno Petralli	.04	.02	.00
☐ 600 Checklist 501-600	.07	.03	.01
☐ 601 Jerry Don Gleaton	.04	.02	.00
☐ 602 Adam Peterson	.04	.02	.00
☐ 603 Craig Grebeck	.04	.02	.00
☐ 604 Mark Guthrie	.04	.02	.00
☐ 605 Frank Tanana	.04	.02	.00
☐ 606 Hensley Meulens	.07	.03	.01
☐ 607 Mark Davis	.04	.02	.00
☐ 608 Eric Plunk	.04	.02	.00
☐ 609 Mark Williamson	.04	.02	.00
☐ 610 Lee Guetterman	.04	.02	.00
☐ 611 Bobby Rose	.04	.02	.00
☐ 612 Bill Wegman	.04	.02	.00
☐ 613 Mike Hartley	.04	.02	.00
☐ 614 Chris Beasley	.15	.06	.01
☐ 615 Chris Bosio	.04	.02	.00
☐ 616 Henry Cotto	.04	.02	.00
☐ 617 Chico Walker	.04	.02	.00
☐ 618 Russ Swan	.04	.02	.00
☐ 619 Bob Walk	.04	.02	.00
☐ 620 Billy Swift	.04	.02	.00
☐ 621 Warren Newson	.10	.04	.01
☐ 622 Steve Bedrosian	.04	.02	.00
☐ 623 Ricky Bones	.10	.04	.01
☐ 624 Kevin Tapani	.07	.03	.01
☐ 625 Juan Guzman	.25	.10	.02
☐ 626 Jeff Johnson	.10	.04	.01
☐ 627 Jeff Montgomery	.04	.02	.00
☐ 628 Ken Hill	.04	.02	.00
☐ 629 Gary Thurman	.04	.02	.00
☐ 630 Steve Howe	.04	.02	.00
☐ 631 Jose DeJesus	.04	.02	.00
☐ 632 Bert Blyleven	.07	.03	.01
☐ 633 Jaime Navarro	.04	.02	.00
☐ 634 Lee Stevens	.07	.03	.01
☐ 635 Pete Harnisch	.07	.03	.01
☐ 636 Bill Landrum	.04	.02	.00

☐ 637 Rich DeLucia .04 .02 .00
☐ 638 Luis Salazar .04 .02 .00
☐ 639 Rob Murphy .04 .02 .00
☐ 640 Diamond Skills .15 .06 .01
Checklist
Jose Canseco
Rickey Henderson
☐ 641 Roger Clemens DS .15 .06 .01
☐ 642 Jim Abbott DS .10 .04 .01
☐ 643 Travis Fryman DS .15 .06 .01
☐ 644 Jesse Barfield DS .07 .03 .01
☐ 645 Cal Ripken DS .20 .08 .02
☐ 646 Wade Boggs DS .15 .06 .01
☐ 647 Cecil Fielder DS .15 .06 .01
☐ 648 Rickey Henderson DS .20 .08 .02
☐ 649 Jose Canseco DS .20 .08 .02
☐ 650 Ken Griffey Jr. DS .50 .20 .05
☐ 651 Kenny Rogers .04 .02 .00
☐ 652 Luis Mercedes .25 .10 .02
☐ 653 Mike Stanton .04 .02 .00
☐ 654 Glenn Davis .07 .03 .01
☐ 655 Nolan Ryan .50 .20 .05
☐ 656 Reggie Jefferson .15 .06 .01
☐ 657 Javier Ortiz .07 .03 .01
☐ 658 Greg A. Harris .04 .02 .00
☐ 659 Mariano Duncan .04 .02 .00
☐ 660 Jeff Shaw .04 .02 .00
☐ 661 Mike Moore .07 .03 .01
☐ 662 Chris Haney .10 .04 .01
☐ 663 Joe Slusarski .07 .03 .01
☐ 664 Wayne Housie .17 .07 .01
☐ 665 Carlos Garcia .07 .03 .01
☐ 666 Bob Ojeda .04 .02 .00
☐ 667 Bryan Hickerson .15 .06 .01
☐ 668 Tim Belcher .07 .03 .01
☐ 669 Ron Darling .07 .03 .01
☐ 670 Rex Hudler .04 .02 .00
☐ 671 Sid Fernandez .07 .03 .01
☐ 672 Chito Martinez .15 .06 .01
☐ 673 Pete Schourek .10 .04 .01
☐ 674 Armando Reynoso .15 .06 .01
☐ 675 Mike Mussina .20 .08 .02
☐ 676 Kevin Morton .10 .04 .01
☐ 677 Norm Charlton .04 .02 .00
☐ 678 Danny Darwin .04 .02 .00
☐ 679 Eric King .04 .02 .00
☐ 680 Ted Power .04 .02 .00
☐ 681 Barry Jones .04 .02 .00
☐ 682 Carney Lansford .07 .03 .01
☐ 683 Mel Rojas .07 .03 .01
☐ 684 Rick Honeycutt .04 .02 .00
☐ 685 Jeff Fassero .10 .04 .01
☐ 686 Cris Carpenter .04 .02 .00
☐ 687 Tim Crews .04 .02 .00
☐ 688 Scott Terry .04 .02 .00
☐ 689 Chris Gwynn .04 .02 .00
☐ 690 Gerald Perry .04 .02 .00
☐ 691 John Barfield .04 .02 .00
☐ 692 Bob Melvin .04 .02 .00
☐ 693 Juan Agosto .04 .02 .00
☐ 694 Alejandro Pena .07 .03 .01
☐ 695 Jeff Russell .04 .02 .00
☐ 696 Carmelo Martinez .04 .02 .00
☐ 697 Bud Black .04 .02 .00
☐ 698 Dave Otto .04 .02 .00
☐ 699 Billy Hatcher .04 .02 .00
☐ 700 Checklist 601-700 .07 .03 .01

WE ARE BUYING!!!

LARRY FRITSCH CARDS, INC.

Before you sell, talk to us! Our 45 years in card collecting is unchallenged by anyone, and our reputation is beyond repute. We do not make wild, unsubstantiated claims: WE BUY CARDS AT A HIGHER PRICE THAN ANYONE!! All purchases made are strictly confidential; we are private individuals and don't brag about our "buys." Try us!

Our experience and knowledge give us the edge. With a mailing list of over 95,000 active collectors, we have more exposure and can pay higher prices. One card or 100,000 - we treat each purchase alike!

Our primary areas of interest are as follows:

- all Tobacco cards (T3 thru T332 including Plow Boy Tobacco)
- all "E" Early Candy & Gum cards, including Cracker Jacks, Colgans, JuJu Drums & Zeanuts
- all 19th Century cards
- all Goudys and Canadian Goudeys
- 1939, 1940 & 1941 Play Balls
- all other cards from 1930s including Batter-Ups, Diamond Stars, Delongs, etc.
- all meats including Glendale, Rodeo, Kahns, Wilson, Stahl-Meyer, Briggs, Esskay & Hunters, etc.
- other foods including Bell Brand, Bond Bread, Hage's Dairy, 1947 Tip Top Bread, etc.
- 1948-49 Leaf Baseball & Football • 1952 Topps
- 1953-60 Spic & Span Braves • 1954 Red Heart
- complete baseball sets prior to 1968
- 1935 National Chicle Football • 1933 Sports Kings
- all Sporting News issues including M101-4, M101-5, M101-6
- any other meat, bakery product cards including those before 1920 & any unusual card issues.

We are interested in all cards issued prior to 1955. Funds are available for immediate purchases, and we also take items on consignment. Call us for details!

(715) 344-8687 • FAX # (715) 344-1778
735 Old Wausau Rd.
P.O. Box 863, Dept. 903
Stevens Point, WI 54481

1st FULL TIME DEALER - STARTING May 1, 1970 - 50,000,000 cards in stock!

REPRINT SETS — WHO BUYS REPRINT SETS? THE TRUE COLLECTOR!

Can you afford an original 1922 E120 American Caramel set for $15,000 or a 1947 Tip Top set for $12,000? You can have your own reprint set for less than $30 - today! True collectors appreciate reprint sets for what they are - beautiful, complete sets that they might otherwise never see. Recapture the great eras of baseball with your own complete sets! The following are all available from Larry Fritsch Cards.

1909 E95 Philadelphia Caramels (25 cards)	$6.95	1927 Middy Bread (42)	5.95	1955 Johnston Cookies (35)	9.95
1910 Plow Boy Tobacco (42)	5.95	1947 Tip Top Bread (163)	24.95	1957 Spic and Span Braves (20)	3.95
1911 D304 General Baking (25)	6.95	1953 Johnston Cookies (25)	8.95	1960 Lake to Lake Braves (28)	6.95
1922 E120 American Caramel (240)	29.95	1954 Johnston Cookies (35)	9.95	1970 Flavor-est Milk Brewers (24)	5.95
		1954 Wilson Franks (20)	8.95		

NEGRO LEAGUE

Available now, a set of the great stars of the Negro Leagues. For the first time ever a set of cards on the Negro League using actual photographs. From 1898 until 1946, black men were barred from organized baseball. The set of 119 cards includes Satchell Paige, Josh Gibson, Cool Papa Bell, Buck Leonard. Also shown are many historic Negro League uniforms.

Complete Set of Negro League (119 cards) ..9.95
2 Complete Sets (238 cards) 17.50
5 Complete Sets (595 cards) 37.50

1953 BRAVES

Limited Edition Collectors Set

- Special limited edition collectors set marking the 30th anniversary of the Milwaukee Braves' move from Boston.
- 33-card set. Custom-printed in two color. Same 2⅝"x3¾" size as the great baseball cards of the mid-1950s.
- Made from original spring training photos.

Complete Set - Only $4.95

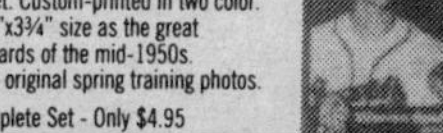

Call for our FREE CATALOG - A must for the novice as well as the serious collector!

SHIPPING AND INSURANCE TABLE

$.01 to $25.00	add $4.50
$25.01 to $50.00	add 5.50
$50.01 and over	add 6.50

All prices subject to change. Call to verify prices.

CHECK POLICY:
All personal checks will be held 15 working days for clearance. For faster service, please send Postal Money Orders.

CANADA CUSTOMERS:
Please send Postal Money Order in U.S. Funds only and an additional $7.00 per set for sets over 250 cards. $3.50 per set for sets under 250 cards for shipping your sets.

LARRY FRITSCH CARDS, INC.

735 OLD WAUSAU RD., P.O. BOX 863, DEPT. 509
STEVENS POINT, WI 54481

(715) 344-8687
FAX # (715) 344-1778

See our ad on page 698 for other items we have in stock

ALASKA, HAWAII, PUERTO RICO, FPO & P.O. CUSTOMERS: Add an additional $5.00 per set for sets over 250 cards and $3.00 per set for sets under 250 cards for shipping your set (if you have a P.O. Box and want your order shipped via UPS, please include your UPS shipping address.)

WITH OVER 55 MILLION CARDS IN STOCK... WE HAVE AMERICA'S MOST COMPLETE STOCK OF SPORTS TRADING CARDS. Full money back guarantee if you are not completely satisfied with our service and products. YOU, the customers are always NO. 1 to us!

To receive Super Service it is necessary to send a POSTAL MONEY ORDER with your order. (All personal checks are held 15 days for clearance.) (Charge orders add 5% to total.) Minimum charge order $20.00 WI residents add 5.5% sales tax.

SAN DIEGO SPORTS COLLECTIBLES
659 Fashion Valley Dept.V
SAN DIEGO, CA. 92108

COMPLETE MINT BASEBALL SETS

BASEBALL SETS	1981	1982	1983	1984	1985	1986	1987	1988	1989	1990	1991
DONRUSS	$68.75	$84.75	$132.75	$419.75	$189.75	$248.75	$144.75	$24.75	$24.75	$24.75	$39.75
FLEER	$68.75	$79.75	$118.75	$229.75	$188.75	$178.75	$129.75	$48.75	$32.75	$25.75	$29.75
TOPPS	$125.75	$144.75	$174.75	$119.75	$118.75	$43.75	$53.75	$24.75	$24.75	$24.75	$29.75
FLEER TRADED	-	-	-	$749.75	$38.75	$37.75	$21.75	$14.75	$23.75	$11.75	$13.75
TOPPS TRADED	$44.75	$275.00	$138.75	$123.75	$39.75	$39.75	$19.75	$34.75	$15.75	$11.75	$13.75

SATISFACTION GUARANTEED OR YOUR MONEY BACK *PRICES SUBJECT TO CHANGE WITHOUT NOTICE*

ORDER TOLL-FREE 1-800-227-0483

"1988 BASEBALL SPECIAL"
Save! Buy All Three Complete Sets, Topps, Fleer and Donruss For Only: $ 94.75

"1989 BASEBALL SPECIAL"
Save! Buy All Three Complete Sets, Topps, Fleer and Donruss For Only: $ 79.75

"1990 BASEBALL SPECIAL"
Save! Buy All Three Complete Sets, Topps, Fleer and Donruss For Only: $ 69.75

"1991 BASEBALL SPECIAL"
Save! Buy All Three Complete Sets, Topps, Fleer and Donruss For Only: $ 89.75

Protect Your Cards

WILL STORE OVER 16,000 CARDS!

- Indestructo Storage Boxes (800 count)
- Each Box Holds 800 Cards
- Shipped in Bundles of 21 Boxes

ORDER TOLL FREE 1-800-227-0483

$14.95
POSTPAID

SPECIAL!

Super deluxe 3-inch card album with 100 -pocket sheets Only $13.95

100 9-pocket top loading sheets $10.95

Super deluxe 3" card album $3.95

When ordering albums please indicate baseball, football, hockey or basketball

Add $3.75 P&H per 100 sheets and $2.75 per album

CLASSIC REPRINT SETS

- 1887 Lone Jack 6.75
- 1887 Allen & Ginter 6.75
- 1895 Mayo Cut & Plug 9.75
- 1910 T-206 ....69.75
- 1911 Mecca T-201 ....19.75
- 1911 T-205 ....39.75
- 1913 T-200 Team Cards 6.75
- 1915 M-104-4 Sporting News 24.75
- 1915 Cracker Jack 44.75
- 1933 Sport Kings 12.75
- 1933 Goudey 49.75
- 1933 Goudey Babe Ruth Card 3.00
- 1933 Goudey Lou Gehrig Card 2.00
- 1934 Goudey ....CALL
- 1935 Diamond Stars 34.75
- 1935 Goudey 8.75
- 1936 Goudey 10.75
- 1937 Diamond Stars 7.75
- 1938 Goudey 13.75
- 1940 Play Ball 34.75
- 1941 Goudey 10.75
- 1948 Bowman 9.75
- 1949 Bowman 34.75
- 1949 Bowman P.C.L. 7.75
- 1951 Bowman 59.75
- 1948 Home Run Derby 6.75
- 1948 Bowman Basketball 29.75
- 1948 Bowman Football 29.75
- 1910 T-206 Honus Wagner 5.00
- 1910 T-206 Ty Cobb 3.00
- 1910 T-206 Walter Johnson 2.00
- 1910 T-206 Nap Lajoie 2.00

SPECIALIZING IN BUYING & SELLING SPORTS CARDS AND COLLECTIBLES SINCE 1979

SportsCards Plus®

We Want To Buy!

- *our 10,000+ store and mail order customers need your cards*
- *we have a six-figure bank balance to support our buying commitment*
- *all transactions and payments are mailed within 24 hours*

Founding Member SCA International™

We will pay cash for the following:

Large and small collections -- Star cards -- Baseball sets Unopened boxes & cases -- Football, Basketball, Hockey sets Hartland statues -- All Sports Memorabilia -- Tobacco cards League issued awards -- Game used equipment -- Rings, etc.

PLEASE FEEL FREE TO CALL AND DISCUSS ANY TRANSACTION

(714)895-4401

Send $1.00 for illustrated catalog. Included in it is a variety of material 1910-1990's, including stars, complete sets, unopened material, rookie cards, Hartlands, bulk lots and more.

14038 Beach Blvd. B-1
Westminster, CA 92683
(714)895-4401 • Fax (714)891-8078
Call David Kohler or Kevin Struss

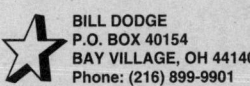

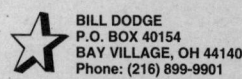